D0849639

THE
GENEALOGIST'S GUIDE

By

GEORGE W. MARSHALL

Reprinted from the last edition of 1903

With A New Introduction By

ANTHONY J. CAMP

Director of Research
Society of Genealogists, London

GENEALOGICAL PUBLISHING CO., INC.
BALTIMORE   1973

First Edition, 1879
Second Edition, 1885
Third Edition, 1893
Fourth Edition, 1903

Reprinted
Genealogical Publishing Co., Inc.
Baltimore, 1967 and 1973

English Publisher
HERALDRY TODAY
London, 1967 and 1973

Library of Congress Catalogue Card Number 66-23581
International Standard Book Number 0-8063-0235-6

Made in the United States of America

Introduction

Since the first published English family history* appeared nearly three hundred years ago an ever growing number of pedigrees have found their way into print. Local and county histories, biographical studies, national and local periodicals, transactions of county archaeological and record societies, and a multitude of out-of-the-way or forgotten books contain pedigrees and family histories although from their titles many would not be expected to contain genealogical information.

Over a period of forty years Dr. Marshall searched through works of this nature and made notes of every tabular pedigree or account of a family that he came across which gave at least three generations in the male line. He first indexed the pedigrees in all the then printed Heralds' Visitations and published his "Index to the Pedigrees contained in the printed Heralds' Visitations" in 1866, following this with "Catalogue of Pedigrees" hitherto unindexed in 1867. These he combined with additional material in the first edition of "The Genealogist's Guide" (1879). Further editions of the latter appeared in 1885, 1893 and 1903, this latter superceding all the other works as well as the similar indexes published by James Coleman ("General Index to Printed Pedigrees," 1866), and Charles Bridger ("Index to Printed Pedigrees contained in County and Local Histories, the Heralds' Visitations, etc.," 1867).

Genealogical research in England thus begins with this volume for it provides the first part of the answer to any question as to what material has already been compiled and is readily available on a particular family. It is a monument of laborious effort which could only have been performed by a man of indomitable perseverance and energy. It was privately printed in a limited edition and has for many years been exceedingly difficult to obtain.

George William Marshall was born at Ward End House, Aston, Warwickshire, on 19th April 1839, the only son of a partner in the Birmingham banking house of Spooner and Attwood. He took his first interest in

---

* *Succinct Genealogies of the Noble and Ancient Houses of Alno, Broc, and Mordaunt, by Robert Halstead (1685).*

genealogy while an undergraduate at Cambridge, he having entered Magdalene College there in 1858. He passed to the Middle Temple in 1862 and was called to the Bar in 1865. The following year he published a history of his mother's family, "Collections for a Genealogical Account of the Family of Comberbach," and in 1868 "A Pedigree of the Descendants of Isaac and Rebecca Marshall, of Perlethorpe, co. Nottingham." In 1883 and 1888 he published the two volumes of his great "Miscellanea Marescalliana" which was one of the first works to deal generally with all families of a certain surname. In 1887 he published two other family histories, "Notes on the Surname of Hall," and "Collections relating to the Surname of Feather." For the Harleian Society he edited "The Visitations of Nottinghamshire, 1569 and 1614" (1871), and "Le Neve's Pedigrees of Knights" (1873). "The Visitation of Wiltshire, 1623" (1878), and "The Visitation of Northumberland, 1615" (1878) which he also edited were privately printed.

His interest in his ancestral county of Nottingham led him to edit and publish the registers of seven parishes there (those of Perlethorpe, Carburton, Edwinstow, Worksop, Wellow, Ollerton, and Walesby). When he bought the Sarnesfield Court estate in Herefordshire in 1891 it was not long before he had transcribed and published the Parish Registers of that place.

But this was not all. His extensive experiences in examining old wills and his practical knowledge of the places where particular records might be found enabled him to print his "Handbook to the Ancient Courts of Probate" (1889, revised 1895) and this remained the standard text-book for forty-five years until B. G. Bouwens published "Wills and Their Whereabouts" in 1939.* Moreover, between 1891 and 1904 he published various lists of published and manuscript copies of Parish Registers which were not altogether superceded until the Society of Genealogists published a "Catalogue of the Parish Registers" in its possession in 1937 and the "National Index of Parish Register Copies" in 1939.

In 1877 he founded "The Genealogist" and edited

---

* Superceded by Mr. Camp's *Wills and Their Whereabouts* published in 1963.

the first seven annual volumes setting high standards which were maintained until that periodical had to cease publication in 1922.

G. W. Marshall became an LL.D. of his old University in 1874, having been elected a Fellow of the Society of Antiquaries two years previously. He was one of the founders of the Harleian Society (1869) and of the Parish Register Society, and was appointed Rouge Croix Pursuivant of Arms at the College of Arms in 1887, becoming York Herald in 1904. He died at Holmbush, Barnes, on 12th September 1905 and was buried at Sarnesfield having bequeathed his extensive collection of manuscripts, many relating to Nottinghamshire, to the College in which he had always taken a great interest.

It was fifty years before a successor was found to carry on his work. Between 1947 and 1953 the Harleian Society published in four volumes John Beach Whitmore's "Genealogical Guide: An Index to British Pedigrees in continuation of Marshall's Genealogist's Guide (1903)," and this was reprinted in one volume with an extra Final Addenda in 1953 under the same title. Both the first of the Harleian Society Volumes (Vol. 99) and the 1953 edition contain a Corrigenda to Dr. Marshall's work. Additions of pedigrees published before 1903 and not noticed by Dr. Marshall are included in the body of Major Whitmore's "Guide" where they came to his notice.

The two volumes together form an immensely useful index to material on English families which appeared in published sources before 1953, but the following small points should be taken into consideration after the Prefaces to both volumes have been read.

Although Dr. Marshall indexed the pedigrees in the most important of the older Peerages and Baronetages he did not include references to those published by Burke, Debrett or Lodge, but referred readers to Richard Sims's "A Manual for the Genealogist" (1888) which contains a list of works of this nature, and to Edward Solly's "An Index of Hereditary English, Scottish, and Irish Titles of Honour" (1880). Major Whitmore devotes a most useful Appendix to a continuation of Solly's "Index" down to 1950 and both should be consulted as they provide the key to the further information hidden in the Peerages under titles which are quite different to the original family names or to families which appeared for a short time when one of their members was enobled and were later removed from the Peerages when they became extinct in that particular branch. The great works of "The Complete Peerage" (13 vols., 1910-1959), "The Complete Baronetage" (6 vols., 1900-1909), and "The Scots Peerage" (9 vols., 1904-1914) are not indexed by either Dr. Marshall or Major Whitmore. Similarly no references are given to the various editions of A. C. Fox-Davies's "Armorial Families" (7th, last and best edition, 1929), Edward Walford's "County Families of the United Kingdom" (published regularly between 1860 and 1920), Kelly's "Handbook to the Titled, Landed and Official Classes" (published regularly since 1880), and other biographical works such as "Who's Who," "Who Was Who," and the "Dictionary of National Biography," all of which contain much genealogical information.

Dr. Marshall did not include new pedigrees which appeared in the various editions of Burke's "Landed Gentry" after the 8th (1894) edition, and Major Whitmore just missed the 1952 (or 17th) edition with all its new material, although of course he indexed the new pedigrees in the 1914 (12th) and 1937 (15th) editions omitting those which appeared in the 8th edition. Thus it should be remembered that any pedigrees which only appeared in the intervening editions would not have been indexed, and more important that a pedigree which is only indexed as appearing in the 8th edition may well also appear in a later one in much fuller detail and showing the results of later scholarship.

It may be noted here that Whitmore compiled his "Guide" in the period 1945-8 and pedigrees printed in serial and periodical publications after those dates are not always included. It is difficult to single out particular works but important volumes of pedigrees published since that time include Burke's "Landed Gentry of Ireland" (1958), the first volume of the 18th edition of Burke's "Landed Gentry" (1965), the "Wiltshire Visitation Pedigrees 1623" (1954) and the "Visitation of London 1568" (1963) both published by the Harleian Society (vols., 105/6 and 109/10), and, of course, the various volumes of the Victoria County History so far published which contain information on innumerable manorial families. The more recent editions of Burke's "Peerage" should not be overlooked for their new families and the new accounts of old ones which they contain.

It seems likely that Marshall and Whitmore cover all the works mentioned in T. R. Thomson's "A Catalogue of British Family Histories" (1928, 2nd edition 1935) and no further editions of this work have appeared. Family histories published since 1951 may be found listed each year under the classification number 929 in the "British National Bibliography," and those received by the English Society of Genealogists are listed quarterly in "The Genealogists' Magazine." The latter (volume VII, pages 645-8) also has an Addenda to T. R. Thomson's "Catalogue."

Marshall and Whitmore made no detailed search for Scottish material and for the pedigrees of Scottish families one should always consult in addition Margaret Stuart's "Scottish Family History" (1930) and Joan Ferguson's "Scottish Family Histories held in Scottish Libraries" (1960). Similarly for Ireland reference should be made to the three volumes by Edward Mac-Lysaght, "Irish Families" (1957), "More Irish Families" (1960), and "A Guide to Irish Surnames" (1964) all of which contain extensive bibliographies of Irish family histories.

As long ago as 1906 a writer in "The Genealogist" said of Dr. Marshall's "Guide," "In every part of the world where the history of English families excites any interest this book is well known and highly appreciated." Generations of genealogists yet unborn will be in his debt, and the Genealogical Publishing Company is to be congratulated on making his work available to many more of them.

Anthony J. Camp
Director of Research
Society of Genealogists

London, 1967

Publisher's Preface

The admirable introduction by Mr. Anthony J.
Camp, Director of Research, Society of Genealogists,
London, points up the great value of this work and the
continuation by John B. Whitmore, as the beginning
point for research on English ancestry. His observations
have been underlined by the many requests we have
had from genealogical researchers and librarians in
America for copies of this book. Apparently only a
small printing was made of the 1903 edition and librarians inform us that their copies are generally badly
worn.

American librarians are also aware of the value
of MARSHALL as a prime source for genealogists, and
correspondence and personal requests have invariably
reflected constant use of this publication by researchers.
We have been informed that reference to this volume
saves librarians and researchers many hours of work,
and it is therefore with great pleasure that we bring to
the public a reprint which we feel will meet with uni-
versal acclaim. It remains only to mention that Mr.
Camp's modesty forbade him to state that he has
written a completely revised and enlarged edition of
BOUWENS' work, also entitled WILLS AND THEIR
WHEREABOUTS published in 1963 for the Society of
Genealogists.

Genealogical Publishing Company

Baltimore, Maryland 1967

PREFACE.

—◦—

THE 'Genealogist's Guide' having been accepted by the public
as a useful book of reference renders it almost unnecessary to
do more by way of preface than recapitulate the plan which
has been followed in constructing it.

It will be asked what kind of genealogy I have considered a
pedigree of sufficient importance to be catalogued here. My
answer is, that as a general rule, I have included any descent of
three generations in male line. A pedigree, therefore, which
sets forth the descendants of A in the families of B, C, and D, is
referred to under such of the families of B, C, and D, as happen
to have three generations in male line given in it; if there be
only two and an heiress, it is not noticed. Exceptions to this
rule are, however, frequent in references to works such as
Peerages and Baronetages, my object being not so much to
index every existing genealogy as to place the intelligent
student in a position to find out the sources from which he
may obtain a clue to the particular pedigree he is searching
for. This observation also applies to the references given to
'Notes and Queries,' which in no degree pretend to supersede
the necessity of consulting for purposes of genealogical reference the general indexes to that periodical. So far, indeed,
as 'Notes and Queries' is concerned, reference is often made
only to one or two out of many articles relating to a particular
family; but it will be found sufficient to give those consulting
the book a clue to further information, as the articles in that
publication are headed by references to such as have previously
appeared in it.

'Pulls' from the publications of Archæological Societies,

and Periodicals have been *carefully excluded* from this book, unless they contain additional matter to that given in the work in which their contents originally appeared.

When, as is frequently the case with county histories, a book has passed through more than one edition, reference is made to the best or most easily accessible edition. In consulting the following pages it is therefore necessary to bear in mind that references to

Dugdale's Warwickshire	are to the 2nd Edition (Thomas's).		
Chauncy's Hertfordshire	,,	1st	,,
Erdeswicke's Survey of Stafford-shire	,,	3rd	,,
Whitaker's Deanery of Craven[1]	,,	1st	,,
Thoresby's Ducatus Leodiensis	,,	1st	,,
Hunter's Hallamshire	,,	New	,, 1869 fol.
Ashmole's Berkshire	,,	2nd	,,
Morant's Essex	,,	2nd	,,
Blomefield's Norfolk	,,	8vo.	,,
Hasted's Kent	,,	fol.	,,
Hutchins' Dorset	,,	3rd	,,
Gregson's Portfolio of Fragments	,,	3rd	,,
Dallaway's Sussex	,,	1st	,,
Burton's Leicestershire	,,	2nd	,,
Thoroton's Nottinghamshire	,,	2nd	,,
Whitaker's History of Whalley	,,	4th	,,
Baines's Lancaster[2]	,,		,, of 1836.
T. Nicholas's County Families of Wales	,,	2nd	,,
Ormerod's Cheshire	,,	2nd	,, (Helsby's).
Watson's History of Halifax	,,	1st	,,
Wotton's English Baronetage	,,		,, of 1741.

The references to 'Glover's Derbyshire' are to the 4to. edition, and the figures in parentheses refer to the 8vo. edition.

Those portions of the publications of the Powys-land Club which have been re-issued as 'The History of Llangurig' and

---

[1] The pages in parentheses refer to the third edition, which has been published since the first edition of this work was compiled.

[2] References to *Croston's Edition* have been added to this edition of the Guide.

'The Sheriffs of Montgomeryshire,' are referred to under those headings.

The references to 'Topographical Miscellanies,' 1792, 4to., of which work, edited by Sir E. Brydges, only one volume was issued, have the *places* under which pedigrees will be found in parentheses, there being no continuous pagination.

When a pedigree is on a folding table, the page which it faces is given. To some books no page is cited ; in such cases it must be understood that they are not paged.

It should be remembered when consulting the references to Burke's ' History of the Commoners,' that the second and subsequent editions of that work bear the title ' Landed Gentry.' In these the pedigrees (except in a few instances) being in alphabetical order, the page where a pedigree will be found is not given, the number appended being that of the *edition* in which it is contained. When, as often happens, more than one family of the same name occurs, its place of residence is given in parentheses, a plan necessary to avoid confusion, and to show that more that one genealogy will be found in the edition referred to. The abbreviation add. = addenda ; supp. = supplement ; corr. − corrigenda. To the fifth edition there are two supplements. The sixth edition was re-issued in 1882, with an amended supplement. This book contains references to only the first eight editions. The Landed Gentry being now issued at much more frequent intervals than formerly it seems unnecessary to index each edition as it comes out.

Burke's ' Extinct Baronetcies' contains a large number of pedigrees not to be found elsewhere. These pedigrees being in alphabetical order, no page is given ; but to those of Baronets of Ireland and Scotland, and descents which are subsidiary to others, the page has been added.

The words 'Caermarthenshire Pedigrees,' ' Cardiganshire Pedigrees,' and ' Pembrokeshire Pedigrees,' refer to a book entitled ' Pedigrees of Caermarthenshire, Cardiganshire, and Pembrokeshire, in continuation of Lewis Dwnn, to about the years 1700-10. From the MS. of John Philipps Allen Lloyd Philipps, Esq., of Dale Castle, co. Pembroke. Typis Medio Montanis, 1859.' Fol. Privately printed by Sir Thomas Phillipps, Bart. Sir Thomas Phillipps printed a considerable

number of pedigrees on separate sheets, many of them signed
with his initials and sometimes the date of the year when
printed thus—T. P., 1870. I have marked all those I know
with the initials T. P., and the date when given. An extensive
collection of them will be found in the Bodleian Library, from
which most of my references are taken.

As a general rule, the surname of a family is the heading
under which its genealogy should be sought; but to this one
exception is frequently made, viz., where there is a *peerage title.*
In searching, therefore, for titled families, it is necessary to
look both under the surname and also under the title, reference
being avoidably made now to the one and again to the other.
When a family has a double surname the references to both
names should be consulted. It must also be borne in mind
that many names are spelt in several different ways, so that it
is necessary to look under all the various ways in which any
name can be spelt. Cross references have been added to assist
the reader, especially to such as are not familiar to those who
are unaccustomed to genealogical researches.

To have given references in this work to the pedigrees contained in all the Peerages and Baronetages which have been
published during the last two hundred years would have
increased its cost and size without being a proportionate aid
to the reader. But references to the most important Peerages
and Baronetages, *e.g.*, Dugdale's ' Baronage,' Brydges' ' Collins,'
Edmondson's ' Baronagium Genealogicum,' etc., have been
added. Lists of the principal works of this class will be found
in Mr. Richard Sims's ' Manual for the Genealogist,' a book so
well known as to render it unnecessary to repeat them here.
Peerages of England at p. 180, Scotland at p. 187, and Ireland
at p. 188. There is also a list of Royal Genealogies at p. 178.
Since my first edition was issued, the Index Society has published (vol. v.) ' An Index of Hereditary English, Scottish, and
Irish Titles of Honour,' by Edward Solly, F.R.S., F.S.A., a
valuable work, and indispensable to every genealogical inquirer
who wishes to make a complete search in reference to any
name one of whose bearers has been raised to the dignity of a
Peer or Baronet.

Private Acts of Parliament frequently contain much genealogical information ; a collection in thirty-nine folio volumes is in the Guildhall Library, with MS. pedigrees by Sir George Naylor, an index to them will be found in 'Genealogical Queries,' by G. F. T. Sherwood, vol. i., p. 21, etc.

The numbers of the Session Papers, printed by order of the House of Lords, which are given as references to the evidence taken on claims to Peerages and to vote at the elections of Irish Peers, refer to the number at the bottom of each paper. The *volume* in which the paper will be found can be ascertained by referring to the General Indexes to the Sessional Papers. Though these give the page as well as the volume, it would be useless here to refer to the page, because it is the MS. page of the copy arranged for the library of the House of Lords, and not the page at which the particular paper inquired for would be found. An explanatory note to this effect will be seen at the commencement of the General Indexes.

Mention of other works of the same kind as this may not be considered out of place. Sims's 'Index to the Heralds' Visitations' is a useful guide to the MS. collections in the British Museum, though inaccurate and incomplete. The 'Heraldic Calendar,' by William Skey, published in 1846, gives a list of pedigrees and arms recorded in Ulster's Office at Dublin Castle. Whitmore's 'Handbook of American Genealogy' contains much information relative to the pedigrees of English families whose descendants have settled in America. Durrie's 'Alphabetical Index to American Genealogies' gives references to the pedigrees in books published in America, and may frequently be consulted with advantage by English readers. There is a useful list of claims to Scottish Peerages, from 1788-1838, in the 'Gentleman's Magazine' for April, 1839. A catalogue of foreign genealogies will be found in Moule's 'Bibliotheca Heraldica,' pp. 619-648. 'L'Art de vérifier les Généalogies des Families Belges et Hollandaises,' par J. Huyttens (Brussels, 1865, 8vo.), is a work similar to several of those already mentioned. A work, entitled 'A Guide to Printed Books and Manuscripts relating to English and Foreign Heraldry and Genealogy,' by George Gatfield, containing *inter alia* a list of family histories, pedigrees, and peerage cases, will be found useful. As I have not been able to discover the method pursued by the author of this compilation, I refer the reader to it, merely remarking that by including in his list of pedigrees such works as 'DEVIL. The Pedigree of the Devil, by Frederic T. Hall. Lond., 1883, 8vo.,' it will be obvious that his researches into genealogical literature take a much lower range than mine.

The following pedigree indexes are useful, and should be borne in mind :

Genealogical Memoranda. List of Pedigrees in the Candler MS., Harleian MS. 6,071. By G. F. T. Sherwood. Brechin, 1895, 8vo., pp. 4.

Tyssen Library Pedigrees. Genealogical Queries. By G. F. T. Sherwood, i. 7, 15.

Glover's Collection. Harleian MS. 245. Genealogical Queries. By G. F. T. Sherwood, i. 29.

Hasted and Rowe More's Kentish Pedigrees. Add. MS. 5,528. Genealogical Queries. By G. F. T. Sherwood, i. 63, 69.

In inquiries of a genealogical nature, biographical memoirs should not be overlooked, as they often supply information of great value. Phillip's 'Dictionary of Biographical Reference' is an index to the best-known biograpical dictionaries. The dictionary of National Biography is an indispensable work, and should find a place on the shelves of every genealogist. 'The Scottish Nation,' by William Anderson, Edinburgh, 1863, 8vo., three vols., though professedly a biographical dictionary, contains extensive pedigrees of many Scottish families.

In deference to the wishes of many persons who have told me that they have derived advantage from this book, I give a list of the volumes issued by the Harleian Society explanatory of their contents :

Vol. i. The Visitation of London, 1568.
„ ii. The Visitation of Leicestershire, 1619.
„ iii. The Visitation of Rutland, 1618.
„ iv. The Visitations of Nottingham, 1569 and 1614.
„ v. The Visitations of Oxford, 1566, 1574, and 1634.
„ vi. The Visitation of Devon, 1620.
„ vii. The Visitation of Cumberland, 1615.
„ viii. Le Neve's Catalogue of Knights.

It should also be added that Surtees Soc., vol. xli., is Tonge's Visitation of the Northern Counties, and vol. xxxvi. Dugdale's Visitation of Yorkshire in 1665-6. Camden Soc., vol. xliii., is the Visitation of Huntingdon, 1613. The Visitations of Lancashire, 1533, 1567, 1613, and 1664-5, will be found in the vols. of the Chetham Soc., lxxxi., lxxxii., lxxxiv., lxxxv., lxxxviii., xcviii., and cx.

An index, embracing as this does the pedigrees contained in every important genealogical and topographical work, as well as those in many of minor importance, is certain to contain some errors both of omission and commission. For such I crave indulgence, and to use the expression of an old heraldic writer, ' All errors and mistakings as shall fall out, I entreat the Learned-modest Reader to correct with his Pen.'

G. W. M.

THE

GENEALOGIST'S GUIDE.

ABADAM. Burke's Landed Gentry, 2, 3, 4, 5. *See* AP ADAM.
ABAROUGH, or ABARROW. Collinson's Somerset, ii. 63. Berry's
Hampshire Genealogies, 265. Visitation of Somerset, printed by
Sir T. Phillipps, 1. Harleian Society, xi. 1. Hampshire Visita-
tions, printed by Sir T. Phillipps, 1. Weaver's Visitations of
Somerset, 1.
ABBIS, or ABBYS. Harleian Society, xix. 73; xxxii. 1.
ABBOT, or ABBOT. Pedigree of Abbot of Suffolk. Single sheet,
1862. Surrey Archæological Collections, ii.; iii. 265. Visitation
of Devonshire, 1620, printed by Sir Thomas Phillipps, (Middle
Hill, fol.) 1. Visitation of Wiltshire, 1677, printed by Sir T.
Phillipps, (Middle Hill, 1854, fol.). Harleian Society, vi. 1;
xxxix. 1137; xliii. 90. Visitatio Comitatus Wiltoniæ, 1623,
printed by Sir T. Phillipps. Abram's History of Blackburn, 589.
Notes and Queries, 1 S. ix. 105, 233, 458. The Visitations of
Devon, edited by J. L. Vivian, 1, 704. Burke's Colonial Gentry,
ii. 420. Oliver's History of Antigua, i. 1.
ABDY. Hasted's Kent, iii. 510. Morant's Essex, i. 177; ii. 152.
Berry's Essex Genealogies, 7. Jewitt's Reliquary, vii. 17. Visita-
tion of London, 1634, printed by Sir T. Phillipps, 1. Burke's
Landed Gentry, 2. Manning and Bray's Surrey, iii. 203. Wright's
Essex, ii. 411. Surrey Archæological Collections, vii. Harleian
Society, xiv. 627; xliii. 148. Wotton's English Baronetage, ii.
187; iii. 26. Betham's Baronetage, i. 390. Burke's Extinct
Baronetcies. Bysshe's Visitation of Essex, edited by J. J.
Howard, 3.
A BECKETT. Burke's Colonial Gentry, i. 145.
ABEELS. Harleian Society, xv. 1.
ABELL, or ABELLS. Morant's Essex, ii. 228, 230. Visitation of
London, 1634, printed by Sir T. Phillipps, 1. Lipscombe's His-
tory of the County of Buckingham, i. 164. Harleian Society,
xv. 2. Bysshe's Visitation of Essex, edited by J. J. Howard, 4.
ABERCROMBY. Burke's Commoners, iii. 1. Nisbet's Heraldry, ii.

1

app. 130. Walter Wood's East Neuk of Fife, 247. Wood's Douglas's Peerage of Scotland, i. 626. Brydges' Collins' Peerage, ix. 149. A short memoir of James Young, 21. Foster's Collectanea Genealogica, (MP's Scotland,) 1. Burke's Extinct Baronetcies. Northern Notes and Queries, x. 67.

ABERDEEN. *See* GORDON.

ABERGAVENNY. Hasted's Kent, ii. 196, 198, 269. Manning and Bray's Surrey, i. 577. Banks' Baronies in Fee. i. 97. Banks' Dormant and Extinct Baronage, ii. 1. *See* NEVILLE.

ABERGWILI. Dwnn's Visitations of Wales, i. 26, 97, 235.

ABERMAED. Dwnn's Visitations of Wales, i. 26, 51.

ABERMARLIES. Glamorganshire Pedigrees, edited by Sir T. Phillipps, 17.

ABERNETHY. Balmerino and its Abbey, by James Campbell, 389. Wood's Douglas's Peerage of Scotland, ii. 466. The Genealogist, New Series, xvii. 150 ; xviii. 16.

ABERNON. Surrey Archæological Collections, v. 53. *See* D'ABERNON.

AB HARRI. History of Powys Fadog, by J. Y. W. Lloyd, vi. 48.

ABINGDON. Visitation of Gloucestershire, 1583 and 1623, printed by Sir T. Phillipps, (1864, fol.) 1. Visitation of Gloucestershire, 1569, (Middle Hill, 1854, fol.) 1. (Earl of,) Burke's Royal Families, (London, 1851, 8vo.) ii. 135.

ABINGTON. Nash's Worcestershire, i. 588. Hutchins' Dorset, iv. 168. Harleian Society, xx. 5; xxi. 194; xxvii. 13. Weaver's Visitation of Herefordshire, 2. The Genealogist, New Series, ii. 219.

ABLETT. Burke's Landed Gentry, 2.

ABNET. Visitations of Staffordshire, 1614 and 1663-4. Williams's Salt Society, 1.

ABNEY. Harleian Society, ii. 153, 154; viii. 287. Nichols' History of the County of Leicester, iii. 1032. Burke's Commoners, i. 572, Landed Gentry, 2, 3, 4, 5, 6, 7, 8. Visitation of Staffordshire, 1663-4, printed by Sir Thos. Phillipps, 1. Stemmata Britannica, by Joseph Foster, (London, 1877, 8vo.) 1. The Genealogist, v. 87. Jewitt's Reliquary, xxii. 255. East Barnet, by F. C. Cass, Part i. 68.

ABNEY-HASTINGS. Burke's Landed Gentry, 5, 6.

ABOYNE. Claim of George Earl of Aboyne to title of Marquis of Huntley, etc., Sess. Papers, 197 of 1838.

ABRAHALL. Robinson's Mansions of Herefordshire, 124. Harleian Society, xv. 3; xxi. 201. Weaver's Visitation of Herefordshire, 2.

ABRAHAM, Foster's Lancashire Pedigrees. Stemmata Britannica, by Joseph Foster, (London, 1877, 8vo.) 1. Foster's Pedigree of the Forsters and Fosters, Part ii. 10.

ABRINCIS. Burke's Dormant and Extinct Baronage, i. 1.

ACHERLEY. Antiquities and Memoirs of the Parish of Myddle, written by Richard Gough, 1700, (fol.) 21.

ACHESON. Archdall's Lodge's Peerage, vi. 81. Foster's Collectanea Genealogica, (MP's Ireland,) 1 ; (Funeral Certificates, Ireland,) 1.

ACHMUTY. Burke's Commoners, iv. 734 ; Landed Gentry, 2.

ACHYM. Maclean's History of Trigg Minor, i. 291. The Visitations of Cornwall, edited by Lt.-Col. J. L. Vivian, 1.

ACKERS. Notices of the Family of Acres or Ackers, by J. P. Rylands, Liverpool, 1881, 8vo. Burke's Landed Gentry, (of Moreton Hall,) 2, 3, 4, 5, 6, 7, 8, (of Prinknash Park,) 5, 6, 7, 8.

ACKROYD. Burke's Landed Gentry, 7, 8.

ACLAM, ACCLOM, ACKLOM, or ACKLAM. Surtees Society, xli. 65. Poulson's Holderness, i. 334, 454. Foster's Visitations of Yorkshire, 109, 203. Harleian Society, xvi. 1, 368. Banks' Baronies in Fee, i. 40.

ACLAND. Hasted's Kent, i. 533. Collinson's Somerset, i. 256. Berry's Sussex Genealogies, 207. Tuckett's Devonshire Pedigrees, 153. Harleian Society, vi. 2-4. Visitation of Devonshire, 1620, printed by Sir T. Phillipps, (Middle Hill, fol.) 2. Stemmata Britannica, by Joseph Foster, (London, 1877, 8vo.) 2. An Historical Survey of Cornwall, by C. S. Gilbert, i. 559. Wotton's English Baronetage, ii. 407. Betham's Baronetage, ii. 28. Foster's Collectanea Genealogica, (MP's England,) 5. The Visitation of Devon, edited by J. L. Vivian, 3. Weaver's Visitations of Somerset, 93. Burke's Colonial Gentry, i. 357. Somersetshire Wills, printed from F. A. Crisp, ii. 86.

A'COMBE. See COMBE.

A'COURT. Hoare's Wiltshire, I. ii. 121. Betham's Baronetage, iv. 301. Foster's Collectanea Genealogica, (MP's England,) 8. Burke's Extinct Baronetcies.

ACTON. Bigland's Observations on Marriages, 31. Visitation of Gloucestershire, 1583 and 1623, printed by Sir T. Phillipps, (1864, folio) 2. Burke's Commoners, (of Wolverton,) iv. 686, Landed Gentry, 2, 3, 4, 5, 6, 7, 8, (of West Aston,) 2, 3, 4, 5, 6, 7, 8, (of Gatacre Park,) 3, 4, 5, 6, 7, 8, (of Acton Scott,) 7, 8. Stemmata Britannica, by Joseph Foster, (London, 1877, 8vo.) 2. Page's History of Suffolk, 581. Ormerod's Cheshire, ii. 124; iii. 582. The Sheriffs of Montgomeryshire, by H. V. Lloyd, 18, 87. Harleian Society, xv. 4; xxi. 1; xxvii. 3-8; xxviii. 7. Notes and Queries, 1 S. x. 265, 371. Wotton's English Baronetage, ii. 398. Betham's Baronetage, ii. 13. Foster's Collectanea Genealogica, (MP's England,) 11. Metcalfe's Visitations of Northamptonshire, 163. Visitation of Gloucester, edited by T. F. Fenwick and W. C. Metcalfe, 1. The Genealogist, New Series, vi. 77, 253; xiv. 257.

ADAIR. The Agnews of Lochnaw, by Sir A. Agnew, 616. Herald and Genealogist, iv. 552. Burke's Landed Gentry, (of Bellegrove,) 2, 3, 4, 5, 6; (of Heatherton Park,) 2, 3, 4, 5, 6, 7, 8, (of Loughanmore), 2, 3, 4, (of Rathdaire,) 7. Suckling's History of Suffolk, i. 201. Lands and their Owners in Galloway, by P. H. M'Kerlie, i. 91. Burke's Royal Families, (London, 1851, 8vo.) ii. 29.

ADAM. Cambridgeshire Visitation, edited by Sir T. Phillipps, 1. Burke's Landed Gentry, 2, 3, 4, 5, 6 and supp. Herald and Genealogist, viii. 129. Stemmata Britannica, by Joseph Foster,

(London, 1877, 8vo.) 3. Douglas's Baronage of Scotland, 255.
Paterson's History of Ayr and Wigton, iii. 476. Foster's Collec-
tanea Genealogica (MP's Scotland), 5. Harleian Society, xli. 99.
ADAMS. Pedigree of Adams of Paterchurch, Holyland, etc., co.
Pembroke, T. P. 1862. 3 pedigrees. Morant's Essex, ii. 571.
Dwnn's Visitations of Wales, i. 130, 131, 172. Surtees Society,
xxxvi. 17, 176, 268. Visitation of London, 1634, printed by Sir
T. Phillipps, 1. Blomfield's Norfolk, x. 461. Burke's Com-
moners, (of Ansty,) iv. 388, Landed Gentry, 2, 3, 4, 5, 6, 7, 8 ; (of
Bowdon,) Commoners, iv. 443, Landed Gentry, 2, 3, 4, 5, 6, 7 ;
(of Hollyland,) Commoners, iii. 630, Landed Gentry, 2, 3, 4, 5, 6,
7, 8 ; (of Northlands,) Landed Gentry, 3, 4, 5 and add., 6, 7, 8 ;
(of Jamesbrook,) 3, 4, 5, 6, 7, 8 ; (of Annagurrah,) 3, 4 ; (of
Clifton,) 5 supp. 7, 8 ; (of Shercock,) 6. See under Hyett in Landed
Gentry. More about Stifford, by W. Palin, 49. Cockayne
Memoranda, by A. E. Cockayne, (Congleton, 1873, 8vo.) at end.
Foster's Visitations of Yorkshire, 485. Burke's Royal Families,
(London, 1851, 8vo.) ii. 203. Harleian Society, viii. 188 ;
xiv. 537 ; xv. 5, 6 ; xxviii. 11, 14 ; xxxix. 931. Burke's
Royal Descents and Pedigrees of Founders' Kin, folding
table. Pembrokeshire Pedigrees, 151. Hunter's Deanery of
Doncaster, ii. 478. Baker's Northampton, i. 298, 459 ; ii.
52. Stemmata Britannica, by Joseph Foster, (London, 1877,
8vo.) 4-8. History of Ecclesfield, by J. Eastwood, 432.
T. Nicholas's County Families of Wales, 893. Foster's Lincolnshire Pedigrees, 1. Wotton's English Baronetage, iii. 29.
Burke's Extinct Baronetcies. The Visitations of Devon, edited by
J. L. Vivian, 9. Yorkshire Genealogist, i. 19. Burke's Colonial
Gentry, i. 149. Genealogical Records of the Family of Woodd,
46. Metcalfe's Visitations of Northamptonshire, 59. New England Register, vii. 39, 351 ; viii. 41 ; ix. 127 ; x. 89 ; xi. 53 ;
xiv. 360 ; xviii. 244 ; xxii. 20 ; xxxiii. 410 ; xliv. 209 ; xlviii.
190 ; xlix. 342. The Genealogist, New Series, x. 94. Family
Notes, by J. M. Browne, 9. Croston's edition of Baines's Lan-
caster, ii. 230. See GILL.
ADAMSON. Stemmata Britannica, by Joseph Foster, (London, 1877,
8vo.) 8. Burke's Landed Gentry, 6, 7, 8. The Parish of
Cramond, by J. P. Wood, 34. Harleian Society, xxxviii.
661.
ADCOCK. Bib. Top. Brit. ix. Part 4, 242-248. History of the
Wilmer Family, 205.
ADDENBROOKE. The Genealogist, i. 391. Burke's Landed Gentry,
6 supp., 7, 8. Genealogy of Henzey, Tyttery, and Tyzack, by
H. S. Grazebrook, 32.
ADDERLEY. Burke's Commoners, (of Hams Hall,) ii. 279, Landed
Gentry, 2, 3, 4, 5 ; (of Barlaston,) Commoners, ii. 281, Landed
Gentry, 2, 3, 4, 5, 6, 7, 8. Shaw's Staffordshire, i. 82. Visitation
of Staffordshire, 1663-4, printed by Sir Thos. Phillipps, 1. Dug-
dale's Warwickshire, 1096. Notes and Queries, 7 S. i. 486.
Harleian Society, xii. 263 ; xxxix. 1012. Stemmata Britannica,

by Joseph Foster, (London, 1877, 8vo.) 8. Visitations of Staffordshire, (Willm. Salt Soc.) 2, 4, 33.

ADDINGTON. Visitation of Devonshire, 1620, printed by Sir Thos.
Phillipps, (Middle Hill, fol.) 1. Wright's Essex, ii. 287. Foster's
Collectanea Genealogica, (MP's England,) 17. New England
Register, iv. 117.

ADDIS. Harleian Society. xv. 7.

ADDISON. Burke's Landed Gentry, 2. Surtees' Durham, i. 194.
Notes and Queries, 5 S. vi. 236, 349 ; vii. 31. Foster's Visitations of Northumberland, 4. Nicolson and Burn's Westmoreland
and Cumberland, i. 503.

ADDY. Notes and Queries, 6 S. xi. 272.

ADDYES. Burke's Commoners, iii. 666.

ADEY. Weaver's Visitation of Herefordshire, 44.

ADEANE. Burke's Landed Gentry, 2, 3, 4, 5, 6, 7, 8. Burke's Royal
Descents and Pedigrees of Founders' Kin, 82. Stemmata Britan-
nica, by Joseph Foster, (London, 1877, 8vo.) 9. Account of the
Mayo and Elton families, by C. H. Mayo, 149.

ADINGTON, or ADDINGTON. Morant's Essex, ii. 483. Harleian
Society, vi. 5. Brydges' Collins' Peerage, vi. 423. The Visitations of Devon, edited by J. L. Vivian, 10.

ADKINS Metcalfe's Visitations of Northamptonshire, 60.

ADLAM. Burke's Landed Gentry, 5, 6, 7, 8.

ADLER. Bysshe's Visitations of Essex, edited by J. J. Howard, 4.

ADLERCRON. Genealogy of Adlercron and D'arabin, privately printed
by Sir Thos. Phillipps, one page folio.

ADLINGTON. Burke's Landed Gentry, 5, 6, 7, 8. Chetham Society,
lxxxi. 70 ; lxxxii. 119 ; lxxxiv. 1 ; cx. 192. Croston's edition of
Baines's Lancaster, iv. 239.

ADWICK. Harleian Society, xl. 1267.

ADYE Hasted's Kent, ii. 694. Surrey Archæological Collections, x.
Harleian Society, xlii. 225 ; xliii. 131.

AELWARD. Genealogies of Morgan and Glamorgan, by G. T. Clark,
336.

AFFLECK. Betham's Baronetage, iv. app. 18.

AFFORDBY. Foster's Lincolnshire Pedigrees, 2. The Genealogist, iii.
337 ; iv. 262.

AGAR. Burke's Landed Gentry, 2. Stemmata Britannica, by Joseph
Foster, (London, 1877, 8vo.) 9. Archdall's Lodge's Peerage, vi.
74. Brydges' Collins' Peerage, viii. 362. Foster's Collectanea
Genealogica, (MP's Ireland,) 4. The Irish Builder, xxix. 155.

AGARD. Surtees Society, xxxvi. 217. Visitation of Derbyshire,
1663-4, (Middle Hill, 1854, fol.) 1. The Genealogist, iii. 61.

AGAR-ELLIS. Baker's Northampton, i. 199. The Ellis Correspondence, by G. A. Ellis, i. xxiii.

AGLIONBY. Gent. Mag., lxiv. 686, 799, 814 ; lxv. 367, 460, 475.
Burke's Commoners, (of Newbiggen Hall,) i. 524, Landed Gentry,
2 ; (of Nunnery,) Landed Gentry, 5 supp., 6, 7, 8. Hutchinson s
History of Cumberland, i. 195. Jefferson's History of Leath
Ward, Cumberland, 243. Harleian Society, xii. 329. Foster's

Collectanea Genealogica, (MP's England,) 22. Foster's Visitations of Cumberland and Westmorland, 1. Nicolson and Burn's Westmorland and Cumberland, ii. 327.

AGMONDESHAM. Visitation of Sussex, 1570, printed by Sir T. Phillipps, (Middle Hill, fol.) 1. Manning and Bray's Surrey, iii. 29. Harleian Society, xliii. 53. The Genealogist, New Series, xvii. 174.

AGNEW. The Agnews of Locknaw, by Sir Andrew Agnew, Bart., M.P., Edinburgh, 1864, 8vo. Burke's Royal Families, (London, 1851, 8vo.) i. 173. Lands and their Owners in Galloway, by P. H. M'Kerlie, i. 104, 140, 164. O'Hart's Irish Pedigrees, 2nd Series, 140. Foster's Collectanea Genealogica (MP's Scotland,) 7. Miscellanea Genealogica et Hereldica, New Series, iv. 5. Burke's Colonial Gentry, ii. 591. *See* VANS-AGNEW.

AGUILLON. Clutterbuck's Hertford, ii. 484. Castles, Mansions, and Manors of Western Sussex, by D. G. C. Elwes, and C. J. Robinson, 257. Burke's Dormant and Extinct Baronage, i. 2.

AIKEN. Burke's Landed Gentry, 8 supp.

AIKIN. Burke's Royal Families, (London, 1851, 8vo.) ii. 188. Harleian Society, xxxvii, 183.

AIKINS. Burke's Colonial Gentry, i. 200.

AIKMAN. Burke's Landed Gentry, 6, 7, 8. Douglas's Baronage of Scotland, 441. Alexander Nisbet's Heraldic Plates, 22.

AILESBURY. *See* AYLESBURY.

AILSA. Burke's Royal Families, (London, 1851, 8vo.) ii. 183. *See* KENNEDY.

AINSLIE. Burke's Landed Gentry, 6. 7, 8. Douglas's Baronage of Scotland, 300. The Parish of Cramond, by J. P. Wood, 22. Notes and Queries, 2 S. x. 133, 220. Betham's Baronetage, v. 592. Alexander Nisbet's Heraldic Plates, 102.

AINSWORTH. The Ainsworths of Smithills, by W. Brimelow. Bolton, 1881, 8vo. Burke's Landed Gentry, (of Smithills Hall,) 2, 3, 4, 5, 6, 7, 8 ; (of Spotland.) 2 supp. ; (of the Flosh,) 6, 7, 8. Chetham Society, lxxxi. 29 ; lxxxii. 83. Foster's Lancashire Pedigrees. Stemmata Britannica, by Joseph Foster, (London, 1877, 8vo.) 10. Abram's History of Blackburn, 386, 614, 623. Fishwick's History of Rochdale, 382.

AIRD. Paterson's History of the County of Ayr, ii. 426, 433. Paterson's History of Ayr and Wigton, i. 689, 702.

AIRLIE. Angus or Forfarshire, by A. J. Warden, 419-431. *See* OGILVY.

AIRMINE. *See* ARMIN.

AIRTH. Airth Papers (in reference to claim of R. B. Allardice to Earldom of Airth), by H. Gurney, London, 1839. *See* ALLARDICE, BARCLAY-ALLARDICE, STRATHERN.

AIRY, or AIREY. Stemmata Britannica, by Joseph Foster, (London, 1877, 8vo.) 10. Burke's Colonial Gentry, ii. 501. Burke's Family Records, 1. Howard's Visitation of England and Wales, vii. 116.

AISLABIE. A Genealogical Account of the Lords of Studley Royal, by J. R. Walbran. Burton's History of Hemingborough, 332. Harleian Society, xxxvii. 190.

AITCHISON. Stemmata Britannica, by Joseph Foster, (London, 1877, 8vo.) 10.

AITON. Inquiry into the Origin, Pedigree, and History, of the Family or Clan of Aiton, by William Aiton. Hamilton, 1830, 8vo. *See* AYTON.

AKERMAN. Burke's Colonial Gentry, ii. 778.

AKEROYD, or AKROYD. Pedigree of Akroyd, by H. E. Smith, 1878, 4to. Burke's Landed Gentry, 4 supp., 5, 6, 7. Foster's Yorkshire Pedigrees. Stemmata Britannica, by Joseph Foster, (London, 1877, 8vo.) 11. Foster's Visitations of Yorkshire, 485. Thoresby's Ducatus Leodiensis, 260. Harleian Society, xxxix. 1013. Annals of Smith of Balby, by H. E. Smith, 73. *See* ECROYD.

AKERS. Burke's Landed Gentry, 2, 3, 4, 5, 6, 7, 8. Stemmata Britannica, by Joseph Foster, (London, 1877, 8vo.) 11.

AKNEY. The Genealogist, iii. 62.

ALABASTER. Visitation of Devon, edited by F. T. Colby, 1. Musketts Suffolk Manorial Families, i. 49-55.

ALAN. Fisher's History of Masham, 209. Manx Society, x. app. A. Munfords Analysis of Domesday Book of Co. Norfolk, 11, 12. *See* ALLAN.

ALBANY. Harleian Society, i. 48; xvi. 336; xix. 73; xxi. 2; xxviii. 14; xliii. 25. Surrey Archæological Collections, iv. Manning and Bray's Surrey, iii. 141. *See* DE ALBANY.

ALBEMARLE. Hasted's Kent, (Hund. of Blackheath, by H. H. Drake,) xxvi. Morant's Essex, ii. 317. Whitaker's History of Craven, st edn., 212. History of Lambeth, by Thos. Allen, 274. Collectanea Topographica et Genealogica, vi. 264. Poulson's Holderness, i. 24, 37; ii. 351. Whitaker's Deanery of Craven, 212. Manning and Bray's Surrey, iii. 496. Baker's Northampton, i. 672. Jones's History of Harewood, 27. *See* AUMERLE, DE ALBEMAILE.

ALBERT, HR.H. PRINCE. Burke's Heraldic Illustrations, Pl. 1.

ALBIN. Fishwick's History of Bispham, 55.

ALBINI. East Anglian, ii. 43, 55, 69, 86, 100, etc. Fisher's History of Masham, 210. Berry's Buckinghamshire Genealogies, 65. Berry's Essex Genealogies, 67. History of Castle and Town of Arundel by M. A. Tierney, 168. Lipscombe's History of the County of Buckingham, i. 455. Blore's Rutland, 114. Nichols' History of the County of Leicester, ii. 27. Memorials of the Church of Attleborough, by J. T. Barrett, 12, 179. Banks' Dormant and Extinct Baronage, i. 3, 7. Berry's Genealogical Peerage 86. Notes and Queries, 6 S. iv. 114. History of the House of Arundel, by J. P. Yeatman, 154. R. Ussher's Historical Sketch of Croxall, 170. The Genealogist, New Series, ix. 80; xv. 219 *See* ARUNDEL, DE ALBINI.

ALCHORNE. Berry's Sussex Genealogies, 96. Berry's Kent Genealogies, 176. Harleian Society, xlii. 85.

ALCOCK, or ALCOCKE. Berry's Sussex Genealogies, 108. Visitation of London, 1634, printed by Sir T. Phillipps, 1. Burke's Landed Gentry, (of Wilton,) 2, 3, 4, 5, 6, 7, 8; (of Kingswood Warren,)

2, 3, 4 ; (of Ballynoe,) 4. Burke's Heraldic Register, (published
with St. James's Magazine,) 57. Dallaway's Sussex, i. 219.
Stemmata Britannica, by Joseph Foster, (London, 1877, 8vo.) 12.
Harleian Society, xv. 11, 14. Foster's Collectanea Genealogica,
(MP's Ireland,) 6. New England Register, xxxvi. 400.

ALCOCK-STAWELL. Burke's Landed Gentry, 3, 4, 5, 6, 7, 8.

ALDAM. Foster's Yorkshire Pedigrees. Stemmata Britannica, by
Joseph Foster, (London, 1877, 8vo.) 12. Burke's Landed Gentry,
5, 6, 7, 8. Harleian Society, xxxix. 1089. Pease of Darlington, by
Joseph Foster, 16. Annals of Smith of Balby, by H. E. Smith, 17.

ALDBOROUGH. See STRATFORD.

ALDBURGH, or ALDEBURGH. Foster's Visitations of Yorkshire, 279.
Plantagenet-Harrison's History of Yorkshire, i. 508. Harleian
Society, xvi. 2. Banks' Baronies in Fee, i. 38.

ALDELYME. Ormerod's Cheshire, iii. 465.

ALDEN. Harleian Society, xxii. 25. New England Register, li. 427 ;
lii. 54, 162, 362, 435.

ALDER. Raine's History of North Durham, 301. The Genealogist,
ii. 251 ; New Series, vii. 180. Foster's Visitations of Northumberland, 5.

ALDERFORD. Harleian Society, xii. 59 ; xxvii. 8.

ALDERLEY. Ormerod's Cheshire, iii. 582.

ALDERNE. Account of the Mayo and Elton Families, by C. H. Mayo,
141.

ALDERSEY. The Family of Aldersey of Aldersey and Spurstow, by
C. G. O. Bridgeman. London, 1899, 8vo. Hasted's Kent, ii. 585.
Berry's Kent Genealogies, 290. Harleian Society, i. 32 ; xv. 8 ;
xviii. 13, 14 ; xlii. 160. Ormerod's Cheshire, ii. 73). Burke's
Commoners, i. 99 ; Landed Gentry, 2, 3, 4, 5, 6, 7, 8. Stemmata
Britannica, by Joseph Foster, (London, 1877, 8vo.) 13

ALDERSON. Stemmata Britannica, by Joseph Foster, (London, 1877,
8vo.) 13. Pedigrees of the Leading Families of Lancashire, published by Joseph Foster, (London, 1872, fol.). Plantagenet-Harrison's History of Yorkshire, i. 332. Harleian Society, xxxviii. 701.

ALDHAM. Visitation of Norfolk, published by Norfolk Arhæological
Society, i. 122. Baker's Northampton, i. 432. Harlean Society,
xxxii. 2. The Genealogist, New Series, xiii. 179.

ALDITHLEY. Erdeswicke's Survey of Staffordshire, 9℄. Banks'
Dormant and Extinct Baronage, ii. 6. See AUDLEY.

ALDOUS. Muskett's Suffolk Manorial Families, i. 388.

ALDRED. Harleian Society, xxxvii. 19. Old Yorkshir, ed. by
Willm. Smith, New Series, iii. 190. See ALURED.

ALDRICH-BLAKE. Stemmata Britannica, by Joseph Foster, (London,
1877, 8vo.) 13. Burke's Landed Gentry, 7, 8.

ALDRICHE. Visitations of Staffordshire, 1614 and 1663-4 William
Salt Society, 5. Harleian Society, xxxii. 2, 4.

ALDRIDGE. Castles, Manors, and Mansions of Western Sussex, by
D. G. C. Elwes and C. J. Robinson, 28. Burke's Landed Gentry,
5, 6, 7, 8. Howard's Visitation of England and Wales, vii. 67.
Stemmata Britannica, by Joseph Foster, (London, 1877, 8vo.) 14.

ALDWARK. Hunter's Deanery of Doncaster, ii. 52.

ALDWORTH. Burke's Landed Gentry, 2 supp., 3, 4, 5, 6, 7, 8.
Visitations of Berkshire, printed by Sir Thos. Phillipps, 1.
Stemmata Britannica, by Joseph Foster, (London, 1877, 8vo.) 14.
The Genealogist, v. 225, 226. Foster's Collectanea Genealogica,
(MP's Ireland,) 7. Miscellanea Genealogica et Heraldica, New
Series, iv. 173.

ALEIGH. Visitation of Cornwall, edited by Sir N. H. Nicholas, 1.
Harleian Society, ix. 1. See LEIGH.

ALEN. Burke's Commoners, ii. 363. Burke's Extinct Baronetcies,
599.

ALESBURY, or ALESBURYE. Berry's Buckinghamshire Genealogies,
20. Dugdale's Warwickshire, 671. See AYLESBURY.

ALEXANDER. Claim of Willm. Alexander to the Earldom of Stirling,
Sess. Papers, May 1760—March 1762. An Analytical Statement
of the Case of Alexander, Earl of Sterling and Doran, by Sir T. C.
Banks, London, 1832, 8vo. Case of the Rt. Hon. Alexander,
Earl of Stirling, by F. J. Burn, London, 1833, 8vo. Narrative
of the Proceedings to overthrow the Earl of Stirling,[1] etc., by
E. Lockhart, Esq., Edinburgh, 1836, 4to. The Stirling Peerage,
Trial of Alexander Humphreys, or Alexander, styling himself Earl
of Stirling, for Forgery, edited by W. B. D. D. Turnbull, Esq.,
Edinburgh, 1839, 8vo. Report of the Trial by Archibald Swinton,
Esq., Edinburgh, 1839, 8vo. Memorials of the Earl of Stirling
and of the House of Alexander, by the Rev. C. Rogers, Edinburgh,
1877, 2 vols., 8vo. Alexander, Earl of Stirling; original case of
the Appellant, and appendix. Reprinted, 1867, London, 4to. The
Respondent's Case. Reprinted, Edinburgh, 1867, 4to. Supplemental Case of the Appellant, London, n. d. 4to. Supplemental
Case for the Respondents. Edinburgh, 1868, 4to. Morant's Essex,
i. 129, 132. Hasted's Kent, iii. 84. Herald and Genealogist, iv.
554. Burke's Commoners, (of Powis,) ii. 170, Landed Gentry, 2,
3; (of Ahilly,) 4, 5, 6, 7, 8; (of Boydstone), 3 supp., 4, 5, 6; (of
Westerton), 4, 5, 6, 7, 8; (of Ballochmyle,) 4 and supp., 5, 6 and
supp., 7; (of Milford,) 5, 6, 7. 8; (of Holwood,) 6. Hampshire
Visitations, printed by Sir T. Phillipps, 1. Stemmata Britannica,
by Joseph Foster, (London, 1877, 8vo.) 15-20. Wright's Essex, ii.
332. Paterson's History of the Co. of Ayr, ii. 336. The
Genealogist, ii. 196, Paterson's History of Ayr and Wigton, i. 553,
668; ii. 224; iii. app. 531. Burke's Extinct Baronetcies, 617.
Walter Wood's East Neuk of Fife, 277. Bigland's Gloucestershire, ii. par. Sapperton. Wood's Douglas's Peerage of Scotland,
ii. 535. Foster's Collectanea Genealogica, (MP's Ireland,) 8.
Notes and Queries, 5 S. ii. 27. Nicholl's account of the Company
of Ironmongers, 2nd edn., 613. Harleian Society, xviii. 14.
Genealogical Record of King and Henham, 16. Howard's Visitation of Ireland, iii. 69. See ALLEXANDER.

ALEYN. Harleian Society, vi. 5; xiii. 133, 333; xv. 9, 10. Visita-

---

[1] This work was published in French at the same time.

tion of Devonshire, 1620, printed by Sir Thos. Phillipps, (Middle
Hill, fol.) 1. The Visitations of Devon, edited by J. L. Vivian,
11. Bysshe's Visitation of Essex, edited by J. J. Howard, 5. *See*
ALLEYN.

ALFORD. Berry's Buckinghamshire Genealogies, 82. Berry's Sussex
Genealogies, 302. Foster's Visitations of Yorkshire, 486. Collec-
tanea Topographica et Genealogica, iv. 177. Dallaway's Sussex,
II. ii. 30. Poulson's Holderness, ii. 315. Visitations of Berk-
shire, printed by Sir Thos. Phillipps, 1. Harleian Society, xv. 11.
Miscellanea Genealogica et Heraldica, 2nd Series, i. 208.

ALFOUNDER. Nichol's History of the County of Leicester, iii. 1049.
Bysshe's Visitation of Essex, edited by J. J. Howard, 5, 6.

ALFREY. Berry's Sussex Genealogies, 244. *See* ALLFREY.

ALGER. New England Register, xxxi. 101.

ALIBOND. Harleian Society, viii. 407.

ALICOCK. Metcalfe's Visitations of Northamptonshire, 60.

ALINGTON. Cambridgeshire Visitation, edited by Sir. T. Phillipps, 2.
Visitation of Suffolk, edited by J. J. Howard, ii. 182. Burke's
Commoners, i. 570, Landed Gentry, 2, 3, 4, 5, 6, 7, 8. Clutter-
buck's Hertford, ii. 541. Stemmata Britannica, by Joseph Foster,
(London, 1877, 8vo.) 21. Chauncy's Hertfordshire, 363. Suffolk
Institute of Archæology, iv. 111. Bank's Dormant and Extinct
Baronage, iii. 7. The Genealogist, v. 187. Howard's Visitation
of England and Wales, vii. 28. *See* ALLINGTON.

ALIS. *See* ELLIS.

ALISON, or ALLISON. Burke's Royal Descents and Pedigrees of
Founders' Kin, 28. Burke's Colonial Gentry, i. 223. Stemmata
Britannica, by Joseph Foster, (London, 1877, 8vo.) 26. Foster's
Visitations of Cumberland and Westmoreland, 2.

ALKIN. Burke's Landed Gentry, 2.

ALKINGTON. Harleian Society, xxviii. 15.

ALKSTEDE. Manning and Bray's Surrey, ii. 258.

ALLAN. Parentalia Memoranda ; Lineage of the Allans of Staffordshire, Hyltons of Westmoreland, Clervaux and Chaytor families
of Croft in Richmondshire, by W. H. Longstaffe, Esq., Newcastle-
on-Tyne, 1852, 8vo. Wills of several members of the Family of
Allan of Darlington. Privately printed at the Darlington Press,
4to. Some Old Families, by H. B. McCall, 3. Burke's Family
Records, 2. Ontarian Families, by E. M. Chadwick, i. 79.
Burke's Commoners, i. 39. Landed Gentry, 2, 3, 4, 5, 6, 7.
Foster's Yorkshire Pedigrees. Burke's Heraldic Illustrations, 2,
109. History of Darlington, by W. Hylton Dyer Longstaffe, not
paged, and iii—xxxii. Burke's Authorized Arms, 2. Ord's
History of Cleveland, 499. Burke's Royal Families, (London,
1851, 8vo.) i. 67 ; ii. 15. Surtees' Durham, iii. 373. Stemmata
Britannica, by Joseph Foster, (London, 1877, 8vo.) 22. *See*
ALAN.

ALLANBY. Burke's Landed Gentry, 7, 8. Howard's Visitation of
England and Wales, viii. 17.

ALLANSON, or ALLENSON. Surtees Society, xxxvi. 230. W. Paver's

Pedigrees of Families of the City of York, 7. Burke's Landed Gentry, 2. Harleian Society, xv. 12 ; xxxix. 937.

ALLARDICE, or ALLARDYCE. Case of Robert Barclay Allardice, claiming the title of Earl of Airth. Folio, pp. 10, and pedigree, 1838. Appendix to this Case. Folio, pp. 15, 1838. Claim of R. B. Allardice, Esq., to be Earl of Airth. Sess. Papers, 162 of 1839. Burke's Royal Families, (London, 1851, 8vo.) ii. 33. A short Memoir of James Young, app. 19. *See* AIRTH.

ALLAUNSON. Harleian Society, i. 96.

ALLCROFT. Burke's Landed Gentry, 6, 7, 8. Howard's Visitation of England and Wales, viii. 58.

ALLEN. Pedigrees of Allen of Cresselly, Co. Pembroke, and of Gellyswick, etc., Co. Pembroke, T.P., 1863, 1864, 1865, 6 folio pages. Hasted's Kent, ii. 247*, 568, 605. Gent. Mag., 1847, i. 370. Visitation of Somerset, printed by Sir T. Phillipps, 2 Berry's Buckinghamshire Genealogies, 5. Berry's Sussex Genealogies, 361. Berry's Kent Genealogies, 76, 192. Cambridgeshire Visitation, edited by Sir T. Phillipps, 1. Harleian Society, i. 6, 53 ; ii. 109, 195 ; xi. 2 ; xv. 3 ; xxviii. 16 ; xxxvii. 207 ; xlii. 16. Chetham Society, lxxxiv. 2. Hampshire Visitations, printed by Sir T. Phillipps, 1. Burke's Landed Gentry, 2 supp. p. 195 ; (of Cresselly,) 2, 3, 4, 5, 6, 7, 8 ; (of Bicton,) 2, 3, 4, 5, 6, 7, 8 ; (of the Rhydd,) 5 ; (of Clifford Priory,) 5, 6, 7, 8 ; (of Inchmartine,) 5, 6 ; (of Hoyland,) 2 ; (of Bathampton,) 6, 7, 8 ; (of Lyngford,) 7, 8 ; (of Robeston,) 7, 8. Visitation of Staffordshire, 1663-4, printed by Sir T. Phillipps, 1. Visitations of Berkshire, printed by Sir Thos. Phillipps, 2. Visitation of Derbyshire, 1663-4, (Middle Hill, 1854, fol.) 1. Nichols' History of the County of Leicester, iv. 163, 804. Visitation of London in Transactions of the London and Middlesex Archæological Society, 26. Stemmata Britannica, by Joseph Foster, (London, 1877, 8vo.) 22, 24. Notices of Great Yarmouth, by J. H. Druery, 167. The Genealogist, iii. 62, 338 ; v. 226. Foley's Records of the English Province, S. J., ii. 133. Foster's Lincolnshire Pedigrees, 3. An Historical Survey of Cornwall, by C. S. Gilbert, ii. 1. O'Hart's Irish Pedigrees, 2nd Series, 141. The Tyldesley Diary, edited by J. Gillow and A. Hewitson, 143. Eastwood's History of Ecclesfield, 430. Burke's Extinct Baronetcies. Omerod's Cheshire, iii. 374. Archdall's Lodge's Peerage, v. 181. Foster's Collectanea Genealogica, (MP's Ireland,) 10. Metcalfe's Visitations of Suffolk, 84, 179. Notes and Queries, 3 S. ix. 488 ; 5 S. vi. 171 ; 6 S. iv. 33. New England Register, x. 225 ; xxv. 144 ; xxx. 444 ; li. 152, 212. Visitations of Staffordshire, 1614 and 1633-4. William Salt Society, 6. Burke's Colonial Gentry, ii. 563. Oliver's History of Antigua, i. 5. Howard's Visitation of England and Wales, v. 72. The Genealogical Magazine, i. 23. Family Records, by Charlotte Sturge, 4-68. Sussex Archæological Collections, xxx. 249. *See* HARDWICKE.

ALLENBY. Burke's Landed Gentry, 6.

ALLENSON. The Genealogist, New Series, xv. 47.

ALLERTON. New England Register, viii. 270 ; xliv. 290.

ALLESTRY. Visitation of Derbyshire, 1663-4, (Middle Hill, 1854, fol.) 1. The Genealogist, iii. 61. Foster's Collectanea Genealogica, (MP's England,) 34. Harleian Society, xxxix. 1038.

ALLETT. Visitation of Somerset, printed by Sir T. Phillipps, 3. Harleian Society, xi. 2.

ALLEXANDER. Berry's Hampshire Genealogies, 316. *See* ALEXANDER.

ALLEY. Harleian Society, xxi. 1.

ALLEYN, or ALLEYNE. Morant's Essex, i. 180, 343 ; ii. 99, 131. Surrey Archæological Collections, ii. Burke's Landed Gentry, 2 corr., p. 426. Jewitt's Reliquary, xiv. 64 ; xv. 253 ; xx. 256 ; xxii. 256 ; xxiii. 208 ; xxiv. 108. Hampshire Visitations, printed by Sir T. Phillipps, 1. Visitatio Comitatus Wiltoniæ, 1623, printed by Sir T. Phillipps. Wright's Essex, i. 209, 245. Harleian Society, xiii. 333 ; xxxix. 1032 ; xliii. 144. Wotton's English Baronetage, ii. 150. Betham's Baronetage, iii. 363. The Rector's of Loughborough, by W. G. D. Fletcher, 27. Burke's Extinct Baronetcies. Miscellanea Genealogica et Heraldica, 3rd Series, i. 147. *See* ALEYN.

ALLFREY. Burke's Landed Gentry, 2 supp., 3, 4, 5, 6, 7, 8. Stemmata Britannica, by Joseph Foster, (London, 1877, 8vo.) 25. *See* ALFREY.

ALLGOOD. Burke's Landed Gentry, 2, 3, 4, 5, 6, 7, 8. Stemmata Britannica, by Joseph Foster, (London. 1877, 8vo.) 25.

ALLHUSEN. Stemmata Britannica, by Joseph Foster, (London, 1877, 8vo.) 25. Burke's Landed Gentry, 7, 8.

ALLIN. Berry's Berkshire Genealogies, 103. Page's History of Suffolk, 327. Burke's Extinct Baronetcies. Wotton's English Baronetage, iv. 80.

ALLINGTON. The Topographer, (London, 1789-91, 8vo.) i. 187. Nichols' History of the County of Leicester, iv. 468. Foster's Lincolnshire Pedigrees, 4. Harleian Society, xli. 14. *See* ALINGTON.

ALLISTON. Herald and Genealogist, v. 401.

ALLIX. Burke's Commoners, (of Willoughby,) i. 482, Landed Gentry, 2, 3, 4, 5, 6, 7, 8 ; (of Swaffham,) 2, 3, 4, 5, 6, 7, 8. Stemmata Britannica, by Joseph Foster, (London, 1877, 8vo.) 26. Foster's Lincolnshire Pedigrees, 6. Howard's Visitation of England and Wales, viii. 137.

ALLOTT. Burke's Landed Gentry, 2 supp., 3, 4, 5, 6, 7. Hunter's Deanery of Doncaster, ii. 366, 450. Stemmata Britannica, by Joseph Foster, (London, 1877, 8vo.) 27. Foster's Lincolnshire Pedigrees, 2. Harleian Society, xxxviii. 494, 498.

ALLOWAY. Herald and Genealogist, v. 78. Burke's Landed Gentry, 2 supp., 3, 4, 5, 6. Burke's Heraldic Illustrations, 100.

ALLSOP, ALSOP, or ALSOPP. J. H. Hill's History of Langton, 63. Jewitt's Reliquary, vii. 17 ; xii. 127, 188. Glover's History of Derbyshire, ii. 21. Burke's Landed Gentry, 5, 6. Harleian Society, ii. 105 ; xxxix. 984, 1038. Visitation of Derbyshire, 1663-4, (Middle Hill, 1854, fol.) 1. Nichols' History of the

County of Leicester, ii. 694*; iv. 802. Stemmata Britannica, by Joseph Foster, (London, 1877, 8vo.) 27. The Genealogist, iii. 63 ; New Series, vii. 1. New England Register, xliv. 92.

ALLYSONN. Harleian Society, vii. 26. *See* ALISON.

ALMACK. Stemmata Britannica, by Joseph Foster, (London, 1877, 8vo.) 28.

ALMAN. Berry's Sussex Genealogies, 81. Carthew's Hundred of Launditch, Part ii. 702.

ALMER, or ALMOR. Dwnn's Visitations of Wales, ii. 355. *See* AYLMER.

ALMERY. Foster's Lincolnshire Pedigrees, 8. Harleian Society, xv. 15.

ALMEY. Metcalfe's Visitations of Northamptonshire, 61.

ALMONT. Oxford Historical Society, xxiv. 133.

ALNO. Succinct Genealogies of the Ancient Houses of Alno or De Alneto, Broc of Shephale, Latimer of Duntish, Drayton of Drayton, Mauduit of Werminster, Greene of Drayton, Vere of Addington, Fitz-Lewes of West Hornedon, Howard of Effingham, and Mordaunt of Turvey, by Rob. Halstead. London, 1685, folio. Baker's Northampton, ii. 44. *See* DE ALNO.

ALPE. Hawes' (Loders') History of Framlingham, 401. Carthew's Hundred of Launditch, Part iii. 188.

ALPHE. Berry's Hampshire Genealogies, 247. Hampshire Visitations, printed by Sir T. Phillipps, 1.

ALPHEGH. A Royal Descent, by T. E. Sharpe, (London, 1875, 4to.) 123.

ALPORT, or ALLPORT. Visitation of Staffordshire, 1663-4, printed by Sir T. Phillipps, 1. Ormerod's Cheshire, ii. 668. Miscellanea Genealogica et Heraldica, New Series, iii. 288, 290. Harleian Society, xv. 15. Visitations of Staffordshire, 1614 and 1663-4. William Salt Society, 7. Burke's Landed Gentry, 7, 8.

ALPRAM. Harleian Society, xviii. 15.

ALSAGER. Omerod's Cheshire, iii. 322.

ALSPATH. Dugdale's Warwickshire, 985. The Genealogist, New Series, x. 137 ; xvii. 19.

ALSTANTON. The Genealogist, New Series, xv. 221.

ALSTON. Hasted's Kent, ii. 538. East Barnet, by F. C. Cass, Part i. 84. Berry's Hertfordshire Genealogies, 217. Burke's Landed Gentry, (of Elmdon,) 3, 4, 5, 6, 7, 8 ; (of Odell Castle,) 6, 7, 8. Harleian Society, viii. 109-111 ; xiii. 335 ; xv. 16 ; xix. 74. Stemmata Britannica, by Joseph Foster, (London, 1877, 8vo.) 28. Page's History of Suffolk, 120, 938, 957. Wotton's English Baronetage, ii. 309 ; iii. 698. Burke's Extinct Baronetcies. Bysshe's Visitation of Essex, edited by J. J. Howard, 6. History of Chipping, by Tom C. Smith, 234. Growse's History of Bildeston.

ALTA RIPA. Berry's Buckinghamshire Genealogies, 38. Lipscombe's History of the County of Buckingham, ii. 192. Whitaker's Deanery of Craven, 3rd edn., 116.

ALTHAM. Morant's Essex, i. 24, 405 ; ii. 60, 488. Berry's Hertford-

shire Genealogies, 172. Burke's Landed Gentry, 5 supp., 6, 7, 8.
Clutterbuck's Hertford, i. 248. Whitaker's History of Whalley,
ii. 268. Stemmata Britannica, by Joseph Foster, (London, 1877,
8vo.) 28. Harleian Society, xiv. 538. Burke's Royal Families,
(edn. of 1876,) 212. Hasted's Kent, (Hund. of Blackheath, by
H. H. Drake,) 248. Miscellanea Genealogica et Heraldica, 2nd
Series, v. 62. Bysshe's Visitation of Essex, edited by J. J.
Howard, 7.

ALUNTON. History of P.owys Fadog, by J. Y. W. Lloyd, iii. 220.

ALURED. Foster's Visitations of Yorkshire, 144. Foster's Collectanea
Genealogica, (MP's England,) 39. Yorkshire Genealogist, i. 1-12,
93. Harleian Society, xxxix. 991.

ALWENT. The Antiquities of Gainford, by J. R. Walbran, 50.
Surtees' Durham, iv. 24.

ALWAY. Harleian Society, xix. 1.

ALWIN. Berry's Sussex Genealogies, 167.

ALYBURTON. Fosbrooke's History of Gloucestershire, ii. 175, 181.

ALYE. Visitation of Gloucestershire, 1583, and 1623, printed by Sir
T. Phillipps, (1864, fol.) 2. Herald and Genealogist, vi. 223.
Hutchins' Dorset, iii. 546. Harleian Society, xx. 5; xxi. 2.
The Genealogist, New Series, ii. 219. See HARWARD.

AMADAS, or AMADYS. Visitation of Devon, edited by F. T. Colby,
2. The Visitations of Devon, edited by J. L. Vivian, 12. Hasted's
Kent, (Hund. of Blackheath, by H. H. Drake,) xxii.

AMBLER. Lincolnshire Notes and Queries, i. 235. Foster's Lincolnshire Pedigrees, 8.

AMBROSE. Morant's Essex, i. 194. Chetham Society, lxxxi. 64;
lxxxiv. 3; cv. 156; New Series, xxv. 183, 185. Local Gleanings,
July 1879—June 1880, (all published,) 99. Bardsley's Registers
of Ulveston, liv.

AMCOATS, AMCOTES, or AMCOTTS. Burke's Landed Gentry, 4, 5, 6,
7, 8. Read's History of the Isle of Axholme, edited by T. C.
Fletcher, 384. Surtees' Durham, i. 197. Stemmata Britannica,
by Joseph Foster, (London, 1877, 8vo.) 29. Memoirs of the
Family of Chester, by R. E. C. Waters, 652. Foster's Lincolnshire Pedigrees, 10. The Genealogist, iii. 339; v. 187. Notes
and Queries, 1 S. viii. 387, 518.

AMERDITH. Harleian Society, vi. 6. Visitation of Devonshire, 1620,
printed by Sir Thos. Phillipps, (Middle Hill, fol.) 4. Westcote's
Devonshire, edited by G. Oliver and Pitman Jones, 596. The
Visitations of Devon, edited by J. L. Vivian, 13.

AMERY. Burke's Landed Gentry, 2, 3, 4. Harleian Society, xiii.
393. See DAMER.

AMES. Genealogical Memoranda of the Family of Ames. By Reginald
Ames. London, 1889, 4to. Burke's Landed Gentry, 2, 3, 4, 5,
6, 7, 8. Cussans' History of Hertfordshire, Parts xi. and xii. 234.
Stemmata Britannica, by Joseph Foster, (London, 1877, 8vo.) 29.
Antiquities and Memoirs of the Parish of Myddle, written by
Richard Gough, 1700, (fol.) 55. The Genealogist, ii. 273. Gene-
alogical Gleanings in England, by H. F. Waters, 279. Johnson's

Typographia, ii. 246.   New England Register, xvi. 255 ; xlii. 270.
A History of Banking in Bristol, by C. H. Cave, 212.
AMESON. Earwaker's History of Sandbach, 222.
AMEY. J. B. Payne's Armorial of Jersey, 26.
AMHERST, or AMHURST. Hasted's Kent, i. 353 ; ii. 143, 145, 358.
Berry's Sussex Genealogies, 212.   Berry's Kent Genealogies, 191,
494.   Burke's Landed Gentry, 3, 4, 5, 6.   Edmondson's Baronagium
Genealogicum, vi. 67.   Miscellanea Genealogica et Heraldica, 2nd
Series, ii. 97.   Brydges' Collins' Peerage, viii. 161.   Burke's
Colonial Gentry, ii. 515.   See TYSSEN-AMHURST.
AMNEVILLE. Herald and Genealogist, iv. 194.
AMORY. New England Register, x. 59.   Tuckett's Devonshire
Pedigrees, 23.   Visitation of London, 1634, printed by Sir T
Phillipps, 2.   Harleian Society, vi. 7.   The Visitations of Devon,
edited by J. L. Vivian, 15.
AMOS. Burke's Landed Gentry, 2 supp., 3.   Stemmata Britannica,
by Joseph Foster, (London, 1877, 8vo.) 30.
AMPHLETT. Pedigree of Amphlett of Hadsor and Clent, 1872, 4to.
Nash's Worcestershire, i. 481.   Burke's Landed Gentry, 2, 3, 4,
5, 6, 7, 8.   Burke's Royal Families, (London, 1851, 8vo.) i. 135.
Stemmata Britannica, by Joseph Foster, (London, 1877, 8vo.) 30.
Visitations of Staffordshire, 1614 and 1663-4, William Salt Society,
8.   Howard's Visitation of England and Wales, i. 152 ; iii. 156 ;
iv. 50.
AMSDEN. New England Register, xv. 21.
AMSON. Earwaker's History of Sandbach, 274.
AMUNDEVILL. Thoroton's Nottinghamshire, i. 360.
AMY, or AMYE. Cambridgeshire Visitation, edited by Sir T. Phillipps,
3.   Maclean's History of Trigg Minor, i. 652.   Harleian Society,
xli. 61.
AMYAND. Bethan's Baronetage, iii. 314.   Miscellanea Genealogica
et Heraldica, New Series, iv. 180.
AMYOT. Miscellanea Genealogica et Heraldica, 3rd Series, ii. 26.
AMYS, or AMYCE. Harleian Society, xiii. 19.
ANCASTER. Case upon the Petition of his Grace the Duke of Ancaster
and Lord Robert Bertie concerning the office of Lord Great
Chamberlain of England, 1780, fol., pp. 4.
ANCKETILL. See ANKETELL.
ANDERDON. Oliver's History of Antigua, ii. 234.
ANDERSON. Berry's Essex Genealogies, 19.   Pedigrees from Visitation of Northumberland, printed by Sir T. Phillipps, (Middle Hill,
1858, fol.) 1.   Lipscombe's History of the County of Buckingham,
i. 325.   Burke's Landed Gentry, (of Grace Dieu,) 2 supp., 3, 4, 5,
6, 7, 8 ; (of Jesmond House,) 2, 3, 4 ; (of Havering Grange,) 2 ;
(of Little Harle Tower,) 6, 7, 8.   Account of the Parish of Lea
with Lea Wood, (London, 1841, 8vo.) 17.   Surtees' Durham, i.
98, 122 ; ii. 269.   Clutterbuck's Hertford, i. 285.   The Genealogist, i. 380 ; ii. 220 ; v. 205.   Stemmata Britannica, by Joseph
Foster, (London, 1877, 8vo.) 32.   Foster's Lincolnshire Pedigrees,
9, 12.   Harleian Society, xiv. 631 ; xvi. 4 ; xxii. 109.   Notes and

Queries, 2 S. viii. 515. Burke's Extinct Baronetcies. Brydges'
Collins' Peerage, viii. 393. Wotton's English Baronetage, ii. 384 ;
iii. 191, 427. Betham's Baronetage, ii. 177 ; iv. 390. Foster's
Collectanea Genealogica, (MP's England,) 46. Massingherd's
History of Ormsby, 241. Foster's Visitations of Northumberland,
5, 6. New England Register, xliii. 198. Ilkley, Ancient and
Modern, by R. Collyer, and J. H. Turner, 207. Oliver's History
of Antigua, i. 7.

ANDERTON. Kent's British Banner Displayed, 725. Burke's Commoners, i. 607. Landed Gentry, 2, 3, 4, 5, 6, 7, 8. Foster's Lancashire Pedigrees. Burke's Royal Families, (London, 1851, 8vo.) ii.
148. Lydiate Hall and its Associations, by Rev. T. E. Gibson,
(1876, 4to.) 49, 165. Chetham Society, lxxxiv. 4-7. Thoresby's
Ducatus Leodiensis, 184. Baines's History of the Co. of Lancaster, iii. 452 ; Croston's edn., iv. 175, 241. Stemmata Britannica, by Joseph Foster, (London, 1877, 8vo.) 32. Foley's Records
of the English Province, S. J. iii. 744 ; iv. 713. Wotton's English
Baronetage, iii. 632. Burke's Extinct Baronetcies. Historic
Society of Lancashire and Cheshire, New Series, vi. 181.

ANDRÉ. Betham's Baronetage, iv. app. 16. Burke's Extinct
Baronetcies.

ANDREW, ANDREWS, or ANDREWES. Visitation of Norfolk, published
by Norfolk Archæological Society, i. 352. Visitation of Warwickshire, 1619, published with Warwickshire Antiquarian Magazine,
113, 182. Maclean's History of Trigg Minor, ii. 530. Visitations
of Berkshire, printed by Sir Thos. Phillips, 2. Baker's Northampton, i. 167, 295. Metcalfe's Visitations of Northamptonshire,
1, 2, 62. J. H. Hill's History of Langton, 228. Berry's Buckinghamshire Genealogies, 47. Berry's Hampshire Genealogies,
330. History of Newenham Abbey, by James Davidson, 168.
Burke's Landed Gentry, 2 supp., 3, 4. More about Stifford, by
William Palin, 8, 70. Topographer, (London, 1789-91, 8vo.) i.
497. Chetham Society, lxxxiv. 8. Lipscombe's History of the
County of Buckingham, iv. 198. Wright's History of Rutland,
34. Bridge's Northamptonshire, by Rev. Peter Whalley, i. 38,
108. Hampshire Visitations, printed by Sir T. Phillipps, 2.
Nichols' History of the County of Leicester, ii. 473 ; iii. 456.
Proceedings of the Essex Archæological Society, New Series,
i. 55. Surtees' Durham, iv. 145. Harleian Society, xii. 50, 395 ;
xv. 16, 17 ; xxii. 123 ; xxvii. 9 ; xxxii. 4. Miscellanea Genealogica et Heraldica, New Series, iii. 177. Wotton's English Baronetage, i. 271. Betham's Baronetage, i. 458 ; iii. 341. Metcalfe's
Visitations of Suffolk, 1. Burke's Extinct Baronetcies. Metcalfe's
Visitation of Worcester, 1683, 1. Burke's Colonial Gentry, i. 229.
Genealogies of Morgan and Glamorgan, by G. T. Clark, 336.
New England Register, xxiii. 11 ; xl. 21 ; li. 455 ; lii. 16. Cyclostyle Pedigrees, by J. J. Green. Croston's edn. of Baines's Lancaster, iii. 230. The Genealogist, New Series, xviii. 32.

ANDROS. Chronicle of the Family of De Havilland.

ANDROWES. Morant's Essex, ii. 212.

ANES. Harleian Society, i. 65.

ANGAS. Burke's Colonial Gentry, ii. 649.

ANGELL. Hasted's Kent, iv. 35. Surrey Archæological Collections, iii. Visitation of London, 1634, printed by Sir T. Phillipps, 2. Harleian Society, xv. 18, 20; xliii. 138. Notes and Queries, 4 S. v. 476.

ANGER. The Genealogist, iii. 234. Harleian Society, xli. 17. *See* AUNGER.

ANGERSTEIN. Burke's Landed Gentry, 4, 5, 6, 7, 8; Stemmata Britannica, by Joseph Foster, (London, 1877, 8vo.) 33. Foster's Collectanea Genealogica, (MP's England,) 48.

ANGEVILE. The Genealogist, iii. 340.

ANGEVIN. Collectanea Topographica et Genealogica, v. 334, 345. Foster's Lincolnshire Pedigrees, 8. Harleian Society, xliii. 57.

ANGIEL. Dwnn's Visitations of Wales, i. 193.

ANGLESEA, (Earldom of). *See* ANNESLEY, MOUNTNORRIS, MULGRAVE, VALENTIA.

ANGUISH. Burke's Commoners, ii. 419, Landed Gentry, 2. Notices of Great Yarmouth, by J. H. Druery, 167. Carthew's Hundred of Launditch, Part iii. 317. Harleian Society, xxxii. 6.

ANGUS (Earls of). Angus or Forfarshire, by A. J. Warden, 264—309. Banks' Baronies in Fee, ii. 191. *See* DOUGLAS, HAMILTON.

ANION. Visitation of London, 1634, printed by Sir T. Phillipps, 2.

ANJOU, (Counts of). The Genealogist, New Series, xiii. 10.

ANKETELL, or ANKETILL. Pedigree of the Anketell Family [by Rev. H. K. Anketell, Vicar of Seagry, *circa* 1883,] Broadside. Memoir of the Family of Anketell (1885, 8vo.) Burke's Commoners, iv. 529, Landed Gentry, 2, 3, 4, 5, 6, 7, 8. Hutchins' Dorset, iii. 62; iv. 513. Stemmata Britannica, by Joseph Foster, (London, 1877, 8vo.) 32. Shirley's History of the County of Monaghan, 158. Harleian Society, xv. 21; xx. 6. The Genealogist, New Series, ii. 220. Miscellanea Genealogica et Heraldica, 2nd Series, ii. 267.

ANLABY. Surtees Society, xxxvi. 334. Foster's Visitations of Yorkshire, 122, 123, 486. History of Beverley, by G. Poulson, i. 393.

ANNAND. Burke's Landed Gentry, 2. Genealogical Notes anent some Ancient Scottish Families, by J. B. Brown Morrison, 7.

ANNANDALE. *See* CAMPBELL, HOPETOUN, JOHNSTONE.

ANNE. (Seize Quartiers of Queen,) Gentleman's Magazine, 1851, ii. 284.

ANNE. Surtees Society, xxxvi. 285; xli. 10. Foster's Yorkshire Pedigrees. Foster's Visitations of Yorkshire, 360, 361. Harleian Society, v. 191; xvi. 5. Hunter's Deanery of Doncaster, ii. 148. Stemmata Britannica, by Joseph Foster, (London, 1877, 8vo.) 33. Burke's Landed Gentry, 6, 7, 8. Metcalfe's Visitations of North-amptonshire, 2. The Genealogist, New Series, xvi. 249.

ANNESLEY. Gentleman's Magazine, xiv. 24; 1831, i. 503; ii. 405. The Tyndale Pedigree, by B. W. Greenfield. Case of Arthur Annesley, Viscount Valentia, upon his claim to be Earl of Anglesea, and Baron Annesley, fol., pp. 4. Claim of James Annesley, Esq., to the Earldom of Anglesea, before the Irish Court of Exchequer

1743. Newcastle, 1744, fol. Claim of William Richard, Earl of Annesley, to Vote at Elections of Irish Peers, Sess. Papers, K of 1855. Visitation of Oxfordshire, 1634, printed by Sir T. Phillipps, (Middle Hill, fol.) 12, 33. Burke's Commoners, (of Bletchington,) i. 7, Landed Gentry, 2 ; (of Arley Castle,) 2 supp., 3. Harleian Society, iv. 125 ; v. 201, 217, 263 ; xxxviii. 575 ; Lipscombe's History of the County of Buckingham, iv. 280. Visitations of Berkshire, printed by Sir Thos. Phillipps, 2. Baker's Northampton, i. 502. Burke's Royal Families, (London, 1851, 8vo.) i. 118. Edmondson's Baronagium Genealogicum, ii. 139. Archdall's Lodge's Peerage, iv. 99 ; v. 299. Banks' Dormant and Extinct Baronage, iii. 11. Foster's Collectanea Genealogica, (MP's Ireland,) 12. Burke's Extinct Baronetcies, 138. The Genealogist, vii. 116 ; New Series, i. 1. Hasted's Kent, (Hund. of Blackheath, by H. H. Drake,) 247. *See* AUNSLEY.

ANNWILL. Dwnn's Visitations of Wales, ii. 92.

ANQUETIL. J. B. Payne's Armorial of Jersey, 31.

ANSELL. Clutterbuck's Hertford, iii. 57. Harleian Society, xix. 2.

ANSLEY. The Genealogist, ii. 142.

ANSON. Pedigree of the Rt. Hon. Viscount Anson, of Shugborough, Co. Stafford. London, 1806, fol., in three folding tables. Genealogical tables of the Family of the Rt. Hon. Viscount Anson, Baron Soberton, fol. (privately engraved). Burke's Royal Families, (London, 1851, 8vo.) ii. 101. Brydges' Collins' Peerage, vi. 426. Banks' Dormant and Extinct Baronage, iii. 19. Visitations of Staffordshire, 1614 and 1663-4, William Salt Society, 9. Croston's edn. of Baines' Lancaster, ii. 230.

ANSTEY, or ANSTIE. Berry's Sussex Genealogies, 361. Aubrey's Collections for Wilts, (London, 1821, 4to.) printed by Sir T. Phillipps, ii. 6. Notes and Queries, 6 S. iv. 324.

ANSTIS. Maclean's History of Trigg Minor, i. 68.

ANSTRUTHER. Case of Dame Anne Paterson Anstruther claiming title of Baroness Polewart or Polwarth, 1818, fol., pp. 5. Claim of Dame Ann Paterson Anstruther to the title of Baroness Polewart or Polwarth, Sess. Papers, 101 of 1818. Burke's Landed Gentry, 3, 4, 5, 6, 7, 8. Burke's Royal Families, (London, 1851, 8vo.) ii. 56. Nisbet's Heraldry, ii. app. 65. Douglas's Baronage of Scotland, 313, 536. Walter Wood's East Neuk of Fife, 243, 302, 303. Betham's Baronetage, iv. 391. Foster's Collectanea Genealogica, (MP's Scotland,) 13.

ANSTRUTHER-THOMPSON. Burke's Landed Gentry, 3, 4, 5, 6, 7, 8.

ANTHONY, or ANTONIE. Harleian Society, i. 43 ; xix. 75. Visitation of London, 1634, printed by Sir T. Phillipps, 2. Lipscombe's History of the County of Buckingham, ii. 309. New England Register, xxxi. 416.

ANTILL. New England Register, xix. 165.

ANTON. Foster's Lincolnshire Pedigrees, 9. The Genealogist, v. 188.

ANTRIM. Earls of Antrim, 'The Macdonells of Antrim,' by Rev. G. Hill, 1873, 4to. Claim of Mark, Earl of Antrim, to Vote at Elections of Irish Peers, Sess. Papers, G of 1857-8.

ANTROBUS. Burke's Landed Gentry, 2, 3, 4, 5, 6, 7, 8. Ormerod's Cheshire, i. 658. Harleian Society, xv. 22 ; xxii. 123. Earwaker's East Cheshire, ii. 650.

ANTRON. The Visitations of Cornwall, edited by Lt.-Col. J. L. Vivian, 353.

ANTYNGHAM. The Genealogist, New Series, xv. 30.

ANWYL. T. Nicholas's County Families of Wales, 699. History of Powys Fadog, by J. Y. W. Lloyd, v. 301; vi. 224.

AP ADAM. Memoir of the Family of Sir John ap Adam ; Ormerod's Strigulensia, Art. xii. Blunt's Dursley and its Neighbourhood, 109, 112. See ABADAM.

AP EIGNON. Harleian Society, xxi. 13.

APERDALE. Manning and Bray's Surrey, ii. 653.

APETON. Morant's Essex, i. 315.

AP HARRI, or APPARY. Dwnn's Visitations of Wales, i. 56, 57. Weaver's Visitation of Herefordshire, 3, 5. Harleian Society, xxi. 3.

AP JOHN. Surrey Archæological Collections, x. Harleian Society, xliii. 212.

APPELGARTH, or APPLEGARTH. Plantagenet-Harrison's History of Yorkshire, i. 55, 210.

APPLEBY, or APLEBY. Surtees Society, xxxvi. 209. Foster's Visitations of Yorkshire, 487. Harleian Society, ii. 11. Topographer, (London, 1789-91, 8vo.) ii. 66. Burton's Description of Leicestershire, 12. Hutchinson's History of Durham, iii. 3. Nichols' History of the County of Leicester, iv. 442. Surtees' Durham, i. 53. Plantagenet-Harrison's History of Yorkshire, i. 466. Nicholson and Burn's Westmoreland and Cumberland, ii. 462.

APPLETHWAITE. Stemmata Britannica, by Joseph Foster, (London, 1877, 8vo.) 33.

APPLETON, or APPULTON. Hasted's Kent, i. 206, 253. Morant's Essex, i. 263. Burke's Visitation of Seats and Arms, i. 73. The Archæological Mine, by A. J. Dunkin, i. 142. Harleian Society, xiii. 134. Metcalfe's Visitations of Suffolk, 85, 108, 180. Burke's Extinct Baronetcies. Muskett's Suffolk Manorial Families, i. 322-335.

APPLEWHAITE. Burke's Landed Gentry, 6, 8.

APPLEYARD, or APLYARD. Amye Robsart, by George Adlard, 10. Visitation of Norfolk, published by Norfolk Archæological Society, i. 38. Foster's Visitations of Yorkshire, 146. Poulson's Holderness, ii. 364. Foster's Lincolnshire Pedigrees, 17, 18. The Suffolk Records, by H. W. Aldred, 109. Yorkshire Genealogist, i. 118-138. Harleian Society, xxxii. 6.

APPLYNDEN. Surtees' Durham, i. 217.

AP POWELL. Harleian Society, xliii. 37.

APREECE, APRYCE, AP REES, AP RYS, AP RICE, or AP RHESE. Camden Society, xliii. 31. Berry's Sussex Genealogies, 203. Lipscombe's History of the County of Buckingham, iv. 126. Betham's Baronetage, iv. 114. Dwnn's Visitations of Wales, i. 252, 263. The Genealogist, vii. 116. Cooke's Continuation of Duncumb's Hereford, (Hund. of Grimsworth,) Part ii. 154. *See* PRICE.

APSLEY. Hutchinson's Memoirs of the Life of Col. Hutchinson, (1806, 4to.) 144. Berry's Sussex Genealogies, 150. Harleian Society, viii. 372. Gyll's History of Wraysbury, 281. Lipscombe's History of the County of Buckingham, iv. 520. Dallaway's Sussex, II. i. 320 ; ii. 243. Sussex Archæological Collections, iv. 220 ; xxviii. 197. Castles, Mansions, and Manors of Western Sussex, by D. G. C. Elwes and C. J. Robinson, 176, 235. Notes and Queries, 8 S. i. 295, 379 ; ii. 115. Memoir of the Molyneux Family, by G. Molineux, 70.

APULDERFIELD, or APULDREFIELD. Hasted's Kent, ii. 686. Topographer and Genealogist, iii. 178.

AQUILA. Banks' Dormant and Extinct Baronage, i. 3.

ARABIN. Burke's Landed Gentry, 2 supp., 3, 4, 5, 6.

ARBLASTER, or ARBALESTER. Bib. Top. Brit., ix., Part 4, 161. Morant's Essex, i. 470. Shaw's Staffordshire, i. 225. Visitation of Staffordshire, 1663-4, printed by Sir Thos. Phillipps, 1. Visitation of Staffordshire, (Willm. Salt Soc.) 34. Visitations of Staffordshire, 1614 and 1663-4, William Salt Society, 10.

ARBUTHNOT. Stemmata Britannica, by Joseph Foster, (London, 1877, 8vo.) 33. Nisbet's Heraldry, ii. app. 86. Wood's Douglas's Peerage of Scotland, i. 78. Burke's Landed Gentry, 7, 8.

ARCHARD. Visitation of Gloucester, edited by T. F. Fenwick and W. C. Metcalfe, 2.

ARCHBOLD. Burke's Landed Gentry, 2, 3, 4, 5, 6, 7, 8. Harleian Society, viii. 242 ; xv. 23.

ARCHDALE, or ARCHDALL. Stemmata Britannica, by Joseph Foster, (London, 1877, 8vo.) 35. Burke's Commoners, ii. 107 ; Landed Gentry, 2, 3, 4, 5, 6, 7, 8. Harleian Society, xv. 24. Foster's Collectanea Genealogica, (MP's Ireland,) 15. Genealogical Gleanings in England, by H. F. Waters, 318. New England Register, xliii. 160. Parliamentary Memoirs of Fermanagh, by Earl of Belmore, 58.

ARCHDEACON, ARCEDECKNE, or ARCHDEKNE. Maclean's History of Trigg Minor, iii. 259. Miscellanea Genealogica et Heraldica, ii. 234. Burke's Landed Gentry, 2, 3, 4, 5. A Complete Parochial History of the County of Cornwall, iv. 237. An Historical Survey of Cornwall, by C. S. Gilbert, i. 529; ii. 7. Banks' Baronies in Fee, i. 106. Banks' Dormant and Extinct Baronage, i. 228. Harleian Society, xxxvii. 140. *See* LERCEDEKNE.

ARCHER. Memorials of Families of the surname of Archer. London, 1861, 4to. Morant's Essex, i. 161, 218. Berry's Sussex Genealogies, 235. Monumental Inscriptions of the British West Indies, by J. H. Lawrence-Archer, 393. Visitation of Oxfordshire, 1634, printed by Sir T. Phillipps, (Middle Hill, fol.) 12. Burke's Commoners, i. 576, Landed Gentry, 2, 3, 4, 5, 6, 7, 8. Harleian Society, v. 319; viii. 388 ; xii. 309 ; xiii. 136 ; xiv. 632; xxvii. 11; xl. 1257. Dugdale's Warwickshire, 781. Stemmata Britannica, by Joseph Foster, (London, 1877, 8vo.) 35. Turnor's History of

Town and Soke of Grantham, 85, 132. Warwickshire Pedigrees from Visitation of 1682-3, (privately printed, 1865, 8vo.). Herald and Genealogist, ii. 523. Maclean's History of Trigg Minor, ii. 180-193. A Complete Parochial History of the County of Cornwall, iii. 115. Journal of Kilkenny Archæological Society, New Series, vi. 220. Edmondson's Baronagium Genealogicum, v. 446. Banks' Dormant and Extinct Baronage, iii. 20. Notes and Queries, 5 S. ii. 21, 94, 196. Metcalfe's Visitation of Worcester, 1683, 2. Genealogical Table of John Stratford Collins. Burke's Colonial Gentry, i. 188 ; ii. 443.

ARCHER-BURTON. Burke's Landed Gentry, 2, 3, 4.

ARCHER-HIND. Burke's Landed Gentry, 7, 8.

ARCHER-HOUBLON. Berry's Essex Genealogies, 163.

ARCHIBALD. Burke's Landed Gentry, 2 and supp. at p. 227, 3, 4, 5, 6, 7. Stemmata Britannica, by Joseph Foster, (London, 1877, 8vo.) 36. Burke's Colonial Gentry, i. 235. Oliver's History of Antigua, i. 8.

ARDDWYFAEN. Archæologia Cambrensis, 4 Series, viii. 195.

ARDEN, or ARDERNE. Memoir on the connection of Arderne, or Arden, of Cheshire, with the Ardens of Warwickshire, by George Ormerod. London, 1843, 8vo. Edmondson's Account of the Greville Family, 7. Visitation of Staffordshire, 1663-4, printed by Sir T. Phillipps, 1. Ormerod's Miscellanea Palatina, Part 2. Drummond's History of Noble British Families, Parts i. and ii. *Shakespeareanea Genealogica, by G. R. French, 416-503. Dwnn's Visitations of Wales, ii. 92. Berry's Sussex Genealogies, 207. Sir T. Phillipp's Topographer, No. 1, (March, 1821, 8vo.) 37. Visitation of Oxfordshire, 1574, printed by Sir T. Phillipps, (Middle Hill, fol.) 1. Burke's Commoners, (of Longcroft,) i. 636, Landed Gentry, 2, 3 and corr., 4, 5, 6, 7, 8 ; (of Sunbury,) 4, 5, 6 ; (of East Burnham,) 7, 8. Topographer and Genealogist, i. 212, 214. Shaw's Staffordshire, i. 102. Harleian Society, v. 161, 207 ; viii. 90 ; xii. 73, 176-182 ; xviii. 16 ; xix. 3. Baker's Northampton, i. 66. The Monumental Effigies in Elford Church, Staffordshire, by E. Richardson, (London, 1852, fol.) 1. Bartlett's History of Manceter, being No. 1 of Nichols' Miscellaneous Antiquities, 165*. Bridge's Northamptonshire, by Rev. Peter Whalley, i. 587. Shakespere's Home, by J. C. M. Bellew, 38. Dugdale's Warwickshire, 925, 952, 1056. Stemmata Britannica, by Joseph Foster, (London, 1877, 8vo.) 36. J. P. Earwaker's East Cheshire, i. 328, 473. Ormerod's Cheshire, i. 548 ; ii. 85, 250 ; iii. 345, 566. The Forest and Chace of Sutton Coldfield, (London, 1860, 8vo.) 114. Brydges' Collins' Peerage, ix. 143. Banks' Baronies in Fee, ii. 40. Ormerod's Parentalia, 76-101. Visitations of Staffordshire, 1614 and 1663, William Salt Society, 11. Burke's Colonial Gentry, ii. 533. The Genealogical Magazine, i. 88, 571, 614, 670 ; ii. 28, 61, 100, 151, 199. The Genealogist, xiv. 22 ; xv. 212.

ARDES. Lipscombe's History of the County of Buckingham, iv. 334. The Genealogist, vii. 117.

ARDYNGTON. Surtees Society, xli. 21.
ARDROSSAN. Geo. Robertson's Account of Families in Ayrshire, i. 9,
AREYNS. Poulson's Holderness, i. 440.
ARGALL. Hasted's Kent, ii. 418. Harleian Society, xiii. 137, 335. Bysshe's Visitation of Essex, edited by J. J. Howard, 8.
ARGENTEIN, ARGENTINE, or ARGENTON. Chauncy's Hertfordshire, 363. Visitation of Suffolk, edited by J. J. Howard, ii. 181. Topographer, (London, 1789-91, 8vo.) i. 184. Lipscombe's History of the County of Buckingham, i. 13. Clutterbuck's Hertford, ii. 541. Cussan's History of Hertfordshire, Parts xi. and xii. 51. Norfolk Archæology, iii. 267. Page's History of Suffolk, 231. Joseph Hunter's History of Ketteringham, 23. Banks' Dormant and Extinct Baronage, i. 229. The Genealogist, New Series, xiii. 242.
ARGLES. Pedigree of Wilson, by, S. B. Foster, 45. Burke's Landed Gentry, 7, 8.
ARGUM. Foster's Visitations of Yorkshire, 178.
ARGYLE. The Argyle Papers, edited by James Maidment. Edinburgh, 1834, 4to. Hasted's Kent, i. 373. Life of John Duke of Argyle, etc., by Robert Campbell, Esq. London, 1745, 8vo. The Mac-Callum More, a history of the Argyll family from the earliest times. By H. H. A. Smith. London, 1871, 8vo. *See* CAMPBELL.
ARKELL. *See* CAPEL.
ARKENSTALL. Cambridgeshire Visitation, edited by Sir T. Phillipps, 3. Harleian Society, xli. 13.
ARKILGARTH. Plantagenet-Harrison's History of Yorkshire, i. 274.
ARKNEY. Visitation of Derbyshire, 1663-4, (Middle Hill, 1854, fol.) 1.
ARKWRIGHT. S. Glover's Peak Guide, edited by Thomas Noble, 122. Burke's Landed Gentry, (of Sutton Scarsdale,) 3, 4, 5, 6, 7, 8; (of Willersley,) 2, 3, 4, 5, 6, 7, 8; (of Hampton Court,) 3, 4, 5, 6, 7, 8; (of Mark Hall,) 3, 4, 5, 6, 8. Stemmata Britannica, by Joseph Foster, (London, 1877, 8vo.) 37. Burke's Colonial Gentry, i. 324. Harleian Society, xxxviii. 470. Howard's Visitation of England and Wales, vii. 17.
ARLUSH. Harleian Society, xl. 1260.
ARMENTERS. Baker's Northampton, i. 443.
ARMERER, or ARMORER. The Genealogist, ii. 219. Harleian Society, xvi. 6. Bateson's History of Northumberland, i. 390.
ARMESTON. Harleian Society, ii. 176. Nichols' History of the County of Leicester, iv. 467.
ARMIGER. Harleian Society, viii. 76. Metcalfe's Visitations of Suffolk, 108, 214.
ARMIN, or ARMINE. Foster's Lincolnshire Pedigrees, 19. Burke's Extinct Baronetcies. *See* ARMYNE, ST. MEDARD.
ARMISTEAD. Burke's Landed Gentry, 2 add., 7. Stemmata Britannica, by Joseph Foster, (London, 1877, 8vo.) 39.
ARMITAGE, or ARMYTAGE. Some account of the Family of the Armitages from 1662 to the present time. By Cyrus Armitage.

London, 1850, 8vo. Miscellanea Genealogica et Heraldica, ii. 87-94, 181 ; New Series, i. 436. Surtees Society, xxxvi. 25, 251. Burke's Landed Gentry, of Atherdee,) 2, 3, 4, 5 ; (of Milnsbridge House,) 2, 3, 4, 5, 6, 7, 8. Foster's Yorkshire Pedigrees. Foster's Visitations of Yorkshire, 488. Thoresby's Ducatus Leodiensis, 91. Hunter's Deanery of Doncaster, i. 210. Stemmata Britannica, by Joseph Foster, (London, 1877, 8vo.) 39. History of Barnsley, by Rowland Jackson, 150. Harleian Society, xv. 25 ; xxxviii. 785 ; xxxix. 895. Wotton's English Baronetage, iv. 245. Betham's Baronetage, iii. 228. Burke's Extinct Baronetcies. Hulbert's Annals of Almondbury, 239, 250. Howard's Visitation of England and Wales, i. 234 ; viii. 71. Burke's Colonial Gentry, i. 230.

ARMITSTEAD. Earwaker's History of Sandbach, 218.

ARMORER. Foster's Visitations of Northumberland, 7.

ARMSTRONG. Burke's Commoners, (of Garry Castle,) iv. 346, Landed Gentry, 2, 3, 4, 5, 6, 7, 8 ; (of Castle Iver,) Commoners, iv. 350, Landed Gentry, 2, 3, 4, 5, 6 ; (of Ballycumber,) Commoners, iv. 343, Landed Gentry, 2, 3, 4 ; (of Gallen,) Commoners, iv. 337 ; (of Killylea,) Landed Gentry, 2, 3, 4, 5, 6, 7, 8 ; (of Mealiffe,) 3, 4, 5, 8 ; (of Hemsworth,) 3, 4, 5 ; (of Willow Bank,) 5, 6 ; (of Co. Clare,) 3, 4 ; (of Lismoher,) 7, 8 ; (of Cheffpool,) 7, 8 ; (of Farney Castle,) 8. Betham's Baronetage, v. 504. Stemmata Britannica, by Joseph Foster, (London, 1877, 8vo.) 40, 42. Thoroton's Nottinghamshire, i. 76. Foster's Lincolnshire Pedigrees, 22. The Genealogist, iii. 341. Memoirs of the House of White of Wallingwells, 43. Stodart's Scottish Arms, ii. 256. History of the Wilmer Family, 197. Ontarian Families, by E. M. Chadwick, ii. 7.

ARMSTRONG-MACDONNELL. Burke's Landed Gentry, 3, 4, 5.

ARMYNE. Blore's Rutland, 176. See ARMIN.

ARNALL. Thoroton's Nottinghamshire, i. 238.

ARNEWAY. Harleian Society, xxviii. 17.

ARNEY. Burke's Landed Gentry, 4 supp. Harleian Society, xx. 7.

ARNOLD. Burke's Landed Gentry (of Ashby St. Ledgers,) 2, 3 supp., 4, 5, 6 ; (of Little Missenden,) 2, 3, 4, 5 supp., 6, 7 ; (of Wolvey,) 7, 8. Hutchins' Dorset, ii. 618 ; iii. 711. Clutterbuck's Hertford, i. 99. Baker's Northampton, i. 247. Stemmata Britannica, by Joseph Foster, (London, 1877, 8vo.) 43. Harleian Society, xv. 25 ; xxi. 4 ; xxii. 1 ; xxxii. 7. Genealogies of Morgan and Glamorgan, by G. T. Clark, 337. Pedigree of the Family of Boddington, by R. S. Boddington, 4. New England Register, xxxiii. 427, 432 ; xxxiv. 196. Muskett's Suffolk Manorial Families, i. 377-388.

ARNOT. Brief notices of the Families of Arnot, Reid, Boswell, Seton, Fyler, Dickens. By a Kinsman. London, 1872, 12mo. Paterson's History of the Co. of Ayr, ii. 457. Paterson's History of Ayr and Wigton, iii. 599. George Robertson's Account of Families in Ayrshire, i. 13. Walter Wood's East Neuk of Fife, 305. Burke's Extinct Baronetcies, 617.

ARNWOOD. Berry's Hampshire Genealogies, 247. Hampshire Visitations, printed by Sir Thomas Phillipps, 2.

ARON. Harleian Society, xxviii. 17.

ARPE. Manning and Bray's Surrey, iii. 231. The Genealogist, iii. 271.

ARRAGH. Burke's Extinct Baronetcies, 599.

ARRAGON (Queen Kath. of). Gentleman's Magazine, 1829, i. 397.

ARRIS. Visitation of Gloucester, edited by T. F. Fenwick and W. C. Metcalfe, 3. Annals of the Barber Surgeons, by S. Young, 550.

ARROWSMITH. Metcalfe's Visitations of Suffolk, 2. Gloucestershire Notes and Queries, v. 432.

ARSCOTT. Harleian Society, vi. 9-11 ; ix. 286. Visitation of Devonshire, 1620, printed by Sir Thomas Phillipps, (Middle Hill, fol.) 3. Westcote's Devonshire, edited by G. Oliver and P. Jones, 489-491. Visitation of Devon, edited by F. T. Colby, 3. The Visitations of Devon, edited by J. L. Vivian, 16.

ARSIC, or ARSICK. Hasted's Kent, ii. 572. Bibliotheca Topographica Britannica, i. Part i. 11. Banks' Dormant and Extinct Baronage, i. 4. Harleian Society, xxxii. 144.

ARTHINGTON. Foster's Visitations of Yorkshire, 272. Herald and Genealogist, vi. 132. Thoresby's Ducatus Leodiensis, 5. Stemmata Britannica, by Joseph Foster, (London, 1877, 8vo.) 44. Harleian Society, xvi. 7. Jones's History of Harewood, 233.

ARTHUR. Collinson's Somerset, iii. 177. Burke's Landed Gentry, 3, 4, 5, 6, 7, 8. Maclean's History of Trigg Minor, i. 574. Stemmata Britannica, by Joseph Foster, (London, 1877, 8vo.) 44. Weaver's Visitations of Somerset, 1. Harleian Society, xxi. 5 ; xxxviii. 632. Historical Notices of Doncaster, by C. W. Hatfield, 2nd Series, 136.

ARUNDEL, or ARUNDELL. History of House of Arundel, being an account of the origin of the families of Montgomery, Albini, Fitzalan, and Howard. By John Pym Yeatman. London, 1882, folio. Bird's Magazine of Honour, 78. Kent's British Banner Displayed, 393. Collectanea Topographica et Genealogica, i. 306, 316. Gough's Sepulchral Monuments, ii. 90. Gentleman's Magazine, 1829, ii. 215 ; 1833, ii. 498. Topographer and Genealogist, ii. 312-339 ; iii. 240-255. Morant's Essex, i. 168, 294 ; ii. 465. Savage's History of the Hundred of Carhampton, 160, 569. Miscellanea Genealogica et Heraldica, ii. 163 ; New Series, ii. 74. Visitation of Cornwall, edited by Sir N. H. Nicholas, 1, 2. Burke's Commoners, i. 512. Topographer and Genealogist, ii. 312. Carthew's Hundred of Launditch, Part i. 17. Visitation of Devonshire, 1620, printed by Sir Thos. Phillipps, (Middle Hill, fol.) 4. Maclean's History of Trigg Minor, ii. 39 ; iii. 80. Collectanea Topographica et Genealogica, vi. 16. Harleian Society, ix. 2, 3, 271 ; xiv. 560 ; xx. 7. Dallaway's Sussex, II. i. 109. Westcote's Devonshire, edited by G. Oliver and P. Jones, 476, 477. Notes and Queries, 3 S. vii. 167, 249. Hutchins' Dorset, ii. 257. Hoare's Wiltshire, IV. i. 179. Manning and Bray's Surrey, i. 27,

282, 311, 553 ; ii. 471. Baker's Northampton, i. 547 ; ii. 243.
Stemmata Britannica, by Joseph Foster, (London, 1877, 8vo.) 44.
Archæologia, xviii. 99 ; xl. 420. Colby of Great Torrington, by
F. T. Colby, 32. Fosbrooke's History of Gloucestershire, i. 328.
The Visitations of Cornwall, edited by Lt.-Col. J. L. Vivian, 2-14,
631, 632. A Complete Parochial History of the County of Corn-
wall, iii. 294, 416 ; iv. 78. An Historical Survey of Cornwall, by
C. S. Gilbert, i. 470, 537 ; ii. 3. Banks' Dormant and Extinct
Baronage, i. 5 ; iii. 24. Brydges' Collins' Peerage, vii. 40.
Edmondson's Baronagium Genealogicum, iv. 376, 398. Jewers'
Wells Cathedral, 118. Roman Catholic Families of England,
by J. J. Howard and H. F. Burke, Part iii. The Genealogist,
New Series, xv. 216 ; xvi. 162, 164. *See* HOWARD, HUNTER-
ARUNDEL.

ARVOS. The Visitations of Cornwall, edited by Lt.-Col. J. L. Vivian,
218. Weaver's Visitations of Somerset, 30.

ASCOUGH. *See* AYSCOUGH.

ASFORDBY. The Genealogist, New Series, xvii. 249.

ASGILL. Betham's Baronetage, iii. 294. Burke's Extinct Baronetcies.

ASH, or ASHE. Jewitt's Reliquary, vii. 157. Tuckett's Devonshire
Pedigrees, 80. Visitation of Somerset, printed by Sir T. Phillipps,
5. Burke's Commoners, (of Ashfield,) ii. 577, Landed Gentry, 2,
3, 4 ; (of Ashbrook,) 2, 3, 4 ; (of Langley,) 5, 6. Westcote's
Devonshire, edited by G. Oliver and P. Jones, 633. Hoare's Wiltshire, I. ii. 118 ; III. i. 41. Wiltshire Archæological Magazine,
v. 382. Weaver's Visitations of Somerset, 95. Foster's Lincolnshire Pedigrees, 20. Harleian Society, xv. 26. Burke's Extinct
Baronetcies. The Visitations of Devon, edited by J. L. Vivian,
25. Oliver's History of Antigua, i. 9. Somerset and Dorset
Notes and Queries, iii. 179. *See* AYSSHE, ESSE.

ASHAWE. Chetham Society, lxxxii. 6 ; cx. 188. Croston's edn. of
Baines's Lancaster, iii. 304.

ASHBROOK. Gyll's History of Wraysbury, 91.

ASHBURNER. Miscellanea Genealogica et Heraldica, New Series,
i. 224.

ASHBURNHAM, or ASHBORNHAM. Drummond's History of Noble
British Families, Parts i. and ii. Berry's Sussex Genealogies, 28,
185. Visitation of Sussex, 1570, printed by Sir T. Phillipps,
(Middle Hill, fol.) 1. Edmondson's Baronagium Genealogicum,
iii. 236. Brydges' Collins' Peerage, iv. 249. Wotton's English
Baronetage, iii. 283. Betham's Baronetage, ii. 256.

ASHBY. Burke's Visitation of Seats and Arms, 2nd Series, i. 25.
Collectanea Topographica et Genealogica, v. 125-141. Notes on
the Parish of Harefield, by W. F. Vernon, 27. Harleian Society,
ii. 13, 14. Topography and History of New and Old Sleaford,
(Sleaford, 1825, 8vo.) 140. Burke's Commoners, (of Quenby,) iv.
175, Landed Gentry, 2, 3, 4, 5, 6, 7, 8 ; (of Naseby,) 5, 6, 7, 8.
Collectanea Topographica et Genealogica, v. 125. Burton's
Description of Leicestershire, 213. Nichols' History of the
County of Leicester, iii. 298, 299, 493. Stemmata Britannica,

by Joseph Foster, (London, 1877, 8vo.) 45. Notes and Queries, 2 S. xii. 102. Burke's Extinct Baronetcies. Metcalfe's Visitation of Worcester, 1683, 3. Fletcher's Leicestershire Pedigrees and Royal Descents, 111.

ASHBY-MADDOCK. Burke's Visitation of Seats and Arms, 2nd Series, i. 25.

ASHBWL. Dwnn's Visitations of Wales, ii. 351.

ASHCOMB, or ASHCOMBE. Visitation of Somerset, printed by Sir T. Phillipps, 4. Oxfordshire Pedigrees, fol., *n. d.*, printed by Sir T. Phillipps. Visitation of Oxfordshire, 1634, printed by Sir T. Phillipps, (Middle Hill, fol.) 12. Harleian Society, v. 318; xi. 3.

ASHCROFT. Bedfordshire Notes and Queries, iii. 384.

ASHEHOW. Chetham Society, lxxxi. 73.

ASHELDON. Weaver's Visitations of Somerset, 30.

ASHENHURST. Jewitt's Reliquary, viii. 97. The Genealogist, iii. 62. Visitation of Staffordshire, (Willm. Salt Soc. 35). Visitations of Staffordshire, 1614 and 1663-4, William Salt Society, 12. *See* ASSHENHURST.

ASHETON. Chetham Society, lxxxi. 63, 64. Nichols' History of the County of Leicester, iv. 370. Fishwick's History of Rochdale, 353. *See* ASHTON.

ASHFEILD, or ASHFIELD. Sir T. Phillipps's Topographer, No. 1, (March, 1821, 8vo.) 40. Visitation of Oxfordshire, 1574, printed by Sir T. Phillipps, (Middle Hill, folio,) 1. Visitation of Oxfordshire, 1634, printed by Sir T. Phillipps, (Middle Hill, folio,) 12. Harleian Society, v. 163, 165, 170, 220; xii. 165. Notices of Swyncombe and Ewelme, in Co. Oxford, by H. A. Napier, 347. Sussex Archæological Collections, xxv. 114. Foster's Lincolnshire Pedigrees, 20. Page's History of Suffolk, 747, 804. Metcalfe's Visitations of Suffolk, 181. Burke's Extinct Baronetcies. The Genealogist, New Series, xvi. 87.

ASHFORD. Harleian Society, vi. 15. Westcote's Devonshire, edited by G. Oliver and P. Jones, 481. Visitation of Devon, edited by F. T. Colby, 5. *See* AYSHFORDE.

ASHFORDBY. Burke's Landed Gentry, 4th edn. 1537; 5th edn. 1411.

ASHFORDBY-TRENCHARD. Burke's Commoners, iv. 75. Burke's Royal Families, (London, 1851, 8vo.) i. 199.

ASHHURST. East Barnet, by F. C. Cass, Part i. 68. Burke's Extinct Baronetcies. Burke's Landed Gentry, 2, 3, 4, 5, 6, 7, 8. Foster's Lancashire Pedigrees. Stemmata Britannica, by Joseph Foster, (London, 1877, 8vo.) 46. *See* ASHURST.

ASHLEY. Visitation of Wiltshire, 1677, printed by Sir T. Phillipps, (Middle Hill, 1854, folio). Visitatio Comitatus Wiltoniæ, 1623, printed by Sir T. Phillipps. Hoare's Wiltshire, V. i. 24. Baker's Northampton, i. 246. Ormerod's Cheshire, i. 557. Harleian Society, xv. 27. Visitation of Wiltshire, edited by G. W. Marshall, 80. Burke's Extinct Baronetcies. Bysshe's Visitation of Essex, edited by J. J. Howard, 8. The Genealogist, New Series, ii. 220; xii. 111; xiii. 183. New England Register, ii. 394; xxxi. 318.

ASHLEY-COOPER, Hutchins' Dorset, iii. 594. Edmondson's Baronagium Genealogicum, ii. 147.

ASHMALL, or ASMALL. Surtees' Durham, iii. 87. Foster's Visitations of Durham, 1.

ASHMAN. Hampshire Visitations, printed by Sir T. Phillipps, 14. Visitatio Comitatus Wiltoniæ, 1623, printed by Sir T. Phillipps.

ASHMOLE. Visitation of Staffordshire, 1663-4, printed by Sir T. Phillipps, 1. Erdeswicke's Survey of Staffordshire, xlix. Oxford Historical Society, xxvi. 334. Visitations of Staffordshire, 1614 and 1663-4, William Salt Society, 13.

ASHPOOLE. History of Powys Fadog, by J. Y. W. Lloyd, v. 383.

ASHTON. Collectanea Topographica et Genealogica, viii. 147. Harleian Society, ii. 198; xiii. 336; xix. 76; xxxviii. 460. Chetham Society, lxxxi. 8, 20, 28, 112; lxxxii. 7, 14, 17, 20, 45, 95; lxxxiv. 10-18; cx. 206. Foster's Lancashire Pedigrees. Butterworth's Account of the Town, etc., of Oldham, 157. Corry's History of Lancashire, i. 450. Thoresby's Ducatus Leodiensis, 131. Hunter's History of the Parish of Sheffield, 360. Clutterbuck's Hertford, i. 251. Baines's History of the County of Lancaster, ii. 532, 591, 596; iii. 190. Stemmata Britannica, by Joseph Foster, (London, 1877, 8vo.) 46. South Mimms, by F. C. Cass, 62. Jewitt's Reliquary, xvii. 254. Abram's History of Blackburn, 500. The Genealogist, ii. 327; v. 192; New Series, vii. 2. Foster's Lincolnshire Pedigrees, 21, 24. Omerod's Cheshire, ii. 175. Burke's Landed Gentry, 5, 6 and supp., 7, 8. Historic Society of Lancashire and Cheshire, New Series, ii. 1-14. The Ashton Family of Penketh, by J. Venn, 1887, 8; pp. 16. See ASSHETON, ASHETON.

ASHTOWN. See TRENCH.

ASHURST. Morant's Essex, ii. 296. Burke's Royal Families, (London, 1851, 8vo.) i. 194. Harleian Society, viii. 414. Chetham Society, lxxxii. 97; lxxxiv. 9. Burke's Visitations of Seats and Arms, ii. 11. Manning and Bray's Surrey, ii. 656. Wright's Essex, i. 518. Local Gleanings, by J. P. Earwaker, ii. 799, 803. Burke's Extinct Baronetcies, Add. See ASHURST.

ASHWELL. Visitation of London, 1634, printed by Sir T. Phillipps, 2. Harleian Society, xv. 28.

ASHWIN. Pedigree of Ashwin of Bretforton, Corbet of Quinton, and Rawlings, on a folio sheet, privately printed by Sir Thomas Phillipps, Bart. Stemmata Britannica, by Joseph Foster, (London, 1877, 8vo.) 47. Pedigree of Ashwin of Bretforton, Co. Wigorn, printed by Sir Thos. Phillipps, (Middle Hill, 1837,) folio page. Burke's Landed Gentry, 6, 7, 8.

ASHWORTH. Visitation of Oxfordshire, 1634, printed by Sir T. Phillipps, (Middle Hill, folio,) 12. Burke's Landed Gentry, 3, 4, 5. Harleian Society, v. 307. Burke's Family Records, 9, 12.

ASK, or ASKE. Surtees Society, xli. 64. Foster's Visitations of Yorkshire, 107, 118. Whitaker's History of Richmondshire, i. 116. Plantagenet - Harrison's History of Yorkshire, i. 70.

Whitaker's Deanery of Craven, 3rd edn., 335. Harleian Society, xvi. 7, 365. Banks' Baronies in Fee, ii. 40.

ASKEW. Burke's Commoners, (of Redheugh,) ii. 292, Landed Gentry, 2, 3, 4, 5, 6 ; (of Conishead Priory,) 7, 8 ; (of Palinsburn,) Commoners, ii. 294, Landed Gentry, 2, 3, 4, 5, 6, 7, 8. Foster's Lancashire Pedigrees. Raine's History of North Durham, 186. Hodgson's Northumberland, II. ii. 198. Stemmata Britannica, by Joseph Foster, (London, 1877, 8vo.) 47. Notes and Queries, 3 S. ii. 348, 514 ; iii. 36 ; vi. 218, 400, 525. Webb's Fells of Swarthmore Hall. Nicholson and Burn's Westmorland and Cumberland, i. 257. *See* AYSCOUGH, BOSANQUET.

ASKWITH. W. Paver's Pedigrees of Families of the City of York, 8. Foster's Visitations of Yorkshire, 211, 487.

ASLACTON. Thoroton's Nottinghamshire, i. 262.

ASLAKE. Visitation of Norfolk, published by Norfolk Archæological Society, i. 336. Harleian Society, xxxii. 7.

ASLAKEBY. Harleian Society, xvi. 3. The Genealogist, New Series, xvi. 238.

ASLINE. Harleian Society, xxxviii. 719.

ASMALL. *See* ASHMALL.

ASPDEN. Abram's History of Blackburn, 686. History of the Chapel, Tockholes, by B. Nightingale, 190.

ASPINALL. Burke's Landed Gentry, 2, 3, 4, 5, 6, 7, 8. Whitaker's History of Whalley, ii. 107. Stemmata Britannica, by Joseph Foster, (London, 1877, 8vo.) 48. Abram's History of Blackburn, 475. Independency at Brighouse, by J. H. Turner, 81.

ASPINWALL. Gregson's Fragments relative to the County of Lancaster, 212. New England Register, xlvii. 342.

ASPLAND. Berry's Hertfordshire Genealogies, 58.

ASSHENHURST. Visitation of Derbyshire, 1663-4, (Middle Hill, 1854, folio,) 1. *See* ASHENHURST.

ASSHETON. Chetham Society, xiv. iii. ; xcviii. 59. Burke's Landed Gentry, 2, 3, 4, 5, 6, 7, 8. Foster's Lancashire Pedigrees. Whitaker's History of Whalley, ii. 2, 121. Stemmata Britannica, by Joseph Foster, (London, 1877, 8vo.) 48. Abram's History of Blackburn, 464. Wotton's English Baronetage, iii. 150. Burke's Extinct Baronetcies. Howard's Visitation of England and Wales, i. 71 ; Notes, ii. 91. Croston's edn. of Baines's Lancaster, ii. 306, 337, 396. *See* ASHTON.

ASSLOSS. Paterson's History of Ayr and Wigton, iii. 424.

ASTBURY. Ormerod's Cheshire, iii. 60. Burke's Family Records, 13.

ASTELL. Burke's Commoners, i. 540, Landed Gentry, 2, 3, 4, 5, 6, 7, 8. Visitation of Norfolk, published by Norfolk Archæological Society, ii. 45. Foster's Visitations of Northumberland, 9. Harleian Society, xxxii. 8.

ASTEN. Surrey Archæological Collections, x.

ASTHULL. Ormerod's Cheshire, iii. 712.

ASTIN. Miscellanea Genealogica et Heraldica, New Series, ii. 338.

ASTLE. Berry's Essex Genealogies, 80. Harleian Society, xiv. 636.

ASTLEY. Case of Sir Jacob Astley on his claim as co-heir to the title of Baron Hastings, 1840, folio, pp. 47. Claims of Sir Jacob Astley, Bart., and of H. Le-S. Styleman Le Strange, Esq., to be co-heirs to the title of Baron Hastings, Sess. Papers 211 of 1840, and 55 of 1841. Blomefield's Norfolk, ix. 417. Beltz's Review of the Chandos Peerage Case, App. 13. Hasted's Kent, ii. 184, 579. Morant's Essex, ii. 64. Berry's Essex Genealogies, 79, 135. Berry's Kent Genealogies, 372. Burke's Landed Gentry, (of Felfoot,) 3, 4, 5, 6 ; (of Dukinfield Lodge,) 7, 8 ; (of Ansley Park,) 5, 6, 7, 8. Visitation of Warwickshire, 1619, published with Warwickshire Antiquarian Magazine, 72. Chetham Society, lxxxii. 83 ; lxxxiv. 19 ; xcv. 43. Eyton's Antiquities of Shropshire, iii. 154. Visitation of Staffordshire, 1663-4, printed by Sir T. Phillipps, 1, 2. Shaw's Staffordshire, ii. 284. Burton's Description of Leicestershire, 55. Nichols' History of the County of Leicester, iv. 59, 811. Dugdale's Warwickshire, 19, 68, 107. Hoare's Wiltshire, II. ii. 9. Harleian Society, xii. 365 ; xiii. 138, 337 ; xiv. 541, 635 ; xxviii. 18, 57 ; xxxvii.170 ; xlii. 143. Norfolk Archæology, iv. 19. Abram's History of Blackburn, 571, 590. Miscellanea Genealogica et Heraldica, New Series, iii. 73. Collections for a History of Staffordshire, William Salt Society, ii. part 2, 128. Wotton's English Baronetage, iii. 63, 368. Banks' Baronies in Fee, i. 108. Betham's Baronetage, ii. 71. Banks' Dormant and Extinct Baronage, ii. 10; iii. 26. Ormerod's Cheshire, iii. 712, 819. Burke's Extinct Baronetcies. Visitation of Staffordshire, (Willm. Salt Soc.) 36. Earwaker's East Cheshire, ii. 24. Visitations of Staffordshire, 1614 and 1663-4, William Salt Society, 15, 17. The Genealogist, New Series, viii. 33. The Gresley's of Drakelowe, by F. Madan, 235.

ASTON. Clifford's Description of Tixall, 145-153. Berry's Hertfordshire Genealogies, 10. Chronicle of the Family of De Havilland. Burke's Landed Gentry, 2 and corr., 3. Shaw's Staffordshire, i. 105. Visitation of Staffordshire, 1663-4, printed by Sir Thos. Phillipps, 2. Erdeswick's Survey of Staffordshire, 71. Manning and Bray's Surrey, ii. 627. Clutterbuck's Hertford, iii. 229. Chauncy's Hertfordshire, 219. Ormerod's Cheshire, i. 721. Foster's Lincolnshire Pedigrees, 24. See under Pudsey in Burke's Landed Gentry. Wood's Douglas's Peerage of Scotland, i. 124. Wotton's English Baronetage, ii. 102. Harleian Society, xv. 29 ; xviii. 15 ; xxvii. 11 ; xliii. 176. Burke's Extinct Baronetcies. Collections for a History of Staffordshire, William Salt Society, ii. part 2, 28, 130. Betham's Baronetage, i. 338. Visitation of Staffordshire, (Willm. Salt Soc.) 37. Visitations of Staffordshire, 1614 and 1663-4, William Salt Society, 18-21. Surrey Archæological Collections, x. The Gresley's of Drakelowe, by F. Madan, 236.

ASTRIE, or ASTRY. Camden Society, xliii. 98. Harleian Society, i. 58 ; viii. 382, 303 ; xix. 3, 59, 77, 157. See CHESTER.

ATCHERLEY. Burke's Landed Gentry, 2, 3, 4, 5, 6, 7, 8. Burke's Heraldic Illustrations, 16.

AT CHURCH. Harleian Society, xxxii. 155.

AT FORDE. *See* FORD.

ATHENRY. *See* BIRMINGHAM, SEWELL.

ATHERLEY. Burke's Landed Gentry, 5, 6, 7, 8.

ATHERTON. Foster's Visitations of Yorkshire, 70. Chetham Society, lxxxiv. 20; xcviii. 86. New England Register, xxxv. 67. Croston's edn. of Baines's Lancaster, iv. 338.

ATHILL. Oliver's History of Antigua, i. 10.

ATHLUMNEY. Claim of W. M. S., Baron Athlumney, to Vote at Elections of Irish Peers, Sess. Papers, C of 1864.

ATHOL, or ATHOLL. The Earldom of Atholl, by J. A. Robertson, Edinburgh, 1860, 8vo. Case of Charlotte, Duchess Dowager of Atholl, respecting her claim to the office of Great Chamberlain of England, pp. 5, folio. Case of the Duke of Atholl claiming the Barony of Strange, 1736, folio, with Pedigree. Claim of the Duke of Atholl to the Barony of Strange, Sess. Papers, Feb. and March, 1736. Manx Society, x. app. E. Nisbet's Heraldry, ii. app. 175. Wood's Douglas's Peerage of Scotland, i. 131-157. Banks' Baronies in Fee, i. 110; ii. 192, 194. *See* MURRAY.

ATHORPE. Burke's Landed Gentry, 2, 3, 4, 5, 6, 7, 8. Hunter's Deanery of Doncaster, i. 137. Harleian Society, xl. 1261.

ATHOW. Blomefield's Norfolk, vii. 293. Carthew's Hundred of Launditch, Part iii. 43. Harleian Society, xxxii. 9.

AT HULL. Manning and Bray's Surrey, ii. 56.

ATHY. Burke's Landed Gentry, 2, 3, 4, 5, 6, 7.

ATKIN. Burke's Landed Gentry, 2 supp., 3, 4.

ATKINS, or ATKYNS. Rudder's Gloucestershire, 643. Burke's Commoners, (of Firville,) iv. 567, Landed Gentry, 2, 3, 4, 5, 6; (of Waterpark,) Landed Gentry, 2, 3, 4, 5, 6, 7, 8; (of Kingston Lisle,) 6, 7. Harleian Society, viii. 11, 332; xv. 30; xxxii. 9. Manning and Bray's Surrey, iii. 362. Clutterbuck's Hertford, ii. 131. South Mimms, by F. C. Cass, 56. Fosbrooke's History of Gloucestershire, i. 362. Joseph Hunter's History of Ketteringham, 50. Wotton's English Baronetage, iii. 38. Daily Telegraph, newspaper, of 9 January, 1897, p. 4. Burke's Extinct Baronetcies. *See* MARTIN-ATKINS.

ATKINS-BOWYER. Burke's Landed Gentry, 5, 6.

ATKINSON. Topographer and Genealogist, ii. 86. Berry's Hertfordshire Genealogies, 65. Surtees Society, xxxvi. 364. Visitation of London, 1634, printed by Sir T. Phillipps, 3. Visitation of Gloucestershire, 1583 and 1623, printed by Sir T. Phillipps, (1864, folio,) 2. Burke's Landed Gentry, (of Lorbottle,) 2 supp., 3, 4, 5, 6, 7; (of Rehins,) 2, 3, 4, 5, 6, 7, 8; (of Cangort,) 2, 3, 4, 5, 6, 7, 8; (of Ashley Park,) 2, 3, 4, 5, 6, 7, 8; (of Angerton,) 2, 3, 4, 5, 6; (of Morland,) 2 add., 3, 4, 5 and 2nd supp., 6, 7, 8; (of Woolley Grange,) 6 supp., 8. Foster's Visitations of Yorkshire, 489. Harleian Society, iv. 129; viii. 120; xv. 31, 32; xxi. 5. Hodgson's Northumberland, II. ii. 193. Burke's Royal Descents and Pedigrees of Founders' Kin, *Founders' Kin*, 9. Thoresby's Ducatus Leodiensis, 80. Whitaker's Deanery of Craven, 3rd edn., 256. Burke's Colonial Gentry, i. 150. Robinson of the White

House, Appleby, by C. B. Norcliffe, 85. Family Notes, by. J. M. Browne, 13. Thoresby Society, i. 248.

ATKIRK. The Genealogist, New Series, lx. 55.

ATMORE. History of the Hundred of Bray, by Charles Kerry, 124. Brocas of Beaurepaire, by M. Burrows, 324.

ATON. Foster's Visitations of Yorkshire, 609. Tate's History of Alnwick, i. 406. Harleian Society, xvi. 10. Bank's Baronies in Fee, i. 109. Bank's Dormant and Extinct Baronage, ii. 15. Burton's History of Hemingborough, 357. Pedigrees of the Lords of Alnwick, by W. H. D. Longstaffe, 22. *See* DE ATON.

ATTEGARE. Berry's Hertfordshire Genealogies, 155.

ATTE SEE. Boyle's Lost Towns of the Humber.

ATTEHOOKE. Berry's Hampshire Genealogies, 97.

ATT FENNE. Dallaway's Sussex, i. 16.

ATTHILL. Burke's Commoners, i. 164, Landed Gentry, 2, 3, 4, 5.

ATT MILNE. Dallaway's Sussex, II. i. 239.

ATTON. Church Bells of Buckinghamshire, by A. H. Cocks, 211.

ATTREE. Howard's Visitation of England and Wales, i. 153, 156. Burke's Family Records, 13.

ATTSLOW. Morant's Essex, i. 205. Harleian Society, xiii. 337.

ATTWATER. Hutchin's Dorset, iv. 66.

ATTWOOD-MATTHEWS. *See* MATTHEWS.

ATTY, ATTYE, or ATYE. Burke's Landed Gentry, (of Ingon Grange,) 3, 4, 5, 6, 7, 8; (of Penley Hall,) 2, 3, 4, 5, 6, 7. History of Hampstead, by J. J. Park, 198. Harleian Society, xv. 32.

ATWELL. Harleian Society, iv. 105. Foster's Lincolnshire Pedigrees, 31. The Genealogist, iii. 345.

ATWILL. Tuckett's Devonshire Pedigrees, 88, 95. Harleian Society, vi. 12. Visitation of Devonshire, 1620, printed by Sir Thomas Phillipps, (Middle Hill, fol.) 1. Westcote's Devonshire, edited by G. Oliver and P. Jones, 612. The Visitations of Devon, edited by J. L. Vivian, 27, 29.

ATWOOD, or ATTWOOD. Pedigree of the Family of Attwood of Hawne, etc., by T. A. C. Attwood. London, 1888, Broadside. Morant's Essex, i. 155. Berry's Surrey Genealogies, 44. Visitation of Gloucestershire, 1583 and 1623, printed by Sir T. Phillipps, (1864, folio,) 3. Westcote's Devonshire, edited by G. Oliver and P. Jones, 591. Manning and Bray's Surrey, ii. 570. Harleian Society, xiii. 338; xxi. 6; xxviii. 19. Metcalfe's Visitations of Suffolk, 2. Bysshe's Visitation of Essex, edited by J. J. Howard, 19. The Visitations of Devon, by J. L. Vivian, 160. Weaver's Visitations of Somerset, 95. Burke's Family Records, 15. The Genealogist, New Series, xiv. 256. *See* WOOD.

AUBERVILLE. Planché's Corner of Kent, 290. Bank's Dormant and Extinct Baronage, i. 18.

AUBREY, or AWBREY. Caermarthenshire Pedigrees, 59. Visitatio Comitatus Wiltoniæ, 1623, printed by Sir T. Phillipps. Robinson's Mansions of Herefordshire, 65. Berry's Buckinghamshire Genealogies, 87, 91. Dwnn's Visitations of Wales, ii. 39, 57. Glamorganshire Pedigrees, edited by Sir T. Phillipps, 23. Burke's

Landed Gentry, 2, 6, 7, 8. Gyll's History of Wraysbury, 229.
Lipscombe's History of the County of Buckingham, i. 67-74.
Dunkin's History of Bullington and Ploughley, ii. 137. Memoir
of John Aubrey, by John Britton, 24. Jones's History of the
County of Brecknock, ii. 368, 567, 607, 655. Wotton's English
Baronetage, iii. 109. Betham's Baronetage, ii. 137. Harleian
Society, xx. 8. Genealogies of Morgan and Glamorgan, by G. T.
Clark, 337-348. The Genealogist, New Series, xiii. 183. Frag-
menta Genealogica, by F. A. Crisp, ii. 22.

AUCHER. Hasted's Kent, ii. 501. Berry's Kent Genealogies, 223.
Burke's Extinct Baronetcies. Harleian Society, xlii. 180.

AUCHINLECK. Burke's Landed Gentry, 5, 6, 7, 8. Paterson's History
of Ayr and Wigton, i. 188. Oliver's History of Antigua, i. 14.

AUCHMUTY. Burke's Landed Gentry, 2. Walter Wood's East Neuk
of Fife, 275.

AUDBOROUGH. Surtees Society, xli. 53.

AUDLEY, or AUDELEY. J. Wilkinson's History of Broughton Gifford,
folding plate. Morant's History of Colchester, 138. Morant's
Essex, i. 412; ii. 32, 205, 549. Herald and Genealogist, v. 65.
Collinson's Somerset, iii. 552. Camden Society, xliii. 54. Berry's
Essex Genealogies, 134. Jewitt's Reliquary, vii. 18. Lord Braybrooke's History of Audley End, 24. Visitation of Norfolk, pub-
lished by Norfolk Archæological Society, i. 129. The Borough of
Stoke-upon-Trent, by John Ward, 148. Erdeswicke's Survey of
Staffordshire, 93. Nichol's History of the County of Leicester, iv.
17. Hoare's Wiltshire, I. ii. 227. Wiltshire Archæological Maga-
zine, v. 267. Foster's Lincolnshire Pedigrees, 25. Page's History
of Suffolk, 703. Harleian Society, xiii. 338; xviii. 19; xix. 78.
The Genealogist, iii. 346; iv. 69; vi. 18; New Series, x. 86.
Edmondson's Baronagium Genealogicum, iv. 353. Bank's Baronies
in Fee, i. 100. Bank's Dormant and Extinct Baronage, iii. 28.
Notes and Queries, 4 S. iv. 44. Duncumb's Hereford, (J. H.
Cooke,) iii. 10. Cooke's Continuation of Duncumb's Hereford,
(Hund. of Grimsworth,) Part ii. 133. Malet's Notices of the
Malet Family, 133. Miscellanea Genealogica et Heraldica, 2nd
Series, iii. 349. *See* AWDELEY, ALDITHLEY.

AUDHAM. Baker's Northampton, i. 432.

AUFRERE. Burke's Landed Gentry, 2 supp. and add., 3, 4, 5 and
supp., 6.

AUGHTON. Chetham Society, lxxxi. 68; xcix. 80.

AUMERLE. Bank's Dormant and Extinct Baronage, iii. 30. *See*
ALBEMARLE.

AUNEBY. Foster's Visitations of Yorkshire, 489. *See* AWNBY.

AUNGER. Cambridgeshire Visitation, edited by Sir T. Phillipps, 3.
The Genealogist, New Series, xvi. 44. *See* ANGER.

AUNSLEY. Ashmole's Antiquities of Berkshire, iii. 33. *See*
ANNESLEY.

AUSTEN. Hasted's Kent, i. 161; ii. 387; iii. 95. Berry's Hampshire
Genealogies, 47. Berry's Kent Genealogies, 127, 350. Berry's
Surrey Genealogies, 95. Visitation of London, 1634, printed by

Sir T. Phillipps, 3. Burke's Commoners, i. 444, 465, Landed
Gentry, 2, 3, 4, 5, 6, 8 ; (of Capel Manor,) Landed Gentry, 5, 6,
7, 8; 8 at p. 1125. Brayley's History of Surrey, v. 139. Man-
ning and Bray's Surrey, ii. 100. Clutterbuck's Hertford, iii. 139.
Chauncy's Hertfordshire, 414. Miscellanea Genealogica et
Heraldica, New Series, ii. 339. Harleian Society, xv. 33, 34;
xlii. 89 ; xliii. 63. Wotton's English Baronetage, iii. 94. Burke's
Extinct Baronetcies.
AUSTIN. Burke's Landed Gentry, 5, 6, 7, 8. Harleian Society, viii.
147. Miscellanea Genealogica et Heraldica, New Series, ii. 339.
The Genealogist, iii. 235.
AUSTREY. Camden Society, xliii. 98.
AUSTWICK, Surtees Society, xxxvi. 23. The Genealogist, New
Series, ix. 73.
AUSTYN AP REES (Children of). Dwnn's Visitations of Wales, i.
277.
AVAN. Glamorganshire Pedigrees, edited by Sir T. Phillipps, 9, 11.
Genealogies of Morgan and Glamorgan, by G. T. Clark, 77.
AVELAND. See WILLOUGHBY.
AVELINE, AVELYN, or AVELYNE. Notices of Swyncombe and Ewelme
in Co. Oxford, by H. A. Napier, 255. Visitations of Berkshire,
printed by Sir T. Phillipps, 2.
AVENANT. Metcalfe's Visitation of Worcester, 1683, 4.
AVENEL, or AVENELL. Nichols' History of the County of Leicester,
ii. 217. Caledonia, by Geo. Chalmers, 513. Harleian Society,
xxxii. 93.
AVENON. Harleian Society, i. 3. Account of the Company of Iron-
mongers, by John Nicholl, 2nd edn., 519. Visitation of London,
in Transactions of London and Middlesex Archæological Society,
14.
AVERY, or AVEREY. Visitation of Somerset, printed by Sir T.
Phillipps, 6. Visitation of Middlesex, (Salisbury, 1820, folio,) 25.
Visitation of Warwickshire, 1619, published with Warwickshire
Antiquarian Magazine, 32. Maclean's History of Trigg Manor, i.
655. Harleian Society, xi. 3 ; xii. 407. Notes and Queries, 4 S.
vii. 433. Robinson's History of Enfield, ii. 74. Weaver's Visita-
tions of Somerset, 3. Foster's Visitation of Middlesex, 48. New
England Register, xxvi. 197.
AVRANCHES. History of the House of Arundel, by J. P. Yeatman, 81
See DE AVERINGES.
AWBRE. Dwnn's Visitations of Wales, i. 235, 237.
AWDELEY. Herald and Genealogist, vi. 152, 351. Harleian Society,
xiii. 139 ; xxxii. 10. Visitation of Devon, edited by F. T. Colby
124. See AUDLEY.
AWDRY. Burke's Landed Gentry, (of Seend,) 2, 3, 4, 5, 6, 7, 8 ; (ot
Notton,) 2, 3, 4, 5, 6, 7, 8.
AWNBY. Surtees Society, xxxvi. 313. The Genealogist, New Series,
xv. 84. See AUNEBY.
AWSITER. Visitation of Middlesex, Salisbury, 1820, folio, 21.
Foster's Visitation of Middlesex, 40.

AXTELL. New England Register, xxii. 143.

AYALA. Croke's History of the Family of Croke, No. 2.

AYER. New England Register, xvii. 307.

AYLEF. Annals of the Barber Surgeons, by S. Young, 516.

AYLESBURY, or AILESBURY. Collectanea Topographica et Genealogica, vii. 256. Harleian Society, iv. 125. Bridge's Northamptonshire, by Rev. Peter Whalley, i. 52. Dugdale's Warwickshire, 828. Baker's Northampton, i. 355. *See* ALESBURY.

AYLESFORD. Gentleman's Magazine, liii. 576. Manning and Bray's Surrey, ii. 125.

AYLET, or AYLETT. Morant's Essex, i. 142 ; ii. 148, 393. Harleian Society, xiii. 339. Bysshe's Visitation of Essex, edited by J. J. Howard, 10.

AYLEWAY. Harleian Society, xxi. 229. The Perverse Widow, by A. W. Crawley-Boevey, 263.

AYLEWORTH. Berry's Kent Genealogies, 312. Harleian Society, xlii. 149.

AYLIFF, or AYLYFFE. Berry's Hampshire Genealogies, 284. Hampshire Visitations, printed by Sir Thos. Phillipps, 2. Visitation of Wiltshire, edited by G. W. Marshall, 29.

AYLMER. Case of Udolphus Lord Aylmer on his claim to vote at Elections of Irish Peers. London, 1859, 4to. Claim of Lord Aylmer to vote at Elections of Irish Peers, Sess. Papers, 16 of 1859 sess. 1 ; 222 of 1860. Morant's Essex, ii. 136. Hasted's Kent, iv. 29. Burke's Commoners, (of Walworth Castle,) i. 177, Landed Gentry, 2, 3, 4, 5, 6, 7, 8 ; (of Courtown,) Landed Gentry, 4, 5, 6, 7, 8; (of Lyons,) 2, 3, 4, 5 supp., 6. Burke's Royal Descents and Pedigrees of Founders' Kin, 39. Nichols' History of the County of Leicester, iii. 908. Foster's Lincolnshire Pedigrees, 26. Harleian Society, xv. 35. Notes and Queries, 2 S. x. 287, 394, 481. Archdall's Lodge's Peerage, vii. 44. Foster's Collectanea Genealogica, (Funeral Certificates Ireland,) 7. Bysshe's Visitation of Essex, edited by J. J. Howard, 12. History of Powys Fadog, by J. Y. W. Lloyd, iii. 217. Burke's Colonial Gentry, ii. 754. The Irish Builder, xxxv. 32, 44. *See* ELMER.

AYLOFFE. Morant's Essex, i. 69 ; ii. 138. Wright's Essex, ii. 443. Harleian Society, xiii. 20, 141, 340 ; xiv. 543 ; xli. 129. Burke's Extinct Baronetcies. Wotton's English Baronetage, i. 249. Bysshe's Visitation of Essex, edited by J. J. Howard, 12.

AYLWARD. Burke's Landed Gentry, 2, 3, 4, 5, 6, and 6 p. 962, 7, 8, and 8 p. 1198.

AYLWAY. Visitation of Oxfordshire, 1634, printed by Sir T. Phillipps, (Middle Hill, fol.) 13. Harleian Society, v. 311.

AYLWIN. Dallaway's Sussex, i. 200.

AYLWORTH. Visitation of Gloucestershire, 1583, and 1623, printed by Sir T. Phillipps, (1864, fol.) 3. Harleian Society, v. 216 ; xxi. 7. Visitations of Berkshire, printed by Sir T. Phillipps, 3. The Genealogist, v. 227. Visitation of Gloucester, edited by T. F. Fenwick, and W. C. Metcalfe, 4.

AYNSCOMBE. Berry's Sussex Genealogies, 98.

AYNSLEY. Burke's Commoners, i. 588. Hodgson's Northumberland, I. ii. 110. Foster's Visitations of Northumberland, 8.

AYNSWORTH, or AYNESWORTH. Harleian Society, viii. 441. Chetham Society, lxxxiv. 22.

AYOTE. Baker's Northampton, i. 355.

AYRE. Visitation of Cornwall, edited by Sir N. H. Nicolas, 3. Cambridgeshire Visitation, edited by Sir Thomas Phillipps, 3. Harleian Society, vi. 13 ; ix. 3 ; xli. 53. The Visitations of Cornwall, edited by J. L. Vivian, 15. The Visitations of Devon, edited by J. L. Vivian, 31. *See* EYR.

AYSCOUGH, or ASCOUGH. Gentleman's Magazine, 1830, ii. 594. Surtees Society, xxxvi. 147, 153, 342. W. Paver's Pedigrees of Families of the City of York, 10. Harleian Society, iv. 77 ; vii. 37, 38 ; viii. 59. Foster's Lincolnshire Pedigrees, 27, 29, 30. History of Richmond, by C. Clarkson. 252. Surtees' Durham, iii. 227, 318. Thoroton's Nottinghamshire, ii. 253. The Genealogist, iii. 342-345 ; v. 189. Fisher's History of Masham, 297. Hasted's Kent, (Hund. of Blackheath, by H. H. Drake,) xv. Foster's Visitations of Cumberland and Westmorland, 3.

AYSHCOMBE. Visitations of Berkshire, printed by Sir T. Phillipps, 3. The Genealogist, v. 228.

AYSHFORDE. Harleian Society, vi. 15. Visitation of Devon, edited by F. T. Colby, 219. The Visitations of Devon, edited by J. L. Vivian. 22. *See* ASHFORD.

AYSON. Harleian Society, xiii. 336.

AYSSHE. Harleian Society, vi. 14 ; xi. 4. *See* ASH.

AYSTERBY. Foster's Lincolnshire Pedigrees, 24.

AYTON, AYTOUN, or AYTONE. Monipenny *v.* Aytone, Case for Respondent, Appendix, 1757. Surtees' Durham, i. 186. Burke's Landed Gentry, 5, 6, 7, 8. Record of the service of John Aytoun. By J. Riddell, 1829, fol. *See* AITON.

BAARD. Harleian Society, xiii. 22.

BABCOCK. New England Register, xiv. 23.

BABER. Visitation of Somerset, printed by Sir T. Phillipps, 7, 9. Harleian Society, viii. 129 ; xi. 5. South Mimms, by F. C. Cass, 56. Weaver's Visitation of Somerset, 3.

BABINGTON. Burke's Landed Gentry, 4th edn., 1729. Harleian Society, ii. 205 ; iv. 150 ; v. 145 ; xv. 36. Gentleman's Magazine, 1856, i. 565. Topographer and Genealogist, i. 133-141, 333-343. Jewitt's Reliquary, ii. 186. Burke's Commoners, iv. 513 ; Landed Gentry, 2, 3, 4, 5, 6, 7, 8. Collectanea Topographica et Genealogica, ii. 94 ; viii. 313. Dickinson's History of Southwell, 2nd edition, 177. Shaw's Staffordshire, ii. 27. Visitation of Staffordshire, 1663-4, printed by Sir T. Phillipps, 2. Westcote's Devonshire, edited by G. Oliver and P. Jones, 473. Nichols' History of the County of Leicester, iii. 954, 964, 965, 967. Thoroton's Nottinghamshire, iii. 243. Visitation of Devon, edited by F. T. Colby, 8. The Visitations of Devon, edited by J. L. Vivian, 32. Visitations of Staffordshire, 1614 and 1663-4. William Salt Society, 23.

Archæological Journal, xxxvi. 219. Cambridge University Association of Brass Collectors, ii. 61. Burke's Family Records, 17. Howard's Visitation of England and Wales, viii. 89. The Genealogist, New Series, xvi. 238.

BABTHORPE. Camden Society, iv. ci. Foster's Visitations of Yorkshire, 102, 598. Monasticon Eboracense, by John Burton, 435. Clutterbuck's Hertford, ii. 424. Foley's Records of the English Province S. J., iii. 192. Burton's History of Hemingborough, 173, 311.

BACCHUS. Howard's Visitation of England and Wales, i. 241.

BACH, or BACHE. Glamorganshire Pedigrees, edited by Sir T. Phillipps, 35. Visitation of Derbyshire, 1663-4, (Middle Hill, 1854, fol.) 1. The Genealogist, iii. 64. The Midland Antiquary, i. 169. Genealogies of Morgan and Glamorgan, by G. T. Clark, 131. Earwaker's History of Sandbach, 270.

BACHESWORTH. Clutterbuck's Hertford, i. 442.

BACHET. Notes and Queries, 2 S. i. 382, 457.

BACK. Burke's Family Records, 21. Howard's Visitations of England and Wales, vi. 117, 122, 124.

BACKHOUSE. The Descendants of John Backhouse, by Joseph Foster. London, 1894, 4to., 2 vols. Select Family Memoirs, by James Backhouse, York, 1831, 8vo. Harleian Society, i. 63. Visitation of London, 1634, printed by Sir T. Phillipps, 3. Foster's Lancashire Pedigrees. Visitations of Berkshire, printed by Sir Thos. Phillipps, 3. Burke's Lauded Gentry, 6 and supp., 7, 8. Monken Hadley, by F. C. Cass, 30. The Genealogist, v. 228. Burke's Extinct Baronetcies. Burke's Colonial Gentry, ii. 491. Pease of Darlington, by Joseph Foster, 66. Annals of Smith of Balby, by H. E. Smith, 172. Berks Archæological and Architectural Soc. Journal, ii. 37, 109. Nicolson and Burn's Westmorland and Cumberland, i. 447.

BACKUS. Cambridgeshire Visitation, edited by Sir T. Phillipps, 3. Harleian Society, xli. 73.

BACKWELL. Berry's Buckinghamshire Genealogies, 24. Lipscombe's History of the County of Buckingham, iv. 376.

BACON. Gentleman's Magazine, 1825, i. 509 ; 1826, i. 394. Blomefield's Norfolk, vi. 503. Berry's Hampshire Genealogies, 305. Harleian Society, i. 9 ; viii. 14 ; xv. 37, 38 ; xxxii. 11 ; xxxviii. 795, 797. Fitzwalter Peerage Evidence, folding at 211. East Anglian, ii. 273. Chronicle of the Family of De Havilland. Visitation of Norfolk, published by Norfolk Archæological Society, i. 24. Blomefield's Norfolk, vii. 165. Burke's Commoners, iv. 122. Notices of Swyncombe and Ewelme, in Co. Oxford, by H. A. Napier, 42. Dickinson's History of Southwell, second edition, 165. Hodson's Northumberland, III. ii. 374. Visitations of Berkshire, printed by Sir T. Phillipps, 5. Nichols' History of the County of Leicester, iv. 711. Hoare's Wiltshire, V. ii. 45. Hampshire Visitations, printed by Sir T. Phillipps, 2. Visitatio Comitatus Wiltoniæ, 1623, printed by Sir T. Phillipps. Clutterbuck's Hertford, i. 93. Foster's Lincolnshire Pedigrees, 32.

Page's History of Suffolk, 179, 569, 712. Burke's Landed Gentry, 6 at p. 694. Wotton's English Baronetage, i. 1 ; ii. 72. Betham's Baronetage, i. 1. Banks' Dormant and Extinct Baronage, iii. 1. Metcalfe's Visitations of Suffolk, 2, 109, 110. Notes and Queries, 5 S. x. 232. Burke's Extinct Baronetcies. Metcalfe's Visitations of Northamptonshire, 66. New England Register, xxxvii. 189. Somerset and Dorset Notes and Queries, iii. 16, 52. The Genealogical Magazine, ii. 514.

BADCOCK. Burke's Commoners, iii. 77. Harleian Society, vi. 15 ; xiii. 340. Lipscombe's History of the County of Buckingham, ii. 115. The Visitations of Devon, edited by J. L. Vivian, 33. New England Register, xix. 215.

BADD. Burke's Extinct Baronetcies.

BADDA. Dwnn's Visitations of Wales, i. 194.

BADELEY, BADDELEY, or BADDULEY. Burke's Landed Gentry, 5 supp., 6. The Borough of Stoke-upon-Trent, by John Ward, 87. Visitations of Staffordshire, 1614 and 1663-4. William Salt Society, 25.

BADEN. Pedigree of Family of Powell, by Edgar Powell, 80.

BADEW. Morant's Essex, ii. 19.

BADGER. Bigland's Gloucestershire, ii. 323. Harleian Society, xxi. 223.

BADLESMERE. G. P. Scrope's History of Castle Combe, 56, 65, 69. Hoare's Wiltshire, I. ii. 86. Clutterbuck's Hertford, iii. 102. Stemmata Baronialia, by Francis Townsend, 1. Banks' Baronies in Fee, i. 112. Banks' Dormant and Extinct Baronage, ii. 23. Aldred's History of Turville, 45.

BADY. History of Llangurig, by E. Hamer and H. W. Lloyd, 284. History of Powys Fadog, by J. Y. W. Lloyd, iii. 123.

BAESH. Clutterbuck's Hertford, iii. 243. Chauncy's Hertfordshire, 192, 284.

BAGEHOT, or BAGHOTT. Pedigree of Baghott of Prestbury, T. P., 1866, Broadside. Harleian Society, ii. 150 ; xxi. 223. Nichols' History of the County of Leicester, i. 548. Visitation of Gloucestershire, 1569, (Middle Hill, 1854, fol.) 1. Bigland's Gloucestershire, ii. 323. Visitation of Gloucester, edited by T. F. Fenwick and W. C. Metcalfe, 5. See BAGOT.

BAGENHALL, BAGNALL, or BAGENAL. Burke's Landed Gentry, 5, 6, 7, 8. Jewitt's Reliquary, x. 111. The Borough of Stoke-upon-Trent, by John Ward, 346. Harleian Society, xv. 38. Notes and Queries, 4 S. ii. 292.

BAGGE, or BAGG. Burke's Commoners, iii. 227, Landed Gentry, 2, 3, 4. Harleian Society, vi. 16. The Visitations of Devon, edited by J. L. Vivian, 34. Burke's Family Records, 26.

BAGGILEY, or BAGULEY. Ormerod's Cheshire, i. 550. Harleian Society, xviii. 150.

BAGLEY. North's Church Bells of Northamptonshire, 41-47.

BAGNALL. Notes and Queries, 1 S. xi. 85, 172 ; 4 S. ii. 291 ; 6 S. v. 494. Burke's Landed Gentry, 7, 8. See BAGENHALL.

BAGNALL-WILD. Burke's Landed Gentry, 5, 6, 7, 8.

BAGOT, or BAGOTT. Memorials of the Bagot Family. Blythfield, 1824, 4to. Berry's Buckinghamshire Genealogies, 15. Burke's Commoners, (of Pype Hall,) i. 503, Landed Gentry, 2, 3 ; (of Ard,) Landed Gentry, 2, 3, 4, 5, 6, 8 ; (of Kilcoursey,) 2, 3, 4, 5, 6 ; (of Castle Bagot,) 3 ; (of Elford,) 5, 6 ; (of Levens,) 8. Erdeswicke's Survey of Staffordshire, 264. Baker's Northampton, i. 532. Collections for a History of Staffordshire, William Salt Society, i. 293 ; ii. part 2, 28. Edmondson's Baronagium Genealogicum, vi. 90. Brydges' Collins' Peerage, vii. 522. Wotton's English Baronetage, ii. 47. Foster's Collectanea Genealogica, (Funeral Certificates, Ireland,) 9. Visitation of Staffordshire, (Willm. Salt Society) 39. Visitations of Staffordshire, 1614 and 1663-4, William Salt Society, 26. The Genealogist, New Series, ix. 85. *See* BAGEHOT, DE BAGOT.

BAGSHAW, or BAGSHAWE. The Bagshawes of Ford, by W. H. G. Bagshawe. London, 1886, 4to. Pedigree of the Family of Bagshawe of the Ridge, single sheet. Harleian Society, xix. 79 ; xxviii. 20 ; xxxvii. 244, 251. Jewitt's Reliquary, vii. 18 ; viii. 240. Pedigrees of Bagshaw, '*ex verbis Arthuri Bagshawe de Weston Subedge*,' privately printed by Sir Thos. Phillipps, 1858. Glover's History of Derbyshire, ii. 245, (213). Burke's Commoners, ii. 28 ; (of Ford,) Landed Gentry, 2, 3, 4, 5, 6, 7, 8 ; (of the Oaks,) 7, 8. Miscellanea Genealogica et Heraldica, New Series, i. 171. Visitation of Derbyshire, 1663-4, (Middle Hill, 1854, fol.) 1. Hunter's History of the Parish of Sheffield, 354. The Genealogist, iii. 64 ; New Series, vii. 2. Foster's Lincolnshire Pedigrees, 31. Whitaker's Deanery of Craven, 3rd edn., 88. Metcalfe's Visitation of Worcester, 1683, 5. Visitation of Staffordshire, (Willm. Salt Soc.) 41. Howard's Visitation of England and Wales, i. 142 ; Notes, iii. 3.

BAGUE. Visitations of Staffordshire, 1614 and 1663-4, William Salt Society, 28.

BAGWELL. Burke's Commoners, iii. 141, Landed Gentry, 2, 3, 4, 5, 6, 7, 8. Foster's Collectanea Genealogica, (MP's Ireland,) 24.

BAIGNARD. Morant's Essex, ii. 322.

BAIJER. Oliver's History of Antigua, i. 18.

BAIKIE. Burke's Landed Gentry, 3 supp., 4, 5, 6, 7, 8.

BAILEIFFE. *See* BAYLIFF.

BAILEY. Burke's Landed Gentry, (of Nant-y-Glo,) 5, 6, 7, 8 ; (of Ightham,) 5 supp., 6, 7, 8 ; (of Aberaman,) 3, 4 ; (of Glenusk Park,) 2 and add. Burke's Heraldic Illustrations, 36. Cambrian Journal, Vol. for 1862(4), 277. Howard's Visitation of England and Wales, vii. 48.

BAILIE. Burke's Landed Gentry, 5, 6. 7.

BAILLIE. Lives of the Baillies, by J. W. Baillie. Edinburgh, 1872, 4to. Case of A. D. R. C. W. Baillie, M.P., on his claim for the title of Baron Wharton, 1843, fol., pp. 16. Burke's Landed Gentry, (of Dochfour,) 2 supp., 3, 4, 5, 6, 7, 8 ; (of Redcastle,) 2, 3, 4, 5, 6, 7, 8 ; (of Jerviswood,) 2, 3 ; (of Leys,) 5, 6 ; (of Duntisbourne Abbots,) 6, 7, 8. Lands and their Owners in Galloway, by P. H.

M'Kerlie, i. 177. Paterson's History of the Co. of Ayr, ii. 384.
Burke's Commoners, iii. 277. Nisbèt's Heraldry, ii. app. 135.
Paterson's History of Ayr and Wigton, i. 593. Biggar and the
House of Fleming, by W. Hunter, 2nd edn., 573, 592. The Upper
Ward of Lanarkshire, by G. V. Irving, i. 234 ; ii. 321. Geo.
Robertson's Account of Families in Ayrshire, i. 24. Letters and
Journals of Robt. Baillie, (Bannatyne Club,) i. cxiv. Burke's
Extinct Baronetcies, and p. 617. Burke's Colonial Gentry, i. 152,
182. Alexander Nisbet's Heraldic Plates, 106. Burke's Family
Records, 29. A History of Banking in Bristol, by C. H. Cave,
216. *See* TYNTE.

BAILLEUL. *See* BAYLEY.

BAILWARD. Burke's Landed Gentry, 6, 7, 8.

BAILY. Burke's Landed Gentry, 3, 4, 5. Visitatio Comitatus
Wiltoniæ, 1623, printed by Sir T. Phillipps. *See* BAYLEY.

BAIN. Genealogical Chart of the Family of Bain, by Rev. C. Rogers,
February, 1871, Broadside. Burke's Landed Gentry, 4 supp., 5.
Burke's Family Records, 32.

BAINARD. Munford's Analysis of Domesday Book of Co. Norfolk,
45. Proceedings of the Essex Archæological Society, v. 265. *See*
BAYNARD.

BAINBRIDGE, BAINBRIG, or BAINBRIGGE. Topographer and Genealogist, ii. 75. Visitation of Durham, 1615, (Sunderland, 1820,
fol.,) 24. Visitation of Durham, 1575, (Newcastle, 1820, fol.,) 5,
47. Glover's History of Derbyshire, ii. 575, (552). Surtees'
Durham, i. 101 ; iv. 141. Harleian Society, ii. 181, 190 ; xv. 57.
The Genealogist, iii. 236. Burke's Commoners, iv. 52, Landed
Gentry, 2, 3, 4, 5, 6 supp., 7, 8. Nichols' History of the County
of Leicester, iii. 632, 882, 883, 883*. Notes and Queries, 3 S. iv.
15, 178. Miscellanea Genealogica et Heraldica, New Series, iv.
245. Howard's Visitation of England and Wales, i. 212, 214.
Leicestershire Architectural Society, vii. 132. Fletcher's Leicestershire Pedigrees and Royal Descents, 169. New England Register,
xxii. 19.

BAINBRIGGE-LE HUNT. Burke's Landed Gentry, 2 supp., 3, 4.

BAINES. Notes and Queries, 6 S. i. 517. Burke's Family Records,
33. *See* BAYNES.

BAIRD. Account of the surname of Baird, edited by W. N. Frazer,
Edinburgh, 1856, 4to. The 2nd edn., London, 8vo., is called
Genealogical Collections concerning the Sirname of Baird.'
Burke's Landed Gentry, 3, 4, 5, 6, 7, 8. Paterson's History of
Ayr and Wigton, ii. 436. Drumlanrig Castle and the Douglases,
by C. T. Ramage, 213. Scottish Journal, i. 241.

BAKE. The Visitations of Cornwall, edited by J. L. Vivian, 334.

BAKEPUIZ. Nichols' History of the County of Leicester, iii. 6. The
Gresleys of Drakelowe, by F. Madan, 237.

BAKEPUZ. The Genealogist, New Series, vii. 243. Publications of
the William Salt Society, New Series, i. 237.

BAKER. A Memoir of the Family of Baker, by T. Y. Baker. Westminster, 1878, 4to. Botfield's Stemmata Botevilliana, 147. Hasted's

Kent, ii. 281 ; iii. 49. Morant's Essex, i. 231, 258, 301, 303. Berry's Hertfordshire Genealogies, 83, 87. Dwnn's Visitations of Wales, i. 284. Berry's Kent Genealogies, 216, 353. Berry's Sussex Genealogies, 225. Visitation of Norfolk, published by Norfolk Archæological Society, i. 45. Burke's Commoners, (of Elemore Hall,) i. 546, Landed Gentry, 3, 4, 5, 6, 7, 8 ; (of Bayfordbury,) Landed Gentry, 2, 3, 4, 5, 6, 7, 8 ; (of West Hay,) 2, 3, 4, 5, 6, 7, 8 ; (of Fenton,) 4, 5, 6 ; (of Hardwicke Court,) 2, 3, 5, 6, 7, 8 ; (of Sweeney,) 5 supp., p. 47, 6 p. 949 ; (of Cottesmore,) 2. 3 ; (of Orsett Hall,) 3, 6 ; (of Lismacue,) 5 supp., 6, 7, 8 ; (of Hasfield Court,) 8 ; (of Fort William,) 5 supp., 7 at p. 1086. Harleian Society, iv. 36 ; xiii. 145 ; xiv. 544 ; xv. 39, 42 ; xxviii. 21 ; xxxii. 11 ; xlii. 63, 178. Lipscombe's History of the County of Buckingham, iv. 530. Burke's Visitation of Seat and Arms, i. 18. Burke's Royal Families, (London, 1851, 8vo.) i. 78. History of Hartlepool, by Sir C. Sharp, (1816, 8vo.) 83. Burke's Authorised Arms, 22. Visitations of Berkshire, printed by Sir T. Phillipps, 4. Hutchins' Dorset, iv. 93. Surtees' Durham, i. 121 ; ii. 358. Cussan's History of Hertfordshire, Parts ix. and x. 144. Thoroton's Nottinghamshire, ii. 251. Scott of Scot's Hall, by J. R. Scott, 207. The Genealogist, v. 230 ; New Series, xiii. 252. Notes and Queries, 1 S. ii. 67, 244 ; 6 S. xii. 89. Metcalfe's Visitation of Worcester, 1683, 5. Betham's Baronetage, iv. 14, 363. Foster's Collectanea Genealogica, (Funeral Certificates, Ireland,) 10. Burke's Extinct Baronetcies. The Visitations of Devon, edited by J. L. Vivian, 61. Genealogies of Morgan and Glamorgan, by G. T. Clark, 475. Burke's Colonial Gentry, i. 100. New England Register, xliii. 279. Howard's Visitation of England and Wales, vii. 156.

BAKER-CRESSWELL. Burke's Commoners, ii. 290.

BALAM. Visitation of Norfolk, published by Norfolk Archæological Society, i. 49. Harleian Society, xxxii. 12.

BALCARRES. See CRAWFURD, MONTROSE.

BALCH, or BALCHE. Visitation of Somerset, printed by Sir T. Phillipps, 10. Harleian Society, xi. 5. New England Register, ix. 233.

BALDEN. Visitation of Norfolk, published by Norfolk Archæological Society, i. 44. Harleian Society, xxxii. 14.

BALDERS. Burke's Landed Gentry, 6.

BALDERSTONE. Abram's History of Blackburn, 413. Alexander Nisbet's Heraldic Plates, 110.

BALDOCK. Harleian Society, viii. 265.

BALDWIN, or BALDWYN. Pedigree of Baldwin of Ashton-under-Hill, Co. Glouc., T. P., 1865, folio page. Camden Society, xliii. 58. Burke's Commoners, ii. 695, Landed Gentry, 2, 3, 4 ; (of Aqualate,) Commoners, iii. 196 ; Landed Gentry, 7, p. 337 ; 8, p. 326. Harleian Society, viii. 238 ; xii. 377 ; xxii. 125 ; xxvii. 103 ; xxviii. 21. Visitation of Warwickshire, 1619, published with Warwickshire Antiquarian Magazine, 122. Metcalfe's Visitations of Suffolk, 111. Notes and Queries, 5 S. vii. 187. Woodcock of

Cuerden, by A. E. P. Gray, 12. Miscellanea Genealogica et
Heraldica, 2nd Series, iii. 136. Burke's Colonial Gentry, i. 295.
New England Register, xxv. 153; xxxviii. 161, 289, 372.
Ontarian Families, by E. N. Chadwick, ii. 34.

BALDWYN-CHILDE. Burke's Landed Gentry, 8.

BALE. J. H. Hill's History of Langton, 240. Harleian Society, ii.
141. Topographer, (London, 1789-91, 8vo.) ii. 27. Burke's
Extinct Baronetcies. Nichols' History of the County of Leicester,
ii. 539. Miscellanea Genealogica et Heraldica, New Series, iii.
221.

BALFE. Burke's Landed Gentry, 4, 5, 6, 7, 8. Foster's Collectanea
Genealogica, (Funeral Certificates, Ireland,) 10.

BALFOUR. Claim of Robert Bruce of Kennet to be Lord Balfour of
Burley, Sess. Papers, 237, 237² of 1861. Case of F. W. Balfour
claiming title of Lord Balfour, pp. 31, *n. d.* Supplemental case of
same, pp. 26, 1864, fol. Claim of F. W. Balfour to dignity of
Lord Balfour of Burley, Sess. Papers, G of 1862; A of 1864; D
of 1867; C of 1867-8; F of 1868-9. Burke's Commoners, iii. 133;
7 at p. 1957; 8 at p. 2171; (of Towneley Hall,) Landed Gentry,
2, 3, 4, 5, 6, 7, 8; (of Whittinghame,) 3, 4, 5, 6, 7, 8; (of Balbirnie,) 3, 4, 5, 6 and supp., 7, 8; (of Balfour,) 3, 4, 5, 6, 8; (of
Fernie Castle,) 5, 6, 7, 8. Burke's Royal Families, (London, 1851,
8vo.) i. 60. Balmerino and its Abbey, by James Campbell, 307,
386, 396. Lindores Abbey, by Alexr. Laing, 354. Wood's
Douglas's Peerage of Scotland, i. 176. Foster's Collectanea Genealogica, (Funeral Certificates, Ireland,) 11. Burke's Colonial
Gentry, ii. 503.

BALFOUR-MELVILLE. Burke's Landed Gentry, 7, 8.

BALFOUR-OGILVY. Burke's Landed Gentry, 5.

BALGEY, or BALGUY. Burke's Landed Gentry, 2, 3, 4, 5, . 6, 7,
8. The Genealogist, New Series, vii. 3. Notes and Queries, 7
S. iii. 143, 243, 270, 316; iv. 263. Harleian Society, xxxviii.
564.

BALIDON. Visitation of Derbyshire, 1663-4, (Middle Hill, 1854, fol.)
1. The Genealogist, iii. 63.

BALIOL, or BALLIOL. Heirs of the Royal House of Baliol, by Alexr.
Sinclair, Edinburgh, *n. d.*, 8vo. The Antiquities of Gainford, by
J. R. Walbran, 147. Burke's Patrician, iii. 174, 264. Hodgson's
Northumberland, II. ii. 41. Hutchinson's History of Durham, iii.
232. Ord's History of Cleveland, 395. Surtees' Durham, iv. 59,
60. Clutterbuck's Hertford, iii. 17. Geo. Robertson's Description
of Cunninghame, 48. Plantagenet-Harrison's History of Yorkshire, i. 390. Geo. Robertson's Account of Families in Ayrshire,
i. 36. Notes and Queries, 3 S. ii. 200. The Genealogist, vi. 1.
Banks' Baronies in Fee, i. 113. Banks' Dormant and Extinct
Baronage, i. 19.

BALL, or BALLE. Account of the Family of Druce of Goreing, 21.
Jewitt's Reliquary, vii. 18; xi. 33. Cambridgeshire Visitation,
edited by Sir T. Phillipps, 4. Visitation of London, 1634, printed
by Sir T. Phillipps, 4. Miscellanea Genealogica et Heraldica, New

Series, i. 315; iii. 184; 2nd Series, iv. 40. Harleian Society, vi. 16; xv. 40; xviii. 263; xxxii. 14; xxxviii. 701; xli. 43. Ormerod's Cheshire, ii. 658. Visitation of Devon, edited by F. T. Colby, 9. Betham's Baronetage, v. 452. Foster's Collectanea Genealogica, (Funeral Certificates, Ireland,) 11; (MP's Ireland,) 26. The Visitations of Devon, edited by J. L. Vivian, 35. The Wolfes of Forenaghts, 94. Records of the Anglo-Irish Families of Ball, by W. B. Wright. Dublin, 1887, 8vo. Burke's Family Records, 34. The Genealogist, New Series, xiii. 253. Howard's Visitation of Ireland, iii. 5. The Gresleys of Drakelowe, by F. Madan, 238.

BALLANTINE, or BALLANTYNE. Burke's Landed Gentry, 3, 4, 6, 7, 8. Paterson's History of the Co. of Ayr, i. 208. New England Register, vi. 371.

BALLANTINE-DYKES. *See* DYKES.

BALLARD. Pedigrees of Ballard of Weston Subedge, etc., [T. P.,] 4 folio pages. Berry's Sussex Genealogies, 116. Visitation of Wiltshire, 1677, printed by Sir T. Phillipps, (Middle Hill, 1854, folio). Burke's Landed Gentry, 5 supp. Harleian Society, iv. 104; xv. 41. Nichols' History of the County of Leicester, iii. 507. Hoare's Wiltshire, III. iv. 3. Genealogical Records of the Family of Woodd, 30. Hasted's Kent, (Hund. of Blackheath, by H. H. Drake,) 48. Notts and Derbyshire Notes and Queries, iv. 106.

BALLEINE. J. B. Payne's Armorial of Jersey, 34.

BALLET. Morant's Essex, ii. 508. Harleian Society, xiii. 341. Metcalfe's Visitations of Suffolk, 111. Bysshe's Visitation of Essex, edited by J. J. Howard, 13.

BALLOWE. F. G. Lee's History of Thame, 552.

BALLS. Burke's Colonial Gentry, i. 251.

BALLY. Burke's Visitation of Seats and Arms, 2nd Series, ii. 29.

BALME. Burke's Landed Gentry, 5, 6, 7. Yorkshire Genealogist, i. 16. Histories of Bolton and Bowling, by Wm. Cudworth, 285. *See* WHEATLEY-BALME.

BALUN. Banks' Dormant and Extinct Baronage, i. 21.

BAMBER. Fishwick's History of Bispham, 118.

BAMBURGH. Foster's Visitations of Yorkshire, 85. Burke's Extinct Baronetcies. Metcalfe's Visitations of Suffolk, 3.

BAMFIELD. Excerpta e cartis, et stemma Familiæ de Bamfield, Sir Thos. Phillipps' Topographer, No. 1, (March, 1821, 8vo.) 60. Pedigree of Bamfylde of Poltimore, and Foster of Meere [T. P.,] Broadside. Visitation of Somerset, printed by Sir T. Phillipps, 11. Tuckett's Devonshire Pedigrees, 161. Harleian Society, vi. 17; xi. 6. Visitation of Staffordshire, 1663-4, printed by Sir T. Phillipps, 2. Visitation of Devon, edited by F. T. Colby, 10. The Visitations of Devon, edited by J. L. Vivian, 38. *See* BAMP-FIELD.

BAMFORD. Chetham Society, lxxxii. 34; lxxxiv. 22. Hunter's Deanery of Doncaster, ii. 270.

BAMFORD-HESKETH. Burke's Commoners, iv. 523; Landed Gentry, 2, 3, 4, 5, 6, 7, 8.

BAMFORTH. Hunter's History of the Parish of Sheffield, 387. Harleian Society, xxxviii. 684, 686.

BAMME. Hasted's Kent, ii. 84.

BAMPFIELD, or BAMPFYLDE. Pedigree of Bampfield, of Hardington, Co. Somerset, privately printed by Sir Thomas Phillipps, Bart., London. Westcote's Devonshire, edited by G. Oliver and P. Jones, 491. Wotton's English Baronetage, ii. 188. Betham's Baronetage, i. 395. Collinson's Somerset, ii. 90; iii. 263. *See* BAMFIELD.

BAMVILE. Harleian Society, xviii. 212.

BANASTER, or BANASTRE. J. H. Hill's History of Langton, 19*. Chetham Society, lxxxiv. 23, 25; xcv. 16; cx. 125. Nichols' History of the County of Leicester, iv. 505, 621. Baker's Northampton, ii. 190. Whitaker's History of Whalley, ii. 268. Abram's History of Blackburn, 705. Ormerod's Cheshire, ii. 574. Visitation of Gloucester, edited by T. F. Fenwick and W. C. Metcalfe, 8. Metcalfe's Visitations of Northamptonshire, 163. Foster's Visitation of Middlesex, 80. Harleian Society, xxviii. 24. Croston's edition of Baines' Lancaster, iv. 133. *See* BANESTER, STOKEPORT.

BANBURY. Case of William, Earl of Banbury, as to Earldom of Banbury, 1809, fol., pp. 24. Proceedings relating to the case of the Earl of Banbury, Sess. Papers, July 1660—Feb. 1697. The true Countess of Banbury's case, London, 1696, fol. The Arguments in the controverted point of Peerage in the case of Charles Knowles otherwise Earl of Banbury. London, 1716, fol. Claim of the Earls of Banbury to that Earldom, Sess. Papers, 14, 48, 87, 126, of 1808 ; 20, of 1809 ; 64, of 1810 ; 11, 33, of 1811 ; 111, of 1812. Law of Adulterine Bastardy, with report of the claim of the Earldom of Banbury, by Sir N. H. Nicolas, London, 1836, 8vo.

BANCKS. Savage's History of the Hundred of Carhampton, 643. Hutchins' Dorset, iv. 385. *See* BANKES.

BANCKYS. Harleian Society, xv. 43. *See* BANCKS.

BANCROFT. Harleian Society, v. 279.

BAND. Burke's Commoners, ii. 303, Landed Gentry, 2, 3, 4, 5, 6, 7.

BANDINEL. J. B. Payne's Armorial of Jersey, 40.

BANDON. Claim of Francis Earl of Bandon to vote at elections of Irish Peers, Sess. Papers, B of 1857, sess. 1.

BANESTER, BANYSTER, or BANNISTER. Surrey Archæological Collections, ii. Berry's Hampshire Genealogies, 81. Visitation of Middlesex, (Salisbury, 1820, fol.,) 45. Harleian Society, ii. 164 ; xv. 44 ; xix. 157 ; xxviii. 25 ; xliii. 120. Foster's Visitations of Yorkshire, 291. Chetham Society, lxxxi. 35, 67 ; lxxxii. 23. Baines' History of the Co. of Lancaster, iii. 406. Abram's History of Blackburn, 726. Hampshire Visitations, printed by Sir Thos. Phillipps, 3. Whitaker's Deanery of Craven, 3rd edn., 236. The Genealogist, v. 308. Lym's Chronicles of Finchampstead, 189. Oliver's History of Antigua, i. 31. *See* BANASTER.

BANGER. Oxford Historical Society, xix. 202.

BANGOR. Genealogies of Morgan and Glamorgan, by G. T. Clark, 97.

BANGS. New England Register, viii. 368 ; x. 157.

BANINGE. Harleian Society, xiii. 142.

BANKE. Foster's Visitations of Yorkshire, 270, 490. Whitaker's Deanery of Craven, 170, (236). Harleian Society, xvi. 12.

BANKES, or BANKS. Hasted's Kent, ii. 742. Harleian Society, ii. 150 ; viii. 465 ; xiv. 544 ; xv. 42. Visitation of London, 1634, printed by Sir T. Phillipps, 4. Burke's Commoners, (of Winstanley,) iv. 213, Landed Gentry, 2, 3, 4, 5, 6 ; (of Kingston Hall), Commoners, iii. 307, Landed Gentry, 2, 3, 6 ; (of Ravesby,) Commoners, iv. 215 ; (of Corfe Castle,) Landed Gentry, 4, 5, 7, 8 ; (of Highmoor,) 6, 7, 8. Jewitt's Reliquary, xii. 255. Chetham Society, lxxxiv. 26. Gregson's fragments relative to the County of Lancaster, 232. Nichols' History of the County of Leicester, iv. 876. Hutchins' Dorset, iii. 240. Memoir of Gabriel Goodman, by R. Newcome, app. S. Notes and Queries, 1 S. iii. 390, 458, 507, 524 ; 5 S. iv. 87, 150, 377. Betham's Baronetage, iv. 76. Burke's Extinct Baronetcies, and add. Woodcock of Cuerden, by A. E. P. Gray, 14. Miscellanea Genealogica et Heraldica, 2nd Series, v. 62. New England Register, xliv. 258 ; li. 262. Croston's edn. of Baines' Lancaster, iv. 306. See BANCKS.

BANNATINE, or BANNATYNE. Geo. Robertson's Description of Cunninghame, 82. Geo. Robertson's Account of Families in Ayrshire, i. 49, 71. J. E. Reid's History of the Co. of Bute, 246.

BANNERMAN. Some Account of the Family of Bannerman of Elsick. Aberdeen, 1812. Nisbet's Heraldry, ii. app. 151. Burke's Family Records, 38.

BANNING. Morant's Essex, ii. 93, 95.

BANTRY. Claim of the Rt. Hon. Richd. Earl of Bantry, etc., to vote at elections of Irish Peers. Sess. Papers, 216 of 1851.

BANYARD. Visitation of Norfolk, published by Norfolk Archæological Society, i. 362. Harleian Society, xxxii. 15.

BARBER, BARBOR, BARBOUR, or BARBOURE. Bibliotheca Topographica Britannica, ix., Part iv. 59. Jewitt's Reliquary, ix. 18. Dwnn's Visitations of Wales, i. 79. Oxfordshire Pedigrees, fol., n. d., printed by Sir T. Phillipps. Visitation of Oxfordshire, 1634, printed by Sir T. Phillipps, (Middle Hill, fol.) 13. Miscellanea Genealogica et Heraldica, i. 58. Harleian Society, v. 324 ; xxii. 25. Visitation of Staffordshire, 1663-4, printed by Sir T. Phillipps, 2. Nichols' Miscellaneous Antiquities, ‘No. 4, 59. Norfolk Archæology, iii. 128. Burke's Landed Gentry, 5, 6, 7. Notes and Queries, 2 S. i. 150, 275. Metcalfe's Visitations of Suffolk, 85. Visitations of Staffordshire, 1614 and 1663-4. William Salt Society, 29, 31.

BARBER-STARKEY. Burke's Landed Gentry, 6, 7, 8.

BARBY. Tuckett's Devonshire Pedigrees, 130. Harleian Society, vi. 18. The Visitations of Devon, edited by J. L. Vivian, 42.

BARCHAM. Historical Notices of the Barcham Family, by T. Barcham. 1857, 8vo.

BARCHARD. Burke's Landed Gentry, 5, 6, 7.

BARCLAY. A Genealogical Account of the Barclays of Urie, formerly of Mather, by R. Barclay. Aberdeen, 1740, 8vo. Brief Memoirs of the Barclay Family. London, 1851, 12mo. Genealogical Account of the Barclays of Urie, 1812, 8vo. The Barclays de Tollie and their descendants; a tabular pedigree. Edinburgh, 1878. Cussan's History of Hertfordshire, i. 138. Burke's Landed Gentry, (of Mathers and Urie), 4, 5, 6, 7, 8 ; (of Leyton,), 4, 5, 6, 7, 8 ; (of Wavertree Lodge,) 2, 3, 4 ; (of Bury Hill,) 2, 3, 4, 6. Manning and Bray's Surrey, iii. cxxxi. Paterson's History of the Co. of Ayr, i. 447 ; ii. 121. Nisbet's Heraldry, ii. app. 245. Paterson s History of Ayr and Wigton, iii. 198, 204, 297. George Robert-son's Account of Families in Ayrshire, i. 72. W. R. Fraser's History of Laurencekirk, 18, 107. Wood's Douglas's Peerage of Scotland, i. 244. Harleian Society, xxxviii. 432. *See* BERKELEY.

BARCLAY-ALLARDICE. Claim of Mrs. Barclay-Allardice to Earldom of Airth, Sess. Papers, G of 1870 ; E of 1871 ; F of 1874. Burke's Landed Gentry, 2, 3, 4, 8. Burke's Colonial Gentry, ii. 409. Burke's Family Records, 5.

BARCROFT. Chetham Society, lxxxiv. 27. Whitaker's History of Whalley, ii. 219.

BARD, or BARDE. Burke's Extinct Baronetcies. Gentleman's Magazine, 1837, i. 52. Visitation of London, 1634, printed by Sir T. Phillipps, 4. Collectanea Topographica et Genealogica, iv. 59, 61. The Genealogist, iii. 347 ; v. 308.

BARDEN. Harleian Society, xvi. 137, 324.

BARDOLF. Morant's Essex, i. 375. Jewitt's Reliquary, vii. 19. Car-thew's Hundred of Launditch, Part i. 51. Clutterbuck's Hertford, i. 407 ; ii. 484. Cussan's History of Hertfordshire, Parts xi. and xii. 174. Thoroton's Nottinghamshire, iii. 11. Harleian Society, xv. 45 ; xvi. 25 ; xxii. 2, 26. Banks' Dormant and Extinct Baronage, ii. 26. The Genealogist, New Series, xvii. 247.

BARDSEY. Harleian Society, xv. 45 ; xxviii. 26.

BARDWELL. Burke's Landed Gentry, 7, 8.

BAREFOOT. Morant's Essex, i. 172.

BARENTINE, or BARENTYNE. Visitation of Sussex, 1570, printed by Sir T. Phillipps, (Middle Hill, fol.) 1. Hoare's Wiltshire, V. i. 21. Notes and Queries, 2 S. vi. 485. *See* DE BARRENTINE.

BARFORD. Nichols' History of the County of Leicester, iv. 343.

BARGRAVE. Hasted's Kent, iii. 721 ; iv. 217. Archæologia Cantiana, iv. 252. Harleian Society, xlii. 6.

BARHAM. Berry's Kent Genealogies, 404. Burke's Landed Gentry, 4, 5 and add., 6. Burke's Royal Descents and Pedigrees of Founders' Kin, 72. Foster's Collectanea Genealogica, (Funeral Certificates, Ireland,) 12. Harleian Society, xlii. 161. *See* FORSTER-BARHAM.

BARING. The Great Governing Families of England, ii. 121. Berry's Hampshire Genealogies, 345. Betham's Baronetage, iv. 254. History of St. Leonard's, Exeter, by Robert Dymond. Burke's Landed Gentry, (of Highbeach,) 8 ; (of Norman Court,) 8.

BARING-GOULD. Burke's Landed Gentry, 6, 7, 8. Howard's Visitation of England and Wales, iv. 23.

BARKER. Miscellanea Genealogica et Heraldica, New Series, ii. 505. 513, 576; iv. 354. Harleian Society, xii. 361; xiii. 143, 341; xv. 47-49; xxviii. 26; xxxvii. 214, 256, 369, 405; xxxviii. 423; xxxix. 962. Page's History of Suffolk, 69, 613. Baker's Northampton, i. 704; ii. 45. Wright's Essex, ii. 26. Nichols' Illustrations of Literary History, iv. 164. Croke's History of the Family of Croke, No. 41. Morant's Essex, ii. 384. Berry's Buckinghamshire Genealogies, 95. Berry's Berkshire Genealogies, 40. Burke's Landed Gentry, 2, p. 1086; (of Kilcooly Abbey), 2, 3, 4, 5, 6; (of Fairford Park,) 2, 3, 4, 5, 6, 7, 8; (of Albrighton Hall,) 8; (of Hemsby Hall,) 8; (of Stanlake Park,) 5, 6, 7, 8; (of Stirling,) 5 supp.; (of Croboy,) 4, 6, 7; (of Brooklands,) 7, 8; (of Needham House,) 8. Visitation of Warwickshire, 1619, published with Warwickshire Antiquarian Magazine, 82. Wright's History of Rutland, 84. Hodgson's Northumberland, II. ii. 353. Visitations of Berkshire, printed by Sir Thos. Phillipps, 4, 5. Surrey Archæological Collections, ii. 105. Wotton's English Baronetage, i. 501; iii. 595. Betham's Baronetage, v. app. 11. The Genealogist, v. 231, 232; New Series, vii. 4. Metcalfe's Visitations of Suffolk, 112, 182. Burke's Extinct Baronetcies. F. G. Lee's History of Thame, 146. Metcalfe's Visitations of Northamptonshire, 164. Visitation of Gloucester, edited by T. F. Fenwick, and W. C. Metcalfe, 9. Notes and Queries, 6 S. xii. 443. Howard's Visitation of England and Wales, iv. 4; v. 25. Miscellanea Genealogica et Heraldica, ii. 337; 3rd Series, iii. 142, 201.

BARKESWORTH. Foster's Visitations of Yorkshire, 217.

BARKHAM. Harleian Society, xiii. 342; xv. 50; xx. 9. Burke's Extinct Baronetcies.

BARKLEY. Bird's Magazine of Honour, 79. Berry's Hampshire Genealogies, 209. Harleian Society, ix. 287; xv. 46; xxi. 8; xxii. 26; xxvii. 12; xxviii. 29. The Visitations of Devon, edited by J. L. Vivian, 43. See BERKELEY.

BARKSTED. Visitation of London, 1634, printed by Sir T. Phillipps, 4.

BARLEE, BARLEY, or BARLYE. Morant's Essex, i. 410; ii. 86, 570, 612. Cussan's History of Hertfordshire, Parts iii. and iv. 148. Berry's Hertfordshire Genealogies, 75. Jewitt's Reliquary, vii. 209. Bysshe's Visitation of Essex, edited by J. J. Howard, 14. The Genealogist, New Series, vii. 4. East Anglian, i. 226. Clutterbuck's Hertford, iii. 67, 333. Wright's Essex, ii. 149. Harleian Society, xiii. 1; xiv. 545; xxii. 27. Chauncy's Hertfordshire, 148.

BARLOW, or BARLOE. Berry's Berkshire Genealogies, 77. Berry's Sussex Genealogies, 164. Dwnn's Visitations of Wales, i. 117. Chetham Society, xlii. 294; lxxxi. 5; lxxxiv. 28. Thoresby's Ducatus Leodiensis, 253. Pembrokeshire Pedigrees, 139, 158. Baines' History of the Co. of Lancaster, ii. 396. Notes and

Queries, 1 S. vi. 147, 392, 439. Wotton's English Baronetage, iii·
614. Betham's Baronetage, v. 536. Burke's Extinct Baronetcies·
Documentary Notes relating to the District of Turton, by J. C.
Scholes, 118. The Genealogist, New Series, vii. 5. The Gresleys
of Drakelow, by F. Madan, 239.

BARNABY. Burke's Commoners, iv. 1. Harleian Society, xiii. 20 ;
xxvii. 13. New England Register, xviii. 361.

BARNAK, or BARNACKE. Morant's Essex, ii. 217. Harleian Society,
xix. 14.

BARNARD. Visitation of Somerset, printed by Sir Thos. Phillipps,
12. Visitation of Gloucestershire, 1569, (Middle Hill, 1854, fol.)
1. Burke's Commoners, (of Cave Castle,) ii. 253, Landed Gentry,
2, 3, 4, 5, 6, 7, 8 ; (of Bartlow,) Landed Gentry, 2, 3, 4, 5, 6 ; (of
Prestbury,) 7, 8. Harleian Society, iv. 177 ; v. 159 ; xi. 6 ; xiii.
20, 144 ; xxi. 202 ; xxxix. 936, 1096. Pedigree of Wilson of
High Wray, etc., by Joseph Foster, 25. Banks' Baronies in Fee,
ii. 76. The Genealogist, v. 308 ; New Series, ix. 120. Metcalfe's
Visitations of Suffolk, 3. Jewers' Wells Cathedral, 97. The
Genealogical Magazine, ii. 161.

BARNARDISTON. Burke's Landed Gentry, 2, 3, 4, 5, 6, 7, 8. Suffolk
Institute of Archæology, iv. 123. The Genealogist, iii. 348.
Harleian Society, xiv. 545 ; xv. 51 ; xix. 4, 79. Wotton's English
Baronetage, iii. 396. Metcalfe's Visitations of Suffolk, 112.
Burke's Extinct Baronetcies. Howard's Visitation of England
and Wales, viii. 41.

BARNBY, or BARNEBY. Burke's Commoners, iv. 1, Landed Gentry,
2, 3, 4, 5, 6, 7, 8. Foster's Visitations of Yorkshire, 339. Burke's
Royal Families, (London, 1851, 8vo.) i. 121. Hunter's Deanery of
Doncaster, ii. 233. Duncumb's History of the Co. of Hereford,
ii. 68. Harleian Society, xvi. 12. Metcalfe's Visitation of
Worcester, 1683, 8. See LUTLEY.

BARNE. Harleian Society, i. 25 ; xiv. 538. Burke's Commoners, i.
139, Landed Gentry, 2, 3, 4, 5, 6, 7, 8. Suckling's History of
Suffolk, i. 95. Miscellanea Genealogica et Heraldica, 2nd Series,
v. 62. Howard's Visitation of England and Wales, vii. 158.

BARNEHOUSE. Visitation of Devon, edited by F. T. Colby, 182.
Visitations of Devon, by J. L. Vivian, 647.

BARNEIS. Harleian Society, xiv. 547.

BARNES. Life of Ambrose Barnes, Alderman of Newcastle, 1828,
8vo. Visitation of Durham, 1615, (Sunderland, 1820, fol.,) 20.
Cambridgeshire Visitation, edited by Sir T. Phillipps, 4. Mis-
cellanea Genealogica et Heraldica, New Series, i. 78. Foster's
Visitations of Yorkshire, 50. History of Darlington, by W.
Hylton Dyer Longstaffe, lxxxi. Hutchins' Dorset, iii. 708.
Surtees' Durham, i. lxxxii. ; iii. 355. Harleian Society, xiii. 2, 21 ;
xx. 10 ; xxvii. 14. Burke's Landed Gentry, 6, 7, 8. Hasted's
Kent, (Hund. of Blackheath, by H. H. Drake,) 160. Foster's
Visitations of Durham, 3. Oliver's History of Antigua, i. 34.
Memoir of Richard Haines, by C. R. Haines, table vii. f.

BARNET, or BARNETT. Topographer and Genealogist, ii. 548. Burke's

Commoners, (of Stratton Park,) i. 498, Landed Gentry, 2, 3, 4, 5, 6, 7, 8; (of Glympton Park,) Landed Gentry, 5, 6, 8. Archæological Sketches of Ross, by T. D. Fosbroke, 156.

BARNEWALL. Case of Matthew Barnewall, Esq., claiming the titles of Viscount Barnewall and Baron Turvey, folio, pp. 7, and Appendix, p. 1, 1814. Claim of Matthew Barnewall, Esq., to be Visct. Barnewall of Kingsland and Baron of Turvey, Sess. Papers, 44 of 1812; 27 of 1812-13; 61 of 1813-14. Burke's Landed Gentry, 4, 5, 6, 7. John D'Alton's History of Co. Dublin, 301. O'Hart's Irish Pedigrees, 2nd Series, 141. Archdall's Lodge's Peerage, v. 29. Foster's Collectanea Genealogica, (Funeral Certificates, Ireland,) 13-17.

BARNEY. Harleian Society, i. 59; xxxii. 15, 16. Visitation of Norfolk, published by Norfolk Archæological Society, i. 7. See BERNEY.

BARNFIELD. Visitations of Staffordshire, 1614 and 1663-4. William Salt Society, 32. Harleian Society, xxviii. 34.

BARNHAM. Hasted's Kent, ii. 466; iii. 469. Berry's Hampshire Genealogies, 166. Harleian Society, i. 88; xlii. 168. Burke's Extinct Baronetcies. Notes and Queries, 6 S. ix. 1. East Barnet, by F. C. Cass, 218. Genealogical Records of the Family of Woodd, 48.

BARNHOUSE. The Visitations of Cornwall, edited by J. L. Vivian, 413.

BARNINGHAM, or BERNINGHAM. Pedigrees of the Leading Families of Lancashire, published by Joseph Foster, (London, 1872, fol.). Plantagenet-Harrison's History of Yorkshire, i. 280, 281.

BARNS. Burke's Landed Gentry, 7 p. 773.

BARNS-GRAHAM. Burke's Landed Gentry, 8.

BARNSLEY, or BARNESLEY. Shaw's Staffordshire, ii. 209. Visitation of Staffordshire, 1663-4, printed by Sir T. Phillipps, 2. Harleian Society, xv. 51; xxvii. 15; xliii. 168. Visitations of Staffordshire, 1614 and 1663-4, William Salt Society, 33. Visitation of Gloucester, edited by T. F. Fenwick and W. C. Metcalfe, 4. Surrey Archæological Collections, x.

BARNSTON. Burke's Landed Gentry, 2, 3, 4, 5, 6, 7, 8. Ormerod's Cheshire, ii. 747. Howard's Visitation of England and Wales, vii. 23.

BARNWALL, or BARNWELL. Blomefield's Norfolk, x. 20. Burke's Landed Gentry, 3, 4, 5, 6, 7, 8. Carthew's Hundred of Launditch, Part ii. 388. Metcalfe's Visitations of Northamptonshire, 3. Harleian Society, xxii. 110; xxxii. 17; xxxvii. 320.

BARON, or BARRON. Harleian Society, i. 87, 91, 94; xiii. 342; xv. 52; xl. 1222; xli. 107. Baker's Northampton, ii. 295. Burke's Commoners, (of Belmont,) ii. 497; Landed Gentry, (of Glenview,) 2, 3, 4, 5, 6, 7; (of Carrig Barron,) 4 supp., 5, 6. Abram's History of Blackburn, 388, 501. Maclean's History of Trigg Minor, iii. 266. The Genealogist, v. 233. Burke's Colonial Gentry, ii. 708. See LE BARON.

BARONS. Morant's Essex, i. 7.

BAROW, or BARROW. Cambridgeshire Visitation, edited by Sir T. Phillipps, 4. Visitation of Norfolk, published by Norfolk Archæological Society, i. 114. Burke's Landed Gentry, 2, 3, 4, 5, 6, 7, 8. Harleian Society, xiii. 344 ; xxxii. 18 ; xli. 46. Fosbrooke's History of Gloucestershire, i. 299. Notes and Queries, 3 S. viii. 148 ; 5 S. i. 436. Metcalfe's Visitations of Suffolk, 113. Weaver's Visitation of Herefordshire, 6. Metcalfe's Visitations of Northamptonshire, 67. Burke's Family Records, 39. The Perverse Widow, by A. W. Crawley-Boevey, 287.

BARR. Paterson's History of Ayr and Wigton, iii. 123. Paterson's History of the Co. of Ayr, i. 293. See BUNTINE-BARR.

BARRE. Lipscombe's History of the County of Buckingham, iv. 345. Baker's Northampton, i. 19. See BARRY.

BARREL. Hasted's Kent, ii. 695. Visitation of Middlesex, Salisbury, 1820, fol., 15. Foster's Visitation of Middlesex, 31.

BARRET, BARETT, or BARRETT. Morant's Essex, i. 78, 86. Hasted's Kent, iii. 665. Visitation of Cornwall, edited by Sir N. H. Nicolas, 3, 4. Dwnn's Visitations of Wales, i. 68, 70, 146, 153, 154. Cambridgeshire Visitation, edited by Sir T. Phillipps, 4. Burke's Landed Gentry, (of Milton House,) 3, 4, 5, 6, 7, 8 ; (of Court Lodge,) 6, 7, 8. Suckling's History of Suffolk, ii. 160. Harleian Society, ii. 107 ; viii. 379 ; ix. 4 ; xiii. 145 ; xiv. 548 ; xli. 92. Nichols' History of the County of Leicester, iv. 407. Caermarthenshire Pedigrees, 61. Visitatio Comitatus Wiltoniæ, 1623, printed by Sir Thos. Phillipps. Thoroton's Nottinghamshire, i. 227. The Visitations of Cornwall, edited by J. L. Vivian, 16. Maclean's History of Trigg Minor, iii. 406. O'Hart's Irish Pedigrees, 2nd Series, 304. Wood's Douglas's Peerage of Scotland, i. 199. Metcalfe's Visitations of Suffolk, 4. Visitations of Wiltshire, edited by G. W. Marshall, 31. Burke's Extinct Baronetcies, 599. Archæologia Cantiana, xiv. 124. Carthew's Hundred of Launditch, Part iii. 233. Genealogies of Morgan and Glamorgan, by G. T. Clark, 476. New England Register, xlii. 257. Howard's Visitation of England and Wales, viii. 57.

BARRETT-LENNARD. Berry's Essex Genealogies, 166. Burke's Royal Families, (London, 1851, 8vo.) ii. 22. Shirley's History of the County of Monaghan, 180. Edmondson's Baronagium Genealogicum, iv. 358. Betham's Baronetage, v. 462.

BARRI. Evidences of the Barri Family, by Sir Geo. Duckett, Bart. Kendal, 1890, 8vo.

BARRIFF. Harleian Society, xv. 53.

BARRINGTON, or BARINGTON. Noble's Memoirs of the House of Cromwell, ii. 44-66. Grandison Peerage Evidence, 356. Morant's Essex, i. 166 ; ii. 23, 503. Miscellanea Genealogica et Heraldica, ii. 161. Berry's Essex Genealogies, 124. Visitation of Sussex, 1570, printed by Sir T. Phillipps, (Middle Hill, fol.) 1. Burke's Royal Families, (London, 1851, 8vo.) ii. 192. Harleian Society, viii. 92 ; xiii. 22, 87, 147, 343 ; xiv. 549. Lipscombe's History of the County of Buckingham, ii. 75. Clutterbuck's Hertford, ii.

299. Wright's Essex, ii. 311. Chauncy's Hertfordshire, 366.
Essex Archæological Society, New Series, i. 251. Archdall's
Lodge's Peerage, v. 200. Wotton's English Baronetage, i. 65.
Banks' English Baronage, i. 321. Betham's Baronetage, i. 71.
Foster's Collectanea Genealogica, (MP's Ireland,) 30; (Funeral
Certificates, Ireland,) 19. Burke's Extinct Baronetcies. Bysshe's
Visitation of Essex, edited by J. J. Howard, 14.

BARRITT. Jewitt's Reliquary, ix. 144; xiii. 40.

BARRY. Claim of James R. Barry to vote at Elections of Irish Peers
as Visct. Buttevant, Sess. Papers, 215 of 1825. Topographer and
Genealogist, ii. 548. Visitation of Oxfordshire, 1634, printed by
Sir T. Phillipps, (Middle Hill, fol.) 13. Burke's Commoners, (of
Lemlara) ii. 456, Landed Gentry, 2, 3, 4, 5, 6, 7, 8; (of Bally-
clough), Landed Gentry, 2, 3, 4, 5, 6, 7, 8; (of Foaty), 2, 3, 4,
5, 6; (of Castle Cor,) 5, 6, 7, 8; (of Kilbolane), 8; (of Keiss Castle),
8; (of Balleydmond,) 5; (of Rocklaveston Manor), 2, 3; (of Sand-
ville,) 8, supp.; Harleian Society, v. 198, 326; vi. 18; xiii. 81.
Westcote's Devonshire, edited by G. Oliver and P. Jones, 556.
Hampshire Visitations, printed by Sir T. Phillipps, 21. Baker's
Northampton, i. 19. Thoroton's Nottinghamshire, i. 171; ii. 304.
O'Hart's Irish Pedigrees, 2nd Series, 103. Archdall's Lodge's
Peerage, i. 285. Banks' Baronies in Fee, ii. 42. Visitation of
Devon, edited by F. T. Colby, 12. Foster's Collectanea Genea-
logica, (Funeral Certificates, Ireland,) 20. F. G. Lee's History of
Thame, 117. History of Santry and Cloghran, by B. W. Adams,
97. The Visitations of Devon, edited by J. L. Vivian, 44. Burke's
Family Records, 40. Berks Archæological and Architectural
Society Journal, iii. 128. Howard's Visitation of Ireland, iii. 40.
See BARRE.

BARSHAM. Carthew's Hundred of Launditch, Part iii. 79. Harleian
Society, xxxii. 18.

BARSTOW. Burton's History of Hemingborough, 217. Burke's
Family Records, 43.

BARTELOTT, BARTTELOT, or BARTTELOTT. Berry's Sussex Genealogies,
179, 201. Burke's Landed Gentry, 5 supp. Visitation of Sussex,
1570, printed by Sir T. Phillipps, (Middle Hill, fol.) 2. Dallaway's
Sussex, i. 28. Sussex Archæological Collections, xxvii. 50.
Castles, Mansions, and Manors of Western Sussex, by D. G. C.
Elwes, and C. J. Robinson, 218.

BARTER. Oliver's History of Antigua, i, 36.

BARTHELMEW. Berry's Hampshire Genealogies, 49.

BARTHOLEMEW. Hasted's Kent, ii. 262.

BARTHOLOMEW. Topographer and Genealogist, iii. 221.

BARTLETT, or BARTLET. Berry's Sussex Genealogies, 178. Nash's
Worcestershire ii. 110. Visitation of Gloucestershire, 1583, and
1623, printed by Sir T. Phillipps. (1864, folio) 4. Visitation of
Gloucestershire, 1569, (Middle Hill. 1854, fol.) 1. Topographer,
(London, 1789-91, 8vo.) iv. 347. Visitatio Comitatus Wiltoniæ,
1623, printed by Sir T. Phillipps. Hutchins' Dorset, iii. 387.
Wiltshire Archæological Magazine, xi. 34. Visitation of Wiltshire,

edited by G. W. Marshall, 89, 93. Howard's Visitation of England and Wales, i. 65 ; vi. 27, 30 ; Notes, ii. 85. Bradford Antiquary, i. 188. Harleian Society, xxi. 203. New England Register, xl. 197. Burke's Family Records, 44. Burke's Landed Gentry, 8. The Visitations of Devon, by J. L. Vivian, 843. The Genealogical Magazine, iii. 360, 404. Bloom's History of Preston-on-Stour, 28.

BARTON. Memoir of the Family of Barton, etc., continued through that of Mowbray, and that of Stedman. By John Stedman. Bath, 1857, 8vo. Surtees Society, xxxvi. 124. Burke's Commoners, (of Stapleton Park,) iv. 405, Landed Gentry, 2, 3, 4, 5, 6, 7, 8 ; (of Threxton House), Landed Gentry, 2 supp., 3, 4, 5, 6, 7 ; (of Grove), 2, 3, 4, 5, 6, 7, 8 ; (of Clonelly), 2, 3, 4, 5 ; (of the Waterfoot), 2, 3, 4, 5, 6, 7 ; (of Straffan), 2, 3, 4, 5, 6, 7, 8 ; (of Glendalough), 2, 3, 4, 5, 6, 7, 8 ; (of Greenfort,) 4 supp., 5, 6, 7, 8 ; (of Rochestown), 2, 3, 4. Miscellanea Genealogica et Heraldica, New Series, i. 174 ; iii. 239 ; 2nd Series, iii. 177 ; iv. 178, 220 ; 3rd Series, i. 230. Foster's Visitations of Yorkshire, 5, 133, 182. Chetham Society, lxxxi. 21, 57 ; xcv. 87 ; cx. 197. Foster's Lancashire Pedigrees. Dickinson's History of Southwell, 2nd edition, 170. Hampshire Visitations, printed by Sir T. Phillipps, 3. Whitaker's History of Whalley, ii. 319. Abram's History of Blackburn, 252, 502. Ormerod's Cheshire, ii. 749. Harleian Society, xvi. 13, 14 ; xxviii. 55. Notes and Queries, 1 S. viii. 543, 590. Howard's Visitation of England and Wales, i. 90 ; Notes, ii. 98. Metcalfe's Visitations of Northamptonshire, 164. Burke's Colonial Gentry, ii. 467, 623, 779. Oliver's History of Antigua, i. 38. Annals of Smith of Balby, by H. E. Smith, 241. Croston's edition of Baines's Lancaster, iii. 156. The Genealogist, New Series, xiii. 97.

BARTRAM. Visitation of Staffordshire, (Willm. Salt Soc.) 42.

BARTTELOTT-SMYTH. Burke's Commoners, ii. 628, Landed Gentry, 2, 3, 4, 5.

BARWELL. Nichols' History of the County of Leicester, iii. 853.

BARWICK. Gentleman's Magazine, 1844, i. 29. Harleian Society, iv. 180 ; xl. 1191. Visitatio Comitatus Wiltoniæ, 1623, printed by Sir T. Phillipps. Burke's Landed Gentry, 2 supp. p. 43. Historical Notices of Doncaster, by C. W. Hatfield, 2nd Series, 8 ; 3rd Series, 330.

BARWIKE. Metcalfe's Visitations of Suffolk, 86.

BARWIS. Burke's Landed Gentry, 2, 3, 4, 5, 6, 7. Foster's Visitations of Cumberland and Westmorland, 2.

BARY. Dwnn's Visitation of Wales, i. 77.

BARZEY. Dwnn's Visitations of Wales, i. 23.

BASFORTH. Foster's Visitations of Yorkshire, 217.

BASH, or BASHE. Harleian Society, viii. 28 ; xx. 125.

BASHETT. See BACHET.

BASKERVILE, BASKERVILLE, or BASKERVYLE. Pedigree of Baskerville of Riccarston, [T. P.] Gentleman's Magazine, 1824, ii. 579 ; 1825, ii. 314, 421. Berry's Hampshire Genealogies, 7. Dwnn's

Visitations of Wales, i. 256. Burke's Commoners, (of Clyro
Court,) i. 87, 89, Landed Gentry, 2, 3, 4, 5, 6, 7, 8; (of Crowsley
Park,) Landed Gentry, 2 supp., 3, 4, 5, 6, 7, 8; Burke's Heraldic
Illustrations, 79. Bridge's Northamptonshire, by Rev. Peter
Whalley, i. 72. Burke's Royal Families, (London, 1851, 8vo.) i. 18.
Visitations of Berkshire, printed by Sir T. Phillipps, 5. Eyton's
Antiquities of Shropshire, v. 102. Hampshire Visitations, printed
by Sir Thos. Phillipps, 3. Visitatio Comitatus Wiltoniæ, 1623,
printed by Sir T. Phillipps. Baker's Northampton, i. 397.
Robinson's Mansions of Herefordshire, 106. Harleian Society,
xv. 53; xxix. 387. The Genealogist, v. 234; New Series, xvi. 44,
86. Ormerod's Cheshire, iii. 718. Earwaker's East Cheshire,
ii. 372. Cooke's Continuation of Duncumb's Hereford, (Hund. of
Grimsworth,) Part ii. 158. Visitation of Gloucester, edited by
T. F. Fenwick, and W. C. Metcalfe, 10. Weaver's Visitation of
Herefordshire, 7. Miscellanea Genealogica et Heraldica, 2nd
Series, v. 85.

BASKET, or BASKETT. Berry's Hampshire Genealogies, 160. Berry's
Sussex Genealogies, 218. Hampshire Visitations, printed by Sir
T. Phillipps, 3. Hutchins' Dorset, ii. 608; iii. 172. Harleian
Society, xx. 11.

BASNETT. Berry's Berkshire Genealogies, 64, 93. Notes and Queries,
1 S. iii. 495; iv. 77. Harleian Society, xxxvii. 371.

BASPOOLE. Harleian Society, xxxii. 19.

BASS. Burke's Landed Gentry, 5, 6. New England Registers,
lii. 435.

BASSANO. Glover's History of Derbyshire, ii. 592, (575). Visitation
of London, 1634, printed by Sir T. Phillipps, 5. Harleian Society,
xiii. 344, xv. 54.

BASSET, or BASSETT. Herald and Genealogist, iv. 437. J. H. Hill's
History of Langton, 76. Collectanea Topographica et Genealogica,
vii. 257. The Visitations of Cornwall, edited by J. L. Vivian,
17. Stemmata Shirleiana, by E. P. Shirley, 2nd edn., 27. A
complete Parochial History of the County of Cornwall, ii. 227.
An Historical Survey of Cornwall, by C. S. Gilbert, i. 486. Ellacombe's History of Bitton, 100, 119. Topographical Miscellanies,
1792, 4to., (Drayton Bassett.) Edmondson's Baronagium Genea-
logicum, vi. 39. Brydges' Collins' Peerage, viii. 502. Burke's
Extinct Baronetcies. Glamorganshire Pedigrees, edited by Sir T.
Phillipps, 2, 4, 21, 34. Visitation of Cornwall, edited by Sir N.
H. Nicolas, 5. Visitation of Gloucestershire, 1583 and 1623,
printed by Sir T. Phillipps, (1864, folio,) 4. Burke's Landed
Gentry, (of Umberleigh and Watermouth,) 2, 3, 4, 5, 6, 7, 8; (of
Beaupré,) 2, 3, 4, 5, 6, 7, 8; (of Tehidy), 2, 3, 4, 5, 6, 7, 8; (of
Bonvilstone,) 3, 4, 5, 6, 7. Harleian Society, iii. 18; iv. 41, 42,
124, 170; vi. 335; viii. 89; ix. 5; xxi. 204; xl. 1188. Topo-
grapher, (London, 1789-91, 8vo.) ii. 318. George Oliver's History
of Beverley, 564. Lipscombe's History of the County of Buckingham, i. 69; iv. 258. Bridge's Northamptonshire, by Rev. Peter
Whalley, ii. 122. Shaw's Staffordshire, ii. 2, 12. Westcote's

Devonshire, edited by G. Oliver and P. Jones, 485. Burton's
Description of Leicestershire, 228. Nichols' History of the County
of Leicester, iv. 904-906, 968. Dugdale's Warwickshire, 1004.
Baker's Northampton, i. 9. Thoroton's Nottinghamshire, i. 162;
iii. 188. T. Nicholas's County Families of Wales, 620. Fosbrooke's History of Gloucestershire, i. 124. Banks' Baronies in
Fee, i. 114. Banks' Dormant and Extinct Baronage, i. 22, 231;
ii. 31. Notes and Queries, 5 S. iv. 68, 98, 134. Visitation of
Staffordshire, (William Salt Soc.) 45. The Visitations of Devon,
edited by J. L. Vivian, 45. Visitation of Gloucester, edited by
T. F. Fenwick, and W. C. Metcalfe, 11. Leicestershire Architectural Society, iv. 25. Genealogies of Morgan and Glamorgan,
by G. T. Clark, 348, 362. Oxfordshire Historical Society, xxiv.
10. The Genealogist, New Series, vii. 245; x. 34, 136; xiii. 255;
xiv. 26; xvi. 40; xvii. 240.

BASSINGBURN, or BASSINGBURNE. Clutterbuck's Hertford, ii. 345.
Baker's Northampton, i. 9. Banks' Dormant and Extinct Baronage,
i. 24. The Genealogist, New Series, vii. 245; x. 88.

BASTARD. Visitation of Cornwall, edited by Sir N. H. Nicolas, 5.
Tuckett's Devonshire Pedigrees, 182. Visitation of Norfolk,
published by Norfolk Archæological Society, i. 52, 439. Burke's
Commoners, (of Kitley), i. 17, Landed Gentry, 2, 3, 4, 5, 6, 7, 8;
(of Charlton Marshall,) Landed Gentry, 2 supp., 3, 4, 5, 6, 7, 8;
Harleian Society, vi. 19; ix. 6; xxxii. 20. Carthew's Hundred of
Launditch, Part ii. 801. Burke's Royal Families, (London, 1851,
8vo.) ii. 159. Hutchins' Dorset, iii. 523. The Visitations of
Cornwall, edited by Lt.-Col. J. L. Vivian, 20. A Complete
Parochial History of the County of Cornwall, iv. 290. Visitation
of Devon, edited by F. T. Colby, 13. Burke's Extinct Baronetcies.
The Visitations of Devon, edited by J. L. Vivian, 49.

BASYNGES, or BASINGES. Savage's History of the Hundred of Carhampton, 267. Blore's Rutland, 127.

BATAILE. Morant's Essex, i. 131.

BATCHCROFT. Blomefield's Norfolk, vii. 308. See BATISCROFT.

BATE. Surtees Society, xxxvi. 80. Foster's Visitations of Yorkshire,
192. Herald and Genealogist, i. 421-430. Ord's History of
Cleveland, 409. Nichols' History of the County of Leicester, iii.
636. Hunter's Deanery of Doncaster, ii. 167. Miscellanea Genea-
logica et Heraldica, New Series, ii. 488, 576. Genealogy of Henzey,
Tyttery, and Tysack, by H. S. Grazebrook, 64. Harleian Society,
xvi. 15; xxxii. 21; xl. 1193. Burke's Extinct Baronetcies.
Fletcher's Leicestershire Pedigrees and Royal Descents, 81.
Howard's Visitation of England and Wales, iv. 173. Burke's
Landed Gentry, 8. New England Register, li. 268.

BATEMAN. Pedigree of Bateman, Parker, and Levinge, by John
Sleigh, Single sheet, 1865. Jewitt's Reliquary, ii. 88; v. 245;
vi. 105; vii. 18. Visitation of London, 1634, printed by Sir
T. Phillipps, 5. History of the Parish of Leek, by John Sleigh,
108. Burke's Commoners, (of Knypersley Hall,) i. 18, Landed
Gentry, 2, 3, 4, 5, 6, 7, 8; (of Middleton Hall,) Commoners, iii.

598, Landed Gentry, 2, 3, 4, 5, 6, 7, 8; (of Hartington,) Commoners, iii. 349, Landed Gentry, 2, 3, 4, 5, 6, 7, 8; (of Guilsborough,) Landed Gentry, 2 add., 3, 4, 5; (of Bartholey House,) 2, 3, 4, 5, 6, 7, 8; (of Oak Park,) 2, 3; (of Moor Park,), 5 supp., 6, 7, 8. Harleian Society, viii. 47, 463; xv. 55; xxxviii. 477. Visitation of Derbyshire, 1663-4, (Middle Hill, 1854, fol.) 1. The Borough of Stoke-upon-Trent, by John Ward, 181. The Genealogist, iii. 120. Archdall's Lodge's Peerage, v. 245. Metcalfe's Visitations of Suffolk, 4. Burke's Extinct Baronetcies. Notes and Queries, 7 S. vii. 364, 437. Burke's Family Records, 46.

BATEMAN-CHAMPAIN. Burke's Landed Gentry, 5 supp., 6. Foster's Lancashire Pedigrees.

BATES. Burke's Commoners, (of Denton,) i. 556, Landed Gentry, 2, 3, 4, 5 supp.; (of Milbourne,) Commoners, i. 623, Landed Gentry, 2, 3, 4, 5, 6, 7; (of Heddon)) 6, 8; (of Manydown Park,) 6. Burke's Royal Families, (London, 1851, 8vo.) 2, 86. Historical Notices of Doncaster, by C. W. Hatfield, 2nd Series, 132. Foster's Visitations of Northumberland, 10.

BATESCOMB. Harleian Society, xx. 11.

BATH. Gentleman's Magazine, 1835, ii. 375. Burke's Extinct Baronetcies, 599. Notes and Queries, 2 S. x. 54, 137. Banks' Dormant and Extinct Baronage, iii. 57. Foster's Collectanea Genealogica, (Funeral Certificates, Ireland,) 21. Burke's Family Records, 51.

BATHER. Jewitt's Reliquary, vi. 28. Burke's Landed Gentry, 8 supp.

BATHURST. Rudder's Gloucestershire, 354. Hasted's Kent, i. 59, 296; iii. 35. Berry's Kent Genealogies, 198. Burke's Landed Gentry, 2, 3, 4, 5, 6, 7, 8. Burke's Commoners, ii. 63. Harleian Society, viii. 188, 341, 360; xv. 56; xxi. 9; xlii. 162, 175. Visitations of Berkshire, printed by Sir T. Phillipps, 6. Hampshire Visitations, printed by Sir T. Phillipps, 3. Thoresby's Ducatus Leodiensis, 13. Archæologia Æliana, 2nd Series, v. 75. Hoare's Wiltshire, V. i. 172. Notes and Queries, 3 S. viii. 127, 177, 217. Bakers' Northampton, ii. 203. The Citizens of London and their Rulers, by B. B. Orridge, 193. Plantagenet-Harrison's History of Yorkshire, i. 207. The Genealogist, iv. 58; v. 234. Yorkshire Archæological and Topographical Journal, vi. 267. Edmondson's Baronagium Genealogicum, v. 416; vi. 11. Brydges' Collins' Peerage, v. 80. Wotton's English Baronetage, ii. 394. Betham's Baronetage, ii. 10. Burke's Extinct Baronetcies. Gloucestershire Notes and Queries, i. 369. Visitation of Gloucester, edited by T. F. Fenwick, and W. C. Metcalfe, 12. Leicestershire Architectural Society, ii. 358.

BATISCROFT. Harleian Society, xxxii. 21. See BATCHCROFT.

BATMAN. Dwnn's Visitations of Wales, i. 173.

BATSON, or BATTESON. Burke's Landed Gentry, 5, 6, 7, 8. Visitation of Gloucester, edited by T. F. Fenwick, and W. C. Metcalfe, 13.

BATT, or BATTE. Surtees Society, xxxvi. 233. Visitation of Wiltshire, 1677, printed by Sir T. Phillipps, (Middle Hill, 1854, fol.). Burke's Landed Gentry, 3, 4, 5, 6, 7, 8. Annual Register, lxxiii. 23u. The Genealogist, New Series, xv. 86. New England Register, li. 348; lii. 46, 321.

BATTAILE. Morant's Essex, i. 346, 376.

BATTELL. Harleian Society, xiii. 23, 227.

BATTEN. Burke's Landed Gentry, 2 supp., 3, 4, 5, 6, 7, 8. Visitations of Berkshire, printed by Sir Thos. Phillipps, 6. Visitation of Devon, edited by F. T. Colby, 13. The Genealogist, v. 235.

BATTERSBY. Visitation of Cornwall, edited by Sir N. H. Nicolas, 6. Burke's Landed Gentry, (of Lislin), 2, 3, 4, 5; (of Lough Bane), 2, 3, 4, 5, 6, 7, 8. Harleian Society, ix. 6. The Visitations of Cornwall, edited by Lt.-Col. J. L. Vivian, 21.

BATTIE, BATTYE, or BATTY. Surtees Society, xxxvi. 167. Burke's Commoners, (of Warmsworth,) ii. 184; (of Ballyhealy,) Landed Gentry, 2, 3, 4, 5, 6; (of Tingrith,) 8; (of Crossland Hill,) 5, 6, 7, 8. Foster's Yorkshire Pedigrees. Hunter's Deanery of Doncaster, i. 127. Hulbert's Annals of Almondbury, 162. The Genealogist, New Series, xiv. 45. Ilkley, Ancient and Modern, by R. Collyer, and J. H. Turner, 223. Harleian Society, xxxvii. 224; xxxviii. 644. Howard's Visitation of England and Wales, v. 4.

BATTIN. Harleian Society, xv. 52.

BATTISCOMBE. Harleian Society, xiv. 561. Notes and Queries, 2 S. x. 99. See BATESCOMB.

BATTISFORD. Harleian Society, xli. 110.

BATTISHILL, or BATTESHULL. Harleian Society. vi. 19. Westcote's Devonshire, edited by G. Oliver and P. Jones, 540. Miscellanea Genealogica et Heraldica, New Series, iii. 334. Visitation of Devon, edited by F. T. Colby, 14. The Visitations of Devon, edited by J. L. Vivian, 52.

BATTLEY, BATTELY, or BATLEY. Berry's Surrey Genealogies, 10. Nichols' Illustrations of Literary History, iv. 85. Burke's Landed Gentry, 7, 8.

BATTYE-TREVOR. Howard's Visitation of England and Wales, ii. i.

BAUD, BAUDE, or BAWDE. Morant's Essex, i. 241. Chauncy's Hertfordshire, 154. The Genealogist, iii. 349. Metcalfe's Visitations of Northamptonshire, 67. Harvey's Hundred of Willey, 322. Harleian Society, xix. 5.

BAUGH. Botfield's Stemmata Botevilliana, 146. Visitation of Oxfordshire, 1634, printed by Sir T. Phillipps, (Middle Hill, fol.) 13. Harleian Society, v. 320; xxi. 11; xxviii. 36. Metcalfe's Visitation of Worcester, 1683, 10.

BAUMGARTNER. Burke's Landed Gentry, 5, 6, 7, 8.

BAUNFIELD. Pedigree of Baunfield of Weston Baunfield, Co. Somerset, [by Sir Thos. Phillipps]. Visitation of Devon, edited by F. T. Colby, 10.

BAVAND. Harleian Society, xviii. 266.

BAVE. Miscellanea Genealogica et Heraldica, 2nd Series, i. 189.

BAVENT. Hoare's Wiltshire, III. ii. 77; IV. ii. 120. Banks'

Baronies in Fee, i. 117. Banks' Dormant and Extinct Baronage, i. 237. *See* DE BAVENT.

BAVERSTOCK. Burke's Commoners, i. 515. Dallaway's Sussex, 2nd edition, II. i. 53.

BAWDEN. An Historical Survey of Cornwall, by C. S. Gilbert, ii. 35. Pedigree of Family of Powell, by Edgar Powell, 80.

BAWDEWYN. Miscellanea Genealogica et Heraldica, 2nd Series, iii. 136. The Genealogist, New Series, xv. 92.

BAWDRIP. Glamorganshire Pedigrees, edited by Sir T. Phillipps, 3. Archæologia Cambrensis, 3 S. vii. 19. Genealogies of Morgan and Glamorgan, by G. T. Clark, 363.

BAWME. *See* BALME.

BAWNE. Foster's Visitations of Yorkshire, 489.

BAWSON. Genealogies of Morgan and Glamorgan, by G. T. Clark, 364.

BAXENDALE. Burke's Colonial Gentry, ii. 673. Burke's Landed Gentry, 8 supp.

BAXTER. Visitation of Norfolk, published by Norfolk Archæological Society, i. 397. Foster's Visitations of Yorkshire, 316. Burke's Visitation of Seats and Arms, i. 31. Hunter's Deanery of Doncaster, i. 384. Surtees' Durham, iii. 292. Harleian Society, xvi. 15 ; xxxii. 23, 24. Notes and Queries, 1 S. ii. 89, 206. Metcalfe's Visitations of Northamptonshire, 165. Foster's Visitations of Northumberland, 11. Burke's Landed Gentry, 7, 8, 8 supp.

BAYARD. Burke's Colonial Gentry, ii. 644.

BAYEAUX. Banks' Dormant and Extinct Baronage, i. 25. The Genealogist, New Series, xii. 174, 175.

BAYER. Oliver's History of Antigua, i. 18

BAYES. Harleian Society, xxxix. 832.

BAYLDON. Foster's Visitations of Yorkshire, 303.

BAYLEGH. Chetham Society, xcv. 45.

BAYLES. Berry's Essex Genealogies, 37. Harleian Society, xiv. 638 Burke's Colonial Gentry, i. 174.

BAYLEY, or BAYLY. The Bailleuls of Flanders and the Bayleys of Willow Hall. By Francis Bayley. London, 1881, 8vo. Topographer and Genealogist, i. 531 ; ii. 541. Berry's Hampshire Genealogies, 8, 239. Visitation of London, 1634, printed by Sir T. Phillipps, 5. Burke's Landed Gentry, (of Ballyarthur),. 2, 3, 4, 5, 6, 7, 8 ; (of Debsborough,) 2, 3, 4, 5, 6, 7, 8 ; (of Allertonshire,) 2 add. ; (of Norelands,) 2, 3, (under *Savage*) ; (of Willaston,) 8. Hampshire Visitations, printed by Sir T. Phillipps, 4. Hutchins' Dorset, iii. 672. Burke's Commoners, iii. 278. Visitation Comitatus Wiltoniæ, 1623, printed by Sir T. Phillipps. Miscellanea Genealogica et Heraldica, New Series, ii. 288. Harleian Society, xiii. 345 ; xv. 56 ; xxii. 27 ; xxviii. 36 ; xxxvii. 280. Brydges' Collins' Peerage, v. 196. Edmondson's Baronagium Genealogicum, vi. 47. The Genealogist, v. 309. Visitation of Wiltshire, edited by G. W. Marshall, 48, 76. Visitation of Gloucester, edited by T. F. Fenwick, and W. C. Metcalfe, 15. The Bayleys of Hope. By Ernest Axon. Stockport, 4to. Burke's Family Records, 52.

Croston's edn. of Baines's Lancaster, iii. 278. A History of Banking in Bristol, by C. H. Cave, 214. Howard's Visitation of Ireland, iii. 29. *See* BAILY.

BAYLIFF, or BAILEIFFE. Visitatio Comitatus Wiltoniæ, 1623, printed by Sir T. Phillipps. Visitation of Wiltshire, edited by G. W. Marshall, 26.

BAYMAN. Metcalfe's Visitations of Suffolk, 183.

BAYNARD. Morant's Essex, ii. 176, 404. Gentleman's Magazine, 1826, i. 418. Visitatio Comitatus Wiltoniæ, 1623, printed by Sir T. Phillipps. Wiltshire Archæological Magazine, iv. 6. Carthew's Hundred of Launditch, Part ii. 651. Banks' Baronies in Fee, ii. 41. Somersetshire Wills, printed for F. A. Crisp, ii. 32. The Genealogist, New Series, xii. 211 ; xv. 91. Visitation of Wiltshire, edited by G. W. Marshall, 34, 79. *See* BAINARD.

BAYNBRIGE, BAYNBRIGG, or BAYNBRIGGE. Foster's Visitations of Durham, 5, 7, 9. *See* BAINBRIDGE.

BAYNE, or BAYNES. Historical Genealogy of the Family of Bayne. By Joseph Lucas. 1896, 8vo. Foster's Visitations of Yorkshire, 491. Surtees Society, xxxvi. 44. Thoresby's Ducatus Leodiensis, 106. Foster's Pedigree of the Forsters and Fosters, Part ii. 5. Whitaker's Deanery of Craven, 3rd edn., 215. Betham's Baronetage, v. 453. W. Wheaters' History of Sherburn and Cawood, 319. Bysshe's Visitation of Essex, edited by J. J. Howard, 16. Burke's Family Records, 57. *See* BAINES.

BAYNHAM. Visitation of Gloucestershire, 1569, (Middle Hill, 1854, fol.) 1. Fosbrooke's History of Gloucestershire, ii. 157. Harleian Society, xxi. 12. Genealogies of Morgan and Glamorgan, by G. T. Clark, 205.

BAYNING. Burke's Extinct Baronetcies. Morant's Essex, i. 446, 482. Visitation of London, 1634, printed by Sir T. Phillipps, 5. Wright's Essex, ii. 762. Fosbrooke's History of Gloucestershire, ii. 357. Banks' Dormant and Extinct Baronage, iii. 52.

BAYNTON, or BAYNTUN. Burke's Extinct Baronetcies. Visitation of Wiltshire, edited by G. W. Marshall, 8, 44. Burke's Commoners, iv. 684. Harleian Society, viii. 32. Kite's Monumental Brasses of Wiltshire, 47. Visitatio Comitatus Wiltoniæ, 1623, printed by Sir T. Phillipps. Hoare's Wiltshire, III. iv. 7. Foster's Collectanea Genealogica, i. 17. Banks' Dormant and Extinct Baronage, ii. 511.

BAYNTUN - ROLT. Burke's Extinct Baronetcies, 452. Betham's Baronetage, iii. 300.

BAZLEY. Foster's Lancashire Pedigrees.

BEACH. Berry's Hampshire Genealogies, 256. Burke's Landed Gentry, 2, 3, 4, 5, 6, 7, 8. Hoare's Wiltshire, II. ii. 30. *See* BEECH.

BEACON. Carthew's Hundred of Launditch, Part. ii. 674.

BEADLE. Bysshe's Visitation of Essex, edited by J. J. Howard, 16.

BEADNELL. Burke's Landed Gentry, 5, 6.

BEADON. Burke's Landed Gentry, 2 supp., 3, 4. Jewers' Wells Cathedral, 198.

BEAKBANE. Pedigree of Wilson of High Wray, etc., by Joseph Foster, 34. The Descendants of John Backhouse, by J. Foster, 57. Pedigree of Wilson, by S. B. Foster, 141.

BEALE. Berry's Kent Genealogies, 18, 22, 203. Surtees Society, xxxvi. 189. Burke's Landed Gentry, (of Heath House,) 2, 3, 4, 5, 6, 7, 8; (of Brettenham,) 5 supp., 6, 7. Foster's Visitations of Yorkshire, 493. Hampshire Visitations, printed by Sir T. Phillipps, 4. Maclean's History of Trigg Minor, iii. 146. Burke's Extinct Baronetcies. Duchetiana, by Sir G. F. Duckett, 2nd edn., 238. Harleian Society, xv. 57, 58; xliii. 78. Metcalfe's Visitations of Suffolk, 184.

BEALING. Foster's Collectanea Genealogica, (Funeral Certificates, Ireland,) 22. Archdall's Lodge's Peerage, iv. 67.

BEALOTT. Jewitt's Reliquary, ix. 18.

BEAMISH. Pedigrees of the Families of Beamish, by R. P. Beamish. Cork, 1892, 8vo. Burke's Landed Gentry, (of Kilmalooda,) 3, 4, 5, 6, 7, 8; (of Mount Beamish,) 3, 4, 5, 6, 7, 8; (of Willsgrove), 3, 4, 5, 6, 8; (of Raheroon,) 3, 4. Burke's Royal Descents and Pedigrees of Founders' Kin, 50.

BEAMOND. Visitation of Devon, edited by F. T. Colby, 14, 16.

BEAMONT. Harleian Society, ii. 60. Bridge's Northamptonshire, by Rev. Peter Whalley, ii. 5.

BEAN, or BEANE. Harleian Society, xv. 58. New England Register, v. 202.

BEANLANDS. Ilkley, Ancient and Modern, by R. Collyer, and J. H. Turner, 225, 226. Burke's Colonial Gentry, ii. 414.

BEAPLE. The Visitations of Devon, edited by J. L. Vivian, 81.

BEARCROFT. Burke's Landed Gentry, 3, 4, 5, 6, 7, 8. Metcalfe's Visitation of Worcester, 1683, 12, 14. See LONGCROFT.

BEARD. Berry's Sussex Genealogies, 111. An Account of the Families of Boase, (Exeter, 1876, 4to.) 24. The Genealogist, New Series, vii. 6. Harleian Society, xl. 1264.

BEARDMORE. Burke's Landed Gentry, 2 supp., 3, 4, 5.

BEARE, or BEAR. Harleian Society, vi. 20. Westcote's Devonshire, edited by G. Oliver and P. Jones, 461. Visitation of Devon, edited by F. T. Colby, 17. Howard's Visitation of England and Wales, vi. 39. See BEER, BERE.

BEART. Metcalfe's Visitations of Suffolk, 184.

BEATSON. Genealogical History of the Family of Beatson, by A. J. Beatson. Edinburgh, 1854; another edn., 1860, 4to.; a pedigree, 1892. Herald and Genealogist, ii. 231. Burke's Landed Gentry, 3, 4. The Genealogical Magazine, iii. 435.

BEATTIE, or BEATTY. W. R. Fraser's History of Laurencekirk, 172. Ontarian Families, by E. M. Chadwick, i. 160. O'Hart's Irish Pedigrees, 2nd Series, 142.

BEAUBOYS. Hutchins' Dorset, iii. 421.

BEAUCHAMP, or BECHAM. Bird's Magazine of Honour, 77. Croke's History of the Family of Croke, No. 5, and ii. 126. Hasted's Kent, ii. 196. Gentleman's Magazine, 1826, ii. 19. Visitation of Cornwall, edited by Sir N. H. Nicolas, 7, 8. Nash's Worcester-

shire, i. 64; ii. 263, 264. Herald and Genealogist, viii. 192, 518.
Maclean's History of Trigg Minor, i. 65, 316. Notices of Swyn-
combe and Ewelme in Co. Oxford, by H. A. Napier, 67. Harleian
Society, ix. 7, 8; xv. 59; xvi. 245, 259; xix. 52. Lipscombe's
History of the County of Buckingham, i. 240, 255; iv. 174, 530.
Wright's History of Rutland, 39. Hutchinson's History of
Durham, iii. 240. Kite's Monumental Brasses of Wiltshire, 36,
47. Dugdale's Warwickshire, 48, 387, 763. Hoare's Wiltshire,
III. iv. 5, 50. Surtees' Durham, iv. 65. Manning and Bray's
Surrey, ii. 461. Clutterbuck's Hertford, i. 159, 358. Baker's
Northampton, ii. 218. The Visitations of Cornwall, by J. L.
Vivian, 22, 24. An Historical Survey of Cornwall, by C. S.
Gilbert, ii. 17. Banks' Baronies in Fee, i. 118, 120; ii. 137.
Banks' Dormant and Extinct Baronage, i. 26, 238; ii. 4, 36, 507;
iii. 64, 717. Jewitt's Reliquary, xx. 26. Weaver's Visitations of
Somerset, 4, 136. Harvey's Hundred of Willey, 4. Miscellanea
Genealogica et Heraldica, 2nd Series, iii. 317. The Genealogist,
New Series, xiv. 251; xvi. 43, 159. See DE BEAUCHAMP.

BEAUCHAMP-PROCTER. Betham's Baronetage, iii. 234.

BEAUCLERK. Berry's Sussex Genealogies, 1. Burke's Landed Gentry,
(of Ardglass,) 3, 4, 5, 6, 7 ; (of St. Leonard's Forest,) 2. Ormerod's
Cheshire, ii. 328. Edmondson's Baronagium Genealogicum, i. 23;
v. 450. Brydges' Collins' Peerage, i. 244. J. T. Godfree's
History of Lenton, 378.

BEAUFITZ. Scott of Scot's Hall, by J. R. Scott, 124.

BEAUFOE. Metcalfe's Visitations of Northamptonshire, 199.

BEAUFOREST. Sir T. Phillipps' Topographer, No. 1, (March, 1821,
8vo.) 19. Visitation of Oxfordshire, 1574, printed by Sir T.
Phillipps, (Middle Hill, fol.) 1. Harleian Society, v. 126.

BEAUFORT. Rudder's Gloucestershire, 256. History of Monmouth-
shire, by D. Williams, App. 129. Notices of Swyncombe and
Ewelme in Co. Oxford, by H. A. Napier, 68. Clutterbuck's
Hertford, iii. 31. Baker's Northampton, i. 55. Berry's Genea-
logical Peerage, 28. A complete Parochial History of the County
of Cornwall, i. 1. Edmondson's Baronagium Genealogicum, i. 19.
Banks' Dormant and Extinct Baronage, iii. 665. East Barnet, by
F. C. Cass, 230.

BEAUFORT, Duke of. T. Nicholas's County Families of Wales, 770.

BEAUFOY. Dugdale's Warwickshire, 278. Harleian Society, viii.
262, 307; xii. 203. Baker's Northampton, i. 232. Visitation of
Warwickshire, 1619, published with Warwickshire Antiquarian
Magazine, 168. Carthew's Hundred of Launditch, Part ii. 812.
Norfolk Antiquarian Miscellany, i. 413.

BEAUHARNAIS. Gentleman's Magazine, 1840, ii. 21.

BEAUMAN. Burke's Commoners, ii. 601, Landed Gentry, 2, 3, 4,
5, 6, 7.

BEAUMES, or BEAUMEYS. Camden Society, xliii. 78. The Genealogist, New Series, xiv. 101.

BEAUMONT. Burke's Extinct Baronetcies. J. H. Hill's History of
Langton, 77. Visitation of Middlesex, (Salisbury, 1820, fol.) 29.

Berry's Kent Genealogies, 140. Surtees Society, xxxvi. 253.
East Anglian, i. 74, 114. Glover's History of Derbyshire, ii. 97,
(88). Foster's Yorkshire Pedigrees. Harleian Society, ii. 169;
vi. 21; xii. 90; xvi. 18; xlii. 57. Westcote's Devonshire, edited
by G. Oliver and P. Jones, 498. Whitaker's Loidis and
Elmete, 338. Burke's Commoners, (of Barrow on Trent,) iv. 204,
Landed Gentry, 2, 3, 4, 5, 6, 7, 8; (of Whitley Beaumont,) Com-
moners, ii. 319, Landed Gentry, 2, 3, 4, 5, 6, 7, 8; (of Bretton,)
Commoners, ii. 323, Landed Gentry, 2, 3, 4, 5, 6, 7, 8; (of Buck-
land Court,) Landed Gentry, 5, 6, 7, 8. Foster's Visitations of
Yorkshire, 302, 491, 492. J. H. Hills' History of Market Har-
borough, 304. Maclean's History of Trigg Minor, i. 554. W.
Robinson's History of Hackney, i. 299. Burton's Description of
Leicestershire, 35, 111, 199. Nichols' History of the County of
Leicester, ii. 861; iii. 66, 661*, 662*, 663*, 743; iv. 621.
Hunter's Deanery of Doncaster, ii. 249. Surtees' Durham, i. xlv.
Manning and Bray's Surrey, ii. 182. Whitaker's History of
Whalley, ii. 24. Armorial Windows of Woodhouse Chapel, by
J. G. Nichols, 37. Stemmata Baronialia, by Francis Townsend,
5. The Visitations of Cornwall, edited by Lt.-Col. J. L. Vivian,
17. Wotton's English Baronetage, iii. 230. Banks' Baronies in
Fee, i. 121, 128. Visitation of Devon, edited by F. T. Colby, 17.
Betham's Baronetage, ii. 212. Banks' Dormant and Extinct
Baronage, ii. 38. Metcalfe's Visitations of Suffolk, 5. Notes and
Queries, 4 S. vii. 470; xi. 16. The Visitations of Devon, edited
by J. L. Vivian, 46, 63, 65. Leicestershire Architectural Society,
i. 333. Foster's Visitation of Middlesex, 59. *See* STAPLETON.
BEAUMONT-NESBITT. Burke's Landed Gentry, 8.
BEAUPLE. The Visitations of Devon, edited by J. L. Vivian, 101.
BEAUPRE. Carthew's Hundred of Launditch, Part ii. 778. Harleian
Society, xxxii. 33.
BEAUVOIR. W. Robinson's History of Hackney, i. 177. *See* DE
BEAUVOIR.
BEAVAN. *See* BEVAN.
BEAVOT. Surtees Society, xxxvi. 26. Foster's Visitations of York-
shire, 491.
BEBYNTON. Ormerod's Cheshire, ii. 449.
BEC. Gentleman's Magazine, 1832, i. 27. Topographer, (London,
1789-91, 8vo.) i. 337. Sussex Archæological Collections, xxiv.
188. Brydges' Collins' Peerage, vi. 591. Banks' Baronies in Fee,
i. 122. Banks' Dormant and Extinct Baronage, ii. 45. *See* BEKE.
BECHER, or BEECHER. Burke's Landed Gentry, 2. Dickinson's
History of Southwell, 2nd edition, 344. Harleian Society, xix. 81.
BECHFIELD. Harleian Society, xxviii. 37.
BECK. Chetham Society, lxxxiv. 29. Miscellanea Genealogica et
Heraldica, New Series, ii. 285. Harleian Society, xv. 59.
Wotton's English Baronetage, iv. 154. Burke's Extinct Baronet-
cies. Pedigrees of the Lords of Alnwick, by W. H. D. Langstaffe,
24. Burke's Family Records, 60.
BECKET or BECKETT. Harleian Society, i. 31; xxxix. 896. Burke's

Landed Gentry, (of the Knoll), 3, 4 ; (of Barnsley,) 2. Foster's Yorkshire Pedigrees. Westcote's Devonshire, edited by G. Oliver and P. Jones, 458, 459. Visitatio Comitatus Wiltoniæ, 1623, printed by Sir T. Phillipps. History of Barnsley, by Rowland Jackson, 113. The Visitations of Cornwall, edited by J. L. Vivian, 25. A Complete Parochial History of the County of Cornwall, iv. 230. The Visitation of Wiltshire, edited by G. W. Marshall.

BECKFORD. Genealogical tables of the Beckford Family, History of Fonthill Abbey, by John Rutter. London, 1823, 4to. Berry's Hampshire Genealogies, 105, 274. Graphical and Literary Illustrations of Fonthill Abbey, by John Britton, 42, 44, 46, 49, 50, 56, 65, 66, 68. Burke's Commoners, (of Fonthill,) i. 678 ; (of Basing Park,) Commoners, ii. 599, Landed Gentry, 2, 3, 4. Account of the Company of Ironmongers, by John Nicholl, 2nd. edn., 592. Burke's Royal Families, (London, 1851, 8vo.) ii. 116. Hoare's Wiltshire, IV. i. 21. Notes and Queries, 6 S. iv. 311, 374.

BECKHAM. Visitation of Norfolk, published by Norfolk Archæological Society, i. 8. Carthew's Hundred of Launditch, Part ii. 757. Harleian Society, xxxii. 24.

BECKINGHAM. Morant's Essex, i. 390. Sir T. Phillipps' Topographer, No. 1, (March, 1821, 8vo.) 33. Visitation of Oxfordshire, 1574, printed by Sir T. Phillipps, (Middle Hill, fol.) 1. Harleian Society, v. 156 ; xiii. 24, 149 ; xxxii. 32.

BECKLEY. New England Register, xvi. 20.

BECKWITH. Surtees Society, xxxvi. 274, 383. Visitation of Durham, 1615, (Sunderland, 1820, fol.) 86. Burke's Commoners, ii. 636, Landed Gentry, 2, 3, 4, 5, 6, 7, 8. Foster's Yorkshire Pedigrees. Foster's Visitations of Yorkshire, 101, 280, 494. Graves' History of Cleveland, 345. Thoresby's Ducatus Leodiensis, 132. Hunter's Deanery of Doncaster, i. 294. Plantagenet-Harrison's History of Yorkshire, i. 207. Harleian Society, xvi. 20 ; xliii. 132. Wotton's English Baronetage, iii. 677. Betham's Baronetage, iii. 36. Burke's Extinct Baronetcies. Foster's Visitations of Durham, 11. The Genealogist, New Series, xiv. 51 ; xvii. 120.

BECONSALL. Chetham Society, lxxxi. 130.

BECONSHAW. Berry's Hampshire Genealogies, 124. Hampshire Visitations, printed by Sir T. Phillipps, 4.

BEDELL, or BEDLE. Morant's Essex, ii. 67. Camden Society, xliii. 38 ; New Series, iv. 259. Harleian Society, xiii. 24 ; xv. 60, 61. Notes and Queries, 4 S. v. 311, 591 ; vii. 104, 199 ; 5 S. ii. 8, 334, 418. Burke's Extinct Baronetcies.

BEDENELL. Pedigrees from Visitation of Northumberland, printed by Sir T. Phillipps, (Middle Hill, 1858, fol.) 4. The Genealogist, i. 301. Foster's Visitations of Northumberland, 12.

BEDFORD. Pedigree of Bedford of Sarum [T. P.]. Berry's Surrey Genealogies, 61. Visitatio Comitatus Wiltoniæ, 1623, printed by Sir T. Phillipps. Surtees' Durham, iv. 99. Miscellanea Genealogica et Heraldica, New Series, iii. 189, 332. Burke's Landed Gentry, 6, 7, 8. The Forest and Chase of Sutton Coldfield,

(London, 1860, 8vo.) app. An Historical Survey of Cornwall, by
C. S. Gilbert, ii. 13. Harleian Society, xv. 61; xl. 1221. Banks'
Dormant and Extinct Baronage, iii. 71. The Visitation of Wilt-
shire, edited by G. W. Marshall, 4. *See* RUSSELL.

BEDINGFIELD, or BEDINGFELD. Case on behalf of Sir E. P. Bedingfeld, claiming the Barony of Grandison. Folio, pp. 32, and 4
folding pedigrees. Seize Quartiers of Sir H. P. Bedingfeld, Bart.
Folio Sheet. Claim of Sir H. P. Bedingfeld of Oxborough, Bart.,
to the Barony of Grandison, Sess. Papers, 82, of 1854; B of
1854-5; M of 1856; C of 1857-8. Blomefield's Norfolk, vi. 175;
ix. 206. Visitation of Norfolk, published by Norfolk Archæological Society, i. 9, 155. Burke's Commoners, iii. 508, Landed
Gentry, 2, 3, 4, 5, 6, 7, 8. Harleian Society, viii. 389; xv. 62;
xxxii. 25-31. Norfolk Archæology, iv. 134. Carthew's Hundred
of Launditch, Part ii. 721. Page's History of Suffolk, 378.
Foley's Records of the English Province, S. J., v. 568. Wotton's
English Baronetage, iii. 212. Betham's Baronetage, ii. 193. Metcalfe's Visitations of Suffolk, 114. Norfolk Antiquarian Miscellany,
ii. 600, 604. Annals of the English Benedictines of Ghent, 186.

BEDO. Surrey Archæological Collections, x. Harleian Society,
xliii. 207.

BEDOW. Maclean's History of Trigg Minor, ii. 525.

BEE. Berry's Hampshire Genealogies, 9. Poulson's Holderness, ii.
503. Hampshire Visitations, printed by Sir T. Phillipps, 5.
Visitation of Devon, edited by F. T. Colby, 18.

BEECH. Burke's Landed Gentry, 3, 4, 5, 6, 7, 8. *See* BEACH.

BEECHER. Harleian Society, i. 9; viii. 118. Manning and Bray's
Surrey, ii. 309.

BEECROFT. Burke's Landed Gentry, 4, 5.

BEEDHAM. Burke's Landed Gentry, 2.

BEER. Hasted's Kent, i. 223. Berry's Kent Genealogies, 327. *See*
BEARE.

BEESTON. Kent's British Banner Displayed, 427. Berry's Hamp-
shire Genealogies, 290. Foster's Visitations of Yorkshire, 322.
Thoresby's Ducatus Leodiensis, 207. The Genealogist, i. 175.
Ormerod's Cheshire, ii. 272. Burke's Landed Gentry, 3, p. 1382.
Harleian Society, xvi. 21; xviii. 15, 20; xxviii. 38. Ilkley,
Ancient and Modern, by R. Collyer and J. H. Turner, 219.

BEETHAM. Burke's Colonial Gentry, i. 97.

BEEVOR. Burke's Visitation of Seats and Arms, 2nd Series, ii. 13.
Betham's Baronetage, iv. 150.

BEHRENS. Burke's Family Records, 61.

BEIGHTON. Harleian Society, xxxviii. 646, 648.

BEILBY. Jewitt's Reliquary, vii. 192. Surtees Society, xxxvi. 4.

BEISINE. Harleian Society, xviii. 15.

BEIST. Harleian Society, xxviii. 38.

BEK, or BEKE. Tate's History of Alnwick, i. 410. F. G. Lee's
History of Thame, 552. Collectanea Topographica et Genealogica, iv. 331-345. Croke's History of the Family of Croke, No.
34. Harleian Society, xx. 13; xxxii. 32. Topographer and

Genealogist, iii. 175. Herald and Genealogist, vii. 449. Lips-combe's History of the County of Buckingham, ii. 309. Hutchins' Dorset, ii. 376. *See* BEC.

BEKERING. Thoroton's Nottinghamshire, iii. 220. *See* DE BEKER-ING.

BEKYSWELL. Harleian Society, xxxii. 248.

BELASYSE, BELLASIS, or BELLASISE. Visitation of Durham, 1615, (Sunderland, 1820, fol.) 69. Foster's Yorkshire Pedigrees. Mis-cellanea Genealogica et Heraldica, New Series, i. 308. Foster's Visitations of Yorkshire, 231. Graves' History of Cleveland, 57. Hutchinson's History of Durham, ii. 574, 575. Surtees' Durham, i. 203. Clutterbuck's Hertford, ii. 425. Abram's History of Blackburn, 254. Harleian Society, xvi. 21. Edmondson's Baron-agium Genealogicum, iii. 295. Brydges' Collins' Peerage, vi. 23. Banks' Dormant and Extinct Baronage, iii. 74, 294. Burke's Extinct Baronetcies. Foster's Visitations of Durham, 13. Howard's Visitation of England and Wales, ii. 57. Croston's edn. of Baines's Lancaster, iii. 156.

BELCH. Family Records, by Charlotte Sturge, 89.

BELCHER, or BELCHIER. Berry's Kent Genealogies, 281. Bridge's Northamptonshire, by Rev. Peter Whalley, i. 570. Harleian Society, xii. 65. Metcalfe's Visitations of Northamptonshire, 68, 165. New England Register, xxvii. 239. Burke's Colonial Gentry, ii. 654.

BELDAM. Burke's Landed Gentry, 8.

BELDING. New England Register, xv. 295.

BELER. Nichols' History of the County of Leicester, ii. 278.

BELESME. History of the House of Arundel, by J. P. Yeatman, 16.

BELET. Banks' Dormant and Extinct Baronage, i. 31. The Genea-logist, New Series, vii. 244.

BELEVERGE. The Genealogist, New Series, xvii. 245.

BELFIELD. Clutterbuck's Hertford, i. 497. Burke's Landed Gentry, 8. Harleian Society, xxii. 3, 28; xxxix. 1010. Fishwick's History of Rochdale, 348.

BELGRAVE. Harleian Society, ii. 67, 95. The Genealogist, ii. 221. Nichols' History of the County of Leicester, iii. 177; iv. 201, 207. Burke's Landed Gentry, 2, 3, 4, 5, 6, 7, 8. Burton's Des-scription of Leicestershire, 38. Foster's Visitations of North-umberland, 13.

BELHAVEN. *See* HAMILTON.

BELHOUSE. Harleian Society, xiv. 549. *See* DE BELHUS.

BELKNAP. Hasted's Kent, i. 135. Dallaway's Sussex, II. ii. 77. Dugdale's Warwickshire, 1073. New England Register, xiii. 17.

BELL. A Genealogical Account of the descendants of John of Gaunt, by J. G. Bell. London, 1855, 4to. Croke's History of the Family of Croke, No. 41. Blomefield's Norfolk, vii. 460. W. Paver's Pedigrees of Families of the City of York, 10. Burke's Landed Gentry, (of Woolsington), 2, 3, 4, 5, 6, 7, 8; (of Melling Hall), 2, 3, 4, 5; (of Thirsk), 2 supp., 4, 5, 6, 7, 8; (of Bourne Park), 4, 5, 6, 7, 8; (of Yewhurst), 8. Foster's Visita-

tions of Yorkshire, 495. Hodgson's Northumberland, II. ii. 290.
Visitations of Berkshire, printed by Sir T. Phillipps, 6. Memoirs
of the Family of Chester, by R. E. C. Waters, 120. The Genealogist, ii. 143; iv. 180; v. 40. Harleian Society, xiii. 25, 150;
xv. 63; xxi. 17; xxxii. 33; xliii. 91, 221. Fosbrooke's History
of Gloucestershire, i. 293. An Historical Survey of Cornwall, by
C. S. Gilbert, ii. 20. Metcalfe's Visitations of Suffolk, 6, 114.
F. G. Lee's History of Thame, 146. Ancient Families of Lincolnshire, in 'Spalding Free Press,' 1873-5, No. xxiv. Cyclostyle
Pedigrees, by J. J. Green. Foster's Visitations of Northumberland,
14. New England Register, xxiii. 253. Howard's Visitation of
England and Wales, iv. 88. The Genealogical Magazine, i. 476;
iii. 103. *See* HARDWICKE.

BELLAIRS. Burke's Landed Gentry, 3, 4, 5, 6, 7, 8. J. H. Hill's
History of Market Harborough, 262. Burke's Visitation of Seats
and Arms, 2nd Series, i. 63. Blore's Rutland, 53. Fletcher's
Leicestershire Pedigrees and Royal Descents, 22, 55.

BELLAMONT. Harleian Society, xvi. 17. *See* BELLOMONT.

BELLAMY. Foster's Visitations of Yorkshire, 495. Hunter's Deanery
of Doncaster, i. 259. Harleian Society, xv. 64. Monken Hadley,
by F. C. Cass, 138.

BELLAY. Camden Society, xliii. 122.

BELLENDEN. Gentleman's Magazine, lxxiii. 712. Walter Wood's
East Neuk of Fife, 276.

BELLERS. Harleian Society, ii. 29. Blore's History of South Winfield,
in Nichols' Miscellaneous Antiquities, No. 3, 36.

BELLEW, or BELLEWE. Tuckett's Devonshire Pedigrees, 157.
Burke's Commoners, ii. xx. 532, Landed Gentry, 2, 3, 4, 5, 6, 7, 8.
Foster's Visitations of Yorkshire, 104. Harleian Society, vi. 22.
Claim of Patrick, Baron Bellew to vote at elections of Irish Peers,
Sess. Papers, J. of 1856. Ormerod's Cheshire, ii. 721. Banks'
Baronies in Fee, ii. 44. Visitation of Devon, edited by F. T.
Colby, 19. The Visitations of Devon, edited by J. L. Vivian,
68. Burke's Family Records, 61.

BELLINGHAM. Berry's Sussex Genealogies, 190, 318. Visitation
of Westmorland, 1615, (London, 1853), 20. English Church
Furniture, by Edward Peacock, 116. Dallaway's Sussex, II. i.
51; ii. 116, 245. Visitatio Comitatus Wiltoniæ, 1623, printed
by Sir T. Phillipps. The Genealogist, iii. 350; v. 310. Harleian
Society, xvi. 22. Betham's Baronetage, iv. 323. Burke's Extinct
Baronetcies, and p. 600. History of Santry and Cloghran, by B.
W. Adams, 34. Foster's Visitations of Cumberland and Westmorland, 4-9. Nicolson and Burn's Westmorland and Cumberland, i. 125, 204.

BELLOMONT, or BELLOMONTE. Nichols' History of the County of
Leicester, i. 98. Clutterbuck's Hertford, iii. 287. Baker's
Northampton, i. 563. *See* DE BELLOMONTE.

BELLOT, or BELLOTT. Tuckett's Devonshire Pedigrees, 186. Miscellanea Genealogica et Heraldica, New Series, i. 9. Harleian
Society, vi. 23; xviii. 22. The Visitations of Cornwall, edited

by J. L. Vivian, 26. An Historical Survey of Cornwall, by
C. S. Gilbert, ii. 18. Notes and Queries, 2 S. iii. 413, 469,
497. Ormerod's Cheshire, iii. 43. Burke's Extinct Baronetcies.
The Visitations of Devon, edited by J. L. Vivian, 71.

BELLWOOD. Surtees Society, xxxvi. 213. *See* BELWOOD.

BELMAIN, or BELLMAINE. Tuckett's Devonshire Pedigrees, 192.
Harleian Society, vi. 23. The Visitations of Devon, edited by J.
L. Vivian, 67.

BELMEIS. Eyton's Antiquities of Shropshire, ii. 208. History of the
House of Arundel, by J. P. Yeatman, 67.

BELMORE. Claim of Somerset Richard, Earl Belmore, to vote at elections of Irish Peers, Sess. Papers, G of 1856.

BELMORE (Earl of). Howard's Visitation of Ireland, i. 1.

BELSON, or BELSONN. Berry's Hampshire Genealogies, 316. Harleian
Society, v. 190, 221. Lipscombe's History of the County of
Buckingham, i. 103. The Genealogist, vii. 118; New Series, xiv.
253. F. G. Lee's History of Thame, 266.

BELT. Gentleman's Magazine, 1823, i. 489. Surtees Society, xxxvi.
152. Harleian Society, xxxix. 944. The Genealogist, New
Series, xvi. 170.

BELTOFT. The Genealogist, New Series, xiv. 192.

BELVERGE. Harleian Society, xix. 199. The Genealogist, New
Series, xvii. 112.

BELWOOD. Stonehouse's History of the Isle of Axholme, 343. *See*
BELLWOOD.

BEMAND. *See* HARDWICKE.

BENAK. Harvey's Hundred of Willey, 458.

BENDOWE. Harleian Society, xxviii. 39.

BENCE. Burke's Commoners, ii. 651, Landed Gentry, 2, 3, 4, 5, 6,
7, 8. The Registers of Thorington, by T. S. Hill, 101.

BENDALL. Oliver's History of Antigua, i. 40.

BENDENGES. Herald and Genealogist, v. 430.

BENDISH, or BENDYSHE. Jewitt's Reliquary, x. 169. Morant's Essex,
i. 16 ; ii. 350, 604. Visitation of Suffolk, edited by J. J. Howard,
ii. 304. Burke's Landed Gentry, 2, 3, 4, 5, 6, 7, 8. Wright's Essex,
i. 627. Harleian Society, xiii. 316, 346 ; xxxii. 34 ; xxxviii. 440.
Burke's Extinct Baronetcies. London Magazine, 1774, 330.

BENDLOWES. Morant's Essex, ii. 387, 521. Harleian Society, xiii.
347 ; xxxix. 921.

BENDRY. Pedigree of Bendry of Cowbridge, Co. Wilts, [T. P.]
1862.

BENEST. J. B. Payne's Armorial of Jersey, 124.

BENESTED. Banks' Baronies in Fee, i. 122.

BENET, BENETT, BENNET, or BENNETT. Miscellanea Genealogica et
Heraldica, i. 294. Morant's Essex, i. 115; ii. 107. Croke's
History of the Family of Croke, No. 30. Surrey Archæological
Collections, ii. ; x. Berry's Hampshire Genealogies, 157. Visita-
tion of Cornwall, edited by Sir N. H. Nicolas, 10. Berry's Hert-
fordshire Genealogies, 205. Berry's Surrey Genealogies, 104.
Tuckett's Devonshire Pedigrees, 88. T. Faulkner's History of

Hammersmith, 183. Visitation of London, 1634, printed by Sir
T. Phillipps, 6. Burke's Commoners, (of Pyt House,) i. 248,
Landed Gentry, 2, 4, 5, 6, 7, 8 ; (of Laleston,) Commoners, ii. 23,
Landed Gentry, 2, 3, 4 ; (of Rougham Hall,) Landed Gentry, 2,
3, 4, 5, 6, 7, 8; (of Thomastown,) 2, 3, 4, 5, 6, 7, 8; (of Thorpe
Place,) 3, 4, 5, 6, 7, 8; (of Kilvilcorris,) 8 supp.; (of Faringdon
House,) 2, 3, 4, 5, 6, 7, 8 ; (of Bennett's Court,) 3, 4, 5 and supp.,
6, 7, 8 ; (of Stourton Hall,) 3, 4, 5 ; (of Sparkford Hall,) 5, 6, 7 ;
(of Cadbury,) 5, 6, 7, 8. Harleian Society, vi. 25 ; viii. 145, 493;
ix. 10 ; xiii. 150, 347 ; xv. 64 ; xvi. 23 ; xx. 14 ; xxxii. 35 ;
xxxviii. 485 ; xliii. 101, 206. Lipscombe's History of the County
of Buckingham, i. 134 ; ii. 529. Hodgson's Northumberland, II.
ii. 331. Westcote's Devonshire, edited by G. Oliver and P. Jones,
619. Visitations of Berkshire, printed by Sir Thos. Phillipps, 6.
Nichols' History of the County of Leicester, ii. 285. Visitatio
Comitatus Wiltoniæ, 1623, printed by Sir T. Phillipps. Hoare's
Wiltshire, III. ii. 78, 107 ; IV. i. 132 ; V. iii. 57. Visitation of
Derbyshire, 1663-4, (Middle Hill, 1854, fol.) 1. Clutterbuck's Hert-
ford, i. 411. Baker's Northampton, ii. 342. Wilson's History of the
Parish of St. Laurence Pountney, 255. The Genealogist, i. 381 ;
iii. 64, 237, 350 ; iv. 144; v. 235 ; New Series, xiii. 184. The
Visitations of Cornwall, edited by J. L. Vivian, 27. A Com-
plete Parochial History of the County of Cornwall, iv. viii.
Duchetiana, by Sir G. F. Duckett, 2nd edn., 68. Records of
Buckinghamshire, v. 142. Edmondson's Baronagium Genea-
logicum, iii. 201. Brydges' Collins' Peerage, iv. 125. Banks'
Dormant and Extinct Baronage, iii. 22. Burke's Extinct
Baronetcies, and p. 617. The Visitations of Devon, edited by
J. L. Vivian, 72. Northern Notes and Queries, iii. 59, 159.
Northamptonshire Notes and Queries, i. 18, 44, 76. New
England Register, xxix. 165. Genealogies of Morgan and Gla-
morgan, by G. T. Clark, 477-9. The Visitations of Cornwall, by
J. L. Vivian, 633. Historic Society of Lancashire and Cheshire,
ii. frontispiece, and 37-148. Foster's Visitations of Northumber-
land, 15, 48. Phillimore's London and Middlesex Note Book, 55,
257. Burke's Family Records, 64. Berkshire Notes and Queries,
i. 108, 110. Northern Notes and Queries, vi. 140 ; ix. 93.

BENGER. Berry's Kent Genealogies, 228. Harleian Society, xlii. 54.
BENGOUGH. Burke's Landed Gentry, 5, 6, 7, 8.
BENHALL. Notes and Queries, 5 S. xii. 511 ; 6 S. i. 299.
BENINGWORTH. The Genealogist, New Series. xv. 12, 68, 140.
BENION. Berry's Sussex Genealogies, 119. Dallaway's Sussex, i. 77.
See BENYON.
BENN, or BENNE. Harleian Society, i. 60. Betham's Baronetage, v.
582*. Miscellanea Genealogica et Heraldica, 2nd Series, i. 141.
Surrey Archæological Collections, x.
BENNING. Visitation of Middlesex, (Salisbury, 1820, fol.) 5. Foster's
Visitation of Middlesex, 11.
BENSLEY. Betham's Baronetage, v. 452. Burke's Extinct
Baronetcies.

BENSON. De Scales Peerage Evidence, 482. Burke's Visitation of Seats and Arms, 2nd Series, i. 43. Visitation of Westmoreland, 1615, London, 1853, 22. Burke's Landed Gentry, (of Lutwyche,) 2 supp., 3, 4, 5, 6, 7, 8; (of Utterby House,) 3, 4. Harleian Society, viii. 494; xv. 65; xxxviii. 537; xxxix. 1135. Foster's Lancashire Pedigrees. Lipscombe's History of the County of Buckingham, iv. 126. Burke's Visitation of Seats and Arms, 2nd Series, i. 43. Visitatio Comitatus Wiltoniæ, 1623, printed by Sir T. Phillipps. Baker's Northampton, i. 296, 355. Foster's Pedigree of the Forsters and Fosters, Part ii. 35. Pedigree of Wilson of High Wray, etc., by Joseph Foster, 62. Pedigree of Wilson, by S. B. Foster, 106. Notes and Queries, 6 S. xi. 351. Foster's Visitations of Cumberland and Westmorland, 10. Howard's Visitation of England and Wales, v. 122.

BENSTED, or BENSTEDE. Morant's Essex, i. 35, 318. Clutterbuck's Hertford, ii. 280. See DE BENSTED.

BENT. Harleian Society, ii. 158. Nichols' History of the County of Leicester, iv. 144, 150, 163. Burke's Commoners, (of Basford,) ii. 408; (of Wexham Lodge,) Landed Gentry, 3, 4. New England Register, xlviii. 288.

BENTALL. Bysshe's Visitation of Essex, edited by J. J. Howard, 17. Harleian Society, xxviii. 40.

BENTHALL. Harleian Society, xxxviii. 700.

BENTHAM. The History, etc., of the Cathedral Church of Ely, by James Bentham, 2nd edn., 20. Shaw's Staffordshire, ii. app. 4.

BENTINCK. The Great Governing Families of England, i. 162. Gentleman's Magazine, lxxix. 1205; lxxx. i. 609. Jacob's Peerage, i. 358. Glover's History of Derbyshire, ii. 140, (123). Burke's Landed Gentry, 3, 4, 5, 6, 7, 8. Edmondson's Baronagium Genealogicum, i. 62. Berry's Genealogical Peerage, 104. Brydges' Collins' Peerage, ii. 29. Nicolson and Burn's Westmorland and Cumberland, ii. 399.

BENTLEY. Burke's Commoners, (of Birch House,) iii. 683, Landed Gentry, 2, 3, 4, 5; (of West House,) Landed Gentry, 5, 6, 7. Foster's Yorkshire Pedigrees. Shaw's Staffordshire, ii. 93. Miscellanea Genealogica et Heraldica, New Series, iii. 95, 120. Howard's Visitation of England and Wales, i. 137; Notes, iii. 1. Visitations of Staffordshire, 1614, and 1663-4, William Salt Society, 34. The Genealogist, New Series, vii. 7; xiv. 27. Bysshe's Visitation of Essex, edited by J. J. Howard, 17. Fishwick's History of Rochdale, 518. Harleian Society, xxxviii. 485. Monograph of the Family of Folkard, ii. 65. Burke's Family Records, 64.

BENTON. New England Register, xvi. 18.

BENYON, or BENYAN. Morant's Essex, ii. 165. Berry's Hertfordshire Genealogies, 93. Berry's Berkshire Genealogies, 139. Burke's Landed Gentry, 2, 3, 4, 5, 6, 7, 8. Blore's Rutland, 170. Harleian Society, xv. 65; xxxvii. 413, 414. Bysshe's Visitation of Essex, edited by J. J. Howard, 18. See BENION.

BERE. Pocock's History of Gravesend, 10. Visitation of Cornwall,

edited by Sir N. H. Nicolas, 9. Archæologia Cantiana, iv. 250.
Berry's Kent Genealogies, 33. Burke's Landed Gentry, (of More-
bath,) 2, 3, 4, 5, 6, 7, 8; (of Timewell House,) 2, 3, 4, 5, 6, 7, 8.
Maclean's History of Trigg Minor, i. 311. Harleian Society, vi.
21; ix. 9; xlii. 5, 188. The Visitations of Cornwall, edited by
J. L. Vivian, 28. The Visitations of Devon, edited by J. L.
Vivian, 59, 62. See BEARE.

BEREFORD. Dugdale's Warwickshire, 487, 922. Baker's Northampton, i. 682. The Forest and Chase of Sutton Coldfield, (London,
1860, 8vo.) app. Plantagenet-Harrison's History of Yorkshire,
i. 473, 475. Banks' Baronies in Fee, ii. 45.

BERENGER. Hoare's Wiltshire, V. ii. 5, 119. The Genealogist, vii.
118.

BERENS. Burke's Landed Gentry, 5, 6, 7, 8.

BERESFORD. Eight Centuries of a Gentle Family, by E. A., S. B.,
and Wm. Beresford. London, 1893-5. Miscellanea Genealogica
et Heraldica, i. 36, 213. Weaver's Visitations of Somerset, 5.
Jewitt's Reliquary, vii. 19; ix. 177; x. 64. Hasted's Kent, i.
385. Gentleman's Magazine, lxxiv. 519, 915, 1194. Visitation
of Somerset, printed by Sir Thomas Phillipps, 13. Berry's Kent
Genealogies, 437. Harleian Society, ii. 178; iv. 169; xv. 66;
xlii. 172. Glover's History of Derbyshire, ii. 46, (44). Burke's
Landed Gentry, 2, 3, 4, 5, 6, 7, 8. Visitation of Derbyshire,
1663-4, (Middle Hill, 1854, fol.) 1. Nichols' History of the
County of Leicester, iii. 51. The Genealogist, iii. 121; New
Series, vii. 8-10. Pilkington's View of Derbyshire, ii. 287.
Archdall's Lodge's Peerage, ii. 289. Brydges' Collins' Peerage,
viii. 74. Account of the Mayo and Elton Families, by C. H.
Mayo, 163. The Irish Builder, xxxv. 220. The Genealogical
Magazine, i. 619, 660; ii. 8, 57, 109.

BERESFORD-HOPE. Burke's Landed Gentry, 5, 6, 8.

BEREW. Visitation of Gloucestershire, 1569 (Middle Hill, 1854,
fol.) 2. Harleian Society, xxi. 18. The Perverse Widow, by
A. W. Crawley-Boevey, 286.

BERFORD. Bridge's Northamptonshire, by Rev. Peter Whalley,
ii. 15.

BERGH. The Genealogist, New Series, xii. 227. See BURGH.

BERGHES. The Genealogist, New Series, xvi. 42.

BERHAM. Hasted's Kent, ii. 291.

BERIE. Harleian Society, iii. 31. See BERY.

BERIFF. Morant's Essex, i. 450. Harleian Society, xiii. 24, 348.

BERIMAN. The Visitations of Devon, edited by J. L. Vivian, 82.
See BERYMAM.

BERINGTON. Berry's Berkshire Genealogies, 23. Ashmole's Antiquities of Berkshire, iii. 297. Burke's Commoners, iv. 336; (of
Little Malvern Court,) Landed Gentry, 3 and corr., 4, 5, 6, 7, 8;
(of Winsley,) 2 supp., 3, 4, 6, 7, 8. Visitations of Berkshire,
printed by Sir Thos. Phillipps, 7. Ormerod's Cheshire, iii. 113.
Harleian Society, xviii. 21; xxviii. 42. Cooke's continuation of
Duncumb's Hereford, (Hundred of Grimsworth,) Part. i. 10.

The Genealogist, New Series, i. 2. Weaver's Visitation of Herefordshire, 8. Earwaker's History of Sandbach, 131.
BERKELEY, BERKLEY, or BERKELE. Case of Norborne Berkeley, Esq., in relation to Barony of Botetourt, fol. pp. 5, and page of pedigree. Claim of N. Berkeley, Esq., to the Barony of Botetourt, Sess. Papers, Dec. 1763—April 1764. Case of W. F. Berkeley for the Earldom of Berkeley, Feb. 1811, folio, pp. 4, and Pedigree. Additional case, 44 pp. fol. Claim of W. F. Berkeley to be Earl of Berkeley, Sess. Papers, May, 1799—June 1802; 14, 16, of 1811; 115, of 1829. Claim of Sir M. F. F. Berkeley to be Baron Berkeley, Sess. Papers, H of 1857-8; D of 1859; C of 1859 sess. 2; A of 1860; A and B of 1861. Evidence respecting the Claim to the Berkeley Peerage, London, 1811, 8vo., pp. 289. Address to the Peers of the United Kingdom, by Mary, Countess of Berkeley. London, 1811, 8vo. The B——y Family, a Narrative, by Mary Tudor, Sister-in-law to the Countess. London, 8vo. Abstracts of Smith's Lives of the Berkeleys, by T. D. Fosbrooke. London, 1821, 4to. FitzAlleyne of Berkeley, A Romance of the present Times, by Bernard Blackmantle. London, 1825, 2 vols. 8vo. Speech of Mr. Fonblanque, May 1829, pp. 74, folio. Case of Sir Maurice F. F. Berkeley, K.C.B., claiming to be Baron Berkeley, pp. 19. Supplemental Case, 1860. Appendix to ditto, 1860, Containing, 1, Earldom of Arundel; 2, Barony of Abergavenny; 3, Notes of Evidence. Argument of the Attorney-General on behalf of the Crown upon the claim of Sir M. F. F. Berkeley, K.C.B., on his Claim to the Honour of Baron Berkeley, 1860, fol. pp. 59. Authorities and Precedents in support of the claim to the dignity of Baron of Berkeley as a peerage by Tenure. London, 1862, fol. Judgments delivered on it, 26 Feb., 1861, pp. 36. Translations of Documents relating to the Barony of Greystock, pp. 3. Entry relating to the discharge of the Amerciament charged against Thomas de Furnival, pp. 3. Argument of Mr. Fleming, July 1860, pp. 209. All folio. Pedigree of Berkeley of Dursley, eight Generations, single sheet. Pedigree of Berkeley of Berkeley Castle Co. Glouc. [T. P.] 1861. See also Lowndes's Bibliographers' Manual, vol. i. p. 161, (Bohn's edition.) Burke's Extinct Baronetcies. Rudder's Gloucestershire, 272-279, 698. Collinson's Somerset, ii. 281; iii. 275. Morant's Essex, ii. 555. Maclean's History of Trigg Minor, iii. 161. Jacob's Peerage, i. 595. Berry's Hampshire Genealogies, 125. Visitation of Somerset, printed by Sir T. Phillipps, 14. Illuminated supplement to Burke's Heraldic Illustrations, 12. Harleian Society, ii. 2; xi. 7. Hampshire Visitations, printed by Sir T. Phillipps, 5. Glover's History of Derbyshire, ii. 195. Nash's Worcestershire, i. 258; ii. 358. Burke's Commoners, i. 63; (of Spetchley,) Commoners, i. 469, Landed Gentry, 2, 3, 4, 5, 6, 7, 8; (of Cotheridge,) Commoners, ii. 226, Landed Gentry, 2, 3, 4, 5, 6, 7, 8; (of Cedar Hill,) 5 supp., 6. Lipscombe's History of the County of Buckingham, iv. 276. Blore's Rutland, 210. Burton's Description of Leicestershire, 291. Nichols' History of the County of Leicester,

ii, 413. Burke's Royal Families, (London, 1851, 8vo.) ii. 51.
Kite's Monumental Brasses of Wiltshire, 31. Hoare's Wiltshire,
V. ii. 49. Clutterbuck's Hertford, ii. 516. J. H. Blunt's History
of Dursley, 135. Fosbrooke's History of Gloucestershire, i. 411,
426, 451, 455 ; ii. 86. Nisbet's Heraldry, ii. app. 245. Blunt's
Dursley and its Neighbourhood, 7, 114, 135, 141. The Genea-
logist, iv. 182. W. R. Fraser's History of Laurencekirk, 18.
Harleian Society, xvi. 246. Notes and Queries, 2 S. v. 256.
Metcalfe's Visitation of Worcester, 1683, 17. Edmondson's
Baronagium Genealogicum, ii. 151 ; iv. 360, 394. Brydges'
Collins' Peerage, iii. 591. Banks' Baronies in Fee, i. 123. Visita-
tion of Devon, edited by F. T. Colby, 20. Banks' Dormant and
Extinct Baronage, ii. 48, 54 ; iii. 76, 291. The Visitations of
Cornwall, edited by J. L. Vivian, 399. Visitation of Gloucester,
edited by T. F. Fenwick and W. C. Metcalfe, 15. Weaver's
Visitations of Somerset, 5. Records of Yarlington, by T. E.
Rogers, 39. East Barnet, by F. C. Cass, Part i. 58. Jewers'
Wells Cathedral, 118. Gloucestershire Notes and Queries, v. 75 ;
vii. 127, 153. *See* BARKLEY, BARCLAY.

BERKELEY-PORTMAN. Hutchins' Dorset, i. 253.

BERKEROLLES. Genealogies of Morgan and Glamorgan, by G. T.
Clark, 365.

BERMINGHAM. Dugdale's Warwickshire, 898. O'Hart's Irish Pedi-
grees, 2nd Series, 305. Betham's Dignities Feudal and Parlia-
mentary, 374. Banks' Dormant and Extinct Baronage, i. 242.
Foster's Collectanea Genealogica, (Funeral Certificates, Ireland,)
26-30. Pedigrees of the Leading Families of Yorkshire, by Joseph
Foster. Memoirs of the Family of French, by John D'Alton, *App.*
The Genealogist, New Series, xii. 233 ; xvi. 94. *See* BIRMING-
HAM.

BERNAK. Memorials of the Church of Attleborough, by J. T.
Barrett, 182. The Genealogist, New Series, xv. 149.

BERNARD. Burke's Commoners, (of Palace Anne,) iv. 32, Landed
Gentry, 2, 3, 4 ; (of Castle Bernard,) Landed Gentry, 2, 3, 4, 5,
6, 7, 8. Harleian Society, viii. 316. Bridge's Northamptonshire,
by Rev. Peter Whalley, i. 401. Baker's Northampton, i. 10.
Lipscombe's History of the County of Buckingham, i, 519, 521.
Wotton's English Baronetage, iii. 363. Betham's Baronetage, iii.
360. Burke's Extinct Baronetcies. Metcalfe's Visitations of
Northamptonshire, 3.

BERNERS. An abstract of several Records, etc., to prove the Claim
and Title of Katherine, wife of Richard Bokenham, to the Barony
of Berners, *n. d.* folio, pp. 26. Morant's Essex, ii. 474, 564.
Burke's Landed Gentry, 2, 3, 4, 5, 6, 7, 8 ; Manning and Bray's
Surrey, iii. 37. Wright's Essex, i. 656. Chauncy's Hertfordshire,
160. Harleian Society, xiii. 349 ; xv. 68 ; xxii. 28. Camden
Society, xiii. 145. Banks' Dormant and Extinct Baronage, i. 32.
Chancellor's Sepulchral Monuments of Essex, 221. *See* BOKEN-
HAM, WILSON.

BERNES. Harleian Society, xli. 103.

BERNESTON. Ormerod's Cheshire, iii. 902.
BERNEY. Blomefield's Norfolk, xi. 125. Burke's Landed Gentry,
2, 3, 4, 5, 6, 7, 8. Carthew's Hundred of Launditch, Part ii. 429,
465. Wotton's English Baronetage, i. 378. Betham's Baronetage,
i. 181. *See* BARNEY.
BEROWE. Visitation of Oxfordshire, 1634, printed by Sir T. Phillipps,
(Middle Hill, fol.) 13. Harleian Society, v. 262.
BERRIDGE. Harleian Society, xxxviii. 617.
BERSHAM. History of Llangurig, by E. Hamer and H. W. Lloyd,
265. History of Powys Fadog, by J. Y. W. Lloyd, iii. 19.
BERTIE. Memoir of Peregrine 11th Ld. Willoughby D'Eresby.
London, 1828, 8vo. Five Generations of a Loyal House, by Lady
Georgina Bertie. London, 1845, 4to. Jacob's Peerage, i. 324,
328, 602. Appendix to Case of Sir J. S. Sidney, claiming to be
Lord Lisle. Morant's Essex, ii. 8. Croke's History of the
Family of Croke, No. 40. Gentleman's Magazine, 1827, i. 587.
Lipscombe's History of the County of Buckingham, 233-236.
Page's History of Suffolk, 140, 142. Edmondson's Baronagium
Genealogicum, i. 54 ; ii. 155 ; vi. 43. Brydges' Collins' Peerage,
ii. 1 ; iii. 307, 628. Banks' Dormant and Extinct Baronage,
ii. 596. Burke's Extinct Baronetcies. F. G. Lee's History of
Thame, 443.
BERTON. The Genealogist, New Series, xiv. 255 ; xv. 96.
BERTRAM. Hodgson's Northumberland, II. ii. 39, 125. Archæologia
Æliana, 2 Series, iii. 75. Plantagenet-Harrison's History of
Yorkshire, i. 193. The Upper Ward of Lanarkshire, by G. V.
Irving, iii. 154. J. B. Payne's Armorial of Jersey, 43, 44.
Banks' Baronies in Fee, ii. 47. Banks' Dormant and Extinct
Baronage, i. 33. Burke's Landed Gentry, 7, 8.
BERWICK. Burke's Royal Families, (London, 1851, 8vo.) i. 113.
Foster's Visitations of Yorkshire, 229. Harleian Society, xlii.
152.
BERWIS. Harleian Society, vii. 15.
BERY, BERYE, BERRY, or BERRYE. Berry's Berkshire Genealogies,
59. Tuckett's Devonshire Pedigrees, 41, 43, 46. Berry's Kent
Genealogies, 264. Burke's Landed Gentry, 3, 7, 8. Harleian
Society, ii. 207 ; vi. 25-28 ; xxviii. 45 ; xlii. 109. Westcote's
Devonshire, edited by G. Oliver and P. Jones, 495, 496, 497.
Norfolk Archæology, iv. 16. Burke's Colonial Gentry, i. 207.
Burke's Extinct Baronetcies, *Add*. Miscellanea Genealogica et
Heraldica, New Series, iv. 213. The Visitations of Devon, edited
by J. L. Vivian, 74-80. Howard's Visitation of Ireland, iii. 21.
See BERIE, BURY.
BERYMAN. Tuckett's Devonshire Pedigrees, 127. *See* BERIMAN.
BESEILLE. The Genealogist, New Series, xv. 149.
BESLEY. Foster's Visitations of Yorkshire, 218.
BESMEADE. Berry's Hampshire Genealogies, 272.
BESSELLS. Jewitt's Reliquary, xxiii. 214.
BEST, or BESTE. Burke's Heraldic Illustrations, Pl. 96. Camden
Society, xliii. 65. Archæologia Cantiana, iv. 268. Berry's Kent

Genealogies, 14, 382. Burke's Commoners, (of Chilston,) i. 259, Landed Gentry, 2, 3, 4, ; (of Eastbury House,) Landed Gentry, 2, 3, 4, 5, 6 ; (of Donnington,) 2 supp., 3, 4, 5, 6, 7, 8 ; (of Park House,) 2, 3, 4, 5, 6, 7, 8 ; (of Botleigh Grange,) 4, 5, 6, 7, ·8 ; Foster's Yorkshire Pedigrees. Miscellanea Genealogica et Heraldica, New Series, i. 44 ; iv. 202, 234. Burke's Royal Families, (London, 1851, 8vo.) ii. 212*. Burke's Heraldic Illustrations, 96. Visitation of Staffordshire, 1663-4, printed by Sir T. Phillipps, 2. Scott of Scot's Hall, by J. R. Scott, 253. Surtees Society, xxxiii. 170. Harleian Society, xv. 72 ; xxxvii. 101 ; xlii. 13. Visitations of Staffordshire, 1614 and 1663-4, William Salt Society, 35. *See* DE BEST.

BESTNEY. Harleian Society, xxii. 126.

BESWICK. Berry's Kent Genealogies, 281. Burke's Landed Gentry, 2, 4, 5, 6, 7, 8. Wilson's History of the Parish of St. Laurence Pountney, 238. Fishwick's History of Rochdale, 441. Harleian Society, xlii. 152.

BESYN. Harleian Society, xxvii. 73. *See* BEYSIN.

BETENSON, or BETINSON. Morant's Essex, i. 354. Maclean's History of Trigg Manor, ii. 426 ; iii. 354. Harleian Society, xiv. 550 ; xv. 69. Wright's Essex, ii. 674. An Historical Survey of Cornwall, by C. S. Gilbert, ii. 21. Wotton's English Baronetage, iii. 513. Burke's Extinct Baronetcies. *See* BETTENSON.

BETHAM. Warwickshire Antiquarian Magazine, Part ii. Burke's Landed Gentry, 5 supp., 6. Harleian Society, xii. 215. Nicolson and Burn's Westmorland and Cumberland, i. 626.

BETHEL, or BETHELL. Surtees Society, xxxvi. 132, 155. Berry's Hampshire Genealogies, 300. Burke's Commoners, i. 451, Landed Gentry, 2, 3, 4, 5, 6, 7, 8. Foster's Yorkshire Pedigrees. Foster's Visitations of Yorkshire, 241. George Oliver's History of Beverley, 533. Poulson's Holderness, i. 408. Hampshire Visitations, printed by Sir T. Phillipps, 5. Thoresby's Ducatus Leodiensis, 110. Account of the Mayo and Elton families, by C. H. Mayo, 147. Harleian Society, xxxix. 916. Oliver's History of Antigua, i. 42.

BETHOME. Oxfordshire Pedigrees, fol. *n. d.*, privately printed by Sir T. Phillipps. Harleian Society, v. 216.

BETHUNE. An Historical and Genealogical Account of the Bethunes of the Island of Sky. Edinburgh, 1788, 8vo. [By Thomas Whyte.] Histoire Genealogique de la Maison de Bethune, par Andre du Chesne. Paris, 1639, fol. Case of Sir J. T. Bethune on his claim to be Lord Lindsay of the Byres. Edinburgh, 1877, fol. Burke's Commoners, (of Balfour,) iii. 376, Landed Gentry, 2, 7, 8 ; (of Blebo,) Landed Gentry, 5, 6, 7, 8. Walter Wood's East Neuk of Fife, 261, 298. *See* LINDSAY, STUART.

BETT. Lipscombe's History of the County of Buckingham, i. 315.

BETTENHAM. Berry's Kent Genealogies, 265, 456. Harleian Society, xlii. 110.

BETTENSON. Archæologia Cantiana, xiii. 395, 402. History of Chislehurst, by Webb, Miller, and Beckwith, 156. *See* BETENSON.

BETTES, or BETTS. Berry's Hampshire Genealogies, 244. Burke's Landed Gentry, (of Preston Hall,) 3, 4, 5 ; (of Wortham,) 2, 3, 4, 5, 6, 7. Hampshire Visitations, printed by Sir T. Phillipps, 5. Cambridgeshire Visitation, edited by Sir T. Phillipps, 1. Burke's Colonial Gentry, ii. 691. Harleian Society, xxxii. 36 ; xli. 78.

BETTESWORTH, or BETTSWORTH. Berry's Sussex Genealogies, 34, 304. Berry's Hampshire Genealogies, 208. Dallaway's Sussex, i. 212, 220, 226, 228. Castles, Mansions, and Manors of Western Sussex, by D. G. C. Elwes and C. J. Robinson, 126.

BETTESWORTH-TREVANION. Burke's Commoners, i. 253.

BETTINGTON. The Borough of Stoke-upon-Trent, by John Ward, 177.

BETTISCOMB. Hutchins' Dorset, ii. 241.

BETTISFIELD. See BECKFIELD.

BETTISON. W. Dickinson's History of Newark, 106.

BETTON. Burke's Commoners, iii. 219, Landed Gentry, 2, 3, 4, 5, 6, 7. Nicholls' Account of the Company of Ironmongers, 2nd edn., 587. Harleian Society, xxviii. 45.

BETUN. Baker's Northampton, ii. 59, 273.

BEVAN, or BEAVAN. Beavan of Llwngwilliam, of Tyn-yr-cwm, and Bevan of Castle Cradock, privately printed by Edward Beavan, of the Middle Temple, on a roll of paper seven feet long by eight inches wide. Dwnn's Visitations of Wales, i. 201. Glamorgan-shire Pedigrees, edited by Sir T. Phillipps, 16. Burke's Landed Gentry, 2, 3, 4, 5, 6, 7, 8. Caermarthenshire Pedigrees, 72, 73. T. Nicholas's County Families of Wales, 621, 921. Notes and Queries, 6 S. xii. 52. Genealogies of Morgan and Glamorgan, by G. T. Clark, 106. Burke's Archæological and Architectural Society Journal, iii. 192.

BEVER. Harleian Society, xxxviii. 748.

BEVERCOTES, or BEVERCOTTS. Harleian Society, iv. 171. Thoroton's Nottinghamshire, iii. 356.

BEVERLEY. Surtees Society, xxxvi. 35. Burke's Landed Gentry, 2, 3, 4, 5. Foster's Visitations of Yorkshire, 496. Harleian Society, viii. 92, 159 ; xix. 82.

BEVILL, or BEVILLE. Camden Society, xliii. 8. Baker's Northampton, i. 433. Couch's History of Polperro, 216, 220. The Visitations of Cornwall, edited by J. L. Vivian, 30. A Complete Parochial History of the County of Cornwall, iv. 203. An Historical Survey of Cornwall, by C. S. Gilbert, ii. 16. The Genealogist, New Series, x. 138.

BEVINGTON. Burke's Family Records, 66.

BEVOT. Thoresby's Ducatus Leodiensis, 20.

BEWES. Maclean's History of Trigg Minor, i. 68. Burke's Landed Gentry, 6, 7, 8. An Historical Survey of Cornwall, by C. S. Gilbert, ii. 15.

BEWICK, or BEWICKE. Burke's Commoners, (of Close House,) iii. 497, Landed Gentry, 2 and add., 3, 4, 5, 6, 7, 8 ; (of Hallaton Hall,) Landed Gentry, 2 add., 3, 4, 5, 6, 7, 8. Surtees' Durham, ii. 193. Foster's Visitations of Northumberland, 16.

BEWLEY. Visitation of London, 1634, printed by Sir T. Phillipps, 6. Burke's Commoners, iv. 308. Harleian Society, xv. 69.

BEWSHIN. Visitatio Comitatus Wiltoniæ, 1623, printed by Sir T. Phillipps.

BEXLEY. Berry's Buckinghamshire Genealogies, 52.

BEXWELL. Visitation of Norfolk, published by Norfolk Archæological Society, i. 222. Blomefield's Norfolk, vii. 307.

BEXWICKE. Croston's edition of Baines Lancaster, ii. 248.

BEYNON. Berry's Surrey Genealogies, 11. Burke's Landed Gentry, 2, 4, 6, 7, 8. Genealogies of Morgan and Glamorgan, by G. T. Clark, 480. See CROWTHER.

BEYSIN. Shropshire Archæological Society, i. 288. See BESYN.

BEYVILL. Dugdale's Warwickshire, 82. The Genealogist, New Series, xv. 93.

BIBBESWORTH. Morant's Essex, ii. 410. Clutterbuck's Hertford, iii. 67. Wright's Essex, ii. 46. Harleian Society, xiii. 1.

BIBBY. Burke's Landed Gentry, 8 supp.

BIBER. Burke's Landed Gentry, 8 supp.

BICCOMBE. Collinson's Somerset, iii. 516. Weaver's Visitations of Somerset, 7.

BICKERSTETH, or BICKERSTAFFE. Surrey Archæological Collections, v. Burke's Family Records, 67. Harleian Society, xliii. 106.

BICKERTON. A Concise Account of the Fall and Rise of the Family of the Bickertons of Maiden Castle, by John Bickerton, 1777, 8vo. Burke's Extinct Baronetcies. Harleian Society, ii. 173; xiii. 151. Nichols' History of the County of Leicester, iii. 170. Betham's Baronetage, iv. 16.

BICKFORD. Burke's Commoners, i. 459.

BICKLEY. Berry's Sussex Genealogies, 77. Visitation of Sussex, 1570, printed by Sir T. Phillipps, (Middle Hill, fol.) 2. Dallaway's Sussex, i. 83. Antiquities and Memoirs of the Parish of Myddle, written by Richard Gough, 1700, (folio,) 55. Memorials of the Church of Attleborough, by J. T. Barrett, 192. Harleian Society, xv. 70. Wotton's English Baronetage, iii. 331. Burke's Extinct Baronetcies.

BICKLIFFE. Visitation of London, 1634, printed by Sir T. Phillipps, 6.

BICKNELL. Excerpta Biconyllea, notes for a History of the Somerset-shire Family of Biconylle. By A. S. Bicknell. Taunton, 1900, 8vo.

BID. Dwnn's Visitations of Wales, i. 78.

BIDDELL. Howard's Visitation of England and Wales, iii. 97.

BIDDER. Caermarthenshire Pedigrees, 66.

BIDDIC. Hutchinson's History of Durham, iii. xxv.

BIDDULPH, or BIDDULPHE. Life of Bishop Hough, by John Wilmot, 140. Additional Case of T. Stonor claiming the Barony of Camoys. Berry's Sussex Genealogies, 219. Visitation of London, 1634, printed by Sir T. Phillipps, 6. Burke's Commoners, (of Biddulph,) iii. 280; (of Ledbury,) Commoners, iii. 286, Landed Gentry, 2, 3, 4, 5, 6, 7, 8; (of Burton,) Landed Gentry, 2, 3, 4, 5, 6, 7, 8;

(of Chirk Castle,) 2, 3, 4, 5, 6, 7, 8 ; (of Burghill,) 2 ; (of Amroth,)
2. Shaw's Staffordshire, i. 352. Dallaway's Sussex, II. i. 251.
Visitation of Staffordshire, 1663-4, printed by Sir Thos. Phillipps,
2. The Borough of Stoke-upon-Trent, by John Ward, 278.
Dugdale's Warwickshire, 324. Wotton's English Baronetage, iii.
442. Betham's Baronetage, ii. 357. Visitation of Staffordshire,
1614 and 1663-4, Willm. Salt Soc., 36-42, 50.
BIDLAKE. Harleian Society, vi. 30. The Visitations of Devon,
edited by J. L. Vivian, 83.
BIDWILL. Burke's Colonial Gentry, i. 345.
BIERD. Dwnn's Visitations of Wales, i. 193.
BIFLEETE. Visitation of Somerset, printed by Sir T. Phillipps, 15.
BIGG, or BIGGE. J. H. Hill's History of Langton, 48. Morant's
Essex, ii. 264, 359. Surtees Society, xxxvi. 151. Nash's Worcestershire, ii. 198. W. Paver's Pedigrees of Families of the City
of York, 11. Burke's Commoners, ii. 402 ; (of Linden,) Com-
moners, i. 630, Landed Gentry, 2 and corr., 3, 4, 5, 6, 7, 8.
Hodgson's Northumberland, II. ii. 97. Visitations of Berkshire,
printed by Sir Thos. Phillipps, 7. Harleian Society, xiii. 349.
The Genealogist, v. 236. Burke's Extinct Baronetcies.
BIGGS. Pedigree of Biggs of Beausale, Co. Warwick, [T. P.] 1866,
4to. Burke's Commoners, iv. 253, Landed Gentry, 2, 3, 4, 5, and
supp., 6, and supp., 7, 8. Hunter's Deanery of Doncaster, ii. 25.
Wiltshire Archæological Magazine, xii. 202. Harleian Society,
xxvii. 16.
BIGG-WITHER. Burke's Heraldic Illustrations, 26.
BIGLAND. Burke's Commoners, iii. 238, Landed Gentry, 2, 3, 4, 5,
6, 7, 8. Foster's Lancashire Pedigrees. Baines' History of the
Co. of Lancaster, iv. 734. Stockdale's Annals of Cartmel, 499.
BIGOD, or BIGOT. Gentleman's Magazine, 1827, i. 588. Blomefield's
Norfolk, v. 225. Morant's Essex, ii. 425. Carthew's Hundred of
Launditch, Part i. 39. Foster's Visitations of Yorkshire, 174, 595.
Mumford's Analysis of Domesday Book of Co. Norfolk, 22. Col-
lectanea Topographica et Genealogica, i. 408. Graves' History of
Cleveland, 298. History and Antiquities of Harwich and Dover-
court, by Silas Taylor, 71, 121. Plantagenet-Harrison's History
of Yorkshire, i. 254. Banks' Dormant and Extinct Baronage, iii.
553. Annals of Chepstow Castle, by J. F. Marsh, 268. Genea-
logical Memoranda of the Family of Ames, *unpaged*. Genealogical
Table of John Stratford Collins. *See* BYGOD.
BIGSBY. Burke's Landed Gentry, 2 supp. Burke's Visitation of
Seats and Arms, 2nd Series, ii. 61.
BIKESTROP. F. G. Lee's History of Thame, 377.
BILBIE. Jewitt's Reliquary, xiv. 111.
BILGAY. Visitation of Derbyshire, 1663-4, (Middle Hill, 1854, fol.) 2
The Genealogist, iii. 63.
BILL. Burke's Landed Gentry, 5 supp., 6, 7. Cussan's History of
Hertfordshire, Parts v. and vi. 28. Sussex Archæological Collec-
tions, vii. 137. Notes and Queries, 1 S. xi. 49, 129. Account of
the Mayo and Elton Families, by C. H. Mayo, 148. Burke's

Landed Gentry, (of Storthes Hall,) 8 ; (of Farley Hall,) 8. *See*
BYLL.
BILLAM. Burke's Landed Gentry, 2 supp., 3, 4.
BILLERS. Nichols' History of the County of Leicester, iii. 188. Clut-
terbuck's Hertford, iii. 270. Chauncy's Hertfordshire, 172.
BILLESBY. The Genealogist, iii. 351.
BILLING, BILLINGE, or BILLINGS. Visitation of Cornwall, edited by
Sir N. H. Nicolas, 11. Dwnn's Visitations of Wales, ii. 303.
Harleian Society, v. 223 ; ix. 10. Chetham Society, lxxxiv. 30.
Maclean's History of Trigg Minor, i. 385 ; ii. 549 ; iii. 359.
Baker's Northampton, i. 736. The Visitations of Cornwall, edited
by J. L. Vivian, 32. New England Register, vii. 272.
BILLINGFORD. Visitation of Norfolk, published by Norfolk Archæo-
logical Society, i. 21. Harleian Society, xxxii. 37.
BILLINGHAM. Visitation of Durham, 1575, (Newcastle, 1820, fol.)
40. Hutchinson's History of Durham, ii. 318. Surtees' Durham,
iv. 139. Foster's Visitations of Durham, 15.
BILLINGHURST. Miscellanea Genealogica et Heraldica, New Series,
i. 412.
BILLINGSLEY. Miscellanea Genealogica et Heraldica, i. 299. Visita-
tion of Somerset, printed by Sir T. Phillipps, 16. Harleian
Society, i. 69 ; xi. 7 ; xv. 71 ; xxviii. 46. Notes and Queries, 6 S.
xi. 513.
BILLON. Maclean's History of Trigg Minor, iii. 364.
BILLOTT. History of Powis Fadog, by J. Y. W. Lloyd, iii. 230.
BILSON. Hampshire Visitations, printed by Sir T. Phillipps, 6.
BINDLOSS, or BINDLOSSE. Burke's Extinct Baronetcies. Chetham
Society, lxxxiv. 31. Whitaker's History of Richmondshire, ii.
311. Surtees' Durham, i. 106. *See* BYNDLOS.
BING. Hasted's Kent, ii. 514. Harleian Society, xlii. 27. *See*
BYNG.
BINGHAM. Burke's Commoners, (of Melcombe Bingham,) iv. 350,
Landed Gentry, 2, 3, 4, 5, 6, 7, 8 ; (of Bingham Castle,) 5, 6, 7, 8.
Harleian Society, iv. 121, 144 ; xiii. 152, 350 ; xv. 72 ; xx. 15 ;
xliii. 142. Burton's Description of Leicestershire, 177. Hutchins'
Dorset, iv. 374. Thoroton's Nottinghamshire, i. 242, 272. Surrey
Archæological Collections, vii. Duchetiana, by Sir G. F. Duckett,
2nd edn., 62, 81. Burke's Royal Families, (edn. of 1876,) 213.
Archdall's Lodge's Peerage, vii. 104. The Genealogist, New Series,
ii. 221 ; xv. 98. Miscellanea Genealogica et Heraldica, 2nd Series,
ii. 265. New England Register, xlix. 333.
BINGLEY. Harleian Society, iv. 155 ; xv. 73.
BINNING-HOME. Burke's Landed Gentry, 2 supp., 3, 4, 5, 6. Burke's
Royal Families, (London, 1851, 8vo.) i. 195.
BINWIN. Harleian Society, xv. 73.
BIRBECK. Harleian Society, xxxviii. 822.
BIRCH, or BIRCHE. Miscellanea Genealogica et Heraldica, i. 305.
Chetham Society, xlvii. 102, 120 ; lxxxiv. 32, 34. Burke's Com-
moners, (of Garnstone,) iv. 27 ; Landed Gentry, (of Wretham,)
2, 3, 4, 5, 6, 7 ; (of Henley Park,) 3, 4 ; (of Armitage,) 6 supp.,

7, 8 ; (of Clare Park,) 7, 8. Gregson's Fragments relative to the County of Lancaster, 359. Baines' History of the Co. of Lancaster, ii. 531 ; Croston's edn., ii. 230. Archæologia Cambrensis, 3 S. xv. 273. Collections for a History of Staffordshiree, (William Salt Society,) ii. Part 2, 30. Visitations of Staffordshire, 1614 and 1663-4, (William Salt Society,) 42. Harleian Society, xix. 158 ; xxviii. 47, 48 ; xxxviii. 483 ; xxxix. 1140. *See* BYRCH, DE BIRCHE.

BIRCHALL. Pedigree of Wilson, by S. B. Foster, 180. Burke's Family Records, 72.

BIRCHELLS. *See* BIRTLES.

BIRCH-REYNARDSON. Burke's Royal Families, (London, 1851, 8vo.) ii. 146.

BIRCHENSTEY. Berry's Sussex Genealogies, 112.

BIRD, or BIRDE. Pedigree of Bird of Bretforton, and of Mansel of Bretforton, [T. P.] folio page. Morant's Essex, ii. 596. Berry's Kent Genealogies, 10. Visitation of Middlesex, (Salisbury, 1820, fol.) 7. Harleian Society, i. 68 ; vii. 7 ; xviii. 23, 265 ; xxi. 20. Ormerod's Cheshire, ii. 675. Burke's Landed Gentry, (of Dinas Mowddwy,) 2 ; (of Drybridge,) 2, 3, 4. Foster's Visitations of Yorkshire, 180. Visitation of Staffordshire, 1663-4, printed by Sir T. Phillipps, 2. Master's Notices of the Family of Master, 100. Metcalfe's Visitation of Worcester, 1683, 17. Metcalfe's Visitations of Northamptonshire, 166. Visitations of Staffordshire, 1614 and 1663-4, (William Salt Society,) 44. Foster's Visitation of Middlesex, 15. Bysshe's Visitation of Essex, edited by J. J. Howard, 18. Foster's Visitations of Cumberland and Westmorland, 11. New England Register, xxv. 21. *See* BYRD.

BIRKBECK. The Birkbecks of Westmorland. By R. Birkbeck. London, 1900, 4to. Surtees Society, xxxvi. 312. The Antiquities of Gainford, by J. R. Walbran, 106. Surtees' Durham, iv. 25. Foster's Pedigree of the Forsters and Fosters, Part ii. 27. Pedigree of Wilson of High Wray, etc., by Joseph Foster, 31, 133. Foster's Visitations of Cumberland and Westmorland, 12. Pedigree of Wilson, by S. B. Foster, 79. Burke's Landed Gentry, 7, 8. Nicolson and Burn's Westmorland and Cumberland, i. 399.

BIRKBY. W. Paver's Pedigrees of Families of the City of York, 11. Foster's Visitations of Yorkshire, 496.

BIRKENHEAD, or BIRKHENED, Burke's Commoners, ii. 237. Harleian Society, viii. 162 ; xv. 75 ; xviii. 25. Ormerod's Cheshire, ii. 368.

BIRKET. Foster's Lancashire Pedigrees.

BIRKIN. Foster's Visitations of Yorkshire, 302. Burke's Landed Gentry, 7, 8.

BIRKS, or BIRKES. The History of Woodhouse, by W. J. Le Tall, 19. Historical Notices of Doncaster, by C. W. Hatfield, 3rd Series, 333. Harleian Society, xxxix. 1080.

BIRLEY. Burke's Landed Gentry, 2 add., 3, 4, 5, 6, 7, 8. Foster's Lancashire Pedigrees. Abram's History of Blackburn, 389.

BIRMINGHAM. Manual of Origin, Descent, etc., of Barony of Athenry.

Dublin, 1820, (?) fol. Case of Edward Birmingham, of Dalgin, claiming to be Lord Birmingham, 1836. Claim of John Birmingham of Dalgin, Esq., to the Baronry of Athenry, Sess. Papers, 17, 269, of 1836. Archdall's Lodge's Peerage, iii. 30. The Midland Antiquary, ii. 41, 67, 124. D'Alton's Memoir of the Family of French, *at end.* A Manual of the Origin and Descent of the Barony of Athenry, fol. pp. 6. *See* ATHENRY, BERMINGHAM, DE BERMINGHAM.

BIRNIE. Account of the Families of Birnie and Hamilton of Bromhill, edited by W. B. D. D. Turnbull. Edinburgh, 1838, 4to. Nisbet's Heraldry, ii. app. 68. Alexander Nisbet's Heraldic Plates, 24. Family Notes, by J. M. Browne, 15.

BIRSTY. Berry's Sussex Genealogies, 112.

BIRT. Cardiganshire Pedigrees, 100. The Genealogist, New Series, ii. 222. *See* BYRT.

BIRTLES. Ormerod's Cheshire, iii. 710. Harleian Society, xviii. 22. Earwaker's East Cheshire, ii. 358.

BIRTLEY. Hutchinson's History of Durham, ii. 411. Surtees' Durham, ii. 189.

BIRTWISTLE. Chetham Society, lxxxiv. 35. Whitaker's History of Whalley, ii. 284. *See* BYRTWESYLL.

BISCHOFF. Harleian Society, xxxvii. 17.

BISCOE. Pedigree of the Family of Biscoe, by J. C. C. Smith. London, 1887, 4to. Burke's Landed Gentry, 5, 6, 7, 8.

BISH. Manning and Bray's Surrey, ii. 286. *See* BYSH.

BISHBURY. Shaw's Staffordshire, ii. 178.

BISHOP, or BISSHOPP. Minutes of the evidence relative to the Claims of Sir Cecil Bisshopp, Bart., of Parham Park, to the Title of Baron Zouche, Sess. Papers, vol. viii. 259. Additional Case of T. Stonor, claiming the Barony of Camoys. Berry's Sussex Genealogies, 213. English Church Furniture, by Edward Peacock, 102. Topographer and Genealogist, iii. 361. Foster's Visitations of Yorkshire, 132. Visitation of Warwickshire, 1619, published with Warwickshire Antiquarian Magazine, 208. Westcote's Devonshire, edited by G. Oliver and P. Jones, 557. Hutchins' Dorset, iv. 8. Harleian Society, xii. 223 ; xv. 74 ; xvi. 371 ; xx. 15 ; xxxii. 59. Wotton's English Baronetage, i. 416. Visitation of Devon, edited by F. T. Colby, 21. Betham's Baronetage, i. 194. The Genealogist, v. 311. Herald and Genealogist, viii. 10. The Visitations of Devon, edited by J. L. Vivian, 85. Miscellanea Genealogica et Heraldica, 2nd Series, v. 84. Berks Archæological and Architectural Journal, ii. 86. *See* BYSSHOPP.

BISHOPSDON. Dugdale's Warwickshire, 701.

BISHOPSTON. Harleian Society, xii. 131.

BISHTON. Botfield's Stemmata Botevilliana, 150.

BISLEY. Visitations of Berkshire, printed by Sir Thos. Phillipps, 7. The Genealogist, v. 236.

BISSE. Visitation of Somerset, printed by Sir Thos. Phillipps, 17, 18. Harleian Society, xi. 8. Clutterbuck's Hertford, ii. 307. Miscellanea Genealogica et Heraldica, 2nd Series, i. 283 ; ii. 139-152

BISSET, or BISET. Notes and Queries, 5 S. vi. 389. Banks' Dormant and Extinct Baronage, i. 35. Burke's Landed Gentry, 8.

BISSON. J. B. Payne's Armorial of Jersey, 47.

BISTON. Harleian Society, i. 30.

BITHEL. History of Powys Fadog, by J. Y. W. Lloyd, v. 246.

BITTON. Herald and Genealogist, iv. 195.

BIX. Berry's Kent Genealogies, 284.

BLAAUW. Burke's Landed Gentry, 2 add., 3, 4, 5, 6, 7, 8. Burke's Royal Families, (London, 1851, 8vo.) ii. 175.

BLABY. Nichols' History of the County of Leicester, iv. 51.

BLACHFORD. Berry's Sussex Genealogies, 161.

BLACK. Burke's Family Records, 73.

BLACKADER. Burke's Extinct Baronetcies, 617. Memoirs of Rev. John Blackader, by Andrew Crichton, 1. Life of Col. Blackader, by Andrew Crichton, Chapter I. Genealogical tree of the Family of Blackader of Tulliallan, by George Begbie. Folio sheet.

BLACKALL. Tuckett's Devonshire Pedigrees, 89. Harleian Society, vi. 30; ix. 288, The Visitations of Devon, edited by J. L. Vivian, 86.

BLACKBURN, or BLACKBURNE. Burke's Landed Gentry, (of Hale,) 2, 3, 4, 5, 6, 7, 8; (of Rathfarnham,) 4, 5, 6, 7; (of Haine,) 6, 7, 8; (of Tankardstown,) 8. History of Richmond, by C. Clarkson, 257. Foster's Lancashire Pedigrees. Chetham Society, lxxxiv. 36; xcix. 15. Gregson's fragments relative to the County of Lancaster, 194, 210. Whitaker's History of Whalley, ii. 30. Miscellanea Genealogica et Heraldica, New Series, ii. 78, 585. Paterson's History of Ayr and Wigton, i. 146. Plantagenet-Harrison's History of Yorkshire, i. 221. The Tyldesley Diary, edited by J. Gillow and A. Hewitson, 172. Harleian Society, xxxviii. 769. Croston's edn. of Baines's Lancaster, v. 54. See IRELAND.

BLACKDON. Harleian Society, vi. 31. See BLAGDON.

BLACKER. Burke's Commoners, (of Carrick Blacker,) ii. 48, Landed Gentry, 2, 3, 4, 5, 6; (of Woodbrook,) Landed Gentry, 3, 4, 5, 6, 7, 8; (of Elm Park,) 6. Visitatio Comitatus Wiltoniæ, 1623, printed by Sir T. Phillipps. The Visitation of Wiltshire, edited by G. W. Marshall, 96. Burke's Family Records, 74.

BLACKER-DOUGLAS. Burke's Landed Gentry, 7, 8.

BLACKET, or BLACKETT. Memoirs of the Life of Sir Walter Blackett, Bart., with Pedigree of the Calverleys of Calverley, etc. Newcastle, 1819, 12mo. Obsequies of certain of the Family of Blackett of Newcastle. Newcastle, 1846, 12mo. Burke's Extinct Baronetcies. Visitation of Durham, 1575, (Newcastle, 1820, fol.) 17. Visitation of Durham, 1615, (Sunderland, 1820, fol.) 9. Nash's Worcestershire, ii. 4. Burke's Commoners, i. 257; Landed Gentry, 2, 3, 4, 5, 6, 7, 8. Hodgson's Northumberland, I. ii. 258. Wotton's English Baronetage, iii. 551. Betham's Baronetage, ii. 427. Bateson's History of Northumberland, i. 281. Foster's Visitations of Durham, 17.

BLACKETT-ORD. Burke's Landed Gentry, 8.

BLACKHALL. Visitation of Cornwall, edited by Sir N. H. Nicolas, 10. Carthew's Hundred of Launditch, Part iii. 348.

BLACKHAM. Burke's Extinct Baronetcies.

BLACKLEECH. Harleian Society, xv. 76.

BLACKLEY. The Genealogist, iii. 238.

BLACKMAN. Pedigree of Blackman of East Sussex, by Mrs. Stephen Batson. 1901, Broadside. Harleian Society, v. 193. Oliver's History of Antigua, i. 48. Memoir of Richard Haines, by C. R. Haines, table vii.e.

BLACKMORE. or BLACKEMORE. Pedigree of the Blackmore Family, by C. E. B. Bowker. London, 1888. Single sheet. Hasted's Kent, iii. 98. Berry's Kent Genealogies, 316. Harleian Society, vi. 31. The Visitations of Devon, edited by J. L. Vivian, 88.

BLACKNALL. Visitation of London, 1634, printed by Sir T. Phillipps, 6. Harleian Society, iv. 113. Visitations of Berkshire, printed by Sir T. Phillipps, 7. Burke's Landed Gentry, 7.

BLACKSTONE. Gentleman's Magazine, 1827, ii. 224. Berry's Berkshire Genealogies, 97. Burke's Commoners, iii. 544 ; Landed Gentry, 2. Notes and Queries, 6 S. i. 243. See BLAKESTON.

BLACKWALL. Jewitt's Reliquary, vii. 20. Harleian Society, xv. 76. Burke's Landed Gentry, 8.

BLACKWELL. Harleian Society, viii. 459 ; xv. 77. Clutterbuck's Hertford, i. 335. Wotton's English Baronetage, iv. 191. Burke's Extinct Baronetcies.

BLACKWOOD. Account of the Printinghouse family of Blackwood, See ' THE CRITIC,' Nos. 522-528. Claim of the Rt. Hon. F. T. Blackwood Baron Dufferin and Claneboye to Vote at Elections of Irish Peers, Sess. Papers, 245 of 1848.

BLADEN. Blore's Rutland, 180. Notes and Queries, 3 S. vii. 258, 326. Oliver's History of Antigua, i. 51.

BLADWELL. Carthew's Hundred of Launditch, Part ii. 499. Harleian Society, xv. 77. See BLODWELL.

BLAENY. Dwnn's Visitations of Wales, i. 134, 283, 284, 299.

BLAGDON. The Visitations of Devon, edited by J. L. Vivian, 91. See BLACKDON.

BLAGE. Visitation of Norfolk, published by Norfolk Archæological Society, ii. 1.

BLAGGE. Gage's History of Thingoe Hundred, Suffolk, 521.

BLAGRAVE, or BLAGROVE. Berry's Berkshire Genealogies, 145. Ashmole's Antiquities of Berkshire, iii. 329. Burke's Landed Gentry, 2, 3, 4, 5, 6, 7, 8. Visitations of Berkshire, printed by Sir Thos. Phillipps, 7, 8. Gyll's History of Wraysbury, 24. The Genealogist, v. 237, 238 ; New Series, i. 2.

BLAGUE. Burke's Commoners, iii. 663.

BLAIR. Five Generations of the Family of Blair. By A. T. Michell. Exeter, 1895, 4to. Burke's Commoners, (of Blair,) iv. 392 ; Landed Gentry, 2, 3, 4, 5, 6, 7, 8; (of Penninghame,) Landed Gentry, 4, 5, 6, 7, 8 ; (of Balthayock,) 2, 3, 4. Geo. Robertson's Description of Cunninghame, 221, 234. Lands and their Owners in Galloway, by P. H. M'Kerlie, i. 86 ; iii. 180, 217. Paterson's

History of the Co. of Ayr, i. 413, 429; ii. 255, 358, 382, 475.
Douglas's Baronage of Scotland, 186-198, 442. Paterson's History
of Ayr and Wigton, i. 577 ; ii. 409; iii. 158, 175. Geo. Robertson's Account of Families in Ayrshire, i. 77-102.
BLAIR-IMRIE. Burke's Landed Gentry, 5, 6, 7, 8.
BLAKE. Morant's Essex, ii. 24. Visitation of Cornwall, edited by
Sir N. H. Nicolas, 12. Berry's Hampshire Genealogies, 145, 306.
Visitation of Norfolk, published by Norfolk Archæological Society,
ii. 1. Burke's Landed Gentry, (of Ballinafad,) 3 supp., 4, 5, 6, 7,
8 ; (of Horsted,) 2 supp., 3, 4, 5, 6, 7 ; (of Swanton Abbots,) 3, 4,
5, 6, 7, 8 ; (of Renvyle,) 2, 3, 4, 5, 6, 7, 8 ; (of Ballyglunin,) 3, 4
and supp., 5, 6, 7, 8 ; (of Towerhill,) 3, 4, 5, 6, 7, 8 ; (of Cregg
Castle,) 2, 3, 4, 5, 6, 7 ; (of Kiltullagh,) 3, 4, 5, 6, 7 ; (of Furbough,)
2, 3, 4 ; (of Merlin Park,) 3 ; (of Coolcon,) 5 supp., 6 supp., 7 ;
(of Ballinacourty,) 6 supp., 7 ; (of Danesbury,) 5, 6 ; 5 at p. 319,
7, 8. Harleian Society, viii. 299 ; ix. 11 ; xi. 121 ; xiii. 152 ;
xv. 78 ; xxxii. 38 ; xxxvii. 89. Raine's History of North Durham,
316. Hampshire Visitations, printed by Sir T. Phillipps, 6.
Visitatio Comitatus Wiltoniæ, 1623, printed by Sir T. Phillipps.
The Visitations of Cornwall, edited by J. L. Vivian, 34. Description of West Connaught, edited by James Hardiman, (Irish
Archl. Society,) 213. Notes and Queries, 1 S. iii. 389 ; 2 S. x.
419 ; xi. 512 ; 3 S. i. 423 ; ii. 14, 58 ; 6 S. xii. 239, 297. Betham's
Baronetage, iii. 374, 436. Foster's Collectanea Genealogica,
(Funeral Certificates, Ireland,) 32. The Visitation of Wiltshire,
edited by G. W. Marshall, 81. Carthew's West and East Braden-
ham, 161. The Howard Papers, by H. K. S. Causton, 664. New
England Register, vi. 372 ; ix. 176. Pedigree of the Family of
Biscoe, by J. C. C. Smith, 19. Bysshe's Visitation of Essex,
edited by J. J. Howard, 19. Burke's Colonial Gentry, ii. 412.
Oliver's History of Antigua, i. 54. Burke's Family Records, 75.
The Genealogical Magazine, i. 499, 563, 609, 682. See ALDRICH-
BLAKE.
BLAKE-HUMPHREY. Burke's Landed Gentry, 8.
BLAKEMORE. Burke's Landed Gentry, 2. Collections for a History
of Staffordshire, (William Salt Society,) ii. part 2, 120, 124.
Miscellanea Genealogica et Heraldica, New Series, iv. 233.
BLAKENEY. Burke's Landed Gentry, 2, 3, 4, 5, 6, 7, 8.
BLAKER. Berry's Sussex Genealogies, 87.
BLAKESTON, or BLAKISTON. Burke's Extinct Baronetcies. Visita-
tion of Durham, 1615, (Sunderland, 1820, fol.) 65, 74. Burke's
Royal Families (London, 1851, 8vo.) ii. 21. Hutchinson's History
of Durham, iii. 119. Surtees' Durham, i. 246, 276 ; ii. 231, 255 ;
iii. 162, 163, 402. Betham's Baronetage, iii. 310. Foster's
Visitations of Durham, 19, 21, 23, 25. Burke's Colonial Gentry,
ii. 498. See BLACKSTONE, BLAYKESTON.
BLAKETT. Harleian Society, xxii. 128.
BLAKEY. Metcalfe's Visitations of Suffolk, 184.
BLAKISTON-HOUSTON. Burke's Landed Gentry, 3, 4, 5.
BLAKNEY. Harleian Society, xxxii. 38.

BLAMIRE. Burke's Landed Gentry, 2, 3, 4.

BLANCHARD, or BLANSHARD. Visitation of Somerset, printed by Sir T. Phillipps, 19. Burke's Commoners, iii. 437, Landed Gentry, 2. Harleian Society, xi. 9. Visitations of Berkshire, printed by Sir T. Phillipps, 8. Notes and Queries, 3 S. i. 408 ; ii. 14, 75. New England Register, x. 152.

BLANCHFIELD, or BLANCHVILLE. History of St. Canice, Kilkenny, by J. Graves, 301.

BLANCK. Harleian Society, i. 12.

BLANCKS. Lipscombe's History of the County of Buckingham, ii. 116. F. G. Lee's History of Thame, 604.

BLAND. Collections for a History of the Ancient Family of Bland, by N. Carlisle. London, 1826, 4to. Index to Nicholas Carlisle's History of the Family of Bland, by Fanny Bland. Kendal, 1890, 4to. Kent's British Banner Displayed, 693. Surtees Society, xxxvi. 350. Burke's Commoners, (of Kippax Park,) iii. 326, Landed Gentry, 2, 3, 4, 5, 6, 7, 8 ; (of Blandsfort,) Landed Gentry, 3, 4, 5, 6, 7, 8 ; (of Derriquin Castle,) 2, 3, 4, 5, 6, 7, 8. Harleian Society, iv. 89, 182 ; xv. 79 ; xxxviii. 421 ; xli. 111. Thoresby's Ducatus Leodiensis, 93, 208. Boothroyd's History of Pontefract, 159. Wotton's English Baronetage, ii. 348. Burke's Extinct Baronetcies. The Wolfe's of Forenaghts, 69. Yorkshire Genealogist, i. 188.

BLANDY. Berry's Berkshire Genealogies, 144.

BLANDY-JENKINS. Burke's Landed Gentry, 5, 6, 7, 8.

BLANE, or BLAYNE. Glamorganshire Pedigrees, edited by Sir T. Phillipps, 19. Dwnn's Visitations of Wales, ii. 23.

BLASHFORD. Harleian Society, xv. 80.

BLASSE. Foster's Visitation of Middlesex, 66. New England Register, xli. 298.

BLATHWAYT. The Family of Blathwayt, broadside, with 4to. page of notes by G. W. W. B. May, 1888. Burke's Landed Gentry, 2 supp., 3, 4, 5, 6, 7, 8. Burke's Royal Families, (London, 1851, 8vo.) i. 54. Burke's Heraldic Illustrations, 33.

BLAW. Northern Notes and Queries, viii. 64.

BLAXLAND. Hasted's Kent, iii. 18. Burke's Colonial Gentry, i. 287.

BLAXTON. The Antiquities of Gainford, by J. R. Walbran, 49. The Genealogist, v. 312.

BLAYDES. Burke's Commoners, i. 667, Landed Gentry, 2 and corr., 3, 4. Poulson's Holderness, ii. 483. Surtees Society, liv. xxxii. Miscellanea Genealogica et Heraldica, New Series, iii. 444. Howard's Visitation of England and Wales, i. 54 ; Notes, ii. 59. Harleian Society, xxxix. 1000.

BLAYKESTON. Visitation of Durham, 1575, (Newcastle, 1820, fol.) 18, 50, 51. See BLAKESTON.

BLAYNEY. Burke's Commoners, iv. 632, Landed Gentry, 2, 3, 4. Shirley's History of the County of Monaghan, 248, 251. Visitations of Berkshire, printed by Sir T. Phillipps, 8. The Genealogist, v. 238. The Sheriffs of Montgomeryshire, by W. V. Lloyd,

186, 495. Collections by the Powysland Club, x. 1. Archdale's
Lodge's Peerage, vi. 299.

BLEASDALE. History of Chipping, by Tom C. Smith, 259.

BLENCOWE. Pedigree of Blencowe of Blencowe, Co. Cumb., and of
Marston St. Lawrence, Co. North'ton, [T. P.] 1869, two pedigrees,
Broadsides. Burke's Commoners, (of Marston St. Lawrence,) i.
414, Landed Gentry, 2, 3, 4, 5, 6, 7, 8 ; (of Blencowe,) Landed
Gentry, 3, 4, 5, 6, 7 ; (of the Hooke,) 3, 4, 5, 6, 7, 8. Hutchinson's
History of Cumberland, i. 413. Jefferson's History of Leath
Ward, Cumberland, 383. Bridge's Northamptonshire, by Rev.
Peter Whalley, i. 182. Baker's Northampton. i. 640. Metcalfe's
Visitations of Northamptonshire, 69. Foster's Visitations of
Cumberland and Westmorland, 13. Nicolson and Burne's West-
morland and Cumberland, ii. 376.

BLENKINSOP, BLENKINSOPP, or BLENKINSOPPE. Visitation of Dur-
ham, 1575, (Newcastle, 1820, fol.) 48. Burke's Landed Gentry,
2, 3, 4, 5, 6, 7, 8. Hodgson's Northumberland, III. ii. 131, 345.
Surtees' Durham, ii. 189. The Genealogist, ii. 143, 256. Harleian
Society, xv. 81. Foster's Visitations of Durham, 27. Foster's
Visitations of Northumberland, 17, 18. Nicolson and Burne's
Westmorland and Cumberland, i. 489, 582.

BLENNERHASSET, or BLENNERHASSETT. Morant's Essex. ii. 153.
Burke's Landed Gentry, 2, 3, 4, 5, 6, 7, 8. Suckling's History of
Suffolk, i. 37. Norfolk Archæology, vii. 86. Charles Smith's
History of Kerry, 53. Metcalfe's Visitations of Suffolk, 7. Mis-
cellanea Genealogica et Heraldica, New Series, iv. 329. Harleian
Society, xix. 159. Parliamentary Memoirs of Fermanagh, by
the Earl of Belmore, 36.

BLETHYN. Glamorganshire Pedigrees, edited by Sir T. Phillipps, 42.
Genealogies of Morgan and Glamorgan, by G. T. Clark, 129.

BLETSOE. Harleian Society, xix. 83.

BLEVERHASSETT. Harleian Society, xxxii. 39.

BLEWETT, or BLEWITT. Visitation of Somerset, printed by Sir T.
Phillipps, 20. Chronicle of the Family of De Havilland. Burke's
Landed Gentry, 2. The Visitations of Cornwall, edited by J. L.
Vivian, 35, 637. An Historical Survey of Cornwall, by C. S.
Gilbert, ii. 25. Visitations of Devon, edited by F. T. Colby, 21.
The Visitations of Devon, edited by J. L. Vivian, 92. Weaver's
Visitations of Somerset, 7. 8.

BLEYNEY. Weaver's Visitation of Herefordshire, 10.

BLIGH, or BLIGHT. Pocock's History of Gravesend, 58. Hasted's
Kent, i. 496. Visitation of Cornwall, edited by Sir N. H.
Nicolas, 13, 14. Maclean's History of Trigg Minor, i. 289.
Harleian Society, ix. 12, 13. The Visitations of Cornwall, edited
by J. L. Vivian, 36, 38. A complete Parochial History of
the County of Cornwall, iv. 66. Notes and Queries, 2 S. ii. 411,
472. Edmondson's Baronagium Genealogicum, iv. 379. Archdall's
Lodge's Peerage, ii. 207. Brydges' Collins' Peerage, vii. 58. The
Irish Builder, xxix. 71.

BLIN. New England Register, xvi. 19.

BLINCKARNE. Visitation of Middlesex, (Salisbury, 1820, fol.) 51. Foster's Visitation of Middlesex, 95.

BLISS. J. H. Hill's History of Langton, 63. Burke's Landed Gentry, 2 supp., 3, 4, 5. Nichols' History of the County of Leicester, ii. 693*. New England Register, xxxi. 320, 417 ; xxxii. 67, 175.

BLITH, or BLITHE. Visitation of Derbyshire, 1663-4, (Middle Hill, 1854, fol.) 2. Dugdale's Warwickshire, 1021, 1051. The Genealogist, iii. 121. See BLYTHE.

BLIZARD. Oliver's History of Antigua, i. 58.

BLODWELL. Harleian Society, viii. 264. Metcalfe's Visitations of Suffolk, 8, 86. History of Powys Fadog, by J. Y. W. Lloyd, iv. 198. See BLADWELL.

BLOFELD, or BLOFIELD. Burke's Landed Gentry, 2 supp., 3, 4, 5, 6, 7, 8.

BLOIS. Burke's Royal Families, (London, 1851, 8vo.) ii. 52. Page's History of Suffolk 53, 286. Wotton's English Baronetage, iv. 9. Betham's Baronetage, iii. 72.

BLOME. Harleian Society, xv. 81.

BLOMEFIELD. Blomefield's Norfolk, i. 101. Carthew's West and East Bradenham, 161.

BLOMER. Harleian Society, xxi. 20.

BLOMMART. Burke's Landed Gentry, 5, 6, 7.

BLONDELL, or BLONDEL. Chronicle of the Family of De Havilland. Chetham Society, lxxxi. 113, 114. See BLUNDELL.

BLONDEN. Harleian Society, xxviii. 48.

BLONDESTON. Harleian Society, iv. 157.

BLOOD. Burke's Landed Gentry, 2 at p. 1253. Howard's Visitation of Ireland, ii. 15.

BLOOM. Caermarthenshire Pedigrees, 14. Howard's Visitation of England and Wales, i. 211.

BLOOMFIELD. Burke's Landed Gentry, 5, 6 and supp., 7, 8. See DOUGLAS.

BLORE. See BLOWER.

BLOSSE. Visitation of Middlesex, (Salisbury, 1820, fol.) 38. Metcalfe's Visitations of Suffolk, 114.

BLOUNT, or BLUNT. Pedigree of Blunt of Heathfield Park, Co. Sussex, and of Lydiard Milicent, Co, Wilts, privately printed by Sir T. Phillipps, Bart. Single Sheet. Collections for a History of the Ancient Family of Blount. London, 1826, 4to. Herald and Genealogist, iv. 194. Morant's Essex, ii. 48. Berry's Sussex Genealogies, 285. Berry's Kent Genealogies, 417. Harleian Society, i. 28; xiii. 153; xv. 82 ; xxi. 22, 231 ; xxii. 29, 128 ; xxvii. 16-23 ; xxviii. 50-57; xxix. 305 ; xlii. 178. Nichols' History of the County of Leicester, iv. 253*, 524. Nash's Worcestershire, ii. 163. Burke's Commoners, iii. 199 ; (of Maple Durham,) Commoners, iii. 163, Landed Gentry, 2, 3, 4, 5, 6, 7, 8 ; (of Orleton,) 2, 3 and corr., 4, 5, 6, 7, 8. Gyll's History of Wraysbury, 234. Dallaway's Sussex, II. i. 354. Hutchins' Dorset, iii. 296. Clutterbuck's Hertford, i. 211 ; ii. 350 ; iii. 195. Robinson's Mansions of Herefordshire, 222. The Genealogist, ii. 19, 44. Ellacombe's History of Bitton, 80.

Wotton's English Baronetage, ii. 367 ; iii. 665 ; iv. 192. Bank's
Baronies in Fee, i. 126. Betham's Baronetage, i. 499; iii. 196.
Banks' Extinct and Dormant Baronage, i. 36, 243 ; iii. 535.
Burke's Extinct Baronetcies. Metcalfe's Visitation of Worcester,
1683, 19. The Genealogist, New Series, ii. 223, 303. Weaver's
Visitation of Herefordshire, 11. Peacham's Complete Gentleman,
230. The Gresley's of Drakelow, by F. Madan, 240. *See* BLUNT,
LE BLUND.

BLOW. Northern Notes and Queries, viii. 64.

BLOWER. Visitations of Berkshire, printed by Sir T. Phillipps, 8.
Harleian Society, xiii. 351. The Genealogist, v. 239.

BLOXHAM. Pedigree of the Family of Bloxham. Oxford, *n. d.*, 4to.
Metcalfe's Visitation of Worcester, 1683, 20,

BLOYOU. Maclean's History of Trigg Minor, iii. 159.

BLUDDER. Society Archæological Collections, iii. Harleian Society,
viii. 48 ; xliii. 125. Manning and Bray's Surrey, i. 306. Aubrey's
Antiquities of Surrey, iv. 210.

BLUETT, or BLUET. Burke's Landed Gentry, 2, 3, 4, 8 supp.
Harleian Society, iv. 32. Westcote's Devonshire, edited by G.
Oliver and P. Jones, 512. The Genealogist, iii. 352. An Historical
Survey of Cornwall, by C. S. Gilbert, ii. 25.

BLUMER. Howard's Visitation of England and Wales, ix. 73, 76.

BLUNDELL. Account of the Parish of Sandford, by Rev. E. Marshall,
20. Baines' History of the Co. of Lancaster, iv. 218 ; Croston's
edn., v. 232. Burke's Commoners, ii. 527, Landed Gentry, 2, 3,
4, 5, 6, 7, 8. Miscellanea Genealogica et Heraldica, i. 67. Lydiate
Hall and its Associations, by Rev. T. E. Gibson, (1876, 4to.) 84.
Harleian Society, viii. 135 ; xix. 160. Foster's Lancashire Pedi-
grees. Chetham Society, lxxxii. 76 ; lxxxiv. 37-40. Gregson's
Fragments relative to the County of Lancaster, 223. Burke's
Extinct Baronetcies, 600. Donations of Peter Blundell, by Benjn.
Incledon, (Exeter, 1804, 8vo.) folding at xlv. Sefton, by W. D.
Caröe, folding at xx. *See* BLONDELL.

BLUNDELL-WELD. Burke's Royal Families, (London, 1851, 8vo.)i. 101.

BLUNDEN. *See* BLONDEN.

BLUNDEVILLE. Harleian Society, iv. 99 ; xxxii. 40.

BLUNT. Pedigree of Blunt of Wotton, Co. Wilts, [T. P.] 1860, folio
page. Visitation of Oxfordshire, 1634, printed by Sir T. Phillipps,
(Middle Hill, fol.) 14. Burke's Landed Gentry, (of Wallop House,)
2, 3, 4, 5, 6 ; (of Kempshott,) 2, 3, 4, 5, 6. Harleian Society, v.
221, 296 ; xxviii. 135. Shaw's Staffordshire, i. 80. Dallaway's
Sussex, II. ii. 342. Notes and Queries, 5 S. xi. 9. Burton's
Description of Leicestershire, 201. Chauncy's Hertfordshire, 503.
See BLOUNT.

BLYKE. Harleian Society, xxviii. 58.

BLYTHE. Jewitt's Reliquary, v. 203. Lincolnshire Tradesmen's
Tokens, by Justin Simpson, (London, 1872, 8vo.) 55. Foster's
Visitations of Yorkshire, 321, 627. The Genealogist, iii. 352.
Harleian Society, xv. 83 ; xxxviii. 451. Hunter's Hallamshire,
Gatty's Edn., 415 note. Burke's Colonial Gentry, i. 40. *See* BLITH.

BLYTHMAN. Morant's Essex, ii. 281. Surtees Society, xxxvi. 179. Thoresby's Ducatus Leodiensis, 7. The Genealogist, New Series, xiv. 183.

BLYTON. Harleian Society, xvi. 25.

BOADE. Harleian Society, xiv. 551.

BOARD. Burke's Landed Gentry, 5 supp., 6, 7, 8 supp. Sussex Archæological Collections, vi. 202.

BOARDMAN. Abram's History of Blackburn, 578. Harleian Society, xxxviii. 582.

BOASE. An Account of the Families of Boase, or Bowes, etc. Printed for Chas. Willm., Geo. Clement, and Fredk. Boase. Exeter, 1876, 4to. ; 2nd Edition, 1893, 4to.

BOCKETT. Berry's Berkshire Genealogies, 78.

BOCKING. Carthew's Hundred of Launditch, Part ii. 423.

BOCKLAND. Hoare's Wiltshire, III. iv. 50.

BODDAM. Burke's Landed Gentry, 3, 4, 5, 6.

BODDAM-WHETHAM. Burke's Landed Gentry, 6, 7, 8.

BODDINGTON. Boddington Pedigree, by R. S. Boddington, 1890, broadside. Pedigree of the Family of Boddington, by R. S. Boddington. Exeter, 1889, oblong 4to. Burke's Landed Gentry, 8. Harleian Society, xxxix. 1110. Pedigree of Bodington, by W. F. Carter, 1895, single sheet. Miscellanea Genealogica et Heraldica, New Series, i. 428 ; ii. 163, 244, 545 ; 2nd Series, i. 211 ; iii. 348. The Midland Antiquary, i. 80, 121 ; ii. 90. Howard's Visitation of England and Wales, i. 121.

BODDYE. Harleian Society, xiii. 155.

BODE. Hasted's Kent, ii. 726. Berry's Kent Genealogies, 136. Harleian Society, xlii. 51. Muskett's Suffolk Manorial Families, i. 131.

BODEN. Burke's Landed Gentry, 5 supp., 6, 7, 8.

BODENHAM. Burke's Commoners, iv. 83; Landed Gentry, 2, 3, 4, 5, 6. Wright's History of Rutland, 112. Blore's Rutland, 49. Hoare's Wiltshire, III. iv. 61. Weaver's Visitation of Hereford-shire, 81.

BODKIN. Burke's Landed Gentry, 2 supp., 3, 4, 5, 6, 7, 8. Oliver's History of Antigua, i. 64.

BODLE. Berry's Essex Genealogies, 87. Nichols' History of the County of Leicester, iv. 802. Harleian Society, xiv. 706.

BODLEIGH, or BODLEY. Westcote's Devonshire, edited by G. Oliver and P. Jones, 499. Harleian Society, vi. 33 ; xliii. 147. Notes and Queries, 6 S. iv. 85. The Visitations of Devon, edited by J. L. Vivian, 96. Surrey Archæological Collections, x.

BODRIGAN, or BODRUGAN. Maclean's History of Trigg Manor, i. 548-555. Banks' Baronies in Fee, ii. 48. Miscellanea Genealogica et Heraldica, ii. 234. Archdall's Lodge's Peerage, vi. 38. The Genealogist, New Series, x. 213.

BODULGATE. Maclean's History of Trigg Minor, ii. 363.

BODVEL. Dwinn's Visitations of Wales, ii. 173. History of Powys Fadog, by J. Y. W. Lloyd, vi. 197.

BODY. Muskett's Suffolk Manorial Families, i. 48.

BODYAM. Sussex Archæological Collections, iii. 93. *See* DE BODIAM.

BODYCHEN. Archæologia Cambrensis, 4 S. ii. 241, 333.

BOEVEY. The Perverse Widow, by A. W. Crawley-Boevey. London, 1898, 4to. Fosbrooke's History of Gloucestershire, ii. 178. Betham's Baronetage, iv. 187. *See* BOVEY.

BOGAN, or BOGANS. Tuckett's Devonshire Pedigrees, 96. Harleian Society, vi. 37; ix. 14. Visitation of Cornwall, edited by Sir N. H. Nicolas, 24. The Visitations of Cornwall, edited by J. L. Vivian, 40. The Visitations of Devon, edited by J. L. Vivian, 98.

BOGAS. Metcalfe's Visitations of Suffolk, 115.

BOGER. Burke's Landed Gentry, 5, 6, 7, 8. A Complete Parochial History of the County of Cornwall, iii. 252.

BOGGIS-ROLFE. Burke's Family Records, 513. Howard's Visitation of England and Wales, vii. 120.

BOGIE. Some old Families, by H. B. McColl, 162.

BOGLE. Airth Peerage Evidence, 116.

BOHUN. The Diary of Edmund Bohun, edited by S. W. Rix. Beccles, 1853, 4to. Gentleman's Magazine, 1826, i. 130; 1827, i. 587. Morant's Essex, ii. 451, 455. Herald and Genealogist, vi. 253, 429; vii. 289. Maclean's History of Trigg Minor, i. 459; ii. 188. Munford's Analysis of Domesday Book of Co. Norfolk, 50. Lipscombe's History of the County of Buckingham, i. 206. Dallaway's Sussex, i. 282; II. i. 22. Nichols' History of the County of Leicester, i. app. 33. Manning and Bray's Surrey, ii. 762. Baker's Northampton. i. 544. Page's History of Suffolk, 393. The Genealogist, iii. 353; vii. 59. Antiquities in Westminster Abbey, by Thomas Moule, 24. Banks' Baronies in Fee, i. 129. Banks' Extinct and Dormant Baronage, i. 244; iii. 354. Metcalfe's Visitations of Suffolk, 10. Notes and Queries, 6 S. vi. 289, 353. Woodcock of Cuerden, by A. E. P. Gray, 19. Harleian Society, xxxvii. 323. The Visitations of Devon, by J. L. Vivian, 747. *See* BOUN, DE BOHUN.

BOIS. Jones's History of the County of Brecknock, ii. 319. *See* DE BOIS.

BOISSIER. The Genealogist, vi. 168.

BOKELAND. Hoare's Wiltshire, III. iv. 44.

BOKENHAM. Abstract of Records, etc., to prove the Claims and Title of Katherine, wife of Richard Bokenham, of Weston Mercate, Co. Suffolk, to the Barony of Berners, 1717, folio, pp. 55. Claim of Mrs. Bokenham to the Barony of Berners, Sess. Papers, March-June 1720. Harleian Society, xiii. 351. Notes and Queries, 2 S. iii. 12, 195. *See* BUCKENHAM.

BOKETON. Baker's Northampton, i. 32.

BOKINGE. Metcalfe's Visitations of Suffolk, 86. *See* BOCKING.

BOLAM. Hodgson's Northumberland, I. ii. 333.

BOLAN. Oliver's History of Antigua, i. 65.

BOLCKOW. Burke's Landed Gentry, 7, 8.

BOLD. Burke's Commoners, iii. 84. Chetham Society, lxxxi. 110; lxxxii. 15; lxxxiv. 41; cx. 147. Gregson's Fragments relative to the County of Lancaster, 182. Baines' History of the Co. of Lancaster, iii. 717; Croston's edn., v. 24. Ormerod's Cheshire, ii. 484. Harleian Society, xviii. 33; xli. 28. *See* BOULD.

BOLDEN. Burke's Landed Gentry, 2, 3, 4, 5, 6, 7, 8.

BOLDERO. Burke's Landed Gentry, 3, 4, 5, 6, 7, 8. Gage's History of Thingoe Hundred, Suffolk, 253. Page's History of Suffolk, 718. Metcalfe's Visitations of Suffolk, 115, 116. Harleian Society, xxxix. 936. Muskett's Suffolk Manorial Families, i. 176-188.

BOLDING. Pedigree of the Bolding Family, by W. B. Bickley. Birmingham, 1898, 8vo. Appendix to same, pp. 14, *n. d.*, 8vo. Howard's Visitation of England and Wales, viii. 73.

BOLEBEC, or BOLBECK. Hodgson's Northumberland, I. ii. 239. Lipscombe's History of the County of Buckingham, ii. 493, 526; iii. 510. Clutterbuck's Hertford, ii. 261. Banks' Extinct and Dormant Baronage, i. 38. *See* DE BOLEBECK.

BOLEIGH. The Visitations of Cornwall, edited by J. L. Vivian, 273.

BOLES. Chauncy's Hertfordshire, 48.

BOLEYNE. Historical Anecdotes of the Family of the Boleynes, Careys, Mordaunts, Hamiltons, and Joscelyns, by E. G. S. Reilly. Newry, 1839, 4to. Gentleman's Magazine, 1829, i. 397; 1849, ii. 155. Blomefield's Norfolk, vi. 386. Gough's Sepulchral Monuments, ii. 184. Clutterbuck's Hertford, iii. 94. The Citizens of London and their Rulers, by B. B. Orridge, 186. Banks' Extinct and Dormant Baronage, iii. 754. Hasted's Kent, (Hund. of Blackheath, by H. H. Drake,) xviii. Notes and Queries, 6 S. ix. 457; xii. 444. *See* BULLEN.

BOLGER. Burke's Landed Gentry, 2, 3, 4, 5.

BOLINGBROKE. Foster's Visitations of Yorkshire, 346.

BOLITHO. Burke's Landed Gentry, 5, 6, 7, 8. The Visitations of Cornwall, by J. L. Vivian, 569. The Visitations of Devon, by J. L. Vivian, 845.

BOLLAND. Harleian Society, xvi. 147.

BOLLE, or BOLLES. Anecdotes of the Family of Bolle, in Illingworth's Account of Scampton, 1810, 4to. Berry's Hertfordshire Genealogies, 40. Burke's Commoners, ii. 389. Harleian Society, iv. 94. The Genealogist, iii. 353-355; v. 312. Holland's History of Worksop, 184. Burke's Extinct Baronetcies, and 617. East Barnet, by F. C. Cass, Part i. 58. Phillimore's London and Middlesex Note-Book, 265.

BOLLERON. Chetham Society, xcix. 70.

BOLLING. Harleian Society, xv. 83, 84. Bradford Antiquary, ii. 117. Ilkley, Ancient and Modern, by R. Collyer and J. H. Turner, 205.

BOLNEY. Visitations of Berkshire, printed by Sir T. Phillipps, 9. Metcalfe's Visitations of Suffolk, 10.

BOLRON. Pedigrees of the Leading Families of Lancashire, published by Joseph Foster, (London, 1872, 4to.). Plantagenet-Harrison's History of Yorkshire, i. 397.

BOLSWORTH. Harleian Society, xix. 83.

BOLT. An Historical Survey of Cornwall, by C. S. Gilbert, ii. 35.

BOLTER. Miscellanea Genealogica et Heraldica, New Series, i. 25. Harleian Society, xxxii. 41. *See* BOULTER.

BOLTON. Camden Society, xliii. 55. Visitation of Norfolk, published by Norfolk Archæological Society, i. 101. Burke's Landed Gentry, (of Bective Abbey,) 3, 4, 5, 6; (of Mount Bolton,) 3, 4, 5, 6, 7, 8; (of the Island,) 5, 6, 7, 8; (of Tullydonnell,) 5 supp., 6, 7; (of Curraghduff,) 2 and corr.; (of Nenagh,) 6. Burke's Heraldic Register, (published with St. James's Magazine,) 50. Foster's Visitations of Yorkshire, 563. Burke's Visitation of Seats and Arms, i. 60. Abram's History of Blackburn, 262, 561, 655. Jordan's History of Enstone, 351. Harleian Society, xv. 82, 84; xxxii. 42. Metcalfe's Visitations of Suffolk, 185. Burke's Family Records, 83.

BOLTWOOD. New England Register, v. 101.

BOMFORD. Burke's Landed Gentry, 2, 3, 4, 5, 6, 7, 8. *See* NORTH-BOMFORD.

BONAMY. Chronicle of the Family of De Havilland.

BONAR. Popular Genealogists, 55-82. Burke's Landed Gentry, (of Bonare,) 2 supp., 3, 4; (of Camden,) 2 supp., 3, 4. Burke's Royal Families, (London, 1851, 8vo.) i. 179. Herald and Genealogist, v. 541. Burke's Heraldic Illustrations, 118. The Theology of Consolation, by D. C. A. Agnew, 209. Burke's Colonial Gentry, ii. 530.

BONATRE. Visitation of Cornwall, edited by Sir N. H. Nicolas, 21.

BONBURY. Harleian Society, xviii. 26.

BOND. Pedigree of the Family of Bond of the Isle of Purbeck. London, 1839. Another edition, 1858, fol. Visitation of Cornwall, edited by Sir N. H. Nicolas, 15, 16. Burke's Commoners, (of Creech Grange,) i. 240, Landed Gentry, 2, 3, 4, 5, 6, 7, 8; (of Ardglass,) Landed Gentry, 2; (of Bondville,) 3. Harleian Society, ix. 15; xv. 86; xx. 16; xliii. 62. Hutchins' Dorset, i. 603; iv. 328. An Historical Survey of Cornwall, by C. S. Gilbert, ii. 30. Wotton's English Baronetage, iii. 3. Burke's Extinct Baronetcies, and 600. The Visitations of Cornwall, edited by J. L. Vivian, 41. East Barnet, by F. C. Cass, Part i. 38. Visitation of Gloucester, edited by T. F. Fenwick and W. C. Metcalfe, 16. Howard's Visitation of England and Wales, iii. 72. Notes and Queries, 8 S. iv. 229, 356, 492, 538.

BONEBURI. The Genealogist, New Series, xiii. 99.

BONER. Burke's Heraldic Register, (published with St. James's Magazine,) 79. *See* BONNER.

BONETH. Castles, Manors, and Mansions of Western Sussex, by D. G. C. Elwes and C. J. Robinson, 285.

BONFOY. Visitation of Middlesex, (Salisbury, 1820, fol.) 19. Harleian Society, viii. 191. Carthew's Hundred of Launditch, Part ii. 549, 550. Herald and Genealogist, vi. 153, 358. Foster's Visitation of Middlesex, 37.

BONHAM. Morant's Essex, ii. 156, 178, 191, 606. Berry's Essex Genealogies, 78, 167. Burke's Landed Gentry, 4, 5, 6, 7, 8. Harleian Society, xiii. 352; xiv. 639, 738.

BONHAM,CARTER. Burke's Landed Gentry, 7, 8.

BONINGTON. Visitation of Derbyshire, 1663-4, (Middle Hill, 1854, fol.) 2. The Genealogist, iii. 121.

BONITHON, or BONYTHON. Visitation of Cornwall, edited by Sir N. H. Nicolas, 17, 21. Harleian Society, ix. 16. The Western Antiquary, i. 200. The Visitations of Cornwall, edited by J. L. Vivian, 43, 44, 572. Burke's Colonial Gentry, i. 91. Gentleman's Magazine, Feb. 1868, 179. The Antiquary for April, 1881, 91. New England Register, xxxviii. 50.

BONNE. Visitations of Staffordshire, 1614 and 1663-4, William Salt Society, 45.

BONNELL. Visitation of Middlesex, (Salisbury, 1820, fol.) 2. Foster's Visitation of Middlesex, 6. The Perverse Widow, by A. W. Crawley-Boevey, 198.

BONNER. Visitation of Somerset, printed by Sir T. Phillipps, 21. Harleian Society, xi. 9; xviii. 205. New England Register, v. 174. *See* BONER.

BONNIN. Oliver's History of Antigua, i. 68.

BONNOR-MAURICE. Burke's Landed Gentry, 5, 6, 7, 8. Collections by the Powys-land Club, v. 266.

BONSALL. Burke's Landed Gentry, 5, 6, 7, 8.

BONSOR. *See* HEWSON.

BONTEIN. Burke's Landed Gentry, 8.

BONVILE, or BONVILLE. Toulman's History of Taunton, new edn. by James Savage, (Taunton, 1822, 8vo.) 69. Maclean's History of Trigg Minor, i. 394*. Dallaway's Sussex, i. 65. Westcote's Devonshire, edited by G. Oliver and P. Jones, 465. Miscellanea Genealogica et Heraldica, New Series, ii. 75. Castles, Mansions, and Manors of Western Sussex, by D. G. C. Elwes and C. J. Robinson, 149. Foster's Account of Families descended from Francis Fox, 26. Colby of Great Torrington, by F. T. Colby, 33. An Historical Survey of Cornwall, by C. S. Gilbert, i. 531. A Description of the Monument and Effigies in Porlock Church, by M. Halliday, *at end*. Banks' Baronies in Fee, i. 129. Visitation of Devon, edited by F. T. Colby, 23. Banks' Extinct and Dormant Baronage, ii. 51. Notes and Queries, 5 S. vi. 447; vii. 52, 231; viii. 17, 430. The Visitations of Devon, edited by J. L. Vivian, 101, 161. Weaver's Visitations of Somerset, 96. Genealogies of Morgan and Glamorgan, by G. T. Clark, 365. The Genealogist, New Series, xvi. 94; xvii. 19, 251.

BONYNGE. Burke's Landed Gentry, 8.

BOODE. Harleian Society, xiii. 26, 73.

BOOKER. Burke's Landed Gentry, 2 add., 3, 4, 5, 6, 7, 8. Harleian Society, xv. 87.

BOOMER. Ontarian Families, by E. M. Chadwick, i. 87.

BOONE. Hasted's Kent, (Hund. of Blackheath, by H. H. Drake,) 223. Oliver's History of Antigua, i, 70.

BOORDE. Berry's Sussex Genealogies, 270. Sussex Archæological Collections, vi. 202.

BOORMAN. Genealogical Record of King and Henham, 19.

BOOSEY. Harleian Society, xiii. 352.

BOOTH, or BOOTHE. The Tyndale Pedigree, by B. W. Greenfield. Gentleman's Magazine, 1848, ii. 608. Surtees Society, xxxvi. 17, 358. Visitation of Durham, 1615, (Sunderland, 1820, fol.) 103. Ashmole's Antiquities of Berkshire, iii. 308. Visitation of Durham, 1575, (Newcastle, 1820, fol.) 52. Jewitt's Reliquary, vii. 242. Eastwood's History of Ecclesfield, 380. Burke's Landed Gentry, 2, 3, 4, 5, 6, 7, 8. Harleian Society, iii. 5 ; viii. 342 ; xxviii, 58 ; xxxviii. 745 ; xxxix. 901. History of the Ancient Chapel of Blackley, by Rev. J. Booker, 26, 27. Chetham Society, lxxxii. 10 ; lxxxiv. 44 ; xcviii. 78. Visitation of Berkshire, printed by Sir T. Phillipps, 9. Hutchinson's History of Durham, ii. 306. Surtees' Durham, i. 246 ; iv. 92. Baines' History of the County of Lancaster, iii. 113 ; Croston's edition, iii. 242. J. P. Earwaker's History of East Cheshire, i. 53. Ormerod's Cheshire, i. 523 ; ii. 382 ; iii. 137, 641. Earwaker's Local Gleanings, ii. 642, 649, 683. Butterworth's History of Stockport, etc., 29. The Genealogist, iii. 356 ; v. 239, 313 ; New Series, i. 2 ; iii. 135. Edmondson's Baronagium Genealogicum, iv. 396. Banks' Extinct and Dormant Baronage, iii. 230. Burke's Extinct Baronetcies. Foster's Visitations of Durham, 29, 31. History of Altrincham and Bowdon, by A. Ingham, 112. Notes and Queries, 6 S. x. 27, 130, 275. Earwaker's History of Sandbach, 269. See BOTHE, BOUTH.

BOOTHBY. Boothby of Hawkesbury, Co. Glouc., [T. P.] 1866. Broadside. Morant's Essex, i. 57. Berry's Surrey Genealogies, 58. Glover's History of Derbyshire, ii. 43. Visitation of Staffordshire, 1663-4, printed by Sir T. Phillipps, 2. Visitation of Derbyshire, 1663-4, (Middle Hill, 1854, fol.) 2. Nichol's History of the County of Leicester, iv. 171, 177-179. The Genealogist, iii. 122. Pilkington's View of Derbyshire, ii. 280. Harleian Society, xv. 87, 88. Wotton's English Baronetage, iii. 99. Betham's Baronetage, iii. 123. Burke's Extinct Baronetcies. Visitations of Staffordshire, 1614 and 1663-4, William Salt Society, 45. Foster's Visitation of Middlesex, 20.

BOOTLE. Chetham Society, lxxxiv. 45. Baines' History of the Co. of Lancaster, iv. 247 ; Croston's edition, v. 262.

BORARD. Lipscombe's History of the County of Buckingham, iv. 105. Nichols' History of the County of Leicester, ii. 360.

BORASTON. Harleian Society, xxii. 110. Oliver's History of Antigua, i. 71.

BORDE. Sussex Archæological Collections, vi. 202.

BORDON. John Brewster's History of Stockton-upon-Tees, 46.

BOREEL. Burke's Extinct Baronetcies.

BOREHED. Metcalfe's Visitations of Suffolk, 116.

BOREMAN. Harleian Society, xi. 11. Weaver's Visitations of Somerset, 9. See BOUREMAN.

BORHUNTE. Brocas of Beaurepaire, by M. Burrows, 334.

BORLACE, or BORLASE. Berry's Buckinghamshire Genealogies, 80. History of the Hundred of Desborough, by Thomas Langley, 317.

Lipscombe's History of the County of Buckingham, i. 309. An Historical Survey of Cornwall, by C. S. Gilbert, ii. 42. Betham's Baronetage, iv. 4. Burke's Extinct Baronetcies, and 554. The Genealogist, New Series, ii. 1, 129, 225, 283 ; iii. 53 ; iv. 160 ; v. 29. Burke's Landed Gentry, 7, 8.

BOROUGH, BOROUGHS, or BORROUGH. Maclean's History of Trigg Minor, i. 394. Cambridgeshire Visitation, edited by Sir T. Phillipps, 5. Surtees Society, xli. 44. Glover's History of Derbyshire, ii. 581, (555). Burke's Landed Gentry, 2 add., 3, 4, 5, 6, 7, 8. Foster's Visitations of Yorkshire, 3. Topographer, (London, 1789-91, 8vo.) ii. 237. Hodgson's Northumberland, II. ii. 41. Clutterbuck's Hertford, iii. 131. The Genealogist, iii. 357 ; v. 317. Harleian Society, xvi. 26 ; xxviii. 59 ; xl. 1205. F. G. Lee's History of Thame, 245.

BORRADAILE. Sketch of the Borradailes of Cumberland, by A. B. London, 1881, 4to.

BORRER. Burke's Landed Gentry, 3, 4, 5, 6, 7, 8. Burke's Visitation of Seats and Arms, i. 41.

BORRET. Hasted's Kent, i, 317.

BORRON. Miscellanea Genealogica et Heraldica, New Series, i. 354.

BORROW, or BOROW. Miscellanea Genealogica et Heraldica, New Series, iv. 260.. Metcalfe's Visitations of Suffolk, 185. Knapp's Life of George Borrow, i. 26.

BORROWES. Burke's Landed Gentry, 4, 5, 6, 7, 8. Burke's Royal Families, (London, 1851, 8vo.) i. 86.

BORTHWICK. Claim of Henry Borthwick to the title of Lord Borth-wick, Sess. Papers, Jan.-April, 1762. Claim of John Borthwick to the same, Sess. Papers, Feb., 1774—Nov. 1776. Claim of Archibald Borthwick to the same, Sess. Papers, 83 of 1812 ; 26 of 1812-13 ; 77 of 1813-14 ; 49 of 1814-15. Claim of Cunning-hame Borthwick to same, Sess. Papers, C of 1868-9 ; B of 1870. Case of Henry Borthwick, claiming the title of Lord Borthwick, March, 1762, folio, reprinted 1868. Case of John Borthwick of Crookstown, claiming the Title of Lord Borthwick, March, 1762, folio, reprinted 1868. Burke's Landed Gentry, 2, 3, 4, 5, 6, 7, 8. Lands and their Owners in Galloway, by P. H. M'Kerlie, ii. 446. Nisbet's Heraldry, ii. app. 111. Walter Wood's East Neuk of Fife, 269, 270. Wood's Douglas's Peerage of Scotland, ii. 651.

BORTON. Surtees Society, xli. 61, 79.

BOSANQUET. The Genealogy of the Family of Bosanquet. By Louisa Clara Meyer, 1877, fol. [Contains pedigrees of Askew, Commerell, Gaussen, Holford, Hunter, Hayes, Pole, Vander Notten, and Whatman.] Berry's Hertfordshire Genealogies, 254. Burke's Commoners, (of Forest House,) iii. 316. Landed Gentry, 2, 3, 4, 5, 6, 7, 8; (of Broxbournbury,) 2, 3, 4, 5, 6, 7, 8. Cussan's History of Hertfordshire, Parts ix. and x., 176. T. Nicholas's County Families of Wales, 772.

BOSAVERN, or BOSAVARNE. Visitation of Cornwall, edited by Sir N. H. Nicolas, 12. Harleian Society, ix. 17. The Visitations of Cornwall, edited by J. L. Vivian, 45.

BOSCAWEN. Visitation of Cornwall, edited by Sir N. H. Nicolas, 18. Harleian Society, ix. 20. Lipscombe's History of the County of Buckingham, i. 447. A Complete Parochial History of the County of Cornwall, iii. 346. An Historical Survey of Cornwall, by C. S. Gilbert, i. 452. Edmondson's Baronagium Genealogicum, iv. 330. Brydges' Collins' Peerage, vi. 62. The Visitations of Cornwall, edited by J. L. Vivian, 46.

BOSEVILLE, or BOSSEVILLE. Surtees Society, xxxvi. 297.

BOSGRAVE. Harleian Society, xix. 5.

BOSON. An Account of the Families of Boase, (Exeter, 1876, 4to.) 26. The Genealogist, New Series, xiv. 199.

BOSSAWSACH, or BOSSAWSACKE. Visitation of Cornwall, edited by Sir N. H. Nicolas, 22. Harleian Society, ix. 22. The Visitations of Cornwall, edited by J. L. Vivian, 50.

BOSSLEY. Harleian Society, xxxvii. 256.

BOSSOM. The Visitations of Devon, by J. L. Vivian, 697.

BOSTOCK. Visitations of Berkshire, printed by Sir Thos. Phillipps, 9, 10. Harleian Society, xv. 90; xviii. 26-32; xxviii. 61. The Genealogist, v. 240. Ormerod's Cheshire, iii. 259. Surrey Archæological Collections, ix. 162.

BOSUM. Harleian Society, xii. 89; xxxii. 43.

BOSUSTOWE. Visitation of Cornwall, edited by Sir N. H. Nicolas, 23. Harleian Society, ix. 23. The Visitations of Cornwall, edited by J. L. Vivian, 51.

BOSVIL, BOSVILE, BOSVILL, or BOSVILLE. Genealogical Tables of the Bosville Family, in Baverstock's Account of Maidstone, 1832, 8vo., 14-22. Surtees Society, xxxvi. 276. Berry's Buckinghamshire Genealogies, 32. Berry's Kent Genealogies, 480. Burke's Commoners, i. 516; (of Ravenfield,) Landed Gentry, 2, 3, 4, 5, 6, 7, 8. Foster's Yorkshire Pedigrees. Foster's Visitations of Yorkshire, 338, 356, 368. Harleian Society, iv. 64; viii. 180; xvi. 27; xlii. 169. Wainwright's Wapentake of Strafford and Tickhill, 90, 122. Hunter's Deanery of Doncaster, i. 123, 127, 133; ii. 111, 245, 393. Thoroton's Nottinghamshire, i. 348. Douglas' Baronage of Scotland, 307, 458. Burke's Family Records, 84.

BOSWELL. Berry's Buckinghamshire Genealogies, 32. Burke's Landed Gentry, (of Crawley Grange,) 2, 4 supp., 5; (of Garrallan,) 7; (of Iver,) 4 supp., 5; (of Balmuto,) 4 supp.; 4, p. 1523; 7, 8. Paterson's History of the Co. of Ayr, i. 237. Douglas' Baronage of Scotland, 307, 458. Paterson's History of Ayr and Wigton, i. 190-199. Boswelliana, by Rev. C. Rogers, 1. See ARNOT, DOUGLAS-BOSWELL.

BOSWORTH. Descent of children of John Bosworth from Edward I. Privately printed by W. G. D. Fletcher, folio page, circa 1883.

BOSYNE. Harleian Society, xvi. 358.

BOTELER, BOTILLER, or BOTILER. Hasted's Kent, ii. 291; iv. 219, 223. Morant's Essex, i. 295-310. Visitation of Somerset, printed by Sir T. Phillipps, 22. Surrey Archæological Collections, iii. Berry's Buckinghamshire Genealogies, 11. Burke's Commoners,

i. 516, Landed Gentry, 2, 3, 4, 5, 6, 7, 8. Harleian Society, vi.
36 ; viii. 25 ; xi. 11 ; xix. 6, 84 ; xxii. 29, 111 ; xli. 96 ; xlii. 41,
222, 223 ; xliii. 120, 220. Camden Society, xcix. 83. Nichol's
History of the County of Leicester, ii. 172 ; iv. 814. Collectanea Topographica et Genealogica, vii. 1. Lipscombe's
History of the County of Buckingham, i. 596. Dugdale's
Warwickshire, 854, 1073. Manning and Bray's Surrey, i. 533.
Clutterbuck's Hertford, ii. 46, 347, 475. Chauncy's Hertford-
shire, 309, 330, 333, 515. Thoroton's Nottinghamshire, i. 191 ;
iii. 123. Memoirs of the Family of Chester, by R. E. C. Waters,
138. Ormerod's Cheshire, ii. 728. Chetham Society, lxxxii. 74.
Wotton's English Baronetage, ii. 180. Banks' Baronies in Fee,
i. 130 Banks' Extinct and Dormant Baronage, i. 245. Burke's
Extinct Baronetcies. The Visitations of Devon, edited by J. L.
Vivian, 104. Devonshire Notes and Notelets, by Sir W. R.
Drake, 50. Aldred's History of Turville, 60. The Genealogist,
New Series, xiii. 175, 245, 250 ; xv. 27, 30 ; xvi. 93 ; xviii. 26.
See BUTLER, LE BOTELER.

BOTERELL. Maclean's History of Trigg Minor, i. 631-641. Harleian
Society, xxviii. 61.

BOTETOURT, or BOTTETOURT. Lipscombe's History of the County of
Buckingham, iv. 276. Blore's Rutland, 90, 209. Edmondson's
Baronagium Genealogicum, iv. 360. Banks' Baronies in Fee, i. 131.
Banks' Extinct and Dormant Baronage, ii. 53. The Genealogist,
New Series, xiv. 251. *See* BERKELEY, DE BOUTETORT.

BOTFIELD. Stemmata Botevilliana, Memorials of the Families of De
Boteville, Thynne, and Botfield, by Byriah Botfield. First edn.,
1843, 8vo., 2nd edn. Westminster, 1858, 4to. Burke's Landed
Gentry, (of Decker Hill,) 2, 3, 4, 5, 6, 7, 8 ; (of Norton Hall,) 2,
3, 4 ; (of Hopton Court,) 2. Topographer and Genealogist, iii.
468. Burke's Visitation of Seats and Arms, 2nd series, i. 52.
Burke's Heraldic Illustrations, 31. Edmondson's Baronagium
Genealogicum, iv. 326.

BOTHBY. Visitation of Middlesex, (Salisbury, 1820, fol.) 14. W.
Robinson's History of Tottenham, ii. 162.

BOTHE. Baines' History of the Co. of Lancaster, iii. 113. *See*
BOOTH.

BOTHOM. Harleian Society, ii. 165. Jewitt's Reliquary, vii. 22.

BOTHWELL. Nisbet's Heraldry, ii. app. 242. Wood's Douglas's
Peerage of Scotland, i. 728.

BOTONER. Dallaway's Antiquities of Bristow, 18.

BOTREAUX. The Genealogist, New Series, xii. 226. Collinson's
Somerset, ii. 67. Eyton's Antiquities of Shropshire, vii. 159.
Dugdale's Warwickshire, 768. Hoare's Wiltshire, I. ii. 92.
Clutterbuck's Hertford, ii. 32. Banks' Baronies in Fee, i. 131.
Banks' Extinct and Dormant Baronage, ii. 55. Miscellanea
Genealogica et Heraldica, 2nd Series, ii. 314. *See* HASTINGS,
LOUDOUN.

BOTRY, or BOTRY. Baker's Northampton, i. 641. Metcalfe's Visitations of Suffolk, 87.

BOTSFORD. Burke's Colonial Gentry, i. 99.
BOTT. Oliver's History of Antigua, i. 72. The Gresley's of Drake-
low, by F. Madan, 241.
BOTTEN. Monograph of the Family of Folkard, ii. 65.
BOTTOMLEY. Independency at Brighouse, by J. H. Turner, 83.
BOTVILE. See BOTFIELD.
BOUCAUT. Burke's Colonial Gentry, i. 344.
BOUCHE. Foster's Visitations of Cumberland and Westmorland, 14.
BOUCHER. Monken Hadley, by F. C. Cass, 166.
BOUCHERETT. Burke's Landed Gentry, 2, 3, 4, 5, 6, 7, 8.
BOUCHIER. Berry's Berkshire Genealogies, 85. See BOURCHIER.
BOUDAEN. The Perverse Widow, by A. W. Crawley-Boevry, 183.
BOUDIER. J. B. Payne's Armorial of Jersey, 49.
BOUGE. Nichols' History of the County of Leicester, iv. 1006.
BOUGHTON. Morant's Essex, i. 259. Visitation of Warwickshire,
1619, published with Warwickshire Antiquarian Magazine, 84.
History of the Town and School of Rugby, by N. H. Nicolas, 38.
Nichols' History of the County of Leicester, iv. 302. Dugdale's
Warwickshire, 100. Harleian Society xii. 83. Scott of Scot's
Hall, by J. R. Scott, 176. Wotton's English Baronetage, ii. 220.
Betham's Baronetage, i. 415.
BOUGHTON-ROUSE. Betham's Baronetage, iv. 213.
BOULD. Dwnn's Visitations of Wales, i. 246; ii. 245, 317. See
BOLD.
BOULDERSON. An Historical Survey of Cornwall, by C. S. Gilbert,
ii. 31.
BOULDWAS. The Genealogist, New Series, ix. 149.
BOULEN. Burke's Extinct Baronetcies.
BOULTBEE. Burke's Landed Gentry, 3, 4, 5, 6, 7, 8.
BOULTER. Two brief Genealogical Tables showing certain descents
in the family of Boulter of Worcestershire and Kingston-upon-
Hull. Hull, printed for a few friends by W. C. B., 20 June,
1871. See BOLTER.
BOULTON. Dwnn's Visitations of Wales, i. 133. Burke's Commoners,
(of Moulton,) ii. 378, Landed Gentry, 2, 3, 4; (of Tew Park,)
Landed Gentry, 6, 7, 8. Pembrokeshire Pedigrees, 123.
Manning and Bray's Surrey, ii. 670. Jordan's History of
Enstone, 351.
BOUN. Nichols' History of the County of Leicester, iv. 644. Dug-
dale's Warwickshire, 133. Thornton's Nottinghamshire, iii. 126.
See BOHUN.
BOUNTAYNE. The Genealogist, v. 313.
BOURBON. Notes and Queries, 4 S. iv. 435; v. 121.
BOURCHIER. Collinson's Somerset, ii. 391. Hasted's Kent, i. 130.
Morant's Essex, i. 145, 353, 380, 383, 401; ii. 76, 80, 135, 149,
254, 448. Berry's Berkshire Genealogies, 55. Surtees Society,
xxxvi. 140. Toulmin's History of Taunton, new edn., by James
Savage, (Taunton, 1822, 8vo.) 70. Foster's Visitations of York-
shire, 62. History of Leeds Castle, by C. Wykeham-Martin, 140.
Harleian Society, vi. 34; viii. 310; xiii. 353; xvi. 30. Topo-

grapher, (London, 1789-91, 8vo.) ii. 372. Herald and Genealogist, viii. 367. Lipscombe's History of the County of Buckingham, iv. 258. Westcote's Devonshire, edited by G. Oliver and P. Jones, 460. Thoresby's Ducatus Leodiensis, 123. Wright's Essex, i. 463. Carthew's Hundred of Launditch, Part ii. 651. Burke's Landed Gentry, 6, 7. Antiquities in Westminster Abbey, by Thomas Moule, 29. Edmondson's Baronagium Genealogicum, vi. 39. Banks' Baronies in Fee, i. 132, 213. Visitation of Devon, edited by F. T. Colby, 24. Banks' Extinct and Dormant Baronage, ii. 50, 57, 121, 217 ; iii. 274. The Visitations of Devon, edited by J. L. Vivian, 106, 750. East Barnet, by F. C. Cass, Part i. 96. Chancellor's Sepulchral Monuments of Essex, 90. Visitation of Gloucester, edited by T. F. Fenwick, and W. C. Metcalfe, 20. Burke's Family Records, 85. The Genealogist, New Series, xiv. 186. *See* BOUCHIER.

BOUREMAN. Visitation of Somerset, printed by Sir T. Phillipps, 24. Harleian Society, xv. 92. *See* BOREMAN.

BOURKE. Burke's Landed Gentry, (of Thornfields,) 2, 3, 4, 5, 6, 7, 8 ; (of Carrowkeel,) 4 supp. ; (of Curraghleagh,) 4 supp., 6, 7 ; (of Urey,) 7 ; (of Heathfield,) 8 supp. O'Hart's Irish Pedigrees, 2nd Series, 306-314. Archdall's Lodge's Peerage, iii. 414 ; iv. 227. The Irish Builder, xxxv. 246.

BOURNE. Pedigrees of the Family of Bourne, by J. H. Bloom. Hemsworth, 1900, 4to., 2nd edn. Hasted's Kent, ii. 692. Morant's Essex, i. 149. Visitation of Somerset, printed by Sir T. Phillipps, 23. Berry's Kent Genealogies, 128. Glover's History of Derbyshire, ii. 64, (56). Visitation of Oxfordshire, 1574, printed by Sir T. Phillipps, (Middle Hill, fol.) 1. Visitation of Oxfordshire, 1634, printed by Sir T. Phillipps, (Middle Hill, fol.) 14. Burke's Commoners, (of Hilderstone,) ii. 31, Landed Gentry, 2 and final add., 3, 4, 5, 6, 7, 8 ; (of Wyersdale,) Landed Gentry, 3, 4, 5 ; (of Hackinsall,) 2 supp., 3, 4, 5, 6 ; (of Testwood,) 2, 5. Harleian Society, v. 183, 316 ; xi. 13 ; xiii. 4, 354; xv. 89 ; xxxvii. 300, 346 ; xlii. 43. Jewitt's Reliquary, xv. 235. Foster's Lancashire Pedigrees. Burke's Visitations of Seats and Arms, 2nd Series, i. 9. Dunkin's History of Bullington and Ploughley, i. 273. Nichols' History of the County of Leicester, iv. 34. Metcalfe's Visitation of Worcester, 1683, 19. Visitation of Gloucester, edited by T. F. Fenwick and W. C. Metcalfe, 22. Weaver's Visitations of Somerset, 10. Sepulchral Memorials of Bobbingworth, 30. History of Ribchester, by T. C. Smith and J. Shortt, 258. Howard's Visitation of England and Wales, iii. 148.

BOURSTAL. Chauncy's Hertfordshire, 324.

BOUTEFORT. Chancellor's Sepulchral Monuments of Essex, 208.

BOUTEVELEYN, or BUTTEVELYN. Banks' Baronies in Fee, ii. 49.

BOUTH. Jewitt's Reliquary, vii. 19. Chetham Society, lxxxi. 129. Harleian Society, xviii. 35. *See* BOOTH.

BOUVERIE. Rudder's Gloucestershire, 611. Hasted's Kent, iii. 373. Burke's Commoners, ii. 7, Landed Gentry, 2, 3, 4, 5, 6, 7, 8.

Hoare's Wiltshire, III. v. 35. Manning and Bray's Surrey, ii. 208. Edmondson's Baronagium Genealogicum, iii. 307. Brydges' Collins' Peerage, v. 29. Wotton's English Baronetage, iv. 150. *See* DESBOUVERIE.

BOVER. Gentleman's Magazine, 1843, i. 371; ii. 31. Earwaker's Local Gleanings, ii. 807, 815.

BOVEY, or BOVY. Burke's Extinct Baronetcies. Harleian Society, xii. 187. *See* BOEVEY.

BOVILE. Page's History of Suffolk, 376, 385. The Genealogist, New Series, xiv. 24. *See* DE BOVILE.

BOVINGTON. The New History of Yorkshire, commencing with Richmondshire, by Genl. Plantagenet-Harrison. (London, 1872, fol.) Part i. 17.

BOWATER. Miscellanea Genealogica et Heraldica, New Series, ii. 177. Harleian Society, xv. 91.

BOWCHER. Visitation of Somerset, printed by Sir T. Phillipps, 27. Harleian Society, xi. 11. Visitation of Gloucester, edited by T. F. Fenwick and W. C. Metcalfe, 23.

BOWDEN. Jewitt's Reliquary, vii. 20. Glover's History of Derbyshire, ii. 338, (304). Nichols' History of the County of Leicester, ii. 262*. Burke's Landed Gentry, 6 p. 1824, and 1832 in 2nd edn. of supp., 8. *See* BUTLER-BOWDEN.

BOWDITCH. Hutchins' Dorset, ii. 83. Harleian Society, xx. 17.

BOWDLER. Dwnn's Visitations of Wales, i. 277. The Genealogist, i. 279. The Sheriffs of Montgomeryshire, by W. V. Lloyd, 333. Harleian Society, xxviii. 63.

BOWDOIN. New England Register, x. 79 ; xi. 43.

BOWDON. Burke's Landed Gentry, 2, 3, 4, 5, 6, 7 ; (of Southgate,) 7. Abram's History of Blackburn, 620. The Genealogist, New Series, vii. 10. Harleian Society, xxxix. 1039. Baddesley Clinton, by H. Norris, 146.

BOWELES. Willmore's Records of Rushall, 25. Harleian Society, xxviii. 218. Willmore's History of Walsall, 254.

BOWEN. Dwnn's Visitations of Wales, i. 110, 116-120, 162, 163, 166-170, 180, 222. Burke's Landed Gentry, (of Bowen's Court,) 4, 5, 6, 7, 8 ; (of Camrose,) 2, 3, 4, 5, 6, 7 ; (of Courtwood,) 4, 5, 6, 7 ; (of Llwyngwair,) 4, 5, 6, 7, 8 ; (of Troedyrawr,) 2, 3, 5 supp., 6, 7, 8 ; (of Hollymount,) 7, 8. Caermarthenshire Pedigrees, 21, 47, 51. Cardiganshire Pedigrees, 98, 112, 117. Pembrokeshire Pedigrees, 119, 120, 121, 124, 130, 134, 138, 154, 158, 159, 162, 163. Meyrick's History of the Co. of Cardigan, 175, 194. T. Nicholas's County Families of Wales, 895. Collections by the Powys-land Club, vii. 51. Harleian Society, xv. 92. Genealogies of Morgan and Glamorgan, by G. T. Clark, 227. Burke's Colonial Gentry, ii. 510. New England Register, xlviii. 453.

BOWEN-COLTHURST. Howard's Visitation of Ireland, i. 66.

BOWEN-DAVIES. Burke's Landed Gentry, 2, 3, 4.

BOWER. Visitation of Somerset, printed by Sir T. Phillipps, 25, 26. Visitation of Durham, 1615, (Sunderland, 1820, fol.) 52. Jewitt's Reliquary, vii. 241 ; viii. 63. Glover's History of Derbyshire,

ii. 391, (358). Burke's Landed Gentry, (of Broxholme,) 4, 5, 6, 7 ; (of Iwerne House,) 2, 3, 4, 5, 6, 7, 8 ; (of Welham,) 2, 3, 4, 5, 6, 7, 8. Foster's Yorkshire Pedigrees. History of Darlington, by W. Hylton Dyer Longstaffe, lxxxv. Burke's Royal Families, (London, 1851, 8vo.) i. 181. Harleian Society, xi. 12 ; xv. 93 ; xxxix. 946. Burke's Authorized Arms, 124. 'Archæologia Æliana, 2nd Series, v. 80. Visitatio Comitatus Wiltoniæ, 1623, printed by Sir T. Phillipps. Hutchins' Dorset, iii. 538. Surtees' Durham, iii. 367. Plantagenet-Harrison's History of Yorkshire, i. 203. Yorkshire Archæological and Topographical Journal, vi. 274. The Visitation of Wiltshire, edited by G. W. Marshall, 42. Notes and Queries, 5 S. vi. 183 ; vii. 51, 194. Bower Family of Gloucestershire,|by Hubert Bower, 1871, 4to., 2 leaves. Yorkshire Genealogist, i. 198. Foster's Visitations of Durham, 33. Staniforthiana, by F. M. H., at end.

BOWERMAN, or BOWREMAN. Berry's Hampshire Genealogies, 78. Westcote's Devonshire, edited by G. Oliver and P. Jones, 518. Hampshire Visitations, printed by Sir T. Phillipps, 6. Visitation of Devon, edited by F. T. Colby, 25. The Visitations of Devon, edited by J. L. Vivian, 108.

BOWES. Claim of the Rt. Hon. Thomas Lyon Bowes to be Earl of Strathmore, Sess. Papers, 39 of 1821. Morant's Essex, i. 442. Visitation of Durham, 1615, (Sunderland, 1820, fol.) 70, 84. Visitation of Durham, 1575, (Newcastle, 1820, fol.) 2. Burke's Commoners, (of Bradley Hall,) i. 181, Landed Gentry, 2 ; (of Streatham Castle,) Landed Gentry, 2, 3, 4, 5, 6, 7 ; (of Monkend,) 8. Foster's Yorkshire Pedigrees. Foster's Visitations of Yorkshire, 497, 596. Burke's Royal Families, (London, 1851, 8vo.) ii. 137. Shaw's Staffordshire, i. 381. Visitation of Staffordshire, 1663-4, printed by Sir T. Phillipps, 2. History of Darlington, by W. Hylton Dyer Longstaffe, xci. Hutchinson's History of Durham, iii. 253. Surtees' Durham, i. 236 ; iii. 383 ; iv. 107, 110, 116. The Monumental Effigies in Elford Church, Staffordshire, by E. Richardson, (London, 1852, fol.) 1. Wright's Essex, ii. 758. Harleian Society, i. 29 ; viii. 383 ; xiii. 5, 27, 355 ; xvi. 31 ; xxxix. 938. Pedigrees of the Leading Families of Lancashire, published by Joseph Foster, (London, 1872, fol.). Plantagenet-Harrison's History of Yorkshire, i. 329. Notes and Queries, 1 S. x. 127, 209, 348 ; xii. 109, 230. Visitation of Staffordshire, (Willm. Salt Soc.) 51. Foster's Visitations of Durham, 34-41. Burton's History of Hemingborough, 193. Pedigrees of the Leading Families of Yorkshire, by Joseph Foster. Hasted's Kent, (Hund. of Blackheath, by H. H. Drake,) 149. Visitations of Staffordshire, 1614 and 1663-4, William Salt Society, 46. New England Register, x. 82, 129. The Genealogist, New Series, viii. 58. See BOASE.

BOWETT. Sussex Archæological Collections, xi. 88.

BOWKER. Burke's Colonial Gentry, i. 24.

BOWLBY. Topographer and Genealogist, ii. 100. Burke's Landed Gentry, 8.

BOWLE. Berry's Kent Genealogies, 357. Visitation of Wiltshire, 1677, printed by Sir T. Phillipps, (Middle Hill, 1854, fol.) Visitatio Comitatus Wiltoniæ, 1623, printed by Sir T. Phillipps. Hoare's Wiltshire, V. i. 63. Harleian Society, xlii. 114.

BOWLES. Burke's Landed Gentry, (of North Aston,) 2, 3, 4, 5, 6 ; (of Milton House,) 5, 6, 7, 8 ; (of Enfield,) 5 ; (of Abney,) 7, 8 ; (of Ahern,) 7, 8. Visitation of Warwickshire, 1619, published with Warwickshire Antiquarian Magazine, 77. Shaw's Staffordshire, ii. 63, 69. Hoare's Wiltshire, II. ii. 145; IV. ii. 36. Clutterbuck's Hertford, iii. 596. Harleian Society, xxii. 112. Baker's Northampton, i. 612. Cussan's History of Hertfordshire, Parts v. and vi. 81. Notes and Queries, 3 S. ii. 254 ; 5 S. vii. 373. History of Chislehurst, by Webb, Miller, and Beckwith, 227.

BOWMAN. Visitation of Wiltshire, 1677, printed by Sir T. Phillipps, (Middle Hill, 1854, fol.). James Hall's History of Nantwich, 508. Harleian Society, xxxvii. 111.

BOWNEST. Berry's Hertfordshire Genealogies, 226.

BOWRE. Harleian Society, xx. 19. Miscellanea Genealogica et Heraldica, 2nd Series, ii. 204.

BOWRING. Burke's Landed Gentry, 5, 6, 7, 8. Howard's Visitation of England and Wales, vi. 1.

BOWRNE. Sir T. Phillipps' Topographer, No. 1, (March, 1821, 8vo.) 25. Harleian Society, xiii. 156.

BOWSER, Harleian Society, xxi. 25.

BOWSTEAD. Howard's Visitation of England and Wales, Notes iii. 42.

BOWYER. Burke's Extinct Baronetcies. Gentleman's Magazine, 1825, ii. 586. Surrey Archæological Collections, iii., and iii. 220 ; x. Berry's Hampshire Genealogies, 250. Berry's Sussex Genealogies, 134, 363. Visitation of Sussex, 1570, printed by Sir T. Phillipps, (Middle Hill, fol.) 2. Burke's Royal Families (London, 1851, 8vo.) i. 33. Visitations of Staffordshire, 1614, and 1663-4, William Salt Society, 47. Harleian Society, vi. 37 ; xv. 94 ; xx. 19 ; xliii. 31, 193. Lipscombe's History of the County of Buckingham, iv. 446. History of the Parish of St. Leonard, Shoreditch, by Henry Ellis, 329. Collectanea Topographica et Genealogica, iii. 151. Dallaway's Sussex, i. 61. Visitation of Staffordshire, 1663-4, printed by Sir T. Phillipps, 3. The Borough of Stoke-upon-Trent, by John Ward, 563. Hampshire Visitations, printed by Sir T. Phillipps, 6. Ord's History of Cleveland, 341. Hutchins' Dorset, iii. 518. Manning and Bray's Surrey, iii. 409. Castles, Mansions, and Manors of Western Sussex, by D. G. C. Elwes and C. J. Robinson, 156. Wotton's English Baronetage, iii. 69. Betham's Baronetage, ii. 78. Visitation of Staffordshire, (Willm. Salt Soc.) 53. The Visitations of Devon, edited by J. L. Vivian, 110. Notes and Queries, 7 S. xii. 422. The Gresley's of Drakelowe, by F. Madan, 242. Sussex Archæological Collections, xlii. 36.

BOX, or BOXE. Harleian Society, i. 10 ; xv. 95. The Genealogist, i. 97.

BOX 100 BOY

BOXTED. Morant's Essex, ii. 239, 265.

BOXWELL. Burke's Landed Gentry, (of the Hermitage,) 5 ; (of Sarshill,) 5.

BOYCOTT. Burke's Commoners, iv. 470, Landed Gentry, 2 supp., 3, 4, 5, 6, 7, 8.

BOYD. History of Kilmarnock, by Archibald M'Kay, 19-37. Burke's Landed Gentry, (of Rosslare,) 2, 3, 4, 5 ; (of Moor House,) 6 supp., 7, 8 ; (of Merton Hall,) 2, 4, supp., 5, 6, 7 ; (of Ballymacool,) 2, 3, 4, 5, 6, 7, 8 ; (of Ballycastle,) 4 ; (of Middleton Park,) 2, 3, 4, 5, 6, 7, 8. George Robertson's Description of Cunninghame, 125, 139, 247, 433. Lands and their Owners in Galloway, by P. H. M'Kerlie, i. 320 ; ii. 301. Paterson's History of the Co. of Ayr, i. 394, 421 ; ii. 80, 135, 171. Paterson's History of Ayr and Wigton, i. 748 ; ii. 235, 255 ; iii. 186, 317, 415. George Robertson's Account of Families in Ayrshire, i. 102. Wood's Douglas's Peerage of Scotland, ii. 30. Notes and Queries, 2 S. vii. 523. Betham's Baronetage, iv. 7. Northern Notes and Queries, iv. 75. Burke's Colonial Gentry, i. 209 ; ii. 486. Ontarian Families, by E. M. Chadwick, ii. 126. Howard's Visitation of England and Wales, viii. 161.

BOYDELL. Ormerod's Cheshire, ii. 848 ; iii. 358. The Genealogist, New Series, xii. 107, 108 ; xvi. 36, 240.

BOYLAND. Harleian Society, xv. 95.

BOYLE. Memorials of the Illustrious Family of Boyle, by E. Budgell, 1732, 8vo. Kent's British Banner Displayed, 753. Burke's Landed Gentry, 2, 3, 4, 5, 6, 7. Thoresby's Ducatus Leodiensis, 65. Robinson's Mansions of Herefordshire, 94. Geo. Robertson's Description of Cunninghame, 102, 106. Paterson's History of the Co. of Ayr, ii. 37, 303. 64 'Quartiers' of Captn. Gerald Edmund Boyle, compiled by E. M. Boyle, 1874, broadside, printed at Torquay ; a second edition of this pedigree was issued in Jan. 1883. Paterson's History of Ayr and Wigton, i. 495 ; iii. 531. Geo. Robertson's Account of Families in Ayrshire, i. 127. O'Hart's Irish Pedigrees, 2nd Series, 143. Keating's History of Ireland, Plate 23. J. E. Reid's History of the Co. of Bute, 229. Wood's Douglas's Peerage of Scotland, i. 627. Edmondson's Baronagium Genealogicum, iv. 405. Archdall's Lodge's Peerage, i. 144 ; ii. 363. Brydges' Collins' Peerage, vii. 134 ; viii. 101. Banks' Dormant and Extinct Baronage, iii. 128. Foster's Collectanea Genealogica, (MP's Scotland,) 32. Weaver's Visitation of Herefordshire, 83.

BOYLSTON. New England Register, vii. 145, 351.

BOYNE. Claim of G. F. Visct. Boyne, to vote at Elections of Irish Peers, Sess. Papers, O of 1855.

BOYNTON. Surtees Society, xxxvi. 126, 127 ; xli. 42. Burke's Royal Families, (London, 1851, 8vo.) ii. 114. Foster's Yorkshire Pedigrees. Foster's Visitations of Yorkshire, 4, 8. History of Richmond, by C. Clarkson, 280. Poulson's Holderness, i. 196. Surtees' Durham, ii. 211. Pedigrees of the Leading Families of Lancashire, published by Joseph Foster, (London, 1872, fol.).

The New History of Yorkshire, commencing with Richmondshire, by Genl. Plantagenet-Harrison, (London, 1872, fol.) Part i. 17. Plantagenet-Harrison's History of Yorkshire, i. 115. Harleian Society, xvi. 33; xxxviii. 779. Wotton's English Baronetage, i. 301. Betham's Baronetage, i. 155, app. 3. Pedigrees of the Leading Families of Yorkshire, by Joseph Foster. The Genealogist, New Series, xvii. 260; xviii. 37.

BOYS, or BOYES. Surtees' Durham, iii. 288. Pedigree of Boys of Coggleshall, Co. Essex, [T. P.] 1867, folio page. Morant's Essex, i. 408. Hasted's Kent, iii. 70, 565; iv. 184, 223. Visitation of Somerset, printed by Sir T. Phillipps, 28. Berry's Kent Genealogies, 16, 438-447, 453. Berry's Sussex Genealogies, 318. Berry's Hampshire Genealogies, 129. Pedigree of the Family of Boys, by W. Boys and W. Boteler, large sheet. Burke's Landed Gentry, 2 supp. Harleian Society, xi. 14; xv. 89; xvi. 35; xxxii. 43; xlii. 38, 92. Dallaway's Sussex, II. ii. 245. Monken Hadley, by F. C. Cass, 138. See DE BOIS.

BOYSE. Burke's Landed Gentry, 2, 3, 4, 5, 6, 7, 8. Hampshire Visitations, printed by Sir T. Phillipps, 7.

BOYSTARD. The Genealogist, New Series, iii. 137.

BOYTON. Harleian Society, xxxii. 44. The Genealogist, New Series, xiii. 96.

BOYVILL, or BOYVILLE. J. H. Hill's History of Langton, 170. J. H. Hill's History of Market Harborough, 260. Hutchinson's History of Cumberland, ii. 568. Jefferson's History of Allerdale Ward, Cumberland, 152. Nichol's History of the Co. of Leicester, ii. 916. Nicolson and Burn's Westmorland and Cumberland ii. 10, 461. Banks' Dormant and Extinct Baronage, i. 113. See DE BOIVILE.

BOZOM, BOZON, BOZUN, or BOZOUN. Thoroton's Nottinghamshire, i. 247, 328. Carthew's Hundred of Launditch, Part i. 276; Part iii. 462, Nichols' History of the County of Leicester, ii. 132. Visitation of Norfolk, published by Norfolk Archæological Society, i. 409. The Genealogist, iii. 357; New Series, x. 30, 137; xiv. 255. Harleian Society, xxxii. 45.

BRABANT. Foster's Visitations of Durham, 43. Burke's Colonial Gentry, i. 297.

BRABAZON. Fragment sur la Maison De Barbançon en Hainaut et de Brabazon en Angleterre. Par M. le Chevalier de Courcelles, n. d., 4to. Genealogical History of the Family of Brabazon, by H. Sharpe. Paris, 1825, 4to. Burke's Landed Gentry, (of Brabazon Park,) 3, 4, 5, 6, ; (of Mornington,) 4, 5, 6, 7, 8; (of Tara House,) 8; (of Louth,) 2. Harleian Society, ii. 47. Nichols' History of the County of Leicester, ii. 171, 345. Archdall's Lodge's Peerage, i. 263. Banks' Baronies in Fee, ii. 51. Burke's Extinct Baronetcies, 601. Northamptonshire Notes and Queries, ii. 194.

BRABOURNE. Harleian Society, xv. 96.

BRABY. Burke's Family Records, 87.

BRABYN. Chetham Society, lxxxiv. 46. The Visitations of Cornwall, edited by J. L. Vivian, 52.

BRACE. Metcalfe's Visitations of Worcester, 1683, 22. Howard's Visitation of England and Wales, vi. 88.

BRACEBRIDGE. Shakespeareana Genealogica, by G. R. French, 511. Warwickshire Antiquarian Magazine, Part ii. Burke's Commoners, (of Atherstone,) i. 270, Landed Gentry, 2, 3, 4, 5; (of Morville,) Landed Gentry, 3, 4, 5. Bartlett's History of Mancetter, being No. 1 of Nichols' Miscellaneous Antiquities, 166*. Burke's Heraldic Illustrations, 8. Nichols' History of the County of Leicester, iii. 1145, 1146. Dugdale's Warwickshire, 1056. Miscellanea Genealogica et Heraldica, New Series, ii. 419; iv. 231. Harleian Society, xii. 9. Chance of Bromsgrove, by J. F. Chance, 99. *See* BRASBRIDGE.

BRACEY. Harleian Society, xxvii. 23.

BRACKENBURY. Visitation of Durham, 1575, (Newcastle, 1820, fol.) 7. Burke's Landed Gentry, (of Skendleby,) 2 supp., 3, 4, 5, 6, 7; (of Scremby,) 2 supp., 3, 4, 5. Hutchinson's History of Durham, iii. 240. Foster's Visitations of Durham, 45, 51. *See* BRAKENBURY.

BRACTON. Collinson's Somerset, ii. 32.

BRADBERY, or BRADBURY. Morant's Essex, ii. 527, 587, 596, 614. East Anglian, i. 228, Jewitt's Reliquary, vii. 21. Chauncy's Hertfordshire, 139. Harleian Society, i. 65; xiii. 28, 157; xiv. 552; xxii. 129. The Genealogist, New Series, vii. 13.

BRADBOURNE. Harleian Society, xv. 97.

BRADBRIDGE, or BRADBRUGE. Berry's Sussex Genealogies, 287. Surrey Archæological Collections, ii. Dallaway's Sussex, II. i. 355. Harleian Society, xliii. 204.

BRADBURNE. The Genealogist, New Series, vii. 11.

BRADDEN. Baker's Northampton, ii. 36.

BRADDOCK. Visitations of Staffordshire, 1614 and 1663-4, William Salt Society, 51. Harleian Society, xxxii. 46. Notes and Queries, 1 S. xii. 73.

BRADDON. Burke's Landed Gentry, (of Treglith,) 2 add., 3, 4, 5, 6, 7; (of Skisdon,) 2 supp. and add., 3, 4, 5, 6, 7, 8. Maclean's History of Trigg Minor, ii. 267. An Historical Survey of Cornwall, by C. S. Gilbert, ii. 37. Burke's Colonial Gentry, i. 331.

BRADDYLL, or BRADDILL. Burke's Landed Gentry, 2, 8. Miscellanea Genealogica et Heraldica, New Series, i. 310. Chetham Society, lxxxiv. 47. Corry's History of Lancashire, i. 449-456. Whittaker's History of Whalley, ii. 3. Abram's History of Blackburn, 438, 663. Bardsley's Registers of Ulverston, lxiii. History of Samlesbury, by James Croston, 201. *See* BRADHULL.

BRADESTON. Morant's Essex, i. 77. Visitation of Gloucestershire, 1569. (Middle Hill, 1854, fol.) 2. Banks' Baronies in Fee, i. 132. The Genealogist, New Series, xiv. 199. *See* DE BRADESTON.

BRADEWALL. Ormerod's Cheshire, iii. 110. The Genealogist, New Series, xiii. 247.

BRADFELD. Harleian Society, xviii. 37.

BRADFORD, or BRADFORTH. Surtees' Society, xxxvi. 229. Visitation of Wiltshire, 1677, printed by Sir T. Phillipps, (Middle Hill, 1854,

fol.). Foster's Visitations of Yorkshire, 326. Hunter's Deanery
of Doncaster, i. 330. An Historical Survey of Cornwall, by C. S.
Gilbert, ii. 32. Harleian Society, xvi. 35. The Genealogist, i.
378 ; v. 293. Bateson's History of Northumberland, 281, 297.
Leicestershire Architectural Society, vii. 13. Bradford Antiquary,
ii. 127. New England Register, iv. 39, 233 ; ix. 127 ; xiv. 174.
Foster's Visitations of Northumberland, 19. *See* ATKINSON of
Angerton in Burke's Landed Gentry.
BRADGATE. Nichols' History of the County of Leicester, iv. 122,
330.
BRADHULL. Chetham Society, lxxxi. 27 ; lxxxii. 30. *See* BRAD-
DYLL.
BRADKIRK. Chetham Society, xcii. 177.
BRADLEY. Visitation of Westmoreland, 1615, (London, 1853,) 23.
Burke's Commoners, (of Gore Court,) iv. 203, Landed Gentry, 2 ;
(of Slyne House,) Landed Gentry, 2, 3 ; (of Acton,) 7 ; Chetham
Society, lxxxi. 38 ; lxxxiv. 49. Foster's Visitations of Cumber-
land and Westmorland, 15. History of Chipping, by Tom C.
Smith, 231. Visitation of Warwickshire, 1619, published with
Warwickshire Antiquarian Magazine, 126. Harleian Society, xii.
355 ; xv 98 ; xxxvii. 71. The Genealogist, iii. 358 ; New Series,
xiv. 102.
BRADNEY. Berry's Berkshire Genealogies, 67. Burke's Commoners,
iii. 607. Shaw's Staffordshire, ii. 222*. Howard's Visitation of
England and Wales, i. 1. Harleian Society, xxxvii. 374. Burke's
Family Records, 88.
BRADSHAIGH, or BRADSHAGH. Burke's Authorized Arms, 144.
Burke's Landed Gentry, 4. Chetham Society, lxxxiv. 52.
Baines's History of the Co. of Lancaster, iii. 553. Burke's Extinct
Baronetcies. Wotton's English Baronetage, iii. 655. Ormerod's
Cheshire, iii. 843. Lancashire and Cheshire Antiquarian Notes,
edited by W. D. Pink, 68.
BRADSHAW, or BRADSHAWE. Jewitt's Reliquary, ii. 223 ; vii. 22 ;
viii. 235. Glover's History of Derbyshire, ii. 101, (90), 248, (218).
Burke's Commoners, (of Barton,) iv. 367, Landed Gentry, 2, 3, 4,
5, 6, 7, 8 ; (of Bradshaw,) Landed Gentry, 6, 7 page 193 ; 8 p.
203 ; (of Milicross,) 7 ; (of Lifton Park,) 6, 7, 8. Foster's Visitations of Yorkshire, 204. Harleian Society, ii. 44, 161 ; viii. 284 ;
xv. 98. Chetham Society, lxxxi. 88 ; lxxxii. 57, 58 ; lxxxiv.
50-55 ; cx. 174. Nichols' History of the County of Leicester, iv.
853*. Hunter's Deanery of Doncaster, ii. 180. Earwaker's
Local Gleanings, i. 195, 202, 219, 229, 232. Earwaker's East
Cheshire, ii. 65. Notes and Queries, 6 S. x. 371. The Genealogist, New Series, vii. 14 ; xvii. 14. Nooks and Corners of Lancashire and Cheshire, by James Croston, 25. History of the Wilmer
Family, 275. Oliver's History of Antigua, i. 73. Croston's edn.
of Baines's Lancaster, iv. 594. *See* DE BRADSHAGH.
BRADSHAW-ISHERWOOD. Foster's Lancashire Pedigrees. Burke's
Landed Gentry, 6.
BRADSTOCK. Hutchin's Dorset, iii. 478. Harleian Society, xx. 20.

BRADSTON. Fosbrooke's History of Gloucestershire, ii. 100.

BRADSTONE. Dallaway's Sussex, i. 250.

BRADSTREET. New England Register, viii. 312 ; ix. 113.

BRADWAY. Visitation of Gloucestershire, 1569, (Middle Hill, 1854, fol.) 2. Harleian Society, xxi. 207.

BRADY. Burke's Landed Gentry, 3, 4, 5, 6, 7. O'Hart's Irish Pedigrees, 2nd Series, 144. Notes and Queries. 2 S. vii. 33, 137.

BRAEMES. Harleian Society, xlii. 215.

BRAGDEN. Harleian Society, i. 48.

BRAGE. Morant's Essex, ii. 313. Wright's Essex, i. 548.

BRAGG. Pedigree of Wilson of High Wray, etc., by Joseph Foster, 52. Pedigree of Wilson, by S. B. Foster, 146.

BRAHAM, or BRAHAMS. Harleian Society, viii. 55 ; xliii. 29. Visitations of Berkshire, printed by Sir T. Phillipps, 10. The Genealogist, v. 241. Metcalfe's Visitations of Suffolk, 116. Burke's Extinct Baronetcies.

BRAIBROC. Banks' Dormant and Extinct Baronage, i. 40.

BRAILSFORD. Harleian Society, xxxix. 1021; xl. 1246, 1249. Burke's Commoners, iii. 139, Landed Gentry, 2. See BRAYLESFORD.

BRAINE. Beltz's Review of the Chandos Peerage Case, Appendix 23. Antiquities and Memoirs of the Parish of Myddle, written by Richard Gough, 1700, (folio,) 25.

BRAITHWAITE. Foster's Lancashire Pedigrees. Foster's Pedigree of the Forsters and Fosters, Part ii. 25. Pedigree of Wilson of High Wray, etc., by Joseph Foster, 56. Betham's Baronage, v. 496. Burke's Extinct Baronetcies. Burke's Family Records, 90. Burke's Landed Gentry, 7, 8. See BRATHWAITE.

BRAKENBURY, or BRAKYNBURY. Surtees Society, xli. 41. Surtees' Durham, iv. 19, 20. Harleian Society, xvi. 37. Metcalfe's Visitation of Northamptonshire, 4. See BRACKENBURY.

BRAKYN. Harleian Society, xli. 68. Cambridgeshire Visitation, edited by Sir T. Phillipps, 5.

BRAMHALL. Burke's Extinct Baronetcies, 601.

BRAMLEY-MOORE. Burke's Landed Gentry, 5, 6, 7.

BRAMMAL. Harleian Society, xxxviii. 795.

BRAMPTON. Blomefield's Norfolk, i. 245 ; vi. 433. Visitation of Norfolk, published by Norfolk Archæological Society, i. 68-74, 446. Harleian Society, xxviii. 139 ; xxix. 304 ; xxxii. 46. The Register of Brampton, by A. T. Michell, vii. Muskett's Suffolk Manorial Families, i. 285.

BRAMSTON. Camden Society, xxxii. 17. Hasted's Kent, iii. 510. Morant's Essex, ii. 72, 539. Berry's Hampshire Genealogies, 258. Berry's Essex Genealogies, 50. Harleian Society, i. 56 ; viii. 14 ; xiii. 157, 356 ; xiv. 641. Burke's Commoners, ii. 430, Landed Gentry, 2, 3, 4, 5, 6, 7. The Citizens of London and their Rulers, by B. B. Orridge, 205. Bysshe's Visitation of Essex, edited by J. J. Howard, 19.

BRAMWELL. Notes and Queries, 1 S. ix. 171.

BRANAN. Dwnn's Visitations of Wales, ii. 274.

BRANAS. Poetical Works of Lewis Glyn Cothi, (Oxford, 1837,) 411. History of Powys Fadog, by J. Y. W. Lloyd, vi. 47.

BRANCHE. Harleian Society, i. 13. *See* DE BRANCHE.

BRANCKER, or BRANKER. Burke's Landed Gentry, 2 supp. Foster's Lancashire Pedigrees. Visitation of Wiltshire, edited by G. W. Marshall, 49. *See* BROUNCKER.

BRAND. Harleian Society, viii. 330 ; xiii. 357. Clutterbuck's Hertford, iii. 73. Cussan's History of Hertfordshire, Parts vii. and viii. 136. The Genealogist, v. 314.

BRANDER. Burke's Landed Gentry, 2. *See* DUNBAR-BRANDER.

BRANDESTON. Dugdale's Warwickshire, 786. Harleian Society, xii. 127.

BRANDLING. Surtees Society, xxxvi. 26. Visitation of Durham, 1615, (Sunderland, 1820, fol.) 3. Burke's Commoners, ii. 39, Landed Gentry, 2. Burke's Royal Families, (London, 1851, 8vo.) ii. 71. Surtees' Durham, ii. 90, 91, 92. Harleian Society, xvi. 38. Bateson's History of Northumberland, i. 247. Foster's Visitations of Durham, 47. Foster's Visitations of Northumberland, 20. The Genealogist, New Series, xviii. 48.

BRANDON. Miscellanea Genealogica et Heraldica, ii. 164. Copies of Various Papers, etc., relating to the Peerages of Brandon and Dover, *n. d. (circa* 1769) 4to. pp. 30, printed by the Duke of Hamilton. Wright's History of Rutland, 126. Whitaker's Deanery of Craven, 3rd edn., 337. The Visitations of Cornwall, edited by J. L. Vivian, 135. Hasted's Kent, (Hund. of Blackheath, by H. H. Drake,) xvii.

BRANDRAM. Notts and Derbyshire Notes and Queries, iv. 158.

BRANDRETH. Bibliotheca Topographica Britannica, ix., Part 4, 39. Burke's Commoners, (of Stullach,) iv. 137, Landed Gentry, 2 ; (of Houghton,) Landed Gentry, 5, 6, 7. Nichols' Miscellaneous Antiquities, No. 4, 38. Shaw's Staffordshire, ii. 42. Visitation of Staffordshire, 1663-4, printed by Sir T. Phillipps, 2. Visitations of Staffordshire, 1614 and 1663-4, William Salt Society, 52.

BRANDT. Harleian Society, xv. 99.

BRANDWOOD. Abram's History of Blackburn, 502.

BRANFILL, or BRANFIL. Morant's Essex, i. 109. Burke's Landed Gentry, 2 supp., 3, 4, 5, 6, 7, 8. Burke's Royal Families, (London, 1851, 8vo.) i. 111. *See* HARRISON.

BRANFORD. Howard's Visitation of England and Wales, ix. 121.

BRANSBY. Foster's Visitations of Yorkshire, 212.

BRANSPETH. The Genealogist, v. 314.

BRANT. Ontarian Families, by E. N. Chadwick, i. 67.

BRANTESTON. Genealogist, New Series, xii. 106.

BRANTHWAYTE. Blomefield's Norfolk, v. 110. Foster's Visitations of Cumberland and Westmorland, 16. *See* BRATHWAITE.

BRAOSE. Lipscombe's History of the County of Buckingham, i. 69, 202, 394. Dallaway's Sussex, i. xlvii. ; II. ii. 174. Manning and Bray's Surrey, ii. 77. Baker's Northampton, ii. 239. Sussex Archæological Collections, v. 5 ; viii. 102 ; xxvi. 261. Stemmata Shirleiana, by E. P. Shirley, 2nd edn., 30. Notes and Queries,

2 S. iii. 331, 412, 476; iv. 76; 3 S. i. 489; ii. 38; viii. 197, 257, 343, 400, 436; 5 S. ii. 168; iii. 458, 516; iv. 311; v. 427. Banks' Baronies in Fee, i. 133. Banks' Dormant and Extinct Baronage, i. 43, 246. See BRUCE.
BRASBRIDGE. Harleian Society, ii. 43. See BRACEBRIDGE, DE BRAOSE.
BRASEY. Visitation of Oxfordshire, 1634, printed by Sir T. Phillipps, (Middle Hill,) fol.) 14.
BRASIER. Burke's Visitation of Seats and Arms, 2nd Series, ii. 25.
BRASSE. Surtees' Durham, i. 82.
BRASSEY. Burke's Landed Gentry, 5 supp., 6, 7, 8. Miscellanea Genealogica et Heraldica, New Series, ii. 577.
BRASTOW. New England Register, xiii. 249.
BRATHWAITE. Visitation of Westmorland, 1615, (London, 1853,) 3. Foster's Visitations of Cumberland and Westmorland, 18. Pedigree of Wilson, by S. B. Foster, 98. Nicolson and Burn's Westmorland and Cumberland, i. 127, 190, 604. See BRANTHAWYTE, BRAITHWAITE.
BRATTLE. Account of some Descendants of Capt. Thomas Brattle, by E. D. Harris, 1867, 4to.
BRATTON. Collinson's Somerset, ii. 32. Harleian Society, vi. 115. Weaver's Visitations of Somerset, 11. The Visitations of Devon, by J. L. Vivian, 375.
BRAWNE. Bloom's History of Preston-on-Stour, 32.
BRAY, or BRAYE. Rudder's Gloucestershire, 263. Gentleman's Magazine, lix. 424; lxix. 277. Berry's Surrey Genealogies, 37. Visitation of Cornwall, edited by Sir N. H. Nicolas, 24. Visitation of Oxfordshire, 1634, printed by Sir T. Phillipps, (Middle Hill, fol.) 14. Burke's Commoners, (of Shere,) iii. 241, Landed Gentry, 2, 3, 4, 5, 6, 7, 8; (of Langford Hill,) Landed Gentry, 2, 3, 4, 5. Miscellanea Genealogica et Heraldica, New Series, i. 62. Harleian Society, v. 316; ix. 23; xiv. 553; xv. 99; xix. 162; xliii. 29, 50, 177. Shaw's Staffordshire, ii. 34. Burke's Royal Families, (London, 1851, 8vo.) ii. 6. Jewitt's Reliquary, xiv. 64. Bridge's Northamptonshire, by Rev. Peter Whalley, i. 176. Manning and Bray's Surrey, i. 517, 523. Burke's Colonial Gentry, i. 222. Baker's Northampton, i. 162, 169, 685. Banks' Dormant and Extinct Baronage, ii. 60. The Visitations of Cornwall, edited by J. L. Vivian, 53, 54, 55. The Genealogist, New Series, viii. 241; ix. 148. Surrey Archæological Collections, x. Berks, Bucks, and Oxon, Archæological Journal, i. 89. See CAVE, HART-DYKE.
BRAYBROKE, or BRAYBROOKE. J. H. Hill's History of Langton, 19. Bridge's Northamptonshire, by Rev. Peter Whalley, ii. 10. Visitations of Berkshire, printed by Sir T. Phillipps, 10. Proceedings of the Essex Archæological Society, v. 297. Clutterbuck's Hertford, iii. 58. Miscellanea Genealogica et Heraldica, New Series, ii. 72; 3rd Series, iii. 242.
BRAYLESFORD. Account of Beauchief Abbey, in No. 3 of Nichols' Miscellaneous Antiquities, 94. Visitation of Derbyshire, 1663-4,

(Middle Hill, 1854, fol.) 2. The Genealogist, iii. 122; New Series, vii. 14; xvii. 22. *See* BRAILESFORD.

BRAYNE. Visitation of Gloucestershire, 1569, (Middle Hill, 1854, fol.) 3. Fosbrooke's History of Gloucestershire, ii. 160. Harleian Society, xxi. 208. Shropshire Notes and Queries, iii. 50.

BRAYTOFTE. The Genealogist, iii. 359.

BREADALBANE. The Breadalbane succession case, how it rose and how it stands, by James Paterson. Edinburgh, 1863, 8vo. Statement of the Breadalbane Peerage Case. By A. Sinclair. Glasgow, 1866, 8vo. Claim to Earldom of Breadalbane (in the House of Lords), Appellant's Case, 4to. pp. 488, Edinburgh, *n. d.* Respondent's Case, 4to. pp. 153. Burke's Royal Families, (London, 1851, 8vo.) i. 192. Address to the Peers by the Dowager Countess of Breadalbane and Holland, Feb. 1877, fol. pp. 14. *See* CAMPBELL.

BREAKENRIDGE. Ontarian Families, by E. M. Chadwick, ii. 31.

BREAREY. Surtees Society, xxxvi. 210. Thoresby's Ducatus Leodiensis, 126.

BRECHIN. Wood's Douglas's Peerage of Scotland, i. 243.

BRECK. New England Register, v. 396.

BRECKNOCK. Gyll's History of Wraysbury, 59.

BREDBURY. Ormerod's Cheshire, iii. 820.

BREE. Howard's Visitation of England and Wales, i. 280.

BREEN. O'Hart's Irish Pedigrees, 2nd Series, 144.

BREIN. Dwnn's Visitations of Wales, i. 19.

BREKLES. The Genealogist, New Series, xvii. 175.

BREMER. Burke's Landed Gentry, 2. Harleian Society, xv. 100.

BREMPTON. The Genealogist, New Series, ix. 82.

BREND. Metcalfe's Visitations of Suffolk, 11.

BRENDISLEY. Harleian Society, iv. 140.

BRENT. Collinson's Somerset, iii. 435. Hasted's Kent, iii. 214. Weaver's Visitations of Somerset, 96. Oxford Historical Society, xxiv. 123, 358. Harleian Society, xlii. 211.

BREOSE. *See* BREWS.

BREREHAUGHE. Thoresby Ducatus Leodiensis, 125.

BRERES. Chetham Society, lxxxii. 93, 95. Thoresby's Ducatus Leodiensis, 71. Whitaker's Craven, 3rd edn., 42.

BRERETON. Observations on the History of one of the old Cheshire Families, by Sir Fortunatus Dwarris, Archæologia, vol. 33. Jewitt's Reliquary, xiii. 191. Visitation of Somerset, printed by Sir T. Phillipps, 29. Surrey Archæological Collections, ii. Burke's Landed Gentry, (of Brinton,) 2, 3, 4, 5; (of Carrigslaney,) 4 supp. Harleian Society, xi. 14; xviii. 41-46; xxviii. 67; xxix. 426; xxxii. 53; xliii. 99. Visitation of Staffordshire, 1663-4, printed by Sir Thos. Phillipps, 3. J. P. Earwaker's East Cheshire, i. 260. Ormerod's Cheshire, i. 442, 556; ii. 195, 686; iii. 88, 644. History of Llangurig, by E. Hamer and H. W. Lloyd, 359. Visits to the Fields of Battle in England, by Richd. Brooke, 282. Collections for a History of Staffordshire, (William Salt Society,) i. 304. Burke's Extinct Baronetcies, *supp.* History of Powys

Fadog, by J. Y. W. Lloyd, iii. 92. Visitation of Gloucester, edited by T. F. Fenwick and W. C. Metcalfe. Visitations of Staffordshire, 1614 and 1663-4, William Salt Society, 53. Croston's edn. of Baines's Lancaster, iii. 287.

BREREWOOD. Lipscombe's History of the County of Buckingham, iv. 511. Harleian Society, xviii. 267.

BRESBY. Foster's Visitations of Cumberland and Westmoreland, 17.

BRESLIN. O'Hart's Irish Pedigrees, 2nd Series, 145.

BRESSY. Harleian Society, xviii. 38 ; xix. 85.

BRET, or BRETT. The Brett Family, by Frederick Brown, 1882, 8vo. Collinson's Somerset, iii. 543. Berry's Kent Genealogies, 325. Harleian Society, i. 47 ; ii. 206 ; xvi. 324. Hutchins' Dorset, ii. 158. Visitation of Staffordshire, 1663-4, printed by Sir T. Phillipps, 3. Nichols' History of the County of Leicester, iii. 400. Thoroton's Nottinghamshire, i. 162. Morant's Essex, i. 83. Visitation of Staffordshire, (Willm. Salt Soc.) 55. Carthew's Hundred of Launditch, Part iii. 344. Visitation of Gloucester, edited by T. F. Fenwick and W. C. Metcalfe, 25. Visitations of Staffordshire, 1614 and 1663-4, William Salt Society, 54. Burke's Colonial Gentry, ii. 828.

BRETAGNE. Carthew's Hundred of Launditch, Part i. 28.

BRETESCHE. Savage's History of the Hundred of Carhampton, 300. See DE BRETESCHE.

BRETEUIL. Berks Archæological and Architectural Journal, i. 84.

BRETHER. Harleian Society, xiii. 158.

BRETHERTON. Chetham Society, lxxxiv. 56. Burke's Landed Gentry, 7, 8.

BRETLAND. Earwaker's East Cheshire, ii. 148.

BRETON. Hasted's Kent, iii. 117. East Anglian, iii. 85. Berry's Kent Genealogies, 205. Bibliotheca Topographica Britannica, vii. Parts i. and ii. 348*. Harleian Society, ii. 161 ; xxxii. 54. Bridge's Northamptonshire, by Rev. Peter Whalley, i. 78. Nichols' History of the County of Leicester, iv. 484. Visitatio Comitatus Wiltoniæ, 1623, printed by Sir T. Phillipps. Baker's Northampton, i. 220. Wilson's History of the Parish of St. Laurence Pountney, 253. See DE BRETON, LE BRETON.

BRETTARGHE. Chetham Society, lxxxiv. 57.

BRETTELL. Burke's Landed Gentry, 5 supp. Herald and Genealogist, i. 421-430. Genealogy of Henzey, Tyttery, and Tyzack, by H. S. Grazebrook, 69.

BRETTON. Morant's Essex, i. 410. Metcalfe's Visitations of Northamptonshire, 4, 69.

BRETTRIDGE. Harleian Society, xv. 100.

BRETUN. Dugdale's Warwickshire, 33.

BREWER. Collinson's Somerset, i. 53 ; iii. 78. Harleian Society xv. 101. Burton's History of Hemingborough, 355. New England Register, xxx. 424. See BRIWERE.

BREWIS. Burke's Landed Gentry, 7, 8.

BREWOSE. The Genealogist, New Series, xv. 92.

BREWS, or BREWSE. Blomefield's Norfolk, viii. 267. Page's History of Suffolk, 35. Fosbrooke's History of Gloucestershire, i. 394, 395. Metcalfe's Visitations of Suffolk, 117. *See* BRUCE.

BREWSTER. Burke's Landed Gentry, 2 supp. and add., 3, 4, 6, 7. Metcalfe's Visitations of Suffolk, 117. Metcalfe's Visitations of Northamptonshire, 70.

BREYNTON. Weaver's Visitation of Herefordshire, 12.

BRIAN. Harleian Society, xlii. 2.

BRIANZON. Morant's Essex, i. 77.

BRICE. Visitation of Somerset, printed by Sir T. Phillipps, 30. Harleian Society, xi. 14. Weaver's Visitations of Somerset, 11. *See* RUGGLES BRICE.

BRICKDALE. Burke's Royal Families, (London, 1851, 8vo.) i. 91. Burke's Landed Gentry, 2, 3, 4, 5 supp.

BRICKENDEN. Visitations of Berkshire, printed by Sir T. Phillipps, 10. The Genealogist, v. 241.

BRICKWOOD. Morant's Essex, i. 336.

BRIDGE. Burke's Colonial Gentry, i. 346.

BRIDGEMAN, or BRIDGMAN. Visitation of Gloucestershire, 1569, (Middle Hill, 1854, fol.) 3. Harleian Society, viii. 288 ; xxi. 26 ; xxviii. 68. Foster's Lancashire Pedigrees. Brydges' Collins' Peerage, viii. 367. Wotton's English Baronetage, iii. 13, 550. Burke's Extinct Baronetcies. Willmore's History of Walsall, 107. Burke's Landed Gentry, 8 at p. 1797. William Salt Society, New Series, ii. 238.

BRIDGER. Berry's Sussex Genealogies, 109. Burke's Landed Gentry, (of Buckingham House,) 2, 3, 4, 5, 6, 7, 8 ; (of Halnaker,) 2 supp., 3, 4. Horsfield's History of Lewes, ii. 130. Dallaway's Sussex, II. ii. 265.

BRIDGES. Hasted's Kent, iii. 704, 762. Bray Peerage Evidence, 1836, 304. Visitation of Somerset, printed by Sir T. Phillipps, 31. Topographer, (London, 1789-91, 8vo.) i. 158. Case of Sir Brook W. Bridges, Bart., 1842. Claim of Sir Brook W. Bridges, Bart., to be Baron Fitzwalter, Sess. Papers, 159 of 1842 ; 104 of 1843 ; 51 of 1844. Harleian Society, v. 200 ; viii. 37, 179 ; xi. 15 ; xiii. 29, 158, 358 ; xxi. 210, 233 ; xxvii. 25 ; xxxix. 1057. Notes and Queries, 1 S. iii. 278 ; vi. 34, 280. Topographical Miscellanies, 1792, 4to., (Avington.) Wotton's English Baronetage, iv. 188. Betham's Baronetage, iii. 192. Visitation of Gloucester, edited by T. F. Fenwick and W. C. Metcalfe, 26. Weaver's Visitation of Herefordshire, 13. New England Register, viii. 252. *See* BRUGES, BRYDGES.

BRIDGEWATER. *See* EGERTON.

BRIDSON. Burke's Family Records, 93.

BRIERS. Harleian Society, xix. 86.

BRIERWOOD. Gyll's History of Wraysbury, 227.

BRIGG, BRIGGS, or BRIGGES. Blomefield's Norfolk, viii. 270. Morant's Essex, ii. 484. Visitation of Westmoreland, 1615, London, 1853, 22. Blomefield's Norfolk, iv. 220. Foster's Yorkshire Pedigrees. Foster's Visitations of Yorkshire, 497. J. H. Hill's History of Market Harborough, 81. Nichols' History of the County of

Leicester, ii. 529. Abram's History of Blackburn, 390. Partial Record of the Descendants ef Walter Briggs, by Sam. Briggs. U.S.A., 1878, 4to. Burke's Landed Gentry, 5, 6, 7, 8. Wotton's English Baronetage, ii. 251. Betham's Baronetage, i. 438. Notes and Queries, 5 S. vii. 507; viii. 15. Burke's Extinct Baronetcies. Harleian Society, xxii. 30; xxviii. 68; xxxii. 55. Ilkley, Ancient and Modern, by R. Collyer and J. H. Turner, 217. Foster's Visitations of Cumberland and Westmorland, 19.

BRIGGINSHAW. Visitation of Middlesex, (Salisbury, 1820, fol.) 20. Foster's Visitation of Middlesex, 38.

BRIGHAM. Surtees Society, xxxvi. 136. Visitation of Oxfordshire, 1634, printed by Sir T. Phillipps, (Middle Hill, fol.) 14. Burke's Landed Gentry, 3, 4. Foster's Visitations of Yorkshire, 167. Harleian Society, v. 301. Poulson's Holderness, ii. 268.

BRIGHOUSE. The Genealogist, v. 315.

BRIGHT. The Brights of Colwall, co. Hereford, 1872. Surtees Society, xxxvi. 263. Burke's Landed Gentry, 5 supp., 6, 7. Foster's Yorkshire Pedigrees. Herald and Genealogist, vii. 503-511. Burke's Authorized Arms, 43. Thoresby's Ducatus Leodiensis, 78. Hunter's History of the Parish of Sheffield, 353, 355, 359, 417. Hunter's Deanery of Doncaster, i. 365; ii. 189, 437. Surtees' Durham, iv. 145 Robinson's Mansions of Herefordshire, 73. Burke's Extinct Baronetcies. Life and Times of Rt. Hon. John Bright, by Wm. Robertson, folding at p. 4. Fishwick's History of Rochdale, 473. New England Register, xiii. 97. Historical Notices of Doncaster, by C. W. Hatfield, 2nd Series, 129, 156. Burke's Colonial Gentry, i. 294; ii. 450. Harleian Society, xxxvii. 135; xxxviii. 671. Howard's Visitation of England and Wales, ii. 16. Annals of Smith of Balby, by H. E. Smith, 95. Burke's Family Records, 94. A History of Banking in Bristol, by C. H. Cave, 220. The Genealogist, New Series, xv. 172. *See* MOORE.

BRIGHTRIDGE. The Genealogist, vii. 119.

BRIGHTWELL. Lipscombe's History of the County of Buckingham, i. 122. Harleian Society, xv. 102. The Genealogist, vii. 119.

BBIGNALL. Plantagenet-Harrison's History of Yorkshire, i. 306.

BRIGSTOCK. Pedigree of William Brigstocke, Esq., [T. P.] 1860, folio page. Caermarthenshire Pedigrees, 47. The Sheriffs of Cardiganshire, by J. R. Phillips, 49. Burke's Landed Gentry, 7, 8. The Genealogical Magazine, iii. 461.

BRINCKMAN. Hutchins' History of Dorset, ii. 397.

BRIND. Pedigree of Brind of London, [T. P.] 1871, folio page. Pedigree of Brind of Stanton Fitzherbert, [T. P.] 1866, folio page. Pedigree of Brind of London, [T. P.] 1867, folio page. Visitatio Comitatus Wiltoniæ, 1623, printed by Sir T. Phillipps. Visitation of Wiltshire, edited by G. W. Marshall, 23.

BRINDLE. History of the Chapel, Tockholes, by B. Nightingale 191.

BRINDLEY, or BRINLEY. Harleian Society, xv. 101; xviii. 40. Genealogical Gleanings in England, by H. F. Waters, i. 14. New England Register, xxxvii. 382.

BRINE. Table of the Descendants of Admiral James Brine of Bland-
ford, 1892, Broadside. Howard's Visitation of England and
Wales, iv. 17. Burke's Family Records, 99.

BRINKLEY. Burke's Landed Gentry, 3, 4, 5, 6, 7, 8.

BRINSLEY. Thoroton's Nottinghamshire, ii. 260.

BRINTON. Burke's Family Records, 102.

BRISBANE. A Genealogical Table of Genl. Sir T. M. Brisbane, Bart.,
etc., by William Fraser. Edinburgh, 1840, large sheet. Genealogical Table of the Families of Brisbane of Bishoptoun, etc., Makdougall of Makerstoun, and Hay of Alderstoun, by William Fraser.
Edinburgh, 1840, large sheet. Burke's Commoners, ii. 332,
Landed Gentry, 5, 6, 7, 8. Geo. Robertson's Description of Cunninghame, 90. Paterson's History of the Co. of Ayr, ii. 305.
Paterson's History of Ayr and Wigton, iii. 525. Geo. Robertson's Account of Families in Ayrshire, i. 136.

BRISCO, BRISCOE, or BRISKO. Hutchinson's History of Cumberland,
ii. 459. Harleian Society, iii. 33; vii. 11; xiii. 496; xv. 103;
xxii. 31. Foster's Visitations of Cumberland and Westmorland,
20. Metcalfe's Visitations of Northamptonshire, 71. Nicolson
and Burn's Westmorland and Cumberland, ii. 202. Burke's Commoners, (of Coghurst,) iii. 235, Landed Gentry, 2; (of Fox Hills,)
Landed Gentry, 4, 5; (of Riverdale,) 4, 5, 6, 7, 8; (of Tinvane,)
3, 4, 5, 6 7. Clutterbuck's Hertford, i. 158. John Watson's
History of Halifax, 159. Plantagenet-Harrison's History of
Yorkshire, i. 383. Betham's Baronetage, iv. 109; v. app. 83.

BRISE. See RUGGLES-BRISE.

BRISET. Hasted's Kent, (Hund. of Blackheath, by H. H. Drake,)
188.

BRISTOW, or BRISTOWE. Burke's Landed Gentry, 2 and corr., 3,
4, 5, 6, 7, 8. Hoare's Wiltshire, V. ii. 11, 31*, 32*, 33*, 34*.
Surtees' Durham, ii. 167. Clutterbuck's Hertford, ii. 254.
Cussan's History of Hertfordshire, Parts vii. and viii. 139.
Chauncy's Hertfordshire, 324. Harleian Society, xiii. 359;
xxii. 130. Miscellanea Genealogica et Heraldica, New Series,
iii. 248; 2nd Series, iii. 35. Foster's Visitations of Durham,
49.

BRITAMIA. Banks' Baronies in Fee, ii. 52.

BRITON. Banks' Baronies in Fee, ii. 52.

BRITTAIN. Harleian Society, xxxviii. 668. Burke's Landed Gentry, 8.

BRITTANY (Dukes of). Registrum Honoris de Richmond, (by Roger
Gale,) folding table after preface. Clutterbuck's Hertford, ii.
84.

BRITTON. Howard's Visitation of England and Wales, ii. 77. Burke's
Family Records, 103.

BRIWERE. Collinson's Somerset, i. 53; iii. 78. Baker's Northampton,
ii. 239. See BREWER, BRUERE.

BROAD, or BROADE. Burke's Authorized Arms, 186. Burke's
Landed Gentry, 4, 5, 6, 6 at p. 1510, 7 at p. 1720. The Borough
of Stoke-upon-Trent, by John Ward, 550. Burke's Colonial
Gentry, i. 292.

BROADBENT. Harleian Society, xxxviii. 430; xl. 1277. Burke's Family Records, 106.

BROADGATE. Harleian Society, xv. 104.

BROADHEAD. Hunter's Deanery of Doncaster, ii. 397.

BROADHURST. Burke's Landed Gentry, 5. Harleian Society, xxxvii. 377.

BROADLEY. Burke's Landed Gentry, (of Welton House,) 3 supp., 4, 5, 6, 7, 8; (of Kirkella,) 2, 3 and supp., 4. Howard's Visitation of England and Wales, viii. 85.

BROADMEAD. Burke's Landed Gentry, 3, 4, 5, 6, 7, 8.

BROADNAX. Hasted's Kent, iii. 159. Lord Brabourne's Letters of Jane Austen, i. 8. See BRODNAX.

BROADRICK. Burke's Family Records, 107.

BROADWOOD. Burke's Landed Gentry, (of Lyne,) 5, 6, 7, 8; (of Holmbush,) 5, 6, 7.

BROC, or BROCK. Burke's Landed Gentry, 2, 3, 4, 5. Herald and Genealogist, v. 508. Lipscombe's History of the County of Buckingham, i. 399. Harleian Society, xiv. 554. Ormerod's Cheshire, i. 820. Life of Sir Isaac Brock, by F. B. Tupper, 457. See ALNO, DE BROC.

BROCAS. History of the Family of Brocas of Beaurepaire, by M. Burrows. London, 1886, 8vo. Brydges' Topographer, iv. 53. Berry's Hampshire Genealogies, 90. The Topographer, (London, 1789-91, 8vo.) iv. 55. J. H. Hill's History of Market Harborough, 273. Hampshire Visitations, printed by Sir T. Phillipps, 7, 22. Nichols' History of the County of Leicester, ii. 832. Manning and Bray's Surrey, ii. 4, 29.

BROCHWELL YSGITHROG. Dwnn's Visitations of Wales, i. 319.

BROCK-HOLLINSHEAD. Abram's History of Blackburn, 685.

BROCKDISH. Blomefield's Norfolk, v. 336.

BROCKEDON. Harleian Society, xv. 104.

BROCKET, BROKETT, BROCKETT. Berry's Hertfordshire Genealogies, 132. The Antiquities of Gainford, by J. R. Walbran, 106. Burke's Landed Gentry, 2, 3, 4, 5, 6, 7, 8. Clutterbuck's Hertford, ii. 360. Harleian Society, xiii. 30; xv. 105; xxii. 32. Metcalfe's Visitations of Suffolk, 11.

BROCKHILL. Hasted's Kent, ii. 497.

BROCKHOLES, or BROKHOLES. History of Merchant Taylors' School, by Rev. H. B. Wilson, 1173. Burke's Commoners, iii. 384, Landed Gentry, 2, 3, 4, 5, 6, 7, 8. Chetham Society, lxxxii. 31, 56; lxxxiv. 58; cv. 242. Whitaker's History of Richmond, ii. 449.

BROCKHULL. Hasted's Kent, iii. 406. Berry's Kent Genealogies, 106.

BROCKLEBANK. Howard's Visitation of England and Wales, ix. 141.

BROCKLEHURST. Burke's Landed Gentry, (of Hurdsfield,) 3 supp., 4, 5, 6, 7, 8. Earwaker's East Cheshire, ii. 423.

BROCKLESBY. The Genealogist, iii. 360.

BROCKMAN. Hasted's Kent, iii. 394. Berry's Kent Genealogies, 118. Burke's Commoners, iii. 367, Landed Gentry, 2, 3, 4, 5, 6, 7, 8. Harleian Society, xiii. 161; xlii. 72.

BRODBELT. Fishwick's History of Bispham, 40-49.

BRODERICK, or BRODRICK. Claim of Rt. Hon. Charles Brodrick, Visct. Middleton, to Vote at Elections of Irish Peers, Sess. Papers, 161 of 1854. Miscellanea Genealogica et Heraldica, ii. 359. Harleian Society, viii. 102. Manning and Bray's Surrey, ii. 33. Archdall's Lodge's Peerage, v. 159. Brydges' Collins' Peerage, viii. 460. Surrey Archæological Collections, x. Howard's Visitation of England and Wales, v. 95.

BRODERIP. Burke's Landed Gentry, 6, 7.

BRODERWICK. Visitations of Berkshire, printed by Sir T. Phillipps, 11. The Genealogist, v. 242.

BRODIE. The Genealogy of the Brodie Family, by William Brodie. London, 1862, 4to. Burke's Commoners, (of Brodie,) iii. 594, Landed Gentry, 2 supp., 3, 4, 5, 6, 7, 8; (of Lethen,) Landed Gentry, 2 supp., 3, 4, 5, 6, 7, 8 ; (of Eastbourne,) 4 supp., 5 ; (of Milton Brodie,) 8. Burke's Heraldic Illustrations, 39. Caithness Family History, by John Henderson, 308. Burke's Royal Families, (London, 1851, 8vo.) i. 109. Shaw's History of Moray, 105. Diary of Alexander Brodie of Brodie, (Spalding Club,) 15. Notes and Queries, 2 S. xi. 518. Foster's Collectanea Genealogica, (MP's Scotland,) 34.

BRODIE-INNES. Burke's Landed Gentry, 5 supp., 6, 7.

BRODNAX, or BRODNIX. Berry's Hampshire Genealogies, 46. Berry's Kent Genealogies, 126. Harleian Society, viii. 186 ; xlii. 73. Dallaway's Sussex, II. i. 50. See BROADNAX.

BRODREPP. Hutchins' Dorset, ii. 159.

BRODRIBB. Burke's Colonial Gentry, ii. 440.

BRODWAY. Visitation of Gloucester, edited by T. F. Fenwick and W. C. Metcalfe, 27.

BROGRAVE. Berry's Hertfordshire Genealogies, 31. Berry's Kent Genealogies, 272. Clutterbuck's Hertford, iii. 154. Chauncy's Hertfordshire, 227. Betham's Baronetage, iv. 242. Burke's Extinct Baronetcies. Carthew's Hundred of Launditch, Part iii. 72. Harleian Society, xxii. 33, 131 ; xlii. 115. Metcalfe's Visitations of Northamptonshire, 4, 71.

BROKE. Burke's Royal Families, (London, 1851, 8vo.) ii. 47. Collectanea Topographica et Genealogica, i. 22. Hampshire Visitations, printed by Sir T. Phillipps, 8. Page's History of Suffolk, 61. Burke's Extinct Baronetcies. Metcalfe's Visitations of Northamptonshire, 5, 72. Burke's Family Records, 107.

BROKEMAN. Morant's Essex, ii. 108, 386.

BROKESBORNE. Harleian Society, xiii. 96.

BROKESBY. Harleian Society, ii. 49. Nichols' History of the County of Leicester, iii. 406 ; iv. 725.

BROME. Blomefield's Norfolk, x. 108. Hasted's Kent, i. 115. Berry's Kent Genealogies, 289. Genealogical Memoranda of the Family of Ames, 2. The Gresley's of Drakelowe, by F: Madan, 243. The Genealogist, New Series, xvii. 113. Visitation of Oxfordshire, printed by Sir T. Phillipps, (Middle Hill, fol.) 15. Burke's Commoners, iv. 604, Landed Gentry, 2, 3, 4, 5. Harleian Society,

iv. 134 ; v. 229, 263 ; xii. 97 ; xxviii. 70. Visitation of Warwickshire, 1619, published with Warwickshire Antiquarian Magazine, 86. Gyll's History of Wraysbury, 22. Dugdale's Warwickshire, 853, 971. Brome of Wolferlow ; Brome of Avenbury ; Pedigree of the Bromes of Avenbury and Wolferlow, Co. Hereford ; three tables, printed for late Gordon Gyll.

BROMEG. Dwnn's Visitations of Wales, i. 160.

BROMFIELD. Dwnn's Visitations of Wales, ii. 361. Hampshire Visitations, printed by Sir T. Phillipps, 8. Harleian Society, xv. 105, 106. Burke's Extinct Baronetcies. History of Powys Fadog, by J. Y. W. Lloyd, ii. 326, 353. New England Register, xiii. 35 ; xxv. 182, 329 ; xxvi. 37, 141.

BROMFLETE. Banks' Dormant and Extinct Baronage, ii. 61.

BROMHALL, or BROMHALE. Harleian Society, xviii. 73 ; xix. 87. Ormerod's Cheshire, iii. 823.

BROMHEAD. Harleian Society, xxxvii. 334 ; xxxviii. 793 ; xxxix. 1015.

BROMILOW. Fletcher's Leicestershire Pedigrees and Royal Descents, 196. Burke's Landed Gentry, 7, 8.

BROMLEY. Noble's Memoirs of the House of Cromwell, ii. 203. Berry's Buckinghamshire Genealogies, 86. Nash's Worcestershire, i. 595 ; ii. 445 ; supp. 42. Burke's Landed Gentry, 4. Surtees' Durham, i. 48. Clutterbuck's Hertford, i. 304. Ormerod's Cheshire, ii. 642 ; iii. 371. Edmondson's Baronagium Genealogicum, v. 432. Collections for a History of Staffordshire, (William Salt Society,) ii. part 2, 106. Brydges' Collins' Peerage, vii. 247. Metcalfe's Visitation of Worcester, 1683, 24. Harleian Society, xviii. 47 ; xxii. 34 ; xxviii. 71 ; xxix. 492. Genealogical Records of the Family of Woodd, 34. A Collection of Original Royal Letters, by Sir George Bromley, Bart., xxxii. Howard's Visitation of England and Wales, v. 136.

BROMPTON. Eyton's Antiquities of Shropshire, iv. 244. Weaver's Visitations of Somerset, 97.

BROMWICH. Visitations of Gloucestershire, 1569, (Middle Hill, 1854, fol.) 2. Dugdale's Warwickshire, 886. Visitatio Comitatus Wiltoniæ, 1623, printed by Sir T. Phillipps. Banks' Baronies in Fee, ii. 123. Visitation of Wiltshire, edited by G. W. Marshall, 43. Weaver's Visitation of Herefordshire, 14. Harleian Society, xxi. 29 ; xxvii. 24.

BROND. Harleian Society, xv. 108 ; xxxii. 55.

BRONKER. Visitation of Middlesex, (Salisbury, 1820, fol.) 23.

BRONSDON. New England Register, xxxv. 361.

BRONTISTON. Shaw's Staffordshire, i. 22.

BROOK, or BROOKE. Rudder's Gloucestershire, 457. J. H. Hill's History of Langton, 22. East Anglian, ii. 130, 142. Notes and Queries, 3 S. iv. 81, 136 ; 7 S. iv. 87 ; vi. 43. Hasted's Kent, i. 492. Berry's Surrey Genealogies, 58. Visitation of Somerset, printed by Sir T. Phillipps, 32. Berry's Kent Genealogies, 45. Berry's Hampshire Genealogies, 339. Burke's Commoners, (of Mere,) iii. 625, Landed Gentry, 2, 3, 4, 5, 6, 7, (of Ufford Place,)

Commoners, i. 336, Landed Gentry, 2, 3, 4, 5, 6, 7, 8; (of
Handford,) Landed Gentry, 2 add., 3, 4, 5, 6 ; (of Sibton Park,)
4, 5, 6, 7, 8 ; (of Haughton,) 2 supp., 3, 4, 5, 6, 7, 8 ; (of Droma-
vana,) 4, 5, 6, 7, 8; (of Church Minshull,) 5, 6 ; (of Summerton,)
6 supp., and at p. 1826, 7, 8 ; (of Hinton Abbey,) 7, 8 ; (of Wexham Park,) 7, 8. Harleian Society, ii. 65 ; xi. 15 ; xv. 109 ;
xviii. 51 ; xxviii. 79 ; xxxviii. 491, 763 ; xxxix. 919, 1097, 1098 ;
xlii. 16. Nichols' History of the County of Leicester, ii. 698.
J. H. Hill's History of Market Harborough, 147. Shaw's
Staffordshire, i. 389. Bridge's Northamptonshire, by Rev. Peter
Whalley, ii. 326. Burke's Royal Families, (London, 1851, 8vo.)
i. 24. Poulson's Holderness, i. 240. Howard's Visitation of
England and Wales, i. 73 ; Notes, ii. 95. Hunter's Deanery of
Doncaster, ii. 262. Ormerod's Cheshire, i. 465, 680 ; iii. 454.
Page's History of Suffolk, 159. Wotton's English Baronetage,
iii. 393 ; iv. 403. Betham's Baronetage, ii. 334 ; v. 514. Banks'
Dormant and Extinct Baronage, ii. 107. Metcalfe's Visitations
of Suffolk, 118, 185. Visitation of Staffordshire, (Willm. Salt
Soc.) 56. Hulbert's Annals of Almondbury, 313, 319, 480.
Visitations of Staffordshire, 1614 and 1663-4, (William Salt
Society,) 55, 58. Miscellanea Genealogica et Heraldica, 2nd
Series, v. 255. Burke's Colonial Gentry, ii. 852. The Genealogist,
New Series, xiii. 222. Parliamentary Memoirs of Fermanagh, by
Earl of Belmore, 56. Oliver's History of Antigua, ii. 142. *See*
VERNEY.

BROOKER. Berry's Kent Genealogies, 225. Harleian Society, xliii.
139.

BROOKES, or BROOKS. Warwickshire Antiquarian Magazine, Part ii.
Burke's Landed Gentry, (of Flitwick,) 2 supp., 3, 4, 5, 6, 7, 8 ; (of
Barlow Hall,) 5, 6 ; (of Crawshaw Hall,) 7 ; (of Croft,) 8 'supp.
Visitations of Berkshire, printed by Sir T. Phillipps, 11. Abram's
History of Blackburn, 390. Liverpool as it was, etc., by Richd.
Brooke, 474. Wotton's English Baronetage, iii. 596. The
Genealogist, v. 243. Burke's Extinct Baronetcies. Fletcher's
Leceistershire Pedigrees and Royal Descents, 56. New England
Register, v. 355 ; xxix. 153. Harleian Society, xxxix. 919. *See*
CLOSE-BROOKS.

BROOKESBY. Harleian Society, ii. 201 ; iv. 133.

BROOKMAN. Harleian Society, xiii. 161.

BROOKSBANK. W. Robinson's History of Hackney, i. 447. Burke's
Landed Gentry, 6, 7, 8. Harleian Society, xl. 1283. *See* LAMPLUGH.

BROOME. Pedigree of the Family of Broome, formerly of the Brook,
printed by C. Symms and Co. Manchester, *n. d.*, broadside.
Earwaker's History of Sandbach, 276. Burke's Family Records,
113.

BROOMHALL. Harvey's Hundred of Willey, 152.

BROOMHEAD. Hunter's Deanery of Doncaster, ii. 189. Harleian
Society, xxxviii. 718.

BROTHERS. Visitatio Commitatus Wiltoniæ, 1623, printed by Sir
T. Phillipps. Visitation of Wiltshire, edited by G. W. Marshall, 18.

BROUGH. Poulson's Holderness, i. 366. W. Dickinson's History of Newark, 276.

BROUGHAM. Burke's Commoners, i. 265. Burke's Royal Families, (London, 1851, 8vo.) ii. 204. Hutchinson's History of Cumberland, i. 301. Foster's Visitations of Cumberland and Westmorland, 22. Nicolson and Burn's Westmorland and Cumberland, i. 396.

BROUGHTON. Morant's Essex, ii. 218. Visitation of Somerset, printed by Sir T. Phillipps, 33. Dwnn's Visitations of Wales, i. 329; ii. 315. Camden Society, xliii. 81. Burke's Landed Gentry, 2, 3, 5, 6, supp., 7, 8. Seize Quartiers of the Family of Bryan Cooke, (London, 1857, 4to.) 92. Harleian Society, iii. 28; vi. 38; xi. 16; xiii. 161; xv. 109; xviii. 268; xix. 13; xxviii. 81, 85. Shaw's Staffordshire, i. 226. Visitation of Staffordshire, 1663-4, printed by Sir T. Phillipps, 3. Westcote's Devonshire, edited by G. Oliver and P. Jones, 632. Visitations of Berkshire, printed by Sir T. Phillipps, 11. Clutterbuck's Hertford, ii. 529. Independency at Brighouse, by J. H. Turner, 73. Wotton's English Baronetage, iii. 259. Betham's Baronetage, ii. 242. The Genealogist, v. 243; New Series, xiii. 39; xiv. 102; xvi. 42. Ormerod's Cheshire, iii. 522. Visitation of Staffordshire, (Willm. Salt Soc.) 58. The Visitations of Devon, edited by J. L. Vivian, 111. History of Powys Fadog, by J. Y. W Lloyd, ii. 384; iii. 332. Visitations of Staffordshire, 1614, and 1663-4, (William Salt Society,) 59, 62. New England Register, xxxvii. 298. Weaver's Visitations of Somerset, 12. Harvey's Hundred of Willey, 458. Burke's Colonial Gentry, ii. 612.

BROUN. Genealogical Notes anent some Ancient Scottish Families, by J. B. Brown-Morison, 17-97. A Monograph on the notice of the Ancient Family of Broun of Colstoun in Crawford's M.S. Baronage, by J. B. Brown-Morison of Finderlie, 1881, 4to. Burke's Landed Gentry, 7, 8.

BROUNCKER. Pedigree of Brouncker of Boveridge, Co. Dorset, [T. P.] 1866. Pedigree of Brouncker of London, Bath Easton, etc., [T. P.] 1866. Burke's Commoners, iv. 404, Landed Gentry, 2, 3 and corr., 4, 5, 6, 7, 8. Visitatio Comitatus Wiltoniæ, 1623, printed by Sir T. Phillipps. See BRANCKER.

BROUNING. Hutchin's Dorset, ii. 659.

BROWN-MORRISON. Burke's Landed Gentry, 8.

BROWELL. Diary of Mark Browell, gent. Newcastle Reprints, by H. A. Richardson, 1847, Vol. i.

BROWKER. Surrey Archæological Collections, viii.

BROWN. A Monograph on the notice of the ancient family of Brown. By John Brown Brown-Morison, 1881, 4to. The Browns of Cultermains, Edinburgh, 1866. Jewitt's Reliquary, viii. 237. Collectanea Topographica et Genealogica, i. 240. Bibliotheca Topographica Britannica, ix. Part 4, 143. Topographer and Genealogist, ii. 102. Hasted's Kent, ii. 440. East Anglian, i. 145, 182, 200. Berry's Surrey Genealogies, 81. Burke's Commoners, iii. 382; (of Harehill's Grove,) Commoners, iv. 34, Landed Gentry,

2, 3 ; (of Brandon,) Commoners, iv. 128 ; (of Woodthorpe Hall,) Landed Gentry, 4, 5, 6, 7, 8; (of Clonboy,) 2, 3, 4, 5, 6, 7, 8; (of Mount Brown,) 4, 5, 6, 7, 8 ; (of Rossington,) 4, 5, 6 ; (of Unthank Hall,) 4, 5, 6, 7, 8 ; (of Kingston Blount,) 5, 6, 7, 8 ; (of Jarrow Hall,) 2, 3, 4, 5, 6 ; (of Beilby Grange,) 2, 3, 4 ; (of Arncliffe Hall,) 6 ; 5 at p. 1413 ; 6 at pp. 1127, 1623 ; 7, 7 at p. 1856 ; (of Loftus Hall,) 7, 8 ; (of Newhall,) 7, 8 ; (of Brent Eleigh,) 7, 8 ; (of Ashley,) 7.   J. H. Hill's History of Market Harborough, 224. Foster's Lancashire Pedigrees.   Shaw's Staffordshire, ii. 50. Wright's History of Rutland, 118, 129.   Blore's Rutland, 51. Westcote's Devonshire, edited by G. Oliver and P. Jones, 589. Manning and Bray's Surrey, i. 149, 560.   The Genealogist, i. 220. Memoirs of the Family of Chester, by R. E. C. Waters, 632, 666. Lands and their Owners in Galloway, by P. H. M'Kerlie, iii. 224, 372.   Paterson's History of Ayr and Wigton, i. 653.   Biggar and the House of Fleming, by W. Hunter, 2nd edn., 579.   Harleian Society, xiv. 554 ; xxxix. 1023 ; xlii. 164, 217.   O'Hart's Irish Pedigrees, 2nd Series, 315.   Wotton's English Baronetage, iv. 79. Betham's Baronetage, iii. 219.   Burke's Extinct Baronetcies, and 618.   Howard's Visitation of England and Wales, i. 51 ; ii. 25; Notes, ii. 55.   Ancient Families of Lincolnshire, in 'Spalding Free Press,' 1873-5, No. v.   Northern Notes and Queries, i. 94. Bysshe's Visitation of Essex, edited by J. J. Howard, 20. Foster's Visitations of Durham, 51.   Oliver's History of Antigua, i. 74.   *See* MONTAGUE.

BROWN-MORRISON.   Burke's Landed Gentry, 5, 6, 7.

BROWN-WESTHEAD.   Burke's Family Records, 623.

BROWNE.   Statement of the claim of Henry Browne, Esq., to the dignity of Viscount Montague, by H. Prater.   London, 1849, 8vo. Case of Henry Browne, Esq., on his claim to the title of Viscount Montague, 1851, 4to.   Memorials of the Browns of Fordell, etc., by R. R. Stodart.   Edinburgh, 1887, 4to.   Genealogical Memoirs of the Browne Family, and of the Peploe Family of Garnstone, by G. B. Morgan, 1888-91, 4to.   Pedigree of Browne of Winterborne Basset, [T. P.]   Burke's Extinct Baronetcies.   Morant's History of Colchester, 111.   Morant's Essex, i. 10, 118, 137, 349, 417 ; ii. 64, 470.   Hasted's Kent, i. 297 ; iii. 357, 588 ; iv. 40.   Harleian Society, i. 20, 24, 25, 62 ; viii. 27, 183, 267, 380 ; xi. 16 ; xiii. 5, 31, 163, 165, 359 ; xv. 110-115 ; xx. 20 ; xxi. 31 ; xxvii. 26 ; xxviii. 90, 267 ; xliii. 8, 19.   Dallaway's Sussex, i. 241, 251. Dugdale's Warwickshire, 90.   Berry's Essex Genealogies, 73. East Anglian, i. 182.   Camden Society, xliii. 95.   Berry's Sussex Genealogies, 254, 350, 354.   Berry's Kent Genealogies, 377. Visitation of Middlesex, (Salisbury, 1820, fol.) 36.   Glover's History of Derbyshire, ii. 320, (295).   Visitation of Oxfordshire, 1634, printed by Sir T. Phillipps, (Middle Hill, folio.) 15.   Burke's Commoners, iii. 382, 529, 539 ; (of Higham Hall,) Landed Gentry, 4, 5, 6 ; (of Morley Hall,) 2 supp., 3, 4, 5, 6 ; (of Janeville,) 2 supp., 3, 4, 5 ; (of Bronwylfa,) 2, 3, 4, 5, 6, 7 ; (of Browne's Hill,) 2, 3, 4, 5, 6, 7 ; (of Mount Kelly,) 3, 4, 5 ; (of Browne Hall,) 2, 3,

4, 5, 6, 7, 8 ; (of Raheens,) 3, 4, 5 ; (of Braeffey,) 3, 4, 5, 6, 7, 8; (of
Caughley,) 3, 4, 5, 6 ; (of Salperton,) 2, 3, 4, 5, 6, 7, 8 ; (of Rath-
bane,) 3, 4, 5 ; (of Tallantire,) 2, 3, 5, 6 ; (of Ballinvoher,) 5, 6, 7,
8 ; (of Elsing Hall,) 5, 6, 7, 8 ; (of Mellington,) 5, 6 ; (of Aughen-
taine,) 5 supp., 6, 7, 8 ; (of Sweeney,) 5 supp. at p. 47 ; (of
Manulla,) 4 ; (of Kilskeagh,) 3, 4 ; (of Moyne,) 3, 4 ; (of Monkton
Farleigh,) 2, 5 ; (of New Grove,) 2 ; (of Doxford,) 7, 8 ; (of Hall
Court,) 7, 8 ; (of Greenville,) 3 ; (of Mount Hazel,) 5 supp. ; (of
Riverstown,) 6 ; 6 at p. 949, 7 ; 7 at p. 1086 ; 8 at p. 1177.
Maclean's History of Trigg Minor, i. 323, 333. Burke's Visitation
of Seats and Arms, 2nd Series, i. 1. Burke's Heraldic Illustrations, 143. Blore's Rutland, 93, 220. Bridge's Northamptonshire,
by Rev. Peter Whalley, ii. 497. Visitations of Berkshire, printed
by Sir T. Phillipps, 12. Visitation of Derbyshire, 1663-4, (Middle
Hill, 1854, fol.) 2. Nichols' History of the County of Leicester, ii.
874, 888 ; iii. 1029. Visitatio Comitatus Wiltoniæ, 1623, printed
by Sir T. Phillipps. Hutchins' Dorset, i. 165, 583 ; ii. 298.
Manning and Bray's Surrey, ii. 182. Clutterbuck's Hertford, i.
448 ; ii. 130. Wright's Essex, ii. 669, 735. The Genealogist, iii.
70, 122, 377 ; iv. 128 ; v. 316 ; New Series, ii. 224 ; vii. 15, 16 ;
xiii. 28. Foley's Records of the English Province S. J., ii. 428.
Carthew's Hundred of Launditch, Part ii. 464. Miscellanea
Genealogica et Heraldica, New Series, iii. 42 ; 2nd Series, i. 123 ;
ii. 60 ; iii. 5, 129, etc. ; iv. 180. Charles Smith's History of
Kerry, 39. Notes and Queries, 1 S. vii. 528, 608 ; viii. 114, 243,
301, 639 ; ix. 41 ; 3 S. viii. 292 ; 5 S. vi. 383 ; 7 S. iv. 463, 506;
v. 24, 224, 302. Edmondson's Baronagium Genealogicum, iv. 318.
Archdall's Lodge's Peerage, iii. 271. Brydges' Collins' Peerage,
ix. 276. Wotton's English Baronetage, iii. 4, 466 ; iv. 132, 235.
Visitation of Devon, edited by F. T. Colby, 26. Betham's
Baronetage, iii. 219. Banks' Dormant and Extinct Baronage,
iii. 525. Metcalfe's Visitations of Suffolk, 186. Visitation of
Wiltshire, edited by G. W. Marshall, 56. The Rectors of Lough-
borough, by W. G. D. Fletcher, 19. Registers of Ecclesfield, by
A. S. Gatty, 142. Jewitt's Reliquary, xxiv. 71. The Visitations
of Devon, edited by J. L. Vivian, 112. Metcalfe's Visita-
tions of Northamptonshire, 167. Somersetshire Wills, printed for
F. A. Crisp, iii. 67. Visitation of Gloucester, edited by T. F.
Fenwick, and W. C. Metcalfe, 28. Foster's Visitation of Middle-
sex, 63. The Suffolk Records, by H. W. Aldred, 21. Burke's
Colonial Gentry, i. 257. New England Register, vi. 232, 272,
278 ; vii. 312 ; xx. 243 ; xliv. 281 ; xlviii. 269. Original Poems,
by Willm. Browne, 2nd app. to preface. Family Notes, by J. M.
Browne. Hobart, Tasmania, 1887, 8vo. The Irish Builder, xxxv.
126. Burke's Family Records, 113, 119. Muskett's Suffolk
Manorial Families, i. 77-82. *See* DU MOULIN-BROWNE, WOGAN-
BROWNE.

BROWNE-CLAYTON. Burke's Landed Gentry, 6, 8.
BROWNELL. Harleian Society, xxxviii. 668. A Chapter in Mediocrity, by W. J. Stavert, 8.

BROWNE-MOSTYN. Burke's Commoners, iii. 381.
BROWNFIELD. Burke's Landed Gentry, 5.
BROWNING. Fosbrooke's Abstracts of Smith's Lives of the Berkeleys, 76. Fosbrooke's History of Gloucestershire, i. 434. Visitation of Gloucester, edited by T. F. Fenwick, and W. C. Metcalfe, 30. Harleian Society, xxi. 32.
BROWNLESS. Burke's Colonial Gentry, ii. 547.
BROWNLOW, or BROWNLOWE. Gentleman's Magazine, 1826, i. 26. Jewitt's Reliquary, vii. 22. Turnor's History of Town and Soke of Grantham, 100. The Genealogist, iii. 360. Burke's Extinct Baronetcies.
BROWNRIGG. The Wolfe's of Forenaghts, 84.
BROXHOLME. The Genealogist, iii. 360 ; v. 316.
BRUCE. Case on behalf of Robert Bruce of Kennet, claiming dignities of Lord Balfour of Burleigh, etc., (London, n. d., fol.). Genealogy of the branch of the Bruce Family settled in Ireland, Heirs Male of the Bruces of Newtoune, and eldest Cadets of Airth, folio broadside. The Bruces of Airth and their Cadets, by W. B. Armstrong. Edinburgh, 1892, 4to. A genealogical view of the origin and descent of the Bruce Family, in the History of Scotland, by R. Kerr, i. xxv-xlix. Family records of the Bruces and the Cumyns, by M. E. Cumming Bruce. Edinburgh, 1870, 4to. Scottish Peerages, their limitations, particularly with reference to the Barony of Bruce of Kinloss, by J. E. B. Bruce. London, 1867, 8vo. Fauconberge Memorial, 62. Drummond's History of Noble British Families, iii. and iv. Burke's Commoners, ii. 369; (of Kennet,) Commoners, ii. 485, Landed Gentry, 2 and supp., 3, 4, 5 ; (of Clackmannan,) Commoners, iv. 618 ; (of Kinnaird,) Landed Gentry, 2, 3, 4, 5 ; (of Miltown,) 4, 5, 6, 7, 8 ; (of South Park,) 5 supp. ; (of Scoutbush,) 2, 3, 4 ; (of Arnot,) 7 ; (of Norton Hall,) 8 supp. Herald and Genealogist, viii. 338. Paterson's History of the Co. of Ayr, ii. 270. The Genealogist, iii. 19, 38 ; vi. 162, 205 ; vii. 131, 224. Burke's Royal Families, (London, 1851, 8vo.) i. 34. Ord's History of Cleveland, 249. Douglas' Baronage of Scotland, 238-246, 510. Paterson's History of Ayr and Wigton, ii. 358. Burke's Extinct Baronetcies, 618. The Ulster Journal of Archæology, v. 1, 128 ; vi. 66. Peter Chalmers' Account of Dunfermline, i. 287 ; ii. 291. Wood's Douglas's Peerage of Scotland, i. 316, 511. Notes and Queries, 2 S. vii. 374. Edmondson's Baronagium Genealogicum, v. 440. Brydges' Collins' Peerage, v. 107. Banks' Baronies in Fee, ii. 98. Betham's Baronetage, v. 588, app. 45. Banks' Dormant and Extinct Baronage, i. 44 ; iii. 39. Foster's Collectanea Genealogica, (MP's Scotland), 38. Caithness Family History, by John Henderson, 262. Burke's Family Records, 119. See BALFOUR, BRUS, BREWS, BRAOSE.
BRUCE-DUNDAS. Burke's Heraldic Illustrations, 121.
BRUCE-GARDYNE. Burke's Royal Families, (London, 1851, 8vo.) i. 189.
BRUCKSHAW. Burke's Landed Gentry, 3, 4.
BRUDENELL, or BRUDNELL. J. H. Hill's History of Langton, 186.

Camden Society, xliii. 88. Berry's Hampshire Genealogies, 109.
Harleian Society, ii. 143; iii. 48; xv. 116; xxviii. 81. Gyll's
History of Wraysbury, 206. Lipscombe's History of the County
of Buckingham, ii. 447. Wright's History of Rutland, 119.
Bridge's Northamptonshire, by Rev. Peter Whalley, ii. 302.
Thoresby's Ducatus Leodiensis, 153. Nichols' History of the
County of Leicester, ii. 807, 913. Edmondson's Baronagium
Genealogicum, ii. 140; vi. 86. Brydges' Collins' Peerage, iii.
487. The Genealogist, vii. 120. Visitations of Staffordshire,
1614 and 1663-4, William Salt Society, 63. Metcalfe's Visita-
tions of Northamptonshire, 6, 168.
BRUDENELL-BRUCE. Edmondson's Baronagium Genealogicum, vi. 15.
BRUEN. Burke's Landed Gentry, 3, 4, 5, 6, 7, 8. Ormerod's
Cheshire, ii. 309, 322. See BRUYN.
BRUERE. Miscellanea Genealogica et Heraldica, i. 326. Manning
and Bray's Surrey, ii. 670. Baker's Northampton, ii. 239. See
BRIWERE.
BRUERTON. Dwnn's Visitations of Wales, ii. 353.
BRUGES. Harleian Society, i. 79; viii. 179; xiii. 158. Burke's
Landed Gentry, (Ludlow-Bruges,) 2, 3, 4, 5, 6, 8. Hampshire
Visitations, printed by Sir T. Phillipps, 9. Miscellanea Genea-
logica et Heraldica, 2nd Series, iii. 350. See BRIDGES, BRYDGES.
BRUGGE. Braye Peerage Evidence, 304. Fosbrooke's History of
Gloucestershire, ii. 160.
BRULEY. Harleian Society, v. 186.
BRUMMELL. Notes and Queries, 1 S. ii. 264.
BRUMPTON. Plantagenet-Harrison's History of Yorkshire, i. 81.
BRUNE. Burke's Commoners, i. 205; Landed Gentry, 3 page 976.
Maclean's History of Trigg Minor, ii. 214, 237, 241. Burke's
Royal Descents and Pedigrees of Founders' Kin, 71. Hampshire
Visitations, printed by Sir T. Phillipps, 10. Hutchins' Dorset,
iv. 190. Banks' Baronies in Fee, ii. 55. Harleian Society, xx.
21. See LE BRUNE.
BRUNING, or BRUNINGE. Herald and Genealogist, iii. 519. Hamp-
shire Visitations, printed by Sir T. Phillipps, 8. Visitatio Comi-
tatus Wiltoniæ, 1623, printed by Sir T. Phillipps. Foley's
Records of the English Province, S. J., v. 814.
BRUNSKELL, or BRUNSKILL. Surtees Society, xxxvi. 44. Visitation
of Middlesex, (Salisbury, 1820, fol.) 17. Surtees' Durham, iv. 93.
Pedigrees of the Leading Families of Lancashire, published by
Joseph Foster, (London, 1872, fol.). Plantagenet-Harrison's
History of Yorkshire, i. 341, 343. Monken Hadley, by F. C.
Cass, 34. Pedigrees of the Leading Families of Yorkshire, by
Joseph Foster. Foster's Visitation of Middlesex, 32.
BRUNSWICK (House of). Memoirs of the House of Brunswick, by
H. Rimius, 1750, 4to. Jacob's Peerage, i. 8, 44.
BRUNWIN. Burke's Landed Gentry, 4, 5, 6.
BRUS, or BRUSE. Hoare's Wiltshire, II. i. 162; III. ii. 77. Foster's
Visitations of Yorkshire, 130. Herald and Genealogist, viii. 336.
Maclean's History of Trigg Minor, i. 651. History of Hartlepool,

by Sir C. Sharp, (1816, 8vo.) 14. Surtees' Durham, iii. 94, 328.
Duchetiana, by Sir G. F. Duckett, 2nd edn., 153. Harleian
Society, xvi. 39, 40, 90 ; xxviii. 152 ; xxix. 424. Burke's Baronies
in Fee, i. 137. *See* BRUCE, DE BRUS.

BRUTON. Burke's Royal Families, (London, 1851, 8vo.) ii. 181.
Harleian Society, vi. 336. The Visitations of Devon, edited by
J. L. Vivian, 113.

BRUYN. Morant's Essex, i. 99. Lipscombe's History of the County
of Buckingham, i. 66. Eyton's Antiquities of Shropshire, v. 102.
Burton's Description of Leicestershire, 186. Nichols' History of
the County of Leicester, iii. 349. Harleian Society, xiv. 555 ;
xviii. 52. Miscellanea Genealogica et Heraldica, 2nd Series, v.
129. *See* BRUEN.

BRUYS. The Genealogist, New Series, viii. 244 ; xiii. 97 ; xvii. 113.

BRYAN. Case of George Bryan claiming the Barony of Slane, folio.
Additional case of George Bryan claiming the Barony of Slane,
1831, fol., pp. 63. Supplemental case, pp. 7. Claim of George
Bryan, Esq., of Jenkinstown, to be Lord Baron of Slane, Sess.
Papers, 157 of 1830 ; 64 of 1830-31 ; 41 of 1831 ; 75 of 1831-2.
Berry's Sussex Genealogies, 110. Berry's Kent Genealogies, 5.
Archæologia Cantiana, iv. 244. Burke's Landed Gentry, (of
Jenkinstown,) 3, 4, 5, 6, 7, 8 ; (of Upton,) 3 supp., 4, 5, 6, 7, 8.
Collectanea Topographica et Genealogica, iii. 250. Hutchins'
Dorset, i. 448. Notes and Queries, 3 S. i. 176. The Genealogist,
vi. 140 ; New Series, xv. 98. Banks' Baronies in Fee, i. 138.
Banks' Dormant and Extinct Baronage, ii. 63. The Irish Builder,
xxix. 322. Fletcher's Leicestershire Pedigrees and Royal Descents,
57. Muskett's Suffolk Manorial Families, i. 53.

BRYANT. Manning and Bray's Surrey, ii. 437. New England
Register, xxiv. 315 ; xxxv. 37 ; xlviii. 46. Burke's Landed
Gentry, 8.

BRYCH. Chetham Society, lxxxi. 121.

BRYCHAN. Jones's History of the County of Brecknock, i. App.
1-30, at 341.

BRYDGES. The Case of Edward Tymewell Brydges claiming the
Barony of Chandos of Sudeley, with Appendices, fol. Further
case of the Rev. E. T. Brydges, 1795, pp. 8, fol. Sess. Papers, 1790
—1802-3. General Pedigree of the Rev. Edward Tymewell
Brydges, fol. Single Sheet. Claim of E. T. Brydges Clerk, to the
Barony of Chandos, 1790, fol. Pedigree of the descendants of
John Brydges of Harbledown, fol., single sheet. Proofs of the
pedigree of John Brydges of Harbledown, fol., single sheet.
Ataviæ Regiæ, by Sir E. Brydges. Florence, 1820, 4to. Stemmata
illustria præcipue Regia, auctore Sir Egerton de Bruges, Bart.
Paris, 1825, fol. Pedigree of Brydges of Wilton Castle, compiled
by Sir T. Phillipps, 1856, folio page. Harleian Society, xiii.
160. Burke's Commoners, iv. 552. Hampshire Visitation, printed
by Sir T. Phillipps, 8. Clutterbuck's Hertford, ii. 450. Jacob's
Peerage, i. 392. Hasted's Kent, iv. 301. Gentleman's Magazine,
1826, i. 110. Berry's Kent Genealogies, 492. Edmondson's

Baronagium Genealogicum, i. 68. Brydges' Collins' Peerage, vi. 704. Banks' Dormant and Extinct Baronage, iii. 161. East Barnet, by F. C. Cass, Part i. 41. *See* BRIDGES, LEE-WARNER, BRUGES.

BRYDIMAN. Harleian Society, xix. 163.

BRYERS. Chetham Society, lxxxiv. 59.

BRYMER. Burke's Landed Gentry, 7, 8.

BRYNKIR. History of Powys Fadog, by J. Y. W. Lloyd, vi. 249.

BUBWITH. Harleian Society, xvi. 41.

BUCHAN. Case of Sir Colin Mackenzie, Bart., on his claim to the Title of Earl of Buchan, with Appendix, 1832, fol. Sir Colin Mackenzie's claim to the Title and Dignity of Earl of Buchan and Lord Auchterhouse, *n. d.* (circa 1840) fol. Burke's Landed Gentry, 3, 4, 5, 6, 7. Burke's Colonial Gentry, ii. 849.

BUCHANAN. A Statement of the Claim of the Family of Buchanan of Spittal. Edinburgh, 1826, 4to. A genealogical essay upon the Family of Buchanan, by W. Buchanan. Glasgow, 1723, 4to. History of the ancient surname of Buchanan, by W. Buchanan. Glasgow, 1793, 8vo. Inquiry into the Genealogy, etc., of Highland Clans and Families of Buchanan, by W. Buchanan. Edinburgh, 1755, 8vo.; 2nd edn., Glasgow, 1820. Burke's Commoners, (of Auchintorlie,) iii. 654, Landed Gentry, 2, 3, 4, 5, 6, 7 ; (of Ardoch,) Commoners, ii. 336 ; Landed Gentry, 2, 3, 4, 5, 6 ; (of Drumpellier House,) Landed Gentry, 4, 5, 6, 7, 8 ; (of Hales Hall,) 2 final add., 3 supp., 4, 5, 6, 7, 8 ; (of Powis,) 5 supp., 6, 7, 8 ; (of Waldens,) 7 ; (of Edenfels,) 8. Herald and Genealogist, v. 516 ; vi. 93. Genealogy of Henzey, Tyttery, and Tyzack, by H. S. Grazebrook, 50. The Genealogical Magazine, ii. 311, 356, 497. *See* GRAY-BUCHANAN.

BUCHANAN-BAILLIE-HAMILTON. Burke's Landed Gentry, 6, 7.

BUCHANAN-HAMILTON. Burke's Landed Gentry, 2 supp., 3, 4, 5, 6, 7, 8.

BUCHI. Sussex Archæological Collections, xii. 107.

BUCK, or BUCKE. Burke's Visitations of Seats and Arms, 2nd Series, i. 17. Morant's Essex, ii. 618, 622. Berry's Kent Genealogies, 99, 100. Surtees Society, xxxvi. 69, 70. Cambridgeshire Visitation, edited by Sir T. Phillipps, 4. Nash's Worcestershire, ii. 19. History and Antiquities of Filey, by John Cole, (Scarborough, 1828, 8vo.) Visitation of Gloucestershire, 1569, (Middle Hill, 1854, fol.) 3, 4. Burke's Landed Gentry, (of Denholme,) 3, 4, 5, 6 ; (of Agecroft Hall,) 2 ; (of Moreton,) 2, 3. Hunter's Deanery of Doncaster, ii. 178. Surtees' Durham, iii. 269. Clutterbuck's Hertford, i. 251. History of the Life and Reigne of Richard the Third, by Geo. Buck, (London, 1647, fol.) 68. The Genealogist, iii. 238 ; New Series, xvii. 180. Notes and Queries, 1 S. ii. 38, 73. Burke's Extinct Baronetcies. Wotton's English Baronetage, iii. 205. Harleian Society, xxi, 211, 212 ; xxvii. 26 ; xxxvii. 192 ; xxxviii. 428 ; xli. 69, 123 ; xlii. 26. Visitation of Gloucester, edited by T. F. Fenwick and W. C. Metcalfe, 31. The Visitations of Devon, by J. L. Vivian, 723.

BUC 123 BUC

BUCKBY. Fletcher's Leicestershire Pedigrees and Royal Descents, 63.
BUCKENHAM. The Buckenham Family of Norfolk, 'to the glory of
God, by Faith, Hope, and Love in Jesus Christ, and Comfort of
the Holy Ghost.' Privately printed by Henry Maudslay—folio
broadside. Another edition marked 'Sixth trial.' Notes and
Extracts respecting the Family of Bukenham or Bokenham, by
Henry Maudslay. London, 1884, 8vo. *See* BOKENHAM.
BUCKERIDGE. Pedigree of Buckeridge of Pangborn, Co. Berks,
[T. P.] folio page. Berry's Berkshire Genealogies, 49, 153. The
Genealogical Magazine, ii. 177.
BUCKETT. Harleian Society, xv. 117.
BUCKHURST. Case of the Right Hon. R. W. S. Earl Delawarr
Claiming the Barony of Buckhurst. London, 1876, pp. 33. Claims
of M. S. West, and Lord de la Warr, to Barony of Buckhurst,
Sess. Papers, E of 1876.
BUCKINGHAM. Case of Richard Plantagenet Duke of Buckingham
and Chandos, on his claim to the dignity of Lord Kinloss, 1867,
fol. pp. 10. Supplemental case of same, 1867, pp. 30. Petition
of G. W. F. Marquis of Aylesbury in opposition to the said claim,
1867, fol., pp. 2. The Family of Buckingham and Chandos,
Stowe Catalogue, 1848, 4to. Lord Braybrooke's History of Audley
End, 7. Gyll's History of Wraysbury, 273. *See* VILLIERS.
BUCKLAND. Miscellanea Genealogica et Heraldica, New Series, i.
341. Harleian Society, xi. 16.
BUCKLE. Berry's Surrey Genealogies, 19. Berry's Sussex Gene-
alogies, 22. Burke's Commoners, ii. 573, Landed Gentry, 2, 3, 4,
5, 6, 7, 8. Harleian Society, viii. 356; xliii. 207. Manning and
Bray's Surrey, ii. 587. Surrey Archæological Collections, vi.
The Genealogist, iii. 251.
BUCKLER. Bucleriana, Notices of the Family of Buckler. By C. A.
Buckler. London, 1886, 4to. Hutchins' Dorset, ii. 479. Har-
leian Society, xx. 23. The Genealogist, New Series, ii. 224.
Miscellanea Genealogica et Heraldica, 2nd Series, ii. 204.
Howard's Visitation of England and Wales, ii. 163.
BUCKLEY. Burke's Landed Gentry, (of New Hall,) 3, 4, 5, 6, 7, 8 ;
(of Ardwick,) 2 supp., 3, 4; (of Minesteed Lodge,) 2. Chetham
Society, lxxxiv. 60. Fishwick's History of Rochdale, 390.
T. Nicholas' County Families of Wales, 281. Harleian Society,
xxxix. 999. Oliver's History of Antigua, i. 82.
BUCKLEY-MATHEW. Maclean's History of Trigg Minor, i. 572.
BUCKLEY-WILLIAMES. Collections by the Powys-land Club, ix. 351.
BUCKNALL, or BUCKNELL. Harleian Society, viii. 241. Clutterbuck's
Hertford, i. 247. Notes and Queries, 2 S. x. 348. Metcalfe's
Visitation of Northamptonshire, 73. *See* LINDSAY-BUCKNALL.
BUCKNER. A Royal Descent, by T. E. Sharpe, (London, 1875, 4to.)
49.
BUCKSTON. Glover's History of Derbyshire, ii. 155, (134). Burke's
Commoners, ii. 406, Landed Gentry, 2, 3, 4, 5, 6, 7.
BUCKWORTH. Cambridgeshire Visitation, edited by Sir T. Phillipps,
5. Burke's Landed Gentry, 5, 6, 7, 8. Wotton's English

Baronetage, iv. 58. Betham's Baronetage, iii. 114. Ancient Families of Lincolnshire, in 'Spalding Free Press,' 1873-5, Nos. ix. and x. Harleian Society, xli. 49.

BUCTON. Harleian Society, xvi. 41.

BUDDICOM. Burke's Landed Gentry, 8.

BUDGE. Caithness Family History, by John Henderson, 181.

BUDGEN. Berry's Surrey Genealogies, 64. Burke's Landed Gentry, 4, 5, 6, 7, 8. Manning and Bray's Surrey, ii. 173.

BUDOKSHED, or BUDOKESIDE. Westcote's Devonshire, edited by G. Oliver and P. Jones, 465. Visitation of Devon, edited by F. T. Colby, 27. The Visitations of Devon, edited by J. L. Vivian, 114.

BUDWORTH. Burke's Landed Gentry, 4, 5, 6. Memorials of the parishes of Greensted-Budworth, Chipping Ongar, etc., by P. J. Budworth, (Ongar, 1876, 8vo.) 21.

BUFKIN. Berry's Kent Genealogies, 470.

BUGAN. Visitation of Cornwall, edited by Sir N. H. Nicolas, 24.

BUGG, or BUGGE. Burton's Description of Leicestershire, 272. Wright's Essex, ii. 290. Thoroton's Nottinghamshire, i. 47. The Genealogist, iii. 239. Harleian Society, xiii. 167, 363.

BUGGIN. Berry's Hertfordshire Genealogies, 219.

BUISLY. Blore's Rutland, 15. Bank's Dormant and Extinct Baronage, i. 46.

BULBEC, or BULBECK. Kennet's Parochial Antiquities, ii. 452. Weaver's Visitations of Somerset, 98

BULBROKE. Metcalfe's Visitations of Suffolk, 119.

BULKELEY-OWEN. Howard's Visitation of England and Wales, viii. 140.

BULKLER. Berry's Hampshire Genealogies, 21.

BULKLEY, or BULKELEY. Dwnn's Visitations of Wales, i. 112; ii. 90, 133, 145, 211. Surtees Society, xxxvi. 247. Burke's Commoners, iii. 336, Landed Gentry, 2 supp. Harleian Society, viii. 455; xv. 117; xviii. 38, 54, 57; xix. 164; xxxviii. 446, 463. Visitation of Staffordshire, 1663-4, printed by Sir T. Phillipps, 3. Hampshire Visitations, printed by Sir T. Phillipps, 10, 11. Visitatio Comitatus Wiltoniæ, 1623, printed by Sir T. Phillipps. Hoare's Wiltshire, V. ii. 28. J. P. Earwaker's East Cheshire, i. 181. T. Nicholas' County Families of Wales, 38. Omerod's Cheshire, ii. 652; iii. 269, 627. Edmondson's Baronagium Genealogicum, vi. 113. Archdall's Lodge's Peerage, v. 14. Brydges' Collins' Peerage, viii. 8. Burke's Extinct Baronetcies, 601. History of Powis Fadog, by J. Y. W. Lloyd, v. 278; vi. 250. Genealogical Gleanings in England, by H. F. Waters, 286. Visitations of Staffordshire, 1614 and 1663-4, William Salt Society, 64. Harvey's Hundred of Willey, 365. New England Register, vii. 269; xxiii. 299; xlii. 277. The Genealogist, xii. 18.

BULL. Visitation of Oxfordshire, 1634, printed by Sir T. Phillipps, (Middle Hill, fol.) 15. Miscellanea Genealogica et Heraldica, New Series, i. 286. Harleian Society, v. 306; xi. 17; xxii. 3, 34; xxxii. 57. Metcalfe's Visitations of Suffolk, 119. Metcalfe's Visitation of Worcester, 1683, 25. Jewer's Wells Cathedral, 45.

BULLAKER. Berry's Hampshire Genealogies, 17.
BULLEN, or BULLEYNE. Sir T. Phillipps' Topographer, No. 1, (March,
1821, 8vo.) 54. Westcote's Devonshire, edited by G. Oliver and
P. Jones, 482. Jones' History of the County of Brecknock, ii.
698. Berry's Buckinghamshire Genealogies, 21. Harleian Society,
xvi. 42 ; xxxii. 51. Notes and Queries, 2 S. ix. 249, 331. See
BOLEYNE, TATCHELL-BULLEN.
BULLER. Visitation of Cornwall, edited by Sir N. H. Nicolas, 25.
Visitation of Somerset, printed by Sir Thos. Phillipps, 34.
Burke's Landed Gentry, (of Downes,) 2, 3, 4, 5, 6, 7, 8; (of
Morval,) 2, 3, 4, 5, 6, 7, 8 ; (of Pelynt,) 2, 3, 4, 5, 6 ; (of Erle
Hall,) 5, 6. Harleian Society, ix. 24 ; xxii. 35. A Complete
Parochial History of the County of Cornwall, iii. 379. An His-
torical Survey of Cornwall, by C. S. Gilbert, ii. 38. Banks'
Baronies in Fee, i. 139. Betham's Baronetage, iv. 190. Burke's
Extinct Baronetcies. The Visitations of Cornwall, edited by
J. L. Vivian, 56. Weaver's Visitations of Somerset, 12. See
DUNBOYNE.
BULLINGHAM. Blore's Rutland, 180. Lincolnshire Notes and Queries,
ii. 98.
BULLIVANT. Burke's Colonial Gentry, ii. 642.
BULLMER. Surtees Society, xli. 25. See BULMER.
BULLOCH. Northern Notes and Queries, viii. 42.
BULLOCK. Morant's Essex, ii. 118. Harleian Society, i. 82 ; xiii.
168 ; xiv. 645 ; xxviii. 91 ; xxxviii. 445, 450. Berry's Essex
Genealogies, 105. Burke's Commoners, (of Shipdam,) iv. 129,
Landed Gentry, 2, 3, 4 ; (of Falkborne,) Commoners, ii. 621,
Landed Gentry, 2, 3, 4, 5, 6, 7, 8; (of North Coker,) Landed
Gentry, 2 final add., 3, 4, 5, 6, 7, 8. Foster's Visitations of York-
shire, 498. Maclean's History of Trigg Minor, i. 299. Visitations
of Berkshire, printed by Sir T. Phillipps, 12. Wright's Essex,
i. 229. Memoirs of the Family of Chester, by R. E. C. Waters,
285. G. W. Johnson's History of Great Totham, 44. The Genealogist, vii. 121 ; New Series, i. 3 ; vii. 65. Jewitt's Reliquary,
xx. 31. Bysshe's Visitation of Essex, edited by J. J. Howard, 20.
BULLOCK-WEBSTER. Burke's Landed Gentry, 6, 8.
BULLOIGNE (Earls of). Collinson's Somerset, ii. 80 ; iii. 4.
BULMAN. Berry's Sussex Genealogies, 361.
BULMER. Visitation of Durham, 1615, (Sunderland, 1820, fol.) 21.
Blomefield's Norfolk, ix. 199. Foster's Visitations of Yorkshire,
175, 193. Foster's Visitations of Durham, 53. Graves' History
of Cleveland, 407-410. Hutchinson's History of Durham, iii.
xxvi. Ord's History of Cleveland, 385. Surtees' Durham, i. 79.
Plantagenet-Harrison's History of Yorkshire, i. 222. Harleian
Society, xvi. 43. Banks' Baronies in Fee, i. 140. Bank's Dormant
and Extinct Baronage, i. 47, 248.
BULSTRODE. Aungier's History of Syon Monastery, 495. Croke's
History of the Family of Croke, No. 34. Ashmole's Antiquities
of Berkshire, iii. 310. Harleian Society, viii. 373. Gyll's History
of Wraysbury, 217. Lipscombe's History of the County of Buck-

ingham, iv. 503, 572. Visitations of Berkshire, printed by Sir T.
Phillipps, 12. Memoirs, British and Foreign, of Illustrious Per-
sons who died in 1711, 551. Visitation of Gloucester, edited by
T. F. Fenwick and W. C Metcalfe, 31.

BULTEEL. Burke's Landed Gentry, 2, 3, 4, 5, 6, 7, 8. Harleian
Society, xv. 118.

BULWER. Blomefield's Norfolk, viii. 332. Burke's Commoners, i.
445, Landed Gentry, 2, 3, 4, 5, 6, 7, 8. Burke's Royal Families,
(London, 1851, 8vo.) i. 72. Harleian Society, xxxii. 57, 92.

BUNBURY. Burke's Landed Gentry, (of Moyle,) 3, 4, 5, 6 supp., 7, 8 ;
(of Lisnevagh,) 2 supp., 3, 4, 5, 6 ; (of Marlston House,) 5 supp.,
6, 7. Ormerod's Cheshire, ii. 395. Harleian Society, xv. 119.
Wotton's English Baronetage, iii. 687. Betham's Baronetage,
iii. 47. The Correspondence of Sir Thomas Hanmer, Bart., edited
by Sir Henry Bunbury, Bart., 1. See BONBURY.

BUNCE. Herald and Genealogist, iv. 282. Hasted's Kent, i. 331 ;
ii. 505, 507. Berry's Kent Genealogies, 379. Burke's Commoners,
iii. 369. Harleian Society, viii. 42, 44 ; xv. 120 ; xlii. 121.

BUND. Burke's Landed Gentry, 2, 3, 5, 6, 7, 8. Burke's Heraldic
Illustrations, 22. Burke's Royal Descents and Pedigrees of
Founders' Kin, *Founders' Kin,* 1.

BUNDEY. Burke's Colonial Gentry, i. 64.

BUNGAY, or BUNGEY. Berry's Kent Genealogies, 319. Surrey
Archæological Collections, vii. Harleian Society, xlii. 121 ; xliii.
152.

BUNNY, or BUNNEY. Berry's Berkshire Genealogies, 46. Surtees
Society, xxxvi. 279 ; xli. 82. Visitation of Durham, 1615,
(Sunderland, 1830, fol.) 90. Burke's Landed Gentry, 2, 3, 4, 5.
Foster's Visitations of Yorkshire, 77, 411. Surtees' Durham, iv. 41.
Yorkshire Archæological and Topographical Journal, iii. 8. The
Castles, Manors, and Mansions of Western Sussex, by D. G. C.
Elwes and C. J. Robinson, 206. Harleian Society, xvi. 44 ;
xxxviii. 608. Foster's Visitations of Durham, 55. The Genealo-
gist, New Series, x. 41.

BUNTEN. Burke's Landed Gentry, 8 supp.

BUNTINE. Paterson's History of the Co. of Ayr, i. 293. Paterson's
History of Ayr and Wigton, iii. 123.

BUNTINE-BARR. Geo. Robertson's Account of Families in Ayrshire,
i. 155.

BUNTING. Topographer and Genealogist, ii. 82. Visitation of Norfolk,
published by Norfolk Archæological Society, ii. 46. Harleian
Society, xxxii. 58 ; xl. 1207.

BUNYAN. Notes and Queries, 1 S. ix. 223 ; xii. 491 ; 2 S. i. 170 ; ix.
69, 470. Bedfordshire Notes and Queries, iii. 225.

BURBAGE. Harleian Society, xv. 121. Monken Hadley, by F. C.
Cass, 128.

BURCHALL. Burke's Landed Gentry, 2 supp., 3, 4.

BURCHAM. New England Register, xl. 406.

BURCHELL-HERNE. Burke's Commoners, ii. 689, Landed Gentry
2, 3, 4, 5, 6, 7, 8.

BURCHILL. Jones' History of the County of Brecknock, ii. 441.
BURCHINSHAW. Dwinn's Visitations of Wales, ii. 300, 346.
BURDEN. The Genealogist, iii. 145. Historical Notices of Doncaster,
by C. W. Hatfield, 2nd Series, 144. Alexander Nisbet's Heraldic
Plates, 156.
BURDET, or BURDETT. Appendix to the Case of Sir J. S. Sidney,
claiming to be Lord Lisle. Surtees Society, xxxvi. 2. Burke's
Landed Gentry, (of Ballymany,) 2, 3, 4, 5, 6, 7, 8; (of Cush-
callow,) 8; (of Hunstanton,) 2, 3, 4, 5, 6; (of Shrubhurst,) 5, 6.
Foster's Yorkshire Pedigrees. Foster's Visitations of Yorkshire,
242, 336, 338. Harleian Society, ii. 18, 23; xii. 101; xv. 122;
xvi. 45. Ord's History of Cleveland, 319. Visitation of Warwickshire, 1619, published with Warwickshire Antiquarian Magazine,
177. Burton's Description of Leicestershire, 129, 182. Nichols'
History of the County of Leicester, iii. 351; iv. 608, 630*,
820, 866. Dugdale's Warwickshire, 847. Hunter's Deanery of
Doncaster, ii. 350, 376. Hoare's Wiltshire, II. i. 153. Pilkington's View of Derbyshire, ii. 85. Wotton's English Baronetage,
i. 327; iii. 491. Betham's Baronetage, i. 160; ii. 386; v. app.
81. Fletcher's Leicestershire Pedigrees and Royal Descents, 104.
The Gresley's of Drakelow, by F. Madan, 244. The Genealogist,
New Series, xv. 81.
BURDON. Topographer and Genealogist, ii. 73. Burke's Commoners,
i. 359, Landed Gentry, 2, 3, 4, 5, 6, 7, 8. Harleian Society, vi.
39. Maclean's History of Trigg Minor, i. 394*. Hoare's Wilt-
shire, V. iii. 46. Surtees' Durham, iii. 416. Thoroton's Notting-
hamshire, iii. 130. The Visitations of Cornwall, edited by J. L.
Vivian, 31. The Visitations of Devon, edited by J. L. Vivian,
115.
BURE. Harleian Society, xiii. 6.
BURELL. Visitation of Cornwall, edited by Sir N. H. Nicolas, 26.
Harleian Society, ix. 25. The Visitations of Cornwall, edited by
J. L. Vivian, 61.
BURES. The Genealogist, New Series, xvi. 159.
BURFORD (Barony of). Eyton's Antiquities of Shropshire, iv. 303.
Journal of the British Archæological Association, xxiv. 136. See
CORNEWALL.
BURGAINE. Harleian Society, vi. 40.
BURGANEY. Ormerod's Cheshire, ii. 858.
BURGATE. Notices of Swyncombe and Ewelme in Co. Oxford, by
H. A. Napier, 66.
BURGES, or BURGESS. Visitation of Cornwall, edited by Sir N. H.
Nicolas, 27. Burke's Landed Gentry, 2, 3, 4, 5, 6, 7, 8. Harleian
Society, ix. 26; xiii. 159. Independency at Brighouse, by J. H.
Turner, 82. Betham's Baronetage, iv. 318. Burke's Extinct
Baronetcies. The Genealogist, vi. 140; New Series, xvii. 251.
The Visitations of Cornwall, edited by J. L. Vivian, 63.
BURGH. Hasted's Kent, ii. 496. Catterick Church, by Rev. James
Raine, (London, 1834, 4to.) 22. Foster's Visitations of Yorkshire,
268, 415. History of Gainsburgh, by Adam Stark, 2nd edn. 369.

Thoroton's Nottinghamshire, iii. 237. Banks' Baronies in Fee, i. 141. Banks' Dormant and Extinct Baronage, ii. 66. The Genealogist, vi. 141 ; New Series, xii. 233. Surrey Archæological Collections, viii. A Monograph on the Gainsborough Parish Registers, by J. Gurnhill, 104. The Irish Builder, xxxv. 258. History of Doddington, by R. E. G. Cole, 50. Harleian Society, xliii. 40, 137. See DE BURG.

BURGHERSH. Gentleman's Magazine, xxxiii. 193, 584 ; 1827, i. 202. Hasted's Kent, i. 404. Blore's Rutland, 204. Hoare's Wiltshire, I. ii. 88. Sussex Archæological Collections, xxi. 126. Excerpta Cantiana, by Rev. T. Streatfield, 6. Banks' Baronies in Fee, i. 142. Banks' Dormant and Extinct Baronage, ii. 72.

BURGHERST. Gough's Sepulchral Monuments, ii. 108.

BURGHILL. Weaver's Visitation of Herefordshire, 15.

BURGOIN, BURGOINE, or BURGOYNE. Surtees Society, xxxvi. 27. Cambridgeshire Visitation, edited by Sir T. Phillipps, 6. Harleian Society, vi. 41 ; xix. 7, 87 ; xli. 24. Westcote's Devonshire, edited by G. Oliver and P. Jones, 476, 551. Cussan's History of Hertfordshire, Parts v. and vi. 29. Wotton's English Baronetage, ii. 199. Visitation of Devon, edited by F. T. Colby, 28. Betham's Baronetage, i. 406, app. 27. The Visitations of Devon, edited by J. L. Vivian, 117.

BURKE. Chronicle of the Family of De Havilland. Burke's Landed Gentry, (of Beaconsfield,) 4, 5 ; (of Ballydugan,) 2, 3, 4, 5, 6, 7, 8 ; (of Elm Hall,) 2, 3, 4, 5, 6, 7, 8 ; (of St. Clerans,) 2, 3, 4, 5, 6, 7, 8; (of Knocknagur,) 3, 4 ; (of Ower,) 2 add., 3, 4, 5, 6, 7, 8 ; (of Tyaquin,) 2, 3 ; (of Prospect Villa,) 2 supp., 3, 4 ; (of Slatefield,) 4. Burke's Visitation of Seats and Arms, i. 20. Burke's Authorized Arms, 138. O'Hart's Irish Pedigrees, 2nd series, 315. Notes and Queries, 1 S. xi. 185 ; 3 S i. 161, 212, 221, 429, 495. Howard's Visitation of England and Wales, iii. 43. Oliver's History of Antigua, i. 84. Burke's Family Records, 122. Howard's Visitation of Ireland, i. 23. See GALL-BURKE.

BURLACY. Berry's Buckinghamshire Genealogies, 81. Lipscombe's History of the County of Buckingham, i. 309.

BURLAND. Hutchins' Dorset, iii. 257. Collinson's Somerset, i. 257. Somerset and Dorset Notes and Queries, iii. 269.

BURLETSON. Surtees' Durham, i. 110.

BURLEY. or BURLEIGH. Burke's Landed Gentry, 2, 3, 4, 5, 6, 7. Berry's Hampshire Genealogies, 289. Burke's Commoners, iii. 527. Topographer and Genealogist, iii. 486. Hampshire Visitations, printed by Sir T. Phillipps, 11. Visitatio Comitatus Wiltoniæ, 1623, printed by Sir T. Phillipps. Surrey Archæological Collections, vii. Peck's Desiderata Curiosa, i. 79. Notes and Queries, 4 S. ix. 464, 512 ; 6 S. vii. 47. The Wolfes of Forenaghts, 61, 71. Journal of Ex-Libris Society, iv. 63, 64. Harleian Society, xxviii. 254 ; xxxviii. 657 ; xliii. 176, 199. The Genealogist, New Series, xii. 19 ; xv. 97.

BURLIMACHI. Harleian Society, xv. 122.

BURLINGTON. Case of Richard Earl of Burlington, claiming the

Barony of Clifford, folio, pp. 4. Claim of the Earl of Burlington to the Barony of Clifford, Sess. Papers, May 1737.

BURLTON. Metcalfe's Visitation of Worcester, 1683, 27.

BURLZ. Metcalfe's Visitations of Suffolk, 120.

BURMAN. The Warwickshire Family of Burman. By R. H. Burman. Birmingham. 1895, 8vo.

BURN. Burke's Landed Gentry, 5, 6, 7.

BURN-CALLANDER. Burke's Landed Gentry, 7, 8.

BURN-MURDOCH. Burke's Landed Gentry, 2 supp., 3, 4, 5, 6, 7, 8.

BURNABY, BURNBY, or BURNEBY. Burke's Commoners, (of Baggrave Hall,) iv. 702, Landed Gentry, 2, 3, 4, 5, 6, 7, 8; (of Langford Hall,) Landed Gentry, 5. J. H. Hill's History of Market Harborough, 99, 335. Metcalfe's Visitations of Northamptonshire, 7, 172. Bridge's Northamptonshire, by Rev. Peter Whalley, i. 587. History of the Town and School of Rugby, by N. H. Nicolas, 36. Tuckett's Devonshire Pedigrees, 134. Harleian Society, vi. 42; xii. 146. Westcote's Devonshire, edited by G. Oliver and P. Jones, 494. Visitation of Devon, edited by F. T. Colby, 28. Betham's Baronetage, iii. 354. Foster's Collectanea Genealogica, i. 20-26. Jewitt's Reliquary, xxi. 256. The Visitations of Devon, edited by J. L. Vivian, 119.

BURNABY-ATKINS. Burke's Landed Gentry, 5 supp., 6, 7, 8.

BURNARD. Collectanea Topographica et Genealogica, vi. 200. Bedfordshire Notes and Queries, iii. 343. Burke's Landed Gentry, 7. The Visitations of Devon, edited by J. L. Vivian, 849.

BURNE. Burke's Landed Gentry, 2 supp., 3, 4, 5. Burke's Royal Families, (London, 1851, 8vo.) ii. 15.

BURNEL, or BURNELL. Collinson's Somerset, ii. 422. Morant's Essex, ii. 12, 92, 577. Bird's Magazine of Honour, 75. Hasted's Kent, i. 168. Visitation of Middlesex, (Salisbury, 1820, fol.) 25. Burke's Landed Gentry, 2, 3, 4, 5, 6, 7, 8. Harleian Society, iv. 99; xv. 123; xxi. 33; xxviii. 91, 94. Dugdale's Warwickshire, 728. Gyll's History of Wraysbury, 13. Dickenson's History of Southwell, 2nd edition, 308. Eyton's Antiquities of Shropshire, vi. 134. Manning and Bray's Surrey, i. 222. Banks' Baronies in Fee, i. 143. Banks' Dormant and Extinct Baronage, ii. 75. New England Register, xlvi. 156. Foster's Visitation of Middlesex, 49. Hasted's Kent, (Hund. of Blackheath, by H. H. Drake) 151. The Genealogist, New Series, xv. 102.

BURNET, or BURNETT. Genealogical Account of the Family of Burnett of Burnet-land. By Montgomery Burnett, 1845, 4to. Another edn., Edinburgh, 1880, 4to. East Anglian, iii. 94. Berry's Surrey Genealogies, 90. Burke's Landed Gentry, (of Gadgirth,) 5, 6, 7, 8; (of Monboddo,) 5, 6, 7, 8; (of Barns,) 2 supp.; (of Kemnay,) 6, 7, 8. Harleian Society, xiii. 364; xxxii. 58; xxxviii. 490. Douglas' Baronage of Scotland, 41. Inverurie and the Earldom of the Garioch, by John Davidson, 485. Notes and Queries, 3 S. vi. 47, 333.

BURNETT-STUART. Burke's Landed Gentry, 7, 8.

9

BURNHAM. Burke's Colonial Gentry, ii. 837. Ontarian Families, by E. M. Chadwick, ii. 21.

BURNOPP. Surtees' Durham, ii. 334.

BURNS, or BURNES. Notes on his Name and Family, by James Burnes, K. H. Edinburgh, 1851, 8vo. Chronicle of 100th Birthday of Robert Burns, by J. Ballantine, 1859, 8vo. Genealogical Memoirs of the Family of Robert Burns, by Rev. C. Rogers. Edinburgh, 1877, 8vo. O'Hart's Irish Pedigrees, 2nd Series, 145. Memorials of Angus and the Mearns, by Andrew Jervise, 97. Burke's Landed Gentry, 2 supp., 7, 8.

BURNSIDE. Burke's Landed Gentry, 6, 7.

BURNYNGHILL. Surtees' Durham, i. 199 ; iii. 310.

BURR, or BURRE. Harleian Society, xiii. 32, 169 ; xv. 124. Burke's Landed Gentry, 2, 3, 4, 5, 6, 7, 8. Duncombe's Hereford, (J. H. Cooke,) iii. 173. Weaver's Visitations of Somerset, 13.

BURRARD. Berry's Hampshire Genealogies, 154. Records of the Corporation of the Borough of New Lymington, by Charles St. Barbe. Burke's Royal Families, (London, 1851, 8vo.) ii. 35. Hampshire Visitations, printed by Sir T. Phillipps, 11. Betham's Baronetage, iii. 356.

BURRAWAY. Notes and Queries, 5 S. i. 339.

BURRELL. Case of Peter Burrell, Esq., and his wife, Baroness Willoughby d'Eresby, upon their claim to the office of Lord High Chamberlain of England, with Appendix, 1787, pp. 10. Burrell, of Dowsby, Co. Lincoln. By C. W. Foster. Rotherham, 1885, 4to. Hasted's Kent, i. 85. Berry's Sussex Genealogies, 42. Burke's Commoners, (of Broomepark,) iv. 633, Landed Gentry, 2, 3, 4, 5, 6, 7, 8 ; (of Stoke Park,) Landed Gentry, 4, 5. Harleian Society, vii. 34 ; xv. 125 ; xliii. 179. Blore's Rutland, 50. Herald and Genealogist, viii. 203. Horsfield's History of Lewes, i. 329. Dallaway's Sussex, II. ii. 295. Manning and Bray's Surrey, i. 308. The Genealogist, ii. 226. Page's History of Suffolk, 142. Brydges' Collins' Peerage, viii. 496. Betham's Baronetage, v. app. 29. Foster's Visitations of Northumberland, 21. Foster's Visitations of Cumberland and Westmorland, 19. Surrey Archæological Collections, x. Sussex Archæological Collections, xliii. 1-43. Howard's Visitation of England and Wales, ix. 103.

BURRINGTON. The Visitations of Devon, edited by J. L. Vivian, 120.

BURRON. Chetham Society, lxxxiv. 65.

BURROUGH. Burke's Family Records, 127. Muskett's Suffolk Manorial Families, i. 294-314.

BURROUGHES, or BURROUGHS. Burke's Commoners, (of Burlingham,) iii. 553, Landed Gentry, 2 and corr., 3, 4, 5, 6, 7, 8 ; (of Long Stratton,) Commoners, iii. 554, Landed Gentry, 2, 3, 4, 5, 6, 7, 8 ; (of Rousay,) Landed Gentry, 4 supp., 5, 6, 7, 8. Burke's Royal Families, (London, 1851, 8vo.) ii. 8. Betham's Baronetage, v. 599. Burke's Extinct Baronetcies.

BURROW. Nichol's History of the County of Leicester, ii. 528. Notes and Queries, 7 S. i. 229, 336.

BURROWES. Burke's Landed Gentry, (of Stradone,) 2, 3, 4, 5, 6, 7, 8; (of Dangan Castle,) 4. F. G. Lee's History of Thame, 250.

BURROWS. History of the Family of Burrows. By Montagu Burrows. Oxford, 1877, 8vo.

BURSHELL. Surrey Archæological Collections, viii. Harleian Society, xliii. 161.

BURSLEM. The Borough of Stoke-upon-Trent, by John Ward, 194.

BURSTON. Harleian Society, xv. 126.

BURT. Berry's Kent Genealogies, 40. New England Register, xxxii. 400. Burke's Colonial Gentry, ii. 601. Oliver's History of Antigua, i. 88. *See* BIRT.

BURTCHAELL. The Irish Builder, xxix. 338. Howard's Visitation of Ireland, i. 77.

BURTON. Pedigree of Burton of Longner, Co. Salop, [T. P.] 1856. Account of the township of Iffley, by Rev. Edwd. Marshall, (1870, 8vo.) 92. J. H. Hill's History of Langton, 259. Reports and Papers of the Associated Architectural Societies, V. part i. 196. Harleian Society, i. 31 ; ii. 56, 160 ; iii. 6 ; xv. 127, 128 ; xvi. 45 ; xxviii. 95 ; xxxvii. 337 ; xxxix. 933, 1024 ; xliii. 98. Berry's Sussex Genealogies, 333. Glover's History of Derbyshire, ii. 324, (288, 555). Burke's Commoners, (of Longner,) iv. 261, Landed Gentry, 2, 3, 4, 5, 6, 7, 8 ; (of Mount Anville,) Commoners, iii. 269, Landed Gentry, 2 ; (of Sackett's Hill House,) Commoners, iii. 312, Landed Gentry, 2 supp., 3 ; (of Burton Hall,) Landed Gentry, 2, 3, 4, 5, 6, 7, 8 ; (of Carrigaholt,) 3, 4, 5, 6, 7, 8 ; (of Cherry Burton,) 5, 6, 7, 8 ; (of Somersby,) 5, 6, 7, 8 ; (of Tun-stall,) 4 ; (of Foggathorpe,) 6 ; 6 at p. 1175 ; 7 ; 7 at p. 1359 ; 8 ; 8 at p. 1494. Miscellanea Genealogica et Heraldica, i. 38 ; New Series, iv. 257. Foster's Visitations of Yorkshire, 7, 277, 498. J. H. Hill's History of Market Harborough, 261. Burke's Heraldic Illustrations, 57. Wright's History of Rutland, 25. Visitation of Sussex, 1570, printed by Sir T. Phillipps, (Middle Hill, fol.) 2. Burke's Royal Families, (London, 1851, 8vo.) ii. 207. Topographer and Genealogist, i. 493, 579. Blore's Rutland, 91, 217. Shaw's Staffordshire, i. 78. Visitation of Derbyshire, 1663-4, (Middle Hill, 1854, fol.) 2. Burton's Description of Leicestershire, 161. Hunter's History of the Parish of Sheffield, 401. Nichols' History of the County of Leicester, ii. 820 ; iv. 635, 644. Historical Notices of Doncaster, by C. W. Hatfield, 3rd Series, 351. Visitations of Staffordshire, 1614 and 1663-4, William Salt Society, 67. Leicestershire Architectural Society, i. 383. Dugdale's Warwickshire, 289. Hunter's Deanery of Don-caster, ii. 434. Manning and Bray's Surrey, ii. 509. The Gene-alogist, iii. 123 ; New Series, xiii. 96 ; xiv. 32. Notes and Queries, 1 S. iii. 106, 157 ; iv. 22, 124 ; ix. 19, 183 ; xi. 124 ; 3 S. v. 140 ; 5 S. iii. 366, 507 ; iv. 200, 212. Archdall's Lodge's Peerage, vii. 173. Wotton's English Baronetage, i. 523. Betham's Baronetage, i. 264. Burke's Extinct Baronetcies. Jewitt's Reliquary, xx. 241. Oliver's History of Antigua, i. 93. Burke's Family Records, 129. *See* ARCHER-BURTON.

BURTON-MACKENZIE. Burke's Landed Gentry, 8 supp.
BURTON-PHILLIPSON. Burke's Landed Gentry, 5.
BURWASH. Harleian Society, xv. 129.
BURWELL. Harleian Society, viii. 165. Surtees' Durham, iv. 168.
Metcalfe's Visitations of Suffolk, 119. Foster's Visitations of
Durham, 57.
BURY, or BURYE. Morant's Essex, i. 221. Tuckett's Devonshire
Pedigrees, 9. Cambridgeshire Visitation, edited by Sir Thomas
Phillipps, 6. Burke's Landed Gentry, 5, 6, 7, 8. Harleian Society,
v. 142, 214 ; vi. 42 ; xii. 265 ; xiii. 364 ; xv. 130 ; xix. 8 ; xxxix.
1144. Westcote's Devonshire, edited by G. Oliver and P. Jones,
495, 496. Herald and Genealogist, i. 338. The Genealogist, New
Series, i. 4. Visitations of Berkshire, printed by Sir T. Phillipps,
12. Memoirs of the Family of Chester, by R. E. C. Waters, 63.
Abram's History of Blackburn, 503. Metcalfe's Visitations of
Suffolk, 12. Visitation of Devon, edited by F. T. Colby, 29, 32, 92.
The Visitations of Devon, edited by J. L. Vivian, 123. Notes and
Queries, 8 S. iv. 461. The Irish Builder, xxxv. 77. Howard's
Visitation of England and Wales, ix. 113. See BERY.
BURYNGTON. Tuckett's Devonshire Pedigrees, 55. Harleian Society,
vi. 41.
BUSBRIDGE. Berry's Sussex Genealogies, 3.
BUSBY. Croke's History of the Family of Croke, No. 43. Harleian
Society, iii. 12 ; viii. 144. Lipscombe's History of the County of
Buckingham, ii. 507. Surtees' Durham, i. 75.
BUSFEILD, or BUSFIELD. Burke's Commoners, iv. 701, Landed Gentry,
2, 3, 4, 5, 6, 7, 8. Foster's Yorkshire Pedigrees. Thoresby's
Ducatus Leodiensis, 6. Kent's British Banner Displayed,
290.
BUSH, or BUSHE. Burke's Landed Gentry, 3, 4, 5, 6, 7, 8. Howard's
Visitation of England and Wales, i. 216 ; vi. 73 ; Notes, iii. 63.
Weaver's Visitations of Somerset, 14. Burke's Colonial Gentry,
ii. 590. History of the Wilmer Family, 230. Burke's Family
Records, 130. The Genealogist, xii. 19.
BUSHELL. Rudder's Gloucestershire, 600. Surtees Society, xxxvi.
82. Fishwick's History of Goosnargh, 120. Foster's Visitations
of Yorkshire, 498. Visitation of Warwickshire, 1619, published
with Warwickshire Antiquarian Magazine, 146. Chetham Society,
lxxxiv. 62. Harleian Society, xii. 139 ; xxi. 238 ; xxvii. 27. The
Tyldesley Diary, edited by J. Gillow and A. Hewitson, 56. See
BUSSELL.
BUSK. The Genealogy of the Busk Family, by Hans Busk. London,
1864, fol. Burke's Landed Gentry, (of Fords Grove,) 2, 3, 4, 5, 6,
7, 8 ; (of Culverden,) 5 supp., 6. Cussan's History of Hertfordshire, Parts vii. and viii. 150. Harleian Society, xxxvii. 11.
BUSKELL. Nicolson and Burn's Westmorland and Cumberland, i.
200.
BUSKIN. Berry's Sussex Genealogies, 103.
BUSLI. History of House of Arundel, by J. P. Yeatman, 38. See
DE BUSLI.

BUSSELL. Visitation of Devon, edited by F. T. Colby, 215. Pedigrees of Bussell of Brodemerston, etc. [T. P.] 1871, 2 fol. pages. *See* BUSHELL.

BUSSERE. Harleian Society, xii. 136.

BUSSEW. Blore's Rutland, 15.

BUSSIE, or BUSSY. Thoroton's Nottinghamshire, i. 360. The Genealogist, iii. 361. Banks' Baronies in Fee, ii. 59. Harleian Society, xxii. 132.

BUSTARD. Visitation of Oxfordshire, 1574, printed by Sir T. Phillipps, (Middle Hill, fol.) 2, Harleian Society, v. 196.

BUSVARGUS. Visitation of Cornwall, edited by N. H. Nicolas, 27. Burke's Commoners, iv. 296. Harleian Society, ix. 27. An Historical Survey of Cornwall, by C. S. Gilbert, ii. 46. The Visitations of Cornwall, edited by J. L. Vivian, 64.

BUSWELL. Bridge's Northamptonshire, by Rev. Peter Whalley, ii. 24. Nichols' History of the County of Leicester, iv. 578. Burke's Extinct Baronetcies.

BUTCHER. Berry's Buckinghamshire Genealogies, 95. Harleian Society, xxxvii. 382. Howard's Visitation of Ireland, ii. 68.

BUTLER. Some Account of the Family of the Butlers, particularly of the late Duke of Ormond. London, 1716. 8vo. Pedigree of Butler of Bremhill and others, [T. P.] 2 folio pages. Claim of Garret Butler, Esq., to the title of Viscount Galmoye, fol. Genealogical Memoranda of the Butler Family, by W. Butler. Sibsagor, Assam, 1845, 8vo. Herald and Genealogist, iv. 209. Morant's Essex, ii. 310. Bibliotheca Topographica Britannica, v. Part i. 9 app.; ix. Part 4, 191. Dwnn's Visitations of Wales, i. 76, 132, 179, 180. Sir Thos. Phillipps' Topographer, No. 1, (March, 1821, 8vo.) 26. Visitation of Durham, 1575, (Newcastle, 1820, fol.) 49. Berry's Kent Genealogies, 83, 229. Cambridgeshire Visitation, edited by Sir T. Phillipps, 5. Visitation of Durham, 1615, (Sunderland, 1820, fol.) 100. Berry's Sussex Genealogies, 176. Visitation of Oxfordshire, 1574, printed by Sir T. Phillipps, (Middle Hill, fol.) 2. Visitation of Oxfordshire, 1634, printed by Sir T. Phillipps, (Middle Hill, fol.) 15. Visitation of Gloucestershire, 1569, (Middle Hill, 1854, fol.) 12. Burke's Commoners, iii. 253 ; (of Warminghurst,) iii. 517 ; (of Cazenoves House,) Landed Gentry, 4 supp., 5, 6, 7 ; (of Ballyline,) 4, 5, 6, 7, 8 ; (of Castle Crine,) 4, 5, 6, 7 ; (of Cregg,) 2, 3, 4 ; (of Faskally,) 7 ; (of Pendeford,) 4, 5, 6 ; (of Bourton House,) 8 supp. ; (of Priestown,) 2 add., 3, 4, 6, 7. Harleian Society, iii. 4 ; v. 141 ; viii. 362 ; xii. 357 ; xiii. 32, 169, 365 ; xiv. 564 ; xix. 9 ; xx. 24 ; xxi. 241 ; xxvii. 301 ; xxviii. 96 ; xl. 1196. Chetham Society, lxxxi. 43, 105 ; lxxxiv. 63, 64 ; lxxxv. 113 ; xcviii. 93, 96 ; cv. 223-230 ; New Series, xxv. 158-161. Dallaway's Sussex, II. ii. 255. Jewitt's Reliquary, xiii. 256. Visitation of Warwickshire, 1619, published with Warwickshire Antiquarian Magazine, 162. Lipscombe's History of the County of Buckingham, ii. 7 ; iv. 334. Gregson's Fragments relative to the County of Lancaster, 266. Whitaker's History of Richmondshire, ii. 454, 455. Bridge's Northamptonshire, by Rev. Peter Whalley, i. 82, 101.

Westcote's Devonshire, edited by G. Oliver and P. Jones, 483.
Hunter's History of the Parish of Sheffield, 257. Pembrokeshire
Pedigrees, 148. Visitatio Comitatus Wiltoniæ, 1623, printed by
Sir T. Phillipps. Hutchins' Dorset, iii. 543. Surtees' Durham,
iii. 49. Clutterbuck's Hertford, ii. 222. Baker's Northampton,
i. 427, 470, 475. Baines' History of the Co. of Lancaster, iii.
660 ; iv. 450, 471 ; Croston's edn., iv. 400. Archæologia Cam-
brensis, 1 S. ii. 279. Abram's History of Blackburn, 619.
Castles, Mansions, and Manors of Western Sussex, by D. G. C.
Elwes, and C. J. Robinson, 235. O'Hart's Irish Pedigrees, 2nd
Series, 318. Journal of the Historical and Archæological Association of Ireland, 3rd Series, i. 62. The Tyldesley Diary, edited by
J. Gillow and A. Hewitson, 186. Ellacombe's History of Bitton,
85. Notes and Queries, 1 S. xii. 30, 146 ; 5 S. xi. 69. Burke's
Extinct Baronetcies, 601. Archdall's Lodge's Peerage, ii. 313,
389 ; iv. 1 ; vi. 215. Brydges' Collins' Peerage, ix. 58. Banks'
Baronies in Fee, i. 146, 360. Visitation of Devon, edited by
F. T. Colby, 32. Banks' Dormant and Extinct Baronage, ii. 78 ;
iii. 119. The Genealogist, vi. 141 ; New Series, xii. 20 ; xv. 218.
Genealogies of Morgan and Glamorgan, by G. T. Clark 366, 368.
Harvey's Hundred of Willey, 10, 460. Foster's Visitations of
Northumberland, 22. Burton's History of Hemingborough, 293.
Metcalfe's Visitations of Northamptonshire, 8, 74. East Barnet,
by F. C. Cass, Part i. 26. Foster's Visitations of Durham, 59.
New England Register, i. 167 ; ii. 355 ; iii. 73, 353 ; xvi. 17.
Chance of Bromsgrove, by J. F. Chance, 74. The Perverse Widow,
by A. W. Crawley-Boevey, 221. *See* BOTELER.

BUTLER-BOWDEN. Burke's Landed Gentry, 2, 3, 4, 5, 6, 8. Foster's
Lancashire Pedigrees.

BUTLER-DANVERS. Burke's Commoners, i. 148.

BUTT. Berry's Hertfordshire Genealogies, 41. Burke's Royal
Families, (London, 1851, 8vo.) i. 124.

BUTTER. Burke's Landed Gentry, 2, 3, 4, 5, 6, 7, 8.

BUTTERFIELD. New England Register, xliv. 33.

BUTTERWICKE. Berry's Sussex Genealogies, 271.

BUTTERWORTH. Chetham Society, lxxxii. 12 ; lxxxiv. 65. Harleian
Society, xv. 129 ; xl. 1183, Fishwick's History of Rochdale, 339,
347, 356. New England Register, xli. 191.

BUTTERY. Metcalfe's Visitations of Northamptonshire, 9, 76.

BUTTES. Surrey Archæological Collections, x.

BUTTEVANT. Claim of J. R. B. Viscount Buttevant to vote at elections of Irish Peers, Sess. Papers, 215 of 1825. *See* BARRY.

BUTTON. Pedigree of Button of Alton, Wilts. [T. P.] Herald and
Genealogist, iv. 195. Berry's Hampshire Genealogies, 33. Glamorganshire Pedigrees, edited by Sir T. Phillipps, 34. Hampshire Visitations, printed by Sir T. Phillipps, 12. Visitatio
Comitatus Wiltoniæ, 1623, printed by Sir T. Phillipps. Ellacombe's History of Bitton, 80. Burke's Extinct Baronetcies.
Harleian Society, xix. 89 ; xxi. 231. Genealogies of Morgan
and Glamorgan, by G. T. Clark, 369. Jenver's Wells Cathedral,

288. The Genealogist, New Series, xiii. 185. *See* GRANT,
D'AUNVILLE.
BUTTS. Berry's Kent Genealogies, 257. Visitation of Norfolk,
published by Norfolk Archæological Society, i. 343. Burke's
Landed Gentry, 2 supp., 3, 4. Notes and Queries, 2 S. ii. 17,
478; iii. 16, 75; iv. 257; viii. 435; ix. 61, 149. Harleian
Society, xxxii. 61; xlii. 115; xliii. 38, 178.
BUXTON. Blomefield's Norfolk, v. 283. Jewitt's Reliquary, vii. 243.
Burke's Heraldic Illustrations, 60. Visitation of Derbyshire,
1663-4, (Middle Hill, 1854, fol.) 2. The Genealogist, iii. 123.
Harleian Society, xv. 130; xxxii. 61; xxxix, 957. Betham's
Baronetage, iv. 410. Burke's Landed Gentry, 7.
BWL. Dwnn's Visitations of Wales, i. 266.
BYAM. Memoirs of the Revs. H. J. and E. Byam, by E. S. Byam.
Ryde, 1854; 2nd edn. Tenby, 1862, 8vo. Savage's History of
the Hundred of Carhampton, 171. Gentleman's Magazine, 1848.
i. 39. Burke's Landed Gentry, 2, 3, 4, 5. Maclean's History of
Trigg Minor, i. 570. Burke's Heraldic Illustrations, 22. Burke's
Royal Families, (London, 1851, 8vo.) i. 196. Harleian Society,
xi. 17. Cambrian Journal, 2 Series, v. 1-82. Pedigree of Byam
of Luccombe, etc., priv. printed by Sir T. Phillipps, 4 leaves, *circa*
1841. Oliver's History of Antigua, i. 95.
BYBY. Dwnn's Visitations of Wales, ii. 288.
BYDE. Berry's Hertfordshire Genealogies, 11. Harleian Society,
viii. 131. Clutterbuck's Hertford, iii. 297.
BYELBY. Foster's Visitations of Yorkshire, 499.
BYER. Hasted's Kent, i. 223.
BYERLEY. Foster's Visitations of Yorkshire, 499. Nichols' History
of the County of Leicester, iii. 178. Surtees' Durham, iii. 313.
Foster's Visitations of Durham, 61. Harleian Society, xxxvii.
102.
BYERS. Surtees' Durham, i. 180.
BYFLETE. Harleian Society, xi. 18.
BYGOD. Surtees Society, xli. 67. Harleian Society, xvi. 24, 222.
The Genealogist, New Series, xvii. 23. *See* BIGOD.
BYLEY. New England Register, lii. 50.
BYLL. Visitation of Cornwall, edited by N. H. Nicolas, 6. Harleian
Society, ix. 27. The Visitations of Cornwall, edited by J. L.
Vivian, 65. *See* BILL.
BYLLETT. Harleian Society, xliii. 47.
BYNCHESTRE. Surtees' Durham, iii. 310.
BYND. Berry's Sussex Genealogies, 186. Surrey Archæological
Collections, ii. Harleian Society, xliii. 115.
BYNDLOS, BYNDLOSE, or BYNDLOSSE. Berry's Sussex Genealogies, 48.
Visitation of Westmoreland, 1615, (London, 1853,) 1. Foster's
Visitations of Cumberland and Westmorland, 23. Nicolson and
Burn's Westmorland and Cumberland, i. 86. *See* BINDLOSS.
BYNE. Berry's Surrey Genealogies, 83. Berry's Sussex Genealogies,
186. Burke's Landed Gentry, 2 add. Dallaway's Sussex, II. ii.
131. Manning and Bray's Surrey, ii. 513.

BYNG. Hasted's Kent, ii. 235. Burke's Commoners, i. 14, Landed Gentry, 2. Clutterbuck's Hertford, i. 160. Edmondson's Baronagium Genealogicum, iv. 332. Brydges' Collins' Peerage, vi. 80. *See* BING.

BYRBECK. Dwnn's Visitations of Wales, i. 191.

BYRCH, or BYRCHE. Life of Bishop Hough, by John Wilmot, 140. Harleian Society, xv. 131. Willmore's History of Walsall, 221. *See* BIRCH.

BYRCHET. Berry's Kent Genealogies, 346. Harleian Society, xlii. 193.

BYRD, or BYRDE. Visitation of Cornwall, edited by N. H. Nicolas, 28. Lord Braybrooke's History of Audley End, 292. Burke's Landed Gentry, 5, 6, 7, 8. Harleian Society, ix. 28; xiii. 365. Nichols' History of the County of Leicester, i. 614. The Visitations of Cornwall, edited by J. L. Vivian, 66. Hasted's Kent, (Hund. of Blackheath, by H. H. Drake,) 230. *See* BIRD.

BYRES. *See* MOIR.

BYRLEY. Harleian Society, xliii. 6.

BYRNE. Burke's Commoners, (of Cabinteely,) i. 462, Landed Gentry, 2, 3, 4, 5; (of Allardstown,) Landed Gentry, 4, 5, 6. Journal of the Historical and Archæological Association of Ireland, 4th Series, iii. 487. The Irish Builder, xxix. 114, 288. *See* O'BYRNE.

BYROM. Burke's Landed Gentry, 5 supp., 6, 7, 8. Harleian Society, iv. 11. Chetham Society, xliv. at end; lxxxii. 35; lxxxiv. 66-68. Lancashire and Cheshire Genealogical and Historical Notes, ii. 108. Journal of the British Archæological Association, xxviii. 396. Nooks and Corners of Lancashire and Cheshire, by James Croston, 361. Croston's edition of Baines's Lancaster, iii. 6.

BYRON. Pedigree of George Gordon, 6th Lord Byron, by Edward Bernard. London, 1870, fol. sheet. Surtees Society, xli. 5. Foster's Visitations of Yorkshire, 4. Harleian Society, iv. 9. Chetham Society, lxxxi. 4; xcviii. 55. Thoroton's Nottinghamshire, ii. 285. Yorkshire Archæological and Typographical Journal, vii. 276. Edmondson's Baronagium Genealogicum, iv. 390. Brydges' Collins' Peerage, vii. 89. Deering's Nottingham, 292.

BYRT, or BYRTE. Dwnn's Visitations of Wales, i. 83. Hutchins' Dorset, iv. 142. Meyrick's History of the Co. of Cardigan, 130. *See* BIRT.

BYRTH. Howard's Visitation of England and Wales, i. 224.

BYRTWESYLL. Chetham Society, lxxxi. 32. *See* BIRTWISTLE.

BYSH, BYSHE, or BYSSHE. Surrey Archæological Collections, iii. Berry's Sussex Genealogies, 199. Harleian Society, viii. 135; xliii. 103. Manning and Bray's Surrey, ii. 318. *See* BISH.

BYSSHOPP, or BYSSHOP. Berry's Sussex Genealogies, 213. Dallaway's Sussex, II. i. 204. *See* BISHOP.

BYTHESEA. Burke's Commoners, (of the Hill,) iv. 603, Landed Gentry, 2, 3, 4, 5, 6, 7, 8; (of Week House,) Commoners, ii. 663, Landed Gentry, 2. Burke's Heraldic Illustrations, 20. Burke's Royal Families, (London, 1851, 8vo.) i. 165.

BYTHEWOOD. New England Register, xl. 299.

CABBELL, or CABELL. Burke's Landed Gentry, 5 supp., 6, 7, 8. Tuckett's Devonshire Pedigrees, 110. Harleian Society, vi. 43. The Visitations of Devon, by J. L. Vivian, 125.

CACHMAID. Harleian Society, xxi. 242.

CADDELL, or CADELL. Burke's Landed Gentry, 6, 7, 8.

CADE. Harleian Society, vi. 43 ; xxii. 133. Nichols' History of the County of Leicester, iv. 399. The Visitations of Devon, by J. L. Vivian, 126.

CADENHEAD. The Family of Cadenhead, by George Cadenhead. Aberdeen, 1887, 8vo.

CADIVOR AB DINAVAL (Descendants of). Meyrick's History of the Co. of Cardigan, 156.

CADMAN. Berry's Kent Genealogies, 116. Burke's Landed Gentry, 4. Foster's Yorkshire Pedigrees. Harleian Society, xxxviii. 712 ; xlii. 193.

CADOGAN. Burke's Landed Gentry, 3, 4, 5, 6, 7, 8. Lipscombe's History of the County of Buckingham, i. 353. Edmondson's Baronagium Genealogicum, v. 422. Brydges' Collins' Peerage, v. 410.

CADURCIS. Herald and Genealogist, vi. 249. Nichols' History of the County of Leicester, i. app. 33. Baker's Northampton, ii. 239.

CADWALADYR. Dwnn's Visitations of Wales, ii. 228, 248.

CÆSAR. The Life of Sir Julius Cæsar, Knt., by Charles Cæsar. London, 1810, 4to. Life of Sir Julius Cæsar, Knt., with Memoirs of his Family and Descendants, by Edmund Lodge. London, 1827, 4to. Berry's Kent Genealogies, 489. Burke's Commoners, ii. 18. Harleian Society, viii. 88 ; xxii. 35, 133 ; xlii. 57. Chauncy's Hertfordshire, 345. W. Robinson's History of Hackney, i. 302. Clutterbuck's Hertford, ii. 286.

CAFE. Burke's Family Records, 133.

CAGE. Cussan's History of Hertfordshire, Parts iii. and iv. 66. Hasted's Kent, ii. 487. Berry's Kent Genealogies, 273. Cambridgeshire Visitation, edited by Sir T. Phillipps, 7. Chauncy's Hertfordshire, 136. Harleian Society, xiii. 367 ; xxi. 33 ; xxii. 35 ; xli. 35; xliii. 203. Fosbrooke's History of Gloucestershire, i. 324. Metcalfe's Visitations of Suffolk, 186. Surrey Archæological Collections, xi.

CAHILL. Burke's Landed Gentry, 4 supp., 5. O'Hart's Irish Pedigrees, 2nd Series, 116.

CAILLI. Banks' Dormant and Extinct Baronage, i. 249.

CAIRNCROSS. Private papers relating to the Cairncross Family of Hilslop, 1769, fol.

CAIRNES, or CAIRNS. Shirley's History of the County of Monaghan, 216. O'Hart's Irish Pedigrees, 2nd Series, 146. Wotton's English Baronetage, iv. 130. Burke's Extinct Baronetcies.

CAITHNESS. Wood's Douglas's Peerage of Scotland, i. 292. Henderson's Caithness Family History, 1. See SINCLAIR.

CALAMY. Gentleman's Magazine, lxxxvi., ii. 90, 296 ; lxxiv. 123.

CALCOFT. The Genealogist, New Series, xii. 227.

CALCOTT. Sir T. Phillipps' Topographer, No. 1, (March, 1821, 8vo.)

28. Visitation of Oxfordshire, 1574, printed by Sir T. Phillipps, (Middle Hill, fol.) 2. Burke's Landed Gentry, 2, 3, 4. Harleian Society, iii. 31; v. 150; xv. 133; xviii. 57; xxviii. 96. Nichols' History of the County of Leicester, iv. 79.

CALCRAFT. Burke's Landed Gentry, (of Ancaster Hall,) 2, 3, 4, 5, 6, 7, 8; (of Rempstone,) 2, 3, 4, 5, 6, 7, 8. Hutchins' Dorset, i. 534.

CALDBECK. *See* ROPER CALDBECK.

CALDECOT, CALDECOTE, or CALDECOTT. Burke's Commoners, (of Rugby,) i. 626, Landed Gentry, 2, 3, 4, 5; (of Holbrook Grange,) Landed Gentry, 3, 4, 5, 6, 7, 8; 8 at p. 943; (of Holton,) 3, 4; 5 page 616, 6 page 775. Burke's Royal Descents and Pedigrees of Founders' Kin, 14. History of the Town and School of Rugby, by N. H. Nicolas, 40-43. Nichols' History of the County of Leicester, iv. 79. Ormerod's Cheshire, ii. 693.

CALDER. Nisbet's Heraldry, ii. app. 237. Shaw's History of Moray, 113. Betham's Baronetage, iv. 401. Burke's Extinct Baronetcies. Henderson's Caithness Family History, 209, 215.

CALDERWOOD. Coltness Collections, 393. `Calderwood's History of the Kirk of Scotland, (Wodrow Society,) viii. xxi.

CALDWALL, or CALDWELL. Burke's Commoners, (of Linley Wood,) iv. 597, Landed Gentry, 2, 3, 4, 5, 6, 7; (of New Grange,) Landed Gentry, 2 supp., 3, 4, 5, 6, 7, 8; (of Beechlands,) 2 add., 3, 4. Visitation of Staffordshire, 1663-4, printed by Sir Thomas Phillipps, 3. Nichols' History of the County of Leicester, iv. 370. Harleian Society, ii. 192; xiii. 368; xxvii. 32. Visitations of Staffordshire, 1614 and 1663-4. William Salt Society, 70. Miscellanea Genealogica et Heraldica, 2nd Series, iii. 104.

CALEW. *See* CALO.

CALEY. Surtees Society, xxxvi. 125.

CALFIELD. Oxford Historical Society, 41.

CALL. Visitation of Norfolk, published by Norfolk Archæological Society, i. 22. A Complete Parochial History of the County of Cornwall, iv. 188. An Historical Survey of Cornwall, by C. S. Gilbert, i. 576. Betham's Baronetage, iv. 227. Harleian Society, xxxii. 62.

CALLAGHAN. Burke's Commoners, iii. 608, Landed Gentry, 2.

CALLAN. O'Hart's Irish Pedigrees, 2nd Series, 147.

CALLANDER. Burke's Landed Gentry, 2 supp., 3, 4, 5, 6, 7, 8. Betham's Baronetage, iv. 398. Burke's Extinct Baronetcies.

CALLARD. Harleian Society, vi. 336. Westcote's Devonshire, edited by G. Oliver and P. Jones, 582. Visitation of Devon, edited by F. T. Colby, 33. The Visitations of Devon, by J. L. Vivian, 127.

CALLEY. Burke's Commoners, (of Burderop,) iv. 153, Landed Gentry, 2, 3, 4, 5, 6, 7, 8; (of Blunsdon,) Landed Gentry, 2 supp. Visitatio Comitatus Wiltoniæ, 1623, printed by Sir T. Phillipps. Miscellanea Genealogica et Heraldica, New Series, iii. 233. Visitation of Wiltshire, edited by G. W. Marshall, 22. Harleian Society, xxvii. 35. The Genealogist, xii. 20.

CALLIS. English Church Furniture, by Edward Peacock, 31.

CALMADY, or CALMADYE. Pedigree of Calmady of Langdon Hall,

etc., [T. P.] 1857, folio page. Burke's Commoners, i. 268, Landed Gentry, 2, 3, 4, 5, 6, 7, 8. Burke's Royal Families, (London, 1851, 8vo.) ii. 206. Harleian Society, vi. 43, 44 ; ix. 288. An Historical Survey of Cornwall, by C. S. Gilbert, ii. 75. The Visitations of Devon, by J. L. Vivian, 128.

CALO. Harleian Society, xxi. 24.

CALROW. Burke's Landed Gentry, 2, 3, 4, 5, 6, 7. Abram's History of Blackburn, 727.

CALTHORP, CALTHORPE, or CALTHROP. Blomefield's Norfolk, vi. 514 ; vii. 58 ; ix. 216, 305, 322. Gentleman's Magazine, 1831, ii. 406 ; 1832, i. 109. Visitation of Somerset, printed by Sir Thomas Phillipps, 35. Burke's Landed Gentry, (of Stanhoe,) 2, 3, 4, 5, 6, 7, 8 ; (of Gosberton,) 2, 3, 4, 5. Harleian Society, viii. 9 ; xi. 20 ; xxxii. 63. Carthew's Hundred of Launditch, Part ii. 615. Page's History of Suffolk, 698. Notes and Queries, 3 S. iv. 55. Norfolk Archæology, ix. 154.

CALTON. Camden Society, xliii. 40. Visitations of Berkshire, printed by Sir T. Phillipps, 13. Harleian Society, xxxvii. 380 ; xxxix. 842.

CALVELEY. Ormerod's Cheshire, ii. 285, 768. Chetham Society, cx. 228. Harleian Society, xviii. 58, 259.

CALVERLEY. Burke's Patrician, iv. 1. Surtees Society, xxxvi. 61, 382 ; xli. 85. Visitation of Durham, 1615, (Sunderland, 1820, fol.) 39. Burke's Commoners, (of the Broad,) i. 673 ; (of Oulton Hall,) Landed Gentry, 3, 4, 5, 6, 7, 8. Foster's Yorkshire Pedigrees. Foster's Visitations of Yorkshire, 9. Harleian Society, viii. 305 ; xvi. 47. Chetham Society, lxxxii. 69. Thoresby's Ducatus Leodiensis, 116. Archæologia Æliana, 1st Series, ii. 176. Notes and Queries, 2 S. viii. 198. Burke's Extinct Baronetcies. Wotton's English Baronetage, iv. 136. Foster's Visitations of Durham, 63. The Genealogist, New Series, xiii. 167, 259. See BLACKETT.

CALVERT. Morant's Essex, ii. 621. Berry's Hertfordshire Genealogies, 13-24. Burke's Commoners, (of Albury Hall,) iii. 399, Landed Gentry, 2 ; (of Ockley Court,) Landed Gentry, 5, 6, 7, 8 ; (of Hundson,) 2, 3. Foster's Visitations of Yorkshire, 500. Jewitt's Reliquary, xiv. 84. Lipscombe's History of the County of Buckingham, i. 184. Manning and Bray's Surrey, ii. 613. Clutterbuck's Hertford, iii. 182, 335. Notes and Queries, 2 S. xii 343. Burke's Colonial Gentry, i. 53.

CALWODELEY, or CALWOODLEIGH. Harleian Society, vi. 44. Maclean's History of Trigg Minor, ii. 38, 40. Westcote's Devonshire, edited by G. Oliver and P. Jones, 514. The Visitations of Devon, by J. L. Vivian, 132. See CAWOODLEY.

CALY. Blomefield's Norfolk, x. 178.

CALYBUTT. Carthew's Hundred of Launditch, Part ii. 681. Harleian Society, xxxii. 67.

CALYSTON. The Genealogist, New Series, xvi. 232.

CALZ. Dickinson's History of Southwell, 2nd edition, 274. Thoroton's Nottinghamshire, iii. 267. See CAULX.

CAM. Harleian Society, xxi. 253.

CAMBELL. Morant's Essex, i. 7, 19. Account of the Company of Ironmongers, by John Nicholl, 2nd edn., 536. Burke's Extinct Baronetcies. Phillimore's London and Middlesex Note-Book, 157. *See* CAMPBELL.

CAMBO. Hodgson's Northumberland, I. ii. 284.

CAMBRAY. The Family of Cambray, by J. A. Dunbar-Dunbar. London, 1898, 4to.

CAMBRIDGE. Burke's Landed Gentry, 2. Fosbrooke's History of Gloucestershire, i. 325. Banks' Dormant and Extinct Baronage, iii. 133. *See* PICKARD-CAMBRIDGE.

CAMDEN. Hasted's Kent, i. 102. Harleian Society, xv. 133.

CAMELFORD. *See* PITT.

CAMERON. Memoirs of Sir Ewen Cameron, etc., with account of the History of the Family, by James Macknight. Edinburgh, 1842, 4to. Life of Dr. A. Cameron, by Archibald Cameron. London, 1752, 8vo. History of the Camerons,· by Alexander Mackenzie. Inverness, 1884, 8vo. Burke's Landed Gentry, (of Lochiel,) 2, 3, 4, 5, 6, 7, 8 ; (of Worcester,) 2 ; (of Murton House,) 6. Miscellanea Genealogica et Heraldica, New Series, i. 159. Douglas's Baronage of Scotland, 328. Burke's Colonial Gentry, i. 221.

CAMILLA. Miscellanea Genealogica et Heraldica, ii. 234.

CAMMEL. Hutchins' Dorset, iii. 166. Burke's Landed Gentry, 6, 7, 8.

CAMOCK, or CAMOCKE. Morant's Essex, i. 408. Harleian Society, xiii. 170.

CAMOYS. Case of Sophia della Cainea to the Barony of Camoys. London, 1838, fol. Visitation of Suffolk, edited by J. J. Howard, ii. 264. Carthew's Hundred of Launditch, Part i. 241. Dallaway's Sussex, i. 217. Sussex Archæological Collections, iii. 94. Banks' Baronies in Fee, i. 147. Banks' Dormant and Extinct Baronage, i. 250. Notes and Queries, 6 S. i. 234, 298, 341, 401. The Genealogist, New Series, xvii. 115. *See* DE CAMOYS, STONOR.

CAMPAGNE. Journal of British Archæological Association, xxx. 123.

CAMPBELL. The Book of the Thanes of Cawdor. Edinburgh, 1859, 4to. Case on the part of Sir Hugh Hume Campbell of Marchmont, Bart., in relation to Claim of F. D. Home, Esq., to titles of Earl of Marchmont, etc., 1843, fol. pp. 76. Pedigree of all Branches of Campbell, by James Duncanson. Inverary, 1777. Genealogy of Breadalbane Family, by Joseph M'Intyre, 1752. Pedigree of J. R. Campbell, and G. D. Gibb. Folding table, 1872. The MacCallum Mòre, by the Rev. Hely Smith. London, 1871, 8vo. A Memorial History of the Campbells of Melfort, by M. O. Campbell. London, 1882, 4to. The Marquis of Lorne and the Clan Campbell. London, *n.d.*, 8vo. The Black Book of Taymouth, by Cosmo Innes. Edinburgh, 1855, 4to. Case of Charles William Campbell claiming to be Earl of Breadalbane, 1864, 4to. The Clan Campbell, by J. H. London, 1871, 8vo. Case, and further case, of Dougal Campbell, M.D., claiming title, etc., of Earl of Annandale, 1844, fol. The House of Argyll, and collateral branches of the Clan Campbell. Glasgow, 1871, 8vo. Claim of John Campbell to be Earl of Breadalbane, Sess. Papers, C of 1867 ; A of 1867-8. Claim of Gavin Campbell to be Earl of Breadalbane, Sess. Papers, B of 1872 ; F of 1877. 'The Spectator,' for 1864, pp. 1357, 1385, 1413, 1442, 1469. Hasted's Kent, i. 373. Herald and Genealogist, iv. 257 ; v. 267. Munro Appellant and Campbell Respondent ; Respondent's Case in House of Lords, 1798. Jacob's Peerage, i. 442. A letter to Mrs. Campbell of Barbreck, containing an account of the Campbells of Barbreck, by F. W. Campbell. Ipswich, 1830, 4to. Burke's Commoners, (of Cessnock,) ii. 359, Landed Gentry, 2, 3, 4, 5, 6 ; (of Barquharrie,) Commoners, ii. 158, Landed Gentry, 2, 3, 4 ; (of Fairfield,) Commoners, ii. 362, Landed Gentry, 2, 3, 4, 5 and supp., 6, 7, 8 ; (of Barbreck,) Commoners, i. 563, Landed Gentry, 2, 5, 6, 8 ; (of Gatcombe,) Commoners, ii. 187 ; (of Auchmannoch,) Commoners, iv. 14, Landed Gentry, 2, 3, 4, 5, 6, 7, 8 ; (of Ormidale,) Landed Gentry, 2 final add., 3, 4, 5, 6, 7, 8 ; (of Monzie,) 2, 3, 4, 5, 6 ; (of Lochnell,) 2 add., 3, 4, 5, 6, 7, 8 ; (of Ardchattan,) 2, 3, 4, 5 ; (of Colgrain,) 3, 4, 5, 6, 7, 8 ; (of Islay,) 2, 3, 4, 5, 6, 7 ; (of Skerrington,) 2, 3, 4, 5, 6, 7, 8 ; (of Jura,) 2, 3, 4, 5, 6, 7, 8 ; (of Sonachan,) 4, 5 ; (of Stonefield,) 4, 5, 6, 7, 8 ; (of Stracathro,) 2 add., 3, 4, 5, 6, 7, 8 ; (of Blythswood,) 5, 6 ; (of Edenwood,) 5, 6, 7 ; (of Ardpatrick,) 5, 6, 7, 8 ; (of Dunoon,) 2, 3, 4, 6, 7, 8, 8 supp., (of Glenfalloch,) 2, 3, 4 ; (of Skipness Castle,) 2, 3 ; (of Inverneil,) 6, 7, 8 ; (of Ballochyle,) 6, 7, 8 ; (of South Hall,) 6, 7, 8 ; (of Tullichewan,) 6, 7, 8 ; (of Woodseat,) 6, 7, 8 ; (of Buscot Park,) 6, 7 ; (of Craigie,) 6, 7, 8 ; (of Treesbank,) 7, 8 ; (of Dunstaffnage,) 8. Burke's Visitation of Seats and Arms, 2nd Series, i. 44. Burke's Royal Descents and Pedigrees of Founders' Kin, 49, 118. George Robertson's Description of Cunninghame, 359. Burke's Royal Families, (London, 1851, 8vo.) ii. 73, 81, 85, 192. Paterson's History of the Co. of Ayr, i. 359, 443 ; ii. 69, 319, 331, 388, 392, 428. Nisbet's Heraldry, ii. app. 174, 221, 238. Douglas's Baronage of Scotland, 57, 61, 537. Paterson's History of Ayr and Wigton, i. 297, 312, 335, 338, 347, 410, 416, 515, 527, 561-72, 600, 607, 610, 655, 684, 692 ; iii. 545. Appendix to fourth Report of Commission on Historical Manuscripts, 470. Caledonia, by Geo. Chalmers, 597. Memoirs of Sir James Campbell, written by himself, (London, 1832, 8vo.) 6. Wood's Douglas's Peerage of Scotland, i. 84, 234 ; ii. 144. Notes and Queries, 2 S. x. 193, 335 ; 3 S. iv. 242, 427 ; vi. 94, 171 ; 6 S. i. 384, 425 ; 7 S. i. 109, 158, 211. The Genealogist, v. 132, 298. Edmondson's Baronagium Genealogicum, v. 504. Brydges' Collins' Peerage. vii. 416 ; viii. 530 ; ix. 371. Foster's Collectanea Genealogica, (MP's Scotland,) 45-62. Burke's Extinct Baronetcies, and p. 618. Nicholls' Account of the Company of Ironmongers, 2nd edn. 536. The Master Masons of Scotland, by R. S. Mylne, at end. Caithness Family History, by John Henderson, 275. Burke's Colonial Gentry, i. 48, 219 ; ii.

844. Alexander Nisbet's Heraldic Plates, 60. New England Register, xxxii. 275. Burke's Family Records, 134. Ontarian Families, by E. M. Chadwick, ii. 5. Northern Notes and Queries, viii. 3. *See* ARGYLE, BREADALBANE, CAMBELL, HOME, COCKBURN-CAMPBELL, HAMILTON-CAMPBELL.

CAMPBELL-DAVYS. Burke's Landed Gentry, 2 add., 4, 5, 6, 7, 8.

CAMPBELL-DOUGLAS. Burke's Landed Gentry, 7.

CAMPBELL-LAMBERT. Burke's Family Records, 369.

CAMPBELL-RENTON. Burke's Landed Gentry, 5, 6, 7, 8.

CAMPERDOWN. (Earls of,) Angus or Forfarshire, by A. J. Warden, 436.

CAMPION. Hasted's Kent, iii. 40. Berry's Sussex Genealogies, 9, 82. Burke's Landed Gentry, 2, 3, 4, 5, 6, 7, 8. Horsfield's History of Lewes, ii. 171. Harleian Society, xiv. 556 ; xv. 134; xlii. 95 ; xliii. 202. Sussex Archæological Collections, x. 34. Surrey Archæological Collections, x.

CAMPTON. Berry's Hampshire Genealogies, 177.

CAMVILE, CAMVILL, or CAMVILLE. Harleian Society, ii. 23. Nichols' History of the County of Leicester, iii. 350. Dugdale's Warwickshire, 847. Hoare's Wiltshire, II. i. 153. Baker's Northampton, i. 694. Banks' Baronies in Fee, i. 148. Banks' Dormant and Extinct Baronage, i. 49, 253. *See* DE CAMVILE.

CANAVAN. O'Hart's Irish Pedigrees, 2nd Series, 147.

CANDLER. Harleian Society, i. 33. Baker's Northampton, ii. 51. Burke's Commoners, i. 105, Landed Gentry, 2, 3, 4, 5.

CANDYSHE. Metcalfe's Visitations of Suffolk, 12.

CANN. Rudder's Gloucestershire, 801. Harleian Society, viii. 338. Wotton's English Baronetage, iii. 381. Burke's Extinct Baronetcies.

CANNAN. Lands and their Owners in Galloway, by P. H. M'Kerlie, iii. 98.

CANNEY. New England Register, v. 452.

CANNING, or CANYNGE. Memorials of the Canynges family, by George Pryce. Bristol, 1854, 8vo. Pedigree of Canning of Foxcote, and Le Marshall of Foxcote, Co. Warwick, [T. P.] 1850. Morant's Essex, ii. 571. Some Account of the Worshipful Company of Grocers, by J. B. Heath, 1st edn., 201, 291. Burke's Commoners, iii. 262, Landed Gentry, 2, 3, 4, 5, 6, 7, 8. Herald and Genealogist, i. 273. Account of the Company of Ironmongers, by John Nicholl, 2nd edn., 545. Dugdale's Warwickshire, 634. Harleian Society, xii. 225 ; xiii. 369. Jordan's History of Enstone, 356. O'Hart's Irish Pedigrees, 2nd Series, 148. The Genealogist, iv. 157. Robert Bell's Life of George Canning, 368. Notes and Queries, 6 S. ii. 364, 431. Burke's Family Records, 137. Dallaway's Antiquities of Bristow, 79, 168.

CANON. Pembrokeshire Pedigrees, 144.

CANT. Shaw's Staffordshire, ii. 222*.

CANTELUPE, CANTALUPE, or CANTILUPE. Historical Notices of the Parish of Withyham, Co. Sussex, by R. W. Sackvill-West, 41. J. H. Hill's History of Market Harborough, 37. Dickinson's History of Southwell, 2nd edn., 314. The Genealogist, New

Series, xiii. 242. Lipscombe's History of the County of Buckingham, i. 176. Bridge's Northamptonshire, by Rev. Peter Whalley, i. 24. Nichols' History of the County of Leicester, ii. 493. Dugdale's Warwickshire, 661, 833. Thoroton's Nottinghamshire, ii. 240, 246. Banks' Baronies in Fee, i. 148; ii. 63. Banks' Dormant and Extinct Baronage, i. 50, 254. *See* DE CANTILUPE.

CANTILLON. Burke's Heraldic Illustrations, 51.

CANTRELL. History of Melbourne, by J. J. Briggs, 2nd edn., 175. Visitations of Berkshire, printed by Sir T. Phillipps, 13. The Genealogist, v. 244. Metcalfe's Visitations of Suffolk, 121. *See* HUBBERSTY.

CANUN. Hunter's Deanery of Doncaster, ii. 231.

CAPEL, CAPLE, or CAPELL. Pedigrees of Capell of How Capel, Dover, Morgan, Arkell, Cox, and Harris [T. P.] 2 folio pages. Jacob's Peerage, i. 560. Morant's Essex, i. 137; ii. 220, 401. Berry's Hertfordshire Genealogies, 1. Visitation of Somerset, printed by Sir Thomas Phillipps, 36. Edmondson's Baronagium Genealogicum, ii. 138. Brydges' Collins' Peerage, iii. 474. History and Description of Cassiobury Park, by John Britton, 29. T. Faulkner's History of Hammersmith, 183. Burke's Landed Gentry, 2, 3, 4, 5. Maclean's History of Trigg Minor, ii. 500. Harleian Society, xi. 20; xiii. 32, 171, 370; xxi. 36; xxii. 36, 113. Clutterbuck's Hertford, i. 243. Wright's Essex, ii. 35. Chauncy's Hertfordshire, 155, 158. Carthew's Hundred of Launditch, Part ii. 479; Part iii. 159. Duncumb's History of the Co. of Hereford, ii. 354, 366. Weaver's Visitation of Herefordshire, 16. Bysshe's Visitation of Essex, edited by J. J. Howard, 21. The Genealogist, New Series, vii. 66. Archæological Journal, xl. 64-79. *See* DE CAPELL.

CAPEN. New England Register, xx. 246.

CAPENHURST. Ormerod's Cheshire, ii. 570.

CAPES. Baker's Northampton, i. 378.

CAPLIN. Memoir of Richard Haines, by C. R. Haines, Table A.

CAPPE. Harleian Society, xxxvii. 188.

CAPPER. Burke's Landed Gentry, 5, 6, 7, 8.

CAPPES. Harleian Society, xxxii. 68.

CAPRON. Burke's Landed Gentry, 2 add., 3, 4, 5, 6, 7, 8.

CARAFA. Notes and Queries, 6 S. xii. 46.

CARAUNTE. Visitatio Comitatus Wiltoniæ, 1623, printed by Sir T. Phillipps. The Genealogist, xii. 21.

CARBERY, or CARBURY. O'Harts Irish Pedigrees, 2nd Series, 148. British Antiquities Revived, by Robert Vaughan. 40. *See* VAUGHAN.

CARBONEL. Page's History of Suffolk, 376.

CARDALE. Genealogy of Henzey, Tyttery, and Tyzack, by H. S. Grazebrook, 55.

CARDEN. Burke's Landed Gentry, (of Barnard,) 5 supp., 6 and supp., 7, 8; (of Fishmoyne,) 8. Ormerod's Cheshire, ii. 669.

CARDEW. Pedigree of Cardew of Truro, [T. P.] 1871, folio page. Hutchinson's History of Cumberland, ii. 449. Nicolson and Burn's Westmorland and Cumberland, ii. 317.

CARDIGAN (Earl of). Burke's Royal Families, (London, 1851, 8vo.) i. 141.

CARDINAL, or CARDINALL. Morant's Essex, i. 442. Burke's Landed Gentry, 3, 4, 5, 6, 7, 8. Harleian Society, xiii. 33, 172, 370. Metcalfe's Visitations of Suffolk, 121.

CARDWELL. Burke's Landed Gentry, 4, 5. Foster's Lancashire Pedigrees. Abram's History of Blackburn, 390.

CARE. Visitation of Gloucestershire, 1569, (Middle Hill, 1854, fol.) 3.

CARÉE. Chronicle of the Family of De Havilland.

CARENT. Collinson's Somerset, ii. 203, 366, 383 ; iii. 207. Hutchin's Dorset, iv. 112.

CARESWELL. Visitation of Devon, edited by F. T. Colby, '42. Visitations of Staffordshire, 1614 and 1663-4. William Salt Society, 71.

CAREW. Pedigree of Carewe of Carew Castle, Co. Pembroke, privately printed by Sir Thos. Phillipps, Bart., double-page folio. Pedigree of Carew of Haccombe, Co. Devon, [T. P.] 1862, single sheet. Collinson's Somerset, iii. 331, 516. Lyson's Environs of London, i. 53.[1] Collectanea Topographica et Genealogica, v. 93. Chronicle of the Family of De Havilland. Dwnn's Visitations of Wales, i. 78, 89. Berry's Surrey Genealogies, 3. Visitation of Cornwall, edited by Sir N. H. Nicolas, 28. Surrey Archæological Collections, i. Tuckett's Devonshire Pedigrees, 121, 124. Burke's Commoners, (of Crowcombe,) i. 266, Landed Gentry, 2, 3, 4, 5, 6, 7, 8 ; and 8, p. 2050 ; (of Ballinamona,) Commoners, iv. 644, Landed Gentry, 2, 3, 4, 5, 6, 7, 8 ; (of Beddington,) Landed Gentry, 2, 3, 4 ; (of Antony,) 6, 7, 8. Harleian Society, vi. 45, 46 ; viii. 263 ; ix. 28, 33 ; xiii. 371 ; xliii. 17, 213. Westcote's Devonshire, edited by G. Oliver and P. Jones, 528. Manning and Bray's Surrey, iii. 523. Burke's Royal Families, (London, 1851, 8vo.) ii. 151. Herald and Genealogist, vii. 19. Maclean's History of Trigg Minor, i. 319 ; ii. 240, 365. Pembrokeshire Pedigrees, 147. Life of Sir Peter Carew, by John Maclean, App. 1. A Complete Parochial History of the County of Cornwall, i. 1, 23 ; iv. 1. An Historical Survey of Cornwall, by C. S. Gilbert, i. 581. Wotton's English Baronetage, i. 231 ; iii. 323 ; iv. 159. Banks' Baronies in Fee, ii. 64. Visitation of Devon, edited by F. T. Colby, 34-41, 124. Betham's Baronetage, ii. 283. Banks' Dormant and Extinct Baronage, iii. 146. Burke's Extinct Baronetcies. Metcalfe's Visitations of Suffolk, 187. The Visitations of Cornwall, edited by J. L. Vivian, 67. Hasted's Kent, (Hund. of Blackheath, by H. H. Drake,) xvii. The Visitations of Devon, by J. L. Vivian, 133-145. The Genealogist, New Series, xviii. 31, 32.

CAREY. Claim of W. F. Carey to the Barony of Hunsdon, Sess. Papers, Feb.—March, 1707. Herald and Genealogist, iv. 33-48, 129-144, 385-398. Morant's Essex, i. 271. Chronicle of the Family of De Havilland. Burke's Landed Gentry, (of Careysville,)

---

[1] A corrected copy of this pedigree was afterwards given to the subscribers to that work.

2 supp., 3, 4, 5 ; (of Rozel,) 2 supp., 3, 4, 5, 6, 7. Raine's History
of North Durham, 30. Westcote's Devonshire, edited by G. Oliver
and P. Jones, 510. Wainwright's Wapentake of Strafford and
Tickhill, 197. Ord's History of Cleveland, 474. Hunter's
Deanery of Doncaster, i. 115. Banks' Dormant and Extinct
Baronage, iii. 383, 519. Visitations of Staffordshire, 1614 and
1663-4, William Salt Society, 72. Gloucestershire Notes and
Queries, ii. 73. The Visitations of Devon, by J. L. Vivian, 150.
See BOLEYNES, CARY.

CARINGTON, or CARRINGTON. Berry's Hertfordshire Genealogies, 124.
Berry's Buckinghamshire Genealogies, 83. Berry's Essex Genea-
logies, 128. Harleian Society, ii. 130, 145 ; xiii. 33, 173 ; xviii. 60.
Nichols' History of the County of Leicester, iii. 29. Ormerod's
Cheshire, i. 544. The Genealogist, New Series, xiii. 101.
Fletcher's Leicestershire Pedigrees and Royal Descents, 126. *See*
CARRINGTON.

CARIQUE. Surrey Archæological Collections, vi. Harleian Society,
xliii. 141.

CARKEREDGE. Berry's Kent Genealogies, 137. Harleian Society,
xlii. 57.

CARLEIL, or CARLEILL. Surtees Society, xxxvi. 115. Burke's Commoners, iii. 587, Landed Gentry, 2, 3, 4, 5. Poulson's Holderness,
i. 277. Harleian Society, xxxvii. 350. *See* CARLISLE.

CARLELE. Surtees' Durham, i. 196.

CARLELL. Berry's Kent Genealogies, 123. Harleian Society, xlii. 30.

CARLETON, or CARLTON. Memorials of the Carletons, by P. A.
Carleton. London, 1869, 4to. Camden Society, lxxix. xii.
Berry's Sussex Genealogies, 232. Cambridgeshire Visitation,
edited by Sir T. Phillipps, 6. Sir T. Phillipps' Topographer,
No. 1, (March, 1821, 8vo.) 17. Visitation of Oxfordshire, 1574,
printed by Sir T. Phillipps, (Middle Hill, fol.) 2. Visitation of
Oxfordshire, 1634, printed by Sir T. Phillipps, (Middle Hill, fol.)
15, 16. Burke's Commoners, iii. 259 ; (of Market Hill,) Landed
Gentry, 2, 3, 4, 5, 6, 7, 8 ; (of Clare,) 4 supp., 5, 6, 8 ; 6 at
p. 1532 ; 7 ; 7 at p. 1749 ; 8 at p. 1177. Foster's Visitations
of Yorkshire, 234. Harleian Society, v. 122 ; xv. 135 ; xli. 59.
Gyll's History of Wraysbury, 95. Hutchinson's History of Cumberland, i. 340. Jefferson's History of Leath Ward, Cumberland,
95. Manning and Bray's Surrey, i. 458*. Thoroton's Nottinghamshire, iii. 414. Plantagenet-Harrison's History of Yorkshire, i. 518.
O'Hart's Irish Pedigrees, 2nd Series, 149. Notes and Queries,
3 S. iii. 295, 379. Brydges' Collins' Peerage, viii. 109. Burke's
Extinct Baronetcies. Metcalfe's Visitations of Northamptonshire,
9. Foster's Visitations of Cumberland and Westmorland, 24.
Robinson of the White House, Appleby, by C. B. Norcliffe, 88.
Parliamentary Memoirs of Fermanagh, by Earl of Belmore, 101.
Nicolson and Burn's Westmorland and Cumberland, ii. 403. The
Genealogist, New Series, xiv. 20.

CARLILLE. Weaver's Visitations of Somerset, 14.

CARLISLE, or CARLILE. The Seize Quartiers of G. W. F. Howard,

7th Earl of Carlisle. Folio sheet. Collections for a History of the Family of Carlisle, by Nichs. Carlisle. London, 1822, 4to. Review of the History of the Family of Carlisle, by T. J. Carlyle. Dumfries, 1881. Burke's Royal Descents and Pedigrees of Founders' Kin, 112. Banks' Dormant and Extinct Baronage, iii. 148. Oliver's History of Antigua, i. 113. Burke's Landed Gentry, 7, 8. *See* CARLEIL.

CARLOS. The Boscobel Tracts, edited by J. Hughes, 2nd edn., 397.

CARLYLE. Journal of the British Archæological Association, ix. 174. Burke's Patrician, iii. 563. Wood's Douglas's Peerage of Scotland, i. 306.

CARLYON. Burke's Commoners, iv. 22, Landed Gentry, 2, 3, 4, 5, 6, 7, 8. Burke's Royal Families, (London, 1851, 8vo.) ii. 48. Burke's Heraldic Illustrations, 18. A Complete Parochial History of the County of Cornwall, i. 65; iv. 119 supp. An Historical Survey of Cornwall, by C..S. Gilbert, ii. 51. Burke's Colonial Gentry, i. 79. Howard's Visitation of England and Wales, ii. 113. Burke's Family Records, 138. The Genealogical Magazine, ii. 457.

CARMARDEN. Harleian Society, xv. 136. History of Chislehurst, by Webb, Miller, and Beckwith, 267.

CARMARTHEN. *See* OSBORN.

CARMICHAEL. Burke's Visitation of Seats and Arms, 2nd Series, i. 44. The Upper Ward of Lanarkshire, by G. V. Irving, ii. 9. Wood's Douglas's Peerage of Scotland, i. 752. Notes and Queries, 3 S. xi. 120, 483; xii. 53; 6 S. vii. 77; x. 350, 396, 477; xi. 12, 58, 133, 212. Foster's Collectanea Genealogica, (MP's Scotland,) 63. Burke's Extinct Baronetcies, 619. Burke's Colonial Gentry, i. 316. Burke's Landed Gentry, 7, 8, 8 supp. Northern Notes and Queries, vii. 55.

CARMICHAEL-FERRALL. Burke's Landed Gentry, 5.

CARMINO, CARMINOW, or CARMYNOWE. Collectanea Topographica et Genealogica, i. 319. Maclean's History of Trigg Minor, i. 317; iii. 158. Polwhele's History of Cornwall, ii. 43. Harleian Society, ix. 33, 296. A Complete Parochial History of the County of Cornwall, i. 1; iii. 286. Weaver's Visitations of Somerset, 31. The Genealogist, New Series, xvii. 170, 246. An Historical Survey of Cornwall, by C. S. Gilbert, ii. 55. The Visitations of Cornwall, edited by J. L. Vivian, 72, 267, 399.

CARMOND. Ashmole's Antiquities of Berkshire, iii. 42.

CARN. Glamorganshire Pedigrees, edited by Sir T. Phillipps, 5, 6. Burke's Commoners, iv. 479, Landed Gentry, 2, 3, 4, 5.

CARNABY. Pedigrees from Visitation of Northumberland, printed by Sir T. Phillipps, (Middle Hill, 1858, fol.) 2. Surtees' Durham, ii. 266. The Genealogist, i. 310; ii. 257. Harleian Society, xvi. 48. Foster's Visitations of Northumberland, 23, 24.

CARNAGIE, CARNEGY, or CARNEGIE. History of the Carnagies, Earls of Southesk, by William Fraser. Edinburgh, 1867, 4to. 2 vols. Case of Sir James Carnegie, of Southesk, Bart., on his claim to be Earl of Southesk, etc., 1848, fol., pp. 30. Supplemental Case of same, Westminster, 1853, fol. Case of Sir James Carnegie on his

claim to the title of Earl of Southesk. Westminster, 1855, fol.
Claim of Sir James Carnegie, of Southesk, Bart., to be Earl of
Southesk, Sess. Papers, 283 of 1847-8 ; 164 of 1854 ; 164 of
1854-5 ; A of 1854-5. Kent's British Banner Displayed, 484.
Burke's Landed Gentry, (of Boysack,) 2 supp., 3, 4, 5, 6 ; (of Lour,)
5, 6, 7, 8 ; (of Seaton House,) 5, 6 ; (of Tarrie,) 7, 8 ; (of Stronvar,)
7, 8. Burke's Royal Families, (London, 1851, 8vo.) ii. 177. Nisbet's
Heraldry, ii. app. 252. Wood's Douglas's Peerage of Scotland, ii.
322, 512. Foster's Collectanea Genealogica, (MP's Scotland,) 64.
CARNARVON (Earl of). Burke's Royal Families, (London, 1851, 8vo.)
ii. 43.
CARNE. *See* STRADLING CARNE.
CARNE. Burke's Landed Gentry, (of Dimland Castle,) 3, 4, 5, 6, 7 ;
(of Penzance,) 4 supp. Genealogies of Morgan and Glamorgan,
by G. T. Clark, 374.
CARNEGIE-ARBUTHNOTT. Burke's Landed Gentry, 7, 8.
CARNEY. O'Hart's Irish Pedigrees, 2nd Series, 150.
CARNSEW. Maclean's History of Trigg Minor, ii. 169, 172. Pol-
whele's History of Cornwall, iv. 112. Harleian Society, ix. 35,
217. A Complete Parochial History of the County of Cornwall,
ii. 363. An Historical Survey of Cornwall, by C. S. Gilbert, ii. 53.
The Visitations of Cornwall, edited by J. L. Vivian, 76, 452.
CARPENDER. Visitation of Gloucester, edited by T. F. Fenwick and
W. C. Metcalfe, 33.
CARPENTER. Burke's Landed Gentry, 2 supp., 3, 4, 5, 6. Visitatio
Comitatus Wiltoniæ, 1623, printed by Sir T. Phillipps. An His-
torical Survey of Cornwall, by C. S. Gilbert, ii. 49. Harleian
Society, xv. 137-139 ; xxi. 243 ; xxxvii. 417. Archdall's Lodge's
Peerage, iii. 88. Visitation of Wiltshire, edited by G. W. Marshall,
39. New England Register, ix. 52. Oliver's History of Antigua,
i. 118. Burke's Family Records, 143.
CARPENTER-GARNIER. Burke's Landed Gentry, 5, 7, 8.
CARPENTIER. Burke's Extinct Baronetcies.
CARR, or CARRE. The History of the Family of Carr, by R. E. Carr.
London, 4to. 3 vols. The Family of Carre of Sleford, Co. Lincoln,
Proceedings of Lincoln Diocesan Architectural Society, 1863, 8vo.
Berry's Sussex Genealogies, 40. Topography and History of
New and Old Sleaford, (Sleaford, 1825, 8vo.) 112. Pedigrees from
Visitation of Northumberland, printed by Sir T. Phillipps, (Middle
Hill, 1858, fol.) 3. Visitation of Gloucestershire, 1569, (Middle
Hill, 1854, fol.) 3. Burke's Commoners, ii. 354, Landed Gentry,
2, 8 ; (of Cavers,) Landed Gentry, 5, 6, 8 ; 6, page 510 ; 7, 7 page
571 ; 8 supp. at p. xi, and 8 at p. 1218. Foster's Yorkshire Families.
Bateson's History of Northumberland, i. 217. Foster's Visitation
of Yorkshire, 500, 602. Hunter's History of the Parish of Sheffield, 439, 503. Surtees' Durham, i. 208, 209. The Genealogist,
i. 306 ; iii. 88, 110, 193, 365, 380 ; iv. 169 ; New Series, vi. 88 ;
viii. 190 ; x. 127. Sleaford, by the Ven. Edward Trollope, 134.
Castles, Mansions, and Manors of Western Sussex, by D. G. C.
Elwes and C. J. Robinson, 161. Abram's History of Blackburn,

392. Whitaker's Deanery of Craven, 3rd edn., 162. Eastwood's History of Ecclesfield, 389. Harleian Society, xvi. 49, 50 ; xxi. 37, 224 ; xxxvii, 140 ; xxxviii. 513, 634, 791. Notes and Queries, 1 S. vii. 408, 512, 558 ; viii. 327, 423 ; xi. 240. Burke's Extinct Baronetcies. Registers of Ecclesfield, by A. S. Gatty, 8. Foster's Visitations of Northumberland, 26-28. Foster's Visitations of Durham, 65. Howard's Visitation of England and Wales, vii. 121. *See* KER.

CARR-ELLISON. Burke's Landed Gentry, 8. Howard's Visitation of England and Wales, vi. 159.

CARR-LLOYD. Burke's Landed Gentry, 6, 7.

CARREG. History of Powys Fadog, by J. Y. W. Lloyd, vi. 234.

CARRELL, or CARILL. Berry's Sussex Genealogies, 358. Dallaway's Sussex, i. 190. Harleian Society, xliii. 88.

CARRIC, or CARRICK. Claim of the Earl of Carrick to Vote at Elections of Irish Peers, Sess. Papers, 269 of 1857-8. Some Account of the Earldom of Carric, by Dr. A. Carrick, with Notices of the Earldom after it came into the families of Bruce and Stewart, by James Maidment. Edinburgh, 1857, 8vo. Morant's Essex, ii. 62. Paterson's History of Ayr and Wigton, ii. 356. Wood's Douglas's Peerage of Scotland, i. 314, 324.

CARRINGTON. Morant's Essex, ii. 113. Surtees Society, xxxvi. 66. Visitation of Norfolk, published by Norfolk Archæological Society, i. 233. Burke's Landed Gentry, 5, 6, 7. Foster's Visitations of Yorkshire, 500. Harleian Society, xii. 71. Annals of the English Benedictines of Ghent, 187. *See* CARINGTON.

CARRINGTON-SMITH. Burke's Commoners, iv. 740.

CARRIQUE. Harleian Society, xv. 140.

CARROLL. Burke's Landed Gentry, (of Ashford,) 4, 5, 6, 7, 8 ; (of Ballynure,) 2, 3, 4, 5. Howard's Visitation of Ireland, ii. 83.

CARROW, or CARROWE. Harleian Society, i. 45. Hutchinson's History of Durham, ii. 417. Surtees' Durham, iii. 131.

CARRUTHERS. Burke's Landed Gentry, 5 supp., 6 and supp. ; 7, 8. Annandale Observer, (newspaper,) 5 July, 1878. Fosbrooke's History of Gloucestershire, i. 352. Burke's Colonial Gentry, ii. 517.

CARRYLL. Berry's Sussex Genealogies, 72. *See* CARYL.

CARSEY. Visitation of Norfolk, published by Norfolk Archæological Society, i. 123. The Genealogist, iii. 366. Massingberd's History of Ormsby, 227. Harleian Society, xxxii. 69.

CARSON. Some descents of Carson of Shanroe, County Monaghan, attempted by N. D. and T. W. C. Dublin, 1879, 4to. [This contains pedigrees of Waggett, and Deane.] Burke's Landed Gentry, 5, 6 and supp., 7, 8. Miscellanea Genealogica et Heraldica, New Series, iii. 156. *See* WILSON.

CARSTAIRS, or CARSTARES. Letters and Correspondence of Rev. J. Carstairs, by Rev. Wm. Ferrie, 1846, 8vo. Alexander Nisbet's Heraldic Plates, 138. Walter Wood's East Neuk of Fife, 297.

CARSWELL. Harleian Society, xv. 141. The Visitations of Devon, by J. L. Vivian, 146.

CART. Harleian Society, xxxvii. 284.

CARTARET, or CARTERET. Kent's British Banner Displayed, 743. A
History of the Noble Family of Carteret, by Arthur Collins, 1756,
8vo. Burke's Authorized Arms, 156. Burke's Extinct Baronetcies.
An Historical Survey of Cornwall, by C. S. Gilbert, i. 476.
Edmondson's Baronagium Genealogicum, iii. 208 ; vi. 109. Banks'
Dormant and Extinct Baronage, iii. 156. Visitation of Gloucester,
edited by T. F. Fenwick and W. C. Metcalfe, 34. *See* DE CARTERET.
CARTER. Hasted's Kent, iii. 182. Morant's Essex, ii. 411. Berry's
Kent Genealogies, 414. Surtees Society, xxxvi. 363. Burke's
Landed Gentry, 2, 3, 4, 5, 6, 7, 8, 8 supp. Harleian Society, viii.
65 ; ix. 36 ; xv. 142 ; xix. 90, 165 ; xxii. 37. Lipscombe's
History of the County of Buckingham, i. 133. Manning and
Bray's Surrey, i. 15. The Visitations of Cornwall, edited by
J. L. Vivian, 78. New England Register, xvii. 51. Metcalfe's
Visitations of Northamptonshire, 76. The Irish Builder, xxxv.
148. Burke's Family Records, 143.
CARTHEW. Burke's Landed Gentry, 2 supp. and add., 3, 4, 5, 6, 7, 8.
A Complete Parochial History of the County of Cornwall, i. 387 ;
ii. 241 ; iv. 119 supp. An Historical Survey of Cornwall, by
C. S. Gilbert, ii. 52. The Visitations of Cornwall, by J. L. Vivian,
574. Howard's Visitation of England and Wales, viii. 6.
CARTHEW-YORSTOUN. Burke's Landed Gentry, 5, 6, 7, 8.
CARTLEGE. Harleian Society, xxxix. 984.
CARTUTHER. The Visitations of Cornwall, edited by J. L. Vivian, 25.
CARTWRIGHT. Burke's Commoners, (of Aynhoe,) ii. 437, Landed
Gentry, 2, 3, 4, 5, 6, 7, 8 ; (of Norwell,) Commoners, ii. 435,
Landed Gentry, 2, 3, 4, 6, 7 ; (of Ixworth Abbey,) 2 ; (of Lough-
borough,) 8 supp. Foster's Visitations of Yorkshire, 501. Harleian
Society, iv. 109 ; xv. 143 ; xxi. 38. Bridge's Northamptonshire,
by Rev. Peter Whalley, i. 137. Hutchins' Dorset, ii. 99. Baker's
Northampton, i. 548. Thoroton's Nottinghamshire, iii. 173.
Doncaster Charities, by Charles Jackson, 87. The Genealogist,
vi. 142. Visitation of Gloucester, edited by T. F. Fenwick and
W. C. Metcalfe, 34. Burke's Colonial Gentry, i. 180. Notts and
Derbyshire Notes and Queries, iv. 71, 125. Ontarian Families,
by E. M. Cartwright, i. 63.
CARUS. Visitation of Westmoreland, 1615, (London, 1853,) 11.
Chetham Society, lxxxi. 60 ; lxxxiv. 69. The Tyldesley Diary,
edited by J. Gillow and A. Hewitson, 72. Foster's Visitations of
Cumberland and Westmorland, 25.
CARUS-WILSON. Genealogical Memoirs of the Carus-Wilson Family.
By H. Carus-Wilson. Hove, 1899, 8vo. Burke's Landed Gentry,
5, 6, 7, 8.
CARVELL. Burke's Colonial Gentry, ii. 607.
CARVER. Harleian Society, xxxviii. 207, 347 ; xxxix. 838.
CARVETH. A Complete Parochial History of the County of Cornwall,
iv. 119 supp.
CARVICK. Burke's Landed Gentry, 2.
CARVILL. Foster's Visitations of Yorkshire, 501. W. Wheater's
History of Sherburn and Cawood, 320.

CARWARDINE. Berry's Essex Genealogies, 114. Harleian Society, xiv. 667. Metcalfe's Visitation of Worcester, 1683, 28. *See* CAWARDEN.

CARWITHAM, CARWYTHAM, or CARWITHEN. Harleian Society, vi. 337. Westcote's Devonshire, edited by G. Oliver and P. Jones, 552. Visitation of Devon, edited by F. T. Colby, 42. The Visitations of Devon, by J. L. Vivian, 147.

CARY. Records of the Family of Cary, Viscts. Falkland, by C. J. Robinson, M.A. Westminster, 1864, 8vo. Visitation of Somerset, printed by Sir Thomas Phillipps, 37. Tuckett's Devonshire Pedigrees, 141-145. Burke's Commoners, (of Torr Abbey,) ii. 33, Landed Gentry, 2, 3, 4, 5, 6, 7, 8 ; (of ·Follaton,) Commoners, ii. 38, Landed Gentry, 2, 3, 4, 5, 6, 7, 8 ; (of White Castle,) Landed Gentry, 2 supp., 3, 4, 5 ; (of Munfin,) 4 supp. Harleian Society, vi. 47-51 ; viii. 103 ; ix. 37 ; xi. 20. Visitation of Devon, edited by F. T. Colby, 43. Lipscombe's History of the County of Buckingham, i. 152. Clutterbuck's Hertford, i. 129 ; iii. 181. Burke's Royal Families, (London, 1851, 8vo.) ii. 105. Herald and Genealogist, ii. 341, 344 ; iii. 33, 129 ; vi. 1-32, 477 ; vii. 19 ; viii. 81-128. Westcote's Devonshire, edited by G. Oliver and P. Jones, 507, 509, 510. Thoresby's Ducatus Leodiensis, 178. Wood's Douglas's Peerage of Scotland, i. 566. New England Register, xlix. 401-403. Notes and Queries, 3 S. v. 398, 468, 525 ; vi. 115, 173, 312, 397 ; vii. 117, 170, 203, 424, 466 ; 4 S. i. 273 ; vii. 376 ; 6 S. ix. 413 ; x. 178, 213, 245. The Visitations of Cornwall, edited by J. L. Vivian, 79. Miscellanea Genealogica et Heraldica, 2nd Series, iii. 373. Old Yorkshire, edited by William Smith, New Series, ii. 174 ; iii. 194. Oliver's History of Antigua, i. 125. Fragmenta Genealogica, by F. A. Crisp, i. 20. *See* CAREY.

CARYL, or CARYLL. Manning and Bray's Surrey, ii. 109. Foley's Records of the English Province S. J., iii. 534. A Royal Descent, by T. E. Sharpe, (London, 1875, 4to.) 79. Dallaway's Sussex, i. 190. Castles, Mansions, and Manors of Western Sussex, by D. G. C. Elwes and C. J. Robinson, 253. Harleian Society, xv. 144 ; xxii. 134. Notes and Queries, 3 S. i. 203, 278. Surrey Archæological Collections, x. *See* CARRYLL.

CARYSFORT. Claim of the Earl of Carysfort to Vote at Elections of Irish Peers, Sess. Papers, 212 of 1857, Sess. 2.

CASAMAJOR. Miscellanea Genealogica et Heraldica, New Series, i. 87. Oliver's History of Antigua, ii. 29.

CASANOVA. Notes and Queries, 8 S. viii. 401.

CASBERD. Burke's Landed Gentry, 2.

CASBORNE. Burke's Landed Gentry. 2 supp., 3, 4, 5, 6.

CASE. Burke's Landed Gentry, 2, 3, 4, 5, 7, 8. Chetham Society, lxxxiv. 70. Gregson's Fragments relative to the County of Lancaster, 176. Carthew's Hundred of Launditch, Part iii. 171.

CASEMENT. Burke's Landed Gentry, (of Ballee House,) 4, 5, 6, 7, 8 ; (of Invermore,) 4, 5, 6.

CASE-WALKER. Burke's Landed Gentry, 8.

CASEY. Burke's Landed Gentry, 5. Burke's Colonial Gentry, i. 73.

CASLOCK. Hasted's Kent, ii. 597.

CASON. Chauncy's Hertfordshire, 144. Harleian Society, xxii. 37.

CASS. Burke's Landed Gentry, 3, 4, 5. Burke's Visitation of Seats and Arms, i. 38. Burke's Heraldic Illustrations, 142. Howard's Visitation of England and Wales, i. 114. East Barnet, by F. C. Cass, Part i. 120. Burke's Family Records, 145.

CASSAN. Burke's Commoners, i. 648, Landed Gentry, 2, 3, 4, 5, 6, 7, 8.

CASSELS. Records of the Family of Cassels, by Robt. Cassels. Edinburgh, 1870, 4to. Burke's Colonial Gentry, ii. 465. Ontarian Families, by E. M. Chadwick, i. 26.

CASSEY. Harleian Society, xxi. 244.

CASSIDY. Burke's Landed Gentry, 5, 6, 7, 8.

CASSILLIS. Reports of Claims preferred to the House of Lords in the Cases of the Cassillis, Sutherland, Spynie, and Glencairn Peerages, by James Maidment. Edinburgh, 1840, 8vo. *See* KENNEDY, RUGLEN.

CASTELION. The Genealogist, vi. 136.

CASTELL, or CASTELLO. East Anglian, ii. 171, 272, 282. Blomefield's Norfolk, viii. 47. Cambridgeshire Visitation, edited by Sir T. Phillipps, 7. Visitation of Norfolk, published by Norfolk Archæological Society, i. 12. Carthew's Hundred of Launditch, Part i. 181-186. Dugdale's Warwickshire, 214, 881. Harleian Society, xiii. 371; xxxii. 69; xli. 42, 81. *See* DE CASTELLO.

CASTILLION. Visitations of Berkshire, printed by Sir T. Phillipps, 13. The Genealogist, New Series, xvii. 73, 199, 225.

CASTILTON. Metcalfe's Visitations of Suffolk, 87. Harleian Society, xliii. 60.

CASTLE. Camden Society, xliii. 111. Burke's Landed Gentry, 5 supp., 6 supp., 7. Howard's Visitation of England and Wales, v. 43.

CASTLEFORD. Foster's Visitations of Yorkshire, 344. Whitaker's Loidis and Elmete, 263. History of Ecclesfield, by J. Eastwood, 432. Harleian Society, xxxix. 901.

CASTLEMAN. Visitation of Gloucester, edited by T. F. Fenwick and W. C. Metcalfe, 36.

CASTLE-STEWART. Claim of Lord Castle-Stewart to the Title of Lord Ochiltree, Sess. Papers, April 1790—June 1793.

CASTLETON. Wotton's English Baronetage, i. 239. Burke's Extinct Baronetcies.

CASTON. Metcalfe's Visitations of Suffolk, 122.

CASWALL, or CASWELL. Berry's Essex Genealogies, 33. Burke's Landed Gentry, 3, 4. Cussan's History of Hertfordshire, Parts xi. and xii. 161. Visitation of Middlesex, (Salisbury, 1820, fol.) 22. Harleian Society, xiv. 699. Foster's Visitation of Middlesex, 43.

CATCHER. Harleian Society, xv. 145.

CATELYN. Harleian Society, viii. 161; xix. 11. *See* CATLEYN.

CATER. Ashmole's Antiquities of Berkshire, iii. 286. Harleian Society, ii. 1; viii. 116; xix. 89. Visitations of Berkshire, printed by Sir T. Phillipps, 13. Cyclostyle Pedigrees, by J. J. Green. The Genealogist, New Series, i. 4.

CATERALL, CATTERALL, CATHERAL, or CATHRALL. Fishwick's History of Goosnargh, 150. Foster's Visitations of Yorkshire, 291, 502. Chetham Society, lxxxi. 39 ; lxxxiv. 71 ; cv. 236. Poulson's Holderness, ii. 394. Ormerod's Cheshire, ii. 709. Whitaker's Deanery of Craven, 3rd edn., 163. Harleian Society, xvi. 50. Whitaker's History of Whalley, ii. 22. Croston's edn. of Baines's Lancaster, iii. 350. *See* DE CATTERALL.

CATERICK. Foster's Visitations of Yorkshire, 255. Plantagenet-Harrison's History of Yorkshire, i. 498.

CATESBY. Harleian Society, iii. 33 ; xii. 125, 142. Bridge's Northamptonshire, by Rev. Peter Whalley, i. 16. Dugdale's Warwickshire, 788. Baker's Northampton, i. 244. Metcalfe's Visitations of Northamptonshire, 9, 172.

CATHCART. Burke's Landed Gentry, (of Carbiston,) 2 supp., 3, 4, 5, 6, 7, 8 ; (of Knockdolian,) 2 supp., 3, 4, 5, 6. Lands and their Owners in Galloway, by P. H. M'Kerlie, i. 194. Paterson's History of the Co. of Ayr, i. 304, 306, 329 ; ii. 365. Paterson's History of Ayr and Wigton, i. 218 ; ii. 135, 162, 394. Wood's Douglas's Peerage of Scotland, i. 338. Brydges' Collins' Peerage, vi. 454.

CATLEYN. Blomefield's Norfolk, viii. 31. Metcalfe's Visitation of Northamptonshire, 11, 77. *See* CATELYN.

CATLIN. Pedigree of Catlin of Wyoming, Pennsylvania, [T. P.] 1854, folio page. Howard's Visitation of England and Wales, vi. 33.

CATON. Burke's Commoners, iv. 305, Landed Gentry, 2, 3, 4, 5 supp., 6, 7, 8. Carthew's Hundred of Launditch, Part iii. 467.

CATOR. Burke's Landed Gentry, 3, 4, 5, 6, 7, 8. Howard's Visitation of England and Wales, v. 55.

CAUDLE. Howard's Visitation of England and Wales, viii. 121.

CAULFIELD. Burke's Landed Gentry, (of Donamon Castle,) 2, 3, 4, 5, 6, 7, 8 ; (of Drumcairne,) 2, 3, 4 ; (of Raheenduff,) 2, 3, 4 ; (of Bloomfield,) 2, 3, 4. O'Hart's Irish Pedigrees, 2nd Series, 150. Archdall's Lodge's Peerage, iii. 127.

CAULX. Visitation of Somerset, printed by Sir T. Phillipps, 38. *See* CALZ.

CAURTHYN. Ormerod's Cheshire, ii. 699.

CAUSTON. Bysshe's Visitation of Essex, edited by J. J. Howard, 21.

CAVE. Case of Sarah Otway Cave on her Claim to be Baroness Braye. London, 1836, fol. Additional Case of same. London, 1836, fol. Claim of Sarah Otway Cave, of Stamford Hall, to be Baroness Braye, Sess. Papers, 40 of 1836 ; 91 of 1838 ; 171 of 1839. Collinson's Somerset, iii. 87. Croke's History of the Family of Croke, No. 22. Berry's Buckinghamshire Genealogies, 10. Berry's Surrey Genealogies, 60. Sir Thomas Phillipps' Topographer, No. 1, (March, 1821, 8vo.) 29. Visitation of Oxfordshire, 1574, printed by Sir T. Phillipps, (Middle Hill, fol.) 3. Burke's Landed Gentry, 4, 5, 6, 7, 8. Harleian Society, ii. 120, 122, 125, 133 ; v. 154 ; xvi. 51. Bridge's Northamptonshire, by Rev. Peter Whalley, i. 580. Nichols' History of the County of Leicester, ii. 888 ; iii. 68, 290, 293, 345 ; iv. 359, 371, 420. Baker's Northampton, i. 348. Robinson's Mansions of Herefordshire, 213.

Memoirs of the Family of Chester, by R. E. C. Waters, 73.
Wotton's English Baronetage, ii. 164. Betham's Baronetage, i.
375. Metcalfe's Visitation of Worcester, 1683, 29. F. G. Lee's
History of Thame, 245. Weaver's Visitations of Somerset, 99.
Notes and Queries, 6 S. xii. 90. Associated Architectural Society's
Reports and Papers, xvii. 125. Oxford Historical Society, xix.
37. Metcalfe's Visitations of Northamptonshire, 11. A History
of Banking in Bristol, by C. H. Cave, 224. History of Longridge,
by Tom C. Smith, 73.

CAVE-BROWNE. Howard's Visitations of England and Wales, ix. 21.

CAVE-BROWN-CAVE. History of Longridge, by T. C. Smith, 73.

CAVELL. Maclean's History of Trigg Minor, ii. 157. Harleian
Society, ix. 37. The Visitations of Cornwall, edited by J. L.
Vivian, 81.

CAVENDISH. Memoir of the Family of Cavendish, by W. Kennett.
London, 1708, 8vo. Historical Collections of the Noble Families
of Cavendish, Holles, Vere, Harley, and Ogle, by A. Collins.
London, 1752, fol. The Lives of the Dukes of Devonshire,
descended from Sir William Cavendish, by Joseph Grove. London,
1764, 8vo. Pedigree of Cavendish. Broadside. Privately printed
by C. G. S. Foljambe, circa 1891. The Great Governing Families
of England, i. 137. Berry's Genealogical Peerage, 48. Jacob's
Peerage, i. 240, 254. Morant's Essex, ii. 323. Gentleman's Magazine, 1835, i. 611. S. Glover's Peak Guide, edited by Thos. Noble,
53. Glover's History of Derbyshire, ii. 140, 276, (123, 252).
Burke's Landed Gentry, 5, 6, 7, 8. Munford's Analysis of Domesday Book of Co. Norfolk, 47. Hodgson's Northumberland, I. ii.
386. Wright's Essex, i. 564. Archæologia, xi. 52, 62. Whitaker's
Deanery of Craven, 3rd edn., 310. Pilkington's View of Derbyshire, ii. 252, 441. Edmondson's Baronagium Genealogicum, i.
35. Brydges' Collins' Peerage, i. 302. Banks' Baronies in Fee, i.
359. Betham's Baronetage, iii. 256. Banks' Dormant and Extinct
Baronage, iii. 547. Jewitt's Reliquary, xxi. 184; xxii. 160.
Howard's Visitation of England and Wales, i. 129. The Irish
Builder, xxix. 127; xxxv. 257. The Genealogist, New Series,
vii. 66.

CAVERSALL. William Salt Society, New Series, ii. 154.

CAWARDEN. Burke's Commoners, iii. 441. Shaw's Staffordshire, i.
180. See CARWARDINE.

CAWLEY. Berry's Sussex Genealogies, 284. Dallaway's Sussex, i.
app. to Chichester.

CAWOOD. Harleian Society, xvi. 369. W. Wheater's History of
Sherburn and Cawood, 311.

CAWOODLEY. Visitation of Devon, edited by F. T. Colby, 44. See
CALWODELEY.

CAWTON. Foster's Visitations of Yorkshire, 502.

CAY. Burke's Commoners, i. 384, Landed Gentry, 2, 3, 4.

CAYLEY. Surtees Society, xxxvi. 196. Burke's Landed Gentry, 2, 3,
4, 5, 6, 7, 8. Burke's Royal Families, (London, 1851, 8vo.) i.
164. Foster's Yorkshire Pedigrees. Harleian Society, viii. 72.

Wotton's English Baronetage, iii. 274. Betham's Baronetage, ii. 250. Burke's Colonial Gentry, ii. 750. Ontarian Families, by E. M. Chadwick, i. 51.

CECIL. Burleigh, The Life of Wm. Cecil Lord Burleigh, etc., by W. H. Charlton, M.A., (Stamford, 1847, 8vo.) 1. The Great Governing Families of England, ii. 61. Jacob's Peerage, i. 491, 496. De Scales' Peerage Evidence, 492. Drummond's History of Noble British Families, i. and ii. The Life of Cecil Lord Burleigh, with Memoirs of the Family of Cecil, by A. Collins. London, 1732, 8vo. Berry's Hertfordshire Genealogies, 208. A Guide to Burleigh House, by T. Blore, 7. Clutterbuck's Hertford, ii. 339. Wright's History of Rutland, 63. Blore's Rutland, 24, 25, 80, 82. Bridge's Northamptonshire, by Rev. Peter Whalley, ii. 592. Manning and Bray's Surrey, iii. 274. Chauncy's Hertfordshire, 308. Miscellanea Genealogica et Heraldica, New Series, iii. 286. Notes and Queries, 2 S. i. 437 ; 6 S. vii. 384 ; xi. 69. Edmondson's Baronagium Genealogicum, ii. 104, 106. Brydges' Collins' Peerage, ii. 484, 582. The King of Arms, 53. Weaver's Visitation of Herefordshire, 17. Metcalfe's Visitations of Northamptonshire, 78. Harleian Society, xxxii. 275. *See* SITSILT.

CELY, or CEELYE. Harleian Society, ix. 38 ; xliii. 56. The Visitations of Cornwall, edited by J. L. Vivian, 82.

CENAN AB COEL GODHEBAWG. Dwnn's Visitations of Wales, ii. 243.

CENCI. Notes and Queries, 5 S. ix. 1, 21, 62, 141.

CERISEAUX. *See* DE CERISIS.

CERJAT. Miscellanea Genealogica et Heraldica, New Series, iv. 222.

CERNE. Wiltshire Archæological Magazine, iii. 178. The Genealogist, New Series, xiii. 248.

CERVINGTON. Hoare's Wiltshire, III. v. 27. *See* SERVINGTON.

CHABNOR. Weaver's Visitation of Herefordshire, 84.

CHAD. Burke's Landed Gentry, 4, 5, 6, 7, 8. Betham's Baronetage, iv. 241. *See* SCOTT-CHAD.

CHADBOURNE. New England Register, xiii. 339.

CHADDOCK, or CHATTOCK. Miscellanea Genealogica et Heraldica, New Series, i. 134. Warwickshire Antiquarian Magazine, edited by John Featherston, 457. Chetham Society, lxxxiv. 72.

CHADERTON, CHADDERTON, or CHATTERTON. Gentleman's Magazine, 1854, ii. 460. Miscellanea Genealogica et Heraldica, i. 160. Surtees Society. xxxvi. 314. W. Paver's Pedigrees of Families of the City of York, 12. Visitation of Sussex, 1570, printed by Sir T. Phillipps, (Middle Hill, fol.) 2. History of the Ancient Chapel of Blackley, by Rev. J. Booker, 147. Chetham Society, lxxxii. 5 ; xcv. 55. Notes and Queries, 1 S. 6, 273, 423 ; viii. 564; xi. 231. Betham's Baronetage, v. 477. Cambridgeshire Visitation, edited by Sir T. Phillipps, 8.

CHADWELL. Harleian Society, xx. 25.

CHADWICK. A Genealogical Account of the Families of Chadwick, of Chadwick, by Joseph Howard. Manchester, 1840, 4to. Reports on the Estate of Sir Andrew Chadwick, by J. O. Chadwick. London, 1881, 4to. Whitaker's History of Whalley, 441.

Glover's History of Derbyshire, ii. 220, (189). Burke's Commoners, (of New Hall,) iii. 438, 444, Landed Gentry, 2, 3, 4, 5, 6, 7, 8 ; (of Pudleston Court,) Commoners, iv. 456, Landed Gentry, 3, 4, 5, 6, 7 ; (of Swinton Hall,) iv. 456, Landed Gentry, 2, 8 ; (of Daresbury Hall,) Landed Gentry, 3, 4, 5, 6, 7, 8 ; (of High Bank,) 3, 4, 5, 6, 7 ; (of Ballinard,) 5 supp., 6, 7, 8. Foster's Lancashire Pedigrees. Chetham Society, lxxxii. 110 ; lxxxiv. 73, 74. Shaw's Staffordshire, i. 182. Burke's Royal Families, (London, 1851, 8vo.) i. 160. Visitation of Staffordshire, 1663-4, printed by Sir T. Phillipps, 3. Corry's History of Lancashire, ii. 542-651, and app. Baines' History of the Co. of Lancaster, ii. 655 ; Croston's edn. iii. 84. Visitations of Staffordshire, 1614 and 1663-4, William Salt Society, 73. Fishwick's History of Rochdale, 384. Burke's Colonial Gentry, ii. 586. Howard's Visitation of England and Wales, v. 134. Ontarian Families, by E. M. Chadwick, ii. 119.

CHAFIN. Visitation of Wiltshire, 1677, printed by Sir T. Phillipps, (Middle Hill, 1854, fol.). .Visitatio Comitatus Wiltoniæ, 1623, printed by Sir T. Phillipps. Hutchins' Dorset, iii. 565. Burke's Commoners, iii. 670. Visitation of Wiltshire, edited by G. W. Marshall, 51. The Genealogist, xii. 21.

CHAFY. Pedigree of the Family of Chafy of Chaffecombe, Co. Somerset, etc. Broadside, circa 1877. Burke's Landed Gentry, 5 and supp., 6, 7, 8. Howard's Visitation of England and Wales, vii. 110.

CHAFYN-GROVE. Burke's Landed Gentry, 8.

CHAKER. Lipscombe's History of the County of Buckingham, ii. 192.

CHALDECOTT. Hutchins' Dorset, i. 591. Hoare's Wiltshire, IV. ii. 32. Harleian Society, xx. 26.

CHALFHUNT. Hasted's Kent, ii. 695.

CHALKE. Visitation of Somerset, printed by Sir T. Phillipps, 39. Harleian Society, xi. 22.

CHALLEN. Burke's Commoners, i. 646, Landed Gentry, 2, 3, 4. Dallaway's Sussex, II. ii. 323.

CHALLENOR, CHALLONOR, CHALLONER, CHALONER, or CHALENER. Visitation of Sussex, 1570, printed by Sir T. Phillipps, (Middle Hill, fol.) 3. Berry's Sussex Genealogies, 73, 345. Surtees Society, xxxvi. 201. Burke's Landed Gentry, (of Portnall,) 2, 3, 4, 5 ; (of Guisborough,) 2, 3, 4, 5 ; (of Kingsfort,) 3, 4, 5. Foster's Yorkshire Pedigrees. Lipscombe's History of the County of Buckingham, iii. 80. Horsfield's History of Lewes, ii. 246. Graves' History of Cleveland, 412. Kent's British Banner Displayed, 192. Surtees Society, xxxvi. 201. Harleian Society, viii. 282 ; xxxviii. 684. Burke's Landed Gentry, 6. Ord's History of Cleveland, 221. Burke's Extinct Baronetcies. History of Powys Fadog, by J. Y. W. Lloyd, iv. 347. Sussex Archæological Collections, xlv. 128.

CHALLONS, or CHALONS. Maclean's History of Trigg Minor, ii. 42. Westcote's Devonshire, edited by G. Oliver and P. Jones, 614. The Visitations of Cornwall, edited by J. L. Vivian, 83. Weaver's Visitations of Somerset, 99. The Genealogist, New Series, xvi. 41.

CHALMER, or CHALMERS. Paterson's History of the Co. of Ayr, i. 323. Burke's Landed Gentry, 5 at p. 1321; 6 at p. 1530; 7, 7 at p. 1746; 8. Nisbet's Heraldry, ii. app. 20, 121. Paterson's History of Ayr and Wigton, i. 228, 633. Notes and Queries, 2 S. xii. 157. Memoirs of Thomas Chalmers, D.D., by Wm. Hanna, LL.D., i. 2. Burke's Landed Gentry, 2, 3, 4, 5, 6.

CHAMBER. Surtees Society, xxxvi. 366. Visitation of Durham, 1615, (Sunderland, 1820. folio) 28. Harleian Society, vii. 5; xiii. 372; xxi. 38; xxii. 137. Nichols' History of the County of Leicester, iii. 969. Surtees' Durham, ii. 55. Foster's Visitations of Durham, 67. Foster's Visitations of Cumberland and Westmorland, 26. Bysshe's Visitation of Essex, edited by J. J. Howard, 21.

CHAMBERLAIN, CHAMBERLAINE, CHAMBERLEN, CHAMBERLAYN, CHAMBERLAYNE, CHAMBERLEYNE, or CHAMBERLYN. Burke's Extinct Baronetcies. Rudder's Gloucestershire, 705. Morant's Essex, i. 342; ii. 261, 534. Sir Thos. Phillipps' Topographer, No. 1, (March, 1821, 8vo.) 44. Cambridgeshire Visitation, edited by Sir T. Phillipps, 8. Berry's Hampshire Genealogies, 337. Visitation of Norfolk, published by Norfolk Archæological Society, i. 92. Visitation of Suffolk, edited by J. J. Howard, ii. 211. Visitation of Oxfordshire, 1634, printed by Sir T. Phillipps, (Middle Hill, fol.) 16. Burke's Landed Gentry, (of Maugersbury,) 2 and corr., 3, 4, 5, 6, 7, 8; (of Stoney Thorpe,) 2, 3, 4, 5, 6, 7, 8; (of Cranbury Park,) 2, 3, 4, 5, 6, 7, 8; (of Dee House,) 2 supp. at p. 252. Miscellanea Genealogica et Heraldica, i. 24; 3rd Series, ii. 278. Burke's Royal Families, (London, 1851, 8vo.) i. 198. Foster's Visitations of Yorkshire, 176. Harleian Society, ii. 137; v. 235, 253, 271; viii. 50; xii. 259; xv. 146, 148; xvi. 52; xxxii. 70; xli. 41. Visitation of Warwickshire, 1619, published with Warwickshire Antiquarian Magazine, 88. J. H. Hill's History of Market Harborough, 128. Collectanea Topographica et Genealogica, iii. 95. Burke's Visitation of Seats and Arms, i. 63. Visitation of Berkshire, printed by Sir T. Phillipps, 14. Nichols' History of the County of Leicester, ii. 881; iii. 475. Clutterbuck's Hertford, i. 376. Hampshire Visitations, printed by Sir T. Phillipps, 12. Notes and Queries, 1 S. ii. 326; 3 S. vi. 151, 403. Wotton's English Baronetage, ii. 374. The Irish Builder, xxix. 251, 264. Visitation of Gloucester, edited by T. F. Fenwick and W. C. Metcalfe, 37. The Chamberlens and the Midwifery Forceps, by J. H. Aveling, 1. Aldred's History of Turville, 34. The Genealogist, New Series, xii. 140.

CHAMBERS. Hasted's Kent, iii. 25. Berry's Kent Genealogies, 360. Visitations of Middlesex, (Salisbury, 1820, fol.) 32. Burke's Commoners, (of Bredgar House,) ii. 179, Landed Gentry, 2; (of Hafod,) Landed Gentry, 4, 5; (of Fox Hall,) 3, 4; (of Loughveagh,) 2 supp.; (of Clough House,) 6 supp., 7, 8. Foster's Visitations of Yorkshire, 503. Harleian Society, ii. 51; iv. 157; xv. 149; xxii. 38; xxviii. 97. Burke's Heraldic Illustrations, 140. Jewitt's Reliquary, xiv. 63, 126. W. Robinson's History of

Hackney, i. 299. Burke's Royal Descents and Pedigrees of Founders' Kin, 20. Nichol's History of the County of Leicester, iii. 1029. Memoir of Gabriel Goodman, by R. Newcome, App. S. Weaver's Visitation of Herefordshire, 85. Foster's Visitation of Middlesex, 60. Notes and Queries, 6 S., xii. 256. Burke's Colonial Gentry, ii. 765.

CHAMBRE, or CHAMBRES. Burke's Commoners, ii. xv. 240 ; (of Hawthorn Hill,) Landed Gentry, 2, 3, 4, 5, 6, 7, 8 ; (of Halhead Hall,) 2 add. J. H. Hill's History of Market Harborough, 285. Nichols' History of the County of Leicester, ii. 831. Baker's Northampton, i. 66. Records of Denbigh and its Lordship, by John Williams, 167. History of Powys Fadog, by J. Y. W. Lloyd, v. 385. Nicolson and Burn's Westmorland and Cumberland, i. 84. *See* CHAMBERS.

CHAMIER. Burke's Visitation of Seats and Arms, i. 33. *See* DESCHAMPS.

CHAMOND. Harleian Society, ix. 40. An Historical Survey of Cornwall, by C. S. Gilbert, ii. 65. The Visitations of Cornwall, edited by J. L. Vivian, 84.

CHAMPAGNE, CHAMPAIGNE, CHAMPAIN, or CHAMPAYNE. Burton's Description of Leicestershire, 272. Hutchins' Dorset, iii. 160. Historical Account of the Church of Stoke Golding, by T. L. Walker, 22. Nichols' History of the County of Leicester, iv. 1006. *See* BATEMAN-CHAMPAIGN.

CHAMPANTI. Harleian Society, viii. 219. *See* CIAMPANTI.

CHAMPERNON, or CHAMPERNOWNE. Tuckett's Devonshire Pedigrees, 129, 131. History of Clyst St. George, by Rev. H. T. Ellacombe, 65. Burke's Commoners, ii. 271, Landed Gentry, 3, 4, 5, 6, 7, 8. Harleian Society, vi. 53. Maclean's History of Trigg Minor, i. 554 ; ii. 241. Nichols' History of the County of Leicester, ii. 132. An Historical Survey of Cornwall, by C. S. Gilbert, ii. 60. Visitation of Devon, edited by F. T. Colby, 45. The Visitations of Devon, by J. L. Vivian, 160. Hasted's Kent, (Hund. of Blackheath, by H. H. Drake,) xvii. The Genealogist, New Series, ix. 210.

CHAMPION. Harleian Society, i. 3 ; ii. 53 ; xliii. 82. Berry's Hampshire Genealogies, 311. Visitation of London, in Transactions of London and Middlesex Archæological Society, 8. Visitation of Berkshire, printed by Sir Thos. Phillipps, 14. The Genealogist, v. 244. Surrey Archæological Collections, x.

CHAMPION-DE CRESPIGNY. Burke's Royal Families, (London, 1851, 8vo.) i. 84. Burke's Heraldic Illustrations, 124.

CHAMPLEY. Foster's Yorkshire Pedigrees.

CHAMPLIN. New England Register, xiv. 24.

CHAMPNEYS, CHAMPNES, or CHAMPNEIS. Hasted's Kent, i. 127 ; iii. 326. Visitation of Somerset, printed by Sir Thos. Phillipps, 40. Berry's Kent Genealogies, 40. Burke's Commoners, iii. 555, Landed Gentry, 2. Harleian Society, vi. 52 ; xi. 21. Hutchins' Dorset, ii. 616. Betham's Baronetage, iii. 347. Burke's Extinct Baronetcies, Supp. The Visitations of Devon, by J. L. Vivian,

166. Miscellanea Genealogica et Heraldica, 2nd Series, ii. 169. Weaver's Visitations of Somerset, 100.

CHANCE. Chance of Bromsgrove and of Birmingham, by J. F. Chance. London, 1892, 8vo. Harleian Society, xxxvii. 127. Howard's Visitation of England and Wales, iii. 61-70. Burke's Family Records, 148.

CHANCELLER, or CHANCELLOR. Nisbet's Heraldry, ii. app. 84. The Upper Ward of Lanarkshire, by G. V. Irving, i. 439. Burke's Landed Gentry, 5 supp., 6 and supp., 7, 8. Hutchinson's History of Durham, iii. xxiv. Biggar and the House of Fleming, by W. Hunter, 2nd edn., 600. *See* CHAUNCELER.

CHANCEUX. Morant's Essex, i. 314. *See* CHAUNCEUX.

CHANDLER. Berry's Hampshire Genealogies, 52. Surtees' Durham, i. cxxi. Cyclostyle Pedigrees, by J. J. Green. New England Register, xxxiii. 68. Church Bells of Buckinghamshire, by A. H. Cocks, 238. *See* CHAUNDLER.

CHANDOS. A letter relative to the Barony of Chandos, by Sir N. H. Nicolas, 8vo. Rudder's Gloucestershire, 718. Papers on the Chandos Peerage, *n. d.*, fol. Review of the Chandos Peerage Case, by G. F. Beltz. London, 1834, 8vo. Fosbrooke's History of Gloucestershire, i. 266 ; ii. 356. Pilkington's View of Derbyshire, ii. 114. Brydges' Collins' Peerage, vi. 704. Banks' Dormant and Extinct Baronage, i. 256. Cooke's Continuation of Duncumb's Hereford, (Hund. of Grimsworth,) Part ii. 171. Miscellanea Genealogica et Heraldica, 2nd Series, iii. 350. *See* BUCKINGHAM, BRYDGES.

CHANDOS-POLE. Burke's Royal Families, (London, 1851, 8vo.) ii. 198. Burke's Landed Gentry, 2, 3, 4, 5, 6, 7, 8.

CHANON. Harleian Society, vi. 53. The Visitations of Devon, by J. L. Vivian, 167.

CHANTRELL. Harleian Society, xviii. 61.

CHANU. *See* CHENEY.

CHANWORTH. Berry's Buckinghamshire Genealogies, 21.

CHAPLIN, CHAPLEYN, or CHAPLYN. Pedigree of Chaplin of Geldeston, co. Norfolk, [T. P.] 1860. Burke's Landed Gentry, (of Blankney,) 2, 3, 4, 5, 7, 8 ; (of Tathwell Hall,) 2 add., 3, 4, 5, 6. Harleian Society, viii. 221. Morant's Essex, ii. 365. Burke's Extinct Baronetcies. Foster's Account of Families Descended from Francis Fox, 20. Metcalfe's Visitations of Northamptonshire, 80.

CHAPMAN. Hasted's Kent, ii. 513. Berry's Sussex Genealogies, 88. Cambridgeshire Visitation, edited by Sir T. Phillipps, 8. Berry's Kent Genealogies, 98. Visitation of Norfolk, published by Norfolk Archæological Society, i. 94. Burke's Landed Gentry, (of Whitby,) 2 supp., 3, 4, 5, 6, 7, 8 ; (of Hill End,) 6, 7, 8. Foster's Yorkshire Pedigrees. Miscellanea Genealogica et Heraldica, New Series, i. 6. Bibliotheca Topographica Britannica, vii. Parts i. and ii. 360*. Harleian Society, ix. 40 ; xv. 150 ; xxii. 4 ; xxxii. 72 ; xli. 83, 87. Burke's Visitation of Seats and Arms, 2nd Series, i. 17. Burke's Heraldic Illustrations, 27. Chauncy's Hertfordshire, 210. Wotton's English Baronetage, iv. 196. Metcalfe's

Visitations of Suffolk, 122. Burke's Extinct Baronetcies. The
Visitations of Cornwall, edited by J. L. Vivian, 85, 86. Burke's
Colonial Gentry, ii. 658. Burke's Family Records, 153.
CHAPPEL, or CHAPPELL. Visitation of Somerset, printed by Sir T.
Phillipps, 41. Harleian Society, xi. 21; xv. 152. History of
Barnsley, by Rowland Jackson, 65. The Visitations of Devon,
by J. L. Vivian, 169, 170.
CHARD. Harleian Society, xv. 153.
CHARDIN. Burke's Extinct Baronetcies. Wotton's English Baronet-
age, iv. 192.
CHARK. Harleian Society, xv. 154.
CHARLEMAGNE. Gregson's Fragments relative to the County of Lan-
caster, 57.
CHARLES. Dwnn's Visitations of Wales, i. 112. Westcote's Devon-
shire, edited by G. Oliver and P. Jones, 541. Page's History of
Suffolk, 110. Plantagenet-Harrison's History of Yorkshire, i. 308.
Visitation of Devon, edited by F. T. Colby, 48. The Visitations
of Devon, by J. L. Vivian, 168.
CHARLESWORTH. Burke's Landed Gentry, (of Chapelthorpe,) 3, 4,
5, 6, 7, 8; (of Lofthouse,) 8.
CHARLETON, or CHARLTON. Burke's Landed Gentry, (of Hesleyside,)
2, 3, 4, 5, 6, 7, 8; (of Apley Castle,) 2, 3, 4, 5, 6; (of Chilwell,)
2, 3, 4, 5 and supp., 6, 7, 8; (of Wytheford Hall,) 2; (of Ludford,) 2, 3. Burke's Heraldic Illustrations, 76. Visitation of
Derbyshire, 1663-4, (Middle Hill, 1854, fol.) 2. Genealogist, iii.
157; New Series, vii. 67. Harleian Society, xv. 155, 156; xxviii.
100-110. Wotton's English Baronetage, iv. 13. Burke's Extinct
Baronetcies. Account of the Guildhall of London, by J. E. Price,
116.
CHARLEVILLE. Claim of the Rt. Hon. C. W. G., Earl of Charleville,
to vote at elections of Irish Peers, Sess. Papers, 198 of 1852-3.
CHARLEY. Burke's Landed Gentry, (of Finaghey House,) 4, 5, 6, 7,
8; (of Seymour Hill,) 4, 5, 6, 7, 8.
CHARMAN. Gage's History of Thingoe Hundred, Suffolk, 75. Memoir
of Richard Haines, by C. R. Haines.
CHARNEL, CHARNELS, or CHARNELLS. Burton's Description of
Leicestershire, 92, 177. Nichols' History of the County of
Leicester, ii. 295; iii. 1047*, 1049*; iv. 984*. Harleian Society,
ii. 122; xii. 53; xxxix. 1016. Dugdale's Warwickshire, 26,
119.
CHARNOCK. Burke's Landed Gentry, 2. Chetham Society, lxxxi. 65,
76; lxxxii. 8, 104. Harleian Society, xv. 156; xix. 12, 92. See
CHERNOCK.
CHARRON. Hodgson's Northumberland, II. ii. 260. Surtees' Durham,
ii. 225. Plantagenet-Harrison's History of Yorkshire, i. 167.
CHARTERS, or CHARTERIS. Nisbet's Heraldry, ii. app. 142. Douglas's
Baronage of Scotland, 150. Burke's Landed Gentry, 7, 8.
CHARTON. Eyton's Antiquities of Shropshire, ix. 319.
CHASE. Berry's Hertfordshire Genealogies, 25. Account of the
Mayo and Elton families, by C. H. Mayo, 157. New England

Register, i. 68 ; x. 45. Howard's Visitation of England and Wales, v. 74.

CHASSEREAU. Miscellanea Genealogica et Heraldica, New Series, iv. 149.

CHASTELIN. Harleian Society, xiii. 226.

CHASTILLON. The Genealogist, New Series, xiv. 250 ; xviii. 27.

CHATFEILD, or CHATFIELD. Berry's Sussex Genealogies, 5. Visitation of Sussex, 1570, printed by Sir T. Phillipps, (Middle Hill, fol.) 3. Dallaway's Sussex, i. 69. History of Ditchling, by Henry Cheal, at end.

CHATOR. The Genealogist, iii. 366.

CHATTAN. See MACKINTOSH.

CHATTERTON. Antiquarian Magazine, iv. 196. New Facts relating to the Chatterton Family, by William George. Bristol, 1883, 8vo. Harleian Society, xli. 93. See CHADERTON.

CHATTOCK. Antiquities, etc., by Christopher Chattock. Birmingham, 1884, 4to. The Genealogical Magazine, i. 491. See CHADDOCK.

CHAUCER. Plate at commencement of Speght's edn. of Chaucer's Works, 1602, folio. The Athenæum, No. 2779, 165. Hasted's Kent, (Hund. of Blackheath, by H. H. Drake,) 47. Oxford Historical Society, xxiv. 354.

CHAUNCELER. Surtees' Durham, iii. 329. See CHANCELLOR.

CHAUNCEUX. Baker's Northampton, i. 224. See CHANCEUX.

CHAUNCEY, or CHAUNCY. Visitation of Norfolk, published by Norfolk Archæological Society, i. 113. Burke's Landed Gentry, 2 supp., 3, 4. Harleian Society, viii. 353 ; xxii. 4, 38 ; xxxii. 72. Bridge's Northamptonshire, by Rev. Peter Whalley, i. 119. Clutterbuck's Hertford, ii. 400. Baker's Northampton, i. 494. Chauncy's Hertfordshire, 60, 189. Banks' Baronies in Fee, ii. 61. Miscellanea Genealogica et Heraldica, 2nd Series, i. 21. Metcalfe's Visitations of Northamptonshire, 12. New England Register, x. 251, 323 ; xi. 148.

CHAUNDLER. Hampshire Visitations, printed by Sir T. Phillipps, 12. Harleian Society, xv. 157. See CHANDLER.

CHAUNTERELL, or CHAUNTRELL. Hutchins' Dorset, i. 667. Ormerod's Cheshire, ii. 775.

CHAWNER. Burke's Landed Gentry, 2, 3, 4, 5, 6, 7, 8.

CHAWORTH. The Tyndale Pedigree, by B. W. Greenfield. Foster's Visitations of Yorkshire, 503. Harleian Society, iv. 123; viii. 179; xxxvii. 349. Hunter's Deanery of Doncaster, i. 141. Account of Beauchief Abbey, in No. 3 of Nichols' Miscellaneous Antiquities, 110. A Royal Descent, by T. E. Sharpe, (London, 1875, 4to.) 13. Baker's Northampton, ii. 239. Thoroton's Nottinghamshire, i. 198. Banks' Baronies in Fee, i. 151. Banks' Dormant and Extinct Baronage, i. 263. Genealogies of Morgan and Glamorgan, by G. T. Clark, 372.

CHAYTOR. Surtees Society, xxxvi. 302. Burke's Commoners, ii. 139, Landed Gentry, 5, 6, 7, 8. Foster's Yorkshire Pedigrees. Foster's Visitations of Yorkshire, 414. A Royal Descent, by T. E. Sharpe, (London, 1875, 4to.) 51. Whitaker's History of Richmondshire,

i. 240. History of Darlington, by W. Hylton Dyer Longstaffe, not paged, and lix.-lxxvi. Hutchinson's History of Durham, ii. 327. Surtees' Durham, iv. 111. Burke's Extinct Baronetcies. Foster's Visitations of Durham, 69. *See* ALLAN, CHEYTOR.

CHEALE. Castles, Mansions, and Manors of Western Sussex, by D. G. C. Elwes and C. J. Robinson, 95.

CHEALES. Burke's Landed Gentry, 4, 8. Burke's Family Records, 155.

CHEAPE. Burke's Landed Gentry, 6, 7, 8. Douglas's Baronage of Scotland, 575.

CHEARNLEY. Burke's Landed Gentry, 6 and supp., 7, 8.

CHEATLE. *See* CHETLE.

CHECKFORD. Hutchin's Dorset, i. 633. Harleian Society, xx. 27.

CHECKLAND. Burke's Landed Gentry, 6, 7.

CHECKLEY. New England Register, ii. 349.

CHEDLE. Ormerod's Cheshire, iii. 622. The Genealogist, New Series, xiii. 102.

CHEDYOK. Hoare's Wiltshire, III. i. 3. *See* CHIDIOCK.

CHEEK, CHEEKE, or CHEKE. Morant's Essex, i. 61. Ashmole's Antiquities of Berkshire, iii. 318. Visitation of Somerset, printed by Sir T. Phillipps, 42. Berry's Hampshire Genealogies, 98. Berry's Berkshire Genealogies, 43. Harleian Society, xi. 21 ; xiii. 91, 176, 373. Hampshire Visitations, printed by Sir T. Phillipps, 12. Wright's Essex, ii. 430. Page's History of Suffolk, 513. Metcalfe's Visitations of Suffolk 13, 187. Notes and Queries, 4 S. xi. 165, 223, 533. Hasted's Kent, (Hund. of Blackheath, by H. H. Drake,) xxii.

CHEERE. Betham's Baronetage, iii. 340. Notes and Queries, 4 S. vi. 525. Burke's Extinct Baronetcies.

CHEESE. Burke's Landed Gentry, 2, 3, 4.

CHEESMENT-SEVERN. Burke's Landed Gentry, 2, 3, 4.

CHEEVER. New England Register, xxxiii. 164 ; xxxvi. 305 ; xxxviii. 170.

CHEEVERS. Burke's Landed Gentry, 2 supp., 3.

CHELMICK. Harleian Society, xxviii. 110.

CHELREY. Clutterbuck's Hertford, iii. 86.

CHELWORTH. Visitation of Somerset, printed by Sir Thomas Phillipps, 43.

CHENDUIT. Baker's Northampton, i. 649. *See* CHEYNDUIT.

CHENEVIX-TRENCH. Howard's Visitation of Ireland, ii. 1.

CHENEY. T. Willement's Historical Sketch of Davington, 17. Collinson's Somerset, i. 244 ; ii. 375. Jewitt's Reliquary, xi. 115. Gough's Sepulchral Monuments, ii. 375. Morant's Essex, ii. 121. Hasted's Kent, ii. 661; iii. 469. Berry's Buckinghamshire Genealogies, 21. Berry's Kent Genealogies, 125. Burke's Landed Gentry, (of Badger Hall,) 3, 4, 5, 6 ; (of Gaddesby,) 4, 5, 6, 7, 8 ; (of Monyash,) 2. Foster's Visitations of Yorkshire, 148. Topographical Collections of John Aubrey, edited by J. E. Jackson, 401. Visitatio Comitatus Wiltoniæ, 1623, printed by Sir T. Phillipps. Baker's Northampton, i. 714. Bibliotheca Topographica Britannica, i. Part i. 38. Visitation of Devon, edited by

F. T. Colby, 48. Banks' Dormant and Extinct Baronage, i. 264.
Ormerod's Cheshire, 490. The Visitations of Devon, by J. L.
Vivian, 171. Harleian Society, xix. 12, 91 ; xxxviii. 697 ; xli.
118 ; xlii. 43. Harvey's Hundred of Willey, 304. Fletcher's
Leicestershire Pedigrees and Royal Descents, 196. The Genea-
logist, xii. 22. *See* CHEYNE.
CHENOUTH. Harleian Society, ix. 41. The Visitations of Cornwall,
edited by J. L. Vivian, 88.
CHEPSTOW (Lords of). Journal of British Archæological Association,
x. 265.
CHERLECOTE. Dugdale's Warwickshire, 507.
CHERLETON. Collections by the Powys-land Club, i. 259, 266, 365.
Banks' Baronies in Fee, i. 153. Banks' Dormant and Extinct
Baronage, ii. 85.
CHERNOCK. Burke's Commoners, ii. 104. Lipscombe's History of
the County of Buckingham, i. 132. Wotton's English Baronetage,
iii. 292. Burke's Extinct Baronetcies. *See* CHARNOCK.
CHERRY. Berry's Berkshire Genealogies, 72. Burke's Landed
Gentry, (of Denford,) 2, 3, 4, 5, 6, 7, 8 ; (of Buckland,) 2, 3, 4.
History of the Hundred of Bray, by Charles Kerry, 64. Collec-
tanea Topographica et Genealogica, iii. 158. Surrey Archæological
Collections, vi. Burke's Family Records, 156. Harleian Society,
xliii. 145.
CHESELDEN, CHESELDON, CHESELTON, or CHESILDEN. Harleian
Society, ii. 20, 107 ; iii. 21. Wright's History of Rutland, 24.
Nichols' History of the County of Leicester, iii. 19 ; iv. 408.
Metcalfe's Visitations of Northamptonshire, 174.
CHESENHALL, or CHESNALL. Chetham Society, lxxxi. 71. Harleian
Society, viii. 247. *See* CHISENHALL.
CHESHULL. Harleian Society, xiv. 557. *See* CHISHULL.
CHESLEY. New England Register, v. 205, 454.
CHESLYN. Collectanea Topographica et Genealogica, iii. 314.
Nichols' History of the County of Leicester, iii. 864.
CHESTER (Earldom of). Journal of British Archæological Association,
vii. 123. Jewitt's Reliquary, ix. 80. Collectanea Topographica
et Genealogica, ii. 249. Miscellanea Genealogica et Heraldica,
New Series, i. 412. Baker's Northampton, i. 121. Ormerod's
Cheshire, i. 48, 167. A defence of Amicia, daughter of Hugh
Cyvelock, Earl of Chester, against Sir Peter Leycester's declara-
tion of her illegitimacy, by Sir Thomas Mainwaring, Bart. London,
1673, 12mo. [A long list of works on this celebrated controversy
will be found in Sims' Guide to the Genealogist, Topographer, and
Antiquary, p. 250.] History of Repton, by Robert Bigsby, 1.
Lancashire and Cheshire Historic Society, ii. 212 ; iv. 88. Banks'
Dormant and Extinct Baronage, i. 210. Harleian Society, xviii. 1 ;
xxi. 275.
CHESTER. Genealogical Memoirs of the extinct family of Chester of
Chicheley, by R. E. C. Waters. London, 1878, 4to., 2 vols. Genea-
logical Memoirs of the families of Chester, descended from Henry
Chester, and of the families of Astry, by R. E. C. Waters. London,

1879, 4to. Genealogical Notes of the Families of Chester of Blaby, etc., by R. E. Chester Waters. Leicester, 1886, 8vo. Leicestershire Architectural Society, vi. 176. New England Register, xvi. 136 ; xxii. 338. Oliver's History of Antigua, i. 126. Harleian Society, i. 1 ; ii. 138 ; viii. 16 ; xiii. 374 ; xv. 158 ; xix. 165 ; xxi. 39 ; xxii. 39. Clutterbuck's Hertford, iii. 363. Berry's Buckinghamshire Genealogies, 10 - 15. Berry's Hertfordshire Genealogies, 82. Visitation of London in Transactions of the London and Middlesex Archæological Society, 2. Burke's Commoners, (of Bush Hall,) ii. 17, Landed Gentry, 2, 3, 4 ; (of Chicheley Hall,) Landed Gentry, 3, 4, 5, 6, 7, 8 ; (of Poyle,) 6, 7, 8. Burke's Royal Families, (London, 1851, 8vo.) ii. 68. Herald and Genealogist, vi. 265. Gage's History of Thingoe Hundred, Suffolk, 391. The Archæological Mine, by A. J. Dunkin, i. 92. Nichols' History of the County of Leicester, iv. 52. Cussan's History of Hertfordshire, Parts xi. and xii. 7. Chauncy's Hertfordshire, 91. D. Royce's History of Stow on the Wold. Dugdale's Warwickshire, 469, 1083. Fosbrooke's History of Gloucestershire, i. 489. Wotton's English Baronetage, i. 368. Burke's Extinct Baronetcies.

CHESTERFIELD. Case on behalf of George Philip Stanhope, claiming to be Earl of Chesterfield. London, 1873, fol. Claim of George Philip Stanhope to be Earl of Chesterfield, Sess. Papers, E of 1873.

CHESTON. Metcalfe's Visitations of Suffolk, 123.

CHESWICK. Raine's History of North Durham, 228.

CHETHAM. Jewitt's Reliquary, ix. 107, 220. Visitation of Suffolke, edited by J. J. Howard, ii. 59. History of the Ancient Chapel of Blackley, by Rev. J. Booker, 148, 155, 204. Chetham Society, lxxxii. 87 ; lxxxiv. 75-77. Baines' History of the County of Lancaster, ii. 395 ; Croston's edn., ii. 230. Harleian Society, xv. 158 ; xxxviii. 579, 583. Notes and Queries, 1 S. xi. 182. Metcalfe's Visitations of Suffolk, 13.

CHETHAM-STRODE. Burke's Commoners, ii. 117, Landed Gentry, 2, 3, 4, 5, 6, 7, 8.

CHETILTON. Harleian Society, xxviii. 73.

CHETLE. Metcalfe's Visitation of Worcester, 1683, 31.

CHETTINGE. Metcalfe's Visitations of Suffolk, 14, 123.

CHETWIN, CHETWINDE, or CHETWYND. The Chetwynds of Ingestre, by H. E. Chetwynd-Stapleton. London, 1892, 8vo. Dugdale's Warwickshire, 101. Miscellanea Genealogica et Heraldica, New Series, iii. 317. Harleian Society, xiii. 22. Archdall's Lodge's Peerage, v. 148. Betham's Baronetage, iv. 270. Visitations of Staffordshire, 1614 and 1663-4, William Salt Society, 76.

CHETWODE, or CHETWOOD. Case of J. Chetwood claiming the title of Baron de Wohul. Burke's Landed Gentry, 2, 3, 4, 5, 6, 7. Burke's Royal Families, (London, 1851, 8vo.) ii. 197. Bibliotheca Topographica Britannica, iv. Part v. 46. Lipscombe's History of the County of Buckingham, iii. 2. Visitation of Staffordshire, 1663-4, printed by Sir Thos. Phillipps, 3. Bridge's Northamptonshire, by Rev. Peter Whalley, i. 217. Baker's Northampton,

i. 739. Ormerod's Cheshire, i. 662. Wotton's English Baronetage, iv. 82. Betham's Baronetage, iii. 121. The Genealogist, vii. 121. Harleian Society, xviii. 62; xix. 59. Miscellanea Genealogica et Heraldica, 2nd Series, i. 69, 85. Visitations of Staffordshire, 1614 and 1663-4, William Salt Society, 74. Oxford Historical Society, xxiv. 328.

CHEVERCOURT. Nichols' History of the County of Leicester, ii. 396.

CHEVEREL. Nichols' History of the County of Leicester, iii. 510. Hutchins' Dorset, i. 414. The Genealogist, New Series, ii. 224.

CHEVERS. Burke's Landed Gentry, 4, 5, 6, 7, 8.

CHEW. Abrams' History of Blackburn, 442.

CHEWITT. Ontarian Families, by E. M. Chadwick, ii. 78. See CHUTE.

CHEYNDUIT. Maclean's History of Trigg Minor, i. 541. See CHENDUIT.

CHEYNE, or CHEYNEY. Miscellanea Genealogica et Heraldica, ii. 134. Collectanea Topographica et Genealogica, i. 314, 409. Herald and Genealogist, iii. 290. Poulson's Holderness, ii. 495. Bridges' Northamptonshire, by Rev. Peter Whalley, i. 204, 348. Westcote's Devonshire, edited by G. Oliver and P. Jones, 518. Hoare's Wiltshire, III. i. 3. Clutterbuck's Hertford, i. 133. Baker's Northampton, i. 714. Sussex Archæological Collections, xxv. 108. Fosbrooke's History of Gloucestershire, ii. 222. Records of Buckinghamshire, ii. 128. Annals of Peterhead, by P. Buchan, 61. Wood's Douglas's Peerage of Scotland, ii. 310. The Genealogist, vii. 172. Notes and Queries, 7 S. x 223, 348, 441, 496. See CHENEY.

CHEYTOR. Visitation of Durham, 1575, (Newcastle, 1820, fol.) 30. Visitation of Durham, 1615, (Sunderland, 1820, fol.) 34. See CHAYTOR.

CHIBBORNE. Morant's Essex, ii. 177. Harleian Society, xiii. 374.

CHIBNALL. Harvey's Hundred of Willey, 283. Metcalfe's Visitations of Northamptonshire, 81. Harleian Society, xix. 16.

CHICHELE, CHICHLEY, or CHICHELEY. Stemmata Chicheleana, by Dr. Buckler. Oxford, 1765, 4to. Supplement to the Stemmata Chicheleana. Oxford, 1775, 4to. Hasted's Kent, i. 44, 54. The Topographer, (London, 1789-91, 8vo.) iii. 70. History of the Colleges and Halls of Oxford, by Anthony A'Wood, edited by John Gutch, 259. Bridges' Northamptonshire, by Rev. Peter Whalley, ii. 179. Cambridgeshire Visitation, edited by Sir T. Phillipps, 9. Harleian Society, viii. 234 ; xiv. 735 ; xli. 33 ; xliii. 13. Hasted's Kent, (Hund. of Blackheath, by H. H. Drake,) 219.

CHICHESTER. History of the Family of Chichester, by Sir A. P. Bruce Chichester, Bart. London, 1871, 4to. Berry's Sussex Genealogies, 6. Burke's Landed Gentry, (of Hall,) 2, 3, 4, 5, 6, 7, 8 ; (of Calverleigh,) 8. Burke's Royal Families, (London, 1851, 8vo.) ii. 209. History of Carrickfergus, by Saml. M'Skimin, 2nd edn. 363, etc. Harleian Society, vi. 55, 56; xx. 27. Herald and Genealogist, vii. 174, 276. Shaw's Staffordshire, i. 368, 374. Westcote's Devonshire, edited by G. Oliver and P. Jones, 604,

607, 608, 609. Foley's Records of the English Province S. J., iv. 646. G. Benn's History of Belfast, 680. Notes and Queries, 2 S. iv. 169, 195, 210, 335. Archdall's Lodge's Peerage, i. 314. Brydges' Collins' Peerage, viii. 177. Wotton's English Baronetage, ii. 226. Visitation of Devon, edited by F. T. Colby, 15, 50. Betham's Baronetage, i. 425. Devonshire Notes and Notelets, by Sir W. R. Drake, 225-378. The Visitations of Devon, by J. L. Vivian, 172-184, 750.

CHIDIOCK. Hutchins' Dorset, ii. 257. Banks' Baronies in Fee, i. 210. *See* CHEDYOK.

CHILCOT, or CHILCOTT. Visitation of Somerset, printed by Sir T. Phillipps, 44. Visitation of Middlesex, (Salisbury, 1820, fol.) 12. Harleian Society, xi. 22. Maclean's History of Trigg Minor, iii. 265, 299. An Historical Survey of Cornwall, by C. S. Gilbert, ii. 63. Notes and Queries, 1 S. iii. 38, 73, 212. Foster's Visitation of Middlesex, 2.

CHILD, or CHILDE. English Merchants, by H. R. Fox Bourne, i. 332. Morant's Essex, i. 30. Nash's Worcestershire, i. 99. Burke's Commoners, (of Bigelly House,) iii. 692, Landed Gentry, 2, 3, 4, 5, 6, 7 ; (of Kinlet,) Commoners, iii. 195, Landed Gentry, 2, 3, 4, 5, 6, 8 ; (of Newfield,) 2, 3, 4. Harleian Society, viii. 139, 285, 424 ; xii. 205 ; xv. 159 ; xix. 92 ; xx. 28 ; xxii. 138 ; xxvii. 36 ; xliii. 210. Visitation of Warwickshire, 1619, published with Warwickshire Antiquarian Magazine, 112. The Borough of Stoke-upon-Trent, by John Ward, 87. Clutterbuck's Hertford, i. 171. Jordan's History of Enstone, 353. Wotton's English Baronetage, iii. 714. Betham's Baronetage, iii. 71. Burke's Extinct Baronetcies. Surrey Archæological Collections, x.

CHILDE-PEMBERTON. Burke's Landed Gentry, 3, 4, 5, 6, 7.

CHILDERS. Hunter's Deanery of Doncaster, i. 65. *See* WALBANKE-CHILDERS.

CHINN. *See* CHEYNE.

CHINNERY. Burke's Landed Gentry, 6, 7, 8.

CHIPMAN. New England Register, xv. 79.

CHIPPELEGH. The Genealogist, New Series, ix. 80.

CHIPPENHAM. Weaver's Visitation of Herefordshire, 19.

CHIPPINGDALE. Harleian Society, ii. 157. Nichols' History of the County of Leicester, iii. 278.

CHISENHALL. Burke's Landed Gentry, 2 supp. Chetham Society, lxxxii. 24 ; lxxxiv. 78. *See* CHESENHALL.

CHISHENHALE-MARSH. Howard's Visitation of England and Wales, iv. 6.

CHISHOLM, or CHISHOLME. History of the Chisholms, by A. Mackenzie, 1891, 8vo. Burke's Colonial Gentry, ii. 497. Malcolm's Memoir of the House of Drummond, 117. Burke's Landed Gentry, (of Erchless Castle,) 2, 3, 4, 5, 6, 7, 8 ; (of that Ilk,) 4, 5, 6, 7, 8.

CHISHULL. Harleian Society, xix. 93. *See* CHESHULL.

CHISLEDON. The Visitations of Cornwall, edited by J. L. Vivian, 35.

CHISWELL. Morant's Essex, ii. 562.

CHITTOKE. Metcalfe's Visitations of Suffolk, 88.

CHITTY. Sussex Archæological Collections, xli. 108.

CHIVER, or CHIVERS. Visitatio Comitatus Wiltoniæ, 1623, printed by Sir T. Phillipps. Duchetiana, by Sir G. F. Duckett, 2nd edn., 235. Visitation of Wiltshire, edited by G. W. Marshall, 37.

CHIVERTON. Harleian Society, viii. 176 ; ix. 42 ; xv. 160. The Visitations of Cornwall, edited by J. L. Vivian, 87.

CHOATE. New England Register, xv. 293.

CHOKE, CHOKKE, CHOKES, or CHOLKE. Genealogical Notes on Family of 'Choke, by F. Brown. Newbury, 1882, 8vo. Collinson's Somerset, ii. 292, 434. Visitation of Berkshire, printed by Sir T. Phillipps, 14. The Genealogist, v. 245; New Series, i. 5 ; vii. 250. Baker's Northampton, ii. 273. Harleian Society, xi. 22. Dallaway's Antiquities of Bristow, 163.

CHOLMLEY, CHOLMELEY, CHOLMONDELEY, or CHOLMUNDELEY. Miscellanea Genealogica et Heraldica, ii. 218. Memoir of Sir Hugh Cholmley, Knt., with some account of his family, 1787, 4to. Burke's Landed Gentry, (of Brandsby,) 2, 3, 4, 5, 6, 7, 8 ; (of Whitby,) 2, 3, 4 ; (of Condover,) 7, 8. Foster's Yorkshire Pedigrees. Foster's Visitations of Yorkshire, 219, 221. Harleian Society, vi. 57 ; xv. 160 ; xvi. 52 ; xviii. 63 ; xliii. 127. Turnor's History of Town and Soke of Grantham, 152. Hunter's Deanery of Doncaster, ii. 454. Ormerod's Cheshire, i. 672 ; ii. 157, 637 ; iii. 400. Surtees Society, xli. 21. Surrey Archæological Collections, v. Boothroyd's History of Pontefract, 275. Edmondson's Baronagium Genealogicum, ii. 185. Archdall's Lodge's Peerage, v. 54. Brydges' Collins' Peerage, iv. 16. Burke's Extinct Baronetcies. Visitation of Staffordshire, (Willm. Salt Soc.) 62. The Visitations of Devon, edited by J. L. Vivian, 185. The Genealogist, New Series, xiii. 101 ; xv. 221.

CHOLWILL. Harleian Society, vi. 58. The Visitations of Devon, by J. L. Vivian, 187.

CHORLEY. Chetham Society, lxxxi. 72 ; lxxxii. 48, 121 ; lxxxiv. 80-82. Foster's Lancashire Pedigrees. Harleian Society, xxxvii. 170.

CHOWNE. Hasted's Kent, ii. 241. Berry's Sussex Genealogies, 133. Berry's Kent Genealogies, 85. Burke's Landed Gentry, 3, 4. Horsfield's History of Lewes, ii. 7. Harleian Society, xlii. 27.

CHRISTIAN. Burke's Landed Gentry, 2, 3, 4, 5, 6, 7, 8. J. H. Hill's History of Market Harborough, 37. Hutchinson's History of Cumberland, ii. 146. Nichols' History of the County of Leicester, ii. 494. Burke's Colonial Gentry, ii. 826. Oliver's History of Antigua, i. 134.

CHRISTIE. Genealogical Memoirs of the Scottish House of Christie, by Rev. C. Rogers, London, 1878, 8vo. Burke's Landed Gentry, (of Langcliffe,) 7, 8 ; (of Melbourne Hall,) 7 ; (of Stenton,) 7 ; (of Durie,) 2 supp., 3, 4, 5, 6, 7, 8 ; (of Preston Deanery,) 5, 6 and supp., 7, 8. Walter Wood's East Neuk of Fife, 306.

CHRISTIE, or CHRISTY. Burke's Commoners, iv. 364, Landed Gentry, 2, 3, 4, 5, 6, 7, 8. Howard's Visitation of England and Wales, ii. 125.

CHRISTMAS. Burke's Landed Gentry, 3, 4, 7. Harleian Society, xv. 162.

CHRISTOPHER. Topographer and Genealogist, ii. 110, 555. Burke's Landed Gentry, 2, 3, 4, 5, 8. Metcalfe's Visitation of Worcester, 1683, 32.

CHRISTOPHER-NISBET-HAMILTON. Burke's Landed Gentry, 3, 4, 5, 6.

CHUBB. An Historical Survey of Cornwall, by C. S. Gilbert, ii. 62. Miscellanea Genealogica et Heraldica, 2nd Series, ii. 188.

CHUDLEIGH. Harleian Society, vi. 59. Westcote's Devonshire, edited by G. Oliver and P. Jones, 462. Hutchins' Dorset, iv. 4. Wotton's English Baronetage, i. 526. Visitation of Devon, edited by F. T. Colby, 52. Burke's Extinct Baronetcies. The Genealogist, New Series, ii. 296. Weaver's Visitations of Somerset, 15. The Visitations of Devon, by J. L. Vivian, 189.

CHUNE. Harleian Society, xxii. 40.

CHURCH. Harleian Society, xiii. 177, 375 ; xxviii. 112. James Hall's History of Nantwich, 446. Jewers' Wells Cathedral, 276. New England Register, xi. 154. The Genealogist, New Series, xiii. 219. Records and Recollections, by A. H. Church, 53.

CHURCHAR. Berry's Sussex Genealogies, 48. Dallaway's Sussex, II. i. 359.

CHURCHILL. Hasted's Kent, iv. 4. Burke's Landed Gentry, 5, 6, 7, 8. Lipscombe's History of the County of Buckingham. i. 563. Hutchins' Dorset, ii. 417 ; 2nd edition, iii. 325 ; 3rd edn., iv. 469. Hoare's Wiltshire, I. ii. 253. Clutterbuck's Hertford, i. 217. Baker's Northampton, i. 198. Foster's Account of Families descended from Francis Fox, 25. Wood's Douglas's Peerage of Scotland, i. 349. Banks' Dormant and Extinct Baronage, iii. 505. Harleian Society, xx. 28. New England Register, xxxiv. 301.

CHURCHMAN. Harleian Society, xv. 163.

CHUTE. Berry's Hampshire Genealogies, 117. Berry's Kent Genealogies, 172, 491. Burke's Commoners, iii. 42, Landed Gentry, 2, 3, 4, 5, 6, 7, 8. Harleian Society, viii. 91 ; xv. 163 ; xlii. 96. Topographer, (London, 1789-91, 8vo.) i. 56. Hampshire Visitations, printed by Sir T. Phillipps, 13. Burke's Extinct Baronetcies. New England Register, xiii. 123. Archæologia Cantiana, xviii. 55. See WIGGETT-CHUTE, CHEWITT.

CHYNOWETH. See CHENOUTH.

CIAMPANTI. Berry's Hampshire Genealogies, 233. Hampshire Visitations, printed by Sir T. Phillipps, 13. See CHAMPANTI.

CIBBER. Baker's Northampton, i. 356.

CIL SANT. Poetical Works of Lewis Glyn Cothi, (Oxford, 1837,) 297.

CIOCHES. Baker's Northampton, ii. 273.

CLAN-DONALD. Monro's Description of the Western Isles of Scotland, (Edinburgh, 1805,) 38.

CLANCHY. Burke's Landed Gentry, 4, 5, 7.

CLANCY. O'Hart's Irish Pedigrees, 2nd Series, 53, 104.

CLANMORRIS. Claim of Lord Clanmorris to Vote at Elections of Irish Peers, Sess. Papers, 17 of 1859, Sess. 1.

CLANNA-RORY. A History of the Clanna Rory, or Rudicians, by R. F. Cronnelly. Dublin, 1864, 8vo.

CLANRICARDE. Burke's Royal Families, (London, 1851, 8vo.) i. 123.

CLANRONALD. Vindication of the Clanronald of Glengarry, with Remarks as to the Descent of the Family who style themselves of Clanronald. Edinburgh, 1821, 8vo.

CLAP. New England Register, vi. 373; vii. 163, 270, 325; xiv. 275; xv. 225.

CLAPCOTT. Burke's Landed Gentry, 4, 5.

CLAPHAM. Gentleman's Magazine, 1853, ii. 384. Surtees Society, xxxvi. 43. Burke's Landed Gentry, 2, 3, 4. Foster's Yorkshire Pedigrees. Foster's Visitations of Yorkshire, 12. Harleian Society, vi. 59; viii. 67; xii. 367; xv. 164; xvi. 54. Thoresby's Ducatus Leodiensis, 218. Visitation of Warwickshire, 1619, published with Warwickshire Antiquarian Magazine, 140. Poulson's Holderness, ii. 42. Foster's Pedigree of the Forsters and Fosters, Part ii. 41. Pedigree of Wilson of High Wray, etc., by Joseph Foster, 86. The Visitations of Devon, by J. L. Vivian, 191. Metcalfe's Visitations of Northamptonshire, 13, 14. Yorkshire Genealogist, i. 189, 224. Old Yorkshire, ed. by Wm. Smith, i. 219. Pedigree of Wilson, by S. B. Foster, 152.

CLARE. A Small Specimen of the Many Mistakes in Sir Wm. Dugdale's Baronage. London, 1730-8, 8vo. Strigulensia, by George Ormerod, 62. Berry's Hampshire Genealogies, 125. Lipscombe's History of the County of Buckingham, i. 200. Hutchins' Dorset, iii. 462. Manning and Bray's Surrey, i. 220; ii. 90, 299. Clutterbuck's Hertford, iii. 225. Banks' Dormant and Extinct Baronage, iii. 179. Metcalfe's Visitation of Worcester, 1683, 33. Harleian Society, xxvii. 37; xxviii. 113. Fletcher's Leicestershire Pedigrees and Royal Descents, 59. Journal of the British Archæological Association, xviii. 272; xx. 270; xxvi. 150. See DE CLARE.

CLARELL, or CLAREL. Foster's Yorkshire Pedigrees. Hunter's Deanery of Doncaster, ii. 53. The Gresleys of Drakelowe, by F. Madan, 245.

CLARENAULX. Burton's Description of Leicestershire, 99. See CLERVAUX.

CLARENCE. Claim of Wm. Henry, Duke of Clarence, to Vote at Elections of Irish Peers, Sess. Papers, 1805.

CLARGES. Burke's Extinct Baronetcies. Wotton's English Baronetage, iii. 569. Betham's Baronetage, ii. 431.

CLARK. Berry's Kent Genealogies, 7. Visitation of Somerset, printed by Sir T. Phillipps, 45. Burke's Commoners, (of Belford Hall,) i. 596, Landed Gentry, 2, 3, 4, 5, 6, 7, 8; (of Buckland Toussaints,) Landed Gentry, 2, 3, 4, 5, 6, 7, 8; (of Largantogher,) 4, 5, 6, 7, 8; (of Tal-y-Garn,) 5, 6, 7, 8; (of Speddoch,) 5, 6, 7, 8; (of Frimhurst,) 4; (of Bellefield House,) 6 supp., 7, 8. Harleian Society, viii. 56, 246; xi. 23; xii. 199; xl. 1269. Burke's Royal Descents and Pedigrees of Founders' Kin, 123. Life of Joseph Clark, by H. E. Clark, 1. The Genealogist, New Series, vii. 68. Pedigree of the Family of Powell, by Edgar Powell, 93. New

England Register, xxxiii. 19. Burke's Colonial Gentry, ii. 514.
Annals of Smith of Balby, by H. E. Smith, 113. *See* CLERK.
CLARKE. Pedigree of Clarke of Bridwell House, Co. Devon, [T. P.],
1863, single sheet. Pedigree of Clarke of Ardington, Co. Berks,
[T. P.], single sheet. Miscellanea Genealogica et Heraldica, ii.
237. Morant's Essex, ii. 459. Berry's Kent Genealogies, 131.
Burke's Commoners, (of Welton Place,) iv. 254, Landed Gentry,
2, 3, 4, 5, 6, 7, 8 ; (of Hyde Hall,) Commoners, ii. 189, Landed
Gentry, 2, 3, 4, 5 ; (of Ardington,) Commoners, i. 110, Landed
Gentry, 2 ; (of Comrie Castle,) Commoners, i. 225, Landed Gentry,
2 ; (of Achareidh,) Landed Gentry, 4, 5, 6, 7, 8 ; (of Bridwell,) 2,
3, 4, 5, 6, 7, 8 ; (of Knedlington,) 2, 3, 4, 5, 6, 7, 8 ; (of Swake-
leys,) 3, 4, 5, 6, 7, 8 ; (of Tremlett,) 5, 6, 7 ; (of Kingsdowne,) 5,
6, 7 ; (of Handsworth,) 2, 3, 4. Topographer and Genealogist, ii.
10. Harleian Society, viii. 387 ; xv. 165, 166 ; xxii. 41, 42 ;
xxviii. 114 ; xxxvii. 250, 309, 315, 335 ; xxxix. 1010 ; xlii. 42 ;
xliii. 148, 165. Visitation of Berkshire, printed by Sir T. Phillipps,
14. Baker's Northampton, i. 460. Burke's Royal Families,
(London, 1851, 8vo.) ii. 24. Suckling's History of Suffolk, ii. 377.
Burke's Heraldic Illustrations, 25. Visitation of Derbyshire,
1663-4, (Middle Hill, 1854, fol.) 2. Hampshire Visitations,
printed by Sir T. Phillipps, 13. Nicholls' History of the County
of Leicester, iii. 468. Manning and Bray's Surrey, i. 474*; ii. 783 ;
iii. cxli. Antiquities and Memoirs of the Parish of Myddle,
written by Richard Gough, 1700, (folio,) 27. Wright's Essex, ii.
263. History of Barnsley, by Rowland Jackson, 65, 113. Surrey
Archæological Collections, vi. Some Account of the Taylor
Family, by P. A. Taylor, 696. History of Willoughby, by Thomas
Deacon, 19. The Genealogist, ii. 169 ; iii. 124, 158, 367 : v. 246 ;
vii. 172. An Historical Survey of Cornwall, by C. S. Gilbert, ii.
89. Topographical Miscellanies, 1792, 4to., (Avington). Wotton's
English Baronetage, i. 280 ; iv. 63. Betham's Baronetage, i. 151;
iii. 117; v. 587. Burke's Extinct Baronetcies. Notes and Queries,
5 S. ii. 67 ; xii. 67, 97. Duncombe's Hereford, (J. H. Cooke,) iii.
204. Jewitt's Reliquary, xxii. 126. Earwaker's East Cheshire,
ii. 47. Somersetshire Wills, printed for F. A. Crisp, iii. 34.
Weaver's Visitations of Somerset, 101. Metcalfe's Visitations of
Northamptonshire, 14, 82. Weaver's Visitation of Herefordshire,
85. Burke's Colonial Gentry, i. 18. New England Register, xiv.
25. Surrey Archæological Collections, x. Howard's Visitation
of England and Wales, iii. 51. Burke's Family Records, 157.
CLARKE-JERVOISE. Berry's Hampshire Genealogies, 341. Nichols'
History of the County of Leicester, iv. 602.
CLARKE-WARDLOW. Burke's Landed Gentry, 2.
CLARKE-WELLWOOD. Burke's Royal Families, (London, 1851, 8vo.)
i. 64. Burke's Commoners, ii. 276, Landed Gentry, 2, 3, 4, 5.
CLARKSON. Harleian Society, iv. 92. Yorkshire Genealogist, i. 163.
CLAVELL, or CLAVILL. Hutchins' Dorset, i. 570, 695 ; iii. 510.
Harleian Society, xx. 29.
CLAVER, or CLAVOR. Lipscombe's History of the County of Buck-

ingham, i. 376. The Genealogist, vii. 173. Harleian Society, xix. 94.

CLAVERING. The Titular Barony of Clavering. London, 1891, fol. Burke's Commoners, i. 237, Landed Gentry, 2, 3, 4, 5. Burke's Royal Families, (London, 1851, 8vo.) i. 82. Herald and Genealogist, iii. 513. Raine's History of North Durham, 213. Hodgson's Northumberland, I. ii. 372. Hutchinson's History of Durham, ii. 442. Surtees' Durham, ii. 228, 248, 280. Baker's Northampton, i. 546. The Genealogist, ii. 221. Wotton's English Baronetage, iii. 295. Banks' Baronies in Fee, i. 153. Betham's Baronetage, ii. 265. Banks' Dormant and Extinct Baronage, i. 266. Harleian Society, xviii. 91. Foster's Visitations of Durham, 71. Foster's Visitations of Northumberland, 30. Chancellor's Sepulchral Monuments of Essex, 354. Burke's Family Records, 158. *See* DE CLAVERING.

CLAVESHAY, or CLAVISHAY. Visitation of Somerset, printed by Sir T. Phillipps, 61. Weaver's Visitations of Somerset, 15. Miscellanea Genealogica et Heraldica, 2nd Series, ii. 188.

CLAXTON. Visitation of Somerset, printed by Sir T. Phillipps, 46. Visitation of Durham, 1615, (Sunderland, 1820, fol.) 18. Visitation of Durham, 1575, (Newcastle, 1820, fol.) 54. Harleian Society, iv. 183 ; xi. 24 ; xv. 167. Hutchinson's History of Durham, iii. xxxi. Surtees' Durham, i. 28, 57 ; iii. 79, 299 ; iv. 97. Page's History of Suffolk, 216, 725. Metcalfe's Visitations of Suffolk, 14, 123, 124. Foster's Visitations of Durham, 73, 75.

CLAY. Jewitt's Reliquary, x. 145, 253, 254 ; xi. 64 ; xxv. 51. Burke's Landed Gentry, 5, 6, 7, 8 ; Dickinson's History of Southwell, 2nd edition, 344. Hunter's History of the Parish of Sheffield, 395. Harleian Society, xv. 168 ; xxviii. 114 ; xxxix. 837. Howard's Visitations of England and Wales, i. 68.

CLAYDON. Harleian Society, xv. 169.

CLAYFIELD-IRELAND. Burke's Landed Gentry, 4, 5, 6, 7, 8.

CLAYHILLS. Burke's Landed Gentry, 5, 6, 7, 8.

CLAY-KER-SEYMER. Hutchins' Dorset, iv. 66.

CLAYTON. Some Account of the Clayton Family of Thelwall, by J. Paul Rylands, F.S.A. Liverpool, 1880, 8vo. Topographer and Genealogist, i. 384. Pedigree of the Family of Sheppard, 14. Berry's Buckinghamshire Genealogies, 77. Surtees Society, xxxvi. 260. Burke's Landed Gentry, (of Hedgerley Park,) 2, 3, 4, 5, 6 ; (of Adlington,) 2, 3, 4, 5, 6, ; (of Enfield,) 2, 3, 4, 5, 6 ; (of Bradford Abbas,) 8 ; (of Chesters,) 8 ; (of Norfolk,) 2. Foster's Visitations of Yorkshire, 504. Harleian Society, viii. 86, 130, 187, 270 ; xviii. 64. Chetham Society, lxxxii. 47 ; lxxxiv. 83-85. The Genealogist,, iii. 240 ; vi. 142. Gregson's Fragments relative to the County of Lancaster, 167. Hodgson's Northumberland, III. ii. 419. Thoresby's Ducatus Leodiensis, 256. Manning and Bray's Surrey, ii. 304. Baines' History of the Co. of Lancaster, iii. 467. Whitaker's History of Whalley, ii. 274. Abram's History of Blackburn, 557, 591. Wotton's English Baronetage, iv. 232. Betham's Baronetage, iii. 212, 409 ; iv. 187. Burke's Extinct

Baronetcies, *Add.* Family Notes, by Justin M. Browne, 31. Memoir of Richard Haines, by C. R. Haines, table vi. *See* BROWNE-CLAYTON, DE CLAYTON.

CLEALAND. Burke's Commoners, iv. 220.

CLEASBY. Burke's Landed Gentry, 8.

CLEATHER. An Historical Survey of Cornwall, by C. S. Gilbert, ii. 68.

CLEAVER. Miscellanea Genealogica et Heraldica, ii. 304. Harleian Society, viii. 66. Chauncy's Hertfordshire, 45.

CLEBURNE. Foster's Visitations of Yorkshire, 255. Notes and Queries, 4 S. viii. 331.

CLEE. Harleian Society, xv. 170.

CLEEVE. Memorials of the Parishes of Greensted-Budworth, Chipping Ongar, etc., by P. J. Budworth, (Ongar, 1876, 8vo.) 6.

CLEGG. Burke's Landed Gentry, 2 p. 824 *note*, 8. Fishwick's History of Rochdale, 452. Harleian Society, xl. 1222.

CLEGHORN. Burke's Landed Gentry, 5, 6, 7.

CLEIVELAND. Bibliotheca Topographica Britannica, vii. Parts i. and ii. 134. Nichols' History of the County of Leicester, iv. 707, 708, 727.

CLELAND. Herald and Genealogist, v. 79. Burke's Commoners, (of Rath Gaol,) iv. 218, Landed Gentry, 2, 3, 4, 5, 6, 7, 8 ; (of Stormont Castle,) Landed Gentry, 5, 6, 7, 8. Notes and Queries, 3 S. x. 192, 299.

CLEMENT. Dwnn's Visitations of Wales, ii. 266. Visitation of Norfolk, published by Norfolk Archæological Society, i. 11. Harleian Society, vi. 338 ; xxxii. 73. Pembrokeshire Pedigrees, 132. Meyrick's History of the Co. of Cardigan, 253. History of the Princes of South Wales, by G. T. O. Bridgeman, 230. The Genealogist, v. 40. The Visitations of Devon, edited by J. L. Vivian, 193.

CLEMENTS. Burke's Landed Gentry, (of Ashfield Lodge,) 2, 3, 4, 5 and supp., 6, 7, 8 ; (of Rathkenny,) 3, 4, 5, 6, 7, 8. History of Carrickfergus, by Saml. M'Skimin, 2nd edn., 398. Carthew's Hundred of Launditch, Part ii. 425. An Historical Survey of Cornwall, by C. S. Gilbert, ii. 89. Archdall's Lodge's Peerage, vii. 219. The Irish Builder, xxxv. 148. Burke's Family Records, 162. Howard's Visitation of Ireland, iii. 1.

CLENCHE. Metcalfe's Visitations of Suffolk, 124, 125. Harleian Society, xxviii. 115.

CLENDINNING. Burke's Landed Gentry, 2.

CLENDON. Bridges' Northamptonshire, by Rev. Peter Whalley, ii. 15.

CLENHILL, CLENNELL, or CLENHELL. The Genealogist, i. 302. Pedigrees from Visitation of Northumberland, printed by Sir T. Phillipps, (Middle Hill, 1858, fol.) 4. Foster's Visitations of Northumberland, 29.

CLEOBURY. Visitation of Devon, edited by F. T. Colby, 54.

CLEPHANE. Douglas's Baronage of Scotland, 317.

CLERBECKE. Collectanea Topographica et Genealogica, ii. 125.

CLERE. Blomefield's Norfolk, vi. 389 ; xi. 234. Visitation of Suffolk, edited by J. J. Howard, ii. 258, 321. A Royal Descent, by T. E.

Sharpe, (London, 1875, 4to.) 52. Burke's Authorized Arms, 4.
The Genealogist, iii. 291 ; iv. 99. Burke's Extinct Baronetcies.
Harleian Society, xxxii. 73.

CLERK, or CLERKE. Hasted's Kent, ii. 239, 424 ; iii. 107. Morant's
Essex, ii. 372. Berry's Hampshire Genealogies, 315. Berry's
Kent Genealogies, 84. Archæologia Cantiana, iv. 246. Burke's
Royal Families, (London, 1851, 8vo.) ii. 182. Topographer and
Genealogist, ii. 9. Visitation of Warwickshire, 1619, published
with Warwickshire Antiquarian Magazine, 216. Lipscombe's
History of the County of Buckingham, i. 446. Nichols' History
of the County of Leicester, iii. 266 ; iv. 407. Clutterbuck's Hert-
ford, ii. 301. Harleian Society, xii. 156 ; xv. 170, 172 ; xvi. 57 ;
xlii. 2. Visitation of Middlesex, (Salisbury, 1820, fol.) 18. Burke's
Landed Gentry, 5, 6, 8. Douglas's Baronage of Scotland, 420.
Peter Chalmers' Account of Dunfermline, ii. 383. Wotton's
English Baronetage, iii. 311. Betham's Baronetage, ii. 118.
Burke's Extinct Baronetcies. F. G. Lee's History of Thame, 310.
Miscellanea Genealogica et Heraldica, New Series, iv. 73. Pedi-
gree of the Family of Sheppard, 17. Foster's Visitation of
Middlesex, 36. Foster's Visitations of Northumberland, 29. See
CLARKE.

CLERK-RATTRAY. Burke's Commoners, iii. 186.

CLERMONT. See FORTESCUE.

CLERVAUX. The House of Clervaux, its Descents and Alliances, by
W. H. D. Longstaffe. Newcastle-upon-Tyne, 1852, 4to. Burke's
Commoners, ii. 139. Foster's Visitations of Yorkshire, 412.
Whitaker's History of Richmondshire, i. 240. History of Dar-
lington, by W. Hylton Dyer Longstaffe, not paged, and lix.-lxxvi.
Nichols' History of the County of Leicester, iv. 174. Harleian
Society, xvi. 58. See ALLAN, CLARENAULX.

CLESEBY. Archæologia Æliana, 2nd Series, v. 33. Plantagenet-
Harrison's History of Yorkshire, i. 194, 473. Yorkshire Archæological and Topographical Journal, vi. 221. Harleian Society,
xvi. 76.

CLEVELAND. W. Mortimer's History of the Hundred of Wirral, 321.
New England Register, xxxix. 213.

CLEVES (Q. Anne of). Gentleman's Magazine, 1829, i. 397.

CLEVLAND. Burke's Landed Gentry, 3, 4,̇5, 6, 7, 8, p. 333.

CLEY. The Genealogist, New Series, vii. 69.

CLEYBROOKE. Berry's Kent Genealogies, 148. Harleian Society,
xlii. 78.

CLEYPITT. Genealogies of Morgan and Glamorgan, by G. T. Clark,
482.

CLEYPOOLE. Metcalfe's Visitations of Northamptonshire, 82.

CLIBBORN. Burke's Landed Gentry, 2, 6 supp. Burke's Colonial
Gentry, i. 72.

CLIDEROW, or CLIDEROWE. Chetham Society, xcviii. 42. Clutterbuck's Hertford, iii. 121. Whitaker's History of Whalley. ii. 376.
See CLITHEROW.

CLIFFE. Burke's Landed Gentry, 2, 3, 4, 5, 6, 7, 8. Harleian

Society, xiii. 35, 178, 376; xviii. 66. Burton's History of Hemingborough, 257.

CLIFFORD. Collectanea Cliffordiana, by A. Clifford, 3 parts. Paris, 1817, 8vo. Cliffordiana, an account of the Cliffords of Chudley, by G. Oliver. Exeter, 1827, 12mo. Claim of the Countess Dowager of Dorset and the Earl of Thanet to the Barony of Clifford, Sess. Papers May, 1663—Nov. 1694. Hasted's Kent, ii. 412, 558, 636, Gentleman's Magazine, lxvii. 842; lxviii. 18; lxxxvii. ii. 207. Clifford's description of Tixall, 154. Berry's Buckinghamshire Genealogies, 17. Burke's Commoners, iii. 660. Foster's Visitations of Yorkshire, 111. Burke's Landed Gentry, (of Frampton,) 2 supp., 3, 4, 5, 6, 7, 8; (of Perristone,) 2, 3, 4, 5, 6; (of Castle Annesley,) 2, 3, 4. Foster's Yorkshire Pedigrees. Harleian Society, vi. 62; xvi. 60, 62. Erdeswicke's Survey of Staffordshire, 73. Bibliotheca Topographica Britannica, i. Part i. 40. History of Hartlepool, by Sir C. Sharpe, (1816, 8vo.) 28. Visitation of Berkshire, printed by Sir T. Phillipps, 15. Eyton's Antiquities of Shropshire, v. 147. Thoresby's Ducatus Leodiensis, 62. Whitaker's Deanery of Craven, 209, 363, (310, 335.) Visitatio Comitatus Wiltoniæ, 1623, printed by Sir T. Phillipps. Hunter's Deanery of Doncaster, ii. 170. Hoare's Wiltshire, II. ii. 115; V. iii. 46. Thoroton's Nottinghamshire, i. 4. Mornings in Spring, by Nathan Drake, i. 53, etc. Fosbrooke's History of Gloucestershire, i. 327. Plantagenet-Harrison's History of Yorkshire, i. 303. Foley's Records of the English Province, S. J. v. 981. The Genealogist, iii. 367; v. 246; New Series, x. 213. Edmondson's Baronagium Genealogicum, iv. 364, 402. Brydges' Collins' Peerage, vii. 117. Banks' Baronies in Fee, i. 155. Banks' Dormant and Extinct Baronage, ii. 87. Visitation of Wiltshire, edited by G. W. Marshall, 65. Cooke's Continuation of Duncumb's Hereford, (Hund. of Grimsworth,) Part i. 24. The Visitations of Devon, by J. L. Vivian, 194. Harleian Society, xxi. 40. Visitation of Gloucester, edited by T. F. Fenwick and W. C. Metcalfe, 39. Nicolson and Burn's Westmorland and Cumberland, i. 274-304. *See* BURLINGTON, DE CLIFFORD.

CLIFFORD-CONSTABLE. Foster's Yorkshire Pedigrees.

CLIFTON. Collectanea Topographica et Genealogica, vii. 144. Camden Society, xliii. 4. Surrey Archæological Collections, ii. Visitation of Norfolk, published by Norfolk Archæological Society, i. 296, 341. Burke's Commoners, (of Clifton and Lytham,) ii. 54, Landed Gentry, 2, 3, 4, 5, 6, 7, 8; (of Clifton Hall,) Landed Gentry, 5, 6, 7, 8. Carthew's Hundred of Launditch, Part i. 173. Foster's Visitations of Yorkshire, 6. Harleian Society, iv. 16; xvi. 176; xxxii. 75; xliii. 75. Chetham Society, lxxxi. 42; lxxxii. 88; lxxxiv. 86. Foster's Lancashire Pedigrees. History of Blyth, by Rev. J. Raine, 138, 139. Baines' History of the Co. of Lancaster, iv. 404. Thoroton's Nottinghamshire, i. 104, 153. Norfolk Archæology, iii. 127. Memorials of the Church of Attleborough, by J. T. Barrett, 183. Notes and Queries, 2 S. ix. 364, 411. Edmondson's Baronagium Genealogicum, iv. 379. Wotton's

English Baronetage, i. 34. Banks' Baronies in Fee, i. 157.
Betham's Baronetage, i. 49. Banks' Dormant and Extinct Baronage, i. 268 ; ii. 99. Burke's Extinct Baronetcies. Carthew's West
and East Bradenham, 5, 6. *See* DE CLIFTON, GREY DE RUTHYN.

CLINCH. Hasted's Kent, iii. 13.

CLINTON. Memoirs of the Clinton Family, by Henry Fynes-Clinton.
London, *n. d.*, 4to. The Great Governing Families of England,
i. 189. Hasted's Kent, ii. 299. Jacob's Peerage, i. 480. Topographer and Genealogist, i. 349, 492. Dugdale's Warwickshire,
651, 993, 1007. Hutchins' Dorset, ii. 99. Clutterbuck's Hertford,
iii. 119. Harleian Society, xii. 137 ; xxvii. 28. Edmondson's
Baronagium Genealogicum, ii. 99 ; vi. 5. Berry's Genealogical
Peerage, 79. Banks' Baronies in Fee, i. 159, 386. Banks' Dormant and Extinct Baronage, ii. 101. *See* CLYNTON, TREFUSIS.

CLINTS. Plantagenet-Harrison's History of Yorkshire, i. 206.

CLIPPESBY, or CLIPSBYE. Blomefield's History of Norfolk, xi. 160.
Harleian Society, xiii. 67 ; xxxii. 77.

CLIPPINGDALE. Howard's Visitations of England and Wales, ix. 169.

CLIPSHAM. Miscellanea Genealogica et Heraldica, 2nd Series, iii. 81.

CLITHEROW, CLITHEROWE, or CLITHEROE. Foster's Visitations of
Yorkshire, 238. Account of the Company of Ironmongers, by
John Nicholl, 2nd. edn., 534. Clutterbuck's Hertford, ii. 551.
Whitaker's History of Whalley, ii. 376. *See* CLIDEROW, DE
CLIDERHOU, STRACEY-CLITHEROW.

CLIVE. Claim of Edwd. James, Earl of Powis, to vote as Baron
Clive at elections of Irish Peers, Sess. Papers, 238 of 1861. Gen-
tleman's Magazine, 1833, ii. 27. Hasted's Kent, ii. 806. Jewitt's
Reliquary, vi. 27. Berry's Kent Genealogies, 111. Burke's
Landed Gentry, 2 supp., 3, 4, 5, 6, 7, 8. Robinson's Mansions of
Herefordshire, 313. Archdall's Lodge's Peerage, vii. 80. Brydges'
Collins' Peerage, v. 543. Ormerod's Cheshire, iii. 215. Harleian
Society, xlii. 24. *See* CLYVE.

CLIVEDON. Banks' Baronies in Fee, ii. 66.

CLOBERRY. Harleian Society, vi. 60 ; viii. 66 ; xv. 173. Westcote's
Devonshire, edited by G. Oliver and P. Jones, 555. The Visitations of Devon, by J. L. Vivian, 200.

CLODESHALL. Harleian Society, xii. 74.

CLODSHALE. Dugdale's Warwickshire, 884.

CLOGSTOWN. Oliver's History of Antigua, i. 139. New England
Register, lii. 25.

CLONCURRY. Claim of the Rt. Hon. Edw. Baron Cloncurry to vote
at elections of Irish Peers, Sess. Papers, 160 of 1854.

CLONVILLE. Morant's Essex, ii. 37.

CLOPTON. Morant's Essex, i. 276 ; ii. 321, 540. Visitation of Suffolk,
edited by J. J. Howard, i. 20-135, 314. Visitation of Durham,
1615, (Sunderland, 1820, fol.) 102. Visitation of Gloucestershire,
1569, (Middle Hill, 1854, fol.) 4. Bibliotheca Topographica
Britannica, v. Part ii. 101. (2nd edn. 112.) Harleian Society,
viii. 159 ; xii. 109 ; xiii. 179, 377 ; xv. 172 ; xxi. 225 ; xxvii. 73.
Hutchinson's History of Durham, iii. 228. Nichols' History of

the County of Leicester, iv. 171. Shakespere's Home, by J. C. M. Bellew, 20, 66. Dugdale's Warwickshire, 698. Surtees' Durham, iv. 48. Wright's Essex, i. 561. Metcalfe's Visitations of Suffolk, 15-17, 126. Foster's Visitations of Durham, 77. New England Register, xviii. 184. Muskett's Suffolk Manorial Families, i. 136-145, 390. The Genealogist, New Series, xvi. 160.

CLOSE. Burke's Commoners, iii. 247, Landed Gentry, 2, 3, 4, 5, 6 and supp., 7, 8. Topographer and Genealogist, i. 557. Burke's Extinct Baronetcies. Burke's Colonial Gentry, i. 78.

CLOSE-BROOKS. Burke's Family Records, 110.

CLOTHALL. Berry's Sussex Genealogies, 319. Dallaway's Sussex, II. ii. 245.

CLOTHERAM. Foster's Visitations of Yorkshire, 234.

CLOTTERBOOK. See CLUTTERBUCK.

CLOTWORTHY, or CLOTWORTHIE. Chronicle of the Family of De Havilland. Harleian Society, vi. 61. Westcote's Devonshire, edited by G. Oliver and P. Jones, 480, 563. A Complete Parochial History of the County of Cornwall, iv. xi. Visitation of Devon, edited by F. T. Colby, 55. The Visitations of Devon, by J. L. Vivian, 203.

CLOUGH. Dwnn's Visitations of Wales, i. 319. Burke's Commoners, (of Plas Clough,) iii. 515, Landed Gentry, 2, 3, 4, 5, 6, 7, 8 ; (of Clifton House,) Landed Gentry, 5, 6, 7, 8. Foster's Visitations of Yorkshire, 504. Thoresby's Ducatus Leodiensis, 225. Earwaker's Local Gleanings, ii. 802. Records of Denbigh and its Lordship, by John Williams, 171. Harleian Society, xv. 174 ; xxviii. 116. Annals of Smith of Balby, by H. E. Smith, 246.

CLOUGH-TAYLOR. Burke's Landed Gentry, 7, 8. Howard's Visitation of England and Wales, vi. 44.

CLOVILL. Morant's Essex, ii. 59. Harleian Society, xiii. 36, 180, 377. Bysshe's Visitation of Essex, edited by J. J. Howard, 22. See DE CLOVILL.

CLOWES. Burke's Commoners, (of Delaford,) iv. 724, Landed Gentry, 2, 3, 4 ; (of Broughton Hall,) Landed Gentry, 5, 6, 7, 8. Foster's Lancashire Pedigrees. Harleian Society, xv. 175, 176 ; xxxviii. 583. The Suffolk Records, by H. W. Aldred, 167-170. Annals of the Barber Surgeons, by S. Young, 538.

CLUDD, or CLUDDE. Burke's Commoners, i. 483, Landed Gentry, 2, 3, 4. Harleian Society, iv. 103 ; xxviii. 118. Notts and Derbyshire Notes and Queries, iv. 172.

CLUN, or CLUNN. Collections by the Powys-land Club, viii. 192. Harleian Society, xxviii. 120.

CLUTTERBUCK. Berry's Hertfordshire Genealogies, 177-184. Burke's Commoners, (of Warkworth,) ii. 224, Landed Gentry, 2, 3, 4, 5, 6, 7, 8 ; (of Newark Park,) Landed Gentry, 2, 3, 4, 5, 6, 7, 8 ; (of Hardenhuish,) 8. Harleian Society, viii. 225 ; xxi. 42. Clutterbuck's Hertford, iii. 300. Fosbrooke's History of Gloucestershire, i. 416. The Visitation of Gloucester, edited by T. F. Fenwick, and W. C. Metcalfe, 41. Gloucestershire Notes and Queries, v. 378, 426, 454, 511, 547 ; vi. 13.

CLUTTON. Burke's Landed Gentry, 2, 3. Metcalfe's Visitation of Worcester, 1683, 33. Harleian Society, xviii. 67.

CLUTTON-BROCK. Burke's Landed Gentry, 2 supp., 3, 4, 5, 6.

CLYBORNE. Harleian Society, vii. 29. Foster's Visitations of Cumberland and Westmorland, 27.

CLYF. The Genealogist, New Series, xvii. 118.

CLYNTON. Robinson's Mansions of Herefordshire, 110. Weaver's Visitation of Herefordshire, 19. See CLINTON.

CLYVE. Ormerod's Cheshire, ii. 800. Harleian Society, xxviii. 121. See CLIVE.

CLYVEDON. Jewers' Wells Cathedral, 293.

COATES. Jewitt's Reliquary, vii. 245. Burke's Landed Gentry, 4, 5, 6, 7, 8. Cyclostyle Pedigrees, by J. J. Green. Annals of Smith of Balby, by H. E. Smith, 205.

COBB, COBBE, or COBBES. Burke's Extinct Baronetcies. Blomefield's Norfolk, ix. 68. Hasted's Kent, iii. 137, 462. Berry's Kent Genealogies, 149. Surtees Society, xxxvi. 332. Berry's Hampshire Genealogies, 292. Visitation of Norfolk, published by Norfolk Archæological Society, i. 317. Oxfordshire Pedigrees, fol., *n. d.*, printed by Sir T. Phillipps. Visitation of Oxfordshire, printed by Sir T. Phillipps, (Middle Hill, fol.) 16. Burke's Landed Gentry, 2, 3, 4, 5, 6, 7, 8. Burke's Royal Families, (London, 1851, 8vo.) ii. 133. Harleian Society, v. 320 ; viii. 125 ; xix. 16, 94 ; xxxii. 77 ; xlii. 148. Poulson's Holderness, ii. 426. Hampshire Visitations, printed by Sir T. Phillipps, 14. Topographical Miscellanies, 1792, 4to. (Adderbury). Wotton's English Baronetage, iii. 392. Harvey's Hundred of Willey, 464. The Genealogist, New Series, xv. 151.

COBBELEIGH. Visitation of Devon, edited by F. T. Colby, 57.

COBBOLD. Burke's Landed Gentry, 5, 6, 7, 8.

COBDEN. Notes and Queries, 7 S., xi. 426, 510.

COBHAM. Collectanea Topographica et Genealogica, vii. 320-354. Pocock's History of Gravesend, 35-46. Collinson's Somerset, iii. 303. Morant's Essex, ii. 535. Hasted's Kent, i. 402, 489, 490, 562 ; ii. 496. Burke's Landed Gentry, 5, 6, 7, 8. Surrey Archæological Collections, ii. 169. Clutterbuck's Hertford, iii. 131. Wright's Essex, ii. 92. Archæologia Cantiana, xi. 81 ; xii. 113. Banks' Baronies in Fee, i. 160. Banks' Dormant and Extinct Baronage, i. 270 ; ii. 104. Notes and Queries, 4 S. iv. 197, 348 ; 5 S. i. 294. The Genealogist, New Series, xiv. 192 ; xvi. 41, 166. See BROOKE.

COBLER. Chronicle of the Family of De Haviland.

COCHRAN, COCHRANE, or COCKRANE. Burke's Landed Gentry, 4. Geo. Robertson's Description of Cunninghame, 264. Paterson's History of the Co. of Ayr, ii. 124, 400. Paterson's History of Ayr and Wigton, i. 135, 208, 444, 629, 634 ; iii. 300. Geo. Robertson's Account of Families in Ayrshire, i. 157. Peter Chalmers' Account of Dunfermline, ii. folding table No. 2 *at end*. Wood's Douglas's Peerage of Scotland, i. 471. Foster's Collectanea Genea-

logica, (MP's Scotland,) 71. Oliver's History of Antigua, i. 139.
See COCKRAM.
COCK. Berry's Hertfordshire Genealogies, 120. Jewitt's Reliquary,
xi. 215. Maclean's History of Trigg Minor, i. 576 ; ii. 369.
Harleian Society, ix. 43; xiv. 558 ; xv. 177 ; xxii. 5. Clutter-
buck's Hertford, ii. 55. Chauncy's Hertfordshire, 296. The
Visitations of Cornwall, edited by J. L. Vivian, 89. Essex
Archæological Society, New Series, ii. Burke's Family Records,
164.
COCKAIN, or COCKAYNE. Cockayne Memoranda, by A. E. Cockayne.
Congleton, 1869, 8vo.; 2nd edn., Congleton, 1873, 8vo. Nichols'
History of the County of Leicester, iv. 607. Dugdale's Warwick-
shire, 1120. Cussans' History of Hertfordshire, Parts vii. and
viii. 27. Topographer and Genealogist, iii. 437-461. Gentleman's
Magazine, 1863, ii. 223. Pilkington's View of Derbyshire, ii. 277.
Harleian Society, xv. 178 ; xix. 17, 95. Glover's History of
Derbyshire, ii. 41 (32). Archdall's Lodge's Peerage, iv. 322.
Journal of the Derbyshire Archæological Society, iii. 109. J. B.
Marsh's Story of Harecourt, 270. The Genealogist, New Series,
vii. 69. *See* COKAYNE.
COCKBURN. House of Cockburn of that Ilk, and the Cadets thereof,
by T. H. C. Hood. Edinburgh, 1888, 4to. Burke's Landed Gentry,
8 supp. Burke's Royal Families, (London, 1851, 8vo.), ii. 185*.
Foster's Collectanea Genealogica, (MP's Scotland,) 74. Burke's
Colonial Gentry, i. 46.
COCKBURN-CAMPBELL. Burke's Colonial Gentry, i. 108.
COCKBURN-HOOD. Burke's Landed Gentry, 6.
COCKCROFT. Harleian Society, xxxviii. 543.
COCKE. Topographer and Genealogist, ii. 107. Visitation of War-
wickshire, 1619, published with Warwickshire Antiquarian Maga-
zine, 214. Harleian Society, xii. 261.
COCKER. Harleian Society, xviii. 67. History of the Chapel, Tock-
holes, by B. Nightingale, 193.
COCKERELL. Foster's Visitations of Yorkshire, 505. H. B. Wheat-
ley's edition of Pepys's Diary. Supplementary vol., 13.
COCKES. Visitation of Somerset, printed by Sir T. Phillipps, 43.
Harleian Society, xi. 24.
COCKESFIELD. Harleian Society, xii. 109.
COCKET. Blomefield's Norfolk, vii. 6. Carthew's Hundred of Laun-
ditch, Part ii. 680. Harleian Society, xxvii. 38 ; xxxii. 80. *See*
COKET.
COCKFIELD. Blomefield's Norfolk, ix. 422 ; x. 256.
COCKRAM, or COCKERAM. Harleian Society, vi. 63 ; xx. 29. Hutchins'
Dorset, i. 672. The Visitations of Devon, by J. L. Vivian, 205.
See COCHRAN.
COCKREIN. Burke's Extinct Baronetage, 351.
COCKS. Rudder's Gloucestershire, 421. Hasted's Kent, ii. 552.
Manning and Bray's Surrey, i. 286. Clutterbuck's Hertford,
i. 457. Harleian Society, xv. 177. Edmondson's Baronagium
Genealogicum, vi. 117. Brydges' Collins' Peerage, viii. 19.

12

Wotton's English Baronetage, iii. 359. Burke's Extinct Baronetcies. Metcalfe's Visitation of Worcestershire, 1683, 34.

COCKSEY. Harleian Society, xxix. 425.

COCKSHED. Harleian Society, vi. 63. The Visitations of Devon, by J. L. Vivian, 207.

COCKSHUTT. Nichols' History of the County of Leicester, iv. 524. Abram's History of Blackburn, 541. Harleian Society, xxxviii. 429.

COCKSON. Harleian Society, xv. 178.

COCTON. Betham's Baronetage, i. 497. See DE COCTON.

CODDINGTON. Burke's Landed Gentry, 2, 3, 4, 5, 6, 7, 8.

CODE. Polwhele's History of Cornwall, iv. 112. See COODE.

CODRINGTON. Bennett's History of Tewkesbury, 435. Burke's Landed Gentry, 2, 3, 4, 5, 6, 7. Fosbrooke's History of Gloucestershire, ii. 23. The Genealogist, iv. 120. Wotton's English Baronetage, iv. 201. Betham's Baronetage, iii. 198. Visitation of Gloucester, edited by T. F. Fenwick and W. C. Metcalfe, 43. Oliver's History of Antigua, i. 146.

COE. Morant's Essex, ii. 279. Harleian Society, xliii. 169. See COO.

COELL. Harleian Society, viii. 194.

COETMOR. Dwnn's Visitations of Wales, ii. 65. History of Powys Fadig, by J. Y. W. Lloyd, vi. 200.

COETON. Harleian Society, xxix. 303.

COFFEY. O'Hart's Irish Pedigrees, 2nd Series, 105.

COFFIN. Burke's Landed Gentry, 2, 3, 4, 5, 6. Harleian Society, vi. 64. Visitation of Devon, edited by F. T. Colby, 57. Betham's Baronetage, v. 584*. Burke's Extinct Baronetcies, supp. The Visitations of Devon, by J. L. Vivian, 208. Burke's Colonial Gentry, i. 62. New England Register, ii. 337 ; xxiv. 149, 305; xxxv. 376. Burke's Colonial Gentry, ii. 693. See PINE-COFFIN.

COGAN. Sir T. Phillipps' Topographer, No. 1, (March, 1821, 8vo.) 24. Visitation of Somerset, printed by Sir T. Phillipps, 47. Visitation of Oxfordshire, 1574, printed by Sir T. Phillipps, (Middle Hill, fol.) 3. Burke's Landed Gentry, 4, 5, 6, 7, 8. Harleian Society, v. 132 ; xi. 26 ; xv. 179. Banks' Baronies in Fee, ii. 67. Visitation of Devon, edited by F. T. Colby, 58. Notes and Queries, 5 S. iv. 291. Hasted's Kent, (Hund. of Blackheath, by H. H. Drake,) 79. The Visitations of Devon, by J. L. Vivian, 212. Genealogies of Morgan and Glamorgan, by G. T. Clark, 378. New England Register, xliii. 310.

COGGLESHALL, or COGSHALL. Morant's Essex, i. 261, 263. Wright's Essex, ii. 584. Harleian Society, xiii. 37. Metcalfe's Visitations of Suffolk, 126. See DE COGGLESHALL.

COGHILL. The Family of Coghill, 1377-1879, with some Sketches of their Maternal Ancestors, the Slingsbys of Scriven Hall, by J. H. Coghill. Cambridge, U.S.A., 1879, 4to. Visitation of Oxfordshire, printed by Sir T. Phillipps, (Middle Hill, fol.) 17. Foster's Visitations of Yorkshire, 505. Harleian Society, v. 285 ; xxii. 42. Betham's Baronetage, iv. 41. Burke's Extinct Baronetcies. Caithness Family History, by John Henderson, 253.

COGHLAN. O'Hart's Irish Pedigrees, 2nd Series, 54.

COGHULL. Ormerod's Cheshire, ii. 817.

COHAM. Burke's Commoners, i. 458, Landed Gentry, 2, 3, 4, 5, 6, 7, 8. Burke's Royal Families, (London, 1851, 8vo.) ii. 176. Burke's Heraldic Illustrations, 122. Burke's Authorized Arms, 36. The Visitations of Devon, by J. L. Vivian, 476.

COHEN. Burke's Colonial Gentry, ii. 559.

COKAYNE. Miscellanea Genealogica et Heraldica, 3rd Series, iii. 221. See COCKAYNE.

COKE. Coke of Trusley, by J. T. Coke, 1880, 4to. Pedigree of Coke of Ellingham, Co. Northumberland, [T. P.] 1856, folio page. Hasted's Kent, i. 288. History of Melbourne, by J. J. Briggs, 2nd edn., 161. Blomefield's Norfolk, ix. 237. Burke's Commoners, (of Trusley,) iv. 268, Landed Gentry, 2, 3, 4, 5, 6, 7, 8 ; (of Holkham,) Commoners, i. 3 ; (of Lower Moor House, or Lemore,) Landed Gentry, 2, 3, 4, 5, 6, 7, 8 ; Miscellanea Genealogica et Heraldica, New Series, i. 35, 170, 299. Harleian Society, vi. 69 ; ix. 44 ; xxxviii. 570 ; xliii. 46. Nichols' History of the County of Leicester, iii. 784*. Burke's Royal Families, (London, 1851, 8vo.) ii. 124. Maclean's History of Trigg Minor, ii. 369. Dugdale's Warwickshire, 523. Clutterbuck's Hertford, iii. 208. Baker's Northampton, i. 141. Robinson's Mansions of Herefordshire, 108. History and Antiquities of Harwich and Dovercourt, by Silas Taylor, 217. Pilkington's View of Derbyshire, ii. 265. Banks' Dormant and Extinct Baronage, iii. 468. Burke's Extinct Baronetcies. Jewitt's Reliquary, xxi. 256. Carthew's Hundred of Launditch, Part iii. 109. See COOK.

COKEFELD. The Genealogist, New Series, xiii. 175. Thoroton's Nottinghamshire, ii. 253. See DE COKEFELD.

COKENAGE. Visitation of Staffordshire, (Willm. Salt Soc.) 42.

COKER. Collinson's Somerset, ii. 343. Burke's Landed Gentry, 2 add., 3. 4, 5, 6, 7, 8. Hutchins' Dorset, i. 310 ; iii. 723. Hoare's Wiltshire, I. ii. 30. Baker's Northampton, ii. 266. History of Bicester, by John Dunkin, 134. Miscellanea Genealogica et Heraldica, 2nd Series, ii. 189. The Genealogist, New Series, ii. 297. Harleian Society, xx. 30.

COKESEY. Nash's Worcestershire, ii. 50. Notices of Swyncombe and Ewelme in Co. Oxford, by H. A. Napier, 46. See COOKSEY.

COKET. Gentleman's Magazine, 1831, i. 417. Page's History of Suffolk, 700. Metcalfe's Visitations of Suffolk, 187. See COCKET.

COLBECK. The Genealogist, iii. 81. Harleian Society, xix. 18.

COLBORNE. Visitation of Somerset, printed by Sir T. Phillipps, 49. Harleian Society, xi. 26. The Genealogist, iii. 241.

COLBRAND, or COLBROND. Berry's Sussex Genealogies, 183. Dallaway's Sussex, i. app. to Chichester. Nichols' History of the County of Leicester, iv. 394. Burke's Extinct Baronetcies.

COLBY, or COLBYE. Colby of Great Torrington, Devon, some account of that family and its alliances for five generations, by F. T. Colby, F.S.A. Exeter, *n. d.*, 4to. ; 2nd. edn., Exeter, 1878, 4to. Appendix to same, 1880, 4to. ; 2nd appendix, 1894, 4to. Burke's Extinct

Baronetcies. Surtees Society, xxxvi. 47. Visitation of Norfolk, published by Norfolk Archæological Society, i. 95. Miscellanea Genealogica et Heraldica, New Series, ii. 73, 76. Metcalfe's Visitations of Suffolk, 17, 18, 127. Howard's Visitation of England and Wales, i. 4. The Genealogist, New Series, vii. 243. Harleian Society, xxxii. 82. Burke's Family Records, 165. Burke's Landed Gentry, 8.

COLCHESTER. Harleian Society, viii. 295. Duncumb's History of the Co. of Hereford, ii. 400. Visitation of Gloucester, edited by T. F. Fenwick and W. C. Metcalfe, 45. Burke's Landed Gentry, 8.

COLCLOUGH, COLECLOGH, or COLECLOUGH. Case of J. S. Boyse claiming the Wexford Estates under the will of Cæsar Colclough. London, 1853, 4to. Harleian Society, i. 52. Visitation of Staffordshire, 1663-4, printed by Sir T. Phillipps, 3. Miscellanea Genealogica et Heraldica, i. 182. Burke's Landed Gentry, 3, 4, 5 and supp., 6, 7, 8. Burke's Royal Descents and Pedigrees of Founders' Kin, 59 ; Founders' Kin, 17. The Borough of Stoke-upon-Trent, by John Ward, 340. Erdeswick's Survey of Staffordshire, 506. Burke's Extinct Baronetcies, 602. Visitations of Staffordshire, 1614 and 1663-4, William Salt Society, 86, 88.

COLDHAM. Berry's Sussex Genealogies, 2. Burke's Landed Gentry, 2 supp., 3, 4, 5, 6, 7, 8. Dallaway's Sussex, i. 230. Manning and Bray's Surrey, iii. 153. Harleian Society, xiii. 378. ; xxxix. 1131 ; xliii. 174. Bysshe's Visitation of Essex, edited by J. J. Howard, 22. Surrey Archæological Collections, x.

COLDWELL. Harleian Society, xxxvii. 116.

COLE. Genealogy of the Family of Cole, by J. E. Cole. London, 1867, 8vo. Miscellanea Genealogica et Heraldica, ii. 234-250 ; New Series, iv. 182. Morant's Essex, i. 489 ; ii. 478. Visitation of Somerset, printed by Sir T. Phillipps, 48. Surrey Archæological Collections, ii. ; x. Berry's Sussex Genealogies, 307. Burke's Commoners, (of Twickenham,) i. 192 ; Landed Gentry, 2, 3, 4, 5, 6, 7, 8 ; (of Holybourn,) Landed Gentry, 3, 4, 5 ; (of Brandrum,) 2, 3, 4, 5, 6 ; (of Leixlip Castle,) 5, 6 ; (of Marazion,) 2 add., 3, 4 ; (of Woodview,) 6, 7, 8 ; (of Hill House,) 6, 7. Harleian Society, v. 190 ; xi. 27 ; xiii. 38, 378 ; xv. 180 ; xxi. 43 ; xxii. 42 ; xxviii. 125 ; xliii. 134, 184. Chetham Society, lxxxiv. 88. Burke's Royal Families, (London, 1851, 8vo.) ii. 171. Burke's Visitation of Seats and Arms, ii. 68. Westcote's Devonshire, edited by G. Oliver and P. Jones, 519. Hampshire Visitations, printed by Sir T. Phillipps, 14. Nichols' History of the County of Leicester, iv. 272. Shirley's History of the County of Monaghan, 227. Jordan's History of Enstone, 360. A Complete Parochial History of the County of Cornwall, ii. 200. An Historical Survey of Cornwall, by C. S. Gilbert, ii. 71. The Genealogist, iii. 289. The Tyldesley Diary, edited by J. Gillow and A. Hewitson, 85. Archdall's Lodge's Peerage, vi. 37. Visitation of Devon, edited by F. T. Colby, 59. Burke's Extinct Baronetcies, and 603. The Visitations of Cornwall, edited by J. L. Vivian, 90. Howard's Visitation of England and Wales, i. 12. Visitation of Gloucester, edited by T. F. Fenwick and W. C. Metcalfe, 45. The Visitations of Devon, by J. L. Vivian, 213. Newcastle Courant for 20 August, 1886. Oxford Historical Society, xix. 180. New England Register, xxxv. 65 ; l. 517. Burke's Family Records, 166. Parliamentary Memoirs of Fermanagh, by Earl of Belmore, 16, 34, 39, 50.

COLEBROOK, or COLEBROOKE. Hasted's Kent, ii. 756. Berry's Sussex Genealogies, 94. Lipscombe's History of the County of Buckingham, i. 134. Dallaway's Sussex, II. i. 52. Betham's Baronetage, iii. 281.

COLEGRAVE. Burke's Landed Gentry, 2 supp., 3, 4, 5, 6.

COLEIRE. Visitations of Staffordshire, 1614 and 1663-4, William Salt Society, 88.

COLEMAN. Plantagenet-Harrison's History of Yorkshire, i. 465. Bysshe's Visitation of Essex, edited by J. J. Howard, 22. New England Register, xi. 347 ; xii. 129.

COLEMORE. Visitation of Warwickshire, 1619, published with Warwickshire Antiquarian Magazine, 90. Harleian Society, xii. 335.

COLEPEPER. History of Leeds Castle, by C. Wykeham Martin, 173. Hasted's Kent, ii. 174, 188, 356, 466, 476 ; iii. 36, 89. Berry's Kent Genealogies, 77. Harleian Society, xlii. 11, 61. Berry's Sussex Genealogies, 136. Herald and Genealogist, viii. 337. Baker's Northampton, ii. 124. Banks' Dormant and Extinct Baronage, iii. 201. See CULPEPER.

COLERIDGE. Burke's Landed Gentry, 5. The Visitations of Devon, by J. L. Vivian, 313.

COLES. Visitation of Wiltshire, 1677, printed by Sir T. Phillipps, (Middle Hill, 1854, fol.). Burke's Landed Gentry, (of Ditcham,) 3, 4, 5 ; (of Parrock's Lodge), 2, 3, 4, 5. Baker's Northampton, i. 433. Burke's Family Records, 168.

COLESHILL. An Historical Survey of Cornwall, by C. S. Gilbert, ii. 82.

COLESWORTHY. New England Register, xv. 330.

COLET. Life of Dr. John Colet, by Samuel Knight, (Oxford, 1823, 8vo.) xx. Berry's Buckinghamshire Genealogies, 46.

COLETHURST. Visitation of Somerset, printed by Sir T. Phillipps, 50. Weaver's Visitations of Somerset, 16.

COLEVILLE. Memoirs of the family of Chester, by R. E. C. Waters, 197.

COLEWORTH. Baker's Northampton, i. 607.

COLFE. Bibliotheca Colfanæ Catalogus, by W. H. Black, (1831, 8vo.) 17. Berry's Kent Genealogies, 368. Harleian Society, xlii. 156.

COLGAN. O'Hart's Irish Pedigrees, 2nd Series, 151.

COLINS, or COLLINGS. Tuckett's Devonshire Pedigrees, 119. Burke's Landed Gentry, 2 add., 3, 4. Harleian Society, vi. 67. Westcote's Devonshire, edited by G. Oliver and P. Jones, 562. See COLLINS.

COLLAMORE. Harleian Society, vi. 65. The Visitations of Devon, by J. L. Vivian, 216.

COLLARD. The Genealogist, v. 24. History of Chislet, Kent, by F. Haslewood, 195. Bysshe's Visitation of Essex, edited by J. J. Howard, 23.

COLLAS. J. B. Payne's Armorial of Jersey, 54,
COLLEN. Harleian Society, xiii. 182. *See* COLLIN.
COLLES. Records of the Colles Family, by R. W. Colles, Dublin, 1892, 8vo. Pedigree of Colles of Lye, co. Worcester, [T. P.] 1867, folio page. Visitation of Somerset, printed by Sir T. Phillipps, 51. Visitation of Warwickshire, 1619, published with Warwickshire Antiquarian Magazine, 92. Harleian Society, xii. 247; xxii. 43; xxvii. 40. Weaver's Visitation of Somerset, 16.
COLLET, or COLLETT. Visitation of Middlesex, (Salisbury, 1820, fol.) 4, 47. Metcalfe's Visitations of Suffolk, 18. Foster's Visitation of Middlesex, 9, 89. Gloucestershire Notes and Queries, ii. 437. Notes and Queries, 6 S., ix. 437.
COLLETON. Pedigree and Memoir of the Colleton Family. By David Ross, 1844, 12mo. Tuckett's Devonshire Pedigrees, 168. Harleian Society, vi. 66. Westcote's Devonshire, edited by G. Oliver and P. Jones, 619. Wotton's English Baronetage, iii. 228. Betham's Baronetage, ii. 209. The Visitations of Devon, by J. L. Vivian, 218.
COLLEY. Gentleman's Magazine, 1822, ii. 325; 1823, i. 40. Burke's Authorized Arms, 172. Surtees' Durham, i. 198. Archdall's Lodge's Peerage, iii. 59. Brydges' Collins' Peerage, viii. 532. Harleian Society, xxii. 5. Gloucestershire Notes and Queries, iv. 563. *See* COWLEY.
COLLIER. Burke's Landed Gentry, 5. Topographer and Genealogist, iii. 568. Visitation of Staffordshire, 1663-4, printed by Sir T. Phillipps, 4. Bibliotheca Topographica Britannica, iv. Part i. 6. Burke's Royal Descents and Pedigrees of Founders' Kin, *Founders' Kin*, 20. Hutchins' Dorset, iv. 486. Foster's Account of Families descended from Francis Fox, 16. Miscellanea Genealogica et Heraldica, New Series, iii. 125. An Historical Survey of Cornwall, by C. S. Gilbert, ii. 80. Burke's ExtinctBaronetcies. Howard's Visitation of England and Wales, i. 56; iii. 74. Harleian Society, xx. 32. Burke's Family Records, 171.
COLLIN. Jewitt's Reliquary, xv. 162. History of the Family of Smith, by Augustus Smith, M.P., (London, 1861, fol.) 25. Harleian Society, xiii. 182, 379; xiv. 559. Bysshe's Visitation of Essex, edited by J. J. Howard, 23. *See* COLLEN.
COLLING, or COLLINGE. Harleian Society, ix. 44. Visitation of Suffolke, edited by J. J. Howard, ii. 47. Burke's Landed Gentry, 3, 4, 5, 7, 8. Metcalfe's Visitations of Suffolk, 88. The Visitations of Cornwall, edited by J. L. Vivian, 91.
COLLINGWOOD. Foster's Visitations of Northumberland, 32-34. Pedigrees from Visitation of Northumberland, printed by Sir T. Phillipps, (Middle Hill, 1858, fol.) 4. Burke's Commoners, (of Dissington,) i. 472, Landed Gentry, 2, 3, 4, 5, 6, 7, 8; (of Chirton,) Landed Gentry, 3, 4, 5, 6, 7, 8; (of Cornhill House), 2 and corr., 3, 4, 5, 7, 8. Burke's Royal Families, (London, 1851, 8vo.) ii. 189. Surtees' Durham, i. 7. The Genealogist, i. 301, 304; ii. 225. Brydges' Collins' Peerage, ix. 389.

COLLINS. A Genealogical Table showing the Descent of John Stratford Collins, Esq., etc., broadside. Morant's Essex, i. 346 ; ii. 27,
130. Hasted's Kent, ii. 254. Berry's Sussex Genealogies, 89.
Berry's Kent Genealogies, 433, 458. Burke's Commoners, (of
Betterton,) iv. 616, Landed Gentry, 2, 3, 4, 5, 6, 7, 8 ; (of Hatch
Beauchamp,) Commoners, iii. 536, Landed Gentry, 2 ; (of
Truthan,) Landed Gentry, 2, 3, 4, 5, 6, 7, 8 ; (of Walford,) 2
supp., 3, 4, 5, 6, 7, 8 ; (of Ardnalee,) 7, 8 ; (of Kelvindale,) 8 ;
(of Simmons Court,) 2 supp. ; of Knaresborough,) 6, 7, 8.
Maclean's History of Trigg Minor, i. 325-335. Burke's Heraldic
Illustrations, 97. Burke's Royal Descents and Pedigrees of
Founders' Kin, 34. Visitation of Berkshire, printed by Sir T.
Phillipps, 15. A Complete Parochial History of the County of
Cornwall, i. 353. Harleian Society, xv. 181 ; xxviii. 48,82,127 ;
xlii. 147, 178. The Genealogist, v. 247. The Visitations of
Devon, by J. L. Vivian, 220. Genealogical Memoranda of the
Family of Ames, 1. Burke's Colonial Gentry, ii. 862. Oliver's
History of Antigua, i. 175. Howard's Visitation of England
and Wales, iv. 113. See COLINS, STRATFORD-COLLINS, COLLYNS.
COLLINS-TRELAWNY. Burke's Landed Gentry, 5 supp., 6, 7, 8.
COLLINSON. Burke's Commoners, ii. 538.
COLLIS, or COLLYS. The Collis Family, compiled January, 1892 [by
W. H. Collis], broadside. The Genealogist, vii. 173. Burke's
Landed Gentry, (of Castle Cooke,) 3, 4, 5, 6 ; (of Lismore,) 3, 4 ;
(of Fort William,) 2 supp., 3, 4 ; (of Tieraclea,) 6, 7, 8. See
COOKE-COLLIS.
COLLISON. Carthew's Hundred of Launditch, Part iii. 6.
COLLY. Harleian Society, iii. 25. Wright's History of Rutland, 65.
COLLYER. Burke's Landed Gentry, 2, 3, 4, 5, 6, 7, 8, (of Hackford
Hall,) 7. Harleian Society, xxxix. 1165. A Kentish Country
House, Hawkhurst, by Mary Adelaide, Lady Jennings. Guildford,
1894, 4to. Howard's Visitation of England and Wales, ix. 17.
COLLYMORE. Harleian Society, xv. 182.
COLLYNS. Tuckett's Devonshire Pedigrees, 118. Harleian Society,
vi. 67.
COLMAN. Memoirs of the Colman Family, by R. B. Peake, (London,
1841, 8vo.). Harleian Society, vi. 65 ; xv. 182. The Visitations
of Devon, by J. L. Vivian, 221. Miscellanea Genealogica et
Heraldica, 2nd Series, i. 249. Burke's Landed Gentry, 7, 8.
Howard's Visitation of England and Wales, viii. 142 ; ix. 5.
COLMER. Harleian Society, xi. 28.
COLMORE. Visitation of Durham, 1615, (Sunderland, 1820, fol.) 47.
Visitation of Somerset, printed by Sir T. Phillipps, 52. Burke's
Landed Gentry, 3, 4, 5, 6, 7, 8. Harleian Society, xi. 28.
Foster's Visitations of Durham, 79.
COLNET, or COLNETT. Berry's Hampshire Genealogies, 16. Hamp-
shire Visitations, printed by Sir T. Phillipps, 14.
COLOGAN. Burke's Heraldic Illustrations, 37.
COLOMB. Burke's Landed Gentry, 8.
COLQUHOUN. The Chiefs of Colquhoun, by William Fraser. Edin-

burgh, 1869, 4to. 2 vols. Burke's Commoners, ii. 345 ; (of Kil-lermont,) Landed Gentry, 2, 3, 4, 5, 6, 7, 8. Miscellanea Genealogica et Heraldica, New Series, ii. 533. History of Dum-bartonshire, by Joseph Irving, 381. Douglas's Baronage of Scotland, 23, 27, 438. The Book of Dumbartonshire, by Joseph Irving, ii. 244-263. Betham's Baronetage, iv. 158. Foster's Col-lectanea Genealogica, (MP's Scotland,) 77. Northern Notes and Queries, iv. 75 ; vii. 158.

COLQUIT. Harleian Society, ix. 45. The Visitations of Cornwall, edited by J. L. Vivian, 92. Bygone Lancashire, by Ernest Axon, 146-156.

COLRICHE. The Genealogist, New Series, xvii. 20.

COLSHILL. Harleian Society, xiv. 560.

COLSTON. Harleian Society, i. 32, 74 ; viii. 223. Burke's Landed Gentry, 2 and add., 3, 4, 5, 6, 7, 8. Phelps' History of Somerset, i. 470. Burke's Heraldic Illustrations, 45. Weaver's Visitations of Somerset, 102. Miscellanea Genealogica et Heraldica, 2nd Series, v. 61.

COLT. Genealogical Memoirs of the families of Colt and Coutts, by Rev. C. Rogers, LL.D., 1879, 8vo. History of the Colts of that Ilk. Edinburgh, 1887, 4to. Gough's Sepulchral Monuments, ii. 253. Visitation of Suffolke, edited by J. J. Howard, ii. 27-44. Morant's Essex, i. 6, 313 ; ii. 485, 492. Berry's Hampshire Genealogies, 293. Burke's Landed Gentry, 2, 3, 4, 5, 6, 7, 8. Harleian Society, viii. 392 ; xxii. 43 ; xxxix. 1124. Wright's Essex, ii. 300. Wotton's English Baronetage, iv. 44. Betham's Baronetage, iii. 102. Metcalfe's Visitations of Suffolk, 18.

COLTHURST. Surtees Society, xxxvi. 370. Burke's Landed Gentry, 2 add., 3, 4, 5, 6, 7, 8. Graves' History of Cleveland, 378. The Genealogist, New Series, xiii. 111. See COULTHURST, COLT.

COLTHURST-VESEY. Burke's Landed Gentry, 4. See VESEY.

COLTMAN. Burke's Landed Gentry, (of Naburn Hall,) 5 ; (of Hagnaby,) 5. Harleian Society, xv. 183.

COLTON. New England Register, xxxiv. 31, 264. Burke's Colonial Gentry, ii. 613.

COLTRANE. Lands and their Owners in Galloway, by P. H. M'Kerlie, i. 496.

COLUMBELL. Jewitt's Reliquary, vii. 23. Nichols' History of the County of Leicester, iii. 1134. Harleian Society, xv. 183 ; xxxvii. 237. The Genealogist, vi. 143 ; New Series, vii. 72.

COLUMBERS. Banks' Baronies in Fee, i. 163. Banks' Dormant and Extinct Baronage, i. 272. See DE COLUMBERS.

COLUMBINE. Carthew's West and East Bradenham, 160.

COLVELL. Miscellanea Genealogica et Heraldica, ii. 73.

COLVILE, COLVILL, or COLVILLE. Claim of Charles John Colville Baron Colville of Culross to vote at the elections of Scotch Peers, Sess. Papers, 36, 84 of 1850. Miscellanea Genealogica et Heraldica, ii. 171. Blomefield's Norfolk, ix. 123. Foster's Yorkshire Pedigrees. Cambridgeshire Visitation, edited by Sir T. Phillipps, 9. Burke's Commoners, (of Lullington,) iii. 543 ; Landed Gentry, 2, 3, 4, 5,

6, 7, 8; (of Ireland,) Landed Gentry, 2 supp.; (of Monkhams Hall,) 7, 8; (of Bellaport,) 8. Foster's Visitations of Yorkshire, 164, 200. Harleian Society, iv. 138; xiii. 180, 377; xv. 181; xli. 3, 73, 103. Ord's History of Cleveland, 457. W. Watson's Acccount of Wisbeach, 482. Collectanea Topographica et Genealogica, vi. 153. Baker's Northampton, i. 9. Paterson's History of the Co. of Ayr, ii. 397. Page's History of Suffolk, 599. Paterson's History of Ayr and Wigton, i. 623. Original Letters of Mr. John Colville, (Bannatyne Club,) ix. Wood's Douglas's Peerage of Scotland, i. 350, 360. Banks' Baronies in Fee, i. 163. Banks' Dormant and Extinct Baronage, i. 273. Metcalfe's Visitations of Suffolk, 127. Bateson's History of Northumberland, i. 181. The Genealogist, New Series, ix. 81, 84; xiii. 35; xv. 155.

COLWELL. Harleian Society, xiv. 563; xxvii. 42; xlii. 120.

COLWICH, or COLWYCHE. Visitation of Derbyshire, 1663-4, (Middle Hill, 1854, fol.) 3. Genealogist, iii. 157. Harleian Society, xvi. 63. Foster's Visitations of Northumberland, 34.

COLYARE, COLYAR, or COLYER. Howard's Visitation of England and Wales, iv. 127. Bibliotheca Topographica Britannica, ix. Part 4, 84. Burke's Landed Gentry, 7, 8. Nichols' Miscellaneous Antiquities, No. 4, 82, 84. Visitation of Staffordshire, (Willm. Salt Soc.) 64.

COLYEAR. Wood's Douglas's Peerage of Scotland, ii. 371. Miscellanea Genealogica et Heraldica, New Series, iv. 65.

COLYER-FERGUSSON. Howard's Visitation of England and Wales, iv. 127.

COLYN. Maclean's History of Trigg Minor, ii. 36.

COMB, or COMBE. Visitation of Somerset, printed by Sir T. Phillipps, 53. Burke's Landed Gentry, (of Cobham Park,) 5, 6, 7, 8; (of Oaklands,) 5, 6, 7, 8; (of Earnshill,) 5, 6, 7, 8. Visitation of Warwickshire, 1619, published with Warwickshire Antiquarian Magazine, 204. Harleian Society, xi. 28; xii. 291; xxii. 6, 44. Clutterbuck's Hertford, i. 418. Shakespeare's Home, by J. C. M. Bellew, 66. Registers of Ecclesfield, by A. S. Gatty, 8. The Visitations of Devon, edited by J. L. Vivian, 83.

COMBEMARTIN. Baker's Northampton, ii. 241. See COUMBEMARTIN.

COMBER. Gentleman's Magazine, 1831, i. 504. Berry's Sussex Genealogies, 142. Burke's Visitation of Seats and Arms, i. 58. Castles, Mansions, and Manors of Western Sussex, by D. G. C. Elwes and C. J. Robinson, 191. Surtees Society, lxii. 344. Dallaway's Sussex, II. ii. 323. Notes and Queries, 7 S., iv. 111, 235. Harleian Society, xxxviii. 767; xliii. 159. Surrey Archæological Collections, x. Miscellanea Genealogica et Heraldica, 2nd Series, v. 261. Howard's Visitation of England and Wales, vii. 145.

COMBERBACH. Collections for a Genealogical Account of the Family of Comberbach, by George W. Marshall, LL.B. London, 1866, 8vo. James Hall's History of Nantwich, 495. Earwaker's East Cheshire, ii. 648.

COMBERFORD. Shaw's Staffordshire, i. 434. A History of Wednesbury, (Wolverhampton, 1854, 8vo.) 161. Erdeswicke's Survey of Staffordshire, 397. Harleian Society, xii. 35. Visitations of Staffordshire, 1614 and 1663-4. William Salt Society, 91. *See* CUMBERFORD.

COMBES. Harleian Society, viii. 127.

COMEE, or COMEY. New England Register, l. 210.

COMER. Burke's Landed Gentry, 2 add., 3, 4, 5.

COMIN, or COMYN. Visitation of Middlesex, (Salisbury, 1820, fol.) 12. Visitation of Durham, 1615, (Sunderland, 1820, fol.) 16. Surtees Society, xxxvi. 72. Burke's Landed Gentry, 3, 4, 5, 6. Manx Society, x. app. D. Dugdale's Warwickshire, 368. Clutterbuck's Hertford, ii. 432. J. B. Pratt's Buchan, 401. Notes and Queries, 4 S. i. 608 ; ii. 84, 210, 302 ; 5 S. viii. 94. Nichols' History of the County of Leicester, iii. 66. Banks' Dormant and Extinct Baronage, i. 54. Foster's Visitation of Middlesex, 2. Foster's Visitations of Durham, 81. Burke's Landed Gentry, 7. *See* CUMIN.

COMMERELL. Berry's Sussex Genealogies, 93. Burke's Landed Gentry, 2, 3, 4. *See* BOSANQUET.

COMPORT. Fragmenta Genealogica, by F. A. Crisp, i. 29.

COMPTON. The Descent of Charlotte Compton, daughter of James Compton, fifth Earl of Northampton, by J. G. C. Clifford, London, 1892, 4to. Jacob's Peerage, i. 504. Gentleman's Magazine, lix. 111, 491. Morant's Essex, i. 24. Drummond's History of Noble British Families, i. and ii. Berry's Sussex Genealogies, 364. Visitation of Somerset, printed by Sir T. Phillipps, 54. Berry's Hampshire Genealogies, 328. Visitation of Gloucestershire, 1569, (Middle Hill, 1854, fol.) 4. Burke's Commoners, iv. 311, Landed Gentry, 2, 3, 4, 5, 6, 7, 8. Harleian Society, xi. 29 ; xxi. 44. Bridge's Northamptonshire, by Rev. Peter Whalley, i. 344. Hampshire Visitations, printed by Sir T. Phillipps, 14, 15. Thoroton's Nottinghamshire, i. 354. Fosbrooke's History of Gloucestershire, i. 284. History of Colmer, by Thomas Hervey, 206. Edmondson's Baronagium Genealogicum, ii. 109 ; vi. 39. Brydges' Collins' Peerage, 223. Wotton's English Baronetage, iv. 12. Banks' Baronies in Fee, i. 164. Banks' Dormant and Extinct Baronage, ii. 114. Burke's Extinct Baronetcies. Somersetshire Wills, printed for F. A. Crisp, iii. 104. Weaver's Visitations of Somerset, 17, 103.

COMYNS. Hasted's Kent, iii. 148. Morant's Essex, ii. 60. Burke's Landed Gentry, 5, 6, 7, 8. Wright's Essex, i. 164. Bysshe's Visitation of Essex, edited by J. J. Howard, 24.

CONANT. Burke's Landed Gentry, 5, 6, 7, 8. History of Sandwich, by W. Boys, 274.

CONCANON. Burke's Landed Gentry, 3, 4. O'Hart's Irish Pedigrees, 2nd Series, 151.

CONDER. Howard's Visitation of England and Wales, i. 18. Miscellanea Genealogica et Heraldica, 2nd Series, i. 61. Harleian Society, xxxvii. 13. Burke's Landed Gentry, 7, 8.

CONGALTON. Douglas's Baronage of Scotland, 521. Burke's Commoners, iii. 380.

CONGLETON. Metcalfe's Visitations of Northamptonshire, 15.

CONGREAVE, or CONGREVE. Berry's Berkshire Genealogies, 27. Burke's Commoners, (of Congreve,) i. 15, Landed Gentry, 2, 3, 4, 5, 6, 7, 8; (of Mount Congreve,) Landed Gentry, 3, 4, 5, 6, 7, 8; (of Flichity House,) 5. Visitation of Staffordshire, 1663-4, printed by Sir T. Phillipps, 4. Harleian Society, xii. 45. Ormerod's Cheshire, ii. 555. Visitations of Staffordshire, 1614 and 1663-4, William Salt Society, 93.

CONIERS. Surtees Society, xli. 46. Hutchinson's History of Durham, ii. 417; iii. 88. Whitaker's Deanery of Craven, 3rd edn., 523. Banks' Dormant and Extinct Baronage, ii. 115. See CONYERS.

CONINGSBY. Berry's Hertfordshire Genealogies, 2, 161. Blomefield's Norfolk, vii. 413. Harleian Society, viii. 69; xxii. 45; xxvii. 43; xxviii. 129. Dugdale's Warwickshire, 760. Clutterbuck's Hertford, i. 444. Chauncy's Hertfordshire, 462, 531. Robinson's Mansions of Herefordshire, 148. Memoirs of the Family of Chester, by R. E. C. Waters, 259. South Mimms, by F. C. Cass, 70. Notes and Queries, 1 S. vi. 406; xii. 222, 312, 414; 4 S. viii. 165. Banks' Dormant and Extinct Baronage, iii. 203. Account of the Guildhall of London, by J. E. Price, 116.

CONLIFFE. Harleian Society, xv. 190. See CUNLIFFE.

CONN. Burke's Landed Gentry, 4, 8.

CONNELLAN. Burke's Landed Gentry, 2, 3, 4, 5, 6, 7, 8. O'Hart's Irish Pedigrees, 2nd Series, 152.

CONNER. Burke's Landed Gentry, 2 add., 3, 4, 5, 6, 7, 8.

CONNOCK. Harleian Society, ix. 46. An Historical Survey of Cornwall, by C. S. Gilbert, ii. 79. The Visitations of Cornwall, edited by J. L. Vivian, 93.

CONNOR. Burke's Colonial Gentry, ii. 535.

CONNY. Harleian Society, iii. 10. The Genealogist, iii. 368.

CONOLLY. Burke's Commoners, (of Castletown,) ii. 159. Landed Gentry, 2, 3, 4, 5, 6, 7, 8; (of Cottles,) Landed Gentry, 2, 3, 4, 5. Burke's Royal Descents and Pedigrees of Founders' Kin, *Founders' Kin,* 21.

CONQUEST. Poceedings of the Archæological Institute, (York, 1847,) 229. Foley's Records of the English Province, S. J. v. 598. Harleian Society, xix. 19, 97.

CONRAN. Burke's Family Records, 174.

CONROY. Burke's Commoners, i. 491. O'Hart's Irish Pedigrees, 2nd Series, 153.

CONSETT. Ord's History of Cleveland, 564.

CONSTABLE. Gentleman's Magazine, 1835, i. 152. Surtees Society, xxxvi. 119, 137, 323, 335, 339; xli. 68. Burke's Commoners, i. 328, iv. 183; (of Wassand,) Commoners, i. 547, Landed Gentry, 2, 6, 7, 8; (of Otley,) Landed Gentry, 5, 6, 7. Foster's Yorkshire Pedigrees. Foster's Visitations of Yorkshire, 56, 146, 177-179, 195-198, 306, 416, 506, 507. Harleian Society, iv. 40; xvi. 63, 68. Graves' History of Cleveland, 243. Poulson's Holderness,

i. 431, 437 ; ii. 227-235. A List of Roman Catholics in the County of York in 1604, by Edward Peacock, 127. Plantagenet-Harrison's History of Yorkshire, i. 303. Wood's Douglas's Peerage of Scotland, i. 455. Wotton's English Baronetage, ii. 322. Burke's Extinct Baronetcies. The Genealogist, New Series, xiv. 96. *See* ROGER.

CONSTABLE-MAXWELL. Burke's Commoners, i. 225, Landed Gentry, 2, 3.

CONSTANTINE. Harleian Society, viii. 217 ; xxviii. 131. Hutchins' Dorset, iii. 304. E. J. Climenson's History of Shiplake, 335.

CONTRY. Berry's Kent Genealogies, 45. Archæologica Cantiana, v. 235.

CONVERSE. New England Register, 1. 346.

CONWAY, or CONWY. Visitation of Warwickshire, 1619, published with Warwickshire Antiquarian Magazine, 177. Dugdale's Warwickshire, 847 Harleian Society, xii. 27. Banks' Dormant and Extinct Baronage, iii. 205. Burke's Extinct Baronetcies. History of Powys Fadog, by J. Y. W. Lloyd, vi. 245, 247, 259. Dwnn's Visitations of Wales, ii. 85, 118, 296, 324, 340. Burke's Landed Gentry, 2 *bis*, 3, 4, 5, 6, 7, 8. The Rawdon Papers, by Edward Berwick, 14. Somerset and Dorset Notes and Queries, iii. 312.

CONYERS. J. H. Hill's History of Langton, 216. Morant's Essex, i. 49. Hasted's Kent, i. 35. Harleian Society, i. 33 ; xiv. 649 ; xv. 184 ; xvi. 69, 74, 77 ; xxii. 139 ; xxxix. 932. Graves' History of Cleveland, 49, 330, 439. Berry's Essex Genealogies, 141. Surtees Society, xxxvi. 340 ; xli. 48. Visitation of Durham, 1575, (Newcastle, 1820, fol.) 53. Visitation of Durham, 1615, (Sunderland, 1820, fol.) 12, 104. Burke's Landed Gentry, 2. Foster's Visitations of Yorkshire, 71, 164, 244, 508. History of Hampstead, by J. J. Park, 124. Whitaker's History of Richmondshire, ii. 42. Ord's History of Cleveland, 555. Nichols' History of the County of Leicester, ii. 456, 457. Archæologia Æliana, 2nd Series, v. 36. Surtees' Durham, i. 28 ; iii. 37, 79, 81, 219, 247, 401. Wright's Essex, ii. 460. Thoroton's Nottinghamshire, ii. 293. Pedigrees of the Leading Families of Lancashire, published by Joseph Foster, (London, 1872, fol.). Visitation of Sussex, 1570, printed by Sir T. Phillipps, (Middle Hill, fol.) 3. The New History of Yorkshire commencing with Richmondshire, by Genl. Plantagenet-Harrison, (London, 1872, fol.) Part i. 35. Plantagenet-Harrison's History of Yorkshire, i. 108. Yorkshire Archæological and Topographical Journal, vi. 225. Edmondson's Baronagium Genealogicum, vi. 45. Wotton's English Baronetage, ii. 99. Banks' Baronies in Fee, i. 164, 179. Betham's Baronetage, i. 334. Metcalfe's Visitations of Suffolk, 154. Burke's Extinct Baronetcies. Bateson's History of Northumberland, i. 245. East Barnet, by F. C. Cass, Part i. 58. Bysshe's Visitation of Essex, edited by J. J. Howard, 24. Foster's Visitations of Durham, 83, 85, 87, 203. Hasted's Kent, (Hund. of Blackheath, by H. H. Drake,) 122. Howard's Visitation of England and Wales, v. 1.

The Genealogist, New Series, xiv. 54; xvi. 181; xvii. 109. *See*
CONIERS, NORTON, OSBORN.
CONYNGHAM. Hasted's Kent, iv. 320. Burke's Landed Gentry, 2,
3, 4, 5, 6, 7, 8. Burke's Royal Families, (London, 1851, 8vo.)
ii. 207. Archdall's Lodge's Peerage, vii. 173. The Irish Builder,
xxxv. 129. Notes and Queries, 4 S. xi. 78, 488; 5 S. i. 329;
iv. 282, 518; 6 S. ii. 175. *See* CUNINGHAM.
COO, or COOE. Morant's Essex, ii. 307. Harleian Society, xiii. 182,
380. Metcalfe's Visitations of Suffolk, 89, 128. Surrey Archæo-
logical Collections, x. *See* COE.
COODE. Harleian Society, ix. 46, 48. Burke's Landed Gentry, 6,
7, 8. A Complete Parochial History of the County of Corn-
wall, i. 45, 52. An Historical Survey of Cornwall, by C. S.
Gilbert, ii. 72. The Visitations of Cornwall, edited by J. L.
Vivian, 94, 96. Howard's Visitation of England and Wales, ii. 18.
See CODE.
COOK, or COOKE. The Seize Quartiers of the Family of Bryan Cooke,
Esq., etc., 1857, 4to. Topographer and Genealogist, ii. 81, 551.
Hasted's Kent, i. 156. Morant's Essex, i. 66, 230; ii. 607. Notes
on the Parish of Harefield, by W. F. Vernon, 62. Berry's Kent
Genealogies, 472. Berry's Sussex Genealogies, 105. Surtees
Society, xxxvi. 299. Edward Miller's History of Doncaster, 206.
Burke's Commoners, (of Peak,) ii. 266 ; (of Owston,) Commoners,
ii. 276, Landed Gentry, 2, 3, 4, 5, 6, 7, 8; (of Kiltinan Castle,)
Landed Gentry, 2 supp., 3, 4, 5, 6, 7, 8; (of Cordangan,) 2 supp.,
3, 4, 5, 6, 7, 8; (of Cookesborough,) 4, 5 ; (of Camerton,) 5 supp.,
6, 7, 8; (of Gurrangrony,) 4 ; (of Retreat,) 2 add., 3, 4 ; (of Farm
Hill,) 2 supp. ; 5 at p. 1441, 6 at p. 1659, 1739 ; (of Harefield
Park,) 7 at p. 1892, 2097 ; (of Castle Cooke,) 7, 8 ; (of Kiltenan,)
7. Foster's Yorkshire Pedigrees. Visitation of Sussex, 1570,
printed by Sir T. Phillipps, (Middle Hill, fol.) 3. Burke's Royal
Families, (London, 1851, 8vo.) i. 9 ; (edn. of 1876,) 216. Miscellanea Genealogica et Heraldica, New Series, i. 346 ; 2nd Series,
iv. 152. Harleian Society, ii. 108 ; vi. 69 ; viii. 290, 434, 475 ;
xii. 299; xiii. 39, 183, 381 ; xiv. 564 ; xv. 184, 186 ; xxi. 45 ;
xxxii. 323 ; xxxvii. 157, 173 ; xxxviii. 581, 728 ; xlii. 117.
Visitation of Warwickshire, 1619, published with Warickshire
Antiquarian Magazine, 94. J. H. Hill's History of Market Har-
borough, 287. Burke's Visitation of Seats and Arms, ii. 16.
Burke's Heraldic Illustrations, 54. Dallaway's Sussex, II. i. 23,
36, 236. Westcote's Devonshire, edited by G. Oliver and P.
Jones, 555. Visitation of Derbyshire, 1663-4, (Middle Hill, 1854,
fol.) 3. Wainwright's Wapentake of Stratford and Tickill, 124.
Thoresby's Ducatus Leodiensis, 75, 210. Nichols' History of the
County of Leicester, iv. 468. Transactions of the London and
Middlesex Archæological Society, iii. 307. Hunter's Deanery of
Doncaster, i. 56, 57, 58. Particulars of Alderman Philip Malpas
and Alderman Sir Thomas Cooke, K.B., by B. B. Orridge, 22, 23.
Wright's Essex, ii. 440. The Picards, or Pychards, (London,
1878, 8vo.) 173. Illustrations of Jack Cade's Rebellion, by B. B.

Orridge and W. D. Cooper, (1869, 4to.) 23. The Genealogist, iii.
14, 158. O'Hart's Irish Pedigrees, 2nd Series, 320. Doncaster
Charities, by Charles Jackson, 20. Notes and Queries, 2 S. xii.
480; 4 S. v. 266, 371. Wotton's English Baronetage, iii. 279.
Visitation of Devon, edited by F. T. Colby, 59. Betham's
Baronetage, ii. 253. Ormerod's Cheshire, iii. 380. Metcalfe's
Visitations of Suffolk, 19, 89, 128. Burke's Extinct Baronetcies,
and 604. Metcalfe's Visitation of Worcester, 1683, 35. The
Visitations of Cornwall, edited by J. L. Vivian, 99. Carthew's
Hundred of Launditch, Part iii. 108. Visitation of Gloucester,
edited by T. F. Fenwick and W. C. Metcalfe, 46, 47. Private
Correspondence of Lady Jane Cornwallis, 132. Historical Notices
of Doncaster, by C. W. Hatfield, 3rd Series, 319-328. East
Barnet, by F. C. Cass, Part i. 26. The Visitations of Devon, by
J. L. Vivian, 222. Chancellor's Sepulchral Monuments of Essex,
247. *See* COKE.

COOKE-COLLIS. Burke's Landed Gentry, 2 supp., 4, 5, 6, 7, 8.

COOKE-HURLE. Burke's Family Records, 341.

COOKES. Nash's Worcestershire, i. 440. Burke's Commoners, iv.
519 ; Landed Gentry, 2, 3, 4, 5, 6, 7, 8. Warwickshire Pedigrees
from Visitation of 1682-3, (privately printed, 1865). History of
the Colleges and Halls of Oxford, by Anthony à Wood, edited by
John Gutch, 632. Burke's Extinct Baronetcies. Metcalfe's
Visitation of Worcestershire, 1865, 36, 38.

COOKSEY. Gough's Sepulchral Monuments, ii. 45. Herald and
Genealogist, vi. 654. Notes and Queries, 4 S. vii. 523 ; viii. 186,
332. Metcalfe's Visitation of Worcestershire, 1685, 38. Harleian
Society, xxvii. 44. *See* COKESEY.

COOKSON. Burke's Commoners, (of Whitehill,) ii. 506, Landed
Gentry, 2, 3, 4, 5 and supp., 6, 7, 8 ; (of Meldon Park,)
Landed Gentry 2, 3, 4, 5, 6, 7, 8 ; (of Neasham Hall,) 7, 8.
Howard's Visitation of England and Wales, iii. 129 ; viii. 48 ;
ix. 145.

COOKWORTHY. Foster's Account of Families descended from Francis
Fox, 18.

COOLEY. New England Register, xxxiv. 266, 386 ; xxxv. 25, 159.

COONAN. O'Hart's Irish Pedigrees, 2nd Series, 154.

COOPER. Bibliotheca Topographica Britannica, ix. Part 4, 196.
Harleian Society, i. 66 ; ii. 90 ; iv. 140 ; xxxviii. 486, 582 ;
xxxix. 868 ; xliii. 181. Chetham Society, lxxxiv. 89. Berry's
Sussex Genealogies, 99, 377. Visitation · of Durham, 1615,
(Sunderland, 1820, fol.) 55. Burke's Commoners, (of Toddington,)
i. 158, Landed Gentry, 2, 3, 4, 5, 6, 7, 8 ; (of Failford,) Landed
Gentry, 3, 4, 5, 6, 7, 8 ; (of Cooper's Hill,) 3 supp., 4, 5, 6, 7, 8 ;
(of Cooper's Hill,) 3, 4, 5, 6 ; (of Markree Castle,) 2, 3, 4, 5, 6, 7, 8 ;
(of Pain's Hill,) 5 ; (of Killenure,) 5, 6, 7, 8 ; (of Finchley,) 3
supp., 4. More about Stifford, by Willm. Palin, 49. Foster's
Visitations of Yorkshire, 602. Herald and Genealogist, viii. 193.
Foster's Lancashire Pedigrees. Dickinson's History of Southwell,
2nd edition, 302. Burke's Visitations of Seats and Arms, 2nd

Series, i. 40; ii. 72. Burke's Royal Descents and Pedigrees of
Founders' Kin, 42. Burke's Authorized Arms, 87. Hampshire
Visitations, printed by Sir T. Phillipps, 15. Nichols' History of
the County of Leicester, iv. 974. Surtees' Durham, iv. 150.
The Genealogist, i. 257. Thoroton's Nottinghamshire, iii. 59.
Notes and Queries, 5 Series, ix. 246. Paterson's History of Ayr
and Wigton, i. 767. Edmondson's Baronagium Genealogicum, ii.
147. Brydges' Collins' Peerage, iii. 543. Burke's Extinct Baronet-
cies. Weaver's Visitations of Somerset, 103. Cyclostyle Pedi-
grees, by J. J. Green. New England Register, xliv. 53. Foster's
Visitations of Durham, 89. Burke's Colonial Gentry, i. 54.
Howard's Visitation of Ireland, i. 59. Howard's Visitation of
England and Wales, v. 112. See COUPER, GILL.

COOPER-HERRING. Burke's Landed Gentry, 2, 7.

COORE. Burke's Landed Gentry, 2, 3, 4, 5, 6, 7. Foster's Yorkshire
Pedigrees.

COOTE. Visitation of Norfolk, published by Norfolk Archæological
Society, i. 85. Burke's Landed Gentry, (of Mount Coote,) 2, 3,
4, 5, 6, 7, 8; (of Ballyclough,) 6, 7, 8; (of West Park,) 6, 7, 8.
Burke's Royal Families, (London, 1851, 8vo.) i. 180. Harleian
Society, xiv. 565; xv. 186; xxxii. 82. Archdall's Lodge's Peerage,
ii. 62; iii. 207. Howard's Visitation of Ireland, iii. 57.

COPE. Memoirs of the Copes of Wiltshire, by J. C. Biddle-Cope. 1881,
4to. Berry's Hampshire Genealogies, 301. T. Faulkner's History
of Kensington, 62. Burke's Landed Gentry, (of Drummilly,) 2
supp., 3, 4, 5, 6, 7, 8; (of Loughgall,) 3, 4, 5, 6, 7, 8; (of Osbaston
Hall,) 5, 6, 7, 8. A Royal Descent, by T. E. Sharpe, (London,
1875, 4to.) 15, 53. Bridge's Northamptonshire, by Rev. Peter
Whalley, i. 122. Visitation of Staffordshire, 1663-4, printed by
Sir T. Phillipps, 4. Hampshire Visitations, printed by Sir T.
Phillipps, 16. Baker's Northampton, i. 748; ii. 13, 51. Wotton's
English Baronetage, i. 112; iv. 152. Betham's Baronetage, i. 87;
iii. 177. Burke's Extinct Baronetcies. Visitations of Staffordshire,
1614 and 1663-4, William Salt Society, 95. Metcalfe's Visitations of Northamptonshire, 15, 175. Harleian Society, xxxvii.
25. Miscellanea Genealogica et Heraldica, 2nd Series, v. 11.

COPELEY. Surtees Society, xli. 73, 81. See COPLEY.

COPEMAN. Burke's Landed Gentry, 5, 6, 7, 8.

COPLAND. Burke's Landed Gentry, 7, 8.

COPLEDIKE, or COPULDYKE. Visitation of Norfolk, published by
Norfolk Archæological Society, i. 10. The Genealogist, iii. 369;
vi. 144; New Series, xiii. 39. Metcalfe's Visitations of Suffolk,
20. Harleian Society, xxxii. 83; xli. 117.

COPLESTON, or COPLESTONE. Tuckett's Devonshire Pedigrees, 165.
Harleian Society, vi. 70, 72, 340; xx. 32. Maclean's History of
Trigg Minor, i. 394*. Visitation of Devon, edited by F. T. Colby,
60-68. Westcote's Devonshire, edited by G. Oliver and P. Jones,
503, 505, 506. Hutchins' Dorset, ii. 282. Miscellanea Genealogica et Heraldica, New Series, ii. 73. Foster's Account of
Families descended from Francis Fox, 25. Colby of Great

Torrington, by F. T. Calby, 4, 32. The Visitations of Devon, by J. L. Vivian, 224-233.

COPLEY. Surtees Society, xxxvi. 259, 272, 275. Surrey Archæological Collections, iii. ; xi. 180. Berry's Sussex Genealogies, 296. Berry's Surrey Genealogies, 85. Edward Miller's History of Doncaster, 163, 222. Burke's Commoners, ii. 155. Foster's Yorkshire Pedigrees. Foster's Visitations of Yorkshire, 10, 11, 508, 526. Dallaway's Sussex, II. ii. 339. Wainwright's Wapentake of Strafford and Tickhill, 113. Thoresby's Ducatus Leodiensis, 9. Hunter's Deanery of Doncaster, i. 51, 251, 342 ; ii. 548. Manning and Bray's Surrey, ii. 231. Thoroton's Nottinghamshire, i. 133. Aubrey's Antiquities of Surrey, iv. 219. Haworth, Past and Present, by J. H. Turner, 143. A Complete Parochial History of the County of Cornwall, ii. 63. John Watson's History of Halifax, 284. Harleian Society, xv. 188 ; xvi. 78, 80 ; xxvii. 45 ; xliii. 121. Banks' Baronies in Fee, i. 169. Burke's Extinct Baronetcies. Historical Notices of Doncaster, by C. W. Hatfield, 3rd Series, 313. The Genealogist, New Series, ix. 161 ; xii. 52 ; xvi. 110. Records of Batley, by M. Sheard, 266. Burke's Family Records, 177. See COPELEY.

COPP. New England Register, x. 369.

COPPET. The Genealogist, New Series, xiv. 261.

COPPIN. Clutterbuck's Hertford, i. 347. Harleian Society, xxii. 45. Burke's Colonial Gentry, ii. 599. Bedfordshire Notes and Queries, iii. 197.

COPPING. Visitation of Norfolk, published by Norfolk Archæological Society, i. 11. Harleian Society, xxxii. 84.

COPPINGER, or COPINGER. The Copingers or Coppingers, edited by W. A. Copinger. New Edition. Manchester, 1884, 8vo. Gentleman's Magazine, 1831, i. 12, 110, 112. Burke's Commoners, iii. 501 ; (of Ballyvolane,) Commoners, ii. 326, Landed Gentry, 2, 3, 4, 5, 6, 7, 8 ; (of Midleton,) Landed Gentry, 3, 4, 5, 6, 7, 8 ; (of Leemount,) 2 supp., 3, 4 ; 8 at 1510. Page's History of Suffolk, 523. Harleian Society, xv. 187, 188. Metcalfe's Visitations of Suffolk, 20, 129.

COPPOCK. Harleian Society, xxxvii. 180.

COPWOOD. East Barnet, by F. C. Cass, Part i. 90. Harleian Society, xxii. 6.

CORAM. Harleian Society, vi. 73. The Visitations of Devon, by J. L. Vivian, 234.

CORBALLY. Burke's Landed Gentry, 2, 3, 4, 5.

CORBET, or CORBETT. Blomefield's Norfolk, x. 459. Morant's Essex, i. 341 ; ii. 109. Gentleman's Magazine, lxxix. 599, 825, 903. Surtees Society, xxxvi. 359. Visitation of Norfolk, published by Norfolk Archæological Society, i. 35. Blomefield's Norfolk, x. 459. Burke's Commoners, (of Sundorne,) iii. 627, Landed Gentry, 2, 3, 4, 5, 6, 7, 8 ; (of Ynysymaengwyn,) Commoners, ii. 91, Landed Gentry, 5, 6, 7, 8 ; (of Elsham,) Commoners, iii. 189, Landed Gentry, 2, 3, 4, 5, 6, 7, 8 ; (of Longnor,) Landed Gentry, 2, 3, 4, 5, 6, 7, 8 ; (of Admington,) 2 supp., 3, 4, 5, 6, 7, 8 ; (of

Adderley Hall,) 6, 7, 8 ; (of Ashfield Hall,) 6 supp., 7, 8. Harleian Society, ii. 17, 48, 177 ; iii. 4; xii. 63 ; xv. 189 ; xxviii. 133 ; xxxii. 84 ; xl. 1247. Lipscombe's History of the County of Buckingham, i. 271. Burke's Heraldic Illustrations, 45. Burke's Royal Families, (London, 1851, 8vo.) i. 7 ; ii. 128. Hodgson's Northumberland, II. ii. 112. Eyton's Antiquities of Shropshire, i. 100 ; iii. 183 ; vii. 40 ; x. 182. Nichols' History of the County of Leicester, iii. 1100 ; iv. 520. Pembrokeshire Pedigrees, 140. Baker's Northampton, i. 130. Carthew's Hundred of Launditch, Part ii. 672. The Sheriffs of Montgomeryshire, by W. V. Lloyd, 247. Collections by the Powys-land Club, viii. 90. Wotton's English Baronetage, ii. 74, 312. Betham's Baronetage, iv. 172 ; v. app. 1. Banks' Dormant and Extinct Baronage, i. 275, 389. Ormerod's Cheshire, iii. 548. Burke's Extinct Baronetcies. Visitation of Staffordshire, (Willm. Salt Soc.) 64. The Suffolk Records, by H. W. Aldred, 133. See ASHWIN.

CORBET-WINDER. Burke's Landed Gentry, 8.

CORBIN, or CORBYN. Shaw's Staffordshire, ii. 230. Dugdale's Warwickshire, 1119. Harleian Society, xii. 312.

CORBOULD. The Genealogist, New Series, ii. 94.

CORBROND. Eyton's Antiquities of Shropshire, viii. 184.

CORBY. Foley's Records of the English Province, S. J., iii. 59.

CORDALL. Visitation of Norfolk, published by Norfolk Archæological Society, i. 91. Harleian Society, xxxii. 85.

CORDELL. Visitation of Suffolke, edited by J. J. Howard, i. 245-266. Harleian Society, i. 91 ; xv. 189. Monken Hadley, by F. C. Cass, 198. Burke's Extinct Baronetcies. Metcalfe's Visitations of Suffolk, 20.

CORDRAY. Visitatio Comitatus Wiltoniæ, 1623, printed by Sir T. Phillipps. Visitation of Wiltshire, edited by G. W. Marshall, 71. The Genealogist, xii. 22.

CORFIELD. Burke's Landed Gentry, 8.

CORHAM. Berry's Hampshire Genealogies, 172.

CORINDON. The Visitations of Devon, by J. L. Vivian, 236.

CORKEN. Harleian Society, xv. 190.

CORNDON. The Visitations of Devon, by J. L. Vivian, 236.

CORNEWALL, or CORNWALL. Pedigree of Cornwall, Barons of Burford, Co. Salop, of Berrington and Moccas, Co. Hereford, and of Diddlebury, Co. Salop, [T. P.] Middle Hill, 1842. 2 sheet pedigrees. Pedigree of Sir Rowland Cornewall of Berrington, Co. Hereford, [T. P.] Broadside. Burke's Landed Gentry, 2 add., 3, 4, 5, 6. Burke's Royal Families, (London, 1851, 8vo.) ii. 199. Lipscombe's History of the County of Buckingham, i. 112. Baker's Northampton, i. 415. Robinson's Mansions of Herefordshire, 118. Miscellanea Genealogica et Heraldica, New Series, ii. 445, 461 ; 2nd Series, v. 76. The Genealogist, iii. 225, 295 ; iv. 76. Harleian Society, xiii. 6 ; xxviii. 145. Nash's Worcestershire, i. 241. Notes and Queries, 1 S. x. 282 ; xi. 240. Banks' Baronies in Fee, ii. 69. Banks' Dormant and Extinct Baronage, iii. 207. Metcalfe's Visitations of Northamptonshire, 15. Weaver's

13

Visitations of Somerset, 83. New England Register, xlix. 39.
See BURFORD.

CORNEY. Visitation of Oxfordshire, 1634, printed by Sir T. Phillipps,
(Middle Hill, fol.) 17. Harleian Society, v. 244. Burke's Colonial
Gentry, i. 290.

CORNISH. Morant's Essex, ii. 87. Burke's Landed Gentry, (of Black
Hall,) 3, 4, 5, 6 and supp., 7, 8; 8 at p. 196; (of Marazion,) 2;
7 p. 188. Harleian Society, xiii. 8; xv. 191. Burke's Extinct
Baronetcies. An Historical Survey of Cornwall, by C. S. Gilbert,
ii. 81. The Visitations of Cornwall, edited by J. L. Vivian, 265.

CORNOCK. Burke's Landed Gentry, 2, 3, 4, 5, 6, 7, 8.

CORNWALL (Earls of). D. Gilbert's History of Cornwall, iv. 346.
Brydges' Collins' Peerage, i. 1. (Dukes of,) An Historical Survey
of Cornwall, by C. S. Gilbert, i. 413.

CORNWALLIS. Gentleman's Magazine, 1826, i. 406, 502. Harleian
Society, iv. 161. Edmondson's Baronagium Genealogicum, iii.
289. Notes and Queries, 4 S. i. 505. Brydges' Collins' Peerage,
ii. 537. Metcalfe's Visitations of Suffolk, 21. Burke's Landed
Gentry, 8. A Description to accompany the Tables of Descent of
the Cornwallis Family, by Louisa, Marchioness Cornwallis.
London, *n. d.*, 8vo., pp. 64. Private Correspondence of Lady
Jane Cornwallis, xxxii.

COROUN. Ormerod's Cheshire, iii. 654.

CORRANCE. Burke's Commoners, iii. 370, Landed Gentry, 2, 3, 4, 5,
6, 7, 8.

CORRIE. Records of the Corrie Family, by J. E. Corrie. London,
1899, 4to. Burke's Family Records, 178.

CORRIGAN. O'Hart's Irish Pedigrees, 2nd Series, 155.

CORRY. The History of the Corry Family of Castle Coole, by the
Earl of Belmore. London, 1891. Burke's Landed Gentry, 3, 4, 5,
6, 7. Paterson's History of the Co. of Ayr, ii. 291. Shirley's
History of the County of Monaghan, 189. Paterson's History of
Ayr and Wigton, ii. 352. Archdall's Lodge's Peerage, vii. 193.
See CORY.

CORSANE. Lands and their Owners in Galloway, by P. H. M'Kerlie,
ii. 247. Nisbet's Heraldry, ii. app. 119.

CORSELLIS. Morant's Essex, i. 407; ii. 188. Berry's Essex Genealogies, 44. Burke's Landed Gentry, 3, 4, 5, 6. Wright's Essex, i.
397. Harleian Society, xiv. 650.

CORSETT. The Visitations of Devon, by J. L. Vivian, 704.

CORSTORPHINE. Burke's Landed Gentry, 4, 5, 6, 7, 8.

CORTINGSTOCK. Thoroton's Nottinghamshire, i. 55.

CORY, CORYE, or CORRIE. Harleian Society, vi. 73; xxxii. 86; xliii.
44. Dawson Turner's Sepulchral Reminiscences of Great Yarmouth, 108. Colby of Great Torrington, by F. T. Colby, 29.
Burke's Landed Gentry, 2 at p. 542; 8 supp. The Visitations of
Devon, by J. L. Vivian, 235. Genealogies of Morgan and Glamorgan, by G. T. Clark, 379. Parliamentary Memoirs of Fermanagh, by the Earl of Belmore, 34, 54. *See* CORRY.

CORYN. The Visitations of Cornwall, edited by J. L. Vivian, 100.

CORYNDON. Harleian Society, vi. 74.

CORYTON. Burke's Commoners, i. 232, Landed Gentry, 2, 3, 4, 5, 6, 7, 8. Harleian Society, ix. 49. A Complete Parochial History of the County of Cornwall, iv. 82. An Historical Survey of Cornwall, by C. S. Gilbert, i. 589 ; ii. 69. Burke's Extinct Baronetcies. The Visitations of Cornwall, edited by J. L. Vivian. 101.

COSBY. Herald and Genealogist, v. 335. Gentleman's Magazine, 1834, i. 179. Burke's Commoners, iii. 153, Landed Gentry, 2, 3, 4, 5, 6, 7, 8. Oliver's History of Antigua, i. 242. Ontarian Families, by E. M. Chadwick, i. 162.

COSIN, or COSYN. Morant's Essex, i. 291. Surtees' Durham, i. cxiv. Foster's Visitations of Durham, 91. Visitation of Gloucester, by T. F. Fenwick and W. C. Metcalfe, 48.

COSSEN. Harleian Society, ix. 51. The Visitations of Cornwall, edited by J. L. Vivian, 103.

COSSINGTON. Surrey Archæological Collections, iii. Visitation of Devon, edited by F. T. Colby, 89.

COSTELLO. Burke's Landed Gentry, 3 supp., 4, 5, 6, 7. O'Hart's Irish Pedigrees, 2nd Series, 323.

COSTON. Harleian Society, xxviii. 148.

COSWARTH, or COSWORTH. Harleian Society, i. 16 ; ix. 50. An Historical Survey of Cornwall, by C. S. Gilbert, ii. 83. The Visitations of Cornwall, edited by J. L. Vivian, 104.

COTEEL. Harleian Society, xv. 192. See COTTLE.

COTES. History of Tetbury, Co. Gloucester, by A. T. Lee, 249. Burke's Landed Gentry, 2, 3, 4, 5, 6, 7, 8. Harleian Society, ii. 94 ; xxviii. 149. Nichols' History of the County of Leicester, iv. 35, 212. Dugdale's Warwickshire, 359. The Genealogist, New Series, xvii. 117.

COTGREAVE. Burke's Commoners, i. 530. Harleian Society, xviii. 68, 80.

COTON. Warwickshire Antiquarian Magazine, Part 1. See COTTON.

COTTAM. Berry's Kent Genealogies, 83. Chetham Society, lxxxii. 100; cv. 256. History of Longridge, by T. C. Smith, 144. History of Ribchester, by T. C. Smith, 242.

COTTERELL. Pedigrees of Cotterell of Seynbury, Harward of Hartlebury, etc., [T. P.] 4 folio pages. Pedigree of Cotterell of Campden, [T. P.] Broadside. Harleian Society, viii. 409; xxxii. 87. History of St. Canice, Kilkenny, by J. Graves, 254. Notes and Queries, 6 S. iv. 384. Cooke's Continuation of Duncumb's Hereford, (Hund. of Grimsworth,) Part ii. 124. Pedigree of Wilson, by S. B. Foster, 201. See COTTRELL.

COTTESFORD. Visitation of Oxfordshire, 1634, printed by Sir T. Phillipps, (Middle Hill, fol.) 17. Harleian Society, v. 284. Dunkin's History of Bullington and Ploughley, i. 316.

COTTESMORE, or COTTISMORE. Harleian Society, v. 195. F. G. Lee's History of Thame, 302.

COTTINGHAM. Ormerod's Cheshire, ii. 541. The Irish Builder, xxix. 347. Harleian Society, xxviii. 153.

COTTINGTON. Hoare's Wiltshire, IV. i. 24. Visitation of Somerset,

printed by Sir T. Phillipps, 55. Harleian Society, xi. 29. Banks'
Dormant and Extinct Baronage, iii. 213. Burke's Extinct
Baronetcies.

COTTLE, COTELE, or COTTELL. A History of the Cotel, Cottell, or
Cottle Family, by W. H. Cottell. London, 1871, 8vo. Pedigree of
the Family of Cotell or Cottle, by W. H. Cottell. London, 1891,
large sheet. Pedigree of Cottell of Yeolmbridge, Co. Devon,
single sheet, privately printed by Sir T. Phillipps, Bart., 1867.
Pedigree of Cottle of Round Hill, Nevis, etc., [T. P.] 1864, 2 folio
pages. Pedigree of Cottle of Round Hill and of Ash Hall, Co.
Glamorgan, [T. P.] 1864, folio page. Westcote's Devonshire,
edited by G. Oliver and P. Jones, 475. Visitatio Comitatus
Wiltoniæ, 1623, printed by Sir T. Phillipps. The Genealogist,
i. 340. Harleian Society, vi. 75 ; xiii. 383. Maclean's History of
Trigg Minor, i. 667, 670. Visitation of Devon, edited by F. T.
Colby, 69. Visitation of Wiltshire, edited by G. W. Marshall, 16.
Notes and Queries, 4 S. v. 212, 325. The Visitations of Devon,
by J. L. Vivian, 238. See COTEEL.

COTTON. Jewitt's Reliquary, ix. 177. Gentleman's Magazine, 1825,
i. 581 ; 1833, i. 400. The Tyndale Pedigree, by B. W. Greenfield.
The trial of the second issue in Bere *versus* Ward, 1823, fol., *at
end*. Morant's Essex, i. 422 ; ii. 406, 528. Glover's History of
Derbyshire, ii. 152. Camden Society, xliii. 26. Berry's Hampshire Genealogies, 52. Cambridgeshire Visitation, edited by Sir
T. Phillipps, 10. Berry's Kent Genealogies, 476. Burke's Landed
Gentry, (of Etwall,) 3, 4, 5, 6, 7, 8 ; (of Knolton,) 5, 6 ; 6 at p.
619, 7, 8. Harleian Society, ii. 191 ; vi. 341 ; viii. 171 ; xii. 305 ;
xiii. 40, 384 ; xv. 193 ; xviii. 69 ; xxi. 45 ; xxii. 46 ; xxviii. 154 ;
xxxvii. 122 ; xli. 20 ; xlii. 158. Visitation of Warwickshire, 1619,
published with Warwickshire Antiquarian Magazine, 96. Herald
and Genealogist, viii. 337. J. H. Hill's History of Market
Harborough, 137, 278. Maclean's History of Trigg Minor,
i. 642-662. Shaw's Staffordshire, i. 157*. Visitation of Staffordshire, 1663-4, printed by Sir T. Phillipps, 4. Visitation of Berkshire, printed by Sir T. Phillipps, 15. Hampshire Visitations,
printed by Sir T. Phillipps, 17. Nichols' History of the
County of Leicester, ii. 694, 834 ; iv. 64, 636, 724. Hunter's
Deanery of Doncaster, ii. 375. Wilson's History of the parish of
St. Laurence Pountney, 239. Notices of Great Yarmouth, by
J. H. Druery, 124. Catalogue of Manuscripts in the Cottonian
Library, (1800, fol.) Preface, xiii. Ormerod's Cheshire, ii. 786 ;
iii. 126, 414. Erdeswicke's Survey of Staffordshire, 276. An
Historical Survey of Cornwall, by C. S. Gilbert, ii. 85. Notes
and Queries, 2 S. i. 250, 298, 324, 459 ; 3 S. vi. 449 ; 4 S. i. 70.
Wotton's English Baronetage, i. 128 ; ii. 195 ; iii. 611. Betham's
Baronetage, i. 401 ; iii. 6. The Genealogist, v. 247 ; vi. 144.
Metcalfe's Visitations of Suffolk, 129, 130. Burke's Extinct
Baronetcies. Visitations of Staffordshire, 1614 and 1663-4,
William Salt Society, 95. The Visitations of Devon, by J. L.
Vivian, 240. The Suffolk Records, by H. W. Aldred, 161. East

Barnet, by F. C. Cass, Part i. 107. Genealogical Gleanings in England, by H. F. Waters, i. 92. Burke's Colonial Gentry, i. 76. Earwaker's History of Sandbach, 190, 194. New England Register, i. 164; iv. 92; xxxix. 64. Burke's Family Records, 181. *See* COTON.

COTTON-SHEPPARD. Burke's Royal Families, (London, 1851, 8vo.) i. 203.

COTTRELL. Burke's Commoners, iv. 745, Landed Gentry, 2, 3, 4. Burrows' History of the Family of Burrows, 208. Monken Hadley, by F. C. Cass, 113. New England Register, xiv. 25. F. G. Lee's History of Thame, 518. *See* COTTERELL.

COTTRELL-DORMER. Lipscombe's History of the County of Buckingham, i. 119. Burke's Landed Gentry, 7. 8.

COUCHMAN. Berry's Kent Genealogies, 260. Harleian Society, xlii. 112.

COUCY. Duchetiana, by Sir G. F. Duckett, 2nd edn., 138.

COULL. Oliver's History of Antigua, i. 178.

COULSON. Surtees Society, xxxvi. 323. Burke's Commoners, ii. 525, Landed Gentry, 2, 3, 4, 5, 6, 7, 8. Hodgson's Northumberland, III. ii. 131. Ord's History of Cleveland, 411.

COULT. Harleian Society, xiv. 566. *See* COLT.

COULTHART. A Genealogical Account of the Coultharts of Coulthart and Collyn, chiefs of the name, etc., by George Parker Knowles. London, 1855, 8vo. Coulthart, of Coulthart, Collyn, and Ashton-under-Lyne, derived from the Family Muniments, and brought down to A.D. 1853, by Alex. Cheyne and George Parker Knowles, broadside sheet. Notes and Memoranda to the Coulthart and Ross Pedigrees, 1864, 8vo., pp. 11. Popular Genealogists, 22-51. Manchester Guardian (newspaper), May 30, 1865. Herald and Genealogist, iii. 17, 151, 252. Burke's Visitation of Seats and Arms, i. 39; 2nd Series, i. 18. Burke's Landed Gentry, 2 supp., 3 and corr., 4. Foster's Lancashire Pedigrees. Burke's Royal Families, (London, 1851, 8vo.) ii. 212.

COULTHURST. Burke's Landed Gentry, 5, 6, 7, 8. Foster's Yorkshire Pedigrees. Ord's History of Cleveland, 350. Whitaker's Deanery of Craven, 172, (240). *See* COLTHURST.

COUMBEMARTIN. Bridge's Northamptonshire, by Rev. Peter Whalley, i. 324. *See* COMBMARTIN.

COUNDON. Foster's Visitations of Yorkshire, 507. Surtees' Durham, iii. 262.

COUNSEL. History of Gloucester, by T. D. Fosbrooke, vi.

COUPER. Ashmole's Antiquities of Berkshire, iii. 19. Harleian Society, xxxii. 87; xli. 108; xliii. 75. The Genealogist, New Series, i. 6. *See* COOPER.

COUPLAND. Burke's Landed Gentry, 7, 8. Plantagenet-Harrison's History of Yorkshire, i. 550.

COURADUS. Harleian Society, xv. 195.

COURCI, or COURCY. Claim of John de Courcy to be Baron Kingsale and Baron Courcy of Ringrone, Sess. Papers, 144 of 1831-32. Baker's Northampton, i. 619. Banks' Dormant and Extinct Baronage, i. 56. *See* DE COURSEY.

COURT. Court of Blockley, Co. Worcester, and of Bourton on the Hill, Co. Gloucester, [T. P.] 1871. Somersetshire wills, printed for F. A. Crisp, iii. 15, 16. Burke's Landed Gentry, 7, 8.

COURTAULD. Burke's Landed Gentry, 5, 6. Some Account of the Taylor Family, by P. A. Taylor, 699.

COURTEN. Harleian Society, xv. 194. Miscellanea Genealogica et Heraldica, 2nd Series, ii. 158. The Perverse Widow, by A. W. Crawley-Boevey, 180.

COURTENAY, COURTNAY, or COURTNEY. Discours sur la Généalogie et Maison de Courtenay. Paris, 1603, 8vo. De stirpe et Origine Domus de Courtenay. Paris, 1607, 8vo. A Genealogical History of the Noble Family of Courtenay, by Ezra Cleaveland, B.D. Exeter, 1735, fol. Case of William, Viscount Courtenay, on his Claim to the Earldom of Devon. 1830, fol., pp. 24. Minutes of Evidence taken before the Committee for Privileges on the Petition of William, Viscount Courtenay, 1831, fol. Sess. Papers, 27 of 1830-31. Histoire Généalogique de la Maison de Courtenay, par Jean du Bouchet, 1661, fol. Gibbon's Decline and Fall of the Roman Empire, Chapter LXI. Letter to Lord Brougham on the late decision of the Earldom of Devon, by T. C. Banks. London, 1831. Report of Proceedings in the claim to the Earldom of Devon, by Sir N. H. Nicolas. London, 1832, 8vo. Collinson's Somerset, ii. 160, 341. Savage's Hundred of Carhampton, 343-514. Herald and Genealogist, iv. 279. Journal of the Archæological Institute, x. 52. Burke's Commoners, ii. 306 ; (of Ballyedmond,) Landed Gentry, 2, 3, 4, 5, 6. Harleian Society, vi. 76 ; ix. 51-53 ; xxxvii. 59. Topographer, (London, 1789-91, 8vo.) i. 133. Maclean's History of Trigg Minor, i. 76, 459, 656 ; ii. 189, 240. Polwhele's History of Cornwall, iv. 9. Lipscombe's History of the County of Buckingham, i. 466, 471. Westcote's Devonshire, edited by G. Oliver and P. Jones, 570, 573, 574-576. Whitaker's Loidis and Elmete, 166. Harding's History of Tiverton, i. Part 2, 19. Jewitt's Reliquary, xvii. 17, 97, 135, 213. Dunsford's Historical Memoirs of Tiverton, 74-100. A Complete Parochial History of the County of Cornwall, i. 1. An Historical Survey of Cornwall, by C. S. Gilbert, i. 497. Collectanea Archæologica, (Brit. Arch. Assn.) i. 232. Exmouth Ancient and Modern, (1868, 8vo.) 254. Edmondson's Baronagium Genealogicum, iv. 340. A description of the Monument and Effigies in Porlock Church, by M. Halliday, at end. Brydges' Collins' Peerage, vi. 214. Banks' Baronies in Fee, i. 165, 193. Visitation of Devon, edited by F. T. Colby, 72. Banks' Dormant and Extinct Baronage, ii. 118 ; iii. 247. Notes and Queries, 6 S. iii. 1, 52 ; 8 S. vii. 441, 503. The Genealogist, vi. 198 ; New Series, xv. 29 ; xvi. 167. The Visitations of Cornwall, edited by J. L. Vivian, 105-118, 576. Hasted's Kent, (Hund. of Blackheath, by H. H. Drake,) xvii., xxiii., xxv. Miscellanea Genealogica et Heraldica, 2nd Series, iii. 349 ; v. 179. The Visitations of Devon, by J. L. Vivian, 243-53, 747. See TRACY.

COURTHOP, or COURTHOPE. Hasted's Kent, ii. 375, 387 ; iii. 650.

Berry's Sussex Genealogies, 216. Berry's Kent Genealogies, 476. Burke's Landed Gentry, 5, 6, 7, 8. Harleian Society, viii. 134 ; xlii. 194. Collectanea Topographica, et Genealogica, ii. 279, 393.

COURTIER. Pedigree of Courtier, privately printed by F. W. Courtier, folio sheet.

COURTOWN. Claim of the Earl of Courtown to vote at elections of Irish Peers, Sess. Papers, 87 of 1859. sess. 1.

COUTTS. Memoirs of a Banking-house, by Sir W. Forbes, 1. *See* COLT.

COVELL. Plantagenet-Harrison's History of Yorkshire, i. 261. Harleian Society, xv. 195.

COVEN. Collections for a History of Staffordshire, (William Salt Society,) i. 320.

COVENTRY. Account of Croome D'Abitot, with Biographical notices of the Coventry family. By W. Dean. Worcester, 1824, 8vo. The Family of Darby-Coventry of Greenlands. By S. G. Fell. London, 1892, 4to. Warwickshire Pedigrees from Visitation of 1682-3, (privately printed, 1865,) App. Herald and Genealogist, vii. 97. Hutchins' Dorset, iii. 358. Edmondson's Baronagium Genealogicum, ii. 174. Brydges' Collins' Peerage, iii. 744. Banks' Dormant and Extinct Baronage, iii. 215. Burke's Landed Gentry, 8. Historic Gleanings, by E. M. Hance and T. N. Morton, 91. The Gresley's of Drakelowe, by F. Madan, 246.

COVERT. Morant's Essex, i. 291. Berry's Kent Genealogies, 428 Berry's Sussex Genealogies, 18, 323. Manning and Bray's Surrey, ii. 65, 441. Castles, Mansions, and Manors of Western Sussex, by D. G. C. Elwes and C. J. Robinson, 227. Burke's Extinct Baronetcics. Weaver's Visitations of Somerset, 18. Surrey Archæological Collections, x. Harleian Society, xlii. 138 ; xliii. 4, 39, 129.

COWAN. Burke's Family Records, 182.

COWARD. Visitation of Somerset, printed by Sir T. Phillipps, 56. Harleian Society, xi. 30. Somersetshire Wills, printed for F. A. Crisp, ii. 32.

COWDRAY, or COWDREY. Berry's Hampshire Genealogies, 324. Lipscombe's History of the County of Buckingham, iv. 251. Hampshire Visitations, printed by Sir T. Phillipps, 17.

COWELL-STEPNEY. Burke's Landed Gentry, 4, 5. Burke's Authorized Arms, 174. T. Nicholas' County Families of Wales, 282.

COWIE. W. R. Fraser's History of Laurencekirk, 176. Burke's Colonial Gentry, ii. 633.

COWLES. Memorials of the Prichards, by Isabell Southall, 113.

COWLEY. Pedigree of Cowley of Eastington, Co. Gloucester, [T. P.] 1868, folio page. Transactions of Kilkenny Archæological Society, ii. 102. Harleian Society, xv. 196. Notes and Queries, 4 S. xi. 340, 429. Gloucestershire Notes and Queries, iv. 563. *See* COLLEY.

COWLIN. Harleian Society, ix. 54. The Visitations of Cornwall edited by J. L. Vivian, 119.

COWPER. Claim of F. T. de G., Earl Cowper, to be Lord Dingwall, and Lord Butler of Moore Park, Sess. Papers, C of 1870 ; C of 1871. Harleian Society, i. 83 ; ii. 152 ; xv. 197 ; xxxix. 938. Visitation of Berkshire, printed by Sir T. Phillipps, 15. Manning and Bray's Surrey, i. 597. Berry's Hertfordshire Genealogies, 167. Berry's Sussex Genealogies, 145, 276. Miscellanea Genealogica et Heraldica, i. 51 ; New Series, i. 330. Burke's Landed Gentry, 2 corr., p. 426, 4, 5, 6, 7, 8. Dallaway's Sussex, i. 194 ; II. i. 356. Nichols' History of the County of Leicester, iv. 974. Clutterbuck's Hertford, ii. 194. The Citizens of London and their Rulers, by B. B. Orridge, 194. Ormerod's Cheshire, i. 375. Surrey Archæological Collections, vi. The Castles, Manors, and Mansions of Western Sussex, by D. G. C. Elwes and C. J. Robinson, 207. Edmondson's Baronagium Genealogicum, iii. 216. Brydges' Collins' Peerage, iv. 162. Metcalfe's Visitations of Northamptonshire, 176. Bysshe's Visitation of Essex, edited by J. J. Howard, 25. Sepulchral Memorials of Bobbingworth, 35. Burke's Colonial Gentry, ii. 748. The Genealogist, New Series, xiv. 121.

COWPER-ESSEX. Howard's Visitation of England and Wales, vi. 11.

COX, or COXE. 'Edward Townsend Cox, Birmingham.'[1] Privately printed, London, *n. d.*, 4to., 16. Pedigree of Coxe of Ellingham, Co. Northumberland, etc., [T. P.] 1856, fol. page. Herald and Genealogist, v. 84 ; viii. 64. Glover's History of Derbyshire, ii. 163, (140). Berry's Sussex Genealogies, 8. Berry's Berkshire Genealogies, 37. Visitation of Somerset, printed by Sir Thos. Phillipps, 57. Burke's Landed Gentry, (of Ballynoe,) 3, 4, 5, 6, 7, 8 ; (of Coolcliffe,) 2, 3, 4, 5 ; (of Hillingdon,) 7, 8 ; (of Min-y-Garth,) 8 ; (Baronets,) 8 at p. 1949 ; (of Broxwood,) 3, 4, 5, 6, 6 at p. 1543, 7, 7 at p. 1763, 8. Visitation of Berkshire, printed by Sir T. Phillipps, 15. Nichols' History of the County of Leicester, iv. 864. The Genealogist, v. 248. An Account of the Families of Boase, (Exeter, 1876, 4to.) 27. Clutterbuck's Hertford, i. 114. Fosbrooke's History of Gloucestershire, i. 384. Family of Sir Richard Cox, created Baronet, 1706, a broadside pedigree, *n. d.* A second edition of this, signed E. G. Cox, October, 1890. Copy of Declaration of Sir George W. Cox, Bart. Poona, 1889, 4to., pp. 13. Genealogical Memoranda relating to the Family of King, by W. L. King, 6. Account of the Family of Hallen, by A. W. C. Hallen, table viii. Visitation of Gloucester, edited by T. F. Fenwick and W. C. Metcalfe, 49. Harleian Society, xxii. 7, 46 ; xxviii. 156. Visitations of Staffordshire, 1614 and 1663-4, William Salt Society, 97. Burke's Colonial Gentry, i. 74 ; ii. 781. Gloucestershire Notes and Queries, iii. 299. Burke's Family Records, 183. Genealogical Record of King and Henham, 8. Staniforthiana, by F. M. H., at end. *See* CAPEL.

COXETER. Oxford Historical Society, xix. 42.

COXWELL. Burke's Commoners, iii. 471, Landed Gentry, 2, 3, 4, 5. Harleian Society, xxi. 47. Visitation of Gloucester, edited by T. F. Fenwick and W. C. Metcalfe, 51, 146.

---

[1] This is the title of the publication.

COXWELL-ROGERS. Miscellanea Genealogica et Heraldica, i. 265. Burke's Landed Gentry, 2, 3, 4, 5, 6, 7, 8.
COYNEY, or COYNY. Burke's Commoners, ii. 42, Landed Gentry, 2, 3, 4, 5, 6, 7, 8. Visitation of Staffordshire, 1663-4, printed by Sir T. Phillipps, 4. Dwnn's Visitations of Wales, i. 25. Visitation of Staffordshire, (Willm. Salt Soc.) 65. Visitations of Staffordshire, 1614 and 1663-4, William Salt Society, 98.
COYS. Morant's Essex, i. 103. Harleian Society, xiii. 184, 385. Bysshe's Visitation of Essex, edited by J. J. Howard, 25.
COZENS. F. G. Lee's History of Thame, 229.
CRABB, or CRABBE. Harleian Society, ix. 55. East Anglian, ii. 259. The Genealogist, iii. 241. The Visitations of Cornwall, by J. L. Vivian, 577. Oliver's History of Antigua, i. 181.
CRACHERODE. Bysshe's Visitation of Essex,, edited by J. J. Howard, 26. Morant's Essex, ii. 360. Wright's Essex, i. 644. See CROCHRODE.
CRACKANTHORPE, or CRAKENTHORP. Burke's Royal Descents and Pedigrees of Founders' Kin, 40. Burke's Landed Gentry, 2, 3, 4, 5, 6, 8. Foster's Visitations of Cumberland and Westmorland, 28. Nicolson and Burn's Westmorland and Cumberland, i. 367, 448.
CRACROFT. Cambridgeshire Visitation, edited by Sir T. Phillipps, 12. Burke's Landed Gentry, 2, 3, 4, 5, 6, 8 at p. 25. Lincolnshire Tradesmen's Tokens, by Justin Simpson, (London, 1872, 8vo.) 13. Stemmata Britannica, by Joseph Foster, (London, 1877, 8vo.) 29. The Genealogist, iii. 370. Harleian Society, xli. 68.
CRADOCK, or CRADOCKE. Descent of J. D. Cradock from Edw. I. Privately printed by W. G. D. Fletcher, (circa 1883), folio page. Collinson's Somerset, iii. 588. Berry's Sussex Genealogies, 218. Dwnn's Visitations of Wales, i. 143, 201. Glamorganshire Pedigrees, edited by Sir T. Phillipps, 20. Burke's Commoners, iv. 256, Landed Gentry, 2, 5, 6 and supp., 7, 8. Burke's Patrician, iv. 481. Harleian Society, ii. 149 ; xv. 198 ; xxi. 114. Surtees' Durham, iv. 13. History of Richmond, by C. Clarkson, 177. Bridges' Northamptonshire, by Rev. Peter Whalley, ii. 31. Nichols' History of the County of Leicester, ii. 466 ; iii. 1149, 1150 . iv. 802, 807*. Pedigrees of the Leading Families of Lancashire, published by Joseph Foster, (London, 1872, fol.). The New History of Yorkshire, commencing with Richmondshire, by Genl. Plantagenet-Harrison, (London, 1872, fol.) Part i. 33. Plantagenet-Harrison's History of Yorkshire, i. 110. Historical Notices of Sir M. Cradock, Kt., by J. M. Traherne, 4. Notes and Queries, 1 S. ii. 376, 427, 465 ; vi. 532 ; vii. 51. The Genealogist, vi. 19. Visitations of Staffordshire, 1614 and 1663-4, William Salt Society, 100. Fletcher's Leicestershire Pedigrees and Royal Descents, 74. Pedigrees of the Leading Families of Yorkshire, by Joseph Foster. Genealogies of Morgan and Glamorgan, by G. T. Clark, 174. Weaver's Visitation of Somerset, 104. New England Register, viii. 25 ; ix. 122 ; x. 231.
CRADOCK-HARTOPP. Fletcher's Leceistershire Pedigrees and Royal Descents, 91.

CRAFORD. Berry's Kent Genealogies, 109, 133. Harleian Society, xv. 199 ; xlii. 34. *See* CRAYFORD.

CRAFTE. Dugdale's Warwickshire, 27.

CRAFTON. Cyclostyle Pedigrees, by J. J. Green.

CRAGGS. Miscellanea Genealogica et Heraldica, ii. 34. Hasted's Kent, i. 42. Hasted's Kent, (Hund. of Blackheath, by H. H. Drake,) 138.

CRAIG. O'Hart's Irish Pedigrees, 2nd Series, 155. Burke's Family Records, 185. Howard's Visitation of England and Wales, v. 34; vi. 146.

CRAIGIE. Walter Wood's East Neuk of Fife, 301.

CRAIG-LAURIE. Burke's Landed Gentry, 5, 6, 7, 8.

CRAKE. Harleian Society, xvi. 81. *See* CREKE.

CRAKPOT. Plantagenet-Harrison's History of Yorkshire, i. 272.

CRAMER. Burke's Landed Gentry, 4, 5, 6, 7, 8.

CRAMER-ROBERTS. Burke's Landed Gentry, 8.

CRAMLINGTON. The Genealogist, ii. 184. Burke's Landed Gentry, 2. Foster's Visitations of Northumberland, 35.

CRAMOND. The Parish of Cramond, by J. P. Wood, 51.

CRAMPE. Bysshe's Visitation of Essex, edited by J. J. Howard, 26.

CRANCH. New England Register, xxvii. 40.

CRANE. Memorials of an old Preston family (the family of Crane). Reprinted from *The Preston Guardian*, 1877. By W. A. Abram. Preston, 1877, 8vo. Visitation of Suffolke, edited by J. J. Howard, i. 137-162. Baker's Northampton, ii. 243. Burke's Landed Gentry, 6, 7, 8. The Visitations of Cornwall, edited by J. L. •Vivian, 120. Metcalfe's Visitations of Suffolk, 22. Burke's Extinct Baronetcies. Genealogical Gleanings in England, by H. F. Waters, i. 226. New England Register, iv. 180 ; xvi. 139 ; xxvii. 76 ; xli. 177 ; xlvi. 216 ; xlvii. 78, 325. Harleian Society, xxxii. 87.

CRANESLEY. Bridges' Northamptonshire, by Rev. Peter Whalley, ii. 89.

CRANFIELD. Banks' Dormant and Extinct Baronage, iii. 513.

CRANFORD. Baker's Northampton, i. 244. Harleian Society, xii. 129.

CRANMER. Genealogical Memoirs of the Kindred Families of Thomas Cranmer and Thomas Wood, by R. E. C. Waters. London, 1877, 4to. Nicholas' edition of Walton's Complete Angler, i. 142. H. J. Todd's Life of Archbishop Cranmer, 1831, 8vo. Gentleman's Magazine, lxii. 991 ; lxiii. 120, 230. Harleian Society, iv. 70 ; viii. 327, 430 ; xv. 199. Gage's History of Thingoe Hundred, Suffolk, 391. Manning and Bray's Surrey, ii. 497 ; iii. clii. Thoroton's Nottinghamshire, i. 262. Memoirs of the family of Chester, by R. E. C. Waters, 367, etc. Notes and Queries, 1 S. iii. 8, 153, 188 ; 5 S. ix. 414. Miscellanea Genealogica et Heraldica, 2nd Series, v. 63.

CRANSTOUN. Burke's Landed Gentry, 3, 4, 5, 6, 7, 8 ; Burke's Royal Families, (London, 1851, 8vo.) i. 139. Wood's Douglas's Peerage of Scotland, i. 366.

CRASHAW. Surtees Society, xxxvi. 212.

CRASTER, or CRASTRE. Burke's Landed Gentry, 2, 3, 4, 5, 6, 7, 8. The Genealogist, ii. 16. Foster's Visitations of Northumberland, 36.

CRATHORNE. Surtees Society, xxxvi. 145. Foster's Visitations of Yorkshire, 207. Graves' History of Cleveland, 105. Ord's History of Cleveland, 490. The Genealogist, iii. 371; New Series, xiv. 179. Harleian Society, xv. 200.

CRAUFUIRD, CRAUFURD, CRAWFORD, or CRAWFURD. Claim of Mr. John Lindsay Crawfurd to the Title and Estates of Crawfurd and Kilbirny, Paisley, 1819, 4to. The Crawfurd Peerage, with genealogical particulars relating to the Illustrious Houses of Crawfurd and Kilbirnie, by Dr. A. M. Adams. Edinburgh, 1829. An Examination of the Claim of J. L. Crawfurd, by J. Dobie. Edinburgh, 1831, 4to. Sketch of the Case of John Lindsay Crawfurd, by Dr. A. M. Adams. Edinburgh, 1834, 4to. Case of* John Lindsay Crawfurd, fol., pp. 50, and Appendix pp. 44 ; reprinted with additions in 3 vols. 8vo., 1849. Lives of the Lindsays, or a Memoir of the Houses of Crawford and Balcares, by Lord Lindsay. Wigan, 1840, 8vo. 4 vols. Claim of James, Earl of Balcarres, to be Earl of Crawfurd, and Lord Lindsay ; and Petition of Robert Lindsay Crawfurd, Esq., claiming the same title, Sess. Papers, 206 of 1845 ; 47 of 1846 ; 231 of 1847 ; 135 of 1847-8 ; 347 of 1852-3. Report of Speeches of Counsel, etc., upon the Claim of James, Earl of Crawfurd and Balcarres, to the original Dukedom of Montrose, by Lord Lindsay. London, 1855, fol. [A bibliographical catalogue of the Cases and Papers printed is given at p. ix. of the Introduction.] Herald and Genealogist, v. 172. Burke's Commoners, (of Crosby,) i. 551, ii. 385 ; Commoners, (of Craufurdland,) ii. 230, Landed Gentry, 2, 3, 4, 5, 6, 7, 8 ; (of Auchinames,) Commoners, ii. 384, Landed Gentry, 2, 3, 4, 5, 6, 7, 8 ; Commoners, (of Kilbirnie,) iii. 181, Landed Gentry, 2, 3, 4, 6, at p. 1464, 8. Landed Gentry, (of Milton,) 3, 4, 5, 6 ; (of Crawfurd,) 2 ; (of Saint Hill,) 2, 3 ; (of Cartsburn,) 6, 7, 8 ; (of Fort Singleton,) 6 at p. 1464, 8 supp. ; (of Ardmillan,) 2 supp., 3, 4, 5, 6, 7, 8 ; (of Overton,) 7 ; (of Crawfordsburn,) 8 ; (of Stonewold,) 8. Nisbet's Heraldry, ii. app. 94. Burke's Heraldic Illustrations, 42. Douglas's Baronage of Scotland, 429-434. George Robertson's Description of Cunninghame, 130, 257, 335. Paterson's History of the County of Ayr, i. 277, 327, 355, 403, 418, 428, 430, 437 ; ii. 39, 77, 114, 139, 195, 318, 335, 368, 440. Burke's Patrician, vi. 272. Burke's St. James's Magazine, i. 242. Paterson's History of Ayr and Wigton, i. 223, 323, 326, 378, 399, 705, 719 ; ii. 248, 427, 444 ; iii. 149, 176, 293, 321, 426, 543. Geo. Robertson's Account of Families in Ayrshire, i. 159-245. Crawford's Renfrewshire, 122. Wood's Douglas's Peerage of Scotland, i. 370. (Earls of,) Angus or Forfarshire, by A. J. Warden, 310-336. Notes and Queries, 7 S., ii. 383. Burke's Colonial Gentry, i. 292. Howard's Visitation of England and Wales, ii. 8 ; Notes, iii. 123. Oliver's History of Antigua, i. 182. Burke's Family Records, 188. Howard's Visitation of Ireland, ii. 29. See MONTROSE, SHARMAN-CRAWFORD.

CRAUNACHE. Ormerod's Cheshire, iii. 127.
CRAVEN. Notes on the Pedigree of the Cravens of Appletreewick,
by W. J. Stavert. Skipton, 1894, 8vo. Surtees Society, xxxvi.
33. Burke's Commoners, i. 180; Landed Gentry, (of Brock-
hampton Park,) 2, 3, 4, 5, 6, 7, 8; (of Brambridge,) 4, 5; (of
Richardston,) 2 supp., 3, 4. Foster's Visitations of Yorkshire,
174. Harleian Society, viii. 143, 151. Burke's Royal Descents
and Pedigrees of Founders' Kin, 6, 111. Abram's History of
Blackburn, 749. Memoirs, British and Foreign, of Illustrious
persons who died in 1711, 546. Notes and Queries, 4 S. i. 52,
128; 8 S. iv. 219, 333. Burke's Extinct Baronetcies. Edmondson's Baronagium Genealogicum, iv. 400. Brydges' Collins' Peerage,
v. 446. Banks' Dormant and Extinct Baronage, iii. 216. Phillimore's London and Middlesex Note Book, 161. The Genealogist, New Series, xiii. 56.
CRAW. Alexander Nisbet's Heraldic Plates, 86.
CRAWLEY. Morant's Essex, ii. 604. Burke's Landed Gentry, 4, 5,
7, 8. Baker's Northampton, i. 185. Notes and Queries, 4 S.
xii. 383. Harvey's Hundred of Willey, 523. Harleian Society,
xix. 98, 192. Bedfordshire Notes and Queries, iii. 124, 195.
The Perverse Widow, by A. W. Crawley-Boevey, 301.
CRAWSHAW. Hunter's Deanery of Doncaster, i. 330.
CRAWSHAY. Burke's Landed Gentry, 5, 6, 7, 8.
CRAY, or CRAYE. Cambridgeshire Visitation, edited by Sir T.
Phillipps, 10. Hampshire Visitations, printed by SirT. Phillipps,
17. Harleian Society, xli. 76.
CRAYFORD. Hasted's Kent, iv. 137. Burke's Visitation of Seats and
Arms, ii. 30. Harleian Society, xix. 167. See CRAFORD.
CREAGH. Burke's Landed Gentry, (of Bally Andrew,) 2 supp., 3, 4,
5, 6, 7, 8; (of Dangan,) 2 supp., 3, 4, 5, 6, 7, 8; (of Creagh
Castle,) 2, 3, 4, 5, 6, 7, 8; (of Cahirbane,) 5, 6, 7, 8; (of Carri-
gerry,) 2. Burke's Visitation of Seats and Arms, 2nd Series,
i. 63. Burke's Royal Descents and Pedigrees of Founders'
Kin, 29.
CREAN. Burke's Landed Gentry, 3. O'Hart's Irish Pedigrees, 2nd
Series, 156.
CREE. Burke's Landed Gentry, 2 supp., 3, 4, 5, 6, 7, 8.
CREFFEL. The Visitations of Cornwall, edited by J. L. Vivian, 121.
See CRESSEL.
CREFFIELD. The Genealogist, New Series, xiv. 80.
CREGOE. Burke's Landed Gentry, 2, 3, 4, 5, 6, 7, 8. See COLMORE-
CREGOE in Landed Gentry.
CREIGHTON. Burke's Commoners, iii. 636. Archdall's Lodge's
Peerage, vi. 65. See CRICHTON.
CREKE. Cambridgeshire Visitation, edited by Sir T. Phillipps, 8.
Clutterbuck's Hertford, ii. 495. Banks' Baronies in Fee, ii. 145.
Harleian Society, xix. 20; xli. 57. See CREYKE, DE CREKE,
CRAKE.
CREMER. Harleian Society, viii. 89. Burke's Family Records, 190.
Howard's Visitation of England and Wales, ix. 79.

CREON. Nichol's History of the County of Leicester, ii. 28. Banks'
Dormant and Extinct Baronage, i. 62.
CRESACRE. Burke's Commoners, iii. 452. Hunter's Deanery of Don-
caster, i. 372. Harleian Society, xvi. 81.
CRESFEILD. Harleian Society, viii. 507.
CRESPIN. Camden Society, xliii. 54. Hutchins' Dorset, iii. 626.
Burke's Landed Gentry, 6.
CRESSEL. Harleian Society, ix. 55. *See* CREFFEL.
CRESSENER. Morant's Essex, ii. 264, 266. Berry's Essex Genea-
logies, 121. Wright's Essex, i. 477. Harleian Society, xiv. 721.
Burke's Commoners, ii. 182. Bysshe's Visitation of Essex, edited
by J. J. Howard, 27.
CRESSETT. Miscellanea Genealogica et Heraldica, New Series, i. 31.
Harleian Society, xxviii. 157.
CRESSWELL, or CRESWELL. Berry's Hampshire Genealogies, 24, 248.
Burke's Commoners, (of Ravenstone,) iii. 475, Landed Gentry,
2, 3, 4, 5, 6, 7; (of Pinkney Park,) Landed Gentry, 2, 3, 4, 5, 6,
7, 8; (of Cresswell,) 7, 8. Foster's Visitations of Yorkshire, 149.
Shaw's Staffordshire, ii. 210. Bridges' Northamptonshire, by
Rev. Peter Whalley, i. 191. Hodgson's Northumberland, II. ii.
200. Baker's Northampton, i. 668. Hampshire Visitations,
printed by Sir T. Phillipps, 19. Metcalfe's Visitations of Northamptonshire, 83. Visitations of Staffordshire, 1614 and 1663-4,
William Salt Society, 101.
CRESSWELL-BAKER. Burke's Commoners, ii. 290, Landed Gentry,
2, 3, 4, 5, 6.
CRESSY, or CRESSI. Lipscombe's History of the County of Buckingham, i. 120. Surtees Society, xxxvi. 269. Foster's Visitations
of Yorkshire, 509. Harleian Society, iv. 41, 95; xxii. 2; xxxviii.
523. History of Blyth, by Rev. John Raine, 135. Dugdale's
Warwickshire, 671. New England Register, xxxi. 197. Clutter-
buck's Hertford, i. 407. Baker's Northampton, i. 355. Thoro-
ton's Nottinghamshire, iii. 416, 419. The Genealogist, iv. 249;
vi. 145. Banks' Dormant and Extinct Baronage, i. 227. Notes
and Queries, 6 S. vi. 169, 464. *See* DE CRESSY.
CRESVILLE. Hampshire Visitations, printed by Sir T. Phillipps, 18.
CRESWICK. Harleian Society, viii. 175. History of Ecclesfield, by
J. Eastwick, 408.
CREUZÉ. Herald and Genealogist, i. 259.
CREVEQUER, or CREVECŒUR. Planché's Corner of Kent, 286.
Clutterbuck's Hertford, i. 280. Archæologia Cantiana, iii. 273.
Banks' Dormant and Extinct Baronage, i. 60. *See* DE CREVECŒUR.
CREW, or CREWE. Glover's History of Derbyshire, ii. 216, (184).
Bridges' Northamptonshire, by Rev. Peter Whalley, i. 198.
Erdeswicke's Survey of Staffordshire, 85. Nichols' History of
the County of Leicester, iv. 303, 839. Baker's Northampton,
i. 685. Wilson's History of the parish of St. Laurence Pountney,
224. Hinchliffe's Barthomley, 241, 371. Notes and Queries,
3 S. iii. 164, 197. Brydges' Collins' Peerage, ix. 326. Banks'
Dormant and Extinct Baronage, iii. 217. Ormerod's Cheshire,

iii. 313. Harleian Society, xviii. 70 ; xxi. 47. Miscellanea Genealogica et Heraldica, 2nd Series, i. 71. Metcalfe's Visitations of Northamptonshire, 176. *See* CRUE.

CREWDSON. Fosters Pedigree of the Forsters and Fosters, Part ii. 29. Pedigree of Wilson of High Wray, etc., by Joseph Foster, 66. Pedigree of Wilson, by S. B. Foster, 117.

CREWE-READ. Burke's Landed Gentry, 2 supp., 3, 4, 5, 6, 7, 8.

CREWER. Foster's Visitations of Yorkshire, 213.

CREWES, or Crews. Harleian Society, ix. 56. Visitation of Devon, edited by F. T. Colby, 74. Bibliotheca Topographica Britannica, iv. Part vi. 112. The Visitations of Cornwall, edited by J. L. Vivian, 122. The Visitations of Devon, edited by J. L. Vivian, 59. Metcalfe's Visitations of Northamptonshire, 16. *See* CRUWYS.

CREYKE. Surtees Society, xxxvi. 328. Burke's Commoners, iv. 24 ; Landed Gentry, 2, 3, 4, 5, 6, 7, 8. Foster's Yorkshire Pedigrees. Burke's Royal Families, (London, 1851, 8vo.) i. 21. Foster's Visitations of Yorkshire, 163. Harleian Society, xxxix. 950. Old Yorkshire, edited by William Smith, New Series, ii. 144. *See* CREKE.

CRICH. Harleian Society, xxxix. 1170.

CRICHTON. Burke's Landed Gentry, 2 supp., 3, 4, 5, 6, 7, 8 Paterson's History of Ayr and Wigton, i. 331. Balmerino and its Abbey, by James Campbell, 261, 301, 385. Wood's Douglas's Peerage of Scotland, i. 295, 448, 608. Parliamentary Memoirs of Fermanagh, by Earl of Belmore, 42. *See* CREIGHTON.

CRICHTON-MAKGILL. Burke's Royal Families, (London, 1851, 8vo.) i. 107.

CRICK. The Midland Antiquary, i. 136, 170 ; ii. 87, 117. Fletcher's Leicestershire Pedigrees and Royal Descents, 183.

CRIGAN. Burke's Landed Gentry, 2.

CRICKLADE. The Genealogist, New Series, xiii. 148.

CRIKETOT. Page's History of Suffolk, 788. Banks' Dormant and Extinct Baronage, i. 61.

CRIOL, or CRYEL. Planché's Corner of Kent, 291. Nichols History of the County of Leicester, ii. 147. Clutterbuck's Hertford, i. 280. Archæologia Cantiano, v. 304. Banks' Baronies in Fee, i. 167. Banks' Dormant and Extinct Baronage, i. 278. The Genealogist, New Series, x. 30.

CRIPS, or CRIPPS. Extracts from the Registers of Chipping Norton, printed by Sir T. Phillipps, (Middle Hill, pp. 4,) 4. Sussex Archæological Collections, xxviii. 186. Burke's Landed Gentry, 6, 7, 8. Howard's Visitation of England and Wales, ii. 119 ; iv. 73.

CRIPPS-DAY. Howard's Visitation of England and Wales, viii. 50.

CRISPE. The Pedigree and Arms of the Family of Crispe, folio sheet, 1734. Collections relating to the family of Crispe, by F. A. Crisp. London, 1882-4, 8vo., 3 vols. Gentleman's Magazine, 1847, i. 598. Hasted's Kent, iv. 333. Berry's Sussex Genealogies, 360. Berry's Kent Genealogies, 154, 491. Harleian Society, v. 207 ; xv. 201, 202 ; xlii. 73. Some account of the Taylor Family, by P. A. Taylor, 697. John Lewis's History of Tenet,

69. Burke's Extinct Baronetcies. Howard's Visitation of England and Wales, vii. 101.

CRISPIN. Gentleman's Magazine, 1832, i. 27.

CRITCHLAW. Harleian Society, xxxvii. 67.

CRIVILL. The Suffolk Records, by H. W. Aldred, 103.

CROC. Herald and Genealogist, v. 512.

CROCHRODE. Harleian Society, xiii. 184, 385. Metcalfe's Visitations of Suffolk, 130. *See* CRACHERODE.

CROCKER. Harleian Society, vi. 78 ; ix. 57. Westcote's Devonshire, edited by G. Oliver and P. Jones, 550. Visitation of Devon, edited by F. T. Colby, 74. The Visitations of Cornwall, edited by J. L. Vivian, 124.

CROCKETT. Collections for a History of Staffordshire, (William Salt Society,) ii. Part 2, 126.

CROCKHAY. Harleian Society, ix. 57. The Visitations of Cornwall, edited by J. L. Vivian, 125.

CROFT. Notices of the Ancient Family of Croft, by N. Carlisle. London, 1841, 8vo. Pedigree of Croft, of Croft Castle, Co. Hereford, privately printed by Sir T. Phillipps, Bart., single sheet, folio. Burke's Landed Gentry, (of Stillington Hall,) 2, 3, 4, 5, 6, 7, 8 ; (of Fanhams Hall,) 8 ; (of Aldborough Hall,) 4, 5, 6, 7, 8 ; (of Greenham Lodge,) 2 supp., 3, 4, 5, 6. Foster's Yorkshire Pedigrees. Harleian Society, ii. 140 ; xv. 203 ; xxxviii. 778. Burke's Royal Families, (London, 1851, 8vo.) ii. 16. Nichols' History of the County of Leicester, iv. 483, 876. Robinson's Mansions of Herefordshire, 81. Chetham Society, xcix. 5. Burke's Landed Gentry, 6th edn., p. 821. Wotton's English Baronetage, iii. 535. Betham's Baronetage, ii. 417. Weaver's Visitation of Herefordshire, 20.

CROFTES, or CROFTS. Surtees Society, xxxvi. 91. Burke's Landed Gentry, (of Velvetstown,) 2, 3, 4, 5, 6, 7, 8 ; (of Churchtown,) 2, 3, 4, 5, 6, 7 ; (of Sompting Abbots,) 5, 6, 7, 8 ; Harleian Society, viii. 293 ; xv. 203 ; xxxii. 88. Gage's History of Thingoe Hundred, Suffolk, 134. Page's History of Suffolk, 684, 761, 818. Burke's Extinct Baronetcies. Metcalfe's Visitations of Suffolk, 96, 131.

CROFTON. Burke's Landed Gentry, 2, 3, 4, 5, 6, 7, 8. Betham's Baronetage, v. 465.

CROFTS-READ. Harleian Society, viii. 293.

CROKE. A Genealogical History of the Croke Family, originally named Le Blount, by Sir A. Croke. Oxford, 1823, 4to., 2 vols. Kennet's Parochial Antiquities, ii. 473-498. Berry's Buckinghamshire Genealogies, 39. Burke's Commoners, i. 354, Landed Gentry, 2, 3, 4, 5, 6, 7, 8. Harleian Society, v. 280 ; xv. 204. Lipscombe's History of the County of Buckingham, i. 131, 368 ; ii. 189, 194. Hoare's Wiltshire, IV. ii. 122. Herald and Genealogist, i. 338. Hutchins' Dorset, iii. 628. Memoirs of the Family of Chester, by R. E. C. Waters, 79. F. G. Lee's History of Thame, 526. The Genealogist, New Series, xiv. 23. *See* CROOKE.

CROKER. Burke's Commoners, iv. 315 ; (of Westmoulsey,) Commoners, i. 340, Landed Gentry, 3; (of Ballynagarde,) Landed Gentry, 2, 3, 4, 5, 6, 7, 8; (of the Grange,) 5, 6, 7, 8. Harleian Society, v. 185; vi. 78; xxi. 48. Herald and Genealogist, viii. 377-391. Foster's account of the Families descended from Francis Fox, 23. The Visitations of Devon, by J. L. Vivian, 254. *See* FOX.

CROLL. W. R. Fraser's History of Laurencekirk, 185.

CROLLY. O'Hart's Irish Pedigrees, 2nd Series, 157.

CROMARTIE. The Earls of Cromartie, their Kindred, Country, and Correspondence, by William Frazer. Edinburgh, 1876, 2 vols. 4to.

CROMBIE. Burke's Landed Gentry, 6, 7, 8.

CROMBLEHOLME. Chetham Society, cv. 259-263. History of Ribchester, by T. C. Smith and J. Shortt, 237.

CROMBOCK. Chetham Society, lxxxiv. 89.

CROMER. Hasted's Kent, ii. 575. Berry's Sussex Genealogies, 318.

CROMMELIN. Burke's Commoners, iv. 422, Landed Gentry, 2, 3, 4, 5, 6.

CROMPE. Berry's Kent Genealogies, 165. Pedigree of Crompe of Bretforton, Co. Wigorn, privately printed by Sir T. Phillipps. Harleian Society, xiii. 386.

CROMPTON. Glover's History of Derbyshire, ii. 593, (578). Surtees Society, xxxvi. 161, 322. Burke's Commoners, (of Duffield Hall, and Lilies,) iii. 689, Landed Gentry, 2 supp., 3, 4, 5, 6, 7, 8, (of Little Lever,) Landed Gentry, 6, 7, 8; (of Hacking,) 2 supp. Butterworth's Account of the Town, etc., of Oldham, 130. Pilkington's View of Derbyshire, ii. 179. Ormerod's Parentalia, 22. Visitation of Staffordshire, (Willm. Salt. Soc.) 66. Visitations of Staffordshire, 1614 and 1663-4, William Salt Society, 101-104. Harleian Society, xxviii. 159; xxxvii. 20, 68.

CROMPTON-ROBERTS. Burke's Landed Gentry, 6, 7, 8.

CROMPTON-STANSFIELD. Burke's Commoners, iii. 59, Landed Gentry, 2, 3, 4, 5, 7, 8. Foster's Yorkshire Pedigrees.

CROMWELL. A sermon preached on the death of Wm. Cromwell, Esq., with a brief Account of the Cromwell Family, by Thomas Gibbons. London, 1773, 8vo. Anecdotes and observations relating to Oliver Cromwell and his Family, by Sir James Burrow. London, 1763, 4to. The House of Cromwell, by James Waylen, London, 1880. The Patrician, edited by J. Burke, i. 121-128. Burke's Vicissitudes of Families, 1st Series, 26-39. Gough's edition of Camden's Britannia, ii. 161*. Reports and Papers of the Associated Architectural Societies, iv. Part ii. 228. Memoirs of the Protectoral House of Cromwell, by Mark Noble. Birmingham, 1787, 8vo. 2 vols. A Review of Noble's 'Memoirs of the Protectoral House of Cromwell,' by W. Richards. Lynn, 1787, 8vo. The Genealogical Line, or Paternal Descent of Oliver Cromwell, Sir John Prestwick's 'Respublica,' 1787, 4to. Bibliotheca Topographica Britannica, vi. Part iii.; see additions to this, Gentleman's Magazine, lvi. 44. Berry's Buckinghamshire Genealogies, 9, 40. Berry's Hertforshire Genealogies, 77, 106. Camden Society, xliii. 79. Burke's Commoners, i. 428, Landed Gentry,

2, 3, 4, 5, 6, 7, 8. Harleian Society, iv. 5 ; xxxviii. 434. Blore's History of South Winfield, in Nichols' Miscellaneous Antiquities, No. 3, 36. Clutterbuck's Hertford, ii. 95. The Citizens of London and their Rulers, by B. B. Orridge, 190. The Antiquary, edited by E. Walford, ii. 164. Notes and Queries, 2 S. v. 128, 224, 339 ; vii. 180, 477 ; viii. 16, 135; xi. 184; 4 S. ii. 74; viii. 431, 550 ; 5 S. vi. 466 ; viii. 445 ; 7 S. iii. 48, 137, 276, 327, 413, 415 ; iv. 11, 33, 177, 337. Banks' Baronies in Fee, i. 167. Banks' Dormant and Extinct Baronage, ii. 120; iii. 276. F. G. Lee's History of Thame, 410. The Genealogist, New Series, xv. 218. New England Register, li. 210. *See* CRUMWELL.

CRONIN-COLTSMAN. Burke's Landed Gentry, 4, 5, 6, 7, 8.

CROOKE. Visitation of Oxfordshire, 1634, printed by Sir T. Phillipps, (Middle Hill, fol.) 17. Earwaker's Local Gleanings, ii. 513, 526, 543, 549, 749, 756, 765. Burke's Extinct Baronetcies, 604. Harleian Society, xxxviii. 821 ; xl. 1300. Genealogies of Morgan and Glamorgan, by G. T. Clark, 379. *See* CROKE.

CROOKER. Jewitt's Reliquary, vii. 23. New England Register, xii. 68.

CROOKSHANK. Burke's Landed Gentry, 8 supp.

CROOME. Burke's Landed Gentry, 5, 6, 7.

CROONE. Harleian Society, xv. 205.

CROPHULL. Banks' Baronies in Fee, ii. 70.

CROPLEY. Camden Society, xliii. 59. Visitation of Middlesex, (Salisbury, 1820, fol.) 8. Harleian Society, xv. 206. Burke's Extinct Baronetcies. Foster's Visitation of Middlesex, 17.

CROPPER. Memorials of the Family of Cropper, Cubham, and Wolsey, by N. Waterhouse. Liverpool, 1864, 4to. Burke's Landed Gentry, 5, 6. Foster's Lancashire Pedigrees. Burke's Family Records, 192.

CROSBY, or CROSBIE. Gentleman's Magazine, 1833, i. 208. Archdall's Lodge's Peerage, iii. 325. Some Account of the Worshipful Company of Grocers, by J. B. Heath, (1st edn.) 204. Burke's Landed Gentry, (of Ballyheigue,) 2, 3, 4, 5, 6, 7, 8 ; (of Ardfert Abbey,) 2, 3, 4, 5, 6, 7, 8. Charles Smith's History of Kerry, 54. Harleian Society, xxii. 47.

CROSIER. Visitation of Durham, 1615, (Sunderland, 1820, fol.) 25. Burke's Commoners, ii. 658. Surtees' Durham, iii. 310. Foster's Visitations of Durham, 93. *See* CROYSER.

CROSLAND. Surtees Society, xxxvi. 133, 188. Foster's Visitations of Yorkshire, 509. The Genealogist, New Series, xii. 199.

CROSS, or CROSSE. Fishwick's History of Goosnargh, 42. Chetham Society, lxxxi. 107. The Tyldesley Diary, edited by J. Gillow and· A. Hewitson, 79. Burke's Commoners, i. 531 ; (of Shaw Hill,) Landed Gentry, 2, 3, 4, 5, 6, 7, 8 ; (of Broomfield,) 2 add., 3, 4 ; (of Red Scar,) 5, 6, 7, 8 ; (of Eccle Riggs,) 5, 6 ; (of Dartan,) 5, 6, 7, 8. Foster's Lancashire Pedigrees. Lipscombe's History of the County of Buckingham, ii. 116. Abram's History of Blackburn, 503. Wotton's English Baronetage, iv. 142. Ormerod's Cheshire, iii. 663. Burke's Extinct Baronetcies. Earwaker's

East Cheshire, ii. 253. Bysshe's Visitation of Essex, edited by
J. J. Howard, 27. Weaver's Visitations of Somerset, 105. The
Visitations of Devon, by J. L. Vivian, 471.

CROSSING. Harleian Society, vi. 342. The Visitations of Devon,
by J. L. Vivian, 255.

CROSSLEY. Burke's Commoners, ii. 536, Landed Gentry, 2, 3, 4, 5,
and supp., 6, 7, 8. Foster's Lancashire Pedigrees. Corry's
History of Lancashire, ii. 653-655. Baines' History of the Co. of
Lancaster, ii. 649 ; Croston's edn., iii. 76. Fishwick's History of
Rochdale, 475. Harleian Society, xxxviii. 538.

CROSSMAN, or CROSMAN. Maclean's History of Trigg Minor, i. 298.
Harleian Society, ix. 58. The Visitations of Cornwall, edited by
J. L. Vivian, 126.

CROSTON. Surtees Society, xxxvi. 60. Croston's edn. of Baines's
Lancaster, iv. 123.

CROUCH, or CROWCH. Morant's Essex, ii. 345. Clutterbuck's Hertford, iii. 429. Harleian Society, xv. 207. Hasted's Kent, (Hund.
of Blackheath, by H. H. Drake,) 122.

CROW. Caermarthenshire Pedigrees, 6.

CROWDER. Dwnn's Visitations of Wales, i. 259. Harleian Society,
xxxvii. 262.

CROWE. Burke's Landed Gentry, 3, 4, 5, 6, 7, 8. Carthew's Hundred
of Launditch, Part ii. 621. Burke's Extinct Baronetcies.

CROWFOOT. Howard's Visitation of England and Wales, i. 26.
Burke's Family Records, 195.

CROWLEY. East Anglian, iii. 95, 121 ; iv. 171. Harleian Society,
viii. 495.

CROWMER. Bibliotheca Topograhia Britannica, i. Part i. 22.

CROWTHER. Harleian Society, xv. 208. Burke's Landed Gentry,
7, p. 135 ; 8, p. 147.

CROXALL. Shaw's Staffordshire, ii. 107*.

CROXTON. Ormerod's Cheshire, ii. 144 ; iii. 207, 213. Harleian
Society, xviii. 70.

CROYSER, or CROZIER. Visitation of Durham, 1575, (Newcastle,
1820, fol.) 20. Hutchinson's History of Durham, iii. 165. Burke's
Landed Gentry, 5 supp., 6, 7, 8. Burke's Family Records, 195.
Howard's Visitation of Ireland, ii. 39.

CRUE. Ormerod's Cheshire, iii. 356, 364. Harleian Society, xxxvii.
189. See CREW.

CRUIKSHANK. Burke's Landed Gentry, 3 supp., 4, 5, 6, 7, 8. Burke's
Royal Descents and Pedigrees of Founders' Kin, 89.

CRUKERN. The Genealogist, New Series, ii. 298.

CRUM-EWING. Burke's Landed Gentry, 4, 5, 6, 7, 8.

CRUMP, or CRUMPE. Berry's Sussex Genealogies, 337. Burke's Commoners, iv. 282 ; Landed Gentry, 5 supp., 7, 8. Miscellanea
Genealogica et Heraldica, New Series, ii. 528. Genealogies of
Morgan and Glamorgan, by G. T. Clark, 482. Oliver's History
of Antigua, i. 184.

CRUMWELL. Thoroton's Nottinghamshire, iii. 170. Carthew's Hundred of Launditch, Part ii. 522. See CROMWELL.

CRUSE. The Visitations of Devon, by J. L. Vivian, 256.
CRUSO. Harleian Society, xv. 209 ; xxxviii. 458. Notes and Queries,
4 S. i. 319.
CRUTCHLEY. Burke's Landed Gentry, 2, 3, 4, 5, 6, 7, 8.
CRUTTENDEN. The New England Register, lii. 466.
CRUWYS, CRUIS, or CRUES. Tuckett's Devonshire Pedigrees, 177.
Harleian Society, vi. 79. Burke's Landed Gentry, 5, 6, 7, 8.
Westcote's Devonshire, edited by G. Oliver and P. Jones, 516.
The Genealogist, New Series, viii. 242. Howard's Visitation of
England and Wales, vii. 25. *See* CREWS.
CRUX. Berry's Kent Genealogies, 363.
CRYCHE. Thoroton's Nottinghamshire, iii. 125.
CRYMBLE. History of Carrickfergus, by Sam. M'Skimin, 2nd edn.,
330. Muskett's Suffolk Manorial Families, i. 131.
CRYMES. Harleian Society, vi. 79. Surrey Archæological Collections,
x. The Visitations of Devon, by J. L. Vivian, 258.
CUBHAM. *See* CROPPER.
CUBITT. Burke's Landed Gentry, (of Catfield,) 2, 3, 4, 5 ; (of
Honing,) 2, 3, 4, 5, 6, 7, 8. Collections for a History of the
Family of Cubitt, in the Norfolk Antiquarian Miscellany, by
W. Rye, i. 215.
CUDDON. Suckling's History of Suffolk, ii. 294. Metcalfe's Visitations
of Suffolk, 23, 131. Burke's Family Records, 199.
CUDMORE. Morant's Essex, ii. 163. Harleian Society, vi. 80 ;
xiii. 386. The Visitations of Devon, by J. L. Vivian, 260.
Bysshe's Visitation of Essex, edited by J. J. Howard, 28.
Burke's Colonial Gentry, ii. 674.
CUDNER. Harleian Society, xv. 210.
CUDWORTH. Some Account of the Family of Cudworth, by J. J.
Green. London, 1898, 4to. Chetham Society, lxxxi. 15 ; lxxxii.
80 ; lxxxiv. 90. Butterworth's Account of the Town, etc., of
Oldham, 69. Hunter's Deanery of Doncaster, ii. 270. Croston's
edn. of Baines's Lancaster, ii. 378.
CUFAUDE. Gentleman's Magazine, lviii. 574 ; lix. 551. *See*
CUFFOLD.
CUFFE. Visitation of Somerset, printed by Sir T. Phillipps, 58.
Descent of William Cuffe, Esq., from King Edward III. London,
small 4to. 1876. Harleian Society, xi. 30. Archdall's Lodge's
Peerage, vi. 55. Weaver's Visitations of Somerset, 18.
CUFFOLD. Berry's Hampshire Genealogies, 281. Hampshire Visita-
tions, printed by Sir T. Phillipps, 19. *See* CUFAUDE.
CUKENEY. Thoroton's Nottinghamshire, iii. 373.
CULCHETH. Chetham Society, lxxxi. 82 ; lxxxiv. 91, 92. Miscel-
lanea Genealogica et Heraldica, New Series, ii. 209. Lancashire
and Cheshire Genealogical and Historical Notes, ii. 135, 229 ;
iii. 129.
CULLEN. Burke's Landed Gentry, 2, 3, 4, 5, 6, 7, 8. Burke's
Royal Descents and Pedigrees of Founders' Kin, 26. O'Hart's
Irish Pedigrees, 2nd Series, 55. Burke's Extinct Baronetcies.
Howard's Visitation of Ireland, ii. 48.

CULLEY. Burke's Landed Gentry, (of Fowberry Tower,) 2, 3, 4, 5, 6, 7, 8 ; (of Coupland Castle,) 5, 6, 7, 8.

CULLIFORD. Visitation of Somerset, printed by Sir T. Phillipps, 59. Harleian Society, xi. 31 ; xx. 33. Hutchin's Dorset, i. 516.

CULLINYNFYD. Dwnn's Visitations of Wales, ii. 22.

CULLOW. Harleian Society, ix. 58. Maclean's History of Trigg Minor, iii. 252. The Visitations of Cornwall, edited by J. L. Vivian, 127.

CULLUM. Bibliotheca Topographica Britannica, (Cullum's Hawsted,) v. Part ii. 152, (2nd edn., 179). Gage's History of Thingoe Hundred, Suffolk, 478. Page's History of Suffolk, 647. Harleian Society, xv. 210. Wotton's English Baronetage, iii. 41. Betham's Baronetage, ii. 53. Howard's Visitation of England and Wales, i. 171. Miscellanea Genealogica et Heraldica, 2nd Series, i. 181, 183, 197 ; ii. 356. See MILNER-GIBSON-CULLUM in Burke's Landed Gentry, 7, 8. Muskett's Suffolk Manorial Families, i. 169.

CULLY, or CULY. Nichols' History of the County of Leicester, iv. 941. Dugdale's Warwickshire, 123.

CULME. Camden Society, cv. at end. Harleian Society, vi. 81. Westcote's Devonshire, edited by G. Oliver and P. Jones, 515. Visitation of Devon, edited by F. T. Colby, 75. The Visitations of Devon, by J. L. Vivian, 262.

CULPEPER. Gentleman's Magazine, lxvii. 294, 476, 543, 563, 645. Archæologia Cantiana, iv. 264. Berry's Kent Genealogies, 56. Berry's Sussex Genealogies, 136. Bartlett's History of Manceter, being No. 1 of Nichols' Miscellaneous Antiquities, 50. Dugdale's Warwickshire, 1080. Baker's Northampton, ii. 124. Sussex Archæological Collections, x. 154. Scot of Scot's-Hall, by J. R. Scott, 228. Notes and Queries, ii. 177. Burke's Extinct Baronetcies. Harleian Society, xxxii. 89. See COLEPEPER.

CULWORTH. Baker's Northampton, i. 607.

CUMBERBATCH. See COMBERBACH.

CUMBERFORD. Bibliotheca Topographica Britannica, ix. Part 4. 257. See COMBERFORD.

CUMBERLAND. Banks' Dormant and Extinct Baronage, iii. 220.

CUMIN, CUMYN, CUMINE, or CUMMINE. Hodgson's Northumberland, II. ii. 41. Dugdale's Warwickshire, 661. Paterson's History of the Co. of Ayr, i. 442. Nisbet's Heraldry, ii. app. 59. Shaw's History of Moray, 91. Wood's Douglas's Peerage of Scotland, i. 160, 262. See BRUCE, COMIN.

CUMING, CUMMING, or CUMMINGS. A Table showing the families [Tomkins, Leith,] descended from Sir Alexander Cumming of Coulter, etc. Compiled in 1868-70, and brought down to 1877, broadside. Burke's Royal Families, (London, 1851, 8vo.) ii. 88. The Genealogist, iii. 1. Douglas's Baronage of Scotland, 331-339. Ontarian Families, by E. M. Chadwick, ii. 172.

CUMING-GORDON. Betham's Baronetage, v. 547.

CUNINGHAM, CUNNINGHAM, or CUNNINGHAME. Burke's Commoners, (of Caddell,) ii. 349, 526, Landed Gentry, 2, 3, 4, 5, 6 ; (of Lain-

shaw,) Landed Gentry, 3, 4, 5, 6, 8; (of Balgownie,) 5, 6, 7, 8; (of Caprington,) 5, 6, 7, 8; (of Craigends,) 6, 7, 8; (of Bandalloch,) 6; 6 at p. 1788, and 72, 7; and 7 at p. 2042, and 8 at p. 1722. Geo. Robertson's Description of Cunninghame, 128, 172, 200, 224, 321, 434. Burke's Royal Families, (London, 1851, 8vo.) ii. 60. Lands and their Owners in Galloway, by P. H. M'Kerlie, iii. 151. Paterson's History of the Co. of Ayr, i. 210, 232, 427, 451; ii. 37, 49, 117, 143, 212, 248, 252, 408, 446, 455, 459. Nisbet's Heraldry, ii. app. 43, 297. Douglas's Baronage of Scotland, 265. Paterson's History of Ayr and Wigton, i. 149, 239, 436, 631, 645, 739, 766; iii. 56, 155, 205, 222, 289, 326, 466, 475, 489, 512, 563, 580, 607. Burke's Extinct Baronetcies, 619. Geo. Robertson's Account of Families in Ayrshire, i. 246-330. O'Hart's Irish Pedigrees, 2nd Series, 158. Walter Wood's East Neuk of Fife, 259. Wood's Douglas's Peerage of Scotland, i. 631. Caithness Family History, by John Henderson, 201. *See* CONYNGHAM.
CUNLIFFE. Miscellanea Genealogica et Heraldica, ii. 22. Foster's Lancashire Pedigrees. Gregson's Fragments relative to the County of Lancaster, 168, 169. Whitaker's History of Whalley, ii. 259. Abram's History of Blackburn, 392, 445. Harleian Society, xv. 211; xxxvii. 60; xxxviii. 581. Betham's Baronetage, iii. 273. Ilkley, Ancient and Modern, by R. Collyer and J. H. Turner, 203. Descendants of the Cunliffes of Wycoller and Acton, by Major Owen, 1887, 8vo. History of Chislehurst, by Webb, Miller, and Beckwith, 271. *See* CONLIFFE.
CUNNINGHAME-GRAHAM. Burke's Landed Gentry, 3, 4, 5, 6, 7, 8.
CUNTRY. Harleian Society, xlii. 17.
CUPPAGE. Burke's Landed Gentry, 4, 8.
CUPPER. Visitation of Somerset, printed by Sir T. Phillipps, 60. Harleian Society, v. 204; xi. 31; xxviii. 159.
CURDIE. Burke's Colonial Gentry, ii. 764.
CURE. Burke's Landed Gentry, 2, 3, 4, 5, 6, 7, 8. History of Powys Fadog, by J. Y. W. Lloyd, vi. 488. Sepulchral Memorials of Bobbingworth, 38. Howard's Visitation of England and Wales, ii. 22. Surrey Archæological Collections, x. Harleian Society, xliii. 209.
CURGENVEN. Maclean's History of Trigg Minor, ii. 265.
CURL, or CURLL. Nichols' History of the County of Leicester, ii. 262*. Burke's Extinct Baronetcies.
CURLI. Dugdale's Warwickshire, 656.
CURLING. Berry's Kent Genealogies, 5. Burke's Landed Gentry, 4, 5. Harleian Society, xlii. 22.
CURRANCE. Harleian Society, xv. 211.
CURRE. Burke's Landed Gentry, 2, 3, 4, 5, 6, 7, 8.
CURRER. A Skeleton Pedigree to illustrate the Descent [Richardson] of the late Miss Currer of Eshton Hall, and of John George Smyth of Heath, Esq., from Jane, the sister of John Hopkinson of Lofthouse, the Antiquary. Long slip, *n. d.* Surtees Society, xxxvi. 231, 252. Burke's Commoners, (of Clifton,) iii. 94, Landed Gentry, 2, 3, 4; (of Kildwick,) Landed Gentry, 2, 3, 4. Foster's

Yorkshire Pedigrees. Burke's Royal Descents and Pedigrees of Founders' Kin, *Founders' Kin,* 2. Whitaker's Deanery of Craven, 152, (213). Burke's Royal Families, (London, 1851, 8vo.) ii. 63. Foster's Visitations of Yorkshire, 510. Ilkley, Ancient and Modern, by R. Collyer and J. H. Turner, 147, 150. The Genealogist, New Series, xv. 249.

CURRIE. Herald and Genealogist, v. 175. Burke's Landed Gentry, (of West Horsley,) 5, 6 ; (of Bishop Oak,) 8 ; (of Rushden House,) 8 ; (of Minley Manor,) 5, 6, 7, 8 ; (of Bush Hill,) 2, 3, 4 ; (of Linthill,) 6, 7, 8. Burke's Royal Families, (London, 1851, 8vo.) ii. 205. Burke's Colonial Gentry, i. 390 ; ii. 471. Burke's Family Records, 201.

CURRY. Burke's Landed Gentry, 6, 7. O'Hart's Irish Pedigrees, 2nd Series, 55.

CURSON, or CURSONE. Sir T. Phillipps' Topographer, No. 1, (March, 1821, 8vo.) 22. Visitation of Norfolk, published by Norfolk Archæological Society, ii. 17. Visitation of Oxfordshire, 1574, printed by Sir T. Phillipps, (Middle Hill, fol.) 3. Visitation of Oxfordshire, 1634, printed by Sir T. Phillipps, (Middle Hill, fol.) 17. Harleian Society, v. 131 ; xxxii. 89. Carthew's Hundred of Launditch, Part ii. 747. Pilkington's View of Derbyshire, ii. 130. Wotton's English Baronetage, iii. 276. Burke's Extinct Baronetcies. Miscellanea Genealogica et Heraldica, 3rd Series, i. 209. The Genealogist, New Series, xiv. 198. *See* CURZON.

CURTEIS. Hasted's Kent, iii. 89. Berry's Kent Genealogies, 65, 69. Berry's Sussex Genealogies, 214. Burke's Commoners, i. 314 ; Landed Gentry, 2, 3, 4, 5, 6, 7, 8. Harleian Society, viii. 213 ; xlii. 89.

CURTIN. O'Hart's Irish Pedigrees, 2nd Series, 117.

CURTIS. Burke's Landed Gentry, 2, 3, 4. Foster's Account of Families descended from Francis Fox, 21. Betham's Baronetage, iv. 259 ; v. 509. The Visitations of Cornwall, edited by J. L. Vivian, 128. New England Register, xvi. 137.

CURTIS-HAWARD. Visitation of Gloucester, edited by T. F. Fenwick and W. C. Metcalfe, 51.

CURTIUS. Burke's Extinct Baronetcies.

CURTLER. Burke's Landed Gentry, 5, 6, 7, 8.

CURTOIS. Burke's Landed Gentry, 4, 5, 6, 7. Howard's Visitation of England and Wales, i. 172.

CURWEN, or CURWYN. Surtees Society, xli. 97, 100. Burke's Commoners, i. 577 ; Landed Gentry, 2, 3, 4, 5, 6, 7, 8. Foster's Visitations of Yorkshire, 8, 11. Harleian Society, vii. 30 ; xv. 212 ; xvi. 82. Chetham Society, lxxxii. 28, 68. Hutchinson's History of Cumberland, ii. 143. Jefferson's History of Allerdale Ward, Cumberland, 251. Burke's Extinct Baronetcies. Nicolson and Burn's Westmorland and Cumberland, i. 465 ; ii. 54. Pedigree of the Family of Curwen of Workingham, single sheet, *n. d.* Foster's Visitations of Cumberland and Westmorland, 29-32. New England Register, x. 304. Papers and Pedigrees relating to Cumberland and Westmorland, by Willm. Jackson, i. 288.

CURZON. Case of Sir Nathaniel Curzon, claiming the Barony of Powes, 1731. Topographical Miscellanies, 1792, 4to., (Bredsall). Glover's History of Derbyshire, ii. 179, 587, (566). Burke's Landed Gentry, 3, 4, 5, 6, 7, 8. Harleian Society, iv. 163. Page's History of Suffolk, 914. Burke's Extinct Baronetcies, 22. Collections by the Powys-land Club, i. 388. Edmondson's Baronagium Genealogicum, v. 475. Brydges' Collins' Peerage, vi. 397 ; vii. 294. Wotton's English Baronetage, ii. 243. R. Ussher's Historical Sketch of Croxall, 10. Fletcher's Leicestershire Pedigrees and Royal Descents, 94, 97. The Genealogist, New Series, vii. 73. Howard's Visitation of England and Wales, iv. 79. The Gresleys of Drakelowe, by F. Madan, 247. *See* CURSON.

CUSACK. Burke's Landed Gentry, (of Gerardstown,) 2 supp., 3, 4, 5, 6, 7, 8 ; (of Moyangher,) 2. Burke's Patrician, vi. 59. Burke's Royal Families, (London, 1851, 8vo.) ii. 157. O'Hart's Irish Pedigrees, 2nd Series, 324. The Irish Builder, xxix. 192. Devonshire Notes and Notelets, by Sir W. R. Drake, 93.

CUSHING. New England Register, xix. 39.

CUSSE. Visitatio Comitatus Wiltoniæ, 1623, printed by Sir T. Phillipps. Visitation of Wiltshire, edited by G. W. Marshall, 98.

CUST. The Cust Family, by Lady Elizabeth Cust. London, 1898, 4to. Cockayne Memoranda, 1869, Part i. 38. Turnor's History of Town and Soke of Grantham, 101. Edmondson's Baronagium Genealogicum, vi. 69. Brydges' Collins' Peerage, vii. 476. Wotton's English Baronetage, iii. 629. Notes and Queries, 3 S. iii. 437 ; 7 S. ii. 72, 113.

CUSTABODIE. Harleian Society, xxxix. 991.

CUSTANCE. Burke's Commoners, i. 492, Landed Gentry, 2, 3, 4, 5, 6, 7, 8.

CUTCLIFFE. Burke's Landed Gentry, 2 supp., 7, 8. Harleian Society, vi. 81. The Visitations of Devon, by J. L. Vivian, 264. Devonshire Notes and Notelets, by Sir W. R. Drake, 61-95.

CUTHBERT. Burke's Landed Gentry, 4, 5, 6, 7, 8. Hutchinson's History of Durham, iii. 305. Paterson's History of the Co. of Ayr, i. 365. Paterson's History of Ayr and Wigton, i. 324.

CUTHBERT-KEARNEY. Burke's Landed Gentry, 4, 5, 6.

CUTHBERTSON. Hodgson's Northumberland, III. ii. 117, 435. Burke's Family Records, 202.

CUTLER. Surtees Society, xxxvi. 4. Some Account of the Worshipful Company of Grocers, by J. B. Heath, 253. Burke's Commoners, iv. 688, Landed Gentry, 2, 3, 4 ; (of Upton,) Commoners, iv. 690, Landed Gentry, 2, 3, 4. Foster's Visitations of Yorkshire, 510, 511. Burke's Royal Families, (London, 1851, 8vo.) ii. 113. Harleian Society, ii. 138 ; viii. 151, 362. Nichols' History of the County of Leicester, iii. 634. Hunter's Deanery of Doncaster, ii. 266. Midland Counties Historical Collector, published by Architectural and Archæological Society of Leicester, 1855-1856, ii. 306. Metcalfe's Visitations of Suffolk, 23, 188. Burke's Extinct Baronetcies. New England Register, iv. 175. Visitation of

Gloucester, edited by T. F. Fenwick and W. C. Metcalfe, 53. The Genealogist, New Series, ix. 164.

CUTT, CUTTE, CUTTES, or CUTTS. Morant's Essex, ii. 439, 497, 583, 589. Hasted's Kent, ii. 495. Cambridgeshire Visitation, edited by Sir T. Phillipps, 7. Proceedings of the Essex Archæological Society, iv. 25. Harleian Society, xiii. 44; xv. 213; xli. 30. Notes and Queries, 6 S. iv. 157, 215. Burke's Extinct Baronetcies.

CYFFIN. Dwnn's Visitations of Wales, i. 307.

D'ABBETOT. Harleian Society, xii. 136.

D'ABERNON. Manning and Bray's Surrey, ii. 721. Miscellanea Genealogica et Heraldica, ii. 161. Harleian Society, xliii. 220. See ABERNON.

DABORNE. Jewitt's Reliquary, xix. 231.

DABRIDGECOURT. Berry's Hampshire Genealogies, 70. Topographer and Genealogist, i. 197. Harleian Society, iv. 37; xii. 47. Topographer, (London, 1789-91, 8vo.) i. 191. Lipscombe's History of the County of Buckingham, i. 69. Hampshire Visitations, printed by Sir T. Phillipps, 19. Dugdale's Warwickshire, Index. Notes and Queries, 5 S. iii. 275.

DABYTON. Weaver's Visitation of Herefordshire, 22.

D'ABZAC. The Genealogist, New Series, xviii. 57.

DACCOMB, or DACKOMBE. Hutchins' Dorset, i. 146, 229, 510. Harleian Society, xx. 34, 36. The Genealogist, New Series, ii. 299. Miscellanea Genealogica et Heraldica, 2nd Series, ii. 238.

DACKHAM. See DACCOMB.

DACRE, or DACRES. Hasted's Kent, i. 121; ii. 162. Berry's Hertfordshire Genealogies, 66. Collectanea Topographica et Genealogica, i. 302. Hutchinson's History of Cumberland, i. 60, 468; ii. 568. Jefferson's History of Leath Ward, Cumberland, 167, 170, 172, 175, 345. Hodgson's Northumberland, II. ii. 375. Archæologia Æliana, 2nd Series, ii. 137. Cussan's History of Hertfordshire, Parts vii. and viii. 136. Chauncy's Hertfordshire, 301. Surtees Society, lxviii. 393. Plantagenet-Harrison's History of Yorkshire, i. 399. Edmondson's Baronagium Genealogicum, iv. 357. Brydges' Collins' Peerage, vi. 558. Banks' Baronies in Fee, i. 171. Banks' Dormant and Extinct Baronage, ii. 129, 139. Harleian Society, viii. 320; xvi. 83; xxii. 47. Clutterbuck's Hertford, ii. 101. Foster's Visitations of Cumberland and Westmorland, 34. Croston's edn. of Baines's Lancaster, v. 3. Nicolson and Burn's Westmorland and Cumberland, i. 338, 487; ii. 351, 378, 503. The Genealogist, New Series, xvii. 115.

DACUS. Collinson's Somerset, iii. 55.

DADE. Berry's Kent Genealogies, 460. Metcalfe's Visitations of Suffolk, 132. Miscellanea Genealogica et Heraldica, 2nd Series, i. 199. Harleian Society, xxxii. 91.

D'AETH. Hasted's Kent, iv. 211. Berry's Kent Genealogies, 249. Burke's Commoners, iii. 85, Landed Gentry, 2, 3, 4, 5, 6, 7, 8. Wotton's English Baronetage, iv. 183. Betham's Baronetage, iii. 185. Burke's Extinct Baronetcies. See DEATH.

DAGGE. Maclean's History of Trigg Minor, i. 295; ii. 179; iii. 168. Harleian Society, ix. 59. The Visitations of Cornwall, edited by J. L. Vivian, 129.

DAGWORTH, or DAGGEWORTH. Morant's Essex, ii. 155, 262, 598. Banks' Baronies in Fee, i. 175. Banks' Dormant and Extinct Baronage, i. 279. Blomefield's Norfolk, vi. 384.

DAINES, DENES, or DINES. Morant's Essex, i. 460.

DAKEYNE, DAKINS, DAKYNS, or DAKIN. Glover's History of Derbyshire, ii. 393, (361). Burke's Landed Gentry, 2 supp. Visitation of Derbyshire, 1663-4, (Middle Hill, 1854, fol.) 3. The Genealogist, iii. 57 ; New Series, vii. 75. Foster's Visitations of Yorkshire, 169, 511. Warwickshire Pedigrees, from Visitation of 1682-3, (privately printed, 1865). Harleian Society, xxxix. 1017. Burke's Family Records, 203.

DALBY. Visitation of Warwickshire, 1619, published with Warwickshire Antiquarian Magazine, 54. Visitations of Berkshire, printed by Sir T. Phillipps, 16. Harleian Society, xii. 369. The Genealogist, v. 248.

DALDEN. Surtees' Durham, i. 6. Genealogies of Morgan and Glamorgan, by G. T. Clark, 380.

DALE. Jewitt's Reliquary, vii. 181. Topographer and Genealogist, ii. 105. Burke's Heraldic Illustrations, Pl. 14. Morant's Essex, i. 437. Glover's History of Derbyshire, ii. 53, (46). Burke's Commoners, (of Ashborne,) iv. 115, Landed Gentry, 2, 3, 4 ; (of Glanville's Wootton,) Landed Gentry, 2, 3, 4, 5, 6, 7, 8 ; (of Tunstall,) 2 supp. Harleian Society, i. 55, 94 ; xiii. 186 ; xxxix. 1026, 1039. Surtees' Durham, i. 251, 307; iv. 145. Burke's Royal Families, (London, 1851, 8vo.) i. 16 ; ii. 142. Lincolnshire Tradesmen's Tokens, by Justin Simpson, (London, 1872, 8vo.) 61. Blore's Rutland, 61. Bysshe's Visitation of Essex, edited by J. J. Howard, 28.

DALGETY. Burke's Landed Gentry, 6, 7, 8. Burke's Colonial Gentry, ii. 484.

DALGLEISH. Burke's Landed Gentry, 5, 7, 8, 8 supp.

DALISON. Berry's Kent Genealogies, 182. Burke's Landed Gentry, 2, 3, 4, 5, 6, 7, 8. Burke's Royal Families, (London, 1851, 8vo.) ii. 183. The Genealogist, iii. 372. Burke's Extinct Baronetcies. Archæologia Cantiana, xv. 402. Miscellanea Genealogica et Heraldica, 2nd Series, ii. 40, 56. Notes and Queries, vii. S. iv. 25. See DALYSON.

DALLAS. Monumental Inscriptions of the British West Indies, by J. H. Laurence-Archer, 123. The Genealogist, iii. 406 ; iv. 121. Betham's Baronetage, iv. 396.

DALLAS-YORKE. Burke's Landed Gentry, 5, 6, 7, 8.

DALLAWAY. Miscellanea Genealogica et Heraldica, i. 286.

DALLENDER. Surrey Archæological Collections, x. Harleian Society, xliii. 128.

DALLING. Betham's Baronetage, iv. app. 19. Harleian Society, xxxii. 92.

DALMAHOY. The Family of Dalmahoy, of Dalmahoy, Ratho, Co.

Edinburgh, [by Thomas Falconer,] London, 1867, 8vo., pp. 55.
Also thirty-five pages relating to surname of Falconer, published
with it. Douglas's Baronage of Scotland, 549. Burke's Extinct
Baronetcies, 619. Alexander Nisbet's Heraldic Plates, 92.

DALRYMPLE. The Dalrymples of Langland, by John Shaw. Bath,
8vo. Lands and their Owners in Galloway, by P. H. M'Kerlie,
i. 153, 184. Paterson's History of the Co. of Ayr, ii. 435.
Paterson's History of Ayr and Wigton, i. 140, 597, 725. Burke's
Extinct Baronetcies, 620. Wood's Douglas's Peerage of Scotland,
ii. 519. Foster's Collectanea Genealogica, (MP's Scotland,) 91.
Memoir of Chancellor Seton, by Geo. Seton, App. II. Some Old
Families, by H. B. McCall, 27. Notes and Queries, 8 S. vii. 301.
See STAIR.

DALSTON. Visitation of Westmoreland, 1615, (London, 1853,) 5.
Harleian Society, vii. 5. Hutchinson's History of Cumberland,
ii. 447. Plantagenet-Harrison's History of Yorkshire, i. 340.
Wotton's English Baronetage, ii. 154. Burke's Extinct Baronetcies.
Foster's Visitations of Cumberland and Westmorland, 35, 36.
Nicolson and Burn's Westmorland and Cumberland, i. 383, 555.

DALTON. Morant's Essex, ii. 377. Harleian Society, i. 44; viii. 311;
xvi. 85; xxxix. 912; xli. 41. Surtees Society, xxxvi. 47, 143.
Cambridgeshire Visitation, edited by Sir T. Phillipps, 12. Burke's
Commoners, (of Sleningford,) i. 528, Landed Gentry, 2, 3, 4, 5, 6,
7, 8; (of Dunkirk,) Landed Gentry, 2, 3, 4; (of Thurnham,)
Commoners, i. 522, Landed Gentry, 2, 3, 4. Foster's Yorkshire
Pedigrees. Chetham Society, lxxxii. 32; lxxxiv. 94. Burke's
Royal Families, (London, 1851, 8vo.) ii. 134. Foster's Visitations
of Yorkshire, 141. Whitaker's History of Richmondshire, i. 328.
Visitation of Derbyshire, 1663-4, (Middle Hill, 1854, fol.) 3.
Hoare's Wiltshire, IV. ii. 33. Baines's History of the Co. of Lan-
caster, iv. 543. The Genealogist, iii. 16, 90. Memoirs of Captn.
J. Dalton, by C. Dalton, i. 2; ii. 88. O'Hart's Irish Pedigrees, 2nd
Series, 324. Plantagenet-Harrison's History of Yorkshire, i. 160.
Miscellanea Genealogica et Heraldica, New Series, iii. 438; 2nd
Series, ii. 81. Bysshe's Visitation of Essex, edited by J. J.
Howard, 28. Historic Society of Lancashire and Cheshire, New
Series, vi. 97-124. Burke's Colonial Gentry ii. 505.

DALWAY. Burke's Landed Gentry, 3, 4, 5, 6, 7, 8. History of Carrickfergus, by Saml. M'Skimin, 2nd edn., 317.

DALY. Burke's Landed Gentry, (of Castle Daly,) 2, 3, 4, 5, 6, 7, 8;
(of Raford,) 5, 6, 7, 8; (of Cooliney,) 3, 4; (of Dunsandle,) 2.
O'Hart's Irish Pedigrees, 2nd Series, 159. Burke's Colonial
Gentry, ii. 492, 612. The Irish Builder, xxxv. 138.

DALYELL, or DALYELL. Burke's Landed Gentry, 3 supp., 4, 5, 6, 7, 8.
Burke's Royal Descents and Pedigrees of Founders' Kin, 106.
Walter Wood's East Neuk of Fife, 304.

DALYNGRUGE, or DALYNGRUDGE. Sketch of Bodyam Castle in
Sussex, by Willm. Cotton, 11. Sussex Archæological Collections,
iii. 93; ix. 287.

DALYSON. Hasted's Kent, ii. 260. See DALISON.

DALZELL. Burke's Landed Gentry, 5 supp., 6, 7, 8. Wood's Douglas's Peerage of Scotland, i. 309. Alexander Nisbet's Heraldic Plates, 30. Berks Archæological and Architectural Journal, iii. 166, 190.

DAMER. Hutchins' Dorset, iv. 387. Edmondson's Baronagium Genealogicum, v. 489. Archdall's Lodge's Peerage, vii. 72. *See* AMERY, D'AMORIE.

DAMES. Burke's Landed Gentry, 2, 3, 4, 5, 6, 7, 8. The Irish Builder, xxix. 218. Howard's Visitation of Ireland, ii. 53.

DAMMARTIN. Manning and Bray's Surrey, ii. 324.

DAMORY, D'AMERY, or D'AMORIE. Manning and Bray's Surrey, iii. 485. Fosbrooke's History of Gloucestershire, i. 391. Banks' Baronies in Fee, i. 176. Banks' Dormant and Extinct Baronage, i. 280. Harleian Society, xxi. 244. *See* DAMER.

DAMPORT. Chetham Society, lxxxi. 133. *See* DAVENPORT.

DANA. New England Register, xxiii. 253.

DANBY. J. Fisher's History of Masham, 244. Surtees Society, xxxvi. 93 ; xli. 87. Burke's Commoners, i. 200. Foster's Visitations of Yorkshire, 262, 264, 292. Harleian Society, viii. 436 ; xvi. 88. Whitaker's History of Richmondshire, i. 254 ; ii. 98. Thoresby's Ducatus Leodiensis, 202. The Genealogist, vi. 145.

DANCASTELL. Visitation of Berkshire, printed by Sir T. Phillipps, 16.

DANCE. Burke's Extinct Baronetcies, 266. History of the Wilmer Family, 202.

DANCE-HOLLAND. Betham's Baronetage, iv. 417.

DAND. Harleian Society, iv. 131 ; xxxix. 1003.

DANDY. East Anglian, ii. 164. Harleian Society, ix. 60. Page's History of Suffolk, 528. The Visitations of Cornwall, edited by J. L. Vivian, 131. *See* DAUNDY.

DANE. Harleian Society, i. 10. Visitation of Somerset, printed by Sir T. Phillipps, 62. Burke's Landed Gentry, 2, 3. Weaver's Visitations of Somerset, 19. New England Register, viii. 148 ; xviii. 263.

DANET. Nash's Worcestershire, i. 347. Nichols' History of the County of Leicester, iv. 571. Dugdale's Warwickshire, 523. *See* DANNET.

DANEYS. Blore's Rutland, 61.

DANFORTH. New England Register, vii. 315.

DANGAR. Burke's Colonial Gentry, i. 21.

D'ANGLE. Archæologia Courtiana, xv. 31.

DANIEL, or DANIELL. Morant's Essex, ii. 176, 310. Gentleman's Magazine, 1826, i. 130. Berry's Hertfordshire Genealogies, 102. Visitation of Suffolk, edited by J. J. Howard, i. 231-243. Burke's Landed Gentry, (of Stoodleigh,) 4, 5, 6, 7, 8 ; (of Newforest,) 2 supp., 3, 4, 5, 6, 7, 8 ; (of Auburn,) 5, 6, 7, 8 ; (of Trelissick,) 2 ; (of Kenbury,) 6, 7, 8 ; (of Cwmgelly,) 8. Foster's Visitations of Yorkshire, 124. Harleian Society, viii. 157, 384, 501 ; xv. 214 ; xviii. 71 ; xix. 98. Chetham Society, lxxxiv. 95. Account of Beauchief Abbey, in No. 3 of Nichols' Miscellaneous Antiquities, 148. Ormerod's Cheshire, i. 472, 734. The Genealogist, ii. 27.

Page's History of Suffolk, 914. A Complete Parochial History of the County of Cornwall, ii. 6. An Historical Survey of Cornwall, by C. S. Gilbert, ii. 90. Metcalfe's Visitations of Suffolk, 24, 25, 132. Visitation of Wiltshire, edited by G. W. Marshall, 72. Carthew's Hundred of Launditch, Part iii. 376. New England Register, xxviii. 185. Oliver's History of Antigua, i. 188. The Genealogist, xii. 23. A History of Banking in Bristol, by C. H. Cave, 228. *See* DANYEL.

DANNATT. Harleian Society, xxviii. 160.

DANNET, or DANNETT. Harleian Society, ii. 64. Nichols' History of the County of Leicester, iii. 235, 969. Robinson's Mansions of Herefordshire, 34. *See* DANET.

D'ANNVILLE. Collections relating to the Family of D'Annville of Bitton and Le Grand, *alias* Button, by 'Alton.' London, 1888, 4to.

DANNY. *See* DANDY.

DANSEY, or DANSIE. Burke's Landed Gentry, 2 supp., 3, 8. Robinson's Mansions of Herefordshire, 45. Cook's Continuation of Duncumb's Hereford, Hund. of Grimsworth, Part i. 40. Harleian Society, xv. 215. The Genealogist, New Series, x. 87.

DANSON. Whitaker's History of Craven, 1st edn. 73.

DANVERS. Claim of G. J. Danvers Butler Danvers, Earl of Lanesborough, to vote at Elections of Peers, Sess. Papers, 96 of 1848. Gentleman's Magazine, 1830, ii. 607. Potter's History of Charnwood Forest, 140. Appendix to Case of Sir J. S. Sidney claiming to be Lord Lisle. Sir Thomas Phillipps' Topographer, No. 1, (March, 1821, 8vo.) 28. Berry's Buckinghamshire Genealogies, 95. Oxfordshire Pedigrees, fol., *n. d.*, printed by Sir T. Phillipps. Visitation of Oxfordshire, 1574, printed by Sir T. Phillipps, (Middle Hill, fol.) 3. Visitation of Oxfordshire, 1634, printed by Sir T. Phillipps, (Middle Hill, fol.) 17. Burke's Commoners, i. 149. Harleian Society, ii. 86 ; v. 172, 187, 188, 265, 304 ; xii. 115 ; xv. 217 ; xxxix. 1139. Collectanea Topographica et Genealogica, i. 324. Lipscombe's History of the County of Buckingham, i. 280 ; iv. 530. Topographical Collections of John Aubrey, edited by J. E. Jackson, 217. Bridge's Northamptonshire, by Rev. Peter Whalley, i. 163. Burton's Description of Leicestershire, 102. Nichols' History of the County of Leicester, iv. 188, 189. Dugdale's Warwickshire, *Index*. Baker's Northampton, i. 443, 605. Wotton's English Baronetage, ii. 381 ; iv. 392. Metcalfe's Visitations of Suffolk, 90. Burke's Extinct Baronetcies. Metcalfe's Visitations of Northamptonshire, 83. Memorials of the Danvers Family, by F. N. Macnamara. London, 1895, 8vo. Howard's Visitation of England and Wales, viii. 60.

DANVILL. The Genealogist, vi. 97.

DANYEL, or DANYELL. Morant's Essex, i. 361. Visitatio Comitatus Wiltoniæ, 1623, printed by Sir T. Phillipps. Harleian Society, xvi. 89. *See* DE ANYERS, DANIEL.

DANYERS, or DANIERS. Chetham Society, xcvii. 124. Harleian

Society, xviii. 199. Historic Society of Lancashire and Cheshire, New Series, vi. 72. The Genealogist, New Series, xvi. 85.
DAPIFER. Munford's Analysis of Domesday Book of Co. Norfolk, 25, 38. Ilkley, Ancient and Modern, by R. Collyer and J. H. Turner, 54.
D'ARABIN. *See* ALDERCRON.
D'ARANDA. Miscelleanea Genealogica et Heraldica, New Series, i. 83.
DARBISHIRE. Harleian Society, xxxvii. 301. Burke's Family Records, 206.
DARBY. Burke's Commoners, (of Colebrookdale,) ii. 310, Landed Gentry, 2, 3, 4, 5, 6, 7, 8; (of Leap Castle,) 2, 3, 4, 5, 6, 7. Pedigree of Wilson of High Wray, etc., by Joseph Foster, 29. The Genealogist, iii. 373. Metcalfe's Visitations of Suffolk, 133. The Family of Darby-Coventry of Greenlands, by S. G. Fell. London, 1892, 4to. Genealogical Memoranda of the Family of Ames, 10. Annals of Smith of Balby, by H. E. Smith, 268. Pedigree of Wilson, by S. B. Foster, 61. Howard's Visitation of England and Wales, iv. 48. Dallaway's Antiquities of Bristow, 75. *See* COVENTRY.
D'ARCI, DARCY, or D'ARCY. Herald and Genealogist, iv. 449. Jacob's Peerage, i. 612. Morant's Essex, i. 314, 391, 396, 398, 458, 476; ii. 28, 139. Surtees Society, xxxvi. 108, 209. Burke's Commoners, (of Kiltullagh,) iii. 142, Landed Gentry, 2, 3, 4, 5, 6, 7, 8; (of Corbetstown,) 7, 8; (of New Forest,) Landed Gentry, 2, 3, 4, 5, 6, 7, 8; (of Hyde Park,) 2, 3, 4, 5, 6, 7, 8; (of Lacken,) 2; (of Kilcroney,) 6, 7, 8. Foster's Visitations of Yorkshire, 47. Graves' History of Cleveland, 49, 140. Burke's Royal Families, (London, 1851, 8vo.) ii. 160. Burke's Heraldic Illustrations, 43. Whitaker's History of Richmondshire, ii. 45. Poulson's Holderness, ii. 200. Thoresby's Ducatus Leodiensis, 226. Ord's History of Cleveland, 445. Surtees' Durham, i. 182. Hunter's Deanery of Doncaster, ii. 164, 391. Clutterbuck's Hertford, i. 324. Wright's Essex, ii. 775. Thoroton's Nottinghamshire, ii. 293. Pedigrees of the Leading Families of Lancashire, published by Joseph Foster, (London, 1872, fol.). Memoirs of the Family of Chester, by R. E. C. Waters, 664. Harleian Society, xiii. 44, 186, 387; xvi. 90. Whitaker's Deanery of Craven, 3rd edn., 71. O'Hart's Irish Pedigrees, 2nd Series, 325. Metcalfe's Visitations of Northamptonshire, 85. Pedigrees of the Leading Families of Yorkshire, by Joseph Foster. Chancellor's Sepulchral Monuments of Essex, 158. The New History of Yorkshire, commencing with Richmondshire, by Genl. Plantagenet-Harrison (London, 1872, fol.), Part i. 22. Plantagenet-Harrison's History of Yorkshire, i. 118. Edmondson's Baronagium Genealogicum, ii. 160; vi. 45. Banks' Baronies in Fee, i. 177-182. Banks' Dormant and Extinct Baronage, ii. 143; iii. 226. Burke's Extinct Baronetcies. J. Watney's Account of St. Osyth's Priory, 117. Burke's Colonial Gentry, ii. 468. The Genealogist, New Series, xiii. 40; xiv. 133; xvi. 241. Howard's Visitations of England and Wales, ix. 175.

D'ARCY-EVANS. Burke's Commoners, ii. 26, Landed Gentry, 2, 3, 4, 5.

DARELL, or DARRELL. Hasted's Kent, ii. 380; iii. 224. Morant's Essex, i. 370. Berry's Kent Genealogies, 102. Berry's Sussex Genealogies, 165. Burke's Commoners, i. viii., 369; (of Calehill,) Commoners, i. 133, Landed Gentry, 2, 3, 4, 5, 6, 7; 7 at p. 1847; 8. Foster's Visitations of Yorkshire, 78. Harleian Society, iv. 90; viii. 240; ix. 61; xlii. 186. Collectanea Topographica et Genealogica, vi. 124. Visitation of Berkshire, printed by Sir T. Phillipps, 16. Clutterbuck's Hertford, iii. 86. Wiltshire Archæological Magazine, iv. 226. Foley's Records of the English Province, S.J., iii. 475. Maclean's History of Trigg Minor, iii. 81. An Historical Survey of Cornwall, by C. S. Gilbert, ii. 91. Betham's Baronetage, iv. 294. Burke's Extinct Baronetcies. The Visitations of Cornwall, edited by J. L. Vivian, 135. Archæologia Cantiana, xvii. 46. The Genealogist, New Series, xiii. 186; xv. 95. The Gresley's of Drakelow, by F. Madan, 248. See DAYRELL, DORRELL.

DARES. Harleian Society, xxxii. 93.

D'ARGENTEIN. The Genealogist, New Series, x. 90.

D'ARGUES. Planché's Corner of Kent, 256.

DARLASTON. The History of Darlaston, by F. W. Hackwood, 27.

DARLEY. Jewitt's Reliquary, vii. 23. Burke's Landed Gentry, (of Aldby Park,) 2, 3, 4, 5, 6, 7, 8, (of Muston,) 6, 7, 8. Foster's Visitations of Yorkshire, 87. Harleian Society, ix. 60; xv. 216; xxxix. 994. The Visitations of Cornwall, edited by J. L. Vivian, 133. Burke's Colonial Gentry, ii. 513.

DARLING. Harleian Society, xv. 216; xxxvii. 248. Burke's Family Records, 208.

DARLINGTON. Burke's Landed Gentry, 7, 8.

DARNALL, or DARNELL. The Genealogist, iii. 374; vi. 146. Burke's Extinct Baronetcies. Notes and Queries, 1 S. v. 489, 545. Miscellanea Genealogica et Heraldica, New Series, iv. 144.

DARNLEY. Burke's Royal Descents and Pedigrees of Founders' Kin, 81.

DARROCH. Burke's Landed Gentry, 3, 4, 5, 6, 7, 8.

DARSETT. Harleian Society, xii. 79.

DART, or DARTE. Harleian Society, ix. 279. The Visitations of Cornwall, edited by J. L. Vivian, 136.

DARTMOUTH (Lord). Hasted's Kent, i. 71.

DARWIN. Glover's History of Derbyshire, ii. 178, (154). Burke's Landed Gentry, (of Breadsall Priory,) 2, 3, 4, 5, 6, 7, 8; (of Elston Hall,) 3, 4, 5, 6, 7, 8; (of Creskeld,) 8, and 8 supp. Life and Letters of Charles Darwin, by Francis Darwin, i. 1. Miscellanea Genealogica et Heraldica, 2nd Series, iii. 12, 17, 33, 62, 65. Howard's Visitation of England and Wales, iv. 116. Burke's Family Records, 209.

DASENT. Oliver's History of Antigua, i. 190. Burke's Landed Gentry, 7, 8.

DASHWOOD. Hasted's Kent, ii. 333. Berry's Buckinghamshire

Genealogies, 98. Burke's Landed Gentry, 3, 4, 5, 6, 7, 8. Harleian
Society, viii. 388. Lipscombe's History of the County of Buckingham, ii. 222. Cussan's History of Hertfordshire, Parts vii.
and viii., 52. Edmondson's Baronagium Genealogicum, iv. 347.
Wotton's English Baronetage, iii. 712 ; iv. 125. Betham's
Baronetage, iii. 68, 148. Banks' Dormant and Extinct Baronage,
ii. 168. Jewers' Wells Cathedral, 157. Notes and Queries,
7 S. x. 350.

DASSETT. Foster's Visitations of Yorkshire, 98.

DASTON. Harleian Society, xii. 21.

DAUBENEY, DAUBIGNY, or DAUBENY. The Genealogist, New Series,
xvii. 26. Collinson's Somerset, iii. 109. Burke's Commoners,
iv. 738, Landed Gentry, 2, 3, 4, 5, 6, 7, 8. Collectanea Topographica et Genealogica, i. 314. Banks' Baronies in Fee, i. 183.
Banks' Dormant and Extinct Baronage, i. 281 ; iii. 106.
Harleian Society, xxi. 274 ; xxvii. 45, 117. A History of Banking in Bristol, by C. H. Cave, 230. Memoir of Richard Haines,
by C. R. Haines, table xa. See DAWBNEY.

DAUGLISH. Burke's Family Records, 214.

DAUNDELYN. The Genealogist, New Series, xv. 93.

DAUNDY. Page's History of Suffolk, 91. See DANDY.

DAUNSEY. Weaver's Visitation of Herefordshire, 23.

DAUNT, or DAUNTE. Some Account of the Family of Daunt, by
John Daunt. Newcastle - upon - Tyne, 1881, 8vo. Rudder's
Gloucestershire, 586. Visitation of Gloucestershire, 1569, (Middle
Hill, 1854, fol.) 4. Burke's Landed Gentry, (of Owlpen,) 2 supp.,
3, 4, 5, 6, 7, 8 ; (of Fahalea,) 2 supp., 3, 4, 5, 6, 7, 8 ; (of Newborough,) 3, 4, 5, 6, 7 ; (of Sliveron,) 2 supp., 3, 4, 5 ; (of Tracton
Abbey,) 2 supp., 3, 4, 5, 6, 7, 8 ; (of Kilcascan,) 2 supp., 3, 4, 5, 6,
7, 8. Fosbrooke's History of Gloucestershire, i. 422, 427. O'Hart's
Irish Pedigrees, 2nd Series, 326. Visitation of Gloucester, edited
by T. F. Fenwick and W. C. Metcalfe, 55. Harleian Society,
xxi. 213. Gloucestershire Notes and Queries, ii. 286.

DAUNTESEY, or DAUNTSEY. Burke's Landed Gentry, 5, 7. Visitatio
Comitatus Wiltoniæ, 1623, printed by Sir T. Phillipps. Hoare's
Wiltshire, V. i. 83. Clutterbuck's Hertford, iii. 33. The
Genealogist, xii. 23.

DAUVERGNE. J. B. Payne's Armorial of Jersey, 59.

DAVALL. Morant's Essex, i. 492. History and Antiquities of Harwich and Dovercourt, by Silas Taylor, 209. The Perverse Widow,
by A. W. Crawley-Boevey, 234.

DAVENANT. Hoare's Wiltshire, V. ii. 85, 125. Harleian Society,
xiii. 388.

DAVENPORT. History and Genealogy of the Davenport Family, by
A. B. Davenport. New York, 1851, 8vo. Supplement to the
same. Stamford, Conn. 1876, 8vo. Burke's Landed Gentry, (of
Capesthorne,) 2, 3, 4, 5, 6, 7, 8 ; (of Davenport,) 2, 3, 4, 5, 6, 7,
8 ; (of Bramall Hall,) 2 add., 3, 4, 5 and supp., 6, 7, 8 ; (of
(Foxley,) 5, 6, 7, 8. Visitation of Warwickshire, 1619, published with Warwickshire Antiquarian Magazine, 160. Burke's

Royal Families, (London, 1851, 8vo.) ii. 112. Chetham Society, lxxxiv. 96 ; cx. 232. Surtees' Durham, i. 170. Burke's Royal Descents and Pedigrees of Founders' Kin, 122. Earwaker's East Cheshire, i. 164, 436; ii. 270, 377, 385, 411, 417. Harleian Society, xii. 373 ; xv. 217 ; xviii. 72-77, 259. Ormerod's Cheshire, ii. 285, 771 ; iii. 68, 602, 690, 707, 721, 827. Cooke's Continuation of Duncumb's Hereford, (Hund. of Grimsworth,) Part ii. 194. Fletcher's Leicestershire Pedigrees and Royal Descents, 32. Burke's Colonial Gentry, i. 23. New England Register, iv. 111, 351 ; ix. 146; xxxiii. 25. The Genealogist, New Series, xiii. 186. *See* DAMPORT.

DAVENTRE. Baker's Northampton, i. 309.

DAVERS. Burke's Extinct Baronetcies. Harleian Society, xv. 217. Wotton's English Baronetage, iii. 708. Betham's Baronetage, iii. 58.

DAVES. Bysshe's Visitation of Essex, edited by J. J. Howard, 29.

DAVEY. Burke's Landed Gentry, 2, 3, 4, 5, 6, 7, 8.

DAVID. Dwnn's Visitations of Wales, i. 82, 103, 155, 217. Glamorganshire Pedigrees, edited by Sir T. Phillipps, 7, 41, 42. Cardiganshire Pedigrees, 113. Meyrick's History of the Co. of Cardigan, 152. Genealogies of Morgan and Glamorgan, by G. T. Clark, 482.

DAVID AB MORGAN. Dwnn's Visitations of Wales, ii. 124.

DAVID AP EINION. Dwnn's Visitations of Wales, i. 195.

DAVID, GRIFFITH. Dwnn's Visitations of Wales, i. 279.

DAVID, JEVAN. Dwnn's Visitations of Wales, i. 80.

DAVID, OWEN. Dwnn's Visitations of Wales, i. 281, 309.

DAVID, RYS. Dwnn's Visitations of Wales, i. 224.

DAVID, RYTHERCH. Dwnn's Visitations of Wales, i. 16, 239.

DAVIDS. Dwnn's Visitations of Wales, ii. 300, 321.

DAVIDSON. Davidson Genealogy, a broadside sheet signed C. T. M'Creedy, 2nd Sept. 1867. Herald and Genealogist, v. 368. Burke's Landed Gentry, (of Inchmarlo,) 3, 4, 5, 6, 7, 8 ; (of Tulloch,) 4, 5, 6, 7, 8 ; (of Cantray,) 2 add., 3, 4, 5, 6, 7, 8 ; (of Muirhouse,) 8. Hodgson's Northumberland, III. ii. 337. Paterson's History of Ayr and Wigton, ii. 434. Burke's Extinct Baronetcies, 620. O'Hart's Irish Pedigrees, 2nd Series, 160. Caithness Family History, by John Henderson, 283, 301.

DAVIE. Wotton's English Baronetage, ii. 263. Betham's Baronetage, i. 453, app. 29. The Visitations of Devon, by J. L. Vivian, 269-272.

DAVIES. A Genealogical History of the House of Gwysaney, by J. Bernard Burke. London, 1847, folio. Camden Society, lxviii. xiii. Berry's Sussex Genealogies, 153. Dwnn's Visitations of Wales, i. 77, 96, 307 ; ii. 86, 119, 312. Visitation of Somerset, printed by Sir T. Phillipps, 63. Burke's Commoners, i. 324 ; ii. 277 ; iv. 384 ; (of Marrington Hall,) Commoners, ii. 642, Landed Gentry, 2, 3, 4, 5, 7, 8 ; (of Elmley Castle and Danehurst,) Commoners, ii. 259, Landed Gentry, 2, 5, 6, 7, 8 ; (of Moor Court,) Landed Gentry, 2 add., 3, 4, 5, 6, 7, 8 ; (of Alltyr Odin), 3, 4, 5,

6 ; (of Croft Castle,) 5, 6, 7, 8 ; (of Cardigan,) 4, 5, 6, 7, 8 ; (of Pentre,) 2, 3, 4, 5, 6, 7, 8 ; (of Gwysaney,) 3 supp., 4 ; (of Eton House,) 2 supp. ; (of Birmingham,) 2 add. ; (of Vronheulog,) 2 ; (of Cranbrooke,) 6, and p. 524. Burke's Heraldic Register, (published with St. James's Magazine,) 67. Harleian Society, viii. 212, 162 ; xv. 218, 220 ; xxvii. 47. Burke's Royal Families, (London, 1851, 8vo.) i. 94 ; ii. 214. Seize Quartiers of the Family of Bryan Cooke, (London, 1857, 4to.) 67. Herald and Genealogist, vi. 155, 356. Polwhele's History of Cornwall, iv. 94. Burke's Visitation of Seats and Arms, i. 69. Burke's Heraldic Illustrations, 18. Caermarthenshire Pedigrees, 56. Pembrokeshire Pedigrees, 128, 129, 135. Hoare's Wiltshire, IV. ii. 36. T. Nicholas' County Families of Wales, 193. Works of Sir John Davies, (Fuller Worthies Library,) ii. xx. The Sheriffs of Cardiganshire, by J. R. Phillips, 40. Collections by the Powysland Club, iv. 155 ; vii. 107 ; x. 33. Brady's Records of Cork, Cloyne, and Ross, i. 332. Notes and Queries, 1 S. iii. 82, 336 ; v. 331. Ormerod's Cheshire, iii. 380, 725. Burke's Extinct Baronetcies. History of Powys Fadog, by J. Y. W. Lloyd, iii. 108, 222, 379 ; iv. 232, 368 ; v. 134, 201. The Visitations of Cornwall, by J. L. Vivian, 634. Burke's Colonial Gentry, ii. 641.

DAVIES-EVANS. Burke's Landed Gentry, 6, 7, 8.

DAVILE. Surtees Society, xxxvi. 101. *See* DEYVILL.

DAVILS, or DAVILES. Visitation of Devon, edited by F. T. Colby, 76. Westcote's Devonshire, edited by G. Oliver and P. Jones, 611. The Visitations of Devon, by J. L. Vivian, 273.

DAVIN. O'Hart's Irish Pedigrees, 2nd Series, 161.

DAVIS. Pedigree of Davis of Evesham, [T. P.] fol. page. Dwnn's Visitations of Wales, i. 70, 96, 179, 194, 244. Burke's Landed Gentry, 5, 7, 8. Harleian Society, viii. 162 ; xi. 32 ; xv. 221 ; xxviii. 161. Phelps' History of Somersetshire, ii. 24. Burke's Royal Descents and Pedigrees of Founders' Kin, 69. Visitations of Berkshire, printed by Sir T. Phillipps, 16. Fosbrooke's History of Gloucestershire, ii. 42. Dorothea Scott, by G. D. Scull, (1882, 4to.) folding at end. The Genealogist, v. 249. Ormerod's Cheshire, iii. 725. Visitation of Gloucester, edited by T. F. Fenwick and W. C. Metcalfe, 54. The Irish Builder, xxix. 113. New England Register, vi. 35 ; xx. 212, 299 ; xxi. 65. Burke's Colonial Gentry, i. 296. Oliver's History of Antigua, i. 194.

DAVISON. Harleian Society, viii. 101. Hutchinson's History of Durham, iii. 120. Surtees' Durham, ii. 227 ; iii. 166, 167. Foster's Visitations of Durham, 95. Burke's Landed Gentry, 8.

DAVISON-BLAND. Burke's Landed Gentry, 8.

D'AVRENCHES. Archæologia Cantiana, ii. 142 ; iii. 273.

DAVY, or DAVYE. Tuckett's Devonshire Pedigrees, 93, 97, 99. Surtees Society, xxxvi. 386. Visitation of Norfolk, published by Norfolk Archæological Society, 275-290. Burke's Landed Gentry, (of Ingoldsthorpe, 2, 3, 4, 5, 6, 7, 8 ; (of Lesketh How,) 4, 5 ; (of

15

Rose Ash,) 6, 7 ; (of Burstone,) 8. Harleian Society, vi. 83-85 ;
xv. 221 ; xvi. 93 ; xxxii. 93 ; xlii. 155. Westcote's Devonshire
edited by G. Oliver and P. Jones, 598. Burke's Royal Families,
(London, 1851, 8vo.) ii. 66. Visitatio Comitatus Wiltoniæ, 1623,
printed by Sir T. Phillipps. Burke's Extinct Baronetcies. Visitation of Wiltshire, edited by G. W. Marshall, 2. Carthew's
Hundred of Launditch, Part iii. 281, 397. The Visitations of
Devon, by J. L. Vivian, 269, 274.

DAVYS. Hoare's Wiltshire, IV. i. 136. The Genealogist, v. 25.
Jewitt's Reliquary, xx. 34. The Irish Builder, xxix. 113.
Fletcher's Leicestershire Pedigrees and Royal Descents, 77.
Parliamentary Memoirs of Fermanagh, by Earl of Belmore, 23.

DAWBNEY. Harleian Society, i. 58 ; xxxii. 98. See DAUBENEY.

DAWE. Burke's Commoners, iv. 577, Landed Gentry, 2, 3, 4, 5, 6,
7, 8. Hutchins' Dorset, ii. 654. Miscellanea Genealogica et
Heraldica, 2nd Series, ii. 255.

DAWES. Morant's Essex, ii. 397. Burke's Landed Gentry, 5 supp.
Burke's Royal Families, (London, 1851, 8vo.) ii. 117. Harleian
Society, ii. 98 ; viii. 270 ; xv. 222. Foster's Lancashire Pedigrees.
Burke's Heraldic Illustrations, 146. Nichols' History of the
County of Leicester, iv. 484. Archæologia Æliana, 1st Series, ii.
139. Dwnn's Visitations of Wales, i. 128. Wotton's English
Baronetage, iii. 401. Burke's Extinct Baronetcies.

DAWKINS, or DAWKYNS. Dwnn's Visitations of Wales, i. 145.
Burke's Landed Gentry, 4 supp., 5, 6, 7, 8. Genealogies of
Morgan and Glamorgan, by G. T. Clark, 483.

DAWLEY. Berry's Hampshire Genealogies, 321. Hampshire Visitations, printed by Sir T. Phillipps, 20.

DAWNEY, or DAWNAY. Berry's Buckinghamshire Genealogies, 60.
Surtees Society, xxxvi. 264. Foster's Yorkshire Pedigrees.
Foster's Visitations of Yorkshire, 79-84. A Complete Parochial
History of the County of Cornwall, i. 1. An Historical Survey
of Cornwall, by C. S. Gilbert, i. 457. Harleian Society, xvi. 94.
Archdall's Lodge's Peerage, v. 72. Brydges' Collins' Peerage,
viii. 453. Banks' Baronies in Fee, ii. 71.

DAWSON. Nichols' Literary Illustrations, vi. 851. Miscellanea
Genealogica et Heraldica, ii. 51. Gentleman's Magazine, 1841, i.
583. Berry's Berkshire Genealogies, 124. Visitation of Durham,
1615, (Sunderland, 1820, fol.) 73. Burke's Commoners, (of Castle
Dawson,) iii. 580, Landed Gentry, 2, 3, 4, 5, 6 ; (of Groton House,)
2, 3, 4, 5, 6, 7, 8 ; (of Charlesfort,) 8 ; (of Launde Abbey,)
4, 5, 6, 7, 8. Foster's Visitations of Yorkshire, 184, 512.
Nichols' History of the County of Leicester, iii. 1106. Burke's
Royal Families, (London, 1851, 8vo.) ii. 121. Whitaker's
Deanery of Craven, 130, (175). Shirley's History of the County
of Monaghan, 184. Jewitt's Reliquary, xvii. 127. Archdall's
Lodge's Peerage, iii. 383 ; vi. 78. Foster's Visitations of Durham,
97. Burton's History of Hemingborough, 327. Harleian Society,
xxxvii. 97 ; xxxviii. 520. Howard's Visitation of England and
Wales, Notes, iii. 75. See MASSY-DAWSON, WESTROPP-DAWSON.

DAWSON-DUFFIELD. Burke's Visitation of Seats and Arms, 2nd Series, ii. 23.

DAWTREY, or DAWTRY. Berry's Sussex Genealogies, 46. Berry's Hampshire Genealogies, 112. Burke's Commoners, iv. 10. Visitation of Sussex, 1570, printed by Sir T. Phillipps, (Middle Hill, fol.) 4. Dallaway's Sussex, II. i. 296. Hampshire Visitations, printed by Sir T. Phillipps, 20. Castles, Mansions, and Manors of Western Sussex, by D. G. C. Elwes and C. J. Robinson, 173. The Genealogist, New Series, xviii. 33.

DAY, or DAYE. Gentleman's Magazine, 1832, ii. 417, 598. Cambridgeshire Visitation, edited by Sir T. Phillipps, 9. Burke's Landed Gentry, 2 supp., 3, 4. Harleian Society, viii. 447; xix. 99; xxviii. 162; xli. 39; xliii. 156. Visitatio Comitatus Wiltoniæ, 1623, printed by Sir T. Phillipps. Visitation of Wiltshire, edited by G. W. Marshall, 53. Harvey's Hundred of Willey, 519. Cyclostyle Pedigrees, by J. J. Green. Surrey Archæological Collections, xi.

DAYLWYN. Weaver's Visitations of Somerset, 19.

DAYMAN. Burke's Landed Gentry, 3, 4, 5, 6, 7, 8.

DAYNCOURT. Thoroton's Nottinghamshire, i. 212. See D'EINCOURT.

DAYRELL. The History of the Dayrells of Lillingston Dayrell, by E. Dayrell. Jersey, 1885, 8vo. Burke's Commoners, (of Lillingston Dayrell,) iii. 147, Landed Gentry, 2, 3, 4, 5, 6, 7, 8; (of Shudy Camps,) Commoners, iii. 152, Landed Gentry, 2, 3, 4, 5, 6, 7. Harleian Society, viii. 274. Lipscombe's History of the County of Buckingham, iii. 32. Burke's Royal Families, (London, 1851, 8vo.) ii. 192. The Genealogist, New Series, xv. 124. See DARELL.

DAYVELL. Berry's Buckinghamshire Genealogies, 18.

DEACON. Burke's Landed Gentry, 2. Harleian Society, xv. 222. See DAKEYNE.

DEAKIN. Pedigree of the Family of Deakin of Soulton Hall, Co. Salop. By W. A. Abram. (No place or date.) 8vo. pp. 7. Burke's Landed Gentry, 6. Burke's Colonial Gentry, i. 270.

DE ALBANY. Berry's Buckinghamshire Genealogies, 19. See ALBANY.

DE ALBEMARLE. Colby of Great Torrington, by F. T. Colby, 33. See ALBEMARLE.

DE ALBINI. Collinson's Somerset, iii. 108. Lipscombe's History of the County of Buckingham, iv. 102. Dallaway's Sussex, II. i. 111. Harleian Society, xiv. 731. Banks' Dormant and Extinct Baronage, i. 281. See ALBINI.

DEALE. The Genealogist, New Series, xiv. 125.

DE ALEMAN. Whitaker's Deanery of Craven, 391, (537).

DE ALFRETON. Jewitt's Reliquary, vii. 194.

DE ALNETO, or DE ALNO. Collinson's Somerset, ii. 290, 421. Harvey's Hundred of Willey, 186. See ALNO.

DE ALTA RIPA. Berry's Hampshire Genealogies, 112. Collectanea Topographica et Genealogica, vi. 124. Dallaway's Ssssex, II. i. 296.

DEALTRY. Burke's Commoners, (of Lofthouse,) i. 252, Landed Gentry, 2; (of Lincolnshire,) 4 supp. Foster's Visitations of Yorkshire, 512.

DEAN. John Watson's History of Halifax, 313.

DEANE. Herald and Genealogist, v. 356; vii. 55, 546. Morant's Essex, ii. 278. Berry's Hampshire Genealogies, 270. Visitation of Norfolk, published by Norfolk Archæological Society, i. 56. Burke's Landed Gentry, (of Berkeley,) 3, 4, 5, 7, 8; (of Boyce Court,) 6, 7, 8. Foster's Visitations of Yorkshire. 513. Collectanea Topographica et Genealogica, iii. 190. Shaw's Staffordshire, ii. 289. Hampshire Visitations, printed by Sir T. Phillipps, 20. Wright's Essex, i. 492. Harleian Society, xiii. 47, 188, 388; xxxii. 99. Life of Richard Deane, by J. B. Deane, 47. Archdall's Lodge's Peerage, vii. 190. F. G. Lee's History of Thame, 274. Visitations of Staffordshire, 1614 and 1663-4, William Salt Society, 104. Genealogical Gleanings in England, by H. F. Waters, i. 242. The Genealogist, New Series, vii. 76. Robinson of the White House, Appleby, by C. B. Norcliffe, 93. New England Register, iii. 375; vi. 103; ix. 93; xviii. 263; xxv. 358; xxxvii. 288. Muskett's Suffolk Manorial Families, i. 154. See CARSON, DENE.

DEANE-DRAKE. Howard's Visitation of Ireland, iii. 80.

DEANE-FREEMAN. Burke's Commoners, ii. 690.

DE ANESTY. Morant's Essex, ii. 137.

DE ANYERS. Burke's Landed Gentry, 6 at p. 1756. See DANYEL.

DEARBORN. New England Register, ii. 81, 297; vi. 60.

DE ARCHES. Berry's Berkshire Genealogies, 23. Whitaker's Deanery of Craven, 3rd edn., 562.

DEARDEN. Burke's Commoners, (of Rochdale Manor,) ii. 356, Landed Gentry, 2, 3, 4, 5, 6, 7, 8; (of The Hollins,) Landed Gentry, 5 supp., 6, 7, 8. Popular Genealogists, 95. Fishwick's History of Rochdale, 449.

DE ARDEN. See ARDEN.

DEARHAM. Visitation of Durham, 1615, (Sunderland, 1820, fol.) 54. Surtees' Durham, iv. 152. Foster's Visitations of Durham, 99.

DEARMAN. Annals of Smith of Balby, by H. E. Smith, 222.

DEASE. Burke's Landed Gentry, 3, 4, 5, 6, 7, 8. See O'REILLY-DEASE.

DE ASPALE. Gage's History of Thingoe Hundred, Suffolk, 47.

DE ASSEWELL. The Genealogist, New Series, x. 212.

DE ASTELEYE. The Genealogist, New Series, ix. 150.

DEATH. Harleian Society, xv. 223; xlii. 112. See D'AETH.

DE ATON. History of the Town and Port of Hull, by C. Frost, 74. See ATON.

DE AUBERNON. Westcote's Devonshire, edited by G. Oliver and P. Jones, 517.

DE AUMARI. Nichols' History of the County of Leicester, iv. 188.

DE AVERINGES. Burton's History of Hemingborough, 243.

DE BADLESMERE. G. P. Scrope's History of Castle Combe, 65, 69.

DE BAGOTT. Berry's Hertfordshire Genealogies, 162. See BAGOT.

DE BAGSORE. Eyton's Antiquities of Shropshire, ii. 65.

DEBANCK. The Genealogist, New Series, vii. 77.

DE BARRENTINE, or DE BARENTON. Morant's Essex, ii. 503. J. B. Payne's Armorial of Jersey, 65. Notes and Queries, 2 S. vi. 485. *See* BARENTINE.

DE BARY. Burke's Landed Gentry, 5, 6, 7, 8.

DE BASINGS. Hasted's Kent, iii. 116. Harleian Society, iii. 49.

DE BATAILE. Morant's Essex, i. 166.

DE BATHE. Gentleman's Magazine, 1835, ii. 375. Betham's Baronetage, v. 467.

DE BAVENT. Dallaway's Sussex, II. ii. 139. *See* BAVENT.

DEBDEN. Metcalfe's Visitations of Suffolk, 133.

DE BEAUCHAMP. Collinson's Somerset, i. 44. Morant's Essex, ii. 329. Carthew's Hundred of Launditch, Part i. 92. *See* BEAUCHAMP.

DE BEAUVOIR. Chronicle of the Family of De Havilland. Notes and Queries, 1 S. ix. 349, 596 ; x. 51 ; 2 S. vii. 383. *See* BEAUVOIR.

DE BECKBURY. Eyton's Antiquities of Shropshire, viii. 160.

DE BEK. The Genealogist, New Series, ix. 208.

DE BEKERING. Hodgson's Northumberland, I. ii. 334. *See* BEKERING.

DE BELHUS. Morant's Essex, i. 78, 202 ; ii. 190. *See* BELHOUSE.

DEBELL. Foster's account of Families descended from Francis Fox, 19. *See* DEEBLE.

DE BELLA. Thoroton's Nottinghamshire, iii. 97.

DE BELLOMONTE. Camden Society, xiii. 144. *See* BELLOMONT.

DE BENSTED. Morant's Essex, ii. 495. *See* BENSTED.

DE BERGHAM. Account of the Family of De Bergham, by Thomas Chatterton, at end of 1803 edn. of vol. ii. of Chatterton's works.

DE BERMINGHAM. Journal of the Historical and Archæological Association of Ireland, 4th Series, i. 634. *See* BIRMINGHAM.

DE BESILLES. Collinson's Somerset, iii. 504.

DE BEST. Harleian Society, xv. 224. *See* BEST.

DE BEYSIN. Eyton's Antiquities of Shropshire, ii. 12.

DE BIDOLF. The Genealogist, New Series, ix. 147.

DE BIRCHE. Morant's Essex, ii. 182. *See* BIRCH.

DE BLAKEHAM. Gage's History of Thingoe Hundred, Suffolk, 32.

DE BLAQUIÈRE. Claim of Baron de Blaquière to vote at elections of' Irish Peers, Sess. Papers, 224 of 1863 ; B of 1864.

DE BOCLOND. The Genealogist, New Series, ix. 7.

DE BODIAM. Sussex Archæological Collections, ix. 277. *See* BODYAM.

DE BODMIN. Maclean's History of Trigg Minor, i. 271.

DE BOHUN. Morant's Essex, ii. 21, 151, 515. Bridges' Northamptonshire, by Rev. Peter Whalley, i. 159. Eyton's Antiquities of Shropshire, iv. 184. Sussex Archæological Collections, xx. 22. *See* BOHUN.

DE BOIS, or DE BOYS. Blomefield's Norfolk, i. 78. Nichols' History

of the County of Leicester, ii. 372 ; iv. 102. Morant's Essex, i.
395 ; ii. 108. *See* WOOD, BOIS, BOYS.
DE BOIVILE. Burton's Description of Leicestershire, 256. *See*
BOYVILL.
DE BOLEBEC. Records of Buckinghamshire, i. 246, *See* BOLEBEC.
DEBONNAIRE. Miscellanea Genealogica et Heraldica, New Series, iii.
245.
DE BORSELE. Notes and Queries, 5 S. xi. 270.
DE BOSCO. Blomefield's Norfolk, i. 78. Westcote's Devonshire,
edited by G. Oliver and P. Jones, 589. Dugdale's Warwick-
shire, 9.
DE BOTEVILLE. *See* BOTFIELD.
DE BOTREAUX. Maclean's History of Trigg Minor, i. 631-641. *See*
BOTREAUX.
DE BOULERS. *See* BOWDLER.
DE BOUTETORT. Morant's Essex, ii. 306, 330, 332. *See* BOTETOURT.
DE BOVILE. Page's History of Suffolk, 137. *See* BOVILE.
DE BRADESTON. Manning and Bray's Surrey, ii. 97. *See* BRADE-
STON.
DE BRADEWELL. The Genealogist, New Series, x. 135.
DE BRADSHAGH. Chetham Society, xcv. 111. *See* BRADSHAW.
DE BRANCHE. Manning and Bray's Surrey, ii. 25. *See* BRANCHE.
DE BRAOSE, or DE BREOSE. Eyton's Antiquities of Shropshire, iv.
184. Castles, Mansions, and Manors of Western Sussex, by
D. G. C. Elwes and C. J. Robinson, 48, 50, 263, 283. Manning
and Bray's Surrey, i. 455*. The Genealogist, iv. 133, 235 ; v.
65, 147, 161, 318 ; vi. 16, 236 ; vii. 51 ; New Series, x. 86. *See*
BRAOSE.
DE BRETESCHE. Collinson's Somerset, ii. 314. *See* BRETESCHE.
DE BRETON. Morant's Essex, ii. 240. *See* BRETON.
DE BROC. Eyton's Antiquities of Shropshire, i. 190. *See* BROC.
DE BROMPTON. The Genealogist, New Series, ix. 207.
DE BRUG. Eyton's Antiquities of Shropshire, viii. 165.
DE BRUS. Fauconberge Memorial, 62. Herald and Genealogist,
viii. 336. Graves' History of Cleveland, 47, 273. *See* BRUS.
DE BURES. Morant's Essex, ii. 326. Manning and Bray's Surrey,
ii. 584.
DE BURG, or DE BURGH. Manning and Bray's Surrey, i. 533.
Journal of the Historical and Archæological Association of Ireland,
4th Series, iv. 34. Herald and Genealogist, iv. 338. Burke's
Commoners, iii. 500, Landed Gentry, (of West Drayton,) 2, 3, 4,
5, 6, 7, 8 ; (of Oldtown,) 8 ; (of Dromkeen,) 8 ; Burke's Royal
Families, (London, 1851, 8vo.) i. 155. Munford's Analysis of
Domesday Book of Co. Norfolk, 8. Lipscombe's History of the
County of Buckingham, i. 159. Bridges' Northamptonshire, by
Rev. Peter Whalley, ii. 342. Clutterbuck's Hertford, ii. 463 ; iii.
225. Archdall's Lodge's Peerage, i. 117. Banks' Dormant and
Extinct Baronage, i. 63 ; iii. 5, 413. Notes and Queries, 4 S.
ix. 219, 286, 330, 356, 431 ; x. 132 ; 6 S., xi. 156, 330. Archæ-
ologia Cantiana, xv. 3. Harleian Society, xli. 124. *See* BURGH.

DE BURGHERSH. Excerpta Cantiana, by Rev. T. Streatfield, 6.
DE BURGO. Bibliotheca Topographica Britannica, i. Part i. 44.
DE BURHUNTE. *See* BORHUNTE.
DE BURI. Eyton's Antiquities of Shropshire, viii. 176.
DE BURSER. Morant's Essex, ii. 253.
DE BURSTOW. Manning and Bray's Surrey, ii. 286.
DE BUSLI. Hunter's History of the Parish of Sheffield, 35. *See*
BUSLI.
DE BUSSY. The Genealogist, New Series, vii. 245.
DE CAILY. Norfolk Archæology, iii. 126.
DE CALVERHALL. Miscellanea Genealogica et Heraldica, New Series,
ii. 511.
DE CAM. Blunt's Dursley and its Neighbourhood, 168.
DE CAMOYS. Morant's Essex, ii. 360. *See* CAMOYS.
DE CAMPANIA. History of Town and Port of Hull, by C. Frost, 9.
DE CAMVILE. Collinson's Somerset, ii. 356. Burton's Description
of Leicestershire, 185. *See* CAMVILE.
DE CANNVILLE. The Genealogist, New Series, viii. 34.
DE CANTILUPE. Collinson's Somerset, iii. 80. *See* CANTELUPE.
DE CAPELL. Betham's Baronetage, v. 525. *See* CAPELL, SUPPLE.
DE CAPELL-BROOKE. Berry's Sussex Genealogies, 274.
DE CAPRECURIA. History of Barnsley, by Rowland Jackson, 50.
DE CARBURRA. Maclean's History of Trigg Minor, i. 276.
DE CARDIFF. Genealogies of Morgan and Glamorgan, by G. T.
Clark, 373.
DE CARDURCIS. Harleian Society, iv. 122. *See* CHAWORTH.
DE CARRU, or CARREW. The Genealogist, New Series, viii. 35 ;
ix. 147.
DE CARTERET. Gentleman's Magazine, 1830, ii. 397. J. B. Payne's
Armorial of Jersey, 67, 88, 92, 111, 118. The King of Arms, 145.
See CARTERET.
DE CASTELLA. Burke's Colonial Gentry, ii. 770.
DE CASTELLO. The Genealogist, New Series, ix. 206, 213. Eyton's
Antiquities of Shropshire, i. 375. *See* CASTELL.
DE CASTILLON. Hasted's Kent, (Hundred of Blackheath, by H. H.
Drake,) xxvi.
DE CASTHORP. The Genealogist, New Series, x. 91.
DE CATTERALL. Chetham Society, xcv. 67. *See* CATERALL.
DE CAUSE. Foster's Visitations of Yorkshire, 302.
DECCAF. History of Powys Fadog, by J. Y. W. Lloyd, ii. 375.
DE CERISIS, CERISEAUX, SERGEAULX, or SERGEAUX. Mullyon, its
History, etc., by E. G. Harvey, 115.
DE CERNE. The Genealogist, New Series, ix. 12.
DE CHATULTON. The Genealogist, New Series, x. 136.
DE CHEDDER. Collinson's Somerset, iii. 575.
DECKER. Harleian Society, viii. 516. Burke's Extinct Baronetcies.
DE CLARE. Collinson's Somerset, iii. 148. Rudder's Gloucester-
shire, 739. Gentleman's Magazine, 1819, ii. 411 ; 1820, i. 33 ;
ii. 103 ; 1821, 215 ; 1822, i. 599 ; 1865, ii. 4. Hasted's Kent, ii.
323. Morant's Essex, i. 59 ; ii. 339, 437. Carthew's Hundred

of Launditch, Part i. 85. Munford's Analysis of Domesday Book of Co. Norfolk, 51. Notes and Queries, 1 S. v. 126, 204, 261, 300, 594 ; 5 S. x. 349 ; xi. 406, 424, 473 ; 6 S., xi. 156. Bridges' Northamptonshire, by Rev. Peter Whalley, ii. 61. Nichols' History of the County of Leicester, ii. 344. Chauncy's Hertfordshire, 214. Banks' Baronies in Fee, ii. 66. Norfolk Antiquarian Miscellany, i. 413. Annals of Chepstow Castle, by J. F. Marsh, 266. Hasted's Kent, (Hundred of Blackheath, by H. H. Drake.) xxvi. The Genealogist, New Series, xii. 232 ; xiii. 98. See CLARE.

DE CLAVERING. Morant's Essex, ii. 611. The Genealogist, New Series, viii. 154. See CLAVERING.

DE CLAYTON. Chetham Society, xcv. 143. See CLAYTON.

DE CLIDERHOU. Abram's History of Blackburn, 645. See CLITHE-ROW.

DE CLIFFORD. Burke's Royal Families, (London, 1851, 8vo.) ii. 185. Blore's Rutland, 15. Hodgson's Northumberland, III. ii. 28. See CLIFFORD.

DE CLIFTON. Morant's Essex, ii. 90. See CLIFTON.

DE CLIVEDEN. The Genealogist, New Series, ix. 206.

DE CLOVILL. Morant's Essex, ii. 37. See CLOVILL.

DE COCTON. Dugdale's Warwickshire, 749. See COCTON.

DE COGGESHALL. Morant's Essex, i. 261, 289, 312, 452 ; ii. 162, 373. See COGGESHALL.

DE COKEFELD. Camden Society, xiii. 144. See COKEFELD.

DE COLUMBERS. Collinson's Somerset, iii. 551. See COLUMBERS.

DECONS. Visitation of Warwickshire, 1619, published with Warwickshire Antiquarian Magazine, 98. Harleian Society, xii. 231.

DE CORONA. Harleian Society, xviii. 150.

DE COTHERCOTE. Eyton's Antiquities of Shropshire, vi. 264.

DE COURCY. Drummond's History of Noble British Families, Part viii. Whitaker's Loidis and Elmete, 166. An Historical Survey of Cornwall, by C. S. Gilbert, i. 493. Archdall's Lodge's Peerage, vi. 132. See COURCY.

DE CREKE. Camden Society, xiii. 144. See CREKE.

DE CREOUN. Manning and Bray's Surrey, i. 359.

DE CRESPIGNY. Burke's Heraldic Illustrations, Pl. 124. Burke's Royal Families, (London, 1851, 8vo.) i. 84.

DE CRESSY. Carthew's Hundred of Launditch, Part i. 70, 156. See CRESSY.

DE CREVECŒUR. Archæologia Cantiana, iii. 273. See CREVEQUER.

DE CUILEY. Burton's Description of Leicestershire, 218.

DE DAVENTRE. Baker's Northampton, i. 306.

DE DEEN. The Genealogist, New Series, ix. 86.

DE DENUM. Surtees' Durham, i. 192.

DE DOL. The Genealogist, New Series, ix. 206.

DE DONZI. Proceedings of the Suffolk Institute of Archæology, ii. 407.

DE DOVER. Morant's Essex, i. 72. See DOVER.

DE DREUX. Carthew's Hundred of Launditch, Part i. 29. *See* DREUX.

DE DUNSTANVILLE. Gentleman's Magazine, 1825, ii. 417. G. P. Scrope's History of Castle Combe, 19. Hoare's Wiltshire, IV. i. 98. *See* DUNSTANVILLE.

DE DURMERS. Morant's Essex, ii. 426.

DE DYNE. Bridges' Northamptonshire, by Rev. Peter Whalley, i. 329. *See* DYNE.

DE DYNEHAM. The Genealogist, New Series, x. 136.

DE DYNELEY. Whitaker's History of Whalley, 335. *See* DYNELEY.

DEE. Genealogical Account of some of the Families derived from Bedo Dee, London, 1815, 4to. Berry's Sussex Genealogies, 161. History of Merchant Taylors' School, by Rev. H. B. Wilson, 1169-1171.

DEEBLE. A Complete Parochial History of the County of Cornwall, iii. 252. *See* DEBELL.

DEEDES. Hasted's Kent, iii. 413. Burke's Landed Gentry, 2, 3, 4, 5, 6, 7, 8. Cussan's History of Hertfordshire, Parts ix. and x. 42.

DEERE. Genealogies of Morgan and Glamorgan, by G. T. Clark, 380.

DE ERLEIGH. Collinson's Somerset, ii. 198.

DE ESLYNTON. The Genealogist, New Series, ix. 212.

DE ESSEBY. Burton's Description of Leicestershire, 23. *See* ESSEBY.

DE ETTON. Vallis Eboracensis, comprising the History, etc., of Easingwold, by Thomas Gill, 257.

DE EYTON. Eyton's Antiquities of Shropshire, ii. 12. *See* EYTON.

DE FAY. Manning and Bray's Surrey, ii. 84. The Genealogist, v. 318.

DE FERARIIS. Harleian Society, xxxii. 239.

DE FERRARS, or DE FERRERS. Nichols' History of the County of Leicester, i. 545. Transactions of the Bristol and Gloucester Archæological Society for 1876, 88. *See* FERRERS.

DE FERRY. Burke's Landed Gentry, 8.

DE FIEULES. Collinson's Somerset, iii. 4.

DE FLANDERS. Burton's Description of Leicestershire, 240. *See* FLANDERS.

DE FOE. Notes and Queries, 1 S. v. 392, 476 ; viii. 51, 94, 197.

DE FORTIBUS. History of the Town and Port of Hull, by C. Frost, 9. Whitaker's Deanery of Craven, 3rd edn., 297. 26th Report of Dep. Keeper of Public Records, app. 64. Banks' Dormant and Extinct Baronage, iii. 32. Nicolson and Burn's Westmorland and Cumberland, ii. 72. *See* FORTIBUS.

DE FOURCHES. The Genealogist, New Series, ix. 212.

DE FOURNEAUX. Collinson's Somerset, i. 262 ; iii. 213. *See* FURNEAUX.

DE FREVILE. Carthew's Hundred of Launditch, Part i. 343. *See* FREVILE.

DE FRIVILL. The Genealogist, New Series, viii. 242.

DE FURNIVAL. Hunter's History of the Parish of Sheffield, 44. *See* FURNIVAL.

De Gant. Bridges' Northamptonshire, by Rev. Peter Whalley, i. 88. *See* Gant.

De Gatesden. Carthew's Hundred of Launditch, Part i. 241. *See* Gatesdene.

De Gatton. Hasted's Kent, ii. 763. Berry's Kent Genealogies, 269. Manning and Bray's Surrey, i. 85 ; ii. 228. *See* Gatton.

De Geney. The Genealogist, New Series, viii. 241.

Degge. Harleian Society, viii. 231 ; xxxix. 982. Visitation of Derbyshire, 1663-4, (Middle Hill, 1854, fol.) 3. Erdeswicke's Survey of Staffordshire, lx. The Genealogist, iii. 187. Jewitt's Reliquary, xxii. 238.

De Goldington. Morant's Essex, ii. 197, 219, 346. *See* Golding-ton.

De Gorram. *See* Gorham.

De Gostre. Ormerod's Cheshire, iii. 132.

De Gournay, or De Gurnai. Morant's Essex, ii. 319. Collinson's Somerset, ii. 138 ; iii. 340. *See* Gurnay.

De Gras. Morant's Essex, ii. 24.

De Gray. Gentleman's Magazine, 1825, ii. 9. *See* Gray.

De Grenville. Lipscombe's History of the County of Buckingham, i. 589. *See* Grenville.

De Grey. Hasted's Kent, ii. 670. History of Town and Port of Hull, by C. Frost, 29. Lipscombe's History of the County of Buckingham, i. 160. Bridges' Northamptonshire, by Rev. Peter Whalley, i. 187, 397, 497. Chauncy's Hertfordshire, 338. Page's History of Suffolk, 929. Controversey between Reginald Lord Grey de Ruthin and Sir Edward Hastings, by Sir C. G. Young, (1841, small fol.) 3. Edmondson's Baronagium Genealogicum, vi. 88. Brydges' Collins' Peerage, vii. 510. Norfolk Antiquarian Miscellany, ii. 604. *See* Grey.

De Gruchy. J. B. Payne's Armorial of Jersey, 120.

De Haccombe. Miscellanea Genealogica et Heraldica, ii. 234.

De Hackenneshawe. Chetham Society, xcv. 83.

De Hadynton. The Genealogist, New Series, viii. 35.

De Hally. Jewitt's Reliquary, viii. 44.

De Hastings. Collinson's Somerset, ii. 337. Morant's Essex, ii. 35. *See* Hastings.

De Havilland. Burke's Landed Gentry, (of Havilland Hall,) 2 supp., 3, 4, 5, 6, 7, 8. *See* Havilland.

De Helwell. Nichols' History of the County of Leicester, ii. 345.

De Helyon. Morant's Essex, ii. 531.

De Hemegrave. Gage's History of Hengrave, 80. Gage's History of Thingoe Hundred, Suffolk, 167. Page's History of Suffolk, 295.

De Hesding. Herald and Genealogist, vi. 245.

De Hethe. Gage's History of Hengrave, 95. Page's History of Suffolk, 842. *See* Hethe.

De Hilton. Hunter's Deanery of Doncaster, ii. 141. *See* Hilton.

De Hodinge. Morant's Essex, ii. 277.

De Hoghton. Foster's Lancashire Pedigrees. *See* Hoghton.

De Holand. Abram's History of Blackburn, 667. *See* Holand.

DE HOOTON. Hunter's Deanery of Doncaster, i. 399. *See* HOOTON.
DE HORNE. Collectanea Topographica et Genealogica, ii. 287. Burke's
    Landed Gentry, 2 and corr., 3, 4, 5, 6, 7, 8. Foster's Account of
    Families descended from Francis Fox, 17. *See* HORNE.
DE HORSEY. Burke's Family Records, 330.
DE HOTHOM. Chetham Society, xcv. 142. *See* HOTHAM.
DE HOUBY. Burton's Description of Leicestershire, 125. *See*
    HOUBY.
DE HOXHAM. The Genealogist, New Series, ix. 211.
DE HUNTINGFIELD, or DE HUNTINGFELD. Morant's Essex, ii. 136.
    Hasted's Kent, ii. 752. Carthew's Hundred of Launditch, Part i.
    349. Page's History of Suffolk, 241. *See* HUNTINGFIELD.
DE ICKLESHAM. Sussex Archæological Collections, viii. 84.
DE ICKWORTH. Gage's History of Thingoe Hundred, Suffolk, 276.
DEIGHTON. Pedigree of Deighton of Worcester, [T. P.] folio page.
D'EINCOURT. Blore's Rutland, 150. Harleian Society, xvi. 95.
    Edmondson's Baronagium Genealogicum, v. 483. Banks' Baronies
    in Fee, i. 184. Banks' Dormant and Extinct Baronage, ii. 149.
    See DAYNCOURT.
DE INSULA. Case of Sir J. S. Sidney, Bart., in relation to the Barony
    of Lisle, Pedigree No. 1. Berry's Hampshire Genealogies, 173,
    193, 271. New England Register, xxxix. 63. Hampshire Visita-
    tions, printed by Sir T. Phillipps, 22. Dugdale's Warwickshire,
    938. *See* LISLE.
DE INTEBERG. Journal of the Historical and Archæological Associa-
    tion of Ireland, 4th Series, i. 634.
DE IRELAND. Lydiate Hall and its Associations, by Rev. T. E.
    Gibson, (1876, 4to.) 27. *See* IRELAND.
DE ISLE. The Genealogist, New Series, xvii. 110.
DE ISNEY. Berry's Essex Genealogies, 1. Hutchins' Dorset, ii. 99.
    See DISNEY.
DE IVERI. Croke's History of the Family of Croke, No. 23. *See*
    IVERY.
D'EIVILL. Banks' Dormant and Extinct Baronage, i. 65.
DE JERSEY. Chronicle of the Family of De Havilland.
DE KEN. Collinson's Somerset, iii. 592. *See* KENN.
DE KENDALE. Cussan's History of Hertfordshire, Parts iii. and iv.
    97. Berry's Sussex Genealogies, 173. *See* KENDAL.
DE KILKENNY. Surtees' Durham, i. 229.
DE KIRKBY THORE. Nicolson and Burn's Westmorland and Cumber-
    land, i. 375.
DE KNYPERSLEY. The Borough of Stoke-upon-Trent, by John Ward,
    563.
DE LA BARR. Miscellanea Genealogica et Heraldica, i. 283. Harleian
    Society, xv. 224.
DE LA BERE. Pedigree of De la Bere, [T. P.] 1868, broadside.
    Topographer and Genealogist, i. 30. Hampshire Visitations,
    printed by Sir T. Phillipps, 21. Burke's Landed Gentry, 7, 8.
    The Genealogist, New Series, viii. 243 ; xv. 154. Weaver's
    Visitation of Herefordshire, 24. Visitation of Gloucester, edited

by T. F. Fenwick and W. C. Metcalfe, 56. Harleian Society, xxi. 49. Genealogies of Morgan and Glamorgan, by G. T. Clark, 479. Miscellanea Genealogica et Heraldica, 2nd Series, v. 89. *See* DELEBERE.

DE LABILLIÈRE. Burke's Colonial Gentry, ii. 418.

DE LA BRUER. Miscellanea Genealogica et Heraldica, New Series, ii. 73. Colby of Great Torrington, by F. T. Colby, 33.

DE LA CHAMBRE. · Berry's Sussex Genealogies, 17. Horsfield's History of Lewes, ii. 203.

DE LA CHEROIS. Burke's Landed Gentry, 6, 7, 8.

DE LA CHEROIS-CROMMELIN. Burke's Commoners, iv. 422, Landed Gentry, 2, 3, 4, 5, 6, 7, 8.

DE LACHINDON. Morant's Essex, i. 353.

DELACOUR. Burke's Landed Gentry, 5 supp., 6, 7, 8.

DE LACY. Pedigree of the Family of De Lacy. Broadside, *n. d.* Eyton's Antiquities of Shropshire, v. 240. Nichols' History of the County of Leicester, ii. 344. Hunter's Deanery of Doncaster, i. 332. Ormerod's Cheshire, i. 692. Baines' History of the Co. of Lancaster, iii. 207. *See* LACY.

DELAFIELD, or DE LA FIELD. Burke's Commoners, i. 542 ; Landed Gentry, 2. John D'Alton's History of Co. Dublin, 396.

DE LA FORD. Croke's History of the Family of Croke, No. 13.

DE LA FOYLE. Hoare's Wiltshire, V. iii. 44. *See* FOYLE.

DE LA GARDE. J. B. Payne's Armorial of Jersey, 123.

DE LA GRAVE. The Visitations of Devon, edited by J. L. Vivian, 76.

DELAHAY. Blore's Rutland, 150. Archæologia Æliana, 2nd Series, iii. 78. Notes and Queries, 5 S. ix. 517.

DELAHYDE. Ashmole's Antiquities of Berkshire, iii. 296. Shaw's Staffordshire, ii. 97. Collections for a History of Staffordshire, (William Salt Society,) i. 326. The Genealogist, v. 249 ; New Series, i. 6.

DE LA LAUNDE. Dugdale's Warwickshire, 949.

DE LA LAUNE. The Visitations of Cornwall, edited by J. L. Vivian, 426.

DE LA LEE. Cussan's History of Hertfordshire, Parts iii. and iv. 148. Morant's Essex, ii. 625. Berry's Hertfordshire Genealogies, 74. Clutterbuck's Hertford, iii. 333. Chauncy's Hertfordshire, 147. *See* LEE.

DE LA LEGH. Collectanea Topographica et Genealogica, vi. 307. *See* LEGH.

DE LA LEIGH. Harvey's Hundred of Willey, 502.

DE LA LEY. Bateson's History of Northumberland, i. 178.

DE LA LEYGRAND. Visitation of Devon, edited by F. T. Colby, 31.

DE LA LUZERNE. Gentleman's Magazine, 1840, ii. 45.

DE LA LYNDE. Hutchins' Dorset, iv. 479. Miscellanea Genealogica et Heraldica, 2nd Series, iii. 325.

DE LA MARE, DELAMARE, DELAMERE, or DELAMORE. Bridges' Northamptonshire, by Rev. Peter Whalley, ii. 528. Clutterbuck's Hertford, iii. 100. Banks' Dormant and Extinct Baronage, i. 284. Collinson's Somerset, i. 186 ; ii. 218. Hoare's Wiltshire, I. ii

256. Herald and Genealogist, iv. 194. Berry's Hampshire Genealogies, 70. Harleian Society, iv. 37; vi. 494; xxxii. 100. Ellacombe's History of Bitton, 80. Edmondson's Baronagium Genealogicum, v. 484. Genealogies of Morgan and Glamorgan, by G. T. Clark, 497, 498. The Genealogist, New Series, xv. 152.

DE LA MATER. New England Register, xiv. 41.

DELAP. Burke's Landed Gentry, 2, 3, 4, 5, 6, 7, 8. Oliver's History of Antigua, i. 197.

DE LA PLACE. J. B. Payne's Armorial of Jersey, 125.

DE LA PLANCHE. Harvey's Hundred of Willey, 250.

DE LA PLANK. The Genealogist, New Series, xvi. 90.

DE LA POLE. Gentleman's Magazine, 1866, ii. 292. Morant's Essex, ii. 244. Gough's Sepulchral Monuments, ii. 321. History of Kingston-upon-Hull, by George Hadley, 256. History of Town and Port of Hull, by C. Frost, 31. Notices of Swyncombe and Ewelme, in Co. Oxford, by H. A. Napier, 291, 322. Lipscombe's History of the County of Buckingham, i. 66. T. Nicholas's County Families of Wales, 792. Banks' Baronies in Fee, i. 186. Banks' Dormant and Extinct Baronage, i. 233; ii. 153. The Genealogist, New Series, iii. 112; ix. 207. Oxford Historical Society, xxiv. 30. Harleian Society, xxxii. 313. Notes and Queries, 7 S. ix. 407, 491; x. 49. Muniments of the Family of Wingfield, 65. *See* POLE.

DE LA POMERAY. The Genealogist, New Series, ix. 147.

DE LA PORTE. Minet's Account of the Family of Minet, 206.

DE LA POYLE. Herald and Genealogist, i. 337. Manning and Bray's Surrey, iii. 174.

DE LA PUTTE. The Genealogist, New Series, xiv. 27.

DE LA ROCHE. Banks' Baronies in Fee, ii. 123.

DELARYVER, DE LA RIVER, or DE LA RYVERE. Surtees Society, xli. 18. Foster's Visitations of Yorkshire, 38, 601. Manning and Bray's Surrey, ii. 220. Burke's Commoners, iv, 229. Harleian Society, xvi. 95; xliii. 128.

DE LA SEE. Poulson's Holderness, i. 195.

DE LA TASTE. J. B. Payne's Armorial of Jersey, 127.

DE LA TOUR. The Genealogist, New Series, ix. 11.

DE LA TWYER. Harleian Society, xvi. 96.

DELAUME. Hasted's Kent, ii. 693. Harleian Society, viii. 179. *See* DELAWNE.

DE LAUTOUR. Burke's Heraldic Illustrations, 107.

DE LA VACHE. Miscellanea Genealogica et Heraldica, ii. 134.

DE LA VAL, or DELAVALE. Pedigrees from Visitation of Northumberland, printed by Sir T. Phillipps, (Middle Hill, 1858, folio). Harleian Society, viii. 432; xvi. 97. The Genealogist, i. 297; New Series, xv. 156; xvii. 18. Archdall's Lodge's Peerage, vii. 225. Banks' Dormant and Extinct Baronage, i. 66; iii. 246. Burke's Extinct Baronetcies. Foster's Visitations of Northumberland, 38. History of Doddington, by R. E. G. Cole, 182.

DE LA WARDE. Banks' Baronies in Fee, i. 187.

DE LA WARR, or DE LA WARRE. Bird's Magazine of Honour, 81. Collinson's Somerset, ii. 412. Berry's Hampshire Genealogies, 198-205. Blore's Rutland, 100. Bridges' Northamptonshire, by Rev. Peter Whalley, ii. 342. Baines' History of the Co. of Lancaster, ii. 172. Banks' Baronies in Fee, i. 188. Banks' Dormant and Extinct Baronage, ii. 159. *See* BUCKHURST, WEST.

DELAWNE. Harleian Society, xv. 225. Notes and Queries, 1 S. xii. 166, 235, 498; 5 S. xii. 29, 53, 98, 117, 158; 6 S. i. 46, 65. *See* DELAUME.

DELAWOOD. Berry's Hertfordshire Genealogies, 225.

DE LA ZOUCH. Gentleman's Magazine, 1827, i. 487; ii. 8. Burke's Royal Families, (London, 1851, 8vo.) ii. 75. Burton's Description of Leicestershire, 168. *See* ZOUCH.

DE LAYLOND. The Genealogist, New Series, ix. 82.

DEL CHAUMBRE. Surtees' Durham, ii. 345.

DELEBERE. Topographer and Genealogist, i. 30. *See* DE LA BERE.

DE LEE. Berry's Hertfordshire Genealogies, 161. Eyton's Antiquities of Shropshire, ix. 294. *See* LEE.

DE LERLING. Blomefield's Norfolk, i. 285.

DE LE ROKELE. Carthew's Hundred of Launditch, Part i. 99.

DE LE SALE. Eyton's Antiquities of Shropshire, viii. 160.

DE LEYBURN. Archæologia Cantiana, v. 193. *See* LEYBORNE.

DEL HOPE. Ormerod's Cheshire, iii. 895.

DE LIGNE. Turnor's History of Town and Soke of Grantham, 113. Gage's History of Thingoe Hundred, Suffolk, 493.

DE LIMESI. Blomefield's Norfolk, vi. 170. Morant's Essex, i. 165; ii. 316. Banks' Baronies in Fee, ii. 109. *See* LIMESI.

DE LIONS. Collinson's Somerset, ii. 290.

DE LISLE. Chronicle of the Family of De Havilland. Blomefield's Norfolk, ii. 243. Burke's Landed Gentry, 5, 6, 7, 8. Maclean's History of Trigg Minor, ii. 500. Hunter's Deanery of Doncaster, ii. 128. Duchetiana, by Sir G. F. Duckett, 2nd edn., 229. The Genealogist, New Series, xiii. 180, 240; xiv. 26. Harleian Society, xliii. 66. *See* LISLE, SIDNEY.

DE LISTON. Morant's Essex, ii. 320.

DE LIZOURS. History of Blyth, by Rev. John Raine, 160. Whitaker's History of Whalley, i. 240. *See* LIZURES.

DELL. Lipscombe's History of the County of Buckingham, ii. 71.

DELMEGE. Burke's Landed Gentry, 5 supp., 6, 7, 8.

DELMÉ. Burke's Landed Gentry, 3, 4, 5, 6, 7, 8. Cussan's History of Hertfordshire, Parts vii. and viii. 44.

DELMÉ-RADCLIFFE. Berry's Hertfordshire, Genealogies, 113. Burke's Landed Gentry, 8.

DELMORE. O'Hart's Irish Pedigrees, 2nd Series, 328.

DE LODBROK. The Genealogist, New Series, ix. 208.

DE LODELOWE. The Genealogist, New Series, x. 28.

DE LONDRES. Genealogies of Morgan and Glamorgan, by G. T. Clark, 418.

DE LONGLEY. Chetham Society, xcv. 53.

DE LOTBINIERES. New England Register, l. 53.

DE LOUNDERS. Harleian Society, iv. 122.
DE LOVAIN. Morant's Essex, i. 466. *See* LOUVAINE.
DE LOVETOT. Hunter's History of the Parish of Sheffield, 37. *See* LOVETOT.
DELPRATT. Miscellanea Genealogica et Heraldica, 2nd Series, iii. 344.
DE LUCCUMBE. Collinson's Somerset, ii. 22.
DE LUCY. Morant's Essex, i. 128, 153. *See* LUCY.
DE LUMINE. Westcote's Devonshire, edited by G. Oliver and P. Jones, 579.
DE LUVERAY. Hoare's Wiltshire, V. ii. 70.
DELVES. Tuckett's Devonshire Pedigrees, 169. Harleian Society, vi. 86; xviii. 77. Ormerod's Cheshire, iii. 522. Burke's Extinct Baronetcies. The Visitations of Devon, by J. L. Vivian, 276. Genealogical Records of the Family of Woodd, 34.
DELVIN. *See* NUGENT.
DE LYMERSTON. Journal of the British Archæological Association, ii. 277.
DE MAGMINOT. Hasted's Kent, i. 2.
DE MALEBISSE. Foster's Yorkshire Pedigrees.
DE MALESOURS. The Genealogist, New Series, x. 215.
DE MALO LACU. Burton's History of Hemingborough, 253. *See* DE MAULAY.
DE MANDEVILLE. Morant's Essex, ii. 75, 123, 543. Bridges' Northamptonshire, by Rev. Peter Whalley, i. 158. *See* MANDEVILLE.
DE MANLEY, or DE MANLAY. Hunter's Deanery of Doncaster, i. 12. Archæologia, xxxi. 241. Wainwright's Wapentake of Strafford and Tickill, 25. *See* MANLEY.
DE MARISCO. *See* MAREYS, MONTMORENCY.
DE MAULAY. The Genealogist, New Series, xiii. 178. Archæologia, xxxi. 241. *See* DE MALO LACU, MORLEY.
DE MAUREWARD. Burton's Description of Leicestershire, 109. *See* MAUREWARD.
DE MEDEWE. Burke's Landed Gentry, 2, 3, 4. *See* MEADOW.
DE MEDUANA. Bibliotheca Topographica Britannica, i. Part i. 19.
DE MERCLESDEN. Whitaker's History of Whalley, ii. 260.
DE MERLAY. Hodgson's Northumberland, I. ii. 315. *See* MERLAY.
DE MERSKE. Plantagenet-Harrison's History of Yorkshire, i. 76.
DE MERTON. Gregson's Fragments relative to the County of Lancaster, 210. *See* MERTON.
DE MESCHIN. Notes and Queries, 4 S. xii. 141, 194, 291, 331, 475.
DE MICHELGROVE. Dallaway's Sussex, II. ii. 75.
DE MILLOM. Jefferson's History of Allerdale Ward, Cumberland, 152.
DEMING. New England Register, xvi. 264.
DE MOELS. Collinson's Somerset, ii. 66. *See* MOELS.
DE MOLYNS. *See* HASTINGS, MOLINS.
DEMONFRYART. Maclean's History of Trigg Minor, i. 304.
DE MONTALT. Ormerod's Miscellanea Palatina, 106. Ormerod's Parentalia, 102. *See* MONTALT.
DE MONTE. Baker's Northampton, i. 751.
DE MONTFORT. The Genealogist, New Series, ix. 12; x. 135.

DE MONTMORENCY. Burke's Landed Gentry, 3, 4, 5, 6, 7, 8. *See* MONTMORENCY.

DE MORA. Dugdale's Warwickshire, 678.

DE MORLE. Thoroton's Nottinghamshire, i. 97. *See* MORLEY.

DE MORTAYNE, or DE MORTEIN. Herald and Genealogist, iii. 176. Thoroton's Nottinghamshire, ii. 209. Notts and Derbyshire Notes and Queries, iv.⋅37. *See* MORTAYNE.

DE MORVILLE. George Robertson's Description of Cunninghame, 45. *See* MORVILLE.

DEMPSEY. O'Hart's Irish Pedigrees, 2nd Series, 161.

DEMPSTER. Burke's Landed Gentry, (of Skibo Castle,) 2, 3, 4, 5 ; (of Durmichon,) 5. Douglas's Baronage of Scotland, 531.

DE MUCHEGROS. Transactions of Bristol and Gloucestershire Archæological Society for 1876, 88.

DE MULES. The Genealogist, New Series, viii. 36.

DE MULTON. Hodgson's Northumberland, III. ii. 364. The Genealogist, New Series, viii. 153 ; ix. 209 ; x. 89. *See* MULTON.

DE NALINGHURST. Morant's Essex, ii. 19.

DE NAPTON. The Genealogist, New Series, ix. 151, 213.

DENBOW. Oliver's History of Antigua, i. 198.

DENDY. Howard's Visitation of England and Wales, vii. 70.

DENE. Herald and Genealogist, v. 354. Harleian Society, i. 89 ; vi. 86. Berry's Hampshire Genealogies, 20. Bridges' Northamptonshire, by Rev. Peter Whalley, ii. 300, 337. Visitation of Devon, edited by F. T. Colby, 77. The Visitations of Devon, by J. L. Vivian, 277. *See* DEANE.

DENEBAND. Weaver's Visitations of Somerset, 20.

DE NEUFVILLE. Burke's Extinct Baronetcies.

DE NEVILLE. Morant's Essex, ii. 371. Hunter's Deanery of Doncaster, i. 388 ; ii. 228. *See* NEVILE.

DENEW. Berry's Kent Genealogies, 359.

D'ENGAYNE. Harleian Society, xxxii. 103.

DENHAM. Coltness Collections, 281. Burke's Landed Gentry, 2. Independency at Brighouse, by J. H. Turner, 75. Notes and Queries, 4 S. i. 552, 617.

DENIS, or DENNIS. Fosbrooke's Abstracts of Smith's Lives of the Berkeleys, 169. Berry's Hampshire Genealogies, 197. Burke's Landed Gentry, 2, 3, 4, 5, 6, 7, 8. Burke's Royal Families, (London, 1851, 8vo.) ii. 55. Westcote's Devonshire, edited by G. Oliver and P. Jones, 615, 616, 617. Bigland's Gloucestershire, ii. 332. Ellacombe's History of Bitton, 85. Notes and Queries, 3 S. xii. 456, 531. Burke's Extinct Baronetcies. The Visitations of Cornwall, edited by J. L. Vivian, 137. Harleian Society, xxi. 49. Genealogies of Morgan and Glamorgan, by G. T. Clark, 381. The Visitations of Devon, by J. L. Vivian, 279. New England Register, xlix. 441. Burke's Family Records, 215. *See* DENNYS.

DENISON. Pedigree of Denison of Methley, [by Samuel Denison, 1890,] broadside. Burke's Commoners, (of Rushholme Park,) i. 383 ; (of Grimthorpe,) Landed Gentry, 2, 3, 4, 5 ; (of Ossington,) 2 supp., 3, 4, 5, 6, 7, 8 ; (of Denbies,) 2 ; 8 at p. 1589. Miscellanea Genealogica et Heraldica, 2nd Series, i. 180. Burke's Colonial Gentry, i. 168. Harleian Society, xxxviii. 772. Ontarian Families, by E. N. Chadwick, i. 103.

DENMAN. Foster's Visitations of Yorkshire, 346. Hunter's Deanery of Doncaster, ii. 75. Piercy's History of Retford, 196. Foster's Lincolnshire Pedigrees, 14. Harleian Society, xxxix. 959. Derbyshire Times (newspaper) of 7 Sept., 1889 ; and 16 July, 1898.

DENNE. Hasted's Kent, iii. 751. Berry's Kent Genealogies, 154, 194, 269. Burke's Commoners, iii. 19, Landed Gentry, 2, 3, 4, 5, 6, 7, 8. Harleian Society, xlii. 99.

DENNETT. Dallaway's Sussex, II. ii. 284.

DENNISTOUN. Burke's Commoners, iii. 322, Landed Gentry, 2, 3, 4, 5, 6, 7, 8. History of Dumbartonshire, by Joseph Irving, 437. The Book of Dumbartonshire, by Joseph Irving, ii. 320-343. Wood's Douglas's Peerage of Scotland, i. 411. Burke's Colonial Gentry, ii. 437. Burke's Family Records, 216.

DENNY. Morant's Essex, i. 43. Topographer and Genealogist, iii. 210. Clutterbuck's Hertford, ii. 107. Chauncy's Hertfordshire, 300. Miscellanea Genealogica et Heraldica, New Series, iii. 76, 113, 158, 197, 293. Burke's Extinct Baronetcies. Charles Smith's History of Kerry, 49. Chancellor's Sepulchral Monuments of Essex, 332. Sketch of the Royal Presents to the Denny Family. Dublin, 1868, 8vo. Harleian Society, xxxii. 101. Notes and Queries, 8 S. iv. 294. Burke's Landed Gentry, 7, 8.

DENNYS, or DENYS. Herald and Genealogist, iv. 209. Morant's Essex, i. 345. Berry's Hampshire Genealogies, 271. Bibliotheca Topographica Britannica, ii. Part iii. 28. Harleian Society, vi. 87 ; ix. 61. Hampshire Visitations, printed by Sir T. Phillipps, 22. Baker's Northampton, ii. 142. Plantagenet-Harrison's History of Yorkshire, i. 263. Visitation of Devon, edited by F. T. Colby, 78. See DENIS.

DENOM. Hodgson's Northumberland, II. ii. 15.

DE NORTHWOOD. Hasted's Kent, ii. 663. Morant's Essex, ii. 374. See NORTHWOOD.

DE NORWICH. Carthew's Hundred of Launditch, Part i. 167. Suckling's History of Suffolk, i. 171. See NORWICH.

DENT. J. H. Hill's History of Langton, 283. The Antiquities of Gainford, by J. R. Walbran, 58. Burke's Landed Gentry, (of Ribston Hall,) 2, 3, 4, 5, 6, 7, 8 ; (of Sudeley Castle,) 3, 4, 5, 6, 7, 8 ; (of Shortflatt Tower,) 2, 3, 4, 5, 6, 7, 8. Surtees' Durham, iv. 33. The Genealogist, iii. 242. Harleian Society, xv. 227 ; xvi. 99. Foster's Visitations of Northumberland, 37. Annals of Smith of Balby, by H. E. Smith, 35.

DENTON. Surtees Society, xxxvi. 63. Berry's Kent Genealogies, 451. Oxfordshire Pedigrees, fol., n. d., printed by Sir T. Phillipps. Visitation of Oxfordshire, 1634, printed by Sir T. Phillipps, (Middle Hill, fol.) 18. Burke's Landed Gentry, 2 supp. Harleian Society, v. 228, 264 ; xv. 226; xlii. 171. Lipscombe's History of the County of Buckingham, iii. 17. Dunkin's History of Bullington and Ploughley, i. 85. Archæologia Æliana, 2nd

Series, iii. 94. Burke's Extinct Baronetcies. Foster's Visitations of Cumberland and Westmorland, 37, 38. Nicolson and Burn's Westmorland and Cumberland, ii. 318.

DENUNE. Douglas's Baronage of Scotland, 456.

DENVER. Harleian Society, xiii. 189.

DENYSELL. Maclean's History of Trigg Minor, iii. 385.

DE ODINGSELLS. Blomefield's Norfolk, vi. 170. Shaw's Staffordshire, ii. 23. Burton's Description of Leicestershire, 240. *See* ODINGSELLS.

DE ORBY. Morant's Essex, i. 369. *See* ORBY.

DE ORLESTONE. Scott of Scott's-Hall, by J. R. Scott, 104.

DE ORWEY. Harleian Society, vi. 212.

DE PEARSALL. Burke's Royal Descents and Pedigrees of Founders' Kin, folding table. *See* PERSHALL.

DE PENTHENY. Burke's Heraldic Illustrations, 46.

DE PIMPE. Hasted's Kent, ii. 286. *See* PIMPE.

DE PIRYE. The Genealogist, New Series, viii. 245.

DE PLAIZ, or DE PLAYZ. Morant's Essex, ii. 578. Blomefield's Norfolk, ii. 162. Carthew's Hundred of Launditch, Part i. 299. *See* PLAYZ.

DE PLESINGTON. Chetham Society, xcv. 75. Abram's History of Blackburn, 612. *See* PLESSINGTON.

DE PLESSETIS, or DE PLACETIS. Collinson's Somerset, iii. 64. Hoare's Wiltshire, III. v. 12. Archæologia, Cantiana, xii. 314. Weaver's Visitations of Somerset, 92. *See* PLESSITIS.

DE PLEYS. 26th Report of Dep. Keeper of the Public Records, app. 64. *See* PLAYZ.

DE POICTOU. Rev. Robt. Simpson's History of the Town of Lancaster, 212.

DE PRAYERS. Archæologia, xxix. 407. *See* PRAYERS.

DE PRIDIAS. Maclean's History of Trigg Minor, ii. 194.

DE QUESTER. Harleian Society, xv. 228.

DE QUINCY. Burton's Description of Leicestershire, 35. Notes and Queries, 4 S. xi. 138, 239, 305, 368, 445; xii. 132; 5 S. ii. 129, 170. *See* QUINCY.

DE RAEDT. Burke's Extinct Baronetcies.

DE RALEIGH. Collinson's Somerset, iii. 536. *See* RALEGH.

DE RAMVILE. The Genealogist, New Series, viii. 154.

DERAUGH. Metcàlfe's Visitations of Suffolk, 189.

DERBY (Earl of). Gentleman's Magazine, 1825, ii. 422, 484. Morant's Essex, ii. 31, 413. Glover's History of Derbyshire, ii. 545, 565, (524, 545). Manx Society, x. app. E.

DERBY. Harleian Society, ii. 18. Chetham Society, lxxxi. 78. Jewitt's Reliquary, xiv. 256. Nichols' History of the County of Leicester, iii. 968.

DE REDE. Gage's History of Thingoe Hundred, Suffolk, 371. *See* REDE.

DEREHAM, or DERHAM. Blomefield's Norfolk, vii. 324. Visitation of Norfolk, published by Norfolk Archæological Society, i. 227. Burke's Extinct Baronetcies. Harleian Society, xxxii. 105.

DE RESKEMMER. The Genealogist, New Series, ix. 208.
DE RIDLESWORTH. Blomefield's Norfolk, i. 279.
DE RILLESTONE. *See* RILLESTONE.
DERING. Genealogical Memoranda relating to the Family of Dering of Surrenden Dering, Kent. By Rev. F. Haslewood, 1876, 4to. Hasted's Kent, iii. 228. Berry's Sussex Genealogies, 241. Berry's Hampshire Genealogies, 219. Berry's Kent Genealogies, 397-403. Burke's Landed Gentry, 2 supp., 3, 4, 5, 6, 7, 8. Burke's Royal Families, (London, 1851, 8vo.) ii. 136. Hampshire Visitations, printed by Sir T. Phillipps, 23. Surrey Archæolgical Collections, ii. 276. Cussan's History of Hertfordshire, Parts xi. and xii. 208. Archæologia Cantiana, x. 327. Harleian Society, xiii. 389; xv. 229; xlii. 139, 206, 209. Wotton's English Baronetage, ii. 13. Betham's Baronetage, i. 287. *See* FITZ DERING.
DE RINZY. Burke's Landed Gentry, 2, 3, 4.
DE RIPARIIS. Baker's Northampton, i. 619.
DE RISBY. Gage's History of Thingoe Hundred, Suffolk, 76. *See* RISBY.
DERLEY. Foster's Visitations of Yorkshire, 88. Jewitt's Reliquary, xxiv. 16.
DERNELEY. A view of the Evidence for proving that the present Earl of Galloway is the heir male of Sir William Stuart. By E. Williams, 1796, 4to. 37. Fishwick's History of Rochdale, 357.
DE ROCHES. Berry's Hampshire Genealogies, 90. Brocas of Beaurepaire, by M. Burrows, 323, 324.
DE RODES. Foster's Yorkshire Pedigrees. Notes and Queries, 7 S. ix. 413. *See* RODES.
DE ROHAND. Nichols' History of the County of Leicester, ii. 132.
DE ROLLOS. Plantagenet-Harrison's History of Yorkshire, i. 74.
DE ROOS, or DE ROS. Morant's Essex, ii. 526. Carthew's Hundred of Launditch, Part i. 249. Thoroton's Nottinghamshire, i. 221. Bridge's Northamptonshire, by Rev. Peter Whalley, i. 29. Brydges' Collins' Peerage, vi. 483. The Genealogist, New Series, ix. 83 ; x. 90. *See* ROOS.
DE ROSDOUREK. The Genealogist, ix. 151.
DE ROSIER. Berry's Kent Genealogies, 35.
DE ROTHERFIELD. Hunter's Deanery of Doncaster, ii. 134.
DE RUDA. Harleian Society, xvi. 16.
DERWENTWATER. Hutchinson's History of Cumberland, ii. 227. Notes and Queries, 2 S. xii. 405, 481. *See* RADCLIFFE.
DE RYE. Carthew's Hundred of Launditch, Part i. 67. *See* RYE.
DE RYTHRE. Burke's Landed Gentry, 3, 4. *See* RYTHER.
DE RYVERS. Burke's Commoners, iv. 229. *See* RIVERS, RYVERS.
DE SACVILL. Morant's Essex, ii. 224. *See* SACKVILL.
DESAGULIERS. The Genealogist, v. 117.
DE STE. CROIX. J. B. Payne's Armorial of Jersey, 129.
DE SALESBURY. Abram's History of Blackburn, 644.
DE SALIS. Burke's Landed Gentry, 5 supp., 6, 7, 8. Burke's Colonial Gentry, ii. 574.
DE SALYNG. Morant's Essex, ii. 412.

DE SARS. A Royal Descent, by T. E. Sharpe, (London, 1875, 4to.) 259.

DE SAUSMAREZ. Chronicle of the Family of De Havilland. *See* SAUMAREZ.

DE SAXHAM. Gage's History of Thingoe Hundred, Suffolk, 372.

DE SAY. Hasted's Kent, i. 2, 118; ii. 195. Lipscombe's History of the County of Buckingham, i. 158. Eyton's Antiquities of Shropshire, iv. 303. Dugdale's Warwickshire, 528. Banks' Dormant and Extinct Baronage, i. 169. Hasted's Kent, (Hund. of Blackheath, by H. H. Drake,) xxvi. *See* SAY.

DESBOUVERIE. Hasted's Kent, iii. 373. Harleian Society, viii. 396. *See* BOUVERIE.

DE SCACCARIO. Morant's Essex, ii. 261, 270.

DE SCALES. Carthew's Hundred of Launditch, Part i. 333. *See* SCALES, TEMPEST.

D'ESCHALERS. Clutterbuck's Hertford, iii. 471. *See* SCALES.

DESCHAMPS. Memoirs of D. Chamier, by W. Courthope, (London, 1852, 8vo.) 56. Burke's Landed Gentry, 2 supp. *See* CHAMIER.

DESCHAMPS DE LA TOUR. Burke's Landed Gentry, 5 supp.

DE SHAPWICK. History of Newnham Abbey, by James Davidson, 161.

DE SHEPEY. Burton's Description of Leicestershire, 238. *See* SHEPEY.

DE SMIDT. Burke's Colonial Gentry, ii. 720.

DES MAISTRES, or DESMAISTRIS. Pedigree of Des Maistres of Flanders, London, etc., [T. P.] fol. page. Harleian Society, xv. 229.

DESMOND. Westcote's Devonshire, edited by G. Oliver and P. Jones, 477. (Earls of) Journal of the Historical and Archæological Association of Ireland, 3rd Series, i. 461. The Ulster Journal of Archæology, vi. 91. The Olde Countesse of Desmonde, by A. B. Rowan, D.D.

DESMOND (Earls of). Unpublished Geraldine Documents. By Samuel Hayman. Dublin, 1870-81, 8vo. The Geraldines, Earls of Desmond. By C. P. Meehan. Dublin, 1847, 12mo.

DES MYNIERS. History of St. Canice, Kilkenny, by J. Graves, 327. The Irish Builder, xxix. 71, 339.

DE SNYTERTON. The Genealogist, New Series, ix. 212.

DE SOMERY. Nichols' History of the County of Leicester, iii. 67. Banks' Dormant and Extinct Baronage, ii. 169. *See* SOMERI.

DESPENSER. Collectanea Topographica et Genealogica, v. 6. Gentleman's Magazine, xxxiii. 193, 584. Blore's Rutland, 200. Hunter's Deanery of Doncaster, i. 71. Banks' Baronies in Fee, i. 191. Banks' Dormant and Extinct Baronage, ii. 164. *See* SPENSER.

DE SPINETO. Dugdale's Warwickshire, 749.

DE STAUNTON. Burton's Description of Leicestershire, 251. *See* STAUNTON.

D'ESTE. A Letter to a Noble Lord explanatory of a Bill filed on behalf of Sir Augustus D'Este, from Sir J. J. Dillon. London, 1831, 8vo. Case of Augustus Frederick D'Este on his claim to the Dukedom of Sussex, etc. Folio, 1844, pp. 28. Claim of Augustus Fredk. D'Este to be Duke of Sussex, Sess. Papers, 142 of 1844; 177 of 1844. The History of. the House of Este, London, 1681, 8vo. Papers elucidating the claim of Sir Augustus D'Este, K.C.H., by J. T. Dillon. London, 1831, 8vo. Case of the Children of H.R.H. the Duke of Sussex elucidated, by J. J. Dillon. 1832, 2 vols. 4to. *See* ESTE.

DE STODDEN. Harleian Society, vi. 81.

DE STODHAGH. The Genealogist, New Series, ix. 83..

DE STOKE. Ormerod's Cheshire, iii. 359.

DE STOKES. Berry's Buckinghamshire Genealogies, 1. *See* STOKES.

DE STRETTON. The Genealogist, New Series, ix. 150.

DE SUTTON. Morant's Essex, i. 470; ii. 187. Ormerod's Cheshire, i. 729. *See* SUTTON.

DE TANY. Morant's Essex, i. 179, 443. *See* TANY.

DE TATTESHALL, or DE TATESHALE. Morant's Essex, ii. 90. Carthew's Hundred of Launditch, Part i. 171. Munford's Analysis of Domesday Book of Co. Norfolk, 42. *See* TATESHALE.

DE TEISSIER. Burke's Landed Gentry, 3, 4.

DE TEMPLE. Burton's Description of Leicestershire, 264. *See* TEMPLE.

DE TERLING. Morant's Essex, ii. 126.

DETHICK. Topographical Miscellanies, 1792, 4to., (Bredsall). Glover's History of Derbyshire, ii. 179. Dwnn's Visitations of Wales, i. 133. Visitation of Durham, 1615, (Sunderland, 1820, fol.) 26. Visitation of Norfolk, published by Norfolk Archæological Society, i. 237. Blomefield's Norfolk, vii. 505. Harleian Society, ii. 88; viii. 134; xv. 227; xxvii. 47; xxxii. 106. Surtees' Durham, iii. 87. Collectanea Topographica et Genealogica, ii. 94. Hutchinson's History of Durham, iii. 101. Notes and Queries, 2 S. xii. 383. Visitation of Staffordshire, (Willm. Salt Soc.) 44. Foster's Visitations of Durham, 101. The Genealogist, New Series, vii. 78. The Gresley's of Drakelowe, by F. Madan, 249.

DE THORPE. Camden Society, xiii. 144. The Genealogist, New Series, x. 135. *See* THORPE.

DE THURNHAM. Notes and Queries, 1 S. vii. 261, 364.

DE TINSLEY. Hunter's Deanery of Doncaster, i. 399. *See* TINSLEY.

DE TOCKA. Shaw's Staffordshire, i. 35.

DE TOENI, or DE TONY. Morant's Essex, i. 32. Carthew's Hundred of Launditch, Part i. 89. Harvey's Hundred of Willey, 317. Norfolk Antiquarian Miscellany, i. 413. *See* TODENI.

DE TORKINGTON. Ormerod's Cheshire, iii. 836.

DE TRAFFORD. History of the De Traffords of Trafford, by W. S. G. Richards. 1896, fol. (only 25 copies printed). Pedigree of De Trafford. By H. F. Burke. London, 1890, 4to. Burke's Royal Families, (London, 1851, 8vo.) i. 25. Foster's Lancashire Pedigrees. *See* TRAFFORD.

DE TUDENHAM. Page's History of Suffolk, 834. *See* TUDENHAM.

DE TYES. Banks' Baronies in Fee, i. 436.

DE TYNTEN. History of Newnham Abbey, by James Davidson, 163.

DE UFFORD. Memoirs of the Family of Chester, by R. E. C. Waters, 323. Page's History of Suffolk, 158. *See* UFFORD.

DE UMFREVILLE. Burke's Commoners, ii. 191. Hodgson's Northumberland, I. ii. 6-59. *See* UMFRAVILLE.

DE UPTON. Eyton's Antiquities of Shropshire, i. 144. *See* UPTON.

DE URSWYK. Chetham Society, xcv. 136. *See* URSWICK.

DE VALOINES, or DE VALOIGNS. Carthew's Hundred of Launditch, Part i. 108. Munford's Analysis of Domesday Book of Co. Norfolk, 48. *See* VALOINES.

DE VALLE. Dugdale's Warwickshire, 704.

DE VALLIBUS. *See* VAUX.

DE VALMER. Burke's Royal Descents and Pedigrees of Founders' Kin, 12.

DE VALORI. Croke's History of the Family of Croke, No. 23.

DEVAS. Burke's Family Records, 217. Burke's Landed Gentry, 7, 8.

DEVENISH. Burke's Landed Gentry, 2, 3, 4, 5, 6, 7, 8. Dallaway's Sussex, i. 96, and i. app. to Chichester. Visitation of Sussex, 1570, printed by Sir T. Phillipps, (Middle Hill, fol.) 4. Harleian Society, xv. 230.

DEVER. Burke's Colonial Gentry, i. 291.

DE VERDON. Croke's History of the Family of Croke, No. 6. Nichols' History of the County of Leicester, ii. 344 ; iv. 279. Banks' Baronies in Fee, ii. 151. The Genealogist, New Series, ix. 147. *See* VERDON.

DE VERE. Miscellanea Genealogica et Heraldica, ii. 237. Gentleman's Magazine, 1827, i. 587. Morant's Essex, i. 191, 439, etc. ; ii. 58. T. Faulkner's History of Kensington, 39. Carthew's Hundred of Launditch, Part i. 340. Topographer, (London, 1789-91, 8vo.) iii. 20 supp. Proceedings of the Essex Archæological Society, i. 83. Wright's Essex. i. 511. Memoirs of the Family of Chester, by R. E. C. Waters, 48, 50. Harleian Society, xiii. 47. Page's History of Suffolk, 142. History and Antiquities of Harwich and Dovercourt, by Silas Taylor, 62, 115. Records of Buckinghamshire, iii. 56. Banks' Baronies in Fee, ii. 151. Banks' Dormant and Extinct Baronage, iii. 582, 710. Notes and Queries, 4 S. ii. 134. Genealogical Records of the Family of Woodd, 30. Chancellor's Sepulchral Monuments of Essex, 10. Hasted's Kent, (Hund. of Blackheath, by H. H. Drake,) 147. Archæological Journal, vii. 313 ; ix. 17. *See* VERE.

DEVEREL. Hoare's Wiltshire, I. ii. 9. Burke's Landed Gentry, 7, 8. The Genealogist, New Series, xv. 92.

DEVEREUX. Lives and Letters of the Devereux, Earls of Essex, by the Hon. W. B. Devereux, London, 1853, 2 vols. 8vo. Hasted's Kent, i. 409. Gentleman's Magazine, 1817, ii. 100 ; 1848, ii. 268. Funeral Sermon preached in the Parish Church of Carmarthen at the Burial of Walter, Earl of Essex, (London, 1577, 4to.) 1. Dwnn's Visitations of Wales, i. 109. Reports and Papers of the Associated Architectural Societies, 1852-1853, 445. Burke's Landed Gentry, 4, 5, 6, 7, 8. Lipscombe's History of the County of Buckingham, iv. 258. Nichols' History of the County of Leicester, iv. 147. Clutterbuck's Hertford, i. 245, 371. Baker's Northampton, i. 123. Duncumb's History of the Co. of Hereford, ii. 36 ; Cooke's Continuation, (Hund. of Grimsworth,) Part i. 70. Harleian Society, xii. 279. Shirley's History of the County of Monaghan, 280. Transactions of the Bristol and Gloucestershire Archæological Society for 1876, 88, Stemmata Shirleiana, by E. P. Shirley, 2nd edn., 103. Collections by the Powys-land Club, viii. 252. Edmondson's Baronagium Genealogicum, iv. 315; vi. 39. Brydges' Collins' Peerage, vi. 1. Banks' Baronies in Fee, i. 205. Banks' Dormant and Extinct Baronage, i. 287 ; iii. 279. Notes and Queries, 4 S. x. 299. Genealogical Table of John Stratford Collins. *See* ESSEX.

DE VERLEY. Morant's Essex, i. 423.

DE VERNAI. Collinson's Somerset, i. 253. *See* VERNEY.

DEVEROYS. The Genealogist, New Series, viii. 34.

DE VESCI. Hasted's Kent, i. 49. Claim of Thomas, Visct. De Vesci, to Vote at Elections of Irish Peers, Sess. Papers, B. of 1856. Burke's Royal Descents and Pedigrees of Founders' Kin, 41. Whitaker's History of Whalley, i. 240. Memoirs of Northumberland, communicated to Archæological Institute, 1858, ii. 155. Banks' Baronies in Fee, i. 446. Hasted's Kent, (Hund. of Blackheath, by H. H. Drake,) xxvi. Pedigrees of the Lords of Alnwick, by W. H. D. Longstaffe, 11, 16. *See* VESCI.

DE VETERIPONTE, or DE VIPONT. History of Blyth, by Rev. John Raine, 174. Jefferson's History of Leath Ward, Cumberland, 112. Hodgson's Northumberland, III. ii. 26. Hunter's Deanery of Doncaster, i. 70. Whitaker's Deanery of Craven, 3rd edn., 312. *See* VIPONT.

DE VIC. Chronicle of the Family of De Havilland. Burke's Extinct Baronetcies.

DEVISHER. Harleian Society, xv. 230.

DE VISME. Burke's Commoners, iv. 320.

DE VIVONIA. Hutchins' Dorset, iii. 338.

DEVON. Manning and Bray's Surrey, iii. 496. Banks' Dormant and Extinct Baronage, iii. 243.

DEVON (Earls of). Collectanea Archæologia, (Brit. Arch. Assn.) i. 263. The History of the House of Arundel, by J. P. Yeatman, 106.

DEVONSHIRE. Lives of the Earls and Dukes of Devonshire, by Joseph Grove. London, 1764, 8vo. *See* CAVENDISH.

DEW, or DEWE. Howard's Visitation of England and Wales, i. 281. The Genealogical Magazine, i. 643.

DE WACHESHAM. The Genealogist, New Series, viii. 36.

DE WAHUL. Banks' Baronies in Fee, i. 447. *See* WAHUL.

DE WALCOTE. The Genealogist, New Series, viii. 155.

DE WALDEN. Gyll's History of Wraysbury, 9. *See* WALDEN.

DE WALLUR. Berry's Buckinghamshire Genealogies, 1.

DE WALSHAM. Gage's History of Thingoe Hundred, Suffolk, 351. *See* WALSHAM.

DE WALTON. Fisher's History of Masham, 219. *See* WALTON.

DE WANTON. Morant's Essex, ii. 349. *See* WANTON.

DEWAR. Oliver's History of Antigua, i. 201. Burke's Family Records, 218.

DE WARMWELL. Hutchins' Dorset, i. 428.

DE WARREN. Wainwright's Wapentake of Strafford and Tickhill, 195. Hunter's Deanery of Doncaster, i. 105, 140. Notes and Queries, 6 S. iii. 431. *See* SURREY, WARREN.

DE WATEVILLE. Morant's Essex, ii. 405, 528.

DE WAUTON. Eyton's Antiquities of Shropshire, iii. 183.

DE WEDON. Notes and Queries, 3 S. ix. 67.

DEWELL. Burke's Commoners, iv. 328.

DE WELLES. Morant's Essex, i. 51, 158. *See* WELLS.

DEWEN, or DEWIN. Harleian Society, ix. 62. The Visitations of Cornwall, edited by J. L. Vivian, 139.

DEWES, or D'EWES. Morant's Essex, i. 108. Burke's Commoners, iii. 7. Page's History of Suffolk, 806. Notes and Queries, 3 S. ix. 294 ; x. 33. Burke's Extinct Baronetcies. *See* GRANVILLE.

DEWHURST. Berry's Hertfordshire Genealogies, 66. Chetham Society, lxxxii. 96 ; lxxxiv. 97. Abram's History of Blackburn 750. Harleian Society, xxii. 48. History of Longridge, by T. C Smith, 151. History of Ribchester, by T. C. Smith, and J. Shortt, 236, 260. Burke's Landed Gentry, 7, 8.

DEWICK. Surtees Society, xxxvi. 136.

DE WIGORNIA. Journal of the Historical and Archæological Association of Ireland, 4th Series, i. 634. The Genealogist, New Series, xiii. 98.

DE WILILEY. Eyton's Antiquities of Shropshire, ii. 51.

DE WINDSOR. Berry's Buckinghamshire Genealogies, 47. Manning and Bray's Surrey, i. 627. *See* WINDSOR.

DE WINTON. Burke's Landed Gentry, (of Wallsworth Hall,) 4, 5, 6, 7, 8 ; (of Maesderwen,) 2, 3, 4, 5, 6, 7, 8 ; (of Maesllwch,) 2, 3, 4, 5, 6, 7, 8 ; (of Glamorganshire,) 2, 3, 4 ; (of Graftonbury,) 8. Burke's Royal Families, (London, 1851, 8vo.) ii. 67. *See* WILKINS.

DE WISTON. Sussex Archæological Collections, v. 3.

DE WITT. Oliver's History of Antigua, i. 202.

DE WODECHURCHE. Ormerod's Cheshire, ii. 521.

DE WODEHOUSE. Hunter's Deanery of Doncaster, ii. 81. *See* WODEHOUSE.

DE WORKESLEY. Chetham Society, xcv. 118. *See* WORKESLEY.

DE WROTHAM. Collinson's Somerset, i. 41 ; iii. 64, 66. Archæologia Cantiana, xii. 314.

DE WYLEBY. The Genealogist, New Series, viii. 35.

DEXTER. New England Register, viii. 248.

DEYNCOURT. Bird's Magazine of Honour, 73. Burke's Landed Gentry, 2 add., 3, 4, 5. Thoroton's Nottinghamshire, i. 212. Burke's Royal Families, (London, 1851, 8vo.) i. 4. Lipscombe's History of the County of Buckingham, iii. 634. The Genealogist, New Series, xiv. 19 ; xvii. 161. *See* TENNYSON-D'EYNCOURT.

DEYNES. Page's History of Suffolk, 591.

DEYVILL. Foster's Visitations of Yorkshire, 215, 602. *See* DAVILE.

D'EYVILLE. Burton's History of Hemingborough, 288.
DIAMOND. Harleian Society, vi. 88. The Visitations of Devon, by
J. L. Vivian, 283.
DICCONSON. Burke's Landed Gentry, 5, 6, 7, 8. The Tyldesley
Diary, edited by J. Gillow and A. Hewitson, 111. Harleian
Society, xv. 231.
DICEY. Burke's Landed Gentry, 3 supp., 4, 5.
DICHFIELD. Harleian Society, xiii. 189 ; xxviii. 162. *See* DYCHE-
FEILD.
DICHFORD. Harleian Society, xii. 91.
DICK. Burke's Landed Gentry, 3, 8 at p. 1014. Herald and Gene-
alogist, viii. 257. Douglas's Baronage of Scotland, 268-274.
DICKEN. Visitations of Staffordshire. 1614 and 1663-4, William
Salt Society, 106. Howard's Visitation of England and Wales,
vii. 138.
DICKENSON. Bibliotheca Topographica Britannica, ix., Part 4, 222.
Chetham Society, xlvii. 105 ; lxxxiv. 98. Burke's Landed Gentry,
5, 6, 7, 8, 8 supp. Collections for a History of Staffordshire,
(William Salt Society,) i. 332. Visitations of Staffordshire,
1614 and 1663-4, William Salt Society, 107. Harleian Society,
xxxvii. 75.
DICKER. Berry's Sussex Genealogies, 277. Howard's Visitation of
England and Wales, i. 12. Miscellanea Genealogica et Heraldica,
2nd Series, iv. 208.
DICKEY. Burke's Colonial Gentry, i. 382.
DICKIN. Burke's Landed Gentry, 2, 3, 4, 5, 6, 7, 8.
DICKINS, or DICKENS. Berry's Sussex Genealogies, 367. Nash's
Worcestershire, i. 191. Burke's Landed Gentry, 3, 4, 5, 6, 7, 8.
Shaw's Staffordshire, ii. 278. Harleian Society, xv. 231, 232.
Visitation of Staffordshire, (Willm. Salt Soc.) 67. Visitations of
Staffordshire, 1614 and 1663-4, William Salt Society, 107. *See*
ARNOT, SCRASE-DICKINS.
DICKINSON. Berry's Hertfordshire Genealogies, 93. Burke's Landed
Gentry, (of Kingweston,) 3, 4, 5, 6, 7, 8 ; (of Abbot's Hill,) 3, 4 ;
(of Hartford,) 7 ; (of Bamborough,) 8 ; (of the Elms,) 8 ; (of
Farley Hill,) 2, 3 ; (of Windlesham,) 6 supp. Phelps' History of
Somersetshire, i. 481. Dickinson's History of Southwell, 2nd
edition, 165. Thoresby's Ducatus Leodiensis, 259. Baker's
Northampton, ii. 295. Pedigree of Wilson of High Wray, etc.,
by Joseph Foster, 26. Harleian Society, xv. 232. Howard's
Visitation of England and Wales, i. 292 ; Notes, iii. 109. New
England Register, xvi. 263. Annals of Smith of Balby, by H. E.
Smith, 272. Pedigree of Wilson, by S. B. Foster, 51. Harleian
Society, xl. 1181. Burke's Family Records, 220. Croston's
edition of Baines' Lancaster, ii. 230.
DICK-LAUDER. Burke's Royal Families, (London, 1851, 8vo.) ii.
173.
DICKSON. Dickson Genealogy, by C. T. M'Cready. Dublin, 1868,
long sheet. Burke's Landed Gentry, (of Woodville,) 3, 4, 5, 6, 7,
8 ; (of Ballyfree,) 3 ; (of Limerick,) 2, 3, 4 ; (of Hartree,) 7, 8 ;

(of Monybine,) 7, 8 ; (of Chatto,) 8.   Notes and Queries, 1 S. ix.
221. Burke's Extinct Baronetcies, 620. Betham's Baronetage,
v. 493.   Burke's Colonial Gentry, i. 166.   Burke's Family
Records, 221.
DIDHAM. Howard's Visitation of England and Wales, vi. 147.
DIG. Berry's Kent Genealogies, 142.   See DYGGS.
DIGBY. Hasted's Kent, ii. 597.   Gentleman's Magazine, lxiv. 791,
918, 1077 ; lxv. 743, 840, 1077.   Topographer, (London, 1789-91,
8vo.) ii. 212.   Pedigree of the Family of Sheppard. 7.   Visitations
of Staffordshire, 1614 and 1663-4, William Salt Society, 107.
Visitation of Norfolk, published by Norfolk Archæological
Society, i. 408.   Burke's Commoners, (of Osbertstown,) iv. 460,
Landed Gentry, 2, 3 ; (of Sherborne Castle,) Landed Gentry, 4, 5,
6, 7, 8 ; (of Landenstown,) 2.   Harleian Society, ii. 40, 87, 199 ;
iii. 17, 20 ; iv. 168; xii. 17 ; xxxii. 111.   Visitation of War-
wickshire, 1619, published with Warwickshire Antiquarian
Magazine, 30.   Gyll's History of Wraysbury, 209.   Shaw's
Staffordshire, ii. 23.   Lipscombe's History of the County of
Buckingham, iv. 145.   Wright's History of Rutland, 79, 115.
Blore's Rutland, 62.   Visitation of Staffordshire, 1663-4, printed
by Sir T. Phillipps, 4.   Nichols' History of the County of
Leicester, ii. 261 ; iii. 473, 475, 933.   Dugdale's Warwickshire,
1012.   Hutchins' Dorset, iv. 472.   Edmondson's Baronagium
Genealogicum, v. 502.   Archdall's Lodge's Peerage, vi. 262.
Brydges' Collins' Peerage, v. 348.   Banks' Baronies in Fee, ii.
107.   Banks' Dormant and Extinct Baronage, iii. 103.   Rocking-
ham Castle and the Watsons, Ped. 3.   Annals of the English
Benedictines of Ghent, 183.   See WINGFIELD-DIGBY.
DIGBY-BESTE. Burke's Landed Gentry, 5 supp., 6.
DIGGES, or DIGGS. Burke's Extinct Baronetcies.   Visitation of
Wiltshire, edited by G. W. Marshall, 20.   Hasted's Kent, ii. 513 ;
iii. 130, 756.   Berry's Kent Genealogies, 143.   Surrey Archæo-
logical Collections, i.   Visitatio Comitatus Wiltoniæ, 1623, printed
by Sir T. Phillipps.   Miscellanea Genealogica et Heraldica, 2nd
Series, i. 37.   Harleian Society, xlii. 64 ; xliii. 140.   See DYGGS.
DIGGLES. History of the Ancient Chapel of Blackley, by Rev. J.
Booker, 38.   Harleian Society, xxxvii. 279.
DIGHTON. Harleian Society, xv. 233 ; xxvii. 48.   The Genealogist,
vi. 147.   Miscellanea Genealogica et Heraldica, 2nd Series, ii. 95.
Records of Batley, by M. Sheard, 278.
DIGNUM. O'Hart's Irish Pedigrees, 2nd Series, 163.
DILKE. Warwickshire Antiquarian Magazine, Part i.   Burke's
Landed Gentry, 2 supp., 4, 5, 6.   Harleian Society, xii. 269.
Miscellanea Genealogica et Heraldica, i. 4.   Visitation of War-
wickshire, 1619, published with Warwickshire Antiquarian
Magazine, 62.
DILKES. East Anglian, i. 127.
DILLINGHAM. J. H. Hill's History of Langton, 47.   Nichols' History
of the County of Leicester, i. 615.   Monken Hadley, by F. C.
Cass, 92.

DILLINGTON. Berry's Hampshire Genealogies, 116, 308. Visitations of Hampshire, printed by Sir T. Phillipps, 23. Burke's Extinct Baronetcies. Miscellanea Genealogica et Heraldica, 2nd Series, i. 380.

DILLON. Epitome of the Case on the Claim of the Dillon Family of Proudston, by Sir J. J. Dillon, Kt. London, 1829, 4to. Harleian Society, vi. 88. Westcote's Devonshire, edited by G. Oliver and P. Jones, 549. Baker's Northampton, i. 621. Jordan's History of Enstone, 132. An Historical Survey of Cornwall, by C. S. Gilbert, ii. 95. O'Hart's Irish Pedigrees, 2nd Series, 164. Journal of the Historical and Archæological Association of Ireland, 4th Series, ii. 372. Notes and Queries, 1 S. ii. 325, 468, 498, 521; 2 S. vii. 154. Betham's Baronetage, v. 474. Archdall's Lodge's Peerage, iv. 135. Visitation of Devon, edited by F. T. Colby, 82. The Visitations of Devon by J. L. Vivian, 284. Metcalfe's Visitations of Northamptonshire, 177. The Irish Builder, xxxv. 20, 130.

DILLON-TRENCHARD. Burke's Landed Gentry, 5, 6, 7, 8.

DILLWYN. Burke's Landed Gentry, 5, 6, 7.

DILLWYN-LLEWELYN. Burke's Landed Gentry, 2, 3, 4, 5, 6, 7.

DILSTON. Surtees' Durham, i. 34.

DILWORTH. History of Chipping, by Tom C. Smith, 250.

DIMOCK. Gloucestershire Notes and Queries, v. 240, 269. See DYMOCK.

DIMSDALE. Berry's Hertfordshire Genealogies, 211. Burke's Royal Families, (London, 1851, 8vo.) ii. 125. Clutterbuck's Hertford, ii. 35.

DINELEY. Pedigree of Dineley of Charlton, Co. Worcester, [T. P.] 1842. Broadside. Nash's Worcestershire. i. 272. Metcalfe's Visitation of Worcester, 1683, 40-44. See DYNELEY.

DINGLEY. Camden Society, xciv. 24. Berry's Hampshire Genealogies, 17, 213. Berry's Kent Genealogies, 120. Hampshire Visitations, printed by Sir T. Phillipps, 23. Harleian Society, xlii. 45.

DINGWALL. See COWPER.

DINHAM. Collinson's Somerset, ii. 362. Maclean's History of Trigg Minor, ii. 376. Westcote's Devonshire, edited by G. Oliver and P. Jones, 494. An Historical Survey of Cornwall, by C. S. Gilbert, i. 526. Banks' Baronies in Fee, i. 195. Visitation of Devon, edited by F. T. Colby, 83. Jewitt's Reliquary, xxiv. 75. Nicholl's Account of the Company of Ironmongers, 2nd edn., 513. The Visitations of Cornwall, edited by J. L. Vivian, 490. The Visitations of Devon, by J. L. Vivian, 316. See DYNHAM.

DINSDALE. Burke's Landed Gentry, 2, 3.

DINWIDDIE. Notes and Queries, 6 S. viii. 13.

DIODATE. New England Register, xxxv. 167.

DIOT. Visitation of Staffordshire, 1663-4, printed by Sir T. Phillipps, 4. See DYOTT.

DIRDO. Visitatio Comitatus Wiltoniæ, 1623, printed by Sir T. Phillipps. Harleian Society, xx. 36.

DIROM. Burke's Landed Gentry, 3, 4, 5, 6, 7, 8.

DIRWYN. Weaver's Visitations of Somerset, 112. Malet's Notices of the Malet Family, 133.

DISBROW. Morant's Essex, i. 207. Genealogical Gleanings in England, by H. F. Waters, i. 250. Chancellor's Sepulchral Monuments of Essex, 180. New England Register, xli. 360.

DISHINGTON. Walter Wood's East Neuk of Fife, 254.

DISNEY. Pedigree of Disney. London, 1815, fol. Claim of Molyneux Disney, Esq., to the Barony of Hussey, by W. B. D. D. Turnbull. Edinburgh, 1836, 8vo. Remarks on the Hussey Peerage, with Pedigrees, by W. B. D. D. Turnbull. Edinburgh, 1842, 8vo. Berry's Essex Genealogies, 5. Burke's Commoners, (of the Hyde,) ii. 151, Landed Gentry, 2, 3, 4, 5, 6, 7, 8 ; (of Ireland,) 2, 3, 4. Harleian Society, iv. 33 ; xiv. 653. Burke's Royal Families, (London, 1851, 8vo.) i. 79. The Genealogist, iii. 375 ; iv. 18. Lincolnshire Notes and Queries, Supplement on Brasses to Vols. i. and ii. 17, 75. See DE ISNEY.

DISRAELI. Burke's Landed Gentry, 5. Foster's Collectanea Genealogica, i. 6, 60.

DISTON. Pedigree of Diston of Esthrop in Highworth, Co. Wilts. [T. P.] on fol. page.

DITCHFIELD. Chetham Society, lxxxii. 131. See DICHFIELD.

DIXEY. Metcalfe's Visitations of Northamptonshire, 177.

DIXIE. Betham's Baronetage, ii. 127. Harleian Society, ii. 116. Nichols' History of the County of Leicester, iv. 506. Wotton's English Baronetage, iii. 102. See DYXYE.

DIXON. Hasted's Kent, ii. 334. Visitation of Middlesex, (Salisbury, 1820, fol.) 6. Berry's Kent Genealogies, 392. Visitation of Norfolk, published by Norfolk Archæological Society, ii. 16. History of Ecclesfield, by J. Eastwood, 384. Burke's Commoners, (of Gledhaw,) iii. 334 ; (of Rheda,) 7, 8 ; (of Cherkley Court,) 7, 8 ; (of Unthank Hall,) Commoners, iv. 671, Landed Gentry, 2, 3 ; (of Astle Hall,) Landed Gentry, 2, 3, 4, 5, 6, 7, 8 ; (of Page Hall,) 3, 4, 5 ; (of Seaton Carew,) 2 supp., 3 supp., 4 ; (of Knells,) 2, 3, 4, 5 ; (of Holton,) 2 add., 3, 4. Foster's Yorkshire Pedigrees. Harleian Society, ii. 195 ; xxii. 48 ; xxxii. 112 ; xxxvii. 103, 202, 203 ; xxxix. 840 ; xlii. 176. J. H. Hill's History of Market Harborough, 48. History of Bradford, by John James, 431. Burke's Royal Descents and Pedigrees of Founders' Kin, 78, 79. Whitaker's Loidis and Elmete, 130. Nichols' History of the County of Leicester, ii. 891. Genealogy of Henzey, Tyttery, and Tyzack, by H. S. Grazebrook, 45. Notes and Queries, 3 S. iii. 43. Ormerod's Cheshire, iii. 714. Earwaker's East Cheshire, ii. 365. Foster's Visitation of Middlesex, 14. Robinson's History of Enfield, ii. 46. Miscellanea Genealogica et Heraldica, 2nd Series, i. 253. Burke's Colonial Gentry, i. 242 ; ii. 490. Pease of Darlington, by Joseph Foster, 32. Annals of Smith of Balby, by H. E. Smith, 191. Burke's Family Records, 222. Ontarian Families, by E. M. Chadwick, i. 58.

DIXWELL. Berry's Kent Genealogies, 469. Harleian Society, xii. 41,

297. Wotton's English Baronetage, iii. 44 ; iv. 181. Burke's Extinct Baronetcies. Metcalfe's Visitations of Northamptonshire, 85. The Gresley's of Drakelowe, by F. Madan, 250.

DOBBIN, or DOBBINS. Burke's Landed Gentry, 4, 5, 6, 7, 8. Harleian Society, xv. 234.

DOBBS. Burke's Landed Gentry, 2, 3, 4, 5, 6, 7, 8. History of Carrickfergus, by Saml. M'Skimin, 2nd edn., 326.

DOBELL. Berry's Sussex Genealogies, 166.

DOBREE. Chronicle of the Family of De Havilland. Notes and Queries, 4 S. xii. 231. Burke's Family Records, 223.

DOBSON. Harleian Society, iv. 130. The Genealogist, New Series, iii. 147. Foster's Visitations of Northumberland, 40. Burke's Colonial Gentry, i. 32. Family Notes, by J. M. Browne, 32.

DOBYNS. Burke's Commoners, iv. 397. Fosbrooke's History of Gloucestershire, ii. 251. Visitation of Gloucester, edited by T. F. Fenwick and W. C. Metcalfe, 211.

DOCKER. Burke's Colonial Gentry, i. 79.

DOCKINFELD. Chetham Society, lxxxi. 133. See DUCKENFIELD.

DOCKWRA, or DOCWRA. Cambridgeshire Visitation, edited by Sir T. Phillipps, 13. Clutterbuck's Hertford, iii. 82. Chauncy's Hertfordshire, 406. Harleian Society, xix. 191 ; xxii. 18, 139; xli. 44.

DOCTON. Harleian Society, vi. 89. The Visitations of Devon, by J. L. Vivian, 286.

DOD, or DODD. Miscellanea Genealogica et Heraldica, i. 169. Burke's Heraldic Illustrations, 129. Harleian Society, i. 22 ; iv. 43 ; viii. 515 ; xviii. 78, 80; xxii. 50 ; xxviii. 163; xliii. 84, 104. The Genealogist, iii. 242. Burke's Commoners, (of Edge,) iii. 548, Landed Gentry, 2, 3, 4, 5, 6, 7, 8 ; (of Cloverley,) Commoners, i. 297, Landed Gentry, 2, 3, 4 ; 2 at p. 1637. Ormerod's Cheshire, ii. 673, 682, 688. Surrey Archæological Collections, iv. Berks Arch. and Architectural Journal, iii. 146, 164, 190.

DODDERIDGE. Howard's Visitation of England and Wales, viii. 52.

DODDS. Burke's Colonial Gentry, i. 296.

DODGE. Visitation of Norfolk, published by Norfolk Archæological Society, ii. 58. New England Register, xv. 254 ; xxxix. 52 ; xlvi. 383. Harleian Society, xxxii. 107.

DODINGE, or DODDING. Chetham Society, lxxxii. 72 ; lxxxiv. 99. Corry's History of Lancashire, i. 398, 451. Bardsley's Registers of Ulverston, xxxiv.

DODSHON. Foster's Pedigree of the Forsters and Fosters, Part ii. 21. Notes and Queries, 3 S. i. 130.

DODSON. Burke's Landed Gentry, 4, 5, 6. Harleian Society, ix. 63 ; xxxviii. 777. The Visitations of Cornwall, edited by J. L. Vivian, 104. Sussex Archl. Collections, xxxiii. 39, 45.

DODSWORTH, or DODWORTH. Surtees Society, xxxvi. 88, 287, 313. Visitation of Durham, 1615, (Sunderland, 1820, fol.) 56. Burke's Royal Families, (London, 1851, 8vo.) ii. 104. Foster's Yorkshire Pedigrees. Harleian Society, xxxvii. 418. Foster's Visitations of Yorkshire, 266. Surtees' Durham, iii. 123. Yorkshire Archæological and Topographical Journal, vii. 409. Foster's Visitations of Durham, 103.

DODWELL. Burke's Landed Gentry, 3, 4, 5. Memoirs, British and Foreign, of Illustrious Persons who died in 1711, 355. Visitation of Gloucester, edited by T. F. Fenwick and W. C. Metcalfe, 57.

DODYNGTON, DODINGTON, or DODDINGTON. Collinson's Somerset, iii. 518. Bibliotheca Topographica Britannica, ix. Part 4, 85. Visitation of Somerset, printed by Sir T. Phillipps, 64. Topographer and Genealogist, iii. 568. Jewitt's Reliquary, xiii. 244 ; xv. 86. Harleian Society, xi. 33 ; xxviii. 165. Hampshire Visitations, printed by Sir T. Phillipps, 24. The Genealogist, i. 23, 155 ; xii. 25. Weaver's Visitations of Somerset, 21. See DORINGTON, MARRIOTT-DODINGTON.

DOE. Harleian Society, viii. 195.

DOGETT. Visitation of Norfolk, published by Norfolk Archæological Society, i. 361. Harleian Society, xxxii. 107. Muskett's Suffolk Manorial Families, i. 335-344.

DOHERTY, or DOCHERTY. Burke's Landed Gentry, 2 supp., 3, 4. O'Hart's Irish Pedigrees, 2nd Series, 166. See O'DOHERTY.

DOIG. Oliver's History of Antigua, i. 204.

DOILY, or D'OILLY. See D'OYLEY.

DOKENFELD. Harleian Society, xviii. 81. See DUCKENFIELD.

DOLBEARE. Harleian Society, vi. 152. The Visitations of Devon, by J. L. Vivian, 471. New England Register, xlvii. 24.

DOLBEN, or DOLBYN. Harleian Society, viii. 314. Wotton's English Baronetage, iv. 95. Betham's Baronetage, iii. 131. Burke's Extinct Baronetcies, add. History of Powys Fadog, by J. Y. W. Lloyd, iv. 169. Miscellanea Genealogica et Heraldica, 3rd Series, ii. 223.

DOLE. New England Register, xxxviii. 74.

DOLLIFFE. Harleian Society, viii. 513.

DOLLING. Burke's Landed Gentry, 2, 3, 4, 5, 7, 8. Hutchins' Dorset, i. 693. Harleian Society, xxv. 36.

DOLMAN, or DOLEMAN. Surtees Society, xxxvi. 138. Burke's Royal Families, (London, 1851, 8vo.) i. 8. Burke's Landed Gentry, 2, 4. Foster's Yorkshire Pedigrees. Foster's Visitations of Yorkshire, 86. Harleian Society, viii. 126 ; xxii. 140. Hunter's Deanery of Doncaster, ii. 437. The Genealogist, v. 250.

DOLPHANBY. Surtees' Durham, ii. 117.

DOLPHIN, or DOLPHYN. Bibliotheca Topographica Britannica, ix. Part 4, 135. Burke's Landed Gentry, (of Turoe,) 3, 4, 5, 6, 7, 8 ; (of Corr,) 3, 4. Shaw's Staffordshire, ii. 48.

DOLSHILL. Manning and Bray's Surrey, iii. 413.

DOMVILLE. Burke's Landed Gentry, 3, 4, 5, 6. Burke's Royal Descents and Pedigrees of Founders' Kin, 61, 73. Ormerod's Cheshire, i. 581 ; ii. 433. History of Santry and Cloghran, by B. W. Adams, 109. Harleian Society, xviii. 82.

DONALDSON. Raine's History of North Durham, 228. Burke's Colonial Gentry, ii. 495.

DONALDSON-HUDSON. Burke's Landed Gentry, 5, 6, 7, 8.

DONCASTLE. The Genealogist, v. 250, 251.

DONE. Ormerod's Cheshire, ii. 136, 248. A short Account of the possessors of Dalton, by Sir P. de M. Grey-Egerton, 1. Harleian Society, xviii. 83-86. *See* DONNE.

DONEGAL. Burke's Royal Families, (London, 1851, 8vo.) i. 169.

DONELAN, or DONNELLAN. Burke's Landed Gentry, (of Hillswood,) 2, 3, 4, 5 ; (of Sylane,) 3, 4, 5, 6, 7 ; (of Killagh,) 2, 3 and 3, p. 307, 4. O'Hart's Irish Pedigrees, 2nd Series, 168. The Irish Builder, xxix. 85, 202. *See* O'DONNELLAN.

DONHAM. Surtees Society, xli. 6. Foster's Visitations of Yorkshire, 37. Harleian Society, iv. 160. *See* DUNHAM.

DONING, DONINGE, or DONYNGE. Berry's Sussex Genealogies, 260. Visitation of Sussex, 1570, printed by Sir T. Phillipps, (Middle Hill, fol.) 4. Dallaway's Sussex, i. app. to Chichester.

DONKIN. Burke's Commoners, ii. 69, Landed Gentry, 2.

DONNE. Gentleman's Magazine, 1835, i. 610 ; ii. 150. Morant's Essex, i. 377. Miscellanea Genealogica et Heraldica, New Series, i. 330 ; 3rd Series, i. 89. Westcote's Devonshire, edited by G. Oliver and P. Jones, 515. Caermarthenshire Pedigrees, 57, 58. Notes and Queries, 1 S. vi. 273 ; 2 S. vii. 241. Visitation of Devon, edited by F. T. Colby, 84. Howard's Visitation of England and Wales, v. 110. *See* DONE.

DONNELLY. O'Hart's Irish Pedigrees, 2nd Series, 170. *See* O'DONNELLY.

DONNITHORNE. Burke's Landed Gentry, 4, 5, 6, 7, 8.

DONOVAN. Burke's Commoners, (of Ballymore,) iv. 708, Landed Gentry, 2, 3, 4, 5, 6, 7, 8 ; (of Framfield,) Commoners, i. 76, Landed Gentry, 2, 3, 4, 5, 6, 7. Oliver's History of Antigua, i. 207. *See* O'DONOVAN.

DONYNGTON, or DONINGTON. Surtees Society, xli. 55. Foster's Visitations of Yorkshire, 38. Harleian Society, xvi. 101.

DOOLE. Genealogies of Morgan and Glamorgan, by G. T. Clark, 485.

DOOLITTLE. New England Register, vi. 293.

DOPPING-HEPENSTAL. Burke's Landed Gentry, 6, 7, 8.

DORE. Account of the Family of Dore, of Compton Beauchamp, Co. Wilts, 4to. Account of the Family of Dore, of Longcot, etc., Co. Berks, 4to. Account of the Family of Dore, of Longleat, Co. Wilts, 4to.

DORESLAER, or DORISLAUS. Notes and Queries, 4 S. iv. 40. Peacock's Lists of Roundheads and Cavaliers, etc., 21.

DOREWARD. Morant's Essex, i. 441, 452, 470 ; ii. 299, 385, 472. Proceedings of the Essex Archæological Society, iii. 100. Harleian Society, xiii. 104. Wright's Essex, i. 525 ; ii. 27. Memoirs of the family of Chester, by R. E. C. Waters, 300. *See* DURWARD.

DORINGTON. Burke's Landed Gentry, 6. Harleian Society, xv. 235.

DORMER. Gentleman's Magazine, 1828, ii. 204. Généalogie de la Maison des Lords Dormers, Comtes de Caernarvon, etc., par M. D——. Antwerp, 1771, fol. Nobiliare De Brabant, iv. 79. Burke's Landed Gentry, 2, 3, 4, 5, 6. Herald and Genealogist, i. 338. Lipscombe's History of the County of Buckingham, i. 118,

415. Clutterbuck's Hertford, i. 494. Baker's Northampton, i. 620, 667. Burke's Royal Families, (London, 1851, 8vo.) ii. 110. Edmondson's Baronagium Genealogicum, iv. 381. Brydges' Collins' Peerage, vii. 66. Banks' Dormant and Extinct Baronage, iii. 152. Burke's Extinct Baronetcies. The Genealogist, vii. 173. F. G. Lee's History of Thame, 504. Miscellanea Genealogica et Heraldica, New Series, iv. 97. Aldred's History of Turville, 24-33. Church Bells of Buckinghamshire, by A. H. Cocks, 619.

DORRELL, or DORRIL. Berry's Surrey Genealogies, 30. Manning and Bray's Surrey, i. 244. Harleian Society, xlii. 186.

DORSET, or DORSETT. Collectanea Topographica et Genealogica, i. 318. Hasted's Kent, i. 65. Morant's Essex, ii. 32, 414. Collections by the Powys-land Club, iv. 146.

DOTCHEN. Harleian Society, xxvii. 49.

DOTTIN. Berry's Hampshire Genealogies, 10. Burke's Commoners, i. 360, Landed Gentry, 2.

DOUBLEDAY. Surtees' Durham, iv. 112.

DOUCE. Berry's Sussex Genealogies, 96. Berry's Kent Genealogies, 176. Burke's Landed Gentry, 2, 3.

DOUGAL, or DOUGALL. Burke's Landed Gentry, (of Glenferness,) 4, 5 ; (of Scotscraig,) 4, 5, 6, 7. Burke's Family Records, 227.

DOUGHTIE, or DOUGHTY. Burke's Commoners, (of Theberton,) ii. 540, Landed Gentry, 2, 3, 4, 5, 6, 7, 8 ; (of Snarford Hall,) 2, and p. 855. Foster's Visitations of Yorkshire, 316. Page's History of Suffolk, 267. The Genealogist, vi. 148. Harleian Society, xxxii. 108.

DOUGLAS. History of the Family of Douglas of Tilwhilly or Tilquhillie. Bath, n. d., 8vo. Letters to Lord Mansfield, by Andrew Stewart, Esq., London, 1773, 8vo. The Douglas Book, by Wm. Fraser. Edinburgh, 1885, 4to., 4 vols. The Genealogy of the Families of Douglas of Mulderg and Robertson of Kindeace. Dingwall, 1895, 8vo. Gentleman's Magazine, 1857, i. 201. Jacob's Peerage, i. 308. Blore's Rutland, 181. The History of the Houses of Douglas and Angus, by D. Hume. Edinburgh, 1644, fol. (the 4th edn. of this work was published in 1748, 2 vols., 8vo.). A Synopsis of the Genealogy of the Noble Family of Brigantes or Douglas, by P. Pineda, 1754, 8vo. Speeches and Judgments of the Lords in the Douglas Cause, by William Anderson. Edinburgh, 1768, 8vo. The Case of Archibald Douglas against the Duke of Hamilton, 1769, 4to. Abstract of the Evidence taken in the service of the Rt. Hon. Sylvester Douglas, Lord Glenbervie, etc., with a Genealogical Table. Edinburgh, 1815, 4to. Claim of J. A. Douglas, Baron Bloomfield, to vote at Elections of Scotch Peers, Sess. Papers, 109 of 1849. Burke's Commoners, (of Gyrn,) iv. 600 ; (of Mains,) Landed Gentry, 5, 6, 7, 8 ; (of Grace Hall,) 7, 8 ; (of Cavers,) 5, 6, 7, 8 ; (of Dervoch,) 3, 4 ; (of Mountain Lodge,) 3, 4 ; (of Bonjedward,) 6, 7, and 7 p. 12, 8 ; (of Salwarpe,) 8 ; (of Douglas Support,) 8. Lands and their Owners in Galloway, by P. H. M'Kerlie, iii. 118, 444. Burke's Royal Families, (London, 1851, 8vo.) i. 185. Nisbet's Heraldry,

ii. app. 57. Douglas's Baronage of Scotland, 18. Paterson's History of Ayr and Wigton, i. 336. The Upper Ward of Lanarkshire, by G. V. Irving, ii. 57-144. Jeffrey's History of Roxburghshire, ii. 227 ; iii. 183. Border Memories, by W. R. Carre, 1. Memoirs, British and Foreign, of Illustrious Persons who died in 1711, 443. Edmondson's Baronagium Genealogicum, i. 47. Hawick and its old Memories, by James Wilson, 178. Wood's Douglas's Peerage of Scotland, i. 200, 269, 308, 418, 458, 597 ; ii. 263, 376, 487. Brydges' Collins' Peerage, viii. 58, 227, 271. Drumlanrig Castle and the Douglases, by C. T. Ramage, 74, 85, 320. A short Memoir of James Young, app. 11. Notes and Queries, 3 S. ix. 157, 326, 439, 441, 515 ; x. 71 ; 4 S. x. 169. The Genealogist, v. 193-203. Betham's Baronetage, iv. 166 ; v. 473. Foster's Collectanea Genealogica, (MP's Scotland,) 99. Burke's Extinct Baronetcies, and 620. Alexander Nisbet's Heraldic Plates, 2. New England Register, xxviii. 69 ; xxxi. 166. Oliver's History of Antigua, i. 212. Burke's Family Records, 227. Northern Notes and Queries, viii. 41, 88. *See* PYE.

DOUGLAS-BOSWELL. Burke's Landed Gentry, 5 supp., 6, 8.

DOUGLAS-GRESLEY. Burke's Landed Gentry, 4 supp., 5, 6, 7 *bis*.

DOUGLAS-HAMILTON. Blore's Rutland, 181.

DOUGLAS-HOME. Alexander Nisbet's Heraldic Plates, 6.

DOUGLASS. Burke's Landed Gentry, 2, 3, 4, 5, 6, 7.

DOULL. Caithness Family History, by John Henderson, 324.

DOVE. East Anglian, ii. 203, 235. Harleian Society, i. 58. Visitation of Wiltshire, 1677, printed by Sir T. Phillipps, (Middle Hill, 1854, fol.). Collectanea Topographica et Genealogica, iii. 142. Notes and Queries, 6 S. ix. 417.

DOVER. Carthew's Hundred of Launditch, Part iii. 3. Banks' Dormant and Extinct Baronage, iii. 259. *See* CAPEL, DE DOVER.

DOVOR. Banks' Dormant and Extinct Baronage, i. 69.

DOVRE. Surtees' Durham, iv. 61.

DOW, or DOWE. Collectanea Topographica et Genealogica, iii. 142. Oliver's History of Antigua, i. 216.

DOWDALL. Burke's Landed Gentry, 2 supp., 3, 4.

DOWDESWELL. Bennett's History of Tewkesbury, 439. Burke's Commoners, (of Pull Court,) i, 376, Landed Gentry, 2, 3, 4, 5, 6, 7, 8 ; (of Redmarley,) Commoners, iv. 544, Landed Gentry, 2, 3, 4, 5. Gloucestershire Notes and Queries, ii. 410, 530. Howard's Visitation of England and Wales, vii. 80.

DOWELL. Fosbrooke's History of Gloucestershire, i. 490. Harleian Society, xxi. 153.

DOWLING. O'Hart's Irish Pedigrees, 2nd Series, 170. Burke's Colonial Gentry, i. 166, 167 ; ii. 546. Howard's Visitations of England and Wales, iv. 9.

DOWNE, or DOWNES. Case on behalf of Hugh Richard Viscount Downe. 1871, fol. Claim of Hugh Richard Viscount Downe to vote at Elections of Irish Peers, Sess. Papers, B of 1871. Visitation of Norfolk, published by Norfolk Archæological Society, i. 13, 37. Harleian Society, vi. 90 ; ix. 206 ; xv. 236 ; xviii. 86 ; xxxii.

109, 110; xxxviii. 693 ; xliii. 40. Gregson's Fragments relative to the County of Lancaster, 210. Manning and Bray's Surrey, ii. 735. Keating's History of Ireland, Plate 25. Visitation of Durham, 1615, (Sunderland, 1820, fol.) 53. Chetham Society, lxxxii. 133 ; lxxxiv. 100. O'Hart's Irish Pedigrees, 2nd Series, 56. The Genealogist, v. 251. Ormerod's Cheshire, iii. 775, 781. Earwaker's East Cheshire, ii. 319, 530. Visitations of Devon, by J. L. Vivian, 288. Foster's Visitation of Durham, 105. Weaver's Visitation of Herefordshire, 25. Surrey Archæological Collections, x. Burke's Landed Gentry, 7, 8.

DOWNHALL. Metcalfe's Visitations of Northamptonshire, 16.

DOWNHAM. Morant's Essex, ii. 404.

DOWNING. Gentleman's Magazine, 1833, i. 400. Visitation of Norfolk, published by Norfolk Archæological Society, i. 14. Carthew's Hundred of Launditch, Part ii. 750. Burke's Landed Gentry, 3 p. 422. Notes and Queries, 1. S. ii. 464, 497 ; iii. 68, 213 ; viii 221 ; x. 2 ; 7 S. ix. 172. Wotton's English Baronetage, iii. 414. Burke's Extinct Baronetcies. Harleian Society, xxxii. 113. Muskett's Suffolk Manorial Families, i. 96.

DOWNSHIRE. Burke's Royal Families, (London, 1851, 8vo.) i. 167.

DOWNTON. Antiquities and Memoirs of the Parish of Myddle, written by Richard Gough, 1700, (folio) 58. Harleian Society, xxviii. 152, 167.

DOWRICHE, or DOWRISH. Tuckett's Devonshire Pedigrees, 113. Harleian Society, vi. 91, 92. Maclean's History of Trigg Minor, i. 318. Westcote's Devonshire, edited by G. Oliver and P. Jones, 618. A Complete Parochial History of the County of Cornwall, i. 1. Visitation of Devon, edited by F. T. Colby, 85. The Visitations of Cornwall, edited by J. L. Vivian, 490. Visitations of Devon, by J. L. Vivian, 289.

DOWSE. Berry's Hampshire Genealogies, 312. Hampshire Visitations, printed by Sir T. Phillipps, 24. J. B. Payne's Armorial of Jersey, 83.

DOWSING. East Anglian, i. 146, 162, 218, 246, 259 ; ii. 256, 258, 359-362.

DOWTHWAITE. Surtees' Durham, iv. 42.

DOYLE. Case of Rt. Hon. Lady Susan Doyle in relation to the Barony of North, with Appendix, 1837, fol., pp. 12. Claim of the Rt. Hon. Lady Susan Doyle to the Barony of North, Sess. Papers, 72 of 1837. Burke's Extinct Baronetcies.

D'OYLEY, D'OYLY, D'OILEY, or DOYLEY. Topographer and Genealogist, i. 366-378, 567 ; ii. 18-27, 88, 543. Blomefield's Norfolk, v. 507. Bibliotheca Topographica Britannica, ix. Part 4, 298-306. History of the House of D'Oyly, by W. D. Bayley. London, 1845, 8vo. 2 parts. Sir T. Phillipps' Topographer, No. 1 (March, 1821, 8vo.) 50, 51, 52. Oxfordshire Pedigrees, fol. n.d., printed by Sir T. Phillipps. Visitation of Oxfordshire, 1574, printed by Sir T. Phillipps, (Middle Hill, fol.) 3. Visitation of Oxfordshire, 1634, printed by Sir T. Phillipps, (Middle Hill, fol.) 18. Harleian Society, v. 224, 266, 272, 325 ; xv. 237 ; xxxii. 113. Lipscombe's

History of the County of Buckingham, iii. 77 ; iv. 516. Baker's
Northampton, i. 709. Page's History of Suffolk, 996. Castles,
Mansions, and Manors of Western Sussex, by D. G. C. Elwes and
C. J. Robinson, 218. Wotton's English Baronetage, iii. 417, 498.
Betham's Baronetage, ii. 338, 400. Banks' Dormant and Extinct
Baronage, i. 67. Burke's Extinct Baronetcies. Oxfordshire
Historical Society, xxiv. 7. Aldred's History of Turville, 62.
Burke's Family Records, 607.
DOYNE. Burke's Landed Gentry, (of Wells,) 2, 3, 4, 5, and add., 6,
7, 8 ; (of Waltham Grove,) 2 supp.
DOYNGELL. The Visitations of Cornwall, edited by J. L. Vivian, 28.
DOYVELLE. The Genealogist, New Series, xvii. 169.
DRAKE. Life of Sir Francis Drake, with Historical and Genealogical
Account of his Family ; containing also an account of the Rich-
mond Family. London, 1828, 8vo. Genealogical and Bio-
graphical Account of the Family of Drake in America, with some
Notices of the same Family-name in England, 1845, 8vo. Some
unpublished papers relating to the Family of Sir Francis Drake,
by Rev. Thos. Hervey. Colmer, 1887, 8vo. Hasted's Kent, ii.
613. Berry's Hertfordshire Genealogies, 158. Maclean's History
of Trigg Minor, i. 320. Surrey Archæological Collections, ii.
Surtees Society, xxxvi. 59. Visitation of Norfolk, published by
Norfolk Archæological Society, i. 36. Burke's Commoners, (of
Roriston,) iv. 192, Landed Gentry, 2, 3, 4, 5 ; (of Ashe,) Landed
Gentry, 2, 3, 4, 5 ; (of Stokestown,) 3, 4, 5, 6, 7, 8 ; (of Oatlands),
6, 7, 8. Harleian Society, vi. 93-96 ; viii. 219 ; xv. 238 ; xxxii.
114 ; xxxviii. 505 ; xxxix. 1154 1163 ; xliii. 102. Lipscombe's
History of the County of Buckingham, iii. 154. Herald and
Genealogist, viii. 433, 476. Westcote's Devonshire, edited by
G. Oliver and P. Jones, 467. Manning and Bray's Surrey, i.
310. Clutterbuck's Hertford, i. 514. The Cistercian Houses of
Devon, by J. B. Rowe, 38. Ormerod's Cheshire, ii. 599. A Complete Parochial History of the County of Cornwall, i. 1. John
Watson's History of Halifax, 247. Boothroyd's History of Pontefract, 158. Notes and Queries, 3 S. iv. 189, 241, 330 ; 5 S. xi.
310 ; xii. 175 ; 8 S. i. 167, 339, 384. Wotton's English Baronetage, i. 531. Visitation of Devon, edited by F. T. Colby, 86.
Betham's Baronetage, i. 267. The Antiquary, (London, 1872,)
ii. 237, 282. Burke's Extinct Baronetcies, and supp. The Visitations of Cornwall, edited by J. L. Vivian, 496. The Visitations
of Devon, by J. L. Vivian, 267, 291-304. Hasted's Kent, (Hund.
of Blackheath, by H. H. Drake,) xxi. Devonshire Notes and
Notelets, by Sir W. R. Drake, 53. Cyclostyle Pedigrees, by
J. J. Green. New England Register, xvi. 107. Old Yorkshire,
by Willm. Smith, v. 186. See TYRWHITT-DRAKE.
DRAKE-BROCKMAN. Berry's Kent Genealogies, 118.
DRAKE-CUTCLIFFE. Howard's Visitation of England and Wales, viii.
108.
DRAKE-GARRARD. Burke's Commoners, i. 591, Landed Gentry,
2, 3, 4, 5.

DRAKES. Harleian Society, xvi. 102. *See* DRAX.

DRANSFELD, or DRANSFIELD. Surtees Society, xli. 47. Foster's Visitations of Yorkshire, 37. Harleian Society, xvi. 101.

DRAPER. Harleian Society, i. 4; ii. 52; iv. 136; xv. 239, 240; xxviii. 168. The Genealogist, ii. 226; iii. 56. History of the Parish of St. Leonard, Shoreditch, by Henry Ellis, 329. The Antiquities of Gainford, by J. R. Walbran, 106. Jewitt's Reliquary, xv. 192. Collectanea Topographica et Genealogica, iii. 150. Visitation of Derbyshire, 1663-4, (Middle Hill, 1854, fol.) 3. Nichol's History of the County of Leicester, ii. 263. Visitation of London in Transactions of London and Middlesex Archæological Society, 18. Surtees' Durham, iv. 31. Thoroton's Nottinghamshire, i. 253. Miscellanea Genealogica et Heraldica, New Series, ii. 302; iii. 322. Burke's Extinct Baronetcies. Nicholl's Account of the Company of Ironmongers, 2nd edn., 520. Foster's Visitation of Durham, 107. Foster's Visitations of Northumberland, 41.

DRAX. Pedigree of Drax of Shetterden. T. P., 1870, folio page. Visitation of Middlesex, (Salisbury, 1820, fol.) 33. Foster's Visitations of Yorkshire, 342. Harleian Society, viii. 76. W. Robinson's History of Hackney, i. 300. Hunter's Deanery of Doncaster, ii. 108. Foster's Visitation of Middlesex, 62. Oliver's History of Antigua, i. 149. Burke's Landed Gentry, 7. *See* DRAKES, ERLE-DRAX, SAWBRIDGE-ERLE-DRAX.

DRAYCOT, or DRAYCOTT. Visitation of Derbyshire, 1663-4, (Middle Hill, 1854, fol.) 3. Erdeswicke's Survey of Staffordshire, 253. The Genealogist, iii. 56; New Series, vii. 80; xiii. 181. Visitations of Staffordshire, 1614 and 1663-4, William Salt Society, 111. Harleian Society, xl. 1253.

DRAYNER. Howard's Visitation of England and Wales, vi. 49.

DRAYTON. Lipscombe's History of the County of Buckingham, i. 29. Bridge's Northamptonshire, by Rev. Peter Whalley, ii. 197, 251. Archæologia, xxix. 407. Memoirs of the Family of Chester, by R. E. C. Waters, 48. Miscellanea Genealogica et Heraldica, 3rd Series, iii. 236. *See* ALNO.

DREUX. Bank's Dormant and Extinct Baronage, iii. 623. *See* DE DREUX.

DREW, or DREWE. Tuckett's Devonshire Pedigrees, 62, 64. Berry's Hampshire Genealogies, 53. Burke's Commoners, (of the Grange,) iv. 672, Landed Gentry, 2, 3, 4, 5, 6, 7, 8; (of Drewscourt,) Landed Gentry, 2 supp., 3, 4, 5, 6, 7, 8; (of Heathfield Towers,) 5, 6. Topographer and Genealogist, ii. 209. Burke's Royal Families, (London, 1851, 8vo.) i. 13, 14. Harleian Society, vi. 96, 98; xxii. 50. Burke's Heraldic Illustrations, 126. Visitation of Devon, edited by F. T. Colby, 87, 88. Visitation of Wiltshire, edited by G. W. Marshall, 43. Westcote's Devonshire, edited by G. Oliver and P. Jones, 582, 583. Hampshire Visitations, printed by Sir T. Phillipps, 25. Visitatio Comitatus Wiltoniæ, 1623, printed by Sir T. Phillipps. New England Register, vi. 36. The Visitations of Devon, by J. L. Vivian, 305. The Genealogist, New Series, xiii. 149.

DREWETT. Burke's Landed Gentry, 5, 6, 7, 8.
DREYER. Howard's Visitation of Ireland, i. 95.
DRIFFIELD. Surtees Society, xxxvi. 384. History of Easingwold, by
Thomas Gill, 78.
DRING. Burke's Landed Gentry, 4, 5, 6, 7, 8.
DRINKWATER. Burke's Commoners, (of Salford,) iii. 420, Landed
Gentry, 2; (of Shrewsbury,) Commoners, iii. 668, Landed Gentry,
2; (of Irwell,) Commoners, iii. 669, Landed Gentry, 2, 3.
DRIVER. Visitation of Gloucester, edited by T. F. Fenwick and
W. C. Metcalfe, 59.
DROGHEDA. Burke's Royal Families, (London, 1851, 8vo.) i. 158.
DROKENSFORD. Jewers' Wells Cathedral, 86, 293.
DROPE. Oxford Historical Society, xix. 285.
DROUGHT. Burke's Landed Gentry, (of Lettybrook,) 2, 3, 4, 5, 6, 7,
8; (of Whigsboro',) 3, 4, 5, 6, 7, 8; (of Glencarrig,) 5, 6, 7, 8.
DRUCE. Genealogical Account of the Family of Druce, of Goreing,
Co. Oxon. London, 1735, 4to. Reprinted 1853, 4to.
DRUITT. An account of the Mayo and Elton families, by C. H.
Mayo, 136.
DRUMMOND. A Genealogical Memoir of the Noble House of Drum-
mond, by David Malcolm. Edinburgh, 1808, 8vo. An Interesting
Statement of the Claims of Thomas Drummond to the Earldom of
Perth, interspersed with copious Memoirs of the Noble House of
Drummond. Newcastle-on-Tyne, 1830, 8vo. Sequel to the above
Work, pp. 3, 8vo. Genealogy of the Most Noble House of
Drummond, collected by Hon. W. Drummond, edited by D.
Laing. Edinburgh, 1831, 4to. Case on behalf of George
Drummond, claiming to be Earl of Perth, n.d., 22 pp. fol. Case
of Thomas Drummond claiming the title of Earl of Perth, 1832,
fol. Claim of George Drummond, Duke of Melfort, to the Earl-
dom of Perth, Sess. Papers, 233 of 1846; 107 of 1847; 326 of
1847-8; 432 of 1852-3. Drummond's History of Noble British
Families, Part vii. Burke's Commoners, (of Stanmore,) iii. 561,
Landed Gentry, 2, 3, 4; (of Cadlands,) Commoners, iii. 560,
Landed Gentry, 2, 3, 4, 5, 6, 7, 8; (of Megginch Castle,) Landed
Gentry, 3, 4, 5, 6, 7, 8; (of Concraig,) 2, 3, 4, 5, 6; (of Blair
Drummond,) 2, 3, 4, 5, 6, 7, 8; (of Albury Park,) 3. Ormerod's
Cheshire, ii. 328. Douglas's Baronage of Scotland, 570. The
Red Book of Menteith, by Wm. Fraser, i. 467, 470. Wood's
Douglas's Peerage of Scotland, ii. 220, 357, 550. Fletcher's
Leicestershire Pedigrees and Royal Descents, 18. Alexander
Nisbet's Heraldic Plates, 14, 88, 98. Northern Notes and Queries,
x. 100. See INNES.
DRURY, or DRUREY. Gentleman's Magazine, 1831, ii. 594. Hasted's
Kent, ii. 689. Morant's Essex, i. 471, 475. Cambridgeshire
Visitation, edited by Sir T. Phillipps, 11. Berry's Sussex Gene-
alogies, 202. Berry's Essex Genealogies, 72. Blomefield's Nor-
folk, i. 278. Bibliotheca Topographica Britannica, (Cullum's
Hawsted,) v. Part ii. 115, (2nd edn. 128). Burke's Landed
Gentry, 2 supp., 3, 4. Gage's History of Thingoe Hundred,

Suffolk, 429. Dallaway's Sussex, i. 161. Baker's Northampton,
i. 57. Page's History of Suffolk, 653, 745. Harleian Society,
xiii. 190, 389; xiv. 736; xxxii. 115; xli. 107. Wotton's English
Baronetage, iv. 247. Metcalfe's Visitations of Suffolk, 91, 133.
Burke's Extinct Baronetcies. Bysshe's Visitation of Essex, edited
by J. J. Howard, 29. Burke's Colonial Gentry, ii. 834. Muskett's Suffolk Manorial Families, i. 345-372.

DRYDEN. Pedigree of Dryden of Canons Ashby, [T. P.] 1851.
Broadside. Gentleman's Magazine, ii. 122. Bridges' North-
amptonshire, by Rev. Peter Whalley, i. 226. Baker's Northamp-
ton, ii. 6. Burke's Extinct Baronetcies. Wotton's English
Baronetage, i. 349. Betham's Baronetage, iv. 272. Metcalfe's
Visitations of Northamptonshire, 178.

DRYHURST. Records of Denbigh and its Lordship, by John Williams,
168.

DRYWOOD. Harleian Society, xiii. 389.

DUBBER. Surrey Archæological Collections, v. Harleian Society,
xliii. 109.

DUBERLEY. Burke's Landed Gentry, 2, 3, 4, 5, 6, 7, 8.

DU BOIS. Blomefield's Norfolk, i. 78. Harleian Society, xv. 240.
The Genealogist, New Series, xv. 97.

DU BOULAY. Burke's Landed Gentry, 4, 5, 6, 7, 8. Burke's Visitation of Seats and Arms, 2nd Series, i. 45.

DU BOURDIEU. Pedigree of the noble family of Du Bourdieu, [by
Rev. C. T. Wilmshurst,]. Ashby-de-la-Zouch, 1864, 8vo. Notes
and Queries, 7 S. iii. 329, 458.

DU BUISSON. Burke's Landed Gentry, 4, 5, 6, 8.

DU CANE. Some Account of the Family of Du-Quesne, by E. F.
Du Cane. London, 1876, 4to. Berry's Essex Genealogies, 15.
Burke's Landed Gentry, 3, 4, 5, 6, 7, 8. Harleian Society, xiv.
658. See DU-QUESNE.

DUCK. Tuckett's Devonshire Pedigrees, 146. Visitation of Norfolk,
published by Norfolk Archæological Society, i. 13. Miscellanea
Genealogica et Heraldica, New Series, i. 317. Harleian Society,
vi. 98; xxxii. 115. Surtees' Durham, iv. 156. Burke's Extinct
Baronetcies. The Visitations of Devon, by J. L. Vivian, 309.

DUCKENFIELD, or DUKENFIELD. Chetham Society, lxxxiv. 100.
Wotton's English Baronetage, iii. 487. Betham's Baronetage, ii.
376. Ormerod's Cheshire, iii. 817. See DUKINFIELD, DOCKIN-
FELD, DOKENFELD.

DUCKET, or DUCKETT. Duchetiana, or a Genealogical Memoir of the
Family of Ducket, by Sir G. F. Duckett, Bart. London, 1869, 4to.
(2nd edition, 1874, 4to.). Duckett of Hartham House, Wilts, pp.
9, printed by E. Haenel, Berlin. Herald and Genealogist, iv. 461;
vi. 212, 320. Harleian Society, i. 7; xv. 241. Burke's Royal
Descents and Pedigrees of Founders' Kin, 56. Visitation of Westmoreland, 1615, (London, 1853,) 15. Burke's Landed Gentry,
2, 3, 4, 5, 6, 7, 8. Visitatio Comitatus Wiltoniæ, 1623, printed
by Sir T. Phillipps. Burke's Royal Families, (London, 1851,
8vo.) ii. 207. Visitation of London in Transactions of the

London and Middlesex Archæological Society, 28. Chetham Society, xcix. 143. Betham's Baronetage, v. app. 33. Visitation of Wiltshire, edited by G. W. Marshall, 82. Foster's Visitations of Cumberland and Westmorland, 39. Nicolson and Burn's Westmorland and Cumberland, i. 111. *See* DUKET.

DUCKWORTH. Burke's Landed Gentry, (of Over Darwen,) 3, 4, 5, 6, 7, 8; (of Mount Erris,) 3, 4. Foster's Lancashire Pedigrees. Manning and Bray's Surrey, ii. 682.

DUCY, or DUCIE. Rudder's Gloucestershire, 776, 842. Bibliotheca Topographica Britannica, ix. Part 4, 175. Shaw's Staffordshire, ii. 50. Visitation of Staffordshire, 1663-4, printed by Sir T. Phillipps, 4. Fosbrooke's History of Gloucestershire, ii. 46. Edmondson's Baronagium Genealogicum, v. 424 ; vi. 59. Brydges' Collins' Peerage, vii. 410. Banks' Dormant and Extinct Baronage, iii. 260. Burke's Extinct Baronetcies. Hasted's Kent, (Hund. of Blackheath, by H. H. Drake,) 121. Visitations of Staffordshire, 1614 and 1663-4, William Salt Society, 113.

DUDDINGSTON. Douglas's Baronage of Scotland, 477. Walter Wood's East Neuk of Fife, 272. The Genealogist, New Series, xv. 7.

DUDDLESTON. Wotton's English Baronetage, iv. 35. Burke's Extinct Baronetcies.

DUDGEON. Burke's Landed Gentry, 5, 6, 7, 8.

DUDLEY. The Sutton-Dudleys of England, and the Dudleys of New England, by George Adlard. London, 1862, 8vo. The Italian Biography of Sir Robert Dudley, Knt., Oxford, *n.d.* 8vo. Herald and Genealogist, ii. 420, 497 ; v. 97, 207, 250. Visitation of Durham, 1615, (Sunderland, 1820, fol.) 60. Harleian Society, vii. 36 ; xv. 241; xvi. 104 ; xix. 100. Blore's Rutland, 207. Shaw's Staffordshire, ii. 140. Bridge's Northamptonshire, by Rev. Peter Whalley, ii. 370. Nichols' History of the County of Leicester, i. 544. Dugdale's Warwickshire, 388. Surtees' Durham, ii. 280. Baker's Northampton, i. 470, 479 ; ii. 32. Dud Dudley's Metallum Martis, the quarto reprint, 1854. faces title-page. Collections for a History of Staffordshire, William Salt Society, ii. Part 2, 37. Notes and Queries, 3 S. ii. 325, 396 ; iii. 357. Burke's Extinct Baronetcies. Harvey's Hundred of Willey, 323. Wotton's English Baronetage, iii. 124. Banks' Dormant and Extinct Baronage, ii. 170. Visitations of Staffordshire, 1614 and 1663-4, William Salt Society, 114. Foster's Visitation of Durham, 109. Metcalfe's Visitations of Northamptonshire, 17, 86. Foster's Visitations of Cumberland and Westmorland, 40. New England Register, i. 71 ; vi. 280 ; x. 130, 337. Papers and Pedigrees relating to Cumberland and Westmorland, by Willm. Jackson, ii. 137. Nicolson and Burn's Westmorland and Cumberland, i. 413.

DUDMASTON. Harleian Society, xxix. 509.

DUDSON. The Genealogist, v. 252.

DUER. Notes and Queries, 3 S. ii. 319, 379. Oliver's History of Antigua, i. 217.

DUFF. Genealogical Memoirs of the Duffs, by L. D. Gordon Duff.
Aberdeen, 1869, 8vo.   Burke's Landed Gentry, (of Hatton,) 3,
4, 5, 6, 7, 8; (of Wellington Lodge,) 4, 5, 6; (of Orton,) 3, 4, 5;
(of Fetteresso,) 2, 3, 4, 5, 6, 7, 8; (of Woodcote House,) 2 supp.;
8 supp. at p. ix.   Douglas's Baronage of Scotland, 136.   Shaw's
History of Moray, 26.   Archdall's Lodge's Peerage, iii. 54.
Foster's Collectanea Genealogica, (MP's Scotland,) 106.   The
Genealogist, New Series, iii. 209.   Memoir of Richard Haines, by
C. R. Haines, table vii^a.   *See* GORDON.

DUFFIELD. Burke's Visitation of Seats and Arms, 2nd Series, i. 23.
Berry's Buckinghamshire Genealogies, 45.   Burke's Landed
Gentry, 5, 6, 7, 8.   History of the Hundred of Desborough, by
Thomas Langley, 481.

DUFFY. Burke's Colonial Gentry, ii. 462.

DUGAN. O'Hart's Irish Pedigrees, 2nd Series, 118.

DUGDALE. Hamper's Life of Dugdale.   Burke's Commoners, (of
Merevale,) i. 488, Landed Gentry, 2, 3, 4, 5, 6, 7, 8; (of Wroxall,)
5, 6, 8.   Harleian Society, viii. 319; xii. 327; xv. 242.   Abram's
History of Blackburn, 393.   Burke's Royal Families, (London,
1851, 8vo.) i. 63.   Warwickshire Pedigrees from Visitation of
1682-3, (privately printed, 1865.)   Visitation of Warwickshire,
1619, published with Warwickshire Antiquarian Magazine, 60.
Foster's Lancashire Pedigrees.   Dugdale's Warwickshire, 1051.
Miscellanea ' Genealogica et Heraldica, 2nd Series, ii. 128.
Howard's Visitation of England and Wales, ii. 73, 105; iv. 13.
Burke's Family Records, 230.

DUHEAUME. J. B. Payne's Armorial of Jersey, 132.

DUIGENAN. Genealogy of the Duigenan Family.   By W. H. Duignan
of Walsall, Staffordshire.   No place or date, 8vo.

DUKE. Burke's Extinct Baronetcies.   Berry's Sussex Genealogies,
275.   Surrey Archæological Collections, iii.   Burke's Commoners,
(of Lake House,) i. 285, Landed Gentry, 2, 3, 4, 5, 6, 7, 8; (of
Newpark,) 8.   Harleian Society, vi. 98, 342; xliii. 70, 167.
Visitatio Comitatus Wiltoniæ, 1623, printed by Sir T. Phillipps.
Collectanea Topographica et Genealogica, iii. 155.   Suckling's
History of Suffolk, ii. 186.   Westcote's Devonshire, edited by
G. Oliver and P. Jones, 559.   Hutchins' Dorset, iv. 231.   Hoare's
Wiltshire, II. ii. 139.   Chauncy's Hertfordshire, 181.   Page's
History of Suffolk, 169, 208, 783.   Visitation of Devon, edited
by F. T. Colby, 88.   Metcalfe's Visitations of Suffolk, 25, 26.
Visitation of Wiltshire, edited by G. W. Marshall, 64.   Notes and
Queries, 3 S. xii. 21.   Bysshe's Visitation of Essex, edited by J. J.
Howard, 30.   The Visitations of Devon, by J. L. Vivian, 311.

DUKET. Herald and Genealogist, vii. 252.   *See* DUCKET.

DUKINFIELD. Berry's Berkshire Genealogies, 74.   Butterworth's
History of Stockport, etc., 352.   Earwaker's East Cheshire,
ii. 18.   *See* DUCKENFIELD.

DUMARESQ. J. B. Payne's Armorial of Jersey, 139.   Burke's
Colonial Gentry, i. 328.   New England Register, xvii. 317.

DUMBLETON. Harleian Society, xxvii. 63.   Burke's Family Records, 232.

DUMFRIES (Earl of). Paterson's History of the Co. of Ayr, i. 357.
DU MOULIN. Archæologia Cantiana, xv. 34. Burke's Family Records, 116.
DU MOULIN-BROWNE. Howard's Visitation of England and Wales, i. 118.
DUMMER. Brocas of Beaurepaire, by M. Burrows, 324. Somerset Archæological Society, xvii. 114. New England Register, xxxv. 254, 321. The Genealogist, New Series, xiv. 172.
DUN. Genealogical Records of the Families of Dun, Meeson, Muddle, Soffe, Tucker, and Mauvesyn. By F. Meeson. London, 1888, fol. Morant's Essex, i. 159. Wright's Essex, ii. 376. Harleian Society, xiv. 567.
DUNBAR. Sketch of the Succession of the Ancient Historical Earldom of March, by Alex. Sinclair. Edinburgh, 1870. Herald and Genealogist, v. 243 ; vi. 289-311. The Agnews of Lochnaw, by Sir A. Agnew, 619. Drummond's History of Noble British Families, Part vi. Burke's Commoners, ii. 109. Burke's Royal Descents and Pedigrees of Founders' Kin, 30. Lands and their Owners in Galloway, by P. H. M'Kerlie, i. 254, 384 ; ii. 289. Paterson's History of the Co. of Ayr, i. 353, 366. Douglas's Baronage of Scotland, 113-126. Paterson's History of Ayr and Wigton, i. 316, 341, 761. Shaw's History of Moray, 81. Walter Wood's East Neuk of Fife, 253. Wood's Douglas's Peerage of Scotland, ii. 166, 252. Burke's Extinct Baronetcies, 621. Caithness Family History, by John Henderson, 219. Stodart's Scottish Arms, ii. 7-18. Alexander Nisbet's Heraldic Plates, 124. Olivœr's History of Antigua, i. 224. The Genealogical Magazine, iii. 298.
DUNBAR-BRANDER. Burke's Landed Gentry, 5, 6, 7, 8.
DUNBOYNE. Case of Theobald Fitzwalter Butler on his claim to the title of Baron Dunboyne. London, 1858, 4to. Claim of T. Fitz-W. Butler, Lord Dunboyne, claiming the dignity of Lord Baron Dunboyne, Sess. Papers, C of 1859; A of 1859, Sess. 2; C of 1860.
DUNCALFE. Foster's Visitations of Yorkshire, 141. Harleian Society, xviii. 87. Earwaker's East Cheshire, ii. 258.
DUNCAN. Burke's Landed Gentry, 3, 4, 5, 8. Paterson's History of the Co. of Ayr, ii. 432. Paterson's History of Ayr and Wigton. i. 701. O'Hart's Irish Pedigrees, 2nd Series, 171. Brydges' Collins' Peerage, vi. 378. Burke's Extinct Baronetcies. Burke's Colonial Gentry, i. 46. Alexander Nisbet's Heraldic Plates, 32.
DUNCH. Noble's Memoirs of the House of Cromwell, ii. 189-203. Banks' Baronies in Fee, i. 146. The Genealogist, v. 252. Berkshire Notes and Queries, i. 2. Miscellanea Genealogica et Heraldica, 3rd Series, ii. 43.
DUNCOMBE, DUNCOMBE, or DUNCUMB. Berry's Surrey Genealogies, 47. Berry's Buckinghamshire Genealogies, 92, 100-102. Burke's Commoners, i. 151, Landed Gentry, 2, 8. Foster's Yorkshire Pedigrees. Miscellanea Genealogica et Heraldica, New Series, i. 412. Harleian Society, viii. 468; xv. 243; xix. 100; xliii. 200. Lipscombe's History of the County of Buckingham, i. 163. Nichols'

History of the County of Leicester, iii. 255; iv. 853. History of Wiltshire, III. iv. 45. Manning and Bray's Surrey, i. 629; ii. 127. Clutterbuck's Hertford, i. 222. The Genealogist, vii. 174. Banks' Dormant and Extinct Baronage, iii. 297. Burke's Extinct Baronetcies. Surrey Archæological Collections, x. Oliver's History of Antigua, i. 225. *See* PAUNCEFORT-DUNCOMBE.

DUNDAS. The Arniston Memoirs, by G. W. T. Omond. Edinburgh, 1887, 8vo. Dundas of Dundas, by Walter Macleod. Edinburgh, 1897, 4to. Dundas of Arniston, 1570-1880, by Louisa Lilias Forbes. Edinburgh, 1880, folding sheet. Drummond's History of Noble British Families, Part vi. Berry's Berkshire Genealogies, 31. Burke's Commoners, (of Dundas,) i. 642, Landed Gentry, 2, 3, 4, 5, 6, 7, 8; (of Barton Court,) Commoners, iii. 113, Landed Gentry, 2, 3, 4, 5, 6; (of Duddingston,) Commoners, iii. 178, Landed Gentry, 2, 3, 4; (of Blair Castle,) Commoners, ii. 368, Landed Gentry, 2, 3; (of Carron Hall,) Landed Gentry, 4, 5, 6, 7; (of Arniston,) 2, 3, 4, 5, 6, 7, 8; (of Clobemon Hall,) 5, 6, 8. Foster's Yorkshire Pedigrees. Ord's History of Cleveland, 351. Nisbet's Heraldry, ii. app. 11, 269. Douglas's Baronage of Scotland, 171-182. Plantagenet-Harrison's History of Yorkshire, i. 73. John Penney's Account of Linlithgowshire, 190. Notes and Queries, 1 S. ix. 311. Brydges' Collins' Peerage, vi. 399; viii. 380. Foster's Collectanea Genealogica, (MP's Scotland,) 111, 114. Memoir of Chancellor Seton, by Geo. Seton, App. II. The *Edinburgh Review*, Oct., 1887. Alexander Nisbet's Heraldic Plates, 36. Burke's Family Records, 233.

DUNDERDALE. History of Chipping, by Tom C. Smith, 267.

DUNDONALD. Case on behalf of the Earl of Dundonald in support of, etc., his succession to be Earl of Dundonald, etc., and folding pedigree, 1861, folio. Minutes of Evidence on the Earl of Dundonald's Petition to be Lord Dundonald, Sess. Papers, 203 of 1861; A and H of 1862; A of 1863.

DUNGAN. Foster's Account of Families descended from Francis Fox, 21.

DUNGIE. Harleian Society, vi. 99.

DUNHAM. Thoroton's Nottinghamshire, iii. 97. Harleian Society, xvi. 100. *See* DONHAM.

DUNHEVED. The Genealogist, New Series, vii. 244.

DUNLEVY. O'Hart's Irish Pedigrees, 2nd Series, 172.

DUNLOP. Burke's Commoners, i. 434; (of Drumhead,) Landed Gentry, 3, 4, 5, 6, 8; (of Corsock,) 4, 5, 6, 7, 8; (of Doonside,) 8; (of Craigton,) 4; (of Monasterboice,) 4, 5, 6. Geo. Robertson's Description of Cunninghame, 298, 306. Paterson's History of the Co. Ayr, i. 208; ii. 46, 50, 53. Paterson's History of Ayr and Wigton, i. 150; iii. 226, 239, 423. Geo. Robertson's Account of Families in Ayrshire, i. 331.

DUNLOP-WALLACE. Burke's Royal Families, (London, 1851, 8vo.) i. 202.

DUNMERE. The Genealogist, New Series, x. 92.

DUNMOLL. Berry's Sussex Genealogies, 100.

DUNN, or DUNNE. Glover's History of Derbyshire, ii. 179. Burke's Landed Gentry, (of Brittas,) 2, 3, 4, 5, 6, 7, 8; (of Birchen Hall,) 7, 8. O'Hart's Irish Pedigrees, 2nd Series, 174, 175. Burke's Colonial Gentry, ii. 700.

DUNN-GARDENER. Burke's Landed Gentry, 4, 5, 6, 7, 8.

DUNNING. Edmondson's Baronagium Genealogicum, vi. 97. Brydges' Collins' Peerage, vii. 543. Oliver's History of Antigua, i. 229. The New England Register, lii. 38.

DUNNINGTON-JEFFERSON. Burke's Landed Gentry, 6 supp., 7, 8.

DUNRAVEN. Burke's Royal Families, (London, 1851, 8vo.) ii. 202.

DUNSANDLE. Claim of the Rt. Hon. D. St. G., Baron Dunsandle, etc., to Vote at Elections of Irish Peers, Sess. Papers, 211 of 1849.

DUNSANY. Case of Randall, styling himself Lord Baron Dunsany. Folio, pp. 2. Claim of the Rt. Hon. Edward, Baron Dunsany, to Vote at Elections of Irish Peers, Sess. Papers, 49, of 1823; 158 of 1854.

DUNSCOMBE. Burke's Landed Gentry, (of King William's Town,) 3, 4, 5, 6, 7; (of Mount Desert,) 2, 3, 4, 5, 6, 7, 8.

DUNSFORD. Pedigree of the Family of Dunsford, by G. L. Dunsford. Exeter, large sheet, [1866.] Genealogical Memoranda of the Family of Ames, 6. Ontarian Families, by E. M. Chadwick, i. 112.

DUNSTANVILLE. J. Wilkinson's History of Broughton Gifford, folding plate. Scrope's History of Castle Combe, 1852, 4to. Wiltshire Archæological Magazine, v. 267. The Visitations of Cornwall, edited by J. L. Vivian, 17. Banks' Dormant and Extinct Baronage, i. 71. The Visitations of Devon, edited by J. L. Vivian, 45. E. J. Climenson's History of Shiplake, 60. See DE DUNSTANVILLE.

DUNSTER. Clutterbuck's Hertford, ii. 183. New England Register, xxvii. 307.

DUNSTERVILE. Harleian Society, xv. 243.

DUNTEITH. See EDNEM.

DUNTZE. Betham's Baronetage, iv. 1.

DUPORT. Harleian Society, ii. 123; vi. 224. Nichols' History of the County of Leicester, iii. 1023. The Visitations of Devon, by J. L. Vivian, 691.

DUPPA. Burke's Commoners, iv. 483, Landed Gentry, 2, 3, 4, 5, 6, 7, 8.

DU PRÉ. Pedigree of Du Pré of Temple Guiting, Co. Glouc., [T. P.] 1860, fol. page. Burke's Landed Gentry, 2, 3, 4, 5, 6, 7, 8.

DUPUIS. Miscellanea Genealogica et Heraldica, New Series, iii. 248.

DU QUESNE. Notes and Queries, 2 S. vii. 73. See DU CANE.

DURANT, or DURRANT. Berry's Hampshire Genealogies, 261. Visitation of Oxfordshire, 1634, printed by Sir T. Phillipps, (Middle Hill, fol.) 19. Burke's Landed Gentry, 4, 5, 6, 7, 8. Harleian Society, iii. 40-43; v. 217. Wright's History of Rutland, 40. Archæologia Cantiana, xii. 315. Betham's Baronetage, iv. 145. Weaver's Visitation of Somerset, 92.

DURANTHORP. Nichols' History of the County of Leicester, iii. 997.

DURDIN. Burke's Landed Gentry, 5, 6, 7, 8 at p. 1723.

DURELL, (le Vavasseur dit). J. B. Payne's Armorial of Jersey, 155.
DURHAM. Pedigree of Durham of Weston Subedge, [T. P.] 1848,
folio paȝe. Pedigrees of Durham of Willersley, Co. Gloucester,
[T. P.] 2 folio pages. Murray's Life of Admiral Sir P. C. H. C.
Durham, 1. Burke's Commoners, i. 287. Landed Gentry, 2.
Douglas's Baronage of Scotland, 472. Walter Wood's East Neuk
of Fife, 294. Bigland's Gloucestershire, ii. par. Willersley.
DURIE. Walter Wood's East Neuk of Fife, 254.
DURKIN. O'Hart's Irish Pedigrees, 2nd Series, 57.
DURNFORD. Notes and Queries, 3 S. i. 492 ; ii. 57.
DURWARD. Proceedings of the Essex Archæological Society, iii. 100.
See DOREWARD.
DURWASSALL. Dugdale's Warwickshire, 757. The Genealogist,
New Series, x. 31.
DURY. Burke's Landed Gentry, 4, 5. Miscellanea Genealogica et
Heraldica, 3rd Series, iii. 164.
DUSTON. Baker's Northampton, i. 140.
DUTILH. Miscellanea Genealogica et Heraldica, 3rd Series, iii. 24.
DUTRY. Burke's Extinct Baronetcies. Miscellanea Genealogica et
Heraldica, 2nd Series, i. 226.
DUTTON. Memorials of the Duttons. London and Chester, 1891,
4to. Rudder's Gloucestershire, 649. Collections for a Genea-
logical Account of the Family of Comberbach, 55. Burke's
Landed Gentry, 3, 4. Foster's Visitations of Yorkshire, 241.
Burke's Royal Descents and Pedigrees of Founders' Kin, 48.
Ormerod's Cheshire, i. 643 ; ii. 795 ; iii. 622. Fosbrooke's
History of Gloucestershire, ii. 388. Edmondson's Baronagium
Genealogicum, vi. 123. Brydges' Collins' Peerage, viii. 39.
Wotton's English Baronetage, iii. 642. Burke's Extinct Baronet-
cies. Chetham Society, cx. 223. Harleian Society, xviii. 87,
237, 260 ; xxi. 53, 54 ; xxxix. 1013, 1018. Visitation of Glouces-
ter, edited by T. F. Fenwick and W. C. Metcalfe, 19. Burke's
Colonial Gentry, ii. 529. The Genealogist, New Series, xii. 112 ;
xiii 99. See EGERTON-WARBURTON.
DUTTON-COLT. Harleian Society, viii. 392.
DUVAL. See SYKES.
DUXBURY. Abram's History of Blackburn, 542.
DWIGHT. Notes and Queries, 8 S. vi. 129.
DWNN. Dwnn's Visitations of Wales, i. 20, 26, 91, 199, 222, 294
ii. 49, 58, 59, 61.
DWYER. O'Hart's Irish Pedigrees, 2nd Series, 175.
DYCER. Burke's Extinct Baronetcies. Visitation of Middlesex,
(Salisbury, 1820, fol.) 29. W. Robinson's History of Hackney,
i. 300. Foster's Visitation of Middlesex, 58.
DYCHFEILD. Chetham Society, lxxxi. 123. See DICHFIELD, DITCH-
FIELD.
DYCON. The Genealogist, New Series, xvi. 37.
DYER. Pedigree of Sir Thomas Dyer, Bart. (T. B. Shenton, printer,
Cheltenham, Nov. 1854,) folio broadside. Burke's Patrician, iv.
7, 264, 420 ; v. 75, 218. Morant's Essex, ii. 424. Visitation of

Somerset, printed by Sir T. Phillipps, 65. Tuckett's Devonshire Pedigrees, 101. Harleian Society, vi. 100 ; xi. 33, 35 ; xxii. 7. Phelps' History of Somersetshire, i. 563. Pembrokeshire Pedigrees, 153. Camden Society, xliii. 69. Wotton's English Baronetage, iii. 652. Weaver's Visitations of Somerset, 21. Foster's Visitation of Middlesex, 57. The Visitations of Devon, by J. L. Vivian, 315. Betham's Baronetage, iii. 33. Account of the Mayo and Elton Families, by C. H. Mayo, 159. Burke's Extinct Baronetcies.

DYGGS. Hasted's Kent, ii. 513. See DIG.

DYKE. Berry's Surrey Genealogies, 61. Berry's Sussex Genealogies, 148, 196. Harleian Society, xv. 233, 244. Wotton's English Baronetage, iii. 608. Betham's Baronetage, iii. 1. Archæologia Cantiana, xvi. 239. See HART-DYKE.

DYKES. Burke's Commoners, i. 263, Landed Gentry, 2, 3, 4, 5, 6, 7, 8. Burke's Visitation of Seats and Arms, 2nd Series, i. 12 ; ii. 36 Burke's Royal Descents and Pedigrees of Founders' Kin, 35, 50* ; *Founders' Kin*, 12. Harleian Society, xvi. 105. Foster's Visitations of Cumberland and Westmorland, 41.

DYMER. Visitation of Gloucester, edited by T. F. Fenwick and W. C. Metcalfe, 60.

DYMOCK, or DYMOKE. Scrivelsby, the Home of the Champions, with some account of the Marmyon and Dymoke Families. By S. Lodge. London, 1894, 4to. 2nd edition. Dwnn's Visitations of Wales, ii. 313. Harleian Society, viii. 132. History of Powis Fadog, by J. Y. W. Lloyd, iii. 392. Case of Lewis Dymoke, Esq., claiming the Barony of Marmyon, 1814, folio, pp. 7. Additional Case of L. Dymoke, claiming the Barony of Marmion, 1817, folio, pp. 13. Claim of Lewis Dymoke to the Barony of Marmyon, Sess. Papers, 47 of 1818, 48 of 1819. Topographical Account of Wainfleet, by Edmd. Oldfield, 190. Burke's Commoners, i. 32 ; iii. 87, Landed Gentry, 2, 3, 4, 5, 6, 7, 8. Burke's Heraldic Illustrations, 48. Banks' History of the Family of Marmyun, 117-132. Gentleman's Magazine, 1821, ii. 395. The Genealogist, ii. 181, 213 ; iii. 326 ; iv. 19, 98. Banks' Dormant and Extinct Baronage, i. 129. See DIMOCK.

DYNE. Gentleman's Magazine, 1829, ii. 20, 124, 202, 321. Berry's Sussex Genealogies, 162. Berry's Kent Genealogies, 452. Burke's Commoners, iii. 237 ; iv. 203. Archæologia Cantiana, xvi. 72. Burke's Landed Gentry, 3, 4. See DE DYNE.

DYNELEY, or DYNLEY. Foster's Yorkshire Pedigrees. Foster's Visitations of Yorkshire, 122, 297, 298, 301. Thoresby's Ducatus Leodiensis, 33. Whitaker's Loidis and Elmete, 198. Whitaker's History of Whalley, ii. 200. Chetham Society, xcv. 122. Harleian Society, xiv. 548 ; xvi. 106 ; xxvii. 50. See DE DYNELEY, DINELEY.

DYNHAM. Tuckett's Devonshire Pedigrees, 135. Harleian Society, vi. 100. Lipscombe's History of the County of Buckingham, i. 66. Dunkin's History of Bullington and Ploughley, ii. 137. Banks' Dormant and Extinct Baronage, i. 288. Genealogical

Records of the Family of Woodd, 32. The Genealogist, New Series, xii. 228. *See* DINHAM.

DYNNE. Harleian Society, xxxii. 111.

DYOS. Harleian Society, xv. 244.

DYOTT. Burke's Commoners, ii. 425, Landed Gentry, 2, 3, 4, 5, 6, 7, 8. Shaw's Staffordshire, i. 362. Erdeswicke's Survey of Staffordshire, 310. Visitations of Staffordshire, 1614 and 1663-4, William Salt Society, 117. The Gresley's of Drakelowe, by F. Madan, 251. *See* DIOT.

DYSON. Visitations of Staffordshire, 1614 and 1663-4, William Salt Society, 120. Harleian Society, xxvii. 51 ; xxxix. 1133. Burke's Landed Gentry, 8.

DYVE. Baker's Northampton, i. 82, 160, 163, 169 ; ii. 254. Harvey's Hundred of Willey, 44. Harleian Society, xix. 21.

DYX. Harleian Society, xxxii. 112.

DYXYE. Harleian Society, i. 16. *See* DIXIE.

EAGAR. Burke's Landed Gentry, 4.

EAGER. A Genealogical History of the Eager Family. By F. J. Eager. Dublin, 1861, 12mo. Burke's Authorised Arms, 210-222.

EAGLES. Berry's Buckinghamshire Genealogies, 95.

EAGLESFIELD. Foster's Visitations of Cumberland and Westmorland, 42.

EAKINS. Harleian Society, xxii. 51.

EALES. Notes and Queries, 3 S. ii. 292. Howard's Visitation of England and Wales, i. 58; Notes, ii. 74. Burke's Family Records, 235.

EARBY. *See* IRBY.

EARLE. Foster's Lancashire Pedigrees. Hutchins' Dorset, iii. 502. Burke's Extinct Baronetcies. Burke's Landed Gentry, 8. Miscellanea Genealogica et Heraldica, 2nd Series, ii. 213. Harleian Society, xx. 37. Historic Society of Lancashire and Cheshire, New Series, vi. 15-70. Berks Archæological and Architectural Society Journal, iii. 193. *See* ERLE.

EARLSMAN. Berry's Hampshire Genealogies, 309.

EARTH. Visitatio Comitatus Wiltoniæ, 1623, printed by Sir T. Phillipps. Visitation of Wiltshire, edited by G. W. Marshall, 5.

EAST. Berry's Berkshire Genealogies, 9. Burke's Royal Families, (London, 1851, 8vo.) ii. 145- Burke's Heraldic Illustrations, 106. Harleian Society, xv. 245. Betham's Baronetage, iii. 339. Burke's Extinct Baronetcies. The Genealogist, vii. 175.

EASTMAN. New England Register, xxi. 229.

EASTON. Visitation of Devon, edited by F. T. Colby, 90. The Visitations of Devon, by J. L. Vivian, 317. The Genealogical Magazine, iii. 478. *See* ESTON.

EASTWOOD. Burke's Landed Gentry, 2, 3, 4, 8. Harleian Society, iv. 91. Howard's Visitation of England and Wales, v. 157.

EATON. Surtees Society, xxxvi. 287. Burke's Landed Gentry, (of Stetchworth Park,) 4, 5 ; (of Tolethorpe,) 5, 6, 7, 8. Ormerod's Cheshire, i. 657. Burke's Extinct Baronetcies, 604. Miscellanea

Genealogica et Heraldica, New Series, iv. 354; 2nd Series, ii. 54.
Earwaker's History of Sandbach, 261. Harleian Society, xxxix.
1149, 1152. Shropshire Notes and Queries, New Series, iii. 50.
Howard's Visitation of England and Wales, vi. 86. *See* ETON.

EAYRE. North's Church Bells of Northamptonshire, 47-51. North's
Church Bells of Leicestershire, 93-95.

EBBEWORTHYE. Harleian Society, vi. 101.

EBORALL. Warwickshire Pedigrees, from Visitation of 1682-3,
(privately printed, 1865).

EBSWORTHY. The Visitations of Devon, by J. L. Vivian, 318.

ECCLES. Descendants of John Eccles of Worley, by R. J. H. Eccles.
Lithograph. London, 1880. Burke's Landed Gentry, (of Fin-
tona,) 4, 5, 6, 7, 8; (of Cronroe,) 2, 3, 4. Abram's History of
Blackburn, 475. Douglas's Baronage of Scotland, 436. History
of Chipping, by Tom C. Smith, 254. The Genealogical Magazine,
i. 353.

ECCLESTON. Visitation of Sussex, 1570, printed by Sir T. Phillipps,
(Middle Hill, fol.) 4. Chetham Society, lxxxi. 97; lxxxiv. 101.
The Tyldesley Diary, edited by J. Gillow and A. Hewitson, 45.
The Genealogist, vi. 148.

ECHINGHAM. Echyingham of Echyngham, by Spencer Hall. London,
1850, 8vo. Banks' Baronies in Fee, i. 197. Banks' Dormant and
Extinct Baronage, i. 291.

ECHLIN. Memoirs of the Ancient Family of the Echlins, by G.
Crawfurd. This work has been reissued as, Genealogical Memoirs
of the Echlin Family, by John R. Echlin, second edition. Edinburgh, [1882,] 8vo. Burke's Landed Gentry, (of Ardquin,) 2, 3,
4, 5, 6, 7, 8; (of Kirlish,) 4, 5.

ECKERSLEY. Burke's Landed Gentry, 6, 7, 8.

ECKLEY. Burke's Landed Gentry, 2, 3, 4.

ECKROYD. Life of Joseph Clark, by H. E. Clark, 1. Annals of
Smith of Balby, by H. E. Smith, 101. Burke's Landed Gentry,
7, 8. *See* AKEROYD.

EDDINGTON. Burke's Landed Gentry, 5, 6, 7, 8. Burke's Colonial
Gentry, i. 269.

EDDOWES. James Hall's History of Nantwich, 506. Fletcher's
Leicestershire Pedigrees and Royal Descents, 190. Harleian
Society, xxxvii. 109.

EDDY. Burke's Royal Families, (London, 1851, 8vo.) i. 124. Burke's
Colonial Gentry, ii. 450.

EDEN. Morant's Essex, ii. 275, 315. The Antiquities of Gainford,
by J. R. Walbran, 51. Visitation of Suffolke, edited by J. J.
Howard, i. 1-18, 313. Visitation of Durham, 1575, (Newcastle,
1820, fol.) 12. Burke's Landed Gentry, 5, 6. History of Hartlepool, by Sir C. Sharp, (1816, 8vo.) 76. Hutchinson's History of
Durham, iii. 339. Brydges' Collins' Peerage, viii. 287. Wotton's
English Baronetage, iii. 546. Betham's Baronetage, iv. 15, app.
5. Foster's Visitations of Durham, 111. Bysshe's Visitation of
Essex, edited by J. J. Howard 30. *See* STUART.

EDGAR. Account of the Surname of Edgar, by J. H. Lawrence-

EDG 272 EDM

Archer, 1873, 4to. Genealogical Collections concerning the
Scottish House of Edgar. London, 1873, 4to. Alexander
Nisbet's Heraldic Plates, 80. Herald and Genealogist, iii. 466.
Burke's Landed Gentry, 2 supp., 3, 4, 5, 6, 7, 8. Notes and
Queries, 2 S. ix. 248, 373, 451; xi. 254; xii. 94, 330; 3 S. ii.
315; 5 S. i. 192, 355. Metcalfe's Visitations of Suffolk, 134.
EDGBURY. Berry's Kent Genealogies, 339. Harleian Society, xlii.
191.
EDGCOMBE, or EDGCUMBE. Burke's Landed Gentry, 3, 4, 5, 6, 8.
Harleian Society, vi. 102, 103; viii. 25; ix. 63, 64. Westcote's
Devonshire, edited by G. Oliver and P. Jones, 494. A Complete
Parochial History of the County of Cornwall, i. 181. An Historical
Survey of Cornwall, by C. S. Gilbert, i. 444. Edmondson's
Baronagium Genealogicum, v. 436; vi. 23. Brydges' Collins'
Peerage, v. 306. The Visitations of Cornwall, edited by J. L.
Vivian, 141. The Visitations of Devon, by J. L. Vivian, 319-326,
866.
EDGE. Burke's Landed Gentry, (of Strelley,) 2 add., 3, 4, 5 and
supp., 6, 7, 8; (of Clonbrock House,) 4, 5, 6, 7, 8. Visitation of
Staffordshire, 1663-4, printed by Sir T. Phillipps, 4. Parish of
Benenden, Kent, by F. Haslewood, 159. The Visitations of
Staffordshire, 1614 and 1663-4, William Salt Society, 122. Har-
leian Society, xxviii. 170.
EDGELL. Burke's Landed Gentry, 3, 4, 5, 8.
EDGERLEY. Harleian Society, v. 164. New England Register, xv.
337; xxxiv. 282.
EDGEWORTH, or EDGWORTH. Burke's Commoners, (of Edgeworths-
town,) iv. 753, Landed Gentry, 2, 3, 4, 5, 6, 7, 8; (of Kilshrewly,)
iv. 755, Landed Gentry, 2, 3, 4, 5, 6, 7, 8; Landed Gentry, 5
supp. Harleian Society, viii. 280. Burke's Colonial Gentry, ii. 744.
EDISBURY. History of Powys Fadog, by J. Y. W. Lloyd, iii. 60.
Hasted's Kent, (Hund. of Blackheath, by H. H. Drake,) 21.
EDMANDS. Burke's Landed Gentry, 3, 4, 5 supp., 6.
EDMERSTON. Harleian Society, ix. 193. The Visitations of Corn-
wall, edited by J. L. Vivian, 413.
EDMONDES, or EDMONDS. Berry's Sussex Genealogies, 44. Berry's
Hampshire Genealogies, 120. Harleian Society, v. 218; ix. 65;
xv. 246; xli. 72. Westcote's Devonshire, edited by G. Oliver and
P. Jones, 524. Hampshire Visitations, printed by Sir T. Phillipps,
25. Visitation of Devon, edited by F. T. Colby, 91. The Visi-
tations of Cornwall, edited by J. L. Vivian, 144. History of
Powys Fadog, by J. Y. W. Lloyd, iv. 423. Hasted's Kent,
(Hund. of Blackheath, by H. H. Drake,) 254. The Visitations of
Devon, by J. L. Vivian, 327. History of the Wilmer Family, 251.
EDMONDSON, or EDMONSON. W. Paver's Pedigrees of Families of the
City of York, 12. Foster's Visitations of Yorkshire, 513.
EDMONDSTONE, or EDMONSTON. The Genealogy of the Lairds of Ednem
and Dunteith [name Edmondstone]. Glasgow, 1699; reprinted by
James Maidment, Edinburgh, 1824, 18mo. Genealogical Ac-
count of the Family of Edmonstone, by Sir Archibald Edmonstone,

Bart. Edinburgh, 1875, 4to. Nisbet's Heraldry, ii. app. 163, 299, (155, 290). Betham's Baronetage, iii. 414. Foster's Collectanea Genealogica, (MP's Scotland,) 119. Burke's Commoners, ii. 385. EDMONDSTOWNE-CRANSTOUN. Burke's Landed Gentry, 7, 8. EDMUNDES, or EDMUNDS. Surtees Society, xxxvi. 9. Foster's Yorkshire Pedigrees. Dallaway's Sussex, II. i. 43. Hunter's Deanery of Doncaster, ii. 290. History of Worsborough, by Joseph Wilkinson, 54. Castles, Mansions, and Manors of Western Sussex, by D. G. C. Elwes and C. J. Robinson, 140.

EDMUNDSON. O'Hart's Irish Pedigrees, 2nd Series, 176.

EDNOWEN BENDEW. Dwnn's Visitations of Wales, ii. 22.

EDOLPHE. Berry's Kent Genealogies, 124. Miscellanea Genealogica et Heraldica, New Series, iv. 169. Harleian Society, xlii. 54.

EDON. Harleian Society, xiii. 390. Metcalfe's Visitations of Suffolk, 27, 135.

EDWARD. Dwnn's Visitations of Wales, i. 67, 152, 200. Alexander Nisbet's Heraldic Plates, 140.

EDWARD VI. (Seize Quartiers of King). Gentleman's Magazine, 1849, ii. 157.

EDWARD, MORGAN. Dwnn's Visitations of Wales, i. 286.

EDWARDES. Dwnn's Visitations of Wales, i. 152, 327. Burke's Commoners, ii. xvi. ; (of Rhyd y Gôrs,) Landed Gentry, 3, 4, 5, 6, 7, 8 ; (of Gileston Manor,) 2 supp., 3, 4, 5, 6 ; (of Sealy Ham,) 5, 6, 8. Harleian Society, ix. 65. Pembrokeshire Pedigrees, 148. The Visitations of Cornwall, edited by J. L. Vivian, 145. See HOPE EDWARDES.

EDWARDS. J. H.-Hill's History of Langton, 301. Morant's Essex, ii. 91. Glover's History of Derbyshire, ii. 589, (570). Berry's Sussex Genealogies, 325. Dwnn's Visitations of Wales, i. 323, 327 ; ii. 232, 327. Camden Society, xliii. 113. Tuckett's Devonshire Pedigrees, 29. Glamorganshire Pedigrees, edited by Sir T. Phillipps, 33. Cambridgeshire Visitation, edited by Sir T. Phillipps, 12. Burke's Commoners, (of Ness Strange,) ii. 78, Landed Gentry, 2, 3, 4, 5, 6, 7, 8 ; (of Arlesey Bury,) Landed Gentry, 2 supp., 3, 4, 5 ; (of Trevor Hall,) 8 ; (of Old Court,) 2, 3, 4, 5 ; (of Dolserau,) 5, 6, 7, 8 ; (of Trematon Hall,) 5, 6, 7, 8 ; (of Hardingham,) 5, 6, 7, 8 ; (of Roby Hall,) 2 supp., 3, 4 ; (of Pyenest,) 3, 4 ; (of Llandaff House,) 4 ; (of Nanhoron,) 2 supp., 3, 4, 5, 6, 7, 8 ; (of The Hayes,) 2 ; (of Henlow Grange,) 2. Foster's Yorkshire Pedigrees. Harleian Society, vi. 104 ; viii. 242, 336 ; xv. 247-250 ; xix. 101 ; xxviii. 170, 174 ; xli. 83, 106, 112. Burke's Visitation of Seats and Arms, ii. 73. Collectanea Topographica et Genealogica, vi. 290. Blore's Rutland, 182. Burke's Royal Descents and Pedigrees of Founders' Kin, 86. Nichols' History of the County of Leicester, ii. 868. Caermarthenshire Pedigrees, 13. Wotton's English Baronetage, ii. 415 ; iv. 34. Betham's Baronetage, ii. 36. Burke's Extinct Baronetcies. Howard's Visitation of England and Wales, i. 257 ; Notes, iii. 87. History of Powys Fadog, by J. Y. W. Lloyd, iii. 80 ; iv. 63, 68, 89, 98, 348, 425 ; v. 242 ; vi. 275, 423. Bysshe's Visitation of

18

Essex, edited by J. J. Howard, 30. Genealogies of Morgan and Glamorgan, by G. T. Clark, 382, 485. Visitation of Gloucester, edited by T. F. Fenwick and W. C. Metcalfe, 7. The Visitations of Devon, by J. L. Vivian, 328. The Genealogist, New Series, x. 184. Oliver's History of Antigua, i. 231. A History of Banking in Bristol, by C. H. Cane, 236.

EDWARDS-MOSS. Burke's Landed Gentry, 4.

EDWIN, or EDWYN. Miscellanea Genealogica et Heraldica, ii. 136. Herald and Genealogist, vi. 54. Harleian Society, viii. 414. Manning and Bray's Surrey, ii. 640. Duncumb's History of the Co. of Hereford, ii. 132. Weaver's Visitation of Herefordshire, 86. Memorials of Adare Manor, by Caroline, Countess of Dunraven, 11.

EDYVEAN. Maclean's History of Trigg Minor, i. 285.

EEDES. Harleian Society, xix. 102.

EELES. History of the Wilmer Family, 255.

EFFINGHAM (Earl of). Hasted's Kent, ii. 755.

EGAN. O'Hart's Irish Pedigrees, 2nd Series, 177. See MAC-EGAN.

EGEBASTON. Dugdale's Warwickshire, 894.

EGERLEY. Sir T. Phillipps' Topographer, No. 1, (March, 1821, 8vo.) 31. Visitation of Oxfordshire, 1574, printed by Sir T. Phillipps, (Middle Hill, fol.) 3.

EGERTON. A Short Account of the possessors of Oulton, by Sir P. de M. Grey-Egerton, 1. Descent and Alliances of William Egerton, by Sir S. E. Brydges. London, 1805, fol. Miscellanea Genealogica et Heraldica, i. 293; ii. 16. Harleian Society, i. 17; xviii. 89-98; xxviii. 174. Jacob's Peerage, i. 432. Bibliotheca Topographica Britannica, ix. Part 4, 117. History of the College of Bonhommes, at Ashridge, Co. Bucks, (London, 1823, folio) 93. Surtees Society, xxxvi. 71. Burke's Commoners, iii. 36, Landed Gentry, 2, 3. Topographer (London, 1789-91, 8vo.) i. 561, 476; ii. 136. Burke's Royal Families, (London, 1851, 8vo.) ii. 30. Foster's Lancashire Pedigrees. Chetham Society, lxxxiii. 8; lxxxiv. 102. Shaw's Staffordshire, i. 93. Bridges' Northamptonshire, by Rev. Peter Whalley, i. 149. Butterworth's Account of the Town, etc., of Oldham, 126. Clutterbuck's Hertford, i. 391. Baker's Northampton, i. 564, 621. Baines' History of the Co. of Lancaster, ii. 563; iii. 143; Croston's edn., ii. 347; iii. 287, 304. Chauncy's Hertfordshire, 553. Ormerod's Cheshire, i. 445; ii. 222, 301, 628, 691. Edmondson's Baronagium Genealogicum, i. 74; vi. 115. Brydges' Collins' Peerage, iii. 170; v. 528. Wotton's English Baronetage, i. 271. The Gresley's of Drakelowe, by F. Madan, 252.

EGERTON-WARBURTON. Burke's Commoners, ii. 1, Landed Gentry, 2, 3, 4, 5, 6, 7, 8. Ormerod's Cheshire, ii. 144. Burke's Colonial Gentry, ii. 617.

EGGERDON. Hutchins' Dorset, ii, 175.

EGGERDS. Harleian Society, xx. 37.

EGGERTON. The Genealogist, New Series, xiii. 98.

EGGINTON. Foster's Yorkshire Pedigrees.

EGIOKE. Harleian Society, xxvii. 52.
EGLESFIELD. Foster's Visitations of Yorkshire, 155, 514. Harleian
Society, xiii. 191 ; xvi. 107.
EGLESTON. Surtees' Durham, ii. 367. Harleian Society, xv. 251.
EGLINGTON, or EGLINTOUN. Burke's Royal Families, (London, 1851,
8vo.) i. 39. Paterson's History of the Co. of Ayr, ii. 228. Geo.
Robertson's Account of Families in Ayrshire, i. 342. See MONT-
GOMERY.
EGLIONBY. Visitation of Warwickshire, 1619, published with War-
wickshire Antiquarian Magazine, 70.
EGREMONT (Earl of). Collinson's Somerset, ii. 234 ; iii. 490.
EINION. Caermarthenshire Pedigrees, 67.
EKERSLEY. Burke's Landed Gentry, 5.
EKINS. Hodgson's Northumberland, II., ii. 527. Bridges' North-
amptonshire, by Rev. Peter Whalley, i. 469. Hutchins' Dorset,
i. 122. Baker's Northampton, i. 73. Metcalfe's Visitations of
Northamptonshire, 178.
ELAND. Surtees Society, xli. 69. Foster's Visitations of Yorkshire,
514, 603-606. Whitaker's Loidis and Elmete, 401. Baines'
History of the Co. of Lancaster, ii. 620 ; Croston's edn., iii. 3.
The Genealogist, ii. 217 ; New Series, ix. 11. John Watson's
History of Halifax, 166. Harleian Society, xvi. 107, 108.
Records of Batley, by M. Sheard, 272. Lincolnshire Notes and
Queries, ii. 117, 153.
ELCOCKE. Burke's Commoners, iii. 49. Whitaker's History of Rich-
mondshire, ii. 122. Ormerod's Cheshire, iii. 353. Harleian
Society. xl. 1261.
ELD. Burke's Landed Gentry, 2 supp., 3, 4, 5, 6, 7, 8. Burke's
Royal Families, (London, 1851, 8vo.) i. 56. Visitation of Staf-
fordshire, 1663-4. by Sir T. Phillipps, 4. Visitations of Stafford-
shire, 1614 and 1663-4, William Salt Society, 122.
ELDER. Burke's Colonial Gentry, ii. 585.
ELDRED. Gentleman's Magazine, 1837, i. 487. Morant's Essex, ii.
193. Gage's History of Thingoe Hundred, Suffolk, 106. Page's
History of Suffolk, 679. Harleian Society, xiii. 391 ; xv. 251.
Burke's Extinct Baronetcies. Bysshe's Visitation of Essex, edited
by J. J. Howard, 31.
ELDREDGE. New England Register, li. 46.
ELERS. Burke's Commoners, iv. 418, Landed Gentry, 2, 3, 4, 5.
Burke's Royal Families, (London, 1851, 8vo.) ii. 187. Miscellanea
Genealogica et Heraldica, New Series, iii. 246.
ELERS-NAPIER. Burke's Landed Gentry, 2 add.
ELFECK. Berry's Sussex Genealogies, 320, 372.
ELFORD, or ELFORDE. Harleian Society, vi. 105 ; ix. 66. An His-
torical Survey of Cornwall, by C. S. Gilbert, ii. 100. Betham's
Baronetage, iv. 415 ; v. app. 13. Burke's Extinct Baronetcies,
Add. The Visitations of Cornwall, edited by J. L. Vivian, 146.
The Visitations of Devon, by J. L. Vivian, 329.
ELIOT, ELIOTT, ELLIOT, or ELLIOTT. The Border Elliots and the
Family of Minto, by G. F. S. Elliot. 1892, 4to. Miscellanea
18—2

Genealogica et Heraldica, ii. 44. Berry's Surrey Genealogies, 23. Dwnn's Visitations of Wales, i. 122, 204. Tuckett's Devonshire Pedigrees, 192. Visitation of Wiltshire, 1677, printed by Sir T. Phillipps, (Middle Hill, 1854, fol.). Burke's Landed Gentry, (of Binfield,) 2, 3, 4, 5; (of Wolfelee,) 7, 8; (of Busbridge,) 2, 3, 4; (of Harwood,) 6, 7, 8. Harleian Society, vi. 105; ix. 66; xiii. 48, 191; xv. 252; xliii. 23. Burke's Royal Descents and Pedigrees of Founders' Kin, 31. Pembrokeshire Pedigrees, 150. Hoare's Wiltshire, V. i. 78. Manning and Bray's Surrey, i. 619. History of the Carnegies, by Willm. Fraser, (Edinburgh, 1867, 4to.) ii. 460. A Complete Parochial History of the County of Cornwall, ii. 62. Border Memories, by. W. R. Carre, 132. An Historical Survey of Cornwall, by C. S. Gilbert, i. 449. Hawick and its old Memories, by James Wilson, 185. Notes and Queries, 2 S. xi. 260. Edmondson's Baronagium Genealogicum, vi. 111. Brydges' Collins' Peerage, viii. 3, 119, 559. Foster's Collectanea Genealogica, (MP's Scotland,) 121. The Visitations of Cornwall, edited by J. L. Vivian, 147. The Visitations of Devon, by J. L. Vivian, 332, 334. Hasted's Kent, (Hund. of Blackheath, by H. H. Drake,) 138. Stodart's Scottish Arms, ii. 274.ˇ New England Register, viii. 45; x. 355; xxiii. 336; xxviii. 143; xxxix. 365; xliv. 112. Oliver's History of Antigua, i. 240. A chapter in Mediocrity, by W. J. Stavert, 15. See ELYOT, STUART, SCOTT-ELLIOTT.

ELIOTH. Foster's Visitations of Yorkshire, 132.

ELIS. Dwnn's Visitations of Wales, ii. 94. See ELLIS.

ELIZABETH (Queen), (Seize Quartiers of). Gentleman's Magazine, 1849, i. 482.

ELKINGTON. Harleian Society, ii. 153; xv. 253. Nichols' History of the County of Leicester, iv. 342.

ELLACOT, or ELLACOTT. Tuckett's Devonshire Pedigrees, 36. Harleian Society, vi. 106. Westcote's Devonshire, edited by G. Oliver and P. Jones, 479. The Visitations of Devon, by J. L. Vivian, 333.

ELLERCAR, or ELLERKER. J. E. Jackson's History of St. George's Church at Doncaster, 77. Surtees Society, xxxvi. 295; xli. 71. Foster's Visitations of Yorkshire, 110, 136, 515. George Oliver's History of Beverley, 508. Poulson's Holderness, i. 394. Harleian Society, xvi. 109.

ELLERTON. Burke's Royal Descents and Pedigrees of Founders' Kin, 75.

ELLERY. Herald and Genealogist, v. 37. New England Register, xliii. 313. Pedigree of Ellery, by Harrison Ellery. Boston, U.S.A., 1881, large sheet.

ELLESDON. Hutchins' Dorset, ii. 78.

ELLESFELD. The Genealogist, New Series, xv. 24.

ELLETSON. Foster's Lancashire Pedigrees. Burke's Landed Gentry, 8.

ELLICE. Burke's Landed Gentry, 5, 6, 7, 8.

ELLICOTT. Foster's account of families descended from Francis Fox, 22.

ELLINGTHORPE. Abram's History of Blackburn, 623.

ELLIS, or ELLYS. Notices of the Ellises of France and England, by W. S. Ellis, Esq. London, 1857, etc., 8vo. Claim of C. A. Ellis to be Lord Howard of Walden, Sess. Papers, 3 of 1806-7. Topographer and Genealogist, iii. 270-297. Berry's Kent Genealogies, 64. Thoresby Society, ii. 57. Berry's Sussex Genealogies, 342. Surtees Society, xxxvi. 373. W. Paver's Pedigrees of Families of the City of York, 13. Burke's Commoners, (of Kiddall,) iii. 554; (of Ponsbourne,) Landed Gentry, 4, 5; (of Wyddial Hall,) 3, 4, 5, 6, 7, 8; (of Glasfryn,) 2, 3, 4, 5, 6, 7, 8; (of Sea Park,) 6, 7, 8; (of Bodychan,) 3 p. 846; (of Leicester,) 8; (of Anstey Grange,) 8. History of Carrickfergus, by Saml. M'Skimin, 2nd edn., 320. Foster's Visitations of Yorkshire, 135, 328, 515. Harleian Society, viii. 487; xv. 254; xxxviii. 774, 798, 826. A Royal Descent, by T. E. Sharpe, (London, 1875, 4to.) 64. The Genealogist, iv. 20; New Series, xiv. 105. The Ellis Correspondence, by G. A. Ellis, i. ix-xxiii. Brydges' Collins' Peerage, vi. 752. Wotton's English Baronetage, iii. 89. Burke's Extinct Baronetcies. History of Powys Fadog, by J. Y. W. Lloyd, iii. 68, 125, 335; v. 396, 413; vi. 193. Cambrian Journal, vol. for 1860, 247. History of Chislehurst, by Webb, Miller, and Beckwith, 265. See ELIS, FITZ-ELLIS.

ELLIS-JERVOISE. Burke's Landed Gentry, 2 add.

ELLIS-NANNEY. Burke's Landed Gentry, 8.

ELLIS-VINER. Burke's Landed Gentry, 2, 3, 4, 5, 6, 7.

ELLISON. Burke's Commoners, (of Hebburn,) i. 77, Landed Gentry, 2, 3, 4, 6, 7, 8; (of Sudbrooke Holme,) Landed Gentry, 4, 5; (of Boultham,) 4, 5, 6, 7, 8; Hodgson's Northumberland, III. ii. 346. Hunter's Deanery of Doncaster, i. 179. Surtees' Durham, ii. 78, 79. Harleian Society, xvi. 110; xxxvii. 196; xxxviii. 576. Foster's Visitations of Northumberland, 42. See CARR-ELLISON.

ELLISON-MACARTNEY. Burke's Landed Gentry, 3, 4, 5, 6, 7, 8.

ELLISTON. Camden Society, New Series, iv. 259. Morant's Essex, ii. 287, 306. Herald and Genealogist, v. 401. Wright's Essex, i. 537. Harleian Society, xiii. 392. Bysshe's Visitation of Essex, edited by J. J. Howard, 31.

ELLNER. Harleian Society, xv. 254.

ELLYATT. Oliver's History of Antigua, i. 237.

ELMEDEN. Surtees' Durham, iii. 55.

ELMER. The Genealogist, vi. 149. Harleian Society, xxii. 141.

ELMERUGGE. Collectanea Topographica et Genealogica, v. 169. Oxford Historical Society, xxiv. 23.

ELMES. Harleian Society, v. 221. Lipscombe's History of the County of Buckingham, i. 394. Bridges' Northamptonshire, by Rev. Peter Whalley, ii. 242. Metcalfe's Visitations of Northamptonshire, 18. Oliver's History of Antigua, i. 243.

ELMHIRST, or ELMHURST. Surtees Society, xxxvi. 199. Burke's Landed Gentry, (of Elmhurst,) 2 supp., 3, 4, 5, 6, 7, 8; (of West Ashby,) 2 supp., 3, 4, 5, 6, 8. Foster's Yorkshire Pedigrees.

Hunter's Deanery of Doncaster, ii. 291. History of Worsborough, by Joseph Wilkinson, 126.

ELMSALL. Harleian Society, xxxix. 904.

ELMY. Metcalfe's Visitations of Suffolk, 135. Muskett's Suffolk Manorial Families, i. 196.

ELPHICK. Sussex Archæological Collections, vii. 131.

ELPHINSTONE, or ELPHINGSTON. A Genealogical tree of the Noble House of Elphinstone, by J. Brown, 1808, fol. sheet. Kent's British Banner Displayed, 360. Burke's Commoners, ii. 369. Nisbet's Heraldry, ii. app. *Ragman's Roll*, 22. Inverurie and the Earldom of the Garioch, by John Davidson, 470. Balmerino and its Abbey, by James Campbell, 283, 391. The Parish of Cramond, by J. P. Wood, 266. Wood's Douglas's Peerage of Scotland, i. 182, 362, 536. Brydges' Collins' Peerage, ix. 168. Burke's Extinct Baronetcies, 621.

ELRINGTON, or ELRYNGTON. Morant's Essex, ii. 566. Excerpta Cantiana, by Rev. T. Streatfield, 5. Harleian Society, xiii. 49, 392. The Genealogist, New Series, ii. 300. Bysshe's Visitation of Essex, edited by J. J. Howard, 32.

ELSFIELD. Dugdale's Warwickshire, 922. The Forest and Chase of Sutton Coldfield, (London, 1860, 8vo.) app.

ELSLEY. Burke's Landed Gentry, 5, 6, 7, 8.

ELSON. Berry's Sussex Genealogies, 40. Dallaway's Sussex, i. 68. Castles, Mansions, and Manors of Western Sussex, by D. G. C. Elwes and C. J. Robinson, 161.

ELSTOB, or ELSTOBBE. Visitation of Durham, 1615, (Sunderland, 1820, fol.) 101. Visitation of Durham, 1575, (Newcastle, 1820, fol.) 27. Hutchinson's History of Durham, iii. 71. Surtees' Durham, iii. 47. Foster's Visitations of Durham, 113.

ELSTON. Doncaster Charities, by Charles Jackson, 86.

ELTOFT. Foster's Visitations of Yorkshire, 301. Whitaker's Deanery of Craven, 3rd edn., 220.

ELTON. Pedigree of Elton of Ledbury, [T. P.] folio page. Burke's Landed Gentry, 2 supp., 6, 7, 8. Ormerod's Cheshire, ii. 28. Harleian Society, xv. 255 ; xliii. 212. Wotton's English Baronetage, iv. 187. Betham's Baronetage, iii. 189. Weaver's Visitation of Herefordshire, 26. Miscellanea Genealogica et Heraldica, 2nd Series, i. 182. A History of Banking in Bristol, by C. H. Cave, 232. *See* MAYO.

ELTONHEAD. Chetham Society, lxxxi. 119 ; lxxxii. 115 ; lxxxiv. 103. Harleian Society, xiii. 393.

ELVIN. Burke's Landed Gentry, 4. *See* ELWIN.

ELWES, or ELWIS. Pedigree of the Family of Elwes, by J. E. Cussans. London, 1881, fol. Genealogical notices relating to the Elwes Family. London, 1867, 8vo. Cussan's History of Hertfordshire, Parts iii. and iv. 110. Morant's Essex, ii. 340. Burke's Commoners, (of Great Billing,) ii. 463, Landed Gentry, 2, 3, 4, 5, 6 and supp., 7, 8 ; (of Stoke College,) ii. 465, Landed Gentry, 2, 3, 4, 5, 6, 7, 8 ; (of Colesbourne,) 5, 6, 8 ; (of Congham,) 6, 7, 8. Harleian Society, iv. 29 ; viii. 199 ; xv. 256. Burke's

Authorized Arms, 38. Clutterbuck's Hertford, iii. 465. Miscellanea Genealogica et Heraldica, i. 68-70 ; New Series, iv. 133. The Genealogist, i. 149 ; v. 254. Wright's Essex, i. 593. Chauncy's Hertfordshire, 118. Page's History of Suffolk, 895. Wotton's English Baronetage, iii. 55. Notes and Queries, 5 S. iv. 520 ; 6 S. ix. 435. Burke's Extinct Baronetcies. Phillimore's London and Middlesex Note-Book, 107.

ELWICK. Foster's Visitations of Yorkshire, 133, 618.

ELWILL. Burke's Extinct Baronetcies. Harleian Society, viii. 454. Manning and Bray's Surrey, iii. 252. Wotton's English Baronetage, iv. 131. Notes and Queries, 5 S. ix. 15.

ELWIN, or ELWYN. Berry's Kent Genealogies, 300. *See* ELVIN.

ELWON. Burke's Landed Gentry, 4, 5, 8.

ELWOOD. Burke's Landed Gentry, (of Strand Hill,) 2, 3, 4, 5 ; (of Clayton Priory,) 2, 3, 4. Brydges' Collins' Peerage, ix. 234.

ELY. New England Register, xxxv. 236.

ELYOT. Berry's Surrey Genealogies, 24. Surrey Archæological Collections. vi. *See* ELIOT.

ELYSTAN GLODRYDD. Poetical Works of Lewis Glyn Cothi, (Oxford, 1837,) 170.

EMAN. Harleian Society, xv. 257. The Genealogist, v. 254.

EMERIS. Burke's Landed Gentry, 4, 5, 6, 7, 8. Burke's Visitation of Seats and Arms, ii. 8. Howard's Visitation of England and Wales, i. 88 ; Notes, ii. 96.

EMERSON. The English Emersons, by P. H. Emerson. London, 1898, 4to. Burke's Landed Gentry, 2 supp., 3, 4, 6, 7, 8.

EMERSON-TENNENT. Burke's Commoners, ii. 21, Landed Gentry, 2, 3, 4.

EMERTON. Burke's Landed Gentry, 8.

EMERY. Burke's Landed Gentry, 2 supp., 3, 4, 5. Burke's Heraldic Illustrations, 108. Visitation of Derbyshire, 1663-4, (Middle Hill, 1854, fol.) 3. Harleian Society, xiii. 393. New England Register, xxiii. 414.

EMILDON. Surtees' Durham, i. 243.

EMILY, or EMYLEY. Berry's Surrey Genealogies, 89. Manning and Bray's Surrey, i. 143. Baker's Northampton, i. 629. Metcalfe's Visitations of Northamptonshire, 86.

EMMETT. Notes and Queries, 2 S. iii. 31, 97, 248 ; iv. 233 ; v. 366.

EMMOT. Whitaker's History of Whalley, ii. 257.

EMMOTT-GREEN. Burke's Landed Gentry, 2 supp., 3, 4, 6, 7, 8.

EMPSON, or EMSON. Surtees Society, xxxvi. 19. Baker's Northampton, ii. 141. Burke's Landed Gentry, 6, 7, 8. F. G. Lee's History of Thame, 322. *See* LISTER.

ENDERBY. Massingberd's History of Ormsby, 207.

ENDESORE. Erdeswicke's Survey of Staffordshire, 444. Visitation of Staffordshire, (Willm. Salt Soc.) 68.

ENDICOTT. New England Register, i. 335.

ENFIELD. Harleian Society, xiii. 23, 227.

ENGAINE. Collinson's Somerset, iii. 615. Morant's Essex, i. 106 ; ii. 121, 217. Bridges' Northamptonshire, by Rev. Peter Whalley,

ii. 275. Clutterbuck's Hertford, iii. 178. Baker's Northampton, i. 9. Harleian Society, xiv. 568. Banks' Baronies in Fee, i. 199. Banks' Dormant and Extinct Baronage, i. 292. The Genealogist, xii. 29. Nicolson and Burn's Westmorland and Cumberland, i. 216.

ENGHAM. Berry's Kent Genealogies, 141. Harleian Society, xl. 1298 ; xlii. 50.

ENGLAND. Harleian Society, viii. 266. Dawson Turner's Sepulchral Reminiscences of Great Yarmouth, 111.

ENGLEFIELD. Burke's Commoners, ii. 646. Visitation of Warwickshire, 1619, published with Warwickshire Antiquarian Magazine, 195. Harleian Society, xii. 123. Wotton's English Baronetage, i. 254. Betham's Baronetage, i. 145. The Genealogist, v. 254. .Burke's Extinct Baronetcies.

ENGLER. Surrey Archæological Collections, xi. Harleian Society, xliii. 114.

ENGLEYS. Hoare's Wiltshire, V. ii. 31.

ENGLISH, or ENGLYSHE. Harleian Society, vi. 106 ; xv. 258. Visitatio Comitatus Wiltoniæ, 1623, printed by Sir T. Phillipps. Hoare's Wiltshire, V. ii. 31. Visitation of Wiltshire, edited by G. W. Marshall, 84. Visitation of Gloucester, edited by T. F. Fenwick and W. C. Metcalfe, 60. Weaver's Visitations of Somerset, 22. The Visitations of Devon, by J. L. Vivian, 335. Nicolson and Burn's Westmorland and Cumberland, i. 427, 511.

ENNIS. Burke's Landed Gentry, 3, 4.

ENSIGN, or ENSYNGE. Visitation of Norfolk, published by Norfolk Archæological Society, i. 40. Harleian Society, xxxii. 116.

ENSOR. Herald and Genealogist, ii. 295, 301. Burke's Landed Gentry, 2, 3, 4, 5, 6, 7, 8. Burke's Patrician, v. 76.

ENT. Harleian Society, viii. 190.

ENTWHISTLE, or ENTWISLE. Burke's Commoners, iv. 41, Landed Gentry, 2, 3, 4, 5, 6, 7, 8. Foster's Lancashire Pedigrees. Chetham Society, lxxxiv. 104. Baines' History of the Co. of Lancaster, iii. 95 ; Croston's edn., iii. 60. History of Ribchester, by T. C. Smith and J. Shortt, 253. Fishwick's History of Rochdale, 408. Oliver's History of Antigua, i. 245.

ENYON. Baker's Northampton, i. 153. Burke's Extinct Baronetcies.

ENYS. Burke's Commoners, iv. 373, Landed Gentry, 2, 3, 4, 5, 6, 7, 8. Harleian Society, ix. 67. An Historical Survey of Cornwall, by C. S. Gilbert, ii. 98. The Visitations of Cornwall, edited by J. L. Vivian, 151.

EOGHAN. A History of the Clan Eoghan, by R. F. Cronnelly. Dublin, 1864, 8vo. Journal of the Historical and Archæological Association of Ireland, 4th Series, iv. 408.

EPPES. Gloucestershire Notes and Queries, iv. 127.

EPPLYNGDEN. Surtees' Durham, i. 217.

ERCALL. William Salt Society, New Series, ii. 154.

ERDDIG. History of Powys Fadog, by J. Y. W. Lloyd, iii. 62.

ERDESWICK. Harleian Society, i. 55. Miscellanea Genealogica et

Heraldica, New Series, iii. 4. Visitations of Staffordshire, 1614 and 1663-4, William Salt Society, 123.

ERDINGTON. Gentleman's Magazine, lxv. 990. Burton's Description of Leicestershire, 30. Nichols' History of the County of Leicester, iii. 67. Dugdale's Warwickshire, 889. Banks' Baronies in Fee, i. 200. Banks' Dormant and Extinct Baronage, i. 295. Genealogist, New Series, xii. 106.

ERESBY. Memoir of P. Bertie, by C. H. Parry, (1838, 8vo.) at end. *See* WILLOUGHBY.

ERGADIA. Manx Society, x. app. B.

ERISEY. Harleian Society, ix. 67. An Historical Survey of Cornwall, by C. S. Gilbert, ii. 99. The Visitations of Cornwall, edited by J. L. Vivian, 154.

ERLE. Blomefield's Norfolk, vi. 245. Burke's Landed Gentry, 4, 5, 6. Hutchins' Dorset, iii. 468. Banks' Baronies in Fee, ii. 73. Bysshe's Visitation of Essex, edited by J. J. Howard, 32. The Genealogist, New Series, ii. 300. *See* EARLE.

ERLE-DRAX. Burke's Commoners, iv. 207, Landed Gentry, 2, 3, 4, 5, 6, 8. Burke's Heraldic Illustrations, 5. Hutchins' Dorset, iii. 502.

ERLESMAN. Hampshire Visitations, printed by Sir T. Phillipps, 25.

ERLYS. History of Powis Fadog, by J. Y. W. Lloyd, iii. 109.

ERMINE. The Genealogist, iv. 20. *See* ARMINE.

ERNELEY, ERNELY, ERNLEY, or ERNLE. Burke's Commoners, iii. 619; iv. 209. Visitation of Sussex, 1570, printed by Sir. T. Phillipps, (Middle Hill, fol.) 4. Harleian Society, viii. 199; xx. 38. Dallaway's Sussex, i. 25. Visitatio Comitatus Wiltoniæ, 1623, printed by Sir T. Phillipps. Hutchins' Dorset, iii. 543. Wiltshire Archæological Magazine, xi. 192. Castles, Mansions, and Manors of Western Sussex, by D. G. C. Elwes and C. J. Robinson, 75. Private Memoirs of John Potenger, Esq., by C. W. Bingham, *at end*. Wotton's English Baronetage, iii. 217. Visitation of Wiltshire, edited by G. W. Marshall, 74. Burke's Extinct Baronetcies. The Genealogist, New Series, xii. 26. *See* ERLE-DRAX.

ERNHAM. The Genealogist, New Series, xiv. 25.

ERNST. Burke's Landed Gentry, 8.

ERPINGHAM. Blomefield's Norfolk, vi. 412.

ERRINGTON. Visitatio Comitatus Wiltoniæ, 1623, printed by Sir T. Phillipps. Gentleman's Magazine, 1832, i. 581. Burke's Landed Gentry, (of High Warden,) 2 supp., 3, 4, 5, 6, 7, 8; (of Lexden Park,) 4, 5, 6, 7; (of Sandhoe,) 4; (of Chadwell Hall,) 8. Hodgson's Northumberland, III. ii. 413. Harleian Society, xv. 258. Hoare's Wiltshire, II. ii. 142. Surtees' Durham, iii. 209. The Genealogist, ii. 114, 216, 254; xii. 26. Visitation of Wiltshire, edited by G. W. Marshall, 55. Foster's Visitations of Northumberland, 43-46.

ERROL. Burke's Royal Descents and Pedigrees of Founders' Kin, 23.

ERSKINE. The Erskine Halcro Genealogy, by E. E. Scott. Edinburgh, 1895, 4to. New Edition. Genealogy of the Erskines of

Pittodrie, by Alexr. Sinclair. Edinburgh, *n. d.*, 8vo. Erskine of
Dun, and Erskine and Cunninghame, by Alexr. Sinclair. Edinburgh, *n. d.*, 8vo. Claim of J. F. M. Erskine, Earl of Mar, to the
title of Earl of Kellie, etc. Sess. Papers, 133 of 1831-2; 212 of
1834; 206 of 1835. The origin, increase, etc., of the Family of
Erskine of that Ilk. Large tabular pedigree printed on seven
sheets of paper, *circa* 1896. Burke's Landed Gentry, (of Pittodrie,)
5, 6, 7, 8; (of Cardross,) 6, 7, 8; (of Dun,) 8; (of Kirk-
buddo,) 7, 8; (of Balhall,) 7. Inverurie and the Earldom of
the Garioch, by John Davidson, 473. Walter Wood's East Neuk
of Fife, 291, 296. Miscellany of the Spalding Ciub, iv. lxix.
Peter Chalmers' Account of Dunfermline, ii. folding table No. 2,
at end. Wood's Douglas's Peerage of Scotland, i. 270; ii. 16, 206.
The Theology of Consolation, by D. C. A. Agnew, 263. Brydges'
Collins' Peerage, v. 427; ix. 251. Betham's Baronetage, iv. 209.
Foster's Collectanea Genealogica, (MP's Scotland,) 125. Memoir
of Chancellor Seton, by Geo. Seton, App. II. Burke's Family
Records, 237. The Genealogist, New Series, iii. 3; ix. 6.
Northern Notes and Queries, i. 181; iii. 27; iv. 116, 183; vi.
50, 62. Burke's Colonial Gentry, i. 267. The Genealogical
Magazine, i. 533. *See* MAR.

ESCHALES. Harleian Society, xii. 75.

ESCOT. Harleian Society, xvi. 111. *See* ESTCOTT.

ESDAILE. Burke's Commoners, iii. 604, Landed Gentry, 2, 3, 4, 5,
6, 7, 8. Miscellanea Genealogica et Heraldica, 2nd Series, i. 211.
Harleian Society, xxxix. 1123.

ESEBY. Plantagenet-Harrison's History of Yorkshire, i. 58. *See*
ESSEBY.

ESHELBY. Howard's Visitation of England and Wales, i. 225.
The Genealogist, New Series, x. 20, 116, 146. *See* EXELBY.

ESPEC. Nichols' History of the County of Leicester, ii. 27.
Harvey's Hundred of Willey, 2.

ESPEUT. Burke's Colonial Gentry, ii. 528.

ESPINASSE. Berry's Kent Genealogies, 333.

ESSE, or ESSHE. Visitation of Somerset, printed by Sir T. Phillipps,
5. Harleian Society, v. 199. Westcote's Devonshire, edited by
G. Oliver and P. Jones, 633. A Complete Parochial History of
the County of Cornwall, iii. 123. Visitation of Devon, edited by
F. T. Colby, 92. The Visitations of Devon, edited by J. L.
Vivian, 25. Weaver's Visitations of Somerset, 2. *See* ASH.

ESSEBY. Nichols' History of the County of Leicester, iv. 15. Baker's
Northampton, i. 277. *See* DE ESSEBY, ESEBY.

ESSEX (Earls of). Collinson's Somerset, ii. 79, 156. Funeral
Sermon preached at Carmarthen, at Burial of Walter, Earl of
Essex. (London, 1577, 4to.) 1. Morant's Essex, i. 203; ii. 431.
Appendix to case of Sir J. S. Sidney, claiming to be Lord Lisle.
Archæologia, xxi. 197. Baker's Northampton, i. 123, 544. *See*
DEVEREUX.

ESSEX. Harleian Society, i. 81. Burke's Royal Families, (London,
1851, 8vo.) i. 172. Topographical Collections of John Aubrey,

edited by J. E. Jackson, 239. Wiltshire Archæological Magazine, iv. 76. Banks' Dormant and Extinct Baronage, i. 72 ; iii. 268. Burke's Extinct Baronetcies. The Genealogist, New Series, i. 6.

ESSINGTON. Harleian Society, xv. 259. Visitation of Gloucester, edited by T. F. Fenwick and W. C. Metcalfe, 61.

ESTCOTT. Harleian Society, ix. 69. The Visitations of Cornwall, edited by J. L. Vivian, 158. *See* ESCOT.

ESTCOURT. Rudder's Gloucestershire, 654. History of Tetbury, Co. Gloucester, by A. T. Lee, 196-208. Burke's Commoners, iv. 155, Landed Gentry, 2, 3, 4, 5, 6, 7, 8. Harleian Society, viii. 127 ; xv. 260 ; xxi. 55. Burke's Extinct Baronetcies. Visitation of Gloucester, edited by T. F. Fenwick and W. C. Metcalfe, 61. A History of Devizes, (1859, 8vo.,) 554.

ESTDAY. Berry's Kent Genealogies, 145. Harleian Society, xlii. 79.

ESTE. Plantagenet-Harrison's History of Yorkshire, i. xxv. *See* D'ESTE.

ESTENEYE. The Genealogist, New Series, xiv. 97.

ESTON. Westcote's Devonshire, edited by G. Oliver and P. Jones, 565. Harleian Society, xix. 24. *See* EASTON.

ESTOUTEVILLE. Foster's Visitations of Yorkshire, 516. *See* STUTE-VILL.

ESTRIDGE. Burke's Colonial Gentry, ii. 560.

ESTSAX. Account of the Parish of Lea with Lea Wood, (London, 1841, 8vo.) 21.

ESTURMY. Hoare's Wiltshire, I. i. 117.

ESTWICK, or ESTWICKE. Miscellanea Genealogica et Heraldica, New Series, i. 195. Nichols' History of the County of Leicester, iv. 888.

ETHELSTON. Burke's Landed Gentry, 3, 4, 5, 6, 7, 8. Chetham Society, lxxxii. 56.

ETHEREGE, or ETHEREDGE. Gentleman's Magazine, 1835, ii. 581. Miscellanea Genealogica et Heraldica, New Series, i. 197, 211, 232, 369.

ETHERINGTON. Foster's Visitations of Yorkshire, 516. Betham's Baronetage, iv. 11. Burke's Extinct Baronetcies.

ETON. Dwnn's Visitations of Wales, ii. 360, 362. Dugdale's Warwickshire, 539. Ormerod's Cheshire, ii. 841 ; iii. 793. Harleian Society, xiii. 50, 192 ; xviii. 242. Miscellanea Genealogica et Heraldica, 2nd Series, ii. 54. *See* EATON.

ETTERICK, ETERICKE, ETTORICK, or ETTRICK. Berry's Hampshire Genealogies, 282. Hutchins' Dorset, iii. 245. Burke's Commoners, iii. 15, Landed Gentry, 2, 3, 4, 5, 6. Burke's Royal Families, (London, 1851, 8vo.) i. 97. Surtees' Durham, i. 238, 245. Harleian Society, xx. 39.

ETTY. Foster's Yorkshire Pedigrees. Notes and Queries, 1 S. iii. 496 ; iv. 27.

EU. Morant's Essex, ii. 431. Sussex Archæological Collections, x. 67. *See* EWE.

EURE. The direct pedigree of Eure of Witton. London, 1880, 8vo. Kent's British Banner Displayed, 777. Foster's Visitations of Yorkshire, 204, 607-617. Harleian Society, v. 308 ; xvi. 111.

Graves' History of Cleveland, 234. Hodgson's Northumberland, I. ii. 372. Hutchinson's History of Durham, iii. 304. Banks' Dormant and Extinct Baronage, iii. 285. Foster's Visitations of Durham, 115. Yorkshire Genealogist, i. 67, 109. Northern Genealogist, iv. 6. *See* EWER, EVER.

EUSTACE. Burke's Landed Gentry, (of Castlemore,) 2, 3, 4, 5, 6, 7, 8 ; (of Newstown,) 3, 4, 5, 6, 7, 8 ; (of Baltinglass,) 2, 3, 4, 5, 6, 7, 8. Munford's Analysis of Domesday Book of Co. Norfolk, 14. John D'Alton's History of Co. Dublin, 745. Burke's Extinct Baronetcies, 604. The Irish Builder, xxviii. 22. Notes and Queries, 8 S. x. 131.

EUSTIS. New England Register, xxxi. 204.

EVAN. Cardiganshire Pedigree, 111.

EVAN AP OWEN. Dwnn's Visitations of Wales, i. 294.

EVAN AP PHILIP. Dwnn's Visitations of Wales, i. 316.

EVAN, THOMAS. Dwnn's Visitations of Wales, i. 309.

EVANCE. Harleian Society, viii. 435.

EVANS. Evans. By M. C. Jones, F.S.A. Newcastle - on - Tyne, 1865, 8vo. Herald and Genealogist, iii. 368. Gentleman's Magazine, 1826, ii. 395. Glover's History of Derbyshire, ii. 19, (18). Dwnn's Visitations of Wales, i. 306, 327 ; ii. 322. Glamorganshire Pedigrees, edited by Sir T. Phillipps, 11, 20, 32. Burke's Commoners, iv. 384 ; (of Hill Court,) Commoners, ii. 242, Landed Gentry, 2, 5, 6 ; (of Ash Hill,) Commoners, i. 593, Landed Gentry, 2, 3, 4, 5, 6, 7, 8 ; (of Portrane,) Commoners, ii. 15, Landed Gentry, 2, 3, 4, 5 ; (of Tuddenham,) Landed Gentry, 2 supp., 3, 4, 5, 6, 7, 8 ; (of Eyton,) 2, 3, 4, 5, 6, 7, 8 ; (of Allestree,) 2, 3, 4, 5, 6, 7, 8 ; (of Lough Park,) 3, 4, 5, 6 ; (of Gortmerron House,) 2 add., 3, 4, 5, 6, 7, 8 ; (of Carker,) 4, 5, 6, 7. 8 ; (of Hereford and Moreton Court,) 3, 4, 5, 6, 7, 8 ; (of Farm Hill,) 3, 4 ; (of Rockfield,) 7, 8 ; (of Llwynarthan,) 7, 8 ; (of Nash Mills,) 8 ; (of Henblas,) 8 ; (of Darley Abbey,) 6, 7, 8 ; (of Forde Abbey,) 6, 7, 8 ; (of Haydock Grange,) 6, 7, 8 ; (of Whitbourne,) 6, 7, 8 ; of Knockaderry,) 5, 6, 7, 8 ; (of Hatley Park,) 6, 7, 8 ; (of Glascoed,) 6 supp., 7, 8. A Royal Descent, by T. E. Sharpe, (London, 1875, 4to.) 45. Burke's Visitations of Seats and Arms, 2nd Series, i. 62. Burke's Heraldic Illustrations, 3, 51, 87. Burke's Royal Descents and Pedigrees of Founders' Kin, 114 ; *Founders' Kin*, 21. Cardiganshire Pedigrees, 104, 105. Meyrick's History of the Co. of Cardigan, 208, 282. T. Nicholas' County Families of Wales, 193, 195, 353, 774. Collections by the Powysland Club, iv. 146, 147 ; v. 268. An eccho to the Voice from Heaven, by Arise Evans, (London, 1652, 12mo.) 1. Historical Notices of Sir M. Cradock, Kt., by J. M. Traherne, 4. Harleian Society, xv. 260 ; xxi. 57 ; xxviii. 175-178 ; xxxvii. 105, 142. Archdall's Lodge's Peerage, vii. 39. Duncombe's Hereford, (J. H. Cooke) iii. 204. Burke's Extinct Baronetcies, 604. Carthew's Hundred of Launditch, Part iii. 403. History of Powys Fadog, by J. Y. W. Lloyd, v. 232, 243 ; vi. 23, 344. Companion to the Wye Tour, by T. D. Fosbroke, 156. Pedigree of the Evans

Family, by P. F. S. Evans. Clifton, 1875, folding sheet. Archæ-
ological Sketches of Ross, by T. D. Fosbroke, 156. Genealogies
of Morgan and Glamorgan, by G. T. Clark, 82, 184, 306.
Minet's Account of the Family of Minet, 208. Cambrian Journal,
vol. for 1864, 108. Howard's Visitation of England and Wales,
iv, 89, 95. Ontarian Families, by E. M. Chadwick, ii. 75. *See*
DAVIES-EVANS.
EVANSON. Oliver's History of Antigua, i. 245.
EVATT. Shirley's History of the County of Monaghan, 232.
EVE. Hasted's Kent, ii. 738.
EVEAS. Hasted's Kent, ii. 609.
EVELEIGH, or EVELEGH. Westcote's Devonshire, edited by G. Oliver
and P. Jones, 563. Visitation of Devon, edited by F. T. Colby,
93. The Savages of Ards, 382, 383. The Visitations of Devon,
by J. L. Vivian, 336.
EVELYN. Memoirs and Diary of J. Evelyn, by W. Bray, i., at begin-
ning ; in new edn., edited by H. B. Wheatley, 1879, i. 96.
Hasted's Kent, i. 5. Berry's Surrey Genealogies, 74. Burke's
Landed Gentry, 2 supp., 3, 4, 5, 6, 7, 8. Brayley's History of
Surrey, v. 25. Hoare's Wiltshire, II. ii. 7 ; V. i. 22. Manning
and Bray's Surrey, ii. 150, 329 ; iii. 14 ; cxliv. Surrey Archæo-
logical Collections, v. Aubrey's Antiquities of Surrey, iv. 128.
The Evelyns in America, by G. D. Scull, (2nd edn., 1881,) 208.
Wotton's English Baronetage, iv. 143. Betham's Baronetage, iii.
159. Burke's Extinct Baronetcies. Miscellanea Genealogica, 2nd
Series, i. 82, 100 ; iv. 121, 296, 312, 328, 337 ; v. 145, 173, 201,
209, 225. Hasted's Kent, (Hund. of Blackheath, by H. H.
Drake,) 8. The Irish Builder, xxviii. 152. N. Dews' History of
Deptford, 36. Harleian Society, xliii. 43, 79.
EVER, or EVERS. South Mimms, by F. C. Cass, 62. *See* EURE,
EVRE.
EVERARD. Savage's Hundred of Carhampton, 255. Bibliotheca
Topographica Britannica, ix. Part 4, 107. Noble's Memoirs
of the House of Cromwell, ii. 76. Morant's Essex,
ii. 87. Chronicle of the Family of De Havilland. Ashmole's Antiquities of Berkshire, iii. 292. Visitation of Norfolk,
published by Norfolk Archæological Society, i. 46. Burke's
Landed Gentry, (of Middleton,) 3, 4, 5 ; (of Randlestown,) 4
supp., 5 and supp., 6, 7, 8 ; (of Bardon Hall,) 8 ; (of Fulney
House,) 5 supp., 6. Harleian Society, ii. 12, 142, 175 ; xiii. 7,
193, 394 ; xix. 25, 103 ; xxxii. 116 ; xli. 116. Burke's Authorized Arms, 135. Nichols' History of the County of Leicester, iv.
522*. Wright's Essex, i. 195. Wotton's English Baronetage, ii.
141. Betham's Baronetage, i. 368. Metcalfe's Visitations of
Suffolk, 27, 92, 136, 189. Burke's Extinct Baronetcies, and 604.
Visitation of Staffordshire, (Willm. Salt Soc.) 69. Bysshe's
Visitation of Essex, edited by J. J. Howard, 33, 34. Chancellor's
Sepulchral Monuments of Essex, 258. Metcalfe's Visitations of
Northamptonshire, 19. The Genealogist, New Series, i. 7.
EVERDON. Shaw's Staffordshire, ii. 186.

EVERED. Burke's Landed Gentry, 5 supp., 6, 7, 8, 8 supp. *See* EVERARD.

EVERETT. Gentleman's Magazine, 1830, ii. 87. New England Register, xiii. 234 ; xiv. 215.

EVERING. Berry's Kent Genealogies, 262. Miscellanea Genealogica et Heraldica, 2nd Series, i. 213 ; ii. 33. Harleian Society, xlii. 108.

EVERINGHAM. Kent's British Banner Displayed, 431. Surtees Society, xli. 12. Foster's Visitations of Yorkshire, 38, 178. Dickinson's History of Southwell, 2nd edn., 274. Thoresby's Ducatus Leodiensis, 185. Ord's History of Cleveland, 274. Thoroton's Nottinghamshire, iii. 207. Duchetiana, by Sir G. F. Duckett, 2nd edn., 133. Harleian Society, xvi. 114. Banks' Baronies in Fee, i. 200. Banks' Dormant and Extinct Baronage, i. 296. The Genealogist, vi. 149 ; New Series, xiv. 101. W. Wheater's History of Sherburn and Cawood, 324.

EVERSFIELD. Burke's Landed Gentry, 4, 5, 6, 7, 8.

EVERTON. Visitation of Warwickshire, 1619, published with Warwickshire Antiquarian Magazine, 52. Harleian Society, xii. 301. Metcalfe's Visitations of Suffolk, 28.

EVERY. Visitation of Somerset, printed by Sir T. Phillipps, 66. History of Repton, by Robert Bigsby, 361. Harleian Society, xi. 35. Visitation of Derbyshire, 1663-4, (Middle Hill, 1854, fol.) 4. The Genealogist, iii. 59. Pilkington's View of Derbyshire, ii. 244. Wotton's English Baronetage, ii. 156. Betham's Baronetage, i. 370 ; v. app. 49.

EVESHAM. Weaver's Visitation of Herefordshire, 27-31.

EVINGTON. Visitation of Middlesex, (Salisbury, 1820, fol.) 17. The Genealogist, ii. 263. Foster's Visitation of Middlesex, 34.

EVRE. Thoresby's Ducatus Leodiensis, 17. *See* EVER.

EWART. Burke's Landed Gentry, (of Craigcleugh,) 7, 8 ; (of Northbrook,) 8.

EWBANK, or EWBANKE. Visitation of Durham, 1615, (Sunderland, 1820, fol.) 13. Burke's Landed Gentry, 2 supp., p. 146, 3, 4. Burke's Visitation of Seats and Arms, ii. 44. Surtees' Durham, iv. 141. Foster's Visitations of Durham, 117.

EWE. Banks' Dormant and Extinct Baronage, i. 74. *See* EU.

EWEN. Howard's Visitation of England and Wales, i. 127.

EWENS. Visitation of Somerset, printed by Sir T. Phillipps, 67. Harleian Society, xi. 36. Miscellanea Genealogica et Heraldica, 2nd Series, ii. 213.

EWER, or EWRE. Visitation of Oxfordshire, 1634, printed by Sir T. Phillipps, (Middle Hill, fol.) 19. Harleian Society, xix. 104 ; xxii. 51. Clutterbuck's Hertford, i. 255. *See* EURE.

EWIN. The Genealogist, iii. 243. Carthew's Hundred of Launditch, Part iii. 411.

EWING. Burke's Landed Gentry, 4, 5, 6, 7, 8. Glasgow Past and Present, (Glasgow, 1856, 8vo.) iii. 550. *See* ORR-EWING, CRUM-EWING.

EWYAS. Hoare's Wiltshire, III. ii. 54.

EXELBY. Notes and Queries, 5 S. ix. 447. *See* ESHELBY.
EXETER. Banks' Dormant and Extinct Baronage, iii. 288.
EXHERST. Berry's Kent Genealogies, 179.
EXTON. Harleian Society, viii. 303.
EYANS. Jordan's History of Enstone, 373. Oxford Historical
Society, xxiv. 348.
EYFFORD. The Visitations of Devon, by J. L. Vivian, 338.
EYLES. Morant's Essex, i. 67. Harleian Society, viii. 413. Notes and
Queries, 2 S. xii. 436, 483. Burke's Extinct Baronetcies. Wotton's
English Baronetage, iv. 155. Betham's Baronetage, iii. 179.
EYNES. Harleian Society, xxvii. 146.
EYR, or EYRE. Case of Thomas Eyre in support of his claim to be
Earl of Newburgh, 1830, fol. pp. 6, and pedigree. Claim of
Thomas Eyre to be Earl of Newborough, etc., Sess. Papers, A of
1857, Sess. 2; F of 1857-8. A short Account of Eyre of Eyre
Court, by Allen S. Hartigan, 1899, 8vo. Jewitt's Reliquary, x. 232;
xi. 238; xii. 40. Gentleman's Magazine, lxv. 41, 121, 212; 1821,
ii. 313. Rutland and Wakeman, Apellants' Case, 1798, 1. Visitation
of Cornwall, edited by Sir N. H. Nicolas, 3. Surtees Society, xxxvi.
13. Visitation of Middlesex, (Salisbury, 1820, fol.) 1. Burke's
Commoners, i. 594; (of Rampton,) Commoners, iv. 233, Landed
Gentry, 2, 3, 4, 5, 6, 7, 8; (of Wiltshire,) Commoners, iii. 290,
Landed Gentry, 2, 3, 4, 5, 6, 7 ; (of Shaw House,) Landed Gentry,
4, 5, 6, 7, 8 ; (of Welford,) 2, 3, 4, 5, 6, 7, 8, and at p. 995 ; (of
Lindley Hall,) 4, 5, 6, 7, 8 ; (of Eyre Court Castle,) 2, 3, 4, 5,
6, 7, 8 ; (of Galway,) 2, 3, 4, 5, 6 ; (of Warrens,) 5, 6, 7, 8.
Seize Quartiers of the Family of Bryan Cooke, (London, 1857,
4to.) 102. Foster's Visitations of Yorkshire, 362. Harleian
Society, ii. 193; iv. 43, 92 ; viii. 187, 426, 445; xv. 261 ; xxxvii.
402 ; xxxviii. 543-564 ; xxxix. 884. Burke's Royal Families,
(London, 1851, 8vo.) ii. 120. Dickinson's History of Southwell,
2nd edition, 177. Lipscombe's History of the County of Buckingham, iii. 211. Burke's Heraldic Illustrations, 70. Visitation
of Derbyshire, 1663-4, (Middle Hill, 1854, fol.) 3, 4. Nichols'
History of the County of Leicester, iii. 649 ; iv. 398. Visitatio
Comitatus Wiltoniæ, 1623, printed by Sir T. Phillipps. Hunter's
Deanery of Doncaster, i. 136, 288; ii. 355. Hoare's Wiltshire,
II. ii. 116 ; III. iv. 50 ; V. ii. 56, 107. Baker's Northampton,
i. 740. Thoroton's Nottinghamshire, iii. 248, 404. The Genealogist, iii. 57 ; vii. 175; xii. 27 ; xvi. 55. Case in House of Lords,
the Duchess of Rutland and others appellants, and W. Wakeman
and V. Eyre respondents, Appellants' Case, 1. The Visitations of
Cornwall, edited by J. L. Vivian, 15. Betham's Baronetage, v.
441*. Visitation of Wiltshire, edited by G. W. Marshall, 56,
76, 89. Foster's Visitation of Middlesex, 3. The Genealogist,
New Series, vii. 129. Journal of the British Archæological Association, xxx. 401. The Livingstones of Callendar, by E. B.
Livingston, 151. Notes and Queries, 8 S. xii. 461. Thomas
Smith's Historical Account of St. Mary-le-bone, 45. *See* AYRE,
NEWBOROW, DEERE.

EYRES. Burke's Landed Gentry, 6 supp., 7, 8.

EYRICK. J. H. Hill's History of Market Harborough, 123. Nichols' History of the County of Leicester, ii. 615.

EYSTON. Pedigree of the Family of Eyston of East Hendred. London, 1875, 4to. Ashmole's Antiquities of Berkshire, iii. 362. Berry's Berkshire Genealogies, 22. Burke's Commoners, i. 12, Landed Gentry, 2, 3, 4, 5, 6, 7, 8. Burke's Royal Descents and Pedigrees of Founders' Kin, 102. The Genealogist, v. 255, 256 ; New Series, i. 8.

EYTON. Dwnn's Visitations of Wales, i. 324. Burke's Landed Gentry, (of Eyton,) 2, 3, 4, 5, 6, 7, 8 ; (of Leeswood,) 2, 3, 4, 5, 6, 7, 8. Harleian Society, ii. 183 ; viii. 298; xxviii. 179. Nichols' History of the County of Leicester, iii. 968. Baker's Northampton, i. 114. The Sheriffs of Montgomeryshire, by W. V. Lloyd, 507. History of Powys Fadog, by J. Y. W. Lloyd, ii. 150-64, 175-81, 188 ; iii. 6, 324, 355, 401; v. 205. Miscellanea Genealogica et Heraldica, 2nd Series, i. 174, 187, 261. *See* DE EYTON.

EYTYN. Dwnn's Visitations of Wales, ii. 320, 357.

EYVES. Chetham Society, lxxxv. 105.

EYWOOD. *See* HEYWOOD.

FABER. Howard's Visitation of England and Wales, i. 98. Weaver's Visitation of Somerset, 23.

FABIAN. Morant's Essex, ii. 392. Harleian Society, xv. 262.

FAGAN. Burke's Commoners, iv. 626, Landed Gentry, 2, 3. John D'Alton's History of Co. Dublin, 215. The Irish Builder, xxix. 85.

FAGGE, or FAGG. Hasted's Kent, iii. 488, 492. Berry's Sussex Genealogies, 262. Dallaway's Sussex, II. ii. 151. Wotton's English Baronetage, iii. 193. Betham's Baronetage, ii. 182.

FAIR. Howard's Visitation of England and Wales, iii. 49.

FAIRBAIRN. Burke's Landed Gentry, 5, 8 supp. Foster's Yorkshire Pedigrees. Foster's Lancashire Pedigrees. Burke's Colonial Gentry, ii. 675.

FAIRBORNE. Harleian Society, viii. 268.

FAIRBROTHER. Notes and Queries, 8 S. xii. 249.

FAIRCLOUGH. Chauncy's Hertfordshire, 375. Harleian Society, xv. 263 ; xxii. 52.

FAIRER. Foster's Visitations of Cumberland and Westmorland, 43.

FAIRFAX. The Fairfax Correspondence, by R. Bell. London, 1848-9, 4 vols. 8vo. Case of the Rev. Bryan Fairfax, claiming the title of Lord Fairfax of Cameron. 1800, folio, pp. 5. History of Leeds Castle, by C. Wykeham-Martin, 207. Hasted's Kent, ii. 477. Harleian Society, i. 23 ; xvi. 117 ; xxxii. 118; xl. 1295. Foster's Visitations of Yorkshire, 39, 96. Surtees Society, xxxvi. 8, 229, 230, 232. Vallis Eboracensis, comprising the History, etc., of Easingwold, by Thos. Gill, 257. Burke's Commoners, (of Gilling Castle,) ii. 113, Landed Gentry, 2, 3, 4, 5, 6 ; (of Steeton.) Landed Gentry, 2, 3, 4, 5, 6, 7, 8. Foster's Yorkshire Pedigrees. Herald and Genealogist, vi. 385, 604 ; vii. 145, 276, 384 ; viii. 225. Drake's Eboracum, or History, etc., of York, 326, 395. Thoresby's Ducatus Leodiensis, 67. Plantagenet-Harrison's History of Yorkshire, i. 257. Wood's Douglas's Peerage of Scotland, i. 558. The Genealogist, v. 34 ; New Series, xvii. 170. Notes and Queries, 1 S. ix. 10, 156, 379, 572 ; x. 74, 200 ; 2 S. i. 17 ; 3 S. i. 431 ; ii. 310, 339, 390, 456 ; 4 S. iv. 49 ; 6 S. viii. 52 ; 7 S. ix. 321. Foster's Visitations of Cumberland and Westmorland, 44. Arcana Fairfaxiana Manuscripta, edited by George Weddell, xxv. Old Yorkshire, edited by William Smith, New Series, iii. 196. Burke's Archæological and Architectural Society's Journal, ii. 122. See FAYREFAX.

FAIRFOUL. Walter Wood's East Neuk of Fife, 289.

FAIRHOLME. Burke's Landed Gentry, 3, 4, 5, 6.

FAIRLES-HUMPHREYS. Burke's Landed Gentry, 8.

FAIRLIE. Burke's Landed Gentry, (of Holmes,) 4, 5, 6, 7, 8 ; (of Coodham,) 4, 5. Paterson's History of the Co. of Ayr, ii. 23, 73. Paterson's History of Ayr and Wigton, i. 475, 526 ; iii. 527.

FALCONER. Potter's History of Charnwood Forest, 132. Burke's Landed Gentry, 3, 4. Maclean's History of Trigg Minor, i. 650. Burke's Royal Descents and Pedigrees of Founders' Kin, 66. Nichol's History of the County of Leicester, iii. 1056. W. R. Fraser's History of Laurencekirk, 37, 68. Wood's Douglas's Peerage of Scotland, ii. 53. Burke's Extinct Baronetcies, 621. See DALMAHOY, FAUCONER, FAULKNOR, FAWCONER.

FALDS. Harleian Society, xix. 104, 168.

FALKENER, or FALKINER. Burke's Landed Gentry, 3, 4, 5. Burke's Extinct Baronetcies. Fletcher's Leicestershire Pedigrees and Royal Descents, 45.

FALKLAND. Burke's Royal Families (London, 1851, 8vo.) ii. 91.

FALLON. Burke's Landed Gentry, 3, 5, 6, 7, 8. O'Hart's Irish Pedigrees, 2nd Series, 177.

FALLOWES. Earwaker's East Cheshire, ii. 619.

FALMOUTH. Burke's Royal Families (London, 1851, 8vo.) ii. 58.

FALSHAW. Thoresby Society, ii. 51.

FALSTAFF. Harleian Society, xii. 75.

FANE. Jacob's Peerage, i. 516. Hasted's Kent, ii. 250, 265, 315. Surtees Society, xxxvi. 293. Burke's Commoners, iv. 92, Landed Gentry, (of Warmsley,) 2, 3, 4, 5, 6, 7, 8 ; (of Fulbeck,) 8 ; of Moyles Court,) 8 ; (of Boyton,) 8. Harleian Society, viii. 7. Blore's Rutland, 20, 103, 222. Notes and Queries, 7 S. ii. 158. Edmondson's Baronagium Genealogicum, ii. 119. Brydges' Collins' Peerage, iii. 283. The Genealogist, New Series, xiii. 81, 209. See VANE, HAMLYN-FANE.

FANSHAW, or FANSHAWE. Miscellanea Genealogica et Heraldica, i. 320 ; ii. 115, 280. Morant's Essex, i. 4, 10. Account of Family of Fanshawe in 'Memoirs of Lady Fanshawe.' London, 1829, 8vo. Burke's Landed Gentry, (of Dengey Hall,) 2, 3, 4, 5, 6, 7, 8 ; (of Parsloes,) 4, 5, 6, 7, 8. Harleian Society, viii. 124 ; xiii. 194 ; xv. 264 ; xxii. 114. Manning and Bray's Surrey, ii. 246 ; iii.

cxxvi. Clutterbuck's Hertford, iii. 294. Wright's Essex, ii. 479. Burke's Extinct Baronetcies. East Barnet, by F. C. Cass, Part i. 96. Howard's Visitation of England and Wales, vi. 113.

FANSTON. Visitation of Wiltshire, edited by G. W. Marshall, 7. *See* FAUXTON.

FARDELL. Burke's Commoners, iv. 246, Landed Gentry, 2, 3, 4.

FARENDEN. Berry's Sussex Genealogies, 372.

FAREWELL. Pedigree of Farewell of Hillbishop, Co. Somerset, [T.P.] 1856. Broadside. Hasted's Kent, iii. 3. Visitation of Somerset, printed by Sir T. Phillipps, 69. Harleian Society, xi. 36 ; xv. 263. Weaver's Visitations of Somerset, 23.

FARIE. Burke's Landed Gentry, 8.

FARINDON. Manning and Bray's Surrey, iii. 349.

FARINGDON. Visitation of Devon, edited by F. T. Colby, 94. *See* FARRINGDON.

FARINGTON. Corrected Pedigree of Farington of Farington, and Farington of Worden, compiled from Documents, broadside, printed by Mitchell and Hughes, London, *n. d.* Berry's Sussex Genealogies, 41. Miscellanea Genealogica et Heraldica, i. 63. Harleian Society, viii. 350 ; xv. 265, 267. Chetham Society, lxxxi. 45, 48, 75 ; lxxxv. 106, 107. Foster's Lancashire Pedigrees. Gregson's Fragments relating to the County of Lancaster, 255. Corry's History of Lancashire, ii. 722-724. Burke's Extinct Baronetcies. Croston's edn. of Baines's Lancaster, iv. 170. *See* FARRINGTON, FFARINGTON.

FARLEY. Weaver's Visitation of Herefordshire, 87. Oliver's History of Antigua, i. 247.

FARMAR. Burke's Commoners, ii. 569, Landed Gentry, 2, 3, 4, 5, 6, 7, 8.

FARMBOROUGH. Burke's Landed Gentry, 4 supp.

FARMER, FARMOR, or FARMOUR. Visitation of Middlesex (Salisbury, 1820, fol.) 50. Burke's Landed Gentry, (of Nonsuch,) 3, 4, 5, 6, 7, 8 ; (of Coworth,) 8. Harleian Society, ii. 177, 179 ; viii. 93 ; xxviii. 182, 219. Warwickshire Pedigrees, from Visitation of 1682-3, (privately printed, 1865). Burke's Visitation of Seats and Arms, ii. 8. Nichols' History of the County of Leicester, iv. 760, 950. The Genealogist, iii. 244. Betham's Baronetage, iv. 74. Foster's Visitation of Middlesex, 92. New England Register, i. 21. Metcalfe's Visitations of Northamptonshire, 19, 87.

FARNABY. Harleian Society, xv. 265. Wotton's English Baronetage, iv. 212.

FARNALL, or FARNELL. Burke's Landed Gentry, 2, 3, 4, 5, 6. Burke's Royal Families, (London, 1851, 8vo.) ii. 182*. Burke's Visitation of Seats and Arms, i. 21.

FARNHAM. Royal Descent of Lord Farnham from Henry VII., King of England, folio. Royal Descent of Lord Farnham from Edward III., King of England, through—1st, Lionel of Antwerp, Duke of Clarence ; 2nd, John of Gaunt, Duke of Lancaster (through—1st, the heiress of Lancaster ; 2nd, Catherine Roet) ; 3rd, Edmond of Langley, Duke of York ; and, 4th, Thomas of Woodstock, Duke of

Gloucester; distinguishing in red characters the descent through Kings Edward IV. and Henry VII., compiled from Authentic Records. Long folio. Royal Descent of Lord Farnham from Edward I., King of England, (through BOTH his Queens,) compiled from authentic sources. Long folio. Royal Descent of Lord Farnham from Henry VIII., King of England, (through three of his children—1st, King Edward I.; 2nd, Edmond, surnamed Crouchback, Earl of Lancaster; and, 3rd, the Princess Beatrice Plantagenet, Princess of Brittany), including numerous Plantagenet Descents, and those through Edward IV. and Henry VII., Kings of England; James I., King of Scotland; Charles V. and VI., Kings of France; through the issue of BOTH the Queens of King Edward I., and ALL THE FOUR SONS of King Edward III. who left issue; showing also the common Descents from Beatrice, Princess of Brittany, of King Henry VII., and of his Queen (the Princess Elizabeth Plantagenet, of York); and also the combined Descents of three of the daughters of Richard Widvile, K.G., Earl Rivers; including that from Lady Elizabeth Widvile, through both her husbands, 1st, Sir John Grey, 7th Lord Ferrers de Groby; and, 2nd, King Edward IV., etc. Long folio. Royal Descent of Lord Farnham from Henry III., King of England; illustrated with the Seize Quartiers of distinguished persons included in the Descents. 2 vols. 4to. Royal Descent of Lord Farnham, from Henry III., Edward I., and the subsequent Kings of England, etc., etc., and from Robert Bruce, King of Scotland; to which are added Descents from a few other distinguished personages. Cavan, 1850, 8vo. Royal Descent of Lord Farnham, from Henry II., King of England, through three of his children (1st, King John; 2nd, the Princess Eleanor, Queen of Castile; and 3rd, the Princess Maud, Duchess of Saxony and Bavaria), including (besides numerous royal, noble, and illustrious Descents in England, Scotland, and Ireland) those through the Kings of Castile and Leon; the Kings of Portugal; the Kings of Sicily; the Kings of France, of the Capetian and Valesian dynasties; the whole showing a curious combination of Descents, etc. Long folio. Royal Descents of Lord Farnham from Henry II., King of England, forming an introduction to the Royal Descents from Henry III. 4to. Seize Quartiers (92 all complete), connected with the Royal Descents of Lord Farnham. Cavan, 1850, 8vo. Royal Descent (double) of Lord Farnham from Robert Bruce, King of Scotland, 4to. Royal Descents of Lord Farnham (through the Howards, Dukes of Norfolk), showing the double Descent, through *seven* successive Knights of the Garter, in the *first* line; and through *four* successive Knights of the Garter, in the *second* line. 4to. Lord Farnham's paternal Royal Descent from Henry III., King of England. Long folio. Royal Descents of Anna Frances Hesther, Baroness Farnham, from Edward III., King of England, through ALL HIS FOUR SONS, who left issue. Long folio. Royal Descents of Henry Maxwell, K.P., seventh Lord Farnham, etc., 2 vols. 8vo. Burke's Commoners, iii. 502, Landed Gentry, 2, 3, 4, 5, 6, 7, 8.

Burke's Royal Families, (London, 1851, 8vo.) i. 1, 153. Harleian Society, ii. 77. Fletcher's Leicestershire Pedigrees and Royal Descents, 107. Burton's Description of Leicestershire, 215. Burke's Royal Descents and Pedigrees of Founders' Kin, 36, *Founders' Kin*, 7. Nichols' History of the County of Leicester, iii. 103, 104. *See* MAXWELL.

FARQUHAR. Burke's Commoners, (of Gilminscroft,) iii. 22, Landed Gentry, 2, 3, 4, 5, 6, 7, 8; (of Drumnagesk,) 8. Paterson's History of the Co. of Ayr, ii. 425, 430. Paterson's History of Ayr and Wigton, i. 690, 697. A short Memoir of James Young, 31. Betham's Baronetage, iv. app. 20.

FARQUARSON. Burke's Commoners, (of Invercauld,) ii. 98, Landed Gentry, 2, 3, 4, 5, 6, 7, 8; (of Haughton,) Commoners, ii. 261, Landed Gentry, 2, 3, 4, 5, 6, 7, 8; (of Langton,) Landed Gentry, 5, 6, 7, 8; (of Whitehouse,) 2 supp., 3, 5 supp., 6, 7, 8; (of Baldovie,) 2; (of Finzean,) 7, 8. Hutchins' Dorset, i. 285. Douglas's Baronage of Scotland, 339, 545. Shaw's History of Moray, 43. Alexander Nisbet's Heraldic Plates, 40.

FARR, or FARRE. Morant's Essex, i. 197, 239; ii. 50. Suckling's History of Suffolk, i. 50. Harleian Society, xiii. 395; xxxix. 1009. Notes and Queries, 1 S. ix. 32. Burke's Colonial Gentry, ii. 857.

FARRAN. Jewitt's Reliquary, xii. 62.

FARRANT. Surrey Archæological Collections, ii. Burke's Landed Gentry, 8. Harleian Society, xliii. 100.

FARRAR. Harleian Society, xxii. 53. New England Register, vi. 313.

FARRELL. Burke's Heraldic Illustrations, 129. Burke's Landed Gentry, 2 at p. 1637; (of Moynalty,) 4, 5, 6, 7, 8; (of Dalyston,) 3, 4.

FARREN, or FARRENT. Miscellanea Genealogica et Heraldica, New Series, i. 34. Nichols' History of the County of Leicester, iv. 272. Harleian Society, ii. 202.

FARRER. Edward Miller's History of Doncaster, 272. Burke's Landed Gentry, (of Ingleborough,) 2, 3, 4, 5, 6, 7, 8; (of Brayfield,) 4, 5, 6, 7, 8. Foster's Yorkshire Pedigrees. Burke's Royal Descents and Pedigrees of Founders' Kin, 67. Thoresby's Ducatus Leodiensis, 196. Surtees' Durham, iii. 43. Harleian Society, xv. 266; xxxix. 859. John Watson's History of Halifax, 244. Carthew's Hundred of Launditch, Part iii. 227. Surrey Archæological Collections, xi.

FARRINGDON. Westcote's Devonshire, edited by G. Oliver and P. Jones, 464, 609. The Visitations of Devon, by J. L. Vivian, 292, 339. *See* FARINGDON.

FARRINGTON. Hasted's Kent, i. 102. Harleian Society, i. 48. Chetham Society, lxxxii. 19, 103. Dallaway's Sussex, i. app. to Chichester. *See* FARINGTON.

FARROW. New England Register, vi. 313.

FARSIDE, or FARSYDE. Surtees Society, xxxvi. 85. Burke's Landed Gentry, 2, 3, 4, 5, 6.

FARWELL Notes and Queries, 4 S. viii. 437, 537; 5 S. iv. 173, 413.

FARYNTON. Baines' History of the Co. of Lancaster, iii. 446. *See* FARINGTON.

FASHIN, or FASHION. Berry's Hampshire Genealogies, 129. Hampshire Visitations, printed by Sir T. Phillipps, 25. The Genealogist, vii. 236. Chronicle of the Family of De Havilland.

FASTOLF. Suckling's History of Suffolk, ii. 41. Notices of Great Yarmouth, by J. H. Druery, 228. Metcalfe's Visitations of Suffolk, 28, 136.

FAUCONBERGE, or FAULCONBERG. Account of Henry Fauconberge, LL.D., of Beccles, with Pedigree, and also Pedigree of Revett, of Brandeston, by S. W. Rix. Ipswich, 1849, 4to. Graves' History of Cleveland, 48. Poulson's Holderness, i. 403. Baker's Northampton, ii. 296. The New History of Yorkshire commencing with Richmondshire, by Genl. Plantagenet-Harrison, (London, 1872, fol.) Part i. 27. Plantagenet-Harrison's History of Yorkshire, i. 100. Notes and Queries, 1 S. viii. 155. Banks' Baronies in Fee, i. 203. Banks' Dormant and Extinct Baronage, i. 298; ii. 176. Collinson's Somerset, iii. 5.

FAUCONBRIDGE. Foster's Visitations of Yorkshire, 71, 516. Harleian Society, xvi. 120.

FAUCONER, or FAULCONER. Dallaway's Sussex, II. ii. 75. Burton's Description of Leicestershire, 270. The Genealogist, New Series, i. 129, 241. Metcalfe's Visitations of Northamptonshire, 20. Genealogical Gleanings in England, by H. F. Waters, i. 99. New England Register, xxxix. 71. Howard's Visitation of England and Wales, iv. 83. Fragmenta Genealogica, by F. A. Crisp, vii. 113. *See* FALCONER, FAWKENER, FAWCONER.

FAULKES. The Genealogist, iii. 244.

FAULKNER. Burke's Landed Gentry, 3, 4, 5 supp. *See* FALCONER.

FAULKNOR. Burke's Landed Gentry, 5 supp.

FAUNCE. Burke's Landed Gentry, 2, 3, 4, 5, 6, 7, 8.

FAUNT. J. H. Hill's History of Langton, 84. Harleian Society, ii. 28; xliii. 193. Burton's Description of Leicestershire, 99. Nichols' History of the County of Leicester, iv. 173. Surrey Archæological Collections, vii.

FAUNTLEROY. Hutchins' Dorset, iv. 180. The Genealogist, New Series, ii. 300; xii. 31. Fragmenta Genealogica, by F. A. Crisp, vii. 44-48.

FAUSSETT. Berry's Kent Genealogies, 138. Burke's Landed Gentry, 2 and add., 3, 4, 5, 6, 7, and p. 741, 8.

FAUXTON. Visitatio Comitatus Wiltoniæ, 1623, printed by Sir T. Phillipps. *See* FANSTON.

FAVEL, or FAVELL. Surtees Society, xxxvi. 348. Foster's Yorkshire Pedigrees. Bridges' Northamptonshire, by Rev. Peter Whalley, i 467. Baker's Northampton, i. 73. Harleian Society, xxxix. 908.

FAVER. Visitation of Somerset, printed by Sir T. Phillipps, 68.

FAWCETT. Burke's Landed Gentry, 2 supp., 3, 4, 5, 6, 7, 8. Surtees' Durham, ii. 60. Burke's Colonial Gentry, i. 16. Howard's Visitation of England and Wales, vi. 52.

FAWCON. Surtees' Durham, iii. 267.

FAWCONER. Lipscombe's History of the County of Buckingham, i. 16. Hampshire Visitations, printed by Sir T. Phillipps, 26. Visitatio Comitatus Wiltoniæ, 1623, printed by Sir T. Phillipps. Visitation of Wiltshire, edited by G. W. Marshall, 11. *See* FALCONER, FAUCONER.

FAWKENER, FAWKNER, or FAWKNOR. Maclean's History of Trigg Minor, i. 651. Wright's History of Rutland, 131. Camden Society, xliii. 36. Berry's Hampshire Genealogies, 239, 297. *See* FALCONER.

FAWKES. The Fawkes's of York in the 16th Century, by Robert Davies. Westminster, 1850, 8vo. Surtees Society, xxxvi. 29. Burke's Landed Gentry, 2, 3, 4, 5, 6, 7, 8. Foster's Yorkshire Pedigrees. Foster's Visitations of Yorkshire, 100. Thoresby's Ducatus Leodiensis, 136. Whitaker's Loidis and Elmete, 191. Burton's History of Hemingborough, 219. The Genealogist, New Series, xiii. 46. Howard's Visitation of England and Wales, vii. 91.

FAWSLEY. Baker's Northampton, i. 379.

FAY. O'Hart's Irish Pedigrees, 2nd Series, 329.

FAYRAM. Historical Notices of Doncaster, by C. W. Hatfield, 3rd Series, 376.

FAYREFAX. Surtees Society, xli. 57, 58. *See* FAIRFAX.

FAYREHARE. Surtees Society, ii. 317.

FAZAKERLEY. Burke's Landed Gentry, 2, 4, 5. Chetham Society, lxxxii. 78; lxxxv. 108, 109.

FEAKE. Surrey Archæological Collections, vi. Harleian Society, xv. 268; xliii. 107. Visitations of Staffordshire, 1614 and 1663-4, William Salt Society, 126.

FEARNLEY. Burke's Landed Gentry, 2 final add., 3, 4, 5, 6, 7, 8.

FEARNLEY-WHITTINGSTALL. Burke's Landed Gentry, 5, 6, 7, 8.

FEATHER. Collections relating to the Surname of Feather. By George W. Marshall. Worksop, 1887, 8vo.

FEATHERSTONE. Clutterbuck's Hertford, iii. 299. Burke's Colonial Gentry, ii. 703. *See* FETHERSTON.

FEATHERSTONHAUGH. Visitation of Durham, 1615, (Sunderland, 1820, fol.) 78. Hutchinson's History of Cumberland, i. 207. Hutchinson's History of Durham, iii. 291. *See* FETHERSTON-HAUGH.

FEEHAN. O'Hart's Irish Pedigrees, 2nd Series, 178.

FEILDE, or FEILD. Foster's Visitations of Yorkshire, 317. Harleian Society, viii. 354. Clutterbuck's Hertford, iii. 243. Herald and Genealogist, vi. 144. History of Bradford, by John James, 433. Burke's Landed Gentry, 2, p. 1459.

FEILDEN. Pedigree of the Family of Feilden, by Ralph Assheton, London, 1879, 8vo. Burke's Commoners, (of Mollington,) ii. 446, Landed Gentry, 2 ; (of Feniscowles,) Commoners, ii. 446, Landed Gentry, 2 ; (of Witton,) Commoners, ii. 444, Landed Gentry, 2, 3, 4, 5, 6, 7, 8. Foster's Lancashire Pedigrees. Abram's History of Blackburn, 621, 638, 752, 756.

FEILDING. History of the illustrious Family of the Feildings, etc., by Nathaniel Wanley, in Nichols' Leicester, iv. 273-293. Surtees

Society xxxvi. 60. Burke's Royal Families, (London, 1851, 8vo.)
i. 47. Visitation of Warwickshire, 1619, published with Warwickshire Antiquarian Magazine, 74. Wright's History of Rutland, 89. Nichols' History of the County of Leicester, iv. 293,
394. Plantagenet-Harrison's History of Yorkshire, i. 392. Harleian Society, xv. 269. Edmondson's Baronagium Genealogicum,
ii. 113. Brydges' Collins' Peerage, iii. 265. The Genealogist,
New Series, x. 193. *See* FIELDING.
FELBRIGG. Blomefield's Norfolk, viii. 108, 110. Page's History of
Suffolk, 65.
FELD, or FIELD. Foster's Yorkshire Pedigrees. Foster's Visitations
of Yorshire, 317. Harleian Society, xxi. 58. *See* FEILDE, FIELD.
FELDEN. Nichols' History of the County of Leicester, iv. 275.
FELGATE. Metcalfe's Visitations of Suffolk, 92.
FELL. The Fells of Swarthmoor Hall, by Maria Webb. London,
1865, 8vo. Hunter's History of the Parish of Sheffield, 401.
Foster's Pedigree of the Forsters and Fosters, Part ii. 8. Notes
and Queries, 1 S. iii. 142; iv. 256; vi. 233, 279; 5 S. iv. 187,
393. Miscellanea Genealogica et Heraldica, New Series, iv. 368;
2nd Series, ii. 288. Bardsley's Registers of Ulverston, 1. Har-
leian Society, xxxix. 902. Burke's Landed Gentry, 7, 8.
FELLOWES. Burke's Landed Gentry, (of Ramsey Abbey,) 2, 3, 4, 5,
6, 7, 8; (of Shotesham,) 5, 6, 7, 8. Hutchins' Dorset, ii. 565.
Howard's Visitation of England and Wales, viii. 97.
FELLOWS. Burke's Landed Gentry, 6 supp., 7. Burke's Colonial
Gentry, ii. 827. Harleian Society, xxxviii. 691.
FELSTEAD. The Genealogist, iii. 296.
FELTHAM. Metcalfe's Visitations of Suffolk, 137.
FELTON. Morant's Essex, i. 371; ii. 323, 337. Carthew's Hundred
of Launditch, Part i. 157. Foster's Visitations of Yorkshire, 372.
Surtees' Durham, ii. 285. Baker's Northampton, i. 478. Wright's
Essex, i. 565, 589. Suffolk Institute of Archæology, iv. 49.
Banks' Baronies in Fee, i. 203. Banks' Dormant and Extinct
Baronage, i. 298. Metcalfe's Visitations of Suffolk, 190, 191.
Burke's Extinct Baronetcies. Collins' Baronetage, ii. 242. Chan-
cellor's Sepulchral Monuments of Essex, 223. Historical M.S.
Commission, 10th Report, app. 2, 177. Burke's Landed Gentry, 8.
FENAY. Hulbert's Annals of Almondbury, 155. Harleian Society,
xxxviii. 634.
FENIS, or FENYS. Croke's History of the Family of Croke, No. 42.
The Genealogist, New Series, xvii. 249.
FENN. Harleian Society, xv. 270.
FENNELL. Notes and Queries, 7 S. vii. 128, 212, 353.
FENNER. Harleian Society, vi. 107. Dallaway's Sussex, i. 16. The
Visitations of Devon, by J. L. Vivian, 341.
FENNO. The New England Register, lii. 448.
FENTON. Pedigree of Fenton of Glynamel, [T. P.] 1860, folio page.
Burke's Landed Gentry, (of Underbank,) 2, 3, 4, 5, 6, 7, 8; (of
Castlerigg,) 3, 4 and supp.; (of Dutton Manor,) 7, 8; (of Cow-
thorpe and Loversall,) 7. Foster's Visitations of Yorkshire, 227.

Harleian Society, iv. 33, 113 ; xxxvii. 286 ; xxxviii. 823. The
Borough of Stoke-upon-Trent, by John Ward, 422. Thoresby's
Ducatus Leodiensis, 2nd edition, 221. Hunter's Deanery of Don-
caster, ii. 357. Thoroton's Nottinghamshire, iii. 295. Memorials
of Angus and the Mearns, by Andrew Jervise, 270. Burke's
Extinct Baronetcies, 605.

FENTOUN. Notes and Queries, 8 S., i. 227 ; ii. 271.

FENWICK, or FENWICKE. Pedigree of Fenwick of East Haddon, etc.,
[T. P.] 1852, broadside. Pedigrees of Fenwick of East Haddon,
Fenwick, Wallington, etc., [T. P] 1860, 3 pedigrees, 4 folio pages.
J. H. Hill's History of Langton, 218. Pedigrees from Visitation
of Northumberland, printed by Sir T. Phillipps, (Middle Hill,
1858, fol.) 1. Burke's Landed Gentry, (of Longframlington,) 2,
3, 4, 5, 6, 7, 8 ; (of Burrow Hall,) 5, 6, 7, 8 ; (of Stockerston,)
6, 7, 8 ; (of Thirlestane House,) 6, 7, 8. Burke's Visitation of
Seats and Arms, i. 60. Burke's Royal Families, (London, 1851,
8vo.) ii. 140. Hodgson's Northumberland, I. ii. 200, 205, 209,
254, 368 ; II. ii. 17, 75, 113, 115. History of Darlington, by
W. Hylton Dyer Longstaffe, (in pedigree of Chaytor,) not paged.
Surtees' Durham, i. 193, 222 ; ii. 64. The Genealogist, i. 380 ;
ii. 17, 121, 144, 183. Harleian Society, xv. 270 ; xvi. 121.
Burke's Extinct Baronetcies. Genealogical Gleanings in England,
by H. F. Waters, i. 42. Foster's Visitations of Northumberland,
47-52, 54. New England Register, xxxviii. 199.

FENWICK-BISSET. Burke's Landed Gentry, 5, 6.

FENWICK-CLENNELL. Burke's Landed Gentry, 7, 8.

FERBY. Hasted's Kent, i. 146. Berry's Kent Genealogies, 365.
Harleian Society, xlii. 161.

FERGUSHILL. Paterson's History of the Co. of Ayr, ii. 402. Paterson's History of Ayr and Wigton, i. 618.

FERGUSON, or FERGUSSON. Records of the Clan Fergusson, by
James and R. M. Fergusson. Edinburgh, 1895, 8vo., 2 vols.
Case of Sir Adam Fergusson, of Kilkerran, Bart., claiming the
title of Earl of Glencairn, etc., 1797, fol. Burke's Heraldic Illustrations, 106. Burke's Landed Gentry, (of Raith,) 4, 5, 6 and
supp., 7, 8 ; (of Kinmundy,) 3, 4, 5, 6, 7, 8 ; (of Harker Lodge,)
2, 3, 4, 5, 6 ; (of Isle,) 7, 8 ; (of Broadfield,) 8 ; (of Carlisle,) 8 ;
(of Craigdarroch,) 2, 3, 4, 5, 6, 7, 8 ; (of Pitfour,) 5, 6, 7. Paterson's History of the Co. of Ayr, i. 250, 390 ; ii. 369. Nisbet's
Heraldry, ii. app. 97. Paterson's History of Ayr and Wigton,
ii. 101, 228, 426. Inverurie and the Earldom of the Garioch, by
John Davidson, 474. Betham's Baronetage, v. 490. Northern
Notes and Queries, iv. 45.

FERGUSON-DAVIE. The Visitations of Devon, by J. L. Vivian, 271.

FERMOR. Gentleman's Magazine, 1827, i. 580. Appendix to Case
of Sir J. S. Sidney, claiming to be Lord Lisle. Berry's Sussex
Genealogies, 180. Bridges' Northamptonshire, by Rev. Peter
Whalley, i. 290. Baker's Northampton, i. 599 ; ii. 142. Notes
and Queries, 3 S. viii. 424, 463. Burke's Extinct Baronetcies.
Edmondson's Baronagium Genealogicum, iii. 225. Brydges'

Collins' Peerage, iv. 197. Wotton's English Baronetage, iv. 209.
Roman Catholic Families of England, by J. J. Howard and H. F.
Burke, Part i. Annals of the English Benedictines of Ghent, 190.
See FARMER.
FERMOY. Gentleman's Magazine, 1855, ii. 43. Claim of Edmund
Burke, Baron Fermoy, to vote at Elections of Irish Peers, Sess.
Papers, C. C 2, 111 of 1856 ; G of 1857, Sess. 2.
FERNE. Jewitt's Reliquary, vii. 23. Stonehouse's History of the
Isle of Axholme, 350. Visitation of Staffordshire, 1663-4, printed
by Sir T. Phillipps, 5. Erdeswicke's Survey of Staffordshire, 510.
Hoare's Wiltshire, IV. i. 56. The Genealogist, iv. 22 ; New
Series, xii. 251. Harleian Society, xv. 271 ; xxxvii. 141. Visita-
tion of Staffordshire, (Willm. Salt Soc.) 70. The Visitations of
Staffordshire, 1614 and 1663-4, William Salt Society, 127.
Jewitt's Reliquary, xxvi. 32. Historical Notices of Doncaster, by
C. W. Hatfield, 2nd Series, 5.
FERNELEY. Metcalfe's Visitations of Suffolk, 29, 137.
FERNELL. Howard's Visitation of England and Wales, ii. 117.
FERRALL. Burke's Landed Gentry, 6, 7, 8.
FERRAND. Surtees Society, xxxvi. 27, 31, 48. Burke's Commoners,
iv. 698, Landed Gentry, 2, 3, 4, 5, 6, 7, 8. Foster's Yorkshire
Pedigrees. Foster's Visitations of Yorkshire, 517. Burke's
Heraldic Illustrations, 14. Whitaker's Deanery of Craven, 161,
194, 224, 243. Ilkley, Ancient and Modern, by R. Collyer and
J. H. Turner, 222. Yorkshire Genealogist, i. 240.
FERRAR. Harleian Society, xliii. 157.
FERRARIIS. Munford's Analysis of Domesday Book of Co. Nor-
folk, 26.
FERRARS, or FERRERS. Nichols' History of the County of Leicester,
iv. 633*. Baker's Northampton, i. 103, 123, 732. Collinson's
Somerset, iii. 40. Jewitt's Reliquary, viii. 229 ; x. 225. Clifford's
Description of Tixall, 125. Foster's Crown Cases, (Dublin, 1791,)
154. Gentleman's Magazine, 1826, ii. 409. Bird's Magazine of
Honour, 71. Morant's Essex, ii. 32, 48, 119, 424. Warwickshire
Antiquarian Magazine, Part i. Burke's Commoners, iii. 127,
Landed Gentry, 2, 3, 4, 5, 6, 7, 8. Burke's Royal Families,
(London, 1851, 8vo.) i. 90 ; ii. 65, 172. Bibliotheca Topographica
Britannica, vii. Parts i. and ii. 300. Harleian Society, viii. 246 ;
xii. 5, 7 ; xv. 271, 272 ; xxi. 59 ; xxii. 141. Shaw's Staffordshire,
i. 39 ; ii. 195. Topographer, (London, 1789-91, 8vo.) i. 487.
Lipscombe's History of the County of Buckingham, i. 252.
Bridges' Northamptonshire, by Rev. Peter Whalley, ii. 171.
Dugdale's Warwickshire, 971, 1089, 1135. Hutchins' Dorset, iii.
337. Manning and Bray's Surrey, iii. clxiv. Clutterbuck's Hertford, i. 360. Wright's Essex, ii. 50. Chetham Society, xcix. 52.
Stemmata Shirleiana, by E. P. Shirley, 2nd edn., 103. Edmondson's Baronagium Genealogicum, iv. 361* ; vi. 39. Banks' Baronies
in Fee, i. 204. Banks' Dormant and Extinct Baronage, i. 75, 312 ;
ii. 181-197 ; iii. 238. The Genealogist, v. 256 ; New Series, ix.
151 ; xvi. 46. Burke's Extinct Baronetcies. Genealogical Table

of John Stratford Collins. Baddesley Clinton with some account of the Family of Ferrers. By Henry Norris. London, 1897, 4to. The Gresley's of Drakelow, by F. Madan, 253, 254. *See* DE FERRARS.

FERRER. Visitation of Devon, edited by F. T. Colby, 96.

FERRIER. Burke's Landed Gentry, 5 supp., 6, 7, 8. Dawson Turner's Sepulchral Reminiscences of Great Yarmouth, 116. The Palatine Note Book, ii. 66.

FERRIS, or FERRYS. Berry's Sussex Genealogies, 319. Burke's Landed Gentry, 2. Dallaway's Sussex, II. ii. 245. Visitatio Comitatus Wiltoniæ, 1623, printed by Sir T. Phillipps. Oliver's History of Antigua, i. 250. The Genealogist, New Series, xii. 89.

FERROUR, or FERRAR. Carthew's Hundred of Launditch, Part iii. 218, 222.

FESSENDEN. New England Register, xxv. 105.

FETHERSTON. Miscellanea Genealogica et Heraldica, ii. 229. Morant's Essex, i. 239. Berry's Sussex Genealogies, 233. Warwickshire Antiquarian Magazine, Part ii. Burke's Landed Gentry, 2, 3, 4, 5, 6. Burke's Visitation of Seats and Arms, 2nd Series, i. 27. The London Money, by W. M. Egglestone, (Stanhope, 1876, 8vo.) 20. Harleian Society, xv. 273; xvi. 121. Wotton's English Baronetage, iii. 185. The Wolfes of Forenaghts, 49. Burke's Extinct Baronetcies. Foster's Visitations of Cumberland and Westmorland, 45. *See* FEATHERSTONE.

FETHERSTONEHALGHE, or FETHERSTONHAUGH. The Genealogist, ii. 254. Visitation of Durham, 1575, (Newcastle, 1820, fol.) 9. Burke's Commoners, (of Bracklyn Castle,) i. 629, Landed Gentry, 2, 3, 4, 5, 6, 7, 8; (of Rockview,) Landed Gentry, 4, 5, 6, 7, 8; (of Carrick,) 4, 5, 6, 7, 8; (of Staffield Hall,) 3, 4, 5, 6, 7; (of Kirkoswald,) 2 supp., 3, 4, 5, 6, 7, 8; (of Hopton Court,) 3, 4, 5, 6, 7, 8. Jefferson's History of Leath Ward, Cumberland, 290. Hodgson's Northumberland, III. ii. 68, 353. Betham's Baronetage, iii. 242. Foster's Visitations of Durham, 119, 121. Foster's Visitations of Northumberland, 53. Nicolson and Burn's Westmorland and Cumberland, ii. 424. *See* FEATHERSTONEHAUGH.

FETTES. Betham's Baronetage, v. 581*. Burke's Extinct Baronetcies, supp.

FETTIPLACE, FETTYPLACE, or FETYPLACE. Journal of the British Archæological Association, xvi. 201. Croke's History of the Family of Croke, No. 24. Ashmole's Antiquities of Berkshire, iii. 307. Bibliotheca Topographica Britannica, iv. Part ii. 67. Harleian Society, v. 299. Parochial Topography of the Hundred of Wanting, by W. N. Clarke, 68, 107. Notices of Swyncombe and Ewelme, in Co. Oxford, by H. A Napier, 408. Blore's Rutland, 61. Wotton's English Baronetage, iii. 266. The Genealogist, v. 257, 258; New Series, i. 8. Burke's Extinct Baronetcies. *See* PHETIPLACE.

FEWTRELL. Harleian Society, xxviii. 183. Howard's Visitation of England and Wales, viii. 65.

FFARINGTON. Burke's Commoners, (of Worden,) iii. 339, Landed

Gentry, 2, 3, 4, 5, 6, 7, 8 ; (of Woodvale,) Landed Gentry, 3, 4, 5.
Burke's Royal Families, (London, 1851, 8vo.) i. 12. *See* FAR-
INGTON.

FFER. Dwnn's Visitation of Wales, i. 150.

FFERIOR. Dwnn's Visitations of Wales, i. 67.

FFINANT. Collections by the Powys-land Club, iv. 149.

FFOGERTY. Burke's Landed Gentry, 6 at p. 1395.

FFOLK. Dwnn's Visitations of Wales, i. 87.

FFOLLIOTT. Burke's Landed Gentry, 3, 4, 5, 6, 7, 8. *See* FOLIOT.

FFOULKES. Burke's Landed Gentry, 2, 3, 4, 5, 6, 7, 8. Miscellanea
Genealogica et Heraldica, New Series, ii. 25.

FFYLIP. Dwnn's Visitations of Wales, i. 109, 232.

FFYLIPS. Dwnn's Visitations of Wales, i. 78, 92, 105, 142, 158, 171,
197, 203, 208, 211.

FFYLP. Dwnn's Visitations of Wales, i. 72.

FFYLPIN. Dwnn's Visitations of Wales, i. 67, 193.

FFYTCHE. Burke's Landed Gentry, 4, 5, 6, 7. *See* FYTCHE.

FICHET. Maclean's History of Trigg Minor, ii. 42.

FIELD. The Fields of Sowerby, by Osgood Field. London, 1895,
fol. Burke's Commoners, (of Heaton,) ii. 145, Landed Gentry, 2 ;
(of Laceby,) 7, 8 ; (of the Grove,) 8 ; (of Ashurst Park,) Landed
Gentry, 5, 6, 7, 8. The Genealogist, ii. 344 ; v. 179 ; New Series,
i. 92. New England Register, xvii. 106, 293 ; xviii. 260 ; xxii.
166 ; xxxv. 356. Fosbrooke's History of Gloucestershire, i. 340.
Harleian Society, xxxviii. 438, 513 ; xxxix. 885, 1119. History
of the Wilmer Family, 141. Howard's Visitation of England and
Wales, iii. 82. *See* FELD.

FIELDEN. Burke's Landed Gentry, 6 supp., 8. Fishwick's History
of Rochdale, 431.

FIELDER. Hampshire Visitations, printed by Sir T. Phillipps,
26, 27.

FIELDING. Jacob's Peerage, i. 510. Dugdale's Warwickshire, 64.
Harleian Society, xii. 11. Archdall's Lodge's Peerage, i. 251.
Burke's Landed Gentry, 7. *See* FEILDING.

FIENNES, or FIENES. Jewitt's Reliquary, viii. 45. Croke's History of
the Family of Croke, No. 42. Kent's Banner Displayed, 437.
Visitation of Oxfordshire, 1634, printed by Sir T. Phillipps,
(Middle Hill, fol.) 19. Lipscombe's History of the County of
Buckingham, ii. 470. Hampshire Visitations, printed by Sir
T. Phillipps, 27. Nichols' History of the County of Leicester,
iv. 805. Manning and Bray's Surrey, ii. 507. Clutterbuck's
Hertford, ii. 9. Baker's Northampton, ii. 273. Page's History of
Suffolk, 789. Edmondson's Baronagium Genealogicum, iv. 320,
357. Banks' Baronies in Fee, i. 387. Banks' Dormant and
Extinct Baronage, ii. 134, 469. Notes and Queries, 4 S. vii. 438.
See FINES.

FIFE. Claim of Earl of Fife to vote at Elections of Irish Peers, Sess.
Papers, 216 of 1857 Sess. 2.

FIFE-COOKSON. Burke's Landed Gentry, 6 supp., 8.

FIFHIDE. Hampshire Visitations, printed by Sir T. Phillipps, 27.

FIFIELD. Harleian Society, i. 76; xxi. 60; xlii. 116. Berry's Kent Genealogies, 450. Miscellanea Genealogica et Heraldica, 2nd Series, v. 61.

FIHILLY. O'Hart's Irish Pedigrees, 2nd Series, 179.

FILBATCH. Pembrokeshire Pedigrees, 137.

FILDES. Foster's Lancashire Pedigrees.

FILGATE. Burke's Landed Gentry, 5 supp., 6, 7, 8. Howard's Visitation of Ireland, iii. 42.

FILKIN. Harleian Society, xviii. 99.

FILLEALL, or FILIOL. Morant's Essex, ii. 21, 151, 404. Hutchins' Dorset, iii. 152; iv. 315. Harleian Society, xiii. 195, 396; xx. 39. The Genealogist, New Series, ii. 301.

FILLEUL. J. B. Payne's Armorial of Jersey, 158.

FILLIMORE. New England Register, xi. 141.

FILLINGHAM. Burke's Landed Gentry, 6, 7, 8.

FILLOLL. Miscellanea Genealogica et Heraldica, 2nd Series, ii. 190. The Genealogist, New Series, x. 28; xv. 91.

FILMER. Hasted's Kent, ii. 418. Berry's Hertfordshire Genealogies, 136. Berry's Kent Genealogies, 13, 186. Clutterbuck's Hertford, i. 172. Harleian Society, xv. 274; xlii. 167. Wotton's English Baronetage, iii. 581. Betham's Baronetage, ii. 439. See FYNMORE.

FINAGHTY. O'Hart's Irish Pedigrees, 2nd Series, 179.

FINCH, or FINCHE. Morant's Essex, i. 47. Jacob's Peerage, i. 532. Hasted's Kent, ii. 118, 592, 689; iii. 96, 198. Berry's Sussex Genealogies, 336. Surrey Archæological Collections, ii. Berry's Kent Genealogies, 165, 207. Visitation of Middlesex, (Salisbury, 1820, fol.) 10. Berry's Kent Genealogies, 48. Burke's Landed Gentry, (of Red Heath,) 4, 5, 6, 7, 8; (of Tullamore,) 2 supp., 2, 3, 4, 5, 7; (of Burley-on-the-Hill,) 4, 5, 6, 7, 8. Miscellanea Genealogica et Heraldica, ii. 327. Harleian Society, viii. 143; xxi. 61; xxii. 142; xlii. 14, 30, 67; xliii. 118. Manning and Bray's Surrey, ii. 125. Baker's Northampton, i. 307. Scott of Scot's Hall, by J. R. Scott, 105. Edmondson's Baronagium Genealogicum, ii. 126; iii. 203. Brydges' Collins' Peerage, iii. 371; iv. 134. Archæologia Cantiana, xiii. 321. Foster's Visitation of Middlesex, 1. Burke's Family Records, 241. See FYNCHE.

FINCHAM. Blomefield's Norfolk, vii. 348, 462. East Anglian, i. 96. Historical Notices of the Parish of Fincham, by William Blyth, 108-134. Cambridgeshire Visitation, edited by Sir T. Phillipps, 14. Carthew's Hundred of Launditch, Part i. 226. Harleian Society, xv. 275; xxxii. 119; xli. 50.

FINCHER. Metcalfe's Visitation of Worcester, 1683, 44.

FINDERNE, or FINDERN. Morant's Essex, ii. 564. History of Repton, by Robert Bigsby, 102. Harleian Society, xiii. 107. Jewitt's Reliquary, xxii. 64. Visitation of Staffordshire, (Willm. Salt Soc.) 71. See FYNDERNE.

FINDLAY. Burke's Landed Gentry, (of Easterhill,) 2, 3 supp., 4, 5, 6, 7, 8; (of Aberlour,) 8.

FINES. Berry's Buckinghamshire Genealogies, 95. Berry's Berkshire Genealogies, 40. *See* FIENNES, FYNES.

FINET. Berry's Kent Genealogies, 449. Harleian Society, xlii. 166.

FINEUX. Berry's Kent Genealogies, 110. Harleian Society, xlii. 29.

FINGON. Memoirs of Clan Fingon, by D. D. Makinnon. Tunbridge Wells, *circa* 1884, 8vo. *See* MACKINNON.

FINISTON. Miscellanea Genealogica et Heraldica, New Series, iii. 420.

FINLAY. Burke's Landed Gentry, (of Castle Toward,) 4, 5, 6, 7, 8 ; (of Deanston House,) 5, 6, 7 ; (of Corkagh,) 5 supp., 6, 7, 8. Walter Wood's East Neuk of Fife, 278.

FINLAYSON. Burke's Colonial Gentry, i. 169.

FINNEY. Harleian Society, xxxviii. 686. J. P. Earwaker's East Cheshire, i. 154. *See* FYNNEY.

FINNIMORE. *See* FYNMORE.

FINSHER. An Historical Survey of Cornwall, by C. S. Gilbert, ii. 359.

FINUCANE. Burke's Landed Gentry, 2.

FINZEL. Burke's Landed Gentry, 4, 5, 6.

FIOTT. Chronicle of the Family of De Havilland. Lipscombe's History of the County of Buckingham, ii. 309.

FIRBANK. Burke's Landed Gentry, 8.

FIREBRACE. Nichols' History of the County of Leicester, iv. 726. Wotton's English Baronetage, iv. 64. Burke's Extinct Baronetcies.

FIRMAN. Burke's Landed Gentry, 6 and supp., 7, 8. Burke's Royal Families, (edn. of 1876,) 215.

FIRMIN. New England Register, xxv. 52.

FIRTH. Burke's Landed Gentry, 2, 3, 4, 5. Life of Joseph Clark, by H. E. Clark, 20. Howard's Visitation of England and Wales, iv. 141.

FISH. Pedigree of Fish, broadside, *n. d.*, printed for H. Fish. Cussan's History of Hertfordshire, Parts xi. and xii. 244. Abram's History of Blackburn, 505, 598. Harleian Society, xv. 274 ; xix. 106, 170 ; xxii. 54. Burke's Extinct Baronetcies, 605.

FISHBOURNE. The Genealogist, v. 258, 323.

FISHER. Life of Bishop Hough, by John Wilmot, 140. Berry's Hampshire Genealogies, 234. Berry's Kent Genealogies, 324. Burke's Landed Gentry, (of Cossington,) 2 supp., 3, 4, 5 ; (of Higham on the Hill,) 8 supp. ; (of Thorncombe,) 5, 6, 7 ; (of Chetwynd,) 2 supp., 3, 4 ; (of Caldecote,) 5 supp. ; (of Spring Dale,) 6, 7, 8. Burke's Heraldic Register, (published with St. James's Magazine,) 88. Warwickshire Pedigrees, from Visitation of 1682-3, (privately printed, 1865,) app. Visitation of Warwickshire, 1619, published with Warwickshire Antiquarian Magazine, 28, 174. Hampshire Visitations, printed by Sir T. Phillipps, 25, 28. Dugdale's Warwickshire, 990. Visitatio Comitatus Wiltoniæ, 1623, printed by Sir T. Phillipps. Harleian Society, xii. 20, 217 ; xiv. 568 ; xv. 275, 276 ; xix. 107 ; xxviii. 184 ; xxxvii. 380 ; xxxix. 1055 ; xlii. 159. Memoirs of the Family of Chester, by R. E. C. Waters, 273. The Genealogist, iv. 42 ; v. 259.

Visitation of Wiltshire, edited by G. W. Marshall, 27. Burke's Extinct Baronetcies. Harvey's Hundred of Willey, 247. Metcalfe's Visitations of Northamptonshire, 20. Foster's Visitations of Cumberland and Westmorland, 48.

FISHER-ROWE. Burke's Landed Gentry, 8.

FISHWICK, or FYSHWYK. Fishwick's History of Goosnargh, 152, 154.

FISKE. Metcalfe's Visitations of Suffolk, 191. New England Register, iv. 180 ; xi. 221.

FISKE-HARRISON. Burke's Landed Gentry, 2, 3, 4, 5, 6.

FITCH. Morant's Essex, ii. 445. Berry's Essex Genealogies, 146. Harleian Society, viii. 232 ; xiii. 51, 197, 397 ; xli. 74. Burke's Landed Gentry, 8 supp. Miscellanea Genealogica et Heraldica, New Series, iii. 396. See FYTCHE, FITZ.

FITTON. Hodgson's Northumberland, II. ii. 260. Nichols' History of the County of Leicester, iv. 343. Earwaker's East Cheshire, i. 50, 121 ; ii. 564. Ormerod's Cheshire, i. 522 ; iii. 552, 593. Burke's Extinct Baronetcies. Harleian Society, xviii. 99. See FYTTON.

FITTS. New England Register, xxii. 70, 161.

FITZ. Cambridgeshire Visitation, edited by Sir T. Phillipps, 14. Westcote's Devonshire, edited by G. Oliver and P. Jones, 466. Visitations of Devon, edited by F. T. Colby, 96. Hasted's Kent, (Hund. of Blackheath, by H. H. Drake,) 251. Miscellanea Genealogica et Heraldica, 2nd Series, iii. 326. New England Register, xxii. 70, 161. The Visitations of Devon, by J. L. Vivian, 342. See FITCH.

FITZ AER. Eyton's Antiquities of Shropshire, ix. 318.

FITZ AILWARD. Collectanea Topographica et Genealogica, vii. 1.

FITZ ALAN, or FITZ ALLAN. Collectanea Topographica et Genealogica, vi. 1-20. Miscellanea Genealogica et Heraldica, ii. 161. Gough's Sepulchral Monuments, ii. 360. Berry's Essex Genealogies, 67. History of Castle and Town of Arundel, by M. A. Tierney, 192. Carthew's Hundred of Launditch, Part i. 17. Dallaway's Sussex, i. xlv. ; II. i. 114. Eyton's Antiquities of Shropshire, vii. 228. Hutchins' Dorset, iii. 322. Manning and Bray's Surrey, i. 116, 282, 311. Baker's Northampton, i. 547. Plantagenet-Harrison's History of Yorkshire, i. 364. Harleian Society, xiv. 731 ; xvi. 337 ; xliii. 8. Archæological Journal, No. 52, Decr. 1856. Berry's Genealogical Peerage, 86. Banks' Baronies in Fee, i. 304. Banks' Dormant and Extinct Baronage, i. 8, 75, 300. The Antiquary, (London, 1873,) iii. 237. See ARUNDEL.

FITZ AUCHER. Morant's Essex, i. 48, 140. Dallaway's Sussex, i. 87.

FITZ DERING. Berry's Kent Genealogies, 397. See DERING.

FITZ DERMOT. Journal of the Historical and Archæological Association of Ireland, 4th Series, iii. 487.

FITZ DUNCAN. Jefferson's History of Allerdale Ward, Cumberland, 36.

FITZ ELLIS. Topographer and Genealogist, iii. 270. Hoare's Wiltshire, V. ii. 119. See ELLIS.

FITZ EUSTACE. Gage's History of Thingoe Hundred, Suffolk, 410.

FITZ GEOFFRY, or GEFFREY. Cussan's History of Hertfordshire, Parts v. and vi. 155. Harleian Society, xix. 25, 108, 171. Harvey's Hundred of Willey, 515. Metcalfe's Visitations of Northamptonshire, 88.

FITZ GERALD, or FITZ GEROLD. Claim of the Rt. Hon. Lady Henry Fitz Gerald, and Sir H. Hunloke, Bart., to the Barony of Ross, Sess. Papers, 15 of 1803-4; 32 of 1805. Burke's Visitation of Seats and Arms, 2nd Series, ii. 46. Burke's Authorized Arms, 66. Burke's Commoners, (of Glin Castle,) iv. 179, Landed Gentry, 2, 3, 4, 5, 6, 7, 8; (of Turlough,) Commoners, iv. 312, Landed Gentry, 2, 3, 4, 5, 6, 7, 8; (of Holbrook,) Landed Gentry, 3, 4, 5, 6, 7, 8; (of Valentia,) 2, 3, 4, 5, 6; (of Adelphi,) 2, 3, 4; (of Moyvane,) 7, 8; (of Moyriesk,) 6, 7, 8; (of Coolanowle,) 6 supp., 7. Burke's Royal Families, (London, 1851, 8vo.) ii. 107. Burke's Royal Descents and Pedigrees of Founders' Kin, 83. Whitaker's Loidis and Elmete, 166. Irish Pedigrees, by John O'Hart, 212. Journal of the Historical and Archæological Association of Ireland, 3rd Series, i. 517; 4th Series, iv. 159, 161 and addenda. Edmondson's Baronagium Genealogicum, iv. 335. Archdall's Lodge's Peerage, i. 55. Brydges' Collins' Peerage, vi. 100. Banks' Dormant and Extinct Baronage, i. 81. Clutterbuck's Hertford, iii. 198. Baker's Northampton, i. 619. Charles Smith's History of Kerry, 237. Burke's Colonial Gentry, i. 184. Irish Antiquarian Researches, by Sir W. Betham, 221. Burke's Family Records, 242. The Ancestor, No. 119. See KILDARE, PENROSE-FITZGERALD, PURCELL-FITZGERALD, WILSON-FITZGERALD, GERALDINE.

FITZGIBBON. Pedigree of the White Knight, by James Graves, large sheet, n. d. O'Hart's Irish Pedigrees, 2nd Series, 332. Journal of the Historical and Archæological Association of Ireland, 4th Series, iv. 16, 35, 53, 299. Brydges' Collins' Peerage, viii. 605. Burke's Landed Gentry, 6 supp., 7, 8. The Irish Builder, xxxv. 100. Ontarian Families, by E. M. Chadwick, ii. 25.

FITZ GISLEBERT. Morant's Essex, iii. 519.

FITZHAMON. Hoare's Wiltshire, V. ii. 32*. Banks' Dormant and Extinct Baronage, i. 82.

FITZ HARDING. Notes and Queries, 5 S. xii. 363; 6 S. i. 20, 203; ii. 10.

FITZHARRIS. Burke's Extinct Baronetcies, 605. The Genealogical Magazine, iii. 539.

FITZ HENRY. Banks' Baronies in Fee, ii. 77. Harleian Society, xix. 171.

FITZHERBERT. Miscellanea Genealogica et Heraldica, ii. 135. History of Merchant Taylors' School, by Rev. H. B. Wilson, 1173. Visitation of Oxfordshire, 1634, printed by Sir T. Phillipps, (Middle Hill, fol.) 19. Burke's Commoners, (of Norbury,) i. 78. Landed Gentry, 2, 3, 4, 5, 6, 7, 8; (of Black Castle,) Landed Gentry, 5, 6, 7, 8. Topographer and Genealogist, i. 362. Harleian Society, v. 243; xiii. 63; xv. 276; xxxvii. 252. Jewitt's Reliquary, xv. 7. The Topographer, (London, 1789-91,

8vo.) ii. 226 ; iii. 57. Records of the English Province of the Society of Jesus, (Manresa Press, 1875, 8vo.) 198. Shaw's Staffordshire, i. 155*. Eyton's Antiquities of Shropshire, vii. 148. Visitation of Derbyshire, 1663-4, (Middle Hill, 1854, fol.) 4. Hampshire Visitations, printed by Sir T. Phillipps, 28. Burton's Description of Leicestershire, 275. Nichols' History of the County of Leicester, iii. 1028; iv. 853, 964*. Hutchins' Dorset, ii. 540. Hoare's Wiltshire, IV. ii. 52. The Genealogist, iii. 59; New Series, vii. 131, 132 ; ix. 85 ; x. 29 ; xiv. 22. Foley's Records of the English Province S. J., ii. 198 ; iii. 792. Dugdale's Warwickshire, 566. Erdeswicke's Survey of Staffordshire, 278. Pilkington's View of Derbyshire, ii. 297. Brydges' Collins' Peerage, ix. 156. Betham's Baronetage, iv. 148. Banks' Dormant and Extinct Baronage, i. 301. Notes and Queries, 6 S. ii. 313. Visitation of Staffordshire, (Willm. Salt Soc.) 72. Visitations of Staffordshire, 1614 and 1663-4, William Salt Society, 128. Oxford Historical Society, xxiv. 340.

FITZHUGH. Berry's Hampshire Genealogies, 144. Burke's Landed Gentry, 2, 3, 4, 5, 6, 7, 8. Whitaker's History of Richmondshire, i. 124 ; ii. 167. Thoroton's Nottinghamshire, iii. 412. Plantagenet-Harrison's History of Yorkshire, i. 136. Banks' Baronies in Fee, i. 208. Banks' Dormant and Extinct Baronage, ii. 197. Harleian Society, xix. 26.

FITZ-HUMPHREY. Morant's Essex, ii. 322.

FITZ-JAMES. Harleian Society, viii. 90. Hutchins' Dorset, iv. 130. Herald and Genealogist, iii. 424. Notes and Queries, 2 S. ii. 296; iii. 310 ; 3 S. v. 202. Weaver's Visitations of Somerset, 24, 106. Somerset Archæological Society, New Series, iv. Part ii. 32.

FITZ JOHN. Baker's Northampton, i. 47. Banks' Baronies in Fee, ii. 78. The Genealogist, New Series, xvii. 28.

FITZ-LAMBERT. Harleian Society, xli. 125.

FITZ LEWIS. Morant's Essex, i. 213. Wright's Essex, ii. 552. See ALNO.

FITZ MARTIN. Collinson's Somerset, ii. 132.

FITZ MAURICE. Berry's Buckingham Genealogies, 59. Burke's Landed Gentry, 2 supp., 3, 4, 5, 6. O'Hart's Irish Pedigrees, 2nd Series, 334. Charles Smith's History of Kerry, 237. Edmondson's Baronagium Genealogicum, v. 463. Archdall's Lodge's Peerage, ii. 182. History of the Wilmer Family, 329.

FITZ-NICOLL. Fosbrooke's Abstracts of Smith's Lives of the Berkeleys, 74. The Genealogist, New Series, xiii. 97.

FITZ-NIGEL. Lipscombe's History of the County of Buckingham, i. 66.

FITZ ODO. Eyton's Antiquities of Shropshire, vi. 83.

FITZOOTH. Robin Hood, edited by Joseph Ritson, 6.

FITZ OSBERN. Norfolk Antiquarian Miscellany, i. 413. Annals of Chepstow Castle, by J. F. Marsh, 265. Berks Archæological and Architectural Society's Journal, i. 83.

FITZ OSBERT. Banks' Baronies in Fee, ii. 80.

FITZ PAIN, FITZ PAINE, or FITZ PAYN. Collinson's Somerset, i. 59 ;

iii. 245. Collectanea Topographica et Genealogica, iii. 250, 398.
Manning and Bray's Surrey, iii. 117. Banks' Baronies in Fee,
i. 209. Banks' Dormant and Extinct Baronage, ii. 203. Genealogies of Morgan and Glamorgan, by G. T. Clark, 397. The
Genealogist, New Series, vii. 244.

FITZ PATRICK. Irish Pedigrees, by John O'Hart, 131. Keating's
History of Ireland, *Plate* 19. Archdall's Lodge's Peerage, ii. 333.
Brydges' Collins' Peerage, viii. 293.

FITZ-PEN, or PHIPPEN. Harleian Society, ix. 71. The Visitations of
Cornwall, edited by J. L. Vivian, 160. New England Register,
xlix. 245.

FITZ PIERS. Manning and Bray's Surrey, ii. 92. Baker's Northampton, i. 47, 544. Banks' Dormant and Extinct Baronage, iii. 271.

FITZ-RALPH, or FITZ-RALF. Morant's Essex, ii. 261. Banks' Dormant
and Extinct Baronage, i. 83. Harleian Society, xxxii. 71.

FITZ-RANDOLPH, or FITZ RANDOLFE. Harleian Society, iv. 187.
Thoroton's Nottinghamshire, ii. 296.

FITZ-RANULPH. Banks' Dormant and Extinct Baronage, i. 83.

FITZ REGINALD. Banks' Baronies in Fee, ii. 80.

FITZ ROBERT. Eyton's Antiquities of Shropshire, i. 381.

FITZ-ROGER. A description of the Monument and Effigies in Porlock
Church, by Maria Halliday, *at end.* The Genealogist, New Series,
x. 29. *See* ROGERS, STOKEPORT.

FITZ-ROY. The Great Governing Families of England, i. 344.
Jacob's Peerage, i. 163, 171. Burke's Landed Gentry, 5, 8 supp.
Baker's Northampton, ii. 71, 169. Edmondson's Baronagium
Genealogicum, i. 13, 17; vi. 93. Berry's Genealogical Peerage,
56. Brydges' Collins' Peerage, i. 213; vii. 540. Banks' Dormant and Extinct Baronage, iii. 197. Burke's Colonial Gentry,
i. 111.

FITZ SEWIN. Baker's Northampton, i. 224.

FITZSIMON. Morant's Essex, i. 303. Burke's Landed Gentry, 4.
See FRAZER, SYMONS.

FITZ-SIMOND. Harleian Society, xiii. 100.

FITZ-SIMONS. Burke's Landed Gentry, 4.

FITZ SYMON. Chauncy's Hertfordshire, 311. Harleian Society
xvi. 328.

FITZ URSE. Savage's Hundred of Carhampton, 280. Collinson's
Somerset, ii. 47; iii. 487.

FITZWALTER. Journal of the British Archæological Association,
xv. 26. Gough's Sepulchral Monuments, ii. 101. Morant's Essex,
i. 338; ii. 428. Carthew's Hundred of Launditch, Part i. 105.
Maclean's History of Trigg Minor, i. 394*. Bridges' Northamptonshire, by Rev. Peter Whalley, i. 44. Clutterbuck's Hertford,
ii. 277, 432, 463. Baker's Northampton, i. 56. Wright's Essex,
ii. 658. Banks' Dormant and Extinct Baronage, ii. 205. Banks'
Baronies in Fee, i. 210; ii. 83. Chancellor's Sepulchral Monuments of Essex, 31. The Genealogist, New Series, xiii. 246.

FITZ WARIN, FITZWARINE, or FITZWARYN. Eyton's Antiquities of
Shropshire, ii. 12; xi. 39. Hutchins' Dorset, iv. 174. Collin-

son's Somerset, iii. 271. Collectanea Topographica et Genealogica, i. 329. Toulman's History of Taunton, new edn., by James Savage, (Taunton, 1822, 8vo.) 70. Banks' Baronies in Fee, i. 212. Banks' Dormant and Extinct Baronage, i. 304; ii. 214. Notes and Queries, 3 S. vii. 55; 4 S. viii. 337. The Genealogist, vi. 18; New Series, xiv. 99; xvi. 234. History of Powys Fadog, by J. Y. W. Lloyd, vi. 180. Archæologia Cambrensis, New Series, iii. 282.

FITZWILLIAM, or FITZWILLIAMS. The Great Governing Families of England, i. 112. Gough's Sepulchral Monuments, ii. 328. Morant's Essex, i. 160. Visitation of Staffordshire, (Willm. Salt Soc.) 76. Foster's Yorkshire Pedigrees. Foster's Visitations of Yorkshire, 7, 411, 517. Comment upon the 5th journey of Antoninus, etc., by Kennet Gibson, (Nichols' Miscellaneous Antiquities, 1800, 4to.) 206. Bridges' Northamptonshire, by Rev. Peter Whalley, ii. 517. Hunter's Deanery of Doncaster, i. 251, 330, 332, 339; ii. 56, 93. Thoroton's Nottinghamshire, i. 133; iii. 170, 286. Memorials of the Church of Attleborough, by J. T. Barrett, 184. Harleian Society, xiii. 197; xvi. 27, 122; xix. 27; xliii. 5. The Genealogist, iv. 23; vi. 150; New Series, xvi. 239. Yorkshire Archæological and Topographical Journal, vi. 369. Notes and Queries, 3 S. ii. 123, 349. Banks' Dormant and Extinct Baronage, i. 305. Edmondson's Baronagium Genealogicum, iii. 259. Archdall's Lodge's Peerage, ii. 158; iv. 306. Brydges' Collins' Peerage, iv. 374, 542. Banks' Baronies in Fee, i. 169, 323. Historical Notices of Doncaster, by C. W. Hatfield, 2nd Series, 130. Metcalfe's Visitations of Northamptonshire, 88. Massingberd's History of Ormsby, 264. Bedfordshire Notes and Queries, iii. 47. Burke's Landed Gentry, 8.

FLACKE. The Genealogist, iii. 296.

FLACKET. Miscellanea Genealogica et Heraldica, New Series, i. 134.

FLAMANK, or FLAMOCK. Maclean's History of Trigg Minor, i. 279. Polwhele's History of Cornwall, ii. 44. Harleian Society, ix. 71. A Complete Parochial History of the County of Cornwall, i. 85. An Historical Survey of Cornwall, by C. S. Gilbert, ii. 103. The Visitations of Cornwall, edited by J. L. Vivian, 161.

FLAMBAUD. The Genealogist, New Series, xiv. 24.

FLAMBOROUGH. Foster's Visitations of Yorkshire, 246.

FLAMSTEAD. Jewitt's Reliquary, xvi. 189.

FLAMVILE, or FLAMVILL. Bibliotheca Topographica Britannica, vii. Parts i. and ii. 252. Harleian Society, ii. 53. Nichols' History of the County of Leicester, iv. 447, 973.

FLANAGAN. Burke's Landed Gentry, 3, 4, 5, 6, 8. See O'FLANAGAN.

FLANDERS. Nichols' History of the County of Leicester, iv. 636. See DE FLANDERS.

FLANDERS, Counts of. Genealogical Table of John Stratford Collins. New England Register, xxvii. 170.

FLATT. Howard's Visitation of England and Wales, viii. 34.

FLAVEL. Howard's Visitation of England and Wales, i. 207; Notes, iii. 52. Burke's Family Records, 244.

FLAY. Harleian Society, vi. 343. The Visitations of Devon, by
J. L. Vivian, 343.
FLEATHAM. Topographer and Genealogist, ii. 85.
FLEET, or FLEETE. Harleian Society, viii. 417; xv. 277; xl. 1297.
Cussan's History of Hertfordshire, Parts ix. and x. 16. Burke's
Landed Gentry, 8.
FLEETWOOD. Noble's Memoirs of the House of Cromwell, ii. 334.
Blomefield's Norfolk, vi. 325. Burke's Commoners, iv. 521.
Bibliotheca Topographica Britannica, ii. Part ii. 28. Topo-
grapher, (London, 1789-91, 8vo.) i. 475. Chetham Society,
lxxxv. 110, 111. Lipscombe's History of the County of Bucking-
ham, ii. 377; iii. 227. Whitaker's History of Richmondshire,
ii. 344. Baines' History of the Co. of Lancaster, iv. 440;
Croston's edn., iv. 208. Harleian Society, xv. 278. Notes and
Queries, 2 S. vii. 317, 403; 4 S. ix. 363; 6 S. xi. 116. Wotton's
English Baronetage, i. 193. Betham's Baronetage, i. 121. Burke's
Extinct Baronetcies. The Visitations of Staffordshire, 1614 and
1663-4, William Salt Society, 129. See FLETEWOOD.
FLEMING, FLEMINGE, FLEMYING, or FLEMYNG. Historical and
Genealogical Memoir of the Family of Fleming of Slane, Co.
Meath, by Sir W. Betham. Dublin, 1829, fol. Biggar and the
House of Fleming, by Willm. Hunter. Biggar, 1862, 8vo. Edin-
burgh, 2nd edn., 1867, 8vo. Claim of C. R. Fleming to be Earl
of Wigtown, Sess. Papers, Jan.-Mar., 1762. Service of B. H.
Gyll as nearest and lawful heir of line of Alexander Flemyng,
1842, 4to. pp. 14. Burke's Extinct Baronetcies, and 621. Mis-
celleanea Genealogica et Heraldica, ii. 141. Morant's Essex, i. 113.
Gentleman's Magazine, 1832, i. 206, 495. Berry's Hampshire
Genealogies, 126, 259. Berry's Hertfordshire Genealogies, 53.
Glamorganshire Pedigrees, edited by Sir T. Phillipps, 42. Foster's
Visitations of Yorkshire, 328, 358. Burke's Commoners, (of
Stoneham,) ii. 372, Landed Gentry, 2, 3, 4, 5, 6, 7, 8; (of Rayrigg,)
Landed Gentry, 5, 6, 8; (of Cumbernauld,) 2, 3; (of Barochan,) 2.
Herald and Genealogist, vi. 350. Gyll's History of Wraysbury,
101. Harleian Society, ix. 72; xiii. 397; xiv. 569; xv. 278.
Lipscombe's History of the County of Buckingham, iv. 598.
Hampshire Visitations, printed by Sir T. Phillipps, 28. Corry's
History of Lancashire, i. 401-411. Caermarthenshire Pedigrees,
53. Baines' History of the Co. of Lancaster, iv. 648. Shirley's
History of the County of Monaghan, 221. The Upper Ward of
Lanarkshire, by G. V. Irving, i. 306. Bigland's Gloucestershire,
ii. par. Saperton. Wood's Douglas's Peerage of Scotland, ii. 628.
Notes and Queries, 3 S. ix. 157, 438; 7 S. i. 116. Wotton's
English Baronetage, iv. 105. Visitation of Devon, edited by
F. T. Colby, 19, 82. Betham's Baronetage, iii. 139. The Visita-
tions of Cornwall, edited by J. L. Vivian, 164. The Visitations
of Devon, edited by J. L. Vivian, 68, 284. Genealogies of
Morgan and Glamorgan, by G. T. Clark, 383. Foster's Visita-
tions of Cumberland and Westmorland, 47. Alexander Nisbet's
Heraldic Plates, 110. Oliver's History of Antigua, i. 252.

Burke's Family Records, 246. Nicolson and Burn's Westmorland and Cumberland, i. 151-174. The Genealogist, New Series, xvi. 88.

FLETCHER. Dwnn's Visitations of Wales, ii. 121. Berry's Kent Genealogies, 488. Surtees Society, xxxvi. 19. Burke's Commoners, (of Lawnswood,) iv. 50, Landed Gentry, 2, 3, 4, 5, 6, 7, 8 ; (of Salton,) Landed Gentry, 2, 3, 4, 5, 6, 7, 8 ; (of Dunans,) 3, 4, 5 ; (of Carsock,) 2, 3, 4, 5 ; (of Dale Park,) 5, 6, 7, 8 ; (of Tarn Bank,) 5, 6 ; (of Garr,) 3, 4 ; (of Rosehaugh,) 8 ; (of Brigham Hill,) 8 ; (of Kevan Ila,) 2, 3 ; (of Nerquis Hall,) 6, 7, 8 ; (of Kenward,) 6, 7, 8. Foster's Visitations of Yorkshire, 30. Visitation of Warwickshire, 1619, published with Warwickshire Antiquarian Magazine, 138. Harleian Society, ix. 73 ; xii. 353 ; xv. 279 ; xxviii. 185. Hutchinson's History of Cumberland, i. 508. Burke's Heraldic Illustrations, 97. Jefferson's History of Leath Ward, Cumberland, 427. Thoresby's Ducatus Leodiensis, 179. Hunter's History of the Parish of Sheffield, 293. Pembrokeshire Pedigrees, 139. Hunter's Deanery of Doncaster, ii. 464. Jewitt's Reliquary, xvii. 128. Poems of Phineas Fletcher, (Fuller Worthies Library,) i. xxi. Poems of Giles Fletcher, (Fuller Worthies Library,) 1. Pedigree of Wilson of High Wray, etc., by Joseph Foster, 90. Betham's Baronetage, iv. 101, 402. Notes and Queries, 6 S. i. 511 ; iv. 392. Burke's Extinct Baronetcies. Miscellanea Genealogica et Heraldica, New Series, iv. 214. The Visitations of Cornwall, edited by J. L. Vivian, 165. History of Powys Fadog, by J. Y. W. Lloyd, iii. 356. Stockdale's Annals of Cartmel, 487. Fletcher's Leicestershire Pedigrees and Royal Descents, 163. Foster's Visitations of Cumberland and Westmorland, 49, 50. New England Register, xxii. 389 ; xxiii. 377. History of the Wilmer Family, 217. Howard's Visitation of England and Wales, iii. 77. Nicolson and Burn's Westmorland and Cumberland, ii. 389. See LONGRIDGE.

FLETCHER-VANE. Jefferson's History of Leath Ward, Cumberland, 430.

FLETEWOOD. Chetham Society, lxxxi. 59 ; lxxxii. 89, 122. Visitation of Staffordshire, 1663-4, printed by Sir T. Phillipps, 5. See FLEETWOOD.

FLETTEWYKE. The Genealogist, New Series, xiv. 195.

FLINN. O'Hart's Irish Pedigrees, 2nd Series, 182.

FLINT. Burke's Colonial Gentry, i. 193. New England Register, xiv. 58.

FLINTON. Poulson's Holderness, ii. 52.

FLOOD. Burke's Commoners, (of Flood Hall and Paulstown,) i. vii. 122, Landed Gentry, 2, 3, 4, 5, 6, 7, 8 ; (of Slaney Lodge,) Landed Gentry, 3, 4, 5, 6, 7. Harleian Society, xv. 279, 280. Burke's Extinct Baronetcies, 605.

FLORY. Howard's Visitation of England and Wales, i. 207. Burke's Family Records, 246.

FLOWER. Pedigree of Flower of Cheltenham, [T. P.] 1870, 2 folio pages. Pedigrees of Flower of Steple Ashton, and of Pottern,

2 folio pages. Berry's Hampshire Genealogies, 37. Cambridgeshire Visitation, edited by Sir T. Phillipps, 13. Foster's Visitations of Yorkshire, 518, 618. Harleian Society, iii. 29; iv. 121;
xv. 280; xxxvii. 357; xli. 86. Wright's History of Rutland,
136. Visitatio Comitatus Wiltoniæ, 1623, printed by Sir T.
Phillipps. Thoroton's Nottinghamshire, iii. 286. Archdall's
Lodge's Peerage, v. 279. Burke's Landed Gentry, 6 supp., 7.
Burke's Family Records, 247. The Genealogist, New Series,
xii. 89.

FLOWERDEW. Amye Robsart, by George Adlard, 19.

FLOYD. Archæologia Cambrensis, 3 S. iv. 408. Surrey Archæological Collections, x. Harleian Society, xliii. 206. Duchetiana,
by Sir G. F. Duckett, 2nd edn., 75.

FLOYER. Cussan's History of Hertfordshire, Parts iii. and iv. 137.
Bibliotheca Topographica Britannica, ix. Part 4, 141. Visitation
of Somerset, printed by Sir T. Phillipps, 70. Burke's Commoners,
(of West Stafford,) i. 605, Landed Gentry, 2, 3, 4, 5, 6, 7, 8; (of
Martin Hall,) Landed Gentry, 5, 6; (of Hints,) 2, 3, 4. Miscellanea Genealogica et Heraldica, New Series, i. 123; 2nd Series,
iv. 129; v. 137. Harleian Society, vi. 343; xi. 36. Shaw's
Staffordshire, ii. 21, 49. Westcote's Devonshire, edited by G.
Oliver and P. Jones, 566. Hutchins' Dorset, ii. 513. Visitation
of Devon, edited by F. T. Colby, 97. Visitations of Staffordshire,
1614 and 1663-4, William Salt Society, 131. The Visitations of
Devon, by J. L. Vivian, 344. Howard's Visitation of England
and Wales, iii. 115.

FLUDD. Hasted's Kent, ii. 491. Berry's Kent Genealogies, 304, 448.

FLUDYER. Betham's Baronetage, iii. 289. Hasted's Kent, (Hund.
of Blackheath, by H. H. Drake,) 223.

FLYER. Cussan's History of Hertfordshire, Parts iii. and iv. 137.
Berry's Hertfordshire Genealogies, 146. Visitation of Staffordshire, 1663-4, printed by Sir T. Phillipps, 5. Clutterbuck's Hertford, iii. 446. Chauncy's Hertfordshire, 142. Harleian Society,
xv. 281.

FOCHE. Berry's Kent Genealogies, 132. Harleian Society, viii. 442;
xlii. 33.

FODEN. Visitation of Staffordshire, 1663-4 printed by Sir T.
Phillipps, 5. Visitations of Staffordshire, 1614 and 1663-4,
William Salt Society, 132.

FODERINGEY. Gage's History of Thingoe Hundred, Suffolk, 354.

FODRINGHEY. Harleian Society, xiii. 52.

FOGARTY. Burke's Commoners, iii. 700. O'Hart's Irish Pedigrees,
2nd Series, 180.

FOGGE. Hasted's Kent, iii. 151, 260. Berry's Kent Genealogies,
471. Burke's Visitation of Seats and Arms, ii. 30. Archæologia
Cantiana, v. 125. Scott of Scot's-Hall, by J. R. Scott, 175. The
Antiquary, (London, 1873,) iv. 313.

FOGG-ELLIOT. Burke's Landed Gentry, 4, 5, 6, 7, 8. Foster's Lancashire Pedigrees.

FOIX. Notes and Queries, 2 S. xi. 395.

FOLEY. Nash's Worcestershire, ii. 465 ; supp. 82. Burke's Landed Gentry, (of Prestwood,) 3, 4, 5, 6, 7, 8 ; (of Tetworth,) 3, 4 ; (of Wistow Manor,) 6. Shaw's Staffordshire, ii. 235. Edmondson's Baronagium Genealogicum, vi. 75. Brydges' Collins' Peerage, vii. 493. Notes and Queries, 5 S. ii. 262. Burke's Extinct Baronetcies. The Genealogist, vi. 117. Metcalfe's Visitation of Worcester, 1683, 46. The Visitations of Cornwall, edited by J. L. Vivian, 197.

FOLGER. New England Register, xvi. 269.

FOLIFATE, or FOLIFOOT. Notes and Queries, 7 S i., 44, 115 ; iii. 71, 481.

FOLIOT, FOLYOTT, or FOLLIOTT. Nash's Worcestershire, ii. 258. Carthew's Hundred of Launditch, Part i. 195. Hutchins' Dorset, iv. 438. Clutterbuck's Hertford, iii. 58. Thoroton's Nottinghamshire, iii. 202. Burke's Landed Gentry, 2, 3, 4, 5. Burke's Heraldic Illustrations, 34. Notes and Queries, 3 S. i. 338. Visitation of Devon, edited by F. T. Colby, 98. Banks' Dormant and Extinct Baronage, i. 84. Metcalfe's Visitation of Worcester, 1683, 47. Harleian Society, xxvii. 53. Parliamentary Memoirs of Fermanagh, by Earl of Belmore, 5. See FFOLLIOTT.

FOLJAMBE. Pedigree of Foljambe of Cockglode, etc., by C. G. S. Foljambe, 1892, broadside. Pedigree of Foljambe of Osberton, by C. G. S. Foljambe, 1892, broadside. Collectanea Topographica et Genealogica, i. 91-111, 333-361 ; ii. 68-90. Camden Society, iv. xxviii. Glover's History of Derbyshire, ii. 392, (359). Surtees Society, xxxvi. 53. Burke's Commoners, iv. 438, Landed Gentry, 2, 3, 4, 5, 6 and supp., 7, 8. Foster's Yorkshire Pedigrees. Jewitt's Reliquary, xiv. 239 ; xv. 25. Howard's Visitation of England and Wales, i. 44, 46. Miscellanea Genealogica et Heraldica, 2nd Series, v. 34. Hunter's Deanery of Doncaster, ii. 57, 60. Holland's History of Worksop, 182. Burke's Extinct Baronetcies. Visitation of Staffordshire, (Willm. Salt Soc.) 77. Supplement to Hunter's Hallamshire, edited by Gatty, xxxix. The Genealogist, New Series, vii. 132 ; xii. 253. Ilkley, Ancient and Modern, by R. Collyer and J. H. Turner, 117. Harleian Society, xxxvii. 198.

FOLKARD. A Monograph of the Family of Folkard of Suffolk. Printed by R. Folkard and Son. London, circa 1895, 2 Parts, 4to. No title-page.

FOLKES. Betham's Baronetage, iii. 441.

FOLKINGHAM. Foster's Visitations of Yorkshire, 225. Thoresby's Ducatus Leodiensis, 112. Harleian Society, xvi. 129.

FOLKRAY, or FOLKEROY. Harleian Society, vi. 152. The Visitations of Devon, by J. L. Vivian, 471.

FOLLET. Burke's Landed Gentry, 8 supp.

FOLSOM. New England Register, xxx. 207.

FOLTHEROP. Surtees Society, xli. 47.

FOLVILLE, or FOLVILE. Camden Society, xliii. 76. Nichols' History of the County of Leicester, iii. 23. Harleian Society, xviii. 101.

FONES. Muskett's Suffolk Manorial Families, i. 83.

FONNEREAU. Burke's Commoners, ii. 110, Landed Gentry, 2, 3, 4, 5, 6, 7, 8.

FOORD. Harleian Society, xiii. 53.

FOOTE. Berry's Kent Genealogies, 26. Burke's Commoners, i. 372. New England Register, ix. 272 ; li. 252. Oliver's History of Antigua, i. 256. Howard's Visitation of England and Wales, vii. 130.

FOOTT. Burke's Landed Gentry, 3, 4, 5, 6, 7, 8.

FORBES. The Earls of Granard, a Memoir of the Noble Family of Forbes, edited by G. A. Hastings, Earl of Granard, K.P. London, 1868, 8vo. The Genealogy of the House of Forbes, by M. Lumsden. Inverness, 1819, 8vo. Another edn., 1883. Forbes of Monymusk and Pitsligo, 1460-1880, by Louisa Lilias Forbes. Edinburgh, 1880. Folding sheet. Genealogy of the House of Tolquhoun, by J. Davidson. Aberdeen, 1839, 8vo. Memoranda relating to the Family of Forbes of Waterton, by J. Forbes. Aber deen, 1857, 4to. Burke's Commoners, (of Culloden,) iv. 620, Landed Gentry, 2, 3, 4, 5, 6, 7, 8; (of Kingareloch,) Landed Gentry, 2, 3, 4, 5, 6, 8; (of Tolquhoun,) 2, 3, 4, 5, 6, 7, 8 ; (of Callendar,) 2, 3, 5, 6, 7, 8 ; (of Balgownie,) 3, 4, 5, 6, 7, 8 ; (of Echt House,) 2, 3, 4 ; (of Boyndlie,) 7, 8 ; (of Callendar,) 8, 8 supp. ; (of Medwyn,) 8 ; (of Rothiemay,) 8. Burke's Visitation of Seats and Arms, 2nd Series, ii. 18. Burke's Royal Families, (London, 1851, 8vo.) i. 176 ; ii. 208. Douglas's Baronage of Scotland, 39, 75. Inverurie and the Earldom of the Garioch, by John David son, 232, 236. Walter Wood's East Neuk of Fife, 256. Col lections for History of Aberdeen and Banff, (Spalding Club,) i. 331, 436. Wood's Douglas's Peerage of Scotland, i. 589 ; ii. 367. A short Memoir of James Young, app. 19. J. B. Pratt's Buchan, 386, 424. Archdall's Lodge's Peerage, ii. 139. Brydges' Collins' Peerage, ix. 311. Foster's Collectanea Genealogica, (MP's Scot land, 139. The Wolfes of Forenaghts, 64. Burke's Colonial Gentry, i. 125, 128.

FORBES-GORDON. Burke's Landed Gentry, 5, 6, 7, 8.

FORBES-LEITH. See FORBES, of Tolquhoun.

FORBES-MITCHELL. Burke's Landed Gentry, 2, 3, 4, 5, 6, 7, 8.

FORCER, or FORSER. Hutchinson's History of Durham, ii. 335. Surtees' Durham, i. 65. Visitation of Durham, 1575, (Newcastle, 1820, fol.) 31. Foster's Visitations of Durham, 123.

FORCETT. Plantagenet-Harrison's History of Yorkshire, i. 456.

FORD, or FORDE. Parentalia : Reminiscences of the Family of Fforde, by Frederick Forde, 1878, 4to. Burke's Landed Gentry, 4th edition, 264. Berry's Sussex Genealogies, 182. Tuckett's Devonshire Pedigrees, 156, 158. Burke's Commoners, (of Sea forde,) iv. 190, Landed Gentry, 2, 3, 4, 5, 6, 7, 8 ; (of Abbeyfield,) Landed Gentry, 2, 3, 4, 5 ; (of Enfield Old Park,) 3, 4, 5, 6, 7, 8 ; (of Ellell Hall,) 2, 3, 4, 5, 6, 7, 8. Harleian Society, vi. 107, 108 ; viii. 49 ; xxviii. 49. Burke's Visitation of Seats and Arms, 2nd Series, i. 21. Foster's Lancashire Pedigrees. Dallaway's Sussex, i. 192. The Visitations of Devon, by J. L. Vivian, 347. West-

cote's Devonshire, edited by G. Oliver and P. Jones, 527, 528.
Pembrokeshire Pedigrees, 125. Visitation of Devon, edited by
F. T. Colby, 7, 47, 99. Betham's Baronetage, iv. 252. Ormerod's
Cheshire, iii. 101. Pease of Darlington, by Joseph Foster, 22.
Croston's edn. of Baines's Lancaster, v. 496. Miscellanea Genea-
logica et Heraldica, 3rd Series, iii. 44.

FORDEN. Harleian Society, xxvii. 79.

FORDHAM. Cussan's History of Hertfordshire, Parts v. and vi. 148.
Burke's Landed Gentry, 7, 8.

FORDYCE. Burke's Landed Gentry, 3, 4, 5, 6, 7, 8.

FORDYCE-BUCHAN. Burke's Landed Gentry, 8 supp.

FORESTER, or FORRESTER. Pedigree of the Foresters of Arngibbon.
Edinburgh, 1880, broadside. Clutterbuck's Hertford, iii. 517.
Walter Wood's East Neuk of Fife, 267. Wood's Douglas's Peer-
age of Scotland, i. 598. Harleian Society, xxviii. 187.

FORMAN. Harleian Society, xv. 281.

FORMBY. Foster's Lancashire Pedigrees. Burke's Landed Gentry,
6 and supp., 7, 8.

FORMESTON. Antiquities and Memoirs of the Parish of Myddle,
written by Richard Gough, 1700, (folio,) 61.

FORREST. The Pedigree of the Forrest, Lowther, and Monk families,
by A. R. Forrest. Derby, 1864, 4to. Burke's Colonial Gentry,
i. 244; ii. 744.

FORSTER. Some Account of the Pedigree of the Forsters of Cold
Hesleden, Co. Durham, by Joseph Foster. Sunderland, 1862, 4to.
A Pedigree of the Forsters and Fosters of the North of England,
etc., by Joseph Foster. London, 1871, 4to. Burke's Extinct
Baronetcies. Hasted's Kent, ii. 568. Camden Society, xliii. 56.
Ashmole's Antiquities of Berkshire, iii. 311. Berry's Sussex
Genealogies, 7, 192, 320, 329, 375. Archæologia Cantiana, iv. 269.
Berry's Kent Genealogies, 44. Surtees Society, xxxvi. 71, 204.
Burke's Landed Gentry, (of Lysways Hall,) 3, 4, 5; (of Walthamstow,) 2; (of Exbury,) 7, 8. Foster's Visitations of Yorkshire,
316, 618. Bateson's History of Northumberland, i. 156, 228,
252, 288. Harleian Society, viii. 122; xii. 133; xv. 282, 286;
xix. 13; xxii. 143; xxvii. 56; xxviii. 185. Raine's History of
North Durham, 306, 322. Burke's Visitation of Seats and Arms,
ii. 13. Graves' History of Cleveland, 225. Hodgson's Northumberland, III. ii. 375. Dallaway's Sussex, i. 219. Ord's History
of Cleveland, 397. Shakespere's Home, by J. C. M. Bellew, 349.
Surtees' Durham, iii. 357; iv. 152. Shirley's History of the
County of Monaghan, 224. The Genealogist, ii. 14; v. 259;
New Series, i. 9. Pedigree of Wilson of High Wray, etc., by
Joseph Foster, 50. Metcalfe's Visitations of Suffolk, 29. Foster's
Visitations of Durham, 125. Notes and Queries, 6 S. ix. 310.
Foster's Visitations of Northumberland, 58, 59. Foster's Visita-
tions of Cumberland and Westmorland, 51. Burke's Colonial
Gentry, i. 55. Surrey Archæological Collections, xi. The Gres-
ley's of Drakelowe, by F. Madan, 255. See FOSTER, HARDWICKE.

FORSTER-BARHAM. Burke's Commoners, iv. 550.

FORSYTH. Burke's Colonial Gentry, ii. 554. Burke's Landed Gentry, 8, and 8 supp.

FORSYTH-GRANT. Burke's Landed Gentry, 5, 6, 7 and at p. 776, 8.

FORT. Visitation of Somerset, printed by Sir T. Phillipps, 71. Burke's Landed Gentry, 5 supp., 6, 7, 8. Harleian Society, xi. 37. Whitaker's History of Whalley, ii. 41.

FORTE. Pedigree of Forte of Barbados, printed by J. Lavars. Bristol, single page, *circa* 1876. Burke's Colonial Gentry, ii. 436.

FORTEATH. Burke's Landed Gentry, 3.

FORTERIE. Harleian Society, xv. 284.

FORTESCUE, or FORTESCU. Sir John Fortescue, Knight, his life, works, and family history, by Lord Clermont. London, 1869, 4to. 2 vols. and supplement. 2nd edn. London, 1880, 4to. Claim of the Right Hon. Thos. Fortescue, Baron Clermont in Ireland, to vote at elections of Irish Peers, Sess. Papers, 330 of 1852-3. Morant's Essex, ii. 117, 120. Harleian Society, vi. 109-112 ; ix. 73 ; xiii. 398 ; xiv. 570 ; xxvii. 56 ; xliii. 14. Burke's Commoners, (of Fallapit,) ii. 541, Landed Gentry, 2, 3, 4, 5, 6, 7, 8 ; (of Buckland Filleigh,) Commoners, ii. 544, Landed Gentry, 2, 3 ; (of Dromisken,) Commoners, iv. 125, Landed Gentry, 2 ; (of Stephenstown,) 8 supp. ; (of Boconnoc,) 8 ; (of Kingcausie,) 8. Notices of Swyncombe and Ewelme, in Co. Oxford, by H. A. Napier, 390. Westcote's Devonshire, edited by G. Oliver and P. Jones, 498, 625, 626. Nichols' History of the County of Leicester, iv. 451. Clutterbuck's Hertford, ii. 348. Foley's Records of the English Province S. J., iv. 275 ; v. 961. Edmondson's Baronagium Genealogicum, v. 442. Archdall's Lodge's Peerage, iii. 340. Brydges' Collins' Peerage, v. 335. Visitation of Devon, edited by F. T. Colby, 100, 103. Burke's Extinct Baronetcies, and 621. The Visitations of Cornwall, edited by J. L. Vivian, 166. The Visitations of Devon, by J. L. Vivian, 352-367, 850. Hasted's Kent, (Hund. of Blackheath, by H. H. Drake,) xviii.

FORTH. Metcalfe's Visitations of Suffolk, 137. Suffolk Manorial Families, by J. J. Muskett, 9, 108-131, 315-321. New England Register, xviii. 184.

FORTHO. Bridges' Northamptonshire, by the Rev. Peter Whalley, i. 297.

FORTIBUS. Clutterbuck's Hertford, ii. 261. *See* DE FORTIBUS.

FORTNUM. Burke's Landed Gentry, 8.

FORTREY, or FORTRYE. Nichols' History of the County of Leicester, ii. 446*. Hasted's Kent, i. 440. The Genealogist, iii. 297. Harleian Society, xv. 285.

FORWOOD. Burke's Landed Gentry, 8.

FOSBERY. Burke's Landed Gentry, (of Clorane,) 2, 3, 4, 5, 6, 7, 8 ; (of Curraghbridge,) 3, 4, 5.

FOSBROOKE. Burke's Commoners, ii. 626, Landed Gentry, 2, 3, 4, 5, 6, 7, 8. T. D. Fosbrooke's British Monachism, 21. Fosbrooke's History of Gloucestershire, i. 407. Fosbrooke's Companion to the Wye Tour, 178. Metcalfe's Visitations of Northamptonshire, 20,

89. Archæological Sketches of Ross, by T. D. Fosbrooke, 172, 178. Fletcher's Leicestershire Pedigrees and Royal Descents, 153.
FOSSARD. Wainwright's Wapentake of Strafford and Tickhill, 7, 25. Banks' Dormant and Extinct Baronage, i. 87.
FOSTER. Pedigree of Foster of Meere, [T. P.] Broadside. Gentleman's Magazine, 1821, i. 295, 387. Camoys Peerage Evidence, 152. Berry's Sussex Genealogies, 154. Visitation of Somerset, printed by Sir T. Phillipps, 72, 73. Burke's Commoners, (of Brickhill House,) iv. 549, Landed Gentry, 2, 3, 4, 5, 6, 7; (of Hornby Castle,) 7, 8; (of Lanwithan,) 7, 8; (of Clewer Manor,) 7, 8; (of Kempstone,) 7, 8; (of Apley,) 7, 8; (of Co. Louth,) 8 at p. 666; (of Kilhow,) 8; (of Jamaica,) Landed Gentry, 3, 4, 5, 6, 7; (of Ballymascanlan,) 3, 4, 5, 6, 7; (of Dunleer,) 7 at page 647; (of Wadsworth Banks,) 2, 3, 4, 5, 6; (of Pontlands,) 6, 7, 8; (of Horton in Ribblesdale,) 6. Topographer, (London, 1789-91, 8vo.) i. 34. Herald and Genealogist, viii. 204. Harleian Society, xi. 37; xix. 108; xxxvii. 77, 269, 404; xxxix. 1118. Lipscombe's History of the County of Buckingham, iv. 174. Blore's Rutland, 50. Nichols' History of the County of Leicester, iv. 725, 726. Wiltshire Archæological Magazine, iii. 224. Miscellanea Genealogica et Heraldica, New Series, ii. 201. Burke's Landed Gentry, 6th edn., 565. Foley's Records of the English Province S. J., ii. 445. Metcalfe's Visitations of Suffolk, 30. The Genealogist, vii. 176. Weaver's Visitations of Somerset, 24. The Curio, (New York,) i. 68. New England Register, i. 352; xx. 227, 308; xxv. 67; xxvi. 394; xxx. 83; lii. 194, 336. Visitations of Staffordshire, 1614 and 1663-4, William Salt Society, 276. The descendants of J. Backhouse, by J. Foster, 43*. The Irish Builder, xxxv. 258. Genealogy of the descendants of Roger Foster, of Edreston, Northumberland. By A. H. Foster-Barham. London, 1897, 4to. See FORSTER.
FOSTER-MELLIAR. Burke's Landed Gentry, 5, 6, 7, 8.
FOTHERBY. The Antiquities of Gainford, by J. R. Walbran, 87. Berry's Kent Genealogies, 268. Harleian Society, xlii. 111.
FOTHERGILL. Notes and Queries, 2 S. v. 170, 321, 487; vi. 215. Burke's Landed Gentry, 8.
FOTHERLEY. Harleian Society, viii. 355; xxii. 144. Clutterbuck's Hertford, i. 188.
FOTHRINGHAM. Burke's Landed Gentry, 7, 8.
FOUCHER. Nichols' History of the County of Leicester, iv. 1006.
FOULIS. Surtees Society, xxxvi. 193. Foster's Yorkshire Pedigrees. Graves' History of Cleveland, 249. Ord's History of Cleveland, 432. Nisbet's Heraldry, ii. app. 18. Douglas's Baronage of Scotland, 86. Burke's Extinct Baronetcies, 621. Annals of Colinton, by Thomas Murray, 29. Wotton's English Baronetage, i. 365. Betham's Baronetage, i. 177. Foster's Collectanea Genealogica, (MP's Scotland,) 143. The Genealogist, New Series, xii. 46.
FOULKE. Harleian Society, xxi. 245.
FOULKES. History of Powis Fadog, by J. Y. W. Lloyd, v. 377; vi. 235, 238.

FOULSHURST. Eyton's Antiquities of Shropshire, v. 102. Baker's Northampton, i. 397. Ormerod's Cheshire, iii. 301, 385. Harleian Society, xviii. 102.

FOUNTAINE, FOUNTAIN, or FOUNTAYNE. Blomefield's Norfolk, vi. 233. Burke's Commoners, i. 224, Landed Gentry, 2, 3, 4, 5, 6, 7, 8. Westcote's Devonshire, edited by G. Oliver and P. Jones, 548. Chauncy's Hertfordshire, 531. Visitation of Devon, edited by F. T. Colby, 103. Tuckett's Devonshire Pedigrees, 109. Harleian Society, vi. 112 ; viii. 472 ; xix. 109 ; xxxii. 120. Hunter's Deanery of Doncaster, i. 367. The Visitations of Devon, edited by J. L. Vivian, 368.

FOUNTAYNE-WILSON. Burke's Commoners, ii. 268, Landed Gentry, 5. Foster's Yorkshire Pedigrees.

FOURBOUR. Gentleman's Magazine, 1838, ii. 21.

FOURDRINIER. Miscellanea Genealogica et Heraldica, New Series, iii. 385.

FOURNESS. Harleian Society, xxxvii. 93.

FOWBERY, or FOWBERYE. Camden Society, xliii. 104. Foster's Visitations of Yorkshire, 117.

FOWEL, or FOWELL. Burke's Commoners, iv. 424, Landed Gentry, 2. Harleian Society, vi. 113, 114 ; xv. 286. Westcote's Devonshire, edited by G. Oliver and P. Jones, 521. Visitation of Devon, edited by F. T. Colby, 104. Burke's Extinct Baronetcies, and add. The Visitations of Devon, by J. L. Vivian, 369.

FOWKE. Bibliotheca Topographica Britannica, iv. Part 4, 170. Burke's Landed Gentry, 4 at p. 1378, 5 at p. 1267, 6 at p. 1463. Berry's Berkshire Genealogies, 27. Visitation of Gloucestershire, 1569, (Middle Hill, 1854, fol.) 5. Burke's Heraldic Illustrations, 144. Shaw's Staffordshire, ii. 60. Visitation of Staffordshire, 1663-4, printed by Sir T. Phillipps, 5. Harleian Society, xv. 288 ; xxii. 54. Visitations of Staffordshire, 1614 and 1663-4, William Salt Society, 133. The Genealogist, New Series, ii. 301. Fletcher's Leicestershire Pedigrees and Royal Descents, 52.

FOWLE. Berry's Sussex Genealogies, 194, 230. Berry's Kent Genealogies, 112. Harleian Society, viii. 407 ; xv. 289. The Genealogist, iii. 299.

FOWLEHURST. Bridges' Northamptonshire, by Rev. Peter Whalley, i. 72. See FOULSHURST.

FOWLER. Topographer and Genealogist, ii. 77. Berry's Kent Genealogies, 121. Blomefield's Norfolk, ii. 167. Burke's Commoners, (of Abbey-cwm-hir,) ii. 375; (of Pendeford,) Commoners, iv. 390, Landed Gentry, 2, 4, 5, 6, 7, 8 ; (of Rahinston,) Landed Gentry, 3, 4, 5, 6, 7, 8 ; (of Braemore,) 5, 6, 7 ; (of Gunton Hall,) 5, 6, 7 ; (of Walliscote House,) 5, 6 ; (of Preston Hall,) 6 ; (of Southgate,) 8. Harleian Society, iii. 47 ; xix. 29 ; xxi. 61 ; xxviii. 189 ; xxxii. 121 ; xlii. 201. Visitation of Staffordshire, 1663-4, printed by Sir T. Phillipps, 5. Herald and Genealogist, vii. 559. Burke's Visitation of Seats and Arms, ii. 58. Shaw's Staffordshire, ii. 203. Fosbrooke's History of Gloucestershire, i. 313. History of Llangurig, by E. Hamer and H. W. Lloyd, 59, 93. The Salopian,

ix. 36. Pedigree of Wilson of High Wray, etc., by Joseph Foster,
31. Miscellanea Genealogica et Heraldica, New Series, iii. 345.
Eastwood's History of Ecclesfield, 448. Wotton's English Baronetage, iv. 102. The Genealogist, v. 296, 298 ; vii. 4, 177. Burke's
Extinct Baronetcies. F. G. Lee's History of Thame, 294. Visita-
tion of Staffordshire, (Willm. Salt Soc.) 78. Gloucestershire Notes
and Queries, i. 223, 282, 450; ii. 55, 172, 324, 405. History of
Powis Fadog, by J. Y. W. Lloyd, iii. 366. New England Register,
xi. 247. Visitation of Gloucester, edited by T. F. Fenwick and
W. C. Metcalfe, 62. Visitations of Staffordshire, 1614 and 1663-4,
William Salt Society, 134-141. Pedigree of Wilson, by S. B.
Foster, 67.

FOWLER-BUTLER. Burke's Landed Gentry, 4, 5, 6.

FOWNE. Glover's History of Derbyshire, ii. 5, (7).

FOWNES. Burke's Commoners, iii. 514. Phelps' History of Somersetshire, iii. 194. Harleian Society, ix. 289 ; xv. 287. Burke's Extinct Baronetcies, 606. Metcalfe's Visitation of Worcester, 1683,
48. The Visitations of Devon, by J. L. Vivian, 373. New England Register, xviii. 185. See LUTTRELL.

FOX. A Revised Genealogical Account of the various Families descended from Francis Fox, of St. German's, Cornwall, by Joseph
Foster. London, 1872, 4to. A short genealogical account of some
of the families of Fox, to which is appended a pedigree of the
Crokers, by C. H. Fox. Bristol, 1864, 4to. Chronicles of Tonedale,
by C. H. Fox. Taunton, 1879, 4to. Glover's History of Derbyshire, ii. 596, (581). Berry's Buckinghamshire Genealogies, 78.
Burke's Commoners, (of Chacombe Priory,) i. 423; (of Grove Hill,)
Commoners, iv. 314, Landed Gentry, 2, 4, 5, 6, 7, 8 ; (of Kil-
coursey,) Landed Gentry, 4, 5, 6, 7, 8; (of Fox Hall,) 4, 5, 6, 7, 8.
Miscellanea Genealogica et Heraldica, New Series, i. 114, 283 ;
2nd Series, iii. 35. Foster's Visitations of Yorkshire, 518. Harleian
Society, ii. 149 ; xxviii. 191 ; xxxviii, 681 ; xxxix. 896, 1021 ; xl.
1173. Phelps' History of Somersetshire, i. 253. Nichols' History
of the County of Leicester, iv. 504. Hutchins' Dorset, ii. 668.
Hoare's Wiltshire, V. i. 37. Baker's Northampton, i. 590. Some
Account of the Taylor Family, by P. A. Taylor, 693. Foster's
Pedigree of the Forsters and Fosters, Part ii. 58. The Sheriffs of
Montgomeryshire, by W. V. Lloyd, 438. Pedigree of Wilson of
High Wray, etc., by Joseph Foster, 129. O'Hart's Irish Pedigrees,
2nd Series, 180. The Genealogist, iii. 299. Notes and Queries,
1 S. i. 214, 250 ; xi. 325, 395 ; 2 S. i. 301. Edmondson's Baronagium Genealogicum, iii. 298 ; v. 496, 498. Brydges' Collins'
Peerage, iv. 529 ; vii. 308. Genealogical Records of the Family
of Woodd, 49. Miscellany of the Irish Archæological Society,
i. 185. History of Ribchester, by T. C. Smith and J. Shortt, 260.
Metcalfe's Visitations of Northamptonshire, 21. Pease of Darlington, by Joseph Foster, 67. Pedigree of Wilson, by S. B. Foster,
35. See LANE-FOX.

FOXALL. Burke's Landed Gentry, 2, 3, 4. Harleian Society, xv.
289.

FOXCROFT. Miscellanea Genealogica et Heraldica, i. 283. Surtees Society, xxxvi. 48. Thoresby's Ducatus Leodiensis, 156. Harleian Society, xv. 290. Records of Batley, by M. Sheard, 279. New England Register, viii. 171. Burke's Landed Gentry, 8.

FOX-LANE. Manning and Bray's Surrey, iii. 32. *See* LANE-FOX.

FOXLE, or FOXLEY. Topographer and Genealogist, iii. 180. History of the Hundred of Bray, by Charles Kerry, 104. Baker's Northampton, ii. 31. Lyon's Chronicles of Finchhampstead, 95. Brocas of Beaurepaire, by M. Burrows, 368. Metcalfe's Visitations of Northamptonshire, 21, 90. The Genealogist, New Series, xvi. 45.

FOXLOWE. Harleian Society, xxxix. 1164.

FOX-STRANGWAYS. Hutchins' Dorset, ii. 662, 668.

FOXTON. Cambridgeshire Visitations, edited by Sir T. Phillipps, 13. Nichols' History of the County of Leicester, ii. 562. Harleian Society, xli. 48.

FOXWIST. Dwnn's Visitations of Wales, ii. 286.

FOYE. Harleian Society, xxxviii. 358.

FOYLE. Berry's Hampshire Genealogies, 334. Miscellanea Genealogica et Heraldica, 2nd Series, ii. 239. *See* DE LA FOYLE.

FRAASER. Burke's Landed Gentry, 5 supp.

FRAMLINGHAM. Metcalfe's Visitations of Suffolk, 192. Historical M.S. Commission, 10th Report, App. 2, 53.

FRAMPTON. Burke's Commoners, iv. 193, Landed Gentry, 2, 3, 4, 5, 6. Burke's Royal Families, (London, 1851, 8vo.) ii. 165. Hutchins' Dorset, i. 398. Hoare's Wiltshire, II. ii. 145 ; IV. ii. 35. Miscellanea Genealogica et Heraldica, 2nd Series, ii. 214. The Genealogist, New Series, ii. 302. Harleian Society, xx. 40. Dallaway's Antiquities of Bristow, 87.

FRANCE. Burke's Commoners, ii. 32, Landed Gentry, 2, 4, 5. Chetham Society, xcii. 195.

FRANCE-HAYHURST. Burke's Landed Gentry, 5 supp., 6, 7, 8.

FRANCEIS, FRANCIS, FRAUNCIS, or FRAUNCEIS. Topographer and Genealogist, i. 361. Westcote's Devonshire, edited by G. Oliver and P. Jones, 462. Hutchins' Dorset, iv. 528. Harleian Society, xiii. 200. Visitation of Somerset, printed by Sir T. Phillipps, 74. Harleian Society, xi. 37 ; xxii. 55. Burke's Landed Gentry, 2 at p. 518. Visitation of Devon, edited by F. T. Colby, 104. Weaver's Visitation of Somerset, 25. Genealogies of Morgan and Glamorgan, by G. T. Clark, 488. The Genealogist, New Series, vii. 134. The Gresley's of Drakelowe, by F. Madan, 256.

FRANCHE. The Master Masons of Scotland, by R. S. Mylne, 305.

FRANCHVIL. Carthew's Hundred of Launditch, Part i. 233.

FRANCK. Berry's Sussex Genealogies, 326.

FRANK. Cussan's History of Hertfordshire, Parts iii. and iv. 148. Berry's Hertfordshire Genealogies, 75. Burke's Commoners, ii. 575, Landed Gentry, 2, 3, 4, 5, 6, 7, 8. Foster's Yorkshire Pedigrees. Hunter's Deanery of Doncaster, ii. 465. Clutterbuck's Hertford, iii. 333. Harleian Society, xiv. 572. Pease of Darlington, by Joseph Foster, 28.

FRANKCHEYNEY. Westcote's Devonshire, edited by G. Oliver and

P. Jones, 517. Visitation of Devon, edited by F. T. Colby, 106. The Visitations of Devon, by J. L. Vivian, 292.

FRANKE. Surtees Society, xxxvi. 3, 79. Foster's Visitations of Yorkshire, 519, 619. Harleian Society, xiii. 200, 399.

FRANKLAND. Noble's Memoirs of the House of Cromwell, ii. 416-426. Surtees Society, xxxvi. 78, 206. Herald and Genealogist, vii. 258, 383, 397, 431. Lipscombe's History of the County of Buckingham, ii. 197. Dallaway's Sussex, II. ii. 90. Sussex Archæological Collections, ii. 79. Wotton's English Baronetage, iii. 207. Betham's Baronetage, ii. 185. Harleian Society, xli. 111.

FRANKLAND-RUSSELL-ASTLEY. Burke's Landed Gentry, 6, 8.

FRANKLIN, FRANKLING, FRANKLYN, FRANCKLEN, FRANCKLIN, or FRANCKLYN. Herald and Genealogist, v. 27. Hasted's Kent, ii. 171. Harleian Society, viii. 300, 302 ; xv. 290; xix. 31, 110, 172. Clutterbuck's Hertford, i. 194. Glamorganshire Pedigrees, edited by Sir T. Phillipps, 41. Burke's Landed Gentry, (of Gonalston,) 2, 3, 4, 5, 6, 7, 8 ; (of Old Dalby,) 8. Notes and Queries, 4 S. v. 70, 518. Burke's Extinct Baronetcies. Genealogies of Morgan and Glamorgan, by G. T. Clark, 486. Harvey's Hundred of Willey, 518. Northamptonshire Notes and Queries, ii. 34, 117, 157. New England Register, xi. 17. Oliver's History of Antigua, i. 257.

FRANKS. Burke's Landed Gentry, (of Ballyscaddane,) 4, 5, 6, 7, 8 ; (of Carrig,) 3, 4, 5, 6, 7, 8.

FRASER, or FRAZER. Case of T. Frazer, of Lovat, Esq., claiming the title of Baron Lovat, Folio pp. 11. Additional Case. Folio pp. 9, and folding pedigree, 1854. Claim of Thos. A. Frazer, of Lovat, Esq., to the Barony of Lovat, Sess. Papers, 93, 178 of 1826-7 ; G of 1854-5 ; L of 1856 ; H of 1857. Annals of the Family of Frazer, Frysell, Simson, or Fitz-Simon, edited by Col. A. Fraser. Edinburgh, 1795, (2nd edn., 1805,) 8vo. Historical Account of the Family of Frisel, or Fraser, by John Anderson. Edinburgh, 1825, 4to. The Frasers of Philorth, by Alex. Fraser. Edinburgh, 1879, 4to., 3 vols. The Lovat Peerage and Estates, a short statement of John Fraser the Claimant, etc. London, 1885, 8vo. A second issue of this has as title 'The Lovat Peerage and Estates, a short history of the Case,' etc. London, 1885, 4to. Burke's Commoners, (of Lovat,) iii. 294 ; Landed Gentry, (of Skipness Castle,) 3, 4, 5 ; (of Hospitalfield,) 3, 4, 5, 6, 7, 8 ; (of Castle Fraser,) 2, 3, 4, 5, 6, 7, 8 ; (of Findrack,) 3, 4, 5, 6, 7, 8 ; (of Moniack,) 2, 7, 8 ; (of Ford,) 6. Paterson's History of the Co. of Ayr, ii. 309. Nisbet's Heraldry, ii. app. 114. Burke's Extinct Baronetcies, 621. Caledonia, by Geo. Chalmers, 552. Shaw's History of Moray, 133. Miscellany of the Spalding Club, ii. ix. Wood's Douglas's Peerage of Scotland, i. 607 ; ii. 155, 471. J. B. Pratt's Buchan, 381. Notes and Queries, 4 S. xi. 56 ; 5 S. xii. 385. Scottish Journal, 1847, i. 396. Lives of Scotch Officers of State, by Geo. Crauford, 268-285. Oliver's History of Antigua, i. 259. See LOVAT.

FRASER-MACKINTOSH. Burke's Landed Gentry, 8.
FRASER-TYTLER. Burke's Landed Gentry, 2, 3, 4, 5, 6, 7, 8.
FRAUNSHAM. The Genealogist, New Series, xvi. 160.
FRAY. Clutterbuck's Hertford, ii. 391.
FREAME. Visitation of Gloucester, edited by T. F. Fenwick and
W. C. Metcalfe, 63. Harleian Society, xxi. 62. *See* FREME.
FRECHEVILLE, or FRECHVILE. Collectanea Topographica et Genea-
logica, iv. 1-28, 181-218. Visitations of Derbyshire, 1663-4,
(Middle Hill, 1854, fol.) 4. Thoroton's Nottinghamshire, i. 86.
The Genealogist, iii. 60 ; New Series, vii. 135.
FREDERICK. Harleian Society, viii. 81. Manning and Bray's Surrey,
ii. 767. Wotton's English Baronetage, iv. 203. Betham's Baronet-
age, iii. 200.
FREEBODY. Berry's Sussex Genealogies, 327. Harleian Society,
xv. 292.
FREELAND. Berry's Sussex Genealogies, 52. Berry's Hampshire
Genealogies, 108. Burke's Landed Gentry, 4, 5, 6, 7.
FREEMAN, or FREMAN. Pedigree of Freeman of Eberton, Blockley,
and other places, from Harleian MSS. Privately printed by Sir
T. Phillipps, Bart., large folio, double page. Pedigree of Freeman
of Batsford, Co. Glouc., [T. P.] 1867, folio page. Pedigree of
Freeman of Todenham, [T. P.] folio page. Pedigree of Freeman
of Todenham and Batsford, [T. P.] folio page. Rudder's Gloucestershire, 265. Harleian Society, i. 93 ; viii. 13 ; xiii. 399 ;
xv. 292-295 ; xl. 1220. Berry's Sussex Genealogies, 291. History
of Henley-on-Thames, by J. S. Burn, 254. Burke's Commoners,
(of Castle Cor,) ii. 690-2, Landed Gentry, 2, 3 ; (of Gaines,) Commoners, iii. 642, Landed Gentry, 2, 3, 4, 5, 6, 7, 8 ; (of Pylewell,)
Landed Gentry, 3, 4, 5 ; (of Fawley Court,) 2, 7, 8. Manning
and Bray's Surrey, ii. 208. Baker's Northampton, i. 20, 233.
Fosbrooke's History of Gloucestershire, ii. 331. Eastwood's
History of Ecclesfield, 437. Clutterbuck's Hertford, iii. 348.
The Genealogist, v. 261. Bysshe's Visitation of Essex, edited by
J. J. Howard, 34. Metcalfe's Visitations of Northamptonshire,
91. Visitation of Gloucester, edited by T. F. Fenwick and W. C.
Metcalfe, 64. Notes and Queries, 6 S. xii. 188, 476. Gloucester-
shire Notes and Queries, iii. 168. New England Register, xx. 59,
353. Oliver's History of Antigua, i. 260, 270. Howard's Visita-
tion of England and Wales, viii. 75 ; ix. 9. *See* ROGERS.
FREEMAN-MITFORD. Burke's Landed Gentry, 8.
FREER, or FREERE. Miscellanea Genealogica et Heraldica, ii. 70.
Morant's Essex, ii. 353. Burke's Commoners, iv. 752, Landed
Gentry, 2, 3, 4, 5, 8. Herald and Genealogist, v. 427. Harleian
Society, i. 82 ; xiii. 200, 400 ; xxviii. 194. Memoirs of the
Family of Chester, by R. E. C. Waters, 72. Burke's Extinct
Baronetcies. Jewitt's Reliquary, xxiii. 217. Fletcher's Leicester-
shire Pedigrees and Royal Descents, 139. *See* FRERE.
FREESTON. Foster's Visitations of Yorkshire, 309. Harleian Society,
xxxii. 121.
FREHER. Miscellanea Genealogica et Heraldica, New Series, ii. 237.

FREKE. A Pedigree or Genealogy of the Family of the Frekes, by R. and Rev. J. and W. Freke, Middle Hill, 1825, folio. Burke's Landed Gentry, 2, 3, 4, 5, 6, 7, 8. Harleian Society, xi. 38; xx. 40, 42. Hutchins' Dorset, iv. 87. Visitation of Somerset, printed by Sir T. Phillipps, 75. Wotton's English Baronetage, iv. 141. Betham's Baronetage, iii. 158. Burke's Extinct Baronetcies.

FREMBAND. The Genealogist, New Series, xv. 213.

FREME. Fosbrooke's History of Gloucestershire, i. 339. *See* FREAME.

FREMINGHAM. Topographer and Genealogist, i. 516.

FREMINGTON. Plantagenet-Harrison's History of Yorkshire, i. 259.

FRENCH. Pedigree of the Family of French, by Nathl. Bogle French. 1866, folio. Memoir of the Family of French, by John D'Alton. Dublin, 1847, 8vo. Burke's Commoners, (of French Park,) iv. 539; (of Cuskinny,) Landed Gentry, 3, 4, 5, 6, 8; (of Cloonyquin,) 3, 4, 5, 6, 7; (of Monivea Castle,) 3, 4, 5, 6, 7, 8; (of Frenchgrove,) 3, 4; (of Frenckland,) 2 supp., p. 303. Burke's Royal Families, (London, 1851, 8vo.) i. 61. Chetham Society, lxxxv. 112. Alexander Nisbet's Heraldic Plates, 84. New England Register, xliv. 367. Burke's Colonial Gentry, i. 171. Oliver's History of Antigua, i. 272-3.

FRENCH-BREWSTER. Burke's Landed Gentry, 5 supp., 6, 7.

FREND. Burke's Landed Gentry, 3 supp., 4, 5, 6, 7, 8.

FRENINGHAM. Topographer and Genealogist, iii. 178.

FRERE. Pedigree of the Family of Frere, of Roydon in Norfolk, and Finningham in Suffolk, compiled by Horace Frere. 1874, 4to. Berry's Hampshire Genealogies, 12. Sir T. Phillipps' Topographer, No. 1, (March, 1821, 8vo.) 23. Visitation of Oxfordshire, 1574, printed by Sir T. Phillipps, (Middle Hill, fol.) 4. Burke's Landed Gentry, (of Roydon,) 2 supp., 3, 4, 5, 6, 7, 8; (of Twyford,) 2 supp., 3, 4, 5. Herald and Genealogist, v. 427. Harleian Society, v. 138; xxxii. 122. Metcalfe's Visitations of Suffolk, 138. Oxford Historical Society, xxiv. 108. Burke's Family Records, 247. *See* FREER.

FRESCHEVILLE. Banks' Baronies in Fee, i. 216. Banks' Dormant and Extinct Baronage, i. 308.

FRESE. Harleian Society, xv. 296.

FRESHFIELD. Burke's Landed Gentry, 7, 8.

FRESHWATER. Morant's Essex, i. 380. Wright's Essex, ii. 698. Harleian Society, xiii. 401. Bysshe's Visitation of Essex, edited by J. J. Howard, 35. Chancellor's Sepulchral Monuments of Essex, 265.

FRESKIN. Caledonia, by Geo. Chalmers, 604.

FRESTON. Blomefield's History of Norfolk, v. 378. Thoresby's Ducatus Leodiensis, 124.

FRETWELL. Foster's Visitations of Yorkshire, 519. Hunter's Deanery of Doncaster, i. 260. Surtees Society, lxv. 244, 330. Historical Notices of Doncaster, by C. W. Hatfield, 3rd Series, 32. Harleian Society, xl. 1184, 1286, 1303. *See* SWIFT.

FREVILE, FREVILL, or FREVILLE. Pedigree of the Freville Family,

folio sheet, privately printed for E. H. G. De Freville, Esq.
Genealogical History of the Freville Family, by A. W. Franks,
Cambridgeshire Antiquarian Society, ii. 21. Clifford's Description
of Tixall, 144. Gentleman's Magazine, lxix. 1017 ; lxxii. 723.
Hutchinson's History of Durham, iii. 68. Dugdale's Warwick-
shire, 1135. Hoare's Wiltshire, II. i. 31. Surtees' Durham,
iii. 36. Manning and Bray's Surrey, ii. 627. Clutterbuck's
Hertford, ii. 398. Harleian Society, xii. 75. Edmondson's
Baronagium Genealogicum, iv. 360. Banks' Baronies in Fee,
i. 217. Banks' Dormant and Extinct Baronage, i. 310. Foster's
Visitations of Durham, 127. *See* DE FREVILE.

FREWEN. History of Sapcote, by Rev. H. Whitley, 61. Burke's
Commoners, iv. 654, Landed Gentry, 2, 3, 4, 5, 6, 7, 8. Harleian
Society, viii. 395. A Royal Descent, by T. E. Sharpe, (London,
1875, 4to.) 74. Nichols' History of the County of Leicester,
ii. 142.

FREWEN-TURNER. Burke's Commoners, iii. 530; iv. 657, Landed
Gentry, 2, 3, 4, 5.

FRIAR. Harleian Society, xxvii. 57.

FRIEND. Harleian Society, viii. 398. Burke's Landed Gentry, 8.

FRIER. *See* FRERE.

FRISEL. *See* FRAZER.

FRISKNEY. The Genealogist, iv. 24.

FRITH. Morant's Essex, i. 110. Cockayne Memoranda, by A. E.
Cockayne, (Congleton, 1873, 8vo.) at end. Harleian Society,
xiii. 201. Bysshe's Visitation of Essex, edited by J. J. Howard,
35. *See* FRYTH.

FROBISHER. Wainwright's Wapentake of Strafford and Tickhill, 145.
Hunter's Deanery of Doncaster, i. 33. Harleian Society, xvi. 129.
Historical Notices of Doncaster, by C. W. Hatfield, 2nd Series, 3 ;
3rd Series, 329.

FRODSHAM. Ormerod's Cheshire, ii. 30, 48. Harleian Society,
xviii. 102.

FROGENHALL. Hasted's Kent, ii. 681, 737.

FROGGAT. Harleian Society, xxxviii. 446. Croston's edn. of Baines's
Lancaster, iv. 329.

FROME. Pedigree of Frome, from a pedigree entered at Heralds'
College in 1681, [T. P.] folio broadside. Visitation of Wiltshire,
1677, printed by Sir T. Phillipps, (Middle Hill, 1854, fol.).
Burke's Commoners, iii. 670, Landed Gentry. 2. Hutchins'
Dorset, ii. 771 ; iv. 185.

FROMOND. Surrey Archæological Collections, xi. Harleian Society,
xliii. 30. Manning and Bray's Surrey, ii. 284, 473.

FROST. Burke's Landed Gentry, (of St. John's House,) 4, 5, supp.,
6, 7, 8 ; (of Westwratting,) 8. Antiquarian Notices of Lupset, by
J. H., (1851 edn.), 91. Harleian Society, xvi. 130 ; xxxix. 1130.
New England Register, v. 165 ; x. 45. *See* MEADOWS.

FROTHINGHAM. Foster's Visitations of Yorkshire, 147. Poulson's
Holderness, ii. 409. The Genealogist, New Series, xv. 214.

FROWDE. Harleian Society, viii. 190.

21

FROWICK, or FROWYKE. Manning and Bray's Surrey, ii. 211.
Clutterbuck's Hertford, i. 476. Chauncy's Hertfordshire, 462.
South Mimms, by F. C. Cass, 70. Harleian Society, xix. 53 ;
xxxii. 264. Account of the Guildhall of London, by J. E. Price,
116.

FROXMERE. Harleian Society, xxvii. 39.

FRY, or FRYE. Harleian Society, vi. 115 ; xi. 38 ; xx. 42. . Westcote's Devonshire, edited by G. Oliver and P. Jones, 562.
Hutchins' Dorset, iii. 537. Visitation of Somerset, printed by
Sir T. Phillipps, 76. Visitation of Devon, edited by F. T.
Colby, 107. New England Register, viii. 226. The Visitations
of Devon, by J. L. Vivian, 375. Oliver's History of Antigua, i.
278, 285.

FRYER. Visitation of Oxfordshire, 1574, printed by Sir T. Phillipps,
(Middle Hill, fol.) 4. Burke's Commoners, (of the Wergs,) iii. 490.
Landed Gentry, 2, 3, 4, 5 ; (of Chatteris,) Landed Gentry, 2, 3,
4, 5, 6, 7, 8. Burke's Extinct Baronetcies. Bateson's History
of Northumberland, i. 399. Pedigree of Wilson, by S. B. Foster,
169.

FRYSBY. The Genealogist, New Series, xv. 95.

FRYSELL. See FRASER.

FRYSTON. Plantagenet-Harrison's History of Yorkshire, i. 362.

FRYTH. Bibliotheca Topographica Britannica, ix. Part 4, 318. Shaw's
Staffordshire, ii. 35. See FRITH.

FULFORD. Burke's Commoners, iv. 158, Landed Gentry, 2, 3, 4, 5,
6, 7, 8. Harleian Society, vi. 117-119. Westcote's Devonshire,
edited by G. Oliver and P. Jones, 612. Hutchins' Dorset, ii. 698.
Visitation of Devon, edited by F. T. Colby, 107. The Visitations
of Devon, by J. L. Vivian, 378. Miscellanea Genealogica et
Heraldica, 2nd Series, ii. 76.

FULHAM. Collectanea Topographica et Genealogica, i. 17. Manning
and Bray's Surrey, ii. 5.

FULLARTON, or FULLARTOUN. Case of Willm. Fullarton, Esq.,
Claiming the Title of Lord Spynie, 1785. Charters referred to
on part of the Crown, etc., pp. 8 and 2. Burke's Landed Gentry,
4, 5, 8. Geo. Robertson's Description of Cunninghame, 127, 405.
Paterson's History of the Co. of Ayr, ii. 12. Alexander Nisbet's
Heraldic Plates, 116. Paterson's History of Ayr and Wigton,
i. 410, 451, 747 ; iii. 320. J. E. Reid's History of the Co. of
Bute, 237.

FULLER. Some Fuller Descents. By J. F. Fuller. Dublin, 1880, 4to.
Miscellanea Genealogica et Heraldica, i. 165, 215, 288, 323 ; New
Series, i. 326 ; ii. 56. Berry's Sussex Genealogies, 278-281.
Berry's Hampshire Genealogies, 286. Visitation of Middlesex,
(Salisbury, 1820, fol.) 11. Burke's Landed Gentry, (of Rose
Hill,) 2, 3, 4, 5 ; (of Neston Park,) 3, 4, 5, 6, 8, 5 p. 917 ; (of
Glashnacree,) 6, 8 ; (of Hyde House,) 8 ; (of the Rookery,) 8.
Harleian Society, viii. 176. Herald and Genealogist, vi. 319.
Manning and Bray's Surrey, ii. 670. Sussex Archæological Col-
lections, xiii. 98. Burke's Royal Families, (edn. of 1876,) 218.

Burke's Extinct Baronetcies. Foster's Visitation of Middlesex,
25. New England Register, xiii. 351; xviii. 198. Burke's
Colonial Gentry, ii. 665. Surrey Archæological Collections, ix.
165, 168; x. Ontarian Families, by E. M. Chadwick, i. 49. *See*
FULWER.

FULLERTON. Burke's Commoners, (of Ballintoy Castle,) iv. 298,
Landed Gentry, 2 supp., 3, 4, 5, 6, 8; (of Thrybergh,) Landed
Gentry, 2 supp., 3, 4, 5, 6; 6 at p. 968, 7, 7 at p. 776, and 1109;
8. Foster's Yorkshire Pedigrees. Herald and Genealogist, viii.
196.

FULMERSTON. Harleian Society, xxxii. 123.

FULNETBY. Visitation of Suffolk, edited by J. J. Howard, i. 305.
The Genealogist, iv. 25. Metcalfe's Visitations of Suffolk, 30.
Notes and Queries, 3 S. ix. 370.

FULTHORPE. Surtees Society, xxxvi. 118. Visitation of Durham,
1615, (Sunderland, 1820, fol.) 82. Herald and Genealogist, vii.
140. Poulson's Holderness, i. 420. Hutchinson's History of
Durham, iii. 45. Surtees' Durham, iii. 126. Plantagenet-Harrison's History of Yorkshire, i. 394. Harleian Society, xvi. 130.
Foster's Visitation of Durham, 129, 131.

FULTON. Burke's Landed Gentry, 4 supp., 5, 6, 7. Paterson's
History of the Co. of Ayr, i. 278. Paterson's History of Ayr and
Wigton, iii. 95. Burke's Colonial Gentry, i. 338; ii. 713.

FULWER. Berry's Hampshire Genealogies, 53. Harleian Society,
xiii. 401; xliii. 126. The Genealogist, New Series, xv. 119. *See*
FULLER.

FULWODE, or FULWOOD. Harleian Society, xii. 237. Visitation of
Warwickshire, 1619, published with Warwickshire Antiquarian
Magazine, 186. Dugdale's Warwickshire, *Index.* Nichols' History
of the County of Leicester, iii. 860*. The Genealogist, New
Series, vii. 137. Historical Notices of Doncaster, by C. W. Hatfield, 3rd Series, 366. Visitations of Staffordshire, 1614 and
1663-4, William Salt Society, 141.

FURGUSSON. Burke's Heraldic Illustrations, 106.

FURLANG, or FURLONGE. Harleian Society, vi. 120. Visitation of
Devon, edited by F. T. Colby, 55. The Visitations of Devon, by
J. L. Vivian, 382.

FURNEAUX, or FURNEUS. Miscellanea Genealogica et Heraldica,
New Series, ii. 171; 3rd Series, iii. 272. Cussan's History of
Hertfordshire, Parts iii. and iv. 148. Collectanea Topographica
et Genealogica, i. 243. Account of Beauchief Abbey, in No. 3 of
Nichols' Miscellaneous Antiquities, 152. Weaver's Visitations of
Somerset, 108. Howard's Visitation of England and Wales, vi.
34. *See* DE FOURNEAUX.

FURNELL. Burke's Landed Gentry, 3, 4.

FURNESE. Burke's Extinct Baronetcies.

FURNIVAL, or FURNIVALL. Gough's Sepulchral Monuments, i. 184.
Account of Beauchief Abbey, in No. 3 of Nichols' Miscellaneous
Antiquities, 160. Clutterbuck's Hertford, ii. 390. Worksop, the
'Dukery,' and Sherwood Forest, (London, 1875, 8vo.) 19. East-

wood's History of Ecclesfield, 59. Holland's History of Worksop, 18. Harleian Society, xvi. 311; xxvii. 54. Banks' Baronies in Fee, i. 218. Banks' Dormant and Extinct Baronage, ii. 220. Miscellanea Genealogica et Heraldica, 2nd Series, v. 85; 3rd Series, ii. 299. Earwaker's History of Sandbach, 151. *See* DE FURNIVAL.

FURSDON. Burke's Landed Gentry, 2, 3, 4, 5, 6, 7, 8. Harleian Society, vi. 120. The Visitations of Devon, by J. L. Vivian, 383.

FURSE. Burke's Landed Gentry, 2, 3, 4, 5, 6, 7, 8. Harleian Society, vi. 121. The Visitations of Devon, by J. L. Vivian, 385.

FURSLAND. Tuckett's Devonshire Pedigrees, 72. Harleian Society, vi. 122. Westcote's Devonshire, edited by G. Oliver and P. Jones, 598. Visitation of Devon, edited by F. T. Colby, 108. The Visitations of Devon, by J. L. Vivian, 387.

FURTHO. Baker's Northampton, ii. 157.

FURTHS. Metcalfe's Visitations of Northamptonshire, 22, 91.

FURVILE. Nichols' History of the County of Leicester, iv. 451.

FURYE. Notes and Queries, 1 S. vi. 175, 255, 327, 473.

FUSSELL. Burke's Colonial Gentry, ii. 483. The Genealogical Magazine, iii. 554.

FUST. Burke's Extinct Baronetcies. Fosbrooke's History of Gloucestershire, i. 500. Wotton's English Baronetage, iii. 374. Visitation of Gloucester, edited by T. F. Fenwick and W. C. Metcalfe, 67. Gloucestershire Notes and Queries, iii. 587; iv. 104. *See* JENNER-FUST.

FUTTER. Visitation of Norfolk, published by Norfolk Archæological Society, i. 145. Harleian Society, xv. 296; xxxii. 123. Metcalfe's Visitations of Suffolk, 138. Norfolk Antiquarian Miscellany, ii. 607. Carthew's Hundred of Launditch, Part iii. 275. Visitation of Gloucester, edited by T. F. Fenwick and W. C. Metcalfe, 68.

FYCHAN. Collections by the Powys-land Club, viii. 404.

FYDELL. Burke's Commoners, ii. 260, Landed Gentry, 2.

FYFFE, or FYFE. Burke's Landed Gentry, 2, 3, 4, 5. Chetham Society, lxxxv. 113; cv. 221.

FYLER. Burke's Landed Gentry, 2, 3, 4, 5, 6, 7, 8. Hutchins' Dorset, i. 418. *See* ARNOT.

FYLIP AP HOWEL. Dwnn's Visitations of Wales, i. 105.

FYNCHE. Collectanea Topographica et Genealogica, iii. 308. *See* FINCH.

FYNDERNE. Morant's Essex, i. 429; ii. 234. Jewitt's Reliquary, iii. 191. Chancellor's Sepulchral Monuments of Essex, 97. *See* FINDERNE.

FYNES. Hasted's Kent, i. 328. Berry's Sussex Genealogies, 331. Visitation of Sussex, 1570, printed by Sir T. Phillipps, (Middle Hill, fol.) 5. Nicolson and Burn's Westmorland and Cumberland, ii. 379. Harleian Society, v. 213, 296; vi. 356. *See* FINES.

FYNMORE. Memorials of the Family of Fynmore. By W. P. W. Phillimore. London, 1886, 8vo. Howard's Visitation of England and Wales, vi. 41.

FYNNEY. Jewitt's Reliquary, viii. 45. Gentleman's Magazine, li. 147, 172, 261, 365, 503. *See* FINNEY.

FYTCHE. Morant's Essex, i. 340 ; ii. 463. Burke's Extinct Baronetcies. Bysshe's Visitation of Essex, edited by J. J. Howard, 35. Fragmenta Genealogica, by F. A. Crisp, i. 29. *See* FFYTCHE, FITCH.

FYTTON. Miscellanea Genealogica et Heraldica, ii. 140. Abram's History of Blackburn, 531. The Genealogist, New Series, xii. 109. *See* FITTON.

GABB. Burke's Landed Gentry, 2. Burke's Heraldic Illustrations, 18.

GABBETT. Burke's Landed Gentry, 2 supp., 3, 4, 5, 6, 7, 8.

GABBITT. Harleian Society, xxxiii. 195.

GABOTT. Harleian Society, i. 95.

GABOURELL. J. B. Payne's Armorial of Jersey, 161.

GADARN. Dwnn's Visitations of Wales, i. 135.

GAEL. Burke's Landed Gentry, 2, 3.

GAERDDIN. History of Powys Fadog, by J. Y. W. Lloyd, ii. 339.

GAGE. Gage's History of Hengrave, 225-252. Collectanea Topographica et Genealogica, ii. 147. Chronicle of the Family of De Havilland. Berry's Sussex Genealogies, 295. Visitation of Suffolk, edited by J. J. Howard, ii. 104. Burke's Commoners, iii. 640 ; (of Rathlin,) Landed Gentry, 3, 4, 5, 6, 7, 8 ; (of Ballinacree,) Landed Gentry, 5, 6, 7, 8 ; (of Streeve Hill,) 4. Horsfield's History of Lewes, i. 340. Gage's History of Thingoe Hundred, Suffolk, 205. Nichols' History of the County of Leicester, iii. 149. Manning and Bray's Surrey, ii. 279. Some Account of the Taylor Family, by P. A. Taylor, 698. Edmondson's Baronagium Genealogicum, vi. 84. Archdall's Lodge's Peerage, v. 206. Brydges' Collins' Peerage, viii. 249. Wotton's English Baronetage, i. 503 ; iii. 366. Betham's Baronetage, ii. 313. Banks' Dormant and Extinct Baronage, i. 87. The Suffolk Records, by H. W. Aldred, 118. Metcalfe's Visitations of Northamptonshire, 22, 92. Harleian Society, xxi. 246. The Manor of Haling, by G. S. Steinman, 15-74.

GAINES. Dwnn's Visitations of Wales, ii. 36. Glamorganshire Pedigrees, edited by Sir T. Phillipps, 21, 29, 37.

GAINFORD, or GAINSFORD. Sir T. Phillipps' Topographer, No. 1, (March 1821, 8vo.) 31. Visitation of Oxfordshire, 1574, printed by Sir T. Phillipps, (Middle Hill, fol.) 4. Manning and Bray's Surrey, iii. 174. Surrey Archæological Collections, vi. Miscellanea Genealogica et Heraldica, 2nd Series, iv. 201. Burke's Landed Gentry, 8. *See* GAYNESFORD.

GAINSBOROUGH. Rudder's Gloucestershire, 320.

GAIRDNER. Paterson's History of Ayr and Wigton, i. 582.

GAIRE. Harleian Society, viii. 23.

GAISFORD. Burke's Landed Gentry, 4, 5, 6, 7, 8. Hoare's Wiltshire, III. i. 34.

GALBRAITH. Burke's Landed Gentry, (of Clanabogan,) 4, 5, 6, 7, 8 ; (of Machrianish,) 2, 3. Burke's Extinct Baronetcies.

GALE. Sussex Archæological Collections, xii. 45. Nichols' Literary Anecdotes, iv. 536. Bibliotheca Topographica Britannica, iii. Part ii. Burke's Commoners, ii. 623. Burke's Landed Gentry, (of Bardsey,) 5, 6, 7, 8 ; (of Scruton,) 8. Foster's Yorkshire Pedigrees. Foster's Lancashire Pedigrees. Westcote's Devonshire, edited by G. Oliver and P. Jones, 567. Corry's History of Lancashire, i. 453. Thoresby's Ducatus Leodiensis, 203. History of Samlesbury, by James Croston, 201. Harleian Society, xvi. 131. Monken Hadley, by F. C. Cass, 161. Visitation of Devon, edited by F. T. Colby, 109. The Genealogist, vii. 3. Howard's Visitation of England and Wales, i. 277. Bardsley's Registers of Ulverston, lxvii. New England Register, i. 97 ; xviii. 189. Visitation of Gloucester, edited by T. F. Fenwick and W. C. Metcalfe, 89. The Visitations of Devon, by J. L. Vivian, 389. Burke's Family Records, 255. Oliver's History of Antigua, ii. 1.

GALE-BRADDYLL. Burke's Heraldic Illustrations, 34. Burke's Landed Gentry, 8.

GALLAGHER. O'Hart's Irish Pedigrees, 2nd Series, 183.

GALLARD. Harleian Society, xv. 298.

GALL-BURKE. Journal of Kilkenny Archæological Society, New Series, iii. 97.

GALLE. The Genealogist, New Series, ii. 302.

GALLEY. Visitation of Somerset, printed by Sir T. Phillipps, 77. Harleian Society, xi. 38.

GALLIARD. Hunter's Deanery of Doncaster, ii. 180.

GALLIARDELLO. Visitations of Staffordshire, 1614 and 1663-4, William Salt Society, 142.

GALLOP. Harleian Society, xx. 43, 44.

GALLOWAY. Wood's Douglas's Peerage of Scotland, i. 482, 612. Notes and Queries, 3 S. ii. 466 ; 7 S. i. 255, 395.

GALLY-KNIGHT. Burke's Commoners, iv. 710.

GALT. Ontarian Families, by E. M. Chadwick, ii. 138. Howard's Visitation of Ireland, iii. 72.

GALTON. Burke's Commoners, (of Claverdon,) iv. 200, Landed Gentry, 2 supp., 3, 4, 5, 6, 7, 8; (of Claverdon Leys,) 8 ; (of Warley Tor,) Commoners, iv. 201 ; Landed Gentry, 2, 3, 4 ; (of Hadzor House,) Commoners, iv. 201, Landed Gentry, 2, 3, 4, 5, 6, 7, 8. Burke's Royal Families, (London, 1851, 8vo.) ii. 12. Miscellanea Genealogica et Heraldica, 2nd Series, iii. 64.

GALWEY. Burke's Commoners, iv. 681, Landed Gentry, 2, 3, 4, 5. Burke's Extinct Baronetcies, 606. Family Notes, by J. M. Browne, 40. Oliver's History of Antigua, ii. 2. See PAYNE-GALLWEY.

GAM. Poetical Works of Lewis Glyn Cothi, (Oxford, 1837,) 1.

GAMADGE, or GAMAGE. Harleian Society, i. 14. Glamorganshire Pedigrees, edited by Sir T. Phillipps, 4, 44. Dwnn's Visitations of Wales, ii. 58. Notes and Queries, 2 S. ii. 48, 135, 336, 473. Genealogies of Morgan and Glamorgan, by G. T. Clark, 388, 392.

GAMBIER. Brydges' Collins' Peerage, ix. 387. Harvey's Hundred of Willey, 461.

GAMBLE. Oliver's History of Antigua, ii. 4. Ontarian Families, by
E. M. Chadwick, i. 74. Historical Notices of Doncaster, by C. W.
Hatfield, 2nd Series, 140. Burke's Landed Gentry, (of Windle-
hurst,) 7, 8; (of Killooly,) 7, 8.

GAMBONE. Harleian Society, ix. 74. See GAMON.

GAMES. Jones' History of the County of Brecknock, ii. 164-169.
The Genealogies of Morgan and Glamorgan, by G. T. Clark, 194.

GAMLYN. The Genealogist, ii. 386; iv. 26. Ancient Families of
Lincolnshire, in 'Spalding Free Press,' 1873-5, No. xi.

GAMMELL. Burke's Landed Gentry, 7, 8.

GAMMIE. Burke's Landed Gentry, 4, 5.

GAMMIE-MAITLAND. Burke's Landed Gentry, 5.

GAMON. Harleian Society, ix. 74. An Historical Survey of Cornwall, by C. S. Gilbert, ii. 106. Betham's Baronetage, iv. 289.
The Visitations of Cornwall, edited by J. L. Vivian, 171. Genealogies of Morgan and Glamorgan, by G. T. Clark, 488.

GAMUL, or GAMULL. Visitation of Staffordshire, 1663-4, printed by
Sir T. Phillipps, 5. Ormerod's Cheshire, ii. 577; iii. 475.
Harleian Society, xv. 298; xviii. 268. Visitations of Stafford-
shire, 1614 and 1663-4, William Salt Society, 144.

GANDOLFI. Burke's Landed Gentry, 5th edn. p. 650; 6th edn. p.
810. Roman Catholic Families of England, by J. J. Howard and
H. F. Burke, Part iv.

GANDY. Burke's Landed Gentry, 4 supp., 5, 8.

GANNON. Burke's Landed Gentry, 3, 4, 5.

GANS. Burke's Extinct Baronetcies.

GANT. Plantagenet - Harrison's History of Yorkshire, i. 229.
Edmondson's Baronagium Genealogicum, v. 484. Banks' Dormant
and Extinct Baronage, i. 313. See DE GANT, GAUNT.

GAPE. Berry's Hertfordshire Genealogies, 114. Clutterbuck's Hertford, i. 112. Harleian Society, xxii. 144. Burke's Landed Gentry,
7, 8.

GARAWAY. Surrey Archæological Collections, xi.

GARBED. Harleian Society, xxviii. 195.

GARDE. Burke's Landed Gentry, 3, 4, 5, 6, 7, 8.

GARDEN-CAMPBELL. Burke's Landed Gentry, 2 supp., 3, 4, 5, 6, 7, 8.

GARDENER. Visitation of Norfolk, published by Norfolk Archæological Society, i. 342. Harleian Society, xxii. 56; xxxii. 124.
Metcalfe's Visitations of Suffolk, 92. See DUNN-GARDENER.

GARDENOR. Harleian Society, i. 42.

GARDINER. Whitaker's History of Whalley, 235. Gentleman's
Magazine, 1821, i. 578, 395; 1831, ii. 138; 1855, i. 495. Morant's
Essex, i. 402. Berry's Hampshire Genealogies, 170. Memoirs of
R-ch-d G-rdn-r, Esq. London, 1782, 1-10. Berry's Buckingham-
shire Genealogies, 95. Burke's Landed Gentry, (of Coombe
Lodge,) 2 supp., 3, 4, 5, 6, 7, 8; (of Farmhill,) 3, 4. Harleian
Society, viii. 94; xiii. 402; xv. 299; xx. 44; xxii. 57; xxviii.
196; xxxix. 840; xliii. 60, 66. Dallaway's Sussex, II. ii. 374.
Collectanea Topographica et Genealogica, iii. 14. Burke's
Heraldic Illustrations, 63. Manning and Bray's Surrey, iii. 415.

Clutterbuck's Hertford, ii. 183 ; iii. 279. Whitaker's History of Whalley, ii. 18. Chauncy's Hertfordshire, 213, 264. Memoirs of the Family of Chester, by R. E. C. Waters, 478. Master's Notices of the Family of Master, 98. Wotton's English Baronetage, iii. 209. Metcalfe's Visitations of Suffolk, 31. Burke's Extinct Baronetcies. Visitation of Gloucester, edited by T. F. Fenwick and W. C. Metcalfe, 69. Brocas of Beaurepaire, by M. Burrows, folding table at end. Bysshe's Visitation of Essex, edited by J. J. Howard, 36. Surrey Archæological Collections, xi. The Manor of Haling, by G. S. Steinman, 75. The Irish Builder, xxxv. 160.

GARDNER. Report of the Proceedings of the House of Lords on the claims to the Barony of Gardner of Uttoxeter in the Co. of Stafford, by D. Le Marchant. London, 1828, 8vo. Case of A. L. Gardner, claiming Barony of Gardner, folio, pp. 8. Claim of A. L. Gardner, an infant, to the Barony of Gardner, Sess. Papers, 175 of 1825 ; 32 of 1826. Harleian Society, i. 87 ; xv. 300 ; xli. 64. Cambridgeshire Visitation, edited by Sir T. Phillipps, 13. Berry's Sussex Genealogies, 334. Burke's Landed Gentry, 6, 7, 8. The Genealogist, iv. 26 ; vi. 151. Brydges' Collins' Peerage, ix. 381. *See* DUNN-GARDNER.

GARDYNE. Burke's Landed Gentry, 2 supp. and add., 3, 4, 5, 6, 7, 8.

GARFIELD. The Garfield Family in England, by W. P. W. Phillimore, 1883, 8vo. Visitation of Middlesex, (Salisbury, 1820, fol.) 22. New England Register, xxxvii. 253 ; xlix. 194, 300, 449. Northamptonshire Notes and Queries, ii. 115, 152. Foster's Visitation of Middlesex, 42. Phillimore's London and Middlesex Note-Book, 14.

GARFIT. Burke's Landed Gentry, 8.

GARFOOT, or GARFORTH. Harleian Society, xiii. 403. Burke's Landed Gentry, 5, 6. Whitaker's Deanery of Craven, 156, (215).

GARGRAVE. Burke's Commoners, iii. 91. Foster's Visitations of Yorkshire, 68. Hunter's Deanery of Doncaster, ii. 214. Whitaker's Deanery of Craven, 3rd edn., 234. Harleian Society, xvi. 132.

GARLAND. Tuckett's Devonshire Pedigrees, 140. Burke's Landed Gentry, 3, 4, 5, 6, 7, 8. Harleian Society, vi. 123; xv. 301; xxxix. 1074. Burke's Visitations of Seats and Arms, 2nd Series, ii. 34. Burke's Royal Descents and Pedigrees of Founders' Kin, 100. J. T. Godfrey's History of Lenton, 212. Devonshire Notes and Notelets, by Sir W. R. Drake, 121, 129. The Visitations of Devon, by J. L. Vivian, 390.

GARMOND. The Genealogist, New Series, i. 10.

GARNET, or GARNETT. Visitation of Durham, 1615, (Sunderland, 1820, fol.) 10. Burke's Landed Gentry, (of Summerseat,) 3, 4, 5, 6, 7, 8 ; (of Wyreside,) 3, 4, 5, 6 and supp., 7, 8 ; (of Quernmore Park,) 2, 3, 4, 5, 6, 7, 8 ; (of Williamston,) 6, 7, 8 ; (of Arch Hall,) 8. Burke's Visitation of Seats and Arms, i. 52. Poulson's Holderness, i. 420. Surtees' Durham, iii. 198. Foster's Visitation of Durham, 133.

GARNETT-BOTFIELD. Burke's Landed Gentry, 5, 6, 7, 8.

GARNEY. Harleian Society, xiv. 573.

GARNEYS. Blomefield's Norfolk, v. 291. Burke's Commoners, iv. 564. Suckling's History of Suffolk, i. 64. Page's History of Suffolk, 114, 239. Metcalfe's Visitations of Suffolk, 32, 33, 139. Muskett's Suffolk Manorial Families, i. 189-194.

GARNHAM. The Genealogist, v. 261 ; New Series, xvi. 96.

GARNIER. Burke's Landed Gentry, 2, 3, 4, 5, 6, 7, 8.

GARNON. Jewitt's Reliquary, x. 192. Harleian Society, iv. 135 ; xxi. 63.

GARNONS. Dwnn's Visitations of Wales, i. 159. Burke's Commoners, i. 374. Robinson's Mansions of Herefordshire, 195.

GARRAD. Harleian Society, xv. 301.

GARRARD. Hasted's Kent, ii. 613. Harleian Society, i. 5 ; xxii. 144; xxxii. 125. Clutterbuck's Hertford, i. 514. Berry's Hertford-shire Genealogies, 155. Visitation of London in Transactions of the London and Middlesex Archæological Society, 22. Burke's Landed Gentry, 6. Wotton's English Baronetage, i. 492. The Genealogist, v. 262-264. Burke's Extinct Baronetcies.

GARRATT. Burke's Landed Gentry, 5, 6, 7, 8. Harleian Society, xxxviii. 466.

GARRAWAY. Harleian Society, xliii. 201.

GARRET, or GARRETT. Burke's Landed Gentry, 2 supp., 3, 4, 5, 6, 7, 8. Manning and Bray's Surrey, ii. 706. Harleian Society, xv. 302. Howard's Visitation of England and Wales, v. 139. Oliver's History of Antigua, ii. 7.

GARRICK. Percy Fitz Gerald's Life of David Garrick, i. 1. Gentle-man's Magazine, 1857, ii. 234.

GARRISON. New England Register, xxx. 418.

GARROW. Burke's Landed Gentry, 6 at p. 1729, 7 at p. 1974, 8 at p. 2191.

GARSHALE. Dugdale's Warwickshire, 289.

GARSTIN. Burke's Landed Gentry, 2 supp., 3 and supp., 4, 5, 6, 7, 8.

GARSTON. Abram's History of Blackburn, 683.

GARTER. Harleian Society, xv. 303. Metcalfe's Visitations of North-amptonshire, 93.

GARTH, or GARTHE. The Antiquities of Gainford, by J. R. Walbran, 110. Berry's Sussex Genealogies, 368. Berry's Surrey Genea-logies, 73. Surrey Archæological Collections, ii. Surtees' Durham, iv. 28, 29. Manning and Bray's Surrey, iii. 488. Wiltshire Archæological Magazine, ii. 332. Burke's Commoners, iii. 557 ; Landed Gentry, 6, 7. Harleian Society, xv. 303; xliii. 189. Foster's Visitations of Durham, 135. The Perverse Widow, by A. W. Crawley-Boevey, 176.

GARTHSHORE. Nisbet's Heraldry, ii. app. 301.

GARTHWAITE. Burke's Landed Gentry, 2 supp. Miscellanea Genea-logica et Heraldica, New Series, iv. 423.

GARTON. Berry's Sussex Genealogies, 152. Visitation of Sussex, 1570, printed by Sir T. Phillipps, (Middle Hill, fol.) 5. Dalla-way's Sussex, II. i. 244. Castles, Mansions, and Manors of

Western Sussex, by D. G. C. Elwes and C. J. Robinson, 272.
Burke's Commoners, iv. 723 ; Landed Gentry, 2 supp., p. 312.
GARTSHORE. Burke's Landed Gentry, 2 supp., 3, 4, 5, 6.
GARTSIDE. Chetham Society, lxxxv. 115. Fishwick's History of
Rochdale, 495.
GARVALY. O'Hart's Irish Pedigrees, 2nd Series, 184.
GARVEY. Burke's Landed Gentry, (of Thornvale,) 3 ; (of Murrisk
Abbey,) 3. O'Hart's Irish Pedigrees, 2nd Series, 185. Miscel-
lanea Genealogica et Heraldica, New Series, iv. 329.
GARWAY. Dallaway's Sussex, II. i. 48. Harleian Society, xv. 304.
GASCOIGNE, GASKON, or GASCOYN. Pedigree of Gascoine in accord-
ance with Wills and Registers to the Death of Sir Edward Gas-
coyne, Bart., 1750, printed on vellum. Surtees Society, xxxvi.
289 ; xli. 14. Visitation of Suffolk, edited by J. J. Howard, ii.
162. Burke's Landed Gentry, 2, 3, 4, 5, 6, 7, 8. Foster's Yorkshire Pedigrees. Foster's Visitations of Yorkshire, 68, 238, 292,
297, 384, 520. History of Richmond, by C. Clarkson, 280.
Thoresby's Ducatus Leodiensis, 176. Dugdale's Warwickshire,
855. Hunter's History of Doncaster, ii. 484. Surtees' Durham,
ii. 211. Thoroton's Nottinghamshire, i. 266 ; iii. 266. Pedigrees
of the Leading Families of Lancashire, published by Joseph
Foster, (London, 1872, fol.) Burke's Extinct Baronetcies, 621.
The New History of Yorkshire, commencing with Richmondshire,
by Genl. Plantagenet-Harrison, (London, 1872, fol.) Part i. 18.
Plantagenet-Harrison's History of Yorkshire, i. 116. Harleian
Society, xvi. 133, 138 ; xix. 172 ; xxi. 273 ; xxxii. 125. Wotton's
English Baronetage, iv. 334. Betham's Baronetage, v. (Barts. of
Scotland,) 8. Burton's History of Hemingborough, 219. Pedi-
grees of the Leading Families of Yorkshire, by Joseph Foster.
Harvey's Hundred of Willey, 508. Old Yorkshire, ed. by Willm.
Smith, ii. 162.
GASKELL. Burke's Landed Gentry, (of Kiddington Hall,) 3, 4, 5, 6 ;
(of Thorne's House,) 2, 3, 4, 5, 6, 7, 8 ; (of Lupset Hall,) 2, 3, 4 ;
(of Ingersley Hall,) 7, 8 ; (of Kiddington Hall,) 8. Burke's Visita-
tions of Seats and Arms, 2nd Series, ii. 52. Harleian Society,
xxxvii. 54, 302.
GASON. Burke's Landed Gentry, 2, 3, 4, 5, 6, 7, 8.
GASSIOT. Burke's Landed Gentry, 7, 8.
GASTNEYS. Visitation of Staffordshire, (Willm. Salt Soc.) 88. See
WASTNEYS.
GASTRELL. Pedigree of Gastrell of Cranham, Co. Glouc., [T. P.]
1866, folio page. Visitation of Gloucestershire, 1569, (Middle
Hill, 1854, fol.) 5. Baker's Northampton, ii. 101. Visitation of
Gloucester, edited by T. F. Fenwick and W. C. Metcalfe, 70.
Harleian Society, xxi. 64.
GATACRE, or GATAKER. Burke's Commoners, i. 589, Landed Gentry,
2, 3, 4, 5, 7, 8.
GATE. Morant's Essex, i. 136, 369 ; ii. 146, 374, 457. Wright's
Essex, ii. 260. Burke's Landed Gentry, 6. Metcalfe's Visitations
of Suffolk, 139.

GATEACRE, or GATACRE. Burke's Commoners, iii. 525, Landed
Gentry, 2, 3, 4, 5, 6. Burke's Royal Families, (London, 1851,
8vo.) i. 152. Harleian Society, xxviii. 197.

GATEGANG. Surtees' Durham, ii. 116.

GATES. Surtees Society, xxxvi. 76. Foster's Visitations of Yorkshire, 60. Harleian Society, xiv. 574; xxi. 65; xxxix. 995. New
England Register, xxxi. 401.

GATESDENE. Clutterbuck's Hertford, i. 376. See DE GATESDEN.

GATTON. Archæologia Cantiana, v. 222. See DE GATTON.

GATTY. Maclean's History of Trigg Minor, i. 322. Howard's Visitation of England and Wales, ii. 153.

GATWICK. Manning and Bray's Surrey, ii. 188.

GAUDEN. Harleian Society, viii. 212.

GAUNT. Burke's Landed Gentry, 2, 3, 4. History of Richmond, by
C. Clarkson, 309. Nichols' History of the County of Leicester,
ii. 303. Baker's Northampton, i. 440. Blunt's Dursley and its
Neighbourhood, 106. See GANT.

GAUNTLET. Harleian Society, xv. 305.

GAURY. The Genealogist, New Series, ix. 184.

GAUSSEN. Burke's Landed Gentry, (of Brookman's Park,) 3, 4, 5, 6,
7, 8; (of Lakeview,) 3, 4, 6, 7, 8. See BOSANQUET.

GAVEL, or GAVELL. Blomefield's Norfolk, viii. 29. Manning and
Bray's Surrey, ii. 734. Surrey Archæological Collections, xi.
Harleian Society, xliii. 46.

GAVRIGAN. An Historical Survey of Cornwall, by C. S. Gilbert, ii.
107. The Visitations of Cornwall, edited by J. L. Vivian, 463.

GAWDEY, or GAWDY. Harleian Society, xiii. 67; xxxii. 125. Burke's
Extinct Baronetcies. Clutterbuck's Hertford, ii. 345. Page's
History of Suffolk, 512. Metcalfe's Visitations of Suffolk, 33.
Historical MS. Commission, 10th Report, app. 2.

GAWEN. Visitation of Somerset, printed by Sir T. Phillipps, 78.
Harleian Society, xi. 39. Visitatio Comitatus Wiltoniæ, 1623,
printed by Sir T. Phillipps. Hoare's Wiltshire, I. ii. 165; IV. i.
100; ii. 84. Foley's Records of the English Province S. J., v.
468. The Genealogist, New Series, xii. 89.

GAWLEY. O'Hart's Irish Pedigrees, 2nd Series, 186.

GAWSELL. Visitation of Norfolk, published by Norfolk Archæological Society, ii. 7. Blomefield's Norfolk, vii. 491. Norfolk
Archæology, iii. 126. Harleian Society, xxxii. 132.

GAY. Hasted's Kent, iii. 308. Tuckett's Devonshire Pedigrees, 171.
Burke's Landed Gentry, (of Alborough,) 2, 3, 4, 5, 6, 7, 8; (of
Thurning Hall,) 3, 4, 5, 6, 7, 8. Harleian Society, vi. 125, 126.
Westcote's Devonshire, edited by G. Oliver and P. Jones, 564.
Notes and Queries, 1 S. iii. 425, 508; iv. 388; v. 36, 197. Visi-
tation of Devon, edited by F. T. Colby, 110. The Visitations of
Devon, by J. L. Vivian, 392. New England Register, vi. 373;
xxxiii. 45. Howard's Visitation of England and Wales, v. 165.

GAYER. Memoirs of the Family of Gayer, by A. E. Gayer, Q.C.,
LL.D. Westminster, 1870, 8vo. Ashmole's Antiquities of Berkshire, iii. 316, 334. Maclean's History of Trigg Minor, i. 669.

Colby of Great Torrington, by F. T. Colby, 27. Harleian Society, xv. 306. Notes and Queries, 2 S. x. 175, 238, 521. The Visitations of Cornwall, edited by J. L. Vivian, 172. The Genealogist, New Series, i. 10. New England Register, xxxi. 296.

GAYFER. Miscellanea Genealogica et Heraldica, 2nd Series, iv. 201.

GAYNESFORD, or GAYNSFORD. Harleian Society, i. 41; v. 154; xv. 297; xlii. 173; xliii. 11, 91. Berry's Kent Genealogies, 451. Herald and Genealogist, i. 337. Gyll's History of Wraysbury, 205. Brayley's History of Surrey, v. 303. Surrey Archæological Collections, iii. 59. Manning and Bray's Surrey, ii. 512. Visitation of Gloucester, edited by T. F. Fenwick and W. C. Metcalfe, 72. See GAINSFORD.

GAYNOR. Oliver's History of Antigua, ii. 9.

GAYTON. Baker's Northampton, ii. 275.

GAYWOOD. Visitation of Staffordshire, 1663-4, printed by Sir T. Phillipps, 5. Visitations of Staffordshire, 1614 and 1663-4, William Salt Society, 145.

GEALE. Burke's Commoners, iii. 200; Landed Gentry, 2nd edn. p. 1217.

GEARE. Westcote's Devonshire, edited by G. Oliver and P. Jones, 565. See GEERE, GERE.

GEARINGE, or GERING. Harleian Society, xv. 309. The Genealogist, vi. 153.

GEARY. Betham's Baronetage, iv. 123.

GEAST. Burke's Commoners, i. 489. Hamper's Life of Dugdale, at end.

GEDDES. Ontarian Families, by E. M. Chadwick, i. 81.

GEDDYNG. Gage's History of Thingoe Hundred, Suffolk, 47.

GEDNEY. The Genealogist, iv. 27; vi. 152. New England Register, i. 169. Massingberd's History of Ormsby, 212.

GEE. Berry's Sussex Genealogies, 368. Surtees Society, xxxvi. 321. Burke's Commoners, ii. 254. Foster's Yorkshire Pedigrees. Harleian Society, ii. 180. George Oliver's History of Beverley, 496. History of Beverley, by G. Poulson, i. 398. Nichols' History of the County of Leicester, iii. 954. Metcalfe's Visitations of Suffolk, 140.

GEERE. Tuckett's Devonshire Pedigrees, 173. Harleian Society, vi. 126; xv. 307. The Visitations of Devon, by J. L. Vivian, 395. See GERE.

GEERS. Cooke's continuation of Duncumb's Hereford, (Hund. of Grimsworth,) Part i. 30.

GEFFEREYS. Harleian Society, xxvii. 58.

GEFFRAYS. Harleian Society, xv. 308.

GEFFRY. Harleian Society, xxvii. 58.

GELDART. Surtees Society, xxxvi. 213. Burke's Landed Gentry, 8.

GELL. Jewitt's Reliquary, xi. 225. Visitation of Derbyshire, 1663-4, (Middle Hill, 1854, fol.) 4. Hunter's History of the Parish of Sheffield, 371. The Genealogist, iii. 60. Pilkington's View of Derbyshire, ii. 308. Burke's Extinct Baronetcies. Harleian Society, xxxvii. 46; xxxviii. 564; xxxix. 834.

GELLYBRAND, or GELIBROND. Chetham Society, lxxxii. 114, 124. See GILLIBRAND.

GEMMELL. Paterson's History of the Co. of Ayr, ii. 52. Paterson's History of Ayr and Wigton, iii. 238. Northern Notes and Queries, vii. 92.

GENESTE. Miscellanea Genealogica et Heraldica, 2nd Series, iv. 226.

GENEVILL. Banks' Baronies in Fee, i. 220. Banks' Dormant and Extinct Baronage, i. 320.

GENNYS. Burke's Landed Gentry, 7, 8.

GENT. Harleian Society, xiii. 202, 403; xiv. 661. Morant's Essex, ii. 354. Berry's Essex Genealogies, 88. Burke's Commoners, i. 370, Landed Gentry, 2, 3, 4, 5, 6. Bridges' Northamptonshire, by Rev. Peter Whalley, i. 77. Baker's Northampton, i. 416. Wright's Essex, i. 633. Bysshe's Visitation of Essex, edited by J. J. Howard, 36. Metcalfe's Visitations of Northamptonshire, 23.

GENTLEMAN. Burke's Landed Gentry, 4, 5, 6, 7, 8.

GEOGHEGAN. Burke's Commoners, iii. 535; Landed Gentry, 2, p. 965.

GEORGE. Harleian Society, ix. 75; xxi. 247. The Visitations of Cornwall, edited by J. L. Vivian, 174. Visitation of Gloucester, edited by T. F. Fenwick and W. C. Metcalfe, 72. Burke's Family Records, 259. A History of Banking in Bristol, by G. H. Cave, 238.

GEORGE OWAIN HARRI. Dwnn's Visitations of Wales, i. 32.

GERAGHTY. O'Hart's Irish Pedigrees, 2nd Series, 186.

GERALDINE. Journal of Historical and Archæological Association of Ireland 3rd Series, i. 461, 591 ; 4th Series, iv. 15, 299. See FITZGERALD.

GERARD, or GERRARD. Berry's Essex Genealogies, 43. Ashmole's Antiquities of Berkshire, iii. 320. Burke's Commoners, i. 278 ; Landed Gentry, 2 p. 1501 ; Landed Gentry, (of Rochsoles,) 2 supp., 3, 4, 5, 6, 7, 8 ; (of Kinwarton,) 8 ; (of Rochsoles,) 8 ; (of Ditton Grove,) 2 ; (of Gibbstown,) 5 supp., 6, 7, 8. Chetham Society, lxxxi. 81, 101 ; lxxxii. 25 ; lxxxv. 116, 118 ; cx. 182. Lipscombe's History of the County of Buckingham, ii. 75. Burke's Royal Families, (London, 1851, 8vo.) ii. 191. Topographer, (London, 1789-91, 8vo.) iv. 310. Foster's Lancashire Pedigrees. Gregson's Fragments relative to the County of Lancaster, 239. Hutchins' Dorset, i. 609. Baines' History of the Co. of Lancaster, iii. 641. Ormerod's Cheshire, i. 549, 653 ; ii. 131. Harleian Society, xiii. 94 ; xiv. 728 ; xviii. 103 ; xx. 45. Burke's Extinct Baronetcies. Monken Hadley, by F. C. Cass, 138. Wotton's English Baronetage, i. 51. Betham's Baronetage, i. 58. Banks' Dormant and Extinct Baronage, iii. 302. Earwaker's East Cheshire, ii. 567. Notes and Queries, 8 S. ii. 243, 415. Croston's edn. of Baines's Lancaster, iv. 374. The Genealogist, New Series, xvii. 240. Howard's Visitation of England and Wales, ix. 108.

GERBERD. Hoare's Wiltshire, III. v. 20. The Genealogist, New Series, xvi. 232 ; xvii. 17.

GERBRIDGE. Visitation of Norfolk, published by Norfolk Archæological Society, i. 396. Harleian Society, xxxii. 128.

GERE. Surtees Society, xxxvi. 81. Harleian Society, xv. 312.

Visitation of Devon, edited by F. T. Colby, 110. *See* GEERE, GEARE.

GEREARDY. New England Register, lii. 313.

GERING. *See* GEARING.

GERLINGTON. Chetham Society, lxxxv. 119. *See* GIRLINGTON.

GERMAIN, or GERMAINE. Brydges' Collins' Peerage, vi. 306. Burke's Extinct Baronetcies.

GERMIN. Camden Society, xliii. 106. Visitation of Warwickshire, 1619, published with Warwickshire Antiquarian Magazine, 176. Harleian Society, xii. 169. *See* JERMIN.

GERNEGAN. The Genealogist, New Series, xvi. 39. *See* JER-NINGHAM.

GERNET. *See* STOKEPORT.

GERNON. Morant's Essex, i. 13, 158; ii. 100, 179, 181, 232. Burke's Landed Gentry, 3, 4, 5, 6, 7, 8. History of the Parish of St. Leonard, Shoreditch, by Henry Ellis, 98. Proceedings of the Essex Archæological Society, v. 173. Wright's Essex, ii. 157. Memoirs of the family of Chester, by R. E. C. Waters, 187, 199. Banks' Baronies in Fee, ii. 85. Harleian Society, xli. 3. The Gresley's of Drakelow, by F. Madan, 257.

GERNONS. Weaver's Visitation of Herefordshire, 31.

GERNOUN. The Genealogist, New Series, ix. 212.

GERUNDE. Notes and Queries, 6 S. v. 5.

GERVIS, GERVAIS, GERVEIS, GERVEYS, GEIRVEIS, or GERVYS. Cambridgeshire Visitation, edited by Sir T. Phillipps, 15. Dwnn's Visitations of Wales, ii. 350. Burke's Commoners, ii. 340. Burke's Landed Gentry, 3, 4, 5, 7, 8. Harleian Society, ii. 71; ix. 75, 77; xli. 12, 32. Maclean's History of Trigg Minor, ii. 423, 427. Burke's Royal Descents and Pedigrees of Founders' Kin, 93. Nichols' History of the County of Leicester, ii. 671. An Historical Survey of Cornwall, by C. S. Gilbert, ii. 108. J. B. Payne's Armorial of Jersey, 162. The Visitations of Cornwall, edited by J. L. Vivian, 175. Miscellanea Genealogica et Heraldica, 3rd Series, ii. 59. The Genealogist, New Series, xvi. 231.

GERY. Burke's Commoners, ii. 379, Landed Gentry, 2, 3, 4, 5, 6, 7, 8. Nichols' History of the County of Leicester, iii. 1041. Harleian Society, xix. 110.

GESTE. *See* GEAST.

GETHIN. Glamorganshire Pedigrees, edited by Sir T. Phillipps, 36, 46. Visitatio Comitatus Wiltoniæ, 1623, printed by Sir T. Phillipps. Harleian Society, xiii. 404. History of Powys Fadog, by J. Y. W. Lloyd, iii. 353; iv. 234. The Genealogist, New Series, xii. 90.

GETTINS. Bysshe's Visitation of Essex, edited by J. J. Howard, 37.

GHERARDINI. Journal of the Historical and Archæological Association of Ireland, 4th Series, iv. 246-264.

GHEST. Harleian Society, xxvii. 59.

GHISNES. Baker's Northampton, ii. 273. Banks' Baronies in Fee, i. 221. Banks' Dormant and Extinct Baronage, i. 321.

GIB, or GIBB. Pall Mall Gazette, of 7 Feb. 1868. Pedigree of the

Family of Gibb of Carriber, folding sheet, 1874. The Life and
Times of Robert Gib, by Sir G. Duncan Gibb, Bart. London,
1874, 8vo. 2 vols. Paterson's History of Ayr and Wigton, i. 549.
Burke's Extinct Baronetcies, 623. Genealogies of Morgan and
Glamorgan, by G. T. Clark, 488. Burke's Landed Gentry, 8.
See CAMPBELL.
GIBAUT. J. B. Payne's Armorial of Jersey, 164.
GIBBARD. Burke's Landed Gentry, 2 add., 3, 4, 5, 6, 7, 8. Harvey's
Hundred of Willey, 466.
GIBBES. Visitation of Warwickshire, 1619, published with Warwick-
shire Antiquarian Magazine, 34. Harleian Society, xii. 213 ; xiii.
405. Betham's Baronetage, iii. 445. Account of the Mayo and
Elton Families, by C. H. Mayo, 151. Miscellanea Genealogica et
Heraldica, 2nd Series, i. 3. *See* GIBBS.
GIBBINGS. Burke's Landed Gentry, 4, 5, 6, 7.
GIBBINS. Howard's Visitation of England and Wales, vii. 113.
GIBBON. Hasted's Kent, iv. 29. Dwnn's Visitations of Wales,
i. 179. Berry's Kent Genealogies, 408. Glamorganshire Pedi-
grees, edited by Sir T. Phillipps, 22. Burke's Landed Gentry,
5, 6, 7, 8. Harleian Society, xv. 310, 312. Gentleman's Magazine,
lviii. 699 ; lix. 584 ; lxvi. 271 ; lxvii. 915, 1104. Genealogies of
Morgan and Glamorgan, by G. T. Clark, 134, 138, 140, 397.
Archæologia Cantiana, xvi. 84. The Autobiographies of Edward
Gibbon, by John Murray, Chapter I.
GIBBONS. Family Notes, by A. W. Gibbons. Westminister, 1884,
8vo. Sir T. Phillipps' Topographer, No. 1, (March, 1821, 8vo.)
36. Glamorganshire Pedigrees, edited by Sir T. Phillipps, 40.
Visitation of Oxfordshire, 1574, printed by Sir T. Phillipps,
(Middle Hill, fol.) 4. Burke's Landed Gentry, 5, 6 and supp.,
7, 8. Harleian Society, v. 161 ; xxviii. 198. Betham's Baronetage,
iii. 245. Howard's Visitation of England and Wales, ix. 45.
GIBBS. Morant's Essex, ii. 238. History of Clyst St. George, by
Rev. H. T. Ellacombe, 70 Berry's Kent Genealogies, 418.
Burke's Landed Gentry, (of Belmont,) 3, 4, 5 ; (of Aldenham,)
3, 4, 5, 6, 7, 8 ; (of Tyntesfield,) 3, 4, 5, 6, 7, 8 ; (of Derry,) 3
and corr., 4, 5, 6, 7. Burke's Visitation of Seats and Arms,
2nd Series, ii. 53, 63. Burke's Royal Descents and Pedigrees
of Founders' Kin, folding table, and 121. Visitatio Comitatus
Wiltoniæ, 1623, printed by Sir T. Phillipps. Hoare's Wiltshire,
III. i. 34. Harleian Society, xv. 313 ; xx. 46 ; xlii. 182. Bysshe's
Visitation of Essex, edited by J. J. Howard, 38. *See* GIBBES.
GIBON. Harleian Society, xlii. 102.
GIBSON, or GYBSON. Surtees Society, xxxvi. 73. Burke's Com-
moners, (of Quernmore Park,) iii. 657, Landed Gentry, 2 ; (of
Whelprigg,) Landed Gentry, 2, 3, 4, 5, 6, 7, 8 ; (of Sandgate
Lodge and Shalford,) 2, 3, 4, 5, 6, 7, 8. Fishwicke's History of
Goosnargh, 159. Foster's Visitations of Yorkshire, 520. Harleian
Society, iii. 13 ; xvi. 140 ; xxxii. 128 ; xliii. 205. Hodgson's
Northumberland, III. ii. 393. Warwickshire Pedigrees, from
Visitation of 1682-3, (privately printed, 1865). Douglas's Baronage

of Scotland, 568. Pedigree of Wilson of High Wray, etc., by Joseph Foster, 94. Walter Wood's East Neuk of Fife, 289. Notes and Queries, 6 S. iii. 447; v. 116; 8 S. ix. 81. Burke's Extinct Baronetcies, 623. Pedigree of Gibson of Bampton, Co. Westmorland, by C. Dalton, single sheet, 1886. Henderson's Caithness Family History, 304. Stodart's Scottish Arms, ii. 397. Northern Notes and Queries, i. 88, 107, 131; iii. 4. Yorkshire Genealogist, i. 78. Jewers' Wells Cathedral, 277. Historical Notices of Doncaster, by C. W. Hatfield, 2nd Series, 135. New England Register, xxxvii. 388. Howard's Visitation of England and Wales, ii. 88. Surrey Archæolgical Collections, x. Pedigree of Wilson, by S. B. Foster, 31. Muskett's Suffolk Manorial Families, i. 175. The Genealogist, New Series, xv. 242. *See* MILNER-GIBSON.

GIBSONE. Burke's Landed Gentry, 2 add., 3, 4, 5, 6, 7, 8.

GIBSON-WATT. Burke's Landed Gentry, 5, 6, 7, 8.

GIBTHORPE. Foster's Visitations of Yorkshire, 624. The Genealogist, iv. 246.

GIDDY. Berry's Sussex Genealogies, 153. A Complete Parochial History of the County of Cornwall, i. 336. An Historical Survey of Cornwall, by C. S. Gilbert, ii. 120.

GIDEON. Burke's Extinct Baronetcies.

GIFFARD. Pedigree of Giffard and Solers of Weston Subedge, and Harward of Weston Subedge and Bretforton, privately printed by Sir T. Phillipps, 1837. Brewood Chancel, by J. H. Smith, (Wolverhampton, 1870, 8vo.). Rudder's Gloucestershire, 310. Collectanea Topographica et Genealogica, i. 129. Kennet's Parochial Antiquities, ii. 447. Burke's Commoners, (of Chillington,) i. 206, Landed Gentry, 2, 3, 4, 5, 6, 7, 8; (of Brightley,) Commoners, iv. 293, Landed Gentry, 2, 3, 4. Jewitt's Reliquary, xv. 7. Herald and Genealogist, vii. 64. Maclean's History of Trigg Minor, ii. 34, 40, 151. Munford's Analysis of Domesday Book of Co. of Norfolk, 39. Lipscombe's History of the County of Buckingham, i. 200; iii. 131; iv. 326. Westcote's Devonshire, edited by G. Oliver and P. Jones, 627, 628. Hoare's Wiltshire, I. ii. 201, 238. Wiltshire Archæological Magazine, ii. 100. Miscellanea Genealogica et Heraldica, New Series, ii. 312; iii. 326. Wood's Douglas's Peerage of Scotland, ii. 649. Notes and Queries, 3 S. xi. 455; xii. 189. Visitation of Staffordshire, (Willm. Salt Soc.) 80. Banks' Dormant and Extinct Baronage, i. 323; iii. 108. Visitations of Staffordshire, 1614 and 1663-4, William Salt Society, 146-150. Brewood, Supplement, by J. H. Smith, folding table. The Visitations of Devon, by J. L. Vivian, 396, 401. The Genealogist, New Series, x. 87, 88; xii. 91; xiii. 177; xiv. 19; xvi. 24. The Gresley's of Drakelowe, by F. Madan, 258. *See* GYFFARD.

GIFFORD. J. Wilkinson's History of Broughton Gifford, folding plate. Gentleman's Magazine, lxviii. 5, 121, 668, 931; 1827, ii. 590. Visitation of Durham, 1615, (Sunderland, 1820, fol.) 87. Berry's Hampshire Genealogies, 285. Burke's Landed Gentry. 3, 4, 5, 6, 7, 8. Foster's Visitations of Yorkshire, 521. Harleian Society,

v. 176; vi. 127, 135; ix. 206; xv. 314; xxi. 249; xliii. 220. Herald and Genealogist, iii. 420. Visitation of Staffordshire, 1663-4, printed by Sir T. Phillipps, 5. Nichols' History of the County of Leicester, iii. 188. Visitatio Comitatus Wiltoniæ, 1623, printed by Sir T. Phillipps. Hoare's Wiltshire, III. ii. 76. Surtees' Durham, iii. 356. Baker's Northampton, i. 151, 396. Wiltshire Archæological Magazine, v. 267. Notes and Queries, 2 S. ii. 74. Burke's Extinct Baronetcies, and 607. Visitation of Devon, edited by F. T. Colby, 78, 80, 92, 111. Topographical Miscellanies, 1792, 4to, (Crundall). The Visitations of Cornwall, edited by J. L. Vivian, 137, 430. Metcalfe's Visitations of Northamptonshire, 93. Foster's Visitations of Durham, 137. *See* GYFFARD.

GIGGER. Hutchins' Dorset, i. 122.

GILBERD. The Genealogist, New Series, viii. 34.

GILBERT. Genealogical Memoir of the Gilbert Family in both Old and New England, by J. W. Thornton. Boston, 1850, 8vo. Harleian Society, i. 39 ; ii. 189; vi. 128; xi. 126; xiii. 405 ; xxxii. 129 ; xxxix. 868 ; xlii. 180. Dwnn's Visitations of Wales, i. 300. Berry's Kent Genealogies, 341. Berry's Sussex Genealogies, 154, 320, 372. Tuckett's Devonshire Pedigrees, 87, 95. Burke's Commoners, (of Tredrea,) i. 323, Landed Gentry, 2, 3, 4, 5, 6, 7, 8 ; (of Cantley,) Landed Gentry, 2, 3, 4, 5, 6, 7, 8 ; (of The Priory,) 2, 3, 4, 5, 6, 7, 8. Miscellanea Genealogica et Heraldica, ii. 384. Dickinson's History of Southwell, 2nd edition, 302. Burke's Royal Families, (London, 1851, 8vo.) i. 140. Maclean's History of Trigg Minor, i. 303. Westcote's Devonshire, edited by G. Oliver and P. Jones, 566. Visitation of Derbyshire, 1663-4, (Middle Hill, 1854, fol.) 4. Nichols' History of the County of Leicester, iii. 1138. Baker's Northampton, ii. 308. The Genealogist, iii. 60 ; New Series, vii. 138. A Complete Parochial History of the County of Cornwall, i. 110, 366. An Historical Survey of Cornwall, by C. S. Gilbert, ii. 109-120. Visitation of Devon, edited by F. T. Colby, 111. The Visitations of Cornwall, edited by J. L. Vivian, 347. Visitations of Staffordshire, 1614 and 1663-4, William Salt Society, 151. Weaver's Visitations of Somerset, 108. New England Register, iv. 223, 339 ; xvi. 107; xlii. 280. The Visitations of Devon, by J. L. Vivian, 160, 405, 408. Oliver's History of Antigua, ii. 12.

GILBEY, or GILBY. The Genealogist, iv. 28 ; vi. 154. Howard's Visitation of England and Wales, iii. 143. Harleian Society, xl. 1227.

GILBORNE. Hasted's Kent, iii. 213. Berry's Kent Genealogies, 345. Harleian Society, xlii. 192.

GILCHRIST. Burke's Landed Gentry, 2, 3, 4, 5, 6, 7, 8. Burke's Colonial Gentry, ii. 557, 676. Oliver's History of Antigua, 16.

GILDART. Berry's Kent Genealogies, 366. East Barnet, by F. C. Cass, 160.

GILDEA. Burke's Landed Gentry, 2, 3, 4, 5, 6, 7, 8.

GILDEFORD. Surtees' Durham, ii. 359. *See* GUILDFORD.

GILDERIDGE. Berry's Sussex Genealogies, 155.

GILES. Tuckett's Devonshire Pedigrees, 126. Harleian Society, vi.
129. Westcote's Devonshire, edited by G. Oliver and P. Jones,
530. Visitation of Devon, edited by F. T. Colby, 113. Genealogies of Morgan and Glamorgan, by G. T. Clark, 400. The
Visitations of Devon, by J. L. Vivian, 409.

GILKELLY. O'Hart's Irish Pedigrees, 2nd Series, 187.

GILL. Pedigree of Gill of Jenkins, and of Spicer, Adams, and Cooper,
of New Jenkins, co. Essex. 1872, 4to. Miscellanea Genealogica et
Heraldica, ii. 24. Collectanea Topographica et Genealogica, viii.
274-297, 410. Berry's Hertfordshire Genealogies, 56-65. Surtees
Society, xxxvi. 277. Burke's Landed Gentry, (of Blairythan,)
3, 4, 5, 6, 7, 8 ; (of Bickham,) 7, 8 ; (of Savock,) 8. More about
Stifford, by Will'm. Palin, 49. Thoresby's Ducatus Leodiensis,
78. Hunter's History of the Parish of Sheffield, 399. Hunter's
Deanery of Doncaster, ii. 30. Harleian Society, xv. 314 ; xxii.
58 ; xxxvii. 13 ; xxxviii. 209. Foster's Visitations of Durham,
139. East Barnet, by F. C. Cass, 140. Burke's Colonial Gentry,
i. 37. The Genealogist, New Series, xii. 49 ; xv. 243. *See* GYLL.

GILLANDERS. Burke's Landed Gentry, 4, 5, 6, 7, 8.

GILLBANKS. Burke's Landed Gentry, 2, 3, 4, 5.

GILLESPIE. Burke's Landed Gentry, 5, 6, 7, 8. Walter Wood's
East Neuk of Fife, 290.

GILLETT. Burke's Landed Gentry, (of Halvergate,) 4 supp., 5, 6,
7, 8 ; (of Banbury,) 5 supp., 6, 7, 8. New England Register,
xlvii. 168.

GILLIAT. Burke's Landed Gentry, 7, 8.

GILLIBRAND. Chetham Society, lxxxv. 120-122. Abram's History
of Blackburn, 629. *See* GELLYBRAND.

GILLING. Plantagenet-Harrison's History of Yorkshire, i. 88.

GILLINGHAM. Hasted's Kent, ii. 81.

GILLIOTT. Whitaker's Deanery of Craven, 80, (105).

GILLMAN, or GILMAN. Searches into the History of the Gillman
Family, by A. W. Gillman. London, 1895, 4to. The Gillmans
of Highgate, by A. W. Gillman. London, 1895, 4to. Burke's
Landed Gentry, (of Oakmount,) 3, 4 ; (of The Retreat,) 4 ; (of
Anne Mount,) 8. The Genealogist, New Series, xiv. 152. Visita-
tion of Staffordshire, 1663-4, printed by Sir T. Phillipps, 5.
Burke's Extinct Baronetcies, 607. Harleian Society, xv. 315.
Howard's Visitation of Ireland, i. 46. Hasted's Kent, (Hund. of
Blackheath, by H. H. Drake,) 21. Visitations of Staffordshire,
1614 and 1663-4, William Salt Society, 152. New England
Register, xviii. 258.

GILLON. Burke's Landed Gentry, 2, 3, 4, 5, 6, 7, 8.

GILLOTT. Harleian Society, xxxii. 129. ; xxxvii. 334 ; xxxviii. 811.

GILLOW. Berry's Kent Genealogies, 487. Chetham Society, cv. 258.
Burke's Landed Gentry, 7, 8.

GILLUM. Burke's Landed Gentry, 2, 3, 4, 5. Bateson's History of
Northumberland, i. 399.

GILLYATT. Burke's Landed Gentry, 5. Oliver's History of Antigua,
ii. 17.

GILMOUR. Burke's Landed Gentry, 6, 7, 8. Burke's Extinct
Baronetcies, 623. *See* LITTLE-GILMOUR.
GILPIN. Burke's Landed Gentry, 2 supp., 3, 4, 5, 6 supp. Hutchin-
son's History of Durham, ii. 549. Pedigrees of the Leading
Families of Lancashire, published by Joseph Foster, (London,
1872, fol.). Memoirs of Dr. Richard Gilpin, by William Jackson,
F.S.A., folding table at end. The New History of Yorkshire,
commencing with Richmondshire, by Genl. Plantagenet-Harrison,
(London, 1872, fol.) Part i. 21. Plantagenet-Harrison's History
of Yorkshire, i. 120. Foster's Visitations of Cumberland and
Westmorland, 52. Pedigrees of the Leading Families of York-
shire, by Joseph Foster. Harleian Society, xxxix. 1099. Nicol-
son and Burns' Westmorland and Cumberland, i. 136.
GILSTRAP. Burke's Landed Gentry, 5, 6, 7.
GINKELL. Archdall's Lodge's Peerage, ii. 153.
GIPPS. Berry's Kent Genealogies, 462. Harleian Society, viii. 309,
367; xv. 315. Gage's History of Thingoe Hundred, Suffolk,
522.
GIRARDOT, or GIRAUDOT. Burke's Landed Gentry, 5. J. B. Payne's
Armorial of Jersey, 166.
GIRDLER. Shaw's Staffordshire, i. 389. Visitatio Comitatus Wil-
toniæ, 1623, printed by Sir T. Phillipps. Genealogist, New
Series, xii. 91.
GIRLING. Visitation of Norfolk, published by Norfolk Archæological
Society, i. 202. Carthew's West and East Bradenham, 44.
Carthew's Hundred of Launditch, Part iii. 349, 435. Harleian
Society, xxxii. 142.
GIRLINGTON, or GYRLINGTON. Foster's Visitations of Yorkshire,
284, 619. Collectanea Topographica et Genealogica, vi. 190.
Chetham Society, lxxxii. 36. Plantagenet-Harrison's History of
Yorkshire, i. 436. Harleian Society, xvi. 140. The Genealogist,
v. 297. *See* GERLINGTON.
GIROIE. History of the House of Arundel, by J. P. Yeatman, 20.
GISBORNE. Glover's History of Derbyshire, ii. 246, 392, (216, 359).
Burke's Landed Gentry, 2, 3, 4, 5. Burke's Colonial Gentry, ii.
448. Harleian Society, xxxviii. 480.
GISLINGE. Harleian Society, xv. 316.
GISLINGHAM. Metcalfe's Visitations of Suffolk, 92. Harleian Society,
xxxii. 129.
GISNES. Baker's Northampton, ii. 273.
GISORS. Notes and Queries, 7 S. vi. 201; viii. 36.
GIST. Burke's Landed Gentry, 6, 7, 8.
GITTINS. Harleian Society, xxviii. 199.
GLADSTONE. Foster's Lancashire Pedigrees. Burke's Royal Descents
and Pedigrees of Founders' Kin, 70. Biggar and the House of
Fleming, by W. Hunter, 2nd edn., 141.
GLADWIN. Burke's Landed Gentry, 2 supp., 3, 4, 5, 6, 7, *sub voc.*,
Goodwin. Harleian Society, xxxviii. 613, 616.
GLANVILL, GLANVILE, or GLANVILLE. Pedigree of the Norman
Family of Glanville, *n. d.*, 8 leaves. Records of the Anglo-

Norman House of Glanville, by W. U. S. Glanville-Richards.
London, 1882, 4to. Tuckett's Devonshire Pedigrees, 133. Burke's
Landed Gentry, 2, 4, 5, 6, 7, 8. Foster's Visitations of Yorkshire,
620. Harleian Society, vi. 130; ix. 77, 78. An Historical
Survey of Cornwall, by C. S. Gilbert, ii. 121. Visitation of
Devon, edited by F. T. Colby, 114. Banks' Dormant and Extinct
Baronage, i. 89. Notes and Queries, 6 S. iv. 368. The Visita-
tions of Cornwall, edited by J. L. Vivian, 77. Oliver's History
of Antigua, ii. 18.

GLAPTHORNE. Cambridgeshire Visitation, edited by Sir T. Phillipps,
15. Harleian Society, xli. 75.

GLASCOCK, or GLASCOTT. Morant's Essex, ii. 456, 508, 580, 625.
Harleian Society, viii. 141, 368; xiii. 54, 406; xiv. 575; xv. 316.
Burke's Landed Gentry, 3, 4, 5, 6 and supp., 7, 8. Bysshe's
Visitation of Essex, edited by J. J. Howard, 38.

GLASGOW. Case of Alex. Glasgow, claiming to be heir male of the
Lords Gray; for the opinion of Counsel, 1880. Burke's Landed
Gentry, 3, 4. Paterson's History of the Co. of Ayr, ii. 252.
Paterson's History of Ayr and Wigton, iii. 513. Geo. Robertson's
Account of Families in Ayrshire, i. 344.

GLASIER. Ormerod's Cheshire, ii. 386. Harleian Society, xviii. 104.
Burke's Colonial Gentry, ii. 829.

GLASSON. An Account of the Families of Boase, (Exeter, 1876, 4to.)
28.

GLAZEBROOK. Foster's Lancashire Pedigrees. Howard's Visitation
of England and Wales, iii. 56.

GLEANE. Notes and Queries, 2 S. viii. 187, 218; ix. 411. Wotton's
English Baronetage, iii. 494. Burke's Extinct Baronetcies.

GLEDHILL. John Watson's History of Halifax, 150.

GLEDSTANES. Burke's Landed Gentry, 6, 7, 8. The Genealogist,
New Series, ix. 153. See UPTON-GLEDSTANES.

GLEDSTON. Whitaker's History of Craven, 1st edn., 73.

GLEGG. Burke's Commoners, (of Irbie,) ii. 235, Landed Gentry, 2,
3, 4, 5, 6; (of Backford,) 7, 8; (of Old Withington,) Landed
Gentry, 2, 3, 4, 5, 6, 7, 8. Harleian Society, viii. 473; xviii.
103. Ormerod's Cheshire, ii. 178, 369, 492, 519; iii. 719. Earwaker's East Cheshire, ii. 374.

GLEMHAM. Page's History of Suffolk, 181. Metcalfe's Visitations of
Suffolk, 34, 140.

GLEN. Burke's Landed Gentry, 6, 7. Poetical Remains of William
Glen, with Memoir by C. Rogers, 9-16.

GLENCAIRN. Claims preferred to the House of Lords in the case of
the Glencairn Peerage, by J. Maidment. Edinburgh, 1840.

GLENDONWYN, or GLENDONING. History of Liddesdale, by R. B.
Armstrong, 160. Nisbet's Heraldry, i. 147. Douglas's Baronage
of Scotland, 223. Burke's Landed Gentry, 2 final add., 3, 4, 5.

GLENDOWER (Owen). Memoirs of Owen Glendower, by Thos.
Thomas, (Haverfordwest, 1822,) Chapter ii. 36. The History of
the Island of Anglesey, with a Genealogical Account of Owen
Glendour, 1775, 4to.

GLENE. Harleian Society, xxxii. 130.

GLEYVE. Harleian Society, xviii. 104.

GLISSON. Visitation of Somerset, printed by Sir T. Phillipps, 79. Harleian Society, xi. 39 ; xx. 46.

GLOSSOP. Burke's Landed Gentry, 5, 6, 7, 8.

GLOSTER. Oliver's History of Antigua, ii. 20.

GLOUCESTER. The Genealogist, New Series, xiv. 96.

GLOUCESTER (Earls of). Rudder's Gloucestershire, 93. Proceedings of the Archæological Institute, 1853, 65. (Dukes of) Gentleman's Magazine, 1851, ii. 619. Banks' Dormant and Extinct Baronage, iii. 307.

GLOVER. Pedigree and Arms of the Glovers of Mount Glover, by D. O. C. Fisher and Sir J. B. Burke. London, 1858, 8vo. Chronicle of the Family of De Havilland. Berry's Surrey Genealogies, 106. Burke's Landed Gentry, 2 add., 3, 4. Burke's Visitation of Seats and Arms, 2nd Series, i. 70. Nichols' History of the County of Leicester, ii. 129. Manning and Bray's Surrey, ii. 437. Harleian Society, xv. 317, 318. Notes and Queries, 3 S. i. 182 ; ii. 256. The Rectors of Loughborough, by W. G. D. Fletcher, 42. Oliver's History of Antigua, ii. 20.

GLUBB. Notes and Queries, 6 S. i. 285, 359 ; ii. 175. The Visitations of Cornwall, by J. L. Vivian, 580.

GLUSBURNE. Collectanea Topographica et Genealogica, vi. 304.

GLYD, or GLYDD. Manning and Bray's Surrey, ii. 307. Harleian Society, xv. 317.

GINN, GLYNN, or GLYNNE. Dwnn's Visitations of Wales. i. 311 ; ii. 147, 150. Maclean's History of Trigg Minor, ii. 58-74. Hutchins' Dorset, iii. 246. Berry's Hampshire Genealogies, 132. Visitation of Somerset, printed by Sir T. Phillipps, 80. Burke's Commoners, ii. 339. Burke's Landed Gentry, 3, 4, 5, 6, 7, 8. Harleian Society, ix. 79, 80 ; xi. 40. Manning and Bray's Surrey, iii. 72. T. Nicholas' County Families of Wales, 447. A Complete Parochial History of the County of Cornwall, i. 118, 200. An Historical Survey of Cornwall, by C. S. Gilbert, ii. 123. Collections by the Powys-land Club, viii. 198. Wotton's English Baronetage, iii. 289. Betham's Baronetage, ii. 260 ; iii. 278 ; iv. 406. The Visitations of Cornwall, edited by J. L. Vivian. 178. History of Powys Fadog, by J. Y. W. Lloyd, vi. 485.

GLYN AERON. Dwnn's Visitations of Wales, i. 27, 80.

GOADE. Gyll's History of Wraysbury, 284.

GOBARD. Harleian Society, xii. 293.

GOBION, or GOBYON. Nichols' History of the County of Leicester, iv. 225. Clutterbuck's Hertford, ii. 217. Memoirs of the Families of Chester, by R. E. C. Waters, 155. Devonshire Notes and Notelets, by Sir W. R. Drake, 45. Hodgson's Northumberland, II. ii. 452. Gibbon's Family Notes, 156. The Genealogist, New Series, xiv. 254.

GOBLE. Dallaway's Sussex, II. ii. 342. Oliver's History of Antigua, ii. 21.

GOCH. Dwnn's Visitations of Wales, i. 231. Glamorganshire Pedigrees, edited by Sir T. Phillipps, 37. History of Powys Fadog, by J. Y. W. Lloyd, ii. 216 ; iii. 396. *See* GOOCH.

GODARD, or GODDARD. A Memoir of the Goddards of North Wilts, by Richard Jefferies. Swindon, *n. d.* sm. 4to. Pedigree of Goddard of Swindon, Clive Pipard, and Purton, Co. Wilts, by Sir T. Phillipps, Bart., folio sheet. Blomefield's Norfolk, vi. 437. Illuminated Supplement to Burke's Heraldic Illustrations, 16. Dwnn's Visitations of Wales, i. 179. Berry's Hampshire Genealogies, 186. Burke's Commoners, (of Cliffe Pypard,) iv. 323, Landed Gentry, 2, 3, 4, 5, 6, 7, 8 ; (of Swindon,) Commoners, iv. 326, Landed Gentry, 2, 3, 4, 5, 6, 7, 8 ; (of Brookline,) Landed Gentry, 2 add. Harleian Society, ii. 190 ; xv. 318 ; xix. 111. Nichols' History of the County of Leicester, iii. 170. Visitation of Wiltshire, edited by G. W. Marshall, 18, 19, 25, 33, 81, 84. Notes and Queries, 3 S. iii. 319. Miscellanea Genealogica et Heraldica, 2nd Series, i. 37. The Genealogist, New Series, xii 91. Howard's Visitation of England and Wales, vi. 65.

GODDE. Miscellanea Genealogica et Heraldica, New Series, iii. 221.

GODDEN. Howard's Visitation of England and Wales, iii. 54.

GODEBOLD, or GODBOLD. Morant's Essex, ii. 126, 133. Harleian Society, xiii. 407. Bysshe's Visitation of Essex, edited by J. J. Howard, 39.

GODERYCHE. Visitation of Gloucestershire, 1569, (Middle Hill, 1854, fol.) 5.

GODFREY. Hasted's Kent, iii. 450, 498, 508. Visitation of Kent (reprinted from Archæologia Cantiana, vol. vi.), 71, 81. Berry's Kent Genealogies, 146. Burke's Commoners, (of Brook Street House,) i. 408, Landed Gentry, 2, 3, 4, 7, 8 ; (of Kennet,) Landed Gentry, 5, 6, 7, 8 ; (of Old Hall,) 2 ; (of Heppington,) 5, p. 425. Harleian Society, viii. 207 ; xlii. 131. Jewitt's Reliquary, xxiii. 195. Burke's Family Records, 261.

GODFREY-FAUSSETT-OSBORNE. Burke's Landed Gentry, 6, 7, 8.

GODLEY. Burke's Landed Gentry, 2, 3, 4, 5, 6, 7, 8.

GODMAN. Berry's Sussex Genealogies, 347. Burke's Landed Gentry, 2, 3, 5, 6, 7, 8. Sussex Archæological Collections, xxxv. 44.

GODMANSTON. Morant's Essex, i. 439.

GODOLPHIN. Maclean's History of Trigg Minor, ii. 522. Harleian Society, ix. 80-83. Lipscombe's History of the County of Buckingham, iv. 559. An Historical Survey of Cornwall, by C. S. Gilbert, i. 520. Edmondson's Baronagium Genealogicum, ii. 182. Banks' Dormant and Extinct Baronage, iii. 315. Burke's Extinct Baronetcies. The Visitations of Cornwall, edited by J. L. Vivian, 182. Records of Yarlington, by T. E. Rogers, 60. Miscellanea Genealogica et Heraldica, iii. 326.

GODRED THE BLACK. Manx Society, x. app. C.

GODRICK. Harleian Society, viii. 154.

GODSAL. Burke's Landed Gentry, 3, 4, 5, 6, 7, 8.

GODSALVE. Blomefield's Norfolk, vii. 213. Foster's Visitations of Cumberland and Westmorland, 53. Harleian Society, xxxii. 130.

GODSCHALK. Harleian Society, xv. 319.

GODWIN,⁕ GODWINE, or GODWYN. Collinson's Somerset, iii. 84.
Westcote's Devonshire, edited by G. Oliver and P. Jones, 540.
Genealogy of Henzey, Tyttery, and Tyzack, by H. S. Grazebrook,
41. Visitation of Somerset, printed by Sir T. Phillipps, 81.
Harleian Society, xi. 40; xxxvii. 299. Notes and Queries, 3 S. i.
503; ii. 94. Weaver's Visitations of Somerset, 25. The Visitations of Devon, by J. L. Vivian, 417. See GOODWIN.

GOET. The Genealogist, New Series, iv. 159.

GOFF. Burke's Landed Gentry, (of Hale Park,) 2 supp., 3, 4, 5, 6,
7, 8; (of Horetown House,) 2 supp., 3, 4, 5, 6, 7, 8; (of Oakport,)
4, 5, 6, 7, 8.

GOGILL. Harleian Society, xxxii. 131.

GOING. Burke's Landed Gentry, (of Ballyphilip,) 3, 4, 5, 6, 7, 8; (of
Traverston,) 2, 3, 4, 5, 6, 7, 8.

GOKIN. Berry's Kent Genealogies, 113. Miscellanea Genealogica et
Heraldica, New Series, iv. 170. Harleian Society, xlii. 48. See
GOOKIN.

GOLAFRE. Lipscombe's History of the County of Buckingham, i. 394.
Baker's Northampton, i. 417; ii. 22. Leland's Itinerary, (3rd edn.
1769,) iv. 5.

GOLBORNE. Ormerod's Cheshire, ii. 670; iii. 387. Harleian Society,
xviii. 105. Lancashire and Cheshire Genealogical and Historical
Notes, iii. 29.

GOLD. Harleian Society, viii. 302; xv. 320. Visitatio Comitatus
Wiltoniæ, 1623, printed by Sir T. Phillipps. Hoare's Wiltshire,
IV. ii. 94. Visitation of Wiltshire, edited by G. W. Marshall, 59.
See GOULD.

GOLDESBOROUGH, or GOLDISBOROUCH. Foster's Visitations of Yorkshire, 369. Burke's Commoners, ii. 241; Landed Gentry, 2,
p. 1469. Harleian Society, xvi. 142.

GOLDFINCH. Burke's Landed Gentry, 6 supp., 7, 8.

GOLDIE. Lands and their Owners in Galloway, by P. H. M'Kerlie,
iii. 84. Burke's Landed Gentry, 7, 8. See TAUBMAN-GOLDIE.

GOLDING. Morant's Essex, ii. 328. Gentleman's Magazine, lxv. 284.
Burke's Landed Gentry, 2, 3, 4, 5. Harleian Society, iv. 107;
xiii. 8, 55; xiv. 580. Wright's Essex, i. 574. Metcalfe's Visitations of Suffolk, 93. Burke's Extinct Baronetcies.

GOLDINGHAM. Morant's Essex, ii. 311. Visitation of Norfolk, published by Norfolk Archæological Society, i. 86. Wright's Essex,
i. 544. Metcalfe's Visitations of Suffolk, 35. Harleian Society,
xxxii. 131.

GOLDINGTON. Morant's Essex, ii. 8. Lipscombe's History of the
County of Buckingham, iv. 352. See DE GOLDINGTON.

GOLDNEY. Burke's Landed Gentry, 6. Howard's Visitation of
England and Wales, Notes, i. 59. Beavan's Reports, xxiv. 199.

GOLDSBURGH. Morant's Essex, i. 129.

GOLDSMITH, or GOLDSMYTH. Gentleman's Magazine, 1837, i. 242.
Berry's Hampshire Genealogies, 88. Harleian Society, xv. 321.
Notes and Queries, 3 S. v. 325. James Hall's History of Nant-
wich, 478. Howard's Visitation of England and Wales, v. 106.

GOLDSTON. Visitatio Comitatus Wiltoniæ, 1623, printed by Sir T. Phillipps. Hoare's Wiltshire, V. i. 202.

GOLDTHORPE. Hunter's Deanery of Doncaster, i. 387. Harleian Society, xvi. 143.

GOLDWILL. Blomefield's Norfolk, iii. 542.

GOLLOP. Burke's Commoners, i. 600, Landed Gentry, 2, 3, 4, 5, 6, 7, 8. Hutchins' Dorset, ii. 111, 113.

GOLOFRE. Harleian Society, xii. 74.

GOMELDON. Visitation of Middlesex, (Salisbury, 1820, fol.) 9. Hoare's Wiltshire, V. i. 62. Foster's Visitation of Middlesex, 23.

GOMM. Letters and Journals of F.M. Sir W. M. Gomme, by F. C. Carr-Gomm, 1.

GOMOND. Robinson's Mansions of Herefordshire, 59. Weaver's Visitation of Herefordshire, 33.

GONNING. Harleian Society, viii. 209.

GONSON. Harleian Society, xiii. 360. Miscellanea Genealogica et Heraldica, 2nd Series, i. 123.

GONVILLE. Blomefield's Norfolk, i. 286. Suckling's History of Suffolk, i. 314.

GONYS. The Genealogist, New Series, xv. 219.

GOOCH, or GOCHE. Herald and Genealogist, vii. 141. Suckling's History of Suffolk, ii. 125. Carthew's Hundred of Launditch, Part ii. 701, 734. Page's History of Suffolk, 204, 370. Harleian Society, xiii. 56. The Genealogist, iv. 29; vi. 155. Betham's Baronetage, iii. 237. See GOCH. .

GOOD. Hutchins' Dorset, ii. 685. The Genealogist, iv. 29. Notes and Queries, 3 S. iii. 319. Harleian Society, xx. 47.

GOODALL. Burke's Landed Gentry, 3, 4, 5, 6, 7, 8. Nichols' History of the County of Leicester, iv. 780. Harleian Society, xii. 204. An Historical Survey of Cornwall, by C. S. Gilbert, i. 590.

GOODAY, or GOODDAY. Morant's Essex, ii. 324. Hasted's Kent, i. 127. Berry's Essex Genealogies, 117. Gage's History of Thingoe Hundred, Suffolk, 244. Harleian Society, xiii. 203, 408; xiv. 663; xv. 322. Metcalfe's Visitations of Suffolk, 140. Metcalfe's Visitations of Northamptonshire, 95.

GOODCHILD. Surtees' Durham, i. 240. Burke's Landed Gentry, 8.

GOODDEN. Burke's Landed Gentry, 2 supp., 3, 4, 5, 6, 7, 8. Hutchins' Dorset, iv. 169.

GOODE. Harleian Society, ix. 83. The Visitations of Cornwall, edited by J. L. Vivian, 189.

GOODERE. Gentleman's Magazine, 1825, ii. 136. Harleian Society, iv. 175; xii. 67; xviii. 240; xxii. 8, 58. Burke's Extinct Baronetcies.

GOODERHAM. Ontarian Families, by E. M. Chadwick, i. 154.

GOODEVE. A Pedigree of the Goodeve Family. By Stephen Miall. London, 1891, fol. pp. 8.

GOODFORD. Burke's Commoners, iii. 146, Landed Gentry, 2, 3, 4, 5, 6, 7, 8.

GOODHALL. The Genealogist, iv. 30.

GOODHAND. The Genealogist, vi. 156.

GOODHART. Burke's Commoners, i. 369, Landed Gentry, 2.

GOODINGE. Metcalfe's Visitations of Suffolk, 94, 141. Muskett's Suffolk Manorial Families, i. 201-240. *See* JOHNSTONE.

GOODLAD. Burke's Landed Gentry, 5, 6, 7.

GOODLAKE. Burke's Landed Gentry, 2, 3, 4, 5, 6, 7, 8. The Genealogist, v. 265.

GOODLAW. Chetham Society, lxxxii. 50.

GOODMAN. J. H. Hill's History of Langton, 217. Dwnn's Visitations of Wales, i. 243 ; ii. 337. Harleian Society, ii. 84 ; xviii. 105 ; xxii. 145. Nichols' History of the County of Leicester, ii. 455. Memoir of Gabriel Goodman, by R. Newcome, app. S. Metcalfe's Visitations of Northamptonshire, 95.. Burke's Family Records, 261.

GOODRICH. New England Register, xvii. 357.

GOODRICK, or GOODRICKE. History of the Goodricke Family, by C. A. Goodricke. London, 1885, 8vo. Cambridgeshire Visitation, edited by Sir T. Phillipps, 14. Surtees Society, xxxvi. 159. Foster's Visitations of Yorkshire, 40. The Genealogist, iv. 31 ; vi. 157 ; New Series, x. 96. Harleian Society, xvi. 143 ; xli. 48. Wotton's English Baronetage, ii. 257. Betham's Baronetage, i. 445. Burke's Extinct Baronetcies, *Add.* Abstracts of Goodricke Wills, by C. A. Goodricke, 1887. Lincolnshire Notes and Queries, i. 122 ; v. 75.

GOODRICKE-HOLYOAKE. Burke's Commoners, ii. 597.

GOODRIDGE. Tuckett's Devonshire Pedigrees, 94. Harleian Society, iv. 131 ; xxi. 250. The Visitations of Devon, by J. L. Vivian, 115.

GOODWIN, or GOODWYN. Berry's Buckinghamshire Genealogies, 71. Berry's Sussex Genealogies, 332. Surtees Society, xxxvi. 278. Burke's Landed Gentry, 3, 4, 5, 6, 7. History of the Hundred of Desborough, by Thomas Langley, 442. Hunter's Deanery of Doncaster, ii. 48. Miscellanea Genealogica et Heraldica, New Series, ii. 217. Visitation of Devon, edited by F. T. Colby, 115. Cambridgeshire Visitation, edited by Sir T. Phillipps, 15. Harleian Society, vi. 131 ; xii. 90 ; xv. 324, 328 ; xxxviii. 604, 716, 747 ; xli. 100 ; xliii. 124. Surrey Archæological Collections, viii. *bis.* The Visitations of Devon, by J. L. Vivian, 416. Muskett's Suffolk Manorial Families, i. 201-240. The Genealogist, New Series, xiv. 116. *See* GODWIN.

GOODWIN-GLADWIN. Burke's Landed Gentry, 8.

GOODYER, or GOODYERE. Berry's Hertfordshire Genealogies, 185. Manning and Bray's Surrey, i. 15. Monken Hadley, by F. C. Cass, 138.

GOOKIN. Hasted's Kent, iv. 161. Notes and Queries, 1 S. i. 385, 492 ; ii. 44, 127 ; iv. 103 ; vii. 238 ; 3 S. ii. 324, 397, 472 ; iv. 438. New England Register, i. 345 ; ii. 167 ; iv. 185. *See* GOKIN.

GOOLD. Burke's Landed Gentry, 3, 4, 5. Harleian Society, viii. 446. Betham's Baronetage, v. 483.

GOORE. Staniforthiana, by F. M. H., *at end.*

GOOSTREY. Earwaker's History of Sandbach, 254.

GOPHILL. Harleian Society, xliii. 45.

GORDON. The History of the Ancient Family of Gordon, by William
Gordon. Edinburgh, 1726, 8vo. 2 vols. A History of the Ancient
House of Gordon, by C. A. Gordon. Aberdeen, 1754, 12mo.
Another edn., 1890, 8vo. Case of Sir Robert Gordon, Bart.,
claiming the title of Earl of Sutherland, 1769, folio, pp. 15.
Supplemental Case of same, 1770, folio, pp. 40. Claim of Sir
Charles Gordon to the Earldom of Sutherland, Sess. Papers,
Decr. 1767—Jan. 1768. Case of John Campbell, Earl of Aber-
deen, 1872, fol. Claim of the Earl of Aberdeen to be Visct.
Gordon, Sess. Papers, A of 1872. Pedigree of Gordon of Huntley
and Abergeldie, [T. P.] folio page. Burke's Commoners, iv. 8 ;
(of Culvennan) Commoners, iii., 610, Landed Gentry, 2, 3, 4, 5, 6 ;
(of Pitlurg,) Commoners, iv. 45, Landed Gentry, 2, 3, 4, 5, 6, 7, 8 ;
(of Florida,) Commoners, iv. 376, Landed Gentry, 2, 3, 4, 6 supp.,
7, 8 ; (of Haffield and Abergeldie,) Commoners, ii. 219, Landed
Gentry, 2, 3, 4, 5, 6, 7, 8 ; (of Cairnfield,) Landed Gentry, 2, 3,
4, 5, 6, 8 ; (of Balmaghie,) 2, 3, 4, 5 ; (of Cairnbulg,) 2, 3, 4, 5 ;
(of Park House,) 2, 3, 4, 5 ; (of Cluny,) 4, 5, 6 ; (of Newtimber
Place,) 5, 6, 7, 8 ; (of Knokespoch,) 2, 3 ; (of Manar,) 6, 7, 8 ; (of
Wardhouse,) 6, 7, 8 ; (of Esslemont,) 6, 7, 8 ; (of Wincombe Park,)
6, 7, 8 ; (of Cairnfield,) 7 ; (of Auchendolly,) 7, 8 ; (of Kenmure,)
8 ; (of Threave,) 8 ; (of Drimmin,) 8. Burke's Royal Descents
and Pedigrees of Founders' Kin, 90, 116. Lands and their Owners
in Galloway, by P. H. M'Kerlie, i. 224 ; ii. 331 ; iii. 17, 70, 75,
81, 112, 191, 366, 414. Paterson's History of the Co. of Ayr,
i. 220. Malcolm's Memoirs of the House of Drummond, 165.
Burke's Visitation of Seats and Arms, 2nd Series, i. 47. Douglas's
Baronage of Scotland, 2, 30. Shaw's History of Moray, 12, 70.
Wood's Douglas's Peerage of Scotland, i. 16, 24, 641 ; ii. 23, 222.
Edmondson's Baronagium Genealogicum, vi. 28*. Brydges'
Collins' Peerage, v. 201. Notes and Queries, 2 S. ii. 344.
Betham's Baronetage, iii. 316. Burke's Extinct Baronetcies, and
623. Metcalfe's Visitations of Suffolk, 141. Caithness Family
History, by John Henderson, 326. Burke's Colonial Gentry, i.
132. Oliver's History of Antigua, ii. 22. The Genealogical
Magazine, ii. 248. See FORBES-GORDON, HAY-GORDON, PRINGLE,
SUTHERLAND.

GORDON-DUFF. Burke's Landed Gentry, 7, 8.

GORE. Collinson's Somerset, ii. 311. Chronicle of the Family of
De Havilland. Burke's Landed Gentry, (of Tyredagh,) 2, 3, 4, 5,
6, 7 ; (of Barrow Court,) 4, 5 ; (of Derryluskan,) 6 and supp.,
7, 8 ; (of Fedney,) 8 ; (of Goremount,) 6 supp., 7. Harleian
Society, ii. 85 ; viii. 100, 107, 164 ; xv. 326 ; xl. 1280. Topographical Collections of John Aubrey, edited by J. E. Jackson, 47.
Burke's Royal Families, (London, 1851, 8vo.) i. 150. Bibliotheca
Topographica Britannica, i. Part. i. 40. Nichols' History of the
County of Leicester, iv. 128. Visitatio Comitatus Wiltoniæ, 1623,
printed by Sir T. Phillipps. Hoare's Wiltshire, I. ii. 183. Manning and Bray's Surrey, ii. 664. Clutterbuck's Hertford, i. 502 ;
iii. 170. Baker's Northampton, i. 84. J. E. Jackson's History

of Grittleton, (Wiltshire Topographical Society,) 7. Notes and
Queries, 2 S. v. 129, 223. Archdall's Lodge's Peerage, iii. 110,
277. Visitation of Wiltshire, edited by G. W. Marshall, 34.
Phillimore's London and Middlesex Note Book, 263. The Gene-
alogist, New Series, xv. 192. *See* ORMSBY-GORE.
GORE-LANGTON. Burke's Commoners, i. 145, Landed Gentry, 2, 3,
4, 5, 6, 7, 8. Burke's Royal Families, (London, 1851, 8vo.) i. 71.
GOREING, or GOREINGE. Additional Case of T. Stonor, claiming
Barony of Camoys, on a folding table. Visitation of Sussex, 1570,
printed by Sir T. Phillipps, (Middle Hill, fol.) 5. *See* GORING.
GORGE, or GORGES. Visitation of Middlesex, (Salisbury, 1820, fol.) 5.
Visitation of Somerset, printed by Sir T. Phillipps, 82, 148. Har-
leian Society, xi. 41, 42, 122. Visitatio Comitatus Wiltoniæ, 1623,
printed by Sir T. Phillipps. Pedigree of Sir Ferdinando Gorges,
by Rev. F. Brown, M.A. Boston, U.S.A. 1875, 8vo. Pedigree
of Gorges of Chelsea, etc., by Sir T. Phillipps, Bart., 2 sheets.
Pedigree of Gorges from Robert Gorges, LL.D., [T. P.] folio page.
Collinson's Somerset, iii. 156. Berry's Hampshire Genealogies,
127. Berry's Buckinghamshire Genealogies, 63. Herald and
Genealogist, vi. 94. Burke's Extinct Baronetcies. Hutchins
Dorset, ii. 154 ; iii. 341. Hoare's Wiltshire, III. v. 30. Miscel-
lanea Genealogica et Heraldica, New Series, ii. 75. Robinson's
Mansions of Herefordshire, 88. Colby of Great Torrington, by
F. T. Colby, 33. Banks' Baronies in Fee, i. 223. Visitation of
Devon, edited by F. T. Colby. 116. Banks' Dormant and Extinct
Baronage, i. 326. Weaver's Visitations of Somerset, 26, 72, 110.
Burke's Extinct Peerage, edn. of 1883, 237. Foster's Visitation
of Middlesex, 12. New England Register, xv. 18 ; xxix. 42, 112.
Parliamentary Memoirs of Fermanagh, by Earl of Belmore, 61.
The Genealogist, New Series, xv. 23 ; xvii. 241.
GORHAM. Collectanea Topographica et Genealogica, v. 182, 329 ; vi.
284 ; viii. 81. Burke's Visitation of Seats and Arms, ii. 20.
Northamptonshire Notes and Queries, ii. 156, 214, 248. New
England Register, lii. 357, 445.
GORING, or GORINGE. Hasted's Kent, ii. 523. Berry's Sussex Gene-
alogies, 138, 154. Visitation of Suffolk, edited by J. J. Howard,
ii. 265. Burke's Commoners, i. 387. Burke's Landed Gentry,
3, 4, 5, 6, 7, 8. Dallaway's Sussex, II. i. 249 ; II. ii. 133, 151.
Scott of Scot's-Hall, by G. R. Scott, 235. Castles, Mansions, and
Manors of Western Sussex, by D. G. C. Elwes and C. J. Robin-
son, 157, 267. Monken Hadley, by F. C. Cass, 128. Notes and
Queries, 1 S. ii. 22, 65, 86 ; vi. 33 ; vii. 143, 317 ; xi. 487 ; xii.
92. Wotton's English Baronetage, ii. 71. Betham's Baronetage,
i. 315. Banks' Dormant and Extinct Baronage, iii. 574. Burke's
Extinct · Baronetcies. Visitations of Staffordshire, 1614 and
1663-4, William Salt Society, 153. Camoys Peerage Evidence,
57. *See* GOREING.
GORING-THOMAS. Burke's Landed Gentry, 7, 8.
GORSUCH. Chetham Society, lxxxv. 123. Harleian Society, xv. 327.
Notes and Queries, 3 S. i. 213.

GORT. Claim of Viscount Gort to vote at Elections of Irish Peers, Sess. Papers, 2 of 1857-8.

GORTON. The Gortons of Gorton, by J. Higson. London, 1873, 8vo. Miscellanea Genealogica et Heraldica, New Series, i. 321, 378. Burke's Family Records, 264.

GOSHALL. Planche's Corner of Kent. 350.

GOSLING. Burke's Landed Gentry, 4 supp., 5, 6, 7, 8.

GOSNELL. Metcalfe's Visitations of Suffolk, 36.

GOSSAGE *See* GORSUCH.

GOSSE. Genealogies of Morgan and Glamorgan, by G. T. Clark, 489.

GOSSELIN. Chronicle of the Family of De Havilland. Berry's Hertfordshire Genealogies, 192. Burke's Commoners, (of Ware Priory,) i. 301, Landed Gentry, 2, 3, 4, 5, 6 and supp., 7, 8; (of Mount Ospringe,) Landed Gentry, 5.

GOSSETT, or GOSSET. Burke's Landed Gentry, 4, 5, 6, 7, 8. Gyll's History of Wraysbury, 230. J. B. Payne's Armorial of Jersey, 172.

GOSSIP. Burke's Heraldic Illustrations, 113. Burke's Landed Gentry, 2; 6 at p. 753; 7 at p. 860; 8 at p. 916. Foster's Yorkshire Pedigrees. History of the Wilmer Family, 129. Burke's Family Records, 265.

GOSTELOW. Baker's Northampton, i. 719.

GOSTLETT. Miscellanea Genealogica et Heraldica, New Series, iii. 436. Visitation of Gloucester, edited by T. F. Fenwick and W. C. Metcalfe, 73. Harleian Society, xxi. 67.

GOSTLIN. Muskett's Suffolk Manorial Families, i. 88-95.

GOSTLING-MURRAY. Burke's Landed Gentry, 8.

GOSWICK, or GOSTWICK. Bedfordshire Notes and Queries, iii. 44. Burke's Extinct Baronetcies. Raine's History of North Durham, 182. Wotton's English Baronetage, i. 238. Harleian Society, xix. 32.

GOTHURST. Visitation of Devon, edited by F. T. Colby, 118.

GOTT, or GOTTES. Berry's Hertfordshire Genealogies, 98. Berry's Sussex Genealogies, 242. Burke's Landed Gentry, 5, 6, 7, 8. Cambridgeshire Visitation, edited by Sir T. Phillipps, 16. Harleian Society, xli. 97.

GOUGE. Genealogical Memoranda of the Family of Ames, 11.

GOUGH. Rudder's Gloucestershire, 308. Berry's Essex Genealogies, 47. Berry's Hertfordshire Genealogies, 220. Visitation of Somerset, printed by Sir T. Phillipps, 83. Burke's Commoners, ii. 392, Landed Gentry, 2, 6 supp., 8. Harleian Society, xi. 43; xiii. 408; xxi. 67; xxviii. 201; xxxix. 932. Burke's Royal Descents and Pedigrees of Founders' Kin, 124. Shaw's Staffordshire, ii. 188. Visitation of Staffordshire, 1663-4, printed by Sir T. Phillipps, 5. Westcote's Devonshire, edited by G. Oliver and P. Jones, 547. Dugdale's Warwickshire, 896. Antiquities and Memoirs of the Parish of Myddle, by Richard Gough, 1700, (folio,) 42. Wiltshire Archæological Magazine, xi. 34. Pedigree of Wilson of High Wray, etc., by Joseph Foster, 96. Burke's Royal Families, (edn. of 1876,) 217. Wotton's English Baronetage, iv.

219. Visitation of Wiltshire, edited by G. W. Marshall, 44.
Brydges' Collins' Peerage, viii. 481. Visitations of Staffordshire,
1614 and 1663-4, William Salt Society, 154. Visitation of
Gloucester, edited by T. F. Fenwick and W. C. Metcalfe, 74.
Weaver's Visitations of Somerset, 110.

GOULBURN. Burke's Landed Gentry, 2, 4, 5, 6, 7, 8.

GOULD. Tuckett's Devonshire Pedigrees, 27. Burke's Landed
Gentry, (of Frampton,) 4, 5, 6, 7, 8; (of Lew Trenchard,) 2, 3, 4,
5, 6, 7, 8; (of Upwey,) 5 supp., 6, 7, 8. Harleian Society, vi.
132; xx. 47. Jewitt's Reliquary, xii. 45. Phelps' History of
Somersetshire, i. 564. Gyll's History of Wraysbury, 75. Hutchins'
Dorset, ii. 842. Clutterbuck's Hertford, ii. 189. The Genealogist,
ii. 332. Miscellanea Genealogica et Heraldica, New Series, iii. 355.
Harleian Society, xv. 328. Notes and Queries, 3 S. ii. 146, 199,
299; 6 S. ix. 292. Burke's Extinct Baronetcies. Weaver's Visitations of Somerset, 111, 114. Jewers' Wells Cathedral, 285.
The Visitations of Devon, by J. L. Vivian, 418-432, 472. Healey's
History of Part of West Somerset, 174. *See* GOLD.

GOULD-ADAMS. Stemmata Britannica, by Joseph Foster, (London,
1877, 8vo.) 8.

GOULDESBURG. Bysshe's Visitation of Essex, edited by J. J. Howard,
40.

GOULDING. Berry's Kent Genealogies, 160. Harleian Society,
xlii. 71.

GOULDSMITH, or GOULDSMYTH. Berry's Kent Genealogies, 432. A
Royal Descent, by T. E. Sharpe, (London, 1875, 4to.) 17. The
Genealogist, ii. 309. Harleian Society, xlii. 198.

GOULDSTON. Harleian Society, xxviii. 203.

GOULDWELL. Cambridgehire Visitation, edited by Sir T. Phillipps,
15, 16. The Genealogist, iii. 299. Harleian Society, xli. 71, 84.

GOULSTON. Morant's Essex, ii. 607. Hasted's Kent, ii. 296. Berry's
Hertfordshire Genealogies, 202. Harleian Society, viii. 335.
Clutterbuck's Hertford, iii. 472. East Barnet, by F. C. Cass, 130.

GOULTON. Burke's Landed Gentry, 7, 8.

GOUNTER. Berry's Sussex Genealogies, 13. Visitation of Sussex,
1570, printed by Sir T. Phillipps, (Middle Hill, fol.) 5. Dallaway's Sussex, i. 154. Sussex Archæological Collections, xxiii. 2.
See GUNTER.

GOURLAY, or GOURLEY. Memorials of the Scottish House of Gourlay
by Rev. C. Rogers. Edinburgh, 1888, 4to. Burke's Landed
Gentry, 2, 4, 5, 6, 7, 8. Foster's Visitations of Yorkshire, 168.
Douglas's Baronage of Scotland, 469. Walter Wood's East Neuk
of Fife, 257.

GOURNARDE. Collectanea Topographica et Genealogica, iv. 91.

GOURNAY, or GOURNEY. Harleian Society, vi. 133; xxxii. 132.
Visitation of Somersetshire, printed by Sir T. Phillipps, 150.
J. H. Blunt's Dursley and its Neighbourhood, 109. Collectanea
Archæologica, (Brit. Archl. Assn.) ii. 174. Edmondson's Barona-
gium Genealogicum, v. 484. Bysshe's Visitation of Essex, edited
by J. J. Howard, 40. Weaver's Visitation of Somerset, 26. The

Visitations of Devon, by J. L. Vivian, 433. Harleian Society
xxii. 58. The Genealogist, New Series, xii. 172. *See* GURNEY.

GOUSHILL. Thoroton's Nottinghamshire, iii. 62. The Genealogist,
New Series, x. 90; xiv. 19.

GOUTON. Foster's Visitations of Yorkshire, 521.

GOVE. Westcote's Devonshire, edited by G. Oliver and P. Jones,
547. Visitation of Devon, edited by F. T. Colby, 118. The
Visitations of Devon, by J. L. Vivian, 434.

GOVIS. Hutchins' Dorset, iii. 703.

GOWER, or GOWRE. Burke's Commoners, (of Bill Hill,) i. 320,
Landed Gentry, 2, 3, 4, 5; (of Glandovan,) 8; (of Titsey Park,)
3, 4, 5. Foster's Visitations of Yorkshire, 144, 226, 267. His-
tory of Richmond, by C. Clarkson, 380. Graves' History of
Cleveland, 478. Poulson's Holderness, ii. 51. Ord's History of
Cleveland, 505. Surtees' Durham, iii. 209. T. Nicholas' County
Families of Wales, 900. Surtees Society, xli. 62. Harleian
Society, xvi. 145; xxvii. 59, 82. Edmondson's Baronagium
Genealogicum, iii. 254. Brydges' Collins' Peerage, ii. 441. Met-
calfe's Visitations of Worcester, 1683, 49. My Reminiscences, by
Lord Ronald Gower, i. 67-96. Croston's edn. of Baines's Lan-
caster, iii. 287.

GOWIZ. The Genealogist, New Series, xiv. 254.

GOWSELL. *See* GAWSELL.

GOW-STEUART. Burke's Landed Gentry, 4, 5, 6, 7, 8.

GOYDER. Burke's Colonial Gentry, ii. 689.

GOZELIN. Baker's Northampton, i. 130.

GRACE. A Survey of Tullaroan, etc., being a Genealogical History
of the Family of Grace. Dublin, 1819, 8vo. Memoirs of the
Family of Grace, by Sheffield Grace, 1823, 2 vols., 4to. Bibliotheca Topographica Britannica, vii. Part ii. 360; ix. Part iv. 96.
Camden Soctety, xliii. 21. Burke's Commoners, (of Mantua,)
ii. 350, Landed Gentry, 2, 3, 4, 5, 6, 7, 8; (of Knole,) 2. Harleian Society, xv. 329. A Letter from the Countess of Nithsdale,
by Sheffield Grace, (London, 1827, 8vo.) 36. The Yorkshire
Genealogist, i. 192.

GRADELL. The Tyldesley Diary, edited by J. Gillow and A. Hewitson, 67.

GRADWELL. Burke's Landed Gentry, 3, 4, 5, 6, 7, 8.

GRÆME. Burke's Commoners, (of Garvock,) iii. 125, Landed Gentry,
2, 3, 4, 5, 6, 7, 8; (of Orchill,) Landed Gentry, 3 supp., 4, 5, 6, 7;
(of Inchbrakie,) 2 supp., 3, 4, 5, 6, 7, 8. Burke's Royal Families,
(London, 1851, 8vo.) ii. 174. *See* GREAME.

GRAFTON. Dwnn's Visitations of Wales, i. 119. The Genealogist,
New Series, xiii. 98.

GRAHAM. A Genealogical Tree of the Illustrious Family of Graham,
by J. Brown, folio sheet. Graham *v.* Hope-Weir, Appellants
Case in House of Lords, 1803. Herald and Genealogist, iv. 277;
v. 535. Surtees Society, xxxvi. 41. Burke's Commoners, (of
Fintry,) iii. 120, Landed Gentry, 2, 3, 4, 5, 6, 7, 8; (of Leitch-
town,) Commoners, iv. 576, Landed Gentry, 2, 3, 4; (of Dun-

trune,) Landed Gentry, 2, 3, 4, 5, 6, 7, *see* under LACON; (of Airth
Castle,) 2 supp., 3, 4, 5, 6, 7, 8; (of Tamrawr,) 2 supp., 3, 4, 5, 6;
(of Mossknow,) 2, 3, 4, 5, 6, 7, 8; (of Edmond Castle,) 3, 4, 5, 6,
7, 8; (of Drumgoon,) 3, 4, 5, 6, 7, 8; (of Murrayshall,) 5, 6, 7, 8;
(of Balgowan,) 2 add., 3; (of Meiklewood,) 2, 3, 4; 6 at p. 919;
and 2nd edn. of supp.; (of Larchfield,) 7, 8; (of Craigallian,) 7;
7 at p. 1660; (of Airthrey Castle,) 8; (of Morphie,) 8. Foster's
Yorkshire Pedigrees. Hutchinson's History of Cumberland, ii.
531. Burke's Royal Families, (London, 1851, 8vo.) i. 92; ii. 37,
122. Jefferson's History of Leath Ward, Cumberland, 239.
Whitaker's History of Richmondshire, ii. 184. Burke's Royal
Descents and Pedigrees of Founders' Kin, 8. Paterson's History
of Ayr and Wigton, ii. 159. Burke's Extinct Baronetcies, 623,
624. Caledonia, by Geo. Chalmers, 545. Wood's Douglas's Peer-
age of Scotland, i. 36, 468; ii. 227, 233, 374. Wotton's English
Baronetage, iii. 385. The Red Book of Menteith, by Wm. Fraser,
i. 464. Edmondson's Baronagium Genealogicum, iii. 228. Brydges'
Collins' Peerage, iv. 209. Betham's Baronetage, ii. 326; iv. 126.
Northern Notes and Queries, i. 119, 152; vii. 90; ix. 160. Sir
Robert Douglas's Peerage of Scotland, 1st edn., 476. Foster's
Visitations of Cumberland and Westmorland, 54, 55. Notes and
Queries, 8 S. viii. 162, 390. Burke's Family Records, 267-275,
563. The Genealogical Magazine, i. 67-82; iii. 301, 338. Nicol-
son and Burns' Westmorland and Cumberland, ii. 431, 465. *See*
CUNNINGHAME-GRAHAM, MAXWELL-GRAHAM, MAXTONE-GRAHAM,
BARNS-GRAHAM.
GRAHAM-CAMPBELL. Burke's Landed Gentry, 7, 8.
GRAHAM-CLARKE. Burke's Landed Gentry, 4, 5, 6, 7, 8.
GRAHAME. Burke's Landed Gentry, 7, 8. Notes and Queries, 8 S.
xi. 383.
GRAHAM-FOSTER-PIGOTT. Burke's Landed Gentry, 5, 6, 7.
GRAHAM-STIRLING. Burke's Landed Gentry, 5, 6, 7, 8.
GRAHME. Nicolson and Burn's Westmorland and Cumberland, ii. 466.
GRAINGER. Burke's Landed Gentry, 5 at p. 1055.
GRAMARY. Harleian Society, xvi. 298.
GRAMMER. Miscellanea Genealogica et Heraldica, New Series, ii.
306. Harleian Society, xii. 51. The Gresley's of Drakelowe, by
F. Madan, 259.
GRAMMONT. Notes and Queries, 1 S. ix. 204.
GRANARD. Claim of the Earl of Granard to vote at Elections of
Irish Peers, Sess. Papers, 217 of 1867, sess. 2. *See* FORBES.
GRANDISON. Fosbrooke's History of Gloucestershire, ii. 235. Banks'
Baronies in Fee, i. 224; ii. 137. Banks' Dormant and Extinct
Baronage, i. 330. The Genealogist, New Series, xiii. 173. *See*
BEDINGFIELD.
GRANDORGE. The Genealogist, iv. 32.
GRANGE. Harleian Society, i. 67; xli. 94.
GRANGER. Burke's Visitation of Seats and Arms, i. 49.
GRANT. Account of the rise and offspring of the name of Grant, by
Sir A. Grant, 1876, 8vo. The Chiefs of Grant, by Wm. Fraser.

Edinburgh, 1883, 4to., 3 vols. Mémoires Historiques, Généalo-
giques, etc., de la Maison de Grant, [by Charles Grant, Visct. de
Vaux,] 1796, 8vo. Pedigree of Grant *alias* Button of Cotterell,
Co. Glamorgan, [T. P.] 1860, broadside. Reminiscences of the
Grants of Glenmoriston, by A. Sinclair. 1887, 4to. Burke's
Commoners, (of Kilgraston,) ii. 613, Landed Gentry, 2, 3, 4, 5, 6,
7, 8 ; (of Glenmoriston,) Landed Gentry, 2, 3, 4, 5, 6, 7, 8 ; (of
Kilmurry,) 3, 4, 5, 6, 7, 8 ; (of Arndilly,) 5, 7, 8 ; (of Hillersdon
House,) 5, 6, 7, 8 ; of Litchborough,) 5, 6, 7, 8 ; (of Kincorth,)
5, 6 ; (of the Gnoll,) 2, 3 ; (of the Hill,) 2 add. ; (of Druminor,)
7, 8 ; (of Ecclesgreig,) 8. Hampshire Visitations, printed by Sir
T. Phillipps, 17. Baker's Northampton, ii. 46. Douglas's Baronage of Scotland, 341. Shaw's History of Moray, 18, 40. Betham's
Baronetage, v. (Barts. of Scotland,) 32. Foster's Collectanea
Genealogica, (MP's Scotland,) 160. F. G. Lee's History of Thame,
378. Genealogies of Morgan and Glamorgan, by G. T. Clark,
402. Burke's Colonial Gentry, i. 247 ; ii. 861. New England
Register, xxi. 173. Burke's Family Records, 275. Oliver's History
of Antigua, ii. 29.

GRANT-DALTON. Burke's Landed Gentry, 3 supp., 4, 5, 6, 7, 8.

GRANT-DUFF. Burke's Landed Gentry, 4, 5, 6, 7, 8.

GRANT-IVES. Burke's Landed Gentry, 8.

GRANT-THOROLD. Burke's Landed Gentry, 5, 6, 8.

GRANTHAM. Morant's Essex, i. 93. Burke's Landed Gentry, 2, 3, 4.
The Genealogist, iv. 32 ; vi. 157. Miscellanea Genealogica et
Heraldica, 2nd Series, i. 204. Burke's Family Records, 276.

GRANTHAM-HILL. Burke's Colonial Gentry, ii. 597.

GRANVILLE. The History of the Granville Family, by R. Granville.
Exeter, 1895, 8vo. Pedigree of Granville of Stowe, Co. Devon,
and of D'Ewes of Wellesborn, Co. Warwick, by Sir T. Phillipps,
Bart., folio broadside. Payne's Monograph of the House of
Lempriere, *at end.* Burke's Commoners, iii. 3, Landed Gentry
2, 3, 4, 5, 6, 7, 8. Burke's Royal Families, (London, 1851, 8vo.)
i. 44. T. Nicholas' County Families of Wales, 780. An Historical
Survey of Cornwall, by C. S. Gilbert, i. 505. Memoirs, British
and Foreign, of Illustrious Persons who died in 1711, 314. Banks'
Dormant and Extinct Baronage, iii. 64. The Visitations of Corn-
wall, edited by J. Vivian, 190. *See* GRENVILLE, LEVESON-
GOWER.

GRASETT. Ontarian Families, by E. M. Chadwick, ii. 63.

GRATTAN. Burke's Landed Gentry, 2, 3, 4.

GRATTAN-GUINNESS. Burke's Landed Gentry, 3, 4.

GRATWICK, or GRATWICKE. Berry's Sussex Genealogies, 169, 170,
256. Dallaway's Sussex, II. i. 66, 79. Jewitt's Reliquary, xviii.
220.

GRAUNT. Foster's Visitations of Yorkshire, 256. Harleian Society,
xxix. 489.

GRAUNTKORT. Bridges' Northamptonshire, by Rev. Peter Whalley,
ii. 369.

GRAVELEY. Harleian Society, xxii. 8. Thoresby Society, ii. 54.

GRAVENOR. Herald and Genealogist, iv. 482 ; v. 33-50, 498. Harleian Society, xv. 331; xviii. 107. Oliver's History of Antigua, ii. 32. *See* GROSVENOR.

GRAVES. Pedigree of Graves of Bath, by Sir T. Phillipps, Bart. London, fol. sheet, 1831. Pedigree of Graves of Derry and Bath, [T. P.] 1870. Broadside. Pedigree of Graves of Mickleton, Co. Glouc. [T. P.] 1848. Broadside. Gentleman's Magazine, 1825, ii. 208. Nash's Worcestershire, i. 198. Burke's Landed Gentry, 3, 4, 5, 6, 7, 8. Foster's Visitations of Yorkshire, 620. Herald and Genealogist, vi. 648. Visitation of Derbyshire, 1663-4, (Middle Hill, 1854, fol.) 4. The Genealogist, iii. 177. A Complete Parochial History of the County of Cornwall, i. 44. An Historical Survey of Cornwall, by C. S. Gilbert, i. 488. Miscellanea Genealogica et Heraldica, New Series, iii. 444. Notes and Queries, 1 S. vii. 130, 319 ; xi. 406. *See* STEELE-GRAVES.

GRAVETT. Harleian Society, xv. 330.

GRAY. Kent's British Banner Displayed, 419. Pratt and Morkill's Records of Whitkirk, 92. Dwnn's Visitations of Wales, ii. 214. Berry's Buckinghamshire Genealogies, 18. Berry's Hampshire Genealogies, 253. Burke's Commoners, iii. 24; (of Carntyne,) iii. 8, Landed Gentry, 2, 3, 4 ; (of Darcey Lever Hall,) Landed Gentry, 4, 5, 6 ; (of Graymount,) 5 supp., 6, 7, 8 ; (of East Bolton,) 5, 6 ; (of Farley Hill Place,) 7, 8 ; (of Carse,) 7, 8 ; (of Nunraw,) 8. Hutchinson's History of Cumberland, ii. 101. Burke's Royal Families, (London, 1851, 8vo.) ii. 23, 115. Foster's Lancashire Pedigrees. Burke's Visitation of Seats and Arms, ii. 36. Burke's Heraldic Illustrations, 73. Nichols' History of the County of Leicester, iii. 863. Harleian Society, ii. 74 ; xiii. 57 ; xv. 331 ; xix. 62, 112. Glasgow Past and Present, (Glasgow, 1856, 8vo.) iii. 305. Wood's Douglas's Peerage of Scotland, i. 664. Burke's Extinct Baronetcies, 624. The Genealogist, vi. 158. Weaver's Visitation of Herefordshire, 88. New England Register, xxxiv. 253. Bysshe's Visitation of Essex, edited by J. J. Howard, 41. Burke's Colonial Gentry, ii. 835. Oliver's History of Antigua, ii. 34. Northern Notes and Queries, vii. 182 ; xii. 179. *See* DE GRAY.

GRAY-BUCHANAN. Burke's Landed Gentry, 6 supp., 7, 8.

GRAYSTAYNES. Surtees' Durham, iv. 24.

GRAYSTOCK. Nicolson and Burn's Westmorland and Cumberland, ii. 349.

GRAZEBROOK. Burke's Landed Gentry, 3, 4, 5 add., 6, 7, 8. Miscellanea Genealogica et Heraldica, 3rd Series, iii. 117, 158, 212, 246.

GREAME. Burke's Commoners, ii. 590, Landed Gentry, 2. Foster's Yorkshire Pedigrees. Burke's Colonial Gentry, ii. 795. *See* GRÆME.

GREAR. Oliver's History of Antigua, ii. 36.

GREATHEAD, or GREATHED. Plantagenet-Harrison's History of Yorkshire, i. 85, 495. Harleian Society, xxxviii. 789. Burke's Landed Gentry, 2 supp., 3, 4, 5 and supp., 6, 7, 8. Hutchins' Dorset, iii. 115.

GREATRAKES. Jewitt's Reliquary, iv. 81, 220 ; v. 94; ix. 162. Burke's Patrician, ii. 255.

GREAVES. History of the Parish of Ecclesfield, by Rev. J. Eastwood,

383. Burke's Commoners, (of Irlam Hall,) iv. 105, Landed Gentry, 2; (of Page Hall,) Landed Gentry, 2 final add., 4, 5, 6, 7, 8; (of Staffordshire,) Commoners, i. 386, Landed Gentry, 2, 4, 5, 6; (of Avonside and the Cliff,) 3, 4, 5, 6, 7; (of Bron Eifion,) 8. Burke's Visitations of Seats and Arms, ii. 63. Butterworth's Account of the Town, etc., of Oldham, 74. Burke's Royal Families, (London, 1851, 8vo.) ii. 166*. Eastwood's History of Ecclesfield, 383. Metcalfe's Visitation of Worcester, 1683, 50. Harleian Society, xxxviii. 717, 800; xxxix. 1082, 1086. Essex Institute Historical Collections, (Salem, Mass.,) xxxi. 166-180. *See* GREVE.

GREAVES-BAGSHAWE. Burke's Landed Gentry, 4, 5, 6.

GREEKE. Harleian Society, xli. 108.

GREEN. Hasted's Kent, ii. 639. Morant's Essex, i. 147. Memoir of Thomas Green, Esq., of Ipswich, and an Account of his Family, etc., (Ipswich, 1825, 4to.). Berry's Berkshire Genealogies, 41. Burke's Landed Gentry, (of Dunsby,) 5 supp., 6; (of Odstone Hall,) 2; (of Pavenham,) 2 supp., 3, 4, 8; (of The Whittern,) 8; (of Hainault Lodge,) 8; (of Wilby,) 7, 8; (of Poulton,) 7, 8; (of Wyvenhoe,) 8. Foster's Visitations of Yorkshire, 258, 342, 522, 523. Harleian Society, viii. 497; xxi. 69; xxii. 59; xxxviii. 791; xxxix. 888. Poulson's Holderness, ii. 30. Hunter's History of the Parish of Sheffield, 449. Nichols' History of the County of Leicester, iv. 709. Hunter's Deanery of Doncaster, i. 80; ii. 234. Baker's Northampton, i. 32. The Genealogist, i. 55, 395. Wright's Essex, ii. 71, 355. Castles, Mansions, and Manors of Western Sussex, by D. G. C. Elwes and C. J. Robinson, 95. Betham's Baronetage, iv. 170. Notes and Queries, 6 S. i. 283, 445; 8 S. x. 270, 371. Burke's Extinct Baronetcies. Carthew's West and East Bradenham, 106. The 36 Royal Descents, of Charles Martin and Emily Frances Green. By Everard Green and A. R. Maddison, 1882. Broadside. Visitation of Gloucester, edited by T. F. Fenwick and W. C. Metcalfe, 76. Foster's Visitations of Northumberland, 60. Bysshe's Visitation of Essex, edited by J. J. Howard, 41. Visitations of Staffordshire, 1614 and 1663-4, William Salt Society, 155. Burke's Colonial Gentry, i. 41. East Barnet, by F. C. Cass, 140. Cyclostyle Pedigrees, by J. J. Green. New England Register, iv. 75; xv. 105; xxix. 170. Green of Worlingworth, Suffolk. Woodbridge, *n. d.*, 8vo., 4 pages. History of the Wilmer Family, 233. Howard's Visitation of England and Wales, iv. 45. Burke's Family Records, 280. Ontarian Families, by E. M. Chadwick, i. 25. *See* ALNO, GRENE.

GREENACRES. Whitaker's History of Whalley, ii. 116.

GREENALL. History of Ribchester, by T. C. Smith and J. Shortt, 261.

GREENAWAY. Burke's Landed Gentry, 2, 3, 4.

GREEN-EMMOTT. Burke's Landed Gentry, 5 supp.

GREENE. Herald and Genealogist, iii. 419; iv. 449; vi. 255. East Anglian, iii. 86, 286. Gough's Sepulchral Monuments, ii. 215. Morant's Essex, i. 183; ii. 286, 525, 526. Visitation of Norfolk, published by Norfolk Archæological Society, i. 89. Berry's Hertforshire Genealogies, 228. Surtees Society, xxxvi. 1, 49, 306,

379. Visitation of Somerset, printed by Sir T. Phillipps, 84.
Burke's Commoners, (of Thundercliffe,) iii. 589 ; (of Rolleston,)
Commoners, i. 521, Landed Gentry, 2, 3, 4 ; (of Slyne,) Landed
Gentry, 2, 3, 4, 5, 6, 7, 8 ; (of Greenville,) 4, 5, 6, 8 ; (of Kilma-
nahan Castle,) 2, 3 ; (of Midgham,) 7, 8. Foster's Visitations of
Yorkshire, 315. Harleian Society, v. 222 ; xi. 43 ; xiii. 57, 204,
409 ; xv. 332 ; xviii. 262 ; xxxii. 133. Burke's Royal Families,
(London, 1851, 8vo.) ii. 197. J. H. Hill's History of Market
Harborough, 49. Foster's Lancashire Pedigrees. Lipscombe's
History of Buckinghamshire, i. 29. Hodgson's Northumberland, II. ii. 333. Bridges' Northamptonshire, by Rev. Peter
Whalley, i. 240 ; ii. 137, 251. Nichols' History of the County
of Leicester, ii. 446* ; iii. 851. Hoare's Wiltshire, III. iv.
50. Clutterbuck's Hertford, iii. 80. J. E. Jackson's History
of Grittleton, (Wiltsh. Topl. Soc.) 14. Ormerod's Cheshire,
ii. 444. Eastwood's History of Ecclesfield, 364. Notes and
Queries, 2 S. iv. 287, 421 ; x. 234, 292, 333, 394 ; xi. 39 ; 3 S.
i. 371, 434. Metcalfe's Visitations of Suffolk, 193. Old Yorkshire, edited by Willm. Smith, iv. 221. Howard's Visitation of
Ireland, i. 15. The Genealogist, New Series, xii. 56, 92, 121 ;
xiii. 265. The Genealogical Magazine, iii. 452, 488. Memoir
of Richard Haines, by C. R. Haines.
GREENFIELD. Burke's Landed Gentry, 2, 3, 4. Abram's History of
Blackburn, 759. Burke's Family Records, 281.
GREENHALGH. Memoranda of the Greenhalgh Family. By J. D.
Greenhalgh. Bolton, 1869, 8vo. Notes and Queries, 2 S. x. 28,
76. Pedigree of Greenhalgh of Brandlesome, Manx Society's
Publications, vol. xxx. See GRENEHALGHE.
GREENHALL. Bibliotheca Topographica Britannica, ix. Part iv. 103.
GREENHAUGH. Thoroton's Nottinghamshire, ii. 304.
GREENHILL. Croke's History of the Family of Croke, No. 25.
Hoare's Wiltshire, I. ii. 247. Wiltshire Archæological Magazine,
xii. 119. Harleian Society, xxxix 1137. Burke's Landed Gentry,
(of Knowle Hall,) 8 ; (of Puriton Manor,) 8.
GREENLEAF. New England Register, xxviii. 473 ; xxxviii. 299.
GREENLY. Burke's Commoners, i. 292 ; Landed Gentry, 6 supp., 7, 8.
GREENOUGH. New England Register, xvii. 167.
GREENSMITH. Harleian Society, xl. 1264.
GREENSTREET. Memorials of the Ancient Kent Family of Green-
street, collected by James Greenstreet, 8vo. Hasted's Kent,
ii. 753.
GREENWAY. Abram's History of Blackburn, 506. Miscellanea
Genealogica et Heraldica, New Series, iii. 395. Oliver's History
of Antigua, ii. 36.
GREENWELL. Burke's Commoners, (of Greenwell Ford,) i. 114 ;
Landed Gentry, 2, 3, 4, 5, 6, 7, 8 ; (of Broomshields,) Landed
Gentry, 2, 3, 4, 5, 6, 7, 8 ; (of Greenwell,) Landed Gentry, 5, 6,
7, 8. Surtees' Durham, ii. 318.
GREENWICH. Banks' Dormant and Extinct Baronage, iii. 323.
GREENWODE, or GREENWOOD. Pedigree of Greenwood, [T. P.] 1866.

Folio page. Surtees Society, xxxvi. 246, 311. Thoresby's Ducatus Leodiensis, 167. Visitation of Oxfordshire, 1634, printed by Sir T. Phillipps, (Middle Hill, fol.) 19. Burke's Landed Gentry, (of Swarcliffe Hall,) 2, 3, 4, 5, 6, 7, 8 ; (of Broadhanger,) 5, 6, 7 ; (of Brookwood,) 5, 6, 7, 8. Foster's Visitations of Yorkshire, 524. Harleian Society, v. 256 ; vi. 133. Miscellanea Genealogica et Heraldica, 2nd Series, v. 253. The Visitations of Devon, by J. L. Vivian, 435. Oxford Historical Society, xix. 267. Howard's Visitation of England and Wales, v. 129.

GREER. Burke's Landed Gentry, (of the Grange Macgregor,) 2, 3, 4, 5, 6, 7, 8 ; (of Tullylagan,) 3, 4, 5, 6, 7, 8 ; (of Sea Park,) 7, 8. Herald and Genealogist, vi. 137. Howard's Visitation of Ireland, i. 9. *See* MACGREGOR.

GREEVES. Howard's Visitation of Ireland, i. 69.

GREG, GREGG, or GREGGE. Burke's Landed Gentry, (of Norcliffe Hall and Coles Park,) 2, 3, 4, 5, 6, 7, 8 ; (of Ballymenoch,) 3, 4. Herald and Genealogist, v. 468. Butterworth's Account of the Town, etc., of Oldham, 72. Ormerod's Cheshire, ii. 34. Harleian Society, xxxix. 1141. Burke's Family Records, 283.

GREGGE-HOPWOOD. Foster's Lancashire Pedigrees. Burke's Landed Gentry, 2, 3, 4, 5, 6, 8.

GREGOR. Historical Notices of the Clan Gregor, by Donald Gregary. 1831, 4to. Burke's Commoners, ii. 617, Landed Gentry, 2, 3, 4, 5, 7, 8. *See* MACGREGOR.

GREGORSON. Burke's Landed Gentry, 2, 3.

GREGORY. A short account of the family of Gregorie from the time they gave up the name of MacGregor, and took that of Gregorie. 1873. (25 copies, privately printed by Miss Gregory ' for my grand-nephew Henry Gregory.') Pedigree of Gregory of How Caple, Co. Hereford, [T. P.] folio page. Burke's Landed Gentry, (of Styvechale,) 2, 3, 4, 5, 6, 7, 8 ; (of Coole Park,) 3, 4, 5, 6, 7, 8 ; 2 supp. p. 192. Foster's Visitations of Yorkshire, 525. Harleian Society, ii. 187 ; xii. 155, 159 ; xv. 334 ; xxviii. 204. Thoroton's Nottinghamshire, ii. 41. Chetham Society, lxxxi. 7. Nichols' History of the County of Leicester, i. 587 ; iii. 19. Hunter's Deanery of Doncaster, i. 211. Turnor's History of Town and Soke of Grantham, 114. The Genealogist, v. 265 ; vi. 159. Duncombe's Hereford, (J. H. Cooke,) iii. 233. J. T. Godfree's History of Lenton, 34. Notes and Queries, 7 S. iii. 147. Oxford Historical Society, xix. 245. Visitation of Gloucester, edited by T. F. Fenwick and W. C. Metcalfe, 76. Burke's Colonial Gentry, i. 45. New England Register, xxiii. 304.

GREGSON. Burke's Landed Gentry, 2, 3, 4, 5, 6, 7, 8. Raine's History of North Durham, 206. Visitation of Derbyshire, 1663-4, (Middle Hill, 1854, fol.) 4. The Genealogist, iii. 158. Earwaker's Local Gleanings, i. 134, 190, 236. Harleian Society, xvi. 147 ; xxxvii. 215. History of the old Chapel, Tockholes, by B. Nightingale, 196.

GREIG. Burke's Landed Gentry, 5, 6, 7, 8. Notes and Queries, 2 S. xi. 88.

GREISBROOKE. Visitations of Staffordshire, 1614 and 1663-4, William Salt Society, 157. *See* GRAZEBROOKE.

GRELLEY. Blore's Rutland, 100-102. Observations on the Armorial Bearing of the Town of Manchester, by W. R. Whatton, 26.

GREME. Hutchinson's History of Cumberland, i. 190. *See* GREAME.

GRENDON. Shaw's Staffordshire, ii. 34. Dugdale's Warwickshire, 1101. Baker's Northampton, ii. 339. Banks' Dormant and Extinct Baronage, i. 331. Harvey's Hundred of Willey, 37. Metcalfe's Visitations of Northamptonshire, 96.

GRENDOURE. Harleian Society, xxi. 13.

GRENE. Morant's Essex, ii. 469. Burke's Landed Gentry, 3, 4. Visitation of Staffordshire, 1663-4, printed by Sir T. Phillipps, 5. Harleian Society, xvi. 145; xxxii. 134. Monken Hadley, by F. C. Cass, 128. *See* GREEN.

GRENEFIELD. Visitation of Devon, edited by F. T. Colby, 119.

GRENEHALGHE. Chetham Society, lxxxv. 124. *See* GREENHALGH.

GRENFELL. Burke's Landed Gentry, 4, 5, 6, 7, 8.

GRENON. Munford's Analysis of Domesday Book of Co. Norfolk, 47.

GRENTEMAISNELL, GRENTEMAISNIL, or GRENTMESNILL. J. H. Hill's History of Langton, 12. History of the House of Arundel, by J. P. Yeatman, 20. Bibliotheca Topographica Britannica, vii. Parts i. and ii. 299. Nichols' History of the County of Leicester, i. 21. Clutterbuck's Hertford, iii. 287. Baker's Northampton, i. 241. Banks' Dormant and Extinct Baronage, i. 90.

GRENVILLE, or GRENVILE. Pedigree of the Family of Grenville. By Ernest Axon. Manchester, 1893, 8vo. The Great Governing Families of England, ii. 1. Berry's Buckinghamshire Genealogies, 81. Berry's Genealogical Peerage, 44. Harleian Society, ix. 84, 87. Lipscombe's History of the County of Buckingham, i. 589, 596, 599. Westcote's Devonshire, edited by G. Oliver and P. Jones, 630, 631. Clutterbuck's Hertford, iii. 512. Baker's Northampton, i. 735. A Complete Parochial History of the County of Cornwall, ii. 370. An Historical Survey of Cornwall, by C. S. Gilbert, i. 482. Notes and Queries, 1 S. x. 417; xi. 71, 128. Edmondson's Baronagium Genealogicum, iii. 276; vi. 10*. Archdall's Lodge's Peerage, iii. 298. Brydges' Collins' Peerage, ii. 390; viii. 553. Hasted's Kent, (Hund. of Blackheath, by H. H. Drake,) xx. Devonshire Notes and Notelets, by Sir W. R. Drake, 115. The Genealogist, New Series, x. 92. *See* DE GRENVILLE, GRANVILLE, NEVILLE-GRENVILLE.

GRESHAM. Botfield's Stemmata Botevilliana, 144. Harleian Society, i. 15; xxxii. 134; xliii. 77. Manning and Bray's Surrey, ii. 403. Visitation of Norfolk, published by Norfolk Archæological Society, i. 355. Berry's Sussex Genealogies, 238. Miscellanea Genealogica et Heraldica, ii. 311-320, etc. ; New Series, iv. 80, 90, 251, 262, 269, 281, 301. Burgon's Life of Sir T. Gresham, i. 455. Wotton's English Baronetage, iii. 113. Burke's Extinct Baronetcies. Malcolm's Londinum Redivivum, iii. 559. Howard's Visitation of England and Wales, Notes, i. 75.

GRESLEY, GRESLEI, or GRESELEY. The Gresley's of Drakelowe. By

Falconer Madan. Oxford, 1899, 8vo. Clutterbuck's Hertford,
ii. 463. Lipscombe's History of the County of Buckingham,
i. 176. Jewitt's Reliquary, vi. 32. Burke's Commoners, iii. 528;
Landed Gentry, 2 p. 1573 *note*. The Borough of Stoke-upon-
Trent, by John Ward, 563. Erdeswick's Survey of Staffordshire,
208. Nichols' History of the County of Leicester, iii. 1009*.
Baines' History of the Co. of Lancaster, ii. 172. Pilkington's
View of Derbyshire, ii. 70. Wotton's English Baronetage, i. 121.
Betham's Baronetage, i. 92. Banks' Dormant and Extinct
Baronage, i. 332. The Genealogist, vi. 159. Visitation of Stafford-
shire, (Willm. Salt Soc.) 85. Howard's Visitation of England
and Wales, viii. 116. The Ancestor, No. i. 195. *See* GRISLING.
GRESSON. Burke's Colonial Gentry, ii. 704.
GRESWOLD, or GRESWOLDE. Dugdale's Warwickshire, *Index*. Har-
leian Society, xii. 61. Burke's Commoners, ii. 673, Landed
Gentry, 2 ; 6 at p. 1749 ; 7 at p. 1996 ; 8 at p. 2216. Visitation
of Warwickshire, 1619, published with Warwickshire Antiquarian
Magazine, 77. Collections for a History of Staffordshire, (William
Salt Society,) ii. part 2, 129.
GRETHEAD. Plantagenet-Harrison's History of Yorkshire, i. 495.
GREVE. Botfield's Stemmata Botevilliana, 149. Harleian Society,
xxii. 9. *See* GREAVES.
GREVIL, GREVILL, or GREVILLE. A Genealogical Account of the
Noble Family of Greville, by J. Edmondson. London, 1766,
8vo. Pedigree of Greville of Campden, etc., [T. P.] 1850, broad-
side. Visitation of Gloucestershire, 1569, (Middle Hill, 1854, fol.)
5. Shakespeareana Genealogica, by G. R. French, 506. Burke's
Landed Gentry, 3, 4. Lipscombe's History of the County of
Buckingham, i. 267. Warwickshire Pedigrees, from Visitation of
1682-3, (privately printed, 1865). Bridges' Northamptonshire, by
Rev. Peter Whalley, i. 535. Dugdale's Warwickshire, 706, 763.
Harleian Society, xii. 29, 143 ; xxi. 70, 214 ; xxix. 425. Edmond-
son's Baronagium Genealogicum, iii. 251 ; iv. 369. Brydges'
Collins' Peerage, iv. 330. Visitation of Gloucester, edited by
T. F. Fenwick and W. C. Metcalfe, 78.
GREVIS. The Genealogist, vi. 304.
GREVIS-JAMES. Burke's Commoners, i. 397, Landed Gentry, 2, 3, 4,
5, 6, 7. Burke's Family Records, 343.
GREY. The Great Governing Families of England, i. 47. Collectanea
Topographica et Genealogica, viii. 185. Jacob's Peerage, i. 528.
Hasted's Kent, i. lxxi. ; ii. 168. Morant's Essex, i. 47, 95, 345,
355 ; ii. 382. Harleian Society, i. 70 ; ii. 17, 139 ; xii. 43 ; xvi.
148 ; xix. 35, 173 ; xx. 48 ; xxviii. 105 ; xxxii. 137. Glover's
History of Derbyshire, ii. 342, (308). Dwnn's Visitations of
Wales, i. 282, 301. Surtees Society, xxxvi. 333. Berry's Sussex
Genealogies, 208, 374. Pedigrees from Visitation of Northumber-
land, printed by Sir T. Phillipps, (Middle Hill, 1858, fol.) 4.
Toulman's History of Taunton, new edn. by James Savage,
(Taunton, 1822, 8vo.) 69. Burke's Commoners, (of Morwick,)
i. 610, Landed Gentry, 2 ; (of Milfield,) 7, 8 ; (of Styford,)

Landed Gentry, 4, 5, 6, 7, 8 ; (of Norton,) 2 supp., 3, 4, 5 ; (of
Chipchase Castle,) 4. Foster's Visitations of Yorkshire, 70. Topo-
grapher, (London, 1789-91, 8vo.) iv. 23. Maclean's History of
Trigg Minor, i. 394*. Raine's History of North Durham, 326,
337, 387. Bibliotheca Topographica Britannica, i. Part i. 114 ;
vii. Part iii. 428. Burke's Patrician, v. 171. Herald and Genea-
logist, vi. 105. Notices of Swyncombe and Ewelme in Co.
Oxford, by H. A. Napier, 389. Shaw's Staffordshire, ii. 269.
Bridges' Northamptonshire, by Rev. Peter Whalley, i. 300, 559.
Blore's Rutland, 162-167. Hodgson's Northumberland, I. ii. 330 ;
II. ii. 331. Burke's Royal Descents and Pedigrees of Founders'
Kin, 9, 68. Dallaway's Sussex, i. 235. Visitation of Staffordshire,
1663-4, printed by Sir T. Phillipps, 6. Erdeswicke's Survey of
Staffordshire, 380, 522. Burton's Description of Leicestershire,
113. Nichols' History of the County of Leicester, ii. 217 ; iii.
682, 683 ; iv. 245, 481, 633*. Dugdale's Warwickshire, 107,
1024, 1029. Hutchins' Dorset, ii. 564. Surtees' Durham, ii. 19.
Baker's Northampton, i. 103, 140, 658, 685. The Genealogist,
i. 300 ; ii. 515 ; New Series, ii. 302 ; viii. 153, 240 ; xiv. 260.
Thoroton's Nottinghamshire, i. 144 ; ii. 183. Ormerod's Cheshire,
i. 534. Collections by the Powys-land Club, i. 327, 365, 367, 382,
388. Edmondson's Baronagium Genealogicum, i. 77 ; ii. 123 ; v.
483. Brydges' Collins' Peerage, iii. 340 ; v. 676. Banks' Baronies
in Fee, i. 227-240. Betham's Baronetage, iii. 237 ; iv. app. 10.
Banks' Dormant and Extinct Baronage, ii. 191, 224-256, 305 ;
iii. 325, 419. Metcalfe's Visitations of Suffolk, 95. Burke's
Extinct Baronetcies. F. G. Lee's History of Thame, 297. The
Visitations of Devon, edited by J. L. Vivian, 102. Bateson's
History of Northumberland, i. 305, 317. History of Altrincham
and Bowdon, by A. Ingham, 112. Visitations of Staffordshire,
1614 and 1663-4, William Salt Society, 158. Fletcher's Leicester-
shire Pedigrees and Royal Descents, 68. Miscellanea Genealogica
et Heraldica, 2nd Series, ii. 290 ; v. 76. Foster's Visitations of
Northumberland, 61-65. Burke's Colonial Gentry, ii. 582.
Nicolson and Burn's Westmorland and Cumberland, ii. 50.
Healey's History of West Somerset, 258. *See* DE GREY.
GREY (Lady Jane). Potter's History of Charnwood Forest, 123.
GREY DE RUTHYN. Case of B. L. Clifton, etc., in the Barony of
Grey de Ruthyn. Westminster, 1876, fol. Claim of Bertha L.
Clifton to Barony of Grey de Ruthyn. Sess. Papers, B of 1876.
Lipscombe's History of the County of Buckingham, iv. 60.
GREY DE WILTON. Chetham Society, lxxxiii. 7.
GREYSTOCK, or GREYSTOKE. Collectanea Topographica et Genea-
logica, ii. 160. Hodgson's Northumberland, I. ii. 239 ; II. ii. 375.
Poulson's Holderness, ii. 2. Plantagenet-Harrison's History of
Yorkshire, i. 372. Harleian Society, xvi. 151. Banks' Baronies
in Fee, i. 240. Banks' Dormant and Extinct Baronage, ii. 256.
Foster's Visitations of Cumberland and Westmorland, 56. The
Genealogist, New Series, xiii. 96.
GRICE. Foster's Visitations of Yorkshire, 323. Dawson Turner's

Sepulchral Reminiscences of Great Yarmouth, 133. Harleian Society, xv. 332.

GRIERSON. Howard's Visitation of Ireland, ii. 8. *See* MACGREGOR.

GRIESBROOK. Bibliotheca Topographica Britannica, ix. Part iv. 98.

GRIFFETH. Visitation of Oxfordshire, 1634, printed by Sir T. Phillipps, (Middle Hill, fol.) 20. Visitation of Warwickshire, 1619, published with Warwickshire Antiquarian Magazine, 212.

GRIFFIES. Pembrokeshire Pedigrees, 130.

GRIFFIN, or GRIFFYN. Case of Sir John Griffin, in relation to the Barony of Howard of Walden, 1784, fol. pp. 4. Claim of Sir John Griffin to the Barony of Howard de Walden, Sess. Papers, 3 and 9 of 1806-7. Morant's Essex, ii. 550. Berry's Sussex Genealogies, 233. Burke's Landed Gentry, 5, 6, 8. Bridges' Northampton-shire, by Rev. Peter Whalley, i. 114 ; ii. 12, 54. Nichols' History of the County of Leicester, 592. Baker's Northampton, i. 73. Harleian Society, xii. 167 ; xviii. 106, 186 ; xix. 113 ; xliii. 135. Ormerod's Cheshire, ii. 99 ; iii. 500. Edmondson's Baronagium Genealogicum, vi. 48*. Banks' Baronies in Fee, i. 280. Banks' Dormant and Extinct Baronage, iii. 328. F. G. Lee's History of Thame, 286. Metcalfe's Visitations of Northamptonshire, 23. New England Register, xiii. 108. Surrey Archæological Col-lections, xi.

GRIFFITH. Observations on the Snowdon Mountains, etc., by John Thomas, A.M. London, 1802, 8vo. Pedigree of Griffith of Pentherne, [T. P.] 1861, 2 fol. pages. Dwnn's Visitations of Wales, i. 281, 306, 328. Glamorganshire Pedigrees, edited by Sir T. Phillipps, 15, 18, 25. Burke's Landed Gentry, (of Castle Neynoe,) 2 supp., 3, 4, 5, 6, 7, 8 ; (of Trevalyn,) 2, 3, 4, 5, 6, 7, 8 ; (of Padworth,) 5, 6, 7, 8 ; (of Braich y Celyn,) 8 ; (of Garn,) 8. Foster's Visitations of Yorkshire, 524. Harleian Society, ii. 205 ; v. 294 ; xii. 15 ; xiii. 410 ; xv. 334. Hodgson's Northumberland, I. ii. 315. Shaw's Staffordshire, i. 107, 122, 126. Nichols' History of the County of Leicester, iii. 67. Dugdale's Warwick-shire, 341. Cæmarthenshire Pedigrees, 68. Surtees' Durham, i. 151. Archæologia Cambrensis, 2 S. v. 41. T. Nicholas' County Families of Wales, 41. History of Llangurig, by E. Hamer and H. W. Lloyd, 280. Collections by the Powys-land Club, v. 260. Visitation of Oxfordshire, 1634, printed by Sir T. Phillipps. Burke's Extinct Baronetcies. Metcalfe's Visitation of Worcester-shire, 1683, 50. History of Powys Fadog, by J. Y. W. Lloyd, ii. 184 ; iii. 222 ; iv. 202 ; v. 262, 294, 399 ; vi. 232. Genea-logies of Morgan and Glamorgan, by J. T. Clark, 107, 146, 489. Betham's Baronetage, iv. 208. Burke's Colonial Gentry, i. 348.

GRIFFITH AP DAVID. Dwnn's Visitations of Wales, ii. 195.

GRIFFITH AP LLEWELLYN. Notes and Queries, 7 S. x. 103.

GRIFFITH GWYR. Genealogies of Morgan and Glamorgan, by G. T. Clark, 205.

GRIFFITHS. Dwnn's Visitations of Wales, i. 308. Collections by the Powys-land Club, iv. 146 ; x. 151. Metcalfe's Visitation of Wor-cestershire, 1683, 51. Burke's Family Records, 283.

GRIGBY. Page's History of Suffolk, 713.

GRIGG. Burke's Colonial Gentry, i. 118. Muskett's Suffolk Manorial Families, 198, 265.

GRIGSON. Visitation of Suffolk, edited by J. J. Howard, ii. 80. Burke's Landed Gentry, 2, 3, 4, 5.

GRILLS. Harleian Society, ix. 88. The Visitations of Cornwall, edited by J. L. Vivian, 202. *See* GRYLLS.

GRIMALDI. The Genealogy of the Family of Grimaldi, by S. (Grimaldi). London, *circa* 1834, single sheet folio. Gentleman's Magazine, 1832, i. 26; ii. 508; 1837, i. 247. Burke's Royal Families, (London, 1851, 8vo.) ii. 167.

GRIMBALD. Nichols' History of the County of Leicester, ii. 372.

GRIMLEY. O'Hart's Irish Pedigrees, 2nd Series, 187.

GRIMSDITCH. Berry's Hertfordshire Genealogies, 176.

GRIMSHAW, or GRYMSHAW. Burke's Landed Gentry, (of High Bank,) 3 ; (of Andenshaw,) 2. Chetham Society, lxxxi. 31 ; lxxxii. 26. Foster's Lancashire Pedigrees. Whitaker's History of Whalley, ii. 274, 276. *See* GRYMESHAWE.

GRIMSTEAD, or GRIMSTED. Hoare's Wiltshire, IV. i. 80 ; V. i. 10, 202.

GRIMSTON, or GRIMSTONE. Croke's History of the Family of Croke, No. 31. Morant's Essex, i. 464, 480. Visitation of Norfolk, published by Norfolk Archæological Society, i. 175. Berry's Hertfordshire Genealogies, 140. Burke's Commoners, iii. 69, Landed Gentry, 2, 3, 4, 5, 6, 7, 8. Foster's Yorkshire Pedigrees. Weale's Quarterly Papers on Architecture, iii. (Suckling Papers), 85. Burke's Royal Families, (London, 1851, 8vo.) i. 187. Foster's Visitations of Yorkshire, 154. History of Beverley, by G. Poulson, i. 432. Page's History of Suffolk, 483. Clutterbuck's Hertford, i. 95, 247. Berry's Essex Genealogies, 148. Harleian Society, xiii. 205, 410. Archdall's Lodge's Peerage, v. 188. Brydges' Collins' Peerage, viii. 209. Burke's Extinct Baronetcies. *See* GRYMSTON.

GRISLING. The Genealogist, iv. 110.

GROAT. History of Caithness, by J. T. Calder, 245.

GROBHAM. Hoare's Wiltshire, II. i. 46. The Genealogist, New Series, xiii. 187.

GROGAN. Howard's Visitation of Ireland, iii. 73.

GROGAN-MORGAN. Burke's Landed Gentry, 3, 4.

GROME. Metcalfe's Visitations of Suffolk, 95.

GRONOW. Burke's Landed Gentry, 3, 4, 8.

GRONWY. Dwnn's Visitation of Wales, i. 176.

GROOM. Notes on the Pedigree of Her Most Serene Highness, Ann Groom, and of her son, Charles Ottley Groom Napier, Prince of Mantua, etc., by the late John Riddell, Esq. London, 1879, 8vo. Burke's Colonial Gentry, ii. 767. Howard's Visitation of England and Wales, v. 21.

GROSSE. Harleian Society, ix. 89. The Visitations of Cornwall, edited by J. L. Vivian, 198.

GROSVENOR. Account of the Descent of William de Grosvenor, 1776, 8vo. Herald and Genealogist, iv. 482, 490 ; v. 33-50, 322, 498 ;

vi. 93. The Great Governing Families of England, i. 112. Burke's
Heraldic Illustrations, 39, 81. Burke's Commoners, ii. 215;
iv. 406; Landed Gentry, 8. Visitation of Warwickshire, 1619,
published with Warwickshire Antiquarian Magazine, 38. Burke's
Visitation of Seats and Arms, ii. 32. Gregson's Fragments
relative to the County of Lancaster, 211. Shaw's Stafford-
shire, ii. 178. Visitation of Staffordshire, 1663-4, printed by Sir
T. Phillipps, 6. Harleian Society, xii. 385-388; xviii. 107, 260;
xxii. 10. Ormerod's Cheshire, ii. 216, 841; iii. 151. Edmond-
son's Baronagium Genealogicum, v. 473; vi. 32*. Brydges'
Collins' Peerage, v. 239. Wotton's English Baronetage, i. 497.
Visitation of Staffordshire, (Willm. Salt Soc.) 90. Chetham
Society, cx. 226. Visitations of Staffordshire, 1614 and 1663-4,
William Salt Society, 159, 163. The Genealogist, New Series,
xiii. 100. The Ancestor, No. i. 166-188. *See* GRAVENOR, SCROPE.
GROTE. Burke's Commoners, i. 609, Landed Gentry, 2.
GROVE. Pedigree of Thomas Grove, of Ferne House, Co. Wilts.
Evesham, 1819, (by Sir T. Phillipps, Bart.). Pedigree of Grove
of Ferne and Sedghill, Co. Wilts, [T. P.] 1859, folio page. Pedi-
gree of Grove of Weston Subedge, etc., [T. P.] 1857, folio page.
Appendix to Case of Sir J. S. Sidney, claiming to be Lord Lisle.
Burke's Landed Gentry, (of Ferne,) 2 and corr., 3, 4, 5; (of Zeals,)
4 supp., 5, 6, 7, 8; (of Castle Grove,) 5, 6, 7, 8; (of Shenstone
Park,) 2. Bibliotheca Topographia Britannica, i. Part i. 115.
Foster's Visitations of Yorkshire, 620. Visitatio Comitatus Wil-
toniæ, 1623, printed by Sir T. Phillipps. Hutchins' Dorset, iii.
568. Hoare's Wiltshire, IV. i. 58. Metcalfe's Visitations of
Suffolk, 142. Harleian Society, xx. 49. Burke's Colonial Gentry,
i. 333. The Genealogist, New Series, xii. 92.
GROVE-ANNESLEY. Burke's Landed Gentry, 5, 6, 7.
GROVER. Grover Pedigree, by G. E. Grover. London, 1884, broad-
side; with 3 pp. of letter press and four shields of arms in colours.
Sussex Archæological Collections, xxxvii. 133.
GRUB, or GRUBBE. Burke's Landed Gentry, 2, 3, 4. Harleian
Society, xxii. 59. Lipscombe's History of the County of Buck-
ingham, ii. 332, 444. Visitatio Comitatus Wiltoniæ, 1623, printed
by Sir T. Phillipps. Visitation of Wiltshire, edited by G. W.
Marshall, 99, Howard's Visitation of England and Wales, i. 27.
GRUEBER. Burke's Colonial Gentry, i. 243.
GRUFFYDD, or GRYFFYDD. Burke's Commoners, i. 251. Dwnn's
Visitations of Wales, i. 44, 65, 69, 130, 151, 199; ii. 73, 130-132,
144-147, 154, 167, 175, 186, 203, 213, 296, 308, 322. Archæo-
logia Cambrensis, 3 S. vi. 168. History of Powys Fadog, by
J. Y. W. Lloyd, iii. 37; v. 233; vi. 208, 210.
GRUFFYTH. History of Powys Fadog, by J. Y. W. Lloyd, iv. 341.
GRUNDY. Burke's Landed Gentry, 2. Harleian Society, xl. 1225.
GRYLLS. Burke's Commoners, ii. 338, Landed Gentry, 2, 3, 4, 5, 6,
7, 8. Harleian Society, vi. 134; ix. 88. Maclean's History of
Trigg Minor, ii. 421, 428. An Historical Survey of Cornwall, by
C. S. Gilbert, ii. 130. The Visitations of Cornwall, edited by

J. L. Vivian, 199. The Visitations of Devon, edited by J. L. Vivian, 436. *See* GRILLS.

GRYME. Harleian Society, xxxii. 139.

GRYMELAND. Harleian Society, xxviii. 154.

GRYMES. Collectanea Topographica et Genealogica, iii. 155. Harleian Society, xliii. 144.

GRYMESHAWE. Chetham Society, lxxxv. 127. Abram's History of Blackburn, 477. *See* GRIMSHAW.

GRYMSTON. Surtees Society, xxxvi. 64, 121, 129. Harleian Society, xvi. 152; xxxii. 140. *See* GRIMSTON.

GRYNDALL. The Genealogist, New Series, x. 214.

GRYNNE. Lincolnshire Notes and Queries, v. 74.

GUBBINS. Memoirs of the Gubbins' Family, by G. G. Gubbins. Limerick, 1891, 8vo. Burke's Landed Gentry, (of Kenmare Castle,) 3, 4, 5; (of Kilfrush,) 5, 6, 7, 8; (of Maidstown,) 6.

GUERDAIN. J. B. Payne's Armorial of Jersey, 174.

GUEST. Hutchins' Dorset, iii. 299. Harleian Society, xxi. 71.

GUIBON. Visitation of Warwickshire, 1619, published with Warwickshire Antiquarian Magazine, 209. Harleian Society, xii. 160. *See* GUYBON.

GUIDOTTI. Notes and Queries, 2 S. iv. 328, 392, 438.

GUILDFORD, or GUILFORD. Hasted's Kent, iv. 191. Burke's Royal Families, (London, 1851, 8vo.) i. 138. Manning and Bray's Surrey, i. 47. Baker's Northampton, i. 526. Camden Society, li. 1. Morant's Essex, i. 441; ii. 483. Roman Catholic Families of England, by J. J. Howard, i. 79. *See* GULDEFORD.

GUILLAMORE. Claim of Standish, Baron O'Grady and Visct. Guillamore, to Vote at Elections of Irish Peers, Sess. Papers, I. of 1856.

GUILLE. Guille of the Rohais and St. George. Exeter, 1882, 4to. Colby of Great Torrington, by F. T. Colby, 2nd edn. J. B. Payne's Armorial of Jersey, 175. Howard's Visitation of England and Wales, i. 38; Notes, ii. 36.

GULLEMARD. Miscellanea Genealogica et Heraldica, New Series, iii. 388.

GUILLIM. Harleian Society, xxi. 251, 261. Weaver's Visitation of Herefordshire, 34.

GUINNESS. Pedigree of Magennis (Guinness) Family. By R. Linn. Christchurch, New Zealand, 1897, 12mo. Burke's Landed Gentry, 3, 4. Burke's Authorized Arms, 169. Irish Pedigrees, by John O'Hart, 89. Burke's Royal Families, (edn. of 1876,) 219, 220. Howard's Visitation of Ireland, ii. 76.

GUISE. Pedigree of Guise of Elmore, Co. Glouc., [T. P.] 1866, folio page. Pedigree of Guise of Elmore, etc., from emblazoned pedigree at Elmore, [T. P.] 1867. Broadside. Chronicle of the Family of De Havilland. Fosbrooke's History of Gloucestershire, i. 277. Betham's Baronetage, iv. 134. Burke's Extinct Baronetcies. Visitation of Gloucester, edited by T. F. Fenwick and W. C. Metcalfe, 80. Somersetshire Wills, printed for F. A. Crisp, i. 48. *See* GYSE.

GULDEFORD. Hasted's Kent, iii. 83. Berry's Buckinghamshire

Genealogies, 2. Herald and Genealogist, iii. 420. Wotton's English Baronetage, iv. 1. Burke's Extinct Baronetcies. Archæologia Cantiana, xiv. 4. Hasted's Kent, (Hund. of Blackheath, by H. H. Drake,) xvii. *See* GILDEFORD, GUILDFORD.

GULDENE. Hutchins' Dorset, i. 282.

GULIAM. Harleian Society, xiii. 208.

GULL. Berry's Kent Genealogies, 294. Harleian Society, xlii. 134.

GULLY. Burke's Landed Gentry, 2, 3, 4 5.

GULSON. Harleian Society, xv. 335.

GULSTON. Cussan's History of Hertfordshire, Parts iii. and iv. 121. Burke's Landed Gentry, 4, 5, 6, 7, 8. Burke's Royal Descents and Pedigrees of Founders' Kin, 125. T. Nicholas' County Families of Wales, 286. Harleian Society, xxii. 60. Bysshe's Visitation of Essex, edited by J. J. Howard, 42. Annals of Smith of Balby, by H. E. Smith, 50, 62.

GUMBLETON. Burke's Landed Gentry, 2 supp., 3, 4, 5, 6, 7, 8.

GUN, or GUNN. The Gunns, by Thomas Sinclair. Wick, 1890, 4to. Burke's Landed Gentry, (of Rattoo,) 2, 3, 4, 5, 6, 7, 8; (of Ballybunion,) 2, 3, 4. Charles Smith's History of Kerry, 59. Caithness Family History, by John Henderson, 319.

GUN-CUNINGHAME. Burke's Landed Gentry, 7, 8.

GUNDRY. Burke's Landed Gentry, 2 add., 7, 8.

GUNMAN. History of Doddington, by R. E. G. Cole, 205.

GUNNING. Documents relating to the Gunning Family, by Lt. George Gunning. Cheltenham, 1834, 8vo. Annals of Swainswick, by R. E. M. Peach, 25-30. Burke's Landed Gentry, (of Torney's Court,) 4; (of Woolley,) 4; (of Swainswick,) 4. Edmondson's Baronagium Genealogicum, vi. 61. Betham's Baronetage, iv. 70.

GUNSON. Harleian Society, xv. 335.

GUNSTON. East Barnet, by F. C. Cass, Part i. 68.

GUNTER. Dwnn's Visitations of Wales, ii. 36. Berry's Hampshire Genealogies, 177. Glamorganshire Pedigrees, edited by Sir T. Phillipps, 23, 24. Ashmole's Antiquities of Berkshire, iii. 315. Berry's Sussex Genealogies, 13. Dallaway's Sussex, i. App. to Chichester. Jones' History of the County of Brecknock, ii. 343. The Genealogist, v. 266; New Series, i. 11; iii. 88. The Visitation of Wiltshire, edited by G. W. Marshall, 68. Pedigree and Arms of Sir Peter Gunter, of Tregunter, etc., from 1088 to the present time. Compiled by J. E. Thomas, F.S.A. Single page. Genealogies of Morgan and Glamorgan, by G. T. Clark, 404. *See* GOUNTER.

GUNTHORPE. Oliver's History of Antigua, ii. 38.

GUNTON. Metcalfe's Visitations of Northamptonshire, 96. Harleian Society, xli. 120.

GUNWARDBY. Plantagenet-Harrison's History of Yorkshire, i. 83.

GURDON. Burke's Commoners, (of Letton,) i. 395, Landed Gentry, 2, 3, 4, 5, 6, 7, 8; (of Assington Hall,) 2, 3, 4, 5, 6, 7, 8. Page's History of Suffolk, 918. Muskett's Suffolk Manorial Families, i. 273-288.

GURNAY, or GURNEY. The Record of the House of Gournay, by

Daniel Gurney, 1848, 4to. Supplement to the Record of the House of Gournay, by Daniel Gurney, 1858, 4to. Three Hundred Years of a Norman House, by James Hannay. London, 1867, 8vo. The Gurneys of Earlham, by A. J. C. Hare. London, 1895, 8vo., 2 vols. Burke's Heraldic Illustrations, 27. Fosbrooke's Abstracts of Smith's Lives of the Berkeleys, 78. Collectanea Topographica et Genealogica, iv. 91. Burke's Commoners, i. 484; Landed Gentry, (of Keswick and Sprowston,) 2, 3, 4, 5, 6, 7, 8. An Historical Survey of Cornwall, by C. S. Gilbert, ii. 131. Harleian Society, xv. 336; xxxii. 140. Notes and Queries, 1 S. ix. 232 ; 6 S. iv. 212. Banks' Dormant and Extinct Baronage, i. 91, 99. Burke's Extinct Baronetcies. *See* DE GOURNAY, GOURNAY.

GURNELL. Cyclostyle Pedigrees by J. J. Green. History of the Wilmer Family, 190. Curriculum Vitæ, or the birth of Henry Lamp, by J. J. Green, 65.

GUTHRIE. Guthrie of Guthrie. Tabular Pedigree. By Rev. J. G. Shaw. Forfar. Burke's Commoners, (of Guthrie,) ii. 414, Landed Gentry, 2, 3, 4, 5, 6, 7, 8; (of Haukerton,) Landed Gentry, 2 supp. ; (of Craigie,) 7, 8. Herald and Genealogist, v. 538. Burke's Royal Families, (London, 1851, 8vo.) ii. 27. Burke's Colonial Gentry, i. 133.

GUTTYNS. *See* HARDWICKE.

GUY. Berry's Sussex Genealogies, 54. Baddesley Clinton, by H. Norris, 144.

GUYDON. Blomefield's Norfolk, viii. 539; x. 178. Visitation of Norfolk, published by Norfolk Archæological Society, i. 178. Harleian Society, viii. 364 ; xxxii. 141. *See* GUIBON.

GUYDOTT. *See* GUIDOTTI.

GUYON. Morant's Essex, ii. 279. Burke's Family Records, 285.

GWATKIN. Howard's Visitation of England and Wales, ii. 1, 166. Burke's Family Records, 287.

GWIDIGADA. Dwnn's Visitations of Wales, i. 27.

GWILLIM VYCHAN. Genealogies of Morgan and Glamorgan, by G. T. Clark, 489.

GWIN. Glamorganshire Pedigrees, edited by Sir T. Phillipps, 41. *See* GWYN.

GWINIONYDD. Dwnn's Visitations of Wales, 27.

GWINNETT, or GWYNNETT. Fosbrooke's History of Gloucestershire, i. 259. Harleian Society, xxi. 252. Visitation of Gloucester, edited by T. F. Fenwick and W. C. Metcalfe, 84.

GWRGENEY AB KADWGAN (Descendants of). Dwnn's Visitations of Wales, ii. 56.

GWYDIR The History of the Gwydir Family, by Sir J. Wynne. London, 1770, 8vo. New edn., Ruthen, 1827, 4to. ; another edn. Oswestry, 1878, 4to. ; also in Barrington's Miscellanies. *See* WYNNE.

GWYLIM. Dwnn's Visitations of Wales, i. 138, 159. Pennant's Tour in Wales, ii. 45.

GWYLT, or GWILT. Burke's Landed Gentry, 2. Collections relating to Henry Smith, 167.

GWYN, GWYNE, GWYNN, or GWYNNE. Poetical Works of Lewis
Glyn Cothi, (Oxford, 1837,) 320. Dwnn's Visitations of Wales,
ii. 172, 221. Glamorganshire Pedigrees, edited by Sir T. Phillipps,
1, 41, 42. Burke's Landed Gentry, (of Barons Hall,) 2, 3, 4, 5 ;
(of Abercrave,) 2 ; (of Duffryn,) 2, 3, 4, 5, 6, 7, 8 ; (of Ford Abbey,)
2 ; (of Monachty, 2, 3, 4, 5, 6, 7, 8 ; (of Glanlery,) 2, 3, 4. Jones'
History of the County of Brecknock, ii. 262. Hutchins' Dorset,
iv. 528. Meyrick's History of the Co. of Cardigan, 292, 302.
T. Nicholas' County Families of Wales, 114, 629, 945. Dwnn's
Visitations of Wales, i. 18, 22, 31, 81, 86, 92, 99, 184, 195, 268,
309, 317. Caermarthenshire Pedigrees, 16, 17, 24, 35, 37, 63, 64,
72. Cardiganshire Pedigrees, 107, 109. Manning and Bray's
Surrey, ii. 112. Military Memoirs of the Great Civil War, and
of John Gwynne, 1822, 4to. Burke's Royal Families, (London,
1851, 8vo.) ii. 100. The Sheriffs of Montgomeryshire, by W. V.
Lloyd, 211. Collections by the Powys-land Club, vii. 37. Harleian
Society, xv. 338. History of Powys Fadog, by J. Y. W. Lloyd,
v. 59. Genealogies of Morgan and Glamorgan, by G. T. Clark,
35, 270. Ontarian Families, by E. M. Chadwick, i. 35. *See* GWIN.
GWYNNE-HOLFORD. Burke's Landed Gentry, 2, 8. Burke's Heraldic
Illustrations, 32.
GWYR Y TOWYN. Dwnn's Visitations of Wales, i. 59, 61.
GWYSANEY. *See* DAVIES.
GYBBON, or GYBON. Hasted's Kent, iii. 87. Metcalfe's Visitations
of Suffolk, 37.
GYBBON-MONYPENNY. Burke's Landed Gentry, 2, 3, 4, 5, 6, 8.
GYFFARD, or GYFFORDE. Harleian Society, vi. 135, 136. The
Genealogist, New Series, xvi. 92. *See* GIFFARD, GIFFORD.
GYLES. Metcalfe's Visitation of Worcester, 1683, 52.
GYLL. Miscellanea Genealogica et Heraldica, ii. 26-32. Cussan's
History of Hertfordshire, Parts iii. and iv. 118. Collectanea
Topographica et Genealogica, viii. 274-297, 410. Berry's Hert-
fordshire Genealogies, 56, 65, 68. Surtees Society, xxxvi. 280.
Burke's Landed Gentry, 2, 3, 4, 5, 6, 8 supp. Burke's Royal
Familes, (London, 1851, 8vo.) ii. 97. Topogapher and Genealogist,
ii. 560. Gyll's History of Wraysbury, 99, 125. Lipscombe's
History of the County of Buckingham, iv. 598, 606. Burke's
Heraldic Illustrations, 134. Surtees' Durham, iii. 338. Notes
and Queries, 2 S. x. 75. *See* GILL.
GYNES. Baker's Northampton, ii. 273. Harleian Society, xiii. 411.
GYNEY. Blore's Rutland, 188.
GYON. Harleian Society, viii. 303.
GYSE. Visitation of Gloucestershire, 1569, (Middle Hill, 1854, fol.),
5. Harleian Society, xxi. 72. The Genealogist, xii. 28. *See*
GUISE.

HABERGHAM. Whitaker's History of Whalley, ii. 180.
HABINGTON. Nash's Worcestershire, i. 588. Harleian Society,
xxvii. 62.
HACHE. Malet's Notices of the Malet Family, 133.

HACK. New England Register, xlviii. 453.
HACKER. Burke's Landed Gentry, 2, 3, 4, 5, 6. Hutchins' Dorset,
ii. 100. Notes and Queries, 2 S. ix. 288. Old Nottinghamshire,
by J. P. Briscoe, i. 130.
HACKET, or HACKETT. Bibliotheca Topographica Britannica, ix.
Part iv. 181. Burke's Landed Gentry, (of Riverston, and Moor
Park,) 3, 4, 5, 6, 7, 8 ; (of Moor Hall,) 6, 7, 8. Harleian Society,
viii. 244 ; xv. 339. Shaw's Staffordshire, ii. 51. Nichols' History
of the County of Leicester, iii. 238. Miscellanea Genealogica et
Heraldica, New Series, ii. 402. The Forest and Chase of Sutton
Coldfield, (London, 1860, 8vo.) app.
HACKEWILL. Tuckett's Devonshire Pedigrees, 127.
HACKLUIT. Weaver's Visitation of Herefordshire, 35.
HACKSHAW. Visitation of Somerset, printed by Sir T. Phillipps, 85.
Harleian Society, xi. 44.
HACON. Harleian Society, xxxii. 143.
HADDE. Hasted's Kent, ii. 512. Berry's Kent Genealogies, 217.
Harleian Society, xlii. 97. See LE HADD.
HADDEN. A short memoir of James Young, 21. The Genealogist,
New Series, xvi. 95. Macmillan's Magazine, Nov., 1863, 61.
HADDESLEY. Burton's History of Hemingborough, 229.
HADDOCK. Scott of Scot's-Hall, by J. R. Scott, 248. Correspond-
ence, Camden Society, New Series, xxxi. 1.
HADDON. Harleian Society, iii. 8. Blore's Rutland, 28. Hutchins'
Dorset, iii. 665. Oliver's History of Antigua, ii. 41.
HADHAM. Surtees' Durham, i. 273.
HADINGTON. Harleian Society, xxvii. 118.
HADLEY. Collinson's Somerset, ii. 48. Harleian Society, xviii. 57.
East Barnet, by F. C. Cass, Part i. 74.
HADSLEY. Berry's Hertfordshire Genealogies, 52.
HAFFENDEN. Burke's Commoners, ii. 301, Landed Gentry, 2, 3.
HAFFRENGUE. Minet's account of the Family of Minet, 205.
HAGAR. Harleian Society, xxviii. 169.
HAGART. Burke's Landed Gentry, 4 supp., 5, 6, 7, 8.
HAGEN. Annals of Smith of Balby, by H. E. Smith, 259.
HAGGARD. Burke's Landed Gentry, 3, 4, 5, 6, 7, 8. Miscellanea
Genealogica et Heraldica, New Series, iii. 247. Carthew's West
and East Bradenham, 96, 116.
HAGGER. Cambridgeshire Visitation, edited by Sir T. Phillipps, 16.
Harleian Society, xli. 56.
HAGGERSTON. Herald and Genealogist, iii. 513. Raine's History of
North Durham, 224. Hutchinson's History of Durham, iii. 378.
Wotton's English Baronetage, ii. 388. Betham's Baronetage, i.
511. Foster's Visitation of Durham, 141.
HAGGETT, or HAGGITT. Burke's Landed Gentry, 2 supp. The
Suffolk Records, by H. W. Aldred, 97.
HAGTHORP, or HAGTHORPE. Visitation of Durham, 1575, (Newcastle,
1820, fol.) 41. Hutchinson's History of Durham, ii. 415. Surtees
Durham, ii. 204. Burton's History of Hemingborough, 191
Foster's Visitations of Durham, 143.

HAIG. The Haigs of Bemersyde, a Family History, by John Russell.
Edinburgh, 1881, 8vo. Burke's Landed Gentry, (of Bemerside,)
5, 6, 7, 8; (of Blairhill,) 6, 7, 8; (of Pen Ithon,) 7, 8.
Douglas's
Baronage of Scotland, 132. Alexander Nisbet's Heraldic Plates,
46. Burke's Family Records, 291. *See* VEITCH-HAIG.

HAIGH. Burke's Landed Gentry, 4, 5, 7, 8. Hulbert's Annals of
Almondbury, 159. Harleian Society, xxxviii. 627, 642.

HAILSTONE. Continuations and Additions to the History of Bradford, by John James, App. ix.

HAINES. A Complete Memoir of Richard Haines. By C. R. Haines.
London, 1900, 8vo. Miscellanea Genealogica et Heraldica, 2nd
Series, iii. 38. New England Register, xxiii. 148, 430; xxiv.
422; xxx. 185. Burke's Landed Gentry, 7, 8. *See* HAYNE.

HAIRE. Burke's Landed Gentry, 3, 4.

HAKE. Metcalfe's's Visitations of Northamptonshire, 97.

HAKEWILL, or HAKEWELL. Harleian Society, vi. 137. Westcote's
Devonshire, edited by G. Oliver and P. Jones, 545. The Visitations of Devon, by J. L. Vivian, 437.

HALCOTT. Carthew's Hundred of Launditch,, Part ii. 732.

HALCRO. *See* ERSKINE.

HALDANE. Memoranda relating to the family of Haldane, by Alexr.
Haldane. London, 1880. Burke's Visitation of Seats and Arms,
ii. 19. Burke's Landed Gentry, 6, 7, 8. Memoirs of R. Haldane
and J. A. Haldane, by Alexr. Haldane. Chapter I. Foster's Collectanea Genealogica, (MP's Scotland,) 166. Douglas's Peerage
of Scotland, ii. 87. *See* ROGER.

HALDEN. Miscellanea Genealogica et Heraldica, ii. 330.

HALDENBY. Foster's Visitations of Yorkshire, 305. Harleian Society,
xvi. 158. *See* HAWDONBY.

HALDIMAND. Miscellanea Genealogica et Heraldica, New Series, iv.
369.

HALE. Morant's Essex, i. 398. Berry's Hertfordshire Genealogies,
34-38. Burke's Commoners, (of Kings Walden,) iii. 12, Landed
Gentry, 2, 3, 4, 5, 6, 7, 8; (of Alderley,) Landed Gentry, 2, 3, 4,
5, 6, 7, 8; (of Somerton Hall,) 6. Harleian Society, viii. 80, 152;
xiii. 209; xix. 113; xxii. 61, 62. Gyll's History of Wraysbury,
62. Lipscombe's History of the County of Buckingham, iv. 530,
609. Ord's History of Cleveland, 232. Clutterbuck's Hertford,
iii. 132. The Citizens of London and their Rulers, by B. B.
Orridge, 188. Visitations of Staffordshire, 1614 and 1663-4,
William Salt Society, 164. Visitation of Gloucester, edited by
T. F. Fenwick and W. C. Metcalfe, 87. New England Register,
vii. 271; xxxi. 83; xxxv. 358, 367; xxxvi. 75. *See* HALL.

HALES. Savage's Hundred of Carhampton, 237. Kent's British
Banner Displayed, 682. Hasted's Kent, ii. 577; iii. 104, 584,
716; iv. 440. History of Henley-on-Thames, by J. S. Burn, 270.
Berry's Kent Genealogies, 12, 210. Visitation of Somerset, printed
by Sir T. Phillipps, 86. Bibliotheca Topographica Britannica, i.
Part i. 36. Miscellanea Genealogica et Heraldica, New Series,
i. 69. Harleian Society, viii. 29; xi. 44; xii. 95, 209, 273; xl.

1298 ; xlii. 58. Shakespere's Home, by J. C. M. Bellew, 246, 249. Notes and Queries, 2 S. iii. 291, 416. Burke's Extinct Baronetcies. Wotton's English Baronetage, i. 219 ; iii. 96, 162. Betham's Baronetage, i. 131 ; ii. 111, 168. The Genealogist, v. 267. Archæologia Cantiana, xiv. 61. Howard's Visitation of England and Wales, i. 289 ; Notes, iii. 105. Weaver's Visitations of Somerset, .27. The Gresley's of Drakelowe, by F. Madan, 260.

HALES-TOOKE. Burke's Landed Gentry, 8.

HALFACRE. The Visitations of Cornwall, edited by J. L. Vivian, 203.

HALFORD. Pedigrees of Halford of Broadway, and of Leach of Broadway, [T. P.] 1862. 2 folio pages. J. H. Hill's History of Langton, 26, 324. Burke's Commoners, iii. 559, Landed Gentry, 2, 8. Harleian Society, ii. 144 ; iii. 25 ; viii. 286. J. H. Hill's History of Market Harborough, 328. Wright's History of Rutland, 42. Nichols' History of the County of Leicester, ii. 864, 874, 876 ; iv. 272. Wotton's English Baronetage, ii. 273. Burke's Extinct Baronetcies. Notes and Queries, 6 S. vii. 387. Leicestershire Architectural Society, iv. 83. Fletcher's Leicestershire Pedigrees and Royal Descents, 137.

HALHEAD. Burke's Royal Families, (London, 1851, 8vo.) ii. 131. Pedigree of Wilson of High Wray, etc., by Joseph Foster, 97.

HALIBURTON, or HALYBURTON. Memorials of the Haliburtons, edited by Sir Walter Scott. Edinburgh, 1820, 4to. Reprinted 1824, 8vo. ; and 1842, 4to. Genealogical Memoirs of the Family of Sir W. Scott, by Rev. C. Rogers, 63. Burke's Extinct Baronetcies, 624.

HALIDAY. Burke's Landed Gentry, 3, 4, 5 supp. *See* HALLIDAY.

HALIFAX. History of Barnsley, by Rowland Jackson, 145. *See* HALLIFAX.

HALKERSTON. Some Old Families, by H. B. McCall, 37.

HALKETT. Burke's Commoners, i. 338, Landed Gentry, 2, 3, 4, 5, 6, 7, 8. Douglas's Baronage of Scotland, 284. Peter Chalmers' Account of Dunfermline, i. 293 ; ii. 300. Foster's Collectanea Genealogica, (MP's Scotland,) 167.

HALL. Notes on the Surname of Hall, by George W. Marshall. Exeter, 1887, 8vo. Pedigree of the Family of Hall of West Stockwith, in the Parish of Misterton, Notts. Broadside, *n. d.* Miscellanea Genealogica et Heraldica, ii. 255 ; New Series, i. 20, 127, 457-476 ; iv. 197. East Anglian, iii. 213 ; iv. 205. Burke's Landed Gentry, 4th edn., 1152. Morant's Essex, i. 254. Visita tion of Kent, (reprinted from Archæologia Cantiana, vol. vi.) 64. Hasted's Kent, iii. 267. Harleian Society, i. 50 ; ii. 204 ; v. 270 ; xv. 340; xxi. 73; xxvii. 64; xxviii. 205; xxxii. 143; xxxviii. 566, 570, 735 ; xxxix. 941; xl. 1175; xli. 97; xlii. 12, 131 ; xliii. 171. Nichols' History of the County of Leicester, iv. 402. Visitation of Norfolk, published by Norfolk Archæological Society, i. 346. Archæologia Cantiana, iv. 267. Berry's Kent Genealogies, 25. 285. Visitation of Durham, 1615, (Sunderland, 1820, fol.) 51, 59. Visitation of Durham, 1575, (Newcastle, 1820, fol.) 44. Surtees Society, xxxvi. 149, 214. Cambridgeshire Visitation, edited by Sir T. Phillipps, 16. Visitation of Oxfordshire, 1634, printed by Sir T.

24

Phillipps, (Middle Hill, fol.) 20. Burke's Commoners, (of Aber-
carne,) i. 202 ; (of Arrows Foot,) Commoners, iv.
741, Landed
Gentry, 2 ; (of Scorboro' Hall,) Landed Gentry, 4, 5, 6 ; (of
Whatton Manor,) 2, 3, 4, 5, 6, 7, 8 ; (of Narrow Water,) 2, 3, 4,
5, 6, 7, 8 ; (of Mairwarra,) 3, 4, 5, 6 ; (of Barton Hall and Holly
Bush,) 5, 6, 7, 8 ; (of Barton Abbey,) 5, 6, 7, 8 ; (of Walton-on-
the-Hill,) 5, 6, 7, and 7 at p. 1421 ; (of Westbank House,) 2
add., 3 ; (of Grappenhall,) 2, 3, 4 ; (of Six Mile Bottom,) 6, 7, 8 ;
(of Hallstead,) 6 ; (of Park Hall,) 6 ; 6 at p. 1235, 7, 8 ; (of Farn-
ham Chase,) 7, 8 ; (of Knockbrack,) 8 ; (of Foscott,) 8. Foster's
Visitations of Yorkshire, 298, 322, 621. Jewitt's Reliquary,
xv. 39. Hodgson's Northumberland, I. ii. 154. Burke's Royal
Families, (London, 1851, 8vo.) i. 126 ; ii. 94. Graves' History of
Cleveland, 354. Blore's Rutland, 131, 225. Burke's Royal
Descents and Pedigrees of Founders' Kin, 97. Visitatio Comi-
tatus Wiltoniæ, 1623, printed by Sir T. Phillipps. Surtees'
Durham, i. 99, 121 ; ii. 215, 291, 297, 323 ; iii. 207 ; iv. 154.
Midland Counties Historical Collector, published by Architectural
and Archæological Society of Leicester, 1855-1856, ii. 351. Wilt-
shire Archæological Magazine, v. 360. J. H. Blunt's Dursley and
its Neighbourhood, 157. The Genealogist, iii. 125 ; iv. 23, 110 ;
New Series, xii. 93 ; xiii. 51, 54. Ormerod's Cheshire, iii. 130.
Account of the Mayo and Elton Families, by C. H. Mayo, 20.
Metcalfe's Visitations of Suffolk, 193. The Visitation of Wilt-
shire, edited by G. W. Marshall, 34, 78. The Rectors of Lough-
borough, by W. G. D. Fletcher, 21. Registers of Ecclesfield, by
A. S. Gatty, 26. Midland Antiquary, iii. 12. Visitations of
Staffordshire, 1614 and 1663-4, William Salt Society, 164.
Northern Notes and Queries, iii. 89. Foster's Visitations of
Durham, 145-149. \ Burke's Colonial Gentry, i. 52. Life of
Joseph Hall, D.D., by Rev. Geo. Lewis, 426. Earwaker's History
of Sandbach, 216. New England Register, vi. 259 ; xiii. 15 ; xv.
59, 238 ; xlvii. 245. Notes and Queries, 7 S. ix. 302. Family
Notes, by J. M. Browne, 45. Howard's Visitation of England
and Wales, iv. 29 ; vi. 108. *See* HAULE.
HALL-DARE. Berry's Essex Genealogies, 76. Burke's Landed Gentry,
5, 6, 7, 8. Harleian Society, xiv. 740.
HALL-MAXWELL. Burke's Landed Gentry, 6.
HALL-SAY. Burke's Landed Gentry, 5.
HALLAMORE. Harleian Society, ix. 90. The Visitations of Cornwall,
edited by J. L. Vivian, 204.
HALLAMSHIRE (Lords of). Hunter's History of the Parish of Shef-
field, 34.
HALLE. Northern Notes and Queries, iii. 89.
HALLELY. Harleian Society, xv. 342.
HALLEN, or HALEN. An Account of the Family of Hallen, or Hol-
land, etc., with pedigrees of the Families of Hatton of Newent,
Shakespeare of Stratford-on-Avon, and Weight of Clingre, by
A. W. C. Hallen. Edinburgh, 1885, 4to. Northern Notes and
Queries, iii. 89 ; ix. 88.

HALLETT. East Anglian, iv. 81. Morant's Essex, ii. 428. Berry's Kent Genealogies, 246. Harleian Society, viii. 496.

HALLEWELL. Burke's Landed Gentry, 7, 8.

HALLIDAY. Burke's Commoners, (of Rodborough,) ii. 131; (of Chapel Cleeve,) Commoners, ii. 127, Landed Gentry, 2, 3, 4, 5, 6, 7, 8; (of Glenthorne,) 6, 7, 8. Phillimore's London and Middlesex Note-Book, 99, 267. Oliver's History of Antigua, ii. 43. *See* HALIDAY, HOLLIDAY.

HALLIFAX. Burke's Landed Gentry, 2, 3, 4, 5, 6. *See* HALIFAX.

HALLIMAN. Surtees' Durham, ii. 397. Foster's Visitations of Durham, 151.

HALLIWELL, or HALLYWELL. Abram's History of Blackburn, 687. Notes and Queries, 6 S. iii. 324. Fishwick's History of Rochdale, 440.

HALLORAN. Oliver's History of Antigua, ii. 48.

HALLOWELL. Berry's Surrey Genealogies, 9.

HALLOWES. Burke's Landed Gentry, 5, 6, 7, 8. Harleian Society, xxxvii. 412; xxxviii. 467.

HALLUM. Harleian Society, xviii. 111.

HALS. Harleian Society, vi. 136. A Complete Parochial History of the County of Cornwall, iii. 324. An Historical Survey of Cornwall, by C. S. Gilbert, ii. 132. The Visitations of Devon, by J. L. Vivian, 439.

HALSALL. Chetham Society, lxxxi. 93; lxxxii. 59; lxxxv. 129; xcix. 91; cx. 166. Staniforthiana, by F. M. H., *at end.*

HALSE. Visitation of Devon, edited by F. T. Colby, 92, 119.

HALSEY, or HAULSEY. Berry's Hertfordshire Genealogies, 88. Burke's Commoners, ii. 619, Landed Gentry, 2, 3, 4, 5, 6, 7, 8. Harleian Society, viii. 233; xv. 365; xxii. 62. Clutterbuck's Hertford, i. 378. Notes and Queries, 3 S. ii. 133.

HALSHAM. Hasted's Kent, 727. Visitation of Suffolk, edited by J. J. Howard, ii. 264. Scott of Scott's Hall, by J. R. Scott, 144. The Castles, Mansions, and Manors of Western Sussex, by D. G. C. Elwes and C. J. Robinson, 109, 284. Notes and Queries, 5 S. vii. 407; viii. 13, 239, 435; xi. 315; 6 S. iii. 316; iv. 198.

HALSTED. Corry's History of Lancashire, ii. 318. Whitaker's History of Whalley, ii. 168. Harleian Society, xv. 343; xxxvii. 10. Notes and Queries, 3 S. iv. 295.

HALSWELL. Visitation of Somerset, printed by Sir T. Phillipps, 87. Harleian Society, xi. 45. Weaver's Visitations of Somerset, 28.

HALTON. Morant's Essex, ii. 524. Jewitt's Reliquary, v. 64. Visitation of Gloucestershire, 1569, (Middle Hill, 1854, fol.) 6. History of South Winfield, in Nichols' Miscellaneous Antiquities, No. 3, 78. Maclean's History of Trigg Minor, ii. 42. Whitaker's Deanery of Craven, 121, (157). Burke's Extinct Baronetcies. Wotton's English Baronetage, ii. 365. Betham's Baronetage, i. 497. Banks' Dormant and Extinct Baronage, i. 200. The Genealogist, vi. 160. Harleian Society, xxi. 75; xxii. 62.

HALTON (Barons of). Ormerod's Cheshire, i. 689. Harleian Society, xviii. 5. History of the Castle of Halton, by Wm. Beamont, 6-87.

HALYBURTON. Wood's Douglas's Peerage of Scotland, i. 686.

HAM. Burke's Colonial Gentry, ii. 824. New England Register, vi. 329 ; xxvi. 388.

HAMBRO. Burke's Landed Gentry, 8.

HAMBROUGH. Burke's Landed Gentry, 3, 4, 5, 6, 7, 8.

HAMBURY. Harleian Society, xxvii. 65.

HAMBY. Harleian Society, viii. 221. The Genealogist, iv. 111 ; vi. 160.

HAMDEN. Morant's Essex, i. 156.

HAMEE. Harleian Society, xv. 344.

HAMEL. The Visitations of Devon, by J. L. Vivian, 761.

HAMELEY. Maclean's History of Trigg Minor, ii. 540-553.

HAMER. Fishwick's History of Rochdale, 395.

HAMERSLEY. Burke's Landed Gentry, 5, 6 and supp., 7, 8. Burke's Colonial Gentry, i. 246. Harleian Society, xxxviii. 504.

HAMERTON. Surtees Society, xxxvi. 354. Burke's Commoners, i. 519, Landed Gentry, 2, 3, 4, 8. Foster's Yorkshire Pedigrees. Foster's Visitations of Yorkshire, 526. Burke's Heraldic Illustrations, 15. Whitaker's Deanery of Craven, 118, (150). John Watson's History of Halifax, 239. Harleian Society, xvi. 152. Notes and Queries, 7 S. ii. 302. The Genealogist, New Series, ix. 168.

HAMES. Burke's Landed Gentry, 4, 5 and supp., 6, 7, 8. See HAYMES.

HAMILTON. Case of the Most Noble Douglas, Duke of Hamilton and Brandon, touching the Peerage of Brandon, 1782, folio, pp. 4. Case of Willm. Hamilton of Wishaw, claiming to be Lord Belhaven and Stenton, 1795, pp. 10 ; Supplementary case, 1795. The Pedigree of the Hamilton Family, by 'Audi alteram partem.' London, 1867, 8vo. Memoirs of the Life and Family of James, Duke of Hamilton, 1717, 8vo. Claim of the Duke of Hamilton and Brandon to the Earldom of Angus, Sess. Papers, Jan.—Mar. 1762. Claim of William Hamilton, Esq., to the Barony of Belhaven and Stenton, Sess. Papers, Jan. 1795—April 1799. Claim of James Hamilton and R. W. Hamilton to Dignity of Lord Belhaven, Sess. Papers, C of 1874 ; B of 1875. State of the Evidence produced for proving the Claim of William Hamilton of Wishaw, to be lawful Heir Male of James, last Lord Belhaven, 1796, 4to. Genealogical Memoirs of the House of Hamilton, by John Anderson. Edinburgh, 1825, 4to. An inquiry into the Pedigree, Descent, etc., of the Chiefs of the Hamilton Family, by William Aiton. Glasgow, 1827, 8vo. Memoirs of the House of Hamilton, corrected by Dr. F. H. Buchanan. Edinburgh, 1828, 4to. Reply to Memoirs, etc., by J. Riddell, Esq. Edinburgh, 1828, 4to. The Olivestob Hamiltons. By A. W. H. Eaton. New York, 1893, 4to. Memorials of the Earls of Haddington, by Sir Willm. Fraser. Edinburgh, 1889, 4to., 2 vols. The Hamilton Manuscripts, edited by T. K. Lowry, (Belfast, 1867, 4to.) 158-166. Berry's Essex Genealogies, 65. Burke's Commoners, iii. 10, 179 ; (of Killyleagh,) Commoners, i. 348, Landed Gentry, 3, 4, 5, 6, 7, 8 ; (of Cornacassa,) Landed Gentry, 4, 5, 6, 7, 8 ;

(of Orbiston,) 3, 4, 5, 6 ; (of Craiglaw,) 2, 3, 4, 5, 6, 7, 8 ; (of Sundrum,) 3, 4, 5, 6, 7, 8 ; (of Cairn Hill,) 3, 4, 5, 6, 7, 8 ; (of Beltrim,) 3, 4, 5, 6, 7, 8 ; (of St. Ernans,) 3, 4, 5, 6 ; (of Abbotstown,) 2, 3, 4, 5, 6, 7, 8 ; (of Hampton Hall,) 3, 4, 5, 6, 7, 8 ; (of Hamwood,) 4, 5, 6, 7, 8 ; (of The Retreat,) 5, 6, 7, 8 ; (of Holyfield Hall,) 5, 6 ; (of Fynecourt,) 5, 6, 7, 8 ; (of Holmhead,) 2 ; (of Kames,) 2 supp. ; (of Evandale,) 3, 4 ; (of Bangour,) 2, 3, 4 ; (of Barnes,) 3 supp., 4, 7, 8 ; (of Rathoe House,) 3, 4 ; (of Westburn,) 3 supp., 4 ; (of Castle Hamilton,) 6 and supp., 7, 8 ; (of Wilton,) 6 ; (of Hilston,) 7, 8 ; (of Brown Hall,) 7. 8 ; 8 at p. 1921. Burke's Visitation of Seats and Arms, 2nd Series, i. 20, 24, 34, 38 ; ii. 74. Burke's Royal Descents and Pedigrees of Founders' Kin, 96. Burke's Authorized Arms, 48, 166. Geo. Robertson's Description of Cunninghame, 168. Lands and their Owners in Galloway, by P. H. M'Kerlie, i. 217. Paterson's History of the Co. of Ayr, i, 205, 207, 319, 382 ; ii. 123, 201, 247. Shirley's History of the County of Monaghan, 237. Hasted's Kent, ii. 435, 440. Jacob's Peerage, i. 318. Beatson's Account of the Family of Beatson, 61. Nisbet's Heraldry, ii. app. 38. Douglas's Baronage of Scotland, 424, 459-467, 479. Paterson's History of Ayr and Wigton, i. 131, 152, 242, 313, 556 ; ii. 199 ; iii. 83, 117, 298, 433. John D'Alton's History of Co. Dublin, 470. Geo. Robertson's Account of Families in Ayrshire, i. 356. O'Hart's Irish Pedigrees, 2nd Series, 57. Harleian Society, xiv. 678. The Ulster Journal of Archæology, iii. 68, 129, 236 ; v. 21. Walter Wood's East Neuk of Fife, 297. J. E. Reid's History of the Co. of Bute, 176-193. Edmondson's Baronagium Genealogicum, i. 50. The Wolfe's of Forenaghts, 91. Wood's Douglas's Peerage of Scotland, i. 195, 201, 677, 689 ; ii. 342, 457, 487. Berry's Genealogical Peerage, 44. The Theology of Consolation, by D. C. A. Agnew, 282. Notes and Queries, 1 S. i. 216, 270 ; v. 371 ; vii. 285, 333 ; x. 61 ; xii. 306, 413, 521 ; 2 S. i. 115 ; iii. 338 ; x. 343 ; 3 S. xii. 10 ; 5 S. v. 472, 526 ; vi. 373 ; 7 S. x. 131. Archdall's Lodge's Peerage, iii. 1 ; v. 88, 172 ; vi. 27. Brydges' Collins' Peerage, i. 491 ; ii. 513. Burke's Extinct Baronetcies, and 607, 624. Alexander Nisbet's Heraldic Plates, 126. Scottish Journal, i. 5. Stodart's Scottish Arms, ii. 418. Miscellanea Genealogica et Heraldica, 2nd Series, iii. 370. Burke's Colonial Gentry, i. 59, 248. R. P. Graves' Life of Sir W. R. Hamilton, i., xviii. Archdall's Lodge's Peerage, vi. 27. New England Register, xliv. 361. The Irish Builder, xxxv. 70. Burke's Family Records, 292. Ontarian Families, by E. M. Chadwick, i. 137, 143. Oliver's History of Antigua, ii. 50, 52. The Genealogist, New Series, xiv. 264 ; xvi. 73. See BIRNIE, BOLEYNES, BUCHANAN-HAMILTON.

HAMILTON-CAMPBELL. Burke's Landed Gentry, 8.

HAMILTON-DOUGLAS. The Spectator (newspaper) 1864, pages 1209, 1238, 1270, 1298, 1325.

HAMILTON-JONES. Burke's Landed Gentry, 3, 4, 5, 6.

HAMILTON-ROWAN. Burke's Commoners, i. 348, Landed Gentry, 2.

HAMILTON-STARKE. Burke's Landed Gentry, 7.

HAMILTOUN. Paterson's History of the Co. of Ayr, i. 277, 369.

HAMLEY. Maclean's History of Trigg Minor, i. 576; ii. 540-553. A Complete Parochial History of the County of Cornwall, ii. 243. An Historical Survey of Cornwall, by C. S. Gilbert, ii. 133.

HAMLYN. Burke's Landed Gentry, 3, 4, 5, 6, 7, 8. Betham's Baronetage, iv. 304. The Visitations of Devon, by J. L. Vivian, 481. Devonshire Notes and Notelets, by Sir W. R. Drake, 215.

HAMLYN-FANE. Burke's Colonial Gentry, 5, 6, 7, 8.

HAMMERSLEY. The Genealogist, New Series, xvi. 263.

HAMMETT. Burke's Landed Gentry, 2 supp., p. 15. Devonshire Notes and Notelets, by W. R. Drake, 217.

HAMMIL. Geo. Robertson's Description of Cunninghame, 289.

HAMMON. Harleian Society, xxxii. 144.

HAMMOND, or HAMOND. Surtees Society, xxxvi. 378. Visitation of Middlesex, (Salisbury, 1820, fol.) 23. Cambridgeshire Visitation, edited by Sir T. Phillipps, 17. Whitaker's History of Whalley, ii. 19. Chetham Society, xiv. 116. Noble's Memoirs of the House of Cromwell, ii. 151-167. Topographer and Genealogist, i. 512; ii. 541. Berry's Kent Genealogies, 95. Burke's Commoners, (of St. Alban's Court,) i. 130, Landed Gentry, 2, 3, 4, 5, 7, 8; (of Wistaston,) Commoners, i. 367, Landed Gentry, 2, 3, 4, 5, 6; (of Firby,) Landed Gentry, 2 supp.; (of Over Dimsdale,) 4; (of Haling House,) 3, 4, 5, 6, 7, 8; (of Westacre,) 2, 3, 4, 5, 6, 7, 8; (of Needham Hall,) 8. Topographer and Genealogist, i. 512. Collectanea Topographica et Genealogica, iii. 16. Burke's Royal Families, (London, 1851, 8vo.) ii. 183. Gage's History of Thingoe Hundred, Suffolk, 395. J. B. Payne's Armorial of Jersey, 176. Harleian Society, xv. 344; xxxix. 877; xli. 71; xlii. 47. Notes and Queries, 2 S. xii. 33, 195, 323. Topographical Miscellanies, 1792, 4to., (St. Alban's in Nonington). Betham's Baronetage, iv. 136. W. Wheater's History of Sherburn and Cawood, 50. Foster's Visitations of Middlesex, 44. New England Register, xxx. 28. The Manor of Haling, by G. S. Steinman, 78. Muskett's Suffolk Manorial Families, i. 251-272. The Genealogist, New Series, xvi. 264.

HAMON. Berry's Kent Genealogies, 245. Burke's Extinct Baronetcies, 608. Harleian Society, xlii. 68.

HAMON AUX DENTS. The History of the House of Arundel, by J. P. Yeatman, 104.

HAMPDEN. Gentleman's Magazine, 1828, ii. 125, 197, 320, 395; 1829, i. 30, 125, 487. Kennet's Parochial Antiquities, ii. 458. Noble's Memoirs of the House of Cromwell, ii. 81-123. Berry's Hertfordshire Genealogies, 77. Berry's Buckinghamshire Genealogies, 9. Lipscombe's History of the County of Buckingham, i. 295; ii. 296, 302, 374. Memoirs of the Family of Chester, by R. E. C. Waters, 90. Genealogical Records of the Family of Woodd, 30. Brydges' Collins's Peerage, vi. 296-301. Metcalfe's Visitations of Northamptonshire, 25. Edmondson's Baronagium Genealogicum, v. 412. Notes and Queries, 4 S. vii. 189. The

Genealogist, vii. 177. Ædes Hartwellianæ, by W. H. Smith. Genealogical Table of John Stratford Collins. *See* TREVOR-HAMPDEN.

HAMPER. Dallaway's Sussex, II. ii. 4.

HAMPSHIRE. Visitation of Oxfordshire, 1634, printed by Sir T. Phillipps, (Middle Hill, fol.) 20. Harleian Society, v. 319.

HAMPSON. Wotton's English Baronetage, ii. 293. Betham's Baronetage, i. 5.

HAMPTON, or HAMPTONNE. Dwnn's Visitations of Wales, ii. 189. Visitation of Middlesex, (Salisbury, 1820, fol.) 11. Herald and Genealogist, iv. 437. Collectanea Topographica et Genealogica, vi. 294. Shaw's Staffordshire, ii. 174. J. B. Payne's Armorial of Jersey, 179, 181. Harleian Society, xv. 345. Ellacombe's History of Bitton, 100. Foster's Visitation of Middlesex, 24.

HAMSHAR. Miscellanea Genealogica et Heraldica, New Series, iii. 56.

HAMSON. Visitation of Oxfordshire, 1634, printed by Sir T. Phillipps, (Middle Hill, fol.) 20. Harleian Society, v. 293.

HANBURY. Pedigree of Hanbury of Elmley Lovett, Co. Worcester, [T. P.] 1868, Broadside. History of Monmouthshire, by D. Williams, App. 192. Historical Tour in Monmouthshire, by Wm. Coxe, 244. Berry's Hampshire Genealogies, 133. Burke's Landed Gentry, (of Poles,) 3, 4, 5, 6, 7, 8 ; (of Holfield Grange,) 3, 4, 5, 6, 7, 8 ; (of Ponty-Pool,) 5, 6, 7, 8 ; (of Ilam,) 7, 8. Archæologia Cambrensis, 3 S. ix. 304. The Genealogist, New Series, xvi. 265. Visitations of Staffordshire 1614 and 1663-4, William Salt Society, 166. Metcalfe's Visitations of Northamptonshire, 179. Harleian Society, xxi. 76. Fletcher's Leicestershire Pedigrees and Royal Descents, 121. The Monthly Visitor, xiv. 236. Pedigree of Wilson, by S. B. Foster, 202.

HANBURY-WILLIAMS. Burke's Landed Gentry, 8.

HANBY. Metcalfe's Visitations of Suffolk, 194. *See* HAMBY.

HANCHET. Morant's Essex, ii. 605. Harleian Society, xxii. 63.

HANCOCK, or HANCOCKE. Visitation of Somerset, printed by Sir T. Phillipps, 88. Harleian Society, xi. 45. Surtees' Durham, ii. 234. Visitation of Wiltshire, 1677, printed by Sir T. Phillipps, (Middle Hill, 1854, fol.). Metcalfe's Visitation of Worcester, 1683, 53. Metcalfe's Visitations of Northamptonshire, 97. The Visitations of Devon, by J. L. Vivian, 441. New England Register, ix. 352 ; xxxvi. 76.

HANCOCKS. Burke's Landed Gentry, 3, 4, 5, 6, 7, 8.

HAND. Ormerod's Cheshire, ii. 771.

HANDCOCK. Herald and Genealogist, iii. 409. Burke's Landed Gentry, 4, 5, 6, 8. Westcote's Devonshire, edited by G. Oliver and P. Jones, 560. Visitation of Devon, edited by F. T. Colby, 121.

HANDFIELD. Burke's Colonial Gentry, i. 347.

HANDFORD. Harleian Society, xxvii. 68.

HANDLEY. Burke's Landed Gentry, 2, 3, 4, 5 and supp., 6, 7, 8. Harleian Society, iv. 156 ; xxxviii. 665. W. Dickinson's History of Newark, 291. Thoroton's Nottinghamshire, ii. 187.

HANDLO. Morant's Essex, i. 14, 478 ; ii. 133. Lipscombe's History of the County of Buckingham, i. 66. Banks' Baronies in Fee, i. 243.

HANDSACRE. Shaw's Staffordshire, i. 207.

HANDVILE. Berry's Kent Genealogies, 117. Harleian Society, xlii. 46.

HANDYSIDE. Burke's Colonial Gentry, ii. 693.

HANFORD. Nash's Worcestershire, ii. 182. Burke's Royal Families, (London, 1851, 8vo.) i. 103. Burke's Landed Gentry, 2, 3, 4.

HANGER. Harleian Society, viii. 453 ; xxxvii. 4. Archdall's Lodge's Peerage, vii. 78. Visitation of Gloucester, edited by T. F. Fenwick and W. C. Metcalfe, 88.

HANHAM. Morant's Essex, i. 472. Hutchins' Dorset, iii. 231 ; iv. 24. Wotton's English Baronetage, iii. 524. Betham's Baronetage, ii. 410. Metcalfe's Visitations of Suffolk, 142.

HANINGSTON. Berry's Kent Genealogies, 131. Harleian Society, xlii. 33.

HANKEY. Burke's Heraldic Illustrations, 106. Burke's Commoners, iv. 117, Landed Gentry, 2, 3, 4, 5, 6, 7, 8. Harleian Society, xviii. 109.

HANKFORD. Gentleman's Magazine, 1849, ii. 491. A Complete Parochial History of the County of Cornwall, i. 1.

HANLY. O'Hart's Irish Pedigrees, 2nd Series, 188.

HANMER. A Memorial of the Parish and Family of Hanmer, by John Lord Hanmer. London, 1877, 8vo. Dwnn's Visitations of Wales, ii. 311, 314. Harleian Society, viii. 104 ; xxviii. 208-213. Lipscombe's History of the County of Buckingham, iv. 341. The Sheriffs of Montgomeryshire, by W. V. Lloyd, 127. Wotton's English Baronetage, i. 411. Betham's Baronetage, iii. 426. The Correspondence of Sir T. Hanmer, Bart., edited by Sir Henry Bunbury, Bart., 1. Burke's Extinct Baronetcies. History of Powys Fadog, by J. Y. W. Lloyd, vi. 345. See JENNENS.

HANNAM. Berry's Kent Genealogies, 328. Harleian Society, xx. 50. The Genealogist, New Series, iii. 89. Miscellanea Genealogica et Heraldica, 2nd Series, ii. 291.

HANNAY. Burke's Landed Gentry, (of Kingsmuir,) 3, 4, 5, 6, 7, 8 ; (of Kirkdale,) 3, 4, 5, 6, 7, 8. Burke's Visitation of Seats and Arms, ii. 70. Lands and their Owners in Galloway, by P. H. M'Kerlie, i. 82*, 456. . Burke's Family Records, 294.

HANNING. Burke's Landed Gentry, 3.

HANRAGHAN. O'Hart's Irish Pedigrees, 2nd Series, 59.

HANS. Foster's Visitations of Yorkshire, 138.

HANSARD. Hutchinson's History of Durham, iii. xxiv. Surtees' Durham, iii. 318. The Genealogist, iv. 112 ; vi. 161.

HANSBY. Foster's Visitations of Yorkshire, 138. Hunter's Deanery of Doncaster, i. 234.

HANSCOMBE. Fragmenta Genealogica, by F. A. Crisp, vii. 10.

HANSLAP. Visitation of Warwickshire, 1619, published with Warwickshire Antiquarian Magazine, 161. Harleian Society, xii. 257.

HANSON. Yorkshire Archæological and Topographical Journal, i. 79.

Surtees Society, xxxvi. 257.   Burke's Landed Gentry, 2 supp., 3, 4.
Foster's Yorkshire Pedigrees.   Harleian Society, viii. 201 ; xl.
1213.   John Watson's History of Halifax, 263.   Yorkshire
Genealogist, i. 86, 156, 201, 214.   Topography of Lofthouse, by
George Roberts, 42.   New England Register, v. 213 ; vi. 329.
Oliver's History of Antigua, ii. 58.   Miscellanea Genealogica et
Heraldica, 3rd Series, i. 120.   The Genealogist, New Series, xvii. 56.
HAPPESFORD. Ormerod's Cheshire, ii. 32.
HARBART. Surtees' Durham, ii. 205.
HARBIN. Burke's Landed Gentry, 2, 3, 4, 5, 6, 7, 8.   Harleian
Society, xi. 46.   Burke's Royal Families, (London, 1851, 8vo.)
i. 41.   Burke's Royal Descents and Pedigrees of Founders' Kin,
Founders' Kin, 5.
HARBORD. Blomefield's Norfolk, viii. 121.   Baker's Northampton,
ii. 172.   Page's History of Suffolk, 548.   Brydges' Collins' Peerage,
viii. 107.
HARBORNE, or HARBOURNE. Harleian Society, i. 83; v. 308; xv. 347.
Visitation of Oxfordshire, 1634, printed by Sir ·T. Phillipps,
(Middle Hill, fol.) 20.
HARBOROUGH. Nichols' History of the County of Leicester, ii. 346.
Miscellanea Genealogica et Heraldica, 3rd Series, iii. 116.
HARBOTEL, HARBOTELL, HARBOTLE, or HARBOTTLE. Harleian
Society, iii. 1.   Sussex Archæological Collections, xiv. 113.
Hodgson's Northumberland, II. ii. 260.   Surtees' Durham, ii. 225.
Thoroton's Nottinghamshire, iii. 177.   Visitation of Sussex, 1570,
printed by Sir T. Phillipps, (Middle Hill, fol.) 6.   Plantagenet-
Harrison's History of Yorkshire, i. 167.   Metcalfe's Visitations of
Suffolk, 37.
HARBY, or HARBYE. Harleian Society, i. 86 ; viii. 221.   Visitation
of Somerset, printed by Sir T. Phillipps, 90.   Clutterbuck's
Hertford, i. 130.   Baker's Northampton, ii. 19.   Harleian Society,
xv. 346.   Burke's Extinct Baronetcies.   Metcalfe's Visitations of
Northamptonshire, 25.
HARCOURT. Histoire Genealogique de la Maison de Harcourt, par
Mons. De la Roque.   Paris, 1662, fol., 4 vols.   Visitations of
Staffordshire, 1614 and 1663-4, William Salt Society, 168.
Notes and Queries, 7 S., viii. 181, 278, 392.   The Genealogist,
New Series, xvii. 175.   Cussan's History of Hertfordshire, Parts
iii. and iv. 23.   Gentleman's Magazine, 1831, i. 394.   Burke's
Commoners, (of Ankerwycke,) ii. 221, Landed Gentry, 2, 3, 4, 5,
6, 7, 8 ; (of Nuneham Park,) Landed Gentry, 4, 5, 6, 7, 8.
Harleian Society, ii. 39, 166 ; viii. 61, 479 ; xviii. 142.   Eyton's
Antiquities of Shropshire, iii. 142.   Gyll's History of Wraysbury,
45, 128.   Lipscombe's History of the County of Buckingham,
iv. 589.   Nichols' History of the County of Leicester, iv. 519*-
521*, 723, 1025.   Hoare's Wiltshire, V. i. 21.   Clutterbuck's
Hertford, i. 285.   Ormerod's Cheshire, i. 629.   Miscellanea
Genealogica et Heraldica, New Series, iii. 358.   Collections for a
History of Staffordshire, William Salt Society, ii. part 2, 70, 72.
Edmondson's Baronagium Genealogicum, iii. 280.   Brydges'

Collins' Peerage, iv. 428. Visitation of Staffordshire, (Willm. Salt Soc.) 91. *See* HARECOURT.

HARCOURT-VERNON. Burke's Landed Gentry, 8.

HARDCASTLE. Burke's Landed Gentry, (of Blidworth Dale,) 3, 4, 5 ; (of Nether Hall and Headlands,) 5, 6 ; (of New Lodge,) 7, 8.

HARDEN. Burke's Landed Gentry, (of Crea,) 2 ; (of Harrybrook,) 4, 8. *See* ARDERNE.

HARDFELD. Harleian Society, xiv. 561.

HARDING. J. Wilkinson's History of Broughton Gifford, 79. Fosbrooke's History of Gloucestershire, i. 435. Harleian Society, i. 18, 54 ; viii. 297 ; xix. 114 ; xxi. 253. Burke's Landed Gentry, (of Baraset,) 2, 3, 4, 5, 6, 7, 8 ; (of Upcott,) 3, 4, 5, 6, 7, 8 ; (of Old Springs,) 8 ; (of Tamworth,) 2 supp., 3, 4. Visitation of Derbyshire, 1663-4, (Middle Hill, 1854, fol.) 4. Visitatio Comitatus Wiltoniæ, 1623, printed by Sir T. Phillipps. Surtees' Durham, ii. 252. Manning and Bray's Surrey, i. 537. Wiltshire Archæological Magazine, vi. 11. J. H. Blunt's Dursley and its Neighbourhood, 168. The Genealogist, iii. 178. Burke's Colonial Gentry, ii. 639.

HARDINGE. Memoirs of George Hardinge, Esq., with Anecdotes of the Hardinge Family, by John Nichols, F.S.A. London, 1818, 8vo. Nichols' Literary Illustrations, iii. 1. The History of Melbourne, by J. J. Briggs, 2nd edn., 167. Visitation of Durham, 1575, (Newcastle, 1820, fol.) 32. Manning and Bray's Surrey, i. 383. Betham's Baronetage, v. 478. The Visitation of Wiltshire, edited by G. W. Marshall, 39. Foster's Visitations of Durham, 153. Burke's Landed Gentry, 7.

HARDMAN. Jewitt's Reliquary, xv. 190. Gregson's Fragments relative to the County of Lancaster, 167. Fishwick's History of Rochdale, 52. Harleian Society, xl. 1224.

HARDREDESHULL, or HARDRESHULL. Bartlett's History of Manceter, being No. 1 of Nichols' Miscellaneous Antiquities, 50. Dugdale's Warwickshire, 1080. Nichol's History of the County of Leicester, iv. 316. Baker's Northampton, ii. 124. Banks' Baronies in Fee, ii. 97.

HARDRESS, or HARDRES. Gentleman's Magazine, lvii. 384 ; lxiii. 862, 911. Archæologia Cantiana, iv. 56. Harleian Society, xiii. 211. Wotton's English Baronetage, ii. 300. Burke's Extinct Baronetcies.

HARDS. The Genealogical Magazine, i. 421.

HARDWARE. Ormerod's Cheshire, ii. 333.

HARDWICK, or HARDWICKE. History of the Family of Hardwicke, with Pedigrees of the Families of Guttyns, Forster, Purton, Bemand, Bell, Wright, and Allen, by H. J. Hardwicke. Sheffield, 1878, 8vo. The Genealogist, New Series, vii. 141. Howard's Visitation of England and Wales, iv. 129. Burke's Landed Gentry, 8. Burton's Description of Leicestershire, 160. Thoresby's Ducatus Leodiensis, 122. Harleian Society, xiii. 412. Genealogy of the Family of Hardwicke of Hardwick and Chilton, 1866, folio sheet. Cussan's History of Hertfordshire, Parts iii. and iv.

44. History of Hardwicke Hall, by P. F. Robinson, 2. Topo-
; rapher, (London, 1789-91, 8vo.) iii. 323. Notes and Queries,
1 S. i. 276, 339 ; ii. 283. Jewitt's Reliquary, xxii. 241 ; xxiii.
232. *See* HERDWICK.

HARDY. A Pedigree of Hardy of Barbon, by C. F. Hardy, 1888,
8vo. Surtees Society, xxxvi. 68. Burke's Landed Gentry, (of
Letheringsett,) 2, 3, 4, 5, 6, 7, 8 ; (of Dunstall Hall,) 5, 6.
Hutchins' Dorset, ii. 645 ; iv. 433. Burke's Extinct Baronetcies,
supp. Harleian Society, xx. 51. Some Old Families, by H. B.
McCall, 51. The Genealogist, New Series, iii. 89. Platt and
Morkill's Records of Whitkirk, 92.

HARE, R. R. Dyson's History of Tottenham High Cross, 31.
Blomefield's Norfolk, i. 414 ; vii. 440. Herald and Genealogist,
ii. 474. Burke's Landed Gentry, (of Docking Hall,) 2, 4, 5, 6,
7, 8 ; (of Court Grange, etc.) 5, 6 and supp., 7, 8 ; (of Tetworth,)
4 supp. ; (of Gresford,) 2 add., 3, 4 ; (of Calder Hall,) 8. Clutterbuck's Hertford, ii. 353, 454. Carthew's Hundred of Launditch,
Part ii. 657. Page's History of Suffolk, 338. Memorials of a
Quiet Life, by A. J. C. Hare, i. 66. Wotton's English Baronetage,
ii. 208. Account of the Mayo and Elton families, by C. H.
Mayo, 139. Metcalfe's Visitations of Suffolk, 37. Burke's Extinct Baronetcies.

HAREBRED. Foster's Visitations of Yorkshire, 527. Thoresby's
Ducatus Leodiensis, 236.

HARECOURT. Visitation of Staffordshire, 1663-4, printed by Sir T.
Phillipps, 6. Visitation of Staffordshire, (William Salt Soc.)
119. The Genealogist, New Series, xii. 231 ; xiv. 196. *See*
HARCOURT.

HARESTON. Nichols' History of the County of Leicester, ii. 217.

HAREWEDEN. The Genealogist, New Series, xvi. 166.

HAREWELL. Nash's Worcestershire, i. 77. Dugdale's Warwickshire,
809. Harleian Society, xv. 348 ; xxvii. 72. Visitations of
Staffordshire, 1614 and 1663-4, William Salt Society, 170.

HAREWOOD. Harleian Society, vi. 137 ; xv. 349. The Visitations
of Devon, by J. L. Vivian, 442. *See* HARWOOD.

HARFLEET, or HARFLETE. Planché's Corner of Kent, 307-350.
Hasted's Kent, iii. 587, 679. The Antiquary, (London, 1873,)
iv. 311.

HARFORD. Weaver's Visitation of Herefordshire, 38. Burke's
Commoners, iv. 638, Landed Gentry, (of Falcondale,) 2, 3, 4, 5,
6, 7, 8 ; (of Down Place,) 6, 7, 8 ; (of Oldown.) 8. History of
the Wilmer Family, 245. A History of Banking in Bristol, by
C. H. Cave, 240.

HARGADAN. O'Hart's Irish Pedigrees, 2nd Series, 189.

HARGILL. Foster's Visitations of Yorkshire, 371.

HARGRAVE. Burke's Landed Gentry, 5 supp. p. 54 ; 6 p. 1244 ;
7 p. 1431.

HARGREAVE. Abram's History of Blackburn, 506.

HARGREAVES. Burke's Commoners, ii. 685, Landed Gentry, 2 and
corr., 3, 4, 5, 6, 7, 8. Foster's Lancashire Pedigrees. Whitaker's

History of Whalley, ii. 12, 175. Abram's History of Blackburn, 395.

HARINGTON. Herald and Genealogist, iv. 276, 370 ; viii. 338. J. E. Jackson's History of St. George's Church at Doncaster, 38. Harleian Society, ii. 59 ; iii. 38 ; vii. 33 ; xiii. 412 ; xvi. 360. Wright's History of Rutland, 51. Burton's Description of Leicestershire, 209. Thoresby's Ducatus Leodiensis, 199, 200. Miscellanea Genealogica et Heraldica, New Series, iii. 236, 271, 333 ; iv. 3, 191, 275, 291, 378, 381. Banks' Baronies in Fee, i. 244. Banks' Dormant and Extinct Baronage, ii. 261. The Genealogist, New Series, x. 32. See HARRINGTON.

HARKNESS. Burke's Landed Gentry, 6 supp., 7, 8.

HARLAKENDEN. Topographer and Genealogist, i. 228-258, 395; ii. 215-223. Morant's Essex, ii. 211, 579. Berry's Kent Genealogies, 465. Berry's Essex Genealogies, 113. Bibliotheca Topographica Britannica, i. Part i. 39. Wright's Essex, i. 421. Harleian Society, xiii. 211, 412 ; xiv. 665. Archæologia Cantiana, xiv. 360. Bysshe's Visitation of Essex, edited by J. J. Howard, 42. New England Register, xv. 327.

HARLAND. Burke's Commoners, iii. 194, Landed Gentry, 2, 3, 4. Betham's Baronetage, iii. 372. Burke's Extinct Baronetcies.

HARLE. Hodgson's Northumberland, I. ii. 239.

HARLESTONE, or HARLSTONE. Morant's Essex, i. 100 ; ii. 349. Archæologia Cantiana, iv. 257. Berry's Kent Genealogies, 4. Harleian Society, xlii. 8.

HARLEWYN. Harleian Society, vi. 138. The Visitations of Devon, by J. L. Vivian, 443.

HARLEY. Camden Society, lviii. Introduction. Drummond's History of Noble British Families, Parts i. and ii. Glover's History of Derbyshire, ii. 140, (123). Harleian Society, viii. 21 ; xxviii. 213, 304. Nichols' History of the County of Leicester, iii. 923. Edmondson's Baronagium Genealogicum, ii. 188. Brydges' Collins' Peerage, iv. 37. Weaver's Visitations of Somerset, 135. Fletcher's Leicestershire Pedigrees and Royal Descents, 188. The Genealogist, New Series, ix. 146 ; xv. 22. Burke's Family Records, 296. Burke's Landed Gentry, 8. See CAVENDISH.

HARLOW. Bysshe's Visitation of Essex, edited by J. J. Howard, 43. New England Register, xiv. 227.

HARMAN. Howard's Visitation of Ireland, iii. 98. Sir T. Phillipps' Topographer, No. 1, (March, 1821, 8vo.) 36. Visitation of Oxfordshire, 1574, printed by Sir T. Phillipps, (Middle Hill, fol.) 4. Burke's Landed Gentry, 4, 5 supp., 6, 7, 8. Oliver's History of Antigua, ii. 62. Harleian Society, v. 157 ; xii. 105. Visitation of Warwickshire, 1619, published with Warwickshire Antiquarian Magazine, 100. The Forest and Chase of Sutton Coldfield, (London, 1860, 8vo.) 56, and app. Metcalfe's Visitations of Suffolk, 143. History of the Wilmer Family, 204. Ontarian Families, by J. M. Chadwick, i. 184. See KING-HARMAN.

HARNAGE. Harleian Society, xxviii. 215. Oliver's History of Antigua, i. 48.

HAROLD. Visitatio Comitatus Wiltoniæ, 1623, printed by Sir T. Phillipps. The Visitation of Wiltshire, edited by G. W. Marshall, 23.

HAROLD-BARRY. Burke's Landed Gentry, 8.

HARPER. Surrey Archæolgical Collections, v. ; vii. Harleian Society, i. 4; vi. 138; xv. 350; xxviii. 216; xliii. 140. Topographical Miscellanies, 1792, 4to., (Bredsall). Weaver's Visitation of Herefordshire, 39. The Visitations of Devon, by J. L. Vivian, 445. Willmore's History of Walsall, 267. Family Notes, by J. M. Browne, 46.

HARPERLEY. Topographer and Genealogist, ii. 79.

HARPESFIELD. Herald and Genealogist, v. 127.

HARPETRE. Banks' Dormant and Extinct Baronage, i. 94.

HARPUR. Glover's History of Derbyshire, ii. 179, 216, (184). Burke's Landed Gentry, 2 supp., 3, 4, 5. Shaw's Staffordshire, ii. 69. Nichols' History of the County of Leicester, iii. 884, 855*. Dugdale's Warwickshire, 478. Pilkington's View of Derbyshire, ii. 78. Wotton's English Baronetage, ii. 1. Betham's Baronetage, i. 277. The Genealogist, New Series, vii. 142. Willmore's Records of Rushall, 38. Harleian Society, xxviii. 217. The Gresley's of Drakelowe, by F. Madan, 261.

HARPWAY. Genealogies of Morgan and Glamorgan, by G. T. Clark, 444.

HARPYN. Hutchinson's History of Durham, iii. 339. Surtees' Durham, i. 84.

HARRI. Dwnn's Visitations of Wales, i. 231.

HARRI AP SION. Dwnn's Visitations of Wales, i. 62.

HARRIE. The Visitations of Cornwall, edited by J. L. Vivian, 205.

HARRIES. Pedigree of Harries of Priskilly, [T. P.] 1859. Burke's Commoners, (of Priskilly,) i. 256, Landed Gentry, 2, 3, 4, 5, 6, 7, 8; (of Cruckton,) Landed Gentry, 2, 3, 4, 5, 6; (of Cwmwdig,) 5 supp., 6; (of Rickestone,) 8. Pembrokeshire Pedigrees, 134. Burke's Extinct Baronetcies. Genealogies of Morgan and Glamorgan, by G. T. Clark, 103.

HARRINGTON, or HARRYNGTON. J. H. Hill's History of Langton, 204. Morant's Essex, ii. 279. Edward Miller's History of Doncaster, 163. Burke's Commoners, i. 461, Landed Gentry, 2. Chetham Society, lxxxii. 73; lxxxv. 130; xcv. 111. Hutchinson's History of Cumberland, ii. 101. Gregson's Fragments relative to the County of Lancaster, 220, 265. Burke's Royal Families, (London, 1851, 8vo.) ii. 78. Jefferson's History of Allerdale Ward, Cumberland, 7. Whitaker's History of Richmondshire, ii. 250. Corry's History of Lancashire, i. 450. Wainwright's Wapentake of Strafford and Tickhill, 113. Nichols' History of the County of Leicester, ii. 584. Hunter's Deanery of Doncaster, ii. 402. Baines' History of the Co. of Lancaster, iv. 648; Croston's edn. v. 74. Whitaker's History of Whalley, ii. 509. Maclean's History of Trigg Minor, iii. 260. Banks' Baronies in Fee, ii. 98. Betham's Baronetage, i. 106. Banks'

Dormant and Extinct Baronage, iii. 339. A Description of the Monument and Effigies in Porlock Church, by M. Halliday, *at end*. Harleian Society, xviii. 140; xxviii. 220. Metcalfe's Visitations of Northamptonshire, 180. Bysshe's Visitation of Essex, edited by J. J. Howard, 43. Foster's Visitations of Cumberland and Westmorland, 57. Nicholson and Burn's Westmorland and Cumberland, i. 228; ii. 50. Healey's History of Part of West Somerset, 258. *See* HARINGTON.

HARRINGWORTH. Nichols' History of the County of Leicester, iii. 1146.

HARRIS. A Narrative of the Descendants of Samuel Harris, of Fordingbridge, Hants, together with a Notice of the Family of Masterman of London. London, 1878, 4to. Pedigree of Harris of Tregwynt, etc., Co. Pembroke, [T. P.] 1861, folio page. Morant's Essex, i. 342. Gentleman's Magazine, 1828, ii. 317. Dwnn's Visitations of Wales, i. 161. Berry's Hampshire Genealogies, 88, 332. Surrey Archæological Collections, ii. (*bis*). Visitation of Wiltshire, 1677, printed by Sir T. Phillipps, (Middle Hill, 1854, fol.). Burke's Commoners, ii. 401; iv. 430; (of Hayne,) Commoners, i. 559, Landed Gentry, 2, 3, 4, 5, 6, 7, 8; (of Rosewarne,) 2; (of Halwill,) 8; (of Bowden Hill House,) 8; (of Tylney Hall,) 6, 7, 8; Harleian Society, ii. 66; vi. 139; viii. 437; ix. 90; xiii. 9, 59, 213, 414; xv. 351; xxi. 77, 254; xxii. 63; xxvii. 74, 109; xxviii. 222; xli. 107; xliii. 101, 185. Westcote's Devonshire, edited by G. Oliver and P. Jones, 531, 532. Maclean's History of Trigg Minor, ii. 444. An Historical Survey of Cornwall, by C. S. Gilbert, ii. 135. Brydges' Collins' Peerage, v. 421. Burke's Extinct Baronetcies. The Visitations of Cornwall, edited by J. L. Vivian, 206. Hasted's Kent,(Hund. of Blackheath, by H. H. Drake,) xx. The Genealogist, New Series, iii. 235. Bysshe's Visitation of Essex, edited by J. J. Howard, 44. Visitation of Gloucester, edited by T. F. Fenwick and W. C. Metcalfe, 89. Genealogical Records of the Family of Woodd, 28a. The Visitations of Devon, by J. L. Vivian, 447-452. New England Register, ii. 218; viii. 172. Family Notes by J. M. Browne, 69. Family Records, by Charlotte Sturge, 75. The Ancestor, No. 1., 1-27. *See* CAPEL, HARRYS.

HARRISON, or HARISON. Family Notes showing the Descendants of the Great-grandfathers of T. Harrison and J. E. Branfill. 1873, 8vo. 2nd. edn. Chew Magna, 1897, 8vo. Berry's Hertfordshire Genealogies, 249. Surtees Society, xxxvi. 132, 172, 216, 217. Collections for a Genealogical Account of the Family of Comberbach, by Geo. W. Marshall, 53. Foster's Visitations of Yorkshire, 527. Gregson's Fragments relative to the County of Lancaster, 269. Poulson's Holderness, i. 319. Thoresby's Ducatus Leodiensis, 12. Archæologia Æliana, 2nd Series, iii. 52. Burke's Landed Gentry, (of Castle Harrison,) 4, 5, 6, 7, 8; (of Greenbank,) 2, 3, 4, 5, 7; (of Winscales,) 2 supp., 3, 4, 5, 6; (of Snelston Hall,) 2 add., 3, 4, 5, 6, 7, 8; (of Merton Hall,) 3, 4, 5, 6, 7, 8; (of Ramsay,) 3, 4, 5 supp., 6; (of Copford Hall,) 7, 8; (of Scale-

How,) 8 ; (of Maer,) 8 ; (of Linethwaite,) 5 ; (of Caerhowel,) 6, 7, 8. Turnor's History of Town and Soke of Grantham, 146. Surtees' Durham, ii. 257 ; iv. 93. Clutterbuck's Hertford, ii. 186. Sussex Archæological Collections, vii. 133. Chetham Society, xcii. 189. An Historical Survey of Cornwall, by C. S. Gilbert, ii. 141. Pedigree of Wilson of High Wray, etc., by Joseph Foster, 98. Plantagenet-Harrison's History of Yorkshire, i. xiv. 348. Collections by the Powys-land Club, viii. 253. Harleian Society, xv. 352-356 ; xxxix. 829, 985. Visitation of Devon, edited by F. T. Colby, 122. The Genealogist, v. 268 ; vi. 256. North's Church Bells of Lincoln, 60. Notes and Queries, 3 S. vi. 152 ; 5 S. x. 175, 212, 270 ; xi. 114, 229, 451, 512 ; 6 S. i. 278 ; ii. 383 ; iii. 303, 345, 446, 505 ; iv. 26, 66 ; x. 272. Miscellanea Genealogica et Heraldica, New Series, iv. 118. History of Powys Fadog, by J. Y. W. Lloyd, vi. 441. Abstract of the Pedigree of F. M. G. H. de S. Plantagenet-Harrison. London, *circa* 1850, 4to. A Pedigree of the Harrison Family, co. Norfolk. Broadside, *n. d.* Petition of General Plantagenet-Harrison to the House of Lords touching the Duchy of Lancaster. London, 1858. Foster's Visitations of Durham, 155. Metcalfe's Visitations of Northamptonshire, 98. New England Register, xliv. 199. Bysshe's Visitation of Essex, edited by J. J. Howard, 44. East Barnet, by F. C. Cass, Part i. 74. A Lancashire Pedigree Case, by J. P. Earwaker, folding table. Earwaker's History of Sandbach, 202. Lyon's Chronicles of Finchampstead, 111. Pedigree of Wilson, by S. B. Foster, 158. Ontarian Families, by E. M. Chadwick, i. 16. Healey's History of Part of West Somerset, 149. *See* FISKE-HARRISON, PLANTAGENET-HARRISON, ROGERS-HARRISON.

HARRISSON. Burke's Landed Gentry, 2, 3, 4, 5, 6, 7, 8.

HARROP. *See* HULTON-HARROP.

HARRY. Genealogies of Morgan and Glamorgan, by G. T. Clark, 490.

HARRY AB JOHN. Dwnn's Visitations of Wales, ii. 196.

HARRYS. Morant's Essex, i. 310, 322, 362, 366 ; ii. 54. Tuckett's Devonshire Pedigrees, 120, 126. Harleian Society, vi. 139. Wright's Essex, ii. 682. Visitation of Devon, edited by F. T. Colby, 123. *See* HARRIS.

HARSICK. Blomefield's History of Norfolk, vi. 77. Carthew's Hundred of Launditch, Part i. 160. Harleian Society, xxxii. 144.

HARSNET. Carthew's Hundred of Launditch, Part iii. 160.

HART, or HARTE. Shakespereana Genealogica, by G. R. French, 397. Hasted's Kent, i. 137. Topographer and Genealogist, ii. 80. Case of Sir P. Hart-Dyke on his claim to title of Baron Braye, 13. Visitation of Norfolk, published by Norfolk Archæological Society, i. 54. Berry's Kent Genealogies, 424. Berry's Surrey Genealogies, 60. Burke's Landed Gentry, (of Kilderry,) 3, 4, 5, 6, 7, 8 ; (of Yarnacombe,) 2 ; (of Netherbury,) 7, 8 ; (of Esperanza,) 8. Foster's Visitations of Yorkshire, 621. Nichols'

History of the County of Leicester, ii. 281. Harleian Society, xiii. 416 ; xv. 356 ; xxxii. 145 ; xlii. 198. O'Hart's Irish Pedigrees, 2nd Series, 189-196. Notes and Queries, 3 S. v. 341. The Visitations of Cornwall, edited by J. L. Vivian, 210. Hasted's Kent, (Hund. of Blackheath, by H. H. Drake,) xx. Bysshe's Visitation of Essex, edited by J. J. Howard, 44. Archæologia Cantiana, xvi. 238. Oliver's History of Antigua, ii. 67. *See* SHAKESPEARE.

HART-DAVIS. Howard's Visitation of England and Wales, ix. 28.

HART-DYKE. Case of Sir Percival Hart-Dyke, Bart., on his claim to the title of Baron Braye. London, 1836, fol., pp. 20. *See* BRAYE, CAVE.

HARTCUP. Burke's Landed Gentry, 2 add., 3, 4, 7, 8. Burke's Visitation of Seats and Arms, i. 18.

HARTER. Burke's Landed Gentry, 7, 8.

HARTFORD. Harleian Society, i. 37.

HARTGILL. Visitation of Somerset, printed by Sir T. Phillipps, 89. Phelps' History of Somersetshire, i. 177. Harleian Society, xi. 46.

HARTHILL. Harleian Society, xviii. 58.

HARTLAND. Burke's Landed Gentry, 5, 6, 7.

HARTLEY. Whitaker's History of Craven, 1st edn., 73. Appendix to Case of Sir J. S. Sidney, claiming the Barony of Lisle. Berry's Berkshire Genealogies, 149. Burke's Commoners, i. 343 ; (of Bucklebury,) iv. 726, Landed Gentry, 2, 3, 4, 5, 6, 7 ; (of Beech Park,) Landed Gentry, 4, 5, 6, 7, 8 ; (of Gillfoot,) 2, 3, 4, 5, 6, 8 ; (of The Oaks,) 5, 6 ; (of Wheaton Aston,) 7, 8 ; (of Hartley,) 8 supp. Chetham Society, lxxxv. 131. Burke's Royal Families, (London, 1851, 8vo.) i. 77. Harleian Society, xxxviii. 615 ; xxxix. 1002.

HARTLEY-KENNEDY. Burke's Visitation of Seats and Arms, 2nd Series, ii. 29.

HARTOPP, or HARTOP. J. H. Hill's History of Langton, 266. Burke's Commoners, iii. 401, Landed Gentry, 2, 3, 4, 5, 6, 7, 8. Harleian Society, ii. 9, 196 ; viii. 78. Nichols' History of the County of Leicester, ii. 128, 159, 267. Wotton's English Baronetage, i. 359. Betham's Baronetage, iv, 365. Notes and Queries, 4 S. ix. 363. Burke's Extinct Baronetcies. Fletcher's Leicestershire Pedigrees and Royal Descents, 85. *See* CRADOCK-HARTOPP, VAUX.

HARTSTONGE. Burke's Extinct Baronetcies, 608. Harleian Society, xxxii. 146.

HARTWELL. Metcalfe's Visitations of Northamptonshire, 25.

HARTY. Berry's Kent Genealogies, 52. Harleian Society, xlii. 36.

HARVEST. Burke's Family Records, 299.

HARVEY, HARVIE, or HARVY. Collinson's Somerset, ii. 121 ; iii. 82. Morant's Essex, i. 166. Hasted's Kent, iv. 199, 205. East Anglian, i. 208, 241 ; ii. 141. Berry's Kent Genealogies, 252-256. Berry's Essex Genealogies, 24, 127. Cambridgeshire Visitation, edited by Sir T. Phillipps, 17. Visitation of Middlesex, (Salisbury,

1820, fol.) 42. Burke's Commoners, i. 319; ii. 433; (of Ickwell Bury,) Commoners, iv. 507, Landed Gentry, 2, 3, 4, 5, 6, 7, 8; (of Thorpe,) Commoners, i. 399, Landed Gentry, 2, 3, 4; (of Bargy Castle,) Landed Gentry, 2, 3, 4, 5, 6, 7, 8; (of Kyle,) 2, 3, 4, 5, 6, 7; (of Castlesemple,) 2, 3, 4, 5, 6, 7, 8; (of Malin Hall,) 3, 4, 5, 6, 7, 8; (of Inishowen,) 5; (of Dundridge,) 8; (of Carnousie,) 3, 4, 5, 6, 7, 8. Harleian Society, i. 13; vi. 140; viii. 53; ix. 91; xi. 47; xiii. 214, 416; xiv. 668; xv. 358, 360; xix. 36, 116; xx. 52; xxii. 10, 146; xxxii. 146; xxxix. 976; xliii. 13. Herald and Genealogist, vi. 154, 352. Lipscombe's History of the County of Buckingham, i. 437. Bridges' North-amptonshire, by Rev. Peter Whalley, i. 362. Nichols' History of the County of Leicester, iv. 608. Hutchins' Dorset, iii. 574. Manning and Bray's Surrey, i. 402; ii. 208. Baker's North-ampton, i. 74. Pedigree of the Family of Sheppard, 9. Wilson's History of the Parish of St. Laurence Poultney, 228. Carthew's Hundred of Launditch, Part ii. 549. Paterson's History of Ayr and Wigton, iii. 171. Notes and Queries, 3 S. v. 247, 326. The Visitations of Cornwall, edited by J. L. Vivian, 211. Howard's Visitation of England and Wales, i. 6. Foster's Visi-tation of Middlesex, 79. Miscellanea Genealogica et Heraldica, 2nd Series, iii. 329, 362, 381. Metcalfe's Visitations of North-amptonshire, 26, 98. Hasted's Kent, (Hund. of Blackheath, by H. H. Drake,) xvii. The Visitations of Devon, by J. L. Vivian, 453. Weaver's Visitations of Somerset, 28. Harvey's Hundred of Willey, 510. Transactions of the Cambridge University Asso-ciation of Brass Collectors, ii. 19. Jewers' Wells Cathedral, 28. New England Register, xii. 313. Ontarian Families, by E. M. Chadwick, ii. 99. Oliver's History of Antigua, ii. 68. *See* HERVEY.

HARVEY-ASTON. Ormerod's Cheshire, i. 726.

HARVEY-THURSBY. Baker's Northampton, i. 11.

HARVIE-BROWN. Burke's Landed Gentry, 8.

HARWARD. Pedigrees of Harward of Hartlebury, [T. P.] folio page. Pedigrees of Harward of Harvington, and Alye of London, [T. P.] 2 folio pages. *See* COTTERELL, GIFFARD.

HARWARE. Visitation of Warwickshire, 1619, published with War-wickshire Antiquarian Magazine, 102. Harleian Society, xii. 267.

HARWEDON. Bridges' Northamptonshire, by Rev. Peter Whalley, i. 254, 324. Baker's Northampton, ii. 96.

HARWOOD. Bibliotheca Topographica Britannica, ix. Part iv. 70. Burke's Commoners, iii. 406; Landed Gentry, 2. Foster's Visita-tions of Yorkshire, 528. Erdeswicke's Survey of Staffordshire, 425. Abram's History of Blackburn, 477, 579. *See* HAREWOOD.

HARYS. Glamorganshire Pedigrees, edited by Sir T. Phillipps, 15.

HASELDEN. Metcalfe's Visitations of Northamptonshire, 76. Harleian Society, xix. 115; xli. 88.

HASELE. Dugdale's Warwickshire, 507.

HASELFOOTE. Harleian Society, xv. 361.

HASELL, HASSEL, or HASSELL. Surtees Society, xxxvi. 75. Collec-

tanea Topographica et Genealogica, viii. 405. Gyll's History of
Wraysbury, 77. Lipscombe's History of the County of Bucking-
ham, iv. 604. Burke's Commoners, iv. 183*n.*; Landed Gentry,
2 and add., 3, 4, 5, 6, 7, 8. Hutchinson's History of Cumberland,
i. 467. Jefferson's History of Leath Ward, Cumberland, 193.
Nicholson and Burn's Westmorland and Cumberland, ii. 383.
HASELRIG. Harleian Society, ii. 15 ; iv. 153. *See* HESELRIG.
HASELWALL. Ormerod's Cheshire, ii. 507. The Genealogist, New
Series, xiii. 100.
HASELWOOD, or HASLEWOOD. Nash's Worcestershire, ii. 203. Har-
leian Society, iii. 44; viii. 226 ; xxvii. 75. Bridges' Northamp-
tonshire, by Rev. Peter Whalley, ii. 47. Nichols' History of
the County of Leicester, ii. 569. The Genealogist, i. 43. Miscel-
lanea Genealogica et Heraldica, New Series, ii. 129. Howard's
Visitation of England and Wales, vii. 133.
HASILDEN, or HASSYLDEN. Hutchins' Dorset, iii. 445. Morant's
Essex, ii. 557. Memoirs of the Family of Chester, by R. E. C.
Waters, 217.
HASKETT. Hutchins' Dorset, iv. 460.
HASLAM. Fishwick's History of Rochdale, 510.
HASLER. Burke's Landed Gentry, 2 supp., 3, 4, 5, 6, 7, 8.
HASLING. Archæologia Cantiana, iv. 254. Harleian Society, xlii. 7.
HASLINGTON. Ormerod's Cheshire, iii. 130.
HASSALL. Ormerod's Cheshire, iii. 296. Harleian Society, xviii. 109.
Earwaker's History of Sandbach, 118.
HASSAM. New England Register, xxiv. 414 ; xliii. 320.
HASSARD. History and Genealogy of the Hassards, by H. Short.
York, 1858, 4to. Burke's Landed Gentry, (of Gardenhill,) 3, 4,
5, 6 ; (of Waterford,) 3, 4, 5, 6, 7 ; (of Skea,) 2, 3, 4. Burke's
Visitations of Seats and Arms, ii. 14. Harleian Society, xl. 1190.
Burke's Family Records, 300.
HAST. Visitation of Norfolk, published by Norfolk Archæological
Society, i. 41. Harleian Society, xxxii. 147.
HASTANG. Nash's Worcestershire, i. 157. Dugdale's Warwickshire,
316. Banks' Dormant and Extinct Baronage, i. 335. The Genea-
logist, New Series, xviii. 30. *See* HASTINGS.
HASTED. Hasted's Kent, ii. 563, 753.
HASTINGS. Case of Hans Francis Hastings, claiming the Titles, etc.,
of Earl of Huntingdon, edited by Sir Samuel Romilly, 1817, 8vo.
Descent of the Barony of Hastings, Sess. Papers, 148 of 1857.
Case of Edith Maud, Countess of Loudoun, etc., pp. 67. 1873, fol.
Case of C. E. Hastings, supplementary to above, pp. 17. 1874,
fol. Claim of Edith Maud, Countess of Loudoun, wife of C. A.
Hastings, to the Baronies of Botreaux, Hungerford, De Malyns,
and Hastings, Sess. Papers, D of 1870 ; D of 1871. Account of
the Controversy between Lord Grey of Ruthyn and Sir Edward
Hastings, by C. G. Young. 1841, fol. Kent's British Banner
Displayed, 612. Jacob's Peerage, i. 468. Gentleman's Magazine,
lxxxii. ii. 626 ; lxxxiii. i. 126, 608 ; lxxxiv. i. 453 ; 1825, i. 390 ;
1829, i. 125 ; 1865, ii. 622. Gough's Sepulchral Monuments, ii.

370. Blomefield's Norfolk, ix. 513. Grandison Peerage Evidence, 337, 344. Montacute Peerage Evidence, 159. Bell's Huntingdon Peerage. London, 1820, 4to. Sir T. Phillipps' Topographer, No. 1, (March, 1821, 8vo.) 33. Cambridgeshire Visitation, edited by Sir T. Phillipps, 11. Berry's Buckinghamshire Genealogies, 18. Visitation of Oxfordshire, 1574, printed by Sir T. Phillipps, (Middle Hill, fol.) 4. Burke's Landed Gentry, 4, 5, 6. Carthew's Hundred of Launditch, Part i. 198. Foster's Visitations of Yorkshire, 372. Harleian Society, ii. 72 ; v. 155, 262 ; xv. 362 ; xvi. 153, 154 ; xx. 52 ; xxxii. 147. Burke's Heraldic Illustrations, 103. Topographer, (London, 1789-91, 8vo.) i 82. Maclean's History of Trigg Minor, i. 383. Hodgson's Northumberland, I. ii. 239. Poulson's Holderness, ii. 22. Bridges' Northamptonshire, by Rev. Peter Whalley, i. 397, 592. Eyton's Antiquities of Shropshire, v. 135 ; x. 221. Burton's Description of Leicestershire, 19. Thoresby's Ducatus Leodiensis, 244. Dugdale's Warwickshire, 1024, 1029. Nichols' History of the County of Leicester, iii. 278, 607 ; iv. 447, 627. Hutchins' Dorset, iii. 155. Hunter's Deanery of Doncaster, ii. 472. Baker's Northampton, i. 478, 538. Thoroton's Nottinghamshire, iii. 202. Norfolk Archæology, vi. 76, 78, 90, 97. Surtees Society, xli. 73. Controversy between Reginald Lord Grey de Ruthin and Sir Edward Hastings, by C. G. Young, (1841, sm. fol.) 3. Burke's Commoners, iv. 573 ; Landed Gentry, 7, 8. Edmondson's Baronagium Genealogicum, ii. 92. Brydges' Collins' Peerage, vi. 643. Banks' Baronies in Fee, i. 245 ; ii. 98. Banks' Dormant and Extinct Baronage, i. 337 ; ii. 4, 263, 264 ; iii. 396. Burke's Extinct Baronetcies. Metcalfe's Visitation of Worcester, 1683, 54. Carthew's Hundred of Launditch, Part iii. 278. Harvey's Hundred of Willey, 317. New England Register, xxi. 350. Woodcock of Cuerden, by A. E. P. Gray, 14. The Genealogist, New Series, xii. 232 ; xiii. 242. The Gresley's of Drakelowe, by F. Madan, 262. See ASTLEY, DE HASTINGS.

HASTLEN. Dwnn's Visitations of Wales, i. 26.

HATCH. Burke's Landed Gentry, (of Ardee Castle,) 3, 4 ; (of Sutton,) 2 supp. Harleian Society, vi. 141 ; ix. 91. Westcote's Devonshire, edited by G. Oliver and P. Jones, 603. The Genealogist, i. 313, 368. Visitation of Devon, edited by F. T. Colby, 124. The Visitations of Cornwall, edited by J. L. Vivian, 212. Visitations of Devon, by J. L. Vivian, 455. Devonshire Notes and Notelets, by Sir W. R. Drake, 193-210. New England Register, xiv. 197 ; li. 34.

HATCHELL. Burke's Landed Gentry, 5, 6, 7, 8.

HATCHER. Blore's Rutland, 134. The Genealogist, iv. 114.

HATCHETT. Antiquities and Memoirs of the Parish of Myddle, written by Richard Gough, 1700, (folio,) 54.

HATCLIFFE. The Genealogist, iv. 114 ; vi. 256. Hasted's Kent, (Hund. of Blackheath, by H. H. Drake,) xv. 219.

HATFIELD. Surtees Society, xxxvi. 185, 270. Burke's Landed Gentry, (of Newton Kyme,) 2 ; (of Thorp Arch,) 2 supp., 3, 4, 5,

6, 7, 8. Foster's Yorkshire Pedigrees. Burke's Heraldic Illustrations, 113. Poulson's Holderness, i. 442. Hunter's Deanery of Doncaster, i. 178, 291. Eastwood's History of Ecclesfield, 370. Harleian Society, xvi. 157 ; xxxvii. 31 ; xl. 1204. Registers of Ecclesfield, by A. S. Gatty, 80. History of the Wilmor Family, 134.

HATHAWAY, HATHEWEY, or HATHEWY. The Genealogist, New Series, ix. 213 ; x. 91. Shakespere's Home, by J. C. M. Bellew, 38, 376.

HATHERELL. Burke's Family Records, 302.

HATHORNE. Lands and their Owners in Galloway, by P. H. M'Kerlie, i. 402, 492. Burke's Landed Gentry, 7, 8.

HATHORNTHWAITE. The Tyldesley Diary, edited by J. Gillow and A. Hewitson, 103.

HATLEY. Cambridgeshire Visitation, edited by Sir T. Phillipps, 17. Harleian Society, xv. 363 ; xli. 54.

HATSALL. Harleian Society, viii. 460.

HATT. Morant's Essex, i. 223. Harleian Society, xv. 364. Bysshe's Visitation of Essex, edited by J. J. Howard, 45.

HATTON. Burke's Landed Gentry, 2, 3, 4, 5, 6, 7, 8. Harleian Society, viii. 125, 317 ; xviii. 110-120 ; xxviii. 225 ; xliii. 71. Bridge's Northamptonshire, by Rev. Peter Whalley, i. 528. Baker's Northampton, i. 196. Ormerod's Cheshire, i. 744 ; ii. 795. Notes and Queries, 2 S. x. 54, 95. Burke's Extinct Baronetcies. Wotton's English Baronetage, ii. 182. Betham's Baronetage, i. 386. Banks' Dormant and Extinct Baronage, iii. 342. Metcalfe's Visitations of Northamptonshire, 27. Parliamentary Memoirs of Fermanagh, by Earl of Belmore, 35. Howard's Visitation of Ireland, iii. 33. See HALLEN.

HAUBEDENE. The Genealogist, New Series, xvii. 173.

HAUGHTON. Ormerod's Cheshire, ii. 291. Harleian Society, xviii. 121 ; xxviii. 230.

HAUKESLOWE. The Genealogist, New Series, xv. 146.

HAUKIN. The Visitations of Cornwall, by J. L. Vivian, 635.

HAULE. Berry's Kent Genealogies, 311. Harleian Society, xlii. 141. See HALL.

HAULSEY. See HALSEY.

HAUSTED. Collectanea Topographica et Genealogica, viii. 182. Baker's Northampton, i. 177.

HAUT, or HAUTE. Hasted's Kent, iii. 741, 745. Hasted's Kent, (Hund. of Blackheath, by H. H. Drake,) xvii. Harleian Society, xlii. 212.

HAUTEYN. Blomefield's Norfolk, x. 427.

HAUTRIVE. The Genealogist, New Series, ix. 148.

HAVARD. Dwnn's Visitations of Wales, i. 102, 264 ; ii. 43. Glamorganshire Pedigrees, edited by Sir T. Phillipps, 29. Jones' History of the County of Brecknock, ii. 127, 132. Genealogies of Morgan and Glamorgan, by G. T. Clark, 405. Cambrian Journal, Vol. for 1864, 109. The Genealogist, New Series, xiv. 142.

HAVERBURGH. Morant's Essex, i. 275.

HAVERING. Collectanea Topographica et Genealogica, viii. 79.
HAVERS. Blomefield's Norfolk, i. 100, 151. Burke's Commoners,
i. 381 ; Landed Gentry, 2, 3, 4, 5, 6. Wilson's History of the
Parish of St. Laurence Poultney, 226. Harleian Society, xv. 365 ;
xxxii. 148.
HAVERSHAM. Lipscombe's History of Buckinghamshire, iv. 187,
188.
HAVILAND, HAVILLAND, or HAVELLAND. A Chronicle of the Ancient
and Noble Norman Family of De Havilland, etc. ; including the
English branches of Havelland of Dorsetshire, Haviland of Hawkes-
bury, and Haviland of Somersetshire. Compiled by Lieut.-Col.
Thomas Fiott de Havilland. Guernsey, 1852, 4to. A Chronicle
of the Ancient and Noble Family of De Havilland. Folio. [By
John Von S. De Havilland, York Herald. No place or date, pp.
122.] Burke's Landed Gentry, 2 supp., 3, 4, 5, 6, 7, 8. Hutchins'
Dorset, i. 640. Harleian Society, xxi. 78. See DE HAVILLAND.
HAVILAND-BURKE. Burke's Landed Gentry, 5.
HAVILE. Blomefield's Norfolk, vii. 139.
HAW. Visitation of Staffordshire, 1663-4, printed by Sir T. Phillipps,
6. Collections for a History of Staffordshire, William Salt Society,
ii. part 2, 42. Visitations of Staffordshire, 1614 and 1663-4,
William Salt Society, 171.
HAWARD. Visitation of Kent, (reprinted from Archæologia Cantiana,
vol. vi.,) 107. Surrey Archæological Collections, xi. Harleian
Society, xlii. 24.
HAWARDEN. Claim of Visct. Hawarden to vote at Elections of Irish
Peers, Sess. Papers, C of 1857, Sess 1. Chetham Society, lxxxi.
87 ; lxxxii. 88 ; lxxxv. 132.
HAWBERK. Nichols' History of the County of Leicester, ii. 344.
HAWDON. Burke's Colonial Gentry, i. 373.
.HAWDONBY. Surtees Society, xli. 74. See HALDENBY.
HAWE. Harleian Society, xxxii. 148. Willmore's History of Walsall,
288.
HAWEIS. Polwhele's History of Cornwall, iv. 112. A Complete
Parochial History of the County of Cornwall, iv. 101. An His-
torical Survey of Cornwall, by C. S. Gilbert, ii. 142. Parish
Registers of Redruth, by T. C. Peter, 108. The Visitations of
Cornwall, by J. L. Vivian, 583.
HAWES. Harleian Society, i. 7 ; xii. 405 ; xv. 366, 368 ; xliii. 181.
Metcalfe's Visitations of Northamptonshire, 99. Surrey Archæo-
logical Collections, xi. Oliver's History of Antigua, ii. 69.
HAWFORD. Cambridgeshire Visitation, edited by Sir T. Phillipps, 17.
Harleian Society, xli. 94.
HAWICK. Foster's Visitations of Yorkshire, 130. See HAWYK.
HAWKE. Harleian Society, ix. 92 ; xxxix. 879. Edmondson's
Baronagium Genealogicum, vi. 65. Brydges' Collins' Peerage,
vii. 458. The Visitations of Cornwall, edited by J. L. Vivian, 213.
HAWKER. Burke's Commoners, iii. 50 ; Landed Gentry, 2, 6, 7, 8.
Burke's Heraldic Register, (published with St. James's Magazine,)
85. Burke's Visitation of Seats and Arms, 2nd Series, i. 4.

Visitatio Comitatus Wiltoniæ, 1623, printed by Sir T. Phillipps.
Visitation of Wiltshire, edited by G. W. Marshall, 58. Burke's
Colonial Gentry, ii. 776.
HAWKES. Burke's Heraldic Illustrations, 136. Visitation of Stafford-
shire, (Wilm. Salt Soc.) 97. Burke's Colonial Gentry, ii. 461.
Harleian Society, xxxix. 1118.
HAWKESTON. Harleian Society, xviii. 92.
HAWKESWELL. Jewitt's Reliquary, xviii. 72.
HAWKESWORTH, HAUXWORTH, or HAWKSWORTH. Burke's Extinct
Baronetcies. Visitation of Middlesex, (Salisbury, 1820, fol.) 13.
Surtees Society, xxxvi. 244. Burke's Landed Gentry, 3, 4, 5, 6,
and page 549. Foster's Yorkshire Pedigrees. Foster's Visita-
tions of Yorkshire, 299. Thoresby's Ducatus Leodiensis, 170.
Harleian Society, xvi. 159 ; xxi. 19 ; xxxix. 971. Ilkley, Ancient
and Modern, by R. Collyer and J. H. Turner, 218. Foster's
Visitation of Middlesex, 27. History of Woodhouse, by W. J.
Le Tall, 18. The Genealogist, New Series, xiii. 161.
HAWKINS. The Hawkins Family, by M. W. S. Hawkins. London,
1890, 4to. Hasted's Kent, iii. 4. Berry's Berkshire Genealogies,
59. Berry's Kent Genealogies, 266. Burke's Commoners, ii. 215 ;
Landed Gentry, (of Tredunnoc,) 2, 3, 4, 5 ; (of Bignor Park,) 2 ;
(of Middlesex,) 2 supp., 3, 4 ; (of Alresford Hall,) 3, 4 ; (of Tre-
withen,) 7, 8. Account of the Company of Ironmongers, by John
Nicholl, 2nd edn., 553. Miscellanea Genealogica et Heraldica,
New Series, ii. 526 ; iii. 43, 111. Foley's Records of the English
Province S. J., iii. 491 ; iv. 700. The Hawkins' Voyages, edited
by C. R. Markham, 50. A Complete Parochial History of the
County of Cornwall, i. 262 ; iv. 103. An Historical Survey of
Cornwall, by C. S. Gilbert, i. 575. Betham's Baronetage, iv. 46,
225. Notes and Queries, 4 S. v. 347, 430. Burke's Extinct
Baronetcies. Hasted's Kent, (Hund. of Blackheath, by H. H.
Drake,) xxii., xxiii. Bysshe's Visitation of Essex, edited by J. J.
Howard, 45. Weaver's Visitation of Herefordshire, 40. Harleian
Society, xxviii. 170 ; xlii. 203.
HAWKS. See LONGRIDGE.
HAWKSLEY. Harleian Society, xxxviii. 696, 702.
HAWKWOOD. Morant's Essex, ii. 288. Memoirs of the Family of
Chester, by R. E. C. Waters, 300.
HAWLES. Harleian Society, viii. 450 ; xx. 53. Hutchins' Dorset,
iii. 389. The Genealogist, New Series, iii. 89.
HAWLEY. Berry's Sussex Genealogies, 272. Berry's Hampshire
Genealogies, 340. Burke's Landed Gentry, 2, 3, 4, 5, 6. Maclean's
History of Trigg Minor, i. 394*. Baker's Northampton, ii. 276.
The Genealogist, i. 161. Harleian Society, xv. 370 ; xl. 1188.
Betham's Baronetage, iv. 297. Burke's Extinct Baronetcies.
Weaver's Visitations of Somerset, 113. Healey's History of Part
of West Somerset, 111.
HAWORTH. Miscellanea Genealogica et Heraldica, New Series, i. 58.
Whitaker's History of Whalley, ii. 404. Jewitt's Reliquary, xviii.
29. Abram's History of Blackburn, 396, 470, 479. Weaver's

Visitation of Herefordshire, 41. Croston's edn. of Baines' Lancaster, iii. 64.

HAWORTH-BOOTH. Burke's Landed Gentry, 5, 6, 7, 8. Foster's Yorkshire Pedigrees. Howard's Visitation of England and Wales, viii. 129.

HAWTAYNE. Harleian Society, v. 137, 295.

HAWTHORNE. Berry's Berkshire Genealogies, 41.

HAWTREY. Croke's History of the Family of Croke, No. 25. Berry's Buckinghamshire Genealogies, 38. Visitations of Oxfordshire, 1634, printed by Sir T. Phillipps, (Middle Hill, fol.) 21. Harleian Society, v. 269. Herald and Genealogist, i. 338. Lipscombe's History of the County of Buckingham, iii. 212. Notes and Queries, 1 S. iii. 459. The Genealogist, vii. 179.

HAWTTON. Sir T. Phillipps' Topographer, No. 1 (March, 1821, 8vo.) 27. Visitation of Oxfordshire, 1574, printed by Sir T. Phillipps, (Middle Hill, fol.) 5. Harleian Society, xv. 369.

HAWYK. Surtees' Durham, i. 36. *See* HAWICK.

HAY. Origo gentis Hayorum. By James Ross. Edinburgh, 1700, 8vo. Hay of Smithfield and Haystoun, 1712-1880. By Louisa Lilias Forbes. Edinburgh, 1880. Folding sheet. Genealogy of the Family of Hay of Leys, by Alexr. Deuchar, folding sheet. Historical Account of the Family of Hay of Leys. Edinburgh, 1832, folio. Berry's Sussex Genealogies, 118, 311. Burke's Commoners, iii. 434; (of Pitfour,) Commoners, i. 507, Landed Gentry, 2 ; (of Leys,) Commoners, i. 504, Landed Gentry, 2, 3, 4 ; (of Scggieden,) i. 509, Landed Gentry, 2, 3, 4, 5, 6, 7, 8 ; (of Hopes,) Landed Gentry, 2, 3, 4, 5 ; (of Duns Castle,) 3, 4, 5, 6, 7, 8. Burke's Visitation of Seats and Arms, ii. 10. Horsfield's History of Lewes, ii. 122, 134. Sussex Archæological Collections, xx. 65. Lands and their Owners in Galloway, by P. H. M'Kerlie, i. 189, 289. Nisbet's Heraldry, ii. app. 140. Douglas's Baronage of Scotland, 481, 587. Balmerino and its Abbey, by James Campbell, 251, 268, 383, 386. Chambers' History of Peebleshire, 333. Wood's Douglas's Peerage of Scotland, i. 544 ; ii. 44, 602. Edmondson's Baronagium Genealogicum, v. 407. Harleian Society, xvi. 365. J. B. Pratt's Buchan, 313. Topographical Collections, 1792, 4to., (Glynde.) Brydges' Collins' Peerage, vii. 197. Betham's Baronetage, iv. 390. Burke's Extinct Baronetcies, 625. Northern Notes and Queries, i. 40, 57, 77. Burke's Colonial Gentry, i. 77. Alexander Nisbet's Heraldic Plates, 70. *See* BRISBANE, HAYE.

HAY-DRUMMOND. Hunter's Deanery of Doncaster, i. 316.

HAY-GORDON. Burke's Landed Gentry, 5, 6, 7, 8.

HAY-MACDOUGAL. Burke's Commoners, iii. 430.

HAY-NEWTON. Burke's Commoners, iii. 26 ; Landed Gentry, 2.

HAYDOCK, or HAYDOK. The Haydock Papers, by Joseph Gillow. London, 1888, 4to. Berry's Hampshire Genealogies, 216. Harleian Society, v. 219. Whitaker's History of Whalley, ii. 176. Chetham Society, lxxxii. 108. The Tyldesley Diary, edited by J. Gillow and A. Hewitson, 164.

HAYDON. Harleian Society, i. 78; vi. 142; xxii. 11; xxvii. 75

Westcote's Devonshire, edited by G. Oliver and P. Jones, 579.
Visitation of Devon, edited by F. T. Colby, 126. Notes and
Queries, 4 S. vii. 143 ; viii. 149; x. 370; xi. 111. Visitations of
Devon, by J. L. Vivian, 458, 460.

HAYE. Genealogy of the Hayes of Tweeddale, by Father Hay,
edited by James Maidment, Esq. 1835, 4to. Chetham Society,
lxxxv. 133. *See* HAY.

HAYES. J. R. Bloxham's Register of the Presidents, Fellows, etc.,
of Magd. Coll., Oxon, ii. 221. History of the Hundred of Bray,
by Charles Kerry, 48. Nichols' History of the County of Leicester,
ii. 271. Harleian Society, xv. 370; xviii. 121 ; xxii. 64. Monken
Hadley, by F. C. Cass, 66. Betham's Baronetage, iv. 372. Account of the Mayo and Elton Families, by C. H. Mayo, 135.
Phillimore's London and Middlesex Note Book, 258. New
England Register, vi. 333; xxvii. 79; xxxvi. 387. *See* BOSANQUET.

HAYHURST. Burke's Landed Gentry, 6. Ormerod's Cheshire, iii.
257. History of Ribchester, by T. C. Smith and G. Shortt, 233.
See FRANCE-HAYHURST.

HAYLEY. Gentleman's Magazine, 1827, i. 204. The Worthies of
Sussex, by M. A. Lower, 154. Notes and Queries, 6 S. v.
119.

HAYMAN. Burke's Landed Gentry, (of Myrtle Grove,) 2 and supp.,
3, 4, 5, 6, 7. Jewitt's Reliquary, xxi. 113, 140.

HAYMES. Fletcher's Leicestershire Pedigrees and Royal Descents, 28.
Burke's Landed Gentry, 8. *See* HAMES.

HAYNE. Hutchin's Dorset, ii. 376. Harleian Society, xx. 54 ; xxxix.
1015. The Genealogist, v. 269. *See* SEALE-HAYNE.

HAYNES. Morant's Essex, ii. 195, 327. Burke's Landed Gentry,
2 supp., 3, 4, 5, 6, 7, 8. Harleian Society, xv. 371. Bysshe's
Visitation of Essex, edited by J. J. Howard, 46. New England
Register, ix. 349; xxxii. 310; xlvii. 71 ; xlix. 304.

HAYRUN. Dugdale's Warwickshire, 30.

HAYTER. Burke's Landed Gentry, 5 supp., page 37 ; 8. Hutchins'
Dorset, i. 587. Burke's Colonial Gentry, i. 335.

HAYWARD. Botfield's Stemmata Botevilliana, 145. Berry's Berk-
shire Genealogies, 37. Visitation of Somerset, printed by Sir T.
Phillipps, 91. Burke's Commoners, iv. 246 ; Landed Gentry, 2, 3,
4, 5, 6, 7, 8. Herald and Genealogist, vi. 373. Harleian Society,
xi. 48; xxxviii. 484; xliii. 152. Burke's Royal Descents and
Pedigrees of Founders' Kin, 44. Antiquities and Memoirs of the
Parish of Myddle, by Richard Gough, 1700, (folio,) 60, 76.
Earwaker's Local Gleanings, ii. 520. Fosbrooke's History of
Gloucestershire, i. 245, 251. Blunt's Dursley and its Neighbourhood, 162. The Sheriffs of Montgomeryshire, by W. V. Lloyd,
501. Visitation of Gloucester, by T. F. Fenwick and W. C. Metcalfe, 49. Weaver's Visitation of Herefordshire, 42. The Genealogist, New Series, xvii. 207.

HAYWOOD. Burke's Landed Gentry, 6, 7, 8.

HAYWORTH. Foster's Lancashire Pedigrees. Earwaker's Local
Gleanings, ii. 554.

HAZELL. Pedigree of Hazell of Ford, Co. Glouc., [T. P.] 1864.

HAZEN. New England Register, xxxiii. 229.

HAZLERIGG. Fletcher's Leicestershire Pedigrees and Royal Descents, 8.

HEAD. Pedigree of Rev. Geo. Head, of Aston Somerville, Co. Glouc., [T. P.] 1854, folio page. Burke's Landed Gentry, (of Modreeny House,) 3, 4, 5, 6, 7, 8 ; (of Seaton,) 5, 6, 7. Wotton's English Baronetage, iii. 597. Betham's Baronetage, ii. 444. Archæologia Cantiana, xiv. 116.

HEADLAM. The Antiquities of Gainford, by J. R. Walbran, 56. Surtees Society, xxxvi. 204. Burke's Colonial Gentry, i. 252.

HEADLEY. Claim of Charles, Baron Headley, to Vote at Elections of Irish Peers, Sess. Papers, I of 1857, Sess. 2.

HEADON. The Genealogist, iv. 115.

HEALD. Harleian Society, xxxvii. 130 ; xxxviii. 642.

HEALE. Harleian Society, xxviii. 231.

HEALEY. English Church Furniture, by Edward Peacock, 228, 229. Fishwick's History of Rochdale, 501.

HEANE. Miscelleanea Genealogica et Heraldica, 2nd Series, ii. 209. Gloucestershire Notes and Queries, iii. 232.

HEAPE. Fishwick's History of Rochdale, 326.

HEARD. Burke's Landed Gentry, 3, 4, 5, 6, 7, 8. Miscellanea Genealogica et Heraldica, 2nd Series, iv. 210. New England Register, v. 179, 187 ; vii. 47.

HEARLE. Weaver's Visitations of Somerset, 29-31.

HEARNE. Genealogies of Morgan and Glamorgan, by G. T. Clark, 490. Burke's Colonial Gentry, i. 106. Gyll's History of Wraysbury, 233.

HEARST. Visitation of Wiltshire, 1677, printed by Sir T. Phillipps, (Middle Hill, 1854, fol.).

HEATH. Heathiana, Notes Genealogical and Biographical of the Family of Heath, by Sir W. R. Drake. London, 1881, 4to. Morant's Essex, ii. 579. Harleian Society, i. 37 ; v. 208 ; viii. 18, 182, 408 ; xlii. 163. Berry's Sussex Genealogies, 256. Visitation of Durham, 1615, (Sunderland, 1820, fol.) 7. Hutchinson's History of Durham, ii. 302. Dugdale's Warwickshire, *Index.* Surtees' Durham, i. 38; iv. 70*. Manning and Bray's Surrey, i. 498 ; ii. 395 ; iii. 47. Foster's Pedigree of the Forsters and Fosters, Part ii. 6. Burke's Colonial Gentry, ii. 435. Foster's Visitations of Durham, 157. The History of Brasted, by J. Cave-Browne, 56. Devonshire Notes and Notelets, by Sir W. R. Drake, 133-170. Burke's Landed Gentry, 7, 8.

HEATHCOTE. Account of some of the Families of Heathcote. By E. D. Heathcote. Winchester, 1899, 4to. Glover's History of Derbyshire, ii. 393, (293, 360). Berry's Hampshire Genealogies, 83. Notes and Queries, 2 S. i. 238. Burke's Landed Gentry, (of Connington Castle,) 2 supp., 4, 5, 6, 7, 8 ; (of Apedale Hall,) 5, 6, 7, 8. *See* HACKER in Landed Gentry. Harleian Society, viii. 481 ; xxxvii. 324; xxxviii. 471-477. Jewitt's Reliquary, xvi. 141 ; xviii. 32 ; xxii. 156. The Borough of Stoke-upon-

Trent, by John Ward, 563. Nichols' History of the County of
Leicester, iii. 428. The Citizens of London and their Rulers, by
B. B. Orridge, 191. Wotton's English Baronetage, iv. 240.
Betham's Baronetage, iii. 220. The Gresley's of Drakelowe, by
F. Madan, 263. Howard's Visitation of England and Wales,
viii. 1.

HEATLIE. Burke's Colonial Gentry, i. 278.

HEATON. Burke's Landed Gentry, 2, 3, 4, 5, 6, 7, 8. Foster's
Yorkshire Pedigrees. Foster's Visitations of Yorkshire, 238.
Records of Denbigh and its Lordship, by John Williams, 190.
Chetham Society, cx. 195. History of Powys Fadog, by
J. Y. W. Lloyd, vi. 241. Historical Notices of Doncaster, by
C. W. Hatfield, 3rd Series, 345. See HEITON, HETON, HEYTON.

HEBB. Harleian Society, xv. 372.

HEBBES. The Genealogist, New Series, iii. 90. Harleian Society,
xliii. 87.

HEBBORNE. Visitation of Durham, 1575, (Newcastle, 1820, fol.) 24.
Pedigrees from Visitation of Northumberland, printed by Sir T.
Phillipps, (Middle Hill, 1858, fol.) 3. Foster's Visitations of
Yorkshire, 528, 621. Hutchinson's History of Durham, iii. 67.
Surtees' Durham, iii. 35. The Genealogist, i. 303. Foster's
Visitations of Northumberland, 66. Foster's Visitations of
Durham, 159.

HEBDEN. Burke's Landed Gentry, 2, 8.

HEBDON. Harleian Society, viii. 169.

HEBER. Surtees Society, xxxvi. 34, 54. Burke's Commoners, iv.
132; Landed Gentry, 2, 3, 4, 5, 6, 7, 8. Foster's Yorkshire
Pedigrees. Foster's Visitations of Yorkshire, 529. Whitaker's
Deanery of Craven, 68, (93.) Baker's Northampton, i. 720.
Keating's History of Ireland, Plate 1. Ilkley, Ancient and
Modern, by R. Collyer and J. H. Turner, 140, 149. The Genea-
logist, New Series, xv. 89.

HEBERDEN. Burke's Family Records, 302. Howard's Visitation of
England and Wales, ix. 57.

HEBERT. The New England Register, li. 316.

HEBLETHWAYTE, or HEBBLETHWAYTE. Harleian Society, viii. 68.
Surtees Society, xxxvi. 205. Miscellanea Genealogica et Heral-
dica, New Series, i. 418. Foster's Visitations of Yorkshire, 240.
The Genealogist, New Series, xiv. 48.

HECHINS. The Visitations of Cornwall, edited by J. L. Vivian,
214.

HECTOR. Botfield's Stemmata Botevilliana, 155.

HEDDING. Burke's Visitation of Seats and Arms, ii. 61.

HEDDLE. Burke's Landed Gentry, 3, 4, 5, 6, 7, 8.

HEDE. Visitation of Devon, edited by F. T. Colby, 122.

HEDGES. Gentleman's Magazine, 1836, i. 376. Harleian Society,
viii. 415. F. G. Lee's History of Thame, 651. The Genealogist,
New Series, xvii. 209, 210.

HEDLAM. Archæologia Æliana, 2nd Series, iii. 87. Surtees' Durham,
iv. 99.

HEDLEY. Cyclostyle Pedigrees, by J. J. Green. Harleian Society, xxviii. 232. Annals of Smith of Balby, by H. E. Smith, 166.

HEDON. Foster's Visitations of Yorkshire, 151. Poulson's Holderness, ii. 259.

HEDWORTH. Surtees Society, xli. 38. Visitation of Durham, 1575, (Newcastle, 1820, fol.) 42. Hutchinson's History of Durham, iii. xxi. Surtees' Durham, ii. 151, 184, 197, 261. Harleian Society, xvi. 159 ; xliii. 65. Foster's Visitations of Durham, 161.

HEFFERNAN. O'Hart's Irish Pedigrees, 2nd Series, 60.

HEIDE. Dwnn's Visitations of Wales, i. 113.

HEIGHAM. Visitation of Suffolk, edited by J. J. Howard, ii. 210-324. Burke's Landed Gentry, 2 supp., 3, 4, 5, 6, 7, 8. Gage's History of Thingoe Hundred, Suffolk, 9. Page's History of Suffolk, 632.

HEIGHINGTON. Visitation of Durham, 1615, (Sunderland, 1820, fol.) 95. Surtees' Durham, i. 99 ; iii. 275. Foster's Visitations of Durham, 163. Burke's Landed Gentry, 8.

HEITON. Chetham Society, lxxxi. 129. See HEATON.

HELBECK. Notes and Queries, 7 S., vi. 281. Nicolson and Burn's Westmorland and Cumberland, i. 580.

HELDER. Clutterbuck's Hertford, iii. 107.

HELDT. Harleian Society, xv. 372.

HELE. Tuckett's Devonshire Pedigrees, 187-191. Harleian Society, vi. 145-149 ; ix. 92. Westcote's Devonshire, edited by G. Oliver and P. Jones, 533-535. Manning and Bray's Surrey, i. 306. Burke's Commoners, iv. 434. Visitation of Devon, edited by F. T. Colby, 127. Burke's Extinct Baronetcies. The Visitations of Cornwall, edited by J. L. Vivian, 215. Hasted's Kent, (Hund. of Blackheath, by H. H. Drake,) 21. The Visitations of Devon, by J. L. Vivian, 461.

HELEY. Croston's edn. of Baines's Lancaster, iii. 83.

HELGOT. Eyton's Antiquities of Shropshire, iii. 183 ; iv. 56.

HELLARD. Surtees Society, xxxvi. 118. Foster's Visitations of Yorkshire, 531. See HIGHLORD.

HELLEGAN, or HELIGAN. Maclean's History of Trigg Minor, i. 317 ; ii. 512, 518. Harleian Society, ix. 276. The Visitations of Cornwall, edited by J. L. Vivian, 30.

HELLELEY. See HOYLAND.

HELLESBY, or HELSBY. Miscellanea Genealogica et Heraldica, ii. 55. Jewitt's Reliquary, ix. 231. Ormerod's Cheshire, ii. 123. Harleian Society, xviii. 111.

HELLIER. Berry's Hampshire Genealogies, 77.

HELMAN. The Visitations of Devon, by J. L. Vivian, 468.

HELMBRIDGE, Weaver's Visitations of Somerset, 113.

HELME. Fishwick's History of Goosnargh, 185. History of Chipping, by Tom C. Smith, 265.

HELSHAM. Burke's Landed Gentry, 5 supp., 6, 7, 8.

HELTON. History of Darlington, by W. Hylton Dyer Longstaffe, not paged, and xxxiii-lvi. Hutchins' Dorset, iv. 354. See HYLTON, HILTON.

HELY. Claim of the Rt. Hon. Richard John Hely-Hutchinson, Earl of Donoughmore, of Ireland, to vote at Elections of Irish Peers, Sess. Papers, 195 of 1852-3; 178 of 1854. Burke's Landed Gentry, 6, 7, 8. Archdall's Lodge's Peerage, vii. 235.

HELYAR. Burke's Commoners, (of Coker Court,) i. 281 ; Landed Gentry, 2, 3, 4, 5, 6, 7, 8; (of Poundisford Lodge,) 2, 3, 4.

HELYER. Burke's Royal Families, (London, 1851, 8vo.) i. 104.

HEMENHALE. Blomefield's Norfolk, v. 185.

HEMINGWAY. Bradford Antiquary, i. 252.

HEMMING, or HEMYNGE. Burke's Landed Gentry, 6, 7, 8. Harleian Society, xv. 373. Notes and Queries, 3 S. v. 268, 426, 489. Metcalfe's Visitation of Worcester, 1683, 55.

HEMPHILL. Burke's Landed Gentry, 4, 5, 6, 7, 8.

HEMSWORTH. Burke's Landed Gentry, (of Abbeville,) 4, 5, 6, 7 ; (of Shropham Hall,) 2, 3, 4, 5, 6, 7, 8 ; (of Monk Fryston,) 6, 7, 8. Foster's Visitations of Yorkshire, 529.

HENCHMAN. Hutchins' Dorset, ii. 831. Harleian Society, xv. 374. Notes and Queries, 3 S. iii. 256, 316.

HENDE. Morant's Essex, i. 491 ; ii. 155. Harleian Society, xiii. 34.

HENDEN. Berry's Kent Genealogies, 436. Harleian Society, xv. 375.

HENDER. Harleian Society, ix. 93. The Visitations of Cornwall, edited by J. L. Vivian, 217.

HENDERSON. Burke's Landed Gentry, (of Stemster,) 3, 4, 5, 6, 7 ; (of Westerton,) 2 add., 3, 4 ; (of Sedgwick Park,) 8. Douglas's Baronage of Scotland, 518. Caithness Family History, by John Henderson, 283. Burke's Family Records, 306. Ontarian Families, by E. M. Chadwick, ii. 134. See MERCER-HENDERSON.

HENDLEY. Berry's Kent Genealogies, 174. Chetham Society, lxxxi. 125. Surrey Archæological Collections, vii. Monken Hadley, by F. C. Cass, 198. Burke's Extinct Baronetcies. Harleian Society, xlii. 95 ; xliii. 139. Sussex Archæological Collections, xlii. 36.

HENDOUR. Collections by the Powys-land Club, vii. 389.

HENDRICK. The Wolfe's of Forenaghts, 43.

HENDURE. Weaver's Visitations of Somerset, 84.

HENE. The Genealogist, v. 270. Burke's Extinct Baronetcies.

HENEAGE, or HENNEGE. History of Merchant Taylors' School, by Rev. H. B. Wilson, 1173. Burke's Commoners, iv. 103 ; Landed Gentry, 2, 3, 4, 5, 6, 7, 8. Harleian Society, viii. 184 ; xl. 1299. The Register, (London, 1869, 8vo.) ii. 9. Herald and Genealogist, iii. 419. The Genealogist, vi. 257. East Barnet, by F. C. Cass, 140. See WALKER-HENEAGE.

HENGESCOTT. Visitation of Devon, edited by F. T. Colby, 128. See HENSCOT.

HENHAM. Genealogical Memoranda relating to the Family of King, by W. L. King, 10. See KING.

HENLEY. Burke's Extinct Baronetcies. Hasted's Kent, ii. 492. Visitation of Somerset, printed by Sir T. Phillipps, 93. Burke's Landed Gentry, (of Waterpery,) 2, 3, 4, 5, 6, 7, 8 ; (of Leigh

House,) 2 add. Harleian Society, viii. 171 ; xi. 48 ; xv. 375. Hutchins' Dorset, iii. 742. Topographical Miscellanies, 1792, 4to., (The Grange). Edmondson's Baronagium Genealogicum, iii. 305. Banks' Dormant and Extinct Baronage, iii. 563. The Visitation of Gloucester, edited by T. F. Fenwick and W. C. Metcalfe, 90.

HENN. Burke's Landed Gentry, 3, 4, 5, 6, 7, 8.

HENN-GENNYS. Burke's Landed Gentry, 3, 4, 5, 6.

HENNAH. Maclean's History of Trigg Minor, i. 321. A Complete Parochial History of the County of Cornwall, iv. 119 supp.

HENNESSY. Burke's Landed Gentry, 2.

HENNEZEL. Northern Notes and Queries, vii. 146.

HENNIKER. Morant's Essex, i. 17. Hasted's Kent, iii. 31. See MAJOR.

HENNIKER-MAJOR. Page's History of Suffolk, 439.

HENNING. Genealogical Tree showing the Presumed Descent of the Family of Henning of Poxwell House, by T. P. Henning. Westminster, 1869, Broadside. Genealogical Tree showing Descent of Earl Beauchamp and Families of Biddulph and Henning, by T. P. Henning. Westminster, 1869, Broadside. Burke's Family Records, 306. Hutchins' Dorset, i. 408. Harleian Society, xx. 54.

HENRIX. Harleian Society, xv. 376.

HENRY. The Descendants of Philip Henry, M.A., Incumbent of Worthenbury, Co. Flint, by Sarah Lawrence. London, 1844, 8vo. Burke's Landed Gentry, (of Lodge Park,) 5 supp. 6, 7, 8 ; (of East Dene,) 7, 8. O'Hart's Irish Pedigrees, 2nd Series, 196. Harleian Society, xxxvii. 358.

HENSCOT. Westcote's Devonshire, edited by G. Oliver and P. Jones, 589. The Visitations of Devon, by J. L. Vivian, 584. See HENGESCOTT.

HENSHAW. Miscellanea Genealogica et Heraldica, i. 182. Collections for a Genealogical Account of the Family of Comberbach, 56. Berry's Sussex Genealogies, 53. Burke's Landed Gentry, 2 supp. Burke's Heraldic Illustrations, 134. Dallaway's Sussex, II. i. 345. Castles, Mansions, and Manors of Western Sussex, by D. G. C. Elwes and C. J. Robinson, 35. Harleian Society, xiii. 417 ; xviii. 122. Ormerod's Cheshire, iii. 733. Earwaker's East Cheshire, ii. 399. Notes and Queries, 6 S., ix. 349, 368, 376, 436, 511; x. 39, 78, 155. New England Register, xvii. 334 ; xxii. 105.

HENSLEY, or HENSLIE. The Visitations of Devon, by J. L. Vivian, 390. Visitation of Sussex, 1570, printed by Sir T. Phillipps, (Middle Hill, fol.) 6. Harleian Society, vi. 123. Nichols' History of the County of Leicester, iv. 272.

HENTY. Burke's Colonial Gentry, i. 1.

HENVILLE. Hutchins' Dorset, ii. 727.

HENZEY. Collections for a Genealogy of Henzy, Tyttery, and Tyzack, by H. S. Grazebrook. Stourbridge, 1877, 8vo. Gentleman's Magazine, 1856, ii. 728. Herald and Genealogist, i. 421. Burke's Visitation of Seats and Arms, 2nd Series, i. 7.

HEPBURN. Memoirs and Adventures of Sir J. Hepburn, by James Grant. Edinburgh, 1857, 8vo. Burke's Royal Families, (London, 1851, 8vo.) ii. 84. Burke's Landed Gentry, 2, 6 supp., 7, 8. Wood's Douglas's Peerage of Scotland, i. 222. The Genealogical Magazine, i. 412.

HEPDEN. Berry's Sussex Genealogies, 303.

HEPENSTAL. Burke's Landed Gentry, 4, 5. *See* DOPPING-HE-PENSTAL.

HEPWORTH. Burke's Landed Gentry, 2, 3, 4, 8. Burke's Family Records, 313. The Genealogist, New Series, xvi. 87.

HERBERT. Pedigrees of Herbert of Ragland, [T. P.] 1861, 3 pedigrees. Yorkshire Archæological and Topographical Journal, i. 214. The Great Governing Families of England, ii. 155. Jacob's Peerage, i. 476. Herald and Genealogist, i. 30. Banks' History of the Family of Marmyun, 28. Gentleman's Magazine, 1849, ii. 583. Hasted's Kent, ii. 622, 663. History of Monmouthshire, by D. Williams, App. 128, 156. Historical Tour in Monmouthshire, by Wm. Coxe, 131. Dwnn's Visitations of Wales, i. 30, 137, 196, 292, 295, 312 ; ii. 37, 45, 54, 58. Camden Society, xliii. 17. Glamorganshire Pedigrees, edited by Sir T. Phillipps, 15, 42. Surtees Society, xxxvi. 148, 165. Berry's Sussex Genealogies, 336. Berry's Hampshire Genealogies, 209. Burke's Commoners, (of Llanarth,) iv. 727, Landed Gentry, 2, 3, 4, 5, 6, 7, 8 ; (of Muckross,) Landed Gentry, 2, 3, 4, 5, 6, 7, 8 ; (of Cahirnane,) 3, 4, 5, 6, 7, 8 ; (of Pill House,) 3, 4, 5 ; (of Glan Hafren,) 8 ; (of Upper Helmsley,) 5 supp., 6, 7. Miscellanea Genealogica et Heraldica, ii. 325. Foster's Visitations of Yorkshire, 530. Harleian Society, viii. 340 ; xv. 376. Lipscombe's History of the County of Buckingham, i. 297. Burke's Royal Families, (London, 1851, 8vo.) ii. 103. Jones' History of the County of Brecknock, ii. 451-458. Caermarthenshire Pedigrees, 39. Cardiganshire Pedigrees, 85, 86. Hoare's Wiltshire, II. i. 139. Baker's Northampton, i. 184. Meyrick's History of the Co. of Cardigan, 351. Cambrian Journal, 1st Series, iv. 114-137, 162-177. Archæologia Cambrensis, 3 S. vi. 272. T. Nicholas' County Families of Wales, 777. Works of Geo. Herbert, (Fuller Worthies Library,) i. xxvi. The Sheriffs of Montgomeryshire, by W. V. Lloyd, 35, 89, 118, 184, 299, 321. Charles Smith's History of Kerry, 34. Collections by the Powys-land Club, v. 153, 353 ; vi. 197, 409 ; vii. 125 ; viii. 1 ; ix. 381. Edmondson's Baronagium Genealogicum, ii. 96 ; iii. 263 ; vi. 95. Historical Notices of Sir M. Cradock, Kt., by J. M. Traherne, 4. A letter from the Countess of Nithsdale, by Sheffield Grace, (London, 1827, 8vo.) 36. Notes and Queries, 2 S. ii. 168. Annals of Chepstow Castle, by J. F. Marsh, 270. Brydges' Collins' Peerage, iii. 104 ; v. 390. Banks' Dormant and Extinct Baronage, ii. 271 ; iii. 347, 610. Burke's Extinct Baronetage, and 608. F. G. Lee's History of Thame, 570. Genealogies of Morgan and Glamorgan, by G. T. Clark, 250-309. Howard's Visitation of England and Wales, iii. 121, 125. Cambrian Journal, iv. 114, 161. Oliver's

History of Antigua, ii. 70. The Genealogist, New Series, xiv. 118.

HERCY, or HERCYE. Surtees Society, xli. 7. Visitation of Oxfordshire, 1634, printed by Sir T. Phillipps, (Middle Hill, fol.) 21. Burke's Commoners, iv. 679 ; Landed Gentry, 2, 3, 4, 5, 6, 7, 8 supp. Foster's Visitations of Yorkshire, 41. Harleian Society, iv. 14 ; v. 298 ; xvi. 160. Blore's Rutland, 130. Thoroton's Nottinghamshire, iii. 262. The Genealogist, v. 270.

HERDE. The Genealogist, New Series, xvii. 276.

HERDEDERGH. Dugdale's Warwickshire, 73, 92.

HERDMAN. Burke's Landed Gentry, 8.

HERDWICK. Nichols' History of the County of Leicester, iv. 643. Dugdale's Warwickshire, 322. See HARDWICK.

HEREFORD. Rudder's Gloucestershire, 692. Morant's Essex, ii. 562. Burke's Commoners, iii. 343 ; Landed Gentry, 2, 3, 4, 5, 6, 7, 8. Burke's Royal Families, (London, 1851, 8vo.) i. 197. Visitation of Devon, edited by F. T. Colby, 128. Banks' Dormant and Extinct Baronage, iii. 351. Duncombe's Hereford, (J. H. Cooke) iii. 85. Harleian Society, xxvii. 76.

HEREFORD (Earl of). Nichols' History of the County of Leicester, i. App. 33.

HEREMON. Keating's History of Ireland, *Plate* 14.

HERENDEN. Harleian Society, iii. 30 ; xv. 377.

HEREWARD. Harleian Society, xii. 98 ; xxvii. 77 ; xliii. 35.

HERGEST. Dwnn's Visitations of Wales, i. 193.

HERINGE. Harleian Society, xxviii. 232.

HERIOT. The Case and Genealogy of Miss Elizth. Heriot. Edinburgh, 1841, fol. Memoirs of George Heriot, (Edinburgh, 1822, 8vo.) 3. History of Heriot's Hospital, by F. W. Bedford, 3rd edn., 1.

HERIZ. Morant's Essex, i. 119. Blore's History of South Winfield, in Nicholas' Miscellaneous Antiquities, No. 3, 36. Thoroton's Nottinghamshire, ii. 191 ; iii. 50. Banks' Dormant and Extinct Baronage, i. 100.

HERLE. Visitation of Somerset, printed by Sir T. Phillipps, 92. Harleian Society, v. 231 ; vi. 220 ; ix. 94. Westcote's Devonshire, edited by G. Oliver and P. Jones, 514. Burton's Description of Leicestershire, 138. Nichols' History of the County of Leicester, iv. 627. A Complete Parochial History of the County of Cornwall, iii. 123, 191. An Historical Survey of Cornwall, by C. S. Gilbert, ii. 145. Banks' Baronies in Fee, ii. 92. The Visitations of Cornwall, edited by J. L. Vivian, 218, 640. The Genealogist, New Series, xvi. 166.

HERLING. Blomefield's Norfolk, i. 319.

HERN, or HERNE. East Anglian, iv. 123. Burke's Commoners, ii. 689. Camden Society, xliii. 97. Harleian Society, viii. 291, 433 ; xv. 378. W. Robinson's History of Hackney, i. 302. Annals of the Barber Surgeons, by S. Young, 555. See BURCHELL-HERNE.

HERON. Gentleman's Magazine, 1852, i. 53. Hasted's Kent, iii.

133. Morant's Essex, i. 26; ii. 345. Genealogical Tables of the Herons of Newark, with a map of Northumberland, *n. d.* fol. Genealogical Tables of the Family of Heron of Newark, (by Sir R. Heron,) 1797, fol. Visitation of Durham, 1575, (Newcastle, 1820, fol.) 15. Burke's Landed Gentry, 2, 3, 4, 5, 6, 7. Harleian Society, iv. 182; viii. 26; xiii. 417; xv. 379; xliii. 16. Hutchinson's History of Durham, iii. 206. Clutterbuck's Hertford, iii. 195. The Genealogist, ii. 119; iv. 115; v. 271; New Series, vi. 87. George Oliver's History of Beverley, 340. Collectanea Topographica et Genealogica, ii. 166. Raine's History of North Durham, 304. Hodgson's Northumberland, II. ii. 16. W. Dickinson's History of Newark, 303. Surtees' Durham, i. 218. Topographer and Genealogist, ii. 80. Wotton's English Baronetage, iii. 390. Betham's Baronetage, iv. 17. Banks' Dormant and Extinct Baronage, i. 339. Burke's Extinct Baronetcies. F. G. Lee's History of Thame, 334. Foster's Visitations of Durham, 165. Notes and Queries, 7 S., i. 149, 239; ii. 157, 158, 353. Foster's Visitations of Northumberland, 67. *See* MAXWELL-HERON.

HERONVILLE. History of Wednesbury, (Wolverhampton, 1854, 8vo.) 22.

HERRICK, or HERICKE. Burke's Commoners, (of Beaumanor,) iii. 637. Landed Gentry, 2, 3, 4, 5, 6, 7, 8; (of Shippool,) Commoners, iii. 641, Landed Gentry, 2, 3, 4, 5, 6, 7, 8. Nichols' History of the County of Leicester, iii. 148. Harleian Society, xv. 377. Notes and Queries, 6 S., xi. 265; xii. 143. Miscellanea Genealogica et Heraldica, 2nd Series, i. 63. Leicestershire Architectural Society, vi. 118, 163.

HERRIES. Wood's Douglas's Peerage of Scotland, i. 726. Burke's Landed Gentry, 7, 8. *See* MAXWELL.

HERRING. Hutchin's Dorset, ii. 520. *See* COOPER-HERRING.

HERRIS, or HERRYS. Morant's Essex, i. 336. Hasted's Kent, i. 364. Harleian Society, iv. 49; xv. 379. Bysshe's Visitation of Essex, edited by J. J. Howard, 46.

HERTFORD. Burke's Royal Families, (London, 1851, 8vo.) ii. 32. Pedigree of the Leading Families of Lancashire, published by Joseph Foster, (London, 1872, fol.) The New History of Yorkshire, commencing with Richmondshire, by Genl. Plantagenet-Harrison, (London, 1872, fol.) Part i. 24. Plantagenet-Harrison's History of Yorkshire, i. 98. Pedigrees of the Leading Families of Yorkshire, by Joseph Foster.

HERTHILL. J. H. Hill's History of Market Harborough, 91. Nichols' History of the County of Leicester, ii. 532.

HERTHULL. Dugdale's Warwickshire, 229, 469. Ormerod's Cheshire, ii. 712. The Genealogist, New Series, xv. 220; xvii. 118.

HERTLINGTON. Whitaker's Deanery of Craven, 2nd edition, 441; 3rd edn., 514.

HERTWELL. Bridges' Northamptonshire, by Rev. Peter Whalley, i. 381.

HERVART. Miscellanea Genealogica et Heraldica, New Series, iv. 221.

HERVEY, or HERVY. Account of the Parish of Ickworth, and of the Family of Hervey, by Lord Arthur Hervey. Lowestoft, 1858, 8vo. Sketches of the Life of the Rev. James Hervey. Scarborough, 1823. Hasted's Kent, i. 41. Gough's Sepulchral Monuments, ii. 347. Morant's Essex, i. 68. Visitation of Suffolk, edited by J. J. Howard; ii. 133-205. Berry's Essex Genealogies, 68. Burke's Landed Gentry, 2, 3, 4, 5, 6, 7, 8. Lipscombe's History of Buckinghamshire, i. 132, 326. Proceedings of the Suffolk Institute of Archæology, ii. 294-425. Gage's History of Thingoe Hundred, Suffolk, 287. Manning and Bray's Surrey, i. 407. Baker's Northampton, i. 74. Wright's Essex, ii. 442. Page's History of Suffolk, 667. Harleian Society, xiv. 581, 735 ; xli. 60. Edmondson's Baronagium Genealogicum, iii. 205. Brydges' Collins' Peerage, iv. 139. Metcalfe's Visitations of Suffolk, 38, 39. Burke's Extinct Baronetcies. *See* HARVEY.

HERWARD. Visitation of Norfolk, published by Norfolk Archæological Society, i. 300. Berry's Hampshire Genealogies, 280. Burke's Commoners, iii. 408. Harleian Society, xxxii. 149 ; xliii. 35.

HERYING. Wiltshire Archæological Magazine, iii. 178.

HESELRIG, HESILRIGE, HESLERIGG, HESILRIGG, or HESELRIGE. J. H. Hill's History of Market Harborough, 194. Burton's Description of Leicestershire, 194. Nichols' History of the County of Leicester, ii. 756. The Genealogist, i. 377. Harleian Society, xv. 380. Wotton's English Baronetage, i. 520. Betham's Baronetage, i. 260. Foster's Visitations of Northumberland, 68. Leicestershire Architectural Society, ii. 266. *See* HASELRIG.

HESKETH, or HESKAITH. Miscellanea Genealogica et Heraldica, ii. 140-154. Fishwick's History of Goosnargh, 162. Chetham Society, lxxxi. 80 ; lxxxii. 21, 22, 112, 128 ; lxxxv. 134-137 ; xcii. 197 ; xcix. 68 ; cx. 120. Foster's Lancashire Pedigrees. Baines' History of the Co. of Lancaster, iii. 426 ; Croston's edn., iv. 155. Abram's History of Blackburn, 532. Burke's Landed Gentry, 6, 7, 8. The Tyldesley Diary, edited by J. Gillow and A. Hewitson, 77. Betham's Baronetage, iii. 295. Howard's Visitation of England and Wales, i. 159 ; Notes, iii. 36. Harleian Society, xxxvii. 295. *See* BAMFORD-HESKETH.

HESKETH-FLEETWOOD. Burke's Commoners, iv. 521.

HESLARTON. Foster's Visitations of Yorkshire, 173.

HESLOP. Surtees' Durham, iv. 156.

HESTER. Visitation of Oxfordshire, 1634, printed by Sir T. Phillipps, (Middle Hill, fol.) 21. Harleian Society, v. 276.

HETH, or HETHE. Visitation of Norfolk, published by Norfolk Archæological Society, i. 75. Gage's History of Thingoe Hundred, Suffolk, 126. Harleian Society, xviii. 254 ; xxxii. 150. *See* DE HETHE.

HETHERINGTON. Harleian Society, vii. 34 ; xvi. 161. Foster's Visitations of Cumberland and Westmorland, 68.

HETLEY. Camden Society, xliii. 108.

HETON. Gentleman's Magazine, 1831, i. 585. Harleian Society,

i. 40, 59. Dwnn's Visitations of Wales, ii. 349. *See* HEATON, HEYTON.

HEVENINGHAM. Blomefield's Norfolk, v. 92. Morant's Essex, i. 98, 283, 292, 386, 388 ; ii. 73. Harleian Society, viii. 290. Suckling's History of Suffolk, ii. 386. Erdeswicke's Survey of Staffordshire, 39. Wright's Essex, ii. 715. Norfolk Archæology, iii. 284. Page's History of Suffolk, 237. Joseph Hunter's History of Ketteringham, 5. Visitations of Staffordshire, 1614 and 1663-4, William Salt Society, 172.

HEVER. Berry's Sussex Genealogies, 330.

HEWER. Visitation of Norfolk, published by Norfolk Archæological Society, i. 149. Blomefield's Norfolk, viii. 410. Harleian Society, xxxii. 150.

HEWES. Harleian Society, i. 26. Visitatio Comitatus Wiltoniæ, 1623, printed by Sir T. Phillipps.

HEWETT, HEWITT, or HEWYT. Morant's Essex, ii. 500. Harleian Society, viii. 119 ; xix. 37, 117 ; xxii. 64 ; xxxix. 1009, 1028. Burke's Landed Gentry, 6 at p. 1201. Berry's Hampshire Genealogies, 325. Berry's Hertfordshire Genealogies, 215. Burke's Landed Gentry, 2, 3, 4, 5, 6, 7. J. H. Hill's History of Market Harborough, 113. Nichols' History of the County of Leicester, ii. 581 ; iv. 156. Archdall's Lodge's Peerage, vi. 53. Wotton's English Baronetage, i. 448. Burke's Extinct Baronetcies. Clutterbuck's Hertford, iii. 202. Memoirs of the Family of Chester, by R. E. C. Waters, 237. Holland's History of Worksop, 175. Notes and Queries, 2 S. vi. 331, 421, 465, 535 ; viii. 391, 455, 519; xii. 409; 3 S. ii. 398; v. 528; vi. 397. Betham's Baronetage, i. 220. Norfolk Archæology, viii. 316. Bysshe's Visitation of Essex, edited by J. J. Howard, 48. *See* LUDLOW-HEWITT.

HEWGILL. Burke's Landed Gentry, 2, 3, 4. Burke's Colonial Gentry, ii. 762.

HEWISH. Visitation of Somerset, printed by Sir T. Phillipps, 94. Harleian Society, xi. 49. Weaver's Visitations of Somerset, 31. *See* HUISH.

HEWISON. Geo. Robertson's Description of Cunninghame, 348.

HEWLEY. Kent's British Banner Displayed, 160. W. Paver's Pedigrees of Families of the City of York, 13. Harleian Society, viii. 172. Thoresby's Ducatus Leodiensis, 211.

HEWSON. A narrative of the Hewson and Bonsor Families, by Thomas Hewson. Croydon, 1822, 4to. Burke's Landed Gentry, 2, 5, 6, 7, 8.

HEXT. Visitation of Somerset, printed by Sir T. Phillipps, 95. Burke's Commoners, (of Trenarren,) ii. 428, Landed Gentry, 2 and add., 3, 4, 5, 6, 7, 8 ; (of Tredethy,) Landed Gentry, 2 add., 3, 4, 5, 6, 7, 8. Maclean's History of Trigg Minor, ii. 526. Harleian Society, ix. 96 ; xi. 49. Westcote's Devonshire, edited by G. Oliver and P. Jones, 503. A Complete Parochial History of the County of Cornwall, iii. 29, 206. Visitation of Devon, edited by F. T. Colby, 129. The Visitations of Cornwall, edited by J. L. Vivian, 221. Howard's Visitation of England and Wales, i. 203. Somerset-

shire Wills, printed for F. A. Crisp, ii. 56. The Visitations of
Devon, by J. L. Vivian, 484. Staniforthiana, by F. M. H., *at end.*
HEXTALL. Willmore's History of Walsall, 144.
HEYBORNE. Harleian Society, xiv. 583.
HEYCOCK. Burke's Commoners, iii. 643; Landed Gentry, 2, 3, 4, 5,
6, 7, 8.
HEYDEY. Weaver's Visitation of Herefordshire, 44.
HEYDON. Hasted's Kent, i. 108. Morant's Essex, ii. 140. Blome-
field's Norfolk, vi. 504. Harleian Society, v. 219; xxxii. 151.
Clutterbuck's Hertford, i. 250. Bigland's Gloucestershire, ii. par.
Shipton Moyne.
HEYFORD. Baker's Northampton, i. 167.
HEYGATE. Berry's Hertfordshire Genealogies, 166. J. H. Hill's
History of Market Harborough, 64. Nichols' History of the County
of Leicester, iv. 628. Harleian Society, xv. 380.
HEYLAND. Burke's Landed Gentry, 3, 4, 5, 6.
HEYLIN. Nichols' Account of the Company of Ironmongers, 2nd
edn. 560. Harleian Society, xxviii. 233.
HEYMAN. Hasted's Kent, iii. 449. Scott of Scot's-Hall, by J. R.
Scott, 207. Wotton's English Baronetage, ii. 253. Betham's
Baronetage, i. 442. Burke's Extinct Baronetcies. Harleian
Society, xlii. 185.
HEYNES. Botfield's Stemmata Botevilliana, 138. Harleian Society,
xxviii. 234, 279.
HEYRAZ. Hoare's Wiltshire, V. ii. 47.
HEYRICK. J. H. Hill's History of Market Harborough, 124. Chetham
Society, lxxxv. 138. Nichols' History of the County of Leicester,
ii. 615.
HEYSHAM. Berry's Hertfordshire Genealogies, 92. Clutterbuck's
Hertford, ii. 399. Miscellanea Genealogica et Heraldica, New
Series, iv. 373.
HEYTESBURY. Burke's Royal Families, (London, 1851, 8vo.) i.
182.
HEYTON. The Genealogist, vi. 258. *See* HEATON, HETON.
HEYWARD. Harleian Society, xxviii. 235; xxxii. 153.
HEYWOOD. Works of Rev. O. Heywood, (1827, 8vo.) i. 506-514.
Burke's Landed Gentry, (of Hope End,) 2, 3, 4, 5, 6, 7, 8; (of
Stanley Hall,) 2, 3, 4, 5. Foster's Lancashire Pedigrees. Chetham
Society, vii. 22; lxxxv. 139, 140. Baines' History of the Co. of
Lancaster, iii. 85; Croston's edn., iii. 207. Heywood's Diaries,
edited by J. H. Turner, i. 3, 114. The Revd. O. Heywood, His
Autobiography, by J. H. Turner, 3-127. Harleian Society,
xxxvii. 61, 382.
HIBBARD. History of Woodhouse, by W. J. Le Tall, 19.
HIBBERT. Burke's Landed Gentry, 2, 3, 4, 5, 6, 7, 8. Miscellanea
Genealogica et Heraldica, New Series, i. 367. Ormerod's Cheshire,
iii. 841. Earwaker's East Cheshire, ii. 55. Harleian Society,
xxxvii. 270.
HIBBERT-WARE. Burke's Commoners, iv. 493; Landed Gentry, 2.
Burke's Heraldic Illustrations, 10.

HIBBINS. Harleian Society, xxviii. 236.

HICHENS. *See* SIKES.

HICKES, or HICKS. Morant's Essex, i. 24, 166. Fosbrooke's
Abstracts of Smith's Lives of the Berkeleys, 4. Rudder's
Gloucestershire, 837. Berry's Hampshire Genealogies, 254.
Burke's Commoners, i. 510. Burke's Landed Gentry, 2 supp., 3,
4, 5, 6, 7, 8. Harleian Society, ix. 96 ; xv. 381 ; xxi. 80 ; xxxix.
867. Thoresby's Ducatus Leodiensis, 138. Hoare's Wiltshire,
II. ii. 30. Surtees' Durham, ii. 54. A Complete Parochial
History of the County of Cornwall, iii. 193. Miscellanea Genea-
logica et Heraldica, New Series, iii. 361 ; 2nd Series, i. 84.
Wotton's English Baronetage, i. 341. Betham's Baronetage,
i. 171. Banks' Dormant and Extinct Baronage, iii. 139. Burke's
Extinct Baronetcies. Metcalfe's Visitation of Worcester, 1683,
56. Howard's Visitation of England and Wales, iii. 100. Burke's
Family Records, 314. The Visitations of Cornwall, edited by
J. L. Vivian, 225. Notes and Queries, 8 S. x. 130, 280.

HICKEY. O'Hart's Irish Pedigrees, 2nd Series, 60.

HICKIE. Burke's Landed Gentry, 2 supp., 4, 5, 6, 7, 8.

HICKLING. Metcalfe's Visitations of Northamptonshire 27.

HICKMAN. Burke's Landed Gentry, (of Fenloe,) 2, 3, 4, 5, 6, 7, 8 ;
(of Whightwick,) 8 ; (of Chorlton House,) 8 ; (of Tyredagh,) 8.
Lipscombe's History of Buckinghamshire, ii. 52. History of
Gainsburgh, by Adam Stark, 1st edition, 123. The Genealogist,
iv. 116 ; New Series, xvii. 279. Wotton's English Baronetage, ii.
391. Notes and Queries, 5 S. i. 250. Burke's Extinct Baronetcies. *See* WINDSOR-HICKMAN.

HICKS-BEACH. Burke's Royal Descents and Pedigrees of Founders'
Kin, 21.

HICKSON. Burke's Landed Gentry, (of Ballintaggart Grange,) 2, 3,
4, 5, 6, 7 ; (of Letterough,) 2 supp., 3, 4, 5, 6 and supp. ; (of
Fermoyle,) 8.

HIERN. Burke's Family Records, 316.

HIGATT, or HIGATTE. Harleian Society, xiii. 61. Metcalfe's Visitations of Suffolk, 39, 143.

HIGDEN. Foster's Visitations of Yorkshire, 531.

HIGFORD. Descendants of Higford of Dixton, and Alderton, Co.
Gloucester, 1839, [T. P.]. Broadside. Fosbrooke's History of
Gloucestershire, ii. 260. Duncumbe's Hereford, (J. H. Cooke,)
iii. 38, 173. Burke's Landed Gentry, 8.

HIGGENS. Berry's Sussex Genealogies, 71. Harleian Society, xxviii.
239. *See* HYGONS.

HIGGES. Pedigree of Higges of Cheltenham, and Sloper of Cheltenham, [T. P.] 1865, 2 pages folio. Harleian Society, xxviii. 239.

HIGGINBOTTOM. Notes and Queries, 2 S. i. 268, 417.

HIGGINS. Howard's Visitation of England and Wales, i. 99. Burke's
Commoners, (of Skellow Grange,) ii. 155, Landed Gentry, 2, 3, 4 ;
(of Turvey House,) Landed Gentry, 3, 4, 5, 6, 7, 8 ; (of Turvey
Abbey,) 2, 3, 4, 5, 6, 7, 8; (of Bosbury,) 2, 3, 4, 5, 6 ; (of Westport,)
2, 3, 4, 5. *See* Burke's Landed Gentry under BURNE and BRA-

BAZON. Burke's Heraldic Illustrations, 32. Dallaway's Sussex, II. i. 236. Hunter's Deanery of Doncaster, ii. 482. Robinson's Mansions of Herefordshire, 110. O'Hart's Irish Pedigrees, 2nd Series, 197. Metcalfe's Visitation of Worcester, 1683, 57. Harvey's Hundred of Willey, 191, 192. Harleian Society, xxviii. 240, 262. Burke's Family Records, 316.

HIGGINSON. Burke's Landed Gentry, 3, 4, 7, 8.

HIGGON. Pedigree of Higgon of Haverford West, [T. P.] 1866, a 4to. page. Burke's Landed Gentry, 8.

HIGGONS. Botfield's Stemmata Botevilliana, 137. Harleian Society, viii. 172 ; xxviii. 240.

HIGGS. Visitation of Gloucester, edited by T. F. Fenwick and W. C. Metcalfe, 89. Harleian Society, xxi. 81. Berks Archl. and Architectural Society's Journal, ii. 46. The Genealogical Magazine, iii. 158.

HIGHAM. Morant's Essex, i. 15, 391. Berry's Essex Genealogies, 404. Berry's Sussex Genealogies, 338. Cambridgeshire Visitation, edited by Sir T. Phillipps, 17. Harleian Society, xiii. 62, 216, 418 ; xli. 75. Metcalfe's Visitations of Suffolk, 40-42, 143, 144. Bysshe's Visitation of Essex, edited by J. J. Howard, 48.

HIGHETT. Burke's Colonial Gentry, i. 258.

HIGHLORD. Harleian Society, xv. 382.

HIGHMORE. Harleian Society, vii. 4. Foster's Visitations of Cumberland and Westmorland, 59.

HILCOMBE. The Genealogist, New Series, xiv. 259.

HILDERSHAM. Notes and Queries, 2 S. ix. 30. Metcalfe's Visitations of Suffolk, 42. Harleian Society, xli. 115.

HILDESLEY. Ashmole's Antiquities of Berkshire, iii. 317. Sir T. Phillipps' Topographer, No. 1, (March, 1821, 8vo.) 18. Visitation of Oxfordshire, 1574, printed by Sir T. Phillipps, (Middle Hill, fol.) 5. Foster's Visitations of Yorkshire, 532. The Genealogist, v. 271, 272 ; New Series, i. 11. See HYLDESLEY.

HILDRETH. New England Register, xi. 7.

HILDYARD. Burke's Patrician, iv. 67. Burke's Authorized Arms, 77. Surtees Society, xxxvi. 144. W. Paver's Pedigrees of Families of the City of York, 14. Burke's Landed Gentry, (of Horsley,) 4 supp., 5, 6, 7, 8 ; (of Winestead,) 2, 3, 4, 5, 6, 7, 8 ; (of Flintham Hall,) 2 supp., 3, 4, 5, 6, 7, 8. Foster's Yorkshire Pedigrees. Foster's Visitations of Yorkshire, 50. Poulson's Holderness, i. 341 ; ii. 221, 426, 466, 498. Burke's Royal Families, (London, 1851, 8vo.) i. 100. Surtees' Durham, iv. 151. Wotton's English Baronetage, iii. 58. Betham's Baronetage, ii. 66. Burke's Extinct Baronetcies. Old Yorkshire, edited by Will'm. Smith, iv. 232. See HILLIARD.

HILL, or HYLL. Collinson's Somerset, i. 444; ii. 457. Harleian Society, i. 29; vi. 344 ; viii. 217; ix. 97-100; xi. 50 ; xv. 384; xix. 118 ; xx. 55; xxi. 82; xxii. 12 ; xxviii. 242 ; xxxii. 153 ; xxxvii. 274 ; xl. 1199; xlii. 117. Berry's Hampshire Genealogies, 185, 319. Berry's Kent Genealogies, 320. Evans, (Newcastle-on-Tyne, 1865, 8vo.) 13. Burke's Patrician, iii. 172.

Bibliotheca Topographica Britannica, ix. Part iv. 52-69. Visitation of Somerset, printed by Sir T. Phillipps, 96, 97. Burke's Commoners, iv. 677; (of Court of Hill,) Commoners, i. 654, Landed Gentry, 2, 5, 6, 7, 8; (of Stallington Hall,) Commoners, ii. 318, Landed Gentry, 2, 3, 4; (of Doneraile,) Landed Gentry, 2, 3, 4, 5, 6, 7, 8; (of Gressenhall,) 2, 3, 4, 8; (of Thornton Hall,) 6 and supp., 7; (of Rockhurst,) 8; (of Catherine Hill House,) 6, 7, 8. Maclean's History of Trigg Minor, ii. 514, 523. Collectanea Topographica et Genealogica, i. 409. Burke's Royal Descents and Pedigrees of Founders' Kin, 119. Visitation of Gloucester, edited by T. F. Fenwick and W. C. Metcalfe, 94. Weaver's Visitations of Somerset, 32. Metcalfe's Visitations of Northamptonshire, 100. Hasted's Kent, (Hund. of Blackheath, by H. H. Drake,) 257. Visitations of Staffordshire, 1614 and 1663-4, William Salt Society, 174. Shaw's Staffordshire, i. 355; ii. 44. Westcote's Devonshire, edited by G. Oliver and P. Jones, 503. Burke's Royal Families, (London, 1851, 8vo.) i. 174. Visitation of Staffordshire, 1663-4, printed by Sir T. Phillipps, 6. Thoresby's Ducatus Leodiensis, 210. Nichols' History of the County of Leicester, iii. 1012*, 1144. Clutterbuck's Hertford, ii. 196. Pedigree of Hill (from Humphrey Hill of Little Witley to Thos. Rowley Hill, Mayor of Worcester,) broadside. Cumberland and Westmoreland Archæological Society, ii: 197. Genealogy of Henzey, Tyttery, and Tyzack, by H. S. Grazebrook, 69. An Historical Survey of Cornwall, by C. S. Gilbert, ii. 149. Edmondson's Baronagium Genealogicum, v. 458; vi. 13, 121. Archdall's Lodge's Peerage, ii. 320; v. 292. Brydges' Collins' Peerage, v. 96; viii. 33. Wotton's English Baronetage, iv. 213. Visitation of Devon, edited by F. T. Colby, 140. Betham's Baronetage, iii. 208. The Genealogist, v. 272. Metcalfe's Visitations of Suffolk, 144. Metcalfe's Visitation of Worcester, 1683, 58. Visitation of Staffordshire, (Willm. Salt Soc.) 98. The Visitations of Cornwall, edited by J. L. Vivian, 226-232. The Visitations of Devon, by J. L. Vivian, 485, 486. Miscellanea Genealogica et Heraldica, 2nd Series, iv. 266. New England Register, xii. 139, 258. Burke's Colonial Gentry, ii. 597, 632. Howard's Visitation of England and Wales, iv. 107. Burke's Family Records, 318. Oliver's History of Antigua, ii. 72. Memoir of Richard Haines, by C. R. Haines, table x^a. The Genealogist, New Series, xv. 103, 178, 228.

HILLARY. Visitation of Norfolk, published by Norfolk Archæological Society, ii. 6. Harleian Society, xv. 383. Willmore's History of Walsall, 246.

HILLE. Maclean's History of Trigg Minor, ii. 42.

HILLERSDON. Tuckett's Devonshire Pedigrees, 136. Harleian Society, vi. 149; xix. 174. Westcote's Devonshire, edited by G. Oliver and P. Jones, 529. Visitation of Devon, edited by F. T. Colby, 129. Visitations of Devon, by J. L. Vivian, 469.

HILLES. Harleian Society, i. 50. Muskett's Suffolk Manorial Families, i. 100.

HILLIARD, or HILLYARD. Visitation of Durham, 1615, (Sunderland, 1820, fol.) 92. Miscellanea Genealogica et Heraldica, New Series, ii. 40. Harleian Society, xv. 386 ; xvi. 170. Foster's Visitations of Durham, 167. *See* HILDYARD.

HILLION. Visitation of Devon, edited by F. T. Colby, 52, 130.

HILLS. Burke's Landed Gentry, 2, 3, 4, 5, 6, 7, 8. Harleian Society, xiv. 636 ; xv. 385. New England Register, xxxvi. 165.

HILLSBOROUGH. Hasted's Kent, i. 387.

HILMAN. Harleian Society, vi. 150.

HILTON. History of the Castle, Family, etc., of the Hiltons, by W. P. Swaby. Sunderland, 1884, 8vo. New England Register, vii. 50, 155; xxxi. 179. Foster's Visitations of Durham, 169, 171. Foster's Visitations of Cumberland and Westmorland, 60, 61. Nicolson and Burn's Westmorland and Cumberland, i. 353, 611. Burke's Patrician, iii. 557-561 ; vi. 398-406. Gentleman's Magazine, 1821, i. 234. Herald and Genealogist, iv. 353. View of the Parishes of Monk-Wearmouth and Bishop's Wearmouth, by George Garbutt, 99. Berry's Sussex Genealogies, 102. Visitation of Durham, 1615, (Sunderland, 1820, fol.) 80. Surtees Society, xli. 36. Burke's Commoners, iii. 704; Landed Gentry, 2 supp., 3, 4, 8. Chetham Society, lxxxv. 141. Hutchinson's History of Durham, iii. xvii. Thoroton's Nottinghamshire, i. 118. Abram's History of Blackburn, 507. Dallaway's Sussex, II. i. 348. Poulson's Holderness, ii. 197. Nichols' History of the County of Leicester, iv. 865. Archæologia Æliana, 2nd Series, iii. 134. Surtees' Durham, ii. 26, 28, 29, 35 ; iv. 167-170. The Genealogist, iv. 184 ; New Series, ix. 81. Banks' Baronies in Fee, i. 250. *See* DE HILTON, HELTON, HYLTON.

HINCHCLIFFE, or HINCHLIFFE. Notes and Queries, 3 S. ii. 97, 119.

HINCKLEY. New England Register, xiii. 208.

HINCKS. Burke's Commoners, iv. 366 ; Landed Gentry, 2, 3, 4, 5, 6, 7, 8 and supp. Harleian Society, xxxvii. 363.

HINDE. Burke's Commoners, (of Acton House,) iv. 309, Landed Gentry, 2, 3, 4 ; (of Caton,) Landed Gentry, 2 add. Burke's Royal Families, (London, 1851, 8vo.) ii. 31. Harleian Society, xv. 386; xxxix. 841. Visitations of Staffordshire, 1614 and 1663-4, William Salt Society, 175.

HINDLE. Abram's History of Blackburn, 397, 482, 507, 639.

HINDLEY. Chetham Society, lxxxii. 117.

HINDS. New England Register, xviii. 267.

HINGSTON. Burke's Commoners, (of Aglis,) iv. 43, Landed Gentry, 2 ; (of Holbeton,) Landed Gentry, 2, 3, 4. Foster's Account of Families descended from Francis Fox, 18.

HINSON. Visitation of Middlesex, (Salisbury, 1820, fol.) 30. Harleian Society, xxii. 82 ; xli. 125. Foster's Visitation of Middlesex, 52, 53.

HINTON, or HYNTON. Ashmole's Antiquities of Berkshire, iii. 327. Dallaway's Sussex, 2nd edition, II. i. 53. Ormerod's Cheshire, ii. 242. Burke's Commoners, i. 443, 515. The Genealogist, v. 273 ; New Series, i. 12; xii. 109; xv. 26, 28. Miscellanea

Genealogica et Heraldica, New Series, iv. 148. Visitations of Staffordshire, 1614 and 1663-4, William Salt Society, 176. Harleian Society, xix. 119 ; xxviii. 248.

HINXMAN. Hoare's Wiltshire, II. ii. 129. Burke's Landed Gentry, 8.

HIPPESLEY. Pedigree of Hippesley of Stone Easton, [T. P.], folio page. Berry's Buckinghamshire Genealogies, 80. Visitation of Somerset, printed by Sir T. Phillipps, 98. Burke's Commoners, iv. 80. Burke's Landed Gentry, 3, 4, 5, 6. Burke's Royal Families, (London, 1851, 8vo.) i. 186. Harleian Society, xi. 52. Visitatio Comitatus Wiltoniæ, 1623, printed by Sir T. Phillipps.

HIPPISLEY. Burke's Landed Gentry, 4th edn., p. 1537. Burke's Commoners, (of Lamborne,) i. 538, Landed Gentry, 2, 3, 4, 5, 7, 8; (of Shobrooke Park,) Landed Gentry, 3, 4, 5 ; (of Cameley,) 2 add. Betham's Baronetage, iv. 327. Weaver's Visitations of Somerset, 114.

HIPPON. Surtees Society, xxxvi. 15. Foster's Visitations of York shire, 532. The Genealogist, New Series, ix. 62. Harleian Society, xl. 1265.

HIPSLEY. Genealogical Memoranda relating to the Family of Parker, by E. M. S. Parker, 14.

HIRD. History of Bradford, by John James, 442.

HIRNE. Harleian Society, xxxii. 154. The Genealogist, New Series, xviii. 61.

HIRST. Miscellanea Genealogica et Heraldica, ii. 257. Foster's Yorkshire Pedigrees. Harleian Society, xiii. 420.

HIRVRYN. Dwnn's Visitations of Wales, i. 27.

HITCH. Sir T. Phillipps' Topographer, No. 1, (March, 1821, 8vo.) 48. Visitation of Oxfordshire, 1574, printed by Sir T. Phillipps, (Middle Hill, fol.) 5. Harleian Society, v. 233 ; xix. 175. The Genealogist, iii. 300.

HITCHCOCK. Visitatio Comitatus Wiltoniæ, 1623, printed by Sir T. Phillipps. Hoare's Wiltshire, V. ii. 74. Visitation of Wiltshire, edited by G. W. Marshall, 93. New England Register, xl. 307.

HITCHING. Surtees Society, xxxvi. 18. The Genealogist, New Series, xvi. 254.

HIWIS, or HIWYSSHE. Miscellanea Genealogica et Heraldica, New Series, ii. 73. Colby of Great Torrington, by F. T. Colby, 32. The Genealogist, New Series, xiv. 199 ; xv. 32.

HIXON. Surtees' Durham, iii. 45.

HOAR, or HOARE. Pedigrees and Memoirs of the Family of Hoare, by Sir R. C. Hoare, Bart. Bath, 1819, 4to. Some Account of the Early History and Genealogy of the Families of Hore and Hoare, by Edward Hoare. London, 1883, 4to. Gentleman's Magazine, 1838, ii. 28. Burke's Landed Gentry, (of Cliff,) 5 supp., 6, 7, 8 ; (of Kelsey,) 8. Harleian Society, viii. 481 ; ix. 100. Lipscombe's History of the County of Buckingham, iv. 390. Hoare's Wiltshire, I. i. 61, 62 ; V. iii. 13. Betham's Baronetage, iv. 177. The Visitations of Cornwall, edited by J. L. Vivian, 232. New England Register, xvii. 149. History of the Wilmer Family], 259. Aldred's History of Turville, 47. See HORE.

HOARD. Miscellanea Genealogica et Heraldica, New Series, iv. 141, 267, 289. *See* HORD.

HOBART, or HOBERT. Gentleman's Magazine, 1828, i. 307; 1851, ii. 382. Blomefield's History of Norfolk, vii. 243; viii. 19. Noble's Memoirs of the House of Cromwell, ii. 151-167. Burke's Commoners, iii. 206. Harleian Society, viii. 141; xxxii. 155, 164. Lipscombe's History of the County of Buckingham, ii. 276. Edmondson's Baronagium Genealogicum, iii. 257. Brydges' Collins' Peerage, iv. 362. Metcalfe's Visitations of Suffolk, 145. Visitation of Norfolk, published by Norfolk Archæological Society, ii. 59-168.

HOBBES, or HOBBS. Surrey Archæological Collections, ii. Harleian Society, xi. 53; xliii. 149. Kite's Monumental Brasses of Wiltshire, 79. Visitation of Somerset, printed by Sir T. Phillipps, 99. Maclean's History of Trigg Minor, i. 315. The Genealogist, v. 274. Weaver's Visitations of Somerset, 34. New England Register, ix. 255. Burke's Landed Gentry, 8.

HOBE. Dwnn's Visitations of Wales, ii. 317.

HOBHOUSE. Burke's Commoners, iv. 360; Landed Gentry, 2, 3, 4, 5, 6, 7, 8. Phelps' History of Somersetshire, i. 259. Jewers' Wells Cathedral, 77.

HOBLEDAY. Harleian Society, xii. 175.

HOBLYN. Burke's Royal Families, (London, 1851, 8vo.) ii. 41. Maclean's History of Trigg Minor, i. 473. Harleian Society, ix. 101. An Historical Survey of Cornwall, by C. S. Gilbert, ii. 152. The Visitations of Cornwall, edited by J. L. Vivian, 234. Howard's Visitation of England and Wales, i. 183. Burke's Family Records, 319. *See* PETER-HOBLYN.

HOBSON, or HOBSONN. Miscellanea Genealogica et Heraldica, i. 50. Harleian Society, xiii. 420; xv. 387; xxxix. 926. Surtees Society, lxv. 330. Berry's Hampshire Genealogies, 269. Visitation of Sussex. 1570, printed by Sir T. Phillipps, (Middle Hill, fol.) 6. Ancient Families of Lincolnshire, in 'Spalding Free Press,' 1873-5, No. i. New England Register, xi. 237.

HOBY. Burke's Extinct Baronetcies. Hasted's Kent, ii. 649. Miscellanea Genealogica et Heraldica, i. 141; 2nd Series, iii. 351. Wotton's English Baronetage, iii. 504. The Genealogist, v. 274. Harleian Society, xxvii. 77.

HOCHPIED. Documents relating to the De Hochepied Family. Antwerp, 1827, 8vo.

HOCKENHULL, or HOCKNELL. Ormerod's Cheshire, ii. 316, 532. Harleian Society, xviii. 122.

HOCKIN. A Complete Parochial History of the County of Cornwall, ii. 158. An Historical Survey of Cornwall, by C. S. Gilbert, ii. 155. Burke's Colonial Gentry, ii. 483.

HOCKLETON. Harleian Society, xxviii. 249.

HOCKMORE. Harleian Society, vi. 152. Visitations of Devon, by J. L. Vivian, 471.

HODDER. Burke's Landed Gentry, 5, 6, 7, 8. Burke's Family Records, 324. *See* MOORE-HODDER.

HODDESDON. Harleian Society, xix. 175.

HODDINOT. Pedigree of Hoddinot of Frome, [T. P.] 1870, 4to. page.

HODESAK. Thoroton's Nottinghamshire, iii. 418.

HODGE. Genealogy of Morgan and Glamorgan, by G. T. Clark, 490. Oliver's History of Antigua, ii. 75.

HODGES. Rudder's Gloucestershire, 653. Visitation of Middlesex, (Salisbury, 1820, fol.) 15. Visitation of Somersetshire, printed by Sir T. Phillipps, 100, 101. Burke's Landed Gentry, 2, 3. Harleian Society, ii. 154 ; xi. 53. Nichols' History of the County of Leicester, iii. 516. Hutchins' Dorset, iv. 460. Baker's Northampton, i. 515. Fosbrooke's History of Gloucestershire, ii. 44. Burke's Extinct Baronetcies. Metcalfe's Visitation of Worcester, 1683, 59. Gloucestershire Notes and Queries, i. 455. The Gentleman's Magazine, 1826, i. 291. Visitation of Gloucester, edited by T. F. Fenwick and W. C. Metcalfe, 91. Weaver's Visitations of Somerset, 34. Foster's Visitation of Middlesex, 19. Oliver's History of Antigua, ii. 80.

HODGESON. Harleian Society, i. 46. Surrey Archæological Collections, vii.

HODGETTS. Burke's Landed Gentry, 2, 3. Collections for a History of Staffordshire, (William Salt Society) ii. part 2, 79.

HODGKIN. Pease of Darlington, by Joseph Foster, 67.

HODGKINSON. Jewitt's Reliquary, xii. 255. Chetham Society, lxxxv. 142. Burke's Colonial Gentry, ii. 636.

HODGKIS. Harleian Society, xix. 176.

HODGSON. Berry's Sussex Genealogies, 339. Visitation of Durham, 1615, (Sunderland, 1820, fol.) 91. Burke's Landed Gentry, (of Newby Grange,) 4, 5 ; (of Houghton House,) 2, 3, 4, 5, 7, 8 ; (of Clopton House,) 5 supp. 6, 7, 8 ; (of Highthorne,) 5, 6, 7 ; (of Brafferton Hall,) 3 supp., 4 ; (of Ovington,) 8, at p. 963 ; (of Ashgrove,) 8. Foster's Yorkshire Pedigrees. Thoresby's Ducatus Leodiensis, 75. Surtees' Durham, ii. 77, 319. Burke's Colonial Gentry, ii. 407. Foster's Visitations of Durham, 173. Foster's Visitations of Cumberland and Westmorland, 62. Harleian Society, xxxvii. 88, 187 ; xliii. 143. Memoir of the Molyneux Family, by G. Molyneux, 66. See ARCHER-HIND.

HODGSON-HINDE. Burke's Commoners, iv. 309 ; Landed Gentry, 5, 6, 7.

HODILOW. Topographer and Genealogist, ii. 28-72, 544. Burke's Landed Gentry, 2 add. p. 330.

HODINGTON. Visitation of Gloucester, edited by T. F. Fenwick and W. C. Metcalfe, 205. Harleian Society, xxi. 271, 279; xxvii. 118.

HODLESTON. The Genealogist, iii. 300. See HUDDLESTON.

HODNET. Burke's Commoners, iv. 134. Eyton's Antiquities of Shropshire, ix. 334. Harleian Society, xxviii. 83.

HODSDON. Harleian Society, i. 36.

HODSOLL. Jewitt's Reliquary, xviii. 217 ; xix. 161. Archæologia Cantiana, xiv. 223.

HODSON. Foster's Visitations of Yorkshire, 533. Ormerod's Cheshire, ii. 31. Harleian Society, xv. 388 ; xxxix. 1024. Burke's Family Records, 324.

HODY. Collectanea Topographica et Genealogica, vii. 22. Hutchins' Dorset, ii. 233. The Visitations of Devon, by J. L. Vivian, 490. Burke's Landed Gentry, 8.

HOEL. Dwnn's Visitations of Wales, ii. 44.

HOESE. Berry's Sussex Genealogies, 344. Dallaway's Sussex, i. 188. Sussex Archæological Collections, viii. 46. Banks' Baronies in Fee, i. 253, 265. Banks' Dormant and Extinct Baronage, i. 343. *See* HUSSEY.

HOEY. The Irish Builder, xxix. 202.

HOG. Burke's Landed Gentry, 2, 3, 4, 5, 6, 7, 8. The Theology of Consolation, by D. C. A. Agnew, 294.

HOGAN. Harleian Society, i. 32. Carthew's Hundred of Launditch, Part ii. 695, 804. O'Hart's Irish Pedigrees, 2nd Series, 61. Carthew's West and East Bradenham, 108.

HOGARTH. Notes and Queries, 4 S. ii. 254 ; 6 S. i. 196.

HOGG. Burke's Landed Gentry, (of Norton House,) 2, 3, 4, 5, 8 ; (of Church View,) 2 supp. Burke's Heraldic Illustrations, 80. Alexander Nisbet's Heraldic Plates, 148. Visitation of Gloucester, edited by T. F. Fenwick and W. C. Metcalfe, 123.

HOGH. Ormerod's Cheshire, iii. 502.

HOGHTON. Burke's Royal Families, (London, 1851, 8vo.) i. 125. Chetham Society, lxxxv. 155 ; xcix. 13, 130. Baines' History of the Co. of Lancaster, iii. 230, 348 ; Croston's edn., iv. 182. Abram's History of Blackburn, 687, 711. Ormerod's Cheshire, ii. 575. Wotton's English Baronetage, i. 15. Betham's Baronetage, i. 34. *See* DE HOGHTON.

HOLAHAN. O'Hart's Irish Pedigrees, 2nd Series, 199.

HOLAND. Bridges' Northamptonshire, by Rev. Peter Whalley, ii. 602. History of Samlesbury, by James Croston, 33. Clutterbuck's Hertford, i. 371 ; iii. 287. Baker's Northampton, i. 563. Chetham Society, xcv. 28 ; xcix. 135. Banks' Dormant and Extinct Baronage, ii. 274. Harvey's Hundred of Willey, 146. Visitations of Devon, by J. L. Vivian, 475. The Genealogist, New Series, xiii. 34. *See* DE HOLAND, HOLLAND.

HOLANT. Dwnn's Visitations of Wales, i. 113.

HOLBEACH. Collinson's Somerset, ii. 441. Visitation of Somerset, printed by Sir T. Phillipps, 102. Harleian Society, xi. 54. The Genealogist, vi. 258.

HOLBEAM, or HOLBEME. Maclean's History of Trigg Minor, ii. 501. Westcote's Devonshire, edited by G. Oliver and P. Jones, 502. Visitation of Devon, edited by F. T. Colby, 131. Visitations of Devon, by J. L. Vivian, 473.

HOLBECH, HOLBECHE, or HOLBEECH. Burke's Commoners, i. 659 ; Landed Gentry, 2, 3 and supp., 4, 5, 6, 7, 8. Warwickshire Pedigrees, from Visitation of 1682-3, (privately printed, 1865). Baker's Northampton, i. 674. Harleian Society, xii. 323, 351. The Genealogist, iv. 179. History of Powys Fadog, by J. Y. W. Lloyd, iv. 93.

HOLBECK. Harleian Society, xxxii. 156.

HOLBROOKE. Berry's Kent Genealogies, 73. Archæologia Cantiana,

v. 225. Harleian Society, xii. 75 ; xlii. 16. The Genealogist, New Series, x. 29 ; xiii. 96.

HOLBROW. Account of the Family of Holbrow. By W. P. W. Phillimore. Devizes, 1901, 4to.

HOLCOMB, or HOLCOMBE. Westcote's Devonshire, edited by G. Oliver and P. Jones, 531. Burke's Commoners, iv. 95. Harleian Society, vi. 345. Visitations of Devon, by J. L. Vivian, 474.

HOLCOT. Camden Society, xliii. 21.

HOLCROFT. Notes on the Family of Holcroft, by J. Paul Rylands. Leigh, Lancashire, 1877, 8vo. Earwaker's Local Gleanings, ii. 602, 612, 620, 624, 629, 634, 647, 650, 655, 658, 662, 665, 667, 693, 699, 703. Ormerod's Cheshire, ii. 154. Harleian Society, xiii. 421 ; xviii. 124. Berry's Hampshire Genealogies, 304. Chetham Society, lxxxi. 117 ; lxxxv. 145 ; xcviii. 84. Baines' History of the Co. of Lancaster, iii. 130. The Tyldesley Diary, edited by J. Gillow and A. Hewitson, 113. Bysshe's Visitation of Essex, edited by J. J. Howard, 48.

HOLDEN. Glover's History of Derbyshire, ii. 68, 384, (60, 351). Berry's Kent Genealogies, 362. Burke's Landed Gentry, (of Aston,) 2, 3, 4, 5, 6, 7, 8 ; (of Palace House and Holden,) 2, 3, 4, 5, 6, 7, 8 ; (of Nuttall Temple,) 6, 7, 8. Foster's Lancashire Pedigrees. Chetham Society, lxxxii. 82 ; lxxxv. 144. History of Wednesbury, (Wolverhampton, 1854, 8vo.) 173. Visitation of Derbyshire, 1663-4, (Middle Hill, 1854, fol.) 4. Nichols' History of the County of Leicester, iv. 935. Dugdale's Warwickshire, 893. Baker's Northampton, i. 317. Whitaker's History of Whalley, ii. 304, 305. Abram's History of Blackburn, 579, 760, 762. The Genealogist, iii. 178. Jordan's History of Enstone, 359.

HOLDENBY. Bridges' Northamptonshire, by Rev. Peter Whalley, i. 528. Baker's Northampton, i. 196, 197. Harleian Society, xv. 389.

HOLDER. Harleian Society, xli. 115.

HOLDICH-HUNGERFORD. Burke's Landed Gentry, 8.

HOLDITCH. Blomefield's Norfolk, x. 113. Harleian Society, xxxii. 157.

HOLDSWORTH. Surtees Society, xxxvi. 255. Burke's Landed Gentry, (of Sandall Hall,) 5 and supp., 6, 7, 8 ; (of Widdicombe,) 6, 7, 8. Foster's Yorkshire Pedigrees. The Genealogist, New Series, xvii. 64.

HOLE. Burke's Landed Gentry, 6, 7, 8. Howard's Visitation of England and Wales, vii. 128.

HOLES. J. Wilkinson's History of Broughton Gifford, folding plate. Clutterbuck's Hertford, i. 246. Wiltshire Archæological Magazine, v. 267. Ormerod's Cheshire, ii. 433.

HOLFORD. Rudder's Gloucestershire, 809. Burke's Heraldic Illustrations, 91. Morant's Essex, i. 93. Cambridgeshire Visitation, edited by Sir T. Phillipps, 18. History of Tetbury, Co. Gloucester, by A. T. Lee, 218-220. Burke's Landed Gentry, (of Westonbirt,) 2 supp., 3, 4, 5, 6, 7, 8 ; (of Buckland,) 2, 3, 4, 5, 6, 7 ; (of Castle Hill,) 8 supp. Ormerod's Cheshire, i. 671 ; iii. 239. Harleian

Society, xiii. 218 ; xv. 390 ; xviii. 125 ; xxi. 83 ; xli. 77. Burke's Royal Families, (London, 1851, 8vo.) i. 129. Miscellanea Genealogica et Heraldica, New Series, iii. 254. The Genealogist, New Series, xii. 110. *See* BOSANQUET, GWYNNE.

HOLGATE. Berry's Essex Genealogies, 114. Foster's Visitations of Yorkshire, 533. Harleian Society, xiii. 421 ; xiv. 666 ; xvi. 161 ; xl. 1282. Bysshe's Visitation of Essex, edited by J. J. Howard, 49.

HOLIWELL. Collectanea Genealogica, (Family of Holiwell.) By W. C. Holiwell. *Circa* 1880, 8vo. The Genealogist, New Series, xiv. 101.

HOLKER. Harleian Society, xl. 1225.

HOLL. Harleian Society, xxxii. 157.

HOLLAND. Pedigree of Holland of Dumbleton, [T. P.] 1854, folio page. Another of same, folio page. Gentleman's Magazine, 1822, i. 303. Harleian Society, i. 56 ; vi. 345 ; xv. 389 ; xxviii. 250 ; xxxii. 158 ; xxxvii. 177 ; xli. 39. Gregson's Fragments relative to the County of Lancaster, 207. Dwnn's Visitations of Wales, ii. 117, 210, 337, 364. Berry's Sussex Genealogies, 185, 378. Cambridgeshire Visitation, edited by Sir T. Phillipps, 17; Blomefield's Norfolk, i. 344. Burke's Commoners, i. 459 ; (Landed Gentry,) 8. Chetham Society, lxxxi. 16, 18, 115 ; lxxxv. 146, 147 ; cx. 214. Archæologia Cambrensis, 3 S. xii. 183 ; xiii. 170. Notices of Swyncombe and Ewelme, in Co. Oxford, by H. A. Napier, 323. History of the Ancient Chapel of Denton, by Rev. J. Booker, 24. Nichols' History of the County of Leicester, ii. 424. Independancy at Brighouse, by J. H. Turner, 72. Plantagenet-Harrison's History of Yorkshire, i. 7. The Genealogist, iv. 179. Edmondson's Baronagium Genealogicum, v. 483. Banks' Baronies in Fee, i. 255. Visitation of Devon, edited by F. T. Colby, 132. Banks' Dormant and Extinct Baronage, iii. 416. Burke's Extinct Baronetcies. Carthew's Hundred of Launditch, Part iii. 80. History of Powys Fadog, by J. Y. W. Lloyd, iii. 50 ; v. 402 ; vi. 437. Notes and Queries, 7 S. ix. 341, 476. Croston's edn. of Baines's Lancaster, ii. 347 ; iii. 282 ; iv. 300. Sussex Archæological Society, xliii. 60. *See* HOLLOND, HOLAND, HALLEN.

HOLLAND-CORBETT. *See* CORBETT of Admington, in Burke's Landed Gentry.

HOLLED. Nichols' History of the County of Leicester, iv. 342.

HOLLES. Jacob's Peerage, i. 348. Glover's History of Derbyshire, ii. 140, (123). Topographer, (London, 1789-91, 8vo.) i. 143. Shaw's Staffordshire, i. 98. Erdeswicke's Survey of Staffordshire, 273. Manning and Bray's Surrey, ii. 32. Clutterbuck's Hertford, i. 131. Memoirs, British and Foreign, of Illustrious Persons who died in 1711, 362. Berry's Genealogical Peerage, 80. Banks' Dormant and Extinct Baronage, iii. 188, 373. Burke's Extinct Baronetcies. *See* CAVENDISH.

HOLLEY. Burke's Landed Gentry, 3, 4, 5, 6 and supp., 7, 8.

HOLLIDAY. Visitation of Middlesex, (Salisbury, 1820, fol.) 38. Foster's Visitation of Middlesex, 70. *See* HALLIDAY.

HOLLIMAN. Visitation of Durham, 1615, (Sunderland, 1820, fol.) 30.
HOLLINGBERY. Berry's Kent Genealogies, 196.
HOLLINGS. Burke's Landed Gentry, 5, 6, 7, 8.
HOLLINGTON. Metcalfe's Visitation of Worcester, 1683, 60.
HOLLINGWORTH. Burke's Landed Gentry, 2. Harleian Society, ii.
184; xv. 391. Nichols' History of the County of Leicester, iv.
166. Ormerod's Cheshire, iii. 870. Earwaker's East Cheshire,
ii. 143, 145.
HOLLINSHEAD. Burke's Landed Gentry, 2 supp., 3, 4, 5. Ormerod's
Cheshire, iii. 767. Earwaker's East Cheshire, ii. 617.
HOLLIS. Memoirs of Thomas Hollis. London, 1780, 2 vols., 4to.
Blomefield's Norfolk, viii. 417. Burke's Landed Gentry, 2, 3, 4.
Harleian Society, iv. 61. Hunter's History of the Parish of
Sheffield, 320. Thoroton's Nottinghamshire, iii. 358.
HOLLIST. Burke's Landed Gentry, 2, 3, 4, 5, 6, 7, 8.
HOLLOND. Collectanea Topographica et Genealogica, i. 296. Burke's
Landed Gentry, 2 supp., 3, 4, 5, 6, 7, 8. See HOLLAND.
HOLLOWAY. Pedigree of Holloway of Hollington, Co. Derby, [T. P.]
1869, folio page. Ashmole's Antiquities of Berkshire, iii. 298.
Visitation of Oxfordshire, 1634, printed by Sir T. Phillipps,
(Middle Hill, fol.) 21. Harleian Society, v. 290; viii. 378.
The Genealogist, New Series, i. 12. Notes and Queries, 6 S. x.
409, 523.
HOLMAN. Berry's Surrey Genealogies, 71. Surrey Archæological
Collections, iv.; vii. Manning and Bray's Surrey, ii. 307.
Baker's Northampton, i. 740. Harleian Society, xv. 390, 391;
xliii. 95, 153. Burke's Extinct Baronetcies. The Visitations of
Cornwall, edited by J. L. Vivian, 496.
HOLME. Cheshire and Lancashire Historic Society, Session i. 86.
Surtees Society, xxxvi. 129. Burke's Commoners, iv. 215, 250;
Landed Gentry, 2, 3, 4, 5, 6, 7, 8. Harleian Society, i. 34; xvi.
162; xviii. 126. Foster's Lancashire Pedigrees. Poulson's
Holderness, ii. 488. Foster's Yorkshire Pedigrees. Foster's
Visitations of Yorkshire, 152, 224. Ormerod's Cheshire, ii. 456.
Plantagenet-Harrison's History of Yorkshire, i. 270. Moule's
Bibliotheca Heraldica, 240. Woodcock of Cuerden, by A. E. P.
Gray, 13. Fishwick's History of Rochdale, 507. The Genealo-
gist, New Series, xvii. 129.
HOLMEDEN. Surrey Archæological Collections, vii. Harleian Society,
xliii. 128.
HOLMER. Chance of Bromsgrove, by J. F. Chance, 93.
HOLMES. Cambridgeshire Visitation, edited by Sir T. Phillipps,
18. Berry's Hampshire Genealogies, 350. Burke's Landed
Gentry, (of St. David's,) 3, 4, 5, 6, 7, 8; (of Scole House,) 2 add.,
3, 4, 5, 6, 7, 8; (of Gawdy Hall,) 6, 7, 8; (of Brooke Hall,) 6, 7,
8. Foster's Visitations of Yorkshire, 361. Harleian Society,
viii. 3, 204; xli. 98. Dallaway's Sussex, 2nd edition, II. i, 213.
Surtees' Durham, iv. 93. Plantagenet-Harrison's History of
Yorkshire, i. 271. Notes and Queries, 3 S. ii. 294. Burke's
Colonial Gentry, i. 201; ii. 722.

HOLME-SUMNER. Burke's Commoners, i. 60 ; Landed Gentry, 4, 5. Burke's Landed Gentry, 7.

HOLROYD. Archdall's Lodge's Peerage, vii. 200. Brydges' Collins' Peerage, ix. 233. Burke's Colonial Gentry, i. 25.

HOLSTOCK. Harleian Society, xiii. 422. Bysshe's Visitation of Essex, edited by J. J. Howard, 49.

HOLT, or HOLTE. A History of the Holtes of Aston, by A. Davidson. Birmingham, 1854, 4to. Visitation of Suffolk, edited by J. J. Howard, ii. 45-58. Morant's Essex, ii. 536. Berry's Hampshire Genealogies, 210. Sir T. Phillipps' Topographer, No. 1, (March, 1821, 8vo.) 21. Cambridgeshire Visitation, edited by Sir T. Phillipps, 18. Visitation of Oxfordshire, 1574, printed by Sir T. Phillipps, (Middle Hill, fol.) 5. Burke's Commoners, i. 273. Burke's Landed Gentry, (of Stubbylee,) 2, 3, 4, 5, 6, 7, 8; (of Enfield,) 2 supp., 3, 4; (of Farnborough Grange,) 8; (of Sefton Park,) 8; 6 at p. 1761. Harleian Society, v. 173; viii. 336; xii. 19; xv. 392; xli. 65. Chetham Society, lxxxi. 13, 22; lxxxii. 39, 91; lxxxv. 148-151; xcviii. 47, 53. Visitation of Warwickshire, 1619, published with Warwickshire Antiquarian Magazine, 174. Herald and Genealogist, ii. 156. Dugdale's Warwickshire, 871. Whitaker's History of Whalley, ii. 24. Notes and Queries, 1 S. ii. 244, 451, 506; 6 S. iv. 156; viii. 356. Wotton's English Baronetage, i. 263. The Genealogist, v. 275; New Series, xvii. 242. Ormerod's Cheshire, iii. 88, 218. Metcalfe's Visitations of Suffolk, 42. Burke's Extinct Baronetcies. Burke's Colonial Gentry, i. 251. Fishwick's History of Rochdale, 330. Burke's Family Records, 327. Croston's edn. of Baines's Lancaster, iii. 352.

HOLTBY. Foster's Visitations of Yorkshire, 230.

HOLTHAM. Pedigree of Holtham of Saintbury Hill; etc., [T. P.] 1865, folio page.

HOLTOFTE. Harleian Society, iv. 103.

HOLWAY, HOLLWAY, or HOLWEY. Visitation of Somerset, printed by Sir T. Phillipps, 103. Harleian Society, vi. 155; xi. 55. Tuckett's Devonshire Pedigrees, 86. The Visitations of Devon, by J. L. Vivian, 447. See CALTHROP, (of Stanhoe).

HOLWELL. Descent of Hugh Martin Short, M.A., from the Ancient Family of Holwell, long slip, circa 1877.

HOLWICK. Plantagenet-Harrison's History of Yorkshire, i. 374.

HOLWORTHY. Harleian Society, viii. 193.

HOLY. Harleian Society, xxxviii. 705.

HOLYDAY. Account of the Township of Iffley, by Rev. Edw. Marshall, 71.

HOLYNGWORTHE. Burke's Landed Gentry, 3, 4, 5.

HOLYOAKE. Burke's Commoners, ii. 597.

HOMAN. Betham's Baronetage, v. 475.

HOMAN-MULOCK. Burke's Landed Gentry, 6. Howard's Visitation of Ireland, iii. 89.

HOME. Case of Alexander Home, claiming to be Earl of Marchmont, London, 1820, fol.; and Westminster, 1822, folio, pp. 17. Claim of Alexander Home to the Title of Earl of Marchmont, Sess. Papers, 40 of 1822. Case, and additional Case for F. D. Home, claiming the Titles of Earl of Marchmont, etc. Westminster, 1842, fol. Claim of Francis Home, Esq., to the Title of Earl of Marchmont, Sess. Papers, 113 of 1838 ; 141 of 1839 ; 67 of 1840 ; 33 of 1842 ; 103 of 1843. Genealogical Account of the Family of Home of Wedderburne. 1776, 4to. Burke's Landed Gentry, (of Wedderburne,) 2 ; (of Argaty,) 7 at p. 1286, 8 at p. 1412 ; (of Whitfield,) 5 ; (of Broom House,) 2 add., 4, 5, 6, 7, 8 ; (of Bassendean,) 5, 6, 7. A. A. Carr's History of Coldingham Priory, 87. Wood's Douglas's Peerage of Scotland, i. 453, 731 ; ii. 173. Foster's Collectanea Genealogica, (MP's Scotland,) 181. Burke's Extinct Baronetcies, 626. Notes and Queries, 6 S., xii. 17. Scottish Journal, i. 353 ; ii. 43. Alexander Nisbet's Heraldic Plates, 48, 94. *See* BINNING-HOME, CAMPBELL, HUME, MILNE-HOME, DOUGLAS-HOME.

HOMER. Chance of Bromsgrove, by J. F. Chance, 43, 93.

HOMERSLEY. Visitations of Staffordshire, 1614 and 1663-4, William Salt Society, 177.

HOMFRAY. Burke's Commoners, (of Penlyne Castle,) i. 236, Landed Gentry, 2, 3, 4, 5, 6, 7, 8 ; (of The Place, Suffolk,) Landed Gentry, 3, 4, 5. Genealogy of Henzey, Tyttery, and Tyzack, by H. S. Grazebrook, 52. Harleian Society, xxxvii. 395.

HONDFORD. J. P. Earwaker's East Cheshire, i. 250.

HONE. Westcote's Devonshire, edited by G. Oliver and P. Jones, 538. Harleian Society, xiii. 220, 423.

HONFORD. Cheshire and Lancashire Historic Society, ii. 54. Visits to the Fields of Battle in England, by Richd. Brooke, 282. Ormerod's Cheshire, iii. 602, 644.

HONING, or HONNINGE. Collectanea Topographica et Genealogica, vii. 394. Page's History of Suffolk, 382. Metcalfe's Visitations of Suffolk, 96.

HONKYLOWE. Ormerod's Cheshire, iii. 477.

HONY. Burke's Royal Families, (London, 1851, 8vo.) i. 154.

HONYCHURCH. Harleian Society, vi. 347. Westcote's Devonshire, edited by G. Oliver and P. Jones, 591. Visitation of Devon, edited by F. T. Colby, 135. The Visitations of Devon, by J. L. Vivian, 478.

HONYMAN. Betham's Baronetage, v. 546.

HONYWOOD. Topographer and Genealogist, i. 397, 568 : ii. 169, 189, 256, 312, 433. Morant's Essex, ii. 167. Croke's History of the Family of Croke, No. 38. Hasted's Kent, ii. 218, 449 ; iii. 213, 308, 588. Berry's Sussex Genealogies, 37. Berry's Essex Genealogies, 72. Berry's Kent Genealogies, 226. Burke's Landed Gentry, 3. G. W. Johnson's History of Great Totham, 31. Harleian Society, xiii. 423 ; xiv. 733 ; xv. 393, 394 ; xl. 1296 ; xlii. 47. Notes and Queries, 3 S. iv. 285, 322. Wotton's English Baronetage, iii. 105. Betham's Baronetage, ii. 131. The Genealogist, New Series, iv. 22. Chancellor's Sepulchral Monuments of Essex, 121. *See* KNATCHBULL.

Hoo. Sir T. Phillipps' Topographer, No. 1, (March, 1821, 8vo.) 53. Berry's Hertfordshire Genealogies, 148, 213. Blomefield's Norfolk, x. 40. Shaw's Staffordshire, ii. 172. Dallaway's Sussex, II. ii. 339. Visitation of Staffordshire, 1663-4, printed by Sir T. Phillipps, 6. History of Wednesbury, (Wolverhampton, 1854, 8vo.) 163. Clutterbuck's Hertford, iii. 72, 94. Chauncy's Hertfordshire, 510. Sussex Archæological Collections, viii. 130. Banks' Dormant and Extinct Baronage, iii. 375. Carthew's Hundred of Launditch, Part iii. 310. The Genealogist, New Series, iv. 77; xiv. 256; xvii. 245. Harleian Society, xxii. 12, 65; xxxii. 158. Visitations of Staffordshire, 1614 and 1663-4, William Salt Society, 178.

Hood. Burke's Commoners, (of Bardon Park,) iv. 166, Landed Gentry, 2, 3, 4, 5; (of Stoneridge,) Landed Gentry, 2 supp., 3, 4, 5, 6, 7, 8; (of Nettleham Hall,) 2 add., 3, 4, 5, 6, 7, 8. Lipscombe's History of the County of Buckingham, i. 280. Nichols' History of the County of Leicester, iv. 806. Archdall's Lodge's Peerage, vii. 213. Brydges' Collins' Peerage, vi. 324, 366. Burke's Colonial Gentry, ii. 544, 677. Harleian Society, xxxix. 1138.

Hoogan. Carthew's Hundred of Launditch, Part ii. 804, 806.

Hook, or Hooke. Berry's Hampshire Genealogies, 212. Visitation of Gloucestershire, 1569, (Middle Hill, 1854, fol.) 6. Harleian Society, xv. 394; xxi. 84. Notes and Queries, 2 S. ix. 466; 6 S. viii. 436. Burke's Extinct Baronetcies. Visitation of Gloucester, edited by T. F. Fenwick and W. C. Metcalfe, 91.

Hooker. Harleian Society, viii. 202. Westcote's Devonshire, edited by G. Oliver and P. Jones, 526. Visitation of Devon, edited by F. T. Colby, 136. The Visitations of Devon, by J. L. Vivian, 479. New England Register, xlvii. 192.

Hookes. Dwnn's Visitations of Wales, ii. 162.

Hookwood. Manning and Bray's Surrey, ii. 190.

Hoolahan. O'Hart's Irish Pedigrees, 2nd Series, 199.

Hoole. Harleian Society, xl. 1201.

Hooper. Berry's Kent Genealogies, 477. Visitation of Somerset, printed by Sir T. Phillipps, 104. Harleian Society, xi. 56; xx. 55. Visitatio Comitatus Wiltoniæ, 1623, printed by Sir T. Phillipps. Hutchins' Dorset, iii. 384. Visitation of Wiltshire, edited by G. W. Marshall, 54. Howard's Visitation of England and Wales, i. 176. New England Register, xxii. 287. Burke's Family Records, 327. The Genealogist, New Series, xii. 93.

Hoord. Harleian Society, xxviii. 251; xliii. 222.

Hooton. Ormerod's Cheshire, ii. 410. Harleian Society, xviii. 214. See De Hooton.

Hope. Jewitt's Reliquary, ii. 6. Glover's History of Derbyshire, ii. 585, (563). Dwnn's Visitations of Wales, ii. 316. Burke's Commoners, (of Deepdene,) iv. 457, Landed Gentry, 2, 3, 4, 5, 6, 7, 8; (of Carriden,) Landed Gentry, 2, 3, 4, 5, 6; (of Luffness,) 7, 8. Pedigrees of the Leading Families of Lancashire, published by Joseph Foster, (London, 1872, fol.). Nisbet's Heraldry, ii.

27

app. 97. Douglas's Baronage of Scotland, 58. The Parish of
Cramond, by J. P. Wood, 132. Plantagenet-Harrison's History
of Yorkshire, i. 304. Wood's Douglas's Peerage of Scotland,
i. 741. Brydges' Collins' Peerage, ix. 392, Foster's Collectanea
Genealogica, (MP's Scotland,) 187. Burke's Extinct Baronetcies,
626. Memoir of Chancellor Seton, by Geo. Seton, App. II.
Pedigrees of the Leading Families of Yorkshire, by Joseph Foster.
Burke's Colonial Gentry, i. 253. A Chapter in Mediocrity, by
W. J. Stavert, 10.

HOPE-EDWARDES. Howard's Visitation of England and Wales, ii. 47.
Burke's Landed Gentry, 8.

HOPEGOOD. Monken Hadley, by F. C. Cass, 187.

HOPER. Burke's Landed Gentry, 3, 4. Westcote's Devonshire,
edited by G. Oliver and P. Jones, 525. The Genealogist, v. 275.

HOPES. Burke's Landed Gentry, 2, 3, 4, 5, 6.

HOPETOUN. Claim of James, Earl of Hopetoun, to the Title of
Marquis of Annandale, Sess. Papers, April and May, 1794;
Decr. 1795. Burke's Colonial Gentry, i. 362.

HOPKINS. Glamorganshire Pedigrees, edited by Sir T. Phillipps, 33,
42. Burke's Landed Gentry, 3, 4, 5, 6, 7, 8. Harleian Society,
viii. 108. Lipscombe's History of the County of Buckingham,
i. 377. Shaw's Staffordshire, ii. 84. Visitation of Staffordshire,
1663-4, printed by Sir. T. Phillipps, 6. History of Wednesbury,
(Wolverhampton, 1854, 8vo.) 169. Manning and Bray's Surrey,
iii. 278. Visitations of Staffordshire, 1614 and 1663-4, William
Salt Society, 180. Metcalfe's Visitations of Northamptonshire,
100. Genealogies of Morgan and Glamorgan, by G. T. Clark, 331.
Miscellanea Genealogica et Heraldica, 2nd Series, iii. 260. New
England Register, v. 43. Burke's Family Records, 328. Howard's
Visitation of England and Wales, viii. 32. See NORTHEY-HOPKINS.

HOPKINSON. Surtees Society, xxxvi. 51. The Genealogist, iii. 179;
New Series, ix. 65. Visitation of Derbyshire, 1663-4, (Middle
Hill, 1854, fol.) 4. See CURRER.

HOPPER. Berry's Kent Genealogies, 7. Burke's Landed Gentry, 2
and supp., 3, 4, 5, 6 at p. 1451.

HOPPER-WILLIAMSON. Burke's Landed Gentry, 2, 3, 4, 5, 6.

HOPPERTON. Foster's Visitations of Yorkshire, 534.

HOPTON. Visitation of Somerset, printed by Sir T. Phillipps, 105.
Burke's Commoners, iv. 172, Landed Gentry, 2, 3, 4, 5, 6, 7, 8.
Foster's Yorkshire Pedigrees. Foster's Visitations of Yorkshire,
42. Suckling's History of Suffolk, ii. 137. Harleian Society, xi.
56; xvi. 164; xxviii. 135, 253, 256; xxxii. 160. Blore's Rutland,
133. Thoresby's Ducatus Leodiensis, 186. Duncumb's History
of the Co. of Hereford, ii. 20. Page's History of Suffolk, 279.
Duchetiana, by Sir G. F. Duckett, 2nd edn., 63. Collections by
the Powys-land Club, x. 43. Notes and Queries, 1 S. iv. 97; 3
S. iv. 95, 255. Metcalfe's Visitations of Suffolk, 43. Weaver's
Visitation of Herefordshire, 45. Old Yorkshire, edited by
William Smith, ii. 160. Miscellanea Genealogica et Heraldica,
3rd Series, iii. 9.

HOPWOOD. Morant's Essex, ii. 192. Chetham Society, lxxxi. 19 ; lxxxv. 152 ; xcviii. 57. Baines' History of the Co. of Lancaster, ii. 611 ; Croston's, edn. ii. 416. Robinson's Mansions of Herefordshire, 229. Abram's History of Blackburn, 398. Genealogical Memoranda relating to the Family of King, by W. L. King, 7. Fishwick's History of Rochdale, 515. Burke's Landed Gentry, 7. Genealogical record of King and Henham, 6. *See* GREGGE-HOPWOOD.

HORD, or HORDE. Visitation of Somerset, printed by Sir T. Phillipps, 106. The Genealogist, New Series, ii. 47. Visitation of Oxfordshire, 1634, printed by Sir T. Phillipps, (Middle Hill, fol.) 21. Topographer and Genealogist, i. 33 ; ii. 515. Harleian Society, v. 261 ; xi. 58. Miscellanea Genealogica et Heraldica, New Series, iv. 138. *See* HOARD.

HORDERN. Burke's Landed Gentry, 2, 3, 4.

HORE. Burke's Commoners, iv. xxi. ; (of Pole Hore,) Commoners, iv. 712, Landed Gentry, 2, 3, 4, 5, 6 ; (of Harperston,) Commoners, iv. 716, Landed Gentry, 2, 3, 4, 5. Harleian Society, vi. 156. Dugdale's Warwickshire, 348, 922. The Forest and Chase of Sutton Coldfield, (London, 1860, 8vo.) app. The Visitations of Devon, by J. L. Vivian, 480. Howard's Visitation of Ireland, i. 84. *See* HOARE.

HORLOCK. Burke's Royal Families, (London, 1851, 8vo.) i. 190. Burke's Landed Gentry, 2.

HORN, or HORNE. Surtees Society, xxxvi. 353. Nisbet's Heraldry, ii. app. 73. Berry's Kent Genealogies, 175. Visitation of Warwickshire, 1619, published with Warwickshire Antiquarian Magazine, 58. Hunter's Deanery of Doncaster, i. 391. Harleian Society, xii. 343 ; xxviii. 260. Genealogical Gleanings in England, by H. F. Waters, i. 155. Burke's Colonial Gentry, i. 256. New England Register, vii. 156 ; xl. 47. Oliver's History of Antigua, ii. 82. *See* DE HORNE, MANTELL.

HORNBY. Burke's Commoners, (of Dalton,) iii. 698, Landed Gentry, 2, 3, 4, 5, 6, 7, 8 ; (of Little Green,) Landed Gentry, 3, 4, 5, 7, 8 ; (of Ribby Hall,) 2 supp., 3, 4, 5, 6, 7, 8 ; (of Liverpool,) 2 supp., 3, 4, 5, 6, 7 ; (of Raikes Hall,) 2 supp., 3, 4, 5, 6, 7 ; (of the Hook,) 5, 6, 7, 8 ; (of St. Michaels,) 2, supp., 3, 4. Foster's Lancashire Pedigrees. Abram's History of Blackburn, 398.

HORNCASTLE. Harleian Society, xxxix. 1168.

HORNDON. Burke's Landed Gentry, 5, 6, 7, 8.

HORNER. The Horner Family of Wakefield, Co. York. Sheffield, 1879, 8vo. Collinson's Somerset, ii. 463. Visitation of Somerset, printed by Sir T. Phillipps, 107. Burke's Landed Gentry, 3, 4, 5, 6, 7, 8. Harleian Society, viii. 79 ; xi. 57. Hutchins' Dorset, ii. 667. Miscellanea Genealogica et Heraldica, New Series, iv. 161.

HORNICOTE. Maclean's History of Trigg Minor, iii. 158.

HORNIDGE. Burke's Landed Gentry, 4. Blunt's Dursley and its Neighbourhood, 161. The Irish Builder, xxix. 304.

HORNOR. Burke's Landed Gentry, 3, 4.

HORNYOLD. Nash's Worcestershire, i. 558. Burke's Commoners,

i. 283 ; Landed Gentry, 2, 3, 4, 5, 6, 7, 8. Burke's Royal Families, (London, 1851, 8vo.) i. 177. Metcalfe's Visitation of Worcester, 1683, 61. Roman Catholic Families of England, by J. J. Howard and H. F. Burke, Part iv.

HORROCKS. Burke's Landed Gentry, 2, 6, 7, 8. Notes and Queries, 1 S. iii. 421, 475. Burke's Colonial Gentry, ii. 734.

HORSBRUGH. Burke's Landed Gentry, 7, 8.

HORSEMAN. Sir T. Phillipps' Topographer, No. 1 (March, 1821, 8vo.) 15. Visitation of Oxfordshire, 1574, printed by Sir T. Phillipps, (Middle Hill, fol.) 5. Harleian Society, v. 172. The Genealogist, iii. 271.

HORSEY. Visitation of Warwickshire, 1619, published with Warwickshire Antiquarian Magazine, 190. Visitatio Comitatus Wiltoniæ, 1623, printed by Sir T. Phillipps. Hutchins' Dorset, iv. 427. Clutterbuck's Hertford, ii. 321. Harleian Society, xii. 195 ; xxii. 114. The Genealogist, New Series, vii. 244 ; xii. 94. Miscellanea Genealogica et Heraldica, 2nd Series, ii. 43. Weaver's Visitations of Somerset, 35. Burke's Family Records, 330.

HORSFALL. Surtees Society, xxxvi. 231. Burke's Landed Gentry, 5, 6, and at p. 128, 7, p. 139. Foster's Visitations of Yorkshire, 534. Independancy at Brighouse, by J. H. Turner, 79. Doncaster Charities, by Charles Jackson, 50. Burke's Colonial Gentry, ii. 637. Harleian Society, xl. 1182.

HORSFORD. Oliver's History of Antigua, ii. 86.

HORSLEY. Foster's Visitations of Northumberland, 69. The Genealogist, New Series, xv. 101. Surtees Society, xxxvi. 169, 362. Burke's Commoners, iii. 210. Foster's Visitations of Yorkshire, 180. Hodgson's Northumberland, I. ii. 235 ; II. ii. 103, 104. Archæologia Æliana, 2nd Series, vi. 181. Surtees' Durham, ii. 266. The Genealogist, ii. 258. Bateson's History of Northumberland, i. 203.

HORSMAN. Burke's Landed Gentry, 6.

HORSMANDEN. Berry's Kent Genealogies, 363.

HORSNAILE. Account of the Family of Druce of Goreing, 10.

HORSPOOLE. Harleian Society, i. 46 ; xlii. 143. Berry's Kent Genealogies, 318.

HORT. Betham's Baronetage, iii. 353.

HORTON. J. Wilkinson's History of Broughton Gifford, 53. Surtees Society, xxxvi. 233. Burke's Commoners, (of Howroyde,) i. 283, Landed Gentry, 2, 3, 4, 5, 6, 7, 8 ; (of the Holt,) Landed Gentry, 6, 7, 8. Foster's Yorkshire Pedigrees. History of Bradford, by John James, 439. Burke's Authorized Arms, 122. Butterworth's Account of the Town, etc., of Oldham, 158. Visitation of Derbyshire, 1663-4, (Middle Hill, 1854, fol.) 5. Visitatio Comitatus Wiltoniæ, 1623, printed by Sir T. Phillipps. Wiltshire Archæological Magazine, v. 233, 267, 317, 357. The Genealogist, iii. 179 ; New Series, xii. 94. Ormerod's Cheshire, ii. 99, 708. John Watson's History of Halifax, 151-157, 296. Glover's Derbyshire, 8vo. edn., ii. 204. Betham's Baronetage, iii. 311. Visitation of Wiltshire, edited by G. W. Marshall, 88. Burke's

Extinct Baronetcies. R. Ussher's Historical Sketch of Croxall, 174. Journal of the Derbyshire Archæological Society, iii. 67. Harleian Society, xviii. 127, 186 ; xxi. 84 ; xxix. 426. Visitation of Gloucester, edited by T. F. Fenwick and W. C. Metcalfe, 93. Burke's Family Records, 332. Yorkshire Archæological Society, Record Series, xxx. 385.

HORWOOD. Maclean's History of Trigg Minor, i. 73.

HOSATUS. Dallaway's Sussex, i. 188. *See* HUSSEY.

HOSIER. Baker's Northampton, ii. 255. Notes and Queries, 6 S. x. 435. Harleian Society, xxviii. 261.

HOSKEN. Burke's Commoners, i. 94 ; Landed Gentry, 2, 3, 4, 5, 6, 7.

HOSKEN-HARPER. Burke's Landed Gentry, 4, 5, 6.

HOSKING. An Account of the Families of Boase, (Exeter, 1876, 4to.) 28. The Visitations of Cornwall, edited by J. L. Vivian, 347.

HOSKINS. Berry's Surrey Genealogies, 32. Surrey Archæological Collections, iii. Burke's Landed Gentry, (of Higham,) 3, 4, 5, 6, 7, 8 ; (of North Perrott,) 5, 6, 7, 8 ; (of Birch House,) 2. Harleian Society, viii. 158, 215 ; xx. 56 ; xliii. 58. Hutchins' Dorset, ii. 123. Manning and Bray's Surrey, ii. 386. Master's Notices of the Family of Master, 90.

HOSKYN, or HOSKYNS. Harleian Society, i. 38. Burke's Royal Families, (London, 1851, 8vo.) i. 66. Burke's Landed Gentry, 2, 3, 4. Robinson's Mansions of Herefordshire, 133. Wotton's English Baronetage, iii. 604. Betham's Baronetage, ii. 451. Genealogies of Morgan and Glamorgan, by G. T. Clark, 490.

HOSTE. Burke's Landed Gentry, 2, 3, 4. Harleian Society, xv. 395.

HOTCHKIN. Burke's Landed Gentry, 7, 8.

HOTHAM, or HOTHUM. Bridges' Northamptonshire, by Rev. Peter Whalley, ii. 434. Surtees Society, xxxvi. 336. Foster's Yorkshire Pedigrees. Foster's Visitations of Yorkshire, 89. George Oliver's History of Beverley, 509. History of Beverley, by G. Poulson, 351. Dugdale's Warwickshire, 942. Wotton's English Baronetage, i. 470 ; iv. 385. Harleian Society, xxxvii. 128. Banks' Baronies in Fee, i. 256. Betham's Baronetage, i. 243. Banks' Dormant and Extinct Baronage, i. 346. The Genealogist, v. 33 ; New Series, xii. 228 ; xiv. 94. *See* DE HOTHOM.

HOTHERSALL. Chetham Society, lxxxv. 153. The Tyldesley Diary, edited by J. Gillow and A. Hewitson, 154. History of Longridge, by T. C. Smith, 136. History of Ribchester, by T. C. Smith, 225. Croston's edn. of Baines's Lancashire, iv. 110.

HOTOT. Bridges' Northamptonshire, by Rev. Peter Whalley, ii. 369. Thoroton's Nottinghamshire, i. 254. The Genealogist, New Series, xiii. 246.

HOTTON. Plantagenet-Harrison's History of Yorkshire, i. 441.

HOUBLON. Morant's Essex, ii. 513. Berry's Essex Genealogies, 164. Burke's Landed Gentry, 2, 4, 5, 6, 7, 8. Miscellanea Genealogica et Heraldica, New Series, i. 171. Harleian Society, xiv. 633. Ellacombe's History of Bitton, 100.

HOUBY. Nichols' History of the County of Leicester, iii. 264. The

Genealogist, New Series, xii. 174 ; xiv. 190 ; xvii. 108. *See* DE
HOUBY.

HOUGH. Life of Bishop Hough, by John Wilmot, 140. Ormerod's
Cheshire, ii. 552. Harleian Society, xviii. 127.

HOUGHAM. Planché's Corner of Kent, 390. Hasted's Kent, iv. 231.
Berry's Kent Genealogies, 164. History of Sandwich, by W.
Boys, 367. Harleian Society, xlii. 97.

HOUGHTON. Berry's Sussex Genealogies, 163. Berry's Hampshire
Genealogies, 236. Burke's Landed Gentry, 3, 4. Harleian Society,
iii. 6 ; xiii. 510 ; xv. 369 ; xxxii. 160. Chetham Society, lxxxi.
25 ; lxxxii. 51, 116 ; lxxxv. 154 ; xcviii. 48 ; xcix. 44. Wright's
History of Rutland, 71. Gage's History of Thingoe Hundred,
Suffolk, 93. Blore's Rutland, 156. Whitaker's History of
Whalley, ii. 28. Ormerod's Cheshire, iii. 901. Genealogical
Gleanings in England, by H. F. Waters, i. 258. History of Rib-
chester, by T. C. Smith, 241. New England Register, xxii. 115 ;
xlii. 66. History of Chipping, by Tom C. Smith, 21.

HOULDSWORTH. Burke's Landed Gentry, 5 supp., 6, 7, 8. Facts
and Traditions, by D. C. M'Connel, 141, 152.

HOULTON. Burke's Commoners, iv. 602 ; Landed Gentry, 2, 3, 4, 5,
6, 7, 8. J. E. Jackson's History of Grittleton, (Wiltsh. Topl.
Soc.), 8. Genealogical Memoranda of the Family of Ames.

HOUND. Cambridgeshire Visitation, edited by Sir T. Phillipps, 18.

HOUNSFIELD. Burke's Landed Gentry, 4. Supplement to Gatty's
edition of Hunter's Hallamshire, xlvi.

HOURD. *See* HORD.

HOUSE. The Genealogist, v. 276. *See* HULSE.

HOUSTON, or HOUSTOUN. Burke's Landed Gentry, (of Johnstone,)
2, 3, 4, 5, 6, 7, 8 ; (of Clerkington,) 5, 6, 7, 8 ; (of Coneywarren,)
2, 3, 4 ; (of Orangefield,) 6, 7, 8. Lands and their Owners in
Galloway, by P. H. M'Kerlie, i. 494, 500. The Genealogist,
v. 22. Foster's Collectanea Genealogica, (MP's Scotland,) 189.
Notes and Queries, 4 S. ix. 473. Burke's Extinct Baronetcies,
627. Northern Notes and Queries, vi. 94.

HOVEDEN, or HOVENDEN. Topographer, (London, 1789-91, 8vo.)
ii. 115.

HOVELL. Blomefield's Norfolk, viii. 466. Harleian Society, viii. 62 ;
xv. 396 ; xxxii. 161. Metcalfe's Visitations of Suffolk, 146, 194.
Burke's Colonial Gentry, ii. 688.

HOW. Rudder's Gloucestershire, 708. Harleian Society, xiii. 425 ;
xv. 396. Archdall's Lodge's Peerage, v. 78. *See* HOWE.

HOWARD. The Howard Papers, by H. K. S. Causton. London, 1863,
8vo. Lives of Earls of Arundel, in C. Wright's History of
Arundel. London, 1818, 8vo. Antiquities of Arundel, with an
Abstract of the Lives of the Earls of Arundel, by C. Carraccioli.
London, 1766, 8vo. Historical Anecdotes of the Howard Family,
by the Hon. Charles Howard. London, 1769, 8vo., 2nd edition,
1817. An Analysis of the Genealogical History of the Family of
Howard, by Sir T. C. Banks. London, 1812, 8vo. The Mysterious
Heir, being the case of Mr. Walter Howard, claiming the Dukedom

of Norfolk. London, 1816, 8vo. Genealogical History of the Noble House of Howard. London, 1830, 8vo. History and Antiquities of the Castle and Town of Arundel, including the Biography of its Earls, by M. A. Tierney. London, 1834, 2 vols., 8vo. Indication of Memorials, etc., of the Howard Family, by H. Howard of Corby Castle, 1834. Records of the Ashtead Estate and of its Howard possessors. Lichfield, 1873. The Worthies of Cumberland, (The Howards,) by Henry Lonsdale. London, 1872, 8vo. The Noble and Illustrious Family of Howard. By Rev. A. Gatty, D.D. Sheffield, 1879, 8vo. Hodgson's Northumberland, I. ii. 6, 79; II. ii. 375, 477. Jacob's Peerage i. 73, 108, 487, 574. Gentleman's Magazine, 1829, i. 397; 1833, i. 405. Morant's Essex, i. 65, 402, 420. Hasted's Kent, i. 170. Appendix to Case of Sir J. S. Sidney, claiming to be Lord Lisle. Clifford's Description of Tixall, 144. Blomefield's Norfolk, i. 81, 91; v. 337; ix. 191. East Anglian, ii. 341. Visitation of Norfolk, published by Norfolk Archæological Society, i. 15. Berry's Essex Genealogies, 73. Berry's Buckinghamshire Genealogies, 21, 63. Berry's Kent Genealogies, 87. History of Castle and Town of Arundel, by M. A. Tierney, 350. Burke's Commoners, (of Corby,) i. 196, Landed Gentry, 2, 3, 4, 5, 6, 7, 8; (of Greystoke,) Landed Gentry, 2, 3, 4, 7, 8; (of Broughton Hall,) 4, 5, 6, 7, 8; (of Clapham Park,) 6, 7; (of Kempstone Grange,) 8; (of Wygfair,) 8; (of Ashmore,) 8; (of Stone House,) 8. Topographer and Genealogist, ii. 91. Burke's Royal Families, (London, 1851, 8vo.) ii. 46, 161. Foster's Yorkshire Pedigrees. A Royal Descent, by T. E. Sharpe, (London, 1875, 4to.) 6. Maclean's History of Trigg Minor, ii. 508. Gyll's History of Wraysbury, 102. Hutchinson's History of Cumberland, i. 165, 353. Jefferson's History of Leath Ward, Cumberland, 346. Burke's Royal Descents and Pedigrees of Founders' Kin, *Founders' Kin*, 13. Dallaway's Sussex, i. xlvi. xlvii.; II. i. 142; II. ii. 185. Burke's Authorized Arms, 60. Thoresby's Ducatus Leodiensis, 146. Hunter's History of the Parish of Sheffield, 129. Hunter's Deanery of Doncaster, ii. 11. Surtees' Durham, i. 80. Manning and Bray's Surrey, i. 282, 302, 533; ii. 355, 630, 631, 690. Baker's Northampton, i. 589. The Monumental Effigies in Elford Church, Staffordshire, by E. Richardson, (London, 1852, fol.) 1. Wright's Essex, ii. 109. Surrey Archæological Collections, v. 208; ix. 395. The Genealogist, ii. 337, 349; v. 106; New Series, iii. 90. Page's History of Suffolk, 967. History and Antiquities of Harwich and Dovercourt, by Silas Taylor, 180. Plantagenet-Harrison's History of Yorkshire, i. 371. Edmondson's Baronagium Genealogicum, i. 2; ii. 102, 143; iii. 239; vi. 48*. Bedford and its Neighbourhood, by Dudley G. Cary Elwes, 44. Eastwood's History of Ecclesfield, 77. Holland's History of Worksop, 133. Archdall's Lodge's Peerage, vi. 85. Brydges' Collins' Peerage, i. 50; iii. 147, 501; iv. 264. Berry's Genealogical Peerage, 89. Banks' Baronies in Fee, i. 257, 343, 391. Banks' Dormant and Extinct Baronage, ii. 276, 533; iii. 81, 379, 578. Foster's Collectanea Genealogica, (MP's Eng-

land,) 47. Notes and Queries, 5 S. v. 348; 6 S. i. 235, 281.
Nicholls' Account of the Company of Ironmongers, 2nd edn., 608.
Howard's Visitation of England and Wales, i. 92, 185. Foster's
Visitations of Cumberland and Westmorland, 63. My Reminiscences, by Lord Ronald Gower, i. 97-116. Harleian Society,
xxxii. 162; xli. 117. Pedigree of Howard of Compton Place,
Sussex, by C. G. S. Foljambe, *circa* 1891, broadside. Burke's
Family Records, 254. The Visitations of Devon, by J. L. Vivian,
537. Annals of the English Benedictines of Ghent, 188. Nicolson and Burn's Westmorland and Cumberland, i. 206; ii. 336,
353, 498. *See* ALNO, ARUNDEL, CARLISLE, HOARD.

HOWARD-VYSE. Burke's Landed Gentry, 5, 6, 7, 8.

HOWARTH. Robinson's Mansions of Herefordshire, 286.

HOWBY. Harleian Society, ii. 29.

HOWE. Harleian Society, viii. 165, 329. History of Richmond, by
C. Clarkson, 386. Hoare's Wiltshire, II. i. 46; IV. i. 3. Clutter-
buck's Hertford, i. 479. Thoroton's Nottinghamshire, i. 205.
Edmondson's Baronagium Genealogicum, v. 134; vi. 27. Brydges'
Collins' Peerage, viii. 133. Banks' Dormant and Extinct Baronage,
iii. 177, 381. Metcalfe's Visitations of Suffolk, 97, 146. Burke's
Extinct Baronetcies. Howard's Visitation of England and Wales,
i. 288. A Collection of Original Royal Letters, by Sir George
Bromley, Bart., xxxii. Weaver's Visitations of Somerset, 35.
Harleian Society, xxxviii. 443. *See* HOW, JENNENS.

HOWEL, or HOWELL. Dwnn's Visitations of Wales, i. 177. Berry's
Kent Genealogies, 385. Glamorganshire Pedigrees, edited by
Sir Thomas Phillipps, 20. Burke's Landed Gentry, 2, 3, 4.
Harleian Society, v. 217; xlii. 124. Carthew's Hundred ol
Launditch, Part ii. 691. Genealogies of Morgan and Gla-
morgan, by G. T. Clark, 491.

HOWEL COETMOR. History of Powys Fadog, by J. Y. W. Lloyd, iv.
275, 370.

HOWENHULL. Shaw's Staffordshire, i. 85.

HOWES. Burke's Commoners, i. 412; Landed Gentry, 2, 3, 4, 5, 6,
7. The Genealogist, v. 277.

HOWISON. Burke's Commoners, ii. 234. The Parish of Cramond,
by J. P. Wood, 62, 289.

HOWLAND. Morant's Essex, ii. 464. Manning and Bray's Surrey,
iii. 386. Wilson's History of the Parish of St. Laurence
Pountney, 235. Wright's Essex, ii. 268. Harleian Society, xv.
397; xxii. 65; xliii. 146. Notes and Queries, 1 S. xi. 484; xii.
18. New England Register, xxxiv. 192. Surrey Archæological
Collections, xi.

HOWLDEN. Chetham Society, lxxxi. 53.

HOWLETT. East Anglian, ii. 263.

HOWLIN. Burke's Landed Gentry, 3, 4, 5, 6, 7, 8.

HOWMAN. East Anglian, ii. 99.

HOWND. Harleian Society, xli. 95.

HOWORTH. Chetham Society, lxxxii. 1; lxxxv. 156, 157. Burke's
Landed Gentry, 2, p. 1628.

HOWPER. Visitation of Somerset, printed by Sir T. Phillipps, 104. Visitation of Devon, edited by F. T. Colby, 137. Weaver's Visitations of Somerset, 35. The Visitations of Devon, by J. L. Vivian, 488.

HOWPILL. Visitation of Devon, edited by F. T. Colby, 137. The Visitations of Devon, by J. L. Vivian, 489.

HOWSLEY. Harleian Society, xxxviii. 820.

HOWTH. Burke's Royal Families, (London, 1851, 8vo.) i. 171.

HOY. Burke's Landed Gentry, 4, 5.

HOYLAND. A Pedigree of Hoyland, Marshall, Stacey, Helleley, etc. Large sheet, lithographed. (No heading, date, or name.)

HOYLE. Burke's Landed Gentry, (of Ferham House,) 4, 5, 6 ; (of Kames Castle,) 4 ; (of Soyland,) 6, 7 ; (of Hooton Levet,) 7. Foster's Yorkshire Pedigrees. The Yorkshire Genealogist, i. 190. Harleian Society, xl. 1286.

HOZIER. Burke's Landed Gentry, 3, 4, 5, 6, 7.

HUBAND. Burke's Heraldic Illustrations, 82. Burke's Landed Gentry, 2, 3, 4, 5. Dugdale's Warwickshire, 737. Burke's Extinct Baronetcies.

HUBARD. See HOBART.

HUBBARD. Miscellanea Genealogica et Heraldica, New Series, iii. 107.

HUBBERSTEY. Abram's History of Blackburn, 672. Burke's Landed Gentry, 8.

HUBBERT. Harleian Society, xxxvii. 26. See HOBART.

HUBECK. Harleian Society, xviii. 58.

HUBERD. Harleian Society, xiv. 584.

HUBERT. Harleian Society, ii. 38. Nichols' History of the County of Leicester, ii. 353. Bysshe's Visitation of Essex, edited by J. J. Howard, 50.

HUCKAMORE, or HUCKMORE. Tuckett's Devonshire Pedigrees, 181. Westcote's Devonshire, edited by G. Oliver and P. Jones, 501. Visitation of Devon, edited by F. T. Colby, 138.

HUDDART. Burke's Commoners, ii. 348.

HUDDISFIELD. Westcote's Devonshire, edited by G. Oliver and P. Jones, 500. Visitation of Devon, edited by F. T. Colby, 139.

HUDDLESTON, or HUDLESTON. Morant's Essex, ii. 173. Cambridge-shire Visitation, edited by Sir T. Phillipps, 19. Burke's Com-moners, (of Sawston,) ii. 582, Landed Gentry, 2, 3, 4, 5, 6, 7, 8 ; (of Upwell Hall,) Landed Gentry, 5, 6, 7, 8 ; (of Hutton John,) 5, 6, 7, 8 ; (of Knaresborough,) 7, 8. Burke's Royal Families, (London, 1851, 8vo.) ii. 130. Harleian Society, vii. 22 ; xxi. 254 ; xxvii. 109 ; xli. 26. Herald and Genealogist, iii. 418. Hutchinson's History of Cumberland, i. 416, 527. Jefferson's History of Leath Ward, Cumberland, 372 ; of Allerdale Ward, Cumberland, 155. Miscellanea Genealogica et Heraldica, New Series, ii. 408, 551. Foley's Records of the English Province, S. J., v. 583. Plantagenet-Harrison's History of Yorkshire, i. 366. The Genealogist, iv. 181 ; New Series, ix. 83. Banks' Baronies in Fee, i. 323 ; ii. 93. Foster's

Visitations of Cumberland and Westmorland, 64. Papers and Pedigrees relating to Cumberland and Westmorland, ii. 330. Nicholson and Burn's Westmorland and Cumberland, ii. 11, 367. *See* HODLESTON.

HUDDY. Visitation of Somerset, printed by Sir T. Phillipps, 108. Visitation of Devon, edited by F. T. Colby, 140. Weaver's Visitations of Somerset, 36, 115. The Visitations of Devon, by J. L. Vivian, 490. The Genealogist, New Series, iii. 91.

HUDESWELL. Harleian Society, xvi. 165.

HUDSON. Foster's Yorkshire Pedigrees. Foster's Visitations of Yorkshire, 535. Nichols' History of the County of Leicester, ii. 264 ; iii. 1102. Harleian Society, xv. 397. Betham's Baronetage, ii. 109 ; iv. 239. Notes and Queries, 6 S. v. 171. Burke's Landed Gentry, 8.

HUDSON-KINAHAN. Howard's Visitation of Ireland, ii. 36.

HUES. Visitation of Wiltshire, edited by G. W. Marshall, 46.

HUFFAM. History of Sandwich, by W. Boys, 367.

HUGESON, HUGESSEN, or HUGESSON. Hasted's Kent, ii. 689, 742. Berry's Hertfordshire Genealogies, 98. Burke's Landed Gentry, 2 add., 3, 4, 5, 6. Harleian Society, viii. 101.

HUGFORD, HUGEFORT, or HUGGEFORD. Rudder's Gloucestershire, 220. Gough's Sepulchral Monuments, ii. 326. Nash's Worcestershire, ii. 183. Dugdale's Warwickshire, 278. Harleian Society, xii. 337 ; xxi. 85. Harvey's Hundred of Willey, 250. The Genealogist, New Series, xii. 229.

HUGH, AB EDWARD. Dwnn's Visitations of Wales, i. 309 ; ab William, ii. 251 ; ap Richard, ii. 178.

HUGHAN. Burke's Landed Gentry, 5, 6, 7, 8.

HUGHES. Poetical Works of Lewis Glyn Cothi, (Oxford, 1837,) 411. Burke's Visitation of Seats and Arms, i. 10. Dwnn's Visitations of Wales, i. 150, 234 ; ii. 77, 142, 237, 249, 252, 272, 282, 299. Berry's Kent Genealogies, 38, 93. Visitation of Somerset, printed by Sir T. Phillipps, 109. Visitation of Oxfordshire, 1634, printed by Sir T. Phillipps, (Middle Hill, fol.) 22. Burke's Commoners, iii. xii. 87 ; Landed Gentry, 5 supp. p. 47. Burke's Landed Gentry, (of Alltlwyd,) 2, 3, 4, 5, 6, 7, 8 ; (of Donnington Priory,) 2, 3, 4, 5 ; (of Ely House,) 3, 4, 5, 6 and supp. ; (of Plas Coch,) 2 supp., 3, 4, 5, 6 ; (of Plas-yn Llangoed,) 2 supp., 3, 4, 5, 6, 7, 8 ; (of Middleton Hall,) 8 ; (of Co. Wexford,) 7, 8 ; (of Ystrad,) 3, 4, 5, 6, 7, 8 ; (of the Grove,) 2 supp., 3, 4, 5 ; (of Tregib,) 5 supp., 6, 7, 8 ; (of Cohelheleur,) 7 *sub* Thomas ; (of Sherdley Hall,) 5, 6, 7, 8 ; (of Kinmel,) 3, 4, 5, 6, 7, 8 ; (of Gwerclas,) 2, 3, 4 ; 2, p. 1110. Harleian Society, v. 251 ; xi. 58 ; xxviii. 262 ; xxxix. 1053. Lipscombe's History of the County of Buckingham. i. 402. Burke's Royal Families, (London, 1851, 8vo.) i. 52, 74. Burke's Visitation of Seats and Arms, 2nd Series, i. 10. Burke's Heraldic Illustrations, 23. Burke's Royal Descents and Pedigrees of Founders' Kin, 11. Caermarthenshire Pedigrees, 67. Memoirs of the Family of Chester, by R. E. C. Waters, 442. Fosbrooke's History of Gloucester-

shire, ii. 374. History of Llangurig, by E. Hamer and H. W.
Lloyd, 239, 274. O'Hart's Irish Pedigrees, 2nd Series, 201.
Betham's Baronetage, iii. 403. History of Powys Fadog, by
J. Y. W. Lloyd, ii. 182 ; iii. 57 ; iv. 261 ; v. 94, 311 ; vi. 46, 416.
Genealogical Memoranda relating to the Family of King, 9.
Genealogies of Morgan and Glamorgan, by G. T. Clark, 276.
Minet's account of the Family of Minet, 207. Burke's Family
Records, 335. Oliver's History of Antigua, ii. 88. Genealogical
Record of King and Henham, 14.

HUGHES-HALLETT. Berry's Kent Genealogies, 246.

HUGHES-LE FLEMING. Burke's Landed Gentry, 5.

HUISH. Burke's Commoners, iv. 417 ; Landed Gentry, (of Smalley
Hall,) 5 supp., 6, 7. Westcote's Devonshire, edited by G. Oliver
and P. Jones, 488. See HEWISH, HUYSHE.

HUIT. Visitation of Staffordshire, 1663-4, printed by Sir T. Phillipps,
6.

HULBERT. Burke's Landed Gentry, 2 p. 1227.

HULCOTE. Baker's Northampton, ii. 153.

HULEY. Surtees Society, xxxvi. 161.

HULGREVE. Ormerod's Cheshire, iii. 222. The Genealogist, New
Series, xii. 231.

HULKE. Berry's Kent Genealogies, 300.

HULL, or HULLE. Visitation of Durham, 1575, (Newcastle, 1820,
fol.) 43. Burke's Landed Gentry, 4. Westcote's Devonshire,
edited by G. Oliver and P. Jones, 517. Surtees' Durham, ii. 331.
Manning and Bray's Surrey, i. 607 ; ii. 56. Harleian Society,
xv. 398 ; xxi. 82 ; xxviii. 243 ; xliii. 5, 172. Maclean's History
of Trigg Minor, ii. 42. Visitation of Devon, edited by F. T.
Colby, 140. The Visitations of Devon, by J. L. Vivian, 492.
Foster's Visitations of Durham, 175. Visitation of Gloucester,
edited by T. F. Fenwick and W. C. Metcalfe, 94. Surrey
Archæological Collections, x.

HULLOCK. Camden Society, xliii. 108.

HULLS. Dwnn's Visitations of Wales, ii. 92.

HULME. Chetham Society, xlii. 226 ; lxxxv. 158. Baines' History
of the Co. of Lancaster, ii. 394 ; Croston's edn., ii. 230. Harleian
Society, xv. 399. The Visitations of Staffordshire, 1614 and
1663-4, William Salt Society, 181.

HULSE. Hasted's Kent, iii. 239. Berry's Hampshire Genealogies,
342. Berry's Kent Genealogies, 326. Ashmole's Antiquities of
Berkshire, iii. 303. Wotton's English Baronetage, iv. 247.
Betham's Baronetage, iii. 232. Ormerod's Cheshire, iii. 464.
Harleian Society, xviii. 128. The Genealogist, New Series, i. 12.
Archæologia Cantiana, xvi. 71. See HOUSE.

HULTON. Genealogy of the Family of Hulton of Hulton, Co. Lanc.,
8vo., pp. 48. Berry's Hampshire Genealogies, 150. Burke's
Commoners, iv. 29, Landed Gentry, 2, 3, 4, 5, and supp. (p. 44,)
6, 7, 8. Chetham Society, lxxxi. 11, 130 ; lxxxv. 159 ; xcix. 6 ;
cx. 209. Foster's Lancashire Pedigrees. Archæologia Æliana,
2nd Series, iii. 89. Baines' History of the Co. of Lancaster, iii.

40 ; Croston's edn., iii. 138, 161. The Genealogist, iv. 184 ;
New Series, ix. 86. Harleian Society, xv. 400 ; xvi. 166 ;
xxxvii. 67, 367.

HULTON-HARROP. Burke's Landed Gentry, 5, 6, 7, 8.

HUMBERSTONE. Harleian Society, xv. 400 ; xxii. 66 ; xxxii. 166.

HUMBLE. Harleian Society, xiii. 220 ; xv. 401. Monken Hadley,
by F. C. Cass, 34. Burke's Extinct Baronetcies. Wotton's
English Baronetage, iii. 48.

HUME. Davidis Humii de Familia Humia Wedderburnensi Liber,
edited by Dr. John Miller, (Abbotsford Club,) Edinburgh, 1839,
4to. Drummond's History of Noble British Families, Part vi.
Kent's British Banner Displayed, 409. History of the Town and
School of Rugby, by N. H. Nicolas, 38. Burke's Commoners, (of
Humewood, now Dick,) iii. 388, Landed Gentry, 2, 3, 4, 5, 6, 7,
8 ; (of Ninewells,) Landed Gentry, 2, 3, 4, 5, 6, 7, 8 ; (of Auchen-
dolly,) 8. Cussan's History of Hertfordshire, Parts ix. and x.
250. Paterson's History of Ayr and Wigton, iii. app. 549.
Douglas's Baronage of Scotland, 587. Betham's Baronetage, iii.
357. Burke's Extinct Baronetcies, supp. and 608. Alexander
Nisbet's Heraldic Plates, 154. Marchmont and the Humes of
Polwarth, by M. Warrender, 179. Parliamentary Memoirs of
Fermanagh, by Earl of Belmore, 17, 52. See HOME.

HUMERSTON. Metcalfe's Visitations of Suffolk, 146.

HUMETT. Visitation of Staffordshire, (Willm. Salt Soc.) 99.

HUMFFREYS. Burke's Landed Gentry, 2, 3, 4.

HUMFINE, or HUMFINES. Hutchins' Dorset, ii. 99. The Genealogist,
iii. 375.

HUMFRESTON. Harleian Society, xxviii. 263.

HUMFREY. Morant's Essex, ii. 524. Surtees Society. xxxvi. 177.
Burke's Landed Gentry, (of Wroxham,) 2 supp., 3, 4, 5 ; (of
Cavanacor,) 3, 4, 5, 6, 7, 8. Bridges' Northamptonshire, by Rev.
Peter Whalley, ii. 218. Harleian Society, xiii. 425 ; xli. 65.
The Visitations of Cornwall, edited by J. L. Vivian, 240. Met-
calfe's Visitations of Northamptonshire, 28. Bysshe's Visitation
of Essex, edited by J. J. Howard, 50. The Genealogical Maga-
zine, i. 396.

HUMFRIE. Morant's Essex, ii. 38, 40.

HUMPHREY. Dwnn's Visitations of Wales, ii. 274. Cambridgeshire
Visitation, edited by Sir T. Phillipps, 18. Harleian Society, ii.
62 ; xx. 57. Nichols' History of the County of Leicester, iii.
1050*. Sussex Archæological Collections, vi. 191.

HUMPHREYS, or HUMPHRYS. Miscellanea Genealogica et Heraldica,
i. 185. Morant's Essex, i. 4. J. P. Earwaker's East Cheshire,
i. 440. Burke's Extinct Baronetcies. Burke's Landed Gentry,
3, 4, 5, 6, and page 430, 7, 8. History of Powys Fadog, by
J. Y. W. Lloyd, v. 289 ; vi. 9. Oliver's History of Antigua,
ii. 91.

HUNCKES. Pedigree of Hunckes of Gloucestershire, etc. [T. P.]
Broadside. Bloom's History of Preston on Stour, 17.

HUNGATE. Surtees Society, xxxvi. 296. Foster's Yorkshire Pedigrees.

Foster's Visitations of Yorkshire, 114, 223. Thoresby's Ducatus
Leodiensis, 247. Harleian Society, xv. 402; xvi. 166; xxxix.
954. Wotton's English Baronetage, ii. 335. Burke's Extinct
Baronetcies. W. Wheater's History of Sherburn and Cawood,
45. The Genealogist, New Series, xvi. 105.

HUNGERFORD. Hungerfordiana, or Memoirs of the Family of Hungerford, by Sir R. C. Hoare, Bart. Shaftesbury, 1823, 8vo. Pedigree
of Hungerford of Wiltshire, etc., [T. P.] 1855. Broadside.
Pedigree of Hungerford of Cadenham Lea, etc., [T. P.,] folio
page. Collinson's Somerset, iii. 353. Morant's Essex, i. 14.
Gentleman's Magazine, 1820, ii. 583; 1823, ii. 307; 1824, i. 9,
606; 1851, ii. 625. Gough's Sepulchral Monuments, ii. Appendix. Guide to Farleigh Hungerford, by Rev. J. E. Jackson,
13. Berry's Berkshire Genealogies, 35. Maclean's History of
Trigg Minor, i. 383. Hutchins' Dorset, iv. 175. Visitation of
Oxfordshire, 1634, printed by Sir T. Phillipps, (Middle Hill,
fol.) 22. Burke's Landed Gentry, (of Inchodony,) 3, 4, 5, 6, 7, 8;
(of Cahirmore,) 2 supp., 3, 4, 5, 6, 7, 8; (of Dingley Park,) 2, 3,
4, 5, 6, 7. Harleian Society, v. 258; viii. 33, 312; xxi. 87, 277.
Topographical Collections of John Aubrey, edited by J. E. Jackson, 234. Visitatio Comitatus Wiltoniæ, 1623, printed by Sir T.
Phillipps. Hoare's Wiltshire, I. ii. 117; IV. i. 123. Manning
and Bray's Surrey, iii. 422. Banks' Baronies in Fee, i. 145,
260. Banks' Dormant and Extinct Baronage, ii. 281. The
Genealogist, v. 277; New Series, xii. 95. Visitation of Wiltshire, edited by G. W. Marshall, 25, 74, 77. Burke's Colonial
Gentry, ii. 858. See HASTINGS.

HUNKES. Harleian Society, xxvii. 81.

HUNKIN. Harleian Society, ix. 290. The Visitations of Devon, by
J. L. Vivian, 493.

HUNLOCK. The Genealogist, New Series, vii. 143.

HUNLOKE. Burke's Royal Families, (London, 1851, 8vo.) i. 120.
Herald and Genealogist, iii. 422. Pilkington's View of Derby-
shire, ii. 329. Wotton's English Baronetage, ii. 378. Betham's
Baronetage, i. 508. Roman Catholic Families of England, by
J. J. Howard and H. F. Burke, Part ii., 97.

HUNSTON. The Genealogist, iv. 184. Harleian Society, xxxii.
167.

HUNT. Cussan's History of Hertfordshire, Parts iii. and iv. 175.
Miscellanea Genealogica et Heraldica, ii. 23. Bibliotheca Topographica Britannica, ix. Part iv. 225. Berry's Kent Genealogies,
260. Tuckett's Devonshire Pedigrees, 146. Surtees Society,
xxxvi. 152. Burke's Landed Gentry, (of Pittencrief,) 2, 3, 4, 5,
6, 7, 8; (of Boreatton,) 2 add., 3, 4, 5, 6, 7, 8; (of Shermanbury
Park,) 4, 5, 6; (of Ketton,) 4 and supp.; (of Ballysinode,) 6, 7,
8. Harleian Society, iii. 14; iv. 167; vi. 155; xiv. 585; xv.
402, 404; xix. 38, 118; xxviii. 263; xxxii. 167; xxxvii. 169;
xlii. 116. Phelps' History of Somersetshire, i. 409. Suckling's
History of Suffolk, ii. 41. Wright's History of Rutland, 83.
Metcalfe's Visitations of Suffolk, 146. Metcalfe's Visitation of

Worcester, 1683, 62. Visitation of Staffordshire, (Willm. Salt
Soc.) 100. The Visitations of Devon, by J. L. Vivian, 494.
The Genealogist, New Series, vii. 144. *See* LE HUNT.
HUNTBACH. Shaw's Staffordshire, ii. 187. Visitation of Stafford-
shire, 1663-4, printed by Sir T. Phillipps, 6. The Visitations of
Staffordshire, 1614 and 1663-4, William Salt Society, 183.
HUNTER. Berry's Hertfordshire Genealogies, 256. Berry's Berkshire
Genealogies, 126. Surtees Society, xxxvi. 87. History of the
Parish of Ecclesfield, by Rev. J. Eastwood, 372. Burke's Com-
moners, (of Hunterston,) ii. 500, Landed Gentry, 2 and supp.,
3, 4, 5, 6, 7, 8 ; (of Straidarran,) Landed Gentry, 3, 4, 5, 6, 7, 8 ;
(of Medomsley,) 2, 3, 4, 5, 6, 7 ; (of Blackness,) 3, 4, 5, 6 ; (of
Bonnytoun,) 2, 3, 4 ; (of Seaside,) 2, 3, 4, 7, 8 ; (of Burnside,) 6
supp. ; (of Mount Severn,) 7, 8 ; (of Thurston,) 8 ; (of Beach
Hill,) 8 ; (of Medomsley,) 8. Foster's Visitations of Yorkshire,
535. Burke's Heraldic Illustrations, 108. Burke's Royal
Descents and Pedigrees of Founders' Kin, 55. Poulson's Holderness, i. 355. Nichols' History of the County of Leicester, iv. 333.
Surtees' Durham, ii. 289. Geo. Robertson's Description of Cunninghame, 121, 141. Paterson's History of the Co. of Ayr,
i. 202 ; ii. 133, 145, 473. The Genealogist, iii. 273. Paterson's
History of Ayr and Wigton, i. 144 ; iii. 327. Collections by the
Powys-land Club, viii. 223. Walter Wood's East Neuk of Fife,
266. Eastwood's History of Ecclesfield, 372. Harleian Society,
xv. 405 ; xxi. 91 ; xxxvii. 354 ; xxxix. 1013. Betham's Baronetage, iv. 178. Burke's Family Records, 336. *See* BOSANQUET.
HUNTER-ARUNDELL. Burke's Landed Gentry, 2, 3, 4, 5, 6, 7, 8.
HUNTER-BLAIR. Paterson's History of Ayr and Wigton, ii. 470.
HUNTERCOMBE. Morant's Essex, i. 29 ; ii. 277. Banks' Dormant
and Extinct Baronage, i. 347.
HUNTINGDON. The Huntingdon Peerage, by H. N. Bell. London,
1820, 4to. ; 2nd edn. 1821. Visitation of Oxfordshire, 1634,
printed by Sir T. Phillipps, (Middle Hill, fol.) 22, Burke's Royal
Families, (London, 1851, 8vo.) i. 36. Banks' Dormant and
Extinct Baronage, iii. 388. Robin Hood, edited by Joseph
Ritson, 6. New England Register, i. 343 ; v. 163 ; viii. 186.
The Genealogist, New Series, xiv. 190. *See* HASTINGS.
HUNTINGFIELD. Hasted's Kent, i. 107. Page's History of Suffolk,
241, 412. Banks' Baronies in Fee, i. 263. Banks' Dormant and
Extinct Baronage, i. 348. Carthew's West and East Bradenham,
103. *See* DE HUNTINGFIELD.
HUNTINGTON. Morant's Essex, ii. 365.
HUNTLEY. Rudder's Gloucestershire, 306. Fosbrooke's Abstracts of
Smith's Lives of the Berkeleys, 171. History of Tetbury, Co.
Gloucester, by A. T. Lee, 208-218. Burke's Commoners, ii. 468 ;
Landed Gentry, 2, 3, 4, 5. Hutchins' Dorset, ii. 592. Surrey
Archæological Collections, vii. Fosbrooke's History of Gloucester-
shire, ii. 3. Miscellanea Genealogica et Heraldica, 2nd Series,
ii. 291. The Genealogist, New Series, iii. 92. Visitation of
Gloucester, edited by T. F. Fenwick and W. C. Metcalfe, 95.

Weaver's Visitations of Somerset, 38. Harleian Society, xx.
57 ; xxi. 92 ; xliii. 158. Burke's Family Records, 337.

HUNTON. Visitatio Comitatus Wiltoniæ, 1623, printed by Sir T.
Phillipps. Plantagenet-Harrison's History of Yorkshire, i. 176.
Visitation of Wiltshire, edited by G. W. Marshall, 24. The
Genealogist, New Series, xii. 95.

HUNTSMAN. Burke's Landed Gentry, 8.

HUNWICK. Harleian Society, xiv. 587.

HURD. Kindred of Rt. Rev. Richd. Hurd, D.D., Bishop of Worcester,
[T. P.] folio page. New England Register, xix. 123.

HURDIS. Sussex Archæological Collections, vii. 134.

HURFORD. Miscellanea Genealogica et Heraldica, New Series, iii.
268.

HURLBATT. Berry's Hampshire Genealogies, 322.

HURLE. See COOKE-HURLE.

HURLESTON, or HURLTON. Chetham Society, lxxxii. 135. Ormerod's
Cheshire, ii. 815. Harleian Society, xviii. 129, 130 ; xix. 177.

HURLOCK. Morant's Essex, i. 444.

HURLY. Burke's Landed Gentry, 3 supp., 4, 5, 6, 7, 8. Topographer and Genealogist, iii. 464. Burke's Visitation of Seats and
Arms, 2nd Series, ii. 48.

HURRY. Memorials of the Hurry Family, by C. J. Palmer. Norwich,
1873, 8vo.

HURST. Burke's Landed Gentry, 2, 5, 6, 7, and 7 at p. 2047, 8.
Blore's Rutland, 52. Westcote's Devonshire, edited by G. Oliver
and P. Jones, 487. Earwaker's Local Gleanings, ii. 812. The
Genealogist, iii. 301 ; v. 139. Harleian Society, xxii. 66 ; xl.
1200. Croston's edn. of Baines's Lancaster, ii. 335. Oliver's
History of Antigua, ii. 92. Memoir of Richard Haines, by C. R.
Haines.

HURT, or HURTE. Glover's History of Derbyshire, ii. 5, (7). Berry's
Kent Genealogies, 101. Burke's Landed Gentry, 2, 3, 4, 5, 6, 7,
8. Burke's Royal Descents and Pedigrees of Founders' Kin, 58.
Visitation of Staffordshire, 1663-4, printed by Sir T. Phillipps, 6.
Eastwick's History of Ecclesfield, 410. Harleian Society, xv. 407 ;
xxxvii. 144 ; xlii. 31. Collections for a History of Staffordshire,
(William Salt Society,) ii. part 2, 44. Registers of Ecclesfield,
by A. S. Gatty, 31. Journal of the Derbyshire Archæological
Society, iii. 6. Visitations of Staffordshire, 1614 and 1663-4,
William Salt Society, 184. The Genealogist, New Series, vii. 144.

HUSBAND. Morant's Essex, ii. 235. Bysshe's Visitation of Essex,
edited by J. J. Howard, 51.

HUSEE, HUSSE, HUSEY, or HUSSEY. Remarks on the Hussey Peerage,
by W. B. D. D. Turnbull, 1842, 8vo. Morant's Essex, ii. 359.
Hasted's Kent, ii. 381. Burke's Heraldic Illustrations, 144.
Topography and History of New and Old Sleaford, (Sleaford,
1825, 8vo.) 108. Surtees Society, xli. 22. Berry's Surrey Genea-
logies, 57. Berry Sussex Genealogies, 126, 286, 344. Berry's
Kent Genealogies, 220, 241. Burke's Commoners, (of Scotney
Castle,) i. 262, Landed Gentry, 2, 3, 4, 5, 6, 7, 8 ; (of Wood-

walton and Upwood,) Commoners, ii. 358, Landed Gentry, 2, 3, 4, 5, 6, 7, 8 ; (of Edenburn,) 7, 8 ; (of Bredy,) 8 ; (of Nash Court,) Landed Gentry, 2, 3, 4, 5, 6, 7 ; (of Wyrley Grove,) 2 supp., 3, 4, 5, 6, 7 ; (of Westown,) 2, 3, 4, 5, 6, 7, 8 ; (of Rathkenny,) 5, 6, 7, 8 ; (of Dingle,) 3, 4 ; 7 at p. 1921 ; 8 at p. 1316, 2127. Foster's Visitations of Yorkshire, 92. Harleian Society, iv. 136 ; viii. 432 ; xv. 407 ; xvi. 168 ; xx. 58 ; xxviii. 265. History of Boston, by Pishey Thompson, 2nd edn. 398. Herald and Genealogist, i. 526. Blore's Rutland, 107-109. Shaw's Staffordshire, ii. 60. Dallaway's Sussex, i. 188 ; II. i. 355. Hutchins' Dorset, i. 302 ; ii. 99, 166 ; iii. 162, 424 ; iv. 312, 313. Hoare's Wiltshire, IV. i. 123. Manning and Bray's Surrey, i. 497. Sussex Archæological Collections, viii. 46 ; xiii. 107. Thoroton's Nottinghamshire, i. 253. Sleaford, by the Venble. Edward Trollope, 123. The Sheriffs of Montgomeryshire, by W. V. Lloyd, 273, 298. An Historical Survey of Cornwall, by C. S. Gilbert, ii. 158. The Genealogist, iv. 182 ; New Series, iii. 92 ; xiv. 190. Bigland's Gloucestershire, ii. par. Saperton. Edmondson's Baronagium Genealogicum, v. 491 ; vi. 34*. Banks' Dormant and Extinct Baronage, ii. 288 ; iii. 69. Notes and Queries, 4 S. vi. 575 ; 6 S. ii. 206. Burke's Extinct Baronetcies. New England Register, vii. 157. The Irish Builder, xxxv. 8. History of Doddington, by R. E. G. Cole, 84, 120. See HOESE, DISNEY.

HUSKARL. The Genealogist, New Series, xv. 152.

HUSSEY DE BURGH. Burke's Landed Gentry, 2, 3, 4, 5, 6.

HUSSEY-FREKE. Burke's Landed Gentry, 5.

HUSSEY-WALSH. Howard's Visitation of Ireland, iii. 85.

HUSTLER. Topographer and Genealogist, ii. 497, 540. Burke's Landed Gentry, 2 supp., 3, 4, 5, 6, 7, 8. Foster's Yorkshire Pedigrees. Poulson's Holderness, i. 441. Ord's History of Cleveland, 529. The Bradford Antiquary, i. 32.

HUTCHENSON. Surtees Society, xxxvi. 83.

HUTCHINS. Burke's Landed Gentry, 3 supp., 4, 5, 6, 7, 8. Harleian Society, viii. 427.

HUTCHINSON. Jewitt's Reliquary, ix. 240. Hutchinson's Memoirs of the Life of Col. Hutchinson, (1806, 4to.) 144. Burke's Commoners, iv. v., 101 ; (of Whitton House,) Commoners, ii. 100, Landed Gentry, 2, 3, 4 ; (of Timoney,) Landed Gentry, 2, 3, 4, 5, 6 ; (of Ballymoney,) 5 supp. ; (of Howden,) 6 supp., 7, 8. Foster's Visitations of Yorkshire, 183. Harleian Society, iv. 115 ; xv. 408 ; xxxix. 979. Surtees' Durham, iv. 155. Clutterbuck's Hertford, ii. 437. Thoroton's Nottinghamshire, i. 159. The Genealogist, ii. 305. Plantagenet-Harrison's History of Yorkshire, i. 183. Notes and Queries, 2 S. vii. 344 ; 5 S. ix. 209. Brydges' Collins' Peerage, ix. 179. Foster's Visitations of Durham, 177. New England Register, xix. 13 ; xx. 355 ; xxii. 236 ; xxvii. 81 ; xxviii. 83. See MARTIN.

HUTCHISON. Burke's Landed Gentry, 2 add., 3, 4. Paterson's History of Ayr and Wigton, i. 299 ; ii. 371. Howard's Visitation of England and Wales, v. 67.

HUTH. Burke's Landed Gentry, 7, 8.
HUTTOFT. Visitatio Comitatus Wiltoniæ, 1623, printed by Sir T. Phillipps. Visitation of Wiltshire, edited by G. W. Marshall, 65.
HUTTON. Account of the Family of Hutton of Gate Burton, by A. W. Hutton. Devizes, 1898, 4to. Life of William Hutton, and the History of his Family. London, 1817, 8vo.; another edn., edited by his daughter, 1841, 4to.; the last edn. was edited by Llewellyn Jewitt. Visitation of Durham, 1615, (Sunderland, 1820, fol.) 57, 62, 72. Visitation of Durham, 1575, (Newcastle, 1820, fol.) 14. Surtees Society, xxxvi. 173. Burke's Commoners, (of Marske,) iii. 303, Landed Gentry, 2, 3, 4, 5, 6, 7, 8; (of Over-thwaite,) Landed Gentry, 2, 3, 4, 5, 6, 7, 8; (of Gate Burton,) 2 add., 3, 4, 5, 6, 7, 8; (of Houghton Hall,) 5, 6, 7, 8; (of Solberge,) 7, 8. Foster's Yorkshire Pedigrees. Foster's Visitations of York-shire, 536. Harleian Society, vii. 1. Hutchinson's History of Cumberland, i. 339. Archæologia Æliana, 2nd Series, v. 11, 49, 51. Jewitt's Reliquary, xi. 215. History of Richmond, by C. Clarkson, 267. Chetham Society, lxxxv. 160. Jefferson's History of Leath Ward, Cumberland, 89. Hutchinson's History of Durham, i. 470; iii. 522. Thoresby's Ducatus Leodiensis, 173. Hunter's Deanery of Doncaster, ii. 143. Surtees' Durham, i. lxxxv. 149; iii. 19, 333. Fisher's History of Masham, 289. Plantagenet-Harrison's History of Yorkshire, i. 200. Yorkshire Archæological and Topographical Journal, vi. 192, 238, 241. Foster's Visitations of Durham, 179, 181, 183. Foster's Visita-tions of Cumberland and Westmorland, 66, 67. Burke's Colonial Gentry, ii. 526. Old Yorkshire, ed. by Willm. Smith, i. 220. Burke's Family Records, 342. Nicolson and Burn's Westmorland and Cumberland, ii. 401. The Genealogist, New Series, xiv. 110.
HUW AP DAVID. Dwnn's Visitations of Wales, i. 53, 105, 215.
HUW VYCHAN. Dwnn's Visitations of Wales, i. 37.
HUXLEY. Burke's Landed Gentry, 2 add., p. 366. Harleian Society, viii. 166; xviii. 131. Ormerod's Cheshire, ii. 800.
HUYGHUE. Oliver's History of Antigua, ii. 93.
HUYSHE. Gentleman's Magazine, 1831, ii. 488. Burke's Com-moners, iv. 409, Landed Gentry, 2, 3, 4, 5, 6, 7, 8. Burke's Royal Families, (London, 1851, 8vo.) ii. 179. Harleian Society, vi. 157. The Visitations of Devon, by J. L. Vivian, 495. See HUISH.
HWVA AB KYNDDELW (descendants of). Dwnn's Visitations of Wales, ii. 22.
HYDE, or HIDE. Gentleman's Magazine, 1829, i. 322. Ashmole's Antiquities of Berkshire, iii. 322, 340. Berry's Hampshire Genea-logies, 264. Berry's Berkshire Genealogies, 106. Burke's Com-moners, ii. 189; Landed Gentry, 2nd edn., 1406; (of Hyde End,) Commoners, iv. 675, Landed Gentry, 2, 5, 6; (of Castle Hyde,) Landed Gentry, 2, 3, 4, 5, 6, 7, 8; (of Syndale House,) 4. Chetham Society, lxxxi. 14, 17; lxxxii. 52, 53, 55; lxxxv. 161; xcix. 41. Nichols' History of the County of Leicester, iii. 109. Harleian Society, viii. 58, 138, 174; xv. 405, 409, 410; xviii. 131; xxii. 64, 67; xxviii. 237; xxxviii. 820. Hutchins' Dorset, iii.

135. Visitatio Comitatus Wiltoniæ, 1623, printed by Sir T. Phillipps. Parochial Topography of the Hundred of Wanting, by W. N. Clarke, 86. History of the Ancient Chapel of Denton, by Rev. J. Booker, 36. Blore's Rutland, 50. Hoare's Wiltshire, II. ii. 145 ; IV. i. 131 ; ii. 33. Baines' History of the Co. of Lancaster, iii. 167 ; Croston's edn., iii. 311. Cussan's History of Hertfordshire, Parts v. and vi. 152. Wiltshire Archæological Magazine, ix. 282. Annals of Swainswick, by R. E. M. Peach, 74. Butterworth's History of Stockport, etc., 290. Banks' Dormant and Extinct Baronage, iii. 193, 636. The Genealogist, v. 278, 279 ; New Series, i. 13, 14 ; iii. 93. Ormerod's Cheshire, iii. 810. Visitation of Wiltshire, edited by G. W. Marshall, 21. Registers of Ecclesfield, by A. S. Gatty, 81. Berks Archl. and Architectural Society's Journal, ii. 111. Berkshire Notes and Queries, i. 92. Archæologia Cantiana, xxii. 112-122. Clutterbuck's Hertford, i. 447. Memoirs, British and Foreign, of Illustrious Persons who died in 1711, 90. Burke's Extinct Baronetcies. Earwaker's East Cheshire, ii. 44. *See* DELAHYDE.

HYETT. Visitation of Somerset, printed by Sir T. Phillipps, 109. Burke's Landed Gentry, 2, 3, 4, 5, 6, 7, 8. Visitation of Gloucester, edited by T. F. Fenwick and W. C. Metcalfe, 96. Weaver's Visitations of Somerset, 38. Harleian Society, xxi. 254. Howard's Visitation of England and Wales, viii. 122.

HY-FIACHIACH. The Genealogies, Tribes, and Customs of Hy-Fiachiach, by John O'Donovan. Dublin, 1844, 4to.

HYGONS. Visitation of Sussex, 1570, printed by Sir T. Phillipps, (Middle Hill, fol.) 6. Dallaway's Sussex, II. i. 236. *See* HIGGENS.

HYLDEHARD. Collectanea Topographica et Genealogica, i. 10.

HYLDESLEY. Harleian Society, v. 182. *See* HILDESLEY.

HYLLARYE. Harleian Society, xxxii. 168.

HYLTON. Topographer and Genealogist, ii. 99, 553, Harleian Society, xvi. 169. Herald and Genealogist, iv. 353. *See* ALLAN, HELTON, HILTON.

HY-MANY. The Tribes and Customs of Hy-many, by John O'Donovan. Dublin, 1843, 4to.

HYNDE. Harleian Society, iv. 129 ; xxviii. 268 ; xli. 113.

HYNDMAN. Geo. Robertson's Description of Cunninghame, 139. Robertson's Crauford's Renfrewshire, 425.

HYNES. O'Hart's Irish Pedigrees, 2nd Series, 202.

HYSLOP. Burke's Landed Gentry, 5, 6, 7, 8.

HYWEL. Dwnn's Visitations of Wales, i. 265.

IAGO. An Historical Survey of Cornwall, by C. S. Gilbert, ii. 160. Maclean's History of Trigg Minor, iii. 424. The Visitations of Cornwall, by J. L. Vivian, 585.

IAGO AB OWAIN GWYNEDD (descendants of). Dwnn's Visitations of Wales, ii. 259. *See* JAGO.

I'ANS. An Historical Survey of Cornwall, by C. S. Gilbert, ii. 159.

I'ANSON. Herald and Genealogist, iv. 280. Hasted's Kent, ii. 342. Burke's Landed Gentry, 2 supp. Hutchins' Dorset, i. 546. Notes and Queries, 5 S. x. 169, 231, 448; 6 S. ii. 112. Howard's Visitation of England and Wales, vii. 65. *See* JANSON.

IARDDUR (descendants of). Dwnn's Visitations of Wales, i. 12, 22, 75.

IBBETSON, or IBBOTSON. Burke's Royal Families, (London, 1851, 8vo.) i. 201. Foster's Yorkshire Pedigrees. Thoresby's Ducatus Leodiensis, 148. Betham's Baronetage, iii. 244. Harleian Society, xxxviii. 650, 654.

IBGRAVE. Harleian Society, xxii. 13.

ICKWORTH. Gage's History of Thingoe Hundred, Suffolk, 276.

IDEN. Genealogical Memoranda relating to the Family of King, by W. L. King, 17. Genealogical Record of King and Henham, 24.

IDLE. Thoresby's Ducatus Leodiensis, 139. Harleian Society, xxxix. 867.

IERMONGER. Ashmole's Antiquities of Berkshire, iii. 290.

IEUAN, AP GRUFYDD. Dwnn's Visitations of Wales, i. 80; ap Howel, i. 97; ap Hugh, ii. 246; ap Robert, ii. 224.

IEUANS. Dwnn's Visitations of Wales, i. 112.

IFANS. Dwnn's Visitations of Wales, ii. 72, 185.

IFIELD. Topographer and Genealogist, iii. 178.

ILBERT. Burke's Commoners, iv. 135, Landed Gentry, 2, 3, 4, 5, 6, 7, 8.

ILDERTON. Burke's Landed Gentry, 6, 7, 8.

ILE. History of Darlington, by W. Hylton Dyer Longstaffe, lxxxvii. Surtees' Durham, iii. 355. Foster's Visitations of Northumberland, 70.

ILES. Oliver's History of Antigua, ii. 95.

ILIFFE. Nichols' History of the County of Leicester, iv. 709.

ILKETSHALLE. Blomefield's Norfolk, ix. 403.

ILLINGWORTH. Topographical Miscellanies, (Bredsall) 1792, 4to. Thoroton's Nottinghamshire, i. 89. Jewitt's Reliquary, xviii. 140. Harleian Society, xliii. 16.

IMAGE. Burke's Landed Gentry, 8.

IMPERVILL. Morant's Essex, i. 89.

INCE. Pedigree of Ince of Mansfield, in the County of Nottingham, etc., by Thomas Norris Ince of Wakefield, etc. Doncaster, printed by Wm. Atock, Baxter-gate, *circa* 1857, 4to., pp. 6. Jewitt's Reliquary, vii. 183. Chetham Society, lxxxv. 163. Monken Hadley, by F. C. Cass, 174. Historical Notices of Doncaster, by C. W. Hatfield, 3rd Series, 381.

INCH. Maclean's History of Trigg Minor, ii. 257.

INCHIQUIN. Claim of Lucius, Baron Inchiquin, to Vote at Elections of Irish Peers, Sess. Papers, 275 of 1861; C of 1862. Case of Lucius, Lord Inchiquin, on his Right to Vote at Elections of Peers for Ireland, 1861, fol. Burke's Royal Descents and Pedigrees of Founders' Kin, 98.

INCLEDEN, or INCLEDON. Tuckett's Devonshire Pedigrees, 11. Harleian Society, vi. 158. The Visitations of Devon, by J. L. Vivian, 497. Burke's Landed Gentry, 7 at p. 1949, 8 at p. 2163.

INGALDESTHORP. Blomefield's Norfolk, vii. 123.

INGE. Burke's Commoners, i. 322, Landed Gentry, 2, 3, 4, 5, 6, 8. Shaw's Staffordshire, i. 409. Visitation of Staffordshire, 1663-4, printed by Sir T. Phillipps, 6. The Visitations of Staffordshire, 1614 and 1663-4, William Salt Society, 185. The Gresley's of Drakelowe, by F. Madan, 264.

INGHAM. Burke's Landed Gentry, 2 supp., 3, 4, 5, 7, 8. Hoare's Wiltshire, I. ii. 230 ; V. i. 21. Doncaster Charities, by Charles Jackson, 45. Banks' Baronies in Fee, i. 266. Banks' Dormant and Extinct Baronage, i. 349. Weaver's Visitations of Somerset, 116. The Genealogist, New Series, x. 34.

INGLEBY, or INGILBY. Thoresby's Ducatus Leodiensis, 191. Morant's Essex, i. 231. Surtees Society, xxxvi. 30, 46. Foster's Yorkshire Pedigrees. Foster's Visitations of Yorkshire, 282. Burke's Landed Gentry, (of Lawkland Hall,) 6 and supp., 7, 8 ; (of Valentines,) 7, 8. Harleian Society, xvi. 171. Wotton's English Baronetage, ii. 293. Betham's Baronetage, iv. 79. Burke's Extinct Baronetcies.

INGLES. Pedigree of Ingles, [T. P.] folio page. Pedigree of Ingles of Macclesfield, [T. P.] 1868, folio page.

INGLETT. Harleian Society, vi. 158. The Family of Fortescue, by Lord Clermont, 2nd edn., 167. The Visitations of Devon, by J. L. Vivian, 500.

INGLIS. Historical and Genealogical Notices of the Family of Inglis, of Milton Bryant, by C. H. Wilson, 1874, 4to. Burke's Landed Gentry, 6, 7, 8. Nisbet's Heraldry, ii. app. 60. Douglas's Baronage of Scotland, 198, 264. Burke's Extinct Baronetcies, 627. The Parish of Cramond, by J. P. Wood, 47, 265. Walter Wood's East Neuk of Fife, 280. Betham's Baronetage, v. 438. Harleian Society, xvii. 1. The Scottish Journal, ii. 180. See ROBERTSON.

INGLOSE. Blore's Rutland, 188.

INGOE. Morant's Essex, i. 290.

INGOLDSBY. Noble's Memoirs of the House of Cromwell, ii. 216-230. Croke's History of the Family of Croke, No. 33. Lipscombe's History of the County of Buckingham, ii. 169. Burke's Extinct Baronetcies. Metcalfe's Visitations of Northamptonshire, 28. The Genealogist, New Series, iii. 136.

INGOLDSTHORP. Hunter's Deanery of Doncaster, ii. 230. Banks' Baronies in Fee, i. 322.

INGOW. Harleian Society, xiii. 103. See YNGOE.

INGPEN. Berry's Hampshire Genealogies, 220.

INGRAM. Surtees Society, xxxvi. 146. Nash's Worcestershire, i. 243. Burke's Landed Gentry, (of Swinshead,) 3, 4, 5, 6, 7 ; (of Ades,) 6, 7, 8. Foster's Yorkshire Pedigrees. Collectanea Topographica et Genealogica, viii. 140. Monasticon Eboracense, by John Burton, 441. Graves' History of Cleveland, 164. Thoresby's Ducatus Leodiensis, 230. Ord's History of Cleveland, 466. Dugdale's Warwickshire, 595. Hunter's Deanery of Doncaster, i. 173. Forrest's History of Knottingley, add. iv. Collections by the Powys-land Club, viii. 211. Wood's Douglas's Peerage of Scotland, ii. 1. Bysshe's Visitation of Essex, edited by J. J. Howard, 51. Harleian Society, xxvii. 82. See MEYNELL-INGRAM.

INGUERSBY. Baker's Northampton, i. 66.

INKEPENNE. Maclean's History of Trigg Minor, ii. 42.

INKERSALL, or INKERSOLE. Harleian Society, xxii. 68. Genealogical Memoranda relating to the Family of Parker, by E. M. S. Parker, 32.

INMAN. Burke's Royal Descents and Pedigrees of Founders' Kin, 77. Burke's Landed Gentry, 6, 7, 8.

INNES. Account of the Origin of the Family of Innes. Edinburgh, 1820, 4to.; and 1864, 4to. Claims of Sir J. N. Innes, Bart., Walter Ker, Esq., and the Rt. Hon. William Drummond, to the Titles of Duke and Earl of Roxburghe, Sess. Papers, 124 of 1808; 15 of 1809; 1 and 66 of 1810; 39 of 1812. Berry's Berkshire Genealogies, 109-122. Burke's Landed Gentry, (of Raemoir,) 2, 3, 4, 5, 6, 7, 8; (of Dromantine,) 4, 5, 6, 7, 8; (of Ayton,) 5, 6, 7, 8. Douglas's Baronage of Scotland, 13, 78. Shaw's History of Moray, 59. Betham's Baronetage, v. (Barts. of Scotland) 1. Burke's Extinct Baronetcies. Caithness Family History, by John Henderson, 238. Alexander Nisbet's Heraldic Plates, 100. Burke's Colonial Gentry, ii. 580. Berks Archl. and Architectural Society's Journal, iii. 113.

INSLIE. Nichols' History of the County of Leicester, iv. 272.

IOHNSON. Burke's Landed Gentry, 8.

ION. The Genealogist, vi. 259.

IONG. Dwnn's Visitations of Wales, i. 117, 156, 162, 243.

IPSTONE, or IPSTONES. History of Llangurig, by E. Hamer and H. W. Lloyd, 359. Herald and Genealogist, vi. 43. Collections by the Powys-land Club, ix. 125. Collections for a History of Staffordshire, William Salt Society, i. 300. History of Powys Fadog, by J. Y. W. Lloyd, iii. 99. Genealogical Records of the Family of Woodd, 35. The Genealogist, New Series, viii. 244.

IRBY. Burke's Commoners, iv. 563, Landed Gentry, 2, 3, 4, 5. Gyll's History of Wraysbury, 78. History of Boston, by Pishey Thompson, 2nd edn., 391. Edmondson's Baronagium Genealogicum, v. 477. Brydges' Collins' Peerage, vii. 301. Wotton's English Baronetage, iv. 99. The Genealogist, iii. 364. Burke's Colonial Gentry, i. 203.

IREBY. Nicolson and Burn's Westmorland and Cumberland, ii. 128.

IRELAND. Hale Hall, with Notes on the Family of Ireland-Blackburne. 1881, 4to. Dwnn's Visitations of Wales, i. 285. Burke's Landed Gentry, (of Owsden Hall,) 2, 3, 4, 5; (of Roberstown,) 2; (of Hutt and Hale,) 6 page 135, 7 page 147. Lydiate Hall and its Associations, by Rev. T. E. Gibson, (1876, 4to.) 163. Chetham Society, lxxxi. 95, 122; lxxxii. 165. Harleian Society, viii. 74; xvii. 2; xxviii. 269, 275; xxxvii. 180. Gregson's Fragments relative to the County of Lancaster, 210, 220. Hunter's Deanery of Doncaster, ii. 215. Baines' History of the County of Lancaster, iii. 753; Croston's edn., v. 50. The Sheriffs of Montgomeryshire, by W. V. Lloyd, 510. The Genealogist, New Series, xvii. 21. See CLAYFIELD-IRELAND, DE IRELAND.

IREMONGER, or IRONMONGER. Berry's Hampshire Genealogies, 14. Burke's Landed Gentry, 2, 3, 5, 6, 7, 8. Burke's Visitation of Seats and Arms, ii. 15. Visitations of Staffordshire, 1614 and

1663-4, William Salt Society, 186. The Genealogist, New Series, ii. 71.

IRETON. Jewitt's Reliquary, x. 169, 254. Harleian Society, vii. 29. Stemmata Shirleiana, by E. P. Shirley, 2nd edn., 326. Notes and Queries, 5 S. vi. 390, 429, 457, 492, 541; xii. 124. Metcalfe's Visitations of Northamptonshire, 100. Foster's Visitation of Cumberland and Westmorland, 68.

IREYS. Dugdale's Warwickshire, 123. Visitatio Comitatus Wiltoniæ, 1623, printed by Sir T. Phillipps.

IRISH. Visitation of Somerset, printed by Sir T. Phillipps, 109. Harleian Society, xi. 60.

IRONSIDE. Burke's Landed Gentry, 5, 6, 7, 8. Hutchins' Dorset, ii. 282. Surtees' Durham, i. 150. Harleian Society, xxii. 68.

IRTON. Berry's Hampshire Genealogies, 116. Burke's Commoners, iii. 675, Landed Gentry, 2, 3, 4, 8. Foster's Visitations of Yorkshire, 42. Harleian Society, vii. 16; xvi. 173. Hutchinson's History of Cumberland, i. 573. Jefferson's History of Allerdale Ward, Cumberland, 195. Visitatio Comitatus Wiltoniæ, 1623, printed by Sir T. Phillipps. Visitation of Wiltshire, edited by G. W. Marshall, 8. Nicolson snd Burn's Westmorland and Cumberland, ii. 23. See YRTON.

IRVINE, or IRVING. The Original of the Family of the Irvines, by Dr. Ch. Irvine. 1678 (?), 12mo. Burke's Commoners, (of Drum Castle,) ii. 680, Landed Gentry, 2, 3, 4, 5, 6, 7, 8; (of Castle Irvine,) Landed Gentry, 4, 5, 6, 7, 8; (of Killadeas,) 2 supp., 3, 4, 5 and supp., 6, 7, 8; (of Inveramsay,) 3; (of Greenhill,) 2, 3, 4; (of Bonshaw,) 7, 8; (of Barwhinnock,) 7; (of Newton,) 4 supp., 5, 6, 7. Burke's Heraldic Illustrations, 5. Nisbet's Heraldry, ii. app. 69. Burke's Extinct Baronetcies, 608. Burke's Colonial Gentry, i. 155. Parliamentary Memoirs of Fermanagh, by the Earl of Belmore, 47.

IRWIN. Burke's Commoners, (of Tanragoe,) iii. 101, Landed Gentry, 2, 3, 4; (of Derrygore,) Landed Gentry, 4, 5, 6, 7, 8; (of Justustown,) 2, 3, 4, 5, 6, 7, 8; (of Richmount,) 8; (of Rathmoyle,) 5 supp. 6, 7, 8. Oliver's History of Antigua, i. 192.

ISAAC, ISAACK, ISACKE, ISAAK, or ISAAKE. Tuckett's Devonshire Pedigrees, 5, 11. Harleian Society, vi. 150. The Genealogist, iv. 118. The Visitations of Devon, by J. L. Vivian, 501, 502. Miscellanea Genealogica et Heraldica, 3rd Series, iii. 54, 56.

ISAACSON. Gentleman's Magazine, 1831, ii. 502. Harleian Society, xvii. 3. Bysshe's Visitation of Essex, edited by J. J. Howard, 51.

ISABELLA II. (Queen of Spain). Gentleman's Magazine, 1834, i. 177.

ISHAM. J. H. Hill's History of Langton, 316. Harleïan Society, i. 17. Visitation of Somerset, printed by Sir T. Phillipps, 110. Burke's Royal Descents and Pedigrees of Founders' Kin, 17. Bridges' Northamptonshire, by Rev. Peter Whalley, i. 112, 124. Baker's Northampton, i. 264, 270. Memoirs of the Family of Chester, by R. E. C. Waters, 51. The Genealogist, ii. 241; iii. 274. Wotton's English Baronetage, ii. 28. Betham's Baronetage, i. 298. Weaver's Visitations of Somerset, 39. Metcalfe's Visitations of Northamptonshire, 181. Somerset and Dorset Notes and Queries, iii. 126.

ISHERWOOD. Burke's Commoners, i. 101, Landed Gentry, 2, 3, 4, 5, 6, 7, 8. Ormerod's Cheshire, iii. 786. Earwaker's East Cheshire, ii. 66.

Is KENNEN. Dwnn's Visitations of Wales, i. 92.

Is KERDYN. Dwnn's Visitations of Wales, i. 27.

ISLEY. Topographer and Genealogist, i. 516 ; iii. 196.

ISMAY. Burke's Landed Gentry, ·8.

ISNEY. See DISNEY.

ISONS. Foster's Visitations of Yorkshire, 536.

ISTED. Burke's Commoners, ii. 462, Landed Gentry, 2, 3, 4, 5, 6.

ITHELL. Cambridgeshire Visitation, edited by Sir T. Phillipps, 19. Harleian Society, xli. 92.

IVER. Account of the Clan Iver, by Very Rev. Principal Campbell. Aberdeen, 1868, 8vo.

IVERY. A Genealogical History of the House of Ivery, or Yvery, (*i.e.*, Percival) by J. Anderson. London, 1742, 2 vols., 8vo. Visitation of Somerset, printed by Sir T. Phillipps, 110. Weaver's Visitations of Somerset, 39. See DE IVERI, YVERY.

IVES. Burke's Landed Gentry, (of Braddon,) 3, 4, 5, 6, 7, 8 ; (of Bentworth Hall,) 3, 4, 5, 6 and supp., 7, 8. Dawson Turner's Sepulchral Reminiscences of Great Yarmouth, 129. Baker's Northampton, ii. 38.

IVESON. Kent's British Banner Displayed, 532. Thoresby's Ducatus Leodiensis, 110.

IVORY. Notes and Queries, 7 S. ix. 447.

IVYE, or IVIE. Visitation of Oxfordshire, 1634, printed by Sir T. Phillipps, (Middle Hill, fol.) 23. Harleian Society, v. 260.

IWARDBY. Lipscombe's History of the County of Buckingham, i. 394..

IZOD. Burke's Landed Gentry, 3, 4, 5, 6, 7, 8. Visitation of Gloucester, edited by T. F. Fenwick and W. C. Metcalfe, 97. Harleian Society, xxi. 95.

JACKMAN. Harleian Society, i. 72 ; xiii. 426. Camden Society, xliii. 105. Visitations of Staffordshire, 1614 and 1663-4, William Salt Society, 187.

JACKSON. Pedigree of Jacksonne of Edderthorpe, Hickleton, and Barnsley. Compiled by Rowland Jackson, 1863. Large sheet. Herald and Genealogist, ii. 78 ; v. 270. Miscellanea Genealogica et Heraldica, ii. 129 ; iii. 408. Ducketiana, by Sir G. F. Duckett, Bart. (London, 1869, 4to.) 2. Bibliotheca Topographica Britannica, ix. Part iv. 260, 278. Morant's Essex, ii. 357. Visitation of Middlesex, (Salisbury, 1820, fol.) 26. Surtees Society, xxxvi. 5, 117. Harleian Society, i. 40; xi. 60; xvi. 173; xxxvii. 77; xxxix. 1070; xl. 1263. Burke's Heraldic Illustrations, 41. Visitation of Somerset, printed by Sir T. Phillipps, 110. Burke's Landed Gentry, (of Duddington,) 2 supp., 3, 4, 5, 6, 7, 8 ; (of Fanningstown,) 3, 4, 5, 6; (of Enniscoe,) 2, 3, 4, 5, 6, 7, 8 ; (of

Ahanesk,) 4, 5, 6, 7, 8; (of Normanby Hall,) 5, 6, 7; (of Manor
House,) 3, 4; (of Glanbeg,) 2, 3; (of Doncaster,) 2; (of Swor-
dale,) 8. Foster's Yorkshire Pedigrees. Foster's Visitations of
Yorkshire, 43, 185, 308, 537, 538. Shaw's Staffordshire, ii. 56.
Burke's Royal Descents and Pedigrees of Founders' Kin, 91.
Archæologia Æliana, 1st Series, ii. 139. Hunter's Deanery of
Doncaster, ii. 79, 136. Surtees' Durham, ii. 183; iii. 271. The
Genealogist, ii. 252; New Series, ix. 71. Yorkshire Archæological and Topographical Journal, vi. 189. Betham's Baronetage,
iv. 232. Metcalfe's Visitations of Suffolk, 147. Notes and
Queries, 4 S. xi. 424; xii. 71; 6 S. viii. 139, 433; ix. 195;
xi. 9. Burke's Colonial Gentry, i. 158, 164; ii. 434. Pedigree
of Jackson, (Baronet). Windsor, 1877. Broadside. Foster's Visitation of Middlesex, 51. Historical Notices of Doncaster, by
C. W. Hatfield, 3rd Series, 240. Visitations of Staffordshire,
1614 and 1663-4, William Salt Society, 187. Foster's Visitations of Northumberland, 71. Foster's Visitations of Durham,
185. Earwaker's History of Sandbach, 139. Howard's Visitation of Ireland, i. 73. The Genealogical Magazine, iii. 310.

JACOB. An Historical and Genealogical Narrative of the Families of
Jacob, by A. H. Jacob and J. H. Glascott. Dublin, 1875, 8vo.
Morant's Essex, ii. 256. Visitation of Middlesex, (Salisbury, 1820,
fol.) 13. Burke's Landed Gentry, 2. Harleian Society, viii. 379;
xvii. 4. Burke's Visitation of Seats and Arms, ii. 28. Burke's
Authorized Arms, 49. Wotton's English Baronetage, iii. 449.
Betham's Baronetage, ii. 366; iv. 413. Notes and Queries, 3 S.
v. 445. Burke's Extinct Baronetcies. Foster's Visitation of
Middlesex, 21. History of the Wilmer Family, 154. The
Genealogist, New Series, xiii. 188.

JACOBSON. Harleian Society, xvii. 5.

JACOMB. Burke's Royal Descents and Pedigrees of Founders' Kin,
Founders' Kin, 3. Burke's Commoners, iv. 168. Hasted's Kent,
(Hund. of Blackheath, by H. H. Drake,) 14. Harleian Society,
xxxix. 1139.

JACQUES. Burke's Extinct Baronetcies.

JACSON. Burke's Landed Gentry, 2, 3, 4, 5, 6, 7, 8. Foster's
Lancashire Pedigrees.

JADWYN. Harleian Society, xvii. 6. New England Register, xlvi.
312.

JAFFREY. New England Register, xv. 16.

JAGO, or IAGO. A Complete Parochial History of the County of
Cornwall, iv. 1. An Historical Survey of Cornwall, by C. S.
Gilbert, ii. 160.

JAKES. Nichols' History of the County of Leicester, iv. 964*.

JAKSON. Surtees' Durham, i. 246.

JALLAND. Account of the Family of Jalland of Whatton, 1535-
1878. Nottingham, 1878, 8vo. Burke's Landed Gentry, 5 supp.,
6, 7, 8.

JAMES. Burke's Extinct Baronetcies. Morant's Essex, ii. 604.
Hasted's Kent, ii. 247. East Anglian, i. 330. Surrey Archæo-

logical Collections, iii. ; xi. Dwnn's Visitations of Wales, i. 111, 231. Visitation of Durham, 1615, (Sunderland, 1820, fol.) 99. Archæologia Cantiana, iv. 242. Berry's Kent Genealogies, 209. Berry's Hampshire Genealogies, 188. Glamorganshire Pedigrees, edited by Sir T. Phillipps, 35. Visitation of Somerset, printed by Sir T. Phillipps, 110. Burke's Landed Gentry, (of Barrock,) 2, 3, 4, 5, 6, 7, 8 ; (of Otterburn,) 2, 3, 4, 5, 6, 7, 8 ; (of Pant-saison,) 2, 3, 4, 5, 6, 7, 8. Harleian Society, viii. 192; xi. 61 ; xiii. 426 ; xvii. 385; xxii. 69 ; xxxvii. 360 ; xlii. 1 ; xliii. 194. Jones' History of the County of Brecknock, ii. 254. Surtees' Durham, i. 216. Burke's Royal Families, (London, 1851, 8vo.) ii. 39. Hutchinson's History of Durham, i. 479. Caermarthen-shire Pedigrees, 54. Manning and Bray's Surrey, i. 326. Chetham Society, vii. 5. The Genealogist, iii. 302 ; v. 279. Notes and Queries, 2 S. xii. 244, 354, 402. Metcalfe's Visitation of Worcester, 1683, 65. Wotton's English Baronetage, iii. 709. Betham's Baronetage, iv. 207. Howard's Visitation of England and Wales, i. 265. Miscellanea Genealogica et Heraldica, 2nd Series, ii. 292. Visitation of Gloucester, edited by T. F. Fenwick and W. C. Metcalfe, 98. Bysshe's Visitation of Essex, edited by J. J. Howard, 52. Foster's Visitations of Durham, 187. Genealogies of Morgan and Glamorgan, by G. T. Clark, 257. Burke's Colonial Gentry, ii. 645. Burke's Family Records, 345. *See* GREVIS-JAMES.

JAMES I. (Seize Quartiers of King.) Gentleman's Magazine, 1849, i. 483.

JAMES AP OWEN. Dwnn's Visitations of Wales, i. 81.

JAMESON. Burke's Landed Gentry, 3, 4, 5, 6, 7, 8.

JAMIESON. J. E. Reid's History of the Co. of Bute, 255.

JANE, or JANES. The Visitations of Cornwall, edited by J. L. Vivian, 241, 587.

JANSON, or JANSSEN. Baker's Northampton, i. 245. Wotton's English Baronetage, iv. 169. Hutchins' Dorset, i. 458. Burke's Extinct Baronetcies. Notes and Queries, 6 S. vi. 369. Harleian Society, xvii. 7. *See* I'ANSON.

JANVRIN. J. B. Payne's Armorial of Jersey, 184.

JAQUES. Surtees Society, xxxvi. 162. Burke's Landed Gentry, 3, 4, 5, 6, 7, 8. Foster's Yorkshire Pedigrees. Plantagenet-Harrison's History of Yorkshire, i. 66.

JARRATT. Doncaster Charities, by Charles Jackson, 50.

JARRETT. Burke's Landed Gentry, 2, 3, 4, 5, 6, 7, 8.

JARVIS, or JARVYS. J. H. Hill's History of Langton, 73. Cambridgeshire Visitation, edited by Sir T. Phillipps, 19. Burke's Landed Gentry, (of Doddington,) 2, 3, 4, 5, 7, 8 ; (of Middleton,) 8. Visitation of Staffordshire, 1663-4, printed by Sir T. Phillipps, 6. Nichols' History of the County of Leicester, ii. 671. Visitation of Devon, edited by F. T. Colby, 140. The Visitations of Devon, by J. L. Vivian, 504. Ontarian Families, by E. M. Chadwick, i. 122. Oliver's History of Antigua, ii. 98. *See* GERVEIS.

JARY. Burke's Landed Gentry, 5, 6, 7, 8.

JASON. Burke's Extinct Baronetcies.
JASSON. Visitations of Staffordshire, 1614 and 1663-4, William Salt Society, 188.
JAUNCYE. Account of the Mayo and Elton Families, by C. H. Mayo, 147.
JAWDRELL. Camden Society, xliii. 66. Cambridgeshire Visitation, edited by Sir T. Phillipps, 19. Harleian Society, xli. 13. See JODRELL.
JAY. Visitation of Gloucester, edited by T. F. Fenwick and W. C. Metcalfe, 99. Weaver's Visitations of Somerset, 40. Phillimore's London and Middlesex Note-Book, 258. Harleian Society, xxviii. 273; xliii. 155. Surrey Archæological Collections, xi.
JAYNE. Genealogies of Morgan and Glamorgan, by G. T. Clark, 305.
JEAFFRESON. Burke's Landed Gentry, 2, 3, 4, 5, 6, and 6 page 1363. Howard's Visitation of England and Wales, ii. 52. Oliver's History of Antigua, ii. 106.
JEAKE. Sussex Archæological Collections, xiii. 78.
JEAMES. Berry's Berkshire Genealogies, 2.
JEBB. Burke's Landed Gentry, (of Walton,) 2 supp., 4 supp., 6, 7, 8; (of Notts,) 2, 4 supp., 5 supp., 6. Burke's Extinct Baronetcies. Life of John Jebb, by Charles Forster, 3rd edn., 3.
JEE. Nichols' History of the County of Leicester, iv. 876.
JEFFERAY. Berry's Sussex Genealogies, 156. Visitation of Sussex, 1570, printed by Sir T. Phillipps, (Middle Hill, fol.) 6. Horsfield's History of Lewes, ii. 66. Sussex Archæological Collections, xiv. 219.
JEFFERIES. Nash's Worcestershire, i. 245, 267.
JEFFERSON. Surtees' Durham, iv. 156. Burke's Landed Gentry, 8.
JEFFERY. Burke's Landed Gentry, 5.
JEFFERYS. Banks' Dormant and Extinct Baronage, iii. 405.
JEFFREYS. Burke's Commoners, iv. 202; Landed Gentry, (of Wem,) 2, 3, 4; (of Burkham,) 8. Harleian Society, viii. 405, 470; xiii. 427; xxvii. 83. Lipscombe's History of the County of Buckingham, iv. 505. Nichols' History of the County of Leicester, ii. 114. Jones' History of the County of Brecknock, ii. 117-121. Burke's Extinct Baronetcies. History of Powys Fadog, by J. Y. W. Lloyd, iii. 68. Visitations of Staffordshire, 1614 and 1663-4, William Salt Society, 189. New England Register, xv. 14.
JEKYLL, or JECKYLL. Topographer and Genealogist, ii. 82. Harleian Society, viii. 461; xiii. 427. Lipscombe's History of the County of Buckingham, iv. 356. Clutterbuck's Hertford, i. 458. Baker's Northampton, i. 132. Bysshe's Visitation of Essex, edited by J. J. Howard, 53. Burke's Family Records, 347.
JELF. Pedigree of Jelf of Bushley and Eckington, [T. P.] 1866, folio page.
JENINGES. Visitation of Staffordshire, 1663-4, printed by Sir T. Phillipps, 6. See JENNENS.
JENISON, or JENYSON. Visitation of Norfolk, published by Norfolk Archæological Society, i. 348. Harleian Society, viii. 318; xvi.

174. W. Dickinson's History of Newark, 219. Surtees' Durham, iii. 263, 320, 322, 412. The Genealogist, ii. 223; vi. 259. C. Brown's Annals of Newark-upon-Trent, 202. Foster's Visitations of Durham, 189. Metcalfe's Visitations of Northamptonshire, 101. Foster's Visitations of Northumberland, 72, 73.

JENKENSON. Harleian Society, i. 52. Visitation of Oxfordshire, 1634, printed by Sir T. Phillipps, (Middle Hill, fol.) 23. Visitation of Norfolk, published by Norfolk Archæological Society, ii. 94. *See* JENKINSON.

JENKES. Harleian Society, xxviii. 275.

JENKIN, or JENKYN. Dwnn's Visitations of Wales, i. 49, 135, 192. Surtees Society, xxxvi. 363. Lipscombe's History of the County of Buckingham, iv. 223. Harleian Society, ix. 103; xiii. 63, xlii. 84. Clutterbuck's Hertford, i. 229. Berry's Kent Genealogies, 482-485. Berry's Sussex Genealogies, 250-253. Foster's Visitations of Yorkshire, 371. A Royal Descent, by T. E. Sharpe, (London, 1875, 4to.) 73. Cardiganshire Pedigrees, 83, 88. The Sheriffs of Montgomeryshire, by W. V. Lloyd, 180. The Visitations of Cornwall, edited by J. L. Vivian, 242.

JENKINS, or JENKYNS. Dwnn's Visitations of Wales, i. 29. Glamorganshire Pedigrees, edited by Sir T. Phillipps, 22. Burke's Commoners, (of Bicton Hall,) iii. 255, Landed Gentry, 2, 3, 4, 5, 6; (of Clanacombe,) 8; (of Charlton Hill,) 2 supp., 3, 4, 5, 6, 7, 8; Miscellanea Genealogica et Heraldica, New Series, i. 84, 122. Cardiganshire Pedigrees, 115. Meyrick's History of the Co. of Cardigan, 133, 159, 194, 332, 334. T. Nicholas' County Families of Wales, 196. Burke's Royal Families, (London, 1851, 8vo.) i. 23. Jewers' Wells Cathedral, 76. Harleian Society, xxxix. 928.

JENKINSON, or JENKYNSON. Berry's Sussex Genealogies, 248. Miscellanea Genealogica et Heraldica, New Series, i. 455; 2nd Series, v. 7, 27, 33, 61, 76, 84. Harleian Society, i. 51; v. 270. Lipscombe's History of the County of Buckingham, i. 315. Horsfield's History of Lewes, ii. 44. Brydges' Collins' Peerage, v. 392. Wotton's English Baronetage, iii. 288. Burke's Extinct Baronetcies. Jewitt's Reliquary, xx. 128. The Monthly Visitor, iv. 145.

JENMAN. Dallaway's Sussex, i. 186.

JENNENS, or JENNINGS. The Great Jennens Case, being an Epitome of the History of the Jennens Family, by Messrs. Harrison and Willis. Sheffield, 1879, 8vo. Pedigrees of Jennens, Howe, Hanmer, Lygon, and other families, published by James Coleman, and numbered 1 and 2, single sheets. Nichols' History of the County of Leicester, iv. 859. Baker's Northampton, i. 720. Cussan's History of Hertfordshire, Parts iii. and iv. 23, 196. Jennings' Wills and Administrations at Litchfield, England, etc. London, *n.d.*, 8vo., pp. 17. Berry's Kent Genealogies, 181. Surtees Society, xxxvi. 58. Visitation of Somerset, printed by Sir T. Phillipps, 111. Burke's Commoners, iii. 585, Landed Gentry, 2 supp., 8. Harleian Society, viii. 325; xi. 61; xvii. 9;

xxii. 147; xxviii. 277; xxxvii. 180; xxxviii. 577; xl. 1268; xliii. 79. Clutterbuck's Hertford, i. 217. Notes and Queries, 1 S. iv. 424; v. 163; vi. 362; vii. 95, 119, 477; xi. 10, 55; 2 S. ii. 466; viii. 57. Metcalfe's Visitations of Suffolk, 46. Statement of Facts in connection with the Pedigree of William Jennens, Esq., printed for J. C. Jennens. London, *n.d.*, folio. Somersetshire Wills, printed for F. A. Crisp, iii. 55. Burke's Colonial Gentry, ii. 626. E. J. Climenson's History of Shiplake, 335. *See* JENINGES, JENNYNS, JEYNENS.

JENNER. Fosbrooke's Abstracts of Smith's Lives of the Berkleys, 220. Berry's Sussex Genealogies, 275. Burke's Landed Gentry, (of Wenvoe Castle,) 2, 3, 4, 5, 6, 7, 8; (of Berkeley,) 2. Harleian Society, viii. 381. Fosbrooke's History of Gloucestershire, ii. 44. Notes and Queries, 3 S. iii. 34. New England Register, xix. 246.

JENNER-FUST. Burke's Landed Gentry, 5, 6, 7, 8.

JENNEY. Visitation of Norfolk, published by Norfolk Archæological Society, i. 132. Burke's Commoners, iii. 446, Landed Gentry, 2, 3, 4, 8. Page's History of Suffolk, 245, 267. The Genealogist, iv. 185. Metcalfe's Visitations of Suffolk, 44, 45. Harleian Society, xvii. 8; xxxii. 169.

JENNISON. New England Register, vii. 71.

JENNYNS, or JENYNS. Burke's Commoners, (of Bottisham,) iii. 582, Landed Gentry, 2, 3, 4, 5, 6, 7, 8; (of Gelli-Dêg,) 7, 8. Visitation of Warwickshire, 1619, published with Warwickshire Antiquarian Magazine, 104. Manning and Bray's Surrey, i. 88; ii. 9. Harleian Society, xii. 241; xiii. 428; xxviii. 275. *See* JENNENS.

JENOUR. Morant's Essex, ii. 110, 426. Harleian Society, xiii. 63, 221, 429. Wotton's English Baronetage, ii. 112. Burke's Extinct Baronetcies. Bysshe's Visitation of Essex, edited by J. J. Howard, 53.

JENYSON. Harleian Society, xxxii. 172.

JERARD. Visitation of Somerset, printed by Sir T. Phillipps, 111. Harleian Society, xi. 62; xvii. 9.

JERMIN, or JERMYN. Berry's Sussex Genealogies, 184. Herald and Genealogist, v. 435. Dallaway's Sussex, i. 155. Page's History of Suffolk, 739. The Genealogist, iii. 302. Betham's Baronetage, iii. 58. Banks' Dormant and Extinct Baronage, iii. 407. Metcalfe's Visitations of Suffolk, 75, 147, 197. Harleian Society, xvii. 10; xxxii. 174. Bysshe's Visitation of Essex, edited by J. J. Howard, 54. Howard's Visitation of England and Wales, iii. 170. *See* GERMIN.

JERMY. Blomefield's Norfolk, v. 386. Visitation of Norfolk, published by Norfolk Archæological Society, i. 107. Page's History of Suffolk, 44, 416. Metcalfe's Visitations of Suffolk, 196. Harleian Society, xxxii. 172.

JERNINGHAM, or JERNEGAN. The Case of Sir Wm. Jerningham, Bart., claiming the two Baronies of Stafford, June, 1808, folio, pp. 10. List of proofs of the Case of Sir Wm. Jerningham, Bart., as to the two Stafford Baronies, folio, pp. 6. Claim of Sir Wm.

Jerningham, Bart., to the Barony of Stafford, Sess. Papers, 80 of 1808 ; 107 of 1809 ; 18 of 1812 ; 129 of 1825. Blomefield's Norfolk, ii. 416. Page's History of Suffolk, 396. Suckling's History of Suffolk, ii. 46. Notices of Great Yarmouth, by J. H. Druery, 166. Burke's Landed Gentry, 6, 7, 8. Wotton's English Baronetage, i. 450. Betham's Baronetage, i. 223. Metcalfe's Visitations of Suffolk, 46. Notes and Queries, 7 S., vii. 89. The Genealogist, New Series, x. 216. *See* GERNEGAN, STAFFORD.

JERSEY. Claim of George, Earl of Jersey, to Vote at Elections of Irish Peers as Viscount Grandison, Sess. Papers, 102 of 1829. Burke's Colonial Gentry, i. 297.

JERVEIS, or JERVIS. Pedigree of Jervis, Viscount St. Vincent, [T. P.] broadside. Nichols' History of the County of Leicester, ii. 671 ; iv. 334. Burke's Landed Gentry, 6, 7, 8. Genealogy of Henzey, Tyttery, and Tyzack, by H. S. Grazebrook, 47. Brydges' Collins' Peerage, v. 399. Earwaker's History of Sandbach, 140. Visitations of Staffordshire, 1614 and 1663-4, William Salt Society, 190. Harleian Society, xl. 1177.

JERVOISE. Burke's Landed Gentry, 2 add., 3, 4, 5, 6, 7, 8. Lipscombe's History of the County of Buckingham, iii. 71. Nichols' History of the County of Leicester, iv. 602. Gentleman's Magazine, lix. i. 21. *See* ELLIS-JERVOISE.

JESSE. Burke's Landed Gentry, (of Llanbedr Hall,) 3, 4, 5, 6, 7, 8 ; (of Maisonette,) 5.

JESSEL. Howard's Visitation of England and Wales, ix. 71.

JESSON. Burke's Landed Gentry, 4, 5. Burke's Authorized Arms, 34. The Forest and Chase of Sutton Coldfield, (London, 1860, 8vo.) app. Harleian Society, xvii. 11.

JESSOP. Surtees Society, xxxvi. 163. Burke's Commoners, ii. 251, Landed Gentry, (of Doory Hall,) 2, 3, 4, 5, 6, 7, 8 ; (of Overton,) 8. Harleian Society, iv. 94. Hunter's History of the Parish of Sheffield, 366. Hutchins' Dorset, ii. 494. Independency at Brighouse, by J. H. Turner, 76. Carthew's West and East Bradenham, 43. Miscellanea Genealogica et Heraldica, 2nd Series, ii. 312. New England Register, xxvi. 403. The Genealogist, New Series, xvii. 52.

JESTON. Genealogy of Henzey, Tyttery, and Tyzack, by H. S. Grazebrook, 56. The Genealogical Magazine, ii. 43.

JESTYN AP GURGAN. Glamorganshire Pedigrees, edited by Sir T. Phillipps, 28. Genealogies of Morgan and Glamorgan, by G. T. Clark, 77-130.

JETER. Metcalfe's Visitations of Suffolk, 147.

JEUNE. Burke's Landed Gentry, 6 supp., 7, 8.

JEVAN, or JEVANS. Cardiganshire Pedigrees, 114. Harleian Society, xxviii. 278.

JEVON. Shaw's Staffordshire, ii. app. 19. Miscellanea Genealogica et Heraldica, New Series, iv. 384.

JEWELL. Westcote's Devonshire, edited by G. Oliver and P. Jones, 536. Visitation of Devon, edited by F. T. Colby, 141. The Visitations of Devon, by J. L. Vivian, 505.

JEWETT. Harleian Society, xviii. 263.

JEX-BLAKE. Burke's Landed Gentry, 2, 3, 4, 5, 6, 7, 8.

JEYNENS. Harleian Society, ix. 104. The Visitations of Cornwall, edited by J. L. Vivian, 243. *See* JENNENS.

JHONES. The Genealogist, v. 280.

JOANES. Harleian Society, xxi. 96.

JOBBER. Collections for a History of Staffordshire, (William Salt Society,) ii. part 2, 113. Harleian Society, xxviii. 279.

JOBSON. Morant's Essex, ii. 186. Morant's History of Colchester, 137. Hunter's Deanery of Doncaster, ii. 399. Harleian Society, xiii. 64. Antiquarian Notices of Lupset, by J. H., (1851 edn.) 59.

JOCELIN, or JOCELYN. Clutterbuck's Hertford, iii. 203. Chauncy's Hertfordshire, 183. Harleian Society, xiii. 65, 223-230, 430. Wotton's English Baronetage, iii. 481. *See* BOLEYNES, JOSCELYN.

JODRELL. Burke's Commoners, i. 226, Landed Gentry, 2, 3, 4, 5 supp., 6, 7, 8. Earwaker's East Cheshire, ii. 538. Burke's Royal Families, (London, 1851, 8vo.) i. 40. Gyll's History of Wraysbury, 23. Ormerod's Cheshire, iii. 786. Harleian Society, xvii. 11. Howard's Visitation of England and Wales, i. 33 ; Notes, i. 110. Visitations of Staffordshire, 1614 and 1663-4, William Salt Society, 191. Harleian Society, xxxvii. 275. *See* JAWDRELL.

JOHN. Cardiganshire Pedigrees, 115, 116.

JOHN, AP DAVID. Dwnn's Visitations of Wales, i. 179, 241 ; ii. 338 ; ap Howel, ii. 94 ; ap Hugh, i. 29 ; ap Huw, ii. 255 ; ap Lewis, ii. 215 ; ap Robert, ii. 216.

JOHN DAVID AB GRIFFITH. Dwnn's Visitations of Wales, i. 279.

JOHNES. Pedigree of Johnes of Dolau Cothi, by John Rowland, 1878, 8vo. Pedigree of Johnes of Abermarles, Co. Caermarthen, [T. P.] 1861, four folio pages. Dwnn's Visitations of Wales, ii. 26, 58, 290, 301, 333, 348. Burke's Commoners, iv. 59, Landed Gentry, 2, 3, 4, 5, 6, 7, 8. Meyrick's History of the Co. of Cardigan, 352-359. Archæologia Cambrensis, 3 S. vi. 178. T. Nicholas' County Families of Wales, 291.

JOHNS. Dwnn's Visitations of Wales, i. 33, 55, 78, 89, 109, 123, 174, 178, 189, 194, 209, 212, 235. Genealogies of Morgan and Glamorgan, by G. T. Clark, 491.

JOHNSON. Hasted's Kent, iv. 371. Burke's Authorized Arms, 191. Visitation of Middlesex, (Salisbury, 1820, fol.) 37, 40. Claim of Martha, wife of Sir Henry Johnson, Knt., to the Barony of Wentworth, Sess. Papers, Mar. and April, 1702. Berry's Kent Genealogies, 153, 384. Visitation of Durham, 1615, (Sunderland, 1820, fol.) 85. Burke's Landed Gentry, (of Ascoughfee Hall,) 2 supp., 3, 4, 5, 6, 7, 8 ; (of Burleigh Field,) 4, 7 ; (of Rockenham,) 4, 5, 6, 7, 8 ; (of Wytham on the Hill,) 5, 6, 7, 8 ; (of Ulverscroft,) 5, 6, 8 ; (of Deanery,) 2, 3, 4 ; (of Monk's Field,) 2 supp., 3, 4 ; (of Aykleyheads,) 6, 7 ; (of Temple Belwood,) 6, 7, 8 ; (of Winkleigh,) 6, 7, 8 ; (of Walton,) 6, 8. Howard's Visitation of England and Wales, i. 85 ; ii. 5 ; iii. 17. Miscellanea Genealogica et Heraldica, New Series, i. 450 ; ii. 122. Harleian Society, iii. 14 ;

viii. 266, 456; xiii. 430; xvii. 12-17; xix. 119; xxi. 97; xlii.
75, 122; xliii. 91. Chetham Society, lxxxv. 164. Stonehouse's
History of the Isle of Axholme, 344. W. Robinson's History of
Hackney, i. 301. Dawson Turner's Sepulchral Reminiscences of
Great Yarmouth, 47. Burke's Heraldic Illustrations, 133.
Wright's History of Rutland, 38. Read's History of the Isle of
Axholme, edited by T. C. Fletcher, 64. Surtees' Durham, ii. 200,
218; iv. 45. The Genealogist, i. 105; vi. 260; New Series, vii.
225. Baines' History of the Co. of Lancaster, iii. 609. Whitaker's
History of Whalley, i. 214. Colby of Great Torrington, by F. T.
Colby, 22. Plantagenet-Harrison's History of Yorkshire, i. 175.
Betham's Baronetage, iii. 257. Metcalfe's Visitations of Suffolk,
97. Ormerod's Parentalia, 11. Foster's Visitation of Middlesex,
67, 74. Ancient Families of Lincolnshire, in 'Spalding Free
Press,' 1873-5, Nos. xii. and xiii. Visitations of Staffordshire,
1614 and 1663-4, William Salt Society, 192. Foster's Visita-
tions of Durham, 191. Fletcher's Leicestershire Pedigrees and
Royal Descents, 119, 157. Burke's Colonial Gentry, i. 343.
New England Register, vii. 158; viii. 232, 359; xxxiii. 81, 333;
xxxiv. 60; xxxviii. 407. Essex Institute Historical Collections,
(Salem, Mass.,) xxxi. 204. Oliver's History of Antigua, ii. 111.
See IOHNSON.

JOHNSON-FERGUSON. Burke's Landed Gentry, 8.

JOHNSTON. Genealogical Account of the Family of Johnston of that
Ilk, by Alexander Johnston. Edinburgh, 1832, 4to. Surtees
Society, xxxvi. 6. Burke's Landed Gentry, (of Carnsalloch,) 2
supp., 3, 4, 5, 6, 7, 8; (of Fort Johnston,) 2, 3, 4, 5, 6, 7, 8; (of
Magheremena,) 3, 4, 5, 6, 7, 8; (of Holly Park,) 4, 5; (of Kin-
cardine,) 3, 4, 5, 6, 8; (of Co. Dublin,) 5 supp.; (of Brookhill,) 5;
(of Ballykilbeg,) 5, 6, 7, 8; (of Shieldhall,) 3, 4; (of Cowhill,) 6,
7, 8; (of Kilmore,) 6, 7, 8; (of Glynn,) 6, 7, 8; (of Knappagh,)
2; (of Annandale,) 7, 8; (of Alva,) 8; (of Galabank,) 8; (of Bignor
Park,) 8; (of Snow Hill,) 8. Burke's Visitation of Seats and
Arms, i. 56. Burke's Heraldic Illustrations, 80. Shirley's History
of the County of Monaghan, 163. Douglas's Baronage of Scotland, 35, 232. Inverurie and the Earldom of the Garioch, by
John Davidson, 223, 448. Walter Wood's East Neuk of Fife,
305. Wood's Douglas's Peerage of Scotland, i. 70. A short
memoir of James Young, app. 38-46. Foster's Collectanea Genealogica, (MP's Scotland,) 198. Burke's Extinct Baronetcies, 628.
Foster's Visitations of Durham, 193. Burke's Colonial Gentry,
ii. 701. Harleian Society, xxxix. 926. Notes and Queries, 7 S.
xi. 329, 450. Ontarian Families, by E. M. Chadwick, i. 45.

JOHNSTONE. The Johnstones of Annandale. London, 1853, 8vo.
Claim of John P. Goodinge Johnstone to be Earl of Annandale,
1839, folio, pp. 58. Case of Sir F. G. Johnstone, claiming the
Earldom of Annandale. Additional Case of same, 1838, fol. pp.
82. Claim of Sir J. L. Johnstone, Bart., to the title of Marquess
of Annandale, Sess. Papers, June, 1805. Claim of J. J. H. Johnstone of Annandale, Esq., to the Earldom of Annandale, Sess,

Papers, 128 of 1825 ; 34 of 1826 ; 56 of 1834 ; 100 of 1838 ; 101 of 1844. Case of Sir F. J. W. Johnstone on his Claim to Honours, etc., of Marquess of Annandale. London, *n.d.*, fol. pp. 66. Additional Case of same. London, *n.d.*, fol. pp. 114. Appendix to Additional Case of same. London, *n.d.*, fol. pp. 50. Claim of F. J. W. Johnstone and others to Dignity of Marquess of Annandale, Sess. Papers, C of 1876 ; B of 1877. Case of John Henry Goodinge Johnstone, claiming to be Earl of Annandale, 20 pp. fol. Supplemental Case, 5 pp. fol. Case for J. J. Hope Johnstone, claiming title of Marquis of Annandale. Edinburgh, 1876, fol. pp. 69. Additional Case of same. Edinburgh, 1878, fol. pp. 29. Case of Edward Johnstone, claiming title of Marquess of Annandale. Westminster, 1876, fol. pp. 14. Appendix of proofs to same, 1877, fol. pp. 39. Supplemental Case of same, 1879, fol. pp. 22. Claim of Service of John Henry Goodinge, Esq., as the nearest and lawful heir of the body, and of line, and Provision in general to the Deceased John Johnstone of Stapleton, his Great Grandfather, 1830, folio, pp. 2 and pedigree. Burke's Commoners, (of Alva,) ii. 302, Landed Gentry, 2, 3, 4, 5, 6, 7 ; (of Galabank,) Commoners, iv. 556, Landed Gentry, 2, 3, 4, 5, 6, 7 ; (of Snow Hill,) Landed Gentry, 2, 3, 4, 5, 6, 7 ; (of Mainstone Court,) 2 supp., 3 ; (of Raehills and Annandale,) 2, 6, 7 ; (of Hilton in the Merse,) 2 supp. Burke's Extinct Baronetcies, 609.

JOHNSTOUN. Harleian Society, xvii. 17.

JOHONNOT. New England Register, vi. 357 ; vii. 141.

JOICEY. Burke's Landed Gentry, 8.

JOLIFFE, or JOLLIFFE. Berry's Essex Genealogies, 122. Burke's Commoners, i. 517, Landed Gentry, 2, 3, 4, 5. Hutchins' Dorset, iii. 633. Burke's Royal Families, (London, 1851, 8vo.) i. 70. Harleian Society, ix. 105 ; xx. 60. Nash's Worcestershire, i. 251. The Visitations of Cornwall, edited by J. L. Vivian, 244. Genealogical Gleanings in England, by H. F. Waters, i. 262. New England Register, xlii. 71. *See* JOLLEY.

JOLLIE, or JOLLEY. Metcalfe's Visitation of Worcester, 1683, 65. Burke's Colonial Gentry, i. 385. Harleian Society, xxxix. 1048.

JONES. Pedigree of Jones of Nanteos, Co. Cardigan, etc., [T. P.] 1857, folio page. Pedigree of Sir William Jones of Castle March, [T. P.] 1870. Broadside. Burke's Patrician, ii. 255. Jewitt's Reliquary, vii. 24. Dwnn's Visitations of Wales, i. 196, 281, 304, 324, 330 ; ii. 95, 116, 305. The History of Monmouthshire, by D. Williams, App. 156. Visitation of Suffolk, edited by J. J. Howard, ii. 296. Glamorganshire Pedigrees, edited by Sir T. Phillipps, 36, 38. Visitation of Middlesex, (Salisbury, 1820, fol.) 19, 38. Oxfordshire Pedigrees, fol., *n.d.*, printed by Sir T. Phillipps. Visitation of Somerset, printed by Sir T. Phillipps, 110. Visitation of Oxfordshire, 1634, printed by Sir T. Phillipps, (Middle Hill, fol.) 23. Burke's Commoners, iii. 385; (of Llanarth, now HERBERT,) iv. 727, Landed Gentry, 2, 3, 4, 5, 6 ; (of Bealanamore,) Commoners, iii. 267, Landed Gentry, 2, 3, 4 ; (of Gwynfryn,) Landed Gentry, 2, 3, 4, 5, 6, 7, 8 ; (of Gurrey,) 2 add., 3, 4, 5 ; (of

Hartsheath,) 2, 3, 4, 5, 6, 7, 8 ; (of Llanerchrugog,) 3, 4, 5, 6, 7, 8 ;
(of Nass,) 3, 4, 5, 6, 7 ; (of Pantglas,) 2 add., 3, 4, 5, 6, 7, 8 ; (of
Trewythen,) 2, 3, 4, 5 ; (of Moneyglass,) 7, 8 ; (of Chastleton,) 3,
4, 5, 6, 7, 8 ; (of Badsworth,) 3, 4, 5, 6, 7, 8 ; (of Lisselan,) 3, 4,
5, 6, 7 ; (of Mullinabro',) 3, 4, 5, 6, 7, 8 ; (of Kelston Park,) 4, 5,
6, 8 ; (of Clytha,) 4, 5, 6 ; (of Derry Ormond,) 5, 6, 7, 8 ; (of
Poulstone,) 5 ; (of Ynysfor,) 8 ; 8 at p. 1341 ; (of Beneda Abbey,)
2 ; (of Sandford,) 2 supp. ; (of Fonmon Castle,) 2, 3, 4, 5, 6, 7, 8 ;
(of Wepre Hall,) 2 supp., 3, 4 ; (of Ystrad,) 2, 3, 4 ; (of Esgair
Evan,) 3 supp., 4 ; (of Larkhill,) 5, 6, 7 ; (of Shackerley,) 5, 6 ;
(of Loynrvre,) 2 supp. at p. 156 ; (of Donington,) 6 supp., 7.
Herald and Genealogist, v. 422. Harleian Society, v. 292 ; viii.
109, 249, 269 ; xi. 63 ; xvii. 18-21 ; xix. 120 ; xxviii. 279-282 ;
xxxvii. 299. Burke's Visitation of Seats and Arms, i. 19, 28.
Burke's Heraldic Illustrations, 25, 71, 141. Jones' History of
the County of Brecknock, ii. 524. Caermarthenshire Pedigrees,
7, 21, 27, 30, 49, 50, 69. Cardiganshire Pedigrees, 106. Pembrokeshire Pedigrees, 136, 137, 140, 151, 157. Meyrick's History of the
Co. of Cardigan, 402. Miscellanea Genealogica et Heraldica,
New Series, ii. 249. Archæologia Cambrensis, 3 S. vii. 17 ; 4 S.
ix. 40. T. Nicholas' County Families of Wales, 292, 353, 355,
631, 776, 941. Fosbrooke's History of Gloucestershire, ii. 473.
Memoirs of Gabriel Goodman, by R. Newcome, App. S. History
of the Gwydir Family, by Sir J. Wynne, the edn. printed at
Oswestry in 1878, *at end.* The Sheriffs of Cardiganshire, by J. R.
Phillipps, 42. An Historical Survey of Cornwall, by C. S. Gilbert,
ii. 164. Collections by the Powys-land Club, viii. 250, 254, 260.
Banks' Baronies in Fee, i. 393. Notes and Queries, 1 S. x. 445 ;
xi. 38 ; 6 S. ii. 370 ; 8 S. xii. 101. The Genealogist, vii. 179.
Archdall's Lodge's Peerage, iv. 300. Burke's Extinct Baronetcies.
Visitation of Wiltshire, edited by G. W. Marshall, 19, 42, 85.
Metcalfe's Visitation of Worcester, 1683, 66, 68. Records of
Upton Bishop, by F. T. Havergal, 10. The Visitations of Cornwall, edited by J. L. Vivian, 245. Carthew's Hundred of Launditch, Part iii. 382. Howard's Visitation of England and Wales,
i. 286. History of Powys Fadog, by J. Y. W. Lloyd, ii. 122 ; iii.
11, 38, 40, 66, 124 ; iv. 124, 323-9, 347, 425 ; v. 68, 226 ; vi.
223, 439. Somersetshire Wills, printed for F. A. Crisp, iii. 115.
Visitation of Gloucester, edited by T. F. Fenwick and W. C.
Metcalfe, 100. Foster's Visitation of Middlesex, 33, 69. Genealogies of Morgan and Glamorgan, by G. T. Clark, 138, 215, 257,
259, 262, 264, 278. Phillimore's London and Middlesex Note
Book, 61. New England Register, vi. 278 ; xiii. 34 ; xlix. 310.
Burke's Colonial Gentry, ii. 737. Burke's Family Records, 350.
Burke's Landed Gentry, 7 at p. 1230. Ontarian Families, by
E. M. Chadwick, i. 167. Transactions of the Shropshire Archæo-
gical Society, v. 338, 340 ; xi. 76. *See* HAMILTON-JONES, JHONES,
JOHNES, MATHIAS, JOANES.

JONES, (THOMAS). Dwnn's Visitations of Wales, i. 45.

JONES-PARRY. Burke's Landed Gentry, (of Madryn and Llwyn Onn,)

2, 3, 4, 5, 6, 7, 8. Burke's Visitation of Seats and Arms, 2nd Series,
i. 4. Burke's Royal Descents and Pedigrees of Founders' Kin, 13.
JONET (Daughter Morgan Jenkin). Dwnn's Visitations of Wales, ii. 56.
JONNS, (THOMAS). Dwnn's Visitations of Wales, i. 98.
JOPE. Harleian Society, ix. 108. The Visitations of Cornwall, edited
by J. L. Vivian, 247.
JOPSON. Foster's Visitations of Yorkshire, 622.
JORCE. The Genealogist, New Series, xviii. 29.
JORDAN, or JORDEN. Berry's Kent Genealogies, 431, 463. Berry's
Surrey Genealogies, 28. Dwnn's Visitations of Wales, i. 72.
Burke's Landed Gentry, (of Pigeonsford,) 2, 3, 4, 5, 6 ; (of Ross-
levin Castle,) 5, 6, 7. Harleian Society, vi. 265 ; xxviii. 282 ;
xliii. 123. Shaw's Staffordshire, ii. 107*. Pembrokeshire Pedi-
grees, 149, 162. Westcote's Devonshire, edited by G. Oliver and
P. Jones, 538. Miscellanea Genealogica et Heraldica, New Series,
iv. 227. Burke's Colonial Gentry, ii. 678. Surrey Archæological
Collections, xi. The Genealogical Magazine i. 692. The Visitations of Devon, by J. L. Vivian, 691.
JORTIN. History and Pedigree of the Lee Jortin Family, 1858, 8vo.
JOSCELYN. The Genealogical History of the Ancient Family of
Josselyn, by J. H. Josselyn. Ipswich, 1880, 8vo. Morant's Essex,
ii. 466, 478. Berry's Essex Genealogies, 119. The Genealogist,
iii. 303. Wright's Essex, ii. 270. Archdall's Lodge's Peerage,
iii. 258. The Genealogical Magazine, iii. 105. Harleian Society,
xvii. 22 ; xxii. 14, 69. Bysshe's Visitation of Essex, edited by
J. J .Howard, 54. New England Register, ii. 306]; xiv. 15; xl. 290.
Howard's Visitation of England and Wales, ii. 42. See JOCELIN.
JOSLIN. Howard's Visitation of England and Wales, iv. 65.
JOURDAN. Notes and Queries, 5 S. ii. 70, 113.
JOWETT, or JOWITT. Pedigree of Wilson of High Wray, etc., by
Joseph Foster, 77. Histories of Bolton and Bowling, by Wm.
Cudworth, 84. Pedigree of Wilson, by S. B. Foster, 167.
JOYCE. Burke's Landed Gentry, (of Mervue,) 2, 3, 4, 5, 6, 7, 8 ; (of
Rahasane,) 3, 4, 5, 6. O'Hart's Irish Pedigrees, 2nd Series, 338.
Harleian Society, xxi. 13.
JOYNER. Oxford Historical Society, xxvi. 259.
JOYNSON. Howard's Visitation of England and Wales, ii. 54.
JUBB. Howard's Visitation of England and Wales, ii. 79.
JUCKES. The Sheriffs of Montgomeryshire, by W. V. Lloyd, 194, 462.
JUDD. Burke's Visitation of Seats and Arms, ii. 30. Thomas Judd
and his Descendants, by S. Judd. Northampton, 1856, 8vo.
JUDKYN. Metcalfe's Visitations of Northamptonshire, 101.
JUKES. Antiquities and Memoirs of the Parish of Myddle, written
by Richard Gough, (1700, folio,) 23, 29.
JULIUS. Burke's Colonial Gentry, ii. 688.
JULL. Berry's Kent Genealogies, 396.
JULLIAN. The Genealogist, vi. 47.
JURDEYNE. Harleian Society, xxii. 13.
JUSTICE. Burke's Landed Gentry, 2, 3, 4, 5. Notes and Queries,
2 S. ii. 413, 514. Visitations of Staffordshire, 1614 and 1663-4,

William Salt Society, 192. Alexander Nisbet's Heraldic Plates, 152.
JUXON. Berry's Kent Genealogies, 464. Harleian Society, viii. 170 ; xvii. 23. Dallaway's Sussex, i. App. to Chichester ; II. ii. 289. Wilson's History of the Parish of St. Laurence Pountney, 136. Some Account of the Taylor Family, by P. A. Taylor, 693. Castles, Mansions, and Manors of Western Sussex, by D. G. C. Elwes and C. J. Robinson, 2. Notes and Queries, 3 S. ii. 147. 231, 290 ; iii. 257 ; vi. 74. Burke's Extinct Baronetcies. Visitation of Gloucestershire, edited by T. F. Fenwick and W. C. Metcalfe, 100.

KADWELL. Hasted's Kent, iii. 90. Berry's Kent Genealogies, 314.
KADWGAN HÊN. Dwnn's Visitations of Wales, i. 95.
KAERWEDROS. Dwnn's Visitations of Wales, i. 27, 80.
KAIS. Dwnn's Visitations of Wales, i. 26.
KANE. Burke's Landed Gentry, (of Drumreaske,) 4 supp., 5, 6 and supp., 7, 8 ; (of Saunderscourt,) 8. O'Hart's Irish Pedigrees, 2nd Series, 202.
KANON. Dwnn's Visitations of Wales, i. 209.
KARNWILLON. Dwnn's Visitations of Wales, i. 26.
KAROG. Dwnn's Visitations of Wales, i. 28.
KARR. Burke's Landed Gentry, 7, 8.
KATER. Burke's Colonial Gentry, i. 165.
KAULL. Visitation of Devon, edited by F. T. Colby, 143.
KAVANAGH. Burke's Landed Gentry, 2, 3, 4, 5, 6 and supp., 7, 8. O'Hart's Irish Pedigrees, 2nd Series, 204. Journal of the Historical and Archæological Association of Ireland, 4th Series, ii. 282 ; iii. 183.
KAY, or KAYE. Surtees Society, xxxvi. 171. Burke's Landed Gentry, 2, 3, 4, 5, 6, 7. Foster's Visitations of Yorkshire, 320, 323, 334, 538, 615. Harleian Society, iii. 23 ; xvi. 175 ; xxxviii. 580 ; xl. 1222. Camden Society, xliii. 33. Foster's Yorkshire Pedigrees. Hulbert's Annals of Almonbury, 193. Doncaster Charities, by Charles Jackson, 45. Supplementary notes on Turton Tower, by J. C. Scholes. Wotton's English Baronetage, ii. 274. Betham's Baronetage, i. 460. Burke's Extinct Baronetcies. Documentary notes relating to the District of Turton, by J. C. Scholes, 78. The Genealogist, New Series, x. 168.
KAYLE. Maclean's History of Trigg Minor, iii. 384.
KAYNES. Harleian Society, iv. 125. Hutchins' Dorset, i. 320.
KEAN, or KEANE. Burke's Landed Gentry, 3, 4, 5, 6, 7, 8. O'Hart's Irish Pedigrees, 2nd Series, 205. Betham's Baronetage, v. 476. See KENE.
KEARNE. See KERNE.
KEARNEY. Burke's Landed Gentry, (of Blanchville,) 4, 5, 6, 7 ; (of Ballinvilla,) 4 supp., 5 ; (of Drom,) 8 supp. ; (of the Ford,) 6 supp., 7. See CUTHBERT-KEARNEY.
KEARSLEY. Visitation of Middlesex, (Salisbury, 1820, fol.) 51. Foster's Visitation of Middlesex, 96.

KEAT, or KEATE. Hasted's Kent, ii. 627. Berry's Hertfordshire
Genealogies, 149, 214. Parochial Topography of the Hundred of
Wanting, by W. N. Clarke, 151. Clutterbuck's Hertford, iii. 72.
Harleian Society, xvii. 24. Notes and Queries, 1 S. viii. 293,
525 ; ix. 19. Burke's Extinct Baronetcies. Wotton's English
Baronetage, iii. 27. The Genealogist, v. 281. The Visitations of
Cornwall, edited by J. L. Vivian, 250. Bysshe's Visitation of
Essex, edited by J. J. Howard, 55. Genealogical Records of the
Family of Woodd, 32. See KETE.
KEATES. Burke's Landed Gentry, 6, 7, 8.
KEAY. Harleian Society, xxxvii. 361.
KEAYS-YOUNG. Burke's Landed Gentry, 8.
KEBLE, or KEBELL. Harleian Society, ii. 56. Burton's Description
of Leicestershire, 128. Nichols' History of the County of
Leicester, iii. 273. Baker's Northampton, i. 659.
KECK. Pedigree of Keck of Mickleton, Co. Glouc., [T. P.] 1857,
folio page. Pedigree of Keck of Long Marston, Co. Gloucester,
etc., [T. P.] 1857, folio page. Harleian Society, viii. 418. Burke's
Landed Gentry, 2, 3, 4. The Genealogist, iii. 173. See POWYS-
KECK.
KEDERMINSTER. Gyll's History of Wraysbury, 89.
KEDINGTON. Page's History of Suffolk, 915.
KEDWELLEY. Berry's Hampshire Genealogies, 51.
KEEFER. Ontarian Families, by E. M. Chadwick, ii. 90.
KEELING, or KELING. Jewitt's Reliquary, xiv. 190 ; xv. 127, 239 ;
xvi. 190 ; xvii. 63 ; xx. 127 ; xxiv. 47. Harleian Society, viii.
150 ; xvii. 25. Visitations of Staffordshire, 1614 and 1663-4,
William Salt Society, 193. Burke's Family Records, 354. Oliver's
History of Antigua, ii. 116.
KEELY. O'Hart's Irish Pedigrees, 2nd Series, 62.
KEENE. Notes and Queries, 1 S. ix. 493. See RUCK-KEENE.
KEEP. New England Register, xxxvi. 166, 313.
KEERMER. Harleian Society, xvii. 25.
KEIGHLEY. Foster's Visitations of Yorkshire, 546.
KEIGHLEY-PEACH. Burke's Landed Gentry, 4, 5, 6, 7.
KEIGHTLEY. Harleian Society, xvii. 30.
KEIGWIN. Burke's Commoners, iv. 287, Landed Gentry, 2. Maclean's
History of Trigg Minor, ii. 264. A Complete Parochial History of
the County of Cornwall, iv. 31. An Historical Survey of Corn-
wall, by C. S. Gilbert, ii. 169. The Visitation of Cornwall, by
J. L. Vivian, 588.
KEILEWAY. Hoare's Wiltshire, V. ii. 44. The Genealogist, New
Series, iii. 94 ; xii. 96. See KEELEWAY.
KEINES. Collinson's Somerset, i. 37 ; iii. 120. See KEYNES.
KEIR. Burke's Landed Gentry, 2, 3, 4, 5, 6, 7, 8. Sketch of the
Life of James Keir, Esq., F.R.S., by Amelia Moilliet, (London,
circa 1870, 8vo.) 29.
KEITH. Account of the Noble Family of Keith, Earls Marischal of
Scotland, by P. Buchan. Peterhead, 1820, 12mo. A Vindication
of Mr. Robert Keith, etc. Edinburgh, 1750, 8vo. Nisbet's

Heraldry, ii. app., 1. Douglas's Baronage of Scotland, 73, 443. Inverurie and the Earldom of the Garioch, by John Davidson, 435. Burke's Extinct Baronetcies, 628. W. R. Fraser's History of Laurencekirk, 27. Wood's Douglas's Peerage of Scotland, i. 61, 413 ; ii. 53, 184. Notes and Queries, 2 S. x. 235. J. B. Pratt's Buchan, 354.

KEITH-FALCONER. Alexander Nisbet's Heraldic Plates, 64.

KEKEWICH, or KEKWICK. Chetham Society, xcv. 11. Burke's Landed Gentry, 2 and supp., 3, 4, 5, 6, 7, 8. Harleian Society, ix. 108. The Genealogist, vi. 8. The Visitations of Cornwall, edited by J. L. Vivian, 252.

KELHAM. Burke's Landed Gentry, 2 and supp., 3, 4, 5, 6, 7, 8. Ormerod's Cheshire, ii. 740. Pedigree of the Longdale Family, 17.

KELKE. The Genealogist, iv. 186. Weaver's Visitations of Somerset, 117.

KELLAM. Surtees Society, xxxvi. 356. Hunter's Deanery of Doncaster, ii. 135. See KILHAM.

KELLAND. The Visitations of Devon, by J. L. Vivian, 506, 508.

KELLAW. Archæologia Æliana, 2nd Series, iii. 84.

KELLET. Betham's Baronetage, v. 481.

KELLIE. See ERSKINE, MAR.

KELLOGG. New England Register, xii. 199 ; xiv. 125 ; xlviii. 59.

KELLOWAY. Berry's Hampshire Genealogies, 338. The Visitations of Devon, by J. L. Vivian, 510.

KELLY. Tuckett's Devonshire Pedigrees, 1. Burke's Commoners, (of Kelly,) ii. 95, Landed Gentry, 2, 3, 4, 5, 6, 7, 8 ; (of Newtown,) Landed Gentry, 2, 3, 4, 5, 6, 7, 8 ; (of Glencara,) 5, 6, 7, 8 ; (of Rockstown,) 6, 7, 8. Harleian Society, vi. 160. Westcote's Devonshire, edited by G. Oliver and P. Jones, 540. A Royal Descent, by T. E. Sharpe, (London, 1875, 4to.) 43. Visitation of Devon, edited by F. T. Colby, 143. The Visitations of Cornwall, edited by J. L. Vivian, 257. The Visitations of Devon, by J. L. Vivian, 511. See O'KELLY.

KELLYGREN. Maclean's History of Trigg Minor, iii. 356.

KELSALL. J. P. Earwaker's East Cheshire, i. 194. Ormerod's Cheshire, iii. 635.

KELSEY. Harleian Society, xiv. 588. Bysshe's Visitation of Essex, edited by J. J. Howard, 55.

KELSICK. Oliver's History of Antigua, ii. 117.

KELSO. Burke's Commoners, ii. 534, Landed Gentry, 2 supp., 3, 4, 5, 6, 7, 8. Paterson's History of the Co. of Ayr, ii. 448, 479. Nisbet's Heraldry, ii. app. 108. Paterson's History of Ayr and Wigton, i. 741 ; iii. 568.

KELSOLT. Thoroton's Nottinghamshire, iii. 116.

KELTON. Harleian Society, xxix. 283.

KELWAY. Hutchins' Dorset, iv. 194. Notes and Queries, 1 S. vii. 529, 608. Weaver's Visitations of Somerset, 118.

KEMBLE. Pedigree of Kemble of Swindon, Co. Wilts, etc., [T. P.] 1862. The Genealogist, v. 281. Burke's Landed Gentry, 7, 8.

KEMES, KEMEYS, KEMIS, or KEMMIS. Dwnn's Visitations of Wales,

i. 156, 164. Glamorganshire Pedigrees, edited by Sir T. Phillipps, 31. Burke's Landed Gentry, (of Shaen,) 3, 4, 5, 6, 7, 8 ; (of Ballinacor,) 3, 5, 6, 7, 8. Burke's Extinct Baronetcies. Weaver's Visitations of Somerset, 118. Harleian Society, xxi. 97. Genealogies of Morgan and Glamorgan, by G. T. Clarke, 407-417.

KEMEYS-TYNTE. Burke's Commoners, iv. 182, Landed Gentry, 2, 3, 4, 5, 6, 7, 8. T. Nicholas' County Families of Wales, 645.

KEMP, or KEMPE. Blomefield's Norfolk, i. 177. Visitation of Suffolk, edited by J. J. Howard, ii. 1-8. Gentleman's Magazine, 1826, ii. 594 ; 1827, i. 123 ; 1845, ii. 482. Hasted's Kent, iii. 170. Morant's Essex, ii. 323, 363. Jewitt's Reliquary, vii. 246. Harleian Society, i. 30 ; xiii. 230, 431 ; xvii. 26 ; xxxii. 175 ; xlii. 32; xliii. 118. Surrey Archæological Collections, ii. Berry's Hampshire Genealogies, 89. Berry's Sussex Genealogies, 75. Berry's Kent Genealogies, 97, 486. Visitation of Middlesex, (Salisbury, 1820, fol.) 46. Burke's Commoners, (of Rosteage,) ii. 530, Landed Gentry, 2 ; (of Lewes,) Landed Gentry, 2, 3, 4. The Worthies of Sussex, by M. A. Lower, 108. Burke's Royal Families, (London, 1851, 8vo.) i. 114, 143. Maclean's History of Trigg Minor, i. 74. Polwhele's History of Cornwall, iv. 112. Burke's Visitation of Seats and Arms, ii. 30. Dallaway's Sussex, i. 59, 150. Wright's Essex, i. 651. Miscellanea Genealogica et Heraldica, New Series, ii. 194. Scott of Scot's-Hall, by J. R. Scott, 106, 184. Page's History of Suffolk, 270. A Complete Parochial History of the County of Cornwall, ii. 75. An Historical Survey of Cornwall, by C. S. Gilbert, ii. 171. Topographical Miscellanies, 1792, 4to., (Slindon). Wotton's English Baronetage, ii. 283. Betham's Baronetage, i. 467. Metcalfe's Visitations of Suffolk, 48, 148. Burke's Extinct Baronetcies. Foster's Visitation of Middlesex, 84. The Visitations of Cornwall, by J. L. Vivian, 589. Chancellor's Sepulchral Monuments of Essex, 229. Ontarian Families, by E. M. Chadwick, ii. 152.

KEMPENFELT. Notes and Queries, 2 S. viii. 427 ; x. 434.

KEMPSALL. Fragmenta Genealogica, by F. A. Crispe, i. 49.

KEMPSON. Visitation of Warwickshire, 1619, published with Warwickshire Antiquarian Magazine, 136. Harleian Society, xii. 411. Burke's Landed Gentry, 8.

KEMPTHORNE. Maclean's History of Trigg Minor, i. 314. Harleian Society, ix. 129. An Historical Survey of Cornwall, by C. S. Gilbert, ii. 173. Mullyon, its History, etc., by E. G. Harvey, 116. The Visitations of Cornwall, edited by J. L. Vivian, 288. The Western Antiquary, iv. 175.

KEMPTON. Cambridgeshire Visitation, edited by Sir T. Phillipps, 20. Harleian Society, xli. 87.

KEMSEY. Harleian Society, xxix. 283.

KEMYELL. The Visitations of Devon, by J. L. Vivian, 748.

KEN. Banks' Baronies in Fee, ii. 95. Harleian Society, xvii. 27.

KENDAL, KENDALE, or KENDALL. J. H. Hill's History of Langton, 78*. Whitaker's History of Richmondshire, ii. 477. Westcote's Devonshire, edited by G. Oliver and P. Jones, 598. Visitation of Derbyshire, 1663-4, (Middle Hill, 1854, fol.) 5. Hutchinson's History of Durham, iii. 89. Nichols' History of the County of Leicester, iv. 985. Surtees' Durham, iii. 81. Clutterbuck's Hertford, iii. 18. Sussex Archæological Collections, xx. 59. Tuckett's Devonshire Pedigrees, 16. Visitation of Durham, 1575, (Newcastle, 1820, fol.) 25. Burke's Landed Gentry, (of Austry,) 2 final add., 3, 4, 5 ; (of Pelyn,) 4, 5, 6, 7, 8. Burke's Visitation of Seats and Arms, ii. 35. The Genealogist, iii. 179 ; New Series, xvi. 89. Harleian Society, ii. 90 ; vi. 161 ; ix. 109, 111, 112 ; xii. 325 ; xvii. 28 ; xxxvii. 128. A Complete Parochial History of the County of Cornwall, iv. 119 supp. An Historical Survey of Cornwall, by C. S. Gilbert, ii. 176. Visitation of Devon, edited by F. T. Colby, 144. The Visitations of Cornwall, edited by J. L. Vivian, 258. Bysshe's Visitation of Essex, edited by J. J. Howard, 56. The Visitations of Devon, by J. L. Vivian, 514. Foster's Visitations of Durham, 195. Fletcher's Leicestershire Pedigrees and Royal Descents, 159. New England Register, xxxix. 17. Nicholson and Burn's Westmorland and Cumberland, i. 29-64. *See* DE KENDALE.

KENDRICK. Notes and Queries, 2 S. x. 455 ; 6 S. viii. 10. *See* KENRICK.

KENE. Metcalfe's Visitations of Suffolk, 48, 148. Harleian Society, xxxii. 176. *See* KEAN.

KENION. Oxfordshire Pedigrees, fol., *n.d.*, printed by Sir T. Phillipps. *See* KENYON.

KENISHAM. Westcote's Devonshire, edited by G. Oliver and P. Jones, 566. *See* KEYNSHAM.

KENN. Visitation of Somerset, edited by Sir T. Phillipps, 111. Harleian Society, xi. 64. Baker's Northampton, i. 747. Notes and Queries, 6 S., x. 501 ; xi. 178. *See* DE KEN.

KENNARD. Burke's Landed Gentry, 5, 6, 7, 8. Burke's Visitation of Seats and Arms, ii. 7.

KENNAWAY. Betham's Baronetage, iv. 203.

KENNEDY. Genealogical Account of the Principal Families of the name of Kennedy, by B. Pitcairn. Edinburgh, 1830, 4to. Anecdotes of the Noble Family of Kennedy, by Hugh Blair. Edinburgh, 1849, 4to. Case of Sir Thos. Kennedy, claiming to be Earl of Cassilis. 8vo. Book of the Kennedies of Cassilis, by John Riddell. Claim of Sir Thomas Kennedy to be Earl of Cassilis, Sess. Papers, March, 1760 — Jan., 1762. Burke's Visitation of Seats and Arms, 2nd Series, ii. 29. Burke's Heraldic Illustrations, 93. Paterson's History of the Co. of Ayr, i. 251, 378, 385 ; ii. 272, 292, 372, 374, 471. Burke's Landed Gentry, (of Bennane,) 2, 3, 4, 5, 6, 7, 8 ; (of Dunure,) 3, 4, 5, 6, 7, 8 ; (of Underwood,) 8 ; (of Hill Foot,) 8 ; (of Romanno,) 7, 8 ; (of Knocknalling,) 2, 3, 4, 5, 6, 7, 8 ; (of Cultra,) 3, 4, 5, 6, 7, 8 ; (of Knockgray,) 2 supp., 3, 4, 5, 6, 7, 8 ; 5 at p. 1270 ; 6 at p. 1467 ; 7 at p. 1678. Burke's Patrician, v. 373. Lands and their Owners in Galloway, by P. H. M'Kerlie, iii. 309. Nisbet's Heraldry, ii. app. 38. Paterson's History of

Ayr and Wigton, ii. 94, 104, 177-199, 204-223, 246, 277, 295—
351, 421, 431, 437, 461; iii. app. 537. Burke's Extinct Baronetcies, 628. O'Hart's Irish Pedigrees, 2nd Series, 62. Wood's
Douglas's Peerage of Scotland, i. 324. Notes and Queries, 3 S.
i. 246, 413 ; ii. 466. Brydges' Collins' Peerage, ix. 346. Caithness Family History, by John Henderson, 328. Burke's Colonial
Gentry, i. 279. Northern Notes and Queries, xi. 43. *See* CAS-
SILLIS.

KENNETT, or KENNET. Burke's Landed Gentry, 5 supp., 7, 8.
Surtees' Durham, i. 72. Miscellanea Genealogica et Heraldica,
New Series, ii. 287. Notes and Queries, 5 S. viii. 117. Foster's
Visitations of Durham, 197. Harleian Society, xxxviii. 521.

KENNEY. Pedigree of the Kenney Family of Kilclogher, Co. Galway,
by J. C. F. Kenney. Dublin, 1868, 4to. Burke's Landed Gentry,
(of Kilclogher,) 3, 4, 5, 6 and p. 773, 7, 8. Burke's Royal Descents and Pedigrees of Founders' Kin, *Founders' Kin*, 10. Burke's
Authorized Arms, 67.

KENNY. Burke's Landed Gentry, (of Ballinrobe,) 3, 4, 5, 6, 7, 8 ;
(of Rocksavage,) 2 supp. Burke's Royal Descents and Pedigrees
of Founders' Kin, 45.

KENNY-HERBERT. Burke's Landed Gentry, 5 supp., 6, 7, 8.

KENRICK, or KENWRICK. Berry's Surrey Genealogies, 96. Burke's
Landed Gentry, 3, 4, 5. Herald and Genealogist, vii. 550.
Manning and Bray's Surrey, ii. 306. Cambrian Journal, 1 Series,
ii. 188. Hasted's Kent, iii. 9. Berry's Kent Genealogies, 457.
Baker's Northampton, i. 694. Edward Townsend Cox, Birming-
ham, (London, *n.d.*, 4to.) 15. The Genealogist, v. 282. Burke's
Extinct Baronetcies. History of Powys Fadog, by J. Y. W.
Lloyd, iii. 339. Harleian Society, xxix. 284 ; xxxvii. 185.
Howard's Visitation of England and Wales, v. 125. *See* KEN-
DRICK.

KENT. Gage's History of Thingoe Hundred, Suffolk, 51. Visitatio
Comitatus Wiltoniæ, 1623, printed by Sir T. Phillipps. Hunter's
Deanery of Doncaster, i. 254. Hoare's Wiltshire, II. ii. 115.
Manning and Bray's Surrey, iii. 19. Baker's Northampton, i. 121,
685 ; ii. 296. The Genealogist, ii. 185. Ormerod's Cheshire, ii.
445. Betham's Baronetage, iv. 120. Banks' Dormant and Extinct
Baronage, iii. 411. Visitation of Wiltshire, edited by G. W.
Marshall, 47. Harleian Society, xvii. 27 ; xix. 178 ; xxii. 148 ;
xl. 1216. The Suffolk Records, by H. W. Aldred, 11, 88. 'Not-
tingham Daily Guardian' Newspaper, 27 Jan., 1887, 6. Metcalfe's
Visitations of Northamptonshire, 137.

KENTISH. Clutterbuck's Hertford, i. 229 ; ii. 308.

KENTON. Burke's Commoners, iv. 564. Harleian Society, xvii. 28.

KENYON. Visitation of Oxfordshire, 1634, printed by Sir T.
Phillipps, (Middle Hill, fol.) 23. Harleian Society, v. 293.
Foster's Lancashire Pedigrees. Chetham Society, lxxxv. 166.
Baines' History of the Co. of Lancaster, iii. 634 ; Croston's edn.,
iii. 146. Abram's History of Blackburn, 752. Brydges' Collins'
Peerage, viii. 127. Philips' Old Halls of Lancashire and Cheshire,

62. Burke's Landed Gentry, (of Pradoe,) 8; (of Gillingham Hall,) 8. *See* KENION.

KEOGH. Burke's Landed Gentry, 3, 4, 5, 6, 7. Burke's Visitation of Seats and Arms, 2nd Series, ii. 59. O'Hart's Irish Pedigrees, 2nd Series, 206. Burke's Family Records, 355.

KEOWN. Burke's Landed Gentry, 5, 6, 7 at p. 197.

KEOWN-BOYD. Burke's Landed Gentry, 8.

KEPPEL. Edmondson's Baronagium Genealogicum, ii. 172; vi. 29. Brydges' Collins' Peerage, iii. 728. Banks' Dormant and Extinct Baronage, iii. 428.

KER, or KERR. Case of Sir James Innes Ker, Bart., claiming the Titles of Duke and Earl of Roxburghe, etc. London, 1808, fol. Additional Case of same. London, 1808, fol. Case of Lady Essex Ker, claiming the Titles of Duchess and Countess of Roxburghe, etc., 1810, folio. Burke's Landed Gentry, (of Gateshaw,) 2, 3, 4, 5; (of Montalto,) 2, 3, 4, 5, 6, 7, 8; (of The Haie,) 6 supp., 7, 8; Herald and Genealogist, vi. 231; vii. 116, 220, 407, 512; viii. 241. George Robertson's Description of Cunninghame, 244. Paterson's History of the Co. of Ayr, i. 425. Shirley's History of the County of Monaghan, 187. Miscellanea Genealogica et Heraldica, New Series, ii. 382; iii. 63. The Genealogist, ii. 137, 176, 282, 380; iii. 246. Paterson's History of Ayr and Wigton, iii. 147, 179. Jeffrey's History of Roxburghshire, ii. 257; iii. 90. Border Memories, by W. R. Carre, 95. Correspondence of Sir R. Kerr, First Earl of Ancrum, and his son William, Third Earl of Lothian, (Edinburgh, 1875, 4to.) i. v. Wood's Douglas's Peerage of Scotland, ii. 130, 439. Edmondson's Baronagium Genealogicum, iii. 231. Banks' Dormant and Extinct Baronage, iii. 430. Burke's Extinct Baronetcies, 628. Notes and Queries, 6 S. iii. 264, 333. Oliver's History of Antigua, ii. 118. *See* INNES.

KERBY. Harleian Society, xvii. 29. Oliver's History of Antigua, ii. 121. *See* KIRKBY.

KER-SEYMER. Burke's Commoners, iii. 495, Landed Gentry, 2, 3, 4, 5.

KERDESTON. Blomefield's Norfolk, x. 112. Notices of Swyncombe and Ewelme in Co. Oxford, by H. A. Napier, 42. Banks' Baronies in Fee, i. 269. Banks' Dormant and Extinct Baronage, i. 350.

KERDIN. Dwnn's Visitations of Wales, i. 27.

KERESFORTH, or KERRESFORTH. Surtees Society, xxxvi. 2. Foster's Visitations of Yorkshire, 335, 622. Hunter's Deanery of Doncaster, ii. 258. History of Barnsley, by Rowland Jackson, 150. The Genealogist, New Series, x. 50.

KERIEL. Planché's Corner of Kent, 291.

KERKAN. Plantagenet-Harrison's History of Yorkshire, i. 488.

KERMOTT. Harleian Society, xvii. 29.

KERNE. The Visitations of Cornwall, edited by J. L. Vivian, 249.

KERREY. Harleian Society, xxix. 285.

KERRICH. Burke's Landed Gentry, 2, 3, 4, 5, 6, 7, 8.

KERRICK-WALKER. Burke's Landed Gentry, 7, 8.

KERRISON. Burke's Landed Gentry, 5.

KERRY. Claim of Henry, Marquis of Lansdowne, Earl of Kerry, etc., to Vote at Elections of Irish Peers, Sess. Papers, A of 1865 ; 62 of 1867. The Sheriffs of Montgomeryshire, by W. V. Lloyd, 46, 447.

KERSHAGH. Gentleman's Magazine, 1844, i. 595.

KERSHAW. Fishwick's History of Rochdale, 466. History of the Old Chapel, Tockholes, by B. Nightingale, 197.

KERVILE, or KERVIL. Visitation of Norfolk, published by Norfolk Archæological Society, i. 57, 189. Blomefield's Norfolk, vii. 490 ; ix. 176. Harleian Society, xxxii. 177.

KESTELL. Maclean's History of Trigg Minor, i. 455. Polwhele's History of Cornwall, ii. 43. Harleian Society, ix. 112, 115. A Complete Parochial History of the County of Cornwall, i. 313. An Historical Survey of Cornwall, by C. S. Gilbert, ii. 180. The Visitations of Cornwall, edited by J. L. Vivian, 263, 266.

KETE. Harleian Society, ix. 116. See KEAT.

KETHINOG. Dwnn's Visitations of Wales, i. 26.

KETSMAE. Dwnn's Visitations of Wales, i. 228.

KETTLE. Burke's Landed Gentry, 5 supp., 6, 7, 8. The Suffolk Records, by H. W. Aldred, 29. Burke's Colonial Gentry, ii. 611.

KETTLEBY, or KETTELBY. The Tyndale Pedigree, by B. W. Greenfield. Visitation of Gloucestershire, 1569, (Middle Hill, 1854, fol.) 6. Harleian Society, xxi. 260 ; xxix. 287.

KETTLEWELL. Burke's Landed Gentry, 8.

KETTON. Burke's Landed Gentry, 5, 6, 7.

KEWRDEN. Chetham Society, lxxxi. 69. See KUERDEN.

KEY. See KAY.

KEYES. Burke's Landed Gentry, 5 supp.

KEYLEWAY. Visitatio Comitatus Wiltoniæ, 1623, printed by Sir T. Phillipps. See KEILEWAY.

KEYNELL. Oliver's History of Antigua, ii. 123.

KEYNES. Collinson's Somerset, iii. 120. Bridges' Northamptonshire, by Rev. Peter Whalley, i. 52. Dugdale's Warwickshire, 671. Baker's Northampton, i. 355. Banks' Dormant and Extinct Baronage, i. 101. The Genealogist, New Series, x. 88 ; xvii. 114.

KEYNSHAM. Visitation of Devon, edited by F. T. Colby, 145. The Visitations of Devon, by J. L. Vivian, 515. Harleian Society, xix. 121. See KENISHAM.

KEYTE, or KEYT. Shakespere's Home, by J. C. M. Bellew, 66. Dugdale's Warwickshire, 693. Hutchins' Dorset, iv. 349. Wotton's English Baronetage, iii. 197. Burke's Extinct Baronetcies. Visitation of Gloucester, by T. F. Fenwick and W. C. Metcalfe, 101. Harleian Society, xx. 61.

KEYWORTH. Jewitt's Reliquary, ix. 191.

KIBBLEWHITE. Pedigree of Kibblewhite of Fawley, Co. Berks, [T. P.] folio page. Pedigree of Kibblewhite of Fawley, [T. P.]. Broadside. Berry's Berkshire Genealogies, 49, 145, 153.

KIDBY. Morant's Essex, i. 427.

KIDD. Memorials of the Prichards, by Isabell Southall, 111.

KIDDALL. The Genealogist, vi. 261.

KIDDER. Sussex Archæological Collections, ix. 130, 138.

KIDNEY. 2 Russell and Mylne's Reports, 172.

KIERNAN. O'Hart's Irish Pedigrees, 2nd Series, 207.

KIGHLEY, or KYGHLEY. Chetham Society, lxxxi. 130; xcviii. 92; New Series, xxv. 174. Ord's History of Cleveland, 474. Harleian Society, xiii. 431; xvi. 178; xxvii. 84. Whitaker's Deanery of Craven, 3rd edn., 205. Bysshe's Visitation of Essex, edited by J. J. Howard, 56.

KILBRIDE. O'Hart's Irish Pedigrees, 2nd Series, 208.

KILBURNE. Hasted's Kent, iii. 71. Harleian Society, xvii. 31.

KILDARE. The Earls of Kildare and their Ancestors, by the Marquess of Kildare, 3rd edition. Dublin, 1858, 8vo. Addenda to the Earls of Kildare and their Ancestors, by the Marquess of Kildare. Dublin, 1862, 8vo. Westcote's Devonshire, edited by G. Oliver and P. Jones, 477. Harleian Society, xvi. 91.

KILGOUR. Burke's Landed Gentry, 5 supp., 6, 7, 8.

KILHAM, KILHOLME, KILLAM, or KELLAM. Historical Notices of Doncaster, by C. W. Hatfield, 3rd Series, 378. Annals of Smith of Balby, by H. E. Smith, 12.

KILLICH. Burke's Landed Gentry, 4.

KILLIGREW. Harleian Society, viii. 39. Archæologia, xviii. 99. An Historical Survey of Cornwall, by C. S. Gilbert, i. 586. Notes and Queries, 5 S. ii. 487; iii. 71. Burke's Extinct Baronetcies. The Visitations of Cornwall, edited by J. L. Vivian, 267. Hasted's Kent, (Hund. of Blackheath, by H. H. Drake,) xxi. Royal Institute of Cornwall, xii. 269.

KILLINGBECK. Surtees Society, xxxvi. 20. Foster's Visitations of Yorkshire, 299. Thoresby's Ducatus Leodiensis, 134.

KILLINGHALL. Burke's Heraldic Illustrations, 109. Hutchinson's History of Durham, iii. 142. Archæologia Æliana, 2nd Series, ii. 69-106. Surtees' Durham, iii. 222. Foster's Visitations of Durham, 199.

KILLINGWORTH. The Genealogist, ii. 146, 256. Harleian Society, xli. 128. Bysshe's Visitation of Essex, edited by J. J. Howard, 56. Foster's Visitations of Northumberland, 74.

KILLIOWE, or KYLLYOWE. Harleian Society, ix. 117. The Visitations of Cornwall, edited by J. L. Vivian, 273.

KILLMOREY. Claim of Robert, Visct. Killmorey, to Vote at Elections of Irish Peers, Sess. Papers, 187 of 1812; 84 of 1812-13.

KILLOM, or KYLLUM. Hunter's Deanery of Doncaster, ii. 135. Harleian Society, xvi. 178.

KILNER. The Descendants of James and Ann Kilner, formerly of Mansergh, Westmoreland. London, 1862, 8vo.

KILPEC. Banks' Dormant and Extinct Baronage, i. 102.

KILVERT. Harleian Society, xvii. 30. Burke's Landed Gentry, 8.

KIMBALL. New England Register, xxviii. 241.

KIMBERE. The Visitations of Devon, by J. L. Vivian, 511.

KIMPTON. Harleian Society, xxii. 69.

KINAHAN. Howard's Visitation of Ireland, ii. 36.

KINARDSLEY. Visitations of Staffordshire, 1614 and 1663-4, William Salt Society, 196.

KINASTON. Burke's Commoners, iv. 357. Harleian Society, viii. 106. Burke's Landed Gentry, 5 at p. 874, 6 at p. 1051, 7 at p. 1214. *See* KYNASTON.

KINCHANT. Burke's Landed Gentry, 2, 3, 4, 5, 6, 7, 8.

KINDER. Burke's Landed Gentry, 5, 6, 7, 8. Jewitt's Reliquary, xv. 167, 253 ; xvi. 64, 125. Harleian Society, xxxvii. 182.

KINDERSLEY. Burke's Landed Gentry, 8.

KINER. Dwnn's Visitations of Wales, i. 109.

KING. Genealogical Record of King and Henham, by W. L. King. London, 1899, 4to. Pedigree of King, Henham, Knowles, and Cox, by W. L. King. 1880, broadside. Genealogical Memoranda relating to the Family of King, by W. L. King. London, 1882, 4to. Savage's Hundred of Carhampton, 133. Memoir of the Life and Death of Sir John King, Knt. London, 1855, 8vo. Burke's Commoners, (of Chadshunt,) ii. 344, Landed Gentry, 2, 3, 4, 5, 6, 7, 8 ; (of Staunton Court,) Commoners, ii. 211, Landed Gentry, 2, 3, 4, 5, 6, 7, 8 ; (of Ballylin,) Landed Gentry, 3, 4, 5, 6, 7, 8 ; (of North Petherton,) 2, 3, 4, 5, 6, 7, 8 ; (of Preston Candover,) 4, 5 ; (of Brinkley Hall,) 8 ; (of Tretowie,) 8. Harleian Society, viii. 295 ; xiii. 10, 66 ; xiv. 588 ; xvii. 32. Lipscombe's History of the County of Buckingham, i. 585 ; iv. 620. Gyll's History of Wraysbury, 19. Burke's Heraldic Illustrations, 15. Whitaker's Deanery of Craven, 179 (251). Nichols' History of the County of Leicester, iv. 626. Manning and Bray's Surrey, iii. 124. Healey's History of Part of West Somerset, 333. Miscellanea Genealogica et Heraldica, New Series, ii. 114. Inverurie and the Earldom of the Garioch, by John Davidson, 103. Wood's Douglas's Peerage of Scotland, i. 557. Monken Hadley, by F. C. Cass, 30. Edmondson's Baronagium Genealogicum, v. 426. Archdall's Lodge's Peerage, iii. 218. Brydges' Collins' Peerage, vii. 223. Betham's Baronetage, iv. 245 Notes and Queries, 5 S. xi. 37. F. G. Lee's History of Thame, 387. The Visitations of Cornwall, edited by J. L. Vivian, 469. Oliver's History of Antigua, ii. 125. Genealogical Memoranda of the Family of Ames, 12. Metcalfe's Visitations of Northamptonshire, 102. Burke's Colonial Gentry, i. 185 ; ii. 596. Somerset and Dorset Notes and Queries, iii. 137, 259. New England Register, xi. 357. The Descendants of John Backhouse, by J. Foster, 39. The Irish Builder, xxxv. 137. Burke's Family Records, 356.

KINGDON. Burke's Commoners, ii. 211, Landed Gentry, 2, 3, 4.

KINGESLEY, or KINGSLEY. Hasted's Kent, iii. 674. Berry's Kent Genealogies, 306. Clutterbuck's Hertford, i. 223. Ormerod's Cheshire, ii. 90. The Wolfe's of Forenaghts, 59. Harleian Society, xxii. 70 ; xlii. 125.

KING-HARMAN. Burke's Landed Gentry, 7, 8.

KINGSBURY. New England Register, xiii. 157 ; xvi. 337.

KINGSCOTE. Fosbrooke's Abstracts of Smith's Lives of the Berkeleys, 218. Burke's Commoners, i. 280, Landed Gentry, 2, 3, 4, 5, 6, 7, 8. Fosbrooke's History of Gloucestershire, i. 419. Visitation of Gloucester, edited by T. F. Fenwick and W. C. Metcalfe, 103. Harleian Society, xxi. 99. *See* KYNGESCOTE.

KINGSMAN. Morant's Essex, i. 217.

KINGSMILL. Morant's Essex, ii. 180. Berry's Hampshire Genealogies, 44, 224. Burke's Landed Gentry, 5, 6, 7, 8. Notes and Queries, 3 S. i. 309, 375. Betham's Baronetage, iv. 408. Burke's Extinct Baronetcies. Weaver's Visitation of Somerset, 40. Hampshire Notes and Queries, vi. 102. The Genealogist, New Series, xii. 77.

KINGSTON. Berry's Hampshire Genealogies, 53. Visitation of Somerset, printed by Sir T. Phillipps, 112. Harleian Society, xi. 65 ; xvii. 32. Burke's Visitation of Seats and Arms, ii. 74. Burke's Royal Descents and Pedigrees of Founders' Kin, 18. Hampshire Visitations, printed by Sir T. Phillipps, 25. Nichols' History of the County of Leicester, iv. 408. Foster's Collectanea Genealogica, i. 17. The Genealogist, vi. 261 ; vii. 180.

KINGSWELL. Berry's Hampshire Genealogies, 322.

KINLOCH. Nisbet's Heraldry, ii. app. 27. Douglas's Baronage of Scotland, 533-536. Burke's Extinct Baronetcies, 628. The Genealogist, New Series, xiv. 200.

KINLOSS. Claim of R. P. C.., Duke of Buckingham and Chandos, to be Lord Kinloss, etc., Sess. Papers, A of 1867 ; B of 1867-68. Case of Marquis of Aylesbury in opposition to this claim, pp. 9.

KINNAIRD. Wood's Douglas's Peerage of Scotland, ii. 40.

KINNEAR, or KINNEIR. Balmerino and its Abbey, by James Campbell, 390. Burke's Colonial Gentry, i. 130. Burke's Landed Gentry, 7, 8.

KINNERSLY. Burke's Landed Gentry, 4, 5, 6, 7. The Genealogist, New Series, ix. 210. Harleian Society, xxxviii. 717. *See* KYNNERSLEY.

KINSELA. O'Hart's Irish Pedigrees, 2nd Series, 209.

KINSEY. Earwaker's History of Sandbach, 258.

KINSMAN. Metcalfe's Visitations of Northamptonshire, 29, 103, 182.

KINTORE. Burke's Colonial Gentry, i. 340.

KIPLING. F. G. Lee's History of Thame, 488.

KIPP. Harleian Society, xvii. 33.

KIPPEN. Burke's Family Records, 359.

KIRBY. Topographer and Genealogist, ii. 13. Burke's Landed Gentry, 2 supp. at p. 226. Chetham Society, New Series, xxv. 164. Harleian Society, xxxvii. 1.

KIRKALDY. Burke's Extinct Baronetcies, 629.

KIRKBRIDE. Hutchinson's History of Cumberland, i. 504. Jefferson's History of Leath Ward, Cumberland, 217. Harleian Society, xvi. 179. Foster's Visitations of Cumberland and Westmorland, 69, 70.

KIRKBY. Morant's Essex, ii. 297. Berry's Hampshire Genealogies, 267. Foster's Visitations of Yorkshire, 43, 309. Chetham Society,

lxxxi. 41 ; lxxxii. 92 ; lxxxv. 169. Corry's History of Lancashire,
i. 412-421. Nichols' History of the County of Leicester, ii. 224.
Harleian Society, xiii. 232 ; xvi. 180 ; xxxviii. 769. Green's
History of Framlingham, 230. Foster's Visitations of Cumberland and Westmorland, 71. The Genealogical Magazine, iii. 494,
531. *See* KYRKEBY.

KIRKE. Jewitt's Reliquary, vi. 219. Burke's Landed Gentry, (of
Markham, 2 supp., 3, 4, 5, 6, 7, 8 ; (of the Eaves,) 5, 6, 7, 8.
Thoresby's Ducatus Leodiensis, 158. Derbyshire Archæological
and Natural History Society, ii. 26. Harleian Society, xvii. 33.
See KYRKE.

KIRKETON. Thoroton's Nottinghamshire, i. 248. Banks' Baronies
in Fee, i. 271.

KIRKHAM. Tuckett's Devonshire Pedigrees, 19. Nash's Worcestershire, ii. 158. Harleian Society, vi. 161. Westcote's Devonshire,
edited by G. Oliver and P. Jones, 458, 523. Visitation of Devon,
edited by F. T. Colby, 145. Metcalfe's Visitations of Northamptonshire, 30, 104. The Visitations of Devon, by J. L. Vivian,
516. *See* KYRKHAM.

KIRKLAND. Miscellanea Genealogica et Heraldica, New Series,
ii. 497. Fletcher's Leicestershire Pedigrees and Royal Descents,
83.

KIRKPATRICK. Memoir respecting the Family of Kirkpatrick of
Closeburn. London, 1858, 4to. Burke's Colonial Gentry, i. 350.
Alexander Nisbet's Heraldic Plates, 42. Ontarian Families, by
J. M. Chadwick, i. 150. Notes and Queries, 4 S. xi. 90, 200, 426,
453.

KIRKSHAW. Croston's edn. of Baines's Lancaster, iii. 69.

KIRKWOOD. Burke's Landed Gentry, (of Woodbrook,) 3, 4, 5, 7, 8 ;
(of Yeo Vale,) 5 supp., 6, 7, 8.

KIRLEW. Burton's History of Hemingborough, 204.

KIRSHAW. Harleian Society, xxxvii. 156.

KIRSOPP. Burke's Landed Gentry, 2, 4, 5, 6, 7, 8.

KIRTLAND. New England Register, xiv. 241 ; xlviii. 66.

KIRTON. Baker's Northampton, i. 719. Harleian Society, xiv. 589.
Notes and Queries, 6 S. viii. 99. Somersetshire Wills, printed for
F. A. Crisp, i. 44. Metcalfe's Visitations of Northamptonshire,
183.

KIRWAN. Burke's Landed Gentry, (of Blindwell,) 2, 4, 5, 6, 7 ; (of
Cregg,) 2, 3, 4, 5, 6, 7, 8 ; (of Castle Hackett,) 2, 3, 4, 5, 6, 7, 8 ;
(of Dalgin,) 2, 3, 4, 5, 6, 7, 8 ; (of Moyne,) 4, 5 ; (of Stowe
Lodge,) 5 ; (of Hillsbrooke,) 2, 3, 4. Oliver's History of Antigua,
ii. 128.

KITCHELL. Miscellanea Genealogica et Heraldica, New Series,
iv. 398.

KITCHEN. Chronicle of the Family of De Havilland.

KITCHENER. Burke's Colonial Gentry, i. 181. Howard's Visitation
of England and Wales, vii. 1.

KITCHIN. Topographer and Genealogist, ii. 76. Harleian Society,
xxii. 70.

KITCHING. Green's Account of the Family of Cudworth, 46.
KITCHINGMAN. Thoresby's Ducatus Leodiensis, 258.
KITSON. Metcalfe's Visitations of Suffolk, 48. *See* KYTSON.
KITTERMASTER. Burke's Landed Gentry, 3, 4. Burke's Visitation of Seat and Arms, 2nd Series, ii. 59.
KLEMENT. Dwnn's Visitations of Wales, i. 108.
KNAPMAN. Tuckett's Devonshire Pedigrees, 7. Harleian Society, vi. 162. The Visitations of Devon, by J. L. Vivian, 518.
KNAPP. The Knapp Pedigree, from Records of College of Arms, by A. B. G., folio sheet, 1876. Burke's Landed Gentry, 5, 6, 7, 8. Lipscombe's History of the County of Buckingham, iv. 231. Miscellanea Genealogica et Heraldica, New Series, iii. 261. Metcalfe's Visitations of Suffolk, 148, 149.
KNAPTON. Burke's Landed Gentry, 4 supp., 5, 6, 7, 8. Howard's Visitation of England and Wales, iv. 16.
KNATCHBULL. Beltz's Review of the Chandos Peerage Case, at end. Hasted's Kent, ii. 444; iii. 286. Memoirs of the Family of Sir Edw. Knatchbull, and Filmer Honeywood, Esq., by R. Pocock. Gravesend, 1802, 8vo. Berry's Kent Genealogies, 297. Burke's Landed Gentry, 2, 3, 4, 5, 6, 7. Wotton's English Baronetage, ii. 228. Betham's Baronetage, i. 430. Annals of the English Benedictines of Ghent, 183. Harleian Society, xlii. 109.
KNATCHBULL-HUGESSON. Burke's Visitation of Seats and Arms, i. 77.
KNAYTH. Genealogies of Morgan and Glamorgan, by G. T. Clark, 491.
KNEESHAW. Burke's Landed Gentry, 5 supp., 6, 7, 8.
KNELLER. Harleian Society, viii. 438. Hoare's Wiltshire, IV. i. 32. Burke's Extinct Baronetcies.
KNEVET. Berry's Berkshire Genealogies, 53. Berry's Kent Genealogies, 359. Memorials of the Church of Attleborough, 185. Harleian Society, xvi. 176. Banks' Baronies in Fee, i. 158. Banks' Dormant and Extinct Baronage, i. 351. Carthew's West and East Bradenham, 5, 6. The Genealogist, New Series, xiii. 237. *See* KNYVETT.
KNIGHT. Burke's Commoners, (of Godmersham,) i. 442, Landed Gentry, 2, 3, 4, 5, 6, 7; (of Glen Parva,) Landed Gentry, 2 supp., 3, 4, 5, 6, 7, 8; (of Wolverley,) 2, 3, 4, 5, 6, 7, 8; (of Downton Castle,) 4, 5, 6, 7, 8; (of Barrels,) 2; (of Firbeck,) 2; (of Chawton,) 8. Burke's Royal Descents and Pedigrees of Founders' Kin, *Founders' Kin*, 15. Dallaway's Sussex, II. i. 51. Hunter's Deanery of Doncaster, i. 299. An Account of the Printing-house Family of Knight, *see* the 'Critic,' No. 624. Berry's Kent Genealogies, 127. Warwickshire Antiquarian Magazine, Part ii. Surtees Society, xxxvi. 272. Berry's Hampshire Genealogies, 46, 261, 306, 320. Harleian Society, viii. 175; xii. 219; xvii. 34, 35; xxii. 14; xxix. 289. T. Nicholas' County Families of Wales, 632. The Genealogist, iii. 304; vi. 262; New Series, iii. 94; ix. 69. Metcalfe's Visitation of Worcester, 1683, 68. Miscellanea Genealogica et Heraldica, New Series, iv. 199. Visitation

of Gloucester, edited by T. F. Fenwick and W. C. Metcalfe, 105.
Memoirs of the House of White of Wallingwells, 29. Burton's
History of Hemingborough, 219. Metcalfe's Visitations of North-
amptonshire, 30, 105. Burke's Family Records, 360. Oliver's
History of Antigua, ii. 132.

KNIGHT-BRUCE. Burke's Landed Gentry, 2 supp., 3, 4, 5, 6, 7, 8.

KNIGHT-ERSKINE. Burke's Landed Gentry, 5.

KNIGHTBRIDGE. Harleian Society, xiii. 432.

KNIGHTLEY. Appendix to Case of Sir J. S. Sidney, claiming to be
Lord Lisle. Noble's Memoirs of the House of Cromwell, ii. 124-
135. Miscellanea Genealogica et Heraldica, i. 129 ; 2nd Series,
i. 245. Bridges' Northamptonshire, by Rev. Peter Whalley, i. 66.
Surrey Archæological Collections, ii. Harleian Society, viii. 17 ;
xii. 309, 401 ; xiii. 67 ; xiv. 590 ; xvii. 35. Baker's Northampton, i. 299, 381. Betham's Baronetage, iv. 385. Burke's
Extinct Baronetcies. Metcalfe's Visitations of Northamptonshire,
31. Oliver's History of Antigua, ii. 133.

KNIGHTON. Clutterbuck's Hertford, ii. 42. Harleian Society, xiv.
586 ; xxii. 70. Metcalfe's Visitations of Suffolk, 49.

KNIPE. Pedigree of Knipe of Imber Court, etc., [T. P.] 1866, folio
page. Chetham Society, lxxxv. 170.

KNIPERSLEY. Visitations of Staffordshire, 1614 and 1663-4, William
Salt Society, 47.

KNIVETON, or KNYFTON. Burke's Landed Gentry, 2, 3, 4, 5, 6.
Jewitt's Reliquary, x. 168. Burke's Extinct Baronetcies. The
Genealogist, New Series, vii. 225.

KNOELL. Visitation of Somerset, printed by Sir T. Phillipps, 112.
Harleian Society, xi. 123. Weaver's Visitations of Somerset, 41.
The Genealogist, New Series, iii. 95.

KNOLL. History of Chipping, by Tom C. Smith, 227.

KNOLLES, or KNOLLYS. Miscellanea Genealogica et Heraldica, ii. 19.
Gentleman's Magazine, lx. 697. Burke's Landed Gentry, (of
Oatlands,) 2 add., 3, 4, 5, 6, 7, 8 ; (of Colston Bassett,) 7, 8.
Herald and Genealogist, vii. 553 ; viii. 289. Lipscombe's History
of the County of Buckingham, i. 527. Westcote's Devonshire,
edited by G. Oliver and P. Jones, 474. South Mimms, by F. C.
Cass, 70. Burke's Extinct Baronetcies. Visitation of Devon,
edited by F. T. Colby, 146. Banks' Dormant and Extinct
Baronage, iii. 44. F. G. Lee's History of Thame, 591. Account
of the Guildhall of London, by J. E. Price, 116. The Visitations
of Devon, by J. L. Vivian, 519. The Genealogist, New Series,
i. 45. Berkshire Notes and Queries, i. 110. Fragmenta Genealogica, by F. A. Crisp, vii. 67-71. See KNOWLES.

KNOTTESFORD. Foster's Visitations of Yorkshire, 349. Ormerod's
Cheshire, iii. 137. Earwaker's History of Sandbach, 264.

KNOVIL. Banks' Dormant and Extinct Baronage, i. 353.

KNOWE. Topographer and Genealogist, iii. 220.

KNOWLER. Hasted's Kent, ii. 794. Harleian Society, xlii. 216.

KNOWLES, or KNOWLYS. The Genealogist, New Series, xiv. 100.
Berry's Hampshire Genealogies, 40. Camden Society, xliii. 101.

Burke's Landed Gentry, 2, 8 supp., (of Newent Court,) 8 ; (of Westwood,) 8. Genealogical Record of King and Henham, 11. Betham's Baronetage, iii. 336. An Account of the Mayo and Elton Families, by C. H. Mayo, 143. Harleian Society, xvii. 36 ; xxxii. 180. Genealogy of the Knowles Family of Edgworth, etc., by J. C. Scholes. 1886, 12mo. Genealogical Memoranda relating to the Family of King, by W. L. King, 4. Croston's edn. of Baines's Lancaster, iii. 222. The Perverse Widow, by A. W. Crawley-Boevey, 274. *See* KNOLLES, SHERIDAN.

KNOWLESLEY. Foster's Visitations of Yorkshire, 539.

KNOWLTON. The New England Register, xv. 344 ; l. 226.

KNOX. Genealogical Memoirs of John Knox, by Rev. C. Rogers. London, 1879, 8vo. Genealogical Chart of John Knox, published by Menzies, Edinburgh. Genealogy of the Family of Knox of Kilbirnie, compiled in 1855 by William Logan. Kilmarnock, 1856, 4to. Gentleman's Magazine, lxxxi. i. 210. Burke's Commoners, (of Rappa Castle,) iv. 580, Landed Gentry, 2, 3, 4, 5, 6 and supp., 7, 8 ; (of Netley Park,) Commoners, iv. 583, Landed Gentry, 2, 3, 4, 5 ; (of Grace Dieu,) 8 ; (of Castlerea,) Commoners, iv. 670, Landed Gentry, 2, 3, 4, 5 ; (of Mount Falcon,) Landed Gentry, 2, 3, 4, 5, 6, 7, 8 ; (of Kilmannock,) 5 ; (of Prehen,) 5, 6, 7, 8. The Works of John Knox, edited by David Laing, vi., lxi. Notes and Queries, 2 S. ix. 347 ; 8 S. vii. 201, 261 ; xii. 464. Archdall's Lodge's Peerage, vii. 195. The Irish Builder, xxxv. 70.

KNOX-GORE. Burke's Commoners, iv. 582, Landed Gentry, 2, 3, 4.

KNYFTON, or KNYVETON. Burke's Landed Gentry, 7, 8. The Genealogist, New Series, xvii. 23.

KNYLL. Weaver's Visitation of Herefordshire, 46.

KNYVETT, KNYVET, KNIVET, or KNEVETT. Thoroton's Nottinghamshire, iii. 170. Gentleman's Magazine, 1819, i. 522. Blomefield's Norfolk, v. 153. Morant's Essex, i. 202, 276 ; ii. 191. Proceedings concerning Baronies by Writ, by A. Collins, 366. Berry's Berkshire Genealogies, 53-57. Harleian Society, viii. 21 ; ix. 117. Gyll's History of Wraysbury, 212. Carthew's Hundred of Launditch, Part ii. 651. Banks' Dormant and Extinct Baronage, ii. 51. Burke's Extinct Baronetcies. The Visitations of Cornwall, edited by J. L. Vivian, 272. Burke's Family Records, 361. *See* KNEVET.

KOLLE. Burke's Landed Gentry, 7 at p. 926.

KONWY. Dwnn's Visitations of Wales, ii. 296, 299, 324, 340.

KRADOC. Dwnn's Visitations of Wales, i. 145.

KREUDDYN. Dwnn's Visitations of Wales, i. 26, 48.

KRYELL, or KRIELL. Camden Society, xliii. 113. Nichols' History of the County of Leicester, ii. 147.

KUERDEN. Chetham Society, lxxxv. 167. Abram's History of Blackburn, 728. *See* KEWRDEN.

KUHN. New England Register, li. 441.

KWM TYTY. Dwnn's Visitations of Wales, i. 27.

KYAN. Burke's Visitation of Seats and Arms, ii. 11. Burke's Landed Gentry, 3, 4, 5.

KYDDALL. Miscellanea Genealogica et Heraldica, 2nd Series, ii. 96.

KYDWELI. Dwnn's Visitations of Wales, i. 26, 94, 188, 217, 230.

KYFFIN. Pedigree of the Descendants of Watkin Kyffin, Esq., of Glascord, [T. P.] 1860, folio page. History of Powys Fadog, by J. Y. W. Lloyd, iv. 257, 262 ; v. 374. Harleian Society, xxix. 290.

KYLE. Burke's Landed Gentry, 8.

KYME. Banks' History of the Family of Marmyun, 126. Topography and History of New and Old Sleaford, (Sleaford, 1825, 8vo.) 274. History of Boston, by Pishey Thompson, 2nd edition, 381. Thoroton's Nottinghamshire, ii. 41. Banks' Baronies in Fee, i. 272. Banks' Dormant and Extinct Baronage, i. 353.

KYMER. Hutchins' Dorset, ii. 638. The Genealogist, New Series, iii. 95. Harleian Society, xliii. 76.

KYMPTON. Monken Hadley, by F. C. Cass, 58.

KYNASTON. Case of John Kynaston of Hardley, claiming the Barony of Powes, 1731, folio, pp. 5. Claim of John Kynaston to the Barony of Powys, Sess. Papers, Feb. 1731—May, 1732. Poetical Works of Lewis Glyn Cothi, (Oxford, 1837,) 368. Dwnn's Visitations of Wales, i. 227. Herald and Genealogist, vi. 105. Collections by the Powys-land Club, i. 382 ; iv. 153. The Sheriffs of Montgomeryshire, by W. V. Lloyd, 471. Burke's Landed Gentry, 6 supp., 7, 8. Harleian Society, xvii. 37, 39 ; xxviii. 233, 291-299. History of Powys Fadog, by J. Y. W. Lloyd, iii. 7 ; iv. 94. *See* KINASTON.

KYNGESCOTE. Visitation of Gloucestershire, 1569, (Middle Hill, 1854, fol.) 6. *See* KINGSCOTE.

KYNGESTON. The Genealogist, New Series, xiii. 173 ; xvi. 236.

KYNNE. Visitation of Gloucestershire, 1569, (Middle Hill, 1854, fol.) 6. Baker's Northampton, ii. 45. Harleian Society, xxi. 226.

KYNNERSLEY. Topographer and Genealogist, ii. 11. Harleian Society, xii. 103, 397 ; xxix. 300. Burke's Landed Gentry, 8. Transactions of Shropshire Archæological Society, vi. 380. *See* KINNERSLEY, SNEYD-KYNNERSLEY.

KYNNESMAN. Bridges' Northamptonshire, by Rev. Peter Whalley, ii. 43.

KYNVIL GAIO. Dwnn's Visitations of Wales, i. 28, 94, 226, 241.

KYRIELL. The Genealogist, New Series, xvii. 176.

KYRKBY. Surtees Society, xli. 92. Harleian Society, xvii. 40. *See* KIRKBY.

KYRKE. Jewitt's Reliquary, vii. 24 ; viii. 239. Burke's Landed Gentry, 8. *See* KIRKE.

KYRKHAM. Maclean's History of Trigg Minor, ii. 501. *See* KIRKHAM.

KYRLE. Burke's Commoners, iii. 615, Landed Gentry, 2, 3, 4, 5, 6. Robinson's Mansions of Herefordshire, 280. Duncombe's Hereford, (J. H. Cooke,) iii. 29, 185. Burke's Extinct Baronetcies. Companion to the Wye Tour, by F. D. Fosbroke, 91. Archæological Sketches of Ross, by T. D. Fosbroke, 91. Genealogical Table of John Stratford Collins. Heath's Excursion down the Wye, 8th edn. (Monmouth, 1826, 8vo.).

KYRYEL. The Genealogist, New Series, xii. 112.

KYTCHEN. Weaver's Visitations of Somerset, 120.

KYTSON. Visitation of Suffolk, edited by J. J. Howard, ii. 83-108. Gage's History of Hengrave, 212. Gage's History of Thingoe Hundred, Suffolk, 184. Page's History of Suffolk, 657. *See* KITSON.
KYWR. Dwnn's Visitations of Wales, ii. 355.

LAAK. Visitation of Devon, edited by F. T. Colby, 147.
LABERTOUCHE. Burke's Colonial Gentry, i. 351.
LABOUCHERE. Burke's Landed Gentry, 2, 3, 4. Notes and Queries, 4 S. xi. 399.
LACHARN. Dwnn's Visitations of Wales, ii. 45.
LA CLOCHE. J. B. Payne's Armorial of Jersey, 189.
LACOCK. Surtees Society, xxxvi. 156. Harleian Society, iv. 95; xl. 1245. *See* LAYCOCK.
LACON. Burke's Commoners, iii. 199. Dawson Turner's Sepulchral Reminiscences of Great Yarmouth, 131. Harleian Society, xiii. 68, 233; xxix. 302, 307; xxxix. 963. Burke's Landed Gentry, 6, 7, 8. The Genealogist, vi. 262. Weaver's Visitations of Somerset, 135. Harvey's Hundred of Willey, 37.
LACY, or LACI. Gentleman's Magazine, 1866, i. 637, 809. History of Barnsley, by Rowland Jackson, 18. Ferne's Blazon of Gentrie, (London, 1586, 4to.) Part ii. Surtees Society, xxxvi. 299. Visitation of Somerset, printed by Sir T. Phillipps, 112. Visitation of Oxfordshire, 1634, printed by Sir T. Phillipps, (Middle Hill, fol.) 24. Foster's Visitations of Yorkshire, 160, 195, 197, 330, 539, 607. Harleian Society, ii. 75, 166, 186; v. 268; xi. 65; xvi. 180; xviii. 5; xxxii. 181. Chetham Society, lxxxv. 171. Shaw's Staffordshire, ii. 107*. Nichols' History of the County of Leicester, ii. 264; iii. 771. Raines' History of the Co. of Lancaster, iii. 207; Croston's edn., iii. 316. Whitaker's History of Whalley, i. 236. John Watson's History of Halifax, 242, 307. O'Hart's Irish Pedigrees, 2nd Series, 342. Boothroyd's History of Pontefract, 60. Ellacombe's History of Bitton, 120. Banks' Baronies in Fee, i. 221. Banks' Dormant and Extinct Baronage, i. 103; iii. 482. Notes and Queries, 4 S. vi. 35. Bysshe's Visitation of Essex, edited by J. J. Howard, 57. The Irish Builder, xxix. 303. The Genealogist, New Series, xvii. 209. Transactions of Shropshire Archæological Society, ii. 33. *See* DE LACY.
LADBROKE, or LADBROOKE. Manning and Bray's Surrey, i. 311. Harleian Society, xii. 128.
LADD, or LADE. Hasted's Kent, ii. 815. Visitation of Norfolk, published by Norfolk Archæological Society, i. 45. Berry's Kent Genealogies, 342. Notes and Queries, 6 S. viii. 395. Berry's Sussex Genealogies, 246. Burke's Landed Gentry, 2, 3, 4, 5. Burke's Extinct Baronetcies, and *supp.* Wotton's English Baronetage, iv. 229. Betham's Baronetage, iii. 266. Harleian Society, xxxii. 182; xlii. 205.
LADKINS. Visitations of Staffordshire, 1614 and 1663-4, William Salt Society, 198.
LAFERTY. Oliver's History of Antigua, ii. 135.
LAFONE. Burke's Landed Gentry, 8.

LAFOREY. Oliver's History of Antigua, ii. 136. Burke's Extinct Baronetcies, *supp.*

LAIDLAY. Burke's Landed Gentry, 8.

LAIDLEY. Burke's Colonial Gentry, i. 138.

LAING. Burke's Landed Gentry, 7, 8.

LAKE. Bibliotheca Topographica Britannica, ix. Part iv. 50. Botfield's Stemmata Botevilliana, 141. Surtees Society, xxxvi. 16. Berry's Kent Genealogies, 219. Foster's Visitations of Yorkshire, 318, 493. Harleian Society, viii. ˎ63, 243 ; xiii. 432 ; xvii. 41 ; xix. 121 ; xxii. 71. New England Register, xiii. 116 ; xviii. 131 ; lii. 275. Lipscombe's History of the County of Buckingham, ii. 75. Clutterbuck's Hertford, i. 505. The Citizens of London and their Rulers, by B. B. Orridge, 201. Brydges' Collins' Peerage, vi. 432. Notes and Queries, 1 S. xi. 282. Burke's Extinct Baronetcies, 609. Wotton's English Baronetage, iv. 134. Visitation of Devon, edited by F. T. Colby, 148. Betham's Baronetage, iii. 153. The Visitations of Devon, by J. L. Vivian, 785.

LAKEN. Thoroton's Nottinghamshire, iii. 286. Transactions of Shropshire Archæological Society, N.S., iv. 6, 236.

LA LEYE. Baker's Northampton, ii. 5.

LALLY. John O'Donovan's Tribes and Customs of Hy-many, 177.

LALOR. Burke's Landed Gentry, 3, 4, 5, 6, 7, 8. A Royal Descent, by T. E. Sharpe, (London, 1875, 4to.) 126. *See* POWER-LALOR.

LALOWEL. Harleian Society, xxxix. 1009.

LAMB. Berry's Kent Genealogies, 288. Burke's Landed Gentry, (of Ryton Hall,) 3, 4, 5, 6, 7, 8 ; (of West Denton,) 8. Burke's Royal Families, (London, 1851, 8vo.) ii. 144. Baker's Northampton, i. 141. Archdall's Lodge's Peerage, vi. 73. Visitation of Gloucester, edited by T. F. Fenwick and W. C. Metcalfe, 105. Harleian Society, xxxvii. 370 ; xlii. 133. *See* LAMBE.

LAMBARD, or LAMBARDE. Hasted's Kent, i. 18. Berry's Kent Genealogies, 349. Archæologia Cantiana, v. 248. Burke's Landed Gentry, 2, 3, 4, 5, 6, 7, 8. Bibliotheca Topographica Britannica, i. Part vi. 530. Hasted's Kent, (Hund. of Blackheath, by H. H. Drake,) 52. Harleian Society, xlii. 167.

LAMBART. Burke's Landed Gentry, 2, 3, 4, 5, 6, 7, 8. Archdall's Lodge's Peerage, i. 343. The Genealogist, vi. 263.

LAMBE. Pedigree of Lambe of Coulston, Co. Wilts., [T. P.] 1855, 2 folio pages. Burke's Landed Gentry, 2 supp., 3, 4. Visitatio Comitatus Wiltoniæ, 1623, printed by Sir T. Phillipps. Surtees' Durham, i. 186. Wiltshire Archæological Magazine, iii. 108. Metcalfe's Visitations of Suffolk, 49, 149, 200. Visitation of Wiltshire, edited by G. W. Marshall, 40. Notes and Queries, 5 S. x. 337. *See* LAMB.

LAMBERT. Pedigree of Lambert of Doulton, Co. Somerset, [T. P.] 1864, folio page. Account of Natural Curiosities in the Environs of Malham, by Thomas Hurtley, Appendix, No. iii. Topographer and Genealogist, ii. 74. Morant's Essex, ii. 556. Bigland's Observations on Marriages, 33. Berry's Surrey Genealogies, 52, 97, 99. Berry's Hampshire Genealogies, 77, 180. Surtees Society,

xxxvi. 367. Visitation of Durham, 1575, (Newcastle, 1820, fol.)
57. Burke's Commoners, (of Boyton,) i. 66 ; (of Carnagh,) Com-
moners, iii. 547, Landed Gentry, 2, 3, 4, 5, 6, 7, 8 ; (of Castle
Ellen,) 8 ; (of Garratts Hall,) 8 ; (of Brookhill,) Landed Gentry,
2, 3, 4, 5, 6, 8 ; (of Waterdale,) 2, 3, 4, 5, 6, 7 ; (of Castle Lambert,) 2, 3, 4, 5, 6, 7 ; (of Lyston Hall,) 2 add., 3, 4, 5, 6 ; (of
Aggard,) 3, 4, 5, 6, 7, 8. Foster's Visitations of Yorkshire, 288.
Harleian Society, i. 26 ; xxii. 121 ; xli. 126, 127 ; xliii. 82, 149.
Whitaker's Deanery of Craven, 183, (256). Visitatio Comitatus
Wiltoniæ, 1623, printed by Sir T. Phillipps. Hoare's Wiltshire,
I. ii. 203. Surtees' Durham, iii. 133. Manning and Bray's Surrey,
ii. 453, 589. Burke's Landed Gentry, 6th edn., p. 538. Plan-
tagenet-Harrison's History of Yorkshire, i. 457. Notes and
Queries, 1 S. vii. 237, 269, 364, 459. Wotton's English Baronet-
age, iv. 132. Betham's Baronetage, iii. 151. Visitation of Wilt-
shire, edited by G. W. Marshall, 60. Ancient Families of Lin-
colnshire, in 'Spalding Free Press,' 1873-5, No. viii. Foster's
Visitations of Durham, 201. Surrey Archæological Collections, xi.
The Manor of Minster, by H. W. Aldred, 53. Burke's Family
Records, 365. The Genealogist, New Series, xiii. 239.

LAMBORNE. Harleian Society, xliii. 173.

LAMBRICK. The Visitations of Devon, by J. L. Vivian, 762.

LAMBTON. Visitation of Durham, 1575, (Newcastle, 1820, folio) 28,
38. Visitation of Durham, 1615, (Sunderland, 1820, fol.) 27.
Foster's Visitations of Yorkshire, 182. History of Hartlepool, by
Sir C. Sharp, (1816, 8vo.) 79. Hutchinson's History of Durham,
iii. xxxii. Archæologia Æliana, 2nd Series, iii. 86. Surtees'
Durham, ii. 174, 201, 397 ; iii. 36, 62. Foster's Visitations of
Durham, 205, 207.

LAMMIN. Burke's Visitation of Seats and Arms, 2nd Series, ii. 13.

LAMONT. Surtees Society, xxxvi. 75. Burke's Landed Gentry, 4, 5,
6, 7, 8.

LAMOTT. Monken Hadley, by F. C. Cass, 30. Harleian Society,
xvii. 42.

LAMPARD. Manning and Bray's Surrey, iii. 141.

LAMPEN. Harleian Society, ix. 119. The Visitations of Cornwall,
edited by J. L. Vivian, 274.

LAMPLEW, or LAMPLUGH. Surtees Society, xli. 94. Foster's Visita-
tions of Yorkshire, 88, 155. Harleian Society, vii. 26 ; xvi. 181.
Hutchinson's History of Cumberland, ii. 95. Jefferson's History
of Allerdale Ward, Cumberland, 84, 437. Foster's Visitations of
Cumberland and Westmorland, 72, 74. Nicolson and Burn's
Westmorland and Cumberland, ii. 37.

LAMPLUGH-RAPER (now Lamplugh-Brooksbank). Burke's Commoners,
iii. 160, Landed Gentry, 2, 3, 4, 5, 6, 7.

LAMPORT. The Genealogist, New Series, iii. 137.

L'AMY. Burke's Landed Gentry, 2, 3, 4, 5, 6, 7.

LANAM. The Genealogist, vi. 265.

LANCASHIRE. Burke's Commoners, iv. 106.

LANCASTER. A Genealogical Account of the Descendants of John

of Gaunt, Duke of Lancaster, by J. G. Bell. London, 1855, 4to.
Visitation of Westmorland, 1615, (London, 1853,) 41. Visitation
of Somerset, printed by Sir T. Phillipps, 113. Harleian Society,
xi. 66. Chetham Society, lxxxi. 118 ; lxxxii. 18 ; lxxxv. 172.
Gregson's Fragments relative to the County of Lancaster, 12, 46.
Blore's Rutland, 98. Baines' History of the Co. of Lancaster, iv.
155, 751. Earls of, (Croston's edition,) 62, 195. Collectanea
Topographica et Genealogica, i. 297, 315. Banks' Baronies in
Fee, i. 273. Banks' Dormant and Extinct Baronage, i. 108, 355.
Ormerod's Cheshire, iii. 898. Metcalfe's Visitations of Suffolk,
201. Foster's Visitations of Cumberland and Westmorland, 46,
75. History of Chipping, by Tom C. Smith, 262. Nicolson and
Burn's Westmorland and Cumberland, i. 151, 386, 401.

LANCASTER-LUCAS. Burke's Landed Gentry, 5, 6.

LANCELYN. Ormerod's Cheshire, ii. 444. *See* LAUNCELIN.

LAND, or LANDE. Tuckett's Devonshire Pedigrees, 16. Harleian
Society, vi. 163; xi. 66. The Visitations of Devon, by J. L.
Vivian, 520.

LANDAFF (Earl of). The Genealogical Magazine, ii. 285, 343.

LANDER, or LANDOR. Burke's Commoners, iii. 682, Landed Gentry,
2, 3, 4, 5, 6, 7, 8. Jewitt's Reliquary, ix. 254. Alexander
Nisbet's Heraldic Plates, 96. *See* LAUNDER.

LANDON. Berry's Hertfordshire Genealogies, 46. Burke's Royal
Families, (London, 1851, 8vo.) ii. 72.

LANE. Burke's Commoners, (of Kings Bromley,) i. 174, Landed
Gentry, 2, 3, 4, 5, 6, 7, 8 ; (of Badgemore,) Landed Gentry, 2, 3,
4, 5, 6; 7, 8 ; (of Coffleet,) 2, 3, 4 ; (of Middleton,) 8 ; (of Grat-
tans,) 8 ; (of Moundsley Hall,) 8 ; (of Ryelands,) 2, 3, 4, 5, 6, 7.
Miscellanea Genealogica et Heraldica, New Series, i. 186. Har-
leian Society, viii. 416. Topographer, (London, 1789-91, 8vo.) i.
549. Visitation of Warwickshire, 1619, published with Warwick-
shire Antiquarian Magazine, 106. Lipscombe's History of the
County of Buckingham, i. 266. Blore's Rutland, 169. Burke's
Royal Descents and Pedigrees of Founders' Kin, 3. Shaw's
Staffordshire, ii. 97. Hutchins' Dorset, iii. 492. Baker's North-
ampton, i. 297. Harleian Society, xii. 307 ; xx. 62 ; xxi. 100.
Archæologia Cantiana, xii. 316. The Boscobel Tracts, edited by
J. Hughes, 2nd edn., 391. O'Hart's Irish Pedigrees, 2nd Series,
209. Collections for a History of Staffordshire, (William Salt
Society,) i. 326. Burke's Extinct Baronetcies. Nicholls' Account
of the Company of Ironmongers, 2nd edn., 577. The Genea-
logical Magazine, i. 131, 201, 278, 347, 402, 458, 509. Metcalfe's
Visitations of Northamptonshire,. 32, 107, 185. Visitation of
Gloucester, edited by T. F. Fenwick and W. C. Metcalfe,
106. New England Register, x. 356 ; xi. 231 ; xxvii. 176 ; xlii.
141. Howard's Visitation of England and Wales, v. 159. *See*
LONE.

LANE-CLAPON. Burke's Landed Gentry, 8.

LANE-FOX. Burke's Commoners, ii. 493, Landed Gentry, 2, 3, 4, 5,
6, 7, 8. Foster's Yorkshire Pedigrees. Whitaker's Deanery of

Craven, 3rd edn., 116. Howard's Visitation of England and
Wales, v. 1.

LANESBOROUGH. Burke's Royal Descents and Pedigrees of Founders'
Kin, 1.

LANFERE. Genealogical Memoranda of the Family of Ames, 5.

LANGDALE. Pedigree of the Langdale Family. London, [1873,] 8vo.
Surtees Society, xxxvi. 82. Burke's Landed Gentry, 2, p. 666,
and supp., 3, 4, 8. Foster's Visitations of Yorkshire, 129, 190.
Harleian Society, viii. 114; xvi. 183. Poulson's Holderness, ii.
254. Edmondson's Baronagium Genealogicum, iv. 392. Banks'
Dormant and Extinct Baronage, iii. 445.

LANGDON. Harleian Society, ix. 119; xxxii. 182. The Visitations
of Cornwall, edited by J. L. Vivian, 275, 276. New England
Register, xxx. 33.

LANGELIER. Oliver's History of Antigua, ii. 138.

LANGESFORD. Tuckett's Devonshire Pedigrees, 8. Harleian Society,
vi. 164.

LANGFIELD. Whitaker's Deanery of Craven, 3rd edn., 150.

LANGFORD. Jewitt's Reliquary, vii. 24. Dwnn's Visitations of
Wales, i. 325. Burke's Landed Gentry, 2. Harleian Society, ix.
121, 122; xvii. 43; xxix. 309. Westcote's Devonshire, edited
by G. Oliver and P. Jones, 462. Dugdale's Warwickshire, 73.
Clutterbuck's Hertford, iii. 33. Thoroton's Nottinghamshire, iii.
145. Wiltshire Archæological Magazine, ix. 282. Maclean's
History of Trigg Minor, iii. 166. Visitation of Devon, by F. T.
Colby, 148. The Visitations of Cornwall, edited by J. L. Vivian,
277, 278. Burke's Extinct Baronetcies, 609. History of Powys
Fadog, by J. Y. W. Lloyd, iii. 207. Notes and Queries, 8 S.
iv. 34. The Visitations of Devon, by J. L. Vivian, 521. Oliver's
History of Antigua, ii. 140, 156.

LANGHAM. Morant's Essex, ii. 406, 528. Berry's Sussex Genealogies, 273. Dwnn's Visitations of Wales, i. 73, 184. Harleian
Society, ii. 12; xii. 388; xiii. 41; xvii. 44, 45. Bridges' Northamptonshire, by Rev. Peter Whalley, i. 555. Nichols' History of
the County of Leicester, iv. 855. Wotton's English Baronetage,
iii. 22. Betham's Baronetage, ii. 48. Muskett's Suffolk Manorial
Families, i. 262, 373.

LANGHARNE. Harleian Society, ix. 122. Pembrokeshire Pedigrees,
145. The Visitations of Cornwall, edited by J. L. Vivian, 279.

LANGHOLME. The Genealogist, iv. 187.

LANGHORNE. History of Hampstead, by J. J. Park, 124. Burke's
Extinct Baronetcies. Harleian Society, xvii. 46; xxii. 71.

LANGLEY. Hasted's Kent, iv. 209. Surtees Society, xxxvi. 205, 234,
300, 301. W. Paver's Pedigrees of Families of the City of York,
14. Burke's Landed Gentry, (of Coal Brook,) 5, 6, 7, 8; (of
Brittas Castle,) 5, 6, 7, 8. Foster's Visitations of Yorkshire, 117.
Harleian Society, i. 6; viii. 344; xiii. 433; xvii. 48; xxi. 102,
255; xxix. 310, 312; xxxviii. 699; xxxix. 980; xliii. 20. Visitation of London in Transactions of the London and Middlesex
Archæological Society, 24. Transactions of Shropshire Archæo-

logicnl Society, N.S., v. 113-150. Chetham Society, lxxxi. 134 ;
xcviii. 70; xcix. 147. Dugdale's Warwickshire, 209. Baker's Northampton, ii. 286. Baines' History of the Co. of Lancaster, ii. 561;
Croston's edn., ii. 370. Meyrick's History of the Co. of Cardigan,
123. Memoirs of the Family of Chester, by R. E. C. Waters, 204.
Wotton's English Baronetage, ii. 158. Betham's Baronetage, i.
372. Burke's Extinct Baronetcies. Visitation of Gloucester,
edited by T. F. Fenwick and W. C. Metcalfe, 107. Account of
the Guildhall of London, by J. E. Price, 131. Yorkshire Genealogist, i. 170. Miscellanea Genealogica et Heraldica, 2nd Series,
ii. 273, 305, 337 ; iii. 75, 141, 158, 169 ; iv. 185. The Genealo-
gist, New Series, viii. 242, 246 ; xiv. 250 ; xvi. 161 ; xvii. 26.
Howard's Visitation of England and Wales, ii. 101. Burke's
Family Records, 370. New England Register, li. 168.
LANGLOIS. J. B. Payne's Armorial of Jersey, 192.
LANGMAN. Howard's Visitation of England and Wales, vi. 24.
LANGMUIR. Ontarian Families, by E. M. Chadwick, i. 44.
LANGRISH. The Family and Manor of Langrishe. Athlone, *n.d.*, fol.
Berry's Hampshire Genealogies, 236.
LANGSTON. Burke's Landed Gentry, 2, 3, 4. Harleian Society,
xxvii. 84. Burke's Family Records, 374.
LANGTON. Memorials of the Family of Langton of Kilkenny, by
J. G. A. Prim. Dublin, 1864, 8vo. J. H. Hill's History of Lang-
ton, 17, 18, 19*. Kent's British Banner Displayed, 449. Topo-
graphical Account of Wainfleet, by Edmd. Oldfield, 207. Burke's
Landed Gentry, (of Liverpool,) 2 ; (of Langton,) 5, 6, 7, 8 ; (of
Danganmore,) 5 supp., 6, 7. Harleian Society, vii. 32 ; viii. 209 ;
xvii. 49 ; xxi. 273, 278 ; xxvii. 148. Chetham Society, lxxxi. 24 ;
lxxxv. 173, 174 ; xcviii. 12 ; xcix. 95. Surtees' Durham, iii. 79.
Baker's Northampton, i. 221. Foster's Lancashire Pedigrees.
Hutchinson's History of Durham, iii. 88. Baines' History of the
Co. of Lancaster, iii. 642 ; iv. 409 ; Croston's edn., iv. 382. Wilt-
shire Archæological Magazine, iv. 77. Abram's History of Black-
burn, 706. Plantagenet-Harrison's History of Yorkshire, i. 444.
The Genealogist, iv. 187 ; v. 282 ; New Series, x. 214 ; xv. 153.
Journal of Kilkenny Archæological Society, New Series, v. 59-108.
The Tyldesley Diary, edited by J. Gillow and A. Hewitson, 85.
Carthew's Hundred of Launditch, Part iii. 247. Foster's Visita-
tions of Durham, 203. Somersetshire Wills, printed for F. A.
Crisp, iv. 30. East Barnet, by F. C. Cass, Part i. 26. Leicester-
shire Architectural Society, ii. 96. Foster's Visitations of Cum-
berland and Westmorland, 76. Burke's Colonial Gentry, ii. 679.
LANGTRE, or LANGTREE. Chetham Society, lxxxi. 66. Metcalfe's
Visitations of Northamptonshire, 33. Croston's edn. of Baines'
Lancaster, iv. 226.
LANGWORTH. Berry's Kent Genealogies, 469. Miscellanea Genea-
logica et Heraldica, New Series, iv. 204.
LANIGAN. Burke's Commoners, iii. 701.
LANION, or LANYON. Polewhele's History of Cornwall, ii. 42. Har-
leian Society, ix. 123. A Complete Parochial History of the

County of Cornwall, ii. 149; iii. 225. An Historical Survey of Cornwall, by C. S. Gilbert, ii. 185. The Visitations of Cornwall, edited by J. L. Vivian, 281.

LANNES. Miscellanea Genealogica et Heraldica, 2nd Series, v. 30.

LANNOY. Miscellanea Genealogica et Heraldica, 3rd Series, ii. 262.

LANSLADRON. Banks' Baronies in Fee, i. 274.

LANT, or LANTE. Tuckett's Devonshire Pedigrees, 13. Harleian Society, vi. 164; xvii. 50. The Visitations of Devon, by J. L. Vivian, 523.

LANVALLEI. Morant's Essex, i. 440. Clutterbuck's Hertford, ii. 463.

LANY, or LANYE. Harleian Society, ii. 196. Nichols' History of the County of Leicester, iii. 400. Metcalfe's Visitations of Suffolk, 50, 149.

LAPP. Visitatio Comitatus Wiltoniæ, 1623, printed by Sir T. Phillipps. Visitation of Wiltshire, edited by G. W. Marshall, 51.

LARDER. Westcote's Devonshire, edited by G. Oliver and P. Jones, 624. Hutchins' Dorset, ii. 638. Visitation of Devon, edited by F. T. Colby, 149. Harleian Society, xvii. 49; xx. 62. The Genealogist, New Series, iii. 96. The Visitations of Devon, by J. L. Vivian, 524.

LARDINER. Drake's Eboracum, or the History, etc., of York, 326.

LARKWORTHY. Tuckett's Devonshire Pedigrees, 13. Harleian Society, vi. 165. The Visitations of Devon, by J. L. Vivian, 525.

LARKYN, or LARKIN. Harleian Society, xli. 61. Genealogical Record of King and Henham, 22. Cambridgeshire Visitation, edited by Sir T. Phillipps, 20.

LARNACH. Burke's Colonial Gentry, ii. 447. Burke's Landed Gentry, 7, 8.

LAROCHE. Betham's Baronetage, iv. 40. Burke's Extinct Baronetcies. Oliver's History of Antigua, ii. 161.

LASCELLES, LASCELLS, or LASSELLS. Nichols' History of the County of Leicester, iii. 169*. Miscellanea Genealogica et Heraldica, ii. 123. History of Harewood, by John Jewell, 17. Foster's Yorkshire Pedigrees. Harleian Society, ii. 155; iv. 57; xvi. 265. Whitaker's History of Richmondshire, i. 264. Thoroton's Nottinghamshire, i. 338. Ingledew's History of North Allerton, 311. Foster's Visitations of Yorkshire, 61, 185. Whitaker's Loidis and Elmete, 168. Brydges' Collins' Peerage, viii. 508. Banks' Dormant and Extinct Baronage, i. 356. Notes and Queries, 4 S. v. 313, 385, 474, 601; vi. 83, 157. Yorkshire Archæological and Topographical Journal, vii. 481. The Genealogist, New Series, xii. 176.

LASLETT. Burke's Landed Gentry, 2, 3, 4, 5, 6, 7.

LASON. Harleian Society, i. 61.

LATHAM, LATHOM, or LATHUM. Morant's Essex, i. 97, 105, 108. Cambridgeshire Visitation, edited by Sir T. Phillipps, 20. Burke's Commoners, i. 190, Landed Gentry, 2, 3, 4, 5, 6, 7. Chetham Society, lxxxii. 4, 106; lxxxv. 175-177; xcv. 20. Gregson's Fragments relative to the County of Lancaster, 242. Baines' History of the Co. of Lancaster, iii. 479; Croston's edn., iv. 199,

200. J. P. Earwaker's East Cheshire, i. 133. Harleian Society,
xiii. 68, 433; xvii. 45; xviii. 214; xxxviii. 459; xli. 55. Mis-
cellanea Genealogica et Heraldica, i. 161. Ormerod's Miscellanea
Palatina, 68. Dwnn's Visitations of Wales, ii. 340. More about
Stifford, by Willm. Palin, 34. Collectanea Topographica et Gene-
alogica, vii. 1. Ormerod's Cheshire, ii. 24, 115. Ormerod's
Parentalia, 55, 63. Earwaker's History of Sandbach, 142. The
Genealogist, New Series, xvi. 206.

LATHBURY. Nichols' History of the County of Leicester, iv. 577.
The Genealogist, New Series, vii. 228.

LATHORPE, or LATHROP. Visitation of Staffordshire, 1663-4, printed
by Sir T. Phillipps, 6. Visitations of Staffordshire, 1614 and
1663-4, William Salt Society, 198.

LATIMER. J. H. Hill's History of Langton, 19. Blomefield's Norfolk,
i. 86. Whitaker's History of Richmondshire, ii. 78. Bridges'
Northamptonshire, by Rev. Peter Whalley, i. 89, 114; ii. 5, 11,
25, 160. Thoresby's Ducatus Leodiensis, 213. Ord's History of
Cleveland, 330. Nichols' History of the County of Leicester, ii.
566. Hutchins' Dorset, iii. 705. Baker's Northampton, i. 525.
Banks' Baronies in Fee, i. 275. Banks' Dormant and Extinct
Baronage, i. 357; ii. 291. Memorials of St. John at Hackney, by
R. Simpson, 300. The Genealogist, New Series, xvi. 42. See
ALNO, LATYMER.

LA TOMBE. Harleian Society, xvii. 51.

LATON. Foster's Visitations of Yorkshire, 546. Surtees' Durham, i.
215. Plantagenet-Harrison's History of Yorkshire, i. 527. See
LAYTON.

LA TOUCHE. Burke's Landed Gentry, (of Bellevue,) 2, 3, 4, 5, 6, 7, 8;
(of Harristown,) 2, 3, 4, 5, 6, 7, 8; (of Marlay,) 2, 3, 4.

LA TROBE-BATEMAN. Burke's Landed Gentry, 8.

LATTIN. Burke's Commoners, iii. 575.

LATTON. Ashmole's Antiquities of Berkshire, iii. 361. Manning and
Bray's Surrey, ii. 753. The Genealogist, v. 283. Harleian
Society, xliii. 225.

LATUS. Hutchinson's History of Cumberland, i. 530. Jefferson's
History of Allerdale Ward, Cumberland, 172.

LATYMER. T. Faulkner's History of Hammersmith, 184. Metcalfe's
Visitations of Suffolk, 50. See LATIMER.

LAUD. The Visitations of Devon, by J. L. Vivian, 520.

LAUDER, or LAWDER. Burke's Landed Gentry, 2. Herald and
Genealogist, iii. 466. Burke's Heraldic Illustrations, 17. Miscellanea Genealogica et Heraldica, New Series, iv. 278.

LAUGHTON. Foster's Yorkshire Pedigrees. Miscellanea Genealogica
et Heraldica, ii. 258. Foster's Visitations of Yorkshire, 542.
Hunter's Deanery of Doncaster, i. 246; ii. 36. Burke's Family
Records, 376.

LAUNCE. A memorable note of the kindred of Robert Launce. [By
Rev. S. B. Turner, London, 1882,] 8vo. Harleian Society, ix.
124. Miscellanea Genealogica et Heraldica, New Series, iv. 104.
The Visitations of Cornwall, edited by J. L. Vivian, 280.

LAUNCELIN. Harleian Society, xviii. 83, 132.

LAUNCELOTT. Harleian Society, xvii. 51.

LAUNDER. Earwaker's Local Gleanings, ii. 590. Master's Notices of the Family of Master, 87. *See* LANDER.

LAURENCE. *See* LAWRENCE.

LAUTOUR. Burke's Landed Gentry, 2, 3, 4.

LAVENDER, or LAVINDER. Miscellanea Genealogica et Heraldica, New Series, iii. 186. Harleian Society, xvii. 52 ; xix. 178 ; xxii. 72. Harvey's Hundred of Willey, 276.

LAVICOURT. Oliver's History of Antigua, ii. 164.

LAVINGTON. Visitatio Comitatus Wiltoniæ, 1623, printed by Sir T. Phillipps. Visitation of Wiltshire, edited by G. W. Marshall, 46, 85. Oliver's History of Antigua, ii. 166.

LAW. Berry's Sussex Genealogies, 121. Popular Genealogists, 88. Horsfield's History of Lewes, ii. 135. Nichols' History of the County of Leicester, iii. 1137. Cumberland and Westmorland Archæological Society, ii. 264. The Parish of Cramond, by J. P. Wood, 43, 161. Notes and Queries, 2 S. i. 56, 141, 176 ; 3 S. iii. 486 ; iv. 31, 132, 151, 214. Brydges' Collins' Peerage, ix. 187. Stodart's Scottish Arms, ii. 246. Jewer's Wells Cathedral, 155. Stockdale's Annals of Cartmel, 192. Metcalfe's Visitations of Northamptonshire, 107. Howard's Visitation of England and Wales, vii. 61.

LAWDAY. Burke's Extinct Baronetcies.

LAWE. Chetham Society, lxxxv. 178. Abram's History of Blackburn, 267.

LAWES. Berry's Hertfordshire Genealogies, 205. Berry's Kent Genealogies, 426. Burke's Landed Gentry, 2, 3, 4, 5, 6, 7, 8. Harleian Society, xlii. 200.

LAWFORD. The Genealogist, iv. 88 ; New Series, viii. 185. Genealogical Memoranda of the Family of Ames, 7.

LAWLESS. History of St. Canice, Kilkenny, by J. Graves, 255. The Irish Builder, xxxv. 256.

LAWLEY. Foster's Yorkshire Pedigrees. Shaw's Staffordshire, ii. 21*. Wotton's English Baronetage, ii. 261. Betham's Baronetage, i. 450. Harleian Society, xvii. 52 ; xxix. 313.

LAWLOR. Burke's Landed Gentry, 3, 4, 5, 6, 7, 8. O'Hart's Irish Pedigrees, 2nd Series, 210.

LAWNDEY. Clutterbuck's Hertford, ii. 302.

LAWRANCE. Burke's Landed Gentry, 8. Harleian Society, xli. 98.

LAWRENCE, or LAURENCE. Pedigree of Lawrence of Sevenhampton, Co. Gloucester, [T. P.] 1867, folio page. Pedigree of Lawrence of Shurdington, [T. P.] folio page. Miscellanea Genealogica et Heraldica, i. 199-212 ; New Series, i. 46, 68. Herald and Genealogist, iv. 465, 529-544 ; viii. 177, 188, 210, 517. Monumental Inscriptions of the British West Indies, by J. H. Lawrence-Archer, 319. Blomefield's Norfolk, v. 335. Gentleman's Magazine, lxxxv. ii. 12, 104, 504 ; lxxxvii. i. 318, 518 ; ii. 126 ; 1829, ii. 105, 312. Collectanea Topographica et Genealogica, iii. 281. Cambridgeshire Visitation, edited by Sir T. Phillipps, 20. Visitation of Gloucestershire, 1569, (Middle Hill, 1854, fol.) 7, Burke's Commoners, (of Sevenhampton,) iii. 64, Landed Gentry, 2, 3, 4, 5, 6, 7, 8; (of Lisreaghan,) Landed Gentry, 2, 3, 4, 5, 6, 7, 8; (of Cowesfield House,) 8. Harleian Society, ii. 27, 102; viii. 75, 474; xvii. 53; xx. 63; xxi. 103, 255; xxii. 72; xxxvii. 363. Nichols' History of the County of Leicester, iii. 1135; iv. 370, 408. Hoare's Wiltshire, III. iv. 68; V. ii. 74. Chetham Society, xcv. 72. Hutchins' Dorset, i. 599; ii. 776. Fosbrooke's History of Gloucestershire, i. 260; ii. 443. Bigland's Gloucestershire, ii. par. Sevenhampton. Notes and Queries, 2 S. vii. 296, 444, 486; x. 292, 480, 493; xi. 13, 87, 495; xii. 177, 196; 3 S. iii. 17, 395, 428; viii. 289; 4 S. xii. 144, 489, 511; 5 S. xi. 501; 6 S. v. 5. Burke's Extinct Baronetcies. The Palatine Note Book, ii. 96. Visitation of Gloucester, edited by T. F. Fenwick and W. C. Metcalfe, 108. The Visitations of Cornwall, by J. L. Vivian, 592. New England Register, x. 297; xlvi. 149. Howard's Visitation of England and Wales, vi. 78.

LAWRENS. Berry's Hampshire Genealogies, 248.

LAWRIE. Lands and their Owners in Galloway, by P. H. M'Kerlie, ii. 256. *See* LOWRY.

LAWSON. Burke's Extinct Baronetcies. Surtees Society, xxxvi. 90. Visitation of Durham, 1575, (Newcastle, 1820, fol.) 35. Burke's Commoners, (of Aldborough,) ii. 247, Landed Gentry, 2, 3, 4, 5, 6, 7, 8; (of Longhirst,) Commoners, ii. 105, Landed Gentry, 2, 3, 4, 5, 6, 7, 8; (of Hall Barn,) 7. Foster's Yorkshire Pedigrees. Foster's Visitations of Yorkshire, 93, 254. Harleian Society, viii. 111, 376; xiv. 590; xvi. 184. Hutchinson's History of Cumberland, ii. 241. Raine's History of North Durham, 237. Hodgson's Northumberland, II. ii. 161. Whitaker's History of Richmondshire, ii. 36. Thoresby's Ducatus Leodiensis, 33, 250. Hunter's History of the Parish of Sheffield, 371. Surtees' Durham, i. 53, 61; ii. 47; iii. 264. Life of Mrs. Dorothy Lawson, by G. B. Richardson, (Newcastle-upon-Tyne, 1855, 8vo.) 1. The Genealogist, ii. 119. Nisbet's Heraldry, ii. app. 98-104. Douglas's Baronage of Scotland, 581. Foley's Records of the English Province, S. J., v. 708. W. R. Fraser's History of Laurencekirk, 182. Wotton's English Baronetage, iii. 489; iv. 18. Betham's Baronetage, ii. 381; iii. 75. Ilkley, Ancient and Modern, by R. Collyer and J. H. Turner, 210. Foster's Visitations of Durham, 209. Foster's Visitations of Northumberland, 75-77. Foster's Visitations of Cumberland and Westmorland, 77. Notes and Queries, 8 S. v. 153. Annals of the English Benedictines of Ghent, 185. Nicolson and Burn's Westmorland and Cumberland, ii. 96. Howard's Visitation of England and Wales, ix. 147.

LAWTON. Burke's Landed Gentry, (of Lawton,) 2, 3, 4, 5, 6, 7, 8; (of Cape View,) 3; (of Lake Marsh,) 2. Erdeswicke's Survey of Staffordshire, 106. Ormerod's Cheshire, iii. 16. Harleian Society, xviii. 133.

LAX. Harleian Society, xxxvii. 379.

LAYBORN, or LAYBOURNE. Surtees Society, xli. 95. Visitation of Westmoreland, 1615, (London, 1853,) 19, 50, 51.

LAYCOCK. Burke's Landed Gentry, 5 supp., 6, 7, 8. *See* LACOCK.

LAYER. Blomefield's Norfolk, vi. 354. Visitation of Norfolk, published by Norfolk Archæological Society, i. 25. Harleian Society, xxxii. 183.

LAYMAN. Burke's Colonial Gentry, ii. 525.

LAYNEY. Harleian Society, xxxii. 184.

LAYTON. Surtees Society, xxxvi. 104, 377. Burke's Landed Gentry, 2, 3, 4. Foster's Visitations of Yorkshire, 258, 540-542. Harleian Society, vii. 31. Graves' History of Cleveland, 171, 172. Thoresby's Ducatus Leodiensis, 261. Ord's History of Cleveland, 474. Plantagenet-Harrison's History of Yorkshire, i. 450, 528. Notes and Queries, 6 S. ii. 351, 457. Foster's Visitations of Cumberland and Westmorland, 78. New England Register, v. 166 ; vii. 255. *See* LATON.

LA ZOUCH. Nichols' History of the County of Leicester, ii. 372. Clutterbuck's Hertford, i. 371 ; iii. 287. Hasted's Kent, ii. 246. Eyton's Antiquities of Shropshire, ii. 208. *See* ZOUCH.

LEA. Herald and Genealogist, v. 212 ; vi. 363. Burke's Landed Gentry, 2 supp., 3, 4, 6 at p. 1477, 7, and at p. 1686, 8, and at p. 1863. Burke's Heraldic Illustrations, 143. Duncumb's History of the Co. of Hereford, ii. 404. The Midland Antiquary, i. 46. Visitations of Staffordshire, 1614 and 1663-4, William Salt Society, 199.

LEACH. Pedigree of Leach of Corston, Co. Pembroke, [T. P.] 1864. Another, 1860. Tuckett's Devonshire Pedigrees, 8. Harleian Society, vi. 166 ; ix. 125 ; xvii. 54 ; xxxvii. 291. An Historical Survey of Cornwall, by C. S. Gilbert, ii. 187. The Visitations of Cornwall, edited by J. L. Vivian, 283. Yorkshire Genealogist, i. 143. Burke's Landed Gentry, 7, 8. The Visitations of Devon, by J. L. Vivian, 526. *See* HALFORD.

LEACHLAND. Harleian Society, xvii. 54.

LEACOCK. Burke's Colonial Gentry, ii. 823.

LEACROFT. Blore's History of South Winfield, in Nichols' Miscellaneous Antiquities, No. 3, 73. Visitation of Staffordshire, 1663-4, printed by Sir T. Phillipps, 7. Visitations of Staffordshire, 1614 and 1663-4, William Salt Society, 200.

LEADBEATER. Earwaker's History of Sandbach, 213.

LEADBITTER. Hodgson's Northumberland, III. ii. 409. Burke's Landed Gentry, 8.

LEADBITTER-SMITH. Burke's Landed Gentry, 6, 7, 8.

LEADER. Burke's Landed Gentry, (of Dromagh Castle,) 2 supp., 3, 4, 5, 6, 7, 8 ; (of Mount Leader,) 2 supp., 3, 4, 5, 6, 7 ; (of Ashgrove,) 5, 6, 7, 8. Notes and Queries, 2 S. iv. 410, 440, 479 ; v. 323. Harleian Society, xxxviii. 710.

LEAHY. Burke's Landed Gentry, 2, 3, 4, 6, 7.

LEAKE, or LEAK. Harleian Society, viii. 483. Dawson Turner's Sepulchral Reminiscences of Great Yarmouth, 133. Collectanea Topographica et Genealogica, v. 51. Nichols' History of the

County of Leicester, ii. 217. Harleian Society, xvii. 55. Burke's Colonial Gentry, ii. 606. Notes and Queries, 8 S. ix. 323, 463. Burke's Landed Gentry, 8. *See* LEKE, MARTIN-LEAKE.

LEAPER. Glover's History of Derbyshire, ii. 601, (592). Harleian Society, xxxviii. 315.

LEAR. Burke's Extinct Baronetcies.

LE ARCHER. Maclean's History of Trigg Minor, ii. 180.

LEARMONTH. Burke's Landed Gentry, 3, 4, 5, 6, 7, 8. Balmerino and its Abbey, by James Campbell, 398. Walter Wood's East Neuk of Fife, 273. Burke's Colonial Gentry, i. 264 ; ii. 663.

LEATHAM. Burke's Landed Gentry, 3, 4, 5, 6, 8. Foster's Yorkshire Pedigrees. Burke's Visitation of Seats and Arms, 2nd Series, i. 58.

LEATHER. Burke's Landed Gentry, 4, 5, 6, 7, 8.

LEATHES. Burke's Landed Gentry, 2, 3, 4, 5, 6, 7, 8. Suckling's History of Suffolk, ii. 14. Burke's Heraldic Illustrations, 25.

LEAVER. Chetham Society, lxxxii. 33. *See* LEVER.

LEAVY. O'Hart's Irish Pedigrees, 2nd Series, 119.

LE BAILLY. J. B. Payne's Armorial of Jersey, 194.

LE BANDY. The Genealogist, New Series, xiv. 99.

LE BARON. Harleian Society, vi. 152. New Register England, xxv. 180. *See* BARON.

LE BASS. Genealogist, i. 218.

LE BLOUNT. *See* CROKE.

LE BLUND. Herald and Genealogist, iv. 194. Morant's Essex, i. 491. Page's History of Suffolk, 788. *See* BLOUNT.

LE BOTILLIER, or LE BOTELER. J. B. Payne's Armorial of Jersey, 195. Hoare's Wiltshire, V. ii. 103. The Genealogist, New Series, ix. 145. *See* BOTELER.

LE BRETON. Plantagenet-Harrison's History of Yorkshire, i. 468. J. B. Payne's Armorial of Jersey, 198. *See* BRETON.

LE BRUNE. Maclean's History of Trigg Minor, ii. 214, 237 ; iii. 142. *See* BRUNE.

LECESNE. Family Notes, by J. M. Browne, 54.

LECESTER. *See* LEYCESTER.

LE CHAMPION-MOLLER. Burke's Landed Gentry, 4.

LECHE. Burke's Commoners, ii. 365, Land Gentry, 2, 3, 4, 5, 6, 7, 8. Burke's Heraldic Illustrations, 42. Ormerod's Cheshire, ii. 207, 381. *See* LEECH.

LECHFORD. Manning and Bray's Surrey, ii. 181. Harleian Society, xliii. 43.

LECHINGHAM. The Genealogist, vii. 181.

LECHLAND. Harleian Society, xi. 67.

LECHMERE. Hanley and the House of Lechmere, by E. P. Shirley. London, 1883, 4to. Berry's Buckinghamshire Genealogies, 99. Nash's Worcestershire, i. 560. Burke's Commoners, i. 146; Landed Gentry, (of Fownhope,) 2, 3, 4, 5, 6, 7, 8 ; (of Hill House,) 2, 3, 4. Harleian Society, viii. 425. Duncumb's History of the Co. of Hereford, ii. 345. Fosbrooke's History of Gloucestershire, ii. 365.

LECKEY. Burke's Landed Gentry, 3, 4, 5.

LECKONBY. The Tyldesley Diary, edited by J. Gillow and A. Hewitson, 155. Chetham Society, New Series, xxv. 188. Croston's
edn. of Baines's Lancaster, iv. 110.

LECKY. Burke's Landed Gentry, (of Ballykeally, 2, 3, 4, 5, 6, 8; (of
Castle Lecky,) 2, 3, 4; (of Beardiville,) 5, 6, 7, 8.

LE COUTEUR. J. B. Payne's Armorial of Jersey, 200.

LEDEATT. Oliver's History of Antigua, ii. 170.

LEDES. The Genealogist, New Series, xviii. 34.

LE DESPENCER, or LE DESPENSER. Collectanea Topographica et
Genealogica, vii. 263. Potter's History of Charnwood Forest, 92.
Morant's Essex, ii. 361. Topographer, (London, 1789-91, 8vo.)
iii. 18 supp. Gage's History of Thingoe Hundred, Suffolk, 4.
Blore's Rutland, 16. Poulson's Holderness, i. 370. Dugdale's
Warwickshire, 942. Hoare's Wiltshire. V. i. 45. Yorkshire
Archæological and Topographical Journal, iii. 216.

LEDET. Clutterbuck's Hertford, iii. 58.

LEDGARD. Berry's Sussex Genealogies, 267. Harleian Society,
xxxvii. 356. Howard's Visitation of England and Wales, vi. 84.

LEDSAM. Burke's Landed Gentry, 2, 3, 4, 5.

LEDSTONE. Yorkshire Archæological Society, Record Series, xxx. 344.

LE DUNE. Hoare's Wiltshire, III. iv. 46.

LEDWELL. Oliver's History of Antigua, ii. 171.

LEDYARD. Life and Travels of John Ledyard, by Jared Sparks, 1.
Pedigree of the Family of Sheppard, 18.

LEE. History and Pedigree of the Lee Jortin Family, 1858, 8vo.
Pedigree of Lee, Earls of Lichfield, by F. G. Lee, 1867, single
sheet. Herald and Genealogist, iii. 113, 289, 481. Croke's
History of the Family of Croke, No. 32. Gentleman's Magazine,
lxxxvii. ii. 602. Chronicle of the Family of De Havilland.
Jacob's Peerage, i. 588. Ædes Hartwellianæ, by W. H. Smyth,
96. Jewitt's Reliquary, vii. 25. History of Clyst St. George, by
Rev. H. T. Ellacombe, 66. Sir T. Phillipps' Topographer, No. 1.
(March, 1821, 8vo.) 26. Dwnn's Visitations of Wales, i. 199, 201,
222. Berry's Sussex Genealogies, 340. Berry's Kent Genealogies,
172. Visitation of Durham, 1615, (Sunderland, 1820, fol.) 23.
Surtees Society, xxxvi. 95; liv. 36. Visitation of Oxfordshire,
1574, printed by Sir T. Phillipps, (Middle Hill, fol.) 5. Burke's
Commoners, iii. 314; Landed Gentry, (of Hartwell,) 2 supp., 3, 4,
5, 6, 7, 8; (of Grove Hall,) 3 supp., 4, 5, 6, 7, 8; (of Knares-
borough,) 2, 3, 4, 5, 6; (of Dillington House,) 2, 3, 4, 5, 6, 8; (of
Holborough,) 3, 4, 5, 6; (of Dynas Powis,) 2, 3, 4, 5, 6, 7, 8; (of
Coton Hall,) 3, 4, 5, 6, 7, 8; (of Barna,) 2, 3, 4, 5, 6, 7, 8; (of
Balsdon,) 2, 3, 4; 8 at p. 910. Foster's Yorkshire Pedigrees.
Miscellanea Genealogica et Heraldica, New Series, i. 421; 2nd
Series, i. 101; iv. 183; v. 61, 107, 124. Harleian Society, i. 56;
v., viii. 133; vi. 348; xvii. 55, 57; xviii. 134; xxii. 149; xxviii.
72; xxix. 314-320; xxxvii. 204; xxxviii. 824, 827; xlii. 55.
Chetham Society, lxxxii. 64. Gyll's History of Wraysbury, 23.
Lipscombe's History of the County of Buckingham, ii. 307, 309,
404; iv. 597. Transactions of Shropshire Archæological Society,

ix. 61. Graves' History of Cleveland, 434. Dallaway's Sussex, II. i. 308. Visitation of Derbyshire, 1663-4, (Middle Hill, 1854, fol.) 5. Ord's History of Cleveland, 241. Hunter's Deanery of Doncaster, i. 177. Surtees' Durham, ii. 7 ; iii. 52. Clutterbuck's Hertford, i. 105 ; ii. 453 ; iii. 333. The Genealogist, i. 177 ; iii. 180 ; v. 283, 284 ; New Series, ix. 18, 157, 227 ; x. 71, 229 ; xii. 186 ; xiii. 29, 120, 229 ; xiv. 193. Chauncy's Hertfordshire, 459. Ormerod's Cheshire, i. 630 ; ii. 574. Foley's Records of the English Province, S. J., i. 456. Jordan's History of Enstone, 59. Records of Buckinghamshire, iii. 203, 241. Notes and Queries, 2 S. iii. 388, 476 ; xi. 469 ; xii. 382 ; 5 S. iii. 294. F. G. Lee's History of Thame, 555-564, 635. Banks' Dormant and Extinct Baronage, iii. 487. Edmondson's Baronagium Genealogicum, ii. 149. Wotton's English Baronetage, iii. 149. Betham's Baronetage, ii. 164. Burke's Extinct Baronetcies. Bysshe's Visitation of Essex, edited by J. J. Howard, 57. Foster's Visitations of Durham, 211. New England Register, xxvi. 61 ; xxviii. 394 ; xliv. 103 ; xlvi. 72, 161 ; xlvii. 21. Foster's Visitations of Cumberland and Westmorland, 79. Cyclostyle Pedigrees, by J. J. Green. Phillimore's London and Middlesex Note-Book, 52. Burke's Colonial Gentry, ii. 550. Howard's Visitation of England and Wales, ii. 63. Burke's Family Records, 380. The Visitations of Devon, by J. L. Vivian, 527. The Gresley's of Drakelowe, by F. Madan, 265. *See* DE LA LEE, DE LEE, LEGA.

LEE-NORMAN. Burke's Landed Gentry, 2 supp., 3, 4, 5, 8.

LEE-WARNER. Burke's Royal Families, (London, 1851, 8vo.) i. 117. Burke's Commoners, (of Walsingham Abbey,) iv. 551, Landed Gentry, 2, 3, 4, 5, 6, 7, 8 ; (of Tibberton Court,) Commoners, iv. 551, Landed Gentry, 2, 3, 4, 5, 6, 7, 8.

LEECH. Pedigree of Leech of Loveston, etc., [T. P.] 1860, folio page. Berry's Sussex Genealogies, 7. Burke's Landed Gentry, (of Clooconra,) 4, 5, 6, 7, 8 ; (of Rathkeale,) 3, 4, 5, 6. Harleian Society, viii. 34 ; xviii. 136. The Sheriffs of Montgomeryshire, by W. V. Lloyd, 53. *See* LECHE, SWIFT.

LEEDES, or LEEDS. Cambridgeshire Visitation, edited by Sir T. Phillipps, 20. Surtees Society, xxxvi. 286. Foster's Visitations of Yorkshire, 302. Thoresby's Ducatus Leodiensis, 112, 113. The Genealogist, vi. 265. Gentleman's Magazine, 1829, i. 503. Berry's Hampshire Genealogies, 272. Burke's Royal Families, (London, 1851, 8vo.) i. 144. Metcalfe's Visitations of Suffolk, 150. Harleian Society, xli. 79.

LEEFE. Burke's Colonial Gentry, ii. 831.

LEEK, or LEEKE. Jewitt's Reliquary, vii. 25 ; x. 69. Surtees Society, xxxvi. 258. Burke's Commoners, iii. 506, Landed Gentry, 2, 3, 4, 5, 6, 7, 8. Harleian Society, iv. 15, 101 ; xvii. 58 ; xxxii. 185 ; xxxix. 1035. W. Dickinson's History of Newark, 213. Thoroton's Nottinghamshire, i. 49, 144, 248 ; iii. 24. C. Brown's Annals of Newark-upon-Trent, 73. Notes and Queries, 6 S. ix. 16, 57, 297. The Genealogist, New Series, vii. 228, 230 ; xvii. 188. *See* LEKE.

LEES. Betham's Baronetage, v. 589. Harleian Society, xxxvii. 138, 416. Howard's Visitation of England and Wales, iv. 151. Burke's Landed Gentry, 7, 8.

LEESON. Bridges' Northamptonshire, by Rev. Peter Whalley, i. 128. Baker's Northampton, i. 517. Archdall's Lodge's Peerage, iii. 124. Metcalfe's Visitations of Northamptonshire, 34, 187.

LEESON-MARSHALL. Burke's Landed Gentry, 8.

LEETE, or LETE. The Family of Leete, by C. Bridger and J. Corbet Anderson. London, 1881, 4to. Camden Society, xliii. 67. Metcalfe's Visitations of Suffolk, 150. Cambridgeshire Visitation, edited by Sir T. Phillipps, 20. Harleian Society, xli. 80.

LEEVES. Berry's Sussex Genealogies, 104. Burke's Landed Gentry, 2. Dallaway's Sussex, II. i. 79. Castles, Mansions, and Manors of Western Sussex, by D. G. C. Elwes and C. J. Robinson, 241.

LEFAUN. See SHERIDAN.

LEFEBVRE, or LEFEVRE. Burke's Landed Gentry, 2. J. B. Payne's Armorial of Jersey, 90, 208.

LEFEILD. Metcalfe's Visitations of Northamptonshire, 107.

LE FLEMING. Eyton's Antiquities of Shropshire, x. 302. Burke's Landed Gentry, 5, 6, 7, 8.

LEFROY. Notes and Documents relative to the Family of Loffroy, by a Cadet [J. H. Lefroy]. Woolwich, 1868, fol. Berry's Kent Genealogies, 17. Burke's Landed Gentry, 2, 3, 4, 5, 6, 7, 8. Herald and Genealogist, vi. 125. Burrow's History of the Family of Burrows, 208. Lord Brabourne's Letters of Jane Austen, i. 31. Burke's Colonial Gentry, ii. 646. Ontarian Families, by E. M. Chadwick, ii. 54. Howard's Visitation of Ireland, iii. 13.

LEFTWICH. Ormerod's Cheshire, i. 628; iii. 273. Harleian Society, xviii. 142. The Genealogist, New Series, xiii. 35.

LEGA. Baker's Northampton, ii. 5. See LEGH, LEYE.

LE GAIT. F. G. Lee's History of Thame, 346.

LE GALLAIS. J. B. Payne's Armorial of Jersey, 211.

LEGARD. Surtees Society, xxxvi. 111. Foster's Yorkshire Pedigrees. Wotton's English Baronetage, iii. 210. Betham's Baronetage, ii. 190. Foster's Visitations of Yorkshire, 54. Harleian Society, ii. 19 ; viii. 365 ; xvi. 185. History of Beverley, by G. Poulson, i. 424. Nichols' History of the County of Leicester, iv. 369. Burke's Landed Gentry, 8. Lincolnshire Notes and Queries, ii. 80.

LEGATT. Harleian Society, xiv. 591.

LE GEYT. J. B. Payne's Armorial of Jersey, 213. Notes and Queries, 8 S. x. 451.

LEGG, or LEGGE. Visitation of Sussex, 1570, printed by Sir T. Phillipps, (Middle Hill, fol.) 6. Edmondson's Baronagium Genealogicum, iii. 197. Hasted's Kent, i. 71. Cambridgeshire Visitation, edited by Sir T. Phillipps, 21. Burke's Landed Gentry, 3, 4, 5, 6. Brydges' Collins' Peerage, iv. 105. Hulbert's Annals of Almondbury, 205. Burke's Colonial Gentry, i. 356. Hasted's Kent, (Hund. of Blackheath, by H. H. Drake,) 244. Old Yorkshire, edited by Willm. Smith, New Series, i. 164. Harleian Society, xli. 92.

LEGH, or LEGHE. History of the House of Lyme, (Legh,) by
W. Beamont. Warrington, 1876, 8vo. Burke's Commoners, (of
Lyme,) ii. 686, Landed Gentry, 2, 3, 4, 5, 6 7 ; (of Norbury
Booths,) Commoners, ii. 44, Landed Gentry, 2, 3, 4, 5, 6, 7, 8 ;
(of Adlington,) Commoners, iii. 453, Landed Gentry, 2, 3, 4, 5, 6,
7, 8 ; (of High Legh,) Landed Gentry, 2, 3, 4, 5, 6, 7, 8 ; (of
Ridge,) 2. Foster's Lancashire Pedigrees. Whitaker's History of
Richmondshire, ii. 246. Thoresby's Ducatus Leodiensis, 221.
Baines' History of the Co. of Lancaster, iii. 644 ; Croston's edn.,
iv. 386. Whitaker's History of Whalley, ii. 63. Ormerod's
Cheshire, i. 461, 499, 550; iii. 661, 676, 765. Earwaker's East
Cheshire, ii. 249, 303, 450. Chetham Society, lxxxii. 51 ; lxxxv.
182 ; xcvii. 115 ; xcix. 11 ; cx. 149. Burgon's Life of Sir Thomas
Gresham, i. 467. Harleian Society, xvi. 187. The Genealogist,
New Series, ix. 210 ; xii. 107, 108. Weaver's Visitations of
Somerset, 41. Woodcock of Cuerden, by A. E. P. Gray, 15.
Cheshire Notes and Queries, New Series, ii. 192. Nooks and
Corners of Lancashire and Cheshire, by James Croston, 291. *See*
DE LA LEGH, LEGA, LIGH.

LE GRAND. Burke's Visitation of Seats and Arms, ii. 30. *See*
D'ANNVILLE.

LE GRAUNT. The Genealogist, New Series, xiv. 257.

LE GRICE. Blomefield's Norfolk, v. 334.

LE GROOS, LE GROS, or LE GROSS. Norfolk Archæology, iii. 90.
J. B. Payne's Armorial of Jersey, 215. Blomefield's Norfolk,
xi. 10. Harleian Society, xxxii. 185.

LE GRYS. Dawson Turner's Sepulchral Reminiscences of Great
Yarmouth, 133. Harleian Society, xxxii. 186.

LE HADD. Berry's Kent Genealogies, 217. *See* HADDE.

LE HARDY. J. B. Payne's Armorial of Jersey, 217.

LE HART. Westcote's Devonshire, edited by G. Oliver and P. Jones,
603.

LE HUNT, or LE HUNTE. Glover's History of Derbyshire, ii. 587,
(567). Burke's Royal Families, (London, 1851, 8vo.) ii. 123.
Gentleman's Magazine, 1832, ii. 599. Burke's Commoners, iii. 365,
Landed Gentry, 2, 3, 4, 5, 6, 7, 8. Harleian Society, xiv. 585.
See HUNT.

LEIBURN. Banks' Dormant and Extinct Baronage, i. 359. *See*
LEYBORNE.

LEICESTER. Gregson's Fragments relative to the County of Lan-
caster, 211. Burton's Description of Leicestershire, 153. Wotton's
English Baronetage, iii. 134. Burke's Extinct Baronetcies. *See*
LEYCESTER.

LEICESTER (Earls of). Nichols' History of the County of Leicester,
i. 18, 98, 212, App. 119. Baker's Northampton, i. 350, 563.
Collectanea Archæologica, (Brit. Arch. Assn.) ii. 30. Edmondson's
Baronagium Genealogicum, vi. 22*. Banks' Dormant and Extinct
Baronage, iii. 451. The Genealogist, New Series, x. 1, 131.
Howard's Visitation of England and Wales, viii. 153.

LEIGH. Stoneleigh Abbey, etc., and a catalogue of the confessed and suspected crimes, by a Solicitor, 1848, 12mo. Pedigree of Leigh of Aldestrop, [T. P.] Broadside. Memoir of the Family of Leigh of Addington, by H. S. Sweetman. Torquay, 1887, 8vo. Case of George Leigh, Esq., claiming the Peerage Dignity of Baron Leigh of Stoneley. London, 1826, folio, pp. 16. Appendix to the Case of George Leigh, claiming to be Baron Leigh of Stoneley, 1828, folio, pp. 17. The Leigh Peerage. London, 1832, 8vo., 2 vols. Petition to the House of Lords. London, 1827, 8vo. Minutes of Evidence taken before the Committee of Privileges, Sess. Papers, 117 of 1828; 59 of 1829. A relation of Facts relating to the Stoneleigh Case, by Charles Griffin, attorney, 1850, 18mo. Pedigrees of the Family of Leigh, see Stoneleigh Abbey, by F. L. Colville. Warwick, 1850, 8vo. The Cistercian Abbey of Stoneley, and its Occupants, by Rev. J. M. Gresley. Ashby De La Zouche, 1854, 8vo. Burke's Extinct Baronetcies, and 609. Gentleman's Magazine, 1823, ii. 585 ; 1864, ii. 365 ; 1865, i. 2. Simon's Cases in Chancery, i. 354. Rudder's Gloucestershire, 217. Miscellanea Genealogica et Heraldica, i. 12, 13, 214. Morant's Essex, i. 54, 146, 343. Berry's Sussex Genealogies, 340. Visitation of Cornwall, edited by Sir N. H. Nicholas, 1. Berry's Surrey Genealogies, 101. Berry's Hampshire Genealogies, 122, 294. Tuckett's Devonshire Pedigrees, 17, 33. History of Lambeth, by Thos. Allen, 277. History of Lambeth, by John Tanswell, 40. Visitation of Somerset, printed by Sir T. Phillipps, 113. Burke's Commoners, ii. 599 ; iii. 223 ; (of West Hall, High Leigh,) Commoners, iv. 530, Landed Gentry, 2 and supp., 3, 4, 5, 6, 7, 8 ; (of Leatherlake House,) Commoners, iv. 533, Landed Gentry, 2, 3, 4 ; (of Bardon,) Commoners, iii. 541, Landed Gentry, 2, 3, 4 and supp. ; (of Luton Hoo,) Landed Gentry, 4, 5 and supp., 6 ; (of Belmont,) 2, 3, 4, 5, 6, 7, 8 ; (of Brownsover Hall,) 2, 3, 4, 5, 6, 7, 8 ; (of Ponty Pool,) 2, 3, 4 ; (of Woodchester,) 5, 6, 7, 8 ; (of Rosegarland,) 5, 6, 7, 8 ; (of Hindley Hall,) 6, 7, 8. Foster's Visitations of Yorkshire, 45. Harleian Society, i. 11 ; ii. 173 ; iv. 100 ; vi. 166 ; viii. 137, 397 ; ix. 125 ; xii. 81 ; xiii. 434 ; xvi. 187 ; xvii. 59 ; xviii. 143-156 ; xix. 179 ; xxviii. 219 ; xxix. 321 ; xxxvii. 276 ; xxxix. 1030 ; xliii. 13, 19, 154. Shaw's Staffordshire, i. 158* ; ii. 69. Burke's Royal Families, (London, 1851, 8vo.) i. 38 ; ii. 138. Warwickshire Pedigrees, from Visitation of 1682-3, (privately printed, 1865,) app. Chetham Society, lxxxv. 179-183. Gregson's Fragments relative to the County of Lancaster, 167. Nichols' History of the County of Leicester, iii. 406 ; iv. 577. Manning and Bray's Surrey, ii. 211, 560, 764 ; iii. cxix. 248, 497. Wilson's History of the Parish of St. Laurence Pountney, 232. The Citizens of London and their Rulers, by B. B. Orridge, 187, 189. Ormerod's Cheshire, i. 451, 587. Surrey Archæological Collections, vii. 77 ; xi. Lancashire and Cheshire Historical and Genealogical Notes, reprinted from the 'Leigh Chronicle,' Part ii. 110. The Genealogist, iv. 40 ; New Series, vii. 230. Notes and Queries, 1 S. vii. 619 ; 2 S. v. 215, 266. Edmondson's Baronagium Genealogicum, iv. 388. Visitation of Devon, edited by F. T.

Colby, 150. Betham's Baronetage, iii. 394. Banks' Dormant and
Extinct Baronage, iii. 471. Visitation of Staffordshire, (Willm.
Salt Soc.) 101. The Visitations of Cornwall, edited by J. L.
Vivian, 284. The Visitations of Staffordshire, 1614 and 1663-4,
William Salt Society, 201. Visitation of Gloucester, edited by T. F.
Fenwick and W. C. Metcalfe, 113. Hasted's Kent, (Hund. of
Blackheath, by H. H. Drake,) 250. Willmore's Records of
Rushall, 82. Cyclostyle Pedigrees, by J. J. Green. History of
the old Chapel, Tockholes, by B. Nightingale, 198. Willmore's
History of Walsall, 270. Parliamentary Memoirs of Fermanagh,
by Earl of Belmore, 66. The Visitations of Devon, by J. L. Vivian,
528, 529. The Gresley's of Drakelowe, by F. Madan, 266. *See*
ALEIGH.
LEIGHTON. Botfield's Stemmata Botevilliana, 157-204. Burke's
Commoners, (of Bewsley,) i. 260, Landed Gentry, 2, 3, 4 ; (of
Sweeney Hall,) Landed Gentry, 5 supp., 6, 7, 8. Nichols' History
of the County of Leicester, iii. 1146. History of the Princes of
South Wales, by G. T. O. Bridgeman, 291. The Sheriffs of Mont-
gomeryshire, by W. V. Lloyd, 57, 242, 277. Collections by the
Powys-land Club, viii. 98, 112. Notes and Queries, 2 S. x. 124,
230, 257, 398, 497. Wotton's English Baronetage, iv. 38.
Betham's Baronetage, iii. 95. Harleian Society, xxvii. 73 ; xxix.
322. New England Register, v. 166 ; vi. 255. Transactions of
the Shropshire Archæological Society, ii. 293 ; vi. 388.
LEIR. Burke's Commoners, (of Jaggards House,) iv. 578, Landed
Gentry, 2, 3, 4, 5, 6, 7 ; (of Ditcheat,) Landed Gentry, 5, 6, 7, 8.
Notes and Queries, 6 S. iv. 318.
LEIR-CARLETON. Burke's Landed Gentry, 8.
LEITH. Burke's Landed Gentry, (of Whitehaugh,) 2, 3, 4, 5, 6 ; (of
Freefield,) 5, 6, 7, 8 ; (of Leith Hall,) 5, 6, 7, 8. Burke's Royal
Families, (London, 1851, 8vo.) ii. 90. Douglas's Baronage of
Scotland, 224-232. Inverurie and the Earldom of the Garioch,
by John Davidson, 458. A short Memoir of James Young,
app. 15. Ontarian Families, by E. M. Chadwick, ii. 109. *See*
CUMMING.
LEITH-HAY. Burke's Commoners, ii. 136, Landed Gentry, 2, 3, 4, 5.
LEITH-ROSS. Burke's Landed Gentry, 7.
LEITRIM. Claim of the Earl of Leitrim to Vote at Elections of Irish
Peers, Sess. Papers, 123 of 1857-8. Howard's Visitation of Ire-
land, iii. 54.
LEKE. Thoresby's Ducatus Leodiensis, 245. Banks' Dormant and
Extinct Baronage, iii. 657. Burke's Extinct Baronetcies. *See*
LEAKE, LEEK.
LE KEUX. Miscellanea Genealogica et Heraldica, New Series, iii. 349.
LELAM. Metcalfe's Visitations of Northamptonshire, 187.
LE LOU. Baker's Northampton, ii. 124.
LELY. Burke's Landed Gentry, 5, 6, 7, 8.
LE MAIRE. Harleian Society, i. 93.
LE MAISTRE. J. B. Payne's Armorial of Jersey, 223.
LEMAN. Pedigree of Edward Godfree Leman, by W. H. A. Fitz-

Stathern, broadside, *n.d.* A correct, brief, and interesting Account of the Leman Case, etc., to which is now added the Pedigrees of the Male and Female Descendants of Sir William Leman, Bart., M.P. ; reprinted from the Nottingham Review. Nottingham, 1840, 8vo. Prospectus of the Leman Estate Fund. London, 12mo., pp. 9 and pedigree. T. Faulkner's History of Hammersmith, 183. Burke's Landed Gentry, 3, 4, 5, 6, 7, 8. Suckling's History of Suffolk, ii. 184. Miscellanea Genealogica et Heraldica, i. 280. Clutterbuck's Hertford, ii. 414. The Suffolk Records, by H. W. Aldred, 119. Notes and Queries, 1 S. iv. 58, 111, 299 ; viii. 150, 234. Wotton's English Baronetage, iii. 458. Burke's Extinct Baronetcies. Harleian Society, xvii. 60.

LE MARCHANT. Chronicle of the Family of De Havilland. Burke's Landed Gentry, 5.

LE MARESCHAL. *See* CANNING, MARSHALL.

LEMING, or LEMYNGE. Foster's Visitations of Yorkshire, 543. Harleian Society, xvii. 61. Bysshe's Visitation of Essex, edited by J. J. Howard, 57.

LE MOIGNE. Hoare's Wiltshire, II. i. 36.

LEMON. Chetham Society, lxxxv. 184. Jewitt's Reliquary, xvii. 169. A Complete Parochial History of the County of Cornwall, ii. 69. An Historical Survey of Cornwall, by C. S. Gilbert, i. 572. Betham's Baronetage, iii. 434.

LE MONTAIS. J. B. Payne's Armorial of Jersey, 227.

LE MOYNE. Morant's Essex, ii. 434. Visitations of Devon, by J. L. Vivian, 568. *See* MOYNE.

LEMPRIÈRE. A Monograph of the House of Lemprière, by J. B. Payne. London, 1862, 4to. Burke's Landed Gentry, (of Pelham,) 4, 5, 6 ; (of Rozel Manor,) 5, 6, 7, 8. J. B. Payne's Armorial of Jersey, 229. Family Notes, by J. M. Browne, 57.

LENCH, or LENCHE. Sir T. Phillipps' Topographer, No. 1, (March, 1821, 8vo.) 49. Harleian Society, xxvii. 85.

LENDRUM. Burke's Landed Gentry, 2, 3, 4, 5, 6, 7, 8.

LE NEVE. Berry's Essex Genealogies, 155. Le Neve's Fasti, edited by T. D. Hardy, i. xii. Norfolk Archæology, ii. 396. Harleian Society, xiv. 683 ; xvii. 62. Carthew's Hundred of Launditch, Part iii. 405. *See* NEAVE.

LENGLEYS. The Genealogist, New Series, xiii. 97.

LENHAM. The Genealogist, New Series, xii. 32 ; xiii. 251.

LENIGAN. Burke's Commoners, iii. 700, Landed Gentry, 2, 4, 5, 6. *See* RYAN-LENIGAN.

LENNARD. Morant's Essex, i. 80. Hasted's Kent, i. 108, 111. Topographer and Genealogist, iii. 217. More about Stifford, by William Palin, 13. Burke's Landed Gentry, 6. Harleian Society, xiv. 673. Notes and Queries, 2 S. viii. 430. Edmondson's Baronagium Genealogicum, iv. 357. Banks' Dormant and Extinct Baronage, ii. 136. Burke's Extinct Baronetcies. Hasted's Kent, (Hund. of Blackheath, by H. H. Drake,) xxv.

LENNARTS. Harleian Society, xvii. 61.

LE NOREIS. Ormerod's Miscellanea Palatina, 8. *See* NORRES.

LENOX, or LENNOX. Memorial relative to the succession of the ancient Earls of Levenax. By ... Wedderburn. History of the Partition of the Earldom of Lennox, with a Vindication of the Antiquities of Merchiston and Thirlestane, by Mark Napier. Edinburgh, 1835, 8vo. Additional Remarks upon the Question of the Lennox or Rusky Representation, by John Riddell. 1835, 8vo. The Lennox, by Willm. Fraser. Edinburgh, 1874, 2 vols., 4to. The Lanox of Auld, an Epistolary Review of 'The Lennox, by Willm. Fraser.' By Mark Napier. Edinburgh, 1880, 4to. Case of Margaret Lennox of Woodhead, in relation to the title, etc. of the Earls of Levenax, by Robt. Hamilton. Edinburgh, 1813, 4to. The Great Governing Families of England, ii. 287. Burke's Landed Gentry, 4. Lands and their Owners in Galloway, by P. H. M'Kerlie, iii. 487, 504. History of Dumbartonshire, by Joseph Irving, 42, 115. Nisbet's Heraldry, ii. app., (*Ragman's Roll*,) 6. Edmondson's Baronagium Genealogicum, i. 15. Cartularium Comitatus de Levenax, (Maitland Club,) ix. Wood's Douglas's Peerage of Scotland, ii. 80, 104. Berry's Genealogical Peerage, 108. Brydges' Collins' Peerage, i. 203.

LENTAIGNE. Burke's Landed Gentry, 4, 5, 6, 7, 8. Burke's Royal Descents and Pedigrees of Founders' Kin, 128.

LENTHALL. Berry's Berkshire Genealogies, 60. Visitation of Oxfordshire, 1634, printed by Sir T. Phillipps, (Middle Hill, fol.) 24. Burke's Commoners, i. 178, Landed Gentry, 2, 3, 4, 5, 6, 7, 8. Harleian Society, v. 199, 318; vi. 169; viii. 324; xiii. 434; xvii. 64. Burke's Royal Families, (London, 1851, 8vo.) i. 122. Ashmole's Antiquities of Berkshire, i. 157. Aubrey's Antiquities of Surrey, v. 86. Gentleman's Magazine, N.S. v. 570.

LEONARD. Burke's Landed Gentry, 6 supp., 7, 8. New England Register, v. 101, 403; vii. 71; xxxii. 269. Oliver's History of Antigua, ii. 175.

LEONS. Miscellanea Genealogica et Heraldica, 2nd Series, i. 70.

LE PALMER. Eyton's Antiquities of Shropshire, i. 365.

LE PETIT. Mullyon, its History, etc., by E. G. Harvey, 114. *See* PETIT.

LEPINGTON, or LEPPINGTON. Foster's Visitations of Yorkshire, 544. Burke's Visitation of Seats and Arms, 2nd Series, ii. 56.

LE POER. Bridges' Northamptonshire, by Rev. Peter Whalley, i. 75. Notes and Queries, 3 S. vii. 377, 446. *See* POER.

LE POWER. Berry's Sussex Genealogies, 318. Harleian Society, xxvii. 62. The Genealogist, New Series, xiii. 245; xiv. 18.

LE PROUZ. The Visitations of Cornwall, edited by J. L. Vivian, 94.

LEPTON. Foster's Visitations of Yorkshire, 214.

LE QUESNE. J. B. Payne's Armorial of Jersey, 250.

LERCEDEKNE. Maclean's History of Trigg Minor, iii. 259. The Genealogist, New Series, xv. 215. *See* ARCHDEACON.

LERMITTE. Burke's Landed Gentry, 7, 8.

LE ROUS. The Genealogist, New Series, ix. 211.

LE ROUX. Oliver's History of Antigua, ii. 177.

LERRIER. J. B. Payne's Armorial of Jersey, 252.

LESCHER. Berry's Essex Genealogies, 21. Burke's Landed Gentry, 5, 6, 7. Harleian Society, xiv. 674. Burke's Family Records, 381.

LESLEY, or LESLIE. Historical Records of the Family of Leslie, by Col. Leslie, K.H. Edinburgh, 1869, 8vo., 3 vols. ; another edn., Aberdeen, 1880, 8vo., 3 vols. Pedigree of the Family of Leslie, by Col. C. Leslie. Bakewell, 1861. Laura Lesleiana explicata, sive enumeratio Personorum utriusque sexus cognomine Leslie. Græcii, 1692, fol. Burke's Commoners, (of Ballibay,) iv. 86, Landed Gentry, 3, 4, 5, 6, 7, 8; (of Leslie Hill,) Commoners, iv. 88, Landed Gentry, 2, 3, 4, 5, 6, 7, 8 ; (of Glasslough,) Commoners, iv. 151, Landed Gentry, 2, 3, 4, 5 ; (of Blaquhain,) Landed Gentry, 2 supp., 3, 4, 5, 6, 7, 8; (of Warthill,) 2, 3, 4, 5, 6, 7, 8; (of Kininvie,) 5, 6, 7, 8. Shirley's History of the County of Monaghan, 152, 253. Nisbet's Heraldry, ii. app. 141. Douglas's Baronage of Scotland, 29. Inverurie and the Earldom of the Garioch, by John Davidson, 219, 440. Sir R. Sibbald's History of Fife, 143. Balmerino and its Abbey, by James Campbell, 312, 399. Walter Wood's East Neuk of Fife, 293. Collections for a History of Aberdeen and Banff, (Spalding Club,) i. 359. Lindores Abbey, by Alexr. Laing, 403. Wood's Douglas's Peerage of Scotland, ii. 110, 120, 304, 424. Archdall's Lodge's Peerage, vii. 179. Burke's Extinct Baronetcies, 609. Miscellanea Genealogica et Heraldica, 2nd Series, v. 178. Burke's Family Records, 382, 384.

LE SOMENUR. Morant's Essex, ii. 369.

LE SORE. Genealogies of Morgan and Glamorgan, by G. T. Clark, 432. The Genealogist, New Series, xv. 94.

LESSLY. Oliver's History of Antigua, ii. 178.

L'ESTRANGE, or LE STRANGE. Case of Henry Le Strange Styleman Le Strange on his claim to the Barony of Hastings, 1840, folio, pp. 47. Camden Society, v. xi. Blomefield's Norfolk, x. 314. J. Wilkinson's History of Broughton Gifford, folding plate. Transactions of the London and Middlesex Archæological Society, i. 125. Visitation of Norfolk, published by Norfolk Archæological Society, i. 61, 443. Visitation of Suffolk, edited by J. J. Howard, ii. 277. Burke's Commoners, iv. 640, Landed Gentry, 2, 6, 7, 8. Carthew's Hundred of Launditch, Part i. 142, 147, 217 ; Part ii. 446. Burke's Royal Families, (London, 1851, 8vo.) ii. 184. Eyton's Antiquities of Shropshire, iii. 142 ; x. 262. Dugdale's Warwickshire, 577. Wiltshire Archæological Magazine, v. 267. Ormerod's Cheshire, i. 528. Reliquiæ Spelmannianæ, (Oxford, 1698,) 200. Wotton's English Baronetage, ii. 144. Banks' Baronies in Fee, i. 419. Burke's Extinct Baronetcies. Howard's Visitation of Ireland, iii. 44. The Genealogist, New Series, xv. 27 ; xvii. 111. Camoy's Peerage Evidence, 175. Transactions of Shropshire Archæological Society, N.S. ii. 201. See STRANGE, STYLEMAN-LE STRANGE.

LE TAILLOUR. Maclean's History of Trigg Minor, i. 311.

LE TALL. History of Woodhouse, by W. J. Le Tall, 20.

LE TAYLOR. Harleian Society, i. 23. See TAYLOR.

LETE. See LEETE.

LETHBRIDGE. Royal Descents of Sir J. H. Lethbridge, Bart., London, 1871, 4to. Burke's Royal Families, (London, 1851, 8vo.) ii. 106. Betham's Baronetage, v. 583*. Burke's Colonial Gentry, i. 275. Burke's Landed Gentry, (of Sherfield Manor,) 8 ; (of Tregeare,) 8.

LETHIEULLIER. Morant's Essex, i. 27. Hasted's Kent, i. 87, 238. Berry's Kent Genealogies, 358. Harleian Society, viii. 294 ; xvii. 64. Hasted's Kent, (Hund. of Blackheath, by H. H. Drake,) 253. Annals of the Barber Surgeons, by S. Young, 556.

LETTICE. Pedigree of Lettice of Polton, Co. Bedford, etc., [T. P.] 1857. Broadside.

LETTIN. The Genealogist, v. 20.

LE VEEL. Banks' Baronies in Fee, ii. 150. The Genealogist, New Series, vii. 244 ; viii. 246.

LEVELIS. Harleian Society, ix. 126. The Visitations of Cornwall, edited by J. L. Vivian, 286.

LEVENS. Visitation of Westmorland, 1615, (London, 1853,) 24. Foster's Visitations of Cumberland and Westmorland, 80. The Genealogist, New Series, xv. 244.

LEVENTHORPE. Cussan's History of Hertfordshire, Parts iii. and iv. 148. Gentleman's Magazine, 1840, i. 142. Morant's Essex, ii. 617. Clutterbuck's Hertford, iii. 333. Wright's Essex, ii. 202. Chauncy's Hertfordshire, 182. Harleian Society, xiv. 593 ; xxii. 149. Burke's Extinct Baronetcies.

LEVER. Appellant's and Respondent's cases in Lever v. Andrews, in House of Lords. Chetham Society, lxxxi. 9 ; lxxxv. 185. Baines' History of the Co. of Lancaster, ii. 566 ; Croston's edn., ii. 352. Harleian Society, xxxvii. 103. Burke's Landed Gentry, 7 at p. 746, 8 at p. 780. See LEAVER.

LEVERETT. New England Register, iv. 121 ; xii. 289.

LEVERICK. Planché's Corner of Kent, 375.

LEVERMORE. Tuckett's Devonshire Pedigrees, 24. Harleian Society, vi. 168. Westcote's Devonshire, edited by G. Oliver and P. Jones, 597. Visitations of Devon, by J. L. Vivian, 530.

LEVERSAGE. Ormerod's Cheshire, iii. 121. Harleian Society, xviii. 156. Earwaker's History of Sandbach, 102.

LEVERSEDGE. Berry's Kent Genealogies, 455. Visitation of Somerset, printed by Sir T. Phillipps, 113. Harleian Society, xi. 67.

LEVESEY. Hasted's Kent, ii. 649. Berry's Kent Genealogies, 197. Chetham Society, lxxxii. 105. Harleian Society, xlii. 102 ; xliii. 36. See LIVESAY.

LEVESON. Morant's Essex, ii. 124, 480. Harleian Society, i. 18. Shaw's Staffordshire, ii. 169. Visitation of Staffordshire, 1663-4, printed by Sir T. Phillipps, 7. Visitation of Staffordshire, (Willm. Salt Soc.) 106. Visitations of Staffordshire, 1614 and 1663-4, William Salt Society, 202. The Genealogist, New Series, xviii. 25. Transactions of Shropshire Archæological Society, ix. 55.

LEVESON-GOWER. The Seize Quartiers of G. G. Leveson-Gower, 2nd Earl Granville, folio sheet. The Great Governing Families of England, i. 266. Burke's Heraldic Illustrations, 6. Baker's

Northampton, i. 564. Howard's Visitation of England and Wales, i. 21. Burke's Landed Gentry, 8.

LEVETT, or LEVITT. Berry's Sussex Genealogies, 229, 373. Dallaway's Sussex, II. i. 309. Burke's Landed Gentry, (of Milford Hall,) 2, 3, 4, 5, 6, 7, 8; (of Wichnor Park,) 2, 3, 4, 5, 6, 7, 8. Foster's Visitations of Yorkshire, 544. Harleian Society, viii. 437. Hunter's Deanery of Doncaster, i. 365. Miscellanea Genealogica et Heraldica, 2nd Series, ii. 354; 3rd Series, i. 5, 116. The Gresley's of Drakelowe, by F. Madan, 268.

LEVETT-PRINSEP. R. Ussher's Historical Sketch of Croxall, 11. Burke's Landed Gentry, 8.

LEVIEN. Burke's Colonial Gentry, ii. 754.

LEVINGE. History of the Levinge Family, by Sir R. Levinge, 1813, 4to. Jottings for early history of the Levinge family, by Sir R. G. A. Levinge, Bart. Dublin, 1873, 4to. Jewitt's Reliquary, v. 245; ix. 177. History of the Parish of Leek, by John Sleigh, 108. Visitation of Warwickshire, 1619, published with Warwickshire Antiquarian Magazine, 154. Nichols' History of the County of Leicester, iv. 952. Harleian Society, xii. 321. The Genealogist, New Series, vii. 231. *See* BATEMAN.

LEVINGSTOUN. Surtees Society, xxxvi. 72.

LEVINGTON. Nicolson and Burn's Westmorland and Cumberland, ii. 461.

LEVINS, LEVYNS, or LEVINZ. Sir T. Phillipps' Topographer, No. 1, (March, 1821, 8vo.) 21. Harleian Society, v. 134; viii. 328. Oxford Historical Society, xxvi. 416. Surtees Society, xxxvi. 330. Burke's Commoners, iv. 489. Visitation of Oxfordshire, 1574, printed by Sir T. Phillipps, (Middle Hill, fol.) 6. Notes and Queries, 2 S. iii. 515. Metcalfe's Visitations of Northamptonshire, 108.

LE WARRE. Visitation of Somersetshire, printed by Sir T. Phillipps, 144, 151. Nichols' History of the County of Leicester, ii. 211. *See* WARRE.

LEWES. Visitation of Somerset, printed by Sir T. Phillipps, 114. Burke's Landed Gentry, 5, 6, 7, 8. Harleian Society, xi. 68. Caermarthenshire Pedigrees, 20, 29, 41, 42, 44, 71. Cardiganshire Pedigrees, 80, 87, 91, 93, 99, 100, 101. Meyrick's History of the Co. of Cardigan, 125, 164, 184, 229, 395. T. Nicholas' County Families of Wales, 293.

LEWEN, LEWIN, or LEWINS. Hasted's Kent, ii. 501. Hutchins' Dorset, iii. 246. Manning and Bray's Surrey, i. 470. Berry's Kent Genealogies, 212. Burke's Landed Gentry, (of the Hollies,) 4, 5, 6, 7, 8; (of Cloghans,) 2, 3, 4, 5, 6, 7, 8; (of Womaston,) 2, 3, 4. Miscellanea Genealogica et Heraldica, New Series, ii. 527. Harleian Society, xvi. 188; xxii. 115; xxxviii. 723; xlii. 103. Poulson's Holderness, i. 478. Foster's Visitations of Northumberland, 78. Historical Notices of Doncaster, by C. W. Hatfield, 2nd Series, 16. Burke's Colonial Gentry, i. 273.

LEWESTON. The Genealogist, New Series, iii. 96.

LEWGAR. Harleian Society, xxxii. 188.

LEWIS. Memoir of W. M. Peyton, by J. L. Peyton, (London, 1872,
8vo.) 375. Appendix to Case of Sir J. S. Sidney, claiming to be
Lord Lisle. Kent's British Banner Displayed, 298. Gentleman's
Magazine, 1833, i. 125. Dwnn's Visitations of Wales, i. 54, 151,
195, 254, 265, 302; ii. 24, 197-200, 223, 325. Glamorganshire
Pedigrees, edited by Sir T. Phillipps, 8, 14, 28, 29, 34, 67. Burke's
Commoners, (of Harpton Court,) i. 335, Landed Gentry, 2; (of
Greenmeadow,) Commoners, iii. 386, Landed Gentry, 2, 3, 4, 5, 6;
(of St. Pierre,) Commoners, i. 221, Landed Gentry, 2, 3, 4, 5, 6,
7, 8; (of Seatown,) Landed Gentry, 3, 4, 5, 6; (of Kilcullen,) 3,
4, 5; (of Henllys,) 2, 3, 4, 5, 6, 7, 8; (of Gwinfe,) 2 supp., 3, 4,
5, 6, 7; (of Stradey,) 2 supp., 3, 4, 5, 6, 7, 8; (of Henllan,) 2
supp., 3, 4, 5, 6, 7, 8; (of Gilfach,) 2, 3, 4, 8; (of Ballinagar,)
6, 8; 2 supp., p. 256; 6 p. 824; 2 p. 931; 7; 8 at p. 1007; (of
Inniskeen,) 7, 8; (of Plas-Drew,) 8. Foster's Visitations of Yorkshire, 545. Topographer, (London, 1789-91, 8vo.) ii. 245.
Burke's Royal Descents and Pedigrees of Founders' Kin, 53.
Hampshire Visitations, printed by Sir T. Phillipps, 17. Jones'
History of the County of Brecknock, ii. 478, 524. Burke's Royal
Families, (London, 1851, 8vo.) i. 43. Hunter's Deanery of Doncaster, i. 361. Meyrick's History of the County of Cardigan, 159,
192, 287. Archæologia Cambrensis, 3 S. vii. 20. T. Nicholas'
County Families of Wales, 634, 904. Memoir of Gabriel Goodman, by R. Newcome, app., S. The Sheriffs of Montgomeryshire, by W. V. Lloyd, 250. Collections by the Powys-land Club,
vii. 48. Notes and Queries, 1 S. viii. 388, 521; ix. 86; 2 S. x.
396. Burke's Extinct Baronetcies. Harleian Society, xvii. 63;
xxix. 325. History of Powys Fadog, by J. Y. W. Lloyd, v. 353.
The Topographer, (1790,) ii. 245. Genealogies of Morgan and
Glamorgan, by G. T. Clark, 34, 38-58, 61, 76, 330, 492. New England Register, viii. 47; x. 97; xvii. 162. Cambrian Journal, Vol.
for 1862(4), 274. Ontarian Families, by E. M. Chadwick, i. 140.
LEWIS AB OWEN. Dwnn's Visitations of Wales, ii. 207; ap Henry,
ii. 33, 56; ap Jenkin Vychan, ii. 271.
LEWKENOR, LEWKNORE, or LEWKNOR. Camoys Peerage Evidence,
451. Visitation of Suffolk, edited by J. J. Howard, ii. 261, 320.
Berry's Sussex Genealogies, 130, 343. Sketch of Bodyam Castle
in Sussex, by William Cotton, 11. Sussex Archæological Collections, iii. 89-102. Additional Case of T. Stonor, claiming the
Barony of Camoys, on folding table. Harleian Society, viii. 16;
xxvii. 86. Visitation of Sussex, 1570, printed by Sir T. Phillipps,
(Middle Hill, fol.) 7. Dallaway's Sussex, i. 167, 218; II. i. 50.
Scott of Scott's-Hall, by J. R. Scott, 141. Castles, Mansions, and
Manors of Western Sussex, by D. G. C. Elwes and C. J. Robin-
son, 103. Page's History of Suffolk, 870. Baker's Northampton,
i. 508. Bridge's Northamptonshire, by Rev. Peter Whalley, ii.
102. The Genealogist, New Series, xiv. 253.
LEWSTON. Nash's Worcestershire, ii. 3. Hutchins' Dorset, iv. 129.
LEWTHWAITE. Burke's Commoners, iv. 98, Landed Gentry, 2, 3, 4, 8.
Jefferson's History of Allerdale Ward, Cumberland, 440.

LEWYS. Dwnn's Visitations of Wales, i. 39 ; ii. 30, 39. Thoresby's Ducatus Leodiensis, 243. Hutchins' Dorset, iii. 684. Burke's Extinct Baronetcies. History of Powys Fadog, by J. Y. W. Lloyd, ii. 382, 383 ; iii. 187, 188 ; iv. 369 ; v. 281.

LEWYS AP HUW. Dwnn's Visitations of Wales, i. 16 ; ap Richard, i. 120 ; ap Thomas, i. 35 ; ii. 60.

LEXINGTON. Baker's Northampton, i. 470. Banks' Dormant and Extinct Baronage, i. 114.

LEY. Harleian Society, ix. 127, 129. Hoare's Wiltshire, IV. i. 110. An Account of the Families of Boase, (Exeter, 1876, 4to.), 29. The Western Antiquary, iv. 175. Banks' Dormant and Extinct Baronage, iii. 476. Burke's Extinct Baronetcies. The Visitations of Cornwall, edited by J. L. Vivian, 288. Burke's Landed Gentry, 7, 8. See LEYE.

LEYBORNE, LEYBOURN, or LEYBURNE. Croke's History of the Family of Croke, No. 20. Foster's Visitations of Yorkshire, 44. Eyton's Antiquities of Shropshire, x. 220. Duchetiana, by Sir G. F. Duckett, 2nd edn., 187. Harleian Society, xvi. 189 ; xvii. 65. The Genealogist, New Series, viii. 36. Foster's Visitations of Cumberland and Westmorland, 81, 82. Notes and Queries, 7 S. xii. 133, 352, 398. Berks Archæological and Architectural Society's Journal, i. 126. Nicholson and Burn's Westmorland and Cumberland, i. 144. See DE LEYBURN, LEIBURN.

LEYCESTER. Burke's Commoners, (of Toft,) i. 73, Landed Gentry, 2, 3, 4, 5, 6, 7, 8 ; (of White Place,) Landed Gentry, 2, 3, 4, 5, 6, 7, 8. Baker's Northampton, i. 426. Ormerod's Cheshire, i. 503, 618 ; iii. 358. Betham's Baronetage, ii. 151. Harleian Society, xviii. 138. See LEICESTER.

LEYDON. O'Hart's Irish Pedigrees, 2nd Series, 119.

LEYE. Bridges' Northamptonshire, by Rev. Peter Whalley, i. 224. See LEGA.

LEYGH. The Genealogist, New Series, ix. 146.

LEYLAND. Chetham Society, lxxxi. 131 ; xcviii. 88 ; xcii. 196. Foster's Lancashire Pedigrees. Abram's History of Blackburn, 399. Burke's Landed Gentry, 8.

LEYNHAM. Harleian Society, xiii. 34.

LIBAERT. Oliver's History of Antigua, ii. 181.

LIBBE. Visitation of Oxfordshire, 1634, printed by Sir T. Phillipps, (Middle Hill, fol.) 24. See LYBBE.

LIDBETTER. Memoir of Richard Haines, by C. R. Haines.

LIDCOTT. Metcalfe's Visitations of Northamptonshire, 109.

LIDDEL, or LIDDELL. Visitation of Durham, 1615, (Sunderland, 1820, fol. 11. Hutchinson's History of Durham, ii. 417. Surtees' Durham, ii. 212, 245. Notes and Queries, 3 S. xi. 276, 404. Edmondson's Baronagium Genealogicum, v. 444. Wotton's English Baronetage, ii. 371. Betham's Baronetage, i. 504. Banks' Dormant and Extinct Baronage, iii. 618. Foster's Visitations of Durham, 213.

LIDDON. Genealogies of Morgan and Glamorgan, by G. T. Clark, 418.

LIDSEY. Harleian Society, xvii. 66.
LIDWILL. Burke's Landed Gentry, 5, 6, 8.
LIFFORD. Claim of the Rt. Hon. James Visct. Lifford to vote at Elections of Irish Peers, Sess. Papers, P of 1855.
LIGH. Harleian Society, xviii. 17. *See* LEGH, LEIGH.
LIGHT. Sir T. Phillipps' Topographer, No. 1, (March, 1821, 8vo.) 27. Harleian Society, v. 141. Visitation of Wiltshire, edited by G. W. Marshall, 28. New England Register, xlvii. 271. *See* LYGHT.
LIGHTBOWNE. History of the Ancient Chapel of Blackley, by Rev. J. Booker, 172, 174. Chetham Society, lxxxv. 187. Harleian Society, xxxvii. 192.
LIGHTFOOT. Oliver's History of Antigua, ii. 181.
LIGHTON. Duncumb's Hereford, (J. H. Cooke,) iii. 243.
LIGHTOWLER. Fishwick's History of Rochdale, 437.
LIGON. Fosbrooke's Abstracts of Smith's Lives of the Berkeleys, 170. *See* LYGON.
LIGONIER. Edmondson's Baronagium Genealogicum, iv. 313. Banks' Dormant and Extinct Baronage, iii. 477. Miscellanea Genealogica et Heraldica, New Series, iv. 219.
LIHON. Chronicle of the Family of De Havilland.
LILBURN, or LILBURNE. Visitation of Durham, 1615, (Sunderland, 1820, fol.) 31. Hutchinson's History of Durham, iii. 342. Foster's Visitations of Durham, 215. Foster's Visitations of Northumberland, 79.
LILE. Harleian Society, viii. 198. *See* LYLE.
LILLINGSTON. Burke's Commoners, i. 186, Landed Gentry, 7, 8. Burke's Royal Families, (London, 1851, 8vo.) ii. 98. Howard's Visitation of England and Wales, ix. 33.
LILLY, or LILY. Harleian Society, xvii. 67 ; xxvii. 87 ; xxxix. 996. Burke's Colonial Gentry, i. 92. Genealogical Memoranda Relating to the Family of Parker, by E. M. S. Parker, 37, 40.
LIMERICK. Burke's Royal Families, (London, 1851, 8vo.) ii. 45.
LIMESI. Munford's Analysis of Domesday Book of Co. Norfolk, 42. Bridges' Northamptonshire, by Rev. Peter Whalley, ii. 434. Dugdale's Warwickshire, 343. Clutterbuck's Hertford, iii. 119. Chauncy's Hertfordshire, 257. Banks' Dormant and Extinct Baronage, i. 115. *See* DE LIMESI.
LIMSEY. Nichols' History of the County of Leicester, iv. 636. *See* LYMSEY.
LINACRE. Jewitt's Reliquary, ix. 29. Harleian Society, xxxix. 837. Visitations of Staffordshire, 1614 and 1663-4, William Salt Society, 203.
LINBREY. Berry's Hampshire Genealogies, 68.
LINCOLN (Earldom of).. Topographer and Genealogist, i. 9-28. Collectanea Topographica et Genealogica, viii. 166. Nichols' History of the County of Leicester, i. App. 33. Banks' Dormant and Extinct Baronage, i. 116 ; iii. 479. The Genealogist, New Series, vi. 129 ; viii. 1, 81. New England Register, xix. 357 ; xli. 153.
LIND, or LINDE. Genealogy of the Family of Lind, by Sir Robert

Douglas, Bart. Windsor, 1795, 8vo. Visitation of Somerset, printed by Sir T. Phillipps, 112. Burke's Royal Families, (London, 1851, 8vo.) i. 80. Burke's Landed Gentry, 2 supp., 3, 4. Weaver's Visitations of Somerset, 42.

LINDALL. New England Register, vii. 15.

LINDESAY. Burke's Landed Gentry, (of Loughry,) 2, 3, 4, 5, 6, 7, 8; (of Cahoo,) 3, 4. *See* LINDSAY.

LINDLEY. Surtees Society, xxxvi. 279. W. Paver's Pedigrees of Families of the City of York, 15. Foster's Visitations of York-shire, 545, 547. Thoresby's Ducatus Leodiensis, 82. Harleian Society, xxxix. 1060. The Genealogist, New Series, xiv. 228. *See* LYNDLEY.

LINDOE. Burke's Heraldic Illustrations, 55.

LINDOW. Burke's Landed Gentry, 4, 5, 6, 7, 8.

LINDSAY. Claim of the Earl of Lindsay to be Earl of Oxford, Sess. Papers, May—Dec. 1660. Claim of Sir John Trotter Bethune to be Lord Lindsay, Sess. Papers, D. of 1877. Burke's Landed Gentry, 2, 3. Harleian Society, iv. 75. Douglas's Baronage of Scotland, 257-262. Burke's Extinct Baronetcies, 629. Walter Wood's East Neuk of Fife, 284, 288, 306. Wood's Douglas's Peerage of Scotland, i. 163, 371-395; ii. 517. Banks' Dormant and Extinct Baronage, i. 108, 118. The Scottish Journal, i. 283. Howard's Visitation of England and Wales, iv. 104. Croston's edn. of Baines's Lancaster, iv. 296. The Genealogist, New Series, xii. 1; xiii. 19. History of Liddesdale, by R. B. Armstrong, 166. *See* CRAWFURD, LINDESAY.

LINDSAY-CARNEGIE. Burke's Landed Gentry, 3, 4, 5, 6, 7, 8.

LINDSELL. Burke's Landed Gentry, 5, 6, and supp., 7, 8.

LINDSEY. Burke's Landed Gentry, 2, 3, 4, 5, 6, 7, 8. Burke's Royal Families, (London, 1851, 8vo.) i. 166, Oliver's History of Antigua, ii. 184. *See* LYNDSEY.

LINDSEY-BUCKNALL. Burke's Landed Gentry, 2, 3, 4, 5, 6, 7.

LINE. Visitation of Sussex, 1570, printed by Sir T. Phillipps, (Middle Hill, fol.) 7. *See* LYNE.

LINFORD. Harleian Society, xviii. 157. *See* LYNFORD.

LINGARD. Visitation of Warwickshire, 1619, published with War-wickshire Antiquarian Magazine, 108. Harleian Society, xii. 347.

LINGEN. Pedigree of Lingen of Radbroke, Co. Glouc. [T. P.] 1856. Pedigree of Lingen of Sutton, Co. Hereford, [T. P.] 1867. Broad-side. Burke's Commoners, iv. 266, Landed Gentry, 2, 3, 4, 5, 6, 7, 8; 2 p. 1454; 7 at p. 262; 6 at p. 235; 8 at p. 261. Duncumb's History of the Co. of Hereford. ii. 184. The Manor of Marden, by Thomas, Earl Coningsby, 1722, folio. Robinson's Mansions of Herefordshire, 179. History of the Princes of South Wales, by G. T. O. Bridgeman, 293. The Genealogist, v. 137. Harleian Society, xxvii. 88; xxix. 327. Visitation of Gloucester, edited by T. F. Fenwick and W. C. Metcalfe, 116. Archæological Journal, xxxiv. 373.

LINGHOKE. Visitation of Norfolk, published by Norfolk Archæo-logical Society, i. 48.

LINGWOOD. Morant's Essex, ii. 391. *See* LYNGWOOD.
LINLEY. Foster's Visitations of Yorkshire, 546. Graves' History of
Cleveland, 173. Thoroton's Nottinghamshire, ii. 302.
LINSEY. Harleian Society, xxxii. 193.
LIONS. Miscellanea Genealogica et Heraldica, 2nd Series, i. 70.
LIPPINCOTT. Harleian Society, vi. 348. Westcote's Devonshire,
edited by G. Oliver and P. Jones, 554. Betham's Baronetage,
iv. 47. Burke's Extinct Baronetcies. Visitations of Devon, by
J. L. Vivian, 531. *See* LUPINGCOTT.
LIPPIT. New England Register, xxvii. 70.
LISLE. Case of the Barony of Lisle. 1790, folio. Report of Proceed-
ings on the Claim to the Barony of Lisle, by N. H. Nicholas.
London, 1829, 8vo. Berry's Hampshire Genealogies, 173-176.
Visitation of Somerset, printed by Sir T. Phillipps, 114. Blomefield's Norfolk, ii. 243. Pedigrees from Visitation of Northumber-
land, printed by Sir T. Phillipps, (Middle Hill, 1858, fol.) 1.
Burke's Landed Gentry, 4, 5, 6. Harleian Society, xi. 69 ; xvii.
68. Hodgson's Northumberland, I. ii. 174. Whitaker's Loidis
and Elmete, 166. Dugdale's Warwickshire, 938. Hutchins'
Dorset, ii. 195. Hoare's Wiltshire, IV. ii. 122. Baker's Northampton, i. 443, 612, 619, 706. The Genealogist, i. 383 ; v. 186 ;
vi. 12 ; vii. 267. Notes and Queries, 3 S. ii. 118, 170. Banks'
Baronies in Fee, i. 281-292. Banks' Dormant and Extinct
Baronage, i. 360 ; ii. 302. Metcalfe's Visitations of Northampton-
shire, 109. Genealogical Gleanings in England, by H. F. Waters,
i. 91. Foster's Visitations of Northumberland, 80. New England
Register, xxxix. 63. Oliver's History of Antigua, ii. 189. The
Genealogist, New Series, xiv. 257 ; xv. 29, 152. *See* DE INSULA,
DE LISLE.
LISLEY. Berry's Hampshire Genealogies, 193, 271. Hampshire
Visitations, printed by Sir T. Phillipps, 14. Harleian Society,
xii. 383. *See* LYSLEY.
LISTER. Chetham Society, xiv. viii. Berry's Hampshire Genealogies,
240. Surtees Society, xxxvi. 128, 246, 316. Burke's Commoners,
(of Armitage Park,) i. 219 ; (of Burwell Park,) Landed Gentry, 2,
3, 4, 5, 6, 7, 8 ; (of Shibden Hall,) 4, 5, 6, 7, 8 ; (of Ousefleet
Grange,) 2, 3, 4 ; (of Hirst Priory,) 5, 6, 7. Foster's Yorkshire
Pedigrees. Foster's Visitations of Yorkshire, 290, 546-548.
History of Bradford, by John James, 440. Burke's Royal Descents
and Pedigrees of Founders' Kin, 99. Hampshire Visitations,
printed by Sir T. Phillipps, 21. Thoresby's Ducatus Leodiensis,
120. Whitaker's Deanery of Craven, 35, 95, (55, 122). Nichols'
History of the County of Leicester, ii. 376. Hunter's Deanery
of Doncaster, i. 72. Surtees' Durham, i. 110. Harleian Society,
xiii. 70, 233 ; xxix. 328 ; xxxviii. 514, 518 ; xl. 1255, 1256.
John Watson's History of Halifax, 254. Brydges' Collins' Peerage,
viii. 584. Some Old Families, by H. B. McCall, 79. The Genealogist, New Series, vii. 232 ; xvii. 252. *See* LYSTER.
LISTER-KAYE. Foster's Yorkshire Pedigrees. Burke's Landed
Gentry, 6.

LISTOWEL. Claim of Willm., Earl of Listowel, to Vote at Elections of Irish Peers, Sess. Papers, F. of 1856.

LITCHFIELD. New England Register, ix. 181, 209.

LITLE, LITTEL, or LITTLE. Morant's Essex, ii. 257, 315. Burke's Landed Gentry, (of Llanvain Grange,) 2, 3, 4, 5, 6, 7, 8 ; (of Stewartstown,) 8 ; (of Pitchcombe,) 8. Poulson's Holderness, ii. 523. Harleian Society, xiii. 435. Bysshe's Visitation of Essex, edited by J. J. Howard, 58. Howard's Visitation of England and Wales, v. 84.

LITTCOTE. Sir T. Phillipps' Topographer, No. 1, (March, 1821, 8vo.) 16. See LYTCOTT.

LITTLEBOY. History of the Wilmer Family, 255.

LITTLEBOYS. Berry's Sussex Genealogies, 166.

LITTLEBURY. The Genealogist, iv. 189 ; vi. 266. Miscellanea Genealogica et Heraldica, 2nd Series, ii. 74.

LITTLEDALE. Burke's Landed Gentry, 2, 3, 4, 5, 8. Howard's Visitation of England and Wales, i. 238 ; Notes, iii. 74 ; Burke's Family Records, 385.

LITTLE-GILMOUR. Burke's Landed Gentry, 5, 6, 7.

LITTLEHALES. Betham's Baronetage, v. app. 42.

LITTLER, or LITLER. The Genealogist, iv. 192. Burke's Landed Gentry, 2. Ormerod's Cheshire, ii. 141.

LITTLETON. Morant's Essex, i. 103. Clifford's Description of Tixall, 140. Gentleman's Magazine, lxxi. 511. Burke's Commoners, i. 389. Harleian Society, viii. 153 ; xxvii. 9, 89, 92. Norfolk Archæology, iv. 19. Wotton's English Baronetage, ii. 59. Betham's Baronetage, i. 306. Banks' Dormant and Extinct Baronage, iii. 490. Notes and Queries, 5 S. ii. 450. Burke's Extinct Baronetcies. Visitation of Staffordshire, (Willm. Salt Soc.) 108. The Visitations of Cornwall, edited by J. L. Vivian, 292. Journal of ex-Libris Society, iv. 63. New England Register, xli. 364. The Visitations of Devon, by J. L. Vivian, 778. The Genealogist, New Series, xv. 100. Transactions of Shropshire Archæological Society, xi. 85. See LYTELTON.

LITTLEWOOD. Burke's Landed Gentry, 5 supp., 6, 7, 8. Genealogy of Henzey, Tyttery, and Tyzack, by H. S. Grazebrook, 66.

LITTON. Surrey Archæological Collections, ii. Burke's Landed Gentry, 4, 5, 6, supp., 7, 8. Foster's Visitations of Yorkshire, 549. Harleian Society, xxii. 73, 115, 151 ; xliii. 117. Burke's Colonial Gentry, ii. 614. See LYTTON.

LIVESAY, or LIVESEY. Chetham Society, lxxxv. 188, 189. Abram's History of Blackburn, 400, 483, 566, 624, 640. Burke's Landed Gentry, 5, 6, 7. Burke's Extinct Baronetcies. Harvey's Hundred of Willey, 431. Croston's edn. of Baines's Lancaster, iv. 36. See LEVESEY.

LIVINGSTONE. Notice Généalogique de famille des Livingstones. Par Monsr. le Maistre Tonnerre, 1856, 8vo. Burke's Landed Gentry, 4, 5, 6, 7, 8. Wood's Douglas's Peerage of Scotland, i. 304 ; ii. 37, 122, 308, 589. Burke's Extinct Baronetcies, 630. The Livingstons of Callendar, by E. B. Livingston. 1887, 4to.

Northern Notes and Queries, iii. 75; iv. 181; v. 12. Oliver's History of Antigua, ii. 190.

LIVIUS. Burke's Landed Gentry, 2 supp.

LIZARS. Ontarian Families, by E. M. Chadwick, ii. 136.

LIZURES. Baker's Northampton, i. 9. Banks' Dormant and Extinct Baronage, i. 118. See DE LIZOURS.

LLAN DYBIE. Dwnn's Visitations of Wales, i. 26.

LLANGURIG. History of Llangurig, by E. Hamer and H. W. Lloyd, 84.

LLAN UFYDD. Dwnn's Visitations of Wales, i. 26.

LLEISAN. Genealogies of Morgan and Glamorgan, by G. T. Clark, 79, 96. See LYSON.

LLEWELLEN. Glamorganshire Pedigrees, edited by Sir T. Phillipps, 45.

LLEWELLIN. Burke's Landed Gentry, (of Tregwynt and Eynant,) 2, 3, 4, 5, 6; (of Hendrescythan,) 5. Notes and Queries, 3 S. i. 28.

LLEWELLYN, or LLEWELYN. Glamorganshire Pedigrees, edited by Sir T. Phillipps, 15, 16, 18. Burke's Landed Gentry, 5, 6, 7, 8. Genealogies of Morgan and Glamorgan, by G. T. Clark, 105, 110. Howard's Visitation of England and Wales, vi. 153. See PURCELL LLEWELLYN.

LLOWDON. Harleian Society, xxviii. 84.

LLOYD. Pedigree of the Lloyds of Dolobran, by Mrs. R. H. Lloyd. Kingston-on-Thames, 1877, 8vo. Lloyd's Farm and its Inhabitants, by R. J. Lowe. London, 1883, 4to. Pedigree of T. D. Lloyd, Esq., of Bronwydd, Co. Cardigan, [T. P.] 1861. Broadside. Pedigree of Lloyd of Cwm Gloyne, Co. Pembroke, [T. P.] 1862, folio page. Rudder's Gloucestershire, 814. Berry's Hertfordshire Genealogies, 27. Dwnn's Visitations of Wales, i. 15-17, 25, 29, 30, 36-38, 40, 41, 49-54, 57, 64, 79, 85, 97, 105, 109, 112, 134, 140, 141, 143-145, 147-149, 166-168, 187, 188, 206, 207, 215, 216, 222, 223, 227, 228, 234, 238, 239, 242, 245-247, 254, 260, 275, 276, 280, 288, 289, 300-302, 311, 317, 322, 323, 328; ii. 25, 30, 31, 33, 34, 36, 38, 47, 53, 74, 80, 95, 99, 112, 141, 142, 185, 197, 198, 214, 225, 226, 232, 233, 238, 239, 241-244, 253, 254, 268, 269, 278, 310, 318, 319, 330, 332, 339, 341, 342, 344-348, 352, 353, 355, 362, 363. Berry's Hampshire Genealogies, 246. Surrey Archæological Collections, ii. Surtees Society, xxxvi. 365. Berry's Kent Genealogies, 189. Glamorganshire Pedigrees, edited by Sir T. Phillipps, 18, 35, 45. Transactions of Shropshire Archæological Society, N.S. iii. 307; v. 319. Visitation of Gloucestershire, 1569, (Middle Hill, 1854, fol.) 6. Burke's Commoners, (of Welcome,) i. 244; (of Ferney Hall,) Commoners, iii. 635, Landed Gentry, 2; (of Dolobran,) Commoners, iv. 107, Landed Gentry, 2, 7, 8; (of Aston,) Commoners, iii. 346, Landed Gentry, 2, 3, 4, 5, 6, 7, 8; (of Dan-yr-Allt,) Commoners, iv. 472, Landed Gentry, 2, 3, 4, 5, 6, 7, 8; (of Croghan,) Commoners, iv. 89, Landed Gentry, 2, 3, 4, 5, 6, 7, 8; (of Gloster,) Commoners, ii. 549, Landed Gentry, 2, 3, 4, 5, 6; 6 at p. 1655; 7 at p. 1887; 8 at p. 1000, 2090; (of Glansevin,) Landed Gentry, 2, 3, 4, 5, 6, 7, 8; (of Leaton Knolls,)

2, 4, 5, 6, 7, 8; (of Coedmore,) 2, 3, 4, 5, 6, 7, 8; (of Trallwyn,)
2, 3, 4, 5, 6, 7, 8; (of Lacques,) 2 supp., 3, 4, 5 and supp., 6 and
supp., 7; (of Strancally,) 4, 5, 6, 7, 8; (of Stockton,) 2, 3, 4, 5,
7, 8; (of Castle Lloyd,) 3, 4, 5, 6, 7; (of Lloydsboro',) 2, 3, 4, 5,
7, 8; (of Tregayan,) 2; (of Ardnagowan,) 2; (of Bronwydd,)
2, 3, 4; (of Peniarth,) 2 supp.; (of Plymog,) 2, 3, 4; (of Cloch-
faen,) 3, 4; (of Pale,) 2, 3, 4; (of Cilcen Hall,) 5, 6, 7; (of
Dinas,) 5, 6, 7, 8; (of Rhagatt,) 5, 6, 7, 8; (of Losset,) 6 supp.,
7, 8; (of Brumont,) 8; (of Rockville,) 8; (of Strancally Castle,) 8;
(of Stockton Manor,) 8; (of Shelton Hall,) 8. Harleian Society, viii.
313; xxi. 101; xxviii. 85, 90; xxix. 329-339; xxxvii. 282; xlii.
56; xliii. 115, 182.   Burke's Royal Families, (London, 1851,
8vo.) i. 42, 191; ii. 53.   Miscellanea Genealogica et Heraldica,
ii. 277.   Foster's Lancashire Pedigrees.   Burke's Visitation of
Seats and Arms, i. 28; ii. 55.   Burke's Heraldic Illustrations, 40.
Burke's Royal Descents and Pedigrees of Founders' Kin, 15.
Dallaway's Sussex, II. ii. 46.   Corry's History of Lancashire, ii.
480. Jones' History of the County of Brecknock, ii. 248, 268, 303.
Caermarthenshire Pedigrees, 6, 12, 14, 19, 20, 23, 32, 36, 41, 44,
51, 53, 54, 56, 60, 62, 63, 68, 71.   Cardiganshire Pedigrees, 76,
78, 79, 84, 86, 87, 88, 89, 90, 94, 95, 96, 99, 102, 103, 105, 113.
Pembrokeshire Pedigrees, 123, 127, 129, 136, 146, 150, 156.
Baker's Northampton, i. 185.   Meyrick's History of the Co. of
Cardigan, 134, 136, 153, 155, 157, 163, 183, 195, 211, 237, 241,
243, 273, 279, 301, 329.   Archæologia Cambrensis, 3 S. vi. 170,
273; vii. 156, 316; xiii. 47, 258; 4 S. vi. 230, 233; vii. 113,
267; viii. 32, 36, 37; ix. 161.   Baronia de Kemeys, printed for
Cambrian Archæological Association, 136.   T. Nicholas' County
Families of Wales, 194, 204, 294, 300, 301, 906.   Castles,
Mansions, and Manors of Western Sussex, by D. G. C. Elwes and
C. J. Robinson, 135.   Foster's Pedigree of the Forsters and
Fosters, Part ii. 49.   Memoir of Col. Lloyd, formerly of Leeds,
Merchant, edited by a Lancashire Vicar. Warrington, 1878, 8vo.
Fosbrooke's History of Gloucestershire, i. 355.   History of Llan-
gurig, by E. Hamer and H. W. Lloyd, 37-78, 266, 290-302.
Memoir of Gabriel Goodman, by R. Newcome, App. S.   Col-
lections by the Powys-land Club, iv. 148, 150, 156; v. 255; vii.
52; viii. 75, 85, 189, 194, 401, 409; ix. 207, 213, 214, 228, 336;
x. 34.   The Sheriffs of Montgomeryshire, by W. V. Lloyd, 3,
183, 201, 229, 280, 378-438, 526, 528.   Pedigree of Wilson of
High Wray, etc., by Joseph Foster, 78.   Wotton's English
Baronetage, iii. 281; iv. 128.   Betham's Baronetage, iv. 45.
Burke's Extinct Baronetcies. Notes and Queries, 3 S. iii. 437;
4 S. xii. 383. History of Powys Fadog, by J. Y. W. Lloyd, ii.
193, 200, 248, 371, 391, 399; iii. 6, 13, 26, 34, 43, 58, 59, 63,
65, 215, 245, 359, 362, 365, 369-375, 404, 406; iv. 60, 69, 116,
122, 127, 136, 163, 166, 173, 182, 201, 234, 254-257, 277, 295, 356,
359-365, 378, 380, 385, 428; v. 95, 100, 121, 130, 133, 146, 237,
290, 300, 302, 349, 354, 410; vi. 11, 51, 71, 73, 85, 99, 103, 126,
151, 209, 248, 347, 348, 351, 414.   Genealogies of Morgan and

Glamorgan, by G. T. Clark, 210. Visitation of Gloucester, edited by T. F. Fenwick and W. C. Metcalfe, 116. Burke's Colonial Gentry, ii. 741. Howard's Visitation of England and Wales, iii. 1. Cambrian Journal, vol. for 1864, 109. Pedigree of Wilson, by S. B. Foster, 189. The Perverse Widow, by A. W. Crawley-Boevey, 241.

LLOYD-BAKER. Blunt's Dursley and its Neighbourhood, 217.

LLOYD-PHILIPPS. Burke's Commoners, iii. 511, Landed Gentry, 2, 3, 4, 5, 7.

LLOYD-PRICE. Burke's Royal Families, (London, 1851, 8vo.) ii. 111.

LLUELLYN. Burke's Landed Gentry, 2, 8.

LLWYN. Dwnn's Visitations of Wales, i. 27.

LLYCHLYN (Bishop of). Dwnn's Visitations of Wales, ii. 103.

LLYSAN. Archæologia Cambrensis, 4 S. ix. 174.

LLYWARCH. Dwnn's Visitations of Wales, ii. 139.

LOCH. Burke's Commoners, ii. 202, Landed Gentry, 2, 3, 4, 5, 6. The Parish of Cramond, by J. P. Wood, 161.

LOCHOR. Pembrokeshire Pedigrees, 426.

LOCK, or LOCKE. A Genealogical Record of the Descendants of Wm. Locke, of Woburn, etc., by J. G. Locke. Boston and Cambridge, 1853, 8vo. Gentleman's Magazine, 1857, i. 331. Burke's Landed Gentry, 2, 3, 4, 5, 7, 8. Poems by Henry Lok, (Fuller Worthies Library,) Miscellanies, ii. 12. Notes and Queries, 1 S. ix. 493 ; xi. 326 ; xii. 391 ; 2 S. i. 141 ; iii. 125 ; v. 12, 177, 297 ; 2 S. iii. 125 ; iv. 12, 177 ; v. 177, 297. Somersetshire Wills, printed for F. A. Crisp, ii. 11. New England Register, xxxv. 59. Harleian Society, xl. 1306. A History of Devizes, 1859, 8vo., 562. Burke's Family Records, 389.

LOCKETT. Glover's History of Derbyshire, ii. 598, (585). Howard's Visitation of England and Wales, ii. 108 ; vi. 37 ; viii. 20. Burke's Family Records, 390.

LOCKEY. Miscellanea Genealogica et Heraldica, New Series, i. 205. Harleian Society, xxii. 151.

LOCKHART. Burke's Landed Gentry, (of Wicketshaw,) 4, 5, 6, 7, 8 ; (of Borthwickbrae,) 3, 4, 5, 6, 7 ; (of Castle Hill,) 5 and supp., 6, 7, 8 ; (of Cleghorn,) 8. Burke's Royal Descents and Pedigrees of Founders' Kin, 85. Paterson's History of the Co. of Ayr, ii. 66. Nisbet's Heraldry, ii. app. 141. Douglas's Baronage of Scotland, 323, 585. Paterson's History of Ayr and Wigton, i. 511, 671. The Upper Ward of Lanarkshire, by G. V. Irving, ii. 292-320. Banks' Baronies in Fee, i. 459. Foster's Collectanea Genealogica, (MP's Scotland,) 218. Alexander Nisbet's Heraldic Plates, 18.

LOCKWOOD. Miscellanea Genealogica et Heraldica, i. 182. Surtees Society, xxxvi. 107. Burke's Commoners, iv. 81 ; Landed Gentry, 2, and see Wood of Bishop's Hall ; (of Bishop's Hall,) 8. Foster's Visitations of Yorkshire, 549. Wright's Essex, ii. 400. Harleian Society, xiv. 676. The Genealogist, New Series, xiv. 258.

LOCKYER, or LOKYER. Burke's Landed Gentry, 2, 3, 4, 5, 6, 7, 8. Harleian Society, xxix. 339.

LOCOCK. Howard's Visitation of England and Wales, ix. 153.

LOCTON. The Genealogist, iv. 192.

LODBROKE, or LODBROC. Nichols' History of the County of Leicester, iv. 51. Dugdale's Warwickshire, 331.

LODER. Burke's Landed Gentry, 6, 7, 8. The Genealogist, v. 284.

LODGE. Burton's History of Hemingborough, 363.

LODINGTON. Lincolnshire Notes and Queries, v. 75.

LOFFROY. Herald and Genealogist, vi. 125.

LOFFT. Burke's Landed Gentry, 7, 8.

LOFTIE. Hasted's Kent, iii. 747 ; iii. 293.

LOFTUS. Burke's Commoners, (of Kilbride,) i. 209, Landed Gentry, 2, 3, 4, 5, 6, 7, 8; (of Woolland,) Landed Gentry, 2; (of Braconash,) 5, 6, 7. Burke's Royal Families, (London, 1851, 8vo.) i. 168. O'Hart's Irish Pedigrees, 2nd Series, 210. Archdall's Lodge's Peerage, vii. 246. Brydges' Collins' Peerage, ix. 33. Notes and Queries, 4 S. viii. 82, 155 ; xi. 18, 186. The Irish Builder, xxxv. 117.

LOGAN. Paterson's History of the Co. of Ayr, i. 369, 404. Paterson's History of Ayr and Wigton, i. 343, 382. Burke's Landed Gentry, 6 supp.

LOGES. Dugdale's Warwickshire, 472.

LOGGE. Manning and Bray's Surrey, iii. 94.

LOGGIN, or LOGGINS. History of the Hundred of Bray, by Charles Kerry, 96. The Visitations of Devon, by J. L. Vivian, 215. The Genealogist, New Series, ii. 71.

LOMAX. Berry's Hertfordshire Genealogies, 103. Burke's Landed Gentry, (of Clayton Hall,) 2, 3, 4, 5, 6, 7 ; (of Childwickbury,) 2 ; (of Grove Park,) 8. Foster's Lancashire Pedigrees. Whitaker's History of Whalley, ii. 275. Harleian Society, xxxvii. 71. See TRAPPES.

LOMAX-GASKILL. Burke's Visitation of Seats and Arms, 2nd Series, ii. 52.

LOMBARD. New England Register, xii. 249.

LOMBE. Burke's Landed Gentry, 6, 7, 8. Betham's Baronetage, iv. 142. Carthew's Hundred of Launditch, Part iii. 402. Harleian Society, xxxix. 1134.

LOMLEY. Miscellanea Genealogica et Heraldica, ii. 277. Harleian Society, xiii. 436 ; xvi. 189. The Genealogist, New Series, xvi. 234. See LUMLEY.

LOMNER. Visitation of Norfolk, published by Norfolk Archæological Society, ii. 35. Harleian Society, xxxii. 189.

LONDON. Morant's Essex, ii. 219. The Genealogist, New Series, xv. 99.

LONDONDERRY. Claim of the Rt. Hon. F. W. R., Marquis of Londonderry, to Vote at Elections of Irish Peers, Sess. Papers, 316 of 1854.

LONDONER. Harleian Society, xvi. 324.

LONE. Berry's Kent Genealogies, 304. Harleian Society, xlii. 138. The Genealogist, New Series, xvi. 94. See LANE.

LONG. Pedigrees of Long, five broadsides, viz., I. Long of Wraxall, Draycote, etc., from the MS. collections of Sir George Naylor, etc., 1828. Reprinted 1878 with Mr. C. E. Long's last corrections and additions, by Willm. Long, Esq., M.A., F.S.A. II. Long of Semington, etc., from MS. Collections of Sir George, Naylor, etc., 1829. Reprinted 1878 with Mr. C. E. Long's latest additions, by Willm. Long, Esq., etc. III. Pedigree of the Longs of Semington, Potterne, etc., curante Gulielmo Long, A.M., A.D. 1878. IV. Pedigree of the Longs of Melksham, Rood Ashton, etc., curante Gulielmo Long, A.M., 1878. V. Pedigree of the Longs of Preshaw, Hants, curante Gulielmo Long, A.M., 1878. Pedigree of the Longs of Semington, Rood Ashton, and Preshaw branches, curante Gulielmo Long, A.M., A.D. 1878. Gentleman's Magazine, 1829, i. 417; 1835, i. 589. Berry's Hampshire Genealogies, 23, 149. Aubrey's Collections for Wilts, (London, 1821, 4to.) printed by Sir T. Phillipps, i. 66. Visitation of Somerset, printed by Sir T. Phillipps. 115. Burke's Commoners, (of Rood Ashton,) iv. 63, Landed Gentry, 2, 3, 4, 5, 6, 7, 8; (of Preshaw,) Commoners, iv. 72, Landed Gentry, 2, 3, 4, 5, 6, 7, 8; (of Monkton Farleigh,) Commoners, iv. 70, Landed Gentry, 2, 3, 4; (of Hampton Lodge,) Commoners, ii. 164, Landed Gentry, 2, 3, 4, 5, 6; (of Dunston Hall,) Landed Gentry, 3, 4, 5, 6, 7, 8; (of Hurts Hall,) 7, 8. Harleian Society, xi. 69. Brayley's History of Surrey, v. 303. Topographical Collections of John Aubrey, edited by J. E. Jackson, 234. Hutchins' Dorset, ii. 584. Burke's Royal Families, (London, 1851, 8vo.) i. 159; ii. 153. Pugin's Examples of Gothic Architecture, 3rd Series, Part III., App. i. and ii. Kite's Monumental Brasses of Wiltshire, 77. Visitatio Comitatus Wiltoniæ, 1623, printed by Sir T. Phillipps. Wiltshire Archæological Magazine, v. 234, 357; xvi. 269. Miscellanea Genealogica et Heraldica, New Series, iii. 34, 46, 58, 70, 397. Page's History of Suffolk, 191. Wotton's English Baronetage, iii. 377. Betham's Baronetage, ii. 322. Notes and Queries, 3 S. vi. 213, 358. Burke's Extinct Baronetcies. East Barnet, by F. C. Cass, Part i. 43. Hasted's Kent, (Hund. of Blackheath, by H. H. Drake,) 256. The Genealogist, New Series, xii. 96, 163. *See* LONGE.

LONG-WELLESLEY. Burke's Commoners, iii. 211.

LONGAN. O'Hart's Irish Pedigrees, 2nd Series, 211.

LONGCHAMP. Banks' Dormant and Extinct Baronage, i. 120.

LONGCROFT. Pedigrees of Longcroft of Wilsford, Co. Wilts, etc., and of Bearcroft of Meer Green Hill, Co. Worc., [T. P.] 1859. 3 folio pages. Illuminated Supplement to Burke's Heraldic Illustrations, 19. Burke's Landed Gentry, 8.

LONGDEN. Notes and Queries, 6 S., v. 277; vi. 138. Howard's Visitation of England and Wales, ix. 41. Gloucestershire Notes and Queries, iii. 214, 244; v. 230. Miscellanea Genealogica et Heraldica, 3rd Series, iii. 101.

LONGE. Tuckett's Devonshire Pedigrees, 104. Burke's Commoners, iii. 361. Landed Gentry, 2, 3, 4, 5, 6, 7, 8. Harleian Society, i. 61; vi. 171. Wiltshire Archæological Magazine, v. 267. Visita-

tion of Wiltshire, edited by G. W. Marshall, 47, 73, 83, 100.
Visitations of Devon, by J. L. Vivian, 532.
LONGEVILE, or LONGEVILLE. Bridges' Northamptonshire, by Rev.
Peter Whalley, i. 324. Claim of . . . Longevile to the Barony
of Hastings and Ruthin, Sess. Papers, Nov. 1640—Feb. 1640-1.
The Genealogist, vii. 181. *See* LONGUEVILLE.
LONGFIELD. Burke's Commoners, (of Longueville,) i. 545, Landed
Gentry, 2, 3, 4, 5, 6, 7, 8; (of Waterloo,) Landed Gentry, 4, 5;
(of Castle Mary,) 4, 5, 6, 7, 8.
LONGFORD. Dwnn's Visitations of Wales, i. 325; ii. 356. Chetham
Society, xlii. 113; xcv. 119. Harleian Society, iv. 32. The
Genealogist, New Series, viii. 17.
LONGLEY. *See* LANGLEY.
LONGMAN. An Account of the Printing House Family of Longman,
see 'THE CRITIC,' Nos. 507, 509, 511. Burke's Landed Gentry, 8.
LONGMER. Harleian Society, xiii. 234.
LONGRIDGE. Genealogical Notes of the Kindred Families of Long-
ridge, Fletcher, and Hawks, by Robt. Edmd. Chester Waters,
B.A., 4to. Herald and Genealogist, vii. 142.
LONGSDEN. Harleian Society, xxxix. 864.
LONGSDON. Jewitt's Reliquary, ix. 32, 126. The Genealogist, New
Series, viii. 19.
LONGSPE. Clutterbuck's Hertford, i. 371. The Genealogist, v. 320.
Baker's Northampton, i. 694. Wiltshire Archæological Magazine,
v. 267; xv. 214. Hutchins' Dorset, iii. 287. *See* SALISBURY.
LONGSTAFF. Howard's Visitation of England and Wales, vi. 70.
LONGUEVILLE. Burke's Landed Gentry, 2, 3, 4, 5, 6, 7, 8. Herald
and Genealogist, vi. 49; vii. 467. Lipscombe's History of the
County of Buckingham, iv. 415. Baker's Northampton, i. 27;
ii. 131. Wotton's English Baronetage, iv. 349. Banks' Dormant
and Extinct Baronage, ii. 241. Notes and Queries, 8 S. iv. 215.
Burke's Extinct Baronetcies. *See* LONGEVILLE.
LONGVILLERS. Harleian Society, iv. 5. Plantagenet-Harrison's His-
tory of Yorkshire, i. 444. *See* LUNGVILLERS.
LONGWORTH, or LONGWORTHE. Burke's Landed Gentry, 3, 4, 5, 6,
7, 8. Chetham Society, lxxxi. 23; lxxxii. 40; lxxxv. 190; New
Series, xxv. 175-9. The Tyldesley Diary, edited by J. Gillow
and A. Hewitson, 16. Croston's edn. of Baines's Lancaster, iii.
220.
LONGWORTH-DAMES. Howard's Visitation of Ireland, ii. 53.
LONSDALE. Fisher's History of Masham, 306. Abram's History of
Blackburn, 753. Burke's Landed Gentry, 8.
LOOBY. Oliver's History of Antigua, ii. 193.
LOPDELL. Burke's Landed Gentry, 3, 4, 5, 6, 7, 8.
LORAINE. Genealogy and other memoirs concerning the Family of
Loraine. Newcastle, 1848, 8vo. (Vol. vi. of Tracts printed by
M. A. Richardson of Newcastle). Hodgson's Northumberland, I.
ii. 246. Wotton's English Baronetage, iii. 433. Betham's Baronet-
age, ii. 350. Foster's Visitations of Northumberland, 81. Har-
leian Society, xxi. 275.

LORANCE. Miscellanea Genealogica et Heraldica, i. 202.
LORD. Dwnn's Visitations of Wales, i. 125. Harleian Society, xxxix. 1094.
LORIMER. Miscellanea Genealogica et Heraldica, New Series, ii. 422.
LORING, or LORYNGE. Harvey's Hundred of Willey, 458. Harleian Society, xix. 13. New England Register, vi. 374 ; vii. 163, 326. Healey's History of Part of West Somerset, 258.
LORT. Pedigree of Lort of Stackpole, [T. P.] 1859. Dwnn's Visitations of Wales, i. 125. Pembrokeshire Pedigrees, 131. Burke's Extinct Baronetcies.
L'ORTI. Collinson's Somerset, i. 18, 26 ; iii. 50, 130. Banks' Baronies in Fee, i. 292. The Genealogist, New Series, xvii. 28, 29.
LOSTOCK. Ormerod's Cheshire, i. 670.
LOTTISHAM. Visitation of Somerset, printed by Sir T. Phillipps, 114. Harleian Society, xi. 70.
LOUBIER. Minet's Account of the Family of Minet, 207.
LOUDHAM. Thoroton's Nottinghamshire, iii. 28. The Genealogist, New Series, xvi. 239.
LOUDON. The Genealogist, New Series, xv. 99.
LOUDOUN. Case of the Rt. Hon. Edith Maud, Countess of Loudoun, co-heiress of Barony of Botreaux, etc., 1870, fol. Case of same on claim to Barony of Montacute, etc., 1870, fol. Claim of the Earl of Loudoun to Vote at Elections of Peers of Scotland, Sess. Papers, E of 1877. Claim of C. E. Hastings, Earl of Loudoun, to Peerages of Montacute, Monthermer, and Montague, Sess. Papers, E of 1874. The Genealogical Magazine, i. 453.
LOUGHER, or LOUGHOR. Dwnn's Visitations of Wales, i. 121. Genealogies of Morgan and Glamorgan, by G. T. Clark, 93.
LOUND. Cambridgeshire Visitation, edited by Sir T. Phillipps, 21. The Genealogist, New Series, xv. 147.
LOUSADA. Burke's Landed Gentry, 4, 5.
LOUTH. Camden Society, xliii. 11 ; lxxvii. 1.
LOUTHER. Plantagenet-Harrison's History of Yorkshire, i. 370. See LOWTHER.
LOUVAINE, or LOVAINE. George Oliver's History of Beverley, 481. Banks' Baronies in Fee, i. 293. Banks' Dormant and Extinct Baronetage, i. 366. See DE LOVAIN.
LOVAT, or LOVATT. Paper on the Lovat Peerage Case, 1727, 4to. Burke's Royal Families, (London, 1851, 8vo.) ii. 63. The Borough of Stoke-upon-Trent, by John Ward, 523. Notes and Queries, 2 S. v. 335, 385 ; vi. 176, 191, 271. See FRASER.
LOVE. Berry's Hampshire Genealogies, 266. Cambridgeshire Visitation, edited by Sir T. Phillipps, 21. Harleian Society, v. 203 ; xli. 78. Paterson's History of the Co. of Ayr, i. 272. Paterson's History of Ayr and Wigton, iii. 118. Metcalfe's Visitations of Northamptonshire, 188.
LOVEBAND. The Visitations of Devon, by J. L. Vivian, 634.
LOVEDAY. Burke's Landed Gentry, 2, 3, 4, 5, 6, 7, 8. Dawson Turner's Sepulchral Reminiscences of Great Yarmouth, 135.

Burke's Heraldic Illustrations, 95. The Genealogist, v. 285.
Metcalfe's Visitations of Suffolk, 150. Harleian Society, xxxii. 189.
LOVEDEN. Ashmole's Antiquities of Berkshire, iii. 289. The Gene-
alogist, v. 285 ; New Series, ii. 72.
LOVEGROVE. Berkshire Notes and Queries, i. 78.
LOVEIS, or LOVEYS. Westcote's Devonshire, edited by G. Oliver and
P. Jones, 629. The Visitations of Cornwall, edited by J. L.
Vivian, 298. The Visitations of Devon, by J. L. Vivian, 534.
See LOVIS.
LOVEL, or LOVELL. Morant's Essex, ii. 13, 93. Bridges' Northamp-
tonshire, by Rev. Peter Whalley, ii. 382. Baker's Northampton,
i. 168, 683. Collinson's Somerset, ii. 54 ; iii. 172. Bird's Magazine
of Honour, 75. Surtees Society, xxxvi. 157 ; xli. 98. Blomefield's
Norfolk, i. 323. Burke's Commoners, iii. 77 ; (of Lincolnshire,)
Landed Gentry, 2, 3, 4, 5 ; (of Wendover Deane House,) 2 ; (of
Cole Park,) 5, 6, 7, 8 ; (of Chilcote Manor,) 5, 6, 7, 8. Foster's
Visitations of Yorkshire, 47, 222. Harleian Society, i. 71 ; xvi.
190 ; xx. 65 ; xxxii. 190 ; xliii. 69. Lipscombe's History of the
County of Buckingham, ii. 115 ; iii. 634. History of the Parish
of St. Leonard, Shoreditch, by Henry Ellis, 196. Shaw's Stafford-
shire, i. 97. Blore's Rutland, 47. Dugdale's Warwickshire, 728.
Visitatio Comitatus Wiltoniæ, 1623, printed by Sir T. Phillipps.
Hutchins' Dorset, i. 325. Hoare's Wiltshire, I. ii. 192; III.
iv. 44. Clutterbuck's Hertford, ii. 463, 484. Chetham Society,
xcix. 3. Abram's History of Blackburn, 668. History of Samlesbury, by James Croston, 33. Hawick and its old Memories, by
James Wilson, 93. Notes and Queries, 2 S. i. 323. Banks' Dormant
and Extinct Baronage, ii. 311. Topographical Miscellanies, 1792,
4to., (Minster Lovell). Edmondson's Baronagium Genealogicum,
v. 483. Banks' Baronies in Fee, i. 294. J. Pym Yeatman's History of the House of Arundel, 268. Earwaker's East Cheshire, ii.
113. The Genealogist, New Series, iii. 97 ; iv. 214 ; xii. 164 ;
xiv. 259. Miscellanea Genealogica et Heraldica, 2nd Series, ii.
262, 355. Weaver's Visitation of Somerset, 42. Oliver's History
of Antigua, ii. 196.
LOVELACE. Croke's History of the Family of Croke, No. 39.
Hasted's Kent, ii. 612. Berry's Kent Genealogies, 474. Burke's
Royal Families, (London, 1851, 8vo.) ii. 70. Archæologia Cantiana,
x. 184 ; xx. 54. Banks' Dormant and Extinct Baronage, iii. 497.
Oxford Historical Society, xxiv. 114. Berks Archæological and
Architectural Society's Journal, ii. 32. Harleian Society, xlii.
125.
LOVELAND. Burke's Landed Gentry, 4.
LOVELINE. Dwnn's Visitations of Wales, i. 78.
LOVET, or LOVETT. Burke's Landed Gentry, (of Liscombe,) 2, 3, 4
and supp., 5, 6, 7, 8 ; (of Belmont,) 2, 3, 4, 5, 6, 7, 8 ; 2 supp.
Lipscombe's History of the County of Buckingham, iii. 457.
Burke's Heraldic Illustrations, 138. Bridges' Northamptonshire,
by Rev. Peter Whalley, i. 215 ; ii. 198. Baker's Northampton,
i. 628, 732. Archæologia, xxix. 407. Memoirs of the Family of

Chester, by R. E. C. Waters, 42, 49. Stemmata Shirleiana, by E. P. Shirley, 2nd edn., 74. Notes and Queries, 1 S. viii. 363, 602. Burke's Extinct Baronetcies. Betham's Baronetage, iv. 87. The Genealogist, vii. 182 ; New Series, viii. 19. Harleian Society, xvii. 68. Metcalfe's Visitations of Northamptonshire, 34. Devonshire Notes and Notelets, by Sir W. R. Drake, 211.

LOVETOT. Clutterbuck's Hertford, ii. 390. Thoroton's Nottinghamshire, i. 63, 235. Holland's History of Worksop, 18. Banks' Dormant and Extinct Baronage, i. 121. The Genealogist, New Series, ix. 84. Miscellanea Genealogica et Heraldica, 2nd Series, v. 85. See DE LOVETOT.

LOVEYN. Morant's Essex, ii. 430.

LOVIBOND. Berry's Essex Genealogies, 65. Burke's Commoners, i. 163, Landed Gentry, 2, 3, 4. Harleian Society, xiv. 678.

LOVIS. A Complete Parochial History of the County of Cornwall, i. 119. See LOVEIS.

LOW, or LOWE. Burke's Landed Gentry, 3, 4, 5, 6. Visitation of Derbyshire, 1663-4, (Middle Hill, 1854, fol.) 5. The Genealogist, iii. 180, 181; New Series, viii. 20 ; xvi. 38. Fosbrooke's History of Gloucestershire, i. 415. J. B. Payne's Armorial of Jersey, 258. Jewitt's Reliquary, xi. 33, 256; xii. 113. Harleian Society, i. 76 ; xvii. 69 ; xxi. 60 ; xxii. 74 ; xxix. 340; xxxvii. 144; xxxix. 1010, 1036 ; xlii. 116. Glover's History of Derbyshire, ii. 5, 398, (7, 367). Berry's Kent Genealogies, 450. Nash's Worcestershire, ii. 94. Burke's Commoners, (of Bromsgrove,) iv. 38, Landed Gentry, 2, 3, 4 ; (of Locko,) Landed Gentry, 2, 3, 4, 5, 6, 7, 8 ; (of Court of Hill,) 3, 4, 5 ; (of Glazebrooke House,) 2 ; (of Highfield,) 5, 6, 7, 8 ; (of Sunvale,) 7, 8. Dickinson's History of Southwell, 2nd edition, 344. Visitatio Comitatus Wiltoniæ, 1623, printed by Sir T. Phillipps. Some Account of the Taylor Family, by P. A. Taylor, 694. Ormerod's Cheshire, iii. 181. Visitation of Wiltshire, edited by G. W. Marshall, 38. Notes and Queries, 6 S. vii. 121, 456. The Journal of the Derbyshire Archæological Society, iii. 157. J. T. Godfree's History of Lenton, 200. Phillimore's London and Middlesex Note Book, 59. Miscellanea Genealogica et Heraldica, 2nd Series, v. 61. Bysshe's Visitation of Essex, edited by J. J. Howard, 59. Visitation of Gloucester, edited by T. F. Fenwick and W. C. Metcalfe, 117.

LOWDE. Chetham Society, lxxxv. 191.

LOWEN. Harleian Society, i. 19. Bysshe's Visitation of Essex, edited by J. J. Howard, 59.

LOWER. Miscellanea Genealogica et Heraldica, i. 13, 266; ii. 18. Polwhele's History of Cornwall, iv. 112. Harleian Society, ix. 132. Archæologia, xviii. 98. Maclean's History of Trigg Minor, iii. 375. A Complete Parochial History of the County of Cornwall, iv. 332. An Historical Survey of Cornwall, by C. S. Gilbert, ii. 191. The Visitations of Cornwall, edited by J. L. Vivian, 298.

LOWES. Foster's Visitations of Yorkshire, 73. Hodgson's Northumberland, III. ii. 337.

LOWIN. Berry's Kent Genealogies, 212.

LOWIS. Tuckett's Devonshire Pedigrees, 5. Harleian Society, vi. 171.

LOWLE, or LOWELL. Herald and Genealogist, iv. 75. Weaver's Visitations of Somerset, 120.

LOWMAN. Tuckett's Devonshire Pedigrees, 15. Harleian Society, vi. 172. Westcote's Devonshire, edited by G. Oliver and P. Jones, 580. Visitation of Devon, edited by F. T. Colby, 151. Visitations of Devon, by J. L. Vivian, 533.

LOWND. The Genealogist, vi. 266. Harleian Society, xli. 95.

LOWNDES. Case of Wm. Selby Lowndes, claiming the Barony of Monthermer, 19 pp. fol., *n.d.* Supplemental Case of same, pp. 16, fol., *n.d.* Claim of Wm. Selby Lowndes to the Title of Lord Monthermer, Sess. Papers, 298 of 1861; D of 1862; E of 1863; F of 1864. Case of same claiming Barony of Montacute, 29 pp. fol., *n.d.* Supplemental Case, 19 pp. fol., *n.d.* Claim of same to the Title of Lord Montacute, Sess. Papers, 297 of 1861; D of 1862 ; D of 1863 ; E of 1864. Dwnn's Visitations of Wales, i. 232. Burke' Commoners, (of Hassall,) iv. 333; (of Barrington Hall,) Landed Gentry, 4, 5, 6, 7, 8; (of Arthurlie,) 2, 3, 4, 5, 6, 7 ; (of Chesham,) 2 supp., 3, 4, 5, 6, 7, 8 ; (of Whaddon,) 2 supp., 3, 4, 5, 6, 7, 8 ; (of Castle Combe,) 5, 6, 7, 8. Lipscombc's History of the County of Buckingham, iii. 544. Burke's Royal Families, (London, 1851, 8vo.) i. 26, 55. Banks' Baronies in Fee, i. 321. Earwaker's History of Sandbach, 122. New England Register, xxx. 141.

LOWNDES-STONE. Burke's Royal Families, (London, 1851, 8vo.) i. 3. Burke's Commoners, iii. 258, Landed Gentry, 2, 3, 4, 5, 6, 7, 8.

LOWNES. Harleian Society, xvii. 70.

LOWRY. Burke's Commoners, (of Pomeroy,) iii. 140, Landed Gentry, 2, 3, 4, 5, 6, 7, 8; (of Rockdale,) Landed Gentry, 3, 4, 5, 6, 7, 8; (of Drumreagh,) 3. Archdall's Lodge's Peerage, vii. 193. Howard's Visitation of Ireland, i. 87.

LOWRY-CORRY. Parliamentary Memoirs of Fermanagh, by Earl of Belmore, 44, 62.

LOWSLEY. Burke's Landed Gentry, 5 supp., 6, 7, 8.

LOWSON. Foster's Visitations of Yorkshire, 550.

LOWTEN. Burke's Landed Gentry, 2, 3, 4.

LOWTHER. The Great Governing Families of England, i. 54. Visitation of Westmoreland, 1615, (London, 1853,) 13. Burke's Landed Gentry, 2 add., 3, 4, 5, 6, 7, 8. Foster's Yorkshire Pedigrees. Foster's Visitations of Yorkshire, 623. Harleian Society, vii. 3 ; viii. 148 ; xvii. 70. Hutchinson's History of Cumberland, ii. 70. Jefferson's History of Allerdale Ward, Cumberland, 369. Thoresby's Ducatus Leodiensis, 5. Whitaker's Loidis and Elmete, 260. Ord's History of Cleveland, 386. Jewitt's Reliquary, xvii. 192. Edmondson's Baronagium Genealogicum, vi. 26*. Brydges' Collins' Peerage, v. 695. Wotton's English Baronetage, ii. 302 ; iv. 61, 170. Banks' Dormant and Extinct Baronage, iii. 493. Burke's Extinct Baronetcies. Foster's Visitations of Cumberland and Westmorland, 83-86. Notes and Queries, 7 S. xi. 307, 358.

Parliamentary Memoirs of Fermanagh, by Earl of Belmore, 105. Nicolson and Burn's Westmorland and Cumberland, i. 428, 437. *See* FORREST, LOUTHER.

LOXDALE. T. Nicholas' County Families of Wales, 205. Burke's Landed Gentry, 6, 7, 8. The Sheriffs of Cardiganshire, by J. R. Phillips, 45.

LOXLEY. Manning and Bray's Surrey, ii. 9.

LOYD. Burke's Landed Gentry, (of Monk's Orchard,) 5, 6, 7, 8; (of Lillesden,) 5, 6, 7; (of Langleybury,) 5, 6, 7.

LOYZELURE. Surtees' Durham, iii. 315.

LUARD. Berry's Essex Genealogies, 101. Burke's Landed Gentry, (of Blyborough,) 2 supp., and add., 3, 4, 5, 6, 7, 8; (of The Lodge,) 4, 5, 6, 7, 8. Harleian Society, xiv. 751.

LUBBOCK. Notes on the History of the Family of Lubbock. By Robert Birkbeck. London, 1891, 4to.

LUCAR. Visitation of Somerset, printed by Sir T. Phillipps, 115. Harleian Society, i. 49; xi. 71. Healey's History of Part of West Somerset, 214.

LUCAS. Morant's Essex, i. 193, 493, 494. Morant's History of Colchester, 123, 135. Visitation of Suffolk, edited by J. J. Howard, ii. 9-26. Glover's History of Derbyshire, ii. 325, (289). Burke's Commoners, (of Hasland,) ii. 171, Landed Gentry, 2, 3, 4; (of Castle Shane,) Commoners, iv. 144, Landed Gentry, 2, 3, 4, 5, 6, 7, 8; (of Mount Lucas,) Landed Gentry, 2, 3, 4, 5; (of Rathealy,) 2 supp., 3, 4, 5, 6, 7, 8; (of Richfordstown,) 2, 4, 5, 6; (of Uplands,) 2, 3; (of Stout Hall, now WOOD,) 4, 6. Gage's History of Thingoe Hundred, Suffolk, 130, 515. Shirley's History of the County of Monaghan, 218. Harleian Society, xiii. 71, 235, 437; xiv. 594; xxxvii. 378; xxxix. 1147. Brydges' Collins' Peerage, vii. 114. Banks' Baronies in Fee, i. 297. Banks' Dormant and Extinct Baronage, iii. 499. Metcalfe's Visitations of Suffolk, 51. Burke's Extinct Baronetcies. Foster's Visitations of Durham, 51. Genealogies of Morgan and Glamorgan, by G. T. Clark, 492-4. Bysshe's Visitation of Essex, edited by J. J. Howard, 60. Chance of Bromsgrove, by J. F. Chance, 34, 87-91. New England Register, xxv. 151. Notes and Queries, 8 S. viii. 416. Burke's Family Records, 394. Oliver's History of Antigua, ii. 200.

LUCAS-WARD. Burke's Commoners, i. 379.

LUCCOMBE. Healey's History of Part of West Somerset, 57.

LUCE. J. B. Payne's Armorial of Jersey, 260.

LUCIEN. Baker's Northampton, i. 113.

LUCK. Berry's Sussex Genealogies, 187.

LUCKER. Bateson's History of Northumberland, i. 234.

LUCKIN, or LUCKYN. Harleian Society, xiii. 237, 437. Morant's Essex, i. 465; ii. 67, 82, 91, 177. Croke's History of the Family of Croke, No. 31. Berry's Hertfordshire Genealogies, 143. Clutterbuck's Hertford, i. 95. Bysshe's Visitation of Essex, edited by J. J. Howard, 60.

LUCY, or LUCIE. Biography of the Lucy Family of Charlecote Park, in the County of Warwick, by Mary Elizabeth Lucy. London,

1862, 4to. Gentleman's Magazine, 1822, i. 130. Visitation of Suffolk, edited by J. J. Howard, ii. 211. Burke's Commoners, iii. 97; Landed Gentry, 2, 3, 4, 5, 6, 7, 8. Lipscombe's History of the County of Buckingham, iv. 188. Jefferson's History of Allerdale Ward, Cumberland, 37, 40. Hodgson's Northumberland, III. ii. 364. Nichols' History of the County of Leicester, iv. 102. Burke's Extinct Baronetcies. Dugdale's Warwickshire, 507, 509. Clutterbuck's Hertford, i. 395. Baker's Northampton, i. 130. Harleian Society, xii. 287. Wotton's English Baronetage, i. 187. Banks' Baronies in Fee, i. 298. Banks' Dormant and Extinct Baronage, i. 122, 363; ii. 323. Harvey's Hundred of Willey, 250. Oliver's History of Antigua, ii. 202. Nicholson and Burn's Westmorland and Cumberland, ii. 76. The Genealogist, New Series, xv. 129. *See* DE LUCY.

LUDDINGTON. Harleian Society, i. 46.

LUDFORD. Bartlett's History of Manceter, being No. 1 of Nichols' Miscellaneous Antiquities, 167*. Nichols' History of the County of Leicester, iv. 1025. Harleian Society, xii. 150. Burke's Commoners, i. 272. Chance of Bromsgrove, by J. F. Chance, 100. *See* NEWDIGATE.

LUDHAM. The Genealogist, v. 191.

LUDLOW. Pedigree of Ludlow of Hill Deverell, etc., Co. Wilts, [T. P.] 2 pages folio. Burke's Heraldic Illustrations, 95. Burke's Landed Gentry, 2, 3, 4, 5. Eyton's Antiquities of Shropshire, ix. 334. Visitatio Comitatus Wiltoniæ, 1623, printed by Sir T. Phillipps. Hoare's Wiltshire, I. ii. 15; III. i. 34. Archdall's Lodge's Peerage, iii. 72. The Genealogist, New Series, xii. 164. Genealogical Gleanings in England, by H. F. Waters, i. 275. Pedigree of Ludlow of Hill Deverell, co. Wilts, 1884, single sheet. New England Register, xlii. 181. Harleian Society, xxix. 340, 342. Transactions of the Shropshire Archæological Society, ix. 267.

LUDLOW-BRUGES. Burke's Landed Gentry, 7, 8. *See* BRUGES.

LUDLOW-HEWITT. Burke's Landed Gentry, 6 supp., 7, 8.

LUDWELL. New England Register, xxxiii. 220.

LUGG. An Account of the Families of Boase, (Exeter, 1876, 4to.) 30.

LUGGER. Maclean's History of Trigg Minor, ii. 527.

LUKE. Camden Society, xliii. 60. An Account of the Families of Boase, (Exeter, 1876, 4to.) 30. Harleian Society, xix. 39, 179.

LUKIN, or LUKYN. Visitation of Oxfordshire, 1634, printed by Sir T. Phillipps, (Middle Hill,) 24. Harleian Society, v. 324 ; xiii. 238, 438 ; xli. 109. Notes and Queries, 3 S. iv. 302. Bysshe's Visitation of Essex, edited by J. J. Howard, 60-62. Howard's Visitation of England and Wales, iii. 46 ; vii. 33.

LUKIS. Pedigree of Lukis of Guernsey, etc., privately printed by Sir T. Phillipps, 1857, folio sheet.

LUM. Burke's Extinct Baronetcies, 610.

LUMB. Burke's Landed Gentry, 4, 5. Harleian Society, xxxvii. 79.

LUMEN. Westcote's Devonshire, edited by G. Oliver and P. Jones, 579.

LUMLEY. Burke's Extinct Baronetcies. Morant's Essex, ii. 369, 520. Edmondson's Baronagium Genealogicum, ii. 167. Archdall's Lodge's Peerage, iv. 250. Brydges' Collins' Peerage, iii. 693. Topographer and Genealogist, ii. 104. Surtees Society, xli. 27. Metcalfe's Visitations of Northamptonshire, 110. Foster's Visitations of Durham, 216. Miscellanea Genealogica et Heraldica, New Series, i. 474. History of Hartlepool, by Sir C. Sharpe, (1816, 8vo.) 46. Bridges' Northamptonshire, by Rev. Peter Whalley, i. 512. Hutchinson's History of Durham, ii. 398, 415. Ord's History of Cleveland, 269. Surrey Archæological Collections, iii. 332. Surtees' Durham, i. 24 ; ii. 168, 211. Manning and Bray's Surrey, i. 456. Baker's Northampton, i. 167. Wright's Essex, ii. 63. Notes and Queries, 1 S. i. 193 ; iv. 194. Wotton's English Baronetage, ii. 153. Banks' Baronies in Fee, i. 300. Banks' Dormant and Extinct Baronage, ii. 328. *See* LOMLEY.

LUMLEY-SAUNDERSON. Hunter's Deanery of Doncaster, i. 275.

LUMSDAINE, or LUMISDAINE. Burke's Landed Gentry, 3, 4, 5, 6, 7, 8. Walter Wood's East Neuk of Fife, 271, 293. *See* SANDYS-LUMSDAINE.

LUMSDEN. Memorials of the Families of Lumsdaine, Lumisden, or Lumsden, by H. W. Lumsden. Edinburgh, 1889, 4to. Burke's Landed Gentry, (of Pitcaple,) 2, 3, 4, 5, 6, 7, 8; (of Cushine,) 2, 3, 4 ; (of Clova,) 2, 3, 4 ; (of Arden,) 8. Burke's Extinct Baronetcies. Northern Notes and Queries, iii. 158.

LUND. Cambridgeshire Visitation, edited by Sir T. Phillipps, 21. The Tyldesley Diary, edited by J. Gillow and A. Hewitson, 69. History of Ribchester, by T. C. Smith and J. Shortt, 262. Burke's Family Records, 395. Harleian Society, xli. 38.

LUNDY, LUNDIE, or LUNDIN. Burke's Landed Gentry, 2 supp., 3, 4, 5. Nisbet's Heraldry, ii. app. 119, 127. Walter Wood's East Neuk of Fife, 239, 279. A short Memoir of James Young, app. 48.

LUNELL. Baker's Northampton, i. 371. Miscellanea Genealogica et Heraldica, 2nd Series, iii. 317.

LUNGVILLERS. Thoroton's Nottinghamshire, iii. 220. The Genealogist, New Series, xv. 22. *See* LONGVILLERS.

LUNNELL. Hoare's Wiltshire, III. iv. 54.

LUNSFORD. Collectanea Topographica et Genealogica, iv. 139-156. Gentleman's Magazine, 1836, i. 350, 602 ; ii. 32, 148. Berry's Sussex Genealogies, 312. Visitation of Sussex, 1570, printed by Sir T. Phillipps, (Middle Hill, fol.) 7. Harleian Society, xii. 85.

LUNT. New England Register, xxii. 232.

LUPINGCOTT. Visitation of Devon, edited by F. T. Colby, 152. *See* LIPPINCOTT.

LUPTON. F. G. Lee's History of Thame, 625.

LUPUS. Munford's Analysis of Domesday Book of Co. Norfolk, 16. Baker's Northampton, ii. 124. (Earl of Chester) Notes and Queries, i. S. vi. 100, 249. The Genealogist, New Series, xiv. 252.

LURKIN. Visitation of Suffolk, edited by J. J. Howard, ii. 306.

LUSCOMBE. Tuckett's Devonshire Pedigrees, 24. Burke's Landed Gentry, 2, 3, 4, 5, 6, 7. Harleian Society, vi. 172. The Visitations of Devon, by J. L. Vivian, 535.

LUSHER. Harleian Society, xvii. 71, 72; xliii. 1.

LUSHINGTON. Cussan's History of Hertfordshire, Parts iii. and iv. 94. Hasted's Kent, ii. 594. Berry's Kent Genealogies, 330. Burke's Commoners, ii. 185, Landed Gentry, 2, 3, 4, 5, 6, 7, 8. Betham's Baronetage, iv. 204.

LUSON. Suckling's History of Suffolk, ii. 7, 454.

LUSSELL. Abram's History of Blackburn, 609.

LUTHER. Morant's Essex, i. 180, 186, 192. Berry's Hampshire Genealogies, 113. Burke's Commoners, iv. 9, Landed Gentry, 2 supp. p. 154. Wright's Essex, ii. 422. Harleian Society, xiii. 439. Bysshe's Visitation of Essex, edited by J. J. Howard, 62

LUTLEY. Burke's Commoners, iv. 6; Landed Gentry, 7, 8. Harleian Society, xxxix 343. Burke's Family Records, 397.

LUTTERELL, LUTTRELL, or LUTEREL. Genealogical Account of the Family of Lutrell, Lotterel, or Luttrell. Milborne Port, 1774, 4to., Collinson's Somerset, ii. 9-13; iii. 499, 534. Savage's Hundred of Carhampton, 490-514. Tuckett's Devonshire Pedigrees, 49, 54. Burke's Commoners, i. 142, Landed Gentry, 2, 3, 4, 5, 6, 7, 8. Harleian Society, vi. 174. Maclean's History of Trigg Minor, ii. 240. Hunter's Deanery of Doncaster, ii. 140. Thoroton's Nottinghamshire, i. 118. The Archæological Journal, xxxvii. 155. Archdall's Lodge's Peerage, iii. 399. Banks' Baronies in Fee, i. 302. Banks' Dormant and Extinct Baronage, i. 364. Notes and Queries, 6 S. iv. 215. The Genealogist, New Series, x. 214. Weaver's Visitations of Somerset, 42. The Irish Builder, xxxv. 222. The Visitations of Devon, by J. L. Vivian, 537.

LUTTON. Tuckett's Devonshire Pedigrees, 40. Surtees Society, xxxvi. 77. Foster's Visitations of Yorkshire, 172. Harleian Society, vi. 173; xxxix. 948. Westcote's Devonshire, edited by G. Oliver and P. Jones, 478. The Visitations of Devon, by J. L. Vivian, 536.

LUTWICH. Harleian Society, viii. 390; xxix. 345. Visitation of Staffordshire, 1663-4, printed by Sir T. Phillipps, 7. Visitations of Staffordshire, 1614 and 1663-4, William Salt Society, 204.

LUTWIDGE. Burke's Royal Families, (London, 1851, 8vo.) ii. 38. Burke's Landed Gentry, 2 supp., 3, 4, 8.

LUTWYCHE. Burke's Landed Gentry, 8.

LUXBOROUGH (Lord). Morant's Essex, i, 169.

LUXFORD. Burke's Landed Gentry, 3, 4, 5, 6, 7, 8, and 8 p. 1720. Burke's Visitation of Seats and Arms, ii. 6.

LUXMOORE. Burke's Landed Gentry, 2, 3, 4, 5, 6, 7, 8.

LYALL. Burke's Landed Gentry, 5, 6, 7, 8.

LYBBE. Sir T. Phillipps' Topographer, No. 1. (March, 1821, 8vo.) 19. Visitation of Oxfordshire, 1574, printed by Sir T. Phillipps, (Middle Hill, fol.) 6. Harleian Society, v. 174, 279. See LIBBE, POWYS-LYBBE.

LYCHWR. Glamorganshire Pedigrees, edited by Sir T. Phillipps, 21.

LYDALL. The Genealogist, v. 286.

LYDCOTT. Harleian Society, v. 121 ; xliii. 199.

LYDE. Visitation of Oxfordshire, 1634, printed by Sir T. Phillipps, (Middle Hill, fol.) 24. Burke's Landed Gentry, 2, 3, 4, 5, 6, 8 at p. 27. Harleian Society, v. 303 ; xvii. 66. Clutterbuck's Hertford, ii. 255. Cussan's History of Hertfordshire, xi. and xii. 234. Burke's Extinct Baronetcies. Oxfordshire Historical Society, xxvi. 259. Genealogical Memoranda of the Family of Ames, xv. 4.

LYDEAT, LYDIAT, or LYDIATE. Visitation of Staffordshire, 1663-4, printed by Sir T. Phillipps, 7. Erdeswicke's Survey of Staffordshire, 370. Gregson's Fragments relative to the County of Lancaster, 220. Visitations of Staffordshire, 1614 and 1663-4, William Salt Society, 205. Harleian Society, xxxvii. 145.

LYDEKKER. Burke's Landed Gentry, 3, 4, 5, 6, 7, 8.

LYDIARD. Pedigree of Lydiard of Cheltenham, [T. P.] 1868, folio page.

LYE, or LYGH. Hoare's Wiltshire, V. ii. 84.

LYELL. Burke's Landed Gentry, 2, 3, 4. Burke's Family Records, 399.

LYFELDE. Jewitt's Reliquary, xiii. 256. Collins' Baronetage, ii. 259.

LYFORD. The Genealogist, v. 286.

LYGHT. Visitation of Oxfordshire, 1574, printed by Sir T. Phillipps, (Middle Hill, fol.) 6. See LIGHT.

LYGON. Nash's Worcestershire, ii. 118. Dugdale's Warwickshire, 1119. Brydges' Collins' Peerage, ix. 337, 507. Metcalfe's Visitations of Worcester, 1683, 69. Harleian Society, xxvii. 90. See JENNENS, LIGON.

LYLE. Burke's Landed Gentry, 4, 5, 6, 7, 8. Wood's Douglas's Peerage of Scotland, ii. 162. Harleian Society, xli. 114. See LILE.

LYMBERGH. Hutchins' Dorset, iv. 66.

LYME. Morant's Essex, ii. 236.

LYMME. Ormerod's Cheshire, i. 451.

LYMMERICK. Harleian Society, xxi. 105.

LYMSEY. Miscellanea Genealogica et Heraldica, New Series, ii. 310. Harleian Society, xxxii. 192. See LIMSEY.

LYNAM. Maclean's History of Trigg Minor, ii. 258, 262. Harleian Society, ix. 134. The Visitations of Cornwall, edited by J. L. Vivian, 303.

LYNBURY. Harleian Society, xxxii. 313.

LYNCH. Notices Historiques sur quelques membres de la Famille de Lynch. Paris, 1842, 8vo. Miscellany of Irish Archæological Society, i. 44-80. Oliver's History of Antigua, ii. 206. Hasted's Kent, iii. 673. Berry's Kent Genealogies, 282. Burke's Landed Gentry, (of Barna,) 2, 3, 4, 5, 6, 7, 8 ; (of Duras,) 2, 3, 4, 5, 6, 7, 8 ; (of Partry,) 3, 4, 5, 6, 7, 8 ; (of Clogher,) 2, 3, 4, 5 ; (of Lavally,) 5, 6, 7. O'Hart's Irish Pedigrees, 2nd Series, 120. Miscellanea Genealogica et Heraldica, New Series, iv. 351.

LYNCH-STAUNTON. Burke's Landed Gentry, 2, 3, 4, 5, 6, 7, 8.

LYNDLEY. Harleian Society, iv. 119. *See* LINDLEY.

LYNDON. History of Carrickfergus, by Saml. M'Skimin, 2nd edition, 319.

LYNDSEY, or LYNDESAY. Berry's Sussex Genealogies, 317. Whitaker's History of Richmondshire, ii. 477. *See* LINDSEY.

LYNE. Berry's Hampshire Genealogies, 344. Notes and Queries, 5 S. xii. 107, 275; 6 S. i. 503; iii. 135; iv. 109, 390. Gloucestershire Notes and Queries, ii. 34, 89. The Visitations of Cornwall, by J. L. Vivian, 594. Fletcher's Leicestershire Pedigrees and Royal Descents, 187. Burke's Colonial Gentry, i. 262. History of the Wilmer Family, 250. *See* LINE.

LYNEALL. Harleian Society, xviii. 271.

LYNES. Burke's Commoners, iv. 511, Landed Gentry, 2, 3, 4. Carthew's Hundred of Launditch, Part iii. 97. Burke's Family Records, 402.

LYNFORD. Lipscombe's History of the County of Buckingham, iv. 334. *See* LINFORD.

LYNGHOKE. Harleian Society, xxxii. 193.

LYNGWOOD. Harleian Society, xiii. 440. Bysshe's Visitation of Essex, edited by J. J. Howard, 64. *See* LINGWOOD.

LYNN, or LYNNE. Tuckett's Devonshire Pedigrees, 15. Harleian Society, vi. 176; xiii. 440; xli. 102. Westcote's Devonshire, edited by G. Oliver and P. Jones, 457. Cambridgeshire Visitation, edited by Sir T. Phillipps, 21. Bridges' Northamptonshire, by Rev. Peter Whalley, ii. 470. The Genealogist, i. 345; New Series, viii. 60. Paterson's History of Ayr and Wigton, iii. 184. Metcalfe's Visitations of Northamptonshire, 35. Notes and Queries, 7 S. ii. 288. The Visitations of Devon, by J. L. Vivian, 542.

LYNS. Plantagenet-Harrison's History of Yorkshire, i. 540.

LYON. Genealogical Tree of the Family of Lyon, by Walter F. K. Lyon. London, 1869. Broadside. Morant's Essex, i. 39. Burke's Commoners, (of Auldbar,) iv. 592, Landed Gentry, 2, 3, 4; (of Appleton Hall,) Landed Gentry 2, 3, 4, 5, 6, 7, 8; (of Goring,) 5, 6, 7, 8; (of Kirkmichael,) 7, 8; (of Tutbury,) 8. Harleian Society, iv. 129; xiii. 441; xvii. 71. Maclean's History of Trigg Minor, iii. 100. Nisbet's Heraldry, i. 444. Wood's Douglas's Peerage of Scotland, ii. 561. Lyon of Ogil (copy of a Genealogical. MS., etc.). No place or date, pp. 13. 4to.

LYONS. Burke's Landed Gentry, (of Ledestown,) 3, 4, 5, 6, 7; (of Old Park,) 3, 4, 5, 6, 7, 8; also 4th edn. p. 264; (of Croome,) 6, 7, 8; (of Ledestown,) 8. Bridges' Northamptonshire, by Rev. Peter Whalley, i. 217. Baker's Northampton, i. 739. Oliver's History of Antigua, ii. 213.

LYRTINGTON. Plantagenet-Harrison's History of Yorkshire, i. 375.

LYS. Berry's Hampshire Genealogies, 69.

LYSAGHT. Archdall's Lodge's Peerage, vii. 76. The Irish Builder, xxxv. 261.

LYSEUX. Visitation of Staffordshire, (William Salt Soc.) 110.

LYSLEY. Burke's Landed Gentry, 2 add., 3, 4, 5, 6, 7, 8. *See* LISLEY.

LYSON, or LYSONS. Glamorganshire Pedigrees, edited by Sir T. Phillipps, 31. Herald and Genealogist, iii. 410. Burke's Commoners, iii. 221, Landed Gentry, 2, 3, 4, 5, 6, 7, 8. Fosbrooke's History of Gloucestershire, i. 275. *See* LLEISAN.

LYSTER. Surtees Society, xxxvi. 32, 178. Burke's Commoners, (of Rowton Castle,) iii. 53, Landed Gentry, 2, 3, 4 ; (of Rocksavage,) 8 ; (of Lysterfield,) Landed Gentry, 4, 5, 6, 7, 8. Harleian Society, xvi. 191. Notes and Queries, 2 S. xii. 358 ; 3 S. vi. 15. Howard's Visitation of England and Wales, iv. 121. The Genealogist, New Series, xvii. 191. Transactions of Shropshire Archæological Society, ix. 26. *See* LISTER.

LYTCOTT. Visitation of Oxfordshire, 1574, printed by Sir T. Phillipps, (Middle Hill, fol.) 6. Surrey Archæological Collections, xi. Berkshire Archæological and Architectural Society's Journal, ii. 13, 35. *See* LITTCOTE.

LYTE. The Lytes of Lytescary, by H. C. Maxwell Lyte. Taunton, 1895, 8vo. Pedigree of Lyte, by H. M. Lyte, 1867, 8vo. sheet. Visitation of Somerset, printed by Sir T. Phillipps, 115. Visitatio Comitatus Wiltoniæ, 1623, printed by Sir T. Phillipps. Wiltshire Archæological Magazine, iv. 79. Lytes Cary Manor House, by William George, (Bristol, [1879,] 8vo.) 5. Weaver's Visitations of Somerset, 44. Howard's Visitation of England and Wales, v. 153.

LYTELTON, or LYTTLETON. Gentleman's Magazine, 1857, i. 709. Nash's Worcestershire, i. 493 ; supp. 35. Westcote's Devonshire, edited by G. Oliver and P. Jones, 621. The Genealogist, iii. 97. Harleian Society, xvi. 192. Archdall's Lodge's Peerage, vii. 121. Edmondson's Baronagium Genealogicum, v. 461. Brydges' Collins' Peerage, viii. 316. Wotton's English Baronetage, i. 306. *See* LITTLETON.

LYTH. Yorkshire Genealogist, i. 55, 201.

LYTTON. Gentleman's Magazine, lxxvi. 1197 ; lxxvii. 632. Berry's Hertfordshire Genealogies, 4. Burke's Commoners, i. 447, Landed Gentry, 2. Harleian Society, viii. 82. Clutterbuck's Hertford, ii. 377. Cussan's History of Hertfordshire, Parts xi. and xii. 113. Chauncy's Hertfordshire, 353. *See* LITTON.

LYVERSEGGE. The Genealogist, New Series, xiii. 96.

MABBE. Harleian Society, i. 39.

MABBS. Visitation of Norfolk, published by Norfolk Archæological Society, i. 347. Harleian Society, xxxii. 193.

MAB EILFYW. Dwnn's Visitations of Wales, i. 27, 101.

MAB WINNION. Dwnn's Visitations of Wales, i. 27.

M'ADAM. Burke's Landed Gentry, (of Waterhead,) 3, 4, 5, 6, 7, 8 ; (of Blackwater,) 2, 3, 4, 5, 6, 7, 8 supp. Lands and their Owners in Galloway, by P. H. M'Kerlie, iii. 288. Paterson's History of the Co. of Ayr, i. 309. Burke's Royal Families, (London, 1851, 8vo.) i. 73. Paterson's History of Ayr and Wigton, ii. 142, 475.

MACALESTER. Burke's Commoners, iii. 687, Landed Gentry, 2, 3, 4, 5, 6, 7, 8.

MACALISTER. Burke's Landed Gentry, 2, 3, 4, 5, 6, 7, 8. Burke's Royal Families, (London, 1851, 8vo.) i. 106.

McCALL. Memoirs of my Ancestors, by H. B. McCall. Birmingham, 1881, 4to. Some Old Families, by H. B. McCall, 121. Burke's Landed Gentry, 2, 3, 4 supp., 5, 6. Burke's Family Records, 403.

M'ALPINE. Burke's Landed Gentry, 2.

M'ALPINE-LENY. Burke's Landed Gentry, 8.

MACAN. Burke's Landed Gentry, 6, 7, 8.

MACANDREW. Burke's Landed Gentry, 8.

MAC ARTAN. O'Hart's Irish Pedigrees, 2nd Series, 121.

McARTHUR. Burke's Landed Gentry, 8.

MACARTNEY. Burke's Landed Gentry, (of Lissanoure,) 2, 2 supp., 3, 4, 5, 6, 7, 8; (of Clogher Park,) 8. The Ulster Journal of Archæology, viii. 196; ix. 1. Archdall's Lodge's Peerage, vii. 87. Burke's Colonial Gentry, ii. 472, 474. Howard's Visitation of Ireland, ii. 44. See ELLISON-MACARTNEY.

M'AULAY, or MACAULAY. History of Dumbartonshire, by Joseph Irving, 418. O'Hart's Irish Pedigrees, 2nd Series, 211. The Ulster Journal of Archæology, viii. 196. The Book of Dumbartonshire, by Joseph Irving, ii. 294. Notes and Queries, 2 S. ix. 44, 86, 465. Fletcher's Leicestershire Pedigrees and Royal Descents, 43. Burke's Landed Gentry, 8. Memoirs of the Clan Aulay. Carmarthen, 1881, 8vo. Ontarian Families, by E. M. Chadwick, i. 55.

MAC AULIFFE. O'Hart's Irish Pedigrees, 2nd Series, 63.

MAC BAIN. Burke's Colonial Gentry, i. 260.

MAC BRAIRE. Burke's Commoners, iv. 598, Landed Gentry, 2, 4, 5, 6.

MAC BRANNEN. O'Hart's Irish Pedigrees, 2nd Series, 212.

MACBRAYNE. Burke's Landed Gentry, 8.

MAC CABE. The Ulster Journal of Archæology, ix. 94.

M'CALL. Burke's Landed Gentry, 7.

McCALMONT. Burke's Landed Gentry, (of Cheveley Park,) 8; (of Abbeylands,) 8.

Mc CANN. O'Hart's Irish Pedigrees, 2nd Series, 239.

MACARTHUR. Burke's Colonial Gentry, i. 223; ii. 843.

MAC CARTAN. O'Hart's Irish Pedigrees, 2nd Series, 122.

M'CARTHY, MAC CARTIE, or MAC CARTY. A Historical Pedigree of the McCarthys, by D. McCarthy. Exeter, 1880, 8vo. The Irish Builder, xxix. 136, 155. Memoir of M. S. J. Mac Carthy, by C. A. Hartshorne, 1885, 8vo., folding at end. Oliver's History of Antigua, ii. 223. Burke's Commoners, (of Cork,) ii. 611; (of Shrub Hill,) 8; (of Drumcar, etc.,) 8; (of Carrignavar,) ii. 606, Landed Gentry, 2, 3, 4, 5, 6, 7, 8. Life and Letters of Florence Mac Carthy Mor, by D. Mac Carthy, (1867, 8vo.) 450-454. Irish Pedigrees, by John O'Hart, 58; 2nd Series, 63-68. O'Donovan's Annals of the Kingdom of Ireland, 2nd edn., vi. 2483. Miscellany of the Celtic Society, edited by John O'Donovan, 402.

Mc CARTHY-O'LEARY. Burke's Landed Gentry, 4, 5, 6.

MACAUSH. Burke's Colonial Gentry, i. 261.

MAC CAUSLAND. Burke's Commoners, (of Strabane,) ii. 58, Landed Gentry, 2, 3, 4, 5, 6; (of Drenagh,) Landed Gentry, 4, 5, 6, 7, 8; (of Bessbrook,) 4, 5.

M'CLELLAN. The Case of Lt. John M'Clellan, claiming the title of Lord Kirkcudbright, with Additional Appendix, 1769, folio, pp. 11. Claim of same, Sess. Papers, Dec. 176...-April 1769. Burke's Colonial Gentry, i. 202.

MACCLESFIELD. Visitation of Staffordshire, (Willm. Salt Soc.) 111. Visitation of Staffordshire, 1663-4, printed by Sir T. Phillipps, 7. Ormerod's Cheshire, iii. 708. Visitations of Staffordshire, 1614 and 1663-4, William Salt Society, 207.

Mc CLINTOCK. Burke's Commoners, (of Drumcar and Seskinore,) ii. 257, Landed Gentry, 2, 3, 4, 5, 6, 7, 8; (of Dunmore,) Landed Gentry, 3, 4, 5, 6, 7, 8; (of Hampstead Hall,) 2, 3, 4. New England Register, x. 99. Parliamentary Memoirs of Fermanagh, by Earl of Belmore, 71.

Mc CLURE. Burke's Landed Gentry, 3, 4, 5.

MAC COMBIE. Memoir of the Family of McCombie, by W. M. Smith. Edinburgh, 1887, 8vo.

M'CONNEL. Facts and Traditions collected for a Family Record, by D. C. M'Connel. Edinburgh, 1861.

M'CONOCHIE. J. E. Reid's History of the Co. of Bute, 241.

Mc CORMICK. Ontarian Families, by E. M. Chadwick, i. 120.

Mc CORQUODALE. Burke's Landed Gentry, 7, 8.

MAC CRAITH. O'Hart's Irish Pedigrees, 2nd Series, 68.

M'CREADY. M'Creery (M'Cready) Genealogy, by C. T. M'Cready. Dublin, 1868, single sheet.

Mc CULLOCH. Burke's Landed Gentry, 2, 3, 4, 5, 6, 7. Lands and their Owners in Galloway, by P. H. M'Kerlie, i. 236, 347; ii. 327; iii. 11, 49. Paterson's History of Ayr and Wigton, ii. 155. Burke's Extinct Baronetcies, 632.

M'CUMMING. Burke's Visitation of Seats and Arms, 2nd Series, i. 26.

MAC DANIEL. Keating's History of Ireland, *Plate* 26.

MAC DERMOTT. Burke's Landed Gentry, (of Alderford House,) 2, 5, 6, 7, 8; (of Coolavin,) 2, 3, 4, 5, 6, 7, 8. Irish Pedigrees, by John O'Hart, 167; 2nd Series, 213.

MACDONALD, or MAC DONALD. A Family Memoir of the Macdonalds of Keppoch, by C. R. Markham. London, 1885, 8vo. A Genealogical table of the potent and independent Sovereigns, Lords of the Isles, etc., comprehending the Macdonnells and Mac Donalds, by John Brown. London, 1816, large sheet. Genealogical and Historical Account of the Clan or Family of Macdonald of Sanda, 1825, 8vo. Sketch of the History of the Macdonalds, by Alexr. Sinclair. Edinburgh, *n.d.*, 8vo. Letters to the Editor of the 'Inverness Journal,' chiefly relating to the Title of Macranald, and the 'Chief of the Clan Macdonald, Lord of the Isles.' Edinburgh, 1818, 8vo. The History of the Macdonalds and Lords of the

Isles, by Alexr. Mackenzie. Inverness, 1880, 8vo. Historical and
Genealogical Account of the Family of Macdonald, in two Parts.
Edinburgh, 1819, 8vo. Extracts from the 'Inverness Courier,'
relative to the Ancient Kindom of the Isles and Ronaldson Controversy. Burke's Landed Gentry, (of Clanranald,) 2, 3, 4, 5, 6,
7, 8; (of Glenaladale,) 4, 5, 6, 7, 8; (of Vallay,) 3; (of Glengarry,) 3; (of Inch Kenneth,) 2, 3, 4, 5; (of Ranathan,) 2 add.,
3, 4; (of Rammerscales,) 2, 3, 4, 5, 6, 7; (of Sandside,) 2, 3, 4
supp., 5, 6, 7; (of Dalchosnie,) 7, 8; (of Largie,) 7, 8; (of St.
Martin's Abbey,) 5, 6, 7, 8. Douglas's Baronage of Scotland, 21,
391. Shaw's History of Moray, 141. Wood's Douglas's Peerage
of Scotland, ii. 5. Archdall's Lodge's Peerage, vii. 108. The
Genealogist, v. 208. Burke's Colonial Gentry, i. 114; ii. 738.
Ontarian Families, by E. M. Chadwick, ii. 1. *See* CLANRONALD,
MAC DONNELL.

M'DONALD. Burke's Landed Gentry, 2, 3, 4, 5, 6.

MAC DONNELL. The Macdonnells of Antrim, by Rev. George Hill,
London, 1873, 4to. Belfast, 1874). Burke's Landed Gentry, (of
New Hall,) 2, 4, 5, 6, 7, 8; (of Murlough,) 5, 6, 7, 8; (of Dun-
fierth,) 5; (of Glengarry,) 8; (of Brackney,) 8. Burke's Royal
Descents and Pedigrees of Founders' Kin, 113. Douglas's Baron-
age of Scotland, 563. Burke's Extinct Baronetcies, 610. Irish
Pedigrees, by John O'Hart, 141; 2nd Series, 214-217. The Ulster
Journal of Archæology, ix. 301. Wood's Douglas's Peerage of
Scotland, ii. 165. Archdall's Lodge's Peerage, i. 199. Burke's
Colonial Gentry, ii. 562, 658, 700. Ontarian Families, by E. M.
Chadwick, i. 1. Northern Notes and Queries, viii. 163. *See*
MACDONALD.

MAC DONOUGH. O'Hart's Irish Pedigrees, 2nd Series, 217. Burke's
Landed Gentry, 8.

MAC DOUALL, or MAC DOUGALL. Burke's Commoners, iii. 430,
Landed Gentry, 2, 3, 4, 5, 6 and supp., 7, 8; (of Mac Dougall,)
7; (of Gallanach,) 7, 8; (of Lunga,) 7, 8; (of M'Dougall,) 8.
Nisbet's Heraldry, ii. app., 53, 104, 253. Jeffrey's History of
Roxburghshire, iii. 360. A Memorial of the Campbells of Mel-
fort, 50. Burke's Colonial Gentry, i. 259, 266.

MC DOWAL-JOHNSTON. Burke's Landed Gentry, 2 supp., 3, 4.

MACDOWALL. The Agnews of Lochnaw, by Sir A. Agnew, 613, 615.
Burke's Landed Gentry, 3, 4, 5, 6, 7, 8. Burke's Royal Descents
and Pedigrees of Founders' Kin, 88. Lands and their Owners in
Galloway, by P. H. M'Kerlie, i. 40, 53; ii. 453. O'Hart's Irish
Pedigrees, 2nd Series, 218. Wood's Douglas's Peerage of Scotland,
i. 452. Northern Notes and Queries, iii. 155. Burke's Colonial
Gentry, ii. 506.

MACDUFF. Wood's Douglas's Peerage of Scotland, i. 573. Burke's
Landed Gentry, 7, 8.

MACE. Tuckett's Devonshire Pedigrees, 23. Berry's Kent Genealogies, 72. Harleian Society, vi. 177. The Visitations of Devon,
by J. L. Vivian, 543.

MAC EGAN. John O'Donovan's Tribes and Customs of Hy-many, 168.

MAC EVOY. Burke's Landed Gentry, 3, 4, 5, 6, 7, 8.

MC FARLAN. Burke's Landed Gentry, 4, 5, 6, 7, 8.

MACFARLANE. Burke's Landed Gentry, 2, 3, 4, 5, 6, 8. Nisbet's Heraldry, ii. app. 61, 85. Douglas's Baronage of Scotland, 93. Burke's Colonial Gentry, ii. 525, 680. Northern Notes and Queries, xi. 7.

MAC FETRIDGE. O'Hart's Irish Pedigrees, 2nd Series, 219.

MACFIE. Burke's Landed Gentry, 6 supp., 7, 8.

MAC GARRY. O'Hart's Irish Pedigrees, 2nd Series, 123.

MAC GEOGHEGAN. O'Hart's Irish Pedigrees, 2nd Series, 219.

M'GHIE. Lands and their Owners in Galloway, by P. H. M'Kerlie, iii. 107.

MACGEORGE. Burke's Landed Gentry, 4, 5, 7.

M'GILDOWNY. Burke's Landed Gentry, 2, 3, 4, 5, 6, 7, 8.

MACGILL. Wood's Douglas's Peerage of Scotland, ii. 345.

MAC GILLCUNNY. O'Hart's Irish Pedigrees, 2nd Series, 220.

MAC GILLICUDDY. Burke's Landed Gentry, 2, 3, 4, 5, 6, 7. The McGillycuddy Papers, by W. M. Brady, 189-204.

MAC GILLIVRAY. Burke's Landed Gentry, 7.

MACGOWN. Geo. Robertson's Description of Cunninghame, 198. Paterson's History of the Co. of Ayr, ii. 245

M'GREGOR, MACGREGOR, or MAC GREGOR. Pedigrees of Mac Gregor, Grierson, and Greer. Large sheet, no place or date. Notes and Queries, 4 S. vi. 31. Burke's Landed Gentry, (of Glengyle,) 2 supp., 3, 4, 5, 6 ; (of Leragan,) 2 supp. Douglas's Baronage of Scotland, 493. Alexander Nisbet's Heraldic Plates, 158. See GREGOR, ROB ROY.

MAC GREGORY. New England Register, xxxvii. 359.

MC GRIGOR. Burke's Landed Gentry, 3 supp., 4, 5, 6, 7, 8. Burke's Visitation of Seats and Arms, ii. 3. Notes and Queries, 4 S. vi. 30, 84.

MACGUARIE. Douglas's Baronage of Scotland, 506.

MAC GUFFIE. Burke's Landed Gentry, 3, 4.

M'GUFFOCK. Lands and their Owners in Galloway, by P. H. M'Kerlie, iii. 37.

MC GUIRE. Burke's Landed Gentry, 5 supp., 6, 7, 8.

MAC HALE. O'Hart's Irish Pedigrees, 2nd Series, 221.

MACHAM. The Genealogist, New Series, xvi. 46.

MC HARDY. Burke's Family Records, 405.

MACHELL. Descent of the Saxon Family of Machell, Lords of Crakanthorpe, by S. Poulson. Broadside. Visitation of Durham, 1615, (Sunderland, 1820, fol.) 68. Burke's Landed Gentry, (of Crackenthorpe,) 2, 3, 4, 5, 6; 7, 8 ; (of Penny Bridge,) 2, 3, 4, 5, 6, 8. George Oliver's History of Beverley, 562. Surtees' Durham, iii. 38. Harleian Society, xiii. 441 ; xvii. 73. The Genealogist, vi. 267. Stockdale's Annals of Cartmel, 512. Robinson of the White House, Appleby, by C. B. Robinson, 86. Bardesley's Registers of Ulverston, xc. Foster's Visitations of Durham, 217. Foster's Visitations of Cumberland and Westmorland, 87. Nicolson and Burn's Westmorland and Cumberland, i. 345.

MACHEN, MACHIN, or MACHON. Burke's Landed Gentry, 2, 3 and corr., 4, 5, 6, 7, 8. Hunter's History of the Parish of Sheffield, 372. Surtees' Durham, i. 143. Foster's Visitations of Durham, 219. Harleian Society, xxi. 106.

MACHETT. History of the Wilmer Family, 185.

MAC HUGH. O'Hart's Irish Pedigrees, 2nd Series, 222.

M'ILVAIN. Paterson's History of Ayr and Wigton, ii. 355.

MACINDEORS. Munro Appellant and Campbell Respondent, Respondent's case in House of Lords, 1798.

MAC INNES. Burke's Landed Gentry, 6, 8. Burke's Colonial Gentry, ii. 772.

MACIVER. Douglas's Baronage of Scotland, 537.

MAC IVER-CAMPBELL. Burke's Landed Gentry, 8.

MAC JORDAN. O'Hart's Irish Pedigrees, 2nd Series, 342.

MACK. Burke's Colonial Gentry, ii. 625. Burke's Landed Gentry, 7, 8.

MACKAY. History of the House of Mackay, and of other Scotch Families, by R. Mackay. Edinburgh, 1829, 4to. J. E. Reid's History of the Co. of Bute, 241. Burke's Royal Families, (London, 1851, 8vo.) ii. 80. Burke's Landed Gentry, 2 supp., 3, 4, 5, 6 and supp., 7, 8. Wood's Douglas's Peerage of Scotland, ii. 389. The Genealogist, v. 20.

MACKELLAR. Burke's Colonial Gentry, i. 14, 258.

MC KENNA. Shirley's History of the County of Monaghan, 140.

MACKENZIE. Genealogical tables of the Clan Mackenzie, by James D. Mackenzie. Edinburgh, 1879, 8vo. (with folding pedigrees). History of the Clan Mackenzie, by Alexr. Mackenzie. Inverness, 1879, 8vo. The Genealogie of the Mackenzies. Edinburgh, 1829, 4to. The Genealogy of the Mackenzies preceding the year 1661, by a person of quality. Dingwall, 1843, 8vo., pp. 19. Burke's Visitations of Seats and Arms, 2nd Series, i. 60; ii. 17. The Earls of Cromartie, etc., by William Fraser. Edinburgh, 1867, 2 vols. Burke's Royal Families, (London, 1851, 8vo.) ii. 2, 17, 162. Burke's Landed Gentry, (of Portmore,) 2, 3, 4, 5, 6, 7, 8; (of Muirton,) 2, 3; (of Grove House,) 3; (of Applecross,) 2; (of Ord,) 2, 3, 4, 5, 6, 7, 8; (of Glack,) 2 supp., 3, 4, 5, 6, 7, 8; (of Flowerburn,) 5, 6, 8; (of Mountgerald,) 5; (of Fawley Court,) 5, 6, 7, 8; (of Findon,) 6; (of Kintail,) 6, 7; (of Mornish,) 6, 7, 8; (of Allangrange,) 8. Nisbet's Heraldry, ii. app. 29. Douglas's Baronage of Scotland, 392-404, 414-418. The Parish of Cramond, by J. P. Wood, 123. Chambers' History of Peeblesshire, 355. Wood's Douglas's Peerage of Scotland, i. 395; ii. 479. Brydges' Collins' Peerage, viii. 593. Foster's Collectanea Genealogica, (MP's Scotland,) 229. Alexander Nisbet's Heraldic Plates, 112. Burke's Colonial Gentry, ii. 644. Notes and Queries, 8 S. vi. 205. Northern Notes and Queries, vi. 35. See BUCHAN, BURTON-MACKENZIE.

MAC KEOGH. O'Hart's Irish Pedigrees, 2nd Series, 223.

MC KERLIE. Herald and Genealogist, vi. 415. Lands and their

Owners in Galloway, by P. H. M'Kerlie, i. 452. Burke's Landed Gentry, 4.

M'KERREL, or MACKERRELL. Burke's Commoners, iii. 173, Landed Gentry, 2, 3, 4, 5, 6, 7, 8. Herald and Genealogist, vi. 411. Paterson's History of Ayr and Wigton, i. 480. Burke's Heraldic Illustrations, 91. Paterson's History of the Co. of Ayr, ii. 32.

MACKESY. Burke's Landed Gentry, 4, 5.

MACKIE. Burke's Landed Gentry, (of Bargaly,) 3, 4, 5, 6, 7, 8 ; (of Auchencairn,) 6, 7, 8 ; (of Heath,) 8.

MC KIERNAN. O'Hart's Irish Pedigrees, 2nd Series, 240.

MACKINNON. Genealogical Account of the Family of Mackinnon, by Sir A. M. Downie. London, 1883, 4to., 2nd edn. Reply from Author of Memoirs of Clan Fingon to a Pamphlet entitled The Family of Mackinnon, by Lauchlin Mackinnon. Tunbridge Wells, n.d., 8vo. Burke's Royal Families, (London, 1851, 8vo.) ii. 18. Burke's Landed Gentry, (of Mackinnon,) 2, 3, 4, 5, 6, 7, 8 ; (of Bittacy House,) 4. Oliver's History of Antigua, ii. 226. Burke's Colonial Gentry, i. 276. See FINGON.

MAC KINSTRY. New England Register, xii. 321 ; xiii. 39.

MACKINTOSH, or MACINTOSH. Memoirs of the House and Clan of Macintosh, and of the Clan Chattan, by A. M. Shaw. 1880, 4to., 2 vols. Burke's Landed Gentry, (of Mackintosh,) 2, 3, 4, 5, 6, 7, 8 ; (of Dalmunzie,) 3, 4, 5, 6, 7, 8 ; (of Balnespick,) 5, 6, 7, 8. Nisbet's Heraldry, ii. app. 46. Douglas's Baronage of Scotland, 347. Shaw's History of Moray, 44. Burke's Extinct Baronetcies.

MC KIRDY. Burke's Landed Gentry, 2 supp., 3, 4, 5, 6, 7, 8. J. E. Reid's History of the Co. of Bute, 254.

MACKNYGHTE. Burke's Visitation of Seats and Arms, 2nd Series, i. 66.

MACKWILLIAM. Morant's Essex, ii. 345, 356. Wright's Essex, i. 639.

MACKWORTH. Berry's Buckinghamshire Genealogies, 28. Burke's Commoners, ii. 481. Harleian Society, iii. 48. Lipscombe's History of the County of Buckingham, iv. 378. Burke's Royal Families, (London, 1851, 8vo.) i. 53. Wright's History of Rutland, 93. Blore's Rutland, 128, 129, 225, 226. Wotton's English Baronetage, i. 337. Betham's Baronetage, i. 167 ; iv. 12. Burke's Extinct Baronetcies.

MACKWORTH-DOLBEN. Burke's Landed Gentry, 5.

MACKWORTH-PRAED. Burke's Landed Gentry, 5 supp., 6, 7, 8. Blore's Rutland, 226.

MACKY. Burke's Landed Gentry, 8.

MACLACHLAN. Burke's Landed Gentry, 2 supp., 3, 4, 5, 6, 7, 8.

M'LAE. Glasgow Past and Present, (Glasgow, 1856, 8vo.) iii. 550.

MACLAINE. Burke's Landed Gentry, (of Lochbuy,) 2, 3, 4, 5, 6, 7, 8 ; (of Kington House,) 2 supp., 3, 4, 5, 6, 7.

MC LAUGHLIN. Burke's Landed Gentry, 3 supp., 4, 7, 8. Irish Pedigrees, by John O'Hart, 150.

MACLEAN. Historical and Genealogical Account of the Clan of
Maclean. London, 1838, 8vo. Burke's Landed Gentry, (of Ard-
gour,) 2 supp., 3, 4, 5, 6, 7, 8; (of Pennycross,) 2 supp., 3, 4, 5,
6, 7, 8 ; (of Haremere Hall,) 4 supp., 5, 6, 7 ; (of Westfield), 8.
Douglas's Baronage of Scotland, 365-373. Paterson's History of
Ayr and Wigton, i. 485. Notes and Queries, 3 S. i. 395.
MACLEAY. Burke's Landed Gentry, 2, 3, 4, 5.
MACLELLAN. Case of Lieut. John M'Clellan, claiming the Title of
Lord Kirkcudbright, with appendices. 1769, fol. Lands and their
Owners in Galloway, by P. H. M'Kerlie, iii. 195, 204. Wood's
Douglas's Peerage of Scotland, ii. 58.
MACLEOD. History of the Macleods, by Alexander Mackenzie. Edin-
burgh, 1888, 4to. and 8vo. Ontarian Families, by E. M. Chadwick,
ii. 48. Burke's Royal Familes, (London, 1851, 8vo.) i. 156. Burke's
Commoners, (of Macleod,) iii. 476, 479, Landed Gentry, 2, 3, 4,
5, 6, 7, 8 ; (of Cadboll,) Commoners, ii. 175, Landed Gentry, 2, 3,
4, 5, 6, 7, 8 ; (of Rasay,) Commoners, iv. 584, Landed Gentry, 2.
Douglas's Baronage of Scotland, 374-388. The Ulster Journal of
Archæology, ix. 94, 317. Celtic Magazine, vol. xiii.
MACLEOD-MOORE. Ontarian Families, by E. M. Chadwick, ii. 52.
MACLIVER. Burke's Landed Gentry, 8.
MAC LOGHLIN. Irish Pedigrees, by John O'Hart, 163 ; 2nd Series,
227.
M'CLUNE. Paterson's History of Ayr and Wigton, i. 485.
MACLURE. Burke's Landed Gentry, 7, 8.
MAC MAHON. Shirley's History of the County of Monaghan, 206.
Burke's Extinct Baronetcies, 611. Irish Pedigrees, by John
O'Hart, 159 ; 2nd Series, 69, 70, 224. Keating's History of
Ireland, *Plate* 9. Notes and Queries, 5 S. ix. 133, 431 ; x. 154.
Burke's Landed Gentry, 8. The Genealogical Magazine, iii. 540.
MAC MANUS. Miscellanea Genealogica et Heraldica, ii. 259 ; New
Series, i. 161, 168. O'Hart's Irish Pedigrees, 2nd Series, 226
Notes and Queries, 4 S. viii. 224. *See* SOTHERON.
MC MASTER. Burke's Coionial Gentry, i. 387.
M'MEIKEN. Lands and their Owners in Galloway, by P. H. M'Kerlie,
i. 213.
MC MICKING. Burke's Landed Gentry, 2 add., 3, 4, 5 and supp., 6,
7, 8. Herald and Genealogist, vi. 140. Foster's Lancashire
Pedigrees. Burke's Colonial Gentry, ii. 481.
MAC MILLAN. Lands and their Owners in Galloway, by P. H.
M'Kerlie, iii. 303, 316. Burke's Colonial Gentry, i. 279. Burke's
Landed Gentry, 8.
MACMILLAN-SCOTT. Burke's Landed Gentry, 5 supp., 6, 7, 8.
M'MINN. Burke's Landed Gentry, 4 supp.
MAC MOROUGH. Irish Pedigrees, by John O'Hart, 161. Visitations
of Devon, by J. L. Vivian, 571.
MC MURRAY. Burke's Landed Gentry, 4, 5, 6. Ontarian Families,
by E. M. Chadwick, i. 47.
MACNAB. Douglas's Baronage of Scotland, 389. Burke's Colonial
Gentry, ii. 578. Ontarian Families, by E. M. Chadwick, i. 19.

MACNAGHTEN, or MACNACHTANE. Gentleman's Magazine, 1827, ii.
495 ; 1828, ii. 600. Burke's Commoners, ii. 307. Douglas's
Baronage of Scotland, 418. The Ulster Journal of Archæology,
viii. 127.

MACNAMARA. Burke's Landed Gentry, (of Caddington Hall,) 4, 5,
6, 7, 8 ; (of Ayle,) 2, 3, 4, 5, 6, 7 ; (of Doolen,) 2, 3, 4, 5, 6, 7, 8.
O'Hart's Irish Pedigrees, 2nd Series, 71. Howard's Visitation of
England and Wales, iii. 91. Burke's Family Records, 407.

MACNAMEE. O'Hart's Irish Pedigrees, 2nd Series, 226.

M'NEIGHT. Paterson's History of the Co. of Ayr, i. 209. Paterson's
History of Ayr and Wigton, i. 130.

MACNEIL. Burke's Commoners, iv. 492, Landed Gentry, 2, 3.

Mc NEILL. Burke's Landed Gentry, (of Parkmount,) 4, 5, 6, 7, 8 ;
(of Colonsay,) 7, 8 ; (of Gigha,) 2 and supp., 3, 4, 5, 6 ; (of Craig-
dunn,) 6, 7, 8. The Ulster Journal of Archæology, viii. 138.
Burke's Family Records, 409.

Mc NEILL-HAMILTON. Burke's Landed Gentry, 4, 5, 6, 7, 8.

MACNEMARRA. Keating's History of Ireland, *Plate* 10.

Mc NISH. Oliver's History of Antigua, ii. 230.

MACONCHY, or MACONKY. Burke's Landed Gentry, 5, 6, 7, 8.
O'Hart's Irish Pedigrees, 2nd Series, 227.

MACONOCHIE. Burke's Landed Gentry, 2, 3, 4, 5, 6, 7, 8.

MACPHERSON. Burke's Commoners, iii. 462, Landed Gentry, 2, 3, 4,
5, 6, 7, 8. Betham's Baronetage, iv. 153. Burke's Extinct
Baronetcies. Douglas's Baronage of Scotland, 354-365. Shaw's
History of Moray, 50. Burke's Colonial Gentry, i. 134 ; ii. 687.
Howard's Visitation of Ireland, i. 49. Ontarian Families, by
E. M. Chadwick, i. 149.

MACQUARIE. Burke's Landed Gentry, 2, 3, 4.

MACQUEEN. Burke's Landed Gentry, 2, 3, 4, 5, 6, 7.

MAC QUILLIN. The Ulster Journal of Archæology, viii. 251 ; ix. 57.

MACRAE. Burke's Landed Gentry, 3, 4. Scottish Journal, i. 19.

MACRANALD. *See* MACDONALD.

MACREDIE. Burke's Landed Gentry, 5, 6, 7, 8 at p. 1454. Paterson's History of the Co. of Ayr, i. 449. Paterson's History of Ayr
and Wigton, iii. 201.

MACRO. Hunter's History of the Parish of Sheffield, 423. Harleian
Society, xxxviii. 497. Staniforthiana, by F. M. H., at end.

MAC SHEEHY. Irish Pedigrees, by John O'Hart, 2nd Series, 228.

MAC SHEELY. Notice Généalogique sur la Famille Mac Sheely, by
A. de la Ponce. Paris, 1848, 8vo.

MAC SWINEY. Irish Pedigrees, by John O'Hart, 166 ; 2nd Series,
229.

M'TAGGART. Lands and their Owners in Galloway, by P. H. M'Kerlie,
i. 79.

Mc TERNAN. Burke's Landed Gentry, 4.

MAC UAIS. Irish Pedigrees, by John O'Hart, 2nd Series, 231.

Mc VEAGH. Burke's Landed Gentry, 2, 3, 4, 5, 6, 7, 8.

MADAN. Nichols' History of the County of Leicester, iv. 760. The
Gresley's of Drakelowe, by F. Madan, 268.

MADDEN. Burke's Landed Gentry, (of Hilton,) 2, 3, 4, 5, 6, 7, 8; (of Inch House,) 3, 4, 5; (of Roslea Manor,) 3, 4, 5, 6, 7, 8. Shirley's History of the County of Monaghan, 191. O'Hart's Irish Pedigrees, 2nd Series, 233. Burke's Colonial Gentry, ii. 610. *See* O'MADDEN.

MADDISON, or MADYSONNE. Visitation of Durham, 1575, (Newcastle, 1820, fol.) 10. Visitation of Durham, 1615, (Sunderland, 1820, fol.) 35. Burke's Landed Gentry, 4, 5, 6, 7, 8. Foster's Visitations of Yorkshire, 274. Hutchinson's History of Durham, iii. 296. Surtees' Durham, ii. 135. The Genealogist, ii. 224 ; iv. 245 ; vi. 267. Foster's Visitations of Durham, 221, 223. Foster's Visitations of Northumberland, 82. Howard's Visitation of England and Wales, v. 150. Lincolnshire Notes and Queries, i. 97 ; iv. 45, 158.

MADDOCK, or MADOCK. Pedigree of Maddock. London, 1898. Broadside. Glamorganshire Pedigrees, edited by Sir T. Phillipps, 45. Visitation of Gloucestershire, 1569, (Middle Hill, 1854, fol.) 7. Burke's Royal Descents and Pedigrees of Founders' Kin, 27. Ormerod's Cheshire, ii. 242, 681. Miscellanea Genealogica et Heraldica, 2nd Series, i. 36. Visitation of Gloucester, edited by T. F. Fenwick and W. C. Metcalfe, 118. Harleian Society, xxi. 108. Howard's Visitation of England and Wales, v. 28.

MADDOCKS, or MADOCKS. Burke's Royal Families, (London, 1851, 8vo.) ii. 87. Burke's Landed Gentry, 2, 3, 4, 5, 6, 7. Jones' History of the County of Brecknock, ii. 602. History of Powys Fadog, by J. Y. W. Lloyd, v. 323. Foster's Visitations of Durham, 225.

MADDOX. Burke's Extinct Baronetcies.

MADEN. Burke's Landed Gentry, 8.

MADERN. Harleian Society, ix. 51. The Visitations of Cornwall, edited by J. L. Vivian, 103.

MADETHERVA, or MATHADERVA. The Visitations of Cornwall, edited by J. L. Vivian, 31.

MADOKES. Visitation of Durham, 1615, (Sunderland, 1820, fol.) 36.

MADRIN, or MADRYN. Dwnn's Visitations of Wales, ii. 177. History of Powys Fadog, by J. Y. W. Lloyd, vi. 219.

MAESMORE. Burke's Landed Gentry, 2 supp. Archæologia Cambrensis, 4 S., viii. 193. History of Powys Fadog, by J. Y. W. Lloyd, vi. 61.

MAGAN. Burke's Landed Gentry, (of Emoe,) 4, 5, 6, 7 ; (of Clonearl,) 2 supp., 3, 4, 5, 6, 7, 8. Burke's Royal Descents and Pedigrees of Founders' Kin, 57.

MAGAURAN. O'Hart's Irish Pedigrees, 2nd Series, 235.

MAGELLAN. O'Hart's Irish Pedigrees, 2nd Series, 236.

MAGENIS. Burke's Landed Gentry, 3, 4, 5, 6, 7, 8. Parliamentary Memoirs of Fermanagh, by Earl of Belmore, 74. *See* GUINNESS.

MAGEOGHEGAN. Keating's History of Ireland, *Plate* 24. Miscellany of the Irish Archæological Society, i. 179.

MAGHULL. Miscellanea Genealogica et Heraldica, i. 300. Chetham Society, lxxxv. 192.

MAGILL. Burke's Landed Gentry, 3, 4, 5, 6, 7; 8. Burke's Extinct Baronetcies, 611.

MAGMINOT. Hasted's Kent, (Hund. of Blackheath, by H. H. Drake,) xxvi.

MAGNAVILLE. Clutterbuck's Hertford, iii. 194.

MAGNE. Harleian Society, xxii. 75.

MAGOFREY. O'Hart's Irish Pedigrees, 2nd Series, 237.

MAGOR. Burke's Landed Gentry, 2, 3, 4, 5.

MAGRATH. O'Hart's Irish Pedigrees, 2nd Series, 237. Burke's Extinct Baronetcies, 611. The Genealogical Magazine, iii. 541.

MAGUIRE. Burke's Landed Gentry, 3, 4, 5, 6, 7. Irish Pedigrees, by John O'Hart, 160.

MAHER. Burke's Landed Gentry, (of Tullemaine,) 2, 3, 4, 5; (of Ballenkeele,) 3, 4, 5, 6, 7, 8; (of Woodlands,) 2, 3, 4. Irish Pedigrees, by John O'Hart, 2nd Series, 73.

MAHEW. Harleian Society, xxxii. 194.

MAHON. Burke's Landed Gentry, 6, 7, 8. O'Hart's Irish Pedigrees, 2nd Series, 238. *See* PAKENHAM-MAHON.

MAHONY. Burke's Landed Gentry, (of Dromore Castle,) 3, 4, 5, 6, 7, 8; (of Dunloe Castle,) 4, 5, 6, 7; (of Castlequin,) 4, 5; (of Kilmona,) 7, 8.

MAIDWELL. Pedigree of Maidwell of Gretton, etc., [T. P.] fol. page. Harleian Society, xvii. 91, 92.

MAINWARING, or MANWARING. A Short History of the Mainwaring Family, by R. M. Finley. London, 1890, 8vo. Burke's Heraldic Illustrations, 129. Burke's Royal Families, (London, 1851, 8vo.) i. 29. Burke's Commoners, (of Whitmore,) iii. 590, Landed Gentry, 2, 3, 4, 5, 6, 7; (of Oteley Park,) Commoners, iv. 356, Landed Gentry, 2, 3, 4, 5, 6, 7, 8. Harleian Society, vi. 177; xvii. 79; xviii. 163; xxi. 272; xxvii. 118; xxix. 347, 426. Herald and Genealogist, vi. 646. The Borough of Stoke-upon-Trent, by John Ward, 519. Memoirs of the Family of Chester, by R. E. C. Waters, 650. Ormerod's Cheshire, i. 478; ii. 178, 429; iii. 80, 214, 229. Wotton's English Baronetage, iii. 174. Betham's Baronetage, v. 568. The Genealogist, v. 287. Burke's Extinct Baronetcies. Visitation of Staffordshire, (Willm. Salt Soc.) 113. James Hall's History of Nantwich, 457. Visitations of Staffordshire, 1614 and 1663-4, William Salt Society, 207, 211. Earwaker's History of Sandbach, 109. New England Register, xxiii. 396. Burke's Family Records, 412. The Visitations of Devon, by J. L. Vivian, 544.

MAIOR. Nichol's History of the County of Leicester, iv. 482.

MAIR. Burke's Colonial Gentry, ii. 640. Howard's Visitations of England and Wales, ix. 137.

MAIRE. Burke's Commoners, iii. 302. Whitaker's History of Richmondshire, i. 140. Hutchinson's History of Durham, iii. 3. Surtees' Durham, i. 52, 53. Plantagenet-Harrison's History of Yorkshire, i. 381. Foley's Records of the English Province, S. J., v. 654. Foster's Visitations of Durham, 227. Cyclostyle Pedigrees, by J. J. Green.

MAIRIS. Burke's Visitation of Seats and Arms, 2nd Series, ii. 31.

MAISNELL. Archæologia Æliana, 2nd Series, iii. 80.

MAISTER. Burke's Landed Gentry, (of Beverley,) 2, 3, 4 ; (of Skeffling,) 5. Poulson's Holderness, ii. 445.

MAISTERSON. Ormerod's Cheshire, iii. 439. James Hall's History of Nantwich, 420.

MAITLAND. Genealogy of the Family of Maitland, Earl of Lauderdale, by A. Dalzel. Edinburgh, 1785, 4to. Short Genealogy of the Family of Maitland, Earl of Lauderdale. Edinburgh, 1875. Genealogical Tree of the Family of Maitland, Earl of Lauderdale, photographic facsimile from original chart drawn up by John Maitland, Esq., to 17 July', 1880. A large sheet. Miscellanea Genealogica et Heraldica, ii. 205-213. Burke's Landed Gentry, (of Dundrennan,) 2, 3, 4, 5, 6, 7, 8 ; (of Hollywich,) Commoners, iii. 600, Landed Gentry, 2 ; (of Freugh,) Landed Gentry, 3, 4, 5, 6, 7, 8 ; (of Eccles,) 5 and supp., 6 ; (of Loughton Hall,) 8. Lands and their Owners in Galloway, by P. H. M'Kerlie, i. 70 ; iii. 339. Wood's Douglas's Peerage of Scotland, ii. 64. Brydges' Collins' Peerage, ix. 296. Foster's Collectanea Genealogica, (MP's Scotland,) 239. Burke's Extinct Baronetcies, 632. Howard's Visitation of England and Wales, iii. 29. Northern Notes and Queries, viii. 91.

MAITLAND-DOUGALL. Burke's Landed Gentry, 8.

MAITLAND-MAKGILL-CRICHTON. Burke's Landed Gentry, 6.

MAJENDIE. Burke's Landed Gentry, 3, 4, 5, 6, 7, 8.

MAJOR. Some Account of the Families of Major and Henniker, by J. H. Major. London, 1803, 4to. Betham's Baronetage, iii. 318. Harleian Society, xvii. 73.

MAKDOUGALL. Genealogical Table of the Makdougal Family, by Willm. Fraser. Edinburgh, 1840, fol., with additions, by Col. Maitland to 17 July 1880. Large sheet in photo-lithographic facsimile. *See* BRISBANE.

MAKENADE. Harleian Society, xlii. 204.

MAKEPEACE. Baker's Northampton, i. 514. Metcalfe's Visitations of Northamptonshire, 111.

MAKGILL. Abstract of the proof which makes out the Case of James Makgill, claiming the title of Viscount Oxford, folio, with pedigree.

MAKINS. Burke's Landed Gentry, 8.

MALBANK. Harleian Society, xviii. 158. The Genealogist, New Series, vi. 193.

MALBON. James Hall's History of Nantwich, 483.

MALBY. Metcalfe's Visitations of Suffolk, 151.

MALCOLM. Burke's Commoners, (of Poltalloch,) iv. 647, Landed Gentry, 2, 3, 4, 5, 6, 7, 8 ; (of Burnfoot,) Landed Gentry, 3, 4, 5, 6, 7, 8. Walter Wood's East Neuk of Fife, 300.

MALDETT. Visitation of Devon, edited by F. T. Colby, 153.

MALEBISE. Yorkshire Archæological Society, Record Series, xxx, lxvii.

MALEFFANT, or MALEFAUNT. Dwnn's Visitations of Wales, i. 164. Genealogies of Morgan and Glamorgan, by G. T. Clark, 419.

MALEGREFFE. Morant's Essex, i. 218.

MALESORS, or MALESORP. The Genealogist, New Series, xiii. 249; xiv. 260.

MALET, MALLETT, or MALLET. Notices of an English Branch of the Malet Family, by Arthur Malet. London, 1885, 8vo. Collinson's Somerset, i. 32, 90; iii. 496. Tuckett's Devonshire Pedigrees, 35. Burke's Landed Gentry, 2 supp., 3, 4, 5. Foster's Visitations of Yorkshire, 325. Harleian Society, vi. 178; viii. 210; xi. 72; xvi. 194; xxxviii. 611. Hoare's Wiltshire, II. ii. 106. The Antiquities of Gainford, by J. R. Walbran, 88. Visitation of Somerset, printed by Sir T. Phillipps, 116, 117. Somerset Archæological Society's Proceedings, xvi. ii. 35. J. B. Payne's Armorial of Jersey, 261. Betham's Baronetage, iv. 197. Banks' Dormant and Extinct Baronage, i. 126. Weaver's Visitations of Somerset, 44, 46. The Visitations of Devon, by J. L. Vivian, 545. Miscellanea Genealogica et Heraldica, 3rd Series, iii. 38.

MALEVERER. Surtees Society, xxxvi. 97; xli. 54. Foster's Visitations of Yorkshire, 64, 68, 200, 266, 550. Harleian Society, xvi. 200, 202. Banks' Baronies in Fee, ii. 100. The Genealogist, New Series, x. 45. See MAULEVERER.

MALGRAVE. Morant's Essex, i. 218.

MALHAM. Foster's Visitations of Yorkshire, 295. Whitaker's Deanery of Craven, 91, (116). Harleian Society, xvi. 193.

MALHERB. Visitation of Devon, edited by F. T. Colby, 69. Jewers' Wells Cathedral, 293. The Genealogist, New Series, xiv. 191.

MALHOME. Collectanea Topographica et Genealogica, vi. 125.

MALIM. The Malim Family. By Rev. Alfred Malim, circa 1897, small 4to., pp. 55.

MALIN. Visitatio Comitatus Wiltoniæ, 1623, printed by Sir T. Phillipps. Visitation of Wiltshire, edited by G. W. Marshall, 20.

MALING. Burke's Landed Gentry, 2. Foster's Yorkshire Pedigrees.

MALLAEN. Dwnn's Visitations of Wales, i. 27.

MALLOCK, or MALLACK. Harleian Society, vi. 178. Visitation of Devon, edited by F. T. Colby, 154. Camden Society, cv. at end. Westcote's Devonshire, edited by G. Oliver and P. Jones, 548. Burke's Landed Gentry, 7, 8. The Visitations of Devon, by J. L. Vivian, 546.

MALLORY, MALORE, or MALORY. Cambridgeshire Visitation, edited by Sir T. Phillipps, 22. Burke's Landed Gentry, 2, 3, 4, 5, 6, 7, 8. Foster's Visitations of Yorkshire, 156. Bridges' Northamptonshire, by Rev. Peter Whalley, i. 604. Whitaker's Deanery of Craven, 391, (537). A Genealogical Account of the Lords of Studley Royal, by J. R. Walbran. Harleian Society, ii. 58; xii. 78; xvi. 195; xix. 122; xli. 39. Ormerod's Cheshire, i. 421. Surtees Society, xli. 51. Burton's Description of Leicestershire, 262. Nichols' History of the County of Leicester, iii. 501; iv. 364, 761. Dugdale's Warwickshire, 82. Banks' Baronies in Fee, ii. 100. The Genealogist, New Series, iv. 118. Metcalfe's Visitations of Northamptonshire, 35, 112.

MALLOWES. Metcalfe's Visitations of Suffolk, 202.

MALMAINS. Notes and Queries, 5 S. iv. 21, 63.

MALMESBURY. Burke's Royal Families, (London, 1851, 8vo.) ii. 61.
MALONE. Burke's Landed Gentry, 5, 6, 7, 8. Archdall's Lodge's
Peerage, vii. 280. The Irish Builder, xxviii. 191.
MALONY. Burke's Commoners, (of Kiltanon,) iv. 766 ; (of Granahan,)
iv. 768.
MALOYSEL. The Genealogist, New Series, xiv. 194.
MALPAS. Ormerod's Cheshire, ii. 641, (Barons of,) 598. Banks'
Dormant and Extinct Baronage, i. 203. Harleian Society, xviii.
159. The Genealogist, New Series, xiii. 36.
MALSTON, or MALSTONNE. Visitation of Devon, edited by F. T.
Colby, 181. Harleian Society, xliii. 73.
MALTBY. Foster's Visitations of Yorkshire, 551.
MALTHUS. Collections for a History of the Family of Malthus, by
J. O. Payne. London, 1890, 4to. Morant's Essex, ii. 543.
MALTRAVERS, or MATRAVERS. Collinson's Somerset, iii. 206. Col-
lectanea Topographica et Genealogica, ii. 77 ; vi. 334. Dallaway's
Sussex, II. i. 132. Burke's Commoners, iv. 142. Banks' Baronies
in Fee, i. 303. Banks' Dormant and Extinct Baronage, ii. 333.
MALUM. See MALHAM.
MALUVAL. Dickinson's History of Southwell, 2nd edition, 177.
MALVESYN. Burke's Commoners, iii. 439. Shaw's Staffordshire, i. 166.
Eyton's Antiquities of Shropshire, vii. 397. Nichols' History of the
County of Leicester, ii. 776.
MALYN. Harleian Society, xxxix. 1033.
MAMINOT. Banks' Dormant and Extinct Baronage, i. 127.
MAN. Jewitt's Reliquary, vii. 26. Berry's Kent Genealogies, i. 92.
Foster's Visitations of Yorkshire, 552, 627. Harleian Society,
xiii. 240, 442 ; xvii. 74 ; xlii. 23. Foster's Visitations of North-
umberland, 83. New England Register, xiii. 325. See MANN.
MANATON. An Historical Survey of Cornwall, by C. S. Gilbert,
ii. 195. The Visitations of Cornwall, edited by J. L. Vivian,
306. Hasted's Kent, (Hund. of Blackheath, by H. H. Drake,) xx.
MANBY. Morant's Essex, i. 121. Surtees Society, xxxvi. 84.
Foster's Visitations of Yorkshire, 552, 624 - 626. Dawson
Turner's Sepulchral Reminiscences of Great Yarmouth, 136.
Norfolk Archæology, iii. 130. The Genealogist, iv. 246. Harleian
Society, xvii. 76. Burke's Colonial Gentry, ii. 605.
MANBY-COLEGRAVE. Burke's Landed Gentry, 8.
MANCESTRE. Dugdale's Warwickshire, 1077.
MANCHEL. The Genealogist, New Series, xiii. 181.
MANCHESTER (Earl of). Morant's Essex, ii. 102. (Barons of) Ear-
waker's Local Gleanings, i. 96, 104, 110, 121. Croston's edn. of
Baines's Lancaster, ii. 28.
MANCKLIN. Harleian Society, xxxviii. 784.
MANDER. Harleian Society, xxxviii. 656.
MANDEVILLE. Miscellanea Genealogica et Heraldica, ii. 161.
Morant's Essex, i. 179, 444 ; ii. 451. Lipscombe's History of
the County of Buckingham, i. 158. Hutchins' Dorset, ii. 261.
Baker's Northampton, i. 544. Wright's Essex, ii. 106. Harleian
Society, xiii. 22 ; xiv. 591. Banks' Dormant and Extinct

Baronage, i. 128; iii. 268. F. G. Lee's History of Thame, 333.
See DE MANDEVILLE, MAUNDEVILLE.

MANIFOLD. Burke's Colonial Gentry, ii. 495.

MANINGHAM, or MANNINGHAM. Archæologia Cantiana, iv. 255.
Cambridgeshire Visitation, edited by Sir T. Phillipps, 22. Berry's
Kent Genealogies, 32. Harleian Society, xli. 97; xlii. 7.

MANINGTON. Harleian Society, ix. 134. The Visitations of Cornwall, edited by J. L. Vivian, 305.

MANLEY. Berry's Kent Genealogies, 463. Burke's Commoners, iv.
707; Landed Gentry, (of Manley Hall,) 2, 3, 4, 5, 6, 7, 8; (of
Spofforth,) 8; (of Hyde Hall,) 8. Visitation of Staffordshire,
1663-4, printed by Sir T. Phillipps, 7. Ormerod's Cheshire, ii.
105. Harleian Society, xviii. 162; xix. 122. Visitations of
Staffordshire, 1614 and 1663-4, William Salt Society, 208. *See*
DE MANLEY, DE MALO LACU.

MANLOR. Visitation of Staffordshire, 1663-4, printed by Sir T.
Phillipps, 7.

MANLOVE. Visitations of Staffordshire, 1614 and 1663-4, William
Salt Society, 210.

MANN. Hasted's Kent, ii. 142, 432. Chronicle of the Family of De
Havilland. Burke's Landed Gentry, (of Linton,) 4, 5, 6, 7; (of
Dunmoyle,) 7, 8. Betham's Baronetage, iii. 254. Burke's Extinct
Baronetcies. Harleian Society, xvii. 75. *See* MAN.

MANNERS. The Great Governing Families of England, i. 290. Jacob's
Peerage, i. 296. Appendix to Case of Sir J. S. Sidney, claiming
to be Lord Lisle. S. Glover's Peak Guide, edited by Thomas
Noble, 100. Turnor's History of Town and Soke of Grantham,
61. Fletcher's Leicestershire Pedigrees and Royal Descents, 1.
History of Belvoir Castle, by J. Eller, *folding table.* Raine's
History of North Durham, 208, 211, 230. Wright's History of
Rutland, 7. Nichols' History of the County of Leicester, ii. 48,
67. Baker's Northampton, i. 269. Thoroton's Nottinghamshire,
i. 222. Edmondson's Baronagium Genealogicum, i. 43. Memoirs,
British and Foreign, of Illustrious Persons who died in 1711, 1.
Berry's Genealogical Peerage, 112. Brydges' Collins' Peerage, i.
454. Banks' Baronies in Fee, i. 379; ii. 101. Betham's
Baronetage, iv. 251. Banks' Dormant and Extinct Baronage, ii.
441, 448. Rockingham Castle and the Watsons, Pedigree 4.

MANNERS-SUTTON. Burke's Commoners, i. 1.

MANNING, or MANNINGE. Visitation of Kent (reprinted from
Archæologia Cantiana, vol. vi.) 87. Topographer and Genealogist,
ii. 534. Hasted's Kent, i. 141. Berry's Sussex Genealogies, 260.
Berry's Kent Genealogies, 406. Tuckett's Devonshire Pedigrees,
80. Burke's Landed Gentry, (of Portland Castle,) 2 supp., 3, 4;
(of Colebrook Park and Diss,) 3, 4, 5, 6; (of Eversfield) 5, 6.
Harleian Society, vi. 179; ix. 214; xiii. 241; xvii. 74, 77, 78;
xlii. 164. Burke's Royal Descents and Pedigrees of Founders'
Kin, 47. O'Hart's Irish Pedigrees, 2nd Series, 124. Collections
for a History of Staffordshire, William Salt Society, i. 310. Burke's
Colonial Gentry, i. 280. Howard's Visitation of England and

Wales, ii. 121. Notes and Queries, 8 S. i. 419, 502. The Visitations of Devon, by J. L. Vivian, 550. Oliver's History of Antigua, ii. 232. New England Register, li. 389.

MANNIX. Burke's Extinct Baronetcies, 611.

MANNOCK, or MANNOKE. Morant's Essex, i. 165 ; ii. 232, 361, 435, 442, 456, 467. Burke's Landed Gentry, 3, 4, 5, 6, 7. Harleian Society, xiii. 72. Foley's Records of the English Province, S.J., v. 546. Wotton's English Baronetage, ii. 57. Metcalfe's Visitations of Suffolk, 151. Burke's Extinct Baronetcies. The Suffolk Records, by H. W. Aldred, 30.

MANNOURS. Harleian Society, iv. 48.

MANNY. Baker's Northampton, i. 54.

MANSBRIDGE. Harleian Society, i. 45 ; xvii. 80.

MANSEL, or MANSELL. Pedigree of Mansell of Trinsaren and Stradey, Co. Carmarthen, Morgan of Coed y Gores, and Shewen of Stradey, and Picton of Nevorne, Co. Pembroke, by Sir T. Phillipps, Bart., folio, pp. 4. Pedigree of Mansell of Hampton near Evesham, [T. P.] 1867, folio page. Pedigree of Mansell of Margam, etc. ; of Modlescombe ; and of Margam, [T. P.] 1859, 4 pages folio. Pedigree of Mansell of Margam and Penrice Castle, [T. P.] Broadside. Pedigrees of Mansell of Frampton Mansell, and others, [T. P.] 1856, 4 folio pages. Pedigree of Mansell of Mudlescombe, etc., [T. P.] Broadside. Pedigree of Mansell of Didbrooke, etc., [T. P.] folio page. Collections of Mancell pedigrees, 2 folio pages. Pedigree of Mansel from Visitation of Berks, 1565, and pedigree of Walrond of Aldborne, [T. P.] folio page. An Historical and Genealogical Account of the Family of Maunsell, Mansell, or Mansel, by W. W. Mansell. London, 1850, 4to. Burke's Extinct Baronetcies. Gentleman's Magazine, 1841, ii. 474. Glamorganshire Pedigrees, edited by Sir T. Phillipps, 2, 12, 32, 51. Dwnn's Visitations of Wales, ii. 43. Burke's Royal Families, (London, 1851, 8vo.) ii. 206. Burke's Landed Gentry, (of Cosgrove Hall,) 2, 3, 4, 6 ; (of Smedmore,) 5, 8. Lipscombe's History of the County of Buckingham, i. 69. Caermarthenshire Pedigrees, 2, 11, 29, 41. Hutchins' Dorset, i. 574. Baker's Northampton, ii. 131. T. Nicholas's County Families of Wales, 296, 641. Bigland's Gloucestershire, ii. par. Sapperton. Wotton's English Baronetage, i. 485 ; iv. 57. Betham's Baronetage, i. 248. Banks' Dormant and Extinct Baronage, iii. 501. Genealogies of Morgan and Glamorgan, by G. T. Clark, 494, 496. See BIRD, MAUNSELL.

MANSERGH. Burke's Landed Gentry, (of Greenane,) 4, 5, 6, 7, 8 ; (of Macroney Castle,) 3, 4. Howard's Visitation of Ireland, iii. 25.

MANSFIELD. Burke's Commoners, (of Birstall House,) ii. 178 ; (of Morristown Lattin,) Landed Gentry, 3, 4, 5, 6, 7, 8 ; (of Castle Wray,) 3, 4, 5, 6, 7, 8.

MANSHIP. Manning and Bray's Surrey, ii. 498.

MANSON. Caithness Family History, by John Henderson, 312.

MANSTONE. The Genealogist, New Series, ix. 13. Platt and Morkill's Records of Whitkirk, 70.

MANSUER. Visitation of Norfolk, published by Norfolk Archæological Society, i. 349. Harleian Society, xxxii. 195.

MANT. Howard's Visitation of England and Wales, i. 193. Burke's Family Records, 417.

MANTELL. Hasted's Kent, iii. 97, 319. Berry's Kent Genealogies, 185, 332. Berry's Sussex Genealogies, 20. Harleian Society, xiii. 72 ; xlii. 87. Burke's Colonial Gentry, i. 174. See MAUNTELL.

MANTUA. (Prince of Mantua.) See GROOM.

MANUEL. J. B. Payne's Armorial of Jersey, 272.

MANVERS. Thoroton's Nottinghamshire, i. 175.

MANWARING. Oliver's History of Antigua, ii. 236. See MAIN-WARING.

MANWOOD. Morant's Essex, ii. 77. Hasted's Kent, iii. 595. Berry's Kent Genealogies, 356. Burke's Landed Gentry, 5 supp., p. 64. History of Sandwich, by W. Boys, 246. Harleian Society, xiii. 443 ; xlii. 144. Bysshe's Visitation of Essex, edited by J. J. Howard, 64.

MANXELL. The Genealogist, New Series, ii. 72.

MAPES. Harleian Society, xxxii. 195.

MAPLES. Burke's Extinct Baronetcies.

MAPLISDEN. Berry's Kent Genealogies, 322. Harleian Society, xlii. 156.

MAPOWDER. Harleian Society, vi. 179. The Visitations of Devon, by J. L. Vivian, 551.

MAR (Earl of). Ancient and Modern. London, 1875, 8vo. Case for J. F. E. Goodeve Erskine, in opposition to W. C., Earl of Kellie, with app. fol. Case of J. F. M. Erskine, Earl of Mar, claiming the titles, etc., of Earl of Kellie, etc. London, fol. 18... Case for Walter Henry, Earl of Kellie, on his claim to be Earl of Mar, pp. 86, fol. Additional case, 114 pp. fol. Case of Walter Coningsby, Earl of Kellie, on his claim to be Earl of Mar, pp. 86, fol. The Mar Peerage Case, by Rev. A. W. Hallen. Alloa, 1875, 4to. New position of the Old Earldom of Mar, by Alexr. Sinclair. Edinburgh, 1875, 8vo. The Earldom of Mar in Sunshine and in Shade, by Alexr., Earl of Crawford. Edinburgh, 1882, 2 vols., 8vo. A Short Account of the Earldom of Mar, by W. A. Lindsay. London and Aylesbury, 1875, 8vo. Claim of Walter Coningsby, Earl of Kellie, to the title of Earl of Mar, Sess. Papers, D. of 1867-8 ; F of 1870 ; A of 1871 ; D of 1872 ; C of 1873 ; B of 1874 ; A and A* of 1875 ; 161 of 1877. Herald and Genealogist, iv. 375 ; vii. 1. Genealogist, ii. 73 ; New Series, iii. 1 ; iv. 177. Wood's Douglas's Peerage of Scotland, ii. 198. See ERSKINE.

MARBURY. The Genealogist, iv. 248. Harleian Society, i. 51 ; xviii. 167 ; xliii. 204. Ormerod's Cheshire, i. 738. Surrey Archæological Collections, x.

MARCET. Miscellanea Genealogica et Heraldica, New Series, iv. 369.

MARCH, or MARCHE. Collinson's Somerset, iii. 14, 149. J. H. Hill's History of Langton, 32. (Earl of,) Jewers' Wells Cathedral, 119. Foster's Visitations of Durham, 229. The Genealogist, New

Series, **xv**. 126. Hasted's Kent, ii. 603. Berry's Hampshire Genealogies, 176, 354. Cambridgeshire Visitation, edited by Sir T. Phillipps, 22. Visitation of Durham, 1575, (Newcastle, 1820, fol.) 16. Topographer and Genealogist, ii. 246. Hutchinson's History of Durham, iii. 205. Surtees' Durham, iii. 308. Burke's Commoners, iv. 98. Harleian Society, xli. 82.

MARCHANT. Sussex Archæological Collections, xxv. 199. Cyclostyle Pedigrees, by J. J. Green. Oliver's History of Antigua, ii. 237.

MARCHMONT. *See* CAMPBELL, HOME.

MARCH-PHILLIPPS DE LISLE. Fletcher's Leicestershire Pedigrees and Royal Descents, 192. Burke's Landed Gentry, 8.

MARCHUMLEY. Harleian Society, xxviii. 73.

MARCON. Burke's Landed Gentry, 4, 5, 6, 7, 8.

MARCY. New England Register, xxix. 301.

MAREDITH. History of Powys Fadog, by J. Y. W. Lloyd, iii. 82.

MAREDYDD. History of Powys Fadog, by J. Y. W. Lloyd, iii. 224 ; iv. 382.

MAREDYDD AB HYWELL. Poetical Works of Lewis Glyn Cothi, (Oxford, 1837,) 382.

MARES. Surtees Society, xxxvi. 45.

MARETT. *See* MARRETT.

MAREYS. Banks' Baronies in Fee, ii. 102. The Genealogist, New Series, x. 32.

MARGARY. Burke's Visitation of Seats and Arms, 2nd Series, ii. 12.

MARGERISON. Surtees Society, lxxvii. 123. Ilkley, Ancient and Modern, by R. Collyer and J. H. Turner, 233.

MARGESSON. Berry's Sussex Genealogies, 258. Berry's Surrey Genealogies, 14, 16. Burke's Commoners, i. 295, Landed Gentry, 2, 3, 4, 5, 6, 7, 8. Castles, Mansions, and Manors of Western Sussex, by D. G. C. Elwes and C. J. Robinson, 96. Sussex Archæological Collections, xxvi. 264. Monken Hadley, by F. C. Cass, 174.

MARGETS. Burke's Colonial Gentry, ii. 691.

MARGETSON. Notes and Queries, 8 S. vi. 1.

MARICHURCH. Dwnn's Visitations of Wales, i. 124. Pembrokeshire Pedigrees, 120.

MARIETT. Dugdale's Warwickshire, 635. Bloom's History of Preston on Stour, 48.

MARINDIN. Burke's Landed Gentry, 2 add., 6.

MARISSAL, or MARISHALL. Gloucestershire Notes and Queries, i. 74.

MARJORIBANKS. Burke's Landed Gentry, 2 supp., 3, 4, 5. Foster's Collectanea Genealogica, ii. 61. *See* STUART.

MARKANT. Carthew's Hundred of Launditch, Part iii. 464.

MARKAUNT. Harleian Society, xiii. 241.

MARKE. Harleian Society, ix. 136. The Visitations of Cornwall, edited by J. L. Vivian, 307, 636.

MARKENFIELD. Harleian Society, xvi. 196.

MARKENTON. Harleian Society, xvi. 197.

MARKER. Burke's Landed Gentry, 6, 7, 8.

MARKES. Visitatio Comitatus Wiltoniæ, 1623, printed by Sir T.

Phillipps. Baker's Northampton, ii. 294. Visitation of Wiltshire, edited by G. W. Marshall, 102. Cyclostyle Pedigrees, by J. J. Green.

MARKESHALL. Morant's Essex, ii. 166.

MARKHAM. A History of the Markham Family, by Rev. D. F. Markham. London, 1854, 8vo. The Markhams of Northampton-shire, by C. A. Markham. Northampton, 1890, 8vo. Genealogy of the Markhams, by C. R. Markham. London, 1872, 8vo. Burke's Commoners, ii. 203, Landed Gentry, 2, 3, 4, 5, 6, 7, 8. Foster's Yorkshire Pedigrees. Harleian Society, iv. 23 ; xvii. 80 ; xxxix. 964. Herald and Genealogist, iii. 516 ; vii. 318, 398. W. Dickin-son's History of Newark, 328. Thoroton's Nottinghamshire, i. 344 ; iii. 348. C. Brown's Annals of Newark-upon-Trent, 40. The Genealogist, iv. 249. Wotton's English Baronetage, ii. 330. Burke's Extinct Baronetcies. Metcalfe's Visitations of Northamp-tonshire, 189. Howard's Visitation of England and Wales, ii. 29.

MARKLAND. Nichols' Literary Anecdotes, iv. 657. Chetham Society, lxxxv. 193. Abram's History of Blackburn, 400.

MARKLOVE. Burke's Landed Gentry, 4, 5.

MARLAND. Fishwick's History of Rochdale, 311. .

MARLAR, or MARLER. Harleian Society, xiii. 242, 444. Morant's Essex, ii. 153. Berry's Kent Genealogies, 405. Harleian Society, xiii. 74 ; xlii. 165.

MARLAY. Burke's Landed Gentry, 3 supp., 4, 5, 6, 7, 8. Burke's Royal Descents and Pedigrees of Founders' Kin, 115. The Irish Builder, xxix. 128.

MARLEY. Archæologia Æliana, 2nd Series, iii. 51. Surtees' Durham, ii. 256. Plantagenet-Harrison's History of Yorkshire, i. 250.

MARLING. Burke's Landed Gentry, 4, 5, 6.

MARLOTT. Berry's Sussex Genealogies, 122. Castles, Mansions, and Manors of Western Sussex, by D. G. C. Elwes and C. J. Robinson, 128.

MARMION, MARMYON, or MARMYUN. History of the Noble Family of Marmyun, by Sir T. C. Banks. London, 1817, 8vo. History of the Baronial Family of Marmion, by C. F. R. Palmer. Tamworth, 1875, 8vo. History of Henley on Thames, by J. S. Burn, 270. J. H. Hill's History of Market Harborough, 107. Whitaker's History of Richmondshire, ii. 167. Bridges' Northamptonshire, by Rev. Peter Whalley, ii. 462. Burton's Description of Leicester-shire, 185. Nichols' History of the County of Leicester, ii. 569 ; iii. 350. Dugdale's Warwickshire, 1043, 1135. Baker's North-ampton, i. 548. Memoirs of the Family of Chester, by R. E. C. Waters, 138. Banks' Baronies in Fee, i. 306. Banks' Dormant and Extinct Baronage, i. 129 ; ii. 337, F. G. Lee's History of Thame, 530. Devonshire Notes and Notelets, by Sir W. R. Drake, 41. The Genealogist, New Series, xvii. 171, 172. See DYMOCK.

MARNEY, or MARNY. Gough's Sepulchral Monuments, ii. 41. Morant's Essex, i. 406. Berry's Essex Genealogies, 73. Maclean's History of Trigg Minor, ii. 504, 507. Lipscombe's History of the

County of Buckingham, i. 295. Proceedings of the Essex Archæological Society, iii. 1. G. W. Johnson's History of Great Totham,
38. Harleian Society, xiv. 738. Banks' Dormant and Extinct
Baronage, iii. 509. Chancellor's Sepulchral Monuments of
Essex, 20.

MAROW. Burke's Extinct Baronetcies. Life of Bishop Hough, by
John Wilmot, 140. Visitation of Warwickshire, 1619, published
with Warwickshire Antiquarian Magazine, 144. Dugdale's Warwickshire, 981. Harleian Society, xii. 69. Jewitt's Reliquary,
xxiii. 50.

MARPLES. Burke's Landed Gentry, 8.

MARRES. Pedigrees of Marres of Bathay, in the Lower End, in Bretforton, Co. Wigorn, privately printed by Sir T. Phillipps.

MARRETT. Maclean's History of Trigg Minor, i. 86, 681. J. B.
Payne's Armorial of Jersey, 273.

MARRIOTT. Burke's Royal Families, (London, 1851, 8vo.) ii. 20.
Burke's Commoners, (of Avonbank,) iv. 583, Landed Gentry, 2, 3,
4, 5, 6, 8; (of Cotesbach,) Landed Gentry, 5, 6, 7, 8. Harleian
Society, xxxviii. 717, 814. Burke's Family Records, 419.

MARRIOTT-DODINGTON. Burke's Landed Gentry, 5, 6, 7, 8. Jewitt's
Reliquary, xiii. 244. The Genealogist, i. 81.

MARROW. Burke's Family Records, 420.

MARRYAT. Burke's Colonial Gentry, ii. 431.

MARSDEN. Abram's History of Blackburn, 484, 508, 689. Independency at Brighouse, by J. H. Turner, 84. History of Chipping, by Tom C. Smith, 243. Burke's Family Records, 421.
Staniforthiana, by F. M. H., at end.

MARSEY. Thoroton's Nottinghamshire, iii. 254.

MARSH.[1] Berry's Kent Genealogies, 460. Visitation of Middlesex,
(Salisbury, 1820, fol.) 4. Burke's St. James's Magazine, i. 243.
Burke's Landed Gentry, (of Snave Manor,) 2, 3, 4, 5, 6, 7 ; (of
Gaynes Park,) 2 supp., 3, 4, 5, 6, 7, 8; (of Springmount,) 3, 4, 5,
6, 7, 8 supp. ; (of Ramridge,) 4, 5, 6 ; (of Winterbourne Park,) 8.
Hunter's Deanery of Doncaster, ii. 370. South Mimms, by F. C.
Cass, 56. Harleian Society, xiii. 10; xvii. 81, 82 ; xix. 184 ;
xxxix. 891. Notes and Queries, 2 S. v. 522 ; vi. 59 ; 4 S. i. 352,
399. The Genealogist, New Series, iv. 118. East Barnet, by
F. C. Cass, Part i. 64. Foster's Visitation of Middlesex, 10.
Family Records, by Charlotte Sturge, 68.

MARSHALL (Earls). Gentleman's Magazine, 1827, i. 588 ; 1837, ii.
21 ; 1838, i. 603. Morant's Essex, ii. 554.

MARSHALL, MARESCHAL, or LE MARISCHAL. Miscellanea Marescalliana, by George W. Marshall, LL.D. London, 1883, 8vo., 2 vols.
Berry's Sussex Genealogies, 357. Surtees Society, xxxvi. 175,
316. Berry's Hampshire Genealogies, 72. Gentleman's Magazine,
1864, i. 781 ; 1865, i. 482. Morant's Essex, ii. 367, 511. Burke's
Authorized Arms, 77. East Anglian, ii. 143 ; iii. 30; iv. 31.
Burke's Heraldic Illustrations, 113. Jewitt's Reliquary, viii. 27 ;

---

[1] 'Some Notice of Various Families of the Name of Marsh' is being issued
with the 'Genealogist.'

ix. 69, 72 ; xx. 169 ; xxi. 39, 101, 179, 245 ; xxii. 25, 102, 217. Collinson's Somerset, ii. 332. Account of Township of Church Enstone, by Rev. Edward Marshall, 78. Miscellanea Genealogica et Heraldica, ii. 62. Notes and Queries, 1 S. vii. 83, 297 ; 2 S. vi. 461, 510 ; viii. 431, 522 ; xii. 81 ; 5 S. i. 187 ; 6 S. i. 131 ; ii. 205 ; iii. 304, 313, 354, 366, 498 ; iv. 183 ; v. 157 ; vi. 123, 142, 387 ; vii. 122 ; xii. 27, 112 ; 8 S. vii. 134. Camden Society, xliii. 34. Visitation of Somerset, printed by Sir T. Phillipps, 115. Visitation of Wiltshire, 1677, printed by Sir T. Phillipps, (Middle Hill, 1854, fol.). Burke's Commoners, (of Patterdale Hall,) i. 294, Landed Gentry, 2, 3, 4, 5, 6, 7, 8 ; (of Treworgey,) Landed Gentry, 2, 3, 4, 5, 6, 7, 8 ; (of Broadwater,) 4, 5, 6, 7, 8 ; (of Penwortham Hall,) 5, 6, 7 ; (of Ward-End and Sarnesfield,) 5, 6, 7, 8 ; of Baronne Court,) 8 ; (of Hambleton Hall,) 8. Foster's Yorkshire Pedigrees. Account of the Parish of Sandford, by Rev. E. Marshall, 62. Lincolnshire Tradesmen's Tokens, by Justin Simpson, (London, 1872, 8vo.) 33. Carthew's Hundred of Launditch, Part i. 68; Part iii. 197. Foster's Visitations of Yorkshire, 130. Harleian Society, ii. 103 ; iv. 166, 182 ; xvii. 83 ; xxii. 15 ; xxxvii. 32, 36, 293 ; xxxviii. 725 ; xxxix. 1169 ; xliii. 132. Hodgson's Northumberland, III. ii. 323. Westcote's Devonshire, edited by G. Oliver and P. Jones, 502. Eyton's Antiquities of Shropshire, viii. 165. Nichols' History of the County of Leicester, iii. 1122. Surtees' Durham, iv. 21. Baker's North-ampton, ii. 59. Wright's Essex, i. 660; ii. 127. Chauncy's Hertfordshire, 372. The Genealogist, iii. 161; iv. 11, 157, 295 ; v. 93, 125 ; New Series, ix. 223 ; xiv. 104; xviii. 28. Earwaker's Local Gleanings, ii. 730, 760, 771. Jordan's History of Enstone, 364-371. Yorkshire Archæological and Topographical Journal, vii. 86-111. Manning and Bray's Surrey, i. 577. Clutterbuck's Hertford, i. 492; ii. 463, 510. Banks' Baronies in Fee, i. 309. Visitation of Devon, edited by F. T. Colby, 154. Banks' Dormant and Extinct Baronage, i. 368. Gloucestershire Notes and Queries, i. 131. Annals of Chepstow Castle, by J. F. Marsh, 267. Lanca-shire and Cheshire Genealogical and Historical Notes, iii. 48, 139. Weaver's Visitations of Somerset, 47. Foster's Visitations of Durham, 230. Burke's Colonial Gentry, i. 137 : ii. 636, 692. Surrey Archæological Collections, xi. Howard's Visitation of England and Wales, iv. 119. Burke's Family Records, 423. *See* MARISSAL, HOYLAND, LEESON-MARSHALL.

MARSHAM. Blomefield's Norfolk, vi. 332. Burke's Commoners, i. 417, Landed Gentry, 2, 3, 4, 5, 6, 7, 8. Harleian Society, xiii. 244, 444; xvii. 84 ; xxxii. 196. Edmondson's Baronagium Genea-logicum, v. 420. Brydges' Collins' Peerage, v. 482. The Ship-wreck of Sir Cloudesley Shovell, by J. H. Cooke, 14. History of Boxley, by J. Cave Browne, 133. The Genealogist, New Series, xvii. 13.

MARSHAM-TOWNSHEND. Burke's Landed Gentry, 8.

MARSKE. Archæologia Æliana, 2nd Series, v. 28. Yorkshire Archæological and Topographical Journal, vi. 216. *See* MERSK.

MARSLAND. Burke's Landed Gentry, 5, 6.
MARSTON, or MARSTONE. J. H. Hill's History of Langton, 194.
Topographer and Genealogist, ii. 14.   Burke's Landed Gentry, 2
supp.   Harleian Society, ii. 101 ; xiii. 244 ; xxii. 74 ; xxix. 349.
Nichols' History of the County of Leicester, ii. 798.   Metcalfe's
Visitation of Worcester, 1683, 71.   New England Register, xxvii.
291, 390.
MARTELL. Morant's Essex, i. 434.   Hoare's Wiltshire, IV. ii. 52.
The Genealogist, New Series, xvi. 235.
MARTEN. Morant's Essex, ii. 490.   Burke's Landed Gentry, 2, 3, 4,
5, 6, 7, 8.   Howard's Visitation of England and Wales, vi. 58.
MARTIN. Genealogical Memoranda relating to the Family of Martyn,
by M. Williams. London, 1873, 4to.   Pedigree showing the descent
of Thomas Martin, Esq., as one of the coheirs of the House of
Vaux, etc. Signed, Chas. Geo. Young, York Herald.   Single sheet.
(Contains Richmond and Hutchinson descents.)   History of
Leeds Castle, by C. Wykeham-Martin, 208.   Hutchins' Dorset,
:i. 582-3, 632.   Pedigree of Martin, by Sir T. Phillipps, Bart.,
1833, one page folio.   Pedigree of Martin of Lombard Street,
banker, [T. P.] folio page.   Morant's Essex, ii. 189, 312.
Chronicle of the Family of De Havilland.   Visitation of
Suffolk, edited by J. J. Howard, i. 207-230.   Visitation of
Somerset, printed by Sir T. Phillipps, 117.   Visitation of Oxford-
shire, 1634, printed by Sir T. Phillipps, (Middle Hill, fol.) 24.
Burke's Royal Families, (London, 1851, 8vo.) i. 132.   Miscellanea
Genealogica et Heraldica, i. 53 ; New Series, i. 385, 387, 388 ;
2nd Series, ii. 312.   Burke's Commoners, (of Anstey,) iii. 469,
Landed Gentry, 2, 3, 4, 5, 6, 7, 8 ; (of Bittern Lodge,) iv. 99,
Landed Gentry, 2, 3, 4 ; (of Hemingstone,) Landed Gentry, 2, 3,
4, 5, 6, 7, 8 ; (of Worsborough Hall,) 2, 3, 4, 5, 6, 7, 8 ; (of Colston Bassett,) 2, 3, 4, 5 ; (of Ham Court and Ledbury,) 2, 3, 4, 5,
6, 7, 8 ; (of Whatton House,) 4, 5, 6, 7 ; (of Blomefield,) 3, 4, 5 ;
(of Cleveragh,) 4, 6, 7, 8 ; (of Ross,) 3, 4, 5, 6, 7, 8 ; (of Wiche,)
3, 4, 6 supp., 7, 8 ; (of Ballinahinch,) 2 supp. ; (of Killeshandra,)
5 ; 6 at p. 1777 ; (of Bideford,) 8.   Harleian Society, v. 291 ;
viii. 372 ; xi. 72 ; xvii. 84 ; xix. 40 ; xx. 66 ; xli. 47.   Dallaway's Sussex, II. i. 51.   Westcote's Devonshire, edited by G.
Oliver and P. Jones, 594.   W. Dickinson's History of Newark,
289.   Pembrokeshire Pedigrees, 141.   Surtees' Durham, iv. 149.
Wright's Essex, i. 547.   Lands and their Owners in Galloway, by
P. H. M'Kerlie, i. 501.   J. B. Payne's Armorial of Jersey, 131.
Walter Wood's East Neuk of Fife, 268.   Bigland's Gloucestershire,
ii. 318.   Wotton's English Baronetage, iii. 520.   Banks' Baronies
in Fee, i. 309.   Visitation of Devon, edited by F. T. Colby, 155.
Betham's Baronetage, ii. 406 ; iv. 210.   Banks' Dormant and Extinct Baronage, i. 370.   Metcalfe's Visitations of Suffolk, 52, 152.
The Visitations of Cornwall, by J. L. Vivian, 597.   Fletcher's
Leicestershire Pedigrees and Royal Descents, 181.   Foster's Visitations of Durham, 233.   The Genealogist, New Series, ii. 73 ; iii.
163.   The Suffolk Records, by H. W. Aldred, 9.   Burke's Colonial

Gentry, ii. 798, 812. Burke's Family Records, 426. Ontarian Families, by E. M. Chadwick, i. 90. Oliver's History of Antigua, ii. 240. *See* MARTYN.

MARTIN-ATKINS. Burke's Landed Gentry, 5, 6, 8.

MARTINDALE. Harleian Society, xxxviii. 724.

MARTINEAU. Burke's Landed Gentry, 2, 3, 4, 8. Harleian Society, xxxix. 1107.

MARTIN-LEAKE. Burke's Landed Gentry, 2, 3, 4, 5, 6, 7, 8.

MARTIVAL. Harleian Society, ii. 129. J. H. Hill's History of Market Harborough, 193. Nichols' History of the County of Leicester, ii. 756. Leicestershire Architectural Society, ii. 265.

MARTON. Burke's Commoners, iv. 157, Landed Gentry, 2, 3, 4, 5, 6, 7, 8. Foster's Visitations of Yorkshire, 287. Foster's Lancashire Pedigrees. Collectanea Topographica et Genealogica, vi. 125. Burke's Royal Descents and Pedigrees of Founders' Kin, 126. Whitaker's Deanery of Craven, 67, (88). Harleian Society, xvi. 198.

MARTYN. Pedigree of Martyn of Whethamsted, Co. Herts, [T. P.], 1869, folio page. Dwnn's Visitations of Wales, i. 75. Cambridge-shire Visitation, edited by Sir T. Phillipps, 22. Visitation of Somerset, printed by Sir T. Phillipps, 117. Burke's Landed Gentry, (of Tullyra,) 2, 3, 4, 5, 6, 7, 8 ; (of Pertenhall,) 3. Harleian Society, i. 2 ; vi. 180, 182 ; ix. 137 ; xiii. 445 ; xliii. 23. Visita-tion of London in Transactions of London and Middlesex Archæo-logical Society, 6. Maclean's History of Trigg Minor, i. 287 ; ii. 438. Lipscombe's History of the County of Buckingham, i. 310, 529. Burke's Visitations of Seats and Arms, ii. 23. The Genea-logist, iii. 305 ; New Series, xiv. 191. The Visitations of Corn-wall, edited by J. L. Vivian, 308, 463. Howard's Visitation of England and Wales, ii. 81. The Visitations of Devon, by J. L. Vivian, 552-559. Memoir of Richard Haines, by C. R. Haines. Visitation of Durham, 1615, (Sunderland, 1820, fol.) 44. *See* MARTIN.

MARVELL. Notes and Queries, 6 S. i. 271, 319 ; ii. 231. Harleian Society, xxxix. 1000.

MARVIN, or MARVYN. Visitatio Comitatus Wiltoniæ, 1623, printed by Sir T. Phillipps. Hoare's Wiltshire, I. i. 180 ; IV. i. 20. New England Register, xvi. 235. Visitation of Wiltshire, edited by G. W. Marshall, 6. History of Ufton Court, by A. M. Sharp, 66. The Genealogist, New Series, xii. 166. *See* MERVYN.

MARWOOD. Surtees Society, xxxvi. 160. Burke's Landed Gentry, 2, p. 1316, 5 and supp., 6, 7, 8. Foster's Yorkshire Pedigrees. Graves' History of Cleveland, 231. Westcote's Devonshire, edited by G. Oliver and P. Jones, 604. Ord's History of Cleveland, 408. Notes and Queries, 1 S. xii. 203 ; 3 S. iv. 143 ; 4 S. ii. 174. Visitation of Devon, edited by F. T. Colby, 155. Burke's Extinct Baronetcies. The Genealogist, New Series, i. 234 ; ii. 15, 123, 225. Harleian Society, xxxix. 934. The Visitations of Devon, by J. L. Vivian, 560.

MARX. Burke's Landed Gentry, 5, 6, 7.

MARYON. Records and Pedigree of the Family of Maryon. By J. E.

Maryon. [London,] 1895, 4to. Hasted's Kent, (Hund. of Black-heath, by H. H. Drake,) 122.

MASCALL. Berry's Sussex Genealogies, 328. Surtees Society, xxxvi. 223. W. Paver's Pedigrees of Families of the City of York, 15. Surtees' Durham, i. 220. Foster's Visitations of Durham, 235.

MASCARENE. New England Register, ix. 239; x. 143.

MASCIE, or MASCY. Ormerod's Cheshire, i. 565; ii. 365; iii. 502. Chetham Society, lxxxv. 194; cx. 220. The Genealogist, xvi. 23, 201. *See* MASSEY.

MASCULIN, or MASKELYNE. Pedigrees of Maskelyne of Lydiard Milicent, [T. P.] 1867, and of Maskelyne of Wotton Bassett, etc., [T. P.] 1867, 2 folio pages. Visitatio Comitatus Wiltoniæ, 1623, printed by Sir T. Phillipps. Burke's Landed Gentry, 6 supp., 7, 8. Visitation of Wiltshire, edited by G. W. Marshall, 22.

MASEFIELD. Burke's Landed Gentry, 8.

MASHAM. Noble's Memoirs of the House of Cromwell, ii. 67. Morant's Essex, i. 141. Edmondson's Baronagium Genealogicum, v. 414. Banks' Dormant and Extinct Baronage, iii. 510. Burke's Extinct Baronetcies.

MASON. Dwnn's Visitations of Wales, ii. 165. Berry's Kent Genea-logies, 336. Bibliotheca Topographica Britannica, vii. Parts i. and ii. 351*. Burke's Commoners, iv. 354; Landed Gentry, (of Aldenham Lodge,) 3, 4, 5, 6; (of Necton Hall,) 2, 3, 4, 5, 6, 7 8; (of Masonbrook,) 2; (of Morton Hall,) 5, 6, 7, 8. Foster's York-shire Pedigrees. Harleian Society, viii. 132; xvii. 85, 86, 87; xxix. 353; xxxvii. 201; xxxviii. 792; xlii. 191. Nichols' History of the County of Leicester, iii. 1148. Surtees Society, liv. 218. Arch-dall's Lodge's Peerage, iii. 177. Notes and Queries, 4 S. xii. 87, 335, 418. Carthew's West and East Bradenham, 159. Hasted's Kent, (Hund. of Blackheath, by H. H. Drake,) 81. New England Register, xv. 117, 217, 318; xvii. 39, 214; xviii. 245. Histories of Bolton and Bowling, by Willm. Cudworth, 218. Annals of Smith of Balby, by H. E. Smith, 217.

MASSEREENE. Burke's Royal Families, (London, 1851, 8vo.) ii. 1.

MASSEY, MASSIE, or MASSY. Claim of H. H. J. Lord Massy to Vote at Elections of Irish Peers, Sess. Papers, H of 1856. Cambridge-shire Visitation, edited by Sir T. Phillipps, 22. Burke's Com-moners, (of Pool Hall,) iii. 48, Landed Gentry, 2, 3, 4, 5, 6, 7, 8; (of Pulford Hall,) Commoners, iii. 44, Landed Gentry, 2, 3, 4; (of Alltyrodin,) 7; (of Ferny Glen,) 8; (of Chester,) Landed Gentry, 2 add., 3, 4; (of Coddington,) Commoners, iii. 44, Landed Gentry, 5, 6, 7, 8; (of Kingswell House,) 3 supp., 4, 5, 6, 7, 8. Harleian Society, viii. 51; xiii. 246; xvii. 87, 88; xviii. 169-176, 261; xli. 28. Chetham Society, lxxxi. 56; lxxxii. 79. Ormerod's Cheshire, i. 441, 520; ii. 561, 676, 706, 731; iii. 353, 467. Archdall's Lodge's Peerage, vii. 160. Banks' Dormant and Extinct Baronage, i. 206. Historic Society of Lancashire and Cheshire, New Series, iii. 59-158. Croston's edn. of Baines's Lancaster, iii. 287; iv. 412. *See* MASCIE.

MASSINGBEARD, or MASSINGBERD. Burke's Commoners, iii. 104,

Landed Gentry, 2, 3, 4, 5, 6, 7, 8. Harleian Society, viii. 153 ; xvii. 89. The Genealogist, iv. 254; vi. 268. Burke's Extinct Baronetcies. Massingberd's History of Ormsby, 116.

MASSINGBERD-MUNDY. Burke's Commoners, i. 661, Landed Gentry, 2, 3, 4, 5, 6, 7, 8.

MASSY-BERESFORD. Burke's Landed Gentry, 8.

MASSY-DAWSON. Burke's Landed Gentry, 6, 7, 8.

MASSY-WESTROP. Howard's Visitation of Ireland, i. 91.

MASTER. Notices of the Family of Master, by G. S. Master. London, 1874, 8vo. Hasted's Kent, iii. 276 ; iv. 122. Glover's History of Derbyshire, ii. 346, (313). Berry's Surrey Genealogies, 32. Berry's Kent Genealogies, 24, 25, 122. Archæologia Cantiana, iv. 259, 266 ; v. 238 ; xv. 404. Burke's Commoners, (of The Abbey and Knowle Park,) i. 657, Landed Gentry, 2, 3, 4, 5, 6, 7, 8 ; (of Barrow Green House,) Landed Gentry, 2, 3, 4, 5, 6, 7, 8. Harleian Society, viii. 462 ; xxi. 111 ; xlii. 10, 12, 30. Miscellanea Genealogica et Heraldica, New Series, ii. 160 ; 2nd Series, iv. 72, 101. Genealogical Memoirs of the Families of Chester and Astry, by R. E. C. Waters, 92. Visitation of Gloucester, edited by T. F. Fenwick and W. C. Metcalfe, 120. Howard's Visitation of England and Wales, vi. 139.

MASTERMAN. See HARRIS.

MASTERSON. Harleian Society, xviii. 176.

MASTERTON. Miscellanea Genealogica et Heraldica, New Series, iii. 135, 141. Douglas's Baronage of Scotland, 320. Notes and Queries, 2 S. v. 395, 445. Burke's Landed Gentry, 2, p. 1126.

MATCHAM. Hoare's Wiltshire, V. ii. 56. Burke's Landed Gentry, 8.

MATHAM. Clutterbuck's Hertford, iii. 503.

MATHAVARN. Dwnn's Visitations of Wales, ii. 318.

MATHER. Jewitt's Reliquary, ix. 128, 190 ; xv. 64. Lancashire and Cheshire Historical and Genealogical Notes, reprinted from the ' Leigh Chronicle,' Part ii. 143, 166. New England Register, vi. 20. Staniforthiana, by F. M. H., at end. Harleian Society, xxxvii. 173 ; xxxix. 1053. Howard's Visitation of England and Wales, iv. 33.

MATHESON. History of the Mathesons, by Alexander Mackenzie. Inverness, 1882, 8vo. Burke's Landed Gentry, (of Ardross,) 2 supp., 3, 4, 5, 6 ; (of Achany,) 2 supp.

MATHEW, MATTHEW, or MATHEWE. Maclean's History of Trigg Minor, i. 564. Bibliotheca Topographica Britannica, ix. Part 4, 115. Kent's British Banner Displayed, 406. Berry's Sussex Genealogies, 9. Glamorganshire Pedigrees, edited by Sir T. Phillipps, 8, 22, 27, 51. Visitation of Gloucestershire, 1569, (Middle Hill, 1854, fol.) 7. Burke's Royal Families, (London, 1851, 8vo.) ii. 11. Burke's Landed Gentry, (of Llandaff,) 2 add. ; (of Tresunger,) 2, 3, 4, 5, 6 ; (of Pentloe Hall,) 3, 4, 5, 6, 7. Foster's Visitations of Yorkshire, 552. Visitation of Warwickshire, 1619, published with Warwickshire Antiquarian Magazine, 158. Harleian Society, ix. 137 ; xii. 349 ; xx. 67. Bridges' Northamptonshire, by Rev. Peter Whalley, i. 237. Westcote's Devonshire, edited by G. Oliver and P. Jones, 599. Hutchinson's

History of Durham, i. 472. Thoresby's Ducatus Leodiensis, 254. Baker's Northampton, ii. 37. Castles, Mansions, and Manors of Western Sussex, by D. G. C. Elwes and C. J. Robinson; 226. Archdall's Lodge's Peerage, vii. 222. Visitation of Devon, edited by F. T. Colby, 156. The Visitations of Cornwall, edited by J. L. Vivian, 309, 310. Genealogies of Morgan and Glamorgan, by G. T. Clark, 7-29, 217. Metcalfe's Visitations of Northamptonshire, 36, 113, 114. Oliver's History of Antigua, ii. 252. The Genealogical Magazine, ii. 285, 343, 384 ; iii. 485.

MATHIAS. Pedigree of Mathias of Trejenkin, etc., and of Jones of Kilwendig, by Sir Thomas Phillipps, 1859, folio page. Burke's Commoners, iii. 542, Landed Gentry, 3, 4, 5, 6, 7, 8. Pembrokeshire Pedigrees, 124.

MATON. Visitatio Comitatus Wiltoniæ, 1623, printed by Sir T. Phillipps. Visitation of Wiltshire, edited by G. W. Marshall, 1.

MATTHEWMAN. Harleian Society, xxxviii. 813, 814.

MATTHEWS, or MATHEWS. Morant's Essex, i. 63. Burke's Landed Gentry, 2, 3 and p. 593, 4 ; 8, 8 at p. 58. Foster's Visitations of Yorkshire, 617. Duncumb's History of the Co. of Hereford, ii. 389. Burke's Extinct Baronetcies. Harleian Society, xvii. 89 ; xxix. 355. History of Powys Fadog, by J. Y. W. Lloyd, iv. 197 ; v. 127. Bysshe's Visitation of Essex, edited by J. J. Howard, 65. Oliver's History of Antigua, ii. 259.

MAUDE. Burke's Commoners, (of The Woodlands,) ii. 90 ; (of Sunnyside,) ii. 91 ; (of Alverthorpe,) ii. 83 ; (of Moor House,) ii. 87, Landed Gentry, 2 ; (of Kendal,) ii. 88, Landed Gentry, 2 ; 6 at p. 1386 ; 7 at p. 1587. Foster's Yorkshire Pedigrees. Foster's Visitations of Yorkshire, 300. Harleian Society, v. 219; xvi. 199 ; xxxviii. 618-625. Foster's Pedigree of the Forsters and Fosters, Part ii. 22. Archdall's Lodge's Peerage, vii. 271. Historical Notices of Doncaster, by C. W. Hatfield, 2nd Series, 14. Ilkley, Ancient and Modern, by R. Collyer and J. H. Turner, 138, 148.

MAUDELEY, MAUDESLEY, MAUDSLAY, or MAUDSLEY. Visitation of Somerset, printed by Sir T. Phillipps, 118. Chetham Society, lxxxii. 75. Abram's History of Blackburn, 268. The Genealogist, vi. 15. Weaver's Visitations of Somerset, 48. See MAWDESLEY.

MAUDUIT, or MAUDIT. Herald and Genealogist, vii. 385. Eyton's Antiquities of Shropshire, iv. 56. Hoare's Wiltshire, III. ii. 2-10. Baker's Northampton, ii. 129. The Genealogist, i. 132 ; iv. 87. Banks' Baronies in Fee, i. 310. Banks' Dormant and Extinct Baronage, i. 371. Genealogical Memoranda of the Family of Ames, 14, 16. Harleian Society, xxxix. 1053. See ALNO.

MAUGER. J. B. Payne's Armorial of Jersey, 277.

MAULE. Registrum de Panmure, edited by John Stuart. Edinburgh, 1874, 2 vols., 4to. Nisbet's Heraldry, ii. 48. Memorials of Angus and the Mearns, by Andrew Jervise, 233. Wood's Douglas's Peerage of Scotland, ii. 349.

MAULEVERER, or MAULIVERER. Miscellanea Genealogica et Heraldica, ii. 73-85. Burke's Commoners, iii. 542, Landed Gentry, 2, 3, 4, 5, 6, 7. Foster's Yorkshire Pedigrees. Burke's Extinct Baronetcies. Herald and Genealogist, ii. 304. Graves' History of Cleveland, 122. Thoresby's Ducatus Leodiensis, 118, 190. Ord's History of Cleveland, 458. Hunter's Deanery of Doncaster, i. 297. *See* MALEVERER.

MAULEY. Graves' History of Cleveland, 298. Ord's History of Cleveland, 309. Banks' Baronies in Fee, i. 311. Banks' Dormant and Extinct Baronage, ii. 341.

MAULOVELL. Thoroton's Nottinghamshire, iii. 243.

MAUNDE. F. G. Lee's History of Thame, 619.

MAUNDEVILLE. Blomefield's Norfolk, vii. 420. *See* MANDEVILL.

MAUNSELL. Pedigree of Maunsell of Margam, Co. Glamorgan, [T. P.] folio page. Ashmole's Antiquities of Berkshire, iii. 304. Visitation of Somerset, printed by Sir T. Phillipps, 117. Burke's Commoners, (of Limerick,) i. 304, Landed Gentry, 2, 3, 4, 5, 6, 7 ; (of Ballywilliam,) Commoners, ii. 274, Landed Gentry, 2, 3, 4, 5, 6, 7, 8 ; (of Fanstown,) Landed Gentry, 4, 5, 6, 7, 8 ; (of Oakly Park,) 2, 3, 4, 5, 6, 7, 8 ; (of Thorpe Malsor,) 2, 3, 4, 5, 6, 7, 8. Collectanea Topographica et Genealogica, i. 389. Burke's Heraldic Illustrations, 129. Harleian Society, xiii. 446 ; xvii. 90. Plantagenet-Harrison's History of Yorkshire, i. 419. Bigland's Gloucestershire, ii. par. Saperton. Weaver's Visitations of Somerset, 48. Burke's Colonial Gentry, i. 349. The Genealogist, New Series, xvi. 95. *See* MANSELL.

MAUNSER. Berry's Sussex Genealogies, 309.

MAUNTELL. Baker's Northampton, i. 183. *See,* MANTELL.

MAUREWARD. Nichols' History of the County of Leicester, ii. 194. *See* DE MAUREWARD.

MAURICE. Dwnn's Visitations of Wales, i. 282, 303, 318, 327. Miscellanea Genealogica et Heraldica, New Series, ii. 289. Archæologia Cambrensis, 4 S. viii. 27. History of Llangurig, by E. Hamer and H. W. Lloyd, 86. Collections by the Powys-land Club, iv. 142 ; viii. 78. History of Powys Fadog, by J. Y. W. Lloyd, iv. 107, 237-242, 252 ; v. 63. *See* BONNOR-MAURICE.

MAUTEBY, or MAWTBY. Blomefield's Norfolk, x. 226. Norfolk Archæology, iii. 159 ; iv. 23. Burke's Extinct Baronetcies.

MAUTRAVERS. Collectanea Topographica et Genealogica, vi. 334. Hutchins' Dorset, iii. 315. Hoare's Wiltshire, I. ii. 181. The Genealogist, New Series, xv. 99. *See* MALTRAVERS.

MAUVESYN. *See* DUN.

MAVERICK. New England Register, xlviii. 207.

MAVESON. Harleian Society, xxix. 513.

MAW, or MAWE. Stonehouse's History of the Isle of Axholme, 436. Metcalfe's Visitations of Suffolk, 152.

MAWBEY. Betham's Baronetage, iii. 322. Notes and Queries, 4 S. xii. 119, 458 ; 5 S. iv. 227 ; vi. 372. *See* MAUTEBY.

MAWDESLEY, or MAWDLEY. Chetham Society, lxxxv. 195, 196. Harleian Society, xi. 73. Lancashire and Cheshire Antiquarian Notes, edited by W. D. Pink, 143. History of Chipping, by Tom C. Smith, 268. Croston's edn. of Baines's Lancaster, iv. 131. *See* MAUDELEY.

MAWHOOD. Harleian Society, xxxviii. 625.

MAWSON. East Barnet, by F. C. Cass, 204.

MAXE. Baker's Northampton, i. 66.

MAXEY. Morant's Essex, ii. 157, 410. Harleian Society, xiii. 75, 246, 446.

MAXTONE. Burke's Landed Gentry, 2 supp., 3, 4, 5.

MAXTONE-GRAHAM. Burke's Landed Gentry, 5, 6, 7, 8.

MAXWELL. The Book of Carlaverock; Memoirs of the Maxwells, Earls of Nithsdale, Lords Maxwell and Herries, by Willm. Fraser. Edinburgh, 1873, 4to. 2 vols. Memoirs of the Maxwells of Pollok, by Willm. Fraser. Edinburgh, 1863, 4to. 2 vols. Case for Wm. Maxwell, Esq., claiming to be Earl Nithsdale, Lord Maxwell, Eskdale, Carlisle, and Herries, 1857, folio, pp. 55. Supplemental Case of same, 93 pp., fol. The Seize Quartiers of Henry Maxwell, 7th Lord Farnham, folio sheet. Case of Wm. C. Maxwell (and supplement to case), claiming to be Lord Herries, 1853, fol. Case of Col. G. B. Maxwell, claiming the Earldom of Nithsdale, fol. Speeches delivered by Counsel upon the claim to the Barony of Herries of Terregles, 1854, fol. Claim of William C. Maxwell, of Nithsdale, Esq., to the Dignity of Lord Herries of Terregles, Sess. Papers, 108 of 1849; 130 of 1851; 154 of 1852-3; 172 of 1854; L of 1854-5; D of 1857-8. Herries Peerage Evidence, 264. Burke's Royal Families, (London, 1851, 8vo.) ii. 3, 74. Burke's Landed Gentry, (of Darvagel,) 4, 5, 6, 7, 8; (of Terraughty,) 4, 5, 6, 7; (of Munches,) 4, 5, 6, 7, 8; (of Finnebrougue,) 2, 5, 6, 7, 8; (of Glenlee,) 4; (of Williamwood,) 2, 5; (of Ballyrolly,) 5 supp., 6, 7, 8; (of Kirkconnell,) 5, 6, 7, 8; 7 at p. 797; (of Middlebie,) 7, 8. Burke's Visitation of Seats and Arms, i. 75. Lands and their Owners in Galloway, by P. H. M'Kerlie, i. 277; ii. 301; iii. 240, 252, 257, 266. Shirley's History of the County of Monaghan, 161. Siege of Caerlaverock, by H. N. Nicolas, xix. Douglas's Baronage of Scotland, 52, 450. Wood's Douglas's Peerage of Scotland, i. 418; ii. 311. Archdall's Lodge's Peerage, iii. 386. A Letter from the Countess of Nithsdale, by Sheffield Grace, (London, 1827, 8vo.) 36. Betham's Baronetage, v. 579. Burke's Extinct Baronetcies, 632. Pedigree of the Family of Maxwell of Springkell, by M. J. M. S. Stewart, 1890. Broadside. Notes and Queries, 8 S. ii. 24. The Genealogical Magazine, i. 262. Oliver's History of Antigua, ii. 260. See FARNHAM, PERCEVAL-MAXWELL.

MAXWELL-GRAHAM. Burke's Landed Gentry, 3, 4.

MAXWELL-HERON. Burke's Landed Gentry, 5, 6, 7, 8.

MAY. Pedigrees of May of Broughton Gifford and Moody of Moodyplace, Co. Worcester, [T. P.] 2 folio pages. J. Wilkinson's History of Broughton Gifford, folding plate. Berry's Hampshire Genealogies, 46. Berry's Buckinghamshire Genealogies, 48. Berry's Sussex Genealogies, 21, 36, 56. Burke's Commoners, i. 443, Landed Gentry, 2 supp., 3, 4. Harleian Society, ii. 180; viii. 229, 348, 350, 458; xi. 73; xiii. 447; xxvii. 95; xxxvii. 169. Nichols' History of the County of Leicester, iv. 548. Wiltshire

Archæological Magazine, v. 267. The Worthies of Sussex, by M. A. Lower, 150. Dallaway's Sussex, i. 114; II. i. 50. Visitatio Comitatus Wiltoniæ, 1623, printed by Sir T. Phillipps. Castles, Mansions, and Manors of Western Sussex, by D. G. C. Elwes and C. J. Robinson, 137. Visitation of Somerset, printed by Sir T. Phillipps, 118. Notes and Queries, 3 S. v. 65, 84, 142, 201, 469, 487; vi. 8, 98. Burke's Extinct Baronetcies, 611. Oxford Historical Society, xxiv. 134. Weaver's Visitations of Somerset, 49. New England Register, xxvii. 113. The Genealogist, New Series, xii. 166.

MAYCOCK. Burke's Landed Gentry, 5.

MAYDSTON. Harleian Society, xiii. 447.

MAYDWELL. See MAIDWELL.

MAYER. Oliver's History of Antigua, ii. 262.

MAYFIELD. The Genealogist, iii. 305.

MAYHEW. Burke's Landed Gentry, 8. The Genealogist, New Series, xiv. 250.

MAYLARD. Metcalfe's Visitation of Worcester, 1683, 72.

MAYNARD. Miscellanea Genealogica et Heraldica, ii. 257. Morant's Essex, i. 34; ii. 432. Glover's History of Derbyshire, ii. 326, (291). Berry's Essex Genealogies, 102. Burke's Commoners, iii. 677, Landed Gentry, 2 supp., 3, 4, 5, 6, 7, 8. Harleian Society, vi. 182; viii. 73, 117; ix. 139, 140; xiii. 76; xiv. 594, 679; xvii. 93; xxii. 15. Clutterbuck's Hertford, iii. 497. Baker's Northampton, ii. 190. Chancellor's Sepulchral Monuments of Essex, 91. Wright's Essex, ii. 225. Chauncy's Hertfordshire, 40, 602. The Genealogist, iii. 306. Edmondson's Baronagium Genealogicum, iv. 345. Brydges' Collins' Peerage, vi. 280. Wotton's English Baronetage, iii. 702. The Visitation of Devon, edited by F. T. Colby, 156. Banks' Dormant and Extinct Baronage, iii. 512. Burke's Extinct Baronetcies. The Visitations of Cornwall, edited by J. L. Vivian, 314. The Visitations of Devon, by J. L. Vivian, 561. The New England Register, lii. 337.

MAYNE. Croke's History of the Family of Croke, No. 34. Warwickshire Antiquarian Magazine, Part ii. Burke's Commoners, iv. 504; (of Powis,) ii. 170; Landed Gentry, 2 corr., 3, 4; (of Glynch House,) 3, 4, 5. Foster's Visitations of Yorkshire, 150. Visitation of Warwickshire, 1619, published with Warwickshire Antiquarian Magazine, 42. Burke's Visitation of Seats and Arms, 2nd Series, i. 58. Poulson's Holderness, i. 365. Hoare's Wiltshire, IV. i. 112. Clutterbuck's Hertford, i. 324. Harleian Society, xii. 331. Archæologia, xxxvi. 225. Douglas's Baronage of Scotland, 262. Archdall's Lodge's Peerage, vii. 119. Burke's Extinct Baronetcies.

MAYNEY. Hasted's Kent, iii. 63. Bibliotheca Topographica Britannica, i. Part i. 19. Burke's Extinct Baronetcies.

MAYNSTON. Harleian Society, xxi. 226; xxix. 446. Weaver's Visitation of Herefordshire, 47.

MAYO, MAIOW, or MAYOWE. A Genealogical Account of the Mayo and Elton families, by C. H. Mayo. London, 1882, 4to. Claim of the Rt. Hon. Robert, Earl of Mayo, to Vote at Elections of Irish

Peers, Sess. Papers, 294 of 1849. W. Robinson's History of Tottenham, ii. 163. Berry's Hertfordshire Genealogies, 48. Visitation of Middlesex, (Salisbury, 1820, fol.) 16. Visitation of Warwickshire, 1619, published with Warwickshire Antiquarian Magazine, 194. Hutchins' Dorset, iv. 186. Some Account of the Taylor Family, by P. A. Taylor, 697. The Visitations of Cornwall, edited by J. L. Vivian, 315. Burke's Landed Gentry, 2, 3, 4, 5, 6, 7, 8. Harleian Society, ix. 140; xii. 248. Visitatio Comitatus Wiltoniæ, 1623, printed by Sir T. Phillipps. Hoare's Wiltshire, V. iii. 66. An Historical Survey of Cornwall, by C. S. Gilbert, ii. 197. Visitation of Wiltshire; edited by G. W. Marshall, 62. Foster's Visitation of Middlesex, 28. New England Register, vi. 169. History of the Wilmer Family, 214. The Genealogist, New Series, xii. 167.

MAYOTT. The Genealogist, v. 287.

MEABURNE. Surtees' Durham, ii. 351.

MEAD, or MEADE. Lipscombe's History of the County of Buckingham, ii. 444. Gentleman's Magazine, 1857, i. 72, 204, 329. Morant's Essex, ii. 366, 434, 590, 593, 599. Cambridgeshire Visitation, edited by Sir T. Phillipps, 23. Burke's Landed Gentry, (of Ballymartle,) 4, 5, 6, 7, 8; (of Ballintober,) 3, 4, 5, 6, 7, 8. Harleian Society, ii. 151; xiii. 448; xvii. 93, 94; xli. 69. Nichols' History of the County of Leicester, iv. 818. Archdall's Lodge's Peerage, iii. 295. Bysshe's Visitation of Essex, edited by J. J. Howard, 65.

MEADE-KING. See KING (of North Petherton).

MEADE-WALDO. Burke's Landed Gentry, 7, 8.

MEADOW, or MEADOWS. The Suffolk Bartholomeans, a memoir of John Meadows, by Edgar Taylor. London, 1840, 8vo. Frost and Meadows Pedigrees, two broadsides, no date or place. Gentleman's Magazine, 1824, ii. 518, 602. Burke's Commoners, ii. 648. Harleian Society, viii. 105, 163; xxxix. 1127. Page's History of Suffolk, 75. Brydges' Collins' Peerage, v. 721. See DE MEDEWE.

MEALE. Gyll's History of Wraysbury, 289.

MEALY (formerly Parry). Burke's Landed Gentry, 3, 4.

MEARES. Burke's Commoners, ii. 533, Landed Gentry, 2, 3, 4, 5, 6, 7, 8. Burke's Colonial Gentry, ii. 737.

MEAUTYS, or MEAUTIS. Morant's Essex, i. 19. Clutterbuck's Hertford, i. 93. Harleian Society, xiii. 10, 76, 247; xxii. 75. Private Correspondence of Lady Jane Cornwallis, xlviii.

MEAUX. Poulson's Holderness, ii. 20.

MEDHOP, or MEDHOPE. Harleian Society, iv. 178; v. 258; xiii. 248; xvi. 211. Visitation of Oxfordshire, 1634, printed by Sir T. Phillipps, (Middle Hill, fol.) 25.

MEDHURST. Burke's Landed Gentry, 3, 4, 5, 6.

MEDICI. Earl of Corke's Letters from Italy, by John Duncombe, (8vo., 1773,) 265. Memoirs of the House of Medici with notes, by Sir R. Clayton, Bart. Bath, 1797, 4to., 2 vols.

MEDLEY. Berry's Sussex Genealogies, 74. Horsfield's History of

Lewes, ii. 45. Harleian Society, xii. 107 ; xiv. 595. Notes and Queries, 6 S. ix. 452. Phillimore's London and Middlesex Note Book, 40. Miscellanea Genealogica et Heraldica, 2nd Series, iv. 353.

MEDLICOTT. Burke's Landed Gentry, 5 supp., 6, 7, 8. Harleian Society, xvii. 94.

MEDLYCOTT. Burke's Landed Gentry, 2, 3, 4, 5, 6, 7, 8. Phelp's History of Somersetshire, i. 298. Miscellanea Genealogica et Heraldica, New Series, ii. 8.

MEDOWCROFT. Chetham Society, lxxxv. 196.

MEE. Herald and Genealogist, iii. 410.

MEEK, or MEEKE. Burke's Landed Gentry, 2 at p. 1365, 5, 6, 7. Harleian Society, xxxviii. 535.

MEEKING. Burke's Landed Gentry, 8.

MEEKINS. Burke's Landed Gentry, 3, 4. Burke's Visitation of Seats and Arms, ii. 7.

MEERE. Hutchins' Dorset, i. 343. Harleian Society, xx. 68.

MEERES, or MEERS. English Church Furniture, by Edward Peacock, 34. Berry's Hampshire Genealogies, 114. Berry's Sussex Genealogies, 255. Harleian Society, viii. 70 ; xxxii. 197. Thoroton's Nottinghamshire, i. 360. The Genealogist, iv. 257.

MEESON. See DUN.

MEETKERKE, or MEETKIRKE. Berry's Hertfordshire Genealogies, 190. Burke's Landed Gentry, 5, 6, 7, 8. Clutterbuck's Hertford, iii. 572. Cussan's History of Hertfordshire, Parts v. and vi. 166.

MEGGOTT. Harleian Society, viii. 434. Notes and Queries, 6 S. xi. 68, 177.

MEGGS. Visitation of Middlesex, (Salisbury, 1820, fol.) 39. Hutchins' Dorset, ii. 535. Foster's Visitation of Middlesex, 72. East Barnet, by F. C. Cass, 130. The Genealogist, New Series, iii. 164. Harleian Society, xx. 69. Miscellanea Genealogica et Heraldica, 2nd Series, ii. 378. Surrey Archæological Collections, ix. 293.

MEGRE. Dugdale's Warwickshire, 353.

MEIGH. Burke's Landed Gentry, 2, 3, 4.

MEIGNELL. J. H. Hill's History of Market Harborough, 91. Burton's Description of Leicestershire, 61. Nichols' History of the County of Leicester, ii. 532. See MEYNELL.

MEIGS. New England Register, iv. 91.

MEIL. Dwnn's Visitations of Wales, i. 263.

MEIN. Burke's Colonial Gentry, i. 13.

MEINELL, MEINILL, or MEYNILL. Graves' History of Cleveland, 70, 71, 139. Ord's History of Cleveland, 444, 513. Dugdale's Warwickshire, 229. Banks' Baronies in Fee, i. 313. Banks' Dormant and Extinct Baronage, i. 372. The Genealogist, New Series, xv. 91.

MEIRIG. Dwnn's Visitations of Wales, ii. 126-129, 138.

MEISNELL. Surtees' Durham, iv. 47. See MENEL.

MELBOURNE. The History of Melbourne, by J. J. Briggs, 2nd edn., 161.

MELDON. Burke's Landed Gentry, 5 supp., 6, 7.

MELDRUM. Burke's Commoners, ii. 298. Douglas's Baronage of Scotland, 157.

MELHUISH. Westcote's Devonshire, edited by G. Oliver and P. Jones, 623. Harleian Society, xvii. 95.

MELL. Metcalfe's Visitations of Suffolk, 52.

MELLAND. Harleian Society, xxxviii. 483.

MELLENT. Description of Nuneham Courtenay, Co. Oxford, (1797,) 54.

MELLER, MELLERS, or MELLOR. Glover's History of Derbyshire, ii. 584, (560). Jewitt's Reliquary, vii. 146, 225; xii. 168, 216. Gentleman's Magazine, 1829, i. 412. Visitation of Derbyshire, 1663-4, (Middle Hill, 1854, fol.) 5. Hutchins' Dorset, ii. 186. History of Ecclesfield, by J. Eastwood, 368. The Genealogist, iii. 180. Registers of Ecclesfield, by A. S. Gatty, 126. Harleian Society, xvii. 95 ; xx. 70 ; xxxix. 1077. Old Nottinghamshire, by J. P. Briscoe, 107. Howard's Visitation of England and Wales, iii. 85 ; vii. 153. Burke's Family Records, 429.

MELLERSH. Pedigree of Mellersh of Shipton Solers, [T. P., *circa* 1862,] 8vo. page.

MELLES. Burke's Family Records, 428.

MELLISH. Surtees Society, xxxvi. 297. History of Blyth, by Rev. John Raine, 83. Harleian Society, xvii. 96 ; xxxix. 975. East Barnet, by F. C. Cass, Part i. 58. Willmore's Records of Rushall, 88.

MELSAMBY. Plantagenet-Harrison's History of Yorkshire, i. 512, 542.

MELSOP. Carthew's West and East Bradenham, 41.

MELTON. Poulson's Holderness, ii. 199. Hunter's Deanery of Doncaster, ii. 162. Baker's Northampton, i. 672. Harleian Society, xvi. 202. Banks' Baronies in Fee, i. 299.

MELVIL, or MELVILLE. Nisbet's Heraldry, ii. app. 29. Douglas's Baronage of Scotland, 527. Leven and Melville Papers, xi. Walter Wood's East Neuk of Fife, 250. Memorials of Angus and the Mearns, by Andrew Jervise, 93. Wood's Douglas's Peerage of Scotland, ii. 110.

MELWARD. Berry's Sussex Genealogies, 156. See MILWYRD.

MENDHAM. Thoroton's Nottinghamshire, i. 196.

MENEL, MENNEL, or MENIL. Foster's Yorkshire Pedigrees. Foster's Visitations of Yorkshire, 250. Archæologia Æliana, 2nd Series, iii. 80. See MEISNELL.

MENIFIE. Tuckett's Devonshire Pedigrees, 48. Harleian Society, vi. 183. The Visitations of Devon, by J. L. Vivian, 562.

MENNIS, MENNES, or MENYS. Berry's Kent Genealogies, 263. History of Sandwich, by W. Boys, 350. Harleian Society, xlii. 107. See MYNNE.

MENTEITH. The Red Book of Menteith, by William Fraser. Edinburgh, 1880, 4to. 2 vols. The Red Book of Menteith Reviewed, by George Burnett, Lyon King of Arms. Edinburgh, 1881, 4to. Wood's Douglas's Peerage of Scotland, ii. 223. The Genealogical Magazine, iii. 301, 338.

MENVILL, or MENVYLE. Plantagenet-Harrison's History of York-shire, i. 394. Surtees' Durham, i. 28.

MENWYNICK. Harleian Society, ix. 141. The Visitations of Corn-wall, edited by J. L. Vivian, 318.

MENZIES. The Red and White Book of Menzies. By D. P. Menzies. Glasgow, 1894, 4to. Burke's Royal Families, (London, 1851, 8vo.) i. 68. Burke's Landed Gentry, 6, 7, 8. Nisbet's Heraldry, ii. app. 245. The Upper Ward of Lanarkshire, by G. V. Irving, iii. 145.

MEOLES. Ormerod's Cheshire, ii. 494.

MERCER. The Mercer Chronicle, by an Irish Sennachy. London, 1866, 8vo. Our Seven Centuries, an account of the Mercers of Aldie and Meikleour, and their branches, by G. R. Mercer. Perth, 1868. Pedigree of the Family of Mercer, by Sir C. W. Blunt, Bart. Broadside. The Mercers of Inner Peffray, by R. S. Fittis. Perth, 1877. Burke's Landed Gentry, 5, 6, 7, 8. Chetham Society, lxxxv. 197. Abram's History of Blackburn, 543. Notes and Queries, 3 S. vi. 537; vii. 40, 350.

MERCER-ELPHINSTONE. See NAIRNE.

MERCER-HENDERSON. Burke's Landed Gentry, 2 add., 3, 4, 5, 6, 7, 8. Burke's Royal Descents and Pedigrees of Founders' Kin, 25.

MERCES. Burke's Extinct Baronetcies.

MERCIA (Earls of). The New History of Yorkshire, commencing with Richmondshire, by Genl. Plantagenet-Harrison, (London, 1872, fol.) Part i. 4. Plantagenet-Harrison's History of Yorkshire, i. 4. Savage's Hundred of Carhampton, 92. Pedigrees of the Leading Families of Lancashire, published by Joseph Foster, (London, 1872, fol.). History of Repton by Robert Bigsby, 7. Pedigrees of the Leading Families of Yorkshire, by Joseph Foster.

MERCLESDEN. See DE MERCLESDEN.

MERE. Ormerod's Cheshire, i. 469; ii. 115. Burke's Commoners, i. 191. Harleian Society, xviii. 178. The Genealogist, New Series, iii. 165.

MEREDITH. Hasted's Kent, ii. 481. Dwnn's Visitations of Wales, i. 285, 307, 320, 328. Burke's Commoners, (of Pentrebychan,) iii. 425, Landed Gentry, 2, 3, 4, 5, 6, 7, 8; (of Cloonamahon,) Landed Gentry, 2, 3, 4, 5; (of Dick's Grove,) 2 add., 3, 4. Harleian Society, v. 218; xxix. 356. Herald and Genealogist, vi. 652. The Sheriffs of Montgomeryshire, by W. V. Lloyd, 244. Duchetiana, by Sir G. F. Duckett, 2nd edn., 233. Wotton's English Baronetage, iv. 358. The Visitation of Devon, edited by F. T. Colby, 157. Ormerod's Cheshire, iii. 708. Burke's Extinct Baronetcies, and 611. The Genealogist, vii. 183. Genealogies of Morgan and Glamorgan, by G. T. Clark, 307. Burke's Colonial Gentry, i. 115; ii. 786.

MEREDYDD. History of Powys Fadog, by J. Y. W. Lloyd, v. 279.

MEREDYDD, AB JOHN. Dwnn's Visitations of Wales, ii. 273; ab Thomas, ii. 247; ab Ivan, i. 183.

MEREFIELD. The Visitations of Cornwall, edited by J. L. Vivian, 319.
MEREHURST. Surrey Archæological Collections, x. Harleian Society, xliii. 159.
MERELL. Harleian Society, xiii. 450.
MERES. Berry's Sussex Genealogies, 81.
MEREWETHER. Burke's Landed Gentry, 5. Harleian Society, xlii. 193.
MERIAM. New England Register, xix. 127.
MERIETT. Collinson's Somerset, ii. 170, 297; iii. 258. Somersèt Archæological Society, xxviii. 99-215.
MERIFIELD. Visitation of Somerset, printed by Sir T. Phillipps, 118. Harleian Society, xi. 74.
MERING. Foster's Visitations of Yorkshire, 304. Harleian Society, iv. 12. Thoroton's Nottinghamshire, i. 371. Notts and Derbyshire Notes and Queries, iv. 7.
MERITON, or MERYTON. Surtees Society, xxxvi. 107. Graves' History of Cleveland, 92. Morant's Essex, ii. 263. Fragmenta Genealogica, by F. A. Crisp, v. 93.
MERIVALE. Family Memorials, by A. W. Merivale. Exeter, 1884, 8vo. Harleian Society, xxxix. 1137.
MERLAND. Manning and Bray's Surrey, ii. 586.
MERLAY. Hodgson's Northumberland, II. ii. 375. See DE MERLAY.
MERLESWAIN. Walter Wood's East Neuk of Fife, 239.
MERLEY. Banks' Dormant and Extinct Baronage, i. 135.
MERLOTT. Dallaway's Sussex, i. 65. Sussex Archæological Collections, xli. 109.
MERRICK. Visitation of Middlesex, (Salisbury, 1820, fol.) 20. Harleian Society, viii. 146; xvii. 97. Foster's Visitation of Middlesex, 39. Weaver's Visitations of Somerset, 121.
MERRILL. New England Register, v. 162; xlv. 304.
MERRIMAN. Berry's Berkshire Genealogies, 58. Burke's Visitation of Seats and Arms, ii. 34. Harleian Society, xxxix. 1114.
MERRITON. See MERITON.
MERRITT. Ontarian Families, by E. M. Chadwick, i. 191.
MERRIWEATHER, or MERRYWEATHER. Berry's Kent Genealogies, 348, 468. Harleian Society, xlii. 193.
MERRY. Burke's Landed Gentry, 2, 3, 4, 5. The Genealogist, iii. 181; New Series, viii. 20.
MERSK. Plantagenet-Harrison's History of Yorkshire, i. 188. See MARSKE.
MERSTON. Manning and Bray's Surrey, ii. 612.
MERTINS. Harleian Society, viii. 505.
MERTON. Ormerod's Cheshire, ii. 178. See DE MERTON.
MERVYN. Fasiculus Mervinensis, Notes Historical, etc., of the Family of Mervyn, by Sir W. R. Drake. London, 1873, 4to. Berry's Sussex Genealogies, 92. Miscellanea Genealogica et Heraldica, New Series, i. 358, 423; ii. 3. Dallaway's Sussex, i. 213. Hoare's Wiltshire, I. i. 180. Devonshire Notes and Notelets, by Sir W. R. Drake, 1-33. Parliamentary Memoirs of Fermanagh, by Earl of Belmore, App. III. See MARVIN.

MERY. Harleian Society, xxii. 152.
MESCHINES, or MESCHENS. Archæologia Æliana, 1st Series, ii. 384.
Banks' Dormant and Extinct Baronage, i. 136.
MESE. Visitation of Oxfordshire, 1634, printed by Sir T. Phillipps,
(Middle Hill, fol.) 25. Harleian Society, v. 250.
MESHAM. Burke's Landed Gentry, 8.
MESSER. Pedigree of Wilson of High Wray, etc., by Joseph Foster,
102. Burke's Colonial Gentry, i. 371.
MESSERVY. Généalogie de la famille Messervy. Jersey, 1899, fol.
J. B. Payne's Armorial of Jersey, 168, 281.
MESSINGER. New England Register, xvi. 308.
METAM. See METHAM.
METCALF, or METCALFE. Records of the Family of Metcalfe, by
W. C. and G. Metcalfe. London, 1891, 4to. Genealogical Table,
showing the Royal Descents of, etc., the Metcalfes of Nappa in
Wensleydale, compiled by J. H. Metcalfe. Broadside, 1872. The
Genealogy of Gilbert Metcalfe, Esq., Barrister-at-Law. London,
[1883,] large sheet. Topographer and Genealogist, ii. 117.
Surtees Society, xxxvi. 105, 107, 325. Burke's Landed Gentry,
(of Hawstead House,) 2, 3, 4, 5, 6, 7 ; (of Roxton House,) 2 ; (of
Northallerton,) 5 supp., at p. 1594, 6 at p. 1073, 7 at p. 1237, 8 at
p. 1350. Foster's Yorkshire Pedigrees. Foster's Visitations of
Yorkshire, 249, 302, 409, 553, 554. Harleian Society, i. 42.
Gage's History of Thingoe Hundred, Suffolk, 446. Whitaker's
History of Richmondshire, i. 407. Thoresby's Ducatus Leodiensis,
22. Surtees' Durham, iv. 22. Ingledew's History of Northaller-
ton, 317. Page's History of Suffolk, 654. Whitaker's Deanery
of Craven, 3rd edn., 514. Betham's Baronetage, v. 505. Bysshe's
Visitation of Essex, edited by J. J. Howard, 65. Genealogical
Memoranda of the Family of Ames, unpaged. New England
Register, vi. 171 ; vii. 168, 328 ; xvi. 180, 279. Lincolnshire
Notes and Queries, i. 200. The Genealogist, New Series, xvii. 177.
METGE. Burke's Landed Gentry, 2 supp., 3, 4, 5, 6, 7, 8. The
Wolfe's of Forenaghts, 81.
METHAM. Surtees Society, xxxvi. 139. Foster's Visitations of York-
shire, 106, 252, 364. Hunter's Deanery of Doncaster, i. 351. The
Genealogist, iv. 258. Harleian Society, xvi. 203, 206. See
MEYTAM.
METHLEY. Harleian Society, iv. 59.
METHOLD, or METHWOLD. Pedigree of the Methwold Family, by
some members of the Family. London, 1870, 4to. Visitation of
Norfolk, published by Norfolk Archæological Society, i. 82.
Herald and Genealogist, vi. 598. Memoirs of the Family of
Chester, by R. E. C. Waters, 696, 708. Howard's Visitation of
England and Wales, i. 145 ; Notes, iii. 22. Harleian Society,
xxxii. 197. Muskett's Suffolk Manorial Families, i. 293.
METHUEN, or METHVEN. Collinson's Somerset, iii. 246. Pedigree of
Methuen of Corsham, Co. Wilts, by Sir T. Phillipps, Bart., Middle
Hill. Burke's Royal Families, (London, 1851, 8vo.) i. 105. Burke's
Commoners, i. 392. Herald and Genealogist, vii. 423. Wilt-

shire Archæological Magazine, v. 378. The Genealogist, iv. 59.
Douglas's Baronage of Scotland, 141.

MEURIG. Pembrokeshire Pedigrees, 160.

MEUX. Berry's Hampshire Genealogies, 55, 58, 135. Berry's Hertfordshire Genealogies, 55. Hampshire Visitations, printed by Sir
T. Phillipps, 25. Burke's Extinct Baronetcies.

MEVERELL. The Genealogist, iii. 181. Visitation of Derbyshire,
1663-4, (Middle Hill, 1854, fol.) 5. Harleian Society, xvii. 98.
The Visitations of Staffordshire, 1614 and 1663-4, William Salt
Society, 211.

MEW, MEWS, or MEWYS. Wilson's History of the Parish of St.
Laurence Pountney, 249. 'Winchester Observer,' (newspaper),
Aug. 7, 1886. The Genealogist, New Series, xii. 167.

MEWCE. Metcalfe's Visitations of Northamptonshire, 114.

MEYE. Harleian Society, xxxii. 198.

MEYER. Harleian Society, viii. 515. Burke's Commoners, i. 191.
East Barnet, by F. C. Cass, 160.

MEYERS. Betham's Baronetage, v. 591.

MEYLER. Burke's Authorized Arms, 232.

MEYNELL, or MEYNILL. Surtees Society, xxxvi. 95, 103. Glover's
History of Derbyshire, ii. 158. Topographer and Genealogist,
i. 349, 357, 492. Burke's Commoners, (of Kilvington,) i. 401,
Landed Gentry, 2, 3, 4, 5, 6 and supp., 7, 8 ; (of Meynell Lang-
ley,) Landed Gentry, 2, 3, 4, 5, 6, 7, 8. Foster's Yorkshire Pedi-
grees. Burke's Heraldic Illustrations, 75. Pilkington's View of
Derbyshire, ii. 296. Foley's Records of the English Province
S. J., v. 722. Visitation of Staffordshire, (Willm. Salt Soc.) 44.
The Genealogist, New Series, xiv. 234. See MEIGNELL, MEINELL,
MEYSNIL.

MEYNELL-INGRAM. Burke's Royal Families, (London, 1851, 8vo.)
i. 99. Burke's Landed Gentry, 2, 3, 4, 5, 6, 7, 8.

MEYRE. Harleian Society, xxix. 357.

MEYRICK. Dwnn's Visitation of Wales, i. 136, 156, 178. Burke's
Commoners, (of Bodorgan,) iii. 631, Landed Gentry, 2, 3, 4, 5 ;
(of Goodrich Court,) Commoners, iii. 633, Landed Gentry, 2, 3,
4, 5 ; (of Bush,) Landed Gentry, 4, 5, 6. Hunter's Deanery of
Doncaster, ii. 399. Archæologia Cambrensis, 4 S. vii. 126. History of Powys Fadog, by J. Y. W. Lloyd, vi. 8, 202.

MEYSEY. Nash's Worcestershire, i. 54. Burke's Commoners, ii. 676.
Metcalfe's Visitation of Worcester, 1683, 72. Harleian Society,
xxvii. 95.

MEYSEY-THOMPSON. Foster's Yorkshire Pedigrees.

MEYSNIL. Nichols' History of the County of Leicester, iii. 707.

MEYTAM. Surtees Society, xli. 63. See METHAM.

MICHAELL. Harleian Society, xi. 124.

MICHE. Hutchins' Dorset, ii. 777.

MICHEL. Burke's Commoners, ii. 650, Landed Gentry, 2, 3, 4, 5, 6,
7, 8. Hutchins' Dorset, ii. 610. See MICHELL.

MICHELBORNE. Berry's Sussex Genealogies, 50. Visitation of
Sussex, 1570, printed by Sir T. Phillipps, (Middle Hill, fol.) 8.

Horsfield's History of Lewes, ii. 217. Sussex Archæological Collections, xiii. 257.

MICHELDEVER. Weaver's Visitations of Somerset, 113.

MICHELL. Michell of Shipley, co. Sussex, by Henry Wagner. 1891. Broadside. Burke's Landed Gentry, 7, 8. Airth Peerage Evidence, 116. Berry's Sussex Genealogies, 123, 137, 346. Harleian Society, viii. 561; ix. 142; xvii. 98. Maclean's History of Trigg Minor, i. 292. Dallaway's Sussex, II. ii. 367. Hoare's Wiltshire, I. ii. 172. Plantagenet-Harrison's History of Yorkshire, i. 464. An Historical Survey of Cornwall, by C. S. Gilbert, ii. 199. The Genealogist, New Series, xii. 167. Visitation of Wiltshire, edited by G. W. Marshall, 98. The Visitations of Cornwall, edited by J. L. Vivian, 321, 322. The Visitations of Devon, by J. L. Vivian, 782. *See* MICHEL, MITCHELL, MYCHELL.

MICHIL. O'Hart's Irish Pedigrees, 2nd Series, 242.

MICKLEHAM. Manning and Bray's Surrey, ii. 653.

MICKLETHWAIT, or MICKLETHWAYTE. Burke's Landed Gentry, (of Taverham,) 2, 3, 4, 5, 6, 7, 8; (of Ardsley,) 2, 3, 4, 5, 6, 7, 8. Foster's Yorkshire Pedigrees. Poulson's Holderness, ii. 201. Hunter's Deanery of Doncaster, ii. 353. The Genealogist, i. 150. Surtees Society, xxxvi. 280. Harleian Society, xxxviii. 759. Miscellanea Genealogica et Heraldica, 3rd Series, ii. 262.

MICKLETON. Surtees' Durham, iv. 140.

MICO. Harleian Society, viii. 190; xvii. 99.

MIDDELWEYE. The Genealogist, New Series, xiii. 251.

MIDDLECOT. Hoare's Wiltshire, III. ii. 43.

MIDDLEMORE. Account of the Family of Middlemore. By W. P. W. Phillimore and W. F. Carter. London, 1901, 4to. Burke's Landed Gentry, 8. Howard's Visitation of England and Wales, viii. 77. *See* MIDLEMORE.

MIDDLETON, MIDELTON, or MIDLETON. The Earls of Middleton and the Middleton Family, by A. C. Biscoe. London, 1876, 8vo. Memoranda, by James Middleton Paton, for the use of those relatives who may succeed him. Montrose, 1875. Notes on the Middleton Family, by W. D. Pink. Chester, 1891, 8vo. Saml. Lewis's History of Islington, 430. Morant's Essex, ii. 578. Gentleman's Magazine, lxii. 291, 422, 590, 698, 700, 720, 897, 903, 1100; lxiii. 134, 418. Berry's Sussex Genealogies, 4, 107, 231. Dwnn's Visitations of Wales, ii. 290, 334, 336, 338, 348. Surtees Society, xxxvi. 57; xli. 34, 87. Visitation of Durham, 1575, (Newcastle, 1820, fol.) 8. Visitation of Durham, 1615, (Sunderland, 1820, folio,) 61, 96. Visitation of Westmorland, 1615, (London, 1853,) 16, 41. Burke's Commoners, (of Leam,) ii. 634, Landed Gentry, 2, 3, 4; (of the Grove,) Landed Gentry, 5; (of Tortington,) 8; (of Bradford Peverell,) 5, 6, 7, 8; (of Stockeld,) Landed Gentry, 2, 3, 4, 5, 6, 7, 8. Jewitt's Reliquary, xii. 50. Horsfield's History of Lewes, ii. 15. Graves' History of Cleveland, 412. Foster's Visitations of Yorkshire, 286. Blore's Rutland, 180. Hodgson's Northumberland, I. ii. 353, 359. Dallaway's Sussex, II. ii. 337. Hutchinson's History of Durham, iii. 339. Surtees' Durham, i.

195, 245 ; iv. 70, 168. The Genealogist, ii. 148. Visitation of Sussex, 1570, printed by Sir T. Phillipps, (Middle Hill, fol.) 7. Chetham Society, lxxxi. 62 ; lxxxii. 29 ; lxxxv. 198. Harleian Society, viii. 303 ; xiii. 451 ; xvi. 206-211 ; xvii. 101, 102 ; xxix. 358 ; xxxvii. 206 ; xliii. 188. Whitaker's Deanery of Craven, 206, (280) ; 3rd edn., 256. Collections by the Powys-land Club, ix. 423. Burke's Commoners, i. 172. W. R. Fraser's History of Laurencekirk, 49. Foster's Yorkshire Pedigrees. Wood's Douglas's Peerage of Scotland, ii. 230. Brydges' Collins' Peerage, ix. 246. Wotton's English Baronetage, iii. 382. Betham's Baronetage, iv. app. 1 ; v. 578. Burke's Extinct Baronetcies. History of Powys Fadog, by J. Y. W. Lloyd, iv. 47, 250. Malcolm's Londinum Redivivum, iv. 490-492. Ilkley, Ancient and Modern, by R. Collyer and J. H. Turner, 93. Foster's Visitations of Durham, 237-241. Foster's Visitations of Northumberland, 84. Foster's Visitations of Cumberland and Westmorland, 87-90. Phillimore's London and Middlesex Note-Book, 252. Surrey Archæological Collections, xi. Howard's Visitation of England and Wales, v. 95 ; ix. 128. Miscellanea Genealogica et Heraldica, 3rd Series, ii. 213, 261. Nicolson and Burn's Westmorland and Cumberland, i. 253, 628. *See* MYDDELTON.

MIDDLEWICH. Ormerod's Cheshire, iii. 176.

MIDELHAM. Raine's History of North Durham, 182.

MIDFORD. Surtees' Durham, i. 21.

MIDGEALL. Fishwick's History of Goosnargh, 169.

MIDGELEY. Thoresby's Ducatus Leodiensis, 21.

MIDLEMORE. Dugdale's Warwickshire, 894. Harleian Society, xii. 333 ; xxvii. 9, 96. *See* MIDDLEMORE.

MIERS. Burke's Landed Gentry, 6, 7, 8. *See* MYERS.

MIGHELLS. Historical Account of Lowestoft, by E. Gillingwater, 401.

MIHILL. Harleian Society, xxxii. 198.

MIKLEFIELD. Foster's Visitations of Yorkshire, 139.

MILBANK, or MILBANKE. Burke's Commoners, iv. 398, Landed Gentry, 2, 3, 4, 5, 6. Foster's Yorkshire Pedigrees. Surtees' Durham, i. 274. Wotton's English Baronetage, iii. 329. Betham's Baronetage, ii. 289. Foster's Visitations of Northumberland, 85.

MILBORNE-SWINNERTON-PILKINGTON. Howard's Visitation of England and Wales, ii. 173.

MILBOURNE, MILBORNE, or MILBURN. Jewitt's Reliquary, vii. 26. Harleian Society, xi. 74 ; xiii. 248, 451 ; xxvii. 55. Visitation of Somerset, printed by Sir T. Phillipps, 119. Notes and Queries, 2 S. v. 149, 286 ; 4 S. x. 298. Miscellanea Genealogica et Heraldica, 2nd Series, v. 86. Bysshe's Visitation of Essex, edited by J. J. Howard, 66. Burke's Landed Gentry, 8.

MILDMAY, or MILDME. Pedigrees of the Families of Mildmay, of Moulsham Hall, Essex ; and of St. John, of Farley, Hampshire. London, 1803, 4to. Miscellanea Genealogica et Heraldica, ii. 193, 262. Fitz-Walter Peerage Evidence, 12, 174. Morant's Essex, i. 30, 346, 370 ; ii. 4, 9, 25, 29, 58. Berry's Essex Genealogies, 69, 74, 150. Visitation of Middlesex, (Salisbury, 1820, fol.) 3.

Berry's Hampshire Genealogies, 225, 226. Burke's Landed Gentry, 5, 6, 7, 8. Phelps' History of Somersetshire, i. 437. Baker's Northampton, i. 56. Wright's History of Essex, i. 89. Chauncy's Hertfordshire, 179. Harleian Society, xiii. 11, 78, 249, 453; xiv. 680, 734; xxii. 153. Banks' Baronies in Fee, i. 212. Betham's Baronetage, iii. 375. Banks' Dormant and Extinct Baronage,\ii. 210. Burke's Extinct Baronetcies. Archæologia, xlviii. 201. Foster's Visitation of Middlesex, 7. Chancellor's Sepulchral Monuments of Essex, 66. Bysshe's Visitation of Essex, edited by J. J. Howard, 66. Muskett's Suffolk Manorial Families, i. 42-48.

MILDRED. History of the Wilmer Family, 219.

MILES. Burke's Landed Gentry, (of Leigh Court,) 2 and supp., 3; (of Kingsweston,) 4, 5, 6, 7, 8; (of Keyham,) 8. Nichols' History of the County of Leicester, i. 587. A History of Banking in Bristol, by C. H. Cave, 244.

MILESON. Foster's Visitations of Yorkshire, 628. Metcalfe's Visitations of Suffolk, 153.

MILFORD. Burke's Royal Families, (London, 1851, 8vo.) ii. 79. An Account of the Families of Boase, (Exeter, 1876, 4to.) 32. Visitations of Devon, by J. L. Vivian, 563. See MYLFORD.

MILL, or MILLE. Additional Case of T. Stoner, claiming the Barony of Camoys, on folding table. Berry's Hampshire Genealogies, 26. Berry's Sussex Genealogies, 90. Dallaway's Sussex, i. 233 ; II. i. 239. Fosbrooke's History of Gloucestershire, i. 268. Wotton's English Baronetage, i. 362. Betham's Baronetage, i. 173. Burke's Extinct Baronetcies. Camoys Peerage Evidence, 134, 141. See MYLLE.

MILLAIS. The Lineage and Pedigree of the Family of Millais, by J. B. Payne. London, 1865, folio. J. B. Payne's Armorial of Jersey, 285.

MILLAR. Nisbet's Heraldry, ii. app. 42.

MILLARD. Miscellanea Genealogica et Heraldica, New Series, iii. 445.

MILLATON. The Visitation of Devon, edited by F. T. Colby, 158.

MILLEAR. Burke's Colonial Gentry, i. 183.

MILLER. Collinson's Somerset, i. 104. Hasted's Kent, ii. 240, 261. Berry's Sussex Genealogies, 292. Berry's Hampshire Genealogies, 147, 323. Burke's Commoners, (of Radway,) iii. 699, Landed Gentry, 2, 3, 4, 5, 6, 7, 8 ; (of Monk Castle,) Commoners, ii. 349, Landed .Gentry, 2, 3, 4, 5 ; (of Colliers Wood,) Landed Gentry, 2, 3, 4 ; (of Milford,) 5, 6, 7, 8. Harleian Society, viii. 354, 431. Dallaway's Sussex, i. App. to Chichester. Clutterbuck's Hertford, iii. 580. Sussex Archæological Collections, ix. 33. Geo. Robertson's Description of Cunninghame, 196. Paterson's History of the Co. of Ayr, ii. 440. Paterson's History of Ayr and Wigton, i. 722; ii. 509. Wotton's English Baronetage, iv. 123. Betham's Baronetage, iii. 147 ; iv. 186. Burke's Extinct Baronetcies. Carthew's West and East Bradenham, 159. Burke's Colonial Gentry, i. 136 ; ii. 761.

MILLES. Hasted's Kent, ii. 728 ; iii. 728. Berry's Kent Genealogies,

309. An Historical Survey of Cornwall, by C. S. Gilbert, ii. 203. Visitation of Gloucester, edited by T. F. Fenwick and W. C. Metcalfe, 121. Harleian Society, xli. 72; xlii. 150. *See* MYLLES.

MILLETT. An Account of the Families of Boase, (Exeter, 1876, 4to.) 34. An Historical Survey of Cornwall, by C. S. Gilbert, ii. 201. Harleian Society, xvii. 102; xliii. 174.

MILLICENT. Memoirs of the Family of Chester, by R. E. C. Waters, 167. Harleian Society, xli. 112.

MILLIGAN. Burke's Landed Gentry, 8.

MILLINGTON. Ormerod's Cheshire, i. 448. Harleian Society, xiii. 455; xviii. 179. Bysshe's Visitation of Essex, edited by J. J. Howard, 67.

MILLOT. Visitation of Durham, 1575, (Newcastle, 1820, fol.) 33. Visitation of Durham, 1615, (Sunderland, 1820, fol.) 77. Hutchinson's History of Durham, ii. 416. Surtees' Durham, ii. 153. Foster's Visitations of Durham, 243.

MILLS. Berry's Hertfordshire Genealogies, 217. Visitation of Sussex, 1570, printed by Sir T. Phillipps, (Middle Hill, fol.) 7. Burke's Royal Families, (London, 1851, 8vo.) i. 107. Burke's Landed Gentry, (of Saxham,) 2, 3, 4, 5, 6, 7, 8; (of Tolmers,) 3, 4, 5, 6, 7, 8; (of Lexden Park,) 2; (of Bisterne,) 5, 6, 7, 8. Gage's History of Thingoe Hundred, Suffolk, 110. Willement's Historical Sketch of Davington, 48. Harleian Society, xvii. 103; xix. 180.

MILLUM. Harleian Society, vii. 22.

MILMAN. Harleian Society, viii. 492. Betham's Baronetage, iv. 404.

MILNE. A short Memoir of James Young, app. 4. Burke's Colonial Gentry, ii. 543.

MILNE-HOME. Burke's Landed Gentry, 2, 3, 4, 5, 6, 7, 8.

MILNER. Visitation of Middlesex, (Salisbury, 1820, fol.) 44. Berry's Kent Genealogies, 82. Foster's Yorkshire Pedigrees. Thoresby's Ducatus Leodiensis, 172, 216. Hunter's Deanery of Doncaster, ii. 277. Wotton's English Baronetage, iv. 186. Betham's Baronetage, iii. 187. Foster's Visitations of Middlesex, 82. Harleian Society, xxxviii. 760, 762. Burke's Landed Gentry, 8. *See* MYLNER.

MILNER-GIBSON. Burke's Landed Gentry, 5, 6, 7, 8. Howard's Visitation of England and Wales, i. 150.

MILNES. Glover's History of Derbyshire, ii. 64, 322, (57, 286). Burke's Landed Gentry, (of Beckingham,) 2, 3; (of Fryston,) 2, 3, 4; (of Stubbing Edge,) 2, 3, 4, 5. Foster's Yorkshire Pedigrees. W. Dickinson's History of Newark, 295. Thoresby's Ducatus Leodiensis, 74. Hunter's Deanery of Doncaster, ii. 130. Antiquarian Notices of Lupset, by J. H. (1851 edn.), 41. Betham's Baronetage, v. 431*. Burke's Extinct Baronetcies, supp. Fishwick's History of Rochdale, 379. Harleian Society, xxxvii. 43, 49; xxxviii. 431. The Visitations of Devon, by J. L. Vivian, 800. *See* WATERHOUSE.

MILNES-GASKELL. Foster's Yorkshire Pedigrees.

MILTON. Milton Genealogical Investigation, by Joseph Hunter.

London, 1850, 12mo. Camden Society, lxxv. 43, 64. Mitford's edition of Milton's Works, i. 1. Burke's Patrician, iii. 424. Harleian Society, viii. 402. Gyll's History of Wraysbury, 242. Nichols' History of the County of Leicester, iii. 413. The Genealogist, ii. 309. Notes and Queries, 2 S. vii. 232, 489 ; 4 S. ix. 275 ; 6 S. vi. 291. James Hall's History of Nantwich, 475.

MILWARD. Pedigree of Milward of Tullogher, etc., with branches and Notes, by C. Milward, Q.C. Westminster, 1880, pp. 8, and folding pedigree. Herald and Genealogist, i. 432. Visitation of Somerset, printed by Sir T. Phillipps, 119. Burke's Landed Gentry, (of Thurgarton,) 2, 3, 4, 5, 6, 7, 8 ; (of Tullogher,) 8 ; (of Lechdale,) 2, 3, 4, 5, 6, 7, 8 ; (of Alice-Holt,) 6, 7 ; (of Redditch,) 8. Harleian Society, xi. 75 ; xvii. 104 ; xxxviii. 577. Visitation of Derbyshire, 1663-4, (Middle Hill, 1854, fol.) 5. Sussex Archæological Collections, xiv. 218. Jewitt's Reliquary, xviii. 88. The Genealogist, ii. 391 ; New Series, viii. 21. Bysshe's Visitation of Essex, edited by J. J. Howard, 67. The Gresley's of Drakelowe, by F. Madan, 269. *See* MELWARD.

MINCHIN. Bibliotheca Topographica Britannica, ix. Part iv. 187. Burke's Landed Gentry, (of Rathclough,) 3, 4, 5 ; (of Busherstown,) 5, 6, 7, 8. Burke's Colonial Gentry, i. 352.

MINET. Account of the Family of Minet. By William Minet. London, 1892, 4to. Burke's Family Records, 431. Howard's Visitation of England and Wales, i. 269.

MINGAY. Harleian Society, xxxii. 199 ; xliii. 133. Surrey Archæological Collections, xi.

MINNITT. Burke's Landed Gentry, 2, 3, 4, 5, 6, 7, 8. The Wolfe's of Forenaghts, 59. Burke's Colonial Gentry, ii. 767.

MINORS. Visitation of Staffordshire, 1663-4, printed by Sir T. Phillipps, 7. Visitations of Staffordshire, 1613 and 1663-4, William Salt Society, 213. Weaver's Visitation of Herefordshire, 89. *See* MYNORS.

MINOT. A Genealogical Record of the Minot Family. By J. G. Minot. Boston, U.S.A., 1897, 4to. New England Register, i. 171, 256.

MINSHULL. Miscellanea Genealogica et Heraldica, ii. 183. Cheshire and Lancashire Historic Society, Session ii. 84, 232. Chronicle of the Family of De Havilland. Tuckett's Devonshire Pedigrees, 124. Visitations of Devon, by J. L. Vivian, 564. Berry's Sussex Genealogies, 376. Harleian Society, vi. 184 ; xviii. 180. Lipscombe's History of the County of Buckingham, ii. 590. An Account of Church Minshull, by Rev. G. B. Sandford, 10. The Genealogist, ii. 309. Ormerod's Cheshire, iii. 225, 340, 362. Notes and Queries, 3 S. iii. 278 ; 4 S. xi. 457. Burke's Extinct Baronetcies, 485. James Hall's History of Nantwich, 470, 477. *See* MYNSHULL.

MINSTERCHAMBER. Metcalfe's Visitations of Suffolk, 98.

MINTERNE. Hutchins' Dorset, iv. 422. Harleian Society, xx. 71 ; xliii. 164. Surrey Archæological Society, x.

MINTO. Hawick and its old Memories, by James Wilson, 188.

MIRABELLE. Northern Notes and Queries, iii. 95.

MIREHOUSE. Burke's Landed Gentry, 2, 3, 4, 5, 6, 7, 8. Howard's Visitation of England and Wales, iii. 153.

MIRFIELD. Foster's Visitations of Yorkshire, 266. Whitaker's Loidis and Elmete, 250. Hunter's Deanery of Doncaster, i. 294. Records of Batley, by M. Sheard, 273.

MIRFINE. Berry's Kent Genealogies, 39.

MISSENDEN. Lipscombe's History of the County of Buckingham, i. 394. See MUSSENDEN.

MITCHELL, or MITCHAEL. Visitation of Somerset, printed by Sir T. Phillipps, 119. Jewitt's Reliquary, xi. 16. Morant's Essex, ii. 583. Burke's Landed Gentry, (of Castlestrange,) 2, 3, 4, 5, 6, 7 ; (of Drumreaske,) 4 ; (of Polmood,) 8 ; (of Carwood,) 8 ; (of Llanfrechfa,) 5, 6, 7, 8. Paterson's History of the Co. of Ayr, ii. 423. Shirley's History of the County of Monaghan, 236. Burke's Extinct Baronetcies. Fosbrooke's History of Gloucestershire, i. 307. Douglas's Baronage of Scotland, 427. Paterson's History of Ayr and Wigton, i. 557, 688, 695, 707. Walter Wood's East Neuk of Fife, 278. Wotton's English Baronetage, iv. 207. Betham's Baronetage, iii. 206. Visitation of Gloucester, edited by T. F. Fenwick and W. C. Metcalfe, 122. See FORBES-MITCHELL, MICHELL.

MITCHELL-GILL. Burke's Landed Gentry, 8.

MITCHELSON. Douglas's Baronage of Scotland, 321.

MITFORD. Berry's Berkshire Genealogies, 12. Burke's Royal Families, (London, 1851, 8vo.) i. 136. Burke's Commoners, (of Mitford Castle,) ii. 282, Landed Gentry, 2, 3, 4, 5, 6 and supp., 7, 8 ; (of Exbury House,) Commoners, ii. 285, Landed Gentry, 2, 3, 4, 5, 6, 7 ; (of Pitshill,) Landed Gentry, 2, 3, 4, 5, 6, 7, 8. Hodgson's Northumberland, I. ii. 152 ; II. ii. 44, 71, 537. Nichols' History of the County of Leicester, ii. 869. The Genealogist, ii. 120, 122, 217. Miscellanea Genealogica et Heraldica, New Series, iii. 137, 151. Castles, Mansions, and Manors of Western Sussex, by D. G. C. Elwes and C. J. Robinson, 239. Harleian Society, xvi. 211. Brydges' Collins' Peerage, ix. 182. Foster's Visitations of Durham, 245. Foster's Visitations of Northumberland, 86-89. Croston's edn. of Baines's Lancaster, iv. 56. See OSBALDESTON-MITFORD.

MITTON. Visitations of Staffordshire, 1614 and 1663-4, William Salt Society, 215. Genealogical Records of the Family of Woodd, 29. Harleian Society, xxix. 360. History of Chipping, by Tom C. Smith, 32. See MYTTON.

MOBBERLEY. Ormerod's Cheshire, i. 416.

MOBBS. Claim of Joshua Mobbs to the Wenlock Estates, 1866, 8vo., pp. 24.

MODYFORD. Burke's Extinct Baronetcies.

MOELS, or MOELES. Visitation of Somersetshire, printed by Sir T. Phillipps, 152. Banks' Dormant and Extinct Baronage, ii. 344. Hoare's Wiltshire, I. ii. 91. Clutterbuck's Hertford, ii. 32. Banks' Baronies in Fee, i. 315. Weaver's Visitations of Somerset, 50. See DE MOELS.

MOENS. Burke's Landed Gentry, 7, 8.
MOFFATT. Burke's Colonial Gentry, i. 184. Burke's Landed Gentry,
7, 8.
MOGG. Burke's Landed Gentry, 6, 7, 8.
MOGGRIDGE. Fosbrooke's History of Gloucestershire, ii. 238.
MOGHAN. O'Hart's Irish Pedigrees, 2nd Series, 245.
MOGRADGE. Visitatio Comitatus Wiltoniæ, 1623, printed by Sir T.
Phillipps. Visitation of Wiltshire, edited by G. W. Marshall, 94.
MOHUN. Collinson's Somerset, ii. 8. Savage's Hundred of Car-
hampton, 458, 484, 489. History of Newenham Abbey, by James
Davidson, 203. Tuckett's Devonshire Pedigrees, 77, 79. Harleian
Society, vi. 185 ; ix. 143 ; xx. 72 ; xxii. 16. Westcote's Devon-
shire, edited by G. Oliver and P. Jones, 610. Hutchins' Dorset,
i. 273 ; ii. 742. Baker's Northampton, ii. 239. An Historical
Survey of Cornwall, by C. S. Gilbert, i. 534. Archæological
Journal, xxxvii. 90-93. Banks' Baronies in Fee, i. 316. Visita-
tion of Devon, edited by F. T. Colby, 159. Banks' Dormant and
Extinct Baronage, i. 373 ; iii. 518. Dunster and its Lords, by
H. C. Maxwell Lyte, (Exeter, 1882, 8vo.), 32-37. Burke's Extinct
Baronetcies. The Visitations of Cornwall, edited by J. L. Vivian,
323. Hasted's Kent, (Hund. of Blackheath, by H. H. Drake,)
xxiii. Visitations of Devon, by J. L. Vivian, 565.
MOILLIET. Burke's Landed Gentry, 4, 5, 6, 7, 8.
MOIR. The Families of Moir and Byres, by A. J. M. Gill. Edin-
burgh, 1885, 4to. Burke's Landed Gentry, 2 supp., 3, 4, 5, 6, 7, 8.
Burke's Extinct Baronetcies, 633.
MOIRA (Earl of). Grandison Peerage Evidence, 344.
MOIR BYRES. Burke's Landed Gentry, 8.
MOISTON. Dwnn's Visitations of Wales, ii. 307-309.
MOLAM. Hutchins' Dorset, i. 671.
MOLDEWORTH. Ormerod's Cheshire, ii. 331.
MOLEDY. O'Hart's Irish Pedigrees, 2nd Series, 125.
MOLESWORTH. Claim of the Rt. Hon. Richard Pigot, Visct. Moles-
worth, to Vote at Elections of Irish Peers, Sess. Papers, 76 of
1821. Chronicle of the Family of De Havilland. Foster's
Lancashire Pedigrees. Maclean's History of Trigg Minor, i. 463-
472. Harleian Society, ix. 147 ; xvii. 116. Miscellanea Genealogica et Heraldica, New Series, ii. 280. A Complete Parochial
History of the County of Cornwall, i. 321. An Historical Survey
of Cornwall, by C. S. Gilbert, i. 571. Archdall's Lodge's Peerage,
v. 127. Wotton's English Baronetage, iv. 25. Betham's Baronetage, iii. 86. The Visitations of Cornwall, edited by J. L. Vivian,
327, 330. Burke's Colonial Gentry, i. 164. Howard's Visitation
of England and Wales, iii. 37. The Irish Builder, xxxv. 124.
Howard's Visitation of England and Wales, iv. 110. Burke's
Landed Gentry, 8.
MOLESWORTH ST. AUBYN. Burke's Landed Gentry, 4, 5, 6.
MOLEYNS, MOLINS, or MOLINES. Visitation of Oxfordshire, 1634,
printed by Sir T. Phillipps, (Middle Hill, fol.) 25. Harleian
Society, vi. 264. Lipscombe's History of the County of Bucking-

ham, iv. 547. Visitatio Comitatus Wiltoniæ, 1623, printed by
Sir T. Phillipps. Hoare's Wiltshire, I. ii. 93. Visitation of
Somerset, printed by Sir T. Phillipps, 119. Notes and Queries,
1 S. x. 444, 532. Banks' Baronies in Fee, i. 317. Banks'
Dormant and Extinct Baronage, ii. 349. Visitation of Wilt-
shire, edited by G. W. Marshall, 67. Weaver's Visitations of
Somerset, 51. The Visitations of Devon, by J. L. Vivian,
691. The Perverse Widow, by A. W. Crawley-Boevey, 274.
See MOLYNS.

MOLFORD. Harleian Society, vi. 187. Westcote's Devonshire, edited
by G. Oliver and P. Jones, 603. Visitations of Devon, by J. L.
Vivian, 567.

MOLINE. Memoir of Richard Haines, by C. R. Haines, table x^b.

MOLINEUX, or MOLYNEUX. Memoir of the Molineux Family, by
Gisborne Molineux. London, 1882, 4to. Pedigree of Molyneux
of Castle Dillon, Co. Armagh, by Sir T. Phillipps, Bart. Evesham,
1819; 2nd edn., 1840; another edn., 1868. Broadside. Molineux
descending from Dovedale of Palmerston, single page, marked
page 3, by Sir T. Phillipps, Bart., the same, 2nd edition, 1840,
folio sheet. Account of the Family and Descendants of Sir
Thomas Molyneux, Kt., by Sir T. Phillipps, Bart. Evesham, 1820,
4to. A History of the Family of Molyneux, by Sir T. Phillipps,
Bart., 1821, 12mo. Shuldham *v.* Smith, Defendant's Case in
House of Lords, 1818, 2 tables. Burke's Heraldic Illustrations,
129. Berry's Surrey Genealogies, 87. Burke's Landed Gentry,
2, 3, 4, 5, 8. Harleian Society, iv. 72. Chetham Society, lxxxi.
99, 103, 108; lxxxii. 131; lxxxv. 200-208; xcv. 30, 71; cx. 135.
Foster's Lancashire Pedigrees. Brayley's History of Surrey, i.
418. Manning and Bray's Surrey, i. 97. Baines' History of the
Co. of Lancaster, iv. 216; Croston's edn., v. 75, 226. Thoroton's
Nottinghamshire, ii. 304. Archdall's Lodge's Peerage, iii. 239.
Wotton's English Baronetage, i. 141. Betham's Baronetage, i.
99. Burke's Extinct Baronetcies. Howard's Visitation of England
and Wales, i. 116. The Genealogist, New Series, iii. 165. The
Irish Builder, xxix. 101. Burke's Family Records, 433. Sefton,
by W. D. Caröe, xxi.

MOLLESLEY. Shaw's Staffordshire, ii. 184, 276.

MOLLEY. Burke's Landed Gentry, 4.

MOLLOY. Burke's Landed Gentry, 6, 7. O'Hart's Irish Pedigrees,
2nd Series, 245.

MOLONY. Burke's Commoners, (of Kiltanon,) iv. 767, Landed
Gentry, 2, 3, 4, 5, 6, 7, 8; (of Cragg,) 8; (of Granahan,) Commoners, iv. 768, Landed Gentry, 2, 3, 4 5.

MOLYNEUX-SEEL. Burke's Landed Gentry, 5, 6, 7, 8.

MOLYNS, or MOLYNES. Berry's Hampshire Genealogies, 249. Harleian Society, v. 233. *See* MOLEYNS.

MOMPESSON. Pedigree of Mompesson of Maiden Bradley, [T. P.]
folio page. Berry's Hampshire Genealogies, 111. Harleian
Society, viii. 154. Hutchins' Dorset, i. 632. Hoare's Wiltshire,
I. ii. 219. Visitation of Wiltshire, edited by G. W. Marshall, 60,

96. History of Ufton Court, by A. M. Sharp, 66. The Genealogist, New Series, xii. 168.

MONBOUCHER, or MONBOCHER. Harleian Society, iv. 50. Hodgson's Northumberland, II. ii. 260. Surtees' Durham, ii. 225. Sussex Archæological Collections, xiv. 113. Thoroton's Nottinghamshire, iii. 177, 254. Plantagenet-Harrison's History of Yorkshire, i. 167.

MONCEAUX. Poulson's Holderness, i. 186.

MONCHENSIE, or MONCHENSY. Lipscombe's History of the County of Buckingham, ii. 141 ; iii. 410. Harvey's Hundred of Willey, 4. *See* MONTCHENSI, MUNCHENSI.

MONCK. Claim of the Rt. Hon. Charles Stanley, Visct. Monck, to Vote at Elections of Peers, Sess. Papers, 121 of 1849. Berry's Berkshire Genealogies, 20. Burke's Commoners, iv. 181, Landed Gentry, 2, 3, 4, 5, 6, 7, 8. Whitaker's History of Whalley, i. 253. Visitation of Devon, edited by F. T. Colby, 160. Howard's Visitation of England and Wales, ii. 134, 137. Howard's Visitation of Ireland, ii. 91. *See* MONK, MUNCK.

MONCK-MASON. Burke's Commoners, iv. 354.

MONCKTON, or MONCTON. A Genealogical History of the Family of Monckton, by D. H. Monckton, M.D. London, 1887, 4to. Berry's Kent Genealogies, 490. Burke's Landed Gentry, (of Somerford,) 5, 6, 7, 8 ; (of Fineshade Abbey,) 5, 6, 7, 8. Archdall's Lodge's Peerage, v. 249. Yorkshire Genealogist, i. 219. Surrey Archæological Society, x. Harleian Society, xliii. 164.

MONCKTON-ARUNDELL. History of Blyth, by Rev. John Raine, 112. Hunter's Deanery of Doncaster, ii. 414.

MONCRIEFF. Nisbet's Heraldry, ii. app. 31. Douglas's Baronage of Scotland, 43. Walter Wood's East Neuk of Fife, 261. Burke's Landed Gentry, 7, 8.

MONDEFORD. Harleian Society, xxxii. 200.

MONEY. Burke's Commoners, (of Much Marcle,) iii. 615, Landed Gentry, 2, 3, 4, 5, 6; (of Walthamstow,) Landed Gentry, 2. Burke's Heraldic Illustrations, 58. Robinson's Mansions of Herefordshire, 281.

MONEY-KYRLE. Burke's Commoners, iii. 615, Landed Gentry, 2, 3, 4, 5, 6, 7. Burke's Heraldic Illustrations, 64. Duncombe's Hereford, (J. H. Cooke,) iii. 29.

MONEYPENNY, or MONYPENNY. Berry's Kent Genealogies, 313. Burke's Landed Gentry, 2, 3, 4, 5. Wood's Douglas's Peerage of Scotland, ii. 247.

MONFODE. Monfode of that Ilk, by R. Malcolm Kerr, LL.D., 1880, 8vo.

MONFORD. Harleian Society, xvi. 213. *See* MOUNTFORD.

MONGER. Harleian Society, xvii. 106.

MONHALT. *See* MONTALT.

MONINGTON. Robinson's Mansions of Herefordshire, 250. The Genealogist, New Series, xii. 9. Weaver's Visitation of Herefordshire, 48.

MONINS. Burke's Extinct Baronetcies. Hasted's Kent, iv. 55, 188. Berry's Kent Genealogies, 179. Burke's Landed Gentry, 2 supp., 3, 4, 8. Harleian Society, xlii. 28.

MONK, or MONKE. The Pedigree and Descent of His Excellency
Genl. George Monck, etc. London, 1659, 4to. Harleian Society,
vi. 189. Gregson's Fragments relative to the County of Lancaster,
274. Westcote's Devonshire, edited by G. Oliver and P. Jones,
468. Berry's Sussex Genealogies, 102. Berry's Berkshire Genealogies, 13-20. Notes and Queries, 2 S. xii. 442, 526 ; 3 S. i. 137,
427. Banks' Dormant and Extinct Baronage, iii. 36. Burke's
Commoners, ii. 304. Visitations of Devon, by J. L. Vivian, 568.
Oliver's History of Antigua, ii. 266. *See* FORREST, MONCK.

MONKETON, or MONKTON. Surtees Society, xxxvi. 163. Foster's
Visitations of Yorkshire, 134, 171. The Genealogist, New Series,
xvi. 167 ; xvii. 257.

MONMOUTH. Banks' Dormant and Extinct Baronage, i. 138.

MONNOUX, MONOUX, or MONOX. Berry's Hertfordshire Genealogies,
174. Transactions of the London and Middlesex Archæological
Society, ii. 145. Harleian Society, xiii. 78, 79, 252 ; xix. 123 ;
xxii. 76. Wotton's English Baronetage, iii. 187. Betham's
Baronetage, ii. 174. Burke's Extinct Baronetcies.

MONRO. Burke's Landed Gentry, (of Edmondsham and Ewell
Castle,) 2 supp., 3, 4, 5, 6, 7, 8 ; (of Ludford Park,) 5 ; (of Auchin-
bowie,) 5, 6, 7, 8 ; (of Allan,) 6, 7, 8 ; (of Ingsdon,) 6, 7, 8.
Annals of Colinton, by Thomas Murray, 87. Burrows' History of
the Family of Burrows, 208. *See* MUNRO.

MONSELL. Burke's Landed Gentry, 2, 3, 4, 5.

MONSON. Hasted's Kent, ii. 784. Berry's Herfordshire Genealogies,
122. Clutterbuck's Hertford, ii. 55. Edmondson's Baronagium
Genealogicum, v. 428. Brydges' Collins' Peerage, vii. 228.
Alexander Nisbet's Heraldic Plates, 135. Rockingham Castle
and the Watsons, ped. 6.

MONTACUTE. Morant's Essex, ii. 378. Visitation of Somersetshire,
printed by Sir T. Phillipps, 151. Lipscombe's History of the
County of Buckingham, ii. 75. Dallaway's Sussex, i. 250. Hutchins'
Dorset, iii. 291. Clutterbuck's Hertford, i. 481 ; iii. 287. Banks'
Baronies in Fee, i. 318, 324. Banks' Dormant and Extinct
Baronage, ii. 350 ; iii. 647. *See* LOUDOUN, LOWNDES.

MONTAGU, MONTAGUE, or MOUNTAGU. Case of Henry Browne,
Esq., on his claim to the Title of Viscount Montague, 1851, 4to.
Pedigree of Montagu of Lackham, [T. P.] fol. page. Collinson's
Somerset, iii. 47. Jacob's Peerage, i. 370, 384, 556, 566. The
Great Governing Families of England, i. 303. Hasted's Kent,
i. 41. Harleian Society, ii. 124 ; vi. 264 ; viii. 488. Herald and
Genealogist, iii. 422. Gregson's Fragments relative to the County
of Lancaster, 274. Westcote's Devonshire, edited by G. Oliver
and P. Jones, 633. Wiltshire Archæological Magazine, iii. 87.
Burke's Commoners, ii. 52. Burke's Landed Gentry, 3, 4, 5, 6, 7,
8. Bridges' Northamptonshire, by Rev. Peter Whalley, i. 368 ;
ii. 117, 352. An Historical Survey of Cornwall, by C. S. Gilbert,
i. 439. Edmondson's Baronagium Genealogicum, i. 64 ; ii. 136 ;
iii. 211. Brydges' Collins' Peerage, ii. 42 ; iii. 448. Berry's
Genealogical Peerage, 64. Banks' Dormant and Extinct Baronage,

iii. 335, 530. Visitation of Wiltshire, edited by G. W. Marshall,
79. Notes and Queries, 3 S. iv. 72. Metcalfe's Visitations of
Northamptonshire, 37, 114. Weaver's Visitations of Somerset,
52. Burke's Colonial Gentry, ii. 806. The Genealogist, New
Series, xiii. 181 ; xiv. 17 ; xvii. 173. The Visitations of Devon,
by J. L. Vivian, 691. Rockingham Castle and the Watsons, ped.
2. *See* LOUDOUN.

MONTALT. Baker's Northampton, i. 516. Ormerod's Cheshire, i. 58.
Page's History of Suffolk, 515. Harleian Society, xvi. 199 ; xviii.
181. Banks' Baronies in Fee, i. 324. Banks' Dormant and
Extinct Baronage, i. 375. The Genealogist, New Series, xiii. 102.
See DE MONTALT.

MONTCHENSI. Hasted's Kent, i. 257. Morant's Essex, i. 411 ; ii. 35.
See MONCHENSIE, MOUNTCHENSY.

MONTEAGLE. Banks' Baronies in Fee, i. 325.

MONTEFERRARD. The Genealogist, New Series, xvii. 117.

MONTEIGNE. Oliver's History of Antigua, ii. 268.

MONTEITH. Burke's Landed Gentry, 3, 4, 5, 6, 7, 8. Glasgow Past
and Present, (Glasgow, 1856, 8vo.) iii. 313.

MONTFITCHET. Morant's Essex, ii. 576. History of the Parish of
St. Leonard, Shoreditch, by Henry Ellis, . 98. Gyll's History of
Wraysbury, 6. Proceedings of the Essex Archæological Society,
v. 173. Clutterbuck's Hertford, ii. 261. Banks' Dormant and
Extinct Baronage, i. 140. Hasted's Kent, (Hund. of Blackheath,
by H. H. Drake,) xxvi.

MONTFODE. Montfode of that Ilk, and Descendants. Glasgow,
1847, 4to.

MONTFORD. The Gresley's of Drakelowe, by F. Madan, 270.

MONTFORT, or MONTFORD. Munford's Analysis of Domesday Book
of Co. Norfolk, 36. Nichols' History of the County of Leicester,
i. 212, App. 118. Dugdale's Warwickshire, 786, 799. Hunter's
Deanery of Doncaster, ii. 50. Manning and Bray's Surrey, ii.
627. Harleian Society, xii. 55 ; xvii. 107. J. E. Jackson's Guide
to Farley Hungerford, 3rd edn., 88. Prothero's Life of Simon de
Montfort, 370. Banks' Baronies in Fee, i. 327. Banks' Dormant
and Extinct Baronage, i. 376. Norfolk Antiquarian Miscellany,
i. 413. Willmore's History of Walsall, 282. The Genealogist,
New Series, xiii. 243, 252 ; xiv. 103, 104.

MONTGOMERIE. Memorials of the Montgomeries, Earls of Eglinton,
by William Fraser. Edinburgh, 1859, 2 vols. 4to. Case of A. W.
Montgomerie, Earl of Eglinton, etc., relating to title of Lord Kil-
winning, pp. 28, fol. A Genealogical Account of the Family of
Montgomerie, by William Anderson. Edinburgh, 1859, 4to.
Historical Memoir of the Family of Eglinton and Winton, by John
Fullarton. Ardrossan, 1864, 8vo. Genealogy of the Montgomeries
of Smithton, by Sir Robt. Douglas, Bart. Windsor, 1795, 8vo.
Burke's Landed Gentry, (of Annick Lodge,) 2, 3, 4 ; (of Gar-
boldisham,) 4 supp., 5, 6, 7, 8. Burke's Visitation of Seats and
Arms, 2nd Series, i. 36. Geo. Robertson's Description of Cunning-
hame, 77, 205, 249, 281-5, 318, 398. Paterson's History of the

Co. of Ayr, i. 230, 279-292 ; ii. 100, 229, 309, 367, 452. Paterson's History of Ayr and Wigton, i. 314 ; ii. 274, 399 ; iii. 71,
86, 98, 173, 213, 275, 278, 491, 533, 594. J. E. Reid's History
of the Co. of Bute, 216-228.

MONTGOMERY. A Genealogical History of the Family of Montgomery,
by E. G. S. Reilly, 1842, 4to. The Curio, (New York,) i. 55.
Hasted's Kent, (Hund. of Blackheath, by H. H. Drake,) xxvi.
Burke's Colonial Gentry, ii. 460. Harleian Society, xxix. 363.
Howard's Visitation of Ireland, ii. 25, 98. Parliamentary Memoirs
of Fermanagh, by Earl of Belmore, 56. The Gresley's of Drakelowe,
by F. Madan, 271. Herald and Genealogist, iv. 462. Shirley's
History of the County of Monaghan, 234. The Montgomery
Manuscripts, etc., by W. Montgomery. Belfast, 1830, 12mo. The
Montgomery Manuscripts, edited by the Rev. George Hill.
Belfast, 1869, 4to. (vol. i. all published.) Tierney's History of
Arundel, 141. Clifford's Description of Tixall, 109. Burke's
Commoners, (of Grey Abbey,) iv. 186, Landed Gentry, 2, 3, 4, 5,
6, 7, 8 ; (of Killee,) 8 ; (of Milton,) Landed Gentry, 2 supp., 3 ;
(of Benvarden,) 3, 4, 5, 6, 7, 8 ; (of Belhavel,) 3, 4, 5, 6, 7, 8 ;
(of Convoy House,) 2, 3, 4, 5, 6, 7, 8 ; (of Crilly House,) 4, 5, 6, 7,
8 ; (of Beaulieu,) 5, 6 and supp., 7, 8 ; (of Blessingbourne,) 6, 7,
8. Jewitt's Reliquary, xv. 7. The Palatine Note Book, i. 185.
Douglas's Baronage of Scotland, 525. The Ulster Journal of
Archæology, ix. 156, 278. Wood's Douglas's Peerage of Scotland,
i. 490. Notes and Queries, 2 S. i. 293, 400 ; ii. 133 ; 4 S. i. 4.
Burke's Extinct Baronetcies, and 633. Brydges' Collins' Peerage,
ix. 283. Betham's Baronetage, v. 471. See ARUNDEL, MOUNT-
GOMERY.

MONTGOMERY-MOORE. Burke's Landed Gentry, 4, 5, 6 and supp., 7, 8.

MONTHERMER. Banks' Baronies in Fee, i. 328. Banks' Dormant and
Extinct Baronage, ii. 355. See LOUDOUN, LOWNDES.

MONTMORENCY. Histoire Généalogique de la Maison de Montmorency,
par André du Chesne. Paris, 1624, folio. A Genealogical Memoir
of the Family of Montmorency, styled De Marisco, or Morres, by
Henry de Montmorency-Morres. Paris, 1817, 4to. Les Montmorency de France et les Montmorency d'Irlande, Précis Historique.
Paris, 1828, 4to. See DE MONTMORENCY.

MONTRESOR. Burke's Landed Gentry, 3, 4, 5, 6, 7, 8.

MONTROSE. Case of James, Duke of Montrose, in opposition to
the case of James, Earl of Crawford and Balcarres, claiming the
title of Duke of Montrose. Edinburgh, n.d., fol. pp. 55, and app.
pp. 16. Supplemental Case of same. Edinburgh, 1853, fol.
Abstract of the Case, drawn up by John Riddell. London, 1850,
8vo. Abstract of the Supplemental Case, by John Riddell.
London, 1852, 8vo. Abstract of Supplemental Case of James,
Duke of Montrose, in answer, etc. Edinburgh, 1853, 8vo. Analysis
of the objections started by the Crown, etc., by John Riddell, in
the matter of, etc., the Earl of Balcarres' claim to the Earldom of
Crawford, 1847, 8vo. Case of James, Earl of Crawford and
Balcarres, claiming the Dukedom of Montrose, 1850, folio, pp. 62.

Supplemental Case of same. London, 1852, folio, pp. 208. Addenda to Supplemental Case of same, 1852, folio, pp. 49. *See* CRAUFUIRD.

MONTSIGROS. The Genealogist, New Series, ix. 10.

MONYPENNY. Burke's Landed Gentry, 6, 7. *See* GYBBON-MONYPENNY.

MOOD. Burke's Landed Gentry, 8.

MOODY. Moody of Moody Place, Co. Worc., etc., [T. P.] folio page. Berry's Hampshire Genealogies, 95. Burke's Commoners, ii. 560, Landed Gentry, 2, 3, 4, 5. Burke's Extinct Baronetcies. Genealogical Gleanings in England, by H. F. Waters, i. 96. New England Register, iv. 179 ; xxxix. 69. *See* SWIFT.

MOONEY. O'Hart's Irish Pedigrees, 2nd Series, 246.

MOORCROFT. Surtees' Durham, iii. 415. *See* MORECROFT.

MOORE, or MOOR. Collinson's Somerset, iii. 246. Miscellanea Genealogica et Heraldica, i. 310 ; New Series, iv. 413. Morant's Essex, i. 254. Burke's Heraldic Illustrations, 96. Glover's History of Derbyshire, ii. 28, (27). Berry's Surrey Genealogies, 87. Berry's Kent Genealogies, 160. Ashmole's Antiquities of Berkshire, iii. 314. Sir T. Phillipps' Topographer, No. 1, (March, 1821, 8vo.) 45. Surtees Society, xxxvi. 54. Berry's Hampshire Genealogies, 192, 296. Visitation of Somersetshire, printed by Sir T. Phillipps, 121. Burke's Commoners, (of Appleby Parva,) i. 169, Landed Gentry, 2, 3, 4, 5, 6, 7, 8 ; (of Tara House,) Commoners, ii. 144 ; (of Grimeshill,) Commoners, iv. 477, Landed Gentry, 2, 3, 4, 5, 6, 7, 8 ; (of Ballyhale,) Commoners, ii. 508, Landed Gentry, 2, 3, 4 ; (of Corswall,) Commoners, iii. 102, Landed Gentry, 2, 3, 4, 5, 6, 7, 8 ; (of Stockwell,) Landed Gentry, 2, 3, 4, 5, 6, 7 ; (of Frampton Hall,) 3, 4, 5, 6, 7, 8 ; (of Maulden,) 4 ; (of Barne,) 2 and supp., 3, 4, 5, 6, 7, 8 ; (of Moore Hall,) 2, 3, 4, 5, 6, 7 ; (of Mooresfort,) 3, 4, 5, 6, 7, 8 ; (of Moore Fort,) 4, 5, 6, 7, 8 ; (of Rowallane,) 5 supp., 6, 7 ; (of Cremorgan,) 5 supp. ; (of Moore Lodge,) 6, 7, 8 ; (of Ballydivity,) 5, 6, 7, 8 ; (of Kilbride,) 7, 8 ; (of Killashee,) 8 ; (of Molenan,) 8. Foster's Yorkshire Pedigrees. Harleian Society, v. 189, 218, 239 ; vi. 193 ; viii. 277 ; xiii. 455 ; xix. 124 ; xxii. 153 ; xxix. 364 ; xxxii. 202 ; xxxvii. 48 ; xliii. 2, 196. Herald and Genealogist, viii. 504. Poulson's Holderness, ii. 23. Visitatio Comitatus Wiltoniæ, 1623, printed by Sir T. Phillipps. Chetham Society, lxxxi. 92. Nichols' History of the County of Leicester, iv. 443, 444. Hutchins' Dorset, iv. 47. Hoare's Wiltshire, I. ii. 118. Manning and Bray's Surrey, i. 483 ; iii. 229. Lands and their Owners in Galloway, by P. H. M'Kerlie, i. 124. Paterson's History of the Co. of Ayr, i. 229. Paterson's History of Ayr and Wigton, iii. 62. O'Hart's Irish Pedigrees, 2nd Series, 125. J. E. Reid's History of the Co. of Bute, 242. Notes and Queries, 1 S. xi. 428 ; 2 S. viii. 195, 235. The Genealogist, v. 288 ; vii. 185. Monken Hadley, by F. C. Cass, 75. Archdall's Lodge's Peerage, ii. 82 ; iii. 364. Brydges' Collins' Peerage, ix. 1. Wotton's English Baronetage, ii. 24. Visitation of Devon, edited by F. T. Colby, 162. Metcalfe's Visitations of Suffolk, 52. Visitation of Wiltshire, edited by G. W. Marshall, 9. Burke's Extinct Baronetcies. Lancashire and Cheshire Genealogical and Historical Notes, iii. 57. Genealogical Memoranda of the Family of De la Moor, by Cecil Moore, Part i. London, 1884, 4to. All published. Somersetshire Wills, printed for F. A. Crisp, ii. 32. Weaver's Visitations of Somerset, 53, 123. Leicestershire Architectural Society, vi. 134. Burke's Colonial Gentry, i. 317, 320, 363; ii. 487. Surrey Archæological Collections, xi. Pedigree of Moore of Winster, co. Derby, (includes Smedley, Bright, Wood, etc.) four pages folio, compiled by T. N. Ince, 1867. Howard's Visitation of England and Wales, v. 90; viii. 105. Berkshire Archæological and Architectural Society's Journal, ii. 94. Visitations of Devon, by J. L. Vivian, 572, 574. New England Register, li. 488; lii. 72. *See* MORE.

MOORE-BRABAZON. Burke's Landed Gentry, 2 supp., 3, 4, 5 supp., 6, 7.

MOORE-HODDER. Burke's Landed Gentry, 2, 3, 4, 5, 6, 7, 8.

MOORE-STEPHENS. Burke's Visitation of Seats and Arms, ii. 73. Burke's Landed Gentry, 6. Howard's Visitation of England and Wales, viii. 110.

MORAN. O'Hart's Irish Pedigrees, 2nd Series, 127.

MORANT, or MOURANT. Burke's Landed Gentry, (of Brokenhurst,) 4, 5, 6, 7, 8; (of Shirley House,) 4, 5. Proceedings of the Essex Archæological Society, iv. 43. J. B. Payne's Armorial of Jersey, 290.

MORAY. Burke's Commoners, i. 619, Landed Gentry, 2, 4, 5, 6, 7 at p. 540, 8. Nisbet's Heraldry, ii. app. 116. Douglas's Baronage of Scotland, 98. Shaw's History of Moray, 74, 100. Wood's Douglas's Peerage of Scotland, i. 217. The Genealogist, New Series, xvi. 137.

MORDAUNT. Jacob's Peerage, i. 520. Morant's Essex, ii. 365, 529, 560. T. Faulkner's Account of the Parish of Fulham, 88. Blomefield's Norfolk, (fol. edn.) iv. 643. Harleian Society, viii. 211; xiii. 253, 456; xix. 40, 125, 180. J. H. Hill's History of Market Harborough, 157. Bridges' Northamptonshire, by Rev. Peter Whalley, ii. 252. Nichols' History of the County of Leicester, ii. 694*. Dugdale's Warwickshire, 577. Baker's Northampton, ii. 255. Edmondson's Baronagium Genealogicum, ii. 119. Brydges' Collins' Peerage, iii. 309. Wotton's English Baronetage, i. 182. Banks' Baronies in Fee, i. 329. Betham's Baronetage, i. 110. The Genealogist, vii. 183. Bysshe's Visitation of Essex, edited by J. J. Howard, 67. Harvey's Hundred of Willey, 186. *See* ALNO, BOLEYNES.

MORDEN. Visitation of Warwickshire, 1619, published with Warwickshire Antiquarian Magazine, 114. Harleian Society, xii. 319. Burke's Extinct Baronetcies. Hasted's Kent, (Hund. of Blackheath, by H. H. Drake,) 126.

MORDOCK. Harleian Society, xxxii. 203.

MORE. Pedigree of More of Lardin, [T. P.] 1868, folio page. Burke's Visitation of Seats and Arms, 2nd Series, ii. 32. Berry's Surrey

36

Genealogies, 87. Surtees Society, xxxvi. 24, 158. Berry's Sussex Genealogies, 119. Visitation of Oxfordshire, 1574, printed by Sir T. Phillipps, (Middle Hill, fol.) 6. Burke's Commoners, (of Linley,) iii. 427, Landed Gentry, 2, 3, 4, 5, 6, 7, 8; (of Burnborough,) Commoners, iii. 449. Foster's Yorkshire Pedigrees. Lydiate Hall and its Associations, by Rev. T. E. Gibson, (1876, 4to.) 160. Foster's Visitations of Yorkshire, 555. Harleian Society, vi. 191, 195; xvi. 212; xvii. 107, 108; xxxix. 1000; xlii. 70. History of the Parish of Sheffield, 479. Brayley's History of Surrey, i. 416. Westcote's Devonshire, edited by G. Oliver and P. Jones, 624. Hunter's Deanery of Doncaster, i. 376. Manning and Bray's Surrey, i. 95, 99, 628. Clutterbuck's Hertford, i. 452. Chauncy's Hertfordshire, 534. Archæologia, xxxv. 27. Foley's Records of the English Province, S. J., v. 702. A Vindication of Elizabeth More, by Richard Hay. (Edinburgh, 1723, 4to.) Notes and Queries, 4 S. ii. 365, 422; iii. 266; iv. 61; v. 347; vii. 226. Wotton's English Baronetage, iii. 582. Visitation of Devon, edited by F. T. Colby, 161. Betham's Baronetage, ii. 442. Burke's Extinct Baronetcies. Visitation of Wiltshire, edited by G. W. Marshall, 7. F. G. Lee's History of Thame, 415. Chetham Society, cx. 138. The Genealogist, New Series, ii. 74; xii. 43. Surrey Archæological Collections, xi. Visitations of Devon, by J. L. Vivian, 571. The Genealogical Magazine, ii. 512. The Gresley's of Drakelowe, by F. Madan, 272. Sussex Archæological Collections, xxxv. 29, 57. Platt and Morkill's Records of Whitkirk, 65. *See* MOORE, MURE.

MORE-MOLYNEUX. Burke's Landed Gentry, 2, 3, 4, 5, 6, 7, 8.

MORE-O'FERRALL. *See* O'FERRALL.

MORECROFT. Visitation of Oxfordshire, 1634, printed by Sir T. Phillipps, (Middle Hill, fol.) 25. Harleian Society, v. 314. Chetham Society, lxxxv. 209. *See* MOORCROFT.

MORES. Hasted's Kent, ii. 580. Bibliotheca Topographica Britannica, i. Part i. xvii.; iv. Part i. 2. The Genealogist, v. 288. Harleian Society, xvii. 109.

MORETOFTE. Harleian Society, xxxii. 203.

MORETON. Bibliotheca Topographica Britannica, ix. Part iv. 179, 317. Surtees Society, xxxvi. 175. Burke's Commoners, i. 345; iv. 503, Landed Gentry, 2. The Register, (London, 1869, 8vo.) ii. 124. Visitation of Staffordshire, 1663-4, edited by Sir T. Phillipps, 7. Baker's Northampton, i. 121. Collections for a History of Staffordshire, (William Salt Society,) ii. part 2, 78. Edmondson's Baronagium Genealogicum, v. 424; vi. 59. Ormerod's Cheshire, iii. 43, 50, 182. Notes and Queries, 5 S. xi. 221. Visitation of Staffordshire, (Willm. Salt Soc.) 114. Visitations of Staffordshire, 1614 and 1663-4, William Salt Society, 216. Burke's Colonial Gentry, ii. 731. Transactions of Shropshire Archæological Society, ii. 265; ix. 2. *See* MORTON.

MOREVILLE. Caledonia, by Geo. Chalmers, 503. *See* MORVILLE.

MOREWICK. Baker's Northampton, i. 167. Banks' Dormant and Extinct Baronage, i. 141.

MOREWOOD. Glover's History of Derbyshire, ii. 14. Burke's Landed Gentry, 2, 3, 4, 5, 6, 7, 8. Visitation of Derbyshire, 1663-4, (Middle Hill, 1854, fol.) 5. History of the Parish of Sheffield, 469. The Genealogist, ii. 392. Harleian Society, xxxix. 1063. The Gresley's of Drakelowe, by F. Madan, 273.

MORGAN. Memoirs of the Morgan Family. By G. B. Morgan. 1891, 4to., 2 vols. Pedigree of Morgan of Pengwern, [T. P.] 1859, folio page. Pedigree of Morgan of Biddlesden Park, [T. P.] folio page. Rudder's Gloucestershire, 443. The Cambrian Register, 1796-9, 8vo., 2 vols. Burke's Visitation of Seats and Arms, 2nd Series, ii. 77. Morgan *v.* Jones and others, Respondents' Case in House of Lords, 1785. Historical Tour in Monmouthshire, by Willm. Coxe, 66. Visitation of Norfolk, published by Norfolk Archæological Society, i. 341. Memorials of the Prichards, by Isabell Southall, 115. Dwnn's Visitations of Wales, i. 30, 80, 103, 159, 198, 205, 218, 221, 230, 233, 236, 300; ii. 71, 140, 221, 297. Glamorganshire Pedigrees, edited by Sir T. Phillipps, 19, 24, 37, 38, 40, 46. Visitation of Durham, 1615, (Sunderland, 1820, fol.) 89. Notices of Pencoyd Castle, by Octavius Morgan, (Monmouthshire and Caerleon Antiquarian Association,) 38. Visitation of Somersetshire, printed by Sir T. Phillipps, 120. Burke's Commoners, (of Cottelstown,) iv. 13; (of Defynog,) 8; (of Nantcaerio,)8 ; (of Woolcombe,) 8 ; (of Golden Grove,) Commoners, ii. 163, Landed Gentry, 2, 3, 4, 5, 6, 7, 8 ; (of Biddlesdon Park,) Landed Gentry, 2, 3, 4, 5, 6, 7, 8 ; 2 supp., p. 255 ; 6, p. 852. Foster's Visitations of Yorkshire, 627. Jones' History of the County of Breeknock, ii. 138, 310, 478, 479. Harleian Society, i. 95 ; xi. 75, 76 ; xiii. 80, 83, 255 ; xvii. 109, 110 ; xx. 73 ; xxii. 76; xxvii. 97; xxviii. 259; xxxii. 204 ; xxxvii. 184 ; xliii. 33. Caermarthenshire Pedigrees, 2, 41, 45, 50, 51. Cardiganshire Pedigrees, 111. Hutchins' Dorset, ii. 158. Manning and Bray's Surrey, ii. 118. Clutterbuck's Hertford, ii. 189. Baker's Northampton, i. 40, 184. Archæologia Cambrensis, 4 S., ix. 178. The Sheriffs of Montgomeryshire, by W. V. Lloyd, 517. O'Hart's Irish Pedigrees, 2nd Series, 247. The Genealogist, iv. 259 ; New Series, iii. 165. Betham's Baronetage, iv. 250. Wotton's English Baronetage, iii. 221. Burke's Extinct Baronetcies. History of Powys Fadog, by J. Y. W. Lloyd, iii. 66 ; iv. 352; v. 118; vi. 229, 413, 425, 475. Genealogy of Morgan of Llantarnam Abbey, Monmouthshire, and of Monasterevan, co. Kildare, by G. B. Morgan. Large sheet, dated at East Croydon, January, 1884. Weaver's Visitations of Somerset, 53. Genealogies of Morgan and Glamorgan, by G. T. Clark, 120, 258, 265, 310-335, 498. Foster's Visitations of Durham, 247. Miscellanea Genealogica et Heraldica, 2nd Series, ii. 134. Cambrian Journal, Vol. for 1861, 334. David Morgan, by W. Llewellin, (Tenby, 1862, 8vo.) 40. Burke's Family Records, 561. Oliver's History of Antigua, ii. 269. *See* CAPEL, MANSELL.

MORGAN, AP FYLIP. Dwnn's Visitations of Wales, i. 341 ; ap John, i. 59 ; Vychan, ii. 71.

MORIARTY. O'Hart's Irish Pedigrees, 2nd Series, 74, 248.

MORICE. Morant's Essex, i. 103, 129. Burke's Landed Gentry, 3, 4, 5, 6, 7, 8. Harleian Society, xiii. 256, 457. An Historical Survey of Cornwall, by C. S. Gilbert, i. 590. Charles Smith's History of Kerry, 58. A short Memoir of James Young, 35, app. 35. Notes and Queries, 3 S. i. 422. Burke's Extinct Baronetcies. Miscellanea Genealogica et Heraldica, New Series, iv. 126. *See* MORRICE.

MORIN. Burke's Landed Gentry, 6 supp., 7, 8.

MORING. Harleian Society, vi. 193.

MORIS. Glamorganshire Pedigrees, edited by Sir T. Phillipps, 37.

MORISON. Burke's Landed Gentry, 6, 7, 8. The Genealogist, vi. 269.

MORKILL. Howard's Visitation of England and Wales, v. 50.

MORLAND. Berry's Kent Genealogies, 366. Burke's Landed Gentry, (of Court Lodge,) 3, 4, 5, 6, 7 ; (of Sheepstead,) 7, 8. Surtees' Durham, iii. 276. Burke's Extinct Baronetcies.

MORLÉ. Clutterbuck's Hertford, ii. 463.

MORLEY. Morant's Essex, ii. 511. Collectanea Topographica et Genealogica, iii. 2. Topographical Miscellanies, 1792, 4to., (Glynde). English Church Furniture, by Edward Peacock, 164, 244, 245. Berry's Sussex Genealogies, 76, 173. Berry's Hampshire Genealogies, 246. Surtees Society, xxxvi. 176. Visitation of Sussex, 1570, printed by Sir T. Phillipps, (Middle Hill, fol.) 8. Burke's Landed Gentry, 2 add., 3, 4, 5, 6, 7, 8. Foster's Yorkshire Pedigrees. Carthew's Hundred of Launditch, Part i. 68. Foster's Visitations of Yorkshire, 194. Harleian Society, viii. 29, 452 ; xvii. 111 ; xxii. 154 ; xxxii. 204, 263. Foster's Lancashire Pedigrees. Chetham Society, lxxxv. 210. Horsfield's History of Lewes, ii. 117. Graves' History of Cleveland, 444. Dallaway's Sussex, i. 132. Ord's History of Cleveland, 563. Wright's Essex, ii. 321. Sussex Archæological Collections, xx. 60. Archæologia Cambrensis, 3 S. ix. 104. Abram's History of Blackburn, 746. Whitaker's Deanery of Craven, 3rd edn., 256. Doncaster Charities, by Charles Jackson, 51. Banks' Baronies in Fee, i. 333. Banks' Dormant and Extinct Baronage, ii. 356. Ilkley, Ancient and Modern, by R. Collyer and J. H. Turner, 151. New England Register, xlvi. 156. East Barnet, by F. C. Cass, Part i. 64. The Genealogist, New Series, xv. 218. *See* DE MALO LACU, DE MORLE, DE MORLEY.

MORNINGTON. Burke's Royal Descents and Pedigrees of Founders' Kin, 4.

MORONY Burke's Landed Gentry, 4, 5, 6.

MORPETH. Surtees' Durham, iii. 74.

MORPHY. Glover's Derbyshire, 8vo. edn., ii. 324. Harleian Society, xxxvii. 344.

MORRALL. Burke's Commoners, ii. 595, Landed Gentry, 2 supp., 3, 4, 5, 6, 7, 8. History of Powys Fadog, by J. Y. W. Lloyd, iv. 90.

MORRELL. Burke's Landed Gentry, (of Headington,) 4, 5, 6, 7, 8 ; (of Milton Nile,) 8.

MORRES. Archdall's Lodge's Peerage, v. 289. Burke's Extinct Baronetcies, 611. *See* MONTMORENCY.

MORRICE. Burke's Commoners, (of Betshanger,) iii. xi., 232, Landed Gentry, 2 ; (of Catthorpe,) 5, 6. Notes and Queries, 3 S. v. 476 ; vi. 16. Wotton's English Baronetage, iii. 269. *See* MORICE.

MORRIS. Pedigree of Morris of Over End in Bretforton, Co. Wigorn, privately printed by Sir T. Phillipps. Hasted's Kent, iii. 317. Dwnn's Visitations of Wales, ii. 156. Surtees Society, xxxvi. 267. Burke's Commoners, iv. xii. ; (of York and Netherby,) iv. 488, Landed Gentry, 2, 3, 4, 5, 6, 7, 8 ; (of The Hurst,) Landed Gentry, 2, 3, 4, 5, 6, 7, 8 ; (of Dunkathel,) 4, 5, 6 ; (of Fishleigh,) 3 ; (of Wood Eaton,) 5, 6, 7, 8. Thoresby's Ducatus Leodiensis, 74. Nichols' History of the County of Leicester, iii. 1148 ; iv. 401. The Sheriffs of Montgomeryshire, by W. V. Lloyd, 46, 192. O'Hart's Irish Pedigrees, 2nd Series, 248. Bigland's Gloucestershire, ii. par. Willersley. Nicholls' Account of the Company of Ironmongers, 2nd edn., 528*. Harleian Society, xvii. 112 ; xxix. 367. Leicestershire Architectural Society, vi. 19. Fletcher's Leicestershire Pedigrees and Royal Descents, 177. Ontarian Families, by E. M. Chadwick, i. 187. Oliver's History of Antigua, ii. 272. Howard's Visitations of England and Wales, viii. 133. The Genealogist, New Series, xiv. 241. *See* O'CONNOR-MORRIS, MORYS.

MORRISON. History and Description of Cassiobury Park, by John Britton, 18. Burke's Landed Gentry, (of Coolegegan,) 4, 5, 6 supp., 7, 8 ; (of Basildon Park,) 5, 6, 7, 8. Clutterbuck's Hertford, i. 238. Balmerino and its Abbey, by James Campbell, 280, 387. Burke's Extinct Baronetcies. Harleian Society, xxii. 76, 116. New England Register, xlviii. 413. *See* MORISON, MORYSON.

MORRITT. Foster's Yorkshire Pedigrees. Burke's Landed Gentry, 3 supp., 4, 5, 6, 7, 8.

MORROGH. Burke's Landed Gentry, 4, 5, 6, 7, 8.

MORRYCE. The Genealogist, New Series, ii. 74. Bibliotheca Topographica Britannica, iv. Part i. 2. *See* MORRICE.

MORSE-BOYCOTT. Burke's Landed Gentry, 4, 5, 6, 7, 8.

MORSHEAD. Burke's Landed Gentry, 3 supp., 4, 5. Maclean's History of Trigg Minor, i. 80. An Historical Survey of Cornwall, by C. S. Gilbert, i. 575 ; ii. 205. The Visitations of Cornwall, by J. L. Vivian, 599.

MORT. Chetham Society, lxxxv. 211, 212. Historic Society of Lancashire and Cheshire, New Series, vi. 76. Croston's edn. of Baines's Lancaster, iv. 328.

MORTAYNE, or MORTEYN. Harleian Society, iv. 14. The Genealogist, New Series, xiv. 194 ; xv. 154. *See* DE MORTAYNE.

MORTHAM. Plantagenet-Harrison's History of Yorkshire, i. 418.

MORTHE. Harleian Society, ix. 147. The Visitations of Cornwall, edited by J. L. Vivian, 331.

MORTIMER, or MORTYMER. Pedigree of Mortimer of Kennet, etc., [T. P.] 1860, folio page. Rudder's Gloucestershire, 290. Morant's Essex, ii. 133. Hasted's Kent, i. 192. Nash's Worcestershire,

i. 241. Harleian Society, vi. 195; xxxii. 71; xxxviii. 440; xlii.
209. Topographer, (London, 1789-91, 8vo.) i. 536. Lipscombe's
History of the County of Buckingham, i. 159, 203. Blore's Rutland, 37, 42, 230. Eyton's Antiquities of Shropshire, iii. 44; iv.
196, 303. Caermarthenshire Pedigrees, 60. Visitatio Comitatus
Wiltoniæ, 1623, printed by Sir T. Phillipps. Clutterbuck's Hertford, iii. 225. Baker's Northampton, i. 415. Meyrick's History
of the Co. of Cardigan, 124. Memorials of the Church of Attleborough, by J. T. Barrett, 187. Banks' Baronies in Fee, i. 335;
ii. 103. Banks' Dormant and Extinct Baronage, i. 379; ii. 364.
Visitation of Wiltshire, edited by G. W. Marshall, 82. Miscellanea Genealogica et Heraldica, 2nd Series, v. 76. History of
Powys Fadog, by J. Y. W. Lloyd, iv. 3. Hasted's Kent, (Hund.
of Blackheath, by H. H. Drake,) 6. J. R. Burton's History of
Bewdley, app. xlvii. Visitation of Gloucester, edited by T. F.
Fenwick and W. C. Metcalfe, 123. Genealogical Memoranda of
the Family of Ames, 5. Burke's Landed Gentry, 8. Visitations
of Devon, by J. L. Vivian, 575. The Genealogist, New Series,
xv. 219; xvii. 174. Transactions of Shropshire Archæological
Society, ii. 33.

MORTLOCK. Burke's Landed Gentry, 2, 7, 8.

MORTMER. Dwnn's Visitations of Wales, i. 34.

MORTOFT. Harleian Society, xvii. 113.

MORTON. Hasted's Kent, iii. 136. Surrey Archæological Collections, ii. Surtees Society, xxxvi. 338. Burke's Landed Gentry, 2.
Harleian Society, ii. 183; ix. 148; xvi. 212; xvii. 110; xviii.
182; xx. 73; xxviii. 260; xxix. 368; xxxvii. 229, 241; xxxviii.
807; xliii. 73, 116. Nichols' History of the County of Leicester,
ii. 397; iv. 505. Hutchins' Dorset, ii. 594; iii. 352. Collectanea
Topographica et Genealogica, iii. 169. Hunter's Deanery of Doncaster, i. 76. Miscellanea Genealogica et Heraldica, New Series,
iii. 22. Independancy at Brighouse, by J. H. Turner, 71. Paterson's History of Ayr and Wigton, i. 778. Brydges' Collins' Peerage, vii. 410. Burke's Extinct Baronetcies. F. G. Lee's History
of Thame, 376. The Visitations of Cornwall, edited by J. L.
Vivian, 333. History of Powys Fadog, ii. 381, 397; iii. 233.
Weaver's Visitation of Herefordshire, 51. Oxford Historical
Society, xxiv. 98. *See* MORETON.

MORUS. Dwnn's Visitations of Wales, ii. 329. Cardiganshire Pedigrees, 116.

MORUS AP GRUFFYD. Dwnn's Visitations of Wales, i. 237; Vachan,
i. 43.

MORVILLE. Gentleman's Magazine, 1856, i. 380. Banks' Dormant
and Extinct Baronage, i. 142. Nicolson and Burn's Westmorland
and Cumberland, ii. 216. *See* MOREVILLE, DE MORVILLE.

MORYS. Metcalfe's Visitations of Suffolk, 98. *See* MORRIS.

MORYSON. Chauncy's Hertfordshire, 484. *See* MORRISON.

MOSELEY. Burke's Commoners, (of Owsden,) iv. 594, Landed Gentry,
2; (of Buildwas,) Commoners, i. 321, Landed Gentry, 2, 3, 4, 5, 6,
7, 8. Harleian Society, viii. 422; xvii. 114. Chetham Society,

lxxxv. 213, 214.   Gage's History of Thingoe Hundred, Suffolk,
244. Burke's Royal Descents and Pedigrees of Founders' Kin,
62. Shaw's Staffordshire, ii. 184, 276.   Visitation of Staffordshire, 1663-4, edited by Sir T. Phillipps, 7.   Page's History of
Suffolk, 889. Notes and Queries, 2 S. xii. 238.   Visitation of
Staffordshire, (Willm. Salt. Soc.) 115.   Visitations of Staffordshire, 1614 and 1663-4, William Salt Society, 217. New England
Register, vii. 329.

MOSLEY. Family Memoirs, by Sir Oswald Mosley, Bart., 1849, 4to.,
pp. 78 and app. xxviii. Chetham Society, xliii. 173 ; lxxxii. 37.
Burke's Commoners, iii. 579, Landed Gentry, 2, 3, 4, 5, 6, 7, 8.
Foster's Visitations of Yorkshire, 555.   Foster's Lancashire Pedi-
grees. Burke's Visitation of Seats and Arms, i. 29.   Corry's
History of Lancashire, ii. 478. Baines' History of the County of
Lancaster, ii. 352 ; Croston's edn., ii. 230.   Wotton's English
Baronetage, iv. 193. Betham's Baronetage, iv. 84.   Burke's Ex-
tinct Baronetcies. Harleian Society, xvii. 112 ; xxxix. 880.

MOSMAN. Burke's Landed Gentry, 7, 8.

MOSSE. Burke's Landed Gentry, 2 and add., 8 supp.   Harleian
Society, xvii. 115.

MOSSOAKE. Chetham Society, lxxxv. 215.

MOSSOCK. The Antiquities of Gainford, by J. R. Walbran, 106.
Burke's Commoners, iii. 229.

MOSSOM. Burke's Visitation of Seats and Arms, ii. 64. History of
St. Canice, Kilkenny, by J. Graves, 326.

MOSTON. Foster's Visitations of Yorkshire, 556.

MOSTYN.[1] Pedigree of George Mostyn, Esq., claiming to be eldest
co-heir to the Barony of Vaux of Harrowden. Lithographed by
C. Impey, 310, Strand. Burke's Royal Families, (London, 1851,
8vo.) ii. 132, 200*. Burke's Landed Gentry, 2 supp., 3, 4, 5.
T. Nichols' County Families of Wales, 451. Foley's Records of
the English Province, S. J., iv. 523. Memoir of Gabriel Goodman, by R. Newcombe, App. S. Wotton's English Baronetage,
iii. 128, 526. Betham's Baronetage, ii. 144, 414. Burke's Extinct Baronetage. History of Powys Fadog, by J. Y. W. Lloyd,
iii. 8 ; iv. 145-62. See VAUX.

MOTE. Pedigree of Mote of London, [T. P.] 1860, folio page.
Hunter's Deanery of Doncaster, i. 365.

MOTON. Harleian Society, ii. 58 ; iv. 138. Burton's Description of
Leicestershire, 208. Nichols' History of the County of Leicester,
iv. 870. Banks' Dormant and Extinct Baronage, i. 233.

MOTT. Morant's Essex, ii. 376. Burke's Landed Gentry, 2, 3, 4, 5,
6, 7, 8. Wright's Essex, i. 680. Harleian Society, xiii. 458.
New England Register, xxi. 216.

MOTTERSHEAD. Earwaker's East Cheshire, ii. 355. Harleian Society,
xxxvii. 299.

MOTTET. Burke's Extinct Baronetcies.

[1] There is a book of Pedigrees, etc., of the Mostyn Family, relating to the titles
to the Mostyn estates, lettered on cover 'Private. Mostyn Estates. January,
1854.' It is printed on one side the paper only, about 200 pages, 4to.

MOTTON. Dwnn's Visitations of Wales, ii. 257.

MOTTRAM. Surtees Society, xxxvi. 222.

MOTTRUM. Ormerod's Cheshire, iii. 693.

MOUAT. Burke's Extinct Baronetcies, 633.

MOUBRAY. W. Peck's Account of the Isle of Axholme, 49-81.
Glover's History of Derbyshire, ii. 195. Berry's Buckinghamshire
Genealogies, 63, 65. Burke's Commoners, i. viii. 125, Landed
Gentry, 2, 3, 4, 5, 6, 7, 8. Blore's Rutland, 114. Nisbet's
Heraldry, ii. app. 22. Banks' Baronies in Fee, i. 339. Banks'
Dormant and Extinct Baronage, ii. 373. *See* MOWBRAY.

MOULD. Surtees Society, xxxvi. 223. W. Paver's Pedigrees of
Families of the City of York, 16.

MOULSOE. Banks' Baronies in Fee, ii. 107.

MOULSON. Harleian Society, xxxvii. 189.

MOULT. Harleian Society, xxxvii. 18.

MOULTON. Harleian Society, vi. 196 ; xxxii. 204. Edmondson's
Baronagium Genealogicum, iv. 357. Visitations of Devon, by
J. L. Vivian, 576.

MOULTRIE. Burke's Landed Gentry, 2 supp., 3, 4, 5.

MOUNSEY. Burke's Landed Gentry, 2 supp., 3, 4, 5, 6, 7, 8.

MOUNSTEVEN. Maclean's History of Trigg Minor, i. 300.

MOUNT. Burke's Landed Gentry, 5, 6, 7, 8.

MOUNTAIGNE. Surtees Society, xxxvi. 362. Surtees' Durham, i. xci.
W. Wheater's History of Sherburn and Cawood, 316. The Genealogist, New Series, xviii. 49.

MOUNTAIN. Burke's Landed Gentry, 2, 3, 4.

MOUNTCHENSY. Clutterbuck's Hertford, i. 442. Harleian Society,
xiii. 83. *See* MONTCHENSI.

MOUNTENEY. Hunter's History of the Parish of Sheffield, 390.
Nichols' History of the County of Leicester, iv. 848*. Hunter's
Deanery of Doncaster, i. 55. Clutterbuck's Hertford, i. 442.
Notes and Queries, 2 S. xii. 169, 197, 238, 254, 335, 403, 526.

MOUNTFORD, or MOUNTFORT. Foster's Visitations of Yorkshire, 248,
415. Visitation of Staffordshire, 1663-4, printed by Sir T. Phillipps,
7. Harleian Society, xii. 127 ; xiii. 84, 256 ; xvi. 214. Dugdale's
Warwickshire, 1007. The Genealogist, vi. 269 ; New Series,
xiii. 175. ; xvi. 89, 231. Visitations of Staffordshire, 1614 and
1663-4, William Salt Society, 219. *See* MONFORD.

MOUNTGARRET. Claim of the Rt. Hon. Henry Edmund, Visct.
Mountgarret, and of Pierre Somerset, Visct. Mountgarret, to Vote
at Elections of Irish Peers, Sess. Papers, 159 of 1854 ; Q of
1855.

MOUNTGOMERY. Botfield's Stemmata Botevilliana, 142. Bridges'
Northamptonshire, by Rev. Peter Whalley, ii. 142. *See* MONT-
GOMERY.

MOUNTJOY. Croke's History of the Family of Croke, No. 7.
Blunt's Dursley and its Neighbourhood, 130. Harleian Society,
xvii. 118.

MOUNTNEY. Surtees Society, xxxvi. 200. Harleian Society, ii. 179 ;
xxxii. 205. Registers of Ecclesfield, by A. S. Gatty, 152.

MOUNTNORRIS. Claim of George, Earl of Mountnorris, in Ireland, to the Titles of Earl of Anglesey and Baron Annesley, of Newport Pagnell, Sess. Papers, 65 of 1819.

MOUNT STEWART. Bute and Others *v.* Wortley, Appellant's Case in House of Lords, 1803.

MOURIER DE LALANDE. The Genealogist, New Series, ix. 183.

MOUTRAY, Burke's Landed Gentry, 2, 3, 4, 5, 6, 7, 8. The Genealogist, vii. 24.

MOWAT. Paterson's History of Ayr and Wigton, iii. 458. Caithness Family History, by John Henderson, 189. Burke's Colonial Gentry, i. 110.

MOWBRAY. Case of A. J., Lord Stourton, claiming Barony of Mowbray, pp. 36, fol. Evidence on Petition of Lord Stourton for termination of Abeyance of Dignity of Lord Mowbray, Sess. Papers, D of 1876 ; A of 1877 ; of same for same of Dignity of Lord Segrave, Sess. Papers, C. of 1877. Fisher's History of Masham, 210. Rudder's Gloucestershire, 764. Morant's Essex, i. 497. Kent's British Banner Displayed, 390. Gentleman's Magazine, 1827, i. 588. East Anglian, ii. 72. Berry's Hampshire Genealogies, 125. Burke's Landed Gentry, 3, 4, 5, 6, 7, 8. A Royal Descent, by T. E. Sharpe, (London, 1875, 4to.) 4, 101. Stonehouse's History of the Isle of Axholme, 141. Bridges' Northamptonshire, by Rev. Peter Whalley, i. 154. Dallaway's Sussex, i. xlvii. ; II. ii. 181. History of Blyth, by Rev. John Raine, 102. Burke's Authorized Arms, 53. Nichols' History of the County of Leicester, ii. 263. Surtees' Durham, i. 242. Clutterbuck's Hertford, ii. 516. Baker's Northampton, i. 588. Sussex Archæological Collections, xxvi. 262. History and Antiquities of Harwich and Dovercourt, by Silas Taylor, 149. Harleian Society, xvi. 259. Notes and Queries, 2 S. vi. 53, 274 ; 6 S. iii. 32. Annals of Chepstow Castle, by J. F. Marsh, 269. J. Pym Yeatman's History of the House of Arundel, 295. Leicestershire Architectural Society, i. 263. Lincolnshire Notes and Queries, ii. 198. The Genealogical Magazine, ii. 225. *See* ALBINI, BARTON, MOUBRAY.

MOWER. Burke's Landed Gentry, 6 at p. 1590, 7 at p. 1814, 8 at p. 2007. Harleian Society, xxxvii. 219 ; xl. 1180.

MOWRY. The New England Register, lii. 207.

MOWSE. Harleian Society, xvii. 117.

MOYER. Morant's Essex, i. 256. Burke's Extinct Baronetcies.

MOYGNE. Harleian Society, xxxii. 205.

MOYLE, or MOYELL. Berry's Kent Genealogies, 205. Harleian Society, iv. 173 ; viii. 55 ; ix. 149, 150. Maclean's History of Trigg Minor, i. 278 ; ii. 265. Lipscombe's History of the County of Buckingham, ii. 595. Dunkin's History of Bullington and Ploughley, i. 199. Wilson's History of the Parish of St. Laurence Pountney, 245. A Complete Parochial History of the County of Cornwall, ii. 53, 63 ; iv. 119 supp. An Historical Survey of Cornwall, by C. S. Gilbert, i. 574. The Visitations of Cornwall, edited by J. L. Vivian, 334, 336.

MOYNE. Berry's Berkshire Genealogies, 13. *See* LE MOYNE.

MOYS. Manning and Bray's Surrey, ii. 590. Surrey Archæological Collections, xi. Harleian Society, xliii. 186.

MOYSER. Surtees Society, xxxvi. 212. Foster's Visitations of Yorkshire, 223.

MOYSEY. Burke's Landed Gentry, 2, 3, 4, 5, 6, 7, 8.

MUCKLESTON. Burke's Commoners, ii. 168. Antiquities and Memoirs of the Parish of Myddle, written by Richard Gough, 1700, (folio,) 52.

MUCKLOWE. Nash's Worcestershire, i. 37. Harleian Society, xxvii. 98 ; xxix. 368.

MUDDLE. *See* DUN.

MUDGE. The Mudge Memoirs, by S. R. Flint. Truro, 1883, 4to. Burke's Landed Gentry, 3, 4, 5, 6, 7, 8.

MUDIE. Burke's Landed Gentry, 2, 3, 4, 5.

MUGG. Harleian Society, xliii. 2.

MUGGLESTON. Harleian Society, xxxvii. 231.

MUILMAN. Notes and Queries, 2 S. xi. 324.

MUIR. *See* MURE.

MUIRHEAD. Burke's Landed Gentry, 4, 5, 6, 7, 8. Nisbet's Heraldry, ii. app. 258. *See* MUREHEAD.

MULBRENNAN. O'Hart's Irish Pedigrees, 2nd Series, 249.

MULCAHY. Burke's Landed Gentry, 8. O'Hart's Irish Pedigrees, 2nd Series, 127-130.

MULCASTER. Berry's Surrey Genealogies, 67. Berry's Kent Genealogies, 62. Burke's Landed Gentry, 3, 4, 8. The Genealogist, New Series, viii. 240. Surrey Archæological Collections, xi. Harleian Society, xliii. 130.

MULES. Burke's Landed Gentry, 2 supp. Burke's Heraldic Illustrations, 136.

MULESSEN. Bateson's History of Northumberland, i. 210.

MULFORD. New England Register, xxxiv. 171.

MULGRAVE. Claim of Constantine, Lord Mulgrave, to the Earldom of Anglesea, Sess. Papers, Feb. 1770—April 1772.

MULHEERAN. O'Hart's Irish Pedigrees, 2nd Series, 251.

MULHOLLAND. Burke's Landed Gentry, 3, 4, 5, 6, 7.

MULLEN. O'Hart's Irish Pedigrees, 2nd Series, 251.

MULLENS. Charles Smith's History of Kelly, 62.

MULLINS. Burke's Landed Gentry, (of Ballyeigan,) 4, 5 ; (of East Court,) 5. Hutchins' Dorset, iv. 181.

MULLOY. Burke's Commoners, iv. 146, Landed Gentry, 2, 3, 4, 5 ; (of Oak Port,) Landed Gentry, 2.

MULNETON. Ormerod's Cheshire, ii. 706.

MULOCK. Burke's Landed Gentry, 6, 7, 8.

MULROY. O'Hart's Irish Pedigrees, 2nd Series, 252.

MULSHO, or MULSO. Harleian Society, ii. 155. J. H. Hill's History of Market Harborough, 81. Burton's Description of Leicestershire, 262. Nichols' History of the County of Leicester, ii. 528. Lipscombe's History of the County of Buckingham, iv. 143. Bridges' Northamptonshire, by Rev. Peter Whalley, ii. 259.

Metcalfe's Visitations of Northamptonshire, 38, 116. The
Gresley's of Drakelowe, by F. Madan, 274.

MULTON. Hasted's Kent, ii. 248. Archæologia Cantiana, v. 243.
Berry's Kent Genealogies, 76. Collectanea Topographica et Genealogica, vii. 389. Jefferson's History of Allerdale Ward, Cumberland, 38. Baker's Northampton, i. 672. Plantagenet-Harrison's
History of Yorkshire, i. 391, 399. Banks' Baronies in Fee, i. 343,
346. Banks' Dormant and Extinct Baronage, ii. 379. The Genealogist, New Series, xiii. 95 ; xv. 31 ; xvi. 43. Harleian Society,
xlii. 18. Nicolson and Burn's Westmorland and Cumberland, ii.
73, 217. See DE MULTON.

MULVY. O'Hart's Irish Pedigrees, 2nd Series, 131, 253.

MULYS. Maclean's History of Trigg Minor, iii. 384.

MUN. Harleian Society, xvii. 118. Parish of Benenden, Kent, by
F. Haslewood, 209. East Barnet, by F. C. Cass, 218.

MUNCHENSI. Manning and Bray's Surrey, ii. 269. Baker's Northampton, ii. 315. Banks' Baronies in Fee, i. 345. Banks' Dormant
and Extinct Baronage, i. 143. Genealogist, New Series, xii. 173.
See MONCHENSIE.

MUNCK. Westcote's Devonshire, edited by G. Oliver and P. Jones,
468. See MONCK.

MUNDAY, or MONDY. Jewitt's Reliquary, vii. 26. Harleian Society,
ix. 151. Visitation of Derbyshire, 1663-4, (Middle Hill, 1854,
fol.) 5. The Genealogist, ii. 392 ; vi. 65 ; New Series, viii. 21.
Burke's Royal Families, (London, 1851, 8vo.) i. 142. Burke's
Commoners, (of Markeaton,) i. 25, 602, Landed Gentry, 2, 3, 4,
5, 6, 7, 8 ; (of Shipley Hall,) Landed Gentry, 2, 3, 4, 5, 6, 7, 8 ;
(of Hollybank,) 5 supp., 6, 7. Topographer, (London, 1789-91,
8vo.) i. 505. Nichols' History of the County of Leicester, iv. 525*,
526*. The Visitations of Cornwall, edited by J. L. Vivian, 337.
See MASSINGBERD-MUNDY.

MUNDEFORD. Blomefield's Norfolk, ii. 182, 193. Wilson's History
of the Parish of St. Laurence Pountney, 245.

MUNDEN. Harleian Society, viii. 370.

MUNN. Burke's Landed Gentry, 7, 8.

MUNNING. Muskett's Suffolk Manorial Familes, i. 103.

MUNNINGS. Carthew's Hundred of Launditch, Part ii. 623.

MUNRO. Genealogy of Munro of Fowlis, in Doddridge's Life of Col.
Gardiner, 1792, 12mo. Burke's Landed Gentry, (of Novar,) 2, 3,
4 ; (of Teaninich,) 2, 3, 4, 5, 6, 7, 8 ; (of Allan,) 5 supp. ; (of
Ingsdon,) 5 supp. ; 6 at p. 1379 ; 7 at p. 1580. Douglas's Baronage
of Scotland, 79. Burke's Colonial Gentry, ii. 638. See MONRO.

MUNSELL. New England Register, xxxiv. 246.

MUNTON. Miscellanea Genealogica et Heraldica, New Series, iv. 54.

MUNTZ. Burke's Landed Gentry, 5, 6, 7, 8.

MURCH. Burke's Landed Gentry, 8.

MURDAC, MURDOCH, or MURDAK. Dugdale's Warwickshire, 563.
Burke's Landed Gentry, 8. Baker's Northampton, i. 492. See
BURN-MURDOCH.

MURDOCH. See BURN-MURDOCH.

MURE. Burke's Commoners, (of Caldwell,) i. 453, Landed Gentry, 2, 3, 4, 5, 6, 7, 8 ; (of Herringswell House,) Landed Gentry, 2 supp., 3, 4, 5 ; (of Livingstone,) 7, 8. Paterson's History of the Co. of Ayr, i. 297 ; ii. 182, 357. Paterson's History of Ayr and Wigton, ii. 402, 413, 440 ; iii. 89, 437, 475. Burke's Extinct Baronetcies, 633. J. E. Reid's History of the Co. of Bute, 242. Selections from the Family Papers preserved at Caldwell, (Maitland Club,) 3-46. *See* MONTGOMERY-MOORE, MOORE, MORE, ROWALLANE.

MUREHEAD. Harleian Society, xvii. 119. *See* MUIRHEAD.

MURIEL. Notes and Queries, 4 S. x, 172.

MURPHY. Burke's Landed Gentry, 3, 4, 5, 6, 7, 8. O'Hart's Irish Pedigrees, 2nd Series, 253.

MURRAY. An Account of the Printing-house Family of Murray, *see* 'The Critic,' Nos. 496-499. Claim of John Murray to the Dukedom of Atholl, Sess. Papers, Feb. 1764. Burke's Visitation of Seats and Arms, 2nd Series, i. 47. Berry's Hertfordshire Genealogies, 53, 69. Burke's Royal Families, (London, 1851, 8vo.) i. 22, 162. Burke's Commoners, (of Philiphaugh,) iii. 56, Landed Gentry, 2, 4, 5, 6, 7, 8 ; (of Polmaise,) Commoners, iii. 67, Landed Gentry, 2, 3, 4, 5, 6, 7, 8 ; (of Danesfield,) Landed Gentry, 2, 3, 4, 5, 6, 7, 8 ; (of Cringletie,) 3, 4, 5, 6, 7, 8 ; (of Caw House,) 3, 4 ; (of Murraythwaite,) 2 supp., 3, 4, 5, 6, 7, 8 ; (of Lintrose,) 2, 3, 4, 5, 6, 7 ; (of Eriswell Lodge,) 2, 3, 4 ; (of Dollerie,) 7, 8 ; (of Wootton Court,) 7, 8 ; (of North Inveramsay,) 8 ; (of Ossemsley Manor,) 8. Lands and their Owners in Galloway, by P. H. M'Kerlie, i. 476 ; ii. 429 ; iii. 72, 496. Nisbet's Heraldry, ii. app. 191, 211. Douglas's Baronage of Scotland, 48, 68, 104-113, 145-149. Chambers' History of Peeblesshire, 345, 358. Wood's Douglas's Peerage of Scotland, i. 66, 143, 483, 486, 524 ; ii. 539, 601. Brydges' Collins' Peerage, v. 133, 272, 388. Notes and Queries, 1 S. vi. 11, 160 ; vii. 192 ; x. 145 ; xi. 72. The Genealogist, vii. 15 ; New Series, xii. 218 ; xv. 193. Edmondson's Baronagium Genealogicum, iv. 386 ; v. 456 ; vi. 19. Betham's Baronetage, iv. 308. New London Magazine, 1790, 174. Burke's Extinct Baronetcies, 633. The Wolfes of Forenaghts, 42. Caithness Family History, by John Henderson, 189. Alexander Nisbet's Heraldic Plates, 52, 146. Burke's Colonial Gentry, i. 4, 135. Ontarian Families, by E. M. Chadwick, i. 181. Oliver's History of Antigua, ii. 280. History of Chislehurst, by Webb, Miller, and Beckwith, 76.

MURRAY-AYNSLEY. Hodgson's Northumberland, I. ii. 209*. Burke's Colonial Gentry, ii. 555. Burke's Landed Gentry, 7, 8. Howard's Visitation of England and Wales, vii. 76.

MURRAY-GRAHAM. Burke's Landed Gentry, 2 supp., 3, 4, 5.

MURRAY-KER. Burke's Landed Gentry, 3, 4, 5, 6, 7, 8.

MURRAY-STEWART. Burke's Landed Gentry, 2, 3, 4, 5, 6.

MURROUGH. Burke's Landed Gentry, 8.

MURTH, or MURTHER. Harleian Society, ix. 147. Couch's History of Polperro, 217. A Complete Parochial History of the County of Cornwall, iv. 202, 204.

MUSARD. Parochial Topography of the Hundred of Wanting, by
W. N. Clarke, 171. Collectanea Topographica et Genealogica,
iv. 1, 181. Lipscombe's History of the County of Buckingham,
i. 398. Yorkshire Archæological and Topographical Journal, vi.
214. Notes and Queries, 2 S. vi. 178, 357. Banks' Dormant
and Extinct Baronage, i. 145.

MUSCHAMP, or MUSCHAMPE. Gentleman's Magazine, 1825, ii. 518.
Banks' Dormant and Extinct Baronage, i. 146. Harleian Society,
i. 41; xliii. 22, 41. Collectanea Topographica et Genealogica,
iii. 148. Raine's History of North Durham, 266, 267. Manning
and Bray's Surrey, iii. 29, 414. The Genealogist, ii. 115; New
Series, ix. 81. Pedigrees of the Lords of Alnwick, by W. H. D.
Longstaffe, 21. Foster's Visitations of Northumberland, 90.
Surrey Archæological Collections, xi.

MUSCOTT. Metcalfe's Visitations of Northamptonshire, 116.

MUSGRAVE. Collinson's Somerset, iii. 37, 548. Gentleman's Magazine, 1825, i. 389. Kent's British Banner Displayed, 588. Surtees
Society, xli. 52. Visitation of Westmorland, 1615, (London,
1853,) 5. Burke's Royal Families, (London, 1851, 8vo.) ii. 64.
Burke's Landed Gentry, 2 supp., p. 15, 5, 6, 7, 8. Foster's Visitations of Yorkshire, 142. Hutchinson's History of Cumberland,
i. 272; ii. 289, 572. Jefferson's History of Leath Ward, Cumberland, 411. Surtees' Durham, i. 215. Plantagenet-Harrison's
History of Yorkshire, i. 180. Harleian Society, xvi. 215, 218;
xvii. 120. Wotton's English Baronetage, i. 74; iv. 354. Banks'
Baronies in Fee, i. 344. Betham's Baronetage, i. 77; v. (Barts.
of Scotland,) 17. Banks' Dormant and Extinct Baronage, i. 382.
Foster's Visitations of Northumberland, 92. Somersetshire Wills,
printed for F. A. Crisp, iii. 41. Foster's Visitations of Cumberland and Westmorland, 91-94. Burke's Colonial Gentry, ii. 810.
Thoresby Society, i. 248. Oliver's History of Antigua, ii. 285.
Nicolson and Burn's Westmorland and Cumberland, i. 590; ii.
154, 459.

MUSKET, or MUSKETT. Burke's Commoners, ii. 102, Landed Gentry,
2, 3, 4, 5, 6, 7, 8. Metcalfe's Visitations of Suffolk, 153.

MUSKHAM. Dickinson's History of Southwell, 2nd edition, 314.
Thoroton's Nottinghamshire, ii. 240, 246; iii. 155.

MUSPRATT. Burke's Landed Gentry, 7.

MUSSELL. Visitatio Comitatus Wiltoniæ, 1623, printed by Sir T.
Phillipps. Visitation of Wiltshire, edited by G. W. Marshall, 52.

MUSSENDEN. Burke's Landed Gentry, 2, 3, 4, 5, 6, 7, 8. Baker's
Northampton, i. 604. The Genealogist, iv. 259; vi. 270. See
MISSENDEN.

MUSSON. Eyton's Antiquities of Shropshire, viii. 160, 165, 176, 184.

MUST. Burke's Colonial Gentry, ii. 596.

MUSTERS. Burke's Landed Gentry, 2, 3, 4, 5, 6, 7, 8. Thoroton's
Nottinghamshire, iii. 266. The Genealogist, New Series,
xiii. 178.

MUTTLEBURY, or MUTTLEBERIE. Visitation of Somersetshire, printed
by Sir T. Phillipps, 120. Harleian Society, vi. 265; xi. 76. The

Pedigree of Smith, by Rev. E. F. N. Smith, (London, 1878, 8vo.) folding table at end. The Visitations of Devon, by J. L. Vivian, 691.

MUTTON. Dwnn's Visitations of Wales, ii. 257. Harleian Society, ii. 80.

MYCHELL. Visitatio Comitatus Wiltoniæ, 1623, printed by Sir T. Phillipps. *See* MICHELL.

MYDDELTON, MYDDLETON, or MYDLETON. Burke's Landed Gentry, 2, 3, 4, 5. Archæologia Cambrensis, 2 S. i. 135; 4 S. viii. 31. T. Nicholas' County Families of Wales, 413. Dwnn's Visitations of Wales, i. 69, 322. S. Lewis's Parish of St. Mary, Islington, 430. Visitation of Durham, 1575, (Newcastle, 1820, fol.) 56. Wotton's English Baronetage, iii. 695. History of Powys Fadog, by J. Y. W. Lloyd, vi. 240. *See* MIDDLETON.

MYDDLETON-BIDDULPH. Burke's Landed Gentry, 8.

MYERS. Burke's Extinct Baronetcies. Burke's Landed Gentry, 5 supp., 6, 7, 8. Foster's Yorkshire Pedigrees. Robinson of the White House, Appleby, by C. B. Norcliffe, 97.

MYHILL. Archdall's Lodge's Peerage, vii. 269.

MYLBOURNE. Weaver's Visitations of Herefordshire, 90.

MYLDMORE. Hutchins' Dorset, i. 671.

MYLES. Dwnn's Visitations of Wales, i. 149.

MYLFORD. Tuckett's Devonshire Pedigrees, 112. Harleian Society, vi. 187. *See* MILFORD.

MYLL, or MYLLE. Visitation of Gloucestershire, 1569, (Middle Hill, 1854, fol.) 8. Harleian Society, xxi. 215. *See* MILL.

MYLLES. Foster's Visitations of Yorkshire, 556. Harleian Society, i. 11. *See* MILLES, MILLS.

MYLLETT. Surrey Archæological Collections, viii.

MYLNE. The Master Masons of Scotland, by R. S. Mylne, 249, 305. History of the Family of Mylne, by R. W. Milne, 1876, 4to. Burke's Landed Gentry, 3, 4.

MYLNER. Berry's Kent Genealogies, 82. Harleian Society, xvii. 120. *See* MILNER.

MYMMES. The Genealogist, New Series, xiv. 18.

MYN, MYNNE, or MYNNES. Harleian Society, iii. 5; xxi. 256; xliii. 18. The Genealogist, i. 38, 151. Carthew's Hundred of Launditch, Part ii. 481-491. *See* MENNIS.

MYNDE. Harleian Society, xxix. 369.

MYNORS. Burke's Royal Families, (London, 1851, 8vo.) i. 81. Burke's Commoners, (of Treago,) i. 86, Landed Gentry, 2, 3, 4, 5, 6, 7, 8; (of Weatheroak,) Landed Gentry, 2, 3, 4, 5, 6, 7. Shaw's Staffordshire, i. 117. Robinson's Mansions in Herefordshire, 296. *See* MINORS.

MYNSHULL. Chetham Society, lxxxv. 199. Notes and Queries, 1 S. ix. 39, 225. Harleian Society, xxxii. 206. *See* MINSHULL.

MYNTRYCHE. Weaver's Visitations of Herefordshire, 52.

MYRTON. Walter Wood's East Neuk of Fife, 274. Burke's Extinct Baronetcies, 634.

MYTTON. Dwnn's Visitations of Wales, ii. 257. Burke's Royal

Families, (London, 1851, 8vo.) i. 146. Burke's Commoners, (of Shipton,) iii. 671, Landed Gentry, 2, 3, 4, 5; (of Halston,) Commoners, ii. 517, Landed Gentry, 2, 5, 6; (of Garth,) Commoners, ii. 523, Landed Gentry, 2, 3, 4, 5, 6, 7, 8; (of Cleobury North,) Landed Gentry, 2, 3, 4, 5, 6, 7. History of the Princes of South Wales, by G. T. O. Bridgeman, 295. Collections by the Powysland Club, vii. 353. Collections for a History of Staffordshire, William Salt Society, i. 366. Ormerod's Cheshire, iii. 735. Harleian Society, xvii. 105. Transactions of Shropshire Archæological Society, viii. 199; ix. 267, 391; x. 412. *See* THORNY-CROFT.

NAAS. The Genealogist, New Series, xv. 1.
NADAULD. Jewitt's Reliquary, x. 116; xvi. 255.
NAGHTEN. O'Hart's Irish Pedigrees, 2nd Series, 254.
NAGLE. Burke's Landed Gentry, (of Calverleigh Court,) 2, 3, 4, 5, 6; (of Clogher House,) 2, 3, 4, 5. The Visitations of Devon, by J. L. Vivian, 182.
NAILOUR. Camden Society, xliii. 96, 109. *See* NAYLOUR.
NAIRNE, or NAIRN. Burke's Landed Gentry, 5, 6, 7, and p. 126, 8. Claim of Emily Jane Mercer-Elphinstone to be Baroness Nairne, Sess. Papers, A and A* of 1873; D of 1874. Burke's Extinct Baronetcies, 634. Walter Wood's East Neuk of Fife, 282. Wood's Douglas's Peerage of Scotland, ii. 279.
NAIS. Dwnn's Visitations of Wales, i. 202.
NAISH. Burke's Landed Gentry, 2, 3, 4, 5.
NALDRETT. Berry's Sussex Genealogies, 92. Visitation of Sussex, 1570, printed by Sir T. Phillipps, (Middle Hill, fol.) 8. Dallaway's Sussex, II. i. 350. Castles, Mansions, and Manors of Western Sussex, by D. G. C. Elwes and C. J. Robinson, 183. Sussex Archæological Collections, xxiv. 288.
NALTON. Foster's Visitations of Yorkshire, 556.
NANDICK. Foster's Visitations of Yorkshire, 557.
NANFAN. Nash's Worcestershire, i. 86. Notes and Queries, 5 S. viii. 472; ix. 129, 457. Metcalfe's Visitation of Worcestershire, 1683, 73. Harleian Society, xxi. 112; xxvii. 99. Visitation of Gloucester, edited by T. F. Fenwick and W. C. Metcalfe, 124.
NANGLE. D'Alton's Memoir of the Family of French, *at end.* Burke's Royal Families, (London, 1851, 8vo.) ii. 50. Burke's Landed Gentry, 2; 6 at p. 1169. Burke's Authorized Arms, 199-209. O'Hart's Irish Pedigrees, 2nd Series, 343. Memoirs of the Family of French, by John D'Alton, App.
NANGOTHAN. The Visitations of Cornwall, edited by J. L. Vivian, 339.
NANKEVELL. Harleian Society, ix. 153. The Visitations of Cornwall, edited by J. L. Vivian, 340.
NANNAN. Dwnn's Visitations of Wales, ii. 226, 233. History of Powys Fadog, by J. Y. W. Lloyd, v. 55, 58.
NANNEY. Burke's Commoners, (of Maes-y-Neuad,) ii. 180, Landed Gentry, 2, 3, 4, 5; (of Cefndeuddur,) Landed Gentry, 2, 3, 4,

5, 6, 7. Burke's Royal Descents and Pedigrees of Founders' Kin, 105. History of Powys Fadog, by J. Y. W. Lloyd, v. 397; vi. 415. *See* ELLIS-NANNEY.

NANSPIAN. Harleian Society, ix. 154. The Visitations of Cornwall, edited by J. L. Vivian, 341.

NANTIAN. Maclean's History of Trigg Minor, i. 311.

NANTON. Oliver's History of Antigua, ii. 288.

NAPER. Burke's Commoners, ii. 639, Landed Gentry, 2, 3, 4, 5, 6, 7, 8.

NAPIER. Memoirs of John Napier of Merchiston, his lineage, life, and times. Edinburgh and London, 1834, 8vo. Genealogical Notices of the Napiers of Kilmahew in Dumbartonshire, by Comr. Kerr. Glasgow, 1849, 4to. Bibliotheca Topographica Britannica, iv. Part iii. 55. Burke's Landed Gentry, 2, 3, 4, 5, 6, 7, 8. Hutchins' Dorset, ii. 770; iii. 125; 2nd edition, iv. 286. History of Dumbartonshire, by Joseph Irving, 458. Border Memories, by W. R. Carre, 288. The Book of Dumbartonshire, by Joseph Irving, ii. 344. Wood's Douglas's Peerage of Scotland, ii. 281. Wotton's English Baronetage, i. 225; ii. 160; iii. 706. Burke's Extinct Baronetcies. Harleian Society, xix. 181. Robertson's Crawford's Renfrewshire, 90, 377; Semple's edn., 136. Oxford Historical Society, xix. 192. The Genealogical Magazine, i. 290. *See* GROOM, NAPPER.

NAPIER-CLAVERING. Burke's Family Records, 158.

NAPLETON. Howard's Visitation of England and Wales, iv. 38.

NAPPER. Tuckett's Devonshire Pedigrees, 114. Visitation of Somersetshire, printed by Sir T. Phillipps, 121. Visitation of Oxfordshire, 1634, printed by Sir T. Phillipps, (Middle Hill, fol.) 25. Harleian Society, v. 253; vi. 197; xi. 77; xx. 74. Hutchins' Dorset, ii. 185, 779. South Mimms, by F. C. Cass, 56. Somersetshire Wills, printed for F. A. Crisp, iii. 101. *See* NAPIER.

NAPTON. Nichols' History of the County of Leicester, iv. 283, 306. Dugdale's Warwickshire, 335. Hoare's Wiltshire, III. iv. 54. Miscellanea Genealogica et Heraldica, 2nd Series, iii. 317.

NARBURGH, or NARBOROUGH. Burke's Extinct Baronetcies. Reliquiæ Spelmannianæ, (Oxford, 1698,) folding table of Spelman Pedigree. Notes and Queries, 7 S. vi. 502.

NARES. Notes and Queries, 5 S. ix. 54, 275.

NARY. Surtees Society, xxxvi. 116.

NASFIELD. Harleian Society, xvi. 219.

NASH. Shakespeareana Genealogica, by G. R. French, 385. Berry's Sussex Genealogies, 103. Nash's Worcestershire, i. 327; supp. 25. Burke's Landed Gentry, 2 supp., 3, 4, 5 and supp. 6, 7. Harleian Society, v. 218; xii. 147; xvii. 121. Visitation of Warwickshire, 1619, published with Warwickshire Antiquarian Magazine, 201. Dallaway's Sussex, II. i. 73, 367. Shakespere's Home, by J. C. M. Bellew, 349. Castles, Mansions, and Manors of Western Sussex, by D. G. C. Elwes and C. J. Robinson, 247.

NASON. New England Register, xvi. 182.

NASSAU. Page's History of Suffolk, 98. Edmondson's Baronagium Genealogicum, ii. 170. The Genealogist, New Series, xiv. 202.

NATHAN. Burke's Colonial Gentry, ii. 760.

NATION. Maclean's History of Trigg Minor, ii. 266.

NAUNTON. Nichols' History of the County of Leicester, iii. 493. Page's History of Suffolk, 123. Metcalfe's Visitations of Suffolk 153.

NAYLINGHERST. Morant's Essex, ii. 395. G. W. Johnson's History of Great Totham, 41. Harleian Society, xiii. 11, 85.

NAYLOR. Berry's Kent Genealogies, 97. Burke's Landed Gentry, 4, 5, 6, 7. Historical Notices of Doncaster, by C. W. Hatfield, 2nd Series, 517. Harleian Society, xxi. 112 ; xxxvii. 116 ; xlii. 32.

NAYLOUR. Harleian Society, i. 90. See NAILOUR.

NEAL, or NEALE. Burton's Description of Leicestershire, 212. Noble's Memoirs of the House of Cromwell, ii. 36-43. Berry's Buckinghamshire Genealogies, 53. Surtees Society, xxxvi. 234. Berry's Hampshire Genealogies, 149. Burke's Landed Gentry, 2, 3, 4, 5, 7 at p. 1884 ; 8 at p. 2087. Harleian Society, ii. 163 ; viii. 408 ; xix. 43, 125, 185. Thoresby's Ducatus Leodiensis, 21. Nichols' History of the County of Leicester, ii. 11. Duchetiana, by Sir G. F. Duckett, 2nd edn., 242. Metcalfe's Visitations of Northamptonshire, 117. Burke's Family Records, 434. The Genealogist, New Series, xiv. 233.

NEALAN. O'Hart's Irish Pedigrees, 2nd Series, 255.

NEAVE. Berry's Essex Genealogies, 156. Wright's Essex, ii. 432. Harleian Society, xiv. 684. Burke's Landed Gentry, 8. Betham's Baronetage, iv. 296. See LE NEVE.

NEDHAM. Burke's Landed Gentry, 2 supp. Harleian Society, iii. 27. Nichols' History of the County of Leicester, iii. 14, 408, 742, 976. Clutterbuck's Hertford, ii. 550. Baker's Northampton, i. 406.

NEED. Burke's Landed Gentry, 2 supp., 3, 4, 5, 6 at p. 1713, 7 at p. 1955, 8 at p. 2170.

NEEDAM, or NEEDHAM. Jewitt's Reliquary, vii. 27, 208. Burke's Landed Gentry, 2, 3, 4. Blunt's Dursley and its Neighbourhood, 158. Archdall's Lodge's Peerage, iv. 218. Ormerod's Cheshire, iii. 127. Harleian Society, ii. 100; xviii. 184 ; xxii. 16, 77 ; xxix. 371. The Genealogist, New Series, viii. 22. Montacute Peerage Evidence, 165. Earwaker's History of Sandbach, 198.

NEEL. J. B. Payne's Armorial of Jersey, 295.

NEELE. Harleian Society, ii. 45.

NEILE. Hodgson's Northumberland, II. ii. 297. Surtees' Durham, i. lxxxix. Notes and Queries, 2 S. vii. 297, 346.

NEILL. Burke's Landed Gentry, 2, 3, 4, 5, 6, 7, 8. Paterson's History of the Co. of Ayr, i. 346. Paterson's History of Ayr and Wigton, i. 266. Burke's Colonial Gentry, i. 380. See O'NEILL.

NEILSON. Douglas's Baronage of Scotland, 434.

NEKETON. The Genealogist, New Series, xvi. 87.

NELE. J. H. Hill's History of Market Harborough, 113. Blore's Rutland, 132. Nichols' History of the County of Leicester, ii. 575 ; iii. 362.

NELLES. Ontarian Families, by E. M. Chadwick, ii. 154.

NELSON. The Royal Descent of Nelson and Wellington from Edw. I., by G. R. French. London, 1853, 8vo. Visitation of Middlesex, (Salisbury, 1820, fol.) 48. Burke's Royal Families, (London, 1851, 8vo.) ii. 119. Burke's Commoners, i. 365, Landed Gentry, 2, 8. Herald and Genealogist, iv. 12. Chetham Society, lxxxii. 64 ; lxxxv. 216. Harleian Society, xiii. 257. Hoare's Wiltshire, III. iv. 50, 72. The Genealogist, vi. 65. Duchetiana, by Sir G. F. Duckett, 2nd edn., 241. Lancashire and Cheshire Genealogical and Historical Notes, i. 398. Notes and Queries, 1 S. v. 176, 236 ; x. 67 ; 3 S. x. 256. Carthew's West and East Bradenham, 115. Brydges' Collins' Peerage, v. 557. Carthew's Hundred of Launditch, Part iii. 350-356. Foster's Visitation of Middlesex, 88. The Nineteenth Century, No. 249, 755. The Genealogical Magazine, i. 49, 106, 162, 449, 518, 629, 638, 651, 687 ; ii. 12, 35, 68 ; iii. 289, 345, 412, 448, 499, 546.

NELTHORPE. Wotton's English Baronetage, iii. 495. Betham's Baronetage, ii. 394.

NERBER. Genealogies of Morgan and Glamorgan, by G. T. Clark, 419.

NEREFORD. Banks' Baronies in Fee, i. 345. Banks' Dormant and Extinct Baronage, i. 384. *See* NEYRFORD.

NEPEAN. An Historical Survey of Cornwall, by C. S. Gilbert, i. 578. Betham's Baronetage, v. 494.

NESBIT, or NESBITT. Surtees Society, xxxvi. 158. W. Paver's Pedigrees of Families of the City of York, 16. Burke's Landed Gentry, 2 supp., 3, 4, 5, 6, 7, 8.

NESHAM. Surtees' Durham, i. 151.

NEST. Visitation of Gloucester, edited by T. F. Fenwick and W. C. Metcalfe, 125.

NETHERCOTE. Burke's Commoners, ii. 93, Landed Gentry, 2, 3, 4, 5, 6, 7. Memoirs of the Family of Chester, by R. E. C. Waters, 661.

NETHERMILL. Visitation of Warwickshire, 1619, published with Warwickshire Antiquarian Magazine, 110. Harleian Society, xii. 253.

NETHERSOLE. Berry's Kent Genealogies, 104. Harleian Society, xlii. 32.

NETTERVILLE (Viscount). Herald and Genealogist, iv. 545. Case of James Netterville, Esq., claiming the title of Viscount Netterville, 1829, folio, pp. 30. Claim of James Netterville, Esq., to the title of Viscount Netterville in Ireland, Sess. Papers, 206 of 1830 ; 35 of 1833 ; 141 of 1834. Case of Arthur James Netterville, claiming to be Visct. Netterville. London, *n.d.*, fol. Claim of Arthur James Netterville to the dignity of Visct. Netterville, Sess. Papers, 273 of 1861 ; E of 1862 ; F of 1863 ; D of 1864 ; B of 1867. Archdall's Lodge's Peerage, iv. 202.

NETTLES. Burke's Landed Gentry, 2, 3, 4, 5, 6, 7, 8.

NETTLETON. Foster's Visitations of Yorkshire, 557. Harleian Society, xxxvii. 127 ; xxxviii. 486, 488.

NEUSUM. Plantagenet-Harrison's History of Yorkshire, i. 175. *See* NEWSAM.

NEVE. Burke's Colonial Gentry, i. 248. *See* LE NEVE.

NEVELL, NEVILE, NEVIL, NEVILL, or NEVILLE. Claim of Henry Neville to the Barony of Abergavenny, Sess. Papers, Apr. 1605—June 1610. A Treatise, whether the Barony of Abergavenny be descended unto the daughter and heire of the Hon. Henry Nevill, the late Baron, etc. London, 1642, 12mo. A Genealogical Account of the Noble Family of Neville, by D. Rowland. London, 1830, folio. A Sketch of the Stock of Nevill, Earls of Northumberland, etc., by W. E. Surtees. Newcastle, 1843, 8vo. De Nova Villa, or the House of Nevill in Sunshine and in Shade, by H. J. Swallow. Newcastle-on-Tyne, 1885, 8vo. Drummond's History of Noble British Families, Part viii. Burke's St. James's Magazine, i. 327. Morant's Essex, i. 383 ; ii. 36, 114, 342, 611. Gentleman's Magazine, 1827, i. 217. Hasted's Kent, ii. 197, 269. Collectanea Topographica et Genealogica, i. 302, 304. Brydges' Topographer, ii. 211. Historical Tour in Monmouthshire, by Willm. Coxe, 181. Surtees Society, xxxvi. 170 ; xli. 15, 20, 28, 80, 83. Berry's Hertfordshire Genealogies, 42. Vallis Eboracensis, comprising the History, etc., of Easingwold, 257. Visitation of Somersetshire, printed by Sir T. Phillipps, 121. Burke's Commoners, (of Thorney,) ii. 8, Landed Gentry, 2, 3, 4, 5, 6, 7, 8 ; (of Walcot,) Landed Gentry, 2, 3, 4, 5, 6, 7, 8 ; (of Skelbrook,) 2 supp., 4, 5, 6, 7, 8 ; (of Nevill Holt,) 3 supp., 4, 5, 6, 7 ; (of Lanlliedi,) 2 supp. ; (of Borrismore House,) 2, 3, 4, 5, 6 ; (of Haselour,) 2 supp., 5, 6, 7 ; (of Belmont Lodge,) 2 supp.; (of Annamult,) 2 ; (of Moyfin,) 7, 8 ; (of Shenstone,) 8 ; (of Westfa,) 8. Foster's Yorkshire Pedigrees. Foster's Visitations of Yorkshire, 6, 246, 340, 628. Harleian Society, ii. 21 ; iv. 64 ; viii. 352 ; xi. 78 ; xiii. 459 ; xvi. 220-230 ; xvii. 121, 122 ; xl. 1232. Lipscombe's History of the County of Buckingham, iv. 143. Excerpta Cantiana, by Rev. T. Streatfield, 6. Herald and Genealogist, iii. 515. J. H. Hill's History of Market Harborough, xiv. 164. Maclean's History of Trigg Minor, i. 316. Stonehouse's History of the Isle of Axholme, 374. Gyll's History of Wraysbury, 82. Graves' History of Cleveland, 274. Jefferson's History of Leath Ward, Cumberland, 68. Whitaker's History of Richmondshire, i. 331 ; ii. 78. Dallaway's Sussex, i. 250. Bridges' Northamptonshire, by Rev. Peter Whalley, ii. 160. Corry's History of Lancashire, i. 422. Thoresby's Ducatus Leodiensis, 182, 200. Ord's History of Cleveland, 330. Nichols' History of the County of Leicester, ii. 730 ; iii. 501 ; iv. 167. Archæologia Æliana, 2nd Series, iii. 51. Dugdale's Warwickshire, 855, 1024. Hunter's Deanery of Doncaster, ii. 393, 401. Surtees' Durham, iv. 158, 162, 163. Manning and Bray's Surrey, iii. 19. Clutterbuck's Hertford, iii. 287. Baker's Northampton, i. 83. 443. Chauncy's Hertfordshire, 281. Thoroton's Nottinghamshire, i. 348, 383 ; iii. 262. The Battle of Stoke Field, by Richd. Brooke, 49. Armorial Windows of Woodhouse Chapel, by J. G. Nichols, *faces title.* Abram's History of Blackburn, 401. Plantagenet-Harrison's History of Yorkshire, i. 444. The Genealogist, iii. 361; vi. 66; New Series, iii. 31, 107; x. 31; xvii. 110; xviii. 33, 39. Edmondson's Baronagium Genealogicum, iv. 350; vi. 20*, 99. Brydges' Collins' Peerage, v. 151; viii. 153. Banks' Baronies in Fee, i. 100, 276, 319, 321, 347; ii. 107. Banks' Dormant and Extinct Baronage, i. 147, 384; ii. 2, 220, 294, 386; iii. 524, 650. Notes and Queries, 4 S. ii. 577; 5 S. ix. 409; 6 S. xii. 356. Burke's Extinct Baronetcies. Visitation of Staffordshire, (Willm. Salt Soc.) 116. Woodcock of Cuerdon, by A. E. P. Gray, 18. Leicestershire Architectural Society, i. 316. Memorials of St. John at Hackney, by R. Simpson, 301. Foster's Visitations of Durham, 248. Chancellor's Sepulchral Monuments of Essex, 354. Old Yorkshire, ed. by Willm. Smith, iv. 240. *See* DE NEVILLE.

NEVILLE-GRENVILLE. Burke's Landed Gentry, 8.

NEVIN. Paterson's History of the Co. of Ayr, ii. 253.

NEVINS. Pedigree of Wilson, by S. B. Foster, 174.

NEVINSON. Hasted's Kent, iv. 217. Berry's Kent Genealogies, 390. Foster's Visitations of Cumberland and Westmorland, 95. Harleian Society, xlii. 146. Nicolson and Burns' Westmorland and Cumberland, i. 451.

NEWALL. Gentleman's Magazine, 1844, i. 594. Fishwick's History of Rochdale, 445. Croston's edn. of Baines's Lancaster, iii. 70. Burke's Landed Gentry, 8.

NEWARK, or NEWARKE. Foster's Visitations of Yorkshire, 92. Surtees Society, xxxvi. 194.

NEWBERIE. Metcalfe's Visitation of Worcester, 1683, 74.

NEWBIGGIN. Nicolson and Burn's Westmorland and Cumberland, i. 365.

NEWBOROW, NEWBOROUGH, or NEWBURGH. Case of Cecilia, Princess Guistiniani, etc., claiming the Dignity of Countess of Newburgh, 1857, folio, pp. 15. Supplemental Case of same. London, fol. pp. 11. Plowden's Disquisition concerning the Law of Alienage, etc., (Paris, 1818, 8vo.). Visitation of Somersetshire, printed by Sir T. Phillipps, 121. Harleian Society, xi. 78; xvi. 245. Edmondson's Account of the Greville Family, 16. Hutchins' Dorset, i. 366, 429. Baker's Northampton, i. 414. Banks' Baronies in Fee, i. 374. Notes and Queries, 6 S. iii. 432. *See* EYRE.

NEWBOTTLE. Bridges' Northamptonshire, by Rev. Peter Whalley, ii. 15.

NEWBOULD, or NEWBOLD. Jewitt's Reliquary, vii. 27. Harleian Society, xvii. 123; xxxviii. 706. Fishwick's History of Rochdale, 313.

NEWBY. Miscellanea Genealogica et Heraldica, i. 282; ii. 95. Foster's Visitations of Yorkshire, 313. Harleian Society, xvii. 124.

NEWCE. Berry's Hertfordshire Genealogies, 175. Harleian Society, xxii. 17, 78; xxxii. 206.

NEWCOMBE, NEWCOMB, or NEWCOME. Tuckett's Devonshire Pedigrees, 39. Harleian Society, vi. 197; xxxix. 1042. Westcote's

Devonshire, edited by G. Oliver and P. Jones, 531. Berry's Hertfordshire Genealogies, 117. Burke's Landed Gentry, 2, 3, 4, 5, 6, 7, 8. Clutterbuck's Hertford, i. 485. North's Church Bells of Leicestershire, 41-59. North's Church Bells of Northamptonshire, 79-87. Miscellanea Genealogica et Heraldica, 2nd Series, ii. 90. Visitations of Devon, by J. L. Vivian, 577.

NEWCOMEN. The Genealogist, iv. 260; v. 181; vi. 270; vii. 229. Burke's Extinct Baronetcies, 612. Harleian Society, xxii. 79.

NEWCOURT. Harleian Society, vi. 197. Westcote's Devonshire, edited by G. Oliver and P. Jones, 478. Visitations of Devon, by J. L. Vivian, 578.

NEWDEGATE, or NEWDIGATE. Notes on the Parish of Harefield, by W. F. Vernon, 1. Warwickshire Antiquarian Magazine, Part i. Burke's Commoners, (of Harefield,) ii. 697, Landed Gentry, 2, 3, 4, 5, 6, 7, 8; (of Kirk Hallam,) Landed Gentry, 4, 5, 6, 7, 8. Manning and Bray's Surrey, ii. 173. Harleian Society, xii. 39; xix. 185; xliii. 26. Surrey Archæological Collections, vi. 227. Aubrey's Antiquities of Surrey, iv. 266. Wotton's English Baronetage, iii. 618. Visitation of Devon, edited by F. T. Colby, 165. Betham's Baronetage, iii. 10. Burke's Extinct Baronetcies. Howard's Visitation of England and Wales, vii. 53.

NEWDIGATE-LUDFORD. Nichols' History of the County of Leicester, iv. 1025.

NEWENHAM. Burke's Landed Gentry, 3 supp., 4, 5, 6, 7, 8.

NEWHAM. Harleian Society, xxxviii. 463.

NEWINGTON. Berry's Sussex Genealogies, 158. Berry's Kent Genealogies, 93, 374.

NEWLAND. Morant's Essex, ii. 74. Harleian Society, viii. 493. Manning and Bray's Surrey, ii. 232.

NEWMAN. Berry's Kent Genealogies, 314, 468. Visitation of Middlesex, (Salisbury, 1820, fol.) 45. Visitation of Somersetshire, printed by Sir T. Phillipps, 122. Burke's Royal Families, (London, 1851, 8vo.) i. 69. Burke's Commoners, (of Thornbury Park,) ii. 111, Landed Gentry, 2, 3, 4, 5, 6, 7, 8; (of Brands House,) Landed Gentry, 2 supp., 3, 4, 5, 6, 7, 8; (of Barwick House,) 2; (of Nelmes,) 8; (of Dromoor,) 3, 4, 5, 6, 7, 8. Harleian Society, xi. 79; xiv. 596; xix. 126. Hutchins' Dorset, iv. 57. Wotton's English Baronetage, iv. 81. Burke's Extinct Baronetcies. Foster's Visitation of Middlesex, 85. Bysshe's Visitation of Essex, edited by J. J. Howard, 68.

NEWMARCH, or NEWMARSH. The Newmarch Pedigree, by G. F. and C. H. Newmarch. Cirencester, 1868, 8vo. Lipscombe's History of the County of Buckingham, i. 202. Jones' History of the County of Brecknock, i. App. 10, at 345. Thoroton's Nottinghamshire, i. 266. Harleian Society, xvi. 223. Stonehouse's History of the Isle of Axholme, 374. Banks' Dormant and Extinct Baronage, i. 150. Yorkshire Archæological Society, Record Series, xxx. 591, 595, 596.

NEWNHAM. Dugdale's Warwickshire, 86. Baker's Northampton, i. 115, 293, 711.

NEWPORT. Genealogical Account of the Family of Newport of High Ercall in the County of Salop, afterwards Earls of Bradford. [By G. T. O. Bridgman.] Bridgnorth, *n.d.*, 4to., pp. 37. Cussan's History of Hertfordshire, Parts iii. and iv. 148. Morant's Essex, i. 393, 423; ii. 597, 621. Clutterbuck's Hertford, iii. 445. Baker's Northampton, i. 459. The Genealogist, i. 202, 213; ii. 250; iii. 144. Wright's Essex, ii. 181, 742. Chauncy's Hertfordshire, 140. Harleian Society, xiii. 460; xxii. 79, 155; xxviii. 77; xxix. 372. History of the Princes of South Wales, by G. T. O. Bridgman, 276-298. Banks' Dormant and Extinct Baronage, iii. 100. Metcalfe's Visitation of Worcester, 1683, 75. Chetham Society, cx. 173. Metcalfe's Visitations of Northamptonshire, 38, 119. Weaver's Visitations of Somerset, 123. Willmore's History of Walsall, 103. William Salt Society, New Series, ii. 168.

NEWPORT-CHARLETT. Burke's Commoners, iv. 355.

NEWSAM. Fishwick's History of Goosnargh, 194. Chetham Society, lxxxi. 51. Harleian Society, xii. 317. *See* NEUSUM.

NEWSHAM. Warwickshire Antiquarian Magazine, Part i. The Genealogical Magazine, i. 555.

NEWSOM. Miscellanea Genealogica et Heraldica, New Series, i. 263. The Genealogist, New Series, xii. 176.

NEWTON. Notices of the Family of Newton, by T. H. Noyes. London, 1857, 8vo. Edinburgh Philosophical Journal, iii. 293. Rudder's Gloucestershire, 296. Herald and Genealogist, iv. 435. Collinson's Somerset, iii. 588. Hasted's Kent, i. 35. Nichols' Illustrations of Literary History, iv. 35. Gentleman's Magazine, 1852, ii. 271. Berry's Sussex Genealogies, 24, 128. Glamorganshire Pedigrees, edited by Sir T. Phillipps, 16. Tuckett's Devonshire Pedigrees, 168. Dwnn's Visitations of Wales, i. 275. Surtees Society, xxxvi. 67. Visitation of Somersetshire, printed by Sir T. Phillipps, 122. Burke's Commoners, (of Newton Hall,) iii. 26, Landed Gentry, 3, 4, 5, 6 supp., 7, 8; (of Cheadle Heath,) Landed Gentry, 3, 4; (of Mickleover,) 2, 3, 4, 5, 6, 7, 8; (of Barton Grange,) 4, 5, 6, 7, 8; (of Croxton Park,) 4, 5, 6, 7, 8; (of Carrickfergus,) 4, 5, 6, 7, 8; (of Hillmount,) 4, 5; (of Dunleckney,) 3, 4, 5, 6, 7, 8. Miscellanea Genealogica et Heraldica, New Series, i. 169, 191. Foster's Visitations of Yorkshire, 274. Harleian Society, vi. 198; viii. 489; xi. 79; xvii. 125; xviii. 184; xix. 127; xxi. 113; xxix. 374; xxxvii. 314; xxxix. 1015. Chetham Society, lxxxv. 217. Turner's History of the Town and Soke of Grantham, 69, 85, 168. Shaw's Staffordshire, i. 147. Horsfield's History of Lewes, i. 247. Burke's Aurthorized Arms, 31. Visitation of Derbyshire, 1663-4, (Middle Hill, 1854, fol.) 5. Nichols' History of the County of Leicester, iv. 807*. Earwaker's East Cheshire, i. 127, 153; ii. 163, 267. Sussex Archæological Collections, ix. 312-341. The Genealogist, ii. 393; iii. 307; New Series, viii. 23. The Sheriffs of Montgomeryshire, by W. V. Lloyd, 259, 533. Ellacombe's History of Bitton, 100. Notes and Queries, 1 S. ii. 465; vii. 600; 2 S. iii. 172; xii. 237, 314, 351, 398, 444; 3 S. i. 17, 97, 158, 191; ii. 217; viii. 120. Burke's

Extinct Baronetcies. Wotton's English Baronetage, iii. 145.
Ormerod's Cheshire, iii. 593, 859. Metcalfe's Visitations of
Suffolk, 53. Weaver's Visitations of Somerset, 54, 105. Visita-
tions of Devon, by J. L. Vivian, 579. Dallaway's Antiquities of
Bristow, 136.

NEWTON-KING. Burke's Landed Gentry, 5, 6.

NEYRFORD. Plantagenet-Harrison's History of Yorkshire, i. 543. See
NEREFORD.

NEYRNUT. Lipscombe's History of the County of Buckingham, i. 326.

NIBBS. Oliver's History of Antigua, ii. 292.

NIBLETT. Burke's Landed Gentry, 2, 3, 4, 5, 6, 7, 8.

NICHOLAS. Genealogical Memoranda relating to the Family of
Nicholas, [by Griffin Nicholas]. Hounslow, 1874, 4to. Gentleman's Magazine, lxxxv. i. 592. Dwnn's Visitations of Wales,
i. 158. Berry's Hampshire Genealogies, 93. Burke's Landed
Gentry, 3, 4. Visitatio Comitatus Wiltoniæ, 1623, printed by
Sir T. Phillipps. Hoare's Wiltshire, V. i. 96, 214. Manning
and Bray's Surrey, iii. 41. Wiltshire Archæological Magazine,
xi. 36. Visitation of Wiltshire, edited by G. W. Marshall, 41, 53,
91. Harleian Society, xvii. 122, 125; xxi. 117. The Visitations of
Cornwall, edited by J. L. Vivian, 601. Burke's Colonial Gentry,
i. 388. The Genealogist, New Series, xii. 170.

NICHOLES. Harleian Society, xiii. 86.

NICHOLETTS. The Genealogist, i. 233 ; ii. 250. Robinson's Mansions
of Herefordshire, 17. Harleian Society, xxvii. 100.

NICHOLL. Gentleman's Magazine, 1836, i. 376. Berry's Essex Genealogies, 46, 47. Burke's Heraldic Illustrations, 137. Berry's Hert-
fordshire Genealogies, 222. Topographer and Genealogist, iii. 533.
Burke's Commoners, (of Dimlands,) iv. 478 ; (of Tredunnock,)
Commoners, iv. 649, Landed Gentry, 2, 3 ; (of Merthyr Mawr,)
Commoners, ii. 143, Landed Gentry, 2, 3, 4, 5, 6, 7, 8 ; (of
Penlline,) Landed Gentry, 2 ; (of the Ham,) 2, 3 and corr., 4, 5,
6, 7, 8. Harleian Society, ix. 156 ; xiv. 685. Chauncy's Hert-
fordshire, 496. T. Nicholas' County Families of Wales, 637.
Genealogies of Morgan and Glamorgan, by G. T. Clark, 421.
Hasted's Kent, (Hund. of Blackheath, by H. H. Drake,) xxiii.
Visitation of Gloucester; edited by T. F. Fenwick and W. C.
Metcalfe, 19.

NICHOLL-CARNE. T. Nicholas' County Families of Wales, 624.

NICHOLLES. Visitation of Norfolk, published by Norfolk Archæological Society, i. 42.

NICHOLLS, or NICHOLS. Topographer and Genealogist, iii. 533-562.
Herald and Genealogist, iii. 308. Burke's Landed Gentry, 2, 5,
6, 7, 8. Visitation of Warwickshire, 1619, published with War-
wickshire Antiquarian Magazine, 194. Maclean's History of Trigg
Minor, ii. 165. Gyll's History of Wraysbury, 83. Harleian
Society, ix. 157 ; xii. 248 ; xix. 63, 186 ; xxxii. 209. A Complete
Parochial History of the County of Cornwall, iii. 219. An
Historical Survey of Cornwall, by C. S. Gilbert, ii. 209. Metcalfe's
Visitations of Suffolk, 53. The Visitations of Cornwall, edited

by J. L. Vivian, 342. Nichols' History of Leicestershire, iv. 709. Metcalfe's Visitations of Northamptonshire, 119. New England Register, xiv. 27. Howard's Visitation of England and Wales, ii. 49.

NICHOLSON, or NICOLSON. Nicholson of Badsworth, etc., originally of Carlton, near Barnsley, compiled from Royston and Badsworth Registers, etc., by T. N. Ince, of Wakefield, August, 1861, 4to. pp. 4. Berry's Kent Genealogies, 329. Burke's Royal Families, (London, 1851, 8vo.) i. 51. Burke's Commoners, (of Roundhay Park,) iv. 615, Landed Gentry, 2, 3, 4 ; (of Ballow,) Commoners, iii. 357, Landed Gentry, 2, 3, 4, 5, 6, 7, 8 ; (of Roe Park,) Landed Gentry, 3, 4 ; (of East Court,) 2 ; (of Thelwall,) 2 ; (of Belrath,) 3, 4, 5, 6, 7, 8 ; (of Waverley Abbey,) 3, 4, 5 ; (of Kinnegoe,) 2 supp. ; (of Eastmore,) 7, 8 ; (of Glenbervie,) 7, 8 ; (of Basing Park,) 8 supp.; (of Arisaig House,) 8. Harleian Society, viii. 344 ; xiii. 461 ; xliii. 83. Raine's History of North Durham, 302. Burke's Heraldic Illustrations, 72. Surtees' Durham, iv. 156. O'Hart's Irish Pedigrees, 2nd Series, 107-113. Notes and Queries, 1 S. iii. 243, 397. Caithness Family History, by John Henderson, 317. Stodart's Scottish Arms, ii. 360. Foster's Visitations of Northumberland, 93. Burke's Colonial Gentry, i. 218, 289. Northern Notes and Queries, iii. 51, 145.

NICOL, or NICOLL. Burke's Landed Gentry, 5, 6, 7, 8. Harleian Society, ix. 156. Maclean's History of Trigg Minor, iii. 366. The Visitations of Cornwall, edited by J. L. Vivian, 344. East Barnet, by F. C. Cass, Part i. 64.

NICOLAS. Burke's Commoners, (of East Looe,) iv. 138, Landed Gentry, 2 ; (of London,) Commoners, iv. 292, Landed Gentry, 2. Harleian Society, viii. 35. An Historical Survey of Cornwall, by C. S. Gilbert, ii. 209.

NICOLLE. J. B. Payne's Armorial of Jersey, 28, 298.

NICOLLS. Visitation of Norfolk, published by Norfolk Archæological Society, i. 43. Burke's Landed Gentry, 5, 6. Harleian Society, i. 66 ; ii. 187 ; xii. 249. Bridges' Northamptonshire, by Rev. Peter Whalley, ii. 95. Nichols' History of the County of Leicester, iii. 480. Burke's Extinct Baronetcies.

NIGEL. Banks' Dormant and Extinct Baronage, i. 200.

NIGHTINGALE, or NIGHTINGALL. Morant's Essex, ii. 587. Burke's Landed Gentry, 3, 4, 5, 6. Harleian Society, xiii. 258, 462 ; xxxvii. 142 ; xli. 54. Cambridgeshire Visitation, edited by Sir T. Phillipps, 23. Betham's Baronetage, ii. 1. History of the old Chapel, Tockholes, by B. Nightingale, 200. Notts and Derbyshire Notes and Queries, iv. 105.

NIHELL. Oliver's History of Antigua, ii. 302.

NIND. Berry's Berkshire Genealogies, 11. Burke's Landed Gentry, 2.

NISBET, or NISBITT. Burke's Landed Gentry, (of Southbroome House,) 2 add., 3, 4, 5, 6 ; (of Derricairne,) 2 ; (of Cairnhill,) 2, 3, 4, 5, 6, 7, 8 ; (of Woodhill,) 2. Paterson's History of Ayr and Wigton, iii. 553. Alexander Nisbet's Heraldic Plates, ix., xlix., li., lv., lviii., 82. Oliver's History of Antigua, ii. 306.

NISBET-HAMILTON. Burke's Landed Gentry, 7.
NISBET-HAMILTON-OGILVY. Burke's Landed Gentry, 8.
NITHSDALE. The Genealogical Magazine, i. 262. *See* MAXWELL.
NIVEN. Burke's Landed Gentry, 2, 8.
NIXON. Burke's Landed Gentry, (of Fermanagh,) 4, 5 ; (of Nixon
Lodge,) 2. Burke's Family Records, 438.
NOBLE. Harleian Society, ii. 114. Shaw's Staffordshire, i. 230.
Westcote's Devonshire, edited by G. Oliver and P. Jones, 561.
Visitation of Staffordshire, 1663-4, printed by Sir T. Phillipps, 7.
Nichols' History of the County of Leicester, i. 616, 617 ; iii. 461.
The Book of Dumbartonshire, by Joseph Irving, ii. 353. Irving's
History of Dumbartonshire, 466. Visitation of Devon, edited by
F. T. Colby, 165. Duncombe's Hereford, (J. H. Cooke,) iii. 20.
Fletcher's Leicestershire Pedigrees and Royal Descents, 50. Visita-
tions of Staffordshire, 1614 and 1663-4, William Salt Society, 221.
Burke's Landed Gentry, 7 at p. 1914, 8. Visitations of Devon, by
J. L. Vivian, 580.
NOCK. New England Register, vii. 258.
NODDER. Harleian Society, xxxviii. 689.
NODES. Clutterbuck's Hertford, ii. 433. Harleian Society, xix. 127 ;
xxii. 18, 80.
NOEL, or NOELL. Edmondson's Baronagium Genealogicum, ii. 157 ;
iv. 338. Burke's Royal Families, (London, 1851, 8vo.) i. 175.
Burke's Landed Gentry, (of Moxhull Park,) 2, 3, 4, 5, 6 ; (of Bell
Hall,) 2, 3, 4, 5, 6, 7, 8. Harleian Society, ii. 3, 113 ; viii. 160,
357. J. H. Hill's History of Market Harborough, 217-223.
History of Hampstead, by J. J. Park, 117. Wright's History of
Rutland, 109. Gage's History of Thingoe Hundred, Suffolk, 410.
Poulson's Holderness, i. 354. Nichols' History of the County of
Leicester, iii. 254 ; iv. 770. Miscellanea Genealogica et Heraldica,
New Series, ii. 353. Surtees Society, xxxvi. 70. Brydges' Collins'
Peerage, vi. 200. Wotton's English Baronetage, iii. 91. Banks'
Dormant and Extinct Baronage, iii. 140. Burke's Extinct
Baronetcies. Visitation of Staffordshire, (Willm. Salt Soc.) 117.
Visitations of Staffordshire, 1614 and 1663-4, William Salt Society,
222. Burke's Colonial Gentry, i. 119. *See* NOWELL.
NOION. Suckling's History of Suffolk, i. 105.
NOKE. The Genealogist, vi. 67 ; New Series, ii. 75.
NOLAN. Burke's Landed Gentry, 5, 6, 7, 8. Burke's Visitation of
Seats and Arms, 2nd Series, i. 54.
NONELEY. Antiquities and Memoirs of the Parish of Myddle, written
by Richard Gough, 1700, (folio) 63.
NOOKE. Ashmole's Antiquities of Berkshire, iii. 20.
NOONE. Harleian Society, ii. 174; xxxii. 207. Nichols' History of the
County of Leicester, iii. 498. Metcalfe's Visitations of Suffolk, 53.
NOOTH. Miscellanea Genealogica et Heraldica, New Series, ii. 9.
Betham's Baronetage, v. 430.
NORBERY. Jewitt's Reliquary, xiii. 256.
NORBORN. Visitatio Comitatus Wiltoniæ, 1623, printed by Sir T.
Phillipps.

NORBURY. Burke's Landed Gentry, 2, 3, 4, 5, 6, 7, 8. Harleian Society, xvii. 126 ; xviii. 186 ; xliii. 220.

NORCLIFF, NORCLIFFE, or NORTHCLIFFE. Surtees Society, xxxvi. 341. Burke's Commoners, ii. 630, Landed Gentry, 2 supp., 3, 4, 5, 6, 7, 8. Foster's Yorkshire Pedigrees. Foster's Visitations of Yorkshire, 558. Harleian Society, viii. 241.

NORCOP. See RADFORD-NORCOP.

NORDEN. Visitatio Comitatus Wiltoniæ, 1623, printed by Sir T. Phillipps. Visitation of Wiltshire, edited by G. W. Marshall, 90. Bysshe's Visitation of Essex, edited by J. J. Howard, 68.

NORFOLK. Harleian Society, xxxix. 998.

NORFOLK (Duke of). Berry's Buckinghamshire Genealogies, 21, 63. Hunter's Deanery of Doncaster, i. 296. Banks' Dormant and Extinct Baronage, iii. 552. See HOWARD.

NORMAN. Morant's Essex, ii. 322. Burke's Landed Gentry, (of Somersetshire,) 2 supp., 3, 4, 5 ; (of Dencombe,) 2, 3, 4, 5, 6, 7 ; (of Glengollan,) 4, 5, 6, 7, 8 ; (of Goadby Marwood,) 5 ; (of Mistley Place,) 7, 8 ; (of the Rookery,) 8. Foster's Visitations of Yorkshire, 558. Erdeswicke's Survey of Staffordshire, 261. Fletcher's Leicestershire Pedigrees and Royal Descents, 35. Burke's Colonial Gentry, ii. 850. Burke's Family Records, 445.

NORMANBY. Howard's Visitation of England and Wales, ix. 54.

NORMANDYS. The Genealogist, New Series, xv. 96.

NORMANTON. Harleian Society, xvi. 147.

NORMANVILL, or NORMANVILLE. Harleian Society, iii. 40. Blore's Rutland, 127, 223. Hunter's Deanery of Doncaster, ii. 127. Foster's Visitations of Yorkshire, 72, 168, 348. The Genealogist, New Series, xiii. 11.

NORMCOTE. Harleian Society, xxix. 376.

NORQUAY. Burke's Colonial Gentry, i. 374.

NORRES, NORREIS, or NORREYS. Ormerod's Miscellanea Palatina, 8, 14, 26, 36, 47. Cheshire and Lancashire Historic Society, Session ii. 138, 240. Topographer and Genealogist, ii. 357-383. Lydiate Hall and its Associations, by Rev. T. E. Gibson, (1876, 4to.) 154. Clutterbuck's Hertford, ii. 484. Baines' History of the Co. of Lancaster, iii. 128, 754 ; Croston's edn., v. 58. Visitation of Kent, (reprinted from Archæologia Cantiana, vol. vi.) 105. Berry's Kent Genealogies, 129. Burke's Royal Families, (London, 1851, 8vo.) ii. 200. Burke's Commoners, i. 310, Landed Gentry, 2 and supp. p. 86, 3, 4, 5, 7. Harleian Society, v. 289, 310 ; xlii. 23. Burke's Heraldic Illustrations, 129. History of the Hundred of Bray, by Charles Kerry, 120. Chetham Society, lxxxv. 218, 219, 220. Gregson's Fragments relative to the County of Lancaster, 198. Thoroton's Nottinghamshire, iii. 11. Plantagenet-Harrison's History of Yorkshire, i. 474. Banks' Dormant and Extinct Baronage, ii. 44. Ormerod's Parentalia, 45. Burke's Extinct Baronetcies. F. G. Lee's History of Thame, 442. History of Ufton Court, by A. M. Sharp, 16.

NORRIS. Hasted's Kent, iii. 83. Visitation of Somersetshire, printed

by Sir T. Phillipps, 123. Visitation of Oxfordshire, 1634, printed
by Sir T. Phillipps, (Middle Hill, fol.) 26. Burke's Landed
Gentry, (of Hackney,) 2 supp., 3, 4, 5, 6, 7, 8; (of Wood Norton,)
8; (of Sudbury House,) 8. Miscellanea Genealogica et Heraldica,
New Series, i. 101. Chetham Society, lxxxi. 83. Harleian
Society, viii. 163; xi. 80; xl. 1174. Lipscombe's History of the
County of Buckingham, i. 233. Notices of Swyncombe and
Ewelme in Co. Oxford, by H. A. Napier, 255, 346. Gyll's
History of Wraysbury, 17. Westcote's Devonshire, edited by
G. Oliver and P. Jones, 541, 626. North's Church Bells of
Leicestershire, 92. North's Church Bells of Northamptonshire,
96-101. Topographical Miscellanies, 1792, 4to., (Witham). Banks'
Baronies in Fee, i. 353. Banks' Dormant and Extinct Baronage,
ii. 395. Weaver's Visitations of Somerset, 55. Genealogies of
Morgan and Glamorgan, by G. T. Clark, 423. The Visitations
of Devon, by J. L. Vivian, 704. Howard's Visitation of England
and Wales, vi. 111.

NORTH. Lives of the Norths, by Hon Roger North. London, 1826.
8vo. 3 vols. Kent's British Banner Displayed, 569. Gentleman's
Magazine, 1829, i. 205. Berry's Sussex Genealogies, 221. Berry's
Hampshire Genealogies, 245. Burke's Royal Families, (London,
1851, 8vo.) i. 115. Burke's Landed Gentry, (of Rougham,) 3, 4,
5, 6, 7, 8; (of Thurland Castle,) 4, 5, 6, 7, 8. Harleian Society,
iv. 82; xxxviii. 641. Baker's Northampton, i. 526. Suckling's
History of Suffolk, ii. 123. Manning and Bray's Surrey, i. 47.
Thoroton's Nottinghamshire, iii. 326. Page's History of Suffolk,
182. Topographical Miscellanies, 1792, 4to., (Catlage). Edmondson's Baronagium Genealogicum, iii. 287. Brydges' Collins'
Peerage, iv. 454. Banks' Baronies in Fee, i. 354. Banks'
Dormant and Extinct Baronage, ii. 401. Burke's Extinct Baronetcies. Hulbert's Annals of Almondbury, 160.

NORTH-BOMFORD. Burke's Landed Gentry, 5, 6, 7, 8.

NORTHAMPTON. Banks' Dormant and Extinct Baronage, iii. 559.

NORTHCOT, or NORTHCOTE. The Life of the Earl of Iddesleigh, with
Complete Genealogy of the Northcote Family, by C. Worthy.
London, 1887, 8vo. Notes and Gleanings, by W. Cotton and
J. Dallas, iv. 133. Tuckett's Devonshire Pedigrees, 29. Burke's
Landed Gentry, 2, 3, 4, 5, 6, 7, 8. Harleian Society, vi. 199.
Westcote's Devonshire, edited by G. Oliver and P. Jones, 599.
Wotton's English Baronetage, ii. 206. Betham's Baronetage, i.
409. The Visitations of Devon, by J. L. Vivian, 581.

NORTHESK (Earls of). Angus or Forfarshire, by A. J. Warden, 431.

NORTHEY. Berry's Surrey Genealogies, 53. Burke's Commoners,
iv. 124, Landed Gentry 2, 3, 4, 5, 6, 7, 8. Harleian Society,
viii. 478, 519; xvii. 127. Manning and Bray's Surrey, ii. 615.
A History of Devizes, (1859, 8vo.) 552.

NORTHEY-HOPKINS. Burke's Royal Families, (London, 1851, 8vo.)
ii. 129. Burke's Commoners, iv. 119, Landed Gentry, 2, 3. Lipscombe's History of the County of Buckingham, i. 377.

NORTHGATE. Harleian Society, xxxii. 208.

NORTHLEIGH. Harleian Society, vi. 200. The Visitations of Devon, by J. L. Vivian, 584.

NORTHMORE. Burke's Landed Gentry, 3 supp., 4, 5, 6, 7, 8. Burke's Royal Descents and Pedigrees of Founders' Kin, 84. The Visitations of Devon, by J. L. Vivian, 851.

NORTHOVER. Visitation of Somersetshire, printed by Sir T. Phillipps, 122. Harleian Society, xi. 80.

NORTHRUP. New England Register, xliii. 242.

NORTHUMBERLAND. Extracts of the History and Genealogy of the Noble Families of the Earl and Countess of Northumberland. By R. Griffith. Dublin, 1764, 8vo. Collectanea Topographica et Genealogica, i. 298. Burke's Royal Families, (London, 1851, 8vo.) i. 85. Hodgson's Northumberland, III. ii. 12. Archæologia, v. 207. Banks' Dormant and Extinct Baronage, iii. 565.

NORTHWICK. Burke's Royal Families, (London, 1851, 8vo.) i. 134.

NORTHWOOD, or NORTHWODE. Archæologia Cantiana, ii. 9-43. Hasted's Kent, ii. 624. Berry's Kent Genealogies, 50. Notes and Queries, 1 S. x. 442. Banks' Baronies in Fee, i. 355. Banks' Dormant and Extinct Baronage, i. 386. Harleian Society, xxi. 117; xlii. 36. The Genealogist, New Series, xii. 32; xvi. 41. See DE NORTHWOOD.

NORTHWYCH. Ormerod's Cheshire, iii. 160.

NORTON. Burke's Extinct Baronetcies, and 634. Collinson's Somerset, iii. 153. Fisher's History of Masham, 285. Hasted's Kent, ii. 626. Berry's Hampshire Genealogies, 106, 194. Berry's Hertfordshire Genealogies, 226. Cambridgeshire Visitation, edited by Sir T. Phillipps, 23. Berry's Kent Genealogies, 158. Surtees Society, xxxvi. 40, 102. Burke's Commoners, iv. 79. Foster's Yorkshire Pedigrees. Harleian Society, viii. 57; xvi. 231; xvii. 128; xix. 128; xxii. 80; xxxii. 208; xxxix. 910; xli. 66; xlii. 79. Whitaker's History of Richmondshire, ii. 182. Surtees' Durham, i. clx. clxi.; iii. 125. Miscellanea Genealogica et Heraldica, i. 51. Foster's Visitations of Yorkshire, 244. History of Richmond, by C. Clarkson, 331. Warwickshire Pedigrees, from Visitation of 1682-3 (privately, printed, 1865). Herald and Genealogist, iii. 277. Burke's Heraldic Illustrations, 49. Plantagenet-Harrison's History of Yorkshire, i. 108. Edmondson's Baronagium Genealogicum, vi. 99. Pedigrees of the Leading Families of Lancashire, published by Joseph Foster, (London, 1872, fol.). The New History of Yorkshire, commencing with Richmondshire, by Genl. Plantagenet-Harrison, (London, 1872, fol.) Part i. 35. Burke's Landed Gentry, 6, 7, 8. Whitaker's Deanery of Craven, 3rd edn., 523. Notes and Queries, 1 S. ii. 216, 250; 2 S. viii. 388; 3 S. iv. 480; 7 S. viii. 324, 394, 456. Brydges' Collins' Peerage, vii. 546. Metcalfe's Visitations of Suffolk, 54, 154. The Visitations of Devon, edited by J. L. Vivian, 59. Pedigrees of the Leading Families of Yorkshire, by Joseph Foster. Burke's Colonial Gentry, i. 368. Hampshire Observer, January 30, 1892. Hampshire Notes and Queries, vi. 124. New England Register, xiii. 225. The Genealogist, New Series, xvi. 181; xvii. 50.

NORWICH. J. H. Hill's History of Market Harborough, 72. Notices of Swyncombe and Ewelme in Co. Oxford, by H. A. Napier, 286. Bridges' Northamptonshire, by Rev. Peter Whalley, ii. 25, 282. Nichols' History of the County of Leicester, ii. 519. Wotton's English Baronetage, ii. 214. Banks' Baronies in Fee, i. 356. Banks' Dormant and Extinct Baronage, i. 387. Burke's Extinct Baronetcies. Metcalfe's Visitation of Northamptonshire, 120. *See* DE NORWICH.

NORWOOD. Rudder's Gloucestershire, 521. Fosbrooke's Abstracts of Smith's Lives of the Berkeleys, 181. Berry's Kent Genealogies, 58. Burke's Landed Gentry, 4, 5. The Genealogist, vii. 185.

NOSWORTHY. The Visitations of Devon, by J. L. Vivian, 782.

NOTLEY. Burke's Landed Gentry, 2, 3, 4, 5, 6, 7, 8.

NOTT. Burke's Landed Gentry, 6, 7, 8. Miscellanea Genealogica et Heraldica, New Series, iii. 233. Weaver's Visitation of Herefordshire, 53. Visitation of Gloucester, edited by T. F. Fenwick and W. C. Metcalfe, 126. Harleian Society, xxvii. 100.

NOTTINGHAM. Hasted's Kent, ii. 203. Banks' Dormant and Extinct Baronage, iii. 577.

NOTTINGHAM (Earls of). Deering's Nottingham, 200.

NOTTON. Hunter's Deanery of Doncaster, ii. 391.

NOURSE. Visitation of Oxfordshire, 1634, printed by Sir T. Phillipps, (Middle Hill, fol.) 26. Burke's Landed Gentry, 2. Harleian Society, v. 282. Duncombe's Hereford, (J. H. Cooke,) iii. 213. Visitation of Gloucester, edited by T. F. Fenwick and W. C. Metcalfe, 127.

NOWELL. Gentleman's Magazine, 1826, i. 221. Churton's Life of Nowell, (Oxford, 1809,) 389. Berry's Sussex Genealogies, 334. Berry's Kent Genealogies, 430. Visitation of Sussex, 1570, printed by Sir T. Phillipps, (Middle Hill, fol.) 8. Burke's Royal Families, (London, 1851, 8vo.) i. 27. Burke's Landed Gentry, 2, 3, 4, 5, 6, 7, 8. Chetham Society, lxxxi. 33, 36 ; lxxxii. 65, 66 ; lxxxv. 221 ; xcix. 40. Foster's Lancashire Pedigrees. Baines' History of the Co. of Lancaster, iii. 303 ; Croston's edn., iii. 420. Whitaker's History of Whalley, ii. 41, 110, 113. Abram's History of Blackburn, 539, 624. Whitaker's Deanery of Craven, 3rd edn., 557. Notes and Queries, 4 S. v. 199 ; xi. 217. The Palatine Note Book, ii. 109. Harleian Society, xlii. 193. *See* NOEL.

NOWELL-USTICKE. Burke's Landed Gentry, 5, 6.

NOWERS. Topographer, (London, 1789-91, 8vo.) ii. 210. Harleian Society, ii. 135. J. H. Hill's History of Market Harborough, 132. Lipscombe's History of the County of Buckingham, ii. 365 ; iv. 143. Nichols' History of the County of Leicester, ii. 655. Banks' Baronies in Fee, ii. 106. The Genealogist, New Series, xii. 177 ; xiii. 38.

NOYE, or NOYES. Berry's Sussex Genealogies, 153. Polwhele's History of Cornwall, iv. 94. Harleian Society, ix. 158. Notes and Queries, 2 S. ii. 169 ; vi. 399 ; vii. 35. Gentleman's Magazine, 1842, i. 671 ; ii. 2. Burke's Landed Gentry, 2, 3, 4, 5, 6.

Sussex Archæological Collections, ix. 341. A Complete Parochial History of the County of Cornwall, i. 366. An Historical Survey of Cornwall, by C. S. Gilbert, ii. 212. The Genealogist, vi. 67. The Visitations of Cornwall, edited by J. L. Vivian, 346. Some Notices of the Family of Newton, by T. H. Noyes, 31. New England Register, xlvii. 71; xlviii. 18.

NUGENT. Case of Wm. Thos. Nugent, Esq., claiming to be Baron Nugent, folio, pp. 37. Claim of Wm. Thos. Nugent to be Baron Nugent of Riverston, in Ireland, Sess. Papers, 208 of 1839. Burke's Patrician, iii. 172. Claim of Governor Nugent, and Andrew Nugent, Esq., to be coheirs of the Barony of Delvin, Sess. Papers, 144 of 1831-32. Burke's Landed Gentry, (of Clonlost,) 3, 4, 5, 6, 7, 8; (of Portaferry,) 2, 3, 4, 5, 6, 7, 8; (of Bobsgrove,) 2, 3, 4, 5, 6, 7, 8. D'Alton's Memoir of the Family of French, at end. Burke's Heraldic Illustrations, 126. O'Hart's Irish Pedigrees, 2nd Series, 343. Archdall's Lodge's Peerage, i. 215. Burke's Extinct Baronetcies, 612. Miscellanea Genealogica et Heraldica, 2nd Series, v. 29. Oliver's History of Antigua, ii. 310. See WESTMEATH.

NUGENT-DUNBAR. Burke's Landed Gentry, 7, 8.

NUN, or NUNN. Burke's Landed Gentry, (of St. Margarets,) 2 supp., 3, 4, 5 and supp., 6, 7; (of Silverspring,) 2 supp., 3, 4, 5. Metcalfe's Visitations of Suffolk, 154. Miscellanea Genealogica et Heraldica, 2nd Series, ii. 89.

NUNWICK. Foster's Visitations of Yorkshire, 156.

NUTBROWNE. Harleian Society, xiv. 597.

NUTCOMBE. Harleian Society, vi. 202. The Visitations of Devon, by J. L. Vivian, 585.

NUTHALL. Chetham Society, lxxxv. 222. Ormerod's Cheshire, ii. 99. Ormerod's Parentalia, 38. Harleian Society, xviii. 187.

NUTHILL. Poulson's Holderness, i. 342.

NUTT. Harleian Society, viii. 86; xxxviii. 745. Sussex Archæological Collections, vi. 238.

NUTTALL. Burke's Commoners, iv. 487, Landed Gentry, 2, 3, 8.

NUTTER. New England Register, vii. 259.

OAKDEN. Burke's Landed Gentry, 4, 5. See OKEDEN.

OAKELEY, or OAKLEY. Burke's Royal Families, (London, 1851, 8vo.) i. 178. Eddowes' Shrewsbury Journal, July 20, 1887, 5. Harleian Society, xxix. 376. The Gresley's of Drakelowe, by F. Madan, 291. Burke's Commoners, i. 250, (of Oakley,) Landed Gentry, 2, 3, 4, 5, 6, 7, 8; (of The Plas,) 7. Betham's Baronetage, iv. 192.

OAKES. Burke's Landed Gentry, 2, 3, 4, 5, 6, 7, 8. Gage's History of Thingoe Hundred, Suffolk, 494. Burke's Extinct Baronetcies.

OATES. Foster's Yorkshire Pedigrees. Whitaker's Loidis and Elmete, 96. Hunter's Deanery of Doncaster, ii. 48. Burke's Landed Gentry, 6, 7, 8. Notes and Queries, 6 S. ix. 445. New England Register, vi. 150. Harleian Society, xxxvii. 260; xxxviii. 788.

OATRIDGE. Visitation of Gloucester, edited by T. F. Fenwick and W. C. Metcalfe, 127.

O'BEIRNE. Burke's Landed Gentry, 5, 6, 7, 8. O'Hart's Irish Pedigrees, 2nd Series, 256.

O'BRANNAN. O'Hart's Irish Pedigrees, 2nd Series, 258.

O'BRASSIL. O'Hart's Irish Pedigrees, 2nd Series, 258.

OBRÉ. Burke's Landed Gentry, 6, 7, 8.

O'BRIEN. Historical Memoir of the O'Briens, by John O'Donoghue, A.M. Dublin, 1860, 8vo. The O'Briens, by W. A. Lindsay. London and Aylesbury, 1876, 8vo. Genealogical Notes of the O'Briens of Kilcor, Co. Cork. *No place.* Privately printed, 1887. Claim of Lady O'Brian to the Barony of Leighton Bromswold, Sess. Papers, Jan.—Feb., 1673. Berry's Buckinghamshire Genealogies, 59. Burke's Commoners, iii. 109. Burke's Landed Gentry, 4, 5, 6, 7, 8. Burke's Visitation of Seats and Arms, 2nd Series, i. 8. Baker's Northampton, i. 21. Irish Pedigrees, by John O'Hart, 71 ; 2nd Series, 75. Edmondson's Baronagium Genealogicum, iv. 379. Archdall's Lodge's Peerage, ii. 1. The Irish Builder, xxxv. 186. Ontarian Families, by E. M. Chadwick, ii. 141.

O'BRIEN-DE-STAFFORD. Burke's Landed Gentry, 5, 6.

O'BRIEN-HOARE. Aldred's History of Turville, 47.

O'BYRNE. Historical Reminiscences of the O'Byrnes, O'Tooles, and O'Kavanahs, and other Irish Chieftains, by O'Byrne. London, 1843, 8vo. Irish Pedigrees, by John O'Hart, 164 ; 2nd Series, 259. Burke's Landed Gentry, 7, 8. *See* BYRNE.

O'CALLAGHAN. Burke's Landed Gentry, (of Maryfort,) 3, 7, 8 ; (of Cadogan,) 4, 5, 6 ; (of Co. Cork,) 6. O'Hart's Irish Pedigrees, 2nd Series, 76. Archdall's Lodge's Peerage, vii. 243.

O'CALLAGHAN-WESTROPP. Howard's Visitation of Ireland, i. 80.

O'CARROLL. Irish Pedigrees, by John O'Hart, 75 ; 2nd Series, 77. Keating's History of Ireland, *Plates* 6, 27. Burke's Landed Gentry, 8.

OCHTERLONY. Burke's Extinct Baronetcies.

OCKLEY. *See* OAKLEY.

O'CLERY. Irish Pedigrees, by John O'Hart, 2nd Series, 260.

O'CONNELL. Gentleman's Magazine, 1839, ii. 359. Burke's Commoners, ii. 565, Landed Gentry, 2, 3, 4, 5, 6, 7, 8. O'Hart's Irish Pedigrees, 2nd Series, 79. Howard's Visitation of Ireland, ii. 50.

O'CONNOR, or O'CONOR. Memoirs of Charles O'Conor of Belanagare, with a Historical Account of the Family of O'Conor, by the Rev. C. O'Conor. Dublin, 1796, 8vo. Memoir of the O'Connor's of Ballintubber, co. Roscommon, by R. O'Conor. Dublin, 1859, 8vo. The O'Conors of Connaught, by C. O. O'Connor Don. Dublin, 1891, 4to. Claim of Maurice O'Connor, Mount Pleasant, in King's Co., Esq., claiming to be Baron of Killeen, Sess. Papers, 144 of 1831-32. Burke's Landed Gentry, (of Mount Druid,) 3, 4, 5, 6, 7, 8 ; (of Milton,) 3, 4, 5, 6 ; (O'Conor Don,) 8 ; (of Charlville,) 8 ; (of Dundermott,) 3, 4, 5, 6, 7. Irish Pedigrees, by John O'Hart, 92, 129, 144, 169 ; 2nd Series, 131, 262. Keating's

History of Ireland, *Plates* 12, 17, 22.   Burke's Colonial Gentry, i. 381.

O'CONNOR-MORRIS. Burke's Landed Gentry, 4, 5, 6, 7, 8.

O'CONOR-DON. Burke's Landed Gentry, 2, 3, 4, 5, 6, 7.   Irish Pedigrees, by John O'Hart, 2nd Series, 261.

O'DALY. Burke's Visitation of Seats and Arms, 2nd Series, ii. 45.

ODDIE, or ODDY. Burke's Colonial Gentry, ii. 769.   Harleian Society, xxxvii. 198.   Annals of Smith of Balby, by H. E. Smith, 127.

O'DEA. O'Hart's Irish Pedigrees, 2nd Series, 79.

ODELL. Visitation of Oxfordshire, 1634, printed by Sir T. Phillipps, (Middle Hill, fol.) 26.   Burke's Landed Gentry, 2, 3, 4, 5, 6, 7.   Burke's Colonial Gentry, ii. 821.

ODIN. New England Register, xii. 223.

ODINGSELLS, or ODINSELLS. Harleian Society, iv. 75.   Nichols' History of the County of Leicester, iv. 636.   Banks' Baronies in Fee, ii. 109.   Blomefield's Norfolk, vi. 170.   Dugdale's Warwickshire, 343, 940.   Clutterbuck's Hertford, iii. 119.   Thoroton's Nottinghamshire, iii. 37.   *See* DE ODINGSELLS.

O'DIRSGEOIL. Keating's History of Ireland, *Plate* 28.

ODLIN. New England Register, xli. 265, 393.

O'DOHERTY, or O'DOCHERTY. O'Donovan's Annals of the Kingdom of Ireland, 2nd edn., vi. 2421.   *See* DOHERTY.

O'DONEL, or O'DONNELL. Burke's Landed Gentry, 2 supp.   Irish Pedigrees, by John O'Hart, 149 ; 2nd Series, 264-269.   O'Donovan's Annals of the Kingdom of Ireland, 2nd edn., vi. 2377-2420.

O'DONNELLAN. John O'Donovan's Tribes and Customs of Hy-many, 169.   *See* DONELAN.

O'DONNELLY. O'Donovan's Annals of the Kingdom of Ireland, 2nd edn , vi. 2426.   *See* DONNELLY.

O'DONOGHUE. Burke's Landed Gentry, 2, 3, 4, 5, 6, 7, 8.   Irish Pedigrees, by John O'Hart, 2nd Series, 80.

O'DONOVAN. Burke's Commoners, (of Clan Cathal,) iii. 397, Landed Gentry, 2, 3, 4, 5, 6, 7, 8 ; (of O'Donovan's Cave,) Landed Gentry, 5.   Irish Pedigrees, by John O'Hart, 2nd Series, 82.   O'Donovan's Annals of the Kingdom of Ireland, 2nd edn., vi. 2430-2483.   Journal of Kilkenny Archæological Society, New Series, iii. 101.   Burke's Colonial Gentry, ii. 324.   *See* DONOVAN.

O'DOWD. Irish Pedigrees, by John O'Hart, 2nd Series, 269.

O'DRISCOLL. O'Hart's Irish Pedigrees, 2nd Series, 114.   Miscellany of the Celtic Society, edited by John O'Donovan, 401.

O'DUINNE. Burke's Landed Gentry, 2, 3, 4, 5.

OEILS. Harleian Society, xvii. 129.

OESTERMAN. Oliver's History of Antigua, ii. 316.

O'FARRELL. Burke's Landed Gentry, 3, 4, 5, 6, 7, 8.   Burke's Heraldic Illustrations, 129.   Irish Pedigrees, by John O'Hart, 84.

O'FELAN. Irish Pedigrees, by John O'Hart, 133.

O'FERRALL. Burke's Landed Gentry, 2, 3, 4, 5, 6, 7, 8.

OFFICER. Burke's Colonial Gentry, ii. 680.

OFFLEY. A True Account of the Alienation and Recovery of the Estates of the Offleys of Norton, by Rev. Joseph Hunter, F.S.A.

London, 1841, 8vo.[1] Harleian Society, i. 64 ; xvii. 130 ; xxxvii. 316 ; xliii. 208. Wilson's History of the Parish of St. Laurence Pountney, 230. The Genealogist, vi. 68. Visitations of Staffordshire, 1614 and 1663-4, William Salt Society, 224. Surrey Archæological Collections, xi.

O'FINAN. Irish Pedigrees, by John O'Hart, 2nd Series, 270.

O'FLAHERTIE, or O'FLAHERTY. Burke's Landed Gentry, 2 and supp., 3, 4, 5, 6, 7. Description of West Connaught, edited by James Hardiman, (Irish Archl. Society,) 362. Irish Pedigrees, by John O'Hart, 162.

O'FLANAGAN. Burke's Visitation of Seats and Arms, 2nd Series, ii. 35. O'Hart's Irish Pedigrees, 2nd Series, 271. *See* FLANAGAN.

O'FLYNN. Irish Pedigrees, by John O'Hart, 2nd Series, 273.

OFSPRING. Miscellanea Genealogica et Heraldica, i. 52. Harleian Society, xvii. 129.

O'GARA. Irish Pedigrees, by John O'Hart, 2nd Series, 87.

OGARD. Carthew's West and East Bradenham, 94.

OGDEN. Notes and Queries, 1 S. ii. 73, 105 ; ix. 541 ; x. 376. Harleian Society, xxxvii. 121, 133.

OGELLTHORPE, or OGLETHORPE. Sir T. Phillipps' Topographer, No. 1, (March, 1821, 8vo.) 17. Surtees Society, xxxvi. 151, 262. Visitation of Oxfordshire, 1574, printed by Sir T. Phillipps, (Middle Hill, fol.) 7. Foster's Visitations of Yorkshire, 275, 314, 315. Harleian Society, v. 125. Manning and Bray's Surrey, i. 614.

OGILBY. Burke's Landed Gentry, (of Ardnargle,) 3, 4, 5, 6, 7, 8 ; (of Altnachree Castle,) 4, 5, 6, 7, 8.

OGILVY, or OGILVIE. Claim of Walter Ogilvy, Esq., to the Title of Earl of Airlie, and Lord Ogilvy, Sess. Papers, 67 of 1812-13 ; 60 of 1813-14. Burke's Landed Gentry, (of Inshewan,) 2, 3, 4, 5, 6, 7, 8 ; (of Chesters,) 6, 8 ; (of Tannadice,) 6. Nisbet's Heraldry, ii. app. 230. Douglas's Baronage of Scotland, 49, 288. Wood's Douglas's Peerage of Scotland, i. 27, 190, 579. Burke's Colonial Gentry, ii. 430, 551, 825, 833. Case of Walter Ogilvy Claiming the Title of Earl of Airlie, etc., 1813, fol. Alexander Nisbet's Heraldic Plates, 128, 150. Northern Notes and Queries, v. 41. Burke's Family Records, 447.

OGLANDER, or OKELANDER. Berry's Hampshire Genealogies, 130. Hutchins' Dorset, ii. 134. Wotton's English Baronetage, iii. 492. Betham's Baronetage, ii. 389.

OGLE. An Account of the Family of Ogle. Edinburgh, 1812, 8vo. Bird's Magazine of Honour, 85. Pedigrees from Visitation of Northumberland, printed by Sir T. Phillipps, (Middle Hill, 1858, fol.) 2. Burke's Commoners, iv. 709. Burke's Landed Gentry, (of Eglingham,) 2, 3, 4, 5, 6, 7 ; (of Kirkley Hall,) 2, 3, 4, 5, 6, 7, 8. Harleian Society, viii. 93 ; xvi. 233. Burke's Heraldic Illustrations, 111. Collectanea Topographica et Genealogica, vi. 194. Raine's History of North Durham, 371. Chetham Society, lxxxv. 223. Gregson's Fragments relative to the County of Lancaster, 176. Hodgson's Northumberland, I. ii. 380-387 ; II. ii.

---

[1] The copy in the British Museum Library has valuable additions.

135, 276, 365. The Genealogist, i. 306, 311, 321 ; iv. 261.
Banks' Baronies in Fee, i. 357. Banks' Dormant and Extinct
Baronage, ii. 402. Foster's Visitations of Northumberland, 94,
95. Croston's edn. of Baines's Lancaster, v. 28. *See* CAVENDISH.

O'GORMAN. Burke's Landed Gentry, 6, 7, 8. O'Hart's Irish Pedigrees, 2nd Series, 274.

O'GRADY. Burke's Commoners, (of Kilballyowen,) ii. 603, Landed
Gentry, 2, 3, 4, 5, 6, 7, 8 ; (of The Grange,) Landed Gentry, 4, 5,
6, 7 ; (of Landscape,) 8. Irish Pedigrees, by John O'Hart, 2nd
Series, 87. Journal of the Historical and Archæological Association of Ireland, 4th Series, iv. 44. Burke's Colonial Gentry, i.
372.

O'HAGAN. Irish Pedigrees, by John O'Hart, 2nd Series, 276.

O'HALLORAN. Burke's Colonial Gentry, i. 81.

O'HANLON. Irish Pedigrees, by John O'Hart, 2nd Series, 277.

O'HARA. Burke's Landed Gentry, (of Crebilly,) 3 supp., 4, 5 ; (of
O'Hara Brook,) 2, 3, 4, 5, 6, 8; (of Annaghmore,) 4, 5, 6, 7, 8 ;
(of Lenaboy,) 6, 7, 8. Irish Pedigrees, by John O'Hart, 2nd
Series, 89.

O'HART. The Last Princess of Tara, or a brief sketch of the O'Hart
Ancient Royal Family, by J. O'Hart. Dublin, 1873, 8vo. Irish
Pedigrees, by John O'Hart, 136 ; 2nd Series, 279.

O'KANE. The Ulster Journal of Archæology, iii. i. 265 ; iv. 139.

O'KAVANAGH. *See* O'BYRNE.

OKEBEARE. Visitation of Devon, edited by F. T. Colby, 165.

OKEDEN. Croston's edn. of Baines's Lancaster, iii. 83. Hutchins'
Dorset, iii. 469. Hoare's Wiltshire, IV. ii. 60. Burke's Landed
Gentry, 5, 6, 7, 8. *See* OAKDEN.

O'KEEFFE. Irish Pedigrees, by John O'Hart, 2nd Series, 92.

OKEHAM. Bysshe's Visitations of Essex, edited by J. J. Howard, 68.

O'KELLEY. Burke's Landed Gentry, 3, 4, 5.

O'KELLY. Burke's Landed Gentry, (of Screen,) 2, 3, 4, 5 supp. ; (of
Gallagh,) 2, 3, 4, 5, 6, 7, 8 ; (of Ballysax,) 2 ; (of Clan Colla,) 2 ;
(of Gurtray,) 5, 6, 7, 8 ; (of Barrettstown,) 5, 6, 7. Burke's Visitation of Seats and Arms, 2nd Series, ii. 43. Irish Pedigrees, by
John O'Hart, 146 ; 2nd Series, 284. John O'Donovan's Tribes
and Customs of Hy-many, 97. *See* KELLY.

OKENDEN. Berry's Hampshire Genealogies, 329.

OKEOVER. Glover's History of Derbyshire, ii. 70, (62). Burke's
Landed Gentry, 2, 3, 4, 5, 6, 7, 8. Harleian Society, i. 62 ; viii.
194. Nichols' History of the County of Leicester, iv. 1039.
Topographer, (London, 1789-91, 8vo.) ii. 316. Visitation of
Staffordshire, (Willm. Salt Soc.) 120. The Genealogist, New
Series, xiii. 182.

OKES. Metcalfe's Visitations of Northamptonshire, 121.

OKETON. The Genealogist, New Series, xvi. 93.

OKEWOLD. Visitation of Gloucestershire, 1569, (Middle Hill, 1854,
fol.) 7. Harleian Society, xxi. 217.

OLDCASTLE. Robinson's Castles of Herefordshire and their Lords,
App. i. The Genealogist, New Series, xv. 22.

OLDENBURGH. Royal House of, Notes and Queries, 8 S. iv. 41.

OLDERSHAW. Nichols' History of the County of Leicester, iii. 859*.

OLDESWORTH. Harleian Society, xxi. 256.

OLDFIELD. Sketch of the Pedigree of the Oldfeilds of Spalding, folio page. Burke's Landed Gentry, (of Oldfield,) 2, 3, 4; (of Oldfield Lawn,) 2 supp., 3, 4. Burke's Heraldic Illustrations, 39, 81. The Genealogist, i. 242; v. 123. Ormerod's Cheshire, iii. 60, 113. North's Church-Bells of Lincoln, 125. Burke's Extinct Baronetcies. Local Gleanings, July 1879—June 1880, (all published,) 197. Ancient Families of Lincolnshire, in 'Spalding Free Press,' 1873-5, Nos. xv., xxv. Old Nottinghamshire, by J. P. Briscoe, 112. Earwaker's History of Sandbach, 138. Burke's Family Records, 447.

OLDHAM. Chetham Society, lxxxv. 224.

OLDMIXON. Visitation of Somersetshire, printed by Sir T. Phillipps, 123. Weaver's Visitations of Somerset, 56.

OLDNALL. Metcalfe's Visitation of Worcester, 1683, 75.

OLDYS. Notes and Queries, 3 S. i. 1, 21, 41, 61, 81.

O'LEARY. Burke's Landed Gentry, 7, 8. O'Hart's Irish Pedigrees, 2nd Series, 115.

OLIPH. Harleian Society, i. 8. Wilson's History of the Parish of St. Laurence Pountney, 232.

OLIPHANT. The Oliphants in Scotland, by Joseph Anderson. Edinburgh, 1879, 4to. Burke's Commoners, (of Condie,) i. 493, Landed Gentry, 2, 3, 4, 5, 6, 8; (of Gask,) Commoners, iv. 258, Landed Gentry, 2, 6, 7, 8; (of Rossie,) 6, 7, 8. Burke's Royal Descents and Pedigrees of Founders' Kin, 76. Walter Wood's East Neuk of Fife, 249. The Jacobite Lairds of Gask, (Grampian Club,) Chapter I. Wood's Douglas's Peerage of Scotland, ii. 330. Notes and Queries, 4 S. ix. 322, 393.

OLIPHANT-FERGUSON. Burke's Landed Gentry, 3, 4, 5, 6, 7, 8.

OLIVE. Howard's Visitation of England and Wales, i. 232. Burke's Landed Gentry, 3 supp., 4.

OLIVER, or OLLIVER. The Olivers of Cloghanodfoy. By Maj.-Gen. J. R. Oliver. London, 1897, 8vo., 2nd edn. Berry's Sussex Genealogies, 170. Hasted's Kent, ii. 210. Berry's Kent Genealogies, 393. Burke's Landed Gentry, 2 supp., 3, 4, 5, 6, 7, 8. Ormerod's Cheshire, ii. 323. Harleian Society, xiv. 562; xxxviii. 633; xlii. 190. Howard's Visitation of England and Wales, i. 82; ii. 145. Sepulchral Memorials of Bobbingworth, 48. Burke's Colonial Gentry, i. 151. New England Register, xix. 100. Notes and Queries, 8 S. iv. 217. Gloucestershire Notes and Queries, v. 158, 322. Oliver's History of Antigua, ii. 318, 346, 354.

OLIVERSON. Burke's Family Records, 449.

OLIVIER. Burke's Landed Gentry, 2, 3, 4, 5, 6.

OLLIVANT. Howard's Visitation of England and Wales, vi. 15.

OLMIUS. Morant's Essex, ii. 395.

OLNEY. Berry's Buckinghamshire Genealogies, 20. Visitation of Warwickshire, 1619, published with Warwickshire Antiquarian Magazine, 130. Lipscombe's History of the County of Buckingham, iv. 398. Harleian Society, xii. 113. The Genealogist, New Series, xvii. 119, 240.

O'LOGHLEN. Burke's Landed Gentry, 2. O'Hart's Irish Pedigrees, 2nd Series, 133. Burke's Colonial Gentry, i. 154.

OLPHERT, or OLPHERTS. Burke's Landed Gentry, 2, 3, 4, 5 and supp., 6, 7, 8.

OLTON. Ormerod's Cheshire, iii. 395. Harleian Society, xvii. 187.

O'MADDEN. Genealogical, Historical, and Family Records of the O'Madden's of Hy-many. Dublin, 1894, 8vo. John O'Donovan's Tribes and Customs of Hy-many, 129.

O'MAHONY. Irish Pedigrees, by John O'Hart, 2nd Series, 92.

O'MALLEY. Burke's Landed Gentry, (of Newcastle,) 4, 5, 6, 7; (of the Lodge,) 2, 4, 8; (of Spence Park,) 2. Irish Pedigrees, by John O'Hart, 2nd Series, 285. Betham's Baronetage, v. 590.

O'MEAGHER. Historical Notices of the O'Meaghers. By J. C. O'Meagher. London, 1886, 4to.

O'MEALLA. Irish Pedigrees, by John O'Hart, 285.

O'MELAGHLIN. Irish Pedigrees, by John O'Hart, 150.

O'MOORE. Irish Pedigrees, by John O'Hart, 94.

O'MULLALLY. John O'Donovan's Tribes and Customs of Hy-many, 177.

O'MULLOY. Burke's Commoners, iv. 146, Landed Gentry, 2, 3, 4, 5.

ONEBY, or ONEBYE. Bibliotheca Topographica Britannica, vii. Parts i. and ii. 142, 347. Nichols' History of the County of Leicester, i. App. 145; iii. 1147; iv. 728. Harleian Society, xvii. 131.

O'NEILL. Burke's Extinct Baronetcies. Gentleman's Magazine, 1833, i. 580; ii. 131. Burke's Commoners, (of Bunowen Castle,) iii. 534, Landed Gentry, 2, (of Shane's Castle,) Landed Gentry, 3, 4; 3, p. 885, 4, p. 862[b]. Burke's Authorized Arms, 112. Irish Pedigrees, by John O'Hart, 100-128; 2nd Series, 286. O'Donovan's Annals of the Kingdom of Ireland, 2nd edn. vi. 2422. Keating's History of Ireland, *Plate* 14. Journal of Kilkenny Archæological Society, New Series, vi. 91. Notes and Queries, 2 S. iii. 117; iv. 38, 75; 5 S. v. 69, 149; vi. 418. Wotton's English Baronetage, ii. 390. Betham's Baronetage, ii. 8. The Irish Builder, xxxv. 148. *See* NEILL.

ONGLEY. Harleian Society, viii. 508.

ONLEY, or ONELEY. Berry's Sussex Genealogies, 197. Dallaway's Sussex, II. i. 319. Metcalfe's Visitations of Northamptonshire, 38, 121. Gentleman's Magazine, 1828, ii. 394; 1829, i. 220. Miscellanea Genealogica et Heraldica, i. 156. Burke's Landed Gentry, 2, 3, 4, 5, 6, 7. Bridges' Northamptonshire, by Rev. Peter Whalley, i. 35. Baker's Northampton, i. 287. The Genealogist, vi. 68. Harleian Society, xvii. 130.

O'NOWLAN. Irish Pedigrees, by John O'Hart, 135.

ONSLOW. Hasted's Kent, i. 141. Surrey Archæological Collections, iii. Burke's Royal Families, (London, 1851, 8vo.) ii. 76. Burke's Landed Gentry, (of Staughton House,) 2 supp., 3, 4, 5, 6; (of Stoke Park,) 4, 5. Harleian Society, viii. 182; xxix. 377; xliii. 154. Dallaway's Sussex, II. i. 340. Manning and Bray's Surrey, iii. 54. Clutterbuck's Hertford, ii. 353. Maclean's History of

Trigg Minor, iii. 391. Miscellanea Genealogica et Heraldica, New Series, iii. 427. Edmondson's Baronagium Genealogicum, v. 418. Brydges' Collins' Peerage, v. 461. Betham's Baronetage, iv. 383. Hasted's Kent, (Hund. of Blackheath, by H. H. Drake,) 248. Genealogical Records of the Family of Woodd, 34. Burke's Colonial Gentry, i. 389 ; ii. 538. Howard's Visitation of England and Wales, v. 39.

OPENSHAW. History of Longridge, by T. C. Smith, 140. Croston's edn. of Baines's Lancaster, iv. 112.

OPIE, or OPY. Maclean's History of Trigg Minor, ii. 50, 53. Harleian Society, ix. 160. The Visitations of Cornwall, edited by J. L. Vivian, 348.

ORANGE, or ORENGE. Visitation of Somersetshire, printed by Sir T. Phillipps, 123. Harleian Society, xi. 81. J. B. Payne's Armorial of Jersey, 301.

ORBELL. Muskett's Suffolk Manorial Families, i. 265.

ORBY. Collectanea Topographica et Genealogica, vii. 144. Manning and Bray's Surrey, iii. 231. The Genealogist, iii. 271. Burke's Extinct Baronetcies. See DE ORBY.

ORCHARD. Harleian Society, xi. 126.

ORD. J. H. Hill's History of Langton, 47. Burke's Landed Gentry, (of Sands Hall,) 8 ; (of Fenham,) 2, 3, 4, 5, 6, 7 ; (of Fornham,) 2 add., 3, 4, 5, 6, 7, 8. Raine's History of North Durham, 159. Burke's Visitation of Seats and Arms, i. 15. Hodgson's Northumberland, III. ii. 107, 433. Hutchinson's History of Durham, iii. 304. Nichols' History of the County of Leicester, i. 615. Surtees' Durham, iii. 41. Page's History of Suffolk, 719. O'Hart's Irish Pedigrees, 2nd Series, 289. See BLACKETT-ORD.

ORDE. Visitation of Durham, 1615, (Sunderland, 1820, fol.) 6. Burke's Commoners, (of Nunnykirk,) i. 561, Landed Gentry, 2, 3, 4, 5, 6, 7, 8 ; (of Weetwood Hall,) Landed Gentry, 2, 3, 4, 5, 6, 7, 8. Raine's History of North Durham, 248, 250, 253, 303, 311, 320. Hodgson's Northumberland, I. ii. 330. Surtees' Durham, iii. 53. Brydges' Collins' Peerage, viii. 555. Betham's Baronetage, iv. 195. Foster's Visitations of Durham, 249.

O'REGAN. O'Hart's Irish Pedigrees, 2nd Series, 291.

O'REILLY. Burke's Royal Families, (London, 1851, 8vo.) i. 151. Burke's Landed Gentry, (of Rahattan,) 2 ; (of Annagh Abbey,) 2 supp. ; (of East Brefney,) 2, 3, 4, 5, 6, 7, 8 ; (of Knock Abbey,) 2, 3, 4, 5, 6, 7, 8 ; (of Baltrasna,) 2, 3, 4, 5, 6, 7, 8 ; (of Scarvagh,) 2, 3, 4, 5, 6, 7 ; (of Scarborough,) 3 supp., 4 ; (of Rathaldron Castle,) 4, 5. Irish Pedigrees, by John O'Hart, 165 ; 2nd Series, 291.

O'REILLY-DEASE. Burke's Landed Gentry, 3, 4, 5, 6, 7.

ORFEUR. Hutchinson's History of Cumberland, ii. 350. Cumberland and Westmoreland Archæological Society, iii. 99. Foster's Visitations of Cumberland and Westmorland, 96. Betham's Baronetage, iii. 40. Papers and Pedigrees relating to Cumberland and Westmorland, by Wm. Jackson, i. 190. Nicolson and Burn's Westmorland and Cumberland, i. 118.

ORGAN. Visitatio Comitatus Wiltoniæ, 1623, printed by Sir T. Phillipps. Visitation of Wiltshire, edited by G. W. Marshall, 69.

ORKNEY. Berry's Buckinghamshire Genealogies, 59. (Earls of) The Orkneyinga Saga, by Joseph Anderson, xxi.-lxxi., cxxxii.

ORLEBAR. Burke's Royal Families, (London, 1851, 8vo.) ii. 139. Burke's Commoners, i. 246, Landed Gentry, 2, 3, 4, 5, 6, 7, 8. Harvey's Hundred of Willey, 392. Miscellanea Genealogica et Heraldica, 2nd Series, iv. 226.

ORME. Surtees Society, xxxvi. 154. Burke's Royal Families, (London, 1851, 8vo.) i. 59. Burke's Landed Gentry, 2 supp. p. 313 ; (of Abbeytown,) 2 supp., 3, 4, 5, 6 ; (of Glenmore,) 2 supp., 3, 4, 5 ; (of Owenmore,) 2, 3, 4, 5, 7, 8 ; (of Ballycorroon,) 5. Visitations of Staffordshire, 1614 and 1663-4, William Salt Society, 227. Shaw's Staffordshire, i. 226. Visitation of Staffordshire, 1663-4, printed by Sir T. Phillipps, 7. Erdeswicke's Survey of Staffordshire, 243. Castles, Mansions, and Manors of Western Sussex, by D. G. C. Elwes and C. J. Robinson, 272. Northern Notes and Queries, viii. 90.

ORMEROD. Visitation of Somerset, printed by Sir T. Phillipps, 123. Burke's Commoners, i. 112, Landed Gentry, 2, 3, 4, 5, 6, 7, 8. Foster's Lancashire Pedigrees. Harleian Society, xi. 81. Baines' History of the Co. of Lancaster, iii. 609 ; Croston's edn. iv. 342. Whitaker's History of Whalley, ii. 220. Ormerod's Cheshire, ii. 377. Independency at Brighouse, by J. H. Turner, 86. Parentalia, by George Ormerod, 1.

ORMONDE. Claim of the Earl of Ormonde and Ossory to Vote at Elections of Irish Peers, Sess. Papers, 104 of 1821. The Genealogist, New Series, xiv. 98.

ORMSBY, or ORMESBY. Burke's Commoners, (of Willowbank,) iii. 288, Landed Gentry, 2 ; (of Gortner Abbey,) 4 supp., 5, 6, 7, 8 ; (of Ballinamore,) 2, 3, 4, 5, 6, 7, 8. Foster's Visitations of Yorkshire, 629. History of Darlington, by W. Hilton Dyer Longstaffe, xciv. The Genealogist, iv. 261 ; vi. 272. Burke's Extinct Baronetcies. Massingberd's History of Ormsby, 35. Miscellanea Genealogica et Heraldica, 2nd Series, ii. 173, 205, 219, 234.

ORMSBY-GORE. Pedigree of Ormesby-Gore, of Porkington, [T. P.] folding sheet. Burke's Commoners, (of Porkington,) i. 82, Landed Gentry, 2, 3, 4, 5 ; (of Derrycarne,) Landed Gentry, 4, 5.

O'RORKE. Burke's Landed Gentry, 4, 5.

O'ROURKE. Irish Pedigrees, by John O'Hart, 158 ; 2nd Series, 293.

ORPEN. Burke's Commoners, iv. 280, Landed Gentry, 2, 3, 4, 5, 6, 7, 8. Burke's Colonial Gentry, ii. 401. Burke's Family Records, 451.

ORPEN-PALMER. Howard's Visitation of Ireland, iii. 93.

ORR. Some Old Families, by H. B. McCall, 145. Burke's Colonial Gentry, ii. 578.

ORREBY. Memorials of the Church of Attleborough, by J. T. Barrett, 181. Banks' Dormant and Extinct Baronage, i. 388. Ormerod's

Cheshire, iii. 548. Harleian Society, xviii. 100, 188. Earwaker's East Cheshire, ii. 564.

ORRED. Burke's Landed Gentry, 3, 4, 5, 6, 7, 8. Burke's Visitation of Seats and Arms, ii. 52.

ORRELL, or ORELL. Cambridgeshire Visitation, edited by Sir T. Phillipps, 23. Chetham Society, lxxxii. 50; cx. 201. Baines' History of the Co. of Lancaster, iii. 91 ; Croston's edn., iii. 217. Harleian Society, xviii. 189 ; xli. 85.

ORR-EWING. Burke's Landed Gentry, 5, 6, 7.

ORROK. Beatson's Account of the Family of Beatson, 58.

ORTON. Nichols' History of the County of Leicester, iii. 395 ; iv. 864. Harleian Society, xvii. 131.

ORWAY, or ORWEY. The Visitations of Devon, by J. L. Vivian, 292, 602. Devonshire Notes and Notelets, by Sir W. R. Drake, 54.

OSBALDESTON. Pedigree of Osbaldestone of Chadlington, Co. Oxon., from Pedigrees in the Heralds' College, etc., [T. P.] Broadside. Surtees Society, xxxvi. 83. Visitation of Oxfordshire, 1634, printed by Sir T. Phillipps, (Middle Hill, fol.) 26. Visitation of Gloucestershire, 1569, (Middle Hill, 1854, fol.) 7. Harleian Society, v. 202, 213 ; xvii. 132 ; xxi. 218 Hunter's Deanery of Doncaster, ii. 413. Chetham Society, lxxxi. 34 ; lxxxii. 84 ; lxxxviii. 225, 226 ; xcviii. 101 ; xcix. 109. Baines' History of the Co. of Lancaster, iii. 343 ; Croston's edn., iv. 56. Whitaker's History of Whalley, ii. 368. Abram's History of Blackburn, 419, 600, 728. Burke's Landed Gentry, 6 at p. 1825, and 2nd edn. of supp., p. 1836, 7th edn., p. 640 ; 8th edn. at p. 659. Wotton's English Baronetage, iii. 425. Burke's Extinct Baronetcies. The Genealogist, New Series, xii. 260.

OSBALDESTON-MITFORD. Burke's Landed Gentry, 5 supp. *See* MITFORD of Mitford Castle.

OSBORNE. Case of G. W. F. Osborn, Marquis of Carmarthen, in relation to his claim to the Barony of Conyers, 1798, folio. Claim of G. W. F. Osborne, called Marquis of Carmarthen, to the Barony of Conyers, Sess. Papers, April, 1797—June, 1798. The Great Governing Families of England, i. 330. Morant's Essex, i. 323, 354. Jacob's Peerage, i. 212. Hasted's Kent, ii. 539. History of Clyst St. George, by Rev. H. T. Ellacombe, 67. Visitation of Norfolk, published by Norfolk Archæological Society, i. 34. Berry's Kent Genealogies, 28. Archæologia Cantiana, v. 227. Burke's Commoners, ii. 383 ; Landed Gentry, 2 supp., 3, 4, 5, 6, 7 p. 741. Foster's Yorkshire Pedigrees. Harleian Society, i. 15 ; iii. 18 ; iv. 31 ; xvii. 132 ; xix. 129 ; xxxii. 210 ; xlii. 15. Bridges' Northamptonshire, by Rev. Peter Whalley, ii. 40. Thoresby's Ducatus Leodiensis, 2. Hunter's Deanery of Doncaster, i. 143. Clutterbuck's Hertford, i. 447. Wright's Essex, ii. 630. Memoirs of the Family of Chester, by R. E. C. Waters, 237. An Historical Survey of Cornwall, by C. S. Gilbert, i. 430. Edmondson's Baronagium Genealogicum, i. 30 ; vi. 51. Wood's Douglas's Peerage of Scotland, i. 459. Berry's Genealogical Peerage, 60. Brydges' Collins' Peerage, i. 253. Notes and Queries, 1 S. viii.

270, 448, 652, 654 ; 3 S. ii. 330 ; 5 S. ii. 493 ; iii. 131. Wotton's English Baronetage, iii. 225. Betham's Baronetage, ii. 205. Archdall's Lodge's Peerage, vii. 70. Metcalfe's Visitations of Northamptonshire, 39, 122. Burke's Colonial Gentry, ii. 707. Oliver's History of Antigua, ii. 368. *See* GODFREY-FAUSSET-OSBORNE.

OSBORNE-GIBBES. Burke's Colonial Gentry, ii. 660.

OSBOURNE. Visitation of Derbyshire, 1663-4, (Middle Hill, 1854, fol.) 5. The Genealogist, ii. 393. Burke's Landed Gentry, 8.

OSGODBY. Burton's History of Hemingborough, 306.

OSGOOD. New England Register, xiii. 117, 200 ; xx. 22.

O'SHAUGHNESSY. Foster's Collectanea Genealogica, (Funeral Certificates, Ireland,) 25, 26. Irish Pedigrees, by John O'Hart, 2nd Series, 295.

O'SHEE. Burke's Commoners, ii. 120, Landed Gentry, 2, 3, 4, 5, 6, 7, 8. *See* SHEE.

OSMAND. Burke's Colonial Gentry, i. 139.

OSMASTON. Burke's Landed Gentry, 8.

OSMOND. Tuckett's Devonshire Pedigrees, 175. Harleian Society, vi. 202. The Visitations of Devon, J. L. Vivian, 586.

OSMUNDERLAW. Foster's Visitations of Cumberland and Westmorland, 97.

OSTLER. Burke's Landed Gentry, 5, 6, 7.

OSTREHAN. Miscellanea Genealogica et Heraldica, New Series, iii. 375.

O'SULLEVAN MORE. Keating's History of Ireland, *Plate* 11.

O'SULLIVAN. Irish Pedigrees, by John O'Hart, 73 ; 2nd Series, 94. Miscellany of the Celtic Society, edited by John O'Donovan, 403.

OSWALD. Burke's Landed Gentry, (of Auchincruive,) 2, 3, 4, 5, 6, 7, 8 ; (of Dunnikier,) 3, 4, 5, 6, and p. 708, 7, 8. Miscellanea Genealogica et Heraldica, New Series, ii. 423. Paterson's History of the Co. of Ayr, ii. 417. Paterson's History of Ayr and Wigton, i. 666. Caithness Family History, by John Henderson, 232.

OSY. Oliver's History of Antigua, i. 170.

OTELEY. Harleian Society, xxix. 380, 386.

OTGER, or OTGHER. Visitation of Middlesex, (Salisbury, 1820, fol.) 9. Harleian Society, xvii. 134. Foster's Visitations of Middlesex, 22.

OTHO, or OTHER. Berry's Surrey Genealogies, 1.

OTIS. New England Register, ii. 281; iv. 143 ; v. 177 ; xlvi. 211. Harleian Society, xxxvii. 264.

OTLEY. Miscellanea Genealogica et Heraldica. 2nd Series, v. 129. Shropshire Notes and Queries, New Series, iii. 72.

O'TOOLE. Irish Pedigrees, by John O'Hart, 156. Journal of the Historical and Archæological Association of Ireland, 4th Series, iii. 487. Burke's Landed Gentry, 6, p. 712. *See* O'BYRNE.

OTTENDUN. F. G. Lee's History of Thame, 346.

OTTER. Jewitt's Reliquary, xiii. 248. Miscellanea Genealogica et Heraldica, New Series, iii. 291, 299, 318, 328. Harleian Society, xxxix. 1026. Ontarian Families, by E. M. Chadwick, i. 100.

OTTLEY. Burke's Landed Gentry, 2 add., 3, 4. Harleian Society, viii. 79; xvii. 134. Oliver's History of Antigua, ii. 372. The Gresley's of Drakelowe, by F. Madan, 291.

OTTO. Morant's Essex, ii. 332.

OTWAY. Surtees Society, xxxvi. 385. Burke's Landed Gentry, 3, 4, 5, 6, 7. Nicolson and Burn's Westmorland and Cumberland, i. 258. The Genealogist, New Series, xvi. 61.

OTWAY-RUTHVEN. Burke's Landed Gentry, 8.

OUGHE. Harleian Society, ix. 160. The Visitations of Cornwall, edited by J. L. Vivian, 351.

OUGHTIBRIDGE. Surtees Society, liv. xxxii.

OUGHTON. Harleian Society, viii. 516. Burke's Extinct Baronetcies.

OULTON. Ormerod's Cheshire, ii. 191.

OUSELEY. Berry's Buckinghamshire Genealogies, 63. Lipscombe's History of the County of Buckingham, iii. 188. Metcalfe's Visitations of Northamptonshire, 190.

OUTHORPE. Thoroton's Nottinghamshire, i. 158.

OUVRY. Howard's Visitation of England and Wales, iii. 167.

OVER. Harleian Society, xix. 187. Bysshe's Visitation of Essex, edited by J. J. Howard, 69.

OVERBECK. Burke's Colonial Gentry, ii. 627.

OVERBURY. The Genealogist, i. 271, 394; ii. 364; iii. 386. Miscellanea Genealogica et Heraldica, New Series, iv. 25.

OVERTON. Visitation of Somersetshire, printed by Sir T. Phillipps, 124. Harleian Society, ii. 193; iii. 16; xi. 82. Poulson's Holderness, ii. 377. Nichols' History of the County of Leicester, iv. 864. Visitations of Staffordshire, 1614 and 1664-5, William Salt Society, 37.

OWDEN. Howard's Visitation of Ireland, i. 5.

OWEIN. Pembrokeshire Pedigrees, 153, 165.

OWEN. Pedigree of Owen of Penrhos and Moynes Court. [T. P.] Sir T. Phillipps' Topographer, No. 1, (March, 1821, 8vo.) 24. Dwnn's Visitations of Wales, i. 23, 62, 113, 156, 247, 261, 265, 272, 286; ii. 46, 75, 132, 133, 164, 169, 170, 180, 181, 191-193, 201-203, 205, 206, 222, 223, 336, 340. Visitation of Somersetshire, printed by Sir T. Phillipps, 124. Visitation of Oxfordshire, 1574, printed by Sir T. Phillipps, (Middle Hill, fol.) 7. Burke's Commoners, i. 84; (of Glensevern,) iv. 380, Landed Gentry, 2, 7, 8; (of Bettws Hall,) Commoners, ii. 512, Landed Gentry, 2, 3, 4, 5, 6, 7, 8; (of Tedsmore,) Commoners, ii. 509, Landed Gentry, 2, 3, 4, 5, 6, 7, 8; (of Condover,) Commoners, ii. 515, Landed Gentry, 2, 3, 4, 5, 6; (of Woodhouse,) Commoners, ii. 513, Landed Gentry, 2, 3, 4, 5, 6, 7, 8; (of Glynafon,) Landed Gentry, 2 add., 3, 4, 5; (of Garthynghared,) 3, 4; (of Broadway Hall,) 2, 3, 4, 5; (of Haverford West,) 6; 6 supp., at p. 1854; (of Ymwlch,) 7, 8; (of Cwmgloyne,) 7; 8 at p. 1131. Harleian Society, v. 127; xi. 82; xiii. 463; xvii. 135; xix. 187; xxviii. 270; xxix. 382-391, 474. Dallaway's Sussex, i. 242. Burke's Royal Families, (London, 1851, 8vo.) i. 98. Cardiganshire Pedigrees, 109. Baker's Northampton, i. 458. Sussex Archæological Collections, vii. 27. T. Nicholas' County Families of Wales, 953. Shirley's History of the County of Monaghan, 226. History of Llangurig, by E. Hamer and H. W. Lloyd, 80. The Sheriffs of Montgomeryshire, by W. V. Lloyd, 46, 137, 315, 450, 482. Collections by the Powys-land Club, vii. 45, 51; viii. 207; ix. 400; x. 23. Wotton's English Baronetage, ii. 248. Betham's Baronetage, i. 435. History of Powys Fadog, by J. Y. W. Lloyd, iv. 100, 284-292, 300, 377, 425; v. 103, 109, 114, 361, 394, 400, 404; vi. 228, 409, 463. Miscellanea Genealogica et Heraldica, 2nd Series, ii. 363. Cyclostyle Pedigrees, by J. J. Green. Transactions of Shropshire Archæological Society, N.S. iv. 237.

OWEN AP BRADWEN. Dwnn's Visitations of Wales, ii. 21; ap Gwallter, i. 95; ap Meredydd, i. 95; ap William, i. 101; Brogyntyn, ii. 109-112; Tudyr, ii. 108, 192; Voel, i. 282.

OWEN GLENDOWER. Notes and Queries, i. S. iii. 222, 356; vii. 205, 288.

OWEN TUDOR. Wynne's History of Wales, 331.

OWENS. Burke's Landed Gentry, 2, 3, 4, 5, 6, 7, 8. Caermarthenshire Pedigrees, 46.

OWGAN. Harleian Society, xxvii. 74.

OWRY. The Visitations of Cornwall, edited by J. L. Vivian, 469.

OWSLEY. Burke's Commoners, iii. 674.

OWTLAW. Harleian Society, xxxii. 211.

OXBOROUGH. Visitation of Norfolk, published by Norfolk Archæological Society, i. 149. Harleian Society, xxxii. 211.

OXENBRIDGE. Sussex Archæological Collections, viii. 214, 231; xii. 203. Historical Notices of Hurstbourn Priors, and St. Mary Bourn, etc., (London, 1861, 8vo.) 44, 46. Berry's Hampshire Genealogies, 214. Gyll's History of Wraysbury, 64.

OXENDEN. Visitation of Kent, (reprinted from Archæologia Cantiana, vol. vi.) 88. Hasted's Kent, iii. 696. Berry's Kent Genealogies, 224. Master's Notices of the Family of Master, 101. Wotton's English Baronetage, iii. 638. Betham's Baronetage, iii. 28. The Genealogist, New Series, viii. 38. Harleian Society, xlii. 19.

OXENFORD. Bridges' Northamptonshire, by Rev. Peter Whalley, i. 324. Baker's Northampton, ii. 241.

OXENHAM. An Account of the Families of Boase, etc. (Exeter, 1876, 4to.) 35.

OXFORD (Earl of). Morant's Essex, ii. 176, 213. Hasted's Kent, ii. 370.

OXLEY. Historical Notices of Doncaster, by C. W. Hatfield, 2nd Series, 431. Burke's Landed Gentry, 8.

OXNARD. New England Register, xxvi. 3.

OXSPRING. Hunter's Deanery of Doncaster, ii. 354.

OYLES. See OEILS.

OZANNE. Burke's Authorized Arms, 102.

PABENHAM. Visitation of Suffolk, edited by J. J. Howard, ii. 211. Berry's Buckinghamshire Genealogies, 19. Harleian Society, iv.

125. Lipscombe's History of the County of Buckingham, iv. 375. Bridges' Northamptonshire, by Rev. Peter Whalley, ii. 179. Baker's Northampton, i. 714. Harvey's Hundred of Willey, 304.

PACE. Harleian Society, ii. 63. Nichols' History of the County of Leicester, i. 548.

PACK. Burke's Landed Gentry, 3, 4, 5, 6, 7, 8. Burke's Royal Descents and Pedigrees of Founders' Kin, 109. History of St. Canice, Kilkenny, by J. Graves, 332-340. Harleian Society, xvii. 136.

PACK-BERESFORD. Burke's Landed Gentry, 3, 4, 5, 6, 7, 8. Howard's Visitations of England and Wales, viii. 168.

PACKE. Burke's Royal Families, (London, 1851, 8vo.) ii. 211. Burke's Commoners, i. 156, Landed Gentry, 2, 3, 4, 5, 6, 7, 8. Nichols' History of the County of Leicester, iii. 362, 557. Howard's Visitation of England and Wales, vii. 165.

PACKENHAM. Burke's Commoners, ii. 160. Burke's Royal Families, (London, 1851, 8vo.) ii. 158. *See* PAKENHAM.

PACKER. Pedigree of Packer of Cheltenham, [T. P.] 4 folio pages. Pedigree of Packer of Charlton Kings, etc., Co. Gloucester, [T. P.] 1863, folio page. The Genealogist, vi. 69. Visitation of Gloucester, edited by T. F. Fenwick and W. C. Metcalfe, 17. East Barnet, by F. C. Cass, Part i. 58. Harleian Society, xxi. 118; xxxix. 835.

PACKINGTON. Reports and Papers of the Associated Architectural Societies, v. Part i. 176. Gentleman's Magazine, 1821, ii. 200, 312, 314 ; 1828, ii. 317. Wotton's English Baronetage, i. 382. Betham's Baronetage, i. 185. Surrey Archæological Collections, xi. *See* PAKINGTON.

PADDOCK. New England Register, xii. 220.

PADDON. Burke's Landed Gentry, 3, 4.

PADDY. Miscellanea Genealogica et Heraldica, i. 216. Harleian Society, xvii. 136.

PAGANEL, or PAGANELL. Herald and Genealogist, v. 100. Foster's Visitations of Yorkshire, 178. Lipscombe's History of the County of Buckingham, iv. 275. Blore's Rutland, 90. Hunter's Deanery of Doncaster, ii. 140. Manning and Bray's Surrey, i. 570. Baker's Northampton, i. 479. Edmondson's Baronagium Genealogicum, iv. 343. Banks' Dormant and Extinct Baronage, i. 153-7. Thoresby Society, iv. 208. *See* PAYNELL, PAINELL.

PAGE. Pedigree of Page of Beccles, [T. P.] 1860. Hasted's Kent, i. 37. Berry's Sussex Genealogies, 141. Visitation of Middlesex, (Salisbury, 1820, fol.) 39. Burke's Landed Gentry, (of Woodbridge,) 2 ; (of Holbrook,) 2 supp., 3, 4, 5, 6. History of the Hundred of Bray, by Charles Kerry, 130. Dallaway's Sussex, i. 54. Burke's Extinct Baronetcies. Wotton's English Baronetage, iv. 158. Ormerod's Cheshire, iii. 172. The Genealogist, vi. 70 ; New Series, xii. 171. Harleian Society, xvii. 137-139 ; xix. 44. Foster's Visitation of Middlesex, 71. Harvey's Hundred of Willey, 177. New England Register, xxvi. 75. Burke's Family Records, 452.

PAGEHAM. The Genealogist, New Series, ix. 85.

PAGE-TURNER. Dunkin's History of Bullington and Ploughley, i. 58. Howard's Visitation of England and Wales, Notes, ii. 63.

PAGET, or PAGITT. The Great Governing Families of England, i. 276. Bird's Magazine of Honour, 83. Burke's Commoners, (of Cranmore,) iii. 423, Landed Gentry, 2, 3, 4, 5, 6; (of Chipping Norton,) Landed Gentry, 3, 4, 5, 6, 7, 8; (of Ruddington,) 2, 3, 4, 5, 6, 7, 8; (of Elford,) 7, 8; (of Loughborough,) 7, 8; (of Ibstock and Thorpe Satchville,) 4, 5, 6 and supp., 7, 8. Shaw's Staffordshire, i. 220. Erdeswicke's Survey of Staffordshire, 197. Nichols' History of the County of Leicester, iv. 481. Hutchins' Dorset, iii. 672. Visitation of Middlesex, (Salisbury, 1820, fol.) 24. Notes and Queries, 1 S. iv. 133; v. 66, 280, 327, 381; vi. 109; viii. 12, 134, 200, 375, 452; xi. 385, 494; xii. 49, 205, 223; 3 S. ii. 513; v. 325. Monken Hadley, by F. C. Cass, 203. Edmondson's Baronagium Genealogicum, iii. 199; vi. 24*, 47. Brydges' Collins' Peerage, v. 174. Banks' Baronies in Fee, i. 360. Banks' Dormant and Extinct Baronage, ii. 408. Visitation of Staffordshire, (Willm. Salt Soc.) 122. Fletcher's Leicestershire Pedigrees and Royal Descents, 14. Foster's Visitation of Middlesex, 46.

PAGGEN. Harleian Society, xvii. 139.

PAGRAVE. See PALGRAVE.

PAILLET. Miscellanea Genealogica et Heraldica, New Series, iii. 321.

PAIN, or PAINE. Jewers' Wells Cathedral, 283. New England Register, xv. 235; xxii. 60, 187, 291.

PAINELL. Banks' Baronies in Fee, ii. 111. See PAGANEL.

PAKE. Miscellanea Genealogica et Heraldica, 3rd Series, i. 146.

PAKENHAM. Blomefield's Norfolk, viii. 403. Turnor's History of the Town and Soke of Grantham, 100. Archdall's Lodge's Peerage, iii. 367. The Genealogist, New Series, xv. 97. See PACKENHAM.

PAKENHAM-MAHON. Burke's Landed Gentry, 8.

PAKINGTON. Nash's Worcestershire, i. 186, 352. Burke's Landed Gentry, 2. Lipscombe's History of the County of Buckingham, ii. 14. Burke's Extinct Baronetcies. The Genealogist, vii. 186. Harleian Society, xxvii. 101; xliii. 198. See PACKINGTON.

PALÆOLOGUS. Gentleman's Magazine, 1843, i. 17. Archæologia, xviii. 96. Notes and Queries, 1 S. v. 173, 280, 357; viii. 408, 256; ix. 312, 572; x. 134, 351, 409, 494; xi. 31; xii. 480; 3 S. xi. 485; xii. 30.

PALAVICINI. Noble's Memoirs of the House of Cromwell, ii. 207-216. Gentleman's Magazine, lxxxv. 298. Harleian Society, viii. 412.

PALEY. Burke's Landed Gentry, 3, 4, 5, 6, 7, 8.

PALFREY. J. H. Hill's History of Langton, 258.

PALGRAVE. Palgrave Family Memorials, by C. J. Palmer and Stephen Tucker. Norwich, 1878, 8vo. East Anglian, iii. 99. Blomefield's History of Norfolk, viii. 95. Visitation of Norfolk, published by Norfolk Archæological Society, ii. 23. Dawson

Turner's Sepulchral Reminiscences of Great Yarmouth, 142.
Burke's Extinct Baronetcies. Harleian Society, xxxii. 212.
PALIN. Transactions of the Shropshire Archæological Society, v. 287.
PALK. Betham's Baronetage, iv. 108.
PALLES. Burke's Landed Gentry, 4 supp., 5, 6, 7.
PALLESER, or PALLISER. Surtees Society, xxxvi. 94. Notes and
Queries, 2 S. viii. 55. Burke's Landed Gentry, 2, 3, 4, 5, 6, 7, 8.
Betham's Baronetage, iii. 399. Life of Sir Hugh Palliser, by
R. M. Hunt, 1.
PALMER. Pedigree of the Ancient Family of the Palmers of Sussex,
etc. London, 1867, 4to. Pedigree of the Palmer Family, by F. T.
Colby. Exeter, 1892, 4to. J. H. Hill's History of Langton, 241.
Collinson's Somerset, i. 254. Hasted's Kent, ii. 537 ; iii. 715.
Berry's Kent Genealogies, 188, 259, 429. Berry's Hertfordshire
Genealogies, 43. Berry's Berkshire Genealogies, 63. Dwnn's
Visitations of Wales, i. 147, 151. Berry's Sussex Genealogies,
206, 276. Visitation of Somersetshire, printed by Sir T. Phillipps,
125. Visitation of Sussex, 1570, printed by Sir T. Phillipps, (Middle
Hill, fol.) 9. Burke's Royal Families, (London, 1851, 8vo.) ii. 9.
Burke's Commoners, (of Holme Park,) i. 65, Landed Gentry, 2, 3,
4, 5, 6, 7, 8 ; (of Woodcourt,) Landed Gentry, 2 ; (of Kilmarc,)
2 ; (of Killowen,) 8 ; (of Boyne House,) 2 ; (of Nazing,) 2, 3, 4,
5, 6 ; (of Summer Hill,) 2, 3, 4, 5 ; (of Clifton Lodge,) 2, 3, 4 ; (of
Withcote Hall,) 5, 6, 7, 8 ; (of Rahan House,) 5, 6, 7, 8. Miscellanea Genealogica et Heraldica, i. 105 ; New Series, i. 257, 280,
297 ; ii. 76 ; 2nd Series, ii. 106. Harleian Society, ii. 39 ; iii. 24 ;
xii. 171, 221, 239 ; xiii. 463 ; xvii. 140 ; xix. 130. Bridges'
Northamptonshire, by Rev. Peter Whalley, ii. 292. Visitation of
Warwickshire, 1619, published with Warwickshire Antiquarian
Magazine, 80, 150. Dallaway's Sussex, i. 53 ; II. i. 62, 204.
Nichols' History of the County of Leicester, ii. 543, 550 ; iii. 923 ;
1101 ; iv. 973. Dugdale's Warwickshire, 632. Colby of Great
Torrington, by F. T. Colby, 14. Monken Hadley, by F. C. Cass,
154. Wotton's English Baronetage, i. 436 ; iii. 19. Betham's
Baronetage, i. 211 ; ii. 44. Burke's Extinct Baronetcies, add.
The Genealogist, vi. 70. Hasted's Kent, (Hund. of Blackheath,
by H. H. Drake,) xxvi. Metcalfe's Visitations of Northampton-
shire, 40, 123, 190. Somersetshire Wills, printed by F. A. Crisp,
ii. 87. Notes and Queries, 7 S., vii. 511. Weaver's Visitations
of Somerset, 57. Fletcher's Leicestershire Pedigrees and Royal
Descents, 98. Genealogical Gleanings in England, by H. F.
Waters, i. 306. Burke's Colonial Gentry, i. 47. New England
Register, xvi. 171 ; xxi. 119 ; xxii. 18 ; xxvii. 104 ; xlii. 106, 199 ;
xliii. 88, 168 ; l. 223. Lyon's Chronicles of Finchampstead, 128.
Ontarian Families, by E. M. Chadwick, ii. 111. See LE PALMER.
PALMES. J. Wilkinson's History of Broughton Gifford, folding plate.
Surtees Society, xxxvi. 222 ; xli. 66. Berry's Hampshire Genea-
logies, 298. Burke's Royal Families, (London, 1851, 8vo.) ii. 77.
Burke's Commoners, i. 611, Landed Gentry, 2, 3, 4, 5, 6, 7, 8.
Foster's Yorkshire Pedigrees. Foster's Visitations of Yorkshire,

91. Wright's History of Rutland, 17. Nichols' History of the County of Leicester, ii. 295. Harleian Society, xvi. 235. Miscellanea Genealogica et Heraldica, 2nd Series, v. 40.

PALTON. Visitation of Somersetshire, printed by Sir T. Phillipps, 124. Weaver's Visitations of Somerset, 57.

PALYNGFORD. The Genealogist, New Series, xvii. 111.

PAMPLIN. The Genealogist, iii. 308.

PANMURE (Earls of). Angus or Forfarshire, by A. J. Warden, 379-419. *See* MAULE.

PANTON. Berry's Sussex Genealogies, 371. Burke's Colonial Gentry, ii. 476.

PANTULF. Banks' Dormant and Extinct Baronage, i. 158. Devonshire Notes and Notelets, by Sir W. R. Drake, 39.

PAPILLON. Hasted's Kent, iii. 346. Morant's Essex, i. 448. Berry's Essex Genealogies, 23. Berry's Kent Genealogies, 114. Burke's Commoners, i. 122, Landed Gentry, 2, 3, 4, 5, 6, 7, 8. J. H. Hill's History of Market Harborough, 146. Scott of Scot's Hall, 225. Harleian Society, xiv. 689. Memoirs of Thomas Papillon, by A. F. W. Papillon, i. 47.

PARADYNE. Bysshe's Visitation of Essex, edited by J. J. Howard, 69. Harleian Society, xix. 130.

PARAMOR, PARAMORE, or PARAMOUR. Planché's Corner of Kent, 379. Nichols' History of the County of Leicester, iii. 988. Berry's Kent Genealogies, 49, 156. Harleian Society, xxix. 392; xlii. 13, 77.

PARBO. Berry's Kent Genealogies, 96. Harleian Society, xlii. 40.

PARDOE. Burke's Landed Gentry, (of Nash Court,) 2, 3, 4, 5, 6, 7, 8; (of Leyton,) 5, 6, 7, 8. Foster's Lincolnshire Pedigrees, 7. Transactions of the Shropshire Archæological Society, New Series, v. 218.

PARDY. Harleian Society, xxviii. 236.

PARES. Burke's Royal Families, (London, 1851, 8vo.) ii. 13. Burke's Commoners, iii. 605, Landed Gentry, 2, 3, 4, 5, 6, 7, 8. Fletcher's Leicestershire Pedigrees and Royal Descents, 123.

PARFITT. Burke's Authorized Arms, 133.

PARGETER, or PARGITER. Bridges' Northamptonshire, by Rev. Peter Whalley, i. 124. Visitation of Staffordshire, 1663-4, printed by Sir T. Phillipps, 8. Baker's Northampton, i. 409, 726. Harleian Society, xiii. 86, 259. Visitations of Staffordshire, 1614 and 1663-4, William Salt Society, 228. Metcalfe's Visitations of Northamptonshire, 40, 123, 124.

PARHAM. Carthew's Hundred of Launditch, Part iii. 410.

PARIS. Camden Society, xliii. 62. Blomefield's Norfolk, vii. 116. Howard's Visitation of England and Wales, ii. 65. *See* PARRIS.

PARK, or PARKE. Baker's Northampton, i. 747. A Chapter in Mediocrity, by W. J. Stavert, 13. Morant's Essex, ii. 309. Burke's Landed Gentry, 2, 3, 4, 5, 6, 7, 8. Hutchins' Dorset, iii. 354. Surtees' Durham, ii. 320. Harleian Society, xiii. 464.

PARKER. Genealogical Memoranda relating to the Family of Parker. By E. M. S. Parker. Bristol, 1899, fol. Jewitt's Reliquary, v. 245; x. 51; xi. 161; xxi. 128; xxii. 139; xxv. 80. Description

of Browsholme Hall, by T. L. Parker, (London, 1815, 4to.) 24.
Morant's Essex, ii. 512. Miscellanea Genealogica et Heraldica,
i. 167; New Series, ii. 451. W. Robinson's History of Tottenham,
ii. 163. Berry's Sussex Genealogies, 12, 219, 228. Surtees Society,
xxxvi. 28. Berry's Kent Genealogies, 373. Visitation of Middlesex, (Salisbury, 1820, fol.) 27. History of the Parish of Leek,
by John Sleigh, 108. Visitation of Sussex, 1570, printed by Sir
T. Phillipps, (Middle Hill, fol.) 8. Burke's Royal Families,
(London, 1851, 8vo.) i. 93. Burke's Commoners, (of Petteril
Green,) ii. 662, Landed Gentry, 2, 3; (of Cuerden,) Commoners,
i. 116, Landed Gentry, 2, 3, 4, 5, 6, 7, 8; (of Dunalley,) 8; (of
Browsholme,) Commoners, iii. 684, Landed Gentry, 2, 3, 4, 5, 6,
7, 8; (of Whiteway,) Commoners, ii. 455, Landed Gentry, 2, 3, 4,
5, 6; (of Woodthorpe,) Commoners, iii. 672, Landed Gentry, 2, 3,
4, 5; (of Rothley Temple,) 8; (of Park Hall,) Landed Gentry,
2; (of Inchigagin,) 2; (of Hareden,) 2, 3, 4; (of Hanthorpe
House,) 4, 5, 6, 7, 8; (of Clopton Hall,) 4, 5, 6, 7, 8; (of
Warwick Hall,) 5 supp., 6, 7, 8; (of Woodham Mortimer,)
5, 7, 8; (of Swannington,) 5, 6, 7; (of Castle Lough,) 5, 6, 7;
3 at p. 514; 6 at p. 948; (of Whitehouse,) 7 at p. 1086; (of
Castle Lough,) 8; (of Passage West,) 8. Foster's Yorkshire Pedigrees. Earwaker's East Cheshire, ii. 363. Howard's Visitation
of England and Wales, i. 163. Fishwick's History of Goosnargh, 189. Carthew's Hundred of Launditch, Part i. 69, 73.
Harleian Society, i. 47; vi. 203, 205; viii. 489; ix. 161; xiii. 87,
259; xvii. 141, 143; xxi. 257; xxxii. 213; xxxvii. 405, 408;
xxxviii. 662, 709; xxxix. 1073; xlii. 173. Chetham Society,
lxxxviii. 227, 228; xcii. 180. Warwickshire Pedigrees, from
Visitation of 1682-3, (privately printed, 1865). Foster's Lancashire Pedigrees. Maclean's History of Trigg Minor, i. 68. Collectanea Topographica et Genealogica, iii. 16. Westcote's Devonshire, edited by G. Oliver and P. Jones, 538, 564. Visitation
of Staffordshire, 1663-4, printed by Sir T. Phillipps, 8. The
Borough of Stoke upon Trent, by John Ward, 561. Thoresby's
Ducatus Leodiensis, 128. Hunter's History of the Parish of
Sheffield, 445, 447, 490. Surrey Archæological Collections, ii.
209. Hunter's Deanery of Doncaster, i. 207, 303. Hoare's
Wiltshire, IV. i. 131; ii. 33. Whitaker's History of Whalley,
i. 340; ii. 226. Abram's History of Blackburn, 655. Page's
History of Suffolk, 4. An Account of the Families of Boase,
(Exeter, 1876, 4to.) 37. The Tyldesley Diary, edited by J. Gillow
and A. Hewitson, 175. Life of Sir W. Parker, by A Phillimore,
i. 1. Topographical Miscellanies, 1792, 4to., (Willingdon).
Edmondson's Baronagium Genealogicum, iii. 223; v. 485; vi.
119. Brydges' Collins' Peerage, iv. 190; viii. 28. Wotton's
English Baronetage, iii. 317, 556, 691. Banks' Baronies in Fee,
i. 326, 334. Visitation of Devon, edited by F. T. Colby, 166.
Betham's Baronetage, iii. 52; iv. 383. Banks' Dormant and
Extinct Baronage, ii. 361. Ormerod's Cheshire, iii. 714. Metcalfe's
Visitations of Suffolk, 155. Visitation of Wiltshire, edited by

G. W. Marshall, 14. Burke's Extinct Baronetcies. The Genea-
logist, vi. 273. The Visitations of Cornwall, edited by J. L.
Vivian, 352. Journal of the Derbyshire Archæological Society,
iv. 23. Foster's Visitations of Middlesex, 56. East Barnet, by
F. C. Cass, Part i. 100. Visitation of Gloucester, edited by T. F.
Fenwick and W. C. Metcalfe, 128. The Suffolk Records, by
H. W. Aldred, 121. Hasted's Kent, (Hund. of Blackheath, by
H. H. Drake,) xxv. 253. Visitations of Staffordshire, 1614 and
1663-4, William Salt Society, 228. Fletcher's Leicestershire Pedigrees and Royal Descents, 151. Jewers' Wells Cathedral, 289.
Burke's Colonial Gentry, i. 236. New England Register, vi. 375 ;
xvi. 41. The Manor of Haling, by G. S. Steinman, 78. Croston's
edn. of Baines's Lancaster, iii. 375. The Visitations of Devon,
by J. L. Vivian, 587. *See* BATEMAN.

PARKES. History of Wednesbury, (Wolverhampton, 1854, 8vo.) 165,
168. Collections for a History of Staffordshire, (William Salt
Society,) ii. part 2, 100. Visitations of Staffordshire, 1614 and
1663-4, William Salt Society, 231.

PARKHOUSE. Burke's Landed Gentry, 2, 3, 4. Burke's Heraldic
Illustrations, 24.

PARKHURST. Visitation of Norfolk, published by Norfolk Archæo-
logical Society, ii. 15. Surrey Archæological Collections, ii.
Harleian Society, viii. 70 ; xvii. 144 ; xliii. 97. Manning and
Bray's Surrey, i. 157. Baker's Northampton, i. 288. Burke's
Family Records, 455.

PARKIN, or PARKYN. History of the Parish of Ecclesfield, by Rev.
J. Eastwood, 432. Gyll's History of Wraysbury, 24. Metcalfe's
Visitations of Suffolk, 202. Registers of Ecclesfield, by A. S.
Gatty, 41, 135. Robinson of the White House, Appleby, by C. B.
Norcliffe, 91. Harleian Society, xxxix. 843; xl. 1178, 1274.

PARKINS, or PARKYNS. Foster's Visitations of Yorkshire, 558.
Harleian Society, iv. 159 ; xxvii. 104. Clutterbuck's Hertford,
ii. 302. Thoroton's Nottinghamshire, i. 89. Wotton's English
Baronetage, iii. 683. Betham's Baronetage, iii. 42. History of
Ufton Court, by A. M. Sharp, 237. *See* PERKINS.

PARKINSON. Visitation of Durham, 1575, (Newcastle, 1820, fol.) 11.
Chetham Society, lxxxii. 134. Surtees' Durham, iv. 144. Burke's
Landed Gentry, (of Ludford,) 6, 7, 8 ; (of Ravendale,) 6, 7, 8 ; (of
Easthill,) 6 supp., 7 ; (of Inglewood,) 8. Harleian Society, xix.
131. Notes and Queries, 6 S. v. 152. The Old Church Clock,
by Richard Parkinson, edited by John Evans, 5th edn., lxxv.
History of Chipping, by Tom C. Smith, 205-217, 247. *See* PER-
KINSON.

PARKINSON-SHARP. Burke's Landed Gentry, 8.

PARLBY. Burke's Landed Gentry, 4, 5, 6, 7, 8. Burke's Royal
Descents and Pedigrees of Founders' Kin, 120. Howard's Visitation of England and Wales, viii. 13.

PARLANE. Burke's Landed Gentry, 8.

PARMIGER. Berry's Hampshire Genealogies, 349.

PARNELL. Pedigree of Parnell of Congleton. By Thos. Cooper.

Congleton, 1896, single sheet. Burke's Landed Gentry, 3, 4, 5, 6, 7, 8. Notes and Queries, 6 S. viii. 509. Congleton Past and Present, by Robert Head, 109-113.

PARNICHEFF. Miscellanea Genealogica et Heraldica, New Series, iii. 361.

PARR, or PARRE. Burke's Patrician, iii. 593. Gentleman's Magazine, 1829, i. 397. Topographer and Genealogist, iii. 352, 597. Berry's Kent Genealogies, 404. Burke's Landed Gentry, 2 p. 779; (of Liverpool,) 2; (of Parr,) 2, 3, 4; (of Ashchurch,) 3, 4; (of Grappenhall Heyes,) 2, 3, 4, 5, 6, 7, 8; (of Stonelands,) 2, 3, 4. Chetham Society, lxxxi. 120. Whitaker's History of Richmondshire, ii. 167. Nichols' History of the County of Leicester, iv. 725, 725*. Baker's Northampton, ii. 61. Memoirs of Rev. Samuel Parr, by W. Field, ii. Appendix 1. Ormerod's Cheshire, ii. 365. Cumberland and Westmorland Archæological Society, ii. 186. Duchetiana, by Sir G. F. Duckett, 2nd edn., 154. Notes and Queries, 1 S. iii. 302; vi. 148; xi. 266. Banks' Dormant and Extinct Baronage, i. 108; iii. 595. Harleian Society, xviii. 193. Croston's edn. of Baines's Lancaster, iii. 292; v. 19-21. Howard's Visitation of England and Wales, viii. 8.

PARRATT. Harleian Society, xiii. 76.

PARRAVICIN. Notes and Queries, 3 S. i. 110, 179, 234.

PARRIS. Cambridgeshire Visitation, edited by Sir T. Phillipps, 24. Harleian Society, xxxii. 214; xli. 37. See PARIS.

PARRY. Pedigree of Parry of Noyadd Trefawr, Co. Cardigan, [T. P.] 1860, folio. Dwnn's Visitations of Wales, i. 332, 341; ii. 332, 337. Burke's Landed Gentry, (of Noyadd Trefawr,) 2, 3, 4, 5; (of Highnam Court,) 2 supp., 3, 4, 5, 6, 7. Jones' History of the County of Brecknock, ii. 557. Cardiganshire Pedigrees, 81. Pembrokeshire Pedigrees, 163. Hutchins' Dorset, iv. 460. Meyrick's History of the Co. of Cardigan, 135, 165, 287, 344. Archæologica Cambrensis, 4 S. vi. 239; vii. 259. Memoir of Gabriel Goodman, by R. Newcome, App. S. The Sheriffs of Cardiganshire, by J. R. Phillipps, 49. Notes and Queries, 4 S. x. 299, 458. History of Powys Fadog, by J. Y. W. Lloyd, iii. 45, 345-352; iv. 373; v. 208-225; vi. 239, 372, 430. Weaver's Visitation of Herefordshire, 3, 5. The Irish Builder, xxviii. 307, 320. Burke's Family Records, 458. See JONES-PARRY, MEALY.

PARRY-CROOKE. Burke's Landed Gentry, 8.

PARRY-OKEDEN. See OKEDEN.

PARRY-PRICE. W. Mortimer's History of the Hundred of Wirral, 321.

PARSONNE, or PERSONN. Cambridgeshire Visitation, printed by Sir T. Phillipps, 24. Harleian Society, xli. 85.

PARSONS. Life and Character of Humphrey Parsons, Esq., by an Impartial Hand. London, 1741, 8vo. Burke's Landed Gentry, 2. Harleian Society, v. 192; viii. 413. Wotton's English Baronetage, iii. 268. Betham's Baronetage, ii. 248. Burke's Extinct Baronetcies. Metcalfe's Visitation of Worcester, 1683, 76. F. G. Lee's History of Thame, 231. Visitation of Gloucester, edited by T. F.

Fenwick and W. C. Metcalfe, 129. New England Register, i. 263.

PARTIN. Harleian Society, xxix. 392.

PARTRIDGE, or PARTRYCHE. Pedigree of Partridge of Stanley St. Leonards, [T. P.] 1866, folio page. Burke's Commoners, (of Hockham Hall,) iii. 332, Landed Gentry, 2, 3, 4, 5, 6, 7, 8; (of Bishop's Wood,) Landed Gentry, 2, 3, 4, 5, 6, 7, 8; (of Horsendon,) 4, 5, 6, 7, 8. Harleian Society, i. 37; xiii. 465; xvii. 145; xxi. 119. Fosbrooke's History of Gloucestershire, i. 354. Visitation of Gloucestershire, 1569, (Middle Hill, 1854, fol.) 8. Metcalfe's Visitations of Suffolk, 99. Duncombe's Hereford, (J. H. Cooke,) iii. 205. Howard's Visitation of England and Wales, vii. 161.

PARVISH. Manning and Bray's Surrey, ii. 99. Harleian Society, xiii. 466.

PASCALL, or PASCHALL. Morant's Essex, ii. 10, 18, 39. Harleian Society, xiii. 11, 88, 260. Bysshe's Visitation of Essex, edited by J. J. Howard, 69.

PASHLEY. Hunter's Deanery of Doncaster, i. 259. Scott of Scot's Hall, by J. R. Scott, 170. Surtees Society, lxv. 330. Harleian Society, xxxviii. 727.

PASLEW, PASHLOW, PASLOWE, or PASSELEW. Thoresby's Ducatus Leodiensis, 121. Whitaker's History of Whalley, ii. 31. Harvey's Hundred of Willey, 37. Harleian Society, xxix. 302.

PASLEY. Betham's Baronetage, iv. 257.

PASMERE, PASSEMORE, or PASSMERE. Tuckett's Devonshire Pedigrees, 35, 39. Harleian Society, vi. 207, 208. Westcote's. Devonshire, edited by G. Oliver and P. Jones, 525. Visitation of Devon, edited by F. T. Colby, 166. The Visitations of Devon, by J. L. Vivian, 589.

PASQUES. The Wolfe's of Forenaghts, 74.

PASSELE. The Genealogist, New Series, xvii. 243.

PASSY. Burke's Landed Gentry, 2 add.

PASTON. Dawson Turner's History of Caister Castle, 138. Blomefield's Norfolk, vi. 479; viii. 329. Morant's Essex, ii. 275, 317. A Royal Descent, by T. E. Sharpe, (London, 1875, 4to.) 11, 76. Notices of Swyncombe and Ewelme in Co. Oxford, by H. A. Napier, 124. Norfolk Archæology, iv. 1, 45, 52. Original Letters, by John Fenn, i. 1. Burke's Extinct Baronetcies. Harleian Society, xxxii. 214.

PASTON-BEDINGFIELD. Burke's Royal Families, (London, 1851, 8vo.) i. 148.

PATE. Harleian Society, ii. 89. Nichols' History of the County of Leicester, ii. 283; iii. 524. Reports and Papers of the Associated Architectural Societies, xii. 282. Burke's Extinct Baronetcies. Leicestershire Architectural Society, iv. 268, 271.

PATERSON. The Birthplace and Parentage of Wm. Paterson, by Wm. Pagan. Edinburgh, 1865, 12mo. Burke's Royal Families, (London, 1851, 8vo.) ii. 194. Burke's Landed Gentry, (of Castle Huntley,) 2 supp., 3, 4, 5, 6, 7, 8; (of Carpow,) 3, 4, 5, 6, 7, 8.

Burke's Visitation of Seats and Arms, ii. 60. Burke's Royal
Descents and Pedigrees of Founders' Kin, 94. Burke's Extinct
Baronetcies, 634. Notes and Queries, 4 S. vi. 207, 243; vii. 218.
Northern Notes and Queries, iv. 95, 141. New England Register,
xxxvii. 148. Howard's Visitation of Ireland, i. 20. Burke's
Family Records, 460.

PATESHALL, or PATESHULL. Burke's Commoners, i. 146, Landed
Gentry, 2, 3, 4, 5, 6, 7, 8. Robinson's Mansions of Herefordshire,
7. Banks' Baronies in Fee, i. 362. Bridges' Northamptonshire,
by Rev. Peter Whalley, i. 267, 350. Clutterbuck's Hertford, ii.
296. Baker's Northampton, ii. 296. Banks' Dormant and Extinct
Baronage, i. 390. Weaver's Visitation of Herefordshire, 54.
Harvey's Hundred of Willey, 4. The Genealogist, New Series,
xvi. 38.

PATMERE. Harleian Society, xiii. 227.

PATON. Burke's Landed Gentry, 2, 3, 4, 5, 6, 7, 8, 8 at p. 2254.
Burke's Family Records, 463.

PATRICK. Burke's Royal Families, (London, 1851, 8vo.) ii. 59.
Burke's Commoners, (of Trearne,) ii. 470, Landed Gentry, 2, 3, 4,
5, 6, 7, 8; (of Ladyland,) Landed Gentry, 3, 4, 5, 6, 7, 8; (of
Dunminning,) 4, 5, 6, 7, 8. Geo. Robertson's Description of
Cunninghame, 287. Paterson's History of the Co. of Ayr, i. 295.
Paterson's History of Ayr and Wigton, iii. 88, 126. Associated
Architectural Societies' Reports and Papers, viii. 274.

PATRICKSON. Burke's Landed Gentry, 2, 3, 4. Harleian Society,
vii. 4; xvii. 145. Jefferson's History of Allerdale Ward, Cumberland, 417, 419. Foster's Visitations of Cumberland and Westmorland, 98.

PATTEN. Burke's Commoners, iii. 79; (of Bishop's Hull,) Landed
Gentry, 5, 6. Chetham Society, lxxxviii. 229. Gregson's Frag-
ments relative to the County of Lancaster, 184. See WILSON-
PATTEN.

PATTENSON. Berry's Kent Genealogies, 204, 315. Burke's Landed
Gentry, 2, 3, 4, 5, 6, 7, 8. Harleian Society, i. 63. Hutchinson's
History of Cumberland, i. 218. Jefferson's History of Leath
Ward, Cumberland, 302.

PATTESON. Burke's Landed Gentry, 8.

PATTINSON. Burke's Visitation of Seats and Arms, ii. 60.

PATTISON. Surtees' Durham, ii. 81. Harleian Society, xxxvii. 15.

PATTON. See PATTEN.

PATTON-BETHUNE. Burke's Landed Gentry, 7, 8.

PATULLO. Walter Wood's East Neuk of Fife, 299.

PAUL, PAULL, or PAULE. History of Tetbury, Co. Gloucester, by
A. T. Lee, 221-227. Burke's Landed Gentry, 2, 3, 4, 5. Harleian
Society, viii. 249; xxix. 393; xliii. 205. Surtees' Durham, iii.
220. Fosbrooke's History of Gloucestershire, i. 398. Betham's
Baronetage, iii. 303. An Account of the Families of Boase,
(Exeter, 1876, 4to.) 43. Notes and Queries, 2 S. ix. 46. Burke's
Extinct Baronetcies. Howard's Visitation of England and Wales,
i. 11. Surrey Archæological Collections, xi.

PAULET. Topographer, (London, 1789-91, 8vo.) i. 171. Gyll's History of Wraysbury, 15. Westcote's Devonshire, edited by G. Oliver and P. Jones, 488. Visitatio Comitatus Wiltoniæ, 1623, printed by Sir T. Phillipps. Edmondson's Baronagium Genealogicum, i. 25. Banks' Dormant and Extinct Baronage, iii. 89. Brocas of Beaurepaire, by M. Burrows, 365. Notes and Queries, 8 S. i. 141, 241, 422. See PAWLET, POULETT.

PAUNCEFOTE, PAUNCEFOOTE, or PAUNCEFORT. Berry's Buckinghamshire Genealogies, 101. Visitation of Somersetshire, printed by Sir T. Phillipps, 124. Burke's Landed Gentry, 4, 5, 6, 7, 8. Duncumb's History of the Co. of Hereford, ii. 100. Fosbrooke's History of Gloucestershire, ii. 416. Betham's Baronetage, v. app. 62. Harleian Society, xvii. 146; xxi. 257. Visitation of Gloucester, edited by T. F. Fenwick and W. C. Metcalfe, 131. Weaver's Visitations of Somerset, 58.

PAUNCEFORT-DUNCOMBE. Burke's Commoners, ii. 74, Landed Gentry, 2, 3.

PAVELEY. Gentleman's Magazine, 1827, i. 202. History of South Winfield, by T. Blore, in Nichols' Miscellaneous Antiquities, No. 3, 13, 81. Excerpta Cantiana, by Rev. T. Streatfield, 6. Bridges' Northamptonshire, by Rev. Peter Whalley, i. 597. Hoare's Wiltshire, III. i. 3. Baker's Northampton, ii. 200. Thoroton's Nottinghamshire, i. 124. Banks' Baronies in Fee, ii. 110. The Genealogist, New Series, xiii. 95.

PAVER. Foster's Visitations of Yorkshire, 559. Banks' Baronies in Fee, i. 369. Notes and Queries, 6 S. vii. 29.

PAVIER. See RUSSELL-PAVIER.

PAWLET, or PAWLETT. Harleian Society, xi. 83; xxi. 121. Westcote's Devonshire, edited by G. Oliver and P. Jones, 474. Visitation of Middlesex, (Salisbury, 1820, fol.) 3. Berry's Hampshire Genealogies, 148, 268. Visitation of Somersetshire, printed by Sir T. Phillipps, 125. Visitation of Devon, edited by F. T. Colby, 167. Visitation of Wiltshire, edited by G. W. Marshall, 92. Foster's Visitation of Middlesex, 8. Weaver's Visitations of Somerset, 59. See PAULET, POULETT, POWLET.

PAWLEY. Burke's Commoners, iv. 296; Landed Gentry, 2, p. 936.

PAWNE. Harleian Society, xiii. 24.

PAWSEY. See PASSY.

PAWSON. Burke's Commoners, ii. 172, Landed Gentry, 5 supp., 6, 7, 8. Thoresby's Ducatus Leodiensis, 77. Thoresby Society, iv. 167.

PAXTON. Burke's Landed Gentry, 2, 3, 4, 5, and 5 p. 994.

PAY, or PAYE. Berry's Sussex Genealogies, 113. Dallaway's Sussex, i. 182.

PAYLER. Surtees Society, xxxvi. 317. Burke's Extinct Baronetcies.

PAYN, or PAYNE. Pedigree of Payne of Beccles, [T. P.] 1860. Chronicle of the Family of De Havilland. Visitation of Suffolk, edited by J. J. Howard, ii. 64-82. Morant's Essex, ii. 264. Camden Society, xliii. 64. Berry's Sussex Genealogies, 164. Berry's Kent Genealogies, 425. Visitation of Somersetshire, printed by Sir T. Phillipps, 125. Burke's Landed Gentry, 2, 3,

4, 8 p. 1576. Harleian Society, viii. 98 ; xxi. 122 ; xxxii. 217 ;
xlii. 201. Gage's History of Thingoe Hundred, Suffolk, 483.
Hutchins' Dorset, iii. 628. Hoare's Wiltshire, IV. ii. 29. Fosbrooke's History of Gloucestershire, i. 364. O'Hart's Irish Pedigrees, 2nd Series, 297. J. B. Payne's Armorial of Jersey, 302.
Wotton's English Baronetage, iv. 244. Betham's Baronetage, iii.
227. Metcalfe's Visitation of Suffolk, 55, 156. New England
Register, v. 331. Visitation of Gloucester, edited by T. F. Fenwick and W. C. Metcalfe, 132. Weaver's Visitations of Somerset,
60. Genealogies of Morgan and Glamorgan, by G. T. Clark, 397.
Burke's Colonial Gentry, i. 180. Annals of Smith of Balby, by
H. E. Smith, 31.

PAYNE-GALLWEY. Foster's Yorkshire Pedigrees.

PAYNELL. Blore's Rutland, 90. Nichols' History of the County of
Leicester, ii. 303. Baker's Northampton, i. 479. The Genealo-
gist, iv. 263. The Visitation of Devon, edited by F. T. Colby, 58.
See PAGANELL.

PAYNTER. Burke's Commoners, (of Boskenna,) i. 38, Landed Gentry,
2, 3, 4, 5, 6, 7, 8 ; (of Camborne House,) 2 supp., 3, 4, 5, 6 ; (of
Dale,) 5 supp. Harleian Society, viii. 184 ; ix. 162 ; xlii. 145.
The Visitations of Cornwall, edited by J. L. Vivian, 353. Burke's
Family Records, 467.

PAYTEFIN. Herald and Genealogist, v. 235. W. Wheater's History
of Sherburn and Cawood, 179. *See* PICTAVENSIS.

PAYTON. Pedigree of Payton of Barton, Co. Warwick, [T. P.] 1867,
folio page. Cambridgeshire Visitation, edited by Sir T. Phillipps,
24. Metcalfe's Visitation of Suffolk, 55. Muskett's Suffolk
Manorial Families, i. 262. *See* PEYTON.

PEABODY. Burke's Visitation of Seats and Arms, i. 11. New England Register, ii. 153, 361 ; iii. 359.

PEACH. Burke's Landed Gentry, 5, 6, 7, 8. Miscellanea Genealogica et Heraldica, ii. 307. Harleian Society, xii. 129. Fosbrooke's
History of Gloucestershire, i. 271. *See* KEIGHLEY-PEACH.

PEACHEY. Cussan's History of Hertfordshire, Parts iii. and iv. 23.
Berry's Sussex Genealogies, 54, 106. Harleian Society, viii. 452.
Dallaway's Sussex, i. 44, 166. Clutterbuck's Hertford, iii. 365.
Bigland's Gloucestershire, ii. par. Shipton Solers. Brydges'
Collins' Peerage, viii. 376. Wotton's English Baronetage, iv. 243.
Burke's Extinct Baronetcies, *supp.* Cooke's Continuation of Dun-
cumb's Hereford, (Hund. of Grimsworth,) Part ii. 177.

PEACOCK, or PEACOCKE. English Church Furniture, by Edward
Peacock, 78. Burke's Landed Gentry, (of South Rauceby,) 2, 3, 4,
5, 6 ; (of Efford Park,) 3, 4, 5, 6, 7, 8 ; (of Fort Etna,) 6, 7. Harleian Society, i. 80 ; xvii. 147. Surtees' Durham, iv. 99. Burke's
Visitation of Seats and Arms, ii. 66. Notes and Queries, 2 S. v.
147, 388. The Genealogist, vi. 72. Betham's Baronetage, v. 513.
Howard's Visitation of Ireland, ii. 66.

PEAKE. Burke's Landed Gentry, 2, 3, 4, 5, 6. Miscellanea Genealogica et Heraldica, ii. 277. Harleian Society, viii. 178 ; xvii.
147 ; xxxvii. 342. The Genealogist, iv. 263 ; vi. 274. *See* PEKE.

PEARCE. Visitation of Middlesex, (Salisbury, 1820, fol.) 50. Burke's Royal Families, (London, 1851, 8vo.) i. 50; ii. 89. Burke's Landed Gentry, 2 supp., 3, 4, 5, 8. Burke's Royal Descents and Pedigrees of Founders' Kin, *Founders' Kin*, 5. An Account of the Families of Boase, (Exeter, 1876, 4to.) 38. An Historical Survey of Cornwall, by C. S. Gilbert, ii. 220. The Genealogist, vi. 73. Lancashire and Cheshire Genealogical and Historical Notes, ii. 135. The Visitations of Cornwall, edited by J. L. Vivian, 245, 603. New England Register, vi. 276; xxxii. 34. Foster's Visitations of Middlesex, 94.

PEARCE-EDGCUMBE. Howard's Visitations of England and Wales, v. 14.

PEARCE-SEROCOLD. Burke's Landed Gentry, 8.

PEARD. Burke's Landed Gentry, 3, 4. Harleian Society, xxix. 411.

PEARETH. Burke's Landed Gentry, 3, 4, 5, 6, 7, 8. Surtees' Durham, ii. 45. Baker's Northampton, i. 720.

PEARS. Miscellanea Genealogica et Heraldica, New Series, iii. 71. Howard's Visitation of England and Wales, vi. 99-107.

PEARSALL. Burke's Landed Gentry, 3, 4. Herald and Genealogist, vii. 270. Jewers' Wells Cathedral, 150. *See* PERSHALL.

PEARSE. Pedigree of Pearse of Minchinhampton, etc., Co. Glouc., and of East Sheen, Co. Surrey. [T. P.] 1871. Burke's Landed Gentry, 2, 3, 4, 5. Harleian Society, vi. 209. An Historical Survey of Cornwall, by C. S. Gilbert, ii. 221. Burke's Colonial Gentry, i. 194. The Visitations of Devon, by J. L. Vivian, 590. *See* PIERCE.

PEARSE-THOMPSON. Burke's Landed Gentry, 7, 8.

PEARSON. Burke's Patrician, vi. 407. Surtees Society, xxxvi. 76. Berry's Kent Genealogies, 493. Burke's Commoners, i. 380, Landed Gentry, 2, 8. Foster's Visitations of Yorkshire, 559. Foster's Lancashire Pedigrees. Burke's Family Records, 471. Burke's Colonial Gentry, i. 87, 391. The Descendants of John Backhouse, by J. Foster, 48. Harleian Society, xl. 1181. *See* PEIRSON.

PEARTE. Morant's Essex, ii. 45. *See* PERTE.

PEASE. Pease of Darlington, by Joseph Foster. *No place* 1891, 4to. The Pease Family of Essex, York, and Durham, by J. H. Bell, 1872, folio. Burke's Landed Gentry, (of Hesslewood,) 2 supp., 3, 4, 5, 6, 7, 8; (of Darlington,) 5, 6, 8. Foster's Yorkshire Pedigrees. History of Darlington, by W. Hylton Dyer Longstaffe, lvii. Pedigree of Wilson of High Wray, etc., by Joseph Foster, 125. Pedigree of Wilson, by S. B. Foster, 136. Cyclostyle Pedigrees, by J. J. Green. New England Register, iii. 27, 169, 233, 390; vii. 12; ix. 91; x. 159. Annals of Smith of Balby, by H. E. Smith, 182.

PEASINGE. Hutchins' Dorset, ii. 719. Weaver's Visitations of Somerset, 124. Harleian Society, xx. 75.

PECHE. Morant's Essex, ii. 568. Hasted's Kent, i. 311. Glover's History of Derbyshire, ii. 152. Harleian Society, ii. 65; xiv. 586. Eyton's Antiquities of Shropshire, ix. 69. Nichols' History of the County of Leicester, iii. 982; iv. 370. Dugdale's Warwickshire, 954. Banks' Baronies in Fee, i. 363. Banks' Dormant and Extinct Baronage, i. 392. The Genealogist, New Series, x. 33;

xiii. 37. Brocas of Beaurepaire, by M. Burrows, 361. Notes and Queries, 6 S. x. 207. Archæologia Cantiana, xvi. 227.

PECHELL. Sussex Archæological Collections, xxvi. 148. Betham's Baronetage, iv. 374.

PECK. Morant's Essex, ii. 524. Berry's Sussex Genealogies, 97. Visitation of Sussex, 1570, printed by Sir T. Phillipps, (Middle Hill, fol.) 8. Burke's Landed Gentry, 3, 4, 5, 6. Foster's Visitations of Yorkshire, 347. Harleian Society, ii. 146-148; iii. 27; xvi. 236; xvii. 148; xxxii. 218. J. H. Hill's History of Market Harborough, 132. Nichols' History of the County of Leicester, ii. 879; iv. 167. F. G. Lee's History of Thame, 114. East Barnet, by F. C. Cass, 140. The Genealogist, New Series, viii. 24.

PECKHAM. Hasted's Kent, ii. 397. Berry's Sussex Genealogies, 58, 305. Burke's Landed Gentry, 2, 3, 4, 5, 6, 7, 8. Harleian Society, viii. 158. Dallaway's Sussex, i. App. to Chichester; i. 78, 143, 180, 183. Genealogical Record of King and Henham, 6.

PECKOVER. Burke's Landed Gentry, 6, 7, 8. Annals of Smith of Balby, by H. E. Smith, 34.

PEDDER. Burke's Landed Gentry, 2, 3, 4. Abram's History of Blackburn, 728.

PEDEN. Paterson's History of the Co. of Ayr, ii. 427. Paterson's History of Ayr and Wigton, i. 683.

PEDLER. Burke's Commoners, iv. 57, Landed Gentry, 2.

PEDLEY. Harleian Society, viii. 273.

PEDWARDYN. Bridges' Northamptonshire, by Rev. Peter Whalley, ii. 18. Nichols' History of the County of Leicester, ii. App. 47.

PEEBLES. Surtees Society, xxxvi. 367. The Genealogist, New Series, ix. 76. Northern Notes and Queries, vii. 128.

PEEL. Pedigree of the Right Hon. Sir Robert Peel, and the Peels of Lancashire, from the year 1600 to 1846, by John Davies. Manchester, May, 1846, broadside. The Peels, a family sketch, by Jonathan Peel, M.A. London, 1877, 8vo. Burke's Landed Gentry, (of Peele Fold,) 2, 3, 4, 5, 6, 7, 8 ; (of Bryn-y-Pys,) 3, 4, 5, 6, 7, 8 ; (of Accrington,) 2, 3, 4 ; (of Aylesmore House,) 2, 3, 4, 5, 6, 7 ; (of Singleton Brook,) 3, 4, 5 ; (of Stone Hall,) 3, 4, 5 ; (of Knowlmere,) 5, 6, 7, 8 ; (of Talioris Park,) 5, 6, 7, 8. Foster's Lancashire Pedigrees. Burke's Heraldic Illustrations, 96. Burke's Royal Descents and Pedigrees of Founders' Kin, 74. Burke's Authorized Arms, 42. Abram's History of Blackburn, 212, 563. Betham's Baronetage, v. 491. Harleian Society, xxxvii. 215.

PEERCE. The Genealogist, New Series, iii. 167.

PEERS, or PEERES. Burke's Landed Gentry, 2 supp. Harleian Society, viii. 497; xii. 233; xiii. 466; xvii. 148. Visitation of Warwickshire, 1619, pub. with Warwickshire Antiquarian Magazine, 206.

PEET. Miscellanea Genealogica et Heraldica, 2nd Series, ii. 32. Peet's Genealogical Memoranda of the family of Wanty, 48.

PEGG. Burke's Landed Gentry, 8.

PEGGE. Glover's History of Derbyshire, ii. 109, (95). Account of Beauchief Abbey, in Nichols' Miscellaneous Antiquities, No. 3, 210. Dickinson's History of Southwell, 2nd edition, 308. Visitation of

Derbyshire, 1663-4, (Middle Hill, 1854, fol.) 5. Hunter's History
of the Parish of Sheffield, 345. The Genealogist, ii. 393. Notes
and Queries, 1 S. i. 59, 90, 142, 200. Derbyshire Archæological
and Natural History Society, ii. 125. Harleian Society, xxxvii. 305.
PEIRCE. Berry's Kent Genealogies, 74. Foster's Visitations of York-
shire, 560. Harleian Society, xi. 83. Miscellanea Genealogica et
Heraldica, New Series, iii. 71. New England Register, xxi. 61,
157, 257, 340; xxii. 73, 174, 304, 428; xxviii. 367; xxix. 273.
PEIRS. Berry's Kent Genealogies, 464. W. Paver's Pedigrees of
Families of the City of York, 17.
PEIRSE. Topographer and Genealogist, i. 510, 525; ii. 541. Surtees
Society, xxxvi. 325. Burke's Landed Gentry, (of Thimbleby,)
2, 4, 5; (of Bedale,) 2, 3, 4, 5. Foster's Yorkshire Pedigrees.
Harleian Society, xvii. 149; xli. 66.
PEIRSON. Harleian Society, viii. 225. Ord's History of Cleveland,
397. Visitations of Staffordshire, 1614 and 1663-4, William Salt
Society, 232. See PEARSON.
PEITON. Harleian Society, xii. 379, 381. See PEYTON.
PEKE. Hasted's Kent, iii. 682. Berry's Kent Genealogies, 116, 351.
Surtees Society, xli. 81. Harleian Society, xlii. 48. See PEAKE.
PEKERYNG. Surtees Society, xli. 97. See PICKERING.
PELHAM. Notices of the Pelham Family, by M. A. Lower, 1873, fol.
Memoirs of the Administration of Henry Pelham, by Wm. Coxe,
1829, 4to. Morant's Essex, ii. 267. Jacob's Peerage, i. 352.
Berry's Sussex Genealogies, 313. Burke's Commoners, iii. 473,
Landed Gentry, 3, 4, 5, 6, 7, 8. Horsfield's History of Lewes,
i. 340. Burke's Visitation of Seats and Arms, 2nd Series, i. 35.
Hutchins' Dorset, ii. 294. Clutterbuck's Hertford, i. 131. Sussex
Archæological Collections, iii. 214. The Genealogist, iv. 213-225,
264; v. 105. Edmondson's Baronagium Genealogicum, i. 60;
vi. 57. Brydges' Collins' Peerage, v. 488; viii. 387. Notes and
Queries, 3 S. x. 21. Harleian Society, xx. 75. New England
Register, xxvi. 399; xxxiii. 285.
PELHAM-CLINTON. Brydges' Collins' Peerage, ii. 181.
PELL. Pedigree of Pell, folio, pp. 11, privately printed by O. C. Pell.
No date, place, or title. Burke's Landed Gentry, 5, 6, 7, 8. The
Genealogist, iv. 264; vi. 274. Harleian Society, xvii. 150; xxxix.
897. Memorials of Smarden, by F. Haslewood, 288. Historical
Notices of Doncaster, by C. W. Hatfield, 2nd Series, 437.
PELLAT, or PELLATT. Berry's Sussex Genealogies, 177. Dallaway's
Sussex, II. i. 217; II. ii. 160. Castles, Mansions, and Manors of
Western Sussex, by D. G. C. Elwes and C. J. Robinson, 34.
Nichols' Account of the Company of Ironmongers, 2nd edn., 602.
Sussex Archl. Collections, xxxviii. 99-128. Howard's Visitations
of England and Wales, ix. 161.
PELLEW. An Historical Survey of Cornwall, by C. S. Gilbert, i. 464.
Betham's Baronetage, iv. 322.
PELSANT. Nichols' History of the County of Leicester, iv. 578.
Burke's Extinct Baronetcies. Harleian Society, xli. 52. Cam-
bridgeshire Visitation, edited by Sir T. Phillipps, 25.

PELYTOT. The Genealogist, xii. 29.

PEMBERTON. Herald and Genealogist, ii. 519. Visitation of Durham, 1615, (Sunderland, 1820, fol.) 88. Burke's Commoners, (of Bainbridge,) ii. 70, 684, Landed Gentry, 2, 3, 4, 5, 6, 7, 8 ; (of Trumpington,) Landed Gentry, 5, 6, 7, 8 ; (of Newton,) 5, 7, 8 ; (of Torry Hill,) 5, 7, 8 ; 8 p. 327 *note.* Harleian Society, viii. 301 ; xxii. 81. Burke's Heraldic Illustrations, 1. Burke's Royal Descents and Pedigrees of Founders' Kin, 51. Bridge's Northamptonshire, by Rev. Peter Whalley, ii. 191. Hutchinson's History of Durham, iii. 138. Surtees' Durham, i. 237 ; iii. 205. Chetham Society, xcv. 104. Metcalfe's Visitations of Northamptonshire, 41, 125. Foster's Visitations of Durham, 251. New England Register, xliii. 295 ; xlvi. 392.

PEMBERTON-LEIGH. Burke's Landed Gentry, 2, 3.

PEMBROKE. East Anglian, iii. 30. Baker's Northampton, ii. 59, 315. Archæologia Cambrensis, 3 S. v. 1, 81, 188, 241 ; vi. 1. 81. 189, 253. Banks' Dormant and Extinct Baronage, iii. 597.

PEMBRUGGE, PEMBRUGE, PEMBRIDGE, or PENEBRUGGE. Lipscombe's History of the County of Buckingham, iv. 590. Shaw's Staffordshire, i. App. 38. Eyton's Antiquities of Shropshire, ii. 226. Nichols' History of the County of Leicester, iv. 36, 422. The Genealogist, New Series, viii. 243 ; ix. 8 ; xv. 26. Fosbrooke's History of Gloucestershire, ii. 239. Weaver's Visitation of Herefordshire, 55. Visitation of Gloucester, edited by T. F. Fenwick and W. C. Metcalfe, 133. Harleian Society, xxix. 394.

PENDARVES, or PENDARVIS. Burke's Commoners, iii. 363, Landed Gentry, 2, 3, 4, 7, 8. Harleian Society, ix. 163, 164. An Historical Survey of Cornwall, by C. S. Gilbert, ii. 222. The Visitations of Cornwall, edited by J. L. Vivian, 355.

PENDER. The Visitations of Cornwall, by J. L. Vivian, 604. Burke's Landed Gentry, 8.

PENDLETON. Harleian Society, xxxii. 219.

PENDOCK. Harleian Society, iv. 107. Thoroton's Nottinghamshire, i. 172.

PENDRELL, PENDERILL, or PENDEREL. Burke's St. James's Magazine, i. 179. Gentleman's Magazine, 1820, ii. 607. Archæologia Cambrensis, 3 S., v. 114, 299. The Boscobel Tracts, edited by J. Hughes, 2nd edn. 368. Notes and Queries, 2 S. xi. 337, 418 ; xii. 296 ; 8 S. i. 107, 178, 232.

PENELL. Nash's Worcestershire, ii. 94.

PENEYSTONE. Bysshe's Visitation of Essex, edited by J. J. Howard, 70.

PENFOLD. Burke's Colonial Gentry, ii. 854.

PENFOUND. Harleian Society, ix. 164. The Visitations of Cornwall, edited by J. L. Vivian, 358.

PENGRIFFIN. Dwnn's Visitations of Wales, i. 244.

PENHALLOW. Maclean's History of Trigg Minor, ii. 537. Harleian Society, ix. 166. The Visitations of Cornwall, edited by J. L. Vivian, 360. New England Register, xxxii. 28.

PENHARGARD. Maclean's History of Trigg Minor, ii. 46.

PENHELLICK. Harleian Society, ix. 167. The Visitations of Cornwall, edited by J. L. Vivian, 363.

PENISTON, PENISTONE, or PENNYSTONE. Sir T. Phillipps' Topographer, No. 1, (March, 1821, 8vo.) 32. Pedigree of Peniston, of Cornwell, Co. Oxon, by Sir T. Phillipps, Bart., London, folding sheet. Burke's Extinct Baronetcies. Visitations of Oxfordshire, 1574, printed by Sir T. Phillipps, (Middle Hill, fol.) 7. Harleian Society, v. 153 ; xiii. 468 ; xvii. 151. Visitation of Norfolk, published by Norfolk Archæological Society, i. 41.

PENKETH. Chetham Society, lxxxi. 124 ; lxxxii. 132.

PENKETT. Miscellanea Genealogica et Heraldica, New Series, iii. 456.

PENKEVILL. Maclean's History of Trigg Minor, iii. 73. The Visitations of Cornwall, edited by J. L. Vivian, 414.

PENN, or PENNE. A Pedigree and Genealogical Notes of the Family of Penn. Compiled and published by James Coleman. London, 1871, 8vo. Genealogical Gleanings, a History of the Family of Penn. By J. H Lea. Reprinted from the Pennsylvania Magazine, April, 1890, 8vo. The Penn's and Peningtons, by Maria Webb. London, 1867, 8vo. Berry's Buckinghamshire Genealogies, 73. Burke's Commoners, iii. 491, Landed Gentry, 2, 3, 4, 8. Harleian Society, viii. 69 ; xix. 45 ; xxii. 82, 116. Herald and Genealogist, vii. 144. Lipscombe's History of the County of Buckingham, iv. 555. Hutchins' Dorset, ii. 92. Clutterbuck's Hertford, ii. 306. Notes and Queries, 1 S. iii. 264, 409, 454 ; iv. 93 ; v. 593 ; 5 S. i. 265 ; 7 S. x. 383. Annals of the Barber Surgeons, by S. Young, 525.

PENN-GASKELL. Burke's Landed Gentry, 5 supp., 6, 7.

PENNANT. Dwnn's Visitations of Wales, ii. 305. Burke's Commoners, (of Downing,) iii. 30, Landed Gentry, 2 ; (of Penrhyn,) Landed Gentry, 2, 3, 4 ; (of Bodfari,) 4, 5, 6, 7, 8. Archdall's Lodge's Peerage, vii. 240. History of Powys Fadog, by J. Y. W. Lloyd, iii. 377, 379.

PENNECK. An Historical Survey of Cornwall, by C. S. Gilbert, ii. 226.

PENNEFATHER, or PENYFATHER. Burke's Commoners, (of New Park,) ii. 551, Landed Gentry, 2, 3, 4, 5, 6, 7 ; (of Ballylanigan,) Landed Gentry, 3, 4 ; (of Rathsallagh,) Landed Gentry, 5, 6, 7, 8. Harleian Society, xvii. 153.

PENNESBY. Ormerod's Cheshire, ii. 530.

PENNING, or PENNINGE. Harleian Society, xiii. 262. Metcalfe's Visitations of Suffolk, 157.

PENNINGTON. Pedigree of Sir Josslyn Pennington, fifth Baron Muncaster, by Joseph Foster. London, 1878, 4to. Visitation of Somersetshire, printed by Sir T. Phillipps, 126. Burke's Landed Gentry, 5. Maclean's History of Trigg Minor, i. 302. Chetham Society, lxxxviii. 231, 232. Hutchinson's History of Cumberland, i. 566. Jefferson's History of Allerdale Ward, Cumberland, 228. Corry's History of Lancashire, i. 422. Harleian Society, xiii. 467 ; xvi. 237 ; xvii. 151, 152. Archdall's Lodge's Peerage, vii. 236. Wotton's English Baronetage, iii. 602. Foster's Collectanea Genealogica, i. 27. Bysshe's Visitation of Essex, edited by J. J.

Howard, 70. Foster's Visitations of Cumberland and Westmorland, 100. Weaver's Visitations of Somerset, 61. New England Register, xxv. 286, 335. Burke's Landed Gentry, 8. Nicolson and Burn's Westmorland and Cumberland, ii. 19. *See* PENN.

PENNY. Corry's History of Lancashire, i. 425. Metcalfe's Visitations of Northamptonshire, 125. Bardsley's Registers of Ulverston, lxxxvi.

PENNYMAN. Surtees Society, xxxvi. 198. Burke's Landed Gentry, 3, 4, 5, 6, 7, 8. Foster's Yorkshire Pedigrees. Foster's Visitations of Yorkshire, 206. Burke's Visitation of Seats and Arms, 2nd Series, ii. 7. Graves' History of Cleveland, 440. Ord's History of Cleveland, 555. Wotton's English Baronetage, iii. 420. Betham's Baronetage, ii. 342. Burke's Extinct Baronetcies.

PENOYRE. Robinson's Mansions of Herefordshire, 68.

PENRHYN. Dwnn's Visitations of Wales, i. 274, 279. Burke's Landed Gentry, 5, 7, 8. The Sheriffs of Montgomeryshire, by W. V. Lloyd, 292. *See* PENRYN.

PENRICE, or PENRISE. Burke's Commoners, (of Yarmouth,) i. 362 ; Landed Gentry, 2, 3, 4, 5 ; (of Kilvrough,) Landed Gentry, 3, 4, 5, 6, 7, 8. Clutterbuck's Hertford, iii. 96. Berry's Hampshire Genealogies, 71. Genealogies of Morgan and Glamorgan, by G. T. Clark, 499.

PENROS, or PENROSE. Burke's Landed Gentry, 2, 3, 4, 5. Harleian Society, ix. 168, 169. An Historical Survey of Cornwall, by C. S. Gilbert, ii. 227. The Visitations of Cornwall, edited by J. L. Vivian, 365, 366, 368. Burke's Family Records, 475.

PENROSE-FITZGERALD. Burke's Landed Gentry, 3, 4, 5, 6, 7, 8.

PENRUDDOCK, or PENRUDDOCKE. Burke's Landed Gentry, 2, 3, 4, 5, 6, 7, 8. Harleian Society, vii. 2. Visitatio Comitatus Wiltoniæ, 1623, printed by Sir T. Phillipps. Hoare's Wiltshire, IV. i. 81. Visitation of Wiltshire, edited by G. W. Marshall, 66. Foster's Visitations of Cumberland and Westmorland, 102. Howard's Visitation of England and Wales, ii. 44. The Genealogist, New Series, xii. 171.

PENRY. Dwnn's Visitations of Wales, i. 24, 131, 305 ; ii. 29, 33. Glamorganshire Pedigrees, edited by Sir T. Phillipps, 14, 17, 37. Caermarthenshire Pedigrees, 34, 57. Genealogies of Morgan and Glamorgan, by G. T. Clark, 102, 107, 211. Burke's Landed Gentry, 8.

PENRYN. Collections by the Powys-land Club, viii. 406. Harleian Society, xvii. 152. *See* PENRHYN.

PENRYN DYFED. Dwnn's Visitations of Wales, i. 27.

PENTHENY. Burke's Heraldic Illustrations, 46.

PENTIRE. Maclean's History of Trigg Minor, i. 563.

PENTLAND. Burke's Landed Gentry, 2 supp.

PENTLOW. Metcalfe's Visitations of Northamptonshire, 125.

PENTON. Burke's Landed Gentry, 5, 6, 7, 8.

PENWARNE, or PENWARREN. Harleian Society, ix. 170. The Visitations of Cornwall, edited by J. L. Vivian, 370.

PENYSTON. Harleian Society, xxxii. 219. Burke's Landed Gentry, 8.

PEPER. Harleian Society, ii. 103.

PEPLER. Ontarian Families, by E. M. Chadwick, ii. 130.

PEPLOE. Burke's Commoners, iv. 27, Landed Gentry, 2, 3, 4, 5, 6, 7, 8. Miscellanea Genealogica et Heraldica, 2nd Series, iii. 114, 129. *See* BROWNE.

PEPPARD. Burke's Landed Gentry, 2, 3, 4, 5.

PEPPER. Burke's Landed Gentry, (of Bally Garth,) 3, 4, 5, 6, 7, 8; (of Lisanisky,) 3, 4, 5. Foster's Visitations of Yorkshire, 560. Nichols' History of the County of Leicester, iii. 187. The Genealogist, iv. 265.

PEPPERELL. Burke's Extinct Baronetcies. Betham's Baronetage, iv. 2. New England Register, xx. 1.

PEPSALL. Berry's Hampshire Genealogies, 333.

PEPWALL, or PEPWELL. Visitation of Gloucestershire, 1569, (Middle Hill, 1854, fol.) 8. Fosbrooke's History of Gloucestershire, ii. 60. Weaver's Visitations of Somerset, 123. Harleian Society, xxi, 219.

PEPYS. A Genealogy of the Pepys Family, by W. C. Pepys. London, 1887, 4to. Cambridgeshire Visitation, edited by Sir T. Phillipps, 23. Genealogical Pedigrees of the Family of Pepys, and of the Impington Branch thereof. Edinburgh, 1844, 4to. 2 sheets. Braybrooke's edition of Pepys' Diary, 1854, iv. 364. Topographer and Genealogist, iii. 109. Visitation of Norfolk, published by Norfolk Archæological Society, i. 380. Blomefield's Norfolk, vii. 81. Betham's Baronetage, iv. 146; v. 435. Harleian Society, xvii. 154; xxxii. 220; xli. 62. Bysshe's Visitation of Essex, edited by J. J. Howard, 70. H. B. Wheatley's edn. of Pepys' Diary, Supplementary Vol., 4-13.

PERCEHAY. Surtees Society, xxxvi. 114; xli. 86. Foster's Visitations of Yorkshire, 186. Harleian Society, xvi. 238. *See* PERCY.

PERCEVAL-MAXWELL. Burke's Landed Gentry, 2, 3, 4, 5, 6, 7, 8.

PERCEVAL, PERCIVAL, or PERCIVALL. A brief account of the Family of Percival, 12mo., pp. 32. Pedigree of the Family of the Earl of Egmont, lithograph, 1877, fol., pp. 45. Collinson's Somerset, iii. 87, 173. Cheshire and Lancashire Historic Society, Session i. 61. Burke's Landed Gentry, 2, 3, 4, 5, 6, 7, 8. Drummond's History of Noble British Families, Part v. Visitation of Somersetshire, printed by Sir T. Phillipps, 126. Burke's Commoners, iv. 609. Harleian Society, xi. 84; xxxvii. 118, 121. Edmondson's Baronagium Genealogicum, v. 484. Archdall's Lodge's Peerage, ii. 214; vii. 86. Brydges' Collins' Peerage, vii. 319; ix. 230. Weaver's Visitations of Somerset, 61. The Irish Builder, xxix. 29, 43, 59. Burke's Colonial Gentry, ii. 816. Howard's Visitation of England and Wales, ii. 68; vi. 89. *See* IVERY.

PERCHARD. J. B. Payne's Armorial of Jersey, 315.

PERCHE. Harleian Society, xxix. 395.

PERCY. Case of Hugh, Baron Percy, etc., on his claim to be Lord Great Chamberlain of England, folio, pp. 5. The Case of James Percy, claymant to the Earldom of Northumberland. London, 1685, folio. Pedigree of Percy or Percehay of East Chaldfield, Co. Wilts, [T. P.] 1862, folio page. Short Account of the Proceedings of James Percy, late of Ireland, in pursuance of his right to the Earl-

dom of Northumberland, folio broadside. A Sketch of the Descendants of Josceline de Louvaine, the second House of Percy, Earls
of Northumberland, etc., by W. E. Surtees. Newcastle-upon-Tyne,
1844, 4to. Chronicle of the Family of Percy. Newcastle, 1845,
4to. Annals of the House of Percy. London, by E. B. de Fonblanque. 1887, 8vo., 2 vols. A Metrical Pedigree, edited by
D. Besley, pp. 44, 8vo. Remarks on the far-descended and
renowned Title of Lord Percy, by Alexander Sinclair, 8vo., pp. 15.
More Percy Anecdotes, Old and New, 1865, pp. 12. Yorkshire
Archæological Journal, i. 145. Hartshorne's History of Alnwick
Castle, 1865, 8vo. The Great Governing Families of England,
i. 21. Collectanea Topographica et Genealogica, ii. 57 ; vi. 266-
283, 370-380. Kent's British Banner Displayed, 383. Hasted's
Kent, i. 152. Surtees Society, xxxvi. 7. George Oliver's History
of Beverley, 481. Burke's Landed Gentry, 2, 3, 4, 5, 6. Burke's
Heraldic Illustrations, 1. Appendix to Case of Sir J. S. Sidney,
claiming to be Lord Lisle. Nash's Worcestershire, i. 587 ; ii. 317.
Foster's Visitations of Yorkshire, 199, 277, 281, 560. Herald and
Genealogist, viii. 504. Graves' History of Cleveland, 439.
Jefferson's History of Allerdale Ward, Cumberland, 41. Hodg-
son's Northumberland, I. ii. 6 ; II. ii. 41 ; III. ii. 365. Dallaway's
Sussex, II. i. 269. Ord's History of Cleveland, 426. Whitaker's
Deanery of Craven, 29, (44). Nichols' History of the County of
Leicester, iv. 174. Archæologia Æliana, 2nd Series, iv. 160.
Hutchins' Dorset, iv. 74. Surtees' Durham, ii. 225. Sussex
Archæological Collections, xiv. 3. Tate's History of Alnwick,
i. 400. An Historical Survey of Cornwall, by C. S. Gilbert, i. 432.
Harleian Society, xvi. 239-248 ; xvii. 154 ; xxxix. 873. Notes
and Queries, 2 S. vii. 34 ; 6 S. vii. 28 ; x. 88. Berry's Genealogical Peerage, 98. Edmondson's Baronagium Genealogicum, iii.
269. Brydges' Collins' Peerage, ii. 217 ; v. 386. Banks' Baronies
in Fee, i. 364. Banks' Dormant and Extinct Baronage, i. 158 ; ii.
415. The Genealogist, New Series, iii. 167 ; ix. 220 ; xiv. 99 ;
xvi. 162. Harvey's Hundred of Willey, 312. Metcalfe's Visitations of Northamptonshire, 41, 191. Ilkley, Ancient and Modern,
by R. Collyer and J. H. Turner, 55, 111. Pedigrees of the Lords
of Alnwick, by W. H. D. Longstaffe, 26, 36. Nicolson and Burn's
Westmorland and Cumberland, ii. 31. *See* NORTHUMBERLAND,
PERCEHAY.

PEREN. Howard's Visitation of England and Wales, ix. 150.

PERERS. Foster's Visitations of Yorkshire, 242. The Genealogist,
New Series, xiv. 197, 256.

PERFECT. Berry's Berkshire Genealogies, 39. Harleian Society,
xxxvii. 259.

PERIAM. Visitation of Devon, edited by F. T. Colby, 168. Weaver's
Visitations of Somerset, 62. The Visitations of Devon, by J. L.
Vivian, 603. *See* PERRIAM.

PERIENT. Clutterbuck's Hertford, ii. 321. Cussan's History of
Hertfordshire, Parts xi. and xii. 252. Harleian Society, xxii. 156.
See PERYENT.

PERIN, or PERINS. Harleian Society, ii. 198 ; xxix. 395. Nichols'
History of the County of Leicester, iii. 633.

PERKES, or PERKS. Robinson's Mansions of Herefordshire, 41. Miscellanea Genealogica et Heraldica, 2nd Series, v. 90. History of
Wednesbury, (Wolverhampton, 1854, 8vo.) 168.

PERKIN. Genealogies of Morgan and Glamorgan, by G. T. Clark,
500. Harleian Society, xxvii. 105.

PERKINS. Burke's Landed Gentry, 2, 3, 4, 5, 6, 7, 8. Visitation of
Warwickshire, 1619, published with Warwickshire Antiquarian
Magazine, 116. Nichols' History of the County of Leicester, iv.
854*. Hunter's Deanery of Doncaster, i. 178. Harleian Society,
xii. 281 ; xxxviii. 815. The Genealogist, vi. 73. The History of
Ufton Court, by A. M. Sharp, 35-65, 205, 220, 241. New England
Register, x. 211, 369 ; xi. 315 ; xii. 79 ; xiv. 113 ; xvii. 63 ; xxxix.
81 ; l. 34. See PARKINS.

PERKINSON. Visitation of Durham, 1575, (Newcastle, 1820,
fol.) 11. Surtees Society, xxxvi. 45. Hutchinson's History of
Durham, iii. 339. Foster's Visitations of Durham, 253. See
PARKINSON.

PERKYN. Dwnn's Visitations of Wales, i. 111.

PERKYNSON. Surtees' Durham, iii. 347.

PERNE. Cambridgeshire Visitation, edited by Sir T. Phillipps, 25.
Harleian Society, xli. 93.

PÉRONNE. The Visitations of Devon, by J. L. Vivian, 761.

PEROT, PERROT, or PERROTT. Perrot Notes, or some Account of the
Various Branches of the Perrot Family, by E. L. Barnwell, M.A.
London, 1867, 8vo. Sir T. Phillipps' Topographer, No. 1, (March
1821, 8vo.) 20. Dwnn's Visitations of Wales, i. 74, 89, 90, 133,
165. Croke's History of the Family of Croke, No. 42. Berry's
Buckinghamshire Genealogies, 95. Nash's Worcestershire, i. 448.
Visitation of Oxfordshire, 1574, printed by Sir T. Phillipps,
(Middle Hill, fol.) 7. Visitation of Oxfordshire, 1634, printed by
Sir T. Phillipps, (Middle Hill, fol.) 26. Ashmole's Antiquities of
Berkshire, iii. 323. Harleian Society, v. 128, 130, 244, 245 ; viii.
105 ; xvii. 155, 156. Herald and Genealogist, viii. 314. Howard's
Visitation of England and Wales, i. 272. Cooke's Continuation
of Duncumb's Hereford, (Hund. of Grimsworth,) Part ii. 146.
Genealogies of Morgan and Glamorgan, by G. T. Clark, 424.
Miscellanea Genealogica et Heraldica, 3rd Series, iii. 13. The
Genealogist, New Series, xvi. 239. Thoresby's Ducatus Leo-
diensis, 76. Caermarthenshire Pedigrees, 3, 146. Pembrokeshire
Pedigrees, 146. Archæologia Cambrensis, 3 S. xi. 1, 101, 229,
371 ; xii. 64, 167, 311, 478 ; 4 S. i. xv. Robinson's Mansions of
Herefordshire, 287. Collections by the Powys-land Club, iv. 143.
J. B. Payne's Armorial of Jersey, 316. Burke's Commoners, iv.
651 ; Landed Gentry, 7 at p. 1354, 8 at p. 1489. Banks' Baronies
in Fee, ii. 116. The Midland Antiquary, i. 57, 114, 157,
ii. 57.

PERRIAM. Westcote's Devonshire, edited by G. Oliver and P. Jones,
584. See PERIAM.

PERRIER. Burke's Landed Gentry, 3, 4, 5.

PERRIN, or PERRINS. Payne's Monograph of the House of Lempriere, 5. J. B. Payne's Armorial of Jersey, 233. New England Register, xxxii. 178. Harleian Society, xxxviii. 665. Burke's Landed Gentry, 7, 8. Howard's Visitation of England and Wales, viii. 118.

PERRONET. The Genealogist, New Series, xiii. 41.

PERRY. Case of Elizabeth Perry, of Penshurst Place, Kent, respecting her claim to the Barony of Sydney of Penshurst. London, 1780, folio. Morant's Essex, i. 321. Berry's Essex Genealogies, 110. Berry's Hertfordshire Genealogies, 238. Visitation of Somerset, edited by Sir T. Phillipps, 126. Burke's Landed Gentry, (of Bitham House,) 4, 5, 6, 7, 8; (of Woodroff,) 2 supp., 3, 4, 5, 6, 7. Harleian Society, xi. 84; xiv. 691; Cardiganshire Pedigrees, 103. Visitation of Gloucester, edited by T. F. Fenwick and W. C. Metcalfe, 133. Burke's Colonial Gentry, ii. 523. Aldred's History of Turville, 36. The Visitations of Devon, by J. L. Vivian, 591.

PERRY-MCCLINTOCK. Burke's Landed Gentry, 4, 5.

PERRY-WATLINGTON. Burke's Landed Gentry, 2, 3, 4, 5, 6.

PERSHALL, or PESHALL. Berry's Kent Genealogies, 347. Notes and Queries, 3 S. vi. 205, 443. Burke's Extinct Baronetcies. Visitations of Staffordshire, 1614 and 1663-4, William Salt Society, 239. Harleian Society, xlii. 179. See DE PEARSALL, PEARSALL.

PERSHOUSE, or PERSEHOUSE. Bibliotheca Topographica Britannica, ix. Part 4, 238. Burke's Commoners, iii. 607. Shaw's Staffordshire, ii. 75, 222, 222*. Visitation of Staffordshire, 1663-4, printed by Sir T. Phillipps, 8. The Midland Antiquary, ii. 133. Visitations of Staffordshire, 1614 and 1663-4, William Salt Society, 233, 238. Willmore's History of Walsall, 295.

PERSSE. Burke's Landed Gentry, (of Roxborough,) 3, 4, 5, 6, 7; (of Moyode,) 5, 6, 7, 8.

PERT, or PERTE. Bysshe's Visitation of Essex, edited by J. J. Howard, 71. Harleian Society, xiii. 263, 468. See PEARTE.

PERTON. Shaw's Staffordshire, ii. 207. J. P. Jones's History of Tettenhall, 131.

PERVEDD. Dwnn's Visitations of Wales, i. 26.

PERWICH. Metcalfe's Visitations of Northamptonshire, 42.

PERY, or PERYE. Westcote's Devonshire, edited by G. Oliver and P. Jones, 545. The Irish Builder, xxxv. 237. Archdall's Lodge's Peerage, vi. 124. Visitation of Devon, edited by F. T. Colby, 169. Harleian Society, xxi. 91.

PERYENT. Berry's Hertfordshire Genealogies, 200. See PERIENT.

PERYNS. Harleian Society, xxviii. 39.

PESCOD. Berry's Hampshire Genealogies, 328.

PESMEADE. Berry's Hampshire Genealogies, 272.

PESTELL. Nichols' History of the County of Leicester, iii. 940.

PETER. Tuckett's Devonshire Pedigrees, 125. Burke's Royal Families, (London, 1851, 8vo.) i. 163. Burke's Commoners, i. 29, Landed Gentry, 2, 3, 4, 5, 6, 7, 8. Harleian Society, vi. 209, 210.

Maclean's History of Trigg Minor, ii. 509. A Complete Parochial History of the County of Cornwall, iii. 208; iv. 128. An Historical Survey of Cornwall, by C. S. Gilbert, ii. 229. Visitation of Devon, edited by F. T. Colby, 169. Burke's Colonial Gentry, ii. 832. The Visitations of Devon, by J. L. Vivian, 592. *See* PETRE.

PETER-HOBLYN. Burke's Landed Gentry, 5. Maclean's History of Trigg Minor, ii. 509.

PETERS. Burke's Royal Families, (London, 1851, 8vo.) ii. 57. Burke's Landed Gentry, 2 add., 3, 4, 5, 6, 6 at p. 1633, 7, 7 at p. 1865, 8, 8 at p. 2063. Topographer, (London, 1789-91, 8vo.) ii. 116. Gyll's History of Wraysbury, 233. New England Register, ii. 58.

PETERSON. Genealogical Memoranda relating to the Family of Parker, by E. M. S. Parker, 35, 39.

PETERSWALD. Burke's Colonial Gentry, i. 194.

PETHICK. Burke's Landed Gentry, 8.

PETIT, PETYT, PETTIT, or PETITT. Hasted's Kent, iii. 5. Berry's Kent Genealogies, 157. Maclean's History of Trigg Minor, i. 317; ii. 252; iii. 161. Harleian Society, ix. 276; xvii. 156; xlii. 76, 101. Shaw's Staffordshire, ii. 52. A Complete Parochial History of the County of Cornwall, iv. 76. O'Hart's Irish Pedigrees, 2nd Series, 345. The Visitations of Cornwall, edited by J. L. Vivian, 30, 267, 399, 494. Metcalfe's Visitations of Suffolk, 56. Visitation of Staffordshire, (Willm. Salt Soc.) 124. Miscellanea Genealogica et Heraldica, New Series, iv. 13. Visitations of Staffordshire, 1614 and 1663-4, William Salt Society, 242. *See* LE PETIT.

PETLEY. Hasted's Kent, ii. 315. Berry's Kent Genealogies, 6, 227, 233, 388. Burke's Landed Gentry, 5, 6, 7, 8. Harleian Society, xlii. 177.

PETO. Dugdale's Warwickshire, 209, 472. Harleian Society, xii. 173.

PETRE. Tables showing the Descent of the Hon. E. M. (Petre), wife of E. S. Trafford, from King Henry VII., etc., 1884, fol. [By E. S. Trafford.] Rudder's Gloucestershire, 721. Morant's Essex, i. 105, 154, 214, 300; ii. 47, 63, 65, 80, 460, 572, 612. Berry's Essex Genealogies, 138. Burke's Commoners, iii. 264, Landed Gentry, 2, 3, 4, 5, 6, 7, 8. Herald and Genealogist, iii. 425. Foley's Records of the English Province S. J., ii. 585; v. 272. Westcote's Devonshire, edited by G. Oliver and P. Jones, 546. Manning and Bray's Surrey, iii. 228. Harleian Society, xiii. 12, 89, 264, 469; xiv. 693; xxi. 123. Edmondson's Baronagium Genealogicum, iv. 374. Brydges' Collins' Peerage, vii. 1. The Visitations of Cornwall, by J. L. Vivian, 605, 608. Chancellor's Sepulchral Monuments of Essex, 321. Morrell's History of Selby, 147. Bysshe's Visitation of Essex, edited by J. J. Howard, 71. Roman Catholic Families of England, by J. J. Howard and H. F. Burke, Part i. 89, 138. *See* PETER.

PETT. Berry's Kent Genealogies, 86, 328. Harleian Society, viii.

155; xiii. 265; xlii. 24; xliii. 197. Surrey Archæological Collections, vi. Hasted's Kent, (Hund. of Blackheath, edited by H. H. Drake,) 20.

PETTEY. Miscellanea Genealogica et Heraldica, New Series, iv. 309, 347.

PETTIWARD. Burke's Landed Gentry, 4, 5, 6, 7, 8.

PETTUS, or PETTOUS. Blomefield's Norfolk, x. 448. Harleian Society, xiii. 469; xxxii. 221. Wotton's English Baronetage, ii. 269. Burke's Extinct Baronetcies.

PETTY. Sir T. Phillipps' Topographer, No. 1, (March, 1821, 8vo.) 50. Visitation of Oxfordshire, 1574, printed by Sir T. Phillipps, (Middle Hill,) fol. 7. Visitation of Oxfordshire, 1634, printed by Sir T. Phillipps, (Middle Hill, fol.) 27. Harleian Society, v. 215, 286; xii. 245. Visitation of Warwickshire, 1619, published with Warwickshire Antiquarian Magazine, 56. Edmondson's Baronagium Genealogicum, vi. 12*. Archdall's Lodge's Peerage, ii. 349. Brydges' Collins' Peerage, ii. 422. F. G. Lee's History of Thame, 86, 217. Ilkley, Ancient and Modern, by R. Collyer and J. H. Turner, 215. Oxford Historical Society, xix. 32-36.

PETTY-FITZMAURICE. The Great Governing Families of England, ii. 133.

PEVER. Harvey's Hundred of Willey, 458. See PEVRE.

PEVEREL, or PEVERIL. Journal of the British Archæological Association, vii. 220; viii. 195. Blore's History of South Winfield in Nichols' Miscellaneous Antiquities, Nos. 3, 13, 81. Maclean's History of Trigg Minor, i. 382. Munford's Analysis of Domesday Book of Co. Norfolk, 46. Blore's Rutland, 143, 226. Dallaway's Sussex, II. ii. 97. Bridges' Northamptonshire, by Rev. Peter Whalley, i. 597. Eyton's Antiquities of Shropshire, ix. 69. Hutchins' Dorset, ii. 533. Hoare's Wiltshire, I. ii. 91. Baker's Northampton, i. 139, 269. Morant's Essex, ii. 413, 447. Banks' Baronies in Fee, ii. 118. Banks' Dormant and Extinct Baronage, i. 160. Miscellanea Genealogica et Heraldica, 2nd Series, ii. 379. The Genealogist, New Series, xii. 232; xiii. 174.

PEVINGTON. Harleian Society, xlii. 211.

PEVRE. Banks' Baronies in Fee, ii. 115. See PEYVER, PEVER.

PEW. Burke's Heraldic Illustrations, 85.

PEXALL. Hampshire Visitations, printed by Sir T. Phillipps, 7. Nichols' History of the County of Leicester, ii. 833.

PEYRSE. Harleian Society, xxxii. 221.

PEYSSUN. See PEASINGE.

PEYTON. Burke's Extinct Baronetcies. Memoir of W. M. Peyton, by J. L. Peyton, (London, 1872, 8vo.) 311-336. Morant's Essex, ii. 179, 182. Gough's Sepulchral Monuments, ii. 386. Hasted's Kent, iv. 210. Visitation of Suffolk, edited by J. J. Howard, ii. 109-132. Berry's Buckinghamshire Genealogies, 11. Berry's Kent Genealogies, 213. Burke's Landed Gentry, (of Wakehurst Place,) 2; (of Driney House,) 2, 3, 4, 5; (of Laheen,) 3, 4, 5, 6, 7, 8. Harleian Society, viii. 239; xli. 3; xlii. 66. W. Watson's Account of Wisbeach, 522. Herald and Genealogist, vi. 63-74,

345. Memoirs of the Family of Chester, by R. E. C. Waters, 183, etc. Page's History of Suffolk, 920. Wotton's English Baronetage, i. 23 ; iii. 515. Banks' Baronies in Fee, ii. 87. Betham's Baronetage, i. 42 ; iv. 13. *See* PAYTON, PEITON.

PEYVER, or PEYVRE. Clutterbuck's Hertford, ii. 529. Lipscombe's History of the County of Buckingham, iv. 210. *See* PEVRE.

PHAIRE. Burke's Landed Gentry, 2, 3.

PHELIP. Clutterbuck's Hertford, ii. 484. Page's History of Suffolk, 385.

PHELIPS. Collinson's Somerset, iii. 314. Visitation of Somersetshire, printed by Sir T. Phillipps, 150. Burke's Commoners, (of Briggins Park,) iii. 647, Landed Gentry, 2, 3, 4, 5, 6, 7, 8 ; (of Montacute,) 2, 3, 4, 5, 6, 7, 8. Hutchins' Dorset, iii. 357. Burke's Extinct Baronetcies. Roman Catholic Families of England, by J. J. Howard and H. F. Burke, Part ii. 120.

PHELPS. Miscellanea Genealogica et Heraldica, i. 164. Burke's Landed Gentry, (of Dursley,) 5, 6, 7, 8 ; (of Waterpark,) 8. Nichols' History of the County of Leicester, ii. 144. Blunt's Dursley and its Neighbourhood, 92. F. G. Lee's History of Thame, 628.

PHESANT. Harleian Society, xvii. 158. East Barnet, by F. C. Cass, Part i. 32.

PHETIPLACE. Visitation of Oxfordshire, 1634, printed by Sir T. Phillipps, (Middle Hill, fol.) 27. Transactions of Shropshire Archæological Society, ix. 32. *See* FETTIPLACE.

PHIBBS. Burke's Landed Gentry, 8.

PHIFFARD. Manning and Bray's Surrey, i. 255.

PHILBRICK. New England Register, xxxviii. 279.

PHILIP. Dwnn's Visitations of Wales, i. 303. Harleian Society, xvii. 159.

PHILIPPA (Queen). Plantagenet-Harrison's History of Yorkshire, i. xxi.

PHILIPPE. History of Richmond, by C. Clarkson, 345. Plantagenet-Harrison's History of Yorkshire, i. 312.

PHILIPPS. Burke's Landed Gentry, (of Penty Park,) 4 ; (of Aberglasney,) 2, 3, 4, 5, 6 ; (of Williamston,) 2, 3, 4 ; (of Cwmgwilly,) 5, 6, 7, 8 ; (of Picton Castle,) 5, 6, 7 ; (of Mabws,) 6 ; (of Dale Castle,) 8. Herald and Genealogist, v. 412. Harleian Society, i. 28, 71 ; xvi. 249. T. Nicholas' County Families of Wales, 298, 908. Wotton's English Baronetage, i. 458.

PHILIPS. Pedigree of Philips of Wanborough, and Cleeve Pipard, by Sir T. Phillipps, Bart., 3 sheets. Camden Society, New Series, iv. 259. Dwnn's Visitations of Wales, ii. 46, 225. Visitation of Somersetshire, printed by Sir T. Phillipps, 126, 127. Burke's Commoners, (of Heath House,) ii. 591, Landed Gentry, 2, 3, 4, 5, 6, 7, 8 ; (of Snitterfield,) Landed Gentry, 3, 4 ; (of Heybridge,) 7, 8 ; (of Lee Priory,) 8. Warwickshire Pedigrees, from Visitation of 1682-3, (privately printed, 1865). Foster's Lancashire Pedigrees. Meyrick's History of the Co. of Cardigan, 161. Archdall's Lodge's Peerage, vii. 95. Philips' Old Halls of Lancashire and

Cheshire, xii. Oxford Historical Society, xxiv. 359. Harleian Society, xxxvii. 272, 276, 277.

PHILIPSE. Burke's Commoners, iv. xv. 491. New England Register, x. 25, 198.

PHILIPSON. Gentleman's Magazine, 1849, ii. 248. Visitation of Westmoreland, 1615, (London, 1853,) 47. Harleian Society, i. 66. Foster's Visitations of Cumberland and Westmorland, 104. Nicolson and Burn's Westmorland and Cumberland, i. 142, 180.

PHILLIMORE. Berry's Berkshire Genealogies, 134. Burke's Landed Gentry, 2 supp., 3, 4, 5, 6, 7. Blunt's Dursley and its Neighbourhood, 202. See FYNMORE.

PHILLIP. Archæologia Æliana, 2nd Series, v. 46. Surtees' Durham, iv. 24. Yorkshire Archæological and Topographical Journal, vi. 236.

PHILLIPPES. Caermarthenshire Pedigrees, 15, 39, 40, 44, 56, 59, 65. Weaver's Visitation of Herefordshire, 56.

PHILLIPPS. Collectanea de Familiis Diversis quibus nomen est Phillipps. Cura et ope T. P. compilata. Middle Hill, n.d., fol. Pedigree of Phillipps of Picton Castle, Co. Pembroke, and its branches of Phillipps of Abertowin, Rushmore, etc., by Sir T. Phillips, Bart. London and Bridgewater, 183—, 4to. pp. 4. Burke's Royal Families, (London, 1851, 8vo.) i. 184. Burke's Commoners, (of Eaton Bishop,) iv. 160, Landed Gentry, 2, 3, 4, 5 ; (of Garendon Park,) Commoners, iv. 97, Landed Gentry, 2, 3, 4, 5, 6 ; (of Longworth,) Commoners, iv. 160, Landed Gentry, 2, 3, 4 ; (of Bryngwyn,) Commoners, iv. 164, Landed Gentry, 2, 3, 4, 5 ; (of Dale Castle,) 7. Maclean's History of Trigg Minor, i. 285. Harleian Society, xi. 85 ; xx. 76 ; xxix. 396. Burke's Heraldic Illustrations, 29, 41. Burke's Authorized Arms, 165. Nichols' History of the County of Leicester, iii. 804. Cardiganshire Pedigrees, 82, 99. Pembrokeshire Pedigrees, 119, 120, 141, 144. Visitatio Comitatus Wiltoniæ, 1623, printed by Sir T. Phillipps. Bigland's Gloucestershire, ii. par. Willersley. Notes and Queries, 2 S. v. 329. New England Register, vi. 273.

PHILLIPS. Dwnn's Visitations of Wales, i. 85, 92, 105, 114, 142, 158, 162, 193, 203, 208, 260. Burke's Landed Gentry, (of Lawrenny Castle,) 2, 3, 4, 5, 6, 7, 8 ; (of Witston House,) 2 supp., 3, 4, 5, 6 ; (of Glenview,) 4, 5, 6, 7, 8 ; (of Culham House,) 5, 6, 7, 8 ; (of the Cedars,) 8. Harleian Society, vi. 210 ; viii. 402 ; xi. 85 ; xvii. 160, 162 ; xxix. 397. Maclean's History of Trigg Minor, ii. 364. Visitatio Comitatus Wiltoniæ, 1623, printed by Sir T. Phillipps. Notes and Queries, 4 S. xii. 98. F. G. Lee's History of Thame, 604. The Visitations of Devon, by J. L. Vivian, 593.

PHILLPOTT, PHILIPOTT, or PHILPOTTS. Harleian Society, xvii. 163 ; xxix. 399. Burke's Landed Gentry, 4, 5, 6, 7.

PHIPPEN. See FITZ-PEN.

PHIPPS. Berry's Sussex Genealogies, 305. Berry's Buckinghamshire Genealogies, 6. Burke's Commoners, iv. 509, Landed

Gentry, 2, 3, 4, 5, 6, 7, 8. Foster's Yorkshire Pedigrees. Hoare's Wiltshire, IV. i. 33. Archdall's Lodge's Peerage, vii. 83. Brydges' Collins' Peerage, viii. 311. Harleian Society, xl. 1288.

PHOWK. Dwnn's Visitation of Wales, ii. 339.

PHULK. Dwnn's Visitations of Wales, i. 87.

PIARD. See PEARD.

PICARD, or PICHARD. The Picards or Pychards, etc., with some Account of the Family of Sapy. London, 1878, 8vo. Cooke's Continuation of Duncumb's Hereford, (Hund. of Grimsworth,) Part ii. 158. The Genealogist, New Series, xii. 34.

PICHFORD. Eyton's Antiquities of Shropshire, vi. 270. Collections for a History of Staffordshire, William Salt Society, ii. Part 2, 84. Harleian Society, xxii. 82. See PYCHEFORD, PITCHFORD.

PICKARD-CAMBRIDGE. Burke's Landed Gentry, 3 supp., 4, 5, 6, 7, 8. Hutchins' Dorset, iii. 326.

PICKERING. J. H. Hill's History of Langton, 37. Kent's British Banner Displayed, 429. Camoys' Peerage Evidence, 256. Berry's Sussex Genealogies, 362. Topographer and Genealogist, i. 442. Burke's Commoners, ii. 191. Miscellanea Genealogica et Heraldica, New Series, i. 456 ; iv. 232, 405. Foster's Visitations of Yorkshire, 120, 281, 627, 630. A Royal Descent, by T. E. Sharpe, (London, 1875, 4to.) 126. Bridges' Northamptonshire, by Rev. Peter Whalley, ii. 384. Thoresby's Ducatus Leodiensis, 212. Nichols' History of the County of Leicester, i. 614. Ormerod's Cheshire, i. 748. Foster's Account of Families Descended from Francis Fox, 21. The Umfrevilles, their Ancestors and Descendants, 43. Harleian Society, xvi. 250 ; xvii. 162. Wotton's English Baronetage, iv. 346. Notes and Queries, 3 S. i. 270 ; 4 S. vi. 47. Burke's Extinct Baronetcies, and 634. Foster's Visitations of Cumberland and Westmorland, 106. Metcalfe's Visitations of Northamptonshire, 42, 126. Burke's Colonial Gentry, i. 379. The Genealogical Magazine, ii. 74, 225. Nicolson and Burn's Westmorland and Cumberland, i. 261, 499. See PEKERYNG, PIKERING.

PICKERSGILL. Burke's Landed Gentry, 4, 5, 6, 7, 8.

PICKFORD. Foster's Yorkshire Pedigrees. Harleian Society, xxxviii. 521.

PICKHAVER. Visitatio Comitatus Wiltoniæ, 1623, printed by Sir T. Phillipps. Visitation of Wiltshire, edited by G. W. Marshall, 99.

PICKOP. Abram's History of Blackburn, 581, 599.

PICKUP. Abram's History of Blackburn, 508.

PICOT, or PICCOT. Morant's Essex, ii. 411. Baker's Northampton, i. 82. See PIGOTT.

PICTAVENSIS. Herald and Genealogist, v. 235. Foster's Visitations of Yorkshire, 325. Gregson's Fragments relative to the County of Lancaster, 50. See PATEFIN.

PICTON. Pedigree of Picton of Iscoed, [T. P.] 1860, folio page. See MANSELL.

PIDCOCK. Burke's Visitation of Seats and Arms, 2nd Series, i. 7.

Burke's Landed Gentry, 3, 4. Genealogy of Henzey, Tyttery, and Tyzack, by H. S. Grazebrook, 80.

PIERCE. Visitation of Somersetshire, edited by Sir T. Phillipps, 127. Burke's Landed Gentry, 8. *See* PEARSE.

PIERCE-SEAMAN. Burke's Landed Gentry, 2, 3, 4.

PIERPOINT, PIERPONT, or PERPONT. Jacob's Peerage, i. 338. Harleian Society, iv. 43. Eyton's Antiquities of Shropshire, i. 218. Sussex Archæological Collections, xi. 84. Thoroton's Nottinghamshire, i. 176. . Edmondson's Baronagium Genealogicum, i. 57. Notes and Queries, 1 S. vii. 65, 606. Brydges' Collins' Peerage, v. 626. Banks' Baronies in Fee, ii. 119. Banks' Dormant and Extinct Baronage, iii. 432. The Genealogist, New Series, xv. 25.

PIERS. Berry's Sussex Genealogies, 261. Cambridgeshire Visitation, edited by Sir T. Phillipps, 25. Archæologia Cambrensis, 4 S., viii. 31. The Sheriffs of Montgomeryshire, by W. V. Lloyd, 521. Burke's Extinct Baronetcies, 634. Burke's Colonial Gentry, ii. 788.

PIERSE. Thoresby's Ducatus Leodiensis, 251.

PIERSON. W. Paver's Pedigrees of Families of the City of York, 18. Harleian Society, i. 31 ; xvii. 163.

PIGEON. Berry's Hampshire Genealogies, 115. Harleian Society, xxxii. 222 ; xlii. 197.

PIGG, or PIGGE. Baker's Northampton, i. 152. Carthew's Hundred of Launditch, Part iii. 97, 451. Genealogies of Morgan and Glamorgan, by G. T. Clark, 500.

PIGOT, PIGOTT, or PIGGOTT. Dallaway's Sussex, i. 228. Morant's Essex, ii. 601. Burke's Royal Families, (London, 1851, 8vo.) i. 147 ; ii. 149. Foster's Visitations of Yorkshire, 234, 302. Jewitt's Reliquary, xv. 15. Chetham Society, lxxxviii. 233 ; xcvii. 70. Lipscombe's History of the County of Buckingham, i. 278, 406, 409, 486 ; ii. 527 ; iv. 237, 326. Thoroton's Nottinghamshire, i. 26. The Genealogist, ii. 294 ; vi. 74, 276 ; vii. 187, 188. Herald and Genealogist, iii. 306. Cambridgeshire Visitation, edited by Sir T. Phillipps, 25. Burke's Commoners, (of Edgmond,) iii. 191, Landed Gentry, 2, 3, 4, 5, 6 ; (of Doddershall Park,) Commoners, iv. 646, Landed Gentry, 2, 3, 4, 5, 6, 7, 8 ; (of Brockley Hall,) Landed Gentry, 2, 3, 4, 5, 6, 7, 8 ; (of Eagle Hill,) 3, 4, 5 ; (of Archer Lodge,) 2 supp., 3, 4, 5, 6 ; (of Slevoy,) 2 supp., 3, 4, 5, 6, 7, 8 ; (of Capard,) 6, 7, 8 ; (of Greywell Hill,) 7 ; (of Sundorne,) 7, 8 ; 8 at 1178. Harleian Society, iv. 115 ; v. 212 ; viii. 115, 203 ; xvii. 164 ; xix. 46, 132, 188 ; xxix. 399 ; xxxix. 1025 ; xli. 100. Thoresby's Ducatus Leodiensis, 114. Miscellanea Genealogica et Heraldica, New Series, iii. 222. Betham's Baronetage, v. app. 26. Ormerod's Cheshire, iii. 667. Harvey's Hundred of Willey, 508. Pedigree of the Family of Boddington, by R. S. Boddington, 4. Burke's Colonial Gentry, ii. 560. Burke's Family Records, 477. History of Doddington, by R. E. G. Cole, 29. Howard's Visitation of Ireland, ii. 95. *See* GRAHAM-FOSTER-PIGOTT, PICOT, PYCOT, PYGOT.

PIKE. Collinson's Somerset, iii. 7. Burke's Landed Gentry, 5 supp., 6, 7, 8. Visitatio Comitatus Wiltoniæ, 1623, printed by Sir T. Phillipps. Notes and Queries, 8 S. iv. 288 ; v. 10. Visitation of Wiltshire, edited by G. W. Marshall, 71. Harleian Society, xliii. 79. *See* PYKE.

PIKERING. Camden Society, xliii. 19. *See* PICKERING.

PILCHER. Burke's Landed Gentry, 8.

PILE. Visitatio Comitatus Wiltoniæ, 1623, printed by Sir T. Phillipps, Wotton's English Baronetage, ii. 122. Visitation of Wiltshire, edited by G. W. Marshall, 69. Burke's Extinct Baronetcies. The Genealogist, vi. 74.

PILEY. Hunter's Deanery of Doncaster, ii. 306.

PILFOLD. Dalloway's Sussex, II. ii. 367. Miscellanea Genealogica et Heraldica, New Series, iv. 85.

PILGRIM. Cyclostyle Pedigrees, by J. J. Green.

PILKINGTON. The History of the Family of Pilkington. By Lt.-Col. John Pilkington. Liverpool, 1894, 8vo. Genealogy of the Pilkingtons of Lancashire, edited by W. E. A. Axon. Manchester, 1875, 4to. Gentleman's Magazine, 1831, i. 294. Jewitt's Reliquary, vii. 28. Visitation of Durham, 1575, (Newcastle, 1820, fol.) 1. Howard's Visitation of England and Wales, i. 254 ; Notes, iii. 86. Burke's Landed Gentry, (of Tore,) 2, 3, 4, 5, 6, 7, 8 ; (of St. Helen's,) 8 ; (of Carrick,) 2 supp., 3, 4, 5, 8 ; (of Park Lane Hall,) 3. Foster's Yorkshire Pedigrees. Foster's Visitations of Yorkshire, 562. Harleian Society, ii. 78 ; viii. 420. Hutchinson's History of Durham, i. 447. Nichol's History of the County of Leicester, i. 606 ; iii. 650. Hunter's Deanery of Doncaster, ii. 394. Surtees' Durham, i. lxxix. Clutterbuck's Hertford, iii. 138. Baines' History of the Co. of Lancaster, iii. 104, 105 ; Croston's edn. ii. 367 ; iii. 226. Chauncy's Hertfordshire, 413. T. Nicholas' County Families of Wales, 454. Chetham Society, xcix. 105, 173. Abram's History of Blackburn, 402. Wotton's English Baronetage, iv. 338. Betham's Baronetage, v. (Barts. of Scotland,) 14. Foster's Visitations of Durham, 255. Metcalfe's Visitations of Northamptonshire, 129.

PILLANS. Burke's Colonial Gentry, i. 386.

PILLSBURY. Essex Institute Historical Collections, (Salem, Mass.,) xxxi. 181-204.

PILSDON. Dwnn's Visitations of Wales, i. 150, 309.

PIMPE. Topographer and Genealogist, i. 516. *See* DE. PIMPE, PYMPE.

PINCERNA. Dugdale's Warwickshire, 854. J. Pym Yeatman's History of the House of Arundel, 233.

PINCHBECK. Lincolnshire Notes and Queries, i. 173. Ancient Families of Lincolnshire, in ' Spalding Free Press,' 1873-5, Nos. iii. and iv. Harleian Society, xli. 104.

PINCHON. Morant's Essex, ii. 65. Harleian Society, xiii. 266, 470 ; xvii. 165. New England Register, xlviii. 260. *See* PYNCHON.

PINCKARD. A Pedigree of George Henry Pinckard of Combe Court, Godalming, J.P. Printed on small sheet of notepaper without date or title, *circa* 1873. Burke's Landed Gentry, 8.

PINCOMB. *See* PYNCOMBE.
PINDAR. Stonehouse's History of the Isle of Axholme, 244. Burke's
Extinct Baronetcies. Notes and Queries, 6 S. xii. 10. Jewers'
Wells Cathedral, 278.
PINDAR, or PINDER. Harleian Society, xvii. 166 ; xxxviii. 485.
PINE. Visitation of Somersetshire, printed by Sir T. Phillipps, 127.
Harleian Society, xi. 86. *See* PYNE.
PINE-COFFIN. Burke's Landed Gentry, 5, 6, 7, 8. The Visitations
of Devon, by J. L. Vivian, 211.
PINEL. J. B. Payne's Armorial of Jersey, 318.
PINELLI. Gentleman's Magazine, 1836, ii. 483.
PINFOLD. Berry's Buckinghamshire Genealogies, 31. Burke's Landed
Gentry, 3 supp., 4, 5.
PINKE. Visitation of Oxfordshire, 1634, printed by Sir T. Phillipps,
(Middle Hill, fol.) 27. Harleian Society, v. 289. Miscellanea
Genealogica et Heraldica, 3rd Series, ii. 105, 185-192, 251.
PINKENEY, PINCKNEY, or PINKNEY. Bridges' Northamptonshire, by
Rev. Peter Whalley, i. 255. Visitatio Comitatus Wiltoniæ, 1623,
printed by Sir T. Phillipps. Clutterbuck's Hertford, iii. 119.
Baker's Northampton, ii. 107. Surtees Society, xxxvi. 326.
Foster's Visitations of Yorkshire, 210. Dugdale's Warwickshire,
343. Visitation of Wiltshire, edited by G. W. Marshall, 87.
Banks' Dormant and Extinct Baronage, i. 395. Burke's Landed
Gentry, 8. Notes and Queries, 8 S. xi. 412 ; xii. 15.
PINKHAM. New England Register, v. 198, 450 ; vii. 353.
PINNER. Metcalfe's Visitations of Suffolk, 157.
PINNEY. Burke's Landed Gentry, 2, 3, 4, 5, 6, 7, 8. Monken
Hadley, by F. C. Cass, 71.
PINNOCK. Monumental Inscriptions of the British West Indies, by
J. H. Lawrence Archer, 239.
PIOT. Visitation of Staffordshire, 1663-4, printed by Sir T. Phillipps,
8. *See* PYOTT.
PIPARD. Banks' Dormant and Extinct Baronage, i. 396.
PIPE. Harleian Society, i. 10. Shaw's Staffordshire, i. 83, 162,
416* ; ii. 172. Visitation of Staffordshire, 1663-4, printed by Sir T.
Phillipps, 8. Erdeswicke's Survey of Staffordshire, 393. Nichol's
History of the County of Leicester, iii. 982*. Dugdale's Warwick-
shire, 892. Visitations of Staffordshire, 1614 and 1663-4, William
Salt Society, 242.
PIPER, or PYPER. Burke's Commoners, iii. 310, Landed Gentry, 2.
The Genealogist, vi. 57, 123.
PIPON. J. B. Payne's Armorial of Jersey, 319.
PIRITON. Dugdale's Warwickshire, 671.
PIRTON. Morant's Essex, i. 444, 446, 468.
PISTAR. Berry's Hampshire Genealogies, 263.
PISTOR. The Genealogist, iv. 265. Surrey Archæological Collec-
tions, x. Harleian Society, xliii. 121.
PITCAIRN. Burke's Landed Gentry, 2. Northern Notes and Queries,
ix. 5, 59.
PITCHER. Harleian Society, xvii. 168.

PITCHFORD. Topographer and Genealogist, ii. 509. Transactions of Shropshire Archæological Society, viii. 123-144; ix. 67. *See* PICHFORD.

PITFIELD. Visitation of Middlesex, (Salisbury, 1820, fol.) 40. Harleian Society, viii. 308. The Genealogist, i. 41. Foster's Visitation of Middlesex, 73.

PITMAN. Burke's Landed Gentry, 2, 3, 4, 5, 6 supp. New England Register, vii. 355.

PITT. Narrative of Thomas Pitt, Lord Camelford, and Proofs of his Claims to the Peerage, 1785, 4to. Rudder's Gloucestershire, 719. Chronicle of the Family of De Havilland. Berry's Hampshire Genealogies, 101-105. Visitation of Somersetshire, printed by Sir T. Phillipps, 127. Visitation of Wiltshire, 1677, printed by Sir. T. Phillipps, (Middle Hill, 1854, fol.). Gyll's History of Wraysbury, 274. Harleian Society, xi. 86; xvii. 167; xxvii. 105; xxix. 402. Blore's Rutland, 170. Nichols' History of the County of Leicester, iv. 962. Hutchins' Dorset, i. 164; ii. 564; iv. 90. Fosbrooke's History ·of Gloucestershire, ii. 531. An Historical Survey of Cornwall, by C. S. Gilbert, i. 540. Edmondson's Baronagium Genealogicum, iv. 311; vi. 71, 107. Brydges' Collins' Peerage, v. 45; vii. 484. Banks' Dormant and Extinct Baronage, iii. 137. Berks Archl. and Architectural Journal, iii. 44. *See* PYTT.

PITTESFORD. Baker's Northampton, i. 61.

PITT-RIVERS. Burke's Landed Gentry, 7, 8.

PITTS. Account of the Township of Iffley, by the Rev. Edw. Marshall, 68. *See* PYTTS.

PIX. Berry's Kent Genealogies, 364. Harleian Society, xlii. 162. Pedigree of the Family of Pix of Hawkhurst, etc., Kent, by A. C. Harvey, 1888. Single sheet. Miscellanea Genealogica et Heraldica, 2nd Series, v. 17, 56, 111.

PIXLEY. Burke's Family Records, 479. Howard's Visitation of England and Wales, vii. 30.

PLACE, or PLAYSE. Visitation of Durham, 1615, (Sunderland, 1820, fol.) 22. Surtees Society, xli. 49. Surtees' Durham, iii. 236. Visitation of Durham, 1575, (Newcastle, 1820, fol.) 23. Hutchinson's History of Durham, iii. 147. Harleian Society, xvi. 251; xxxix. 921. Foster's Visitations of Durham, 257, 258. *See* PLAYZ.

PLANE. Genealogical Record of King and Henham, 23, 35.

PLANT. Harleian Society, xxxviii. 581.

PLANTAGENET. Morant's Essex, ii. 465. Rev. Robt. Simpson's History of the Town of Lancaster, 212. A Royal Descent, by T. E. Sharpe, (London, 1875, 4to.) 1. Blore's Rutland, 37, 98. Baker's Northampton, i. 350. Banks' Dormant and Extinct Baronage, iii. 34, 71, 415, 439, 652.

PLANTAGENET-HARRISON. Plantagenet-Harrison's History of Yorkshire, i. xiv.

PLANTNEY. Visitation of Staffordshire, (Willm. Salt. Soc.) 125.

PLATT. Burke's Landed Gentry, 5, 6 and supp., 7, 8. Manning and Bray's Surrey, i. 609.

PLAUNCHE. The Genealogist, New Series, xvii. 244.

PLAYER. Berry's Hampshire Genealogies, 159.

PLAYFAIR. Herald and Genealogist, viii. 454. *See* ROGER.

PLAYFORD. Burke's Colonial Gentry, i. 195. Notes and Queries, 8 S. vii. 449, 494.

PLAYNE. Burke's Landed Gentry, 5, 6, 7, 8. Metcalfe's Visitations of Suffolk, 158. Genealogical Memoranda relating to the Family of King, by W. L. King, 16.

PLAYS, or PLAYZ. Morant's Essex, i. 488. Clutterbuck's Hertford, ii. 261. Banks' Baronies in Fee, i. 371. Banks' Dormant and Extinct Baronage, i. 397. The Genealogist, New Series, xvii. 244. *See* DE PLAIZ, PLACE.

PLAYSTED. Visitation of Sussex, 1570, printed by Sir T. Phillipps, (Middle Hill, fol.) 9.

PLAYTER, or PLAYTERS. Gentleman's Magazine, 1833, i. 125 ; 1834, i. 276. Suckling's History of Suffolk, i. 86. Page's History of Suffolk, 365. Wotton's English Baronetage, i. 541. Metcalfe's Visitations of Suffolk, 56, 158. Burke's Extinct Baronetcies. The Genealogist, New Series, i. 243 ; iii. 117.

PLEASANCE. Metcalfe's Visitations of Suffolk, 99, 158.

PLECY, or PLESEY. Manning and Bray's Surrey, ii. 638. Berry's Surrey Genealogies, 56. Hutchins' Dorset, iii. 166, 579. The Genealogist, New Series, xii. 34. Harleian Society, xliii. 7.

PLEDGERD. Cambridgeshire Visitation, edited by Sir T. Phillipps, 25. Harleian Society, xli. 99.

PLESLEY. Foster's Visitations of Yorkshire, 73.

PLESSINGTON, or PLESYNGTON. Harleian Society, iii. 29, 35. Chetham Society, lxxxi. 61 ; lxxxii. 75 ; cv. 232, 236. Plantagenet-Harrison's History of Yorkshire, i. 249. Wright's History of Rutland, 29. The Genealogist, New Series, x. 35. Ilkley, Ancient and Modern, by R. Collyer and J. H. Turner, 62. *See* DE PLESINGTON.

PLESSITIS, PLESSIS, or PLESSY. Hoare's Wiltshire, III. v. 12. Hodgson's Northumberland, II. ii. 295. Banks' Dormant and Extinct Baronage, i. 397. *See* DE PLESSETIS.

PLEYDELL. Rudder's Gloucestershire, 229. Burke's Authorized Arms, 21. Ashmole's Antiquities of Berkshire, iii. 319. Bibliotheca Topographica Britannica, iv. Part i. 2. Burke's Landed Gentry, 2 add., 3, 4, 5, 6, 7, 8. Visitatio Comitatus Wiltoniæ, 1623, printed by Sir T. Phillipps. Hutchins' Dorset, i. 198. Wotton's English Baronetage, iv. 235. Visitation of Wiltshire, edited by G. W. Marshall, 100. Burke's Extinct Baronetcies. Visitation of Gloucester, edited by T. F. Fenwick and W. C. Metcalfe, 134. Harleian Society, xxi. 124. The Genealogist, New Series, ii. 76 ; xii. 236.

PLIMLEY. A Royal Descent, by T. E. Sharpe, (London, 1875, 4to.) 37.

PLOMER. Burke's Extinct Baronetcies. Berry's Hertfordshire Genealogies, 198. Topographer and Genealogist, ii. 278. Burke's Landed Gentry, 2 corr. Clutterbuck's Hertford, iii. 550. Baker's Northampton, i. 460. The Genealogist, vi. 75. Harleian Society, xix. 189 ; xxii. 83, 157. *See* PLUMER.

PLOMER-CLARKE. Baker's Northampton, i. 460.

PLOMSTED. Harleian Society, xxxii. 223.

PLOT, or PLOTT. Noble's History of the College of Arms, 326. Erdeswicke's Survey of Staffordshire, liii. Ashmole's Antiquities of Berkshire, iii. 285. The Genealogist, New Series, ii. 76.

PLOWDEN. Records of the Plowden Family. By B. M. P. *No place*, 1887, 4to. Visitation of Oxfordshire, 1634, printed by Sir T. Phillipps, (Middle Hill, fol.) 28. Burke's Commoners, iii. 250, Landed Gentry, 2, 3, 4, 5, 6, 7, 8. Harleian Society, v. 277. Burke's Visitation of Seats and Arms, 2nd Series, i. 6. Baker's Northampton, i. 470. Foley's Records of the English Province S. J., iv. 537, 671. Notes and Queries, 1 S. iv. 58, 165, 319. The Genealogist, New Series, ix. 207. E. J. Climenson's History of Shiplake, 290.

PLUCKLEY. Archæologia Cantiana, xv. 25.

PLUGENET. Topographer and Genealogist, i. 30. Banks' Dormant and Extinct Baronage, i. 400.

PLUMBE. Burke's Commoners, i. 292. Harleian Society, ii. 121. Nichols' History of the County of Leicester, iv. 484. Howard's Visitation of England and Wales, Notes, ii. 1.

PLUMBE-TEMPEST. Burke's Commoners, i. 288, Landed Gentry, 2, 3, 4, 5. Baines' History of the Co. of Lancaster, iv. 230.

PLUME. Wright's Essex, i. 526. Bysshe's Visitation of Essex, edited by J. J. Howard, 72.

PLUMER. Berry's Hertfordshire Genealogies, 198. Clutterbuck's Hertford, iii. 171, Howard's Visitation of England and Wales, i. 218 ; Notes, iii. 67. Harleian Society, xxxix. 943. Burke's Family Records, 484. *See* PLOMER.

PLUMER-WARD. Burke's Commoners, i. 71, Landed Gentry, 2.

PLUMLEIGH. Tuckett's Devonshire Pedigrees, 109. Harleian Society, vi. 211 ; ix. 171. Maclean's History of Trigg Minor, ii. 533. The Visitations of Cornwall, edited by J. L. Vivian, 371. The Visitations of Devon, by J. L. Vivian, 595.

PLUMME. Morant's Essex, ii. 300. Harleian Society, xiii. 470.

PLUMMER. Burke's Landed Gentry, 2 supp., 3, 4, 5, 6, 7, 8.

PLUMPTON. Camden Society, iv., ix. Glover's History of Derbyshire, ii. 392, (359). Surtees Society, xxxvi. 190 ; xli. 55. Foster's Yorkshire Pedigrees. Foster's Visitations of Yorkshire, 386. Harleian Society, iv. 171 ; xvi. 252. Bridges' Northamptonshire, by Rev. Peter Whalley, i. 254. Whitaker's Deanery of Craven, 154, (215). Clutterbuck's Hertford, ii. 424. Baker's Northampton, ii. 96. Thoroton's Nottinghamshire, i. 153. The Genealogist, vi. 76. Ilkley, Ancient and Modern, by R. Collyer and J. H. Turner, 116, 122.

PLUMPTRE, or PLUMPTREE. Hasted's Kent, iii. 710. Berry's Kent Genealogies, 89. Burke's Royal Families, (London, 1851, 8vo.) ii. 127. Burke's Commoners, iii. 73, Landed Gentry, (of Nottingham,) 2, 3, 4, 5, 6, 7, 8 ; (of Goodnestone Park,) 8. Thoroton's Nottinghamshire, ii. 80.

PLUNKETT, or PLUNKET. Harleian Society, viii. 124. Burke's Landed

Gentry, 6, 7, 8. Irish Pedigrees, by John O'Hart, 2nd Series, 95. Archdall's Lodge's Peerage, vi. 160. The Irish Builder, xxxv. 77.

POCHIN. Burke's Commoners, i. 234, Landed Gentry, 2, 3, 4, 5, 6, 7, 8. Harleian Society, ii. 106. Nichols' History of the County of Leicester, iii. 51, 52, 62*. Fletcher's Leicestershire Pedigrees and Royal Descents, 36-42.

POCKLEY. Surtees Society, xxxvi. 15. Poulson's Holderness, i. 240. Harleian Society, xxxix. 1098.

POCKLINGTON. Burke's Landed Gentry, (of Chelsworth,) 5 and supp p. 64, 6 and p. 1596, 7, 8; (of Hagnaby,) 7, 8; 8 at p. 1820. Dickinson's History of Southwell, 2nd edition, 164. Notes and Queries, 2 S. iv. 211.

POCKLINGTON-SENHOUSE. Burke's Commoners, i. 113, Landed Gentry, 2, 3, 4, 5, 6.

POCOCK. Pedigree of Pocock from 1160, lithograph, *circa* 1840, fol. Berry's Berkshire Genealogies, 116-122. History of Hartlepool, by Sir C. Sharp, (1816, 8vo.) 53. Notes and Queries, 2 S. vii. 129.

PODE. Burke's Landed Gentry, 2, 3, 4, 5, 6, 7, 8.

PODYFORD. Maclean's History of Trigg Minor, ii. 503. The Genealogist, xiv. 20.

POE. Burke's Landed Gentry, (of Tipperary and Solsborough,) 4, 5, 6, 7, 8, and 8 supp.; (of Harley Park,) 2 supp., 3, 4, 5, 6, 7; (of Heywood,) 8.

POER, or POHER. Pedigrees of the family of Poher, Poer, etc. Clonmel, *n.d.*, 4to. Baker's Northampton, i. 406, 426. Burke's Royal Families, (London, 1851, 8vo.) i. 200. Burke's Landed Gentry, 2 supp., 3, 4, 5, 6, 7. *See* POWER, LE POER.

POGGE. Thoroton's Nottinghamshire, iii. 286.

POINGDESTRE. J. B. Payne's Armorial of Jersey, 321.

POINTER. The Genealogist, New Series, iii. 101, 232. Harleian Society, xxxii. 224.

POINTINGDON. Westcote's Devonshire, edited by G. Oliver and P. Jones, 547. *See* POYNTINGDON, PONTINGTON.

POINTZ. Morant's Essex, i. 103. Fosbrooke's History of Gloucestershire, ii. 115. Banks' Dormant and Extinct Baronage, i. 401. Visitation of Gloucester, edited by T. F. Fenwick and W. C. Metcalfe, 135. *See* POYNTZ.

POLE. The Beauties of Shute, with a biographical account of the Family of Pole, by D. M. M. Stirling. Exeter, 1834. Morant's Essex, ii. 612. The Visitations of Cornwall, edited by J. L. Vivian, 71. Glover's History of Derbyshire, ii. 356, (323). Visitation of Gloucestershire, 1569, (Middle Hill, 1854, fol.) 11. Burke's Landed Gentry, 2 add. Harleian Society, vi. 212; xxxvii. 343, 348. Clutterbuck's Hertford, iii. 287. Sussex Archæological Collections, xxi. 74. An Historical Survey of Cornwall, by C. S. Gilbert, i. 492. Pilkington's View of Derbyshire, ii. 115. The Life of Reginald Pole, 2nd edn., (London, 1767, 8vo.) i. 1. Liverpool as it was, etc., by Richd. Brooke, 295. Notes and Queries,

1 S. v. 105, 163, 567; vi. 204; 2 S. ix. 29; xi. 77. Betham's
Baronetage, i. 349, app. 26; iv. 235; v. 489. Wotton's English
Baronetage, ii. 124. Banks' Baronies in Fee, i. 320. Banks'
Dormant and Extinct Baronage, ii. 432. Burke's Extinct Baronet-
cies. Minet's account of the Family of Minet, 208. The Visita-
tions of Devon, by J. L. Vivian, 602. *See* CHANDOS-POLE, BOSAN-
QUET, POOLE, DE LA POLE.

POLE-CAREW. Burke's Commoners, i. 557, Landed Gentry, 2, 3, 4, 5.
Howard's Visitation of England and Wales, v. 145.

POLEWART, or POLWARTH. *See* ANSTRUTHER, SCOT.

POLEY. Visitation of Suffolk, edited by J. J. Howard, i. 269-304.
Burke's Landed Gentry, 2, 3, 4, 5, 6, 7, 8. Harleian Society, viii.
120. Page's History of Suffolk, 565. Metcalfe's Visitations of
Suffolk, 57, 58, 99, 159.

POLEYN. · Visitation of Gloucestershire, 1569, (Middle Hill, 1854,
fol.) 8. Harleian Society, xxi. 220.

POLHILL. Topographer and Genealogist, i. 180-193, 577. Hasted's
Kent, i. 316. Berry's Sussex Genealogies, 264-268. Berry's
Kent Genealogies, 334. Burke's Landed Gentry, 2, 3, 4, 5, 6, 7.
Hoare's Wiltshire, IV. ii. 35. Harleian Society, xxxviii. 440;
xlii. 87.

POLIGNAC. Gentleman's Magazine, 1831, i. 7.

POLKINGHORNE, or POLKINHORNE. Harleian Society, ix. 173, 175.
The Visitations of Cornwall, edited by J. L. Vivian, 374.

POLLARD, or POLLARDE. Visitation of Somersetshire, printed by Sir
T. Phillipps, 129. Visitation of Oxfordshire, 1634, printed by Sir
T. Phillipps, (Middle Hill, fol.) 27. Burke's Landed Gentry, (of
Hund Hill,) 5; (of Haynford Hall,) 8 supp.; (of Scarr Hill,) 5,
6, 8. Foster's Visitations of Yorkshire, 188. Harleian Society,
v. 204, 305; vi. 215; ix. 176; xi. 87; xvii. 168. Westcote's
Devonshire, edited by G. Oliver and P. Jones, 493, 552, 553.
Hutchinson's History of Durham, iii. 240. Foster's Account of
Families descended from Francis Fox, 25. An Account of the
Families of Boase, (Exeter, 1876, 4to.) 43. Visitation of Devon,
edited by F. T. Colby, 170. Burke's Extinct Baronetcies. The
Visitations of Cornwall, edited by J. L. Vivian, 372. The Visita-
tions of Devon, by J. L. Vivian, 597.

POLLARD-URQUHART. Burke's Landed Gentry, 2, 3, 4, 5, 6, 7, 8.

POLLEN. Chronicle of the Family of De Havilland. Berry's Hampshire Genealogies, 67. Burke's Commoners, i. 575, Landed Gentry,
2, 3, 4, 5, 6, 7. Betham's Baronetage, iv. 292.

POLLEXFEN. Harleian Society, vi. 216; viii. 419. The Visitations
of Devon, by J. L. Vivian, 600.

POLLEY. Harleian Society, xlii. 87.

POLLOCK. Burke's Landed Gentry, (of Mountainstown,) 3, 4, 5, 6,
7, 8; (of Avening,) 8. Burke's Royal Descents and Pedigrees of
Founders' Kin, 107. Burke's Extinct Baronetcies, 634.

POLLOK. Burke's Landed Gentry, 5, 6, 7, 8. Alexander Nisbet's
Heraldic Plates, 34.

POLSTED. Berry's Sussex Genealogies, 243. Surrey Archæological

Collections, ii. Harleian Society, xvii. 169. Hasted's Kent,
(Hund. of Blackheath, by H. H. Drake,) 247.

POLWHELE. Traditions and Recollections, by Rev. R. Polwhele, 1.
Burke's Royal Families, (London, 1851, 8vo.) i. 10. Burke's
Commoners, i. 424, Landed Gentry, 2, 3, 4, 5, 6, 7, 8. Polwhele's
History of Cornwall, ii. 42. Harleian Society, ix. 172. A
Complete Parochial History of the County of Cornwall, i. 210.
An Historical Survey of Cornwall, by C. S. Gilbert, ii. 239. The
Visitations of Cornwall, edited by J. L. Vivian, 376.

POLY. Memoirs of the Family of Poly, by Antoinette, Baroness de
Poly. Northampton, 1822, 8vo.

POMERAI, POMERAY, or POMEROY. Savage's History of Carhampton,
58. History of Clyst St. George, by Rev. H. T. Ellacombe, 68.
Tuckett's Devonshire Pedigrees, 160. Harleian Society, vi. 216 ;
ix. 177. Maclean's History of Trigg Minor, i. 336. An Historical
Survey of Cornwall, by C. S. Gilbert, i. 459. Archdall's Lodge's
Peerage, vii. 214. Visitation of Devon, edited by F. T. Colby,
171. Banks' Dormant and Extinct Baronage, i. 162. The Visitations of Cornwall, edited by J. L. Vivian, 379-382. Transactions
of the Devonshire Association, xv. 435. The Genealogist, New
Series, xvi. 231. The Visitations of Devon, by J. L. Vivian, 349,
605. New England Register, xliii. 39. The Irish Builder, xxxv.
197.

POMFRET. Hutchins' Dorset, ii. 606. Harleian Society, xx. 77.
Burke's Landed Gentry, 8.

POMPELION. Harleian Society, xliii. 170.

POMPHRETT. Bysshe's Visitation of Essex, edited by J. J. Howard, 72.

PONDER. Suffolk Armorial Families, by J. J. Muskett, 39.

PONSONBY. Burke's Landed Gentry, (of Hale,) 2, 3, 4, 5, 6, 7, 8 ;
(of Inchiquin,) Landed Gentry, 5, 6, 7, 8 ; (of Kilcooly Abbey,)
7, 8. Jefferson's History of Allerdale Ward, Cumberland, 435.
Charles Smith's History of Kerry, 60. Edmondson's Baronagium
Genealogicum, v. 448. Archdall's Lodge's Peerage, ii. 269.
Brydges' Collins' Peerage, vii. 258 ; ix. 343. Foster's Visitations
of Cumberland and Westmorland, 103.

PONSONBY-BARKER. Burke's Landed Gentry, 5, 6.

PONTDELARCH. Herald and Genealogist, v. 140.

PONTESBURY. Harleian Society, xxix. 403.

PONTIFEX. Burke's Family Records, 485.

PONTINGTON. Visitation of Devon, edited by F. T. Colby, 173. The
Visitations of Devon, by J. L. Vivian, 596. *See* POINTINGDON.

PONYNGES. Collectanea Topographica et Genealogica, iii. 250.

POOL, or POOLE. Dwnn's Visitations of Wales, ii. 102. Berry's
Hampshire Genealogies, 168. Burke's Landed Gentry, 2, 3, 4, 5,
6, 7, 8. Foster's Visitations of Yorkshire, 351. Harleian Society,
iv. 27, 139 ; xvii. 170 ; xviii. 191 ; xix. 64 ; xxi. 125 ; xxxvii.
144. Visitation of Derbyshire, 1663-4, (Middle Hill, 1854, fol.) 6.
Thoresby's Ducatus Leodiensis, 74. The Genealogist, iii. 12 ;
New Series, viii. 65, 66. Ormerod's Cheshire, ii. 423. Fosbrooke's
History of Gloucestershire, i. 361. Boothroyd's History of Ponte-

fract, 259. Bigland's Gloucestershire, ii. par, Saperton. Wotton's English Baronetage, iii. 635. Betham's Baronetage, i. app. 22 ; iii. 23 ; v. 453*. Burke's Extinct Baronetcies. Visitation of Gloucester, edited by T. F. Fenwick and W. C. Metcalfe, 136. Bysshe's Visitation of Essex, edited by J. J. Howard, 72. Sepulchral Memorials of Bobbingworth, 49. Howard's Visitation of England and Wales, v. 83. History of Ditchling, by Henry Cheal, *at end*. Lancashire and Cheshire Historic·Society, New Series, xvi. 165-216.

POOLER. Burke's Landed Gentry, 5, 6, 7, 8.

POOLEY. Cambridgeshire Visitation, edited by Sir T. Phillipps, 25. Foster's Collectanea Genealogica, i. 31. Harvey's Hundred of Willey, 8. Harleian Society, xix. 190 ; xli. 94.

POORE. Pedigrees of Poore of Rushall, and of Poore of Amesbury, (fol. page,) by Sir T. Phillipps, Bart., Middle Hill. Visitatio Comitatus Wiltoniæ, 1623, printed by Sir T. Phillipps. Betham's Baronetage, iv. 306. Visitation of Wiltshire, edited by G. W. Marshall, 9.

POPE. Account of the Township of Church Enstone, by Rev. Edw. Marshall, 29. Croke's History of the Family of Croke, No. 17. Berry's Sussex Genealogies, 365. Pope, his Descent and Family Connections, by Joseph Hunter. London, 1857, 8vo. Sir T. Phillipps' Topographer, No. 1, (March, 1821, 8vo.) 29. Berry's Kent Genealogies, 435. Visitation of Oxfordshire, 1574, printed by Sir T. Phillipps, (Middle Hill, fol.) 8. Visitation of Oxfordshire, 1634, printed by Sir T. Phillipps, (Middle Hill, fol.) 28. Harleian Society, v. 151 ; xx. 77 ; xxix. 404. Baker's Northampton, i. 707. History of the Colleges and Halls of Oxford, by Anthony à Wood, edited by John Gutch, 532. Notes and Queries, 2 S. viii. 378, 441. Burke's Extinct Baronetcies. Topographical Miscellanies, 1792, 4to. (Wroxton). Carthew's Hundred of Launditch, Part iii. 348. New England Register, xlii. 45. *See* TURNER.

POPELAY, or POPELEY. Foster's Visitations of Yorkshire, 335. Hunter's Deanery of Doncaster, ii. 385.

POPHAM. Collinson's Somerset, i. 264 ; ii. 483 ; iii. 71. Berry's Hampshire Genealogies, 181, 197. Visitation of Somersetshire, printed by Sir T. Phillipps, 128. Burke's Commoners, (of Littlecote,) ii. 196, Landed Gentry, 2, 3, 4, 5, 6, 7, 8 ; (of Bagborough,) Landed Gentry, 2, 3, 4, 5 ; (of Shanklin,) 4, 5, 6, 7, 8 ; (of Trevarno,) 2, 3, 4, 5. Harleian Society, vi. 217 ; viii. 8 ; xi. 87, 124. J. H. Hill's History of Market Harborough, 47. Burke's Royal Descents and Pedigrees of Founders' Kin, 127. Nichols' History of the County of Leicester, ii. 445*. Hoare's Wiltshire, V. i. 21. Weaver's Visitations of Somerset, 62. Genealogies of Morgan and Glamorgan, by G. T. Clark, 424. Wadham College, Oxford, by T. G. Jackson, 26. The Visitations of Devon, by J. L. Vivian, 610. Healey's History of Part of West Somerset, 268.

POPKIN. Glamorganshire Pedigrees, edited by Sir T. Phillipps, 36.

T. Nicholas' County Families of Wales, 951. Miscellanea Genealogica et Heraldica, 2nd Series, iv. 272.

POPLE, or POPPLE. Notes and Queries, 4 S. vi. 198, 222. The Genealogist, New Series, xii. 236.

POPPLEWELL. Stonehouse's History of the Isle of Axholme, 344. Read's History of the Isle of Axholme, edited by T. C. Fletcher, 64.

PORCH. Burke's Commoners, ii. 694, Landed Gentry, 2, 3, 4, 5, 6, 7, 8. *See* REEVES.

PORCHER. Burke's Landed Gentry, 2, 3, 4, 5.

PORDAGE. Hasted's Kent, ii. 594. Foley's Records of the English Province S. J., v. 566. The Genealogist, vi. 76.

PORMONT. The Genealogist, iv. 266 ; vi. 276.

PORT. History of Repton, by Robert Bigsby, 103. Bibliotheca Topographica Britannica, i. Part i. 7. Banks' Dormant and Extinct Baronage, i. 164. Visitations of Staffordshire, 1614 and 1663-4, William Salt Society, 243. The Genealogist, New Series, xvi. 1.

PORTAL. The Portal Family. London, 1863, 4to. Burke's Landed Gentry, 2, 3, 4, 5, 6, 7, 8.

PORTE. Harleian Society, ii. 48. Visitation of Staffordshire, 1663-4, printed by Sir T. Phillipps, 8.

PORTEOUS. Burke's Landed Gentry, 6, 7, 8.

PORTER. Pedigree of Porter of Aston Subedge, etc. [T. P.] 1866, folio page. Pedigree of Porter of Broadway, [T. P.] folio page. Hasted's Kent, ii. 376. Berry's Sussex Genealogies, 200. Dwnn's Visitations of Wales, i. 297. Berry's Kent Genealogies, 321. Visitation of Durham, 1575, (Newcastle, 1820, fol.) 39. Visitation of Durham, 1615, (Sunderland, 1820, fol.) 45. Burke's Commoners, (of Alfarthing,) iii. 577; (of Kilkerry,) Landed Gentry, 3, 4, 5, 6, 7, 8 ; (of Black Hall,) 6 supp., 7. Harleian Society, vii. 35 ; viii. 401; ix. 178; xii. 99, 117; xiii. 471; xvi. 254; xvii. 170 ; xxi. 126 ; xlii. 155. Hutchinson's History of Cumberland, ii. 300. Maclean's History of Trigg Minor, ii. 554. Turnor's History of the Town and Soke of Grantham, 99. Chetham Society, lxxxviii. 234. Surtees' Durham, ii. 231. Fosbrooke's History of Gloucestershire, i. 249. An Historical Survey of Cornwall, by C. S. Gilbert, ii. 240. The Genealogist, iv. 266 ; vii. 188. Visitation of Devon, edited by F. T. Colby, 2. Metcalfe's Visitation of Worcester, 1683, 77. The Visitations of Cornwall, edited by J. L. Vivian, 383, 384. Howard's Visitation of England and Wales, i. 158 ; Notes, iii. 36. Miscellanea Genealogica et Heraldica, 2nd Series, v. 169. Weaver's Visitations of Somerset, 125. Foster's Visitations of Durham, 261. Visitations of Staffordshire, 1614 and 1663-4, William Salt Society, 244. Bysshe's Visitation of Essex, edited by J. J. Howard, 73. Foster's Visitations of Cumberland and Westmorland, 107, 108. New England Register, ix. 54. Life and Letters of Endymion Porter, by Dorothea Townshend, 11.

PORTERFIELD. Paterson's History of the Co. of Ayr, ii. 51. Paterson's History of Ayr and Wigton, iii. 235. Crawfurd's Renfrewshire, 62, 402.

PORTINGTON. Surtees Society, xxxvi. 120, 168. Foster's Yorkshire Pedigrees. Foster's Visitations of Yorkshire, 561. Thoresby's Ducatus Leodiensis, 99. Hunter's Deanery of Doncaster, i. 214. The Genealogist, vi. 276.

PORTLAND (Earl of). Morant's Essex, ii. 71.

PORTMAN. Collinson's Somerset, i. 62 ; iii. 274, 283. Visitation of Somersetshire, printed by Sir T. Phillipps, 129. Burke's Royal Families, (London, 1851, 8vo.) ii. 143. Burke's Commoners, i. 62. Harleian Society, xi. 126. Blore's Rutland, 211. Hutchins' Dorset, i. 253. Burke's Extinct Baronetcies. Metcalfe's Visitation of Worcester, 1683, 78. Weaver's Visitations of Somerset, 63. Thomas Smith's Historical Account of St. Marylebone, 39.

PORTQUIN. Maclean's History of Trigg Minor, i. 578.

PORTREY. The Genealogies of Morgan and Glamorgan, by G. T. Clark, 501.

PORTSMOUTH (Earl of). Nichols' Illustrations of Literary History, iv. 38.

POST. Berry's Kent Genealogies, 20.

POSTLETHWAITE. Burke's Landed Gentry, 4, 5.

POTE. Harleian Society, vi. 217. The Visitations of Devon, by J. L. Vivian, 611.

POTICARY. Kite's Monumental Brasses of Wiltshire 76.

POTKIN, or POTKYN. Cambridgeshire Visitation, edited by Sir T. Phillipps, 26. Harleian Society, xvii. 172 ; xxii. 158; xli. 119.

POTT. Burke's Landed Gentry, (of Todrig,) 2, 3, 4, 5, 6, 7, 8 ; (of Bentham Hill,) 2, 4, 5. Harleian Society, xvii. 173 ; xl. 1238. Earwaker's East Cheshire, ii. 324. The Genealogist, New Series, viii. 67. Hasted's Kent, (Hund. of Blackheath, by H. H. Drake,) 204.

POTTENGER, or POTTINGER. Burke's Commoners, iv. 442. Burke's Royal Descents and Pedigrees of Founders' Kin, 37. The Genealogist, vi. 77.

POTTER. Glover's History of Derbyshire, ii. 391, (358). Harleian Society, vi. 218 ; xxxviii. 713 ; xxxix. 1047. Burton's History of Hemingborough, 116. New England Register, xxiii. 61. The Visitations of Devon, by J. L. Vivian, 612.

POTTS. Blomefield's Norfolk, vi. 464. Burke's Extinct Baronetcies. Burke's Landed Gentry, 7, 8.

POULETT. Collinson's Somerset, ii. 166; iii. 74. Harleian Society, xi. 88. J. B. Payne's Armorial of Jersey, 81. Edmondson's Baronagium Genealogicum, ii. 180. Brydges' Collins' Peerage, iv. 1. Family Notes, by J. M. Browne, 49.

POULTENEY, or POULTNEY. Burton's Description of Leicestershire, 174. Nichols' History of the County of Leicester, iv. 319. Clutterbuck's Hertford, i. 474. Harleian Society, ii. 70; viii. 60. Wilson's History of the Parish of St. Laurence Poultney, 222. Chauncy's Hertfordshire, 535. *See* PULTENEY.

POULTON. Foley's Records of the English Province S. J., i. 155 ; iv.

676.   Metcalfe's Visitations of Northamptonshire, 191.   Annals of the English Benedictines of Ghent, 182.   Gloucestershire Notes and Queries, vi. 5, 69.   *See* PULTON.

POUNCETT. Morant's Essex, i. 5.   Harleian Society, xiii. 90 ; xliii. 62.

POUNDE. Morant's Essex, i. 254.   Berry's Hampshire Genealogies, 194.

POUNDEN. Burke's Landed Gentry, 3, 4, 5, 6, 7, 8.

POUNT. The Genealogist, vi. 77.

POUTRELL. Thoroton's Nottinghamshire, i. 31, 66.   The Genealogist, New Series, ix. 12.   *See* POWTRELL.

POVERE. F. G. Lee's History of Thame, 348.

POWEL, or POWELL. Dwnn's Visitations of Wales, i. 126, 186, 223, 239, 260, 264, 280, 288, 306, 331; ii. 311, 356, 361.   Glamorganshire Pedigrees, edited by Sir T. Phillipps, 20, 35, 37, 43, 45, 50. Jones' History of the County of Brecknock, ii. 180, 379, 524, 550, 585, 687.   History of the Wilmer Family, 265.   Case of John Kynaston Powell, showing his right to the Barony of Powes, fol., pp. 7.   Hasted's Kent, ii. 398.   Gentleman's Magazine, lxxxv. i. 23 ; 1841, i. 487.   Berry's Sussex Genealogies, 243, 324.   Visitation of Middlesex, (Salisbury, 1820, fol.) 31, 42.   Glamorganshire Pedigrees, edited by Sir T. Phillipps, 16, 45.   Visitation of Oxfordshire, 1634, printed by Sir T. Phillipps, (Middle Hill, fol.) 28. Burke's Commoners, iii. 177 ; (of Nant Eos,) Commoners, i. 230, Landed Gentry, 2, 3, 4, 5, 6, 7, 8 ; (of Brandlesome Hall,) Commoners, iii. 572, Landed Gentry, 2, 3, 4, 5, 6 ; (of Hurdcott House,) Commoners, i. 375, Landed Gentry, 2, 3, 4, 5, 6, 7, 8 ; (of Clonshavoy,) Landed Gentry, 2 supp., 3, 4, 5, 6, 7 ; (of Bellingham Lodge,) 3, 4, 5 ; (of Banlahan,) 5 supp., 6, 7, 8 ; (of Ynysmendny,) 8 ; (of Castle Madoc,) 7, 8 ; (of Brooklands,) 7, 8 ; (of Clapton House,) 8 ; (of Maesgwynne,) 5, 6, 7, 8 ; (of Horton,) 5, 6, 7.   Foster's Lancashire Pedigrees.   Burke's Royal Families, (London, 1851, 8vo.) i. 32 ; ii. 128.   Miscellanea Genealogica et Heraldica, New Series, i. 23.   Harleian Society, v. 287 ; viii. 403, 410 ; xvii. 174 ; xxii. 83 ; xxix. 405 ; xliii. 143.   Nichols' History of the County of Leicester, ii. 85.   Cardiganshire Pedigrees, 108.   Pembrokeshire Pedigrees, 149.   Gyll's History of Wraysbury, 86, 128.   Caermarthenshire Pedigrees, 31, 39, 52.   Hoare's Wiltshire, IV. i. 101.   Meyrick's History of the Co. of Cardigan, 198, 403.   Archæologia Cambrensis, 4 S. vii. 25, 27.   T. Nicholas' County Families of Wales, 206.   Surrey Archæological Collections, vii.   Ormerod's Cheshire, ii. 461.   The Sheriffs of Montgomeryshire, by W. V. Lloyd, 46, 81.   Wotton's English Baronetage, iii. 282.   Burke's Extinct Baronetcies.   History of Powys Fadog, by J. Y. W. Lloyd, ii. 340 ; iii. 104, 253, 338, 405 ; v. 358.   The Pedigree of the Family of Powell, by Edgar Powell.   London, 1891, 4to.   Foster's Visitation of Middlesex, 53, 78.   Genealogies of Morgan and Glamorgan, by G. T. Clark, 160, 181, 229, 264. Burke's Colonial Gentry, ii. 634.   Notes and Queries, 8 S. x. 293. Ontarian Families, by E. M. Chadwick, i. 30.   Muskett's Suffolk Manorial Families, i. 132.   The Genealogist, New Series, xiv.

141. Transactions of Shropshire Archæological Society, N. S., v. 184.

POWELL - COTTON. Howard's Visitation of England and Wales, ix. 60.

POWER. Sir T. Phillipps' Topographer, No. 1, (March, 1821, 8vo.) 43. Visitation of Oxfordshire, 1574, printed by Sir T. Phillipps, (Middle Hill, fol.) 8. Burke's Landed Gentry, (of Faithlegg,) 4, 5, 6, 7, 8; (of Gurteen,) 4, 5, 6, 7, 8; (of the Hill Court,) 2, 3, 4, 5, 6, 7, 8; (of Snow Hill,) 5, 6, 7; (of Bellevue,) 6, 7. Harleian Society, iv. 176; v. 209, 210. Topographical Collections of John Aubrey, edited by J. E. Jackson, 290. Thoresby's Ducatus Leodiensis, 260. Nichols' History of the County of Leicester, iv. 517, 848*. O'Hart's Irish Pedigrees, 2nd Series, 345. Duncumb's Hereford, (J. H. Cooke,) iii. 190. History of Powys Fadog, by J. Y. W. Lloyd, iii. 25. The Genealogical Magazine, i. 140, 207, 270. See POER.

POWER-LALOR. Burke's Landed Gentry, 3, 4, 5, 7, 8.

POWERSCOURT (Viscount). Howard's Visitation of Ireland, i. 57.

POWIS. Claim of Edwd. James, Earl Powis, to Vote at Elections of Irish Peers, 1861, folio, pp. 12. Harleian Society, viii. 403, 506. See POWYS.

POWLE. Harleian Society, viii. 31. The Genealogist, vi. 78.

POWLET, or POWLETT. Jacob's Peerage, 191, 194. Berry's Berkshire Genealogies, 138. Harleian Society, vi. 142; xvii. 175. Collectanea Topographica et Genealogica, v. 256. Brydges' Collins' Peerage, ii. 367. The Genealogist, New Series, iii. 168. See PAWLET.

POWLTER. Harleian Society, xiv. 597.

POWNALL. Burke's Commoners, (of Pownall,) iv. 17, Landed Gentry, 2; (of Woodlands Lodge,) Landed Gentry, 5.

POWNEY. History of the Hundred of Bray, by Charles Kerry, 148. Burke's Landed Gentry, 7, 8.

POWTRELL. Visitation of Derbyshire, 1663-4, (Middle Hill, 1854, fol.) 6. The Genealogist, iii. 12; New Series, viii. 67. See POUTRELL.

POWYS (Princes of). Collectanea Archæologica, (Brit. Arch. Assn.) i. 79, 182. History of Powys Fadog, by J. Y. W. Lloyd, i. 109, 306.

POWYS. The Feudal Barons of Powis, by M. C. Jones. London, 1868, 8vo. Dwnn's Visitations of Wales, ii. 234. Burke's Royal Families, (London, 1851, 8vo.) ii. 192. Burke's Landed Gentry, (of Berwick,) 2, 3, 4; (of Westwood,) 2, 3, 4, 5. Herald and Genealogist, vi. 97. Collections by the Powys-land Club, i. 1, 257-423. Brydges' Collins' Peerage, viii. 577. History of Powys Fadog, by J. Y. W. Lloyd, iii. 381. Burke's Colonial Gentry, ii. 630. See POWIS.

POWYS-KECK. Burke's Landed Gentry, 2, 3, 4, 5, 6, 7, 8.

POWYS-LYBBE. Burke's Landed Gentry, 2, 3, 4, 5, 6, 7, 8.

POYLE. Harleian Society, ix. 180. The Visitations of Cornwall, edited by J. L. Vivian, 386. See DE LA POYLE.

POYNER. Clutterbuck's Hertford, ii. 307. Harleian Society, xxix. 407.

POYNINGS. Hasted's Kent, i. 131 ; ii. 385, 386. Bibliotheca Topographica Britannica, i., Part vi. 464. Blore's Rutland, 163. Manning and Bray's Surrey, iii. 117. Sussex Archæological Collections, xv. 14. Castles, Mansions, and Manors of Western Sussex, by D. G. C. Elwes and C. J. Robinson, 42. Harleian Society, xvi. 244. Topographical Miscellanies, 1792, 4to., (Boxgrove). Banks' Baronies in Fee, i. 374. Banks' Dormant and Extinct Baronage, ii. 436.

POYNTELL. History of Chislehurst, by Webb, Miller, and Beckwith, 261.

POYNTINGDON. Tuckett's Devonshire Pedigrees, 31. Harleian Society, vi. 219. See POINTINGTON.

POYNTON. Miscellanea Genealogica et Heraldica, New Series, ii. 78. Harleian Society, xii. 121.

POYNTZ. Rudder's Gloucestershire, 214. Collinson's Somerset, i. 33. Fosbrooke's Abstracts of Smith's Lives of the Berkeleys, 75. Morant's Essex, ii. 471. Berry's Sussex Genealogies, 352, 356. Sir T. Phillipps' Topographer, No. 1, (March, 1821, 8vo.) 45. Burke's Commoners, iii. 537. More about Stifford, by Wm. Palin, 127. Harleian Society, viii. 202. Dallaway's Sussex, i. 284. Weale's Quarterly Papers on Architecture, iii. (Suckling Papers,) 64. Hutchins' Dorset, ii. 834. Clutterbuck's Hertford, iii. 8. Castles, Mansions, and Manors of Western Sussex, by D. G. C. Elwes and C. J. Robinson, 79. Aubrey's Antiquities of Surrey, iv.* 212. Harleian Society, xiii. 91, 267 ; xxi. 128, 130. Blunt's Dursley and its Neighbourhood, 116. Banks' Baronies in Fee, i. 373. Miscellanea Genealogica et Heraldica, 2nd Series, iii. 326. The Genealogist, New Series, xiv. 252 ; xvii. 21. See POINTZ.

POYSER. Burke's Family Records, 487.

PRAED. Berry's Buckinghamshire Genealogies, 28. Burke's Commoners, iv. 290. Lipscombe's History of the County of Buckingham, iv. 378. A Complete Parochial History of the County of Cornwall, iii. 101. An Historical Survey of Cornwall, by C. S. Gilbert, ii. 241.

PRAERS. Ormerod's Cheshire, iii. 301, 359. Harleian Society, xxviii. 73. The Genealogist, New Series, xv. 220. See PRAYERS.

PRANELL. Harleian Society, xxii. 159.

PRATER. Visitatio Comitatus Wiltoniæ, 1623, printed by Sir T. Phillipps. Somersetshire Wills, printed for F. A. Crisp, ii. 47. The Genealogist, New Series, xii. 237.

PRATT. Blomefield's Norfolk, vii. 395. Hasted's Kent, i. 337 ; ii. 379. Visitation of Norfolk, published by Norfolk Archæological Society, i. 208. Camden Society, xliii. 37. Bibliotheca Topographica Britannica, iv. Part i. 2. Burke's Commoners, (of Ryston,) i. 231, Landed Gentry, 2, 3, 4, 5, 6, 7, 8 ; (of Cabra Castle,) Commoners, iv. 502, Landed Gentry, 2, 3, 5, 6, 7, 8, and 8 supp. ; (of Tuckhill,) Landed Gentry, 2. Harleian Society, viii. 218 ; xvii. 176 ; xxxii. 224. Burke's Royal Descents and Pedi-

grees of Founders' Kin, 92. Nichols' History of the County of
Leicester, iv. 152. Norfolk Archæology, ii. 142. Notes and
Queries, 2 S. viii. 11, 137. Burke's Extinct Baronetcies. Ed-
mondson's Baronagium Genealogicum, v. 500. Brydges' Collins'
Peerage, v. 264. Metcalfe's Visitations of Suffolk, 100. The
Genealogist, vi. 79. Burke's Family Records, 489. History of
Chislehurst, by Webb, Miller, and Beckwith, 77.

PRAYERS. Bridges' Northamptonshire, by Rev. Peter Whalley, ii.
197. The Genealogist, New Series, xvi. 88. *See* PRAERS, DE
,PRAYERS.

PREAUX. The Genealogical Magazine, i. 543 ; ii. 83. *See* PRIAULX.

PREBLE. New England Register, xxii. 311, 404 ; xxiv. 253.

PREECE. Antiquities and Memoirs of the Parish of Myddle, written
by Richard Gough, 1700, (folio,) 35.

PREES. Glamorganshire Pedigrees, edited by Sir T. Phillipps, 18,
19, 43. Genealogies of Morgan and Glamorgan, by G. T. Clark,
501.

PRENDERGAST. Burke's Extinct Baronetcies, 613. Notes and
Queries, 8 S. ix. 341. Burke's Colonial Gentry, iii. 773.

PRENELL. Harleian Society, xxix. 409.

PRENTALL. The Ancestor, No. 1, 271.

PRENTICE, PRENTIS, or PRENTYS. Visitation of Norfolk, published
by Norfolk Archæological Society, i. 260. Harleian Society, xiv.
598 ; xxxii. 225. Howard's Visitation of England and Wales, i.
148. New England Register, vi. 273 ; vii. 74.

PRESCOTT-DECIE. Burke's Landed Gentry, 8.

PRESCOTT, or PRESCOT. Morant's Essex, ii. 46. Jewitt's Reliquary,
vii. 28. Berry's Hertfordshire Genealogies, 104. Harleian
Society, viii. 3, 68 ; xiii. 473 ; xvii. 176. History of Darlington,
by W. Hylton Dyer Longstaffe. Surtees' Durham, iii. 370.
Cussan's History of Hertfordshire, Parts ix. and x. 210. J. P.
Earwaker's East Cheshire, i. 195. Betham's Baronetage, iv. 262.
The Suffolk Records, by H. W. Aldred, 166. Bysshe's Visitation
of Essex, edited by J. J. Howard, 73. Phillimore's London and
Middlesex Note-Book, 208. Burke's Family Records, 493.

PRESTLAND. Ormerod's Cheshire, ii. 289. Harleian Society, xviii.
193 ; xxix. 426.

PRESTLEY. Clutterbuck's Hertford, ii. 129.

PRESTON. Memoirs of W. M. Peyton, by J. L. Peyton, (London,
1872,) 355-374. Memorial to his Grace Bernard Edward, Duke
of Norfolk, etc., viz., the Memorial of Richard Rushton Preston,
1841, 8vo., pp. 37. Visitation of Durham, 1575, (Newcastle,
1820, fol.) 21. Visitation of Somerset, printed by Sir T. Phillipps,
129. Topographer and Genealogist, ii. 471. Burke's Commoners,
(of Westerby House,) i. 478 ; (of Flasby Hall,) Landed Gentry,
2, 3, 4, 5, 6, 7, 8 ; (of Moreby,) 2, 3, 4, 5, 6, 7, 8 ; (of Bellinter,)
3, 4, 5, 6, 7 ; (of Cockerham,) 2 ; (of Askham Bryan,) 5, 6, 7, 8 ;
(of Swainston,) 5, 6, 7, 8 ; (of Dalby Park,) 5, 6, 7, 8 ; (of Valley-
field,) 5, 6, 7, 8 ; (of Burythorpe House,) 8. Foster's Yorkshire
Pedigrees. Harleian Society, vi. 221 ; viii. 448 ; xi. 88 ; xvii.

177; xxii. 84; xxxix. 956. Chetham Society, lxxxii. 25, 56, 60; lxxxviii. 235-237. Westcote's Devonshire, edited by G. Oliver and P. Jones, 588. Corry's History of Lancashire, i. 427. Clutterbuck's Hertford, i. 99. Baker's Northampton, i. 184. Baines' History of the Co. of Lancaster, iv. 658. Douglas's Baronage of Scotland, 91. Peter Chalmers' History of Dunfermline, ii. *at end.* Whitaker's Deanery of Craven, 3rd edn., 242. Walter Wood's East Neuk of Fife, 286. Wood's Douglas's Peerage of Scotland, i. 413. Betham's Dignities, Feudal and Parliamentary, 374. Visitation of Devon, edited by F. T. Colby, 173. Burke's Extinct Baronetcies, and 635. Foster's Visitations of Durham, 263. Howard's Visitation of England and Wales, Notes, i. 64. The Visitations of Devon, by J. L. Vivian, 613. Nicolson and Burn's Westmorland and Cumberland, i. 212, 239.

PRESTWICH, or PRESTWICHE. Harleian Society, ii. 63. J. H. Hill's History of Market Harborough, 145. Nichols' History of the County of Leicester, ii. 698. Chetham Society, lxxxi. 6; lxxxii. 41. Baines's History of the Co. of Lancaster, ii. 393; Croston's edn., ii. 230, 370. Burke's Extinct Baronetcies, and supp. Harleian Society, xvii. 178.

PRESTWOOD, or PRESTWOODE. Tuckett's Devonshire Pedigrees, 112. Harleian Society, vi. 222. Westcote's Devonshire, edited by G. Oliver and P. Jones, 545. Burke's Commoners, iii. 569. Visitation of Devon, edited by F. T. Colby, 174. The Visitations of Devon, by J. L. Vivian, 615.

PRETHEROE. Carthew's Hundred of Launditch, Part iii. 234.

PRETTY, or PRETYE. Jewitt's Reliquary, xii. 124. Metcalfe's Visitations of Suffolk, 159.

PRETYMAN. Harleian Society, viii. 113. Metcalfe's Visitations of Suffolk, 203. Burke's Extinct Baronetcies, 635. Burke's Landed Gentry, 7, 8.

PRIAULX. Visitation of Wiltshire, 1677, printed by Sir T. Phillipps, (Middle Hill, 1854, fol.). Miscellanea Genealogica et Heraldica, 3rd Series, ii. 81. *See* PREAUX.

PRICE, or PRISE. Pedigree of Price of Broadway, etc., [T. P.] 1863, folio page. Poetical Works of Lewis Glyn Cothi, (Oxford, 1837,) 237. Dwnn's Visitations of Wales, i. 283. Berry's Berkshire Genealogies, 99-102. Glamorganshire Pedigrees, edited by Sir T. Phillipps, 12, 22, 32, 38. Burke's Royal Families, (London, 1851, 8vo.) i. 87; ii. 111. Burke's Commoners, (of Castle Madoc,) iii. 176, Landed Gentry, 2, 3, 4, 5; (of Glangwilly,) Landed Gentry, 2, 3, 4, 5, 6; (of Saintfield,) 2, 3, 4, 5, 6, 7, 8; (of Norton, 2, 3, 4, 5; (of Plas Cadnant,) 2, 3, 4, 5, 6, 7, 8; (of Rockfield Park,) 8; (of Broomfield Hall,) 8; (of Tibberton Court,) 8; (of Waterhead House,) 8; (of Triley Court,) 8; (of Birkenhead Priory,) 3; (of Rhiwlas,) 5, 6, 7, 8; 2, p. 517; 8, p. 480. The Wolfe's of Forenaghts, 63. Jones' History of the County of Brecknock, ii. 112, 657. Caermarthenshire Pedigrees, 70. T. Nicholas' County Families of Wales, 300. Ormerod's Cheshire, ii. 461. Nicholls' Account of the Company of Ironmongers, 2nd edn., 597. Harleian

Society, xvii. 179 ; xxi. 136 ; xxxvii. 184 ; xliii. 182. Memoir of Gabriel Goodman, by R. Newcome, app. S. The Sheriffs of Montgomeryshire, by W. V. Lloyd, 3, 46, 130, 144, 148, 190, 238, 323, 469. An Historical Survey of Cornwall, by C. S. Gilbert, i. 579. Collections by the Powys-land Club, ix. 308. Betham's Baronetage, v. 542. Burke's Extinct Baronetcies. Cook's Continuation of Duncumb's Hereford, (Hundred of Grimsworth,) Part ii. 154, 192. History of Powys Fadog, by J. Y. W. Lloyd, iv. 165 ; v. 393. Genealogies of Morgan and Glamorgan, by G. T. Clark, 84, 96, 150, 217. Howard's Visitation of England and Wales, ii. 159 ; vii. 87. *See* APREECE, PARRY-PRICE, PRYCE, PRYS, PRYSE.

PRICHARD, or PRITCHARD. Genealogy of the Descendants of the Prichards, etc., by the Rev. T. G. Smart. Enfield, 1868, 8vo. Memorials of the Prichards of Almeley. By Isabell Southall. Birmingham, 1893, 4to. Herald and Genealogist, ii. 250. Dwnn's Visitations of Wales, i. 38, 240. Glamorganshire Pedigrees, edited by Sir T. Phillipps, 7, 16, 19, 36, 40. Burke's Landed Gentry, 5, 6, 7, 8. Harleian Society, viii. 280. Jones' History of the County of Brecknock, ii. 322. Account of the Mayo and Elton Families, by C. H. Mayo, 26. The Genealogist, New Series, viii. 115. Genealogies of Morgan and Glamorgan, by G. T. Clark, 59, 107, 136, 138, 155. *See* PRITCHARD.

PRICHETT. Robinson's Mansions of Herefordshire, 41.

PRICKART. Dwnn's Visitations of Wales, i. 75.'

PRICKET, or PRICKETT. Surtees Society, xxxvi. 130. Burke's Commoners, iii. 624, Landed Gentry, 2, 3, 4, 5, 6, 7, 8.

PRICKLEY. Pedigree of Prickley of Prickley, etc., [T. P.] folio page. Harleian Society, xvii. 180 ; xxvii. 106.

PRIDEAUX, PRIDIEULX, or PRYDEAUX. Gentleman's Magazine, 1831, ii. 589. History of Clyst St. George, by Rev. H. T. Ellacombe, 70. Burke's Royal Families, (London, 1851, 8vo.) i. 5. Burke's Commoners, iv. 534, Landed Gentry, 2, 3, 4. Harleian Society, vi. 219, 221, 227, 228. Herald and Genealogist, vi. 341. Maclean's History of Trigg Minor, ii. 194-236, 241, 379. Hutchins' Dorset, iv. 528. Westcote's Devonshire, edited by G. Oliver and P. Jones, 470-472, 486. Foster's Account of Families descended from Francis Fox, 17. A Complete Parochial History of the County of Cornwall, iii. 191 ; iv. viii. An Historical Survey of Cornwall, by C. S. Gilbert, i. 542. Notes and Queries, 1 S. iii. 186, 266, 398 ; v. 248. Wotton's English Baronetage, i. 515. Visitation of Devon, edited by F. T. Colby, 175. Betham's Baronetage, i. 254. The Visitations of Cornwall, edited by J. L. Vivian, 218, 610. The Genealogist, New Series, viii. 156. Howard's Visitation of England and Wales, v. 62. The Visitations of Devon, by J. L. Vivian, 616, 618, 624.

PRIDEAUX-BRUNE. Burke's Commoners, i. 203, Landed Gentry, 2, 3, 4, 5, 6, 7, 8. Hutchins' Dorset, iv. 190. A Complete Parochial History of the County of Cornwall, iv. 22. Howard's Visitation of England and Wales, ii. 97.

PRIDHAM. Burke's Heraldic Illustrations, 65.

PRIESTLEY. Burke's Landed Gentry, (of White Windows,) 2, 3 ; (of Boston,) 2, 3. John Watson's History of Halifax, 298. Surtees Society, lxxvii. 1-41. Harleian Society, xxxvii. 9, 81, 94.

PRIM. The Genealogical Magazine, ii. 91.

PRIME. Burke's Landed Gentry, 2, 3, 4, 5, 6, 8. The Genealogist, vi. 138. *See* PRYME.

PRIMROSE. Wood's Douglas's Peerage of Scotland, ii. 401. Alexander Nisbet's Heraldic Plates, 9. Miscellanea Genealogica et Heraldica, 3rd Series, ii. 77.

PRINCE. Pedigree of Prince, [T. P.], 1868, folio page. History of Newenham Abbey, by James Davidson, 215. New England Register, v. 375 ; vi. 234. Harleian Society, xxix. 409 ; xxxviii. 605.

PRINGLE. Memoirs of Walter Pringle of Greenknow, etc., with app. containing account of Families of Gordon and Seton, by Rev. Walter Wood. Edinburgh, 1847. Burke's Landed Gentry, (of Yair,) 2 supp., 3, 4, 5, 6, 7, 8 ; (of Haining,) 2 supp., 3, 4 ; (of Torwoodlee,) 2 supp., 3, 4, 5, 6, 7, 8. Nisbet's Heraldry, ii. app. 71. Douglas's Baronage of Scotland, 208. Notes and Queries, 2 S. xii. 465. Burke's Extinct Baronetcies. Alexander Nisbet's Heraldic Plates, 68.

PRINSEP. Burke's Royal Families, (London, 1851, 8vo.) ii. 4.

PRIOR. Burke's Royal Families, (London, 1851, 8vo.) ii. 196. Burke's Landed Gentry, 2, 3, 4, 5, 6, 7. Howard's Visitation of England and Wales, i. 9. Cussan's History of Hertfordshire, Parts xi. and xii. 40. Burke's Colonial Gentry, i. 49. History of the Wilmer Family, 262. Ilkley, Ancient and Modern, by R. Collyer and J. H. Turner, 220.

PRITCHARD. Burke's Landed Gentry, 8. *See* PRICHARD.

PRITCHARD-RAYNER. Burke's Landed Gentry, 8.

PRITCHETT. Howard's Visitation of England and Wales, i. 197 Miscellanea Genealogica et Heraldica, 2nd Series, v. 90, 103.

PRITT. Burke's Landed Gentry, 8.

PRITTIE. Claim of the Rt. Hon. Henry Prittie, Lord Dunally, to Vote at Elections of Irish Peers, Sess. Papers, N of 1855.

PRIVIAN. Harleian Society, viii. 131.

PROBERT. Dwnn's Visitations of Wales, i. 267.

PROBY. Archdall's Lodge's Peerage, vii. 67. Brydges' Collins' Peerage, ix. 137. Pedigrees of Proby, [T. P.] 1866, 2 folio pages. Burke's Extinct Baronetcies. Harleian Society, xvii. 181. Annals of the Barber Surgeons, by S. Young, 532.

PROBYN. Pedigree of Probyn of Longhope, [T. P.] 1866, folio page. Burke's Landed Gentry, 2, 3, 4, 5, 6, 7, 8. Visitation of Gloucester, edited by T. F. Fenwick and W. C. Metcalfe, 137. Miscellanea Genealogica et Heraldica, 2nd Series, iii. 304.

PROCTER, or PROCTOR. Burke's Commoners, i. 252. The Genealogist, i. 304. Pedigrees from Visitation of Northumberland, printed by Sir T. Phillipps, (Middle Hill, 1858, fol.) 3. Cambridgeshire Visitation, edited by Sir T. Phillips, 26. Lipscombe's

History of the County of Buckingham, iv. 530. Foster's Visitations of Northumberland, 96. Harleian Society, xxxix. 906; xli. 43.

PRODGERS. Burke's Landed Gentry, 2, 3, 4, 5, 6, 7, 8.

PROGER. Glamorganshire Pedigrees, edited by Sir T. Phillipps, 37. Genealogies of Morgan and Glamorgan, by G. T. Clark, 252.

PROSSER. Genealogies of Morgan and Glamorgan, by G. T. Clark, 263.

PROTHERCH. Dwnn's Visitations of Wales, i. 142.

PROTHERO. Burke's Landed Gentry, 2 supp., 3, 4, 5, 6, 7, 8.

PROUDE. Hasted's Kent, ii. 815. Berry's Kent Genealogies, 51. Harleian Society, xlii. 35.

PROUZ. Tuckett's Devonshire Pedigrees, 81. Harleian Society, vi. 223. Westcote's Devonshire, edited by G. Oliver and P. Jones, 568. See PROWSE.

PROVENDER. Visitatio Comitatus Wiltoniæ, 1623, printed by Sir T. Phillipps. Wiltshire Archæological Magazine, xi. 202. Visitation of Wiltshire, edited by G. W. Marshall, 80. The Genealogist, New Series, xii. 237.

PROWER. Miscellanea Genealogica et Heraldica, New Series, ii. 10. Burke's Landed Gentry, 4, 5, 6, 7.

PROWETT. Burke's Landed Gentry, 2 supp.

PROWSE, or PROUSE. Tuckett's Devonshire Pedigrees, 85. Visitation of Somersetshire, printed by Sir T. Phillipps, 129, 148. Harleian Society, i. 49; vi. 223, 224; xi. 89; xxi. 137. Lipscombe's History of the County of Buckingham, iv. 604. Westcote's Devonshire, edited by G. Oliver and P. Jones, 597. Baker's Northampton, ii. 255. Miscellanea Genealogica et Heraldica, New Series, iii. 167. Visitation of Devon, edited by F. T. Colby, 53, 131, 177. Weaver's Visitations of Somerset, 64. The Visitations of Devon, by J. L. Vivian, 626, 627, 628. See PROUZ.

PRUDDERCH. Caermarthenshire Pedigrees, 13.

PRUJEAN. See PRIVIAN.

PRUST. Harleian Society, vi. 225. The Visitations of Devon, by J. L. Vivian, 629.

PRYCE. Dwnn's Visitations of Wales, i. 291, 293, 298, 313-315. Burke's Commoners, (of Gunley,) ii. 654, Landed Gentry, 2, 3, 4, 5, 6 and supp., 7, 8; (of Gogerddan,) Commoners, iii. 466, Landed Gentry, 2, 3, 4; (of Duffryn,) Landed Gentry, 2, 3, 4, 5, 6, 7, 8; (of Cyfronydd,) 5, 6, 7. Cardiganshire Pedigrees, 73. Duncumb's History of the Co. of Hereford, ii. 111. Collections by the Powys-land Club, iv. 151. The Sheriffs of Montgomeryshire, by W. V. Lloyd, 46. Wotton's English Baronetage, ii. 114. Burke's Extinct Baronetcies. Weaver's Visitation of Herefordshire, 58. See PRICE.

PRYCE-JONES. Burke's Family Records, 353.

PRYDDERCH. History of Powis Fadog, by J. Y. W. Lloyd, vi. 203.

PRYE. Tuckett's Devonshire Pedigrees, 55. Harleian Society, vi. 230. Westcote's Devonshire, edited by G. Oliver and P. Jones, 611. The Visitations of Devon, by J. L. Vivian, 631.

PRYME, or DE LA PRYME. Surtees Society, Vol. 54. W. Peck's History of Bawtry and Thorne, 91*-97*. Burke's Commoners, iv. 705, Landed Gentry, 2. Archæologia, xl. 230. Harleian Society, xxxviii. 698. Burke's Family Records, 495. *See* PRIME.

PRYN, PRYNN, or PRYNE. Visitatio Comitatus Wiltoniæ, 1623, printed by Sir T. Phillipps. Visitation of Wiltshire, edited by G. W. Marshall, 31. Weaver's Visitations of Somerset, 125. Harleian Society, xxvii. 110. Burke's Landed Gentry, 8.

PRYOR. *See* PRIOR.

PRYS. Dwnn's Visitations of Wales, i. 44, 71, 74, 77, 79, 82, 257, 266. Caermarthenshire Pedigrees, 12. Cardiganshire Pedigrees, 77.

PRYSE. Dwnn's Visitation of Wales, ii. 23, 116, 240, 288, 289, 344, 351. Meyrick's History of the Co. of Cardigan, 396. T. Nicholas' County Families of Wales, 208. Archæologia Cambrensis, 4 S., ix. 169. The Sheriffs of Cardiganshire, by J. R. Phillipps, 32. Collections by the Powys-land Club, ix. 227 ; x. 6. Burke's Extinct Baronetcies. History of Powys Fadog, by J. Y. W. Lloyd, iii. 48 ; iv. 83, 101, 174, 185, 254, 258, 260, 374 ; vi. 83, 263, 267, 421, 476. *See* PRICE.

PRYTHERCH. Burke's Landed Gentry, 2 supp., 3, 4.

PUCKERING, or PUCKERINGE. Visitation of Warwickshire, 1619, published with Warwickshire Antiquarian Magazine, 120. Clutterbuck's Hertford, ii. 521. Harleian Society, xii. 197 ; xxii. 160. Burke's Extinct Baronetcies.

PUDNER. Hasted's Kent, iv. 428.

PUDSAY, or PUDSEY. Kent's British Banner Displayed, 225. Surtees Society, xxxvi. 29 ; xli. 45. Visitation of Oxfordshire, 1634, printed by Sir T. Phillipps, (Middle Hill, fol.) 28. Burke's Landed Gentry, 2 supp., 3 and p. 284n, 4, 5, 6, 7, 8. Foster's Yorkshire Pedigrees. Foster's Visitations of Yorkshire, 294, 563. Harleian Society, v. 206, 248 ; xii. 251 ; xvi. 255 ; xix. 46. Visitation of Staffordshire, 1663-4, printed by Sir T. Phillipps, 8. Thoresby's Ducatus Leodiensis, 258. Whitaker's Deanery of Craven, 101, (126, 135, 156). Archæologia Æliana, 2nd Series, ii. 173. Dugdale's Warwickshire, 923. Plantagenet-Harrison's History of Yorkshire, i. 482. The Forest and Chase of Sutton Coldfield, (London, 1860, 8vo.) app. Foley's Records of the English Province S. J., v. 767. Notes and Queries, 4 S. ix. 428, 487. Visitations of Staffordshire, 1614 and 1663-4, William Salt Society, 245. Oxford Historical Society, xxiv. 101.

PUFFER. New England Register, xxii. 288.

PUGH, or PUGHE. Dwnn's Visitations of Wales, i. 271, 280, 295. Burke's Landed Gentry, (of Manoravon,) 3, 4, 5, 6, 7 ; (of Llanerchydol,) 2, 3, 4, 5, 6, 7, 8 ; Cambrian Journal, 1st Series, i. 132-140, 356-364. The Sheriffs of Montgomeryshire, by W. V. Lloyd, 304, 490. Collections by the Powys-land Club, viii. 49.

History of Powys Fadog, by J. Y. W. Lloyd, v. 106; vi. 35. Cambrian Journal, i. 132.

PUGSLEY. Burke's Colonial Gentry, i. 153.

PULESDON. Baker's Northampton, ii. 45.

PULESTON. Dwnn's Visitations of Wales, ii. 150, 309. Seize Quartiers of the Family of Bryan Cooke, (London, 1857, 4to.) 48. Harleian Society, viii. 342; xvii. 182; xviii. 191. T. Nicholas' County Families of Wales, 455. History of Powys Fadog, by J. Y. W. Lloyd, iii. 14, 27, 120, 219. The Suffolk Records, by H. W. Aldred, 165.

PULFORD. Ormerod's Cheshire, ii. 857. The Genealogist, New Series, xiii. 100; xvi. 23.

PULL. Harleian Society, vi. 212. The Visitations of Devon, by J. L. Vivian, 602.

PULLAND. The Irish Builder, xxxv. 69.

PULLEINE, PULLEYN, or PULLEYNE. Burke's Commoners, iv. 377, Landed Gentry, 2, 3, 4, 5, 6, 7, 8. Foster's Yorkshire Pedigrees. Surtees Society, xli. 13. Foster's Visitations of Yorkshire, 242, 280. Harleian Society, xxxix. 879.

PULLEN. Harleian Society, xvi. 256. See PULLEINE.

PULLER. Burke's Landed Gentry, 3, 4, 5, 6, 7, 8.

PULLEY. Harleian Society, xiii. 472. Bysshe's Visitation of Essex, edited by J. J. Howard, 74.

PULLING. Burke's Landed Gentry, 5.

PULMAN. Colby of Great Torrington, by F. T. Colby, 14.

PULTENEY. Burke's Landed Gentry, 5, 6, 7. Nichols' History of the County of Leicester, iv. 304, 320. Notes and Queries, 2 S. v. 379. Hasted's Kent, (Hund. of Blackheath, by H. H. Drake,) 147. The Genealogist, New Series, xvii. 25. See POULTENEY.

PULTER. Glover's History of Derbyshire, ii. 599, (588). Camden Society, xliii. 101. Clutterbuck's Hertford, iii. 517. Chauncy's Hertfordshire, 69, 73. Harleian Society, xxii. 85, 116.

PULTON. Bridges' Northampton, by Rev. Peter Whalley, ii. 26. Visitation of Gloucester, edited by T. F. Fenwick and W. C. Metcalfe, 139. See POULTON.

PULVERTOFTE. The Genealogist, iv. 267.

PUNCHARD. Punchard of Heanton Punchardon. By E. G. Punchard, 1894, 4to. Monograph of the Family of Folkard, ii. 129. Howard's Visitation of England and Wales, iii. 136.

PUNSHON. Visitation of Durham, 1575, (Newcastle, 1820, fol.) 46. Visitation of Durham, 1615, (Sunderland, 1820, fol.) 41. Surtees' Durham, i. 182. Doncaster Charities, by Charles Jackson, 51. Foster's Visitations of Durham, 265.

PURCELL. Burke's Landed Gentry, 2 supp., 195; (of Kildare,) 3 supp., 4; (of Burton House,) 3, 4, 5, 6, 7, (of Cromlyn,) 2; (of Altamira,) 3, 4, 5, 6, 7, 8; (of Co. Cork,) 6, 7, 8. Visitation of Staffordshire, 1663-4, printed by Sir T. Phillipps, 8. Collections by the Powys-land Club, iii. 47. The Sheriffs of Montgomeryshire, by W. V. Lloyd, 3, 69, 270, 488. O'Hart's Irish Pedigrees, 2nd Series, 349. History of St. Canice, Kilkenny, by J. Graves,

263. Visitations of Staffordshire, 1614 and 1663-4, William Salt
Society, 246. Harleian Society, xxix. 411.

PURCELL-FITZGERALD. Burke's Landed Gentry, 3 supp., 4, 5, 6, 7, 8.

PURCELL-LLEWELLYN. Burke's Landed Gentry, 7.

PURCHAS. Proceedings of the Essex Archæological Society, iv. 183.

PURDON. Burke's Landed Gentry, (of Tinerana,) 2, 3, 4, 5, 6, 7, 8 ;
(of Lisnabin,) 3, 4, 5, 6, 7, 8 ; (of Curristown,) 5 and supp., 6 ;
2, p. 1084.

PUREFEY, PUREFOY, or PURIFOY. Burton's Description of Leicester-
shire, 86. Dugdale's Warwickshire, 54. Burke's Extinct Baronet-
cies. Adlard's Sutton-Dudleys of England, etc., 16 E. Burke's
Landed Gentry, 3, 4, 5, 6, 7, and at p. 643, 8, 8 at p. 662.
Lipscombe's History of the County of Buckingham, iii. 71.
Nichols' History of the County of Leicester, iv. 599-602. Baker's
Northampton, i. 355. Harleian Society, ii. 32-37 ; xii. 255. The
Genealogist, vi. 79 ; vii. 189 ; xii. 29.

PURLEY. The Genealogist, iv. 268.

PURNELL. Burke's Landed Gentry, (of Stancombe Park,) 2, 3, 4, 5,
6, 7, 8 ; (of Kingshill,) 2, 3, 4, 5, 6, 7, 8.

PURSE. Harleian Society, xliii. 157.

PURSELL. Dwnn's Visitations of Wales, i. 290.

PURSGLOVE, or PURSLOVE. Harleian Society, xxxviii. 531.

PURSHULL. Metcalfe's Visitations of Worcester, 1683, 79.

PURSLOWE. Harleian Society, xxix. 414.

PURTON. Burke's Landed Gentry, 2, 3, 4, 5, 6, 7, 8. Transactions
of Shropshire Archæological Society, N.S. v. 220. See HARD-
WICKE.

PURVES. Douglas's Baronage of Scotland, 566. Alexander Nisbet's
Heraldic Plates, 104.

PURVEY. Harleian Society, xxii. 161.

PURVIS. Suckling's History of Suffolk, ii. 224. Burke's Commoners,
(of Darsham,) iii. 329, Landed Gentry, 2, 3, 4, 5, 6, 7 ; (of Black-
brook,) Landed Gentry, 2 ; (of Kinaldy,) 8 ; (of Plawsworth,) 2.
Hodgson's Northumberland, II. ii. 353. Page's History of
Suffolk, 222.

PURY, or PURIE. Harleian Society, v. 189. Blunt's Dursley and
its Neighbourhood, 151. Notes and Queries, 5 S. ix. 45, 241,
304, 423. Visitation of Gloucester, edited by T. F. Fenwick and
W. C. Metcalfe, 140.

PUSEY. Ashmole's Antiquities of Berkshire, iii. 294. Burke's Royal
Families, (London, 1851, 8vo.) i. 58. Burke's Commoners, i. 347,
Landed Gentry, 2, 3, 4, 5, 6, 7, 8. Archæologia, xii. 400. The
Genealogist, vi. 81 ; New Series, ii. 76.

PUTLAND. Burke's Landed Gentry, 3, 4, 5, 7, 8.

PUTT. Westcote's Devonshire, edited by G. Oliver and P. Jones, 629.
Burke's Extinct Baronetcies.

PUTTENHAM, or PUTTNAM. Topographer and Genealogist, iii. 180.
Berry's Hampshire Genealogies, 288. The Genealogist, vii. 244.

PUXLEY. Burke's Landed Gentry, 3, 4, 5, 6, 7, 8.

PYBUS. Hutchins' Dorset, ii. 237. Betham's Baronetage, iii. 399.

PYCHARD. Weaver's Visitation of Herefordshire, 59. *See* PICARD.
PYCHEFORD. Topographer and Genealogist, ii. 506. *See* PICHFORD.
PYCOT. Clutterbuck's Hertford, i. 442. *See* PIGOTT.
PYE. Herald and Genealogist, v. 130. Berry's Berkshire Genea-
logies, 131. Visitation of Middlesex, (Salisbury, 1820, fol.) 43.
Burke's Commoners, i. 350, Landed Gentry, 2, 3, 4, 5, 6, 7, 8.
Harleian Society, ix. 181 ; xvii. 183. Shaw's Staffordshire, i. 395.
Robinson's Mansions of Herefordshire, 87. Burke's Extinct
Baronetcies. The Genealogist, vi. 81. The Visitations of Corn-
wall, edited by J. L. Vivian, 387. Harvey's Hundred of Willey,
460. History of Ribchester, by T. C. Smith and J. Shortt, 253.
Weaver's Visitation of Herefordshire, 91. Foster's Visitation of
Middlesex, 77.
PYE-DOUGLAS. Burke's Commoners, iv. 704.
PYEMONT, or PYEMOND. Harleian Society, xxxviii. 492. Burke's
Landed Gentry, 5, 6 supp., 8. Foster's Yorkshire Pedigrees.
PYGOT. Plantagenet-Harrison's History of Yorkshire, i. 519. Har-
leian Society, xvi. 258. *See* PIGOTT, PYCOT.
PYKE. Visitation of Somersetshire, printed by Sir T. Phillipps, 129.
Hutchins' Dorset, i. 693. Harleian Society, xi. 47 ; xvii. 183.
Visitation of Gloucester, edited by T. F. Fenwick and W. C.
Metcalfe, 44. Weaver's Visitations of Somerset, 64. The Visita-
tions of Devon, by J. L. Vivian, 503. *See* PIKE.
PYKE-NOTT. Burke's Landed Gentry, 5 supp., 7.
PYM, or·PYMME. Savage's Hundred of Carhampton, 229. Collin-
son's Somerset, i. 233. Berry's Kent Genealogies, 35. Burke's
Landed Gentry, 2, 3, 4, 5, 6, 7, 8. Topographer, (London, 1789-
91, 8vo.) i. 177. Clutterbuck's Hertford, iii. 545. Cussan's
History of Hertfordshire, Parts v. and vi. 75, 76. Notes and
Queries, 3 S. viii. 206. Visitation of Somersetshire, printed by
Sir T. Phillipps, 130. Burke's Extinct Baronetcies. East Barnet,
by F. C. Cass, Part i. 58. Weaver's Visitations of Somerset, 65.
The Genealogical Magazine, ii. 361, 475.
PYMPE. Scott of Scot's-Hall, by J. R. Scott, 171, lxv. *See* PIMPE.
PYN. The Genealogist, New Series, xiv. 198 ; xv. 94.
PYNCHON, or PYNCHEON. Gyll's History of Wraysbury, 21. F. G.
Lee's History of Thame, 322. New England Register, xx. 243.
See PINCHON.
PYNCOMBE. Tuckett's Devonshire Pedigrees, 22. Harleian Society,
vi. 230. The Visitations of Devon, by J. L. Vivian, 594.
PYNE. Burke's Visitation of Seats and Arms, 2nd Series, ii. 57.
Morant's Essex, ii. 371*. Visitation of Somersetshire, printed by
Sir T. Phillipps, 130. Burke's Landed Gentry, 3, 4. Harleian
Society, vi. 231 ; xx. 78. Westcote's Devonshire, edited by
G. Oliver and P. Jones, 544. An Historical Survey of Cornwall,
by C. S. Gilbert, ii. 242. Visitation of Devon, edited by F. T.
Colby, 178. Weaver's Visitations of Somerset, 66. The Visita-
tions of Devon, by J. L. Vivian, 632. *See* PINE.
PYNKENEYE. The Genealogist, New Series, ix. 9.
PYNKERNELL. The Genealogist, New Series, xv. 261.

PYNSENT. Wotton's English Baronetage, iv. 16. Burke's Extinct Baronetcies.

PYOTT. Shaw's Staffordshire, i. 364. Harleian Society, xiii. 473. Visitations of Staffordshire, 1614 and 1663-4, William Salt Society, 247. Phillimore's London and Middlesex Note-Book, 163. *See* PIOT.

PYRAY, or PYRRY. Visitatio Comitatus Wiltoniæ, 1623, printed by Sir T. Phillipps. Harleian Society, xxvii. 144. The Genealogist, New Series, xii. 237.

PYRKE. Pedigree of Pyrke of Little Dean, Co. Glouc., [T. P.] 1869. Broadside. Burke's Landed Gentry, 2, 3, 4, 5, 6, 7, 8. Fosbrooke's History of Gloucestershire, ii. 162.

PYRLEY. The Genealogist, New Series, xvii. 109.

PYRS. Dwnn's Visitations of Wales, ii. 122, 344. Harleian Society, xxix. 416.

PYRTON. Harleian Society, xiii. 92, 473.

PYTT. Hoare's Wiltshire, IV. i. 132. *See* PITT.

PYTTS. Nash's Worcestershire, ii. 71. *See* PITTS.

QUADRING. The Genealogist, iv. 254, 269 ; vi. 277.

QUANTOCK. Burke's Royal Families, (London, 1851, 8vo.) i. 62. Burke's Landed Gentry, 2, 3, 4, 5.

QUARLES. East Anglian, iii. 155, 170, 184, 196, 203, 225, 227, 241, 274, 282, 287, 307; iv. 11, 137. Morant's Essex, i. 67. Berry's Essex Genealogies, 114. Wilson's History of the Parish of St. Laurence Pountney, 234. Wright's Essex, ii. 441. Harleian Society, xiii. 93, 271, 474 ; xxii. 161. Metcalfe's Visitations of Northamptonshire, 192. Burke's Family Records, 23.

QUARME. Harleian Society, ix. 182. The Visitations of Cornwall, edited by J. L. Vivian, 388.

QUARNBY. Thoroton's Nottingham, ii. 41. North's Church Bells of Lincoln, 103.

QUARTERMAIN. F. G. Lee's History of Thame, 293. Journal of Ex-Libris Society, iv. 63. The Genealogist, New Series, xvi. 233.

QUAYLE. Burke's Landed Gentry, 2 supp., 3, 4, 5, 6, 7, 8. Howard's Visitation of England and Wales, ii. 40.

QUEENSBURY. Case of Charles Marquis and Earl of Queensbury, etc., claiming to be enrolled among the Peers of Scotland, 1812, folio, pp. 6, and pedigree.

QUENNELL. Surrey Archæological Collections, x. Harleian Society, xliii. 162.

QUICKE. Burke's Landed Gentry, 2, 3, 4, 5, 6, 7, 8. Weaver's Visitations of Somerset, 67. The Visitations of Devon, by J. L. Vivian, 854.

QUILTER. Burke's Landed Gentry, 8.

QUIN, or QUINN. Irish Pedigrees, by John O'Hart, 2nd Series, 96, 134.

QUINCY. Nichols' History of the County of Leicester, iii. 66. Clutterbuck's Hertford, iii. 287. Baker's Northampton, i. 563. Edmondson's Baronagium Genealogicum, v. 484. The Genealogist,

New Series, vii. 17. New England Register, xi. 71, 157. *See*
DE QUINCY.
QUINEY, or QUYNEY. Warwickshire Antiquarian Magazine, Part ii.
Shakespeareana Genealogica, by G. R. French, 391. Harleian
Society, xvii. 184. Genealogical Gleanings in England, by H. F.
Waters, i. 198.
QUINTIN, QUINTON, or QUINTYN. Hasted's Kent, ii. 210. Berry's
Kent Genealogies, 393. Bibliotheca Topographica Britannica, ix.
Part 4, 274. Visitatio Comitatus Wiltoniæ, 1623, printed by Sir
T. Phillipps. The Genealogist, New Series, xii. 237. Harleian
Society, xlii. 190.
QUIRK. Irish Pedigrees, by John O'Hart, 2nd Series, 298.
QUISENBERRY. Memorials of the Quisenberry Family. By A. C.
Quisenberry. Washington, D.C., 1900, 8vo.
QUITWELL. Harleian Society, xxxii. 88.

RABETT. Burke's Landed Gentry, 2, 3, 4, 5, 6, 7, 8.
RABY. Ormerod's Cheshire, ii. 548.
RADBARD. Visitation of Somerset, printed by Sir T. Phillipps, 131.
Weaver's Visitations of Somerset, 68.
RADCLIFFE, RADCLIFF, or RADCLYFFE. Some Account of Francis
Radcliffe, 1st Earl of Derwentwater, and of his Descendants.
Newcastle, 1856, 4to. Genealogy of the Family of Radclyffe, by
James Ellis. Newcastle-upon-Tyne, 1850, 4to. St. James's Maga-
zine, New Series, (No. 9, Dec., 1868,) 428. Life of Sir G. Rad-
cliffe, Kt., by T. D. Whitaker, 1810, 4to. Hasted's Kent, iii.
281. Morant's Essex, ii. 347. Pedigrees from Visitation of
Northumberland, printed by Sir T. Phillipps, (Middle Hill, 1858,
fol.) 3. Berry's Kent Genealogies, 130. Berry's Hertfordshire
Genealogies, 109-113. Burke's Royal Families, (London, 1851,
8vo.) i. 37. Burke's Commoners, (of Warleigh,) ii. 27, Landed
Gentry, 2 and supp., 3, 4, 5, 6, 7, 8; (of Hitchin Priory,) Landed
Gentry, 2, 3, 4, 5, 6, 7 ; (of Tinnakilly,) 5 supp., 6; (of Little Park,)
8; (of Foxdenton,) 5, 6, 7, 8. Foster's Yorkshire Pedigrees.
Foster's Visitations of Yorkshire, 206, 295. Harleian Society, vii.
15 ; xiii. 274, 474 ; xix. 47, 64 ; xxii. 19, 85 ; xxxvii. 247 ; xxxviii.
522, 737 ; xlii. 70. Chetham Society, lxxxi. 1, 126 ; lxxxii. 43,
44 ; lxxxviii. 239, 240 ; xcv. 149, 150 ; xcix. 34, 93, 104, 125, 152.
Collectanea Topographica et Genealogica, vi. 125. Butterworth's
Account of the Town, etc., of Oldham, 103, 148. Whitaker's
Deanery of Craven, 380, (519, 556). Archæologia Æliana, 2nd
Series, ii. 137. Hutchins' Dorset, i. 141. Surtees' Durham, iii.
129. Clutterbuck's Hertford, iii. 23. Burke's Commoners, iv.
399, Landed Gentry, 2, 3, 4, 5. Foster's Lancashire Pedigrees.
Chetham Society, lxxxii. 130; xcviii. 64. Blore's Rutland, 63.
Surtees' Durham, i. 32. Whitaker's History of Whalley, ii. 81,
110, 292, 319. Memorials of the Church of Attleborough, by
J. T. Barrett, 189. The Genealogist, i. 307. Baines's History of
the Co. of Lancaster, ii. 353 ; iii. 6 ; Croston's edn., ii. 422 ; iii.
156. Cussan's History of Hertfordshire, Parts vii. and viii. 44.

Wright's Essex, ii. 659. Chauncy's Hertfordshire, 391. Miscellanea Genealogica et Heraldica, New Series, ii. 297. Abram's History of Blackburn, 416, 681. Metcalfe's Visitations of Suffolk, 59. Burke's Extinct Baronetcies, and *supp.* Radclyffe Tracts, edited by John Fenwick, pp. 54, 1859, 4to. Notes and Queries, 7 S. iv., 506; v. 118, 209, 414; viii. 287; ix. 32, 132, 216, 313, 376. The Livingstons of Callendar, by E. B. Livingston, 144. Yorkshire Genealogist, i. 150. Foster's Visitations of Cumberland and Westmorland, 109. History of Ribchester, by T. C. Smith and J. Shortt, 246. Fishwick's History of Rochdale, 467. New England Register, l. 30. *See* DERWENTWATER, RATCLIFF.

RADFORD. Burke's Landed Gentry, (of Smalley Hall,) 2 supp., 3, 4, 5, 6, 7, 8; (of Carnfield Hall,) 2 supp.; (of Tansley Wood,) 2 supp. Harleian Society, vi. 232; xx. 78; xxxvii. 367. Hutchins' Dorset, ii. 606. The Visitations of Devon, by J. L. Vivian, 636.

RADFORD-NORCOP. Burke's Landed Gentry, 2, 3, 4, 5, 6, 7, 8.

RADLEY. The Genealogist, vi. 278.

RADMILL, or RADMYL. Visitation of Suffolk, edited by J. J. Howard, ii. 264. Sussex Archæological Collections, iii. 101.

RADSTOCK. Claim of Lord Radstock to Vote at Elections of Irish Peers, Sess. Papers, 213 of 1857, sess. 2.

RAE. Betham's Baronetage, v. 586.

RAFF. Burke's Colonial Gentry, ii. 480.

RAFFLES. Burke's Landed Gentry, 2, 3, 4, 5, 6, 7, 8.

RAFTON. History of Hartlepool, by Sir C. Sharp, (1816, 8vo.) 78.

RAGLAN. Glamorganshire Pedigrees, edited by Sir T. Phillipps, 1. Archæologia Cambrensis, 3 S. xii. 3. Genealogies of Morgan and Glamorgan, by G. T. Clark, 274.

RAGON. Baker's Northampton, i. 163. Visitation of Devon, edited by F. T. Colby, 207. Harvey's Hundred of Willey, 44.

RAIKES. Historical and Biographical Account of the Raikes Family. Northampton, 1881, 8vo. The Pedigree of Raikes, formerly of Kingston-upon-Hill, by Joseph Foster, 1897. Large sheet. Burke's Commoners, (of Welton,) iii. 461, Landed Gentry, 2, 3, 4, 5, 6, 7, 8; (of Hill Ash,) 5, 6; (of Bennington,) 8; (of Llwynegrin,) 5, 6, 7, 8. Foster's Yorkshire Pedigrees.

RAINES. Burke's Landed Gentry, 2 supp., 3, 4, 5. Foster's Yorkshire Pedigrees. Poulson's Holderness, ii. 45, 270. *See* RAYNES.

RAINEVAL. The Genealogical Magazine, i. 463, 504.

RAINSBOROW. Genealogical Gleanings in England; by H. F. Waters, i. 168. New England Register, xl. 163. Muskett's Suffolk Manorial Families, i. 155.

RAINSFORD. Morant's Essex, i. 464. Sir T. Phillipps's Topographer, No. 1, (March, 1821, 8vo.) 41. Harleian Society, xii. 49. Genealogist, ii. 105. *See* RAYNSFORD.

RAINTON. Some Account of the Taylor Family, by P. A. Taylor, 696. *See* RAYNTON.

RAISBECK. Topographer and Genealogist, ii. 97, 553.

RAIT. Burke's Landed Gentry, 2, 3, 4, 5, 6, 7, 8.

RALEGH, or RALEIGH. Life of Sir Walter Raleigh, by Edw. Edwards, i. 3. Miscellanea Genealogica et Heraldica, ii. 155. History of the Family of Chichester, by Sir A. P. B. Chichester, Bart., 15. Gentleman's Magazine, lxviii. 185, 377. Visitation of Somersetshire, printed by Sir T. Phillipps, 131. Westcote's Devonshire, edited by G. Oliver and P. Jones, 535. Dugdale's Warwickshire, 529. Hoare's Wiltshire, III. iv. 37. Harleian Society, xii. 77. Exmouth, Ancient and Modern, 32. Visitation of Devon, edited by F. T. Colby, 124, 179. Weaver's Visitations of Somerset, 68. Genealogies of Morgan and Glamorgan, by G. T. Clark, 426. New England Register, xvi. 107. Visitations of Devon, by J. L. Vivian, 638, 736. Devonshire Association for the Advancement of Science, xxxii. 309-340. The Genealogist, New Series, xiv. 101. *See* DE RALEIGH, RAWLEIGH.

RALLI. Burke's Landed Gentry, 8.

RALSTON, or RALSTOUN. Burke's Landed Gentry, 2 and supp., p. 273, 3. Geo. Robertson's Description of Cunninghame, 276. Paterson's History of the Co. of Ayr, i. 265, 453. Paterson's History of Ayr and Wigton, iii. 129, 211. Burke's Colonial Gentry, i. 378; ii. 623.

RAM. Burke's Landed Gentry, 2, 3, 4, 5, 6, 7, 8.

RAMEY. Dawson Turner's Sepulchral Reminiscences of Great Yarmouth, 144.

RAMSAY, or RAMSEY. Harleian Society, i. 68. Burke's Landed Gentry, (of Barnton,) 2 supp., 3, 4; (of Whitehill,) 3, 4, 5, 6, 7, 8; (of Barra,) 4, 5, 6, 7, 8; (of Hill Lodge,) 2, 3, 4; (of Croughton,) 5, 8; (of Kildalton,) 7, 8. Lands and their Owners in Galloway, by P. H. M'Kerlie, i. 291. Douglas's Baronage of Scotland, 33, 551. Wood's Douglas's Peerage of Scotland, i. 221, 401, 675. Burke's Extinct Baronetcies, 635. Weaver's Visitations of Somerset, 69.

RAMSBOTHAM. Burke's Landed Gentry, 2, 3, 4, 5, 6, 7, 8.

RAMSDEN. Burke's Landed Gentry, (of Carlton Hall,) 2, 3, 4, 5, 6, 7, 8; (of Hexthorpe,) 8. Foster's Yorkshire Pedigrees. Foster's Visitations of Yorkshire, 565. Burke's Royal Descents and Pedigrees of Founders' Kin, 5. Hunter's Deanery of Doncaster, ii. 473. Wotton's English Baronetage, iv. 30. Betham's Baronetage, iii. 92. Hulbert's Annals of Almondbury, 226. Harleian Society, xxxviii. 781; xxxix. 973. Aldred's History of Turville, 50.

RAND. Surtees' Durham, iii. 417. Miscellanea Genealogica et Heraldica, New Series, iv. 179. Harleian Society, xvii. 184.

RANDALL. Harleian Society, vi. 233; ix. 182. Couch's History of Polperro, 217. A Complete Parochial History of the County of Cornwall, iii. 199; iv. 202, 204. The Visitations of Cornwall, edited by J. L. Vivian, 390. The Visitations of Devon, by J. L. Vivian, 640. Pedigree of the Family of Biscoe, by J. C. C. Smith, 18. Howard's Visitation of England and Wales, iii. 164.

RANDES. Harvey's Hundred of Willey, 285. Harleian Society, xix. 48, 133.

RANDOLPH. Hasted's Kent, iii. 64, 268. Berry's Kent Genealogies, 278. Miscellanea Genealogica et Heraldica, New Series, i. 44. Visitation of Warwickshire, 1619, published with Warwickshire Antiquarian Magazine, 210. Sussex Archæological Collections, xiv. 114. Harleian Society, xii. 303. Wood's Douglas's Peerage of Scotland, ii. 249. Notes and Queries, 3 S. i. 483. New England Register, xxvi. 35. Burke's Landed Gentry, 7, 8.

RANDYLL. Manning and Bray's Surrey, ii. 118.

RANFURLY. Claim of Earl of Ranfurly to Vote at Elections of Irish Peers, Sess. Papers, 96 of 1857-8.

RANKEN, RANKIN, RANKINE, or RANKYN. Paterson's History of the Co. of Ayr, i. 371⅓; ii. 373, 425. Burke's Landed Gentry, 6, 7, 8. Paterson's History of Ayr and Wigton, i. 359, 708; ii. 420. Some Old Families, by H. B. McCall, 159.

RANT. Harleian Society, viii. 97; xvii. 185. Carthew's Hundred of Launditch, Part iii. 457, 461.

RAPER. Berry's Sussex Genealogies, 95.

RASBY. Hunter's Deanery of Doncaster, ii. 461. The Genealogist, i. 92; iv. 108.

RASCH. Burke's Landed Gentry, 8.

RASHLEIGH. Pedigree of Rashleigh, compiled by Evelyn W. Rashleigh, Esq., Menabilly, Cornwall, 1876, folio sheet. Burke's Royal Families, (London, 1851, 8vo.) i. 88. Burke's Commoners, i. 495, Landed Gentry, 2, 3, 4, 5, 6, 7, 8. Harleian Society, ix. 183; xvii. 188. A Complete Parochial History of the County of Cornwall, iii. 189; iv. xi. 1. An Historical Survey of Cornwall, by C. S. Gilbert, ii. 244. The Visitations of Cornwall, edited by J. L. Vivian, 391.

RASINE. Harleian Society, xxxix. 893.

RASING. Foster's Visitations of Yorkshire, 181. Harleian Society, xvii. 186. Genealogical Gleanings in England, by H. F. Waters, i. 182. New England Register, xl. 365.

RASTALL. W. Dickinson's History of Newark, 322.

RASTALL-DICKINSON. Burke's Family Records, 220.

RATCLIFF, or RATCLIFFE. Harleian Society, viii. 214; xii. 149; xiii. 94, 274; xvi. 260, 361; xxviii. 93; xxxii. 264. Graves' History of Cleveland, 298. Hutchinson's History of Durham, iii. 45. Hunter's History of the Parish of Sheffield, 336. Morant's Essex, i. 339; ii. 539. Gentleman's Magazine, 1849, i. 471. Visitation of Durham, 1575, (Newcastle, 1820, fol.) 29. Surtees Society, xxxvi. 277. Chetham Society, lxxxviii. 238. Banks' Baronies in Fee, i. 211. Banks' Dormant and Extinct Baronage, ii. 209; iii. 242, 696. The Genealogist, New Series, viii. 68; xii. 204. Foster's Visitations of Durham, 267. Foster's Visitations of Northumberland, 98. Howard's Visitation of England and Wales, iii. 139. Nicolson and Burn's Westmorland and Cumberland, ii. 78. See RADCLIFFE.

RATENBURY. Harleian Society, vi. 233. The Visitations of Devon, by J. L. Vivian, 641.

RATHBONE. Burke's Landed Gentry, 2, 3, 4, 5, 6, 7, 8. Foster's

Lancashire Pedigrees. Pedigrees of Wilson, by S. B. Foster, 72.

RATHDONNELL. Claim of Lord Rathdonnell to Vote at Elections of Irish Peers, Sess. Papers, B of 1868-9.

RATTON. Howard's Visitation of England and Wales, iii. 158.

RATTRAY. Burke's Commoners, (of Craighall Rattray,) iii. 186, Landed Gentry, 2, 3, 4, 5, 6, 7, 8; (of Barford House,) Landed Gentry, 2, 3, 4. Douglas's Baronage of Scotland, 274.

RAUES. Harleian Society, xii. 91.

RAVAUD. Miscellanea Genealogica et Heraldica, New Series, iv. 322.

RAVEN. Harleian Society, xiii. 142; xvii. 187. Metcalfe's Visitations of Suffolk, 160. Earwaker's History of Sandbach, 90.

RAVENING. Harleian Society, v. 234. Oxford Historical Society, xxiv. 62.

RAVENSCROFT. Berry's Sussex Genealogies, 32. Dwnn's Visitations of Wales, i. 281; ii. 315. Miscellanea Genealogica et Heraldica, New Series, i. 475. Ormerod's Cheshire, iii. 207. Harleian Society, xviii. 194. History of Powys Fadog, by J. Y. W. Lloyd, v. 264. Ancient Families of Lincolnshire, in 'Spalding Free Press,' 1873-5, No. xvii. Metcalfe's Visitations of Northampton-shire, 129.

RAVENSWATH, or RAVENSWORTH. Whitaker's History of Richmond-shire, i. 124. Surtees' Durham, ii. 115.

RAWDEN, or RAWDON. Camden Society, lxxxv. xl. Kent's British Banner Displayed, 690. Foster's Yorkshire Pedigrees. Foster's Visitations of Yorkshire, 565. Thoresby's Ducatus Leodiensis, 168. Wright's Essex, ii. 734. Geo. Robertson's Description of Cunninghame, 367. Edmondson's Baronagium Genealogicum, vi. 103. Archdall's Lodge's Peerage, iii. 95. Wotton's English Baronetage, iii. 467. Harleian Society, xvii. 188; xxxvii. 89. The Irish Builder, xxix. 174. The Rawdon Papers, by Edward Berwick, 14. See ROWDON.

RAWE. Surtees' Durham, ii. 234. Miscellanea Genealogica et Heral-dica, New Series, ii. 252.

RAWLEIGH. Harleian Society, vi. 286; viii. 73, 277. Visitatio Comi-tatus Wiltoniæ, 1623, printed by Sir T. Phillipps. Visitation of Wiltshire, edited by G. W. Marshall, 16. See RALEGH.

RAWLES. Hutchins' Dorset, i. 269. Harleian Society, xx. 78.

RAWLIN. Harleian Society, xvii. 190.

RAWLING. Clutterbuck's Hertford, iii. 84. Foster's Visitations of Cumberland and Westmorland, 110.

RAWLINGS. Burke's Commoners, ii. 68, Landed Gentry, 2 supp., 3, 4, 5.

RAWLINS. Warwickshire Pedigrees, from Visitation of 1682-3, (privately printed, 1865). Burke's Landed Gentry, 8. Surrey Archæological Collections, vii. New England Register, viii. 253; x. 306. Harleian Society, xliii. 173. See ASHWIN.

RAWLINSON. Burke's Commoners, ii. 304, (of Graythwaite,) Landed Gentry, 2, 3, 4, 5, 6, 7, 8; (of New Place,) 2. Harleian Society,

viii. 405. Foster's Lancashire Pedigrees. Chetham Society, lxxxviii. 241. Stockdale's Annals of Cartmel, 442. Nicolson and Burn's Westmorland and Cumberland, i. 499.

RAWSON. Surtees Society, xxxvi. 164, 258. Burke's Commoners, (of Nidd Hall,) ii. 47, Landed Gentry, 2, 3, 4, 5, 6, 7; (of Woodhurst,) 8; (of Hope House,) Landed Gentry, 2; (of Mill House,) 4, 5, 6, 7, 8. Foster's Yorkshire Pedigrees. Foster's Visitations of Yorkshire, 351. History of Bradford, by John James, 430. Hunter's History of the Parish of Sheffield, 386, 450. Hunter's Deanery of Doncaster, i. 85, 321. History of Ecclesfield, by Rev. J. Eastwood, 392. Harleian Society, xvi. 261; xxxviii. 518; xl. 1176. Notes and Queries, 2 S. i. 452; ii. 27. Burke's Colonial Gentry, ii. 425. New England Register, iii. 201, 297. Burke's Family Records, 496. The Genealogist, New Series, xiii. 164; xviii. 46. Howard's Visitation of England and Wales, viii. 67.

RAWSTORNE. Burke's Landed Gentry, 2 and supp., 3, 4, 5, 6, 7, 8. Foster's Lancashire Pedigrees. Croston's edn. of Baines's Lancaster, iii. 116. *See* ROSETHORNE.

RAY. Morant's Essex, ii. 580. Wright's Essex, ii. 159. Harleian Society, xiii. 475; xxxix. 891. Miscellanea Genealogica et Heraldica, 3rd Series, iii. 192.

RAYER. Burke's Landed Gentry, 6, 7, 8.

RAYMAN. Berry's Sussex Genealogies, 57.

RAYMES. Hodgson's Northumberland, I. ii. 367.

RAYMOND. Morant's Essex, i. 206; ii. 330. Berry's Essex Genealogies, 26. Visitation of Somersetshire, printed by Sir T. Phillipps, 131. Burke's Landed Gentry, (of Symondsbury,) 2, 3, 4; (of Belchamp Hall,) 3, 4, 5, 6, 7, 8; (of Kilmurry,) 2 supp., 3, 4; (of Heathfield House,) 5 supp., 6, 7, 8. Harleian Society, viii. 331; xi. 90; xiii. 95, 475; xiv. 696; xxxvii. 368; xliii. 163. Burke's Royal Descents and Pedigrees of Founders' Kin, 63. Clutterbuck's Hertford, i. 171. Wright's Essex, i. 578. Surrey Archæological Collections, vii. Notes and Queries, 2 S. ii. 268. Banks' Dormant and Extinct Baronage, iii. 619. Visitation of Gloucester, edited by T. F. Fenwick and W. C. Metcalfe, 141.

RAYNE. Surtees' Durham, iv. 15.

RAYNER. Dwnn's Visitation of Wales, i. 76. Harleian Society, xxxvii. 157.

RAYNES. Camden Society, xliii. 88. Surtees Society, xxxvi. 368. *See* RAINES.

RAYNEY. Hunter's Deanery of Doncaster, ii. 120. History of Worsborough, by Joseph Wilkinson, 318. Burke's Extinct Baronetcies.

RAYNOLDS. Oxford Historical Society, xix. 305.

RAYNSFORD. Visitation of Oxfordshire, 1574, printed by Sir T. Phillipps, (Middle Hill, fol.) 8. Visitation of Gloucestershire, 1569, (Middle Hill, 1854, fol.) 8. Harleian Society, v. 165; xiii. 96; xvii. 191, 192; xxi. 227. Baker's Northampton, i. 131 Miscellanea Genealogica et Heraldica, 3rd Series, ii. 158, 195. *See* RAINSFORD.

RAYNTON. Visitation of Middlesex, (Salisbury, 1820, fol.) 12. Foster's Visitations of Middlesex, 26. *See* RAINTON.

RAYSON. Nichols' History of the County of Leicester, iii. 135.

REA. Harleian Society, viii. 168.

READ. Pedigree of Read of Crowwood, Co. Wilts, [T. P.] 2 folio pages. The Athenæum, No. 3465, 377. Visitation of Norfolk, published by Norfolk Archæological Society, i. 405. Pedigrees from Visitation of Northumberland, printed by Sir T. Phillipps, (Middle Hill, 1858, fol.) 1. Berry's Kent Genealogies, 413. Blomefield's Norfolk, ix. 4. Burke's Commoners, iv. 362, Landed Gentry, 2, 3, 4, 5, 6, 7, 8. Harleian Society, viii. 490; xvii. 192; xxii. 162; xxxii. 226; xxxix, 964, 1149. Surtees' Durham, iii. 121. Chauncy's Hertfordshire, 312. Maclean's History of Trigg Minor, iii. 374. Wotton's English Baronetage, iii. 256. Betham's Baronetage, ii. 238. Visitation of Wiltshire, edited by G. W. Marshall, 61, 79. The Genealogist, vi. 82, 83. Foster's Visitations of Northumberland, 97. Ontarian Families, by E. M. Chadwick, ii. 28. *See* RUDSTON-READ, CREWE-READ.

READE. Copies of all the Papers recorded in the Herald's College connected with the claim made in the year 1810, by a person calling himself Sir William Reade, to the title of Baronet, etc. Sess. Papers, 80, 89, 144, of 1831-2. Berry's Hertfordshire Genealogies, 134. Burke's Royal Families, (London, 1851, 8vo.) i. 130. Burke's Landed Gentry, (of Ipsden,) 2, 3, 4, 5, 6, 7, 8; (of Rossenarra,) 2, 3, 4, 5, 6, 7; (of the Wood Parks,) 2, 3, 4, 5, 6, 7, 8; (of Crowe Hall,) 5 supp., 6, 7, 8. Raine's History of North Durham, 179. Visitatio Comitatus Wiltoniæ, 1623, printed by Sir T. Phillipps. Clutterbuck's Hertford, ii. 360. The Genealogist, i. 382; vii. 244. Burke's Extinct Baronetcies. Harleian Society, xvii. 193; xlii. 195; xliii. 68. Visitations of Devon, by J. L. Vivian, 642. Muskett's Suffolk Manorial Families, i. 160. *See* REDE.

READHEAD. Foster's Visitations of Yorkshire, 566.

READING. Burke's Extinct Baronetcies, 613.

REAMS. Munford's Analysis of Domesday Book of Co. Norfolk, 52.

REAVELEY. Burke's Landed Gentry, 4, 5, 6, 7, 8.

REAY. Burke's Landed Gentry, 2.

REBOW, or REBOE. Berry's Essex Genealogies, 16. Burke's Landed Gentry, 2, 3, 4, 5, 6, 7, 8. Harleian Society, viii. 444; xiv. 698.

RECKITT. Burke's Landed Gentry, 8.

REDDISH, or REDISH. Chetham Society, xlii. 212; lxxxi. 12; xcviii. 75.

REDE. A Record of the Redes, by Compton Reade. Hereford, 1899, 4to. Burke's Landed Gentry, 2, 3, 4. Harleian Society, vi. 234. Suckling's History of Suffolk, i. 30. Lipscombe's History of the County of Buckingham, i. 66. Metcalfe's Visitations of Suffolk, 59, 160. *See* DE REDE, READE.

REDFEARNE. Fishwick's History of Rochdale, 506.

REDHAM. Blomefield's Norfolk, x. 122.

REDHEUGH. Surtees' Durham, ii. 132.

REDICH. Visitatio Comitatus Wiltoniæ, 1623, printed by Sir T. Phillipps. The Genealogist, New Series, xii. 238.

REDINGTON. Burke's Landed Gentry, 2, 3, 4, 5, 6, 7, 8.

REDISHE. The Genealogist, New Series, ii. 77.

REDMAN, or REDMAYNE. Foster's Visitations of Yorkshire, 99, 285. Harleian Society, i. 54 ; xvi. 262. Lipscombe's History of the County of Buckingham, i. 375. Yorkshire Archæological and Topographical Journal, iv. 84. Duchetiana, by Sir G. F. Duckett, 2nd edn., 33, 208, 218. Whitaker's Loidis and Elmete, 166. Miscellanea Genealogica et Heraldica, New Series, iii. 441 ; iv. 156. The Genealogist, vii. 245. Lancashire and Cheshire Genealogical and Historical Notes, iii. 127. History of the old Chapel, Tockholes, by B. Nightingale, 209. The Northern Genealogist, v. 12, 54.

REDMOND. Burke's Landed Gentry, (of the Deeps,) 2, 3, 4, 5 ; (of Killoughter,) 2, 3.

REDVERS. Savage's History of the Hundred of Carhampton, 123. Lipscombe's History of the County of Buckingham, i. 466. The Cistercian Houses of Devon, by J. B. Rowe, 37. Edmondson's Baronagium Genealogicum, iv. 340. The Genealogical Magazine, i. 4.

REDWOOD. Burke's Landed Gentry, 3.

REDYSHE. Ashmole's Antiquities of Berkshire, iii. 293.

REE. Harleian Society, xvii. 195 ; xxvii. 111.

REED, or REEDE. Burke's Landed Gentry, (of Crag,) 3, 4, 6, 7, 8 ; (of Heathpool,) 3, 4. Raine's History of North Durham, 179. Burke's Visitation of Seats and Arms, ii. 6. Surtees' Durham, i. 75. Dwnn's Visitations of Wales, i. 68, 333. New England Register, xxv. 378 ; lii. 52.

REES. Dwnn's Visitations of Wales, ii. 23. Glamorganshire Pedigrees, edited by Sir T. Phillipps, 44. Burke's Commoners, iii. xi. 265, Landed Gentry, 2, 3, 4, 5, 6, 8 at p. 494. Cardiganshire Pedigrees, 110, 114. T. Nicholas' County Families of Wales, 302, 951.

REEVE. Burke's Landed Gentry, 2, 3, 4, 5, 6, 7, 8. Metcalfe' Visitations of Suffolk, 60, 161. Burke's Extinct Baronetcies.

REEVES. Burke's Landed Gentry, (of Burrane,) 2, 3, 4, 5, 6, 7, 8 (of Danemore Park,) 5, 6, 7, 8. Burke's Royal Families, (edn. of 1876,) 211. See PORCH.

REIBEY. Burke's Colonial Gentry, i. 196.

REICHELL. Miscellanea Genealogica et Heraldica, New Series, i. 277. Burke's Landed Gentry, 6, 7, 8. Stemma Vetus Reichelianum, folding table. London, 1872.

REID. Paterson's History of the Co. of Ayr, ii. 335, 336, 431. Paterson's History of Ayr and Wigton, i. 551, 559, 693, 703, 716. Notes and Queries, 4 S. v. 92, 284, 352. East Barnet, by F. C. Cass, 160. Burke's Colonial Gentry, i. 372, 389. Burke's Family Records, 200. Burke's Landed Gentry, 8. See ARNOT.

REIGNE, or REIGNY. Harleian Society, vi. 339. Nichols' History of the County of Leicester, ii. 360. Genealogies of Morgan and Glamorgan, by G. T. Clark, 425.

REIGNES. Lipscombe's History of the County of Buckingham, iv. 105.

REIGNOLDE. Metcalfe's Visitations of Suffolk, 60.

REILLY. Burke's Landed Gentry, 2, 3, 4, 7, 8.

REINBUDECURT. Clutterbuck's Hertford, iii. 58.

RELFE. Berry's Sussex Genealogies, 283. Archæologia Cambrensis, 3 S. ix. 104.

REMICK. New England Register, xlvii. 472.

REMINGTON. Surtees Society, xxxvi. 123. Burke's Landed Gentry, 3, 4, 5, 6, 7, 8. Foster's Visitations of Yorkshire, 566.

REMPESTON. Thoroton's Nottinghamshire, i. 59.

REMPSTON. Hutchins' Dorset, i. 667.

RENCHING. Harleian Society, xl. 1300.

RENNEL. Berry's Hampshire Genealogies, 1.

RENNICK. Harleian Society, xvii. 196. Doncaster Charities, by Charles Jackson, 127.

RENNIE. Burke's Landed Gentry, 8.

RENSHAW. Collections relating to some Renshaws. By W. C. Renshaw. London, 1893, 8vo.

RENWICK. Burke's Colonial Gentry, ii. 830.

REPINGHALE. The Genealogist, New Series, ix. 8.

REPINGTON. Burke's Commoners, ii. 473. Harleian Society, ii. 42 ; xii. 189. Nichols' History of the County of Leicester, iv. 636. Dugdale's Warwickshire, 1143.

REPPS. Visitation of Norfolk, published by Norfolk Archæological Society, i. 193. Blomefield's Norfolk, viii. 150 ; ix. 137. Carthew's Hundred of Launditch, Part iii. 320. Harleian Society, xxxii. 228, 230.

RERESBY. Gentleman's Magazine, 1829, i. 323. Surtees Society, xxxvi. 182. Foster's Visitations of Yorkshire, 72, 74, 76. Hunter's Deanery of Doncaster, ii. 39. Harleian Society, xvi. 262 ; xl. 1289. Wotton's English Baronetage, ii. 290. Burke's Extinct Baronetcies. Registers of Ecclesfield, by A. S. Gatty, 26. The Genealogist, New Series, xv. 33.

RESCASWITHE. Visitation of Devon, edited by F. T. Colby, 208.

RESKYMER, or RESKIMER. Maclean's History of Trigg Minor, i. 555 ; iii. 385. Harleian Society, ix. 185. A Complete Parochial History of the County of Cornwall, iii. 285. The Visitations of Cornwall, edited by J. L. Vivian, 395. See ROSKIMER.

RESTWOLD. Miscellanea Genealogica et Heraldica, ii. 134.

REVE. Morant's Essex, ii. 484. Berry's Sussex Genealogies, 110. Antiquities and Memoirs of the Parish of Myddle, written by Richard Gough, 1700, (folio,) 34. Harleian Society, xiii. 275, 476 ; xvii. 194. See REEVE.

REVELEY. Burke's Commoners, ii. 287, iii. 132, Landed Gentry, 2, 3, 4, 5, 6, 7, 8. Raine's History of North Durham, 221. Hodgson's Northumberland, II. ii. 70. The Genealogist, ii. 148. Foster's Visitation of Northumberland, 100.

REVEL, or REVELL. Dwnn's Visitations of Wales, i. 156. Hunter's

Deanery of Doncaster, ii. 180. Visitation of Derbyshire, 1663-4, (Middle Hill, 1854, fol.) 6. Nichols' History of the County of Leicester, iv. 364. Dugdale's Warwickshire, 82. The Genealogist, iii. 13 ; New Series, viii. 69, 70. The Visitations of Cornwall, edited by J. L. Vivian, 412. Harleian Society, xxxvii. 387, 397.

REVETT. Harleian Society, xi. 91 ; xvii. 197. Clutterbuck's Hertford, ii. 269. *See* FAUCONBERGE.

REYGATE. Foster's Yorkshire Pedigrees.

REYMES. Blomefield's Norfolk, viii. 144. Visitation of Norfolk, published by Norfolk Archæological Society, i. 290. Harleian Society, xxxii. 231.

REYNARD. Howard's Visitation of England and Wales, iii. 163. Burke's Landed Gentry, 8.

REYNARDSON. Burke's Royal Families, (London, 1851, 8vo.) ii. 146. Burke's Landed Gentry, 2 and supp., 3, 4, 5, 6, 7, 8. Harleian Society, viii. 85 ; xvii. 198.

REYNELL. Burke's Landed Gentry, 2nd edn., 1367, 4th edn., 1482. Berry's Sussex Genealogies, 233. Tuckett's Devonshire Pedigrees, 147. Burke's Commoners, iv. 446, Landed Gentry, 2, 3, 4, 5 and 5 p. 1362, 6, 7, 8. Harleian Society, vi. 234, 240; xliii. 73. Westcote's Devonshire, edited by G. Oliver and P. Jones, 576, 578. Visitation of Devon, edited by F. T. Colby, 181. The Visitations of Devon, by J. L. Vivian, 643.

REYNELL-PACK. Howard's Visitation of England and Wales, viii. 165.

REYNER. Harleian Society, xxxvii. 7.

REYNES. Berry's Sussex Genealogies, 335. Harleian Society, iv. 108. Miscellanea Genealogica et Heraldica, 2nd Series, iv. 355.

REYNOLDS. Memoirs of the Reynolds Family, *see* Some Account of the Town of Plympton Maurice, by William Cotton. London, 1859, 8vo. Morant's Essex, i. 419. Jewitt's Reliquary, vii. 139. Burke's Landed Gentry, (of Norfolk,) 3 supp., 4 ; (of Canonsgrove,) 5, 6, 7. Harleian Society, viii. 60 ; xii. 243 ; xxxii. 233 ; xl. 1195. Visitation of Warwickshire, 1619, published with Warwickshire Antiquarian Magazine, 44. Maclean's History of Trigg Minor, i. 70. Miscellanea Genealogica et Heraldica, New Series, ii. 76. Colby of Great Torrington, by F. T. Colby, 26. O'Hart's Irish Pedigrees, 2nd Series, 135. Notes and Queries, 2 S. xii. 18; 3 S. i. 149, 245; iii. 54 ; ix. 463 ; xi. 467 ; 5 S. vi. 246. F. G. Lee's History of Thame, 617. Edmondson's Baronagium Genealogicum, vi. 59. Burke's Colonial Gentry, i. 374.

REYNWARD. The Genealogist, New Series, xv. 23.

RHAM. The Genealogist, New Series, xv. 49.

RHES. Cardiganshire Pedigrees, 101.

RHODES. Pedigree of the Family of Rhodes of New Zealand, by F. W. Hoyle. Sheffield, 1865, 4to. Miscellanea Genealogica et Heraldica, ii. 158. History of Newenham Abbey, by James Davidson, 169. Surtees Society, xxxvi. 266. Burke's Commoners, iii. 566, Landed Gentry, 2, 3, 4, 8. Foster's Yorkshire Pedigrees.

Visitation of Derbyshire, 1663-4, (Middle Hill, 1854, fol.) 6. The Genealogist, iii. 13. Historical Notices of Doncaster, by C. W. Hatfield, 3rd Series, 349. History of Ribchester, by T. C. Smith and J. Shortt, 244. Harleian Society, xxxvii. 91. History of Chipping, by Tom C. Smith, 250.

RHODOCANAKIS. Genealogia della Casa Imperiale dei Rhodocanakis di Scio, four sheets.

RHYS. Pembrokeshire Pedigrees, 142. Meyrick's History of the Co. of Cardigan, 138.

RHYS AP IEUAN. Dwnn's Visitations of Wales, ii. 239.

RHYS AP THOMAS. Dwnn's Visitations of Wales, ii. 32, 57, 104.

RIALL. Burke's Landed Gentry, (of Old Conna Hill,) 3, 4, 5, 6, 7, 8; (of Annerville,) 5, 6, 7, 8.

RIBALD. Banks' Dormant and Extinct Baronage, i. 165.

RIBBESFORD. The Genealogist, New Series, xii. 233.

RICARD, or RICCARD. Foster's Visitations of Yorkshire, 567. Hunter's Deanery of Doncaster, i. 176. The Genealogist, iii. 352. J. B. Payne's Armorial of Jersey, 325. Harleian Society, xvii. 199.

RICARDO. Burke's Commoners, i. 373, Landed Gentry, 2, 3, 4, 5, 6, 7, 8. Cooke's Continuation of Duncumb's Hereford, (Hund. of Grimsworth,) Part i. 35.

RICE. Pedigree of Rice of Newton, etc., [T. P.] 1856, folio page. Dwnn's Visitations of Wales, i. 210, 233; ii. 26. Berry's Hampshire Genealogies, 121. Glamorganshire Pedigrees, edited by Sir T. Phillipps, 16. Burke's Landed Gentry, (of Dane Court,) 2, 3, 4, 5, 6, 7, 8; (of Llwyn-y-Brain,) 4, 5, 6, 7; (of Loughor,) 4; (of Bushmount,) 7, 8. Caermarthenshire Pedigrees, 8. Charles Smith's History of Kerry, 58. Edmondson's Baronagium Genealogicum, vi. 82. Brydges' Collin's Peerage, vii. 504. Harvey's Hundred of Willey, 46.

RICH. Morant's Essex, i. 188; ii. 101. The History of Essex, by N. Tindall, 24. T. Faulkner's History of Kensington, 62. Berry's Hampshire Genealogies, 13. Herald and Genealogist, v. 444. Harleian Society, i. 27; viii. 206, 394; xiii. 13, 276; xvii. 197; xxii. 86; xxxvii. 40. Wright's Essex, i. 211; ii. 424. Page's History of Suffolk, 353. Notes and Queries, 3 S. xi. 257, 392; 5 S. x. 31. Wotton's English Baronetage, iii. 263, 586. Betham's Baronetage, iv. 238. Banks' Dormant and Extinct Baronage, iii. 371, 731. Burke's Extinct Baronetcies. Hasted's Kent, (Hund. of Blackheath, by H. H. Drake,) 182. History of Felsted School, by John Serjeant, 110. Chancellor's Sepulchral Monuments of Essex, 142. Visitation of Gloucester, edited by T. F. Fenwick and W. C. Metcalfe, 142. See RICHE.

RICHARD, AP JOHN. Dwnn's Visitations of Wales, i. 315; ii. 171; ap Rydderch, i. 161.

RICHARDES. Burke's Landed Gentry, 8.

RICHARDS. Berry's Hampshire Genealogies, 18. Visitation of Middlesex, (Salisbury, 1820, fol.) 14. Berry's Berkshire Genealogies, 136. Visitation of Somersetshire, printed by Sir T.

Phillipps, 148. Burke's Commoners, (of Caerynwch,) iii. 552, Landed Gentry, 2, 3, 4, 5, 6, 7, 8; (of Solsborough,) Landed Gentry, 4, 5, 6, 7, 8; (of Ardamine,) 4, 5, 6, 7, 8; (of Macmine,) 4, 5, 6, 7, 8; (of Croft House,) 4, 5, 6, 7, 8; (of Grange,) 5, 6, 7, 8. Harleian Society, xi. 91. Hutchins' Dorset, ii. 499. An Account of the Families of Boase, (Exeter, 1876, 4to.) 44. Wotton's English Baronets, iii. 711. Betham's Baronetage, iii. 67. Burke's Extinct Baronetcies. Foster's Visitation of Middlesex, 29. Weaver's Visitations of Somerset, 127. Howard's Visitation of England and Wales, Notes, i. 60. Burke's Family Records, 503. Berks Archæological and Architectural Society Journal, ii. 84.

RICHARDSON. A Skeleton Pedigree to illustrate the Descent of the late Miss Currer, [Richardson Family]. Annals of the Cleveland Richardsons and their Descendants. Newcastle-on-Tyne, 1850, 12mo. Pedigree of W. R. Richardson of Shortlands, co. Kent, 1896. Broadside. Records of the Richardsons of Cleveland, by A. O. Bryce. London, 1889, 4to. Kent's British Banner Displayed, 459. Berry's Kent Genealogies, 53. Berry's Sussex Genealogies, 49. Visitation of Durham, 1615, (Sunderland, 1820, fol.) 40. Surtees Society, xxxvi. 50. Blomefield's Norfolk, ii. 449. Burke's Commoners, (of Finden Place,) iii. 111, Landed Gentry, 2, 3, 4; (of Chisbury,) 8; (of Aber Hirnant,) Landed Gentry, 2, 3, 4, 5; (of Poplar Vale,) 2 supp., 3, 4, 5, 6, 8; (of Field House,) 2 supp., 3, 4, 5, 6, 7, 8; (of Riccall Hall,) 2 supp., 3, 4; (of Rich Hill,) 4, 5, 6, 7, 8; (of Rossfad,) 4, 5, 6, 7; (of Lameg,) 4, 5; (of Waringstown,) 4; (of Derwen Fawr,) 8; (of Potto Hall,) 8; (of Kirklevington Grange,) 8; (of Shotley,) 6 supp., 7, 8. Foster's Yorkshire Pedigrees. Collectanea Bradfordiana, by A. Holroyd, (Saltaire, 1873, 8vo.) 114. History of Bradford, by John James, 423. Burke's Visitation of Seats and Arms, ii. 27, 42. Dallaway's Sussex, II. i. 30. Thoresby's Ducatus Leodiensis, 20. Whitaker's Loidis and Elmete, App. 38. Whitaker's Deanery of Craven, 152, (213). Nichols' History of the County of Leicester, iv. 964*. Surtees' Durham, iv. 145, 151. Shirley's History of the County of Monaghan, 225. Castles, Mansions, and Manors of Western Sussex, by D. G. C. Elwes and C. J. Robinson, 92. J. B. Payne's Armorial of Jersey, 327. Wood's Douglas's Peerage of Scotland, i. 363. Monken Hadley, by F. C. Cass, 174. Notes and Queries, 3 S. v. 72, 123, 165, 527; xi. 83; 5 S. iv. 18; v. 267, 291. Surrey Archæological Collections, viii. Harleian Society, xvii. 199, 200; xxix. 417; xxxix. 1016; xliii. 136. Foster's Visitations of Durham, 269. East Barnet, by F. C. Cass, 145. Bysshe's Visitation of Essex, edited by J. J. Howard, 74. Burton's History of Hemingborough, 262. New England Register, ix. 68. Burke's Colonial Gentry, ii. 493. Pease of Darlington, by Joseph Foster, 70. History of the old Chapel, Tockholes, by B. Nightingale, 210. History of the Wilmer Family, 351. The Descendants of John Backhouse, by J. Foster, 19. Annals of Smith of Balby, by H. E. Smith, 212. The Northern Genealogist, ii. 12. Burke's

Family Records, 504. Howard's Visitation of England and
Wales, v. 103. *See* CURRER.

RICHARDSON-DICKSON. Burke's Landed Gentry, 7.

RICHE. Morant's Essex, i. 147 ; ii. 75, 84, 418, 503. Hunter's
Deanery of Doncaster, ii. 362. The Genealogist, vi. 83. *See*
RICH.

RICHERS, or RICHARS. Harleian Society, xi. 91 ; xxxii. 233, 234.

RICHES. The Perverse Widow, by A. W. Crawley-Boevey, 229.

RICHEY. Burke's Colonial Gentry, i. 119.

RICHMOND, or RICHMUND. Pedigree of Richmond *alias* Webb of the
Middle Temple, [T. P.] folio page. Pedigree of Richmond *alias*
Webb of Biddleston, etc., [T. P.] 1842. Broadside. Visitation of
Westmorland, 1615, (London, 1853,) 40. Burke's Commoners,
iv. 100. Harleian Society, vii. 37 ; xxxii. 234. Burke's Visitation
of Seats and Arms, 2nd Series, i. 11. Whitaker's History of
Richmond, i. 26. Dallaway's Sussex, i. 137. Burke's Royal Families,
(London, 1851, 8vo.) i. 48. Hutchinson's History of Cumberland,
ii. 429. Corry's History of Lancashire, i. 454. Visitatio Comitatus
Wiltoniæ, 1623, printed by Sir T. Phillipps. Plantagenet-Harrison's History of Yorkshire, i. 35, 46. Cumberland and Westmorland Archæological Society, ii. 144. Paterson's History of
Ayr and Wigton, i. 682. Betham's Baronetage, i. 271. Banks'
Dormant and Extinct Baronage, iii. 620. Historical Notices of
Doncaster, by C. W. Hatfield, 3rd Series, 356. Foster's Visitations of Cumberland and Westmorland, 111. Weaver's Visitations
of Somerset, 69. Papers and Pedigrees relating to Cumberland
and Westmorland, by William Jackson, i. 109. History of
Chipping, by Tom C. Smith, 258. The Genealogist, New Series,
xiii. 239. Nicolson and Burn's Westmorland and Cumberland,
ii. 320. *See* DRAKE, MARTIN.

RICHMOND (Earls of). History of Richmond, by C. Clarkson, 12.
Plantagenet-Harrison's History of Yorkshire, i. 6.

RICKABY. Burke's Landed Gentry, 2. Poulson's Holderness,
i. 229.

RICKARDS. Robinson's Mansions of Herefordshire, 297. Miscellanea
Genealogica et Heraldica, 2nd Series, i. 211. Harleian Society,
xxxix. 1111, 1171.

RICKER. New England Register, v. 308, 464.

RICKETTS. Berry's Hampshire Genealogies, 163. Burke's Commoners, i. 22, Landed Gentry, 2, 3, 4, 5. Howard's Visitation of
England and Wales, i. 273 ; Notes, iii. 89.

RICKFORD. Burke's Landed Gentry, 2.

RICKTHORNE. Visitations of Staffordshire, 1614 and 1663-4, William
Salt Society, 249.

RIDDELL, RIDELL, or RIDEL. Pedigree of Sir James Riddell, Bart.,
(Edinburgh, 1794 ?) 4to. A Genealogical Sketch of the Riddell
Family, by W. P. Riddell. New Orleans, 1852, 8vo. Visitation
of Durham, 1615, (Sunderland, 1820, fol.) 43. Burke's Royal
Families, (London, 1851, 8vo.) i. 45 ; ii. 164. Burke's Com-
moners, (of Felton Park,) iii. 207, Landed Gentry, 2, 3, 4, 5, 6,

7, 8; (of Cheeseburne Grange,) Landed Gentry, 2, 3, 4, 5, 6, 7; (of Camieston,) 5, 6, 7, 8. Raine's History of North Durham, 325. Hodgson's Northumberland, II. ii. 104. Hutchinson's History of Durham, iii. 1. Surtees' Durham, ii. 128. Bridges' Northampton-shire, by Rev. Peter Whalley, ii. 607. Nisbet's Heraldry, ii. app. 303. Douglas's Baronage of Scotland, 63, 201. Border Memories, by W. R. Carre, 181. Betham's Baronetage, iv. 53. Foster's Visi-tations of Durham, 271. The Genealogist, New Series, vi. 1. Foster's Visitations of Northumberland, 101. *See* RYEDALE.

RIDDELL-CARRE. Burke's Landed Gentry, 4, 5, 6, 7.

RIDER. Berry's Kent Genealogies, 395. Harleian Society, vi. 241. The Visitations of Devon, by J. L. Vivian, 646. *See* RYDER.

RIDGE. Berry's Sussex Genealogies, 11. Chetham Society, lxxxviii. 242. Horsfield's History of Lewes, ii. 138. Harleian Society, xxix. 418. Sussex Archæological Collections, xxix. 148 ; xxxvii. 116-132.

RIDGEWAY. Visitation of Devon, edited by F. T. Colby, 182. Burke's Extinct Baronetcies. Burke's Landed Gentry, 7. The Visitations of Devon, by J. L. Vivian, 647.

RIDGLEY. Harleian Society, xxix. 419.

RIDLER. Fosbrooke's History of Gloucestershire, i. 359.

RIDLEY. Burke's Landed Gentry, 2, 3, 4, 5, 6, 7, 8. Foster's Visita-tions of Yorkshire, 569. Hodgson's Northumberland, II. ii. 322; III. ii. 323, 329, 339. Chetham Society, xcix. 166. The Genea-logist, ii. 145, 147. Harleian Society, xvi. 263 ; xvii. 201 ; xxix. 417, 419. Betham's Baronetage, iii. 259. Foster's Visitations of Northumberland, 102-105. *See* RYEDALE.

RIDOUT. Burke's Colonial Gentry, ii. 667, 803. Ontarian Families, by E. M. Chadwick, i. 36.

RIDSDALE. Harleian Society, xxxviii. 598.

RIDWARE. Glover's History of Derbyshire, ii. 152. Maclean's History of Trigg Minor, i. 650. Shaw's Staffordshire, i. 152. Harleian Society, xiii. 41. Thoroton's Nottinghamshire, iii. 24. *See* RYDEWARE.

RIGAUD. Miscellanea Genealogica et Heraldica, 3rd Series, iii. 24.

RIGBY, or RIGBYE. Morant's Essex, i. 462. Fishwick's History of Goosnargh, 141. Chetham Society, lxxxi. 74 ; lxxxii. 24, 65, 113 ; lxxxviii. 243-246. Baines's History of the Co. of Lancaster, iii. 481 ; Croston's edn., iv. 201. Robinson's Mansions of Here-fordshire, 68. The Tyldesley Diary, edited by J. Gillow and A. Hewitson, 118. Philips' Old Halls of Lancashire and Cheshire, 62. Fishwick's History of Bispham, 104. Harleian Society, xxxix. 1106.

RIGGE. Burke's Commoners, ii. 303, Landed Gentry, 2, 3, 4, 5, 6, 7, 8. Annals of Smith of Balby, by H. E. Smith, 99.

RIGGES. The Genealogist, iv. 270.

RIGGS. Berry's Sussex Genealogies, 100. Berry's Hampshire Genea-logies, 306. Dallaway's Sussex, i. 240.

RIGHTON. Pedigree of Righton of Ebrington, Co. Glouc., etc., [T. P.] 1864, folio page.

RIGMAYDEN. Chetham Society, lxxxi. 54; xcv. 67; xcix. 107; cv. 214.

RIKEDON. Morant's Essex, ii. 107. Harleian Society, xiii. 161.

RIKHILL. Bibliotheca Topographica Britannica, i. Part iii. 43.

RILAND. Three Hundred Years of a Family Living, being a History of the Rilands of Sutton Coldfield, by W. K. R. Bedford. Birmingham, 1889, 4to. Burke's Landed Gentry, 7 p. 113. *See* RYLAND.

RILEY. Jewitt's Reliquary, x. 192. Burke's Landed Gentry, 4, 5, 8.

RILLESTONE. Whitaker's Deanery of Craven, 3rd edn., 518.

RIMAN. Visitation of Sussex, 1570, printed by Sir T. Phillipps, (Middle Hill, fol.) 9.

RIMELL. Pedigree of Rimell of Weston Subedge, Co. Glouc., [T. P.] folio page.

RIMINGTON. Hunter's History of the Parish of Sheffield, 476. Harleian Society, xxxviii. 660.

RIMINGTON-WILSON. Burke's Landed Gentry, 5, 6, 7, 8. Foster's Yorkshire Pedigrees. Howard's Visitation of England and Wales, v. 162.

RINGER. Gyll's History of Wraysbury, 86.

RINGROSE. Burke's Commoners, iv. 575 ; Landed Gentry, 8.

RINGWOOD. Berry's Hampshire Genealogies, 237. Hoare's Wiltshire, V. ii. 31.

RIPLEY. Surtees Society, xxxvi. 130.

RIPPON. Burke's Landed Gentry, 2 supp., 3, 4. Burke's Family Records, 504.

RISBY. Metcalfe's Visitations of Suffolk, 100. Muskett's Suffolk Manorial Families, i. 66-73. *See* DE RISBY.

RISDON. Tuckett's Devonshire Pedigrees, 107. Harleian Society, vi. 241, 243. Westcote's Devonshire, edited by G. Oliver and P. Jones, 507. Visitations of Devon, by J. L. Vivian, 648.

RISHTON. Berry's Sussex Genealogies, 306. Chetham Society, lxxxii. 94 ; lxxxviii. 250, 251 ; xcviii. 32. Dallaway's Sussex, i. 28. Whitaker's History of Whalley, ii. 298, 300. Abram's History of Blackburn, 631, 641. The Genealogist, New Series, viii. 243. *See* RUSHTON.

RISLEY. Chetham Society, lxxxviii. 246. Lipscombe's History of the County of Buckingham, iii. 3. Baker's Northampton, i. 62. Miscellanea Genealogica et Heraldica, New Series, ii. 273. Earwaker's Local Gleanings, i. 201, 251, 266, 382 ; ii. 575. The Genealogist, vii. 245, 246.

RITCHIE. Paterson's History of the Co. of Ayr, ii. 219. Paterson's History of Ayr and Wigton, iii. 462.

RITHE. Plantagenet-Harrison's History of Yorkshire, i. 265.

RITHER. *See* RYTHER.

RITHERDON. Visitation of Somersetshire, printed by Sir T. Phillipps, 131. Harleian Society, xi. 92.

RIVELL. Harleian Society, i. 51.

RIVERS. Harleian Society, i. 7. Collinson's Somerset, iii. 556.

Dunford's Historical Memoirs of Tiverton, 66. Morant's Essex, i. 128, 429. Kent's British Banner Displayed, 385. Collectanea Topographica et Genealogica, i. 296. Carthew's Hundred of Launditch, Part i. 74. Baker's Northampton, i. 619. Wotton's English Baronetage, i. 444. Banks' Baronies in Fee, ii. 120. Betham's Baronetage, i. 217. Banks' Dormant and Extinct Baronage, iii. 629. Harleian Society, xvii. 201. The Genealogist, New Series, x. 30. *See* RYVERS.

RIVES. Pedigrees of Rives of Damery Court, etc., [T. P.] 1868. Broadside. Two pedigrees. *See* RYVES.

RIVETT. Harleian Society, i. 19 ; xli. 102. Cambridgeshire Visitation, edited by Sir T. Phillipps, 26. Visitation of Somersetshire, printed by Sir T. Phillipps, 132. The Suffolk Records, by H. W. Aldred, 9.

RIVINGTON. Howard's Visitation of England and Wales, iii. 20.

RIVIS. Burke's Landed Gentry, 6, 7, 8.

RIXTON. Chetham Society, lxxxi. 116.

ROACH. Visitations of Devon, by J. L. Vivian, 651.

ROBART. Dwnn's Visitations of Wales, i. 234.

ROBARTS, or ROBARTES. Bibliotheca Topographica Britannica, vii. Parts i. and ii. 360*. Harleian Society, ix. 186. Burke's Commoners, ii. 316, Landed Gentry, 2, 3, 4, 5, 6, 7, 8. Burke's Extinct Baronetcies. A Complete Parochial History of the County of Cornwall, iii. 10. An Historical Survey of Cornwall, by C. S. Gilbert, i. 517. Banks' Dormant and Extinct Baronage, iii. 616. *See* ROBERTS.

ROBERT AP IEUAN. Dwnn's Visitations of Wales, ii. 221 ; ap John, ii. 113, 245.

ROBERTON. Nisbet's Heraldry, ii. app. 153.

ROBERTS. J. H. Hill's History of Langton, 79, 79*, 80*. Visitation of Sussex, 1570, printed by Sir T. Phillipps, (Middle Hill, fol.) 9. Hasted's Kent, ii. 369 ; iii. 46, 575, 590. Morant's Essex, ii. 144. Berry's Surrey Genealogies, 29. Dwnn's Visitations of Wales, ii. 75, 78, 215. Berry's Kent Genealogies, 177, 181. Burke's Landed Gentry, (of Milford Haven,) 3, 4, 5 ; (of Coeddu,) 4, 5, 6, 7, 8 ; (of Cork,) 4 ; (of Ardmore,) 4, 5, 6, 7, 8 ; (of Llwyndderw,) 2, 3 ; (of Struan,) 7 ; (of Glassenbury Park,) 8 ; (of Plas yn Rhiw,) 8 ; (of Bewdley,) 2 ; (of Dormstown Castle,) 5, 6, 7, 8 ; (of Kilmoney Abbey,) 6 supp., 7. Miscellanea Genealogica et Heraldica, New Series, i. 159. Harleian Society, ii. 117, 203 ; iii. 34 ; viii. 323 ; ix. 186 ; xiii. 97, 279, 478 ; xvii. 202 ; xxi. 137 ; xxix. 420 ; xxxvii. 4, 162 ; xlii. 93. Burke's Visitation of Seats and Arms, 2nd Series, i. 30. Westcote's Devonshire, edited by G. Oliver and P. Jones, 609. Nichols' History of the County of Leicester, ii. 671 ; iv. 452*, 547. Archæologia Cambrensis, 4 S., ix. 177. Annals of Cranbrook Church, by William Tarbutt, 2nd Lecture, 29. Fosbrooke's History of Gloucestershire, ii. 484. Notes and Queries, 2 S. xi. 138. Wotton's English Baronetage, i. 403. The Genealogist, v. 300. Burke's Extinct Baronetcies. The Visitations of Cornwall, edited by J. L. Vivian, 397. History of Powys

Fadog, by J. Y. W. Lloyd, iii. 17, 25, 45, 65 ; iv. 184. Bysshe's Visitation of Essex, edited by J. J. Howard, 75. Weaver's Visitations of Somerset, 128. Genealogical Memoranda of the Family of Ames, 24. Burke's Colonial Gentry, i. 387 ; ii. 510 ; ii. 616. Betham's Baronetage, v. 458. New England Register, vii. 356 ; viii. 63 ; xlii. 242. Howard's Visitation of Ireland, i. 97. Burke's Family Records, 505. The Visitations of Devon, by J. L. Vivian, 502. Howard's Visitation of England and Wales, vii. 160. *See* CROMPTON-ROBERTS.

ROBERTS-WEST. Howard's Visitation of England and Wales, vi. 54.

ROBERTSON. The Descendants of Conan of Glenersdrie, etc., afterwards known as the Robertsons of Strowan, by Sir Noel Paton, Kt., 1873. Pedigree showing the connection between the existing family of Inglis, etc., with the family of Ladykirk, etc., by C. J. L. Inglis, 1880. Broadside. The History of the Robertsons of Strowan. Edinburgh, *circa* 1771, 12mo. Burke's Royal Families, (London, 1851, 8vo.) ii. 190. Burke's Commoners, (of Strowan,) iv. 419, Landed Gentry, 2, 3, 4, 5, 6, 8 ; (of Kindeace,) Commoners, ii. 76, Landed Gentry, 2, 3, 4, 5, 6, 7, 8 ; (of Chilcote,) Landed Gentry, 4, 5, 6 ; (of Hazel Hill,) 4, 5 ; (of Prenderguest,) 3, 4 ; (of Lady Kirk,) 2, 3, 4, 5 ; (of Auchleeks,) 2, 3, 4, 5, 6, 7, 8; (of Inshes,) 2, 3, 4, 5 ; (of Lude,) 2 ; (of Kinlochmoidart,) 2 add., 3, 4, 5, 6 ; (of Tulliebelton,) 5, 6 ; (of Palé,) 8 ; (of Huntington Castle,) 8 ; (of Widmerpool,) 6, 7, 8 ; 6 at p. 1754. Burke's Heraldic Illustrations, 47. Douglas's Baronage of Scotland, 405-414. Peter Chalmers' History of Dunfermline, ii. Table i. *at end*. The Earldom of Athol, by J. A. Robertson, 39. Notes and Queries, 3 S. xi. 240 ; 5 S. ii. 393. Burke's Extinct Baronetcies. Burke's Colonial Gentry, ii. 477. Northern Notes and Queries, xi. 60. *See* STEWART-ROBERTSON, DOUGLAS.

ROBERTSON-GLASGOW. Burke's Landed Gentry, 3, 4, 5, 6, 7, 8.

ROBERTSON-REID. Burke's Landed Gentry, 8.

ROBERTSON-ROSS. Burke's Landed Gentry, 5, 6, 8.

ROBERTSON-WALKER. Burke's Landed Gentry, 2, 3, 4.

ROBIN. Burke's Landed Gentry, 2. J. B. Payne's Armorial of Jersey, 329.

ROBINETT. Miscellanea Genealogica et Heraldica, 3rd Series, i. 98.

ROBIN HOOD. Thoroton's Nottinghamshire, ii. 165. Robin Hood, edited by Joseph Ritson, 6.

ROBINS. Dwnn's Visitations of Wales, ii. 113, 290. Harleian Society, xvii. 203.

ROBINSON. Some Account of the Family of Robinson of the White House, Appleby, Westmoreland. By C. B. Norcliffe. Westminster, 1874, 8vo. Pocock's History of Gravesend, 13. Hasted's Kent, iii. 318. Topographer and Genealogist, ii. 103. Berry's Hertfordshire Genealogies, 7, 229. Archæologia Cantiana, iv. 251. Berry's Kent Genealogies, 37. Surtees Society, xxxvi. 18, 34, 69, 91, 117, 207, 208. *See* under 'Burton of Cherry Burton,' Burke's Landed Gentry, 5 ; and 'Fowler of Preston Hall,' 6. Burke's Landed Gentry, (of Widmerpool,) 3, 4 ; (of Silksworth,) 2 supp.,

3, 4, 5, 6, 7, 8 ; (of Knapton House,) 4, 5, 6, 7, 8 ; (of Rosmead,)
2 supp. ; (of Sudley,) 2 ; (of Lynhales,) 8 ; (of Poston Court,) 8 ;
(of Reedley Hall,) 8 ; (of Denston Hall,) 5, 6, 7, 8. Foster's
Yorkshire Pedigrees. Foster's Visitations of Yorkshire, 568, 631,
632. Harleian Society, ii. 182 ; viii. 84, 323, 520 ; ix. 188 ; xvii.
204-208 ; xxii. 86 ; xxxvii. 278, 355 ; xxxviii. 449, 627 ; xxxix.
990 ; xlii. 5. Chetham Society, lxxxviii. 247. Bridges' Northamptonshire, by Rev. Peter Whalley, ii. 90. Whitaker's History
of Richmondshire, ii. 122. Shaw's Staffordshire, ii. 5. Poulson's
Holderness, ii. 179. Thoresby's Ducatus Leodiensis, 262. Nichols'
History of the County of Leicester, ii. 583 ; iii. 1106. Archæologia Æliana, 2nd Series, v. 84. Surtees' Durham, i. 190, 245,
306. Clutterbuck's Hertford, ii. 377. Chauncy's Hertfordshire,
302. The Genealogist, iii. 259 ; iv. 270 ; vi. 84 ; New Series,
xiv. 112, 231. Plantagenet-Harrison's History of Yorkshire, i.
67, 124, 415. Yorkshire Archæological and Topographical
Journal, vi. 279. Edmondson's Baronagium Genealogicum, v.
471. Archdall's Lodge's Peerage, vii. 165. Brydges' Collins'
Peerage, vii. 286. Wotton's English Baronetage, iii. 56, 700 ; iv.
32, 225. Betham's Baronetage, ii. 63. Burke's Extinct Baronet-
cies. Visitation of Staffordshire, (Willm. Salt Soc.) 125. The
Visitations of Cornwall, edited by J. L. Vivian, 402. History of
Powys Fadog, by J. Y. W. Lloyd, iii. 188. Burton's History of
Hemingborough, 159. Bysshe's Visitation of Essex, edited by
J. J. Howard, 75. Genealogical Memoranda of the Family of
Ames, 17. New England Register, iii. 172 ; xiv. 17 ; xxxix. 323 ;
xliv. 285 ; xlviii. 204. Burke's Colonial Gentry, ii. 757, 793, 822.
Burke's Family Records, 506. Ontarian Families, by E. M. Chad-
wick, ii. 57.

ROBOTHAM. Clutterbuck's Hertford, i. 106. F. G. Lee's History of
Thame, 157. Harleian Society, xvii. 208 ; xxii. 87. See Row-
BOTHAM.

ROB ROY. Historical Memoirs of Rob Roy and the Clan Macgregor,
by K. Macleay. Glasgow, 1818. Another edition, 1881, 8vo.
Notes and Queries, 4 S. vi. 30.

ROBSART. Blomefield's Norfolk, vii. 181.

ROBSERT. Banks' Dormant and Extinct Baronage, i. 403.

ROBSON. Visitation of Durham, 1615, (Sunderland, 1820, fol.) 66.
Burke's Landed Gentry, 2 add., 3, 4, 5. History of Darlington,
by W. Hylton Dyer Longstaffe, lvii. Surtees' Durham, iii. 57.
The Genealogist, iii. 308. Foster's Visitations of Durham, 273.
Cyclostyle Pedigrees, by J. J. Green. Visitation of Gloucester,
edited by T. F. Fenwick and W. C. Metcalfe, 144. Pease of
Darlington, by Joseph Foster, 49. Annals of Smith of Balby, by
H. E. Smith, 147.

ROBY. Nichols' History of the County of Leicester, iii. 784.

ROBYNS. Maclean's History of Trigg Minor, i. 85.

ROBYNSON. Surtees Society, xxxvi. 65, 142.

ROCH, or ROCHE. Pedigree of Roche of Roche Castle, and Roche of
St. Ishmaels, [E. P.] 1859, two pedigrees. Pedigree of Roche of

Butter Hill, [T. P.] 1859. Gentleman's Magazine, 1853, ii. 46 ; 1855, ii. 43, 254. Burke's Commoners, (of Granagh Castle,) i. 669, Landed Gentry, 2, 3, 4, 5, 6, 7, 8 ; (of Carass,) Commoners, iv. 211 ; (of Trabolgan,) Landed Gentry, 2 ; (of Aghado,) 2 ; (of Woodbine Hill,) 2 supp., 3, 4, 5, 6, 7 ; (of Butter Hill,) 2, 6, 7, 8. Harleian Society, vi. 243 ; xiii. 477 ; xvii. 210. Memoirs of the Family of Chester, by R. E. C. Waters, 160. The Genealogist, iv. 272. Burke's Extinct Baronetcies, 613. The Visitations of Cornwall, by J. L. Vivian, 523. Bysshe's Visitation of Essex, edited by J. J. Howard, 76. Burke's Family Records, 511.

ROCHEAD. Burke's Extinct Baronetcies, 635.

ROCHESTER. Morant's Essex, ii. 127, 391. Harleian Society, xiii. 97, 279 ; xiv. 622.

ROCHFORD. Hasted's Kent, ii. 344. Morant's Essex, i. 269 ; ii. 615. Blomefield's Norfolk, ix. 104. The Genealogist, New Series, ix. 13.

ROCHFORT. Burke's Landed Gentry, (of Clogrenane,) 2, 4, 5, 6, 7 ; (of Westmeath,) 5, 6, 7, 8. Archdall's Lodge's Peerage, iii. 13. The Irish Builder, xxix. 289 ; xxxv. 78.

ROCHFORT-BOYD. Burke's Landed Gentry, 5, 6.

ROCK. Memoirs of Captn. Rock, with some Account of his Ancestors. London, 1824, 12mo.

ROCKE. Burke's Landed Gentry, 5, 6, 7, 8. The Sheriffs of Montgomeryshire, by W. V. Lloyd, 455. Harleian Society, xxix. 421.

ROCKLEY, or ROKELEY. Foster's Yorkshire Pedigrees. . Foster's Visitations of Yorkshire, 343. Thoresby's Ducatus Leodiensis, 25. Hunter's Deanery of Doncaster, ii. 286. Surtees Society, xli. 76. Harleian Society, xvi. 264. The Genealogist, New Series, xv. 217.

ROCLIFFE, or ROCLYFFE. Glover's History of Derbyshire, ii. 392, (359). Foster's Visitations of Yorkshire, 285, 383. Whitaker's Deanery of Craven, 154, (215). Surtees Society, xli. 58. Harleian Society, xvi. 265.

RODD. Account of the Township of Church Enstone, by Rev. E. Marshall, 68. Burke's Commoners, i. 260, Landed Gentry, 2, 3, 4, 5, 6, 7, 8. Robinson's Mansions of Herefordshire, 242. A Complete Parochial History of the County of Cornwall, iv. 11. An Historical Survey of Cornwall, by C. S. Gilbert, ii. 249. Cooke's Continuation of Duncumb's Hereford, (Hund. of Grimsworth,) Part ii. 189.

RODDAM. Burke's Commoners, i. 675, Landed Gentry, 2, 3, 4, 5, 6, 7, 8. Harleian Society, xvi. 267. Foster's Visitations of Northumberland, 106.

RODE. Visitation of Staffordshire, 1663-4, printed by Sir T. Phillipps, 8. Ormerod's Cheshire, iii. 53. Harleian Society, xviii. 195. Visitations of Staffordshire, 1614 and 1663-4, William Salt Society, 249.

RODES. Glover's History of Derbyshire, ii. 91, (82). Burke's Commoners, iii. 562, Landed Gentry, 2, 3, 4, 5, 6, 7. Thoresby's Ducatus Leodiensis, 94. Hunter's Deanery of Doncaster, ii. 130.

Pilkington's View of Derbyshire, ii. 366. Boothroyd's History of Pontefract, 268. Wotton's English Baronetage, ii. 255. Burke's Extinct Baronetcies. The Genealogist, New Series, viii. 71 ; xvii. 173. Harleian Society, xxxvii. 38 ; xxxviii. 583. *See* DE RODES.

RODGER. Burke's Landed Gentry, 4, 5, 6, 8.

RODGERS. Foster's Yorkshire Pedigrees. New England Register, x. 352. Harleian Society, xxxix. 1080.

RODHAM. Pedigrees from Visitation of Northumberland, printed by Sir T. Phillipps, (Middle Hill, 1858, fol.) 4. The Genealogist, i. 302.

RODICK. Burke's Heraldic Illustrations, 45.

RODINGTON. Eyton's Antiquities of Shropshire, vii. 380.

RODMAN, Notes on Rodman Genealogy, by W. W. Rodman. London, (?) 1889, 8vo.

RODNEY. Collinson's Somerset, iii. 604. Gentleman's Magazine, 1831, i. 296. Visitation of Somersetshire, printed by Sir T. Phillipps, 132. Harleian Society, xi. 93. Edmondson's Baronagium Genealogicum, vi. 101. Brydges' Collins' Peerage, vii. 555. Weaver's Visitations of Somerset, 70. The Genealogist, New Series, xvi. 169 ; xvii. 6, 100.

RODON. Burke's Landed Gentry, 3, 4, 5, 6. Burke's Visitations of Seats and Arms, i. 61. *See* ROWDEN.

RODRI MAWR (Descendants of). Dwnn's Visitations of Wales, ii. 16, 50, 98, 100, 106.

RODVILE. Nichols' History of the County of Leicester, iv. 643.

ROE. Burke's Landed Gentry, 3, 4, 5. W. Robinson's History of Hackney, ii. 11. Nichols' History of the County of Leicester, iv. 1005. Harleian Society, xiii. 282. Miscellanea Genealogica et Heraldica, New Series, iv. 116. Notes and Queries, 7 S. v. 402.

ROEBUCK. Harleian Society, xxxviii. 702 ; xxxix. 1163.

ROECH (THOMAS LE). Dwnn's Visitations of Wales, i. 71, 164.

ROGAN. O'Hart's Irish Pedigrees, 2nd Series, 299.

ROGER. The Scottish House of Roger, with Notes respecting the Families of Playfair and Haldane, by Rev. C. Rogers. Edinburgh, 1872 ; 2nd edition, 1875, 8vo. An Historical Summary of the Roger Tenants of Coupar, by J. C. Roger. London, 1879, 8vo. Some Account of the Rogers of Coupar Grange, by J. C. Roger. London, 1877. Herald and Genealogist, viii. 452. Four Perthshire Families—Roger, Playfair, Constable, and Haldane, by Rev. C. Rogers. Edinburgh, 1887, 4to.

ROGER AP HARRI. Dwnn's Visitations of Wales, i. 211.

ROGERLEY. Chetham Society, lxxxii. 13.

ROGERS. Pedigree of Rogers of Broadway and Wickhamford, Co. Glouc., [T. P.] 1850, folio page. Pedigrees of Rogers of Dowdeswell, Mauncel, Freeman of Saintbury and Buckland, etc., [T. P.] folio page. John Rogers, by J. L. Chester. London, 1861, 8vo. Miscellanea Genealogica et Heraldica, i. 258. Gentleman's Magazine, 1856, i. 383, 442. Visitation of Middlesex, (Salisbury, 1820, fol.) 2. Berry's Sussex Genealogies, 338. Dwnn's Visita-

tions of Wales, i. 67, 145, 229. Wotton's English Baronetage, iv.
77. Aubrey's Collections for Wilts, (London, 1821, 4to.) printed
by Sir T. Phillipps, ii. 46. Burke's Commoners, (of Yarlington
Lodge,) iv. 625, Landed Gentry, 2, 3, 4, 5, 6, 7, 8; (of River
Hill,) 8; (of Penrose,) Commoners, i. 299, Landed Gentry, 2, 3,
4, 5, 6, 7, 8; (of Rainscombe,) Landed Gentry, 2, 3, 4, 5, 6,
7, 8; (of the Home,) 2, 3, 4, 5, 6, 7, 8; (of Lota,) 2, 3, 4, 5; (of
River Hill,) 5, 6, 7, 8. Maclean's History of Trigg Minor, i. 392.
Harleian Society, ix. 188; xi 128; xii. 202; xvii. 209; xx. 79;
xxi. 139; xxii. 87; xxxvii. 367; xxxviii. 799; xxxix. 1052; xli.
118. Topographical Collections of John Aubrey, edited by J. E.
Jackson, 22. Burke's Heraldic Illustrations, 17. Hampshire
Visitations, printed by Sir T. Phillipps, 22. Visitatio Comitatus
Wiltoniæ, 1623, printed by Sir T. Phillipps. Hutchins' Dorset,
i. 250. Hunter's Deanery of Doncaster, i. 311. Wilson's History
of the Parish of St. Laurence Pountney, 239. Wiltshire Archæological Magazine, v. 357, 366. An Historical Survey of Cornwall,
by C. S. Gilbert, ii. 250. O'Hart's Irish Pedigrees, 2nd Series,
300. Notes and Queries, 1 S. v. 247, 307, 508, 522; vi. 63;
3 S. i. 519; 6 S. i. 462. Betham's Baronetage, iii. 118. The
Genealogist, vi. 84; New Series, xii. 238. The Visitations of
Cornwall, edited by J. L. Vivian, 404. History of Powys Fadog,
by J. Y. W. Lloyd, ii. 343. Visitation of Gloucester, edited by
T. F. Fenwick and W. C. Metcalfe, 145. Foster's Visitations of
Northumberland, 107. Bysshe's Visitation of Essex, edited by
J. J. Howard, 76. Foster's Visitation of Middlesex, 4. Genea-
logical Gleanings in England, by H. F. Waters, i. 209, 213. New
England Register, iv. 179; v. 105, 224; vi. 235; x. 148; xii.
337; xiii. 61; xvii. 43, 326; xxi. 172; xxiii. 273; xxxix. 225;
xli. 158, 165. Ontarian Families, by E. M. Chadwick, ii. 9.
Howard's Visitation of England and Wales, vi. 129, 133. Healey's
History of Part of West Somerset, 292. See COXWELL-ROGERS.
ROGERS-HARRISON. Berry's Hertfordshire Genealogies, 252.
ROGERSON. Burke's Landed Gentry, 8.
ROGES. Healey's History of Part of West Somerset, 240, 252.
ROKEBY. Æconomia Rokebiorum, an account of the family of
Rokeby, by A. W. C. Hallen. Issued with Northern Notes and
Queries, vol. i. 1887. Claim of the Rt. Hon. Matthew Baron
Rokeby to Vote at Elections of Irish Peers, Sess. Papers, 153 of
1830. Surtees Society, xxxvi. 73, 167, 184, 372; xli. 40.
Gentleman's Magazine, 1825, ii. 212. Burke's Commoners, iv.
666, Landed Gentry, 2, 3, 4, 5, 6, 7, 8. Foster's Yorkshire
Pedigrees. Foster's Visitations of Yorkshire, 128, 199, 352.
Harleian Society, viii. 426; xvi. 268; xxxviii. 587, 595. History
of the Town and School of Rugby, by N. H. Nicolas, 3. Thoresby's
Ducatus Leodiensis, 255. Archæologia Æliana, 2nd Series, v. 19.
Dugdale's Warwickshire, 23. Hunter's Deanery of Doncaster,
i. 203; ii. 102. Plantagenet-Harrison's History of Yorkshire,
i. 407, 410. Yorkshire Archæological and Topographical Journal,
vi. 202. Burke's Extinct Baronetcies. Scott's Poetical Works,

(Author's edn. 1869,) app. to Rokeby, 364. The Genealogist, New Series, xv. 253 ; xvi. 48-55.

ROKES. Berry's Buckinghamshire Genealogies, 82.

ROKEWODE. Visitation of Norfolk, published by Norfolk Archæological Society, i. 140. Metcalfe's Visitations of Suffolk, 101. Harleian Society, xxxii. 235. *See* ROOKWOOD.

ROLFE. Morant's Essex, ii. 380. Berry's Hampshire Genealogies, 210, 279. Berry's Kent Genealogies, 427, 455. Burke's Landed Gentry, 2 supp., 3, 4, 5, 6, 7, 8. Visitatio Comitatus Wiltoniæ, 1623, printed by Sir T. Phillipps. Metcalfe's Visitations of Suffolk, 204. Harleian Society, xvii. 210 ; xxii. 88 ; xlii. 175. Hasted's Kent, (Hund. of Blackheath, by H. H. Drake,) 21. New England Register, iii. 149 ; xxxvi. 143. The Genealogist, New Series, xiii. 240.

ROLL, ROLLE, or ROLLES. Westcote's Devonshire, edited by G. Oliver and P. Jones, 593. Visitation of Oxfordshire, 1634, printed by Sir T. Phillipps, (Middle Hill, fol.) 29. Harleian Society, v. 328 ; vi. 244, 323 ; viii. 30 ; ix. 290; xvii. 214. A Complete Parochial History of the County of Cornwall, i. 2. An Historical Survey of Cornwall, by C. S. Gilbert, i. 489. Brydges' Collins' Peerage, viii. 516. Visitation of Devon, edited by F. T. Colby, 184. Banks' Dormant and Extinct Baronage, iii. 641. Visitations of Devon, by J. L. Vivian, 652, 656.

ROLLAND. Burke's Commoners, iii. 611, Landed Gentry, 2.

ROLLESLEY. Jewitt's Reliquary, x. 167. The Genealogist, New Series, viii. 73.

ROLLESTON, or ROLSTON. Burke's Landed Gentry, (of Watnall,) 2, 3, 4, 5, 6, 7, 8 ; (of Franckfort,) 2, 3, 4, 5, 6, 7, 8. Foster's Visitations of Yorkshire, 569. Harleian Society, iv. 169 ; xl. 1278. Shaw's Staffordshire, i. 29. The Genealogist, New Series, viii. 74. The Visitations of Staffordshire, 1614 and 1663-4, William Salt Society, 250. Burke's Colonial Gentry, ii. 603.

ROLLINS. New England Register, viii. 253.

ROLLO. Appendix to Case of Sir J. S. Sidney, claiming to be Lord Lisle. Kent's British Banner Displayed, 361. Burke's Royal Descents and Pedigrees of Founders' Kin, 19. Wood's Douglas's Peerage of Scotland, ii. 396. Northern Notes and Queries, iv. 143.

ROLLS. Burke's Landed Gentry, 2, 3, 4, 5, 6, 7. T. Nicholas' County Families of Wales, 784. *See* ROLL.

ROLT, or ROLTE. Berry's Kent Genealogies, 385. Burke's Extinct Baronetcies. Burke's Landed Gentry, 5. Clutterbuck's Hertford, ii. 426. Cussan's History of Hertfordshire, Parts xi. and xii. 161. Burke's Family Records, 513. Harvey's Hundred of Willey, 520. Harleian Society, xix. 133, 134 ; xlii. 196.

ROMAINE. History of Hartlepool, by Sir C. Sharp, (1816, 8vo.) 77. The Theology of Consolation, by D. C. A. Agnew, 347.

ROMARA. Antiquities of Lacock Abbey, by W. L. Bowles and J. G. Nicholls, 65.

ROMARY. Harleian Society, xx. 275.

ROMESEY. Hoare's Wiltshire, III. v. 13.

ROMILLY. Burke's Landed Gentry, 8.

ROMNEY. Harleian Society, i. 88; xvii. 212. Phillimore's London and Middlesex Note-Book, 58.

ROMPENEY. Harleian Society, xxvii. 111.

ROMSEY. Visitation of Somersetshire, printed by Sir T. Phillipps, 133.

RONALD. Burke's Colonial Gentry, ii. 609.

RONAYNE. Burke's Landed Gentry, 2.

RONDELL. Harleian Society, xxi. 71.

RONE. Harleian Society, xiii. 281; xxix. 422.

RONESHALE. The Genealogist, New Series, xvi. 87.

RONKSLEY. Harleian Society, xxxvii. 230.

ROOE. Camden Society, xliii. 92. Nichols' History of the County of Leicester, iv. 1005. The Genealogist, New Series, viii. 75.

ROOKE. Berry's Kent Genealogies, 301. Burke's Landed Gentry, 4, 5, 6, 7, 8. Harleian Society, viii. 443; xlii. 184. History of Barnsley, by Rowland Jackson, 97. Scott of Scott's Hall, 185. The Genealogist, iv. 195-208. Miscellanea Genealogica et Heraldica, New Series, iii. 323.

ROOKES. Burke's Commoners, iii. 63, Landed Gentry, 2. Foster's Yorkshire Pedigrees. History of Bradford, by John James, 437. Whitaker's Loidis and Elmete, 202. John Watson's History of Halifax, 234. The Bradford Antiquary, i. 25. Harleian Society, xvi. 366; xxxvii. 39. The Genealogist, vii. 247.

ROOKWOOD. Collectanea Topographica et Genealogica, ii. 120-147. Harleian Society, xxxii. 236. Blomefield's Norfolk, viii. 288. Foley's Records of the English Province S. J., iii. 788. See ROKEWODE.

ROOME. Burke's Landed Gentry, 8.

ROOPE, or ROUPE. Tuckett's Devonshire Pedigrees, 180, 182. Burke's Commoners, iv. 136. Harleian Society, vi. 246. Visitations of Devon, by J. L. Vivian, 657, 658.

ROOPER. Burke's Landed Gentry, 3, 4, 5, 6, 7, 8.

ROOS. Appendix to Case of Sir J. S. Sidney, claiming to be Lord Lisle. Foster's Visitations of Yorkshire, 569. Harleian Society, ii. 92; iii. 8; iv. 111. Clutterbuck's Hertford, iii. 393. Herald and Genealogist, vii. 535. Dickinson's History of Southwell, 2nd edn., 274. Baker's Northampton, i. 269. Thoroton's Nottinghamshire, iii. 207. Banks' Baronies in Fee, i. 377. Banks' Dormant and Extinct Baronage, i. 167, 404; ii. 441. The Genealogist, New Series, xvii. 243. See DE ROOS.

ROOTS, or ROOTES. Berry's Sussex Genealogies, 242. Howard's Visitation of England and Wales, i. 290.

ROPE. Ormerod's Cheshire, iii. 497. Howard's Visitation of England and Wales, ii. 91.

ROPER. Hasted's Kent, i. 55; ii. 605. Berry's Kent Genealogies, 214. Burke's Royal Families, (London, 1851, 8vo.) ii. 152. Herald and Genealogist, iii. 417. Visitation of Derbyshire, 1663-4, (Middle Hill, 1854, fol.) 6. Surtees' Durham, i. 107.

Memoirs of the Family of Chester, by R. E. C. Waters, 586. The Genealogist, iii. 14; New Series, xiii. 140. Edmondson's Baronagium Genealogicum, iv. 383. Brydges' Collins' Peerage, vii. 67. Visitation of Norfolk, published by Norfolk Archæological Society, ii. 44. Harleian Society, xxxii. 237; xlii. 81, 83. Burke's Landed Gentry, 8. Annals of the English Benedictines of Ghent, 184. *See* TREVOR-ROPER.

ROPER-CALDBECK. Burke's Landed Gentry, 8.

ROPP. Harleian Society, xviii. 196.

ROS. Burton's History of Hemingborough, 270. *See* ROOS.

ROSCARROCK. Maclean's History of Trigg Minor, i. 546, 556-563; iii. 296. Polwhele's History of Cornwall, ii. 42. Harleian Society, ix. 189. A Complete Parochial History of the County of Cornwall, i. 337. An Historical Survey of Cornwall, by C. S. Gilbert, ii. 251. The Visitations of Cornwall, edited by J. L. Vivian, 399.

ROSCELYN. Banks' Baronies in Fee, ii. 123.

ROSCOMMON. Claim of the Earl of Roscommon to Vote at Elections of Irish Peers, Sess. Papers, 122 of 1823; 62 of 1824; 46 of 1825; 116 of 1826; 40 of 1826-7; 138 of 1828. The Roscommon claim of Peerage explained, by J. S. Taylor, 1829, 8vo.

ROSE. History of the Family of Rose of Kilravock, edited by Cosmo Innes, Esq. Edinburgh, 1848, 4to. Rose *v.* Rose, Appellant's Case in House of Lords, 1787. Berry's Sussex Genealogies, 25. Burke's Commoners, iv. 221; (of Kilravock,) Landed Gentry, 2, 3, 4, 5, 6, 7, 8; (of Cransley Hall,) 4, 5, 6, 7; (of Leiston Old Abbey,) 1, 5; (of the Ferns,) 4, 5, 6, 7, 8; (of Holme,) 2, 3, 4, 5, 6, 7, 8; (of Woolston Heath,) 2, 3, 4, 5, 6 supp., 7, 8; (of Ahabeg,) 4, 5, 6, 7, 8; (of Glastullick,) 4, 5, 6, 7; (of Sandhills,) 2. Burke's Heraldic Illustrations, 7. Dallaway's Sussex, i. 120. History of Wednesbury, (Wolverhampton, 1854, 8vo.) 171. Baker's Northampton, i. 317. Castles, Mansions, and Manors of Western Sussex, by D. G. C. Elwes and C. J. Robinson, 259. Douglas's Baronage of Scotland, 453. Shaw's History of Moray, 118. F. G. Lee's History of Thame, 608, 630. Northern Notes and Queries, iv. 132. Burke's Family Records, 514.

ROSEL. Thoroton's Nottinghamshire, i. 184. *See* ROSSELL.

ROSER. Metcalfe's Visitations of Suffolk, 101.

ROSETHORNE. Chetham Society, lxxxviii. 248. Harleian Society, xliii. 61. *See* RAWSTORNE.

ROSEWARNE, or ROSEWARAN. Harleian Society, ix. 191. The Visitations of Cornwall, edited by J. L. Vivian, 407.

ROSKELL. Burke's Landed Gentry, 2. Burke's Heraldic Illustrations, 99.

ROSKIMER. Westcote's Devonshire, edited by G. Oliver and P. Jones, 632. *See* RESKYMER.

ROSKROWE, or ROSKRUGE. Harleian Society, ix. 192. The Visitations of Cornwall, edited by J. L. Vivian, 408, 409.

ROSS. A Genealogical Account of the Rosses of Dalton, in the County of Dumfries, etc., to the year of our Lord 1854, by John

Parker Knowles. London, 1865, 8vo. Ane Breve Chronicle of
the Earlis of Ross, including Notices of the Family of Ross of
Balnagown. Edinburgh, 1850, 4to. Kent's British Banner Dis-
played, 729. Burke's Commoners, (of Craigie,) iii. 644, Landed
Gentry, 2; (of Rossie Castle,) Landed Gentry, 2 supp.; (of
Dalton,) 2 supp., 3, 4; (of Rosstrevor,) 2, 3, 4, 5, 6, 7, 8; (of
Cromarty,) 4, 5, 6, 7, 8; (of Netherley,) 5, 6, 7, 8; (of Arnage,)
7, 8; (of Glenmoidart,) 7; (of Ross Hill,) 7; 8 at p. 1014; (of
Invercharron,) 5, 6, 6th edn. p. 831, 7; (of Pitcalnie,) 6, 7, 8.
Foster's Visitations of Yorkshire, 213. Burke's Visitation of
Seats and Arms, 2nd Series, i. 45; ii. 20. Nichols' History of
the County of Leicester, ii. 27. Nisbet's Heraldry, ii. app. 24.
A Short Memoir of James Young, app. 16. Wood's Douglas's
Peerage of Scotland, ii. 410, 417. Northern Notes and Queries,
iii. 140; iv. 1, 51, 102, 163; v. 27; vi. 81; vii. 15, 124, 182;
viii. 26; Index facing p. 193. Thirteen Equity Cases, 287. A.D.
1871. Burke's Colonial Gentry, i. 177; ii. 537. Notes and
Queries, 6 S. xi. 31, 256. Ontarian Families, by E. M. Chadwick, i. 165; ii. 105. Rockingham Castle and the Watsons,
ped. 4. *See* COULTHART.

ROSSALL. Transactions of Shropshire Archæological Society, iv. 89.

ROSSANDALL. Dwnn's Visitations of Wales, ii. 333.

ROSSE. Surtees Society, xxxvi. 250. Visitation of Somersetshire,
printed by Sir T. Phillipps, 133. Harleian Society, xi. 95. The
Genealogist, New Series, xvii. 72.

ROSSELL. Harleian Society, iv. 119. *See* ROSEL.

ROSSENDALE. Miscellanea Genealogica et Heraldica, ii. 277.

ROSSETUR, ROSSITER, or ROCETER. Harleian Society, viii. 52. The
Genealogist, iv. 273; vi. 278.

ROSSINGTON. Visitation of Derbyshire, 1663-4, (Middle Hill, 1854,
fol.) 6. The Genealogist, iii. 14. Harleian Society, xxxvii.
341.

ROSS-LEWIN. Burke's Landed Gentry, 2, 3, 4, 5, 6, 7, 8.

ROSUGGAN. Harleian Society, ix. 193. The Visitations of Cornwall,
edited by J. L. Vivian, 411.

ROTCH. Burke's Landed Gentry, 2.

ROTHERAM, or ROTHERHAM. Burke's Landed Gentry, 2 supp., 3, 4,
5, 6, 7, 8. Morant's Essex, ii. 88. Bysshe's Visitation of Essex,
edited by J. J. Howard, 77. Heywood's Diaries, edited by J. H.
Turner, i. 13. Harleian Society, xix. 49, 135, 191; xxii. 88.

ROTHERFORD. Harleian Society, xvi. 269.

ROTHERY. Burke's Landed Gentry, 3, 4, 5, 6. Burke's Royal
Descents and Pedigrees of Founders' Kin, 80.

ROTHSAY. Wood's Douglas's Peerage of Scotland, ii. 436.

ROTHWELL. Burke's Landed Gentry, (of Rockfield,) 2, 3, 4, 5, 6, 7;
(of Shantonagh,) 3, 4, 5, 6, 7, 8. Burke's Authorized Arms, 179.
Shirley's History of the County of Monaghan, 256. Burke's
Extinct Baronetcies. Harleian Society, xxxvii. 71.

ROTSEY. Harleian Society, xxvii. 112.

ROUGHAN. Irish Pedigrees, by John O'Hart, 2nd Series, 97.

ROUGHSEDGE. Burke's Landed Gentry, 2, 3, 4.

ROULT. Harleian Society, viii. 366.

ROUND. Berry's Essex Genealogies, 31. Berry's Kent Genealogies, 191. Burke's Landed Gentry, (of Birch,) 2, 3, 4, 5, 6, 7, 8; (of Danbury Park,) 2, 3, 4, 5, 7; (of Tipton,) 5, 6, 7, 8; (of West Bergholt,) 8. Harleian Society, xiv. 699.

ROUNDELL. Surtees Society, xxxvi. 208. Burke's Commoners, i. 342, Landed Gentry, 2, 3, 4, 5, 6, 7, 8. Foster's Yorkshire Pedigrees. Burke's Visitation of Seats and Arms, ii. 27. Whitaker's Deanery of Craven, 71, (95). Old Yorkshire, ed. by Willm. Smith, v. 191.

ROUNSEVILL. New England Register, xix. 47.

ROUPELL. Burke's Landed Gentry, 2, 3, 4, 5 and supp.

ROUS. Camden Society, lxvi. v.; xliii. 103. Berry's Hampshire Genealogies, 11. Nash's Worcestershire, ii. 85. Burke's Commoners, i. 118, Landed Gentry, 2, 3, 4, 5, 6. Suckling's History of Suffolk, ii. 366. Harleian Society, ix. 193; xiii. 478. Nichols' History of the County of Leicester, ii. App. 45. Dugdale's Warwickshire, 853. A Complete Parochial History of the County of Cornwall, i. 301. An Historical Survey of Cornwall, by C. S. Gilbert, ii. 253. Miscellanea Genealogica et Heraldica, New Series, iii. 346. Brydges' Collins' Peerage, viii. 476. Wotton's English Baronetage, iii. 159. Visitation of Devon, edited by F. T. Colby, 184. Betham's Baronetage, iv. 213. Metcalfe's Visitations of Suffolk, 61, 62, 161. The Visitations of Cornwall, edited by J. L. Vivian, 413. Rysshe's Visitation of Essex, edited by J. J. Howard, 77. The Genealogist, New Series, xiv. 253.

ROUSE. Harleian Society, vi. 350; ix. 206; xxvii. 113. Westcote's Devonshire, edited by G. Oliver and P. Jones, 580. Burke's Extinct Baronetcies. Burke's Landed Gentry, 8.

ROUSWELL. Visitation of Somersetshire, printed by Sir T. Phillipps, 133, 148. See ROWSEWELL.

ROUTH, or ROUTHE. Pedigree of the Rev. Martin Routh of South Elmham, Co. Suffolk, 1850, [T. P.] folio page. Foster's Visitations of Yorkshire, 570. Yorkshire Genealogist, i. 233.

ROUTHMELL. History of Chipping, by Tom C. Smith, 201.

Row, or ROWE. Miscellanea Genealogica et Heraldica, i. 162, 166; New Series, ii. 252. Morant's Essex, i. 35. Berry's Sussex Genealogies, 117. Tuckett's Devonshire Pedigrees, 175, 176. Memoirs of the Family of Row, by James Maidment. Edinburgh, 1828, 4to. Visitation of Middlesex, (Salisbury, 1820, fol.) 16. Burke's Landed Gentry, 2, 3, 4, 5. Harleian Society, i. 5; vi. 247, 248; viii. 374; xiii. 479; xvii. 213; xviii. 197; xix. 193. Nichols' History of the County of Leicester, iv. 1005. Account of the Company of Ironmongers, by John Nicholl, 2nd edn., 531. W. Robinson's History of Hackney, ii. 11. Visitation of London in Transactions of the London and Middlesex Archæological Society, 20. Surtees' Durham, ii. 203. Sussex Archæological Collections, xxiv. 98. Castles, Mansions, and Manors of Western Sussex, by D. G. C. Elwes and C. J. Robinson, 239. Notes and

Queries, 1 S. iii. 408, 470; ix. 371, 449; x. 325, 433; 2 S. vii. 477, 518; 3 S. ii. 459; iii. 74; 5 S. vi. 375, 494; vii. 372. Visitation of Devon, edited by F. T. Colby, 185. Earwaker's East Cheshire, ii. 482. Foster's Visitation of Middlesex, 30. Metcalfe's Visitations of Northamptonshire, 130. Foster's Visitations of Durham, 259. Genealogies of Morgan and Glamorgan, by G. T. Clark, 502. Alexander Nisbet's Heraldic Plates, 120. Phillimore's London and Middlesex Note-Book, 104. Visitations of Devon, by J. L. Vivian, 660.

ROWALLANE. Historie and Descent of the House of Rowallane, by Sir W. Mure, Knt. Glasgow, 1825, 12mo.

ROWAN. Burke's Landed Gentry, 2, 3, 4, 5, 6, 7, 8. Burke's Heraldic Illustrations, 36. Burke's Colonial Gentry, ii. 594.

ROWBORO. Weaver's Visitations of Somerset, 129.

ROWBOTHAM. Harleian Society, xiii. 282. See ROBOTHAM.

ROWCLIFFE. Harleian Society, vi. 248. Visitations of Devon, by J. L. Vivian, 659.

ROWDEN, or ROWDON. Rowdon of Rowdon, County York, [by John Rodon,] Dublin, n.d., 4to., pp. 31. Duncumb's History of the Co. of Hereford, ii. 71. Robinson's Mansions of Herefordshire, 52. Weaver's Visitation of Herefordshire, 60. See RAWDEN, RODON.

ROWLAND. Descent of C. A., wife of T. W. Rowland, from Edw. I. Privately printed (circa 1883) by W. G. D. Fletcher, folio page. Dwnn's Visitations of Wales, ii. 184. Surrey Archæological Collections, v. Harleian Society, xliii. 187.

ROWLAND AP ROBERT. Dwnn's Visitations of Wales, ii. 247.

ROWLATT. Clutterbuck's Hertford, i. 217.

ROWLES. Visitation of Gloucester, edited by T. F. Fenwick and W. C. Metcalfe, 148.

ROWLET. Harleian Society, xii. 13.

ROWLEY. Evans, (Newcastle on Tyne, 1865, 8vo.) 13. Burke's Landed Gentry, (of Maperath,) 2 final add., 3, 4, 5, 6; (of Mount Campbell,) 2; (of De Beauvoir,) 8; (of Glassonby,) 8; (of Morcott,) 5 supp., 8. Archdall's Lodge's Peerage, v. 295. Betham's Baronetage, iv. 171. History of Powys Fadog, by J. Y. W. Lloyd, iv. 376. Harleian Society, xxix. 422. The Irish Builder, xxxv. 221.

ROWLEY-CONWY. Burke's Landed Gentry, 8.

ROWNTREE. Topographer and Genealogist, ii. 120.

ROWSE. Visitation of Sussex, 1570, printed by Sir T. Phillipps, (Middle Hill, fol.) 9. Harleian Society, xxxii. 238.

ROWSWELL. Visitatio Comitatus Wiltoniæ, 1623, printed by Sir T. Phillipps. The Genealogist, New Series, xii. 239. Weaver's Visitations of Somerset, 70. See ROUSWELL.

ROXBY. Burke's Landed Gentry, 3, 4, 5, 6, 7.

ROY. Burke's Landed Gentry, 2, 3, 4, 5, 6, 7, 8. Hutchins' Dorset, ii. 615.

ROYAL. New England Register, xxxix. 348.

ROYDON. Hasted's Kent, ii. 288. Harleian Society, xiv. 598; xliii.

179. History of Powys Fadog, by J. Y. W. Lloyd, iii. 111. Surrey Archæological Collections, xi.

ROYDS. Burke's Landed Gentry, (of Elm House,) 5 ; (of Falinge,) 5, 6, 7, 8. Fishwick's History of Rochdale, 510. Howard's Visitation of England and Wales, iii. 12 ; viii. 25 ; ix. 1.

ROYNON. Visitation of Somersetshire, printed by Sir T. Phillipps, 133. Harleian Society, xi. 95.

ROYS. Harleian Society, xvii. 214.

ROYSE. Burke's Landed Gentry, 2.

RUBENS. Papers illustrative of the life of Sir P. P. Rubens, by W. Noël Sainsbury, 1.

RUCK. Berry's Kent Genealogies, 16.

RUCK-KEENE. Burke's Landed Gentry, 2, 3, 4, 5, 6, 7, 8.

RUDD. Dwnn's Visitations of Wales, i. 79, 93. Caermarthenshire Pedigrees, 3. Surtees' Durham, iv. 107. Harleian Society, xiii. 480. The Genealogist, iv. 273. Burke's Extinct Baronetcies. Metcalfe's Visitations of Northamptonshire, 192.

RUDDER. See RUTTER.

RUDDLE. Cyclostyle Pedigrees, by J. J. Green.

RUDDY. O'Hart's Irish Pedigrees, 2nd Series, 137.

RUDGE. Burke's Commoners, iv. 197, Landed Gentry, 2, 3, 4, 5, 6, 7, 8. Harleian Society, xvii. 215.

RUDHALE, or RUDHALL. Duncombe's Hereford,* (J. H. Cooke,) iii. 165. Weaver's Visitation of Herefordshire, 93.

RUDIARD, or RUDYERD. Berry's Hampshire Genealogies, 50. Harleian Society, ii. 202 ; xvii. 215. Visitation of Staffordshire, 1663-4, printed by Sir T. Phillipps, 8. Jewitt's Reliquary, vii. 211-219. Burke's Extinct Baronetcies, 333. The Genealogist, vi. 85. Visitation of Staffordshire, (Willm. Salt Soc.) 126.

RUDING. Gentleman's Magazine, lxvi. 217. Harleian Society, ii. 104 ; xxvii. 115. Nichols' History of the County of Leicester, iv. 568. Leicestershire Architectural Society, v. 306.

RUDSDELL. Harleian Society, xl. 1289.

RUDSTON. Cambridgeshire Visitation, edited by Sir T. Phillipps, 26. Harleian Society, xli. 100. Surtees Society, xxxvi. 131. Foster's Visitations of Yorkshire, 126. Burke's Extinct Baronetcies. The Genealogist, New Series, x. 93.

RUDSTON-READ. Burke's Commoners, iv. 362, Landed Gentry, 2, 3, 4, 5, 6, 8. Foster's Yorkshire Pedigrees.

RUDYARD. Visitations of Staffordshire, 1614 and 1663-4, William Salt Society, 252.

RUFFORD. The Genealogist, vii. 248. Metcalfe's Visitation of Worcester, 1683, 80. Harleian Society, xxvii. 115.

RUFUS. Nash's Worcestershire, ii. 85. Willmore's History of Walsall, 105.

RUGELEY, or RUGGELEY. Erdeswicke's Survey of Staffordshire, 431. Dugdale's Warwickshire, 934. Bibliotheca Topographica Britannica, ix. Part 4, 29. Topographer and Genealogist, ii. 490. Visitation of Warwickshire, 1619, published with Warwickshire Antiquarian Magazine, 184. Shaw's Staffordshire, i. 211*. Visitation of

Staffordshire, 1663-4, printed by Sir T. Phillipps, 9. Harleian Society, xii. 153, 229 ; xvii. 216. Miscellanea Genealogica et Heraldica, New Series, iii. 201. Visitation of Staffordshire, (Willm. Salt Soc.) 127. Visitations of Staffordshire, 1614 and 1663-4, William Salt Society, 256.

RUGGE. Blomefield's Norfolk, xi. 36.

RUGGLES. Berry's Essex Genealogies, 84.

RUGGLES-BRICE. Berry's Essex Genealogies, 84. Burke's Commoners, i. 486, Landed Gentry, 2, 3, 4, 5, 6, 7, 8. Harleian Society, xiv. 703.

RUGLEN. Claim of William, Earl of Ruglen, to be Earl of Cassilis, Sess. Papers, March 1760—Feb. 1761.

RUMBOLD. Betham's Baronetage, iv. 74, app. 15.

RUMNEY. Metcalfe's Visitation of Worcester, 1683, 81.

RUMSEY. Burke's Landed Gentry, 5 supp., 8. Jones' History of the County of Brecknock, ii. 511.

RUSH, or RUSHE. Morant's Essex, i. 305 ; ii. 300, 302. Berry's Essex Genealogies, 82. Burke's Commoners, ii. 61, Landed Gentry, 2, 3, 4, 5, 6, 7, 8. Collectanea Topographica et Genealogica, ii. 288. Baker's Northampton, i. 622. Harleian Society, xiii. 481 ; xiv. 703. Metcalfe's Visitations of Suffolk, 63.

RUSHALL. Visitation of Warwickshire, 1619, published with Warwickshire Antiquarian Magazine, 77. Shaw's Staffordshire, ii. 69. Harleian Society, xxviii. 217. Willmore's Records of Rushall, 13. Willmore's History of Walsall, 249.

RUSHBROOKE. Burke's Landed Gentry, 2, 3, 4, 5, 6, 7, 8. Metcalfe's Visitations of Suffolk, 197.

RUSHFORTH. Ilkley, Ancient and Modern, by R. Collyer and J. H. Turner, 235.

RUSHOUT. Nash's Worcestershire, i. 99. Blore's Rutland, 171. Brydges' Collins' Peerage, viii. 572. Wotton's English Baronetage, iii. 304. Metcalfe's Visitation of Worcester, 1683, 82.

RUSHTON. Chetham Society, lxxxi. 40 ; lxxxviii. 249. See RISHTON.

RUSKIN. Nichols' History of the County of Leicester, ii. 264.

RUSSEL, or RUSSELL. An Historical Account of the Original and Rise of the Russells, Earls of Bedford. London, 1684, 12mo. Collections for the Pedigree of Russell of Broadway, Co. Wigorn, [T. P.] 1871, folio page. A Sketch of the History of the House of Russell, by David Ross. London, 1848, 8vo. Anecdotes of the House of Bedford, from the Norman Conquest. London, (circa 1800) 8vo. Historical Memoirs of the House of Russell, by J. H. Wiffen. London, 1833, 8vo. 3 vols. Collinson's Somerset, ii. 372. Stephen Dodd's History of Woburn, 72-80. The Great Governing Families of England, ii. 25. Jacob's Peerage, i. 216. Croke's History of the Family of Croke, Nos. 25, 27. Morant's Essex, i. 103. Noble's Memoirs of the House of Cromwell, ii. 381-402. The Will of Richard Russell, Esq. London, 1784, 8vo. Visitation of Norfolk, published by Norfolk Archæological Society, i. 398. Visitation of Suffolk, edited by J. J. Howard, ii. 288.

Berry's Buckinghamshire Genealogies, 36-41. Berry's Sussex Genealogies, 235. Nash's Worcestershire, ii. 141, 395. Bibliotheca Topographica Britannica, vi. Part iii. xv. Burke's Commoners, (of Brancepeth,) i. vi. 104, Landed Gentry, 2 ; (of Dundas Castle,) 8 ; (of Maulside,) 8 ; (of Stubbers,) 8 ; (of Cleveden,) 8 ; (of Killough,) Landed Gentry, 2, 3, 4, 5 ; (of Stone,) 4, 5, 6, 7, 8 ; (of Aden,) 2, 3, 4, 5 and supp., 6, 7, 8 ; (of Ashiesteel,) 2, 3, 4, 5, 6, 7 ; (of Ilam Hall,) 2, 4, 5, 6 ; (of King's Heath,) 2 ; (of Ashford Hall,) 2 ; (of Donamaggan,) 6, 7. Foster's Visitations of Yorkshire, 325. Harleian Society, viii. 276, 334; xvii. 217 ; xxi. 50 ; xxvii. 116, 120 ; xxxii. 239 ; xxxviii. 439. Lipscombe's History of the County of Buckingham, ii. 194, 195 ; iii. 248. Bridges' Northamptonshire, by Rev. Peter Whalley, ii. 596. Hutchins' Dorset, i. 615 ; ii. 189, 782; iii. 242. Clutterbuck's Hertford, i. 193. Whitaker's Deanery of Craven, 3rd edn., 310. An Historical Survey of Cornwall, by C. S. Gilbert, i. 423. Edmondson's Baronagium Genealogicum, i. 32. Memoirs, British and Foreign, of Illustrious Persons who died in 1711, 207. Notes and Queries, 1 S. ix. 416. Berry's Genealogical Peerage, 36. Brydges' Collins' Peerage, i. 262. Wotton's English Baronetage, ii. 138. Banks' Baronies in Fee, ii. 125. Visitation of Devon, edited by F. T. Colby, 116. Betham's Baronetage, i. 364. Notes and Queries, 4 S. x. 190, 279 ; xii. 414 ; 5 S. ix. 461, 491, 510. Burke's Extinct Baronetcies. Metcalfe's Visitation of Worcester, 1683, 84. Miscellanea Genealogica et Heraldica, New Series, iv. 235. New England Register, xxvii. 290. Metcalfe's Visitations of Northamptonshire, 194. Weaver's Visitations of Somerset, 72. Genealogies of Morgan and Glamorgan, by G. T. Clark, 429. Burke's Colonial Gentry, i. 367 ; ii. 522. Howard's Visitation of England and Wales, v. 59. Berks Archæological and Architectural Society's Journal, iii. 194. The Genealogist, New Series, xiv. 27 ; xv. 125.

RUSSELL-PAVIER. Burke's Landed Gentry, 6, 7, 8. Burke's Family Records, 465.

RUST. Burke's Landed Gentry, 3, 4, 5, 6, 7, 8.

RUSTAT. Memoirs of Thomas Rustat, Esq., by Willm. Hewett, junr. London, 1849, 8vo.

RUSTON. Burke's Landed Gentry, 8.

RUTHALL. Lipscombe's History of the County of Buckingham, iv. 416. The Genealogist, vii. 249.

RUTHERFORD, or RUTHERFURD. The Rutherfords of that Ilk. Edinburgh, 1884, 4to. Burke's Landed Gentry, 2, 3, 4, 5, 6, 7, 8. Nisbet's Heraldry, ii. app. 219. Claim of Alexander Rutherford to the title of Lord Rutherford, Sess. Papers, Dec. 1761—March 1762. Jeffrey's History of Roxburghshire, ii. 277, 296. Wood's Douglas's Peerage of Scotland, ii. 458. Notes and Queries, 2 S. x. 55, 178 ; xii. 376. Foster's Visitations of Northumberland, 108.

RUTHVEN. Papers relating to Willm. first Earl of Gowrie, by John Bruce. London, 1867, 8vo. Burke's Landed Gentry, 5, 6, 7. Wood's Douglas's Peerage of Scotland, i. 605, 658 ; ii. 463.

Notes and Queries, 3 S. iii. 50; v. 188, 270; 4 S. i. 237, 496;
6 S. viii. 151. *See* OTWAY-RUTHVEN.

RUTINGTON. Thoroton's Nottinghamshire, i. 125.

RUTLAND. Kite's Monumental Brasses of Wiltshire, 74. Harleian
Society, xliii. 64.

RUTSON. Burke's Landed Gentry, 2 add., 3, 4, 6, 7, 8. Foster's
Yorkshire Pedigrees.

RUTTEN. Berry's Kent Genealogies, 184. History of Sandwich, by
W. Boys, 273.

RUTTER. Pedigree of Rutter of Quinton, [T. P.] 1866, 2 pages folio.
Pedigree of Rutter of Quinton and Bourton-on-the-Hill, Co.
Glouc., [T. P.] 1871, folio page. Foster's Yorkshire Pedigrees.
Jewitt's Reliquary, xii. 128, 229. Harleian Society, xii. 235;
xviii. 197. Ormerod's Cheshire, i. 741; ii. 94. 'Nottingham
Daily Guardian,' Newspaper, Dec. 15, 1886, 2. Gloucestershire
Notes and Queries, ii. 80. Visitation of Gloucester, edited by
T. F. Fenwick and W. C. Metcalfe, 149.

RUTTLEDGE. Burke's Landed Gentry, 2, 3, 4, 5, 6, 7, 8. Burke's
Colonial Gentry, i. 139.

RUXTON. Burke's Landed Gentry, (of Ardee House,) 2, 3, 4, 5, 6, 7,
8; (of Broad Oak,) 3, 4, 5, 6, 7, 8.

RUXTON - FITZHERBERT. Burke's Commoners, iv. 566, Landed
Gentry, 2.

RYAL. Plantagenet-Harrison's History of Yorkshire, i. 168.

RYAN. Burke's Landed Gentry, (of Inch House,) 2, 3, 4, 5, 6, 7; (of
Ballymackeogh,) 4, 5, 6, 7, 8; (of Knocklyon,) 4. O'Hart's Irish
Pedigrees, 2nd Series, 300. Burke's Colonial Gentry, i. 191.

RYAN-LENIGAN. Burke's Landed Gentry, 6, 7, 8.

RYCAUT, or RYCHAUT. Harleian Society, viii. 399; xvii. 219.

RYCE. Metcalfe's Visitations of Suffolk, 205.

RYCROFT. Betham's Baronetage, iv. 140.

RYCULF. Hasted's Kent, (Hund. of Blackheath, by H. H. Drake,)
216.

RYD. Dwnn's Visitations of Wales, i. 18, 79, 91, 93, 96, 198.

RYDDARCH AP RICHARD. Dwnn's Visitations of Wales, ii. 137.

RYDELEGH. Ormerod's Cheshire, ii. 297.

RYDER. Berry's Hertfordshire Genealogies, 230. Burke's Landed
Gentry, 2 supp., 3, 4. Harleian Society, viii. 128; xvi. 367.
Clutterbuck's Hertford, i. 325. Edmondson's Baronagium Genea-
logicum, vi. 73. Brydges' Collins' Peerage, v. 717. *See* RYTHER,
RIDER.

RYDEWARE. Nichols' History of the County of Leicester, iii. 982*.
See RIDWARE.

RYE, or RIE. An Account of the Family of Rye, by Walter Rye.
London, 1876, 8vo. Burke's Landed Gentry, 4, 5, 6, 7, 8.
Herald and Genealogist, vi. 33, 261; vii. 235; viii. 401. The
Genealogist, i. 67, 122. Plantagenet-Harrison's History of Yorkshire, i. 307. Banks' Baronies in Fee, ii. 127. Banks' Dormant
and Extinct Baronage, i. 166. Norfolk Antiquarian Miscellany,
i. 413; ii. 486. *See* DE RYE.

RYEDALE. History of the Ancient Ryedales, comprising the Genea-
logy of the families of Riddell, Ridley, etc., by G. T. Ridlon.
Manchester, N.H. 1884, 8vo.
RYELAND. Bysshe's Visitation of Essex, edited by J. J. Howard, 78.
RYERSON. Ontarian Families, by E. M. Chadwick, ii. 15.
RYHIL. Plantagenet-Harrison's History of Yorkshire, i. 166.
RYKELD. Bibliotheca Topographica Britannica, i. Part iii. 43.
RYKES. Topographer and Genealogist, iii. 178.
RYLAND, or RYLANDS. Foster's Lancashire Pedigrees. Miscellanea
Genealogica et Heraldica, New Series, ii. 558. Earwaker's Local
Gleanings, ii. 299. Burke's Commoners, iv. 406. The Forest
and Chase of Sutton Coldfield, (London, 1860, 8vo.) app. The
Genealogist, iv. 170. Howard's Visitation of England and Wales,
14, 245. Burke's Family Records, 515, 516. Croston's edn. of
Baines's Lancaster, iii. 161.
RYLEY. Chetham Society, lxxxi. 125. Visitatio Comitatus Wiltoniæ,
1623, printed by Sir T. Phillipps. Memoirs of the Family of
Chester, by R. E. C. Waters, 175. Lancashire and Cheshire
Genealogical and Historical Notes, i. 407. Norfolk Archæology,
viii. 317. The Genealogist, New Series, xii. 239.
RYMAN. Dallaway's Sussex, i. 96. Sussex Archæological Collections,
xviii. 81.
RYND. Burke's Landed Gentry, 4, 5, 6, 7, 8.
RYNGEWOOD. Hoare's Wiltshire, V. ii. 31.
RYPERS. The Genealogist, New Series, ix. 14.
RYPPLINGHAM. Plantagenet-Harrison's History of Yorkshire, i. 75.
RYRIE. Burke's Colonial Gentry, ii. 577.
RYS. Dwnn's Visitations of Wales, i. 253, 266.
RYS AP DAVID. Dwnn's Visitations of Wales, i. 151, 184; ap
Morgan, i. 241.
RYSUM. Harleian Society, xvi. 270.
RYTHE. Surrey Archæological Collections, xi. Harleian Society,
xliii. 197.
RYTHER. Surrey Archæological Collections, iii. Surtees Society,
xxxvi. 235. Foster's Visitations of Yorkshire, 145, 303. Stone-
house's History of the Isle of Axholme, 344. Whitaker's Loidis
and Elmete, 166. Read's History of the Isle of Axholme, edited
by T. C. Fletcher, 64. Duchetiana, by Sir G. F. Duckett, 2nd
edn., 221. Banks' Baronies in Fee, i. 383; ii. 39. Banks'
Dormant and Extinct Baronage, i. 405. W. Wheater's History of
Sherburn and Cawood, 322. Harleian Society, xliii. 191. See
DE RYTHRE, RYDER.
RYTON. Harleian Society, xvii. 218.
RYVERS. Carthew's Hundred of Launditch, Part ii. 671. The Genea-
logist, New Series, xiv. 104. See DE RYVERS, RIVERS.
RYVES. Burke's Commoners, iii. 51, Landed Gentry, 2, 3, 4. Har-
leian Society, viii. 177; xx. 80. Hutchins' Dorset, iv. 96. The
Genealogist, New Series, iii. 168. See RIVES.
RYVETT. Notes and Queries, 2 S. v. 188. Metcalfe's Visitations of
Suffolk, 63, 162, 206.

SABIN, or SABINE. Berry's Kent Genealogies, 461. Burke's Extinct Baronetcies. New England Register, xxxvi. 52.

SACHEVERELL. Visitation of Oxfordshire, 1634, printed by Sir T. Phillipps, (Middle Hill, fol.) 29. Harleian Society, ii. 45; iv. 163; xii. 391; xx. 81. Herald and Genealogist, vii. 533. Nichols' History of the County of Leicester, iii. 220, 394, 395, 509, 513, 1140. Thoroton's Nottinghamshire, i. 27, 97. The Genealogist, New Series, ii. 224.

SACHEVILLE. Chronicle of the Family of De Havilland.

SACKVILL, or SACKVILLE. Memoirs of the Noble Family of Sackville, by A. Collins. London, 1741, 8vo. A Topographical Sketch of Knowle in Kent, with a brief Genealogy of the Sackville Family, by J. Bridgman. London, 1797, 8vo. (Several other editions.) Notices of Swyncombe and Ewelme, in Co. Oxford, by H. A. Napier, 296. Collectanea Topographica et Genealogica, iii. 295. Hasted's Kent, i. 344. Jacob's Peerage, i. 408, 428. The Visitor's Guide to Knole, by J. H. Brady, 19. Berry's Sussex Genealogies, 300. Berry's Buckinghamshire Genealogies, 82. Lipscombe's History of the County of Buckingham, iii. 560. Wright's Essex, i. 436. Memoirs of the Family of Chester, by R. E. C. Waters, 200. Burke's Landed Gentry, 6, 7, 8. Edmondson's Baronagium Genealogicum, i. 70. Berry's Genealogical Peerage, 53. Brydges' Collins' Peerage, ii. 90. The Genealogist, New Series, xvii. 251. *See* DE SACVILL.

SADBURY. Plantagenet-Harrison's History of Yorkshire, i. 113.

SADLEIR, or SADLER. Berry's Hertfordshire Genealogies, 9. Berry's Hampshire Genealogies, 95. Burke's Commoners, (of Ballinderry,) ii. 560, Landed Gentry, 2, 3, 4, 5, 6, 7; (of Sadleir's Wells,) 2; (of Keynsham Bury,) 2, 3, 4, 5. Hoare's Wiltshire, II. ii. 198. Clutterbuck's Hertford, iii. 28, 229. Chauncy's Hertfordshire, 398. Fosbrooke's History of Gloucestershire, ii. 76. Gentleman's Magazine, 1835, i. 260. Dwnn's Visitations of Wales, i. 275. Visitation of Warwickshire, 1619, published with Warwickshire Antiquarian Magazine, 68. Visitatio Comitatus Wiltoniæ, 1623, printed by Sir T. Phillipps. Harleian Society, xii. 339; xiii. 481; xix. 136; xxii. 89. The State Papers of Sir Ralph Sadler, edited by Arthur Clifford, ii. 602. Collections by the Powys-land Club, x. 40. Visitation of Wiltshire, edited by G. W. Marshall, 14, 63. Burke's Extinct Baronetcies. Life and Times of Sir Ralph Sadleir, by F. S. Stoney, 247. The Genealogist, New Series, xiii. 240.

SAFFIN. Harleian Society, vi. 249. Jewitt's Reliquary, xiv. 236. Visitation of Gloucester, edited by T. F. Fenwick and W. C. Metcalfe, 151.

SAFFORD. Burke's Landed Gentry, 5.

SAGAR. Thoresby Society, i. 248.

SAGAR-MUSGRAVE. Burke's Landed Gentry, 8.

SAGER. Harleian Society, xxxvii. 149.

SAIES. Glamorganshire Pedigrees, edited by Sir T. Phillipps, 33.

ST. ALBIN, or ST. ALBYN. Collinson's Somerset, i. 264. Visitation

of Somersetshire, printed by Sir T. Phillipps, 137, 151. Burke's
Commoners, iv. 165, Landed Gentry, 2, 3, 4. Somersetshire Wills,
printed for F. A. Crisp, i. 86. *See* ST. AUBYN.

ST. AMAND. Lipscombe's History of the County of Buckingham,
i. 255. Banks' Baronies in Fee, i. 400. Banks' Dormant and
Extinct Baronage, ˄ii. 505. R. Ussher's Historical Sketch of
Croxall, 171.

ST. ANDREW. Harleian Society, iv. 78. Baker's Northampton,
i. 160. Thoroton's Nottinghamshire, i. 39.

ST. AUBIN, or ST. AUBYN. Harleian Society, ix. 212 ; xi. 96. A
Complete Parochial History of the County of Cornwall, i. 272.
An Historical Survey of Cornwall, by C. S. Gilbert, i. 567.
Wotton's English Baronetage, iii. 542. Betham's Baronetage,
ii. 423. The Visitations of Cornwall, edited by J. L. Vivian, 437.
Burke's Extinct Baronetcies, *add.* Weaver's Visitations of Somer-
set, 73. Burke's Landed Gentry, 7, 8. *See* ST. ALBIN.

ST. BARBE. Gentleman's Magazine, 1832, ii. 600 ; 1860, ii. 414.
Berry's Hampshire Genealogies, 2-6. Burke's Commoners, ii.
447, Landed Gentry, 2, 3. Visitatio Comitatus Wiltoniæ, 1623,
printed by Sir T. Phillipps. Hoare's Wiltshire, V. ii. 10. Visitation of Wiltshire, edited by G. W. Marshall, 49. Burke's Extinct
Baronetcies. Weaver's Visitations of Somerset, 73.

ST. CLAIR, SAINTCLAIRE, or ST. CLARE. The Case of Charles
St. Clair, Esq., claiming the Title of Lord Sinclair, 1782, folio, 3
leaves. Genealogie of the Saintclaires of Rosslyn, by Father
R. A. Hay. Edinburgh, 1835, 4to. Nisbet's Heraldry, ii. app. 171.
Burke's Landed Gentry, (of Roslin,) 3 supp., 4 ; (of Staverton,)
2, 3, 4, 5, 6, 8. Collinson's Somerset, iii. 7. The Crkneyinga
Saga, by Joseph Anderson, cxxxvi. The Genealogist, New Series,
x. 216. Caithness Family History, by John Henderson, 1-150,
255, 331. Northern Notes and Queries, ix. 40.

ST. CLERE. Morant's Essex, i. 455. Baker's Northampton, i. 432.
Visitation of Devon, edited by F. T. Colby, 185. *See* SEYNT-
CLERE.

ST. GEORGE. Howard's Visitation of England and Wales, i. 105.
Cambridgeshire Visitation, edited by Sir T. Phillipps, 30. Burke's
Landed Gentry, (of Tyrone,) 2, 3, 4, 5, 6, 7, 8 ; (of Headford
Castle,) 2, 3, 4, 5, 6, 7 ; (of Wood Park,) 2, 3, 4, 5, 6, 7, 8 ; (of
Hatley Manor,) 3, 4. Harleian Society, viii. 223 ; xli. 89. Me-
moirs of the Family of Chester, by R. E. C. Waters, 680. Miscel-
lanea Genealogica et Heraldica, New Series, iii. 77. Noble's
History of the College of Arms, 236, 352. J. B. Payne's Armorial
of Jersey, 99. Burke's Extinct Baronetcies.

ST. GERMANS. Burke's Royal Descents and Pedigrees of Founders'
Kin, 31.

SAINTHILL, or SENTHILL. Miscellanea Genealogica et Heraldica, i.
281. Gentleman's Magazine, 1824, i. 215. Harleian Society, vi.
249, 250 ; xvii. 220. Westcote's Devonshire, edited by G. Oliver,
and P. Jones, 537. Visitation of Devon, edited by F. T. Colby,
187. Visitations of Devon, by J. L. Vivian, 663.

ST. JOHN. Notitia St. Johanniana, Genealogical Memoirs of the Family of St. John, 1713, 8vo. Morant's Essex, ii. 430. Hasted's Kent, i. 82. Noble's Memoirs of the House of Cromwell, ii. 16-32. Lysons' Environs of London, i. 30. The Tyndale Pedigree, by B. W. Greenfield. Berry's Sussex Genealogies, 61. Berry's Hampshire Genealogies, 148, 232. Camden Society, xliii. 2. Burke's Royal Families, (London, 1851, 8vo.) ii. 7. J. H. Hill's History of Market Harborough, 133. Collectanea Topographica et Genealogica, i. 310. Topographical Collection of John Aubrey, edited by J. E. Jackson, 170. Dallaway's Sussex, i. 124. Brydges' Northamptonshire, by Rev. Peter Whalley, i. 254 ; ii. 266. Nichols' History of the County of Leicester, ii. 656. Visitatio Comitatus Wiltoniæ, 1623, printed by Sir T. Phillipps. Manning and Bray's Surrey, ii. 324. Baker's Northampton, ii. 96. Castles, Mansions, and Manors of Western Sussex, by D. G. C. Elwes and C. J. Robinson, 42. Topographical Miscellanies, 1792, 4to., (Boxgrove). Burke's Landed Gentry, 6, 7, 8. Memoirs, British and Foreign, of Illustrious Persons who died in 1711, 541. Notes and Queries, 2 S. ii. 381; vii. 27 ; viii. 386. Edmondson's Baronagium Genealogicum, iv. 328, 372. Brydges' Collins' Peerage, vi. 42, 741. Wotton's English Baronetage, iv. 174. Banks' Baronies in Fee, i. 401. Banks' Dormant and Extinct Baronage, i. 171, 410 ; ii. 512 ; iii. 87. Visitation of Wiltshire, edited by G. W. Marshall, 36. Burke's Extinct Baronetcies. Harleian Society, xvii. 221 ; xix. 51, 194. Hasted's Kent, (Hund. of Blackheath, by H. H. Drake,) xxvi. Harvey's Hundred of Willey, 457, 484. Genealogies of Morgan and Glamorgan, by G. T. Clark, 429. Brocas of Beaurepaire, by M. Burrows, 365. New England Register, xiv. 61. Lyon's Chronicles of Finchampstead, 167. Berks Archæological and Architectural Society's Journal, i. 128. The Genealogist, New Series, xvi. 1. Healey's History of Part of West Somerset, 65. See MILDMAY.

ST. JOHN-MILDMAY. Burke's Landed Gentry, 8.

ST. LAWRENCE. Topographer and Genealogist, iii. 178. John D'Alton's History of Co. Dublin, 156. Archdall's Lodge's Peerage, iii. 180. The Genealogist, New Series, xvii. 27.

ST. LEGER. Claim of the Rt. Hon. Henry Hayes St. Leger, Viscount Doneraile of Ireland, to vote at Elections of Irish Peers, Sess. Papers, 163 of 1854. Stemmata St. Leodegaria, by Edward F. St. Leger, Scotton, Kirton-in-Lindsey. Broadside, dated 1 Feb. 1867. History of Leeds Castle, by C. Wykeham-Martin, 157. Hasted's Kent, ii. 398, 422. Burke's Commoners, (of Hayward's Hill,) iv. 485, Landed Gentry, 2 and corr. ; (of Park Hill,) Landed Gentry, 5, 6, 7, 8. Westcote's Devonshire, edited by G. Oliver and P. Jones, 483. Sussex Archæological Collections, xii. 100. Scott of Scot's-Hall, by J. R. Scott, 228. A Complete Parochial History of the County of Cornwall, i. 1. Notes and Queries, 3 S. ii. 315 ; iii. 15. Archdall's Lodge's Peerage, vi. 92. Visitation of Devon, edited by F. T. Colby, 186. The Irish Builder, xxxv. 198. The Genealogist, New Series, xii. 76.

St. LIZ, or St. LYZ. Burke's Commoners, i. 651. Bridges' Northamptonshire, by Rev. Peter Whalley, i. 44. Banks' Dormant and Extinct Baronage, iii. 389, 560. The Genealogist, New Series, ix. 79.

St. LO, St. LOE, or St. LOWE. Collinson's Somerset, iii. 342. Harleian Society, viii. 208 ; xvii. 222. Visitatio Comitatus Wiltoniæ, 1623, printed by Sir T. Phillipps. Hutchins' Dorset, iv. 81. Visitation of Wiltshire, edited by G. W. Marshall, 54. Miscellanea Genealogica et Heraldica, 2nd Series, ii. 314.

St. MARTIN. Hoare's Wiltshire, V. i. 21. The Genealogist, New Series, x. 34.

St. MAUR. Collinson's Somerset, ii. 54. Visitatio Comitatus Wiltoniæ, 1623, printed by Sir T. Phillipps. Hoare's Wiltshire, I. i. 116 ; III. i. 4. Harleian Society, xvi. 283. Banks' Baronies in Fee, i. 404. Banks' Dormant and Extinct Baronage, ii. 517. Weaver's Visitations of Somerset, 129. *See* SEYMOUR.

St. MEDARD. Bridges' Northamptonshire, by Rev. Peter Whalley, ii. 596.

St. NICHOLAS. Planché's Corner of Kent, 361. Nichols' History of the County of Leicester, iv. 269.

St. OMER. Hoare's Wiltshire, III. iv. 44. The Genealogist, New Series, xiv. 98.

St. OWEN. Weaver's Visitations of Herefordshire, 94. Harleian Society, xxviii. 82, 152.

St. PAUL. Foster's Visitations of Yorkshire, 307, 356. Hunter's Deanery of Doncaster, ii. 464. The Genealogist, iv. 273. Burke's Extinct Baronetcies.

St. PETER. Harleian Society, xxix. 424.

St. PHILIBERT. History of the Hundred of Bray, by Charles Kerry, 86. Gage's History of Thingoe Hundred, Suffolk, 43. Banks' Baronies in Fee, i. 406. Banks' Dormant and Extinct Baronage, i. 411.

St. PIERE. Harleian Society, xiii. 482 ; xvii. 223 ; xviii. 193. Bysshe's Visitation of Essex, edited by J. J. Howard, 78. The Genealogist, New Series, xii. 108.

St. QUINTIN. Burke's Extinct Baronetcies. Surtees Society, xxxvi. 135. Burke's Landed Gentry, (of Scampston,) 4, 5, 6, 7, 8 ; (of Hatley St. George,) 5. Foster's Yorkshire Pedigrees. Foster's Visitations of Yorkshire, 127, 153, 162, 176. Poulson's Holderness, i. 266, 268. Harleian Society, xvi. 361. Bibliotheca Topographica Britannica, ix. Part 4, 274. Wotton's English Baronetage, ii. 280. Banks' Baronies in Fee, i. 406. Banks' Dormant and Extinct Baronage, i. 413.

St. SAUVEUR. History of the House of Arundel, by J. P. Yeatman, 80.

St. VALERY, or St. WALERY. The Genealogist, iv. 240. Lipscombe's History of the County of Buckingham, i. 367. Banks' Dormant and Extinct Baronage, i. 173. *See* YVERY.

SAKER. Berry's Kent Genealogies, 144. Harleian Society, xlii. 45.

SALADIN. Burke's Royal Families, (London, 1851, 8vo.) ii. 168.

44

SALCETO. Baker's Northampton, i. 176.

SALE. Chetham Society, lxxxviii. 252. Visitation of Derbyshire, 1663-4, (Middle Hill, 1854, fol.) 6. The Genealogist, iii. 14. Lancashire and Cheshire Antiquarian Notes, edited by W. D. Pink, 118. The Visitations of Devon, edited by J. L. Vivian, 76.

SALISBERIE, or SALISBURY. Annals and Antiquities of Lacock Abbey, with Memorials of Ela Countess of Salisbury and of the Earls of Salisbury, etc., by W. L. Bowles, and J. G. Nicholls. London, 1835, 8vo. Genealogical Account of the Ancient Earldom of Salisbury, by T. C. Banks. London, 1832, 8vo. Visitation of Somersetshire, printed by Sir T. Phillipps, 134. Burke's Royal Families, (London, 1851, 8vo.) i. 30, 31. Harleian Society, ii. 185; vi. 250. Herald and Genealogist, iv. 149; vi. 253. Nichols' History of the County of Leicester, iii. 940. Hutchins' Dorset, iii. 287. Hoare's Wiltshire, VI. (Old and New Sarum,) 40. Banks' Dormant and Extinct Baronage, iii. 644. Notes and Queries, 4 S. ix. 313, 453. Miscellanea Genealogica et Heraldica, 2nd Series, ii. 17. Weaver's Visitations of Somerset, 75. Visitations of Devon, by J. L. Vivian, 666. See MONTACUTE, SALSBRI, SALUSBURY.

SALKELD. Harleian Society, vii. 25; xvi. 271. Hutchinson's History of Cumberland, ii. 360. Hutchins' Dorset, i. 270. The Genealogist, ii. 18. Plantagenet-Harrison's History of Yorkshire, i. 333. Notes and Queries, 4 S. vii. 236. Foster's Visitations of Northumberland, 109. Foster's Visitations of Cumberland, and Westmorland, 112-114. Nicolson and Burn's Westmorland and Cumberland, ii. 122.

SALKYNS. Harleian Society, i. 22.

SALLEY. Harleian Society, xvi. 167.

SALMON. Burke's Landed Gentry, 5, 6, 7, 8. Chancellor's Sepulchral Monuments of Essex, 399.

SALMOND. Burke's Royal Families, (London, 1851, 8vo.) i. 96. Burke's Landed Gentry, 2, 3, 4, 5, 6, 7, 8.

SALOMONS. Burke's Landed Gentry, 2, 3, 4.

SALSBRI. Dwnn's Visitations of Wales, ii. 89, 111, 114, 115, 330, 331, 332, 334, 347.

SALSO MARISCO. Harleian Society, xii. 140.

SALT. Miscellanea Genealogica et Heraldica, New Series, iv. 15. Howard's Visitation of England and Wales, iii. 104.

SALTER. Gyll's History of Wraysbury, 43, 233. Hutchins' Dorset, i. 347. The Genealogist, vi. 85. Norfolk Antiquarian Miscellany, ii. 614. Harleian Society, xvii. 223; xx. 82; xxix. 427, 428. Metcalfe's Visitations of Northamptonshire, 130. Howard's Visitation of England and Wales, ii. 37. Transactions of Shropshire Archæological Society, ix. 123.

SALTMARSH, SALTMARSHE, or SALTMERSH. Foster's Visitations of Yorkshire, 100. Hutchinson's History of Durham, iii. 461. Burke's Landed Gentry, 2, 3, 4, 5, 6, 7. 8. Foster's Yorkshire Pedigrees. Burke's Royal Descents and Pedigrees of Founders'

Kin, 104. Surtees Society, xxxvi. 94. The Genealogist, iv. 275. Harleian Society, xvi. 272.

SALTONSTALL, or SALTINGSTALL. Foster's Visitations of Yorkshire, 570. Morant's Essex, i. 101. Thoresby's Ducatus Leodiensis, 236. Clutterbuck's Hertford, iii. 362. Baker's Northampton, i. 526. John Watson's History of Halifax, 237. Notes and Queries, 2 S. xi. 513 ; xii. 372, 460 ; 3 S. i. 350. New England Register, xxxiii. 227. Harleian Society, xxii. 90 ; xxxviii. 639.

SALTOUN. Claim of Lord Saltoun to Vote at Elections of Irish Peers, Sess. Papers, E of 1856.

SALUSBURY. Testimonial to the Descent of Foulke Salusbury, and his Claim to be entitled a Gentleman, 5th Annual Report of the Oxford Heraldic Society, 1839, 8vo. Burke's Landed Gentry, 2, 3, 4, 5, 6, 7, 8. Clutterbuck's Hertford, iii. 96, 98. Archæologia Cambrensis, 4 S., ix. 285. Memoir of Gabriel Goodman, by R. Newcome, App. S. Betham's Baronetage, iv. 282. Burke's Extinct Baronetcies. History of Powys Fadog, by J. Y. W. Lloyd, iv. 330, 343 ; v. 99 ; vi. 25. See SALISBERIE.

SALVAGIUS. Dugdale's Warwickshire, 229.

SALVIN, SALVEN, SALVEIN, SALVEYN, or SALVINE. Surtees Society, xxxvi. 96 ; xli. 23. Foster's Visitations of Yorkshire, 367. Visitation of Durham, 1615, (Sunderland, 1820, fol.) 2. Burke's Commoners, (of Croxdale,) i. 532, Landed Gentry, 2, 3, 4, 5, 6, 7, 8 ; (of Hawksfold,) 8 ; (of Sunderland Bridge,) Commoners, i. 537 ; (of Sutton Place,) Landed Gentry, 4, 5, 7, 8. Herald and Genealogist, iii. 428. Hutchinson's History of Durham, ii. 329, 330. Surtees' Durham, iv. 117, 120. Harleian Society, xvi. 273. Graves' History of Cleveland, 289. The Genealogist, New Series, x. 92. Foster's Visitations of Durham, 275. Burton's History of Hemingborough, 297.

SALWAY, or SALWEY. Burke's Royal Families, (London, 1851, 8vo.) i. 28. Burke's Commoners, i. 152, 155, Landed Gentry, 2, 3, 4, 5, 6, 7, 8. The Sheriffs of Montgomeryshire, by W. V. Lloyd, 150. Collections for a History of Staffordshire, William Salt Society, i. 341. Harleian Society, xxvii. 120.

SAMBORNE. Visitation of Somersetshire, printed by Sir T. Phillipps, 134. Harleian Society, v. 232 ; xi. 97. The Genealogist, i. 218 ; vi. 85 ; New Series, xiii. 145. Weaver's Visitations of Somerset, 75. New England Register, xxxix. 245.

SAMBROOKE. Clutterbuck's Hertford, i. 453.

SAMFORD, or SAMPFORD. Visitation of Somersetshire, printed by Sir T. Phillipps, 134. Harleian Society, xi. 97. Hutchins' Dorset, ii. 659. See SANFORD.

SAMON. Berry's Hampshire Genealogies, 278. Harleian Society, iv. 35. Thoroton's Nottinghamshire, ii. 39.

SAMPSON. Ashmole's Antiquities of Berkshire, iii. 302. Burke's Commoners, iv. 188, Landed Gentry, (of Buxhalls,) 2, 3, 4, 5, 6, 7, 8 ; (of Henbury,) 8. Surtees' Durham, ii. 187. Metcalfe's Visitations of Suffolk, 206.

SAMS, SAMES, or SAMMES. Morant's Essex, i. 386, 388, 391. Harleian Society, xiii. 283, 482 ; xvii. 224. Bysshe's Visitation of Essex, edited by J. J. Howard, 79.

SAMUDA. Burke's Landed Gentry, 8.

SAMUEL. Burke's Colonial Gentry, ii. 416. Genealogies of Morgan and Glamorgan, by G. T. Clark, 430.

SAMUELL. Westcote's Devonshire, edited by G. Oliver and P. Jones, 533, 623. Harleian Society, ix. 196. The Visitations of Cornwall, edited by J. L. Vivian, 417.

SAMWAYS. Visitatio Comitatus Wiltoniæ, 1623, printed by Sir T. Phillipps. Hutchins' Dorset, ii. 487, 697. Visitation of Wiltshire, edited by G. W. Marshall, 11. Harleian Society, xx. 82. The Genealogist, New Series, iii. 169.

SAMWELL. Burke's Commoners, i. 440. Bridges' Northamptonshire, by Rev. Peter Whalley, i. 539. Baker's Northampton, i. 224. Wotton's English Baronetage, iii. 584. Burke's Extinct Baronetcies. Metcalfe's Visitations of Northamptonshire, 194.

SANBORN. New England Register, x. 271, 313 ; xii. 271.

SANCROFT. Gentleman's Magazine, 1841, i. 486; ii. 23, 226. Life of William Sancroft, by G. D'Oyly, i. 4.

SANDARS. Burke's Landed Gentry, 4, 8.

SANDBACH. Burke's Commoners, iv. 16, Landed Gentry, 2, 3, 4, 5, 6, 7, 8. Ormerod's Cheshire, iii. 97. Earwaker's History of Sandbach, 5.

SANDBY. The Genealogist, v. 49.

SANDDE. Dwnn's Visitations of Wales, ii. 359.

SANDDEF. History of Powys Fadog, by J. Y. W. Lloyd, iii. 227.

SANDEMAN. Burke's Family Records, 523.

SANDER. Manning and Bray's Surrey, ii. 190.

SANDERS. Berry's Kent Genealogies, 159. Burke's Landed Gentry, 2, 3, 4, 5, 6, 7, 8. Jewitt's Reliquary, xi. 166 ; xii. 10. Shaw's Staffordshire, ii. 107*. Visitation of Staffordshire, 1663-4, printed by Sir T. Phillipps, 9. Manning and Bray's Surrey, i. 459. Harleian Society, xvii. 225-227 ; xxxviii. 440, 442 ; xlii. 77. Visitation of Gloucester, edited by T. F. Fenwick and W. C. Metcalfe, 151. Visitations of Staffordshire, 1614 and 1663-4, William Salt Society, 259. *See* SAUNDERS.

SANDERSON. Hasted's Kent, i. 17. Visitation of Durham, 1615, (Sunderland, 1820, fol.) 17. Burke's Landed Gentry, (of West Jesmond,) 2, 3, 4, 5, 6, 7, 8 ; (of Cloverhill,) 5 supp., 6, 7, 8. Harleian Society, iv. 100 ; viii. 511 ; xix. 194 ; xxxix. 871, 872. Abram's History of Blackburn, 485. Surtees' Durham, ii. 343. The Genealogist, iii. 81 ; vi. 279. Wotton's English Baronetage, iv. 199. Burke's Extinct Baronetcies. Foster's Visitations of Durham, 277, 279. Burke's Colonial Gentry, i. 172. Burke's Family Records, 526. Parliamentary Memoirs of Fermanagh, by the Earl of Belmore, 59.

SANDES. Cambridgeshire Visitation, edited by Sir T. Phillipps, 27. Nash's Worcestershire, ii. 221. Burke's Landed Gentry, (of Carrigafoyle,) 2, 3, 4, 5, 6, 7 ; (of Sallow Glen,) 3, 4, 5, 6, 7 ; (of Greenville,) 2, 3, 4, 5 ; (of Dunowen House,) 2. Manning and

Bray's Surrey, ii. 671. Harleian Society, xiii. 99 ; xli. 5. *See* SANDS, SANDYS.

SANDFORD. Cambridgeshire Visitation, edited by Sir T. Phillipps, 26. Visitation of Gloucestershire, 1569, (Middle Hill, 1854, fol.) 9. Burke's Commoners, (of Sandford,) ii. 665, Landed Gentry, 2, 3, 4, 5, 6, 7, 8 ; (of Isle of Rossall,) Commoners, ii. 670, Landed Gentry, 2, 3, 4, 5, 6, 7, 8 ; (of Reeves Hall,) Landed Gentry, 5, 6. Harleian Society, iv. 168 ; xiii. 285, 484 ; xxi. 142, 220 ; xxix. 429 ; xli. 86. Chetham Society, lxxxviii. 253. History of the Ancient Chapel of Blackley, by Rev. J. Booker, 160. Eyton's Antiquities of Shropshire, ix. 236. Hunter's Deanery of Doncaster, i. 310. D. Royce's History of Stow-on-the-Wold. Collections by the Powys-land Club, ix. 424. Burke's Extinct Baronetcies. The Genealogist, New Series, viii. 75. Visitation of Gloucester, edited by T. F. Fenwick and W. C. Metcalfe, 153. Bysshe's Visitation of Essex, edited by J. J. Howard, 80. Foster's Visitations of Cumberland and Westmorland, 115. The Irish Builder, xxxv. 239. Croston's edn. of Baines's Lancaster, ii. 338. Nicolson and Burn's Westmorland and Cumberland, i. 387, 423, 512.

SANDHAM. Berry's Sussex Genealogies, 17, 307. Dallaway's Sussex, i. 70.

SANDILANDS. Sandilands of Crabstone, 1863, 4to. Privately printed. Walter Wood's East Neuk of Fife, 268. Wood's Douglas's Peerage of Scotland, i. 14 ; ii. 590.

SANDS, or SANDIS. Berry's Kent Genealogies, 244. Burke's Landed Gentry, 2 supp. Manning and Bray's Surrey, iii. cxxxii. Harleian Society, vii. 17 ; xiii. 286; xliii. 34. Burke's Extinct Baronetcies, 614. Bysshe's Visitation of Essex, edited by J. J. Howard, 81. Surrey Archæological Collections, xi.

SANDWICH. Planché's Corner of Kent, 296. Archæologia Cantiana, ii. 39.

SANDWITH. Harleian Society, xxxvii. 415.

SANDYS. Pedigrees of Sandys of the Vine, and Sandys of Fladbury, [T. P.] 1837. Pedigree of Sandys of Hawkshead, [T. P.] 1870, folio page. Rudder's Gloucestershire, 311, 554. Hastèd's Kent, iv. 146. Berry's Kent Genealogies, 41. Nash's Worcestershire, ii. 221 ; Supp. 57. Visitation of Somersetshire, printed by Sir T. Phillipps, 134. Burke's Commoners, (of Graythwaite,) i. 308, Landed Gentry, 2, 3, 4, 5, 6, 7, 8 ; (of St. Minver,) Commoners, i. 658, Landed Gentry, 2, 3. Topographer, (London, 1789-91, 8vo.) 53. Foster's Lancashire Pedigrees. Polwhele's History of Cornwall, iv. 94. Harleian Society, xi. 97 ; xvii. 227, 228 ; xxi. 143 ; xxvii. 122 ; xlii. 147. Chetham Society, lxxxviii. 254. Corry's History of Lancashire, i. 432. Baker's Northampton, i. 685. Fosbrooke's History of Gloucestershire, ii. 531. A Complete Parochial History of the County of Cornwall, ii. 349 ; iii. 373. An Historical Survey of Cornwall, by C. S. Gilbert, ii. 258. Notes and Queries, 4 S. iii. 273. Edmondson's Baronagium Genealogicum, v. 438. Banks' Baronies in Fee, i. 384. Banks'

Dormant and Extinct Baronage, ii. 455 ; iii. 655. Burke's Extinct Baronetcies. Visitation of Gloucester, edited by T. F. Fenwick and W. C. Metcalfe, 154. Brocas of Beaurepaire, by M. Burrows, 363. Somersetshire Wills, printed for F. A. Crisp, iv. 46. Foster's Visitations of Cumberland and Westmorland, 116-118. *See* SANDES.

SANDYS-LUMSDAINE. Burke's Landed Gentry, 2 and add., 3, 4, 5, 6, 7, 8.

SANFORD, or SANFORDE. Tuckett's Devonshire Pedigrees, 146. Burke's Landed Gentry, 2, 3, 4, 5, 6, 7, 8. Harleian Society, i. 60 ; vi. 251, 252 ; xlii. 151. Collectanea Topographica et Genealogica, v. 199. Banks' Baronies in Fee, ii. 129. Burke's Colonial Gentry, i. 266. Visitations of Devon, by J. L. Vivian, 668. *See* SAMFORD.

SANKEY. Memorials of the Family of Sankey, 1207-1880, by C. S. Best-Gardner. Swansea, 1880, 8vo. Herald and Genealogist, v. 190. Burke's Landed Gentry, (of Coolmore,) 2, 3, 4, 5, 6, 7, 8 ; (of Lurganbrae,) 4, 5. The Genealogist, vii. 249.

SANS. *See* SANDYS.

SANTON. The Genealogist, vi. 280.

SANZAVER. The Genealogist, New Series, ix. 79.

SAPCOTTS, or SAPCOTTES. Camden Society, xliii. 12. Harleian Society, iii. 46 ; xxii. 162. Westcote's Devonshire, edited by G. Oliver and P. Jones, 551. The Genealogist, vi. 280. The Visitations of Devon, by J. L. Vivian, 677. *See* SHAPCOTE.

SARE. Berry's Kent Genealogies, 420. Harleian Society, xlii. 183.

SARES. Harleian Society, i. 67.

SARGENT. Burke's Commoners, iv. 723. Castles, Mansions, and Manors of Western Sussex, by D. G. C. Elwes and C. J. Robinson, 272. New England Register, x. 184.

SARGOOD. Burke's Colonial Gentry, i. 129.

SARIS. Berry's Sussex Genealogies, 149.

SARSFIELD. Herald and Genealogist, ii. 205-215. Burke's Landed Gentry, 2, 3, 4, 5, 6, 7, 8. Burke's Extinct Baronetcies, 614.

SARSONN. Harleian Society, xli. 104.

SARTLE. New England Register, vi. 274.

SARTORIS. Burke's Landed Gentry, 5, 6, 7, 8.

SASSOON. Burke's Landed Gentry, 8.

SAS-VAN-BOSCH. Burke's Extinct Baronetcies.

SATTERTHWAITE. Pedigree of Wilson of High Wray, etc., by Joseph Foster, 104.

SAUCHELLE. Minet's Account of the Family of Minet, 206.

SAUMAREZ. Betham's Baronetage, v. 450. *See* DE SAUSMAREZ.

SAUNDER. Berry's Surrey Genealogies, 40.

SAUNDERS. J. H. Hill's History of Langton, 61. Miscellanea Genealogica et Heraldica, i. 159. Berry's Berkshire Genealogies, 50. Burke's Royal Families, (London, 1851, 8vo.) ii. 126. Burke's Commoners, (of Saunders Grove,) iv. 375, Landed Gentry, 2, 3, 4, 5, 6 and supp., 7, 8 ; (of Wennington Hall,) Landed Gentry,

2 supp., 3, 4, 5, 6, 7, 8 ; (of Largay,) 2, 3, 4, 5, 6, 7 ; (of Downs House,) 8. Harleian Society, i. 34 ; vi. 252 ; xii. 371 ; xix. 137 ; xxii. 90 ; xliii. 18, 53, 69. Visitation of Warwickshire, 1619, published with Warwickshire Antiquarian Magazine, 132. Foster's Lancashire Pedigrees. Lipscombe's History of the County of Buckingham, i. 336, 385. Nichols' History of the County of Leicester, ii. 564, 792. Clutterbuck's Hertford, i. 362. Baker's Northampton, i. 153, 293. The Genealogist, vi. 86. Metcalfe's Visitations of Northamptonshire, 44, 131, 195. Collections relating to Henry Smith, 159. Genealogies of Morgan and Glamorgan, by G. T. Clark, 502. Surrey Archæological Collections, xi. Visitations of Devon, by J. L. Vivian, 669. *See* SANDERS.

SAUNDERSON. Burke's Landed Gentry, 2 and supp., 3, 4, 5, 6, 7, 8. History of Blyth, by Rev. John Raine, 75. Hunter's History of the Parish of Sheffield, 398. Hunter's Deanery of Doncaster, i. 274. Thoroton's Nottinghamshire, iii. 427. The Genealogist, iv. 275. Banks' Dormant and Extinct Baronage, iii. 160. Burke's Extinct Baronetcies. Historical Notices of Doncaster, by C. W. Hatfield, 2nd Series, 212. Metcalfe's Visitations of Northamptonshire, 133. Northamptonshire Notes and Queries, i. 113, 140, 160.

SAUNZAVER. Banks' Baronies in Fee, ii. 131.

SAURIN. Burke's Landed Gentry, 6, 7, 8.

SAVAGE. Pedigree of Savage of Elmley Castle and Broadway, Co. Worcester, etc., [T. P.] 1857. Broadside. Morant's Essex, i. 458. Archæologia, xxxiii. 67. Hasted's Kent, ii. 399, 635. Jewitt's Reliquary, vii. 207. Sir T. Phillipps' Topographer, No. 1, (March, 1821, 8vo.) 38. Berry's Sussex Genealogies, 96. Berry's Kent Genealogies, 176. Nash's Worcestershire, i. 384, 385. History of Tilbury, Co. Gloucester, by A. T. Lee, 228, 237. Visitation of Oxfordshire, 1574, printed by Sir T. Phillipps, (Middle Hill, fol.) 8. Burke's Landed Gentry, (of Hunton and St. Leonards,) 2 and corr., 3, 4 ; (of Ballymadun,) 2, 3, 4 ; (of Norelands,) 3 ; *see* Nugent (of Portaferry,) in Burke's Landed Gentry ; also 4 p. 8. Harleian Society, v. 157 ; xviii. 198-205 ; xix. 138 ; xx. 83 ; xxi. 144 ; xxvii. 124 ; xxxvii. 361. Nichols' History of the County of Leicester, iii. 501. Visitatio Comitatus Wiltoniæ, 1623, printed by Sir T. Phillipps. Hutchins' Dorset, i. 180. J. P. Earwaker's East Cheshire, i. 188. Ormerod's Cheshire, i. 712 ; ii. 720. Banks' Dormant and Extinct Baronage, iii. 632. Burke's Extinct Baronetcies. Visitation of Wiltshire, edited by G. W. Marshall, 15, 93. Metcalfe's Visitation of Worcester, 1683, 85. J. Watney's Account of St. Osyth's Priory, 118. The Genealogist, New Series, viii. 76. The Ancient and Noble Family of the Savages of Ards, by G. F. Armstrong. London, 1888, 4to. Visitation of Gloucester, edited by T. F. Fenwick and W. C. Metcalfe, 157. Howard's Visitation of England and Wales, iii. 4. New England Register, xlviii. 311. Burke's Family Records, 527.

SAVEREY, SAVEREYE, or SAVERY. Westcote's Devonshire, edited by

G. Oliver and P. Jones, 562. Tuckett's Devonshire Pedigrees, 101. Burke's Landed Gentry, (of Venn,) 2, 3, 4, 5, 6; (of Fowelscombe,) 2, 3, 4. Harleian Society, vi. 253. Visitation of Devon, edited by F. T. Colby, 186. New England Register, xli. 369. Visitations of Devon, by J. L. Vivian, 670.

SAVIGNAC. Pedigree of Savignac of Southwark and Carshalton. Broadside. [Printed in Texas *circa* 1893.]

SAVILE, SAVELL, SAVILL, or SAVILLE. T. D. Whitaker's Life of Sir George Radcliffe, at end. Surtees Society, xxxvi. 181, 256, 310, 346; xli. 79. Burke's Commoners, iii. 521, Landed Gentry, 2, 3, 4, 5, 6, 7, 8. Foster's Yorkshire Pedigrees. Foster's Visitations of Yorkshire, 184, 324, 329, 341, 358, 371, 372. Jewitt's Reliquary, xiv. 102. Visitation of Derbyshire, 1663-4, (Middle Hill, 1854, fol.) 6. Thoresby's Ducatus Leodiensis, 114, 152. Whitaker's Loidis and Elmete, 272. Nichols' History of the County of Leicester, iv. 51, 421. Hunter's Deanery of Doncaster, i. 393; ii. 41, 67, 301, 374. Harleian Society, ii. 93; iv. 174; xvi. 274; xvii. 228; xxxix. 869. The Genealogist, iii. 15; iv. 276; New Series, x. 156; xiii. 115; xv. 41. Baines' History of the Co. of Lancaster, ii. 620. Camden Society, lxxi. iii. Early Ecclesiastical History of Dewsbury, by J. B. Greenwood, 199-215. Gentleman's Magazine, 1846, ii. 156. Dickinson's History of Southwell, 2nd edition, 304. John Watson's History of Halifax, 165, 182, 184, 208, 277, 306. Forrest's History of Knottingley, add. v. Antiquarian Notices of Lupset, by J. H., (1851 edn.) 32. Archdall's Lodge's Peerage, iii. 156. Wotton's English Baronetage, i. 153. Banks' Baronies in Fee, i. 181. Banks' Dormant and Extinct Baronage, iii. 333, 699. Burke's Extinct Baronetcies. Old Yorkshire, by William Smith, ii. 149. Records of Batley, by M. Sheard, 274.

SAVILL-ONLEY. Burke's Landed Gentry, 2, 3, 4, 5, 6, 7, 8. (*See* Onley of Stisted.)

SAVOURS. Genealogies of Morgan and Glamorgan, by G. T. Clark, 430.

SAWBRIDGE. Burke's Commoners, (of Olantigh,) iv. 210, Landed Gentry, 2; (of East Haddon,) Landed Gentry, 2, 3, 4, 5, 6, 7, 8. Baker's Northampton, i. 161. *See* SYKES.

SAWBRIDGE-ERLE-DRAX. Burke's Landed Gentry, 5, 6, 7, 8.

SAWKINS. Hasted's Kent, iii. 330.

SAWLE. A Complete Parochial History of the County of Cornwall, i. 44. Burke's Royal Families, (London, 1851, 8vo.) i. 20. Harleian Society, ix. 196. An Historical Survey of Cornwall, by C. S. Gilbert, ii. 260. The Visitations of Cornwall, edited by J. L. Vivian, 418.

SAWLEY. Foster's Visitations of Yorkshire, 114.

SAWREY. Burke's Landed Gentry, 2, 3, 4. Chetham Society, lxxxviii. 255. Corry's History of Lancashire, i. 447. Bardsley's Registers of Ulverston, xxxiv. lx.

SAWYER. Berry's Berkshire Genealogies, 87-90, 104. Burke's Royal Families, (London, 1851, 8vo.) ii. 92. Burke's Landed Gentry,

2, 3, 4, 5, 6, 7, 8. Harleian Society, viii. 321; xxxii. 241. Metcalfe's Visitations of Northamptonshire, 133. New England Register, xxviii. 194.

SAXBY. Memoirs of the Family of Chester, by R. E. C. Waters, 76.

SAXE. Yorkshire Archæological Society, Record Series, xxx. 483.

SAXTON. Foster's Visitations of Yorkshire, 327. Hunter's Deanery of Doncaster, i. 122. Harleian Society, xvi. 276; xxxviii. 603. Betham's Baronetage, iv. 255.

SAY, or SAYE. Morant's Essex, i. 436. Nash's Worcestershire, i. 241. Visitation of Oxfordshire, 1634, printed by Sir T. Phillipps, (Middle Hill, fol.) 29. Burke's Landed Gentry, 2 supp., 4, 5, 6, 7, 8. Harleian Society, v. 252; xvi. 277; xxix. 433. Clutterbuck's Hertford, ii. 391; iii. 194. Edmondson's Baronagium Genealogicum, iv. 320. Banks' Baronies in Fee, i. 385. Banks' Dormant and Extinct Baronage, ii. 461. Metcalfe's Visitations of Northamptonshire, 134. See DE SAY.

SAYE and SELE. Burke's Royal Families, (London, 1851, 8vo.) ii. 93.

SAYER, or SAYRE. Hasted's Kent, iii. 213. Morant's Essex, i. 353; ii. 199. Blomefield's Norfolk, v. 401. Morant's History of Colchester, 111. Berry's Kent Genealogics, 496. Burke's Commoners, iii. 504, Landed Gentry, 2, 3, 4, 5, 6, 7, 8. Foster's Visitations of Yorkshire, 572. Harleian Society, viii. 38; ix. 197; xiii. 286, 484; xvii. 229; xxxii. 240; xliii. 209. Surtees' Durham, iii. 190. Plantagenet-Harrison's History of Yorkshire, i. 223. Metcalfe's Visitations of Suffolk, 163. The Visitations of Cornwall, edited by J. L. Vivian, 420. Memorials of Smarden, by F. Haslewood, 229. Surrey Archæological Collections, xi.

SAYLE. Harleian Society, xxxviii. 747.

SAYS. Glamorganshire Pedigrees, edited by Sir T. Phillipps, 44.

SCAIFE. Foster's Visitations of Cumberland and Westmorland, 120.

SCALES, or SCALERS. Clutterbuck's Hertford, ii. 398. The Genealogist, iii. 328. Banks' Baronies in Fee, i. 389. Cussan's History of Hertfordshire, Parts iii. and iv. 28. Morant's Essex, ii. 145. Memoirs of the Family of Chester, by R. E. C. Waters, 253. Banks' Dormant and Extinct Baronage, ii. 476. Hasted's Kent, (Hund. of Blackheath, by H. H. Drake,) 145. See DE SCALES, TEMPEST.

SCAMBLER. Harleian Society, xxxii. 241.

SCAMMON. New England Register, viii. 65.

SCANLAN. O'Hart's Irish Pedigrees, 2nd Series, 301.

SCARBOROUGH. Harleian Society, viii. 226.

SCARDEVILLE. Berry's Hampshire Genealogies, 112. Berry's Sussex Genealogies, 46.

SCARFE. Dwnn's Visitations of Wales, i. 182.

SCARGILL. Herald and Genealogist, iv. 402. Gentleman's Magazine, 1822, ii. 316, 594. Cambridgeshire Visitation, edited by Sir T. Phillipps, 27. Pedigrees of the Leading Families of Lancashire, published by Joseph Foster, (London, 1872, fol.). Plantagenet-

Harrison's History of Yorkshire, i. 83, 292. Yorkshire Archæological and Topographical Journal, viii. 13. W. Wheater's History of Sherburn and Cawood, 177. Pedigrees of the Leading Families of Yorkshire, by Joseph Foster. Harleian Society, xli. 57. *See* SKARGILL.

SCARISBRICK, or SKARESBRICKE. Burke's Landed Gentry, 2 supp., 3, 4, 5, 7, 8. Chetham Society, lxxxi. 89. Baines' History of the Co. of Lancaster, iv. 258.

SCARLET, or SCARLETT. Burke's Landed Gentry, 4, 5, 6, 7, 8. Maclean's History of Trigg Minor, i. 279. Notes and Queries, 2 S. xi. 192. Carthew's Hundred of Launditch, Part iii. 347. Miscellanea Genealogica et Heraldica, 2nd Series, i. 223. Bysshe's Visitation of Essex, edited by J. J. Howard, 81. Harleian Society, xxxi. 242. Howard's Visitation of England and Wales, iii. 52.

SCARSDALE. Howard's Visitation of England and Wales, iv. 79.

SCARTH. Burke's Landed Gentry, 5.

SCATCHERD. Harleian Society, xxxviii. 789. Northern Genealogist, i. 142.

SCAWEN, or SCAWNE. Berry's Surrey Genealogies, 43. Gyll's History of of Wraysbury, 223. Harleian Society, viii. 441 ; ix. 198, 200. Manning and Bray's Surrey, ii. 510. An Historical Survey of Cornwall, by C. S. Gilbert, ii. 261. Notes and Queries, 2 S. xi. 215. The Visitations of Cornwall, edited by J. L. Vivian, 421.

SCHANK. Burke's Landed Gentry, (of Barton House,) 3, 4, 5 ; (of Castlerig,) 5, 6, 7, 8. Nisbet's Heraldry, ii. app. 229. Burke's Visitation of Seats and Arms, ii. 17. Miscellanea Genealogica et Heraldica, 2nd Series, i. 235. *See* SHANK.

SCHAW. Paterson's History of the Co. of Ayr, ii. 67, 469. Paterson's History of Ayr and Wigton, i. 476, 531 ; ii. 478. *See* SHAW.

SCHOLEFIELD, or SCOFIELD. Chetham Society, lxxxi. 127 ; lxxxviii. 256. Fishwick's History of Rochdale, 357. Harleian Society, xxxvii. 114.

SCHOMBERG. History and Antiquities of Harwich and Dovercourt, by Silas Taylor, 252. Banks' Dormant and Extinct Baronage, iii. 659. Howard's Visitation of England and Wales, i. 209.

SCHOMBURGK. Burke's Colonial Gentry, ii. 629.

SCHONSWAR. Burke's Landed Gentry, 2.

SCHOOLCROFT-BURTON. Burke's Landed Gentry, 5.

SCHREIBER. Burke's Landed Gentry, (of Henhurst,) 2, 3, 4 ; (of the Hill House,) 4, 5, 6, 7, 8.

SCLATER, Berry's Hampshire Genealogies, 68. Burke's Landed Gentry, (of Hoddington,) 3, 4, 5, 6, 7 ; (of Newick Park,) 5, 6, 7, 8. Chetham Society, lxxxviii. 256. The Genealogist, iii. 309. Notes and Queries, 1 S. v. 457, 518. Burke's Extinct Baronetcies.

SCOBAND. The Genealogist, New Series, xv. 155.

SCOBELL. Burke's Landed Gentry, 2, 3, 4, 5, 6, 7, 8. Harleian Society, ix. 200. A Complete Parochial History of the County of Cornwall, i. 387 ; iv. 119 supp.

SCOLAND. The Genealogist, New Series, xvi. 40.
SCORAH. J. E. Jackson's History of St. George's Church at Don-
caster, App. lxxvii. Surtees Society, xxxvi. 168. Doncaster
Charities, by Charles Jackson, 78. The Genealogist, New Series,
xiv. 229.
SCOREY. Harleian Society, xxvii. 125.
SCOT, or SCOTT. Genealogical Memoir of the Family of Sir Walter
Scott, Bart., by Rev. Charles Rogers, LL.D. London, 1877, 8vo.
Memorials of the Family of Scott of Scot's-Hall, Kent, by J. R.
Scott. London, 1876, 4to. The History of several Families of
the name of Scott, by Captain Walter Scott. Edinburgh, 1688,
4to. ; 2nd edn., 1776 ; 3rd. edn., 1786 ; new edn. Hawick, 1894,
4to. Case of Hugh Scott of Harden, claiming the title of Baron
Polewart or Polwarth. 1831, fol. pp. 5. The Scotts of Buccleugh,
by Wm. Frazer. Edinburgh, 1878, 4to., 2 vols. Claim of Hugh
Scott, Esq., to be Baron of Polewart, Sess. Papers, 45 of 1831.
Pedigree of Scott of Stokoe, compiled by William Scott. Newcastle, 1783, 8vo. ; 2nd edn., 1827, 4to. ; 3rd edn., 1852, London,
8vo. Jacob's Peerage, i. 580. Visitation of Staffordshire, 1663-4,
printed by Sir T. Phillipps, 9. Hutchins' Dorset, i. 522. Hunter's
Deanery of Doncaster, ii. 287. Manning and Bray's Surrey, iii.
406. Wright's Essex, ii. 388. Jewitt's Reliquary, xviii. 71.
Harleian Society, xiii. 100, 287, 485 ; xiv. 599, 705 ; xvii. 230 ;
xxxviii. 595 ; xxxix. 1121 ; xl. 1301 ; xlii. 91, 127 ; xliii. 48.
Amye Robsart, by George Adlard, 8. ' National Omnibus ' Newspaper, No. 74, Supplement, 379. Hasted's Kent, iii. 292.
Burke's Patrician, iii. 265, 423, 425. Morant's Essex, i. 168,
234 ; ii. 99, 499. Berry's Essex Genealogies, 85. Berry's Sussex
Genealogies, 310, 370. Berry's Kent Genealogies, 161, 170.
Burke's Commoners, iv. 663 ; (of Harden,) Commoners, iii. 372 ;
(of Logie,) Commoners, iv. 543, Landed Gentry, 2, 3 ; (of
Betton,) Commoners, ii. 503, Landed Gentry, 2, 3, 4, 5, 6, 7, 8 ;
(of Stourbridge,) Commoners, iii. 665, Landed Gentry, 2, 3, 4, 5,
6, 7 ; (of Malleny,) Commoners, iii. 170, Landed Gentry, 2 supp.,
3, 4, 5, 6, 7, 8 ; (of Raeburn,) Commoners, iii. 375, Landed
Gentry, 2, 3, 4, 5, 6, 7, 8 ; (of Carbrooke,) Landed Gentry, 2, 3, 4 ;
(of Gala,) 3, 4, 5, 6, 7, 8 ; (of Rotherfield Park,) 4, 5, 6, 7, 8 ; (of
Melby,) 4, 7, 8 ; (of Brotherton,) 2 supp., 3, 4, 5, 6, 7, 8 ; (of
Abbotsford,) 3, 4, 5, 6, 7, 8 ; (of Willsborough,) 3, 4, 5, 6, 7, 8 ;
(of Synton,) 8 ; (of Thorpe,) 8. Visitation of Sussex, 1570,
printed by Sir T. Phillipps, (Middle Hill, fol.) 9. Foster's Yorkshire Pedigrees. Foster's Visitations of Yorkshire, 573. Collectanea Topographica et Genealogica, iii. 144. Burke's Visitation of
Seats and Arms, i. 71. Burke's Heraldic Illustrations, 11.
Gregson's Fragments relative to the County of Lancaster, 274.
Hodgson's Northumberland, II. ii. 193. Shaw's Staffordshire, ii.
107*. Poulson's Holderness, ii. 18. Hunter's History of the
Parish of Sheffield, 442. Lands and their Owners in Galloway,
by P. H. M'Kerlie, iii. 451. Nisbet's Heraldry, ii. app. 58, 133,
291, 297. Douglas's Baronage of Scotland, 213-224, 302. The

Staggering State, etc., with Memoir, by Rev. C. Rogers, 1. Jeffrey's History of Roxburghshire, ii. 341, 359. Border Memories, by W. R. Carre, 46. Walter Wood's East Neuk of Fife, 283, 286, 300. Wood's Douglas's Peerage of Scotland, i. 245 ; ii. 588. Edmondson's Baronagium Genealogicum, ii. 145. Dorothea Scott, by G. D. Scull, (1882, 4to.) folding at end. Archdall's Lodge's Peerage, vii. 242. Brydges' Collins' Peerage, iii. 510 ; viii. 602. Wotton's English Baronetage, iii. 1. Metcalfe's Visitations of Suffolk, 63. Notes and Queries, 5 S. vii. 292, 330, 341, 470, 490, 509 ; viii. 29, 370, 389, 410 ; ix. 369, 391 ; 6 S. iii. 238 ; viii. 229. Registers of Ecclesfield, by A. S. Gatty, 90. Nicholls' Account of the Company of Ironmongers, 2nd edn., 611. Miscellanea Genealogica et Heraldica, New Series, iv. 185 ; 3rd Series, i. 204. Passages from the Letter Book of Wm. Scott, Publications of M. A. Richardson, vol. vi. No. 2. The Master Masons of Scotland, by R. S. Mylne, *at end.* Visitations of Staffordshire, 1614 and 1663-4, William Salt Society, 262. Alexander Nisbet's Heraldic Plates, 108. Bysshe's Visitation of Essex, edited by J. J. Howard, 82. Some Old Families, by H. B. McCall, 171. New England Register, xxii. 13. Burke's Colonial Gentry, ii. 509. Berks, Bucks, and Oxon, Archæological Journal, i. Transactions of Shropshire Archæological Society, ix. 25. *See* MACMILLAN-SCOTT.

SCOTENI. Banks' Dormant and Extinct Baronage, i. 170.

SCOTLAND (Kings of). Hodgson's Northumberland, III. ii. 6.

SCOTNEY. Notes and Queries, 4 S. iii. 332, 395 ; iv. 319, 491, 572 ; v. 68, 131.

SCOTT-CHAD. Burke's Landed Gentry, 4, 5, 6, 7, 8.

SCOTT-ELLIOT. Burke's Landed Gentry, 7, 8.

SCOTT-KERR. Burke's Landed Gentry, 2 supp., 3, 4, 5, 6, 7, 8.

SCOTT-MONCRIEF. Burke's Landed Gentry, 7, 8.

SCOUGALL. Stodart's Scottish Arms, ii. 372.

SCOURFIELD. Burke's Landed Gentry, 4, 5.

SCOVYLLE. The Genealogist, New Series, xiv. 257.

SCRASE. Sussex Archæological Collections, viii. 14. Berry's Sussex Genealogies, 366. Miscellanea Genealogica et Heraldica, New Series, iii. 56.

SCRASE-DICKINS. Burke's Commoners, iv. 279, Landed Gentry, 2, 3, 4, 5.

SCRATTON. Burke's Landed Gentry, 3, 4, 6, 7, 8.

SCRIMGEOUR, or SCRYMGEOUR. Burke's Landed Gentry, 2 supp. and add. Nisbet's Heraldry, ii. app. 49. Balmerino and its Abbey, by James Campbell, 318. Wood's Douglas's Peerage of Scotland, i. 462.

SCRIMGEOUR-WEDDERBURN. Balmerino and its Abbey, by James Campbell, 401. Burke's Landed Gentry, 8.

SCRIMSHIRE. Thoroton's Nottinghamshire, i. 168. *See* SKRIMSHIRE.

SCRIVEN. Cambridgeshire Visitation, edited by Sir T. Phillipps, 27. Burke's Landed Gentry, 4, 5, 6. Foster's Visitations of Yorkshire,

112. Harleian Society, xli. 67 ; xxix. 434. Genealogical Records of the Family of Woodd, 34.

SCRIVENER. Burke's Landed Gentry, 3, 4, 5, 6, 7, 8. Metcalfe's Visitations of Suffolk, 163. Harleian Society, xxxii. 242.

SCROGGS. Cussan's History of Hertfordshire, Parts iii. and iv. 162. Harleian Society, viii. 346 ; xix. 195 ; xxii. 163. Chauncy's Hertfordshire, 151.

SCROOPE, SCROUP, SCROOP, or SCROPE. History of the Family of Scrope. 'No place or date. 8vo. Case of Simon Thomas Scrope, claiming to be Earl of Wilts, 1859, folio, pp. 19. Additional Case of same, folio, pp. 47. The Scrope and Grosvenor Roll, edited by Sir N. H. Nicolas. London, 1832, 8vo. 2 vols. The History of Castle Combe, by G. P. Scrope, 86, 350, 354, 358. Claim of Simon Thomas Scrope to be Earl of Wiltes, Sess. Papers, K of 1862 ; B of 1863 ; B of 1865 ; E of 1867 ; A of 1868-9 ; 100 and 101 of 1868-9. Kent's British Banner Displayed, 445. Morant's Essex, i. 134 ; ii. 237, 240. Hasted's Kent, i. 144. Berry's Hampshire Genealogies, 64. Surtees Society, xxxvi. 36 ; xli. 32. Vallis Eboracensis, comprising the History, etc., of Easingwold, by Thos. Gill, 116. Visitation of Oxfordshire, printed by Sir T. Phillipps, (Middle Hill, fol.) 29. J. H. Hill's History of Langton, 213, 214. Fisher's History of Masham, 221. Foster's Yorkshire Pedigrees. History of Richmond, by C. Clarkson, 354. Burke's Commoners, (of Danby,) i. 450, Landed Gentry, 2, 3, 4, 5, 6, 7, 8 ; (of Castle Combe,) Commoners, iii. 693, Landed Gentry, 2, 3, 4. Foster's Visitations of Yorkshire, 632. Harleian Society, v. 327 ; viii. 31 ; xvi. 278 ; xxix. 475. Blore's Rutland, 5, 198. Herald and Genealogist, iii. 423. Collectanea Topographica et Genealogica, i. 303. Hodgson's Northumberland, I. ii. 373. Whitaker's History of Richmondshire, i. 368. Burke's Royal Descents and Pedigrees of Founders' Kin, 103. Hutchinson's History of Durham, ii. 383. Nichols' History of the County of Leicester, ii. 447. Visitatio Comitatus Wiltoniæ, 1623, printed by Sir T. Phillipps. Hunter's Deanery of Doncaster, i. 92. Thoroton's Nottinghamshire, i. 204, 293 ; iii. 150. Brydges' Collins' Peerage, viii. 556. Banks' Baronies in Fee, i. 391, 394. Banks' Dormant and Extinct Baronage, ii. 484. Visitation of Wiltshire, edited by G. W. Marshall, 28. Burke's Extinct Baronetcies. Memorials of Adair Manor, by Caroline Countess of Dunraven, 22. The Genealogist, New Series, xv. 162.

SCRUBY. Miscellanea Genealogica et Heraldica, 3rd Series, i. 99.

SCRUTEVILLE. Visitation of Durham, 1615, (Sunderland, 1820, fol.) 46. Foster's Visitations of Durham, 281.

SCUDAMORE. Gibson's View of the Churches of Door, Holme Lacey, and Hempsted, 54, 116. Kent's British Banner Displayed, 715. Berry's Kent Genealogies, 34. Burke's Extinct Baronetcies. Surtees Society, xxxvi. 25, 154. Burke's Commoners, iii. 354, Landed Gentry, 2 supp., 3, 4, 5, 6, 7, 8. Foster's Visitations of Yorkshire, 573. Collectanea Topographica et Genealogica, iv. 256. Thoresby's Ducatus Leodiensis, 35. Hoare's Wiltshire, III.

ii. 54; IV. ii. 120. Robinson's Mansions of Herefordshire, 21, 142, 155. Weaver's Visitation of Herefordshire, 62. Visitation of Gloucester, edited by T. F. Fenwick and W. C. Metcalfe, 159. Phillimore's London and Middlesex Note-Book, 101. The Genealogist, New Series, xviii. 29.

SCUDAMORE-STANHOPE. Burke's Royal Families, (London, 1851, 8vo.) ii. 205*.

SCULL, or SCULLE. Miscellanea Genealogica et Heraldica, New Series, ii. 231. Topographer and Genealogist, iii. 178.

SCULLY. Burke's Landed Gentry, 5 supp., 6, 7, 8.

SCURES, or SCURRES. Collectanea Topographica et Genealogica, i. 9. Poulson's Holderness, i. 341.

SCURFIELD. Topographer and Genealogist, ii. 78. Burke's Landed Gentry, 2 supp., 3, 4, 5, 6, 7, 8. Pembrokeshire Pedigrees, 142. Surtees' Durham, i. 194; ii. 218; iii. 65. Foster's Visitations of Durham, 281.

SCURLAGE. Genealogies of Morgan and Glamorgan, by G. T. Clark, 502.

SEA. See DE LA SEE.

SEABRIGHT, or SEBRIGHT. Morant's Essex, ii. 19. Harleian Society, i. 14; xiii. 288; xxvii. 125. Clutterbuck's Hertford, i. 362. Nash's Worcestershire, i. 79. Wotton's English Baronetage, ii. 8. Betham's Baronetage, i. 282.

SEALE. J. B. Payne's Armorial of Jersey, 332.

SEALE-HAYNE. Burke's Landed Gentry, 5, 6, 7, 8.

SEALY. Burke's Landed Gentry, 2, 3, 4, 5, 6, 7, 8.

SEAMAN. Morant's Essex, ii. 408. Wright's Essex, ii. 44. Burke's Landed Gentry, 2 at p. 933.

SEARLE. Morant's Essex, i. 50. Burke's Royal Families, (London, 1851, 8vo.) i. 76. Harleian Society, i. 90; vi. 254; ix. 202. The Visitations of Cornwall, edited by J. L. Vivian, 424. Visitations of Devon, by J. L. Vivian, 673.

SEARS. Herald and Genealogist, viii. 486. Burke's Visitation of Seats and Arms, i. 53; 2nd Series, i. 5. New England Register, xl. 262.

SEATON. J. E. Jackson's History of St. George's Church at Doncaster, 88. Harleian Society, xl. 1292. Historical Notices of Doncaster, by C. W. Hatfield, 1st Series, 344.

SEAVER. Burke's Landed Gentry, 2.

SEAWARD. History of Clyst St. George, by Rev. H. T. Ellacombe, 67.

SEBORNE. Weaver's Visitation of Herefordshire, 64.

SECCOMBE. Harleian Society, vi. 254. Visitations of Devon, by J. L. Vivian, 675.

SECKFORD, or SEKFORD. Page's History of Suffolk, 41. Statutes and Ordinances for the Government of the Almshouses in Woodbridge, by R. Loder, 1. Metcalfe's Visitations of Suffolk, 64.

SECKHAM. Burke's Landed Gentry, 8.

SECORD. Ontarian Families, by E. M. Chadwick, ii. 81.

SEDBOROUGH. Visitation of Somerset, printed by Sir T. Phillipps,

134. Weaver's Visitations of Somerset, 76. Healey's History of Part of West Somerset, 331.

SEDGEWICK, or SEDGWICK. Bibliotheca Topographica Britannica, ix. Part 4, 189. Cambridgeshire Visitation, printed by Sir T. Phillipps, 27. Surtees' Durham, iii. 82. Harleian Society, xiv. 600; xli. 40.

SEDLEY. Hasted's Kent, ii. 170. Visitation of Norfolk, published by Norfolk Archæological Society, i. 111. Nichols' History of the County of Leicester, ii. 415. Clutterbuck's Hertford, ii. 322. Harleian Society, xxii. 91 ; xxxii. 243.

SEED, or SEEDE. Miscellanea Genealogica et Heraldica, 2nd Series, iv. 7. History of Ribchester, by T. C. Smith and J. Shortt, 257.

SEEL. See MOLYNEUX-SEEL.

SEELY. Burke's Landed Gentry, 5, 6, 7, 8.

SEGAR. Tuckett's Devonshire Pedigrees, 173. Harleian Society, vi. 256. Noble's History of the College of Arms, 230. Visitations of Devon, by J. L. Vivian, 674.

SEGINTON. Harleian Society, xii. 249.

SEGRAVE. Glover's History of Derbyshire, ii. 195. Burke's Landed Gentry, 3, 4, 5, 6, 7, 8. Harleian Society, ii. 18; xxxvii. 417. Nichols' History of the County of Leicester, iii. 314 ; iii. 413 ; iv. 577. Baker's Northampton, i. 588. Banks' Baronies in Fee, i. 396. Banks' Dormant and Extinct Baronage, ii. 498. Archæologia Cantiana, ii. 139, 142. Catalogue of Arundel MSS. in Coll. Arms, by C. G. Y., 91b. The Genealogist, New Series, xiv. 96 ; xvii. 108. See MOWBRAY.

SEIGNORET. Miscellanea Genealogica et Heraldica, New Series, iv. 321.

SELBY. Selbyana, an Attempt to Elucidate the History of Selby of Wavendon. Carlisle, 1825, 8vo. Burke's Extinct Baronetcies. Gentleman's Magazine, 1820, i. 588 ; 1821, ii. 315, 508. Hasted's Kent, ii. 248. Berry's Kent Genealogies, 465. Visitation of Durham, 1615, (Sunderland, 1820, fol.) 14. Burke's Royal Families, (London, 1851, 8vo.) i. 49. Burke's Commoners, (of Biddleston,) ii. 703, Landed Gentry, 2, 3, 4, 5, 6, 7, 8 ; (of Yearle), Commoners, ii. 706, Landed Gentry, 2, 3, 4, 5, 6, 7, 8 ; (of the Mote,) Landed Gentry, 3, 4 ; (of Twizell House,) 2 add., 3, 4, 5, 6, 7 ; (of Cheswick House,) 2, 3, 4 ; (of Lindisfarne,) 5 ; (of Pawston,) 7. Herald and Genealogist, iii. 518. Raine's History of North Durham, 206, 315, 338. Harleian Society, viii. 397. Lipscombe's History of the County of Buckingham, iii. 497, 544. Surtees' Durham, ii. 274. The Genealogist, i. 378. A Statement of Facts of the Lawful Coheiresses of John Selby, (1822, 8vo., pp. 60). Tate's History of Alnwick, ii. 412. Foster's Visitations of Durham, 283. Foster's Visitations of Northumberland, 110.

SELFE. Pedigree of Selfe of Melksham, Co. Wilts, etc., [T. P.] 1870. Broadside. Visitatio Comitatus Wiltoniæ, 1623, printed by Sir T. Phillipps.

SELISKE. Harleian Society, xxii. 91.

SELLER. Harleian Society, xvii. 231.

SELLIGOW. Alexander Nisbet's Heraldic Plates, 54.

SELLON. The Genealogist, vi. 169.

SELMAN. Harleian Society, xxix. 435.

SELWIN, or SELWYN. Berry's Sussex Genealogies, 114. Harleian Society, viii. 377 ; xxi. 146. Visitation of Sussex, 1570, printed by Sir T. Phillipps, (Middle Hill, fol.) 10. Burke's Landed Gentry, 5. Fosbrooke's History of Gloucestershire, i. 273. Archæologia Cantiana, xiii. 402 ; xxii. 100. Bristol and Gloucestershire Archæological Society, ii. 251-284. Visitation of Gloucester, edited by T. F. Fenwick and W. C. Metcalfe, 160. History of Chislehurst, by Webb, Miller, and Beckwith, 156.

SELYNGESBY. Surtees Society, xli. 11.

SEMARC. Bridges' Northamptonshire, by Rev. Peter Whalley, ii. 596.

SEMPIL, SEMPLE, or SEMPILL. Burke's Landed Gentry, 3, 4, 5. Douglas's Barouage of Scotland, 467. Wood's Douglas's Peerage of Scotland, ii. 492. Semple's edition of Crawford's Renfrewshire, 161.

SENHOUSE. Burke's Commoners, i. 113, Landed Gentry, 2, 3, 4, 5, 6, 7, 8. Hutchinson's History of Cumberland, ii. 268. Foster's Visitations of Cumberland and Westmorland, 121, 122. Nicolson and Burn's Westmorland and Cumberland, ii. 159.

SENNOKE. Harleian Society, xxii. 92.

SEPHAM. Harleian Society, xliii. 32.

SEPTVANS. Planché's Corner of Kent, 307-350. Archæologia Cantiana, ii. 326. The Antiquary, (London, 1873,) iv. 310. Hasted's Kent, ii. 497.

SERGEANT, SERJAUNT, or SERJEANT. Bibliotheca Topographica Britannica, ix. Part iv. 249. Visitation of Warwickshire, 1619, published with Warwickshire Antiquarian Magazine, 76. Nichols' History of the County of Leicester, ii. 262*. Harleian Society, xii. 211 ; xxi. 258. Abram's History of Blackburn, 729. Plantagenet-Harrison's History of Yorkshire, i. 111. The New History of Yorkshire, commencing with Richmondshire, by Genl. Plantagenet-Harrison, (London, 1872, fol.) Part i. 32. Pedigrees of the Leading Families of Lancashire, published by Joseph Foster, (London, 1872, fol.). Visitation of Gloucester, edited by T. F. Fenwick and W. C. Metcalfe, 166. Pedigrees of the Leading Families of Yorkshire, by Joseph Foster. Visitations of Staffordshire, 1614 and 1663-4, William Salt Society, 263.

SERGEAUX. Maclean's History of Trigg Minor, ii. 502, 507. See DE CERISIS.

SERGISON. Burke's Landed Gentry, 4, 5, 6, 7, 8. Sussex Archæo‑ logical Collections, xxv. 84.

SERJEANTSON. Burke's Landed Gentry, 5, 6, 7, 8. Foster's York‑ shire Pedigrees. Whitaker's Deanery of Craven, 3rd edn., 253. Harleian Society, xxxvii. 40 ; xxxix. 876.

SERLBY, or SERLEBY. Foster's Visitations of Yorkshire, 364. Hunter's Deanery of Doncaster, i. 140. Thoroton's Nottingham‑ shire, iii. 431.

SEROCOLD. Burke's Landed Gentry, 2, 3, 4, 5, 6. *See* PEARCE-
SEROCOLD.

SERVINGTON. Hutchins' Dorset, iii. 422. Hoare's Wiltshire, III. v.
27. Visitation of Devon, edited by F. T. Colby, 187, 188.
Visitations of Devon, by J. L. Vivian, 676. *See* CERVINGTON.

SETON. Case and Evidence in the Service of the Earl of Eglinton,
etc., by John Riddell, 1840, fol. Memoir of Chancellor Seton,
by George Seton. Edinburgh, 1882, 4to. Burke's Commoners, ii.
298, Landed Gentry, 3 p. 450; (of Mounie,) Landed Gentry, 2,
3, 4, 5, 6, 7, 8 ; (of Cariston,) 2, 3, 4, 5, 6, 7, 8. Surtees' Durham,
iii. 190. Burke's Royal Families, (London, 1851, 8vo.) ii. 186.
Nisbet's Heraldry, ii. app. 131. Douglas's Baronage of Scotland,
158, 166, 170, 182-186. Inverurie and the Earldom of the
Garioch, by John Davidson, 463. Collections for History of
Aberdeen and Banff, (Spalding Club,) i. 529. Wood's Douglas's
Peerage of Scotland, i. 480 ; ii. 39, 638. Burke's Extinct Baronet-
cies, 635. Stodart's Scottish Arms, ii. 23. Alexander Nisbet's
Heraldic Plates, 72, 132. *See* ARNOT, PRINGLE, SEYTOUN.

SEVANZ. *See* SEPTVANS.

SEVERN, or SEVERNE. Burke's Commoners, i. 413, Landed Gentry,
2, 3, 4, 5, 6, 7, 8. Baker's Northampton, i. 712. Metcalfe's
Visitation of Worcester, 1683, 86.

SEWARD. Westcote's Devonshire, edited by G. Oliver and P. Jones,
559. Visitation of Devon, edited by F. T. Colby, 188. Genealogies of Morgan and Glamorgan, by G. T. Clark, 503. The
Visitations of Devon, by J. L. Vivian, 696. New England Register,
lii. 323.

SEWELL. Morant's Essex, ii. 273. Burke's Landed Gentry, 2 add.
Wright's Essex, i. 486. Notes and Queries, 1 S. viii. 388, 521,
621; ix. 86. The Genealogical Magazine, ii. 145.

SEWSTER. Cambridgeshire Visitation, edited by Sir T. Phillipps, 28.
Harleian Society, xli. 80.

SEX. Genealogical Record of King and Henham, 13.

SEXTON. Visitation of Norfolk, published by Norfolk Archæological
Society, i. 263. Harleian Society, xxxii. 243. Howard's Visita-
tion of England and Wales, vi. 21. Muskett's Suffolk Manorial
Families, i. 289-293.

SEYCILLE. *See* CECIL.

SEYLIARD, or SEYLYARD. Hasted's Kent, i. 397. Monken Hadley,
by F. C. Cass, 92. Miscellanea Genealogica et Heraldica, 2nd
Series, i. 7. *See* SULIARD.

SEYMER. Burke's Commoners, iii. 495, Landed Gentry, 6, 7, 8.
Hutchins' Dorset, iv. 66, 81. Hoare's Wiltshire, VI. (Old and
New Sarum,) 429. Harleian Society, xiii. 486 ; xx. 83.

SEYMORE. Sir T. Phillipps' Topographer, No. 1, (March, 1821, 8vo.) 35.

SEYMOUR. The Attorney-General's Report of Sir Edward Seymour's
Title to the Dukedom of Somerset, fol. pp. 15. Dated 23 Novr.,
1750. Memoirs of the Life, Family, and Character of Charles
Seymour, Duke of Somerset. London, 8vo. The Great Governing Families of England, ii. 245. Gentleman's Magazine, 1829, i.

397. Jacob's Peerage, i. 152. Burke's Heraldic Illustrations, 134. Tuckett's Devonshire Pedigrees, 91. Visitation of Oxfordshire, 1574, printed by Sir T. Phillipps, (Middle Hill, fol.) 9. Burke's Commoners, (of Castletown,) iii. 200, Landed Gentry, 2, 3, 4; (of Ballymore Castle,) Landed Gentry, 2, 3, 4, 5, 6, 7; (of Knoyle,) 2, 3, 4, 5, 6, 7, 8; (of Brockham Park,) 8. Harleian Society, v. 162; vi. 256. Lipscombe's History of the County of Buckingham, iv. 533. Jefferson's History of Allerdale Ward, Cumberland, 45. Westcote's Devonshire, edited by G. Oliver and P. Jones, 479. Visitatio Comitatus Wiltoniæ, 1623, printed by Sir T. Phillipps. Hoare's Wiltshire, I. i. 117-136; V. ii. 51. The Citizens of London and their Rulers, by B. B. Orridge, 204. Wiltshire Archæological Magazine, xv. 143, 214. T. Nicholas' County Families of Wales, 194. Shirley's History of the County of Monaghan, 283. Edmondson's Baronagium Genealogicum, i. 7. Ellacombe's History of Bitton, 89. Archdall's Lodge's Peerage, vii. 13. Brydges' Collins' Peerage, i. 144; ii. 560. Wotton's English Baronetage, i. 86. Banks' Baronies in Fee, i. 121. Banks' Dormant and Extinct Baronage, iii. 361. Burke's Extinct Baronetcies. The Genealogist, vi. 87. The Visitations of Devon, by J. L. Vivian, 702. *See* ST. MAUR.

SEYMOUR-CONWAY. Edmondson's Baronagium Genealogicum, iii. 285.

SEYNTCLERE. J. H. Hill's History of Market Harborough, 145. Nichols' History of the County of Leicester, ii. 697. *See* ST. CLERE.

SEYS. Burke's Landed Gentry, 2, 3, 4, 5, 6, 7, 8. Genealogies of Morgan and Glamorgan, by G. T. Clark, 218-223.

SEYTON, or SEYTOUN. History of the House of Seyton, by Sir R. Maitland, continued by Alexr. Visct. Kingston. Glasgow, 1829, 4to. Genealogy of the House and Surname of Setoun, by Sir R. Maitland, edited by C. K. Sharpe. Edinburgh, 1830, 4to. Bridges' Northamptonshire, by Rev. Peter Whalley, ii. 47. Metcalfe's Visitations of Northamptonshire, 45.

SGWRFIELD. Dwnn's Visitations of Wales, i. 110, 175.

SHAA. Morant's Essex, i. 217. Visitation of Somerset, printed by Sir T. Phillipps, 135. Harleian Society, i. 77; xi. 98; xiii. 486. Account of the Guildhall of London, by J. E. Price, 185, 186.

SHACKLOCK. History of the Ancient Chapel of Blackley, by Rev. J. Booker, 183.

SHADFORTH. Surtees' Durham, i. 221, 222.

SHADWELL. Berry's Sussex Genealogies, 369. Burke's Landed Gentry, 6, 7, 8. Howard's Visitation of England and Wales, iii. 106. Transactions of Shropshire Archæological Society, ix. 79.

SHAEN. Burke's Extinct Baronetcies, 614.

SHAFTO, or SHAFTOE. Burke's Commoners, (of Whitworth,) i. 47, Landed Gentry, 2, 3, 4, 5, 6, 7, 8; (of Bavington Hall,) 4, 5, 6, 7, 8. Hutchinson's History of Durham, ii. 424. Hoare's Wiltshire, III. iv. 45. Surtees' Durham, ii. 220, 246; iii. 294, 296. Harleian Society, viii. 235; xvi. 284. Visitation of Durham,

1575, (Newcastle, 1820, fol.) 45. Visitation of Durham, 1615, (Sunderland, 1820, fol.) 8, 42. Foster's Visitations of Durham, 285, 287. Foster's Visitations of Northumberland, 111, 112.

SHAIRP. Burke's Landed Gentry, 2, 3, 4, 5, 6, 7, 8. Burke's Royal Descents and Pedigrees of Founders' Kin, 24.

SHAKERLEY. Berry's Kent Genealogies, 261. Burke's Commoners, i. 9. Chetham Society, lxxxi. 128; xcviii. 77. Baker's Northampton, i. 548. Harleian Society, viii. 155; xviii. 206; xlii. 159. Ormerod's Cheshire, iii. 151. The Genealogist, New Series, viii. 77, 78.

SHAKESPEARE, SHAKESPERE, or SHAKSPERE. Original Memoirs of the Families of Shakespeare and Hart, by John Jordan. London, 1865, 4to. Pedigree of Shakespear of London, and of Brookwood, Co. Hants, [T. P.] 1864, folio page. Shakespeareana Genealogica, by G. R French. London, 1869, 8vo. Herald and Genealogist, ii. 295. Shakespere's Home, by J. C. M. Bellew, 38. Proceedings of the Essex Archæological Society, iii. 64. Notes and Queries, 3 S. vi. 64; vii. 175, 498; viii. 33, 124, 184; xii. 81, 161. Nicholl's Account of the Company of Ironmongers, 2nd edn., 594. Outlines of the Life of Shakespeare, by J. O. Halliwell-Phillipps, 5th edn., 614. The Genealogical Magazine, i. 30, 83, 160, 214, 282, 357. See HALLEN.

SHALCROSS. Jewitt's Reliquary, vi. 150. Harleian Society, xvii. 231, 232; xviii. 206. The Genealogist, New Series, viii. 79.

SHAN, or SHANN. Memoirs of the Family of Chester, by R. E. C. Waters, 182. Howard's Visitation of England and Wales, i. 168. Burke's Family Records, 534. Burke's Royal Descents and Pedigrees of Founders' Kin, 7.

SHAND. Some Notices of the Surname of Shand, by Rev. Geo. Shand. Norwich, 1877, 8vo. Burke's Landed Gentry, 8 at p. 910.

SHANE. The Irish Builder, xxxv. 150.

SHANK. Burke's Landed Gentry, 2, 3, 4, 5, 6. The Genealogist, i. 85. Metcalfe's Visitations of Suffolk, 163. Miscellanea Genealogica et Heraldica, 2nd Series, i. 235. See SCHANK.

SHANLY. O'Hart's Irish Pedigrees, 2nd Series, 137.

SHANNON. Burke's Royal Families, (London, 1851, 8vo.) i. 170. New England Register, v. 245.

SHAPCOTE, or SHAPCOTT. Tuckett's Devonshire Pedigrees, 152. Harleian Society, vi. 257. Westcote's Devonshire, edited by G. Oliver and P. Jones, 602. The Visitations of Devon, by J. L. Vivian, 677. See SAPCOTTS.

SHAPLEIGH. Harleian Society, vi. 258. New England Register, v. 345. Visitations of Devon, by J. L. Vivian, 678.

SHAPWYK. The Genealogist, New Series, iv. 68.

SHARD. Harleian Society, viii. 498. Oxford Historical Society, xxiv. 141.

SHARDELOW. Gage's History of Thingoe Hundred, Suffolk, 60. Page's History of Suffolk, 825. Metcalfe's Visitations of Suffolk, 164. Harleian Society, xxxii. 214.

SHARESHULL. Shaw's Staffordshire, ii. 281. The Genealogist, New Series, xvi. 37.

SHARINGTON. Blomefield's Norfolk, x. 201. Carthew's Hundred of Launditch, Part i. 237.

SHARMAN-CRAWFORD. Burke's Landed Gentry, 5, 6, 7. Howard's Visitation of Ireland, ii. 21.

SHARNBORNE, or SHARNBURN. Reliquiæ Spelmannianæ, (Oxon, 1698, folio,) 189. Blomefield's Norfolk, x. 335. Harleian Society, xxxii. 246.

SHAROWE. Gyll's History of Wraysbury, 19. Lipscombe's History of the County of Buckingham, iv. 620. Harleian Society, xvii. 232.

SHARP. J. E. Jackson's History of St. George's Church at Doncaster, App. lvi. Berry's Kent Genealogies, 470. Visitation of Sussex, 1570, printed by Sir T. Phillipps, (Middle Hill, fol.) 10. Burke's Landed Gentry, 4, 5, 6, 7, 8. Collectanea Bradfordiana, by A. Holroyd, (Saltaire, 1873, 8vo.) 93-111. Harleian Society, viii. 509; xiii. 487. Baker's Northampton, ii. 255. History of Bradford, by John James, 426. Thoresby's Ducatus Leodiensis, 36. Whitaker's Loidis and Elmete, 355. Notes and Queries, 3 S. xii. 321, 449; 5 S. ix. 91. Burke's Extinct Baronetcies, 636. Hulbert's Annals of Almondbury, 471. Stodart's Scottish Arms, ii. 369. Northern Notes and Queries, iii. 160. Notes and Queries, 7 S., i. 109, 177, 295, 394, 514. See PARKINSON-SHARP.

SHARPE. Berry's Sussex Genealogies, 220. Burke's Landed Gentry, (of Oaklands,) 2; (of Woodbridge,) 2. Harleian Society, ii. 89; vi. 258; xiii. 100. Nichols' History of the County of Leicester, ii. 443. A Royal Descent, by T. E. Sharpe, (London, 1875, 4to.) 64. J. H. Hill's History of Market Harborough, 48. Burke's Family Records, 535. Visitations of Devon, by J. L. Vivian, 679. Muskett's Suffolk Manorial Families, i. 41.

SHARPLES. Chetham Society, lxxxi. 10; lxxxviii. 257, 269; xcii. 199. Abram's History of Blackburn, 269.

SHARRETT. Midland Counties Historical Collector, published by Architectural and Archæological Society of Leicester, 1855-1856, ii. 351.

SHARROCK. Chetham Society, lxxxviii. 268. The Visitations of Cornwall, edited by J. L. Vivian, 425. Carthew's Hundred of Launditch, Part iii. 197.

SHAW. Memorials of the Clan Shaw, by W. G. Shaw, 1881, 8vo. A Genealogical Account of the Highland Families of Shaw, by A. M. Shaw. London, 1877, 8vo. Hasted's Kent, i. 53. Morant's History of Colchester, 118. Gentleman's Magazine, 1837, ii. 330. Morant's Essex, i. 483. Berry's Hertfordshire Genealogies, 49. Surtees Society, xxxvi. 365; lxv. 162. Burke's Landed Gentry, 2, 3, 4, 5, 6, 7, 8. Harleian Society, viii. 146; xvii. 233; xxxvii. 327, 376; xxxviii 790; xliii. 135. Chetham Society, lxxxviii. 258-262. Hunter's Deanery of Doncaster, ii. 24. Clutterbuck's Hertford, ii. 103. Butterworth's Account of the Town, etc., of

Oldham, 111. Nisbet's Heraldry, ii. app. 301. The Genealogist, iv. 45. Shaw's History of Moray, 41. Wotton's English Baronet- age, iii. 463. Betham's Baronetage, ii. 373. Metcalfe's Visita- tions of Suffolk, 164. Memoirs of Master John Shaw, by J. R. Boyle, 83. Burke's Colonial Gentry, ii. 455. Genealogical Notes anent some Ancient Scottish Families, by J. B. Brown-Morison, 99. Heywood's Diaries, edited by J. H. Turner, i. 15. Bysshe's Visitation of Essex, edited by J. J. Howard, 82. Miscellanea Genealogica et Heraldica, 2nd Series, i. 309. Surrey Archæo- logical Collections, xi. History of the old Chapel, Tockholes, by B. Nightingale, 211. Ontarian Families, by E. M. Chadwick, i. 95. New England Register, li. 191. *See* SCHAW.

SHAWE. Harleian Society, xxxvii. 312. Burke's Commoners, i. 672, Landed Gentry, 2, 3, 4, 7, 8.

SHAWE-TAYLOR. Burke's Landed Gentry, 2, 3, 4, 5, 6, 7, 8.

SHAXTON. Harleian Society, xxxii. 246.

SHEAFE. New England Register, iv. 310.

SHEANE. O'Hart's Irish Pedigrees, 2nd Series, 302.

SHEDDEN. Burke's Commoners, (of Paulerspury Park,) iii. 351, Landed Gentry, 2, 3, 4, 5, 6, 7, 8 ; (of Morris Hill,) 2 supp. and add., 3, 4. Geo. Robertson's Description of Cunninghame, 289. Paterson's History of the Co. of Ayr, i. 274. Paterson's History of Ayr and Wigton, iii. 110, 112.

SHEE. Burke's Commoners, i. 405 ; ii. 124. *See* O'SHEE.

SHEEHY. Burke's Landed Gentry, 4. Literary Life and Corre- spondence of the Countess of Blessington, by R. R. Madden, i. 12.

SHEEPSHANKS. Whitaker's Loidis and Elmete, App. 31. Burke's Landed Gentry, 6, 7, 8.

SHEFFELD, or SHEFFIELD. Harleian Society, iii. 19. A Character of John Sheffield, late Duke of Buckinghamshire, with an Account of the Pedigree of the Sheffield Family. London, 1729, 12mo. Peck's Account of the Isle of Axholme, 82. Gentleman's Maga- zine, lxxx. i. 203 ; ii. 34, 586, 630. Visitation of Middlesex, (Salisbury, 1820, fol.) 1. Burke's Commoners, i. 651. Stone- house's History of the Isle of Axholme, 276. Collectanea Topo- graphica et Genealogica, i. 171; iv. 259. Graves' History of Cleveland, 301. Ord's History of Cleveland, 309. Read's History of the Isle of Axholm, edited by T. C. Fletcher, 160. Betham's Baronetage, iii. 249. Banks' Dormant and Extinct Baronage, iii. 541. The Genealogist, vi. 281 ; New Series, xv. 214. Foster's Visitation of Middlesex, 5. Bysshe's Visitation of Essex, edited by J. J. Howard, 83.

SHEILDS. *See* SHIELDS.

SHEKELL. Burke's Landed Gentry, 2, 3. Howard's Visitation of England and Wales, vi. 68.

SHELBURY. Visitation of Middlesex, (Salisbury, 1820, fol.) 49. Collectanea Topographica et Genealogica, iii. 159. Foster's Visitation of Middlesex, 91.

SHELDON. Pedigree of Sheldon of Rowley, Co. Stafford, etc.,

privately printed by Sir T. Phillipps, folio page. Hasted's Kent,
ii. 497. Nash's Worcestershire, i. 64, 145 ; ii. 357. Visitation
of Gloucestershire, 1569, (Middle Hill, 1854, fol.) 9. Burke's
Royal Families, (London, 1851, 8vo.) i. 17. Burke's Landed
Gentry, 2, 3, 4, 5, 6, 7, 8. Visitation of Warwickshire, 1619,
published with Warwickshire Antiquarian Magazine, 26. Herald
and Genealogist, iii. 423. Visitation of Derbyshire, 1663-4,
(Middle Hill, 1854, fol.) 6. Harleian Society, viii. 208 ; xii. 3 ;
xxi. 221 ; xxvii. 127. Dugdale's Warwickshire, 584. The
Genealogist, iii. 182. Foley's Records of the English Province
S. J., v. 850. Oxford Historical Society, xxvi. 99. Miscellanea
Genealogica et Heraldica, 3rd Series, iii. 124.

SHELLEY. Hasted's Kent, iii. 460. Berry's Sussex Genealogies, 62-
70. Burke's Landed Gentry, 3, 4, 5, 6, 7. Herald and Gene-
alogist, iii. 515. Horsfield's History of Lewes, ii. 176*, 180*.
Dallaway's Sussex, II. i. 38 ; II. ii. 76, 244, 367. Visitatio Comi-
tatus Wiltoniæ, 1623, printed by Sir T. Phillipps. Wiltshire
Archæological Magazine, xi. 35. Castles, Mansions, and Manors
of Western Sussex, by D. G. C. Elwes and C. J. Robinson, 235.
The Antiquary, iii. 53. Miscellanea Genealogica et Heraldica,
New Series, iii. 421. Notes and Queries, 2 S. viii. 199. Betham's
Baronetage, i. 65. Wotton's English Baronetage, i. 59. The
Genealogist, New Series, xii. 240.

SHELTON. Blomefield's Norfolk, v. 264. Burke's Landed Gentry,
2, 3, 6, 7, 8. Visitation of Staffordshire, 1663-4, printed by Sir
T. Phillipps, 9. Erdeswicke's Survey of Staffordshire, 394.
Page's History of Suffolk, 767, 926. The Forest and Chace of
Sutton Coldfield, (London, 1860, 8vo.) 84. Harleian Society,
xxxii. 247. Visitations of Staffordshire, 1614 and 1663-4, William
Salt Society, 264. New England Register, xi. 271.

SHEMELD. Harleian Society, xxxviii. 738.

SHENSTONE. Herald and Genealogist, vi. 366.

SHENTON. Nichols' History of the County of Leicester, iv. 483.
Harleian Society, xxix. 436.

SHEPEY. Nichols' History of the County of Leicester, iv. 932. The
Genealogist, New Series, xiv. 21. See DE SHEPEY.

SHEPHARD, SHEPHEARD, or SHEPPARD. Brief History of the
Sheppard Family, by W. A. Sheppard. Calcutta, 1891, 8vo.
Pedigree of the Family of Sheppard. [By R. S. Boddington.]
London, 1883, 4to. Visitation of Oxfordshire, 1634, printed by
Sir T. Phillipps, (Middle Hill, fol.) 29. Visitation of Sussex,
1570, printed by Sir T. Phillipps, (Middle Hill, fol.) 10. Notes
and Queries, 2 S. vii. 155, 305. Robinson's Mansions of Here-
fordshire, 203. Gentleman's Magazine, 1830, i. 398, 510. Berry's
Sussex Genealogies, 308. Burke's Landed Gentry, (of Frome
Selwood,) 2, 3, 4, 5, 6, 7, 8 ; (of Folkington,) 2, 3, 4 ; (of High
House,) 2, 3, 4 ; (of Campsey Ashe,) 5, ·6 ; (of Clifton,) 8.
Harleian Society, v. 315 ; viii. 446 ; xvii. 234 ; xix. 138 ; xxix.
437 ; xxxii. 248 ; xliii. 171. Page's History of Suffolk, 86. Fosbrooke's History of Gloucestershire, i. 374. Account of the

Mayo and Elton Families, by C. H. Mayo, 145. Duncombe's Hereford, (J. H. Cooke,) iii. 22. Visitation of Gloucester, edited by T. F. Fenwick and W. C. Metcalfe, 167. New England Register, vi. 127 ; xxxii. 332. Historical Notices of Doncaster, by C. W. Hatfield, 2nd Series, 147. Gloucestershire Notes and Queries, ii. 508. Memoir of Richard Haines, by C. R. Haines, table vi.

SHEPHERD. Burke's Landed Gentry, 7, 8.

SHEPLEY. Northern Genealogist, ii. 199.

SHERAR. Harleian Society, xxix. 437.

SHERARD, or SHERRARD. Hasted's Kent, i. 415. Harleian Society, ii. 10, 88. Wright's History of Rutland, 121, 134. Nichols' History of the County of Leicester, ii. 343, 346, 353. Midland Counties Historical Collector, published by Architectural and Archæological Society of Leicester, 1855-1856, ii. 351. Edmondson's Baronagium Genealogicum, iii. 220. Archdall's Lodge's Peerage, vii. 1. Brydges' Collins' Peerage, iv. 180. Wotton's English Baronetage, iii. 563. Burke's Extinct Baronetcies. The Genealogist, xvii. 168.

SHERBROOK, or SHERBROOKE. Burke's Landed Gentry, 4, 5, 6, 7, 8. Harleian Society, iv. 132. Dickinson's History of Southwell, 2nd edition, 156. Some Account of the Taylor Family, by P. A. Taylor, 694.

SHERBURN, SHERBORNE, SHERBOURNE, or SHERBURNE. Chetham Society, lxxxi. 58 ; lxxxii. 27, 109 ; lxxxviii. 263-267. Chauncy's Hertfordshire, 62. Whitaker's History of Whalley, ii. 23. Baines' History of the Co. of Lancaster, iii. 572 ; Croston's edn. iii. 351. Gentleman's Magazine, 1824, i. 513, 588. Harleian Society, viii. 368 ; xvi. 284. Robinson's Mansions of Herefordshire, 228. Whitaker's Craven, 3rd edn., 24. Burke's Extinct Baronetcies. History of Ribchester, by T. C. Smith and J. Shortt, 239. New England Register, ix. 180. History of Chipping, by Tom C. Smith, 229.

SHERD. Foster's Yorkshire Pedigrees. Ormerod's Cheshire, iii. 831. Earwaker's East Cheshire, ii. 87.

SHERIDAN. Memoirs of the Rt. Hon. R. B. Sheridan, by J. Watkins. London, 1817, 4to. Genealogical Tables of the Families of Sheridan, Lefaun, and Knowles, by F. Harvey. London, 1875, 8vo. Camden Society, New Series, iv. 203. Burke's Landed Gentry, 2, 3, 4, 5, 6, 7, 8. Notes and Queries, 7 S., vii. 75.

SHERINGTON, or SHERRINGTON. Lipscombe's History of the County of Buckingham, iv. 334. East Anglian, iii. 342. Bowles' History of Lacock Abbey, 297. Visitatio Comitatus Wiltoniæ, 1623, printed by Sir T. Phillipps. Harleian Society, xxvii. 134. The Genealogist, New Series, xii. 241.

SHERMAN. Cambridgeshire Visitation, edited by Sir T. Phillipps, 28. Harleian Society, ii. 203 ; vi. 260 ; xli. 70. Nichols' History of the County of Leicester, i. 504. Metcalfe's Visitations of Suffolk, 164. New England Register, xxiv. 63, 155 ; xxvii. 73 ; li. 309. Burke's Colonial Gentry, ii. 805. The Visitations of Devon, by J. L. Vivian, 680.

SHERSTON. Burke's Landed Gentry, 3, 4, 8. Phelps' History of Somersetshire, ii. 24. Jewers' Wells Cathedral, 181.

SHERWILL. Burke's Royal Families, (London, 1851, 8vo.) i. 80.

SHERWIN. A Collection of Letters written by his Excellency General George Monk. London, 1714.

SHERWIN-GREGORY. Burke's Landed Gentry, 3, 4, 5.

SHERWOOD. Burke's Landed Gentry, 5, 6, 7. Parochial Topography of the Hundred of Wanting, by W. N. Clarke, 128. A Complete Parochial History of the County of Cornwall, i. 114. Harleian Society, xvi. 285. The Genealogist, vi. 88. Foster's Visitations of Northumberland, 113. Cyclostyle Pedigrees, by J. J. Green.

SHEWEN. Genealogies of Morgan and Glamorgan, by G. T. Clark, 503. *See* MANSELL.

SHIELDS, or SHEILDS. Burke's Landed Gentry, 5 supp., 6 at p. 1667.

SHIENTON. Dwnn's Visitations of Wales, i. 205.

SHIERCLIFFE. Foster's Visitations of Yorkshire, 574. Hunter's History of the Parish of Sheffield, 446. Eastwood's History of Ecclesfield, 422.

SHIERS. Surrey Archæological Collections, v. 42. Burke's Extinct Baronetcies.

SHILLETO, or SHILLITO. Surtees Society, xxxvi. 385. W. Paver's Pedigrees of Families of the City of York, 18.

SHILLINGFORD.. Visitation of Oxfordshire, 1634, printed by Sir T. Phillipps, (Middle Hill, fol.) 30. Harleian Society, v. 303. Westcote's Devonshire, edited by G. Oliver and P. Jones, 468. Dunkin's History of Bullington and Ploughley, i. 100. Visitation of Devon, edited by F. T. Colby, 139.

SHILTON. *See* SHELTON.

SHIPLEY. Berry's Hampshire Genealogies, 207. Burke's Landed Gentry, 2, 3, 4, 5, 6, 7, 8. Burke's Royal Descents and Pedigrees of Founders' Kin, 47. Annals of Smith of Balby, by H. E. Smith, 132.

SHIPMAN. Thoroton's Nottinghamshire, i. 231. The Genealogist, New Series, iii. 156.

SHIPPARDSON. Burke's Heraldic Illustrations, 24. Burke's Royal Descents and Pedigrees of Founders' Kin, 54.

SHIPPERDSON. Burke's Commoners, i. 108, Landed Gentry, 2, 3, 4, 5, 6. Surtees' Durham, i. 114.

SHIPWARD. Harleian Society, ii. 82. Nichols' History of the County of Leicester, iii. 523. Dallaway's Antiquities of Bristow, 39.

SHIRLEY. Stemmata Shirleiana, or Annals of the Shirley Family, by Evelyn Philip Shirley. London, 1841, 4to. ; 2nd edn., 1873, 4to. Historical Memoirs of the Sherley Brothers, by E. P. Shirley, 1848, 4to. Jewitt's Reliquary, ix. 189. Berry's Sussex Genealogies, 172, 204. Visitation of Sussex, 1570, printed by Sir T. Phillipps, (Middle Hill, fol.) 10. Burke's Commoners, i. 49. Landed Gentry, 2, 3, 4, 5, 6, 7, 8. Harleian Society, ii. 25-27 ; xvii. 235, 236 ; xxii. 163 ; xxxvii. 402. Dallaway's Sussex, II. ii. 139, 307. The Topographer, (London, 1789-91, 8vo.) iv. 332. Bridges' Northamptonshire, by Rev. Peter Whalley, i. 215.

Nichols' History of the County of Leicester, iii. 715*-719*, 721*, 727; iv. 1050. Dugdale's Warwickshire, 622. Baker's Northampton, i. 732. Sussex Archæological Collections, xviii. 63. Shirley's History of the County of Monaghan, 282. Edmondson's Baronagium Genealogicum, ii. 191; vi. 39. Brydges' Collins' Peerage, iv. 85. Betham's Baronetage, iv. 167. Banks' Dormant and Extinct Baronage, ii. 183. Notes and Queries, 5 S. ii. 76, 96. Burke's Extinct Baronetcies. *See* SHURLEY.

SHIRT. Miscellanea Genealogica et Heraldica, ii. 258.

SHOLL. An Account of the Families of Boase, (Exeter, 1876, 4to.) 45. Burke's Colonial Gentry, ii. 686.

SHOLMSTED. Harleian Society, xvi. 358.

SHORDICH, or SHORDITCH. Visitation of Norfolk, published by Norfolk Archæological Society, i. 222. History of the Parish of St. Leonard Shoreditch, by Henry Ellis, 93, 94. Harleian Society, xxxii. 248.

SHORE. Burke's Landed Gentry, 2, 3, 4, 5, 6, 7, 8. Visitation of Derbyshire, 1663-4, (Middle Hill, 1854, fol.) 6. Hunter's History of the Parish of Sheffield, 376. The Genealogist, iii. 16. Fishwick's History of Rochdale, 433. Harleian Society, xxxvii. 317; xxxviii. 471. Burke's Family Records, 536.

SHORROCK. Harleian Society, ix. 202. Abram's History of Blackburn, 508, 599.

SHORT. Tuckett's Devonshire Pedigrees, 151. Berry's Kent Genealogies, 61. Burke's Landed Gentry, (of Edlington Grove,) 2 supp., 3, 4, 5, 6, 7, 8; (of Bickham,) 2 supp., 3, 4, 5, 6, 7, 8; (of Newham Hall,) 5, 6, 7; (of Heslerton Hall,) 8. Harleian Society, vi. 259; xvii. 237; xl. 1189; xlii. 90. Visitation of Staffordshire, 1663-4, printed by Sir T. Phillipps, 9. Visitations of Staffordshire, 1614 and 1663-4, William Salt Society, 265. The Visitations of Devon, by J. L. Vivian, 681.

SHORTER. Gyll's History of Wraysbury, 275. Harleian Society, viii. 301. Notes and Queries, 2 S., xi. 455; xii. 14; 3 S., i. 219; 6 S., x. 72.

SHORTGRAVE. Metcalfe's Visitations of Northamptonshire, 135.

SHORTHOSE. Harleian Society, xvi. 286.

SHORTRIDGE. Harleian Society, vi. 260. The Visitations of Devon, by J. L. Vivian, 682.

SHORTT. Burke's Landed Gentry, 2 supp., 4. Burke's Authorized Arms, 105.

SHOTBOLT. Chauncy's Hertfordshire, 61. Harleian Society, xxii. 163.

SHOTTESBROOKE. Ashmole's Antiquities of Berkshire, iii. 301.

SHOULDHAM. Blomefield's Norfolk, vii. 113. Archdall's Lodge's Peerage, vii. 151. Harleian Society, xxxii. 249. *See* SHULDHAM.

SHOVEL. Pedigree of the Descendants of Elizabeth, eldest daughter of Sir Cloudesley Shovel, compiled by Hon. Robert Marsham, January, 1881. Broadside. The Shipwreck of Sir C. Shovell, by J. H. Cooke, 14. Notes and Queries, 7 S. ii. 393; 8 S. vii. 41.

SHOYSWELL. Berry's Sussex Genealogies, 84.

SHREWSBURY. Claim of the Rt. Hon. Bertram Arthur, Earl of

Shrewsbury and Earl of Waterford, to Vote at Elections of Irish
Peers, Sess. Papers, 162 of 1854 ; 328 of 1854-5 ; 284 of 1856 ;
290 of 1857-8. Redfern's History of Uttoxeter, 128. *See* TALBOT.
SHREWSBURY (Earls of). Collectanea Archæologica, (Brit. Arch.
Assn.,) i. 67.
SHRIGLEY. Harleian Society, xviii. 207. Earwaker's East Cheshire,
ii. 323.
SHRUBB. Burke's Visitation of Seats and Arms, 2nd Series, ii. 65.
Burke's Landed Gentry, 2, 3, 4, 5, 6, 7, 8.
SHRUBSOLE. Harleian Society, xlii. 151.
SHUCKBURGH. Burke's Royal Families, (London, 1851, 8vo.) ii. 14.
Burke's Commoners,] ii. 94, Landed Gentry, 7, 8. Visitation of
Warwickshire, 1619, published with Warwickshire Antiquarian
Magazine, 64. Hoare's Wiltshire III. iv. 54. Baker's North-
ampton, i. 62, 371. Harleian Society, xii. 345. Wotton's Eng-
lish Baronetage, iii. 76. Betham's Baronetage, ii. 88. Miscel-
lanea Genealogica et Heraldica, 2nd Series, iii. 317, 352. Met-
calfe's Visitations of Northamptonshire, 46, 135.
SHUDD. Manning and Bray's Surrey, ii. 46.
SHULDHAM. Burke's Landed Gentry, (of Marlesford Hall,) 2, 3, 4, 5,
6 ; (Dunmanway,) Commoners, i. 653, Landed Gentry, 2, 3, 4,
5, 6, 7, 8 ; (of Ballymulvey,) Landed Gentry, 2, 3, 4, 5, 6, 7 ; (of
Kettlestone,) 2 add. Norfolk Archæology, vi. 300. Foster's
Lincolnshire Pedigrees, 16. *See* SHOULDHAM.
SHURLEY. Berry's Sussex Genealogies, 204. Horsfield's History of
Lewes, ii. 145. *See* SHIRLEY.
SHUTE. Morant's Essex, ii. 23. Burke's Landed Gentry, 2, 3, 4, 5.
Harleian Society, xli. 96. Cambridgeshire Visitation, edited by Sir
T. Phillipps, 27.
SHUTTE. Poulson's Holderness, ii. 70.
SHUTTLEWORTH. Surtees Society, xxxvi. 72. Burke's Heraldic
Register, (published with St. James's Magazine,) 68. Burke's
Commoners, (of Gawthorp,) iii. 518, Landed Gentry, 2, 3, 4, 5, 6,
7 ; (of Great Bowden,) Commoners, iv. 665 ; (of Hodsack Park,)
Landed Gentry, 2 add., 3, 4 ; (of Old Warden,) 5 supp., 6, 7, 8 ;
(of Hathersage,) 8 and 8 supp. Chetham Society, lxxxi. 30 ;
lxxxviii. 270-273. Foster's Lancashire Pedigrees. History of
Blyth, by Rev. John Raine, 153. Corry's History of Lancashire,
ii. 655. Whitaker's History of Whalley, ii. 184, 387. Harleian
Society, xii. 38 ; xxxviii. 461. Jewitt's Reliquary, xvii. 254.
Abram's History of Blackburn, 430. Plantagenet-Harrison's
History of Yorkshire, i. 461. The Genealogist, v. 119. Croston's
edn. of Baines's Lancaster, iii. 391.
SHYRARD. Visitations of Staffordshire, 1614 and 1663-4, William
Salt Society, 65.
SIANKIN DAVYDD SION. Dwnn's Visitations of Wales, ii. 47.
SIAR. Harleian Society, xvii. 238.
SIBBALD. Burke's Landed Gentry, 3, 4. Nisbet's Heraldry, ii. app.
127. Burke's Extinct Baronetcies, 636.
SIBTHORPE. Burke's Landed Gentry, 3, 4, 5, 6, 7, 8. Thoroton's

Nottinghamshire, i. 327, 329. The Genealogist, New Series, ix.
149, 213. Harleian Society, xxxii. 276.

SICKLEMORE. Burke's Commoners, iv. 743, Landed Gentry, 2, 3, 4, 5, 6, 7.

SIDDALL. Chetham Society, xlvii. 136.

SIDEBOTTOM. Burke's Landed Gentry, 8.

SIDENHAM. Visitation of Somersetshire, printed by Sir T. Phillipps,
139, 140. Harleian Society, xi. 99. Weaver's Visitations of
Somerset, 76-78. See SIDNAM, SYDENHAM.

SIDLEY. Berry's Kent Genealogies, 230. Wotton's English Baronetage, i. 447 ; iv. 93. Burke's Extinct Baronetcies.

SIDNAM. Harleian Society, xi. 100 ; xx. 84.

SIDNEY. Memoirs of the Lives and Actions of the Sidneys, pp. 180,
forms the first portion of ' Letters and Memorials of State,' by
Arthur Collins, vol. i. Case of Sir J. S. Sidney, Bart., in relation
to the Dignity of Baron L'Isle, 1824, pp. 13; Appendix, pp. 11, all
folio. Claim of Sir J. S. Sidney, Bart., to the Barony of De L'Isle,
Sess. Papers, 140 of 1824 ; 177 of 1825 ; 59 of 1826. Miscellanea
Genealogica et Heraldica, ii. 161; 2nd Series, ii. 345. Hasted's
Kent, i. 411. Gentleman's Magazine, 1832, i. 214, 400, 605 ;
1833, i. 406. Berry's Kent Genealogies, 478. Berry's Sussex
Genealogies, 297. Burke's Landed Gentry, 2, 3, 4, 5, 6, 7, 8.
Wright's History of Rutland, 126. Dallaway's Sussex, i. 195.
Nichols' History of the County of Leicester, i. 544. Hasted's
Kent, (Hund. of Blackheath, by H. H. Drake,) xvii. See SYDNEY.

SIER. Burke's Landed Gentry, 3 supp., 4.

SIFERWAST. Topographer and Genealogist, iii. 178.

SIKES. Gentleman's Magazine, 1839, ii. 544. Burke's Commoners,
i. 406, Landed Gentry, 2, 3. Herald and Genealogist, vi. 193 ;
vii. 481. W. Dickinson's History of Newark, 221. Sikes of
Hackney [by Henry Wagner]. Broadside, 1893. Includes
descents of Sawbridge, Hichens, and Duval. See SYKES.

SILLIFANT. Burke's Landed Gentry, 2, 3, 4, 5, 6, 7, 8.

SILLY. Maclean's History of Trigg Minor, ii. 515, 521.

SILVA. Burke's Landed Gentry, 8.

SILVER. Berry's Hampshire Genealogies, 92.

SILVERLOCK. More about Stifford, by Wm. Palin, 35. Harleian
Society, xiv. 601.

SILVERTOP. Burke's Commoners, iii. 300, Landed Gentry, 2, 3, 4, 5,
6, 7, 8. Surtees' Durham, i. 52. Fishwick's History of Goosnargh, 185.

SILVESTER. Foster's Visitations of Yorkshire, 574. Yorkshire
Archæological and Topographical Journal, v. 279. J. B. Payne's
Armorial of Jersey, 98. Burke's Extinct Baronetcies. Registers
of Ecclesfield, by A. S. Gatty, 24. The Genealogist, New Series,
xiii. 102. See SYLVESTER.

SIMCOCKS. Collections by the Powys-land Club, iv. 143.

SIMCOE. Burke's Landed Gentry, 5, 6, 7, 8. Howard's Visitation
of England and Wales, iii. 112.

SIMCOX. Burke's Landed Gentry, 3, 4, 5, 6, 7, 8. The Midland
Antiquary, i. 41, 90.

SIMEON. Berry's Hampshire Genealogies, 100. Burke's Royal Families, (London, 1851, 8vo.) ii. 192. Herald and Genealogist, iii. 515. Foley's Records of the English Province S. J., iv. 606. Wotton's English Baronetage, iii. 634. Burke's Extinct Baronetcies.

SIMEONS. Vaux Peerage Claim, 62.

SIMON. Notes and Queries, 2 S. ii. 11ç, 276 ; xii. 2, 140, 218, 357 ; 3 S. i. 219, 297, 378. Harleian Society, xl. 1175.

SIMONDS. Harleian Society, xxxii. 250. Burke's Landed Gentry, 8. The Visitations of Devon, by J. L. Vivian, 683.

SIMONET. J. B. Payne's Armorial of Jersey, 335.

SIMONS, or SIMMONS. Vaux Peerage Claim, 62. Berry's Kent Genealogies, 459. Pembrokeshire Pedigrees, 127. Burke's Colonial Gentry, i. 286. Harleian Society, xxxix. 1056 ; xli. 105.

SIMPKINSON. Miscellanea Genealogica et Heraldica, New Series, iii. 389. The Genealogist, New Series, xii. 102.

SIMPSON. Berry's Kent Genealogies, 6, 173. Surtees Society, xxxvi. 9, 39. Burke's Landed Gentry, (of Mellor Lodge,) 2, 3, 4, 5, 6 ; (of Babworth,) 3, 4, 5, 6 ; (of Knaresborough,) 3, 4, 5 ; (of Merklands,) 3, 4 ; (of Cloncorick,) 2, 3, 4, 5, 6, 7 ; (of Westhouse,) 2, 3 ; (of Maypool,) 8 ; (of Walton Hall,) 6, 7, 8 ; Landed Gentry, 7 at p. 938 ; 8 at p. 1003. Foster's Yorkshire Pedigrees. Foster's Visitations of Yorkshire, 98, 574. Burke's Royal Descents and Pedigrees of Founders' Kin, 64. Thoresby's Ducatus Leodiensis, 19. Hunter's Deanery of Doncaster, i. 184. Surtees' Durham, ii. 269. The Genealogist, ii. 224 ; New Series, xii. 205. John Watson's History of Halifax, 236. Fletcher's Leicestershire Pedigrees and Royal Descents, 161. Foster's Visitations of Cumberland and Westmorland, 123. Harleian Society, xxii. 92 ; xxxvii. 27 ; xlii. 86. See SYMPSON.

SIMSON. Burke's Commoners, iii. 102, Landed Gentry, 3, 4, 5, 6, 7, 8. Paterson's History of the Co. of Ayr, ii. 144. Paterson's History of Ayr and Wigton, iii. 365. See FRAZER.

SINCLAIR. The Sinclair Genealogy, by C. T. M'Cready, broadside, dated 1 Feb. 1868. Genealogy of the Sinclairs of Ulbster, by Sir John Sinclair, Bart. 1810. Claim of Wm. Sinclair, Esq., to the title of Earl of Caithness, Sess. Papers, Feb. 1771—Feb. 1790. Proof taken by William Sinclair of Raltu, Esq., etc., with a Tree of the Family of Caithness. 1767, 4to. Genealogy of the Sinclair Family of Ballyrussell, by C. T. MacCready. Dublin, 1867, fol. sheet. The Sinclairs of England. London, 1887, 8vo. Herald and Genealogist, v. 368. Gentleman's Magazine, 1844, i. 590. Burke's Landed Gentry, (of Holyhill,) 3, 4, 5, 6, 7, 8 ; (of Forss,) 2, 3, 4, 5, 6, 7 ; (of Mey,) 8. Douglas's Baronage of Scotland, 89, 246-255. History of Caithness, by J. T. Calder, 256. Wood's Douglas's Peerage of Scotland, i. 296 ; ii. 336, 498. Betham's Baronetage, iv. 151. Stodart's Scottish Arms, ii. 181. Celtic Magazine, vol. xiii. See ST. CLAIR.

SINGLETON. Burke's Landed Gentry, (of Mell,) 3, 4, 5, 6, 7, 8 ; (of

Holyhill,) 7 ; (of Aclare,) 2, 3, 4, 5, 6, 7, 8 ; (of Quinville Abbey,) 2, 3, 4, 5, 6, 7, 8 ; (of Fort Singleton,) 6, 7. Fishwick's History of Goosnargh, 192. Chetham Society, lxxxi. 128 ; lxxxii. 81 ; lxxxviii. 274. Shirley's History of the County of Monaghan, 164. Metcalfe's Visitations of Suffolk, 164. Harleian Society, xxxii. 278.

SION AP RYS. Dwnn's Visitations of Wales, i. 35.

SISON. Jewitt's Reliquary, x. 191.

SITSILT, or SITSYLT. Berry's Herefordshire Genealogies, 207. Duncumb's History of the Co. of Hereford, ii. 304. Harleian Society, xxi. 180. *See* CECILL.

SITWELL. The Sitwell Pedigree, by Sir G. R. Sitwell, Bart. Scarborough, 1890, 4to. Burke's Landed Gentry, (of Stainsby,) 2, 3, 4, 5, 6, 7, 8 ; (of Barmoor Castle,) 2, 5 ; (of Ferney Hall,) 3, 4. Visitation of Derbyshire, 1663-4, (Middle Hill, 1854, fol.) 6. Hunter's History of the Parish of Sheffield, 373. The Genealogist, iii. 15.

SIVEWRIGHT. Burke's Landed Gentry, 2 supp., 3, 4, 7, 8.

SKARGILL. Kent's British Banner Displayed, 129. Thoresby's Ducatus Leodiensis, 224. *See* SCARGILL.

SKEELS. Howard's Visitation of England and Wales, v. 19. Burke's Landed Gentry, 8.

SKEERE. Hasted's Kent, ii. 747.

SKEFFINGTON. Hasted's Kent, ii. 334. Select Views in Leicestershire, by J. Throsby, ii. 210. Berry's Kent Genealogies, 371. Harleian Society, ii. 7, 110 ; xlii. 151. Shaw's Staffordshire, i. 365, 372. Nichols' History of the County of Leicester, iii. 437-450. Archdall's Lodge's Peerage, ii. 368. Betham's Baronetage, iv. 179. Burke's Extinct Baronetcies. Notes and Queries, 6 S., xii. 505.

SKEGGS. Camden Society, xxxvi. 63.

SKELHORNE. Botfield's Stemmata Botevilliana, 149.

SKELLY. Burke's Royal Families, (London, 1851, 8vo.) i. 183.

SKELTON. Surtees Society, xxxvi. 21, 113 ; xli. 98. Burke's Landed Gentry, 2, 3, 4. Foster's Visitations of Yorkshire, 169, 376. Harleian Society, vii. 36 ; xvi. 286. Foster's Lancashire Pedigrees. Hutchinson's History of Cumberland, i. 494. Jefferson's History of Leath Ward, Cumberland, 221. Thoresby's Ducatus Leodiensis, 110. Plantagenet-Harrison's History of Yorkshire, i. 203. Foster's Visitations of Cumberland and Westmorland, 124-126. Nicolson and Burn's Westmorland and Cumberland, ii. 340.

SKENE. Tracts by Dr. Gilbert Skeyne, by W. F. Skene. Edinburgh, 1860, 4to. Memorials of the Family of Skene. By W. F. Skene. Aberdeen, 1887, 4to. Burke's Commoners, iv. 475, Landed Gentry, 2, 3, 4, 5, 6, 7, 8. Douglas's Baronage of Scotland, 555. Burke's Extinct Baronetcies, 636. Burke's Colonial Gentry, i. 312. Alexander Nisbet's Heraldic Plates, 76.

SKEPPER. Visitation of Durham, 1615, (Sunderland, 1820, fol.) 49. Surtees' Durham, iv. 150. Foster's Visitations of Durham, 289. Lincolnshire Notes and Queries, v. 74.

SKERNE. Foster's Visitations of Yorkshire, 108. The Genealogist, v. 33. Harleian Society, xxxviii. 782.

SKERRETT. Burke's Landed Gentry, (of Finavara,) 3, 4, 5, 6, 7, 8; (of Athgoe,) 2, 3, 4, 5, 6, 7.

SKERYT, or SKERRIT. Harleian Society, vi. 261. The Visitations of Devon, by J. L. Vivian, 684.

SKEWYS. Maclean's History of Trigg Minor, iii. 385.

SKEY. Burke's Landed Gentry, 2. Harleian Society, xl. 1250.

SKIERS. Hunter's Deanery of Doncaster, ii. 101.

SKIKELTHORPE. Pedigree of the Family of Skikelthorpe of Southgate, Middlesex, long slip, *n.d.*

SKILLICORNE. Chetham Society, lxxxi. 52 ; xcii. 191.

SKILLING. Visitatio Comitatus Wiltoniæ, 1623, printed by Sir T. Phillipps. The Genealogist, New Series, xii. 241. *See* SKYLLING.

SKINNER. Berry's Surrey Genealogies, 25. Berry's Kent Genealogies, 286. Visitation of Somersetshire, printed by Sir T. Phillipps, 135. Burke's Commoners, (of Shirley Park,) iv. 749, Landed Gentry, 2 ; (of Fordham,) Landed Gentry, 2 add.; (of Carisbrook,) 5 ; (of the Chantry,) 8. Miscellanea Genealogica et Heraldica, New Series, i. 81 ; ii. 188. Visitation of Warwickshire, 1619, published with Warwickshire Antiquarian Magazine, 180. Westcote's Devonshire, edited by G. Oliver and P. Jones, 599. Hutchins' Dorset, ii. 609. Manning and Bray's Surrey, i. 325. Harleian Society, xii. 295 ; xxii. 93 ; xxxvii. 414 ; xlii. 122 ; xliii. 48, 50, 59. Robinson's Mansions of Herefordshire, 235. The Genealogist, v. 34. Duncumb's Hereford, (J. H. Cooke,) iii. 41. The Visitations of Devon, by J. L. Vivian, 685. *See* SKYNNER.

SKIPPE. Robinson's Mansions of Herefordshire, 170.

SKIPPON. Miscellanea Genealogica et Heraldica, New Series, i. 37, 64. Carthew's Hundred of Launditch, Part iii. 438-444. *See* SKYPPON.

SKIPTON. Burke's Landed Gentry, (of the Casino,) 4, 5 ; (of Beech Hill,) 2, 5, 6, 7.

SKIPWITH. A Brief Account of the Skipwiths, by Fulwar Skipwith. Tunbridge Wells, 1867, 8vo. Burke's Royal Families, (London, 1851, 8vo.) ii. 102. Foster's Visitations of Yorkshire, 634. Nichols' History of the County of Leicester, iii. 368. Dugdale's Warwickshire, 84. Burke's Landed Gentry, 6. Wotton's English Baronetage, i. 536 ; iii. 528, 654. Betham's Baronetage, i. 272. The Genealogist, v. 35 ; vi. 281. Burke's Extinct Baronetcies. Massingberd's History of Ormsby, 52. Burton's History of Hemingborough, 241. Harleian Society, xxii. 20 ; xxxii. 249.

SKIPWORTH. Burke's Landed Gentry, 2 supp., 3, 4, 5, 6, 7.

SKIRBROOKE. Foster's Visitations of Yorkshire, 73.

SKITEBY. Plantagenet-Harrison's History of Yorkshire, i. 77, 78.

SKORIE, or SKORY. Harleian Society, ix. 203. The Visitations of Cornwall, edited by J. L. Vivian, 426.

SKRENE. Morant's Essex, i. 131 ; ii. 170.

SKRIMSHIRE, SCRIMSHAW, or SKRYMSHER. Nichols' History of the County of Leicester, iv. 421. Visitation of Staffordshire, 1663-4, printed by Sir T. Phillipps, 9. Collections for a History of Staffordshire, (William Salt Society,) ii. part 2, 96. Visitation of Staffordshire, (Willm. Salt Soc.) 129. Visitations of Staffordshire, 1614 and 1663-4, William Salt Society, 266-271. Notes and Queries, 8 S. x. 377. *See* SCRIMSHIRE.

SKRINE. Burke's Landed Gentry, 2, 3, 4, 5, 6, 7, 8.

SKULL. Weaver's Visitation of Herefordshire, 65.

SKUTT. Visitatio Comitatus Wiltoniæ, 1623, printed by Sir T. Phillipps. Visitation of Wiltshire, edited by G. W. Marshall, 63.

SKYLLING. Berry's Hampshire Genealogies, 299. *See* SKILLING.

SKYNNER. Hasted's Kent, ii. 295. Tuckett's Devonshire Pedigrees, 32. Miscellanea Genealogica et Heraldica, New Series, i. 177. Harleian Society, i. 86 ; vi. 261. *See* SKINNER.

SKYPPON. Harleian Society, viii. 298. *See* SKIPPON.

SKYRES. Foster's Visitations of Yorkshire, 355.

SLACK. Burke's Landed Gentry, 8.

SLACKE. Burke's Landed Gentry, 4, 5, 6, 7, 8.

SLADE. Pedigree of Slade of Worcester, etc., [T. P.] 1871, 4to. page. Camden Society, xliii. 20. Burke's Landed Gentry, 6. *See* GULLY.

SLADEN. Burke's Landed Gentry, 2, 3, 4, 5, 6, 7, 8.

SLADER. Westcote's Devonshire, edited by G. Oliver and P. Jones, 524. Visitation of Devon, edited by F. T. Colby, 189. The Visitations of Devon, by J. L. Vivian, 686.

SLANEY. Pedigree of Robert Aglionby Slaney, Esq., [T. P.] 1863, folio page. Burke's Commoners, iv. 503, Landed Gentry, 2, 3, 4, 5, 6, 7, 8. Harleian Society, xiii. 487 ; xvii. 238 ; xxix. 438. Memoir of the Molineux Family, by G. Molyneux, 69, Transactions of Shropshire Archæological Society, ix. 3.

SLANNING, or SLANNYNGE. Harleian Society, vi. 262. Westcote's Devonshire, edited by G. Oliver and P. Jones, 563. Visitation of Devon, edited by F. T. Colby, 189. Burke's Extinct Baronetcies. Hasted's Kent, (Hund. of Blackheath, by H. H. Drake,) 251. The Visitations of Devon, by J. L. Vivian, 687.

SLATER. Burke's Landed Gentry, (of Chesterfield,) 2 add., 3, 4 ; (of Newick Park,) 3, 4. The Genealogist, vi. 282. Harleian Society, xxxvii. 210 ; xxxix. 1014.

SLATOR. Burke's Landed Gentry, 2, 3, 4, 5, 6, 7, 8.

SLATTERY. O'Hart's Irish Pedigrees, 2nd Series, 97.

SLAUGHTER. Notes and Queries, 4 S., v. 33, 152, 320, 350. Robinson's Mansions of Herefordshire, 28. The Genealogist, New Series, viii. 79. Gloucestershire Notes and Queries, ii. 64.

SLEECH. Burke's Commoners, iii. 571.

SLEEMAN. Burke's Landed Gentry, 2 supp.

SLEFORD. The Genealogist, v. 37.

SLEGGE. Cambridgeshire Visitation, edited by Sir T. Phillipps, 28. Harleian Society, xli. 46.

SLEIGH. Pedigree of the Family of Sleigh, 1864, folio sheet. Jewitt's Reliquary, vii. 29, 147 ; x. 169. The Genealogist, iii. 15. Visitation of Derbyshire, 1663-4, (Middle Hill, 1854, fol.) 6. Harleian Society, xvii. 239 ; xxxix. 1019.

SLIFFIELD. Harleian Society, xliii. 224.

SLINGAR. Surtees Society, xxxvi. 55.

SLINGSBY. Diary of Sir Henry Slingsby of Scriven, Bart., etc., with a Genealogical Memoir, by Daniel Parsons. London, 1836, 8vo. Surtees Society, xxxvi. 228. Burke's Royal Families, (London, 1851, 8vo.) ii. 42. Foster's Yorkshire Pedigrees. Foster's Visitations of Yorkshire, 112. Harleian Society, viii. 40 ; xvi. 287 ; xix. 139. Burke's Landed Gentry, 6, 7, 8. Notes and Queries, 2 S. iii. 331, 378. Burke's Extinct Baronetcies. Wotton's English Baronetage, iv. 341. Betham's Baronetage, v. (Baronets of Scotland,) 25. The Genealogist, New Series, xvi. 174. *See* COGHILL.

SLIPPER. Burke's Landed Gentry, 8.

SLOANE. Wotton's English Baronetage, iv. 179. Burke's Extinct Baronetcies. Burke's Colonial Gentry, ii. 557.

SLOCOCK. Berry's Berkshire Genealogies, 69.

SLOCOMB. Gyll's History of Wraysbury, 233.

SLOCUM. New England Register, xxxiv. 391.

SLOGGATT. Maclean's History of Trigg Minor, ii. 350.

SLOPER. Fosbrooke's History of Gloucestershire, i. 397. *See* HIGGES.

SLOREY, SLORREY, or SLORY. Pedigree of Slorey, and of Wood of Colwick, [T. P.] 1860, folio page. Harleian Society, ii. 45 ; iv. 87. Nichols' History of the County of Leicester, iv. 621.

SLOWLEY. Harleian Society, vi. 262. The Visitations of Devon, by J. L. Vivian, 689.

SLYFIELD. Surrey Archæological Collections, v. 47.

SLYMAN. Harleian Society, xxxviii. 613.

SLYNEHEAD. Earwaker's Local Gleanings, iii. 551, 556, 617.

SMALBONE. The Genealogist, vi. 89.

SMALL, SMALE, or SMALLE. Nichols' History of the County of Leicester, iii. 94. Hutchins' Dorset, ii. 237. Visitation of Gloucester, edited by T. F. Fenwick and W. C. Metcalfe, 168. Genealogical Memoranda of the Family of Ames, 3. Burke's Colonial Gentry, ii. 609. Harleian Society, xxxix. 865 ; xl. 1197.

SMALLCOMBE. Harleian Society, vi. 263. The Visitations of Devon, by J. L. Vivian, 690.

SMALLEY. Jewitt's Reliquary, vii. 28. Harleian Society, ii. 76. Nichols' History of the County of Leicester, iii. 93. Abram's History of Blackburn, 402, 421, 509.

SMALLPIECE, or SMALPECE. Visitation of Norfolk, published by Norfolk Archæological Society, i. 115. Harleian Society, xxxii. 251 ; xliii. 175.

SMALLWOOD. Surtees Society, xxxvi. 371. Graves' History of Cleveland, 378. Ord's History of Cleveland, 350. Earwaker's East Cheshire, ii. 366. The Genealogist, New Series, xiii. 110.

SMALMAN. Harleian Society, xxix. 438.

SMART, or SMARTE. Morant's Essex, i. 162. Burke's Landed Gentry, 3, 4, 5, 6. Herald and Genealogist, ii. 249. Nichols' History of the County of Leicester, iii. 636. Hutchins' Dorset, ii. 496.

Surtees' Durham, iv. 142. Harleian Society, xvii. 239, 240;
xx. 84. The Genealogist, New Series, vii. 180; viii. 57, 111.
SMEATON. Burke's Landed Gentry, 3, 4. The Genealogist, vi. 90.
Thoresby Society, ii. 53. Platt and Morkill's Records of Whit-
kirk, 60.
SMEDLEY. *See* MOORE.
SMELT. Surtees Society, xxxvi. 104. Notes and Queries, 2 S. vi.
432; vii. 154, 246.
SMELTER. Harleian Society, xxxviii. 664.
SMETHURST. Miscellanea Genealogica et Heraldica, ii. 214. Burke's
Landed Gentry, 4, 5, 6, 7, 8. Foster's Lancashire Pedigrees.
SMETHWICK. Ormerod's Cheshire, iii. 92. Harleian Society, xviii. 208.
SMIJTH. Morant's Essex, i. 157. Lord Braybrooke's History of
Audley End, 285. Berry's Hertfordshire Genealogies, 54. Berry's
Essex Genealogies, 11. Gyll's History of Wraysbury, 41. Lips-
combe's History of the County of Buckingham, iv. 598. Burke's
Heraldic Illustrations, 74. Wright's Essex, ii. 369. Harleian
Society, xiv. 709. Betham's Baronetage, ii. 299.
SMIJTH-WINDHAM. Burke's Landed Gentry, 2, 3, 4, 5, 6, 7.
SMILTER. Harleian Society, xxxviii. 795.
SMITH. Annals of Smith of Balby, by H. Ecroyd Smith, 4to. Pedi-
gree of Smith of Campden, [T. P.] Broadside. Some Account of
the Family of Smith. By W. P. W. Phillimore. London, 1900,
4to. History of the Family of Smith, etc., by Augustus Smith,
M.P. London, 1861, fol. Collections relating to Henry Smith,
Esq., sometime Alderman of London, etc. London, 1800, 8vo.
Notices relating to Thomas Smith of Campden, and to Henry
Smith, Alderman of London, by the late Rev. C. P. Gwilt.
London, 1836, 8vo. The pedigree of Smith, (sometime Smyth,
Smythe, and Smithe,) now Smith Marriott, by the Rev. E. F. N.
Smith. London, 1878, 8vo. Notice of the Family of Smith, etc.,
formerly Lindsay, by Rev. P. C. Campbell, 1869. [12 copies
only.] The Smith Family. By Compton Reade. London, 1902,
8vo. The Heraldry of Smith, by H. S. Grazebrook. Herald
and Genealogist, ii. 78; iii. 427; v. 218; vi. 480. Chronicle of
the Family of De Havilland. Blomefield's Norfolk, v. 407;
vi. 325. Topographer and Genealogist, ii. 115. Nichols' Illustrations of Literary History, iv. 38. Hasted's Kent, i. 238.
Morant's Essex, i. 119; ii. 23, 114. Gentleman's Magazine,
1828, ii. 317; 1830, ii. 488; 1837, i. 149. Visitation of Norfolk,
published by Norfolk Archæological Society, i. 87, 90, 233.
Berry's Surrey Genealogies, 65. Sir T. Phillipps' Topographer,
No. 1, (March, 1821, 8vo.) 24. Dwnn's Visitations of Wales,
i. 77; ii. 287. Berry's Sussex Genealogies, 59, 275, 346.
Berry's Essex Genealogies, 158, 160. Berry's Hertfordshire
Genealogies, 78, 124-131. Berry's Kent Genealogies, 113, 454.
Visitation of Durham, 1615, (Sunderland, 1820, fol.) 98. Visita-
tion of Middlesex, (Salisbury, 1820, fol.) 28, 41. Berry's Buck-
inghamshire Genealogies, 83-86. Surtees Society, xxxvi. 116.
History of the Parish of Ecclesfield, by Rev. J. Eastwood, 377,

417. Visitation of Somersetshire, printed by Sir T. Phillipps, 136. Burke's Commoners, (of Elmhurst,) iv. 471, Landed Gentry, 2, 3, 4, 8; (of Lydiate,) Commoners, iv. 201, Landed Gentry, 2, 3, 4, 5; (of Grovehurst,) 8; (of Hammerwood,) 8; (of Annesbrook,) 8; (of Greenland,) 7; (of Horbling,) 7, 8; (of Shortgrove,) 7, 8; (of Tresco Abbey,) Commoners, i. 98, Landed Gentry, 2, 3, 4, 5, 6, 7; (of Jordanhill,) Commoners, iv. 62, Landed Gentry, 2, 3, 4, 5, 6, 7, 8; (of Togston,) Commoners, iii. 257, Landed Gentry, 2, 3; (of Apsley House,) Commoners, ii. 103, Landed Gentry, 2, 3, 4, 5, 6, 7, 8; (of Halesowen Grange,) Landed Gentry, 2, 3, 4, 5, 6, 7, 8; (of Camer,) 2, 3, 4, 5, 6, 7, 8; (of Woodhall Park,) 3, 4, 5, 6, 8; (of Selsdon,) 3, 4, 5; (of Dale Park,) 3, 4; (of Ellingham,) 2 add., 3, 4, 5, 6, 7, 8; (of Vaynol,) 2, 3, 4, 5, 6, 7, 8; (of Ryhope,) 2 supp., 3, 4, 5, 6, 7, 8; (of Bitteswell Hall,) 2; (of Munslows Aston,) 2; (of Great Fenton,) 6 supp., 7, 8; (of Milford,) 2; (of Pendryffryn,) 2; (of Beabeg,) 2, 3, 4, 5, 6, 7; (of Goldicote,) 5 supp., 6, 8; (of Blackwood House,) 5, 6. Harleian Society, ii. 66, 130, 145; vi. 263, 264; viii. 12, 36, 238, 281; ix. 204; xi. 101; xii. 71, 163; xiii. 101, 175; xiv. 707; xvii. 240-246; xviii. 209, 210; xxix. 439; xxxii. 253, 254; xxxvii. 74, 225, 257; xxxviii. 569, 692; xlii. 48, 86, 113, 183, 195. History of Richmond, by C. Clarkson, 386. Visitation of Warwickshire, 1619, published with Warwickshire Antiquarian Magazine, 200. Maclean's History of Trigg Minor, i. 68. History of the Colleges and Halls of Oxford, by Anthony A' Wood, edited by John Gutch, 353. Gregson's Fragments relative to the County of Lancaster, 179. Blore's Rutland, 54. Visitation of Staffordshire 1663-4, printed by Sir T. Phillipps, 9. The Borough of Stoke-upon-Trent, by John Ward, 543. Burton's Description of Leicestershire, 22. Thoresby's Ducatus Leodiensis, 21, 262. Nichols' History of the County of Leicester, ii. 184, 185; iii. 29, 971; iv. 342. Visitatio Comitatus Wiltoniæ, 1623, printed by Sir T. Phillipps. Hutchins' Dorset, i. 166. Surtees' Durham, i. 187; iv. 98. Manning and Bray's Surrey, ii. 44. Clutterbuck's Hertford, ii. 131. Cussan's History of Hertfordshire, Parts ix. and x. 156; Parts xi. and xii. 176. Paterson's History of the Co. of Ayr, i. 429. Reports and Papers of the Associated Architectural Societies, xii. 282. Douglas's Baronage of Scotland, 539-545. Paterson's History of Ayr and Wigton, ii. 406; iii. 189. Walter Wood's East Neuk of Fife, 299. Account of the Estates belonging to the Trustees of Mr. Smith's Charity, (London, 1825, 8vo.) 13-35. The Tyldesley Diary, edited by J. Gillow and A. Hewitson, 28, 78. Burrows' History of the Family of Burrows, 208. Master's Notices of the Family of Master, 100. Notes and Queries, 1 S. vii. 629; 2 S. i. 453; viii. 152; 3 S. iii. 87, 307, 417; 4 S. x. 290, 326. The Genealogist, vi. 213. Brydges' Collins' Peerage, viii. 547. Wotton's English Baronetage, iii. 286; iv. 52. Betham's Baronetage, ii. 371; iii. 449; iv. 9, 141; v. 507, 578*. Banks' Dormant and Extinct Baronage, iii. 154. Ormerod's Cheshire, iii. 231, 503. Metcalfe's Visitations of Suffolk, 165,

206. Visitation of Wiltshire, edited by G. W. Marshall, 33, 67. Burke's Extinct Baronetcies. Leicestershire Architectural Society Transactions, iv. 271. Visitation of Staffordshire, (Willm. Salt Society) 130. Miscellanea Genealogica et Heraldica, i. 52 ; New Series, iv. 61, 127 ; 2nd Series, i. 171 ; iv. 241 ; 3rd Series, i. 177. The Visitations of Cornwall, edited by J. L. Vivian, 427. Surrey Archæological Collections, ii. Carthew's Hundred of Launditch, Part iii. 205. Burke's Colonial Gentry, i. 5, 11, 172, 341 ; ii. 494. Life of Sir Thomas Smith, Kt., by J. S[trype], 1. Visitation of Gloucester, edited by T. F. Fenwick and W. C. Metcalfe, 169-173. Genealogical Records of the Family of Woodd, 32. Pedigree of the Family of Powell, by Edgar Powell, 81. New England Register, vii. 132, 279 ; viii. 65 ; xiv. 29 ; xlv. 222. Foster's Visitation of Middlesex, 55, 76. Visitations of Staffordshire, 1614 and 1663-4, William Salt Society, 271. Stodart's Scottish Arms, ii. 373. Burton's History of Hemingborough, 324. Brewood, supplement, by J. H. Smith, *at end*. Bysshe's Visitations of Essex, edited by J. J. Howard, 83-85. Foster's Visitations of Durham, 291. Oxford Historical Society, xxiv. 86-88, 91, 358. Metcalfe's Visitations of Northamptonshire, 136. Hasted's Kent, (Hund. of Blackheath, by H. H. Drake,) 80, 194. Cyclostyle Pedigrees, by J. J. Green. Chancellor's Sepulchral Monuments of Essex, 113. Burke's Colonial Gentry, ii. 682, 860. Howard's Visitation of England and Wales, ii. 129 ; vi. 81. History of the old Chapel, Tockholes, by B. Nightingale, 211. History of the Wilmer Family, 251. The Irish Builder, xxxv. 196. Burke's Family Records, 538. The Visitations of Devon, by J. L. Vivian, 691, 693. Ontarian Families, by E. M. Chadwick, i. 17 ; ii. 132. Annals of the English Benedictines of Ghent, 187. Muskett's Suffolk Manorial Families, i. 249.

SMITH-BARRY. Burke's Landed Gentry, 5, 7, 8.

SMITH-BOSANQUET. Burke's Landed Gentry, 5, 6, 7. Howard's Visitation of England and Wales, i. 251.

SMITH-CARRINGTON. Burke's Landed Gentry, 7, 8.

SMITH-DORRIEN. Burke's Landed Gentry, 3, 4, 5, 6, 7, 8.

SMITH-MARRIOTT. The Pedigree of Smith, by Rev. E. F. N. Smith. London, 1878, 8vo. Burke's Landed Gentry, 2 supp., 3, 4.

SMITHES. Visitation of Somersetshire, printed by Sir T. Phillipps, 135. Harleian Society, xi. 101.

SMITHSBY. Harleian Society, xvii. 247.

SMITHSON. Surtees Society, xxxvi. 39. Berry's Genealogical Peerage, 101. Tate's History of Alnwick, i. 353. Plantagenet-Harrison's History of Yorkshire, i. 179, 504. Edmondson's Baronagium Genealogicum, vi. 7. Wotton's English Baronetage, iii. 126. Betham's Baronetage, v. 452*. Pedigrees of the Lords of Alnwick, by W. H. D. Longstaffe, 33. Harleian Society, xxxvii. 160 ; xxxix. 912.

SMITHWICK. Burke's Landed Gentry, 4, 5, 6, 8. Harleian Society, xvii. 247 ; xxii. 21.

SMOLLETT. Account of the Family of Smollett of Bonhill, written by

T. Smollett, arranged by J. Irving. Dumbarton, 1859, 4to. Burke's
Landed Gentry, 2, 3, 4, 5, 6, 7, 8. History of Dumbartonshire,
by Joseph Irving, 334. The Book of Dumbartonshire, by Joseph
Irving, ii. 175-208.
SMYTH. Pedigree of the Ancient and Noble Family of Smyth.
London, 1856, 8vo. Genealogia dell' antica e nobile famiglia
Smyth, by Sir William Betham. Lucca, 1868, 8vo. Collinson's
Somerset, ii. 292. Camden Society, xliv. 22. Morant's Essex,
i. 14; ii. 57, 148. Visitation of Suffolk, edited by J. J. Howard,
ii. 206. Berry's Buckinghamshire Genealogies, 42. Berry's Sussex
Genealogies, 201. Berry's Essex Genealogies, 35, 129. Berry's
Hertfordshire Genealogies, 151. Tuckett's Devonshire Pedigrees,
99. Visitation of Oxfordshire, 1574, printed by Sir T. Phillipps,
(Middle Hill, fol.) 9. Burke's Royal Families, (London, 1851,
8vo.) ii. 96. Burke's Commoners, (of Elkington,) ii. 652, Landed
Gentry, 4, 5, 6, 7, 8; (of Heath Hall,) Landed Gentry, 2, 3,
4, 5, 6, 7, 8; (of Ballynatray,) 2, 3, 4, 5, 6, 8; (of Head-
borough,) 4, 5, 6, 7, 8; (of Gaybrook,) 2, 3, 4, 5, 6, 7, 8;
(of Castle Widenham,) 4 supp., 5, 6, 7; (of Castle Fergus,) 2;
(of Kilnalack,) 2 supp.; (of Drumcree House,) 2, 3, 4, 5, 6, 7, 8;
(of Glananea,) 3, 4, 5, 6, 7; (of Ballynegall,) 3, 4, 5, 6, 7, 8; (of
Ashton Court,) 3; (of Mount Henry,) 5, 6, 7, 8; (of Barbavilla,)
6, 7; (of Masonbrook,) 6, 7, 8. Foster's Yorkshire Pedigrees.
Harleian Society, i. 21, 44, 69; v. 136; vi. 263, 264; ix. 204;
xiii. 13, 487; xiv. 712; xvii. 242-246; xix. 139; xxi. 147; xxii. 164;
xxvii. 130, 145; xxxii. 254-258; xxxvii. 318; xxxix. 939; xliii.
98, 136, 172, 180, 223. Herald and Genealogist, vi. 74. History
of Bradford, by John James, 435. Lipscombe's History of the
County of Buckingham, iv. 223. Burke's Heraldic Illustrations,
66. Burke's Royal Descents and Pedigrees of Founders' Kin, 65.
Dallaway's Sussex, i. 167. Whitaker's Loidis and Elmete, 361.
Nichols' History of the County of Leicester, ii. 730; iii. 29; iv.
644. Dugdale's Warwickshire, 809. Clutterbuck's Hertford,
i. 412. Baker's Northampton, i. 56. Surrey Archæological
Collections, vi. Collections for a History of Staffordshire, William
Salt Society, ii. Part 2, 88. Notes and Queries, 3 S. xii. 27; 4 S.
iii. 166, 318. Wotton's English Baronetage, iii. 278, 337, 462;
iv. 156. Betham's Baronetage, iii. 181, 306. The Genealogist, v.
37; vi. 91. Burke's Extinct Baronetcies. Metcalfe's Visitations
of Suffolk, 65. Carthew's West and East Bradenham, 11. Carthew's Hundred of Launditch, Part iii. 471. History of Wakefield
Rectory Manor, by Thomas Taylor, 248. Weaver's Visitation of
Herefordshire, 95. New England Register, xxvi. 190, 198. Churton's Lives of Wm. Smyth and Sir Richard Sutton, 467-469*.
The Irish Builder, xxxv. 196. Howard's Visitation of Ireland,
iii. 77. See CURRER.
SMYTH-STUART. Notes and Queries, 2 S. viii. 495.
SMYTHE. Whitaker's History of Whalley, 235. Gentleman's Maga-
zine, 1830, ii. 437. Berry's Hampshire Genealogies, 169. Berry's
Kent Genealogies, 10, 251. Burke's Royal Families, (London,

1851, 8vo.) ii. 5. Burke's Commoners (of Methven Castle,) i.
228, Landed Gentry, 2, 3, 4, 5, 6, 7 ; (of Hilton,) Landed Gentry,
2, 3, 4, 5, 6, 7 ; (of New Park,) 2, 3, 4, 5 ; (of Barbavilla,) 2, 3,
4, 5, 6, 7, 8. Harleian Society, i. 33. Whitaker's History of
Whalley, ii. 18. Herald and Genealogist, viii. 204. Surtees'
Durham, ii. 338. Scott of Scot's-Hall, by J. R. Scott, 222. Fosbrooke's History of Gloucestershire, i. 469. Miscellanea Genealogica et Heraldica, New Series, iii. 406. Master's Notices of the
Family of Master, 98. Archdall's Lodge's Peerage, iv. 274.
Wotton's English Baronetage, iii. 242. Betham's Baronetage, ii.
226. Metcalfe's Visitations of Suffolk, 65, 165. The Genealogist,
vi. 282, 283. Archæologia Cantiana, xix. 76.

SNAGG. Clutterbuck's Hertford, ii. 386. Notes and Queries, 2 S. xi.
90, 139. Harleian Society, xix. 140 ; xxii. 21.

SNAPPE. Sir T. Phillipps' Topographer, No. 1, (March, 1821, 8vo.)
25. Visitation of Oxfordshire, 1574, printed by Sir T. Phillipps,
(Middle Hill, fol.) 9. Harleian Society, v. 135 ; xiii. 489.

SNASELL, or SNAWSELL. Surtees Society, xxxvi. 150 ; xli. 17.
Foster's Visitations of Yorkshire, 94. Harleian Society, xvi. 289.

SNEADE. Burke's Landed Gentry, 3 p. 1396. Visitations of Staffordshire, 1614 and 1663-4, William Salt Society, 273.

SNEITH. Visitatio Comitatus Wiltoniæ, 1623, printed by Sir T.
Phillipps.

SNELL. Ashmole's Antiquities of Berkshire, iii. 287. Aubrey's Collections for Wilts, (London, 1821, 4to.) printed by Sir T. Phillipps,
i. 113. Burke's Landed Gentry, 4. Lipscombe's History of the
County of Buckingham, i. 102, 280. Topographical Collections of
John Aubrey, edited by J. E. Jackson, 132. Nichols' History of
the County of Leicester, iv. 805. Visitatio Comitatus Wiltoniæ,
1623, printed by Sir T. Phillipps. Clutterbuck's Hertford, i. 483.
Wiltshire Archæological Magazine, iv. 44. Visitation of Wiltshire,
edited by G. W. Marshall, 12, 32. Weaver's Visitations of
Somerset, 89. Harleian Society, xxi. 150. The Genealogist,
New Series, ii. 77 ; xii. 242.

SNELLING, or SNELLINGE. Berry's Sussex Genealogies, 3. Harleian
Society, vi. 266 ; xvii. 248 ; xxii. 164 ; xliii. 160, 167. Tuckett's
Devonshire Pedigrees, 21. Metcalfe's Visitations of Suffolk, 165.
The Visitations of Devon, by J. L. Vivian, 694. Muskett's Suffolk
Manorial Families, i. 240.

SNELSON. Harleian Society, xvii. 249.

SNEYD. Dwnn's Visitations of Wales, ii. 325. Burke's Royal
Families, (London, 1851, 8vo.) ii. 44. Burke's Commoners, (of
Ashcombe,) i. 555, Landed Gentry, 2, 3, 4, 5, 6, 7, 8 ; (of Keele,)
Landed Gentry, 2, 3, 4, 5, 6, 7, 8. Visitation of Staffordshire,
1663-4, printed by Sir T. Phillipps, 9. The Borough of Stoke-
upon-Trent, by John Ward, 82. Ormerod's Cheshire, iii. 492.

SNEYD-KYNNERSLEY. Burke's Commoners, i. 166, Landed Gentry,
2, 3, 4, 5, 6, 7, 8.

SNEYTHE. The Genealogist, New Series, xii. 242.

SNIGG. Weaver's Visitations of Somerset, 130.

SNODGRASS. Paterson's History of the Co. of Ayr, i. 452. Paterson's
History of Ayr and Wigton, iii. 209. Geo. Robertson's Account
of Families in Ayrshire, i. 148.

SNOW, or SNOWE. Burke's Extinct Baronetcies. New England
Register, xlvii. 81, 186, 341; xlviii. 71, 188; xlix. 71, 202, 451;
li. 204.

SNOWBALL. Metcalfe's Visitations of Northamptonshire, 47.

SNYTHALL. Foster's Visitations of Yorkshire, 325.

SOAME. Cussan's History of Hertfordshire, Parts iii. and iv. 100.
Morant's Essex, ii. 602. Harleian Society, viii. 290; xiii. 490;
xvii. 250. Clutterbuck's Hertford, iii. 464. Wright's Essex, ii.
184. Page's History of Suffolk, 907. Wotton's English Baronetage, iii. 715. Burke's Extinct Baronetcies. Carthew's Hundred
of Launditch, Part iii. 61, 62.

SOFFE. See DUN.

SOHIER. J. B. Payne's Armorial of Jersey, 337. The King of
Arms, 6.

SOLERS. Jones' History of the County of Brecknock, ii. 377. Bigland's Gloucestershire, ii. par. Shipton Solers. See GIFFARD.

SOLEY, or SOLLEY. Jewitt's Reliquary, xviii. 207; xix. 28. Metcalfe's Visitation of Worcester, 1683, 87.

SOLLY. Planché's Corner of Kent, 401.

SOLTAU. Burke's Landed Gentry, 2, 3, 4, 5, 6, 7.

SOMASTER. Tuckett's Devonshire Pedigrees, 111. Westcote's Devonshire, edited by G. Oliver and P. Jones, 500, 551. The Visitations
of Devon, by J. L. Vivian, 695. See SUMMASTER.

SOMER. Berry's Kent Genealogies, 81, 121. Harleian Society,
xlii. 55.

SOMERBY. Burke's Visitation of Seats and Arms, i. 50.

SOMERFORD. Visitation of Staffordshire, 1663-4, printed by Sir T.
Phillipps, 9. Ormerod's Cheshire, iii. 60, 151, 560. Visitation
of Staffordshire, (Willm. Salt Soc.) 131. Visitations of Staffordshire, 1614 and 1663-4, William Salt Society, 275.

SOMERI, or SOMERIE. Lipscombe's History of the County of Buckingham, iv. 275. Blore's Rutland, 90. Baker's Northampton, i. 479.
Herald and Genealogist, v. 103. Manning and Bray's Surrey,
i. 570. Edmondson's Baronagium Genealogicum, iv. 343. Banks'
Baronies in Fee, i. 398. Genealogies of Morgan and Glamorgan,
by G. T. Clark, 431. See DE SOMERY, SOMERY, SUMERY.

SOMERS. Nash's Worcestershire, ii. 54. Clutterbuck's Hertford, i. 457.
Harleian Society, xvii. 249. Howard's Visitation of England and
Wales, ii. 15. Burke's Landed Gentry, 8. See SOMMERS.

SOMERSALL. Jewitt's Reliquary, xiv. 256.

SOMERSET, or SOMERSETT. Rudder's Gloucestershire, 253. Journal
of the British Archæological Association, xii. 312. The Great
Governing Families of England, ii. 190. Collectanea Topographica
et Genealogica, i. 308, 310; vii. 196. Jacob's Peerage, i. 178,
180. Visitation of Somersetshire, printed by Sir T. Phillipps, 136.
Lydiate Hall and its Associations, by Rev. T. E. Gibson, 1876,
4to., 151. Surtees' Durham, iv. 33. Foley's Records of the

English Province S. J., iv. 471; v. 906. Fosbrooke's History of Gloucestershire, ii. 9. Edmondson's Baronagium Genealogicum, i. 19; vi. 41. Berry's Genealogical Peerage, 28. Brydges' Collins' Peerage, i. 222. Metcalfe's Visitations of Suffolk, 66. Annals of Chepstow Castle, by J. F. Marsh, 270. Weaver's Visitations of Somerset, 78. The Gresley's of Drakelowe, by F. Madan, 275.

SOMERVELL. Burke's Landed Gentry, 7.

SOMERVILE, or SOMERVILLE. Memorie of the Somervilles, by James, Lord Somerville, edited by Sir Walter Scott. Edinburgh, 1815, 8vo., 2 vols. Dugdale's Warwickshire, 341, 828. Harleian Society, xii. 33. Paterson's History of the Co. of Ayr, ii. 463. Rudder's Gloucestershire, 241. Burke's Landed Gentry, (of Dinder,) 2, 3, 4, 5, 6, 7, 8; (of Drishane,) 4, 5, 6, 7, 8. Visitation of Warwickshire, 1619, published with Warwickshire Antiquarian Magazine, 66. Phelps' History of Somersetshire, ii. 194. Shaw's Staffordshire, i. 126. Fosbrooke's History of Gloucestershire, ii. 349. Nisbet's Heraldry, ii. app. 79, 277. Paterson's History of Ayr and Wigton, iii. 604. The Upper Ward of Lanarkshire, by G. V. Irving, ii. 485. Wood's Douglas's Peerage of Scotland, ii. 504. Banks' Baronies in Fee, i. 399. Banks' Dormant and Extinct Baronage, i. 407. The Genealogist, New Series, ix. 1; xiii. 73, 152. The Irish Builder, xxix. 152. Alexander Nisbet's Heraldic Plates, 130. Howard's Visitation of Ireland, i. 64. The Gresley's of Drakelowe, by F. Madan, 276.

SOMERY. Burton's Description of Leicestershire, 30. Cussan's History of Hertfordshire, Parts v. and vi. 50. See SOMERI.

SOMESTER. Harleian Society, xiv. 561. Visitation of Devon, edited by F. T. Colby, 153.

SOMMERS. Manning and Bray's Surrey, i. 286. See SOMERS, SUMMERS.

SONDE. Manning and Bray's Surrey, i. 567.

SONDEBACH. The Genealogist, New Series, xvi. 87.

SONDES. Hasted's Kent, ii. 760, 764, 784. Rockingham Castle and the Watsons, ped., 7.

SONDS. Burke's Extinct Baronetcies, 614. Harleian Society, xlii. 105.

SONIBANCK. or SONNIBANK. Visitation of Oxfordshire, 1634, printed by Sir T. Phillipps, (Middle Hill, fol.) 30. Harleian Society, v. 275.

SONLLI. Dwnn's Visitations of Wales, ii. 358. History of Powys Fadog, by J. Y. W. Lloyd, ii. 147.

SONTLEY. Harleian Society, xvii. 252.

SORBY. Harleian Society, xxxviii. 688.

SORESBY. Glover's History of Derbyshire, ii. 327, (292). Betham's Baronetage, v. 439*. Harleian Society, xxxvii. 227; xxxix. 1012.

SOROCOLD. Chetham Society, lxxxviii. 276.

SORRELL. Morant's Essex, ii. 86, 416. Harleian Society, viii. 78; xiii. 490. Bysshe's Visitation of Essex, edited by J. J. Howard, 85, 86.

SORROCOLLE. Harleian Society, xvii. 253.

SOTEHILL. Glover's History of Derbyshire, ii. 392, (359). See SOT-HILL.

SOTELL. Harleian Society, xvi. 291.

SOTHEBY. Burke's Landed Gentry, 5, 6, 7, 8. Foster's Yorkshire Pedigrees. Foster's Visitations of Yorkshire, 170, 575. Harleian Society, xxxix. 953. *See* SOUTHBY, SOWTHEBY.

SOTHERAN, SOTHEREN, or SOTHERON. Genealogical Memoranda relating to the Family of Sotheron, and to the Sept of Mac Manus, by Charles Sotheron. London, 1871-3, 4to. Burke's Commoners, iii. 520. Foster's Yorkshire Pedigrees. Miscellanea Genealogica et Heraldica, New Series, i. 137, 219, 223. Jewitt's Reliquary, xv. 55. Hunter's History of the Parish of Sheffield, 421. Harleian Society, xxxviii. 536.

SOTHERNE. Miscellanea Genealogica et Heraldica, New Series, i. 218. Harleian Society, xvii. 255.

SOTHERTON. Blomefield's Norfolk, x. 429. Harleian Society, i. 80 ; xvii. 251, 254 ; xxxii. 269. Norfolk Antiquarian Miscellany, ii. 629.

SOTHEWORTH. Chetham Society, xcix. 46. *See* SOUTHWORTH.

SOTHILL, or SOWTHYLL. Foster's Visitations of Yorkshire, 275, 331. Harleian Society, xvi. 290. *See* SOTEHILL.

SOTWELL. Surtees Society, xxxvi. 304. Visitatio Comitatus Wiltoniæ, 1623, printed by Sir T. Phillipps. Hunter's Deanery of Doncaster, ii. 271. Visitation of Wiltshire, edited by G. W. Marshall, 68. The Genealogist, New Series, xii. 243.

SOUCH. Visitatio Comitatus Wiltoniæ, 1623, printed by Sir T. Phillipps. Visitation of Wiltshire, edited by G. W. Marshall, 52. The Genealogist, New Series, xiii. 21.

SOULNEY. Nichols' History of the County of Leicester, iv. 577.

SOUTH. Berry's Hampshire Genealogies, 145. Visitation of Warwickshire, 1619, published with Warwickshire Antiquarian Magazine, 49. Visitatio Comitatus Wiltoniæ, 1623, printed by Sir T. Phillipps. Harleian Society, xii. 79. Visitation of Wiltshire, edited by G. W. Marshall, 10. The Genealogist, New Series, xii. 243.

SOUTHALL. Memorials of the Prichards, by Isabell Southall, 65.

SOUTHALLS. Metcalfe's Visitations of Suffolk, 166.

SOUTHAM. Burke's Landed Gentry, 2, 8.

SOUTHAMPTON. Baker's Northampton, ii. 71.

SOUTHBY. Berry's Berkshire Genealogies, 36, 38, 140-143. Burke's Landed Gentry, (of Carswell,) 2, 3, 4, 5, 6, 7, 8 ; (of Hodcott,) 2, 3, 4. Harleian Society, xvi. 289. The Genealogist, vi. 93. *See* SOTHEBY.

SOUTHCOMB. Burke's Landed Gentry, 3, 4, 5, 6, 7.

SOUTHCOT, SOUTHCOTT, or SOUTHCOTE. Burke's Extinct Baronetcies. Tuckett's Devonshire Pedigrees, 57. Westcote's Devonshire, edited by G. Oliver and P. Jones, 537. Morant's Essex, ii. 110. Harleian Society, vi. 266, 269 ; xiii. 491 ; xiv. 601. Manning and Bray's Surrey, ii. 260. The Visitations of Devon, by J. L. Vivian, 697.

SOUTHESK (Earls of). Angus or Forfarshire, by A. J. Warden, 357-379. *See* CARNEGIE.

SOUTHEY. Notes and Queries, 8 S. v. 141, 202, 241.
SOUTHILL. J. H. Hill's History of Market Harborough, 260.
Burton's Description of Leicestershire, 256. Nichol's History of
the County of Leicester, ii. 916. The Genealogist, v. 38. *See*
SOTHILL.
SOUTHLAND. Berry's Kent Genealogies, 317. Harleian Society, xlii.
158.
SOUTHMEADE. Tuckett's Devonshire Pedigrees, 76. Harleian Society,
vi. 270. The Visitations of Devon, by J. L. Vivian, 704.
SOUTHWELL. Rudder's Gloucestershire, 493. Visitation of Norfolk,
published by Norfolk Archæological Society, i. 124. Blomefield's
Norfolk, x. 275. Burke's Royal Families, (London, 1851, 8vo.)
i. 119. Burke's Landed Gentry, 2 add. p. 404. Harleian Society,
viii. 200; xxxii. 258. Gage's History of Thingoe Hundred,
Suffolk, 475. Manning and Bray's Surrey, ii. 256. Page's
History of Suffolk, 567. Fosbrooke's History of Gloucestershire,
i. 496. Poems of Robt. Southwell, (Fuller Worthies Library,)
xxxvi. Whitaker's Deanery of Craven, 3rd edn., 310. Edmond-
son's Baronagium Genealogicum, vi. 33. Archdall's Lodge's
Peerage, vi. 1. Brydges' Collins' Peerage, vi. 512. Metcalfe's
Visitations of Suffolk, 66, 166. Norfolk Antiquarian Miscellany,
ii. 612. The Gresley's of Drakelowe, by F. Madan, 277.
SOUTHWORTH. Visitation of Somersetshire, printed by Sir T.
Phillipps, 136. Harleian Society, iv. 114; xi. 102. Chetham
Society, lxxxi. 26; lxxxviii. 277. Jewitt's Reliquary, xv. 256.
Baines' History of the Co. of Lancaster, iii. 354; Croston's edn.,
iv. 64. Abram's History of Blackburn, 658. History of Samles-
bury, by James Croston, 161. *See* SOTHEWORTH.
SOWDEAK. Harleian Society, i. 59.
SOWERBY. Plantagenet-Harrison's History of Yorkshire, i. 171.
Burke's Landed Gentry, 6, 7, 8.
SOWRAY. Surtees Society, xxxvi. 317. W. Paver's Pedigrees of
Families of the City of York, 19.
SOWTELL. Harleian Society, xvi. 290.
SOWTHEBY. Surtees Society, xxxvi. 318. *See* SOTHEBY.
SPAIGHT. Burke's Landed Gentry, 2, 3, 4, 5, 6, 7, 8. Burke's
Heraldic Illustrations, 57.
SPALDING. Lands and their Owners in Galloway, by P. H. M'Kerlie,
iii. 77. Stodart's Scottish Arms, ii. 371. Burke's Landed
Gentry, 8.
SPAN. Burke's Colonial Gentry, ii. 744.
SPANTON. The Spanton Family, by A. T. Spanton. Hanley,
1897, 4to.
SPANY. Harleian Society, xxxii. 261.
SPARCHFORD. Harleian Society, v. 220.
SPARHAM. Blomefield's Norfolk, viii. 259.
SPARKE. Burke's Landed Gentry, 5, 6, 7, 8. The Visitations of
Devon, by J. L. Vivian, 856. Harleian Society, ix. 205; xvii.
256. The Genealogist, vi. 94. Howard's Visitation of England
and Wales, Notes, iii. 54.

SPARKES. Burke's Landed Gentry, 2, 3, 4, 5. The Midland Antiquary, ii. 95.

SPARKHAUKE, or SPARHAWK. Clutterbuck's Hertford, ii. 302. New England Register, xix. 125 ; xxi. 172.

SPARKS. Burke's Landed Gentry, 2, 3, 4. Miscellanea Genealogica et Heraldica, New Series, ii. 469. Howard's Visitation of England and Wales, iii. 126.

SPARLING. Burke's Landed Gentry, 2, 3, 4, 5, 6, 7, 8.

SPARNON. Harleian Society, ix. 205. The Visitations of Cornwall, edited by J. L. Vivian, 428.

SPARREY. Harleian Society, xii. 161.

SPARROW. Morant's Essex, ii. 278, 289. Berry's Essex Genealogies, 53. Burke's Landed Gentry, (of Gosfield Place,) 2, 3, 4, 5, 6 ; (of Penn,) 3, 4, 5, 6, 7, 8 ; (of Red Hill,) 2 and corr., 3, 4, 5, 6, 7, 8 ; (of Preen Manor,) 8. Harleian Society, viii. 213 ; xiii. 492 ; xiv. 714 ; xxxvii. 319. Burke's Visitation of Seats and Arms, ii. 51. Wright's Essex, ii. 6. Howard's Visitation of England and Wales, i. 227 ; Notes, iii. 71. Bysshe's Visitation of Essex, edited by J. J. Howard, 86.

SPATCHURST. Visitatio Comitatus Wiltoniæ, 1623, printed by Sir T. Phillipps. Visitation of Wiltshire, edited by G. W. Marshall, 55.

SPATEMAN. Visitation of Derbyshire, 1663-4, (Middle Hill, 1854, fol.) 6. The Genealogist, iii. 182. Harleian Society, xxxix. 1058.

SPEAR. New England Register, xviii. 158.

SPEARMAN. Burke's Commoners, ii. 452, Landed Gentry, 2, 3, 4, 5, 6, 7, 8. Surtees' Durham, i. 96.

SPECCOTT, or SPECOTE. Harleian Society, vi. 271, 272. Maclean's History of Trigg Minor, ii. 501. Visitation of Devon, edited by F. T. Colby, 190. Miscellanea Genealogica et Heraldica, New Series, iv. 86, 100. The Visitations of Devon, by J. L. Vivian, 706.

SPEDDING. Burke's Landed Gentry, 2, 3, 4, 5 supp., 6, 7, 8.

SPEED, or SPEEDE. Harleian Society, xvii. 256. Miscellanea Genealogica et Heraldica, 3rd Series, ii. 18.

SPEELMAN. Burke's Extinct Baronetcies.

SPEGHT. Harleian Society, xvii. 258.

SPEID. Burke's Landed Gentry, 7.

SPEIR. Burke's Landed Gentry, (of Burnbrae,) 2, 3, 4, 5, 6, 7, 8 ; (of Blackstoun,) 3, 4, 5.

SPEIRS. Burke's Landed Gentry, 3, 4, 5, 6, 7, 8. Burke's Family Records, 541.

SPEKE. Collinson's Somerset, i. 67. Burke's Commoners, iv. 536, Landed Gentry, 2, 3, 4, 5, 6, 7, 8. Harleian Society, xi. 103. Burke's Extinct Baronetcies. Visitation of Somersetshire, printed by Sir T. Phillipps, 137, 149. The Genealogist, New Series, xvii. 21.

SPELMAN. Blomefield's Norfolk, vi. 150. Visitation of Norfolk, published by Norfolk Archæological Society, i. 249, 449. Hoare's

Wiltshire, V. ii. 74. South Mimms, by F. C. Cass, 70. Reliquiæ Spelmannianæ, (Oxford, 1698,) folding table. Notes and Queries, 3 S. v. 523. Harleian Society, xvii. 257 ; xxxii. 263. Account of the Guildhall of London, by J. E. Price, 116.

SPENCE. Berry's Sussex Genealogies, 26. Horsfield's History of Lewes, ii. 172. Chauncy's Hertfordshire, 339. Foster's Pedigree of the Forsters and Fosters, Part ii. 42. Harleian Society, xxxii. 262.

SPENCER, or SPENSER. Gentleman's Magazine, 1842, ii. 138 ; 1855, ii. 605. Surtees Society, xxxvi. 12, 20. The Great Governing Families of England, i. 358. Jacob's Peerage, i. 264. Hasted's Kent, iii. 9. Dwnn's Visitations of Wales, i. 177. Berry's Kent Genealogies, 38, 318. Burke's Patrician, v. 54. Burke's Commoners, ii. 387, Landed Gentry, 2, 3. Foster's Visitations of Yorkshire, 372. Visitation of Warwickshire, 1619, published with Warwickshire Antiquarian Magazine, 170. Gyll's History of Wraysbury, 29. Chetham Society, lxxxviii. 279. Lipscombe's History of the County of Buckingham, i. 565 ; iii. 342. Bridges' Northamptonshire, by Rev. Peter Whalley, i. 481. Thoresby's Ducatus Leodiensis, 104. Hunter's History of the Parish of Sheffield, 416. Hunter's Deanery of Doncaster, ii. 232. Clutterbuck's Hertford, i. 107 ; ii. 356 ; iii. 96. Baker's Northampton, i. 108, 364, 752. Chauncy's Hertfordshire, 405. Harleian Society, xii. 283 ; xix. 55, 141, 195 ; xxii. 22, 165 ; xxix. 441 ; xxxii. 262 ; xlii. 120. Edmondson's Baronagium Genealogicum, i. 39 ; iii. 309. Berry's Genealogical Peerage, 74. Brydges' Collins' Peerage, i. 362 ; v. 42 ; vii. 15. Wotton's English Baronetage, i. 198. Metcalfe's Visitations of Suffolk, 67, 167. Burke's Extinct Baronetcies. Norfolk Antiquarian Miscellany, ii. 595. Typographia, by J. Johnson, at beginning of vol. i. Metcalfe's Visitations of Northamptonshire, 47, 196. Woodcock of Cuerden, by A. E. P. Gray, 12. Genealogical Table of John Stratford Collins. Oxford Historical Society, xxiv. 285. Staniforthiana, by F. M. H., at end. The Genealogist, New Series, xvii. 125. Howard's Visitation of England and Wales, ix. 122. See DESPENCER.

SPENCER-CHURCHILL. Baker's Northampton, i. 198. The Gresley's of Drakelowe, by F. Madan, 278.

SPENCER-STANHOPE. Burke's Commoners, i. 467, Landed Gentry, 2, 3, 4, 5, 6, 7. Foster's Yorkshire Pedigrees.

SPENLUFFE. The Genealogist, v. 39.

SPENS. Burke's Commoners, (of Lathallan,) iv. 168, Landed Gentry, 2, 3, 4, 5, 6, 7, 8 ; (of Craigsanquhar,) Commoners, iv. 506, Landed Gentry, 2, 3, 4, 5, 6. Douglas's Baronage of Scotland, 290-299. Walter Wood's East Neuk of Fife, 260, 270.

SPERINGE. Harleian Society, xvii. 258.

SPERLING. Burke's Landed Gentry, 3, 4, 5, 6, 7, 8.

SPERT. Harleian Society, xxi. 150.

SPICE. Morant's Essex, ii. 75, 123.

SPICER. Dwnn's Visitations of Wales, ii. 120. More about Stifford, by Willm. Palin, 49. Harleian Society, vi. 273. Clutterbuck's Hertford, iii. 107. The Visitations of Devon, by J. L. Vivian, 708. Metcalfe's Visitation of Worcester, 1683, 89. *See* GILL.

SPIER. The Genealogist, vi. 94.

SPIGURNELL. Morant's Essex, i. 148, 187. Banks' Baronies in Fee, ii. 132.

SPILLANE. O'Hart's Irish Pedigrees, 2nd Series, 302.

SPINKS. Burke's Landed Gentry, 4, 5, 6, 7 8.

SPITTY. Burke's Landed Gentry, 6, 7, 8.

SPODE. Burke's Landed Gentry, 3, 4, 5, 6, 7.

SPOFFORD. New England Register, viii. 335 ; ix. 61, 273. *See* SPOFFORTH.

SPOFFORTH. Burke's Landed Gentry, 3, 4. Burke's Visitation of Seats and Arms, 2nd Series, i. 41. Burke's Family Records, 543.

SPOONE. Harleian Society, xxxviii. 812.

SPOONER. Miscellanea Genealogica et Heraldica, New Series, i. 300. Carthew's Hundred of Launditch, Part iii. 136. Burke's Landed Gentry, 7 at p. 1107 ; 8 at p. 1203. New England Register, xxiii. 407.

SPOONER-LILLINGSTON. Burke's Commoners, i. 85, Landed Gentry 2, 3, 4, 5, 6, 7.

SPOOR, or SPOORE. Burke's Visitation of Seats and Arms, 2nd Series, ii. 28. Burke's Landed Gentry, 4, 5, 6. Harleian Society, ix. 206. The Visitations of Cornwall, edited by J. L. Vivian, 430.

SPOTSWOOD, SPOTTISWOOD, or SPOTTISWOODE. The Spottiswoode Miscellany. Edinburgh, 1844, 8vo., 2 vols. Genealogy of the Family of Spotswood, by Charles Campbell. Albany (U.S.A.) 1868, 8vo. Douglas's Baronage of Scotland, 446. Burke's Landed Gentry, 2, 3, 4, 6, 7, 8. Burke's Royal Descents and Pedigrees of Founders' Kin, 95. Paterson's History of Ayr and Wigton, i. 560. Stodart's Scottish Arms, ii. 220.

SPRACKLING. Berry's Kent Genealogies, 369. Harleian Society, xlii. 124, 174.

SPRANGER. Harleian Society, xiii. 289. Bysshe's Visitation of Essex, edited by J. J. Howard, 87.

SPRATT. Burke's Landed Gentry, 4, 5, 6, 7, 8.

SPRENTALL. Harleian Society, xxxix. 1014.

SPREWEL. Nisbet's Heraldry, ii. app. 25.

SPREY. Maclean's History of Trigg Minor, i. 294. Harleian Society, ix. 207. The Visitations of Cornwall, edited by J. L. Vivian, 432.

SPRIGNELL. Burke's Extinct Baronetcies.

SPRING, or SPRINGE. Morant's Essex, i. 228, 414 ; ii. 185, 284. Visitation of Suffolk, edited by J. J. Howard, i. 165-206. Page's History of Suffolk, 729. Plantagenet-Harrison's History of Yorkshire, i. 378. Burke's Landed Gentry, 6. Wotton's English Baronetage, ii. 241. Metcalfe's Visitations of Suffolk, 67, 167. Burke's Extinct Baronetcies.

SPRINGETT. Berry's Sussex Genealogies, 33, 240. Berry's Kent Genealogies, 242, 243. Horsfield's History of Lewes, ii. 194. Sussex Archæological Collections, xx. 34. Burke's Extinct Baronetcies.

SPRINGFIELD. Burke's Landed Gentry, 8.

SPRINTE. Berry's Hampshire Genealogies, 217. Harleian Society, xxxvii. 3.

SPROSTON. Burke's Landed Gentry, 2 supp., 3, 4, 5, 6, 7.

SPROT, or SPROTT. Erdeswicke's Survey of Staffordshire, 241. Burke's Landed Gentry, 6, 7, 8. Burke's Family Records, 549.

SPRY, or SPRYE. Maclean's History of Trigg Minor, i. 72. Burke's Commoners, iv. 691, Landed Gentry, 2, 3, 4. Harleian Society, ix. 208. A Complete Parochial History of the County of Cornwall, ii. 56. The Visitations of Cornwall, edited by J. L. Vivian, 434.

SPURR. Harleian Society, xxxviii. 711.

SPURRIER. Burke's Landed Gentry, 8. Healey's History of Part of West Somerset, 401.

SPURSTOWE. Ormerod's Cheshire, ii. 294. Harleian Society, xvii. 259; xviii. 211.

SPURWAY. Tuckett's Devonshire Pedigrees, 184. Harleian Society, vi. 274. The Visitations of Devon, by J. L. Vivian, 724.

SPYER. Harleian Society, v. 215.

SPYNIE. See CASSILIS.

SQUIBB. Hutchins' Dorset, i 198. The Genealogist, vi. 95.

SQUIRE. Burke's Landed Gentry, 2, 3, 4, 5. Visitation of Devon, edited by F. T. Colby, 190. The Genealogist, New Series, ix. 152. Harleian Society, xix. 142; xxvii. 130. Burton's History of Hemingborough, 110.

STABLES. Surtees Society, xxxvi. 11.

STACÉ. Blore's Rutland, 189.

STACEY, or STACYE. Hunter's History of the Parish of Sheffield, 488. Pedigree of Wilson of High Wray, etc., by Joseph Foster, 109. Annals of Smith of Balby, by H. E. Smith, 211. Harleian Society, xl. 1209. See HOYLAND.

STACK. Burke's Landed Gentry, 8.

STACKHOUSE. An Historical Survey of Cornwall, by C. S. Gilbert, ii. 267.

STACKHOUSE-ACTON. Burke's Landed Gentry, 5, 6.

STACPOOLE. Burke's Landed Gentry, (of Eden Vale,) 2, 3, 4, 5, 6, 7, 8; (of Craigbrian,) 2. Howard's Visitation of Ireland, i. 82.

STAFFERTON. History of the Hundred of Bray, by Charles Kerry, 96. See STAVERTON.

STAFFORD. Papers relating to the two Baronies of Stafford, claimed by Sir W. Jerningham, Bart., 1807, 4to. The Stafford Peerage, by J. Campbell. London, 1818, 4to. Collinson's Somerset, ii. 424. Rudder's Gloucestershire, 753. The Descent of the Ancient and Illustrious Barony of Stafford. Johnson, printer, Southwark, 8vo. sheet. Hasted's Kent, ii. 329. Gentleman's Magazine, 1826, i. 130; 1827, i. 588; 1846, ii. 31. The Tyndale

Pedigree, by B. W. Greenfield. Clifford's Description of Tixall, 117, 194. Morant's Essex, i. 128, 154, 244; ii. 62, 503. Lord Braybrooke's History of Audley End, 7. Berry's Sussex Genealogies, 268. Berry's Buckinghamshire Genealogies, 20. Nash's Worcestershire, i. 157. Burke's Landed Gentry, 2, 3, 4, 5, 6, 7, 8. Jewitt's Reliquary, xvi. 192. Maclean's History of Trigg Minor, i. 316. Collectanea Topographica et Genealogica, i. 249. Suckling's History of Suffolk, ii. 46. Lipscombe's History of the County of Buckingham, iv. 258. Topographical Collections of John Aubrey, edited by J. E. Jackson, 401. Wright's History of Rutland, 127. Bridges' Northamptonshire, by Rev. Peter Whalley, i. 52, 159; ii. 61, 277. Visitation of Staffordshire, 1663-4, printed by Sir T. Phillipps, 9. History of the Town and School of Rugby, by N. H. Nicolas, 96. Visitation of Derbyshire, 1663-4, (Middle Hill, 1854, fol.) 7. Erdeswicke's Survey of Staffordshire, 146. Burton's Description of Leicestershire, 129. Nichols' History of the County of Leicester, iii. 982*; iv. 154, 760, 820. Dugdale's Warwickshire, 316, 1004. Hutchins' Dorset, ii. 179. Manning and Bray's Surrey, ii. 299. Baker's Northampton, i. 355, 532. The Genealogist, iii. 16; vi. 95; vii. 265; New Series, viii. 80; xii. 33, 228. Fosbrooke's History of Gloucestershire, ii. 121. A Complete Parochial History of the County of Cornwall, i. 1. Harleian Society, xiv. 560; xxviii. 139. Collections for a History of Staffordshire, William Salt Society, ii. part 2, 90. Banks' Baronies in Fee, i. 408. Banks' Dormant and Extinct Baronage, i. 171, 408; ii. 519-544; iii. 753. Notes and Queries, 3 S. ix, 375; 4 S. vi. 250; vii. 500; viii. 14, 286, 306; 6 S. iv. 134. Visitation of Staffordshire, (Willm. Salt Soc.) 132. Visitations of Staffordshire, 1614 and 1663-4, William Salt Society, 276. Devonshire Notes and Notelets, by Sir W. R. Drake, 115. Genealogical Table of John Stratford Collins. Jowers' Wells Cathedral, 121. Burke's Colonial Gentry, i. 36. The Visitations of Devon, by J. L. Vivian, 712. Church Bells of Buckinghamshire, by A. H. Cocks, 614. The Gresley's of Drakelowe, by F. Madan, 279, 280. See JERNINGHAM.

STAFFORD-O'BRIEN. Burke's Landed Gentry, 7.

STAFFORT. Dwnn's Visitation of Wales, ii. 75.

STAGG. Hutchins' Dorset, ii. 574. Harleian Society, xx. 85. Genealogical Gleanings in England, by H. F. Waters, i. 61. New England Register, xxxviii. 312.

STAINTON. Jane Stainton and her Family. By J. R[aine]. York, 1888, 8vo.

STAIR. The Case of James Dalrymple to the title of Earl of Stair, 1748, folio, pp. 3. The Case of John, Earl of Stair, etc., claiming the title of Earl of Stair, 1748, fol. Claim of James Dalrymple to the Earldom of Stair, Sess. Papers, March 1747—May 1748.

STALWORTH. Clutterbuck's Hertford, ii. 350.

STAMFORD. Shaw's Staffordshire, ii. 109. Miscellanea Genealogica et Heraldica, New Series, iii. 73. Visitation of Staffordshire, (Willm. Salt Soc.) 133.

STAMPE. Visitation of Oxfordshire, 1574, printed by Sir T. Phillipps, (Middle Hill, fol.) 9. Visitation of Oxfordshire, 1634, printed by Sir T. Phillipps, (Middle Hill, fol.) 30. Harleian Society, v. 273; viii. 311. The Genealogist, vi. 96; New Series, ii. 107. *See* STOMPE.

STANBERY, or STANBURYE. Harleian Society, ix. 213. The Visitations of Cornwall, edited by J. L. Vivian, 443.

STANBRIDGE. Burke's Colonial Gentry, i. 298.

STANCOMB. Burke's Landed Gentry, 8.

STANDARD. Visitation of Oxfordshire, 1634, printed by Sir T. Phillipps, (Middle Hill, fol.) 30. Harleian Society, v. 251. Oxford Historical Society, xxiv. 51.

STANDISH, or STANDYSHE. Burke's Royal Families, (London, 1851, 8vo.) ii. 147. Burke's Commoners, (of Standish,) ii. 64, Landed Gentry, 3, 4, 5, 6, 7, 8 ; (of Duxbury,) Commoners, ii. 642, Landed Gentry, 2, 3, 4, 5, 6, 7, 8 ; (of Scaleby Castle,) Landed Gentry, 4 supp., 5, 6, 7, 8. Chetham Society, lxxxi. 90, 102 ; lxxxii. 70, 71, 123 ; lxxxviii. 290-294 ; xcviii. 52, 103 ; xcix. 126. Foster's Lancashire Pedigrees. Burke's Heraldic Illustrations, 1. Baines' History of the Co. of Lancaster, iii. 519 ; Croston's edn., iv. 223, 243. Earwaker's Local Gleanings, ii. 531, 535, 537, 540, 544, 547, 550, 553, 555, 558, 562, 565, 569, 572, 574, 579, 585, 589, 593. Ashmole's Antiquities of Berkshire, iii. 288. Wotton's English Baronetage, iii. 606. Betham's Baronotage, ii. 453. Burke's Extinct Baronetcies. The Wolfe's of Forenaghts, 53. The Genealogist, New Series, ii. 106.

STANE. Morant's Essex, i. 130. Bysshe's Visitation of Essex, edited by J. J. Howard, 87.

STANFORD. Harleian Society, ii. 160. Visitation of Staffordshire, 1663-4, edited by Sir T. Phillipps, 9. Nichols' History of the County of Leicester, iii. 51. Dugdale's Warwickshire, 809. Howard's Visitation of England and Wales, ix. 91. *See* STAUNFORD.

STANHOPE. Notices of the Stanhopes as Esquires and Knights, and until their first Peerages in 1605 and 1616, by Visct. Mahon, [afterwards Earl Stanhope]. London, 1855, 8vo. The Great Governing Families of England, i. 213. Jacob's Peerage, i. 540. Hasted's Kent, i. 362. Glover's History of Derbyshire, ii. 190, (164). Surtees Society, xxxvi. 294. Burke's Royal Families, (London, 1851, 8vo.) i. 188. Burke's Landed Gentry, 3, 4, 5, 6, 7, 8. Harleian Society, iv. 5 ; xvi. 292 ; xxxix. 986. Thoresby's Ducatus Leodiensis, 166. Manning and Bray's Surrey, i. 440. Stonehouse's History of the Isle of Axholme, 260. Dickinson's History of Southwell, 2nd edition, 177. Lipscombe's History of the County of Buckingham, i. 479 ; iii. 379. Hunter's Deanery of Doncaster, ii. 232. Clutterbuck's Hertford, i. 494. Thoroton's Nottinghamshire, i. 288; iii. 243. Pilkington's View of Derbyshire, ii. 103. Edmondson's Baronagium Genealogicum, ii. 129 ;

iii. 218, 245. Brydges' Collins' Peerage, iii. 407 ; iv. 171, 284.
Banks' Dormant and Extinct Baronage, iii. 674. The Genealogist,
New Series, viii. 80 ; xiii. 106. Historical Notices of Doncaster,
by C. W. Hatfield, 2nd Series, 6, 12. *See* CHESTERFIELD,
SPENCER-STANHOPE.

STANIER. Burke's Landed Gentry, 7, 8.

STANIFORTH. Staniforthiana, or Recollections of the Family of
Staniforth. By F. M. H. Bristol, 1863, 8vo. Hunter's History
of the Parish of Sheffield, 422. Hunter's Deanery of Doncaster,
i. 301. Harleian Society, xxxviii. 728. Howard's Visitation of
England and Wales, v. 132.

STANLEY. The Stanleys of Knowsley, a History of that Noble
Family, by William Pollard. London, 1869, 8vo. The House of
Stanley, by P. Draper. Ormskirk, 1864, 8vo. Historical Sketches
of the House of Stanley, by Thomas Aspden. The History of the
House of Stanley, etc. Liverpool, 1830, 8vo. Sketch of the
History of the House of Stanley, by D. Ross. 1848, 12mo. A
Genealogical Account of the House of Stanley to 1735, by J. Sea-
combe. Liverpool, 1741, 4to. ; 2nd edition, Manchester, 1783 ;
3rd edition, Preston, 1793, 8vo. The Great Governing Families
of England, i. 90. Miscellanea Genealogica et Heraldica, ii. 142;
2nd Series, ii. 57. Gentleman's Magazine, 1854, ii. 250. Kent's
British Banner Displayed, 347. Jacob's Peerage, i. 460, 464.
Glover's History of Derbyshire, ii. 565, (545). Berry's Sussex
Genealogies, 45, 188. Dwnn's Visitations of Wales, i. 266 ; ii.
283, 316. Visitation of Middlesex, (Salisbury, 1820, fol.) 47.
Berry's Kent Genealogies, 140. Burke's Commoners, (of Dale-
garth,) i. 95, Landed Gentry, 2, 3, 4, 5, 6, 7, 8 ; (of Cross Hall,)
Landed Gentry, 2, 3, 4, 5, 6, 7, 8 ; (of Tedworth,) 4, 5 ; (of
Paultons,) 3, 4, 5, 6, 7, 8 ; 2 add. ; (of Longstowe,) 5, 6, 7, 8.
Foster's Visitations of Yorkshire, 247, 576. Harleian Society,
vii. 8 ; viii. 7, 368; xii. 23 ; xiii. 493 ; xiv. 602; xvi. 293 ; xviii.
212-216, 260 ; xxxii. 266 ; xlii. 55. Chetham Society, lxxxi. 78,
79 ; lxxxii. 111, 120 ; lxxxviii. 280-289 ; xcviii. 1 ; cx. 230 ;
New Series, xxv. 187. Herald and Genealogist, iii. 285 ; vi. 348.
Foster's Lancashire Pedigrees. Collectanea Topographica et
Genealogica, vii. 1. Bibliotheca Topographica Britannica, ix.
Part 4, 217. Shaw's Staffordshire, i. 412 ; ii. 128. Bridges'
Northamptonshire, by Rev. Peter Whalley, i. 149. Jefferson's
History of Allerdale Ward, Cumberland, 281. Dallaway's Sussex,
II. i. 309. Visitation of Staffordshire, 1663-4, printed by Sir
T. Phillipps, 10. Erdeswicke's Survey of Staffordshire, 395.
Nichols' History of the County of Leicester, iv. 152. Hunter's
Deanery of Doncaster, ii. 405. Clutterbuck's Hertford, i. 374.
Baker's Northampton, i. 564. Baines' History of the Co. of Lan-
caster, iv. 10, 228; Croston's edn., v. 88. The Monumental
Effigies in Elford Church, Staffordshire, by E. Richardson, (London,
1852, fol.) 1. Earwaker's East Cheshire, i. 328 ; ii. 602. Or-
merod's Cheshire, i. 442; ii. 415; iii. 566, 577. Castles,
Mansions, and Manors of Western Sussex, by D. G. C. Elwes and

C. J. Robinson, 99. Antiquities in Westminster Abbey, by Thomas Moule, 41. The Tyldesley Diary, edited by J. Gillow and A. Hewitson, 18, 21. Edmondson's Baronagium Genealogicum, ii. 87. Brydges' Collins' Peerage, iii. 50. Wotton's English Baronetage, iii. 71, 301 ; iv. 78. Banks' Baronies in Fee, i. 414. Betham's Baronetage, ii. 83, 272. Banks' Dormant and Extinct Baronage, ii. 352, 545. Notes and Queries, 4 S. xii. 298. Burke's Extinct Baronetcies. History of Powys Fadog, by J. Y. W. Lloyd, iii. 242. Visitations of Staffordshire, 1614 and 1663-4, William Salt Society, 277. Genealogical Memoranda of the Family of Ames. Foster's Visitation of Middlesex, 83. Foster's Visitations of Cumberland and Westmorland, 127. History of Chipping, by Tom. C. Smith, 45. The Genealogist, New Series, xiii. 102. The Gresley's of Drakelowe, by F. Madan, 281.

STANLOW. The Genealogist, vi. 284.

STANNARD. Blomefield's Norfolk, xi. 178. Burke's Landed Gentry, (of Grange,) 3 ; (of the Priory,) 2. Harleian Society, xvii. 259. Burke's Family Records, 550.

STANNEY. Harleian Society, xxix. 442.

STANNIER. Harleian Society, viii. 492. Burke's Landed Gentry, 6.

STANNOW. Metcalfe's Visitations of Suffolk, 168. Harleian Society, xxxii. 266.

STANNUS. Stannus Genealogy, by C. T. M'Cready. Dublin, 1873, long sheet. Burke's Landed Gentry, 3, 4, 5, 6, 7, 8.

STANSFELD, or STANSFIELD. History of the Family of Stansfeld, by John Stansfeld. Leeds, 1886, 4to. Stansfeld of Stansfeld Hall, a broadside in lithograph, n.d. Burke's Commoners, iii. 60 ; iv. 756, Landed Gentry, 2, 3, 4, 5, 6, 7, 8. Whitaker's Loidis and Elmete, 202, 203. Stansfeld of Stansfeld Hall, folding sheet, circa 1873. Foster's Yorkshire Pedigrees. History of Bradford, by John James, 436. History of Blyth, by Rev. John Raine, 73. Whitaker's History of Whalley, ii. 230. John Watson's History of Halifax, 281. Harleian Society, xxxvii. 88. Green's Account of the Family of Cudworth, 37.

STANSHALL. Ashmole's Antiquities of Berkshire, iii. 328. The Genealogist, New Series, ii. 106.

STANTER. Visitatio Comitatus Wiltoniæ, 1623, printed by Sir T. Phillipps. Hoare's Wiltshire, I. ii. 48. The Genealogist, New Series, xiii. 21.

STANTON. J. H. Hill's History of Langton, 21. Burke's Landed Gentry, 2 supp., 3, 4, 5, 6, 7, 8. Harleian Society, iv. 179 ; xii. 277, 290 ; xxxii. 267. Visitation of Warwickshire, 1619, published with Warwickshire Antiquarian Magazine, 50. Eyton's Antiquities of Shropshire, ix. 294. Nichols' History of the County of Leicester, i. 614 ; ii. 664. Metcalfe's Visitations of Suffolk, 102. See STAUNTON.

STANWIGGE. Plantagenet-Harrison's History of Yorkshire, i. 492, 538.

STANWIX. Foster's Visitations of Cumberland and Westmorland, 128.

STANWOOD. New England Register, l. 540.

STANYFORTH. Burke's Landed Gentry, 8.
STANYHURST. John D'Alton's History of Co. Dublin, 411.
STAPELEY. Ormerod's Cheshire, iii. 497. *See* STAPLEY.
STAPER. Harleian Society, i. 30.
STAPLEFORD. Thoroton's Nottinghamshire, ii. 194. Harleian Society, xxvii. 18.
STAPLEHILL. Tuckett's Devonshire Pedigrees, 119. Harleian Society, vi. 275. Westcote's Devonshire, edited by G. Oliver and P. Jones, 624. The Visitations of Devon, by J. L. Vivian, 710.
STAPLES. Burke's Landed Gentry, 2 supp., 3, 4, 5, 6, 7. Visitatio Comitatus Wiltoniæ, 1623, printed by Sir T. Phillipps. Sussex Archæological Collections, ii. 105. Visitation of Wiltshire, edited by G. W. Marshall, 65.
STAPLES-BROWNE. Burke's Landed Gentry, 8.
STAPLETON, or STAPILTON. Chronicles of the Yorkshire Family of Stapleton, by H. E. Chetwynd Stapleton. London, 1885, 8vo. Case and Pedigree of Thomas Stapleton of Carlton, Esq., in relation to the Barony of Beaumont, with Additional Case prefixed, 1795, folio, pp. 12. Claim of Thomas Stapleton of Carlton, Esq., to the Barony of Beaumont, Sess. Papers, April 1791—May 1798; 64 of 1840. Royal Descents from Henry III., King of England, of Sir Thomas Stapleton, Bart., 22nd Lord Le Despencer, by Lord Farnham, 4to. Clutterbuck's Hertford, ii. 484. Kent's British Banner Displayed, 396. Surtees Society, xxxvi. 110, 224, 265; xli. 16. Blomefield's Norfolk, ix. 320. Berry's Hampshire Genealogies, 207. Burke's Royal Families, (London, 1851, 8vo.) ii. 10. Foster's Yorkshire Pedigrees. Foster's Visitations of Yorkshire, 332, 333. History of Richmond, by C. Clarkson, 206. Blore's Rutland, 20. Thoresby's Ducatus Leodiensis, 188. Thoroton's Nottinghamshire, iii. 11. Norfolk Archæology, viii. 222. Plantagenet-Harrison's History of Yorkshire, i. 364, 548. Burke's Commoners, ii. 584, Landed Gentry, 6, 7. Memoir of Gabriel Goodman, by R. Newcome, app. S. Harleian Society, xvi. 293. Brydges' Collins' Peerage, vi. 496. Wotton's English Baronetage, iii. 663. Banks' Baronies in Fee, i. 267, 417. Banks' Dormant and Extinct Baronage, i. 409; ii. 44. Notes and Queries, 6 S. v. 53. Yorkshire Archæological and Topographical Journal, viii. 65-116, 223-258. Earwaker's East Cheshire, ii. 344, 484. The Genealogist, New Series, ix. 85; xii. 123-133; 193-199; xvii. 169. Nicolson and Burn's Westmorland and Cumberland, i. 134. *See* STAPULTON.
STAPLEY. Berry's Sussex Genealogies, 85, 371. Horsfield's History of Lewes, ii. 110. Sussex Archæological Collections, ii. 107. Burke's Extinct Baronetcies. *See* STAPELEY.
STAPULTON, or STAPYLTON. Surtees Society, xxxvi. 141; xli. 2. Burke's Commoners, (of Myton,) ii. 207, Landed Gentry, 2, 3, 4, 5, 6, 8; (of Norton,) Commoners, ii. 210; (of Wighill,) Landed Gentry, 4, 5, 6, 8. Foster's Yorkshire Pedigrees. Ord's History of Cleveland, 558. Archæologia Æliana, 2nd Series, v. 12. Hoare's Wiltshire, V. i. 21. Yorkshire Archæological and Topo-

graphical Journal, vi. 193. Wotton's English Baronetage, iii. 49.
Betham's Baronetage, ii. 57. Burke's Extinct Baronetcies. The
Genealogist, New Series, ix. 211.
STARBUCK. New England Register, viii. 68, 129.
STARESMORE. Harleian Society, ii. 5, 99. Burton's Description of
Leicestershire, 102. Nichols' History of the County of Leicester,
iv. 190. Metcalfe's Visitations of Northamptonshire, 137.
STARK-CHRISTIE. Burke's Landed Gentry, 5, 6, 7.
STARK, or STARKE. Burke's Authorized Arms, 147. Burke's Landed
Gentry, 2, 3, 4, 5, 8. Burke's Visitation of Seats and Arms, 2nd
Series, ii. 79. Balmerino and its Abbey, by James Campbell,
304, 394.
STARKEY. Burke's Landed Gentry, (of Wrenbury,) 3, 4, 5, 6, 7, 8;
(of Thornton Lodge,) 2; (of Norwood Park,) 7, 8. Nichols'
History of the County of Leicester, iii. 728. Ormerod's Cheshire,
i. 666; ii. 191, 452; iii. 395. Harleian Society, xvii. 260; xlii. 4.
New England Register, xlvi. 144.
STARKIE. Burke's Commoners, iii. 653, Landed Gentry, 2, 3, 4, 5,
6, 7, 8. Burke's Royal Families, (London, 1851, 8vo.) i. 112.
Harleian Society, ii. 175. Foster's Lancashire Pedigrees. Chetham Society, lxxxviii. 296. Baines' History of the Co. of Lan-
caster, iii. 309; Croston's edn., iii. 415. Whitaker's History of
Whalley, ii. 45, 155. Ormerod's Cheshire, i. 641. Lancashire
and Cheshire Genealogical and Historical Notes, ii. 131; iii. 48.
Berkshire Notes and Queries, i. 110. Howard's Visitation of
England and Wales, vi. 150.
STARKY. Burke's Commoners, iv. 684, Landed Gentry, 2, 3, 4, 5
supp. Chetham Society, lxxxviii. 295. Ormerod's Cheshire, iii.
161. Harleian Society, xviii. 217.
STARLING. Carthew's Hundred of Launditch, Part iii. 375.
STATHAM, STATHOM, or STATHUM. Harleian Society, iv. 163;
xxxviii. 655. Thoroton's Nottinghamshire, i. 98. Journal of
the Derbyshire Archæological Society, iv. 37.
STAUGHTON. Burke's Colonial Gentry, i. 301.
STAUNFORD. Monken Hadley, by F. C. Cass, 154. Visitations of
Staffordshire, 1614 and 1663-4, William Salt Society, 279. See
STANFORD.
STAUNTON.[1] Memoir of the Life and Family of the late Sir G. L.
Staunton, Bart. Havant Press, 1823, 8vo. Berry's Hampshire
Genealogies, 61. Burke's Commoners, (of Staunton,) i. 526,
Landed Gentry, 2, 3, 4, 5, 6, 7, 8; (of Longbridge,) Commoners,
ii. 587, Landed Gentry, 2, 3, 4, 5, 6, 7, 8. Nichols' History of the
County of Leicester, iii. 704. Thoroton's Nottinghamshire, i. 306.
Harleian Society, xiii. 102; xix. 142; xxvii. 131; xxxix. 980.
Stemmata Shirleiana, by E. P. Shirley, 2nd edn., 48. Banks'
Baronies in Fee, ii. 133. The Genealogist, New Series, viii. 155,
156. See DE STAUNTON, LYNCH-STAUNTON, STANTON.
STAVELEY. Bibliotheca Topographica Britannica, vii. Parts i. and ii.

---

[1] There is a valuable account of this family in Mr. Mellish's MS., marked
'Newark,' now at Hodsock Priory, Co. Nottingham.

152. Burke's Landed Gentry, 5, 6, 7, 8. Foster's Visitations of Yorkshire, 635. Harleian Society, ii. 136; v. 192; xvii. 261. Westcote's Devonshire, edited by G. Oliver and P. Jones, 562. Nichols' History of the County of Leicester, ii. 664, 676. Visitation of Devon, edited by F. T. Colby, 191. Ormerod's Cheshire, iii. 867. Earwaker's East Cheshire, ii. 167. The Visitations of Devon, by J. L. Vivian, 714.

STAVERT. A Chapter in Mediocrity, by W. J. Stavert. Skipton, 1896, 8vo.

STAVERTON. Ashmole's Antiquities of Berkshire, 326. Berry's Hampshire Genealogies, 178. Betham's Baronetage, v. 529*. See STAFFERTON.

STAWEL, or STAWELL. Collinson's Somerset, iii. 250, 431, 445. Burke's Landed Gentry, 2, 3. Harleian Society, viii. 173. Hoare's Wiltshire, III. iv. 4. Edmondson's Baronagium Genealogicum, v. 465. Brydges' Collins' Peerage, vii. 269. Banks' Baronies in Fee, ii. 137. Banks' Dormant and Extinct Baronage, iii. 675. Weaver's Visitations of Somerset, 79. Burke's Colonial Gentry, i. 58. See ALCOCK-STAWELL, STOWELL.

STAYNINGE. Weaver's Visitations of Somerset, 79.

STEAD, or STEADE. Hunter's Deanery of Doncaster, ii. 193. Annals of the Cleveland Richardsons and their Descendants. Burke's Commoners, i. 150. Memoirs of Master John Shawe, by J. R. Boyle, 90. Harleian Society, xxxvii. 331.

STEAVENS. Berry's Buckinghamshire Genealogies, 95.

STEBBING. Page's History of Suffolk, 111.

STEBBINS. New England Register, v. 71, 351.

STEDMAN. Dwnn's Visitations of Wales, i. 19, 79, 88. Jones' History of the County of Brecknock, ii. 272. Cardiganshire Pedigrees, 77. Meyrick's History of the Co. of Cardigan, 265. Burke's Landed Gentry, 3 p. 1108. New England Register, xiv. 69. The Genealogical Magazine, iii. 508. See BARTON.

STEEDE, or STEDE. Berry's Kent Genealogies, 105. Hasted's Kent, ii. 457. Harleian Society, viii. 443; xlii. 71.

STEEL. Burke's Landed Gentry, 4, 8. Miscellanea Genealogica et Heraldica, New Series, ii. 38.

STEELE. Pedigree of Steele of Manor House, Mickleton, Co. Glouc., [T. P.] 1854, folio page. Burke's Commoners, iii. 358, Landed Gentry, 3, 4, 5, and 5 at p. 989; 6, and 6 at p. 1169; 7, and 7 at p. 1351; 8 at p. 1485. Nichols' History of the County of Leicester, iv. 853. Miscellanea Genealogica et Heraldica, New Series, ii. 36. Ormerod's Cheshire, iii. 98. Notes and Queries, 4 S. xii. 129, 258. Foster's Visitations of Cumberland and Westmorland, 129. Earwaker's History of Sandbach, 20. Burke's Colonial Gentry, i. 173, 274.

STEELE-GRAVES. Pedigree of Steele-Graves of Mickleton, [T. P.] 1862, folio page.

STEER, or STEERE. Stonehouse's History of the Isle of Axholme, 344. Reed's History of the Isle of Axholme, edited by T. C Fletcher, 64. Eastwood's History of Ecclesfield, 207. Notes and

Queries, 2 S. iv. 90, 219, 297.   Burke's Colonial Gentry, i. 4.
Berry's Surrey Genealogies, 34.   Burke's Landed Gentry, 5 supp.
Dallaway's Sussex, II. i. 334.   Harleian Society, xxxviii. 817.
STEFFE. Miscellanea Genealogica et Heraldica, 2nd Series, iv. 224.
STEIL. Monfode of that Ilk, by R. M. Kerr, 89.
STEINMAN. Burke's Landed Gentry, 2.
STENHOUSE. Burke's Colonial Gentry, i. 300.
STENINGES. Weaver's Visitations of Somerset, 79.
STENTON. Dickinson's History of Southwell, 2nd edition, 344.
STEPHEN. Burke's Colonial Gentry, i. 42.
STEPHENS. Pedigree of Stephens of Estington, etc., Co. Gloucester,
   [T. P.] folio page.   Rudder's Gloucestershire, 430, 677, 713.   The
   Castle Builders, or the History of William Stephens, 1759, 8vo.
   Chavenage, a Tale of the Cotswolds, by R. W. Huntley, 12.
   Berry's Berkshire Genealogies, 21, 91.   Burke's Commoners, (of
   Tregenna,) iii. 609, Landed Gentry, 2, 3, 4, 5, 6, 7 ; (of Easting-
   ton,) Landed Gentry, 3, 4, 6, 7, 8 ; (of Llananno,) 5, 6, 7 ; 7 at p.
   1848 ; (of Bentworth Lodge,) 8 ; (of Trewornan,) 8.   Harleian
   Society, viii. 91 ; ix. 214 ; xiii. 290 ; xvii. 261, 262 ; xxi. 150 ;
   xxix. 443.   Burke's Visitations of Seats and Arms, 2nd Series,
   i. 49.   Nichols' History of the County of Leicester, i. 586, 588,
   607.   Visitatio Comitatus Wiltoniæ, 1623, printed by Sir T.
   Phillipps.   Maclean's History of Trigg Minor, iii. 83.   Fosbrooke's
   History of Gloucestershire, i. 317, 320.   Betham's Baronetage,
   iv. 264.   Burke's Extinct Baronetcies.   History of Sautry and
   Cloghran, by B. W. Adams, 31.   The Visitations of Cornwall,
   edited by J. L. Vivian, 445.   Bysshe's Visitation of Essex,
   edited by J. J. Howard, 87.   Visitation of Gloucester, edited
   by T. F. Fenwick and W. C. Metcalfe, 173-178.   The Genea-
   logist, New Series, xiii. 22.
STEPHENSON. Surtees Society, xxxvi. 221.   Hodgson's Northumber-
   land, III. ii. 85.   Cyclostyle Pedigrees, by J. J. Green.   Harleian
   Society, xxxix. 835.   Burke's Family Records, 552.   See STEVEN-
   SON.
STEPHYN. Harleian Society, vi. 276.   The Visitations of Devon, by
   J. L. Vivian, 715.
STEPNETH. Dwnn's Visitations of Wales, i. 180.   Harleian Society,
   xiii. 291 ; xiv. 603.
STEPNEY. Some Notices of the Stepney Family, by R. Harrison.
   London, 1870, 8vo.   Wotton's English Baronetage, i. 463.
   Betham's Baronetage, i. 233.   Burke's Extinct Baronetcies.
   Annals of Smith of Balby, by H. E. Smith, 57.
STERLING. Harleian Society, viii. 211.   See STIRLING.
STERNE.[1] Henry Sterne's Statement of Facts, 8vo.   Berry's Hertford-
   shire Genealogies, 227.   Cambridgeshire Visitation, edited by Sir
   T. Phillipps, 28.   Burke's Patrician, iii. 68.   Poulson's Holderness,
   i. 411.   Thoresby's Ducatus Leodiensis, 215.   Anthony Wood's
   Fasti Oxonienses, (3rd edn.) ii. 336.   The works of Laurence

---

[1] See a pedigree in Add. MS. 24,458.

Sterne, in four vols., (London, 1808,) i. vii. Life of Lawrence
Sterne, by Percy Fitzgerald, i. 1. . Harleian Society, xxii. 93, 94;
xxxii. 267; xxxviii. 516; xli. 58, 122.

STERRY. Howard's Visitation of England and Wales, i. 180; notes,
iii. 44. History of the Wilmer Family, 228. Burke's Family
Records, 552.

STERT. The Visitations of Devon, by J. L. Vivian, 799.

STEUART. Burke's Royal Families, (London, 1851, 8vo.) ii. 178.
Burke's Commoners, (of Ballechin,) ii. 149, Landed Gentry, 2, 3,
4, 5, 6, 7, 8; (of Dalguise,) Landed Gentry, 2, 3, 4, 5, 6, 7, 8; (of
Auchlunkart,) 2 supp., 3, 4, 5, 6, 7, 8; (of Glenormiston,) 2, 3, 4;
(of Steuart Hall,) 2, 3, 4, 5, 6, 6 at p. 1093, 7, 8. Nisbet's
Heraldry, ii. app. 52. *See* STUART.

STEUART-MENZIES. Burke's Landed Gentry, 2 supp., 3, 4, 5, 6, 7, 8.

STEVEN. Genealogies of Morgan and Glamorgan, by G. T. Clark,
505.

STEVENS. Burke's Landed Gentry, 4, 5, 6, 7, 8. Harleian Society,
xvii. 262; xxix. 444. *See* STEPHENS.

STEVENSON. Burke's Landed Gentry, (of Uffington,) 2, 3, 4, 5, 6, 7;
(of Braidwood,) 8; (of Westoe,) 8; (of Balladoole,) 8; (of Playford
Mount,) 8; (of Foxlease,) 8. Graves' History of Cleveland, 354.
Surtees' Durham, ii. 292. Burke's Colonial Gentry, ii. 521. *See*
STEPHENSON.

STEVENTON. Harleian Society, xxix. 444.

STEWARD. Blomefield's Norfolk, (1st edn. iv. 125, 387;) vii. 384.
Visitation of Norfolk, published by Norfolk Archæological Society,
i. 19. Surtees Society, xxxvi. 326. Notes and Queries, 2 S. ii.
239. Harleian Society, xvii. 263; xix. 181; xxii. 94; xxxii. 268.
Cambridgeshire Visitation, edited by Sir T. Phillipps, 29. Burke's
Commoners, (of Nottington House,) iii. 586, Landed Gentry,
2, 3, 4, 5, 6, 7, 8; (of Blundeston,) Landed Gentry, 2, 3, 4, 5;
(of Newton Manor,) 4, 5, 6, 7. Burke's Heraldic Illustrations, 94.
Ord's History of Cleveland, 276. Hutchins' Dorset, ii. 481.
Clutterbuck's Hertford, iii. 151. Baker's Northampton, ii. 298.
Page's History of Suffolk, 840. The Genealogist, iii. 310; New
Series, ii. 34, 81. Metcalfe's Visitations of Northamptonshire,
138, 197. Burke's Colonial Gentry, ii. 730. *See* STUART.

STEWART. Pedigree of the Family of Stewart (now Stuart) of Castle-
milk, co. Dumfries, by M. J. M. S. Stewart. Worksop, 1890,
broadside. An Abstract of the Evidence to prove that Sir William
Stewart of Jedworth was 2nd Son of Sir Alexander Stewart, etc.
London, 1801, 4to. Historical and Genealogical Account of the
Royal Family of Scotland, and of the Surname of Stewart, by
Duncan Stewart, M.A. Edinburgh, 1739, 4to. Appendix to same,
4to. Memorials of the Stewarts of Fothergill, by C. P. Stewart.
Edinburgh, 1879, 4to. The Stewarts of Appin, by J. H. J.
Stewart and Lt.-Col. Duncan Stewart. Edinburgh, 1880, 4to.
Genealogical Tree of the Royal Family of Stewart, by Robt.
Douglas. Broadside. The Red Book of Grand Tully, by William
Fraser. Edinburgh, 1868, 4to. 2 vols. Case between R. Stewart

of Garth and Anne Stewart of Inchgarth, 1784, fol. The Lennox, by Willm. Fraser, 2 vols. 1874, 4to. Pocock's History of Gravesend, 49. The Agnews of Lochnaw, by Sir A. Agnew, 622. Burke's Commoners, (of St. Fort,) iv. 40, Landed Gentry, 2, 3, 4, 5, 6, 7 ; (of Physgill,) Landed Gentry, 2, 3, 4, 5, 6, 7, 8 ; (of Ardvorlich,) 2, 3, 4, 5, 6, 7, 8 ; (of Cairnsmore,) 2, 3, 4, 5, 6, 7, 8; (of Drumin,) 2, 3, 4 ; (of Murdostoun,) 4, 5, 6, 7, 8 ; (of Tonderghie,) 4 ; (of Ballymenagh,) 3, 4, 5, 6, 7, 8 ; (of Ards,) 2, 3, 4, 5, 6, 7, 8; (of Hornhead,) 4, 5, 6, 7, 8 ; (of Binny,) 2, 8 ; (of Garvocks,) 7 ; (of Blackhouse,) 8 ; (of Lismurdie,) 2 ; (of Alltyrodyn,) 8 ; (of Kinlochmoidart,) 8 ; (of Urrard,) 5, 6, 7 ; (of Coll,) 6, 7, 8. Burke's Royal Descents and Pedigrees of Founders' Kin, 43. Archæologia, viii. 325. Lands and their Owners in Galloway, by P. H. M,Kerlie, i. 412, 479, 511 ; ii. 442 ; iii. 476. Paterson's History of the Co. of Ayr, ii. 399. Douglas's Baronage of Scotland, 483-491. Paterson's History of Ayr and Wigton, i. 626 ; ii. 429. Burke's Extinct Baronetcies, 637. O'Hart's Irish Pedigrees, 2nd Series, 97. Archæological Journal, No. 52, Decr. 1856. J. E. Reid's History of the Co. of Bute, 194-215. The works of John Knox, edited by David Laing, vi. lxvi. Peter Chalmers's Account of Dunfermline, ii. 421. Wood's Douglas's Peerage of Scotland, i. 42, 64, 121, 136, 158, 231, 264, 281, 294, 322, 615 ; ii. 90, 224, 229, 254, 326, 340, 370, 416, 466, 559, 597. Notes and Queries, 2 S. xii. 246 ; 3 S. iii. 51 ; 7 S., ii. 392 ; iv. 145 ; v. 469 ; vi. 69 ; xii. 251. Edmondson's Baronagium Genealogicum, iv. 379. Archdall's Lodge's Peerage, vi. 236. Brydges' Collins' Peerage, viii. 418. Betham's Baronetage, ii. 101; v. 534, app. 44. The Genealogist, New Series, viii. 56 ; xviii. 1. Northern Notes and Queries, iv. 23 ; v. 1 ; vii. 103-8. Exchequer Rolls of Scotland, preface to vol. iv. ciii.-ccxii. Scottish Journal, i. 341. Alexander Nisbet's Heraldic Plates, 142. Burke's Colonial Gentry, i. 336. Ontarian Families, by E. M. Chadwick, ii. 116. *See* STUART.

STEWART-MENZIES. Burke's Landed Gentry, 2, 3, 4, 5, 6, 7, 8.

STEWART-ROBERTSON. Genealogical Table of the Descent of James Stewart-Robertson of Edradynate, etc., July 1878. Folio broadside. Burke's Landed Gentry, 6, 7, 8.

STEWKLEY. Berry's Hampshire Genealogies, 310. Harleian Society, vi. 352. Visitation of Devon, edited by F. T. Colby, 192. Burke's Extinct Baronetcies. Weaver's Visitations of Somerset, 80. The Visitations of Devon, by J. L. Vivian, 721. *See* STUKELEY.

STEYNGREVE. Banks' Baronies in Fee, ii. 136.

STEYNING, or STAYNINGE. Camden Society, cv. *at end.* Visitation of Somersetshire, printed by Sir T. Phillipps, 137. Harleian Society, xi. 103. Metcalfe's Visitations of Suffolk, 68. Healey's History of Part of West Somerset, 198.

STIDOLPH. Harleian Society, xiv. 619. *See* STYDOLF.

STIEGLITZ. Burke's Colonial Gentry, i. 383.

STIFF. Memorials of the Family of Stiff of Norton and Rougham, by W. P. W. Phillimore. Stroud, 1885, 8vo. Gloucestershire Notes and Queries, ii. 614. Collections relating to the Family of Stiff, by W. P. W. Phillimore. Stroud, 1892, 8vo.

STILE. Harleian Society, i. 84. Bysshe's Visitation of Essex, edited by J. J. Howard, 88. *See* STYLE.

STILEMAN-GIBBARD. Burke's Landed Gentry, 6, 7, 8.

STILES. Metcalfe's Visitations of Northamptonshire, 138.

STILL. Gentleman's Magazine, 1840, ii. 496. Visitation of Somersetshire, printed by Sir T. Phillipps, 138. Harleian Society, xi. 104; xxxix. 1113. Visitatio Comitatus Wiltoniæ, 1623, printed by Sir T. Phillipps. Hutchins' Dorset, iii. 73. Hoare's Wiltshire, I. i. 191. Visitation of Wiltshire, edited by G. W. Marshall, 29. Notes and Queries, 3 S. vi. 345. Jewers' Wells Cathedral, 147, 152. Muskett's Suffolk Manorial Families, i. 74.

STILLINGFLEET. Burke's Landed Gentry, 2. Hutchins' Dorset, iii. 404.

STILLINGTON. Surtees Society, xxxvi. 215. Foster's Visitations of Yorkshire, 111, 633. Memoirs of Master John Shawe, by J. R. Boyle, 268.

STILWELL. Manning and Bray's Surrey, ii. 46.

STINT. Harleian Society, xvii. 264.

STINTON. Burke's Royal Families, (London, 1851, 8vo.) ii. 40.

STIRAP. Thoroton's Nottinghamshire, iii. 423.

STIRKLAND. The Genealogist, New Series, xv. 147.

STIRLING. The Stirlings of Keir and their Family Papers, by W. Fraser. Edinburgh, 1858, 4to. Comments in refutation of a recent work, 'The Stirlings of Keir and their Family Papers,' by John Riddell. Edinburgh, 1860, 4to. The Stirlings of Craigbernard and Glorat, by Joseph Bain. Edinburgh, 1883, 4to. Miscellaneous and Juridicial Essays, by — Warton. Burke's Landed Gentry, 7 at p. 1660; 8 at p. 1835; (of Keir,) 3, 4, 7, 8; (of Garden,) 8; (of Fairburn,) 8; (of Kippindavie,) 3, 4, 5, 6, 7, 8; (of Gargunnock,) 5, 6, 7, 8; (of Larbert,) 5, 6, 7, 8. Herald and Genealogist, viii. 6. Betham's Baronetage, iv. 247, 418. Burke's Extinct Baronetcies, 637. *See* ALEXANDER, STERLING.

STISTED. Harleian Society, xvii. 264.

STIVICHALE. Dugdale's Warwickshire, 651.

STOCKDALE. Visitation of Westmorland, 1615, (London, 1853,) 40. Surtees Society, xxxvi. 58. Burke's Landed Gentry, 5, 6, 7, 8. Foster's Visitations of Yorkshire, 410. Foster's Visitations of Cumberland and Westmorland, 130. The Genealogist, New Series, xiv. 58.

STOCKDEN. J. H. Hill's History of Market Harborough, 81. Nichols' History of the County of Leicester, ii. 520.

STOCKER. Visitation of Somersetshire, printed by Sir T. Phillipps, 138. Harleian Society, xi. 105; xix. 143.

STOCKETT. Berry's Kent Genealogies, 303. Harleian Society, xlii. 184.

STOCKING. New England Register, l. 171.

STOCKLEY. Visitation of Warwickshire, 1619, published with Warwickshire Antiquarian Magazine, 77.

STOCKPORT. Harleian Society, xviii. 241. Butterworth's History of Stockport, etc., 222. Miscellanea Genealogica et Heraldica, 2nd Series, ii. 54. *See* STOKEPORT.

STOCKS. Burke's Landed Gentry, 6, 7, 8.

STOCKTON. J. H. Hill's History of Market Harborough, 81. Nichols' History of the County of Leicester, ii. 520. Ormerod's Cheshire, ii. 661. Burke's Colonial Gentry, i. 271. The Genealogist, New Series, xiii. 95.

STOCKWITH. Harleian Society, iv. 176. Berry's Hampshire Genealogies, 114.

STODART. Burke's Landed Gentry, 2, 6 at p. 1635.

STODDARD. Harleian Society, i. 27. Hasted's Kent, (Hund. of Blackheath, by H. H. Drake,) 194. New England Register, v. 21-42.

STODELEGH. Foster's Visitations of Yorkshire, 112, 234.

STOKE. J. H. Hill's History of Market Harborough, 54. Nichols' History of the County of Leicester, ii. 461. Hutchins' Dorset, i. 412. The Genealogist, New Series, xv. 215.

STOKEPORT. J. P. Earwaker's East Cheshire, i. 343. Ormerod's Cheshire, iii. 788. ' The Early Connexion of Stokeport, Fitz-Roger Banastre, and Gernet,' *see* Ormerod's ' Parentalia.' *See* STOCKPORT.

STOKES. Cambridgeshire Visitation, edited by Sir T. Phillipps, 28. Berry's Kent Genealogies, 110. Burke's Landed Gentry, (of Mounthawk,) 2, 3, 4, 5, 6, 7, 8 ; (of Stanshawes Court,) 2 ; (of St. Botolphs,) 8. Bridges' Northamptonshire, by Rev. Peter Whalley, ii. 158. Visitatio Comitatus Wiltoniæ, 1623, printed by Sir T. Phillipps. Harleian Society, xvi. 298 ; xxi. 153 ; xli. 96 ; xlii. 29. Visitation of Wiltshire, edited by G. W. Marshall, 78. Visitation of Gloucester, edited by T. F. Fenwick and W. C. Metcalfe, 178. Miscellanea Genealogica et Heraldica, 2nd Series, ii. 25. The Genealogist, New Series, xiii. 247. Transactions of Shropshire Archæological Society, ix. 25. *See* DE STOKES.

STOMPE. Sir T. Phillipps' Topographer, (March, 1821, 8vo.) 15. Harleian Society, v. 121. *See* STAMPE, STUMPE.

STONARD. Morant's Essex, i. 178. Bysshe's Visitation of Essex, edited by J. J. Howard, 88.

STONE. Berry's Sussex Genealogies, 79, 347. Berry's Kent Genealogies, 473. Visitation of Somersetshire, printed by Sir T. Phillipps, 138. Burke's Commoners, (of Streatley House,) iii. 260, Landed Gentry, 2, 3, 4, 5, 6, 7 ; (of Leigh Park,) Landed Gentry, 5, 8 ; (of Erdington,) 8 ; (of Badbury,) 6 supp., 7, 8. Maclean's History of Trigg Minor, i. 313 ; iii. 76. Harleian Society, ix. 215 ; xi. 105 ; xvii. 265-267 ; xix. 143 ; xxi. 259 ; xxxii. 270. Lipscombe's History of the County of Buckingham, ii. 444. Cussan's History of Hertfordshire, Parts v. and vi. 166. Chauncy's Hertfordshire, 79. F. G. Lee's History of Thame, 578. The Visitations of Cornwall, edited by J. L. Vivian, 446. Howard's Visitation of England and Wales, i. 60. The Genealogist, New Series, viii. 174. Bysshe's Visitation of Essex, edited by J. J. Howard, 89. New

England Register, x. 229 ; xxxvi. 366 ; xlix. 314. Burke's Family Records, 554.

STONEHOUSE. Hasted's Kent, ii. 792. Morant's Essex, ii. 565. Berry's Buckinghamshire Genealogies, 53. Berry's Kent Genealogies, 206. Wotton's English Baronetage, ii. 81. Betham's Baronetage, i. 317, app. 21. Burke's Extinct Baronetcies. Harleian Society, xlii. 71.

STONER. Sir T. Phillipps' Topographer, No. 1, (March, 1821, 8vo.) 16. Harleian Society, v. 143 ; xiii. 493. Metcalfe's Visitations of Suffolk, 77. *See* STONOR.

STONES. Camden Society, xliii. 101. Harleian Society, xvii. 267 ; xxxviii. 457, 824.

STONESTREAT. Berry's Sussex Genealogies, 233-236. Burke's Landed Gentry, 2, 3, 4, 5.

STONEY. Some Old Annals of the Stoney Family, by F. S. Stoney. London, 1879, 8vo. Burke's Landed Gentry, (of Kyle Park,) 2, 3, 4, 5, 6, 7 ; (of Portland,) 2, 3, 4, 5, 6, 7, 8. Burke's Family Records, 555. Howard's Visitation of Ireland, ii. 10.

STONOR. Case of Thomas Stonor claiming the Barony of Camoys, pp. 25. Additional Case of T. Stonor, claiming the Barony of Camoys, pp. 13. Claim of Thomas Stonor, Esq., to the Barony of Camoys, Sess. Papers, 118 of 1838 ; 167 of 1839. Excerpta Historica, Part 4. Visitation of Oxfordshire, 1574, printed by Sir T. Phillipps, (Middle Hill, fol.) 10. Burke's Commoners, ii. 440. Gyll's History of Wraysbury, 59. Lipscombe's History of the County of Buckingham, iv. 609. The Genealogist, New Series, xiv. 199. *See* STONER.

STONOURE. Fosbrooke's History of Gloucestershire, ii. 76.

STONYER. Visitations of Staffordshire, 1614 and 1663-4, William Salt Society, 282.

STOPFORD. Archdall's Lodge's Peerage, iii. 118. Brydges' Collins' Peerage, viii. 445. The Irish Builder, xxix. 72.

STOPFORD-BLAIR. Burke's Landed Gentry, 3, 4, 5, 6.

STOPFORD-SACKVILLE. Burke's Landed Gentry, 3, 4, 5.

STOPHAM. Foster's Visitations of Yorkshire, 235. Sussex Archæological Collections, xxvii. 50. Castles, Mansions, and Manors of Western Sussex, by D. G. C. Elwes and C. J. Robinson, 218. W. Wheater's History of Sherburn and Cawood, 170.

STORER. Burke's Royal Families, (London, 1851, 8vo.) i. 83 ; ii. 169. Burke's Landed Gentry, (of Purley Park,) 2 add., 3, 4, 5, 6, 7, 8 ; (of Combe Court,) 3, 4, 5 ; (of Hawkesworth,) 2 supp. New England Register, vi. 275.

STORETON. Ormerod's Cheshire, ii. 448.

STORIE. Burke's Commoners, i. 275, Landed Gentry, 2.

STORMEY. Graves' History of Cleveland, 243.

STORR. Poulson's Holderness, ii. 79. Yorkshire Archæological and Topographical Journal, vii. 46.

STORY. Burke's Landed Gentry, (of Ralagh Lodge,) 2, 8 ; (of Bingfield,) 3, 4, 5, 6, 7 ; (of Lockington,) 5. Surtees' Durham, i. 233. Harleian Society, xvii. 268.

STORY-MASKELYNE. Miscellanea Genealogica et Heraldica, ii. 11.
STOTE. Harleian Society, viii. 274. Burke's Commoners, iii. 498.
Foster's Visitations of Northumberland, 114.
STOTESBURY. Harleian Society, v. 206. Bridges' Northamptonshire,
by Rev. Peter Whalley, i. 128. Baker's Northampton, i. 517.
STOTEVILL. Cambridgeshire Visitation, edited by Sir T. Phillipps,
28. Thoroton's Nottinghamshire, ii. 291. Metcalfe's Visitations
of Suffolk, 68, 103. Harleian Society, xli. 76. *See* STUTEVILL.
STOTHERT. Burke's Landed Gentry, 2, 3, 4.
STOUGHTON. Burke's Landed Gentry, 2, 3, 4, 5, 6, 7, 8. Visitation
of Warwickshire, 1619, published with Warwickshire Antiquarian
Magazine, 198. Burke's Royal Descents and Pedigrees of
Founders' Kin, 87. Dallaway's Sussex, i. App. to Chichester.
Manning and Bray's Surrey, i. 171. Harleian Society, xii. 141,
315; xvii. 269; xliii. 85. Berry's Kent Genealogies, 108.
Burke's Extinct Baronetcies. New England Register, v. 350.
STOURTON. Burke's Royal Families, (London, 1851, 8vo.) ii. 170.
Foster's Yorkshire Pedigrees. Collectanea Topographica et Genea-
logica, i. 312, 409. Nichols' History of the County of Leicester,
iv. 818. Visitatio Comitatus Wiltoniæ, 1623, printed by Sir T.
Phillipps. Hoare's Wiltshire, I. i. 47. Wiltshire Archæological
Magazine, viii. 244. Edmondson's Baronagium Genealogicum, iv.
367. Brydges' Collins' Peerage, vi. 633. Harleian Society, xx.
85. *See* MOWBRAY, STURTON.
STOUT. Burke's Colonial Gentry, i. 80. Memoir of Richard Haines,
by C. R. Haines, table vii. C.
STOVIN. Burke's Landed Gentry, 2 add. Stonehouse's History of
the Isle of Axholme, 427. Hunter's Deanery of Doncaster, i. 183.
Harleian Society, xxxvii. 321; xl. 1242. Historical Notices of
Doncaster, by C. W. Hatfield, 2nd Series, 149.
STOWE. New England Register, x. 121.
STOWELL. Visitation of Somersetshire, printed by Sir T. Phillipps,
139. Harleian Society, xi. 106. *See* STAWELL.
STOWFORD, or STOFORD. Harleian Society, vi. 276, 277. Westcote's
Devonshire, edited by G. Oliver and P. Jones, 592. Visitation of
Devon, edited by F. T. Colby, 194. The Visitations of Devon,
by J. L. Vivian, 712. *See* STAFFORD.
STOYTE. Stoyte of Lincolnshire. Sheet pedigree. The Genealogist,
iii. 310.
STRABOLGI, or STRABOLGY. Carthew's Hundred of Launditch, Part i.
325. Thoroton's Nottinghamshire, iii. 237. Banks' Dormant and
Extinct Baronage, i. 414.
STRACEY-CLITHEROW. Burke's Landed Gentry, 5, 6, 7, 8.
STRACHAN, or STRAHAN. Memorials of the Families of Strachan and
Wise, by Rev. C. Rogers. Edinburgh, 1877, 4to. Burke's Landed
Gentry, 2. Burke's Extinct Baronetcies, 637. Notes and Queries,
8 S. iv. 242, 323. Ontarian Families, by E. M. Chadwick,
ii. 61.
STRACHEY. Burke's Landed Gentry, 2. Harleian Society, xiv. 604.
Betham's Baronetage, v. 431.

STRADBROKE. Burke's Royal Families, (London, 1851, 8vo.) i. 131.

STRADLING. The History of Wales, by Dr. Powell, (Merthyr Tydvil, 1812, 8vo.) xli. Collinson's Somerset, iii. 335. Glamorganshire Pedigrees, edited by Sir T. Phillipps, 26. Topographical Collections of John Aubrey, edited by J. E. Jackson, 217. Visitatio Comitatus Wiltoniæ, 1623, printed by Sir T. Phillipps. Burke's Extinct Baronetcies. The Stradling Correspondence, by J. M. Traherne, ix.-xxiii. Genealogies of Morgan and Glamorgan, by G. T. Clark, 433-444.

STRADLING-CARNE. Burke's Landed Gentry, 8.

STRAFFORD. Jewitt's Reliquary, ii. 222. (Earl of,) Notes and Queries, 7 S. iii. 71.

STRAKER. Burke's Landed Gentry, 7, 8.

STRANG, or STRANGE. Memoirs of Sir Robt. Strange, by James Dennistoun. London, 1855, 8vo., 2 vols. Walter Wood's East Neuk of Fife, 246, 250. Savage's Hundred of Carhampton, 220. Visitation of Gloucestershire, 1569, (Middle Hill, 1854, fol.) 9. Blore's Rutland, 228. Clutterbuck's Hertford, i. 170. Miscellanea Genealogica et Heraldica, New Series, ii. 189. Banks' Dormant and Extinct Baronage, ii. 548. Harleian Society, xxi. 154, 222 ; xxxii. 271. New England Register, xix. 324. Burke's Colonial Gentry, ii. 846. See ATHOL, L'ESTRANGE.

STRANGEWAYES, STRANGEWAYS, STRANGWAYES, or STRANGWAYS. Burke's Commoners, ii. 311 ; (of Well,) Commoners, i. 135, Landed Gentry, 2 ; (of Alne,) 7, 8 ; (of Shapwick,) 8. Foster's Yorkshire Pedigrees. Miscellanea Genealogica et Heraldica, New Series, i. 132 ; iii. 22. Foster's Visitations of Yorkshire, 71, 202-204. Collectanea Topographica et Genealogica, ii. 161. Raine's History of North Durham, 228. Ord's History of Cleveland, 447, 555. Hutchins' Dorset, i. 149 ; ii. 662. Hoare's Wiltshire, V. i. 37. Surtees Society, xxxvi. 86. Harleian Society, xvi. 299 ; xx. 86 ; xxxviii. 627, 631 ; xxxix. 940. Banks' Baronies in Fee, i. 179. Burton's History of Hemingborough, 189. Jewers' Wells Cathedral, 50, 52. The Genealogist, New Series, iii. 169. See SWAINSTON-STRANGWAYES.

STRANGFORD. Lives of the Lords Strangford, by E. B. De Fonblanque. London, 1877. Hasted's Kent, iii. 259.

STRANGMAN, or STRANGEMAN. Morant's Essex, i. 280. Proceedings of the Essex Archæological Society, iii. 95. Harleian Society, xiii. 73, 103, 291. The Genealogist, New Series, iii. 169.

STRANGWICH. Chetham Society, lxxxii. 13.

STRATFORD. Claim of the Rt. Hon. Benjn. O'Neale Stratford, Earl of Aldborough, to Vote at Elections of Irish Peers, Sess. Papers, 155 of 1854. Burke's Heraldic Illustrations, 97. Warwickshire Antiquarian Magazine, Part i. Visitation of Gloucestershire, 1569, (Middle Hill, 1854, fol.) 9. Baker's Northampton, i. 57. Notes and Queries, 2 S. viii. 376, 477, 522. Archdall's Lodge's Peerage, iii. 336. Visitation of Gloucester, edited by T. F. Fenwick and W. C. Metcalfe, 180. Harleian Society, xxi. 155 ; xxii. 95.

Genealogical Table of John Stratford-Collins. The Irish Builder, xxxv. 51. Burke's Family Records, 559.

STRATFORD-COLLINS. Duncumb's Hereford, (J. H. Cooke,) iii. 205.

STRATHBOLGIE. Hodgson's Northumberland, II. ii. 41.

STRATHERN. History of the Earldoms of Strathern, Monteith, and Airth, by Sir N. H. Nicolas. London, 1842, 8vo. The Genealogist, v. 105.

STRATHMORE. Surtees' Durham, iv. 109. Angus or Forfarshire, by A. J. Warden, 336-357.

STRATHY. Ontarian Families, by E. M. Chadwick, ii. 68.

STRATTON. Burke's Landed Gentry, 5, 6, 7, 8. Visitatio Comitatus Wiltoniæ, 1623, printed by Sir T. Phillipps. Visitation of Wiltshire, edited by G. W. Marshall, 99.

STREAPER. Harleian Society, xvii. 385.

STREATFEILD, or STREATFIELD. Berry's Kent Genealogies, 234-241. Burke's Commoners, (of Chiddingstone,) ii. 422, Landed Gentry, 2 and add., 3, 4, 5, 6, 7, 8; (of Charts Edge,) Landed Gentry, 4, 5, 6, 7. Glover's History of Derbyshire, ii. 109. The Genealogist, v. 118. Harleian Society, xlii. 145.

STREATFIELD-MOORE. Burke's Landed Gentry, 8.

STRECHE. Collinson's Somerset, iii. 26. Hutchins' Dorset, iv. 197.

STRECHLEGH. Westcote's Devonshire, edited by G. Oliver and P. Jones, 514. Visitation of Devon, edited by F. T. Colby, 194. The Visitations of Devon, by J. L. Vivian, 716.

STREET. Harleian Society, xvii. 269; xliii. 76. Oxford Historical Society, xxiv. 78, 358. New England Register, xliv. 183; xlvi. 256. Ontarian Families, by E. M. Chadwick, ii. 174.

STREETER. New England Register, xxxvi. 161.

STRELLEY. J. H. Hill's History of Langton, 21. Miscellanea Genealogica et Heraldica, i. 144. Jewitt's Reliquary, vii. 29. Glover's History of Derbyshire, ii. 109, (95). Burke's Landed Gentry, 2, 3, 4. Harleian Society, ii. 194; iv. 19; xxxvii. 302. Hunter's History of the Parish of Sheffield, 345. Nichols' History of the County of Leicester, ii. 663. Thoroton's Nottinghamshire, ii. 220; iii. 33. Account of Beauchief Abbey, by S. Pegge, being No. 3 of Nichols' Miscellaneous Antiquities, 205. The Gresley's of Drakelowe, by F. Madan, 282.

STRETCH. Burke's Colonial Gentry, ii. 602.

STRETE. J. H. Hill's History of Langton, 278. Nichols' History of the County of Leicester, ii. 602.

STRETHAY. Shaw's Staffordshire, i. 363. Visitation of Staffordshire, (Willm. Salt Soc.) 137.

STRETLEY. Sir T. Phillipps' Topographer, No. 1, (March, 1821, 8vo.) 33. Visitation of Oxfordshire, 1574, printed by Sir T. Phillipps, (Middle Hill, fol.) 10. Harleian Society, v. 184. Metcalfe's Visitations of Northamptonshire, 48.

STRETTON. Harleian Society, iv. 89. Nichols' History of the County of Leicester, iii. 1025, 1028. J. T. Godfrey's History of Lenton, 204.

STREYNSHAM. Notes relating to the Family of Streynsham, of

Faversham, by Rev. G. S. Master, with additional information by
Genl. Sir A. B. Stransham. London, 1879, 4to. Master's Notices
of the Family of Master, 75.

STRICKLAND, or STRIKLAND. Pedigree of Strickland, of Sizergh, Co.
Westmorland, etc., 2 folio pages. Plantagenet-Harrison's History
of Yorkshire, i. 373. Surtees Society, xxxvi. 112. Burke's Commoners, (of Sizergh,) i. 55, Landed Gentry, 2, 3, 4, 5, 6, 7, 8; (of
Cokethorpe,) Landed Gentry, 5, 6, 7. Foster's Yorkshire Pedigrees. Foster's Visitations of Yorkshire, 166. Herald and Genealogist, iii. 428. Wotton's English Baronetage, ii. 218. Betham's
Baronetage, i. 412. Nicolson and Burn's Westmorland and Cumberland, i. 88-103, 129. Howard's Visitation of England and
Wales, ix. 97.

STRICKLAND-CONSTABLE. Burke's Landed Gentry, 5.

STRICKSON. Bibliotheca Topographica Britannica, ix. Part iv. 51.

STRIGUL (Earls of). Journal of British Archæological Association,
x. 265. Strigulensia, by George Ormerod, 62.

STRINGER. Berry's Kent Genealogies, 308. Surtees Society, xxxvi.
282. Foster's Visitations of Yorkshire, 575. Harleian Society,
iv. 85; viii. 228; xvii. 270; xxxix. 1067. Hunter's Deanery of
Doncaster, ii. 181. Thoroton's Nottinghamshire, iii. 260. The
Genealogist, New Series, viii. 174; ix. 224.

STRINGFELLOW. Berry's Hampshire Genealogies, 233.

STROBRIDGE. Tuckett's Devonshire Pedigrees, 128. Harleian Society,
vi. 278. The Visitations of Devon, by J. L. Vivian, 717.

STRODE, or STROWDE. Herald and Genealogist, iv. 437. Collinson's
Somerset, ii. 210. Berry's Hertfordshire Genealogies, 7. Tuckett's
Devonshire Pedigrees, 185. Visitation of Somersetshire, printed
by Sir T. Phillipps, 138. Burke's Royal Families, (London, 1851,
8vo.) ii. 69. Burke's Commoners, ii. 117; Landed Gentry, 2, 3,
4, 5, 6, 7, 8. Harleian Society, vi. 278; viii. 83, 123, 306; xi.
108; xx. 88. Westcote's Devonshire, edited by G. Oliver and
P. Jones, 542. Hutchins' Dorset, ii. 130. Clutterbuck's Hertford,
ii. 377. Foster's Account of Families descended from Francis
Fox, 26. Ellacombe's History of Bitton, 100. Notes and Queries,
2 S. xii. 441, 462. Visitation of Devon, edited by F. T. Colby,
195. The Genealogist, New Series, iii. 170. Hasted's Kent,
(Hund. of Blackheath, by H. H. Drake,) xxi. Weaver's Visitations
of Somerset, 131. Somerset and Dorset Notes and Queries, i. 236.
The Visitations of Devon, by J. L. Vivian, 718.

STRONG. Burke's Royal Families, (London, 1851, 8vo.) ii. 208.
Burke's Landed Gentry, (of Nether Stronge,) 2, 3, 4, 5, 6, 7, 8;
(of Thorpe Hall,) 5, 6, 7, 8. Clutterbuck's Hertford, i. 170.
Betham's Baronetage, v. 535. Gloucestershire Notes and Queries,
ii. 262. Notes and Queries, 7 S., i. 228, 279, 373. New England
Register, vii. 100; viii. 180.

STRONGBOW. Clutterbuck's Hertford, ii. 510.

STROTHER. Records of the Family of Strother, by A. Strother. Bath,
1881, 4to. Hodgson's Northumberland, I. ii. 254. The Genealogist, i. 384. Notes and Queries, 2 S. i. 211; ii. 156. Foster's

Visitations of Northumberland, 115. Miscellanea Genealogica et
Heraldica, 2nd Series, iv. 150. Burke's Landed Gentry, 8.
STROUGHILL. The Genealogist, vi. 97. Berks, Bucks, and Oxon
Archælogical Journal, v. 122.
STRUTT. Glover's History of Derbyshire, ii. 591, (573). Burke's
Landed Gentry, (of Derby,) 2 ; (of Belper,) 2, 3, 4, 5, 6, 7, 8.
Burke's Heraldic Illustrations, 61. Proceedings of the Essex
Archæological Society, v. 147. Harleian Society, xiv. 664. Notes
and Queries, 4 S. vi. 180. Burke's Extinct Baronetcies.
STRYPE. The Perverse Widow, by A. W. Crawley-Boevey, 211.
STUART.[1] A Trewe Description of the Nobill Race of the Stewards.
Amsterdam, 1603, fol. The Descendants of the Stuarts, by William
Townend. London, 1858, 8vo. 2nd edition. A Defence of the
Royal Line of Scotland, by Sir George Mackenzie. London, 1685,
8vo. The Antiquity of the Royal Line of Scotland further de-
fended, by Sir George Mackenzie. London, 1686, 8vo. Memoires
of the Family of the Stuarts. London, 1683, 8vo. La Race et la
Naissance, la Vie et la Mort, de Marie Stuart. Amsterdam, 1695,
18mo. A Chronological, Genealogical, and Historical Dissertation
of the Royal Family of the Stuarts, by Matthew Kenedy. Paris,
1705, 8vo. Les Derniers Stuarts a Saint-Germain en Laye, par la
Marquise Campana de Cavelli. Paris, 1869, 8vo. A Genealogical
History of the Royal Family of the Stewarts, from 1034-1710, by
G. Crawford. Edinburgh, 1710, folio ; 2nd edition, 1782, 4to. ; see
also Crawford's Renfrew, continued by Geo. Robertson. Paisley,
1818, 4to. A Genealogical Account of the Most Illustrious Name
of Stuart, by D. Symson, 1713, 4to. Essay on the Origin of the
Royal Family of the Stewarts, by R. Hay. Edinburgh, 1722 and
1793, 4to. An Historical Genealogy of the Royal House of Stuart,
by Mark Noble. London, 1795, 4to. Genealogical History of the
Stuarts, by A. Stuart, 1798, 4to.; Supplement, London, 1799, 4to.
The Genealogical History of the Stewarts refuted. Edinburgh,
1799, 8vo. Genealogical Account of the Royal House of Stuart,
by Thomas Waterhouse. Grantham, 1816, 8vo. Stuart of Allan-
bank, 1643-1880, by Louisa Lilias Forbes. Edinburgh, 1880,
folding sheet, includes the families of Bethune, Eden, Elliot,
Marjoribanks, and Trotter. The Salt Foot Controversy, involving
the Descent of the Family of Stewart of Allanton, by J. Riddell.
Edinburgh, 1818, 8vo. Coltness Collections, comprising Memorials
of the Stewarts of Allanton, Coltness, etc., by Mrs. Calderwood,
1842, 4to. Stewartiana, containing the Case of Robert II. and
Elizabeth Mure, etc., by J. Riddell. Edinburgh, 1843, 8vo. View
of the Evidence for proving that the Paternal Ancestor of the
present Earls of Galloway was the second son of Sir Alex. Stewart
of Darnley, etc., by E. Williams, 1801, 4to. Claim of the Rt.
Hon. John Stuart, Earl of Darnley, to Vote at Elections of Peers,
Sess. Papers, 293 of 1849. Genealogical Sketch of the Stuarts of
Castle Stuart in Ireland, by Rev. A. G. Stuart. Edinburgh, 1854,

---

[1] See Lowndes' 'Bib. Man.,' part ix., p. 2537.

4to. Noble's Memoirs of the House of Cromwell, ii. 231. Gentleman's Magazine, 1857, i. 201; 1858, i. 378; ii. 299. Berry's Hampshire Genealogies, 189. History of Hardwicke Hall, by P. F. Robinson, 18. Burke's Commoners, (of Aldenham Abbey,) i. 427, Landed Gentry, 2, 3, 4, 5, 6; (of Inchbreck,) Landed Gentry, 2, 3, 4, 5, 6, 7, 8; (of Blairhall,) 4; (of Tempsford,) 7, 8; (of Dalness,) 7, 8; (of Dromana,) 7, 8; (of Castletown,) 6, 7, 8. Eyton's Antiquities of Shropshire, vii. 228. Thoresby's Ducatus Leodiensis, 277. Archæologia Cantiana, xi. 272; xii. 105. Nisbet's Heraldry, ii. app. 157, 169, 181. Douglas's Baronage of Scotland, 513. Balmerino and its Abbey, by James Campbell, 392. Pedigree of Wilson of High Wray, etc., by Joseph Foster, 111. O'Hart's Irish Pedigrees, 2nd Series, 101. Notes and Queries, 1 S. ix. 177; 6 S. iii. 464; iv. 185. Wood's Douglas's Peerage of Scotland, i. 212. Edmondson's Baronagium Genealogicum, v. 469; vi. 63. Brydges' Collins' Peerage, ii. 568; viii. 402. Wotton's English Baronetage, iii. 83. Banks' Dormant and Extinct Baronage, iii. 627. The Genealogist, New Series, i. 150. Harleian Society, xli. 7. The Genealogical Magazine, i. 21, 119. Ontarian Families, by E. M. Chadwick, ii. 102. *See* STEUART, STEWART.

STUART DE DECIES. Claim of H. W. V. Stuart to Dignity of Lord Stuart de Decies, Sess. Papers, A of 1876.

STUART-GRAY. Burke's Landed Gentry, 8.

STUART-MENTETH. Herald and Genealogist, v. 260, 456, 526.

STUART-WORTLEY. Foster's Yorkshire Pedigrees.

STUBBER. Burke's Landed Gentry, 2, 3, 4, 5, 6, 7, 8.

STUBBING. Morant's Essex, ii. 532. Harleian Society, xxxix. 1008.

STUBBS. Pedigree of Wm. Stubbs, Esq., of Salford, Co. Warwick, privately printed by Sir T. Phillipps, Bart., 1849, folio page. Burke's Commoners, iv. 372. Burke's Landed Gentry, 4, 8. A Royal Descent, by T. E. Sharpe, (London, 1875, 4to.) 22. The Genealogist, iii. 311. Archæologia Cantiana, xviii. 209. Howard's Visitation of Ireland, i. 17. The Irish Builder, xxix. 275. Willmore's History of Walsall, 433.

STUBBY. Harleian Society, xxxii. 273.

STUCHE. *See* STYCH.

STUCKEY. Burke's Colonial Gentry, ii. 712. Burke's Landed Gentry, 8.

STUCKLEY. Howard's Visitation of England and Wales, ii. 148. *See* STEWKLEY.

STUDD. Burke's Landed Gentry, 6, 7, 8.

STUDDERT. Burke's Landed Gentry, (of Bunratty Castle,) 2, 3, 4, 5, 6, 7, 8; (of Elm Hill,) 3, 4. Burke's Heraldic Illustrations, 85.

STUDDY. Burke's Landed Gentry, 8.

STUDHOLME. Burke's Landed Gentry, 6, 7, 8. Burke's Colonial Gentry, i. 170.

STUDLEY. Berry's Kent Genealogies, 425. Harleian Society, xxix. 447; xlii. 171.

STUKELEY. Harleian Society, vi. 352. Westcote's Devonshire, edited by G. Oliver and P. Jones, 579, 585. Burke's Extinct

Baronetcies. G. W. Macdonald's Holbeach Register, 84. *See* STEWKLEY.

STUMPE. Collectanea Topographica et Genealogica, vii. 81. *See* STOMPE.

STURDIVANT. Harleian Society, iv. 159.

STURDY. Harleian Society, xxxviii. 513.

STURE. Tuckett's Devonshire Pedigrees, 169. Harleian Society, vi. 279. Westcote's Devonshire, edited by G. Oliver and P. Jones, 512. The Visitations of Devon, by J. L. Vivian, 725.

STURGE. Pedigree of Wilson, by S. B. Foster, 59. Family Records. By Charlotte Sturge. London, 1882, 8vo.

STURGEON. Gage's History of Thingoe Hundred, Suffolk, 385.

STURGES. Weaver's Visitations of Somerset, 81.

STURGES-BOURNE. Berry's Hampshire Genealogies, 336.

STURGIS. Burke's Visitation of Seats and Arms, 2nd Series, i. 9.

STURMY. Morant's Essex, i. 265. Foster's Visitations of Yorkshire, 177, 196.

STURT. Burke's Landed Gentry, 2, 3, 4, 5. Harleian Society, viii. 506. Hutchins' Dorset, iii. 125. Burke's Colonial Gentry, ii. 444.

STURTON. Harleian Society, ii. 119. Miscellanea Genealogica et Heraldica, 2nd Series, iii. 325. The Genealogist, New Series, xiii. 23. *See* STOURTON.

STURY. Harleian Society, xxix. 448.

STUTEVILL, STUTEVILLE, STUTTEVILLE, or STUTEVYLL. Collectanea Topographica et Genealogica, i. 10. George Oliver's History of Beverley, 459. Hutchinson's History of Cumberland, ii. 528. Hodgson's Northumberland, II. ii. 41. Nichols' History of the County of Leicester, ii. 303. Dugdale's Warwickshire, 95. Baker's Northampton, i. 230. Banks' Dormant and Extinct Baronage, i. 174. Morant's Essex, ii. 246. Harleian Society, xvii. 270. Nicolson and Burn's Westmorland and Cumberland, ii. 464. *See* ESTOUTEVILLE, STOTEVILL.

STYCH. Burke's Extinct Baronetcies. Harleian Society, xvii. 271 ; xxix. 445. Bysshe's Visitation of Essex, edited by J. J. Howard, 89.

STYDOLF. Manning and Bray's Surrey, ii. 640, 651. Burke's Extinct Baronetcies. Harleian Society, xliii. 42. *See* STIDOLPH.

STYLE. Hasted's Kent, i. 86 ; ii. 282, 512. Berry's Kent Genealogies, 412. Burke's Landed Gentry, 2 supp., 3, 4. Fosters Visitations of Yorkshire, 576. Burke's Royal Descents and Pedigrees of Founders' Kin, 10 ; *Founders' Kin*, 19. Hutchins' Dorset, ii. 616. Harleian Society, xiv. 605 ; xvii. 272 ; xix. 144 ; xx. 89 ; xlii. 123. Wotton's English Baronetage, ii. 22. Betham's Baronetage, i. 294. Burke's Extinct Baronetcies. F. G. Lee's History of Thame, 626. Hasted's Kent, (Hund. of Blackheath, by H. H. Drake,) 224. Phillimore's London and Middlesex Note-Book, 62, 108. *See* STILE.

STYLEMAN, or STYLLEMAN. Case of H. Le Strange Styleman on his Claim to be Baron Camoys, 1838 (?), fol. Additional Case of T. Stonor, claiming the Barony of Camoys, folding table. Blomefield's Norfolk, x. 114. Visitatio Comitatus Wiltoniæ, 1623 printed by Sir T. Phillipps. Carthew's Hundred of Launditch, Part ii. 448. Berry's Hampshire Genealogies, 60. The Genealogist, New Series, xiii. 23.

STYLEMAN-LE-STRANGE. Burke's Landed Gentry, 2, 3, 4, 5, 6.

STYWARD. *See* STUART.

SUCKLING. Burke's Commoners, iii. 157, Landed Gentry, 2, 3, 5 supp., 6, 7, 8. Suckling's History of Suffolk, i. 40. Hoare's Wiltshire, III. iv. 50. Harleian Society, xxxii. 274. The Genealogical Magazine, i. 164.

SUDBURY. Morant's Essex, ii. 93, 95. Burke's Extinct Baronetcies. Burke's Landed Gentry, 8.

SUDELL. Abram's History of Blackburn, 403.

SUDLEY, or SUDELEY. Dallaway's Sussex, II. ii. 77. Dugdale's Warwickshire, 1073. Harleian Society, xiv. 563; xliii. 220. Banks' Baronies in Fee, i. 423. Collectanea Topographica et Genealogica, v. 10. Banks' Dormant and Extinct Baronage, i. 416. *See* TRACY.

SUDWORTHE. Chetham Society, xcviii. 73.

SUENE. Proceedings of the Essex Archæological Society, v. 101.

SUFFOLK. Morant's Essex, ii. 244, 550. Banks' Dormant and Extinct Baronage, iii. 682.

SULIARD, or SULYARD. Berry's Kent Genealogies, 87. Harleian Society, xiii. 494; xlii. 26. Morant's Essex, i. 140; ii. 42. Berry's Essex Genealogies, 64. Foley's Records of the English Province S. J., iv. 606. Page's History of Suffolk, 556. The Genealogist, iv. 226. Metcalfe's Visitations of Suffolk, 69, 168. *See* SEYLIARD, SYLYARD.

SULIVAN. Burke's Landed Gentry, 2 supp., 3, 4.

SULLIVAN. Burke's Commoners, (of Richings Lodge,) i. 410; (of Curramore,) Landed Gentry, 4, 5, 6, 7, 8; (of Chesterfield,) 2, 3; (of Tullylease,) 5, 6, 7, 8. Lipscombe's History of the County of Buckingham, iv. 519. Betham's Baronetage, v. 556. New England Register, xix. 289. Ontarian Families, by E. M. Chadwick, ii. 44.

SULLY. Banks' Baronies in Fee, ii. 138. The Genealogist, New Series, xiv. 191.

SUMER. Berry's Kent Genealogies, 81, 121. Harleian Society, xlii. 21.

SUMERY Clutterbuck's Hertford, i. 442. *See* SOMERI.

SUMMASTER. Harleian Society, vi. 279. *See* SOMASTER.

SUMMERS. Morant's Essex, ii. 289. *See* SOMMERS.

SUMNER. Burke's Commoners, i. 61, Landed Gentry, 2, 3, 4, 5, 6, 7, 8. Burke's Family Records, 567. New England Register, viii. 128; ix. 303. History of the Old Chapel, Tockholes, by B. Nightingale, 213.

SUNDERLAND. Surtees Society, xxxvi. 21, 380. John Watson's History of Halifax, 255. Antiquarian Notices of Lupset, by J. H. (1851, edn.), 99. The Yorkshire Genealogist, i. 208. Bardsley's Registers of Ulverston, xcvii. Harleian Society, xxxviii. 636.

SUPPLE. J. H Hill's History of Langton, 22. Betham's Baronetage, v. 528.

SURDWAL. Jones' History of the County of Brecknock, ii. 205.

SURMAN. Burke's Landed Gentry, 2 add., 3, 4, 5, 6, 7.

SURREY. Manning and Bray's Surrey, i. xxvii. Banks' Dormant and Extinct Baronage, iii. 687. *See* DE WARREN.

SURRIDGE. Burke's Visitation of Seats and Arms, ii. 10.

SURTEES. Visitation of Durham 1575, (Newcastle, 1820, fol.) 22. Visitation of Durham, 1615, (Sunderland, 1820, fol.) 5. Burke's Royal Families, (London, 1851, 8vo.) ii. 19. Burke's Commoners, (of Redworth,) ii. 656, Landed Gentry, 2, 3, 4, 5, 6, 7, 8 ; (of Newcastle-on-Tyne,) Commoners, iv. 303; (of Hamsterley,) Landed Gentry, 2, 3, 4, 5, 6, 7, 8 ; (of Dinsdale,) 2, 3, 4, 5, 6, 7, 8. Hutchinson's History of Durham, iii. 145. Surtees' Durham, iii. 234; iv. 168. Foster's Visitations of Durham, 293, 295.

SUSSEX. Banks' Dormant and Extinct Baronage, iii. 694. *See* D'ESTE.

SUTCLIFFE. Harleian Society, xxxviii. 541.

SUTHERLAND. Case of George Sutherland of Forse, Esq., claiming the title of Earl of Sutherland, 1769, folio, pp. 7. Additional Case of same, 1770, folio, pp. 11. The Case of Elizabeth, claiming the Title and Dignity of Countess of Sutherland, by D. Dalrymple, 1770, 4to. The Additional Case of Elizabeth, Countess of Sutherland, by D. Dalrymple, 1770, 4to. A Genealogical History of the Earldom of Sutherland, by Sir R. Gordon. Edinburgh, 1813, folio. Wood's Douglas's Peerage of Scotland, i. 445 ; ii. 570. Claims preferred to the House of Lords in the Case of the Sutherland Peerage, by James Maidment. Edinburgh, 1840, 8vo. Caithness Family History, by John Henderson, 151-172, 333. Burke's Landed Gentry, (of Forse,) 7, 8; (of Skibo Castle,) 7, 8. *See* CASSILIS, GORDON.

SUTHERLAND-GRAEME. Burke's Landed Gentry, 7, 8.

SUTHERLAND-WALKER. Burke's Landed Gentry, 6.

SUTTON. Herald and Genealogist, ii. 491 ; v. 109. Churton's Life of Sir Richard Sutton, 533*. History of Dudley Castle, by C. Twamley, 1867, 8vo. Blomefield's Norfolk, x. 61. Collectanea Topographica et Genealogica, vi. 301. Topographer and Genealogist, ii. 99. Adlard's Sutton-Dudleys of England, etc., 16A. Cambridgeshire Visitation, edited by Sir T. Phillipps, 29. Burke's Commoners, (of Elton,) ii. 62, Landed Gentry, 2, 3, 4, 5 ; (of Rossway,) Landed Gentry, 2, 3, 4 ; (of Shardlow Hall,) 3 ; (of Scawby Hall,) 5, 6, 7, 8. Carthew's Hundred of Launditch, Part i. 340. Harleian Society, i. 77 ; iv. 141, 142, 186 ; viii. 476; xii. 78 ; xiii. 105 ; xviii. 220 ; xxii. 29 ; xxxvii. 12 ; xli. 105. History of Town and Port of Hull, by C. Frost, 99. History of the Colleges and Halls of Oxford, by Anthony à Wood, edited by John Gutch, 356. Earwaker's East Cheshire, ii. 443. Dickinson's History of Southwell, 2nd edition, 183. Blore's Rutland, 206, 207. Poulson's Holderness, ii. 326. Eyton's Antiquities of Shropshire, ii. 111. Burton's Description of Leicestershire, 201. Nichols' History of the County of Leicester, iv. 523*. Baker's Northampton, i. 470. Thoroton's Nottinghamshire, iii. 110, 177.

The Genealogist, iii. 351 ; v. 39 ; vi. 284 ; New Series, viii. 175 ; xiii. 40 ; xiv. 21 ; xviii. 30, 31. C. Brown's Annals of Newark-upon-Trent, 311. Collections by the Powys-land Club, vi. 34. Notes and Queries, 2 S. xi. 272 ; 3 S. i. 216 ; v. 447. Metcalfe's Visitation of Worcester, 1683, 90. Edmondson's Baronagium Genealogicum, iv. 343. Brydges' Collins' Peerage, ix. 385. Banks' Baronies in Fee, i. 424 ; ii. 139. Betham's Baronetage, iii. 394. Banks' Dormant and Extinct Baronage, ii. 170 ; iii. 475. Ormerod's Cheshire, iii. 761. Burke's Extinct Baronetcies. History of Powys Fadog, by J. Y. W. Lloyd, iii. 185. Churton's Lives of Wm. Smyth and Sir Richard Sutton, 534. A History of Devizes, 1859, 8vo., 553. Burke's Family Records, 567. The Gresley's of Drakelowe, by F. Madan, 283. Transactions of the Thoroton Society, 1901, *at end.* *See* DE SUTTON.

SUTTOR. Burke's Colonial Gentry, ii. 819.

SWABEY. Berry's Buckinghamshire Genealogies, 56. Burke's Landed Gentry, 2, 3, 4, 5, 6, 8.

SWAIN, or SWAINE. Burke's Landed Gentry, 2. Hutchins' Dorset, i. 515 ; iii. 453. Harleian Society, xxxvii. 297 ; xxxviii. 513. *See* SWAYNE.

SWAINSON. Burke's Landed Gentry, 3, 4, 5, 6.

SWAINSTON. Topographer and Genealogist, ii. 76. The Antiquities of Gainford, by J. R. Walbran, 57.

SWAINSTON-STRANGWAYES. Burke's Commoners, i. 655, Landed Gentry, 2, 3, 4, 5, 6.

SWALE. Surtees Society, xxxvi. 42. Foster's Visitations of York-shire, 276. Miscellanea Genealogica et Heraldica, New Series, ii. 44. Plantagenet - Harrison's History of Yorkshire, i. 236. Wotton's English Baronetage, iii. 45. Burke's Extinct Baronetcies.

SWALLOW. Harleian Society, xiii. 14, 106 ; xxxix. 903. Bysshe's Visitation of Essex, edited by J. J. Howard, 89.

SWAN. Berry's Kent Genealogies, 293. Burke's Landed Gentry, 2 add., 3, 4, 5, 6, 7. Burke's Visitation of Seats and Arms, i. 43. Harleian Society, xiii. 494 ; xxxvii. 256 ; xlii. 130. Burke's Extinct Baronetcies. New England Register, x. 44 ; xxxiii. 403. Burke's Family Records, 568.

SWANLAND. Harleian Society, xii. 39.

SWANLEY. Visitation of Middlesex, (Salisbury, 1820, fol.) 37. Foster's Visitation of Middlesex, 68.

SWANN. Burke's Landed Gentry, 2, 5, 6, 8. Howard's Visitation of England and Wales, i. 95 ; v. 101 ; Notes, ii. 99.

SWANSEY. Chetham Society, lxxxii. 48.

SWANSTON. Family Notes, by J. M. Browne, 95.

SWANTON. Visitation of Wiltshire, 1677, printed by Sir T. Phillipps, (Middle Hill, 1854, fol.).

SWANWICK. The Midland Antiquary, i. 141. Harleian Society, xxxvii. 364.

SWANZY. Burke's Family Records, 569.

SWASH. Collections relating to Henry Smith, 157.

SWAYNE. Visitation of Wiltshire, 1677, printed by Sir T. Phillipps,

(Middle Hill, 1854, fol.). Hoare's Wiltshire, V. iii. 49. Burke's Family Records, 574. *See* SWAIN.

SWEETMAN. Burke's Landed Gentry, 6, 7, 8.

SWETENHAM. Burke's Commoners, ii. 459, Landed Gentry, 2, 3, 4, 5, 6, 7, 8. Ormerod's Cheshire, iii. 560. Earwaker's East Cheshire, ii. 646. The Genealogist, New Series, xii. 110 ; xiii. 176 ; xv. 148 ; xvi. 165.

S WETT. New England Register, vi. 49.

S WETTENHAM. Burke's Royal Families, (London, 1851, 8vo.) i. 116. Burke's Commoners, i. 640, Landed Gentry, 2, 3, 4, 5, 6, 7, 8. Ormerod's Cheshire, iii. 74. Harleian Society, xviii. 220.

S WIFT, or SWIFTE. Burke's Landed Gentry, (of Lynn,) 2, 3, 4, 5 ; (of Swiftsheath,) 5, 6, 7, 8. Foster's Visitations of Yorkshire, 576. A Pedigree of Swift, showing their descent from the Families of Leech, Moody, Frettwell, and others. Large sheet, no heading, date, or printer's name. Harleian Society, xiv. 606 : xvii. 273 ; xx. 90 ; xxxix. 900. W. M. Mason's History of Cathedral of St. Patrick, Dublin, 225-227. Notes and Queries, 2 S. vi. 69, 138 ; 5 S. iv. 150, 269 ; v. 153. Metcalfe's Visitation of Worcester, 1683, 90. *See* SWYFT.

SWILLINGTON. Herald and Genealogist, iv. 225. Nichols' History of the County of Leicester, ii. 227. Thoroton's Nottinghamshire, iii. 50.

SWINBURN, or SWINBURNE. Surtees' Durham, i. 71 ; ii. 278. Harleian Society, xiii. 106. W. Paver's Pedigrees of Families of the City of York, 20. Burke's Landed Gentry, 2, 3, 4, 5, 6, 7, 8. Foster's Visitations of Yorkshire, 578. Hodgson's Northumberland, I. ii. 231, 310 ; II. ii. 230. Wotton's English Baronetage, iii. 167. Betham's Baronetage, ii. app. 1. Foster's Visitations of Durham, 297. Foster's Visitations of Northumberland, 116, 117. Foster's Visitations of Cumberland and Westmorland, 131. Chancellor's Sepulchral Monuments of Essex, 97. *See* SWYNBOURNE.

SWINCY. Chetham Society, lxxxii. 47.

SWINFEN, or SWYNFEN. Bibliotheca Topographica Britannica, ix. Part iv. 289. Harleian Society, ii. 134. Shaw's Staffordshire, ii. 28*. Nichols' History of the County of Leicester, iii. 982* ; iv. 546. Notes and Queries, 6 S. v. 352. Burke's Landed Gentry, 4, 5.

SWINFORD. The Manor of Minster, by H. W. Aldred, 45. The Genealogist, New Series, xiii. 242.

SWINGLEHURST. History of Chipping, by Tom C. Smith, 240.

SWINHOE. Raine's History of North Durham, 184, 237. Bateson's History of Northumberland, i. 212.

SWINNERTON, SWYNERTON, or SWYNNERTON. Burke's Commoners, iii. 601, Landed Gentry, 2. Jewitt's Reliquary, xviii. 167 ; xix. 99, 205 ; xx. 21, 104, 223 ; xxi. 34, 97, 169, 238 ; xxii. 152 ; xxiii. 39, 115. Baker's Northampton, i. 232. Visitation of Middlesex, (Salisbury, 1820, fol.) 28. Collections for a History of Staffordshire, William Salt Society, ii. part 2, 112. Banks' Baronies in

Fee, i. 426. Banks' Dormant and Extinct Baronage, i. 418.
Harleian Society, xvii. 273 ; xviii. 201, 203. Morant's Essex, ii.
184, 191. William Salt Society, New Series, iii. 73-120. Phillimore's London and Middlesex Note Book, 205. Foster's Visitation of Middlesex, 57. The Genealogist, New Series, xii. 225.
The Gresley's of Drakelow, by F. Madan, 284.

SWINTON. The Swintons of that Ilk, by A. C. Swinton. Alnwick,
1878. Another edn., Edinburgh, 1883, 4to. Burke's Royal
Families, (London, 1851, 8vo.) ii. 25. Burke's Commoners, (of
Swinton,) iii. 486, Landed Gentry, 2, 3, 4, 5, 6, 7, 8 ; (of Kim-
merghame,) Landed Gentry, 3, 4, 5, 6, 7, 8. Douglas's Baronage
of Scotland, 127. The Genealogist, New Series, xv. 133.

SWIRE. Burke's Commoners, ii. 342, Landed Gentry, 2, 3, 5, 6, 7, 8.
Foster's Yorkshire Families. Whitaker's Deanery of Craven, 156,
(218).

SWITHINBANK. Howard's Visitation of England and Wales, vii. 151.

SWORTON. Ormerod's Cheshire, i. 542.

SWYFT. Hunter's History of the Parish of Sheffield, 366. Hunter's
Deanery of Doncaster, i. 204. Harleian Society, xvi. 302. See
SWIFT.

SWYNBOURNE, or SWYNBORNE. Morant's Essex, ii. 234. Weale's
Quarterly Papers on Architecture, iii. (Suckling Papers,) 102.
The Genealogist, i. 305. Harleian Society, xvi. 303. See SWIN-
BURN.

SWYNNO. Harleian Society, xvi. 304. Foster's Visitations of Northumberland, 118.

SYBSAY. Harleian Society, xxxii. 275.

SYCILL. See CECIL.

SYDENHALE, or SYDENHALL. Baker's Northampton, i. 371. Miscellanea Genealogica et Heraldica, 2nd Series, iii. 318.

SYDENHAM. Collinson's Somerset, iii. 86, 448, 522, 547. Nichols'
Illustrations of Literary History, iv. 78. Visitation of Somersetshire, printed by Sir T. Phillipps, 140. Hutchins' Dorset, ii. 703,
705. Burke's Extinct Baronetcies. The Genealogist, New Series,
iii. 171. Miscellanea Genealogica et Heraldica, 2nd Series, iii.
325. Oxford Historical Society, xxiv. 101. Healey's History of
Part of West Somerset, 309. See SIDENHAM.

SYDLEY. Berry's Kent Genealogies, 230. Harleian Society, xlii. 60.

SYDNEY. An Account of the Sydney Family. Lee Priory Press,
1816, 8vo. Pedigree of Sydney of Penshurst, etc., [T. P.] 1857,
folio page. Burke's Landed Gentry, 2 supp., 3, 4. Manning and
Bray's Surrey, i. 94. Norfolk Archæology, vi. 263. Banks' Dormant and Extinct Baronage, iii. 462. Genealogies of Morgan and
Glamorgan, by G. T. Clark, 391. See SIDNEY.

SYDNOR. Suckling's History of Suffolk, i. 311. Metcalfe's Visitations
of Suffolk, 169.

SYDSERF. Notes and Queries, 3 S. vii. 21. Burke's Landed Gentry,
7, 8.

SYDYNGTON. Ormerod's Cheshire, iii. 728.

SYER. Burke's Landed Gentry, 5.

SYERSON. Jewitt's Reliquary, x. 191.

SYKES. Pedigree of the Family of Sykes of Bretton West, Co. York, broadside, *circa* 1877, printed for William Sykes, Surgeon. Sykes, sometime of Thornhill, Co. York, and of Basildon, Berks, 1859, 4to. pp. 16. Sykes of Leeds, 1859, 4to. pp. 4. Sykes of Ackworth, broadside, on vellum, *n.d.* Surtees Society, xxxvi. 166. Foster's Yorkshire Pedigrees. Continuations and Additions to the History of Bradford, by John James, App. xvii. Poulson's Holderness, ii. 91. Thoresby's Ducatus Leodiensis, 3, 34. Independancy at Brighouse, by J. H. Turner, 80. Notes and Queries, 2 S. xii. 297 ; 6 S. vi. 236. Betham's Baronetage, iv. 131, app. 16. Harleian Society, xxxvii. 150. Burke's Landed Gentry, 8.

SYLVESTER. Gens Sylvestrina, Memorials of some of my good and religious Ancestors, and Eleven Generations of a Puritan Family, by Joseph Hunter, 1846, 12mo. Bibliotheca Topographica Britannica, ix. Part iv. 129. *See* SILVESTER.

SYLYARD. Burke's Extinct Baronetcies. *See* SULIARD.

SYMCOCK, or SYMCOKE. Harleian Society, iv. 156. Weaver's Visitations of Somerset, 131.

SYMCOTTS. Visitation of Middlesex, (Salisbury, 1820, fol.) 18. Foster's Visitation of Middlesex, 35.

SYMES, or SYMMES. Burke's Landed Gentry, 2, and p. 72. Harleian Society, xi. 110. An Account of the Families of Boase, (Exeter, 1876, 4to.) 49. Metcalfe's Visitations of Northamptonshire, 139. New England Register, xiii. 135.

SYMKIN. Miscellanea Genealogica et Heraldica, New Series, iv. 354.

SYMMER. History of the Carnegies, by Wm. Fraser, (Edinburgh, 1867, 4to.) ii. 458.

SYMMINS, or SYMYNS. Pedigree of Symyns of Martell, Co. Pembroke, [T. P.] 1859, folio page. Dwnn's Visitations of Wales, i. 192.

SYMON. History of Powys Fadog, by J. Y. W. Lloyd, iii. 223.

SYMOND. The Genealogist, New Series, xiv. 255.

SYMONDS. Camden Society, lxxiv. 1. Morant's Essex, ii. 302. Visitation of Norfolk, published by Norfolk Archæological Society, i. 416. Tuckett's Devonshire Pedigrees, 40. Cambridgeshire Visitation, edited by Sir T. Phillipps, 29. Burke's Landed Gentry, 2, 3, 4, 5, 6, 7, 8. Harleian Society, vi. 280 ; xiii. 495 ; xvii. 274 ; xxi. 158 ; xxxii. 277. Hutchins' Dorset, ii. 237. Wright's Essex, i. 529. Burke's Colonial Gentry, ii. 573.

SYMONS. Burke's Commoners, (of Mynde Park,) iv. 645, Landed Gentry, 2, 3, 4, 5, 6, 7, 8 ; (of Hatt,) Landed Gentry, 4, 5, 6, 7, 8 ; (of Chaddlewood,) 2, 3, 4, 5, 6, 7, 8. A Complete Parochial History of the Co. of Cornwall, i. 114 ; iii. 372 ; iv. 113 supp. Visitation of Devon, edited by F. T. Colby, 196. Burke's Extinct Baronetcies. The Visitations of Cornwall, by J. L. Vivian, 614.

SYMPSON. Surtees Society, xxxvi. 124, 173. Harleian Society, iii. 44 ; xiii. 497 ; xvii. 274 ; xxxvii. 156. Surtees' Durham, i. 115, 303. *See* SIMPSON.

SYMS. Visitation of Gloucester, edited by T. F. Fenwick and W. C. Metcalfe, 183.

SYNGE. Burke's Landed Gentry, 2, 3, 4, 5, 6, 7. Notes and Queries, 1 S. viii. 327, 423; xi. 240; 8 S. xii. 316. Betham's Baronetage, v. 486. Harleian Society, xxix. 449.

SYNNOT. Burke's Landed Gentry, (of Drumcondra,) 2 supp.; (of Ballymoyer,) 2, 3, 4, 5, 6, 7, 8. Burke's Heraldic Illustrations, 98.

SYSLEY. Harleian Society, xiii. 14.

SYSTON. Jewitt's Reliquary, viii. 191; x. 191; xii. 124; xiv. 189.

TAAFE, or TAAFFE. Memoirs of the Family of Taaffe. Vienna, 1856, 8vo. Case of C. R. J. F. C., 10th Visct. Taaffe, on his claim to the title of Viscount Taaffe. London, 1856-7, 4to. pp. 57. Claim of Viscount Taaffe to Peerage of Taaffe, Sess. Papers, F of 1857, sess. 2; B of 1857-8; B of 1859, sess. 2; D of 1860. Burke's Landed Gentry, (of Smarmore,) 3, 4, 5, 7, 8; (of Woodfield,) 2, 3; (of Foxborough,) 6 supp. Herald and Genealogist, iii. 471. Notes and Queries, 2 S. x. 90, 136; 4 S. ix. 102, 168; 5 S. ii. 65, 425. Archdall's Lodge's Peerage, iv. 287.

TABER. Cambridgeshire Visitation, edited by Sir T. Phillipps, 30. Harleian Society, xli. 59.

TABLEY. Ormerod's Cheshire, i. 489.

TABOR. Harleian Society, xi. 110. Burke's Landed Gentry, 5, 6. Weaver's Visitations of Somerset, 23.

TACON. Burke's Landed Gentry, 8.

TADDY. Howard's Visitation of England and Wales, iii. 102.

TADLOW. Visitation of Warwickshire, 1619, published with Warwickshire Antiquarian Magazine, 128. Harleian Society, xii. 271.

TAILARD. Nichols' History of the County of Leicester, ii. 360. See TAYLARDE.

TAILBOIS. Banks' History of the Family of Marmyun, 126. Archæologia Æliana, 1st Series, ii. 384. Surtees' Durham, iii. 254, 382. Plantagenet-Harrison's History of Yorkshire, i. 514. The Genealogist, New Series, iii. 31, 107; xiii. 252; xiv. 28. Leicestershire Architectural Society, ii. 187. See TALBOYS, TAYLBOIS.

TAILBY. J. H. Hill's History of Langton, 325. Burke's Landed Gentry, 4, 5, 6, 7, 8. Fletcher's Leicestershire Pedigrees and Royal Descents, 138.

TAILGEBOSC. Munford's Analysis of Domesday Book of Co. Norfolk, 40.

TAILLEFER. The Genealogist, New Series, ii. 10.

TAILYOUR. Burke's Landed Gentry, 2, 3, 4, 5, 6, 7, 8. See TAYLEUR.

TAINTOR. New England Register, iii. 155.

TAIT. Burke's Landed Gentry, (of Millrig House,) 3, 4, 5, 6, 7, 8; (of Harviestoun,) 5, 6. Herald and Genealogist, vii. 381, 470.

TALBOR. Harleian Society, viii. 326.

TALBOT. Case of H. J. C., Earl Talbot, claiming to be Earl of Shrewsbury, 1857, fol. Proceedings before the Committee of Privileges on the Claim of Earl Talbot to the Earldom of Shrewsbury ; speech of Mr. Serjeant Byles, 1857, folio. Case on behalf of Lord E. B. F. Howard, etc., in opposition to the Case of H. J. C., Earl Talbot, claiming the Honour and Dignity of Earl of Shrewsbury. London, 1857 (?), fol. Proceedings before the Committee of Privileges on the claim of Earl Talbot to the Earldom of Shrewsbury ; the Speech of the Solicitor-General. London, 1858, fol. Proceedings, etc., judgment[1] and resolution of the Committee. London, 1858, fol. Claim of H. J. C., Earl Talbot, to the title of Earl of Shrewsbury, Sess. Papers, D. of 1857, sess. 2 ; A of 1857-8. Case of Earl of Shrewsbury to be Lord High Steward of Ireland, 20 pp. fol. Minutes of Evidence on the Earl of Shrewsbury's claim to be Lord High Steward of Ireland, 1863, folio, pp. 18. Additional Statement and Case of Major Talbot of Castle Talbot, in opposition to the claim of Earl Talbot to the Earldom of Shrewsbury. London, 1858, 4to., pp. 3, and three folding pedigrees. Case of Willm. Talbot of Ballimona, Co. Wexford, claiming to be Earl of Shrewsbury, 1857, 4to., pp. 3. Pedigree of Talbot of Lacock Abbey, Co. Wilts, by Sir T. Phillipps, Bart., Middle Hill, 1855, broadside. Pedigree of Talbot, Earl of Shrewsbury, [T. P.] 1856, folio page. Memoirs of the Noble Family of Talbot, by Charles Talbot, 1737, 8vo. Genealogical Memoir of the Ancient and Noble Family of Talbot, of Malahide, Co. Dublin. Dublin, 1829, folio. Claim of the Rt. Hon. James, Baron Talbot of Malahide, to Vote at Elections of Peers, Sess. Papers, 106 of 1851. The Great Governing Families of England, i. 239. Jacob's Peerage, i. 454. Clifford's Description of Tixall, 144. Morant's Essex, i. 341 ; ii. 109. J. Wilkinson's History of Broughton Gifford, folding plate. Berry's Buckinghamshire Genealogies, 19. Surtees Society, xxxvi. 38, 236-244. Nash's Worcestershire, i. 158, 241. Burke's Commoners, (of Castle Talbot,) iii. 359, Landed Gentry, 2, 3, 4, 5, 6, 7, 8 ; (of Ballytrent,) Landed Gentry, 3 ; (of Oakland,) 2, 5 ; (of Talbot Hall,) 2 ; (of Margam,) 3, 4, 5, 6, 7, 8 ; (of Lacock Abbey,) 2, 3, 4, 5, 6, 7, 8 ; (of Mount Talbot,) 3, 4, 5, 6, 7, 8 ; (of Temple Guiting,) 2, 3, 4, 5 ; (of Greenhill,) 2, 3, 4 ; 2nd edn., 740. Foster's Yorkshire Pedigrees. Foster's Visitations of Yorkshire, 46, 577. Chetham Society, lxxxi. 37 ; lxxxviii. 297-299 ; xcviii. 35 ; xcix. 145, 159, 161. Blore's History of South Winfield, in Nichols' Miscellaneous Antiquities, No. 3, 40. Topographer, (London, 1789-91, 8vo.) i. 572. Maclean's History of Trigg Minor, ii. 241. Harleian Society, viii. 63 ; xvi. 305-313 ; xvii. 275 ; xx. 90 ; xxvii. 131 ; xxix. 450, 454 ; xxxii. 279. Lipscombe's History of the County of Buckingham, i. 27. Hunter's History of the Parish of Sheffield, 61. Whitaker's Deanery of Craven, 24, (32). Nichols' History of the County of Leicester, iii. 1123. Dugdale's Warwickshire, 73, 388. Hutchins' Dorset, i. 667 ; ii. 541. Surtees' Durham, i. cxx. Whitaker's History of Whalley, ii. 377, 500, 514. Duncumb's History of the Co. of Hereford, ii. 380. Wiltshire Archæological Magazine, v.

---

[1] A folding pedigree from the Book of Benefactors is annexed to the copy of this in the Library of the Soc. Antiq.

267. Abram's History of Blackburn, 634, 642, 647, 654, 753. John D'Alton's History of Co. Dublin, 198. A Complete Parochial History of the County of Cornwall, i. 1. The Ulster Journal of Archæology, v. 275. Edmondson's Baronagium Genealogicum, ii. 83 ; iii. 303 ; vi. 53. Eastwood's History of Ecclesfield, 67. Holland's History of Worksop, 19. Archdall's Lodge's Peerage, ii. 16. Brydges' Collins' Peerage, iii. 1 ; v. 229. Banks' Baronies in Fee, i. 338, 427. Banks' Dormant and Extinct Baronage, i. 176 ; ii. 220, 304, 557. Burke's Extinct Baronetcies, 614. History of Ribchester, by T. C. Smith and J. Shortt, 251. New England Register, ix. 129. Notes and Queries, 7 S. ix. 447. The Genealogist, New Series, xiv. 20. *See* SHREWSBURY.

TALBOYS. History of the Town and School of Rugby, by N. H. Nicolas, 33. The Genealogist, ii. 51 ; v. 40. Fosbrooke's History of Gloucestershire, i. 398. Banks' Baronies in Fee, i. 429. Banks' Dormant and Extinct Baronage, i. 419, 434. The Visitation of Gloucester, edited by T. F. Fenwick and W. C. Metcalfe, 183. Harleian Society, xxi. 158. *See* TAILBOIS.

TALCOTT. Harleian Society, xiii. 497. Bysshe's Visitation of Essex, edited by J. J. Howard, 90. New England Register, l. 135.

TALK, or TALKE. Berry's Hampshire Genealogies, 224, 324.

TALKERNE. Metcalfe's Visitations of Suffolk, 103.

TALLAKERNE, or TALLAKARNE. Morant's Essex, ii. 340. Harleian Society, xiii. 293.

TALMACH, TALMASH, or TALMACHE. Kent's British Banner Displayed, 652. Gage's History of Thingoe Hundred, Suffolk, 427. Manning and Bray's Surrey, i. 368. Wood's Douglas's Peerage of Scotland, i. 486. Metcalfe's Visitations of Suffolk, 70, 169. F. G. Lee's History of Thame, 378. *See* TOLLEMACHE.

TAME. Baker's Northampton, i. 152. Harleian Society, xxi. 260.

TAMES. Journal of the British Archæological Association, xxvii. 110.

TAMHORNE. Shaw's Staffordshire, i. 93.

TAMLYN. Maclean's History of Trigg Minor, ii. 537.

TAMPION. Metcalfe's Visitations of Northamptonshire, 140.

TAMWORTH. Blore's Rutland, 55. Nichols' History of the County of Leicester, iii. 477. The Genealogist, v. 40.

TANAT. Dwnn's Visitations of Wales, i. 290. Archæologia Cambrensis, 4 S., vii. 29. Collections by the Powys-land Club, iv. 151 ; viii. 417. The Sheriffs of Montgomeryshire, by W. V. Lloyd, 161. History of Powys Fadog, by J. Y. W. Lloyd, iv. 194, 197. Harleian Society, xxix. 455.

TANFIELD. Morant's Essex, ii. 54. Bridges' Northamptonshire, by Rev. Peter Whalley, i. 263. Baker's Northampton, ii. 275. Harleian Society, xiii. 294, 498. Metcalfe's Visitations of Northamptonshire, 49, 140. Bysshe's Visitation of Essex, edited by J. J. Howard, 90.

TANGERD. Dwnn's Visitations of Wales, i. 128.

TANKARD, or TANCRED. Foster's Yorkshire Pedigrees. Foster's Visitations of Yorkshire, 216, 271, 278. Wotton's English

Baronetage, iii. 387. Betham's Baronetage, ii. 330. Surtees Society, xxxvi. 56. Pembrokeshire Pedigrees, 128. Harleian Society, xvi. 313. The Genealogist, New Series, x. 163. Burke's Landed Gentry, 8.

TANKE. Berry's Hampshire Genealogies, 234.

TANKERSLEY. Notes and Queries, 1st Series, x. 162.

TANNER. Burke's Commoners, ii. 214. Burke's Landed Gentry, 4, 5, 6, 7, 8. Harleian Society, vi. 195; ix. 278; xliii. 36. Polwhele's History of Cornwall, iv. 112. Miscellanea Genealogica et Heraldica, New Series, iii. 52. A Complete Parochial History of the County of Cornwall, iv. 164. An Historical Survey of Cornwall, by C. S. Gilbert, ii. 269. The Visitations of Cornwall, edited by J. L. Vivian, 447. Visitations of Devon, by J. L. Vivian, 575.

TANY. Morant's Essex, ii. 487. Banks' Dormant and Extinct Baronage, i. 179, See DE TANY.

TAPPAN. New England Register, xxxiv. 48.

TAPPENDEN. Hasted's Kent, iii. 236. Berry's Kent Genealogies, 487.

TAPPER. Burke's Colonial Gentry, i. 300.

TAPPS. Betham's Baronetage, iv. 240.

TARBOCK. Chetham Society, lxxxi. 91; cx. 131. Gregson's Fragments relative to the County of Lancaster, 242. Baines' History of the Co. of Lancaster, iv. 9. Harleian Society, xviii. 189.

TARBOX. New England Register, xlii. 27, 43, 91.

TARDY. Burke's Landed Gentry, 3, 4.

TARLETON. Burke's Landed Gentry, 5, 8. Ormerod's Cheshire, ii. 677. Liverpool as it was, etc., by Richard Brooke, 376. Burke's Extinct Baronetcies. Burke's Colonial Gentry, i. 299. Harleian Society, xxxvii. 131.

TASBURGH. Suckling's History of Suffolk, i. 198. Metcalfe's Visitations of Suffolk, 71.

TASH. Burke's Heraldic Illustrations, 145. Lipscombe's History of the County of Buckingham, iv. 530.

TASSELL. Metcalfe's Visitations of Suffolk, 72.

TASWELL. Miscellanea Genealogica et Heraldica, New Series, i. 254.

TATCHELL-BULLEN. Burke's Landed Gentry, 3, 4, 5, 6, 7, 8.

TATE. Burke's Commoners, (of Burleigh Park,) ii. 488, Landed Gentry, 2; (of Cheam Hall,) 5 supp., 6. Harleian Society, iv. 84; viii. 411. Brayley's History of Surrey, v. 303. Bridges' Northamptonshire, by Rev. Peter Whalley, i. 365. Nichols' History of the County of Leicester, ii. 888; iii. 1146. Yorkshire Archæological and Topographical Journal, vi. 197. Metcalfe's Visitations of Northamptonshire, 198.

TATESHALE, TATESHALL, TATTERSHALL, or TATTESHALL. Sketch of Tateshale, pedigree, [T. P.] 1851, broadside. Pedigree of Tateshale or Tatershall, [T. P.] fol. page. Collectanea Topographica et Genealogica, vii. 144. Gentleman's Magazine, 1826, ii. 408, 595. Memorials of the Church of Attleborough, by T. J. Barrett, 180.

Reports and Papers of the Associated Architectural Societies, iv. Part ii. 229. Topographical Account of Tattershall. Horncastle, 1813, 8vo. Burke's Landed Gentry, 2. Nichols' History of the County of Leicester, ii. 17*. Banks' Baronies in Fee, i. 430. Banks' Dormant and Extinct Baronage, i. 180. *See* DE TATTES-HALL, TETTERSHALL.

TATHAM. Genealogical Chart of Family of Tatham, by R. E. Tatham. Settle, 1875, fol. Burke's Landed Gentry, 2, 3, 4.

TATLOCK. Burke's Landed Gentry, 2. Chetham Society, lxxxviii. 300.

TATTERSALL. Fosbrooke's History of Gloucestershire, i. 478. History of Ufton Court, by A. M. Sharp, 111. Burke's Family Records, 576.

TATTON. Burke's Royal Families, (London, 1851, 8vo.) i. 6. Burke's Commoners, iii. 39, Landed Gentry, 2, 3, 4, 5, 6, 7, 8. J. P. Earwaker's East Cheshire, i. 318. Ormerod's Cheshire. iii. 609. Harleian Society, xviii. 221.

TAUBMAN-GOLDIE. Burke's Landed Gentry, 5, 6, 7, 8.

TAUNTON. Burke's Commoners, ii. 213, Landed Gentry, 2, 3, 4, 5. Polwhele's History of Cornwall, iv. 112. Burke's Visitation of Seats and Arms, ii. 32. A Complete Parochial History of the County of Cornwall, iii. 154. An Historical Survey of Cornwall, by C. S. Gilbert, ii. 270. Howard's Visitation of England and Wales, iv. 161, 167.

TAVER. Cambridgeshire Visitation, edited by Sir T. Phillipps, 30.

TAVERNER. Morant's Essex, i. 173. Clutterbuck's Hertford, iii. 8. Chauncy's Hertfordshire, 518. Maclean's History of Trigg Minor, iii. 165. Carthew's Hundred of Launditch, Part ii. 579. Harleian Society, xiii. 498; xiv. 606; xvii. 276; xix. 196; xxii. 95; xxxii. 280. Oxford Historical Society, xix. 38, 239, 240. Bysshe's Visitation of Essex, edited by J. J. Howard, 91.

TAWKE. Visitation of Sussex, 1570, printed by Sir T. Phillipps, (Middle Hill, fol.) 10. Dallaway's Sussex, i. 96.

TAWLEY. Tuckett's Devonshire Pedigrees, 125. Harleian Society, vi. 280. The Visitations of Devon, by J. L. Vivian, 726.

TAWYER. Metcalfe's Visitations of Northamptonshire, 49.

TAYLARDE. Camden Society, xliii. 87. Some Account of the Taylor Family, by P. A. Taylor, 3, 689. *See* TAILARD, TAYLOR.

TAYLBOYS. Hodgson's Northumberland, I. ii. 6. 61. *See* TAILBOYS.

TAYLER. Berry's Sussex Genealogies, 306. Surtees Society, xxxvi. 314. Visitation of Derbyshire, 1663-4, (Middle Hill, 1854, fol.) 7. The Genealogist, iii. 183. Harleian Society, xli. 48.

TAYLEUR, or TAILEUR. Burke's Commoners, iv. 156, Landed Gentry, 2, 3, 4, 5, 6, 7, 8. The Genealogist, vi. 97. *See* TAILYOUR.

TAYLOR, or TAILOR. Some Account of the Taylor Family, by P. A. Taylor. London, 1875, 4to. Pedigree of Taylor of Littleton, and Middle Hill, Co. Worc., [T. P.] 1860, folio page. Pedigree of Taylor of Littleton, with Bill of Complaint of Robt. Surman against Francis Taylor, [T. P.] 1860, 2 folio pages. Account of the Parish of Sandford, by Rev. Edw. Marshall, 62. Hasted's Kent, ii. 497; iii. 112. Berry's Berkshire Genealogies, 45. Berry's

Kent Genealogies, 162, 193, 277. Cambridgeshire Visitation, edited by Sir T. Phillipps, 31. Surtees Society, xxxvi. 16, 214. W. Paver's Pedigrees of Families of the City of York, 20. Visitation of Oxfordshire, 1634, printed by Sir T. Phillipps, (Middle Hill, fol.) 30. Burke's Royal Families, (London, 1851, 8vo.) i. 157. Burke's Commoners, (of Bifrons,) iii. 107, Landed Gentry, 2, 3, 4, 5, 6, 8; (of Carshalton Park,) 8; (of Rendcombe Park,) 8; (of Clifton,) Commoners, iv. 7; (of Ogwell,) Commoners, iv. 445, Landed Gentry, 2, 3, 4, 5; (of Pennington,) Commoners, iv. 237, Landed Gentry, 2, 3, 4, 5, 6, 8; (of Dunkerron,) Commoners, iv. 288, Landed Gentry, 3, 4; (of the Brooms,) Landed Gentry, 2; (of Chyknell,) 2, 3, 4, 5, 6; (of Kirkham Abbey,) 2, 3, 4, 5, 6; (of Hillbrook,) 8; (of Erlestoke Park,) 3, 4, 5, 6, 7, 8; (of Moreton Hall,) 3, 4; (of Radcliffe-on-Trent,) 3, 4, 5 and supp., 6, 7, 8; (of Strensham,) 2, 3, 4, 5, 6, 7, 8; (of Moseley Hall,) 2, 3, 4, 5, 6, 7; (of Todmorden,) 2, 3, 4, 5, 6, 7; (of Ardgillan Castle,) 3, 4, 5, 6, 7, 8; (of Burnham,) 5, 6, 7; (of Eccleston,) 5, 6, 7, 8; (of Tyn Llwyn,) 6, 7, 8; (of Chipchase,) 6, 7, 8; (of Castle Taylor,) 7, 8. Harleian Society, v. 296; xvii. 276; xix. 144; xxi. 159; xxii. 165; xxix. 457; xxxvii. 234, 237; xxxviii. 578, 657; xxxix. 1104, 1122; xl. 1198, 1224; xlii. 54, 69. Burke's Visitation of Seats and Arms, ii. 72; 2nd Series, ii. 42. Burke's Heraldic Illustrations, 4, 69, 115. Burke's Royal Descents and Pedigrees of Founders' Kin, *Founders' Kin*, 2. Burke's Authorized Arms, 51. Antiquities and Memoirs of the Parish of Myddle, written by Richard Gough, 1700, (folio,) 64. North's Church Bells of Leicestershire, 73, 74. North's Church Bells of Northamptonshire, 94, 95. Fosbrooke's History of Gloucestershire, i. 386. John D'Alton's History of Co. Dublin, 288. O'Hart's Irish Pedigrees, 2nd Series, 350. Notes and Queries, 1 S. v. 370, 473; 2 S. xii. 519; 3 S. i. 75, 317. The Genealogist, vii. 269. Metcalfe's Visitation of Worcester, 1683, 91. Monken Hadley, by F. C. Cass, 154. Burke's Extinct Baronetcies. Metcalfe's Visitations of Suffolk, 207. Norfolk Archæology, viii. 317. Documentary Notes relating to the District of Turton, by J. C. Scholes, 118. Hulbert's Annals of Almondbury, 247. Bateson's History of Northumberland, i. 339. Harvey's Hundred of Willey, 151. Caithness Family History, by John Henderson, 298. Memoirs of the House of White of. Wallingwells, 27. Pedigree of the Taylors and Barlows, by J. C. Scholes, 1882, single sheet. Metcalfe's Visitations of Northamptonshire, 200. Genealogies of Morgan and Glamorgan, by G. T. Clark, 505. Fishwick's History of Rochdale, 334. New England Register, ii. 398. Miscellanea Genealogica et Heraldica, 2nd Series, v. 169. Howard's Visitation of England and Wales, iii. 95. The Descendants of John Backhouse, by J. Foster, 61. Records of Batley, by M. Sheard, 281. Burke's Family Records, 579. History of Doddington, by R. E. G. Cole, 67. Muskett's Suffolk Manorial Families, i. 241-248. *See* LE TAYLOR, SHAWE-TAYLOR.

TAYLOR-DOMVILLE. Burke's Landed Gentry, 2 add., 3.

TAYLOR-SMITH. Burke's Landed Gentry, 2 add., 3, 4, 5, 6, 7, 8.
TAYSPILL. Cyclostyle Pedigrees, by J. J. Green.
TEASDALE. Surtees' Durham, i. 82. Burton's History of Hemingborough, 114. *See* TESEDALE.
TEBUT. New England Register, viii. 130.
TECON. Clutterbuck's Hertford, ii. 541.
TEGIN. History of Powys Fadog, by J. Y. W. Lloyd, iii. 83.
TEISSONIERE. Miscellanea Genealogica et Heraldica, 3rd Series, ii 292.
TEMMES. Bowles' History of Lacock Abbey, 291. Visitatio Comitatus Wiltoniæ, 1623, printed by Sir T. Phillipps. The Genealogist, New Series, xiii. 24.
TEMPEST, or TEMPESTE. Case of Sir Charles Robert Tempest, claiming to be a co-heir to the Barony of Scales. London, *n.d.*, folio, pp. 49. Claim of Sir C. R. Tempest, to the Barony of De Scales, Sess. Papers, A of 1857 ; C of 1857, sess. 2 ; E of 1857-8 ; D of 1859, sess. 2 ; B of 1860 ; C. of 1863 ; H of 1864 ; C of 1865. Hasted's Kent, iii. 47. Visitation of Durham, 1615, (Sunderland, 1820, fol.) 15. Surtees Society, xxxvi. 319, 360 ; xli. 84, 103. Burke's Royal Families, (London, 1851, 8vo.) i. 19. Burke's Commoners, i. 474, Landed Gentry, 5, 6, 8. Foster's Yorkshire Pedigrees. Foster's Visitations of Yorkshire, 293, 357. History of Hartlepool, by Sir C. Sharp, (1816, 8vo.) 74. Burke's Heraldic Illustrations, 9. Hutchinson's History of Durham, iii. xxx. Thoresby's Ducatus Leodiensis, 205. Whitaker's Loidis and Elmete, 250. Whitaker's Deanery of Craven, 75, 83, 391, (96, 106). A Genealogical Account of the Lords of Studley Royal, by J. R. Walbran. Surtees' Durham, ii. 271, 275, 327 ; iv. 93. Howard's Visitation of England and Wales, i. 35 ; ii. 139 ; Notes, ii. 12. Pedigrees of the Leading Families of Lancashire, published by Joseph Foster, (London, 1872, fol.). The New History of Yorkshire, commencing with Richmondshire, by Genl. Plantagenet-Harrison, (London, 1872, fol.) Part i. 31. Plantagenet-Harrison's History of Yorkshire, i. 105. Fosbrooke's History of Gloucestershire, ii. 241, 244. Foley's Records of the English Province S. J., v. 720. Harleian Society, xvi. 314. Wotton's English Baronetage, i. 538 ; iii. 423 ; iv. 404. Betham's Baronetage, ii. 345. Burke's Extinct Baronetcies. The Northern Genealogist, by A. Gibbons, i. 5. The Genealogist, New Series, x. 52. Pedigrees of the Leading Families of Yorkshire, by Joseph Foster. Foster's Visitations of Durham, 299. Burke's Family Records, 582. Croston's edn. of Baines's Lancaster, iv. 416. Annals of the English Benedictines of Ghent, 189. *See* PLUMBE-TEMPEST.
TEMPLAR. The Genealogist, iii. 311.
TEMPLE. The Family of Temple, reprinted from the ' Cornhill Magazine,' *see* Three Hundred Years of a Norman House, by James Hannay. London, 1867, 8vo. Herald and Genealogist, iii. 385-410, 529 ; iv. 8 ; viii. 510. Burke's Landed Gentry, (of Bishopstrow,) 2, 3, 4, 5, 6, 7, 8 ; (of Over Dinsdale,) 2. Harleian

Society, ii. 167. Lipscombe's History of the County of Buckingham, iii. 85. Nichols' History of the County of Leicester, iv. 958-962. Dugdale's Warwickshire, 523. Hoare's Wiltshire, III. ii. 73. Manning and Bray's Surrey, iii. 139. Baker's Northampton, i. 734. An Historical Survey of Cornwall, by C. S. Gilbert, i. 438. Notes and Queries, 2 S. vi. 157 ; xii, 405, 438 ; 3 S. ii, 391. The Genealogist, vii. 250. Edmondson's Baronagium Genealogicum, iii. 278. Archdall's Lodge's Peerage, v. 225. Betham's Baronetage, i. 136. Banks' Dormant and Extinct Baronage, iii. 198. Burke's Extinct Baronetcies. New England Register, x. 73. *See* DE TEMPLE.

TEMPLER. Burke's Landed Gentry, 2, 3, 4, 5, 6, 7, 8.

TEMYS. Visitation of Sussex, 1570, printed by Sir T. Phillipps, (Middle Hill, fol.) 10.

TENCH. Morant's Essex, i. 25. Burke's Landed Gentry, 4, 5. Monken Hadley, by F. C. Cass, 34. Burke's Extinct Baronetcies. Harleian Society, xvii. 278 ; xlii. 79.

TENCHE. Berry's Kent Genealogies, 145.

TENDERING, or TENDRING. Blomefield's Norfolk, v. 336. Morant's Essex, ii. 16. Berry's Essex Genealogies, 143. Harleian Society, xiii. 107, 296, 499. Metcalfe's Visitations of Suffolk, 181. Bysshe's Visitation of Essex, edited by J. J. Howard, 91, 92.

TENISON, or TENNYSON. Burke's Landed Gentry, (of Loughbawn,) 7, 8 ; (of Kilronan,)·2, 3, 4, 5, 6 supp. ; (of Portnelligan,) 2, 3, 4, 5, 6, 7, 8. Shirley's History of the County of Monaghan, 255. Burke's Colonial Gentry, ii. 507. Burke's Patrician, iv. 67. Foster's Collectanea Genealogica, i. 56. Miscellanea Genealogica ct Heraldica, 3rd Series, ii. 141.

TENNANT, or TENANT. Burke's Landed Gentry, (of Chapel House,) 2, 3, 4, 5, 6, 8 ; (of Cadoxton,) 5 supp., 6, 7, 8 ; (of Needwood House,) 5 supp., 6, 7, 8 ; (of the Glen,) 6 ; (of Scarcroft and Kildwick,) 7, 8. Foster's Visitations of Yorkshire, 578. Shaw's Staffordshire, ii. 107*. Harleian Society, xiii. 500. Burke's Family Records, 589.

TENNYSON-D'EYNCOURT. Genealogical History of the Family of Tennyson-D'Eyncourt, by J. B. Burke. London, 1846, 12mo. Burke's Patrician, iv. 67. Burke's Landed Gentry, 2, 3, 4, 5, 6, 7, 8.

TERNAN. Burke's Visitation of Seats and Arms, ii. 13.

TERRICK. Harleian Society, xvii. 279. Visitations of Staffordshire, 1614 and 1663-4, William Salt Society, 283.

TERRINGHAM. Visitation of Suffolk, edited by J. J. Howard, ii. 212.

TERROT. Notes and Queries, 7 S., iii. 256.

TERRY, or TERREY. Harleian Society, xvii. 278. Burke's Landed Gentry, 8.

TESCHEMAKER. Burke's Colonial Gentry, i. 364.

TESEDALE. Plantagenet-Harrison's History of Yorkshire, i. 387. *See* TEASDALE.

TETLAW, or TETLQW. Butterworth's Account of the Town, etc., of

Oldham, 70. Harleian Society, xiii. 501. Chetham Society, lxxxii. 11. Jacob's Peerage, ii. 337. Croston's edn. of Baines's Lancaster, ii. 379.

TETLEY. Harleian Society, xxxii. 281.

TETTERSHALL. The Genealogist, vi. 98.

TEVEREY. Thoroton's Nottinghamshire, ii. 194. The Genealogist, New Series, xii. 175.

TEW. Burke's Landed Gentry, 5, 6, 7, 8.

TEY. East Anglian, i. 96. Morant's Essex, i. 412, 418, 432; ii. 183, 196, 197, 202. Wright's Essex, i. 413; ii. 730. Harleian Society, xiii. 15, 108, 297.

TEYES. See TYES.

TEYNHAM. Hasted's Kent, ii. 687.

THACKER. History of Repton, by Robert Bigsby, 93. Visitation of Derbyshire, 1663-4, (Middle Hill, 1854, fol.) 7. The Genealogist, iii. 183.

THACKERAY. The Pedigree of Thackeray. Westminster, 1864, 8vo. Burke's Landed Gentry, 4. Herald and Genealogist, ii. 315, 440, 455. Monken Hadley, by F. C. Cass, 74. Burke's Family Records, 592.

THACKWELL. Gentleman's Magazine, 1864, i. 640. Burke's Landed Gentry, 3, 4, 5, 6 and supp., 7. 8. Notes and Queries, 2 S. viii. 310, 439; xii. 528.

THAME. Harleian Society, ii. 130. Nichols' History of the County of Leicester, iv. 370.

THAMENHORNE. Shaw's Staffordshire, i. 162.

THARP. Burke's Landed Gentry, 4, 5, 6, 7, 8.

THATCHAM. Visitatio Comitatus Wiltoniæ, 1623, printed by Sir T. Phillipps. Hoare's Wiltshire, V. i. 58. The Genealogist, New Series, xiii. 24.

THATCHER, or THECCHER. Berry's Sussex Genealogies, 157. Horsfield's History of Lewes, ii. 189. Visitation of Sussex, 1570, printed by Sir T. Phillipps, (Middle Hill, fol.) 11. Harleian Society, xvii. 281. Camoys Peerage Evidence, 453. New England Register, viii. 183; xiii. 245; xiv. 11; xxxvii. 12.

THAXTER. East Anglian, iii. 35.

THAYER. Harleian Society, xvii. 280. Bysshe's Visitation of Essex, edited by J. J. Howard, 92. New England Register, xxvii. 123. Notes and Queries, 6 S., xii. 31, 196.

THEED. Baker's Northampton, i. 435.

THELLUSON. Treatise on the Thelluson Act, by J. F. Hargrave, 1842, 8vo. Burke's Landed Gentry, 5, 6, 7, 8. Hunter's Deanery of Doncaster, i. 318.

THELWAL, or THELWALL. Burke's Landed Gentry, 2. Dwnn's Visitations of Wales, ii. 113, 336. Memoirs of Gabriel Goodman, by R. Newcome, App. S. History of Powys Fadog, by J. Y. W. Lloyd, iv. 305-22; vi. 487.

THEMELBY. Dwnn's Visitations of Wales, ii. 217. See THIMELBY.

THEOBALD. Harleian Society, viii. 222.

THERLAND. Harleian Society, iv. 154; xliii. 190. See THURLAND.

THE   769   THO

THETFORD. Harleian Society, xvii. 281 ; xxxii. 281.
THETOFTE. The Genealogist, v. 41.
THICKBROME. Nichols' History of the County of Leicester, iii. 636.
THICKNES, THICKNESS, or THICKNESSE. Dwnn's Visitations of
Wales, ii. 188. Harleian Society, xii. 145. Burke's Authorized
Arms, 193. Burke's Landed Gentry, 2, 4, 5, 6, 7, 8. Foster's
Lancashire Pedigrees. Visitation of Staffordshire, (Willm. Salt
Soc.) 138. Visitations of Staffordshire, 1614 and 1663-4, William
Salt Society, 286.
THIERY. Notes and Queries, 1 S. xi. 389.
THIMBLEBY. Foster's Visitations of Yorkshire, 578. The Genea-
logist, v. 114; vi. 285. See THYMILBY.
THIMBLETHORP. Visitation of Oxfordshire, 1634, printed by Sir T.
Phillipps, (Middle Hill, fol.) 31. Harleian Society, v. 329.
THIMELBY. Foley's Records of the English Province S. J., v. 598.
See THEMELBY.
THIRKELD. Foster's Visitations of Yorkshire, 120, 166. Archæo-
logia Æliana, 2nd Series, iii. 97, 99. Surtees' Durham, i. 197.
Foster's Visitations of Durham, 301.
THIRKELL. Shaw's Staffordshire, i. 92. Visitation of Staffordshire,
(Willm. Salt Soc.) 127.
THIRLAND. Surtees Society, xli. 8. See THURLAND.
THIRLEWALL, or THIRLWALL. The Genealogist, ii. 253. Hodgson's
Northumberland, III. ii. 145. Foster's Visitations of North-
umberland, 119.
THISTLETHWAYT, or THISTLETHWAITE. Burke's Commoners, iii. 472,
Landed Gentry, 2, 3, 4, 5, 6, 7, 8. Visitatio Comitatus Wil-
toniæ, 1623, printed by Sir T. Phillipps. Hoare's Wiltshire, V.
i. 46. Harleian Society, xiii. 501. Visitation of Wiltshire,
edited by G. W. Marshall, 3, 4. Pedigree of Family of Powell,
by Edgar Powell, 86.
THOATTES. Surtees Society, xli. 96.
THOMAS. Hasted's Kent, ii. 243, 382. Berry's Sussex Genealogies,
290, 299. Dwnn's Visitations of Wales, i. 47, 58, 60, 125, 159,
192, 201 ; ii. 151-153, 190, 271. Glamorganshire Pedigrees,
edited by Sir T. Phillipps, 7, 13, 14, 22, 33, 34, 40, 41. Berry's
Kent Genealogies, 416. Visitation of Middlesex, (Salisbury,
1820, fol.) 44. Burke's Royal Families, (London, 1851, 8vo.) ii.
166. Burke's Commoners, (of Gellywernen,) i. 628, Landed
Gentry, 2, 3, 4, 5, 6 ; (of Hereford,) Landed Gentry, 2, 3 ; (of
Llwyn Madoc,) 2, 3, 4, 5, 6, 7, 8 ; (of Llanbradach,) 4, 5, 6, 7, 8 ;
(of Pwllywrach,) 4 ; (of Trevor,) 7, 8 ; (of Coedhelen,) 7, 8 ; (of
Brooklands,) 7, 8 ; (of Welfield House,) 2, 3, 4, 5, 6, 7, 8 ; (of
Ratton,) 2, 3, 4, 5, 6, 7, 8. Maclean's History of Trigg Minor,
i. 305 ; ii. 171, 174. Gage's History of Thingoe Hundred,
Suffolk, 359. Dallaway's Sussex, II. i. 44, 187. Harleian Society,
ix. 215 ; xlii. 194. Caermarthenshire Pedigrees, 64, 66. Cardiganshire Pedigrees, 114. Hoare's Wiltshire, I. ii. 261. Meyrick's History of the Co. of Cardigan, 160. T. Nicholas' County
Families of Wales, 952. The Genealogist, iii. 312. Castles,

49

Mansions, and Manors of Western Sussex, by D. G. C. Elwes and
C. J. Robinson, 276.   Memoir of Gabriel Goodman, by R. New-
come, App. S.   Collections by the Powys-land Club, viii. 81.
Wotton's English Baronetage, iv. 55.   Betham's Baronetage,
iii. 110, 344.   Burke's Extinct Baronetcies.   The Visitations of
Cornwall, edited by J. L. Vivian, 449-452.   History of Powys
Fadog, by J. Y. W. Lloyd, iv. 121, 371 ; v. 67, 307.   Foster's
Visitatior of Middlesex, 81.   Genealogies of Morgan and Gla-
morgan, by G. T. Clark, 30, 89-92, 108, 191, 263, 272, 444, 505.
Howard's Visitations of England and Wales, vi. 46.   *See* GORING-
THOMAS.

THOMAS YR ARGLWYDD (Prior of Kaervyrddyn).   Dwnn's Visitations of Wales, i. 94.

THOMELEY. Lipscombe's History of the County of Buckingham, i. 585.

THOMLINSON. Visitation of Durham, 1575, (Newcastle, 1820, fol.)
37.   Visitation of Durham, 1615, (Sunderland, 1820, fol.) 58.
Surtees Society, xxxvi. 66, 110, 376.   Burke's Landed Gentry, 2.
Foster's Visitations of Yorkshire, 217.   Burke's Heraldic Illustra-
tions, 93.   Surtees' Durham, ii. 117.   East Barnet, by F. C. Cass,
Part i. 43.   Foster's Visitations of Durham, 303.   The Genealogist,
New Series, xii. 262-268.   *See* TOMLINSON.

THOMPSON. Morant's Essex, ii. 375.   Surtees Society, xxxvi. 122,
143, 219.   Surrey Archæological Collections, iii.   Burke's Landed
Gentry, (of Kirby Hall,) 2, 3, 4, 5 ; (of Sheriff Hutton,) 2, 3, 4,
5, 6 ; (of Annaverna,) 3, 4 ; (of Clonfin,) 2, 3, 4, 5, 6, 7, 8 ; (of Ash-
down Park,) 6, 7, 8 ; (of Muckamore Abbey,) 6, 7, 8.   Foster's
Yorkshire Pedigrees.   Foster's Visitations of Yorkshire, 175.
Herald and Genealogist, vi. 650.   Harleian Society, viii. 45, 189 ;
xvii. 283 ; xxii. 97 ; xxxviii. 531, 649 ; xxxix. 1000.   Lipscombe's
History of the County of Buckingham, iv. 188.   Blore's Rutland,
177.   Poulson's Holderness, ii. 63.   Archæologia Æliana, 1st
Series, ii. 176.   The Citizens of London and their Rulers, by
B. B. Orridge, 185.   The Genealogist, iii. 312 ; v. 47 ; New Series,
xiii. 41.   The Tyldesley Diary, edited by J. Gillow and A. Hewitson, 163.   Betham's Baronetage, iv. 382.   Banks' Dormant and
Extinct Baronage, iii. 345.   Burke's Extinct Baronetcies, and 638.
Carthew's West and East Bradenham, 9, 39.   Nicholl's Account
of the Company of Ironmongers, 2nd edn., 612.   Carthew's Hundred of Launditch, Part iii. 469.   Bysshe's Visitation of Essex,
edited by J. J. Howard, 93.   New England Register, iv. 180.

THOMS. Harleian Society, ix. 216, 217.   Burke's Family Records,
569.

THOMSON. Hasted's Kent, iii. 736.   Berry's Hertfordshire Genealogies, 50.   Berry's Kent Genealogies, 16, 459.   Archæologia
Cantiana, iv. 261.   Burke's Landed Gentry, (of Castleton,) 3, 4,
5, 6 ; (of Banchory,) 2, 3, 4, 5, 6 ; (of Kentfield,) 3, 4 ; (of
Treveryan,) 2, 3, 4 ; (of Broomford,) 5, 6, 7.   Foster's Visitations
of Yorkshire, 300, 634.   Burke's Royal Descents and Pedigrees
of Founders' Kin, 22, 108.   An Account of the Families of Boase,
(Exeter, 1876, 4to.) 50.   An Historical Survey of Cornwall, by

C. S. Gilbert, ii. 272. Walter Wood's East Neuk of Fife, 303.
Harleian Society, xvii. 282; xix. 146; xlii. 10. Genealogical
Gleanings in England, by H. F. Waters, i. 67. New England
Register, xxxviii. 318. Burke's Colonial Gentry, i. 365. *See*
WHITE-THOMSON.

THOMSON-CARMICHAEL. Burke's Landed Gentry, 6.

THONER. Miscellanea Genealogica et Heraldica, 2nd Series, i. 37.

THORESBY. Gentleman's Magazine, 1853, i. 172. Blomefield's Nor-
folk, viii. 422. Kent's British Banner Displayed, 442. Surtees
Society, xxxvi. 248. Foster's Yorkshire Pedigrees. Foster's
Visitations of Yorkshire, 635. Whitaker's History of Richmond-
shire, i. 370. Thoresby's Ducatus Leodiensis, 71. Harleian
Society, xiii. 502; xxxix. 866.

THORN, or THORNE. Harleian Society, vi. 255, 281; xvii. 283;
xxi. 160; xliii. 41. Westcote's Devonshire, edited by G. Oliver
and P. Jones, 525. Visitation of Devon, edited by F. T. Colby,
196. Bedfordshire Notes and Queries, iii. 257. The Visitations
of Devon, by J. L. Vivian, 727.

THORNBOROUGH, or THORNBURGH. Surtees Society, xli. 98. Visitation of Westmorland, 1615, (London, 1853,) 26. Burke's Commoners, iv. 300. Foster's Visitations of Yorkshire, 148. Harleian
Society, xvi. 316. Metcalfe's Visitation of Worcester, 1683, 92.
Berry's Hampshire Genealogies, 86. Visitations of Staffordshire,
1614 and 1663-4, William Salt Society, 286. Stockdale's Annals
of Cartmel, 470. Nicolson and Burn's Westmorland and Cumberland, i. 117.

THORNEHOLME. Foster's Visitations of Yorkshire, 166.

THORNES. Harleian Society, xxix. 458.

THORNETON. Surtees Society, xxxvi. 67. Chetham Society, xcix.
25. Ormerod's Cheshire, ii. 17. *See* THORNTON.

THORNEWILL. Burke's Landed Gentry, 5, 6.

THORNEYCROFT, or THORNICROFT. Burke's Landed Gentry, 3, 4, 5,
6, 7, 8. Earwaker's East Cheshire, ii. 401. Wotton's English
Baronetage, iv. 90. Burke's Extinct Baronetcies. *See* THORNY-
CROFT.

THORNHAUGH, THORNHAGH, or THORNHEGH. Harleian Society, iv.
69. Jewitt's Reliquary, xvi. 41, 103, 197; xvii. 235; xviii. 15.
Thoroton's Nottinghamshire, iii. 296. Transactions of the Thoroton Society, 1901, *at end*.

THORNHILL, or THORNHULL. Hasted's Kent, ii. 580; iii. 170. Berry's
Kent Genealogies, 466. Surtees Society, xxxvi. 308. Burke's
Landed Gentry, (of Woodleys,) 2, 3, 4, 5, 6; (of Stanton,) 2, 3, 4,
5, 6, 7, 8; (of Fixby,) 3, 4, 5, 6, 7; (of Diddington,) 5, 6, 7, 8; (of
Riddlesworth,) 5, 6. Foster's Yorkshire Pedigrees. Foster's
Visitations of Yorkshire, 579. Thoresby's Ducatus Leodiensis, 115.
John Watson's History of Halifax, 188. Harleian Society, xvi.
317; xx. 91; xxxvii. 240. Burke's Extinct Baronetcies. The
Genealogist, vi. 286; New Series, iii. 171; x. 173; xiii. 25.
Visitatio Comitatus Wiltoniæ, 1623, printed by Sir T. Phillipps.
Hutchins' Dorset, iv. 417.

THORNHURST. Burke's Extinct Baronetcies. Hutchins' Dorset, i. 438.

THORNLEY. Burke's Landed Gentry, 2, 3, 4. History of Chipping, by Tom C. Smith, 263.

THORNTON. Pedigree of Thornton of Dover, etc., by H. J. Thornton, 1898. 2 sheets. Surtees Society, xxxvi. 250; lxii. 344. Cambridgeshire Visitation, edited by Sir T. Phillipps, 31. Burke's Commoners, ii. 329. Burke's Royal Families, (London, 1851, 8vo.) i. 193. Burke's Commoners, (of Brockhall,) ii. 495, Landed Gentry, 2, 3, 4, 5, 6, 7, 8; (of Birkin,) Landed Gentry, 2 supp., 3, 4, 5, 6, 7, 8; (of Grenville,) 3, 4; (of Skerton,) 5, 7; (of Highcross,) 8; (of Westbrook,) 8. Foster's Yorkshire Pedigrees. Foster's Visitations of Yorkshire, 210, 265, 296, 579, 580. Foster's Lancashire Pedigrees. Chetham Society, lxxxii. 113. Hodgson's Northumberland, I. ii. 316. Bridges' Northamptonshire, by Rev. Peter Whalley, i. 22. Thoresby's Ducatus Leodiensis, 22. Baker's Northampton, i. 115. Cussan's History of Hertfordshire, Parts ix. and x. 14. The Genealogist, ii. 149; New Series, xv. 246. Independency at Brighouse, by J. H. Turner, 77. Harleian Society, xvi. 318; xviii. 83, 111; xxxvii. 139; xxxviii. 767; xli. 32. Burke's Colonial Gentry, i. 282; ii. 424. Metcalfe's Visitations of Northamptonshire, 142. Bysshe's Visitation of Essex, edited by J. J. Howard, 93. Foster's Visitations of Northumberland, 120. Burke's Family Records, 597. Yorkshire Archæological Society, Record Series, xxx. 385. See THORNETON, TODD-THORNTON.

THORNTON-DUESBURY. Howard's Visitation of England and Wales, ix. 62.

THORNTON-HEYSHAM. Berry's Hertfordshire Genealogies, 91.

THORNYCROFT. Burke's Landed Gentry, 7, 8. Ormerod's Cheshire, iii. 733. J. P. Jones's History of Tettenhall, 279. See THORNEY-CROFT.

THOROLD. The Descent of the Family of Thorold, by the Ven. Edward Trollope, M.A., F.S.A. Lincoln, 1874, 4to. Strype's Stow's Survey, Book v. 155. Cambridgeshire Visitation, edited by Sir. T. Phillipps, 31. Herald and Genealogist, iii. 421. Account of the Company of Ironmongers, by John Nicholl, 2nd edn., 564. Harleian Society, viii. 104, 484; xvii. 284; xli. 63. Burke's Landed Gentry, 6, 7, 8. Foley's Records of the English Province S. J., v. 612. Wotton's English Baronetage, ii. 338; iv. 250. The Genealogist, v. 43. Burke's Extinct Baronetcies. Miscellanea Genealogica et Heraldica, 2nd Series, ii. 297.

THOROTON. Thoroton's Nottinghamshire, i. 235.

THOROWGOOD, or THOROGOOD. Visitation of Middlesex, (Salisbury, 1820, fol.) 34. Harleian Society, xiv. 607; xvii. 286; xxii. 98, 117. Metcalfe's Visitations of Northamptonshire, 143. Foster's Visitation of Middlesex, 68.

THORP, or THORPE. Blomefield's Norfolk, v. 143. Burke's Landed Gentry, (of Headingley,) 2, 3, 4; (of Ryton,) 2, 3, 4; (of Coddington,) 6, 7, 8. Hodgson's Northumberland, III. ii. 336. Poulson's Holderness, ii. 513. Baker's Northampton, i. 176. Page's History of Suffolk, 398, 527. Plantagenet-Harrison's History of Yorkshire, i. 430. Hasted's Kent, ii. 524. Berry's Sussex Genealogies, 348. Surtees Society, xxxvi. 134. Burke's Royal Families, (London, 1851, 8vo.) ii. 155. Foster's Visitations of Yorkshire, 52, 53, 580, 624. Burke's Heraldic Illustrations, 61. History of Beverley, by G. Poulson, i. 393. Hoare's Wiltshire, V. iii. 46. The Genealogist, iv. 246; v. 42; New Series, xiii. 241; xiv. 98. Harleian Society, xvi. 319, 321. Banks' Baronies in Fee, ii. 142. Cyclostyle Pedigrees, by J. J. Green. Metcalfe's Visitations of Northamptonshire, 144. The Gresley's of Drakelowe, by F. Madan, 285. *See* DE THORPE.

THOYTS. Burke's Landed Gentry, 4, 5, 6, 7, 8.

THREELE. Berry's Sussex Genealogies, 132, 273. Dallaway's Sussex, II. i. 341. Castles, Mansions, and Manors of Western Sussex, by D. G. C. Elwes and C. J. Robinson, 262.

THREIPLAND. The Threiplands of Fingask, by R. Chambers, LL.D. Edinburgh, 1880, 8vo.

THRELFALL. Fishwick's History of Goosnargh, 167. The Tyldesley Diary, edited by J. Gillow and A. Hewitson, 22, 107.

THRELKELD. The Threlkelds of Threlkeld, by William Jackson. Kendal, 1888, 8vo. The Threkelds of Melberby, by William Jackson. Kendal, 1889, 8vo. Hutchinson's History of Cumberland, i. 218. Jefferson's History of Leath Ward, Cumberland, 300. Foster's Visitations of Cumberland and Westmorland, 132. Papers and Pedigrees relating to Cumberland and Westmorland, by Willm. Jackson, ii. 120, 282. Nicolson and Burn's Westmorland and Cumberland, i. 498.

THRESHER. Wiltshire Archæological Magazine, v. 240.

THRESHFIELD. Whitaker's Deanery of Craven, 3rd edn., 552.

THRING. Burke's Landed Gentry, 4, 5, 6, 7, 8. Jewers' Wells Cathedral, 80.

THROCKMORTON, THROGMORTON, or THROKMORTON. Burke's Extinct Baronetcies. Surrey Archæological Collections, i. Camden Society, xliii, 123. Surtees Society, xxxvi. 84. Nash's Worcestershire, i. 452. Visitation of Oxfordshire, 1574, printed by Sir T. Phillipps, (Middle Hill, fol.) 10. Burke's Commoners, ii. 161. Lipscombe's History of the County of Buckingham, i. 271; iv. 399. Bridges' Northamptonshire, by Rev. Peter Whalley, i. 312. Dugdale's Warwickshire, 749. Clutterbuck's Hertford, ii. 301. Baker's Northampton, ii. 202. Chauncy's Hertfordshire, 368. Sir T. Phillipps' Topographer, No. 1, (March, 1821, 8vo.) 39. Harleian Society, v. 120; viii. 110, 145; xii. 87, 111, 207; xxi. 162; xxxii. 282; xliii. 214. Fosbrooke's History of Gloucestershire, ii. 41. Wotton's English Baronetage, ii. 351. Betham's Baronetage, i. 486. Metcalfe's Visitations of Suffolk, 208. Burke's Extinct Baronetcies, 101. Hasted's Kent, (Hund. of Blackheath, by H. H. Drake,) 254. Metcalfe's Visitations of Northamptonshire, 200.

THRUSTON. Burke's Landed Gentry, 5 and supp., 6, 7, 8.

THRUXTON. Harleian Society, xxvii. 136.

THUNDER. Burke's Landed Gentry, 3, 4, 5, 6, 7, 8.

THURBAN, or THURBANE. Berry's Buckinghamshire Genealogies, 39. Lipscombe's History of the County of Buckinghamshire, ii. 194.

THURBARNE. History of Sandwich, by W. Boys, 350. Harleian Society, xvii. 287.

THURBURN. The Thurburns, by Lt.-Col. F. A. V. Thurburn. London, 1864, 8vo. Howard's Visitation of England and Wales, v. 114.

THURGARLAND, or THURGERLAND. Surtees Society, xxxvi. 261. Foster's Visitations of Yorkshire, 581. Hunter's Deanery of Doncaster, ii. 269.

THURKETELL. Harleian Society, xvii. 287. Bysshe's Visitation of Essex, edited by J. J. Howard, 94.

THURLAND. Surrey Archæological Collections, ii. Foster's Visitations of Yorkshire, 151. Harleian Society, viii. 191; xvi. 322. See THERLAND, THIRLAND.

THURLEBY, or THURLBY. Harleian Society, xvii. 288. Carthew's Hundred of Launditch, Part iii. 93.

THURLOW. Burke's Landed Gentry, 2, 3, 4, 5. Burke's Royal Descents and Pedigrees of Founders' Kin, 2. Manning and Bray's Surrey, iii. 385. Edmondson's Baronagium Genealogicum, vi. 78. Brydges' Collins' Peerage, viii. 284.

THURSBY. Morant's Essex, ii. 385. Burke's Commoners, i. 318, Landed Gentry, 2, 3, 4, 5, 6, 7, 8. Surtees' Durham, iv. 95. Harleian Society, xiii. 52, 298; xxxii. 283.

THURSTANESTON. Ormerod's Cheshire, ii. 507.

THURSTON. Berry's Kent Genealogies, 202, 203. Metcalfe's Visitations of Suffolk, 169. Harleian Society, xvii. 289; xlii. 58. Burke's Colonial Gentry, i. 17. The Genealogist, New Series, xvii. 114.

THWAITE, THWAITES, THWAYTE, or THWAYTES. Morant's Essex, ii. 74. Visitation of Norfolk, published by Norfolk Archæological Society, i. 118. Foster's Visitations of Yorkshire, 93, 175. Harleian Society, i. 72; viii. 375; xiii. 503; xvi. 322; xxxii. 284. Drake's Eboracum, or the History of York, 326. Plantagenet-Harrison's History of Yorkshire, i. 365. Doncaster Charities, by Charles Jackson, 89. The Genealogist, New Series, viii. 176. Historical Notices of Doncaster, by C. W. Hatfield, 3rd Series, 373. Foster's Visitations of Cumberland and Westmorland, 133.

THWENG, or THWENGE. Burke's Commoners, ii. 147. Foster's Visitations of Yorkshire, 230, 261, 370, 408, 581. Banks' Baronies in Fee, i. 431. Banks' Dormant and Extinct Baronage, i. 426. History of the Wilmer Family, 115. See TWENGE.

THYMBLETHORP. Harleian Society, xxxii. 285.

THYMILBY. Thoroton's Nottinghamshire, i. 118. See THIMBLEBY.

THYNNE, or THINNE. Topographer and Genealogist, iii. 468-491. Reports and Papers of the Associated Architectural Societies, 1852-1853, 445. Visitatio Comitatus Wiltoniæ, 1623, printed by Sir T. Phillipps. Hoare's Wiltshire, I. ii. 60. Duncumb's History of the Co. of Hereford, ii. 40. Shirley's History of the County of Monaghan, 283. Edmondson's Baronagium Genealogicum, iv. 326. Brydges' Collins' Peerage, ii. 496. Visitation of Wiltshire, edited by G. W. Marshall, 59. The Visitations of Cornwall, edited by J. L. Vivian, 195. Harleian Society, xxi. 164 ; xxix. 460. *See* BOTFIELD.

TIBBETS, or TIBBITS. Burke's Landed Gentry, 7, 8. New England Register, viii. 130.

TIBEAUDO. Burke's Landed Gentry, 2.

TIBETOT, or TIBTOT. Hunter's Deanery of Doncaster, i. 325. Hoare's Wiltshire, III. iv. 44. Banks' Baronies in Fee, i. 432. Banks' Dormant and Extinct Baronage, ii. 561. *See* TYBETOT.

TICHBORNE, TICHBOURNE, or TICHBURN. Berry's Hampshire Genealogies, 28-32. Berry's Kent Genealogies, 361. Surrey Archæological Collections, ii. Herald and Genealogist, iii. 424 ; iv. 64. Harleian Society, viii. 230 ; xvii. 289 ; xlii. 177 ; xliii. 107. Visitatio Comitatus Wiltoniæ, 1623, printed by Sir T. Phillipps. Hoare's Wiltshire, V. ii. 31. Wotton's English Baronetage, i. 425. Betham's Baronetage, i. 203. Visitation of Wiltshire, edited by G. W. Marshall, 13. Burke's Extinct Baronetcies.

TICHESEY. Manning and Bray's Surrey, ii. 400.

TICKELL. Miscellanea Genealogica et Heraldica, New Series, ii. 472. Burke's Landed Gentry, 8.

TIDERLEIGH. Harleian Society, vi. 281.

TIDSWELL. Burke's Family Records, 598.

TIFFYN. Morant's Essex, ii. 222.

TIGHE. Burke's Commoners, (of Woodstock,) iii. 513, Landed Gentry, 2, 3, 4, 5, 6, 7 ; (of Michelstown,) Commoners, iv. 12, Landed Gentry, 2, 3, 4, 5, 6, 7 ; and 8. Burke's Visitation of Seats and Arms, 2nd Series, ii. 77. The Irish Builder, xxix. 128.

TILBURY. Morant's Essex, i. 232 ; ii. 335.

TILDEN. Miscellanea Genealogica et Heraldica, 2nd Series, i. 333.

TILDESLEY, or TYLDESLEY. Chetham Society, lxxxi. 44 ; lxxxii. 101 ; lxxxviii. 301, 302. Baines' History of the Co. of Lancaster, iii. 608 ; Croston's edn., iv. 333, 334. The Tyldesley Diary, edited by J. Gillow and A. Hewitson, 182. Harleian Society, xviii. 206 ; xlii. 25.

TILESTON. New England Register, xiii. 121.

TILGHMAN. Hasted's Kent, ii. 191. Berry's Kent Genealogies, 70, 71. Harleian Society, xlii. 37.

TILLARD. Burke's Landed Gentry, 2 and supp., 3, 4, 5, 7, 8.

TILLIARD. Oxford Historical Society, xix. 202.

TILLIOL. Hutchinson's History of Cumberland, ii. 359, 572. Betham's Baronetage, v. (Barts. of Scotland,) 22. Nicolson and Burn's Westmorland and Cumberland, ii. 121, 457. *See* TYLLIOL.

TILLOTSON. Life of Dr. John Tillotson, by T. Birch, (London, 1753, 8vo.) 1. John Watson's History of Halifax, 294. Harleian Society, xxxviii. 711.

TILLY, or TILLIE. Harleian Society, vi. 283. Burke's Colonial Gentry, i. 35. The Visitations of Devon, by J. L. Vivian, 728.

TILNEY. East Anglian, i. 96. Cambridgeshire Visitation, edited by

Sir T. Phillipps, 31. History of Boston, by Pishey Thompson, 2nd edition, 373. Harleian Society, xxxii. 287 ; xli. 38.

TILSTON. Ormerod's Cheshire, ii. 800. Harleian Society, xviii. 222. *See* TILLOTSON.

TILT. Chance of Bromsgrove, by J. F. Chance, 85.

TIMINS. The Genealogist, v. 205.

TIMPERLEY. Herald and Genealogist, iii. 420. Page's History of Suffolk, 21.

TINDAL, TINDALE, or TINDALL. Morant's Essex, ii. 171. Burke's Landed Gentry, (of Chelmsford,) 3, 4 ; (of Hanningfield,) 5 supp., 6 ; (of Aylesbury,) 5 supp., 6, 7, 7 p. 144. Hodgson's Northumberland, III. ii. 364. Burke's Royal Descents and Pedigrees of Founders' Kin, 60. Surtees Society, xxxvi. 352. Harleian Society, xvi. 323. Burke's Colonial Gentry, ii. 478. *See* TYNDAL.

TINDAL-CARILL-WORSLEY. Burke's Landed Gentry, 8.

TINKER. Blore's Rutland, 180.

TINNE. Burke's Family Records, 600.

TINSLEY. Harleian Society, xvi. 324. *See* DE TINSLEY.

TINTEN. Maclean's History of Trigg Minor, iii. 159.

TIPPING, or TIPPINGE. Gentleman's Magazine, 1828, i. 210. Berry's Buckinghamshire Genealogies, 81. Burke's Landed Gentry, 2, 3, 4, 5, 6, 7, 8. Harleian Society, v. 274. Foster's Lancashire Pedigrees. Lipscombe's History of the County of Buckingham, i. 450. Dunkin's History of Bullington and Ploughley, ii. 47. Burke's Extinct Baronetcies. The Genealogist, vi. 98. Annals of Smith of Balby, by H. E. Smith, 97. *See* TYPPING.

TIPTOFT. G. P. Scrope's History of Castle Combe, 56. Gough's Sepulchral Monuments, ii. 141. Blore's Rutland, 44. Clutterbuck's Hertford, iii. 102. Robinson's History of Enfield, ii. 16.

TIPTON. Harleian Society, xliii. 122.

TIRINGHAM. Harleian Society, viii. 24 ; xix. 65, 197. Betham's Baronetage, iv. 267. The Genealogist, New Series, xii. 31. Metcalfe's Visitations of Northamptonshire, 144.

TIRRELL. Surrey Archæological Collections, ii. Aubrey's Antiquities of Surrey, iv. 251. Harleian Society, xiii. 15, 110, 299, 503 ; xxviii. 152 ; xliii. 104. Wotton's English Baronetage, iii. 510. The Genealogist, vii. 252. *See* TYRREL.

TIRRICK. Visitation of Staffordshire, 1663-4, printed by Sir T. Phillipps, 10.

TIRWHIT, or TIRWITT. Baker's Northampton, i. 114. The Genealogist, v. 45. *See* TYRWHITT.

TISDALL, or TISDELL. Burke's Landed Gentry, (of Charlesfort,) 3, 4, 5, 6, 7, 8 ; (of Charleville,) 2.

TISON. Archæologia Æliana, 2nd Series, iii. 130. Pedigrees of the Lords of Alnwick, by W. H. D. Longstaffe, 15.

TITHERLEIGH. Berry's Hampshire Genealogies, 273.

TITLEY. Visitation of Norfolk, published by Norfolk Archæological Society, i. 77. Harleian Society, xxix. 462.

TITTLE. Burke's Landed Gentry, 3, 4.

TIXALL. Erdeswicke's Survey of Staffordshire, 260.

TOBIN. O'Hart's Irish Pedigrees, 2nd Series, 350.

TOCHETT. Harleian Society, xviii. 224. *See* TOUCHET.

TOCKER. Dwnn's Visitations of Wales, i, 152, 192. The Visitations of Cornwall, by J. L. Vivian, 521.

TOCKETTS. Surtees Society, xxxvi. 320. Foster's Visitations of Yorkshire, 195. Graves' History of Cleveland, 429.

TODD. Thoresby's Ducatus Leodiensis, 27. Burke's Landed Gentry, 2, 3, 4, 5, 6, 7, 8. Ontarian Families, by E. M. Chadwick, ii. 73. Bysshe's Visitation of Essex, edited by J. J. Howard, 94. Burke's Colonial Gentry, ii. 791. Harleian Society, xxxvii. 213.

TODD-THORNTON. Burke's Landed Gentry, 2, 5, 6, 7, 8.

TODENHAM. Westcote's Devonshire, edited by G. Oliver and P. Jones, 478. The Genealogist, New Series, xii. 34, 229.

TODENI, or TOENI. Munford's Analysis of Domesday Book of Co. Norfolk, 34. Lipscombe's History of the County of Buckingham, iv. 102. Nichols' History of the County of Leicester, ii. 27. Notes and Queries, 2 S. xi. 154; xii. 131. Maclean's History of Trigg Minor, i. 64. Hoare's Wiltshire, III. v. 5. Banks' Dormant and Extinct Baronage, i. 182. History of the House of Arundel, by J. P. Yeatman, 72. The Gresley's of Drakelowe, by F. Madan, 1-15, 223. *See* DE TOENI, TONI.

TOEY. Dwnn's Visitations of Wales, i. 137.

TOFIELDS. Harleian Society, xl. 1290.

TOFT. Ormerod's Cheshire, i. 501. Harleian Society, xviii. 139.

TOFTES. The Genealogist, New Series, xvi. 162.

TOINKEIN, or TONKIN. Harleian Society, ix. 217. *See* TONKEN.

TOKE. Hasted's Kent, iii. 247 ; iv. 29. Berry's Hertfordshire Genealogies, 70. Berry's Kent Genealogies, 167. Burke's Landed Gentry, 2, 3, 4, 5, 6, 7, 8. Harleian Society, xlii. 153.

TOKER. Maclean's History of Trigg Minor, ii. 54. Burke's Visitation of Seats and Arms, 2nd Series, i. 14. The Visitations of Cornwall, by J. L. Vivian, 521. *See* TOOKER, TUCKER.

TOKY. Nash's Worcestershire, ii. 63. Harleian Society, xxvii. 150.

TOLCHER. Burke's Family Records, 603.

TOLER. The Wolfe's of Forenaghts, 57. The Irish Builder, xxxv. 77.

TOLETHORPE. Blore's Rutland, 217.

TOLHURST. Howard's Visitation of England and Wales, i. 64. Burke's Family Records, 604.

TOLKARNE. The Visitations of Cornwall, edited by J. L. Vivian, 518.

TOLL. Burke's Landed Gentry, 2, 3, 4, 5, 6, 7, 8.

TOLLAR, or TOLLER. Maclean's History of Trigg Minor, ii. 254. Blore's Rutland, 51. The Genealogist, i. 185, 322. Chronicle of the Family of De Havilland. Memoirs of the Family of Chester, by R. E. C. Waters, 624, 672.

TOLLEMACHE. Gentleman's Magazine, 1821, i. 275. Burke's Royal Families, (London, 1851, 8vo.) i. 128. Burke's Landed Gentry, 2, 3, 4, 5. Betham's Baronetage, v. app. 72. Ormerod's Cheshire, iii. 380. Burke's Extinct Baronetcies. Oliver's History of Antigua, ii. 43. *See* TALMACH.

TOLLET. Burke's Commoners, ii. 224, Landed Gentry, 2.

TOLMAN. New England Register, xiv. 247.

TOLSON. Tolson Appeal Case, before the House of Lords, 1828, folio, pp. 60. Burke's Commoners, ii. 133, Landed Gentry, 2. Hunter's Deanery of Doncaster, ii. 68. Foster's Visitations of Cumberland and Westmorland, 134.

TOLTHORPE. The Genealogist, New Series, xii. 31.

TOLWIN. Visitation of Norfolk, published by Norfolk Archæological Society, i. 78. Harleian Society, xxxii. 289.

TOM. Howard's Visitation of England and Wales, viii. 94.

TOMES. Pedigree of Tomes of Marston Sicca, Co. Gloucester, [T. P.] 1860, broadside. Miscellanea Genealogica et Heraldica, New Series, iii. 273.

TOMKINS, or TOMKYNS. Burke's Landed Gentry, 2, 3, 4. Harleian Society, viii. 149. Duncumb's History of the Co. of Hereford, ii. 73. Archæologia Cambrensis, 3 S., xv. 272. Robinson's Mansions of Herefordshire, 293. Pedigree of the Family of Sheppard, 11. Cooke's Continuation of Duncumb's Hereford, (Hund. of Grimsworth,) Part ii. 134. Weaver's Visitation of Herefordshire, 66. See CUMMING.

TOMKINSON. Burke's Landed Gentry, (of Reaseheath,) 2, 3, 4, 5, 6, 7, 8 ; (of Franche Hall,) 8. Ormerod's Cheshire, iii. 480. James Hall's History of Nantwich, 464.

TOMLIN. Burke's Landed Gentry, 2, 3, 4, 5, 6, 7, 8.

TOMLINE. Burke's Landed Gentry, 3, 4, 5, 6, 7.

TOMLINSON. Thoresby's Ducatus Leodiensis, 24. Nichols' History of the County of Leicester, iv. 304. See THOMLINSON.

TOMPSON. Burke's Landed Gentry, 2, 3, 4, 5. New England Register, xv. 113. See THOMPSON.

TONG, or TONGE. Bibliotheca Topographica Britannica, i. Part i. 116. Harleian Society, iv. 84 ; xvi. 325 ; xvii. 290 ; xlii. 17. Whitaker's Loidis and Elmete, 250. Chetham Society, lxxxviii. 303 ; xcv. 58. Visitation of Kent, (reprinted from Archæologia Cantiana, vi.) 67. Surtees Society, xli. 39, Berry's Kent Genealogies, 73. Visitation of Durham, 1575, (Newcastle, 1820, fol.) 4. Visitation of Durham, 1615, (Sunderland, 1820, fol.) 38. Burke's Landed Gentry, 3, 4, 5, 6, 7, 8. Hutchinson's History of Durham, iii. 218. Surtees' Durham, iv. 4. Foster's Visitations of Durham, 305. The Genealogical Magazine, iii. 349, 406.

TONI, or TONY. Morant's Essex, i. 32. Banks' Dormant and Extinct Baronage, i. 420. Hoare's Wiltshire, III. v. 5. Clutterbuck's Hertford, i. 354. See TODENI.

TONKEN, or TONKIN. Mullyon, its History, etc., by E. G. Harvey, 119. An Historical Survey of Cornwall, by C. S. Gilbert, ii. 274. The Visitations of Cornwall, edited by J. L. Vivian, 454. See TOINKEIN.

TONSON. Notes and Queries, 6 S., xi. 157.

TONSTALL. Surrey Archæological Collections, ii.

TOODE. Surtees' Durham, i. 219.

TOOKE. Gentleman's Magazine, 1839, ii. 603. Berry's Hertfordshire Genealogies, 70. Burke's Landed Gentry, 3, 4, 5, 6, 7, 8.

Clutterbuck's Hertford, ii. 351. Cussan's History of Hertford-shire, Parts ix. and x. 249. Harleian Society, xvii. 291 ; xxii. 98, 166.

TOOKER. Burke's Landed Gentry, 2. Visitatio Comitatus Wiltoniæ, 1623, printed by Sir T. Phillipps. Hunter's Deanery of Doncaster, ii. 25. Hoare's Wiltshire, II. i. 37. Visitation of Wiltshire, edited by G. W. Marshall, 3, 101. Burke's Extinct Baronetcies. The Genealogist, vi. 99, 100. *See* TOKER, TUCKER.

TOONE. Nichols' History of the County of Leicester, iii. 650.

TOOSE. Visitation of Somersetshire, printed by Sir T. Phillipps, 141. Harleian Society, xi. 111.

TOOTLE. Historical Notices of Doncaster, by C. W. Hatfield, 2nd Series, 394.

TOPCLIFFE. The Genealogist, v. 49. Harleian Society, xxxii. 290.

TOPESFIELD. Gage's History of Thingoe Hundred, Suffolk, 123. Harleian Society, xiii. 504. Metcalfe's Visitations of Suffolk, 103.

TOPHAM. Surtees Society, xxxvi. 149. Burke's Landed Gentry, (of Caldberg,) 2, 3, 4, 5, 6, 7, 8 ; (of Cockerton Hall,) 8. Foster's Visitations of Yorkshire, 581. Burke's Visitation of Seats and Arms, i. 28. Poulson's Holderness, i. 473. Burton's History of Hemingborough, 225.

TOPLIS. The Gresley's of Drakelowe, by F. Madan, 286.

TOPP. Burke's Landed Gentry, 2, 3, 4, 5, 6. Burke's Visitation of Seats and Arms, i. 75. Visitatio Comitatus Wiltoniæ, 1623, printed by Sir T. Phillipps. Hoare's Wiltshire, I. ii. 242. A Plea for an old Wilts Charity, by J. Baron, (Warminster, *circa* 1879, 8vo.) 24. Visitation of Wiltshire, edited by G. W. Marshall, 64. Burke's Extinct Baronetcies.

TOPPAN. New England Register, xxxiii. 66.

TORBOCK. Jewitt's Reliquary, x. 171, 227 ; xi. 35, 97. Croston's edn. of Baines's Lancaster, v. 76.

TORKYNGTON, or TORKINGTON. Camden Society, xliii. 102. Burke's Landed Gentry, 2 and corr., 3, 4, 5, 6, 7. Metcalfe's Visitations of Northamptonshire, 145.

TORNEY. Berry's Kent Genealogies, 107. The Genealogist, New Series, xiv. 249.

TORR. Burke's Landed Gentry, 8.

TORRE. Burke's Landed Gentry, 2, 3, 4, 5, 6, 7, 8. Foster's York-shire Pedigrees. Stonehouse's History of the Isle of Axholme, 308. Poulson's Holderness, i. 412, 491. Harleian Society, xxxvii. 253.

TORRELL. Morant's Essex, i. 92, 227, 474 ; ii. 476, 478. Harleian Society, xiii. 115.

TORRIANO. Berry's Berkshire Genealogies, 86. Genealogical Memoranda of the Family of Ames.

TOTHILL. Tuckett's Devonshire Pedigrees, 163. Harleian Society, vi. 284 ; xli. 122. Westcote's Devonshire, edited by G. Oliver and P. Jones, 520. Visitation of Devon, edited by F. T. Colby, 197. The Visitations of Devon, by J. L. Vivian, 729.

TOTTENHALL. Miscellanea Genealogica et Heraldica, ii. 277.

TOTTENHAM. Burke's Landed Gentry, (of Woodstock,) 4, 5, 6, 7, 8; (of Ballycurry,) 2, 3, 4, 5, 6, 7, 8; (of Glenfarne,) 4, 5, 6, 7, 8.

TOTTIE. Thoresby's Ducatus Leodiensis, 120.

TOTWORTHY. Harleian Society, ix. 69. The Visitations of Cornwall, edited by J. L. Vivian, 158.

TOTYLL. Dwnn's Visitations of Wales, i. 183. New England Register, xxii. 335.

TOUCHET. Erdeswicke's Survey of Staffordshire, 95. Wiltshire Archæological Magazine, v. 267. Ormerod's Cheshire, i. 662. Edmondson's Baronagium Genealogicum, iv. 353. Brydges' Collins' Peerage, vi. 546. Miscellanea Genealogica et Heraldica, 2nd Series, iii. 349. Harleian Society, xxxvii. 167. *See* TOCHETT, TUCHET.

TOULMIN. Burke's Landed Gentry, 8.

TOUNRAWE. Jewitt's Reliquary, vii. 30.

TOURNAY. Berry's Kent Genealogies, 107. Harleian Society, xlii. 132.

TOVEY-TENNENT. Burke's Landed Gentry, 4, 5.

TOWER. Burke's Royal Families, (London, 1851, 8vo.) i. 137. Burke's Landed Gentry, 2, 3, 4, 5, 6, 7, 8. Gyll's History of Wraysbury, 62. Lipscombe's History of the County of Buckingham, iv. 530. Burke's Heraldic Illustrations, 145. Howard's Visitation of England and Wales, ii. 33.

TOWERS. Cambridgeshire Visitation, edited by Sir T. Phillipps, 32. Burke's Landed Gentry, 2. The Genealogist, v. 49 ; vi. 287. Harleian Society, xvii. 292 ; xli. 73.

TOWLE. New England Register, xliii. 364.

TOWNE. New England Register, xx. 367 ; xxi. 12, 217. Harleian Society, xxxix. 843.

TOWNERAW. The Genealogist, v. 50.

TOWNESHEND. Visitation of Norfolk, published by Norfolk Archæological Society, i. 306. History of Chislehurst, by Webb, Miller, and Beckwith, 156. *See* TOWNSEND.

TOWNLEY, TOUNLEY, or TOWNELEY. Whitaker's History of Whalley, 325*, (Book iv. chap. iii.). Pedigree of the Family of John Townley of Wigan, folio sheet. Burke's Commoners, (of Towneley,) ii. 262, Landed Gentry, 2, 3, 4, 5, 6 supp., 7, 8; (of Fulbourne,) Landed Gentry, 5, 6, 7, 8. Foster's Lancashire Pedigrees. Chetham Society, lxxxii. 61, 62, 99 ; lxxxviii. 304-314 ; xcviii. 43 ; xcix. 157, 165. Baines' History of the Co. of Lancaster, iii. 254 ; Croston's edn., iii. 374, 382 ; iv. 108. Whitaker's History of Whalley, ii. 178, 190, 235, 255. Earwaker's Local Gleanings, i. 195, 202, 219, 223, 229, 232, 237. Notes and Queries, 4 S. xi. 23. History of Longridge, by T. C. Smith, 146. History of Ribchester, by T. C. Smith and J. Shortt, 229. Fishwick's History of Rochdale, 344.

TOWNSEND, or TOWNSHEND. Blomefield's Norfolk, vii. 130-137. Burke's Commoners, (of Trevallyn,) iii. 313, Landed Gentry, 2, 3, 4, 5, 6, 7, 8; Commoners, iv. 130 ; (of Wincham,) Landed Gentry,

5, 6, 7, 8; (of Honington Hall,) 2, 3, 4, 5, 6, 7, 8; (of Castle Townsend,) 2, 3, 4, 5, 6, 7, 8; (of Whitehall,) 2, 3, 4, 5, 6; (of Myross Wood,) 2, 3, 4, 5, 6, 7, 8; (of Derry,) 2, 3, 4, 5, 6, 7, 8; (of Garrycloyne Castle,) 3, 4, 5, 6, 7; (of Woodside,) 2, 3, 4, 5; 2; (of Clifton,) 6, 7, 8; (of Downhills,) 6 supp., 7, 8. Ormerod's Cheshire, i. 631. Page's History of Suffolk, 209. Claim of certain Persons to be Children of the Marquis Townshend, Sess. Papers, 116 of 1842; 46, 97 of 1843. Hasted's Kent, i. 100. Morant's Essex, ii. 188. Nash's Worcestershire, i. 378. Jewitt's Reliquary, xv. 72. Harleian Society, viii. 57; xxix. 463; xxxii. 290; xxxvii. 18, 375. Clutterbuck's Hertford, ii. 186, 315. The Genealogist, iii. 78. Burke's Royal Families, (London, 1851, 8vo.) i. 133. Pedigree of the Family of Sheppard, 18. Edmondson's Baronagium Genealogicum, iv. 323; vi. 39, 105. Brydges' Collins' Peerage, ii. 454; vi. 319; viii. 551. Notes and Queries, 6 S. iv. 301. Metcalfe's Visitation of Worcester, 1683, 92. Archæologia Cantiana, xiii. 402. Miscellanea Genealogica et Heraldica, New Series, iv. 125. Visitation of Gloucester, edited by T. F. Fenwick and W. C. Metcalfe, 184. New England Register, xxix. 97. Burke's Colonial Gentry, ii. 684. *See* MARSHAM-TOWNSHEND, TOWNESHEND.

TOWNSON. Wilson's History of the Parish of St. Laurence Pountney, 238.

TOWRY. Foster's Visitations of Yorkshire, 582. Poulson's Holderness, i. 371; ii. 542. Foster's Visitations of Cumberland and Westmorland, 135.

TOWSE. Morant's Essex, ii. 574. Harleian Society, xi. 112; xiii. 505; xvii. 290.

TOWTHBY. The Genealogist, vi. 287.

TOWY. Poetical Works of Lewis Glyn Cothi, (Oxford, 1837,) 130.

TOY, or TOYE. Dwnn's Visitations of Wales, i. 137. Metcalfe's Visitation of Worcester, 1683, 93.

TRACTON. Notes and Queries, 2 S. ix. 249.

TRACY. Case on behalf of Matthew Tracy, claiming the Title of Viscount Tracy. London, 1862, fol. Case of B. W. Tracy, claiming titles of Viscount and Baron Tracy. London, 1853, fol. Case of James Tracy on his claim to the titles of Viscount and Baron Tracy, folio. Claim of James Tracy, Esq., to be Visct. and Baron Tracy of Rathcoole, Sess. Papers, 46 of 1841; 59 of 1843; 62 of 1847; 156 of 1847-8; 107 of 1849; R of 1854-5. Memoirs Illustrating the Noble Families of Tracy and Courtenay. Canterbury, 1796, 8vo. Pedigree of Tracy of Coscomb, Co. Glouc., [T. P.] 1860, folio page. History of Tewkesbury, by James Bennett, 437. Rudder's Gloucestershire, 770. Bibliotheca Devoniensis, by James Davidson, 147. Hasted's Kent, ii. 557. Visitation of Middlesex, (Salisbury, 1820, fol.) 36. Collectanea Topographica et Genealogica, vi. 153. Lipscombe's History of the County of Buckingham, i. 575. Pedigrees of the Families of Tracy of Toddington, Sudeley of Sudeley, etc., etc., *see* ' Historical and Descriptive Accounts of Toddington, Gloucestershire,' by J.

Britton, F.S.A., (*at end*). Archdall's Lodge's Peerage, v. 1.
Banks' Dormant and Extinct Baronage, i. 184. Burke's Extinct
Baronetcies. Foster's Visitations of Middlesex, 64. Harleian
Society, xxi. 165.

TRADESCANT. Notes and Queries, 1 S. ii. 119, 286; iii. 119, 286,
353, 391, 469; iv. 182; v. 266, 367, 385, 474; vi. 198; vii. 295;
viii. 513.

TRAFFORD. Burke's Royal Families, (London, 1851, 8vo.) ii. 141.
Burke's Commoners, (of Trafford,) iv. 247; (of Swithamley,)
Landed Gentry, 3; (of Oughtrington,) 2, 3, 4, 5; (of Wroxham
Hall,) 2 add., 3, 4, 5, 6; (of Brundall House,) 7, 8; (of Michael-
church Court,) 8. Chetham Society, lxxxi. 2; lxxxii. 10; lxxxviii.
315; xcv. 128; xcviii. 66. Foster's Lancashire Pedigrees. Visitation of Staffordshire, 1663-4, printed by Sir T. Phillipps, 10.
Butterworth's Account of the Town, etc., of Oldham, 148. Corry's
History of Lancashire, ii. 660-667. Baines' History of the Co. of
Lancaster, iii. 110; Croston's edn., iii. 236. Ormerod's Cheshire,
i. 589; ii. 45. The Genealogist, ii. 155. Harleian Society, xiii.
505. Liverpool as it was, etc., by Richd. Brooke, 477. History
of Powys Fadog, by J. Y. W. Lloyd, iii. 32. Visitations of Staffordshire, 1614 and 1663-4, William Salt Society, 288. The
Gresley's of Drakelowe, by F. Madan, 287. *See* DE TRAFFORD,
PETRE.

TRAGETT. Burke's Landed Gentry, 5, 6.

TRAHAIRN AB CARADAWG. History of Powys Fadog, by J. Y. W.
Lloyd, i. 79.

TRAHERNE. Glamorganshire Pedigrees, edited by Sir T. Phillipps, 9.
Burke's Landed Gentry, 2, 3, 4, 5, 6, 7, 8. T. Nicholas' County
Families of Wales, 643. Historical Notices of Sir M. Cradock,
Kt., by J. M. Traherne, 4. *See* TREHANE, TREHERNE.

TRAIL, or TRAILL. Burke's Landed Gentry, (of Ballylough,) 4, 5, 6,
7, 8; (of Holland,) 4, 5, 6, 7; (of Woodwick,) 5, 6, 7; (of
Westeve,) 5, 6. The Theology of Consolation, by D. C. A. Agnew,
359. Caithness Family History, by John Henderson, 229.

TRAILLY. Harvey's Hundred of Willey, 250.

TRANGMAR. Burke's Colonial Gentry, i. 366.

TRANT. Burke's Landed Gentry, 2, 3, 4, 5, 6, 7, 8. Burke's Extinct
Baronetcies, 615.

TRAPPES. Burke's Commoners, iii. 522, Landed Gentry, 2, 5, 6, 7, 8.
Harleian Society, i. 21; xiii. 506. Foster's Lancashire Pedigrees.

TRASCY. Harleian Society, xxi. 262.

TRAVEIS. Harleian Society, xvii. 293.

TRAVELL. Harleian Society, viii. 385; xii. 57, 409; xvii. 294.

TRAVERS. A Collection of Pedigrees of the Family of Travers, etc.,
by S. Smith Travers. Oxford, 1864, 4to. Chetham Society,
lxxxii. 85; cv. 247-51. Plantagenet-Harrison's History of Yorkshire, i. 150. Brady's Records of Cork, Cloyne, and Ross, i. 351.
Notes and Queries, 3 S. i. 231, 296, 378; v. 27. Harleian Society,
xvii. 294.

TRAYNE. Surtees' Durham, iv. 100.

TRAYTON. Berry's Sussex Genealogies, 80.

TREAGE. The Genealogist, New Series, xv. 148.

TREBARFOOTE. Harleian Society, ix. 218. The Visitations of Cornwall, edited by J. L. Vivian, 455.

TREBARTHA. Harleian Society, ix. 206. The Visitations of Cornwall, edited by J. L. Vivian, 430.

TREBY. Burke's Landed Gentry, 2, 3, 4, 5. Harleian Society, viii. 343.

TRECARREL. A Complete Parochial History of the County of Cornwall, iii. 123.

TREDCROFT. Berry's Sussex Genealogies, 16. Burke's Landed Gentry, 2, 3, 4, 5, 6, 7, 8. Dallaway's Sussex, II. ii. 341.

TREDENECK, TREDENNICK, or TREDINICK. Burke's Landed Gentry, 2, 3, 4, 5, 6, 7, 8. The Visitations of Cornwall, edited by J. L. Vivian, 334, 457.

TREDENHAM. Harleian Society, viii. 99. Chauncy's Hertfordshire, 208. A Complete Parochial History of the County of Cornwall, i. 386. The Visitations of Cornwall, edited by J. L. Vivian, 456. Burke's Landed Gentry, 2 p. 189.

TREDIDON. Harleian Society, ix. 105. The Visitations of Cornwall, edited by J. L. Vivian, 244.

TREDURFF. The Genealogical Magazine, iii. 555.

TREDWAY. Blore's Rutland, 175.

TREEBY. Burke's Landed Gentry, 5.

TREFALUN. History of Powys Fadog, by J. Y. W. Lloyd, iii. 221.

TREFFRY, or TREFRIE. Maclean's History of Trigg Minor, ii. 242-256. Harleian Society, ix. 219, 221. A Complete Parochial History of the County of Cornwall, ii. 30. An Historical Survey of Cornwall, by C. S. Gilbert, ii. 277. The Visitations of Cornwall, edited by J. L. Vivian, 459. Burke's Landed Gentry, 7, 8.

TREFUSIS. Case of R. G. W. Trefusis in relation to the Barony of Clinton, folio, pp. 10. Claim of R. G. W. Trefusis, Esq., to the Barony of Clinton, Sess. Papers, June 1793—March 1794. Polwhele's History of Cornwall, ii. 42. Harleian Society, ix. 222. A Complete Parochial History of the County of Cornwall, iii. 125, 397. An Historical Survey of Cornwall, by C. S. Gilbert, i. 468. Brydges' Collins' Peerage, vi. 541. The Visitations of Cornwall, edited by J. L. Vivian, 463.

TREGADECK. The Visitations of Cornwall, edited by J. L. Vivian, 471.

TREGAGLE. Maclean's History of Trigg Minor, ii. 177. Hoare's Wiltshire, V. ii. 79.

TREGARTHYN. Polwhele's History of Cornwall, iv. 112.

TREGEARE. Harleian Society, ix. 225. The Visitations of Cornwall, edited by J. L. Vivian, 469.

TREGENDER. Harleian Society, ix. 155. The Visitations of Cornwall, edited by J. L. Vivian, 341.

TREGIAN. Polwhele's History of Cornwall, iv. 112. An Historical Survey of Cornwall, by C. S. Gilbert, ii. 281.

TREGONING. Burke's Landed Gentry, 6, 7, 8.

TREGONWELL. Illuminated Supplement to Burke's Heraldic Illustra-

tions, 7. Burke's Commoners, (of Anderson,) ii. 403, Landed
Gentry, 2, 3, 4, 5, 6, 7, 8 ; (of Cranbourne,) Landed Gentry, 2, 3,
4. Hutchins' Dorset, i. 161. An Historical Survey of Cornwall,
by C. S. Gilbert, ii. 283. Harleian Society, xx. 92.

TREGOS, TREGOSE, TREGOSSE, or TREGOZE. Castles, Mansions, and
Manors of Western Sussex, by D. G. C. Elwes and C. J. Robinson,
103. Dallaway's Sussex, II. i. 35. Topographer and Genealogist,
ii. 124, 549. Visitation of Suffolk, edited by J. J. Howard, ii. 262.
Hoare's Wiltshire, IV. i. 110. Banks' Baronies in Fee, i. 436 ; ii.
146. Banks' Dormant and Extinct Baronage, i. 422. The Visitations of Cornwall, edited by J. L. Vivian, 472.

TREHAMPTON. Account of the Parish of Lea, with Lea Wood,
(London, 1841, 8vo.) 12.

TREHANE. Harleian Society, ix. 227. The Visitations of Cornwall,
edited by J. L. Vivian, 473. See TRAHERNE.

TREHANNICK. Maclean's History of Trigg Minor, iii. 143.

TREHAWKE. The Visitations of Cornwall, edited by J. L. Vivian, 474.

TREHERNE. Burke's Landed Gentry, 3, 4. See TRAHERNE.

TREISE. Maclean's History of Trigg Minor, i. 79, 83. The Visitations of Cornwall, by J. L. Vivian, 599.

TRELAWDER. Maclean's History of Trigg Minor, i. 385 ; iii. 359.

TRELAWNEY, or TRELAWNY. Burke's Royal Families, (London, 1851,
8vo.) ii. 180. Burke's Commoners, i. 368, Landed Gentry, (of
Coedramick,) 2, 3, 4, 5, 6, 7, 8 ; (of Shotwick,) 7, 8 ; (of Ham,) 8.
Maclean's History of Trigg Minor, ii. 519. Harleian Society, ix.
228. Lipscombe's History of the County of Buckingham, i. 400.
Westcote's Devonshire, edited by G. Oliver and P. Jones, 561.
A Complete Parochial History of the County of Cornwall, ii. 64.
An Historical Survey of Cornwall, by C. S. Gilbert, i. 546 ; ii. 291.
Wotton's English Baronetage, ii. 87. Betham's Baronetage, i. 324.
The Visitations of Cornwall, edited by J. L. Vivian, 475. Hasted's
Kent, (Hund. of Blackheath, by H. H. Drake,) xxiii.

TRELULLA. Maclean's History of Trigg Minor, ii. 155.

TREMAYLE. Weaver's Visitations of Somerset, 82.

TREMAYNE. Tuckett's Devonshire Pedigrees, 114. Burke's Commoners, i. 193, Landed Gentry, 2, 3, 4, 5, 6, 7, 8. Harleian
Society, vi. 284. Westcote's Devonshire, edited by G. Oliver and
P. Jones, 587. An Historical Survey of Cornwall, by C. S. Gilbert,
ii. 292. Visitation of Devon, edited by F. T. Colby, 198. The
Visitations of Cornwall, by J. L. Vivian, 616-620. The Visitations
of Devon, by J. L. Vivian, 730.

TREMENHEERE. Burke's Landed Gentry, 2, 3, 4, 5, 6, 7, 8. An Historical Survey of Cornwall, by C. S. Gilbert, ii. 297. The Visitations of Cornwall, by J. L. Vivian, 621.

TREMILL. Harleian Society, xiv. 608.

TRENANCE. Harleian Society, ix. 231. The Visitations of Cornwall,
edited by J. L. Vivian, 483.

TRENCH. Memoir of the Family of Trench. By T. R. Cooke-Trench.
London, 1897, 8vo. Claim of F. M. Trench, Baron Ashtown, to
Vote at Elections of Peers, Sess. Papers, M of 1855. Burke's

Landed Gentry, (of Cangort Park,) 2, 3, 4, 5, 6, 7, 8 ; (of Heywood,) 3. Harleian Society, xiii. 506 ; xvii. 295. Notes and Queries, 8 S. v. 423 ; vii. 134. Howard's Visitation of Ireland, i. 27; ii. 1; iii. 38.

TRENCHARD. Burke's Royal Families, (London, 1851, 8vo.) i. 199. Burke's Commoners, (of Dorsetshire,) iv. 75, Landed Gentry, 2 add., 3, 4, 5 ; (of Stanton,) Commoners, iv. 75, Landed Gentry, 2, 3, 4, 5, 7, 8. Harleian Society, viii. 429 ; xx. 93. Hutchins' Dorset, i. 430 ; iii. 326. The Genealogist, New Series, iii. 172. The Suffolk Records, by H. W. Aldred, 118.

TRENCHFIELD. History of Chislehurst, by Webb, Miller, and Beckwith, 26.

TRENERTH. Harleian Society, ix. 233. The Visitations of Cornwall, edited by J. L. Vivian, 484.

TRENGOVE. Harleian Society, ix. 233. The Visitations of Cornwall, edited by J. L. Vivian, 485.

TRENORGAS. The Genealogist, New Series, ix. 146.

TRENOWTH, TRENOTHE, or TRENOWITH. Burke's Commoners, iv. 692. Maclean's History of Trigg Minor, i. 72. Harleian Society, ix. 208. The Visitations of Cornwall, edited by J. L. Vivian, 434. Weaver's Visitations of Somerset, 31.

TRENTHAM. Visitation of Staffordshire, (Willm. Salt. Soc.) 139. Visitations of Staffordshire, 1614 and 1663-4, William Salt Society, 289.

TRENWITH. Harleian Society, ix. 238. An Historical Survey of Cornwall, by C. S. Gilbert, ii. 300. The Visitations of Cornwall, edited by J. L. Vivian, 486.

TREPE. Harleian Society, vi. 285. The Visitations of Devon, by J. L. Vivian, 735.

TRESAHAR. Maclean's History of Trigg Minor, i. 317. Harleian Society, ix. 234. A Complete Parochial History of the County of Cornwall, iv. 76. The Visitations of Cornwall, edited by J. L. Vivian, 488-496.

TRESHAM. The Ruins of Liveden, with Historical Notices of the Family of Tresham, by T. Bell. London, 1847, 4to. Bridges' Northamptonshire, by Rev. Peter Whalley, ii. 69, 323. Notes and Queries, 1 S. xi. 49, 131, 200. Burke's Extinct Baronetcies. Metcalfe's Visitations of Northamptonshire, 50, 146, 201. Northamptonshire Notes and Queries, ii. 41, 119, 142.

TRESWALLEN. Visitation of Middlesex, (Salisbury, 1820, fol.) 21. Foster's Visitation of Middlesex, 41.

TRESWELL. Harleian Society, i. 92.

TRETHERFF. The Visitations of Cornwall, edited by J. L. Vivian, 497.

TRETHEWY. Harleian Society, ix. 237. An Historical Survey of Cornwall, by C. S. Gilbert, ii, 303. The Visitations of Cornwall, edited by J. L. Vivian, 498. The Genealogist, New Series, ix. 11.

TREUAVAS. An Account of the Families of Boase, (Exeter, 1876, 4to.) 54.

TREVANION. Burke's Commoners, i. 253, Landed Gentry, 2, 3, 4. Maclean's History of Trigg Minor, i. 568. Polwhele's History of Cornwall, ii. 42. Harleian Society, ix. 239. A Complete Parochial

History of the County of Cornwall, iii. 337 ; iv. 116 supp. An Historical Survey of Cornwall, by C. S. Gilbert, ii. 304. The Visitations of Cornwall, edited by J. L. Vivian, 501.

TREVARTHIAN. The Visitations of Cornwall, edited by J. L. Vivian, 31. Maclean's History of Trigg Minor, iii. 385.

TREVELLIAN, TREVILLIAN, or TREVELYAN. Harleian Society, vi. 286; ix. 242 ; xi. 112 ; xvii. 295. Hodgson's Northumberland, I. ii. 262, 316. Westcote's Devonshire, edited by G. Oliver and P. Jones, 558. Collinson's Somerset, iii. 539. Camden Society, cv. *at end.* Visitation of Somersetshire, printed by Sir T. Phillipps, 141. Burke's Commoners, ii. 329, Landed Gentry, 2, 3, 4, 5, 6, 7, 8. An Historical Survey of Cornwall, by C. S. Gilbert, i. 564. Wotton's English Baronetage, iii. 353. Visitation of Devon, edited by F. T. Colby, 198. Betham's Baronetage, ii. 307. The Visitations of Cornwall, edited by J. L. Vivian, 507. The Visitations of Devon, by J. L. Vivian, 736.

TREVENOR. Maclean's History of Trigg Minor, i. 563.

TREVETT. Harleian Society, xi. 126. *See* TRYVET.

TREVIADOS. The Visitations of Cornwall, edited by J. L. Vivian, 463.

TREVILLE. Duncumb's History of the Co. of Hereford, ii. 112.

TREVISA. Harleian Society, ix. 244. The Visitations of Cornwall, edited by J. L. Vivian, 509.

TREVITHEN. The Visitations of Cornwall, edited by J. L. Vivian, 511.

TREVOR. Noble's Memoirs of the House of Cromwell, ii. 138-150. Dwnn's Visitations of Wales, ii. 317, 328, 354. Berry's Sussex Genealogies, 174. Harleian Society, viii. 245, 438 ; xxix. 465 ; xxxii. 292. Lipscombe's History of the County of Buckingham, ii. 296. Sussex Archæological Collections,, xx. 62. Archæologia Cambrensis, 4 S. viii. 37. Collections by the Powys-land Club, v. 263. Edmondson's Baronagium Genealogicum, v. 411 ; vi. 21. Archdall's Lodge's Peerage, v. 293. Brydges' Collins' Peerage, vi. 291. Burke's Extinct Baronetcies. History of Powys Fadog, by J. Y. W. Lloyd, iii. 196 ; iv. 78, 84, 86, 108, 110, 135 ; v. 259, 276, 398. Harvey's Hundred of Willey, 46. Notes and Queries, 6 S., ix. 403 ; 7 S., i. 225. East Barnet, by F. C. Cass, Part i. 64. Miscellanea Genealogica et Heraldica, i. 78.

TREVOR-BATTYE. Burke's Landed Gentry, 8.

TREVOR-HAMPDEN. Horsfield's History of Lewes, ii. 116.

TREVOR-ROPER. Burke's Landed Gentry, 2, 3, 4, 5, 6, 7, 8.

TREWBODY. Harleian Society, ix. 246. The Visitations of Cornwall, edited by J. L. Vivian, 512.

TREWOLLA. Harleian Society, ix. 244. The Visitations of Cornwall, edited by J. L. Vivian, 514.

TREWREN, or TRYOURNE. Harleian Society, ix. 247. An Historical Survey of Cornwall, by C. S. Gilbert, ii. 311. The Visitations of Cornwall, edited by J. L. Vivian, 515.

TREWYNT. Maclean's History of Trigg Minor, ii. 357.

TRIGGE. Harleian Society, xxxix. 1171.

TRIGOTT, or TRYGOT. Foster's Visitations of Yorkshire, 304. Hunter's Deanery of Doncaster, ii. 447. Harleian Society, xvi. 325.

TRILLESDEN. Surtees' Durham, i. 76.
TRIMNELL. Harleian Society, ii. 176; xxvii. 137.
TRIPCONEY. The Visitations of Cornwall, edited by J. L. Vivian, 517.
TRIPP, or TRIPPE. Archæologia Cantiana, v. 236. Berry's Kent Genealogies, 88. Burke's Landed Gentry, 2, 3, 4, 5, 6, 7, 8. T. Nicholas' County Families of Wales, 954. Burke's Colonial Gentry, i. 237. Harleian Society, xliii. 20.
TRIST. Burke's Landed Gentry, (of Bowdon,) 3, 4; (of Parc Behan,) 3, 4, 5, 6, 7, 8. Burke's Royal Descents and Pedigrees of Founders' Kin, 101, 110. Bridge's Northamptonshire, by Rev. Peter Whalley, i. 248. Baker's Northampton, i. 752; ii. 45. An Historical Survey of Cornwall, by C. S. Gilbert, ii. 312. Metcalfe's Visitations of Northamptonshire, 147.
TRISTRAM. Harleian Society, vi. 287; xvii. 296. The Visitations of Devon, by J. L. Vivian, 737. Miscellanea Genealogica et Heraldica, 3rd Series, i. 229.
TRITTON. Berry's Kent Genealogies, 202.
TROBRIDGE. The Visitations of Devon, by J. L. Vivian, 738. Harleian Society, vi. 288. See TROWBRIDGE.
TROCHES. Harleian Society, xliii. 170.
TROLLOP, or TROLLOPE. The Family of Trollope, by the Venble. Edwd. Trollope, M.A., F.S.A. Lincoln, 1875, 4to. Visitation of Durham, 1615, (Sunderland, 1820, fol.) 37. Surtees' Durham, i. 92, 93. Visitation of Durham, 1575, (Newcastle, 1820, fol.) 26. The Tyndale Pedigree, by B. W. Greenfield. Blore's Rutland, 94, 95. Hutchinson's History of Durham, iii. 339. Wotton's English Baronetage, ii. 278. Betham's Baronetage, i. 464. Foster's Visitations of Durham, 307. Burke's Landed Gentry, 8.
TROMWIN. Harleian Society, xxvii. 120.
TROPNELL. Visitatio Comitatus Wiltoniæ, 1623, printed by Sir T. Phillipps. Hoare's Wiltshire, V. ii. 118.
TROSSE. History of Clyst St. George, by Rev. H. T. Ellacombe, 69. Harleian Society, vi. 288. The Visitations of Devon, by J. L. Vivian, 739.
TROTMAN. Collections relating to the Family of Trotman. By W. P. W. Phillimore Stroud, 1892, 8vo. Fosbrooke's History of Gloucestershire, ii. 55. Harleian Society, xxi. 168. Gloucestershire Notes and Queries, ii. 201, 273, 341, 429; v. 14, 76, 123, 196, 234, 283, 334. Visitations of Gloucester, edited by T. F. Fenwick and W. C. Metcalfe, 186. Howard's Visitation of England and Wales, iii. 161.
TROTT. Harleian Society, xiii. 507; xiv. 609; xvii. 297. Burke's Extinct Baronetcies. New England Register, xliii. 79.
TROTTER. Visitation of Durham, 1615, (Sunderland, 1820, fol.) 64, 67. Surtees Society, xxxvi. 99. Burke's Commoners, (of Ballindean,) iv. 524, Landed Gentry, 2, 3, 4, 5; (of Morton Hall,) Landed Gentry, 2, 3, 4, 5, 6, 7, 8; (of The Bush,) 2, 3, 4, 5, 6, 7, 8; (of Dreghorn,) 2, 3, 4, 5, 6, 7, 8; (of Byers Green Hall,) 4, 6, 7, 8; (of Quansborough,) 4; (of Downpatrick,) 2; (of Horton Manor,)

5, 6, 7, 8. Foster's Visitations of Yorkshire, 582. Graves' History of Cleveland, 354. Douglas's Baronage of Scotland, 204. Walter Wood's East Neuk of Fife, 307. The Genealogist, New Series, ix. 67. Foster's Visitations of Durham, 309, 311. Alexander Nisbet's Heraldic Plates, 58. Burke's Family Records, 604. *See* STUART.

TROTTER-CRANSTOUN. Burke's Landed Gentry, 8.

TROUGHEAR. Berry's Hampshire Genealogies, 351.

TROUGHTON. Burke's Commoners, iv. 379, Landed Gentry, 2, 3, 4.

TROUTBECK. Petition of Right of Catherine Robson and Isabella Ainslie, presented 5 June, 1845, folio, pp. 80, two tables. Debate on the Troutbeck Estate in the House of Lords, (London, 1836, 8vo.) 2. J. Wilkinson's History of Broughton Gifford, folding plate. Petition of Wm. Robson and others, representatives of C. Robson and I. Ainslie, folio, pp. 17, *at end.* Clutterbuck's Hertford, i. 246. Ormerod's Cheshire, ii. 42. Notes and Queries, 4 S. iv. 276, 369. Harleian Society, xviii. 223. 2 Russell and Mylne's Reports, 153.

TROUTON. Burke's Colonial Gentry, ii. 536.

TROWBRIDGE. Betham's Baronetage, iv. 404. *See* TROBRIDGE.

TROWER. Berry's Sussex Genealogies, 233.

TROWLE. Cambridgeshire Visitation, edited by Sir T. Phillipps, 32. Harleian Society, xli. 29.

TROWSDALE. The Genealogist, v. 50.

TROYTE. Burke's Landed Gentry, 3, 4, 5, 6, 7, 8. Burke's Visitation of Seats and Arms, ii. 74.

TROYTE-BULLOCK. Burke's Visitation of Seats and Arms, 2nd Series, i. 45. Burke's Royal Descents and Pedigrees of Founders' Kin, 117.

TRUELL. Burke's Landed Gentry, 2, 3, 4, 5, 6, 7, 8.

TRUMAN. Glamorganshire Pedigrees, edited by Sir T. Phillipps, 8, 10. Genealogies of Morgan and Glamorgan, by G. T. Clark, 446.

TRUMBALL, or TRUMBULL. Gyll's History of Wraysbury, 71. Harleian Society, viii. 391. The Genealogist, vi. 100. New England Register, xlix. 322, 417.

TRUMWYN. Collections for a History of Staffordshire, (William Salt Society,) i. 341.

TRUSBUTT. Blomefield's Norfolk, vii. 405.

TRUSCOTT. Howard's Visitation of England and Wales, iv. 99.

TRUSLOVE. Foster's Visitations of Yorkshire, 582. Poulson's Holderness, i. 365.

TRUSLOWE. Visitatio Comitatus Wiltoniæ, 1623, printed by Sir T. Phillipps. Hoare's Wiltshire, III. iv. 58. Visitation of Wiltshire, edited by G. W. Marshall, 73.

TRUSSEL, or TRUSSELL. Harleian Society, iv. 28 ; xii. 93 ; xiii. 359 ; xvii. 298 ; xviii. 225 ; xxix. 466. Bridges' Northamptonshire, by Rev. Peter Whalley, ii. 51. Dugdale's Warwickshire, 26, 714. Baker's Northampton, i. 154. Burton's Description of Leicestershire, 93. Morant's Essex, i. 84. Berry's Hampshire Genealogies,

143. Banks' Dormant and Extinct Baronage, i. 423. Ormerod's Cheshire, iii. 229. Miscellanea Genealogica et Heraldica, 2nd Series, i. 123. The Genealogist, New Series, xv. 27, 157.

TRY, or TRYE. Rudder's Gloucestershire, 472. Burke's Commoners, i. 603, Landed Gentry, 2, 3, 4, 5, 6, 7, 8. Fosbrooke's History of Gloucestershire, i. 297. Visitation of Gloucester, edited by T. F. Fenwicke and W. C. Metcalfe, 188. Harleian Society, xxi. 169. The Genealogist, New Series, xvii. 241.

TRYAN. Harleian Society, xiii. 303, 506.

TRYCE. Camden Society, xliii. 107.

TRYMNELL. Nichols' History of the County of Leicester, iv. 726.

TRYON. Morant's Essex, ii. 252. Burke's Landed Gentry, (of Bulwick Park,) 3, 4, 5, 6, 7, 8 ; (of Alsager,) 5. Wright's Essex, i. 460. Burke's Extinct Baronetcies. History of Chislehurst, by Webb, Miller, and Beckwith, 277.

TRYOURNE. See TREWREN.

TRYST. Baker's Northampton, i. 752 ; ii. 45.

TRYVET. Excerpta Cantiana, by Rev. T. Streatfield, 6. See TREVETT.

TUBB. Harleian Society, ix. 247. The Genealogist, vi. 101. The Visitations of Cornwall, edited by J. L. Vivian, 519.

TUCHET. J. Wilkinson's History of Broughton Gifford, folding plate. Banks' Baronies in Fee, i. 101. Banks' Dormant and Extinct Baronage, ii. 17. The Genealogist, New Series, xv. 26. See TOUCHET.

TUCK, or TUCKE. Burke's Landed Gentry, 2 supp., 8. Harleian Society, i. 38. New England Register, x. 197.

TUCKER. Pocock's History of Gravesend, 11. Hasted's Kent, i. 155. Berry's Kent Genealogies, 36. Archæologia Cantiana, iv. 248. Burke's Landed Gentry, (of Trematon,) 2 supp., 3, 4, 5, 6 ; (of Kingsnympton,) 4 ; (of Coryton Park,) 2, 5, 6, 7, 8. Harleian Society, vi. 352 ; ix. 248 ; xlii. 3. Maclean's History of Trigg Minor, ii. 54. Polwhele's History of Cornwall, iv. 112. Westcote's Devonshire, edited by G. Oliver and P. Jones, 526. Pembrokeshire Pedigrees, 122. A Complete Parochial History of the County of Cornwall, ii. 168. An Historical Survey of Cornwall, by C. S. Gilbert, ii. 313. The Visitation of Devon, edited by F. T. Colby, 199. The Visitations of Cornwall, by J. L. Vivian, 521. The Genealogist, New Series, iii. 172. Bysshe's Visitation of Essex, edited by J. J. Howard, 94. New England Register, xxvi. 34. See DUN, TOKER, TOOKER.

TUCKER-EDWARDES. Burke's Commoners, ii. 313, Landed Gentry, 2 supp., 3, 4, 5.

TUCKETT. Foster's Account of Families Descended from Francis Fox, 19. History of the Willmer Family, 254.

TUDENHAM. Blomefield's Norfolk, vi. 174. Baker's Northampton, i. 186. Notes and Queries, 5 Series, ix. 83. Banks' Baronies in Fee, i. 363. See DE TUDENHAM.

TUDOR. Gentleman's Magazine, 1825, ii. 422, 484 ; 1826, i. 28, 397. Glamorganshire Pedigrees, edited by Sir T. Phillipps, 25. History of Powys Fadog, by J. Y. W. Lloyd, iii. 23 ; iv. 139, 383 ;

vi. 420. Metcalfe's Visitations of Northamptonshire, 51. Miscellanea Genealogica et Heraldica, 3rd Series, i. 21.

TUDOR-VYCHAN. Dwnn's Visitations of Wales, ii. 235.

TUDWAY. Burke's Landed Gentry, 2, 3, 4, 5, 6, 7, 8. Jewers' Wells Cathedral, 286.

TUESLEY. Surrey Archæological Collections, viii. Harleian Society, xliii. 166.

TUFNELL. Berry's Essex Genealogies, 123. Burke's Commoners, ii. 183, Landed Gentry, 2, 3, 4, 5, 6, 7, 8. Harleian Society, xiv. 721. Monken Hadley, by F. C. Cass, 166.

TUFTON. Memorials of the Family of Tufton, Earls of Thanet, by R. Pocock. Gravesend, 1800, 8vo. Jacob's Peerage, i. 548. Hasted's Kent, ii. 224, 638; iii. 253. Berry's Sussex Genealogies, 237. Berry's Kent Genealogies, 352. Harleian Society, viii. 205, 345; xlii. 118, 219; xliii. 102. Nichols' History of the County of Leicester, ii. 144. Surrey Archæological Collections, iv. Baker's Northampton, i. 606. Whitaker's Deanery of Craven, 3rd edn., 310. Edmondson's Baronagium Genealogicum, ii. 133. Brydges' Collins' Peerage, iii. 435. Burke's Extinct Baronetcies, and 615. Nicolson and Burn's Westmorland and Cumberland, i. 305.

TUFTS. New England Register, xi. 223; li. 299.

TUITE. Burke's Landed Gentry, 3, 4, 5, 6, 8. O'Hart's Irish Pedigrees, 2nd Series, 351.

TUKE. Morant's Essex, i. 407, 420. Foster's Yorkshire Pedigrees. Thoroton's Nottinghamshire, iii. 114. G. W. Johnson's History of Great Totham, 39. Harleian Society, xiii. 508; xiv. 609. Notes and Queries, 2 S. vii. 279, 404; 4 S. v. 266, 517. Burke's Extinct Baronetcies. Howard's Visitations of England and Wales, ii. 84.

TULL. The Genealogist, vi. 101.

TULLOCH. Burke's Colonial Gentry, ii. 519.

TULLY. New England Register, iii. 157.

TUNNARD. Burke's Landed Gentry, 3, 4, 5, 6, 7, 8.

TUNSTAL, or TUNSTALL. Baines' History of the Co. of Lancaster, iv. 616. Plantagenet-Harrison's History of Yorkshire, i. 300, 303, Synopsis of the Newcastle Museum. Newcastle, 1827, 8vo. Surtees Society, xxxvi. 31; xli. 95. Visitation of Durham, 1575. (Newcastle, 1820, fol.) 34. Visitation of Durham, 1615, (Sunderland, 1820, fol.) 32. Foster's Visitations of Yorkshire, 168, 583. Whitaker's History of Richmondshire, ii. 270, 272, 273, 501. Poulson's Holderness, ii. 235. Hutchinson's History of Durham, iii. 240. Surtees' Durham, i. lxvi.; iii. 272. Harleian Society, xvi. 326; xliii. 188. Foster's Visitations of Durham, 313.

TUNSTED. Visitation of Derbyshire, 1663-4, (Middle Hill, 1854, fol.) 7. The Genealogist, iii. 183; New Series, viii. 176.

TUPPER. Chronicle of the Family of De Havilland. Burke's Landed Gentry, 2 supp., 3, 4, 5, 6, 7, 8. Life of Sir Isaac Brock, by F. B. Tupper, 457. Burke's Colonial Gentry, i. 85.

TURBERVILE, TURBERVILL, or TURBERVILLE. Dr. Powell's History of
Wales, (Methyr Tydfil, 1812, 8vo.) xxxvi.   Camden Society,
xliii. 57.   Glamorganshire Pedigrees, edited by Sir T. Phillipps,
4, 5, 44.   Visitation of Wiltshire, 1677, printed by Sir T.
Phillipps, (Middle Hill, 1854, fol.).   Burke's Commoners, iv. 652.
Landed Gentry, 2, 3, 4, 5, 7, 8.   Harleian Society, vi. 289 ; viii.
192 ; xx. 95.   Lipscombe's History of the County of Bucking-
ham, i. 69.   Jones' History of the County of Brecknock, ii. 443.
Hutchins' Dorset, i. 138.   The Genealogist, vi. 102 ; New Series.
iii. 173.   Miscellanea Genealogica et Heraldica, 2nd Series, ii. 133.
Visitation of Gloucester, edited by T. F. Fenwick and W. C.
Metcalfe, 190.   Genealogies of Morgan and Glamorgan, by G. T.
Clark, 447-463.   The Visitations of Devon, by J. L. Vivian, 740.
See TURVILE.
TURBRIDGE. Dwnn's Visitations of Wales, ii. 351.
TURBUTT. Burke's Commoners, i. 666, Landed Gentry, 2, 3, 4, 5, 6,
7, 8.
TURGIS. Manning and Bray's Surrey, ii. 232.   Harleian Society,
xvii. 300.
TURING. The Lay of the Turings, a sketch of the Family History,
by H. M. K. 1830, 4to.
TURNBULL. Jeffrey's History of Roxburghshire, ii. 326.   Burke's
Colonial Gentry, ii. 665.
TURNER. Pope—Additional facts concerning his Maternal Ancestry,
[the Turners,] by Robert Davies. London, 1858, 8vo.   History
of Sapcote, by the Rev. H. Whitley, 68.   Archæologia Cantiana,
vi.   Morant's Essex, ii. 566.   Glover's History of Derbyshire,
ii. 13.   Berry's Sussex Genealogies, 370.   Berry's Kent Genealogies, 111, 274.   Visitation of Middlesex, (Salisbury, 1820, fol.)
49.   Surtees Society, xxxvi. 324.   Burke's Commoners, iv. 662.
Topographer and Genealogist, i. 505.   Burke's Landed Gentry,
(of Menie,) 2, 3, 4, 5 ; (of Glentyre,) 4, 5 ; (of Kippen House,) 6 ;
(of Turner Hall,) 7, 8 ; 8 at p. 2275.   Miscellanea Genealogica et
Heraldica, New Series, i. 158 ; iii. 231 ; iv. 158.   Harleian Society,
ii. 95 ; vi. 289, 290 ; xii. 151 ; xiii. 303, 509 ; xiv. 612 ; xvii.
301, 302 ; xix. 147 ; xxix. 467 ; xxxvii. 175 ; xxxviii. 699 ;
xxxix. 924 ; xlii. 25 ; xliii. 145.   Dallaway's Sussex, II. i. 217.
Ord's History of Cleveland, 368.   Nichols' History of the County
of Leicester, i. 548 ; ii. 142.   Baker's Northampton, ii. 7.
History of Worsborough, by Joseph Wilkinson, 111.   Some
Account of the Taylor Family, by P. A. Taylor, 690.   Sussex
Archæological Collections, xxv. 217.   Abram's History of Black-
burn, 544.   The Genealogist, iv. 150 ; New Series, x. 101.
Notes and Queries, 2 S. xii. 321.   Burke's Extinct Baronetcies.
Wotton's English Baronetage, iv. 217, 242.   Betham's Baronet-
age, iii. 225.   Metcalfe's Visitations of Suffolk, 170.   F. G. Lee's
History of Thame, 610.   Carthew's Hundred of Launditch, Part
iii. 129.   Howard's Visitation of England and Wales, i. 189.
Burke's Colonial Gentry, i. 275 ; ii. 455.   Bysshe's Visitation of
Essex, edited by J. J. Howard, 95.   Foster's Visitation of Mid-

dlesex, 90. New England Register, vii. 185; xli. 215. Turner
Family, Collections and Notes, by Harward Turner. 1895, 4to.
Burke's Family Records, 606. The Visitations of Devon, by J. L.
Vivian, 741. Ontarian Families, by E. M. Chadwick, ii. 148.
See TURNOR.

TURNER-FARLEY. Burke's Landed Gentry, 5.

TURNEY. English Church Furniture, by Edward Peacock, 215. The
Genealogist, vi. 288.

TURNHAM. Banks' Dormant and Extinct Baronage, i. 186.

TURNLY. Burke's Landed Gentry, 3, 4, 5, 6, 7, 8.

TURNOR. Morant's Essex, ii. 495, 569. Burke's Commoners, i. 300,
Landed Gentry, 2, 3, 4, 5, 6, 7, 8. Turnor's History of the Town
and Soke of Grantham, 147. Harleian Society, viii. 87, 160,
386, 404. Surrey Archæological Collections, vi. Metcalfe's Visitations of Suffolk, 72. *See* TURNER.

TURNOUGH. Fishwick's History of Rochdale, 355.

TURNOUR. Pedigree of Turnour, Earl of Winterton, by Sir T.
Phillipps, Bart. London, 1831, folio sheet. Berry's Sussex
Genealogies, 368. Harleian Society, viii. 235. Dallaway's
Sussex, II. i. 332. Manning and Bray's Surrey, ii. 7. Archdall's
Lodge's Peerage, iii. 167. *See* WINTERTON.

TURPIN. Cambridgeshire Visitation, edited by Sir T. Phillipps, 32.
Harleian Society, xli. 81. Nichols' History of the County of
Leicester, iv. 225.

TURSSAR. Harleian Society, xiii. 304.

TURTON. Burke's Landed Gentry, 2 and add., 4, 5, 6, 7, 8. Shaw's
Staffordshire, i. 128, 132. Visitation of Staffordshire, 1663-4,
printed by Sir T. Phillipps, 10. Erdeswicke's Survey of Staffordshire, 395. Betham's Baronetage, iv. 368. Visitations of Staffordshire, 1614 and 1663-4, William Salt Society, 290.

TURVILE, TURVILL, or TURVILLE. Bibliotheca Topographica Britan-
nica, vii. Parts i. and ii. 252. Burke's Commoners, ii. 644,
Landed Gentry, 2, 3, 4, 5, 6, 7, 8. Harleian Society, ii. 53;
xvii. 299. Burton's Description of Leicestershire, 188. Dugdale's
Warwickshire, 33, 119. Thoroton's Nottinghamshire, i. 47.
J. H. Hill's History of Market Harborough, 57, 58. Lipscombe's
History of the County of Buckingham, ii. 493. Nichols' History
of the County of Leicester, ii. 465; iv. 150, 451, 1004. Baker's
Northampton, i. 628. The Genealogist, New Series, xiv. 197.
See TURBERVILE.

TUSSOR. Harleian Society, xiii. 117.

TUTHILL. Harleian Society, xiii. 510. Notes and Queries, 2 S. iv.
150, 294. Howard's Visitation of Ireland, i. 35.

TUTT. Berry's Hampshire Genealogies, 38. Visitatio Comitatus
Wiltoniæ, 1623, printed by Sir T. Phillipps. Visitation of Wilt-
shire, edited by G. W. Marshall, 95. The Genealogist, New
Series, xiii. 25.

TUTTÉ. Berry's Sussex Genealogies, 289. Dallaway's Sussex, i.
App. to Chichester.

TUTTLE. New England Register, viii. 132; xxi. 133.

TWANBROOK, or TWENEBROKE. Historic Society of Lancashire and Cheshire, New Series, i. 1-20.

TWEDDELL. Hodgson's Northumberland, III. ii. 370. Surtees' Durham, iii. 82.

TWEDY, TWEEDIE, or TWEEDY. Harleian Society, xiii. 305. An Account of the Families of Boase, (Exeter, 1876, 4to.) 54. Burke's Landed Gentry, 5, 6, 7, 8. Metcalfe's Visitation of Worcester, 1683, 94.

TWELLS. East Anglian, iv. 34. Jewitt's Reliquary, vii. 146. The Genealogist, i. 35 ; vi. 36 ; vii. 163 ; New Series, xv. 120.

TWEMLOW, or TWEMLOWE. Burke's Commoners, (of Peatswood,) iii. 485, Landed Gentry, 2, 3, 4, 5 ; (of Hatherton,) Commoners, i. 334 ; (of Betley Court,) Landed Gentry, 5, 6, 7, 8. The Borough of Stoke-upon-Trent, by John Ward, 423. Ormerod's Cheshire, iii. 118. Earwaker's History of Sandbach, 110. Burke's Family Records, 608.

TWENGE. Ord's History of Cleveland, 269. *See* THWENG.

TWENTYMAN. W. Dickinson's History of Newark, 315. Harleian Society, xxxix. 983. 'Nottingham Daily Guardian,' newspaper, December 8, 1886, 2.

TWIFORD. Harleian Society, xxix. 468.

TWIGG. Transactions of Shropshire Archæological Society, ix. 5.

TWIGGE, or TWIGGS. The Visitations of Devon, by J. L. Vivian, 742. Glover's History of Derbyshire, ii. 196. Harleian Society, vi. 291.

TWINING. Some Facts in the History of the Twining Family, by W. H. G. Twining. Salisbury, 1895, 4to. New England Register, vii. 280. Burke's Colonial Gentry, ii. 739.

TWINYHOE, or TWYNEHO. Hutchins' Dorset, iii. 468. Bigland's Gloucestershire, ii. par. Shipton Solers. Weaver's Visitations of Somerset, 132. Harleian Society, xx. 95 ; xxi. 262.

TWISDEN, or TWYSDEN. Hasted's Kent, ii. 213, 275, 728. Berry's Kent Genealogies, 310. Willement's Historical Sketch of Davington, 50. Burke's Extinct Baronetcies, add. Wotton's English Baronetage, i. 211 ; iii. 497. Betham's Baronetage, i. 125 ; ii. 398. Hasted's Kent, (Hund. of Blackheath, by H. H. Drake,) 224. Harleian Society, xlii. 134.

TWISS. Burke's Landed Gentry, (of Birdhill,) 2, 3, 4, 5, 6, 7, 8 ; (of Hoseley,) 2 supp.

TWISTLETON, or TWISLETON. Case of Col. Thomas Twistleton, of Broughton Castle, in relation to the Barony of Saye and Sele, 1781, folio, pp. 7. The Case of John Twistleton of Broughton, in the Co. of Oxon, Esq., folio. Claim of John Twistleton, Esq., to the Barony of Saye and Sele, Sess. Papers, March, 1733. Case of Rev. F. B. Twistleton, on his claim to be Baron Saye and Sele, 1848, fol. pp. 72. Claim of the Rev. F. B. Twistleton, to be Baron of Saye and Sele, Sess. Papers, 316 of 1847 ; 101 of 1848. Hasted's Kent, i. 223. Foster's Visitations of Yorkshire, 583. Nichols' History of the County of Leicester, iv. 524. Edmondson's Baronagium Genealogicum, vi. 49. Brydges' Collins' Peerage,

vii. 16. Burke's Extinct Baronetcies. Harleian Society, xxxix. 922.

TWITTY. *See* TWEDY.

TWOMBLEY. New England Register, viii. 263.

TWYER. Poulson's Holderness, ii. 192.

TWYNE. Berry's Hampshire Genealogies, 223.

TYACK. The Visitations of Cornwall, by J. L. Vivian, 523.

TYAS. Metcalfe's Visitation of Worcester, 1683, 95.

TYBALD. Harleian Society, xxxii. 292.

TYBETOT. Blore's Rutland, 44. *See* TIBETOT.

TYDERYNTON. Ormerod's Cheshire, iii. 700.

TYDYR. Dwnn's Visitations of Wales, ii. 8, 192.

TYES. Banks' Dormant and Extinct Baronage, i. 427.

TYGHALL, or TYGEHALL. Ashmole's Antiquities of Berkshire, iii. 305. The Genealogist, New Series, ii. 108.

TYLDEN. Hasted's Kent, ii. 589. Berry's Kent Genealogies, 30. Burke's Commoners, ii. 381, Landed Gentry, 2, 3, 4, 5, 6, 7, 8.

TYLECOTE. Burke's Royal Families, (London, 1851, 8vo.) ii. 48.

TYLER. Pedigree of Tyler of Cottrells, Co. Glamorgan. [T. P.] 1864. Burke's Royal Families, (London, 1851, 8vo.) ii. 193. Burke's Landed Gentry, (of Cottrell,) 2, 3, 4, 5, 6, 7, 8 ; (of Newtownlimavady,) 4, 5, 6 ; (of Linsted,) 8. Antiquities and Memoirs of the Parish of Myddle, written by Richard Gough 1700, (fol.) 25, 49. The Genealogist, vi. 103. Harleian Society, xvii. 302. Burke's Colonial Gentry, ii. 572.

TYLLIOL. Surtees' Durham, i. 215. *See* TILLIOL.

TYLNEY. Metcalfe's Visitations of Suffolk, 73, 170.

TYLSTON. Harleian Society, xxxvii. 366.

TYMPERLEY. Metcalfe's Visitations of Suffolk, 170.

TYNDAL, TYNDALE, or TYNDALL. The Tyndale Pedigree, by B. W. Greenfield. London, 1843, folding sheets. Rudder's Gloucestershire, 696, 756. Morant's Essex, ii. 280. Blomefield's Norfolk, ii. 181. Burke's Commoners, (of Hayling,) iv. 545, Landed Gentry, 2, 3, 4, 5 ; (of Holton,) Landed Gentry, 4, 5 ; 8 at p. 155 ; (of Oaklands,) 6, 7, 8. Foster's Visitations of Yorkshire, 317. Surtees' Durham, i. 34. Memoirs of the Family of Chester, by R. E. C. Waters, 250, 263, 276. Transactions of the Bristol and Gloucestershire Archæological Society, 1877-8, 29. The Genealogist, ii. 1, 38, 123, 159, 227, 319, 356, 369 ; New Series, xiv. 103. Harleian Society, xiii. 511 ; xxi. 263. Banks' Baronies in Fee, i. 391. Bysshe's Visitation of Essex, edited by J. J. Howard, 96. New England Register, xviii. 185. A History of Banking in Bristol, by C. H. Cave, 248. Muskett's Suffolk Manorial Families, i. 146-153. *See* TINDAL.

TYNTE. Case of C. K. K. Tynte on his Claim to the Title of Baron Wharton, 1843, fol. pp. 58. Claim of C. K. K. Tynte, of Halswell, Co. Somerset, to the Barony of Wharton, Sess. Papers, 66 of 1844 ; 202 of 1845. Collinson's Somerset, i. 80 ; ii. 317. Visitation of Somersetshire, printed by Sir T. Phillipps, 141. Harleian Society, xi 113. Burke's Commoners, iv. 182.

Wotton's English Baronetage, iii. 554. Burke's Extinct Baronetcies, and 616. Family Notes, by J. M. Browne, 62. *See* KEMEYS-TYNTE.

TYPPING. Sir T. Phillipps' Topographer, No. 1, (March, 1821, 8vo.) 29. Visitation of Oxfordshire, 1574, printed by Sir T. Phillipps, (Middle Hill, fol.) 10. Visitation of Oxfordshire, 1634, printed by Sir T. Phillipps, (Middle Hill, fol.) 31. Harleian Society, v. 151. *See* TIPPING.

TYRCONNEL. Burke's Royal Families, (London, 1851, 8vo.) i. 11.

TYRINGHAM, or TYRRINGHAM. Camden Society, xliii. 115. Berry's Buckinghamshire Genealogies, 18, 20. Burke's Landed Gentry, 4, 5, 6, 7, 8 ; Topographer, (London, 1789-91, 8vo.) i. 497. Lipscombe's History of the County of Buckingham, i. 519 ; iv. 373, 375. Nichols' History of the County of Leicester, iv. 407. Baker's Northampton, i. 74. Harvey's Hundred of Willey, 304.

TYRREL, TYRRELL, or TYRELL. Morant's Essex, i. 100, 114, 199, 201, 206, 209, 261, 286 ; ii. 8, 50, 541. Croke's History of the Family of Croke, Nos. 36, 37. Berry's Essex Genealogies, 59. Burke's Landed Gentry, 2, 3, 4, 5, 6, 7. Gyll's History of Wraysbury, 236. Lipscombe's History of the County of Buckingham, i. 352 ; iii. 119 ; iv. 175. Wright's History of Essex, i. 108. Archæologia, i. 409. O'Hart's Irish Pedigrees, 2nd Series, 352. Harleian Society, xiv. 717 ; xvi. 328. Wotton's English Baronetage, ii. 76. Metcalfe's Visitations of Suffolk, 74, 171. Notes and Queries, 6 S. iii. 423. Burke's Extinct Baronetcies, and 616. Visitation of Staffordshire, (Willm. Salt Soc.) 141. Chancellor's Sepulchral Monuments of Essex, 173. *See* TIRRELL.

TYRWHITT. Notices and Remains of the Family of Tyrwhitt. Printed 1858, corrected and reprinted 1862, and again with corrections, 1872. By R. P. T. London, 8vo. Appendix to Case of Sir J. S. Sidney, claiming to be Lord Lisle. Gentleman's Magazine, 1835, i. 154. Burke's Commoners, i. 583. Wotton's English Baronetage, i. 178. Burke's Extinct Baronetcies. The Genealogist, vi. 286. East Barnet, by F. C. Cass, Part i. 26. Burke's Colonial Gentry, i. 211. *See* TIRWHIT.

TYRWHITT-DRAKE. Burke's Commoners, i. 580, Landed Gentry, 2, 3, 4, 5, 6, 7, 8.

TYSON. Harleian Society, xvi. 10. Annals of Smith of Balby, by H. E. Smith, 260.

TYSSEN. Berry's Hertfordshire Genealogies, 94-102. Berry's Essex Genealogies, 63. Burke's Landed Gentry, 2, 3, 4, 5, 6. W. Robinson's History of Hackney, i. 323. Harleian Society, xiv. 719. Miscellanea Genealogica et Heraldica, New Series, iii. 380.

TYSSEN-AMHURST. Burke's Landed Gentry, 3, 4, 5, 6, 7. Stemmata Britannica, by Joseph Foster, (London, 1877, 8vo.) 30. Burke's Royal Families, (edn. of 1876,) 214.

TYTHERLEIGH. Berry's Hampshire Genealogies, 273. The Genealogist, New Series, iii. 174.

TYTLER. Burke's Landed Gentry, 3, 5, 6, 7. *See* FRASER-TYTLER.

TYTTERY. *See* HENZEY.

TYWYN. Poetical Works of Lewis Glyn Cothi, (Oxford, 1837,) 282.
TYZACK. *See* HENZEY.

UDNEY, or UDNY. The Genealogist, ii. 33, 87. Udney *v.* Allott;
Supplemental Appendix to Cause in House of Lords, 1860, 4to.,
pp. 13. Burke's Landed Gentry, 6, 7, 8.

UFFENHAM. Herald and Genealogist, viii. 188, 517. Visitatio
Comitatus Wiltoniæ, 1623, printed by Sir T. Phillipps. Hoare's
Wiltshire, III. iv. 68. The Genealogist, New Series, xiii. 26.

UFFLETE. Metcalfe's Visitations of Suffolk, 172. Notes and Queries,
5 S. ii. 255, 412.

UFFORD. Topographer and Genealogist, iii. 271. Notices of Swyncombe and Ewelme, in Co. Oxford, by H. A. Napier, 288. Collectanea Topographica et Genealogica, v. 154; viii. 179. Banks'
Baronies in Fee, i. 437. Banks' Dormant and Extinct Baronage,
i. 429. Harleian Society, xviii. 91. *See* DE UFFORD.

UGHTRED. Banks' Baronies in Fee, i. 440. Banks' Dormant and
Extinct Baronage, i. 430.

ULF. Poulson's Holderness, ii. 2.

ULVINGTON. Plantagenet-Harrison's History of Yorkshire, i. 485.

UMFRAVILLE, or UMFREVILLE. The Umfrevilles, their Ancestors and
Descendants. (No place or date,) 4to. Burke's Commoners, ii.
193. Harleian Society, viii. 140. Hodgson's Northumberland, I.
ii. 35. Surtees' Durham, ii. 325, 394. Wood's Douglas's Peerage
of Scotland, i. 62. Notes and Queries, 2 S. xi. 330. Banks'
Baronies in Fee, i. 103. Banks' Dormant and Extinct Baronage,
i. 431. Bysshe's Visitation of Essex, edited by J. J. Howard, 97.
The Genealogist, New Series, xiv. 195. *See* DE UMFREVILLE.

UNCAS. New England Register, x. 227.

UNDERCOMBE. Morant's Essex, ii. 277.

UNDERHILL. Visitation of Warwickshire, 1619, published with Warwickshire Antiquarian Magazine, 36. Herald and Genealogist, ii.
127. Collectanea Topographica et Genealogica, vi. 380. Shakespere's Home, by J. C. M. Bellew, 87. Dugdale's Warwickshire,
607. Harleian Society, xii. 31; xvii. 304. Notes and Queries,
3 S. i. 285; 4 S. iii. 259. Miscellanea Genealogica et Heraldica,
New Series, iv. 78.

UNDERWOOD. Harleian Society, xvii. 303; xxxii. 293. New England
Register, xxxviii. 400.

UNETT. Burke's Landed Gentry, (of the Woodland,) 2, 3, 4; (of
Freen's Court,) 2, 3, 4, 5. Shaw's Staffordshire, ii. 149. History
of the Princes of South Wales, by G. T. O. Bridgeman, 293.
Weaver's Visitation of Herefordshire, 66. Burke's Family Records,
609.

UNIACKE. Burke's Landed Gentry, (of Mount Uniacke,) 2, 3, 4, 5,
6, 7, 8; (of Woodhouse,) 2, 3, 4. Betham's Baronetage, v. 480.
The Genealogical Magazine, ii. 412.

UNTHANK. Burke's Landed Gentry, 5, 6, 7, 8.

UNTON. The Unton Inventories, with Genealogical Notices of the
Unton Family, by J. G. Nichols. London, 1841, 4to. Croke's

History of the Family of Croke, No. 24. Gentleman's Magazine, 1835, ii. 472. Ashmole's Antiquities of Berkshire, iii. 313. Burke's Commoners, i. 357.

UNWIN, or UNWYNE. Berry's Hampshire Genealogies, 59. Miscellanea Genealogica et Heraldica, New Series, ii. 353. Visitation of Staffordshire, 1663-4, printed by Sir T. Phillipps, 10. Visitation of Staffordshire, (Willm. Salt Soc.) 142. Visitations of Staffordshire, 1614 and 1663-4, William Salt Society, 292. Harleian Society, xxxvii. 381.

UPCHER. Burke's Landed Gentry, 2, 3, 4, 5, 6, 7, 8. Howard's Visitation of England and Wales, iii. 25.

UPHAM. New England Register, xxiii. 33, 130.

UPPETON. Harleian Society, ix. 291.

UPPHILL. Harleian Society, xvii. 304.

UPPLEBY. Burke's Landed Gentry, 2, 3, 4, 5, 6, 7, 8. Pedigree of Wilson of High Wray, etc., by Joseph Foster, 112. Pedigree of Wilson, by S. B. Foster, 37.

UPTON. Upton Family Records. By W. H. Upton. London, 1893, 4to. Hasted's Kent, ii. 766. Berry's Kent Genealogies, 152. Tuckett's Devonshire Pedigrees, 75. Visitation of Somersetshire, printed by Sir T. Phillipps, 141. Burke's Commoners, (of Ingmire Hall,) iv. 385, Landed Gentry, 2, 3, 4, 5, 6, 7, 8 ; (of Glyde Court,) Landed Gentry, 2, 3, 4, 5, 6, 7, 8. Harleian Society, vi. 292 ; ix. 291; xii. 229; xlii. 46. Westcote's Devonshire, edited by G. Oliver and P. Jones, 519. Maclean's History of Trigg Minor, iii. 384. A Complete Parochial History of the County of Cornwall, iii. 116. An Historical Survey of Cornwall, by C. S. Gilbert, i. 462. Notes and Queries, 2 S. ix. 227 ; 6 S. viii. 372. Archdall's Lodge's Peerage, vii. 152. Visitation of Devon, edited by F. T. Colby, 201. The Genealogist, v. 51. Weaver's Visitations of Somerset, 82. New England Register, xl. 147. Somersetshire Wills, printed for F. A. Crisp, i. 7. Miscellanea Genealogica et Heraldica, 2nd Series, ii. 65, 102, 113, 129, 161, 182 ; iv. 21, 45, 73. Notts and Derbyshire Notes and Queries, iv. 144. The Visitations of Devon, by J. L. Vivian, 743. Nicolson and Burn's Westmorland and Cumberland, i. 259. Transactions of the Shropshire Archæological Society, N.S. ii. 174 ; iii. 185. See DE UPTON.

UPTON-GLEDSTANES. Burke's Landed Gentry, 3, 4, 5.

UPWOOD. Miscellanea Genealogica et Heraldica, 2nd Series, iv. 248.

URIEL. Foster's Visitations of Cumberland and Westmorland, 137.

URMESTON, or URMSTON. Collectanea Topographica et Genealogica, viii. 147. Chetham Society, lxxxi. 114 ; lxxxviii. 319 ; xcviii. 91.

URQUHART. Promptuary of Time, with the Pedigree of the Urquharts of Cromartie. London, 1652, 8vo. Reprinted in the 8vo. edn. of Sir Thomas Urquhart's Tracts. Edinburgh, 1774. Burke's Royal Families, (London, 1851, 8vo.) ii. 108. Burke's Commoners, (of Meldrum,) ii. 294, Landed Gentry, 2, 3, 4, 5, 6, 7, 8; (of Craigston,) Commoners, ii. 300, Landed Gentry, 2, 3, 4, 5, 6, 7, 8. Nisbet's Heraldry, ii. app. 132, 274. Douglas's Baronage of

Scotland, 156, 166. Inverurie and the Earldom of the Garioch, by John Davidson, 468. Northern Notes and Queries, vi. 133.

URRICK. Harleian Society, xliii. 138.

URRY, or URREY. Morant's Essex, i. 254. History of Merchant Taylor's School, by Rev. H. B. Wilson, 1172. Berry's Hampshire Genealogies, 356, 357.

URSWICK. Hunter's Deanery of Doncaster, ii. 437. Foster's Visitations of Cumberland and Westmorland, 46. See DE URSWYK.

USBORNE. Burke's Landed Gentry, 6, 7, 8.

USHER, or USSHER. Genealogical Memoirs of the Ussher Families in Ireland, by W. B. Wright. Dublin, 1889, 4to. Foster's Visitations of Yorkshire, 350, 636. History of Barnsley, by Rowland Jackson, 113. Burke's Landed Gentry, (of Eastwell,) 3, 4, 5, 6, 7, 8; (of Cappagh,) 2, 3, 4, 5, 6, 7, 8. Notes and Queries, 2 S. viii. 324, 438. The Irish Builder, xxviii. 111. New England Register, xxiii. 410.

USTICKE. Burke's Landed Gentry, (of Penwarne,) 2 supp.; (of Woodlane,) 7, 8; (of Trenley House,) 3, 4. A Complete Parochial History of the County of Cornwall, iii. 304. See NOWELL-USTICKE.

UTBER. Carthew's Hundred of Launditch, Part ii. 729. Harleian Society, xvii. 305, 306; xxxii. 293.

UTHWATT. Berry's Buckinghamshire Genealogies, 49.

UVEDALE, or UVEDALL. Collectanea Topographica et Genealogica, v. 253. Surrey Archæological Collections, iii. 63-192. Hutchins' Dorset, iii. 144. Hoare's Wiltshire, IV. ii. 60. Manning and Bray's Surrey, ii. 400. Plantagenet-Harrison's History of Yorkshire, i. 220. Berry's Hampshire Genealogies, 76. Banks' Baronies in Fee, ii. 149. The Genealogist, New Series, iii. 175; xvi. 237. Miscellanea Genealogica et Heraldica, 2nd Series, ii. 345; v. 297, 305.

UWCH AERON. Dwnn's Visitations of Wales, i. 26, 88.

VACHELL. Ashmole's Antiquities of Berkshire, iii. 312. Lipscombe's History of the County of Buckingham, i. 336. The Genealogist, vi. 104; vii. 253; New Series, ii. 109. Berks Architectural and Archæological Society's Journal, iii. 2, 32, 44, 87.

VACYE. Harleian Society, ix. 250. The Visitations of Cornwall, by J. L. Vivian, 525.

VAIL, or VAILE. Berry's Kent Genealogies, 292. Burke's Colonial Gentry, ii. 685.

VAIZEY. Burke's Landed Gentry, 6 supp., 7, 8.

VALCKENBURGH. Burke's Extinct Baronetcies. See VAN VAULCONBURGH.

VALE. Burke's Landed Gentry, 8.

VALENCE. History of Gainsburgh, by Adam Stark, 2nd edn., 440. Hodgson's Northumberland, II. ii. 41. Visitatio Comitatus Wiltoniæ, 1623, printed by Sir T. Phillipps. Banks' Baronies in Fee, i. 441.

VALENTIA. Case of Arthur, Viscount Valentia, claiming to be Earl of Anglesea, 1799, folio, pp. 24. Claim of Arthur, Viscount

Valentia, to the Earldom of Anglesea, Sess. Papers, Feb. 1770—
April 1772. Several Claims to the Title of Viscount Valentia,
etc. Dublin, 1773, folio.

VALENTINE, or VALENTYN. Chetham Society, lxxxviii. 320; xcv. 70.
New England Register, xx. 221.

VALLETOURT, or VALETORT. Banks' Dormant and Extinct Baronage,
i. 188. Visitation of Devon, edited by F. T. Colby, 210.

VALOINES, VALOYNES, or VALOIGNS. Jewitt's Reliquary, xvi. 97.
The Genealogist, vi. 7. Clutterbuck's Hertford, ii. 277. Banks'
Dormant and Extinct Baronage, i. 187. The Antiquary, (London,
1873,) iv. 312. Notes and Queries, 6 S. v. 142, 290. See DE
VALOINES.

VALONIIS. Wood's Douglas's Peerage of Scotland, ii. 348.

VALPY. J. B. Payne's Armorial of Jersey, 339. Burke's Family
Records, 611.

VAMPAGE. Nash's Worcestershire, ii. 183. Harleian Society, xxvii.
68, 137.

VAN. Historical Tour in Monmouthshire, by Wm. Coxe, 41. Glamorganshire Pedigrees, edited by Sir T. Phillipps, 3. Genealogies of
Morgan and Glamorgan, by G. T. Clark, 464.

VANACKER. Clutterbuck's Hertford, i. 453. Wotton's English
Baronetage, iv. 89. Burke's Extinct Baronetcies. The Perverse
Widow, by A. W. Crawley-Boevey, 185.

VANBRUGH. Harleian Society, viii. 511. The Genealogist, ii. 237.
Notes and Queries, 2 S. i. 8, 116 ; 4 S. ix. 499 ; x. 17. Sir John
Vanbrugh, (Plays,) by A. E. H. Swaen, 12.

VANCE. A Correct Pedigree of the Vance Family, by Willm. Vance,
London, 1882, large sheet. An Account of the Family of Vance
in Ireland, by W. Balbirnie. Cork, 1860, 4to. O'Hart's Irish Pedigrees, 2nd Series, 352.

VAN CORTLANDT. Burke's Heraldic Illustrations, 115. Burke's
Commoners, iv. 241, Landed Gentry, 4.

VAN COULSTER. Burke's Extinct Baronetcies.

VANDELEUR. Burke's Landed Gentry, 2, 3, 4, 5, 6, 7, 8.

VANDEN-BEMPDE. Betham's Baronetage, iv. 303.

VANDEN-BEMPDE-JOHNSTONE. Foster's Yorkshire Pedigrees.

VANDEPUT. Harleian Society, viii. 389 ; xvii. 307. Wotton's
English Baronetage, iv. 204. Betham's Baronetage, iii. 203.
Burke's Extinct Baronetcies.

VANDER-BRANDE. Burke's Extinct Baronetcies.

VANDER-EYCKEN. Topographer and Genealogist, ii. 471.

VANDER-NOTTEN. See BOSANQUET.

VANDERSTEGEN. Burke's Landed Gentry, 4, 5, 6, 7, 8.

VANDEWALL. Cyclostyle Pedigrees, by J. J. Green.

VANE. The Great Governing Families of England, i. 66. The
Antiquities of Gainsford, by J. R. Walbran. J. H. Hill's History
of Market Harborough, 37. History of Hartlepool, by Sir C.
Sharpe, (1816, 8vo.) 82. Harleian Society, viii. 7. Hutchinson's
History of Cumberland, i. 508. History of Blyth, by Rev.
John Raine, 96. Hutchinson's History of Durham, iii. 264.

Surtees' Durham, iii. 214. W. Fordyce's History of Durham, 104, 323. An Historical Survey of Cornwall, by C. S. Gilbert, i. 442. Edmondson's Baronagium Genealogicum, iii. 293. Brydges' Collins' Peerage, iv. 499. Betham's Baronetage, iv. 117, 175. Burke's Extinct Baronetcies. Foster's Visitations of Durham, 315. The Genealogist, New Series, xiii. 81, 210. Transactions of the Thoroton Society, 1901, *at end. See* FANE.

VAN FREISENDORF. Burke's Extinct Baronetcies, *Add.*

VAN KONGHNET. Burke's Colonial Gentry, ii. 705. Ontarian Families, by E. M. Chadwick, i. 160.

VANLORE. Croke's History of the Family of Croke, No. 26. Burke's Extinct Baronetcies.

VANS. Lands and their Owners in Galloway, by P. H. M'Kerlie, i. 377. Nisbet's Heraldry, ii. app. 250. *See* VANCE, VAUX.

VANS-AGNEW. The Agnews of Lochnaw, by Sir A. Agnew, 617. Burke's Commoners, i. 436, Landed Gentry, 2, 3, 4, 5, 6, 7, 8. Stemmata Britannica, by Joseph Foster, (London, 1877, 8vo.) 9.

VAN SITTART. Berry's Buckinghamshire Genealogies, 51-54. Burke's Landed Gentry, 2, 3, 4, 5, 6, 7, 8.

VAN STRAUBENZEE. Burke's Royal Families, (London, 1851, 8vo.) ii. 82. Burke's Landed Gentry, 2, 3, 4, 5, 6, 7. Foster's Yorkshire Pedigrees.

VAN TROMP. Burke's Extinct Baronetcies.

VAN VAULCONBURGH. Surtees Society, liv. 285. *See* VALCKENBURGH.

VAN WIJCKERSLOOT. Harleian Society, xvii. 307.

VARNEY. Amye Robsart, by George Adlard, 89. *See* VERNEY.

VARNUM. New England Register, v. 79, 250.

VASEY. Visitation of Durham, 1615, (Sunderland, 1820, fol.) 4. Surtees' Durham, iii. 381. Foster's Visitations of Durham, 316.

VASSALL. Burke's Commoners, i. 499, Landed Gentry, 2. Harleian Society, xvii. 308. New England Register, xvii. 56, 113 ; li. 152.

VAUDIN. J. B. Payne's Armorial of Jersey, 343.

VAUGHAN. Miscellanea Genealogica et Heraldica, ii. 254. Morant's Essex, i. 194. Poetical Works of Lewis Glyn Cothi, (Oxford, 1837,) 1. British Antiquity Revived, etc., by Robert Vaughan. Bala, 1834, 4to. Glamorganshire Pedigrees, edited by Sir T. Phillipps, 39, 43. Dwnn's Visitations of Wales, i. 127, 139, 147, 150, 172, 190, 213, 226, 245, 255, 280, 291, 294 ; ii. 27, 55, 58, 219, 229, 232, 275. Visitation of Somersetshire, printed by Sir T. Phillipps, 143. Visitation of Gloucestershire, 1569, (Middle Hill, 1854, fol.) 9. Burke's Royal Families, (London, 1851, 8vo.) ii. 95. Burke's Commoners, (of Nanney and Dolymelynllyn,) ii. 571, Landed Gentry, 2, 4 ; (of Burlton Hall,) Commoners, ii. 238, Landed Gentry, 2, 3, 4, 5, 6, 7, 8 ; (of Humphreston,) 8 ; (of Rheola,) Landed Gentry, 2, 3, 4, 5, 7 at p. 1076, 8 ; (of Caethle,) 2, 3, 4 ; (of Court Field,) 2, 3, 4, 5, 6, 7, 8 ; (of Golden Grove,) 5, 6, 7, 8 ; (of Quilly,) 6 supp., 7, 8 ; (of Brynog,) 8 ; (of Builth,) 8. Foster's Visitations of Yorkshire, 120, 584. History of the Parish of St. Leonard, Shoreditch, by Henry Ellis, 326. Harleian Society, xi. 113 ; xvii. 309, 310 ; xxi. 264 ; xxvii. 79 ; xxviii. 85 ;

xxix. 515 ; xxxix. 993.   Jones' History of the County of Brecknock, ii. 190, 340, 360, 505.   Caermarthenshire Pedigrees, 4, 17,
19, 22, 23, 25, 28, 38, 42, 65.   Cardiganshire Pedigrees, 74, 91,
93, 97.   Pembrokeshire Pedigrees, 122, 158.   Visitatio Comitatus Wiltoniæ, 1623, printed by Sir T. Phillipps.   Hoare's Wiltshire,
III. iv. 8.   Meyrick's History of the Co. of Cardigan, 174, 321, 439.
T. Nichols' County Families of Wales, 201, 955.   Robinson's
Mansions of Herefordshire, 163.   Archæologia Cambrensis, 4 S.,
ix. 164.   Works of Henry Vaughan, (Fuller Worthies Library,)
i. xxv.   The Sheriffs of Montgomeryshire, by W. V. Lloyd, 3,
215, 376.   Collections by the Powys-land Club, ix. 217, 426.
Archdall's Lodge's Peerage, iii. 288.   Betham's Baronetage, iv.
236.   Banks' Dormant and Extinct Baronage, iii. 705.   Visitation
of Wiltshire, edited by G. W. Marshall, 13.   Notes and Queries,
4 S. iii. 579 ; 5 S. ii. 93.   History of Powys Fadog, by J. Y. W.
Lloyd, iv. 95, 293 ; v. 292, 357, 382, 407 ; vi. 75, 113, 164, 265.
382-97, 491.   The Genealogist, New Series, iii. 175.   Weaver's
Visitation of Herefordshire, 68, 97.   Visitation of Gloucester,
edited by T. F. Fenwick and W. C. Metcalfe, 190.   The Genealogies of Morgan and Glamorgan, by G. T. Clark, 233-249, 266,
367.   Fletcher's Leicestershire Pedigrees and Royal Descents, 132.
New England Register, v. 245 ; xix. 343.   A History of Banking
in Bristol, by C. H. Cave, 252.   *See* VYCHAN.
VAUGHAN-JENKINS. Burke's Landed Gentry, 5.
VAUGHAN-LEE. Burke's Landed Gentry, 8.
VAUGHAN-PRYSE-RICE. Burke's Landed Gentry, 8.
VAUNCY. Clutterbuck's Hertford, ii. 495.
VAUX, VAULX, VAUS, or VAUSE. Case of E. B. Hartopp, Esq., on
his claim to the title of Baron Vaux of Harrowden, 1836, folio,
pp. 26.   Case of George Mostyn of Kiddington, on his claim to
the Barony of Vaux of Harrowden, 1836, folio, pp. 21.   Claims
of George Mostyn, and E. B. Hartopp, to the Barony of Vaux of
Harrowden, Sess. Papers, 41 of 1836.   Sketch of a Genealogical
Account of the Family of Vaux, Vaus, or De Vallibus. Pembroke,
1800, 4to.   Speeches delivered upon the Claims to the Barony of
Vaux of Harrowden. London, 1836, 8vo.   Royal and other
original Documents addressed to the Lairds of Barnbarroch, with
sketch of their family history, *n.d.*, 4to.   Burke's Commoners,
iv. 100.   Harleian Society, vii. 27 ; xix. 148 ; xxviii. 152.   Berry's
Hampshire Genealogies, 291.   Foster's Visitations of Yorkshire,
228.   Herald and Genealogist, iii. 515.   Lipscombe's History of
the County of Buckingham, i. 271.   Jefferson's History of Leath
Ward, Cumberland, 145.   Bridges' Northamptonshire, by Rev.
Peter Whalley, ii. 103.   Nichols' History of the County of Leicester, ii. 28 ; iii. 1129.   Visitatio Comitatus Wiltoniæ, 1623, printed
by Sir T. Phillipps.   Clutterbuck's Hertford, iii. 80.   Lands and
their Owners in Galloway, by P. H. M'Kerlie, i. 359.   Edmondson's
Baronagium Genealogicum, iv. 357.   Banks' Baronies in Fee,
i. 442.   Banks' Dormant and Extinct Baronage, i. 189 ; iii. 707.
Visitation of Wiltshire, edited by G. W. Marshall, 17.   Metcalfe's

Visitations of Northamptonshire, 51, 203. Harvey's Hundred of Willey, 266. Foster's Visitations of Cumberland and Westmorland, 136. The Genealogist, New Series, xiii. 174. Nicolson and Burn's Westmorland and Cumberland, ii. 487. *See* MOSTYN, VANCE, VANS.

VAVASOR, or VAVASOUR. Surtees Society, xxxvi. 345; xli. 56. Foster's Visitations of Yorkshire, 107, 116, 235-237, 345, 368, 435. Herald and Genealogist, vi. 416. Bridges' Northamptonshire, by Rev. Peter Whalley, ii. 345. Whitaker's Loidis and Elmete, 206. Miscellanea Genealogica et Heraldica, i. 193, 245, 322, 325; ii. 270-276. Burke's Commoners, i. 51. Foster's Yorkshire Pedigrees. Stonehouse's History of the Isle of Axholme, 343. Hunter's Deanery of Doncaster, i. 395. Foley's Records of the English Province S. J., iv. 690. Harleian Society, xiii. 118, 306, 513; xiv. 611; xvi. 329, 332; xxix. 468. The Sheriffs of Montgomeryshire, by W. V. Lloyd, 133. Wotton's English Baronetage, ii. 130. Banks' Baronies in Fee, i. 444. Betham's Baronetage, i. 355; v. 425. Banks' Dormant and Extinct Baronage, i. 435. Burke's Extinct Baronetcies. W. Wheater's History of Sherburn and Cawood, 159. Ilkley, Ancient and Modern, by R. Collyer and J. H. Turner, 110. Metcalfe's Visitations of Northamptonshire, 148. Fishwick's History of Rochdale, 329. The Gresley's of Drakelowe, by F. Madan, 288. *See* DURELL.

VAWDEY. Harleian Society, xiv. 612.

VAWDREY, or VAWDRY. Burke's Commoners, i. 353, Landed Gentry, 2, 3, 4, 6, 7, 8. Ormerod's Cheshire, i. 549. Miscellanea Genealogica et Heraldica, New Series, iv. 357. The Genealogist, New Series, xv. 211.

VAWER. Somersetshire Wills, printed for F. A. Crisp, iv. 50. Weaver's Visitations of Somerset, 133.

VAZIE. Visitation of Oxfordshire, 1634, printed by Sir T. Phillipps, (Middle Hill, fol.) 31. Harleian Society, v. 256.

VEALE, VEEL, or VELE. Chronicle of the Family of De Havilland. Burke's Landed Gentry, 4, 5, 6, 7, 8. Chetham Society, lxxxviii. 321. The Tyldesley Diary, edited by J. Gillow and A. Hewitson, 170. Rudder's Gloucestershire, 849. Fosbrooke's Abstracts of Smith's Lives of the Berkeleys, 73. Visitation of Gloucestershire, 1569, (Middle Hill, 1854, fol.) 10. Fosbrooke's History of Gloucestershire, ii. 37, 38. Fishwick's History of Bispham, 83-93. Visitation of Gloucester, edited by T. F. Fenwick and W. C. Metcalfe, 191. Genealogies of Morgan and Glamorgan, by G. T. Clark, 468. Harleian Society, xxi. 171.

VEINOR. Harleian Society, xxix. 474. *See* VYNER.

VEITCH. Burke's Landed Gentry, 2, 3, 4, 5, 6, 7, 8.

VEITCH-HAIG. Burke's Landed Gentry, 7, 8.

VELLY. Harleian Society, vi. 293. The Visitations of Devon, by J. L. Vivian, 745.

VENABLES. Berry's Hampshire Genealogies, 221. Burke's Landed Gentry, (of Woodhill,) 2, 3, 4; (of Leftwich,) 4; (of Llysdinam Hall,) 5, 6, 7, 8. Maclean's History of Trigg Minor, i. 651.

J. P. Earwaker's East Cheshire, i. 51. Ormerod's Cheshire, i. 523, 539, 658; iii. 113, 198. Harleian Society, xviii. 226-230. The Genealogist, New Series, xii. 110; xv. 156, 220; xvi. 47. Earwaker's History of Sandbach, 129. Chetham Society, lxxxiii. v. Transactions of Shropshire Archæological Society, v. 332.

VENN. Burke's Landed Gentry, 2, 3. Harleian Society, xvii. 308.

VENNER, or VENNOR. Harleian Society, vi. 294; xxxviii. 725. The Visitations of Devon, by J. L. Vivian, 746.

VENOUR. Berry's Kent Genealogies, 370. Berry's Berkshire Genealogies, 126. Harleian Society, xii. 313; xlii. 136.

VENTRIS. Cambridgeshire Visitation, edited by Sir T. Phillipps, 32. Harleian Society, xix. 148; xli. 53.

VENUZ. Herald and Genealogist, v. 316.

VERDIN. Burke's Landed Gentry, 8.

VERDON. Jewitt's Reliquary, viii. 145. Burton's Description of Leicestershire, 179. Nichols' History of the County of Leicester, iii. 640. Dugdale's Warwickshire, 44. Harleian Society, xvi. 312. Banks' Baronies in Fee, i. 445. Banks' Dormant and Extinct Baronage, i. 191; ii. 566. Visitation of Staffordshire, (Willm. Salt Soc.) 144. Genealogical Table of John Stratford Collins. Burke's Colonial Gentry, i. 232. See DE VERDON.

VERE. Planché's Corner of Kent, 264. East Anglian, i. 115. Morant's Essex, ii. 292. Hasted's Kent, ii. 775. Jacob's Peerage, i. 328. Bird's Magazine of Honour, 82. Blomefield's Norfolk, i. 84. Burke's Commoners, (of Craigie Hall,) iii. 319, Landed Gentry, 2, 3, 4, 5, 6, 7, 8; (of Carlton,) Landed Gentry, 3, 4, 5, 6; (of Managhin,) 2. Gyll's History of Wraysbury, 7. Lipscombe's History of the County of Buckingham, i. 29. Bridge's Northamptonshire, by Rev. Peter Whalley, ii. 251. Clutterbuck's Hertford, iii. 104. Chauncy's Hertfordshire, 135. Harleian Society, xiii. 16; xvi. 227; xx. 12. Douglas's Baronage of Scotland, 153. Metcalfe's Visitations of Suffolk, 74, 80. Maidment's Scottish Songs and Ballads, ii. 267. See ALNO, CAVENDISH, DE VERE, WEIR.

VEREKER. The Irish Builder, xxxv. 196.

VERELST. Hunter's Deanery of Doncaster, ii. 166. The Manor of Minster, by H. W. Aldred, 41. Burke's Landed Gentry, 8.

VERLING. Family Notes, by J. M. Browne, 72.

VERMAN. Harleian Society, ix. 251. The Visitations of Cornwall, by J. L. Vivian, 526.

VERMUYDEN. Harleian Society, xvii. 310. Notes and Queries, 8 S. iv. 152.

VERNATTI. Herald and Genealogist, v. 146. Burke's Extinct Baronetcies, 638.

VERNER. Chronicle of the Family of De Havilland. Burke's Commoners, iv. 56.

VERNEY. Memoirs of the Verney Family, by Lady Verney. London, 1892-9, 8vo., 4 vols. Claim of Sir R. Verney to the Barony of Brooke, Sess. Papers, Dec. 1694—February 1695. Amye Robsart, by George Adlard, 89. Camden Society, lvi. Hasted's Kent,

i. 379. Evidence on Balfour of Burley Peerage, 313. Gentleman's Magazine, 1834, ii. 33, 226, 364. Berry's Surrey Genealogies, 59. Visitation of Somersetshire, printed by Sir T. Phillipps, 142. Visitation of Warwickshire, 1619, published with Warwickshire Antiquarian Magazine, 148. Harleian Society, viii. 37 ; xii. 25 ; xxii. 23, 168. Lipscombe's History of the County of Buckingham, i. 178, 180, 184. Wright's History of Rutland, 22. Bridges' Northamptonshire, by Rev. Peter Whalley, i. 535. Nichols' History of the County of Leicester, iii. 12. Dugdale's Warwickshire, 566. Clutterbuck's Hertford, i. 284 ; iii. 512. Edmondson's Baronagium Genealogicum, iv. 369. Archdall's Lodge's Peerage, ii. 283. Brydges' Collins' Peerage, vi. 691. Burke's Extinct Baronetcies. Weaver's Visitations of Somerset, 83. *See* DE VERNAI, VARNEY.

VERNON. Historical Memoir of the House of Vernon, (by Thomas Stapleton, *n.d.*, unfinished,) 4to. Miscellanea Genealogica et Heraldica, i. 212 ; 2nd Series, iv. 206. Cussan's History of Hertfordshire, Parts iii. and iv. 23. Morant's Essex, i. 335. Gough's Sepulchral Monuments, ii. 264. Burke's Visitation of Seats and Arms, 2nd Series, i. 52. Jewitt's Reliquary, vii. 30 ; xxi. 127. Dwnn's Visitations of Wales, i. 153. Collectanea Topographica et Genealogica, iii. 160. Harleian Society, viii. 358 ; xiii. 118, 307, 512 ; xiv. 612 ; xviii. 230-236, 241 ; xxii. 99 ; xxvii. 138 ; xxix. 469 ; xxxvii. 127. Nash's Worcestershire, i. 549. Burke's Royal Families, (London, 1851, 8vo.) i. 57. Burke's Commoners, (of Hilton Park,) iii. 622, Landed Gentry, 2, 3, 4, 5, 6, 7, 8 ; (of Clontarf Castle,) 3, 4, 5, 6, 7, 8 ; (of Hanbury,) 4, 5, 6. Herald and Genealogist, vi. 105. Lipscombe's History of the County of Buckingham, i. 383. Hodgson's Northumberland, II. ii. 239. Shaw's Staffordshire, i. 87, 404, app. 38. Eyton's Antiquities of Shropshire, ii. 226. Nichols' History of the County of Leicester, iii. 982* ; iv. 36, 283. Clutterbuck's Hertford, ii. 200. Chauncy's Hertfordshire, 272. Ormerod's Cheshire, ii. 795 ; iii. 200, 252, 317. John D'Alton's History of Co. Dublin, 95. Collections by the Powys-land Club, i. 365, 367, 382, 388. Pilkington's View of Derbyshire, ii. 247. Notes and Queries, 1 S. v. 389, 471 ; 3 S. v. 200 ; xii. 147, 258. Burke's Extinct Baronetcies. Metcalfe's Visitation of Worcester, 1683, 96. Edmondson's Baronagium Genealogicum, v. 493. Brydges' Collins' Peerage, vii. 396. Banks' Dormant and Extinct Baronage, i. 202. Burke's Colonial Gentry, i. 196. Chance of Bromsgrove, by J. F. Chance, 92. New England Register, xxxiii. 312. The Genealogist, New Series, xii. 111 ; xiii. 100, 177 ; xvii. 112. The Gresley's of Drakelowe, by F. Madan, 289.

VERNON-WENTWORTH. Burke's Royal Families, (London, 1851, 8vo.) i. 145. Burke's Commoners, ii. 81, Landed Gentry, 2, 3, 4, 5, 6. Burke's Heraldic Illustrations, 76. Baker's Northampton, ii. 244. History of Worsborough, by Joseph Wilkinson, 106.

VERSCHOYLE. The Irish Builder, xxix. 348. Burke's Landed Gentry, 8.

VERSTURME. Miscellanea Genealogica et Heraldica, New Series, iii. 322.

VERTUE. Burke's Landed Gentry, 2 corr., p. 429.

VESCI, VESCY, VESEY, or VESSEY. Tate's History of Alnwick, i. 400. Cambridgeshire Visitation, edited by Sir T. Phillipps, 32. Foster's Visitations of Yorkshire, 585. Hunter's Deanery of Doncaster, ii. 179. Morant's Essex, i. 469. Burke's Landed Gentry, (of Lucan,) 4, 5, 6, 7, 8; (of Derrabard,) 3, 4, 5, 6, 7, 8. Harleian Society, xiii. 513; xvi. 10; xxxii. 294; xl. 1207; xli. 93. Archdall's Lodge's Peerage, vi. 29. Banks' Dormant and Extinct Baronage, ii. 569. Metcalfe's Visitations of Suffolk, 104, 172, 173. Bysshe's Visitation of Essex, edited by J. J. Howard, 96. The Irish Builder, xxxv. 237. Muskett's Suffolk Manorial Families, i. 56-65. See DE VESCI.

VETERIPONT. Plantagenet-Harrison's History of Yorkshire, i. 338. Nicolson and Burn's Westmorland and Cumberland, i. 269, 502. See VIPONT.

VEVERS. Platt and Morkill's Records of Whitkirk, 96.

VIBERT. J. B. Payne's Armorial of Jersey, 346.

VICARS, or VICKERS. Eastwood's History of Ecclesfield, 388. Doncaster Charities, by Charles Jackson, 87. Burke's Commoners, iv. 345. New England Register, xviii. 186. Harleian Society, xxxix. 897, 1079.

VICKERMAN. Burke's Landed Gentry, 8.

VIDAL. Harleian Society, xx. 96.

VIELESTON. Baker's Northampton, i. 105.

VIELL. Maclean's History of Trigg Minor, iii. 364. Harleian Society, xvii. 311. Dallaway's Antiquities of Bristow, 141.

VIGNE. Burke's Colonial Gentry, ii. 780.

VIGNOLES. Burke's Landed Gentry, 4, 5, 6, 7.

VIGORS. Burke's Landed Gentry, (of Erindale,) 2, 3, 4, 5; (of Burgage,) 2, 3, 4, 5, 6, 7, 8. Howard's Visitation of Ireland, i. 41.

VILETT. Burke's Landed Gentry, 2.

VILLA REAL. Transactions of the Thoroton Society, 1901, at end.

VILLIERS, VILERS, or VILLERS. The Case of George Villiers, claiming the title of Earl of Buckingham, etc., 1724, folio. Claim of John Villiers to be Earl of Buckingham, Sess. Papers, April, 1709. Burke's Patrician, vi. 52. The Great Governing Families of England, ii. 96. Appendix to Case of Sir J. S. Sidney, claiming to be Lord Lisle. Wright's History of Rutland, 31. Visitation of Staffordshire, 1663-4, printed by Sir T. Phillipps, 10. Thoroton's Nottinghamshire, i. 153. Burton's Description of Leicestershire, 53. Nichols' History of Leicestershire, iii. 197. Clutterbuck's Hertford, i. 252; ii. 46. Memoirs of the Family of Chester, by R. E. C. Waters, 595. Harleian Society, ii. 29. Historical and Biographical Memoirs of George Villiers. London, 1819, 4to. Memoirs, British and Foreign, of Illustrious Persons who died in 1711, 503. Edmondson's Baronagium Genealogicum, ii. 177; v. 452; vi. 17. Archdall's Lodge's Peerage, iv. 76. Brydges' Collins' Peerage, iii. 762; v. 130. Banks' Dormant and Extinct

Baronage, iii. 111, 613. The Genealogist, v. 52, 297. Notes and Queries, 4 S. vii. 452, 469 ; xi. 284, 508. Burke's Extinct Baronetcies. Visitations of Staffordshire, 1614 and 1663-4, William Salt Society, 293.

VINCENT. Pedigree of Vincent. By R. S. Boddington. London, [1895,] broadside. Nicolas' Memoir of Λ. Vincent. London, 1827, 8vo. Berry's Surrey Genealogies, 62. Surtees Society, xxxvi. 202. Burke's Landed Gentry, (of Boston Lodge,) 5 supp., 6 and supp., 7, 8 ; (of Summerhill,) 7, 8. Foster's Yorkshire Pedigrees. Foster's Visitations of Yorkshire, 636. Harleian Society, ii. 50, 79-82 ; iv. 138 ; vi. 294 ; viii. 47 ; xvii. 312 ; xliii. 55, 219. Burton's Description of Leicestershire, 209, 262. Nichols' History of the County of Leicester, iv. 364, 870, 933, 934, 952. Hunter's Deanery of Doncaster, i. 131, 377. Manning and Bray's Surrey, ii. 725. Miscellanea Genealogica et Heraldica, New Series, ii. 239 ; 3rd Series, i. 10. Pedigrees of the Leading Families of Lancashire, published by Joseph Foster, (London, 1872, fol.). Wotton's English Baronetage, i. 418. Betham's Baronetage, i. 198. Pedigrees of the Leading Families of Yorkshire, by Joseph Foster. Metcalfe's Visitations of Northamptonshire, 149. Howard's Visitation of Ireland, iii. 62. The Gresley's of Drakelowe, by F. Madan, 290. The Genealogist, New Series, xvi. 57. See VYNCENT.

VINER. Burke's Extinct Baronetcies.

VINOUR. Visitatio Comitatus Wiltoniæ, 1623, printed by Sir T. Phillipps. See VYNOR.

VINTON. New England Register, vii. 164.

VIPAN. Burke's Landed Gentry, 4, 5, 6, 7. Burke's Family Records, 613.

VIPONT. Kent's British Banner Displayed, 590. Jefferson's History of Leath Ward, Cumberland, 112. Blore's Rutland, 15. Banks' Dormant and Extinct Baronage, i. 193. See DE VETERIPONTE, VETERIPONT.

VISE. Visitation of Staffordshire, 1663-4, edited by Sir T. Phillipps, 10. Visitation of Staffordshire, (Willm. Salt Soc.) 144. Visitations of Staffordshire, 1614 and 1663-4, William Salt Society, 295. See VYSE.

VITRE. Antiquities of Lacock Abbey, by W. L. Bowles and J. G. Nicholls, 264*.

VITUS. Burke's Extinct Baronetcies.

VIVIAN. Burke's Commoners, i. 407, Landed Gentry, 2, 3, 4, 5, 6, 8, and at p. 1294. Maclean's History of Trigg Minor, i. 307 ; ii. 162. Harleian Society, ix. 252-261. A Complete Parochial History of the County of Cornwall, i. 167, 201 ; iii. 284 ; iv. 119 supp. An Historical Survey of Cornwall, by C. S. Gilbert, ii. 316. The Visitations of Cornwall, by J. L. Vivian, 527-548. The Visitations of Devon, by J. L. Vivian, 747, 753-760, 763. See VYVYAN.

VIZARD. Blunt's Dursley and its Neighbourhood, 94.

VOEL. Dwnn's Visitations of Wales, i. 71, 177, 282. Pembrokeshire Pedigrees, 137.

VOGEL. Burke's Colonial Gentry, ii. 518.

VOLPE. *See* WOLPE.

VON MUELLER. Burke's Colonial Gentry, ii. 444.

VON SONNENTAG. Chronicle of the Family of De Havilland.

VOSE. New England Register, ix. 177.

VOSPER. The Visitations of Cornwall, by J. L. Vivian, 624.

VOSS. Genealogies of Morgan and Glamorgan, by G. T. Clark, 469, 470.

VOUGHTON. Burke's Landed Gentry, 2 supp. p. 191.

VOWE. J. H. Hill's History of Langton, 280. Burke's Commoners, ii. 97, Landed Gentry, 2. Harleian Society, ii. 194. Nichols' History of the County of Leicester, ii. 602.

VOWEL. Visitation of Norfolk, published by Norfolk Archæological Society, i. 340. Westcote's Devonshire, edited by G. Oliver and P. Jones, 526. Visitation of Devon, edited by F. T. Colby, 136. The Visitations of Devon, by J. L. Vivian, 479. Harleian Society, xxxii. 294.

VOWLER. Burke's Landed Gentry, 2, 3, 4, 5.

VOYSEY. Harleian Society, vi. 353. The Visitations of Devon, by J. L. Vivian, 764.

VRRICKE. Surrey Archæological Collections, vi. viii.

VYCHAN. Dwnn's Visitations of Wales, i. 251, 255, 258, 261; ii. 26, 27, 36, 37, 164, 175, 181-183, 204, 218, 219, 236. *See* VAUGHAN.

VYELL. The Visitations of Cornwall, by J. L. Vivian, 549.

VYNCENT. Plantagenet-Harrison's History of Yorkshire, i. 288. *See* VINCENT.

VYNE. Visitation of Oxfordshire, 1634, printed by Sir T. Phillipps, (Middle Hill, fol.) 31. Harleian Society, v. 311; xliii. 4.

VYNER, or VYNOR. Vyner, a Family History, 1885, 8vo. Supplement. 1885, 8vo. [By C. J. Vyner.] The same, revised and enlarged. 1887, 8vo. Pedigree of the Family of Vyner. 1879, single sheet. Vyner Pedigree. 1887, single sheet. Burke's Landed Gentry, 4, 5, 6 and supp., 7, 8. Harleian Society, xvii. 313; xxix. 475. Metcalfe's Visitations of Suffolk, 209. Visitation of Wiltshire, edited by G. W. Marshall, 98. *See* VEINOR, VINER, VINOUR.

VYOLET. Harleian Society, xvii. 314.

VYSE. Burke's Landed Gentry, 2, 3, 4, 5, 6. Erdeswicke's Survey of Staffordshire, 121. Baker's Northampton, i. 33. Collections for a History of Staffordshire, William Salt Society, ii. part 2, 55. *See* VISE.

VYVYAN. Burke's Landed Gentry, 5 supp., 6. Maclean's History of Trigg Minor, i. 570. Polwhele's History of Cornwall, ii. 42. Harleian Society, ix. 259-261. An Historical Survey of Cornwall, by C. S. Gilbert, i. 557. Pedigree of Wilson of High Wray, etc., by Joseph Foster, 106. Wotton's English Baronetage, ii. 411. Betham's Baronetage, ii. 24. *See* VIVIAN.

WAAD. Morant's Essex, ii. 620. History of Hampstead, by J. J. Park, 137. Wright's Essex, ii. 206. Harleian Society, xvii. 315.

WADAMS. Bibliotheca Topographica Britannica, ix. Part 4, 232.

WADDELL. Burke's Landed Gentry, 2.

WADDILOVE. Burke's Landed Gentry, 8.

WADDINGHAM. Burke's Landed Gentry, 6, 7, 8.

WADDINGTON. Burke's Landed Gentry, 3, 4, 5, 6, 7, 8.

WADDON. Visitation of Devon, edited by F. T. Colby, 202. The Western Antiquary, iv. 175. The Visitations of Devon, by J. L. Vivian, 765.

WADDY. Descendants of Edmond Waddy, a Cornet in Cromwell's Army. [Printed for Robert Warren.] Sheet pedigree, *circa* 1853. Burke's Landed Gentry, 3, 4, 5, 6, 7. Burke's Visitation of Seats and Arms, 2nd Series, ii. 8.

WADE. Berry's Sussex Genealogies, 230. Surtees Society, xxxvi. 32, 245. Burke's Landed Gentry, 3, 4, 5, 6, 7, 8. History of Hampstead, by J. J. Park, 137. Thoresby's Ducatus Leodiensis, 155. Cheshire and Lancashire Historic Society, ii. 100. An Account of Church Minshull, by Rev. G. B. Sandford, 18. Maclean's History of Trigg Minor, iii. 267. Whitaker's Deanery of Craven, 3rd edn., 531. John Watson's History of Halifax, 289. Account of the Mayo and Elton Families, by C. H. Mayo, 158. Metcalfe's Visitations of Suffolk, 173. Historical Notices of Doncaster, by C. W. Hatfield, 2nd Series, 141. Metcalfe's Visitations of Northamptonshire, 151. New England Register, xi. 163. Howard's Visitation of England and Wales, iv. 137. The Genealogist, New Series, xiii. 112. Fragmenta Genealogica, by F. A. Crisp, i. 28.

WADESLEY. The Genealogist, New Series, xvii. 244.

WADESON. Foster's Visitations of Yorkshire, 584.

WADHAM. Collinson's Somerset, i. 7, 48. History of the Colleges and Halls of Oxford, by Anthony à Wood, edited by John Gutch, 592. Westcote's Devonshire, edited by G. Oliver and P. Jones, 634. Hutchins' Dorset, ii. 216. Hoare's Wiltshire, IV. ii. 93. Weaver's Visitations of Somerset, 83. Wadham College, Oxford, by T. G. Jackson, 27.

WADLAND. J. H. Hill's History of Market Harborough, 157. Nichols' History of the County of Leicester, ii. 719.

WADMAN. Hoare's Wiltshire, I. ii. 165.

WADSLEY. Hunter's History of the Parish of Sheffield, 465. Eastwood's History of Ecclesfield, 441.

WADSWORTH. Chetham Society, lxxxviii. 322. The Tyldesley Diary, edited by J. Gillow and A. Hewitson, 62. Harleian Society, xxxvii. 8.

WAGGETT. Burkes Landed Gentry, 2 and add.; 3, p. 328; 5, p. 380. Miscellanea Genealogica et Heraldica, New Series, iii. 182. *See* CARSON.

WAGSTAFFE. Pedigree of Wagstaffe of Tachbrook, Co. Warwick, [T. P.] 1837. Visitation of Warwickshire, 1619, published with Warwickshire Antiquarian Magazine, 124. Harleian Society, viii. 96; xii. 289, 403; xvii. 316. The Genealogist, New Series, viii. 177.

WAHUL. Bibliotheca Topographica Britannica, iv. Part v. 46. Banks' Dormant and Extinct Baronage, i. 436. Harleian Society, xix. 67. *See* DE WAHUL.

WAINMAN. Visitation of Oxfordshire, 1574, printed by Sir T. Phillipps, (Middle Hill, fol.) 10. *See* WAYNEMAN, WENMAN.

WAINWRIGHT. Earwaker's Local Gleanings, i. 250, 259, 267, 276, 277, 287. Harleian Society, xxxviii. 797, 798.

WAIT, or WAITE. Burke's Landed Gentry, 2, 3, 4. Harleian Society, viii. 466. Account of the Family of Hallen, by A. W. C. Hallen, Table x. New England Register, xxiv. 103; xxxi. 421; xxxii. 188. A History of Banking in Bristol, by C. H. Cave, 256. *See* WAYTE.

WAITHMAN. Burke's Landed Gentry, 2, 3, 4, 5, 6, 7, 8. Pedigree of Wilson of High Wray, etc., by Joseph Foster, 114. Pedigree of Wilson, by S. B. Foster, 163.

WAKE. A Memoir of Hereward the Saxon Patriot, by E. Trollope, with six Pedigrees of the Family of Wake, by Thomas Close, in Reports and Papers of the Associated Architectural Societies for 1861. A Brief Enquiry into the Antiquity of the Family of Wake, by W. Wake, D.D. Warminster, 1833, 8vo. A Memoir of a branch of the Wake Family of Northamptonshire, by H. T. Wake, Carlisle, 1861, 8vo. Collinson's Somerset, iii. 168. Morant's Essex, i. 44; ii. 221. Stukeley's Itinerarium Curiosum, 9. Berry's Buckinghamshire Genealogies, 63. George Oliver's History of Beverley, 462. Lipscombe's History of the County of Buckingham, iv. 126. Hutchinson's History of Cumberland, ii. 529. Bridges' Northamptonshire, by Rev. Peter Whalley, i. 335. Burton's Description of Leicestershire, 26. Nichols' History of the County of Leicester, iv. 1026. Hoare's Wiltshire, V. iii. 35. Clutterbuck's Hertford, iii. 287. Baker's Northampton, i. 113; ii. 239. Notes and Queries, 2 S. vi. 352, 423; 6 S. vi. 196. Wotton's English Baronetage, i. 465. Banks' Baronies in Fee, i. 449; ii. 153. Betham's Baronetage, i. 238. Banks' Dormant and Extinct Baronage, i. 440. Harvey's Hundred of Willey, 146. Northampton-shire Notes and Queries, ii. 1. Weaver's Visitations of Somerset, 133. Metcalfe's Visitations of Northamptonshire, 52. The Genealogist, New Series, xii. 30. Miscellanea Genealogica et Heraldica, 3rd Series, iii. 72.

WAKEBRIGGE. Glover's History of Derbyshire, ii. 356, (323).

WAKEFIELD. Surtees Society, xxxvi. 218. Foster's Visitations of Yorkshire, 139. Burke's Landed Gentry, 6, 7, 8. Pedigree of Wilson of High Wray, etc., by Joseph Foster, 117. The Descen-dants of John Backhouse, by Joseph Foster, 64. Pedigree of Wilson, by S. B. Foster, 206. Burke's Family Records, 613.

WAKEHURST. Sussex Archæological Collections, x. 152.

WAKELY. Burke's Landed Gentry, 8.

WAKELYN, or WAKLYN. Bridges' Northamptonshire, by Rev. Peter Whalley, i. 122. Visitation of Derbyshire, 1663-4, (Middle Hill, 1854, fol.) 7. Baker's Northampton, i. 504. The Genealogist, iii. 184. Metcalfe's Visitations of Northamptonshire, 54. Visitations of Staffordshire, 1614 and 1663-4, William Salt Society, 296.

WAKEMAN. Tuckett's Devonshire Pedigrees, 56. Burke's Landed Gentry, 2, 3, 4. Harleian Society, vi. 295, 296; xxi. 174. Miscellanea Genealogica et Heraldica, New Series, ii. 183. F. G. Lee's History of Thame, 647. The Visitations of Devon, by J. L. Vivian, 766, 767.

WAKEMAN-NEWPORT. Burke's Landed Gentry, 8.

WAKERING. Morant's Essex, i. 306. Wright's Essex, ii. 616. Harleian Society, xiii. 513; xiv. 613.

WALBANKE-CHILDERS. Burke's Commoners, ii. 229, Landed Gentry, 2, 3, 4, 5, 6, 7, 8.

WALBEC. Glamorganshire Pedigrees, edited by Sir T. Phillipps, 24.

WALBEOF, WALBYF, WALBIEFFE, or WALBEOFFE. Dwnn's Visitations of Wales, ii. 37, 58. Jones' History of the County of Brecknock, ii. 583.

WALCOT, WALCOTE, or WALCOTT.[1] Pedigree of Walcot of Co. Salop, [T. P.] 1846, folio page. Berry's Berkshire Genealogies, 150. Burke's Royal Families, (London, 1851, 8vo.) ii. 54. Burke's Landed Gentry, (of Bitterley,) 2 and corr., 3, 4, 5, 6, 7, 8; (of Winkton,) 3, 4, 5, 6. Harleian Society, iii. 23; viii. 360; xvii. 317; xxix. 476. Notes and Queries, 1 S. vii. 488. Nichols' History of the County of Leicester, iv. 318. Miscellanea Genealogica et Heraldica, 2nd Series, ii. 120. The Gresley's of Drakelowe, by F. Madan, 291.

WALDECHEF. Jewitt's Reliquary, viii. 232.

WALDEGRAVE, WALDGRAVE, or WALGRAVE. Collinson's Somerset, ii. 117. Morant's Essex, i. 182, 417, 436; ii. 232, 318, 592. Lydiate Hall and its Associations, by Rev. T. E. Gibson, 317. Herald and Genealogist, iii. 424. Clutterbuck's Hertford, ii. 391. Wright's Essex, ii. 735. Harleian Society, xiii. 119-122, 307, 514; xiv. 614; xxxii. 295. Blomefield's Norfolk, x. 465. Dugdale's Warwickshire, 665. Page's History of Suffolk, 924. Foley's Records of the English Province S. J., v. 382. Edmondson's Baronagium Genealogicum, iii. 233. Brydges' Collins' Peerage, iv. 232. Metcalfe's Visitations of Suffolk, 75. Chancellor's Sepulchral Monuments of Essex, 200, Transactions of Shropshire Archæological Society, ix. 57.

WALDEN. Morant's Essex, ii. 570. Camden Society, xliii. 18. Harleian Society, xliii. 19. The Genealogist, New Series, xvi. 232. See DE WALDEN.

WALDIE. Burke's Landed Gentry, 2, 3, 4.

WALDO. Herald and Genealogist, ii. 236, 312. Notes respecting the Family of Waldo, by M. C. Jones. 1863, 8vo. Burke's Landed Gentry, 5 supp., 7. Harleian Society, viii. 322. Notes and Queries, 3 S. iii. 191, 397; iv. 136, 199; 4 S. ix. 323. Miscellanea Genealogica et Heraldica, 2nd Series, ii. 254. New England Register, lii. 213.

[1] Add. MS. 29743, is 'Collections for the History of the Family of Walcott, by M. E. C. Walcott.

WALDRON. Visitation of Somersetshire, printed by Sir T. Phillipps, 143. Burke's St. James's Magazine, i. 496. Burke's Landed Gentry, 2, 3, 4. Nichols' History of the County of Leicester, iv. 325. Visitation of Wiltshire, edited by G. W. Marshall, 70. New England Register, v. 182, 205 ; viii. 78 ; ix. 55. *See* WALROND.

WALDY. Burke's Landed Gentry, 2, 3, 4, 5 and supp., 6, 7, 8.

WALDYVE. Dugdale's Warwickshire, 1063.

WALE. Morant's Essex, i. 471 ; ii. 523. Burke's Landed Gentry, 4, 5 and supp., 6, 7, 8. Harleian Society, viii. 46 ; xiii. 515. Baker's Northampton, i. 502 ; ii. 108. Wright's Essex, ii. 69. Bysshe's Visitation of Essex, edited by J. J. Howard, 97.

WALEIS. Collinson's Somerset, iii. 438. *See* WALLIS.

WALERAN, WALERAND, or WALEROND. Topographer and Genealogist, i. 30. Hoare's Wiltshire, II. i. 10 ; III. v. 73. Fosbrooke's History of Gloucestershire, ii. 54. Banks' Dormant and Extinct Baronage, i. 194. *See* WALDRON, WALROND.

WALES (Princes of). Plantagenet-Harrison's History of Yorkshire, i. xx. xxiii.

WALESHALE. Willmore's History of Walsall, 256.

WALEYS. Nichols' History of the County of Leicester, iii. 1100. *See* WALLIS.

WALFORD. East Anglian, i. 127. Burke's Landed Gentry, (of Foxburrow,) 2, 6 supp., 7, 8 ; (of Ruyton Towers,) 8. Wright's Essex, i. 608.

WALKEDEN. Harleian Society, i. 18.

WALKER. Topographer and Genealogist, ii. 119, 558. Berry's Hertfordshire Genealogies, 137. Visitations of Middlesex, (Salisbury, 1820, fol.) 6. Visitation of Somersetshire, printed by Sir T. Phillipps, 143. Burke's Royal Families, (London, 1851, 8vo.) i. 15, 95. Burke's Commoners, i. 312 ; (of Blythe Hall,) ii. 288, Landed Gentry, 2, 3, 4, 5, 6, 7 ; (of Redland,) Landed Gentry, 2, 3, 4, 5 ; (of Sand Hutton,) 2 and supp., 3, 4 ; (of Dalry,) 2, 3, 4, 5, 6, 7, 8 ; (of Gilgarran,) 3, 4 ; (of Berry Hill,) 2, 3, 4, 5, 6 ; (of Tagunnan,) 2, 3, 4 ; (of Crownest,) 3, 4 ; (of the Grange,) 3, 4, 5 ; (of Bushey,) 2 ; of Abererder,) 5 ; (of Bathwick,) 6, 7, 8 ; (of Tykillen,) 6, 7, 8 ; (of Berkswell Hall,) 6, 7, 8 ; (of Crawfordton,) 6, 7, 8 ; (of Bowland,) 7, 8 ; (of Perdiswell,) 8. Foster's Yorkshire Pedigrees. Lincolnshire Tradesmen's Tokens, by Justin Simpson, (London, 1872, 8vo.) 103. Harleian Society, ii. 137 ; iv. 130 ; xi. 114 ; xxxvii. 285, 294 ; xxxviii. 742, 770 ; xxxix. 1006 ; xlii. 113. The Genealogist, iii. 313. J. H. Hill's History of Market Harborough, 37, 261. Burke's Visitation of Seats and Arms, ii. 4. Burke's Royal Descents and Pedigrees of Founders' Kin, *Founders' Kin*, 6. Visitation of Staffordshire, 1663-4, printed by Sir T. Phillipps, 10. Douglas's Baronage of Scotland, 480. An Historical Survey of Cornwall, by C. S. Gilbert, ii. 324. Doncaster Charities, by Charles Jackson, 45. Nichols' History of the County of Leicester, ii. 494 ; iv. 171. Visitatio Comitatus Wiltoniæ, 1623, printed by Sir T. Phillipps. Surtees' Durham, i. 47. Clutterbuck's Hertford, i. 336. Thoroton's Nottinghamshire, iii.

19. Visitation of Wiltshire, edited by G. W. Marshall, 12. Notes and Queries, 5 S. ii. 247 ; iii. 56 ; 7 S. iv. 108 ; 8 S. ii. 293, 457 ; iv. 453. Burke's Extinct Baronetcies. Foster's Visitation of Middlesex, 13. Weaver's Visitations of Somerset, 85. Visitations of Staffordshire, 1614 and 1663-4, William Salt Society, 297. Historical Notices of Doncaster, by C. W. Hatfield, 2nd Series, 14. Miscellanea Genealogica et Heraldica, 2nd Series, ii. 241. Burke's Colonial Gentry, i. 208, 231, 240. Green's Account of Family of Cudworth, 36. Howard's Visitation of England and Wales, vi. 7. *See* CASE-WALKER.

WALKER-ARNOTT. Burke's Landed Gentry, 2, 3, 4.

WALKER-HENEAGE. Burke's Commoners, iv. 368, Landed Gentry, 2, 3, 4, 5, 6, 7, 8.

WALKER-MORISON. Burke's Landed Gentry, 7, 8.

WALKEY. Burke's Landed Gentry, 4.

WALKINSHAW. Notes and Queries, 2 S. xi. 67, 137 ; 3 S. ii. 117, 457 ; iii. 32. Northern Notes and Queries, iv. 191 ; vii. 134. Semple's Crawfurd's Renfrewshire, 23, 34.

WALL. Berry's Hampshire Genealogies, 65, 317. Burke's Commoners, (of Worthy Park,) i. 121, Landed Gentry, 2, 3, 4, 5 ; (of Norman Court,) Landed Gentry, 2. Chetham Society, lxxxi. 49 ; lxxxviii. 323, 324. Baines' History of the Co. of Lancaster, iv. 375. Harleian Society, xviii. 270 ; xxix. 478 ; xxxvii. 217. Visitation of Gloucester, edited by T. F. Fenwick and W. C. Metcalfe, 192. Weaver's Visitation of Herefordshire, 98. Bysshe's Visitation of Essex, edited by J. J. Howard, 98.

WALLACE. Burke's Royal Families, (London, 1851, 8vo.) ii. 156. Burke's Commoners, (of Kelly,) iii. 274, Landed Gentry, 2 ; (of Downpatrick,) 8 ; (of Asholme,) Landed Gentry, 2 supp. and corr., 3, 4, 5 ; 7 p. 820 ; 8 p. 869. Burke's Visitation of Seats and Arms, i. 75 ; 2nd Series, i. 31. Hodgson's Northumberland, III. ii. 91. Burke's Royal Descents and Pedigrees of Founders' Kin, 16. Geo. Robertson's Description of Cunninghame, 73. Paterson's History of the Co. of Ayr, i. 209, 336 ; ii. 25, 35, 39, 203, 220, 337, 498. Paterson's History of Ayr and Wigton, i. 146, 269-297, 440, 486, 558, 654, 663, 673 ; iii. 436, 465. Transactions of Glasgow Archæological Society, 1885, 102. Burke's Colonial Gentry, i. 250. *See* WALLIS.

WALLASCOTT. Visitation of Oxfordshire, 1634, printed by Sir T. Phillipps, (Middle Hill, fol.) 33.

WALLEIS. Nichols' History of the County of Leicester, iii. 1047. *See* WALLIS.

WALLER. Hasted's Kent, i. 430. Glover's History of Derbyshire, ii. 326, (290). Berry's Kent Genealogies, 297. Berry's Hertfordshire Genealogies, 76. Berry's Buckinghamshire Genealogies, 1-9. Berry's Hampshire Genealogies, 109, 358. Surtees Society, xxxvi. 369. Burke's Landed Gentry, (of Farmington,) 3, 4, 5, 6. 7, 8 ; (of Prior Park,) 3, 4, 5, 6, 7, 8 ; (of Finoe,) 3, 4, 5, 6, 7 ; (of Castletown,) 2, 3, 4, 5, 6, 7, 8 ; (of Allenstown,) 2 supp., 3, 4, 5, 6, 7, 8. Lipscombe's History of the County of Buckingham,

iii. 182. Burke's Visitation of Seats and Arms, 2nd Series, ii. 77. Westcote's Devonshire, edited by G. Oliver and P. Jones, 623. Burke's Authorized Arms, 29. Clutterbuck's Hertford, i. 351. Notes and Queries, 1 S. v. 586, 619; vi. 231, 401, 537; xii. 201; 7 S. iii. 189. Visitation of Devon, edited by F. T. Colby, 203. Metcalfe's Visitations of Suffolk, 95, 209. Harleian Society, xix. 149; xxii. 101; xl. 1226; xlii. 129. Howard's Visitation of England and Wales, ix. 177.

WALLERON. Bird's Magazine of Honour, 73. *See* WALROND.

WALLEY. Bysshe's Visitation of Essex, edited by J. J. Howard, 98.

WALLEYS. Topographical Miscellanies, 1792, 4to. (Glynde). Berry's Sussex Genealogies, 173. Sussex Archæological Collections, xx. 59. *See* WALLIS.

WALLINGER. Harleian Society, xiii. 517. The Genealogist, vii. 253. Notes and Queries, 8 S. i. 321; ii. 472; iii. 235.

WALLINGFORD. New England Register, xx. 335.

WALLINGTON. Burke's Landed Gentry, (of Gloucestershire,) 2 supp., 3, 4; (of Dursley,) 2, 3, 4, 5, 6, 7, 8. Fosbrooke's History of Gloucestershire, i. 447. Pedigree of the Family of Sheppard, 6.

WALLIS. Visitation of Sussex, 1570, printed by Sir T. Phillipps, (Middle Hill, fol.) 11. Burke's Landed Gentry, 2, 3, 4, 5, 6, 7, 8. Maclean's History of Trigg Minor, ii. 370; iii. 423. Harleian Society, ix. 279. Hodgson's Northumberland, III. ii. 85. Visitatio Comitatus Wiltoniæ, 1623, printed by Sir T. Phillipps. Hutchins' Dorset, i. 637. Hunter's Deanery of Doncaster, ii. 484. An Account of the Families of Boase, (Exeter, 1876, 4to.,) 56. Banks' Baronies in Fee, ii. 154. Visitation of Wiltshire, edited by G. W. Marshall, 83. The Genealogist, New Series, xiv. 258; xv. 146. *See* WALEIS, WALEYS, WALLACE, WALLEIS.

WALLOP. Berry's Hampshire Genealogies, 41. Edmondson's Baronagium Genealogicum, iii. 247. Brydges' Collins' Peerage, iv. 291. Harleian Society, xxix. 479.

WALLROTH. Burke's Landed Gentry, 8.

WALLS. Metcalfe's Visitation of Worcester, 1683, 98.

WALMESLEY, or WALMSLEY. Berry's Essex Genealogies, 39. Surtees Society, xxxvi. 14. Burke's Commoners, (of Sholley,) iii. 228, Landed Gentry, 2, 3, 4, 7, 8; (of Westwood,) Commoners, i. 278, Landed Gentry, 2, 3, 4, 5, 6, 7, 8; (of the Hall of Ince,) Landed Gentry, 2, 3, 4, 5, 6, 7, 8. Foster's Lancashire Pedigrees. Chetham Society, lxxxii. 67; lxxxviii. 325-328. Gregson's Fragments Relative to the County of Lancaster, 239. Corry's History of Lancashire, ii. 715. Manning and Bray's Surrey, ii. 285. Whitaker's History of Whalley, ii. 280, 406. Abram's History of Blackburn, 433, 458, 593, 690. Harleian Society, xiv. 723; xvii. 318. The Genealogist, New Series, x. 243. Morrell's History of Selby, 138. Fishwick's History of Rochdale, 321.

WALNE. History of Chipping, by Tom C. Smith, 236.

WALPOLE. One Generation of a Norfolk House, by A. Jessop, D.D. London, 1879, 8vo., 2nd edn. Genealogy of Walpole of Whaplode, by A. Jessop and Everard Green, folding sheet, 1874. A brief History of Sir Robert Walpole and Family, by W. Musgrave. London, 1732, 8vo.; 1738, 8vo.; 1745, 8vo. Visitation of Norfolk, published by Norfolk Archæological Society, i. 363, 451. Blomefield's Norfolk, vii. 109. Burke's Landed Gentry, 2, 3, 4, 5, 6. The Norfolk Antiquarian Miscellany, by Walter Rye, i. 267. Harleian Society, viii. 19, 173; xxxii. 300. The Genealogist, i. 6; iii. 79; v. 53; vi. 289; New Series, xvi. 237. The Citizens of London and their Rulers, by B. B. Orridge, 202. Foley's Records of the English Province, S. J., ii. 235. Houghton and the Walpoles, by J. H. Broome, 27. Edmondson's Baronagium Genealogicum, iii. 242; v. 454. Brydges' Collins' Peerage, v. 631. Banks' Dormant and Extinct Baronage, iii. 581. Ancient Families of Lincolnshire in 'Spalding Free Press,' 1873-5, Nos. xx.-xxiii. The Genealogical Magazine, ii. 235, 300, 364, 390, 433, 490, 550; iii. 3.

WALROND, or WALRAUND. Cussan's History of Hertfordshire, Parts xi. and xii. 38. Tuckett's Devonshire Pedigrees, 137. Visitation of Somersetshire, printed by Sir T. Phillipps, 144. Visitation of Gloucestershire, 1569, (Middle Hill, 1854, fol.) 10. Burke's Royal Families, (London, 1851, 8vo.) i. 75; ii. 150. Burke's Commoners, (of Dulford,) ii. 557, Landed Gentry, 2, 3, 4, 5, 6, 7, 8; (of Bradfield,) Commoners, ii. 553, Landed Gentry, 2, 3, 4, 5; (of Calder Park,) Commoners, iv. 444, Landed Gentry, 2, 3, 4. Harleian Society, vi. 296; xi. 114; xvii. 317; xxi. 264. Westcote's Devonshire, edited by G. Oliver and P. Jones, 484. Visitatio Comitatus Wiltoniæ, 1623, printed by Sir T. Phillipps. Notes and Queries, 1 S. ii. 134, 206, 284. Visitation of Devon, edited by F. T. Colby, 203. Visitation of Wiltshire, edited by G. W. Marshall, 70. Somersetshire Wills, printed for F. A. Crisp, iii. 20. Weaver's Visitations of Somerset, 85. The Genealogist, New Series, xiii. 27. The Visitations of Devon, by J. L. Vivian, 768. *See* MANSEL, WALERAND, WALLERON.

WALSALL. *See* WALESHALE.

WALSH, or WALSHE. Rudder's Gloucestershire, 677. Gentleman's Magazine, lxxx. i. 203. Visitation of Somersetshire, printed by Sir T. Phillipps, 144. Burke's Landed Gentry, (of Fanningstown,) 4, 5, 6, 7, 8; (of Walsh Park,) 2; (of Cranagh,) 7, 8; (of Grimblethorpe,) 8; (of Laragh,) 8. Nichols' History of the County of Leicester, iii. 1100. Dugdale's Warwickshire, 1040. Abram's History of Blackburn, 511. Fosbrooke's History of Gloucestershire, ii. 28. The Wolfe's of Forenaghts, 50. Gyll's History of Wraysbury, 59. Lipscombe's History of the County of Buckingham, iv. 609. Metcalfe's Visitation of Worcester, 1683, 99. Weaver's Visitations of Somerset, 86. Harleian Society, xxi. 264; xxvii. 139; xxxii. 302. Notes and Queries, 7 S. iii. 168; iv. 42, 64. Genealogies of Morgan and Glamorgan, by G. T. Clark, 470. The Genealogist, New Series, xiii. 148; xiv. 28, 192; xvii. 36, 90, 153, 217. The Gresley's of Drakelowe, by F. Madan, 292. *See* WELSH.

WALSHALL. Nichols' History of the County, of Leicester, iv. 188.
Burton's Description of Leicestershire, 102.
WALSHAM. Burke's Heraldic Illustrations, 35. The Genealogist,
New Series, xiii. 248. *See* DE WALSHAM.
WALSINGHAM. Hasted's Kent, i. 99. Manning and Bray's Surrey,
ii. 540. Archæologia Cantiana, xiii. 401. History of Chislehurst,
by Webb, Miller, and Beckwith, 112. Harleian Society, xliii. 10.
The Gresley's of Drakelowe, by F. Madan, 293.
WALSTED. Harleian Society, xvii. 318.
WALTER. Pedigree of C. Walter, Esq., of Radford House, Co. War-
wick, [T. P.] 1858, folio page. Dwnn's Visitations of Wales, i.
193, 228, 248 ; ii. 48. Cambridgeshire Visitation, edited by Sir
T. Phillipps, 33. Berry's Kent Genealogies, 380. Burke's
Landed Gentry, 3, 4, 5, 6, 7, 8. Harleian Society, vi. 297 ; xiii.
311, 359 ; xvii. 319 ; xxii. 23 ; xxix. 482 ; xli. 19 ; xliii. 222.
The History of Monmouthshire, by D. Williams, App. 197.
Herald and Genealogist, viii. 1. Miscellanea Genealogica et
Heraldica, New Series, ii. 8 ; 2nd Series, i. 123. Notes and
Queries, 2 S. ii. 375 ; 4 S. v. 407. Burke's Extinct Baronetcies.
Visitation of Gloucester, edited by T. F. Fenwick and W. C. Met-
calfe, 193. New England Register, viii. 209. Notes and Queries,
7 S. ix. 346. The Visitations of Devon, by J. L. Vivian, 771.
WALTERS. Visitation of Middlesex, (Salisbury, 1820, fol.) 26. Mis-
cellanea Genealogica et Heraldica, New Series, iii. 226, 252.
Foster's Visitation of Middlesex, 50. Harleian Society, xxxix. 991.
WALTHALL. Glover's History of Derbyshire, ii. 395, (364). Burke's
Commoners, i. 367, Landed Gentry, (of Wistaston Hall,) 2, 3, 4,
5, 6, 7, 8, in some edns. under ' Hammond ' ; (of Alton Manor,) 8.
Harleian Society, xiii. 311 ; xvii. 320 ; xviii. 236. Ormerod's
Cheshire, iii. 333. Phillimore's London and Middlesex Note-
Book, 103.
WALTHAM. Morant's Essex, ii. 91. Tuckett's Devonshire Pedigrees,
69. Harleian Society, vi. 298. Westcote's Devonshire, edited
by G. Oliver and P. Jones, 583. The Visitations of Devon, by
J. L. Vivian, 772, 857.
WALTHEW. Berry's Kent Genealogies, 340. Harleian Society, xlii.
189. Hasted's Kent, (Hund. of Blackheath, by H. H. Drake,) 21.
WALTON. Pedigree of Walton of Steppes House, Halifax, [T. P.]
Broadside. Morant's Essex, i. 200 ; ii. 558. Visitation of
Somersetshire, printed by Sir T. Phillipps, 143. Harleian Society,
i. 57 ; xi. 115 ; xiii. 517 ; xvii. 320 ; xxxix. 884. Account of the
Company of Ironmongers, by John Nicholl, 2nd edn., 553.
Chetham Society, lxxxviii. 329. Visitatio Comitatus Wiltoniæ,
1623, printed by Sir T. Phillipps. Surtees' Durham, iv. 154.
Whitaker's History of Whalley, ii. 270. Ingledew's History of
North Allerton, 164. Abram's History of Blackburn, 729.
Burke's Landed Gentry, 6, 7, 8. Weaver's Visitations of Somer-
set, 134. The Genealogist, New Series, xiii. 27. *See* DE WALTON.
WALUR. Thoroton's Nottinghamshire, iii. 121.
WALWORTH. Archæologia Æliana, 1st Series, ii. 74.

WALWYN, or WALWIN. Berry's Sussex Genealogies, 376. Visitatio of Gloucestershire, 1569, (Middle Hill, 1854, fol.) 10. Burke's Royal Families, (London, 1851, 8vo.) ii. 152. Burke's Commoners, iii. 678, Landed Gentry, 2. Robinson's Mansions of Herefordshire, 202. Metcalfe's Visitation of Worcester, 1683, 100. Account of the Mayo and Elton Families, by C. H. Mayo, 145. Duncombe's Hereford, (J. H. Cooke,) iii. 21. The Genealogist, vii. 253. Harleian Society, xxi. 175, 265 ; xxvii. 141. Weaver's Visitations of Herefordshire, 69. Genealogical Table of John Stratford Collins. Transactions of Woolhope Naturalists' Field Club, 1889, 272.

WANDESFORD, WANDESFORDE, or WANDYSFORD. T. D. Whitaker's Life of Sir George Radcliffe, at end. Surtees Society, xxxvi. 100 ; xli. 50 ; lxii. 344. The Genealogist, New Series, xv. 75. Foster's Visitations of Yorkshire, 269, 585. Whitaker's History of Richmondshire, ii. 140. Burke's Landed Gentry, 6, 7, 8. Harleian Society, xvi. 333. Burke's Extinct Baronetcies. Notes and Queries, 5 S. iii. 158, 338.

WANKFORD. Morant's Essex, ii. 359. Bysshe's Visitation of Essex, edited by J. J. Howard, 99.

WANLEY. Notes and Queries, 4 S. v. 143. Visitation of Gloucester, edited by T. F. Fenwick and W. C. Metcalfe, 194.

WANNERSILE. Yorkshire Archæological Society, Record Series, xxx. 619.

WANNERTON. Harleian Society, xvii. 361.

WANSEY. Miscellanea Genealogica et Heraldica, 2nd Series, i. 116.

WANTON. Morant's Essex, ii. 558. Harleian Society, i. 62 ; xxxii. 304. See DE WANTON.

WANTY. Genealogical Memoranda relating to the Family of De Vautier anglais Wanty. By Henry Peet. Privately printed, 1902, 8vo. Miscellanea Genealogica et Heraldica, 2nd Series, ii. 32.

WAPENBURY. Dugdale's Warwickshire, 82.

WAPPS. Topographer and Genealogist, ii. 80.

WARBLETON. Topographer and Genealogist, iii. 178. Lyon's Chronicles of Finchampstead, 99. The Genealogist, New Series, xvi. 92.

WARBLINGTON. Manning and Bray's Surrey, ii. 324.

WARBURTON. Memoir of the Family of Warburton, of Garryhinch, King's Co., Ireland. Dublin, 1848, 8vo. Observations on the Snowdon Mountains, by John Thomas, (London, 1802, 8vo.) 185. Visitation of Suffolk, edited by J. J. Howard, i. 308. Berry's Hertfordshire Genealogies, 7. Burke's Landed Gentry, 2, 3, 4, 5, 6, 7, 8. Clutterbuck's Hertford, iii. 82. Ormerod's Cheshire, i. 573 ; ii. 175. C. Brown's Annals of Newark-upon-Trent, 223. Wotton's English Baronetage, iii. 85. Betham's Baronetage, ii. 104. Metcalfe's Visitations of Suffolk, 76. Burke's Extinct Baronetcies. Harleian Society, xviii. 237. The Warburtons of Arley, by J. E. Bailey. Manchester, 1881, 8vo. Burke's Colonial Gentry, ii. 804. The Genealogist, New Series, xv. 211. See EGERTON-WARBURTON.

WARCOP, WARCOPP, WARCUP, WARCUPP, or WARCUPPE. Surtees Society, xli. 100. Visitation of Westmorland, 1615, (London, 1853,) 10. Foster's Visitations of Yorkshire, 376. Harleian Society, v. 163; viii. 393; xvi. 334. Sir T. Phillipps' Topographer, No. 1, (March, 1821, 8vo.) 39. Visitation of Oxfordshire, 1574, printed by Sir T. Phillipps, (Middle Hill, fol.) 10. Visitation of Oxfordshire, 1634, printed by Sir T. Phillipps, (Middle Hill, fol.) 31. Foster's Visitations of Cumberland and Westmorland, 138. Nicolson and Burn's Westmorland and Cumberland, i. 335, 554, 602.

WARD. Pedigree of Ward of Newcastle and Stromshall, Co. Stafford, and Ogborn, Great Bedwin, etc., Co. Wilts. Folio sheet, by Sir T. Phillipps. J. H. Hill's History of Langton, 239. Herald and Genealogist, v. 207. Blomefield's Norfolk, v. 451. History of Dudley Castle, by C. Twamley, 1867, 8vo. Bibliotheca Topographica Britannica, ix. Part 4, 112. Visitation of Norfolk, published by Norfolk Archæological Society, i. 31. Berry's Kent Genealogies, 101. Warwickshire Antiquarian Magazine, Part ii. Visitation of Durham, 1615, (Sunderland, 1820, fol.) 1, 93. Ashmole's Antiquities of Berkshire, iii. 309. Visitation of Middlesex, (Salisbury, 1820, fol.) 48. Cambridgeshire Visitation, edited by Sir T. Phillipps, 33. Burke's Commoners, (of Salhouse,) iv. 19, Landed Gentry, 2, 3, 4, 5, 6, 7, 8 ; (of Willey,) Landed Gentry, 2, 3, 4, 5 ; (of Ogbourne St. Andrew,) 2, 3, 4, 5, 6, 7, 8 ; (of Fern Park,) 3, 4 ; (of Holwood,) 2, 3, 4, 5, 6, 7, 8 ; (of Crabborn,) 2, 3, 4 ; (of Northwood Park,) 3, 4, 5, 6, 7, 8 ; (of Bangor Castle,) 3, 4, 5, 6, 7, 8 ; (of Vianston,) 2 ; (of Oaklands,) 5, 6 ; (of Rodbaston,) 7, 8. Harleian Society, ii. 83 ; xii. 275 ; xiii. 518 ; xvi. 335 ; xvii. 323 ; xxix. 483 ; xxxii. 304 ; xxxviii. 647, 720. Topographer, (London, 1789-91, 8vo.) ii. 27. Shaw's Staffordshire, ii. 46. Blore's Rutland, 54, 207. Hodgson's Northumberland, I. ii. 330. Dallaway's Sussex, II. ii. 311. Bridge's Northamptonshire, by Rev. Peter Whalley, i. 339. Visitation of Staffordshire, 1663-4, printed by Sir T. Phillipps, 10. Hunter's History of the Parish of Sheffield, 375. Nichols' History of the County of Leicester, ii. 636 ; iv. 710. Hunter's Deanery of Doncaster, ii. 189, 445. Surtees' Durham, ii. 297 ; iii. 13. Abram's History of Blackburn, 594. O'Hart's Irish Pedigrees, 2nd Series, 138. Notes and Queries, 2 S. xii. 426. Collections for a History of Staffordshire, William Salt Society, ii. part 2, 59. Edmondson's Baronagium Genealogicum, iv. 343. Archdall's Lodge's Peerage, vi. 68. Bridges' Collins' Peerage, vi. 272. Wotton's English Baronetage, iii. 195. Banks' Baronies in Fee, i. 197. Banks' Dormant and Extinct Baronage, ii. 174. Burke's Extinct Baronetcies, and 616. Ormerod's Cheshire, iii. 723. Earwaker's East Cheshire, ii. 408. Foster's Visitation of Middlesex, 87. The Genealogist, New Series, ii. 109. Metcalfe's Visitations of Northamptonshire, 151. Visitations of Staffordshire, 1614 and 1663-4, William Salt Society, 298. Foster's Visitations of Durham, 145, 317, 319. Burke's Colonial Gentry,

i. 320. New England Register, xli. 282, 284. Parliamentary
Memoirs of Fermanagh, by Earl of Belmore, 64. Howard's
Visitations of England and Wales, ix. 119.
WARD BOUGHTON LEIGH. Burke's Commoners, i. 379, Landed
Gentry, 2, 3, 4, 5.
WARD-JACKSON. Burke's Landed Gentry, 5.
WARDE. Visitation of Norfolk, published by Norfolk Archæological
Society, i. 29. Blomefield's Norfolk, x. 106. Visitation of
Durham, 1615, (Sunderland, 1820, fol.) 59. Burke's Royal
Families, (London, 1851, 8vo.) i. 2. Burke's Landed Gentry, (of
Squerryes,) 2 add., 3, 4, 5, 6, 7, 8 ; (of Clopton House,) 2, 3, 4, 5 ;
(of Hooton Pagnell,) 5, 6, 7, 8. Harleian Society, ii. 87, 177 ;
xvii. 321, 322, 323 ; xxxii. 305 ; xli. 60 ; xlii. 31. Nichols'
History of the County of Leicester, ii. 539 ; iv. 760. Hunter's
Deanery of Doncaster, ii. 143. Surtees' Durham, i. 110.
Wilson's History of the Parish of St. Leonard Pountney, 236.
Metcalfe's Visitations of Suffolk, 173. The Genealogist, New
Series, x. 138. Archæologia Cantiana, xvi. 136. Howard's
Visitation of England and Wales, iv. 55. The Genealogist, New
Series, xv. 214.
WARDEDIEU. Sussex Archæological Collections, ix. 282.
WARDELL. Surtees' Durham, ii. 198. Notes and Queries, 6 S. x.
448. Burke's Landed Gentry, 7 at p. 1488 ; 8 at p. 1637.
WARDEN. Sussex Archæological Collections, xxv. 84.
WARDER. Visitatio Comitatus Wiltoniæ, 1623, printed by Sir T.
Phillipps. Hoare's Wiltshire, V. ii. 96. The Genealogist, New
Series, xiii. 26.
WARDLAW. Memoirs of Ralph Wardlaw, D.D., by W. L. Alexander.
Edinburgh, 1856, 8vo. Peter Chalmers' Account of Dunfermline,
i. 301 ; ii. 303. Burke's Landed Gentry, 8 at p. 1681.
WARDROP. Burke's Landed Gentry, 4, 5.
WARE. Irish Literary Inquirer, conducted by John Power, 16.
Burke's Heraldic Illustrations, 10. Burke's Commoners, iv. 494 ;
(of Hendon Hall,) Landed Gentry, 2, 3, 4, 5, 6 ; (of Woodfort,)
2, 3, 4, 5, 6, 7 ; (of Poslingford,) 7, 8. Harleian Society, xiii.
518 ; xiv. 615. New England Register, vi. 145 ; xli. 21, 394.
See HIBBERT-WARE.
WAREING. See WARING.
WARENTHAM. Bateson's History of Northumberland, i. 213.
WARGRAVE. Reid's History of Wargrave, 109-122.
WARHAM. Hasted's Kent, iii. 699. Berry's Hampshire Genealogies,
252. Collectanea Topographica et Genealogica, iii. 2, 6. Hutchins'
Dorset, ii. 505. Harleian Society, xx. 96 ; xliii. 15. The
Manor of Haling, by G. S. Steinman, 9, 13.
WARING. Gentleman's Magazine, lxiii. 391, 522, 688, 796 ; lxxix.
1191. Burke's Landed Gentry, (of Beenham House,) 8 ; (of
Waringstown,) 2, 3, 4, 5, 6, 7, 8. Fishwicke's History of Goos-
nargh, 189. Visitation of Warwickshire, 1619, published with
Warwickshire Antiquarian Magazine, 156. Pembrokeshire
Pedigrees, 152. Harleian Society, xii. 341, 359 ; xvii. 324 ;

xxviii. 80 ; xxix. 485. Ormerod's Cheshire, ii. 13. Ormerod's
Parentalia, 18. Burke's Colonial Gentry, ii. 757. Transactions
of Shropshire Archæological Society, ix. 50. *See* WARYNG.
WARING-MAXWELL. Burke's Landed Gentry, 2, 3, 4, 5, 6.
WARMOUTH. Pedigrees from Visitation of Northumberland, printed
by Sir T. Phillipps, (Middle Hill, 1858, fol.) 2. The Genealogist,
i. 309. Foster's Visitations of Northumberland, 121.
WARNECOMBE. Weaver's Visitations of Herefordshire, 70.
WARNELL. Visitatio Comitatus Wiltoniæ, 1623, printed by Sir T.
Phillipps.
WARNER. Harleian Society, i. 64 ; xii. 51 ; xvii. 325 ; xxxii. 308.
Hasted's Kent, ii. 663. Morant's Essex, i. 311 ; ii. 84. Visita-
tion of Norfolk, published by Norfolk Archæological Society,
i. 17, Burke's Commoners, (of Ardeer,) ii. 340, Landed Gentry,
2, 3, 4, 5, 6, 7, 8 ; (of Highams,) Landed Gentry, 3, 4, 5, 6, 7, 8 ;
(of Antigua,) 4 ; (of Quorn Hall,) 4, 5, 6, 7, 8. Visitation of
Warwickshire, 1619, published with Warwickshire Antiquarian
Magazine, 192. Geo. Robertson's Description of Cunninghame,
179. Paterson's History of the Co. of Ayr, ii. 448. Page's
History of Suffolk, 843. Paterson's History of Ayr and Wigton,
iii. 570. Metcalfe's Visitations of Suffolk, 174. Burke's Extinct
Baronetcies. Carthew's Hundred of Launditch, Part iii. 125.
Family Notes, by J. M. Browne, 75. Metcalfe's Visitations of
Northamptonshire, 151. Fletcher's Leicestershire Pedigrees and
Royal Descents, 191. New England Register, x. 103 ; xx. 64.
WARNET, or WARNETT. Berry's Sussex Genealogies, 129. Visitation
of Sussex, 1570, printed by Sir T. Phillipps, (Middle Hill, fol.) 11.
Horsfield's History of Lewes, ii. 106. Genealogical Gleanings in
England, by H. F. Waters, i. 40. New England Register,
xxxviii. 198. Surrey Archæological Collections, x. Harleian
Society, xliii. 137.
WARNFORD, or WARNEFORD. Pedigree of Warneford of Seven-
hampton, by Sir T. Phillipps, single page, folio. Berry's
Hampshire Genealogies, 314. Burke's Landed Gentry, 5 supp.,
6, 7, 8. Visitation of Wiltshire, edited by G. W. Marshall, 16.
The Genealogist, vi. 104.
WARRAM. Harleian Society, xxix. 487.
WARRAND. Burke's Landed Gentry, 6 supp., 7, 8.
WARRE. Collinson's Somerset, iii. 259. The Tyndale Pedigree, by
B. W. Greenfield. Burke's Landed Gentry, (of Hestercombe,) 2,
3, 4, 5, 6, 7 ; (of Bindon House,) 5 ; (of Westcliff House,) 5, 6, 7,
8. Harleian Society, xi. 115, 116. Westcote's Devonshire,
edited by G. Oliver and P. Jones, 491. Burke's Extinct Baronet-
cies. Weaver's Visitations of Somerset, 87. Burke's Family
Records, 616. The Genealogist, New Series, xiii. 27 ; xvii. 242.
See LE WARRE.
WARRELL. Harleian Society, xvii. 325.
WARREN. The History of the Ancient Earls of Warren and Surrey,
etc., by the Rev. J. Watson. Warrington, 1776, 4to. ; 2nd edn.,
1782, 2 vols., 4to. Genealogy of Warren, by J. C Warren.

Boston, U.S.A., 1854, 4to. Morant's Essex, i. 368. Berry's Buckinghamshire Genealogies, 80. Dwnn's Visitations of Wales, i. 163, 181. Berry's Essex Genealogies, 66, 96, 98. Berry's Kent Genealogies, 60. Burke's Landed Gentry, (of Sandford's Court,) 2 ; (of Lodge Park,) 4, 5, 6, 7, 8 ; (of Killiney,) 3, 4, 5, 6, 7, 8. Carthew's Hundred of Launditch, Part i. 36. Harleian Society, i. 8 ; vi. 299, 354 ; xiv. 730, 742 ; xvi. 336 ; xvii. 326 ; xviii. 240 ; xix. 149 ; xxi. 176 ; xxii. 100, 169 ; xxix. 347 ; xxxvii. 370 ; xlii. 38. Abram's History of Blackburn, 653. Herald and Genealogist, viii. 70. Munford's Analysis of Domesday Book of Co. Norfolk, 19. Collectanea Topographica et Genealogica, vii. 378. Brayley's History of Surrey, i. 113. Earwaker's East Cheshire, ii. 279, 286. Burke's Visitation of Seats and Arms, 2nd Series, ii. 9. Hodgson's Northumberland, II. ii. 239. Hoare's Wiltshire, V. ii. 104. Manning and Bray's Surrey, i. 483, 553. Sussex Archæological Collections, xi. 84. Chetham Society, xcv. 133. Butterworth's History of Stockport, etc., 232. Notes and Queries, 1 S. x. 66, 231. Berry's Genealogical Peerage, 87. Betham's Baronetage, iv. 4. Banks' Dormant and Extinct Baronage, i. 195. Ormerod's Cheshire, iii. 685. Metcalfe's Visitations of Suffolk, 76, 175. Burke's Extinct Baronetcies. The Genealogist, New Series, iii. 54 ; xiii. 250. *See* DE WARREN.

WARRENDER. Wotton's English Baronetage, iv. 172. Betham's Baronetage, iii. 183.

WARRENER. Burke's Landed Gentry, 2.

WARRINGTON. Burke's Landed Gentry, 2, 4 p. 211. Burke's Heraldic Illustrations, 8. The Visitations of Devon, by J. L. Vivian, 138.

WARRY. Burke's Landed Gentry, 3, 4, 5, 6, 7, 8.

WARTER. Burke's Landed Gentry, 2, 3, 4, 5, 6, 7, 8. Foster's Visitations of Yorkshire, 587. East Barnet, by F. C. Cass, 204.

WARTHECOPE. The Genealogist, New Series, xiv. 95.

WARTNABY. Fletcher's Leicestershire Pedigrees and Royal Descents, 66.

WARTON. Surtees Society, xxxvi. 331. Burke's Landed Gentry, 4. Foster's Visitations of Yorkshire, 586. George Oliver's History of Beverley, 515. Poulson's Holderness, i. 483. History of Beverley, by G. Poulson, i. 498. Hunter's Deanery of Doncaster, i. 248. Harleian Society, xxxviii. 606. *See* WHARTON.

WARWICK. Pedigree of Sir Copleston Warwick, M.P., etc., [T. P.]. Morant's Essex, ii. 102. Hutchinson's History of Cumberland, i. 154. Burke's Royal Descents and Pedigrees of Founders' Kin, 33. Banks' Dormant and Extinct Baronage, iii. 713. The Visitations of Devon, edited by J. L. Vivian, 40. Foster's Visitations of Cumberland and Westmorland, 139. Nicolson and Burn's Westmorland and Cumberland, ii. 328.

WARWICK (Earls of). Dugdale's Warwickshire, 378, 387. Baker's Northampton, i. 414 ; ii. 129, 218. Archæologia, xxi. 200. Plantagenet-Harrison's History of Yorkshire, i. 393. The Forest

and Chase of Sutton Coldfield, (London, 1860, 8vo.) 28-35.
Willmore's History of Walsall, 76, 106.

WARYN. The Genealogist, New Series, ix. 86.

WARYNG. Chetham Society, xcv. 133. *See* WARING.

WASCHETT, or WASHETT. Ormerod's Cheshire, iii. 324. Harleian
Society, xviii. 237.

WASE. Berry's Sussex Genealogies, 125. Harleian Society, ii. 200 ;
iv. 173. Dallaway's Sussex, II. ii. 123. Nichols' History of the
County of•Leicester, iii. 400.

WASHBORN, or WASHBOURNE. The Sheriffs of Montgomeryshire, by
W. V. Lloyd, 159, 497. Burke's Commoners, iii. 621. Harleian
Society, xvii. 328 ; xxvii. 121, 142. Weaver's Visitation of
Herefordshire, 72. Burke's Colonial Gentry, i. 375.

WASHINGTON. Memoir of W. M. Peyton, by J. L. Peyton, (London,
1872,) 380. Surtees Society, xxxvi. 273. Burke's Patrician,
ii. 36. Foster's Visitations of Yorkshire, 587. Herald and
Genealogist, iv. 62. Thoresby's Ducatus Leodiensis, 102. Hunter's
Deanery of Doncaster, i. 353. Baker's Northampton, i. 513.
Plantagenet-Harrison's History of Yorkshire, i. 140-145. Stem-
mata Shirleiana, by E. P. Shirley, 2nd edn., 173. Notes and
Queries, 4 S. ix. 248, 325, 450; 5 S. xi. 232; 6 S. xi. 39, 85,
213 ; 8 S. i. 377, 461, 521 ; iii. 214. Metcalfe's Visitations
of Northamptonshire, 54, 152. Northamptonshire Notes and
Queries, i. 145, 189, 233 ; ii. 111, 148. The Genealogist, New
Series, vii. 145 ; xiii. 157. The Castle Howell School Records,
(Lancaster, 1888, 4to.), 192. New England Register, xvii. 248 ;
xxi. 25 ; xliii. 379, 420 ; xliv. 73, 195, 301. Harleian Society,
xxxviii. 443 ; xl. 1293. Croston's edn. of Baines's Lancaster,
v. 520. The Genealogical Magazine, iii. 392.

WASSAND. Poulson's Holderness, i. 434.

WASSE. Harleian Society, i. 40.

WASTAL. Hodgson's Northumberland, III. ii. 323.

WASTELL. Surtees Society, xxxvi. 227. Metcalfe's Visitations of
Northamptonshire, 153.

WASTENEYS, WASSENES, WASTNEY, or WASTNEYS. Ormerod's
Cheshire, i. 627. Surtees Society, xli. 8. Harleian Society, iv.
67 ; xvi. 339 ; xxxix. 1075. Burke's Extinct Baronetcies.
Thoroton's Nottinghamshire, iii. 251. Wotton's English Baronetage, i. 533. Visitation of Staffordshire, (Willm. Salt Soc.) 156.
The Genealogist, New Series, xiii. 174 ; xiv. 103. The Gresley's
of Drakelow, by F. Madan, 294. *See* GASTNEYS.

WASTFELDE. Harleian Society, xvii. 329.

WATEIS. Harleian Society, xxix. 488.

WATER. *See* WALTER.

WATERER. Surrey Archæological Collections, ii.

WATERFIELD. Monken Hadley, by F. C. Cass, 174.

WATERFORD. Burke's Royal Families, (London, 1851, 8vo.) i. 108.
See SHREWSBURY.

WATERHOUSE. Pedigree of Waterhouse of Woodhouse, Co. York,
[T. P.] Broadside. Pedigrees of Waterhouse of Pontefract, Co.

York, and of Milnes of Higham, Co. York, [T. P.] 1871. Broadside. Burke's Landed Gentry, 2, 3, 4, 5, 6, 7, 8. Foster's Yorkshire Pedigrees. Foster's Visitations of Yorkshire, 353. Lipscombe's History of the County of Buckingham, iii. 512. Hunter's Deanery of Doncaster, i. 117, 118, 132. Clutterbuck's Hertford, i. 418. Chauncy's Hertfordshire, 548. John Watson's History of Halifax, 212, 252. Harleian Society, xvii. 330; xxii. 119; xxxvii. 163; xxxviii. 805; xxxix. 844, 863, 882. Annals of Smith of Balby, by H. E. Smith, 229.

WATERLAND. Harleian Society, xxxix. 875.

WATERMAN. Miscellanea Genealogica et Heraldica, New Series, i. 316, 353. The Genealogist, vi. 105. New England Register, xxiii. 204.

WATERS. Burke's Royal Families, (London, 1851, 8vo.) ii. 118. Burke's Landed Gentry, 2, 3, 4, 5, 6, 7, 8. Herald and Genealogist, vii. 336. Memoirs of the Family of Chester, by R. E. C. Waters, 712, etc. Harleian Society, xvii. 329. New England Register, li. 406.

WATERTON. Burke's Landed Gentry, 2, 3, 4, 5, 6, 7, 8. Foster's Yorkshire Pedigrees. Foster's Visitations of Yorkshire, 104, 312. Stonehouse's History of the Isle of Axholme, 454. Foley's Records of the English Province S. J., v. 737.

WATERVILLE, WATEVIL, or WATEVILLE. Wright's Essex, ii. 41. Banks' Baronies in Fee, ii. 155. Harleian Society, xiii. 41.

WATESON. Harleian Society, xix. 149.

WATHE. Harleian Society, xxii. 101. Metcalfe's Visitations of Northamptonshire, 153.

WATHEN. Burke's Landed Gentry, 2, 3. Pedigree of the Family of Sheppard, 19.

WATKIN. Harleian Society, xvii. 331. Account of the Family of Hallen, by A. W. C. Hallen, 38.

WATKINS. Visitation of Somersetshire, printed by Sir T. Phillipps, 145. Burke's Landed Gentry, (of Pennoyre,) 2, 3, 4; (of Woodfield,) 2, 3, 4, 5, 6, 7, 8; (of Shotton Hall,) 3, 4, 8; (of Badby House,) 3, 4, 5, 6, 7, 8; (of Yorkshire,) 2, 3, 4. Jones' History of the County of Brecknock, ii. 199. Hutchins' Dorset, iv. 521. Antiquities and Memoirs of the Parish of Myddle, written by Richard Gough, 1700, (folio) 29. Miscellanea Genealogica et Heraldica, New Series, iii. 397. Harleian Society, xvii. 332. Weaver's Visitations of Somerset, 89. The Genealogist, New Series, iii. 176. History of the Wilmer Family, 316.

WATKINSON. Surtees Society, xxxvi. 206. W. Paver's Pedigrees of Families of the City of York, 21. Thoresby's Ducatus Leodiensis, 77. Notes and Queries, 2 S. xi. 238, 278. Ilkley, Ancient and Modern, by R. Collyer and J. H. Turner, 210. History of Wakefield, Rectory Manor, by Thomas Taylor, 211. Harleian Society, xxxviii. 481, 722. The Genealogist, New Series, xv. 170.

WATLING. Burke's Landed Gentry, 4.

WATLINGTON. Berry's Hertfordshire Genealogies, 233-238. Berry's Berkshire Genealogies, 80-84. Burke's Landed Gentry, 2.

WATMERE, or WATMOUGH. Berry's Kent Genealogies, 144. Chetham Society, lxxxii. 114. Harleian Society, xlii. 44.

WATNEY. Howard's Visitation of England and Wales, i. 109 ; Notes, ii. 112. Burke's Landed Gentry, 5 supp. 6, 7, 8.

WATNOW. Thoroton's Nottinghamshire, ii. 246.

WATSON. Rockingham Castle and the Watsons. By C. Wise. London, 1891, 4to. Topographer and Genealogist, ii. 81. Cambridgeshire Visitation, edited by Sir T. Phillipps, 33. Surtees Society, xxxvi. 283. Berry's Kent Genealogies, 137. Berry's Hampshire Genealogies, 331. Visitation of Durham, 1615, (Sunderland, 1820, fol.) 76. Visitation of Gloucestershire, 1569, (Middle Hill, 1854, fol.) 10. Burke's Landed Gentry, (of Calgarth Park,) 3, 4, 5, 6, 7, 8 ; (of Kilmanahan•Castle,) 3, 4, 5 ; (of Ayton,) 8 ; (of Burnhead,) 8 ; (of Kilconner House,) 3, 4, 5, 8 ; (of Lumclone,) 3, 4, 5, 6, 7 ; (of Clonbrogan,) 2 ; (of Berwick Hall,) 6, 7 ; (of Langley House,) 6 supp., 7, 8. Foster's Yorkshire Pedigrees. J. H. Hill's History of Market Harborough, 73. Raine's History of North Durham, 186, 319. Hodgson's Northumberland, II. ii. 191. Surtees' Durham, iii. 292. Harleian Society, xiv. 617 ; xxi. 266 ; xxvii. 144 ; xxix. 491 ; xxxviii. 708 ; xli. 56 ; xlii. 22. Edmondson's Baronagium Genealogicum, i. 80. Notes and Queries, 2 S. viii. 76, 94, 119 ; xi. 217. Burke's Extinct Baronetcies. Brydges' Collins' Peerage, vii. 283. Betham's Baronetage, iii. 291 ; v. 540. Banks' Dormant and Extinct Baronage, iii. 638. Metcalfe's Visitation of Worcester, 1683, 101. Alexander Nisbet's Heraldic Plates, 144. Foster's Visitations of Northumberland, 122. Visitations of Staffordshire, 1614 and 1663-4, William Salt Society, 299. Foster's Visitations of Durham, 321. New England Register, xviii. 363.

WATSON-WENTWORTH. Jacob's Peerage, i. 446.

WATT. Letters respecting the Watt Family, by George Williamson, 1840, 8vo. Memoirs of the Lineage, etc., of James Watt, by George Williamson. Edinburgh, 1856, 4to. Burke's Landed Gentry, (of Bell Vale,) 2 ; (of Breckness,) 7, 8 ; (of Abney Hall,) 7 ; (of Bishop Burton,) 5, 6, 7, 8. Burke's Colonial Gentry, ii. 719. See GIBSON-WATT.

WATTON. Hasted's Kent, ii. 227. Archæologia Cantiana, iv. 258. Berry's Kent Genealogies, 8, 477. Harleian Society, xiii. 311 ; xlii. 9.

WATTS. Genealogy of the Family of Watts. By W. P. W. Phillimore. Shrewsbury, 1894, 8vo. Visitation of Somersetshire, printed by Sir T. Phillipps, 145. Burke's Commoners, (of Hawkesdale,) iii. 393, Landed Gentry, 2, 3, 4, 5 ; (of Danet's Hall,) Landed Gentry, 2 add. ; (of Abney Hall, 3, 4, 5, 6, 8 ; (of Hanslope Park,) 4, 5, 6, 7, 8. Hunter's History of the Parish of Sheffield, 442. Harleian Society, xi. 117 ; xvii. 332 ; xxii. 102 ; xxxvii. 224. Clutterbuck's Hertford, iii. 305. Baker's Northampton, ii. 23. Chauncy's Hertfordshire, 210. Scott of Scot's-Hall, by J. R. Scott, 157. North's Church Bells of Leicestershire, 59-72. North's Church Bells of Northamptonshire, 87-93. Eastwood's

History of Ecclesfield, 413. Account of the Mayo and Elton Families, by C. H. Mayo, 22. Metcalfe's Visitations of Northamptonshire, 203. Weaver's Visitations of Somerset, 89. Phillimore's London and Middlesex Note-Book, 101. Bysshe's Visitation of Essex, edited by J. J. Howard, 99. Shropshire Notes and Queries, New Series, iii. 16.

WATTS-RUSSELL. Burke's Landed Gentry, 7, 8.

WAUCHOPE. History and Genealogy of the Family of Wauchope, by James Paterson. Edinburgh, 1858, 4to. Burke's Landed Gentry, (of Niddrie Marischal,) 2, 3, 4, 5, 6, 7, 8 ; (of Edmondstone,) 2, 3.

WAUD. Burke's Landed Gentry, 2, 3, 4, 5, 6, 7, 8.

WAUNCY. Baker's Northampton, i. 731.

WAURE. The Genealogist, New Series, xii. 225.

WAUTON. Harleian Society, xix. 198.

WAVER. Dugdale's Warwickshire, 90.

WAVERTON. Harleian Society, xxix. 492.

WAWEN. Harleian Society, xvii. 333.

WAWGOOD. Dwnn's Visitations of Wales, i. 111.

WAWTON. Foster's Visitations of Yorkshire, 260, 408. *See* WARTON.

WAY, or WAYE. Burke's Commoners, (of Denham,) iv. 676, Landed Gentry, 2, 3, 4, 5, 6, 7, 8 ; (of Spencer Grange,) Landed Gentry, 5, 6, 7, 8 ; (of Spaynes Hall,) 5. Harleian Society, vi. 300. F. G. Lee's History of Thame, 582. Burke's Colonial Gentry, i. 192. The Visitations of Devon, by J. L. Vivian, 773.

WAYER. Harleian Society, i. 63.

WAYLEN. Burke's Landed Gentry, 2 add.

WAYLETT. Morant's Essex, ii. 475.

WAYNE. Burke's Landed Gentry, 4, 5, 6. Burke's Colonial Gentry, i. 144.

WAYNEMAN. Sir T. Phillipps' Topographer, No. 1, (March, 1821, 8vo.) 40. Harleian Society, v. 175, 176. *See* WAINMAN.

WAYTE. Visitation of Norfolk, published by Norfolk Archæological Society, i. 270. Surtees Society, xxxvi. 35. Berry's Hampshire Genealogies, 80. Collections by the Powys-land Club, v. 258. Carthew's Hundred of Launditch, Part iii. 419. Harleian Society, xxxii. 306. The Genealogist, New Series, xvi. 92. *See* WAIT.

WEALE. Harleian Society, xxix. 493.

WEARE. Burke's Landed Gentry, 5 supp., 6, 7, 8. Harleian Society, vi. 301. Visitatio Comitatus Wiltoniæ, 1623, printed by Sir T. Phillipps. Blunt's Dursley and its Neighbourhood, 105. The Genealogist, New Series, xiii. 28. The Visitations of Devon, by J. L. Vivian, 774. *See* WERE.

WEATHORLEY. Cyclostyle Pedigrees, by J. J. Green.

WEAVER. Harleian Society, i. 35 ; xvii. 334 ; xxix. 494 ; xliii. 37. Robinson's Mansions of Herefordshire, 17. Weaver's Visitation of Herefordshire, 99. New England Register, xviii. 257 ; xlvii. 48.

WEBB, or WEBBE. Pedigree of Webb of Gloucester, and Garnstone, Co. Hereford, [T. P.] 1858, folio page. Pedigree of Webb of Norton Court, etc., [T. P.] 1859, folio page. Webb of the Hill,

Painswick, Co. Glouc. Sheet pedigree, privately printed by Sir T. Phillipps. Chronicle of the Family of De Havilland. Dwnn's Visitations of Wales, i. 234. Berry's Kent Genealogies, 302. Berry's Sussex Genealogies, 101. Visitation of Middlesex, (Salisbury, 1820, fol.) 41. Burke's Landed Gentry, (of Newstead Abbey,) 3, 4, 5, 6, 7, 8 ; (of Donnington Hall,) 2, 3, 4, 5, 6, 7, 8 ; (of Woodville,) 2, 3, 4, 5, 6, 7, 8 ; (of Webbsborough,) 2 ; (of Caheragh,) 2, 3, 4 ; (of Knocktoran,) 7 ; (of Odstock,) 8 ; (of The Berrow,) 4, 5, 6. Miscellanea Genealogica et Heraldica, New Series, i. 14 ; iii. 55. Lipscombe's History of the County of Buckingham, ii. 450. Visitatio Comitatus Wiltoniæ, 1623, printed by Sir T. Phillipps. Hutchins' Dorset, iii. 298, 628. Hoare's Wiltshire, III. v. 20 ; IV. ii. 29. Manning and Bray's Surrey, ii. 44. Meyrick's History of the Co. of Cardigan, 195. Memoirs of the Family of Chester, by R. E. C. Waters, 516. Fosbrooke's History of Gloucestershire, i. 285. Notes and Queries, 3 S. i. 131. Harleian Society, vi. 301 ; xvii. 334 ; xli. 63 ; xlii. 123. Betham's Baronetage, ii. 19. Monken Hadley, by F. C. Cass, 74. Wotton's English Baronetage, ii. 403. Visitation of Wiltshire, edited by G. W. Marshall, 87. Cambridgeshire Visitation, edited by Sir T. Phillipps, 33. Tuckett's Devonshire Pedigrees, 128. Foley's Records of the English Province S. J., v. 960. Norfolk Archæology, viii. 316. Foster's Visitations of Cumberland and Westmorland, 140. Annals of an Old Manor House, Sutton Place, by F. Harrison, at end. Foster's Visitations of Middlesex, 75. Visitation of Gloucester, edited by T. F. Fenwick and W. C. Metcalfe, 195-198. Collections relating to Henry Smith, 161. Burke's Colonial Gentry, i. 321. Burke's Family Records, 620. The Genealogist, New Series, xiii. 239. The Visitations of Devon, by J. L. Vivian, 775. Howard's Visitation of England and Wales, viii. 9 ; ix. 25.

WEBB-PEPLOE. Miscellanea Genealogica et Heraldica, 2nd Series, iii. 130.

WEBBE-WESTON. Burke's Landed Gentry, 2, 3, 4, 5.

WEBBER. Chronicle of the Family of De Havilland. Burke's Landed Gentry, (of Buckland,) 4, 5, 6, 7, 8 ; (of Leekfield,) 8. Maclean's History of Trigg Minor, ii. 166, 548. Harleian Society, ix. 262. The Visitations of Cornwall, by J. L. Vivian, 550. Howard's Visitation of England and Wales, iv. 158, 159. Burke's Family Records, 622. The Visitations of Devon, by J. L. Vivian, 812.

WEBLEY. Pedigree of Webley of the Mead, [T. P.] 1861, folio page.

WEBLIN. Harleian Society, xiii. 519.

WEBSTER. Topographer and Genealogist, ii. 113. The Trial of the Second Issue in Bere versus Ward, (1823, folio,) at end. Burke's Landed Gentry, (of Penns,) 3, 4, 5, 6 ; (of Balruddery,) 2 supp. ; (of Pallion Hall,) 5, 6, 7, 8. Foster's Visitations of Yorkshire, 588. Jewitt's Reliquary, xii. 201. Burke's Visitation of Seats and Arms, ii. 49. Wotton's English Baronetage, iv. 94. Betham's Baronetage, iii. 129. Miscellanea Genealogica et Heraldica, 2nd

Series, iii. 37. New England Register, vii. 102 ; ix. 159 ; xxi. 1. Harleian Society, xxxvii. 235, 319 ; xxxix. 1011.

WECHERLIN. Berry's Kent Genealogies, 457.

WEDD. Berry's Hertfordshire Genealogies, 239-243. Burke's Royal Descents and Pedigrees of Founders' Kin, 40.

WEDDELL. Surtees Society, xxxvi. 164. Whitaker's History of Richmondshire, ii. 122. Harleian Society, xvii. 336 ; xl. 1259.

WEDDERBURN. A Genealogical Account of the Wedderburn Family, by James Wedderburn. Nantes, 1819, 8vo. Burke's Landed Gentry, 2, 3, 4, 5, 6, 7. Douglas's Baronage of Scotland, 278-284, 578. Balmerino and its Abbey, by James Campbell, 322. Edmondson's Baronagium Genealogicum, vi. 80. Betham's Baronetage, v. 543. See SCRIMGEOUR-WEDDERBURN.

WEDDERBURN-COLVILLE. Burke's Landed Gentry, 2 supp., 3, 4, 5, 6.

WEDGEWOOD, or WEDGWOOD. Visitation of Staffordshire, 1663-4, printed by Sir T. Phillipps, 10. The Borough of Stoke-upon-Trent, by John Ward, 153, 197, 199-202. Jewitt's Life of Wedgwood, 158. Marks and Monograms on Pottery and Porcelain, by Wm. Chaffers, 3rd edn., 480. Visitations of Staffordshire, 1614 and 1663-4, William Salt Society, 300.

WEDNESTER. Weaver's Visitation of Herefordshire, 100.

WEEDEN. Burke's Landed Gentry, 4, 5.

WEEKES. Berry's Sussex Genealogies, 168. Tuckett's Devonshire Pedigrees, 37. Burke's Landed Gentry, 2, 3, 4, 5, 6, 7, 8. Harleian Society, vi. 318. The Genealogist, i. 192, 222 ; ii. 95. Sussex Archæological Collections, xiv. 116. Dallaway's Sussex, II. i. 68. Foster's Collectanea Genealogica, i. 53. New England Register, xxxix. 234. The Visitations of Devon, by J. L. Vivian, 776.

WEELEY. Morant's Essex, i. 474.

WEEMS. Kent's British Banner Displayed, 379. See WEMYSS.

WEEVER. Harleian Society, xviii. 243 ; xxix. 495.

WEGG PROSSER. Burke's Landed Gentry, 4, 5, 6, 7.

WEIATT. Dwnn's Visitations of Wales, i. 66.

WEIGHT. See HALLEN.

WEIGHTMAN. Burke's Landed Gentry, 4.

WEILD. See WYLDE.

WEIR. Burke's Commoners, iii. 320 ; Landed Gentry, (of Managhin,) 2, 7, 8. Paterson's History of the County of Ayr, i. 233. Paterson's History of Ayr and Wigton, iii. 60. Burke's Extinct Baronetcies, 638. The Upper Ward of Lanarkshire, by G. V. Irving, ii. 207. Alexander Nisbet's Heraldic Plates, 26. New England Register, xxv. 246. See VERE.

WELBECK. Jewitt's Reliquary, vii. 30. Harleian Society, xiv. 599. Metcalfe's Visitations of Suffolk, 105. The Genealogist, vi. 105.

WELBORE. Harleian Society, xli. 34.

WELBORNE. Harleian Society, xxxvii. 416.

WELBURNE. The Genealogist, New Series, iii. 176.

WELBURY. Foster's Visitations of Yorkshire, 588. Surtees' Durham, i. 43.

WELBY. Notices of the Family of Welby. Grantham, 1842, 8vo. Burke's Royal Families, (London, 1851, 8vo.) i. 89. Burke's Patrician, iv. 67. Harleian Society, iii. 7 ; xvii. 335 ; xxxii. 307. Turnor's History of the Town and Soke of Grantham, 124. Dickinson's History of Southwell, 2nd edition, 166. Blore's Rutland, 192. Betham's Baronetage, v. app. 16. The Genealogist, v. 53. Ancient Families of Lincolnshire, in 'Spalding Free Press,' 1873-5, Nos. xviii. and xix. Lincolnshire Notes and Queries, ii. 162, 193 ; iii. 33.

WELCH. Burke's Landed Gentry, 2, 3, 4, 5, 6, 7, 8. Burke's Heraldic Illustrations, 42. New England Register, xxiii. 417.

WELD. Harleian Society, i. 91 ; xvii. 336 ; xviii. 244 ; xxii. 103 ; xxix. 495. Foster's Lancashire Pedigrees. Some Account of the Worshipful Company of Grocers, by J. B. Heath, 224. Visitation of Middlesex, (Salisbury, 1820, fol.) 27. Burke's Commoners, i. 197 ; ii. 677 ; iv. 334 ; Landed Gentry, 2, 3, 4, 5, 6, 7, 8. Miscellanea Genealogica et Heraldica, New Series, i. 113. History of the Parish of St. Leonard, Shoreditch, by Henry Ellis, 128. W. Robinson's History of Hackney, i. 159. Hutchins' Dorset, i. 373. Clutterbuck's Hertford, ii. 358. Foley's Records of the English Province, S. J., iv. 623. Ormerod's Cheshire, ii. 241. East Barnet, by F. C. Cass, Part i. 32. Phillimore's London and Middlesex Note-Book, 154. New England Register, vii. 309 ; viii. 207 ; ix. 42 ; xxii. 381. Foster's Visitation of Middlesex, 54. Earwaker's History of Sandbach, 121. Burke's Colonial Gentry, ii. 650.

WELD-BLUNDELL. Burke's Landed Gentry, 2, 3, 4, 5, 6, 7, 8. Foster's Lancashire Pedigrees.

WELDON. Hasted's Kent, i. 261. The Genealogist, vi. 106. Howard's Visitation of England and Wales, iii. 40.

WELFITT. Burke's Landed Gentry, (of Sherwood Lodge,) 4 ; (of Manby Hall,) 2 supp.

WELFOOTE. Surtees' Durham, iii. 68.

WELFORD. Weaver's Visitation of Herefordshire, 74.

WELISBURNE. Ashmole's Antiquities of Berkshire, iii. 299.

WELLBELOVED. Burke's Commoners, iii. 667, Landed Gentry, 6 at p. 1426 ; 7 at p. 1633 ; 8 at p. 1804. Harleian Society, xxxvii. 182.

WELLER. Hasted's Kent, iii. 91. Berry's Kent Genealogies, 46.

WELLER-POLEY. Visitation of Suffolk, edited by J. J. Howard, i. 291.

WELLES. Banks' History of the Family of Marmyun, 122. Burke's Commoners, ii. 516, Landed Gentry, 2, 3, 4. Burke's Heraldic Illustrations, 48. Hodgson's Northumberland, II. ii. 196. Shaw's Staffordshire, i. 105. Banks' Dormant and Extinct Baronage, ii. 575. Visitation of Staffordshire, (Willm. Salt Soc.) 145. Harleian Society, xvii. 337. See WELLS.

WELLESBOROUGH. Harleian Society, ii. 32.

WELLESLEY. Gentleman's Magazine, 1822, ii. 325 ; 1823, i. 40 ; 1865, i. 87, 130. Notes and Queries, 2 S. vii. 164, 506 ; 3 S.

ix. 291 ; 5 S. xi. 175. Brydges' Collins' Peerage, vi. 462. The Genealogist, New Series, x. 89. *See* WESLEY.

WELLINGTON. The Royal Descent of Nelson and Wellington from Edwd. I., by G. R. French. London, 1853, 8vo. Gentleman's Magazine, 1853, ii. 379, 595.

WELLIS, or WELLYS. Visitation of Staffordshire, 1663-4, printed by Sir T. Phillipps, 10. The Visitations of Staffordshire, 1614 and 1663-4, William Salt Society, 302.

WELLS. The Pedigree of Dymoke Wells, Esq., of Grebby Hall in the County of Lincoln. Printed by William Hunt, Market Place, Pontefract, *n.d.*, broadside. J. H. Hill's History of Langton, 227. Berry's Hampshire Genealogies, 110. Visitation of Sussex, 1570, printed by Sir T. Phillipps, (Middle Hill, fol.) 12. Burke's Landed Gentry, (of Boxford,) 2 ; (of Holme Wood,) 3, 4, 5, 6, 7. Burke's Heraldic Illustrations, 30. Nichols' History of the County of Leicester, ii. 472 ; iii. 60. Hutchins' Dorset, i. 668. Banks' Baronies in Fee, i. 449. Earwaker's History of Sandbach, 22. The Visitations of Cornwall, by J. L. Vivian, 551. New England Register, xii. 157 ; xx. 131 ; xliii. 359 ; xliv. 208. Ontarian Families, by E. M. Chadwick, ii. 145. *See* DE WELLES, WELLES.

WELLWOOD. Burke's Commoners, i. 276, Landed Gentry, 2. Peter Chalmers' History of Dunfermline, ii. 440, and folding table, No. 1, *at end.*

WELMAN. Burke's Commoners, iii. 649, Landed Gentry, 2, 3, 4, 5, 6, 7, 8. Howard's Visitation of England and Wales, iii. 33. Miscellanea Genealogica et Heraldica, 3rd Series, i. 230.

WELSH. Dwnn's Visitations of Wales, i. 124. Burton's Description of Leicestershire, 280. Genealogical Memoirs of John Knox, by C. Rogers, 142. Harleian Society, xxi. 266. Notes and Queries, 8 S., vii. 202. *See* WALSH.

WELSTEAD, or WELSTED. Burke's Landed Gentry, 3, 4, 5, 6, 7, 8.

WELTON. Bridges' Northamptonshire, by Rev. Peter Whalley, i. 96. Baker's Northampton, i. 232.

WEMYSS. Memorials of the Family of Wemyss, by Sir W. Fraser. Edinburgh, 1888, 4to., 3 vols. Burke's Landed Gentry, (of Danesfort and Trefechan,) 2, 3, 4, 5 and supp., 6, 7, 8 ; (of Wemysshall,) 8. Herald and Genealogist, viii. 62, 189. Nisbet's Heraldry, ii. app. 33. Douglas's Baronage of Scotland, 553, 561. Walter Wood's East Neuk of Fife, 255. Wood's Douglas's Peerage of Scotland, ii. 615. The Irish Builder, xxix. 11. *See* WEEMS.

WEMYSS-COLCHESTER. Burke's Landed Gentry, 6, 7.

WENCELAGH. Foster's Visitations of Yorkshire, 150. Poulson's Holderness, i. 277.

WENDELL. New England Register, xxxvi. 242.

WENDESLEY. Jewitt's Reliquary, vii. 208. The Genealogist, New Series, viii. 177.

WENDEY, or WENDY. Cambridgeshire Visitation, edited by Sir T. Phillipps, 33. Harleian Society, viii. 17 ; xli. 40.

WENGETT. New England Register, ix. 143.

WENHAM. Berry's Sussex Genealogies, 257. Harleian Society, xvii. 337.

WENLOCK. Bysshe's Visitation of Essex, edited by J. J. Howard, 99.

WENMAN. Hasted's Kent, ii. 622, 663. Visitation of Oxfordshire, 1634, printed by Sir T. Phillipps, (Middle Hill, fol.) 32. Burke's Commoners, i. 421. Harleian Society, v. 307. Lipscombe's History of the County of Buckingham, iii. 131. Herald and Genealogist, ii. 521. Topograpical Miscellanies, 1792, 4to., (Witney.) Archdall's Lodge's Peerage, iv. 280. Burke's Extinct Baronetcies. F. G. Lee's History of Thame, 434. *See* WAINMAN.

WENTWORTH. The Wentworth Genealogy. By J. Wentworth. 1870, 8vo., 2 vols. Three Branches of the Family of Wentworth, by W. L. Rutton. London, 1891, 4to. Case of R. G. N. M., Viscount Ockham, on his claim to be Lord Wentworth, fol. pp. 14. Supplemental Case of same, fol. pp. 13. Claim of R. G. N. M., Viscount Ockham, to the Barony of Wentworth, Sess. Papers, H of 1863 ; G of 1864. Collectanea Topographica et Genealogica, vii. 263. Morant's Essex, ii. 235, 306, 333, 361, 371, 381, 383, 445. Surtees Society, xxxvi. 3, 10, 284, 288, 307 ; xli. 11, 75, 85. Burke's Commoners, iii. 89, Landed Gentry, 2, 3, 4, 5, 6, 7, 8. Foster's Yorkshire Pedigrees. Foster's Visitations of Yorkshire, 334, 374, 378. J. H. Hill's History of Market Harborough, 102. Harleian Society, viii. 36, 354 ; xiii. 16, 124, 312, 519 ; xiv. 615 ; xvi. 339. Gage's History of Thingoe Hundred, Suffolk, 4. Thoresby's Ducatus Leodiensis, 197, 241. Hunter's Deanery of Doncaster, ii. 81, 89, 243, 267, 388, 453, 456. Edmondson's Baronagium Genealogicum, i. 80 ; iii. 194 ; iv. 338. Burke's Extinct Baronetcies. Baker's Northampton, i. 33. Wright's Essex, ii. 9. History of Barnsley, by Rowland Jackson, 450. History of Worsborough, by Joseph Wilkinson, 106. Yorkshire Archæological and Topographical Journal, vi. 369. Brydges' Collins' Peerage, vi. 200. Wotton's English Baronetage, iii. 436 ; iv. 36. Banks' Baronies in Fee, i. 453. Betham's Baronetage, iv. 300. Banks' Dormant and Extinct Baronage, ii. 582 ; iii. 677. Metcalfe's Visitations of Suffolk, 77, 78, 175. Miscellanea Genealogica et Heraldica, New Series, iv. 340. History of Wakefield Rectory Manor, by Thomas Taylor, 431. Notes and Queries, 7 S., iii. 71. Chancellor's Sepulchral Monuments of Essex, 217. New England Register, iv. 321 ; vi. 213, 291 ; vii. 265, 304 ; viii. 48, 246 ; xix. 65 ; xxii. 120 ; xxxvi. 315. Burke's Colonial Gentry, i. 95. Rockingham Castle and the Watsons, ped. 5. The Genealogist, New Series, xiv. 175 ; xvii. 182. *See* JOHNSON, VERNON-WENTWORTH, WATSON-WENTWORTH.

WEOLEY. Harleian Society, xxi. 177.

WERDEN. Burke's Commoners, iv. 330. Wotton's English Baronetage, iii. 548. Burke's Extinct Baronetcies.

WERE. Burke's Commoners, iv. 140, Landed Gentry, 2. *See* WEARE.

WERGE. Burke's Commoners, i. 378 ; ii. xxii ; Landed Gentry, 2, 3.

WERRY. Plantagenet-Harrison's History of Yorkshire, i. 152.

WESCOMBE, or WESTCOMBE. Wotton's English Baronetage, iv. 82. Betham's Baronetage, iii. 121. Burke's Extinct Baronetcies.

WESLEY. A Biographical History of the Wesley Family, by John Dove. London, 1833, 8vo. Memorials of the Wesley Family, by George J. Stevenson. London, 1876, 8vo. Gentleman's Magazine, 1833, i. 229, 386. Stonehouse's History of the Isle of Axholme, 175. Harleian Society, xxxviii. 576. See WELLESLEY, WESTLEY.

WESSELOWSKI. The Genealogist, New Series, xii. 102.

WESSENHAM. Herald and Genealogist, viii. 337.

WEST. Rudder's Gloucestershire, 819. Berry's Sussex Genealogies, 14. Berry's Hampshire Genealogies, 201. Surtees Society, xxxvi. 292. Berry's Buckinghamshire Genealogies, 96. Burke's Landed Gentry, (of Postern Park,) 2; (of Alscot Park), 2, 3, 4, 5, 6, 7, 8; (of Braywick Lodge,) 2, 3, 4, 5; (of Horham Hall,) 2, 3, 4, 5, 6, 7, 8; (of Ruthin Castle,) 5, 6, 7, 8. Foster's Visitations of Yorkshire, 359, 588. Herald. and Genealogist, iii. 296. Chetham Society, lxxxviii. 330. Lipscombe's History of the County of Buckingham, i. 255. Blore's Rutland, 100. Dallaway's Sussex, II. ii. 27, 284. Hampshire Visitations, printed by Sir T. Phillipps, 21. Nichols' History of the County of Leicester, ii. 211. Dugdale's Warwickshire, 661. Hutchins' Dorset, iii. 141, 450. Hunter's Deanery of Doncaster, i. 301; ii. 173, 357. Clutterbuck's Hertford, i. 338. Harleian Society, xiv. 616; xvi. 346; xvii. 338-9. Topographical Miscellanies, 1792, 4to., (Ossington). Edmondson's Baronagium Genealogicum, iii. 300. Brydges' Collins' Peerage, v. 1. Banks' Baronies in Fee, i. 456. Banks' Dormant and Extinct Baronage, ii. 160. The Genealogist, vii. 254; New Series, xvii. 28. Historical Notices of Doncaster, by C. W. Hatfield, 2nd Series, 128. Metcalfe's Visitations of Northamptonshire, 154. Hampshire Notes and Queries, vi. 96. The Genealogical Magazine, ii. 504. Bloom's History of Preston on Stour, 52, 54, 64. See BUCKHURST, DE LA WARR.

WESTBROOK, or WESTBROOKE. Berry's Sussex Genealogies, 171. Dallaway's Sussex, II. i. 29. Manning and Bray's Surrey, ii. 45. Castles, Mansions, and Manors of Western Sussex, by D. G. C. Elwes and C. J. Robinson, 92. Aubrey's Antiquities of Surrey, iv. 18. Monken Hadley, by F. C. Cass, 174. Memorials of the Prichards, by Isabel Southall, 90. The Genealogist, New Series, xvi. 39.

WESTBURY. Hoare's Wiltshire, III. i. 19.

WESTBY, or WESTBYE. Miscellanea Genealogica et Heraldica, ii. 217; New Series, i. 445. Gentleman's Magazine, lxxxii. i. 4, 111, 622. Surtees Society, xxxvi. 174, 278. Burke's Commoners, (of Mowbreck,) i. 597, Landed Gentry, 2, 3, 4, 5; (of Roebuck Castle,) Commoners, iii. 117, Landed Gentry, 2, 4, 5, 6, 7, 8; (of High Park,) Commoners, iii. 119, Landed Gentry, 2, 3, 4, 5, 6, 7. Foster's Yorkshire Pedigrees. Foster's Visitations of Yorkshire, 363. Chetham Society, lxxxi. 47; lxxxii. 90; lxxxviii. 331, 332; xcii. 174. Foster's Lancashire Pedigrees. Hunter's Deanery of

Doncaster, i. 397. Baines' History of the Co. of Lancaster, iv. 452. Harleian Society, xxxviii. 527. The Genealogist, New Series, xiii. 261, 264.

WESTCAR. Burke's Landed Gentry, 2, 3, 4, 5.

WESTCOTE, or WESTCOTT. Harleian Society, vi. 302. Westcote's Devonshire, edited by G. Oliver and P. Jones, xii. 621, 622. Polwhele's Devon, ii. 49. Visitation of Devon, edited by F. T. Colby, 204. The Visitations of Devon, by J. L. Vivian, 778.

WESTENRA. Shirley's History of the County of Monaghan, 214. The Irish Builder, xxxv. 198.

WESTERN. Morant's Essex, ii. 147. Berry's Essex Genealogies, 91. Burke's Royal Families, (London, 1851, 8vo.) ii. 195. Burke's Landed Gentry, 2 and add., 3, 4. Harleian Society, xiv. 747.

WESTFALING. Cooke's Continuation of Duncumb's Hereford, (Hund. of Grimsworth,) Part ii. 125.

WESTHEAD. See BROWN-WESTHEAD.

WESTHROPPE. Foster's Visitations of Yorkshire, 261, 370, 408.

WESTLED. The Genealogist, vi. 290.

WESTLEY. Jewitt's Reliquary, viii. 188. Notes and Queries, 3 S. xii. 388. Harleian Society, xiii. 316.. See WESLEY.

WESTMEATH. Claim of A. F., Earl of Westmeath, to Vote at Elections of Irish Peers, Sess. Papers, F of 1871. See NUGENT.

WESTMORELAND. Hasted's Kent, ii. 196, 226.

WESTON. Additional Case of Sir T. Stonor claiming the Barony of Camoys, folding table. Morant's Essex, i. 136; ii. 171. Berry's Surrey Genealogies, 54. Burke's Landed Gentry, (of West Horsley,) 2, 3, 4, 5, 6, 7, 8; (of Somerby,) 2 add; (of Wolveton,) 7, 8. Harleian Society, vi. 303; xiii. 125, 318; xvii. 339; xliii. 7, 28, 215. Erdeswicke's Survey of Staffordshire, 164, 165. Visitation of Staffordshire, 1663-4, printed by Sir T. Phillipps, 10. Herald and Genealogist, iii. 426. Brayley's History of Surrey, ii. 81-88. Visitatio Comitatus Wiltoniæ, 1623, printed by Sir T. Phillipps. Hutchins' Dorset, ii. 553, 860; iii. 676. Manning and Bray's Surrey, i. 135, 136; iii. 41. Memoirs of the Family of Chester, by R. E. C. Waters, 94, 108. Miscellanea Genealogica et Heraldica, New Series, iii. 72. Foley's Records of the English Province, S. J. v. 960. Notes and Queries, 2 S. v. 359, 440; vii. 405, 485; 3 S. ix. 105, 261; xi. 27; 4 S. iv. 246, 366; ix. 275. Collections for a History of Staffordshire, William Salt Society, i. 336. Banks' Dormant and Extinct Baronage, iii. 608. Visitation of Wiltshire, edited by G. W. Marshall, 75. Visitations of Staffordshire, 1614 and 1663-4, William Salt Society, 303. New England Register, xli. 285. Annals of an Old Manor House, Sutton Place, by F. Harrison, at end. The Visitations of Devon, by J. L. Vivian, 780. William Salt Society, New Series, ii. 46. Camoys Peerage Evidence, 268.

WESTROPP. Burke's Landed Gentry, (of Attyflin,) 2, 3, 4, 5, 6, 7, 8; (of Coolreagh,) 2; (of Mellon,) 5, 6, 7. Burke's Family Records, 624. Howard's Visitation of Ireland, ii. 57; iii. 65.

WESTROPP-DAWSON. Burke's Landed Gentry, 6 supp., 8.

WESTTHORP. The Genealogist, vi. 106.

WETENHALE, WETENHALL, or WETNALL. Ormerod's Cheshire, ii. 195 ; iii. 367, 479. James Hall's History of Nantwich, 463. Harleian Society, iii. 28 ; xviii. 244, 246.

WETHERALL. Burke's Landed Gentry, 8.

WETHERED. Burke's Landed Gentry, 5 supp., 6, 7, 8.

WETHERELL. Topographer and Genealogist, ii. 75, 550. Burke's Landed Gentry, 6, 7, 8. The Wolfe's of Forenaghts, 46.

WEVER. Dwnn's Visitations of Wales, i. 258. Ormerod's Cheshire, ii. 210.

WEVERHAM. Ormerod's Cheshire, ii. 116.

WEYLAND. Blomefield's Norfolk, vi. 171, 173. Burke's Landed Gentry, 2, 3, 4, 5, 6, 7, 8.

WEYMOUTH (Visct.). Rudder's Gloucestershire, 511.

WEYNMAN. Roman Catholic Families of England, by J. J. Howard, i. 11.

WGAN. Dwnn's Visitations of Wales, i. 42, 90, 106-8, 115, 164, 179, 220, 229, 293 ; ii. 45, 55.

WHADDON. Harleian Society, vi. 304.

WHAITES. Burke's Family Records, 25.

WHALLEY, or WHALEY. Noble's Memoirs of the House of Crom-well, ii. 168-189. Berry's Hampshire Genealogies, 171. Camden Society, xliii. 35. Burke's Commoners, iv. 606. Miscellanea Genealogica et Heraldica, ii. 321. Foster's Visitations of York-shire, 218. Harleian Society, ii. 148 ; iv. 116 ; xl. 1230. J. H. Hill's History of Market Harborough, 175. Nichols' History of the County of Leicester, ii. 736. Whitaker's History of Whalley, ii. 18. Thoroton's Nottinghamshire, i. 168, 248. Abram's History of Blackburn, 405. Master's Notices of the Family of Master, 98. Annals of Smith of Balby, by H. E. Smith, 265.

WHARNCLIFFE (Earls of). Angus or Forfarshire, by A. J. Warden, 442.

WHARTON. Herald and Genealogist, ii. 519. Morant's Essex, i. 481 Surtees Society, xli. 99. Berry's Buckinghamshire Genealogies, 71. Visitation of Durham, 1615, (Sunderland, 1820, fol.) 94. Visitation of Oxfordshire, 1634, printed by Sir T. Phillipps, (Middle Hill, fol.) 32. Burke's Landed Gentry, (of Dryburn,) 2, 3, 4, 5, 6, 7, 8 ; (of Skelton Castle,) 4, 5, 6, 7, 8. Foster's Visi-tation of Yorkshire, 379, 589. Harleian Society, v. 260 ; viii. 205 ; xvi. 347. Lipscombe's History of the County of Bucking-ham, i. 543. History of Richmond, by C. Clarkson, 120. Graves' History of Cleveland, 331, 358. Whitaker's History of Richmond-shire, i. 78. Thoresby's Ducatus Leodiensis, 252. Ord's History of Cleveland, 255. Hunter's Deanery of Doncaster, i. 93. Surtees' Durham, i. 194 ; iii. 300. Pedigrees of the Leading Families of Lancashire, published by Joseph Foster, (London, 1872, fol.). The New History of Yorkshire, commencing with Richmondshire, by Genl. Plantagenet-Harrison, (London, 1872, fol.), Part i. 12. Banks' Baronies in Fee, i. 456. Banks' Dormant and Extinct

Baronage, ii. 585 ; iii. 739. Burke's Extinct Baronetcies. Foster's Visitations of Durham, 323, 325. Pedigrees of the Leading Families of Yorkshire, by Joseph Foster. Foster's Visitations of Cumberland and Westmorland, 141-143. Burke's Colonial Gentry, i. 147. Old Yorkshire, ed. by Willm. Smith, ii. 156. Nicolson and Burn's Westmorland and Cumberland, i. 377, 558. *See* WARTON.

WHARTON-MYDDLETON. Burke's Commoners, i. 171, Landed Gentry, 2. Ord's History of Cleveland, 288. Plantagenet-Harrison's History of Yorkshire, i. 94, 256.

WHATMAN. Burke's Landed Gentry, 2, 3, 4, 5, 6, 7, 8. *See* BOSANQUET.

WHATMORE. Miscellanea Genealogica et Heraldica, 2nd Series, iv. 193.

WHATTON. Gentleman's Magazine, 1825, i. 502 ; ii. 585. Burke's Commoners, iv. 224, Landed Gentry, 2. Harleian Society, viii. 164. Nichols' History of the County of Leicester, iii. 912. Thoroton's Nottinghamshire, i. 268.

WHEATE. Visitation of Oxfordshire, 1634, printed by Sir T. Phillipps, (Middle Hill, fol.) 32. Harleian Society, v. 249 ; xii. 193 ; xxxviii. 429, 431. Visitation of Warwickshire, 1619, published with Warwickshire Antiquarian Magazine, 118. Wotton's English Baronetage, iv. 56. Betham's Baronetage, iii. 112. Burke's Extinct Baronetcies.

WHEATHE. Surtees Society, xxxvi. 123.

WHEATHILL. Nichols' History of the County of Leicester, iv. 932. *See* WHETHILL.

WHEATLEY. Morant's Essex, ii. 108. Visitation of Norfolk, published by Norfolk Archæological Society, i. 354. Berry's Sussex Genealogies, 224. Foster's Visitations of Yorkshire, 590. Hunter's Deanery of Doncaster, ii. 386. Harleian Society, xvii. 343 ; xxxviii. 596. Burke's Landed Gentry, 8.

WHEATLEY-BALME. Foster's Yorkshire Pedigrees.

WHEBLE. Burke's Landed Gentry, 4, 5, 6, 7, 8.

WHEELER, or WHELER. Description of Otterden Place, Co. Kent, by the Rev. T. Rackett, 7. Gentleman's Magazine, 1832, i. 397 ; 1834, i. 276. Burke's Landed Gentry, (of Kyrewood House,) 2, 3, 4, 5, 6, 7, 8 ; (of Otterden Place,) 2, 3, 4, 5, 6, 7, 8 ; (of Bromwich House,) 8. Harleian Society, viii. 366 ; xvii. 341, 342 ; xxix. 496. Wotton's English Baronetage, iii. 143. Hasted's Kent, ii. 502. Burke's Royal Families, (London, 1851, 8vo.) i. 65. Herald and Genealogist, viii. 424. History of the Parish of St. Leonard, Shoreditch, by Henry Ellis, 346. Surtees' Durham, i. 176. Betham's Baronetage, ii. 159. Visitation of Gloucester, edited by T. F. Fenwick and W. C. Metcalfe, 198. Bysshe's Visitation of Essex, edited by J. J. Howard, 100. Harleian Society, xxvii. 144. Howard's Visitation of England and Wales, viii. 81 ; ix. 12.

WHEELOCK. Earwaker's History of Sandbach, 97.

WHEILDON. Burke's Landed Gentry, 8.

WHELLESBURGH. Nichols' History of the County of Leicester, iv. 963*. Burton's Description of Leicestershire, 283.

WHELOCK. Ormerod's Cheshire, iii. 121. Harleian Society, xviii. 156.

WHELTON. *See* WELTON.

WHETCOMBE. Bysshe's Visitation of Essex, edited by J. J. Howard, 100.

WHETENHALL. Foster's Visitations of Yorkshire, 257.

WHETHAM. Burke's Landed Gentry, 2 supp. Hunter's History of the Parish of Sheffield, 421. *See* BODDAM-WHETHAM.

WHETHILL. Harleian Society, ii. 44. Gyll's History of Wraysbury, 205. *See* WHEATHILL.

WHETLEY. Harleian Society, xxxii. 307.

WHETNALL. Visitation of Norfolk, published by Norfolk Archæological Society, i. 17. Harleian Society, xxxii. 308.

WHETSTONE. Morant's Essex, i. 38. Harleian Society, xiii. 520 ; xiv. 617.

WHICHCOTE, or WICHCOTE. Clutterbuck's Hertford, ii. 449. Harleian Society, xvii. 344. The Genealogist, v. 56. Wotton's English Baronetage, iii. 10. Betham's Baronetage, i. 40.

WHICKER. Harleian Society, vi. 356.

WHIDDON. Harleian Society, vi. 354 ; xxxix. 1052. Visitation of Devon, edited by F. T. Colby, 205. The Visitations of Devon, by J. L. Vivian, 781. *See* WHYDDON.

WHIELDON. Burke's Commoners, iii. 116, Landed Gentry, 2, 3, 4, 5 and supp., 6, 7.

WHINYATES. The Genealogist, New Series, viii. 52.

WHIPPLE, or WHYPPLE. New England Register, xi. 238 ; xxxii. 403. Harleian Society, xxxii. 309.

WHIPPY. Burke's Landed Gentry, 2, 3, 4.

WHISTLER. Account of the Family of Druce of Goreing, 3. Sussex Archæological Collections, xxxv. 60. Burke's Landed Gentry, 8.

WHITACRE, or WHITTACRE. Burke's Landed Gentry, 2, 3, 4. Chetham Society, lxxxi. 132. Dugdale's Warwickshire, 1039. The Genealogist, New Series, xiii. 40.

WHITAKER. Burke's Landed Gentry, (of Broadclough,) 2, 3, 4, 5, 6, 7, 8 ; (of Symonstone,) 2, 3, 4, 5 ; (of the Holme,) 2, 3, 4, 5, 6, 7, 8 ; (of Hesley Hall,) 5, 6, 7, 8 ; (of Balkholme,) 5, 6, 7, 8. Jewitt's Reliquary, xii. 81. Foster's Lancashire Pedigrees. Hutchins' Dorset, iii. 628. Hoare's Wiltshire, III. i. 43 Whitaker's History of Whalley, ii. 26, 43, 176, 204. The Genealogist, vi. 14. Surrey Archæological Collections, viii. 218. Harleian Society, xix. 150 ; xx. 97 ; xxii. 103 ; xxxvii. 16, 301 ; xxxviii. 493. Historical Notices of Doncaster, by C. W. Hatfield, 3rd Series, 338. Burke's Family Records, 628.

WHITAPH, or WHITAPHE. Harleian Society, ii. 98. Nichols' History of the County of Leicester, iv. 407.

WHITBREAD, or WHITBRED. Burke's Landed Gentry, (of Southill,) 2 supp., 3, 4, 5, 6, 7, 8 ; (of Loudham,) 2, 3, 4, 5, 6, 7, 8. Harleian Society, xiii. 17, 126, 320, 520.

WHITBROOKE. Camden Society, xliii. 72. Harleian Society, xxix. 497.

WHITBURN. Burke's Landed Gentry, 8.

WHITBY. Glover's History of Derbyshire, ii. 598, (586). Burke's Landed Gentry, 2, 3, 4, 5, 6, 7, 8. Howard's Visitation of England and Wales, vi. 57.

WHITCHESTER. The Genealogist, i. 298.

WHITCHURCH. Berry's Hampshire Genealogies, 25. Burke's Landed Gentry, 2.

WHITCOMBE. Harleian Society, xiii. 320, 521; xiv. 618; xvii. 345.

WHITE. Memoirs of the House of White of Wallingwells. Edinburgh, 1886, 8vo. History of the Family of White, by J. D. White. Cashel, 1887, 4to. Burke's Landed Gentry, 4th edition, 1212. Blomefield's Norfolk, v. 504. Morant's Essex, i. 195; ii. 198. Chronicle of the Family of De Havilland. Dwnn's Visitations of Wales, i. 129, 161. Berry's Sussex Genealogies, 181, 291. Berry's Kent Genealogies, 467. Berry's Hampshire Genealogies, 194, 241, 260, 295. Ashmole's Antiquities of Berkshire, iii. 323-325. Berry's Essex Genealogies, 144. Visitation of Durham, 1575, (Newcastle, 1820, fol.) 36. Visitation of Durham, 1615, (Sunderland, 1820, fol.) 33. Burke's Commoners, iii. 372, Landed Gentry, (of Clements Hall,) 2, 3, 4; (of Kellerstain,) 2, 3, 4, 5, 6, 7, 8; (of Kilbyrne,) 7, 8; (of Arddarroch,) 7, 8; (of Guestingthorpe,) 7, 8; (of Charleville,) 7, 8; 8 at p. 1634; (of Congelow,) 8; (of Gennings,) 8; (of Scardragh,) 2, 3, 4, 5; (of Woodlands,) 2, 3, 4; (of Charlton Marshall,) 2, 3; (of Belmont,) 3; (of Exeter,) 2; (of Yeovil,) 2; (of Castor,) 5 supp., 6, 7, 8; (of Old Elvet,) 5, 6, 7, 8; (of Wateringbury,) 6, 7; 6 at p. 1293, 1586. Miscellanea Genealogica et Heraldica, New Series, i. 60; 2nd Series, i. 37. Harleian Society, i. 2; iv. 96; viii. 93; ix. 262; xiii. 18, 321, 521; xvii. 346; xliii. 212. Jewitt's Reliquary, xiii. 252, 254. Burke's Heraldic Illustrations, 26. Nichols' History of the County of Leicester, iii. 1135; iv. 333. Visitation of London in Transactions of London and Middlesex Archæological Society, 10. Pembrokeshire Pedigrees, 131. Visitatio Comitatus Wiltoniæ, 1623, printed by Sir T. Phillipps. Hutchins' Dorset, iv. 154, 341. Surtees' Durham, ii. 132. Manning and Bray's Surrey, iii. 94, 177. J. E. Jackson's History of Grittleton, (Wiltshire Topl. Soc.), 8. Thoroton's Nottinghamshire, i. 169. T. Nicholas' County Families of Wales, 911. Fosbrooke's History of Gloucestershire, i. 314. Betham's Baronetage, v. 498. Visitation of Wiltshire, edited by G. W. Marshall, 7. The Genealogist, vi. 107; New Series, iii. 177; viii. 178. Visitation of Gloucester, edited by T. F. Fenwick and W. C. Metcalfe, 199. The Visitations of Cornwall, by J. L. Vivian, 552. Foster's Visitations of Durham, 327. Chetham Society, New Series, xxv. 190. Burke's Colonial Gentry, ii. 802. Burke's Family Records, 628. Howard's Visitation of Ireland, ii. 62. The Visitations of Devon, by J. L. Vivian, 784. The Perverse Widow, by A. W. Crawley-Boevey, 270. Sussex Archæological

Collections, xxxiv. 127-166. The New England Register, lii. 421. *See* WHYTE, WIGHT.

WHITE-THOMSON. Burke's Landed Gentry, 8.

WHITEBREAD. Bysshe's Visitation of Essex, edited by J. J. Howard, 101.

WHITEFOORD, or WHITEFORD. Paterson's History of the Co. of Ayr, ii. 471. Paterson's History of Ayr and Wigton, ii. 465. Burke's Landed Gentry, 3, 4, 5, 6. Burke's Extinct Baronetcies, 638. The Genealogist, iv. 141 ; v. 19. Miscellanea Genealogica et Heraldica, 2nd Series, ii. 263. The Genealogical Magazine, ii. 167, 174 ; iii. 221.

WHITEHALGH. Visitations of Staffordshire, 1614 and 1663-4, William Salt Society, 304.

WHITEHALL. Seize Quartiers of the Family of Bryan Cooke, (London, 1857, 4to.) 91. Visitation of Staffordshire, 1663-4, printed by Sir T. Phillipps, 10. Visitations of Staffordshire, 1614 and 1663-4, William Salt Society, 305.

WHITEHEAD, or WHITEHED. Foster's Lancashire Pedigrees. Chetham Society, cv. 254. Berry's Hampshire Genealogies, 287. Fishwick's History of Rochdale, 320. Harleian Society, xxxvii. 68. Burke's Landed Gentry, 8. *See* WHYTEHEAD.

WHITELAW. Burke's Landed Gentry, 6, 7, 8.

WHITELOCKE. Croke's History of the Family of Croke, No. 34. Camden Society, lxx. 2. Burke's Visitation of Seats and Arms, 2nd Series, ii. 72. History of Henley on Thames, by J. S. Burn, 248. Burke's Landed Gentry, 6 supp., 7 at p. 1122 ; 8 at p. 1223. *See* WHITLOCK.

WHITFELD, WHITFEILD, or WHITFIELD. Berry's Sussex Genealogies, 15, 223. Berry's Kent Genealogies, 55. Visitation of Sussex, 1570, printed by Sir T. Phillipps, (Middle Hill, fol.) 11. Harleian Society, vi. 123 ; xvii. 348 ; xlii. 90 ; xliii. 218. Hutchins' Dorset, ii. 412. Clutterbuck's Hertford, i. 189. Sussex Archæological Collections, xviii. 83. Hasted's Kent, iii. 98, 241 ; iv. 427. Hodgson's Northumberland, III. ii. 100, 104. The Visitations of Devon, by J. L. Vivian, 390. Devonshire Notes and Notelets, by Sir W. R. Drake, 122. Archæologia Cantiana, xvi. 81. Burke's Landed Gentry, 7, 8. New England Register, li. 418.

WHITGIFT. Surrey Archæological Collections, ii. 202. Harleian Society, xiii. 522. New England Register, xxiii. 262.

WHITGRAVE, WHITGREAVE, or WHITGREAVES. Visitation of Staffordshire, 1663-4, printed by Sir T. Phillipps, 10. The Boscobel Tracts, edited by J. Hughes, 2nd edn., 378. Burke's Commoners, iv. 558, Landed Gentry, 2, 3, 4, 5, 6, 7, 8. Foley's Records of the English Province S. J., v. 437. Visitation of Staffordshire, (Willm. Salt Soc.) 147. Bysshe's Visitation of Essex, edited by J. J. Howard, 101. Visitations of Staffordshire, 1614 and 1663-4, William Salt Society, 307, 310. Journal of the British Archæological Association, xxix. 24.

WHITHALGH. Abram's History of Blackburn, 594.

WHITHALL. The Genealogist, New Series, viii. 178.

WHITHORNE. Visitation of Gloucester, edited by T. F. Fenwick and W. C. Metcalfe, 200.

WHITHULL. Nichols' History of the County of Leicester, iv. 932.

WHITING. Harleian Society, ii. 92 ; xiii. 522. Nichols' History of the County of Leicester, iv. 571. Suffolk Armorial Families, by J. J. Muskett, 39. New England Register, 1. 132.

WHITLA. Burke's Landed Gentry, 3, 4, 5, 6, 7, 8. Howard's Visitation of Ireland, i. 62.

WHITLEY. Dwnn's Visitations of Wales, ii. 323. Burke's Commoners, iii. 115. History of Powys Fadog, by J. Y. W. Lloyd, v. 272. Harleian Society, xxxvii. 90.

WHITLOCK. Burke's Visitation of Seats and Arms, 2nd Series, ii. 72. Harleian Society, vi. 305 ; viii. 420 ; xvii. 347 ; xxxix. 1124. Westcote's Devonshire, edited by G. Oliver and P. Jones, 583. The Visitations of Devon, by J. L. Vivian, 785. *See* WHITELOCKE.

WHITMORE. Rudder's Gloucestershire, 665. Herald and Genealogist, iv. 21, 398 ; vii. 365, 523 ; viii. 176. Morant's Essex, i. 492. Burke's Commoners, ii. 409, 412. Landed Gentry, 2, 3, 4, 5, 6, 7, 8. History of the Parish of St. Leonard, Shoreditch, by Henry Ellis, 129. Harleian Society, viii. 20 ; xviii. 246 ; xxix. 499. Ormerod's Cheshire, ii. 507. History and Antiquities of Harwich and Dovercourt, by Silas Taylor, 205, 449. Notes and Queries, 3 S. v. 159, 220 ; 6 S. iv. 279. Burke's Extinct Baronetcies. Visitation of Gloucester, edited by T. F. Fenwick and W. C. Metcalfe, 201. The Genealogist, New Series, vi. 16, 74. East Barnet, by F. C. Cass, Part i. 38. New England Register, xxi. 169. Transactions of Shropshire Archæological Society, ix. 6, 78.

WHITMORE-JONES. Burke's Landed Gentry, 6, 7, 8.

WHITNEY. The Ancestry of John Whitney, by H. Melville. New York, 1895, 8vo. Burke's Landed Gentry, 3, 4, 5. Weaver's Visitation of Herefordshire, 75. New England Register, xi. 113, 225 ; xii. 215. Harleian Society, xxi. 267. The Genealogist, New Series, xiii. 133.

WHITTAKER. Berry's Kent Genealogies, 53. Burke's Landed Gentry, 2, 3, 4, 7, 8.

WHITTELL, or WHITLE. Burke's Landed Gentry, 2 supp., 3, 4, 5, 6. History of the Wilmer Family, 149.

WHITTER. Burke's Landed Gentry, (of Ashurst,) 4 ; (of Devon,) 2, 3.

WHITTEWRONG. Lipscombe's History of the County of Buckingham, iv. 347. *See* WITTEWRONGE.

WHITTIER. Genealogy of the Whittier Family, 1882. Large sheet.

WHITTING. Burke's Landed Gentry, 4. Burke's Authorized Arms, 129.

WHITTINGHAM, or WHITYNGHAM. Clutterbuck's Hertford, i. 284. Pedigrees from Visitation of Northumberland, printed by Sir T. Phillipps, (Middle Hill, 1858, fol.) 2. Burke's Landed Gentry, 2. Fishwick's History of Goosnargh, 185. Chetham Society,

lxxxi. 50 ; lxxxii. 63 ; lxxxviii. 333 ; cv. 254.   Hutchinson's
History of Durham, ii. 378.   Surtees' Durham, ii. 330.   Baker's
Northampton, i. 493.   The Genealogist, i. 309.   Miscellanea
Genealogica et Heraldica, New Series, iv. 357.   Harleian Society,
xvii. 342 ; xviii. 248 ; xxi. 267.   Foster's Visitations of Northumberland, 123.   New England Register, v. 149; xxvii. 136 ;
xxxiv. 34.   Howard's Visitation of England and Wales, viii.
145.

WHITTINGSTALL. Burke's Landed Gentry, 2.

WHITTINGTON. The Model Merchant, by Rev. Saml. Lysons, 1860,
8vo. *at end.*   Harleian Society, xi. 117 ; xxi. 178, 267.   Shaw's
Staffordshire, ii. 267.   Erdeswicke's Survey of Staffordshire, 381.
Fosbrooke's History of Gloucestershire, i. 364 ; ii. 60.   Bigland's
Gloucestershire, ii. par. Saperton.   Duncumb's Hereford, (J. H.
Cooke,) iii. 148.   Rudder's Gloucestershire, 598.   Visitation of
Somersetshire, printed by Sir T. Phillipps, 145.   Visitation of
Gloucestershire, 1569, (Middle Hill, 1854, fol.) 11.   Annals of
Swainswick, by R. E. N. Peach, *folding at end.*

WHITTON. Berry's Kent Genealogies, 386.   Sir T. Phillipps' Topographer, No. 1, (March, 1821, 8vo.) 31.   Visitation of Oxfordshire, 1574, printed by Sir T. Phillipps, (Middle Hill, fol.) 10.
Harleian Society, v. 182.

WHITTUCK. Burke's Landed Gentry, 2, 3, 4, 5, 6, 7, 8.

WHITWANGE. Pedigrees from Visitation of Northumberland, printed
by Sir T. Phillipps, (Middle Hill, 1858, fol.) 1.   The Genealogist,
ii. 14.   Foster's Visitations of Northumberland, 124.

WHITWELL. Pedigree of Wilson of High Wray, etc., by Joseph
Foster, 121.   Pedigree of Wilson, by S. B. Foster, 132.   Burke's
Family Records, 629.

WHITWICK. Visitation of Staffordshire, 1663-4, printed by Sir T.
Phillipps, 11.

WHITWORTH. Healey's History of Part of West Somerset, 222.

WHORWOOD. Visitation of Oxfordshire, 1634, printed by Sir T.
Phillipps, (Middle Hill. fol.) 32.   Harleian Society, v. 242.
Shaw's Staffordshire, ii. 129, 276, 278.   Visitation of Staffordshire, (Willm. Salt Soc.) 148, 151.   Visitations of Staffordshire,
1614 and 1663-4, William Salt Society, 311.

WHYDDON. Westcote's Devonshire, edited by G. Oliver and
P. Jones, 581.   *See* WHIDDON.

WHYGHTE, or WHYTE. Tuckett's Devonshire Pedigrees, 32.   Harleian Society, vi. 309 ; xiv. 618 ; xxxvii. 214.   Burke's Landed
Gentry, (of Loughbrickland,) 2 and add., 3, 4, 5, 6, 7, 8 ; (of
Newtown Manor,) 3, 4, 5, 6, 7, 8 ; (of Redhills,) 2, 3, 4, 5, 6,
7, 8.   Burke's Royal Descents and Pedigrees of Founders' Kin,
52.   Thoresby's Ducatus Leodiensis, 257.   Hoare's Wiltshire,
III. iv. 59.   O'Hart's Irish Pedigrees, 2nd Series, 355.   History
of Powis Fadog, by J. Y. W. Lloyd, vi. 195.   *See* WHITE.

WHYTE-MELVILLE. Burke's Commoners, ii. 659, Landed Gentry,
2, 3, 4, 5, 6.

WHYTEHEAD, or WHYTEHED. Burke's Landed Gentry, 2 supp., 3, 4,

5, 6, 8. Poulson's Holderness, i. 168. Surtees' Durham, ii. 8. *See* WHITEHED.

WHYTELL. Plantagenet-Harrison's History of Yorkshire, i. 352.

WHYTT. Dwnn's Visitations of Wales, i. 129, 161. Douglas's Baronage of Scotland, 529.

WIAT. Gentleman's Magazine, 1831, i. 585. Harleian Society, vi. 317. History of Boxley, by J. Cave Browne, 133. *See* WYAT.

WIBBERY. Miscellanea Genealogica et Heraldica, New Series, ii. 75. Colby of Great Torrington, by F. T. Colby, 33. *See* WYBBERY.

WICH. Harleian Society, viii. 50. *See* WYCHE.

WICHALSE. Berry's Kent Genealogies, 362. Harleian Society, vi. 355. Westcote's Devonshire, edited by G. Oliver and P. Jones, 627. The Visitations of Devon, by J. L. Vivian, 786. *See* WYCHEHALSE.

WICHARD. Nichols' History of the County of Leicester, iv. 523*. Burton's Description of Leicestershire, 201. The Genealogist, New Series, xii. 176.

WICHERLEY. Antiquities and Memoirs of the Parish of Myddle, written by Richard Gough 1700, (folio,) 37. Harleian Society, xxix. 500.

WICHINGHAM. Morant's Essex, i. 387. Blomefield's Norfolk, viii. 299. Harleian Society, xxxii. 170.

WICKENS. Annals of a Country Churchyard, by E. M. Thoyts, 8.

WICKHAM. Howard's Visitation of England and Wales, i. 249; Notes, iii. 78. Collectanea Topographica et Genealogica, ii. 225, 368; iii. 178, 345. Topographer and Genealogist, iii. 49. Herald and Genealogist, v. 225. Croke's History of the Family of Croke, No. 42. Berry's Berkshire Genealogies, 40. Surtees Society, xxxvi. 150. Visitation of Oxfordshire, 1634, printed by Sir T. Phillipps, (Middle Hill, fol.) 32. Burke's Commoners, (of Horsington,) iv. 596, Landed Gentry, 2, 3, 4, 5, 6, 7, 8; (of Bradford,) 3, 4, 5, 6, 7; (of Cnestnut Grove,) 8; (of Binsted-Wyck,) 8; (of Fronwnion,) 8. History of Leeds Castle, by C. Wykeham-Martin, 209. Harleian Society, v. 322; vi. 357. Hampshire Visitations, printed by Sir T. Phillipps, 27. Phelps' History of Somersetshire, i. 320. History of Bradford, by John James, 442. Life of Richard Deane, by J. B. Deane, 56. Notes and Queries, 3 S. viii. 465. Miscellanea Genealogica et Heraldica, New Series, iv. 67. The Genealogist, New Series, ix. 14. Oxford Historical Society, xix. 214, 244. Bradford Antiquary, New Series, i. 304. *See* WYKEHAM.

WICKLEY. Metcalfe's Visitations of Northamptonshire, 154.

WICKLOW. Case of C. F. A., Earl of Wicklow, on his claiming to vote as Earl of Wicklow, 1869, 4to., pp. 34. Claim of the Earl of Wicklow to vote at Elections of Irish Peers, Sess. Papers, 102, 274, E of 1868-9; A, E of 1870.

WICKS, or WICKES. Visitation of Middlesex, (Salisbury, 1820, fol.) 24. Foster's Visitation of Middlesex, 47.

WICKSTED. Burke's Commoners, i. 497, Landed Gentry, 2, 3, 4, 5,

6, 7, 8. Ormerod's Cheshire, iii. 442. James Hall's History of Nantwich, 496.

WIDDRINGTON, or WIDDRINTON. Herald and Genealogist, iii. 514. Gentleman's Magazine, 1853, i. 173, 280. Burke's Landed Gentry, 2, 3, 4, 5, 6, 7, 8. Hodgson's Northumberland, I. ii. 200; II. ii. 104, 230, 251, 297. Archæologia Æliana, 2nd Series, iii. 189. Surtees Durham, ii. 8. The Genealogist, i. 312. Banks' Dormant and Extinct Baronage, iii. 741. Burke's Extinct Baronetcies. Harleian Society, xvii. 349. Foster's Visitations of Northumberland, 125, 126. *See* WODERYNGTON.

WIDEVILLE. Baker's Northampton, ii. 166. *See* WYDVILLE.

WIDMERPOLE, or WIDMERPOOLE. Harleian Society, iv. 108. Thoroton's Nottinghamshire, i. 76. The Genealogist, New Series, xvii. 24.

WIDNELL. Harleian Society, xliii. 151.

WIDWORTHY. Notes and Gleanings, by W. Cotton and J. Dallas, iv. 140.

WIEDEMANN. Notes and Queries, 8 S. xi. 261.

WIGFALL. Visitation of Derbyshire, 1663-4, (Middle Hill, 1854, fol.) 7. Memoirs of the Family of Chester, by R. E. C. Waters, 360. The Genealogist, iii. 184. Harleian Society, xxxviii. 464.

WIGGES. Harleian Society, xvii. 349.

WIGGETT. Blomefield's Norfolk, viii. 215. Berry's Hampshire Genealogies, 119. Burke's Commoners, i. 446.

WIGGETT-CHUTE. Burke's Commoners, i. 632, Landed Gentry, 2, 3, 4, 5, 6, 7, 8.

WIGGLESWORTH. New England Register, xv. 334.

WIGHT. Burke's Commoners, (of Brabœuf Manor,) iii. 204, Landed Gentry, 3, 4, 5, 6, 7; (of Ormiston,) 6. Manning and Bray's Surrey, i. 88; ii. 211. Baker's Northampton, ii. 23. The Suffolk Records, by H. W. Aldred, 89. Harleian Society, xliii. 81. *See* WHITE.

WIGHT-BOYCOTT. Burke's Landed Gentry, 7, 8.

WIGHTMAN, or WEIGHTMAN. Burke's Landed Gentry, 4. Harleian Society, iv. 131, 178; xvii. 350. Nichol's History of the County of Leicester, iv. 876. Master's Notices of the Family of Master, 85.

WIGHTWICK. Berry's Hertfordshire Genealogies, 86. Burke's Commoners, iv. 371, Landed Gentry, 2, 4. Shaw's Staffordshire, ii. 201; app. 4. The Genealogist, vi. 108. Visitations of Staffordshire, 1614 and 1663-4, William Salt Society, 312. J. P. Jones's History of Tettenhall, 46. Transactions of Shropshire Archæological Society, ix. 12.

WIGLEY. Jewitt's Reliquary, vii. 31, 247; xii. 16, 48. Burke's Commoners, ii. 674. Harleian Society, ii. 97. Visitation of Derbyshire, 1663-4, (Middle Hill, 1854, fol.) 7. J. H. Hill's History of Market Harborough, 241-244. Nichols' History of the County of Leicester, ii. 787, 789. The Genealogist, iii. 185; New Series, viii. 178. Harleian Society, xxxvii. 379; xxxix. 1035, 1059.

WIGMORE. Herald and Genealogist, v. 556. Foley's Records of the English Province S. J., iv. 420. Harleian Society, xxix. 501; xxxii. 310.

WIGNOLL. Visitatio Comitatus Wiltoniæ, 1623, printed by Sir T. Phillipps. Visitation of Wiltshire, edited by G. W. Marshall, 62.

WIGRAM. Cussan's History of Hertfordshire, Parts iii. and iv. 173.

WIGSTON. Nichols' History of the County of Leicester, i. 504. Harleian Society, xii. 37.

WIKES. Tuckett's Devonshire Pedigrees, 25. Visitation of Somersetshire, printed by Sir T. Phillipps, 146. Foster's Visitations of Yorkshire, 288. Visitation of Devon, edited by F. T. Colby, 206. *See* WYKE.

WILBERFORCE, or WILBERFOSSE. Burke's Commoners, iv. 720, Landed Gentry, 2 and supp., 3, 4, 5, 6, 7, 8. Foster's Yorkshire Pedigrees. Surtees Society, xxxvi. 120. Foster's Visitations of Yorkshire, 158. Castles, Mansions, and Manors of Western Sussex, by D. G. C. Elwes and C. J. Robinson, 272. Master's Notices of the Family of Master, 100.

WILBERHAM. The Genealogist, New Series, xiii. 182.

WILBORE. Cambridgeshire Visitation, edited by Sir T. Phillipps, 34. Historical Notices of Doncaster, by C. W. Hatfield, 3rd Series, 375.

WILBRAHAM. Gentleman's Magazine, 1820, i. 316. Burke's Commoners, i. 315, 635, Landed Gentry, 2, 3, 4, 5, 6, 7, 8. Foster's Lancashire Pedigrees. Gregson's Fragments relative to the County of Lancashire, 246. Visitation of Staffordshire, 1663-4, printed by Sir T. Phillipps, 11. Transactions of the London and Middlesex Archæological Society, iv. 274. Baker's Northampton, i. 606. Ormerod's Cheshire, ii. 137 ; iii. 54, 346, 379. Burke's Extinct Baronetcies. Harleian Society, xvii. 351; xviii. 249, 250. Visitations of Staffordshire, 1614 and 1663-4, William Salt Society, 314. Willmore's History of Walsall, 96, 107. Croston's edn. of Baines' Lancaster, V. 262. William Salt Society, New Series, ii. 140.

WILCOCK. Dwnn's Visitations of Wales, ii. 242.

WILCOCKS. Berry's Buckinghamshire Genealogies, 48. Harleian Society, ii. 135 ; xiii. 523 ; xxvii. 146 ; xxix. 502. Nichols' History of the County of Leicester, ii. 655. J. H. Hill's History of Market Harborough, 132. New England Register, xxix. 25.

WILCOTES. Berks, Bucks, and Oxon Archæological Journal, iii. 97.

WILCOX. Middleton *v.* Welles, Appellant's Case in House of Lords, 1785. Morant's Essex, i. 454. Harleian Society, iii. 10. The Genealogist, vi. 108.

WILD, or WILDE. Hasted's Kent, ii. 753 ; iii. 11. Berry's Kent Genealogies, 108, 189. Historical Account of Lowestoft, by E. Gillingwater, 245. Burke's Extinct Baronetcies. Harleian Society, xxxviii. 665, xlii. 18. *See* BAGNALL-WILD, WYLDE.

WILDBORE. Forrest's History of Knottingley, add. Metcalfe's Visitations of Northamptonshire, 155.

WILDER. Berry's Berkshire Genealogies, 154. Burke's Royal Families, (London, 1851, 8vo.) ii. 36. Burke's Landed Gentry, 2, 3, 4, 5, 6, 7, 8. Burke's Heraldic Illustrations, 46. Burke's Royal Descents and Pedigrees of Founders' Kin, *Founders' Kin*, 16. New England Register, xxi. 120. Howard's Visitations of England and Wales, ii. 127.

WILDIGOS. Berry's Sussex Genealogies, 10.

WILDING. Visitation of Middlesex, (Salisbury, 1820, fol.) 32. W. Robinson's History of Hackney, i. 301. Foster's Visitation of Middlesex, 61.

WILDMAN, or WILEMAN. Burke's Landed Gentry, 2, 3. Nichols' History of the County of Leicester, iii. 379. *See* WYLDMAN.

WILDMAN-LUSHINGTON. Burke's Landed Gentry, 6, 7.

WILFORD. Morant's Essex, ii. 581. Harleian Society, viii. 138; xiii. 18, 127, 322, 523; xliii. 141. Surrey Archæological Collections, vii. The Genealogist, iv. 1. Monken Hadley, by F. C. Cass, 198. Notes and Queries, 5 S. v. 68. *See* WILSFORD.

WILKES. Cambridgeshire Visitation, edited by Sir T. Phillipps, 34. Foster's Visitations of Yorkshire, 288. Lipscombe's History of the County of Buckingham, ii. 44. Shaw's Staffordshire, ii. 149. Visitation of Staffordshire, 1663-4, printed by Sir T. Phillipps, 11. Burke's Landed Gentry, 6, 7, 8. Life of John Wilkes, by P. Fitzgerald, i. 1. Visitations of Staffordshire, 1614 and 1663-4, William Salt Society, 318. Harleian Society, xix. 150; xxix. 503; xli. 84.

WILKIE. Burke's Landed Gentry, 5, 6, 7, 8. Raine's History of North Durham, 233. History of Chislet, Kent, by F. Haslewood, 172. The Parish of Cramond, by J. P. Wood, 64. Some Old Families, by H. B. McCall, 239.

WILKIN. Dwnn's Visitations of Wales, i. 113.

WILKINS. Burke's Commoners, (of Maesllwch,) ii. 216; (of Maesderwen,) ii. 218; (of Clifton,) iii. 391. Jones' History of the County of Brecknock, ii. 139. Genealogies of Morgan and Glamorgan, by G. T. Clark. 471. *See* DE WINTON.

WILKINSON, or WYLKYNSON. Topographer and Genealogist, ii. 105. Croke's History of the Family of Croke, No. 29. Glover's History of Derbyshire, ii. 124, (110). Visitation of Norfolk, published by Norfolk Archæological Society, i. 88. Visitation of Durham, 1615, (Sunderland, 1820, fol.) 81. Surtees Society, xxxvi. 52, 255, 381. Burke's Commoners, ii. 249; (of Coxhoe,) Commoners, i. 69, Landed Gentry, 2, 3, 4, 5, 6, 7, 8; (of White Webbs,) 3, 4, 5, 6, 7; (of Winterburn,) 2, 3, 4, 5, 6, 7, 8; (of Harperley Park,) 2, 3, 4, 5, 6, 7, 8; (of Upper Hare Park,) 5, 6, 7, 8; (of Hilcote,) 2; (of Potterton Hall,) 7, 8. Foster's Visitations of Yorkshire, 366. Burke's Heraldic Illustrations, 89. Hunter's Deanery of Doncaster, i. 384. Surtees' Durham, i. 81; ii. 349; iii. 315; iv. 3. Wilson's History of the Parish of St. Laurence Pountney, 226. Harleian Society, i. 57; xvi. 353; xvii. 352; xxxii. 310; xxxvii. 164; xxxviii. 668; xxxix. 1034, 1077; xlii. 191. Foster's Lincolnshire Pedigrees, 7. Eastwood's History of

Ecclesfield, 386. The Genealogist, vi. 109 ; New Series, x. 241.
Foster's Visitations of Durham, 329. Metcalfe's Visitations of
Northamptonshire, 156. Burke's Colonial Gentry, i. 323.
WILKS. Berry's Surrey Genealogies, 27.
WILLAN. Foster's Visitations of Yorkshire, 637.
WILLANCE. Plantagenet-Harrison's History of Yorkshire, i. 207.
WILLARD. Burke's Landed Gentry, 2. New England Register, iv.
305.
WILLASTON. Harleian Society, xxix. 503.
WILLATS. Burke's Landed Gentry, 6 supp., 7.
WILLES. Berry's Berkshire Genealogies, 2-7. Burke's Landed
Gentry, 2, 3, 4, 5, 6, 7, 8. Baker's Northampton, i. 695. F. G.
Lee's History of Thame, 325. New England Register, xxii. 186.
WILLESBYE. The Genealogist, iii. 138, 405.
WILLESFORD. Tuckett's Devonshire Pedigrees, 178. Harleian Society,
vi. 304. The Visitations of Devon, by J. L. Vivian, 787.
WILLETS. Harleian Society, xxxvii. 175.
WILLETT. Bysshe's Visitation of Essex, edited by J. J. Howard, 101.
Gloucestershire Notes and Queries, ii. 558. History of the Wilmer
Family, 186.
WILLETT-ADYE. Hutchins' Dorset, iii. 306.
WILLEY. Surtees' Durham, ii. 74. Foster's Visitations of North-
umberland, 127. Harleian Society, xxix. 303.
WILLIAM. Dwnn's Visitations of Wales, i. 105 ; ii. 193.
WILLIAM AP DAVID. Dwnn's Visitations of Wales, i. 230, 279 ; ap
Rhys, ii. 196 ; ap Richard, ii. 149 ; ap Sion, ii. 140.
WILLIAMES. Collections by the Powys-land Club, ix. 347.
WILLIAMS. Observations on the Snowdon Mountains, etc., by John
Thomas, A.M. London, 1802, 8vo. Kent's British Banner Dis-
played, 405. Historical Tour in Monmouthshire, by Wm. Coxe,
119. The History of Monmouthshire, by Dr. Williams, App. 194.
Camden Society, xliii. 20. Berry's Sussex Genealogies, 120, 261.
Berry's Hampshire Genealogies, 73, 190. Dwnn's Visitations of
Wales, i. 100, 104, 122, 206, 235, 243, 330 ; ii. 81, 82, 85, 87, 169,
204, 212, 222, 287, 303. Berry's Berkshire Genealogies, 41, 152.
Glamorganshire Pedigrees, edited by Sir T. Phillipps, 12, 15, 17,
34, 35, 36, 39. Visitation of Oxfordshire, 1634, printed by Sir T.
Phillipps, (Middle Hill, fol.) 33. Visitation of Gloucestershire,
1569, (Middle Hill, 1854, fol.) 11. Burke's Commoners, (of Ivy-
tower,) i. 647, Landed Gentry, 2 ; (of Rushden and Warfield,)
Commoners, ii. 14, Landed Gentry, 2, 3, 4 ; (of Herringston,)
Commoners, i. 614, Landed Gentry, 2, 3, 4, 5, 6, 7, 8 ; (of Bride-
head,) Commoners, i. 618, Landed Gentry, 2, 3, 4, 5, 6, 7, 8 ; (of
Temple House,) Commoners, ii. 635, Landed Gentry, 2, 3, 4, 5, 6,
7, 8 ; (of Cowley Grove,) Landed Gentry, 2, 3 ; (of Llangibby
Castle,) 2, 3, 4, 5, 6, 7, 8 ; (of Williamston,) 4 ; (of Coldbrook
Park,) 2, 3, 4, 5, 6, 7, 8 ; (of Pendley,) 7 ; (of Gnaton,) 7, 8 ; (of
Wallog,) 7, 8 ; (of Dolmelynllyn,) 8 ; (of Woolland,) 7, 8 ; (of
Gwernant Park,) 2, 3, 4, 5, 8 ; (of Malvern Hall,) 3, 4, 5, 6, 7, 8 ;
(of Trecastle,) 8 ; (of Burncoose,) 4, 5, 6 ; (of Tregullow,) 4 ; (of

Deudreath Castle,) 4, 5, 6, 7, 8; (of Cwmcynfelin,) 4, 5, 6; (of
Abercamlais,) 4, 5; (of Maesruddud,) 5 supp.; (of Penpont,) 5, 6,
7, 8; (of Bryntirion,) 6, 7, 8; 8 at p. 2253.   Harleian Society,
v. 312; vi. 305; ix. 263; xii. 90; xiii. 524; xvii. 352-354; xx.
97; xxi. 179; xxii. 169; xxviii. 202; xxix. 504.   Dallaway's
Sussex, i. App. to Chichester.   Burke's Royal Descents and Pedigrees of Founders' Kin, 46.   Maclean's History of Trigg Minor,
ii. 432, 443.   Turnor's History of the Town and Soke of Grantham, 125.   Gyll's History of Wraysbury, 228.   Lipscombe's
History of the County of Buckingham, i. 233.   Burke's Visitation
of Seats and Arms, i. 44; 2nd Series, i. 60.   Westcote's Devonshire, edited by G. Oliver and P. Jones, 521.   Thoresby's Ducatus
Leodiensis, 253.   Jones' History of the County of Brecknock, ii.
383, 385, 698, 700, 701, 707, 717.   Caermarthenshire Pedigrees,
10, 33, 35, 37, 43, 45, 55, 70, 72.   Pembrokeshire Pedigrees, 136,
161.   Hutchins' Dorset, i. 617; ii. 524; iii. 520.   Clutterbuck's
Hertford, i. 224.   Meyrick's History of the Co. of Cardigan, 274.
Archæologia Cambrensis, 4 S., i. 309.   Nicholas' County Families
of Wales, 121, 122, 306, 361.   A Complete Parochial History of
the County of Cornwall, iv. 102, 119 supp.   The Sheriffs of
Montgomeryshire, by W. V. Lloyd, 3, 28, 125, 232, 254.
Wotton's English Baronetage, ii. 288, 404; iii. 306, 579; iv. 21,
127.   Banks' Baronies in Fee, i. 460.   Visitation of Devon,
edited by F. T. Colby, 207.   Betham's Baronetage, ii. 22, 276,
437; iii. 80; iv. 397.   Banks' Dormant and Extinct Baronage,
ii. 590.   Burke's Extinct Baronetcies.   F. G. Lee's History of
Thame, 415.   Howard's Visitation of England and Wales, i. 41;
Notes, ii. 41.   History of Powys Fadog, by J. Y. W. Lloyd, iv.
267; v. 117, 329, 330, 407; vi. 248, 427.   Burke's Colonial
Gentry, i. 179, 283; ii. 421.   The Visitations of Cornwall, by
J. L. Vivian, 555.   Visitation of Gloucester, edited by T. F.
Fenwick and W. C. Metcalfe, 202.   The Genealogist, New Series,
ii. 110; iii. 177; xiv. 141.   The Genealogies of Morgan and
Glamorgan, by G. T. Clark, 86, 104, 127, 194, 200.   New
England Register, x. 155; xii. 297; xx. 205; xxxiv. 69; xxxvi.
277; li. 211.   Gloucestershire Notes and Queries, v. 92.   Burke's
Family Records, 631.   The Visitations of Devon, by J. L. Vivian,
789.   Muskett's Suffolk Manorial Families, i. 333, 334.

WILLIAMS-FREEMAN. Burke's Landed Gentry, 6, 7.
WILLIAMS-VAUGHAN. Burke's Landed Gentry, 6, 7.
WILLIAMS-WYNN. Burke's Landed Gentry, 6, 7, 8.
WILLIAMSON. Visitation of Durham, 1615, (Sunderland, 1820, fol.)
29.   Burke's Royal Families, (London, 1851, 8vo.) ii. 62.   Burke's
Landed Gentry, (of Lawers,) 3, 4, 5, 6, 7, 8; (of Whickham,)
2, 6, 7, 8; (of Cardrona,) 7, 8.   Foster's Visitations of Yorkshire,
181.   Harleian Society, iv. 97; v. 238; vii. 14; xiii. 524.   The
Borough of Stoke-upon-Trent, by John Ward, 177.   Hutchinson's
History of Durham, iii. 339.   Surtees' Durham, ii. 9.   Thoroton's
Nottinghamshire, iii. 230.   Wotton's English Baronetage, ii. 297.
Betham's Baronetage, i. 471.   Metcalfe's Visitations of North-

amptonshire, 55. Foster's Visitations of Durham, 331. Caithness Family History, by John Henderson, 295. Foster's Visitations of Cumberland and Westmorland, 144.

WILLILEY. Weaver's Visitations of Somerset, 135.

WILLIMOTT. Harleian Society, xxii. 104.

WILLINGTON. Burke's Commoners, (of Tamworth,) iv. 526, Landed Gentry, 2, 3, 4, 5, 6 ; (of Killoskehane,) Landed Gentry, 2, 3, 4; (of Castle Willington,) 2, 3, 4, 5, 6, 7, 8. Visitation of Warwickshire, 1619, published with Warwickshire Antiquarian Magazine, 134. Dugdale's Warwickshire, 1063. Harleian Society, xii. 375. The Visitations of Cornwall, edited by J. L. Vivian, 17. Visitation of Devon, edited by F. T. Colby, 15. Banks' Dormant and Extinct Baronage, i. 442. *See* WYLYNGTON.

WILLIS. Burke's Landed Gentry, 4th edn., 1748. Berry's Hampshire Genealogies, 127. Burke's Commoners, ii. 374 ; (of Halsnead,) i. 43, Landed Gentry, 2, 3, 4, 5, 6, 7, 8 ; (of Wick House,) Landed Gentry, 4, 5. Visitation of Warwickshire, 1619, published with Warwickshire Antiquarian Magazine, 166. Lipscombe's History of the County of Buckingham, iv. 11. Burke's Authorized Arms, 188. Clutterbuck's Hertford, ii. 184. Harleian Society, xii. 311; xxii. 104 ; xli. 121. Historic Society of Lancashire and Cheshire, New Series, vi. 74. New England Register, xlvi. 329. Family Notes, by J. M. Browne, 80.

WILLIS-BUND. Burke's Landed Gentry, 5, 8.

WILLISCOT. Harleian Society, v. 278.

WILLISONE. Weaver's Visitation of Herefordshire, 76.

WILLMOT. Berry's Hampshire Genealogies, 121. Visitation of Oxfordshire, 1634, printed by Sir T. Phillipps, (Middle Hill, fol.) 33. Harleian Society, v. 301. *See* WILLYMOT, WILMOT.

WILLOUGHBY. Case of Henry Willoughby, Esq., claiming the Title of Willoughby of Parham, 1767, folio, pp. 3. Claim of Henry Willoughby to the Barony of Willoughby of Parham, Sess. Papers, Feb. 1733 ; Mar. 1767. Case of C. E. Dowager Lady Aveland, the elder of the two co-heirs to the Barony of Willoughby D'Eresby. London, 1871, fol. Evidence on Petition of Lady Aveland for determination of Abeyance of Barony of Willoughby de Eresby, Sess. Papers, G of 1871. Camden Society, cv. *at end.* Edmondson's Account of the Greville Family, 68. Hasted's Kent, i. 405. Herald and Genealogist, iii. 144. Memoir of P. Bertie, 11th Lord Willoughby D'Eresby, *at end.* Berry's Kent Genealogies, 9. Tuckett's Devonshire Pedigrees, 71. Archæologia Cantiana, iv. 256. Berry's Hampshire Genealogies, 238. Burke's Commoners, ii. 214, Landed Gentry, 2. Foster's Yorkshire Pedigrees. Harleian Society, iv. 102, 145, 184 ; vi. 306, 308 ; ix. 265 ; xvi. 363 ; xx. 99 ; xlii. 8. Graves' History of Cleveland, 274. Topographer, (London, 1789-91, 8vo.) i. 338. Polwhele's History of Cornwall, iv. 112. Dickinson's History of Southwell, 2nd edition, 162. Topographical Collections of John Aubrey, edited by J. E. Jackson, 401. Bridges' Northamptonshire, by Rev. Peter Whalley, i. 535. Westcote's Devonshire, edited by G. Oliver and

P. Jones, 619, 620. Dugdale's Warwickshire, 1054. Visitatio
Comitatus Wiltoniæ, 1623, printed by Sir T. Phillipps. Hutchins'
Dorset, iv. 103. Clutterbuck's Hertford, iii. 512. Thoroton's
Nottinghamshire, i. 12 ; ii. 209. The Genealogist, ii. 91 ; iv. 34 ;
New Series, iii. 178 ; xiii. 28 ; xv. 147 ; xvii. 23. Earwaker's
Local Gleanings, ii. 496, 509, 514, 518, 523, 528. An Historical
Survey of Cornwall, by C. S. Gilbert, i. 532. Edmondson's
Baronagium Genealogicum, iv. 369, 371* ; v. 409. Brydges'
Collins' Peerage, vi. 591, 691 ; vii. 215. Banks' Baronies in Fee,
i. 462. Betham's Baronetage, iv. 260. Banks' Dormant and
Extinct Baronage, ii. 591 ; iii. 743. Visitation of Wiltshire,
edited by G. W. Marshall, 58. Notes and Queries, 5 S. vi. 535.
Burke's Extinct Baronetcies. Deering's Nottingham, 227. Mis-
cellanea Genealogica et Heraldica, 2nd Series, ii. 190. Metcalfe's
Visitations of Northamptonshire, 157. The Visitations of Cornwall, by J. L. Vivian, 556. New England Register, xxx. 67 ;
xl. 50 ; xlvii. 200. Notts and Derbyshire Notes and Queries,
iv. 37. The Visitations of Devon, by J. L. Vivian, 790. *See*
WYLLOUGHBY.

WILLOUGHBY DE BROKE. Howard's Visitation of England and
Wales, viii. 38.

WILLS. Burke's Landed Gentry, 2, 3, 4, 5, 6, 7. The Visitations of
Cornwall, by J. L. Vivian, 557-563, 626. Harleian Society, ix. 265.

WILLS-SANDFORD. Burke's Landed Gentry, 8.

WILLSHER. Berry's Hertfordshire Genealogies, 244. *See* WYLSHERE.

WILLSON. Burke's Landed Gentry, 3, 4, 5, 6, 7, 8. Harleian
Society, xvii. 355. *See* WILSON.

WILLY. Surtees' Durham, iv. 5.

WILLYAMS. Burke's Commoners, iv. 35, Landed Gentry, 2, 3, 4, 5,
6, 7, 8. A Complete Parochial History of the County of Cornwall, iii. 299. An Historical Survey of Cornwall, by C. S. Gilbert, ii. 331. The Visitations of Cornwall, by J. L. Vivian, 627.

WILLYMOT, or WILLYMOTT. Visitation of Derbyshire, 1663-4, (Middle
Hill, 1854, fol.) 7. Clutterbuck's Hertford, iii. 533. The Genealogist, iii. 185. *See* WILMOT.

WILLYS. Burke's Extinct Baronetcies. New England Register,
xxxviii. 33. Bysshe's Visitation of Essex, edited by J. J. Howard,
102.

WILM. The Genealogist, New Series, xv. 101.

WILMER. History of the Wilmer Family, by C. W. Foster and
J. J. Green. Leeds, 1888, 4to. Burke's Commoners, ii. 148.
Harleian Society, xiii. 525 ; xxxix. 887. Metcalfe's Visitations of
Northamptonshire, 157. Cyclostyle Pedigrees, by J. J. Green.

WILMOT, or WILMOTT. Hasted's Kent, iii. 241, 576. Glover's
History of Derbyshire, ii. 239, (208). Burke's Royal Families,
(London, 1851, 8vo.) ii. 154. Miscellanea Genealogica et Heraldica, New Series, i. 421 ; 2nd Series, iii. 63. Herald and Genealogist, vi. 359. Nichols' History of the County of Leicester, i. 144
app. ; iv. 344, 937. Burke's Landed Gentry, 6 at p. 1465.
Berry's Kent Genealogies, 280. Surtees' Durham, ii. 388. Pil-

kington's View of Derbyshire, ii. 202, 205. Betham's Baronetage, iii. 269, 389. Banks' Dormant and Extinct Baronage, iii. 635. The Genealogist, vi. 109. Metcalfe's Visitation of Worcester, 1683, 104. The Midland Antiquary, ii. 139. Archæologia Cantiana, xvi. 83. Clarke's Hundred of Wanting, 187. The Gresley's of Drakelowe, by F. Madan, 296. *See* WILLMOT.

WILMSHURST. Pedigree of the Noble Family of Du Bourdieu. Ashby de la Zouch, 1864, 8vo.

WILSFORD. Hasted's Kent, iii. 48, 750. Berry's Kent Genealogies, 134, 496. Harleian Society, xxxix. 997 ; xlii. 53, 104. *See* WILFORD.

WILSHERE. Burke's Landed Gentry, 4, 5, 6, 7, 8. Clutterbuck's Hertford, ii. 544. *See* WILLSHER.

WILSON, or WYLSON. Case of Robert Wilson, Esqr., on his claim to be Eldest Co-heir of the Barony of Berners, 1832, folio, pp. 21. Claim of Robert Wilson, Esq., to the Barony of Berners, Sess. Papers, 73 of 1831-32. The Pedigree of Wilson of High Wray and Kendall, by Joseph Foster. London, 1871, 4to. 2nd edition by S. B. Foster. London, 1890, 4to. Pedigree of Wilson of York, Pocklington, etc. [Dorothy Wilson of York, the Benefactress.] Broadside, *n.d.* Jewitt's Reliquary, xi. 33. Topographer and Genealogist, ii. 118, 556. Morant's Essex, ii. 392, 601. Berry's Kent Genealogies, 421. Berry's Sussex Genealogies, 209. Nash's Worcestershire, ii. 317. Burke's Commoners, (of Eshton Hall,) iii. 183, Landed Gentry, 2, 3, 4, 5 ; (of Stowlangtoft,) Landed Gentry, 2, 3, 4, 5, 6, 7, 8 ; (of Brinkcliffe Tower,) 2, p. 1611, 3, 4, 5, 6 ; (of Cahirconlish,) 2, 4 ; (of Knowle Hall,) 2, 3, 4, 5 ; (of Waldershaigh,) 7, 8 ; (of Ercildoune,) 7 ; (of the Grove,) 8 ; (of Dallam Tower,) 2, 3, 4, 5, 6, 7, 8 ; (of Redgrave Hall,) 2, 3, 4, 5, 6, 7, 8 ; (of Evening Hill,) 2, 3 ; (of High Wray,) 2 ; (of Crofton,) 5 supp., 6, 7, 8 ; (of Cliffe Hall,) 5, 6, 7, 8 ; (of Rigmaden,) 6, 7, 8 ; (of Bolton le Moors,) 5, p. 817 ; 7, p. 1823 ; (of Seacroft,) 8 ; (of Broomhead,) 8 ; (of Currygrane,) 8 ; (of Tranby Croft,) 8 ; (of Nunthorpe Hall,) 8. Foster's Yorkshire Pedigrees. Foster's Visitations of Yorkshire, 590, 591. Foster's Lancashire Pedigrees. History of Hartlepool, by Sir C. Sharp, (1816, 8vo.) 80. Burke's Heraldic Illustrations, 7. Hodgson's Northumberland, III. ii. 418. Thoresby's Ducatus Leodiensis, 4. Hunter's History of the Parish of Sheffield, 473. Whitaker's Deanery of Craven, 172, (238). Nichols' History of the County of Leicester, iii. 514, 907. Hunter's Deanery of Doncaster, i. 367. Surtees' Durham, i. 276 ; ii. 133. Manning and Bray's Surrey, i. 263. Clutterbuck's Hertford, ii. 530. Sussex Archæological Collections, xi. 48 ; xii. 240. Miscellanea Genealogica et Heraldica, New Series, ii. 78 ; 3rd Series, iii. 45. Geo. Robertson's Description of Cunninghame, 101. Paterson's History of the Co. of Ayr, ii. 312. Yorkshire Archæological and Topographical Journal, v. 69. Harleian Society, xiii. 525 ; xvi. 354 ; xvii. 356 ; xxii. 105, 121 ; xxxvii. 1, 206 ; xxxviii. 493, 703 ; xxxix. 1014. S. Lewis's Parish of St. Mary, Islington, 184. Wotton's English Baronetage,

iii. 243. Betham's Baronetage, ii. 229. Burke's Extinct Baronetcies, 616. The Genealogist, vi. 290. Howard's Visitation of England and Wales, i. 177; vi. 22. Hasted's Kent, (Hund. of Blackheath, by H. H. Drake,) 123. Bysshe's Visitation of Essex, edited by J. J. Howard, 102. Foster's Visitations of Durham, 333. Foster's Visitations of Cumberland and Westmorland, 145-147. Burke's Colonial Gentry, i. 60, 311, 319, 322; ii. 661. Old Yorkshire, edited by William Smith, iv. 242. The Index Pedigree, case of Stead *v*. Stead, Liverpool, 1891, broadside. This includes CARSON. Burke's Family Records, 631. The Genealogical Magazine, i. 640. Staniforthiana, by F. M. H., *at end*. Nicolson and Burn's Westmorland and Cumberland, i. 227, 248. Platt and Morkill's Records of Whitkirk, 77. *See* CARUS-WILSON, RIMINGTON-WILSON, WILLSON.

WILSON-FITZGERALD. Burke's Landed Gentry, 6, 7.

WILSON-PATTEN. Burke's Commoners, iii. 79, Landed Gentry, 2, 3, 4, 5. Foster's Lancashire Pedigrees.

WILSON-TODD. Burke's Landed Gentry, 2, 3, 4, 5, 6, 8.

WILSTROP, or WYLSTROPE. Foster's Visitations of Yorkshire, 38. Harleian Society, xvi. 355.

WILTES. History of Hereditary Dignities, with reference to the Earldom of Wiltes, by W. F. Finlayson. London, 1869, 8vo. *See* SCROOPE.

WILTON. Visitation of Gloucestershire, 1569, (Middle Hill, 1854, fol.) 11. Harleian Society, xxi. 270.

WILTSHIRE. Pedigree of Wiltshire of Wotton Basset, Co. Wilts, [T. P.] 1861, folio page. Morant's Essex, ii. 601. Berry's Hampshire Genealogies, 177. Berry's Sussex Genealogies, 318. Visitation of Westmoreland, 1615, (London, 1853,) 32. Visitation of Middlesex, (Salisbury, 1820, fol.) 7. Foster s Visitations of Middlesex, 16.

WIMBISH. *See* WYMBISHE.

WIMBLE. Berry's Sussex Genealogies, 60.

WIMONDEFOLD. Thoroton's Nottinghamshire, iii. 86. *See* WYMONDESWOLD.

WINCH. History of the Hundred of Bray, by Charles Kerry, 126. Harleian Society, xiii. 323, 526; xix. 199. Burke's Extinct Baronetcies. The Genealogist, vi. 110.

WINCHELSEA. Baker's Northampton, i. 307.

WINCHESTER. Berry's Kent Genealogies, 80.

WINCHOMBE. Berry's Berkshire Genealogies, 149. Ashmole's Antiquities of Berkshire, iii. 300. Burke's Extinct Baronetcies. The Genealogist, vi. 111.

WINCKLEY. Chetham Society, lxxxviii. 334. Abram's History of Blackburn, 731. Notes and Queries, 3 S. i. 196, 237. *See* WINKLEY.

WINCOLD. Metcalfe's Visitations of Suffolk, 106.

WINCOLE. Morant's Essex, ii. 271.

WINCOLL. Harleian Society, ii. 156. Nichols' History of the County of Leicester, i. 548.

WINDEBANK. Burke's Extinct Baronetcies. Notes and Queries, 8 S. i. 23, 150.

WINDER. Burke's Landed Gentry, 6, 7, 8.

WINDESORE. *See* WYNDESOR.
WINDEYER. Burke's Colonial Gentry, i. 93.
WINDHAM. Pedigree of Windham of Orchard, Co. Somerset, etc., [T. P.] folio page. Burke's Landed Gentry, 2, 3, 4, 8. Harleian Society, viii. 123, 236 ; xvii. 357. Hunter's Deanery of Doncaster, i. 326. Nicholls' Account of the Company of Ironmongers, 2nd edition, 567. Carthew's Hundred of Launditch, Part iii. 288. Weaver's Visitations of Somerset, 90. Notes and Queries, 6 S., ix. 17. Devonshire Notes and Notelets, by Sir W. R. Drake, 184. The Visitations of Devon, by J. L. Vivian, 537. Howard's Visitation of England and Wales, vii. 40. *See* SMIJTH-WINDHAM, WYNDHAM.
WINDOWE. Visitation of Gloucester, edited by T. F. Fenwick and W. C. Metcalfe, 203.
WINDSOR. A Genealogical Account of the Family of Windsor, by A. Collins. London, 1754, 4to. Gyll's History of Wraysbury, 208. Dugdale's Warwickshire, 732. Manning and Bray's Surrey, iii. 37. Edmondson's Baronagium Genealogicum, ii. 165. Metcalfe's Visitation of Worcester, 1683, 105. Monken Hadley, by F. C. Cass, 128. Brydges' Collins' Peerage, iii. 637. Banks' Baronies in Fee, i. 465 ; ii. 158. Banks' Dormant and Extinct Baronage, i. 112 ; ii. 610 ; iii. 540. Harleian Society, xliii. 186. Nicolson and Burn's Westmorland and Cumberland, i. 199, 446. *See* DE WINDSOR, WYNDESOR.
WINDSOR-HICKMAN. Jacob's Peerage, i. 613.
WINDSORE. Berry's Hampshire Genealogies, 36.
WINFIELD. Harleian Society, xxxvii. 231.
WINFORD. Nash's Worcestershire, i. 42. Wotton's English Baronetage, iv. 92. Burke's Extinct Baronetcies. Metcalfe's Visitation of Worcester, 1683, 106. Harleian Society, xvii. 355.
WING. New England Register, xviii. 266 ; xxxviii. 376.
WINGATE. Harleian Society, viii. 276; xix. 151, 152, 199 ; xxii. 105. Clutterbuck's Hertford, ii. 496.
WINGFIELD, WINGFEILD, or WINGFELD. Wingfield Memorials. By M. E., 7th Viscount Powerscourt. London, 1894, fol. Muniments of the Family of Wingfield. By Viscount Powerscourt. London, 1894, 4to. Gough's Sepulchral Monuments, ii. Appendix. Croke's History of the Family of Croke, No. 35. Visitation of Norfolk, published by Norfolk Archæological Society, i. 79. Blomefield's Norfolk, i. 85. Camden Society, xliii. 112, 125, 128, 129, 130, 131. Nash's Worcestershire, ii. 317. Burke's Commoners, (of Tickencote,) ii. 476, Landed Gentry, 2, 3, 4, 5, 6, 7, 8 ; (of Onslow,) Commoners, ii. 483, Landed Gentry, 2, 3, 4, 5, 6, 7, 8. Carthew's Hundred of Launditch, Part i. 161. Harleian Society, iii. 32 ; xxxii. 311 ; xxxvii. 311. Comment upon the 5th Journey of Antoninus, etc., by Kennet Gibson, (Nichols' Miscellaneous Antiquities, 1800, 4to.) 215. Burke's Visitation of Seats and Arms, i. 18. Wright's History of Rutland, 124. Blore's Rutland, 65, 70, 208. Bridges' Northamptonshire, by Rev. Peter Whalley, ii. 508. Archdall's Lodge's Peerage, v. 255. Metcalfe's

Visitations of Suffolk, 79, 175, 176. Burke's Extinct Baronetcies. Metcalfe's Visitations of Northamptonshire, 204. Healey's History of Part of West Somerset, 214.

WINGFIELD-DIGBY. Hutchins' Dorset, iv. 281. Burke's Landed Gentry, 4, 5, 6.

WINKLEY. Documents relating to the Winkley Family, by William Winkley, junr. Harrow, 1863, 8vo. Additional Notes on Winkley Pedigree. Chetham Society, lxxxii. 38. *See* WINCKLEY.

WINN, or WINNE. Burke's Royal Families, (London, 1851, 8vo.) i. 149. Burke's Landed Gentry, 3, 4, 5, 6. Foster's Yorkshire Pedigrees. Foster's Visitations of Yorkshire, 593. Hunter's Deanery of Doncaster, ii. 216. Miscellanea Genealogica et Heraldica, New Series, iv. 224. Morant's Essex, i. 112. Surtees Society, xxxvi. 298. Berry's Kent Genealogies, 471. The Genealogist, New Series, x. 237. *See* WYNN.

WINNINGTON. Familia Wynyngtonorum, A.D. 1847, from a pedigree in the possession of Sir Thomas Winnington of Stanford Court. Privately printed by Sir Thos. Phillipps, three pages folio. Nash's Worcestershire, i. 245 ; ii. 368. Ormerod's Cheshire, ii. 205 ; iii. 136, 166, 839. Betham's Baronetage, iii. 246. Harleian Society, xvii. 250, 253. Earwaker's East Cheshire, ii. 108. Earwaker's History of Sandbach, 208, 209.

WINSLADE. Visitation of Devon, edited by F. T. Colby, 207.

WINSLOW. New England Register, iv. 297 ; xiii. 248 ; xvii. 159 ; xxi. 209 ; xxv. 355 ; xxvi. 69.

WINSTANLEY. Dwnn's Visitations of Wales, i. 257. Burke's Royal Families, (London, 1851, 8vo.) ii. 199*. Burke's Commoners, (of Braunston House,) i. 363, Landed Gentry, 2, 3, 4, 5; (of Chaigeley,) Landed Gentry, 5 supp., 6, 7, 8. Jewitt's Reliquary, xv. 14. Corry's History of Lancashire, ii. 717, 718. Nichols' History of the County of Leicester, iv. 629*.

WINSTON. Fosbrooke's History of Gloucestershire, i. 305. Harleian Society, xvii. 358 ; xxi. 179, 188. Weaver's Visitation of Herefordshire, 77.

WINTER. Blomefield's Norfolk, viii. 97. Burke's Commoners, ii. 547, Landed Gentry, 2, 3, 4, 5, 6, 7, 8. Harleian Society, ii. 42 ; xvii. 359 ; xxi. 182, 271 ; xxvii. 118, 147 ; xxxix. 1016. Nichols' History of the County of Leicester, iii. 650, 732. Jones' History of the County of Brecknock, ii. 135-137. Caermarthenshire Pedigrees, 13. Fosbrooke's History of Gloucestershire, ii. 18, 240. Foley's Records of the English Province S. J., v. 848. Visitation of Gloucester, edited by T. F. Fenwick and W. C. Metcalfe, 205. Burke's Colonial Gentry, ii. 792. The Gresley's of Drakelowe, by F. Madan, 297. Healey's History of Part of West Somerset, 292.

WINTERHAY. Hutchins' Dorset, iv. 453.

WINTERINGHAM. Harleian Society, xxxviii. 487.

WINTERSELL, WINTERSHALL, or WINTERSHULL. Visitatio Comitatus Wiltoniæ, 1623, printed by Sir T. Phillipps. The Genealogist, New Series, xiii. 89 ; xv. 217 ; xvii. 24. Visitation of Oxford-

shire, 1574, printed by Sir T. Phillipps, (Middle Hill, fol.) 11.
Sir T. Phillipps' Topographer, No. 1, (March, 1821, 8vo.) 17.
Harleian Society, v. 184; xliii. 3. Manning and Bray's Surrey,
ii. 9, 84.

WINTERTON. Case on behalf of Edward, Earl of Winterton, to Vote
at Elections of Irish Peers. Dublin, *n.d.*, fol. Claim of Edward
Turnour, Earl of Winterton, to Vote at Elections of Irish Peers,
Sess. Papers, C. of 1872. *See* TURNOUR.

WINTHORPE. Metcalfe's Visitations of Suffolk, 176.

WINTHROP. Burke's Visitation of Seats and Arms, 2nd Series, i. 39.
Burke's Royal Families, (London, 1851, 8vo.) ii. 49. Herald and
Genealogist, vii. 90. Notes and Queries, 3 S. vii. 96, 160, 269.
Suffolk Manorial Families, by J. J. Muskett, i. 33. New England
Register, xviii. 182.

WINTOUR. Burke's Extinct Baronetcies.

WINTRINGHAM. Burke's Extinct Baronetcies.

WINWOOD. Burke's Landed Gentry, 8.

WIRDNAM. The Genealogist, New Series, ii. 110. Clarke's Hundred
of Wanting, 186. *See* WYRDNAM.

WIRIOT. Dwnn's Visitations of Wales, ii. 46.

WIRLEY. Lipscombe's History of the County of Buckingham, iv. 126.
Visitation of Staffordshire, 1663-64, printed by Sir T. Phillipps, 11.
See WYRLEY.

WISDEN. Howard's Visitation of England and Wales, iii. 7.

WISDOM. Jordan's History of Enstone, 345.

WISE. Gentleman's Magazine, 1831, ii. 313. Cambridgeshire Visi-
tation, edited by Sir T. Phillipps, 34. Burke's Commoners, (of
Clayton,) i. 19, Landed Gentry, 2, 3, 4, 5, 6, 7, 8; (of Woodcote,)
Landed Gentry, 2, 3, 4, 5, 6, 7; (of Leamington,) 2, 3, 4, 5, 6,
7, 8; (of Hillbank,) 5, 6, 7. Harleian Society, vi. 358; xli. 62.
Westcote's Devonshire, edited by G. Oliver and P. Jones, 553.
Visitation of Devon, edited by F. T. Colby, 220, 221. Hasted's
Kent, (Hund. of Blackheath, by H. H. Drake,) 250. Burke's
Colonial Gentry, i. 177. The Visitations of Devon, by J. L.
Vivian, 791. *See* STRACHAN.

WISEMAN. The Genealogist, vi. 111. Gentleman's Magazine, lxi.
885, 999; lxii. 308; lxiii. 107; lxxx, i. 202, 530, 623; ii. 628.
Morant's Essex, i. 261; ii. 88, 146, 283, 369, 390, 461, 479, 536,
559, 563. Berry's Berkshire Genealogies, 129. Parochial Topo-
graphy of the Hundred of Wanting, by W. N. Clarke, 144.
Harleian Society, viii. 81, 138, 347; xiii. 18, 129, 324, 526.
Wright's Essex, ii. 265. Foley's Records of the English Province
S. J., ii. 574. Wotton's English Baronetage, ii. 120. Betham's
Baronetage, i. 345. Metcalfe's Visitation of Suffolk, 210. Burke's
Extinct Baronetcies. Bysshe's Visitation of Essex, edited by J. J.
Howard, 103. *See* WYSEMAN.

WISHART. Memoir of Geo. Wishart, by Rev. C. Rogers, 74-108.
W. R. Fraser's History of Laurencekirk, 77.

WISSE. Visitation of Gloucestershire, 1569, (Middle Hill, 1854, fol.)
11. Harleian Society, xxi. 228.

WISTON. Sussex Archæological Collections, v. 3.

WISTONESTON. Dallaway's Sussex, II. ii. 75, 138.

WISWALL. New England Register, xl. 58.

WITHAM. Burke's Commoners, ii. 5, Landed Gentry, 2, 3, 4, 5, 6, 7, 8. Foster's Yorkshire Pedigrees. Foster's Visitations of Yorkshire, 260, 310, 408, 593. Thoresby's Ducatus Leodiensis, 240. Bysshe's Visitation of Essex, edited by J. J. Howard, 104. *See* WYTHAM.

WITHE, or WITHES. Foster's Visitations of Yorkshire, 591. Harleian Society, xxvii. 149.

WITHEN. Harleian Society, xlii. 188.

WITHER. Berry's Hampshire Genealogies, 256, 326. Berry's Kent Genealogies, 389. Burke's Commoners, ii. 397, Landed Gentry, 2, 3, 4, 5. Harleian Society, xiii. 130, 328.

WITHERDEN. Archæologia Cantiana, xvi. 79.

WITHERING. Botfield's Stemmata Botevilliana, 152. Harleian Society, xiv. 619; xvii. 340.

WITHERINGS. Bysshe's Visitation of Essex, edited by J. J. Howard, 104.

WITHERS. Harleian Society, viii. 471; xvii. 360; xxxvii. 195.

WITHERSTONE. Cooke's Continuation of Duncumb's Hereford, (Hund. of Grimsworth,) Part i. 62.

WITHIE. Harleian Society, vi. 359. Miscellanea Genealogica et Heraldica, New Series, 361, 373. The Visitations of Devon, by J. L. Vivian, 814.

WITHINGTON. Burke's Landed Gentry, 5, 6, 7, 8.

WITTEWRONGE. Berry's Hertfordshire Genealogies, 204. Clutterbuck's Hertford, i. 411. Burke's Extinct Baronetcies. Wotton's English Baronetage, iii. 361. *See* WHITTEWRONG.

WITTIE. Surtees Society, xxxvi. 221. W. Paver's Pedigrees of Families of the City of York, 21.

WITTLEBURY. The Genealogist, New Series, x. 35.

WITTON. Surtees Society, xxxvi. 318. W. Paver's Pedigrees of Families of the City of York, 22. Harleian Society, i. 53; xxix. 508; xxxvii. 91, 365. Abram's History of Blackburn, 582. Antiquarian Notices of Lupset, by J. H. (1851 edn.), 33.

WIVELL. Westcote's Devonshire, edited by G. Oliver and P. Jones, 611. *See* WYVELL.

WIVERTON. Thoroton's Nottinghamshire, i. 196.

WLONKESLOW. Harleian Society, xxix. 445.

WODDE. Hulbert's Annals of Almondbury, 218.

WODDROP. Burke's Landed Gentry, 4, 5, 6.

WODEHOUSE. Blomefield's Norfolk, ii. 540-558; ix. 353. Visitation of Norfolk, published by Norfolk Archæological Society, i. 103. Burke's Royal Families, (London, 1851, 8vo.) ii. 205. Burke's Landed Gentry, 3, 4, 5, 6, 7. The Genealogist, iii. 129. Carthew's Hundred of Launditch, Part ii. 417. Brydges' Collins' Peerage, viii. 562. Wotton's English Baronetage, i. 164. The Visitations of Cornwall, edited by J. L. Vivian, 156. *See* DE WODEHOUSE, WOODHOUSE.

WODELOK. The Genealogist, New Series, xv. 23.

WODENOTE, or WODENOTH. Harleian Society, ix. 266. The Visitations of Cornwall, by J. L. Vivian, 629.

WODERYNGTON. Harleian Society, xvi. 348.

WODFORD. Dwnn's Visitations of Wales, i. 135.

WODHAM. The Genealogist, New Series, iii. 179.

WODHULL. Hoare's Wiltshire, II. ii. 128. Baker's Northampton, i. 711. Miscellanea Genealogica et Heraldica, 2nd Series, i. 71. See WOODHULL.

WODLOW. Dugdale's Warwickshire, 469.

WODROFF. Harleian Society, i. 12. See WOODROOFFE.

WODROW. Paterson's History of the Co. of Ayr, ii. 339.

WOFFINGTON. Notes and Queries, 3 S. i. 38, 156.

WOGAN. Pedigree of Wogan of Boulston, Co. Pembroke, and of the descendants of Thomas Wyrriott, Esq., of Orielton, [T. P.] 1867. 2 folio pages. Glamorganshire Pedigrees, edited by Sir T. Phillipps, 39. Harleian Society, viii. 428. Pembrokeshire Pedigrees, 119, 133, 153, 164. Notes and Queries, 2 S. iii. 25 ; v. 329. Banks' Baronies in Fee, ii. 157.

WOGAN-BROWNE. Burke's Landed Gentry, 8.

WOLCOTT, or WOLCOT. Burke's Landed Gentry, 2, 3, 4, 5, 6. Harleian Society, vi. 310. Visitation of Devon, edited by F. T. Colby, 209. New England Register, i. 251. The Visitations of Devon, by J. L. Vivian, 793.

WOLDEDON. Weaver's Visitations of Somerset, 31.

WOLF, WOLFE, or WOLFF. The Wolfe's of Forenaghts. By R. T. Wolfe. Guildford, n.d., 8vo., 2nd edn. Berry's Sussex Genealogies, 55. Dallaway's Sussex, II. ii. 260. Foley's Records of the English Province S. J., v. 960. Tuckett's Devonshire Pedigrees, 170. Burke's Landed Gentry, (of Bishop Land,) 3, 4, 5 ; (of Leighon,) 8 ; (of Wood Hall,) 4, 5, 6, 7, 8 ; (of Forenaghts,) 5 supp., 6, 7, 8. Harleian Society, vi. 313. Nichols' History of the County of Leicester, iv. 188. Baker's Northampton, ii. 124. Berry's Hampshire Genealogies, 319. Dwnn's Visitations of Wales, i. 11. Betham's Baronetage, iii. 346. Notes and Queries, 1 S. iv. 271, 323, 393, 409, 438, 489, 503 ; v. 34, 136, 185, 279. Burke's Extinct Baronetcies. Burke's Colonial Gentry, ii. 723. The Irish Builder, xxxv. 213. The Visitations of Devon, by J. L. Vivian, 794. See WOOLFE, WOULFE.

WOLFERSTAN. Burke's Commoners, i. 187, Landed Gentry, 2, 3, 4, 5, 6, 7, 8. Shaw's Staffordshire, i. 416.

WOLLACOMBE. Harleian Society, vi. 312. Westcote's Devonshire, edited by G. Oliver and P. Jones, 539. Visitation of Devon, edited by F. T. Colby, 208. The Visitations of Devon, by J. L. Vivian, 793.

WOLLASCOTT. The Genealogist, vi. 113.

WOLLASTON. Pedigree of Wollaston [of Staffordshire, etc.] six broadside sheets, circa, 1879. Privately printed. (? at Ipswich.) Genealogical Memoirs of the Wollastons of Shenton, by R. E. C. Waters. London, 1877, 8vo. Bibliotheca Topographica Britannica,

ix. Part iv. 100. Burke's Landed Gentry, 7, 8 ; 3rd edn., 524 ; 4th edn., 655. Berry's Buckinghamshire Genealogies, 11. Burke's Commoners, iii. 415, Landed Gentry, 2 and add., 3, 4, 5 and supp., 6. Visitation of Staffordshire, 1663-4, printed by Sir T. Phillipps, 11. Nichols' History of the County of Leicester, iv. 531, 541. Memoirs of the Family of Chester, by R. E. C. Waters, 545-583. Burke's Extinct Baronetcies. Harleian Society, xvii. 362. Burke's Colonial Gentry, ii. 569. Visitations of Staffordshire, 1614 and 1663-4, William Salt Society, 320. Bysshe's Visitation of Essex, edited by J. J. Howard, 105. Fletcher's Leicestershire Pedigrees and Royal Descents, 144. Willmore's History of Walsall, 292.

WOLLESCOTT. Blore's Rutland, 61.

WOLLEY, or WOOLLEY. Burke's Landed Gentry, 2, 3, 4, 5, 6, 7. Visitation of Derbyshire, 1663-4, (Middle Hill, 1854, fol.) 7. Clutterbuck's Hertford, i. 111. The Genealogist, i. 121 ; iii. 186. Harleian Society, xii. 157 ; xl. 1241. Burke's Family Records, 641. Miscellanea Genealogica et Heraldica, 3rd Series, iii. 124.

WOLLEY-DOD. Burke's Landed Gentry, 8.

WOLLFALL. Harleian Society, xvii. 362.

WOLMER. Nash's Worcestershire, ii. 63. The Genealogist, v. 58. Harleian Society, xxvii. 150.

WOLPE. Notes and Queries, 1 S. iii. 244.

WOLRICH, or WOLRYCH. Pedigree of Wolrich of Dodmarton, Co. Salop, etc., [T. P.] 1860. Broadside. Burke's Commoners, iv. 758. Harleian Society, viii. 142 ; xxix. 508. Visitation of Staffordshire, 1663-4, printed by Sir T. Phillipps, 11. Burke's Extinct Baronetcies. Metcalfe's Visitations of Suffolk, 106. Robinson's Mansions of Herefordshire, 99. Visitations of Staffordshire, 1614 and 1663-4, William Salt Society, 322.

WOLRYCHE-WHITMORE. Burke's Landed Gentry, 7, 8.

WOLSDON. A Complete Parochial History of the County of Cornwall, iii. 253.

WOLSELEY. Erdeswicke's Survey of Staffordshire, 203. Wotton's English Baronetage, ii. 133. Betham's Baronetage, i. 359. Visitations of Staffordshire, 1614 and 1663-4, William Salt Society, 323. The Gresley's of Drakelowe, by F. Madan, 298.

WOLSEY. Life of Robert Wolsey of Ipswich, Gent, by Mr. Grove of Richmond, 1761, 8vo. Wolsey the Cardinal, and his Times, by J. Howard, 1824, 8vo. Visitation of Norfolk, published by Norfolk Archæological Society, 23. Harleian Society, xxxii. 319. *See* CROPPER.

WOLSTENHOLM. Hunter's Deanery of Doncaster, ii. 215. Wotton's English Baronetage, iii. 444. Betham's Baronetage, ii. 361. Burke's Extinct Baronetcies. Robinson's History of Enfield, ii. 98. Fishwick's History of Rochdale, 526.

WOLSTON. Visitation of Westmorland, 1615, (London, 1853,) 45. Tuckett's Devonshire Pedigrees, 183. Harleian Society, vi. 313. Metcalfe's Visitations of Northamptonshire, 55. Foster's Visitations of Cumberland and Westmorland, 147. The Visitations of Devon, by J. L. Vivian, 798.

WOLTON. Howard's Visitation of England and Wales, viii. 127.

WOLVARDINGTON. Dugdale's Warwickshire, 665.

WOLVEDON. Polwhele's History of Cornwall, iv. 112. A Complete Parochial History of the County of Cornwall, iv. 101.

WOLVERIDG. Berry's Hampshire Genealogies, 313.

WOLVERSTON. Visitation of Staffordshire, 1663-4, printed by Sir T. Phillipps, 11. Visitations of Staffordshire, 1614 and 1663-4, William Salt Society, 324.

WOLVERTON. Herald and Genealogist, vi. 48. Bridges' Northamptonshire, by Rev. Peter Whalley, i. 332. Baker's Northampton, ii. 252. Banks' Dormant and Extinct Baronage, i. 196.

WOMBWELL. Hasted's Kent, i. 440. Surtees Society, xxxvi. 180. Berry's Kent Genealogies, 57. Archæologia Cantiana, iv. 253. Burke's Commoners, iii. 589. Foster's Yorkshire Pedigrees. Foster's Visitations of Yorkshire, 365, 366. Thoresby's Ducatus Leodiensis, 69. Hunter's History of the Parish of Sheffield, 449. Hunter's Deanery of Doncaster, ii. 124. Betham's Baronetage, iv. 49. Harleian Society, xlii. 6.

WOOD. Memorials of the Family of Wood of Largo, by Mrs. Montagu, privately printed, 1863, 4to. Pedigree of Wood of Enfield, [T. P.] folio page. Kent's British Banner Displayed, 332. Visitation of Norfolk, published by Norfolk Archæological Society, i. 27. Berry's Sussex Genealogies, 189, 311. Cambridgeshire Visitation, edited by Sir T. Phillipps, 34. Surtees Society, xxxvi. 78. Burke's Commoners, (of Swanwick,) iii. 137 ; (of Brownshills,) iv. 640 ; (of Henley Hall,) 7, 8 ; (of Bodlondeb,) 7, 8 ; (of Freeland,) 8 ; (of Hawnby,) 8 ; (of Hollin Hall,) Commoners, iii. 691, Landed Gentry, 2, 3, 4, 5, 6, 7, 8 ; (of Bishops Hall,) Commoners, iv. 81, Landed Gentry, 2, 3, 4, 5, 6 ; (of Singleton Lodge,) Commoners, iii. 138, Landed Gentry, 3, 4, 5, 6, 7, 8 ; (of Largo,) Burke's Landed Gentry, 4 ; (of Littleton,) 2, 3, 4, 5, 6, 7, 8 ; (of Thoresby,) 2, 3, 4, 5, 6, 7 ; (of the Whitehouse,) 2, 3, 4, 5, 6, 7 ; (of Woodville,) 2, 3, 4, 5, 6 ; (of Wirksworth Hall,) 3, 4 ; 5 at p 62 ; (of Ottershaw Park,) 5, 6, 7 ; (of Osmington House,) 5, 6, 7, 8 ; (of Newton Hall,) 6 and supp:, 7, 8 ; (of Stout Hall,) 6, 7, 8 ; (of Thedden Grange,) 6, 7, 8 ; (of Raasay,) 6 ; (of Woolley,) 8 ; (of Hollyhurst,) 8 ; (of Whitehouse,) 8 ; (of Driffield,) 8 ; (of Robinhoods Bay,) 8 ; (of Newbold Revel,) 6 supp., 7, 8. Foster's Yorkshire Pedigrees. Miscellanea Genealogica et Heraldica, New Series, i. 14. Foster's Visitations of Yorkshire, 124, 592. Harleian Society, iv. 86 ; vi. 314 ; viii. 271, 374 ; xiii. 531 ; xiv. 620 ; xvii. 363, 364 ; xx. 100 ; xxi. 184 ; xxix. 510 ; xxxii. 319, 320 ; xxxvii. 267, 342 ; xxxviii. 481, 600, 784 ; xxxix. 898 ; xli. 101. Herald and Genealogist, viii. 198. Foster's Lancashire Pedigrees. Chetham Society, lxxxii. 49 ; lxxxviii. 335. Gage's History of Thingoe Hundred, Suffolk, 391. Westcote's Devonshire, edited by G. Oliver and P. Jones, 589-591. Visitation of Staffordshire, 1663-4, printed by

Sir T. Phillipps, 11. Oxford Historical Society, xix. 23-31;
xxvi. 94. History of Chislet, by F. Haslewood, 172. Bateson's
History of Northumberland, i. 331. Account of the Parish of
Lea with Lea Wood, (London, 1841, 8vo.) 21. The Borough of
Stoke-upon-Trent, by John Ward, 153. Thoresby's Ducatus
Leodiensis, 207. Hunter's Deanery of Doncaster, ii. 396, 427.
Manning and Bray's Surrey, ii. 543. History of Barnsley, by
Rowland Jackson, 81. Thoroton's Nottinghamshire, iii. 34.
Memoirs of the Family of Chester, by R. E. C. Waters, 468.
The Genealogist, ii. 201. Maclean's History of Trigg Minor, iii.
263. Hinchliffe's Barthomley, 167. Fosbrooke's History of
Gloucestershire, i. 270. An Historical Survey of Cornwall, by
C. S. Gilbert, ii. 332. Walter Wood's East Neuk of Fife, 266,
281. Visitation of Devon, edited by F. T. Colby, 8, 210.
Betham's Baronetage, iv. 146. Ormerod's Cheshire, iii. 182.
Burke's Extinct Boronetcies, supp., and 638. Metcalfe's Visita-
tion of Worcester, 1683, 107. Bysshe's Visitation of Essex,
edited by J. J. Howard, 105. Visitation of Gloucester, edited by
T. F. Fenwick and W. C. Metcalfe, 207. Visitations of Stafford-
shire, 1614 and 1663-4, William Salt Society, 325. Burke's
Colonial Gentry, i. 310. Howard's Visitation of England and
Wales, iv. 69 ; v. 78. Burke's Family Records, 634. The Visi-
tations of Devon, by J. L. Vivian, 799, 801. Healey's History
of Part of West Somerset, 170. *See* CRANMER, MOORE, SLOREY,
WOODE.

WOODALL. Harleian Society, xvii. 364.

WOODBRIDGE. Burke's Family Records, 636.

WOODBURNE. Adlard's Sutton-Dudleys of England, etc., 105. New
England Register, xviii. 302 ; xxxii. 292.

WOODCOCK. Woodcock of Cuerden, of Newburgh and of Wigan.
By A. E. P. Gray. Canterbury, 1882, 4to. Croston's edn. of
Baines's Lancaster, iv. 187. Herald and Genealogist, v. 221.
Jewitt's Reliquary, vii. 31 ; xiv. 146 ; xv. 14. Burke's Landed
Gentry, 4, 5, 6, 7, 8. Harleian Society, viii. 41 ; xiii. 532 ; xvii.
366 ; xxix. 511. Burke's Visitation of Seats and Arms, i. 15.
Nichols' History of the County of Leicester, iii. 983. Abram's
History of Blackburn, 733. Fletcher's Leicestershire Pedigrees
and Royal Descents, 148.

WOODD. Genealogical Records of the Family of Woodd. By Henry
Woodd. London, 1886, fol. Burke's Landed Gentry, 2, 3, 4, 5,
6, 7, 8. Foster's Yorkshire Pedigrees. Miscellanea Genealogica
et Heraldica, New Series, ii. 80. Whitaker's Deanery of Craven,
3rd edn., 574. Howard's Visitation of England and Wales,
ix. 65.

WOODDESON. The Genealogist, vi. 114.

WOODE. Harleian Society, v. 223 ; vi. 314. *See* WODDE.

WOODFORD, or WOODFORDE. Harleian Society, ii. 47, 48. Burton's
Description of Leicestershire, 22. Nichols' History of the
County of Leicester, ii. 345, 376 ; iii. 24. The Genealogist, vii.
255. Burke's Commoners, iv. 760, Landed Gentry, 2, 3, 4, 5, 6,

7, 8. Betham's Baronetage, iv. 234. Burke's Extinct Baronetcies.

WOODGATE. Gentleman's Magazine, 1827, ii. 200. Hasted's Kent, ii. 340. Burke's Landed Gentry, (of Pembury,) 5 supp., 7, 8 ; (of Bellavista,) 8.

WOODHALL. Berry's Hertfordshire Genealogies, 92. Clutterbuck's Hertford, ii. 350, 399. Harleian Society, xiii. 620 ; xix. 67. Genealogical Gleanings in England, by H. F. Waters, i. 53. New England Register, xxxviii. 305.

WOODHAM, or WOODHAMS. Morant's Essex, i. 263, 302 ; ii. 33. Genealogical Record of King and Henham, 21. Genealogical Memoranda relating to the Family of King, by W. L. King, 14.

WOODHEAD. Life of Joseph Clark, by H. E. Clark, 20. Harleian Society, xxxviii. 658.

WOODHOUSE. Blomefield's Norfolk, ix. 353. Burke's Commoners, (of Wombourne Wood-house,) iii. 613, Landed Gentry, 2 ; (of Norley Hall,) 7, 8 ; (of Omeath Park,) Landed Gentry, 4, 5, 6, 7. Burke's Royal Descents and Pedigrees of Founders' Kin, 32. Shaw's Staffordshire, ii. 216. Visitation of Staffordshire, 1663-4, printed by Sir T. Phillipps, 11. Surtees Society, lxv. 244. Harleian Society, xvi. 344 ; xxxii. 321 ; xxxvii. 26 ; xl. 1186. The Genealogist, New Series, viii. 59. Visitations of Staffordshire, 1614 and 1663-4, William Salt Society, 327. See WODEHOUSE.

WOODHULL. Harleian Society, v. 198, 266. Bridges' Northamptonshire, by Rev. Peter Whalley, i. 205, 217, 266. Metcalfe's Visitations of Northamptonshire, 56, 159. See WODHULL.

WOODIWISS. Burke's Landed Gentry, 8.

WOODLEY. Burke's Landed Gentry, 6 and supp., 7, 8. The Visitations of Devon, by J. L. Vivian, 858.

WOODLOCK. Herald and Genealogist, v. 432.

WOODMAN. Hodgson's Northumberland, II. ii. 468. Surrey Archæological Collections, vii. Harleian Society, xliii. 108.

WOODMAN-HASTINGS. Burke's Landed Gentry, 8.

WOOD-MARTIN. Burke's Landed Gentry, 7, 8.

WOODMASS. Burke's Landed Gentry, 7, 8.

WOODNETT. Harleian Society, xviii. 254.

WOODNOTH. Ormerod's Cheshire, iii. 508. Visitations of Staffordshire, 1614 and 1663-4, William Salt Society, 328.

WOODROOFFE, WOODROFFE, WOODROUFFE, WOODRUFFE, or WOODROVE. Pedigree of Woodrooffe, with Memorials and Notes, collected by S. M. Woodroofe. London, 1878, 4to. Surrey Archæological Collections, vi. Miscellanea Genealogica et Heraldica, ii. 378 ; New Series, i. 411 ; iii. 65. Harleian Society, vi. 315 ; viii. 347 ; xvi. 350 ; xvii. 366 ; xxxvii. 322 ; xliii. 54. A Royal Descent, by T. E. Sharpe, (London, 1875, 4to.) 81. Manning and Bray's Surrey, iii. 176. Hunter's Deanery of Doncaster, ii. 387. Foster's Visitations of Yorkshire, 355, 381. Banks' Baronies in Fee, i. 369. Notes and Queries, 6 S. vii. 29. East Barnet, by

F. C. Cass, Part i. 92. Howard's Visitation of England and Wales, ii. 10. Burke's Family Records, 637. The Visitations of Devon, by J. L. Vivian, 802. *See* WODROFF.

WOODS. Dwnn's Visitations of Wales, ii. 203. Burke's Landed Gentry, (of Milverton,) 2, 3, 4, 5, 6, 7, 8; (of Wigan,) 2 supp., 3, 4, 5, 6, 7, 8. Herald and Genealogist, viii. 191. History of the Wilmer Family, 268. Burke's Family Records, 638.

WOODTHORPE. Croke's History of the Family of Croke, ii. 122.

WOODVILLE. Nichols' History of the County of Leicester, ii. 345.

WOODWARD. Botfield's Stemmata Botevilliana, 149. Berry's Kent Genealogies, 52. Visitation of Middlesex, (Salisbury, 1820, fol.) 8. Burke's Landed Gentry, (of Drumbarrow,) 3, 4, 5; (of Hopton Court,) 5, 6, 7, 8; (of Arley Castle,) 5, 6, 7, 8; (of Stafford,) 5 at p. 1040; 6 at p. 1223. Harleian Society, v. 215; xii. 119, 227; xxi. 185; xl. 1300; xlii. 35; xliii. 206. Visitation of Warwickshire, 1619, published with Warwickshire Antiquarian Magazine, 46. Chetham Society, lxxxviii. 336. Fosbrooke's History of Gloucestershire, ii. 221. Notes and Queries, 3 S. vi. 403; vii. 299. The Genealogist, vii. 256. Account of the Mayo and Elton Families, by C. H. Mayo, 153. Harleian Society, xvii. 367, 368; xxxix. 1024. Visitation of Gloucester, edited by T. F. Fenwick and W. C. Metcalfe, 208. New England Register, xviii. 265; l. 300; li. 169. Foster's Visitation of Middlesex, 18.

WOODYEARE. Burke's Commoners, iv. 361, Landed Gentry, 2, 3, 4, 5, 6. Foster's Yorkshire Pedigrees. Hunter's Deanery of Doncaster, i. 124.

WOOLAVINGTON. Collinson's Somerset, iii. 438.

WOOLFALL. Chetham Society, lxxxviii. 337.

WOOLFE, or WOOLFF. Additional Case of T. Stonor, claiming the Barony of Camoys, folding table. Dwnn's Visitations of Wales, i. 11-14, 104, 205. *See* WOLF.

WOOLFRIES. Harleian Society, xx. 101.

WOOLGAR. Berry's Sussex Genealogies, 101.

WOOLHOUSE. Visitation of Derbyshire, 1663-4, (Middle Hill, 1854, fol,) 7. Hutchins' Dorset, ii. 99. The Genealogist, iii. 186; New Series, viii. 179. Harleian Society, xxxviii. 467.

WOOLLAM. Burke's Family Records, 640.

WOOLLCOMBE. Harleian Society, vi. 312. Couch's History of Polperro, 217. Burke's Landed Gentry, 6, 7, 8. The Visitations of Cornwall, edited by J. L. Vivian, 332. Burke's Colonial Gentry, i. 354. The Visitations of Devon, by J. L. Vivian, 803.

WOOLRYCH. Burke's Landed Gentry, 2 and supp, 3, 4, 5, 6, 7, 8.

WOOLSEY. Burke's Landed Gentry, 8.

WOOSNAM. Burke's Landed Gentry, 6, 8. Collections by the Powys-land Club, viii. 219.

WORCESTER. Banks' Dormant and Extinct Baronage, iii. 760.

WORDSWORTH. Burke's Landed Gentry, 4, 5. Miscellanea Genealogica et Heraldica, New Series, iv. 41. Yorkshire Notes and Queries, i. 163, 237. Harleian Society, xxvii. 6; xxxviii. 751-

758. Old Yorkshire, ed. by Willm. Smith, New Series, iii. 202. The Manor of Minster, by H. W. Aldred, 39. Pedigree of Wilson, by S. B. Foster, 201.

WORGE. Berry's Sussex Genealogies, 274. Burke's Landed Gentry, 2.

WORKESLEY. Berry's Hampshire Genealogies, 134. See DE WORKESLEY.

WORLESTON. Ormerod's Cheshire, iii. 356.

WORLEY. Berry's Kent Genealogies, 129. Burke's Landed Gentry, 2 supp. Harleian Society, xlii. 42.

WORLICH. See WOLRICH.

WORMALD, or WORMALL. Miscellanea Genealogica et Heraldica, New Series, ii. 184. Hulbert's Annals of Almondbury, 136. Surrey Archæological Collections, x. Harleian Society, xliii. 169.

WORME. Metcalfe's Visitations of Northamptonshire, 204.

WORMELEY, or WORMLEY. Surtees Society, xxxvi. 211. Foster's Visitations of Yorkshire, 350. Burke's Landed Gentry, 2 supp. Hunter's Deanery of Doncaster, i. 175. Harleian Society, xl. 1190.

WORNELL. Visitation of Somersetshire, printed by Sir T. Phillipps, 147. Harleian Society, xi. 119.

WORRALL. Burke's Visitation of Seats and Arms, 2nd Series, i. 17. Harleian Society, xxxviii. 803. A History of Banking in Bristol, by G. H. Carce, 258.

WORSLEY. Pedigree of the Family of Worsley, by H. A. M. Worsley, single sheet, 1895. Pedigree of the Family of Worsley of Chale, by H. A. M. Worsley, single sheet, 1895. Jewitt's Reliquary, xi. 40. Berry's Hampshire Genealogies, 84, 134, 136-142. Surtees Society, xxxvi. 62. The Genealogical Magazine, ii. 26. Burke's Commoners, ii. 188; iv. 607. Foster's Yorkshire Pedigrees. Chetham Society, xlvii. 67, 68; lxxxi. 120, 131; lxxxii. 72; lxxxviii. 338, 339; xcviii. 81; xcix. 77. Hoare's Wiltshire, IV. i. 55. Whitaker's History of Whalley, 3rd edition, 320. Burke's Royal Families, (London, 1851, 8vo.) ii. 83. Bridges' Northamptonshire, by Rev. Peter Whalley, ii. 525. Duchetiana, by Sir G. F. Duckett, 2nd edn., 20. Wotton's English Baronetage, i. 189. Betham's Baronetage, i. 115. Burke's Extinct Baronetcies. Croston's edn. of Baines's Lancaster, iii. 286, 292. Metcalfe's Visitations of Northamptonshire, 56, 205. Harleian Society, xxxvii. 137. History of the Old Chapel, Tockholes, by B. Nightingale, 215.

WORSLEY-HOLMES. Berry's Hampshire Genealogies, 353.

WORSLEY-TAYLOR. Burke's Landed Gentry, 8.

WORTH. Visitation of Somersetshire, printed by Sir T. Phillipps, 146. Harleian Society, vi. 315; xi. 120; xviii. 256. Westcote's Devonshire, edited by G. Oliver and P. Jones, 561. Mullyon, its History, etc., by E. G. Harvey, 118. Visitation of Devon, edited by F. T. Colby, 212. Ormerod's Cheshire, iii. 700. Visitation of Wiltshire, edited by G. W. Marshall, 39. Earwaker's East Cheshire, ii. 339. Weaver's Visitations of Somerset, 91. The Visitations of Devon, by J. L. Vivian, 805. Healey's History of Part of West Somerset, 153.

WORTHALL, or WORTHYALE. Harleian Society, vi. 361. Westcote's Devonshire, edited by G. Oliver and P. Jones, 629.

WORTHAM. Cussan's History of Hertfordshire, Parts v. and vi. 133. Burke's Landed Gentry, 7, 8.

WORTHEVALE. Maclean's History of Trigg Minor, i. 663. Harleian Society, ix. 267.

WORTHINGTON. Burke's Landed Gentry, (of the Bryn,) 3, 4, 5 ; (of Sandiway Bank,) 2 ; (of Burton,) 6 supp., 7, 8. Chetham Society, lxxxi. 77 ; lxxxii. 125, 126 ; lxxxviii. 341-344. Foley's Records of the English Province S. J., ii. 76, 133. Burke's Heraldic Illustrations, 129. Harleian Society, xiii. 328 ; xvii. 369. The Genealogist, vi. 291. Howard's Visitation of England and Wales, i. 221. New England Register, xliii. 361. Burke's Family Records, 642.

WORTHIVALL. The Visitations of Cornwall, by J. L. Vivian, 630.

WORTHYATE. The Visitations of Devon, by J. L. Vivian, 810.

WORTLEY. Visitation of Durham, 1615, (Sunderland, 1820, fol.) 48. Foster's Visitations of Yorkshire, 592. Hunter's Deanery of Doncaster, ii. 171, 324. Harleian Society, xiii. 329. Burke's Extinct Baronetcies. Foster's Visitations of Durham, 335.

WORTS. Ontarian Families, by E. M. Chadwick, i. 158.

WOTTON. Hasted's Kent, i. 140 ; ii. 428, 614. Tuckett's Devonshire Pedigrees, 133. Harleian Society, vi. 316 ; xvii. 369, 370. The Visitations of Devon, by J. L. Vivian, 811. Notes and Gleanings, by W. Cotton, and J. Dallas, iv. 140. Lipscombe's History of the County of Buckingham, iv. 480. Blore's Rutland, 177. Dugdale's Warwickshire, 523. Banks' Dormant and Extinct Baronage, iii. 763. History of Powys Fadog, by J. Y. W. Lloyd, v. 251.

WOULFE, or WOULPHE. Burke's Landed Gentry, 5 supp., 6, 7, 8. Harleian Society, xiii. 81. *See* WOLF.

WRAGG. Cyclostyle Pedigrees, by J. J. Green.

WRAITH. Abram's History of Blackburn, 408.

WRANGHAM. Burke's Royal Families, (London, 1851, 8vo.) ii. 26. Burke's Commoners, ii. 311.

WRAY. Visitation of Oxfordshire, 1634, printed by Sir T. Phillipps, (Middle Hill, fol.) 33. Burke's Commoners, ii. 632 ; (of Kilfield,) Commoners, iv. 21, Landed Gentry, 2 ; (of Castle Wray,) Landed Gentry, 3, 4, 5, 6, 7, 8. Harleian Society, v. 295 ; xlii. 220. Surtees' Durham, ii. 226. History of Richmond, by C. Clarkson, 256. Hunter's Deanery of Doncaster, i. 349. The Genealogist, iv. 278-285 ; v. 141. Wotton's English Baronetage, i. 242. Visitation of Devon, edited by F. T. Colby, 213. Betham's Baronetage, i. 139. Burke's Extinct Baronetcies. Tuckett's Devonshire Pedigrees, 25. Burke's Colonial Gentry, ii. 642. The Visitations of Devon, by J. L. Vivian, 825. *See* WREY.

WRAYFORD. The Visitations of Devon, by J. L. Vivian, 815.

WREFORD. *See* WRAYFORD.

WREIGHT. Hasted's Kent, ii. 799. *See* WRIGHT.

WREN, WRENN, or WRENNE. Memoirs of the Family of the Wrens, by Stephen Wren. London, 1750, folio. Gentleman's Magazine, 1826, i. 34 ; 1829, i. 324. Visitation of Durham, 1575, (Newcastle, 1820, fol.) 13. Visitation of Durham, 1615, (Sunderland, 1820, fol.) 97. *See* 'Hoskyns,' in Burke's Landed Gentry. Harleian Society, viii. 289 ; xli. 113. The Genealogist, iii. 314 ; v. 330 ; New Series, i. 262 ; vi. 168. Charles Smith's History of Kerry, 61. Notes and Queries, 5 S. x. 288, 434; 6 S. v. 133. The Rectors of Loughborough, by W. G. D. Fletcher, 14. Jewitt's Reliquary, xxii. 67. Foster's Visitations of Durham, 337.

WRENBURY. Ormerod's Cheshire, iii. 395.

WRENCH. Earwaker's Local Gleanings, ii. 708, 713, 739, 772.

WREY. Harleian Society, ix. 268. Westcote's Devonshire, edited by G. Oliver and P. Jones, 567. A Complete Parochial History of the County of Cornwall, ii. 251. An Historical Survey of Cornwall, by C. S. Gilbert, i. 555. Wotton's English Baronetage, ii. 84. Betham's Baronetage, i. 320. The Visitations of Cornwall, by J. L. Vivian, 564. Burke's Landed Gentry, 7, 8. *See* WRAY.

WRIGHT. Topographer and Genealogist, ii. 79. Morant's Essex, i. 62, 105, 121, 185 ; ii. 409, 568. Glover's History of Derbyshire, ii. 201, (170). Blomefield's Norfolk, i. 545. Berry's Kent Genealogies, 264. Surtees Society, xxxvi. 98. Visitation of Durham, 1615, (Sunderland, 1820, fol.) 63. Berry's Hampshire Genealogies, 323, 335. Visitation of Middlesex, (Salisbury, 1820, fol.) 46. Bibliotheca Topographica Britannica, vii. Parts i. and ii. 151, 348*. Burke's Commoners, ii. 125 ; (of Kilverstone,) Commoners, ii. 614, Landed Gentry, 2, 3, 4 ; (of Bolton-on-Swale,) Commoners, ii. 678, Landed Gentry, 2 ; (of Mottram St. Andrew's,) Commoners, iii. 104, Landed Gentry, 2, 5, 6, 7, 8 ; (of Kelvedon,) Landed Gentry, 2, 3, 4, 5, 6, 7, 8 ; (of Osmaston,) 2, 3, 4, 5, 6, 7, 8 at p. 1543; (of Mapperley,) 2, 3, 4, 5, 6, 7, 8; (of Golagh House,) 2, 3, 4, 5, 6 ; (of Longstone Hall,) 2 add.; (of Dulwich,) 2 ; (of Bolton Hall,) 5, 6, 7, 8 ; (of Hatfield Priory,) 5, 6, 7, 8 ; (of Sigglesthorne Hall,) 5, 6, 7, 8; (of Castle Park,) 7, 8 ; (of West Bank,) 7 ; (of Halston,) 7, 8 ; (of Hinton Blewitt,) 7 ; (of Brattleby Hall,) 8 ; (of Wootton Court,) 8 ; (of Highfield,) 8. Foster's Visitations of Yorkshire, 145. Harleian Society, ii. 152 ; viii. 457 ; xiii. 532 ; xiv. 751 ; xvi. 351 ; xvii. 371, 372 ; xviii. 257 ; xx. 101 ; xxxii. 323 ; xxxvii. 57, 226; xxxviii. 509 ; xlii. 127 ; xliii. 134, 150. Poulson's Holderness, ii. 516. Jewitt's Reliquary, xiii. 176. Surtees' Durham, iii. 41 ; iv. 153. Visitation of Staffordshire, 1663-4, printed by Sir T. Phillipps, 11. Visitation of Derbyshire, 1663-4, (Middle Hill, 1854, fol.) 7. Nichols' History of the County of Leicester, iv. 64. A List of Roman Catholics in the County of York in 1604, by Edward Peacock, 124. Antiquities and Memoirs of the Parish of Myddle, written by Richard Gough, 1700, (folio,) 61. Wright's Essex, ii. 422. Shirley's History of the County of Monaghan, 230. Surrey Archæological Collections, vi. The Genealogist, iii. 186 ; vi. 291. Carthew's Hundred of Launditch, Part ii. 500. Ormerod's Cheshire, ii. 711 ; iii. 695. Notes and Queries, 2 S. ix. 313, 355, 414 ; 8 S. vi. 233. Betham's Baronetage, iii. 399. Metcalfe's Visitations of Suffolk, 81, 177. Burke's Extinct Baronetcies. Metcalfe's Visitation of Worcester, 1683, 108. James Hall's

History of Nantwich, 492. Earwaker's East Cheshire, ii. 353. Foster's Visitations of Durham, 339. Genealogical Memoranda of the Family of Ames, 9. Harvey's Hundred of Willey, 460. Visitations of Staffordshire, 1614 and 1663-4, William Salt Society, 329. J. T. Godfrey's History of Lenton, 202. Cheshire Notes and Queries, New Series, i. 29. Foster's Visitation of Middlesex, 86. Bysshe's Visitation of Essex, edited by J. J. Howard, 106. New England Register, iv. 355 ; xx. 208 ; xxxv. 74 ; xxxvii. 76 ; xl. 280. Burke's Colonial Gentry, i. 308 ; ii. 593. Burke's Family Records, 645-648. Howard's Visitation of Ireland, iii. 9. *See* HARWICKE, WREIGHT.

WRIGHT-ARMSTRONG. Burke's Landed Gentry, 5.

WRIGHTE. Burke's Commoners, ii. 245. Lipscombe's History of the County of Buckingham, iv. 151. Nichols' History of the County of Leicester, iii. 219. Baker's Northampton, i. 132. Page's History of Suffolk, 389. Burke's Extinct Baronetcies.

WRIGHTINGTON. Chetham Society, xcix. 134.

WRIGHTSON. Memorials of the Family of Wrightson. By W. G. Wrightson, London, 1894, 8vo. Part i. Burke's Commoners, ii. 184, Landed Gentry, 2, 3, 4, 5, 6, 7, 8. Foster's Yorkshire Pedigrees. Hunter's Deanery of Doncaster, i. 350. The Genealogist, iii. 400. Burke's Family Records, 648.

WRIGLEY. Burke's Landed Gentry, 7.

WRINCH. Howard's Visitation of England and Wales, viii. 113.

WRIOTHESLEY. Banks' Dormant and Extinct Baronage, iii. 671.

WRITELL, or WRITTLE. Morant's Essex, i. 148, 188 ; ii. 156. Harleian Society, xiv. 621.

WRIXON. Burke's Colonial Gentry, i. 142.

WROTH, or WROTHE. Collinson's Somerset, iii. 67. Morant's Essex, i. 163, 165 ; ii. 519. Visitation of Somersetshire, printed by Sir T. Phillipps, 147. History of Hampstead, by J. J. Park, 115. Hoare's Wiltshire, III. iv. 44. Wright's Essex, ii. 62. Archæologia Cantiana, xii. 315. Harleian Society, xiii. 132, 330 ; xvii. 373, 374 ; xxii. 106. Notes and Queries, 7 S. xi. 55, 118 ; 8 S. i. 154 ; iii. 407 ; iv. 282, 394, 454. Metcalfe's Visitations of Suffolk, 210. Burke's Extinct Baronetcies. Hasted's Kent, (Hund. of Blackheath, by H. H. Drake,) xxv. Weaver's Visitations of Somerset, 92. Genealogies of Morgan and Glamorgan, by G. T. Clark, 473. Somersetshire Wills, printed for F. A. Crisp, ii. 86.

WROTTE, or WROTE. Metcalfe's Visitations of Suffolk, 211. Harleian Society, xvii. 372.

WROTTESLEY. Shaw's Staffordshire, ii. 205. Wotton's English Baronetage, ii. 345. Betham's Baronetage, i. 482. Visitation of Staffordshire, (Willm. Salt Soc.) 152. Harleian Society, xviii. 17. The Genealogist, New Series, viii. 155.[1] Visitations of Staffordshire, 1614 and 1663-4, William Salt Society, 330. The Gresley's of Drakelowe, by F. Madan, 299. J. P. Jones's History of Tettenhall, 236.

[1] A History of the family of Wrottesley of Wrottesley is being issued with the ' Genealogist.'

WROUGHTON. Burke's Landed Gentry, 2, 3, 4, 5, 6, 7, 8. Visitatio Comitatus Wiltoniæ, 1623, printed by Sir T. Phillipps. The Genealogist, New Series, xiii. 90.

WROWE-WALTON. Burke's Landed Gentry, 2.

WYAT, or WYATT. Genealogical Memoranda relating to Rd. Wyatt, by E. B. Jupp. Hasted's Kent, ii. 183. Bibliotheca Topographica Britannica, ix. Part iv. 722. Berry's Kent Genealogies, 295. Burke's Commoners, iv. 741, Landed Gentry, (of Court Wick,) 5, 6, 7, 8 ; (of Bryn Gwynant,) 5, 6. Surrey Archæological Collections, iii. 290. Miscellanea Genealogica et Heraldica, New Series, ii. 107. Harleian Society, xiii. 331, 534 ; xiv. 622 ; xxi. 186 ; xlii. 142. Castles, Mansions, and Manors of Western Sussex, by D. G. C. Elwes and C. J. Robinson, 89. Bysshe's Visitation of Essex, edited by J. J. Howard, 106. The Visitations of Devon, by J. L. Vivian, 823. See WIAT.

WYATT-EDGELL. Burke's Landed Gentry, 5, 6, 7, 8.

WYBBE. Harleian Society, xxvii. 9.

WYBBERY. Harleian Society, vi. 348. See WIBBERY.

WYBERD. Morant's Essex, ii. 572. Harleian Society, xvii. 375.

WYBERGH. Burke's Commoners, iii. 702, Landed Gentry, 2, 3, 4, 5, 6 supp. Foster's Visitations of Cumberland and Westmorland, 148. Nicolson and Burn's Westmorland and Cumberland, i. 418.

WYCHE. Cheshire and Lancashire Historical Society, Session i. 12. Hoare's Wiltshire, V. ii. 29. Visits to the Fields of Battle in England, by Richd. Brooke, 245. Wotton's English Baronetage, iv. 222. Earwaker's East Cheshire, ii. 623. Burke's Extinct Baronetcies. See WICH.

WYCHEHALSE, or WYCHALSE. Harleian Society, ix. 292. Visitation of Devon, edited by F. T. Colby, 214. See WICHALSE.

WYCHERLEY. Harleian Society, xxix. 511. Transactions of the Shropshire Archæological Society, N.S., ii. 356.

WYCKER. Berry's Surrey Genealogies, 15.

WYCLIFFE, or WYCLYFF. Visitation of Durham, 1615, (Sunderland, 1820, fol.) 50. Surtees Society, xxxvi. 195 ; xli. 40. Foster's Visitations of Yorkshire, 377. Whitaker's History of Richmond-shire, i. 200. Poulson's Holderness, ii. 239. Surtees' Durham, i. 194 ; iv. 46. Plantagenet-Harrison's History of Yorkshire, i. 157, 424. Harleian Society, xvi. 352 ; xvii. 376. Foster's Visitations of Durham, 340.

WYCOMBE. Harleian Society, xxix. 513.

WYDDEL-OSBORN. Archæologia Cambrensis, 3 S. ix. 38.

WYDELOCK. The Genealogist, New Series, xii. 173.

WYDNELL. Surrey Archæological Collections, v.

WYDVILLE. Bridges' Northamptonshire, by Rev. Peter Whalley, i. 300. Hasted's Kent, (Hund. of Blackheath, by H. H. Drake,) 218. See WIDEVILLE.

WYE. Harleian Society, xxi. 187.

WYER. New England Register, xxv. 246.

WYGLAND. Ormerod's Cheshire, ii. 663.

WYKE. Collinson's Somerset, iii. 267, 617. Visitation of Somersetshire, printed by Sir T. Phillipps, 146. Manning and Bray's Surrey, iii. 93. Blunt's Dursley and its Neighbourhood, 7. Harleian Society, xiii. 535. Weaver's Visitations of Somerset, 94. Weaver's Visitation of Herefordshire, 78. *See* WIKES, WYKES.

WYKEHAM, Herald and Genealogist, v. 225. Lowth's Life of Wm. of Wykeham, folding at end. Topographer and Genealogist, iii. 49, 73. Burke's Landed Gentry, i. 419, Landed Gentry, 2, 3, 4, 5, 6, 7, 8. History of the Colleges and Halls of Oxford, by Anthony à Wood, edited by John Gutch, 172. Lipscombe's History of the County of Buckingham, i. 298. F. G. Lee's History of Thame, 438. *See* WICKHAM.

WYKEHAM-MARTIN. Burke's Commoners, i. 422, Landed Gentry, 2, 3, 4, 5, 7, 8. Baker's Northampton, i. 590.

WYKES. Harleian Society, vi. 319; xi. 120. Westcote's Devonshire, edited by G. Oliver and P. Jones, 557, 558. The Genealogist, i. 192, 222. Peck's Desiderata Curiosa, i. 79. The Visitations of Devon, by J. L. Vivian, 825, 827. *See* WIKES, WYKE.

WYKYS. The Antiquary, edited by E. Walford, ii. 165.

WYLBY. Harleian Society, xxxii. 94.

WYLD, or WYLDE. Morant's Essex, i. 383. Nash's Worcestershire, ii. 331. Burke's Landed Gentry, 2 supp., 3, 4, 5. Foster's Visitations of Yorkshire, 593. Shaw's Staffordshire, ii. 107*. G. W. Johnson's History of Great Totham, 30. Metcalfe's Visitations of Worcester, 1683, 102. Harleian Society, xvii. 376; xix. 152; xxvii. 151; xxxvii. 73, 401; xliii. 15. History of Powys Fadog, by J. Y. W. Lloyd, iii. 91. *See* WILD.

WYLDMAN. Harleian Society, viii. 439. *See* WILDMAN.

WYLIE. Alexander Nisbet's Heraldic Plates, 66.

WYLLEY. The Genealogist, ii. 251.

WYLLOUGHBY. Surtees Society, xli. 4. *See* WILLOUGHBY.

WYLME. Ormerod's Cheshire, i. 587.

WYLMER. Harleian Society, xii. 135.

WYLSHERE. Cussan's History of Hertfordshire, Parts xi. and xii. 212. *See* WILLSHER, WILSHERE.

WYLYNGTON. Maclean's History of Trigg Minor, i. 384. *See* WILLINGTON.

WYMAN. New England Register, iii. 33.

WYMARKE. Harleian Society, iii. 46; xvii. 378.

WYMBERLEY. The Genealogist, iv. 6. 109. Ancient Families of Lincolnshire, in 'Spalding Free Press,' 1873-5, No. ii.

WYMBISHE. A List of Roman Catholics in the County of York, by Edward Peacock, 44. The Genealogist, v. 57.

WYMELDON. Manning and Bray's Surrey, ii. 651.

WYMOND. The Visitations of Cornwall, edited by J. L. Vivian, 297.

WYMONDESWOLD. Harleian Society, iv. 114. *See* WIMONDEFOLD.

WYMONDSELL. Harleian Society, viii. 280.

WYNARD. History of Clyst St. George, by Rev. H. T. Ellacombe, 67.

WYNDESOR, or WYNDSOR. Duchetiana, by Sir G. F. Duckett, Bart.,

2nd edition, (1876, 4to.) 249. Dallaway's Sussex, i. 191. *See* WINDSOR.

WYNDHAM. Claim of the Rt. Hon. E. R. Wyndham, Earl of Dunraven, to Vote at Elections of Peers, Sess. Papers, 107 of 1851. Collinson's Somerset, ii. 234 ; iii. 490. Blomefield's Norfolk, viii. 113. Berry's Hertfordshire Genealogies, 54. Burke's Royal Families, (London, 1851, 8vo.) i. 161. Burke's Commoners, (of Dinton,) i. 160, Landed Gentry, 2, 3, 4, 5, 6, 7, 8 ; (of Cromer,) Commoners, ii. 244 ; (of Sarum,) Landed Gentry, 2 supp., 3, 4, 5, 6, 7. A Royal Descent, by T. E. Sharpe, (London, 1875, 4to.) 9. Gyll's History of Wraysbury, 102. Lipscombe's History of the County of Buckingham, iv. 598. Jefferson's History of Allerdale Ward, Cumberland, 46. Hutchins' Dorset, iv. 48 ; 2nd edition, iii. 330. Hoare's Wiltshire, IV. i. 108 ; ii. 93 ; V. iii. 67. Memorials of the Church of Attleborough, by J. T. Barrett, 193. The Boscobel Tracts, edited by J. Hughes, 2nd edn., 386. Notes and Queries, 3. S. ii. 348, 395, 454 ; iii. 16, 137, 258. Burke's Extinct Baronetcies. Edmondson's Baronagium Genealogicum iii. 273. Brydges' Collins' Peerage, iv. 401. Wotton's English Baronetage, iii. 346. Somersetshire Wills, printed for F. A. Crisp, ii. 43. Genealogies of Morgan and Glamorgan, by G. T. Clark, 474. Memorials of Adare Manor, by Caroline, Countess of Dunraven, 19, 21. Burke's Colonial Gentry, i. 302. Harleian Society, xxxii. 323. Healey's History of Part of West Somerset, 219. *See* WINDHAM.

WYNDOUT. Berry's Hertfordshire Genealogies, 225. Harleian Society, xxii. 106.

WYNDOWE. Burke's Royal Families, (London, 1851, 8vo.) ii. 213. Burke's Landed Gentry, 2 supp.

WYNELL. An Historical Survey of Cornwall, by C. S. Gilbert, ii. 198. Burke's Landed Gentry, 7 at p. 1253.

WYNEVE. Harleian Society, viii. 167. Metcalfe's Visitations of Suffolk, 211.

WYNINGTON. *See* WINNINGTON.

WYNN. Dwnn's Visitations of Wales, i. 293, 321 ; ii. 73, 158-160, 173, 179, 180, 207, 208, 225, 228, 230, 231, 248, 273, 280, 289, 297, 304, 319, 321, 322, 329, 341-343, 345-347, 349, 354, 355. Burke's Landed Gentry, (of Rûgin Edeirnion,) 4; (of Llangedwin,) 2. Archæologia Cambrensis, 4 S., ii. 241, 333 ; vi. 226, 235 ; viii. 26 ; ix. 164. Memoir of Gabriel Goodman, by R. Newcome, app. S. The Sheriffs of Montgomeryshire, by W. V. Lloyd, 3. Collections by the Powys-land Club, vii. 105 ; viii. 96, 401, 419 Harleian Society, xvii. 379 ; xxix. 515. History of Powys Fadog, by J. Y. W. Lloyd, iii. 16, 19, 20, 226, 358, 403 ; iv. 53-58, 243-249, 267, 276, 353, 357, 366, 384 ; v. 91, 112, 116, 145, 230, 236, 244, 280, 317, 320, 322, 365, 391 ; vi. 21, 32, 42, 76, 87, 143, 148-163, 191, 221, 230, 237, 262, 379, 438. Cambrian Journal, vol. for 1860, 247. *See* WINN.

WYNNE. Notes and Queries, 4 S. v. 284. Dwnn's Visitations of Wales, i. 328. Burke's Royal Families, (London, 1851, 8vo.) ii.

34. Burke's Commoners, (of Peniarth,) i. 566, Landed Gentry, 2, 3, 4, 5, 6, 7, 8 ; (of Garthewin,) Commoners, iii. 646, Landed Gentry, 2, 3, 4, 5, 6, 7, 8 at p. 2303 ; (of Voelas,) Landed Gentry, 2 supp., 3, 4, 5, 6, 7 ; (of Llwyn,) 2, 3, 6 at p. 573 ; (of Hasle-wood,) 2, 3, 4, 5, 6, 7, 8 ; (of Coed Coch,) 2 and p. 1021, *note*, 3, 4, 5, 6, 7, 7 at p. 2069, 8 ; (of Rosbriea,) 8. Miscellanea Genea-logica et Heraldica, New Series, i. 265 ; iii. 1. Cambrian Journal, 1 Series, ii. 188. Archæologia Cambrensis, 3 S., vi. 114. T. Nicholas' County Families of Wales, 712. Harleian Society, viii. 166. Collections by the Powys-land Club, viii. 82 ; x. 352, 356. Archdall's Lodge's Peerage, vii. 101. Wotton's English Baronetage, iii. 184 ; iv. 231. Betham's Baronetage, ii. 172. Burke's Extinct Baronetcies. The Gresley's of Drakelowe, by F. Madan, 300. *See* GWYDIR.

WYNNE-FINCH. Burke's Landed Gentry, 8.

WYNNIAT. Pedigree of Wynniat of Dymock, etc., [T. P.] folio page. Descent of Wynniatt of Stanton, etc., [T. P.] folio page. Burke's Landed Gentry, 2, 3, 4, 5, 6, 7, 8.

WYNTER. Pedigree of Wynter of Aldborough, Co. Suffolk, [T. P.] folio page. Rudder's Gloucestershire, 428. Burke's Heraldic Illustrations, 33. Jones' History of the County of Brecknock, ii. 135-137. Maclean's History of Trigg Minor, iii. 260. Harleian Society, xxxii. 325.

WYNYARD. Berry's Hampshire Genealogies, 205. Miscellanea Genea-logica et Heraldica, New Series, ii. 270.

WYOT. Hutchins' Dorset, i. 616.

WYRCESTER. Dallaway's Antiquities of Bristow, 18.

WYRDNAM. Ashmole's Antiquities of Berkshire, iii. 291. *See* WIRDNAM.

WYRLEY. Shaw's Staffordshire, ii. 110, 115. Bridges' Northampton-shire, by Rev. Peter Whalley, i. 52. History of the Town and School of Rugby, by N. H. Nicolas, 35. Baker's Northampton, i. 355. Visitation of Staffordshire, (Willm. Salt Soc.) 153. Har-leian Society, xvii. 379. Visitations of Staffordshire, 1614 and 1663-4, William Salt Society, 333. Metcalfe's Visitation of Northamptonshire, 57, 160, 205. *See* WIRLEY.

WYRRAL, or WYRALL. Rudder's Gloucestershire, 288. Burke's Visi-tation of Seats and Arms, 2nd Series, i. 17. Foster's Visitations of Yorkshire, 349. Hunter's Deanery of Doncaster, i. 62. Trans-actions of the Bristol and Gloucestershire Archæological Society for 1876, 68. Harleian Society, xxi. 189 ; xxix. 516.

WYRRIOTT. *See* WOGAN.

WYSE. Burke's Landed Gentry, 3, 4, 5, 6, 7, 8. Visitation of Gloucester, edited by T. F. Fenwick and W. C. Metcalfe, 209. Harleian Society, xli. 62.

WYSEMAN. Berry's Sussex Genealogies, 107. Berry's Berkshire Genealogies, 129. Dallaway's Sussex, i. 113. *See* WISEMAN.

WYSHAM. Weaver's Visitation of Herefordshire, 79.

WYSKARD. Visitation of Norfolk, published by Norfolk Archæological Society, i. 271. Carthew's Hundred of Launditch, Part iii. 238. Harleian Society, xxxii. 326.

WYTHAM. Surtees Society, xxxvi. 109, 374. Harleian Society, xvi. 355 ; xvii. 380. Burke's Extinct Baronetcies. *See* WITHAM.
WYTHE. Banks' Baronies in Fee, ii. 158.
WYTHEFORD. Transactions of Shropshire Archæological Society, 3 S., ii. 272.
WYTHENS. Hasted's Kent, (Hund. of Blackheath, by H. H. Drake,) 195.
WYTHERNWYKE. The Genealogist, v. 59 ; vi. 292.
WYTHES. Burke's Landed Gentry, 6, 7, 8.
WYTHINS. Hasted's Kent, i. 60. Harleian Society, viii. 338.
WYTHIPOOL. Metcalfe's Visitations of Suffolk, 82, 178.
WYTTLEBURY. Harleian Society, xii. 121.
WYVELL, WYVILE, WYVILL, or WYVILLE. Surtees Society, xxxvi. 37, 89, 329. Surrey Archæological Collections, ii. Harleian Society, ix. 269 ; xvi. 356 ; xliii. 113. Nichols' History of the County of Leicester, ii. 807. Whitaker's History of Richmondshire, i. 322. J. H. Hill's History of Langton, 186. Burke's Royal Families, (London, 1851, 8vo.) ii. 99. Bibliotheca Topographica Britannica, iii. Part ii. 265. Burke's Commoners, iv. 467, Landed Gentry, 2, 3, 4, 5, 6, and at p. 1088, 7, 8, and at p. 1369. Foster's Yorkshire Pedigrees. Foster's Visitations of Yorkshire, 189, 380. Surtees' Durham, iii. 263. Wotton's English Baronetage, i. 232. Visitation of Devon, edited by F. T. Colby, 214. Burke's Extinct Baronetcies. The Visitations of Cornwall, by J. L. Vivian, 567. Foster's Visitations of Cumberland and Westmorland, 149. The Visitations of Devon, by J. L. Vivian, 828. *See* WIVELL.

XIMENES. Burke's Landed Gentry, 7, 8.

YALDWYN, or YALWIN. Burke's Landed Gentry, 2 supp., 3, 4, 5. Dallaway's Sussex, II. i. 326. Castles, Mansions, and Manors of Western Sussex, by D. G. C. Elwes and C. J. Robinson, 142. Berry's Sussex Genealogies, 195.
YALE. Dwnn's Visitations of Wales, ii. 352. Burke's Landed Gentry, 2, 3, 4, 5, 6, 7 8. History of Powys Fadog, by J. Y. W. Lloyd, v. 137-144.
YALLOP. Harleian Society, viii. 183.
YARBOROUGH, YARBROUGH, or YARBURGH. Surtees Society, xxxvi. 169, 186, 260. Burke's Royal Families, (London, 1851, 8vo.) i. 110. Foster's Yorkshire Pedigrees. Burke's Commoners, (of Heslington,) iii. 661, Landed Gentry, 2, 3, 4, 5, 6, 7 ; (of Campsmount,) Landed Gentry, 2, 3, 4, 5, 6, 7, 8. Harleian Society, viii. 166. Hunter's Deanery of Doncaster, ii, 466. History of the Priory and Peculiar of Snaith, by C. B. Robinson, (1861, 8vo.) 55-81. The Genealogist, v. 59 ; vi. 293.
YARD, or YARDE. Tuckett's Devonshire Pedigrees, 65. Westcote's Devonshire, edited by G. Oliver and P. Jones, 601. Burke's Landed Gentry, 4. Harleian Society, ii. 91 ; vi. 319. Nichols' History of the County of Leicester, iv. 145. Visitation of Devon,

edited by F. T. Colby, 215. The Visitations of Devon, by J. L. Vivian, 829.

YARDLEY. Visitation of Warwickshire, 1619, published with Warwickshire Antiquarian Magazine, 153. Harleian Society, xii. 110. Visitation of Staffordshire, (Willm. Salt Soc.) 154. Notes and Queries, 6 S. vii. 212. Miscellanea Genealogica et Heraldica, 2nd Series, iv. 232.

YARKER. The Genealogy of the Surname of Yarker, by John Yarker. Manchester, 1882, 4to. Burke's Landed Gentry, 2, 3, 4, 5 and add. The Yorkshire Genealogist, i. 105. Burke's Family Records, 651.

YARMER. Notes and Queries, 7 S. iv. 75.

YATE. Pedigree of Yate of Weston Subedge, [T. P.] on fol. page. Rudder's Gloucestershire, 233. Ashmole's Antiquities of Berkshire, iii. 295, 321. Sir T. Phillipps' Topographer, No. 1, (March, 1821, 8vo.) 34, 38. Visitation of Oxfordshire, 1574, printed by Sir T. Phillipps, (Middle Hill, fol.) 11. Visitation of Oxfordshire, 1634, printed by Sir T. Phillipps, (Middle Hill, fol.) 33. Topographer and Genealogist, i. 422. Burke's Commoners, iv. 395, Landed Gentry, 2. Harleian Society, v. 158, 163, 219, 257; xii. 363; xvii. 381; xxi. 191; xxxix. 1167. Visitation of Warwickshire, 1619, published with Warwickshire Antiquarian Magazine, 142. Fosbrooke's History of Gloucestershire, i. 438, 439; ii. 209, 251. Bigland's Gloucestershire, ii. par. Willersley. Burke's Extinct Baronetcies. The Genealogist, vi. 115; New Series, ii. 111; xiii. 90. Visitation of Gloucester, edited by T. F. Fenwick and W. C. Metcalfe, 209. Transactions of Shropshire Archæological Society, ix. 32; 3 S., ii. 271.

YATES. Burke's Landed Gentry, 3, 4, 7, 8. Abram's History of Blackburn, 408, 763. The Boscobel Tracts, edited by J. Hughes, 2nd edn., 376. Collections for a History of Staffordshire, (William Salt Society,) ii. part 2, 116. Harleian Society, xvii. 380; xxxviii. 740. Ilkley, Ancient and Modern, by R. Collyer and J. H. Turner, 240. Croston's edn. of Baines's Lancaster, iii. 151. Transactions of Shropshire Archæological Society, ix. 11.

YAXLEY. Page's History of Suffolk, 467, 506. Metcalfe's Visitations of Suffolk, 82. Harleian Society, xxxii. 327.

YEA. History of the Family of Yea, by A. J. Monday. Taunton, 1885, 4to. Collinson's Somerset, iii. 290. Burke's Royal Families, (London, 1851, 8vo.) ii. 210. Betham's Baronetage, iii. 277.

YEALLATON. Harleian Society, vi. 321. The Visitations of Devon, by J. L. Vivian, 833.

YEAMANS. Wotton's English Baronetage, iii. 452. Burke's Extinct Baronetcies.

YEATMAN. Burke's Landed Gentry, 2, 3, 4, 5, 6, 7, 8. Hutchins' Dorset, iii. 688. The Visitations of Cornwall, edited by J. L. Vivian, 188.

YELAND. Surtees' Durham, i. 273.

YELDENTRE. Nichols' History of the County of Leicester, iv. 935. Dugdale's Warwickshire, 893.

YELVERTON. Blomefield's Norfolk, x. 30. Visitation of Norfolk, published by Norfolk Archæological Society, i. 265. Bridges' Northamptonshire, by Rev. Peter Whalley, ii. 164. Carthew's Hundred of Launditch, Part ii. 497. Edmondson's Baronagium Genealogicum, iii. 213. Brydges' Collins' Peerage, vi. 620. Banks' Baronies in Fee, i. 234. Banks' Dormant and Extinct Baronage, ii. 242. Burke's Extinct Baronetcies. Harleian Society, xxxii. 327.

YEO. Tuckett's Devonshire Pedigrees, 103, 105. Burke's Landed Gentry, 5, 6, 7, 8. Harleian Society, vi. 322-325; ix. 292. Westcote's Devonshire, edited by G. Oliver and P. Jones, 592, 593. Foster's Account of Families Descended from Francis Fox, 25. An Historical Survey of Cornwall, by C. S. Gilbert, ii. 335. Miscellanea Genealogica et Heraldica, New Series, iii. 364. Visitation of Devon, edited by F. T. Colby, 217. The Visitations of Devon, by J. L. Vivian, 834-839.

YEOMAN. Burke's Landed Gentry, 5, 6, 7, 8. Harleian Society, xvii. 381.

YERBURGH. Harleian Society, iv. 105. Burke's Landed Gentry, 8.

YERBURY, or YERBERIE. Visitatio Comitatus Wiltoniæ, 1623, printed by Sir T. Phillipps. Wiltshire Archæological Magazine, v. 369, 357. Visitation of Wiltshire, edited by G. W. Marshall, 83.

YERMOUTH. Metcalfe's Visitations of Suffolk, 107.

YERWORTH. Westcote's Devonshire, edited by G. Oliver and P. Jones, 524. Visitatio Comitatus Wiltoniæ, 1623, printed by Sir T. Phillipps. Visitation of Devon, edited by T. F. Colby, 218. The Genealogist, New Series, xiii. 91.

YNGOE. Proceedings of the Essex Archæological Society, iii. 100. See INGOW.

YONG, or YONGE. Berry's Hampshire Genealogies, 318. The Visitation of Surrey, made A°. 1623, edited by J. J. Howard, LL.D. (25 copies printed for private circulation,) at end.[1] Collinson's Somerset, iii. 149. Camden Society, xli. viii. Observations on the Snowdon Mountains, etc., by John Thomas, A.M. London, 1802, 8vo. Berry's Sussex Genealogies, 269. Tuckett's Devonshire Pedigrees, 31, 53. Burke's Landed Gentry, (of Puslinch,) 2 and supp., 3, 4, 5, 6, 7, 8; (of Charnes Hall,) 2, 3, 4, 5, 6, 7, 8; (of Otterbourn,) 2; 2 add. Harleian Society, vi. 325; xiii. 332, 536; xvii. 382, 384; xx. 101; xxvii. 152; xxix. 425, 517. Wotton's English Baronetage, ii. 334. Betham's Baronetage, ii. 292. Burke's Extinct Baronetcies. History of Powis Fadog, by J. Y. W. Lloyd, iii. 376; v. 257. Genealogical Records of the Family of Woodd, 35. The Visitations of Devon, by J. L. Vivian, 840, 842. See YOUNG.

YONGLING. Visitation of Devon, edited by F. T. Colby, 99. The Visitations of Devon, by J. L. Vivian, 349.

YORK, or YORKE. Collectanea Topographica et Genealogica, i. 297. Burke's Commoners, i. 664, Landed Gentry, 2, 3, 4, 5, 6. Foster's

[1] All the other pedigrees in this book will be found in the 'Surrey Archæological Collections.'

Visitations of Yorkshire, 382. Harleian Society, ix. 269. Gregson's Fragments relative to the County of Lancaster, 46. Pedigree of Yorke, of Hildrop and Hannington, Co. Wilts, by Sir T. Phillipps, Bart. London, 1830. Surtees Society, xxxvi. 92. Burke's Royal Families, (London, 1851, 8vo.) i. 102. Burke's Commoners, (of Bewerley,), iv. 744, Landed Gentry, 2, 3, 4, 5, 6, 7, 8 ; (of Hutton Hall,) 7 ; (of Erddig,) Commoners, i. 344, Landed Gentry, 2, 3, 4, 5, 6, 7, 8 ; (of Dyffryn Aled,) Landed Gentry, 2, 3, 4, 5, 6, 7 ; (of Forthampton,) 2, 3, 4, 5, 6, 7, 8. Foster's Yorkshire Pedigrees. Harleian Society, i. 81 ; viii. 74 ; ix. 269 ; xvi. 357 ; xxix. 520. History of Richmond, by C. Clarkson, 332. Burke's Heraldic Illustrations, 70. Whitaker's Deanery of Craven, 376, (156). Visitatio Comitatus Wiltoniæ, 1623, printed by Sir T. Phillipps. Clutterbuck's Hertford, i. 211. Fosbrooke's History of Gloucestershire, i. 298. Burke's Extinct Baronetcies, 616. Edmondson's Baronagium Genealogicum, iii. 291. Brydges' Collins' Peerage, iv. 486. Banks' Dormant and Extinct Baronage, iii. 768. Visitation of Wiltshire, edited by G. W. Marshall, 26. History of Powys Fadog, by J. Y. W. Lloyd, v. 319. Metcalfe's Visitations of Northamptonshire, 206. The Visitations of Cornwall, by J. L. Vivian, 568.

YOUDE. History of Llangurig, by E. Hamer and H. W. Lloyd, 60.

YOUL. Burke's Colonial Gentry, i. 178 ; ii. 789.

YOUNG. A short Memoir of James Young, Merchant Burgess of Aberdeen, and Rachel Cruickshank, his spouse, etc., brought down to the year 1860. [By Alexr. Johnston, Aberdeen.] 1860, 4to. Dwnn's Visitations of Wales, ii. 314. W. Paver's Pedigrees of Families of the City of York, 22. Burke's Landed Gentry, (of Kingerby,) 2 supp., 3, 4, 5, 6, 7, 8 ; (of Orlingbury,) 2, 3, 4, 5, 6, 7, 8 ; (of Cleish,) 2, 3, 4, 5, 6, 7, 8 ; (of Coolkeiragh,) 2, 3, 4, 5, 6, 7, 8 ; (of Brockley Park,) 8 ; (of Galgorm,) 8 ; (of Culdaff House,) 3, 4, 5, 6, 7, 8 ; (of Harristown,) 3 supp., 4, 5, 6, 7, 8. Foster's Visitations of Yorkshire, 327, 593. Harleian Society, i. 70 ; xvi. 364 ; xxxviii. 613 ; xliii. 174. Dallaway's Sussex, i. 280. Westcote's Devonshire, edited by G. Oliver and P. Jones, 600. Pembrokeshire Pedigrees, 128, 163. Visitatio Comitatus Wiltoniæ, 1623, printed by Sir T. Phillipps. Hoare's Wiltshire, II. ii. 125. Surtees' Durham, i. 22. Foley's Records of the English Province S. J., i. 629. Page's History of Suffolk, 707. Paterson's History of Ayr and Wigton, ii. 254. The Parish of Cramond, by J. P. Wood, 70. Walter Wood's East Neuk of Fife, 281. Betham's Baronetage, iii. 371. Burke's Extinct Baronetcies. Metcalfe's Visitation of Worcester, 1683, 109. Visitations of Staffordshire, 1614 and 1663-4, William Salt Society, 336. Bysshe's Visitation of Essex, edited by J. J. Howard, 107. Foster's Visitations of Northumberland, 128. Some Old Families, by H. B. McCall, 263. Alexander Nisbet's Heraldic Plates, 90. Burke's Colonial Gentry, ii. 568. Howard's Visitation of England and Wales, iii. 10. Dallaway's Antiquities of Bristow, 168. *See* YONG.

YOUNGE. Dwnn's Visitations of Wales, i. 162. Harleian Society, vi. 325 ; xvii. 383, 384 ; xxxviii. 713. Hutchins' Dorset, iv. 116. Visitation of Wiltshire, edited by G. W. Marshall, 5.

YOUNGER. Burke's Landed Gentry, 6 supp., 7, 8. Northern Notes and Queries, iii. 6, 35, 134 ; x. 108.

YOUNGHUSBAND. The Genealogist, ii. 7, 53. Bateson's History of Northumberland, i. 188, 414.

YOUNGMAN. New England Register, xxxiv. 401 ; xxxv. 45.

YOWARD. Surtees Society, xxxvi. 327. Foster's Visitations of Yorkshire, 192. Graves' History of Cleveland, 269. Ord's History of Cleveland, 346.

YR HENDWR. Archæologia Cambrensis, 4 S., ix. 277.

YRTON. Surtees Society, xli. 93. See IRTON.

YUILLE. Burke's Landed Gentry, 3, 4, 5, 6, 7, 8.

YVERY. An Epitome of the Genealogical History of the House of Yvery. 8vo. (no title, pp. 36). Edmondson's Baronagium Genealogicum, v. 483. See IVERY, ST. WALERY.

ZACHARY. Nash's Worcestershire, i. 37.

ZEAL. Burke's Colonial Gentry, i. 317.

ZINZAN. Notes and Queries, 5 S., ii. 27. The Genealogist, vi. 116.

ZOUCH, or ZOUCHE. Collinson's Somerset, ii. 55. Kennet's Parochial Antiquities, ii. 463-473. Gentleman's Magazine, lxii. 428 ; lxxxii. i. 212, 619 ; lxvii. 7, 207, 294 ; lxviii. 927 ; lxix. 118, 1013, 1104 ; lxxi. 402, 698 ; lxxviii. 380, 505 ; lxxix. 399. Glover's History of Derbyshire, ii. 342, (308). Berry's Berkshire Genealogies, 34. Lipscombe's History of the County of Buckingham, i. 176. Dallaway's Sussex, II. i. 203. Bridges' Northamptonshire, by Rev. Peter Whalley, ii. 318. Westcote's Devonshire, edited by G. Oliver and P. Jones, 475. Burton's Description of Leicestershire, 18. Nichols' History of the County of Leicester, ii. 372 ; iii. 635, 1146 ; iv. 38, 780, 968. Dugdale's Warwickshire, 58. Visitatio Comitatus Wiltoniæ, 1623, printed by Sir T. Phillipps. Hoare's Wiltshire, V. i. 207. Manning and Bray's Surrey, i. 125. Baker's Northampton, i. 563. Thoroton's Nottinghamshire, ii. 183. Plantagenet-Harrison's History of Yorkshire, i. 7. Banks' Baronies in Fee, i. 229, 469. Banks' Dormant and Extinct Baronage, ii. 616. Visitation of Wiltshire, edited by G. W. Marshall, 50. Notes and Queries, 5 S., iv. 488 ; v. 526. The Genealogist, New Series, viii. 179 ; xiii. 173, 242. Harvey's Hundred of Willey, 146. Harleian Society, xxxviii. 783. See DE LA ZOUCH, LA ZOUCH, SOUCH.

ZULESTEIN. Page's History of Suffolk, 98. Brydges' Collins' Peerage, iii. 721.

ADDENDA.

The following references came to hand during the progress of this work through the press too late for insertion in their proper places.

BAILDON. Registers of Kirkburton, by F. A. Collins, ii. app. cxxxv.
BAILEY. Registers of Kirkburton, by F. A. Collins, ii. app. cxxxviii.
BALDWYN. Transactions of Shropshire Archæological Society, ix. 302.
BARBER. Registers of Kirkburton, by F. A. Collins, ii. app. cxliv.
BARDEN. Registers of Kirkburton, by F. A. Collins, ii. app. cxlvii.
BARKER. Transactions of Shropshire Archæological Society, ii. 293 ; ix. 70.
BARNFIELD. Transactions of Shropshire Archæological Society, ix. 133.
BARRACLOUGH. Registers of Kirkburton, by F. A. Collins, ii. app. cl.
BARROW. Registers of Kirkburton, by F. A. Collins, ii. app. clviii.
BARTLETT. Pedigree of Bartlett of St. Mary Church, Devon. London, 1891, 8vo., 2nd edition.
BATES. Registers of Kirkburton, by F. A. Collins, ii. app. clx.
BATHER. Transactions of Shropshire Archæological Society, 2 S. viii. 123.
BATLEY. Registers of Kirkburton, by F. A. Collins, ii. app. clxiii.
BATTYE. Registers of Kirkburton, by F. A. Collins, ii. app. clxv. cxcii. The Ancestor, No. 1, 264.
BAYLLIE. Transactions of Shropshire Archæological Society, 2 S. ix. 212.
BEAUMONT. Registers of Kirkburton, by F. A. Collins, ii. app. cxcii.-ccxvii.
BEDFORD. Registers of Kirkburton, by F. A. Collins, ii. app. ccxvii.
BEE. Diary of Jacob Bee, 5.
BEEBEE. Howard's Visitation of England and Wales, ix. 49.
BEELEY. Registers of Kirkburton, by F. A. Collins, ii. app. ccxxv.
BELMEIS. Transactions of Shropshire Archæological Society, vi. 91.
BENBOW. Transactions of Shropshire Archæological Society, ix. 63.
BENNETT. Registers of Kirkburton, by F. A. Collins, ii. app. ccxxviii.
BENTHALL. Transactions of Shropshire Archæological Society, xi. 63-69.
BENTINCK. Thomas Smith's Historical Account of St. Mary le bone, 16.
BERDSELL. Registers of Kirkburton, by F. A. Collins, ii. app. ccxxxi.
BERKELEY. Thomas Smith's Historical Account of St. Mary le bone, 41.
BERRY. Registers of Kirkburton, by F. A. Collins, ii. app. ccxxxix.
BEVER. Registers of Kirkburton, by F. A. Collins, ii. app. ccliii.-cclxxvii.
BEWLEY. The Bewleys of Cumberland, their Irish and other descendants. By Sir Edmund T. Bewley. Dublin, 1902, 4to.
BICEDON. Transactions of Shropshire Archæological Society, 3 S. i. 309.
BICKERTON. Transactions of Shropshire Archæological Society, v. 287.
BILCLIFFE. Registers of Kirkburton, by F. A. Collins, ii. app. cclxxvii.

BINGLEY. Registers of Kirkburton, by F. A. Collins, ii. app. cclxxxiii.
BINNS. Registers of Kirkburton, by F. A. Collins, ii. app. cclxxxvi.
BLACKBURN. Registers of Kirkburton, by F. A. Collins, ii. app. ccxciv.
BLACKER. Registers of Kirkburton, by F. A. Collins, ii. app. ccxcix.
BLACKFORD. Healey's History of Part of West Somerset, 317.
BLATHWAYT. Healey's History of Part of West Somerset, 292.
BLOXHAM. Bloxham Pedigree. Oxford, *n.d.*, 4to.
BLYKE. Transactions of Shropshire Archæological Society, 2 S. v. 77.
BOLLAND. Registers of Kirkburton, by F. A. Collins, ii. app. cccii.
BOLLES. Transactions of the Thoroton Society, 1901, 16, *at end.*
BONEL. Transactions of Shropshire Archæological Society, 3 S. i. 294, 302.
BONNOR. Transactions of Shropshire Archæological Society, v. 330.
BONVILE. Healey's History of Part of West Somerset, 258.
BOOTH. Registers of Kirkburton, by F. A. Collins, ii. app. ccciv.-cccxxxi.
BOOTHROYD. Registers of Kirkburton, by F. A. Collins, ii. app. cccxxxi.
BORREY. Transactions of Shropshire Archæological Society, 3 S. i. 159.
BOTTOMLEY. Registers of Kirkburton, by F. A. Collins, ii. app. cccxxxiv.
BOWER. Registers of Kirkburton, by F. A. Collins, ii. app. cccxlii.
BOYLE. Transactions of Shropshire Archæological Society, ix. 75.
BRAMHALL. Registers of Kirkburton, by F. A. Collins, ii. app. cccxlix.
BRATTON. Healey's History of Part of West Somerset, 331.
BRAY. Registers of Kirkburton, by F. A. Collins, ii. app. cccliv.-ccclxxix.
BREARLEY. Registers of Kirkburton, by F. A. Collins, ii. app. ccclxxix.
BRIDGEMAN. Transactions of Shropshire Archæological Society, ix. 65; 3 S. ii. 1.
BRIGGS. Transactions of Shropshire Archæological Society, 2 S. v. 216. Registers of Kirkburton, by F. A. Collins, ii. app. ccclxxx.
BROADBENT. Registers of Kirkburton, by F. A. Collins, ii. app. ccclxxxii.
BROADHEAD. Registers of Kirkburton, by F. A. Collins, ii. app. ccclxxxv.-cccxcvii.
BROGYNTYN, descendants of OWEN. Transactions of Shropshire Archæological Society, 2 S. iii. 290; iv. 236; vii. 134, 173.
BROOKE. Registers of Kirkburton, by F. A. Collins, ii. app. cccxcvii. Platt and Morkill's Records of Whitkirk, 84.
BROUGHTON. Transactions of Shropshire Archæological Society, 2 S. ix. 65.
BROWNE. Transactions of Shropshire Archæological Society, v. 284.

BURNELL. Transactions of Shropshire Archæological Society, xi. 74.
BURTON. Transactions of Shropshire Archæological Society, ix. 17 ;
2 S. vi. 386.
BYAM. Healey's History of Part of West Somerset, 170.

CANTILUPE. Transactions of Shropshire Archæological Society, 2 S.
viii. 102 ; 3 S. i. 175.
CAREW. Transactions of Shropshire Archæological Society, 2 S.
v. 25.
CARR. History of the Family of Carr. By Colonel R. E. Carr.
London, 1893, fol., 3 vols.
CARTER. Platt and Morkill's Records of Whitkirk, 92.
CASSEY. Transactions of Shropshire Archæological Society, xi. 71.
CHARLETON. Transactions of Shropshire Archæological Society, ix. 68.
CHATFIELD. History of Ditchling, by Henry Cheal, at end.
CHAWORTH. Transactions of the Thoroton Society, 1901, at end.
CHEALE. Fragmenta Genealogica, by F. A. Crisp, vii. 115.
CHESTER. Transactions of Shropshire Archæological Society, ix. 15.
CLEMENT. Transactions of Shropshire Archæological Society, 3 S. i. 9.
CLIFTON. Transactions of the Thoroton Society, 1901, at end.
CLIVE. Transactions of Shropshire Archæological Society, 2 S. vii.
154 ; xii. 169.
CLOPTON. Transactions of Shropshire Archæological Society, i. 304.
COLEMORE. Transactions of Shropshire Archæological Society, ix. 51.
CORBETT. Transactions of Shropshire Archæological Society, iv. 81 ;
ix. 35, 38.
CORFIELD. Transactions of Shropshire Archæological Society, 2 S.
vi. 233.
COX. Transactions of Shropshire Archæological Society, 3 S. i. 153.
CRESSWELL. J. P. Jones's History of Tettenhall, 89.
CRESSY. Transactions of the Thoroton Society, 1901, at end.

DAGER, or DAKER. Transactions of Shropshire Archæological Society,
2 S. ix. 53.
DAVENPORT. William Davenport of Reading, and his Descendants.
By Revd. J. Davenport, n.d., 8vo.
DE ALFRETON. Transactions of the Thoroton Society, 1901, at end.
DEANE. Transactions of Shropshire Archæological Society, ix. 42.
DE BOULLI. Yorkshire Archæological Society, Record Series, xxx.
609.
DE BRACY. Transactions of Shropshire Archæological Society, 3 S. i.
177.
DE BUSLI. Transactions of the Thoroton Society, 1901, at end.
DE COLNEHAM. Transactions of Shropshire Archæological Society,
3 S. i. 25.
DE GAUNT. Yorkshire Archæological Society, Record Series, xxx.
480.
DE LACY. Transactions of the Thoroton Society, 1901, at end.
DE LA MERE. Transactions of Shropshire Archæological Society, 2 S.
xi. 179.

DE LA POLE. Transactions of Shropshire Archæological Society, 2 S. iii. 194.

DE LA TOUR. Transactions of Shropshire Archæological Society, 3 S. ii. 270.

DELLA CAINEA. Case of Sophia Della Cainea claiming the Barony of Camoys, 1838, fol.

DE VAUTIER. *See* WANTY.

DE VIPONT. Transactions of the Thoroton Society, 1901, *at end.*

DONNE. Transactions of Shropshire Archæological Society, v. 290.

DOUGLAS. A History of the House of Douglas. By Sir Herbert Maxwell. London, 1902, 8vo., 2 vols.

DUNCH. Transactions of Shropshire Archæological Society, ix. 32.

DUNFOWL. Transactions of Shropshire Archæological Society, 3 S. i. 317.

DURANT. Transactions of Shropshire Archæological Society, ix. 24.

DUTTON. Memorials of the Duttons. London and Chester, 1891, 4to.

EAMONSON. Platt and Morkill's Records of Whitkirk, 80.

EDGCUMBE. Edgcumbe Family Records. By Rev. J. Traherne. Plymouth, 1888, 4to.

EDWARDES. Transactions of Shropshire Archæological Society, vii. 1-48; 3 S. i. 321.

EDWARDS. Transactions of Shropshire Archæological Society, 2 S. v. 159, 205, 289.

EDWIN. Transactions of Shropshire Archæological Society, 3 S. i. 306.

ELDE. Transactions of Shropshire Archæological Society, ix. 26.

ERDESWICKE. Transactions of Shropshire Archæological Society, ix. 42.

ESSEX. Transactions of Shropshire Archæological Society, ii. 33.

EYTON. Transactions of Shropshire Archæological Society, v. 318.

FILILODE. Transactions of Shropshire Archæological Society, 2 S. v. 77.

FITZHERBERT. Transactions of Shropshire Archæological Society, ix. 59; 2 S. v. 232.

FITZWALTER. Healey's History of Part of West Somerset, 258.

FITZ-WIMARCH. Transactions of Shropshire Archæological Society, ii. 33.

FLEEMING. J. P. Jones's History of Tettenhall, 55.

FORESTER. Transactions of Shropshire Archæological Society, 2 S. iii. 151-184.

FORSTER. Transactions of Shropshire Archæological Society, ii. 269.

FOSTER. Camoy's Peerage Evidence, 152.

FOWKE. Transactions of Shropshire Archæological Society, ix. 37.

FOWLER. J. P. Jones's History of Tettenhall, 98. Transactions of Shropshire Archæological Society, ix. 13.

FOXE. Transactions of Shropshire Archæological Society, 2 S. xii. 113, 146, 169, 188.

FRY. Healey's History of Part of West Somerset, 332.

FRYER. J. P. Jones's History of Tettenhall, 55.

GARNEL. Transactions of Shropshire Archæological Society, 3 S. i. 18.
GATACRE. Transactions of Shropshire Archæological Society, ix. 59, 72.
GEFFERY. Transactions of Shropshire Archæological Society, 3 S. ii. 279.
GIFFARD. Transactions of Shropshire Archæological Society, ix. 40.
GOCH. Transactions of Shropshire Archæological Society, 3 S. i. 154.
GODOLPHIN. Transactions of Shropshire Archæological Society, 2 S. iv. 212.
GORE. Transactions of Shropshire Archæological Society, 2 S. iv. 239.
GOUGH. Transactions of Shropshire Archæological Society, 2 S. v. 261-292.
GRAFTON. Transactions of Shropshire Archæological Society, 3 S. ii. 284.
GRANEGOS. Transactions of Shropshire Archæological Society, 3 S. i. 162.
GREY. Transactions of Shropshire Archæological Society, ii. 267 ; ix. 41.

HAINES. Memoir of Richard Haines, with account of his Ancestry. By C. R. Haines. London, 1899, 8vo.
HANBURY. Transactions of Shropshire Archæological Society, iv. 303.
HANMER. Transactions of Shropshire Archæological Society, 2 S. v. 21.
HARCOURT. Transactions of Shropshire Archæological Society, ii. 293 ; ix. 45.
HARLEY. Transactions of Shropshire Archæological Society, 2 S. ix. 168.
HARNAGE. Transactions of Shropshire Archæological Society, iv. 339.
HARRINGTON. Transactions of Shropshire Archæological Society, ix. 31; 2 S. xi. 104.
HARRIS. Transactions of Shropshire Archæological Society, x. 336.
HARTOPP. Hartopp of Little Dalby, etc. By Henry Hartopp. Leicester, n.d., 8vo.
HAUGHTON. Transactions of Shropshire Archæological Society, 2 S. vi. 248.
HERBERT. Transactions of Shropshire Archæological Society, 2 S xii. 169.
HERCY. Transactions of the Thoroton Society, 1901, at end.
HESKETH. Descent of Hesketh of Kenwick, Co. Salop. By Edwin Hobhouse, 1893, broadside.
HEYLIN. Transactions of Shropshire Archæological Society, 2 S. vii. 164.
HEYNES. Transactions of Shropshire Archæological Society, xi. 76.
HILL. Transactions of Shropshire Archæological Society, 2 S. xi. 113.
HOLYOAKE. Transactions of Shropshire Archæological Society, ix. 21.
HOMFRAY. Transactions of Shropshire Archæological Society, ix. 8.
HOUGHTON. Transactions of Shropshire Archæological Society, ix. 43.

HULSE. Transactions of Shropshire Archæological Society, ix. 31.
HUMPHRESTON. Transactions of Shropshire Archæological Society,
ix. 37.
HUTTON. The Northern Genealogist, v. 100.

IRELAND. Transactions of Shropshire Archæological Society, 2 S. vi.
321.
IVE. Transactions of Shropshire Archæological Society, 3 S. i. 22.

JELLICORSE. Transactions of Shropshire Archæological Society, ix. 4.
JESSOP. Transactions of the Thoroton Society, 1901, at end.
JOBSON. Transactions of the Thoroton Society, 1901, at end.
JOHNS. Transactions of Shropshire Archæological Society, 2 S. vii. 225.
JOHNSON. Genealogy of the Family of Johnson of Barkby, from A.D.
1296 to 1898. By T. F. Johnson, 1898.
JONES. Transactions of Shropshire Archæological Society, 2 S. viii.
168.

KNILL. Genealogy of the Knills of Knill. [By J. L. Lambe, 1902.]
Broadside.
KYNASTON. Transactions of Shropshire Archæological Society, 2 S.
vi. 209 ; x. 273.

LAMBE. See Genealogy of the Knills of Knill.
LETON. Transactions of Shropshire Archæological Society, 2 S. vi.
375.
LINGEN. Transactions of Shropshire Aichæological Society, 2 S. vi.
403.
LLOYD. Transactions of Shropshire Archæological Society, 2 S. ix. 69.
LOKER. Transactions of Shropshire Archæological Society, 2 S. vii.
225.
LOWTHER. Cumberland and Westmorland Archæological Society,
2 S. ii.

MACKWORTH. Transactions of Shropshire Archæological Society,
2 S. viii. 119.
MARTIN. Transactions of Shropshire Archæological Society, 3 S. i.
17, 157.
MELLISH. Transactions of the Thoroton Society, 1901, at end.
MORTAYNE. Transactions of the Thoroton Society, 1901, at end.
MUTTON. Transactions of Shropshire Archæological Society, 3 S. ii.
274.

NEWLING. Transactions of Shropshire Archæological Society, 2 S.
vii. 189.
NEWPORT. Transactions of Shropshire Archæological Society, 2 S.
xii. 1.

OFFLEY. Transactions of Shropshire Archæological Society, 2 S. xi.
187.

WARD. Transactions of Shropshire Archæological Society, 2 S. xi. 187.

WELD. Transactions of Shropshire Archæological Society, 3 S. i. 207.

WILDEGOS. Transactions of Shropshire Archæological Society, 3 S. i. 307.

WILDING. Transactions of Shropshire Archæological Society, 2 S. vii. 233.

WOLLASCOT. Transactions of Shropshire Archæological Society, 2 S. ix. 193.

WOLRYCHE. Transactions of Shropshire Archæological Society, 3 S. ii. 324.

WOOD. Pedigree of Wood of Leicester. By H. J. Roby. Manchester, 1890, 8vo.

ZOUCH. Transactions of Shropshire Archæological Society, 2 S. viii. 106.